Founded in 1744 as a book auction house, and now the leading firm of art auctioneers and appraisers in the world.

Sotheby Parke Bernet Inc.,
1334 York Avenue at 72nd Street,
New York, N.Y. 10021 (212) 472-3592.

SOTHEBY'S
Founded 1744

READ THIS NOTICE!!!

The American Book Prices Current Index 1983-1987 will be available at the beginning of April 1988.

It costs $390.00 and is a bargain at the price.

The ABPC Index 1983-1987 is two volumes totalling over 2000 pages. These in sophisticated, reliable, intelligent, and comprehensive fashion detail prices achieved at over 1000 sales in the U.S., the U.K., France, the Netherlands, Monaco, West Germany, Australia, etc. Lots covered include autographs, manuscripts, maps and charts as well as books.

This Index set like all our other publications is published in a limited edition. It will soon be out of print: ABPC volumes always are. Don't hesitate, don't delay, don't procrastinate — ORDER NOW WHILE THE SUPPLY LASTS. Almost 1000 dealers, collectors, jobbers, and institutions have already placed their orders. Do so as well; don't be left out.

REMEMBER!! The last Index set sold out fast, and the next Index set will not appear until 1992.

Send $390.00 for the set and $9.95 for shipping/handling in cash, check, or money order — and we will send you a set. Be sure of getting your set. Don't delay today, and feel sorry tomorrow, and the day after tomorrow, and the day after the day after tomorrow, etc.

This is a test — use the words "Bookline" in your order and we'll pay shipping/handling and you may also deduct an additional $5.00 from your payment. Get payment to us by March 1, 1987 and in addition you need only pay the special pre-pub price of $287.97.

Order now and be sure of getting your two-volume 1983-1987 Index set.

BOOK
PRICES
CURRENT

American Book Prices Current
P.O. Box 236, Washington, CT 06793
(212) 737-2715

American Book Collector

is the monthly magazine for book collectors interested in modern first editions, Americana and Western Americana, illustrated and childrens' books, modern fine printing and press books, autographs and manuscripts, and the myriad specialties that make up bookdom. We offer interesting and well-illustrated articles, auction notes, listings of new dealers' catalogues, reviews of books you won't find elsewhere, exhibition and scholarly conference reports, and news of the book world and the book trade.

A one-year subscription in the U.S. and Canada is only $30, $37.50 elsewhere. Two- and three-year subscriptions also available. Write for our free subscription and advertising leaflets for further details.

Now distributing over 3,000 copies on newsstands throughout the world. No other book-collecting periodical even comes close to our coverage of book collectors, not just the trade.

American Book Collector   P. O. Box 867   Ossining, N. Y. 10562-0867
Telephone (914) 941-0409

During 1986-87, which magazine ran features and reviews of interest to bookmen in U.K. and Eire, America, Australia, Canada, France, Germany, India and more?
Which magazine carried reviews or notices of twelve different Trade Directories world wide?
Where could you read about John Clare or The Grey Walls Press; Pacific explorers or U.S. loyalists; W.W.1. poets or The Data Protection Act; Book Collectors and their Catalogues or W.H.G. Kingston, regular columns and book reviews covering a wide range of subjects?

FOR BOOKMEN OF ALL INTERESTS:
ANTIQUARIAN BOOK MONTHLY REVIEW
52 St Clements Street Oxford OX4 1EW England Tel: (0865) 721615

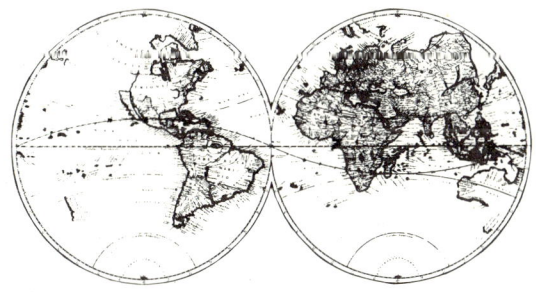

EDITOR: JOHN A. KINNANE **BUSINESS MANAGER: ANN SALMON**

PHOTOCOPY IF YOU PREFER NOT TO CUT THE PAGE

Please register my subscription to ABMR from (month): ....
Name: ....
Address (& ZIP/Post Code): ....
....

I enclose £ ....

ADVERTISING, INSERT & CATALOGUE INSERT RATES AVAILABLE ON REQUEST FROM THE BUSINESS MANAGER

U.K. £14	AUSTRALIA £21	AFRICA £18
U.S.A. £18	CANADA £18	FAR EAST £21
EUROPE (& EIRE) £16	SOUTH AMERICA £18	($ rates on request)

Antiques Trade GAZETTE

Hundreds of book prices every week

Every Week in

* *Extensive coverage of all major and minor Antiquarian Book sales throughout the United Kingdom*

* *Detailed reports on the most important book sales held in the United States*

* *Notices of some of the more important European book sales*

* *A Calendar of forthcoming book auctions in the United Kingdom and Overseas — including those sales which contain 'Book Sections'*

* *A list of Book Fairs and Markets for the coming weeks*

* *Advertisements for forthcoming sales*

Send for a free specimen copy to
ANTIQUES TRADE GAZETTE,
17 WHITCOMB STREET,
LONDON WC2H 7PL

or fill in the subscription form below

For further information on
the Antiquarian Books coverage
offered by
Antique Trade Gazette,
please contact
IAN McKAY on 01-930 9955

Plus the **Gazette's** usual comprehensive coverage of fine art auctions, U.K. and worldwide, the full Auction Calendar, Fairs and Markets, Stolen Goods, News and Views, etc . . .

Antiques Trade GAZETTE

Subscribe to Antiques Trade Gazette for £30 a year

TO: Antiques Trade Gazette, 17 Whitcomb Street, London WC2H 7PL
Please enter my subscription for one year (50 issues)

[ ] Cheque for £30 enclosed
[ ] Charge to the credit card circled here: Visa/Access/American Express/Diners

My card number is: ☐☐☐☐☐☐☐☐☐☐☐☐☐☐

Signature ....
NAME: ....
ADDRESS: ....
....
....

INTERNATIONAL
SUBSCRIPTION
BY AIRMAIL

Australia $A175
Belgique 2850FB
Danmark 525kr
Deutschland 135DM
Eire   IR33
Espana 9500ptas
France 450FF
Hong Kong $HK775
Italia L95,000
Japan 22,000 yen
Nederland 155fl
New Zealand $NZ230
Norge 525kr
Osterreich 1000sch
Suisse 115FS
Sverige 475kr

**NORTH AMERICA
by Airmail**

U.S.A. $100
Canada C$140

THE BIBLIOGRAPHICAL SOCIETY OF AMERICA

The Society was founded in 1904. Membership is open to all who share its aims and interests in the promotion of bibliographical research and publication.

Membership is available at a cost of $20.00 per year, which includes a subscription to the quarterly *Papers* of the Society, as well as substantial discounts for the Society's monographic publications.

The BSA sponsors an annual short-term (one or two months) fellowship program, in support of bibliographical inquiry as well as research in the history of the book trades and publishing history. Details of the program are available from the Executive Secretary.

The *Papers of the Bibliographical Society of America (PBSA)* publishes contributions dealing with books and manuscripts, in any field, which treat them as artifacts of historical evidence, as well as studies of the printing, publishing, and allied trades.

For further information, address the BSA Executive Secretary, P. O. Box 397, Grand Central Station, New York, N. Y. 10163, U. S. A.

Harvey W. Brewer, Bookseller

BOX 322, CLOSTER, NEW JERSEY 07624
Telephone 768-4414. Area Code 201
BY APPOINTMENT

We are interested in the following subjects

FINE ARTS
COLOR PLATE BOOKS
TOPOGRAPHY - VIEW BOOKS
ATLASES
FINE ILLUSTRATED BOOKS
COSTUME & FASHION
ART NOUVEAU
ART DECO

"Bloomsbury Book Auctions surprise by their variety"

Book Collector, Summer 1987

Another successful year for
London's only specialist book auction house.

Highlights include:

* Shakespeare's Fourth Folio – $24,000

* Bibliotheque Latine-Françoise,
  177 volumes of 180, Paris, 1825-38.
  Trollope's own annotated set, – $7,600

* Letter from Byron's mother – $2,240

* MS 17th century verse miscellany
  with poems by Donne, Philip Sidney,
  Ben Jonson and others from
  c. 1580 to 1668 – $6,400

We hold about 20 sales a year. If you have books to
sell or you wish to buy please ring us on
011 441 833 2636/7.

Bloomsbury Book Auctions
3 & 4 Hardwick Street, London EC1R 4RY,
England

THE BOOK COLLECTOR

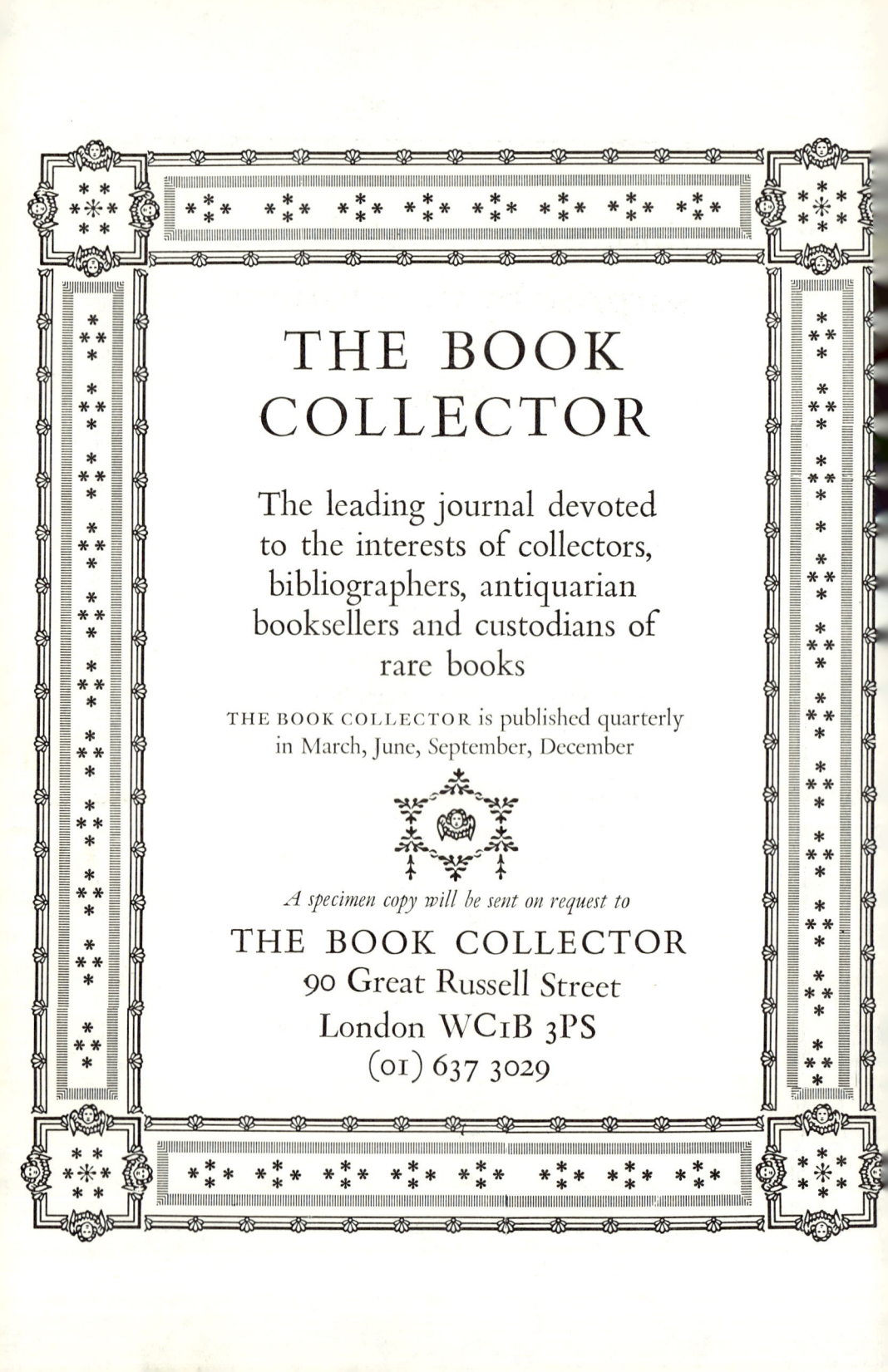

The leading journal devoted to the interests of collectors, bibliographers, antiquarian booksellers and custodians of rare books

THE BOOK COLLECTOR is published quarterly in March, June, September, December

A specimen copy will be sent on request to

THE BOOK COLLECTOR
90 Great Russell Street
London WC1B 3PS
(01) 637 3029

BI-WEEKLY BOOK AUCTIONS
SAN FRANCISCO

California & The West
Fine Press & Illustrated
Modern First Editions
Autographs & Manuscripts
English & American Literature
Detective & Science Fiction
Fine & Rare Books in all fields

Subscription: $90 domestic or $115 foreign.
20-22 catalogues and prices realized.
Individual catalogues and prices realized: $6 domestic or $7 foreign. Quarterly newsletter including sales schedule free to all on mailing list.

CALIFORNIA BOOK AUCTION
GALLERIES

965 Mission Street, Suite 730, San Francisco, California 94103
(415) 243-0650
Cable: Books, San Francisco

Member ABAA and ILAB

CHRISTIE'S

for auctions of the finest rare books, manuscripts and autographs

---

FIFTEENTH-CENTURY PRINTED BOOKS
The Gutenberg Bible $2,000,000
The Eric Sexton collection $1,331,380

AUTOGRAPH MANUSCRIPTS
The Codex Leicester by Leonardo da Vinci $5,126,000

AMERICANA AUTOGRAPHS
Original drawing for the Mason-Dixon Line $360,000
The Sang set of Signers of the Declaration of Independence $320,000

PRINTED AMERICANA
The Declaration of Independence $375,000
The Hudson River Portfolio $80,000

ENGLISH LITERATURE
The Arthur A. Houghton collection $5,759,031
The Marjorie Wiggin Prescott collection $1,341,640

MODERN LITERATURE
The James Gilvarry collection $1,054,640

BOOKBINDINGS
The Leipzig Collection by Robert Riviere & Son $100,000
Manuscript bound by King Henry VIII's Binder $120,000
Fine bindings by T.J. Cobden-Sanderson $76,000

MINIATURE BOOKS
The Arthur A. Houghton collection $605,760

PRIVATE PRESS BOOKS
The John Saks Ashendene collection $301,550
The John Saks Kelmscott collection $703,325

MUSICAL MANUSCRIPTS
Wagner: Rienzi $150,000
Wagner: Tannhauser $220,000
Debussy: Pelleas et Melisande $350,000

HEBREW MANUSCRIPTS
Bible, Ashkenaz 1264 $360,000

HEBREW PRINTED BOOKS
Isaac Aben Sahulah [*Ancient Fables*], Brescia 1491 $160,000

NATURAL HISTORY BOOKS
Audubon: The Birds of America (separate sheets) $1,754,550
Gould: A collection of works in 49 volumes,
the gift of John Pierpont Morgan to Wadsworth Atheneum $400,000

NEW YORK
Christie, Manson & Woods International, Inc.–Stephen Massey
502 Park Avenue, New York, N.Y. 10022
Telephone: 212/546-1000 • International Telex: 620 721

LONDON
Christie, Manson & Woods, Ltd.–Hans Fellner
8 King Street, St. James, London SW1Y 6QT
Telephone: 01/839/9060 • Telex 916 429 • Cable: Christiart, London

Christie's South Kensington
85 Old Brompton Road, London SW7 3J7
Telephone: 01/581/2231 • Telex: 922 061

HARTUNG & KARL

Antiquariat-Auktionen

KAROLINENPLATZ 5 A · D-8000 MÜNCHEN 2
Telephone: (089) 28 40 34 · Cables: Buchauktion
WEST GERMANY

Illuminated Manuscripts · Incunabulas
Books on Medicine and Natural History
Illustrated Books from the 15th to the 20th century
German Literature in First Editions
Autographs · Fine Bindings
Atlases · Decorative Prints · Maps and Views

 # AUCTIONS
as usual twice a year, May and November

Richly illustrated catalogues and lists of results

Dr. Ernst Hauswedell & Co.

Jahrbuch der Auktionspreise für Bücher,
Handschriften und Autographen

*(Central european auction prices for books,
manuscripts and autographs)*

Published every year since 1950.

Vol. 37 (1986) includes prices of 37.500 books, manuscripts, and autographs sold at 65 public sales in Germany, the Netherlands, Switzerland, and other middle european countries in 1986. Among the appendices of the book is to be found a list of antiquarian booksellers according to their specialities and an english/german index of the keywords used in this list. 1987. Royal octavo. 900 pages. Cloth DM 298,-.

A few copies are still in stock of vols. 29 (1978) to 36 (1985) (DM 298,- each), and of the index volumes 11-20 (DM 360,-) and 21-30 (DM 560,-). An index volume 31-35 will come out end of 1987.

We are publishers since 1927:

Books about Books — Typography

Book Trade   Fine Arts

Illustrated Books

Catalogue sent on request
DR. ERNST HAUSWEDELL & CO.
Rosenbergstrasse 113 — D-7 Stuttgart 1

LEO S. OLSCHKI
ANTIQUARIAN BOOKSELLERS

ITALIAN BOOKS

ART · ARCHAEOLOGY
ARCHITECTURE · CLASSICS
HISTORY · HUMANISM · MEDICINE
SCIENCE · THEOLOGY

FINE BOOKS

GRIDLEYS – BELCHAMP OTTEN
SUDBURY – SUFFOLK CO10 7BH
ENGLAND – Tel: 0787-277341

RARE BOOKS
AUTOGRAPH LETTERS & HISTORICAL DOCUMENTS
ATLASES & MAPS

Phillips conducts regular sales worldwide.

For further information about buying and selling at Phillips please contact:

LONDON
7 Blenheim Street
New Bond Street
London W1Y OAS

James Smith
01-629-1824

NEW YORK
406 East 79th St.
New York
NY 10021

Frank Frost
(212) 570-4830

EDINBURGH
65 George Street
Edinburgh EH2 2JL

Peter Nelson
031-225-2266

Charles Robinson
Rare Books

ILLUSTRATED BOOKS

FINE BINDINGS AND SETS

PSYCHOLOGY AND PSYCHIATRY

BOOKS AND PERIODICALS

CONTAINING ORIGINAL ART:
VERVE
XXieme SIECLE
DERRIERE Le MIRROR

By Appointment Only

Box 299, Pond Road
Manchester, Maine 04351
(207) 662-1885

APPRAISALS UNDERTAKEN

Thomas Rowlandson, *A Sale at Sotheby's*, c. 1800.

RECORD RESULTS

The results for the first half of 1987 indicate
that this will be the most successful year to date for the
London Department of Printed Books and Manuscripts.

Sales to the end of July this year have already achieved an
aggregate total of more than the £11.5m for the whole of 1986.

Some notable results are listed here:

Books from the library of Robert de Belder £5,900,000
Bibliothèque Marcel Jeanson, Première partie £4,335,936
Mozart's autograph manuscript of nine symphonies £2,585,000
Archive relating to the Secret Treaty of Dover £313,500
Items from the archive of J.M Dent £750,000
The archive of Giacomo Meyerbeer £176,000
John Gould's own set of his works £397,485

We have also sold by private treaty to the British Library
the archive of Sir John Coke (1563-1644), the friend of Fulke Greville
and Secretary of State, which was formerly owned by the Rt. Hon. the Marquess of Lothian
and was sold on behalf of the Melbourne Garden Charity Trust.

For a calendar of sales and information or advice
about buying and selling at auction please contact. Roy Davids
Sotheby's, 34-35 New Bond Street, London W1A 2AA. Telephone: (01) 493 8080

FOUNDED 1744

"The painter whom Paul Durrieu recognized as pre-eminent in France has begun to attract more attention in recent years, and he emerged in Erwin Panofsky's account of 1953 as a major protagonist in European painting . . . . Since then, the Boucicaut Master has assumed a place alongside the Limbourgs in all accounts of the great renewal in the North" (M. Meiss, *The Boucicaut Master*, 1968, p.5).

Sotheby's, 24th June 1986, lot 100, Book of Hours from the workshop of The Boucicaut Master, c.1415. £572,000.

Sotheby's, 2nd December 1986, lot 56, another Book of Hours from the workshop of The Boucicaut Master, c.1412. £198,000.

Sotheby's, 23rd June 1987, lot 105, yet another Book of Hours from the workshop of The Boucicaut Master, c.1410. £214,500.

SOTHEBY'S

Western and Oriental Illuminated Manuscripts and Miniatures
Dr. C.F.R. de Hamel

Bloomfield Place,
off New Bond Street,
London W1A 2AA
Telephone: 01-493 8080
Telex: 24454 (SPBLON-G)

Titles, Inc.

FLORENCE SHAY
1931 Sheridan Rd.
Highland Park, Ill. 60035

(312) 432-3690

DEALERS IN
RARE & FINE BOOKS
IN ALL CATEGORIES

SEARCH SERVICE

Do you have books to sell us?

SWANN GALLERIES, INC.
104 East 25th Street • New York, New York 10010
Telephone: (212) 254-4710 • Cable: Swannsales

WEEKLY AUCTION SALES

OF

RARE BOOKS

AUTOGRAPHS & MANUSCRIPTS

GRAPHIC ARTS

PHOTOGRAPHS

DRAWINGS & WATERCOLORS

PRINTS • MAPS

Catalogues and prices realized
available by annual subscription or for individual sales

Also Available:
The Trumpet, a quarterly newsletter containing
current schedule and interesting editorial matter, and
Buying and Selling Books at Auction, a comprehensive
brochure for prospective bidders or consignors

FREE SEARCH SERVICE
— O.P. American Imprints

We will undertake, upon request, to search for and supply out-of-print American imprints. No obligation, of course.

Wants lists, inquiries invited.

chip's booksearch
Box 123, Planetarium Station
New York, N.Y. 10024, U.S.A.

Cables: "Wheldwesly, Codicote, Hitchin"
Phone: Stevenage (0438) 820370
Telex: 825562 CHACOM G WHELD

NATURAL HISTORY BOOKS AND PERIODICALS

Wheldon & Wesley Ltd

LYTTON LODGE, CODICOTE
HITCHIN, HERTS., SG4 8TE
ENGLAND

Established 1843 *Catalogues issued*

Walter R. Benjamin
Autographs, Inc.
Established 1887

Specialists in
letters and documents
of literary,
historical, musical
and scientific interest

P.O. Box 255
Scribner Hollow Road
Hunter, N.Y. 12442
Telephone: (518) 263-4133

Publishers of
"THE COLLECTOR"

FINE BINDING
RESTORATIONS
& CASES MADE

FIRST & FINE EDITIONS OF
ENGLISH LITERATURE
IN OLD & NEW BINDINGS
BOUGHT & SOLD

Large General Stock

Museum of Bookbinding

GEORGE BAYNTUN
incorporating
ROBERT RIVIERE
Manvers Street, Bath,
England
Tel: (0225) 66000

BIELEFELD AUCTIONS

Several Auction Sales
each year of Fine Books,
Decorative Graphics
and Modern Art.

*Catalogues may be ordered
according to particular
fields of interest.*

**JOCHEN GRANIER
BOOK AND ART AUCTIONS**
Welle 9 • 4800 Bielefeld 1
West Germany
Tel. 05 21 / 6 71 48

Our antiquarian book firm
ANTIQUARIAT GRANIER GMBH
Welle 9 • 4800 Bielefeld 1
Tel. 05 21 / 6 71 48
*is ready as it has been for more than
15 years, to accommodate your needs
in buying and selling books.*

D & E LAKE

ABAC/ILAB

*Old and Rare Books
Specializing in Americana,
Canadiana and Travel*

CATALOGUES UPON REQUEST

D & E LAKE LTD.
239 King Street East, Toronto
Canada M5A 1J9

416 / 863-9930

NATURAL HISTORY
OUR SPECIALTY
SINCE 1948

Scholarly books wanted
at all times.
We are interested in
single important volumes,
small collections and
complete libraries.

AMPHIBIANS • ANIMALS
BIRDS • BOTANY
CRYPTOGRAMS • DARWIN
FISHES • INSECTS
INVERTEBRATES
PALEONTOLOGY
REPTILES • SNAKES
VOYAGES AND
EXPLORATIONS

John Johnson

NATURAL HISTORY
BOOKS

R.D. #1 — BOX 513
NO. BENNINGTON, VT 05257
(802) 442-6738

WANTED FOR STOCK

ANTIQUE MAPS
ATLASES, ETC.

CARTOGRAPHIC
REFERENCES.

Jonathan Potter Ltd.,
21 Grosvenor Street,
Mayfair, London W1X 9FE
ENGLAND
01 491 3520

DIANA J. RENDELL, INC.
AUTOGRAPH LETTERS
MANUSCRIPTS · DOCUMENTS

From the First Forms of Writing
to the Present Day...
We Are Interested In Buying
Individual Pieces
Or Entire Collections.

177 COLLINS ROAD
WABAN, MASSACHUSETTS 02168
617/969-1774

AMERICAN BOOK PRICES CURRENT VOLUME 93

1986 - 1987

AMERICAN BOOK PRICES CURRENT

1987

VOLUME 93

The auction season September 1986—August 1987

BANCROFT-PARKMAN, INC.

1987

EDITORS

K̲atharine K̲yes L̲eab
D̲aniel J. L̲eab
Managing Editors

M̲arie-L̲uise F̲rings
J̲ane C. M̲allison
S̲ara W̲albridge

Please send all inquiries and suggestions to:
American Book Prices Current
P.O. Box 236
Washington, CT 06793
TEL: (212) RE 7-2715

Copyright © 1987 by Bancroft-Parkman, Inc. All rights reserved.
ISBN: 0-914022-20-2
ISSN: 0091-9357
Library of Congress Card No. 3-14557
Printed in the United States of America

CONTENTS

	Page
Abbreviations	vi
Introduction	vii
Auction Houses	ix
Named Consignors	xii
Season's Sales	xvi
Part I: Autographs & Manuscripts	1
Part II: Books, Broadsides, Maps & Charts	239

ABBREVIATIONS

ad, ads Advertisement(s)
ACs Autograph Card, signed
ADs Autograph Document, signed
ALs Autograph Letter, signed
A Ls s Autograph Letters, signed
Amst. Amsterdam
anr Another
Anon Anonymous
ANs Autograph Note, signed
armorial bdg Binding with coat of arms on cover
Balt. Baltimore
bdg Binding
bds Boards
Birm. Birmingham
Bost. Boston
c. Circa
Cambr. Cambridge
cat Catalogue
cent Century
contemp Contemporary
def Defective
Ds Document, signed
d/j Dust-jacket
Ed Edition; Edited; Editor
Edin. Edinburgh
extra bdg Elaborate binding
f, ff Folio(s)
frontis Frontispiece
H of R House of Representatives
illus, illusts Illustrate(d); Illustrations
imperf Imperfect
inscr Inscribed; Inscription
intro Introduction

L London
lea Leather
lev Levant
litho Lithograph
L.p. Large paper
Ls Letter, signed
Ls s Letters, signed
Ltd Limited
mor Morocco
Ms, Mss Manuscript; Manuscripts
mtd Mounted
n.d. No date
n.p. No place
n.y. No year
NY New York
no, nos Number; Numbers
orig Original
pbd, pbr Published; Publisher
Phila. Philadelphia
port Portrait
pp Pages
prelim Preliminary
pseud. Pseudonym
ptd, ptg, ptr Printed; Printing; Printer
pvtly Privately
Sen. Senate
sgd Signed
syn Synthetic
tp Title-page
trans Translated; Translation; translator
vol, vols Volume; volumes
w.a.f. With all faults
Wash. Washington
wrap, wraps Wrapper; Wrappers

Book sizes are listed as:
folio
4to
8vo
12 mo
16 mo
etc.

INTRODUCTION

Volume 93 of *American Book Prices Current* details a particularly fine and rich year for the auction market. There are quite a number of books in this volume, particularly from the Jeanson sale, which appear in *ABPC* for the first time in this century. As a result of all this activity, our type size has reached its lower limit throughout the book.

Explanatory Notes

Volume 93 of *American Book Prices Current* has been prepared by a team of editors highly experienced in the field of rare books and manuscripts. As its users know, ABPC is not just a transcribed record of titles and prices, copied unquestioningly from the season's auction catalogues. It is, on the contrary, the only work in English in which every listing of printed material has been checked as to title, format, date of publication, edition, and limitations. Bindings are described, with condition when relevant, and whenever possible maps and plates in books are verified. Moreover, sales of autographs and manuscripts are reported. Because of this, ABPC is an essential tool for buying, selling and evaluating books, serials, autographs, manuscripts, broadsides, and maps, based on actual figures realized at auction. In the words of a reviewer in *The Times Literary Supplement,* it is "an accurate, indispensable tool for the antiquarian bookseller and collector." And, in addition to meeting the need for a dependable guide in determining the value of old and out-of-print books, ABPC serves as a reference work and as an aid to scholars in locating printed works and manuscripts of all centuries, from the earliest years to the present.

American Book Prices Current is composed of two parts. Part I, Autographs & Manuscripts, includes original illustrations for printed books, documents, letters, typescripts, corrected proofs, signed photographs, and signatures, as well as manuscripts. Part II, Books, includes broadsides, single-sheet printings, maps and charts, and uncorrected proof copies of books.

Entries are listed alphabetically by author whenever possible, by title when the author's name is unknown, or by Private Press and Club, printer, or publisher headings if such are the associations which attract the collector. In general, illustrated books are listed under the author of the text. Subject headings such as England, Maps & Charts, Hebrew Books and Miniature Books or those for individual U.S. states or cities have also been used. Individual works are in turn listed alphabetically under each heading and include: title; place & date of publication; edition designation; number of volumes when more than one; size, binding, and condition of binding; descriptive material, limitation notes, and the sale record — auction house (in code), date or number of sale, lot number, price, and purchaser (buyers' names are given when and as listed in price lists). There are cross-references to Club or Press books, to books bound together, and to books by more than one author.

INTRODUCTION

Volume 93 lists only those books and manuscripts which sold for at least $50 or its equivalent in another currency. In keeping with previous editorial policy, auction lots consisting of groupings of miscellaneous volumes are not listed, for the prices realized by such lots can give no accurate indication of the value of individual items. Similarly, listings of badly broken runs or seriously incomplete sets of printed books do not appear. Listings of books in non-Western languages realizing less than $100 have been selectively excluded, as have such peripheral works as printings of musical scores, collections of plates, and panoramas. We are selective in approaching German and Dutch sales, for our aim here is to include some items of particular interest to our readers.

Listings of 20th-century books frequently appear without format or binding information. In such instances it may be assumed that these books are octavo or duodecimo and bound in cloth or boards. Items which are sold by auction houses as "a collection of plates" or which are deemed to be bound prints rather than books are excluded from these pages. Considerable effort has been made to secure price lists for all of the relevant sales held by the auction houses listed herein. We make great efforts to be comprehensive, but not all auction houses are equally diligent in sending us price lists, or equally responsive to our inquiries.

Buyers' Surcharges

The following buyers' surcharges should be noted: in England, 10% at most houses; in the Netherlands, 14%; in Monaco, 11%; in Germany, 15%; and in the United States, 10%.

Currency and Exchange Rates

Please note that the figures given below are simplified approximations of the currency fluctuations throughout the 1986-87 season, not a precise bank rate.

The Pound Sterling fluctuated from a low of $1.40 in October 1986 to a high of $1.67 in April, ending the season at $1.63. At the time of the Jeanson sale the French Franc was at about 6.01 to the Dollar. The German Mark varied from a high of 1.77 in April 1987 to a low of 2.06 in October 1986. It took 1.39 Canadian Dollars to make an American Dollar in November 1986. The Australian Dollar ranged from 1.64 to the American Dollar to 1.38. And the Dutch Guilder ranged from 2.01 in April to 2.33 in October.

AUCTION HOUSES

The sales recorded in this volume are from the auction houses listed below and are designated by code letters. On the following pages are a list of the season's sales from each house and a record of the named consignors of merchandise.

AVP   Alfred van Peteghem
422 E. de La Gauchetiere, Montreal, Quebec, Canada H2L 2M5

B   J. L. Beijers
Achter Sint Pieter 140, Utrecht, The Netherlands

bba   Bloomsbury Book Auctions
3 & 4 Hardwick Street, London EC1 England

C   Christie, Manson & Woods, Ltd.
8 King Street, St. James's, London SW1Y 6QT England

CA   Christie, Manson & Woods (Australia) Ltd.
298 New South Head Rd., Double Bay, NSW 2028, Australia

CAM   Christie's Amsterdam B. V.
Cornelis Schuytstraat 57, 1071 JG, Amsterdam, The Netherlands

cb   California Book Auction Galleries
965 Mission Street, Ste. 730, San Francisco, CA 94103

Ck   Christie's South Kensington
85 Old Brompton Road, London SW7 3JS England

CNY   Christie, Manson & Woods International, Inc.
502 Park Avenue, New York, NY 10022

F   Samuel T. Freeman & Co.
1808 Chestnut Street, Philadelphia, PA 19103

ha   Harris Auction Galleries, Inc.
873-875 N. Howard St., Baltimore, MD 21201

AUCTION HOUSES

HK   Hartung und Karl
Karolinenplatz 5a, D 8000 Munich 2, West Germany

HN   Hauswedell und Nolte
Poseldorfer Weg 1, D 2000 Hamburg 13, West Germany

JG   Jochen Granier
4800 Bielefeld 1, Welle 9, West Germany

K   Kane Antiquarian Auction
1525 Shenkel Road, Pottstown, PA 19464

kh   Kenneth Hince Book Auctions
140 Greville Street, Prahran, Victoria 3181, Australia

L   Lawrence Fine Art
South Street, Crewkerne, Somerset TA18 8AB, England

O   Richard E. Oinonen Book Auctions
Box 470, Sunderland, MA 01375

P   Sotheby Parke Bernet, Inc.
1334 York Ave., New York, NY 10021

pn   Phillips, Son & Neale
7 Blenheim at New Bond Street, London W1Y OAS England

pnC   Phillips in Chester
New House, 150 Christleton Road,
Chester, Cheshire CH 3 5TD, England

pnE   Phillips in Scotland
65 George Street, Edinburgh EH2 2JL, Scotland

pnNY   Phillips, Son & Neale, Inc.
406 East 79th Street, New York, NY 10021

rf   Richard C. Frajola, Inc.
85 North Street, Danbury, CT 06810

AUCTION HOUSES

S   Sotheby Parke Bernet & Co.
         34-35 New Bond Street, London W1A 2AA, England

sg   Swann Galleries, Inc.
         104 East 25th Street, New York, NY 10010

SM   Sotheby Parke Bernet Monaco S.A.
         Le Sporting d'Hiver, Place du Casino, Monaco 98001

SSA   Sotheby Parke Bernet South Africa (Pty) Ltd.
         Total House, Cor. Smit & Rissik Streets
         Braamfontein, Johannesburg, South Africa

star   J. A. Stargardt
         Rade-Strasse 10, D-3550 Marburg, West Germany

T   Taviner's Auction Rooms
         Prewett Street, Redcliffe, Bristol BS1 6PB, England

VH   Venator & Hanstein
         Caecilienstrasse 48, 5000 Cologne 1, West Germany

wa   Waverly Auctions
         4931 Cordell Avenue, Suite AA, Bethesda, MD 20814

wd   William Doyle Galleries
         175 East 87th Street, New York, NY 10128

NAMED CONSIGNORS

Abajian, James De Tarr	cb Oct 9	Christian, Peggy	sg Jan. 22 sg Feb. 26
Abercorn, Duke of	CNY May 11	Cruising Association	C Dec. 12
Ambrose, Anthony	pn June 18	de Belder, Robert	S Apr. 27
B. Altman & Co.	pnNY Sept. 13	de Lancy Foundation	S Nov. 10
		Detwiler, Kenneth J.	cb Dec. 4
Barkley, Roy	CNY Dec. 19	East Hampton Free Library	CNY May 11
Barnes, J.F. Lovel	pn July 23	Enniskillen, Earl of	pnE Dec. 17
Benkovitz, Miriam J.	sg Mar. 5		
Berger, Georgette	S July 2	Ernst, Max	S June 29
Besterman, E.M.M.	S Nov. 10	Feinberg, Charles E.	P Dec. 15
Bibliotheque des Fontaines	S Oct. 23	Flack Estate, Elizabeth	wd June 19
		Franklin Institute	F Sept. 12
Binney Estate, Edwin III	CN May 11	Fraser, Alice & Warren H.	wa Nov. 6
Bowood Settlement Collection	C May 13	Gardner, Eric	pn May 21
Brooklyn Public Library	bba Dec. 18 sg Mar. 12	Gibson, John Michael	cb Apr. 24
		Gimbel Family, Richard	P May 13 P June 18
Buchter Estate, Essaye	wd June 19		
Bullock Estate, Calvin	CNY Dec. 19	Harrington Estate, Phyllis	CNY May 11
Carfagno Estate, Simon A.	CNY May 11	Haverschmide, Francois	B Feb. 24
Crahan, Marcus & Elizabeth	P Nov. 25	Heertje, Dr. Arnold	P Sept. 24 P Nov. 25

NAMED CONSIGNORS

Hopkins, Harry L.	wa Dec. 11	Montague of Beaulieu, Lord	C Apr. 8
Howland, Elihu	P May 13		
		Mowbray, Dr. Robert	pnE Dec. 17
Hunt Institute	CNY Nov. 21		pnE Jan. 28
		Newstead Abbey	S Oct. 23
Jeanson, Marcel	SM Feb. 28 SM Mar. 1	Newman, W.H.	Ck May 15 Ck May 29
Kalt, Melissa	CNY Dec. 19	O'Byrne, James	C July 22
Keck Day, Williametta	P Nov. 25	Pforzheimer Library, Carl H.	sg Mar. 5 sg Mar. 12
Kirschner, Bruno	CAM Dec. 3	Pierpont Morgan Library	CNY Dec. 19
Levin, Barry R.	cb Sept. 28	Quaritch, Bernard, Ltd	S Apr. 27
Linden, Samuel	Ck Nov. 7	Ranschburg, Otto	sg May 14
McCarn, Davis Barton	wa Dec. 11	Robb Estate, Eustace	C Dec. 12
McNeese Stat University	sg Mar. 5	Rosenblatt, Ruth	P June 18
Magritte, Rene	S July 2	Ross, Michael Macdonald	pn Mar. 26
Marcus, Stanley	CNY May 11	Salomons, Sir David	C Dec. 3 C May 13
Mayer Memorial Foundation	C Dec. 3	Sang, Mrs. Philip D.	P May 13
Mayer Memorial Trust	C May 13	Sargant, Dr. William	bba May 14
Miller Estate, Flora W.	P June 18	Schocken Books	P June 18
Milligan, Spike	S Nov. 10	Sims, G.F.	bba July 2
Mitchell, Herbert	sg Feb. 26	Sternfeld, Dr. F.W.	bba Dec. 18

xiii

NAMED CONSIGNORS

Stiles, Ed	wa June 25	Wade, Rita W.	P May 13
Thayer, Scofield	P June 19	Warn, John M.	cb Jan. 22
Tranchin, Marjorie Allen	sg Oct. 30	Watkins Estate, Mrs. Sheldon	CNY May 11
Upsher, H.T.S., Trustees	C Apr. 8	Wertheimer, Adele	P Dec. 15
Uzielli Estate, Giorgio	P June 19	Wood, Charles B., III	sg Oct. 23
Van Buren Estate, Maurice P.	wd June 19	Yeates, Robert O.	wa June 25
van der Morwe, P.J.	SSA Oct. 27	Young, John R.	CNY May 11

SEASON'S SALES

(arranged alphabetically by code letters)

ALFRED VAN PETEGHEM

-1986-

| AVP Nov 20 | Americana & Canadiana |

J. L. BEIJERS

-1986-

| B Oct 7 | 1885-1985: A Century of Artful Book-Making |
| B Oct 7 | Dutch Literature |

-1987-

B Feb 24	Ornithology
B Feb 25	Old & Rare Books
B June 2-3	Books

BLOOMSBURY BOOKS AUCTIONS

-1986-

bba Sept 25	Printed Books
bba Oct 16	Printed Books
bba Oct 30	Printed Books
bba Nov 13	Printed Books & Manuscripts
bba Dec 4	Printed Books
bba Dec 18	Printed Books, Music & Manuscripts

-1987-

bba Jan 15	Printed Books
bba Feb 5	Printed Books
bba Feb 19	Valuable Hebrew Books
bba Mar 12	Printed Books
bba Mar 26	Printed Books
bba Apr 9	Printed Books & Manuscripts
bba Apr 23	Printed Books
bba May 14	Printed Books
bba May 28	Printed Books
bba June 18	Printed Books
bba July 2	Library of G.F. Sims
bba July 16	Printed Books
bba Aug 20	Printed Books

SEASON'S SALES

CHRISTIE, MANSON & WOODS, LTD.

-1986-

C Oct 15	Valuable Travel & Natural History Books
C Nov 21	Islamic, Indian, South-East Asian Manuscripts
C Dec 3	French Illustrated Books and Almanacs
C Dec 3	Valuable Autograph Letters, Historical Documents and Music
C Dec 12	Books from the Library of Matthew Boulton
C Dec 12	Printed Books

-1987-

C Apr 8	Books
C May 13	Valuable Printed Books
C June 18	Napoleonic Memorabilia
C June 24	Autograph Letters, Historical Documents & Literary Mss
C June 24	Medieval & Illuminated Manuscripts
C July 22	19th-century Art & Architecture- James O'Byrne

CHRISTIE'S AUSTRALIA

-1986-

CA Oct 7	Australian Paintings & Books

-1987-

CA Apr 12	Australian Paintings, Prints & Books

CHRISTIE'S AMSTERDAM B.V.

-1986-

CAM Dec 3	Fine Judaica

SEASON'S SALES

CALIFORNIA BOOK AUCTION GALLERIES

-1986-

cb Sept 11	Fine Press Books
cb Sept 28	Highlights from Barry R. Levin Science Fiction
cb Oct 9	Western Americana
cb Oct 23	Fall Miscellany
cb Nov 6	Travel, Exploration, Hunting, Sporting
cb Nov 20	Mystery & Detective Fiction
cb Dec 4	Library of Mr. & Mrs. Kenneth J. Detwiler

-1987-

cb Jan 8	Western Americana
cb Jan 22	California Writers
cb Feb 5	Books about Books
cb Feb 19	Fine & Rare Books
cb Mar 5	Art Reference
cb Mar 19	Americana Miscellany Part I
cb Apr 2	Americana Miscellany Part II
cb Apr 24	Sherlock Holmes Centenary: Library of John Michael Gilson
cb May 7	Literature, Detective Fiction
cb May 21	Hunting & Sporting Firearms
cb June 4	Natural History, Travel & Exploration
cb June 18	Fine Press Books
cb July 16	The American West
cb July 30	Summer Miscellany

CHRISTIE'S SOUTH KENSINGTON

-1986-

Ck Sept 5	Printed Books
Ck Sept 26	Maps, Travel Books & British Topography
Ck Oct 17	Printed Books
Ck Oct 31	Printed Books
Ck Nov 7	Printed Books
Ck Nov 21	Printed Books
Ck Nov 28	Art Reference
Ck Dec 5	Art Reference
Ck Dec 10	19th & 20th Century Illustrations & Books

SEASON'S SALES

-1987-

Ck Jan 16	Printed Books
Ck Jan 30	Printed Books
Ck Feb 13	Printed Books
Ck Feb 27	Atlases, Maps & Travel Books
Ck Apr 24	Printed Books
Ck May 8	African Maps, Travel Books & Africana
Ck May 15	Atlases, Maps and Travel Books
Ck May 29	Printed Books
Ck June 5	Printed Books
Ck June 19	Printed Books

CHRISTIE'S NEW YORK

-1986-

CNY Nov 21	Botanical, Horticultural & Natural History Books: from the Hunt Institute for Botanical Documentation
CNY Dec 19	American & European Manuscripts & Printed Books

-1987-

CNY May 11	Printed Books and Manuscripts

S. T. FREEMAN

-1986-

F Sept 12	Rare Book Collection of the Franklin Institute
F Oct 29	Books, Autographs

-1987-

F Jan 15	Books
F June 25	Books

F. DÖRLING

-1986-

FD Dec 2-4	Wertvolle Buecher

SEASON'S SALES

-1987-

FD June 11-13 Wertvolle Buecher

RICHARD C. FRAJOLA INC.

-1986-

fr Nov 15 Autographs

-1987-

fr Mar 14 US & Foreign Postal History
fr May 30 US Postal History

HARRIS AUCTION GALLERIES

-1986-

ha Sept 19 Books
ha Nov 7 Civil War
ha Dec 19 Books

-1987-

ha Mar 13 Books
ha May 22 Books

HARTUNG & KARL

-1986-

HK Nov 4-7 Wertvolle Buecher

-1987-

HK May 12-15 Wertvolle Buecher

HAUSWEDELL & NOLTE

-1986-

HN Nov 26 Wertvolle Buecher

SEASON'S SALES

-1987-

HN May 20-22   Wertvolle Buecher

JOCHEN GRANIER

-1986-

JG Oct 2-4   Autographen, Wertvolle Buecher

-1987-

JG Mar 20-21   Wertvolle Buecher

KANE AUCTIONS

-1986-

K Oct 4   Books
K Dec 13   Books

-1987-

K Mar 22   Books
K June 7   Books

KENNETH HINCE BOOK AUCTIONS

-1987-

kh Mar 16   Books, Maps, Prints

LAWRENCE FINE ART

-1986-

L Dec 11   Valuable Printed Books

-1987-

L July 2   Books, Documents, Maps

SEASON'S SALES

RICHARD E. OINONEN BOOK AUCTIONS

-1986-

O Sept 23	Limited Editions Club, Fore-Edge Paintings
O Oct 21	Americana, Photography
O Nov 18	19th & 20th Century Literature

-1987-

O Jan 6	Art History & Reference
O Feb 24	English & Scottish History
O Mar 24	Natural History
O Apr 28	Children's Books
O May 12	Rare Books, Manuscripts
O June 9	Travel & Exploration
O June 16	Bibliography

SOTHEBY PARKE BERNET INC.

-1986-

P Sept 24	Fine Books & Manuscripts: Dr. Arnold Heertje
P Oct 29	Fine Printed & Manuscript Americana
P Nov 25	Cookery & Gardening
P Dec 15	Fine Books & Manuscripts

-1987-

P May 13	Fine Printed & Manuscript Americana
P June 18	Fine Books & Manuscripts

PHILLIPS, SON & NEALE

-1986-

pn Sept 18	Printed Books
pn Oct 23	Printed Books
pn Dec 11	Autograph Letters & Historical Documents

SEASON'S SALES

-1987-

pn Jan 22	Printed Books
pn Mar 5	Printed Books
pn Mar 26	Chess Library of Michael Macdonald Ross
pn Apr 30	Printed Books
pn May 21	Printed Books
pn June 18	Printed Books
pn July 23	Printed Books

PHILLIPS IN CHESTER

-1987-

pnC Jan 23	Golfing
pnC July 16	Golfing

PHILLIPS IN SCOTLAND

-1986-

pnE Oct 15	Printed Books
pnE Nov 12	Printed Books, Law Books
pnE Dec 17	Good Printed Books

-1987-

pnE Jan 28	Good Printed Books
pnE May 20	Printed Books
pnE June 17	Printed Books

PHILLIPS IN NEW YORK

-1986-

pnNY Sept 13	B. Altman & Co.: Manuscripts, Maps, Rare Books
pnNY Oct 11	Prints & Rare Books
pnNY Dec 10	Maps, Manuscripts

-1987-

pnNY Mar 12	Manuscripts, Books
pnNY Mar 28	Lead Soldiers . . . Sports Memorabilia
pnNY June 11	Books, Autograph Letters

SEASON'S SALES

SOTHEBY'S

-1986-

S Sept 22-23	Printed Books
S Oct 6-7	Printed Books
S Oct 23-24	Topography, Travel
S Nov 10-18	Printed Books
S Nov 20	Fine Oriental Manuscripts
S Nov 27-28	Continental Printed Books
S Dec 2	Western Manuscripts
S Dec 4-5	Illustrated & Children's Books
S Dec 18	English Literature and History

-1987-

S Jan 12-27	Printed Books
S Feb 17	Hebrew Books
S Feb 23-24	Printed Books
S Mar 9-10	Printed Books
S Apr 23-24	Travel, Atlases & Natural History
S Apr 27-28	Magnificent Botanical Books
S May 6-29	Printed Books
S May 21-22	Continental Printed Books, Manuscripts
S May 27	Music, Continental Books & Manuscripts
S May 27	Wolfgang Amadeus Mozart
S June 1	Oriental Manuscripts & Miniatures
S June 17-19	Illustrated & Children's Books
S June 23	Western Manuscripts & Miniatures
S June 25-26	Valuable Printed Books
S June 29	Max Ernst
S July 2	Rene Magritte
S July 13-28	Printed Books

J. A. STARGARDT

-1987-

star Apr 8-9	Autographen

SEASON'S SALES

SWANN GALLERIES, INC.

-1986-

sg **Sept 18**	Americana & Latin America
sg **Sept 25**	Hebraica & Judaica
sg **Oct 2**	Important Bibliographical Reference Library
sg **Oct 9**	Early Printed Books
sg **Oct 23**	Charles B. Wood III Collection of Angling & Shooting
sg **Oct 30**	Marjorie Allen Tranchin Collection of Arthur Rackham
sg **Nov 6**	Autographs
sg **Nov 13**	Photography
sg **Nov 20**	Travel & Exploration
sg **Dec 4**	Rare Books
sg **Dec 11**	Modern Literature
sg **Dec 18**	Military History
sg **Dec 18**	Books with Plates & Engravings

-1987-

sg **Jan 8**	Modern Illustrated & Press Books
sg **Jan 15**	Cookery & Wine
sg **Jan 22**	Books about Books
sg **Feb 5**	Art & Architecture
sg **Feb 12**	Bindings, Literature
sg **Feb 26**	Performing Arts
sg **Mar 5**	Modern Literature
sg **Mar 12**	Americana
sg **Mar 26**	Early Printed Books
sg **Apr 2**	Rare Books
sg **Apr 9**	Autographs
sg **Apr 23**	Travel & Exploration
sg **Apr 30**	Hebraica & Judaica
sg **May 7**	Photography
sg **May 14**	Two Important Reference Libraries
sg **May 21**	Sporting Books
sg **June 4**	Art & Architecture
sg **June 11**	Fine Books
sg **June 18**	American Historical

SEASON'S SALES

SOTHEBY'S MONACO SA

-1986-

SM Oct 20   Livres Anciens et Modernes

-1987-

SM Feb 28   Bibliotheque Marcel Jeanson, Premiere Partie -Chasse

SOTHEBY PARKE BERNET SOUTH AFRICA (PTY) LTD.

-1986-

SSA Oct 28   The Library of the late Professor P.J. van der Merwe

-1987-

SSA Feb 10-11   Collectors' Items and Books

TAVINER'S AUCTION ROOMS

-1986-

T Sept 18	Printed Books
T Oct 15	Modern Literature
T Oct 16	Printed Books
T Nov 20	Printed Books
T Dec 18	Printed Books

-1987-

T Jan 22	Printed Books
T Feb 18	Modern Literature
T Feb 19	Printed Books
T Mar 19	Printed Books & Maps
T Apr 16	Printed Books
T May 20	Modern First Editions
T May 21	Printed Books
T June 18	Printed Books
T July 16	Printed Books

SEASON'S SALES

VENATOR & HANSTEIN

-1986-

VH Sept 12-15	Buecher, Manuskript

WAVERLY AUCTIONS

-1986-

wa Sept 25	Fine Books & Prints
wa Oct 18	Autographs & Manuscripts
wa Nov 6	From the Library of Alice & Warren H. Fraser
wa Dec 11	Fine Books

-1987-

wa Feb 19	Fine Books
wa Mar 5	Fine Books
wa May 30	Fine Books
wa June 25	Fine Books

WILLIAM DOYLE GALLERIES

-1986-

wd Nov 12	Books, Illustrated Works & Autographs

-1987-

wd June 19	Books & Autographs

PART I

Autographs & Manuscripts

A

Abercromby, James, 1st Baron Dunfermline, 1776-1858
[An important collection of more than 2000 letters to Abercromby & his wife, c.1820 to 1867, relating to political activities & family matters, sold at S on 18 Dec 1987, lot 222, for £ 5,000 to Quaritch.]

Adams Family
[A collection of 5 items sgd by or related to the family of John & John Quincy Adams, 1765 to 1891, with an engraved port of J. Q. Adams, sold at P on 29 Oct 1986, lot 25, for $ 550.]

Adams, H. Isobel
Original drawings, tp & 2 illusts for a vol containing the stories of Tom Thumb & Little Red Riding Hood, 1895. In ink. Each initialled; c.205mm by 140mm. Archives of J. M. Dent & Son. S June 19 (732) £260 [Sawyer]

Adams, John, 1735-1826
ALs, 24 Oct 1780. 2 pp, size not stated. To S. C. Johonnot. Requesting that Franklin be Johonnot's guardian in Adams's absence. rf May 30 (1) $1,900
— 8 Mar 1802. 1 p, 4to. To Francis Adrian Van der Kemp. Commenting about his recent "remarks on Jefferson and Buffon." Mtd. P May 13 (26) $2,700
Ls, 24 Aug 1817. 1 p, 4to. To William Bainbridge. Asking that Rufus Davis be compensated for loss of his boat. Also sgd by his son Thomas Boylston & 4 neighbors. P May 13 (27) $1,400
— 8 Aug 1821. 1 p, 4to. To Major J. Worth. Saying he will be happy to receive him with West Point cadets at any time. Autograph salutation. Framed. Altman collection. pnNY Sept 13 (1) $1,600

ADs, 2 Apr 1764. 1 p, 3 by 4.5 inches. Promissory note for 12 shillings; sgd in text. wa May 30 (86) $1,000
— 19 Oct 1788. 1 p, 12mo. Receipt for 21 shillings to Amsa Thomson. Dampstained; laid down. Charlotte Parker Milne collection. wd Nov 12 (25) $450
Ds, 9 Jan 1798. 1 p, folio. Ship's passport for the schooner Variety; partly ptd. Countersgd by Sec of State Pickering. Faded. Framed. P Oct 29 (23) $1,300
— 3 Mar 1798. 1 p, folio. Ship's papers in 4 languages for the schooner Illinois of Philadelphia. Countersgd by Sec of State Timothy Pickering. rf May 30 (2) $1,450
— 9 June 1798. 1 p, folio. Land grant. Countersgd by Timothy Pickering. rf Mar 14 (2) $1,250
Document, 6 Mar 1799. Size not stated. Ptd proclamation that April 25 be observed as day of prayer & thanksgiving. On verso franking signature of Timothy Pickering. Mended with adhesive tape. rf Mar 14 (3) $125
Franking signature, [1796]. Repaired. rf Mar 14 (63) $900

Adams, John Quincy, 1767-1848
ALs, 6 Dec 1830. 3 pp, 4to. To Samuel Southard. Elaborating on his reasons for serving in the House of Representatives. P May 13 (28) $13,000
— 30 June 1834. 1 p, 4to. To Charles P. Curtis & al. Declining to attend a Fourth of July dinner at Boston. P May 13 (29) $1,200
— 17 May 1839. 1 p, 4to. To Edgar S. Van Winkle. Declining to comment on the Presidential question. Framed with a port. P May 13 (30) $1,600
Ds, 6 Aug 1825. 1 p, 4to. Land grant to John Low. wa May 30 (87) $500
— 4 Aug 1827. 1 p, 4to. Land grant to David Wiley. wa May 30 (268) $350

ADAMS

— 19 Sept 1827. 1 p, folio. Grant of land in Ohio to the Bank of the US. pnNY June 11 (2) $425

Franking signature, [1803]. With autograph address. rf Mar 14 (64) $400

— Anr, [Dec 15, n.y.]. As Sec of State. rf Nov 15 (28) $200

— Anr, [16 July 1847]. rf Mar 14 (65) $210

— Anr, [6 Feb n.y.]. rf May 30 (16) $210

Adams, Samuel, Signer from Massachusetts

AL, 26 Mar 1778. 4 pp, 4to. To Elbridge Gerry. Discussing the business of the Massachusetts General Court, the new State Constitution, & the necessity of army discipline. Repaired. P Oct 29 (24) $850

Ds, 8 Dec 1794. 1 p, folio. As Gov. of Massachusetts, affirming Samuel Barrett is a Justice of the Peace. rf Nov 15 (1) $280

— 21 Dec 1795. 1 p, folio. Commission for Capt. Bailey Hall. Charlotte Parker Milne collection. wd Nov 12 (26) $225

Adelaide, Queen of William IV of England, 1792-1849

A Ls s (2), [16 Apr 1829] & [n.d.]. 6 pp, 8vo. To Luise von Parry. Regarding visits. Sgd Adelheid. In German. star Apr 9 (999) DM220

Adelung, Friedrich, 1768-1843

ALs, 16 Jan 1793. 1 p, 4to. To his uncle. Reporting about his work in the Vaticana & about riots in Rome. HK Nov 7 (2160) DM500

Adenauer, Konrad, 1876-1967

Photograph, sgd, [1962]. Postcard size. With covering letter of the Chancellor's Office, 27 July 1962. star Apr 9 (878) DM540

Adler, Alfred, 1870-1937

Series of 6 A Ls s (5 on field postcards), 1913 to 1916. 9 pp, 4to & 8vo. To Dr. Karl Grosz. Concerning pbd work on the use of psychotherapy in treating schizophrenia, etc. S Jan 27 (958) £720 [Maggs]

Afghan War, First

— MACKESON, FREDERICK. - Collection of 15 A Ls s & Ls, 7 June to 22 Oct 1842. 51 pp, various sizes. To Gen. [George] Pollock & Capt. R. Shakespear, & Capt. Lawrence (1). About the preparations for the invasion of Afghanistan & the rescue of captives. Modern cloth bdg. C June 24 (84) £520 [Burgess Browning]

AMERICAN BOOK PRICES CURRENT

Agassiz, Louis, 1807-73

ALs, 6 Sept 1855. 2 pp, 8vo. To John van Lansing Pruyn. Reporting that he has received a sufficient number of subscriptions for a new work. In English. star Apr 8 (298) DM240

Agnew, Spiro T.

Ds, 20 June 1966. 5 pp, 4to. As Baltimore County Executive, contract for road repairs. pnNY June 11 (67) $100

Albert, 1819-61, Prince Consort of Victoria of England

ALs, 30 Oct 1846. 2 pp, 4to. To William Howley, Archbishop of Canterbury. Pledging a donation to a fund. C Dec 3 (207) £150 [Maggs]

Albert, Eugen d', 1864-1932

Collection of ALs & autograph postcard, sgd, 12 Aug 1911 & 21 Nov 1915. 1 p, 4to, & card. To Ludwig Strecker. Regarding corrections for his concert in A major. Requesting a copy of a libretto. star Apr 9 (559) DM220

ALs, 3 May 1913. 1 p, 4to. To Paul Bekker. Expressing his reluctance to give concerts for the Museumsgesellschaft at Frankfurt. star Apr 9 (560) DM240

Albertus Magnus

Ms, Traite de Fauconnerie. [Southwestern France, c.1400] 49 leaves, vellum, 200mm by 145mm, in mor janseniste by Thibaron Jeanson Ms 113 SM Feb 28 (11) FF85,000

Albrecht, Prince of Prussia, 1837-1906

Autograph telegram, [Dec 1891]. 1 p, 4to. To an aide-de-camp at Potsdam. Draft, requesting that the Emperor be notified of his departure to Lisbon. In pencil. With related material. star Apr 9 (957) DM200

Albrecht V, Herzog von Bayern, 1528-79

Document, 15 Apr 1551. 1 p, folio. Vellum. Letter of investiture for Marthan Eckher. star Apr 9 (883) DM780

Alen, Luke. See: West Indies

Alexander II, Emperor of Russia, 1818-81

ALs, 7/19 Sept 1856. 2 pp, 8vo. To Princess Carl von Preussen. Thanking for congratulations on his coronation. star Apr 9 (1228) DM420

Alexander IV, Pope, d.1261

Document, [10 May] 1255. 1 p, 22.5cm by 28cm. Vellum. Confirmation of the privileges of the Benedictine abbey of St. Michael's at Hildesheim. Lead seal. star Apr 9 (1110) DM6,500

Alexander VI, Pope
Letter, 9 Oct 1499. 1 p, 350mm by 123mm. Vellum. To King Louis XII of France. About an appeal for papal protection by the mayor & citizens of Sens. Unsgd; countersgd L. Podocatharus. C Dec 3 (208) £250 [Maggs]

Alfieri, Vittorio, 1749-1803
Collection of AN & ANs, [c.23 July 1783] & 2 Sept 1790. 2 pp, 8vo & 4to. To Count Wiltzach. In 3d person, thanking for loan of a book & sending 2 copies of his Tragedies. To M. Martin, about the rent for a house. In French. C Dec 3 (389) £220 [L'Autographe]

Alfonso the Wise, King of Castile & Leon, 1221-84
— FORGERY. - Ds, 24 Oct 1295 [sic; presumably late medieval]; 1 p, 558mm by 532mm. Vellum. Letters patent confirming a charter of his father Ferdinand III, defining boundaries between Roa & Coriel. With decorative roundels & leaden bulla. Various inconsistencies in dating. C Dec 3 (210) £900 [Gwara]

Alfonso V, King of Aragon & Sicily, 1396-1458
Ds, 26 May 1428. 1 p, 288mm by 157mm. Appointment of Juan Masquessa as deputy governor of Valencia. Several tears. C Dec 3 (209) £160 [De Lucas]

Alice, Princess of Monaco
Series of 31 A Ls s, 1914 to 1925. Size not stated. To her son Armand, Duc de Richelieu. Contents not stated. Sgd Mother. With related material. sg Nov 6 (2) $350

Allan, Anthony Pierce
Autograph Ms, series of journals of voyages between 1826 & 1846, including visits to Australia & Southern Africa, bound in 5 vols. About 800 pp, 4to, in half lea, 2 vols covered in sailcloth. With orig drawings, sketch maps, newspaper cuttings & ptd ephemera. S Oct 23 (314) £9,500 [Perrin]

Allard, Geoffrey, 1912-41. See: World War II

Allston, Washington, 1779-1843
ALs, 30 Sept 1838. 3 pp, 4to. To his mother. About her recovery & his illness; family letter. Fold splits. wa Oct 18 (66) $160

Almanacs
Ms, Almanach curieux et instructif pour l'annee 1758 dedie et presente a monseur Thiery par son tres humble et tres obeissant serviteur et fils Thiery. 44 pp, 8vo, in contemp mor gilt with arms of Thiery de Sainte-Colombe C Dec 3 (75) £3,400 [Quaritch]
— Ms, Amusing French Almanack, [18th cent]. 18 pp, folio. Sewed. Containing comical stories, etc. sg Nov 6 (9) $50
— SEARLE, GEORGE. - Autograph Ms, sgd, A Pack of Cards Turned into an Almanack; Feb 1789. 16 pp, 12mo. Self-wraps; unsewn. Witty description of the meaning of each card. sg Nov 6 (25) $50

Alpenny, J. S.
Original drawing, 3 men with seaman's chest on a rocky shore, sgd & dated 1827. 542mm by 388mm. Identified on verso as scene from Walter Scott's The Pirate. Framed. S Dec 5 (423) £160 [Henderson]

Altenberg, Peter, 1859-1919
Autograph Ms, "La rampa. (Sizilianische Szene)"; [n.d.]. 3 pp, 4to. Ptd port & signature in facsimile at head. star Apr 8 (3) DM530
— Autograph Ms, "Tagebuch einer Mizi", [n.d.]. 1 p, 4to. On hotel letterhead. On verso list of groceries, crossed out. star Apr 8 (2) DM550
Series of 6 A Ls s, 1 June 1918 & [n.d.]. 8 pp, 4to. To an unnamed physician. Mostly relating to his health problems. S Nov 27 (299) £300 [Haas]
ALs, [n.d.] 2 pp, 4to. To the "Internationale Sammlerzeitung". Regarding his collection of picture postcards. star Apr 8 (5) DM580
Lithographed port, handcolored; by Berthold Loeffler. Sgd by Altenberg & dated 9 Mar 1909. In commemorative card issued on his 50th birthday, 4 pp, 35cm by 29cm. star Apr 8 (4) DM950

American Revolution
[A collection of 18 autographs by Signers of the Declaration of Independence & other major figures of the American Revolution sold at P on 13 May 1987, lot 124, for $9,000.]
[A collection of 10 items relating to the Revolutionary War sold at rf on 14 Mar 1987, lot 56, for $400.]
Ms, Orderly book from the headquarters of Sir William Howe during the New York campaign, 5 Aug to 25 Sept 1776. 78 pp, 185mm by 110mm. Modern limp mor; 1 leaf detached. Daily details of General Orders, court martials, etc. With typed transcript. Bullock collection. CNY Dec 19 (216) $18,000
— Ms, record book of pay received 30 Dec 1776 to 6 Jan 1777. 9 pp, 8vo. Unbound. Sgd by Capt Barnardus Swartwout & men of his New York regiment. sg Nov 6 (318) $200
ADs, 16 Oct 1776. 1 p, 8vo. Receipt for 207 gallons of rum for the US Army. Sgd Sam Phillips. sg Nov 6 (6) $100
Ds, 25 Jan 1778. 1 p, 8vo. Permit for Ebbert

AMERICAN REVOLUTION

Willett "to pass the Lines this Day to Phillips's Manner". Sgd by [Zebediah?] Jones. Partly ptd; bottom edge indenture-cut. sg Nov 6 (321) $225

— 26 June 1778. Size not given. Proceedings by the State of New Jersey against John Druler for joining the British Army. Sgd by 17 Justices of the Peace of Cumberland County. sg Nov 6 (304) $200

— ATLEE, SAMUEL JOHN. - ALs, 15 Dec 1779. 1 p, 8vo. To John Gibson, Commissioner of the Treasury. About his inability "to pay the debts contracted for my subsistence whilst in the Hands of the Enemy." With related material. sg Nov 6 (313) $70

— CONTINENTAL CURRENCY. - 4 Ds s, 7 Dec 1775 to 14 Aug 1776; 24mo. Woodcuts, partly ptd; various denominations. Sgd by officials of the Maryland Conventions. Worn. sg Nov 6 (254) $60

— DUPLESSIS-PARSCAU, COUNT. - ALs, 26 Nov 1781. 2 pp, 4to. To the Chevalier de Monteil. Reporting about the joy of the French Court at the news of the English surrender which he brought to Versailles with the Duc de Lauzun. S Dec 18 (339) £650 [Joseph & Sawyer]

— HOPEWELL MILITARY ASSOCIATION, CUMBERLAND COUNTY, NEW JERSEY. - Ds, May 1775. 2 pp, folio. Resolution to form "a well Disciplined Militia" to defend the freedom of the country. 7 signatures. Repaired. sg Nov 6 (305) $700

— MILES, COL. - Transcript, extract of a letter to Col. Hughes, 22 Oct 1781. 1 p, 8vo. About the surrender of Cornwallis. rf Mar 14 (10) $80

— WILLMOT, GEORGE. - Ds, 14 May 1783, receipt for payment received from Timothy Pickering for transporting "a public Ox Cart from West Point to Newburgh". S Jan 27 (921) £120 [Middleton]

— WYLLYS, GEORGE. - ADs, 18 Dec 1776. 1 p, folio. As Sec of the Gen Assembly & Company of the State of Connecticut; copy of a resolution that the Governor be allowed to draw £ 10,000 on the Treasury in compliance with a request by Washington. sg Nov 6 (252) $325

See also: Duportail, Louis Le Begue de Presle
See also: Napoleonic Wars

Amherst, Jeffrey Amherst, Baron, 1717-97

ALs, [n.d.]. 2 pp, 4to. To Lord Dover. About reprimanding Cornet Rainsford. S Jan 27 (923) £120 [Barnes]

Ls, 31 May 1762. 1 p, folio. To Donald Campbell. Encouraging him to enlist new volunteers. wa May 30 (321) $260

AMERICAN BOOK PRICES CURRENT

Amherst, John, 1718?-78

ALs, 7 Dec 1759. 2 pp, folio. To his brother Jeffrey. Reporting about events in England since his return from Quebec. S Jan 27 (924) £70 [Faupel]

Amici, Giovanni Battista, 1786-1863

ALs, 12 Apr 1841. 1 p, 4to. To Prince Dolgorowsky. Regarding the purchase of a microscope. sg Apr 9 (9) $100

Andersen, Hans Christian, 1805-75

Autograph Ms, story, Den sidste Perle, c.1854. 3 pp, folio. Some revisions. Sgd. With note of authenticity by Arthur Abrahams. S Nov 27 (300) £4,200 [Joseph & Sawyer]

Autograph sentiment, Dec 1853. 13 lines, inscription, sgd; in verse. On verso tp of his Gesammelte Werke, vol. 1, Leipzig 1853, 16.5cm by 10cm. Margins cut. JG Oct 2 (3) DM500

Anderson, Sherwood, 1876-1941

Collection of Ns & photograph, sgd. 2 Dec 1931 & [n.d.]. 1 p, 4to, & size not stated. Recipient unnamed. Saying a photograph may be obtained from his pbr Liveright. Photograph sgd on mount. wa May 30 (328) $400

Anhalt-Dessau, Leopold I, Fuerst von, 1676-1747 ("Der alte Dessauer")

Ls, 4 Aug 1728. 3 pp, folio. To Christoph Franz von Hutten-Stolzenberg, Bishop of Wuerzburg. Pressuring him for permission to recruit soldiers in his territory for the Prussian army. star Apr 9 (879) DM850

Anjou, Rene I, Duc d', 1409-80

Ms, L'Abuze en Court. [Northern France, 2d half of 15th cent]. Attributed to Rene d'Anjou on uncertain authority. Bound with Ms of Georges Chastellain, Le Temple de Boccace. Together 118 leaves (2 blank), 264mm by 188mm. 18th-cent calf bdg. Written in 2 distinct parts in brown ink in a lettre batarde. With initials throughout in red. S June 23 (85) £8,000 [Thomas]

Ls, 9 Aug 1453. 1 p, 210mm by 162mm. To Angelo Acciaiolo. Enclosing a copy of a letter to the Duke of Milan (not present). C June 24 (71) £320 [Pryor]

Anne, Queen of James I of England, 1574-1619

Document, 20 June 1614. 1 p, 600mm by 570mm; vellum. Confirming Sir Alexander Hay in his estates at Naetoun. Stamp signatures of Anne & James. With copy of orig wax seal. sg Nov 6 (10) $350

Anne, Queen of England, 1665-1714

Ds, 5 Dec 1710. 1 p, 350mm by 410mm. Appointment for Ellis Cooper as Major in Lord Montjoy's regiment of foot. Countersgd by Lord Dartmouth. C June 24 (14) £220 [Wilson]

— 8 Dec 1710. 1 p, folio. Ordering that Major Leigh be paid for bringing an express from the Duke of Marlborough. Countersgd by Robert Harley & others. S Dec 18 (211) £450 [Kemp]

— 10 July 1713. 1 p, folio. Warrant ordering Robert, Earl of Oxford & Earl Mortimer, High Treasurer, to pay £10,000 for "Expences of Our Stables". C Dec 3 (211) £350 [Bristow]

Anne of Denmark. See: Anne, 1574-1619

Antarctica

— ORDE-LEES, T. - Autograph Ms, journal of Shackleton's expedition, 24 Mar 1915 to 16 Apr 1916. Reporting the loss of the Endurance, etc. Including typewritten continuation concerning the period on Elephant Island. In all c.370 pp, folio. In ink & pencil; revised for possible publication. Spine worn. S Dec 18 (271) £6,200 [Quaritch]

— WILSON, EDWARD ADRIAN. - Orig drawing, Discovery in Winterquarters, McMurdo Strait, 1903. 190mm by 250mm. In pencil. Framed. pn Dec 11 (121) £360 [Buckell & Ballard]

Anthology

Ms, 17th-cent verse miscellany. [c.1667-68] About 260 pp, 8vo, in contemp calf. Comprising nearly 250 poems by Donne, Signey, raleigh, carew, Jonson, Shirley, Waller, Cleveland & many others from c.1580 to 1668. bba Apr 9 (272) £4,000 [Quaritch]

— Ms, The Boke off Marschalse & 7 other medical, culinary & herbal works [North of England?, c.1440 - 1480]. 239 pp, 1 blank; paper with 6 vellum leaves. 1 vol, def contemp calf bdg, 210mm by 140mm. Dampstained. In English & Latin in several 15th cent hands. C Dec 3 (349) £15,000 [Griffiths]

Anthony, Susan B., 1820-1906

ALs, [c.1856]. 2 pp, 8vo. To Mrs. Nichols. About John Brown's insurrection in Kansas. sg Nov 6 (231) $600

Signature, 21 Oct 1900. On card; size not stated. wa May 30 (449) $100

Antiphoner

Ms, Antiphonale Romanum iuxta Breviarium Sacrosancti Concilii Tridentini restitutum. [France, 16th cent]. 178 leaves [& 10 blanks], 268mm by 182mm. In brown & red ink; 9 red 4-line staves per p. Late 16th cent green mor gilt; monogram of Isabella Clara Eugenia, daughter of King Philipp II of Spain. With decorated borders & 10 illuminated miniatures on vellum, taken from an older book of hours [Paris, c.1490] & mtd on paper Ms. FD Dec 2 (1) DM62,000

— Ms, Antiphoner and Hymnal, [Germany, late 15th cent]. 271 leaves & various half-leaves, 187mm by 133mm. Modern marbled bds, with spine made from 15th cent Antiphonal Ms in vellum. In brown ink in a gothic hand; music in black neumes, Hufnagelschrift, on a 5-line brown stave. With calligraphic initials in brown infilled in red & painted initials in red throughout, 6 large or illuminated initials cut from other Mss & very many additions in later hands, including some polyphonic music. S Dec 2 (51) £1,200 [McKittrick]

— Ms, Antiphoner. [Italy, 14th cent]. Of Franciscan Use. 364 leaves, vellum, 408mm by 282mm. 19th-cent blindstamped calf with clasps & catches. With 10 lines each of text in a rounded gothic hand & of music on a 4-line red stave. With decorated initials throughout & c.86 very large initials in red & blue with penwork, 1 partly in gold, 1 in full colors. S June 23 (128) £6,500 [Marcus]

— Ms, Antiphoner. [North central Spain, 1598]. 166 leaves, vellum, 153mm by 107mm. Contemp dark brown lea over wooden bds, stamped. In dark brown ink in a rounded gothic hand in 2 sizes. With 22 very large initials with partial or full borders. Written for the Carthusian Abbey of Paular. S June 23 (127) £3,500 [Perceval]

— Ms, [Central Italy, late 13th cent]. 1 leaf only, vellum, 520mm by 357mm. With 7 lines each of text in a rounded gothic hand & music on a 4 line red stave. With large historiated initial. S June 23 (9) £1,200 [Maggs]

— Ms, portable Antiphoner, [Italy, 17th cent]. Of Dominican Use. 46 leaves, vellum, & 4 paper flyleaves. Contemp calf gilt, worn. In dark brown ink in several sizes of a neat roman hand in imitation of ptd type. With 4 lines of music on each page in black neumes on a 4-line stave. Containing only opening words & first notes of each antiphon. S Dec 2 (53) £260 [McKittrick]

— Ms, [Spain, 1616]. 107 leaves, vellum, 483mm by 350mm. Light brown sheepskin over wooden bds with metal fittings. In brown & red ink. With initials in red or

ANTIPHONER

black & large illuminated initial on f.1. FD June 11 (1) DM22,000

Antoninus Florentinus, Saint, 1389-1459
Ms, Summa confessionalis, [Italy, 1478]. 140 leaves (1 blank), 215mm by 145mm. In light brown ink in a neat gothic bookhand, written by Antonius de Capitalibus at the Monastery of St. Honoferi. Spaces for initials left blank. Contemp wooden bds. C June 24 (256) £2,600 [Maggs]
— Ms, Tractatus de Censuris Ecclesiasticis. [Italy, mid-15th cent]. 124 leaves (3 blank), vellum, 146mm by 96mm. 19th-cent French mor gilt. In dark brown ink in a small gothic bookhand. With painted initials throughout in red. S June 23 (84) £2,000 [Thomas]

Arabic & Persian Manuscripts
Ms, Book of Prayers. [Persia, A.H.1196/A.D.1781-82]. 10 calligraphic panels in concertina form, 6 leaves & 2 flyleaves, 254mm by 171mm. Brown mor bdg. In naskhi script by Muhammad 'Ali Tabrizi for Mirza 'Abbas Khan. On buff, pink & beige ground, with gold scrolling floral pattern between gold margins & heading in red naskhi script within illuminated cartouche. C June 16 (102) £750
— Ms, Tafsir. [India, 16th cent]. 477 leaves, 279mm by 171mm. Brown mor with stamped medallions. In bihari script, with the word Allah picked in red throughout & 3 double pp of illumination. Lacking last leaf. Repaired. S Nov 20 (381) £400

Arabic & Turkish Manuscripts
Ms, Sharh Qasidah Imru'l-Qays. [Ottoman, A.H.1173/A.D.1759]. 68 leaves, 215mm by 120mm. Contemp maroon mor tooled in gold. In naskhi script by Sulayman al-Mawdavi. With illuminated headpiece. S June 1 (148) £110 [Maggs]

Arabic Manuscripts
Ms, Al-Awrad al-Saba. [Ottoman, A.H.926/A.D.1519]. 76 leaves, 232mm by 157mm. Dark maroon mor with gilt lea onlay. In bold & small naskhi script in black & blue. With double page of illumination. S June 1 (137) £400 [Kanoo]
— Ms, Al-Futuhat al-Ilahiya fi Ahadith Khayr al-Bariyah (Hadith). [North Africa, 19th cent]. 198 leaves, 305mm by 210mm. Contemp red mor gilt. In maghribi script. With headings in gold on illuminated panels. Wormed; leaves detached. S Nov 20 (406) £1,000
— Ms, Al-Sahifah al-Sajjadiyah. [Persia, A.H.1124/A.D.1711]. 189 leaves, 206mm by 131mm. Contemp lacquer bdg, re-backed. In naskhi script by Ibn Ali Muhammad Ghulamali. With interlinear Persian trans in red & double page of illumination. Few leaves loose. S Nov 20 (391) £280
— Ms, Al-Sami fi al-Asami. [Konya, A.H.822/A.D.1419]. 104 leaves, 281mm by 180mm. Contemp brown mor tooled in blind. In naskhi script by Mahmud bin Mu'min al-Qunuvi. S June 1 (133) £2,600 [Lake]
— Ms, Al-Tafsir fi taqasim al-amrad wa 'alamatiha wa 'ilajatiha, parts 1 & 2. [Near East, 15th cent]. 118 leaves & 4 flyleaves, 273mm by 210mm. Later bds. In maghribi script. C June 16 (51) £380
— Ms, document of authority concerning a commercial transaction, [Egypt?, c.900]. 1 leaf, papyrus, 410mm by 180mm; written on both sides. In cursive script. Frayed. S June 1 (60) £260 [Lari]
— Ms, Firman of Sultan Mustafa IV. Constantinople, A.H.1222/A.D.1807. 169cm by 76cm. In divani kirmasi script with large tughra in gold within illuminated triangle. Paper scattered with powdered gold leaf. Some repairs. S Nov 20 (247) £10,000
— Ms, Firman of Sultan Mahmud II. Constantinople, A.H.1224/A.D.1809. 75cm by 53cm. In divani kirmasi script with tughra in gold within illuminated triangle. Text interspersed with gold discs. S Nov 20 (248) £2,000
— Ms, Hilyat al-Awliya' (Hadith). [Cairo, A.H.708/A.D.1308]. In maghribi script. Last 2 vols only; 110 leaves, 262mm by 174mm. Red mor tooled in blind, repaired. Ordered by the vizir of the Sultan. S Nov 20 (365) £2,200
— Ms, 'Ilm al-hai'ah. [Herat, A.H.802/A.D.1399-1400]. 164 leaves & flyleaf, 222mm by 145mm. Brown mor bdg. In naskhi & nasta'liq script in several hands. Some leaves detached & copied later. C June 16 (44) £380
— Ms, Kitab al-Wasayit fi al-Munharafat wa al-Basayit. [Levant, probably Syria, A.H.1129/A.D.1716]. 54 leaves, 210mm by 145mm. Patterned bds. In naskhi script by Muhammad bin Khizr. S Nov 20 (398) £260
— Ms, legend of Joseph & Jacob, [13th - 17th cent]. 71 leaves, 18cm by 13cm. In naskhi script in several hands. Lacking bdg. From the Convent of St. Catherine on Mount Sinai. FD June 11 (35) DM15,000
— Ms, list of the dead of the Convent of St. Catherine on Mount Sinai, [17th cent]. 24 leaves, 17.5cm by 11.5cm. In black ink on waxed paper. In wrap, 10th cent Greek vellum Ms, 24.5cm by 18cm. FD June 11 (37) DM16,000
— Ms, Nauruznameh. [Ottoman, A.H.1221/A.D.1806-07]. Scroll, 129.6cm by 10.9cm. In black & red naskhi script by

Suleiman Hikmati. With illuminated heading & headings in gold on red. C June 16 (55) £300
- Ms, Nauruznameh. [Ottoman, A.H.1279/A.D.1862-63]. Scroll, 78cm by 10.2cm. In black & red naskhi script by al-Sayyid Muhammad, known as Hikmati. With illuminated heading & headings in gold on blue. C June 16 (56) £480
- Ms, notes of daily transactions, [Egypt?, c.900]. 1 leaf, papyrus, 410mm by 115mm; written on both sides. In cursive script. Frayed. S June 1 (61) £220 [Seibu]
- Ms, notes of daily transactions, [Egypt?, c.900]. 1 leaf, papyrus, 450mm by 165mm; written on both sides. In cursive script. Frayed. S June 1 (62) £900 [Khalili]
- Ms, Prayer Book, including the Martyrs of Badr. [North Africa, early 19th cent]. 113 leaves, 103mm by 80mm. Contemp red mor tooled in gold; flap detached. In maghribi script. With headings in gold on illuminated panels. S Nov 20 (403) £300
- Ms, Prayer Book. [Qajar, 19th cent]. 24 leaves, 95mm by 58mm. Black mor with stamped panels of gilt lea onlay. In small naskhi script in gold on blue-colored paper. With illuminated headpiece. S Nov 20 (405) £650
- Ms, Prayer Scroll. [Qajar, late 19th cent]; c.440cm, width not stated. In naskhi script with interlinear Persian trans. Illuminated headpiece. Top section probably later replacement. S Nov 20 (253) £400
- Ms, Prayers. [Qajar, 19th cent]. 119 leaves, 155mm by 95mm. Contemp lacquer bdg. In naskhi script. With illuminated headpiece. S June 1 (157) £120 [Kanoo]
- Ms, The Book of The Honorable Law and of The Shining Lamp [Homs, Northern Syria, 4 Jan 1855]. Contemp tooled red calf over wooden bds. In naskhi script by Costantin bin al-Khouri Dawud al-Homsi. With 28 carpet pages in colors & burnished gold & 16 full-page miniatures. S June 23 (134) £5,500 [Franklin]
- Ms, treatise on medicine. [North Africa, 17th cent]. 40 leaves, 210mm by 150mm. Loose patterned paper bds. In maghribi script. S June 1 (140) £190 [Quaritch]
- ABDUL-WAHAB AL-SHA'RAWI. - Al-Mizan al-Sha'raniyah. [Levant, A.H.1086/A.D.1675]. 208 leaves, 295mm by 205mm. Modern buckram bdg. In cursive script. S June 1 (143) £220 [Maggs]
- ABU MA'SHAR JA'FAR BIN MUHAMMAD RABI'. - Al-Nukat fi 'alm Ahkam al-Nujum. [Anatolia or Iraq, 13th cent]. In naskhi script. With illuminated panel on tp. 105 leaves, 239mm by 160mm. 19th cent black mor. Some repairs. S Nov 20 (360) £6,000
- ABU MUHAMMAD AL-HUSAIN BIN MASUD BAGHARI. - Kitab Mishkwat al-Masabih. [Turkey, A.H.1156/A.D.1743]. 343 leaves plus 2 flyleaves, 184mm by 127mm. Brown mor gilt. In naskhi script by Ahmad bin Khalil bin Mustafa. With principal words in red & marginal annotations. C Nov 21 (112) £400
- ABU'L-BAYAN BANNA AL-QARSHI. - Kitab al-Adhkar wa Sharhahu. [Damascus?, 15th cent]. 170 leaves & 2 flyleaves, 254mm by 184mm. Bds. In naskhi script. Some leaves repaired. C June 16 (98) £380
- ABUL-HASAN ALI BIN AHMAD AL-WAHIDI. - Tafsir al-Wajiz. [Mamluk, Egypt or Syria, A H 878/A D 1473] 536 leaves, 348mm by 250mm. Brown mor covered with green paper. In naskhi script by Muhammad bin Muhammad al-Halabi. S June 1 (135) £500 [Kanoo]
- AL-BUSIRI. - Al-Kawakib al-Durriyah fi Madhi Khayr al-Barriyah. [Aleppo, A.H.789/A.D.1378]. 29 leaves, 257mm by 172mm. Brown mor, lacking lower cover. In muhaqqaq, naskhi & thuluth scripts by Abdullah bin Yunis bin Ghanim bin Yahya, with dedication to the Royal Treasury & full page of illumination. Repaired. S Nov 20 (366) £600
- AL-BUSIRI. - Al-Kawakib al-Durriyah fi Madhi Khayr al-Barriyah. [Mamluk, 15th cent]. 28 leaves, 230mm by 150mm; imperfect at end. Contemp brown mor tooled in blind. In large & smaller naskhi script. With 1 page of illumination. Repaired. S Nov 20 (367) £1,100
- AL-JAZULI. - Dala'il al-Khayrat. [North Africa, 18th cent]. 212 leaves, 115mm by 106mm. Contemp red mor tooled in gilt. In maghribi script. With significant words picked out in gold, headings in gold on illuminated panels & numerous illuminated diagrams. S Nov 20 (397) £1,700
- AL-JAZULI. - Dala'il al-Khayrat. [Ottoman, A.H.1213/A.D.1798]. 106 leaves, 168mm by 110mm. Contemp red mor, stamped; rebacked. In naskhi script by Ahmad, known as Khulusi. With 2 illuminated headpieces & double-page drawing of Mecca & Medina. Wormed. S Nov 20 (400) £450
- AL-SUYUTI. - Tarikh al-Khulafa. [Zaghwan, North Africa, A.H.1068/A.D.1657]. 290 leaves, 203mm by 145mm. Brown mor bdg with stamped lea onlay. In maghribi script by Muhammad ibn Ramazan al-Aluwini al-Zaghwani. Crude repairs. S June 1 (142) £550 [Maggs]
- HAFIZ MAHMUD AL-WARDARI. - Kitab fi'ilm al-Qur'an. Tartib-i-Ziba. [Ottoman, 19th cent]. 94 leaves & 3 flyleaves, 273mm by 165mm. Contemp brown mor gilt bdg. In black & red naskhi script by al-Sayyid

ARABIC MANUSCRIPTS

Khalil bin 'Umar al-Qaisari. With 2 half-page illuminated headings. Introduction & notes in Turkish. C June 16 (96) £900
— IBRAHIM BIN MUHAMMAD BIN IBRAHIM AL-HALABI. - Multaqa al-Abhur. [Ottoman, A.H.1044/A.D.1634]. 170 leaves, 162mm by 100mm. Contemp red mor with gilt lea onlay. In nasta'liq script by Abdul Qadir bin Ahmad bin Ramadan known as Sari Naib. With illuminated headpiece. S June 1 (141) £300 [Buxton]
— IBRAHIM HAKKI. - Ma'rifat Namah. [Ottoman, A.H.1251/A.D.1835]. 326 leaves plus 3 flyleaves, 22.2cm by 14cm. Contemp brown mor gilt. In naskhi script by al-Hajj Muhammad Sharif bin Muhammad Ibrahim bin Mustafa bin Ahmad. With headings in white on gold within illuminated cartouche, numerous colored diagrams & tables, & 4 half-page illuminated headings. C Nov 21 (51) £1,050
— JAMSHID BIN MAS'UD BIN MUHAMMAD BIN MAHMUD AL-TABIB AL-KASHI. - Nuzhat al-Hada'iq, & 2 other treatises. [Persia or Levant, A.H.907/A.D.1501]. 47 leaves, 215mm by 132mm. Gold-splattered colored bds. In nasta'liq script, with numerous tables & diagrams. Loose. S Nov 20 (382) £1,200
— KAMAL AD-DIN BADI AZ-ZAMAN. - Kifajat at-tibb. [Persia, c.1800]. 228 leaves, c.305mm by 220mm. Contemp blind-stamped lea, worn. In naskhi script in black & red ink. Lacking some leaves. HK Nov 4 (438) DM5,000
— MUHAMMAD BIN AHMAD AL-KHAFRI. - Al-Takmila fi Sharh al-Tadhkira. [Ottoman, A.H.1027/A.D.1618]. 202 leaves & flyleaf, 215mm by 145mm. Red mor bdg. In naskhi script with annotations in nasta'liq. C June 16 (45) £260
— MUHAMMAD BIN MUHAMMAD AL-LAWALLAWI AL-AFSHANJI. - Haqaiq al-Manduma. [Buthara, A.H.666/A.D.1267-68]. 259 leaves plus 3 flyleaves, 28.5cm by 17cm. Brown lea bdg, stamped; repaired. In naskhi script; holograph copy. C Nov 21 (50) £2,800
— MUHAMMAD BIN MUHAMMAD BIN MAHMUD AL-BUKHARI. - ?Fasl al-Kitab. [Near East, A.H.883/A.D.1478]. 400 leaves & flyleaf, 274mm by 165mm. Brown mor bdg. In naskhi script by Shams al-Din Muhammad bin Ahmad bin 'Abd ul-'Aziz. C June 16 (97) £380
— MUHAMMAD IBN MUHAMMAD AL-QAZWINI. - Kitab 'Aja'ib al-Makhluqat. [Mamluk, A.H.790/A.D.1388]. 167 leaves & 2 flyleaves, 260mm by 178mm. Later brown mor bdg. In naskhi script. With illuminated tp. C June 16 (47) £450
— QADI 'ADUD AL-DAULA. - Usul al-Fiqh.

AMERICAN BOOK PRICES CURRENT

[Eastern Anatolia, A.H.833/A.D.1430]. 176 leaves & flyleaf, 244mm by 145mm. Later brown mor bdg, worn. In naskhi script. C June 16 (53) £400
— SA'D AL-DIN TAFTAZANI. - Sharh al-Kashshaf. [Tabriz, A.H.784/A.D.1382]. 303 leaves & 3 flyleaves, 273mm by 165mm. Brown mor bdg. In naskhi script by Ishaq bin Mas'ud bin Ahmad bin Muhammad al Naushabadi. C June 16 (100) £750
— SHAIKH SA'DULLAH AL-KHILWATI. - Qasidah al-Burdah. [Ottoman, A.H.1157/A.D.1744-45]. 51 leaves, 203mm by 140mm. Brown mor gilt, spine rebound. In naskhi script with marginal versified Turkish trans, 14 archaistic miniatures & opening page with illuminated heading. Possibly holograph. C Nov 21 (111) £140

Ardizzone, Edward, 1900-79
[A complete set of proofs of the lithographed illusts for Great Expectations, 1939, each handcolored & sgd; mtd together in 1 frame, sold at S on June 19, 1987, lot 628, for £1,000 to Contemporary.]
Original drawings, 11 ink illusts for David Copperfield, 1955. Each 292mm by 194mm, with caption & directions for block maker in pencil. S Dec 5 (421) £2,300 [Beetles]
— Original drawings, (22), to illus Maurice Gorham's Londoners, 1951. In ink. 288mm by 388mm & 288mm by 197mm. 3 drawings with rejected designs on backs. S June 19 (629) £9,000 [Contemporary]
— Original drawings, complete set of 16 drawings to illus John Buchan's The Thirty Nine Steps, 1965. Mostly in ink. 290mm by 197mm. With related material. Archives of J. M. Dent & Son. S June 19 (734) £5,800 [Brown]
— Original drawings, complete set of 13 ink drawings to illus John Symonds's The Stuffed Dog, 1967. 200mm by 270mm. Captioned in pencil. With related material. Archives of J. M. Dent & Son. S June 19 (735) £3,200 [Sealhouse]
Original drawing, 2 men running down mountain path. 294mm by 212mm. Ink & wash; initialled. Preparatory drawing for illus in Bunyan's Pilgrim's Progress, 1947. Framed. S Dec 5 (422) £250 [Beetles]

Arens, Hanns, 1901-83
[A collection of c.400 letters & cards addressed to Arens, 1943 to c.1970, by a large number of German authors, with related material, sold at star on 8 Apr 1987, lot 11, for DM10,500.]
[A collection of 53 portraits, mostly photographs, sgd, presented to Arens by German authors, artists & politicians, partly inscr, c.1950 to 1970, sold at star on 8 Apr 1987, lot 12, for DM2,800.]

Aristotle
Ms, Disputationes, commentaries to 6 of his works, 1650-52. 625 & 582 pp, 270mm by 164mm. Blindstamped pigskin over wooden bds with 2 clasps; lacking 1 clasp. In Latin. HK Nov 4 (401) DM750
— Ms, Organon. De anima. [Paris, c.1300]. 182 leaves, vellum; 290mm by 200mm. Vellum over wooden bds, slightly def. Written in small gothic script in 2 hands. With numerous initials in red & blue, partly gilt, 26 large initials with floral borders, sometimes with grotesque figures, & 1 initial depicting Aristotle. Including commentaries. Lacking f.1. VH Sept 12 (910) DM63,000

Armenian Manuscripts
Ms, Casoc. [Isfahan, 1661-1687]. 472 leaves, 380mm by 250mm. Contemp decorated brown lea over wooden bds. In black ink in a regular medium bolorgir hand. Profusely illuminated, with 2 full-page & 19 smaller miniatures & headpieces, probably by Hayrapet. C June 24 (272) £36,000 [Savidjian]

Armfield, Maxwell
Original drawings, (24), to illus the Tales of Hans Andersen, 1953. In ink. Mostly sgd with monogram, some dated [19]50 or 1951. Average sizes 250mm by 190mm or 120mm by 170mm. With related material. Archives of J. M. Dent & Son. S June 19 (739) £2,800 [Edberg]
— Original drawings, (4), probably illusts for Constance Armfield's Sylvia's Travels, 1911. In ink. 3 sgd with initials or rainbow device. 225mm by 185mm & smaller. Archives of J. M. Dent & Son. S June 19 (737) £500 [Piccadilly]
— Original drawings, pictorial title design & 2 illusts for Fairy Tales from Hans Andersen, 1910. 2 sgd; 1 inscr to J. M. Dent. Various sizes. Archives of J. M. Dent & Son. S June 19 (736) £420 [Sawyer]

Armstrong, Neil
Ls, 24 June 1970. 1 p, 4to. Recipient unnamed. Responding to a children's thank you card. On NASA letterhead. With 8 NASA photographs. wa May 30 (5) $300

Armstrong, Neil —& Others
Group photograph, NASA photograph of crew members of 1st manned lunar expedition, [n.d.]. 4to. Sgd by Armstong, Buzz Aldrin & Michael Collins. wa May 30 (7) $230

Arndt, Ernst Moritz, 1769-1860
Autograph Ms, poem, Das runde Lied, draft [c.1808]. 2 pp, 17.4cm by 8.8cm. Nine 4-line stanzas, differing from version ptd 1840. Some autograph revisions. JG Oct 2 (5) DM730

ADs, 1 July 1843. 1 p, 4to. Receipt for salary as university professor. star Apr 8 (13) DM500

Arnim, Bettina von, 1785-1859
AL, [n.d.]. 1 p, 4to. To Herr Klein. Explaining that she will not be able to return a Ms before the next day. HK Nov 7 (2172) DM1,000
— [1841]. 4 pp, 4to. To Adolf Friedrich Rudorff. Draft, defending & recommending Moritz Carriere as philosopher. With 8-line paragraph by Carriere at end. star Apr 8 (14) DM3,000

Arnim, Ludwig Achim von, 1781-1831
ALs, 12 June 1817. 4 pp, 4to. Recipient unnamed. Regarding money matters, & inviting him to visit. S May 21 (221) £260 [Haas]
ANs, 29 July 1828. 1 p, 8vo. To Amtsrat Bartels. Accepting an invitation to a boat trip. With engraving, "Die Rabeninsel", 7.5cm by 8 cm, at head. star Apr 8 (15) DM650

Arnold, Benedict, 1741-1801
ADs, 22 May 1790. 1 p, 8vo. In 3d person, as plaintiff, certifying that Christopher Hatch, defendant, owes him £ 100. Sgd twice sg Nov 6 (232) $1,100
— PAGETT, WILL. - ALs, 12 Oct 1780. 3 pp, size not stated. To Thomas Druce. Account of Arnold's treason & the capture of Major Andre. rf Mar 14 (4) $1,350

Arnold, Matthew, 1822-88
ALs, 1 Sept 1878. 3 pp, 8vo. To Lady Reay. Informing her that he will not be able to visit her. S Jan 27 (692) £70 [Jarndyce]

Artelouche de Alagona
Ms, Fauconnerie. [Southern France, probably Arles], 1504. 49 (of 50) leaves (the 1st leaf in facsimile), 180mm by 121mm, in mor janesniste by Gruel. Dated at end by the scribe, Vincent Philippon. Jeanson Ms 115 SM Feb 28 (72) FF70,000

Arthur, Chester A., 1830-86
Collection of Ls, ANs, ptd check, sgd, & 2 White House cards, sgd; 10 July 1874 to 14 Aug 1884. Various sizes & recipients. P Oct 29 (30) $1,000
Ds, 13 May 1875. 1 p, 8vo. Oath, sgd as Customs Collector. rf Nov 15 (2) $145
— 22 Oct 1881. 1 p, folio. Naval appointment. rf May 30 (3) $300
— 22 Oct 1881. 1 p, 19.5 by 15.75 inches. Vellum. Commission of Edwin L. Reynolds as Master in the Navy. Countersgd by William H. Hunt. S Jan 27 (925) £160 [Blair]

Ashby, Turner, 1828-62
Ds, 28 Feb 1862. 1 p, 16mo. Quartermaster requisition. wa May 30 (208) $250

Astaire, Fred
Photograph, sgd, [c.1935]. 10 by 8 inches. Seated. Slightly def; was mtd. sg Nov 6 (11) $175

Astrological Manuscript
Ms, Pratique abregee des jugemens astrologiques sur les nativitez par H.D.C.C.D.D.E.D.S.S. 16 Aug 1717. About 800 pp, folio, bds, broken. Stamp of the astrologer Julevno. S Nov 27 (304) £250 [Quaritch]

Ms, collection of astrological observations, tables & horoscopes, [Germany, Italy, France, c.1430 to 1485]. 132 leaves, c.30cm by 21cm. In vellum cover. In brown & red ink in several hands. Some leaves def. Mostly in Latin; some German. VH Sept 12 (911) DM5,000

Auber, Daniel Francois, 1782-1871
Autograph music, Andante, for piano; 55 bars; 19 Mar 1862. 2 pp, folio; 12 staves each. Sgd & inscr to Madame Chabrier. With port photograph, 9cm by 5.5cm; glued to corner of Ms. star Apr 9 (563) DM1,100

Auberjonois, Rene, 1872-1957
Series of 10 A Ls s, 9 Oct 1943 to 25 Dec 1946. 19 pp, 8vo (lettercards). To Lukas Lichtenhan. Regarding the sale of his paintings. With related material. star Apr 8 (437) DM1,050

Auden, Wystan Hugh, 1907-73
Autograph Ms, song, Here we come a piping in springtime, music & words; [c.1930-32]. 2 pp, folio, & 10 blanks. Sgd & inscr to Anne Bristow. In pencil. Bristow Estate. S July 23 (129) £600 [Gekoski]

Series of 16 A Ls s, 1930 to 1932. 27 pp, various sizes. To Anne Bristow. Personal correspondence regarding his teaching at Larchfield Academy, his homosexuality, literary matters, etc. 1 ALS with 12-line poem. With 2 photographs, inscr; 1 sgd. Bristow Estate. S July 23 (128) £5,800 [Manyon]

ALs, 7 feb 1949. 1 p, 4to. To Jimmy. About sending him money. sg Mar 5 (8) $150
See also: Isherwood, Christopher & Auden

Auerbach, Berthold, 1812-82
ALs, 14 Aug 1869. 1 p, 8vo. To an unnamed recipient in Munich. Announcing his visit. star Apr 8 (16) DM320

Augereau, Pierre Francois Charles, Duc de Castiglione, 1757-1816
Ls, [6 May 1804]. 1 p, folio. To Gen. Donzelet. Concerning draft of a speech urging Napoleon to become Emperor; with autograph postscript. Including draft speech, 2 pp, 4to. Bullock collection. CNY Dec 19 (157) $380

— [28 June 1804]. 2 pp, 4to. To Gaudin, Minister of Finance. Letter of recommendation for M. Barat. star Apr 9 (881) DM220

Augsburg
Ms, chronicles of the city of Augsburg, c.1810. 285 pp & 24 index leaves, 290mm by 210mm. Contemp half lea. In German. With 6 engraved illusts (3 colored) & 2 double-page engraved tables pasted in. With related material. HK Nov 4 (404) DM800

August Ferdinand, Herzog von Braunschweig, 1677-1704
Ls, 8 Sept 1699. 2 pp, folio. To the mayor of Helmstedt. Ordering the arrest of a deserter. Repaired. star Apr 9 (925) DM340

August II, King of Poland, 1670-1733
Ls, 26 July 1710. 2 pp, folio. To Count Boris Scheremetew. Expressing congratulations on the conquest of Riga. With contemp Russian trans. star Apr 9 (1128) DM1,000

August III, King of Poland, 1696-1763
ALs, 1 June 1752. 1 p, 4to. In French. With ALs, 1 Jan 1750, 1 p, 4to, by his Queen Maria Josepha. In Italian. Both to the King of the Two Sicilies. Congratulating him on the birth of a child. S Nov 27 (450) £280

Auguste Viktoria, Empress of Wilhelm II of Germany, 1858-1921
Series of 4 A Ls s, 1908 to 1912. 13 pp, 8vo. To Hans Karl von Winterfeld. Regarding her children, a wedding, instructions how to use oxygen, & a journey to Switzerland. With further autographs by the empress. star Apr 9 (955b) DM500

ALs, 6 Nov 1901. 2 pp, 8vo (lettercard). To Dr. von Leuthold. About her husband's health. With related material. star Apr 9 (955a) DM300

Augustinian Order
Document, Statutes, in Latin. [South Flanders, c.1556]. 126 leaves, 140mm by 100mm. Limp vellum bdg using leaves of a late 13th-cent & a 15th-cent Ms. In black ink in a cursive bookhand. With painted initials throughout in red. S June 23 (89) £900 [Thomas]

Auric, Georges, 1899-1983

Menu, 16 Aug 1965. Sgd & inscr with 4 bars of music, on verso. Also sgd by Greta Garbo. star Apr 9 (566) DM950

Austen, Jane, 1775-1815

Autograph Ms, play, Sir Charles Grandison or The Happy Man, a Comedy, [1799 or later]. 53 pp, various sizes. With autograph revisions on c.28 pp. S July 23 (38) £28,000 [Quaritch]

AL, [n.d.]. Fragment, 4 lines cut from a letter. Recipient unnamed. About dining at the Great House. Framed with a port; overall size 16 by 14 inches. S July 23 (36) £550 [MacNutt]

B

Bach, Johann Christian, 1743-1814

Autograph music, collection of c.50 works for piano or organ by a number of composers, including himself, [n. d.]. 87 pp, 8vo. Contemp half lea. HK Nov 7 (2174) DM3,500

Bach, Johann Christoph Friedrich, 1732-95

Autograph music, cembalo part for music for the Passion week, combining parts of Reinhard Keiser's Passion according to St. Mark with Handel's Brockes Passion, [1740s]. Tp & 17 pp, 34.5cm by 21.5cm; sewn. Probably executed for a concert directed by Johann Sebastian Bach at Leipzig. With related material. star Apr 9 (567) DM14,000

Bachem, Bele, Pseud. of Renate Gabriele Boehmer

Original drawing, pen-&-ink sketch with watercolors, showing 4 mermaids with boat, [c.1955]. 1 p, folio. On verso ANs, to Peter Zingler. Repaired. With related material. star Apr 8 (438) DM480

Bachmann, Ingeborg, 1926-73

Collection of 5 A Ls s & 25 Ls s, 1964 to 1966. About 37 pp, 4to. To Adolf Opel. Interesting personal correspondence relating to their travels together, her health problems & her work. With related material. FD June 11 (3494) DM24,000

Bacon, Charles, c.1784-1818

Autograph Ms, diary, 11 July 1813 to 28 Feb 1815. About 270 pp, 8vo. Red calf. Referring to his daily life & work as Clerk of the Works at Whitehall, Westminster & St. James's, social affairs, etc. S July 24 (471) £1,500 [Quaritch]

Bacon, Francis, Sir, 1561-1626. See: Proverbs

Baden-Powell of Gilwell, Robert S. S. Baden-Powell, 1st Baron, 1857-1941

Collection of 22 A Ls s, Ls s & cards, sgd, 21 May 1900 to 17 May 1940; c.60 pp, 4to & 8vo. To Sir Alexander & Lady Godley. About the Boer War, the South African Constabulary & the Scouting Movement. S Dec 18 (223) £1,600 [Gekoski]

Badings, Henk

Autograph music, Andante, 12 bars; Allegretto, 24 bars; etc., [n.d.]. 3 pp, 30 staves each. Mostly in pencil. star Apr 9 (568) DM220

Baillie, Joanna, 1762-1851

Series of 17 A Ls s, 26 Oct 1809 to 9 Feb 1833 & [n.d.]. To Mrs. Anne Elliott of Egland. Reporting about her literary work & mentioning friends, including Sir Walter Scott. With related material. C June 24 (88) £1,000 [Quaritch]

Baker, Sir Samuel, 1821-93

ALs, 8 Mar 1867. 12 pp, 8vo. To Sir Roderick Murchison. About the news of Livingstone's death, African exploration & a plan for the annexation of the equatorial Nile basin to Egypt. S Dec 18 (272) £950 [Joseph & Sawyer]

— 29 Apr 1873. 4 pp, 8vo. To Larking. About the slave trade of the White Nile & other African affairs. S July 24 (329) £480 [Joseph & Sawyer]

Baldwin, Stanley, 1867-1947. See: George V, 1865-1936

Balzac, Honore de, 1799-1850

ALs, 25 Dec 1838. 1 p, 8vo. To his publisher Souverain. About the timing of 2 publications. star Apr 8 (18) DM1,500

ADs, 1 July 1838. 1 p, 8vo. Promissory note for 300 francs, payable to M. Hubert. star Apr 8 (17) DM4,000

Bandel, Ernst von, 1800-76

Collection of ALs & autograph sentiment; 2 pp, 8vo. Draft, 1875, to Hofmarschall Jessendor [?], letter of condolences on the death of the prince. On verso calligraphic exercises & self port. Poem, 6 stanzas, dated 31 Jan 1825 & inscr to an unnamed friend. Initialled. JG Oct 2 (297) DM560

Bankhead, Tallulah, 1902-68

Ptd photograph, [n.d.]. 8 by 10 inches. Sgd & inscr to Annie Laurie [Rankin]. Also sgd by her father W. B. Bankhead. wa May 30 (372) $150

Banks, Sir Joseph, 1743-1820
[2 A Ls by Banks, with 2 by Nevil Maskelyne, 20 June 1798 to 27 Mar 1799, 6 pp, 4to, to Messrs. Pearson & Loggen regarding the accounts of Mr. Buckton for ptg the Greenwich Observations for 1796 sold at S on 24 July 1987, lot 373, for £400 to Wilson.]

Barbe-Marbois, Francois, Marquis de, 1745-1837. See: United States

Bargheer, Eduard, 1901-79
Original drawing, sketch, with ball-point pen, showing town in front of mountains, sgd & dated 1966. 14cm by 19.5cm. With ALs, 1969. star Apr 8 (439) DM800

Baring, Maurice, 1874-1946
Autograph Ms, fairy story, Vox Angelica, [1886]. 10 pp, folio. In French. In pencil with pencil & watercolor illusts. Mtd in an album with later typewritten transcript. With related Ls, 24 June 1940, to "H.W.". C June 24 (89) £550 [Rota]

Barker, George
Series of 8 A Ls s, [1940s?]. 14 pp, 4to & 8vo. To Ralph & Julian Orde. About a variety of subjects. S Jan 27 (726) £180 [Rota]

Barlach, Ernst, 1870-1938
Autograph postcard, sgd, 21 Feb 1893. To Friedrich Duesel. Concerning information for articles about art in Hamburg. Sgd E. star Apr 8 (440) DM520

Barlow, Peter, 1776-1862
ALs, 26 Mar 1822. 3 pp, 4to. To Michael Faraday. Informing him about his experiments in magnetism. With 5 A Ls s, 1813 to 1831, & further related material. C June 24 (161) £100 [Sakmyster]

Barnum, Phineas Taylor, 1810-91
ALs, 30 Nov 1878. 2 pp, 8vo, on rectos only. Recipient unnamed. Setting the date for a lecture. Was mtd. wa May 30 (338) $500

Barras, Paul, 1755-1829 —& Others
Ds, [1 Apr 1796]. 5 pp, folio. Authorized copy of a project for revision of the Treaty of Basel of 15 May 1795. Also sgd by Carnot, La Revelliere de Lepeaux, Le Tourneur, & Reubell of the Directory. C Dec 3 (213) £150 [L'Autographe]

Barron, James, 1769-1851
ALs, 25 Nov 1834. 1 p, 4to. Recipient unknown. Withdrawing his request that his nephew be appointed to the Naval Academy. sg Nov 6 (236) $80

Barrow, Clyde. See: Parker, Bonnie & Barrow

Barrymore, Ethel
Photograph, sgd, [c.1895]. 1 p, 4to. Gravure photographic bust port; sgd in pencil. Dampstained. sg Nov 6 (16) $70

Bartholdi, Frederic A., 1834-1904
ALs, 12 Jan 1882. 3 pp, 4to. To William M. Evarts. Reporting about his work on the Statue of Liberty & requesting instructions where to send Evarts's bust. P Oct 29 (31) $3,750

— 2 June 1889. 1 p, 8vo. Recipient unnamed. Accepting a dinner invitation. Framed with a reproduction of the Statue of Liberty. sg Nov 6 (237) $325

— 18 Nov 1903. 2 pp, 8vo. Recipient unnamed. Suggesting 2 paintings for an exposition. With related material. wa May 30 (460) $180

Bartlett, Josiah, Signer from New Hampshire
Ds, 17 June 1790. 1 p, 4to. Appointment of Nathaniel Batchelder as justice of the peace. Charlotte Parker Milne collection. wd Nov 12 (27) $300

Bartok, Bela, 1881-1945
[A picture postcard with autograph address to Adila Aranyi, [3 Apr 1910], sold at star on 9 Apr 1987, lot 570a, for DM300.]

ALs, 15 June 1939. 2 pp, folio. To Erwin Stein. Discussing the publication of his 2d Violin Concerto; with 7 autograph musical quotations. In English. S May 22 (572) £4,200 [Haas]

— [1945?]. 2 pp, 8vo. To [Erwin Stein]. Discussing the publication of the Concerto for Orchestra. Probably incomplete. S May 22 (574) £600 [Bouvier]

Ls, 29 Nov 1921. 2 pp, 4to. Recipient unnamed. Suggesting compositions for Ansermet to direct. In French. star Apr 9 (570b) DM3,600

Autograph postcard, sgd, 22 Dec 1936. To Universal Ed. Establishing the title of his Music for Strings, Percussion and Celesta. File holes. S May 22 (575) £800 [Bouvier]

— 11 Jan 1938. To Concertdirectie A. Kosser. Regarding concerts in The Hague & Luxemburg. File holes. S May 22 (573) £500 [Kruyfhooft]

Bartolomeo da San Concordia, 1250-1347
Ms, Summa Casuum. [Southern Italy], dated 13 May to 24 July 1434. 241 leaves & flyleaf, vellum, 189mm by 133mm. Contemp red-stained lea over bevelled wooden bds. In brown ink in a small gothic bookhand by Guilgelmus Nicolai de Campis for Brother Thomas de Bova. With painted initials throughout. S June 23 (80) £3,800 [Schoyen]

Barton, Clara, 1821-1912
Autograph postcard, sgd, 5 July 1889. To Miss Guernsey. Thanking for "skirts made by your own crippled hands". wa May 30 (339) $190

Christmas card, [n.d.]. 1 p, 8vo. Recipient unnamed. Ptd card, sgd. wa May 30 (9) $100

Baruch, Bernard M., 1870-1965
Collection of 2 Ls s & 2 autograph notes, sgd, 1953 to 1962. 4 pp, 4to & smaller. To Rose Bigman. About Walter Winchell & Truman (2), & contents not stated. sg Apr 9 (22) $300

Baudelaire, Charles, 1821-67
ALs, [c.3 Mar 1846]. 3 pp, 8vo. To his sister-in-law. Sending her one of his earliest pbd works & asking her to be his guide. Sgd Baudelaire Dufays. S Nov 27 (306) £1,600

Baudouin, King of the Belgians —& Fabiola, Queen of Baudouin, King of the Belgians
Group photograph, 17 Nov 1976. 22.8cm by 17.6cm. Sgd by both & inscr by Baudouin to K. B. Andersen, Foreign Minister of Denmark; on mount, 31cm by 23cm. star Apr 9 (888) DM1,300

Bawden, Edward
Original drawings, (30), to illus Robert Paltock's The Life and Adventures of Peter Wilkins, 1928. In ink. 7 sgd & dated 1924 to 1926. Various sizes. Archives of J. M. Dent & Son. S June 19 (740) £2,200 [Contemporary]

Bayer, Wolfgang Balthasar
Ms, Zu Etzlesweiler. Jager jung Alda gewesen Anno 1707. 60 pp, 146mm by 188mm, in 19th-cent lea. Jeanson Ms 154 SM Feb 28 (52) FF8,000

Beardsley, Aubrey, 1872-98
Original drawing, ink drawing for the upper cover of Malory's Le Morte Darthur, preliminary version with title spelled incorrectly. 312mm by 250mm; mtd. Archives of J. M. Dent & Son. S June 19 (742) £10,000 [Edberg]

— Original drawing, ink drawing for the decorated spine of Malory's Le Morte Darthur, 263mm by 74mm. Lettering on 2 separate pieces inset above ornamental panel. With related material. Archives of J. M. Dent & Son. S June 19 (743) £1,500 [Nahum]

— Original drawing, ornamental border for Morte d'Arthur; ink. In card mount with Frederick Evans' note of authenticity on verso, 217mm by 170mm. S Dec 5 (428) £1,400 [Maggs]

— Original drawing, ornamental tp of Fanny Burney's Evelina, 1893. In ink. Sgd with initials. 246mm by 170mm. Ptd title, etc. pasted in. Archives of J. M. Dent & Son. S June 19 (744) £4,400 [Beardsley]

— Original drawing, Pan; ink. Sgd with device at top. In card mount with Frederick Evans' note of autheticity on verso, 85mm by 62mm. Reproduced in Sheridan's Bon Mots, 1893. S Dec 5 (429) £3,200 [Hartnoll]

— Original drawing, "The Achieving of the Sangreal", in ink & wash. Reproduced as frontis for vol 2 of Malory's Le Morte Darthur, 1893-94. Sgd with device. 368mm by 291mm. Framed. Archives of J. M. Dent & Son. S June 19 (741) £95,000 [Fogg]

Series of 7 A Ls s, 8 Oct 1892 & [n.d.]. 17 pp, 8vo. To J. M. Dent. About drawings & terms for Morte d'Arthur. With related material. S July 24 (472) £7,500 [Manyon]

ALs, [c.July 1891]. 4 pp, folio. To [G. F. Scotson-]Clark. Reporting about a letter from Burne-Jones concerning London art schools & his own plans. Including a drawing; man climbing up a mountain to reach the valley of art. S Dec 18 (29) £1,600 [Curry]

— 9 Aug 1891. 2 pp, folio. To [G. F. Scotson-]Clark. Lively letter, reporting about his activities & including a poem. Profusely illustrated with a pen-and-wash drawing of Whistler's port of his mother, 3 self-caricatures, & other drawings. S Dec 18 (31) £18,000 [Curry]

Photograph, sgd, [n.d.]; c.9.75 by 7.5 inches. S Dec 18 (30) £1,000 [Dailey]

— Anr, 1897. c.9 by 6.75 inches. Sgd with his pseud. Giulio Floriani. Photograph by Frederick Evans[?]. S Dec 18 (32) £800 [Dailey]

Photograph, sgd & inscr, [Nov 1897]. c.9.5 by 11.75 inches. Seated in his room. Inscr on mount to H. C. J. Pollitt. With related material. S Dec 18 (33) £1,100 [Dailey]

— BEARDSLEY, ELLEN. - ALs, "Sunday" [1898]. 4 pp, 16mo. To J. M. Dent. About her son's last illness. With related material. S July 24 (473) £1,200

Beatrice of Savoy, Duchess of Modena, 1792-1840
ALs, 1 Aug 1832. 2 pp, 4to. To Marie Louise, Empress of the French, now Duchess of Parma. Sending condolences on the death of her son. star Apr 9 (1078) DM320

Beauharnais, Alexandre, Vicomte de, 1760-94
Ls, 4 Sept 1793. 1 p, 4to. To an unnamed officer. Informing him that his commission must be confirmed by Gen. Hallot. HN May 22 (2942) DM550

BEAUHARNAIS

Beauharnais, Eugene de, 1781-1824
Collection of 9 A Ls s & Ls s, 1806 to 1822; c.20 pp, 4to. To various recipients. About commissioning portraits of his mother & Napoleon, military matters, the administration of Italy, etc. With related material. S Nov 27 (307) £520 [Dr. Sam]

Ls s (2), 11 Jan 1811 & 6 Oct 1812. To the Duc de Feltre. About enlisting new conscripts in Italy & candidates for generals for the Army of Italy. S Nov 27 (308) £200 [Maggs]

Ds, 29 Mar 1813. 1 p, 4to. As Commander in Chief of the French Army in Germany, orders concerning the occupation of towns on the Weser River. Sgd E N. HN May 22 (2943) DM780

Beauharnais Family
[A collection of 20 items by or relating to various members of the Beauharnais family, 1794 to 1835, sold at CNY on 19 Dec 1986, lot 158, for $1,600.]

Beauharnais, Hortense de, 1783-1837
A Ls s (2), 15 brumaire & 17 thermidor [n.y.]. 4 pp, 8vo. To her cousin Lavalette, regarding Hortense's relationship with her mother. To Madame Mere, sending family news; sgd Hortense Bonaparte. S Nov 27 (309) £200 [Dr. Sam]

ALs, 10 June 1826. 2 pp, 4to. To Joseph Bonaparte. Discussing the proposed marriage between her son & his daughter. S Nov 27 (311) £280 [Charavay]

Ds, 14 July 1815. 6 pp, 4to. Establishing her right as part heir to the estate of her mother. Sgd hortense duchesse de st leu. With related material. S Nov 27 (310) £300 [Dr. Sam]

Beauregard, Pierre G. T., 1818-93
ALs, 27 Nov 1838. 1 p, 4to. Recipient unnamed. Expressing disappointment at being unable to visit Europe. wa Oct 18 (70) $120

Beauvoir, Simone de
Autograph Ms, novel, Les Mandarins; 1st draft of chapters III to XI; c.1954. About 500 pp, folio. Some typewritten pp. Extensive revisions. S Nov 27 (312) £4,000 [Bibliotheque Nationale]

Bebel, August, 1840-1913
ALs, 25 Mar 1869. 1 p, 8vo. To a newspaper Ed [Rausche?]. Sending the Ms of a speech. HN May 22 (2944) DM620

Beckett, Samuel
ALs, 13 Jan 1961. 1 p, 4to. To an unnamed graphologist. Complying with a request for his autograph. star Apr 8 (19) DM220

AMERICAN BOOK PRICES CURRENT

Beckford, William, 1760-1844
Autograph Ms, annotations, 115 lines, in pencil, on 2 fly-leaves of B. C. Walpole, Recollections of the Life of the late Right Honourable Charles James Fox. L, 1806; 8vo. pn Dec 11 (33) £200 [Joseph]

Beckwith, Thomas Sidney, Sir. See: Nelson, Horatio Nelson

Bedford, F. D.
Original drawings, (7), to illus The Vicar of Wakefield, 1898. In ink & watercolor. All sgd. 362mm by 266mm. Archives of J. M. Dent & Son. S June 19 (745) £1,000 [Sawyer]

— Original drawings, complete set of 12 ink & watercolor illusts for The History of Henry Esmonde, 1898. All sgd; 10 mtd. 362mm by 266mm. With ink design for tp. Archives of J. M. Dent & Son. S June 19 (746) £2,000 [Edberg]

Beerbohm, Max, 1872-1956
ALs, 31 May 1917. 2 pp, 8vo. To Richard D'Oyly Carte. Agreeing to write a contribution. Was mtd. With related material. S Jan 27 (727) £90 [Sawyer]

— [n.d.]. 2 pp, 8vo. Recipient unnamed. About the opening of an exhibition. S Jan 27 (728) £50 [Maggs]

ANs, [n.d.]. 1 p, 255mm by 200mm. To Sydney Schiff. Note of thanks. With large ink drawing, caricature of Schiff, captioned The Darkness, and the Flashing Eye. Framed. S June 19 (635) £1,300 [Rota]

Beethoven, Ludwig van, 1770-1827
Autograph music, Diabelli-Variations, end of variation 31, [1823]. 1 p, 24cm by 31 cm; 8 staves. Mostly in ink; some pencil. star Apr 9 (572) DM44,000

Ms, song, Kennst du das Land, Op. 75, no 1; 1809. 9 pp, folio, with up to 4 systems, each of 3 staves. Some autograph alterations. Mostly in brown ink. Engraver's copy. S Nov 28 (494) £7,000 [Haas]

Cut signature, [n.d.]. Size not stated. Fragment of ALs; with subscription. S May 22 (333) £1,600 [Wilson]

— Schindler, Anton. - ALs, 14 Mar [n.y.], 4 pp, 8vo. To [Franz Messer]. Discussing Beethoven's intentions regarding measure & tempo in the 9th Symphony. Including Ms, 1 p, 4to, "Metronomisierung der 9ten Symphonie von Beethoven selbst ... gemacht". With related material. star Apr 9 (573) DM3,800

See also: Streicher, Johann Andreas

Beeton, Isabella Mary, 1836-65 —& Beeton, Samuel

[A collection of correspondence, including 5 A Ls s by Isabella Mayson to her fiancee Samuel Beeton, 4 A Ls s by Samuel Beeton to Isabella, 2 letters by Samuel Beeton written after his wife's death, 1856 to 1865, c.35 pp, 8vo, with 2 photographs of Mrs. Beeton & other related material, sold at S on 24 July 1987, lot 289, for £4,000 to Segal.]

Beeton, Samuel. See: Beeton, Isabella Mary & Beeton

Begas, Karl, 1794-1854

ALs, 17 Feb 1843. 1 p, 4to. To the pbr J. D. Sauerlaender. Notifying him that "Direktor von Cornelius" is too busy to sit for a painting. With material relating to his sons. star Apr 8 (441) DM250

Bell, Alexander Graham, 1847-1922

[A collection of 8 items, mostly in Bell's hand, c.1873 to 1876, relating to Bell's experiments & the "Multiple Telegraph", sold at P on 13 May 1987, lot 33, for $6,000.]

Ds s (2) 11 Dec 1885 & 7 May 1886. 2 pp, 4to. Contracts with Richard L. Pease, stating that Pease will provide Bell with information on deaf mutes on Martha's Vineyard, in exchange for Bell subsidizing publication of Pease's History of Martha's Vineyard. Also sgd by Pease. P Oct 29 (33) $750

Bell, Robert Anning

Original drawings, (28), to illus Palgrave's Golden Treasury, 1907. In ink. 1 sgd with initials. Various sizes. Archives of J. M. Dent & Son. S June 19 (748) £500 [A & H]

— Original drawings, (29), to illus Mrs. A. B. Jameson's Shakespeare's Heroines, 1901. In ink. 2 initialled. 196mm by 276mm. With anr drawing. Archives of J. M. Dent & Son. S June 19 (747) £1,600 [Beetles]

— Original drawings, (45), to illus Marian Edwardes' Ed of the Grimms' Household Tales, 1901. In ink. 2 sgd. Various sizes. Archives of J. M. Dent & Son. S June 19 (751) £3,200 [Edberg]

— Original drawings, (9), to illus A Midsummer Night's Dream, 1895. In ink. Various sizes. Archives of J. M. Dent & Son. S June 19 (750) £300 [Edberg]

Original drawing, a man approaching a sleeping woman, to illus Samuel Rogers' The Sleeping Beauty, [n.d.]. In ink & watercolor; sgd. 270mm by 386mm. Archives of J. M. Dent & Son. S June 19 (749) £320 [Parris]

Bellarmine, Roberto Francesco Romolo, Saint, 1542-1621

Ds, 6 Nov 1608. 1 p, folio. As Executor for Cardinal [Zarugi?], about the repayment of a loan. 3 other signatures. HK Nov 7 (2182) DM550

Bellingham, John, d.1812

[2 documents relating to the arrest of Bellingham for the murder of Spencer Perceval, 11 & 12 May 1812, with related material, sold at C on 24 June 1987, lot 15, for £120 to Shutter.]

Bellmer, Hans, 1902-75

ALs, [n.d.]. 1 p, 4to. Recipient unnamed. Thanking for money & describing his financial problems. star Apr 8 (443) DM480

— [n.d.]. 2 pp, folio. To Rene Magritte. Asking for permission to paint Magritte's port for a projected series of portraits of contemp artists & writers. S July 2 (968) £500 [Ducasse F. A.]

Belloc, Hilaire, 1870-1953

Autograph transcript, poem, Halnacker Mill, Sept 1913. 4 pp, size not stated. Sgd & inscr to Juliet. Musical notation on verso of tp. In purple embossed silk covers. C June 24 (90) £380 [Lowndes]

Benedek, Ludwig August, Ritter von, 1804-81

ALs, 30 May 1850. 2 pp, folio. Recipient unnamed. Letter of recommendation for a cousin. star Apr 9 (889) DM220

Benedict XIV, Pope, 1675-1758

ALs, 15 Oct 1710. 4 pp, 8vo. Recipient unnamed. About affairs at Rome. star Apr 9 (1115) DM650

Document, [1 July] 1755. 1 p, folio. Bull; contents not stated. Lead seal. star Apr 9 (1116) DM400

Ben-Gurion, David, 1886-1973

ALs, 1 Jan 1967. 1 p, 8vo. To Ida M. Silverman. Expressing astonishment at the news that his records "are or will be at Brandeis University". wa May 30 (44) $550

Benjamin, Judah P., 1811-84

Series of 3 A Ls s, 5 Jan to 3 Mar 1874. 7 pp, 12mo. To Judge Robert Ludlow Fowler. Contents not stated. Mentioning a court case. sg Nov 6 (18) $800

Benn, Gottfried, 1886-1956

ALs, 28 Apr 1952. 1 p, 8vo. To Gerd Rosen. Authorizing him to add his name to an appeal regarding the founding of a society. HK Nov 7 (2180) DM600

Bennett, Charles Henry, 1829-67

Original drawings, 15 illusts in ink & watercolor for The Frog who would A Wooing Go, 125mm by 181mm. Text opposite each illus; music on last leaf with notes in form of human figures. S Dec 5 (432) £3,000 [Greer]

Berenson, Bernard, 1865-1959

Series of c.60 A Ls s, 28 June 1909 to 30 July 1931. Over 200 pp, 8vo. To the art dealer Rene Gimpel. Giving advice on Italian paintings & the art market; requesting his share of the profits of sales. With related material. S Nov 27 (314) £1,700 [Sims Reed]

Berg, Alban, 1885-1935

Collection of 4 A Ls s (1 fragment) & autograph postcard, sgd, 23 Mar 1929 to [Apr 1935]. 10 pp, mostly 8vo, & card. To Erich Kleiber. Personal correspondence, about Kleiber's operation, concerts directed by him, & about Lulu. star Apr 9 (577) DM22,000

— Collection of 9 A Ls s & autograph postcard, sgd, 17 Jan 1934 to 30 Nov 1935. 35 pp, mostly 8vo, & card. To Arnold Schoenberg. Personal correspondence regarding his life & work, performances of Schoenberg's & his compositions, the music scene in Austria, etc. star Apr 9 (580) DM42,000

ALs, 5 Oct 1923. 3 pp, 8vo. To Erich Kleiber. Letter of recommendation for Josef Schmied. star Apr 9 (575) DM2,800

— 16 June [1932]. 4 pp, 8vo. To an unnamed lady. Regarding a secret meeting in Vienna & describing his schedule. In pencil. Sgd Dein--. star Apr 9 (578) DM3,000

— 26 June 1932. 4 pp, 8vo. To an unnamed lady. Speculating about the possibility of a date later in the year. In pencil. star Apr 9 (579) DM3,200

— June 1935. 2 pp, 8vo. To Karl Boehm. Saying that [Willi] Reich would like to meet him. star Apr 9 (581) DM2,600

Ls, 1 Mar 1928. 2 pp, 8vo. To Arnold Schoenberg. Describing 2 concerts in enthusiastic terms. star Apr 9 (576) DM3,400

Bergengruen, Werner, 1892-1964

Collection of 2 A Ls s, 10 Ls s, & 3 postcards, sgd (1 autograph), 12 July 1928 to 18 May 1930. 13 pp, 4to & 8vo, & cards. To the publishing house J. Engelhorns Nachf. at Stuttgart. Offering a novel written by his wife for print, & about his own publications, fees, etc. HN May 22 (2949) DM440

Bergman, Torbern Olof

Ms, Chemical dissertation on the analysis of Iron, translated from his latin work Dissertatio Chemica de analysi ferri. 100 pp, 8vo, in contemp half calf. C Dec 12 (18) £400 [Bjork & Borjesson]

Berlioz, Hector, 1803-69

Autograph Ms, part of Scene XIV of the libretto of his Beatrice et Benedict, draft, [July 1862]. 2 pp, 8vo. In black ink on blue paper. With authentication [by Prilleux] on top. With related material. C Dec 3 (406) £1,500 [MacNutt]

ALs, [n.d.]. 2 pp, 8vo. To an unnamed lady. Expressing admiration for the violinist Theodore Haumann. S May 22 (348) £380 [MacNutt]

— 20 May 1843. 2 pp, 8vo. To the publishers Breitkopf & Haertel. Asking whether they bought the German rights for his King Lear overture. With port photograph. star Apr 9 (582) DM2,400

— [n.d.], "Vendredi matin". 1 p, 8vo. To [August?] Koempel. Suggesting a meeting to discuss musical matters. Framed. Altman collection. pnNY Sept 13 (156) $425

— [n.d.], "Dimanche matin". 2 pp, 8vo. To M. de St. Georges. Saying his poor health prevented him from attending a dinner. Framed. Altman collection. pnNY Sept 13 (157) $425

— [n.d.]. 1 p, 8vo. To "Mon cher Amiral". Concerning the charges of a music teacher. Framed with autograph envelope. Altman collection. pnNY Sept 13 (158) $375

— [n.d.]. 1 p, 8vo. To M. Gabriel. Saying he has seen Perrin & requesting an interview. S May 22 (354) £250 [Wilson]

— 11 Sept [1855]. 2 pp, 8vo. To Amedee Mereaux. Regarding the arrangement of the trio for 2 flutes & harp from L'enfance du Christ. S May 22 (351) £900 [Johnson]

— 10 Feb 1860. 1 p, 8vo. To Richard Pohl. Requesting information about the publication of his Grotesques de la musique. S May 22 (577) £520 [MacNutt]

— 23 Jan 1868. 4 pp, 8vo. To Ernest Reyer. Reporting about his visit to Russia. S May 22 (355) £1,700 [MacNutt]

— 25 May [n.y.]. 3 pp, 8vo. To his pbr Maurice Schlesinger. Discussing journalistic activities & financial problems. Was mtd. S May 22 (352) £600 [Maggs]

— 5 Sept [n.y.]. 2 pp, 8vo. To an unnamed lady. About staging the ending of Cortez & sending the score from Berlin to Paris & Weimar. Framed. Altman collection. pnNY Sept 13 (155) $750

— 17 Dec [n.y.]. 4 pp, 8vo. To Ernest Reyer. Reporting about a Vienna performance of

La damnation de Faust. S May 22 (353) £1,300 [MacNutt]

ANs, [n.d.]. 1 p, 8vo. Recipient unnamed. Requesting that a note should appear in tomorrow's Gazette. C Dec 3 (407) £220 [Maggs]

Bern

[Sinner, Johann Rudolf. - 3 Mss, detailing annual accounts for land owned by the City of Bern, 1744 to 1747, 110 pp in 3 vols, folio, sold at C on 24 June 1987, lot 16, for £200 to Hoffman.]

Bernadotte, Jean Baptiste, 1763-1844. See: Charles XIV John, 1763-1844

Bernardus de Magdunum

Ms, Ordo dictaminum, [Germany, 2d half of 13th cent]. 16 leaves, vellum, 175mm by 125mm. 18th cent lea, repaired. In black ink in a small gothic bookhand. Some leaves def. HK Nov 4 (406) DM3,800

Bernhardt, Sarah, d.1923

ALs, 1887. 2 pp, 16mo. Recipient unnamed. Saying she is too ill to visit. Mtd on 4to sheet with 2 photographs & a port. Stamped. sg Apr 9 (24) $200

Berry, Charles Ferdinand de Bourbon, Duc de

Ms, Recueil des chasses faites par l'equipage de S.A.R. Monseigneur le Duc de Berri. 1816-19. 4 vols, c.300 pp, 186mm by 154mm, in contemp mor gilt. Jeanson Ms 175 SM Feb 28 (65) FF70,000

Berthier, Alexandre, Prince de Wagram, 1753-1815

Ds, [16 Aug 1797]. 1 p, folio, "Ordre du General en Chef" [Bonaparte] for protection of Turkish subjects in Italy. With large engraved vignette at head. star Apr 9 (890) DM1,000

Bertuch, Friedrich Justin, 1747-1822

ALs, 14 Feb 1806. 1 p, 4to. To the bookseller Jaeger at Frankfurt. Complaining about the poor quality of paper received. star Apr 8 (98) DM220

Berzelius, Jons Jacob von, 1779-1848

ALs, 24 Jan 1832. 2 pp, 8vo. To T. L. von Ertel. Regarding payment for instruments ordered by the Swedish Academy of Science. In German. star Apr 8 (302) DM900

Bessemer, Sir Henry, 1813-98

ALs, 3 May 1896. 1 p, 8vo. To the Ed of The Engineer. Thanking him for ptg 2 of his articles. Matted with a port. With related material. sg Nov 6 (20) $175

Bessieres, Jean Baptiste, Duc d'Istrie, 1768-1813

Ls, 24 May 1807. 1 p, 4to. To Gen. Soules. As commander of the Imperial Guard, sending commissions & marching orders for 3 lieutenants. star Apr 9 (891) DM330

Betjeman, Sir John, 1906-84

Autograph Ms, 4 essays on aspects of London architecture, written for the magazine Ballet; with 5 related letters & 4 drawings by David Thomas. 1951 to 1952; 9 pp, folio & 8vo; & drawings. S Dec 18 (109) £420 [Maggs]

— Autograph Ms, poem, acrostic on the name of Telford, by "The Revd. Archibald Oldys..."; c.1959. With Ls by Betjeman to Richard Buckle, 27 May 1959, thanking for payment for the Telford poem. S Dec 18 (108) £180 [Maggs]

— Autograph Ms, working poetical notebook, including Ellan Vannin, sgd & inscr to "Noel TCX", 12 Nov 1970. About 20 pp, 8vo, on rectos only. With corrected typescript, 14 pp, 4to. S July 23 (131) £900 [Rota]

Series of 3 Ls s, 17 Mar 1966 to 14 Apr 1978. 3 pp, 8vo. To Peter Luke. Mostly about a jubilee history of the Dublin Gate Theatre. Each containing a phrase in Gaelic. C Dec 3 (348) £100 [Burwood]

Beuys, Joseph, 1921-86

[A collection of 2 lithographs, sgd, 1974 & [n.y.], 23cm by 15.6cm & 21.6cm by 15.7cm; autograph Ms, sgd, 1 p, 8vo, regarding national economics; & signature on postcard, sold at star on 8 Apr 1987, lot 445, for DM1,400.]

Autograph Ms, notes regarding national economics, [n.d.]. 1 p, 4to. In pencil. On hotel letterhead. Sgd on verso. With signature on postcard. FD June 11 (3499) DM1,200

Signature, 1974. On inscr lithograph, 23cm by 16cm. star Apr 8 (444) DM750

Bevington, Louisa Sarah, 1845-95

Series of 18 A Ls s, 1893 to 1895. Over 130 pp, 8vo. To Ethel Rolt-Wheeler. Regarding her political ideology & the Anarchist movement. With related material. S Dec 18 (221) £540 [Collins]

Beyle, Marie Henri, ("Stendhal"), 1783-1842

ALs, [9 June 1807]. 4 pp, 4to. To his sister Pauline. About his failure to win the heart of Wilhelmine von Griesheim & urging her to find a husband. Repaired. S Nov 27 (470) £1,800 [Lee]

— 8 Apr 1811. 3 pp, 8vo. To his sister Pauline. About the brevity of her last letter, his plans for visiting Rome, etc. S Nov 27 (469) £1,000

BEYME

Beyme, Karl Friedrich von, 1765-1838
ALs, 8 May 1824. 2 pp, 4to. To [Zelter]. Concerning musical instruction for his daughters. star Apr 9 (892) DM300

Bialas, Guenter
Autograph music, "Partitur-Ausschnitt aus 'Orpheus singt'...", 1981. 14 pp, 33.5cm by 26.5cm. Sgd. With ALs, 10 Mar 1981, 2 pp, 8vo (lettercard). star Apr 9 (583) DM250

Bianca Maria Sforza, Empress of Maximilian I, 1472-1510
Ds, 6 Mar 1506. 1 p, 4to. Pay order to Ulrich Horniger. HK Nov 7 (2183) DM1,400

Bible Manuscripts, Arabic
— [Deir al-Humaira, Mount Lebanon, 1807]. New Testament. 184 leaves, 293mm by 210mm. Contemp repoussee silver bdg, spine with chains. In naskhi script. S Nov 20 (413) £4,000

Bible Manuscripts, Latin
— [Rome, late 9th & late 11th cent]. The Bible of Santa Cecilia. Vol 1, 228 leaves, vellum, 327mm by 240mm, in dark brown in in a very fine Carolingian minuscule probably by more than 1 scribe. With chapter initials throughout & 7 large decorated initials. Vol 2, 290 leaves, vellum, 373mm by 275mm, in brown ink by many different scribes of varying skill in small or large late Carolingian minuscule script. With 12 very large decorated initials. Both vols in 19th-cent marbled paper over pastebds, rebacked in brown mor. Brooklyn Museum collection. S June 23 (72) £210,000 [Schoyen]
— [France, c.1230-60]. 335 leaves & 2 flyleaves, vellum, 205mm by 139mm. 16th-cent blindstamped pigskin over wooden bds. With Prologues attributed to St. Jerome & Interpretation of Hebrew Names. In brown ink in a small gothic bookhand. With large initials at the start of every book, & 2 large illuminated initials. Ownership inscr of the Abbey of St. Maximin at Trier. Library of the Dukes of Manchester at Kimbolton. S June 23 (78) £22,000 [Schoyen]
— [Italy?, c.1250-75]. 316 leaves, vellum, 173mm by 122mm. Def late 16th cent calf bdg, separated into 2 pieces. With Prologues ascribed to St. Jerome. In brown ink in an extremely small gothic bookhand. With decorated initials throughout, large initials at the beginning of each book & some medieval sidenotes. S Dec 2 (36) £3,200 [Schoyen]
— [Paris?, c.1260/70]. 473 leaves, vellum, 152mm by 100mm. In brown & red ink in a very small gothic bookhand; 2 columns, 50 lines each, per p. With red & blue initials throughout, c.80 large illuminated initals & 81 historiated initials executed in the style of the studio of Johannes Grusch. Extra lilac mor bdg "a la cathedrale", c.1820. Paper slipcase. FD Dec 2 (2a) DM85,000
— [Paris, c.1260-80]. 640 leaves, vellum, 137mm by 90mm. Late 17th-cent red mor gilt. With Prologues attributed to St. Jerome & Interpretation of Hebrew Names. In dark brown ink in a small gothic hand by more than 1 scribe. With 64 large illuminated initials & 81 historiated initials. Library of the Dukes of Manchester at Kimbolton. S June 23 (77) £14,000 [Bender]
— [Northern France, 2d half of 13th cent]. 360 leaves, vellum, 175mm by 120mm. 16th cent suede gilt. In a small gothic hand, mainly by 1 scribe. With red & blue initials throughout & 71 large initials in colors. Lacking c.24 leaves. HK Nov 4 (407) DM12,000
— [England, 2d half of 13th cent]. 540 leaves & 5 flyleaves, vellum, 159mm by 106mm. Modern Swedish blindstamped orange-brown mor. Lacking 2 leaves; Prologues ascribed to St. Jerome added at the end. In brown ink by several scribes in very small gothic bookhand. With decorated initials at the beginning of each book. S Dec 2 (37) £11,000 [Schoyen]
— [Northern France, 3d quarter of 13th cent, with some later additions]. 559 leaves, vellum, 208mm by 137mm, in 16th- or 17th-cent blindstamped pigskin over wooden bds, with brass fittings. Talleyrand's copy sg Dec 4 (18) $8,800
— [Normandy, perhaps Rouen, c.1290-1300]. 531 leaves, vellum, 266mm by 190mm. Modern red-brown tooled mor gilt bdg by W. H. Smith, in slipcase. In black ink in a very fine gothic boookhand. With decorated initials throughout with full-length borders, 80 illuminated initials in elaborate leafy & dragon designs in colors, gold & silver & 84 historiated initials with borders extending into 3 or 4 margins. S Dec 2 (38) £160,000 [Maggs]
— [Naples, early 14th cent]. 500 leaves, vellum, 310mm by 220mm, in rebacked 19th cent brown lea gilt. With c.100 large illuminated initials in colors & burnished gold in leafy designs, sometimes with grotesque figures, often with long extensions in similar leafy designs along margins. With prologues attributed to St. Jerome & many sidenotes & glosses. 3-line subscription, sgd, by scribe Phylippus on f.223v. FD Dec 2 (2b) DM110,000
— [East Anglia, Cambridge?, c.1350]. 3 leaves only, vellum, 445mm by 308mm. In brown ink in a large gothic hand. Each leaf with large historiated initial. Framed. S June 23 (17) £1,000 [Maggs]

Ms, [Pontigny or Canterbury, c.1200]. 2 leaves

only, vellum, 295mm by 152mm. Each mtd, in red mor bdg. In black, red & blue gothic bookhand. 2 elaborate large illuminated initials (H & V) with magnificent foliate designs, grotesque animals, flowers, etc.; incipits for Exodus & Leviticus. FD Dec 2 (4) DM130,000

Bible Manuscripts, Russian
— [Russia, late 17th cent]. 73 (of 74) leaves, 30cm by 15.5cm. Contemp dark brown lea over wooden bds, blindstamped with floral & ornamental designs. Lacking spine. In black ink in Cyrillic script. 73 excerpts from the Bible or legends only, each illus with full page pen & ink & watercolor drawing. FD June 11 (2) DM16,000

Bible Manuscripts, Syriac
— [Eastern Syria, 9th to 10th cent]. Peshitta Pentateuch. 204 leaves only, vellum, 240mm by 150mm, in medieval bdg of blindstamped tanned lea over wooden bds. In black ink in more than 1 regular estranglo hand. Some 18th-cent paper replacements. S June 23 (131) £17,000 [Smith]

Bicken, Johann Adam von, Kurfuerst & Erzbischof von Mainz, 1564-1604
Ls, 15 June 1601. 2 pp, folio. To the brothers von Eyb. Confirming their acquisition of Doertzbach & setting a date for the investiture. Fold tears. star Apr 9 (987) DM360

Biedermann, Woldemar von, 1817-1903. See: Goethe, Johann Wolfgang von

Bienek, Horst
Autograph Ms, poem, beginning "Woerter, meine Fallschirme", & autograph postscript, 10 Oct 1977. 1 p, 8vo. Sgd. star Apr 8 (20) DM300

Bischoffwerder, Johann Rudolf von, 1741-1803
ALs, 31 Oct 1790. 2 pp, 4to. To Viktor Amadeus Graf Henckel von Donnersmarck. Discussing the political intentions of Catherine the Great of Russia, the possibility of war, & the lack of horses. In French. star Apr 9 (893) DM320

Bismarck, Otto von, 1815-98
Ms, draft of a newspaper article about current politics, Oct 1870. 2 pp, 4to. With 25 autograph lines & numerous autograph corrections, in pencil. star Apr 9 (897) DM660
— Ms, report to Kaiser Wilhelm I, [1882]. 5 pp, folio. Concerning Russia & Panslavism. With autograph correction, 4 words. With related material. star Apr 9 (898) DM600
ALs, 25 Oct 1864. 1 p, 8vo. To Baron [Edmond de Rothschild?]. Expressing his wish to see him. In French. star Apr 9 (895) DM2,800

Ls, 26 Apr 1888. 3 pp, 4to. To Gen. von Winterfeld. Concerning the conferral of the dignity of a baron to the 4 brothers Stumm. With material related to von Winterfeld. star Apr 9 (899) DM1,080
— 1 May 1888. 2 pp, folio. To Kaiser Friedrich III. Submitting additional lists (not present) for the conferral of dignities & orders. star Apr 9 (900) DM700
— 10 Sept 1890. 1 p, 8vo. Recipient unnamed. Thanking for good wishes. S Jan 27 (960) £100 [Pilli]
— 6 Apr 1891. 1 p, 4to. To Karl Helmerding. Thanking for a birthday telegram. star Apr 9 (902) DM420
Autograph endorsement, 12 Jan 1865. 5 words in pencil, on letter addressed to him regarding the text of his speech for the opening of the Diet, 1 p, 4to. Torn. With ALs by Alfred von Kiderlen-Waechter, 1892. star Apr 9 (896) DM450
Signature, 30 Mar 1889; 8vo. In pencil. Mtd, in gilt lea folder, folio. With 23 A L s s by members of Bismarck's family to F. Witzleben, 1885 to 1894, mostly regarding orders for fur coats, & further related material. star Apr 9 (901) DM850
— Anr, [n.d.], 3 by 3.5 inches. wa Oct 18 (71) $60

Bissier, Julius, 1893-1965
ALs, 30 Nov 1963. 1 p, folio. To Felix H. Man. Regarding the publication of some lithographs. Including a small sketch. star Apr 8 (446) DM820

Bizet, Georges, 1838-75
ALs, [13 July 1867]. 1 p, 8vo. To Bernard [de] Lopez. Apologizing profusely & announcing his visit. star Apr 9 (584) DM2,600
— [n.d.]. 1 p, 8vo. To [Philippe] Gille. About literary matters. S May 22 (578) £800 [MacNutt]

Black, Joseph, 1728-99
Ms, lectures on chemistry. [c.1760-80] Bound in 6 vols of 8vo size with approximately 250 leaves in each, written on rectos only. Bound in 18th-cent calf gilt. C Dec 12 (24) £3,600 [Quaritch]

Blessington, Marguerite, Countess of, 1789-1849
ALs, [c.1840]. 3 pp, 8vo. To Nathaniel Parker Willis. Concerning a dramatization of an engraving. Docketed. sg Apr 9 (25) $100

Bligh, William, 1754-1817 — & Christian, Fletcher
Ds, 1 Dec 1788. 2 pp, 125mm by 100mm; lower half of a 4to sheet. Incomplete; last lines of a document written at Matavai Bay, Tahiti, attesting impartiality of proceedings. Sgd

by Christian & 3 other members of the crew of H.M.S. Bounty. Bligh's subscription on verso. Bullock collection. CNY Dec 19 (10) $8,000

Bliss, Sir Arthur, 1891-1975
Autograph Ms, errata to full score of The Colour Symphony; 15 May 1951. 2 pp, 4to. With 7 musical quotations; sgd. S May 22 (579) £220 [Quaritch]

Bloch, Ernest, 1880-1959
Autograph music, "Night" & "Trois paysages", 2 works for string quartet; sgd several times & dated 8 to 13 Dec 1923. 11 pp, folio. In blue & black ink. S Nov 28 (498) £1,000 [Haas]
— Autograph music, Schelomo, Rhapsodie hebraique; full score. Sgd & dated Jan - Feb 1916. 63 pp, folio. In blue ink on up to 26 staves per page. With many revisions. Inscr to Alexandre & Catherine Barjansky. S Nov 28 (499) £45,000 [Haas]
Collection of 13 A Ls s & 3 autograph postcards, sgd, 8 July 1933 to 9 June 1943. 63 pp, 4to & folio. To Sylvia Glass. Interesting personal correspondence regarding his impressions of the U. S. A., his compositions, the political situation in Europe, etc. Various signatures. With autograph address on Glass's visiting card. star Apr 9 (586) DM4,000

Bloch, Ernst, 1885-1977
Autograph Ms, part of a philosophical work [Das Prinzip Hoffnung?]; [n.d.]. 1 p, folio. Draft, with revisions. star Apr 8 (304) DM1,500

Bloomfield, Robert
ALs, [n.d.]. Size not stated. To Joseph Blackett. Praising his poems. S Jan 27 (694) £150 [Quaritch]

Bluecher von Wahlstatt, Gebhard Leberecht, Fuerst, 1742-1819
ALs, 17 Nov 1810. 1 p, 4to. Recipient unnamed. Concerning a bond deposited with the court of justice at Stettin. JG Oct 2 (362) DM1,100
— [4 Sept 1813]. 1 p, 8vo. To von Eisenhart. Stating his intention to reach Bautzen the next day. Dorow collection. star Apr 9 (905) DM4,500
— 29 Dec 1813. 1 p, 4to. To an unnamed friend. Informing him that he intends to cross the Rhine on 1 Jan, & that he expects a victor's welcome on his return. star Apr 9 (906) DM15,000
— 22 Apr 1814. 2 pp, 4to. To his wife. Informing her that he will be going to London before his return to Berlin. C Dec 3 (214) £850 [Huesken]
Ls, 10 Aug 1807. 1 p, 4to. To an unnamed French general. Regarding an agreement between Bluecher & Marechal Brune. star Apr 9 (903) DM680
— 26 Dec 1808. 1 p, folio. To Capt. von Rottenburg. About F. W. Graf von Goetzen's illness. star Apr 9 (904) DM520
— 29 Jan [1814]. 1 p, 8vo. To an unnamed general [Yorck?]. As Commander-in-Chief of the Silesian Army, stating that he is waiting for further news of the enemy & intends to concentrate troops at Brienne. star Apr 9 (907) DM1,300
— 22 May 1815. 1 p, folio. To the Prussian Army. Regarding Gen. Thielmann. Several endorsements by other officers. Bullock collection. CNY Dec 19 (159) $320
— 17 June 1815. 1 p, folio. To the military government at Muenster. Requesting them to speedily recruit 800 soldiers. star Apr 9 (908) DM800

Blum, Robert, 1807-48
ALs, 11 Feb 1837. 3 pp, 4to. To [K. G. Th. Winkler, Ed of the Abendzeitung at Dresden]. Informing him about the program of the Leipzig theater. star Apr 9 (910) DM420
— 27 May 1840. 1 p, 4to. To August Kahlert. Sending a fee. star Apr 9 (911) DM420

Bode, Johann Elert, 1747-1826
ALs, 27 Oct 1815. 1 p, 4to. To Johann Hieronymus Schroeter. About the price of his Astronomisches Jahrbuch & Schroeter's observations of Mars. star Apr 8 (307) DM550

Bodelschwingh, Friedrich von, 1831-1910
A Ls s (2), 13 Aug 1906 & 4 Jan 1908. 5 pp, 8vo. Recipient unnamed. Concerning church affairs at Bethel. JG Oct 2 (179) DM500

Boell, Heinrich, 1917-85
ALs, 7 Apr 1958. 2 pp, 8vo. To Elisabeth Bergner. About a production of one of his plays, & sending a book. With a copy of his Irisches Tagebuch. Berlin, 1957; sgd, dated [7 Apr] 1958 & inscr to Bergner. C June 24 (137A) £240 [Bender]
— 31 Mar 1960. 1 p, folio. To an unnamed graphologist. Complying with a request for his autograph. star Apr 8 (24) DM340

Boetticher, Hans, 1883-1934. See: Ringelnatz, Joachim

Bogart, Humphrey —& Others
Menu, [n.d.], 8vo, for Congressional party en route to Hawaii, sgd by Bogart, Bette Davis, Kay Francis, Anita Louise & Dick Powell. wa May 30 (380) $375
— Anr, [n.d.], 8vo, for Congressional party en route to Hawaii, sgd by Bogart, Jack Warner & Dick Powell. wa May 30 (381)

$425

Boieldieu, Francois Adrien, 1775-1834

ALs, 4 Nov 1816. 2 pp, 4to. To the management of the Theatre Feydeau. Requesting them not to play his opera in order to avoid a confrontation with the author of the libretto. star Apr 9 (587a) DM360

— 31 Oct 1822. 2 pp, folio. To the members of the committee of the Opera Comique. Concerning free tickets for members of his family. S May 22 (581) £60 [Bouvier]

Bolingbroke, Henry St. John, Viscount, 1678-1751

ALs, 22 Apr 1712. 2 pp, 4to. To J. B. Colbert, Marquis de Torcy. Enclosing a letter (not present) & hoping that their negotiations may bring peace. In French. star Apr 9 (912) DM700

Bolivar, Simon, 1783-1830

Ls, 16 Nov 1821. 3 pp, folio. To Jose de San Martin, Protector of Peru. As President of the Republic of Colombia, repudiating the plan of an imperial government for Mexico & suggesting further efforts "to finish the expulsion of the Spanish from the entire continent". On Republica de Colombia letterhead. Frayed. CNY Dec 19 (11) $9,000

— 21 Nov 1827. 3 pp, folio. To Sec of State Henry Clay. Thanking for his efforts in promoting South American independence. Endorsed by Clay. Framed. P Sept 24 (2) $2,000

— 14 Sept 1830. 4 pp, 4to. To Andres de Santa Cruz, President of Bolivia. Discussing political & military developments. With autograph subscription. Fold tears; some repairs. With related material. sg Apr 9 (26) $3,000

ANs, 30 Jan 1821. 1 p, 4to. 4-line reply note at foot of ALs, 7 Dec 1820, from Gen. Francisco de Paula Santander to Bolivar, concerning claims made against the Colombian Government by Alberto Salazza. C Dec 3 (215) £900 [Emunds]

Ds, 10 Oct 1821. 2 pp, folio. Appointment for Miguel Santamaria as envoy to Mexico. Countersgd by Pedro Gual. P June 18 (15) $1,500

Bolivar, Simon, 1783-1830 — & Sucre, Antonio Jose de, 1795-1830

Ds, 31 Aug 1821. 1 p, folio. Commission for Lieut. Col. Pedro Torres; partly ptd. Repaired. S May 21 (224) £1,100 [Lucas]

Bonaparte, Carlo, 1746-85

Ds, 25 May 1776. 1 p, 4to. Power of attorney for Lorenzo Bono di Porgo to act against persons interfering with the flow of water to windmills belong to him & others. 6 other signatures. C Dec 3 (216) £320 [L'Autographe]

Bonaparte, Caroline, 1782-1839

[A collection of c.20 letters by her & members of her family, 1808 to 1850, c. 40 pp, various sizes, sold at S on 27 Nov 1986, lot 318, for £1,350 to Dr. Sam.]

ALs, 7 Apr [n.y.; 1808 - 1814]. 2 pp, 8vo. To [Regis de Cambaceres, Duke of Parma]. Thanking for news about Napoleon. HN Nov 27 (2218) DM500

— [n.d.]; 4 pp, 8vo. To the Prince of Canino. About politics & family news. sg Nov 6 (21) $60

Bonaparte Family

[A collection of 38 items, mostly A Ls s, by or relating to various members of the Bonaparte family, 1783 to 1873, sold at CNY on 19 Dec 1986, lot 160, for $6,500.]

Bonaparte, Jerome, 1784-1860

ALs, 2 Nov 1836. 2 pp, 8vo. To an unnamed General [Pelet-Clozeau?]. Praising his efforts on behalf of the Bonaparte family. HN Nov 27 (2294) DM550

— [1849 or later]. 1 p, 8vo. To his daughter Pauline Graefin Schoenfeld. About the departure of [his daughter] Jenny [von Pappenheim]. star Apr 9 (1082) DM720

Series of 4 Ls s, 1808 t0 1860. Size not stated. Recipients unnamed. Family matters. With 6 letters by his wives & his son Napoleon Jerome. S Nov 27 (320) £500 [Carroll]

Ds, 16 Oct 1841. 1 pp, folio. Promissory note for 310,000 francs borrowed from his niece "la Princesse Elisa Napoleon Baciocchi Comtesse Camerata" in 1835. Also sgd by Comtesse Camerata. With several attestations. HN May 22 (3057) DM460

Bonaparte, Joseph, 1768-1844

Collection of 15 A Ls s & L s s, c.1797 to 1829. Size not stated. To various recipients. About political & personal matters, & recommendations. With letters by his wife Julie Clary & his children. S Nov 27 (321) £950 [Carroll]

ALs, 4 Oct 1809. 1 p, 4to. To an unnamed French marshal in Spain. Acknowledging receipt of a letter. star Apr 9 (1079) DM600

Bonaparte, Louis, King of Holland, 1778-1846

[A collection of 27 letters, c.50 pp, folio & 4to, 1806 to 1807, pertaining to his installation on the throne of Holland, sold at S on 27 Nov 1986, lot 325, for £200 to

BONAPARTE

Carroll.]
Collection of ALs & 4 Ls s, 1802 to 1831. 7 pp, 4to & folio. Recipients unnamed. Recommending promotion of army members & requesting that his children be allowed back into France. S Nov 27 (324) £250 [Carroll]

Ls, 27 nivose an 13 [17 Jan 1805]. 1 p, 4to. Letter of recommendation for Louis Duterdoir for employment in the Forestry Administration. Framed. Altman collection. pnNY Sept 13 (77) $180

Bonaparte, Lucien, 1775-1840
Collection of 13 A Ls s & Ls s, 1801 to 1839; c.25 pp, various sizes. Recipients unnamed (1 to his mother). About the present state of France, his exile & financial situation, etc. With letters by his wife & children & a journal of his voyage to New York, 1823. S Nov 27 (326) £1,050 [Carroll]

Bonaparte, Maria Anna Elisa, 1777-1820
Collection of 7 A Ls s & Ls s, 1806 to 1819. 9 pp, 4to. To various recipients. Family letters, letters of recommendation, etc. With related material. S Nov 27 (319) £900 [Carroll]

Bonaparte, Maria Letizia Ramolino, 1750-1836
Series of 7 Ls s, 1808 to 1827. 14 pp, 4to. To members of her family & Cardinal Fesch. Family letters. In French & Italian. 1 Ls with 4-line autograph subscription; 1 silked. S Nov 27 (323) £1,900 [Dr. Sam]

Ls, 2 Aug 1789. 2 pp, 4to. Recipient unnamed. Thanking for information concerning the ineligibility of her son for nomination to the Ecole Royale Militaire. Sgd Veuve de Buonaparte. S Nov 27 (322) £950 [Dr. Sam]

Bonaparte, Napoleon, 1769-1821. See: Napoleon I

Bonaparte, Pauline, 1780-1825
Collection of c.30 A Ls s & Ls s, c.1803 to 1823. About 100 pp, 4to. To Madame Michelot. Personal letters to a friend. With related material. S Nov 27 (327) £1,450 [Dr. Sam]

ALs, 27 Oct [n.y., c.1803-1813]. 2 pp, 8vo. To Felix Bacchiocchi. Family letter, reporting about her own & her brothers' health. HN Nov 27 (2219) DM1,300

Ls, 21 July 1813. 3 pp, 4to. To Cambaceres. Sending wishes for his recovery & commenting about her own health. star Apr 9 (1080) DM440

Bonfadini, Vita
Ms, La caccia dell'arcobugio. 1652. 72 pp, 208mm by 154mm, in old vellum. Jeanson Ms 129 SM Feb 28 (82) FF4,500

AMERICAN BOOK PRICES CURRENT

Booth, John Wilkes, 1838-65
ALs, 23 Nov [1861]. 3 pp, 8vo. To Joseph H. Simonds. Reporting about engagements in Buffalo, Detroit & Cincinnati; mentioning [Edwin] Forrest. Bullock collection. CNY Dec 19 (14) $6,000

Borchert, Wolfgang, 1921-47
ALs, 16 Feb 1947. 4 pp, 4to. To Hans [Kirchner]. Reporting about his illness & his literary work. With related material. VH Sept 12 (955) DM1,700

Borges, Jorge Luis
Autograph Ms, story, El hombre de la esquina rosada, sgd; [1933?]. 5 leaves, 4to. With numerous revisions. In wraps bearing autograph Ms of Ensayos classicos. With related material. P June 18 (16) $20,000

Borgia, Lucretia, 1480-1519
Ls, 17 Oct 1515. 1 p, 4to. To "Raynaldo". Acknowledging receipt of his letter & requesting news about the war. P June 18 (17) $10,500

Borromeo, Carlo, Saint, 1538-84
ALs, 11 Aug 1574. 1 p, folio. To the provost & canons of the Milan cathedral. Regarding offices for the Virgin Mary. With authentication by Archbishop Benedict Erba Odescalchi & Johannes Petrus Andrianus, 27 May 1719, on verso. HK Nov 7 (2185) DM1,000

Borrow, George, 1801-81
Autograph Ms (2), Egil's Head Ransome, & When on your Fleet; [n.d.]. 3 pp, 8vo. With related material. sg Apr 9 (27) $1,200

Bosco, Giovanni, Saint, 1815-88
Lottery ticket, [Jan 1873]. 1 p, 4.3cm by 17.7cm. With signature of Don Michele Rua affixed to upper right corner. Mtd. With related material. star Apr 9 (913) DM1,200

Bossuet, Jacques Benigne, 1627-1704
Ms, notes on the life of Bertrand du Guesclin & the campaign in Spain, [n.d.]. 4 pp, 4to. Taken from pp 269-316 of an unnamed work. C June 24 (138) £180 [Castaing]

A Ls (2), 16 Aug & 22 Dec 1694. 8 pp, 4to. To Madame d'Albert de Luynes. Giving spiritual advice. 1st ALs incomplete. S Nov 27 (330) £280 [Charavay]

Boswell Family
[A collection of ALs by James Boswell & 4 A Ls s & A Ns s by Euphemia Boswell, [1836] & n.d., concerning Euphemia's confinement for madness, with related material, sold at CNY on 19 Dec 1986, lot 15, for $1,900.]

Botanical Manuscripts
Original drawings, Collection des Geraniers, Cultives par Mlle. Sidonie Hurtel d'Arboval...Tome 1er; [France, c.1850]. Tp & 99 leaves, each with watercolor drawing of a geranium; ink captions. In gilt-stamped mor album, 218mm by 297mm. Rubbed. Hunt collection. CNY Nov 21 (96) $7,200

Ms, Curiosites de la Nature. Des Fleurs, Paris 1756. 49 leaves (18 blanks], 238mm by 180mm. Tp in black ornamental stencil, 54 pp in neat cursive hand in brown ink, with black capitals; 28 pp with watercolor drawings, 2 pp with wash drawings of flowers. 68 pp with double-ruled black frames. Contemp olive-green mor bdg, gilt, with fleur-de-lys ornaments & arms of Louis Charles [or Louis-Auguste] de Bourbon, Prince de Dombes. CNY Nov 21 (9) $11,000 [John Fleming]

— Ms, Plantes francaises et etrangeres. [N.d.] 3 vols, 4to, in half shagreen. With 238 original watercolors of flowers & fruits. SM Oct 20 (415) FF27,000

— TULIPS. - Ms, tulip grower's catalogue, [Netherlands, early 18th cent], 90 watercolor drawings, of which 81 tulips, on 54 pp (of 40 leaves), 4to; vellum. 45 drawings with contemp captions. Contemp calf; spine gilt-tooled. Hunt collection CNY Nov 21 (271) $40,000

— TULIPS. - Ms, tulip grower's catalogue, [Netherlands, after 1715], 38 watercolor drawings, on rectos only. 80 leaves including blanks, 310mm by 195mm. Contemp captions in crimson ink. Contemp vellum over bds; modern slipcase. Hunt collection. CNY Nov 21 (272) $18,000

Boudin, Eugene, 1824-98
Series of 4 A Ls s, May 1894 to May 1898. 12 pp, 8vo. To Mr. Braquaval. About a Monet exhibition, his intention to visit Venice, his health, etc. 1 ALs with 2 small sketches. S Nov 27 (332) £380 [Quaritch]

A Ls s (2), 17 Oct 1868 & 12 June 1875. 5 pp, 8vo. To his friend Martin, about sales at the Le Havre exhibition. To his brother Louis, about his health. S Nov 27 (331) £280 [Quaritch]

— A Ls s (2), 5 & 8 July 1897. 6 pp, 8vo. To Guyotin. Concerning the sale of 2 paintings. S Nov 27 (334) £320 [Quaritch]

ALs, 23 Oct 1876. 3 pp, 8vo. To his brother Louis. Complaining about the difficulties of his life as an artist. Repaired with adhesive tape. sg Apr 9 (28) $425

— 17 Dec 1894. 4 pp, 8vo. To his brother Louis. Explaining why his plays are not good enough for the theatre. Fold split. S Nov 27 (333) £180 [Quaritch]

Boudinot, Elias, 1740-1821
Ds, 6 Mar [n.y.]. 1 p, 4to. Writ of attachment. Fragment. wa May 30 (25) $55

Boulez, Pierre
Autograph music, 2 staves on verso of restaurant bill, [10 July 1969]. 1 p, 8vo. Music using letters of Schoenberg's name (ArnolD eSCHoenBErG & A eS). Sgd P. B. star Apr 9 (588) DM360

Bourbon-Conti, Prince Louis Francois de
Ms, Recueil de fanfare usitee a l'equipage de S.A.S. Monseigneur le Prince de Conti. [c.1750] 7 leaes plus blanks, 122mm by 200mm, in contemp red mor gilt. Jeanson Ms 220 SM Feb 28 (86) FF8,000

Boutiller, Jean
Ms, La Somme rurale. [Eastern France, end of 15th cent] 228 leaves plus 9 endleaves on paper & 1 on vellum, 289mm by 210mm, in contemp blindstamped calf, with contemp painted edges. Jeanson Ms 116 SM Feb 28 (88) FF160,000

Bowyer, Henry. See: West Indies

Boyle, Kay
ALs, 10 Dec 1965. 1 p, 4to. To Mr. Cohen at Holt, Rinehart & Winston. Reviewing John Ashbery's Rivers and Mountains. sg Apr 9 (29) $200

Braddock, James J.
Menu, 21 Feb 1950. Banquet for Cub Pack 102, with Braddock as guest speaker. 4 pp, 12mo; mimeographed. Sgd on front cover. sg Apr 9 (30) $60

Bradley, Omar. See: Eisenhower, Dwight D. & Others

Braendstroem, Elsa, 1888-1948
ALs, 23 Dec 1936. 2 pp, folio. To Ingeborg Golm. Saying time will heal the bitterness left after her forced emigration. In German. Repaired. star Apr 9 (920) DM400

Bragg, Braxton, 1817-76
ALs, 27 Jan 1861. 3 pp, 8vo. To his wife. Reporting about the Louisiana secession ceremony. On Executive Office stationery. Tipped to larger sheet. Bullock collection. CNY Dec 19 (16) $5,500

Brahms, Johannes, 1833-97
ALs, [n.d., "Friday"]. 4 pp, 8vo. To an unnamed friend. Reporting that he has composed 2 songs for him. Some tears. P Dec 15 (9) $2,000

— 24 Dec 1895. 3 pp, 8vo. To Fritz Simrock. Discussing a quartet by Smetana. star Apr 9 (590) DM5,000

— 21 Sept [n.y.]. 1 p, 8vo. To Max Kalbeck &

BRAHMS

his wife. Referring to a proposal by Kalbeck. S May 22 (580) £800 [Simeone]

Autograph postcard, sgd, [22 May 1886]. To Herr Eylinger of Basel. Declining to undertake a concert. S Nov 28 (501) £300 [Batchelder]

— [21 Dec 1895]. To Ludwig Weber. Thanking for a poem & saying it cannot be set to music. star Apr 9 (589) DM1,500

— 31 Aug 1896. To Eusebius Mandyczewski. Suggesting a meeting. In pencil. star Apr 9 (591) DM650

ANs, [n.d.]. 2 pp, 5.5cm by 8.5cm. Recipient unnamed. Offering congratulations & thanks. 9 lines on both sides of ptd visiting card. S May 22 (360) £320 [Maggs]

AN, [n.d.]. Recipient unnamed. 5 lines, sending compliments. On verso of visiting card. star Apr 9 (592) DM780

Engraving, port by Ludwig Michalek; [n.d]. About 106cm by 75cm. Framed. Showing Brahms standing at his piano in Vienna; sgd by Michalek. S May 22 (361) £1,300 [Bordone]

Braine, John

[A collection of 17 autograph poems & 8 typescripts of poems, all sgd, 1943 to 1948, c.30 pp, various sizes, sold at S on 23 July 1987, lot 132, for £350 to Quaritch.]

Brandeis, Louis D., 1856-1941. See: Taft, William Howard & Brandeis

Brandt, Willy

Ls, 22 May 1959. 1 p, folio. To Karl Boehm. Asking him to join the Bund der Berliner und Freunde Berlins & commenting about the political situation of Berlin. star Apr 9 (921) DM750

Braque, Georges, 1882-1963

Ds, 25 Feb 1956. 1 p, 8vo. Contract granting Jim Tillet exclusive rights for 1 year to use works of art created by Braque for textiles & other products. Framed. Altman collection. pnNY Sept 13 (81) $400

Braun, Lily, 1865-1916

Autograph Ms, notes for a political speech, [n.d.]. 5 pp, 8vo. In pencil. With further material, partly autograph, relating to her family. star Apr 8 (26) DM750

Braxton, Carter, Signer from Virginia

Autograph endorsement, on statement of account of Garland Anderson, 11 Oct 1782. 1 p, 4to. With a port. Charlotte Parker Milne collection. wd Nov 12 (28) $100

AMERICAN BOOK PRICES CURRENT

Brentano, Clemens, 1778-1842

Autograph Ms, poem, Lied auf die Kinder; 1824. 20 8-line stanzas, 4 pp, 8vo. Sgd at head. S May 21 (227) £1,450 [Haas]

Bresgen, Cesar

Autograph music, sketches for his Mass for children, 1970. 4 pp, 29.5cm by 20.5cm, 12 staves each. In ink & pencil. Sgd at head. star Apr 9 (594) DM200

Breton, Andre, 1896-1966

Series of 12 A Ls s, 1 July 1934 to 3 Nov 1964. 24 pp, 4to & 8vo. To Rene Magritte. Important letters discussing his writings, Magritte's paintings, Surrealism, etc. S July 2 (969) £12,000 [Ducasse F. A.]

Breviarium -- Latin Manuscripts

— [Poland, 14th cent]. Of Dominican Use. 246 leaves only, vellum, 204mm by 152mm. Modern lea over wooden bds. In dark brown ink in a gothic liturgical hand. With painted initials throughout in red & blue & very large initial with pen- & brushwork border. S June 23 (95) £2,600 [Niewodniczanski]

— [Paris, c.1400]. The Armagnac Breviary. 2 vols, 336 & 357 leaves, vellum, 205mm by 136mm. Early 20th-cent dark red velvet over pastebds. In dark brown ink in 2 sizes of a gothic liturgical bookhand. Brilliantly illuminated with c.2,800 large illuminated initials, illuminated borders throughout & 47 miniatures comprising 37 very large historiated initials. S June 23 (96) £640,000 [St. Pauls]

— [Cologne, early 15th cent]. Use of Cologne. 147 leaves, vellum, 354mm by 296mm, in modern mor gilt & blind-stamped. In red & brown ink, with decorated initials throughout, in colors; large elaborate initial in blue, red & green with ornamental border on f.1. 2 leaves missing [after f.143]. FD Dec 2 (3a) DM45,000

— [Flanders or Rhineland, possibly Liege, 15th cent]. Of Augustinian Use. 246 leaves only, vellum, 160mm by 110mm. Lacking bdg. In several sections in various gothic hands. With music on a 4-line red stave, large calligraphic initials in black & painted initials throughout in red. Including text of Ars Moriendi. Worn. S June 23 (97) £1,500 [Derry]

— [Southern France, 2d half of 15th cent]. Of Benedictine Use [Abbey of Montmajour]. 349 leaves, vellum, 140mm by 100mm. 19th cent red mor preserving sides of earlier bdg. In light & dark brown ink in a small rounded lettre batarde. With 15 large illuminated initials. C June 24 (260) £3,400 [Schoyen]

— [North-East Italy, 2d half of 15th cent]. Of

Franciscan Use. 369 leaves, vellum, 139mm by 100mm. Lacking 49 leaves. Modern quarter calf over wooden bds. In brown ink in a very small rounded liturgical hand. With 17 large decorated initials in red or blue & 42 illuminated initials in elaborate leafy designs in full colors on burnished gold grounds. Very worn; some leaves def. S Dec 2 (49) £2,200 [Ferrini]

— [Germany, 2d half of 15th cent]. Of Dominican Use. 274 leaves, vellum, 177mm by 120mm. Contemp blindstamped red tanned skin over wooden bds, repaired. Written by several scribes in dark brown ink in a gothic liturgical hand. With decorated initials throughout, c.12 larger initials, c.30 very large illuminated initials in different styles & 7 very large historiated initials with illuminated borders. S Dec 2 (50) £12,000 [Tenschert]

— [Northern Rhineland, early 16th cent]. Of Benedictine Use. 207 leaves, vellum, 13.5cm by 9.2cm. Modern lea with new clasps. With 12 historiated initials, 10 large & numerous small illuminated initials, elaborate floral borders. Lacking several leaves. HN Nov 27 (2196) DM8,000

— [Lombardy, c.1520-30]. Of Augustinian Use. 1 leaf only, 310mm by 232mm, vellum. In red & dark brown ink. With large historiated initial of St. Andrew & full border with elaborate designs of flowers, leaves, animals & IHS monogram within double burnished gold frame. Framed. S Dec 2 (22) £4,500 [Fogg]

Brisbin, James S.

ALs, 18 Aug 1862. 8 pp, folio. To his wife. Reporting about the march to Williamsburg. wa May 30 (211) $425

— 9 May 1863. 4 pp, 4to. To his wife. Reporting about the war. wa May 30 (210) $300

Britten, Benjamin, 1913-76

Collection of 19 A Ls s & postcards, sgd, c.1963 to 1976; c.40 pp, various sizes. To John Culshaw. Regarding the recording & performance of his various works. S Nov 28 (503) £4,500 [Haas]

Autograph postcard, sgd, [15 Aug 1940]. To Ralph Hawkes. About his Diversions for piano & orchestra, contracts with RCA, etc. Sgd Benjie. S Nov 28 (504) £240 [Haas]

Autograph quotation, 2 bars from Peter Grimes, notated on 2 staves, 23 Jan 1949. 1 p, c.18cm by 22cm. Sgd & inscr. With 2 port photographs, sgd, 21cm by 16cm. S May 22 (583) £700 [Friedman]

Broca, Paul, 1824-1880

ALs, [n.d.]. 3 pp, 8vo. To Alexandre Hovelacque. Inviting him to a meeting of the editors of the Revue d'anthropologie. With autograph Ms, regarding a "thermometre a spirale", 1 p, 8vo. star Apr 8 (310) DM500

Brock, Charles Edward

Original drawings, (12), to illus Jane Austen's Mansfield Park, in the English Idylls series. In ink & watercolor. Mostly sgd & dated 1908. 372mm by 264mm. Archives of J. M. Dent & Son. S June 19 (767) £12,000 [Edberg]

— Original drawings, (12), to illus Walter Raymond's Tryphena in Love & Young Sam and Sabina, 1912. In ink. Mostly captioned, sgd & dated 1912. Average size 350mm by 235mm. Archives of J. M. Dent & Son. S June 19 (763) £1,600 [Greer]

— Original drawings, (14), to illus Jane Austen's Northanger Abbey, in the English Idylls series. In ink & watercolor. All sgd & dated 1907. 373mm by 267mm. Archives of J. M. Dent & Son. S June 19 (765) £7,500 [Hartnoll]

— Original drawings, (17), to illus Jane Austen's Sense and Sensibility, in the English Idylls series. In ink & watercolor. All sgd & dated 1908; tp initialled. 373mm by 266mm. With ink drawing of tp of the 1922 Ed. Archives of J. M. Dent & Son. S June 19 (766) £22,000 [Edberg]

— Original drawings, (18), to illus Dickens' The Chimes, 1905. In ink & watercolor, & in ink. Mostly captioned, sgd & dated 1905. 371mm by 270mm (7) & various sizes. With a reprint of the book. Archives of J. M. Dent & Son. S June 19 (760) £6,000 [Beetles]

— Original drawings, (18), to illus Dickens' The Haunted Man, 1907. In ink & watercolor, & in ink. Captioned, sgd & dated 1906 or 1907. 370mm by 269mm (7) & various sizes. With a copy of the book. Archives of J. M. Dent & Son. S June 19 (761) £2,600 [Edberg]

— Original drawings, (18), to illus Jane Austen's Persuasion, in the English Idylls series. In ink & watercolor. Sgd & dated 1909; tp initialled. 379mm by 271mm. Archives of J. M. Dent & Son. S June 19 (769) £30,000 [Edberg]

— Original drawings, (19), complete set of illusts for Dickens' The Cricket on the Hearth, 1905. In ink, & in ink & watercolor. Captioned & sgd, 18 dated 1905. Mostly 372mm by 269mm. With a copy of the book. Archives of J. M. Dent & Son. S June 19 (759) £2,000 [Hartnoll]

— Original drawings, (19), complete set of

BROCK

illusts for Dickens' The Battle of Life, 1907. In ink & watercolor, & in ink. Captioned & sgd, some dated 1907. 372mm by 271mm (8) & various sizes. With a copy of the book. Archives of J. M. Dent & Son. S June 19 (762) £2,400 [Beetles]

— Original drawings, (19), to illus Dickens' A Christmas Carol, 1905. In ink, & in ink & watercolor. Mostly captioned, sgd & dated 1905. 371mm by 270mm (7) & various sizes. With a copy of the book. Archives of J. M. Dent & Son. S June 19 (758) £12,500 [Hartnoll]

— Original drawings, (20), to illus Jane Austen's Pride and Prejudice, in the English Idylls series. In ink & watercolor. All captioned, sgd & dated 1907; tp initialled. 371mm by 269mm. Archives of J. M. Dent & Son. S June 19 (764) £11,500 [Edberg]

— Original drawings, (24), complete set of illusts for Jane Austen's Emma, in the English Idylls series. In ink & watercolor. 23 sgd & dated 1909. 378mm by 271mm. Archives of J. M. Dent & Son. S June 19 (768) £42,000 [Edberg]

— Original drawings, 4 ink & watercolor illusts for Jane Austen's Sense and Sensibility, 1898. Each captioned, sgd & dated 1898. 300mm by 235mm. Archives of J. M. Dent & Son. S June 19 (753) £1,900 [Sawyer]

— Original drawings, 4 ink & watercolor illusts for Jane Austen's Pride and Prejudice, 1898. Each captioned, sgd & dated 1898. 246mm by 150mm. Mtd. With drawings for cover design & endpapers. Archives of J. M. Dent & Son. S June 19 (754) £4,800 [Edberg]

— Original drawings, 4 ink & watercolor illusts for Jane Austen's Persuasion, 1898. Each captioned, sgd & dated 1898. 285mm by 225mm. Archives of J. M. Dent & Son. S June 19 (755) £3,400 [Edberg]

— Original drawings, 47 ink illusts for Dickens' The Holly Tree and the Seven Poor Travellers, 1900. Mostly captioned, sgd & dated 1898. Various sizes. Archives of J. M. Dent & Son. S June 19 (757) £8,000 [Edberg]

— Original drawings, 6 ink & watercolor illusts for Jane Austen's Emma, 1898. Each captioned, sgd & dated 1898. 288mm by 227mm. 2 mtd. With a copy of a later ptg of the book. Archives of J. M. Dent & Son. S June 19 (756) £3,600 [Edberg]

— Original drawings, (9), to illus Sir Walter Scott's Ivanhoe, 1899. In ink. Each with caption in panel below, sgd & dated 1898. 380mm by 280mm. Archives of J. M. Dent & Son. S June 19 (752) £800 [Sawyer]

Brock, Henry Matthew

Original drawings, (11), to illus Sir Walter Scott's Ivanhoe, 1899. In ink. Each captioned & sgd. Average size 300mm by 230mm. Archives of J. M. Dent & Son. S June 19 (770) £2,000 [Sawyer]

— Original drawings, (5), to illus Jane Austen's Northanger Abbey, 1898. In ink & watercolor. Each captioned & sgd, 4 dated 1898. 287mm by 228mm. Archives of J. M. Dent & Son. S June 19 (773) £2,100 [Sawyer]

— Original drawings, (7), to illus Jane Austen's Pride and Prejudice, 1898. In ink & watercolor. Each captioned & sgd, 5 dated 1898. Average size 287mm by 230mm. Archives of J. M. Dent & Son. S June 19 (771) £5,800 [Edberg]

— Original drawings, (9), to illus Jane Austen's Mansfield Park, 1898. In ink & watercolor. Each captioned & sgd, 8 dated 1898. 286mm by 229mm. 2 mtd. With a reprint of the book. Archives of J. M. Dent & Son. S June 19 (772) £4,000 [Edberg]

Brod, Max, 1884-1968

Collection of 6 A Ls s & Ls, 10 May 1964 to 25 Nov 1965. 13 pp, folio & 8vo. To the publisher Karl Borromaeus Glock. Mostly concerning the publication of a collection of essays. star Apr 8 (27) DM380

Broenik de Legnitz, Hieronymus

Ms, Collatiunculae, [Germany, late 15th cent]. 189 leaves, 150mm by 105mm. Contemp blindstamped brown lea, wormed. In black ink; rubricated in red. Sermons addressed to members of a Carthusian convent. HK Nov 4 (409) DM3,600

Broglie, Louis Victor, Prince de, 1892-1987

ALs, 5 May 1946. 1 p, 12mo. Recipient unnamed. Declining an invitation. star Apr 8 (311) DM240

Broglie, Maurice, Duc de, 1875-1960

ALs, 2 June 1936. 2 pp, 8vo (lettercard). To an unnamed colleague. Describing a study of one of his assistants. star Apr 8 (312) DM210

Bronte, Charlotte, 1816-55

— NICHOLLS, A. B. - ALs, 31 Mar 1855. 2 pp, 8vo. To Ellen Nussey. Notifying her of the death of his wife Charlotte. Was mtd. S Dec 18 (34) £1,000 [Bronte Society]

Brooklyn, New York

[A collection of c.145 items relating to the Cortelyou & Van Vechten families in 19th cent Brooklyn sold at sg on 6 Nov 1986, lot 23, for $200.]

Brown, John, of Osawatomie, 1800-59

ALs, 18 June 1855. 1 p, 4to. To "Dear Children". Making plans for moving from Ohio to North Elba. Bullock collection. CNY Dec 19 (22) $950

— BECKHAM, FONTAINE. - 2 Ds s, 2 May 1847 & 25 Aug 1846. Writs. With anr writ, sgd by Israel Russel. wa May 30 (227) $90

Browning, Elizabeth Barrett, 1806-61

Autograph Ms, Poems before Congress, working draft of 8 poems, [c.1859]. 54 pp, 8vo. Bound with 1st Ed, L, 1860; red mor gilt. 7 pp in pencil. Gimbel Family collection. P June 18 (21) $25,000

Collection of ALs & cut signature, [n.d.]. 2 pp, size not stated. To Mrs. Powers. Thanking for the loan of books. Last 2 lines of a letter, sgd Ba. pnNY June 11 (3) $1,000

Browning, Robert, 1812-89

Collection of 8 A Ls s, ANs & telegram, 1879 to 1889 & [n.d.]. 10 pp, mostly 8vo. To Mrs. Hill, regarding dinner invitations. To Mrs. Sitwell, informing her that a port will be on view, & about the movement of some statues. pnNY June 11 (4) $2,300

ALs, "Wednesday Mg." [1842?]. 1 p, 16mo. To [W. C.] Macready. Agreeing "to talk over the matter". pn Dec 11 (35) £320 [Maggs]

— 14 May 1875. 1 p, 8vo. To the Duchess of St. Albans. Sending compliments & photographs. Laid down. S Jan 27 (697) £300 [Maggs]

— [n.d., "Wednesday"]. 2 pp, 8vo. To Lady Castletown. Explaining a misunderstanding about a dinner invitation. C June 24 (92) £320 [Maggs]

— 10 May 1876. 1 p, 8vo. To Moscheles. Arranging a visit. With related material. S Jan 27 (696) £220 [Maggs]

— 9 Dec 1877. 2 pp, 8vo. To Miss Anna Swanwick. Sending her a translation & hoping for her understanding of what he tried to do. Including autograph dedication to Miss Swanwick, 9 Dec [18]77, on half-title of 1st Ed of his trans of The Agamemnon of Aeschylus, 1877. C Dec 3 (350) £550 [Maggs]

— 16 June 1881. 1 p, 8vo. To Lady Reay. Apologizing for apparent negligence. S Jan 27 (695) £190 [Maggs]

— 5 Mar 1887. 1 p, 8vo. To Mrs. Drummond. Declining an invitation. Framed. Altman collection. pnNY Sept 13 (106) $400

ANs, 8 Sept [n.y]. 1 p, size not stated. Recipient unnamed. Acknowledging receipt of a telegram & saying he is at Cortina. Possibly postscript to a longer letter. Framed with a port. wd Nov 12 (2) $75

Brownson, Nathan, c.1740-96

ALs, 1 Dec 1781. 3 pp, folio. To Gen. Nathanael Greene. Describing problems with Indians & the military situation in Georgia. Some paper loss affecting text. Silked. P May 13 (50) $2,300

Bruch, Max, 1838-1920

Series of 16 A Ls s, 4 Apr 1862 to 1 Dec 1866. 61 pp, mostly 8vo. To L. F. C. Bischoff. Letters to a friend, reporting about his life & work & mentioning contemp composers. star Apr 9 (595) DM3,400

ALs, 3 Aug 1872. 3 pp, 8vo. To [C. H.?] Bitter. Asking for the return of the piano score of Hermione. S May 22 (584) £250 [Preussische Staatsbibliothek]

— 23 Aug 1875. 4 pp, 4to. To [Georg Henschel?]. Requesting him to sing in the 1st performance of Hermannsschlacht. Was mtd. With autograph list of his works, [1874], 3 pp, 8vo. star Apr 9 (597) DM550

— 5 Oct 1905. 4 pp, 8vo. Recipient unnamed. Requesting him to print a notice concerning two young musicians. star Apr 9 (598) DM300

Bruell, Ignaz, 1846-1907

Autograph music, 5 songs for male choir, each sgd, [1898]. 7 pp, size not stated. Also sgd at head. star Apr 9 (599) DM920

Bruere (Percy C. Sadleir)

Autograph Ms, Story of the Little Pigs and their Wonderful Adventures; 2 vols, 1851. Ms, watercolour bound 1848, 22 pp, 4to, orig cloth; & Ms, 22 watercolor illusts, c.78mm by 142mm, tp, dramatis personae, etc., mtd in oblong 4to sketchbook; roan-backed cloth. Ink & wash drawing by J. S. S. King mtd on endleaf. Dedicated to Murray John & Robert Albert Hickson. 2d pt presumably unpbd. S Dec 5 (438) £24,000 [Schiller]

Bryan, Henry

Ms, report, Memorandum of History of Gholson's Cavalry Brigade, [Dec 1864]. 2 pp, folio. With 12 autograph lines. Sang collection. wa May 30 (213) $120

Bryan, William Jennings, 1860-1925

ALs, [n.d.]. 2 pp, 4to. To Mr. Berger, father of his son-in-law. About going to Miami together. On Department of State letterhead. wa May 30 (462) $75

Bryant, William Cullen, 1794-1878

ALs, 21 Apr 1862. 1 p, 8vo. To Mr. Lawson. Sending clippings (included) of the burning of [W. Gilmore] Simms's house. On Evening Post letterhead. sg Apr 9 (33) $60

Buber, Martin, 1878-1965
Series of 7 A Ls s, 1905 to 1919 & [n.d.]. 13 pp, 4to. To Hermann Stehr. Asking him to cooperate in a collection of essays. Asking him to chair a meeting. Commenting about Stehr's Die Grossmutter. star Apr 8 (313) DM1,800

ALs, 29 Oct 1933. 1 p, 8vo. To Herr Warburg. Suggesting that he talk to Hermann Gerson about his Palestine scheme. File holes affecting text. C June 24 (163) £180 [Lucas]

Ls, 13 Nov 1961. 1 p, 8vo. To Mrs. Urquart. Agreeing to contribute to a publication. wa May 30 (344) $80

— 28 Feb 1962. 1 p, 8vo. To Mrs. Urquart. Saying he has not written anything for her vol yet. wa May 30 (345) $110

Buchanan, Franklin, 1800-74. See: Perry, Matthew Calbraith

Buchanan, James, 1791-1868
A Ls s (2), 4 Nov 1835, 1 p, 4to, & 12 July 1861, size not stated. To Thomas Elder. Explaining why he could not meet Elder at Reading. To Joseph C. G. Kennedy. Commenting on military affairs. P Oct 29 (34) $550

— A Ls s (2), 8 Dec 1852 & 25 Nov 1856. 3 pp, 4to. To Lewis P. Clover & Rev. Henry Slicer. About Franklin Pierce's selection of a cabinet. As President-elect, thanking for a letter of advice. P May 13 (35) $2,700

ALs, 22 June 1842. 3 pp, 4to. To James McLanahan. About the removal of the postmaster at Chambersburg & the reapportionment of seats in the House of Representatives. P May 13 (34) $1,900

— 4 June 1844. 1 p, 4to. To T. & J. W. Johnson. Concerning amendments to a resolution submitted to the Senate. sg Sept 18 (47) $225

— 25 July 1865. 1 p, 12mo. To Ralph Metcalf. Sending his autograph. Rebacked. sg Nov 6 (24) $175

— 17 Oct 1866. 1 p, 8vo. To an unnamed lady. Looking forward to her visit. wa May 30 (89) $325

Ds, 11 June 1859. 1 p, folio. Ship's passport for the ship Hunter bound for the Pacific. pnNY June 11 (5) $700

Cut signature, [n.d.]. Size not stated. wa May 30 (90) $110

Franking signature, [21 Feb 1827]. rf May 30 (17) $270

— Anr, [27 Mar 1858]; "J. Buchanan Henry", executed by his private secretary. rf Mar 14 (69) $130

— Anr, [29 Dec 1859]. Ptd "President's Message" newspaper enclosure. rf Mar 14 (66) $190

— Anr, [23 Mar 1861]. rf May 30 (18) $200

— Anr, [21 Jan n.y.]. rf Mar 14 (67) $150

— Anr, [11 June n.y.]. rf Mar 14 (68) $130
See also: Polk, James K. & Buchanan

Buchanan, James, 1791-1861. See: Polk, James K. & Buchanan

Buck, Pearl S., 1892-1973
[An important series of 5 drafts of her play Flight into China, later called Plum Blossoms, holograph & typed, 692 pp, 4to, was sold at P on 24 Sept 1986, lot 12, for $500.]

Typescript, novel, Good People; draft. 1936, 446 pp, 4to. With autograph corrections. P Sept 24 (11) $500

— Typescript, story, China Stage, [c.1943]. 136 pp, 4to. Incomplete; with autograph corrections & 13 Ms pp. With revised typescript carbon copy, 93 pp, 4to, & related material. P June 18 (23) $400

Typescript carbon copy, novel, Command the Morning, 1957. 367 pp, 4to. With some autograph corrections. P June 18 (22) $200

Bucke, Richard Maurice. See: Whitman, Walt

Buckingham Castle Iron Works Company
Document, [n.d., 1865?]. 49 leaves, folio. Deed of Settlement, including names of subscribers, etc. Calf bdg. C June 24 (8) £130 [Weng]

Buckingham, George Villiers, 1st Duke of, 1592-1628
[A Ms satirical poem, A proper new ballet upon the naminge of the Duke of Buckingham in the Remonstrance, [1628]; 2 pp, folio, sold at C on 24 June 1987, lot 112, for £170 to Burgess Browning.]

Buelow, Hans von, 1830-94
ALs, 13 Oct [18]59. 3 pp, 8vo. To a concert director. Discussing his plans to perform unpbd works by Liszt, & about Wagner. With ALs by Marie von Buelow. S Jan 27 (1002) £170 [Haas]

— 11 Feb 1860. 4 pp, 8vo. To Julius Schuberth. About Schuberth's Verdi Ed, his concerts, & the reception of Wagner's Tristan und Isolde in Paris. star Apr 9 (600) DM1,000

— 2 Apr 1870. 2 pp, 8vo. To Reinhard Hallwachs. Explaining why he did not visit him. With related material. star Apr 9 (601) DM240

— "20 prairial 99"[June 1891?]. 1 p, 8vo. To Hermann Wolff. Cheerful letter, suggesting a meeting in Berlin. star Apr 9 (602) DM220

Bulwer-Lytton, Edward, 1803-73

Series of 5 A Ls s, 1830 to 1832. 12 pp, 4to & 8vo. To William Godwin. About his own & Godwin's literary work. S July 23 (40) £850 [Quaritch]

Bunsen, Robert Wilhelm, 1811-99

ALs, 7 July 1856. 2 pp, 8vo. To an unnamed young scientist. Asking to be notified if he should arrive after the beginning of the semester. star Apr 8 (314) DM700

— 12 Mar 1862. 3 pp, 8vo. To William Sharpey. Forwarding a letter by J. H. J. Mueller [not present] & supporting a request by Mueller. With related material. HN Nov 27 (2228) DM700

— 26 June 1870. 3 pp, 4to. To Jolly, Minister of the Interior of Baden. Expressing his wish that his colleague Professor Kopp, who has been offered a chair at Leipzig, stay at Heidelberg. HN May 22 (2962) DM2,000

Burghley, William Cecil, 1st Baron, 1520-98

ALs, 26 Sept 1574. 1 p, folio. To Robert Petre. As Lord High Treasurer, arranging for payment of money by Sir Thomas Gresham. C Dec 3 (219) £320 [Bristow]

Ls, 28 Jan 1589. 1 p, folio. To Steven Fullwell. Ordering 3 woods in the county of Huntingdon to be sold to James Hudson. C Dec 3 (220) £190 [Claridge]
See also: Essex, Robert Devereux

Burne-Jones, Sir Edward Coley, 1833-98

Collection of 2 A Ls s & ANs, [n.d.]. 3 pp, 8vo. To "Dear Edward". Social messages. Each with a sketch. Bullock collection. CNY Dec 19 (23) $850

Burne-Jones, Sir Philip

Collection of ALs & orig drawing, 7 Mar 1915 & 1916. 4 pp, 8vo. Recipient & contents not stated. Pen-&-ink sketches in ALs, & separate pen-&-ink sketch. sgd P B-J : all sketches relating to the war. sg Apr 9 (34) $110

Burney Family

Ms, Lines on or by the Burney Family. [N.d.]. 114 pp, 4to, vellum, soiled. In various hands, consisting of 85 poems by members of the Burney family & their circle. d sg Apr 2 (36) $2,600

Burns, Robert, 1759-96

[An album containing 7 autograph letters & Mss by Burns, & related material, sold at pn on 11 Dec 1986, lot 36, for £ 14,000 to Quaritch.]

Burnside, Ambrose E., 1824-81

Signature, [n.d.]. With engraved port, framed. wa May 30 (214) $60

Burr, Aaron, 1756-1836

ALs, 16 Feb [1804]. 1 p, folio. To David Gelston. Concerning a real estate deal with John Jacob Astor. Sgd AB. CNY Dec 19 (24) $950

— 2 Sept 1824. 1 p, 4to. To Capt. Sam Reid. Regarding passage to NY on the steamer Kent. Sgd A.B. rf Mar 14 (7) $260

AL, [20 July 1804]. 1 p, 4to. To Joseph Alston. Regarding the jury deliberations after the duel with Hamilton. With a ciphered note in Burr's hand, 2 pp, 4to; docketed by Alston "A.B. Baltimore 1800". Repaired. Sang collection. P Oct 29 (35) $1,000

Franking signature, [31 Oct 1791]. rf Mar 14 (70) $450

— EDWARDS, TIMOTHY. - ALs, 28 Apr 1783; 1 p, size not stated. To Burr, advising him not to return to NY before the British leave. rf Mar 14 (8) $80

Burton, Sir Richard Francis, 1821-90

Autograph Ms, notes from Disraeli's letters & some Oriental authors, [c.1886-90]. 3 pp, 8vo. In violet & black ink. S Jan 27 (825) £120 [Burton]

— Autograph Ms, notes on Abyssinia, the Emperor Johannes & the tribe of Joseph, [c.1885-90]. 3 pp, on rectos only, 16mo. S Jan 27 (826) £120 [Burton]

ALs, 8 Jan 1867. 4 pp, 16mo. To A[lexander] Findlay. Concerning projected travels in Brazil & literary activities. pn Dec 11 (122) £360 [Buckell & Ballard]

— 1 Jan [n.y.]. 1 p, 8vo. To J. C. Parkinson. Apologizing for being unable to attend a meeting. Framed. Altman collection. pnNY Sept 13 (107) $200

— [n.d., "Tuesday 7"]. 2 pp, 8vo. To his publisher. Returning corrected proofs. bba Nov 13 (154) £90 [Trophy Room]

Busch, Wilhelm, 1832-1908

ALs, 10 Jan 1889. 1 p, 4to. To Alexander Guenther. Thanking for a letter & musing about the importance of contentedness. star Apr 8 (28) DM3,500

— "Sonnabend" [1 May 1897?]. 1 p, 8vo. To his nephew Hermann [Noeldeke]. Notifying him of the date of his arrival. On verso ALs, 28 Nov 1912, from Noeldeke to [Theodor] Hoppe; authentication & covering letter. JG Oct 2 (18) DM730

BUSONI

Busoni, Ferruccio, 1866-1924
A Ls s (2), 14 June & 2 Aug 1921. 3 pp, 4to & 8vo. To Felice Boghen. Talking about his work on Dr. Faust, Turandot & the Fantasia Contrappuntistica. S May 22 (364) £200 [Kruyfhooft]

ALs, [n.d.]. 1 p, 8vo. To an unnamed lady. Agreeing to visit her & her mother. On hotel letterhead. star Apr 9 (604) DM220

— 21 Nov 1918. 1 p, folio. To [Dr. Zeiss] of the Frankfurt Opera. Letter of thanks. star Apr 9 (603) DM550

Butler, Charles, 1750-1832
Ms, Lectures on various aspects of conveyancing and property law, 1819. 173 pp, 8vo. Orig half mor. bba Nov 13 (169) £55 [White]

Butler, Pierce, 1744-1822
ANs, 8 Feb 1816. 1 p, 4to. Recipient unnamed. Request to settle a business "with esteem". With note in anr hand below. wa May 30 (147) $100

Byron, Catherine Gordon, Mother of the poet
ALs, 15 Apr 1799. 4 pp, folio. To her relative Mrs. Duff of Fetteresso. About the operation on Byron's foot by Dr. Baillie & his future education. Apparently unpbd. bba Apr 9 (276) £1,400 [Burgess Browning]

Byron, George Gordon Noel, Lord, 1788-1824
Autograph Ms, poem, Farewell to Malta. Sgd B & dated 26 May 1811. 4 pp, 4to. 56 lines; 2 revisions. S Dec 18 (39) £11,000 [Quaritch]

— Autograph Ms, poem, The Charity Ball; 10 Dec 1820. 2 pp, 4to. 7 stanzas; working Ms. Mostly unpbd. Sgd with a flourish. Bullock collection. CNY Dec 19 (37) $22,000

ALs, 20 Feb 1814. 4 pp, 4to. To [John Hamilton Reynolds]. Praising his poems, offering advice, & remembering his own experience as a young writer. Tipped in gilt brown mor vol. S Dec 18 (40) £7,500 [Joseph & Sawyer]

— 1 Apr 1815. 1 p, 8vo. To Robert John Wilmot. Applauding "the resurrection of Bonaparte". Integral blank partly separated. Bullock collection. CNY Dec 19 (36) $2,200

— [n.d.]. 1 p, 8vo. To John Hanson. Fragment; postscript only. Expressing his consent. Signature affixed on separate slip. S Jan 27 (701) £180 [Dupre]

Address leaf, [n.d.], 8vo; with autograph address to his pbr Galiagnani in Paris. Seal tear. C Dec 3 (351) £70 [Scotchman]

— Forgery. - Letter, 30 Mar 1807, 5 pp, 4to. To Edward Noel Long. Contents not stated. Probably by George Gordon De Luna Byron. Bullock collection. CNY Dec 19 (39) $240

AMERICAN BOOK PRICES CURRENT

— Forgery. - Letter, 2 Mar 1820, 3 pp, 4to, by Maj. George Gordon de Luna Byron, forging Byron's hand, to Thomas Moore. About William Godwin. P Sept 24 (13) $200

— Forgery. - Letter, 1 Sept 1811, 2 pp, 4to, [by Major Byron], purportedly by Byron to James Cawthorn. Contents not stated. Cloth folder. S Jan 27 (702) £170 [Wise]

— Guiccioli, Teresa (nee Gamba). - ALs, 29 Oct 1837. 3 pp, 8vo. To Baron Alibert. Asking him to treat her sick daughter. With related material. sg Apr 9 (36) $80

— Haydon, Benjamin Robert. - ALs, 23 Jan 1839. 4 pp, 4to. To Henry Austen Driver. Denouncing Byron's "lecherous luxury of married Strumpetism" & attacking his Don Juan. Mtd on album leaf. S Dec 18 (38) £650 [Joseph & Sawyer]

C

Calder, Alexander, 1898-1976
A Ls s (2), 10 Jan & 4 Oct 1949. 2 pp, 4to. Recipients unnamed. Invitations. star Apr 8 (447) DM320

Calderon de la Barca, Angel, 1790-1861
Autograph Ms, diary, Oct 1839 to May 1841. 284 pp, 4to. Contemp half calf. Describing voyage from New York to Havana & residence in Mexico. Partly in code. CNY May 11 (8) $4,000

Calhoun, John C., 1782-1850
Franking signature, [9 Nov 1837]. On folded letter of his son to Cadet Patrick Calhoun at West Point. rf Mar 14 (71) $110

— Anr, [22 Mar 1840]. rf Mar 14 (72) $60

California
— Committee of Vigilance of the City of San Francisco. - Document, 25 June 1851. 1 p, folio. Certificate of membership for Lewis W. Sloat; partly ptd. Sgd by 3 officers of the Committee. Bullock collection. CNY Dec 19 (40) $550

Callas, Maria, 1923-77
Photograph, sgd & inscr, [n.d.]. 18cm by 13cm. Full length, as Norma. Was mtd. star Apr 9 (606) DM1,200

Calligraphy
— Bouton, Victor. - Briefue Autourserie...by Charles d'Archssia. [Paris, c.1887] 20 leaves, vellum, 202mm by 142mm, in mor gilt by Chambolle-Duru. Jeanson Ms 212 SM Feb 28 (30) FF32,000

— Bouton, Victor. - Traite Divertissant sur la Chasse...by M. d'Aucour. 1668-94. 26 leaves, vellum, 155mm by 108mm, in mor gilt by Chambolle-Duru. Jeanson Ms 214

SM Feb 28 (46) FF5,000
— BOUTON, VICTOR. - Le dit dou cerf amoureux. La comparaison du faucon. [Paris, Apr 1894] 16 leaves, vellum, 262mm by 190mm, in mor gilt by Chambolle-Duru. With 1 miniature & 1 historiated initial in colors & gold. Jeanson Ms 209 SM Feb 28 (180) FF13,000
— BOUTON, VICTOR. - A Jean de Couci, Baron de Stone, ieune enfant de grande esperance aage de 9 ans...[De la chasse], by francois de L'Alouete. [Paris, c.1880] 10 leaves, vellum, 200mm by 140mm, in half mor gilt. Jeanson Ms 211 SM Mar 1 (317) FF3,000
— BOUTON, VICTOR. - Memento des chasseurs ou dictionnaire des termes de chasse en usage dans la montagne de Reims, la Foret des Ardennez et les Vosges sous le roy Louis XIV.... [Paris, 1899] 68 leaves, vellum, 174mm by 120mm, in mor gilt by Chambolle-Duru. Jeanson Ms 215 SM Mar 1 (403) FF20,000
— HEWITT, GRAILY. - Ms, Psalm 78, [c.1945-50]. 14 pp, & title & blanks, 253mm by 175mm. Brown half mor bdg by A. V. Hughes. In black ink in a fine roman hand. With large illuminated initial with Celtic interlace & 5 initials in gold. S Dec 2 (71) £280 [Maggs]
— MARTICH, RUDOLPH. - Autograph Ms, The Calendar-Stone of the Aztecs, 1933-44. 59 leaves, 258mm by 224mm; thick watercolor paper. 25 leaves of text & 31 full-page illusts, richly illuminated throughout. Leaves in glassine folds in half art lea bds. Rosenblatt collection. P June 18 (121) $3,750
— MUCKE, GEORG. - Devotional book; Luestgertlein, das ist, Wie ein Christlichs hertz durch denn gantzen Psalter...mit schonen reimen und spruchen spatzieren...kann, 1581. 46 leaves, vellum & 10 leaves, paper, 114mm by 70mm. Dark brown contemp lea in half lea case. In brown, red & green ink in calligraphic gothic script. With elaborate colored borders throughout & numerous large initials. Containing calendar, psalms, prayers & ABC with quatrains, lacking 6 letters on 3 leaves. FD Dec 2 (9a) DM5,800
— SANGORSKI, ALBERTO. - The Garland of Love. 1907. 53pp, vellum, 4to, in mor gilt. With double-page opening of large ornamental gold-lettered title & 1st page of text enclosed within richly illuminated borders, tp with borders of scrolling grape-vine & wild rose with cherubs, cupids & a medallion miniature of Cupid & Psyche, 1st page of text with large gilt initial & scrolling foliate borders inhabited by cherubs & doves. C Dec 12 (375) £1,700 [Joseph]
— SANGORSKI, ALBERTO. - The Rubaiyat of Omar Khayyam, translated by Edward Fitzgerald. 1905. 20 leaves plus blanks, 202mm by 138mm, vellum, in contemp mor gilt by Sangorski & Sutcliffe, lacking backstrip. sg Dec 4 (148) $1,500
— SEDELMEYER, ANDREAS GOTTLIEB. - Ms, Probschrifft, [Germany, 1770]. Tp & 14 leaves. Contemp brocade-paper wraps. With 4 initials in 2 colors, large watercolor, & 8 colored engravings. Calligraphic exercises of a 12-year old. HK Nov 4 (426) DM1,700
— WELD, EMMA MARIA. - Illuminations. 1843-45. Series of 24 orig pen, ink & gouache copies of medieval manuscript miniatures, painted in colors & heightened with gold, on 19 leaves, with an additional 3 leaves reproducing medieval calligraphy, mtd on card. In an album on 22 leaves, with additional index on 2 pp with colored decorated outer border. Folio, in contemp vellum gilt over wooden bds, with brass clasps. C Dec 12 (376) £2,400 [Maggs]

Cambaceres, Jean Jacques Regis de, 1753-1824
Ls, 26 May 1807. 1 p, 4to. To Gen. Junot. About his request for officers & the return of the Empress to Paris. With autograph postscript, 6 lines, regarding the court of Caroline Bonaparte. star Apr 9 (930) DM300

Cambridge University
Ms, The Laws & Statutes of the University, [17th cent]. About 110 pp & blanks, folio. Vellum. With illuminated initial letter incorporating the University's coat of arms. In extra blue mor gilt bdg by John Houlden. Bookplate of Robert Montagu, 3d Duke of Manchester. Collection of Elizabeth, Dowager Duchess of Manchester. S July 24 (242) £29,000 [Quaritch]

Campbell, Thomas, 1777-1844
Autograph Ms, poem, Caroline; 10 four-line stanzas, [n.d.]. 3 pp, 8vo. Sgd with initials (crossed out). Some alterations in anr hand. In buckram folder. C Dec 3 (352) £140 [Mitchell Library]

Campendonk, Heinrich, 1889-1957
ALs, 24 Jan 1919. 2 pp, 4to. To [Fritz] Schaefler. Discussing Schaefler's idea of uniting young painters & doubting that Klee will join. star Apr 8 (448) DM580

Camus, Albert, 1913-60
Collection of 8 A Ls s & Ls, 21 Nov 1957 to 2 June 1958. 13 pp, 8vo. To Emma Bikich. About the Nobel Prize & his personal life. S Nov 27 (336) £750 [Lee]
ALs, [n.d.]. 1 p, size not stated. To an unnamed lady. Sending names & addresses. On N[ouvelle] R[evue] F[rancaise] letterhead.

Framed. Altman collection. pnNY Sept 13 (108) $375

Ls, 4 Mar 1946. 1 p, 8vo. To Louis Bardon. Regretting not being able to meet him & mentioning his indifference to the Academie Francaise. Framed. Altman collection. pnNY Sept 13 (109) $300

Caran d'Ache, Pseud. of Emanuel Poire, 1859-1909

ANs, [n.d.]. 1 p, folio. To "Mon cher Directeur". "Priere de mettre des petits numeros sous chaque dessin de 1-20...". With sketch of a quadrangle & calligraphic signature. Repaired. star Apr 8 (449) DM220

Cardozo, Benjamin N., 1870-1938

Collection of ALs & 3 Ls s, 8 Nov 1913 to 6 Feb 1914. 5 pp, various sizes. To Judge Robert Ludlow Fowler. About routine matters. sg Nov 6 (27) $800

ALs, 28 Nov 1919. 2 pp, 4to. To Judge Robert Ludlow Fowler. About Fowler's approaching retirement. Disbound. sg Nov 6 (26) $550

Carlyle, Thomas, 1795-1881

[Carlyle's copy of Sir Thomas Duffus Hardy's General Introduction to the Materials for the History of Britain, 1848, with numerous autograph annotations in pencil, sold at S on 18 Dec 1986, lot 42, for £1,000 to Serendipity.]

Series of 15 A L s s, 5 Dec 1856 to 4 Feb 1861. 40 pp, 8vo. To Vernon Lushington. Relating to the preparation of Carlyle's Collected Works. S Dec 18 (44) £7,500 [Quaritch]

ALs, 23 Jan 1849. 4 pp, 12mo. To Mr. Robertson. Discussing an unnamed revolutionary & disapproving of universal suffrage. Bullock collection. CNY Dec 19 (41) $650

— 10 Apr 1868. 2 pp, 12mo. To Lady Stratford. Declining an invitation. C Dec 3 (353) £190 [Wilson]

ANs, 2 Apr 1859. 2 pp, 16mo. Recipient unnamed. Concerning an earlier book order. wa May 30 (11) $100

Carnegie, Andrew, 1835-1919

Autograph transcript, parts of his article Wealth, published June 1889. 1 p, folio. Sgd. P Oct 29 (36) $2,500

ALs, 22 Dec 1902. 1 p, 4to. To Mr. Jessup. Saying he will see "The Palace" when next in town. Matted with a port. wa May 30 (463) $300

See also: Sherman, William Tecumseh

Caroline, Queen of George IV of England, 1768-1821

ALs, 1817. 3 pp, 4to. To Lucien Bonaparte. Describing the poor health & miserable situation of Marie Louise [Empress of the French]. In French. Bullock collection. CNY Dec 19 (161) $100

Carossa, Hans, 1878-1956

Collection of ALS & autograph postcard, sgd, 13 Nov 1930 & 7 Mar 1951. 2 pp, 8vo (lettercard) & postcard. To Ottmar Endres. Thanking for photographs, & mentioning Ernst Bertram. star Apr 8 (33) DM250

— Collection of 7 A Ls s & 2 autograph postcards, sgd, 18 Dec 1943 to 27 July 1954. 11 pp, various sizes, & cards. To Hanns Arens. Mostly regarding his lecture tours. star Apr 8 (36) DM1,600

ALs, 15 Oct 1934. 2 pp, 8vo (lettercard). To Hans Wolffheim. Saying he will discuss Wolffheim's chances to make a living abroad with friends in Switzerland. star Apr 8 (35) DM310

Carre, Louis

Ms, Inventaire des Meubles, titres et Papiers delaisses par anne Guiot...., 1686. About 40 pp, 4to. Sgd twice. S Jan 27 (965) £130 [Lasalle]

Carriere, Moritz, 1817-95

Autograph Ms, Moses Mendelssohn und die philosophische Gegenwart, [c.1855/60]. 4 pp, 8vo. Fragment; beginning of an essay for the Frankfurter Museum. star Apr 8 (316) DM440

See also: Arnim, Bettina von

Carroll, Charles, Signer from Maryland

ALs, 11 Nov 1767. 1 p, 4to. Recipient unnamed. Concerning payment of goods ordered on company's account. With comments by his partners below & on verso, initialled. wa May 30 (494) $160

— 6 Jan 1818. 1 p, 8vo. To his son Charles. Sending news of his grandson in Europe. Charlotte Parker Milne collection. wd Nov 12 (29) $225

— 15 Aug 1824. 1 p, 4to. To Capt. Francis Foster. About a tenant & requesting collection of rents. Seal tear affecting signature. sg Apr 9 (38) $100

— 12 Sept 1826. 1 p, 4to. To Richard Caton. About financial matters. wa May 30 (130) $240

Carroll, Lewis, 1832-98. See: Dodgson, Charles Lutwidge

Carter, James E. ("Jimmy")

Typescript, 26 Mar 1979. 2 pp, 8vo. Comments about peace between Israel & Egypt. Sgd twice. wa May 30 (311) $150

Ls, 15 Dec 1980. 1 p, 8vo. To Braha Marcus-Ofseyer. As President, concerning her efforts to promote peace in the Middle East. Sgd Jimmy. wa Oct 18 (74) $575

Carus, Carl Gustav, 1789-1869

A Ls s (2), 5 May [1854] & [n.d.]. 3 pp, 8vo. Recipients unnamed. Discussing two books about the psychology of art. Accepting an invitation. JG Oct 2 (190) DM1,300

Caruso, Enrico, 1873-1921

Original drawings, self port, sgd, [n.d.]. 23.1cm by 10.1cm. In pencil. Mtd. star Apr 9 (608) DM900

Collection of 3 A Ls s, AL & 6 telegrams, 1909 to 1911. To Elsa Trauner. Thanking for presents, sending condolences, etc. In French & Italian. 3 Nov 28 (508) £300 [MacNutt]

Series of 11 autograph postcards, sgd, 1909 to 1911. To Elsa Trauner. About his performances in Germany, his health, etc. Various signatures & languages. Including postcard photograph of Caruso. S Nov 28 (511) £950 [MacNutt]

Autograph postcard, sgd, 11 Sept 1911. Port postcard. To Elsa Trauner. Mentioning his travel plans. S Jan 27 (1005) £180 [MacNutt]

AN, [n.d.]. Ptd visiting card with 7-line message to [Elsa Trauner]. S Jan 27 (1007) £100 [Gekoski]

Photograph, sgd, [n.d.]. Postcard size. As Duke in Rigoletto. star Apr 9 (607) DM250

Photograph, [n.d.]. 8 by 6 inches. By Mishkin, "five minutes before his last appearance in La Juive". wa May 30 (347) $55

Self-caricature, as Eleazar, from Halevy's La juive. On Metropolitan Opera House program wrap, dated 22 Sept 1919. Sgd by Caruso & his wife. In pencil. S Nov 28 (509) £250 [Reuter]

Casals, Pablo, 1876-1973

ALs, 2 July 1925. 2 pp, 4to. Recipient unnamed. Informing him that he already has a number of offers for concerts in Germany. star Apr 9 (609) DM220

Casement, Sir Roger, 1864-1916

ALs, 15 Oct 1915. 4 pp, 8vo. To Herr Scheffauer. Enclosing a letter (not present) & mentioning a pamphlet which is to appear in America. C June 24 (18) £300 [Bush]

Cassatt, Mary, 1845-1926

ALs, 1 Aug 1886. 1 p, 8vo. To [Ben W. Austin?]. Thanking for being named honorary member of a society. wa May 30 (1) $500

Catalani, Alfredo, 1854-93

ALs, 27 Jan [1890]. 4 pp, 8vo. To [Signora Castelfranchi]. Requesting her to help "la povera Luisina" who is in love with him. S May 22 (367) £400 [Riskin]

Catalonian Documents

Document, 26 Oct 966. 1 p, 70mm by 295mm. Vellum. Donation of a vineyard to the monastery of Sant Sebastia by the executors of the late Arginric. In Latin; written in Frankish-meridional minuscule. sg Nov 6 (30) $900

— [5?] June 1040. 1 p, 90mm by 420mm. Vellum. Cession of land to Amel & his Gardiza by Abbot Odegar & the monks of Sant Llorenc del Munt. In Latin; written in Frankish-meridional minuscule. With subscription of Ermessenda of Carcassonne, penned by scribe; sign-cross probably in her hand. sg Nov 6 (31) $1,300

— 13 May 1060. 1 p, 75mm by 455mm. Vellum. Exchange of lands between Guadamir & his family & Ramon Ricolf. In Latin; written in Frankish-meridional minuscule. sg Nov 6 (32) $700

— 23 May 1063. 1 p, 105mm by 260mm. Vellum. Guillem & his brothers & sisters recognize the right of Sunyer Argemir to one half of the vineyards in Guillem's allodial property. In Latin; written in Frankish-meridional minuscule. sg Nov 6 (33) $700

— 24 Aug 1126. 1 p, 70mm by 310mm. Vellum. Cession of manses near Eramprunya to Guillem Gerau by Gerau Gombau & his wife. In Latin; written in Frankish-meridional minuscule. Chirograph. sg Nov 6 (29) $550

— 18 Dec 1158. 1 p, 120mm by 280mm. Vellum. Cession of property to the monks of Sant Cugat by Guerau & Arsendis, on condition that their son be received as a monk without further endowment. In Latin; written in Frankish-meridional minuscule. Unusual chirograph. sg Nov 6 (34) $650

— 2 Jan 1183. Size not stated. Vellum. Cession of revenues in the Valley of Argolell to the Hospital of La Seu d'Urgell by Bernat & Saurina de Granana. In Latin; written in quasi-French bookhand minuscule. sg Nov 6 (35) $800

CATHER

Cather, Willa S., 1873-1947
ALs, 28 July [n.y.]. 1 p, 8vo. To Mr. Winslow. Mentioning her departure for Canada. wa May 30 (464) $180
ANs, [21 Nov 1920]. 1 p, 8vo. Recipient unnamed. Answering a request for one of her Mss. With typescript of a 5-line poem, sgd W.C. sg Nov 6 (36) $250

Catherine de Medicis, 1519-89
Ds, 1 Aug 1564. 1 p, 270mm by 480mm. Grant to Claude de Boueahu in recompense for disbursements made by him. C June 24 (19) £320 [American Museum of Hist. Docs.]

Catherine II, Empress of Russia, 1729-96
ALs, 9 Mar 1771. 1 p, 4to. To Maj. Gen. Friedrich Wilhelm von Bauer. Requesting information about a young lady. In German. HK Nov 7 (2265) DM4,600
AL, 14 May 1787. 1 p, 4to. To Master of the Hunt Pohlmann. Sending a message to a princess. star Apr 9 (1225) DM3,800
Ls, 26 May 1772. 3 pp, folio. To Count Orloff. Regarding the strengthening of Russian naval forces. In Russian; sgd in Russian script. wa Oct 18 (75) $375
— 24 May 1784. 2 pp, folio. To the King of the Two Sicilies. Recommending an ambassador. S Nov 27 (337) £480 [Lee]

Catherine of Braganza, Queen of Charles II of England, 1638-1705
Ds, 27 June 1676. 1 p, c.27 by 29 inches. Vellum. Indenture for lease of land in Yorkshire to Matthew Farrow. With 7 other signatures. Chewed by rodents. S July 24 (232) £150 [Bristow]

Catt, Carrie Chapman, 1859-1947
Ls, 29 Jan 1933. 1 p, 4to. To Mrs. Frank A. Vanderlip. Regretting she is unable to attend a dinner for Mrs. Roosevelt. With a port. wa May 30 (497) $55

Cecil, Robert, Earl of Salisbury, 1563-1612
ALs, 16 Apr [1595]. 1 p, folio. To Matthew Hutton, Archbishop of York. About his intercession with the Queen on behalf of Lady Neville. C Dec 3 (218) £480 [Maggs]
Series of 5 Ls s, 13 Oct 1594 to 1 Sept 1600. 7 pp, folio. To Matthew Hutton, Archbishop of York. Mostly requesting favors for his own or the Queen's proteges. 1 Ls also sgd by Sir John Wolley. C Dec 3 (217) £900 [Quaritch]
Ls, 12 Dec 1600. 1 p, folio. To Thomas Buckhurst. Ordering payment of £5,000 for the troops in Ireland. Also sgd by other members of the Privy Council. star Apr 9 (931) DM320

AMERICAN BOOK PRICES CURRENT

Chabrier, Emmanuel, 1841-94
ALs, 6 Feb [18]89. 1 p, 8vo. To Gilles. Urging him to keep an appointment. S May 22 (370) £200 [Rankin]

Chagall, Marc, 1889-1985
Ls, 3 Feb 1953. 1 p, 4to. To an unnamed lady. Suggesting that she contact Galerie Maeght to obtain some of his works. With ptd photograph. wa May 30 (349) $110
Photograph, sgd, [n.d.]. 23.8cm by 17.7cm. Sitting in his studio. star Apr 8 (451) DM600

Chailly, Luciano
Autograph music, Studio per un'orchestra di ragazzi. Abbozzo originale, 1974; sgd. 17 pp, 32.5cm by 23.5cm. In pencil; corrections in ballpoint pen. In folder. With related material. star Apr 9 (610) DM650

Chain, Ernst Boris, 1906-79
ALs, [Apr 1962]. 5 pp, 8vo. To S. J. Goldsmith. Reporting about his contribution to the discovery of Penicillin. With 2 related Ls s. S Dec 18 (330) £900 [Joseph & Sawyer]

Chaliapin, Feodor, 1873-1938
Ls, 2 June 1924. 1 p, 8vo. To an unnamed admirer. Sending a photograph (not included). In French. With engraved port. sg Apr 9 (40) $80
Photograph, sgd, 1928. Postcard size. Mtd. With anr. star Apr 9 (791) DM400
Photograph, sgd & inscr, 8 July [1]914. In costume for Ivan the Terrible. Inscr in French to Edwin Evans. Mtd; overall size 26cm by 16cm. S Nov 28 (513) £300 [Reuter]

Cham, Pseud. of Amedee de Noe, 1819-79
Caricature, 2 ladies at a pool; pen-&-ink, [n.d.]. 1 p, 4to, sketch 11cm by 11cm. With text. Lower margin cut. star Apr 8 (452) DM280

Chamberlain, Eva Wagner
[An extensive collection of A Ls s, Ls s & documents by or pertaining to Eva Chamberlain, including Ms notes made for her husband Houston Stewart Chamberlain, was sold at P on 24 Sept 1986, lot 52, for $950.]

Chamberlain, Houston Stewart, 1855-1927. See: Chamberlain, Eva Wagner

Chambers, Charles Haddon, 1860-1921
Autograph Ms, play, The Tyranny of Tears, sgd & dated 6 Aug 1898. 156 pp, 4to. With numerous autograph revisions & doodles. In purple mor gilt bdg, inscr to Nellie Melba, 1899. With ALs, [n.d.], from Chambers to an unnamed recipient, stating that a play will be produced in NY, & a letter from Chambers's agents concerning roy-

alties. C Dec 3 (355) £450 [Allen]

Char, Rene

Collection of ALs & 2 autograph Ms s, 17 May 1957 & [n.d.]. 3 pp, 4to & 8vo. To Rene Magritte. Thanking for 2 illusts for a vol of his poems & asking him to do a 3d. Poems, La Chaise vide, & Les Amis III; sgd. S July 2 (970) £1,100 [Communaute de Francais de Belgique]

Charles I, King of England, 1600-49

ALs, 15 Mar 1643 [1644]. 1 p, size not stated. To the Earl of Newcastle. Hoping to have good news from him concerning the campaign against the Scots. C Dec 3 (221) £1,500 [Maggs]

Ls, 20 June 1643. 1 p, folio. To Louis II de Bourbon, Prince de Conde. About the death of Louis XIII & saying he has sent an envoy with a message. With autograph subscription. Bullock collection. CNY Dec 19 (44) $1,900

— 24 July 1643. 1 p, folio. To Prince Rupert. About dangerous Parliamentary forces & requesting him to come to Oxford with the cavalry. Sgd at head. With autograph postscript, sgd CR, asking him to restrain plundering. S Dec 18 (207) £2,100 [Maggs]

Ds, 20 May 1628. 1 p, 250mm by 335mm. Vellum. Passport for Lady Elizabeth Wyche to follow her husband to Constantinople. Bullock collection. CNY Dec 19 (43) $1,600

— 22 May 1636. 1 p, c.10.75 by 14 inches. Vellum. License for Thomas Littleton to go abroad for 3 years. Lyttelton Papers. S Jan 27 (749) £380 [Maggs]

— LUCAS, SIR GERVASE. - Ls, 3 Nov 1645. 1 p, folio. Reporting about Prince Rupert's reaction to the King's recent letter. With a Ds by Sir John Dalston, 1707. S July 24 (230) £420 [Burgess & Browning]

— OTTOBON, JEAN BAPTIST. - Ms, diary of a journey [from Venice to England] in 1626; 19th-cent trans by Charlotte Augusta Sneyd. 53 pp, 4to. pnNY June 11 (69) $300

Charles II, King of England, 1630-85

Ds, 17 Mar 1674. 1 p, folio. Order to increase Samuel Pepys's salary. Countersgd by Pepys. sg Nov 6 (165) $1,000

3 July 1674. 1 p, folio. Order to appoint a carpenter & assistant for the ship Armes of Rotterdam. Countersgd by Samuel Pepys. Torn & repaired. sg Nov 6 (167) $475

Document, March 1686. 3 pp, folio. Order that monies in arrears be paid to Samuel Pepys. Sgd in a secretary's hand. Sgd twice by S. Pepys. sg Nov 6 (165) $700

Charles II, King of England, 1630-85
[Treaty of Dover, 1670. - A unique collection of working drafts, memoranda, correspondence & agreements, 1669 to 1672, relating to the secret Treaty of Dover, c.70 items, c.320 pp, mostly folio & 4to, secretly preserved by Thomas Clifford, 1st Baron Clifford of Chudleigh, sold at S on 24 July 1987, lot 243, for £285,000 to Cranmer.]

ALs, 10 May 1660. 2 pp, 4to. To Marshal Turenne. Asking him to thank Mazarin for his good wishes & expressing his gratitude for support given him. In French. S Dec 18 (208) £1,000 [Spiro]

— 5 Dec 1674. 1 p, 8vo, mtd on folio sheet. To Lady Jane Fisher. About the marriage of her niece to Mr. Offley & his gratitude to Lady Jane for her aid at the Battle of Worcester. O May 12 (40) $800

Ls, 12 Mar [1649]. 1 p, folio. To Prince Rupert. Asking him to find places in the navy for three men. C Dec 3 (222) £380 [Wilson]

— 3 July 1674. 1 p, folio. To the principal Officers & Commissioners of the Navy. Ordering that Joseph Smith be entered as master carpenter of H.M.S. Eagle. Sgd at head. Also sgd by Samuel Pepys, at foot. S Dec 18 (302) £800 [Wilson]

Ds, 1 Feb 1660/1. 1 p, c.8.5 by 12 inches. Vellum. Commission for Cornet Ferdinando Littleton. Lyttelton Papers. S Jan 27 (751) £240 [Barnes]

— 18 June 1669. 1 p, c.16 by 23 inches. Vellum. Commission for Sir Thomas Allin as Commander in Chief of the Mediterranean & to treat with Algiers. In Latin. S Jan 27 (752) £300 [Wilson]

— 15 Mar 1670. 2 pp, folio. Warrant to the Attorney General concerning concealed money or jewels belonging to the Crown. Countersgd by Lords Shaftesbury & Clifford. Folds repaired. Bullock collection. CNY Dec 19 (45) $200

— 20 Jan 1671. 1 p, folio. Warrant for payment to Sir Thomas Slingesby for the garrison of Scarborough. S Jan 27 (750) £220 [Dupre]

— 5 Feb 1673. 2 pp, folio. Warrant to Lord Chancellor Heneage Lord Finch to affix the Great Seal to an appointment of commissioners to treat with the Spanish ambassador concerning peace with the Netherlands. C Dec 3 (223) £260 [Wilson]

— 3 May 1674. 1 p, folio. Pay warrant for Henry, Marquess of Worcester. With Worcester's receipt on verso. O May 12 (41) $275

— 13 Dec 1675. 1 p, folio. Warrant to affix the Great Seal to the appointment of Thomas Chudleigh as Secretary of the Embassy "appointed for the Treaty of the generall Peace at Nimeguen". C Dec 3 (224) £260 [Bristow]

CHARLES II

— 8 Jan 1677/78. 1 p, folio. Warrant to affix the Great Seal to an instrument empowering Lawrence Hyde to conclude a treaty with the United Provinces. C June 24 (20) £300 [American Museum of Hist. Docs.]

— 10 Jan 1677. 1 p, folio. Warrant to affix the Great Seal to a commission authorizing Sidney Godolphin to treat with the Governor of the Spanish Netherlands. C Dec 3 (225) £270 [Bristow]

— 14 Feb 1677/78. 1 p, folio. Warrant to affix the Great Seal to a treaty with the Netherlands & to 2 related separate articles. S July 24 (231) £800 [Stewart]

— 21 June 1677. 1 p, folio. Commission for Sir John Narborough to treat with Tripoli. Framed. Altman collection. pnNY Sept 13 (38) $550

— 23 Dec 1677. 1 p, folio. Warrant to affix the Great Seal to an instrument authorizing Lawrence Hyde to treat with the United Provinces. C Dec 3 (226) £320 [Maggs]

— 11 Apr 1678. 2 pp, folio. Warrant to affix the Great Seal to an appointment of commissioners to treat with Spain & the United Provinces. C Dec 3 (227) £260 [Wilson]

— 27 July 1678. 1 p, folio. Warrant to affix the Great Seal to the ratification of the treaty with the United Provinces concluded 15/25 July. C Dec 3 (228) £300 [Maggs]

— 27 Feb 1679/80. 1 p, folio. Warrant to affix the Great Seal to an instrument empowering Robert Southwell to conclude a treaty with the Elector of Brandenburg. C June 24 (21) £280 [Roberts]

— 30 Apr 1679. 1 p, folio. Warrant to issue a writ to John Mannors de Haddon. C Dec 3 (229) £320 [Bristow]

— 17 June 1680. 1 p, folio. Warrant to affix the Great Seal to an instrument empowering Gabriell Sylvius to conclude a treaty with the Duke of Brunswick. C June 24 (22) £250 [Wilson]

— 20 Oct 1680. 1 p, folio. Warrant to affix the Great Seal to a commission empowering James Leslie to conclude a treaty with the Emperor of Morocco. C June 24 (23) £300 [Roberts]

— 31 Oct 1680. 1 p, folio. Warrant to issue a writ of summons to Conniers Darcy "returnable into our House of Peers". C June 24 (24) £280 [Wilson]

— 29 May 1682. 1 p, folio. Warrant to affix the Great Seal to the ratification of a treaty with Morocco. C June 24 (26) £380 [Maggs]

— [n.d.]. 1 p, folio. Warrant to issue a writ. Unaccomplished. C June 24 (25) £280 [Wilson]

AMERICAN BOOK PRICES CURRENT

Charles IX, King of France, 1550-74

Ds, 9 May 1567. 2 pp, folio. List of various royal orders, confirmations of rights, restitutions, privileges, etc. C June 24 (30) £170 [L'Autographe]

Charles V, Emperor, 1500-58

Ls, 8 Oct 1520. 1 p, folio. To Kurfuerst Ludwig V von der Pfalz. Credentials for his envoys Maximilian von Berghe & Georg von Emershofen. Sgd carolus. star Apr 9 (1194) DM4,500

— 7 Mar 1530. 1 p, folio. To the Duque de Arcos. About the situation in Italy after his coronation & his intention to attend the Diet of Augsburg. In Spanish. C June 24 (27) £900 [Joseph]

Ds, 4 May 1544. 1 p, vellum, 440mm by 660mm. Grant of arms to Sebastian & Daniel Stephani. With illuminated coat-of-arms. Seal in tin case. C June 24 (28) £1,100 [Bender]

— DIALOGUS. - Ms, Ein Dialogus oder Gesprech... In welchem...vormeldett wird, Was sich Inn denn Kriegenn, von den .1521.Jhar ann... gegen Kayser Carolo denn fuenfften vorgelauffenn..., [Germany, late 16th cent]. 201 leaves, 290mm by 195mm. Contemp lea gilt. In brown ink in a cursive script. Trans from the Spanish. Description of the wars between Charles V & Francis I. HK Nov 4 (410) DM1,300

Charles VI, Emperor, 1685-1740

Ls, 3 Oct 1715. 2 pp, folio. To Philipp Ferdinand von Gudenus. Inviting him to a diet. Ptd; sgd. star Apr 9 (1205) DM420

Ds, 30 July 1717. 9 pp, 4to. Patent of nobility for Martin Guenther Pechmann & his brother Antonius Ludwig Pechmann. With painted coat-of-arms. Contemp red velvet. HN Nov 27 (2298) DM1,400

— 23 Feb 1723. 12 leaves, 4to, vellum. Patent of nobility for 3 Counts von Kielmannsegg. With full-page illuminated coat of arms. Red velvet bdg. FD June 11 (3641) DM1,200

— 24 Jan 1727. 1 p, folio. Order that Herkules Graf von Montecuccoli be given all possible assistance in his efforts to enlist soldiers for his regiment. Partly ptd. Also sgd by Prince Eugene of Savoy. star Apr 9 (1206) DM1,100

Charles VII, King of France, 1403-61

Ls, 31 Apr [1431?]. 1 p, vellum, 125mm by 320mm. To "Chers biens amis". Requesting their obedience & fidelity to the Seigneur de Sainte Severe. C June 24 (29) £1,500 [Joseph]

Charles VII, Emperor, 1697-1745
Ls, 26 Apr 1743. 2 pp, folio. To Franz Georg von Schoenborn, Archbishop of Trier, & Kurfuerst Karl Theodor von der Pfalz. Requesting them to assist & protect newly enlisted soldiers of his regiments. star Apr 9 (1208) DM950

Charles X, King of France, 1757-1836
AL, 1 Nov 1793. 1 p, 4to. To Comtesse Diane de Polignac. As Comte d'Artois, emotional letter concerning the recent death of Marie Antoinette. Integral leaf torn. C Dec 3 (231) £550 [Joseph]

Ls, 19 Mar 1829. 1 p, folio. To Cardinal Capellari. Thanking for Christmas wishes. With a port. star Apr 9 (977) DM240

Charles XII, King of Sweden, 1682-1718
Ls s (2), 2 Nov & 8 Dec 1699. 4 pp, folio. To Gen. Baron Otto Wellingk. Providing for the widow of Johan Christoph Schwartz. Sgd Carolus. star Apr 9 (1241) DM950

Charles XIV John, King of Sweden, 1763-1844
Series of 3 Ls s, 1799 to 1800. 7 pp, folio & 4to. Recipients unnamed. Concerning military matters. With related material. S Nov 27 (316) £200 [Charavay]

Ls, 26 Jan 1796. 1 p, folio. To the Adjutant Gen. As Gen. of Division, regarding an officer who lost his commission. Repaired. sg Apr 9 (23) $80

Charlotte, Princess, daughter of George IV
Series of 11 A Ls s, 1805 to 1811. 34 pp, 4to & 8vo. To Lady Albermarle. About a variety of personal matters. S Jan 27 (753) £350 [Maggs]

Charpentier, Gustave, 1860-1956
ALs, [n.d.]; 3 pp, 12mo. To an unnamed friend. Discussing changes in part II of an unnamed work. sg Nov 6 (38) $110

Chartrier thereutique
Ms, Chartrier thereutique, un recueil de notes manuscrites sur les pieces originales du chartrier thereutique forme par le Baron Pichon. [c.1870] 57 pp, 4to, in modern half mor Jeanson Ms 225 SM Feb 28 (125) FF500

Chase, Salmon P., 1808-73
ALs, 1 Mar 1861. 2 pp, 8vo. To C. J. Wright. Urging him to give "all the aid possible to the Committee". wa May 30 (12) $120

Chase, Samuel, Signer from Maryland
Ds, 17 Aug 1793. 1 p, 4to. Declaration of naturalization for Leon Chaugeur. Charlotte Parker Milne collection. wd Nov 12 (30) $275

Chastellain, Georges, d.1475.
See: Anjou, Rene I

Chateaubriand, Francois Rene, Vicomte de, 1768-1848
Ls, 9 Sept 1823. 1 p, folio. To an unnamed count. As Foreign Minister, regarding a committee to determine rates to be charged by the Royal printing office. star Apr 8 (37) DM250

Chelard, Hippolyte Andre, 1789-1861
ALs, 1 Dec 1838. 3 pp, 8vo. To Georg Friedrich Treitschke. Suggesting that the Vienna theater play his opera Macbeth. star Apr 9 (611) DM220

Cherubini, Luigi, 1760-1842
Ls, 18 Dec 1835. 1 p, 4to. To Lucien Piette. Regarding the admission of a student to the Paris conservatory. star Apr 9 (613a) DM340

Ds, 17 Nov 1839. 1 p, folio. Certificate that Amedee Artus won "Le Second Prix de Trompette", sgd as Director of the Conservatoire de Musique. star Apr 9 (613b) DM220

Chesapeake-Leopard Affair
[An archive of more than 300 pp, consisting of material pertaining to the court martial of James Barron, Feb 1807 to 1808, sold at P on 13 May 1987, lot 36, for $9,000.]

Chesterfield, Philip Dormer Stanhope, 4th Earl of, 1694-1773
ALs, 2 Sept 1769. 1 p, 4to. To Mr. Fisher. About routine matters. Tipped to tp of vol 1 of his Letters...to his Son, L 1774. 1st Ed. 2 vols. 4to, contemp calf. With errata leaf. Signature of Henry Croker, 1818, on half-titles. sg Nov 6 (39) $300

Chesterton, Gilbert Keith, 1874-1936
Original drawings, 3 crayon & chalk drawings on brown paper, 345mm by 246mm. Sgd in pencil. A painter looking at a town; man shooting from rooftop by moonlight; & merman with sailor's hat. Framed. S Dec 5 (139) £600 [Heneage]

Chirico, Giorgio de, 1888-1978
A Ls s (2), 14 Feb 1953 & 8 Dec 1966. 2 pp, folio. To Rene Magritte. About an exhibition of Magritte's work in Rome, & commenting on Magritte's art. S July 2 (971) £650 [19th Century Shop]

Chodowiecki, Daniel, 1726-1801
ALs, 27 Apr 1799. 2 pp, 8vo. To an unnamed nobleman. Itemized account for works ordered by recipient. S May 21 (229) £320 [Quaritch]

Chopin, Frederic, 1810-49
Autograph music, 2 lines & a few bars; [n.d.]. 1 p, folio; on ptd music paper. In pencil. With note of authenticity by W. Lenz, dated [18]45, & anr endorsement dated 1850. Max Thorek collection. P Dec 15 (15) $5,500

Christian, Fletcher. See: Bligh, William & Christian

Christian VIII, King of Denmark, 1786-1848
ALs, 21 Feb 1810. 1 p, 4to. Recipient & contents not stated. wa May 30 (13) $65

Christina, Queen of Sweden, 1626-89
Letter, [1670]. 3 p, 4to. To King Louis XIV of France. Draft, requesting an explanation for Cardinal d'Estree's behavior. Some autograph revisions. HN May 22 (2970) DM550
— 10 Sept 1675. 4 pp, 4to. To Pierre Michon Bourdelot. Draft, emphasizing that calumnies lately published about her do not affect her. With autograph revision. HN Nov 27 (2236) DM500
Ds, 4 June 1653. 2 pp, folio. Commission for Du Plessis Saumaite as Capt. in her bodyguard. In German. C Dec 3 (233) £300 [L'Echiquier]

Chronicles
Ms, Genealogia deorum, [Italy?, c.1600]. 11 leaves, 443mm by 295mm, on rectos only. Loose in folder. Tracing descent of Roman kings & emperors from Chaos. C June 24 (269) £900 [Amery]
— Ms, historical genealogy, [Netherlands, after 1472]. 32 leaves (2 blanks), vellum, 435mm by 305mm. In red & black ink in a small gothic bookhand. With 3 painted miniatures & large decorated initial. 17th cent panelled calf gilt. C June 24 (261) £14,000 [Bibliotheca Philosophica]

Churchill, Sir Winston L. S., 1874-1965
Autograph Ms, 2 fragments, 17 lines, of a despatch sent to The Morning Post, 20 Nov [1899]. Describing the position of a prisoner of war & referring to the possibility of losing South Africa. Editor's markings. pn Dec 11 (85A) £950 [Fine Art Society]
Typescript, 2d article on the Austo-German Customs Union, 22 May 1931. 10 pp, 4to. Sgd. With autograph revisions. S July 24 (318) £5,800 [FAS]
— Typescript, article on Europe & the League of Nations, 31 Jan 1931. 10 pp, 4to. Sgd. With autograph revisions. S July 24 (314) £3,000 [FAS]
— Typescript, article on political change & the recent General Election, [after 27 Oct 1931]. 11 pp, 4to. Sgd. With autograph revisions. S July 24 (322) £3,000 [FAS]
— Typescript, article on the Austro-German Customs Union, [before 31 Mar 1931]. 8 pp, 4to. Sgd. With autograph revisions. S July 24 (316) £3,000 [FAS]
— Typescript, article on the abdication of Alfonso XIII of Spain, [c.Apr/May 1931]. 10 pp, 4to. Sgd. With autograph revisions. S July 24 (317) £3,000 [FAS]
— Typescript, article on the Great Depression, entitled "America - Beware!" [Summer 1931]. 8 pp, 4to. Sgd. With autograph revisions. S July 24 (319) £3,000 [FAS]
— Typescript, article on the Japanese invasion of Manchuria, [c.Sept 1931]. 7 pp, 4to. Sgd. With autograph revisions. S July 24 (320) £6,000 [FAS]
— Typescript, article on the question of a British General Election, 8 Oct 1931. 9 pp, 4to. Sgd. With autograph revisions. S July 24 (321) £3,000 [FAS]
— Typescript, article on the possibility of a European war, [1931]. 8 pp, 4to. Sgd. With autograph revisions. S July 24 (323) £6,000 [FAS]
— Typescript, article on the political & financial crisis in Britain, [1931]. 8 pp, 4to. Sgd. With autograph revisions. S July 24 (324) £3,000 [FAS]
— Typescript, article, "The Economic Collapse of Europe", [1931]. 13 pp, 4to. Sgd. With autograph revisions. S July 24 (325) £3,000 [FAS]
— Typescript, article, The United States of Europe, [before 11 Jan 1931]. 9 pp, 4to. Sgd. With autograph revisions. S July 24 (313) £3,000 [FAS]
— Typescript, part of his The Second World War, [1950]. 1 p, 12 by 7.5 inches. Describing the bombing of the Guards' Chapel at Wellington Barracks. With autograph revisions in blue pencil & black ink; typed on galley proof of an earlier vol. Framed. S Dec 18 (251) £1,600 [Joseph & Sawyer]
Typescript carbon copy, article attacking The Week End Review's national plan for reorganizing industry, [c.Feb 1931]. 10 pp, 4to. Sgd. With autograph revisions. S July 24 (315) £2,000 [FAS]
Collection of 3 A Ls s & 3 Ls s, 1906 to 1907. 21 pp, 8vo. To Eliot Crawshay-Williams. Relating to his duties as Churchill's assistant private secretary at the Colonial Office. With related material. pn Dec 11 (86) £5,000 [Fine Art Society]
A Ls s (2), 13 Sept 1903 & 28 Nov 1906. 4 pp, 8vo. To Charles Hughes. Agreeing to abandon a project. Thanking for his book & discussing Ireland. S July 24 (305) £1,700 [Maddalena]
ALs, 13 Mar [1895]. 3 pp, 8vo. To Sir Algernon West. Commenting on West's [typescript]

article on Lord Randolph Churchill. L. C. R. West collection. S July 24 (299) £1,700 [FAS]
— 25 Oct [1896]. 5 pp, 4to. To Sir Algernon West. Commenting on West's pbd article on Lord Randolph Churchil & current politics. L. C. R. West collection. S July 24 (300) £2,700 [FAS]
— 18 Feb 1898. 7 pp, 8vo. To Sir Algernon West. About his life in India, his 1st book & current interests. L. C. R. West collection. S July 24 (301) £3,000 [Gekoski]
— 5 Oct 1902. 3 pp, 8vo. To Sir Algernon West. Thanking for papers to be used for his father's biography. L. C. R. West collection. S July 24 (302) £1,200 [Vivalda]
— 5 Mar 1904. 2 pp, 8vo. To Lord Esher. About the report of the Esher Committee, & requesting a meeting to discuss military policy. C June 24 (31) £1,100 [Trihome]
— 21 Apr 1905. 3 pp, 8vo. To [John Edward] Ellis. Sending part of the draft of his biography of his father. S July 24 (306) £1,000 [FAS]
— 4 Sept 1908. 1 p, 8vo. To Sir Algernon West. Thanking for a present. L. C. R. West collection. S July 24 (303) £700 [Dickson]
— 12 July [n.y.]. 1 p, 8vo. To Sir Reginald [?]. Sending a proof. S Jan 27 (772) £400 [Barnes]

Series of 9 Ls s, 14 Aug 1909 to 3 Jan 1910. 22 pp, 8vo & 4to. To Eliot Crawshay-Williams. As President of the Board of Trade, concerning the tariff question, the election campaign at Leicester, etc. With related material. pn Dec 11 (87) £7,500 [Fine Art Society]

Ls s (2), 6 Mar & 26 June 1923. 2 pp, 4to. To Messrs. Knight, Frank & Rutley. Regarding the letting of their house at Sussex Square. With signature on blank sheet of paper & related letter by Clementine Churchill. S July 24 (307) £900 [Lewis]

Ls, 4 June 1908. 3 pp, 8vo. To Austen [Chamberlain]. Concerning the likelihood of the English adopting the French hall marking system. With autograph salutation & subscription. S Dec 18 (246) £700 [F. A. S.]
— 8 Sept 1908. 8 pp, 8vo. To David Lloyd George. Concerning the settlement of the engineering strike & requesting his assistance in finding employment for the shipbuilders. Marked "Secret" by Churchill. Pencil notes by Lloyd George on verso of last leaf. S Dec 18 (247) £1,500 [F. A. S.]
— 21 Aug 1912. 4 pp, 8vo. To David Lloyd George. About Home Rule for Ireland, the Land Question, & other political matters. S Dec 18 (248) £1,400 [F. A. S.]
— 21 Sept 1916. 1 p, folio. To Mr. Watney. Expressing his willingness to talk with him. With autograph subscription. C Dec 3 (235) £450 [Sotheran]
— 27 Apr 1925. 1 p, 8vo. To Sir Mitchell Thomson. About the Budget. Partly autograph, partly in the hand of Eddie Marsh. S July 24 (308) £700 [Maggs]
— 11 Jan 1931. 1 p, 4to. To N[ancy] Pearn of Curtis Brown Ltd. Promising to start working on an article about Moses. C Dec 3 (236) £750 [Sotheran]
— 6 June 1932. 1 p, 4to. To Mr. Harrap. Regarding the progress of his biography of Marlborough. With a copy of Churchill's Marlborough, His Life and Times. L, 1933-38. 1st Ed. 4 vols; no 20 of 155 copies sgd by the author. C June 24 (33) £2,200 [Sotheran]
— 7 Aug 1936. 1 p, 4to. To L. S. Amery. Concerning the situation in Palestine. Sang collection. P Sept 24 (16) $1,200
— 11 May 1943. 1 p, 4to. To Capt. C. G. Illingworth & his staff on R.M.S. Queen Mary. Paying formal tribute for the "efficient conduct" of his journey. With material relating to Illingworth. S July 24 (311) £1,200 [Maddalena]
— 6 Oct 1943. 1 p, 4to. To Sir John Anderson. Discussing the possibility of the destruction of 10 Downing Street by a bomb. S Dec 18 (250) £2,800 [F. A. S.]
— 16 Feb 1953. 1 p, 4to. As Prime Minister, recommending the Rev. W. L. Guyler for a living. Initialled by the Queen in approval. S Jan 27 (776) £600 [Gekoski]
— 21 Oct 1959. 1 p, 4to. To E. E. Fryer. Thanking for a gift bestowed on Churchill College. With related material. P June 18 (25) $700
— 5 Mar [n.y.]. 1 p, 8vo. To [Viscount] Haldane. Asking him to talk to Frederic Villiers "about an interesting Army matter". With autograph superscription & subscription. C June 24 (32) £450 [Wilson]

ANs, 14 Dec 1905. 1 p, 8vo. To "Ronnie". Thanking for his letter. Matted with a photographic port. sg Nov 6 (40) $750

Ns, 19 Apr 1931. 1 p, 4to. To R. D. Blumenfeld. Thanking for a gift. With autograph superscription & subscription. wa May 30 (351) $425

Ds, 27 Dec 1945. 1 sheet, c.11.25 by 27.5 inches. Ptd U.S. declaration form completed before sailing to New York. Text in the hand of a secretary. S July 24 (310) £1,400 [FAS]
— 17 Jan 1963. 25 pp, folio. Contract relating to the film The Finest Hours. Sgd twice. With related material. S Dec 18 (253) £1,800 [F. A. S.]

Photograph, sgd, Sept 1898. 188mm by 125mm.

Almost full length, in uniform. Sepia photograph by J. Heyman, Cairo. Mount trimmed. pn Dec 11 (116) £1,500 [Eker] See also: George V, 1865-1936

Cicero, Marcus Tullius, 106-43 B.C.
Ms, De Officiis, Paradoxica, De Senectute, & De Amicitia. [Rome, late 15th cent]. 172 pp, vellum, 168mm by 108mm. Modern full brown mor bdg dated 1964. In pale brown ink in a calligraphic humanistic cursive minuscule by Jacobus Aurelius Questenberg, previously attributed to Bartolomeo Sanvito. With 6 large illuminated initials & full-page illuminated armorial frontis. S June 23 (93) £13,000 [King]

Cimarosa, Domenico, 1749-1801
Autograph music, operatic scene, beginning Mi poteva succedere, full score; [n.d.]. 10 pp, size not stated. Modern bds. In brown ink on 9 staves per page; some revisions. S May 22 (371) £600 [Dreesman]

Cistercians
Ms, statutes of the Cistercian Order, [France, 1256-88]. 76 leaves, vellum, 175mm by 130mm. Contemp limp lea, wormed. In black ink with red initials & headings. 1st 46 leaves written in a single hand, 1256 to 1259; various addenda. Sketch of a man with a scroll on f.1. Lacking c.7 leaves. HK Nov 4 (469a) DM 10,500

Civil War, American
[A collection of over 50 items, ALs s, ptd orders, certificates, etc., May 1862 to Jan 1865, sold at sg on 6 Nov 1986, lot 247, for $800.]
[A collection of 6 A Ls s, Ls, 2 Ds s, & 2 autograph quotations, sgd, by various figures related to the Civil War, sold at sg on 9 Apr 1987, lot 42, for $225.]
[A collection of 29 carte de visite portraits of naval & military figures of the Civil War, mostly sgd, sold at P on 13 May 1987, lot 37, for $5,500.]
[A collection of 5 carte-de-visite photographs of Civil War figures sold at wa on 30 May 1987, lot 215, for $85.]
[An album containing the signatures of Abraham Lincoln, U. S. Grant, Lincoln's Cabinet & c.60 others, many Union generals & admirals; gilt-stamped contemp mor, sold at wa on 30 May 1987, lot 237, for $4,250.]
Ms, album of 1st Lieut. Joseph Donovan, containing 335 entries of prisoners of war. 8vo. Contemp lea. With 86 carte-de-visite photographs of officers, 77 sgd. wa May 30 (209) $3,500
Single sheet ptg, broadside, [n.d.]. 9 by 11 inches. Recruiting soldiers in Delaware.
Corner torn off. wa May 30 (212) $65
— BURHAUS, HERMANN. - Series of 10 A Ls s, 25 Feb 1862 to 23 Mar 1863. 25 pp, 8vo. To his sister. Soldier's letters, especially about the Sharpsburg & Fredericksburg campaigns. With related photographs. S Jan 27 (918) £620 [19-Century]
— CONFEDERATE ARMY. - Letter; 9 Oct 1864, 1 p, 4to. Circular, contemp copy, sgd by W. H. Taylor; directed to Col. D. A. Weisinger. Order by the Commanding General [R. E. Lee], that all enlisted men not physically disqualified return to duty. Endorsement on verso. wa Oct 18 (76) $55
— GARVIN, O. C., CAPT. - Series of 15 A Ls s, 21 Feb 1861 to 26 Oct 1862. 46 pp, 8vo & 4to. To his parents. Describing life of a Union soldier, including Battle of Antietam. Mtd to album pages; with typescript of contents. sg Apr 9 (43) $300
— HOOKER, GEORGE H. - ALs, 5 Apr 1865. 1 p, 8vo. To an unnamed colonel. Informing him of the fall of Richmond. wa May 30 (228) $325
— KING, LOUIS M. - Ms, soldier's account of the battle of Gettysburg. 3 pp, 4to. With related material. S Jan 27 (917) £220 [19-Century]
— PENROSE, WILLIAM H. - Ls, 12 May 1863. 4 pp, folio. To A. K. Parsons. Report about his brigade in the Battle of Chancellorsville. With related material. wa May 30 (248) $425
— ROBINSON, WILLIAM. - Autograph Ms, poem written on Antietam Battlefield, Oct 1862. 4 pp, 4to. 10 stanzas, 8 lines each. wa May 30 (207) $280
— WOODROFFE, GEORGE WILLIAM P. - Autograph Ms, journal of his tour of Canada & the U.S.A., 20 Aug to 16 Dec 1862. About 200 pp, 8vo. Roan. Including detailed accounts of events during the Fredericksburg campaign. With some photographs & other related material. S July 24 (390) £2,800 [Maggs]
— WREN, MAJOR JAMES. - Series of 7 Ms diaries covering his military service from 17 Apr 1861 to 25 May 1863. Plus 168 pp written by him in speech form & other related material. pnNY Dec 10 (240) $3,100

Claiborne, William C. C., 1775-1817
Ds, 25 Aug 1804. 1 p, 4to. Affirming Certificate, sgd as Gov. of Mississippi Territory, "exercising the powers of Governor General & Intendant of the Province of Louisiana". rf Nov 15 (4) $105

Clare, John, 1793-1864

Autograph Ms, poem, Elizabeth West, sgd & dated 5 July 1851. 2 pp, 8vo. 18 lines. Was mtd. S July 23 (42) £600 [Maggs]

Clark, Abraham, Signer from New Jersey

Ds, 18 June 1766. 1 p, 8vo. Writ for Samuel Jones. Repaired. Charlotte Parker Milne collection. wd Nov 12 (31) $100

Clarke, Harry

Original drawing, man in costume standing on a platform before other people; ink, background in pencil. In card mount, 484mm by 304mm. For an unpbd Ed of J. M. Synge's The Playboy of the Western World. S Dec 5 (441) £3,000 [Glendale]

Claude Gellee, ("Le Lorrain"), 1600-82

Ls, 25 Aug 1668. 1 p, folio. To his patron Count Waldstein. Reporting about the progress of 2 paintings. With autograph subscription. S May 21 (231) £4,000 [Fogg]

Claudel, Paul, 1868-1955

ALs, [n.d.]. 2 pp, 8vo. To Monsieur de Wyzewa. Forwarding a letter answering recipient's question & referring to a newspaper article. star Apr 8 (38) DM210

Claudius, Matthias, 1740-1815

ALs, 24 July 1790. 3 pp, 8vo. To an unnamed professor. Sending copies of one of his works [Asmus, part 5], & referring to some acquaintances. star Apr 8 (39) DM4,000

Clay, Henry, 1777-1852

ALs, 27 Mar 1840. 1 p, 4to. To the Bank of the US at Philadelphia. About a remittance of $500. sg Nov 6 (248) $150

ANs, 4 May 1844. 1 p, 12mo. To S. C. Sample. Responding to a request for his autograph. wa May 30 (466) $55

— 1 July [n.y.]. 1 p, 8vo. Recipient unnamed. Accepting a dinner invitation. Framed. Altman collection. pnNY Sept 13 (3) $160

Franking signature, [5 Nov 1836]. rf Mar 14 (73) $110

Cleland, John, 1709-89

ALs, [n.d.] "Saturday morning". 2 pp, 4to. To Edward Dickinson. Wildly protesting about his mother's refusal to pay his debts to his landlady. S Dec 18 (17) £550 [Quaritch]

— [n.d.]. 2 pp, 4to. To E[dward] Dickinson. Complaining about his mother's "inhuman procedure" against him. S Dec 18 (18) £650 [Quaritch]

Clemens August von Bayern, Erzbischof und Kurfuerst von Koeln, 1700-61

— KERSENBROCK, HERMANN. - Ms, Wahrhafte und kurtze Lehr und Lebens Beschreibung der Wiedertauferen, 1736. Tp & 284 pp, 4to. Lea bdg. In dark brown ink in 2 hands, with calligraphic tp [by Maria Joseph Clemens Kaukol?]. Written for Clemens August or someone at his court, probably a member of the von Kempis family (ownership inscr). VH Sept 12 (926) DM4,100

Clemens, Samuel Langhorne, 1835-1910

Autograph Ms, notes, [n.d.]. 1 p, 8vo. Presumably related to Roughing It & Life on the Mississippi. In ink; pencil notes in unidentified hand. Bullock collection. CNY Dec 19 (49) $650

— Autograph Ms, review essay, English as She is Taught, [1887]. 64 leaves, 8vo, on rectos only. In brown ink with many autograph revisions; copy-editing marks in anr hand. Sgd Mark Twain. With long note on fragment of galley proof, sgd SLC. Crushed red mor gilt bdg. P June 18 (28) $42,500

— Autograph Ms, story, The $30,000 Bequest, [1903]. 81 leaves, 8vo, mostly on rectos. In black & purple ink with numerous autograph revisions. In crushed green mor bdg by MacDonald. Gimbel Family collection. P June 18 (27) $100,000

— Autograph Ms, The Private History of a Campaign That Failed, draft; [pbd Dec 1885]. 2 pp, 8vo, on rectos only. 14 lines of text, & map of battlefield. Tab p sgd by Twain & Clemens. CNY Dec 19 (48) $2,200

Collection of 4 A Ls s, Ls & ANs, [n.d.]. 9 pp, size not stated. To Barbara Mullen. About his prt by Sarony, the school at Hannibal, & thanking for congratulations on his birthday. With 2 envelopes (1 autograph) & photograph, sgd. Laid down together on cardboard. Lue C. Lozier Estate. wd Nov 12 (3) $6,000

— Collection of ALs & autograph postcard, sgd, 13 Oct 1897 & 2 Apr [1901]. 2 pp, 8vo, & card. To J. Henry Harper. Asking for a copy of his Joan of Arc for a granddaughter of Queen Victoria. Confirming a date. P Oct 29 (39) $2,000

Series of 7 A Ls s, 1890 to 1907. 20 pp, 12mo & 8vo. To Jean Clemens. Chatting about his activities. Sgd Father. CNY May 11 (19) $13,000

— Series of 4 A Ls s, 14 May to 12 July 1907. 13 pp, 8vo & 12mo. Reporting about his trip to England. Sgd Father. CNY May 11 (31) $7,500

— Series of 8 A Ls s, [20 Sept 1907] to 15 May 1908. 18 pp, 12mo & 8vo. To Jean Clemens. Chatting about his activities. Sgd Father. CNY May 11 (32) $13,000

CLEMENS

— Series of 3 A Ls s, 20 May to [2 July] 1908. 9 pp, 8vo. To Jean Clemens. About her new home. Sgd Father. CNY May 11 (35) $6,000

— Series of 5 A Ls s, 5 June 1908 to 19 Apr 1909. 13 pp, 8vo. To Jean Clemens. Chatting about naming a house, a family funeral, etc. Sgd Father. CNY May 11 (36) $11,000

A Ls s (2), 7 & 20 July [n.y.]. 4 pp, 8vo. To Lord Monkswell. Requesting information for an article about copyright. Thanking for information. S July 23 (133) £1,300 [Richards]

— A Ls s (2), 17 & 21 Aug 1895. 4 pp, 4to & 8vo. To J. Henry Harper. About disclosing his authorship of Personal Recollections of Joan of Arc, ptd in Harper's Magazine. P Oct 29 (38) $2,500

— A Ls s (2), 25 Feb & 5 Mar 1907. 8 pp, 12mo. About a tomcat having kittens & a premonitory dream. Sgd Father. CNY May 11 (30) $3,800

ALs, 1 Sept 1869. 2 pp, 8vo. To "F.C.". About his lecturing activities. S July 23 (134) £750 [Maggs]

— 13 July [1878]. 4 pp, 4to. To Frank Bliss. Referring to problems with the shareholders of the American Book Company & reporting about the progress of his new book [A Tramp Abroad]. Sgd S L C. P Oct 29 (37) $3,000

— 16 July 1889. 2 pp, 8vo. To Susy [Olivia Susan] Clemens. About the art of writing, her reading, & the lonely house. Sgd Papa. CNY May 11 (18) $2,000

— 24 Mar 1893. 6 pp, 8vo. To Susy Clemens. Telling a story about Charles Eliot Norton introducing Richard Hunt as a speaker. Sgd Papa. CNY May 11 (20) $9,000

— 7 May 1893. 4 pp, 4to. To Susy Clemens. Describing a visit with his sister-in-law at Elmira. Sgd Papa. CNY May 11 (21) $4,800

— 6 Nov 1893. 4 pp, 8vo. To Susy Clemens. Stressing his determination to work "until we are safe from the poor-house". Sgd Papa. CNY May 11 (22) $6,500

— 27 Dec 1893. 8 pp, 8vo. To Susy Clemens. Giving a vivid description of [Lillian W. Aldrich] & saying he loathes her. With small ink sketch. Sgd Papa. CNY May 11 (23) $7,500

— 8 Aug 1894. 8 pp, size not stated. To Susy Clemens. Describing a visit to a palm-reader. With 2 small drawings. Sgd Papa. CNY May 11 (24) $4,000

— 7 Feb 1896. 3 pp, 8vo. To Susy Clemens. Chatting about catching a cold in India. Sgd Papa. CNY May 11 (25) $1,800

— 26 Feb 1896. 2 pp, 8vo. Recipient unnamed. Accepting an invitation. Framed. Altman collection. pnNY Sept 13 (110) $1,100

— 25 July 1904. 2 pp, 12mo. To his sister-in-law Susan L. Crane. About the death of his wife. Sgd S.L.C. CNY May 11 (26) $12,000

— 27 July 1906. 2 pp, 12mo. To his sister-in-law Susan L. Crane. Concerning a funeral & telling about receiving a letter from a sweetheart of 48 years ago. Sgd Samuel. CNY May 11 (27) $5,500

— [7 Dec 1906]. 2 pp, 4to. To Jean Clemens. About attending congressional hearings on the copyright law. Sgd Father. CNY May 11 (28) $1,600

— 14 Feb 1907. 3 pp, 12mo. To Jean Clemens. Reporting about a reading of Shelley & the progress of his autobiography. Sgd Father. CNY May 11 (29) $1,600

— 8 Oct 1907. 2 pp, 8vo. To Jean Clemens. Joking about the benefits of exercise. Sgd Father. CNY May 11 (33) $2,800

— 14 Feb 1908. 3 pp, 8vo. To Jean Clemens. Proudly reporting "about [his daughter] Clara's musicale of last night." Sgd Father. CNY May 11 (34) $1,600

— [19 June 1908]. 3 pp, 4to. To Jean Clemens. Expressing his admiration for Cleveland. Sgd Father. CNY May 11 (37) $4,800

— [28 July 1908]. 3 pp, 12mo. To Jean Clemens. Family letter, & describing the joys of a beautiful day. Sgd Father. CNY May 11 (38) $4,800

— 12 Oct 1908. 4 pp, 12mo. To Jean Clemens. Commenting about the Presidential election. Sgd Father. CNY May 11 (39) $3,200

Cut signature, [n.d.]. wa May 30 (499) $180

Signature, [n.d.]. 1 p, 24mo; card. With brief inscr. Mtd on thinner sheet. sg Nov 6 (212) $225

Clemens Wenzeslaus von Sachsen, Kurfuerst & Erzbischof von Trier, 1739-1812

Ls, 6 Dec 1793. 1 p, folio. To Ferdinand IV of Naples, later King of the Two Sicilies. New Year's wishes. With autograph subscription. In Latin. star Apr 9 (988) DM340

Clement VI, Pope, 1291-1352

Document, 27 May 1351. 1 p, folio. Vellum. Papal Bull, giving permission to Duke Albrecht von Anhalt-Zerbst to select his own confessor. wa May 30 (63) $1,200

Clement VII, Pope, 1478-1534

Ls, 7 July 1521. 1 p, 4to. To the cathedral chapter & canons of San Gimignano. As Cardinal, instructing them about a forthcoming election to fill a vacancy in the chapter. C Dec 3 (238) £380 [L'Autographe]

Cleveland, Frances Folsom, 1864-1947

White House card, sgd, 14 Dec [18]86. 4.5 by 2.75 inches. With related material. wa May 30 (479) $120

Cleveland, Grover, 1837-1908

Collection of 3 A Ls s, 2 A Ls, & 3 signatures, 12 Dec 1899, 1 Nov 1902, & [n.d.]. About 12 pp, mostly 8vo. To A. M. D. Halaway, J. H. Eckels, & unnamed recipients. About work to be done to Cleveland's grounds, some chickens, etc. Signatures on Executive Mansion card, a card, & fragment of a document. With related material. pnNY June 11 (7) $800

ALs, 31 Jan 1890. 2 pp, 8vo. To Judge Robert Ludlow Fowler. Thanking for organizational help. On legal firm letterhead. Was mtd. sg Nov 6 (43) $175

— 11 Nov 1890. 2 pp, 8vo. Recipient unnamed. Thanking for the gift of a cotton stalk. Repaired. wa May 30 (269) $150

— 15 July 1894. 3 pp, 8vo. To William L. Wilson. Enclosing Ls, 2 July 1894, 7 pp, 4to, by Cleveland to Wilson. Stressing the necessity of tariff reform & explaining that the [Wilson Gorham] tariff bill before Congress is a departure from Democratic principles. P Oct 29 (41) $4,500

— 26 Dec 1897. 2 pp, 12mo. To James J. Lampton. Stating that he does not intend to buy real estate. Fold split. wa Oct 18 (82) $80

— 3 Nov 1907. 2 pp, 12mo. To J. Edward Simmons. Thanking for help given to E. C. Benedict. wd Nov 12 (5) $225

A Ls (2), 8 Feb & 25 July 1906. 4 pp, 12mo. To J. Hacker Hall. Enclosing money for repairs to the Remick house. Expressing surprise at the amount of unpaid bills. wa Oct 18 (80) $270

Ls, 18 July 1892. 1 p, 8vo. Recipient unnamed. Thanking for political support. Framed with a photograph. wa Oct 18 (7) $90

ANs, [n.d.], 1 p, 12mo. To J. Hacker Hall. Fragment, 3 lines directing him to do something [about Cleveland's house?]. wa Oct 18 (83) $75

Collection of AD & White House card, sgd. 14 Feb 1889, 1 p. 4to. Draft; Veto Message to the Senate, returning "An Act granting a pension to Charles J. Esty". P Oct 29 (40) $400

Executive Mansion card, sgd. Framed. Altman collection. pnNY Sept 13 (4) $225

Photograph, sgd & inscr, [n.d.]. 6.5 by 4 inches. Inscr on mount. wd Nov 12 (6) $300

Clifford, Thomas, 1st Baron Clifford of Chudleigh, 1630-73

[A collection of more than 100 documents, consisting of Lord Clifford's miscellaneous papers, both official & domestic, [1660s to 1673], c.230 pp, various sizes, sold at S on 24 July, lot 246, for £4,500 to Burgess & Browning.]

[A collection of papers prepared or used by Lord Clifford in his various Treasury offices, mostly 1662 to 1673, c. 100 documents, c.250 pp, chiefly folio, some autograph, sold at S on 24 July 1987, lot 245, for £4,500 to Burgess & Browning.]

[A collection of Lord Clifford's papers concerning the Dutch Wars & related negotiations, [1665 to 1674], c.160 documents, nearly 600 pp, mostly folio, including 7 A Ls s by James, Duke of York [later King James II], sold at S on 24 July 1987, lot 244, for £10,000 to Maggs.]
See also: Charles II, 1630-85
See also: Postal Service

Clinton, George, 1737-1812

ALs, 20 May 1783. 1 p, folio. To George Washington. Draft, concerning the return of Westchester County to New York State authority after the departure of the British. Waterstained. P Oct 29 (42) $850

Clinton, Sir Henry, 1738?-95

Ds, 28 Oct 1778. 1 p, folio. Pay order to Capt. Lawrence Robert Campbell. Countersgd by John Smith. Partly ptd. sg Nov 6 (249) $325

Clinton, James, 1733-1812

ALs, 14 Mar 1790. 1 p, 4to. To Isaac Melcher. Discussing land holdings in western New York. wa May 30 (322) $280

Clive, Robert, Baron Clive, 1725-74

ALs, 15 Apr 1757. 4 pp, 4to. Recipient unnamed. Explaining the removal of French officers at Chandernagore to Calcutta. Bullock collection. CNY Dec 19 (50) $2,000

Clymer, George, Signer from Pennsylvania

ALs, 5 Jan 1805. 3 pp, 8vo. Mentioning a new invention to grind up Indian corn cob. Sgd G.C. Fold splits. wa May 30 (131) $100

Ds, 2 Apr 1802. 1 p, 8vo. Sight draft of Henry Clymer. Charlotte Parker Milne collection. wd Nov 12 (32) $100

Cobden-Sanderson, Thomas James, 1840-1922

ALs, 30 Apr 1912. 2 pp, 8vo. To Henry van de Velde. Asking him to call on Francis Hirst at Weimar. star Apr 8 (453) DM340

Cochin, Charles Nicolas, 1715-90
ALs, 15 May 1783. 1 p, 4to. Recipient unnamed. Commenting on recipient's talents as a draughtsman. With related material. S Jan 27 (949) £350 [Quaritch]

Cocteau, Jean, 1889-1963
ALs, 24 Jan 1930. 1 p, 8vo. To Richard Thomas. Saying he is overworked. Sgd Jean [with star]. S Jan 27 (961) £80 [Rankin]
— [n.d.]. 1 p, 4to. To Kees van Dongen. Sending theater tickets. At bottom of page ANs by van Dongen, inviting friends to use the tickets. star Apr 8 (41) DM320
— 13 Apr 1938. 2 pp, 4to. Recipient unnamed. Enlisting his help for "une entreprise musicale de premiere ordre". star Apr 8 (40) DM400
— 2 Dec 1950. 1 p, 4to. To Mary. About his health & a new Persian cat. Sketch of profile in blue crayon on right hand side of sheet. Sgd Jean. Framed. Altman collection. pnNY Sept 13 (111) $400

Colbert, Jean Baptiste, 1619-83. See: Le Vau, Louis

Coleridge, Samuel Taylor, 1772-1834
Autograph Ms, poem, beginning "The prayer of Hate", 7 lines; [n.d.]. 1 p, c.75mm by 160mm. Fragment; mtd. With a letter from J. Gillman to an unnamed recipient, 26 July [1834], announcing Coleridge's death. C June 24 (104) £600 [Quaritch]
ALs, [c.1815; "Thursday"]. 4 pp, 4to. To Dr. Sainsbury. Describing his opium dependence. With postscript. Bullock collection. CNY Dec 19 (52) $1,600

Colette, Sidonie Gabrielle, 1873-1954
ALs, [18 Oct 1939]. 2 pp, 4to. To Marie-Therese Montaudry. Thanking for offering a retreat in the country. S Jan 27 (962) £120 [Smith]
— [1 July 1948]. 1 p, 8vo. To Andre Barbier. About a dying philocactus & her holiday plans. Framed with envelope. Altman collection. pnNY Sept 13 (112) $400

Colfax, Schuyler, 1823-85
Series of 3 A Ls s, 1875. 4 pp, 8vo. To his cousin [Mrs. Barbour]. Regarding autographs for her collection. With related material. sg Apr 9 (44) $110
Franking signature, [15 Feb n.y.]. As Vice President. rf Mar 14 (75) $90

Collins, Wilkie, 1824-89
Series of 4 A Ls s, 1850 to 1888. 15 pp, 4to & 8vo. To Ward, Palgrave Simpson & Jane. About a variety of subjects. S July 23 (45) £1,100 [Wilson]
ALs, 15 May 1876. 1 p, 8vo. To "Dearest Padronna". Sending "a line of introduction for the abishag of the American King David". wa May 30 (352) $85

Collis, Maurice
Autograph Ms, Lords of the Sunset, draft; [n.d.]. 384 pp. In folder. With ptd 1st Ed & typescript carbon copy, in folder; & autograph Ms, Journal of My Tour to the Shan States, 60 pp, in folder. 8vo & 4to. bba Nov 13 (157) £140 [Burgess Browning]
— Autograph Ms, Nancy Astor, draft. 511 pp, in folder. With typescript carbon copy, Ms notes, page proofs & presentation copy of 1st American Ed, 1960, to his brother John Stewart Collis. 8vo & 4to. bba Nov 13 (158) £140 [Burgess Browning]

Commonplace Books
Ms, containing entries about herbs, animals, voyages of discovery, etc., [17th cent]. 284 pp, 4to. Vellum bdg. C June 24 (9) £160 [Newmarket Gallery]
— Ms, prose works & verse by a number of different authors, [England, c.1700]. About 260 pp, 4to. Contemp vellum bds. Written in a single hand. S July 23 (11) £500 [Quaritch]

Connecticut
[A collection of c.60 autograph & ptd receipts & certificates mainly from the Hartford area, 1813 to 1850s, 8vo & 4to, was sold at sg on 6 Nov 1986, lot 251, for $275.]

Conrad, Joseph, 1857-1924
Collection of 34 A Ls s & Ls s, 1916 to 1923. About 65 pp, 4to & 8vo. To J. M. Dent & Sons. About the publication of The Rescue & a variety of other subjects. With related material. S July 23 (137) £9,000 [Rota]

Constable, John, 1776-1837
ALs, 22 Nov 1830. 2 pp, 4to. To A. Keightley, Jr. Admiring Mr. Lane's copy of Sir Thomas Lawrence's port of George IV. Was mtd. S July 24 (476) £600 [Fogg]
Letter, 20 Feb 1834. 4 pp, 8vo. To his cousin Mary Allen. About his health, an undeserved insult, etc. In the hand of Charles Boner. With related material. C June 24 (186) £280 [Fogg]

Constantinople
— VALERIO, CHRISTOFORO. - Relatione di Constantinopoli, [c.1620]. 44 leaves (5 blanks), 262mm by 205mm. 17th cent bds. Bound with anr Relatione di Constantinopoli, 1639, 28 blanks. Contemp copies of diplomatic reports addressed to the Doge of Venice. HK Nov 4 (427) DM800

Contades, Louis Georges Erasme, Marquis de, 1704-93

Ls, 18 Oct 1758. 3 pp, 4to. To Gen. Fitzjames. Reporting about the military situation in Westfalia. With autograph postscript, 10 lines. star Apr 9 (933) DM400

Cook, Capt. James, 1728-79

— FELICITE, LOUIS LEON, COMTE DE LAURAGUAIS. - Ls, 17 [Mar?] 1772. 2 pp, 4to. To Sir Joseph Banks. Trying to justify his unauthorized ptg of Banks's account of Cook's 1st voyage. S Dec 18 (273) £2,700 [Brooke-Hitching]

Cookery Manuscripts

Ms, A Book of Choice Receipts, In Cookery; belonging to Anne Burton, 1742. About 200 pp, folio. Contemp vellum bds. Also containing medical prescriptions. S Jan 27 (782) £350 [Clark]

— Ms, [c.1595 to c.1750]. 183 pp, 4to. 19th cent brown mor gilt; det. Flyleaf inscr with 17th cent names of Jane Harewell & Wenefride Dormer. Begun by John Eames as collection of herbal remedies; later transformed into cookery notebook. In a variety of hands. C Dec 3 (357A) £150 [Levy]

— Ms, [late 17th to early 18th cent]. 139 pp, folio. Contemp calf. Recipes, remedies & household hints. Flyleaf inscr "Mary Hookes 1680". In 2 hands. C Dec 3 (357) £380 [Hofmann & Freeman]

— Ms, recipe book & herbal of Lady Elizabeth Cotton, [late 17th/early 18th cent]. 568 pp, folio. Contemp reversed calf panelled in blind. In several hands. Also sgd by other members of the Cotton family. C June 24 (165) £450 [Quaritch]

Coolidge, Calvin, 1872-1933

[A collection of 5 White House cards, sgd, & signature on anr card, [n.d.]., sold at pnNY on 11 June 1987, lot 12, for $650.]

Ls, 5 Nov 1915. Size not given. Recipient unnamed. As member of the Massachusetts state senate; thanking for a telegram. wa Oct 18 (8) $80

— 14 Nov 1924. 1 p, 4to. To Mary Shimonek. Thanking for her praise of his writings. P May 13 (38) $1,300

— 19 Aug 1925. Size not given. To Wm. A. Aiken. As President, reciprocating expression of good wishes. wa Oct 18 (86) $130

— 4 Jan 1930. 1 p, 4to. Recipient unnamed. Regarding contact with Phillips Brooks. On personal letterhead. rf Nov 15 (5) $200

Ds s (2) 26 Nov 1927 & 18 Sept 1928. 2 pp, folio. Appointment for Harry Hine as notary public. Recognition for Nestor Mustiga as Honorary Vice Consul. pnNY June 11 (10) $250

Ds, 18 Dec 1923. 1 p, folio. Appointment of B. Ogden Chisholm to the International Prison Commission. Partly ptd. Framed. wd Nov 12 (8) $150

— 5 June 1924. 1 p, folio. Consular appointment. Countersgd by Sec of State Charles E. Hughes. wa Oct 18 (88) $135

— 2 June 1926. 1 p, folio. Foreign Service appointment. Countersgd by Sec of State Frank Kellogg. wa Oct 18 (87) $110

Check, 14 Aug 1916. Drawn on 1st National Bank, Northampton, for $10. wa May 30 (91) $130

Cut signature, [n.d.]. With autograph subscription, 2 words. wa May 30 (92) $55

White House card, [23 Nov 1927]. Sgd. Was mtd. wa May 30 (93) $160

Corbeil

Ms, Memoire de la Ville de Corbeil. 1628. 270pp, 4to, in old calf. SM Oct 20 (430) FF20,000

Corinth, Lovis, 1858-1925

Original drawing, pencil sketch showing vinyards & the Rhine, on autograph postcard, sgd, [11 Sept 1907], to Rudolf Sieger. star Apr 8 (454) DM660

ALs, 20 Sept 1919. 2 pp, 8vo. To Ernst Oppler. Regarding an exhibition. star Apr 8 (456) DM540

Autograph postcard, sgd, [11 Dec 1907]. To the Editors of the magazine Maerz. Declining their request to write an article about R. Wilke. With related material. star Apr 8 (455) DM220

Cornelius, Peter, 1824-74

Autograph Ms, collection of 39 poems. Sgd on tp & dated 17 Dec 1849. 112 pp, 8vo. Contemp brown half cloth bdg. Inscr to his sister Auguste. star Apr 9 (615) DM4,500

Cornwall & Kilsyth Families

[An archive of personal & business papers, 1673 to 1742, 271 items in 2 vols, connected with the Cornwall family of Kilsyth, Scotland & their landlords, descendants of Sir James Livingstone, 1st Viscount Kilsyth, sold at C on 3 Dec 1986, lot 239, for £290 to Bristow.]

Cornwallis, Charles Cornwallis, Marquis, 1739-1805

ANs, 5 Mar 1771. 1 p, 4to. Recipient unnamed. 3 lines, requesting acceptance of bills. rf Mar 14 (9) $260

Ds, 15 Apr 1781. 1 p, folio. Pay order to David Thomas for £2,000. Countersgd by Henry Haldane. Partly ptd. sg Nov 6 (255) $600

Cortes, Hernando, 1485-1547
Ds, 18 Aug 1534. 1 p, folio. Pay order to Antonio de la Cadena in favor of Christoval Pez; sgd El Marques. Pez's receipt, 2 endorsements & arithmetical calculations on verso. Fold tear; waterstained. H. A. Monday collection. P Dec 15 (18) $15,000

Cortot, Alfred, 1877-1962
ALs, 13 Apr 1952. 2 pp, 8vo. To an unnamed lady. Regarding his book Aspects de Chopin. star Apr 9 (616) DM340

Corvisart des Marets, Jean Nicolas, Baron, 1755-1821
ALs, 12 Jan 1808. 2 pp, 4to. Recipient unnamed. Protesting against postal charges. star Apr 8 (318) DM360

Cosway, Richard, 1742-1821
ALs, [c.1805]. 3 pp, 4to. To an unnamed Lord. Notifying him of the arrival of marbles shipped to England by Lord Elgin. S Jan 27 (950) £220 [Quaritch]

Cotman, Joseph. See: Manship, Henry

Cowley, Abraham, 1618-67
ALs, 24 Aug/3 Sept 1650. 3 pp, folio. To an unnamed peer in Poland [John, 1st Lord Colepeper?]. Commenting on the military situation in Great Britain, the treatment of Charles II in Holland, etc. With ALs by Henry Jermyn on 4th p of same sheet; mostly about the financial distress of the exiled royal family. S Dec 18 (3) £5,500 [Quaritch]

Crane, Thomas. See: Sowerby, John G. & Crane

Crane, Walter, 1845-1915
Original drawings, 2 ink & watercolor illusts for Charles Lamb's, A Masque of Days, 1901; a man & a woman at the dinner table. Both with text in panel & artists's monogram. In card mount, 275mm by 188mm. S Dec 5 (444) £1,500 [Hartnoll]

Cranmer, Thomas, 1489-1556
Ds, 16 Feb 1551. 1 p, 360mm by 565mm. Vellum. Award of the estate of Sir John Thymelbye between his sons & executors. Sgd T. Cant. Also sgd by John Cokk. C Dec 3 (240) £1,000 [Harrison]

Cretin, Guillaume Dubois, Called, d. c.1525
Ms, Debat entre deux dames sur le passtemps des chiens et des oiseaux. [Rouen, c.1525] 4 vellum leaves plus 6 pp of vellum flyleaves, 270mm by 200mm, in modern mor gilt by Saulnier. With 4 full-page miniatures in the style of the Master of Petrarch's Triumphs. Jeanson Ms 112 SM Feb 28 (157) FF380,000

Crimean War
— BURNETT, JOHN. - Journal, describing experiences in the Crimea in 1855. About 300 pp, 8vo, in 2 vols. Blue mor & marbled bds. S Jan 27 (848) £280 [Jackson]
— HOPE, LIEUT. J. E. - Autograph sketchbook, c.May 1854 to Sept 1855. About 50 pp, 16mo. Quarter-calf. Containing nearly 30 panoramic views of the theater of war, in watercolors, with some related material. S July 24 (334) £1,100 [Lake]
— SERVANTES, COL. W. F. G. - Series of 3 A Ls s, May to Sept 1855; 31 pp, various sizes. To Gen. Henderson. Discussing military organization during the Crimean campaign & describing assaults on Sebastopol. C Dec 3 (241) £220 [Rutherford]

Crippen, Hawley Harvey, 1862-1910
— LE NEVE, ETHEL. - Series of 6 A Ls s, 29 Oct to 16 Nov 1910. 13 pp, 8vo. To the Governor of Pentonville Prison [Maj. Mytton-Davies]. Concerning Crippen's last weeks & his will. S July 24 (378) £420 [Seyer]

Cromwell, Oliver, 1599-1658
ALs, 22 Apr [1651]. 1 p, folio. To "Sir Henry Vane the younger". Asking him to do his utmost to find good officers. Sgd your faythfull Brother Fountaine. S Dec 18 (226) £6,000 [Henry]
— 15 Dec 1651. 1 p, folio. To his sister Elizabeth Cromwell. Family letter, sending money & mentioning the death of his son-in-law Ireton. S July 24 (255) £3,300 [Wilson]
Ls, 22 Jan 1654/5. 1 p, folio. To the Commissioners of the Admiralty & Navy. Ordering them to hasten the departure of the fleet sailing to Barbados. S Dec 18 (227) £1,100 [Wilson]
— 2 Dec 1657. 1 p, folio. To Lieut. Col. Underwood. Reporting about an expected Royalist insurrection. C Dec 3 (242) £2,400 [Burns Lindley]
Ds, 14 Jan 1649. 1 p, 4to. Granting Hugh Courtney safe passage to return to England. With autograph corrections. 2-line memorandum by Courtney at foot of p. Repaired. P Dec 15 (19) $1,100
— 26 Aug 1649. 1 p, folio. Orders for Col. John Moore to raise recruits for his regiment in England. sg Apr 9 (47) $2,600
— 14 Mar 1650. 1 p, 8vo. Ordering Anthony Playford & his army to return to England. Fold tear. Sang collection. P Sept 24 (20) $1,600
Signature, 3 Nov 1648. On cut address panel directed to Col. Charles Fairfax, c.70mm by 185mm. Set into paper border. With 14

engravings of Cromwell. C June 24 (36) £1,100 [Maggs]

Cromwell, Richard, 1626-1712
Ds, 1 Dec 1658. 1 p, 263mm by 345mm. Vellum. Appointment of Diggory Taylor as Rector of St. Earme. Partly faded. C Dec 3 (243) £520 [Rendell]

Cruikshank, George, 1792-1878
Original drawings, male heads, in pencil & ink, [n.d.]. 3 small pp, 1 sgd, 1 initialled. In frame, 12 by 14.75 inches. wa May 30 (21) $210

Original drawing, 12 male heads, in pencil, 8 with watercolor, [n.d.]. 6.75 by 4.5 inches. Sgd in ink. Framed. wa May 30 (19) $300

— Original drawing, 4 heads, in pencil with watercolors; 3 in Elizabethan costume, [n.d.]. 4.4 by 4.1 inches. Sgd. Framed. wa May 30 (20) $250

— Original drawing, 5 male heads & dog, in ink & wash, [n.d.]. 1 p, 4.6 by 8 inches. Sgd. Framed. wa May 30 (22) $220

— Original drawing, man in profile, in pencil & wash; [n.d.]. 3.5 by 3 inches. Framed. wa May 30 (23) $50

ALs, [c.1840]. 1 p, 4to. Recipient unknown. Fragment; criticizing an article "Men of the Day". With 4 watercolor & ink drawings incorporated into the letter. sg Nov 6 (46) $175

ANs, 7 Oct 1875. 1 p, 8vo. To Miss Elizabeth R. Wright. Saying Bedford House was pulled down c.1798. With engraving of Bedford House. sg Nov 6 (45) $40

Crusade, Third
[A collection of 25 vellum documents issued by members of the armies of Philip Augustus, King of France, & Richard the Lionheart, King of England during the siege of Acre, 1191, mostly concerning loans of money from merchants of Pisa & Genoa, sold at S on 23 June 1987, lot 35, for £20,000 to Brinton.]

Cui, Cesar, 1835-1918
Photograph, sgd & inscr, 1900. Overall size 16cm by 10.5cm. Inscr to Madame Litta. With ALs, 1900, 2 pp, 8vo. S May 22 (590) £160 [McCann]

Culbertson, M. S.
Ls, 1 Jan 1847. 3 pp, 4to. To Professor Joseph Henry. Circular letter, reporting about activities of missionaries in China & Hong Kong. Encapsulated. sg Apr 9 (41) $50

Cummings, Edward Estlin, 1894-1962
Ls, 24 Feb 1952. 1 p, 4to. To Alfred Borrello. About his father's influence on him and his definition of poetry: "a poem is a poem just insofaras it cannot be translated into another language." sg Mar 5 (48) $175

Curie, Marie, 1867-1934
ALs, 22 May 1921. 1 p, 8vo. To Miss Brooks. Letter of thanks. Framed. Altman collection. pnNY Sept 13 (143) $850

ANs, 3 Aug 1927. 1 p, 12mo. Recipient unknown. Giving her signature "a l'appel des intellectuels en faveur de Sacco et Vanzetti". On ptd card of Laboratoire Curie. P Dec 15 (22) $1,500

Curtius (Quintus Curtius Rufus)
Ms, Des Fais d'Alexandre, in French trans by Vasco Fernandez, Count of Lucena, dedicated to Charles the Bold, Duke of Burgundy. [Bruges. c.1470-80]. 287 leaves (4 blank, 1 vellum), 371mm by 262mm. 18th-cent French calf. In dark brown ink in a regular flamboyant lettre batarde. With nine large initials in red & blue & three-quarter page frontispiece miniature in full colors & liquid gold within full illuminated border, possibly by the Master of the Vienna Chronicle of England. S June 23 (86) £15,000 [Brown]

Custer, George Armstrong, 1839-76
Ls, 10 June 1867. 1 p, 4to. To Brevet Brig. Gen. Henry B. Carrington. As Lieut-Col. of the 7th Cavalry, notifying him of the suicide of Major Wickliffe Cooper. S Dec 18 (342) £1,200 [Jeffery]

Czerny, Carl, 1791-1857
Autograph music, Rondeau a la Bacarole, Op. 255 for piano solo; [c.1830]. 16 pp, 250mm by 322mm. Ms tp & 15 pp of music, 14 staves each. Some revisions. Marked by the printer. CNY Dec 19 (137) $1,500

ALs, 10 Nov 1842. 1 p, 4to. To the pbr F. Lucca. Notifying him that he has received money from "la Veuve Mainzer". S May 22 (374) £280 [Schneider]

D

Dahlmann, Friedrich Christoph, 1785-1860
ALs, 4 July 1844. 1 p, 4to. To Joseph Du Mont. Recommending Gustav von Guelich. Repaired. star Apr 8 (319) DM540

Dahn, Felix, 1834-1912
ALs, 2 Jan 1877. 3 pp, 8vo. To an unnamed society in Vienna. Commenting on the cultural bonds between Germans & Austrians, & saying he is unable to attend a commemorative ceremony [for Beetho-

ven?]. star Apr 8 (42) DM500

Dalber, Karl, Reichasfreiherr von, Kurfuerst von Mainz, 1744-1817
ALs, 11 Aug 1813. 2 pp, folio. To Eugene Beauharnais. Suggesting the exploitation of the Spessart woods for the French navy. In French. star Apr 9 (934) DM3,400

Dali, Salvador
Autograph postcard, sgd, [3 Feb 1937]. To Rene Magrittte. Saying that Surrealism "fait un gran 'efet' a New York". Address written in anr hand. S July 2 (972) £220 [Shulson]
Photograph, sgd, [c.1958]. 10 by 8 inches. Posed in front of his The Discovery of America. With untitled color print, [c.1976], sgd; & book, Dali. The Masterworks, 1971; sgd on tp verso under self-port. sg Nov 6 (48) $150

Dallapiccola, Luigi, 1904-75
Ls, 27 Apr 1963. 1 p, 4to. To Rolf Liebermann. Expressing his thanks for efforts to perform his opera Il Prigioniero. In French. star Apr 9 (617) DM270

Dalton, John, 1766-1844
Autograph Ms, draft syllabus of lectures on meteorology, 1835; with ptd sheets of atomic symbols & other related material. About 25 pp, folio. S Jan 27 (902) £500 [Rota]

Dalzell, James
Autograph transcript, poem, The Blue and the Gray, [n.d.]. 2 pp, 4to. Sgd Private Dalzell, twice. With note at end giving history of the writing & publication of the poem. sg Nov 6 (41) $175

D'Annunzio, Gabriele, 1863-1938
Autograph Ms, draft of a political speech, [c.1919]. 6 pp, 4to; each tipped on card mount. To the Romans, referring to a procession the preceding day. C Dec 3 (390) £420 [Bragho]
— Autograph Ms, drama, Il Ferro, 1st draft, sgd G.d.A. & dated 21 Sept 1912 & [31 Oct] 1913. 366 pp, 4to. Including 21 variant pp for finale of Act II. C June 24 (145) £15,000 [Fondazione Banca Credito]
— Autograph Ms, drama, Il Sogno d'un Mattino di Primavera, 1897. 145 pp, 4to, on rectos only. Sgd. Some revisions & instructions for the ptr. In wrap of folded paper. C June 24 (143) £10,000 [Fondazione Banca Credito]
— Autograph Ms, drama, Il Sogno d'un Tramonto d'Autunno, sgd & dated Oct 1897 & Oct 1908. 112 pp, 4to, on rectos only. Final draft. Tied with red silk ribbons. C June 24 (144) £5,000 [Fondazione Banca Credito]
— Autograph Ms, La Contemplazione della Morte, dated 7 to 17 Apr 1912. 199 pp, 4to, on rectos only. Sgd 4 times. Some revisions. Lacking preface included in book Ed ptd 1912. C June 24 (141) £12,000 [Fondazione Banca Credito]
— Autograph Ms, La Vita di Cola di Rienzo, draft of orig version, dated 30 Dec 1905. 278 pp, 4to, on rectos only. With numerous revisions. C June 24 (140) £15,000 [Fondazione Banca Credito]
— Autograph Ms, novel, Le Vergini delle Rocce, dated 30 June [18]95. 600 pp, 4to, on rectos only. With numerous revisions & some instructions for ptg. C June 24 (139) £24,000 [Fondazione Banca Credito]
— Autograph Ms, Preludio alle tre Parabole del bellissimo Nemico -- Il Vangelo secondo l'Avversario, dated 27 Jan 1897. 143 pp, 4to, on rectos only. With revisions & instructions for ptg. Version ptd in Le Faville del Maglio, 1924. C June 24 (142) £15,000 [Fondazione Banca Credito]
Series of 7 A Ls s, 15 Mar to 5 Nov 1920. 14 pp, 4to & folio. To Gen. Cesare Faccini. Regarding the occupation of Fiume, meetings & his opponents in Rome. C Dec 3 (391) £260 [King]
ALs, 19 Oct 1929. 2 pp, folio. To Martino Hurupp. About the tuning of his pianos. star Apr 8 (7) DM300
Photograph, sgd & inscr, Oct 1929. 19.5cm by 17cm. Inscr to Martino Hurupp, on mount, 38cm by 26cm. star Apr 8 (8) DM260

Danton, Georges Jacques, 1759-94
Ds, 2 Sept 1792. 1 p, folio. Passport for William Maxwell going to England on a government mission. Also sgd by 3 other members of the Conseil Executif Provisoire. Tipped to larger sheet, with transcript. Bullock collection. CNY Dec 19 (162) $800
— [n.d.]. 1 p, 4to. Accusation of liberticide against an unknown person for various crimes; also sgd by 2 others. Endorsed "Baudron". C Dec 3 (244) £380 [Rendell]

D'Arboval, Sidonie Hurtel. See: Botanical Manuscripts

Darwin, Charles, 1809-82
Autograph Ms, headings for chapter II of his The Descent of Man, [n.d.]. 1 p, folio. "Comparison of the Mental process of Men & the Lower Animals"; sgd. On blue paper. S Dec 18 (332) £2,800 [Joseph & Sawyer]
Collection of 3 A Ls s & Ls, 25 Feb 1868 to 23 Dec 1871. 6 pp, 8vo. To Henry Lee. About research concerning the sex of trout. Bullock collection. CNY Dec 19 (56) $3,800
ALs, 9 Apr 1859. 3 pp, 8vo. To William Bernhard Tegetmeier. Expressing his gratitude for Tegetmeier's help with poultry specimens & talking about the publication

of his new book. Tipped into a copy of his On the Origins of Species... L 1859. 1st Ed; inscr to Tegetmeier. Further related material also tipped in. S Dec 18 (333) £7,800 [Kohler]

— 10 Jan 1865. 2 pp, 8vo. To Professor Hennesy. Discussing the "case of the Asturian plants". C June 24 (167) £1,200 [Lucas]

— 23 Dec [1866?]. 4 pp, 8vo. To [Thomas Rivers]. Introducing himself & requesting information for his book "on the Variation of Animals & Plants under domestication". S July 24 (354) £1,000 [West]

— 28 Dec [1866?]. 7 pp, 8vo. To [Thomas Rivers]. Commenting on aspects of the physiology of plants. S July 24 (353) £1,500 [West]

— 7 Jan [1867?]. 6 pp, 8vo. To [Thomas Rivers]. Thanking for shoots & discussing several plants. S July 24 (357) £2,400 [Quaritch]

— 11 Jan [1867?]. 5 pp, 8vo. To [Thomas Rivers]. Discussing Rivers's paper about peaches in the Gardener's Chronicle. S July 24 (356) £2,600 [Quaritch]

— 15 Jan [1867?]. 4 pp, 8vo. To [Thomas Rivers]. Discussing information about peaches & requesting samples. S July 24 (355) £2,000 [Quaritch]

— 25 Jan [1867?]. 1 p, 8vo. To [Thomas Rivers]. Thanking for 2 [peach] trees. S July 24 (359) £1,050 [Maggs]

— "Saturday" [Jan 1867?]. 3 pp, 8vo. To [Thomas Rivers]. Discussing information about the Weeping Ash & the Thorn. S July 24 (358) £2,200 [Burr]

— 1 Feb [1867?]. 4 pp, 8vo. To [Thomas Rivers]. Answering a question about stomata & discussing "Weeping trees". S July 24 (360) £1,600 [Caldur]

— 5 Mar [1867?]. 4 pp, 8vo. To [Thomas Rivers]. About the progress of his double peach & almond tree. S July 24 (361) £1,200 [West]

— "Saturday 10th" [Mar 1867?]. 3 pp, 8vo. To [Thomas Rivers]. Thanking for peaches sent to him & requesting other specimens. S July 24 (362) £950 [Quaritch]

— 27 Apr [1867?]. 4 pp, 8vo. To [Thomas Rivers]. Concerning Rivers's article in the Journal of Horticulture & requesting a raceme of Cytisus pupureus elongatus. S July 24 (363) £750 [Richards]

— 8 June [1867?]. 2 pp, 8vo. To [Thomas Rivers]. Discussing the Cytisus. S July 24 (366) £620 [Wilson]

— 17 Aug [1867?]. 4 pp, 8vo. To [Thomas Rivers]. Asking for fruit-bearing almond trees. S July 24 (364) £1,500 [Quaritch]

— 17 [Aug 1867?]. 1 pp, 8vo. To [Thomas Rivers]. Asking whether he can distinguish "a nectarine tree from a Peach before if flowers". S July 24 (365) £750 [Wilson]

— 13 Oct [1867?]. 3 pp, 8vo. To [Thomas Rivers]. About purple nuts. S July 24 (367) £750 [Quaritch]

— 9 Feb 1870. 3 pp, 8vo. To Alfred Newton. About Newton's comments on Darwin's Variation of Animals and Plants under Domestication. Nicholas Wollaston collection. S July 24 (372) £1,300 [Quaritch]

— 31 July [1876]. 1 p, 8vo. To [August Mueller Beeck]. Refusing to send him a copy of a work. C Dec 3 (398) £900 [Maggs]

— 16 Nov 1881. 3 pp, 8vo. Recipient unnamed. Discussing the reproductive system of worms & other scientific questions. C Dec 3 (399) £1,300 [L'Echiquier]

— 8 Oct 1886. 1 p, 8vo. Recipient unknown. Sending a check for subscriptions for himself & his family. Holed. C Dec 3 (400) £480 [Wilson]

— 3 Feb [n.y.]. 1 p, size not stated. Recipient unnamed. Asking him to post a letter. Framed. Altman collection. pnNY Sept 13 (144) $600

Ls, 3 Feb [1865?]. 4 pp, 8vo. To [Max Wichura]. Referring to recipient's work on hybrid willows & admitting he may have to revise what he said about hybrids in his On the Origin of Species. P Dec 15 (24) $3,500

— 19 Jan [1867]. 3 pp, 8vo. To Alfred Newton. Requesting information about the Rhynchoea butterfly. Text in the hand of his wife Emma, with partly autograph postscript. Nicholas Wollaston collection. S July 24 (369) £950 [Quaritch]

— 23 Jan [1867]. 2 pp, 8vo. To Alfred Newton. Discussing "the male plumage" of swans. Text in the hand of his wife Emma. Nicholas Wollaston collection. S July 24 (370) £600 [Quaritch]

— 4 Mar [1867]. 4 pp, 8vo. To Alfred Newton. About evidence regarding the dotterel & Swinhoe's papers. Text in the hand of his wife Emma, with autograph insertion & postscript. Nicholas Wollaston collection. S July 24 (371) £1,300 [Quaritch]

— 2 Apr [1868?]. 7 pp, 8vo. To Sir William Bowman. Scientific letter discussing contraction of the orbicularis during screaming. With 16-line autograph postscript; letter in Emma Darwin's hand. S Dec 18 (334) £1,550 [Maggs]

— 3 Apr 1872. 2 pp, 8vo. To [Thomas Rivers]. Thanking for vines & returning a periodical about Amygdales. Text in the hand of his wife Emma. S July 24 (368) £400 [Wilson]

ANs, [n.d.]. 1 p, 8vo. Recipient unnamed. Acknowledging receipt of a Ms & saying he is ill. star Apr 8 (320) DM950

— 22 May [n.y.]. 1 p, 8vo. To [Mr. Schater?]. Stating he has sgd an enclosure (not present). C June 24 (168) £400 [Wilson]

Daudet, Alphonse, 1840-97
Autograph Ms, La Double Conversion, [c.1860]. 29 pp, on rectos only, 265mm by 195mm. Sgd. Some revisions. With ALs, [n.d.], 2 pp, 8vo, to an unnamed journalist of the Figaro. Covering letter for Ms, & commenting on his earlier Les Amoureuses. Late 19th cent red mor gilt. Previously without dates in me FD Dec 2 (3189) DM17,000

Daun, Leopold, Graf von, 1705-66
Ls, 15 Nov 1764. 1 p, folio. To Graf von Harsch. Concerning a request by the magistrate at Bruenn regarding a canal. star Apr 9 (936) DM360

Dauthendey, Max, 1867-1918
Collection of 2 A Ls s, 8 autograph postcards, sgd, photograph, sgd & inscr, & autograph Ms, 1892 to 1894. 7 pp, various sizes, & cards. To Julius Sommer. Discussing private & literary matters. Poem, Herbstflammen, 45 lines. With inscr offprint from Pan, 1899. VH Sept 12 (956) DM2,300
ALs, 22 Feb 1893. 4 pp, 8vo. To unnamed friends in Munich. Asking for their help to support a poor friend. Sgd Max. star Apr 8 (43) DM480
— 24 & 31 Oct 1894. 8 pp, 8vo. Recipient unnamed. About his friend's literary efforts, his own wish to return to Germany & find a wife, & sending 5 poems (present). star Apr 8 (44) DM2,000

Davis, Jefferson, 1808-89
ALs, [1870s or 1880s]. 6 pp, 8vo. To the Rev. W. M. Green. Describing his capture by Union forces at the end of the Civil War. Bullock collection. CNY Dec 19 (57) $13,000
— [n.d.]. 3 pp, 8vo. To A. D. Mann. Reporting about his travels & his stay in Paris. Fold split. wa May 30 (217) $290
Ls, Apr 1854. 2 pp, 4to. To James Maurice. As Secretary of War, requesting him to supply names of cadets nominated for the Military Academy. sg Apr 9 (48) $750
Autograph endorsement, 13 lines, on verso of integral blank of ALs, 21 May 1864, 1 p, 4to, by Israel Welsh to Davis. Expressing his opinion that publication of his message concerning habeas corpus suspension "would do special injury". Sgd J.D.; in pencil. P Oct 29 (44) $700
Autograph telegram, 30 July 1864. 1 p, 12mo. To Gen. D. H. Maury. Instructing him to inquire into the case of G. W. F. Cook, detained at Mobile. Partly ptd form. wa May 30 (216) $550
— Anr, 9 Aug 1864. 1 p, oblong 32mo. To Gen. R. E. Lee. As President of the Confederacy, discussing relief for Gen. Rauson & defeat at Moorfield. In pencil; partly ptd. wa Oct 18 (91) $750

Davy, Humphry, 1778-1829
ANs, [n.d.]; 1 p, 16mo. In 3d person; accepting an invitation to dine with Lord Stowell on 24 Dec. Matted with a port. sg Nov 6 (50) $110

De Gaulle, Charles, 1890-1970
Autograph Ms, speech about the Free French cause, delivered at the Royal Albert Hall, 18 June 1942. 19 pp, 4to. With numerous corrections; some differences to version ptd 1946. star Apr 9 (981) DM42,000
Typescript, radio broadcast on the fall of Mussolini, 27 July 1945. 4 pp, size not stated. S May 21 (235) £300 [Pervanas]
— Typescript, speech given at Oran, 12 Sept 1943. 6 pp, folio. With numerous autograph revisions & additions. With related material. S May 21 (234) £1,550 [Pervanas]
— Typescript, speech given at Metz after the liberation, [11 Feb 1945]. 2 pp, 4to. Saying the Rhine will be "une route francaise d'un bout a l'autre". Numerous autograph revisions. Not ptd in his Discours et Messages. Paris 1946. star Apr 9 (983) DM5,500
Ls, 13 Jan 1953. 1 p, 4to. To Lucien Rachet. Requesting his further support for the Union Privee. Framed. Altman collection. pnNY Sept 13 (80) $250
— 26 Sept 1957. 1 p, 4to. To Lieut. Col. Coulet. Agreeing "que votre situation soit reglee comme vous le desirez". With autograph postscript, 5 lines. star Apr 9 (984) DM1,600
ANs, 30 Apr 1964. 1 p, 8vo. Recipient unnamed. Sending thanks. wa May 30 (359) $250

De la Mare, Walter, 1873-1956
Collection of 6 A Ls s & Ls s, 1944 to 1945. 10 pp, 4to & 8vo. To Julian Orde. Discussing poetry. S Jan 27 (732) £100 [Sawyer]

De Quincey, Thomas, 1785-1859
Autograph Ms (2), fragment of the opening of "Memorial Chronology", & "3 Capital Distinctions of Kant"; [n.d.]. 4 pp, 4to & 8vo. C June 24 (109) £180 [Wilson]
Autograph Ms, essay, Constituents of Happiness, 18 Aug to 13 Oct 1806. 9 pp on 3 4to sheets. C June 24 (107) £1,200 [Burgess Browning]
ALs, 19 Apr 1824. 3 pp, 4to. To J. A. Hessey. About financial arrangements, proofs, his opium addiction, & the London Magazine. With sgd postscript. Bullock collection.

CNY Dec 19 (58) $2,000
AL, 30 Sept & 1 Oct [1856]. 8 pp, 8vo. To his daughter Emily. About revising his Confessions of an English Opium Eater, mentioning his debts, & family news. S Dec 18 (47) £1,500 [Doyle]

Dearborn, Henry, 1751-1829
Ls, [15 May] 1806. 1 pp, size not stated. To Tench Coxe. As Sec of War, about medals to be sent to Indian Agent Peter Chouteau. With franking signature. rf Nov 15 (29) $90

Debussy, Claude, 1862-1918
[A copy of La Musique Francaise d'Aujourd'hui by G. Jean-Aubry, no 2 of 10 copies, 306 pp, size not stated, extra illus with many A Ls s from French composers & musicians, including Debussy, to Jean-Aubry, 1916, sold at S on 22 May 1987, lot 375, for £1,500 to MacNutt.]
Autograph Ms, critique of Meyerbeer's Huguenots; draft of 1st part of an article about musical life in Paris, Mar 1903. 1 p, 4to. Ptd in Gil Blas, 23 Mar 1903. S Nov 28 (516) £2,200 [Harris]
ALs, [n.d.]. 2 pp, 16mo. To the writer Viele-Griffin. Thanking for a book. S May 22 (591) £400 [Rankin]
— 12 Nov 1907. 2 pp, size not stated. Recipient unnamed. Regretting he does not have time to write the music for a drama. Framed. Altman collection. pnNY Sept 13 (159) $550
— 18 Sept 1910. 1 p, 16mo. To Th. Szanto. About a meeting & a reply to Dr. Hubry. Framed with autograph envelope. Altman collection. pnNY Sept 13 (160) $375
— [n.d., Monday]. 1 p, 8vo. Recipient unnamed. Agreeing to meet at the suggestion of Fromont. Framed. Altman collection. pnNY Sept 13 (162) $550
— 27 Oct 1911. 1 p, size not stated. To Monsieur Bertault. Concerning a [financial?] crisis. Framed with envelope. Altman collection. pnNY Sept 13 (161) $475
— 22 Jan 1917. 1 p, 4to. Recipient unnamed. Regretting that his absence from Paris did not allow him to accept an invitation & referring to his illness. Was mtd. star Apr 9 (618a) DM1,600
— 10 Mar 1917. 1 p, 4to. To Schurmann. Discussing the possibility of a concert tour in England & Scotland. star Apr 9 (618b) DM2,600

Debye, Peter, 1884-1966
Autograph Ms, scientific paper, Arnold Sommerfeld und die Ueberlichtgeschwindigkeit; sgd at head & dated 16 July 1960. 6 pp, 4to. star Apr 8 (321) DM1,400
Ls, 10 Nov 1937. 1 p, folio. Recipient unnamed. As director of the Kaiser-Wilhelm-Institut fuer Physik, answering a question concerning radiation. star Apr 8 (322) DM540

Delacroix, Eugene, 1798-1863
ALs, 17 Sept [n.y.]. 1 p, 8vo. To the President of the Association for the benefit of Mount Carmel. Regretting he is unable to serve in a commission. Framed. Altman collection. pnNY Sept 13 (82) $300

Delaware
— CALL, MARK W. - ADs, 19 Jan 1778. 1 p, 420mm by 325mm. Survey of land on Murtherkill Creek, Kent County, for John Dill; with map. Repaired. sg Nov 6 (257) $110

Delibes, Leo, 1836-91
Autograph transcript, 9 bars of music from his Le Roi l'a dit, 3 staves; 20 Apr 1874. 1 p, size not stated. Inscr to Count Victor of Wimpffen. Sgd by the librettist at a later date. Was mtd. wa May 30 (354) $400

Delius, Frederick, 1862-1934
ALs, 21 Feb 1921. 1 p, 4to. To Paul Bekker. Accepting an invitation. star Apr 9 (620) DM650
— [n.d.; "Saturday"]. 2 pp, 8vo. To Sir Granville Bantock. Regretting that he is unable to hear Bantock's Omar Khayyam. S May 22 (378) £520 [MacNutt]

Dempsey, Jack, 1895-1983
Photograph, sgd & inscr, [n.d.]. 23cm by 18.4cm. Inscr to Evelyn McLean. pnNy Mar 28 (419) $275

Derain, Andre, 1880-1954
Series of 4 A Ls s, 6 July 1917 to 1 Sept 1947. 6 pp, 4to & 8vo. Recipient unnamed. Writing from the front; thanking for photographs, etc. S Nov 27 (344) £300 [Anderson]

Derfflinger, Georg, Freiherr von, 1606-95
Ls, 15 Dec 1684. 1 p, folio. To the estates in Pomerania. Confirming receipt of their resolutions at the Colberg diet. JG Oct 2 (372) DM640

Derrick, Thomas
Original drawings, (74), to illus an Ed of Hakluyt's Voyages in 10 vols, 1927. In pencil, ink & watercolor. Mostly initialled. 465mm by 290mm. With a set of the books. Archives of J. M. Dent & Son. S June 19 (775) £800 [Vincent]

Desmarest, Nicolas, 1725-1815
Autograph Ms, Notes sur les brigues legeres, [13 Sept 1801]. 2 pp, 8vo. Sgd. About a conversation with J.-G. Soufflot in 1764. HN Nov 27 (2243) DM920

DESMOULINS

Desmoulins, Camille, 1760-94
Autograph Ms, Les Vacances d'un philosophe; [n.d.]. 2 pp, 8vo. Collection of ideas for an article; quoting Tertullian & reflecting about the decline of Rome; with corrections. 1 corner cut. star Apr 9 (938) DM2,500

Dibdin, Thomas Frognall, 1776-1847
ALs, 18 Jan [n.y.]. 1 p, 4to. To Thomas Amyot. Returning a letter & about choosing a printer's device. Initialled. C Dec 3 (358) £70 [Bristow]

Dickens, Charles, 1812-70
[A collection of 3 playbills, 1844 to 1847, advertising dramatizations of 3 works by Dickens, sold at S on 23 July 1987, lot 54, for £600 to Joseph & Sawyer.]
ALs, [Jan 1833]. 4 pp, 8vo. To H. W. Kolle. About arrangements for a Hackney Coach outing & Kolle's arrest. S July 23 (47) £2,400 [Wilson]
— [1834]. 3 pp, 8vo. To Count D'Orsay. Praising his port of Maclise & accepting a dinner invitation. S Dec 18 (51) £520 [Sotheran]
— 8 Feb 1836. 3 pp, 4to. To Lord Stanley. Presenting him with a copy of his 1st book. S July 23 (49) £3,800 [Quaritch]
— [23 Dec 1836?]. 2 pp, 8vo. To Charles Hicks. Forwarding the Ms of the end of a number of Pickwick. S July 23 (51) £950 [Jarndyce]
— [1837-1838]. 2 pp, size not stated. To Mrs. [Margaret] Wilson. Apologizing for delay in publishing her poems in Bentley's Miscellany. S Dec 18 (52) £320 [Pickwick]
— 10 Apr 1839. 2 pp, 8vo. To Mrs. Hall. Introducing Mrs. Metze. S Dec 18 (53) £320 [Pickwick]
— 13 Mar 1840. 3 pp, 8vo. To Mrs. Hall. Witty letter, thanking her for a pair of braces. S July 23 (53) £1,500 [Blackwell]
— 18 June 1840. 1 p, 8vo. To [Thomas] Mitton. Instructing him to "let the Miscellany papers go." pn Dec 11 (37) £520 [Joseph]
— 17 Mar 1841. 1 p, 8vo. To [W. C.] Macready. Asking him to accompany him to Evans's. Initialled. pn Dec 11 (38) £380 [Demetzy]
— 16 Aug 1841. 3 pp, 8vo. To Daniel Maclise. Inviting him to enjoy "conveniences of all kinds at Margate". S July 23 (52) £3,600 [Wilson]
— 13 Dec 1841. 3 pp, 8vo. To Count D'Orsay. About a sitting for his port. With autograph envelope, sgd. S Dec 18 (54) £520 [Sotheran]
— 4 Oct 1842. 1 p, 8vo. To Lady Holland. Declining an invitation. On blue paper. wa May 30 (362) $850
— 11 Jan 1844. 2 pp, 8vo. To [Thomas] Mitton.

AMERICAN BOOK PRICES CURRENT

Concerning a legal dispute with printers represented by Mr. Cross. pn Dec 11 (39) £620 [Joseph]
— 26 Jan 1844. 4 pp, 8vo. To Theodore Compton. Declining to join the National Temperance Society & defending the moderate use of alcohol. Bullock collection. CNY Dec 19 (59) $3,200
— [5 July 1845]. 3 pp, 8vo. To Count D'Orsay. Sending his servant & announcing his re-possession of Devonshire House. With autograph envelope. S Dec 18 (56) £400 [Sotheran]
— 6 Nov 1845. 8 pp, 8vo. To the publishers Bradbury & Evans. Expressing his opinion that The Daily News "has received a blow from which it cannot recover", but promising his assistance. S Dec 18 (55) £2,700 [Elliott]
— 7 Nov 1845. 7 pp, 8vo. To the publishers Bradbury & Evans. About financing The Daily News. S Dec 18 (57) £500 [Quaritch]
— 1 May 1846. 2 pp, 8vo. To Count D'Orsay. Thanking for a pipe. S Dec 18 (61) £600 [Pickering & Chatto]
— 25 June 1846. 2 pp, 4to. To John Forster. Discussing the suitability of Bradbury & Evans as publishers for his new books. S July 23 (55) £1,600 [Joseph & Sawyer]
— 21 Oct 1846. 2 pp, 4to. To Thomas Beard. About the completion of [The Battle of Life], the success of Dombey and Son, & his plans. S Dec 18 (60) £3,200 [Elliott]
— 29 Jan 1848. 2 pp, 8vo. To [Thomas] Mitton. About a meeting with a life insurance company regarding a scheme for authors & artists. Initialled. pn Dec 11 (40) £200
— 31 Mar 1848. 3 pp, 8vo. To [Count D'Orsay]. Inviting him to dinner to celebrate the completion of Dombey & Son. In French. S July 23 (56) £1,200 [West]
— 14 Apr 1848. 3 pp, 8vo. To Ann Romer. About fund raising performances to be played at the request of the Shakespeare House Committee. pn Dec 11 (41) £460 [Demetzy]
— 21 Dec 1849. 2 pp, 8vo. To Robert Rogers. Pledging himself to alter a character [in David Copperfield] following a complaint by Mrs. Seymour Hill. With related material. S July 23 (57) £1,100 [Joseph & Sawyer]
— 7 Feb 1850. 3 pp, 8vo. To Mrs. Gaskell. Regarding the publication of her story Lizzie Leigh in the magazine Household Words. S Dec 18 (58) £1,600 [Quaritch]
— 3 May 1852. 2 pp, 8vo. To John T. Lawrence. About his fund raising activities & doubting that he will be able to accept an invitation. pn Dec 11 (42) £580 [Demetzy]
— 27 Sept 1854. 3 pp, 8vo. To Dr. John

Elliotson. Expressing his conviction that there is no need for a proposed society to improve standards in the British theater. C Dec 3 (359) £850 [Quaritch]

— 5 Oct 1854. 2 pp, 8vo. To [Thomas] Mitton. About a date for a visit. Initialled. Fold tear. pn Dec 11 (43) £180 [Joseph]

— 23 Dec 1854. 2 pp, 8vo. To [James Bourne?]. Informing him that he cannot ask Sir Edward Bulwer Lytton to give a speech. C June 24 (110) £420 [Trihome]

— 29 Mar 1855. 1 p, 8vo. To Maria Beadnell, now Mrs. Winter. Sending a pass for a box at the Adelphi for the following night. S July 23 (58) £750 [Maggs]

— Feb 1857. 2 pp, 8vo. To Augustus [Egg]. Concerning the rush for tickets at the Hall of Commerce. Initialled. Framed. Altman collection. pnNY Sept 13 (113) $475

— 20 May 1857. 2 pp, 8vo. To Clarkson Stanfield. Regarding the dedication of Little Dorrit to Stanfield, & sending proofs of the book. S July 23 (59) £1,600 [Caldar]

— 23 Jan 1858. 3 pp, 8vo. To Lady Duff Gordon. Reporting about his emotions when correcting the proofs of The Peril of Certain English Prisoners, & personal news. S Dec 18 (59) £1,300 [Quaritch]

— 21 Apr 1859. 2 pp, 8vo. To Mary Cowden Clarke. About A Tale of Two Cities, & reminiscing about their theatrical days. With ALs by Cowden Clarke to Dickens, 1859, & presentation copy of 1st Ed of A Tale of Two Cities, sgd & inscr to Mrs. Cowden Clarke, Dec 1859. S July 23 (61) £18,000 [Maggs]

— 5 Apr 1860. 1 p, 8vo. To Angela Georgina Burdett Coutts. Declining a reconciliation with his wife. Bullock collection. CNY Dec 19 (60) $1,200

— 12 Apr 1862. 1 p, 8vo. To Mr. Twining. In 3d person, declining to join a committee. C Dec 3 (360) £160 [Wilson]

— 24 May 1862. 1 p, 8vo. To Mr. Ellis. Informing him of the number of his guests for the coming Saturday. S Jan 27 (704) £120 [Maggs]

— 10 May 1867. 1 p, 8vo. To Walter Jones of the Savings Bank. Regretting he is unable to "support Mr. Smith with the Society's Dinner". With autograph envelope, mtd on recto & verso of 1 leaf & inserted in copy of Edwin Drood, 1st Ed, 1870, 8vo. Maroon mor gilt. Extra illus with newspaper cuttings, sale cat of Dickens' effects, etc. C Dec 3 (362) £400 [Demetzy]

— 16 Sept 1867. 2 pp, 8vo. To Lady Molesworth. About his proposed reading tour in America & a variety of subjects. S July 23 (62) £1,350 [Richards]

— 28 Apr 1869. 1 p, 8vo. To Frederic Ouvry. Discussing the terms of his will. S July 23 (60) £1,000 [West]

ANs, 13 Oct 1866. 1 p, 8vo. To the Lord Mayor Elect & the Sheriffs of London & Middlesex. In 3d person, declining an invitation to dinner on Lord Mayor's Day because of a prior engagement. C Dec 3 (361) £90 [Dupre]

Check, sgd, 20 Oct 1868, payable to [Owen J.] Carter. Ptd with Ms insertions. Endorsed by Carter on verso. pn Dec 11 (44) £160 [Joseph]

Diesterweg, Friedrich Adolf Wilhelm, 1790-1866

ALs, 16 Oct 1814 [?]. 2 pp, 4to. To the editors of the magazine Morgenblatt. Covering letter for a novella. With ADs, sgd, 30 June 1806, 1 p, 4to; certificate of university attendance. JG Oct 2 (195) DM540

Directors Guild of America

Single sheet ptg, poster, Directors Guild of America Golden Jubilee 1936-1986, 30 by 22 inches, sgd by 22 Directors including John Huston, Barry Levinson, Vincente Minelli, Sydney Pollack, Stephen Spielberg, etc. wa May 30 (471) $180

— Anr. poster, Directors Guild of America Golden Jubilee 1936-1986, 30 by 22 inches, sgd by 32 Directors including Woody Allen, Elia Kazan, Gene Kelly, etc. wa May 30 (472) $160

Disney Studios, Walt

[A file of over 100 preliminary drawings for The Dog Show, Dec 1936, mostly sgd by contributors, 4to, sold at S on June 19, 1987, lot 646, for £2,400 to V & A.]

Disraeli, Benjamin, 1st Earl of Beaconsfield, 1804-81

Series of 4 A Ls s, 3 Sept 1865 to 27 Mar 1867. 15 pp, 8vo. To William Lowther, 2d Earl of Lonsdale. About the betrothal of Princess Mary, the postmortem on Lord Palmerston, the career of George Bentinck, etc. Sgd D. With 3 draft replies from Lord Lonsdale, 7 pp, 8vo. C Dec 3 (246) £850 [Maggs]

ALs, 3 Feb 1846. 3 pp, 4to. To Richard Taylor. Thanking for a gift & promising to serve his constituents faithfully. S Jan 27 (789) £270 [Maggs]

— 21 Jan 1854. 3 pp, 8vo. To Col. Lowther M.P. Inviting him to a dinner for Lord Derby's supporters. S Jan 27 (792) £120 [Maggs]

— 16 Dec 1868. 4 pp, 8vo. To Sir Henry Edwards. Note of thanks. Sgd D. S Jan 27 (790) £80 [Maggs]

— 25 Apr 1869. 2 pp, 8vo. To Arthur Helps. Thanking for his book. Sgd D. S Jan 27 (791) £180 [Maggs]

DISRAELI

— 24 Dec 1870. 4 pp, 8vo. To the 2d Duke of Wellington. Letter of thanks, & mentioning current political events. Bullock collection. CNY Dec 19 (61) $550
— 24 Aug 1876. 4 pp, 8vo. To Mr. Vernon. Thanking for congratulations. Sgd Beaconsfield. Framed. pn Dec 11 (88) £240 [Maggs]

Dix, John A., 1798-1879
Collection of 2 A Ls s & engraved port, sgd; 2 Apr 1850, 21 Dec 1861, & [n.d.]. 4 pp, 12mo, & port. To Gideon Nye, concerning a National Institute of Art. To Mrs. Pierrepont, sending a lock of hair (present). wa May 30 (218) $210

Dix, Otto, 1891-1969
ALs, [c.1920]. 2 pp, 8vo. To Willi Wolfradt. Sending photographs of 3 of his paintings. star Apr 8 (459) DM750

Dobie, James Frank, 1888-1964
Ls, 11 Apr 1961. 1 p, 4to. To Mr. Lane. Concerning the bdg of books. wa May 30 (363) $55

Doderer, Heimito von, 1896-1966
Collection of 11 A Ls s & 8 Ls s, 20 Aug 1957 to 28 Nov 1963. 23 pp, various sizes. Mostly to his publisher Karl Borromaeus Glock. Concerning reviews, publications & the aims of the Pirkheimer Kuratorium. With a telegram. star Apr 8 (57) DM5,000

Dodgson, Charles Lutwidge, 1832-98
[A collection of 28 ptd examiner's sheets, with name & marks of each candidate entered in Dodgson's hand, 1871 to 1892, with related material, sold at C on 24 June, 1987, lot 97, for £2,000 to Schiller.]
[A collection of 4 proofs for a program for the Royal Cowper Theatre, Nov & Dec 1891, 4 pp each, 8vo, 2 with autograph corrections by Dodgson, sold at C on 24 June 1987, lot 100, for £750 to Schiller.]
Autograph Ms (2), examination paper for a child & explanation of hard words, both relating to a recitation called "The Demon of the Pit"; 21 Oct & 2 Nov 1888. 8 pp, 8vo. Answers to examination paper in anr hand [Isa Bowman's]. S July 23 (66) £1,400 [Demetzy]
Autograph Ms, lists of answers to examination problems in logic, [n.d.]. 7 pp, folio. C June 24 (96) £1,550 [Schiller]
Original drawings, 9 illusts for Alice's Adventures in Wonderland, [c.1865]; based on John Tenniel's drawings. In pen & brown ink; 7 with captions. Each drawn on card & mtd on stiff card, in 19th cent gilt red mor bdg, 4to. Caryl Liddell Hargreaves bookplate. Previously attributed to Tenniel. C Dec 3 (354) £170,000 [Baker]

AMERICAN BOOK PRICES CURRENT

Collection of ALs & 3 autograph postcards [1 sgd], 1894 to 1895. 3 pp, 8vo, & cards. To Edith Lucy, A. H. J. Greenridge & Mrs. Lucy. About Edith Lucy's engagement to Greenridge & other matters. With related material. S July 23 (73) £1,000 [Richards]
A Ls s (2), 10 Apr 1873 & 18 Dec 1877. 6 pp, 8vo. Recipient unnamed; letter of apologies. To [Henry] Jebb, sending congratulations on his new-found wealth. S July 23 (76) £900 [Richards]
— A Ls s (2), [Jan 1884] & 2 Feb 1884. 7 pp, 12mo. To Mrs. Edwin Hatch. About the uncertainty, "as to any young lady, whether to kiss or shake hands." With a photograph of a young girl possibly by Dodgson. Bullock collection. CNY Dec 19 (62) $3,000
ALs, 1 Feb 1873. 1 p, 8vo. To Augustus William Dubourg. Regarding talks about a dramatization of Alice. Matted. In black lea folding case. P June 18 (41) $2,700
— 29 Mar 1874. 3 pp, 8vo. To Rivers. Regarding a meeting to get "up a system of reading in the family circle". Framed. Altman collection. pnNY Sept 13 (114) $700
— 28 Nov 1881. 2 pp, 8vo. To Mrs. Taylor. Concerning the entertainment of her children. With ptd copy of An Easter Greeting to Every Child who Loves Alice, inscr by Dodgson to May [Taylor]. pn Dec 11 (45) £420 [Joseph]
— 18 Aug 1884. 9 pp, 8vo. To Rachel Lowrie. Charming letter to young admirers, answering a question about the meaning of the Snark. Sgd twice ("Lewis Carroll"). With a copy of his game Mischmasch, inscr to "The Lowrie Children". P Sept 24 (22) $31,000
— 18 July 1885. 3 pp, 12mo. To Mrs. H. A. Feilden. Concerning the facsimile of Alice in Wonderland. S July 23 (74) £1,200 [Coleman]
— 12 Feb 1887. 1 p, 8vo. To George Du Maurier. Introducing the Rev. J. Langton Clarke. S Jan 27 (708) £320 [Maggs]
— 15 Feb 1889. 4 pp, 8vo. To Isa Bowman. Expressing sympathy at an accident she suffered at the theater. S July 23 (72) £1,200 [Coleman]
— 4 Apr 1889. 8 pp, 8vo. To "My Lord Duke" [Isa Bowman]. Commenting on her performnce as Duke of York in Richard III. With autograph envelope. S July 23 (64) £3,000 [Coleman]
— 14 Apr 1890. 4 pp, 8vo. To Isa Bowman. Calculating how long it would take her to give him 2,000,000 kisses. S July 23 (70) £2,600 [Coleman]
— 16 May 1890. 3 pp, 12mo. To Isa Bowman. Sending a specially bound copy of [Sylvie and Bruno]. S July 23 (67) £700 [Coleman]

— 22 Aug 1890. 4 pp, 8vo. To Isa Bowman. Regarding a copy of the "French 'Alice'" & a book he has loaned her. S July 23 (68) £950 [Coleman]
— 30 Aug 1890. 2 pp, 8vo. To [Isa Bowman]. Chiding her for not putting a stamp on her letter. S July 23 (69) £1,200 [Coleman]
— 17 Sept 1893. 8 pp, 8vo. To [Isa Bowman]. Whimsical letter, mostly about an intentional misreading of her "sacks full of love & baskets full of kisses" as "a sack full of gloves, and a basket full of Kittens". S July 23 (65) £3,400 [Coleman]

Ls, 21 Aug 1885. 2 pp, 8vo. To Mrs. H. A. Feilden. Thanking for permission to print the preface [to Alice's Adventures Underground] as it stands. Partly ptd, with autograph insertions & 13-line autograph postscript. S July 23 (75) £420 [Coleman]

ANs, 8 July 1894. 1 p, 8vo. To "My dear Fanny". Thanking for writing to him & saying his "memory is very treacherous". Framed. Altman collection. pnNY Sept 13 (115) $800

Dodgson, Charles Lutwidge, 1832-98 —& Tenniel, John, Sir, 1820-1914
[An extra-illus copy of Through the Looking-Glass, and what Alice Found there. L, 1872. 1st Ed, containing a large collection of Tenniel's orig working illusts, ALs by Dodgson to the Dalziel Brothers, 5 Dec 1871, & further related material, sold at C on 24 June 1987, lot 93, for £135,000 to Biggs.]

Doeblin, Alfred, 1878-1957
A Ls s (2), 30 Dec 1933 & 31 Aug 1938. 6 pp, 8vo. To Siegmund Pollag. Mentioning the forthcoming publication of a book. Saying he is unable to support his brother who has left Vienna in France. Including 2 letters by his wife to Pollag, 1947 with autograph postscript by Doeblin, 2 pp, & 1955. star Apr 8 (56) DM1,300

Doenitz, Karl, 1891-1980
Photograph, sgd, 23 Aug 1974. Postcard size. In uniform. wa May 30 (57) $60

Doepfner, Julius, Cardinal, 1913-76
Typescript carbon copy, dissertation, Das Verhaeltnis von Natur und Uebernatur bei John Henry Newman; 1941. 127 pp, 4to. Numerous autograph corrections in ink & pencil. star Apr 9 (958) DM950

Dominguez, Pascual
Ms, Registro de los Actos Recibidos, [Segorbe, eastern Spain, 1417-18]. 109 leaves, 222mm by 150mm. Contemp limp vellum wraps. Notary's notebook containing drafts of legal transactions. In brown ink in a variety of notarial hands; with many alterations. 2 draft documents loosely inserted. S Dec 2 (39) £4,000 [Chiaramonte]

Donizetti, Gaetano, 1797-1848
ALs, 1 Aug [18]33. 4 pp, 4to. To Giovanni Ricordi. Regarding several of his operas. Including 2 autograph musical quotations. Seal tear. S Nov 28 (518) £1,500 [Kent]
— [n.d.]. 1 p, 8vo. To [Ettore Pacini]. Contents not stated. Framed with part of autograph envelope. Altman collection. pnNY Sept 13 (164) $1,000
— [n.d., "Dimanche 12"]. 1 p, size not stated. To M. Antenar Jolly. Promising to talk to a music pbr about his music. In French. S May 22 (592) £320 [Reuter]

Doolittle, James Harold
Photograph, sgd & inscr, [n.d.]. 4to. In military dress. sg Apr 9 (50) $60

Dorst, Tankred
ALs, 8 Sept 1941. 3 pp, folio. To Lulu von Strauss und Torney. Reporting about his literary efforts. With copy of recipient's answer. star Apr 8 (58) DM260

Douglas, Lord Alfred, 1870-1945
Series of 6 A Ls s, 1925 to 1931. 17 pp, 4to & 8vo. To the Countess of Tankerville. About Oscar Wilde, thanking for a stay at her house, offering condolences, etc. pn Dec 11 (46) £180 [Ferret Fantasy]
— Series of 3 A Ls s, 2 July & 24 Aug 1942 & 16 Feb 1943. 5 pp, 4to. To Charles Outcault. Icy letters declining recipient's requests & commenting about Miss Warner & Frank Harris's "filthy book" [about Oscar Wilde]. CNY Dec 19 (256) $220
ALs, 23 Aug 1905. 8 pp, 4to. To his wife. Discussing their marital problems after a fight. With related material. S July 23 (138) £1,600 [Hyde]

Douglas, Robert M.
Franking signature, [n.d.]. As Secretary to President Grant. rf Mar 14 (76) $55

Douglass, Frederick, 1817-95
A Ls s (2), 23 Nov 1887 & 25 Aug 1890. 6 pp, 8vo & 4to. Recipient unnamed. Regarding "inequalities between the races as to school privileges at the South." To "My dear Bassett". About the Van Bakken will & his return to Haiti. P Oct 29 (45) $600

Autograph sentiment, 1868. 1 p, 32mo. Sgd. Was mtd. wa May 30 (26) $425

DOUGLASS

Douglass, Frederick, 1817-95
Signature, 10 Oct 1874. 1 p, size not stated. With subscription. wa May 30 (27) $110

Doyle, Sir Arthur Conan, 1859-1930
[A large collection of c. 100 items, including 4 A Ls s by Doyle, 1920, relating to the hoax of the Cottingley Fairies, sold at S on 23 July 1987, lot 140, for £7,000.]
Autograph Ms, The Adventure of the Mazarin Stone, [pbd Oct 1921]. 19 pp, 4to; on rectos only. Some revisions; lacking an insert of 106 words of ptd version. Few repairs; white cloth bdg in cloth folding case. Kalt collection. CNY Dec 19 (64) $45,000
A Ls s (2), 21 Sept 1900 & [n.d.]. 6 pp, 8vo. Recipient unnamed. Stating his qualifications as a parliamentary candidate for Edinburgh. To Bruce Low. About Mary Queen of Scots's letters & 2 of his works. S July 23 (139) £1,000 [Rosenbaum]
ALs, 5 Aug 1902. 1 p, 8vo. To Robert L. Bremner. Declining a request. HN May 22 (2985) DM480
— [n.d.]. 1 p, 8vo. To Mr. Maude. Declining to assume anr duty. Framed. Altman collection. pnNY Sept 13 (116) $425
— 18 July [n.y.]. 1 p, 8vo. Recipient unnamed. Saying the censor would not permit discussion of points "which you indicate as missing in my history". Framed. Altman collection. pnNY Sept 13 (117) $325

Doyle, James W. E., 1822-92. See: Elizabeth I, 1533-1603

Doyle, Richard, 1824-83
Original drawings, (25), preparatory ink drawings for The Foreign Tour of Brown, Jones and Robinson, mostly with further sketches on backs. Various sizes. S June 19 (625) £450 [Sawyer]
— Original drawings, (3), pencil & ink drawing depicting Punch in the House of Commons, & 2 ink drawings of Punch walking with·2 men & of a nocturnal fairy dance. Illusts for Punch, 1847 & 1848. Various sizes. Framed. S June 19 (618) £420 [Droller]
Original drawing, ink & watercolor drawing of a knight looking at a girl in an eagle's nest, to illus The Eagle's Bride. 202mm by 144mm; rectangle to take text cut out. S June 19 (619) £850 [Edberg]

Dreiser, Theodore, 1871-1945
ALs, 11 Dec 1911. 2 pp, 8vo. To Mr. Daly. Thanking for books. With ANs by Dreiser to Duffy, 1 p, 16mo. sg Apr 9 (52) $150
— 17 Apr [n.y.]. 1 p, 16mo. To Mr. Overton. Thanking for papers & commenting on H. L. M[encken]. sg Nov 6 (53) $175
Ls, 4 Mar 1933. 1 p, 8vo. Authorizing Liveright Publishers to sell the $3.00 Ed of An American Tragedy for $1.00. sg Nov 6 (52) $200

Dreyfus, Alfred, 1859-1935
ANs, [n.d.]. On card, 4.5 by 3.5 inches. Recipient unnamed. Stating that he is preparing himself for the War Academy. wa May 30 (364) $220

Droste-Huelshoff, Annette von, 1797-1848
ALs, [n.d.]. 1 p, 8vo. Recipient unnamed. Explaining at length that she is unable to answer his letter now, because she is preparing to receive the holy sacraments. Sgd A. HK Nov 7 (2195) DM10,500

Du Maurier, George, 1834-96
Series of 12 A Ls s (2 fragments), [1860s] to 1896. 23 pp, 12mo & 8vo. Mostly to Felix Moscheles. Chatty letters to a good friend; including 6 ink sketches. To Bishop Jenner (1); about a Swinburne poem & his novel Trilby. Recipient unnamed (1); social letter. Bullock collection. CNY Dec 19 (65) $650

Dukas, Paul, 1865-1935
Autograph music, sketchbook containing drafts for his works & excerpts from others, [n.d.]. 43 pp, 8vo. In blue ink & pencil on up to 8 staves per page. S May 22 (381) £1,350 [MacNutt]
— Autograph music, sketches, for flute & piano, [before 1912?]. 7 pp only, in 8vo sketchbook. Mostly in ink; some pencil. star Apr 9 (625) DM1,300

Dulac, Edmund
Original drawings, (10), to illus Charlotte Bronte's Jane Eyre, 1905. In watercolor; sgd. Average size 290mm by 210mm. 4 mtd. With a copy of the 1922 Ed. Archives of J. M. Dent & Son. S June 19 (778) £9,000 [Sawyer]
— Original drawings, 2 watercolors, to illus Charlotte Bronte's Shirley, 1905. Captioned & sgd; sgd & dated 1904 on backs. Average size 255mm by 175mm. With a copy of the 1922 Ed. Archives of J. M. Dent & Son. S June 19 (780) £1,700 [White]
— Original drawings, 2 watercolors, to illus Anne Bronte's The Tenant of Wildfell Hall, 1905. Captioned & sgd; also sgd on backs. 220mm by 166mm. With a copy of the 1922 Ed. Archives of J. M. Dent & Son. S June 19 (783) £1,200 [Sawyer]
— Original drawings, 3 watercolors, to illus Emily Bronte's Wuthering Heights, 1905. 2 captioned, all sgd; sgd & dated 1905 on backs. Average size 220mm by 165mm. With a copy of the 1922 Ed. Archives of J. M. Dent & Son. S June 19 (782) £3,000 [Sawyer]
— Original drawings, 5 watercolors, to illus Charlotte Bronte's Villette, 1905. 2 cap-

tioned, all sgd; sgd & dated 1905 on backs. Average size 265mm by 200mm. With a copy of the 1922 Ed. Archives of J. M. Dent & Son. S June 19 (781) £3,800 [Hartnoll]

Original drawing, Florina and the Fairy Pie, watercolor used as an illust in Mme d'Aulnoy's The Fairy Garland. 305mm by 205mm, mtd. sg Apr 2 (76) $1,900

— Original drawing, illus from the 57th quatrain of the Rubaiyat of Omar Khayyam. 32cm by 23cm, watercolor, sgd & dated 1909. Ck Dec 10 (121) £6,600

— Original drawing, watercolor, depicting a couple dancing to the lute, to illus Verlaine's Fetes Galantes. Sgd & dated [19]10. 311mm by 232mm. Framed. S June 19 (650) £4,000 [Baillie]

— Original drawing, watercolor, to illus Charlotte Bronte's The Professor, 1905. Sgd. 211mm by 158mm. With a copy of the 1922 Ed. Archives of J. M. Dent & Son. S June 19 (779) £800 [Southey]

— Original drawing, watercolor, to illus Anne Bronte's Agnes Grey, 1905. Captioned & sgd; sgd & dated [19]05 on back. 220mm by 166mm. Archives of J. M. Dent & Son. S June 19 (784) £750 [Southay]

— Original drawing, watercolor, young woman beside an elderly man, to illus The Story of Princess Deryabar in Stories from the Arabian Nights, 1907. Sgd, 283mm by 201mm. Framed. S June 19 (649) £3,000 [Greer]

Dumas, Alexandre, 1802-70

Autograph Ms, describing Gen. Suvorov's victory over Napoleon in Northern Italy, 1799; [n.d.]. 1 p, folio. Sgd AD. wa May 30 (469) $220

ALs, [n.d.]; 2 pp, 16mo. To Moneau. Making amusing apologies for mistaking him. On personal letterhead. sg Nov 6 (55) $70

Dumas, Alexandre, 1824-95

ALs, [17 Jan 1875]. 4 pp, 16mo. Recipient unnamed. Expressing his belief that recipient's work will not be published for a broad audience. wa May 30 (365) $65

Dunant, Jean Henri, 1828-1910

ALs, 26 Dec 1900. 4 pp, 8vo. To [Professor Rudolf Mueller]. Thanking for a report about activities in Norway. star Apr 9 (960) DM2,400

Dunois, Jean, Comte de, 1403-68 ("Bastard of Orleans")

Ls, 10 July 1450. 1 p, 100mm by 315mm. To Estienne Petit. Authorizing a payment for the campaign in Languedoc. C June 24 (37) £320 [Castaing]

Dunoyer de Segonzac, Andre, 1884-1974

Collection of 3 A Ls s, 2 autograph postcards, sgd, & autograph calling card, sgd A. D. S.; 1929 to 1952 & [n.d.]. 7 pp, various sizes. To Professor Mondor. About various subjects. star Apr 8 (460) DM480

Duportail, Louis Le Begue de Presle, 1743-1802

ALs, 17 Apr 1791. 1 p, folio. Recipient unnamed. As French Minister of War, concerning a military assignment. sg Nov 6 (7) $90

Dvorak, Antonin, 1841-1904

ALs, 13 Apr 1885. 1 p, 8vo. To Alfred Littleton of Novello. Stating the time of his arrival & sending the score of a symphony. In English. S May 22 (593) £650 [Schneider]

— 26 Jan 1887. 4 pp, 8vo. To an unnamed recipient in England. Saying it is difficult to find a good libretto, mentioning his oratorio Ludmila & complaining about his health. In English. star Apr 9 (627) DM3,600

— 3 Mar 1892. 3 pp, 8vo. Recipient unnamed. Notifying him of 1st performance of the Requiem under his own direction. In English. Framed. Altman collection. pnNY Sept 13 (163) $930

Autograph postcard, sgd, 16 June 1883. To "Lieber Herr Dorffel", but addressed to N. Simrock. Saying he has been unable to call on Simrock at Karlsbad due to his children's illness. With autograph musical quotation by Jan Kubelik, 13 Jan 1902. P Dec 15 (25) $800

— 3 Nov 1888. To Oskar Schwalm. Apologizing for his forgetfulness & saying he is now sending the money. With ANs by Franz Lehar. star Apr 9 (628) DM900

— 26 Mar [18]92. To his publishers Novello & Ewer. Regarding his Eighth Symphony. Including musical quotation, 2 bars. In English. Paper loss at corners. S Nov 28 (519) £650 [Batchelder]

Photograph, sgd & inscr, 17 Dec 1883. Carte size. Inscr to [Julius] von Bernuth. star Apr 9 (626) DM2,400

E

Earhart, Amelia, 1898-1937

Photograph, sgd & inscr, 11 Feb 1935. Size not stated. Inscr to Benigna Green. sg Nov 6 (56) $425

East India Company

[A collection of 3 large Mss pertaining to the affairs of the East India Company, 1708, 1791 & 1825, sold at C on 24 June 1987, lot 81, for £380 to Bristow.]

Eckart, Dietrich, 1868-1923
ALs, 2 Jan 1919. 2 pp, 4to. To an unnamed lady. Ranting about politicians & the Emperor who poison the German character. On ptd letterhead of his Wochenschrift fuer Ordnung und Recht. star Apr 9 (961) DM1,400

Eckener, Hugo, 1868-1954
ALs, 6 Feb 1950. 1 p, folio. To Herr Feddersen. Thanking for a review of his book & talking about dirigibles. star Apr 9 (1040) DM460

Eckermann, Johann Peter, 1792-1854
A Ls s (2), 25 July 1843 & 25 Jan 1848. 3 pp, 4to & 8vo. To the bookseller Heinrichshofen at Magdeburg. Contents not stated & regarding the publication of a Ms. With autograph address leaf of anr letter. star Apr 8 (101) DM2,400

Edgcombe, Piers
Ms, The Invisible worlde... Written in Latin by Jeronimus Zanchius and abbreviated into Englishe by Peers Edgcumbe gent.; 1608. Dedicated to Sir George Cary. With A breefe Discoorse of usury, by Zanchius & Edgcombe, 1611. Dedicated to Lady Margaret Denny. Written in the same hand; 358 & 15 pp, 4to. Orig vellum wraps; 93 blank leaves at end. S Dec 18 (5) £1,300 [Quaritch]

Edison, Thomas A., 1847-1931
Autograph Ms, draft of memorandum on marketing of his phonographs in Germany, [1911-1912?]. 7 pp, 4to & folio. In pencil; 6 lines in anr hand. With Ls, 23 Dec 1914, 1 p, 4to; to A. C. Lehmann, regarding the damage done to his plant by a recent fire; & check, sgd, [n.d.], 8 by 3 inches, on the Union National Bank of Newark. P Oct 29 (46) $1,600

ALs, 11 Nov 1875. 1 p, 8vo. To Albert B. Chandler. Requesting payment of a bill. With Ls, 1 Nov 1929, 1 p, 8vo, from Calvin Bullock to Edison, asking whether Chandler paid the bill; autograph endorsement, sgd, by Edison, confirming payment. Bullock collection. CNY Dec 19 (66) $650

Ls, 3 Sept 1890. 1 p, 4to. To George Richards. Declining a proposed real estate deal. With 2 A Ls s by his wife Minna & 2 photographs. P May 13 (39) $800

Check, 10 Dec 1928. Sgd as President of the Edison Botanic Research Corporation. Cancellation holes affecting signature. wa May 30 (30) $190

Photograph, sgd, [1918?]. Frontis port, 6.5 by 4.5 inches, in Edison Pioneers: Constitution and By-Laws 1918. [n.p., n.y.]. 15 pp, 16mo. Green cloth. wa May 30 (28) $425

Photograph, sgd & inscr, [c.1895]. 7 by 9 inches. Inscr to Paul Iogolevitch, on mount, 9.5 by 11.5 inches. sg Apr 9 (54) $475

Signature, [n.d.]. On card. wa May 30 (29) $160

Edward I, King of England
Ms, Statuta quaedam antiqua, including Magna Carta, Charter of the Forest, Statutes of Westminster, Statuta Mercatorum, etc., [early 14th cent]. 132 leaves, vellum, 120mm by 80mm. In a small round legal bookhand by 2 different scribes. 18th cent vellum bdg. Ownership inscr of Edward Cotton, 1787. Contemp Latin epitaph on the death of Edward I on flyleaf. C June 24 (259) £3,400 [Ferrini]

Edward III, King of England, 1312-77
Document, 10 Aug [1336]. 1 p, 325mm by 195mm. Vellum. Letters patent, licence to John Torny & Isabel his wife to enfeoff William Giboun & Robert FitzEdmund of a moiety of the manor of Fighelden. C Dec 3 (247) £260 [Wilson]

— 29 Nov [1360]. 1 p, 430mm by 267mm. Vellum. Letters patent to the abbot & convent of Whalley. C Dec 3 (248) £300 [Claridge]

Edward IV, King of England, 1442-83
Ds, [c.1475]. 1 p, 4to. List of munitions & men required for the invasion of France. Repaired. P Dec 15 (26) $8,000

Edward VI, King of England, 1537-53
Document, 23 Aug 1547. 1 p, 22 by 33 inches, vellum. Granting Sir Walter Hendle & his wife the tenement Northelade & other estates. With initial letter port. S Dec 18 (204) £750 [Spiro]

Edward VII, King of England, 1841-1910
Collection of ALS & Ds, 11 May 1870 & 1 Oct 1906. 4 pp, 8vo & folio. To an unnamed Archbishop. Thanking for an account of his brother's tour in India. Acknowledgment of appointment of W. E. Wheatley as Cuban consul in Sheffield; partly ptd. C Dec 3 (249) £180 [Barnes]

Ds, 1 Apr 1901. 1 p, folio. Appointment of Herbert Arthur Richards as Oriental Secretary to the Legation at Teheran. Framed. Altman collection. pnNY Sept 13 (53) $550

Photograph, sgd, 1896. 4to. Sgd Albert Edward P. Framed. Altman collection. pnNY Sept 13 (52) $225

Edward VIII, King of England, 1894-1972. See: Windsor, Edward

Edwards, Jonathan, 1703-58
Ms, sermon delivered 28 Apr 1745. 34 pp, 32mo. Probably not in his hand. wa Oct 18 (94) $110

Edwards, Lionel

Original drawings, (24), to illus Capt. Marryat's The Children of the New Forest, 1955. In watercolor or ink. 5 initialled. Sizes not stated. Archives of J. M. Dent & Son. S June 19 (787) £1,500 [A & H]

— Original drawings, (24), to illus Primrose Cumming's The Great Horses, 1946. In watercolor, pencil or ink. 14 sgd. Various sizes. Archives of J. M. Dent & Son. S June 19 (785) £600 [A & H]

— Original drawings, (25), to illus R. L. Stevenson's The Black Arrow, 1957. In watercolor or ink. Various sizes. With artwork for dust jacket. Archives of J. M. Dent & Son. S June 19 (788) £800 [A & H]

— Original drawings, (33), to illus R. D. Blackmore's Lorna Doone, 1951. In watercolor or ink. 6 initialled; 1 dated [19]43. Various sizes. 25 mtd in 2 folio sketchbooks, disbound. Archives of J. M. Dent & Son. S June 19 (786) £2,800 [A & H]

Eggers, Friedrich, 1819-72

ALs, 18 Apr 1857. 1 p, 8vo. To Otto Friedrich Gruppe. Asking him to cooperate in a new Ed of Argo. star Apr 8 (325) DM280

Egk, Werner, 1901-83

Collection of ALs & 6 Ls s, 3 July to 16 Dec 1958. 8 pp, 8vo & folio. To an unnamed lady in Paris. Mostly about the possibility of a performance of his ballet Abraxas in Paris. With related material. star Apr 9 (629b) DM1,400

Egremont, Charles Wyndham, Sir, 2nd Earl, 1710-63. See: Wyndham, Sir Charles

Ehrlich, Paul, 1854-1915

— EHRLICH, HEDWIG. - 2 A Ls s & postcard, sgd, 25 Mar to 3 July 1919. 5 pp, 8vo. To Professor Leonor Michaelis. Sending material for a biography of Ehrlich. With enclosures, reminiscences by Franz Oppenheimer & Max Grube. 11 pp. C June 24 (169) £260 [Lucas]

Eich, Guenter, 1907-72

Autograph Ms, poem, Tage mit Haehern; [n.d.]. 1 p, folio. 16 lines. star Apr 8 (62) DM1,200

Eichendorff, Joseph von, 1788-1857

ALs, 5 May 1832. 3 pp, 4to. To [Theodor von Schoen]. Requesting his help to prevent his transfer to a government position at Koenigsberg. HK Nov 7 (2198) DM8,000

— 20 Mar [1850?]. 1 p, 20cm by 16.5cm. To Professor Dr. Friedlaender. Requesting books from the library. JG Oct 2 (30) DM3,200

Einstein, Albert, 1879-1955

Autograph Ms, algebraic equations. On verso discussion of post-war Japan & atomic science; [n.d.]. 2 pp, 4to. S Nov 27 (347) £3,400 [Pervamas]

— Autograph Ms, autobiographical essay, sgd & dated 1 Dec 1940. 1 p, 4to. Written for R. S. Benjamin's I Am An American. 1941. P June 18 (49) $7,500

— Autograph Ms, scientific essay, Ueber die Untersuchung des Aetherzustandes im magnetischen Felde, [1895?]. 6 pp, folio. With covering ALs to his uncle Caesar Koch, [1895?], 1 p, folio; sgd again at head in 1950. C June 24 (170) £15,000 [American Museum of Hist. Docs.]

ALs, 9 Apr 1924. 2 pp, folio. To [Max] Warburg. Supporting the plan to build a Jewish university in Poland. S May 21 (236) £1,600 [Schiff]

— [n.d., "Thursday evening", c.1930]. 1 p, folio. To Dr. Walther Mayer. Discussing the solution of an equation. Sgd A. E. With autograph Ms, 2 pp, folio, probably equations for a unified field theory; & ALs from Elsa Einstein, 1930, concerning Dr. Mayer. C June 24 (171) £3,000 [American Museum of Hist. Docs.]

Ls, 27 Feb 1938. 1 p, 4to. To T. E. Tomlinson. Concerning ESP & the scientific world. In German. With related material. sg Nov 6 (57) $950

— 2 Aug 1939. 2 pp, 4to, on rectos only. To President Franklin Delano Roosevelt. Informing him of recent experiments by Fermi & Szilard, the possiblity of using chain reactions for construction of bombs, & discussing availability & quality of uranium. One of 2 alternative letters; endorsed in pencil by Szilard "Original not sent". With ALs, [c.9 Aug 1939], 1 p, 4to, by Einstein to Szilard. Letter of transmittal stating his preference for more detailed version of letter; in German. Framed with a port. CNY Dec 19 (68) $200,000

— 18 Oct 1939. 1 p, 4to. To Martin A. Paul. Declining an invitation to speak. Sgd in green ink. With carbon copy of Paul's letter, 16 Oct 1939. sg Nov 6 (58) $600

— 12 May 1952. 1 p, 4to. To Kenneth Heuer. Commenting about the Ms of Heuer's The End of the World. In English, with 10-line autograph addition in German. CNY May 11 (42) $4,800

Autograph sentiment, about the importance of devotion & curiosity for scientific studies, sgd & dated 1924. 1 p, 8vo (lettercard). star Apr 8 (326) DM7,000

— Anr, [n.d.]. 3 lines, 8vo. About the grandeur of nature. Sgd. On verso autograph Ms, calculations; in pencil. C June 24 (171A) £1,600 [L'Autographe]

EINSTEIN

Photograph, sgd & inscr, 1954. 12cm by 10cm. Seated in chair on a veranda. S Nov 27 (348) £800 [Dr. Sam]

Signature, [25 Apr 1931]. With 2 autograph words, on postcard to Dr. L. Michaelis. Also sgd & inscr by 4 other hands. pnNY June 11 (70) $275

Eisenhower, Dwight D., 1890-1969

Collection of ALs & autograph Ms, [31 Oct 1952]. 3 pp, 4to. Draft, form letter thanking supporters for their part in a Madison Square Garden rally; list of 4 recipients at head. Memorandum, list of 12 participants in the rally, anr name added by a secretary. P May 13 (42) $2,400

A Ls s (2), [c.31 Oct 1952]. On recto of same 8vo leaf. To Walter Williams & Mary Pillsbury Lord. Thanking for their efforts in organizing a Madison Square Garden rally. With autograph revisions. P Oct 29 (48) $2,200

ALs, [c.31 Oct] 1952. 1 p, 4to. To Thomas E. Dewey. Draft, thanking him for his campaign efforts. Faded. P Oct 29 (47) $3,000

— [c.31 Oct 1952]. 1 p, 8vo. To Tex & Jinx Falkenburg McCrary. Expressing his appreciation of their efforts at organizing the Madison Square Garden rally. P Oct 29 (49) $1,600

— [c.31 Oct 1952]. 1 p, 4to. To [Justus B.] Lawrence. Draft, thanking for his part in a Madison Square Garden rally. P May 13 (40) $2,400

— [31 Oct 1952]. 1 p, 4to. To Sarah Delano Roosevelt. Draft, thanking for her part in a Madison Square Garden rally. Faded. P May 13 (41) $900

— 1 Mar 1961. 1 p, 4to. To Jack C. Toole. Complimenting him on a recent statement concerning Montana's building program. Sgd Ike. Hotel stationery. Matted with a port & a newspaper clipping. P Oct 29 (51) $3,000

Collection of 2 Ls s, signature & 2 port photographs, sgd, & 26 Feb, [Aug] 1953 & [n.d.]. 3 pp, 4to & 8vo, & photographs. To Nelson Cox, thanking for a resolution of congratulations from the Arkansas Legislature. 2nd paragraph crossed out. To Charles R. Howell; arranging a meeting with Joyce & Beverly Carson. Signature in pencil, with signatures of companions at a golf game. P Oct 29 (50) $750

Ls, 27 Oct 1952. 2 pp, 4to. To E. K. Inman. Answering campaign questions from a reporter. wa May 30 (271) $475

— 2 Feb 1957. 1 p, 4to. To Arthur S. Nevins. About the management & image of his farm, & saying he will give a calf to a boy as a present. Sgd D. E. wa May 30 (270) $450

AMERICAN BOOK PRICES CURRENT

Ns, 6 Jan 1964. 1 p, 4to. To Louise [Eisenhower]. Birthday wishes. With Ns by Mamie Eisenhower. wa May 30 (275) $120

Photograph, sgd & inscr, [1953]. 8 by 10 inches. Photograph of Eisenhower & Sergeant John Alton Moaney in fishing gear. Inscr to Moaney on mount by Eisenhower & Aksel Nielsen. Framed. With photographs, fishing gear & golf clubs belonging to Eisenhower. P Oct 29 (52) $2,600

— Anr, [n.d.]. 26cm by 31cm. Inscr to Harry Hershfield. Framed. Altman collection. pnNY Sept 13 (5) $350

Signature, [Dec 1945]. 1 p, 16mo. War Department Card, sent to Irving Sussman. With related material. sg Nov 6 (60) $175

— Anr, [n.d.]. On 1 Yuan note, 3 by 6 inches. wa May 30 (274) $95

— Anr, on detached tp of his Crusade in Europe, 4.5 by 6.5 inches. With inscr, 6 words. With secretarial letter forwarding book. wa May 30 (272) $130

— Anr, on reproduction of Norman Rockwell port of Eisenhower, [n.d.]. Folio. wa May 30 (273) $130

— Anr, [n.d.]; 1 p, 8vo. On broadside, the D-Day message to Allied troops, 6 June 1944. Sgd beneath facsimile signature. sg Nov 6 (59) $300

Eisenhower, Dwight D., 1890-1969 —& Others

Signature, [n.d.]. On a $10.00 bill. Also sgd by Douglas MacArthur & Omar Bradley. P May 13 (43) $600

Eisenhower, Dwight D., 1890-1969 —& Eisenhower, Mamie D.

Group photograph, [n.d., c.1940]. 7.5 by 9.25 inches, on mat 10.75 by 13.5 inches. At a table in a library. Inscr to Josephine & Rick Bay by Mamie Eisenhower; sgd by both. sg Apr 9 (57) $375

Eisenhower, Mamie D. See: Eisenhower, Dwight D. & Eisenhower

Elgar, Sir Edward, 1857-1934

[A large collection of musical Mss, many autograph, 1876 & later, c.240 pp, folio, comprising drafts of compositions & instrumental parts for music by various composers performed at musical gatherings, some initialled, sold at S on 28 Nov 1986, lot 520, for £4,000 to MacNutt.]

Autograph transcript, musical quotation, sgd, from The Dream of Gerontius. In 1st ed of the vocal score of his Coronation Ode, 1909. Lacking covers. S Jan 27 (1016) £170 [Smith]

Series of 3 A Ls s, 1915 & 1924. 4 pp, 8vo. To Gertrude Walker. Concerning appointments to meet. S Nov 28 (525) £250 [Reuter]

60

1986 - 1987 • AUTOGRAPHS & MANUSCRIPTS   ELISABETH

— Series of 4 A Ls s, 1920 & 1927. 5 pp, 4to & 8vo. To Gertrude Jenner, nee Walker. Thanking for condolences on the death of his wife, etc. S Nov 28 (526) £320 [Wilson]

ALs, 14 Dec 1896. 4 pp, 8vo. To Edward Capel-Cure. About The Light of Life, the success of King Olaf, & returning a libretto. S Nov 28 (522) £600 [Brookes]

— 27 Oct 1899. 3 pp, 8vo. Recipient unnamed. About the Enigma Variations, & arranging a fee. C June 24 (190) £170 [Palace]

— [Aug 1900]. 2 pp, size not stated. To George Sinclair. Arranging to visit him shortly. C Dec 3 (412) £75 [Reuter]

— 23 Dec 1904. 4 pp, 8vo. To John E. West. About mistakes in the publication of a score. S Nov 28 (523) £420 [Harris]

— 16 May 1909. 2 pp, 8vo. To John E. West. Discussing West's arrangement for organ of themes from his First Symphony. S Nov 28 (524) £250 [Harris]

— 22 June 1917. 1 p, 4to. To "My dear Agnes". Declining an invitation. Framed. Altman collection. pnNY Sept 13 (166) $180

— 28 Dec 1921. 3 pp, 8vo. To Mr. Phillips. Sending payment for a life membership. Framed & double-glazed. Altman collection. pnNY Sept 13 (167) $170

— 14 May 1924. 3 pp, 8vo. To Lady Radnor. Thanking for a letter & reminiscing about their acquaintanceship. S Jan 27 (1017) £240 [MacNutt]

— 23 Feb 1932. 2 pp, 8vo. To Christine Chaundler. Explaining musical terminology. With related material. S Nov 28 (529) £300 [Harris]

Elgin, Thomas Bruce, 7th Earl, 1766-1841

Series of 6 A Ls s, 9 Nov 1794 to 4 Feb 1797. 18 pp, 4to. To the Right Hon. Henry Dundas. Discussing military & diplomatic matters. With copy of a letter from Elgin to Dundas, 23 Dec 1800. C Dec 3 (250) £190 [Quaritch]

Eliot, George (Mary Anne Evans Lewes), 1819-80

ALs, 27 Feb 1840. 4 pp, 4to. To Martha [Barclay]. About the correspondence of friends & books she has read recently. Sgd Mary Ann. S Dec 18 (63) £650 [Hofmann & Freeman]

— 8 July 1870. 4 pp, 8vo. To Mrs. Lytton. Musing about love, death, & women's affections. S Dec 18 (64) £2,400 [Mrs. Eliot]

— [31 Oct 1879]. 1 p, 8vo. To Mrs. [Stewart] Hodgson. Thanking for a present of game & suggesting a meeting. pn Dec 11 (47) £180 [Dryson]

Eliot, Thomas Stearns, 1888-1965

[A collection of 11 A Ls s & Ls s, 9 Mar 1965 to 27 Jan 1972 to Michael Gonin in response to his request for personal impressions of Eliot by 11 contemporaries, including W. H. Auden, Robert Graves, Bertrand Russell, & others, sold at C on 3 Dec 1986, lot 363A, for £1,700 to Robbins.]

Typescript, poem, II. Virginia [n.d.]. 1 p, 4to. 13 lines, sgd. sg Nov 6 (62) $200

Collection of 2 A Ls s, 22 Ls s, autograph postcard, sgd, & 4 Christmas cards, sgd, [25 Dec] 1939 to 28 Feb 1961. 22 pp, 4to & 8vo. To Margaret Nelson. Thanking for presents, mostly an annual birthday cake, etc. With related material. C June 24 (111) £1,300 [Wilson]

Collection of Ls & Ds, 12 June 1957 & 17 July 1959. 2 pp, 4to. To an unnamed journalist, about the war crimes trials after World War II. Giving permission to quote from letter; with autograph addendum. sg Nov 6 (61) $475

Ls, 9 Feb 1939. 2 pp, 8vo. To Mrs. Muller. About publishing Old Possum's Book of Practical Cats. S Dec 18 (121) £300 [Joseph & Sawyer]

— 29 Aug 1941. 1 p, 4to. To "My dear Reckitt". About his present projects. On The Criterion letterhead. Framed. Altman collection. pnNY Sept 13 (119) $225

— 29 July 1963. 1 p, 4to. To T. O'Keeffe. Informing him that he has recommended a script to Wesleyan [University Press]. With related material. wa May 30 (368) $110

Autograph quotation, sgd & dated 12 Oct 1961. 1 p, 8vo. 3 lines from Four Quartets. Framed. Altman collection. pnNY Sept 13 (121) $700

Ptd photograph, sgd & dated 22 Oct 1950. 8 by 5.5 inches. Framed. Altman collection. pnNY Sept 13 (120) $170

Elisabeth, Princess Palatine, 1618-80

ALs, 2 [12] Aug 1661. 2 pp, 8vo. To her mother [Elizabeth, Queen of Bohemia]. Reporting about the illness of her cousin & predecessor as Abbess of Herford, Elisabeth von Pfalz-Zweibruecken. In English. Repaired. HN Nov 27 (2249) DM2,800

Elisabeth, Empress of Franz Josef I of Austria, 1837-98

Ls, 9 Apr 1882. 1 p, 4to. To Cardinal Angelo Jacobini. Sending congratulations on his nomination as cardinal. In Italian. star Apr 9 (1104) DM850

Elisabeth, Queen of Carol I of Romania, 1843-1916. See: Sylva, Carmen

ELISABETH CHRISTINE

Elisabeth Christine, Queen of Frederick II of Prussia, 1715-97
Collection of 2 A Ls s & 2 Ls s, 4 Dec 1787 to 1789. 8vo. To Woellner. Passing on petitions. A Ls s in French. JG Oct 2 (377) DM520

ALs, 12 May 1782. 1 p, 4to. To [Charlotte Wilhelmine] von der Schulenburg. Chatting about her birthday. In French. star Apr 9 (1156) DM550

Elizabeth Charlotte, Duchesse d'Orleans, 1652-1722
Ds, 30 Mar 1711. 1 p, folio. Vellum. Investing the son of A. Lambotte with the office of "Procureur du Roy pour la police" at Montargis. 2 large slits. HN Nov 27 (2315) DM1,800

Elizabeth I, Queen of England, 1533-1603
Ls, 26 May 1575. 1 p, folio. To Don Luis de Zuniga y Requesens. Requesting him to grant safe passage through the Low Countries to Sir Henry Wallop. In French. Address on verso. Seal tear. Matted with a port. P Dec 15 (28) $7,000

— 26 May 1575. 1 p, folio. To Don Luis de Requezens. Requesting him to grant safe passage through the Low Countries to Sir Henry Wallop. In French. Address on verso. Seal tear. Mtd with a port. S July 24 (228) £4,800 [Maggs]

— 18 July 1598. 1 p, folio. To Matthew Hutton, Archbishop of York. Ordering a levy to suppress the Irish rebellion. C Dec 3 (251) £3,200 [Wilson]

— 24 Aug 1599. 1 p, folio. To Matthew Hutton, Archbishop of York. Granting his discharge from the office of Lord President of the North, & stressing the need to supress religious dissent. C Dec 3 (252) £3,800 [Wilson]

— 25 Oct 1601. 1 p, folio. To Matthew Hutton, Archbishop of York. Granting license to be absent from Parliament & requesting him to send a proxy. C Dec 3 (253) £3,200 [Wilson]

Ds, 5 Nov 1568. 1 p, vellum, 445mm by 285mm. Letters Patent in favor of Bartholomew Jennings regarding repayment of a loan arranged by Thomas Gresham. In Latin. On verso certificate of indemnity sgd by 8 Privy Councillors. C June 24 (38) £3,800 [Weng]

— 24 Apr 1572. 1 p, folio. List of the 25 members of the Order of the Garter. Matted with a port. P Dec 15 (29) $11,500

Document, 7 Apr 1559. 1 p, folio. Proclamation announcing peace between England & France concluded at Cateau Cambresis. S Dec 18 (245) £450 [Joseph & Sawyer]

— DOYLE, JAMES W. E. - Orig drawings,

c.1850. Baptismal procession of Elizabeth I. 7 sections, each 170mm by 520mm. In pen, ink & watercolors. Sgd J. S. Doyle. pn Dec 11 (14) £150 [Heraldry]

— MIDDLEMORE, HENRY. - ALs, 23 Apr 1585. 1 p, folio. To Sir Christopher Hatton. Reporting about his search of the lodgings of Philip Howard, Earl of Arundel, & about interrogating the conspirator Charles Tilney. S Dec 18 (228) £1,600 [Doyle]

— PRIVY COUNCIL. - Ls, 8 Mar 1601 [1602]. 1 p, folio. To the Lord High Treasurer. Requesting £300 to be repaid to Hugh Beeston. Sgd by Robert Cecil, Thomas Egerton, John Fortescue & others. C Dec 3 (255) £320 [Wilson]

— SQUIRE, EDWARD. - Document, possibly autograph & probably sgd, [1598]. 6 pp, folio. Account of his conversion by the Jesuits in Spain & his attempt to poison the Queen. S Dec 18 (242) £2,600 [Collins]
See also: England

Elizabeth II, Queen of England
ALs, 26 Apr 1944. 2 pp, 8vo. To Cousin Dorothy. Thanking for a watch given to her as a birthday present. Sgd Lilibet. Framed & double-glazed. Altman collection. pnNY Sept 13 (60) $1,100

Elizabethan Verse
Ms, poem, beginning "Who wilbe ware in purchasyng"; 24 lines. Written at beginning of Ms book of legal precepts, [c.1595]. About 100 pp, 4to; modern half calf. S Jan 27 (686) £280 [Smallwood]

Ellery, William, Signer from Rhode Island
Autograph endorsement, sgd, 6 lines, 17 June 1768, to the House of Magistrates, action of petition about granting execution of an estate. Torn & repaired. Charlotte Parker Milne collection. wd Nov 12 (33) $50

Ellis, Havelock, 1859-1939
Collection of 27 A Ls s (9 on postcards) & ANs, 1886 to 1888. 75 pp, 8vo to 16mo. To William W. Mackenzie. Literary correspondence, especially relating to the Mermaid series. sg Apr 9 (58) $425

Ellsworth, Oliver, 1745-1807
ADs, 29 May 1778. 1 p, 8vo. Pay order in favor of Job Bates. wa May 30 (31) $75

— 18 Sept 1784. 1 p, oblong 12mo. As State Attorney, draft for 10 shillings on the Treasurer. Repaired. wa Oct 18 (13) $50

Ds, 27 Aug 1775. 1 p, 4to. Pay order to Benjamin Bacon regarding losses at Bunker Hill. rf Mar 14 (6) $250

— 7 Aug 1776. 1 p, 4to. Order to pay Capt. William Coit & his company for losses at Bunker Hill. Endorsed by Coit on verso. rf Mar 14 (5) $220

— 13 Jan 1777. 1 p, 4to. Pay order to Ebenezar Backus regarding pay for Troops of Light Horse under his command. Endorsed by Backus on verso. rf Mar 14 (57) $200
— 28 May 1777. 1 p, 4to. As member of Connecticut's Committee of the Pay Table; pay order to Capt. John Gilbert. Countersgd by John Lawrence. sg Nov 6 (262) $50
— 23 June 1777. 1 p, 8vo. As member of Connecticut's Committee of the Pay Table; pay order to Jedediah Johnson for wages of Stebbins Johnson. Countersgd by John Lawrence & 2 others. sg Nov 6 (263) $90
Franking signature. [2] Jan n,yl, rf Mar 14 (77) $80

Eluard, Paul, 1895-1952
Collection of 7 A Ls s & postcards, sgd, 20 Apr 1940 to 12 Sept 1947. 8 pp, size not stated. To Rene Magritte. About the illusts in the Catalogue surrealiste, André Breton, contributions for Labyrinthe, etc; including 2 poems. With related material. S July 2 (973) £3,200 [Rota]

Emerson, Ralph Waldo, 1803-82
ALs, 3 Dec [n.y.]. 1 p, 8vo. To Rev. James F. Clarke. Letter of invitation. wa Oct 18 (95) $80
Engraving, port, 1878; 14.6 by 10.2 inches, mtd. Engraved by Stephen Alonzo Schoff from a drawing by Samuel W. Rowse. Sgd by Emerson & Schoff, in pencil. wa Oct 18 (14) $150

Emma, Queen of The Netherlands, 1858-1934
ALs, Christmas 1932. 2 pp, 8vo (lettercard). To Julie [Liotard]. Season's greetings. With autograph lettercard, sgd, by Queen Wilhelmina. star Apr 9 (1092) DM300

Englaender, Richard, 1859-1919. See: Altenberg, Peter

England
Ms, comparative abstracts of royal household accounts, Apr 1539 to Apr 1541, Jan 1550 to Jan 1551, July 1556 to July 1558, & Nov 1559 to Nov 1561; [c.1562/63?]. 1 p, 450mm by 580mm. In Latin. C Dec 3 (254) £100 [Griffiths]
— LINCOLNSHIRE. - Ds, 6 Sept 1626, by Francis, Earl of Rutland as Lord Lieut.; commission for Philip Tyrrwhit as captain of foot soldiers within the sessions of Horncastle. 209mm by 310mm. Vellum. In fitted case. pn Dec 11 (64) £55 [Laywood]
— PRISONERS. - Ms, [Nov 1554], 1 p, folio. List of prisoners "in the gatehouse off Westmyster"; drawn up by Geoffrey Harrysson, Bailiff. C Dec 3 (323) £200 [Hofmann & Freeman]
— SUFFOLK. - Court Book of the manor of Kettlebers in Cretingham, 1640 to 1714. 44 leaves plus index, folio. Orig vellum covers. pn Dec 11 (68) £100 [Quaritch]
— SUFFOLK. - Court Book of the manor of Redgrave with Botesdale & Gislingham, 1681 to 1695. 92 leaves, folio. Orig vellum covers. pn Dec 11 (69) £110 [Quaritch]
— TOWER OF LONDON. - Ms, 24 to 31 Dec 1598; accounts submitted by Sir John Peyton for maintenance of 12 prisoners & for salaries from Michelmas to Christmas. Sgd by Peyton & others. 2 pp, folio; in mor-backed case. C Dec 3 (331) £2,100 [Royal Armouries]
— WILTSHIRE. - Document, 4 Nov 1584. 160mm by 390mm. Vellum. Writ directing escheator of Wiltshire to allow Henry Pyke to take possession of his father's land near Pewsey. Framed. pn Dec 11 (71) £440 [Maggs]
— YORKSHIRE, EAST RIDING. - 7 documents, c.1310 to 1541, deeds relating to the manor of Little Kelk in possession of the Boynton family. Vellum. pn Dec 11 (74) £250 [Dryson]

Eon de Beaumont, Charles de, 1728-1810
AD, 25 May 1768. 1 p, 8vo. Agreement with a London gunsmith & receipt for payment. With anr document, 24 Dec 1774, 1 p, folio; receipt for a sword, annotated by D'Eon. S Nov 27 (349) £260 [Royal Armourial]

Epistolary Literature, French
Ms, Correspondance litteraire secrete, Jan to Sept 1779; c.180 pp, 4to. Vellum bds. Anon letters describing literary & social life in Paris. S Nov 27 (355) £300

Erasmus High School
Document, 22 Feb 1786. 3 pp, folio. List of subscribers for Kings County & New York City, etc., for the building of [Erasmus Hall] Academy. Somewhat def. sg Nov 6 (63) $450

Erhard, Ludwig, 1897-1977
Ms, discussion of economic prospects for 1967; 19 Dec 1966. 1 p, folio. Sgd. star Apr 9 (962) DM800

Ernst, Max, 1891-1976
Original drawing, sketch of 3 figures, in ballpoint pen, sgd; [1964]. 1 p, 8vo, on verso of menu. On top of page autograph poem, 5 lines, by Louise de Vilmorin. With Ernst's autograph address, 1 p, 8vo. star Apr 8 (461) DM750

ERZBERGER

Erzberger, Matthias, 1875-1921
Ls s (2), 8 Oct 1918 & 26 June 1920. 2 pp, 4to. To an unnamed lady. Expressing his wish to secure a lasting peace. Saying he is pessimistic about the future. Somewhat def. star Apr 9 (963) DM380

Essex, Robert Devereux, 2d Earl of, 1567-1601
A Ls s (2), 18 Mar 1597[8] & 29 Apr 1598. 3 pp, folio. To Matthew Hutton, Archbishop of York. Giving directions concerning the imprisonment of Sir Robert Ker of Cessfurd. 2d letter also sgd by Burghley. C Dec 3 (256) £1,600 [Metcalf]
ALs, [n.d.]; 1 p, folio. To his sister Penelope Rich. A "fantasticall" letter full of word-play & rhetorical effect. S Dec 18 (230) £4,000 [Quaritch]
See also: Hoby, Sir Thomas

Estabrook, Joseph
[A collection of 18 A Ls s, 1799 - [c.1820], 35 pp, various sizes, mostly by Joseph Estabrook of Massachusetts & his daughter Lucy, to Nathaniel Cushing, depicting family life in the early 19th cent, sold at sg on 6 Nov 1986, lot 64, for $70.]

Estabrook, Mehetabel Cushing. See: Estabrook, Nathaniel & Estabrook

Estabrook, Nathaniel —&
Estabrook, Mehetabel Cushing
Series of 36 A Ls s, 10 Sept 1812 to 7 Mar 1836; c.85 pp, various sizes. Family letters, illustrating New England life & manners. sg Nov 6 (65) $150

Estella, Diego de, 1524-78
Ms, The Contempte of the World, and the Vanitie thereof, [early 17th cent]. About 500 pp, 8vo. 19th cent calf bdg. In a single print-like Italic hand. Trans by George Cotton. Lacking tp & 4 leaves. S July 24 (263) £500 [Thomas]

Ethiopic Manuscripts
[A collection of 3 magical prayer scrolls, [19th or 20th cent], vellum, each with 2 or 3 drawings & geometric ornamentation, sold at C on 24 June 1987, lot 274, for £160 to Ferrini.]
[A collection of 3 magical prayer scrolls, [19th or 20th cent], vellum, each with 2 or 3 drawings & geometric ornamentation, sold at C on 24 June 1987, lot 275, for £100 to Thomas.]
[A collection of 3 magical prayer scrolls, [19th or 20th cent], vellum, each with 2 or 3 drawings & geometric ornamentation, sold at C on 24 June 1987, lot 276, for £130 to Thomas.]
Ms, Discourse of St. Michael & Gospel of St. John. [Ethiopia, 20th cent]. 90 leaves,

AMERICAN BOOK PRICES CURRENT

vellum, 152mm by 112mm. Wooden bds. With headings & significant words in red. S June 23 (149) £100 [Kraus]

— Ms, liturgical Ms, [19th cent]. 137 leaves, vellum, c.160mm by 130mm. Wooden bds, lacking spine. With double-page miniature of St. George. C June 24 (273) £150 [Thomas]

— Ms, Nagara Maryam; History & Miracles of the Virgin Mary. [Ethiopia, c.1750]. 138 leaves, vellum, 247mm by 220mm. Wooden bds backed with pale calf. With 46 full-page miniatures. Written for Asnana Dengel. S June 23 (142) £4,800 [Fogg]

— Ms, Scroll, [18th or 19th cent]. 190cm by 8.5cm, vellum. In black ink with red headings. With 3 ornamental borders & 1 miniature. HK Nov 4 (421) DM650

— Ms, Synaxarium; Book of the Saints. [Ethiopia, 1646]. 127 leaves (2 lacking), vellum, 367mm by 331mm. Wooden bds backed with red lea. With 44 miniatures, mostly full-page. Written for Queen Sabla Wangel. S June 23 (139) £19,000 [Brown]

— Ms, The Acts of Za'mika'el Aragawi, & History of Gabra Krestos. [Ethiopia, c.1750]. 70 leaves, vellum, 247mm by 226mm. Linen over wooden bds. With 14 full- to half-page miniatures & 19 1-column miniatures. S June 23 (143) £5,000 [Thomas]

Eugene of Savoy, Prince, 1663-1736
Ls, 8 Aug 1706. 2 pp, folio. Recipient unnamed. Ordering troop movements. Sgd Eugenio von Savoy. JG Oct 2 (383) DM1,000

— 24 Nov 1725. 1 p, folio. To Daiser von Sillpach. Regarding long overdue payments to recipient. HK Nov 7 (2202) DM1,300

— 16 Jan 1726. 1 p, folio. Recipient unnamed. Thanking for congratulations. Sgd Eugenio di Savoya. In Italian. star Apr 9 (964a) DM530

— 30 Oct 1728. 1 p, folio. To Count von Wratislaw. Regarding a missing report. Sgd Eugenio von Savoy. star Apr 9 (964b) DM530

Ds, 18 Jan 1711 [1712]. 2 pp, folio. Confirmation of a pay order to the Treasurer General of Milan regarding the salary of Carlo Filiberto D'Este. C Dec 3 (257) £160 [Pollak]
See also: Charles VI, 1685-1740

Eugenie, Empress of the French, 1826-1920.
See: Napoleon III & Eugenie

Eulenberg, Herbert, 1876-1949
Autograph Ms, Ikarus und Daedalus. Ein Oratorium, [ptd 1912]. 64 pp, 4to. Some revisions in ink, a few in pencil. Extra red mor gilt bdg by Huebel & Denk. FD Dec 2 (3191) DM4,000

Eustis, William, 1753-1825. See: Leavenworth, Henry

Evelyn, John, 1620-1706
ALs, 23 Nov 1670. 3 pp, folio. To Thomas Clifford, 1st Baron Clifford of Chudleigh. About his career in the service of the Crown & requesting his help in obtaining suitable employment. S July 24 (248) £3,200 [Burgess & Browning]

Exelmans, Josephe Isidore, Comte, 1775-1852
Ls, 13 Apr 1815. 1 p, 4to. To the Minister of War [Davout]. Notifying him that his soldiers would like to continue fighting for Napoleon. star Apr 9 (965) DM300

F

Fabiola, Queen of Baudouin, King of the Belgians. See: Baudouin & Fabiola

Fairfax, Thomas, 3d Baron, 1612-71
Ds, 2 Apr 1645. 1 p, 7.75 by 11.5 inches. Vellum. Commission for Algernon Sidney as Colonel of a regiment of horse. With related material. S Dec 18 (240) £300 [Webb]

Falla, Manuel de, 1876-1946
Ms, musical Ms, Danza ritual del fuego, from El amor brujo, [1939]. 12 pp, folio. Piano score, notated on up to 12 staves per page. With autograph annotations, an autograph musical quotation, sgd, & an addition to the title. S May 22 (388) £1,000 [Johnson]

ALs, 13 Aug 1909. 1 p, 8vo (lettercard). To Ricardo Vines. Mentioning the progress of his Nocturnos, & Debussy. With related material. S May 22 (596) £250 [Joselson]

— 7 Oct 1923. 2 pp, 8vo. To an unnamed lady [Princesse Edmond de Polignac?]. Hoping that she has received the photographs of El retablo. In Spanish; closing sentence in French. Mtd on paper. P June 18 (62) $350

— 31 Jan [19]24. 4 pp, 8vo. To Francisco Lacerda. About a performance of Nights in the Gardens of Spain, & reporting about his current work. In French. S Nov 28 (533) £600 [MacNutt]

— 30 May [1]924. 12 pp, 8vo. To G. Jean-Aubry. Requesting changes to be made in Aubry's trans of El Retablo de Maese Pedro. S Nov 28 (535) £3,100 [Harris]

Ls, 28 June 1932. 1 p, 4to. To the Mayor & President of the Assembly of San Sebastian.

Declining an invitation to participate in the inauguration of a museum & reporting about his work on Atlantida. Framed. Altman collection. pnNY Sept 13 (163) $350

Faneuil, Peter, 1700-43
Ds, [n.d.]. 1 p, 12mo. Sight draft for 650 pounds drawn on Thomas Hancock. Sgd by Hancock on verso. wa May 30 (353) $55

Fantin-Latour, Ignace Henri Jean Theodore, 1836-1904
ALs, 30 July 1891. 2 pp, 12mo (card). Recipient unnamed. Complaining about the heat. sg Apr 9 (60) $100

Faraday, Michael, 1791-1867
Series of 6 A Ls s, 19 June 1849 to 2 Dec 1857. 8 pp, 8vo. To Thomas Twining. Social messages, etc. C Dec 3 (401) £320 [Des Pabilades]

ALs, May 1834. 1 p, size not stated. To "Margrath". Concerning a committee list. pnNY June 11 (13) $140

— 1 June 1835. 1 p, 12mo. To Messrs. Durand & Co. In 3d person, ordering brandy. Integral address leaf torn. sg Nov 6 (66) $80

— 19 Mar 1850. 1 p, 8vo. To Thomas Twining, Jr. Enclosing a copy of a paper by W. Scott Harris (not present). HN May 22 (2997) DM700

— [n.d.]. 1 p, 8vo. To [Magrath]. Asking for information about the provenance of an autograph. star Apr 8 (327) DM320

— 20 Mar 1851. 1 p, 8vo. Recipient unnamed. Declining an invitation. Matted with a port. sg Nov 6 (67) $90

Fargo, William George, 1818-81. See: Wells, Henry & Fargo

Fastolf, Sir John, c.1378-1459
Document, 11 Jan 1425/6. 1 p, c.10.5 by 20 inches. Vellum. Confirming a charter of 25 Feb 1378/9, a grant of lands in Great Yarmouth & elsewhere by Hugh Fastolf to his brother John. S July 24 (256) £500 [Maggs]

Faultrier, J. B.
Ms, Traicte general des oyseaulx divise en sept livres.... 1661. 992 pp, 360mm by 333mm, in contemp red mor gilt with arms of Nicolas Foucquet. Inscr Jeanson Ms 153 SM Mar 1 (218) FF165,000

Faure, Gabriel, 1845-1924
Autograph quotation, Le Secret, 6 bars with piano & vocal notation, Jan 1916. Sgd & inscr to Madame de Rougemont. Framed. Altman collection. pnNY Sept 13 (168) $475

FECHNER

Fechner, Gustav Theodor, 1801-87
ALs, 23 Oct 1837. 1 p, 4to. To [Theodor Mundt]. Concerning a contribution to the magazine Dioskuren. Margins cut. With anr ALs by Fechner, 1827, & related material. star Apr 8 (328) DM240

Fehling, Juergen, 1885-1968
A Ls s (2), 8 & 31 Jan 1960. 3 pp, folio. Recipient unnamed. Reminiscing about their childhood & announcing his visit to Hamburg. In pencil & ink. star Apr 9 (865) DM220

Feininger, Lyonel, 1871-1956
Collection of Ls & ADs, 30 Sept & 11 Dec 1954. 1 p, 4to, & 10 lines on verso of a photograph. To Dr. H. Sommer. Requesting a photograph of a picture supposedly painted by him. Certificate that painting on verso is a forgery. VH Sept 12 (957) DM320
Autograph postcard, sgd, 27 Oct 1919. To Paul Westheim. Describing the ptg of a woodcut at the Bauhaus. star Apr 8 (462) DM700

Felicite, Louis Leon, Comte de Lauraguais. See: Cook, Capt. James

Fell, H. Granville
Original drawings, (27), illusts & ornamental designs for The Book of Job, 1896. In ink. 9 initialled. Various sizes. Archives of J. M. Dent & Son. S June 19 (789) £1,000 [Hartnoll]

Ferdinand Albrecht II, Herzog von Braunschweig-Wolfenbuettel, 1680-1735
Ds, 21 Aug 1734. 1 p, folio. Receipt for 1,000 thalers from the treasury of Braunschweig. With Ds, 1697, by his mother, Herzogin Christine; receipt. star Apr 9 (926) DM340

Ferdinand I, Emperor, 1503-64
Document, 8 Mar 1549. 1 p, folio. Vellum. Title-deed for Heinrich Jastram. star Apr 9 (1196) DM350

Ferdinand I, Emperor of Austria, 1793-1875
ALs, 2 Sept 1808. 3 pp, 4to. To his sister Marie Louise [later Empress of the French]. Looking forward to a family reunion. star Apr 9 (1099) DM520
— 10 May 1816. 3 pp, 4to. To his sister Marie Louise, Empress of the French. Reporting about her son. star Apr 9 (1100) DM1,300
Ds, 28 Dec 1837. 1 p, folio. Dispensatio Litis Matrimonialis for Johann Friedl & Katharina Jaross. star Apr 9 (1101) DM320

Ferdinand II, Emperor, 1578-1637
Ls, 27 Dec 1627. 3 pp, folio. To Cardinal Franz von Dietrichstein. Acceding to a request by Maximilian von Liechtenstein. star Apr 9 (1199) DM480

AMERICAN BOOK PRICES CURRENT

Ferdinand III, Emperor, 1608-57
Ls, 18 Mar 1642. 2 pp, folio. To Graf Jobst Maximilian zu Gronsfeld. Giving orders for the quartering of troops. star Apr 9 (1200) DM600
Ds, 28 May 1653. 32 leaves (3 blank), 315mm by 265mm. Contemp red vellum bdg. Confirmation of an agreement between the Princes of Anhalt & their territorial diet. HN May 22 (2999) DM650

Ferdinand IV, Roman King & King of Bohemia, 1633-54
Ls, 7 Oct 1647. 2 pp, folio. To the magistrate at Moedtling. Ordering them to provide for newly enlisted soldiers. star Apr 9 (1202) DM350

Ferdinand V, King of Spain, 1452-1516 —& Isabella I, Queen of Spain, 1451-1504
Ls, 4 Aug 1484. 1 p, 4to. To Juan de Ribera. Instructing him to carry out orders. S May 21 (239) £1,350 [Maggs]
Ds s (2)[1 sgd by each, both c.1500]. On vellum. vellum. Each 1 p, folio. Contents not stated. Matted, with portraits. Overall size 790mm by 760mm. sg Nov 6 (279) $4,000

Ferdinand von Bayern, Kurfuerst & Erzbischof von Koeln, 1577-1650
Ls, 6 Feb 1640. 1 p, folio. To the Bailli of Condroz. Ordering the collection of taxes for his court. With a letter written in his name, 1634. star Apr 9 (985) DM320

Fesch, Joseph, Cardinal, 1763-1839
Collection of 15 A Ls s & Ls s, 1797 to 1832. 18 pp, various sizes. To various correspondents. About family matters, requests for positions, etc. Some autograph subscriptions. S Nov 27 (352) £350 [Charavay]

Fetis, Francois Joseph, 1784-1871
Autograph Ms, essay, Preface historique d'une dissertation inedite sur les notations musicales du moyen age...; working Ms, with covering ALs. 1845. 14 pp, 8vo. With typescript copies. S May 22 (599) £220 [Maggs]

Feuchtwanger, Lion, 1884-1958
Ls, 25 May 1951. 1 p, 4to. To Dr. Horch. Asking for a copy of a contract with a publishing firm. star Apr 8 (66) DM280

Fidus, Pseud. for Hugo Hoeppener, 1868-1948
ALs, 14 July 1896. 6 pp, 8vo. Recipient unnamed. Providing autobiographical information for an article. With a number of revisions. HN May 22 (3000) DM380

1986 - 1987 · AUTOGRAPHS & MANUSCRIPTS — FLAUBERT

Fidus, Pseud. of Hugo Hoeppener, 1868-1948
Autograph Ms, commentaries about the illusts of Fidus cards 33, 59, 64, 71, 74, 94, 123, 197, & 218; 1932 to 1939 & [n.d.]. On verso of cards. Sgd. star Apr 8 (463) DM300

Field, Cyrus W., 1819-92
Series of 3 A Ls s, 18 June & 28 July 1885. 3 pp, 8vo. To Judge Robert Ludlow Fowler & Sir Henry W. Tyler. Letter of introduction; cover letter & invitation. sg Nov 6 (68) $100

Field, Eugene, 1850-95
Autograph Ms, ballad, The Bottle and the Bird. Sgd & dated 10 May 1891. 4 pp, 4to. Small pencil sketch in margin of 1st p. Printer's copy; disbound. Bullock collection. CNY Dec 19 (85) $320

— Autograph Ms, poem, beginning "Like some avenger, in he strode", [n.d.]. 1 p, 4to. 2 eight-line stanzas from a larger work, about his meeting with Grover Cleveland, addressed to Charley Kern. wa May 30 (371) $280

Fields, W. C., 1880-1946
ALs, 20 Apr 1940. 3 pp, 4to. To a staff member here addressed as Mickey Mouse. Telling him not to come on Monday. Sgd "The brain sapping parsimonious Pantata." Framed with photo. wd June 19 (20) $1,500

Fillmore, Millard, 1800-74
ALs, [24 Dec 1840]. 1 p, 4to. To George Jonson. Regarding a visit. With franking signature. rf May 30 (19) $270

— 10 May 1849. 1 p, 8vo. To his cousin [James E. Eaton]. Saying he has added his recommendation to a petition [for Eaton's appointment as postmaster]. With related material. sg Apr 9 (61) $650

— 18 May 1849. 1 p, 8vo. To George Lunt. Covering letter for a letter of recommendation (not included). Framed. Altman collection. pnNY Sept 13 (6) $275

— 2 Nov 1849. 1 p, 4to. To J. E. Eaton. Saying he has neither patronage nor influence. sg Apr 9 (62) $700

— 2 Jan 1852. 1 p, 8vo. To Dr. Leibis. Expressing his appreciation of a commencement speech. wa May 30 (95) $1,200

— 30 July 1853. 2 pp, 8vo. To Professor Pierce. Concerning a meeting. Autograph envelope with franking signature. rf Mar 14 (78) $425

— 24 Oct 1854. 1 p, 8vo. To Asbury Dickens. Thanking for sending him the Annals of [the 13th] Congress. Framed. Altman collection. pnNY Sept 13 (7) $450

Franking signature, [4 Apr 1861]. rf Mar 14 (79) $260

Finch, Anne, Countess of Winchilsea, 1661-1720. See: Finch, Heneage

Finch, Heneage, 4th Earl of Winchilsea, 1657-1726
Autograph Ms, pocketbook, 1722-1726; interleaved copy of Cardenus Riders' British Merlin, 1722. c.80 pp of miscellaneous notes, including items relating to his wife Anne Finch, Countess of Winchilsea. S Dec 18 (28) £3,300 [Crewe Read]

Firnisbuechlein
Ms, Das ist der Schlissel von dem firnniss bichel..., [Germany, c.1650]. 14 leaves (1 blank), 195mm by 155mm. Bds. Manual explaining varnishing techniques, etc. HK Nov 4 (412) DM1,400

Fitch, Thomas, 1700-74
Ds, 1 Sept 1755. 1 p, folio. As Gov. of Connecticut, military appointment for Nehemiah Dickinson; partly ptd. Silked & spotted. sg Nov 6 (266) $140

Fitzgerald, F. Scott, 1896-1940
Autograph Ms, poem, beginning "My very, very dear Marie...", [30 Jan 1915]. 1 p, 8vo. 3 six-line stanzas, sgd Scott. On stationery with Princeton insignia. With envelope addressed to Marie Louise Hersey. In blue mor Ms case. P June 18 (64) $2,200

— Autograph Ms, poem, Lines on Reading through an Autograph Album, 1937. 1 p, 4to. 24 lines, written for Carmel & Ralph Blum. Sgd. P June 18 (65) $2,500

Fitzherbert, Maria Anne, 1756-1837
Series of 4 retained autograph drafts & copies of letters, [1808] to 15 Aug 1814. 13 pp, 4to. To George IV as Prince & Prince Regent, " apparently the sole surviving letters from Mrs. Fitzherbert to the Prince, the rest having been deliberately destroyed by George IV's executors." S Dec 18 (217) £2,800 [Wallace]

Flamsteed, John, 1646-1719
ADs, 28 June 1694. 1 p, 8vo. Certifying to work at Greenwich Observatory by Samuel Clowes. S Jan 27 (904) £150 [Maggs]

Flaubert, Gustave, 1821-80
Autograph Ms, poem, Apres une lecture, Aug 1852. 1 p, folio; blue paper. 3 four-line stanzas. With anr autograph Ms, 1 p, folio; A Voltaire, 2 lines. FD June 11 (3503) DM3,300

AL, [15 Sept 1846]. 4 pp, 8vo. To Louise Colet. Love letter, & expressing relief that she is not expecting his child. S Nov 27 (356) £2,300 [Wilson]

Fleming, Sir Alexander, 1881-1955

ALs, 2 Aug 1948. 1 p, 8vo. To [Walter] Starkie. About informing the Rector that he had worn Spanish garments at a University of London's function. Framed. Altman collection. pnNY Sept 13 (145) $375
— 10 Sept 1948. 1 p, 8vo. To Mrs. Starkie. Thanking for a box of tea & discussing his holiday & his dress at London University. Framed. Altman collection. pnNY Sept 13 (146) $400

Ls, 22 Jan 1948. 1 p, 8vo. To Dr. P. Lemay. Thanking for a reprint. Framed. Altman collection. pnNY Sept 13 (147) $400
— 15 Nov 1952. 1 p, 8vo. To Dr. Hugh Clegg. Thanking for a document. Matted with a port photograph. sg Nov 6 (70) $300

Flotow, Friedrich von, 1812-83

ALs, 5 Oct 1854. 2 pp, 8vo. To his pbr Andre. Sending the 2d act of his opera Albin, oder der Pflegesohn, & discussing the publication. S May 22 (595) £350 [Schneider]
— 17 Nov 1860. 3 pp, 4to. To an unnamed recipient in Paris. Regarding the lack of interest in his ballet Die Libelle, & sending the libretto. star Apr 9 (634) DM900

Flower, Noel

Original drawings, (39), to illus Rowland Strong's & Pierre Jan's Yoyo's Animal Friends, 1913. Various sizes; 5 framed. With Flower's copy of the book & further drawings. S June 19 (657) £400 [Klugerman]

Floyd, William, Signer from New York

Ls, 29 Mar 1784. 1 p, 4to. To Gerard Bancker. Authorizing payment of state debts for clothing. Inlaid. Charlotte Parker Milne collection. wd Nov 12 (34) $250

Foch, Ferdinand, 1851-1929

Photograph, sgd, [n.d.]. Postcard size. Half-length, in uniform. star Apr 9 (1280) DM240

Fock, Gorch, Pseud. of Johann Kinau, 1880-1916

Autograph postcard, sgd, 19 Dec 1915. To Leon Goldschmidt. Sending Christmas greetings. Sgd as Fock & Kinau (sender's address). star Apr 8 (67) DM360

Folkard, Charles

Original drawings, (10), to illus Helena Nyblom's Jolly Calle and other Swedish Fairy Tales, 1912. In ink & watercolor, & in ink. Mostly sgd & dated 1911 or 1912. Various sizes. Archives of J. M. Dent & Son. S June 19 (796) £10,500 [Ryder]
— Original drawings, (17), to illus George Macdonald's The Princess and the Goblin, 1949. In ink & watercolor, & in ink. Sgd or initialled. 280mm by 190mm (8) & various sizes. Archives of J. M. Dent & Son. S June 19 (798) £15,000 [Edberg]
— Original drawings, (19), to illus The Land of Nursery Rhyme, 1932. In watercolor & ink. Sgd or initialled. 363mm by 260mm (8), & various sizes. Some mtd. With 51 A Ls s from Folkard to Dent, Jan 1931 to June 1933, & further related material. Archives of J. M. Dent & Son. S June 19 (794) £24,000 [Marks]
— Original drawings, (22), to illus George Macdonald's The Princess and Curdie, 1949. In ink & watercolor, & in ink. Sgd or initialled. 286mm by 198mm (8) & various sizes. Archives of J. M. Dent & Son. S June 19 (797) £12,500 [Edberg]
— Original drawings, (26), to illus Wyss's The Swiss Family Robinson, 1910. In watercolor & ink. Sgd; some initialled. Various sizes. With 8 ink drawings for an Ed pbd 1949. Archives of J. M. Dent & Son. S June 19 (791) £11,800 [Edberg]
— Original drawings, (38), to illus Alice Hoffmann's The Children's Shakespeare, 1911. In ink & watercolor, & in ink. Sgd, some initialled; some dated 1910 to 1911. Various sizes. Archives of J. M. Dent & Son. S June 19 (792) £12,000 [Hartnoll]
— Original drawings, (4), to illus The Book of Nonsense, 1956. In ink & watercolor. Sgd or initialled. Average size 275mm by 195mm. Drawn at an earlier date for a similar work. Archives of J. M. Dent & Son. S June 19 (799) £8,500 [Caffy]
— Original drawings, (53), illusts & headpieces for the Grimms' Fairy Tales, 1949. In ink & watercolor, & in ink. Sgd or initialled. 280mm by 203mm (4), & various sizes. Archives of J. M. Dent & Son. S June 19 (795) £8,500 [Beetles]
— Original drawings, (77), to illus Pinocchio, 1911. In ink & watercolor, & in ink. Sgd or initialled; some dated 1910 to 1911. Various sizes. With related material. Archives of J. M. Dent & Son. S June 19 (793) £7,000 [Edberg]

Fontaines-Guerin, Hardouin de. See: Hardouin

Fontane, Theodor, 1819-98

ALs, 19 June 1846. 1 p, 8vo. To the magazine Morgenblatt. Offering poems for print. JG Oct 2 (39) DM2,800
— 13 June 1862. 2 pp, 8vo. To his wife Emilie. Commenting about some other letters, family news, etc. HN May 22 (3003) DM2,600
— 10 July 1862. 4 pp, 8vo. To his wife. Describing an apartment he is thinking of renting & saying a house may be a better investment. star Apr 8 (68) DM2,400

— 2 July 1870. 2 pp, 8vo. Recipient unnamed. Postponing a visit. HN May 22 (3004) DM1,200
— [n.d.]. 2 pp, 8vo. To his son Friedel. Sending congratulations on his birthday & on his 1st engagement at Jena. HN May 22 (3007) DM1,400
— 6 June 1887. 1 p, 8vo. To [Fritz Mauthner]. Sending a poem, as requested. star Apr 8 (69) DM1,700
— 10 Feb 1888. 1 p, 8vo. To his pbr W. L. Hertz. Sending a new Ms. Tipped into a copy of Irrungen, Wirrungen. Leipzig, 1888. 1st Ed. HN May 22 (3005) DM2,200
— 2 July 1894. 1 p, 8vo. To Emil Pindter. Thanking for his valedictory address to the readers of the Norddeutsche Allgemeine Zeitung. star Apr 8 (70) DM1,300
— 1 Nov 1896. 2 pp, 8vo. To an unnamed Ed. Acknowledging receipt of a fee & promising to send 2 poems. HN May 22 (3006) DM1,700

Forbes-Mosse, Irene, 1864-1946
Series of 30 A Ls s, 16 Nov 1901 to 25 May 1903 & [n.d.]. About 250 pp, mostly 8vo. To Lily Braun. Interesting letters about private & literary matters, including 20 poems. star Apr 8 (71) DM900

Ford, Gerald R.
Series of 3 Ls s, 14 & 23 Apr 1962. 3 pp, 4to. Recipients unnamed. Regarding H.R.3745, discharge petition. On congressional committee letterhead. wa May 30 (279) $120

Ford, Henry, 1863-1947
Photograph, sgd & inscr, 10 Dec 1918. 8.25 by 11 inches. Inscr to Paul Iogolevitch. sg Apr 9 (65) $800

Forrest, Edwin, 1806-72
ALs, [c.1845]; 2 pp, 4to. To Mr. Wetmore. Theater news. Torn. With engraved port. sg Nov 6 (74) $90

Forrest, Nathan B., 1821-77
Ds, 1869. 2 pp, folio. Mortgage Bond for Selma, Marian & Memphis Railroad Company. Sgd twice. wa May 30 (219) $325

Forster, Edward Morgan, 1879-1970
Series of 6 A Ls s (1 a postcard), 1956 to 1962. 10 pp, various sizes. To Mr. Bozman of J. M. Dent & Sons. About matters relating to a new Ed of A Passage to India. With autograph Ms, bibliography of his works. S July 23 (142) £350 [Sotheran]
— Series of 3 A Ls s, 11 May to 18 June 1964. 3 pp, 8vo. To [Peter] Luke. Regarding a television production of Where Angels Fear to Tread. C Dec 3 (364) £140 [Bristow]
— ALs, 19 Apr 1950. 2 pp, 12mo. To Mr. Orlansky. About conjectured identifications of houses etc. in recipient's study on Stevenage. With related material. wa May 30 (33) $150

Forster, Georg, 1754-94
ALs, 20 Feb 1791. 2 pp, 8vo. To Archenholtz. Interesting letter, thanking for money & talking about his work. JG Oct 2 (205) DM2,600

Forsyth, John, 1780-1841
Franking signature, [n.d.]. As Sec of State. rf Mar 14 (80) $75

Foscolo, Ugo, 1778-1827
ALs, 3 Nov 1821. 1 p, 4to. To Countess Theotochi Albrizzi. Introducing Mr. Collyer. C Dec 3 (392) £850 [L'Autographe]

Fouche, Joseph, Duc d'Otrante, 1759-1820
Ls, 10 June 1815. 1 p, folio. To Minister of War Davout. Complaining about the failure to execute Napoleon's orders concerning provisions for Boulogne. star Apr 9 (967) DM400

Fouque, Friedrich de la Motte, 1777-1843
ALs, 7 Apr [1827]. 1 p, 4to. To the "Bardua triplets". In verse, thanking for a pleasant evening. With 8-line postscript, in verse. star Apr 8 (72) DM1,050

France
[Revolution. - A collection of 100 A Ls s, Ls s, documents, & other material relating to the Convention, Assembly & Directory sold at CNY on 19 Dec 1986, lot 164, for $2,200.]
[Treaty of Paris, 1815. - A collection of material relating to the indemnity of 700 million francs paid by France to the allies in 1821 & to James Drummond's share in these transactions sold at C on 3 Dec 1986, lot 332, for £850 to Burgess & Browning.]
Ms, Collection de portraits, [c.1793]. 2 vols, 4to. Containing 66 pen & wash portraits of the Kings of France from Pharamond to Louis XVI, each with 3 pp of text. Contemp red mor. C June 24 (34) £3,500 [Beres]
— REVOLUTION. - 4 A Ls s, by Francois Boissy d'Anglas, President of the Jacobin Club, & Ds by Merlin de Douai, both members of the National Assembly; [1790s], 8 pp, 4to & 8vo. Contents not stated. sg Nov 6 (79) $175
— REVOLUTION. - Document, [20 June 1794] 6 pp, folio; orders concerning a military expedition into Holland, sgd by Carnot, Billaud Varenne, Barere de Vieuzac & St. Andre of the Comite de Salut Public. C Dec 3 (263) £160 [L'Autographe]

FRANCE

France, Anatole, 1844-1924

ALs, 31 Jan 1886. 2 pp, 8vo. To the bookbinder M. Vie. Suggesting samples to show a lady. star Apr 8 (73) DM210

Franchieres, Jean de

Ms, Livre de fauconnerie. [Southern France, beginning of the 16th cent] 62 leaves, vellum, 202mm by 138mm, in mor janseniste by Bauzonnet-Trautz. With decorated initials on every page. Jeanson Ms 119 SM Mar 1 (237) FF60,000

— Ms, Livre de Faulconnerie. [Eastern France, c.1500-20] 117 (of 118, lacking f. 98) leaves, 211mm by 145mm, in blindstamped contemp calf with doublures from a vellum scholastic manuscript of the 13th cent. With many illuminated borders. Jeanson Ms 118 SM Mar 1 (236) FF82,000

Francieres, Jehan de. See: Franchieres, Jean de

Francis I, King of France, 1494-1547

Ls, 14 Apr 1532. 1 p, folio. To his Treasurer Jean Laguette. Ordering him to pay 500 ecus to Gaston de Foix. star Apr 9 (968) DM2,000

Ds, 27 Apr 1518. 1 p, vellum, 230mm by 290mm. Instructions for payments to officers in Normandy. C June 24 (40) £280 [Maggs]

Francis I, Emperor, 1708-65

Ls, 1 Feb 1744. 1 p, 4to. To Baron von Gehlen. Returning New Year's wishes in his own & Maria Theresa's name. In French. star Apr 9 (1209) DM420

Ds, 1751. 7 leaves, vellum. Patent of nobility for Felix Emanuel Grosshauser. With full-p illuminated coat-of-arms. Red wax seal in brass case. C Dec 3 (258) £290 [Haas]

Francis II, Emperor, 1768-1835. See: Franz I, 1768-1835

Franck, Cesar, 1822-90

ALs, 16 [no month] 1872. 2 pp, 8vo. To Edouard Colonne. Concerning a concert arrangement. sg Nov 6 (75) $325

— [8 Dec 1887]. 1 p, 8vo. To Georges Serviers. Informing him about the date of his naturalization as a French citizen. S May 22 (597) £180 [Rankin]

— 20 Sept 1888. 3 pp, 8vo. To an unnamed student. Recommending pieces by Tchaikovsky, Beethoven & Mendelssohn for exercise. Possibly fragment. star Apr 9 (637) DM1,900

AMERICAN BOOK PRICES CURRENT

Francke, August Hermann, 1663-1727

ALs, 6 Oct 1712. 2 pp, 4to. To Herr Ehlers. Receipt for money, & about the ptg of a book. HK Nov 7 (2207) DM500

— 15 Apr 1725. 1 p, 4to. To Herr Neubauer. Sending a bottle of wine. In German & Latin. HK Nov 7 (2208) DM520

Frankfurter, Felix, 1882-1965

Collection of 3 Ls s & ANs, 12 Oct 1940 to 23 Mar 1942. 3 pp, 8vo & card, 24mo. To Leon S. Wellstone. About the situation at the beginning of the war; responding to letters of encouragement. On Supreme Court letterhead. sg Nov 6 (76) $700

Autograph sentiment, [n.d.], inscr to Daisy Harriman on reprint of his article on Franklin Delano Roosevelt in The Harvard Alumni Bulletin, 28 Apr 1945. 7 pp, 12mo. Sgd. wa May 30 (480) $200

Photograph, sgd & inscr, 17 May 1948. 9 by 7 inches. Inscr to Daisy Harriman, on mount. wa May 30 (382) $190

Franklin, Benjamin, 1706-90

A Ls s (2), 23 May 1765. 2 pp, folio, on a single leaf. To "Sally" & his daughter. Retained drafts, recommending Mrs. Rollof. S July 24 (392) £3,000 [Burr]

ALs, 27 Apr 1778. 1 p, 4to. To Comte de Milly. In 3d person, arranging for a meeting. rf Mar 14 (13) $1,700

Ls, 19 Oct 1779. 2 pp, 4to. To David Hartley. Providing for an exchange of prisoners of war. With related material. S Dec 18 (343) £5,500 [Joseph & Sawyer]

Ds, 9 July 1787. 1 p, folio. Authorizing commission on bankruptcy petition of Henry Dawson. Repaired. Charlotte Parker Milne collection. wd Nov 12 (35) $2,700

Franklin, Sir John, 1786-1847

ALs, 17 Feb 1829. 2 pp, 4to. To D. Francois Arago. Concerning observations on the Aurora Borealis in his 2d narrative. Bullock collection. CNY Dec 19 (87) $400

Franz Ferdinand, Archduke, 1863-1914

ALs, 7 Jan 1897. 3 pp, 8vo. To Amy Ehrman. Thanking for photographs & complaining about Corsica. On hotel letterhead. S May 21 (241) £400 [Maliye]

ANs, [6 Feb 1901]. To Lieut. Col. Kraus. Encouraging him to go to a dinner at the court. Sgd with paraph. In pencil; on ptd visiting card. star Apr 9 (1107) DM430

Franz I, Emperor of Austria, 1768-1835

ALs, 25 Mar 1808. 1 p, 4to. To his brother Ferdinand. Thanking for efforts in his behalf in Paris & about his new marriage. star Apr 9 (1096) DM1,000

Ds, 30 Apr 1809. 15 pp, 38cm by 32cm. Vellum.

Patent of nobility & grant of arms to Anton von Petz. With full-page illuminated painting of the arms, calligraphic script, floral borders & insignia throughout. Red velvet bdg. star Apr 9 (1097) DM1,500

— 7 July 1809. 1 p, folio. Vellum. Conferring the rank of Commander of the Order of Maria Theresa on Johann Graf von Klenau. Large seal in wooden case. HN Nov 27 (2261) DM1,700

— 26 Sept 1817. 22 pp, 4to. Confirmation of an agreement with Prussia regarding the occupation of Mainz. Countersgd by Metternich. Including text of agreement sgd by 3 commissioners. HN May 22 (3010) DM900

Franz Josef I, Emperor of Austria, 1830-1916
ALs, 25 Aug 1901. 1 p, 8vo. To Katharina Schratt. Cancelling a visit & confirming a date for the following morning. S May 21 (242) £550 [Maliye]

Ls s (2), 7 Jan 1850 & 10 Jan 1865. 3 pp, folio. To Francis II, as Duke of Calabria & King of the Two Sicilies. Offering him his Order of Stephen. Notifying him of the death of Archduke Ludwig. In French & Latin. With autograph subscriptions. S May 21 (243) £300 [Maliye]

Ds, 10 Sept 1888. 7 pp, 38cm by 29cm. Vellum. Grant of arms for Franz Vukovic. With full-page illuminated coat-of-arms. Violet velvet bdg. With related material. star Apr 9 (1103) DM750

Endorsement, in margin of a memorial, 9 Feb 1867. 1 p, folio. Pardon for Joseph Eger, sgd. star Apr 9 (1102) DM460

Freiligrath, Ferdinand, 1810-76
Autograph Ms, poem, Nadel und Draht. Eine Stimme vom Grand Eastern; sgd. [Summer 1866]; 2 pp, 4to. Seven 4-line stanzas. star Apr 8 (76) DM1,700

Collection of 3 A Ls s & autograph poem, 11 & 21 Nov 1839 & [n.d., 1839]. 10 pp, 8vo. To Franziska Schwiter. Enthusiastic & poetical letters about his activities & feelings, & announcing his visit. 1 sgd Ihr blauer Cabinetsminister, anr sgd der Hofmarschall. Poem, Fuer Musik, four 4-line stanzas. star Apr 8 (74) DM3,400

ALs, 30 May 1842. 2 pp, 4to. To Heinrich Schwiter. Sending condolences on the death of his wife & apologizing for his long silence. Fold tears. star Apr 8 (75) DM380

— 2 July 1842. 3 pp, 8vo. To Dr. Hermann Hauff. Inquiring about mail sent to his Darmstadt address after his departure. JG Oct 2 (41) DM1,100

— 25 Mar 1853. 3 pp, 8vo. To the editors of the magazine Morgenblatt. Requesting careful proofreading of an enclosed trans & complaining about recent ptg errors. JG Oct 2 (42) DM1,500

— 18 Dec 1870. 4 pp, 8vo. To Johann Heinrich Kuenzel. About his journey to England & his son's return from the war & projected emigration to America. HK Nov 7 (2211) DM850

ANs, 21 Aug 18[42?]. 1 p, 4to. To the editors of the magazine Morgenblatt. Asking for an early publication of his trans of Longfellow's The Skeleton in Armour. In the margin of an unrelated letter. JG Oct 2 (43) DM850

French & Indian War
— Burk, T. - ALs, 27 June 1758. Folded soldier's letter from "Secanaitady", regarding marching orders. Tape patching. rf Mar 14 (14) $105

— Knap[p], Nathaniel. - Autograph Ms, diary of the Louisburg campaign, 27 Mar 1758 to 4 July 1759. About 133 pp, 8vo, & blanks. With 32 pp recording Knapp family genealogy. Bound with Nathaniel Ames. An Astronomical Diary...1758. Bost., 1758. Contemp vellum; brass clasp & catch. CNY May 11 (44) $7,000

— Morgan, Jacob. - ALs, 14 Mar 1757. Size not stated. To Col. Wheeler. Military news from Philadelphia. rf May 30 (7) $130

Freud, Sigmund, 1856-1939
Autograph Ms, running titles for the 1st 64 pp of his work Das Unbehagen in der Kultur, [c.1929]. 2 pp, folio. With a copy of the book, Wien, 1930. 1st Ed. Bookplate of R. Sterba. HN May 22 (3011a) DM1,400

ALs, 19 July 1938. 2 pp, 8vo. To Mr. Susman. Thanking for an invitation to attend a theater performance & saying he did not feel well. On personalized letter card. P Dec 15 (42) $2,600

— 4 Aug 1938. 1 p, 4to. To an unnamed doctor. Refusing a request for analysis & acceptance as his pupil. In German. P Sept 24 (26) $3,750

Autograph postcard, sgd, 29 Dec 1929. To Georg Sylvester Viereck. Saying Einstein is naive & thanking for an interview with Thomas Mann. star Apr 8 (332) DM4,200

— 9 July 1936. To Dr. Felix Meyer. Notifying him that he has not received the French trans of Traumarbeit. C June 24 (173) £850 [Schulson]

ANs, 22 Jan 1939. 1 p, 8vo (card). To Dr. & Mrs. R. Sterba. Sending good wishes for their emigration. HN May 22 (3011b) DM1,000

Engraving, port by Ferdinand Schmutzer showing Freud half-length. Sgd by Freud & dated 1926; in pencil. 60cm by 45cm. Framed. S Nov 27 (360) £1,200 [Schneider]

FRIEDRICH I

Friedrich I, King of Prussia, 1657-1713
Ls, 22 Dec 1691. 2 pp, folio. To Conrad Barthold von Stille. As Elector, notifying him of appointments to his household. Repaired. star Apr 9 (917) DM220
— 15 June 1695. 1 p, folio. To Col. von Hake. As Elector, regarding the discharge of 2 Pommeranian soldiers. star Apr 9 (919) DM580
— 19 July 1710. 3 pp, folio. To Count Boris Scheremetew. Discussing the military situation in the East. star Apr 9 (1131) DM700
Ds, 10 Mar 1694. 2 pp, folio. As Elector, military commission for Capt. La Viville. star Apr 9 (918) DM280
— 29 Jan 1703. 3 pp, folio. Military commission for [Jean] von Felix. star Apr 9 (1130) DM300

Friedrich I, King of Wuerttemberg, 1754-1816
Ls s (2), 12 Feb & 8 May 1808. 1 p, folio. To his commission for conscriptions. Regarding the enlistment of 2 cadets. With related material. star Apr 9 (1298) DM620

Friedrich II, King of Prussia, 1712-86
ALs, 13 Oct 1736. 3 pp, 4to. To his father Friedrich Wilhelm I. Sending doves & crabs, commenting about a soldier, & discussing family matters. With Friedrich Wilhelm's reply, Ls, 17 Oct 1736, 1 p, 4to; thanking for his son's letter. C Dec 3 (260) £4,800 [Fritz-Denneville]
— 2 Jan 1741. 1 p, 4to. To [his wife Elizabeth Christina of Brunswick?]. Approving of her letter to Duke Anton & announcing his return to Berlin after the campaign. In French. C Dec 3 (261) £1,300 [Haas]
— 27 May 1742. 2 pp, 4to. To Duhan de Jandun. Reporting about the war. In French. Sgd Federic. star Apr 9 (1142) DM14,000
Series of 6 Ls s, 13 Feb 1751 to 31 Dec 1770. 6 pp, 4to. To the directors of the Potsdam gun factory. Regarding the quartering of soldiers, a payment to the factory, financial problems, etc. Sgd Fch & Frdch. star Apr 9 (1144) DM3,200
Ls, 4 Jan 1739. 1 p, 8vo. Recipient unnamed. Returning New Year's wishes. Sgd Friderich. star Apr 9 (1140) DM880
— 25 Apr 1740. 1 p, folio. To the Landgrave of Hesse. Sending congratulations on the birth of a son. Bullock collection. CNY Dec 19 (88) $420
— 31 Oct 1740. 1 p, 4to. To Dr. Kauffmann. Concerning an appointment for his son. Sgd Frederic. In French. star Apr 9 (1141) DM950
— 6 Dec 1746. 1 p, folio. Recipient unnamed. Remitting legacy dues to be paid by Johann Georg Schumann's nephew. Sgd with paraph. HK Nov 7 (2215) DM600
— 30 Aug 1749. 1 p, 4to. To the merchant Splittgerber. Giving permission to order arms for the Graf von Lippe. Sgd Fch. star Apr 9 (1143) DM600
— 6 Nov 1751. 1 p, 4to. To Karl Ludolph von Danckelmann. Concerning a petition (included) by Johann Gottfried Mueller for admission to the Joachimsthal grammar-school. Sgd Fch. star Apr 9 (1145) DM520
— 7 May 1753. 1 p, 4to. To Cammer Praesident Lentz at Aurich. Requesting further information concerning "drey elenden Leuten aus Emden". JG Oct 2 (393) DM900
— 21 Apr 1759. 1 p, 8vo. To Lieut. Col. d'O [commander at Glatz]. Ordering him to supply Gen. von Ramin with arms & provisions. In German. With autograph postscript, in French. Sgd Federic. Margins cut; mtd. star Apr 9 (1146) DM1,200
— 16 Mar 1765. 1 p, 4to. To von Finckenstein. Concerning a financial claim against Graf von Sappia. Sgd Fch. With related material. FD June 11 (3623a) DM1,400
— 22 July 1765. 1 p, 4to. To councillor Niethe. Commenting about a report describing business at the Frankfurt fair. Sgd Frch. star Apr 9 (1149) DM640
— 8 Mar 1766. 1 p, 4to. To Gen. von Tauentzien. Saying he is enclosing a note for Dr Jeckwitz concerning his health. With copy of this note, in contemp hand, on lower part of p. Asking for advice about his gout. C Dec 3 (262) £200 [Haas]
— 10 Sept 1767. 1 p, 4to. To von Finckenstein. Concerning property in Poland inherited by Theodor von Czapski. Sgd Fch. With related material. FD June 11 (3623b) DM1,200
— 19 Oct 1768. 1 p, folio. To a judicial court at Horst. Forwarding a sentence in the trial of Anna, Maria & Joachim Lossow. Sgd Fch. star Apr 9 (1150) DM800
— 3 Aug 1770. 1 p, folio. To Ferdinand IV of Naples. Notifying him of the birth of a nephew. Sgd Federic. In French. star Apr 9 (1151) DM1,100
— 9 Feb 1772. 1 p, 4to. To Freiherr von der Schulenburg. Transmitting a report by Count Solms (not present) regarding financial transactions with a bank at St. Petersburg. Endorsed by Schulenburg; his notes for a reply to Solms attached. HK Nov 7 (2216) DM900
— 18 May 1774. 1 p, 4to. To Heinrich August Karl de la Motte Fouque. Declining a request regarding the last will of recipient's father. Sgd Federic. In French. star Apr 9 (1152) DM900

— 19 July 1782. 1 p, 4to. To the "Cammer Deputation" at Stendal. Ordering them to ensure the supply of Berlin & Potsdam with grains. HK Nov 7 (2217) DM750
— 4 Nov 1783. 1 p, 4to. To Capt. d'Harroy. Sending Ensign Kauffmann for the corps of engineers. Sgd Frch. star Apr 9 (1153) DM750
— 13 Mar 1785. 1 p, 4to. To Counts Cossel & von Stentsch. Regarding the importation of grain from Poland. HK Nov 7 (2218) DM650
— 9 Nov 1785. 1 p, 4to. To Bau-Inspector Unger. Requesting estimates for houses. Sgd Frch. JG Oct 2 (390) DM700
— 19 Nov 1785. 1 p, 4to. To Bau-Inspector Unger. Reprimanding him for his failure to deliver the required estimates for houses. Sgd Frch. JG Oct 2 (391) DM1,000
— 1785. 1 p, size not stated. To Capt. von Schoetzel. Declining a request. With paraph. FD Dec 2 (3288) DM600
— 2 June 1786. 1 p, 4to. To the Bau Comptoir at Berlin. Concerning the estimates for the Berlin city wall. Sgd Frch. JG Oct 2 (392) DM1,500
ANs, "ce 21" [c.1735]. 1 p, 4to. To Wilhelm von Rohwedell. Regarding "La lettre de Truks" Sgd Frederic. star Apr 9 (1138) DM2,200
Autograph endorsement, 3 comments, 1 sgd Fch, in the margin of a memorial addressed to him, 13 Dec 1765, 1 p, folio, sgd by von Anhalt. Deciding questions relating to several Prussian officers. star Apr 9 (1147) DM4,300

Friedrich III, Deutscher Kaiser, 1831-88
A Ls s (2), 8 Apr & 13 May 1888. 3 pp, 8vo. To Gen. von Winterfeld. Asking for a list of duties to be assumed by the crown prince. Regarding the death of Princess Marie von Hohenzollern-Hechingen. With paraph. In pencil. With 2 A Ls s, 26 Feb 1885 & 9 Apr 1886, & 2 telegrams, 1886 & 1887, to von Winterfeld. star Apr 9 (945) DM1,600
ALs, 22 Feb 1881. 7 pp, 8vo. To Princess Amalie von Schleswig-Holstein. About the wedding of her niece & his son [Emperor Wilhelm II]. HK Nov 7 (2219) DM2,100
— 17 Aug 1881. 4 pp, 8vo. To [Georg] von Bunsen. As Crown Prince, expressing condolences on the death of his daughters. star Apr 9 (943) DM750
— 10 Nov 1887. 1 p, 4to. To Gen. von Winterfeld. As Crown Prince, requesting information about Dr. Schmidt. Sgd FW. In pencil. With related material. star Apr 9 (944) DM650
Ls, 17 Jan 1871. 2 pp, 4to. To Marquise Lavaggi. As Crown Prince, answering her inquiry about her captured brother. With autograph subscription. star Apr 9 (1180) DM480
Letter, 21 Sept 1875. 3 pp, 4to. To his father, Kaiser Wilhelm I. As Crown Prince, draft, proposing a decoration for the Lord Mayor of Augsburg. With autograph revisions. star Apr 9 (942) DM260

Friedrich Wilhelm, Kurfuerst von Brandenburg ("The Great Elector"), 1620-88
Ls, 1 Jan 1654. 2 pp, folio. To Herzog Albrecht VI von Bayern. New Year's wishes, & wishing peace to the German nation. With autograph subscription. star Apr 9 (914) DM2,000
— 2 Sept 1662. 2 pp, folio. Recipient unnamed. Confirming an agreement between the chapter of the Magdeburg cathedral & the magistracy at Halberstadt. With letter by the magistracy for the Neumark, 1 Sept 1662, regarding religious controversies among Protestants. star Apr 9 (915) DM650
— 30/20 Dec 1672. 2 pp, folio. To Philipp Wilhelm, Pfalzgraf zu Neuburg. Informing him that he has received his envoy Friedrich Christian von Spee. With 3 A Ls s, 1 each by his wives Louise Henriette & Dorothea, & his aunt Maria Eleonora. HN May 22 (3015) DM3,600
— 22 Mar 1681. 1 p, 4to. To the mayor of Beelitz. Giving orders for an investigation of a case of arson. With related material. star Apr 9 (916) DM480

Friedrich Wilhelm I, King of Prussia, 1688-1740
Ms, draft of a circular to all infantry regiments regarding strength of units, 23 Nov 1718. 4 pp, folio. With extensive autograph comments in the margin, sgd FW. Repaired. star Apr 9 (1133) DM3,200
Ls, 25 Feb 1715. 1 p, folio. To his "Lehns Canzley". Regarding the claim of councillor Fuchs to a judgeship. With contemp copy of letter of condolences from Landgraf Ludwig IX von Hessen-Darmstadt to Friedrich Wilhelm II, 1786. star Apr 9 (1132) DM320
— 10 Aug 1722. 2 pp, folio. To Johann Philipp Franz von Schoenborn, Bishop of Wuerzburg. Notifying him of the birth of a son. star Apr 9 (1134) DM520
— 17 Nov 1722. 1 p, 4to. To von Massow. Approving of an appointment. With autograph postscript regarding Massow's son. star Apr 9 (1135) DM640
— 28 Jan 1738. 1 p, 4to. To Field Marshal von Grumbkow. Approving of a suggestion to facilitate provisioning of troops. Left margin cut. star Apr 9 (1137) DM440
Ds, 14 Mar 1732. 3 pp, folio. Appointment for de Renouard as judge. star Apr 9 (1136) DM580
See also: Friedrich II, 1712-86

Friedrich Wilhelm II, King of Prussia, 1744-97
ALs, 15 May 1788. 1 p, 4to. To an unnamed lady. Suggesting that doctors be consulted about the illness of a lady at court. star Apr 9 (1161) DM850

Series of 6 Ls s, 1787 to 1789. Size not given. To Woellner. Concerning financial matters. With cut signature, 16 Feb 1794, 4to. JG Oct 2 (404) DM530

Friedrich Wilhelm III, King of Prussia, 1770-1840
Ls, 13 May 1790. 1 p, 4to. To L. G. von Wallmoden. As Crown Prince, thanking for drawings of Hanoverian army uniforms. With autograph postscript. star Apr 9 (1162) DM280

— 17 May 1809. 1 p, 4to. To Graf Dohna. About the appointment of Zelter as professor of music at the Academy of Arts & the importance of music for a nation. Countersgd by Wilhelm von Humboldt. star Apr 9 (1165) DM1,600

Ds, 31 Jan 1814. 1 p, folio. Conferral of the Iron Cross on G. von Pelkowsky. star Apr 9 (1166) DM1,300

Friedrich Wilhelm IV, King of Prussia, 1795-1861
Collection of 2 A Ls s & Ls, 6 June 1838 to 25 Oct 1840. 4 pp, 8vo & 4to. To Johann Heusinger. Friendly letters to his former drawing-master, sending birthday congratulations, conferring a decoration, etc. Fold tears. HK Nov 7 (2226) DM850

Ls, 23 June 1837. 1 p, folio. To superintendent Foss at Stettin. Granting leave. star Apr 9 (1170) DM200

— TSCHECH, HEINRICH LUDWIG. - Autograph endorsement, sgd, 10 July 1841, 1 p, folio, on a complaint addressed to the magistrate of Storkow concerning smoking as a fire hazard. star Apr 9 (1172) DM260

Friesz, Othon
Series of 3 A Ls s, [n.d.]. 12 pp, 4to & 8vo. Recipients unnamed. Discussing his style of painting, his projects, etc. 2 A Ls s with pen-and-ink sketches. With autograph draft of a speech concerning his artistic career. S Nov 27 (361) £600 [Quaritch]

Friml, Rudolf, 1879-1972
[3 carbon copies of contracts, sgd, 14 to 17 Apr 1936, 6 pp, folio, sales of motion picture rights to 3 musicals to MGM, sold at wa on 30 May 1987, lot 355, for $200.]

Frisch, Karl von, 1886-1982
Autograph Ms, draft of his speech as Nobel prize winner (p 11); [1973]. 1 p, folio. With ALs, 1974. star Apr 8 (333) DM280

Fromentin, Eugene, 1820-76
ALs, 1 Apr 1857. 4 pp, 8vo. To [George Sand]. Thanking for her praise of his Un Ete dans le Sahara & assessing his merits as a writer & painter. S Nov 27 (362) £450 [Quaritch]

Frost, Robert, 1874-1963
Autograph transcript, poem, The Gift Outright, July 1954. 1 p, 8vo. 16 lines, sgd. P June 18 (68) $1,700

Fuchs, Ernst
Original drawing, pen-&-ink sketch, showing male head. Inscr, sgd & dated 29 Jan 1975. 1 p, 8vo, on recto of mourning envelope. Inscr partly in Hebrew letters. star Apr 8 (464) DM550

Fuessli, Johann Heinrich, 1741-1825. See: Fuseli, Henry

Fulton, Robert, 1765-1815
Autograph Ms, 4 July to 13 Sept 1813. 1 p, 4to. Journal leaf, mostly mentioning his correspondence concerning submarine firing. P Oct 29 (54) $2,000

— Autograph Ms, Notes on the Submarine Vessel, 26 July 1804. 15 pp, folio. Sgd at head & at end. Lacking the drawings. Sewn. In red quarter mor slipcase. P May 13 (45) $9,000

ALs, 12 July 1808. 1 p, 8vo. To Robert McQueen. Requesting him to ensure that no one has access to his models. Laid down. With address panel. P Oct 29 (53) $1,400

— 11 Sept 1810. 1 p, 4to. To Commodore John Rodgers. Arranging for a test of his torpedoes against a naval vessel. P May 13 (46) $1,500

— 17 July 1813. 2 pp, 4to. To Edward Livingston. About payment for shares in the Mississippi Navigation Company. P May 13 (47) $1,500

Furniss, Harry
Collection of 6 A Ls s & a page from a sketchbook, 1888 to 1918. 14 pp, 8vo. Recipient & contents not stated. 5 A Ls s & page from sketchbook with pen-&-ink sketches, mostly self-caricatures. With pen-&-ink drawing by Dorothy Furniss, 1918. sg Apr 9 (69) $200

Furtwaengler, Wilhelm, 1886-1954
ALs, 22 July 1909. 4 pp, 8vo. To an unnamed professor. About his unsuccessful application for a position as conductor in Prague. star Apr 9 (641) DM520

— [n.d.]. 1 p, folio. To Princess Loremarie von Schoenberg-Hartenstein. Looking forward to seeing her in Vienna. star Apr 9 (643) DM240

Ls s (2), 19 Feb & 29 Apr 1950. 3 pp, folio. To Friedrich Pasche. About problems regarding the Berlin Philharmonic Orchestra. star Apr 9 (642) DM900

Fuseli, Henry, 1741-1825
Autograph Ms, [n.d.], 2 pp, folio. About images in contemp English poetry & the work of Raphael & Parmigiano. Originally intended as addition to anr work. Sgd F. S Dec 18 (311) £750 [Wilson]

Futurism
[A collection of letters, Mss & photographs, mostly relating to the Gruppo Futurista Napoletano, c.1924-1933; about 150 pp, 4to & folio, sold at S on 21 May 1987, lot 246, for £5,200 to Rota.]

G

Gace de la Bigne
Ms, Le Roman des oiseaulx. [Lorraint, end of 15th cent] 76 leaves, vellum, 402mm by 278mm, in 18th-cent mor gilt. Written & illuminated for Rene II, 1473-1508 & with a large miniature & full border on f1 showing Gace de la Bigne presenting his manuscript to Philppe le Hardi, Duc de Bourgogne. Jeanson Ms 111 SM Mar 1 (247) FF950,000

Gaffet de la Briffardiere, Antoine
Ms, Livre de chasse royal du cerf, du chevreuil, du sanglier, du loup, et du liepvre. 1661. 258 leaves, 213mm by 144mm, in mor by Affolter. Jeanson Ms 133 SM Mar 1 (248) FF8,900

Gal, Hans
Autograph music, "Minuet" & "Siciliano", from Op. 68b. 2 pp, 31cm by 24.5cm. With ANs, on visiting card. star Apr 9 (644) DM430

Galilei, Galileo, 1564-1642
ADs, 13 Apr 1595. Receipt for part of a debt repaid by Luigi de la Court. 3 lines on folio sheet containing debtor's promissory note, 15 Mar 1595. Matted with a port. P Dec 15 (43) $15,000

Gall, Franz Joseph, 1758-1828
Ls, 10 Dec 1813. 1 p, 4to. To the board of directors of the Athenee. Requesting payment of his salary. star Apr 8 (335) DM200

Gallatin, Albert, 1761-1849
ALs, [n.d.]. 3 pp, size not stated. To an unknown collector in Boston. As Sec of the Treasury, concerning the necessity of removing the collector at Passamaquoddy because of irregularities in his accounts. With postscript, initialled, suggesting division of the public deposits in Boston among several banks. wa Oct 18 (101) $130
Ls, 18 June 1804. 2 pp, 4to. To William R. Lee. Giving orders to set up a facility for sick seamen. Matted with envelope & a port. sg Nov 6 (80) $110
— 20 Oct 1812. 1 p, 4to. To James Wilson, Collector of Customs. Ptd letter; contents not stated. With franking signature. wa May 30 (34) $85

Franking signature, [23 May 1808]. On ptd Treasury Department circular, 20 May 1808; sgd. rf Mar 14 (81) $95
— Anr, [2 Apr, n.y.] As Sec of the Treasury, on address label to William Few, New York. With franking signature by Thomas T. Tucker, on Ls, 1808. rf Nov 15 (30) $60

Galsworthy, John, 1867-1933
Typescript, dedication of the Forsyte Saga to his wife, 16 Aug 1927. 1 p, 8vo. Sgd. C June 24 (113) £120 [Lucas]
Series of 6 A Ls s, 19 Jan 1918 to 5 July 1922. 9 pp, 8vo & 4to. To Mr. & Mrs. Bretherton. Explaining his protest against keeping wild animals caged in zoos. C Dec 3 (365) £210 [Wilson]

Gandhi, Mohandas K., 1869-1948
Autograph Ms, comments on a newspaper article, [c.1938]. 2 pp, 8vo. On verso of an unrelated letter. sg Apr 9 (71) $375
Series of c.260 letters, mostly autograph, 9 Feb 1909 to 5 Dec 1946. To Hermann Kallenbach. Important letters chronicling their relationship, Gandhi's activities & thinking. With 15 letters to Hanna Lazar, c.130 telegrams sent to Gandhi, & further related material. S Dec 18 (255) £140,000 [Indian High Commission]

Ganz, Leopold, 1810-69. See: Ganz, Moritz & Ganz

Ganz, Moritz, 1806-68 —&
Ganz, Leopold, 1810-69
ALs, 14 July 1830. 2 pp, 4to. To the pbr Schlesinger. About some of their compositions & suggesting they should talk about a fee. Sgd Gebrueder Ganz. star Apr 9 (645) DM550

Garbo, Greta. See: Auric, Georges

Garfield, James A., 1831-81
A Ls s (2), 5 Sept 1860 & 15 Jan 1881. 2 pp, 4to & 8vo. To W. J. Ford, reporting about his candidacy for the Ohio state senate. Repaired. To Richard Randolph, thanking for a publication sent to him. Separated at fold. P Oct 29 (55) $650
— A Ls s (2), 25 Oct 1876 & 16 July 1880. 2 pp, 4to. To Postmaster Gen. James N. Tyner. Responding to an inquiry concerning Col. Dudley. Enlisting Tyner's help for the Presidentioal campaign in Indiana. With 2 autograph envelopes. Descendants of J. N.

GARFIELD

Tyner. P May 13 (48) $1,000
ALs, 22 Dec 1863. 4 pp, 4to. To E. B. Taylor. About the death of his child, his 1st term in Congress, & Taylor's financial problems. Bullock collection. CNY Dec 19 (90) $2,600
— 5 Dec 1879. 1 p, 8vo. To [Alfonso Taft?]. Apologizing for being unable to attend a banquet in honor of Gen. Grant. pnNY June 11 (14) $180
Ls, 8 Dec 1880. 1 p, 8vo. To Daniel Lee. Thanking for congratulations [on his election]. Was mtd. wa May 30 (96) $375
ANs, 19 Mar [1881]. 1 p, on Executive Mansion card. To Sec of State James Blaine. Asking him to come for an interview. Sgd J.A.G. Framed with a port. P May 13 (49) $8,000
Autograph endorsement, 4 lines in pencil, in top margin of a letter to Garfield from Lewis L. Pinkerton, 12 Feb 1866, 5 pp, 4to, describing his plight as a Union man in Kentucky. Referring letter to "Bro Emett"[?]. Sgd J.A.G. With cut signature, on part of an envelope. P Oct 29 (56) $500
Cut signature, [c.1880]. 1 p, 50mm by 110mm. In purple ink. Was mtd. sg Nov 6 (267) $60
Franking signature, [30 Oct 1869]. rf Mar 14 (82) $250
— Anr, [4 Jan n.y.]. rf Mar 14 (83) $160
Photograph, sgd, [n.d.], 4 by 6.5 inches. "Pach" imprint on verso. Sgd in red ink. Small tear. rf Mar 14 (15) $400
Signature, on subscription list to a speech ptd by Congressional Globe, Mar 1870. Also sgd by John Sherman & others. rf Nov 15 (6) $150
— BLISS, D. W. - ALs, 14 Sept 1881. 2 pp, 8vo. To an unknown physician. Reporting about the President's condition. With copy of statement, 11 Aug [1881], by Bliss & other physicians, about Garfield's condition. P Oct 29 (57) $750
— THUDOW, WILLIAM. - ALs, 4 July 1881. 2 pp, 8vo. To T. D. Barbour. Informing him of the President's condition. On White House letterhead. sg Nov 6 (81) $150
See also: Hayes, Rutherford B.

Garfield, Lucretia R., 1832-1918
Franking signature, [5 Sept 1889]. rf Mar 14 (85) $200
— Anr, [1902]. rf Mar 14 (84) $120
— Anr, [13 Nov 1909]. On cover to U.S. Trust Co. rf May 30 (20) $90

Garibaldi, Giuseppe, 1807-82
ALs, [May 1860]. 1 p, folio. To Commandante Zambianchi. Ordering him to incite a rebellion in the Papal States & in the states of the King of Naples. S May 21 (247) £1,600 [Johnson]
Ls, 30 Nov 1862. 1 p, 8vo. To J. J. Coleman. Expressing thanks for sympathy with the Italian cause. C Dec 3 (264) £220 [Bragho]

Gariopontus, d.c.1050
Ms, Liber Passionarii, [Italy, c.1200]. 94 leaves plus 2 flyleaves, vellum, 245mm by 150mm. Def medieval bdg of bevelled wooden bds. In brown ink in a rounded late romanesque hand. With small painted initials throughout & many contemp glosses in several hands. S Dec 2 (34) £27,000 [Brown]

Garner, John Nance, 1868-1967
Ls, 10 Nov 1932. 1 p, 4to. To Henry T. Rainey. Thanking for congratulations on his election as Vice President. wa May 30 (385) $65

Garrick, David, 1717-79
Autograph Ms, poem, The Bankrupt Beauty to Mrs. Bouverie; 16 Dec 1777. 2 pp, 8vo. 32 lines, including 3 cancelled. Cloth folder & brown mor-backed slipcase. Houghton Collection. S July 23 (21) £850 [Maggs]

Gaskell, Elizabeth Cleghorn, 1810-65
[An album, c.1851-1908, c.140 pp, 8vo, apparently compiled by Jane Adeane of Llanfawr, containing extracts of a letter from Mrs. Gaskell to Lady Hatherton, 27 Dec 1853, describing the inspiration for her story Morton Hall, & further material relating to Mrs. Gaskell, sold at S on 18 Dec 1986, lot 71, for £450 to Quaritch.]
Series of 6 A Ls s, 31 Dec [1858] to 22 Dec [1864]. 28 pp, 8vo. To Florence Nightingale. About Nightingale's work & writings. S July 24 (297) £1,900 [Quaritch]
ALs, 18 June 1831. 4 pp, 4to. To Harriet Carr. Inquiring about recipient's visits to London & her acquaintances. Sgd Elizabeth Cleghorn Stevenson. S Dec 18 (68) £700 [Quaritch]

Gaston III Phoebus, Count of Foix, 1331-91.
See: Phebus, Gaston

Gates, Horatio, 1728?-1806
ALs, 24 May 1778. 1 p, folio. To George Clinton. Notifying him of an imminent attack by the enemy & requesting the New York militia to join him. S July 24 (393) £650 [Profile]

Gauguin, Paul, 1848-1903
ALs, [c.1903]. 3 pp, 4to. To M. Brault, a lawyer. Concerning an enquiry into an affair at Taoala, with remarks on the corruption of the police. wd June 19 (23) $2,200

Gauss, Carl Friedrich, 1777-1855
ALs, 15 July 1836. 3 pp, 4to. To Kreil. Regarding observations concerning magnetism, galvanic currents & electricity. HK Nov 7 (2232) DM1,800

Gawsworth, John

Typescript, Toreros/ Poems of John Gawsworth selected by Richard Aldington..., [n.d.]. About 75 pp, 4to. Marked typescript, with some proof copy. Possibly unpbd. S July 23 (144) £200 [Quaritch]

— GARDINER, WREY. - Typescript, Gawsworth/ Poet: King/ Sketches towards a Portrait of Terence Ian Fytton Armstrong "John Gawsworth"..., c.1965. About 220 pp, 4to. Unpbd anthology of tributes to Gawsworth by a number of authors, including Dylan Thomas, Edith Sitwell & Lawrence Durrell. S July 23 (143) £650 [Quaritch]

Geibel, Emanuel, 1815-84

ALs, 2 Feb 1875. 4 pp, 8vo. To Ludwig Ziemssen. Thanking for a book & reporting about his health problems. star Apr 8 (78) DM260

Geneva Convention

[2 letters by the Swiss Federal Government, 18 July 1876, sgd by Vice President Heer, & 21 Oct 1879, sgd by President Hammer, 2 pp, folio, to the Foreign Minister of Montenegro, regarding Montenegro's & Bolivia's accession to the Geneva Convention, sold at star on 9 Apr 1987, lot 989, for DM320.]

Gentz, Friedrich von, 1764-1832

Series of 3 A Ls s, 6 June 1808, 8 Aug & 14 Oct [n.y.]. 6 pp, 4to & 8vo. To an unknown lady, requesting a meeting. Some later erasures. To Hofrath von Mueller, news & invitations. JG Oct 2 (48) DM540

Genzmer, Harald

Autograph music, sketch for voice, trumpet & organ, [n.d.]. 4 pp, 34cm by 27cm. Sgd. In pencil. star Apr 9 (647) DM220

Geoffrey, Duke of Brittany & Count of Richemont, 1158-86

Document, [1171-1186]. 1 p, vellum, 157mm by 144mm. Grant of land "in villa Sci Botulfi" to Reiner de Waxtenelham. C June 24 (257) £500 [Quaritch]

Geoffroy, J.

Original drawings, (7), to illus Gulliver's Travels. In ink & watercolor. Sgd. 204mm by 166mm; mtd. S June 19 (659) £1,300 [Edberg]

Geoffroy Saint-Hilaire, Etienne, 1772-1844

Ms, notes on teratology [c. 1830-40]. 24 pp, 4to. Including 6 folio drawings. P Sept 24 (27) $800

George, Prince Consort of Queen Anne of England, 1653-1708

Ls, 26 Mar 1705. Size not stated. To Lord Dysart, Vice Admiral of Suffolk. As Lord High Admiral, instructing him to remove an embargo within his command. Framed. Altman collection. pnNY Sept 13 (41) $160

George I, King of England, 1660-1727

Ds, 26 June 1704. 4 pp, folio. Ptd proclamation concerning improvement of roads in his lands, sgd as Elector. S July 24 (234) £220 [Wilson]

George II, King of England, 1683-1760

Ls, 7 Dec 1759. 1 p, 4to. To the King of the Two Sicilies. Sending good wishes on his accession to the throne. S Dec 18 (213) £320 [Dawson]

Ds, 11 Dec 1733. 2 pp, folio. Warrant to Edward Hughes to hold a court martial to try James McDaniel. C Dec 3 (265) £220 [Cooper]

— 24 Jan 1752. 1 p, 4to. Notifying Gov. George Clinton of the appointment of John Chambers to the Council of the Province of New York. sg Nov 6 (82) $225

— 24 Dec 1755. 1 p, folio. Appointment of Robert Gray as Lieut. in Capt. Benjamin's Company at Sheerness. Seal removed. Framed. Altman collection. pnNY Sept 13 (42) $425

George III, King of England, 1738-1820

Autograph Ms, notes, lists & memoranda in his copy of Rider's British Merlin, 1761. Contemp gilt crimson mor with the King's monogram, 12mo. Partly concerning his arranged marriage with Charlotte Sophia of Mecklenburg-Strelitz. With several notes in later hands. S Dec 18 (216) £1,500

ALs, 3 Apr 1778. 1 p, 4to. To Lord Townshend. Discussing repairs needed at several ports & at Pendennis Castle. Repaired. Framed. Altman collection. pnNY Sept 13 (43) $750

— 9 Sept 1792. 1 p, 4to. Recipient unnamed. About "the French Revolutionists"& a request by Lord Westmorland. Sgd GR. S Dec 18 (215) £550 [Spiro]

— 18 Sept 1801. 1 p, 4to. Concurring with remitment of part of the punishment imposed on Thomas Bailey. S Dec 18 (214) £400 [Bristow]

Collection of Ds & Ls, 23 Mar 1791 & 24 Mar 1807. 3 pp, folio & 4to. Pay order in favor of John & Coutts Trotter; sgd at head. To Lord Tewkesbury, directing him to meet him. pn Dec 11 (16) £120 [Clark]

Series of Ds s, 4 Ds s, 3 Sept 1801 to 29 July 1809. 24 pp, folio. Warrants to affix the Great Seal to 2 commissions & 2 ratifications. pnNY June 11 (72) $1,000

— Series of 3 Ds s, 12 Oct 1804 to 7 July 1810.

GEORGE III

15 pp, folio. Warrants to affix the Great Seal to Mr. Pierrepont's & Sir Gore Ouseley's Full Powers. pnNY June 11 (75) $225
— Series of 3 Ds s, 8 Jan 1805 & 16 May 1807. 17 pp, folio. Warrants to affix the Great Seal to Full Powers for Lord Granville Leveson Gower. pnNY June 11 (74) $400
— Series of 4 Ds s, May 1807 to 7 July 1810. Length not stated. Warrants to affix the Great Seal to commissions. pnNY June 11 (73) $650

Ds s (2) 18 Sept 1792 & 26 Feb 1807. 2 pp, folio. Pay order for money due the 35th Regiment of Foot. Military commission for Chapman Gint; partly ptd. C Dec 3 (266) £210 [Army Museum]

Ds, 10 Dec 1773. 2 pp, folio. Pardon for a native of India accused of stealing. Stained. rf Mar 14 (16) $105
— 25 Feb 1774. 3 pp, folio. As Elector of Hannover, commission for Eberhard Berghoff as councillor of the chancery of Osnabrueck, issued in the name of his son Frederick, Duke of York, designated Bishop of Osnabrueck. star Apr 9 (996) DM280
— 28 Apr 1790. 2 pp, 4to. Authorizing payment to a regiment. sg Nov 6 (83) $175
— 18 Feb 1794. 3 pp, folio. Warrant to issue a license to George Griffin to change his name to Stonestreet. Repaired. Framed. Altman collection. pnNY Sept 13 (45) $350
— 6 Dec 1794. 1 p, folio. Commission for Samuel Sankey as Lieut.; partly ptd. Framed. Altman collection. pnNY Sept 13 (46) $300
— 1 Feb 1798. 1 p, folio. Commission for Robert Boyer as Adjutant in a cavalry regiment. Seal removed. Framed. Altman collection. pnNY Sept 13 (47) $275
— 12 Dec 1798[?]. 1 p, folio. Commission for George Forbes as 1st Lieut. in the Strathdon Volunteers. Framed. Altman collection. pnNY Sept 13 (44) $275
— 6 Mar 1800. 2 pp, folio. Pay order addressed to the tax collector for Barbados & the Leeward Islands in favor of Gen. George Hotham for salaries of servants of the Royal Princes. Countersgd by William Pitt. star Apr 9 (997) DM360
— May 1800. 2 pp, folio. Warrant authorizing George Hazelton MD to be kept on half-pay. Framed with engraved port & double-glazed. Altman collection. pnNY Sept 13 (48) $350
— 10 July 1802. 2 pp, folio. Warrant to affix the Great Seal to 2 instruments containing the ratification of the convention with the United States of 8 Jan 1802. With official copy of the convention, 8 pp, folio; last leaf frayed. C Dec 3 (267) £2,000 [Joseph]

— 27 Aug 1804. 1 p, folio. Commission for John Vicary as Capt. in the 72nd Highland Regiment of Foot. Framed. Altman collection. pnNY Sept 13 (49) $275
— [n.d.]. 2 pp, folio. List concerning costs of military establishments. Sgd twice; countersgd by William Pitt, twice. Lower margin trimmed. pnNY June 11 (16) $225

George III, King of England, 1738-1820
Ds, 14 Sept 1761. 1 p, 4to. Requesting the presence of Camilla, Countess Dowager of Tankerville, at the Queen's coronation. Fold tears. P Sept 24 (28) $650

George IV, King of England, 1762-1830
Collection of ALs & Ds, 24 May & 4 Sept 1827. 2 pp, 4to & folio. To Mr. Sturges Burnes. In 3d person, giving permission for Lady Grantham to "pass through the parks"; sgd GR. Warrant authorizing William Huskisson to countersign military commissions. C Dec 3 (271) £150 [Bristow]

Series of Ds s, 4 Ds s, 26 Oct 1811 to 2 Mar 1818, & 22 Jan 1827. 18 pp, folio. Warrants to affix the Great Seal to commissions for Mr. Lamb, Louis Casamajor, & the Earl of Clarcarty (as Prince Regent), & for Charles Henry Hall. pnNY June 11 (79) $550
— Series of 4 Ds s, 27 Mar 1812, & 3 Mar 1823 to 22 Sept 1826. 19 pp, folio. Warrants to affix the Great Seal to commissions for Mr. Lisbon (as Prince Regent), Algernon Percy, Mr. Hamilton, & G. H. Seymour. pnNY June 11 (78) $550
— Series of 3 Ds s, 12 Feb 1822 to 1 May 1826. 14 pp, folio. Warrants to affix the Great Seal to commissions for Mr. Autobus, R. F. Jameson, & E. C. Disbrowe. pnNY June 11 (76) $325
— Series of 4 Ds s, 4 Nov 1823 to 22 Sept 1826. 19 pp, folio. Warrants to affix the Great Seal to commissions for William Temple, F. R. Forbes, Richard Packerhan, & Charles Manners St. George. pnNY June 11 (77) $550

Ds s (2) 15 & 26 July 1813. 17 pp, folio. As Prince Regent, warrants to affix the Great Seal to a commission for Mr. Douglas & a treaty with Prussia. pnNY June 11 (80) $375
— Ds s (2) 27 Dec 1815. 16 pp, folio. As Prince Regent, warrants to affix the Great Seal to the ratification of treaties with the Grand Duke of Mecklenburgh-Strelitz & the Hanoverian Government; with copies of the treaties. C June 24 (43) £250 [Husken]

Ds, 31 July 1815. 15 pp, folio. As Prince Regent, warrant to affix the Great Seal to the ratification of the Commercial Convention with the USA; sgd at head. Countersgd by Earl Bathurst. Contemp endorsement, sgd R. L., concerning res-

ervation respecting St. Helena. Fold tear. pn Dec 11 (17) £460 [Buckell & Ballard]
— 4 Sept 1815. 7 pp, folio. As Prince Regent, warrant to affix the Great Seal to the appointment of Thomas Barclay as commissioner to effect the stipulations of the Treaty of Ghent; with a copy of the stipulations. C Dec 3 (269) £3,200 [Joseph]
— 31 Dec 1815. 33 pp, folio. As Prince Regent, warrant to affix the Great Seal "to the Ratification of a Treaty of Accession... to the Treaty concluded at Vienna, 18 May 1815"; sgd at head. Countersgd by Castlereagh. pn Dec 11 (18) £260 [Maggs]
— 18 Aug 1818. 6 pp, folio. As Prince Regent, warrant to affix the Great Seal to Castlereagh's & Wellington's Full Powers as negotiators at Aix-la-Chapelle; sgd at head. Countersgd by Earl Bathurst. pn Dec 11 (19) £300 [Maggs]
— 13 Oct 1819. 2 pp, folio. As Prince Regent, license for James Scarlett to plead in the case of Sir Manasseh Lopes. Sgd on verso by Viscount Sidmouth. With cut signature. Framed. Altman collection. pnNY Sept 13 (50) $350
— 1 Oct 1822. 4 pp, folio. Warrant to affix the Great Seal to a commission for Edward Ward to treat with Portugal & Brazil regarding the slave trade; with copy of the full power. Countersgd by George Canning. C Dec 3 (270) £140 [Maggs]
— 13 Sept 1823. 1 p, 4to. Vellum. Commission for Henry Canning as Consul General in Hamburg. Countersgd by George Canning. star Apr 9 (998) DM320
— 19 Jan 1827. 17 pp, 360mm by 240mm. Warrant to affix the Great Seal to the ratification of a convention with Portugal. sg Nov 6 (84) $500
— [n.d.]. 2 pp, folio. Granting a pension to Francois Serra. Sgd at top of 1st p. wa Oct 18 (104) $100

George IV, King of England, 1762-1830 —& Wellington, Arthur Wellesley, 1st Duke, 1769-1852

Ds, 26 June 1823. 1 p, folio. Appointment for William Raynes as 2d Captain in the Royal Artillery; engraved. With an engraving of George IV. Bullock collection. CNY Dec 19 (208) $55

George V, King of England, 1865-1936

[2 photographs, sgd, 1897 & 1921, 9cm by 14.5cm & 20.5cm by 12cm, sold at pnNY on 13 Sept 1986, lot 54, for $425.]

Ds, 1921. Appointment of Sir Percy Cox as High Commissioner of Iraq. Also sgd by Churchill as Sec of State for War. With anr 23 items relating to Cox, some sgd by the King, 1915 to 1935. S Dec 18 (249) £2,000

[F. A. S.]

Autograph endorsement, note of approval, sgd, on petition, initialled, by Stanley Baldwin, 30 Oct 1923. 1 p, 4to, submitting the name of Hugh Langton to the Vicarage of Christ Church, Kilndown. wa May 30 (443) $85

Photograph, sgd, 1933. 10cm by 14.5cm. Framed. Altman collection. pnNY Sept 13 (55) $180

George VI, King of England, 1895-1952

ALs, 25 Apr 1921. 2 pp, 8vo. To Messrs. Hugh Rees Ltd. Ordering a copy of Hammond's The Village Labourer. Sgd Albert. Framed with envelope & double-glazed. Altman collection. pnNY Sept 13 (57) $160

— 22 May 1933. 2 pp, 8vo. To Mr. Young. Giving permission to print part of his letter about Young's carpets in the Factory Magazine. Sgd Albert. Framed. Altman collection. pnNY Sept 13 (58) $170

Photograph, sgd, 1949. 21.5 by 16 inches. Framed. Altman collection. pnNY Sept 13 (59) $650

Germain de Caen

Ms, De la chasse. Bound with: Le Cesne de Coutances. De l'origine de la chasse. [c.1880]. 37 leaves & 19 leaves respectively, 215mm by 135mm, in half mor gilt. Jeanson Ms 203 SM Mar 1 (262) FF2,000

Gernsheim, Friedrich, 1839-1916

Series of 5 A Ls s, 1884 to 1897. 14 pp, 8vo. Recipients unnamed & to Herr Seligmann (1). About his relationship with Brahms & his own compositions. HN Nov 27 (2269) DM560

Gerry, Elbridge, Signer from Massachusetts

ALs, [n.d.]. 1 p, 4to. To John Mason. Fragment, contents not stated. Charlotte Parker Milne collection. wd Nov 12 (36) $100

Ds, 10 July 1810. 1 p, folio. Affirming Certificate, sgd as Gov. of Massachusetts. rf Nov 15 (7) $170

Gerstaecker, Friedrich, 1816-72

ALs, 5 July 1863. 2 pp, 8vo. To Karl Helmerding. Apologizing for not recognizing him at Coburg. star Apr 8 (79) DM460

Giardini, Felice, 1716-96

ALs, 4 July 1774. 1 p, 4to. To Dr. Burney. Arranging for a meeting to discuss a plan to found a musical academy in London. S May 22 (398) £750 [Riskin]

Gibbins, Robert
[Proof impressions of 52 wood-engraved illusts for Sweet Cork of Thee, 1951, 4 initialled, many captioned in pencil, various sizes, sold at S on 19 June 1987, lot 660, for £400 to Marks.]

Gide, Andre, 1869-1951
ALs, 16 Mar 1932. 1 p, 4to. Recipient unnamed. Sending congratulations on a successful operation. With autograph postcard; invitation for A. Silaeff. HN May 22 (3017a) DM440

Gigli, Beniamino, 1890-1957
Photograph, sgd, 1934. Postcard size. Half length. With related material. star Apr 9 (648) DM320

Gilbert, William Schwenck, 1836-1911
[A prompt-book of The Fortune Hunters, interleaved & marked-up [for 1st production, 27 Sept 1897?], including watercolor scene designs, sold at S on 27 Jan 1987, lot 897, for £500 to Quaritch.]

Gill, Eric, 1882-1940
Original drawings, 2 alternative designs, naked girl holding a cloak, sgd & dated 10 & 11 Sept [19]24, for Enid Clay's Sonnets and Verses; ink. Each captioned Dartmoor. 120mm by 101mm & 144mm by 101mm. Mtd in same frame. S Dec 5 (465) £1,300 [Piccadilly]

Giovanni da Bologna, 1529-1608
ALs, [1589]. 1 p, folio. To Giovanni Caccini. Regarding money due Caccini & referring to outstanding payment for two models. star Apr 8 (465) DM10,000

Giraudoux, Jean, 1882-1944
Autograph Ms, short story, Nouvelles Morts d'Elpenor, draft; [1926]. 30 pp, on rectos only; folio. Blue half mor, marbled bds. In blue & violet ink; with autograph revisions. S Nov 27 (366) £850 [Lee]

Gladstone, William E., 1809-98
Collection of 8 A Ls s (2 on postcards) & secretarial letter, 1885 to 1892. 24 pp, 8vo to 16mo. To P. W. Campbell. Political correspondence with his agent in Edinburgh. sg Apr 9 (72) $475

A Ls s (2), 11 & 13 Apr 1880. 6 pp, 8vo. To Lord Reay. Discussing the Austrian occupation of Bosnia & the Hercegovina. S Jan 27 (817) £110 [Subunso]

ALs, 26 May [18]78. 3 pp, 8vo. To Rev. J. N. House. Discussing the Christian hospital system. sg Apr 9 (73) $70

— 29 Dec 1886. 2 pp, 4to. To Lord Fitzgerald. Discussing R. L. Fowler's article on Thomas Pownall. With ALs by Lord Fitzgerald to Robert Ludlow Fowler, 3 Jan 1887, 3 pp, 12mo, about the article on Pownall. sg Nov 6 (86) $150

Glasgow Lecture Association
[A collection of c.120 letters, c.1895 to 1908, mostly to Robert L. Bremner concerning lectures for the Glasgow Lecture Association, sold at C on 3 Dec 1986, lot 272, for £550 to Des Pabilades.]

Gleim, Johann Wilhelm Ludwig, 1719-1803
ALs, 23 Feb 1774. 4 pp, 8vo. To [Heinrich Christian] Boie. Concerning advance payment for his Gedichte nach den Minnesaengern. JG Oct 2 (51) DM1,200

Gneisenau, August, Graf Neithardt von, 1760-1831
ALs, 3 Oct 1826. 3 pp, 4to. To Amalie von Helvig. Talking about the costs of travelling & his financial situation as owner of a big estate. With autograph by Field Marshal von dem Knesebeck. star Apr 9 (992) DM1,200

Ls, 24 June 1809. 1 p, folio. To Capt. von Rottenburg. Concerning problems with Rottenburg's brother. star Apr 9 (990) DM650

Godley, Sir Alexander John, 1867-1957
[The Army Message Books of Major [later Gen.] Godley written during the Siege of Mafeking & later, Sept 1899 to Oct 1900, containing copies of sgd autograph messages, 9 messages sgd by Robert Baden-Powell, 4 booklets, c.300 pp, 4to & 8vo, sold at S on 18 Dec 1986, lot 288, for £ 600 to Hackett.]

Godwin, William, 1756-1836
Series of 4 A Ls s, 27 Mar [n.y.], 12 Dec [n.y.], & [n.d.]. 4 pp, 4to. To John Robinson, Thomas Hill, & 2 unnamed recipients. About a variety of subjects. C June 24 (114) £350 [Quaritch]

Goebbels, Joseph, 1897-1945
ALs, 19 Apr 1940. 1 p, 4to. To Adolf Hitler. Birthday congratulations, wishing him victory & presenting him with a copy of the 1st ptg of Das Lied der Deutschen by Hoffmann von Fallersleben, 1 Sept 1841 (included). sg Apr 9 (74) $3,000

Photograph, sgd & inscr, 12 June [19]44. 9 by 11.25 inches. Inscr to Guenther Schwagermann. Mtd. sg Apr 9 (75) $750

Goering, Hermann, 1893-1946 —& Others
Ds, 21 Aug 1945. 1 p, folio. Certificate of discharge from the German Armed Forces by the Counter Intelligence Corps; in English & German. Sgd by Goering, Wilhelm Keitel, Alfred Jodl, Ernst Mantel & Karl Doenitz. Also sgd by Rolf M.

Wallenstein for the CIC. sg Nov 6 (87) $1,600

Goering, Hermann, 1893-1946. See: Hitler, Adolf & Goering

Goethe, Johann Wolfgang von, 1749-1832
[Biedermann, Woldemar von. - A collection of 124 letters & cards addressed to Biedermann, mostly relating to Goethe, with related material, sold at star on 8 Apr 1986, lot 99, for DM480.]
Autograph Ms, poem, beginning "Der Reiter kommt auf weissem Grund geritten", [c.1781?]. Draft, 4 lines; in pencil. star Apr 0 (01) DM0,500

Ms, essay, Dante, initialled three times & dated Sept 1826 & 9 Sept 1826. 6 pp, folio & 4to. Revised dictation, as ptd in Weimar Ed vol 42 (2d Ed), 70. FD Dec 2 (3193) DM28,000

ALs, 22 June 1781. 2 pp, 8vo. To Geheimrat J. F. von Fritsch. Concerning his admission to the Masonic Lodge at Weimar. VH Sept 12 (949) DM26,000

— 30 May 1823. 1 p, 4to. To Johann Michael Faerber. Requesting him to visit Dr. Koerner & to inquire about his health. Sgd G. star Apr 8 (89) DM10,000

Ls, 28 Mar 1819. 2 pp, 4to. To Johann Michael Faerber. Asking him to send some flower bulbs. star Apr 8 (86) DM4,400

— 14 Nov 1822. 1 p, folio. To Johann Michael Faerber. Notifying him that the student Metius has been admitted as assistant to the veterinary school. star Apr 8 (88) DM3,200

— 26 Jan 1827. 7 pp, 4to. To Adolf Friedrich Karl Streckfuss. Discussing Manzoni's Adelchi, problems of translation & the emergence of a world literature. With autograph subscription. Sophien-Ed vol 42, no 26 (draft). FD Dec 2 (3194) DM15,000

— 26 Nov 1827. 3 pp, 4to. To Adolf Friedrich Karl Streckfuss. Acknowledging receipt of two essays & commenting about 2 Italian works [by Tommaso Grossi]. With autograph subscription. Small repairs. Sophien-Ed vol 42, no 126 (draft). FD Dec 2 (3195) DM15,000

ANs, [n.d., c.1810?]; 1 p, 8vo. Recipient unknown. Requesting information about Saint Filippo Neri. JG Oct 2 (52) DM2,400

— 18 Apr 1817. 1 p, 4to. To [Karl Ludwig von Knebel?], "Im engsten Vertrauen. G." On verso contemp note stating this covering note was sent with letters by [Karl Friedrich] Zelter. star Apr 8 (85) DM2,600

Ns, [8 Nov n.y.]. 1 p, 70mm by 100mm (card). To Herr Foerster. Inviting him to lunch. C June 24 (148) £15,000 [Bender]

ADs, 24 Dec 1806. 1 p, 8vo. Receipt for an advance on his quarterly salary. star Apr 8 (84) DM3,200

Ds, 17 Oct 1794. 1 p, 8vo. Ptd receipt for fees due the Ilmenau mines; also sgd by Christian Gottlob Voigt. star Apr 8 (82) DM7,000

Goethe, Ottilie von, 1796-1872
Autograph Ms, 29 poems & passages in prose, 1826 to 1830. 92 pp, 4to. Stitched; red bds. Last leaf repaired. Partly autobiographical, often addressed to friends. With related material. star Apr 8 (91) DM4,200

— Autograph Ms, "Vermehrungsbuecher", 1 Sept 1852 to Oct 1872, 61 pp in 2 notebooks, 4to, & 424 pp in 3 notebooks, 8vo. Chronological Lists of art treasures bought or presented to her. With 2 further Mss, 93 pp & 61 pp, 4to; inventory of her collections. star Apr 8 (92) DM3,400

Series of 10 A Ls s, 24 Apr 1854 to 22 June 1872 & [n.d.]. 34 pp, 4to & 8vo. To Leo Graf Henckel von Donnersmarck & his wife Emma. Interesting family letters. With related material. star Apr 8 (93) DM1,100

Goethe, Walther von, 1818-85
Autograph Ms, diary, 17 Sept 1853 to 29 Nov 1854. 204 pp, 8vo. Half lea bdg. Chronicling his travels in Italy, his activities at Weimar & a journey to Franzensbad. star Apr 8 (94) DM2,200

ALs, 6 Jan 1875. 3 pp, 8vo. To Emma Graefin Henckel von Donnersmarck. Reporting about Christmas spent with his aunt Ulrike von Pogwisch at Schleswig. With related material. star Apr 8 (95) DM630

Goethe, Wolfgang von, 1820-83
ALs, 12 Nov 1854. 10 pp, 8vo. To Leo Graf Henckel von Donnersmarck. Sending congratulations on the birth of his son & criticizing a publication of letters exchanged between his grandfather & the Grandduke. Sgd W. star Apr 8 (96) DM850

Goffe, Edward. See: Massachusetts

Goldmark, Karl, 1830-1915
Autograph music, sketch leaf of part of the 2nd act of Die Koenigin von Saba, in full & short score, c.1875. 2 pp, folio. 33 bars in all; some revisions. In black ink. S Nov 28 (543) £1,300 [MacNutt]

ALs, 26 Sept 1876. 4 pp, 8vo. To an unnamed friend. Saying his quartet will take some time. star Apr 9 (650) DM220

— 5 Feb 1888. 3 pp, 8vo. Recipient unnamed. Stating that he has not written any music since last summer. star Apr 9 (651) DM200

GOLDSMITHS' GUILD

Goldsmiths' Guild
Ds, certificate of apprenticeship for Martin Sigmund, 6 Nov 1670. 1 p, 41cm by 50cm, vellum. Seal in wooden case. Issued by the goldsmiths' guild at Leipzig. JG Oct 2 (489) DM600

Gommer, Pierre de, Siegneur de Lusancy, fl.1594
Ms, De L'autourserie ou maniere de nourrir et dresser les oyseaulx de poing. Chalons-sur Marne, 1594 [but Paris, 20 Apr 1894] In the hand of Victor Bouton. 67 leaves, vellum, mor gilt by Chambolle-Duru. Jeanson Ms 213 SM Mar 1 (269) FF28,000

Goodall, John S.
Original drawings, (8), medieval scenes to illus Above and Below Stairs, 1983. In ink & watercolor. 4 Sgd. Various sizes. Framed. S June 19 (665) £600 [Kimpton]
— Original drawings, Fieldmouse House; 12 ink & watercolor drawings in book form, 145mm by 113mm. With cut-out doorways revealing part of next room. Text on versos, in pencil. S Dec 5 (466) £1,150

Gordon, Charles George, 1833-85
Collection of 3 A Ls s & AL, 26 Dec 1865 to 22 Apr 1876. 24 pp, 8vo. To "Nugent". About a variety of subjects. AL def. C Dec 3 (275) £380 [Wilson]
— Collection of 4 A Ls s, AL & autograph card, sgd, 1878 to 1884. 11 pp, 8vo. To Amy & Annie Grant. About the slave trade, African animals, his plans, & family news. With related material. pn Dec 11 (90) £340 [Wilson]
Series of 6 A Ls s, 19 June 1867 to [1882]. 30 pp, 8vo. To Sir Gerald Graham. About a variety of subjects. With photograph, 152mm by 112mm; seated in uniform. C Dec 3 (276) £1,100 [Sakmyster]
— Series of 10 Nov 1877 to 20 Dec 1881. 6 pp, 8vo. To his sister Augusta; explaining why he cannot go to Cairo. To "My dear Faulkner"; saying he has heard of the death of his sister & talking about the political scene in Egypt. C Dec 3 (277) £240 [Wilson]
ALs, 11 May 1855. 4 pp, 8vo. To his mother. Describing the siege of Sebastopol. S Jan 27 (871) £160 [Bristol]
— 6 June 1870. 2 pp, 12mo. To "Clarke". Requesting him to find employment for someone at the harbor at Galle. wa May 30 (390) $170
— 3 Oct 1872. 4 pp, 8vo. To Miss Browne. Discussing details of donations he will make. S Jan 27 (870) £80 [Lasalle]
— [c.1874]. 4 pp, 8vo. To Col. Nugent. Describing his proposed itinerary for his voyage down the Nile; including autograph sketch-map. With anr letter from Gordon to Nugent, incomplete. S Dec 18 (282) £500 [Collins]
— [c.1874]. 1 p, 8vo. To Col. Nugent. About slave-traders in the south of the Sudan. S Dec 18 (285) £250 [Maggs]
— 18 Oct 1875. 2 pp, 8vo. To Sir Samuel Baker. About his progress down the Nile & the discovery of Fola Falls; with small sketch plan of the falls. C Dec 3 (274) £500 [Joseph]
— 3 Oct 1877. 4 pp, 8vo. To Sir Charles Hartley. About Hartley's going to the Colonies, & expressing respect for the Khedive. Bullock collection. CNY Dec 19 (91) $300
— 23 Apr [1879]. 4 pp, 4to. To Col. Nugent. Reporting about his campaign against slave-traders; with autograph sketch-map of the Red Sea, Arabia & Abyssinia. S Dec 18 (283) £500 [Pollard]
— 14 June 1879. 2 pp, 8vo. To Col. Nugent. About a campaign against "the son of Zebehr", a slave trader. S July 24 (335) £600 [MacNutt]
— 20 Aug 1879. 2 pp, 4to. To Col. Nugent. Concerning the death of Suleiman & other slave traders, his admiration for the Khedive Ismail & his misgivings about the new Khedive Tewfik. S July 24 (336) £600 [MacNutt]
— 6 Mar 1884. 2 pp, 8vo. To his Aunt Amy. From Khartoum, expressing trust in the Lord. S Jan 27 (869) £150 [Ruskin]

Gorki, Maxim, 1868-1936
ALs, 1 Nov 1923. 1 p, 4to. To Baroness von Foelkersam. Thanking for a sketch dedicated to him & musing about searching for the good in man. HK Nov 7 (2234) DM750
Ls, 23 Oct 1907. 2 pp, 8vo. To Gino Righini. Regarding an Italian Ed of his story The Prison. In French; signature in Cyrillic script. S May 21 (249) £300 [Maggs]

Gospel Manuscripts
Ms, Gospel according to St. Luke, [Northern France, 9th/10th cent]. 1st leaf only, vellum, 360mm by 255mm. In calligraphic Carolingian minuscule in dark brown ink, rubricated in red. With illuminated initial & several initials in red. Framed & double glazed. FD June 11 (12a) DM32,000
— Ms, Gospels in Armenian. [Alt'amar, eastern Turkey, 1420]. 290 leaves (some lacking), 275mm by 180mm. Contemp tooled brown calf over wooden bds. In black bolorgir by the scribe Grigor. With full-page ornamental headpiece, 2 full-page miniatures, 8 full-page decorative canon tables & nine scenes from the life of Christ on 3 leaves. Flyleaf made of vellum sheet

written in 10th-cent uncial. S June 23 (138) £22,000 [Smith]
— Ms, Gospels in Church Slavonic. [Russia, 15th cent]. 181 leaves, 280mm by 210mm. Contemp wooden bds. In pale brown ink in a regular hand. With eight 7- to 9-line initials in colors & 4 very large headings in elaborate designs. S June 23 (69) £2,400 [Smith]
See also: Ethiopic Manuscripts
See also: Greek Manuscripts

Gosse, Sir Edmund W., 1849-1928
ALs, 21 Jan 1890. 9 pp, 4to. To J. M. Dent & Sons. Describing a box of letters, poems & other material of Thomas Beddoes in his possession. S July 23 (79) £250 [Quaritch]

Goulburn, Edward, 1787-1868
Ms, The Bluevial. A Satyrical Poem, [c.1805]. 120 pp, 4to. Roan bdg, worn. About the Royal Horse Guards. C June 24 (115) £170 [Burgess Browning]

Gould, Jay, 1836-92
Ls, 30 Aug 1873. 1 p, 8vo. To Onslow Stearns. Concerning affairs of the Fall River Line. Framed. wd Nov 12 (10) $200

Ds, 9 Sept 1878. 1 p, 8vo. Order for delivery of shares in the Union Pacific Railroad. Partly ptd. sg Apr 9 (76) $250

Gounod, Charles, 1818-93
Autograph music, score of a prayer, [n.d.]. 4 pp (numbered 5 - 8), 8vo. Words in English. wa May 30 (14) $210

ALs, 20 Aug 1872. 3 pp, 8vo. Recipient unnamed. Requesting him to send his suggestions for a libretto. star Apr 9 (653) DM320

— 27 [no month] 1876. 1 p, 4to. To Edouard Colonne. Praising the concerts arranged by him. sg Nov 6 (88) $130

— 23 Apr 1879. 2 pp, 8vo. To Madame Lynen. Presenting her with the score of his Polyeucte & thanking her for her hospitality. star Apr 9 (654) DM320

— 23 Mar [18]83. 2 pp, 8vo. To "Mon cher Henri". Reporting about recipient's son. C June 24 (191) £100 [American Museum of Hist. Docs.]

Goury de Champgrand, Charles Jean
Ms, Traite de venerie et de chasses, [18th cent]219pp, 285mm by 193mm, in 19th-cent half vellum. Jeanson Ms 141 SM Mar 1 (272) FF4,000

Grabbe, Christian Dietrich, 1801-36
ADs, 3 Jan 1827. 1 p, folio. Concerning the lawsuit of some students against the music teacher Neumann. JG Oct 2 (54) DM1,100

Grace, William Gilbert, 1848-1915
Collection of ALs & photograph, 14 Dec 1890. 1 p, 8vo, & 3 by 2.75 inches. To his friend Tinzel. About finding "one to answer the description of man wanted". S Jan 27 (794) £130 [Dupre]

ALs, 28 Aug 1903. 2 pp, 8vo. To G. W. Beldam. Concerning the London County Cricket Club. bba Nov 13 (159) £95 [Grosvenor]

Gracq, Julien
Series of 4 A Ls s, [n.d.]. 4 pp, 8vo. To Rene Magritte. About his writings & Magritte's paintings. 3 July 2 (974) £200 [Communaute de Francais de Belgique]

Gradual
— [Ferrara or Bologna, c.1460-80]. 1 leaf only, vellum, 530mm by 360mm. 8 lines each of text in a rounded gothic hand & of music on a 4-line red stave. With very large historiated initial & full illuminated border painted by Taddeo Crivelli or an artist in his circle. S June 23 (14) £4,800 [Kerr]

— [Northern France or Flanders, c.1475]. 132 leaves only, vellum, & 15 later leaves, paper, 253mm by 175mm. 16th cent panelled calf. With music on every page, mostly on 4-line staves; text in a gothic liturgical hand. With 46 small & 2 large initials in red or blue with penwork decoration. C June 24 (262) £1,800 [Ferrini]

— [Spain, c.1600]. 229 leaves, 52cm by 36cm. Vellum. Lea over wooden bds, def. In dark brown & red ink in several hands. With numerous red & violet initials with ornamental designs; some in black. VH Sept 12 (918) DM7,800

— [Peru, 1609]. Of Franciscan Use. 125 leaves & flyleaf, vellum, 564mm by 340mm. Contemp lea over wooden bds. With 7 lines each of text in brown ink in a rounded gothic hand & music on a 5-line red stave. With c.200 large calligraphic initials in penwork designs, c.100 large & 26 very large painted initials in red or blue, 2 with full length borders. Somewhat def. Written at the Franciscan convent of Santa Clara in Lima by Christobal Munos at the request of the abbess Justina Guevara. S June 23 (129) £3,000 [Ferrini]

— [Poland, 1632]. 14 leaves only, vellum, 605mm by 412mm. 8 to 10 lines of text in a calligraphic gothic hand & of music on a 4-line red stave. With 22 large initials in Celtic designs, 16 very large initials in baroque designs & half-page title with 4 lines of initials. Made by Father Blazeja Dereya for the Dominican Convent in Posen. S Dec 2 (26) £2,300 [Graton]

Graefe, Albrecht von, 1828-70
ALs, 11 May [18]66. 2 pp, 8vo. To an unnamed colleague. Giving advice about an operation. JG Oct 2 (211) DM900

Graf, Oskar Maria, 1894-1967
Ls, 20 May 1921. 1 p, 4to. To [Lulu von Strauss und Torney]. Saying the best time to see him in Munich will be in the morning. star Apr 8 (113) DM370

Grainger, Percy, 1882-1961
ALs, 9 Apr 1949. 1 p, 4to. To Eugene Weintraub. Discussing the publication of one of his works. S Nov 28 (544) £420 [MacNutt]
— 15 May 1949. 2 pp, 4to. To Eugene Weintraub. Regarding the musical notation in the proofs of Hill-song II. Repaired. S Nov 28 (545) £450 [Quaritch]

Granados, Enrique, 1867-1916
ALs, 3 Sept 1912. 3 pp, 8vo. To Ricardo Vines. Jocular letter requesting that he write to people in Lerida. S May 22 (601) £400 [Soley Ramon]

Grant, Ulysses S., 1822-85
[2 ptd checks, accomplished & sgd by Grant, 27 Mar 1866 & 5 Feb 1868, various sizes, drawn on the Washington branch of Jay Cooke & Co., sold at P on 29 Oct 1986, lot 60, for $ 1,600.]
[A collection of 5 autograph Mss, partly sgd, drafts of Presidential communications, 11 pp, 4to & 8vo, mostly in pencil, sold at P on 13 May 1987, lot 51, for $2,100.]
Autograph Ms, speech on the dedication of Lincoln's statue in Springfield, draft; 15 Oct 1874. 4 pp, 4to. Late 19th cent dark purple mor gilt bdg. CNY May 11 (60) $10.000
A Ls s (2), 24 July 1871 & 26 Feb 1872. 5 pp, 8vo. To Sec of the Treasury George S. Boutwell. Revoking an order concerning consolidation of districts in Alabama. Referring a request. P May 13 (53) $1,400
ALs, 18 Feb 1862. 1 p, 4to. To Gen. S. A. Hurlbut. Concerning the prevention of plundering. wa May 30 (221) $2,000
— 7 May 1863. 1 p, 8vo. Recipient unnamed. Ordering protection from further impressments of provisions by the Federal Army for [Mrs. Bagman?]. Framed with color print. wd Nov 12 (11) $800
— 31 May 1863. 1 p, 4to. To Admiral David D. Porter. Requesting him to send steamers to Memphis to bring reinforcements to Vicksburg. P Oct 29 (58) $2,000
— 7 May 1865. 1 p, 8vo. To Sec of War Edwin M. Stanton. Suggesting that public animals be sold. With brief endorsement by Stanton, approving the plan. P Oct 29 (59) $1,300
— 22 Sept 1870. 3 pp, 8vo. To Sec of the Treasury George S. Boutwell. Denouncing dissident Republicans in Missouri & suggesting the removal of a port collector. P May 13 (52) $2,100
— 9 Mar 1877. 2 pp, 8vo. To Postmaster Gen. James N. Tyner. Farewell letter. Repaired. Descendants of J. N. Tyner. P May 13 (56) $900
Collection of AL & ALs, 21 Mar 186[?] & 17 Jan [1868]. 4 pp, 8vo. Recipients unnamed. Inquiring about reasons for deposing Gen. R. Ransom, Jr. In 3d person, thanking for the offer of a box at Wall's Opera House. Bullock collection. CNY Dec 19 (92) $150
ANs, 28 Nov [18]80. Size & contents not stated. Bound opposite tp of 1st vol of his Personal Memoirs. NY 1886. 2 vols, 8vo; 1st Ed. Also bound in these vols, more than 100 plates, mostly engraved portraits, & more than 75 autographs by figures mentioned in the text. P Oct 29 (62) $2,700
Collection of 2 Ds s & autograph endorsement, sgd, 26 Feb 1875 to 26 Dec 1876. 2 pp, folio, & 2 pp, 8vo. Appointments for James Noble Tyner as Second Assistant Postmaster Gen & Postmaster Gen. 7 lines on verso of letter from Tyner to Grant, regarding a request by Nathaniel Page for an advance on his salary. With 2 Ls s by Ulysses S. Grant, Jr., on behalf of Mrs. Grant & the President. Descendants of J. N. Tyner. P May 13 (55) $550
Ds, 17 Sept 1851. 1 p, 4to. Receipt to Lieut. Col. G. Talcott for a sword. pnNY June 11 (18) $375
— 14 Apr 1869. 1 p, 16 by 21 inches. Appointment of Foster Cooper as Collector of Internal Revenue. wa Oct 18 (107) $220
— 7 July 1870. 1 p, 4to. Order to affix the US Seal to a pardon warrant. pnNY June 11 (19) $225
— 6 Aug 1873. 1 p, 4to. Order to affix the US Seal to a Postal Convention with Japan. P May 13 (54) $6,000
Cut signature, "U.S.Grant Bvt. Capt. 4th Infty", [28 Oct 1851]. Tipped into George W. Child's Recollections of General Grant. Phila., 1890. 16mo. wa May 30 (222) $130
Group photograph, [n.d.], oval print 10.5 by 13.5 inches in diameter. Showing Grant with his aides Adam Badeau & Orville E. Babcock. Sgd by Grant as Lieut. Gen. & by his aides. Photograph by Leon Van Loo. P Oct 29 (61) $3,500
Signature, on card. With reproduced sketch of Grant in 1863. Framed; 8.25 by 5.25 inches. wa May 30 (223) $190
— Anr, [c.1870]. On card, 1 p, 24mo. In purple ink. Was mtd. sg Sept 18 (111) $110

— HILL, DAVID B. - Ds, 23 July 1885. 1 p, folio.
As Gov. of New York, announcing Grant's
death. wa May 30 (224) $60

Grant, Ulysses S., 1822-85 —& Others
Signature, [1873/74]. In album also containing
51 signatures of members of his cabinet &
of Congress. 12mo; mor gilt bdg. pnNY
June 11 (82) $275

Grass, Guenter
Typescript, part of Ms (p 85) of his Das Treffen
in Telgte. With autograph revisions. Sgd in
margin. 1 p, folio. star Apr 8 (114) DM380

Graves, Robert
[A collection of papers by Graves, including 3 A Ls s to Michael [Horniman], 1970
to 1972, 3 typescripts with autograph
revisons, & mimeographed material, in a
deed box assigned for Graves's papers, sold
at S on 23 July 1987, lot 213, for £200 to
Maggs.]
Collection of 35 A Ls s & cards, sgd, 1943 to
1959. 55 pp, 8vo & 4to, & 4 cards. To Derek
Savage. Interesting letters concerning
Derek's & his own work. S Dec 18 (122)
£3,200 [Rota]
Series of 14 A Ls s, 1960 to 1971. 15 pp, folio.
To Harry Kemp. About a variety of
subjects. S Dec 18 (123) £1,200 [Rota]
ALs, 17 Mar 1962. 1 p, 4to. To Professor
Strutz. "I don't accept doctorates". sg Nov
6 (89) $110

Greek Manuscripts
Ms, Chronicle of biblical history. [Eastern
Mediterranean, late 18th cent]. Scroll, 56cm
by 1,365cm. In brown ink in a small Greek
minuscule script. With 562 miniatures in
full color, often interlinked with penwork
lines or multicolored vinestem scrolls. S
June 23 (70) £11,000 [Pervanas]
— Ms, compilation of medical & astrological
texts, Dec 1716. 82 leaves, 21cm by 16.5cm.
Contemp dark brown lea, worn; spine def.
Written in dark brown ink (some red) by
Gerasimos of Chios. With 1 ornamental
border, 1 small & 1 full-page drawing in
colors, all pasted down, from an older Ms
From the Convent of St. Catherine on
Mount Sinai. FD June 11 (36) DM16,000
— Ms, Gospel Book. [Jerusalem or Constantinople?, c.1125]. 173 leaves, vellum,
168mm by 125mm. Medieval bdg of wood-
en bds covered with textile in floral patterns. In brown ink in a regular Greek
minuscule script; 50 pp with glosses in
Latin in a 12th-cent European hand. With
full-page miniature of St. Mark in colors &
gold. Burdett-Coutts collection. S June 23
(44) £32,000 [Brown]
— Ms, Gospel Lectionary. [Constantinople?,

11th cent]. 319 leaves, vellum, 270mm by
218mm. Later bds, def. In dark brown ink
in a large Greek minuscule. With c.300
large illuminated initials. Some leaves
lacking, some def. Burdett-Coutts collection. S June 23 (41) £5,500 [Axia]
— Ms, Gospel Lectionary. [Eastern Mediterranean, c.1100]. 144 leaves only, vellum,
246mm by 200mm. Lacking bdg. In dark
brown ink in a large Greek minuscule. With
illuminated initials throughout, "a battered
but once very grand" Ms. Burdett-Coutts
collection. S June 23 (43) £4,000 [Axia]
— Ms, Gospel Lectionary. [Eastern Mediterranean, 13th or 14th cent]. 154 leaves only,
vellum, 232mm by 187mm. Contemp bdg
of thick wooden bds. In dark brown ink in
Greek minuscule script. With decorated
initials throughout in red, yellow & black,
10 decorated headpieces & 2 drawings.
Burdett-Coutts collection. S June 23 (48)
£3,500 [Axia]
— Ms, Gospel Lectionary. [Eastern Mediterranean, 14th cent]. 137 leaves, 238mm by
180mm. Lea covering from old tanned lea
bdg, lacking wooden bds. In brown ink in
Greek minuscule script by more than 1
scribe. With decorated initials throughout.
8 palimpsest leaves originally written in
Greek uncials, [8th or 9th cent]. Burdett-
Coutts collection. S June 23 (51) £4,800
[Mazza]
— Ms, Gospel Lectionary. [Eastern Mediterranean, 15th cent]. 288 leaves only, 323mm
by 258mm. Contemp thick wooden bds,
mostly bare. In brown ink in large rounded
Greek minuscule script. With decorated
initials throughout. Some leaves def.
Burdett-Coutts collection. S June 23 (52)
£2,800 [Axia]
— Ms, Gospel Lectionary. [Eastern Mediterranean, 15th cent]. 156 leaves & 2 flyleaves,
288mm by 195mm. Contemp wooden bds,
repaired. In brown ink in a regular Greek
minuscule script by several scribes. With
painted initials throughout & 6 large decorated headpieces. Inscr pasted to front
flyleaf dated 16 Feb 1477. Burdett-Coutts
collection. S June 23 (53) £8,000 [Pervanas]
— Ms, Hagiasmatarion, [16th cent]. 27 leaves,
13.4cm by 9.6cm. Waxed paper. New
brown lea bdg incorporating fragment of
old bdg. Decorated initials & 3 ornamental
borders. From the Convent of St. Catherine
on Mount Sinai. FD June 11 (38)
DM12,000
— Ms, Hesperinos. [16th cent]. 34 leaves,
13.5cm by 9cm. Brown sheepskin. Written
in black & red ink by the deacon
Ioannikios. Initials in red throughout; 2
colored ornamental borders. From the
Convent of St. Catherine on Mount Sinai.

GREEK MANUSCRIPTS

FD June 11 (34) DM8,000
— Ms, Horologion & Menologion. [Eastern Mediterranean, 1528]. 358 leaves, 100mm by 69mm. 18th-cent dark red mor profusely gilt. In black ink in a small calligraphic Greek miniscule by Georgios of Naupaktos. Many small initials in red. Burdett-Coutts collection. S June 23 (57) £2,600 [Pervanas]
— Ms, Hymnal. [Eastern Mediterranean, 18th cent]. 294 leaves, 150mm by 105mm. Contemp blindstamped calf. In black ink with 9 lines of text in a small hand between lines of music in red & black. With decorated initials throughout. 1 leaf torn. Ownership inscr dated 1792. Burdett-Coutts collection. S June 23 (67) £1,400 [Axia]
— Ms, list of the dead of the Convent of St. Catherine on Mount Sinai. [16th & 17th cent]. 57 leaves, 14cm by 10cm. Contemp brown blindstamped lea. List of names in Arabic at end. FD June 11 (39) DM12,000
— Ms, Liturgies of St. John Chrysostom & St. Basil. [Eastern Mediterranean, 16th or early 17th cent]. 80 leaves, 203mm by 135mm. Contemp blindstamped orange-brown lea over wooden bds. With painted initials throughout in red & 3 decorated headpieces. Ownership inscr of Ioannikios Ierodiakonos. Burdett-Coutts collection. S June 23 (62) £2,000 [Axia]
— Ms, Liturgies of St. John Chrysostom & St. Basil. [Eastern Mediterranean, c.1800]. 58 leaves only, 244mm by 170mm. Bdg of pastebds covered with vellum leaf from a Ms in Greek miniscule script, c.1100. In a flamboyant Greek script. With c.40 very large decorated initials in red & 3 full-page decorations. Some leaves def. S June 23 (71) £600 [Axia]
— Ms, Liturgy of St. John Chrysostom, & other texts. [Eastern Mediterranean, 1623-24]. 104 leaves, 210mm by 152mm. Contemp blindstamped black lea bdg. In black & red ink in a flamboyant Greek cursive script. With c.40 large zoomorphic & decorated initials in full colors or penwork, 4 decorated headpieces (1 pasted in), & full-page drawing of a priest. Scribal prayer on f.63. Burdett-Coutts collection. S June 23 (63) £2,400 [Axia]
— Ms, Menaion, from Sept to Feb. [Eastern Mediterranean, c.1175]. 260 leaves only, vellum, 334mm by 223mm. Lacking bdg. In dark brown ink in a small Greek miniscule script. With initials throughout in carmine, some musical neumes in red, & drawing of a saint. 2 frames left blank for miniatures. Somewhat def. Burdett-Coutts collection. S June 23 (46) £3,500 [Axia]
— Ms, Octoechos. [North-west Greece, probably Janina, 16th cent]. 218 leaves only, 215mm by 145mm. Lacking bdg. In dark brown & red ink in a Greek miniscule script. With initials throughout in red. Dampstained; some leaves detached. From the Monastery of St. John the Baptist on the island in the lake of Ioannina. Burdett-Coutts collection. S June 23 (60) £1,300 [Axia]
— Ms, Octoechos, Triodion, & other liturgical texts. [Eastern Mediterranean, 16th or early 17th cent]. 214 leaves only, 282mm by 212mm. Contemp dark brown lea over wooden bds. In a regular Greek miniscule script by more than 1 scribe. With initials throughout in red & some decorated headpieces. Burdett-Coutts collection. S June 23 (61) £2,200 [Axia]
— Ms, Orologion. [Eastern Mediterranean, c.1100]. 196 leaves, vellum, 105mm by 88mm. Lacking bdg. In brown ink in a small "Perlschrift" miniscule. With initials throughout in red & 8 decorated headpieces. Lacking some leaves; generally somewhat def. Burdett-Coutts collection. S June 23 (42) £2,800 [Axia]
— Ms, St. John Damascene, Michael Psellus, & other patristic texts. [Eastern Mediterranean, 15th or 16th cent]. 99 leaves only, 178mm by 122mm. Black lea bdg, very def. In black ink in a Greek miniscule script by at least 2 scribes. Some headings & small initials in red. Burdett-Coutts collection. S June 23 (55) £500 [Axia]
— Ms, The Grammar of Manuel Chrysoloras, & other grammatical texts. [Greece, 15th cent]. 97 leaves, vellum, 188mm by 122mm. Contemp blind-stamped lea over wooden bds, def. In brown ink in a small Greek miniscule script. With initials throughout in red. Given by the Priest Theodore to the monastery at Meteora. Palimpsest; orig written in "Perlschrift". [2d half of 11th cent]. Burdett-Coutts collection. S June 23 (54) £3,800 [Quaritch]
— Ms, Theotokarion. [Eastern Mediterranean, 13th or 14th cent]. 248 leaves only, vellum, 142mm by 103mm. 1 cover only of bdg of bare wooden bds. In brown ink in small Greek miniscule script. With c.50 large painted initials, 7 large decorated headpieces, & full-page decoration on f.94. Burdett-Coutts collection. S June 23 (49) £3,200 [Axia]
— Ms, Theotokarion. [Eastern Mediterranean, 1st half of 14th cent]. 172 leaves only, vellum, 200mm by 147mm. Contemp dark brown lea over wooden bds. In brown ink in Greek miniscule script. With initials in red. Many early side notes & other signs of much use. Burdett-Coutts collection. S June 23 (50) £3,800 [Pervanas]

— Ms, Treatises on logic, rhetoric, etc., including Aristotle, Michael Psellus, & others. [Eastern Mediterranean, 17th cent]. 261 leaves, 147mm by 102mm. Mottled sheepskin bdg. In very small Greek minuscules by several scribes. With some initials in red & some mathematical & other diagrams. Probably several booklets bound together. Burdett-Coutts collection. S June 23 (65) £3,200 [Axia]

— JOHANNES CHRYSOSTOMUS, SAINT. - Ms, Homilies. [Eastern Mediterranean, 16th cent]. 367 leaves only, 303mm by 205mm. Lacking bdg. In brown ink in a Greek minuscule script. With initials throughout in red. Stained. Burdett-Coutts collection. S June 23 (58) £1,400 [Axia]

— JOHN CLIMACUS, SAINT. - Ms, Ladder of Paradise. [Eastern Mediterranean, c.1300]. 205 leaves only, vellum, 210mm by 155mm. Lacking bdg. In black ink in Greek minuscule script. With initials throughout in red or black & drawing of a ladder. Very worn. Burdett-Coutts collection. S June 23 (47) £1,700 [Axia]

— MANUEL MALAXOS. - Nomimon (manual of canon law). [Eastern Mediterranean, 1651]. 228 leaves, 194mm by 137mm. 19th-cent mottled calf gilt. In red & black ink by Konstantinos Amartolos for Ieromonachos Dositheos. With painted initials throughout in red & decorated headpiece. Some inscriptions. Burdett-Coutts collection. S June 23 (64) £1,400 [Axia]

— SYMEON METAPHRASTES. - Ms, Menologion. [Eastern Mediterranean, 16th cent]. 93 detached leaves only, 296mm by 218mm. In wrap. In dark brown ink in a neat Greek minuscule script. With decorated initials throughout & 3 large painted zoomorphic initials. Stained. Text loss at inner edges. Burdett-Coutts collection. S June 23 (59) £320 [Axia]

Greeley, Horace, 1811-72

ALs, 16 Dec 1856. 2 pp, 12mo. To S. J. Morris. About a speaking engagement. Fold splits. wa May 30 (35) $60

Green, Duff, 1791-1875

Document, Sept 1840. 1 p, folio. Selling 5 houses on Capitol Hill for $3,000 to Benjamin E. Green. Sgd by James H. Hamilton on behalf of Duff Green. wa Oct 18 (73) $110

Green, Winifred

Original drawings, (27), to illus Charles & Mary Lamb's Poetry for Children, 1898. In ink; some tinted. 18 initialled. Mostly 255mm by 140mm. Archives of J. M. Dent & Son. S June 19 (801) £1,300 [Beetles]

— Original drawings, (39), to illus Charles & Mary Lamb's Mrs. Leicester's School, 1899. In ink; 17 handcolored. Various sizes. With proofs of tp. Archives of J. M. Dent & Son. S June 19 (800) £2,000 [Beetles]

Greenaway, Kate, 1846-1901

Original drawings, 11 pen-&-ink illusts for Kate Greenaway's Birthday Book for Children. L, [1880?]. Various sizes. Mtd on tissue sheets inserted into a copy of the book. Gimbel Family collection. P June 18 (76) $2,500

— Original drawings, complete set of 16 watercolor illusts for Mary Annette Russell's The April Baby's Book of Tunes, 1900; each initialled. With calligraphic tp, Ms music & verses of nursery rhymes. Blue mor gilt bdg; large 4to. S Dec 5 (469) £50,000 [Penny Cyllin]

ALs, [1 Mar 1887]. 2 pp, 8vo. To Miss Jenner. Saying she has nothing to lend her. Framed with a reproduction of a drawing. wa May 30 (391) $260

Greene, Nathanael, 1742-86

ALs, 13 Aug 1780. 4 pp, folio. To Joseph Webb. About the military situation & his controversy with Congress. CNY May 11 (62) $1,800

— 9 Jan 1781 [1782]. 4 pp, 4to. To Gen. Anthony Wayne. Draft, giving instructions for Wayne's expedition into Georgia. P May 13 (57) $1,800

Greene, William, 1731-1809

Ls, 7 Jan 1779. 2 pp, 4to. To George Clinton. Concerning the shortage of grain & flour in Rhode Island. S July 24 (394) £320 [Apfelbaum]

Gregory I, Saint, Pope

Ms, Dialogues, in Latin, [Paris?, c.1250-80]. 92 leaves, vellum, 162mm by 114mm. 18th cent calf. In dark brown ink in a small gothic bookhand. With decorated initials throughout in red or blue & 4 very large initials with elaborate penwork in red & blue. S Dec 2 (41) £2,900 [Percival]

— Ms, Libri IV dialogorum. [France, probably Paris, 1250-80]. 92 leaves, vellum, 162mm by 118mm. 18th cent dark calf; spine gilt. In dark brown ink in small gothic bookhand. With initials in red & blue & 4 large illuminated initials. FD June 11 (3) DM15,000

Gretchaninoff, Alexandre, 1864-1956

Autograph quotation, 2 bars from a Russian song, sgd & dated 13 May 1936. 1 p, 8vo (lettercard). star Apr 9 (655a) DM360

Grey, Edward, Viscount Grey of Fallodon, 1866-1933
Collection of c.190 A Ls s & memoranda, sgd, 15 Dec 1905 to 29 June 1910. Over 400 pp, mostly 8vo. To John Morley, Sec of State for India. As Foreign Sec, relating to foreign affairs, the Anglo-Russian entente, the situation in Asia, etc. Including some autograph notes by Morley & further related material. S Dec 18 (257) £3,000 [Pollard]

Grey, Zane, 1875-1939
[A collection of 2 postcard photographs, sgd, & 12 items relating to his financial affairs, checks, check registers, & protest documents, 1923 to 1938, sold at sg on 9 Apr 1987, lot 78, for $250.]
A Ls s (2), 10 June & 2 Sept [1932]. 3 pp, 4to. To [Edward] Cave. Sending samples of literature received. Giving specifications for fishing rods. Both initialled. wa May 30 (386) $190
— A Ls s (2), 24 Sept & 26 Oct [1932]. 3 pp, 4to. To [Edward] Cave. Mostly about fishing rods. wa May 30 (387) $110
— A Ls s (2), 12 Mar & 6 Sept [1933]. 3 pp, 4to. To [Edward] Cave. Regarding the Montague fishing rods. Both initialled. wa May 30 (389) $290
ALs, 17 Nov [1932]. 2 pp, 4to. To [Edward] Cave. Complaining about being sent the wrong fishing rods. wa May 30 (388) $210

Grieg, Edvard, 1843-1907
Autograph Ms, concert program, [1898?]. 3 pp, 4to & 8vo. In German. Including autograph Ms of the German text of his song Ragna & a list of songs with Norwegian titles. S May 22 (403) £520 [MacKinnon]
ALs, 4 Feb [18]86. 1 p, 8vo. To the pbr Hansen. Asking for an account of payments due him. S May 22 (402) £320 [MacKinnon]
— 31 Mar 1886. 1 p, 8vo; on postcard. To Robert Fischhof. Hoping to meet him in Vienna the following winter. S May 22 (603) £350 [University of Oslo]
— 23 Mar 1891. 3 pp, 8vo. To Also Noseda. Insisting on a bigger orchestra for a concert. star Apr 9 (656) DM1,200
— 1 Feb [18]97. 3 pp, 8vo. To a singer [Maria Brema?]. About songs to be performed at a concert. In German. Was mtd. S May 22 (405) £580 [Uni. Lib. Oslo.]
— 30 Dec [18]98. 4 pp, 8vo. To the director of a concert-management in Rome. About a concert to be given in 1899. In German. S May 22 (404) £580 [Amadeus]
— 13 Oct 1906. 1 p, 8vo. To an unnamed concert agent in England. Declining his proposals, having completed arrangements for his visit to England already. star Apr 9

(657) DM650
Ls, 1 Jan 1903. 3 pp, 12mo. Recipient unknown. Discussing a concert program. In French. sg Nov 6 (91) $500

Grimm, Jacob, 1785-1863
Autograph Ms, critical review of Hoepker's essay Ueber den Namen Westfalen, [n.d.]. 4 pp, 4to. With revisions. Fold tears. star Apr 8 (344) DM12,500
ALs, 8 Mar 1822. 2 pp, 4to. To Ludwig Tross. Sending some books & mentioning his search for old Germanic Mss. HK Nov 7 (2235) DM3,800
— 15 May 1827. 1 p, 4to. To the architect Wolff. Informing him that a book is now available at the Goettingen library. HK Nov 7 (2236) DM750
— 14 Jan 1828. 1 p, 4to. To Ritter Heeren at Goettingen. Thanking for a communication & commenting on Russian literature. HK Nov 7 (2237) DM2,000
— 5 July 1846. 2 pp, 8vo. To an unnamed friend. Concerning the subject for a prize essay. JG Oct 2 (213) DM3,200

Grimm, Jacob, 1785-1863 —& Grimm, Wilhelm, 1786-1859
Ds, 25 July 1837. 1 p, 4to. Certifying that the student Wellerding attended their lectures. With anr 4 certificates by different professors. JG Oct 2 (55) DM530

Grimm, Wilhelm, 1786-1859
Series of 45 A Ls s, [7 Apr] 1817 to 22 Mar 1835. 132 pp, 4to & 8vo. To David Theodor August Suabedissen. Interesting & lively correspondence with personal news, political discussions, comments about literature & the arts, etc. star Apr 8 (345) DM120,000
ALs, 14 Sept 1831. 2 pp, 4to. To Karl Georg von Raumer. Reporting about his move to Goettingen. star Apr 8 (346) DM5,500
— 18 Oct 1832. 1 p, 4to. To an unnamed official. Confirming that he is still in possession of a Ms. HK Nov 7 (2238) DM1,400
— 23 Aug 1843. 2 pp, 8vo. To Heinrich Asmus. About illusts for his Ed of fairy tales. HN May 22 (3020a) DM920
See also: Grimm, Jacob & Grimm

Gropius, Walter, 1883-1969
Ls s (2), 16 Jan 1919 & 10 Feb 1923. 3 pp, 4to. To John Schikowski. About an article to be ptd in the magazine Vorwaerts. As director of the Bauhaus, notifying him of a projected exhibition & requesting his cooperation. FD June 11 (3507) DM450
Ls, 10 Feb 1923. 2 pp, 4to. To John Schikowski. As director of the Bauhaus, notifying him of a projected exhibition & requesting his cooperation. With anr Ls to

Schikowski, 16 Jan 1919. star Apr 8 (466) DM500

Grossmith, Weedon
Original drawings, (32), to illus George & Weedon Grossmith's The Diary of a Nobody, 1892. In ink. Many captioned; mostly initialled. Various sizes. With printer's markings. Archives of J. M. Dent & Son. S June 19 (802) £10,000 [V & A]

Grosz, George, 1893-1959
Collection of 2 A Ls s, 2 Ls s & autograph postcard, sgd, 21 July 1954 to 30 June 1959. 6 pp, 4to & 8vo. To Walter G. Oschilewski. Thanking for his book, requesting a copy of his article, arranging a meeting, etc. In German. With copies of Oschilewski's letters to Grosz. C June 24 (192) £200 [L'Autographe]

Groth, Klaus, 1819-99
Autograph transcript, poem, Winters Ende, 6 lines. Sgd & dated 29 Feb 1884. 1 p, 8vo. star Apr 8 (116) DM450
ALs, 9 Nov 1870. 4 pp, 8vo. Recipient unnamed. About the dedication of part 2 of his Quickborn to the Crown Prince of Prussia & commenting about the times. star Apr 8 (117) DM1,100

Guderian, Heinz, 1888-1854
Ls, 8 June 1951. 1 p, 4to. To a former officer of the general staff. Expressing his hope that recipient's book may save the honor of the general staff. star Apr 9 (1285) DM270

Guilbert, Yvette, 1866-1944
Series of 6 A Ls s, 1902 to 1932. 9 pp, various sizes. To various recipients. About her press reception in Germany & financial or personal matters. With 2 ptd portraits. sg Apr 9 (79) $100

Gurk, Paul, 1880-1953
Series of 13 autograph postcards, sgd, 31 May 1931 to 14 Oct 1933. To H. Draws-Tychsen. Mostly about his problems to find a pbr for his works. HN May 22 (3021) DM540

Gustav II Adolf, King of Sweden, 1594-1632
Ls, 19 Nov 1616. 1 p, folio. To a steward. Granting grain for the support of Peder Joensson. Repaired. star Apr 9 (1240) DM850

Gustedt, Jenny von, 1811-90. See: Pappenheim, Jenny von

Gutzkow, Karl Ferdinand, 1811-78
ALs, 15 Apr 1843. 5 pp, 8vo. To [Franz Dingelstedt]. Protesting against a newspaper article & saying he will not visit Vienna. star Apr 8 (119) DM650

Gyrowetz, Adalbert, 1763-1850 —& Umlauff, Michael, 1781-1842
Ds, [1814/1825]. 1 p, 4to. Contract regarding the sale of their ballet Lodoiska to S. A. Steiner & Co. Text in the hand of Tobias Haslinger. star Apr 9 (659) DM650

H

Haber, Fritz, 1868-1934
Ls, 11 Mar 1924. 2 pp, 4to. To Kasimir Fajans. Answering a question regarding one of his earlier studies. star Apr 8 (347) DM550

Hadfield, James
Autograph transcript, verses, sgd. Written on the death of "little Dick my partner dear (kill'd Octr 3rd 1806)". 1 p, 8vo. C June 24 (44) £160 [Burgess Browning]

Haertling, Peter
Autograph Ms, poem, Weise Moeglichkeit. Sgd, inscr & dated 4 Oct 1981. 1 p, folio. star Apr 8 (125) DM260

Hagedorn, Friedrich von, 1708-54
ALs, 16 Dec 1750. 3 pp, 4to. To Nicolaus Dietrich Giseke. Interesting letter about Giseke's situation at Braunschweig, Voltaire, Klopstock, & news from Hamburg. Kuenzel collection. star Apr 8 (120) DM2,600

Hagelstange, Rudolf, 1912-84
Autograph Ms, poem, Memento; three 4-line stanzas. 1 p, 8vo. star Apr 8 (121) DM480

Hahn, Otto, 1879-1968
Ns, 13 Sept 1958. 1 p, 8vo (lettercard). Recipient unnamed. Thanking for reports from the British press. With autograph additions. star Apr 8 (348) DM520

Hahn, Reynaldo, 1875-1947
ALs, [n.d.]. 2 pp, 8vo. To [Maurice Donnay]. Regarding his defense of Hahn in an article. star Apr 9 (660b) DM250

Haiti
Ms, Le Philantrope revolutionnaire ou l'Hecatombe d'Haiti. Drame historique en 4 actes... Copy dated 1 Jan 1811; 70 pp, 8vo. 7 watercolors, somewhat def. Cloth backed vellum bdg. bba Nov 13 (174) £600 [Henderson]

Halevy, Jacques Fromental Elie Levy, 1799-1862
ALs, [n.d.]. 1 p, 8vo. To Maurice Schlesinger. Requesting a copy of the score of Meyerbeer's Robert der Teufel for Mademoiselle Ottmann. star Apr 9 (661) DM240

HALEY

Haley, Bill —& Others
Concert program, [c.1955]. 16 pp, 4to. Illus with photographs. Sgd by Haley & "the Comets" Johnny Grande, Al Rex, Franny Beecher, Rudy Pompelli & Ralph Jones. wa May 30 (488) $160

Hall, Lyman, Signer from Georgia
Ds, 20 Sept 1783. 1 p, 8vo. Certificate that Capt. Gideon Booker is entitled to 300 acres of land. Inlaid. Charlotte Parker Milne collection. wd Nov 12 (37) $650

Hamilton, Alexander, 1739-1802
[A Ms, notes on lectures on midwifery delivered by Hamilton at Edinburgh, [n.d.], c.500 pp, 8vo, sold at S on 27 Jan 1987, lot 910, for £500 to Wellcome.]

Hamilton, Alexander, 1757-1804
Autograph Ms, notes for an insurance case arising from French seizure of an American vessel carrying contraband, 16 Aug 1800. 4 pp, 4to. sg Apr 9 (80) $375
Ls, 27 Aug 1790. 2 pp, 4to. To William Ellery. About a light house in Rhode Island & imports. wa May 30 (37) $500
ADs, 19 June 1792. 1 p, 8vo. Draft on Benjamin Walker for $300. P May 13 (58) $650

Hamilton, Clive, 1898-1963. See: Lewis, Clive Staples

Hamilton, Lady Emma, 1761?-1815
ALs, 27 Sept 1791. 3 pp, 4to. To Mrs. Dickensen. Praising her husband & expressing her happiness in her marriage. With ALs by Sir William Hamilton, 4 Sept 1793. P June 18 (78) $1,000
— [15 Apr 1801]. 1 p, 4to. To Lady Malmesbury. Reporting about Nelson's victory at the Battle of Copenhagen. S July 24 (340) £2,800 [May]
Ls, [c.1813]. 24 pp, folio. To [the Prince Regent, later George IV?]. Petition citing her services to her country & requesting financial help. Last p stained. With 2 engraved portraits. P Dec 15 (47) $2,100

Hamilton, Paul, 1762-1816
Autograph endorsement, sgd, 7 lines at bottom of Ls, 6 June 1812, from David Porter; concerning continuance of a surgeon. Repaired. rf Mar 14 (17) $55

Hamlin, Hannibal, 1809-91
ALs, 29 Mar 1856. 1 p, 8vo. To Ed. Partridge. As Senator, promising to present Partridge's petition. With port photograph. wa Oct 18 (18) $75
Franking signature, 2 Jan [18]65. As Vice President, on cover to Maine. rf Nov 15 (31) $105

AMERICAN BOOK PRICES CURRENT

— Anr, [18 Feb n.y.]. rf Mar 14 (86) $70

Hammett, Dashiell
A Ls s (2), [n.d.]. 2 pp, 8vo. To Miss Wolff. About a secretarial position. One sgd with initials. O May 12 (84) $850

Hamon & Veremond. See: Legenda...

Hamsun, Knut, 1859-1952
Autograph Ms, novel, Men livet lever, c.1933. 213 pp, 8vo. With autograph revisions & corrections. S May 21 (252) £28,000 [Uppstrom]
Photograph, sgd & inscr, 11 Oct 1932. 154mm by 107mm. Inscr to Knut Arens. Mtd. star Apr 8 (123) DM220

Hancock, John, 1737-93
Ls, 31 Oct 1783. 2 pp, 4to. To George Clinton. Notifying him of the appointment of commissioners to ascertain the dividing line between New York & Massachusetts. S July 24 (395) £1,640 [Joseph & Sawyer]
Ds, 27 Apr 1771. 1 p, 8vo. Endorsement on bill of exchange. wa May 30 (133) $800
— 1 July 1781. 1 p, 330mm by 296mm. Commission for Caleb Keep as captain in a Massachusetts militia regiment; partly ptd. Countersgd by John Avery. Repaired. sg Nov 6 (269) $1,400
— 26 Aug 1790. 1 p, folio. Appointment for Lucius Allis as Capt. in the militia. Repaired. Framed with 2 portraits. pnNY June 11 (83) $1,300
Cut signature, [n.d.]; 3 by 6 inches. With Massachusetts seal. rf Mar 14 (18) $450
— Anr, as Gov. of Massachusetts. With blind-stamped state seal. wa May 30 (134) $750
Signature, [n.d.]. On vertical p with impressed seal, size not stated. rf Nov 15 (8) $400
— WADSWORTH, JEREMIAH. - AD, 24 Sept 1777. 1 p, 8vo. Receipt for "Oats for President Hancocks Horses". Sgd by George Haas. sg Nov 6 (270) $120

Hancock, John, 1737-93 —& Others
Ls, 26 Mar 1776, 1 p, 4to. To Capt. John Barry. Giving instructions for the departure of the brig Lexington. Letter in the hand of John Alsop; sgd by the 7 members of the Marine Committee of the Continental Congress. P May 13 (59) $16,000

Hancock, John, 1737-93 —&
Adams, Samuel, Signer from Massachusetts
[A copy of a resolution of the House of Representatives & the Senate of Massachusetts that Adams is accountable for certain sums of money, 6 Mar 1782, 1 p, folio, with attestation by John Avery, sold at wd on 12 Nov 1986, lot 38, for $375.]

Hand, Edward, 1744-1802
Autograph endorsement, 16 Aug 1782. 1 p, folio. 21 words, sgd. On verso of a pay order to the Treasurer of Connecticut for money due soldiers in 2 regiments for their service. sg Nov 6 (325) $100

Handel, George Frederick, 1685-1759
Ms, oratorio, Samson; full score [England, c.1750]. Over 300 pp, unpaginated, in 3 vols, folio. Contemp calf. In contemp scribal hand, written in brown ink on up to 10 staves per p. Bookplate of Henry Sanford. S Nov 28 (547) £750 [MacNutt]

Hardee, William Joseph, 1815-73
Telegram, 19 Jan 1865. 1 p, 4to. To Jefferson Davis. Requesting soldiers & supplies to hold Charleston. Retained Ms copy. Silked. wa May 30 (226) $230

Hardenberg, Karl August, Fuerst von, 1750-1822
ALs, 15 Feb 1819. 1 p, 8vo. To an unnamed count. Sending a bond of the late Kingdom of Westfalia. star Apr 9 (1008) DM350

Ls s (2), 31 Dec 1815 & 25 May 1816. 2 pp, folio. To Generallandschaftsrepraesentant von Goldfus. Concerning war damages to his estates. With related material. star Apr 9 (1007) DM240

Harding, Warren G., 1865-1923
Ls, 16 July 1920. 1 p, 8vo. Recipient unnamed. Thanking for a letter of congratulations (included). On Senate stationery. rf Nov 15 (9) $210

— 7 May 1921. 1 p, 4to. To his tenant Millard Hunt. Declining responsibility for requested repairs. sg Apr 9 (81) $425

Ds, 15 Sept 1897. 1 p, 8vo. Certificate that a notice appeared in 5 issues of The Marion Star. Partly ptd, accomplished in Harding's hand. Sgd twice. wa May 30 (99) $230

— 27 Dec 1921. 1 p, folio. Consular appointment of Thomas M. Wilson. Countersgd by Sec of State Charles E. Hughes. wa Oct 18 (111) $300

Autograph endorsement, on check made out to Harding for $300, from the Harding Publishing Company; 30 Oct 1915. 1 p, 7 by 8.25 inches. Framed. wa Oct 18 (19) $80

Photograph, sgd & inscr, [n.d.]. 9 by 7 inches; sheet size 12 by 9 inches. Sepia photograph, inscr to the western New York newspaper The Express, in white ink. Laid down. wa Oct 18 (112) $320

Hardouin, Seigneur de Fontalnes-Guerin
Ms, Tresor de venerie. [Paris, 1837] In the hand of A. Veinant. 67 leaves, vellum (a few paper leaves), 174mm by 118mm, in mor gilt by Bauzonnet. Jeanson Ms 199 SM Feb 28 (229) FF12,000

Hardwicke, Sir Cedric, 1893-1964
Series of 6 A Ls s, 1935 & 1939. 19 pp, various sizes. To "Jim" [his business manager?]. Relating to his work & future plans. sg Nov 6 (92) $150

Hardy, Oliver, 1892-1957. See: Laurel, Stan & Hardy

Hardy, Thomas, 1840-1928
A Ls s (2), 15 Jan & 26 Apr 1908. 5 pp, 8vo & 16mo. To Mr. Macmillan & Mr. Milne. Outlining the 3d part of his The Dynasts. S July 23 (149) £600 [Rota]

ALs, 23 July 1895. 1 p, 8vo. To Richard Le Gallienne. Thanking for a book. S Jan 27 (733) £190 [Bristow]

— 14 May 1900. 1 p, 8vo. To Mr. Watkins. Insisting to have a paper back for revisions. Framed. Altman collection. pnNY Sept 13 (122) $425

— 22 Nov [n.y.]. 2 pp, 8vo. To [Robert] Collier. Concerning illusts for The Trumpet Major. S July 23 (148) £600 [Rota]

— 17 Dec 1912. 1 p, 8vo. To Mrs. Strickland. Thanking for her condolences on the death of his 1st wife, Emma. With related material. S July 23 (147) £500 [Solomon]

Harrison, Anna Symmes, 1775-1864
ALs, 29 Dec 1855. 2 pp, size not stated. To her son John Scott Harrison. Family news, & about Washington politics. With additional initialed note on verso of integral leaf. wa May 30 (108) $1,100

Harrison, Benjamin, Signer from Virginia
ALs, 3 Apr 1784. 1 p, 4to. To Col. John Fitzgerald. Regarding a land warrant. Also sgd on integral address leaf. Patriotic watermark. rf Mar 14 (19) $900

Ls, 21 Aug 1783. 1 p, 8vo. Recipient unnamed. As Governor of Virginia, order to deliver lead to Indian agent Joseph Martin. Fold tears. wa May 30 (135) $210

Ds, 1 May 1784. 1 p, folio. Land grant. Frayed. wa May 30 (425) $110

— 30 June 1784. 1 p, 8vo. Certificate that William Lunsford is entitled to land for military service. Als sgd by Thomas Meriwether. Charlotte Parker Milne collection. wd Nov 12 (39) $125

Harrison, Benjamin, 1833-1901
[A group of 10 cut signatures sold at wa on 30 May 1987, lot 103, for $475.]

Collection of ALs & Ls, 2 Feb 1889 & 14 Dec 1888. 3 pp, 8vo & 4to. To James N. Tyner. About filling a vacancy likely to occur in the Interstate Commerce Commission. Thanking for political information from NY. ALs def. P May 13 (60) $700

HARRISON

ALs, 26 Dec 1890. 1 p, 12mo. To Anna Harrison Morris. Concerning illness in the family. With autograph envelope. wa May 30 (100) $650

— 24 Aug 1893. 1 p, 12mo. To Maggie Curtis. Sending congratulations on the birth of a son. wa May 30 (101) $210

Ls, 29 Oct 1888. 1 p, 4to. Recipient unnamed. Declining the invitation to a NY State Chamber of Commerce banquet. Repaired. wa May 30 (102) $170

Harrison, John Scott

ALs, 18 Mar 1854. 4 pp, 12mo. To his daughter Anna. About his activities in Washington. wa May 30 (104) $130

Harrison, William Henry, 1773-1841

ALs, 7 Mar 1831. 2 pp, 4to. To Edward T. Taylor. Regarding evidence brought before the government to get Moore dismissed. S Jan 27 (930) £1,000 [Barnes]

— 2 Dec 1839. 3 pp, 8vo. To Col. John O'Hallon. Discussing a real estate transaction & the Whig convention. sg Apr 9 (82) $4,800

Ls, 11 Sept 1797. 1 p, 8vo. To the quartermaster. Requesting writing paper for the garrison. sg Apr 9 (83) $450

— 12 July 1813. 2 pp, size not stated. To Sec of War Armstrong. Discussing readiness of Naval vessels on the Lake. Separate address leaf. rf Mar 14 (20) $2,000

ANs, 25 June [17]95. 1 p, 2.75 by 7.75 inches. About rations of "wiskey for the use of the spies at Greenville". Repaired. Framed with a port. wa May 30 (106) $400

Ds s (2) 30 June 1794 & 29 July 1795; "each a small oblong". As aide de camp to Anthony Wayne; "Return for Whiskey" & order to issue provisions to the Ottawas & Chippewas. P Oct 29 (63) $750

Ds, 16 June 1836. 3 pp, 4to. Land transfer from Zenos Bronson to David Bolles; sgd as Clerk of the County Court. Framed. Altman collection. pnNY Sept 13 (8) $650

Hart, John, Signer from New Jersey

Ds, 25 Mar 1776. 1 p, size not stated. 6 shilling New Jersey colonial currency note. Also sgd by Robert Smith & John Stevens, Jr. Soiled. Tipped to larger sheet. Charlotte Parker Milne collection. wd Nov 12 (40) $100

Harte, Bret, 1836-1902

ALs, 3 July 1881. 2 pp, 12mo (card). To an unnamed lady. Thanking for a present. wa May 30 (481) $90

Hartley, Marsden

Collection of 4 A Ls s, 2 autograph postcards, sgd, & photograph, sgd & inscr; 16 July 1906 to 31 Dec 1915. To Horace & Anne Traubel. Letters to friends, reporting about his life in Maine, etc. Charles E. Feinberg collection. P Dec 15 (96) $1,300

Hasard, John, c.1493-1540. See: Maps & Charts

Hasenclever, Walter, 1890-1940

ALs, 10 Apr 1924. 2 pp, 8vo. To Dr. Hartmann. Asking that a different date be set for a lecture. star Apr 8 (126) DM220

Haslinger, Carl, 1816-68. See: Haslinger, Tobias & Haslinger

Haslinger, Tobias, 1787-1842 —& Haslinger, Carl, 1816-68

[A collection of 43 letters & documents (12 autograph) relating to their publishing business, c.1800 to 1882, sold at HN on 22 May 1987, lot 3026, for DM800.]

[A collection of 35 letters & documents pertaining to their publishing firm, mostly by composers, 1835 to 1876, with related material, sold at star on 9 Apr 1987, lot 662, for DM3,000.]

[A collection of 11 contracts with musicians & composers, 1836 to 1871, sold at HN on 22 May 1987, lot 3027, for DM1,050.]

Haslinger, Tobias, 1787-1842. See: Steiner, Sigmund Anton & Haslinger

Hastings, Henry, 3d Earl of Huntingdon, 1535-95. See: Leicester, Robert Dudley

Hastings, Warren, 1732-1818

Autograph Ms, Importance of obtaining possession of the Island of Perim, in the Straits of Babelmandel, 30 Sept 1798. 7 pp, 4to. With map of the area, possibly by Hastings, 1 p, 8vo. Bullock collection. CNY Dec 19 (165) $1,800

Collection of 3 A Ls s & Ls, 24 Oct 1783 to 21 Aug 1795 & [n.d.]. 13 pp, 4to & 8vo. To the Chevalier d'Eon, declining to write a letter of recommendation for Mr. Bateman. In 3d person, declining an invitation. To J[ohn] Hunter, referring to a pamphlet. Recipient & contents not stated. With related material. C June 24 (82) £300 [Marks]

ALs, 15 May [1794]. 2 pp, size not stated. To Clement Francis. About the forthcoming birth of a child & mentioning his trial. Repaired. sg Apr 9 (84) $110

Hauff, Wilhelm, 1802-27
ALs, [n.d., c.1824]. 2 pp, 4cm by 8.2cm. To his brother Hermann Hauff. About his examination & his current plans. Sgd Wilhelm. Stained. JG Oct 2 (63) DM1,600

Haug, Friedrich, 1761-1829
Autograph Ms, 16 "Apophthegmen", [n.d.]. 2 pp, 8vo. Sgd Hg. star Apr 8 (127) DM420
— Autograph Ms, poem, An Dannecker, [1803]; 12 lines. 1 p, 4to. Sgd Hg. star Apr 8 (128) DM650

Hauptmann, Gerhart, 1862-1946
ALs, [30 Nov 1897]. 1 p, 8vo. To the lawyer Bernstein in Munich. Thanking for congratulations on his birthday. With autograph postcard, sgd, 20 Feb 1892, to Max Loewenfeld. About his literary agents. star Apr 8 (129) DM380
— 23 Jan 1903. 1 p, 8vo. To Toni Neisser. Letter of thanks. star Apr 8 (130) DM270

Hausmann, Manfred, 1898-1986
Autograph Ms, poems, eskimo songs & last stanzas of Naechtlicher Garten. 3 pp, 8vo. With covering letter, 5 Sept 1982. 1 p, 8vo. star Apr 8 (131) DM320

Havemann, Robert, 1910-82
Typescript, declaration regarding GDR currency regulations, [n.d.]. 3 pp, folio. With autograph revisions. With covering Ls, 23 Oct 1980, 1 p, 8vo. star Apr 8 (349) DM600

Hawthorne, Nathaniel, 1804-65
ALs, 8 Oct 1862. 1 p, 4to. To Abraham Lincoln. Recommending Bayard Taylor for the post of U. S. minister to Russia. Mtd. P May 13 (61) $4,250

Haydn, Franz Joseph, 1732-1809
[A collection of autograph memorandum by Ignaz Pleyel, [1799/1800], 2 pp, 4to, concerning the publication of 2 string quartets by Haydn, & ALs by A. C. F. von Koehler to Johann Andreas Streicher, 3 Sept 1800, 3 pp, 4to, about the publication of Die Schoepfung. sold at S on 22 May 1987, lot 410, for £1,300 to Haas.]
ALs, 8 Feb 1780. 1 p, 4to. To his pbr Artaria. Covering letter for the 5th of his 6 sonatas for piano, Op. 30. star Apr 9 (663) DM42,000

Haydon, Benjamin Robert. See: Byron, George Gordon Noel

Hayes, Rutherford B., 1822-93
ALs, 23 Apr 1878. 1 p, 12mo. Recipient unnamed. Complying with a request for his autograph. wa May 30 (109) $700
— 18 Nov 1879. 1 p, 8vo. To Gen. Schofield. Dinner invitation. Framed. Altman collection. pnNY Sept 13 (9) $550
— 12 June 1883. 1 p, 8vo. To Harry N. Ensign. Complying with a request [for his autograph]. Framed. Altman collection. pnNY Sept 13 (10) $350
— 22 July 1889. 1 p, 8vo. To William Groesbeck. Thanking for his sympathy on the death of his wife. sg Nov 6 (94) $250

Ls s (2), 6 & 7 Mar 1877. 2 pp, 8vo. To Postmaster Gen. James N. Tyner. Accepting his resignation. Requesting that he continue in office until his successor shall be named. Descendants of J. N. Tyner. P May 13 (62) $1,000

Series of 4 A Ns s, 8 Aug 1877 to 27 Jan 1879 & [n.d.]. 1 p, 8vo, & on rectos of 3 White House cards. To James N. Tyner. Introducing the bishop of Fort Wayne, & regarding nominations. Descendants of J. N. Tyner. P May 13 (63) $900

Signature, on subscription list to speech ptd by Congressional Globe, Jan 1867. Also sgd by James Garfield & Thaddeus Stevens. rf Nov 15 (10) $250
— Anr, [n.d.]; 1 p, 24mo (card). With carte-de-visite port of Mr. & Mrs. Hayes, [c.1875-80]. sg Nov 6 (271) $50

Hebbel, Friedrich, 1813-63
ALs, 16 Oct 1853. 2 pp, 8vo. Recipient unnamed. Explaining advice given in an earlier letter about a young man's future. FD June 11 (3509) DM3,200
— 29 Nov 1862. 2 pp, 8vo. To an editor of the magazine Die Grenzboten [Julian Schmidt?]. Expressing his appreciation of a review of his Nibelungen. star Apr 8 (132) DM2,400

Hebrew Manuscripts
Ms, Bible. [Toledo or Burgos, c.1260]. 1 leaf only, vellum, 297mm by 260mm. "Carpet page" with text in a large square Spanish Hebrew script, micrographic writing of the Masora & full-page illumination. Apparently written by Menahem bar Abraham ibn Malik of Burgos. S June 23 (40) £28,000 [Ramos]
— Ms, Torah. [Poland, c.1880] In Ashkenazi sq script. scroll on vellum, 10.5cm high. CAM Dec 3 (134) HF13,000
— Ms, Yizkor Buch. Fuerth, 1651-1828. In Hebrew sq & cursive scripts by various hands. 86 leaves, vellum, 185mm by 152mm, in 19th-cent lea with bind-tooled covers of an earlier bdg laid down. sg Apr 30 (366) $18,000
— DAVID BEN ARYEH LEIB OF LIDA. - Sod ha-Shem. [Bohemia/Moravia, 1738] In sq & mashait script. 28 leaves, vellum, 123mm by 75mm, in calf gilt. With 12 illusts. CAM Dec 3 (131) HF100,000

HECKEL

Heckel, Erich, 1883-1970

Collection of 5 A Ls s, 2 Ls s, 1 autograph postcard, sgd & 2 postcards, sgd, 7 Sept 1944 to 23 Oct 1948. 10 pp, 8vo & 4to, & cards. To Dr. Maximilian Klafkowsky. Regarding an order for a watercolor & requests for painting utensils. VH Sept 12 (961) DM650

ALs, 6 May 1917. 2 pp, 4to. To Paul Westheim. Protesting against an unauthorized reprint of an etching. star Apr 8 (468) DM1,500

Heems, Nicolas, c.1470-1532

Ms, Compendium quatuor librorum institutionum secundum ordinem rubricarum..., [Louvain, 1533]. 152 leaves & blanks, 202mm by 140mm. Contemp lea, blind-stamped with acorn design. Copy written by Ulrich Cluts. HK Nov 4 (433) DM4,400

Hegel, Georg Wilhelm Friedrich, 1770-1831

Ds, 22 Feb 1830. 1 p, folio. Sitten-Zeugnis for G. A. T. Schroeder. Sgd as rector of the Frederick William Univesity & countersgd by him as government representative. sg Apr 2 (108) $650

— 25 Feb 1830. 1 p, folio. Certificate of studies for divinity student G. A. T. Schroeder. Sgd by Philipp Marheineke as dean, countersgd by Hegel as government official. sg Apr 9 (85) $550

— 7 Apr 1830. 1 p, folio. University certificate for G. A. Wagner, sgd as government official. star Apr 8 (350) DM1,500

Hegenbarth, Josef, 1884-1962

Series of 5 A Ls s, 28 Oct 1922 to 4 Jan 1925. 9 pp, 4to. To Johannes Reichelt. About Reichelt's article on Hegenbarth, & mentioning some of his etchings. With ALs to Richard von Sichowsky, 30 June 1958. star Apr 8 (469) DM320

Heidegger, Martin, 1889-1976

ALs, 6 Sept 1968. 1 p, 8vo. To Anna Martina Gottschick. Answering a question about one of his works. HN May 22 (3028) DM400

Heiller, Anton, 1923-79

Autograph music, sketches for 4 Stuecke zum Fronleichnamsfest fuer Orgel (1957); 2 pp, 30cm by 21cm. In pencil. Later sgd & dated 2 May [19]78; in ballpoint pen. star Apr 9 (664) DM200

Heinrich, Prinz von Preussen, 1726-1802

Series of 25 A Ls s, 28 July 1783 to 14 June 1802. 34 pp, 4to. To Viktor Amadeus Graf Henckel von Donnersmarck (5) & his widow Ottilie. Personal correspondence, & commenting about political & military affairs. In French. star Apr 9 (1158) DM11,000

AMERICAN BOOK PRICES CURRENT

Heller, Stephen, 1813-88

ALs, 3 Sept 1843[?]. 4 pp, 8vo. To [Jenny Lind]. Defending his prolificacy & asserting he could compose even more. star Apr 9 (665) DM460

Helmerding, Karl, 1822-99

[An archive of c.80 letters & postcards addressed to him, documenting theater life in Berlin, sold at star on 9 Apr 1987, lot 869, for DM1,950.]

Hemingway, Ernest, 1899-1961

Collection of 1 ALs & 3 Ls s, 1943. 6 pp, 4to. To Jane & Robert Joyce. Expressing his loneliness & reporting about his activities. Apologizing for some quarrel. P Sept 24 (29) $4,750

ALs, 21 Apr [1928]. 4 pp, 8vo. To Charles & Lorene Thompson. Reporting about his sea voyage to France, Spanish ports, etc. Sgd Ernest. S Dec 18 (128) £1,500

ANs, 12 April [19]53. 1 p, 4to. To Charlie. Giving his opinion about [Spencer] Tracy & [Leland] Hayward. Sgd Ernest. In pencil. sg Nov 6 (95) $1,500

— [n.d.]; 1 p, 100mm by 213mm. Recipient unnamed. "Please never make me a good man in the book; just a good writer if I am." Sgd EH. sg Nov 6 (96) $250

Ns, [n.d.]; 1 p, 91mm by 160mm. Recipient unnamed. About payment for an article in the magazine True. Sgd EH. sg Nov 6 (97) $225

Henri III, King of France, 1551-89

Ls, 10 Nov 1579. 1 p, folio. To a commissioner of war. Notifying him of a change in command & giving instructions regarding pay. With transcript. HK Nov 7 (2247) DM650

Henri, Robert

Collection of 8 A Ls s & 2 autograph postcards, sgd, 20 May 1909 to 2 Apr 1913. To Horace Traubel. Repeated refusals to speak at dinners commemorating Walt Whitman; & about a New York exhibition of modern art. Charles E. Feinberg collection. P Dec 15 (97) $1,300

Henricus de Bartholomaeis

Ms, Summa de Titulis Decretalium. [Bologna, with miniatures added in Paris, c.1280-1300]. 2 leaves only, vellum, 440mm by 288mm. In brown ink in a rounded gothic hand. With 2 large historiated initials. S June 23 (8) £6,500 [Ferrini]

Henrietta Anne, Duchesse d'Orleans, 1644-70
AL, 23 June [1670]. 2 pp, 4to. To Thomas Clifford, 1st Baron Clifford of Chudleigh. Informing him about her brother's [Charles II of England] promise regarding Clifford & Lord Arlington. In English. Clifford of Chudleigh collection. S July 24 (249) £2,400 [Turner]

Henrik, Prince Consort of Margrethe of Denmark. See: Margrethe, Queen of Denmark & Henrik

Henry III, King of France, 1551-89
Ls, 29 Mar 1572. 1 p, folio. To Mons. de Fourquevaux. Sending greetings from the King & Queen & hoping for a meeting in the near future. C June 24 (45) £220 [American Museum of Hist. Docs.]

Henry IV, King of Castile & Leon
Ds, 1447. 1 p, 4to. Order to deliver the castle of San Martin into the hands of Pedro Suarez de Quinones. C June 24 (46) £240 [Joseph]

Henry, Patrick, 1736-99
Ds, 2 Dec 1785. 1 p, folio. Land grant to Francis & William Doaking; partly ptd. Sgd as Governor of Virginia. Mtd & silked. sg Nov 6 (272) $500

Henry VI, King of England
Document, 1431. 1 p, 10.5 by 5 inches. Vellum. Grant of land to Sillius Strong, John Smyth & John [Benyett?]. P Sept 24 (23) $550

Henry VII, King of England, 1457-1509
Ds, 6 Nov 1498. 1 p, 7 by 9.5 inches. Vellum. Order addressed to Sir Robert Lytton for garments for 3 of his children. P Dec 15 (49) $2,600

Henry VIII, King of England, 1491-1547
Ms, file of over 300 judicial summonses for Easter Term 1528; vellum. Contemp vellum wrap. S June 23 (34) £1,100 [Maggs]

Ls, 1 July 1511. 1 p, 7.5 by 8.5 inches. Vellum. To Sir Andrewe Wyndesore, Keeper of the Great Wardrobe. Ordering him to deliver accoutrements for the Royal horses. P Dec 15 (50) $6,250

Ds, 23 Feb 1513/14. 1 p, c.5 by 9.5 inches. Vellum. Order to Sir Andrew Windsor to deliver canvas to Sir Wistan Browne. S July 24 (225) £1,700 [Wilson]

— 18 Jan 1529 [1530]. 1 p, folio. Introducing his new ambassador [Lord Thomas Boleyn] to Cardinal Benedetto Accolti, Bishop of Ravenna & requesting him to recommend him to Charles V. Matted with a port. P Dec 15 (51) $13,000

— 1 July 1542. 1 p, 17.5 by 34 inches. Vellum. Letters Patent, granting to Nicholas Fortescue the reversion of the messuage & chapel of St. Giles. With inital letter port on separate membrane, 5.5 by 5 inches. S July 24 (226) £400 [Schaetzer]

Henschke, Alfred, 1890-1928. See: Klabund

Henze, Hans Werner
Autograph quotation, 2 bars of music on verso of a picture postcard, [n.d.]. Sgd. star Apr 9 (668) DM280

Heraldic Manuscripts
[A collection of 9 illuminated vols, c. 160 leaves in all, 8vo, presented to Queen Elizabeth I by Sir Gilbert Dethick, Garter King of Arms, 1568 to 1580, containing 294 coats-of-arms, in early 17th cent crimson velvet bdg stamped with crowned cypher CR of Charles I, sold at S on 18 Dec 1986, lot 203, for £70,000 to Owen.]

Ms, 39 coats of arms of Elizabethan nobility in blazon, [n.d.]; folio. With blanks, loose in contemp vellum bds. S July 24 (278) £400 [Heraldry Today]

— Ms, compilation of heraldic sketches relating to a number of European noble families, [France, c.1700-1800]. About 460 pp, 350mm by 260mm, partly interleaved with blanks. With hundreds of armorial sketches in pen-&-ink, & engraving by M. Ogier, 1700. Phillipps Ms. 8557. HK Nov 4 (420) DM1,100

— Ms, Executoria de Hidalguia in favor of Don Ramon Zazo y Ortega; 1766. About 110 pp, folio; contemp velvet bds. In professional calligraphic hand, illuminated. With full-p coat of arms & genealogical table. S May 21 (308) £350 [Dennistoun]

— Ms, genealogical scroll for 17 generations of the Villiers family, [c.1636]. About 212 by 53 inches. Containing 123 small & 2 large illuminated coats-of-arms. Sgd by Henry St. George, Norroy Herald, & Henry Lilly, Rouge-Rose Herald. C June 24 (10) £500 [Waxman]

— Ms, grant of arms to Thomas Wyche, sgd by William Dethick, Garter King of Arms, 15 Aug 1590. 40cm by 55cm. Vellum. Illuminated. pn Dec 11 (1) £240 [Graton]

— Ms, grant of arms to John Tivitoe, sgd by Martin Leake & Charles Townley, Garter & Clarenceux Kings of Arms, 30 Mar 1761. 42cm by 52cm. Vellum. Illuminated. In orig case. pn Dec 11 (2) £270 [Woodcock]

— Ms, grant of arms to John Stables, sgd by Martin Leake & Thomas Browne, Garter & Norroy Kings of Arms, 18 July 1767. 40cm by 51cm. Vellum. Illuminated. In orig case. Damaged. pn Dec 11 (3) £150 [Graton]

— Ms, grant of arms to Arthur Cooper, sgd by Gerald Wollaston, Arthur Cochrane & Algar Howard, Garter, Clarenceux & Norroy Kings of Arms, 8 Oct 1931. 37cm

HERALDIC MANUSCRIPTS

by 53cm. Illuminated. In orig case. pn Dec 11 (4) £95 [Rankin]

— Ms, grant of arms to Richard Garth, 8 July 1564. 1 p, c.12 by 24 inches, vellum. Sgd by William Hervy, Clarenceux King of Arms. With initial letter port of Hervy & illuminated coat of arms. S July 24 (277) £350 [College of Arms]

— Ms, Roll of Arms and Pedigree of John Sutton de Dudley, Duke of Northumberland, 1742. Scroll, c.218mm by 47mm. With 1 large & 18 small coats-of-arms in gold & colors. C June 24 (42) £350 [Solomon]

— BOUTON, VICTOR. - Armorial des grands louvetiers de France.... Paris, 1887. 21 leaves, vellum, mor gilt by Chambolle-Duru. With 36 coats-of-arms. Jeanson Ms 205 SM Feb 28 (89) FF16,000

— BOUTON, VICTOR. - Armorial des grands veneurs depuis l'origine jusqu'a nos jours. Paris, 1887. 26 leaves, vellum, 210mm by 145mm, in mor gilt by Chambolle-Duru. Jeanson Ms 204. SM Feb 28 (90) FF18,000

— IRELAND. - Ms, "Ierish Arms", dated 1609 & 1637; c.96 pp, 4to; disbound & laid down on later paper; later bdg incorporating parts of orig calf. Coats-of-arms in painted emblazonry with identifying notes. In several hands. S Dec 18 (264) £800 [Maggs]

— ORDER OF THE GARTER. - Armes, Noms, surnoms et Qualitez de tous les Chevalliers du trenoble Ordre de la Iartiere... iusques a present l'an 1642. With large armorial woodcut & 432 colored woodcuts of coats-of-arms on 23 tables. Contemp vellum bdg. Ownership inscr Ex Bibliotheca Sammarthanorum Fratrum, De Sainte-Marthe. FD June 11 (17) DM4,600

— ORDER OF THE GOLDEN FLEECE. - Armorial [late 16th cent], listing members of the order from its foundation in 1429 to 1594. With port of Philip the Good of Burgundy; some coats-of-arms painted on separate sheets & affixed. 52 pp, folio. In purple mor case. Chewed by rodents. S Nov 27 (442) £800 [Almond]

Herder, Johann Gottfried von, 1744-1803

Autograph Ms, poem, Das Genesungsmittel, [n.d.]. 1 p, 8vo. 2 stanzas, in all 18 lines. Some revisions. JG Oct 2 (67) DM1,500

ALs, 27 May 1782. 1 p, 4to. To Christian Friedrich von Blankenburg. Regarding his earlier & Blankenburg's current plans of publishing a trans of the works of Hemsterhuis. star Apr 8 (133) DM4,600

Herloszsohn, Karl, 1804-49

Series of 35 A Ls s, 1830 to 1840 & [n.d.]. 44 pp, 4to & 8vo. To the publishing firm Pierer at Altenburg. Concerning literary matters, mostly the magazine Der Komet. With related material. star Apr 8 (134) DM900

AMERICAN BOOK PRICES CURRENT

Herman, Martial Joseph Armand, 1759-95

ALs, [6 Jan 1794]. 2 pp, 4to. To the Comite de Salut Publique. As President of the Tribunal Revolutionnaire, discussing organizational problems regarding the trial of 110 citizens of Nantes. Georges Cain collection. star Apr 9 (1009) DM3,200

Hermine, Princess Reuss, Consort of Wilhelm II of Germany, 1887-1947

Collection of 2 A Ls s, 6 Ls s, 2 autograph postcards, sgd, & 3 postcards, sgd, & 2 telegrams, 10 May 1928 to 7 Sept 1938. 15 pp, 8vo & 4to. To Ernst Freiherr von Maydell. About recipient's paintings & reporting about her travels. HK Nov 7 (2249) DM750

Herschel, Sir John Frederick William, 1792-1871

ALs, 22 Oct 1839. 2 pp, 12mo. To Dr. Tinner. Returning weather registers & denying he received an almanac. Collector's stamp. sg Apr 9 (86) $50

— 1846. 2 pp, 4to. To Sir William J. Hooker. Concerning acquisition of a telescope. Collector's stamp. sg Apr 9 (87) $110

Herschel, Sir William, 1738-1822

Autograph music, song, beginning "Suppose we sing a catch", [n.d.]. 2 pp, 31cm by 23cm. Sgd. On verso beginning of the text of anr song. star Apr 8 (351) DM1,600

AL, [1791]. 1 p, 4to. To Sir William Hamilton. Regarding his wish to observe the planets from Naples. S July 24 (375) £200 [Wilson]

Herwegh, Emma. See: Herwegh, Georg & Herwegh

Herwegh, Georg, 1817-75 —& Herwegh, Emma

[A collection of c.70 A Ls s, c.1842 to 1843, c.200 pp, 8vo, love letters of Herwegh & his fiancee Emma, discussing personal, literary & political matters, with related material, sold at S on 27 Nov 1986, lot 367, for £850 to Haas.]

Herzen, Alexander, 1812-70

ALs, 24 Dec 1854. 1 p, 8vo. Recipient unnamed. Commenting on a report about his journal, & about Russian ministers. C June 24 (48) £80 [Maggs]

Hess, Victor Franz, 1883-1964

Autograph Ms, excerpts from a paper by Walter Rau, 1939, "Intensity variations of the hard compounds in the Lake Constance". 2 pp, 8vo. Including a sketch in text. star Apr 8 (352) DM320

Hesse, Hermann, 1877-1962

[A collection of typescripts of 10 poems, sgd, 1929 to 1944, 12 pp, 4to, some on versos of calendar leaves, sent by Hesse to his nephew Carlo Isenberg, sold at S on 21 May 1987, lot 257, for £500 to Lionheart.]

[A collection of typescripts of 8 poems, sgd, 1944 to 1962, 8 pp, folio & 8vo, some with brief A Ls s at foot, sent by Hesse to Lise Isenberg, sold on 21 May 1987, lot 258, for £260 to Lionheart.]

Autograph Ms, Neuromantik, [before 1900]. 4 pp, 8vo. Sgd. star Apr 8 (135) DM3,600

— Autograph Ms, poem, Ninon, 23 Mar 1926; 10 lines. 1 p, 8vo. In pencil, 3 corrections. Early version of Fuer Ninon. star Apr 8 (136) DM1,600

Autograph sketchbook, containing 8 pencil drawings of his house in Montagnola, each sgd H & dated [19]31. 8vo. S May 21 (254) £1,400 [Bareiss-Ohloff]

Original drawing, pencil & watercolors, showing garden in front of mountain; 13 Aug [19]22. On drawing paper, 23cm by 31cm. star Apr 8 (146) DM13,000

— Original drawing, pen-&-ink sketch, with pencil, showing part of a gnarled tree; 1 July 1930. 238mm by 190mm, on drawing paper, 310mm by 224mm. Stamp of Bruno Hesse. star Apr 8 (148) DM2,000

— Original drawing, pen-&-ink sketch, 2 trees in winter, 16 Feb [19]60. Inscr [to his wife?] "Kleine Gabe von Avis mont." 6cm by 6.7cm. On cardboard. star Apr 8 (149) DM550

— Original drawing, pen-&-ink sketch, landscape (Montagnola), [n.d.]. Sgd H. H. 20.5cm by 17.5cm, on handmade paper, 24cm by 19cm. Spotted in margins. star Apr 8 (150) DM1,750

— Original drawing, pen-&-ink sketch, with watercolors, flowers in a pot, [n.d.]. 7.2cm by 5.5cm, on handmade paper, 17cm by 12cm. star Apr 8 (151) DM1,300

— Original drawing, pen-&-ink sketch, with watercolors, room with a bunch of flowers in front of the window, [n.d.]. 6.9cm by 7.1cm, on handmade paper, 21cm by 13.5cm; double sheet. star Apr 8 (152) DM700

Autograph transcript, 12 poems, [after 1940]. 13 folded leaves, 8vo. Sgd & inscr to Mauricio Boersner. With 13 watercolors. HN May 22 (3034) DM24,000

Typescript, 3 "poetical fragments" by Joseph Knecht (central character in Das Glasperlenspiel), 1935, 1937 & [n.d.]. 3 pp, folio & 8vo. S May 21 (255) £350 [Lucas]

— Typescript, essay, Beim Einzug in's neue Haus, 1st draft, summer 1931. 39 pp, 8vo; sgd. With typescript carbon copy of a slightly different version, 16 pp, folio; in paper wrap illus with watercolor. With privately ptd version, inscr to Hans & Elsy Bodmer; with 2 watercolors. In green case. S May 21 (253) £1,700 [Bareiss-Ohloff]

— Typescript, poem, Ein Traum, 24 lines; [fall 1958]. 2 pp, 8vo. Sgd & inscr. At head watercolored pen-&-ink sketch (house in the mountains). star Apr 8 (138) DM1,100

Series of 3 A Ls s, 14 Mar 1919 to 16 July 1936. 10 pp, 4to & 8vo. To his half-brother Karl Isenberg. About the composition of Das Glasperlenspiel, his unhappiness about being alienated from Germany, etc. 2 A Ls s with small watercolors at head. S May 21 (256) £1,200 [Johnson]

ALs, [Feb 1913]. 2 pp, 8vo. To Frau Lichtenhahn. Thanking for a present & reporting about his family. star Apr 8 (139) DM520

— 16 Sept 1922. 3 pp, 8vo. To H. C. Bodmer. Thanking for money to support Hugo Ball. With watercolor. HN May 22 (3035) DM4,000

— [n.d.]. 2 pp, 8vo. Recipient unnamed. Thanking for material received. With colored woodcut at head. On 3d page typescript carbon copy, poem, Bericht des Schuelers, three 8-line stanzas. Sgd & dated 28 Nov 1941. star Apr 8 (141) DM580

Collection of Ls & 5 autograph postcards, sgd, [1941 to 1949]. 2 pp, 8vo & cards. To Hanna Roehr. About a variety of subjects. star Apr 8 (142) DM1,100

Ls s (2), 7 Feb & 19 Mar 1949. 3 pp, 8vo. To H. Dietrich Mueller-Grote. Sending condolences on the death of his father, & about a reprint of a vol of poems. With related material. HN May 22 (3036a) DM300

Ls, "Ende Sept. 59". 1 p, 8vo. To an unnamed literary society. Explaining that he cannot attend a conference because he is too infirm to travel. star Apr 8 (144) DM320

Autograph postcard, sgd, [9 July 1915]. To Albrecht Keller. About Keller's plans to send him a paper & saying he has not been drafted to the army yet. With related material. star Apr 8 (140) DM360

Heuschele, Otto

Autograph Ms, Wenn uns der Himmel bleibt, [summer] 1962. 9 pp, folio. Radio program about Andreas Gryphius, sgd. With related material. star Apr 8 (153) DM260

Heuss, Theodor, 1884-1963

Series of 4 Ls s, 29 Sept 1950 to 25 July 1957. 4 pp, folio & 4to. To Karl Borromaeus Glock. Thanking for books. With related material. star Apr 9 (1011) DM550

Photograph, sgd, [c.1958]. 17cm by 11.5cm. star Apr 9 (1012) DM420

HEVESY

Hevesy, George Charles de, 1885-1966
Typescript, essay, Iron Transport Rate in the Neoplastic Organism, [n.d.]. 4 pp, folio. Sgd. star Apr 8 (353) DM210

Hewes, Joseph, Signer from North Carolina
ADs, 20 July 1778. 1 p, folio. As Justice of the Peace, acknowledgment of debt by Daniel Hewes to Gov. Richard Caswell; sgd twice. Charlotte Parker Milne collection. wd Nov 12 (41) $1,200

Hewitt, Graily, 1864-1952. See: Calligraphy

Heyward, Thomas, Signer from South Carolina
Ds, 5 July 1788. 1 p, 8vo. Order for the arrest of Dixon Pearce. wa May 30 (136) $230
— 15 July 1788. 1 p, 4to. As Justice of the Peace, summons for William Blamyer. Repaired. Charlotte Parker Milne collection. wd Nov 12 (42) $125

Heyward, Thomas, Signer from South Carolina —& Others
Ds, 5 July 1785. 1 p, 4to. Order to Robert Vardele to appear before the Charleston Court of Common Pleas. Also sgd by Charles Cotesworth Pinckney (twice) & Isaac Huger. wa May 30 (424) $270

Hill, Sir Rowland, 1795-1879
ALs, 20 Jan 1854. 2 pp, 12mo. To Dr. Browning. Sending congratulations on an appointment & inviting him to dinner. wa May 30 (418) $50
Ls, 21 June 1861. 1 p, 8vo. To William Sharpey. Promising an investigation regarding his complaints about postage charges. HN Nov 27 (2287) DM600
Ds, 15 Apr 1859. 2 pp, size not stated. Report addressed to the U.S. Postmaster General regarding accounts between the 2 countries. rf May 30 (8) $115

Hiller, Ferdinand, 1811-85
Autograph music, Namenlose Taenze fuer Pianoforte zu vier Haenden. Op. 169; sgd & dated 4 Apr 1875. 22 pp, 4to. Inscr to H. Seligmann on tp. Extensive revisions. HN Nov 27 (2289) DM800
Collection of 20 A Ls s, 4 autograph postcards, sgd & 2 photographs, sgd & inscr, 1852 to 1884. 67 pp, 8vo. To Herr Schnitzler & other recipients. Contents not stated. Some in French. HN Nov 27 (2288) DM2,400
A Ls s (2), 13 Nov 1849 & [n.d.]. 4 pp, 8vo. To Franz Messer. Informing him of his appointment as conductor in Cologne. Inviting him to a rehearsal of some quartets. With visiting card. star Apr 9 (671) DM1,100
ALs, 6 Dec 1830. 2 pp, 4to. To the music pbr Probst. Offering a composition for print. star Apr 9 (670) DM850

AMERICAN BOOK PRICES CURRENT

Himmler, Heinrich, 1900-45
Ds, 8 Nov 1937. 2 pp, 4to. "Basic Law for Mandatory Saving." Possibly near final draft; some corrections. Sgd in pencil. wa May 30 (411) $325

Hindemith, Paul, 1895-1963
ANs, 5 Oct 1932. 1 p, 8vo. To Herr Saerchinger. Sending pictures. star Apr 9 (672) DM340

Hindenburg, Paul von, 1847-1934
ALs, 26 May 1915. 2 pp, 8vo. To his cousin [Sophie von Hindenburg]. Commenting about politics & the war. star Apr 9 (1014) DM900
Ds, 30 Apr 1894. 3 pp, folio. Confirmation of the sentence in the military trial of Herrmann Bleck. star Apr 9 (1013) DM450
— 24 Nov 1925. 1 p, folio. Discharge of Minister A. Pauli. Countersgd by Gustav Stresemann. star Apr 9 (1015) DM500
— 16 July 1927. 1 p, folio. As President, military promotion for Capt. Windecker. Partly ptd. wa Oct 18 (20) $100
— 30 June 1934. 1 p, 4to. Military discharge for Dr. Wischhusen. wa May 30 (39) $160

Hitchcock, Ethan Allen, 1798-1870
Franking signature, [1866]. Commissary General of Prisoners imprint cover. rf Mar 14 (87) $60

Hitler, Adolf, 1889-1945
Ls, 15 Aug 1939. 3 pp, folio. To the President of Ecuador. Sending congratulations on his election. Countersgd by von Ribbentrop. sg Apr 9 (89) $1,300
Ds, 1 May 1934. 1 p, folio. Appointment for Wilhelm Frick as Minister of the Interior of Prussia. sg Apr 9 (88) $1,500
— 13 Jan 1939. 1 p, 4to. Military discharge for Maj. Mossgraber. Countersgd by von Brauchitsch. wa May 30 (40) $700
— 24 Jan 1942. 3 pp, folio. Promotions for 36 high-ranking officers, including Rommel, Foertsch, Jodl & von Arnim. Countersgd by Keitel. sg Apr 9 (90) $4,400
— 10 June 1943. 9 pp, folio. Promotions for 66 officers. Countersgd by Gen. Schmundt. sg Apr 9 (91) $850
— 12 June 1944. 4 pp, folio. Promotions for 28 officers. With related material. sg Apr 9 (92) $700
— [c.25 Mar] 1945. 3 pp, folio. Working carbon copy draft of a military directive to Army Group Vistula directing the defense of the Oder. With a few words of correction by Hitler. sg Apr 2 (110) $3,000

Hitler, Adolf, 1889-1945 —& Goering, Hermann, 1893-1946
Ds, 28 Jan 1939. 1 p, folio. Appointment for Dr. Georg Schaede as medical officer. Framed with portraits. pnNY June 11 (84) $900

Hitzig, Julius Eduard, 1780-1849
ALs, 28 Jan 1827. 2 pp, 4to. To Wilhelm Hauff. Discussing the plan of a new Ed of E. T. A. Hoffmann's works. JG Oct 2 (70) DM950

Hoban, James, 1762-1831 —& Thornton, William, 1759-1828
Ds, [n.d.]. 2 pp, folio. Lease between James Hoban & Ioppan Webster, witnessed by Thornton. wa May 30 (482) $190

Hobart, Sir James, d.1507
Ds, 20 Oct 1506. Size not stated. Quitclaim, to Hobart's named feoffes, for 2 houses & land in Creeting St. Peter & Earls Stonham. Vellum. Mtd. pn Dec 11 (80) £120

Hoby, Sir Thomas, 1539-66
Autograph Ms, letterbook as ambassador in France, 9 Apr to 21 June 1566; 19 letters to the Queen, William Cecil, & others, & related material. Together with contemp copies of letters of advice to Roger Manners, 5th Earl of Rutland, 1595, supposedly by Robert Devereux, 2d Earl of Essex & Sir Thomas Posthumus Hoby. Together 90 pp, folio, in 1 vol; unbd. C Dec 3 (279) £6,000 [Quaritch]

Hoby, Thomas Posthumus, Sir, 1566-1640. See: Hoby, Sir Thomas

Hoelderlin, Friedrich, 1770-1843
Autograph Ms, poem, Der Mensch, [n.d.]. 1 p, 8vo. 4 lines, sgd. Pasted into 1st Ed of his Gedichte. Stuttgart & Tuebingen, 1826. 8vo. Contemp half lea gilt. With related material. HK Nov 7 (2251) DM32,000

Transcript, poem, beginning "Es kommt der neue Tag aus fernen Hoehn herunter", [n.d.]. 1 p, 16cm by 20,5cm. Possibly in Eduard Moerike's hand. JG Oct 2 (107) DM800

Hoelty, Ludwig Heinrich Christoph, 1748-76
ALs, 28 Sept 1775. 3 pp, 8vo. To his brother. Family news. With related material. JG Oct 2 (72) DM2,200

Hoelzel, Adolf, 1853-1934
ALs, 7 Feb 1930. 1 p, 4to. To Eugen Diederichs. Commenting about Naumann's Das Gruenewald-Problem. star Apr 8 (471) DM700

Hoeppener, Hugo, 1868-1948. See: Fidus, 1868-1948

Hofer, Karl, 1878-1955
Collection of 4 A Ls s & AL, Apr 1954 to 30 Sept 1954. 7 pp, 4to & 8vo. To Dr. Hans Sommer. Commenting about modern art & criticism. VH Sept 12 (964) DM850

ALs, 11 Feb 1954. 2 pp, 4to. To Hans Sommer. Sending photographs of some works & discussing art. star Apr 8 (470) DM480

Hoffmann von Fallersleben, August Heinrich, 1798-1874
ALs, 5 Jan 1840. 2 pp, 8vo. To Dr. Friedlaender. About the augmentation of the Silesian library at Breslau. Sgd H,v,F, HK Nov 7 (2254) DM500

— 2 June 1870. 1 p, 8vo. To [G. J. Compes]. Sending a Ms. Sgd H. v. F. Was mtd. star Apr 8 (154) DM260

Hofmannsthal, Hugo von, 1874-1929
Autograph Ms, book review, fragment; [n.d.]. 1 p, 4to. Some revisions. star Apr 8 (155) DM1,100

— Autograph Ms, program for the 1st performance of Der Buerger als Edelmann at Berlin on 9 Apr 1918; 1 p, 8vo. With envelope addressed to Johannes Oertel of the publishing firm Adolph Fuerstner, postmarked 24 Mar 1918. star Apr 8 (157) DM800

Series of c.40 A Ls s, c.1897 to 1912. About 90 pp, folio & 8vo. To Annie Schindler & her husband Robert von Lieben. About his methods of working, personal views & news. S Nov 27 (369) £4,600 [Haas]

ALs, 5 Nov [1903?]. 3 pp, 8vo. To Rudolf von Poellnitz of Insel Press. Explaining his impatience & agreeing to a possible reprint of Tod des Tizian. star Apr 8 (156) DM2,400

— [31 Dec 1915]. 4 pp, 8vo. To Professor A. Roller. Requesting permission to call upon him with Fraeulein Wiesenthal, & asking for free tickets for the opera. HK Nov 7 (2255) DM1,200

Hofmeister, Friedrich, 1782-1864
Collection of 3 A Ls s & Ls, 1821 to 1855. 6 pp, 4to. To the publishers Schlesinger, Hoffmann & Campe, & Haslinger. Concerning questions of copyright. HN May 22 (3044) DM600

Hohenlohe-Schillingsfuerst, Chlodwig, Fuerst zu, 1819-1901
ALs, 1 June 1880. 1 p, 4to. To Kaiser Wilhelm I. Informing him of the arrival of the Russian ambassador. With autograph endorsement by Wilhelm I, 4 lines, sgd, setting a date for receiving the ambassador. star Apr 9 (1016) DM380

Hokinson, Helen Elna, 1893-1949
Original drawing, pen-and-ink cartoon, 2 ladies at lunch, [n.d.]. 11 by 14 inches, sgd. Framed. wd Nov 12 (9) $75

Holk, Heinrich, Graf von, 1599-1633
ALs, 11 Sept 1630. 1 p, folio. To Christian II von Anhalt-Bernburg. Apologizing for the misbehavior of his troops. With a port. star Apr 9 (1017) DM850

Hollinsworth, John, d.1861. See: Naval Manuscripts

Holmes, Oliver Wendell, 1809-94
ALs, 23 May 1872. 3 pp, size not stated. Recipient unnamed. Commenting on an article on Sir Walter Scott. pnNY June 11 (20) $225
— 20 July 1884. 3 pp, 8vo. To Judge Robert Ludlow Fowler. Commenting on an essay by Fowler & David Dudley Fields's codification of the law. sg Nov 6 (99) $325
— 12 Dec 1886. 3 pp, 12mo. To Judge Robert Ludlow Fowler. Thanking for his article on Thomas Pownall. sg Nov 6 (100) $275
Photograph, sgd, [Aug 1892]. Cabinet size. Mtd. wa Oct 18 (21) $95

Holmes, Oliver Wendell, 1841-1935
ANs, 25 Feb 1910. 1 p, 8vo. Recipient unnamed. Complying with a request. wa May 30 (41) $170

Holtei, Karl von, 1798-1880
Autograph transcript, poem, Deutsche Einigkeit, 1856. 2 pp, 8vo. 38 lines, sgd. star Apr 8 (159) DM220

Holz, Arno, 1863-1929
Collection of 5 A Ls s, 2 autograph Mss, partly autograph Ms & Ms, sgd, 26 Apr 1926 to 30 Jan 1929. 14 pp, various sizes. Letters (3 to Gustav Boess) & lists related to his efforts to find subscribers for a new Ed of his works. With anr ALs, 1928, concerning his illness. star Apr 8 (161) DM1,100

Honegger, Arthur, 1892-1955
Autograph Ms, remarks about the importance of Verdi's operas, [n.d.]. 1 p, 4to. Sgd. star Apr 9 (673) DM1,000
Autograph music, Antigone Scene I; 4 bars in treble & bass clef, [n.d.]. Sgd. 1 p, 4to. In pencil. Framed. Altman collection. pnNY Sept 13 (169) $275
— Autograph music, song, Le chasseur perdu en foret, orchestral version; [n.d.]. 8 pp, folio. Notated in black ink on up to 24 staves per page, with revisions in colored crayon; text in pencil. Sgd. Repaired with translucent tape. With related material. S May 22 (605) £1,500 [Haas]
Typescript, work list of his music, sgd AH & in full, 1931. 8 pp, size not stated. Wraps. Annotated by Honegger; revisions & comments in black ink & pencil. S May 22 (607) £120 [L. I. M.]
Collection of 4 A Ls s, Ls, autograph postcard with musical quotation, & 2 group portraits, sgd, 1923, 1937 & [n.d.]; c.10 pp, various sizes. A Ls s to M. Jobin, concerning the publication of Le roi David. S May 22 (606) £1,000 [Waridel]
— AUGSBOURG, GEA. - Orig drawing, heads of six Swiss musicians with laurel leaves (Ansermet, Bovet, Dalcroze, Doret, Honegger & Hemmerling), [n.d.]. 21cm by 29cm. In pencil. Sgd. S May 22 (608) £320 [Haas]

Hooper, William, Signer from North Carolina
ADs, 15 Feb 1777. 1 p, 2.75 by 3.5 inches. Receipt to John Hancock. Inlaid. With a port. Charlotte Parker Milne collection. wd Nov 12 (43) $800

Hoover, Herbert, 1874-1964
[An autograph card, sgd as President, [n.d.], framed, sold at pnNY on 13 Sept 1986, lot 12, for $250.]
Series of 3 Ls s, 2 Dec 1921 to 31 May 1949. 3 pp, 4to. To Alton Parker, about the relief situation in Russia. To Howard Brown, thanking for a letter of appreciation. To Emil Hurja, about employment in a committee. With related material. pnNY June 11 (24) $120
Ls s (2), 12 Nov 1928 & 3 Oct 1949. 2 pp, 4to. To Dutee Wilcox Flint & Wayne Light. Expressing thanks. 1 Ls mtd. wa May 30 (112) $130
Ls, 28 Dec 1931. 1 p, 8vo. To Adolph Zukor. As President, thanking for a message. wa Oct 18 (113) $180
— 4 June 1932. 1 p, 4to. To Will Hays. Suggesting a meeting to discuss the situation of the film industry. P May 13 (65) $2,400
— 17 June 1932. 1 p, 8vo. Recipient unnamed. About the election campaign. wa May 30 (110) $400
— 13 Mar 1940. 1 p, 4to. To Frances Winwar. Thanking for a contribution to the Finnish Relief Fund. sg Nov 6 (101) $60
— 26 Aug 1949. 1 p, 4to. To Benjamin Strauss. Thanking for a birthday message. wa May 30 (282) $55
— 13 Oct 1949. 1 p, folio. To John Lewis Cochran. About the death of Mr. & Mrs. Ionides. star Apr 9 (1018) DM360
Photograph, sgd & inscr, [n.d.]. 7.25 by 10.5 inches. wa May 30 (111) $220

Hoover, Lou Henry
Photograph, sgd, [n.d.]. 8 by 10 inches. Seated, in white dress. Sepia port by Underwood & Underwood. wa Oct 18 (24) $85

Hopkins, Stephen, Signer from Rhode Island
Ds, 22 Apr 1757. 1 p, 8vo. Fragment, contents not stated. Mtd. Charlotte Parker Milne collection. wd Nov 12 (44) $75

— [n.d.]. 1 p, 12mo. List of Bristol Superior Court costs for April term. wa May 30 (137) $230

Hopkinson, Francis, Signer from New Jersey
Ds, 4 Mar 1780. Sight draft to John Bell. rf Mar 14 (21) $270

— 30 June 1780. 1 p, 8vo. Bill of exchange for 333 Mexican dollars to Joseph Barrell. Charlotte Parker Milne collection. wd Nov 12 (45) $350

— 10 Dec 1780. 1 p, 12mo. Receipt for $1,000. wa May 30 (138) $425

Horace, 65-8 B.C.
Ms, Odes, Epodes, & Carmen Saeculare. [Italy, 2d half of 15th cent]. 80 leaves, vellum & paper, 217mm by 145mm. Modern blind-stamped calf with 15th-cent catches. In dark brown ink in a gothic hand with some humanist features, becoming more cursive throughout the book. With large illuminated initial; other initials left blank. S June 23 (91) £5,500 [Maggs]

Horae B.M.V.
— [Liege, c.1310]. Use of Liege. 266 leaves & 4 flyleaves, vellum, 86mm by 60mm. Lacking 2 leaves. Contemp blindstamped bdg of wooden bds covered with red tanned lea; decorative pierced metal clasp. In dark brown ink in a small gothic liturgical hand. With illuminated borders on verso of text pages, c.155 illuminated initials, 5 historiated initials with elaborate borders & 9 full-page miniatures in full color on burnished gold grounds. 15th cent drawing added on front flyleaf. S Dec 2 (54) £90,000 [Fogg]

— [Paris, c.1407-10]. Use of Soissons. In Latin, with Calendar, Quinze Joyes & Sept Requetes in French. 225 leaves & 5 flyleaves, vellum, 189mm by 132mm, in 15th-cent blindstampd tanned lea over wooden bds. In dark brown ink in a formal gothic liturgical hand. With illuminated initials throughout & 30 large miniatures with 3-sided baguette borders within full foliate borders. Illus within the circle of the Boucicaut Master. S June 23 (105) £195,000 [Kraus]

— [Paris, c.1412]. Use of Rome. 182 leaves & 6 flyleaves, vellum, 169mm by 117mm. Contemp blindstamped bdg of dark brown tanned lea over bevelled wooden bds; orig elaborately painted edges. In dark brown ink in a fine gothic liturgical hand, with horizontal catchwords in a small lettre batarde. With illuminated panel borders on every page, small initials on most pages on highly burnished gold grounds, & 12 large miniatures. Illus by the workshop of the Boucicaut Master. S Dec 2 (56) £180,000 [Ferrini]

— [Paris, c.1415-1420]. Use of Paris. In Latin & French. 258 leaves, 181mm by 127mm, vellum. Modern dark red velvet, somewhat def. With 15 miniatures by the Master of the Harvard Hannibal & 2 by a follower of the Boucicaut Master, full foliate & floral borders throughout & numerous illuminated initials. Carfagno collection. CNY May 11 (141) $130,000

— [Paris, c.1420-30]. Use of Paris. In Latin, with Calendar, Quinze Joyes & Sept Requetes in French. 121 leaves & 5 flyleaves, vellum, 160mm by 108mm, in Parisian calf of c.1540 profusely gilt. In dark brown ink by more than 1 scribe in a gothic liturgical hand. With illuminated panel borders on every page & 14 large miniatures with full borders. S June 23 (106) £14,000 [Fogg]

— [Flanders, 1st half of 15th cent]. Of Dominican Use. 151 leaves only, vellum, 107mm by 83mm, in modern bds covered with 14th-cent vellum leaf with polyphonic music. In dark brown ink in a gothic liturgical hand. With 9 very large illuminated initials with full borders. Nibbled by rodents. S June 23 (118) £1,400 [Marcus]

— [Anjou or Southern Brittany?, c.1430-50]. Use of Rome. In Latin, with Calendar, Quinze Joyes & Sept Requetes in French. 224 leaves, vellum, 190mm by 135mm, in 19th-cent English blue velvet. In dark brown ink in a large calligraphic lettre batarde. With three-quarter illuminated borders throughout & 26 large miniatures with full borders. Small miniature & additional texts at end in later hands. Library of the Dukes of Manchester at Kimbolton. S June 23 (107) £40,000 [Ferrini]

— [Bruges, c.1430-50]. Use of Rome. 147 leaves (2 lacking) & 2 flyleaves, vellum, 247mm by 176mm, in purple velvet over pastebds with silver clasps. In dark brown ink in a formal gothic liturgical hand. With panel borders on every page, & 27 large miniatures with full borders & large illuminated initial below. S June 23 (119) £48,000 [Tenschert]

— [Bruges?, c.1430-50]. Use of Sarum. 178 leaves (3 lacking) & flyleaves, vellum, 189mm by 128mm, in 17th-cent calf gilt. In dark brown ink in a gothic liturgical hand.

HORAE B.M.V.

With 23 very large illuminated initials with three-quarter or full borders; & 15 full-page miniatures with full borders from the workshop of the Master of Otto van Moerdrecht. Long rubric in Middle English added at end. S June 23 (121) £3,500 [Schoenberg]

— [Low Countries, c.1440]. Unidentified Use. 203 leaves (1 blank), vellum, 125mm by 80mm. 17th cent French light tan calf bdg tooled in gilt. In brown ink in an upright gothic liturgical hand. With 17 large illuminated initials & 7 large miniatures, all within full borders. C June 24 (266) £6,800 [Ferrini]

— [Northern France, c.1450]. Use of Paris. In Latin, with some prayers in French. 98 leaves (6 blank), vellum, 155mm by 115mm. 16th cent bdg of an early Ms over bds. In brown ink in a gothic liturgical script. With 5 four-line initials in blue on gold ground. 6 calendar leaves replaced by 16th cent Ms copies on paper. C June 24 (264) £1,300 [Schuster]

— [France, c.1450]. Use not stated. 6 leaves only, vellum, c.185mm by 150mm. 19th cent bds. With 14 larger initials & 19 iluminated line-fillers. HN May 22 (2923) DM800

— [Western France, mid-15th cent]. Of unidentified use. 2 leaves only, 212mm by 155mm, vellum. In a gothic liturgical hand. Each with a large miniature in colors & gold, illuminated initials, line-fillers in burnished gold on red & blue grounds & full borders. S Dec 2 (16) £1,400 [Axel]

— [Paris, mid-15th cent]. Use of Rome. In Latin, with Calendar, Quinze Joyes & Sept Requetes in French. 168 leaves & 6 flyleaves, vellum, 187mm by 138mm. Green velvet over pastebds, restored. In dark brown ink in a gothic liturgical hand. With illuminated initials throughout & 14 large miniatures with full borders above very large illuminated initials. S Dec 2 (57) £65,000 [Tenschert]

— [Nantes or Angers, c.1450]. Use of Rome. In Latin. 84 leaves & 12 blanks, vellum, 105mm by 75mm. Lacking 7 leaves. 17th cent red mor gilt bdg, worn. In dark brown ink in a skilful small lettre batarde. With small illuminated initials throughout, & 24 large miniatures with full borders above large initials. S Dec 2 (59) £10,000 [Percival]

— [Paris, c.1450-60]. Use of Paris. In Latin, with Calendar, Quinze Joyes & Sept Plaies in French. 171 leaves & 7 flyleaves, vellum, 187mm by 133mm, in 17th- or 18th-cent French armorial red mor gilt. In pale black ink in a gothic liturgical hand. With illuminated panel borders throughout & 11 large miniatures with full borders. S June 23 (108) £14,000 [Fogg]

— [Paris?, c.1460]. Use of Rome. In Latin, with Calendar & Quinze Joyes in French. 152 leaves, vellum, 182mm by 128mm. Late 16th cent Parisian tan mor bdg "a la fanfare". In brown ink in a gothic liturgical hand. With four-line illuminated initial, panel borders on every page & 18 large miniatures with full borders. C June 24 (267) £40,000 [Rose]

— [Paris?, c.1460-70]. Use of Langres. 186 leaves, vellum, 205mm by 140mm. Late 18th cent bright red half mor gilt. In brown & red ink in calligraphic textura. With illuminated initials throughout & foliate borders, 8 large initials in blue or pink & burnished gold with gilt borders, & 12 full-page illuminated miniatures. FD June 11 (5) DM60,000

— [Tours?, c.1460]. Use of Rennes. In Latin & French. 238 leaves & 4 flyleaves, vellum, 168mm by 121mm. Wooden bds re-covered with red velvet, worn. In brown ink in 2 sizes of a skilful lettre batarde. With decorated initials, illuminated borders throughout on outer margins of every page, 12 full borders & 23 large miniatures in colors & liquid gold within full borders. Illuminated by the Coetivy Master. S Dec 2 (58) £115,000 [Kraus]

— [Southern France, c.1460]. Use of Rome. In Latin & French [Languedoc?]. 229 leaves, vellum, 160mm by 112mm. 19th cent black mor. In dark brown ink in a gothic liturgical hand by more than 1 scribe. With small illuminated initials throughout, 30 large initials, large miniature & 7 full-page miniatures, all within full borders often historiated with small scenes. S Dec 2 (60) £20,000 [Percival]

— [Flanders, c.1460-80]. Use of Rome. In Latin. 70 leaves only, vellum, 153mm by 104mm. Modern brown mor bdg. In dark brown ink in a gothic liturgical hand. With illuminated initials on most pages, 13 large illuminated initials with full borders & 4 full-page miniatures. S Dec 2 (62) £3,800 [Schuster]

— [Rouen, c.1460-75]. Use of Rouen. In Latin, with Calendar in French. 134 leaves only, vellum, 112mm by 77mm. 18th cent mottled calf. In dark brown ink in 2 sizes of a gothic liturgical hand. With 3 large illuminated initials with 3-quarter borders in gold & colors. S Dec 2 (63) £1,100 [Marshall]

— [Florence, c.1460-80]. 187 leaves & flyleaf, vellum, 113mm by 82mm, in 19th-cent vellum bdg. In dark brown ink in 2 sizes of a rounded gothic hand. With 7 large illuminated initials with full-length borders & 3 large historiated initials with full

borders. S June 23 (104) £1,400 [Schuster]
— [Paris, c.1460]. Use of Chartres. In Latin, with Calendar in French. 190 leaves & 2 flyleaves, vellum, 160mm by 105mm, in 16th-cent French calf profusely gilt. In dark brown ink in a gothic liturgical hand. With 8 large illuminated initials with three-quarter illuminated borders & 11 large miniatures with 3-sided baguette borders. S June 23 (109) £6,000 [Cope]
— [Rouen, c.1460-80]. Fragment, containing Penitential Psalms, Litany, Hours of the Cross & Hours of the Holy Ghost; in Latin. 26 leaves, vellum, 170mm by 120mm, in 19th cent English "divinity" calf over wooden bds. In dark brown ink in a formal gothic liturgical hand. With illuminated initials throughout, panel borders on every page & 2 very large miniatures with full borders. From the workshop of the Master of the Geneva Latini. S June 23 (110) £2,800 [Roberts]
— [Amiens, c.1460-80]. Use of Amiens. In Latin, with Calendar in French. 165 leaves & 2 flyleaves, vellum, 165mm by 117mm, in 17th-cent French brown mor profusely gilt. In dark brown ink in a large lettre batarde. With 4 large illuminated initials with three-quarter illuminated borders & 8 large miniatures with full borders. 20 ptd leaves added in 17th cent. S June 23 (111) £5,200 [Schuster]
— [Low Countries, 3d quarter of 15th cent]. Use of Rome. In Latin, with Calendar in French. 129 leaves & 4 flyleaves, vellum, 213mm by 155mm. 16th cent French brown mor over wooden bds, rebacked. In brown ink in a gothic liturgical hand. With 7 three- or four-line illuminated initials & 4 large miniatures with arched frames. C June 24 (268) £10,000 [Epping]
— [Flanders, probably Bruges, c.1470]. Use of Sarum. 145 leaves, vellum, 202mm by 136mm. 18th cent brown calf gilt. In calligraphic textura. With blue, red & gold initials throughout, numerous initials with burnished gold, 26 large illuminated initials, floral borders, 20 small & 24 full-page miniatures. FD June 11 (4) DM135,000
— [Northern Netherlands, 2d half of 15th cent]. Use of Utrecht. In Dutch. 227 leaves, vellum, 144mm by 98mm, 18th cent red mor gilt. In dark brown & red ink, with hundreds of decorated initials in colors, 20 large initials in burnished gold, 7 large historiated initials, elaborate borders & 14 full-p miniatures. FD Dec 2 (8) DM40,000
— [Savoy, 2d half of 15th cent]. Of unidentified use. In Latin, with Calendar, Quinze Joyes & Sept Requetes in French. 154 leaves, vellum, 205mm by 143mm. Lacking 12 leaves. Contemp blindstamped tanned lea over wooden bds, def. In dark brown ink in a lettre batarde. With small illuminated initials, panel borders on every page & 14 large miniatures. S Dec 2 (61) £13,500 [Marshall]
— [Florence, c.1475-85]. Use of Rome. In Latin. 223 leaves (6 modern replacements), vellum, 98mm by 65mm. 18th cent red mor gilt. In dark brown ink in a regular rounded gothic liturgical hand. With decorated initials throughout & 4 elaborately illuminated opening pages with historiated initials or small miniatures. 5 full-page miniatures & 1st leaf of text modern copies. S Dec 2 (68) £5,500 [Tenschert]
— [Central Italy, Perugia?, 2d half of 15th cent]. 190 leaves, vellum, 86mm by 60mm, in 18th-cent olive-brown sheepskin bdg. In dark brown ink in 2 sizes of a rounded gothic liturgical hand. With 8 large illuminated initials & 2 half-page historiated initials. S June 23 (103) £750 [Hildebrandt]
— [Northern Netherlands, c.1475] Use of Utrecht. In Dutch. 171 leaves (1 lacking) & flyleaves, vellum, 144mm by 108mm, in black lea over wooden bds with metal clasps. In black ink in a small gothic hand. With 28 large illuminated initials & 5 large historiated initials, all with three-quarter illuminated borders, & 6 full-page miniatures with full borders. S June 23 (122) £9,500 [Israel]
— [Northern Netherlands, Delft?, c.1475]. Use of Utrecht. In Latin, with Calendar in Dutch. 90 leaves (1 lacking), vellum, 132mm by 91mm, in 18th-cent calf. In black ink in a small gothic hand; Calendar by a different scribe. With 11 large & 2 very large decorated initials & very large illuminated initial with full illuminated border. S June 23 (123) £2,200 [Marcus]
— [Northern France, c.1480]. [Use of Paris?]. In Latin, with Calendar & some prayers in French. 153 leaves, vellum, 170mm by 115mm. 16th cent dark brown calf gilt. Mostly in black ink in a lettre batarde. With numerous initials in gold & colors, 12 historiated initials & 3 miniatures within full borders. HK Nov 4 (122) DM13,000
— [Paris or Tours, c.1480]. Use of Paris. In Latin, with Calendar in French. 167 leaves & 5 flyleaves, vellum, 162mm by 110mm. Lacking 8 leaves. Late 16th cent red mor gilt, tooled. In dark grey-brown ink in a gothic liturgical hand. With panel borders on every page, 40 small miniatures, 49 pictures & scenes of saints in margins of Calendar, & 14 full-page miniatures. S Dec 2 (65) £42,000 [Schoyen]
— [Tours, c.1480-90]. Use not stated. 175 leaves only, vellum, 124mm by 86mm, in 16th-cent calf gilt. In brown ink in a regular

lettre batarde. With illuminated initials throughout & 13 large miniatures with full borders. S June 23 (101) £5,500 [Fogg]
— [Northeast France or Paris, c.1480-95]. Unidentified Use. In Latin, with Calendar in French. 97 leaves (3 lacking), vellum, 149mm by 105mm, in 19th-cent dark green mor. In dark brown ink in a regular small lettre batarde. With 13 large illuminated initials with three-quarter illuminated borders & 2 large miniatures with full borders. S June 23 (112) £6,500 [Tenschert]
— [Northern Netherlands, Utrecht?, c.1480-1500]. In Dutch. 88 leaves only, vellum, 150mm by 110mm, in 19th-cent half calf. In dark brown ink in a compressed gothic liturgical hand. With 15 large illuminated initials with panel borders & 3 very large historiated initials with full borders. 7 outer margins cut with loss of borders. S June 23 (124) £2,500 [Schwartz]
— [Rouen, late 15th cent]. Use of Rouen. 110 leaves only, vellum, 163mm by 118mm, in an important early 17th-cent mor fanfare bdg, bound for Marie Le Maistre de Gonneville in 1606. With 9 large miniatures & 12 small calendar miniatures. C Dec 3 (185) £13,000 [Kraus]
— [Rouen?, after 1477]. Use of Rouen. 154 leaves (& 4 blanks), vellum, 170mm by 125mm. 17th cent brown calf. In brown ink, calendar in blue, red & gold; rubricated throughout. With numerous elaborate initials & decorated borders, partly gilt. 24 calendar miniatures & 15 almost full-p miniatures. FD Dec 2 (6) DM75,000
— [Tours, c.1485-95]. Use not stated. 96 leaves (6 lacking), vellum, 213mm by 152mm, in 18th-cent red mor gilt. In dark brown ink in a slightly sloping lettre batarde. With 21 small miniatures with three-quarter illuminated borders & 9 very large or full-page miniatures with full borders. Illuminated by a follower of Jean Fouquet & an associate of Jean Bourdichon. S June 23 (113) £48,000 [Kraus]
— [Chartres, late 15th cent]. Use of Chartres. In Latin, with Calendar, Quinze Joyes & Sept Requetes in French. 116 leaves only, vellum, 167mm by 112mm. Late 18th cent red mor gilt. In dark brown ink by more than 1 scribe in a gothic liturgical hand. With illuminated initials & line-fillers throughout & 3 large illuminated initials with full borders. S Dec 2 (64) £1,500 [Bocian]
— [Northern France, probably Auxerre, late 15th cent]. Use of Rome. In Latin, with Les Dictz des Sibilles in French. 136 leaves (12 lacking) & 5 flyleaves, vellum, 190mm by 96mm, in modern red velvet bdg. In black ink in a calligraphic lettre batarde with gothic features. With 16 small miniatures mostly with partial borders & 6 large miniatures with full borders. S June 23 (116) £13,000 [Tenschert]
— [Flanders, late 15th cent]. Use of Rome. 49 leaves, vellum, 117mm by 80mm, in modern limp vellum. In dark brown ink in a small gothic liturgical hand. With 8 small miniatures with panel borders, & large initial & full-page miniature with full borders. S June 23 (120) £2,400 [Schwartz]
— [Paris or Amiens, c.1490-1510]. Use of Amiens. 130 leaves, including 7 blanks, vellum, 175mm by 115mm, in modern lev by Hans Asper. With 10 half-page miniatures in colors within floral borders & 20 large decorated initials in colors & gold. sg Apr 2 (112) $22,000
— [France, c.1500]. [Of unidentified use.] In Latin. 136 leaves, vellum, 197mm by 121mm. Contemp purple velvet over wooden bds. In black & red ink. With numerous illuminated initials & 17 very large miniatures within full borders. HK Nov 4 (423) DM42,000
— [Auvergne?, c.1500]. 124 leaves & 5 flyleaves, vellum, 154mm by 93mm, in 16th-cent Parisian olive-brown mor gilt bdg "a la fanfare". In dark brown ink in a small lettre batarde. With 13 small miniatures with panel borders & 17 large miniatures with full borders. S June 23 (114) £16,000 [Tenschert]
— [Bourges, c.1500]. Use of Bourges. 86 leaves & 5 flyleaves, vellum, 223mm by 123mm, in contemp blindstamped tanned calf over wooden bds. In dark brown ink in a lettre batarde. With 12 large historiated initials & 2 small & 3 large miniatures with full borders. Dates of the Bourgeoys family added on flyleaves. S June 23 (115) £30,000 [Kraus]
— [Troyes, c.1508]. In Latin & French. 50 leaves, vellum, 170mm by 112mm, in 16th-cent roll-tooled calf, repaired. In brown ink in a lettre batarde. With 32 small & 3 large miniatures, all with full borders. Illuminated for Jeanne d'Avally. Possibly a supplement to a family Book of Hours. S June 23 (117) £7,000 [Thomas]
— [Northern France, early 16th cent]. Use not stated. 104 leaves, vellum, 24cm by 16cm. Late 16th cent vellum bdg. With illuminated foliate borders throughout & 10 full-page & 47 smaller miniatures in gold & colors. Lacking 2 leaves. HN May 22 (2922) DM38,000
— [Rouen, early 16th cent]. Use of Rouen. In Latin, with Calendar in French. 81 leaves, vellum, & 1 leaf in facsimile, 185mm by 110mm. 19th cent black mor. In dark brown ink in a formal upright lettre

batarde. With borders on every page, illuminated initials on most pages, 24 calendar miniatures & 14 full-page miniatures. S Dec 2 (66) £16,000 [Tenschert]
— [Paris?, early 16th cent]. Use of Rome. In Latin, with Calendar & a hymn in French. 161 leaves & 2 flyleaves, vellum, 162mm by 107mm. 17th cent chagreen with pierced silver clasp-mounts. In dark brown ink in a lettre batarde. With gold borders on every page, 22 small miniatures & 16 very large or full-page miniatures, mostly above historiated initials. S Dec 2 (67) £20,000 [G. Moss]
— [St. Omer, early 16th cent]. Use of St. Omer. In Latin & French. 76 leaves, vellum, 214mm by 150mm. Lacking 1 leaf. 16th cent blindstamped calf by Nicholas Spierinck, rebacked. In dark brown ink in a large lettre batarde. With illuminated initials, 12 calendar miniatures, 8 full-page & 13 smaller miniatures, mostly retouched, astronomical figures, planetary tables, & a working volvelle with 11 turning discs. S Dec 2 (69) £12,500 [Axel]
— [Netherlands, early 16th cent]. Use of Utrecht. 149 leaves, vellum, 151mm by 103mm, in modern calf. In dark brown ink in a regular gothic hand. With 27 decorated initials (3 very large) & 4 full-page miniatures by the Master of Charles V, with large initials & full borders on facing pages. S June 23 (125) £9,500 [Tenschert]
— [Trier?, early 16th cent]. Use of Rome. In German. 129 leaves only, vellum, 119mm by 85mm, in 19th-cent dark green cloth. In dark brown ink in a calligraphic gothic hand. With 8 large illuminated initials with partial borders & 2 full-page miniatures within ornamental frames, retouched. Last 24 leaves in a much later hand in cursive script. S June 23 (126) £1,400 [Niewodniczanski]
— [Paris or Tours, 1532-1540]. Use of Rome. 93 leaves (5 blank), vellum, 200mm by 135mm. 18th cent English gilt-panelled calf bdg. In brown ink in a fine rounded roman hand. With 152 initials on gold ground within colored floriate decoration & 18 large miniatures within elaborate borders. Made for King Francis I of France. C June 24 (265) £180,000 [H. P. Kraus]

Horman, William, c.1458-1535
Ms, Collectanea Sententiarum et Rerum Notabilium, in Latin with occasional words in English & Greek. [England, 1st half of 16th cent]. 191 leaves, vellum, 160mm by 108mm. Contemp blindstamped calf. In dark brown ink in an English italic or humanistic hand by 1 main scribe with additions in anr hand. Some ownership notes. S June 23 (88) £16,000 [Quaritch]

Horsley, Charles Edward
Autograph music, song, Dreams of the Past, for voice & piano. Sgd & dated 28 Mar 1871. 7 pp, folio. In brown ink on up to 12 staves per p. Last 2 pp nibbled by insects. S Nov 28 (551) £200

Hosemann, Theodor, 1807-75
ALs, [n.d.] 2 pp, 8vo. To [Karl Helmerding]. Asking for permission to wear Helmerding's costume to a ball. star Apr 8 (472) DM260

Houdini, Harry, 1874-1926
Ls, 17 Oct 1914. 1 p, 4to. To "Miss Rodney Richmond". Requesting her telephone no to arrange an appointment. Engraved port in upper corner. pnNY June 11 (25) $375

Howard, Henry, Earl of Northampton, 1540-1614
Ms, An answere to the coppie of a rayling Invective ag[ains]t the regement of woemen in gen[er]all [by John Knox]... written unto Queene Elizabeth; c.1630. About 100 pp, folio; modern bds. Written in a professional hand. S Jan 27 (795) £180 [Quaritch]

Howard, Leslie, 1893-1943
Photograph, sgd, [n.d.]. 5 by 7 inches. wa May 30 (374) $130

Howard, Oliver Otis, 1830-1909
ALs, 6 Dec 1883. 2 pp, 4to. Recipient unnamed. Recommending Thomas F. Barr for a judicial position. wa May 30 (229) $55

Howard, Sir Robert, 1626-98
ALs, 26 July 1668. 2 pp, folio. To Thomas Clifford, 1st Baron Clifford of Chudleigh. Explaining his poem The Duel of the Stags. Clifford of Chudleigh collection. S July 24 (250) £1,200 [Quaritch]

Howe, Julia Ward, 1819-1910
Collection of 2 A Ls s, 2 autograph transcripts, sgd, & 2 photographs, [1866-1867?] to 1901 & [n.d.]. 9 pp, various sizes, & photographs. To Mrs. Bradford, inviting her to a meeting. To Mr. Biddle, requesting a meeting. Transcripts of Battle Hymn of the Republic; five verses & 1st line. With Ls by her husband Gridley Howe [n.y.]; form notice for a meeting. P Oct 29 (68) $4,500

ALs, 16 Oct 1872. 2 pp, 8vo. Recipient unnamed. Ordering tickets for a lecture. Was mtd. wa May 30 (393) $100

Huch, Ricarda, 1864-1947
Collection of 3 A Ls s & autograph postcard, sgd, 1919 to 1927. 4 pp, 8vo. To Wilhelm Kolbe. Declining to give a lecture at Coburg, & regarding a poem about the Harz Mountains. HK Nov 7 (2256) DM750

HUDSON

Hudson, William Henry, 1841-1922
[An extensive collection of material by & pertaining to Hudson, including working papers for A Hind in Richmond Park, partly autograph, c.800 pp, sold at S on 23 July 1987, lot 150, for £4,500 to Caldur.]
Series of 125 A Ls s, 1904 to 1922 & [n.d.]. Over 400 pp, various sizes. To Lady [Margaret] Brooke, Ranee of Sarawak. Important letters chronicling their friendship. C June 24 (116) £6,500 [Quaritch]

Hueffer, Georg, 1851-1922
[A collection of c.330 letters addressed to Hueffer by scholars, politicians, priests, etc., 1869 to 1908, partly relating to the founding of the Goerres Society, sold at star on 8 Apr 1987, lot 356, for DM11,000.]
— EHRLE, FRANZ, CARDINAL. - 2 A Ls s, 1 Nov 1913 & 10 Apr 1915. 5 pp, 8vo. To Hueffer. Thanking for his book about Loreto. Cautioning him about publicizing his results too widely. 1st letter on Bibliotheca Apostolica Vaticana letterhead. With c.35 related letters. star Apr 8 (357) DM1,400

Huettenbrenner, Anselm, 1794-1868
Autograph music, "Fuga a tre voci", 44 bars for piano. 2 pp, 12 staves each. Sgd at head & dated 1832. Inscr to Joseph Deibl. star Apr 9 (675) DM4,200

Hufeland, Christoph Wilhelm, 1762-1836
ADs, 14 Apr [1821?]. 2 pp, 4to. Order permitting Dr. Stapf to produce & prescribe his own homeopathic medicines for a limited period. star Apr 8 (355) DM1,200

Hugenots
[A collection of 29 items, 1790 to 1811, relating to a Royal Bounty for the relief of Hugenots in England, especially to Peter Beuzeville, one of the distributors of the Bounty, with Beuzeville family correspondence, 23 items, sold at C on 3 Dec 1986, lot 280, for £400 to Quaritch.]

Huger, Isaac, d.1797. See: Heyward, Thomas & Others

Hugo, Victor, 1802-85
[An album containing 17 items by or pertaining to Hugo, drafts of poems, letters to Hugo or Juliette Drouet, a pencil port of Hugo, etc, sold at P on 15 Dec 1986, lot 52, for $3,500.]
ALs, 20 Aug [1821]. 3 pp, 8vo. To Pierre Foucher. About his stay at La Roche-Guyon & the illness of his fiancee Adele. S Nov 27 (371) £480 [Chaponniere]
— 20 Nov [1826]. 3 pp, 4to. To a friend in Constantinople. Informing him of the publication of his Odes et Ballades & the birth of his son. S Nov 27 (373) £250 [Lucas]
— 9 Feb 1831. 7 pp, 8vo. To Antoine Fontaney. Reporting that he has completed his Notre Dame de Paris & discussing his memories of Spain. S Nov 27 (374) £680 [Roth]
— [c.1840]. 1 p, 8vo. To Adolphe Chauveau. Congratulating him on a work. HN May 22 (3045a) DM280
— 10 Sept [1849]. 3 pp, 8vo. To Madame Hamelin. Describing a journey through the country. Sgd VH. With related material. S Nov 27 (372) £320 [Lucas]
— 4 Oct [n.y.]. 1 p, 8vo. To an unnamed lady. Promising to work for the pardoning of her husband. star Apr 8 (163) DM500
— 24 Oct [n.y.]. 1 p, 4to. To M. Bertall of Le Soir. Dinner invitation. S Jan 27 (973) £120 [Maggs]
Photograph, sgd & inscr, [n.d.]. 3.75 by 2.25 inches. Sgd on mount. wa May 30 (394) $210

Hull, T. A., 1830-1904
Autograph Ms, The elements of navigation acquired...during his education in the Royal Mathematical School...[n.d.].Fair copy, 355 pp, 4to. Orig calf gilt, repaired. bba Nov 13 (173) £75 [Burgess Browning]

Hull, William, 1753-1825
ADs, 26 June 1812. 1 p, 4to. General Order to "determine what Baggage shall be carried with the Army". wa May 30 (395) $270

Humboldt, Alexander von, 1769-1859
Series of 6 A Ls s, 5 June to 10 Oct 1841. 16 pp, folio. To King Friedrich Wilhelm IV of Prussia. "Rapports" nos 2, 8, 9, 14, 15 & 16 from Paris, analyzing the political situation in France & Europe, reporting about his talks with the French King & his ministers, etc. In French. HN May 22 (3049) DM7,000
ALs, 11 Oct 1807. 3 pp, 4to. To a French diplomat [Caulaincourt?]. Thanking for his intercession regarding interest payments due Humboldt. In French. star Apr 8 (358) DM780
— 23 Dec 1810. 3 pp, 4to. To an unnamed official in France. Recommending the son of his friend Reinhard von Haeften for a military appointment. In French. star Apr 8 (359) DM600
— [n.d.]. 2 pp, 4to. To [Pierre Francois Percy?]. Discussing a report regarding physiology. In French. HN Nov 27 (2293) DM1,000
— [n.d. "Saturday"]. 1 p, 8vo. To an unnamed U. S. consul. About currents in the Pacific & American progress in science. In French. sg Apr 9 (93) $350
— [1832]. 1 p, 12mo. To Julius Froebel. Informing him that he has recommended Froebel to G. R. Baerensprung. Sgd AHt.

star Apr 8 (360) DM210
— 28 June 1841. 1 p, 4to. To King Friedrich Wilhelm IV of Prussia. Reporting about Daguerre's invention. HN May 22 (3048) DM820
— [spring 1842]. 2 pp, 8vo. To an unnamed count. Declining a dinner invitation & mentioning Prussian ministers. In French. star Apr 8 (361) DM450
— 24 Apr 1844. 1 p, 8vo. To [Albert Peter] Lassen. Thanking for his book & commenting on it. star Apr 8 (362) DM850
— 28 May 1846. 1 p, 8vo. Recipient unnamed. Thanking for Schacht's Lehrbuch der Geographie. star Apr 8 (364) DM460
— 10 June 1846. 1 p, 8vo. Recipient unnamed. Reporting about an inspection of recipient's residence prior to his return to Berlin. star Apr 8 (365) DM650
— 23 Dec 1852. 1 p, 8vo. Recipient unnamed. Praising his work. JG Oct 2 (224) DM600
ANs, [n.d.]. 1 p, 3 by 4.5 inches. Recipient & contents not stated. Sgd in text. In French. With 2 portraits. wa May 30 (396) $75

Humboldt, Wilhelm von, 1767-1835
ALs, 22 Nov 1803. 1 p, 8vo. To an unnamed Marquis. Requesting him to forward letters to Baron de Schubart. In French. star Apr 8 (366) DM420
— 4 July 1810. 2 pp, 4to. To Philipp Albert Stapfer. Talking about his diplomatic appointment to Vienna & his efforts on behalf of the new university in Berlin. In French. star Apr 8 (367) DM1,700
— 24 Sept 1815. 4 pp, 4to. To [Princess Radziwill]. About the political situation in Europe after Waterloo. With ANs by Alexander von Humboldt. S May 21 (259) £520 [Lucas]
— 14 June 1825. 1 p, 4to. To von Altenstein. Inviting him to dinner. With draft of Altenstein's reply below, in pencil. star Apr 8 (368) DM500

Hummel, Johann Nepomuk, 1778-1837
[A collection of 2 A Ls s, 2 A Ds s, & Ds, 27 Sept 1830 to 10 Nov 1834, 5 pp, 4to & 8vo, regarding his business contacts with Tobias Haslinger, with related material, sold at star on 9 Apr 1987, lot 674, for DM7,500.]
Ms, Thematisches Verzeichnis der Original-Compositionen..., in the hand of Tobias Haslinger; [n.d.], 6 pp, folio. Listing 40 compositions, each with 1-line musical quotation. With ANs by Haslinger concerning assumption of copyright from S. A. Steiner. With ADs by Hummel, 1836, confirming Haslinger's copyright. FD Dec 2 (3238) DM1,050
ALs, 13 May 1831. 1 p, 4to. To Sir George Smart. Agreeing to play at a concert. C Dec 3 (414) £180 [Andrews]

Humperdinck, Engelbert, 1854-1921
ALs, 13 Dec [18]95. 4 pp, 8vo. To the pbr Gustav Cohen. About differences regarding the rights to the 2d Ed of one of his songs. FD June 11 (3557) DM600

Humphrey, Hubert H.
Series of 4 Ls s, 1954 & 1955. 4 pp, size not stated. To George McCullough. Concerning a bill & the Ladejinsky case. With related material. pnNY June 11 (21) $70

Hundertwasser, Friedensreich
Collection of 2 A Ls s, Ls, 9 autograph postcards, sgd, & art postcard, sgd. 1959 to 1975. 4 pp, 4to, & cards. Recipient unnamed. Personal news & about his work. With related material. FD June 11 (3512) DM2,400
— Collection of 2 A Ls s, Ls, & 11 autograph postcards, 10 sgd, 1959 to 1975. 4 pp, folio & 4to, & cards. Recipient unnamed. Personal news & about his work. With related material. star Apr 8 (473) DM1,400

Hunter, John
Ms, consular letterbook kept at San Lucar de Barrameda, 1786 to 1791. 180 pp, 4to; orig cloth. Copies of letters to Anthony Merry, Consul-General at Madrid & others; reporting about shipping, customshouse business, etc. C Dec 3 (329) £100 [Bristow]

Hunter, William, 1718-83
— Power, J.[?]. - Ms, notes taken in Hunter's lectures on anatomy, [n.d.]. About 400 pp, in 2 vols; calf. Mostly in ink. S Jan 27 (906) £700 [Rota]

Hunting Manuscripts
Ms, Discours sur la chasse du lievre. [17th cent] 12 pp, 256mm by 165mm, in 19th-cent half vellum. Jeanson Ms 151 SM Feb 28 (179) FF2,000
— Ms, Duo de cors de chasse. [c.1760] 2 vols. 31 & 28 leaves, 120mm by 204mm, in contemp mor gilt. Collection of 53 fanfares, with 6 19th-cent fanfares written at the end of the 1st vol. Jeanson Ms 155 SM Feb 28 (201) FF7,000
— Ms, Etat des cerfs pris ou manques, annee par annee. 1741. 18 pp, 115mm by 58mm, in red mor gilt with arms of Louis Charles, Comte d'Eu. Jeanson Ms 148 SM Feb 28 (213) FF22,000
— Ms, Etat general des forets du domaine. 1763. 584 pp, 177mm by 195mm, in red mor gilt with arms of Jean Moreau de Séchelles. Jeanson Ms 160 SM Feb 28 (214) FF13,000
— Ms, Giornale della caccia ussisa da settembre 1827 ad agosto 1828. 90 pp, 230mm by 162mm, in red mor gilt with

HUNTING MANUSCRIPTS

arms of Francois I, King of the Two Sicilies. Jeanson Ms 170 SM Mar 1 (264) FF15,000
— Ms, La Chace dou cerf. [19th cent] 51 leaves, 4to, in contemp half calf. Jeanson Ms 198 SM Feb 28 (117) FF700
— Ms, L'Art d'Archerie. [France, perhaps Picardie, c.1485] 8 leaves, vellum, 306mm by 215mm, in 19th-cent bds. Heber-Pichon-Gallice-Jeanson Ms SM Mar 1 (323) FF75,000
— Ms, Le Livre de la chace dou serf. [c.1860] 10 leaves, vellum, 8vo, in mor extra by Hardy. Jeanson Ms 233 SM Mar 1 (361) FF4,200
— Ms, Le Livre du faucon des dames. [c.1860] 24 leaves, vellum, 8vo, in mor gil by Trautz-Bauzonnet. Jeanson 1804 SM Mar 1 (364) FF5,000
— Ms, Le Livre du faucon des dames. [19th cent] In the hand of A. Veinant. 49 pp, 197mm by 126mm, in half cloth. Jeanson Ms 221 SM Mar 1 (365) FF1,200
— Ms, Les Dictz des bestes & aussi des oyseaulx. [c.1860] 22 leaves, vellum, in mor janseniste by Chambolle-Duru, 1863. With 50 illusts in the text. Jeanson Ms 1803 SM Feb 28 (177) FF2,000
— Ms, Livret des chasse pour 1814, comprenant le budget des depenses du Grand Veneur pour l'an 1814.... 100 pp, 201mm by 145mm, in mor gilt. Jeanson Ms 172 SM Mar 1 (366) FF12,000
— Ms, Proces de chasse a fourquevaux 1550-1551. 30 pp, 285mm by 176mm, in 19th-cent half vellum. Jeanson Ms 150 SM Mar 1 (477) FF3,600
— Ms, Recueil des proces-verbaux de MM Milles, d'Estrees et vaillant des 26 avril 1540, 12 decembre 1672 et 5 may 1690. [end of 17th cent] About 500 pp, 222mm by 165mm, in calf gilt. Jeanson Ms 167 SM Mar 1 (482) FF2,800
— Ms, Sesuyt le deduit des chiens et des oiseaulx et aussi la sentence du conte de tancarville sur le faict diceluy. Paris: Philippe Le Noir [c.1860]. 20 leaves, vellum, 8vo, inmor janseniste by Chambolle-Duru, 1863. Schwerdt-Jeanson Ms SM Feb 28 (166) FF2,200
— Ms, Traite dans lequel il est parle du naturel des oyseaulx de chant qui vivent dans les bois et autour des buissons. [end of 17th cent] 126 pp, 182mm by 125mm, in 19th-cent half calf. Jeanson Ms 131 SM Mar 1 (564) FF3,900
— Ms, Traite de fauconnerie et autres textes sur les oiseaux et la fauconnerie.... [Northeastern Italy, probably Venice, mid 16th cent] 54 leaves, vellum, 212mm by 164mm, in 18th-cent vellum. Jeanson Ms 130 SM Mar 1 (565) FF30,000

AMERICAN BOOK PRICES CURRENT

Huntington, Samuel, Signer from Connecticut

Ds s (2) 10 Apr 1772 & 5 Nov 1793. 2 pp, 12mo & 8vo. As Justice of the Peace, summons. Receipt. pnNY June 11 (22) $50

Ds, 2 Nov 1792. 1 p, folio. Military commission for Joel Hawkins. Foxed. Charlotte Parker Milne collection. wd Nov 12 (46) $100

Huntington, Samuel, 1765-1817

Ds, 18 July 1809. 1 p, 4to. As Governor of Ohio, commission in state militia. rf Mar 14 (22) $95

Hutton, Catherine, 1756-1846

Series of 9 A Ls s, 4 Dec 1821 to 21 Jan 1827 & [n.d.]. 18 pp, 8vo & 4to. To James Belcher. About her literary works & her father. C Dec 3 (367) £65 [Temperley]

Hymnal

Ms, Liber Hymnorum Dominicalium et Festivorum per totum annum. [Naples, between 1461 & 1483]. 103 leaves, vellum, 227mm by 147mm. 18th-cent red mor bdg with crowned monogram PR. In dark brown ink in a rounded slightly clubbed humanistic minuscule attributable to Pietro Ursuleo. With 2-line illuminated initials throughout, 5 large whitevine illuminated initials, 2 half-page miniatures, illuminated tp & facing leaf with historiated initial & full illuminated & historiated border, almost certainly by Cola Rapicano. S June 23 (94) £40,000 [Brown]

See also: Greek Manuscripts

I

Ibert, Jacques, 1890-1962

Autograph music, Cello Concerto, 1925; 9 pp, folio. Cello part only, with autograph p & revisions, & annotations by Ibert & Madeleine Monnier. With related material. S May 22 (414) £650 [Talbot]

Ibsen, Henrik, 1828-1906

A Ls s (2), 8 Dec 1886 & 30 June 1891. 3 pp, 8vo. To the theater directors Julius Petersen & W. Foght. Concerning performing rights & royalties for some of his plays. S May 21 (261) £850 [Uppstrom]

Photograph, sgd & inscr, 20 Jan 1880. 16cm by 11cm. Inscr to Emil Poulsen. Folded. S May 21 (260) £200 [Uppstrom]

Signature, on autograph visiting card; with address. 1885 or later]. star Apr 8 (164) DM270

Iffland, August Wilhelm, 1759-1814

ALs, 8 Sept 1801. 1 p, folio. To Johann Friedrich Reichardt. Asking him to a conference to discuss the opening of the new theater. star Apr 9 (870) DM1,200

Ihering, Rudolf von, 1818-92

ALs, 11 Apr 1882. 4 pp, 8vo. To his daughter Helene & her husband Viktor Ehrenberg. Family news, & about his article regarding the abolition of tipping. star Apr 8 (370) DM500

India

[A collection of 3 journals & letterbooks relating to the 39th Regiment of Foot in the service of the East India Company in India, c.1757 to 1760, c.650 pp, folio, calf & vellum, sold at S on 24 July 1987, lot 337, for £1,100 to Army Museum.]

[Sindh. - A collection of Ms copies of correspondence relating to events in Sindh, 1845 to 1847, & its conquest by Sir Charles Napier, 921 pp, folio, in half calf bdg, sold at C on 24 June 1987, lot 85, for £750 to Bush.]

Ms, Account book of transactions at Mirzapore, Lucknow, Benares, etc., 6 June 1778 to 8 July 1785. 150 pp, folio. Calf bdg. Listing shipping quantities of cotton, opium, indigo, etc., with prices & expenses. C June 24 (83) £300 [Maggs]

— WARING, EDWARD JOHN. - 2 Mss, [c.1853 to 1862], 122 & 60 leaves, 4to, mostly on rectos only. Notes on Indian customs, folklore, etc., some initialed. Wraps. C June 24 (86) £280 [Maggs]

Indian Manuscripts

Ms, collection of 4 Hindu texts, [Northern India, 18th cent]. 274 leaves, 170mm by 130mm. Cloth over bds. In devanagari script. With 13 full-page illusts in gold & colors. HK Nov 4 (440) DM2,100

Indians, North American

Single sheet ptg, 11 Mar 1831. 1 p, 330mm by 190mm. Broadside petition of inhabitants of Tunkhannock, Pa., sgd by Anson Jones & c.46 others, not to remove Indians from Pennsylvania. sg Nov 6 (102) $350

— BIDDLE, CHARLES. - Ls, 15 July 1790; length not stated. To Col. Willett. Mentioning the Creek Indians, Col. McGillivray & a treaty with the U.S. rf Mar 14 (11) $210

Indy, Vincent d', 1851-1931

A Ls s (2), 30 Aug & 11 Nov 1916. 4 pp, folio & 8vo. Recipient unnamed. About his Orfeo & Monteverdi's L'incoronazione di Poppaea. Arranging for a meeting. S May 22 (416) £250 [Haas]

Ingolstadt

Ms, Bericht vnd uberslag dess hauss und underhalltung der befestigung Schloss und Stat Jngellstatt, [Germany, c.1550]. 35 leaves & 3 blanks, 303mm by 205mm. Contemp blindstamped pigskin, wormed. In black cursive script. Ownership inscr of Joachim Graf von Ortenburg, 1591. About fortifications at Inglostadt & their maintenance. HK Nov 4 (424) DM5,000

Innocent IV, Pope, d.1254

Transcript, contemp notarial copy of a bull concerning his fight against heresy, 8 Apr [1254]. 1 p, 330mm by 260mm. Vellum. With 4-line authentication by Rolandinus, imperial notary, 12 June 1254. C Dec 3 (281) £380 [Robbins]

Innocent VIII, Pope, 1432-92

Document, [11 Oct] 1488. 1 p, 33cm by 55cm. Vellum. Bull, addressed to the archdeacon & the treasurer of the church at Cordoba, regarding revenues from taxes, & repeating bull by Paul II, 11 May 1465. Countersgd by Juan de Torquemada. Lead seal. star Apr 9 (1112) DM1,700

Ireland, William Henry, 1777-1835. See: Shakespeare, William

Irving, Washington, 1783-1859

Series of 5 A Ls s, 2 Apr 1832 to 2 Aug 1837. To Col. Thomas Wildman. Sending books, thanking for his hospitality & introducing various countrymen. S July 23 (80) £800 [Jackson]

ALs, 13 May 1829. 3 pp, 4to. To Peter Irving. Describing his moving into one of the vacant apartments of the Alhambra. Seal holes. Bullock collection. CNY Dec 19 (99) $800

— 30 Oct 1849. 1 p, 12mo. To his printer[?]. Asking that the proofs be sent to him because of a carriage accident. Mtd. sg Nov 6 (104) $110

— 22 Nov 1854. 2 pp, 8vo. To A. Featherman. Saying he does not know whether he could find a pbr in NY for his "programme". Framed. Altman collection. pnNY Sept 13 (123) $475

Isabella Clara Eugenia of Austria, Regent of the Netherlands, 1566-1633

Ls, 14 June 1626. 1 p, folio. To Juan Bravo de Lagunas, castellan at Antwerpen. Requesting information about the religious trustworthiness of a person nominated for office. star Apr 9 (1247) DM250

ISABELLA I

Isabella I, Queen of Spain, 1451-1504
Ds, 5 Jan 1501. 1 p, folio. Order to give money to a servant for the setting of a diamond. With receipt sgd by Juan de Tabera below. Repaired. C June 24 (49) £680 [Maggs] See also: Ferdinand V & Isabella I

Isabey, Jean-Baptiste, 1767-1855
ALs, 15 Feb 1815. 2 pp, 4to. To Picard. Complaining about being badly treated by the Academie Royale de Musique. S Nov 27 (376) £280 [Quaritch]

Isherwood, Christopher, 1904-86
[A collection of childhood writings, photographs & memorabilia sold at C on 24 June, lot 118C, for £650 to Zeitlin & Verbrugge.]

Collection of 18 A Ls s & 31 Ls s, 5 Dec 1942 to 22 Apr 1974. 68 pp, various sizes. To his brother Richard Isherwood & his mother Kathleen Bradshaw-Isherwood. Describing the war years in America, talking about his work, his friends, etc. C June 24 (118A) £2,200 [Stone Trough]

— Collection of 3 A Ls s, 5 Ls s, 3 autograph postcards, sgd & 3 A Ns s, 29 Aug 1966 to 9 Oct 1971. 14 pp, various sizes. To Harry Heckford. Giving information for a study of his work begun by Heckford. 1 Ls def. C Dec 3 (368) £360 [Bristow]

— Collection of 4 A Ls s & 6 Ls s, 5 Sept 1967 to 21 Sept 1969. 10 pp, air letters. To Harry Heckford. Providing information for a critical appreciation of his work. C June 24 (119) £500 [Zeitlin & Verbrugge]

Series of 3 A Ls s, 30 Sept [1930] to 31 May [1932]. 8 pp, 8vo. To his brother Richard Isherwood. Reporting about his stay in Berlin, describing one of his pupils, etc. C June 24 (118) £500 [Schiller]

Isherwood, Christopher, 1904-86 —& Auden, Wystan Hugh, 1907-73
[A collection of 9 photographs of Isherwood & W. H. Auden, 1 sgd by Isherwood, 1 by both, [1930s], sold at C on 24 June 1987, lot 118B, for £350 to Schiller.]

Italy
— UNIVERSITY OF BOLOGNA. - Document, 14 Dec 1591. 10 leaves, 245mm by 168mm. Vellum. Grant of a doctorate in canon & civil law to Ettore di Antonio Dosio. In black ink in a very fine italic hand; 1st page, names, & capitals in gold. With miniature, 2 very fine illuminated initials & 1st page with large initial & full border. S June 23 (37) £700 [Licini]

AMERICAN BOOK PRICES CURRENT

Itten, Johannes, 1888-1967
ALs, [n.d., c.1919-1923]. 3 pp, 8vo. To Eugen Diederichs. Regarding the performance of an Indian musician at Weimar. In pencil. star Apr 8 (475) DM580

J

Jackson, Andrew, 1767-1845
ALs, 23 June 1824. 1 p, 4to. To Major Henry Stark. Thanking for a present from his daughters. With copy of letter of presentation. CNY May 11 (63) $1,200

— 29 Jan 1832. 1 p, 8vo. To Amos Kendall. In 3d person, requesting information whether he has a missing report by [George W. Erving] concerning Florida & Louisiana. With note of authentication by Kendall, 6 May 1864, at bottom of p. P Oct 29 (69) $500

— 10 March 1832. 2 pp, 4to. To Andrew Jackson, Jr. Enclosing money & talking about the refurnishing of the Hermitage. P Oct 29 (70) $2,700

AL, [n.d.]. 1 p, size not stated. Recipient unknown. Draft, recommending a revolutionary officer for an appointment. pnNY June 11 (29) $150

Ls, 5 Jan 1813. 2 pp, 4to. To [David Holmes]. Requesting him to forward letters concerning supplies needed by his troops. Paper loss affecting text; repaired. P May 13 (66) $2,400

— 21 Jan 1818. 1 p, 4to. To Edward Livingston. Expressing thanks for a statue of Napoleon. Seal tear. P May 13 (67) $1,300

Ds, 1 June 1829. 1 p, folio. Commission of William Pitt Preble as Minister to the Netherlands. Countersgd by Van Buren. pnNY June 11 (28) $900

— 1 Dec 1830. 1 p, 4to. Land grant. Worn. wa May 30 (113) $350

— [n.d.]. 1 p, 4to. Appointment of Robert Whitaker as boatswain. Countersgd by Mahlon Dickerson. wa May 30 (283) $400

Autograph endorsement, 18 Mar 1829. 1 p, 4to. On integral address leaf of ALs from Charles S. Stewart to Sec of the Navy John Branch, recommending Francis G. McCauley for Purser. Referring letter to Branch. Sgd A.J. sg Nov 6 (105) $225

Franking signature, [23 Mar 1830]. With autograph address. rf May 30 (21) $625

Jackson, Thomas J. ("Stonewall"), 1824-63
Autograph endorsement, sgd, 15 May 1863. On verso of a letter by Col. Willis, 14 Apr 1863, stating his inability to comply with General Orders no 23; 3 lines referring the matter to Capt. Allen. Also endorsed by other army officers. Quarter mor gilt folding case.

CNY Dec 19 (100) $2,200

Jacobi, Hugo, 1842-1906
[A collection of c.90 letters addressed to him by German politicians, industrialists & scholars, 1873 to 1906, with related material, sold at star on 9 Apr 1987, lot 1021, for DM2,600.]

Jahn, Friedrich Ludwig, 1778-1852
ALs, 18 Dec 1844. 2 pp, 8vo. To Heinrich Proehle. Asking him to send yeast. Initialled. star Apr 9 (1022) DM320
— 27 Jan 1850. 2 pp, 8vo. Recipient unnamed. Commenting about the election at Freyburg. star Apr 9 (1023) DM380

Jahnn, Hans Henny, 1894-1959
Ls, 30 June 1956. 1 p, folio. To Hans Wolffheim. Requesting an interview concerning the diaries of Ida Dehmel. star Apr 8 (166) DM380

James, Charles, 1758-1821
[A large collection of his papers, including c.200 letters written to him, c.1788 to 1821, Mss of poems & military proposals, documents, etc., sold at S on 18 Dec 1986, lot 287, for £ 1,400 to White.]

James, Edward
Collection of 2 A Ls s, Ls, 4 telegrams & 3 typescripts, 1937 to 1940. About 20 pp, 4to. To Rene Magritte & his wife Georgette (1). About Magritte's paintings, his travels, art dealers, etc. 3 poems, 2 sgd. S July 2 (975) £900 [Quaritch]

James, Henry, 1843-1916
A Ls s (2), 6 May 1895 & 9 Nov 1902. 3 pp, 4to & 8vo. To Charles F. Keary. Inviting him to dinner. Re-establishing contact. S July 23 (83) £450 [Sotheran]

James I, King of England, 1566-1625
Ls, 28 Dec 1599. 1 p, folio. To George Keith, Earl Marischal of Scotland. Complaining about financial difficulties & calling a convention of the Scotch estates. With quittance, sgd & sealed by the Earl Marischal [1547]. S Dec 18 (205) £520 [Wilson]
— 21 Feb 1603 [1604]. 1 p, folio. To Matthew Hutton, Archbishop of York. Granting leave of absence from Parliament & requesting him to send a proxy. With certified contemp copy of a letter from James to Hutton & Lord Sheffield, 19 Feb 1604, 3 pp, folio, emphasizing the laws concerning religion. C Dec 3 (284) £700 [Wilson]
— 10 Apr 1603. 1 p, folio. To Matthew Hutton, Archbishop of York. Thanking him for his declaration of allegiance. C Dec 3 (283) £1,000 [Joseph]

— 8 Apr 1606. 1 p, folio. To [George Keith,] the Earl Marischal of Scotland. Ordering that hawks are not to be disturbed in their nests. With autograph postscript, 13 words. S Dec 18 (206) £620 [Maggs]
— 15 Sept 1606. 1 p, 4to. Recipient unnamed. Granting a permanent salary to Capt. Robert Jameson. With related ALs by Lord Nottingham. wa May 30 (398) $900
— 16 May 1623. 1 p, folio. To an unnamed counsellor. Discussing the granting of 2 fairs at Hawick to William Douglas of Drumlanrig. Sgd at head. Def. pn Dec 11 (13) £580 [J. Wilson]

Letter, 19 Feb 1612. 2 pp, folio. To Sir James Fullerton. True copy, giving directions regarding the succession of Prince Charles to the Killingworth estate. Copy attested by Fullerton. Docketed. With notes by Fullerton, sgd twice, at bottom. sg Apr 9 (96) $60

Ds, 12 Apr 1578. 1 p, folio. As King of Scotland, instructions to admit Patrick, Master of Gray, as one of the extraordinary Lords of Session. C Dec 3 (282) £380 [Wilson]
— 22 Dec [1614]. 1 p, 4to. Vellum. Grant of hunting rights in the Forest of Waltham to Sir Gawen Hervye. Framed. Altman collection. pnNY Sept 13 (37) $1,400

James II, King of England, 1633-1701
ALs, 25 Aug [1683]. 2 pp, 4to. To his niece Charlotte Fitzroy, Countess of Lichfield. Expressing concern about her health. Sgd J. C Dec 3 (285) £300 [Jackson]
— 8 Sept [1683]. 2 pp, 4to. To Charlotte Fitzroy, Countess of Lichfield. Reporting about hunting as a pastime of his family & a sea trip to Portsmouth. Sgd J. C Dec 3 (286) £260 [Dupre]
— 6 June [n.y.]. 2 pp, 4to. To his niece the Countess of Lichfield. Saying there is little news & asking her to write to him. Sgd J, twice. S July 24 (233) £320 [Stewart]

Ls, 12 July 1686. 1 p, folio. To the Duke of Ormond. Directing him to swear Sir Winston Churchill in the position of 2nd clerk of the Greencloth. S Dec 18 (209) £450 [Maggs]
— 11 June 1688. 2 pp, 4to. To Prince Philip William. Notifying him of the birth of his son. In Latin. P Dec 15 (54) $2,100

Ds, 27 Mar 1686. 1 p, folio. Warrant for payment to the Holland Regiment of Foot. Countersgd by William Blathwayt. S Jan 27 (756) £280 [Bristow]
— 20 Aug 1686. 1 p, folio. Money order to Henry, Duke of Grafton for payment of the 5th Regiment of Foot Guards. Framed.

111

JAMES II

Altman collection. pnNY Sept 13 (39) $600
See also: Clifford, Thomas

James River and Kanawha Company
Ms, minute book of the annual stockholders' meetings, Oct 1859 to 5 Mar 1880. 1 vol, folio. Leather bdg. wa Oct 18 (72) $1,300

Jarry, Alfred, 1873-1907
— COLLEGE DE PATAPHYSIQUE. - Letter, 25 Dec 1953, to Rene Magritte, enclosing results of a survey into the meaning of the word "Poesie" (present). Together 4 pp, 4to & 8vo. S July 2 (976) £900 [Rota]

Jaspers, Karl, 1883-1969
Ls, 22 Oct 1947. 1 p, 8vo. To Georg Wieszner. Declining to lecture in Nuernberg. star Apr 8 (371) DM210

— 3 Oct 1956. 1 p, folio. To Arthur A. Cohen. Declining to contribute to the Handbook of Christian Theology. star Apr 8 (372) DM320

Jaures, Jean Leon, 1859-1914
Autograph Ms, article, Prenez l'offensive, [c.1897]. 10 pp, folio. Attack on anti-semitic elements in France. C June 24 (50) £500 [Castaing]

Jawlensky, Alexej von, 1864-1941
ALs, [n.d.]. 2 pp, 8vo (lettercard). To an unnamed lady. Reporting about tests done in a hospital. star Apr 8 (476) DM440

Jay, John, 1745-1829
Series of 6 A Ls s, 27 May 1780 to 10 Jan 1825. 6 pp, 4to. To Gouverneur Morris (1) & his son Peter Augustus Jay. Reporting from Madrid; partly in cipher. Political & family news. P Oct 29 (71) $3,250

AL, 9 Feb 1779. 1 p, 8vo. Recipient unnamed. Draft. As President of the Continental Congress, covering letter for a Resolution of 30 Jan 1779, concerning warrants on goods taken for the use of troops. sg Nov 6 (280) $200

Ls, 14 Aug 1779. 2 pp, folio. To George Clinton. As President of the Continental Congress, about the need to recruit soldiers in view of British reinforcements. With autograph subscription. S July 24 (396) £820 [Joseph & Sawyer]

Ds, 16 Mar 1779. 1 p, 4to. Commission for Aaron Benjamin as Lieut. in the 8th Connecticut Regiment; partly ptd. Framed with a port. sg Nov 6 (281) $450

— 18 Apr 1800. 1 p, folio. Military appointment for William Clapsaddle. Partly ptd. sg Apr 9 (97) $275

Jean, Grand Duc de Luxembourg —& Josephine Charlotte, Grande Duchesse de Luxembourg
Group photograph, 22 Nov 1971. 18.6cm by 14.5cm. Sgd by both & inscr to K. B. Andersen by Josephine Charlotte, on mount, 26cm by 20cm. star Apr 9 (1045) DM900

Jean Paul. See: Richter, Jean Paul

Jefferies, Richard, 1848-87
Autograph Ms, essay, Grey Sea, draft; [n.d.]. 33 pp, mostly on rectos, 8vo. In ink & pencil; numerous revisions. With related material. S Dec 18 (72) £6,000 [Sotheran]

Jefferson, Thomas, 1743-1826
Autograph Ms, transcription from memory of last p of his letter to William Short, begun 13 April 1800. 9 May 1800; 1 p, 4to. Analyzing the state of parties & discussing the next Presidential elections. Sgd Th:J. Was mtd. P Oct 29 (73) $3,750

A Ls s (2), 7 Sept & 23 Nov 1807. 2 pp, 4to. To George Hay & to the U. S. Congress. Sending an edited copy of Wilkinson's letter of 12 Nov 1806 (not present) for use in the Burr trial. Submitting a copy of the proceedings & the evidence exhibited in the Burr trial (not present). P May 13 (71) $40,000

ALs, 11 Mar 1790. 1 p, size not stated. To A. Donald. Concerning plants to be shipped to France. Encapsulated. wa May 30 (114) $3,250

— 10 Nov 1796. 1 p, 4to. To John Stuart. Acknowledging receipt of fossil "bones of the Great-claw". Expressing his wish to obtain a thigh bone of the animal before reporting the find to the Philosophical Society. Mtd with a port. P Oct 29 (72) $6,000

— 12 June 1801. 1 p, 4to. To Attorney Gen. Levi Lincoln. Suggesting a course of action in a prize case. Mtd. P May 13 (68) $8,000

— 13 June 1802. 1 p, 4to. To Thomas Whitney. As President, ordering an artificial horizon as described in a European cat. Seal tear. CNY Dec 19 (102) $5,000

— 25 July 1803. 1 p, 8vo. To [William] Roberts & Mrs. Taylor. In 3d person, inviting them to dinner. S Dec 18 (345) £600 [Jeffery]

— 14 June 1808. 1 p, 4to. To David Gelston. About a plough being sent to him from France. CNY May 11 (46) $3,200

— 9 Dec 1808. 1 p, 4to. "To the Society of the Methodist Episcopal church at Pittsburg". Thanking for a message of good wishes & commenting on religious freedom & current political problems. P May 13 (72) $15,000

— 15 Jan 1810. 2 pp, 4to. To Samuel

Kercheval. Explaining his rules for donating money to philanthropic institutions. Mtd between plexiglass. P May 13 (73) $17,000

— 7 Dec 1810. 1 p, 4to. To David Gelston. About a plough brought for him by Gen. Armstong. With franking signature. CNY May 11 (47) $3,200

— 14 Nov 1811. 1 p, 4to. To David Gelston. In 3d person, expressing his thanks for information concerning the tonnage of steamboats. With franking signature. Seal hole. CNY Dec 19 (25) $3,000

— 9 Apr 1812. 1 p, 4to. To David Gelston. Concerning the shipping of a spinning machine invented by Ebenezer Herrick. With franking signature. CNY May 11 (48) $3,200

— 2 July 1812. 1 p, 4to. To David Gelston. Giving instructions concerning the shipping [of a spinning machine]. With franking signature. CNY May 11 (49) $7,500

— 3 Apr 1814. 1 p, 4to. To David Gelston. In 3d person, expressing his thanks for pumpkin seed sent to him. With franking signature. Seal tear. CNY Dec 19 (26) $2,400

— 6 Mar 1815. 1 p, 4to. To Philip Mazzei. Letter of introduction for Dr. Benjamin Smith Barton. P May 13 (74) $4,000

— 15 Aug 1815. 1 p, 4to. To David Gelston. Making arrangements for reshipment of packages from Europe. With franking signature. Seal hole. CNY Dec 19 (28) $3,200

— 3 Aug 1816. 1 p, 4to. To David Gelston. Requesting him to reship Barsac wine addressed to his care to Richmond. With franking signature. CNY Dec 19 (27) $4,200

— 18 Sept 1816. 1 p, 4to. To David Gelston. Concerning a shipment of books ordered after "parting with my library to Congress" With franking signature. Torn. CNY Dec 19 (29) $5,000

— 13 Nov 1816. 2 pp, 4to. To Gov. Wilson Cary Nicholas. Regarding a government appointment for Mr. Armistead & trying to reconcile Nicholas & James Monroe. Framed. P May 13 (75) $10,000

— 28 May 1818. 1 p, 4to. To Mordecai M. Noah. Thanking for a discourse on the consecration of a synagogue sent to him. Commenting on the persecution of Jews & the necessity of religious tolerance. Charles J. Rosenbloom collection. P Oct 29 (76) $360,000

— 2 Feb 1819. 1 p, 4to. To William Davenport. Giving instructions for repairing his telescope. Mtd. P Oct 29 (75) $4,350

— 13 Aug 1820. 1 p, 4to. To David Gelston. Asking him to forward letters. With franking signature. CNY May 11 (50) $4,000

— 27 Aug 1820. 1 p, 4to. To David Gelston. About a shipment of books. With franking signature; integral address leaf separated. CNY Dec 19 (30) $3,500

— 1 Oct 1820. 1 p, 4to. To David Gelston. Enclosing a bank note to cover freight & duties on his books. CNY May 11 (51) $2,800

— 19 Jan 1823. 1 p, 4to. To Francis Adrian Van Der Kemp. About old age, his declining health, & the difficulty to write. With franking signature on integral address leaf. P May 13 (76) $9,000

AL, 19 Aug 1803. 1 p, 4to. To Benjamin Lincoln. Requesting him to forward goods ordered from Marseilles. Bottom portion lacking. With franking signature on integral address leaf. With related material. sg Apr 9 (99) $1,200

ANs, 10 Jan 1803. 1 p, small oblong, cut from a larger sheet. To Attorney Gen. Levi Lincoln. In 3d person, requesting him to attend a consultation. P Oct 29 (74) $1,600

— 14 Mar 1807. 1 p, 4to. To the Attorney General [C. A. Rodney]. In 3d person, inviting the cabinet to a consultation at dinner. rf Mar 14 (24) $2,000

Ds, An Act for...Satisfying the Claims of Frederick William de Steuben, approved 4 June 1790. 1 p, folio; ptd. Attested & sgd as Sec of State. wa May 30 (284) $5,000

— 15 June 1801. 1 p, folio. Ship's passport for the brig Paisley of New York. Countersgd by Madison. Large vignette. sg Apr 9 (98) $3,800

— 2 Jan 1804. 1 p, 4to. Naval appointment. rf May 30 (10) $1,600

— [before 30 Jan 1805]. 1 p, folio. Ship's papers in 4 languages for the sloop Eliza. Countersgd by James Madison. Fold tear. Framed. P May 13 (69) $1,200

— 18 Nov 1805. 1 p, folio. Ship's papers for the schooner Lion of New York. Countersgd by Madison. pnNY June 11 (31) $2,800

— 10 Apr 1806. 1 p, folio. Military commission, partly ptd. Countersgd by Sec of War Henry Dearborn. Faded. wa Oct 18 (26) $600

— 13 Nov 1806. 1 p, folio. Passport for the brigantine Fox of Salem. Countersgd by James Madison. P May 13 (70) $2,600

— 13 May 1807. 1 p, folio. Ship's passport for a schooner. Countersgd by Madison. wa May 30 (285) $2,600

— 22 Aug 1807. 1 p, folio. Ship's papers in 4 languages for the Susan of New York. Countersgd by Madison. rf Mar 14 (25) $1,550

— 10 Nov 1807. 1 p, 16.5 by 20.5 inches. Ship's papers in 4 languages for the Sally and Hetty. Countersgd by Madison. S July 24

(397) £2,000 [Maggs]
— 2 June 1808. 1 p, folio. Mediterranean Pass for the ship Tiger of Philadelphia. Countersgd by Madison. rf Mar 14 (26) $2,200
— 26 July 1808. 1 p, folio. Ship's papers in 4 languages for the Sally of Portsmouth. Countersgd by Sec of State James Madison. rf May 30 (9) $1,800
Check, 26 July 1793. 1 p, 8vo. Bank of the U. S. check for $20, payable to Sampson Crosby. Sgd. Charlotte Parker Milne collection. wd Nov 12 (47) $3,000
Franking signature, [19 Mar 1811]. rf Mar 14 (88) $1,250

Jenifer, Daniel, 1723-90
ALs, 23 Aug 1782. 1 p, 8vo. To Mr. Hudson. Stating that his offer has been submitted to the Governing Council. Frayed. wa May 30 (148) $160

Jenings, Edmund, 1659-1727. See: Jennings, Edmund

Jenner, Edward, 1749-1823
A Ls s (2), 16 Feb 1808 & [n.d.]. 8 pp, 4to. To the Rev. J. Joyce, P. Lanell & Miss Carlile. About vaccination, his friends & family, & including a humorous quatrain. S July 24 (376) £2,500 [Joseph & Sawyer]
ALs, [n.d.]; 3 pp, 4to. To Mrs. Tollet. Suggesting a diet, advising baths & prescribing medicine for a patient. S Dec 18 (335) £850 [Maggs]

Jenner, Sir William, 1815-98
ALs, 5 June 1869. 2 pp, 16mo. To Mr. White Cooper. Concerning the medical condition of Princess Louise. sg Nov 6 (109) $50

Jennings, Edmund, 1659-1727
ALs, 25 May 1716. 2 pp, 4to. To William Blathwayt. Describing improvements made at Williamsburg during the years of his absence. Bullock collection. CNY Dec 19 (103) $1,600

Jeritza, Maria
[The complete vocal score of the 2nd version of Richard Strauss' Ariadne auf Naxos, [1916]; 181 pp, folio, sgd by Jeritza & with numerous pencil marks in her own part, sold at P on 15 Dec 1986, lot 55, for $1,400.]

Jermyn, Henry, 1st Earl of St. Albans, d.1684. See: Cowley, Abraham

Jerusalem, Johann Friedrich Wilhelm, 1709-89
ALs, 23 July 1772. 1 p, 4to. Recipient unnamed. Sending a "Promemoria". star Apr 8 (103) DM420

Jessop, Ernest M.
Original drawings, complete set of 35 water-color illusts & others in ink, 20 pp, 382mm by 279mm, for Thomas Barnham's Misadventures at Margate, 1887. Drawn within borders incorporating text; each p sgd with initials or monogram. S Dec 5 (484) £350 [Jones]

Joachim II, Kurfuerst von Brandenburg, 1505-71
Ds, 11 June 1563. 1 p, folio. Letters Patent concerning fishing rights of the town of Landsberg. HN May 22 (3058) DM1,200

Joachim, Joseph, 1831-1907
Series of 14 A Ls s, 1848 to [1850s]. 48 pp, various sizes. Mostly to Ferdinand David. About the problems of the Schumann family & commenting on composers & musical performances. S Nov 28 (554) £1,500 [Harris]
A Ls s (2), [n.d.]. 3 pp, 8vo. To Bernhard Friedel. Discussing changes in a concert program. With ALs by his wife Amalie Weiss. star Apr 9 (676) DM280

Johann Friedrich I, Kurfuerst von Sachsen, 1503-54
Ls, 15 July 1543. 4 pp, folio. To the von Rechberg family & the city of Ulm. In his own & the name of Landgraf Philipp von Hessen, suggesting they accept the decision of an umpire. star Apr 9 (1230) DM560

Johann Salvator, Archduke, 1852-90?
ALs, 5 Nov 1875. 3 pp, 8vo. To Herr Kellner. Sending material relating to the war of 1870. HK Nov 7 (2261) DM500
— 12 Oct 1885. 2 pp, 4to. Recipient unnamed. Sending illusts for a book. star Apr 9 (1269) DM300

Johannes Chrysostomus, Saint, 345?-407. See: Greek Manuscripts

John, Don, of Austria, 1547-78
ALs, 21 Oct 1567. 2 pp, folio. To Bernardino de Cardenas. Reporting about Spanish court intrigues. S Nov 27 (345) £1,000 [Joseph & Sawyer]
— 6 May 1574. 3 pp, folio. To his sister Margaret, Duchess of Parma. Expressing his discontent at being obliged to remain in Lombardy. S Nov 27 (346) £1,000 [Haas]

John, Augustus, 1879-1961
Series of 27 A Ls s, c.1944 to 1959. About 36 pp, 8vo. To H. G. Francis. About an award of a D.Litt. & a Festschrift for Dora Yates. With related material. S July 24 (481) £500 [Quaritch]

John Climacus, Saint, c.570-649. See: Greek Manuscripts

John II, King of Aragon, 1397?-1479
Ls, 28 Aug 1460. 1 p, folio. To his viceroy & other officials in Sicily. Ordering them to refrain from confiscating the property of Antonio de Luna y Peralta. HK Nov 7 (2259) DM900

John III Sobieski, King of Poland, 1624-96
Ls, 21 Oct 1689. 2 pp, folio. To the castellan of Trakken. About the political situation & convoking a meeting of the diet. Sgd Jan Krol. star Apr 9 (1127) DM1,000

Ds, 25 Dec 1600. 1 p, folio. Letters of safe-conduct for Nicolaus Koel & his ship. In Latin. C June 24 (51) £200 [Niewodniczanski]

Johnson, Amy, 1903-41
[A collection including 2 letters by Johnson to her parents, 1933, a 215-page typescript biographical tribute to her by her sister, with related notes, & correspondence & family photographs, sold at S on 24 July 1987, lot 348, for £550 to Apfelbaum.]

Johnson, Andrew, 1808-75
[A series of 3 endorsements, sgd (2 autograph), 19 Aug 1865 & [n.d.], 3 small pp, sold at P on 13 May 1987, lot 78, for $600.]

Series of Ds s, 3 Ds s, 1 June 1865 to 17 Sept 1868. 3 pp, 4to & 8vo. Statement concerning amnesty for Samuel Tate. Orders to affix the US Seal to a treaty with Madagascar & to a pardoning warrant. P May 13 (77) $750

Ds s (2)23 June & 25 Nov 1866. 2 pp, 4to. Orders to affix the US Seal to a pardon warrant & to an order "remitting the interest accruing to the United States in the real and personal property of Clement C. Clay". P Oct 29 (79) $850

Ds, 19 Aug 1865. 1 p, folio. Appointment of Lawrence Leahy as Marshall of the Consular Court of the US at Chin Kiang. Countersgd by Sec of State William H. Seward. wa Oct 18 (115) $220

— 15 Jan 1866. 1 p, 4to. Appointment of Edwin Shaw Deputy Postmaster at Fall River, Mass. Countersgd by Acting Sec of State Hunter. Fold splits. wa Oct 18 (27) $225

Autograph endorsement, c.Mar 1853, recommending J. R. Bennett for consul; on blank following letter, 23 Feb 1853, from Gideon Pillow to Franklin Pierce. Also sgd by other members of the Tennessee Congressional delegation. With Ds, 6 Mar 1864, 1 p, 4to; certificate of election of justices of the peace; partly ptd, sgd as Governor. Also including signature as Governor, cut from ptd document. P Oct 29 (77) $800

— Anr, 7 lines, [n.d.], on letter from Demas Barnes to Henry A. Smith, 21 June 1866, 1 p, 4to. Expressing his willingness to accept Barnes's suggestions for appointments to the Customs Service, sgd; in pencil. With endorsement, sgd, 7 Oct 1868, 9 lines on verso of last p of a letter from William Reid to Johnson. Asking the Sec of War to furnish a copy of the correspondence requested by Reid. P Oct 29 (78) $500

Photograph, sgd, [5 May 1865]. Carte size; by Brady. With orig transmitted cover. rf Mar 14 (27) $1,900

See also: Pierce, Franklin

Johnson, Lyndon B., 1908-73
[A collection of 2 White House photographs, 10.75 by 14 inches, Johnson with his grandson, sgd & inscr by Johnson; & Johnson & Lady Bird Johnson, inscr by Mrs. Johnson & sgd by both, sold at sg on 9 Apr 1987, lot 100, for $450.]

ALs, [24 Oct 1928]. 2 pp, 4to. To Mr. & Mrs. John Gipson. Letter of condolence on the death of their son. On Cotulla Public Schools letterhead. P Oct 29 (80) $6,500

Ls, 5 Dec 1955. 1 p, 4to. To Mrs. J. B. Harriman. Regretting her retirement as National Committeewoman for the District of Columbia. wa May 30 (287) $110

— 12 Aug 1963. 1 p, 4to. Recipient unnamed. Thanking for a letter & sending a copy of a speech. wa May 30 (286) $160

Autograph sentiment, 4 lines addressed to Helen [Hofheinz], above his picture on p 138 of a copy of The Pedagog 1928. P May 13 (79) $3,250

Cut signature, [n.d.]. Lower portion of Ls by Felix Frankfurter; sgd by Johnson. wa Oct 18 (118) $55

White House card, [n.d.]. Sgd in black ink. Also sgd by Lady Bird Johnson, in blue ink. wa Oct 18 (117) $650

Johnson, Samuel, 1709-84
Transcript, his letter to Bennet Langton, 21 Sept 1758, regarding the death of Gen. Drury. Incorporated in ALs by Langton to Mrs. Turner, 15 Oct [1758], 3 pp, 4to. S Dec 18 (24) £650 [Quaritch]

ALs, 12 Apr 1781. 2 pp, 4to. To Mrs. Thrale. About the death of her husband. S July 23 (22) £5,200 [Lord Eccles]

— REYNOLDS, SIR JOSHUA. - Ls, [Jan 1790], 1 p, 4to. To Charles Townley. Soliciting contributions for a monument to Johnson. Also sgd by Burke, Metcalfe & Malone. S July 23 (23) £2,000 [Maggs]

Johnson, Uwe, 1934-84
Collection of autograph Ms & Ls, 3 Jan & 29 Feb 1972. 2 pp, 8vo. List of sources regarding the book Jahrestage & covering letter, recipient unamed. star Apr 8 (170) DM900
Ls, 9 Nov 1972. 1 p, 8vo. Recipient unnamed. Discussing the participation of authors in election campaigns. star Apr 8 (171) DM360

Johnston, Joseph E., 1807-91
ALs, 12 Feb 1863. 1 p, 4to. To Major Gen. William Rosecrans. Declining to conduct a correspondence relating to Gen. Bragg's command. Inlaid; stamped. Bullock collection. CNY Dec 19 (104) $4,200
— [n.d.]. 1 p, 8vo. To Julius Strauser. Responding to a question about his military service. wa May 30 (230) $210

Jones, Allen
ALs, [15 Aug 1969]. 2 pp, 8vo. To Felix H. Man. Asking for further information regarding his contribution to a collection of prints. star Apr 8 (478) DM200

Jones, Anson, 1798-1858. See: Indians, North American

Jongkind, Johan Barthold, 1819-91
Series of 6 A Ls s, 1858 to 1876. 21 pp, 4to & 8vo. To Monsieur Vial (2) & Monsieur Martin. Concerning the sale of pictures. S Nov 27 (377) £800 [Quaritch]

Jordan, Dorothy, 1762-1816
Ds, [June 18, 1814]. 1 p, 24mo. Promissory note for £50, sgd on recto & verso. wa May 30 (76) $130

Jordan, Thomas, 1819-95
Autograph endorsement, on verso of Ms, General Orders No 41, 9 Oct 1861, Army of the Potomac, giving night rocket signals. 1 p, size not stated. rf Mar 14 (29) $90

Joseph I, Emperor, 1678-1711
Ls, 6 May 1705. 2 pp, folio. To Pfalzgraf Christian August von Sulzbach. Notifying him of the death of his father Leopold I. star Apr 9 (1204) DM600

Joseph II, Emperor, 1741-90
Ls, 24 Dec 1773. 2 pp, folio. To Herzog Karl Eugen von Wuerttemberg. Ordering him to deliver a report concerning the complaints of a subject. star Apr 9 (1215) DM450
— 23 Nov 1789. 1 p, 4to. To one of his sisters [Karoline?]. Notifying her of the death of their sister Marianne. In French. star Apr 9 (1217) DM260
Ds, 13 Apr 1768. 14 pp, 4to. Vellum. Patent of nobility & grant of arms to Moritz Julius Heinrich Untzer. With full-page heraldic painting in gold & colors. Red velvet bdg; seal in gilt metal case. star Apr 9 (1214) DM2,800
Autograph endorsement, 8 Mar 1789. 1 p, folio. On memorial addressed to him by Leopold von Kolowrat, 8 pp, folio, regarding commercial privileges in the quicksilver trade with Spain. star Apr 9 (1216) DM360

Josephine, Empress of the French, 1763-1814
ALs, 15 Dec [1806?]. 2 pp, 8vo. To Marshal Berthier. Forwarding some petitions & commending Napoleon to his care in the new campaign. Bullock collection. CNY Dec 19 (166) $1,400
Series of 4 Ls s, 19 Jan 1797 to 15 Jan 1812 & [n.d.]. 4 pp, 4to. To various recipients. Letter of thanks, recommendations, covering letter. Bullock collection. CNY Dec 19 (167) $2,800
Ls, 16 May 1791. 3 pp, 4to. To Captain du Braye. Thanking for his kindness on her voyage back from Martinique & about her financial difficulties. Sgd Lapagerie de Beauharnois. S Nov 27 (378) £420 [Dr. Sam]
— 4 Nov 1811. 1 p, 4to. To the Director-General of Forests. Letter of recommendation for Monsieur Cavalette. S Nov 27 (380) £400 [Maggs]
Ds, 1 prairial an IX [21 May 1801]. 1 p, 4to. Certificate concerning pensions received by the late Francois Beauharnais. Sgd Tascher Lapagerie Bonaparte. S Nov 27 (379) £400 [Dr. Sam]

Josephine Charlotte, Grande Duchesse de Luxembourg. See: Jean & Josephine Charlotte

Juan II, King of Castile, 1405-54
Ds, 23 May 1453. 1 p, 225mm by 315mm. Letters patent in favor of Esteban & Rodrigo Pacheco. Shaved; repaired. C Dec 3 (288) £160 [Lucas]

Juenger, Ernst
Collection of autograph postcard, sgd, & postcard, sgd, 10 Jan 1952 & 7 July 1959. To the publishers Glock und Lutz. Expressing his interest in 2 publications. Ordering books. star Apr 8 (172) DM280
Series of 4 autograph postcards, sgd, 12 Sept 1955 to 26 June 1956. To Rene Magritte. Thanking him for sending works. 2 in French, 2 in German. S July 2 (977) £100 [Communaute de Francais de Belgique]

Julius II, Pope, 1443-1513
ALs, 18 July 1477. 1 p, 4to. To the Duchess of Milan. As Cardinal, reassuring her about the recent visit of the archbishop of Genoa to Rome. In Italian; subscription & address on verso in Latin. C Dec 3 (289) £2,500 [L'Autographe]

Jumonville, Joseph Coulon de Villiers, Sieur de, 1718-54
Ds, 5 Apr 1749. 1 p, 4to. Receipt to Jacques St. Aubin, reciting details of Jumonville's family relationships. With Ds, 24 Mar 1756, 1 p, 8vo, by his brother Louis Coulon de Villiers; in half mor case. Both repaired. With related material. P Oct 29 (147) $1,400

Jung, Carl Gustav, 1875-1961
Autograph postcard, sgd, [n.d., c.1936]. To Dr. W. M. Kranefeldt. Agreeing to see him the coming weekend. Framed. Altman collection. pnNY Sept 13 (125) $300

Ns, 3 Jan 1936. On postcard. To Dr. W. M. Kranefeldt. Saying Kranefeldt should send his essay to Bollingen. Framed. Altman collection. pnNY Sept 13 (124) $275

Jusserand, Jean Jules, 1855-1932
Series of 8 Ls s, 1916 to 1922. 8 pp, 4to. To Armand, Duc de Richelieu. Regarding the Duke's activities for the American Red Cross & the safekeeping of the Richelieu family papers. With related material. sg Nov 6 (110) $80

K

Kaestner, Abraham Gotthelf, 1719-1800
Autograph sentiment, comment about Kepler, [n.d.]. On detached flyleaf of his copy of Kepler's Rudolphinische Tafeln, folio. Sgd. star Apr 8 (177) DM330

Kafka, Franz, 1883-1924
Collection of 327 A Ls s, 15 Ls s, 178 postcards, sgd (145 autograph) & 5 telegrams, 20 Sept 1912 to 16 Oct 1917. Over 1,600 pp, various sizes. To Felice Bauer. Complete collection of letters to his fiancee. With 41 A Ls s to Grete Bloch & further related material. Schocken Books, Inc. P June 18 (97) $550,000

ALs, [late Dec 1917]. 2 pp, 8vo. To Max Brod. Sending some Mss & commenting critically on his novels. star Apr 8 (173) DM7,000

— 16 Aug 1922. 6 pp, 8vo. To Max Brod. Discussing Brod's personal problems. Sgd F. star Apr 8 (174) DM26,000

Kant, Immanuel, 1724-1804
ANs, 19 Nov 1799. 1 p, 8vo. To the Koenigliches Licentcollegium. Concerning a delivery. On verso autograph Ms; several short notes. JG Oct 2 (227) DM4,800

Karl Alexander, Grossherzog von Sachsen-Weimar, 1818-1901
Series of 5 A Ls s, 1856 to 1895 & [n.d.]. 24 pp, 8vo. To Leo Graf Henckel von Donnersmarck & his wife Emma. Contents not stated. With related material, mostly numerous letters by his wife & daughters to Emma Graefin Henckel. star Apr 8 (104) DM2,600

Karl II Eugen, Herzog von Wuerttemberg, 1728-93
[2 autograph endorsements, sgd, 5 Aug 1784 & 15 Oct 1787, on memorials addressed to the Duke, 4 pp, folio, regarding the arsenal at Hohenasperg & bread rations for his guard, with related material, sold at star on 9 Apr 1987, lot 1297, for DM830.]

Ls s (2), 17 & 24 June 1780. 2 pp, 4to. To Col. von Huegel. Regarding Capt. von Pennasse & a lawsuit pending at Cannstatt. With anr Ls, 1781, to Col. von Nicolai. star Apr 9 (1296) DM700

Ds, 11 Sept 1750. Granting a request by Leopold Retti. On Ls by Retti, 7 Sept 1750, 2 pp, folio, requesting remittance of money due him. With related material. star Apr 9 (1295) DM470

Karl Wilhelm Ferdinand, Herzog von Braunschweig-Wolfenbuettel, 1735-1806
ALs, 12 Apr 1791. 2 pp, 4to. To Viktor Amadeus Graf Henckel von Donnersmarck. About the mobilization of troops against Russia. star Apr 9 (927) DM480

Karloff, Boris, 1887-1969
Photograph, sgd, [n.d.]. 8 by 10 inches. wa May 30 (375) $160

Photograph, sgd & inscr, [c.1935]; 7 by 5 inches. Was mtd. sg Nov 6 (111) $140

Kaschnitz, Marie Luise, 1901-74
Series of 4 A Ls s, [1966] to 1973. To Hilde Claasen & the staff of her publishing firm. Refusing to authorize a new Ed of her novels, mentioning her poems, & praising the poems of Rose Auslaender. star Apr 8 (176) DM1,100

Katharina, Queen of Westfalia, 1783-1835
ALs, 28 July 1824. 2 pp, 4to. To Monsieur Girard. Recalling her indebtedness to him for his efforts on behalf of her children. Crawford collection. star Apr 9 (1083) DM620

Keith, Jakob, 1696-1758
Ls, 14 Nov 1757. 1 p, 4to. To Viktor Amadeus Graf Henckel von Donnersmarck. Congratulating him on his promotion to captain. In French. star Apr 9 (1025) DM1,000

Kemp-Welch, Lucy
Original drawings, (25), to illus Anna Sewell's Black Beauty, 1915. 2 oil paintings, 5 watercolors, watercolor & ink, & 17 ink drawings, mostly dated 1915. 6 initialled. Various sizes. Archives of J. M. Dent & Son. S June 19 (803) £11,000 [Davis]

Kennedy, John F., 1917-63
ALs, 24 Aug 1945. 2 pp, 4to. To "Dear Whitey" [E. B. Taylor]. Thanking for a check. CNY Dec 19 (107) $2,500
— 2 Aug [1953]. 4 pp, 4to. To Mrs. R. McCarthy. Expressing his gratitude for her note & her efforts last year. On Senate stationery. CNY Dec 19 (108) $2,000
— [Dec 1958 - Jan 1959]. 2 pp, 4to. To John [McCormack]. Saying he will join [Leverett Saltonstall] in working for the passage of [the Labor and Racketeering Act]. Sgd Jack. P Dec 15 (57) $1,900
Ls s (2), 20 Oct 1952 & 7 Jan 1955. 2 pp, 8vo. To George McCullough. Letters of thanks. pnNY June 11 (33) $200
Ls, 14 Apr 1959. Size not stated. To Dr. Sara M. Jordan. Reporting about his meeting with her granddaughter. Sgd Jack. P Oct 29 (81) $700
Ds, 4 May 1961. 1 p, folio. Appointment for Maxwell Taylor as Member of the President's Foreign Intelligence Advisory Board. Countersgd by Dean Rusk. Framed. Altman collection. pnNY Sept 13 (13) $7,500
— 8 May 1963. 1 p, 4to. Appointment of Leo D. Welch to the Communications Satellite Corporation. wd Nov 12 (12) $425
Menu, 22 Mar 1956, of U. S. Senate Restaurant; 4 pp, 8vo. Sgd & inscr to Pat. wa May 30 (289) $400
— Anr, 14 Sept [1960]; fund raising dinner given by Adlai Stevenson. Folio, folded twice. Sgd on back page; also sgd by cartoonists Osborn & Jules Feiffer. sg Apr 9 (101) $800
— YARBOROUGH, RALPH W. - Ls, 13 July 1964. 2 pp, 4to. Recipient unnamed. Describing what he saw & heard in the 2d car behind the Kennedys at Dallas. On Senate letterhead. wa May 30 (288) $450

Kennedy, Joseph Patrick, 1888-1969
Ns, 18 Oct 1935. 1 p, 8vo. To Joseph Reilly. Expressing appreciation of an article. wa May 30 (291) $70

Kennedy, Rose Fitzgerald
Ds, 13 Dec 1946. Size not stated. Stock transfer. Stapled to United States Lines Company Common Stock certificate. wa May 30 (493) $110

Kennedy, William Robert. See: Naval Manuscripts

Kent, James, 1700-76
Autograph music, cantata, When artfull Damon strikes ye trembling Lyre, full score; [mid-18th cent]. 22 pp, folio. Sgd at end. Orig blue paper wraps. Signature & annotations of John S. Bumpus. S Nov 28 (555) £250

[MacNutt]

Kent, Rockwell, 1882-1971
Collection of 4 A Ls s & 2 A Ns s, 10 Apr 1910 to Oct 1912. 7 pp, 8vo, & 2 correspondence cards. To Hirace Traubel. Inviting him to dinner; commenting on The International Studio; referring to The Conservator, etc. Charles E. Feinberg collection. P Dec 15 (98) $750
Ns, 12 Sept 1928. 1 p, 4to. To C. G. Littell. Contents not stated. On personal letterhead. With a copy of Voyaging Southward from the Strait of Magellan. NY, 1924. Gilt stamped 3/4 mor; Littell bookplate, & with Christmas card designed by Kent. sg Apr 9 (103) $350

Kern, Jerome, 1885-1945
Ls, 4 June 1936. 1 p, 8vo. To "Peggy dear". Expressing his annoyance at delay in the writing of a play. Framed. Altman collection. pnNY Sept 13 (170) $375

Kerner, Justinus, 1786-1862
Autograph Ms, poem, beginning "Herz! ich hab es wohl erwogen..."; sgd & dated 7 Aug 1852. 1 p, 8vo. Inscr to Therese Milanollo. 5 4-line stanzas; last stanza crossed out in pencil. HN Nov 27 (2303) DM750
A Ls s (2), 21 Feb [18]29 [1839?] & Aug [18]31. 3 pp, 4to & 8vo. To an unnamed lady [Fraeulein Huber?]. Concerning a publication in the magazine Morgenblatt. Regretting he did not see her at Baden-Baden. JG Oct 2 (80) DM2,400
ALs, [11 Oct 1839]. 1 p, 4to. To Raphael Hanno. Promising to forward the nightcap Hanno left behind. star Apr 8 (179) DM760

Kerouac, Jack
Autograph Ms, 37 haikus with numerous drawings & quotations, 1963. 14 pp, folio & 4to. With related material. P June 18 (101) $5,500
— Autograph Ms, "Golden Jack"A Testament in the Midst of All; 8 Jan 1949. 8 pp, 8vo. Poetical account about finding God in a rainy night in NY. In pencil, on lined paper from spiral-bound notebook. CNY Dec 19 (109) $3,800

Kersenbrock, Hermann. See: Clemens August von Bayern, 1700-61

Keyes, Sir Roger, Baron Keyes of Zeebrugge & of Dover, 1872-1945
Collection of 4 A Ls s & 1 Ls with autograph postscript, 5 Dec 1917 to 13 Oct 1918. 25 pp, 4to, with 8 pp of enclosures. To Adm. David Beatty. About the Zeebrugge Raid, recent engagements at sea & affairs on the Western Front. S Dec 18 (293) £1,600
[Maggs]

Khevenhueller, Hans, Reichsgraf von, 1537-1606

ALs, 2 Jan 1604. 2 pp, folio. To his brother Bartholomaeus. Concerning family affairs. Sgd with paraph. With ALs by Georg Augustin von Khevenhueller, 1643. star Apr 9 (1027) DM280

Kienzl, Wilhelm, 1857-1941

Photograph, sgd & inscr, Nov 1910. 26cm by 20cm. With 2 bars of music. Inscr to Karl Wildbrunn. In pencil. star Apr 9 (679) DM260

Kinau, Johann, 1880-1916. See: Fock, Gorch

King, Edward

Autograph Ms, diary of his visit to Nagasaki & Ningpo, China; 15 Mar to 13 May 1859. 89 pp, plus blanks, 8vo. Red mor bdg. With contemp map of Nagasaki, woodblock print, c 190mm by 170mm, & further related material. pn Dec 11 (130) £3,800 [Barbican]

King, Jessie M.

Original drawings, (23), ornamental borders, headings & tailpieces to illus The High History of the Holy Graal, 1903. In ink Various sizes. Center compartments of 15 borders cut away. Archives of J. M. Dent & Son. S June 19 (808) £3,500 [Barclay]

— Original drawings, 7 preliminary ink drafts for pictorial borders in Isobel Steele's The Enchanted Capital of Scotland; each captioned. 382mm by 279mm. With a copy of the book. S June 19 (674) £500 [Naum]

Original drawing, "Perceval goeth toward the Deep Forest", to illus The High History of the Holy Graal, 1903. In ink. 239mm by 155mm. Archives of J. M. Dent & Son. S June 19 (807) £8,000 [Edberg]

— Original drawing, "Perceval seeth the Questing Beast", to illus The High History of the Holy Graal, 1903. In ink. 212mm by 151mm. Archives of J. M. Dent & Son. S June 19 (806) £4,500 [Hartnoll]

— Original drawing, pictorial tp for The High History of the Holy Graal, 1903. In ink. 227mm by 143mm. Archives of J. M. Dent & Son. S June 19 (804) £19,000 [Edberg]

— Original drawing, "The Knight of the Burning Dragon", to illus The High History of the Holy Graal, 1903. In ink. 211mm by 124mm. Archives of J. M. Dent & Son. S June 19 (805) £4,000 [Barclay]

Kingsley, Charles, 1819-73

ALs, 26 Apr 1849. 4 pp, 8vo. To Thomas Carlyle. Mentioning his Village Sermons & confessing how much he owes to Carlyle. Bullock collection. CNY Dec 19 (111) $420

Kingsmill, Sir Robert, 1730-1805

[A large collection of naval papers of Admiral Kingsmill, c.1756 to 1803, including letters, accounts, diaries, etc., thousands of pp, sold at S on 18 Dec 1986, lot 295, for £ 1,700 to Maggs.]

Kipling, Rudyard, 1865-1936

[A collection of documents relating to Kipling's copyrights & negotiations for publishing rights, 1903 to 1906, c.60 pp, various sizes, with a black deed box assigned for Kipling's papers, sold at S on 23 July 1987, lot 216, for £150 to Sotheran.]

Collection of 2 A Ls s & Ls, 26 June 1905 to 12 July 1913. 4 pp, 4to & 8vo. To Charles Hughes. Thanking for books, & about motoring. S July 23 (155) £1,150 [Sotheran]

Series of 3 A Ls s, 14 June to 7 Nov 1896. 6 pp, 8vo. To Robert Barr. About the completion of Captains Courageous, an attack on Barr in the NY Sun, etc. C Dec 3 (369) £1,300 [Joseph]

A Ls s (2), 2 Feb & 9 Sept 1935. 3 pp, 8vo. To Miss [Cecily L.] Nicholson. Instructing her to complain about an inadequate car & driver, & to express his views about a light pole. 1 ALs initialled. pn Dec 11 (50) £360 [Sullivan]

ALs, 4 July 1904. 2 pp, 8vo. To Sir John Fisher. Returning "the dynamite... the most cheering & comforting thing I've read in a long time". C June 24 (120) £300 [Lucas]

— 4 May 1935. 2 pp, 8vo. To Miss Lawrence. Regarding a foreword for her book. pn Dec 11 (49) £130 [Sullivan]

Ls, 12 May 1934. 1 p, 8vo. To Nicolas Bentley. Refusing permission to use his quotes for a book. Framed. Altman collection. pnNY Sept 13 (127) $225

Kippenberg, Anton, 1874-1950

Series of 3 Ls s, 10 June 1924 to 18 Aug 1934. 5 pp, 4to. To Karl Klingspor. About a festschrift Ed by his wife. Looking forward to the cooperation of Insel Press & the artists in Klingspor's circle. star Apr 8 (272) DM220

Kirchner, Ernst Ludwig, 1880-1938

ALs, 12 Dec 1914. 1 p, 4to. To [Eugen Diederichs]. Expressing his thanks for a book & mentioning a recent painting. Including pen & ink sketch, three women in a bathtub. star Apr 8 (479) DM10,000

— [1933 or later]. 2 pp, 4to. To Dr. [F. Bauer]. About the sale of a woodcut port of Bauer. star Apr 8 (480) DM950

Kirsch, Sarah
Autograph transcript, poem, Sanfte Jagd, [1980]. 1 p, folio. Sgd. star Apr 8 (180) DM520

Kitchener, Horatio Herbert, Earl Kitchener of Khartoum & of Broome, 1850-1916
ALs, 12 Jan 1903. 4 pp, 8vo. To [St. John] Brodrick. Sending congratulations on his appointment as Sec of State for India, & about his plans. pn Dec 11 (95A) £75 [Barnes]

Klabund, 1890-1928
[A collection containing 28 A Ls s, Ls s & other material addressed to his friend Ernst Levy, numerous poems, mostly autograph, & 3 typescripts, 1917 to 1922, with related material, sold at HK on 7 Nov, lots 2268-2275, for DM10,000.]
Autograph Ms, short story, Im gruenen Salon, [n.d.]. 39 pp, 4to, in 2 exercise books with blue wraps. Some revisions. With related material. S May 21 (263) £350 [Mytze]

Klaproth, Heinrich Julius, 1783-1835
ALs, 15 Aug 1834. 2 pp, 4to. To an unnamed count. Sending a "petit ouvrage" & talking about his projected Ed of Marco Polo. star Apr 8 (375) DM300

Kleist, Heinrich von, 1777-1811
— KRUG, WILHELMINE, NEE VON ZENGE. - Series of 5 A Ls s, 22 Aug 1821 to 5 Sept 1844. 14 pp, 8vo. To David Theodor August Suabedissen, his wife (1), & his son-in-law Hermann Hupfeld (1). Family & society news. star Apr 8 (183) DM520
— ZENGE, LUISE VON. - Series of 23 A Ls s, 1816 to 1833. 75 pp, 8vo. To David Theodor August Suabedissen. Interesting letters about family & friends. star Apr 8 (184) DM780

Klemperer, Otto, 1885-1973
Ls, 26 Jan 1968. 1 p, 8vo. To Rolf Liebermann. Sending a libretto & commenting about Liebermann's interview with Pierre Boulez. With carbon copy of Liebermann's reply, 29 Jan 1968. star Apr 9 (681) DM480

Klinger, Max, 1857-1920
ALs, 2 Dec 1911. 2 pp, 4to. To Walter Tiemann. Expressing his thanks for his honorary membership in the Verein deutscher Buchgewerbe-Kuenstler. star Apr 8 (483) DM260

Klopstock, Friedrich Gottlieb, 1724-1803
ALs, 2 Oct [17]76. 4 pp, 20.5cm by 16.5cm. To B[iester?]. Elaborating on his controversy with H[emmerde?] concerning money & publication rights. Postscript, sgd Kl, relating to his differences with Goethe. JG Oct 2 (86) DM4,300

Knigge, Adolf, Freiherr von, 1752-96
ALs, 15 July 1777. 2 pp, 8vo. To an unnamed lady. Reporting about his move to Hanau. JG Oct 2 (87) DM2,700

Knight, Thomas, 1759-1838
Ms, Pomona Herefordiensis.... 15 ink & watercolor drawings to this work, each with leaf of descriptive text in a secretarial hand. 4to, wraps. S Oct 23 (707) £1,700 [Mrs. Sneya]

Knowles, Charles
[A collection of 10 letters to General Knowles, mostly about military matters, & 2 letters to Lady Knowles, 1896 to 1922, sold at C on 24 June 1987, lot 53, for £280 to Burgess Browning.]

Knox, Henry, 1750-1806
Ds, 3 Aug 1793. 2 pp, folio. Order to John Cochran to pay various pensions. wa May 30 (323) $150
— 5 Aug 1794. 2 pp, folio. Order to John Cochran to pay various pensions. Fold split. wa May 30 (324) $90

Kodaly, Zoltan, 1882-1967
Autograph postcard, sgd, [received 6 Aug 1936]. To Universal Edition in Vienna. Discussing the ptg of [his Budavari Te Deum?]. S May 22 (611) £320 [Kruyfhooft]

Koenig, Samuel, 1712-57
ALs, [1752 or later]. 6 pp, 4to. To an unnamed colleague. Fragment, discussing the importance of hypotheses for progress in science. star Apr 8 (376) DM1,100

Koestlin, Christian Reinhold, 1813-56
ALs, 17 Mar 1842. 3 pp, 4to. To Friedrich List. News from the University of Tuebingen, commenting on List's work, & mentioning his marriage. star Apr 8 (377) DM800

Kokoschka, Oskar, 1886-1980
Autograph Ms, autobiographical essay, Vom Bewusstsein der Geschichte, draft; [1917]. 9 pp, folio; written on rectos only. Sgd. With autograph revisions. Discarded draft on verso of 7th p. S Nov 27 (384) £1,550 [Maliye]
ALs, 14 Mar 1954. 2 pp, 4to. To Ritter von Wissenburg. Thanking for flowers. On hotel letterhead. FD June 11 (3516) DM750
— 14 Mar 1954. 2 pp, 4to. To Ritter von Wissenburg. Thanking for flowers. On hotel letterhead. star Apr 8 (485) DM750

Kollwitz, Kaethe, 1867-1945

Collection of Als & autograph postcard, sgd, 12 July & 24 Aug 1926. 2 p, 4to, & card. To Hildegard Heyne. About the fee for the reproduction of an etching. With material related to Heyne. star Apr 8 (487) DM900

ALs, 2 Mar 1912. 1 p, 4to. To Fritz Pfuhle. Informing him that she will send 3 etchings for an exhibition. star Apr 8 (486) DM380

— 18 Sept 1917. 2 pp, 8vo. To [Erich Bauchwitz]. Criticizing the advertising done by the publishing firm of Erich Steinthal. FD June 11 (3518) DM500

— 18 Oct 1937. 2 pp, 8vo (lettercard). To Gertrud Andresen. Commenting about port photographs. star Apr 8 (488) DM260

— 12 Dec 1941. 2 pp, 8vo. To Dr. M. Klafkowski. Regretting that she does not have any drawings for him. VH Sept 12 (966) DM340

Kopisch, August, 1799-1853

ALs, 23 May 1840. 3 pp, 4to. To [Rudolph Marggraff]. About Platen's letters, the current situation & the sale of one of his paintings to the King. star Apr 8 (187) DM320

Koran

— [Near East, 9th cent]. 21 leaves only, vellum, 111mm by 178mm. In kufic script with gold rosettes between verses & sura heading in gold. 1 leaf replaced; some repairs. C Nov 21 (70) £6,000

— [Near East, 9th cent]. 6 leaves only, 114mm by 165mm. Brown mor bdg. In bold black kufic script; vowels in red. C June 16 (73) £1,900

— [Near East, 9th cent]. 2 leaves only, 124mm by 190mm. In bold black kufic script. Part of Sura al-Qalam. C June 16 (74) £800

— [Persia or Iraq, 10th cent]. 1 vellum leaf in kufic script, 215mm by 303mm. With diacritics in red & green & gold rosettes between verses, added later. Mtd. S Nov 20 (273) £1,500

— [North Africa, 10th cent]. 1 vellum leaf in bold kufic script with diacritics in red & green, cluster of gold dots between verses, 195mm by 255mm. Framed. S Nov 20 (275) £1,000

— [Persia, 10th cent]. 1 vellum leaf in elongated & dispersed kufic script with diacritics in red & illuminated markers between verses; sura heading in gold, 238mm by 332mm. Damaged; framed. S Nov 20 (278) £1,300

— [The Great Mosque, Qairawan, 10th cent]. Single vellum leaf in gold kufic, with diacritics in green, blue & red. 148mm by 207mm. S June 1 (78) £9,500 [Talhouni]

— [Persia, probably Khurasan, 11th or 12th cent]. 50 leaves only, thick brown paper, 203mm by 165mm, detached. In eastern kufic script with diacritics in red, the word Allah in gold outlined in red & sura headings in white within illuminated cartouche. C Nov 21 (73) £10,000

— [Persia, c.1100]. 9 leaves only, 367mm by 235mm. In Eastern kufic script with diacritics in red, yellow, green or blue. With sura headings in gold or white within cartouche & borders of gold rope-work design. C June 16 (77) £15,000

— [Iraq or Persia, 12th cent]. 2 conjugate vellum leaves in eastern kufic script with diacritics in red, gold florets between verses & illuminated circular devices in margins, 123mm by 92mm. Smudged. S Nov 20 (280) £1,300

— [Baghdad, c.1300]. 292 leaves, 89mm by 74mm. In clear naskhi script with diacritics in black, gold discs between verses, illuminated devices in margins & 4 pp of illumination (partly damaged); school of Yaqut al-Musta'simi. Crude repairs. Brown mor tooled in blind. S Nov 20 (304) £2,000

— [Mamluk, 14th cent]. Juz XXVI only. 41 leaves, 210mm by 152mm. Brown mor bdg, worn. In muhaqqaq script. With sura headings in white within illuminated cartouche & double page of illumination. C June 16 (79) £2,800

— [Egypt?, 14th or 15th cent]. Single leaf in clear naskhi script in gold with diacritics in gold, text interspersed with gold florets decorated with red & blue dots, 360mm by 260mm. Some crude repairs. S Nov 20 (293) £450

— [Turkey, A.H.815/A.D.1412]. About 154 leaves plus 3 flyleaves, 53mm by 44mm. Black mor gilt. In naskhi script by Muhammad Ahmad bin al-Hasan bin 'Ali bin Ahmad. With sura headings in red & illuminated page. 1 leaf replaced. C Nov 21 (99) £2,100

— [Near East, A.H.847/A.D.1443-44]. 308 leaves, 305mm by 210mm. Brown mor bdg, worn. In muhaqqaq script by Muhammad bin Aibak bin Shams al-Din. With sura headings in yellow, green & red. Some leaves repaired. C June 16 (80) £650

— [India, 15th cent]. 105 leaves only, 330mm by 280mm. Modern red bdg. In muhaqqaq script in gold & naskhi script in black. With sura headings in gold on illuminated panels. Crude repairs. S June 1 (87) £8,000 [Khalili]

— [Turkey or Persia], A.H.869/A.D.1464. 248 leaves, 307mm by 225mm. In clear naskhi script by Muhammad bin Sharaf al-Katib. With double page of illumination; some repairs. 1st 2 leaves detached, 5 leaves later replacements. Modern black lea with tooled

KORAN

borders. S Nov 20 (315) £1,200
— [Mamluk, A.H.873/A.D.1469]. 282 leaves & 2 flyleaves, size not stated. Later brown mor gilt bdg, def. In naskhi script by Yasin. With sura headings in gold & double page of illumination, partly repainted. 3 leaves replaced. C June 16 (78) £3,800
— [India, c.1500]. 458 leaves, 322mm by 206mm. Red mor, rebacked. In bihari script with diacritics in black & interlinear Persian trans in red. With illuminated panels between suras & 2 double pages of illumination. S June 1 (89) £1,200 [Kanoo]
— [India, A.H.908/A.D.1503]. About 460 leaves plus 10 flyleaves, 7cm by 5cm. Contemp red mor gilt. In naskhi script by Abdullah bin Abu Talib al-Husaini al-Astrabadi. With occasional marginal notes in Persian red & sura headings in gold. Wormed. C Nov 21 (79) £800
— [Safavid, A.H.924/A.D.1518]. 419 leaves, 132mm by 90mm. 19th cent red mor, rebacked. In naskhi script by Muhammad Mu'min bin Abdullah Murwarid. With sura headings in gold thuluth on panels decorated with hatching in pink; double page of illumination added later. S June 1 (91) £500 [Kanoo]
— [Persia, A.H.926/A.D.1519-20]. About 236 leaves, 53mm by 53mm, octagonal. Lacquer bgd. In naskhi script by Shaikh Muhammad bin al-Hajji Muhammad bin Muhammad. With sura headings in gold & 2 double pages of illumination. Some leaves detached. C June 16 (87) £1,300
— [Persia, c.1530]. 261 leaves, 162mm by 100mm. Floral lacquer bdg. On gold-sprinkled paper in naskhi script. With sura headings in white on illuminated panels, 2 illuminated headpieces & 3 double pages of illumination. Crude repairs. S June 1 (92) £1,500 [Kanoo]
— [Tabriz, c.1539]. 1 leaf only, 486mm by 320mm. On gold-sprinkled paper in nasta'liq script with diacritics in black; attributed on verso to Shah Mahmud Nishapuri. Outer border with Koranic verses in naskhi script. S June 1 (85) £3,400 [Kanoo]
— [Mecca], A.H.947/A.D.1540. 450 leaves, 109mm by 77mm. In naskhi script with diacritics in black, gilt discs between verses & double page of illumination. Some crude repairs. Red mor bdg (covered with green cloth) in slipcase with tooled borders. S Nov 20 (317) £825
— [Ottoman, A.H.948/A.D.1541]. 393 leaves & 2 flyleaves, 237mm by 159mm. Later green mor bdg, gilt. On gilt-sprinkled paper in naskhi script by Muhammad bin Abdullah al-Nishaburi al-Ansari. With sura headings in white on gold within illuminated cartouche (retouched) & 2 pp of illumination. C June 16 (86) £4,500
— [Ottoman, c.1550]. 300 leaves plus 3 flyleaves, 24cm by 14cm. Contemp red mor bdg with gold decoupe on blue or cream ground; spine rebound. In naskhi script on gilt-sprinkled buff leaf, with illuminated marginal medallions, sura headings in white on gold with polychrome floral motif within illuminated cartouche & 4 double pp of illumination. Ginsberg collection. C Nov 21 (115) £10,000
— [Ottoman], A.H.957/A.D.1550. 273 leaves, octagonal form, 60mm by 60mm. In ghubari script with double interlinear rules in gold between suras & double page of illumination. Brown mor with stamped medallions of gilt lea onlay, rebacked. S Nov 20 (319) £1,600
— [Persia, late 16th cent]. 308 leaves, 90mm by 56mm. In minute naskhi script by Mir Ali. With illuminated devices in margins & double page of illumination. Colophon gives date A.H.830/A.D.1426. Some repairs. Brown mor with panels of gilt lea onlay, rebacked; in slipcase. S Nov 20 (323) £1,600
— [Damascus], A.H.987/A.D.1579. 204 leaves, 280mm by 190mm. In naskhi script by Ahmad Hasan bin Ali Marau. With clusters of 3 red dots between verses. Some defects. Red mor tooled in blind, rebacked. S Nov 20 (321) £750
— [Ottoman, A.H.989/A.D.1581-82]. About 294 leaves plus 2 flyleaves, 5cm by 5cm. Brown mor gilt bdg in 19th cent octagonal silver box. In naskhi script by Ahmad Israil [?]. With sura headings in gold & double-page illuminated opening. C Nov 21 (101) £900
— [Persia, A.H.991/A.D.1583]. 303 leaves, 197mm by 123mm. Modern brown lea bdg. In naskhi script by Husain bin Hasan al-Husaini. With sura headings in white or gold on blue or gold panels & double page of illumination. Crude repairs. S June 1 (93) £500 [Kanoo]
— [Persia, late 16th cent]. 343 leaves, 141mm by 85mm. Brown mor gilt bdg. In naskhi script with diacritics in black. With sura headings in white on illuminated panels & double page of illumination. Crude repairs. S June 1 (94) £600 [Kanoo]
— [Ottoman], A.H.1001/A.D.1592. 278 leaves, 415mm by 285mm. 1st, 8th & 15th line on each page in bold muhaqqaq script, remainder of text in smaller script; by Khan Ahmad 'Asiri. With double page of illumination. Some crude repairs. Black mor with medallions of gilt lea onlay, worn. S Nov 20 (322) £1,500
— [Safavid or Ottoman, c.1600]. Juz XXIV

only. 15 leaves, 355mm by 242mm. Later cloth bdg. In gold thuluth & black naskhi script. With decorated cartouches with gold floral design, illuminated marginal medallions & opening double-page with illuminated heading. C June 16 (85) £1,500

— [India, 17th cent]. About 330 leaves plus flyleaf, 60mm by 44mm. Green cloth bdg. In naskhi script, with marginal medallions in tree-of-life design, sura headings in gold between gold margins; opening double-page illuminated. C Nov 21 (78) £800

— [Ottoman], A.H.1086/A.D.1657. 359 leaves, 154mm by 90mm. In small naskhi script by Jamal ad-Din, known as Murjan al-Islami. On gold-sprinkled paper with gold discs decorated with blue dots between verses & double page of illumination. 19th cent maroon mor, rebacked. S Nov 20 (325) £700

— [Ottoman], A.H.1082/A.D.1671. 317 leaves, 161mm by 103mm. In elegant naskhi script by Hafiz Usman. With gold discs decorated with red & blue dots between verses, illuminated devices in margins, sura headings in white on illuminated panels & double page of illumination. Contemp brown mor with stamped medallions. S Nov 20 (326) £18,000

— [Afghanistan?, A.H.1084/A.D.1673]. 298 leaves, 264mm by 155mm. Modern red mor bdg. In naskhi script by Muhammad Yusuf. With sura headings in gold & double page of illumination. Crude repairs. S June 1 (95) £500 [Kanoo]

— [Isfahan, A.H.1093/A.D.1682]. 198 leaves (1 blank), 142mm by 82mm. Floral lacquer bdg. In naskhi script by Muhammad Muhsin. With sura headings in red on illuminated panels & double page of illumination. Damaged with loss of 2 lines of text on each page. S June 1 (96) £500 [Kanoo]

— [Ottoman, late 17th cent]. 302 leaves, 228mm by 142mm. Contemp red mor with gilt lca onlay. In naskhi script with dia critics in black. With sura headings in gold & double page of illumination. S June 1 (98) £1,300 [Ziai]

— [Persia], A.H.1103/A.D.1691. 479 leaves, 124mm by 85mm. In naskhi script, probably by Abdullah bin Mulla 'Ashur al-Isfahani. With double page of illumination. Extensively repaired in 19th cent. Qajar lacquer bdg. S Nov 20 (327) £800

— [Persia, A.H.1111/A.D.1699]. 217 leaves, 291mm by 180mm. 19th cent floral lacquer bdg. On gold-sprinkled paper in naskhi script by Muhammad Ibrahim al-Qumi. With sura headings in gold & double page of illumination. S June 1 (97) £1,900 [Talhouni]

— [India, c.1700]. About 465 leaves & 8 flyleaves, 88mm by 57mm. Contemp brown mor gilt bdg. In naskhi script on gold ground. With sura headings in black on gold within illuminated cartouche & double page of illumination. Flyleaves bearing numerous seals. C June 16 (94) £4,000

— [India, c.1700]. 403 leaves, 330mm by 230mm. Contemp lacquer bdg, worn. On gold-sprinkled paper in naskhi script by Hasan al-Urdustani, with interlinear Persian trans in nasta'liq. With sura headings in blue & 2 double pages of illumination. S June 1 (99) £1,000 [Kanoo]

— [Ottoman, c.1700]. 282 leaves, 352mm by 245mm. Brown mor gilt bdg, repaired. In naskhi script with diacritics in black. With sura headings in red & double page of illumination. 1 leaf later replacement. S June 1 (100) £2,000 [Kanoo]

— [India, A.H.1113/A.D.1701-02]. About 450 leaves plus 13 flyleaves, 12cm by 7cm. Red mor gilt, cover detached. In case. In naskhi script on gold ground by Muhammad Mustaqim. With sura headings in white on gold & double page of illumination. C Nov 21 (81) £1,000

— [Ottoman, early 18th cent]. 30 sections with c.22 leaves each, 302mm by 205mm. Brown mor tooled in blind. In naskhi script with diacritics in black. With sura headings in red. Some defects. S June 1 (101) £500 [Kanoo]

— [Persia, A.H.1131/A.D.1718]. 331 leaves, 142mm by 91mm. Qajar lacquer bdg, rebacked. In naskhi script by Muhammad Muhsin al-Isfahani. With sura headings in red on gold panels; double page of illumination added in 19th cent. S June 1 (112) £600 [Kanoo]

— [Persia, Safavid, A.H.1134/A.D.1721-22]. 315 leaves, 240mm by 152mm. Contemp brown mor bdg, def. In naskhi script by Muhammad Taqi bin Muhammad bin 'Ali, at the instance of Sayyid Muhammad Kirmani, with Persian interlinear trans in nasta'liq. With sura headings in red on gold within illuminated cartouche & double page of illumination. Some leaves detached. C June 16 (89) £650

— [India, early 18th cent]. 31 leaves, 283mm by 173mm. In minute naskhi script. With significant words & sura headings picked out in red, outer margins richly decorated throughout, & double page of illumination. Wormed & repaired. Red mor gilt in green velvet case. S Nov 20 (334) £1,500

— [Mehmet Fatih Mosque, Constantinople], A.H.1143/A.D.1730. 463 leaves, 128mm by 82mm. In naskhi script by Dervish Ahmad, known as Qara Javushzadeh. With illuminated devices in margins, sura headings

KORAN

in white on illuminated panels, & double page of illumination. Brown mor with stamped medallions, skilfully repaired. S Nov 20 (336) £1,500

— [Ottoman], A.H.1159/A.D.1746. 303 leaves, 176mm by 115mm. In naskhi script by Muhammad, known as Imamzadeh. With some illuminated devices in margins, sura headings in white on gold panels, & double page of illumination. Some repairs. Red mor gilt. S Nov 20 (337) £200

— [India, 18th cent]. 486 leaves & 2 flyleaves, 172mm by 117mm. Contemp brown mor gilt bdg. In naskhi script within gold cloud-bands. With sura headings in white on gold within illuminated cartouche & 2 double pages of illumination. Some leaves detached. C June 16 (95) £650

— [India, 18th cent]. 490 leaves, 168mm by 100mm. In naskhi script. With some illuminated devices in margins & double page of illumination. Repaired. Modern red bds, worn. S Nov 20 (331) £160

— [India, 18th cent]. 334 leaves, 115mm by 71mm. Modern red lea bdg. In minute naskhi script with diacritics in black. With sura headings in red on gold panels. S June 1 (102) £200 [Kanoo]

— [Afghanistan or North India, 18th cent]. 296 leaves, 165mm by 96mm. 19th cent black lacquer bdg. On gold-sprinkled paper in naskhi script with diacritics in black. With sura headings in white on gold panels & double page of illumination. S June 1 (104) £400 [Kanoo]

— [Persia, 18th cent]. 285 leaves, 100mm by 60mm. Floral lacquer bdg, rebacked. In naskhi script with diacritics in black. With sura headings in blue on illuminated panels & double page of illumination. S June 1 (105) £800 [Kanoo]

— [India, 18th cent]. 362 leaves, 280mm by 210mm. Modern purple lea gilt. In naskhi script with diacritics in black; interlinear Persian trans in red. Margins ruled in blue & red. S June 1 (107) £500 [Kanoo]

— [India, 18th cent]. 398 leaves, 195mm by 115mm. Brown mor gilt bdg. In naskhi script with diacritics in black. With sura headings in white on illuminated panels & 8 double pages of illumination. S June 1 (108) £400 [Kanoo]

— [Anatolia, 18th cent]. 226 leaves, 305mm by 200mm. Brown mor bdg, repaired. In cursive script with diacritics in black. With sura headings in red & double page of illumination. S June 1 (109) £160 [Kanoo]

— [Persia, 18th cent]. 315 leaves, 110mm by 68mm. Green mor bdg with gold lea filigree. In naskhi script with diacritics in black. With sura headings in gold & double page of illumination. Repaired. 2 leaves

AMERICAN BOOK PRICES CURRENT

added later. S June 1 (110) £700 [Kanoo]

— [India, 18th cent]. 484 leaves (1 blank), 262mm by 160mm. Contemp lacquer bdg, worn. On gold-sprinkled paper in naskhi script with diacritics in black; interlinear Persian trans in red. With sura headings in white on gold panels & 8 double pages of illumination. S June 1 (111) £800 [Kanoo]

— [Mughal, 18th cent]. 493 leaves, 315mm by 200mm. Modern buckram bdg. In naskhi script with interlinear trans in red & glosses written diagonally in nasta'liq in margins. With sura headings in red & double page of illumination. Crude repairs. S June 1 (130A) £800 [Kanoo]

— [Persia, Qajar, A.H.1188/A.D.1774]. 402 leaves plus 2 flyleaves, 305mm by 203mm; cream polished paper. Contemp floral lacquer bdg. In naskhi script by Muhammad Mashim ibn Muhammad Salih al-Saigh al-Isfahani; Persian interlinear trans in shafia script by Muhammad Riza ibn 'Abdu'l Aziz. With sura headings in ornamental gold on alternating colored ground with scrolling design within illuminated cartouche & 6 double pp of illumination. Prepared for Sultan Fath 'Ali Shah. C Nov 21 (94) £45,000

— [Persia, late 18th cent]. 371 leaves, 186mm by 115mm. Brown mor with gilt lea onlay. In naskhi script with diacritics in black. With sura headings in gold & double page of illumination. Some leaves later replacements. S June 1 (106) £450 [Kanoo]

— [India, late 18th cent]. 472 leaves, 552mm by 320mm. Contemp laquered bdg with gilt lea onlay, repaired. In cursive script with diacritics in black. With sura headings in red. S June 1 (114) £500 [Kanoo]

— [Qajar, A.H.1208/A.D.1793]. 323 leaves, 144mm by 95mm. Contemp floral lacquer bdg, rebacked. In naskhi script with diacritics in black. With sura headings in red on illuminated panels & 5 double pages of illumination by Ali Asghar. S June 1 (113) £800 [Kanoo]

— [Kashmir, c.1800]. 297 leaves plus 8 flyleaves, text 184mm by 88mm. Contemp lacquer bdg. In naskhi script within gold cloud-bands. With sura headings in blue on gold within illuminated cartouche, 3 double pp of illumination & half-page illuminated heading. C Nov 21 (83) £1,000

— [Persia, Qajar, 19th cent]. 249 leaves plus 2 flyleaves, 124mm by 75mm. Contemp lacquer bdg. In naskhi script with marginal Persian commentary in nast'liq script between cloud-bands. With sura headings in red on gold within illuminated cartouche & double-page illuminated opening. Dated A.H.1112, but year probably added later. C Nov 21 (90) £700

— [Persia, c.1800]. Scroll, 516cm by 8cm. In naskhi script. With bismillah, the names of Muhammad, his descendants & the 12 Imams in white within cartouche & illuminated heading. C Nov 21 (97) £1,700

— [Persia, c.1800]. 223 leaves & 3 flyleaves, 179mm by 102mm. Lacquer bdg with Koranic phrases. In naskhi script. With sura headings in red & double page of illumination. Illuminated borders added later. C June 16 (90) £750

— [Arabic Ms, c.1800]. 296 leaves, 170mm by 112mm. Contemp brown lea gilt. In black with diacritics in gold, each page framed in gold, red & black. 1 double-page of illumination in gold & colors. HK Nov 4 (439) DM1,100

— [India, c.1800]. Scroll, c.330cm by 46cm. In different sizes of naskhi script in black & red. Crude repairs. S June 1 (115) £700 [Kanoo]

— [Qajar, A.H.1217/A.D.1802]. 257 leaves, 196mm by 127mm. Floral lacquer bdg by Murjani al-Talqani. In naskhi script by Muhammad Ibn Baqir al-Musavi al-Lahjani. With sura headings in red on illuminated panels & 2 double pages of illumination. S June 1 (118) £850 [Kanoo]

— [Isfahan], A.H.1218/A.D.1803. 239 leaves, 243mm by 145mm. In naskhi script by Abdul-Ali al-Qazvini. With sura headings in red on illuminated panels & double page of illumination. Floral lacquer bdg. Written for Aqa Abu Taleb Ibn Haji Muhammad Ali Isfahani. S Nov 20 (341) £750

— [Qajar, early 19th cent]. 177 leaves, 109mm by 65mm. Modern brown lea gilt. In naskhi script with diacritics in black. With sura headings in red on gold panels & double page of illumination. S June 1 (116) £350 [Kanoo]

— [Persia, Qajar, A.H.1227/A.D.1812-13]. 229 leaves plus 17 flyleaves, 197mm by 114mm. Contemp lacquer bdg, repaired. In naskhi script by Zain ul'Abidin at the instance of Akhund Mulla Mir. With occasional Persian marginal commentary in nast'liq within gold cloud-bands, sura headings in red on gold within illuminated cartouche & double-page illuminated opening. C Nov 21 (91) £1,100

— [Ottoman, A.H.1227/A.D.1812]. 244 leaves plus 2 flyleaves, 158mm by 102mm. Contemp brown mor gilt. In naskhi script by al-Sayyid Ahmet Nuzhat. With sura headings in white on gold within illuminated cartouche, colophon within illuminated panel & double-page illuminated opening. C Nov 21 (107) £1,600

— [Qajar, A.H.1227/A.D.1812]. 307 leaves, 187mm by 120mm. Floral lacquer bdg, rebacked. In naskhi script by Abdullah bin Ashur al-Isfahani; with interlinear Persian trans in red. With sura headings in gold on illuminated panels & 3 double pages of illumination. S June 1 (119) £800 [Kanoo]

— [Qajar], A.H.1230/A.D.1814. 200 leaves, 144mm by 88mm. In naskhi script by Ali bin Muhammad al-Khavansari. With illuminated markers between verses, sura headings in red on illuminated panels, & double page of illumination. Contemp lacquer bdg, some gatherings loose. S Nov 20 (343) £200

— [Qajar, A.H.1230/A.D.1814]. 357 leaves, 327mm by 210mm. Brown mor gilt bdg, worn. In naskhi script by Hasan al-Khavansari; with interlinear Persian trans in red. With sura headings in white, blue or red on illuminated panels & 2 double pages of illumination. S June 1 (120) £1,800 [Kanoo]

— [Qajar, A.H.1245/A.D.1829]. 250 leaves, 120mm by 70mm. Floral lacquer bdg. In naskhi script by Ibn Muhammad Mahdi Kirmani Muhammad Ali. With sura headings in red on gold panels & 3 double pages of illumination. S June 1 (121) £600 [Kanoo]

— [Kashmir, A.H.1246/A.D.1831]. 544 leaves & 3 flyleaves, 229mm by 140mm. Contemp lacquer bdg sgd amal 'Aziz Mughal. On gilt-sprinkled ground, in naskhi script within gold cloud-bands by Muhammad Hasan at the instance of Amir Shah Dad Khan Talpur; with Persian interlinear trans in nasta'liq. In outer margin Tafsir Mulla Fathullah written diagonally in nasta'liq. With sura headings in blue on gold within illuminated cartouche, 100 pp with illuminated text area, & 3 double pages of illumination. C June 16 (93) £20,000

— [Qajar, A.H.1247/A.D.1831]. 239 leaves, 327mm by 205mm. Contemp floral lacquer bdg. In naskhi script by Ali bin Musa al-Reza Sulayman al-Mashhadi. With sura headings in red on illuminated panels & double page of illumination. S June 1 (122) £3,000 [Kanoo]

— [Qajar, A.H.1250/A.D.1834]. 304 leaves (1 blank), 265mm by 174mm. Contemp floral lacquer bdg. In naskhi script by Ali Askar Arsanjani; with interlinear Persian trans in red. With sura headings in gold on illuminated panels & 3 double pages of illumination. S June 1 (123) £6,500 [Talhouni]

— [Ottoman], A.H.1251/A.D.1835. 4 leaves, 158mm by 107mm. In naskhi script by Husain al-Hamdi; selected verses. With illuminated markers between verses & illuminated headpiece. Red mor gilt, repaired. S Nov 20 (345) £180

— [Ottoman], A.H.1258/A.D.1842. 153 leaves,

197mm by 120mm. In naskhi script by Amrallah al-Wehbi al-Amasi. With illuminated devices in margins, illuminated panels containing the bismillah between suras & double page of illumination. Contemp brown mor gilt, worn. S Nov 20 (346) £320

— [Ottoman, A.H.1260/A.D.1844-45]. 433 leaves plus 7 flyleaves, 172mm by 111mm. Green mor gilt, in slip-case. In naskhi script by al-Shaikh 'Ali. With principal phrases in red, marginal commentary in Arabic, sura headings on gold within illuminated cartouche & double-page illuminated opening. Including a treatise, Sanai al Qur'an, ff.424v-433v. C Nov 21 (108) £700

— [Qajar, A.H.1260/A.D.1844]. 342 leaves, 245mm by 158mm. Lacquer bdg, rebacked. In naskhi script by Muhammad Reza al-Muzzahib. With sura headings in gold & double page of illumination. S June 1 (124) £700 [Kanoo]

— [Ottoman, A.H.1263/A.D.1846]. 368 leaves, 190mm by 115mm. Red mor gilt bdg. In naskhi script by Ibrahim. With sura headings in white on illuminated panels & double page & single page of illumination. Some leaves detached. S June 1 (126) £900 [Kanoo]

— [Ottoman, A.H.1264/A.D.1847-48]. 306 leaves & 4 flyleaves, 190mm by 120mm. Contemp brown mor bdg, gilt. In naskhi script by al-Sayyid Isma'il Najib. With sura headings in white on gold within illuminated cartouche; opening double-pages finely illuminated. C June 16 (82) £2,200

— [Ottoman], A.H.1264/A.D.1847. 297 leaves, 202mm by 120mm. In naskhi script by Mahmud Jalal ad-Din, known as Maqsmallizadeh. With gold panels between suras & double page of illumination. Some repairs. Red mor gilt, rebacked. With anr Koran. S Nov 20 (348) £200

— [Persia or Ottoman, 19th cent]. About 130 leaves, 72mm by 72mm. Later brown mor. In naskhi script. With gold panel marking suras & 2 double pp of illumination. C Nov 21 (98) £600

— [Ottoman, probably 19th cent]. About 101 leaves in 2 parts, 38mm by 38mm. Lacquer bdgs. In naskhi script, each with illuminated opening & final page. C Nov 21 (100) £1,400

— [Ottoman, c.1850]. 305 leaves plus 3 flyleaves, 197mm by 126mm. Contemp brown mor gilt, spine repaired. In naskhi script with sura headings in white on gold with floral swags & double-page illuminated opening. C Nov 21 (104) £700

— [Ottoman, c.1850]. 339 leaves plus 8 flyleaves, 215mm by 133mm. Purple mor gilt. In naskhi script. With marginal medallions in tree-of-life design & double-page illuminated opening. C Nov 21 (109) £550

— [Persia, c.1850]. 302 leaves & 4 flyleaves, 222mm by 146mm. Contemp floral lacquer bdg. In naskhi script between gold cloudbands. With sura headings in gold on alternating colored ground within illuminated cartouche & 2 double pages of illumination. C June 16 (91) £2,800

— [North India, 19th cent]. 346 leaves, 242mm by 140mm. In naskhi script with interlinear Persian trans throughout, sura headings in blue on gold panels, & 3 double pp of illumination. Contemp floral lacquer bdg, rebacked. S Nov 20 (339) £500

— [Qajar, 19th cent]. 176 leaves, 95mm by 55mm. Floral lacquer bdg. In naskhi script with diacritics in black. With sura headings in red on gold panels & double page of illumination. S June 1 (117) £850 [Talhouni]

— [Ottoman, A.H.1270/A.D.1853]. 309 leaves, 173mm by 115mm. Contemp green mor gilt bdg. In naskhi script by Mustafa al-Sururi known as Azanizadeh. With sura headings in white on illuminated panels & double page of illumination. S June 1 (127) £1,700 [Quaritch]

— [Ottoman], A.H.1275/A.D.1858. 308 leaves, 166mm by 114mm. In naskhi script by Mustafa al-Shauqi, known as Qulanjizadeh. With sura headings in white on illuminated panels & 2 double pp of illumination; f.2 torn. Contemp red mor gilt. S Nov 20 (352) £900

— [Ottoman, A.H.1281/A.D.1864-65]. 305 leaves plus 3 flyleaves, 20cm by 14cm. Contemp brown mor gilt. In naskhi script by Hafiz Muhammad Wahbi Efendi. With sura headings in white on gold & colophon in illuminated panel. C Nov 21 (105) £650

— [Qajar, 3d quarter of 19th cent]. Length not stated, 64mm by 43mm. In minute naskhi script. With sura headings in red on illuminated panels & 3 double pp of illumination. Floral lacquer bdg with black mor spine. S Nov 20 (349) £2,200

— [Qajar, A.H.1284/A.D.1867-68]. About 323 leaves & 4 flyleaves, 70mm by 45mm. Contemp floral lacquer bgd. In naskhi script by Muhammad 'Ali at the instance of Hashmat al-Daula Hamza Mirza. With sura headings in red on gold within illuminated cartouche & 3 double pages of illumination. C June 16 (88) £1,800

— [Ottoman], A.H.1284/A.D.1867. 297 leaves, 150mm by 110mm. In naskhi script by Hasan Wehbi. With sura headings in white on gold panels & double page of illumination. Crude repairs. Modern purple lea gilt. With anr Ottoman Koran. S Nov 20 (353) £300

— [Persia, A.H.1285/A.D.1868]. 308 leaves,

113mm by 67mm. Bds painted with flowers, rebacked. In naskhi script by Ahmad Ibn Ramazan al-Murjani. With sura headings in red on gold panels & double page of illumination. Crude repairs. S June 1 (129) £260 [Kanoo]

— [Ottoman], A.H.1287/A.D.1870. 304 leaves, 172mm by 112mm. In naskhi script by Ahmed al-Shauqi. With sura headings in white on gold panels & double page of illumination. Contemp red mor gilt; with case, repaired. S Nov 20 (354) £180

— [Ottoman, A.H.1288/A.D.1871]. 307 leaves, 178mm by 122mm. Red mor gilt bdg, def. In naskhi script by Muhammad Fawzi bin Abu Bakr known as Hamil al-Qur'an. With sura headings in white on gold panels & double page of illumination. Some leaves detached. With anr Koran. S June 1 (130) £380 [Kanoo]

— [Persia, A.H.1291/A.D.1874-75]. 197 leaves plus 4 flyleaves, 107mm by 63mm. Contemp floral lacquer bdg, spine def. In naskhi script between gold cloud-bands. With sura headings in red on gold within illuminated cartouche & 2 double pp of illumination. C Nov 21 (92) £1,000

— [Qajar, late 19th cent]. 183 leaves, 68mm by 40mm. In minute naskhi script. With sura headings in red on gold panels & double page of illumination. Waterstained. Floral lacquer bdg, brown mor spine, in mauve velvet bag. S Nov 20 (355) £300

Korngold, Erich Wolfgang, 1897-1959
Autograph music, 4 themes from the film The Constant Nymph, 1942. 1 p, 35.6cm by 16.6cm. Sgd at head. Erasures. star Apr 9 (682) DM420

Autograph quotation, theme from his Sinfonietta in B major, Op. 5. On verso of photograph of the choir of the Bonner Musikverein; 8vo. Sgd & dated 21 June 1914. Also sgd by Adolf Busch, E. von Gebhardt & others. star Apr 9 (683) DM800

Kosciuszko, Tadeusz, 1746-1817
ALs, [n.d., 9-15 July 1784]. 1 p, 4to. To Richard Varick. Farewell message before embarking to Europe. Silked. P May 13 (80) $600

Kossuth, Lajos, 1802-94
ALs, 23 Oct 1852. 1 p, 4to. Letter of recommendation for Capt. Casselman. Torn. In English. star Apr 9 (1028) DM560

— 19 Apr 1856. 2 pp, 8vo. To Gertrude Rawlins. Expressing gratitude for his reception at her parents' house. wa May 30 (484) $160

Kotzebue, August von, 1761-1819
Autograph Ms, beginning "Eine Dame von Welt will zuerst gefallen", [1804]. 1 p, 8vo. star Apr 8 (188) DM420

ALs, 1 Jan 1808. 3 pp, 8vo. To his publisher Kummer. About forthcoming Mss & concerning items ordered by his wife. Tipped into his Ausgewaehlte Lustspiele. Leipzig, 1863. Half mor bdg. star Apr 8 (189) DM950

Kraus, Karl, 1874-1936
Autograph Ms, poem, Grabstein eines Huendchens, 14 lines; [n.d., 1913?]. 1 p, 8vo. S Nov 27 (385) £450 [Davies]

— Autograph Ms, poem, Wiedersehn mit Schmetterlingen, 1/2 July 1917. 2 pp, 8vo. Sgd at head. 8 stanzas. star Apr 8 (191) DM6,500

ALs, 20 Apr 1905. 1 p, 8vo. To R. Lanyi. Returning a Ms. On Die Fackel letterhead. With related material. star Apr 8 (190) DM1,600

Kreisler, Fritz, 1875-1962
Photograph, sgd, [n.d.]; 12mo. Sgd in blue ink. sg Nov 6 (115) $50

Krenek, Ernst
A Ls s (2), 4 & 9 Sept 1933. 5 pp, 4to. To Willi Reich. Making suggestions for the magazine "23" & talking about true conservatism. star Apr 9 (684) DM900

Kreutzer, Konradin, 1780-1849
ALs, 9 Aug 1820. 2 pp, 4to. To unnamed friends. About a new invention in piano manufacture & a financial matter. S May 22 (613) £200 [L. I. M.]

— [1843]. 2 pp, 8vo. To Mr. Belli. Informing him of their impending move to Mainz. With draft of reply on integral leaf. star Apr 9 (686) DM900

Krolow, Karl
Collection of 4 A Ls s & 8 autograph postcards, sgd, 28 Jan 1945 to 10 Feb 1952. 9 pp, 4to, & cards. To Hanns Arens. About his work, the impossibility to publish after the war & his move to Hannover. With autograph postcard, sgd, to the publisher Bechtle. star Apr 8 (192) DM1,700

Kropotkin, Petr Alekseevich, Prince, 1842-1921
ALs, 26 Dec 1901. 4 pp, 8vo. To [Eugen Diederichs]. Sending some of his works. In German. star Apr 9 (1029) DM340

Krug, Wilhelmine, 1780-1852. See: Kleist, Heinrich von

Kubin, Alfred, 1877-1959
ALs, 5 July 1924. 1 p, 4to. To Wolfgang von Weber. Sending an anecdote regarding Weber's father & acknowledging receipt of a magazine. star Apr 8 (489) DM220
— 3 Oct 1950. 2 pp, 4to. To [Oskar Rotterheim]. Expressing his thanks for an essay & reporting about his current work. star Apr 8 (490) DM650

Kuehnau, Johann Christoph, 1735-1805
ALs, 18 Mar 1789. 4 pp, 4to. To an unnamed churchman. Sending specially bound copies of his works & stating the price. S May 22 (612) £500 [Riskin]

Kurtz, Hermann, 1813-78
Series of 3 A Ls s, 12 & 18 June 1843 & 20 June 1846. 6 pp, 8vo. To the magazine Morgenblatt[?]. Offering Mss. Inviting [H. Hauff?] to Dresden. JG Oct 2 (91) DM500

Kurz, Isolde, 1853-1944
Ds s (2) 1 Sept 1927 & 4 to 24 May 1928. 3 pp, 4to. Contracts with 2 different publishers regarding Die Stunde des Unsichtbaren & Aus fruehen Tagen. With 3 port photographs, sgd. HN Nov 27 (2306) DM500

L

La Fontaine, Jean de, 1621-95
Ms, Contes et nouvelles en vers, vol 1. [France?, 2d half of 18th cent]. Length not given, 210mm by 150mm, vellum. Contemp extra red mor gilt. With 30 full-p erotic miniatures in colors & 30 miniatures in colors as tail pieces. Contemp authentication pasted to front endpaper, stating that Ms was executed "pour Louis XV. par Madame la Duchesse de Dubarry". Minimal repairs to bdg; 1st 15 leaves slightliy dampstained. FD Dec 2 (11a) DM100,000

Lachmann, Karl, 1793-1851
ALs, 9 Apr 1843. 3 pp, 8vo. To [Karl August Hahn]. Commenting on Hahn's grammar of Middle High German. star Apr 8 (378) DM340

Lafayette, Gilbert du Motier, Marquis de, 1757-1834
ALs, 24 Oct 1777. 1 p, 4to. To Thomas-Antoine Du Plessis. Congratulating him on his & Col. Green's success at Fort Mercer. Fold splits. P May 13 (81) $2,100
— 25 July [1781]. 1 p, 4to. To Friedrich Wilhelm von Steuben. As Commander in Virginia, concerning "an Immediate Augmentation of cavalry". S July 24 (398) £1,550 [Hoffman]
— 9 Feb 1825. 1 p, 4to. To Mrs. O. Wilmouth. Sending regards. In English. rf Mar 14 (32) $230
Ls, 23 July 1789. 1 p, 4to. To the French National Assembly. As Commander of the National Guard; asking them to preserve the peace. Framed. Altman collection. pnNY Sept 13 (66) $800
ANs, [n.d.]. 1 p, 4to. Recipient unnamed. Asking that letters be enclosed in a packet. In English. Mtd. rf Mar 14 (31) $260
ADs, [n.d.]; 1 p, 32mo. 7 lines, requesting attention to a report. In French. Mtd with related material. rf Mar 14 (30) $260
Ds, 16 thermidor an 9 [4 Aug 1801]. 1 p, 4to. Recommendation for Citizen Cassin seeking employment in the Forestry Administration. Framed. Altman collection. pnNY Sept 13 (67) $250
Autograph endorsement, 18 Nov 1830. 1 p, 4to. In margin of petition by Andre Sauge to the French Minister of Finance, requesting appointment as tax collector. C. 100 words, suggesting how a position can be made available. Matted with a port. sg Nov 6 (116) $225

Lallemant, Nicolas, 1739-1829
Ms, Plans des forests et buissons de France. [18th cent] 2 vols. 66 plans on vellum, 165mm by 109mm, in contemp mor gilt. Jeanson Ms 164 SM Mar 1 (315) FF85,000

Lalo, Edouard, 1823-92
A Ls s (2), 12 Sept 1880 & 29 Jan 1885. 10 pp, 8vo. To [Otto Goldschmidt]. Complaining about recipient's silence. Mentioning his ballet Namouna & von Buelow. star Apr 9 (689) DM360
ALs, [c.1885/86]. 1 p, 8vo. To the Secretary of the Academie des Beaux-Arts. Accepting a nomination to a jury. star Apr 9 (690) DM360
— 1 Oct 1889. 1 p, 8vo. To Edouard Colonne. About the Krupp family & his work for Colonne. sg Nov 6 (117) $100

Lamar, Mirabeau B., 1798-1859
Ds, Oct 1840. Texas bond with 10 coupons affixed. Also sgd by William Levey. Cancellation slashes. wa May 30 (436) $90

Lamb, Lady Caroline, 1785-1828
Autograph Ms, key to the characters in her novel Glenarvon; [n.d.]. 1 p, 4to. Bullock collection. CNY Dec 19 (38) $1,400

Lamb, Charles, 1775-1834
Series of 20 A Ls s, 1800 to 1808 [& n.d.]. 35 pp, various sizes. To William Godwin. Important literary & personal correspondence. 1 letter possibly incomplete. With 3 A Ls s by Goodwin to Lamb on blank areas of Lamb's letters. S July 23 (85) £9,000 [Caldur]

— Moxon, Edward. - ALs, "Wednesday evening", 1 p, 4to. To [Lamb]. Thanking him for a humorous letter. pn Dec 11 (51) £100 [Flower]

Lampe, Hinrich, 1503-83
ADs, 19 Dec 1571. 1 p, folio. Receipt for a present of 40 thalers given by the Braunschweig magistrate for his son's studies. Sgd at head. In Low German. star Apr 9 (1030) DM1,100

Landor, Walter Savage, 1775-1864
ALs, [n.d.]. 1 p, 8vo. Recipient unnamed. Thanking for a book. With related material. sg Apr 9 (104) $200

Landowska, Wanda, 1877-1959
ALs, [n.d.]. 2 pp, 4to. Recipient unnamed. Saying she would like to see him after her return from Munich. In French. star Apr 9 (691) DM220

Landseer, Sir Edwin Henry, 1802-73
ALs, [n.d.]. 1 p, sized not stated. To Mr. [Henry?] Beckwith. Concerning the loan of a picture of snow sheep for an engraving. wa May 30 (45) $50

Lang, Andrew, 1844-1912
[A collection of 5 A Ls s, 5 autograph Mss, 2 sets of proofs, & further related material, c. 35 pp, sold at CNY on 19 Dec 1986, lot 113, for $300.]

Langdon, John, 1741-1819
ALs, 1 June 1798. 1 p, 4to. To Henry Tazewell. Stating his intention to leave for Philadelphia next Friday. wa May 30 (149) $375

Langlois, J. J.
Ms, Code abrege du baillage et capitainerie royale des chasses de la Varenne du Louvre.... [18th cent] 112 pp, 175mm by 116mm, in contemp calf. Jeanson Ms 149 SM Mar 1 (320) FF2,000

Lanner, Joseph, 1801-43
Series of Ds s, 15 Ds s, 17 Nov 1840 to 31 Oct 1842. 15 pp, folio. Contracts with Tobias Haslinger. Text mostly in Haslinger's hand. With related material. star Apr 9 (692) DM4,200

Ds s (2) 1840 & 1841. 2 pp, folio. Contracts with Tobias Haslinger concerning his waltzes Die naechtlichen Wanderer & K. K. Kammerball-Taenze. Texts in Haslinger's hand. FD Dec 2 (3242) DM1,200

Ds, 21 Sept 1841. 1 p, folio. Contract, ceding rights to his waltz Die Sonderlinge Op. 183 to Tobias Haslinger. Text in Haslinger's hand. HN May 22 (3089) DM420

Lasker-Schueler, Else, 1869-1945
Autograph Ms, poem, O Gott hoere mich, [1920]. 1 p, folio. Four 4-line stanzas, sgd. Repaired with adhesive tape & mtd. 1st version of Gott hoer, pbd Nov 1920. star Apr 8 (193) DM2,800

Collection of 5 A Ls s & 6 autograph postcards, sgd, 30 Mar 1926 to 5 Apr 1930. 16 pp, 4to, & cards. To Dr. Dorsch. Regarding her son's illness. Some letters & cards with small sketches. With related material. star Apr 8 (194) DM4,500

Series of 5 A Ls s, [1943]. 11 pp, various sizes (4 cards). To Mordechai & Miriam Ardon-Bronstein. Letters to friends, mostly about her life in Jerusalem. 1 letter incomplete, 1 sgd Tino, 1 sgd Prinz Jussuf. star Apr 8 (195) DM8,500

Laski, Harold J., 1893-1950
Autograph Ms, article, The Future of Britain, [before 6 July 1945]. 5 pp, 4to. Predicting victory for the Labour Party in the general election. Sgd. With postscript, sgd & dated 26 July 1945, 2 pp, 4to, analyzing the reasons for Labour's success, & 5 A Ls s & autograph postcard, sgd. C Dec 3 (290) £110 [Quaritch]

Lassalle, Ferdinand, 1825-64
ALs, [1845/46?]. 1 p, 8vo. To his brother-in-law Ferdinand Friedlaender. Discussing financial matters. star Apr 9 (1031) DM750

Latini, Brunetto, 1220-95
Ms, Livre de Tresor. [Eastern France, probably Brittany, 2d half of 15th cent] 179 leaves, 263mm by 200mm, in 18th-cent calf, with arms of Goyen de Matignon. With initials in red or blue. Jeanson Ms 117 SM Mar 1 (331) FF55,000

Lauder, Sir Harry, 1870-1950
Autograph music, "appeared first, New York Nov. 4th 1907"; 1 p, 12mo. 2 bars, sgd. With pen-&-ink self-port, 15 May 1930, on postcard to James M. Libby. Sgd & inscr. sg Nov 6 (119) $90

Laurel, Stan, 1890-1965 —&
Hardy, Oliver, 1892-1957
Photograph, sgd & inscr, [c.1940]; 8 by 10 inches. Sgd by both; inscr to Raimundo [Araujo] by Laurel. Was mtd. sg Nov 6 (120) $400

Laurens, Henry, 1724-92
Ds, [1 Nov 1777 to 10 Dec 1778]. 1 p, 4to. "Instructions to the Commanders of Private Ships or Vessels of War..."; ptd with Ms corrections. Dated 3 Apr 1776 in type but sgd as President of the Continental Congress. rf Mar 14 (33) $1,900

LAUSSAT

Laussat, Pierre Clement de, 1756-1835
Ds, "29 Thermidor 11" [1802]. 1 p, size not stated. Regarding the transfer of Louisiana. Soiled. rf Mar 14 (34) $475

Lavater, Johann Kaspar, 1741-1801
ANs, 30 Aug 1792. 1 p, 8vo. Recipient unnamed ("vorausbezahlende guetige Herzogin"). Expressing thanks. star Apr 8 (196) DM250

Autograph sentiment, An einen Freund nach meinem Tode, 3 Oct 1794. Carte size. Sgd L. With anr autograph sentiment, 1793, mtd. star Apr 8 (197) DM530

Lavoisier, Antoine Laurent de, 1743-94
Ds, [7 Mar 1794]. 1 p, 4to. Full power for Citizen Lalleman to satisfy his creditors. S May 21 (265) £780 [Pervanas]

Lawrence, David Herbert, 1885-1930
ALs, 11 July 1915. 4 pp, 8vo. Recipient unnamed. Discussing dialect & spelling in The Prussian Officer. S Dec 18 (160) £1,000 [Meerwen]

Autograph postcard, sgd, [11 Dec 1912]. To Baronin [Frieda] von Richthofen. Sending greetings & news. In German. Initialled. In pencil. With related ALs by Frieda Lawrence Ravagli, 1952. pn Dec 11 (52) £170 [Forster]

Lawrence, Thomas Edward, 1888-1935
Series of 4 A Ls s, 24 Aug & 5 Nov 1923 & [1923]; 18 Jan 1928. 7 pp, various sizes. To To William Edward Marshall (3) & his brother. About his service as a private in the Tank Corps, W. E. Marshall's death & The Seven Pillars of Wisdom. With 2 photographs. C Dec 3 (370) £2,400 [Walker]

— Series of 4 A Ls s, 1931 to 1932. 5 pp, folio & 4to. To G. Brough. About motorcycles & other machines. S July 23 (156) £2,200 [Sotheran]

ALs, 30 Oct 1919. 3 pp, 8vo. To Willmore. Answering some questions & mentioning mutual friends. Sgd TEL. S Dec 18 (159) £420 [Spiro]

— 17 Apr 1931. 1 p, 4to. To T. C. Griffin. Apologizing for not remembering him & saying he wants to forget his time in the Middle East. Sgd T. E. Shaw. C June 24 (55) £1,300 [Spiro]

— 23 Nov 1934. 2 pp, 4to. To the Hon. Francis Rodd. Declining the post of Secretary of the Bank of England & talking about retirement in his cottage. S Dec 18 (163) £2,300 [Wilson]

AMERICAN BOOK PRICES CURRENT

Le Cain, Errol
Original drawing, 12 princesses in ball gowns in a forest, watercolor. Sgd & dated [19]77. In card mount, 252mm by 336mm. Reproduced to illus The Twelve Dancing Princesses, 1978. S Dec 5 (489) £900 [Joseph & Sawyer]

— Original drawing, dust jacket design for Brian Patten's The Sly Cormorant and the Fishes, 1977; watercolor. In card mount, 333mm by 218mm. S Dec 5 (490) £600 [Joseph & Sawyer]

— Original drawing, woman in white fur gown with small child & reindeer, watercolor. Sgd & dated [19]78. 384mm by 232mm. Reproduced to illus Hans Andersen's The Snow Queen, 1979. S Dec 5 (488) £950 [Joseph & Sawyer]

Le Sueur, Jean Francois, 1760-1837 —& Paer, Ferdinando, 1771-1839
Ds, 20 Sept 1811. 3 pp, folio. List of c.50 musicians accompanying Napoleon to Compiegne, with confirmation of actual workdays. star Apr 9 (699) DM300

Le Vau, Louis, 1612-70
Ds, 30 Oct 1665. 7 pp, folio. Contract, Jacques Nicolas Colbert ceding his right to establish a tin plate manufacture to A. Champion. Also sgd by Jean Baptiste Colbert & others. With a notarized Extrait de compte, 1676. 2 pp, 4to. star Apr 8 (495) DM1,600

Lear, Edward, 1812-88
ALs, 8 Feb 1865. 1 p, 4to. To Henry Newbolt. Requesting him to show his landscapes to Mr. Bethell. S Jan 27 (951) £100 [Wise]

— 18 Oct 1883. 4 pp, 8vo. To Gussie. Mourning the loss of friends & talking about his health & work. Illus with pen-&-ink sketch of 3 poodles playing musical instruments. Inlaid. S Dec 18 (74) £1,400 [Curry]

Leavenworth, Henry, 1783-1834
— EUSTIS, WILLIAM. - Ds, 27 Apr 1812. 1 p, 4to. Appointment for Leavenworth as Capt. in the Infantry. wa May 30 (400) $150

Lebourg, Albert, 1849-1928
Series of 30 A Ls s, c.1902 to 1921. About 50 pp, 8vo & 16mo. To Gustave Geoffroy & other recipients. Concerning the loan of pictures, his painting, etc. Including pencil sketch of a yacht, 1909. S Nov 27 (389) £850 [Quaritch]

Lecky, Holsten Sterling
[The printer's draft of the unpbd 5th vol of The King's Ships, [c.1917?], possibly incomplete, comprising marked-up sheets with c.360 illusts of 92 ships, sold at S on 27 Jan, lot 889, for £280 to Maggs.]

130

Lecocq, Alexandre Charles, 1832-1918

[A collection of 5 musical Mss, transcriptions of his own works & of works by Mendelssohn, Mozart & Kastner, [n.d.], 16 pp, folio, sold at S on 22 May 1987, lot 422, for £300 to L. I. M.]

Autograph music, aria, Jupiter tonnant, for bass & orchestra, full score; [n.d.]. 19 pp, folio. Mostly in black ink on up to 22 staves per p. With revisions. S Nov 28 (561) £250 [Haas]

— Autograph music, transcription for piano of Beethoven's String Quartets, comprising Op. 59, nos 1 - 3, Op. 74, Op. 95, Op. 127, & Op. 130-131; c.1906-1908. 223 pp, folio. In brown ink on up to 16 staves per p; many revisions. With autograph tp, sgd, & cancelled preface. S Nov 28 (560) £450 [Haas]

Lecourbe, Claude Jacques, Comte, 1759-1815

ALs, [23 Sept 1799]. 3 pp, folio. To the members of the Directoire. As Commander-in-Chief of the Army of the Rhine, discussing the military situation in Southern Germany. With vignette at head. star Apr 9 (1032) DM550

Lectionary

Ms, in Latin, [Rhineland, 2d quarter of 14th cent]. 224 leaves, vellum, 261mm by 185mm; lacking several leaves. 18th cent mottled calf. In brown ink by more than one scribe in an angular gothic liturgical hand. With 13 pp of music in brown neumes on a 5-line red stave, 284 elaborate illuminated initials in colors & highly burnished gold, 119 historiated initals on burnished gold ground & 63 pp with miniatures in margins. S Dec 2 (42) £95,000 [Axel]

Lee, Fitzhugh, 1835-1905

ALs, 20 Jan 1860. 3 pp, 4to. To Capt. E. K. Smith. Reporting about an action against 2 Indian horse thieves. wa May 30 (233) $2,000

Lee, Francis Lightfoot, Signer from Virginia

ALs, [n.d.]. 2 pp, size not stated. To Mr. Staurt. Asking him for the services of his carpenter. Initialled; [retained copy?]. Foxed. With a port. Charlotte Parker Milne collection. wd Nov 12 (48) $700

Lee, Mary Custis, 1806-73

ALs, [c.1869]. 1 p, 8vo. To Mr. Davies. Commenting about port photographs of her husband. Framed. wa May 30 (235) $300

Lee, Richard Henry, Signer from Virginia

ALs, 19 Apr 1787. 6 pp, 4to. To [his son] Carter. About military history & great generals. Initialled; [retained copy?]. Was mtd. Charlotte Parker Milne collection. wd Nov 12 (49) $450

Lee, Robert E., 1807-70

ALs, 23 Apr 1855. 3 pp, 4to. To Col. S. Cooper. Sending a list of officers whose addresses have not been received & referring to recruiting in the West. Docket in Lee's hand on 4th p. Half gray mor slipcase. CNY Dec 19 (114) $2,000

— 28 Apr 1856. 4 pp, 8vo. To his daughter Agnes. Giving a detailed description of the Comanches. S July 24 (401) £3,800 [Perry]

— 26 Nov 1863. 2 pp, 4to. To Major Gen. Jubal Early. As Commander of the Army of Northern Virginia, ordering troop movements. Silked. P May 13 (82) $6,500

— LEE, FITZHUGH. - ALs, 16 May 1885. 1 p, 8vo. To Mr. Lawsing. Stating he has no autographs of his uncle R. E. Lee. sg Apr 9 (106) $100

Leete, Alfred Chew, 1882-1933

Original drawings, 3 India-ink cartoons, sgd, 6 Feb to 3 Apr 1915. 3 pp, 233mm by 318mm. Each with mtd ptd caption. Printer's markings. sg Apr 9 (107) $100

Legal Manuscripts

[A collection of 20 documents, drafts from a notary's register, relating to financial affairs of the Jews in Apt (Provence), 1346 to 1426, sold at S on 23 June 1987, lot 39, for £2,800 to Hoffman.]

Ms, Cases of Land Holding & Inheritance, [London?, c.1460-70]. 22 leaves & 8 flyleaves, vellum, 202mm by 127mm. Contemp bevelled wooden bds covered with lea; battered. In brown ink in a professional English legal bookhand; in French with some words in English. Paragraph-marks in blue. Many additions in later hands on blanks. S Dec 2 (44) £6,500 [Quaritch]

— PATTINSON, JOHN. - 2 Mss, legal notebooks listing his actions in Chancery, Star Chamber, Court of Wards & elsewhere, & other legal memoranda, 1632 to 1638, c.360 pp, 4to. Contemp calf. S July 24 (379) £900 [Maggs]

Legenda...

Ms, Legenda venerabilium virorum Aymonis et Vermondi. [Abbaye de Meda, near Milan, c.1400] 11 leaves plus 2 contemp flyleaves, vellum, 252mm by 187mm, in 19th-cent vellum. With 11 miniatures by Anovelo da Imbonate & with 30 illuminated initials. Jeanson Ms 126 SM Mar 1

LEGER

(339) FF2,200,000

Leger, Fernand, 1881-1955

A Ls s (2), [n.d.]. 4 pp, 8vo. To Francesca Clausen. Saying he would like to see her & talking about life in Paris. Including 2 simple pen-and-ink sketches. C Dec 3 (415) £380 [L'Autographe]

Legros, Alphonse, 1837-1911

A Ls s (2), 29 Nov 1875 & [n.d.]. 5 pp, 8vo. To Champfleury. About contributions to the journal The Academy. S Nov 27 (390) £180 [Quaritch]

Lehar, Franz, 1870-1948

Autograph music, Das Fuerstenkind, introduction; sgd & dated 4 Nov [1]911. 29 pp, folio. Full score, on up to 30 staves per page. In pencil; annotations in colored crayon. S May 22 (423) £3,200 [MacNutt]

ALs, 30 Jan 1915. 3 pp, 4to. To an unnamed singer. Asking him to participate in a series of concerts for the benefit of the Red Cross. star Apr 9 (693) DM250

Series of 3 autograph postcards, sgd, 3 May 1925 to 17 Aug 1927. To Maria Jeritza. Contents not stated & regarding his "Friederike". star Apr 9 (695) DM250

Photograph, sgd & inscr, 1923. 22.6cm by 15.9cm. Sgd & inscr to Carl Lindau on mount; overall size 33.5cm by 24.5cm. star Apr 9 (694) DM380

Lehmann, Lotte, 1888-1976

Collection of 30 A Ls s & Ls s, 1936 to 1976. Size not stated. To Hugo Burghauser & others. About Elisabeth Schumann, her retirement, etc. With related material. S Nov 28 (562) £320 [Lionheart]

Lehmann, Wilhelm, 1882-1968

A Ls s (2), 2 A Ls s, 14 Dec 1945 & 17 Jan 1945[6]. 3 pp, 4to & 8vo. To Hans Wolffheim. About his collections of poetry & the prosecution of his publishers. star Apr 8 (198) DM320

Leibl, Wilhelm, 1844-1900

ALs, 6 Jan 1884. 1 p, 8vo. To [his friend Kayser?]. Commenting about the death of a friend. star Apr 8 (492) DM470

Leibniz, Gottfried Wilhelm, 1646-1716

ALs, 26 June 1708. 4 pp, 4to. To Jacques Lelong. Providing bibliographical information about an Italian bible & discussing a number of scientific questions. In French. S May 21 (266) £4,000 [Quaritch]

AMERICAN BOOK PRICES CURRENT

Leicester, Robert Dudley, Earl of, 1532-88

Ds, 25 June 1558. 1 p, c.4.5 by 10.5 inches. Vellum. Bond & obligation in £120 to the haberdasher Edward Bradley. In Latin & English. Lyttelton Papers. S Jan 27 (797) £300 [Quaritch]

— HASTINGS, HENRY, 3D EARL OF HUNTINGDON. - ALs, 16 June 1560. 1 p, folio. To Leicester. Requesting his intercession in a money matter. pn Dec 11 (91) £220 [Clark]

Leistikow, Walter, 1865-1908

ALs, 25 Apr 1890. 2 pp, 8vo. To an unnamed art collector. Inviting him to his studio. star Apr 8 (493) DM340

Lemon, Mark

ALs, 3 Nov 1864. 3 pp, 8vo. To Charles Samuel Keene. As Ed of Punch Magazine, concerning the work of John Tenniel, & other matters. sg Apr 9 (159) $60

Lenau, Nikolaus, 1802-50

Autograph transcript, poem, Herbstentschluss, sgd & dated 4 May 1834. 2 pp, 8vo. 7 4-line stanzas. star Apr 8 (200) DM5,500

Leo X, Pope, 1475-1521

Ds, 22 July 1512. 1 p, 4to. As Cardinal, granting Alexandro Mazzolo the usufruct of the Abbey of St. Stephano. Pasted down at corners. C June 24 (54) £2,400 [Joseph]

Leo XII, Pope, 1760-1829

Document, [13 Feb] 1827. 1 p, folio. Vellum. Bull; contents not stated. Lead seal. star Apr 9 (1119) DM330

Leoncavallo, Ruggiero, 1858-1919

Series of 5 A Ls s, 1893 to 1917. 9 pp, 4to & 8vo. To various recipients. On a variety of subjects. S May 22 (426) £360 [Wilson]

ALs, 6 June 1893. 3 pp, 8vo. To Sir Augustus Harris. Expressing his appreciation for his efforts regarding the performance of Pagliacci at Covent Garden. In French. star Apr 9 (697) DM750

Photograph, sgd & inscr, 23 May 1894. Cabinet size. Inscr to Bertha Doepler, with musical quotation from I Medici. With ALs by Leoncavallo, [n.d.]; on postcard. S May 22 (425) £400 [Hoffman]

Leopardi, Giacomo, 1798-1837

AN, [n.d.]. 1 p, 16mo. Recipient unknown. Explaining a dramatic point. Mtd. C Dec 3 (393) £260 [L'Autographe]

Leopold I, Emperor, 1640-1705

Ls, 10 Jan 1658. 2 pp, folio. To Graf Sigmund Friedrich von Sinzendorf. Inviting him to a diet. Partly ptd. star Apr 9 (1203) DM340

Ds, 8 May 1679. 12 leaves, 4to. Vellum. Patent of nobility for 3 Barons von Kielmanseck.

With full-page illuminated coat of arms. FD June 11 (3643) DM1,100

Leopold I, Grossherzog von Baden, 1790-1852
Ls, 10 Mar 1832. 1 p, 4to. To Geheimrat Betz. Regarding a decoration awarded Betz by the Elector of Hesse. With Ls by Grossherzogin Sophie, 1832, & Grossherzog Ludwig, 1822. star Apr 9 (882) DM320

Leopold I, King of the Belgians, 1790-1865
Autograph Ms, account book, 1804 to 1823. 71 leaves (& blanks), 4to. Detailed list of his receipts & expeditures; some entries in a different hand. HN Nov 27 (2309) DM3,800

Leopold II, Emperor, 1747-92
Ls, 15 Apr 1790. 2 pp, 4to. To an unnamed prince. Asking him to stay at his present post at Frankfurt. With autograph subscription. In French. star Apr 9 (1218) DM550

Leopold II, King of the Belgians, 1835-1909
[A vol of 13 photographs, entitled "Funerailles de S. M. Leopold Ier roi des Belges et avenement de Leopold II au throne", sgd on fly-leaf & inscr to Auguste de Saxe Coburg, Dec 1865, sold at S on 27 Nov 1986, lot 313, for £200 to Lionheart.]

Lernet-Holenia, Alexander
Autograph transcript, poem, Heiliger Hubertus, [n.d.]. 2 pp, folio. 5 6-line stanzas, sgd at head. star Apr 8 (201) DM280

Leslie, Walter, Graf von, 1607-67
Ls, 6 Sept 1663. 1 p, folio. To Prince Lobkowitz in Vienna. Asking for a new assignment. Address leaf detached. star Apr 9 (1033) DM520

Lesseps, Ferdinand de, Viscount, 1805-94
ALs, 11 May 1882. 1 p, 8vo. To an unnamed lady. About her letter being read at a meeting of the Societe de Geographie. star Apr 9 (1034) DM200

Lewald, Fanny, 1811-89
Autograph Ms, Josias. Eine Geschichte aus alter Zeit; [ptd 1888]. 59 leaves, 4to. In black & violet ink, with numerous revisions. Marked for the ptr. With 2 A Ls s, 15 Aug 1879 & 17 May 1881. 6 pp, 8vo. HN Nov 27 (2323) DM600

Lewin, William
Ms, copy of the Insects of Great Britain. [Watermarked 1823-25] 2 titles & 50 orig watercolor drawings each accompanied by a text leaf in a neat italic hand & 3 pp index at end. 4to size, bound in 19th-cent mor gilt by S. I. Fuller. C Dec 12 (272) £900 [Spelman]

Lewis, Clive Staples, 1898-1963
Autograph Ms, Clivi Hamiltonis Summae Metaphysices Contra Anthroposophos Libri II, Nov 1928. 138 pp, 4to, in black note-book; spine def. Working Ms, including autograph comments by Owen Barfield & Lewis's critique of Barfield's comments. Unpbd. S Dec 18 (164) £5,800 [Mayou]
Series of 12 A Ls s, Jan to Oct 1933. 17 pp, 4to & 8vo. To Pocock, at J. M. Dent & Sons. Regarding the publication of his The Pilgrim's Progress an allegorical apology for Christianity, Reason, and Romanticism. With related material. S July 23 (159) £850 [Joseph & Sawyer]

Lewis, Francis, Signer from New York
Ls, 24 Apr 1781. 2 pp, size not stated. To Joseph Reed, President of Pennsylvania. Concerning the raising of seamen for the frigate Trumbull. Mtd with a port. Charlotte Parker Milne collection. wd Nov 12 (50) $450

Libro...
Ms, Libro de monteria, compuesto por d. Hernando de Hojeda...dirigado ala magestad del Rey. D. Felipe nro Sr IIII. [c 1640] 100 leaves, 240mm by 165mm, contemp mor gilt with arms of Philip IV of Spain. Jeanson Ms 125 SM Mar 1 (349) FF96,000

Liebermann, Max, 1847-1935
Autograph Ms, speech for the opening of the exhibition commemorating the 10th anniversary of the "Berliner Sezession", [1909]. 4 pp, 8vo. At end ANs to an unnamed Ed, requesting him not to publish speech prior to the opening. star Apr 8 (496) DM6,500
Original drawings, 5 small sketches, drafts for his lithograph Der Marschall / zu Goethes Bassompierre; in pen-&-ink & pencil. On 3 pp of ALs by Karl Scheffler to Liebermann, 7 May 1917, 4to. With related material. Ludwig von Hofmann collection. star Apr 8 (501) DM5,000
Series of 4 A Ls s, 29 Nov 1892 to 6 Mar 1903 & [n.d.]. 8 pp, 8vo. To Hermann Schlittgen. About the death of his mother; declining to switch studios; discussing paintings for an exhibition. star Apr 8 (497) DM2,400
ALs, 20 Apr 1899. 2 pp, 4to. Recipient unnamed. Asking for a painting to be exhibited at the 1st exhibition of the "Berliner Sezession". In French. star Apr 8 (498) DM400
— [7 Apr 1907]. 2 pp, 8vo. To [Richard Graul]. Regarding works by Kolbe, Hartmann & Klinger to be shown at an exhibition of the "Berliner Sezession". star Apr 8 (499) DM850
— 21 Apr 1912. 1 p, 8vo. Recipient unnamed.

LIEBERMANN

Notifying him of his stay at Amsterdam. In French. star Apr 8 (500) DM420
— 3 Dec 1924. 3 pp, 4to. To [Richard Graul]. Discussing paintings which Graul might buy. 2d leaf def. star Apr 8 (502) DM380

Liebig, Justus von, 1803-73
Autograph Ms, essay, Neues Verfahren zur Bestimmung des Sauerstoff-Gehaltes der atmospherischen Luft, [n.d.]. 8 pp, 8vo. Numerous revisions. star Apr 8 (380) DM4,400

Liebknecht, Wilhelm, 1826-1900
ALs, 21 June [1872?]. 1 p, 8vo. Recipient unnamed. From prison, requesting help for his wife & discussing the duration of his imprisonment. HN May 22 (3096) DM660
— 29 Dec [18]94. 2 pp, 8vo. To [Marie] von Buelow. Regarding her wish to see Lassalle's papers, now in the possession of Graf von Hatzfeld. JG Oct 2 (431) DM780

Lifar, Sergei Mihailovich
Collection of 2 A Ls s, ANs & AN, 8 Mar & 8 Oct 1928, c. 1930 & [after 1953]. 11 pp, 8vo & folio. To Sergei Diaghilev, about his own progress, a work by Strauss, Hindemith & a Toscanini concert. Recipients unnamed; describing a conversation with Gordon Craig concerning his relationship with Diaghilev; listing his partners in Giselle, 1932 to 1953. Mostly in Russian. C Dec 3 (416) £800 [Quaritch]

Ligne, Charles Joseph, Prince de, 1735-1814
ALs, 30 Apr [n.y.]. 1 p, 4to. To the French Governor of Vienna. Expressing appreciation of his administration. star Apr 9 (1035) DM1,200

Ligniville, Jean de, Comte de Bey, d. c.1645
Ms, Les Meuttes et veneries de haut et puissnat seigneur Messire Jean de Ligniville.... [17th cent] 702 pp, 304mm by 192mm, in contemp calf gilt. Jeanson Ms 136 SM Mar 1 (350) FF78,000
— Ms, Les Meuttes et veneries de haut et puissnat seigneur Messire Jean de Ligniville.... [17th cent] 482 leaves, 315mm by 198mm, in contemp lea. In many scribel hands. Jeanson Ms 137 SM Mar 1 (351) FF58,000

Liliencron, Detlev von, 1844-1909
ALs, 17 June 1903. 4 pp, 8vo. To Paul Dobert. Offering 2 poems for publication. star Apr 8 (202) DM460
— [18 Dec 1905]. 2 pp, 8vo. To Adolph Meyerdiercks. About a speech by Loewenberg & praising Dehmel as a poet. star Apr 8 (203) DM380

AMERICAN BOOK PRICES CURRENT

Lincoln, Abraham, 1809-65
Autograph Ms, speech on "Discoveries and Inventions", given at Bloomington, Illinois, 6 Apr 1858; draft. 10 pp, folio, on rectos only; blue & white lined paper. Pasted together at top. CNY May 11 (67) $95,000
Autograph transcript, copy of pleas in the case of Robert Irwin v. Ulysses Lindley & Theodore Baker, [31 Mar 1855]. 2 pp, folio. Sgd Lincoln & Herndon, nine times. Also sgd & endorsed by Stephen Logan. Inlaid. P Oct 29 (82) $3,000
ALs, 26 Aug 1861. 1 p, 8vo. To Sec of War Cameron. Requesting that some residents of Kentucky be appointed paymaster. Endorsed by Cameron. Sang collection. P Oct 29 (85) $7,250
— 4 Nov 1862. 1 p, 8vo. To Sec of War Edwin M. Stanton. Suggesting that "a Hebrew" receive an appointment, & nominating Cheme M. Levy as assistant quartermaster. Sang collection. P May 13 (88) $42,500
— 16 Oct 1863. 1 p, 8vo. To Major Gen. George G. Meade. Requesting information concerning Jacob Schwarz, a Swiss deserter. Fold split. P May 13 (89) $3,250
— 12 Sept 1864. 1 p, 8vo. To Maj. Gen. [Lew] Wallace. Requesting him to investigate the complaint of Mrs. & Miss Moore. S July 24 (402) £2,200 [Maddalena]
Ls, 11 June 1860. 1 p, 4to. To H. F. Stodder. Sending his autograph. Framed. P Oct 29 (83) $2,600
— 20 June 1861. 2 pp, 8vo. To "The Lieut. General, Commanding the Armies of the United States". Authorizing him to suspend the writ of habeas corpus in the case of Major Chase. Countersgd by Sec of State Seward. Bullock collection. CNY Dec 19 (117) $4,000
— 10 Feb 1865. 1 p, 4to. To Admiral David D. Porter. Sending the Congressional resolution of 24 Jan, thanking Porter & his men for the victory at Fort Fisher. Repaired. P Oct 29 (91) $4,500
ANs, 27 Feb 1862. 1 p, 8vo. To Sec of War Stanton. Expressing his wish to have Charles A. Gaubert appointed Brigade Quartermaster. Endorsed by Stanton. Bullock collection. CNY Dec 19 (118) $3,200
— 28 Apr 1862. 2 pp, size not stated (card). Recipient unnamed. Providing for an exchange of prisoners. Endorsed by Sec of War Stanton & Gen. McClellan. Framed. P Oct 29 (86) $3,250
— 23 Feb 1863 [1865?]. 3 lines on oblong card. Recipient unnamed. Ordering that a man take the oath of Dec 8, 1863 & be discharged". Was mtd. P Dec 15 (59) $1,400
— 16 Mar 1863. 1 p, small card. To Sec of War Stanton. 2 lines, requesting him to see Capt.

1986 - 1987 • AUTOGRAPHS & MANUSCRIPTS — LINCOLN

Dean. Was mtd. P Oct 29 (88) $1,200

— [n.d.]. 1 p, small card. To the Sec of State. 3 lines, requesting him to see bearers of note. Mtd. P May 13 (96) $1,300

— 13 Sept 1864. 4 lines on small card. Recipient unnamed. Denying any intention to appoint Mr. Carpenter to office. Sang collection. P Oct 29 (90) $1,600

— 13 Mar 1865. 1 p, small card. To Sec of War Stanton. Asking for papers concerning the case of Timothy Pearson. Mtd; marginal holes. P May 13 (95) $1,800

ADs, 3 Mar 1834. 2 pp, folio. Survey of 4 tracts of land belonging to Jesse Gum. P May 13 (83) $15,000

— [16 Oct 1852]. 2 pp, folio. Bill filed for William Coovey before the Champaign County Circuit Court regarding a purchase of land from Margaret Moss. P May 13 (84) $2,300

AD, [Nov 1864]. 1 p, 4to. Response to the Senate committee appointed to notify him of his election. Authenticated by C. W. J. McDonald, Chief Clerk of the Senate. With related material. sg Dec 4 (109) $32,000

Ds, 16 July 1861. 1 p, folio. Commission for William H. De Costa as deputy postmaster. Countersgd by Seward. Framed with a port. P May 13 (85) $1,900

— 27 Sept 1861. 2 pp, folio. Pardon for John Demaine. Countersgd by Seward. P May 13 (86) $1,900

— 16 Jan 1862. 2 pp, folio. Pardon for James Keenan. Countersgd by Seward. Fold split. P May 13 (87) $1,900

— 5 Feb 1862. 1 p, folio. Commission of Francis O. Wyse as Major of the 4th Artillery Regiment; partly ptd. Countersgd by Edwin M. Stanton. Framed. P Dec 15 (58) $1,800

— 21 Feb 1862. 1 p, folio. Appointment of James C. Plaght as Assistant Quartermaster of Volunteers. Countersgd by Edwin M. Stanton. Soiled & faded. Mtd. sg Nov 6 (122) $800

— 21 Feb 1862. 1 p, folio. Commission for Edward C. Boynton as Capt. Countersgd by Edwin M. Stanton. Fold tear. Partly engraved. sg Apr 9 (108) $2,400

— 21 Feb 1863. 1 p, folio. Commission for Leonard Paulding as Lieut. Commander of the Navy. Countersgd by Sec of the Navy Gideon Welles. Framed. P Oct 29 (87) $3,250

— 26 Feb 1863. 1 p, 16.5 by 17.25 inches. Appointment for William H. McAllister as Additional Paymaster. Countersgd by the Sec of War. Trimmed. Framed with portraits. S July 24 (399) £2,800 [Vivalda]

— 3 Mar 1863. 1 p, 285mm by 530mm. Appointment for John G. Treadwell as Assessor of Internal Revenue. Countersgd by Samuel P. Chase. Partly engraved. With orig envelope. sg Nov 6 (288) $2,600

— 10 Mar 1863. 1 p, folio. Appointment for Elyah Sells as Additional Paymaster; partly engraved. Countersgd by Sec of War Stanton. Fold tears. Framed with a port. CNY Dec 19 (119) $1,900

— 7 May 1864. 1 p, 370mm by 455mm. Exequatur for Carlos E. Leland as Consul of Uruguay at New York. Countersgd by William H. Seward. Mtd. sg Apr 9 (109) $1,900

— 7 July 1864. 1 p, 4to. Order to affix the US Seal to a proclamation [declaring the 1st Thursday of August a day of national humiliation & prayer]. P May 13 (91) $2,100

— 5 Aug 1864. 1 p, 278mm by 426mm. Appointment of Andrew Van Dyck as Customs Collector; ptd. CNY Dec 19 (120) $1,800

— 1 Mar 1865. 1 p, folio. Commission for George W. Cushing as assistant quartermaster. Countersgd by Stanton. Was mtd. P May 13 (94) $1,900

Autograph endorsement, sgd, 8 lines on verso of a letter from Kersey H. Fell, 8 July 1859, 1 p, 4to; approving of the proposed settlement of a debt. Separated at fold. With ANs, 1 Nov 1859, 1 p, 4to, to Fell, saying he will be glad to see him in Springfield. P Dec 15 (57A) $3,500

— Anr, sgd, 22 May 1861. 3 lines on integral blank of a letter from William Fullter Tufts to Chauncey Shaffer, 21 May 1861. Requesting that Tufts be put on the list for a Lieutenancy. P Oct 29 (84) $1,600

— Anr, 15 Oct 1862. 1 p, 4to. On integral leaf of a letter from Gen. McClellan. Concerning Lieut. John Sullivan Knapp, "being detached on recruiting service". sg Nov 6 (123) $2,400

— Anr, 13 Dec 1862. 1 p, 65mm by 75mm. 19 words, clipped from Ms document. Sgd. sg Nov 6 (124) $1,500

— Anr, sgd, 14 Dec 1863. 6 lines on verso of integral blank of a Ls by Mary Todd Lincoln to Edward McPherson, 1 p, 4to. Recommending an upholsterer. P Oct 29 (89) $8,000

— Anr, 3 lines on envelope addressed to him by J. C. Henderson, 29 Dec 1863; pardoning 6 men. Sgd. P May 13 (90) $1,500

— Anr, sgd, 3 lines at foot of a letter from F. H. Baldwin, 12 Aug 1864. 1 p, 8vo; on Executive Mansion stationery. Referring the request for promotion of Henry Moore Baldwin to the Sec of War. P May 13 (92) $4,500

— Anr, sgd, 3 lines on recto of an envelope

LINCOLN

addressed to Lincoln, 16 Oct 1864. Referral to the Sec of War. P May 13 (93) $1,500
— Anr, sgd, [18 Feb 1865]. 6 lines on verso of 2nd leaf of a letter to him from Sen. Nathan A. Farwell, 17 Feb 1865, 2 pp, 4to. Pardoning the deserter Edwin Sprague. Framed with a port. P Oct 29 (92) $3,750

Endorsement, 10 Apr 1865. 1 p, 45mm by 80mm. Sgd. Clipped from larger sheet & mtd. sg Nov 6 (125) $1,200

Franking signature, [n.d.]. With autograph address to Henry Janney. Glued to thin card. rf May 30 (22) $1,400

Photograph, sgd, [Dec 1861]. 82mm by 53mm. By Brady; full length, seated. Sgd on mount. Authentication by John Hay on verso. C Dec 3 (292) £3,800 [Hoffman]

Photograph, 3 June 1860. Platinum print photograph made in 1881 from original glass negative taken at Springfield by Alexander Hesler; 6.5 by 8.5 inches. wa May 30 (238) $850

Signature, 1864. 1 p, 8vo; on ptd card "Autographs of the President and Cabinet". Also sgd by 7 cabinet members. Bullock collection. CNY Dec 19 (121) $3,800

Lincoln, Abraham, 1809-65 —& Others

Signature, [c.1863]. In album containing signatures of Seward, Stanton, Chase, Welles, Usher, Bates, Fessenden, Sprague, Wilson, & 44 other members of Congress. Mor gilt bdg, 8vo. pnNY June 11 (87) $1,400

Lincoln, Benjamin, 1733-1810

Ds, 20 Oct 1804. 1 p, 12mo. As Collector of the Port of Marblehead; contents not stated. wa May 30 (325) $55
— 31 July 1807. 1 p, 12mo. As Collector of the Port of Boston; contents not stated. wa May 30 (401) $60

Lincoln, Mary Todd, 1818-82

ALs, 8 Sept [1861]. 3 pp, 8vo. To Sec of the Interior Caleb B. Smith. Defending John Watt against attacks by William Wood. Sang collection. P May 13 (98) $11,000
— [9 Sept 1861]. 1 p, 8vo. To [Oliver Halsted, Jr.?]. Inviting him & Gov. [Newell] to visit. Was mtd. P May 13 (99) $1,300
— 30 Jan [1865]. 3 pp, 8vo. To Abram Wakeman. Inviting him to dinner & alluding to some personal problems. P Oct 29 (93) $6,250
— 16 Mar 1869. 4 pp, 4to. To Mrs. Rhoda White. Complaining about her afflictions, & suggesting they visit Italy together. Silked. P May 13 (100) $4,750

See also: Lincoln, Abraham

AMERICAN BOOK PRICES CURRENT

Lindbergh, Charles A., 1902-77

Ls, 8 Jan 1970. 1 p, 4to. To Miss Cunningham. Concerning his comments on the "Whitman manuscript". Framed. Altman collection. pnNY Sept 13 (148) $450

Group photograph, [n.d.]. 4.5 by 7 inches. With Gaston Doumergue & Myron T. Herrick. Sgd by Lindbergh [& Herrick?]. Mtd on dinner invitation. wd Nov 12 (13) $325

Signature, [18 Feb 1928], on a small oblong piece of canvas from the Spirit of St. Louis. Framed with a photograph, sgd & inscr, & a letter establishing provenance. P May 13 (101) $1,700

Lindpaintner, Peter Joseph von, 1791-1856

Ms, Missa solemnis, no 2 in C minor; c.1842. 107 pp, 235mm by 310mm. Contemp half lea. Full score. HK Nov 4 (428) DM2,400

Linnaeus, Carolus, 1707-78

ALs, [21 Jan 1762]. 1 p, 4to. To his pbr Salvius. Referring to proof reading, & mentioning his work on his Species Plantarum. Pasted down at corners. C June 24 (174) £750 [Rota]

Lipatti, Dinu, 1917-50

Ls, 30 Nov 1950. 1 p, 4to. To his pbr Boosey & Hawkes. Offering his Aubade for wind instruments for publication. S May 22 (614) £450 [Friedman]

Lister, Joseph Lister, Baron, 1827-1912

Series of 46 A Ls s, 18 July 1896 to 18 Nov 1908. 85 pp, 8vo. To George Dean. About the Lister Institute of Preventive Medicine & discussing aspects of research in immunology. With related material. C Dec 3 (403) £6,000 [Rendell]

Ls, 29 June 1903. 1 p, 4to. To Professor Starling. Notifying him of J. C. Martin's appointment as director of the Jenner Institute. Partly faded. sg Nov 6 (129) $200

Liszt, Franz, 1811-86

[A collection of 4 Mss in the hand of Gaetano Belloni, comprising 4 songs for voice & piano from the Buch der Lieder (Lieferung II, nos 7, 9, 11 & 12), 45 pp, folio, with extensive autograph additions & revisions, sold at CNY on 19 Dec 1986, lot 141, for $5,500.]

Autograph music, Fugue Chromatique for piano, subject; 12 Aug [18]44. 1 p, 22cm by 17cm. On 3 systems of 2 staves each. Sgd; with seal. S Nov 28 (565) £1,950 [McGwynn]
— Autograph music, funeral march, 30 Aug 1827. 2 leaves, 4to. Sgd. Written 2 days after the death of his father. Inlaid. P Dec 15 (60) $5,000
— Autograph music, Grand Galop

Chromatique, opening 10 bars; 12 Jan [n.y.]. 1 p, 4to. On 2 systems of 2 staves; sgd. Was mtd. S Nov 28 (563) £1,500 [Conjal]
— Autograph music, Hungaria, version for 2 pianos; [c.1855-56]. 15 pp, 273mm by 342mm, on ptd staff paper, 20 staves each. In brown ink. CNY Dec 19 (143) $8,000
— Autograph music, O Salutaris Hostia, for soprano, tenor, bass & organ; 23 bars, [n.d.]. 1 p, size not stated; 16 staves. Stained. With 2 A Ls s, 6 Aug 1871 & 12 Feb 1872; 3 pp, 8vo. To [Joseph Seiler]. Regarding the publication of the composition. star Apr 9 (702) DM9,000
— Autograph music, opening of the piano arrangement of Salve Polonia from Die Legende vom heiligen Stanislaus, [1884]. 2 pp, 24cm by 31cm; cut from a larger sheet. 24 bars on 3 systems each of 2 staves; in brown ink & red crayon. Stained. S Nov 28 (568) £1,600 [Harris]
— Autograph music, song, Das deutsche Vaterland, for 4-voice men's chorus & orchestra; [c.1841]. 39 pp, 260mm by 348mm & 285mm by 375mm. On 4 different sorts of staff paper; 20 or 18 staves each. Numerous revisions; autograph tp. Last leaf torn. CNY Dec 19 (139) $7,500
— Autograph music, song, Du bist wie eine Blume, for tenor & piano [c.1844-45]. 2 pp, 234mm by 309mm; 12 staves each. Working Ms; sgd. CNY Dec 19 (142) $4,000

Autograph transcript, 8 bars of a theme from Valse melancolique; 28 Nov [18]44. 1 p, 8vo. Sgd & inscr. Split in halves. S May 22 (429) £600 [Bordone]
— Autograph transcript, Etude d'execution transcendante d'apres Paganini, no 6; 16 bars from the introduction; [1884]. 1 p, 8vo. Stave lines faded. Mtd. S May 22 (433) £280 [Wilson]

Ms, song, Mignon's Lied, for voice & piano, [c.1842-43]. 10 pp, 333mm by 265mm. In the hand of Gaetano Belloni; with extensive autograph revisions. With proof of ptd score, corrected by Liszt, 8pp. CNY Dec 19 (140) $2,800

Series of 3 A L s s, 11 Dec 1870 to 21 Nov 1884, 6 pp, 8vo. To Pauline Lichtner, assuring she will be welcome at Pest. To Marie von Saaz, asking for the return of a shell left behind, & praising Buelows concerts. With related material. CNY Dec 19 (147) $1,500

A Ls s (2), 19 Aug 1879 & 6 Oct 1882. 3 pp, 8vo. To Jules Zarembski, saying he will not return to Weimar this year; in French. To Otto Lessman of the Deutsche Musikzeitung, commenting on the miserliness of Th. Kullak; in German. CNY Dec 19 (145) $750

ALs, 27 July 1849. 1 p, 8vo. To Minna Wagner. Sending her money to join her husband. With port photograph. S May 22 (431) £1,550 [Haas]
— [n.d.]. 1 p, 8vo. To the Chevalier Catrufo. Sending a ticket to his concert. C Dec 3 (417) £270 [Grimwood Taylor]
— 17 Feb 1851. 1 p, 8vo. To the banker H. Calmann. Requesting a sight draft in favor of his mother at Paris. Was mtd. star Apr 9 (704) DM480
— 13 Dec 1853. 1 p, 8vo. Recipient unnamed. Covering letter for a Ms. With ANs by Marie d'Agoult. star Apr 9 (705) DM600
— 28 Feb 1856. 1 p, 8vo. To an unnamed baron. Expressing his willingness to put himself at the service of the Great Duchess. In French. Framed. Altman collection. pnNY Sept 13 (171) $375
— [1859?]. 2 pp, 8vo. Recipient unnamed. Agreeing to play in a concert given for the erection of a monument to Carl Maria von Weber. star Apr 9 (706) DM2,000
— 5 June [18]61. 2 pp, 8vo. To an unnamed composer. Concerning his failure to deliver a sgd port. S May 22 (434) £340 [Wilson]
— 19 Nov [18]62. 4 pp, 8vo. To Eduard Liszt. Commenting on death, his children, religion, & the progress of his work. S Nov 28 (566) £2,300 [Kent]
— 15 Apr 1873. 2pp, 8vo. Recipient unnamed. Thanking for his hospitality. S May 22 (615) £280 [Wilson]
— [n.d.]. 8 pp, 8vo. To "Cher Hidalgo" [Carl Tausig]. Commenting on Tausig's letter to the Wiener Musikzeitung & suggesting alterations in a composition; with 5 bars of music. In French, on blue paper. CNY Dec 19 (144) $3,500
— [n.d.]. 2 pp, 8vo. To [Gustav de Pfaffius]. Regretting that they cannot carry out a plan because of his commitments for next winter. In French. HN May 22 (3099) DM620
— 23 Jan [18]76. 3 pp, 8vo. To Eduard Liszt. Referring to his religious feelings & his symphonic poem Hunnenschlacht. S Nov 28 (567) £1,400 [Harris]
— 30 July 1880. 1 p, 8vo. To Karl von Jeniersky. Draft, regarding the 1st performance of Tannhaeuser at Weimar & declining to comment about Wagner's travels in 1849. Sgd FL. star Apr 9 (707) DM620
— [31 Jan 1883]. 2 pp, 8vo. To Eduard Liszt. About his activities in Budapest & his next visit to Vienna. S Nov 28 (569) £300 [Muggs]
— 10 Apr [18]84. 2 pp, 8vo. Recipient unnamed ("Herr Doctor"). About money to be sent to Budapest. S May 22 (437) £300 [Wilson]

LISZT

— 13 Apr [18]86. 2 pp, 8vo. To Madame Lyner. Asking if he may stay with her in Brussels. S May 22 (436) £450 [McCann]
— 17 Mar [n.y.]. 1 p, 8vo. Recipient unnamed. Concerning financial matters. S May 22 (432) £280 [Wilson]

ANs, 25 Aug [18]48. 1 p, 8vo. Recipient unnamed. Agreeing not to part with his Mss without the consent of Belloni. S May 22 (430) £260 [Maggs]

AN, [n.d.]. Ptd visiting card, 6.5cm by 11cm. To Bechstein. Sending compliments by bearer. S May 22 (616) £180 [Maggs]

Corrected page proofs, Gustav Schilling's biography of Liszt, 1844; 256 pp [lacking 2 leaves] & 7 autograph leaves, 8vo. With some autograph & numerous dictated notes & revisions by Liszt. In def contemp cardboard. star Apr 9 (703) DM2,600

Photograph, sgd, [c.1880]. Carte size. Was mtd. With group photograph, 11 June 1881, showing Liszt, Major Klein & Lessmann. star Apr 9 (708) DM1,300

Photograph, sgd & inscr, July 1878. 105mm by 65mm. Inscr to Mlle Pringl. With anr photograph, [1886], 230mm by 161mm, inscr on verso "Derniere sortie de Liszt". CNY Dec 19 (148) $1,100

Signature, 22 July 1884. On copy of Bayreuther Festblaetter in Wort und Bild. Munich, 1884; 60 pp, folio. Inscr to Hedwige von Liszt. S May 22 (438) £300 [West]

Liturgical Manuscripts

[2 Mss in Latin, Psalter & Officium et missa nativitatis domini, [Spain or South America, mid-17th cent], 102 & 104 leaves, 78cm by 45cm, vellum; lea over wooden bds; both incomplete, with numerous initials in red & blue & 2 large initials in colors sold at VH on 12 Sept 1986, lot 917, for DM10,000.]

Ms, chants for various feasts, [Germany, c.1700]. 56 leaves & blanks, 225mm by 150mm. Contemp vellum bdg using 15th cent Ms. In Latin; some German. Music written in brown & red ink. HK Nov 4 (431) DM850

— Ms, Collectar & Office Book, in Latin, [Eastern France, 1st half of 15th cent]. 80 leaves only, vellum, 250mm by 176mm. Old sheepskin bdg, repaired. Of Dominican Use. Written by several different scribes at different periods in the 15th cent, mostly in dark brown ink in large gothic liturgical hand. With 33 pp of music on a 4-line red stave, c.200 decorated initials in red or blue with contrasting penwork & 3 very large initials. S Dec 2 (46) £1,300 [Thomas]

— Ms, collection, containing 3 texts for mass & Officium in agendis mortuorum, [Southern Germany, c.1500]. 36 leaves, 210mm by 143mm. Blindstamped lea over wooden bds. Spine def., lacking clasps. Various scripts; in several hands. With a number of red & blue initials, 3 with floral designs. VH Sept 12 (914) DM1,400

— Ms, Latin Ms, [Italy, late 16th cent]. 89 leaves, 18.5cm by 14cm. Vellum. Contemp calf, def. Using neumatic system of notation for Gregorian chants; red & blue initials. Ownership inscr by a Franciscan monastery near Naples dated 1588. JG Oct 2 (483) DM3,600

— Ms, Manuale sacerdotum, [Paris, c.1510]. Use of Paris. 60 leaves, vellum, 216mm by 156mm, contemp vellum bdg. In black & red ink, with illuminated initials throughout. With 5 large elaborate miniatures illustrating baptism, marriage, blessing of nuptial bed, extreme unction & a procession. FD Dec 2 (3) DM58,000

See also: Greek Manuscripts

Lives of the Saints

Ms, description of the martyrdom of St. George, in Latin, & Translatio Capitis divi Georgii martyris, [Italy, Venice?, 16th cent]. 23 leaves, 21.5cm by 14.5cm. 19th cent violet velvet bdg, worn. In humanistic cursive script, with several illuminated initials. FD June 11 (7) DM4,000

— Ms, Vita beati Anselmi episcopi et confessoris, [France, 13th cent]. Length not stated, 150mm by 105mm. Part of a vol possibly compiled by a divinity student in Paris, early 14th cent. In black ink with red headings. HK Nov 4 (468) DM1,200

Livingston, Philip, Signer from New York

ADs, 8 Mar 1776. 1 p, 8vo. Receipt to Abraham Wendell. Strengthened on verso; tipped to larger sheet. Charlotte Parker Milne collection. wd Nov 12 (51) $200

Livingston, Robert R., 1746-1813. See: United States

Livingston, Walter, 1740-97

Franking signature, [2 Apr 1788]. As Commissioner of Treasury. rf Mar 14 (90) $120

Livingstone, David, 1813-73

ALs, 14 Jan 1851. 6 pp, 4to. To James Hamilton. Reporting about Hamilton's brother Robert, missionary work in South Africa & criticizing the Boers. With related material. pn Dec 11 (123) £1,600 [Quaritch]

— 3 Feb 1858. 4 pp, 8vo. To the Right Hon. H. Labouchere. Declining an invitiation because of a prior commitment. wa May 30 (485) $350

— 24 July 1863. 4 pp, 8vo. To Horace Waller. Describing his experiences during his Zambesi Expedition. Was mtd. S July 24 (330) £500 [Sakmyster]

— 28 Feb 1865. 4 pp, 8vo. To [John] Kirk. Returning a paper & commenting on British colonial policy. Framed. Altman collection. pnNY Sept 13 (149) $600

— 12 May 1865. 4 pp, 8vo. To Arthur Mills. Criticizing Richard Burton's assertions about missionaries. S Dec 18 (276) £1,050 [Joseph & Sawyer]

— 28 July 1865. 4 pp, 8vo. To Mr. Mills. Regretting he has no time to call & thanking Mrs. Mills for a present. C Dec 3 (293) £250 [Reuter]

— 20 Sept 1865. 4 pp, 8vo. To [Sir John] Kirk. Mentioning Col. Playfair's health problems, suggesting he try for his place, & describing Bombay. pn Dec 11 (124) £200 [Dupre]

Corrected proof, Missionary Travels, 1 page only, 8vo; [c. 1857]. With 9-line autograph addition about a chronometer watch carried to the Zambesi, 1852 to 1856. Laid down. S Jan 27 (829) £120 [Dupre]

Lloyd George, David, 1863-1945

[A series of typescripts of 14 articles by Lloyd George on foreign affairs, 1928 to 1935, 74 pp, folio [2 carbon copies], all sgd, sold at S on 24 July, lot 326, for £9,500 to FAS.]

Locke, John, 1632-1704

ALs, 28 July 1698. 1 p, 8vo. To Cornelius Lyde. Explaining an earlier notification that he is in London where he will stay as long as his health permits. S Dec 18 (327) £750 [Jeffrey]

— 16 Feb 1698/9. 2 pp, 8vo. To Cornelius Lyde. Regretting to have missed the opportunity to introduce Lyde's son to London physicians & requesting him to give money to Mary Doleman. S Dec 18 (328) £1,000 [Boyle]

Loens, Hermann, 1866-1914

Autograph transcript, poem, Die Letzten; 2 4-line stanzas. On flyleaf of 1st Ed of his anthology Mein goldenes Buch. Hannover, 1901; inscr to Lulu von Strauss und Torney, sgd & dated 17 Aug 1901. 4to, cloth bdg. star Apr 8 (205) DM1,000

Loens, Hermann, 1866-1914 —& Loens, Lisa

[A collection of 50 A Ls s & 8 autograph postcards, sgd, by Hermann Loens, 14 Feb 1910 to 20 Sept 1914, 143 pp, 4to & 8vo, & cards; & 13 A Ls s by Lisa Loens, 4 Jan 1911 to 18 Oct 1914, 80 pp, 8vo; to Eugen Diederichs, regarding Loens's publications & their personal & financial problems after their separation, with related material, sold at star on 8 Apr, lot 206, for DM11,000.]

Loens, Lisa. See: Loens, Hermann & Loens

Long, Huey Pierce, 1893-1935

Ds, 25 Sept 1928. 15 by 9.4 inches. Louisiana State Bond for Confederate Veterans, for $10,000. Sgd as Governor. wa May 30 (490) $110

Longfellow, Henry Wadsworth, 1807-82

Autograph Ms, poem, Dante; 8 Mar 1881. 1 p, 8vo. 4 lines, sgd. Pasted down at edge. C June 24 (122) £240 [Maggs]

Autograph transcript, quatrain, The night shall be filled with music, sgd & dated Mar 1867. 2 pp, 8vo. S Jan 27 (715) £340 [Middleton]

ALs, 1 Dec 1840. 4 pp, 4to. To Samuel Ward. Discussing Ward's sister Louisa and his own literary endeavors. sg Dec 4 (114) $1,600

— 5 Oct 1860. 1 p, 4to. Recipient unnamed. Sending a transcript of a poem, sgd [at head of page]. With a port. sg Apr 9 (113) $425

— 7 Oct 1873. 1 p, 8vo. To Mr. Osgood. Asking for missing issues of a magazine. With a port. sg Apr 9 (114) $150

Longstreet, James, 1821-1904

ALs, 5 Oct 1862. 4 pp, 8vo. To Gen. J. E. Johnston. Praising Johnston as a leader & describing his command. Fold tears. CNY Dec 19 (123) $1,500

Lopez de Ayala, Pedro

Ms, Libro de la caza de aves.... [Spain, 15th cent] 79 (of 80, lacking f.48) leaves, 209mm by 146mm, in 17th-cent vellum, worn. In brown ink in a rounded gothic hand, with c.50 decorated initials in red with purple & 3 small diagrams. Jeanson Ms 123 SM Mar 1 (370) FF220,000

Lorrain, Claude, 1600-82. See: Claude Gellee, 1600-82

Lorre, Peter, 1904-64

Photograph, sgd, [c.1935]. 10 by 8 inches. Bust view. Was mtd. sg Nov 6 (130) $200

Lortzing, Albert, 1801-51

ALs, 29 Jan 1843. 1 p, 4to. To Greiner, director of the Dessau theater. Enlisting his help in collecting a debt. star Apr 9 (711) DM1,700

Lossing, Benson John, 1813-91

ALs, 29 Sept 1859. 1 p, 8vo. Recipient unnamed. About the publication date of his "book on Mt. Vernon" & the whereabouts of Mr. Tomlinson. With The Pictorial Field-Book of the Revolution. NY, 1855. 2 vols. 4to, cloth. sg Nov 6 (291) $70

LOUIS

Louis, Dauphin, 1729-65

Ms, Etat et Menu General de la Depense ordinaire de Monsieur le Dauphin Annee 1754; 86 pp, 4to. Contemp speckled calf with arms of Louis-Joseph de Bourbon, Prince de Conde. S May 21 (268) £400 [Bouvier]

Louis XI, King of France, 1423-83

Ls, 22 Sept [c.1465]. 1 p, 4to. To [Francesco Sforza], Duke of Milan. Mentioning the return of his envoys & thanking for an offer of help. C Dec 3 (294) £750 [L'Echiquier]

Louis XII, King of France, 1462-1515

Ds, 22 Apr 1510. 1 p, 4to. Address to officials at Gennes, requesting cooperation in assessing the property of the late Anthoine d'Albario. Repaired. C Dec 3 (295) £260 [McCormick]

Louis XIV, King of France, 1638-1715

Ms, Les Plans et figures geometriques des forests royals du departement de Touraine, Anjou et Maine.... 1666-69. 9 pp with 7 plans drawn by Jacques Le Loyer de la Fleche & frontis by Compardet, 623mm by 435mm, in contemp red mor gilt with royal arm. Jeanson Ms 163 SM Mar 1 (372) FF72,000

ALs, 1 Aug 1683. 1 p, 4to. To Queen Catherine of England. Notifying her of the death of his wife. Address leaf detached. Bullock collection. CNY Dec 19 (170) $2,800

Ls, 23 Feb 1658. 1 p, 4to. To an unnamed German prince. Assuring him of his friendship & of his satisfaction with a treaty. star Apr 9 (970) DM1,300

— 16 Dec 1714. 1 p, folio. To the Duc de Guiches. Military letter. sg Nov 6 (132) $250

Ds, 20 Jan 1674. 1 p, folio. Military appointment. Torn. wd Nov 12 (14) $75

— 18 Nov 1679. 6 pp, folio. Marriage contract of Marie Anne Baillet de Vaugrenant, widow of Jean Truchot, & Jean de St. Esteden. Also sgd by c.20 members of the Royal family & the court. Bound with 8 engravings of the Royal family. P Dec 15 (62) $800

— 10 Nov 1682. 1 p, folio. Money order to Louis Poirier to pay the debts of the Departement of Tours. Framed. Altman collection. pnNY Sept 13 (64) £750

— 1700. 1 p, folio. Commission for Chevallier de Cheury as Capt. of Infantry. Indenture cut. Signature faded. sg Nov 6 (131) $200

AMERICAN BOOK PRICES CURRENT

Louis XV, King of France, 1710-74

Ms, Chasses du Roy, et la quantite de lieues que le Roy a fait tant a cheval qu'en carosse pendant l'annee 1726 [1727], par le sieur Mouret. 2 vols, each with 26 pp, 212mm by 138mm, in contemp red or olive mor gilt with arms of Louis XV in mosaic form. Jeanson Ms s 161 & 162 SM Mar 1 (374) FF440,000

— Ms, Etat des depenses de la grande venerie du Roy faites par le grand veneur...depuis janvier 1726 jusqu'en avril 1774. About 300 pp, 370mm by 243mm, in 19th-cent calf gilt. Jeanson Ms 159 SM Mar 1 (375) FF9,000

ALs, 7 Apr 1760. 1 p, 4to. To Sr Henin. Notifying him of secret negotiations in Poland. Framed. Altman collection. pnNY Sept 13 (65) £750

Letter, 22 Sept 1754. 1 p. folio. To Cardinal Giovanni Jacopo Millo. Letter of introduction for Francois Joseph Marquis de Choiseuil-Stainville. With secretarial signature. star Apr 9 (972) DM270

Ds, 25 May to June 1749. 24 pp, folio. Marriage contract of Adelaide Camus de Pontcarre & Henry Francois de Briqueville. Also sgd by the Royal family & numerous court members. In 4to bdg, with related material. P Dec 15 (63) $900

Louis XVI, King of France, 1754-93

Ms, Comte rendu des chasses du cerf faites par le Roi entre le 4 janvier 1775 et le 14 septembre 1790. 17 pp, 177mm by 116mm, in contemp mor. With ANs of Prince Alexandre Labanoff de Rostoff at beginning. Jeanson Ms 139 SM Mar 1 (376) FF380,000

— Ms, Comte rendu des chasses du cerf faites pendant l'annee 1789. 6 pp, 191mm by 149mm, in contemp mor. Jeanson Ms 138 SM Mar 1 (377) FF90,000

— Ms, Etats des forets du Roi dans le departement de la matrise general de Metz ou resultat de la visite qui en a ete faite en 1786 en execution des ordres de M. le controleur general. [c.1786] 330 pp with 80 maps, 410mm by 260mm, in contemp mor gilt. Jeanson Ms 169 SM Mar 1 (378) FF24,000

Ds, 22 Nov 1789. 2 pp, folio. Order of the Royal Council of Finances concerning accounts for 1786. C Dec 3 (296) £180 [L'Echiquier]

— 19 Apr 1791. 1 p, folio. Pay order in favor of harpsicord maker Christophe Chiquelier. S Nov 27 (392) £260 [Maggs]

140

Louis XVII, King of France, 1785-95
— NAUNDORF, KARL WILHELM. - ALs, 9 Aug 1840. 2 pp, 4to. To Modeste Gruau de la Barre. About the people being mislead by others, his letter to the Minister of Police, & his publication. Sgd Charles Louis Duc de Normandie. star Apr 9 (974) DM560

Louis XVIII, King of France, 1755-1824
Autograph Ms, detailed list of the descendants of Emperor Maximilian I, [n.d.]. 4 pp, 4to. star Apr 9 (975) DM3,000

Ms, Livret des chasses du Roi pour 1816. 169 pp, 196mm by 135mm, in contemp red mor gilt. Jeanson Ms 173 SM Mar 1 (380) FF45,000

— Ms, Livret matricule du service du grand veneur. [c.1824] 94 leaves, 203mm by 163mm, contemp bdg. Jeanson Ms 174 SM Mar 1 (381) FF1,400

AL, 24 Oct 1793. 1 p, 8vo. To [Yolande-Martine, Duchesse de Polignac?]. About the recent death of Marie Antoinette. C Dec 3 (297) £320 [Joseph]

Lover, Samuel, 1797-1868
Ms, Occasional Poems, 1819. 60 pp, 4to. In brown ink; titles in gothic lettering. Diced russia gilt with green silk liners; modern mor slip-case. Some of his earliest poems; possibly autograph fair copy. C Dec 3 (371) £300 [Burgess & Browning]

Lowell, James Russell, 1819-91
ALs, 11 June 1850. 1 p, 4to. To A[ndrew] J[ackson] Downing. Reporting about a meeting with Frederika Bremer. sg Nov 6 (133) $80

Check, 19 Jan 1877. Drawn on Charles River National Bank, for $75 payable to the Old South Fund. Sgd. Matted with a photograph. With related material. sg Apr 9 (115) $150

Lucas, Frederic Augustus, 1852-1929
[A collection containing 2 Mss, diaries of his travels to South America & England, 17 Nov 1868 to 30 May 1870, 3 A Ls (2 sgd) to his wife & daughter, 65 orig drawings of fossils & zoological specimens, & further related material, sold at P on 13 May 1987, lot 104, for $4,500]

Ludendorff, Erich, 1865-1937
Series of 6 A Ls s, 18 Mar [1924] to 23 Apr [1925]. 6 pp, 8vo. To Col. von Baumer. Explaining his political opinions & actions. star Apr 9 (1038) DM3,700

A Ls s (2), [c.1928]. 2 pp, 8vo. To Herr von Wangenheim. About his publications & grumbling at the press. With 3 A Ls s by Gen. von Kuhl, 1934 & later. star Apr 9 (1039) DM1,150

ALs, 15 Feb [1919]. 2 pp, 4to. To Col. von Tieschowitz. Requesting a list of officers discharged by him before his resignation. star Apr 9 (1037) DM700

Ludwig, Emil, 1881-1948
Collection of ALs, autograph document, sgd, & 3 documents, sgd, 19 Sept 1927 to 25 Feb 1928. 7 pp, various sizes. Material concerning contracts with Samuel Sidney McClure & Lee Keedick about lectures in the USA & Canada. With related material. star Apr 8 (207) DM280

Ludwig I, King of Bavaria, 1786-1868
Autograph Ms, poem, beginning "Seyd, theure Frauen, herzlich mir willkommen", 15 May 1832. 2 pp, 4to. 3 eight-line stanzas addressed to Luise Herding & Charlotte von Lilien. HK Nov 7 (2285) DM1,500

Ls, 3 Apr 1836. 1 p, 4to. To Ferdinand II, King of the Two Sicilies. Sending condolences on the death of his wife. star Apr 9 (887) DM260

Ludwig II, King of Bavaria, 1845-86
[A collection of 28 A Ls s, 1880 to 1902, about 48 pp, 8vo & 4to, mostly addressed to Richard von Hornig by Ludwig von Buerkel, Lorenz Mayr & Freiherr von Wolffskeel, chiefly concerning the King's orders regarding the furnishing of Herrenwoerth, sold at HK on 7 Nov 1986, lot 2299, for DM5,500.]

Collection of ALs, 16 A Ls, & 6 Ls s & 3 Ls, [May 1884] to 23 July 1884. About 63 pp, 8vo. To Richard von Hornig. Mostly concerning this building projects at Herrenchiemsee & Falkenstein, & about financial problems. Somr autograph corrections & additions. 11 signatures cut with some loss of text. HK Nov 7 (2298) DM40,000

ALs, 3 July 1867. 2 pp, 4to. To Emperor Franz Joseph of Austria. Expressing condolences on the death of his brother, Emperor Maximilian of Mexico. Fold splits. HK Nov 7 (2292) DM7,000

7 Oct 1867. 6 pp, 4to & 8vo. To "Elsa" [Sophie Charlotte Herzogin in Bayern]. Breaking their engagement. Sgd Heinrich. HK Nov 7 (2291) DM52,000

Series of 21 Ls s, 1880 to 1883. About 44 pp, 8vo. To Richard von Hornig. About his building projects & a variety of private matters. Some letters with autograph subscription, additions & corrections, a few def. HK Nov 7 (2297) DM21,000

Ls s (2), 27 Aug 1880 & 5 Feb 1882. 2 pp, 4to & folio. To Dr. Hamberger, in German, & Cardinal Pitra, in Italian. Thanking for good wishes. S May 21 (271) £320 [MacNutt]

Ls, 30 July 1871. 1 p, 4to. To Count

d'Henricourt von Gruenne. Thanking for his kindness to wounded Bavarian soldiers during the Franco-Prussian war. In lea frame inside lea case. S Nov 27 (394) £480 [Pervamas]

— 4 May 1877. 1 p, 4to. To his brother Otto. About Otto's removal to Fuerstenried for the benefit of his health. With related material. HK Nov 7 (2293) DM7,000

— 31 Aug 1883. 1 p, 4to. To Freiherr von Lutz. Thanking for congratulations. HK Nov 7 (2294) DM800

— 2 Jan 1886. 1 p, 4to. To Freiherr von Lutz. Thanking for New Year's wishes. HK Nov 7 (2296) DM650

Series of Ds s, 7 Ds s, 13 July 1864 to 24 June 1872. 11 pp, mostly folio. Documents pertaining to the War Department. HK Nov 7 (2288) DM1,500

— BOMHARD, EDUARD GRAF VON. - Letter, c.1865. 3 pp, folio. To [Franz Seraph von Pfistermeister?] Contemp copy, regarding Freiherr von Lerchenfeld, the investigation of the conduct of the brothers Voelk, grooms of the King, & rumours about the King's homosexuality. HK Nov 7 (2301) DM550

— THURN UND TAXIS, PAUL, FUERST VON. - ALs, 7 Aug 1866. 3 pp, 8vo. To [King Ludwig]. Reporting about his visit with Wagner at Triebschen. Sgd Friedrich. HK Nov 7 (2303) DM800

Ludwig of Bavaria, Duke, 1831-1920
Collection of 9 A Ls s & Ls, 1875 to 1879. To Richard von Hornig & his wife, Ls to King Ludwig II. About life at the Bavarian court, his financial problems, etc. With related material. HK Nov 7 (2300) DM2,000

Ludwig, Paula, 1900-74
Collection of 9 A Ls s & autograph postcard, sgd, 1933 to 1955. 23 pp, 4to & 8vo. To H. Draws-Tychsen. About personal affairs & publication matters, her concept of the mission of a writer, her emigration & return, etc. With related material. HN May 22 (3104) DM600

Luetzow, Adolf, Freiherr von, 1782-1834
Ds, 15 Dec 1814. 1 p, folio. Conferral of a medal commemorating the campaign of 1813/14. Partly ptd. star Apr 9 (1043) DM650

— 18 Apr 1815. 1 p, folio. Certificate of military service for Capt. Staak. star Apr 9 (1044) DM450

Luetzow, Adolph, Freiherr von, 1782-1834
Ms, 4 July [1818?]. 2 pp, folio. List concerning movements of troops. Sgd by Luetzow, Chr. Fr. Petersdorf & Ferdinand B. Schill. JG Oct 2 (435) DM800

Lugosi, Bela, 1882-1956
Photograph, sgd, [n.d.]. Size not stated. wa May 30 (376) $325

Luise, Queen of Frederick William III of Prussia, 1776-1810
ALs, 2 Dec 1809. 1 p, 8vo. Recipient unnamed. Regarding the salary of Fraeulein von Rheinbrecht. star Apr 9 (1168) DM1,300

Ls, 3 Jan 1798. 1 p, 4to. Recipient unnamed. Thanking for New Year's wishes. Lower margin cut. star Apr 9 (1167) DM440

Luther, Martin, 1483-1546
Ms, compilation, Der Regenten Spiegel vonn allerley Historien aus den zwoelff Tomis operum Lutheri gezogen. [Wuerzburg?, 1571]. 76 leaves & 3 flyleaves, 30.2cm by 19.5cm. Contemp red vellum bdg. FD June 11 (6) DM3,400

Lyttleton, George, 1st Baron, 1709-73
Ms, A description of North Wales in a Letter from Ld. Littleton to his Brother the Bp. of Carlisle, [c.1755]. 52 leaves, 8vo. Contemp calf. C June 24 (11) £180 [Palace]

M

MacArthur, Douglas, 1880-1964. See: Eisenhower, Dwight D. & Others

McClellan, George B., 1826-85
ALs, [n.d.]. 4 pp, 8vo. To [William Buel Franklin]. Regarding negotiations for a railroad from Hoboken to Buffalo. wa May 30 (239) $100

ANs, 9 May 1862. 1 p, 8vo. To his wife. Saying John will return via West Point. On Head-Quarters, Army of the Potomac letterhead. In pencil. 2 notes of authentication on verso. wa Oct 18 (130) $80

Macdonough, Thomas, 1783-1825
Autograph Ms, Journal kept on board the United States Frigate 'Guerriere'; 25 Apr 1818 to 5 Aug 1819. 78 pp, size not given. Sgd several times. With 8 autograph topographical profile maps. Last 50 pp in secretary's hand. Contemp suede; joints worn. sg Nov 6 (210) $750

Macdougall, W. B.
Original drawings, (12), illusts, tp & initial letters for The Fall of the Nibelungs, 1897. In ink. Average size 200mm by 150mm. Mostly sgd on mounts & dated 1896 to 1897. Archives of J. M. Dent & Son. S June

19 (810) £2,000 [Edberg]
— Original drawings, (19), illusts, borders & initial letters for The Book of Ruth, 1896. 18 sgd & dated 1896. Mostly 550mm by 425mm. 3 def. Archives of J. M. Dent & Son. S June 19 (809) £600 [Abi]

McDowell, Edward Alexander, 1861-1908
ALs, 28 May 1898. 2 pp, 12mo. To Miss Martin. Saying he cannot make an appointment to see her at this time. wa May 30 (16) $220

Machen, Arthur, 1863-1947
Autograph Ms, The Green Round. [Early 1930s] 308 pp, 4to. In pencil. sg Mar 3 (144) $2,600

McHenry, James, 1753-1816
ALs, 3 June 1800. 2 pp, 4to. To George Simpson. Recommending William Burton for a position in the Bank of the US. sg Nov 6 (293) $200

— 3 June 1800. 2 pp, 4to. To George Simpson. Recommending William Burton for a position in the Bank of the U.S., & about his resignation. sg Apr 9 (116) $100

Ls, 10 June 1785. 1 p, 4to. To the Maryland Convention. Transmitting a letter from Jefferson. Also sgd by John Henry & William Hindman. Fold split. wa May 30 (150) $160

Machiavelli, Niccolo, 1469-1527
ALs, 18 Aug 1515. 1 p, 4to. To his nephew Giovanni Vernacci. Family letter, & asking that he send an item requested by his wife. Repaired. P Dec 15 (66) $6,000

Ds, 20 June 1509. 1 p, folio. Vellum. Confirmation of a letter from the Council of Ten regarding foreign ambassadors in Florence; directed to the Commissioner of Pisa. With 4-line autograph statement at bottom of p. Matted with a port. P Dec 15 (65) $4,000

McIntosh, Lachlan, 1725-1806
Ds, 20 Jan 1791. 1 p, folio. Attestation that Alexander Forester has lived in Georgia for 6 years. Charlotte Parker Milne collection. wd Nov 12 (52) $200

McKean, Thomas, Signer from Delaware
Ds, 12 Apr 1805. 1 p, folio. As Gov. of Pennsylvania, land grant to Philip Nicklin & Robert E. Griffith. Charlotte Parker Milne collection. wd Nov 12 (53) $100

— 29 May 1806. 1 p, folio. Land grant. Countersgd by Timothy Matlack. wa May 30 (426) $200

— 10 Sept 1806. 1 p, folio. Land grant for Robert Blackwell. Countersgd by Timothy Matlack. wa May 30 (139) $260

McKean, Thomas, Signer from Delaware
Autograph endorsement, 3 July 1792. 1 p, 8vo. On verso of partly ptd Ds by Thomas Mifflin, 15 June 1792; pay order to McKean for travel expenses, countersgd by John Nicholson. Fold tear affecting signatures. sg Apr 9 (117) $100

Mackensen, August von, 1849-1945
Ls, 4 Dec 1915. 1 p, folio. To Gen. von Watter. Informing him about accusations against officers & soldiers of a division. Fold tear. With draft of von Watter's reply on verso & on integral leaf. star Apr 9 (1282) DM340

Mackensen, Fritz, 1866-1953
Collection of 3 A Ls s & 3 autograph postcards, sgd, 14 Oct 1894 to [26 July 1906]. 27 pp, 8vo, & cards. To Hans Mueller-Brauel. Giving biographical information & describing the beginnings of the Worpswede colony. Some stains & tears. star Apr 8 (503) DM3,200

— Collection of 2 A Ls s, autograph postcard, sgd, & ANs, 2 May 1926 to Apr 1941. 4 pp, 4to & 8vo. To Frido Witte. Discussing exhibitions & thanking for congratulations. HN May 22 (3107) DM340

Mackeson, Frederick, 1807-53. See: Afghan War, First

McKinley, William, 1843-1901
Ls, 28 Feb 1882. 1 p, 8vo. Recipient unnamed. About a pension claim. wa May 30 (293) $110

ANs, 19 Dec 1900. 1 p, 12mo. To the Sec of the Navy. Order to appoint William Frye Tibbetts Collector at Mobile. Initialled. On White House letterhead. wa Oct 18 (30) $250

Ds, 22 Oct 1898. 1 p, folio. Appointment of William B. Winn to Brigade Surgeon of Volunteers with rank of Major. Countersgd by Sec of War Russel A. Alger. wa Oct 18 (131) $90

Executive Mansion card, [c.1900]. 1 p, 24mo. Sgd. Was mtd. sg Sept 18 (164) $175

McNeile, H. C.
Series of c.100 A Ls s, 1914 to 1918. Size not stated. To A. P. Watt Ltd. Concerning proofs & arrangements. In black deed box assigned for his papers. S July 23 (218) £200 [Minerva]

Madison, Dorothy Payne Todd ("Dolley"), 1768-1849
Franking signature, [16 Jan n.y.]. rf Mar 14 (91) $1,000

Madison, James, 1751-1836

ALs, 15 May 1809. 1 p, 4to. To David Gelston. As President, regarding a shipment of wine from Lisbon. With franking signature. Seal hole. CNY Dec 19 (31) $2,000

— 24 Nov 1809. 1 p, 4to. To David Gelston. As President, regarding a "Pipe of Brandy...sent by Mr. Lee". CNY Dec 19 (32) $2,200

ANs, 9 Feb 1810. 1 p, 4to. To the proprietor of the "American Citizen". In 3d person, sending money for payment. With ALs to Madison by Gabriel Allen, 27 Oct 1808, 2 pp, 4to, concerning a letter opened by Allen. CNY May 11 (55) $280

— 20 Dec 1811. 1 p, 4to. To David Gelston. In 3d person, asking him to forward letters. CNY May 11 (52) $500

— [June 1817]. 1 p, 4to. To David Gelston. In 3d person, asking him to forward an enclosure. With franking signature. CNY May 11 (53) $400

Ds s (2)[before 17 Jan 1812] & 16 Nov 1812. 2 pp, folio. Ship's papers in four languages for the brig Cygnet; countersgd by James Monroe & Henry Dearborn. Commission for the privateer Hunter; countersgd by Monroe. P Oct 29 (95) $1,900

Ds, 25 May 1809. 1 p, folio. Mediterranean Pass for the schooner Two Sisters of Marblehead. Engraved vignettes. rf Nov 15 (11) $400

— 28 Oct 1809. 1 p, folio. Ship's papers for the Nancy, bound for Lisbon. Also sgd by 4 other hands. Framed. Altman collection. pnNY Sept 13 (14) $700

— 20 July 1810. 1 p, folio. Ship's papers in 4 languages for the sloop Frances of Philadelphia. Countersgd by R. Smith. rf Mar 14 (39) $500

— 2 Apr 1811. 1 p, folio. Land grant. Countersgd by Monroe. rf Mar 14 (36) $650

— 2 Apr 1811. 1 p, folio. Land grant. Countersgd by Monroe. rf Mar 14 (37) $650

— 2 Apr 1811. 1 p, folio. Land grant. Countersgd by Monroe. rf Mar 14 (38) $650

— 1 Mar 1817. 1 p, folio. Land grant to Nancy Bledsoe & others. Framed. Altman collection. pnNY Sept 13 (15) $800

— 17 Mar 1818. 1 p, folio. Ship's papers in 4 languages for the schooner Betsy of Marblehead. Countersgd by Monroe. rf Mar 14 (35) $725

Check, 16 Nov 1814. 2.5 by 7.2 inches. Payable to A.B. for $600. P May 13 (105) $600

Franking signature, [13 Dec 1824]. Repaired. rf Mar 14 (94) $300

— Anr, [8 Feb n.y.]. rf Mar 14 (92) $375

— Anr, [1 Nov n.y.]. As Sec of State. rf Mar 14 (93) $325

Magano, Juan

Ms, Defensa canonica dedicada al rey nuestro senor por la dignidad episcopal de la puebla de Los Angeles...parte primera [c.1650]. 348 leaves, 4to; written on recto & verso. In contemp vellum bdg; worn. Jose Maria Andrade collection. sg Sept 18 (180) $250

Magritte, Rene, 1898-1967

[A collection of autograph Mss & drafts of 12 of his writings, 26 pp, mostly folio, sold at S on 2 July 1987, lot 959, for £5,000 to Rota.]

[A collection of preliminary material for Magritte's review La Carte d'apres nature, [c.1952-56], c.100 pp, various sizes, with annotations & corrections by Magritte, sold at S on 2 July 1987, lot 960, for £1,300 to Communaute de Francais de Belgique.]

[A collection of 11 autograph lists of pictures lent to exhibitions, 1964 to 1967, 14 pp, various sizes, with related correspondence, a number of photocopies & some documents pertaining to Magritte sold at S on 2 July 1987, lot 963, for £5,000 to Brachot.]

Autograph Ms (2), notebooks containing an inventory of his paintings, etc., from 1942 onwards; [c.1964]. About 25 pp, in 2 exercise books, 8vo. Also containing some other material. S July 2 (964) £950 [Rota]

Collection of c.60 A Ls s & postcards, sgd, c.1922 to 1946. About 90 pp, various sizes. To his wife Georgette. Love letters before their marriage, others from visits to Paris, mentioning Chirico, Dali, Andre Breton, etc. With related material. S July 2 (958) £11,000 [Morris]

— Collection of over 40 A Ls s & postcards, sgd, c.1934 to 1957. About 50 pp, folio. To Paul Colinet. About appropriate titles for his paintings & discussing works of literature; with a number of ballpoint sketches. With related material. S July 2 (957) £12,000 [Morris]

— Collection of 24 A Ls s & postcards, sgd, 15 Feb to 31 Mar 1937. To his wife Georgette. About his visit to London, his paintings, his host Edward James, etc. S July 2 (955) £6,500 [Morris]

Ls s (2), 26 Feb & 12 Mar 1937. 4 pp, 4to. To [Colinet]. Describing the interpretation of his paintings by 2 Freudian psychoanalysts, & about the progress of his paintings. One Ls in English, 1 partly in English, with pen-&-ink sketch of the typist. S July 2 (956) £2,800 [Communaute de Francais de Belgique]

Autograph postcard, sgd, [5 Mar 1922]. To his fiancee Georgette Berger. Sending greetings from a restaurant. Illus with some sketches.

S July 2 (953) £800 [De Frietas]

— [17 Mar 1922]. To his fiancee Georgette Berger. Describing a practice with gas masks. Illus with sketch of man with gas mask. S July 2 (954) £900 [De Frietas]

Mahler, Gustav, 1860-1911

Autograph music, 1st draft of the 3d movement of his Second Symphony; dated 16 July [18]93. 46 pp, folio; unbound. In black ink on up to 18 staves per page; many revisions. Differing substantially from final version. S May 22 (440) £55,000 [Kirkman]

— Autograph music, song-cycle, Lieder eines fahrenden Gesellen; full score, [1891?-1893]. 58 pp, folio, & 2 blanks. Notated in brown ink on up to 20 staves per p; many revisions & differences from ptd versions. 1 p laid down over anr. With note of authentication by Hermann Behr on flyleaf. Contemp blue wraps. S Nov 28 (574) £180,000 [Haas]

ALs, [4 Oct 1895?]. 2 pp, 8vo. To [Hermann Behn]. Regarding missing corrections & commenting about Massenet's Werther. star Apr 9 (716) DM2,800

— 20 May 1898. 5 pp, 8vo. To [Julius Wolff]. Commenting extensively about Wolff's poetical work Renata. star Apr 9 (717) DM8,500

— [24 Sept 1905]. 2 pp, 8vo. To Richard Wickenhauser. Notifying him of revisions made to his 4th Symphony. star Apr 9 (718) DM3,800

AL, [n.d.]. 2 pp, 8vo (lettercard). To [Otto] Singer. Asking for "Materialien zu meiner Symphonie". HK Nov 7 (2311) DM3,200

Ls, 25 Sept 1907. 2 pp, 8vo. To Ignaz Herbst. Announcing that he will be leaving his post as Director of the Court Opera. S Nov 28 (576) £520 [Maggs]

— 15 Nov 1907. 2 pp, 8vo. Recipient unnamed. Recommending Alexander Kosman for an engagement at Dresden. S May 22 (617) £650 [Haas]

Mahler-Werfel, Alma, 1879-1964

Collection of 13 A Ls s (3 on picture postcards), Ls, 2 autograph postcards, sgd, & telegram, 1925 to 1948. 11 pp, mostly 4to, & cards. To Lotte Czarniawski. Regarding meetings; mentioning Werfel & Stefan Zweig; about a Werfel autograph. star Apr 9 (719) DM1,100

ALs, 6 May 1942. 2 pp, folio. To [Friderike Maria Zweig]. Letter of apology. star Apr 9 (720) DM380

Maidstone, George James Finch-Hatton, Viscount, 1815-87

Autograph Ms (2), Voices through many years, 1856-57, 235 & 153 leaves, & The Poem of the Book of Job in English Verse, [c.1860], 186 pp, 8vo. Together 3 vols, contemp half mor. With 2 commonplace books of poetry. C June 24 (123) £120 [Roberts]

Malherbe, Francois de, 1555-1628

ALs, 15 July 1626. 1 p, folio. To M. de la Berchere. Requesting his protection for his son. S Nov 27 (396) £6,800 [Henry]

Malipiero, Gian Francesco, 1882-1972

ALs, 18 Nov 1959. 1 p, 4to. To Rolf Liebermann. Wondering why he did not hear from him after the performance of his Macbeth at Hamburg. In German. With carbon copy of reply. star Apr 9 (721) DM280

Malta

Original drawings, view of fortifications from entrance of the harbor, c.1800-1820, 260mm by 1100mm, in pen, ink & wash; & sketch, View of the fortifications of the Floriana, 215mm by 310mm. pn Dec 11 (120) £200 [Sinsteden]

Manby, Charles, 1804-84

[A collection of c.500 letters addressed to Manby by civil engineers, actors, etc., 1845 to 1880, concerning his business & private affairs, sold at C on 24 June 1987, lot 12, for £220 to Wilson.]

Manby, George William, 1765-1854

[A collection of autograph Mss, letter books & memoranda, 1813 to 1833, relating to his work to save lives at sea from shipwreck, sold at C on 24 June 1987, lot 56, for £400 to Bush.]

Mandeville, Sir John, d.1372

Ms, Travels, Anglo-Norman French version. [England, mid-14th cent?]. 40 leaves only, vellum, 269mm by 186mm. In brown ink in an English cursive bookhand; proper names in gothic script. With short poem in Middle English. Stitched with part of an Elizabethan Ms chronicle, 9 leaves (4 blank), in a sloping italic hand, & a leaf from an illuminated English Ms Missal, [15th cent]. Library of the Dukes of Manchester at Kimbolton. S June 23 (84) £13,500 [Quaritch]

Manet, Edouard, 1832-83

ALs, [n.d.] "Monday". To Heyman. Requesting money. Framed. Altman collection. pnNY Sept 13 (84) $425

— 18 Apr [n.y.]. 2 pp, 8vo. To an unnamed lady. Inviting her to his studio. Framed. Altman collection. pnNY Sept 13 (83) $450

Mann, Klaus, 1906-49

Collection of 7 A Ls s, 5 Ls s, 4 autograph postcards, sgd & postcard, sgd, 11 May 1929 to 29 Nov 1935. 19 pp, various sizes, & cards. To Franz Goldstein. Interesting letters about personal matters, his own literary work, & other writers. star Apr 8 (209) DM3,400

Photograph, sgd & inscr, 31 Dec 1929. 385mm by 278mm. Inscr to Gert; sgd K. In pencil. Mount def. star Apr 8 (208) DM330

Mann, Thomas, 1875-1955

Autograph Ms, comment about attacks against him in the press, sgd & dated Nov 1928. 1 p, 4to. On verso typescript, dated Nov 1928, regarding festivities at Leipzig. star Apr 8 (210) DM1,300

ALs, 11 May 1926. 3 pp, 8vo. To Hanna Roehr. Commenting angrily about an essay ptd in Hamburger Anzeiger & explaining his feud with Paul Steegemann. On blank draft of a letter to the Hamburger Anzeiger by Hanna Roehr, in pencil. With port postcard. FD Dec 2 (3206) DM1,900

— 14 July 1945. 1 p, 8vo. To Maria T. Salinas Gutierrez-Salinas. Responding to an earlier request for his autograph. FD June 11 (3522) DM600

Ls s (2), 18 Aug 1937 & 20 Apr 1938. 3 pp, 4to. To a publisher in the Netherlands. Regarding a new Ed of Koenigliche Hoheit. With related material. star Apr 8 (213) DM750

— Ls s (2), 20 & 30 June 1949. 4 pp, folio & 8vo. To Georg Wieszner. About attacks against him in Nuernberg. Saying he has declined to visit Nuernberg. With related material. star Apr 8 (214) DM1,300

Ls, 7 Oct 1927. 1 p, 4to. To Hans Wolffheim. Encouraging his poetical efforts. star Apr 8 (211) DM850

— 30 Oct 1945. 1 p, 4to. To Frances Winwar. Congratulating her on her book The Life of the Heart & explaining his nickname. In English. sg Nov 6 (134) $250

Autograph postcard, sgd, 22 Nov 1937. To Fraeulein M. Binder. Thanking for a review of their magazine Mass und Wert. HN May 22 (3109) DM420

Photograph, sgd & inscr, [1930s]. Postcard size. Inscr to Fritz Fehl. star Apr 8 (215) DM520

Manship, Henry

Transcript, History of Great Yarmouth [1619]. Ms transcript by Joseph Cotman, 13 Aug - 20 Sept 1724, 237 pp, folio. Reversed calf, worn. bba Nov 13 (163) £120 [Fiske]

Manuel Malaxos. See: Greek Manuscripts

Manzoni, Alessandro, 1785-1873

[A collection of Ms drafts of poetry & other writings, c. 20 pp, mainly folio, with a carte-de visite size photograph & other related material, including 6 A Ls s by Vittorina Manzoni, sold at C on 3 Dec 1986, lot 394, for £4,000 to Turner.]

ALs, 18 Apr 1844. 1 p, 4to. To Signora Gaetana del Rosso. Disclaiming knowledge of a packet & a letter returned to her. C June 24 (150) £260 [Pittau]

Maps & Charts

Ms, untitled chart of the Mekong Delta. [Portugal, c.1750] 2 sheets joined, 650mm by 975mm, in ink & colors over pencil. S Oct 23 (471) £1,600 [Israel]

— GOUTTES, J. HENRY. - Autograph Ms, Album souvenir de la Patagonie-australe...., 1877-78. 58 leaves, 255mm by 170mm. Containing 8 maps in ink & colors, meteorological chart, watercolor views & watercolors of flora & fauna, mostly sgd. With port mtd on dedication leaf, sgd & dated 24 Oct 1879. Contemp brown mor gilt. P June 18 (75) $5,000

— GRENADA. - Ms, Survey of Montrose Estate, by Richard Biggs, executed by Nutter; 1774. 500mm by 710mm; vellum. In pen & watercolors. With related material. pn Dec 11 (128) £260 [Buckell & Ballard]

— HASARD, JOHN. - Ms, map of part of the manor of Shaw [Heath], Berkshire; c.1528-29. 495mm by 357mm; in brown ink & watercolor. Fold tears. Matted. CNY Nov 21 (135) $12,000

— JUSTI, K. WILHELM. - Totius mundi nova et accurata delineatio, 1781. 28 double-page charts in ink & colors & 2 leaves with explanations. 150mm by 96mm. Contemp half lea. HK Nov 4 (403) DM1,100

— VAN KEULEN, GERARD. - Nette Afteekening vande Rivier Pekingh in Sina heel Groot bestek Geleegen in de Indische Zee. [Amst., c.1706-26]. 590mm by 1,000mm, in ink & colors superimposed on an engraved network of rhumb-lines. S Oct 23 (143) £3,800 [Israel]

— VON WITKEN, JOHANN LUDOLPH. - Geometrischer Grundris der stadt Schleswig.... [North Germany, c.1720]. 620mm by 735mm, in ink & colors. Minor marginal tears repaired. S Oct 23 (105) £1,200 [Christoph]

— WILTSHIRE. - Mss (2), [early 19th cent]. Plan of Spye Park Estate & the Tithing of Chittoe, 181cm by 145cm; orig fitted case. Plan of the Manor of St. Anley, 72cm by 88cm. Both hand-colored on linen-backed paper. pn Dec 11 (73) £130 [Heraldry]

Marconi, Guglielmo
Ls, 5 Aug 1902. 1 p, 4to. To Robert L. Bremner. Declining to give a lecture at Glasgow due to prior commitments. HN May 22 (3112) DM720

Marees, Hans von, 1837-87
ALs, 30 Oct 1879. 2 pp, 8vo. To [Philipp Fiedler]. Sending congratulations on the birth of a son. With port photograph. star Apr 8 (508) DM1,100

Marengus, Joannes Baptista
Ms, Palladis chymice arcana detecta; sive, mineralogia naturlis et artificialis opus plene aureum....[N.p., late 17th or early 18th cent] 294 pp, 4to, 190mm by 135mm, in contemp vellum. sg Dec 4 (122) $650

Margrethe, Queen of Denmark —& Henrik, Prince Consort of Margrethe of Denmark
Group photograph, Dec 1981. 19.9cm by 14.1cm. Sgd by both on mount, 26.5cm by 19cm. star Apr 9 (935) DM1,300

Maria Luisa, Queen of Etruria, 1782-1824
ALs, 22 May 1811. 2 pp, 8vo. To the banker Goupy in Paris. Mostly about her financial problems. HN Nov 27 (2325) DM320

Maria Paulowna, Grossherzogin von Sachsen-Weimar, 1786-1859
ALs, 21 Aug/2 Sept 1810. 1 p, 8vo. To an unnamed Prussian Councillor. Acknowledging his letter regarding the death of Queen Luise. star Apr 8 (105) DM380

Maria Theresa, Empress, 1717-80
Ls, 29 Oct 1740. 3 pp, folio. To Fuerst Froben Ferdinand zu Fuerstenberg. Summoning him to take the oath of fealty. star Apr 9 (1210) DM1,700

— 18 Feb 1744[5]. 1 p, folio; 6 blanks. To Leopold von Weingarten. Requesting that arrangements be made at Prussian staging-posts for the journey of the Prince of Lothringen & Archduchess Maria Anna. C Dec 3 (299) £200 [Pollak]

— 9 Aug 1755. 3 pp, folio. To Johann Moritz, Archbishop of Prague. Requesting financial assistance for a convent in Prague destroyed by fire. HK Nov 7 (2315) DM650

Ds, 23 Dec 1744. 7 pp, folio. Levying a war tax. Ptd & sgd. star Apr 9 (1211) DM860

— 19 July 1748. 6 pp, folio. Vellum. Deed investing Antonius Spissich with an estate. In Latin. Executed in calligraphic script by Stephan Michalek, with ornaments in gold & black. Red velvet bdg; seal in wooden case. star Apr 9 (1212) DM1,300

— 21 Mar 1758. 3 pp, folio. Order addressed to the magistrates in Silesia that Phillipp Polzer & Johann Casimir be dismissed. star Apr 9 (1213) DM700

Maricourt, Rene de
Ms, Livre de chasse. 1627. 56 pp, vellum, 373mm by 281mm, in contemp mor gilt with the initials N & R alternately at corners & 2 interlaced Y's between. Jeanson Ms 132 SM Mar 1 (397) FF64,000

Marie de Medicis, Queen of France, 1573-1642
ALs, 8 Feb 1629. 1 p, 4to. To Cardinal Richelieu. Recommending that the benefices enjoyed by Alexandre de Vendome should be given to one of the children of the Duchesse de Vendome. C Dec 3 (300) f620 [L'Echiquier]

Marie Louise, Empress of the French, 1791-1847
[A collection of 6 items by or pertaining to Marie Louise sold at CNY on 19 Dec 1986, lot 174, for $900.]

ALs, 8 May 1811. 3 pp, 8vo. To Augusta, wife of Prince Eugene. Family news. With related material. S Nov 27 (398) £420 [Maggs]

— 12 Dec 1812. 1 p, 4to. To [Cambaceres]. Forwarding a letter from Napoleon. S May 21 (274) £300 [Haas]

Ds, 15 Dec 1811. 1 p, folio. Nomination to the Societe de la Charite maternelle for Madame Fregeville. Countersgd by Cardinal Fesch. Partly ptd. star Apr 9 (1077) DM450

Marien, Marcel
Collection of ALs & 42 postcards, sgd, c.1938 to 1952. Over 40 pp, folio & 8vo. To Rene & Georgette Magritte. About life as a smuggler in the French West Indies, his travels, titles for paintings, etc. With related material. S July 2 (978) £340 [Brachot]

Marinetti, Emilio Filippo Tommaso, 1876-1944
ALs, [1909-1911?]. 15 pp, 8vo. To an unknown lady. About the Futurist movement in a modern society. C Dec 3 (395) £750 [Quaritch]

Marlborough, John Churchill, 1st Duke, 1650-1722
AL, [4/]15 July 1709. 3 pp, 4to. To [Sidney, Earl of Godolphin]. About negotiations for peace with France, & enclosing (present) a copy of a letter from the Marquis de Torcy to Grand Pensioner Heinsius, the intermediary in the peace negotiations, [16/]27 June 1709, 2 pp, 4to. In red mor-backed folding case. C Dec 3 (234) £300 [Burgess & Browning]

Ls, 7 Oct 1701. 1 p, 4to. To George Stepney. Sending a copy of the project of a treaty between "the King of Sweden & the States". S July 24 (333) £400 [Maggs]

Ds s (2) 3 Dec 1705. 11 pp, folio. Treaty &

MARLBOROUGH

Secret Article concluded between Frederick I of Prussia & Queen Anne of England by their representatives, the Count of Wartenberg & Marlborough; agreeing on a vigorous prosecution of the war against France, on the retaining of Prussian troops in Italy, etc. In French. S Dec 18 (289) £1,100 [Letkemanns]

Marlborough, Sarah Churchill, Duchess of, 1660-1744
Ls, 18 Mar 1728. 3 pp, 4to. To the Viscountess of Longueville. Defending Gay's Beggar's Opera & chatting about the Court & society. S Dec 18 (237) £750

Marradas, Balthasar, 1560-1638
ALs, 7 Mar 1634. 1 p, folio. To King [later Emperor] Ferdinand. Imploring him to trust Ottavio Piccolomini. In Spanish. Margins cut. star Apr 9 (1047) DM800

Marriage Manual
Ms, Brevis Instructio Sponsi et Methodus bene consummandi matrimonii; [17th cent]. 265 pp, 4to. Contemp calf bdg; cover detached. Instructions for newlyweds, some in poetic form. In Latin, French & Dutch. P Dec 15 (10) $200

Marston, John, Cleric of Canterbury
ALs, [1642]. 1 p, folio. To Lord Kimbolton. Written from Gate House prison; asking for help. S Jan 27 (687) £80 [Quaritch]

Martich, Rudolph, c.1883-1951. See: Calligraphy

Martin, Frank, 1890-1974
Autograph music, "Fragment du 1. mouvement du concerto pour violoncelle et orchestre (1966)"; 8 bars. 2 pp, 34.5cm by 25.5cm. In pencil. Sgd later, in ink. star Apr 9 (723) DM460

ALs, 14 May [19]66. 1 p, 4to. To Pierre Fournier. Regarding an alteration to the end of his Cello Concerto; with autograph musical quotation, 7 bars. S May 22 (441) £200 [MacNutt]

Martin, Luther, 1748-1826
ALs, 2 June 1814. 1 p, 4to. To John Stevens. Concerning court cases. wa May 30 (151) $165

Martin V, Pope, 1368-1431
Document, [20 Sept] 1427. 1 p, 30.5cm by 50cm. Vellum. Bull, charging Ludovicus, Abbot of Sancta Justina at Padua, with inspection & reform of a Benedictine abbey at Brescia. star Apr 9 (1111) DM700

AMERICAN BOOK PRICES CURRENT

Martinitz, Jaroslaw, Graf von, 1582-1649
Ls, [1649]. 3 pp, folio. To Emperor Ferdinand III. Petitioning him to refund the ransom money he owes to the Swedish. With autograph endorsement by Ferdinand, 1 word; refusal. With engraved port. star Apr 9 (1048) DM2,400

Martinu, Bohuslav, 1890-1959
Collection of ALs & Ns, 1939 & 1946. 2 pp, folio & 8vo. To his pbr Ralph Hawkes, inquiring about the publication of his Etudes and Polkas; in English. To Desarzens Brothers, wishing someone a speedy recovery; on postcard, in French. S May 22 (619) £500 [Friedman]

ALs, 8 July [19]55. 2 pp, folio. To Pierre Fournier. Discussing his revisions of his First Cello Concerto; with a musical quotation. In French. S Nov 28 (582) £650 [MacNutt]

Marx, Karl
Autograph music, part of Op. 70/1, [1973]. 1 p, 34cm by 27cm. In ink & pencil. With covering ALs, 2 Oct 1977; 1 p, folio. star Apr 9 (724) DM300

Mary II, Queen of England, 1662-94
Ds, 24 Aug 1691. 1 p, folio. Warrant to John Tillotson, Archbishop of Canterbury regarding a dispensation for the Bishop Elect of Bristol to retain other offices. C Dec 3 (302) £550 [Maggs]

Mary of Guise, Queen of James V of Scotland, 1515-60
Ls, 15 Apr 1549. 1 p, folio. To Sir William Edmonston. Discharging him from duties owed to her from the Lordship of Menteith. Tipped to stiff paper. C Dec 3 (301) £170 [Bristow]

Mary of Modena, Queen of James II of England, 1658-1718
Ns, 9 June 1692. Recipient unnamed. Regarding payment to Henry Conquest. On verso of an order sgd by Francesco Monthioni. With Ds by Innocent XII concerning payments to James II & Mary from the Papal Treasury. Together 4 pp, 4to. S Jan 27 (759) £320 [Dr. Sam]

Masaryk, Jan Garrigue, 1886-1948. See: Masaryk, Thomas Garrigue & Masaryk

Masaryk, Thomas Garrigue, 1850-1937 — & Masaryk, Jan Garrigue, 1886-1948
[2 port photographs, sgd, dated 1932 & inscr to Francis Percy Woodcock; 1 each by Thomas & Jan Masaryk, various sizes, sold at pn on 11 Dec, lot 119, for £150 to Reuter.]

Mascagni, Pietro, 1863-1945

ALs, 8 Feb [18]93. 3 pp, 8vo. To "Leonzio". Sending money for various debts & drawing 2 sketches of his children in costumes for Pagliaccio & Trovatore. C June 24 (199) £170 [Yablon]

— 23 Feb 1897. 4 pp, 8vo. To Professor Magrini. Inquiring if he can nominate someone to be Professor at the Liceo Rossini. S May 22 (620) £60 [L. I. M.]

— 16 Apr 1902. 5 pp, 4to. To Tancredi Mantovani. Regarding the program for a concert at Bologna, & quoting his telegram [in French] to Carmen Sylva on her mother's death as well as the queen's reply. star Apr 9 (728) DM850

— 18 Feb 1905. 3 pp, 8vo. To the director of the "Figaro". Describing Victorien Sardou's offering him a libretto. star Apr 9 (729) DM580

Photograph, sgd & inscr, 1 Nov 1895. Cabinet size. Sgd & inscr on verso. star Apr 9 (726) DM320

— Anr, 15 Nov 1895. Cabinet size. With musical quotation in left margin, 3 bars from Cavalleria rusticana. Corners cut. star Apr 9 (727) DM1,250

Anr, 9 May [1]906. 16cm by 11cm. Inscr to Mme Ferdinand Kohn. S Jan 27 (1039) £160 [MacNutt]

Massachusetts

Ms, agreement not to serve wine or wear gloves at funerals, 10 Apr 1706. 1 p, folio. Sgd by c.90 Bostonians. With ADs, 7 Feb 1657, 1 p, folio, by Edward Goffe, recording cases considered at Cambridge County Court. Bullock collection. CNY Dec 19 (131) $750

— LIVERMORE, JOHN, & OTHERS. - Ls, 28 Mar 1679. 1 p, 8vo. To the Massachusetts Legislature. Requesting them to solve the problem of school affairs in Watertown. wa May 30 (422) $100

Massenet, Jules, 1842-1912

[The vocal score of Herodiade. Paris, [1884], with autograph annotations by Massenet, disbound; with 7 A Ls s by Massenet & others relating to Herodiade, 1878 to 1903 & [n.d.], sold at S on 22 May 1987, lot 447, for £250 to Talbot.]

Autograph music, fragment from a religious or dramatic work, possibly from Roma, beginning "Tout homme dans Rome nous fut"; [1912?]. 1 p, folio. In black ink on three systems of four staves each. With ALs by his daughter. S Nov 28 (583) £250 [Billington]

Series of 21 A Ls s, 1873 to 1910. 37 pp, mostly 8vo. To G. Gatteschi. Talking about his operas, new projects, & Gatteschi's restoration of the Forum in Rome. With ptd group photograph, sgd. S May 22 (448) £520 [MacNutt]

ALs, [n.d.]; 3 pp, 12mo. Recipient unnamed. Concerning routine matters. sg Nov 6 (135) $100

Masters, Edgar Lee, 1868-1950

Collection of 4 A Ls s & 7 Ls s, 4 Jan to 14 Apr 1924; 22 Mar 1944 to 15 May 1945. 11 pp, 4to & 8vo. 1 to G. A. Shaw, 10 to Ada McVickar. About literary & routine matters. Some initialled; mostly in pencil. sg Nov 6 (136) $350

Masters, Edgar Lee, 1869-1950

Autograph Ms, poem, Alexander Throckmorton, 16 Dec 1941. 1 p, 4to. 5 lines, sgd. Mtd. wa May 30 (405) $55

Mata Hari, Pseud. of Geertruida Zelle McLeod, 1876-1917

ALs, 29 Sept 1908. 3 pp, 8vo. To Mr. Beaudu. Giving instructions about photographs of her which are to appear in the press. S Nov 27 (404) £500 [Maggs]

— 10 Sept [1912]. 3 pp, 8vo. To a concert agent [Astruc]. Hoping for good contracts. star Apr 9 (1051) DM2,800

— 18 Sept 1914. 2 pp, folio. To her former husband. Asking to see her daughter. Sgd Marguerite. S Nov 27 (402) £580 [Maggs]

— [n.d.]. 1 p, folio. Recipient unnamed. Cancelling an appointment & suggesting they meet the next day. S Nov 27 (403) £650 [Pulido]

— 29 May [1917]. 1 p, folio. To Capt. Bouchardon. Written from prison, concerning her answer to the accusations levelled against her. S Nov 27 (401) £700 [Lucas]

— [n.d.] "mardi". 4 pp, folio. To Capt. Bouchardon. From prison, denying that she was engaged in espionage. S Nov 27 (400) £2,800 [Joseph & Sawyer]

Matisse, Henri, 1869-1954

ALs, 21 Nov 1925. 2 pp, folio. To his printmaker Raquint. Saying he has sent an engraved copper plate & is expecting the proofs for signing. Fold tear. S Nov 27 (405) £380 [Quaritch]

— 5 May 1933. 2 pp, 4to. Recipient unnamed. Regarding some panels he painted & about finishing a job for recipient. Framed. Altman collection. pnNY Sept 13 (85) $650

— 31 Aug 1940. 2 pp, size not stated. To Monsieur Escholier. Discussing the impact of the German invasion of France. Framed. Altman collection. pnNY Sept 13 (87) $1,300

— 6 Dec 1945. 1 p, 8vo. To Monsieur Zervorz. Sending proofs of photographs of drawings to choose an interesting set. Framed.

Altman collection. pnNY Sept 13 (86) $475
Ls, 19 Nov 1948. 1 p, 8vo. To Monsieur Goldschmidt. Thanking for notifying him of publication of vol 4 of Memoire d'Outre Tombe. Framed. Altman collection. pnNY Sept 13 (88) $400

Matthias, Emperor, 1557-1619
Ls, 24 Apr 1613. 3 pp, folio. To the Bishop of Constance. Reporting about the Turkish menace. star Apr 9 (1198) DM720

Matthisson, Friedrich von, 1761-1831
ALs, 22 Sept [n.y.]. 2 pp, 8vo. To the editors of the magazine Morgenblatt. Recommending Herrn Waiblinger. Margin def. JG Oct 2 (103) DM630

Maugham, William Somerset, 1874-1965
Ls s (2), 5 May 1941 & 28 Feb 1963. 2 pp, 8vo. Recipients unnamed. Replies to admirers. sg Nov 6 (138) $130
Ls, 30 Jan 1949. 1 p, 12mo. Recipient unnamed. Invitation to a party. sg Nov 6 (137) $60

Maupertuis, Pierre Louis Moreau de, 1698-1759
ALs, 30 Nov 1754. 3 pp, 4to. To an unnamed lady. About Algarotti's return to Italy. star Apr 8 (383) DM420

Maximilian I, Emperor, 1459-1519
Ls, [Tuesday after Exaudi] 1492. 1 p, folio. To the Council of Innsbruck. Requesting urgent dispatch of iron ordered from Leoben. C Dec 3 (303) £1,300 [L'Autographe]
Document, 13 Apr 1497. 1 p, folio. Vellum. Permission for Bleickard von Gemmingen to establish a criminal court at Gemmingen. star Apr 9 (1192) DM850

Maximilian I, Kurfuerst von Bayern, 1573-1651
Ls, 3 Jan 1607. 1 p, folio. To Count Maximilian Montecuccoli. Returning New Year's wishes. In Italian. Repaired. star Apr 9 (884) DM380

Maximilian I Joseph, King of Bavaria, 1756-1825
Ls, 8 Feb 1805. 1 p, folio. To Cetto, his minister in Paris. As Elector, instructing him to order a newly invented fire-escape for use in Munich. Countersgd by Montgelas. star Apr 9 (886) DM240

Maximilian of Mexico, Emperor, 1832-67
Ls, 14 Oct 1865. 1 p, 4to. Recipient unnamed. Thanking for a document concerning Miguel Hidalgo. With autograph subscription. star Apr 9 (1059) DM920
Autograph sentiment, 13 Aug 1850. 1 p, 8vo. Sgd. HK Nov 7 (2319) DM1,000

Maxwell, William, c.1733-96
Ds, 1 Sept 1777. 2 pp, 4to. Muster roll of Capt. Hollinshead's Company of the 2nd New Jersey Regiment, sgd as Brig. Gen. Countersgd by 2 officers. sg Nov 6 (294) $250

May, Karl, 1842-1912
Autograph postcards (2), sgd, [May 1899]. To Prince Adalbert of Bavaria. Sending greetings from Egypt. 2d card signature only. star Apr 8 (216) DM750

Mayo, Charles Horace, 1865-1939 —& Mayo, William James, 1861-1939
Photograph, sgd, 7 Feb 1938. 10 by 13 inches. 2 photographs ptd side by side. With anr photograph of Charles Mayo, with ptd signature. wa May 30 (406) $260

Mayo, William James, 1861-1939. See: Mayo, Charles Horace & Mayo

Mazarin, Jules, Cardinal, 1602-61
Ls, 20 July 1657. 4 pp, 4to. To the Duc de Gramont. Giving instructions for negotiations with the Electors concerning the election of the Holy Roman Emperor. With lengthy autograph postscript, in margins. S Nov 27 (406) £1,300 [Joseph & Sawyer]
— 26 Oct 1657. 1 p, folio. To Monsieur le Comte de Schwerin. Congratulating him on the Great Elector's entrusting him with "la principale direction de Ses affaires". With autograph postscript, introducing the new French minister Blondel. star Apr 9 (1052) DM2,000

Meade, George Gordon, 1815-72
ALs, 10 Feb 1865. 4 pp, 8vo. To Mrs. Neil. About his family, his duties, & peace proposals. On Army of the Potomac letterhead. sg Apr 9 (118) $850
ANs, 24 Apr 1863. 1 p, 8vo. To Maj. Gen. Hancock. About Hancock's visiting the headquarters of the army. With engraved port. wa May 30 (240) $325

Medical Manuscripts
Ms, notes & extracts from ptd & other sources, of medical recipes & observations, [c.1685]. 349 pp, size not stated. Contemp calf, rebacked. With an early 19th cent vol of Ms medical recipes. S July 24 (377) £380 [Agnew]
— Ms, Of the Birth of Children & how male may be conceaved & not female, [early 17th cent]. 9 pp, folio. Extracts from a larger work. C June 24 (164) £60 [Solomon]
— Ms, The Poetical Farrago [Lincoln?, England, 1790 - c.1816]; 341 pp. Compilation of ballads, satires, etc., including 2 ptd poems & many orig contributions by the compiler "J. C.". 3 watercolor illusts. Contemp

half-calf. C Dec 3 (346) £130 [Burgess & Browning]

— Ms, Treatise on the Plague, in Latin. [Italy, 15th cent]. 5 pp, 216mm by 147mm. Modern marbled wraps & vellum spine. In brown ink in a small rounded gothic hand. Foliated 38-42 in an early hand. S June 23 (79) £850 [Kerr]

— MORAES SOARES, MANOEL DE. - Ms, Epithome Historico-Medico-Politico [Portugal, late 18th cent]. About 600 pp, 8vo. Contemp red mor gilt, covers with floral motif & roll-tooled borders. In several hands. Dedicated to the Duke of Lafoes. S Nov 27 (410) £1,100 [Quaritch]

Medici, Cosimo I de', 1519-74

Ls, 1 Aug 1537. 1 p, folio. To a magistrate. Informing them of his victory over a faction favoring France. Sgd Cosimo medici. star Apr 9 (1267) DM480

— 1 Nov 1553. 2 pp, folio. To Pier Vettori. Assuring him that he has no intention to interfere in educational management. sg Apr 9 (119) $700

Medtner, Anna. See: Medtner, Nikolay & Medtner

Medtner, Nikolay, 1880-1951 —& Medtner, Anna

Series of 6 A Ls s, Aug 1938 to Dec 1944. 15 pp, 8vo. To Archie & Polly Henderson. Joint letters, about his Sonata romantica, Christianity, Renaissance art, life in wartime. S May 22 (621) £180 [Schneider]

Meggendorfer, Lothar, 1847-1925

Original drawings, complete ink & watercolor drawings to illus Helene Schaupp-Horn's Ich Kann Schon Franzoesisch, [c.1899]. 24 leaves, 219mm by 154mm, on rectos only. Over 80 illusts with ptd text pasted in. Cloth folder within cloth folding box. With a copy of the 4th Ed of the book. P June 18 (124) $2,000

Melanchthon, Philipp, 1497-1560

ALs, 1 May [1538]. 1 p, folio. To Veit Dietrich. Letter of recommendation for Erasmus Flock. In Latin. star Apr 9 (1054) DM6,500

Autograph sentiment, Greek distich, on clipping from final page of Johannes Lufft, Ptolemaei Mathematicae constructionis Liber primus... Wittenberg, 1549; 9cm by 9.8cm. Sgd & inscr Philippus Georgio [Georg Fabricius?]. star Apr 9 (1055) DM1,350

Mencken, Henry Louis, 1880-1956

Autograph quotation, 1929. 1 p, 8vo. "Immortality: the condition of a dead man who doesn't believe that he is dead." sg Nov 6 (139) $225

Christmas card, [n.d.]. Inscr & sgd. Pasted on half-title of Mencken's The American Language. NY, 1919. 8vo, cloth. sg Apr 9 (120) $275

Mendelssohn, Moses, 1729-86

ALs, 13 Oct 1772. 1 p, 4to. To Friedrich Nicolai. Sending a bill payable at Hamburg & commenting angrily on changes made to his text by Junker. star Apr 8 (386) DM3,200

— 8 Oct 1775. 1 p, 4to. To the bookseller [Friedrich] Nicolai. Requesting him to forward a parcel to Joseph Gomer. S Nov 27 (407) £780 [Lucas]

AD, [1776 or later]. 1 p, 8vo. Certificate of membership in a "Heiratsverein fuer Toechter" for Eisik Jaffe. Sgd by 6 members of the board of directors. In Hebrew. star Apr 8 (387) DM1,400

Mendelssohn-Bartholdy, Cecile, 1817-53

ALs, 18 Oct 1848. 2 pp, 8vo. To Otto Dresel. Covering letter for a letter of introduction. star Apr 9 (738) DM300

Mendelssohn-Bartholdy, Felix, 1809-47

Autograph music, song, Troestung, Op. 71, no 1; complete transcript. Sgd & dated 30 Aug 1846. In album of Auguste Rosen; contemp green half lea bdg, gilt. Also containing an orig drawing by Mendelssohn-Bartholdy, pencil sketch of Engelberg in Switzerland; & entries by Karl Klingemann, Ch. E. Horsley, Fanny Horsley, & Ignaz & Charlotte Moscheles, & others. star Apr 9 (736) DM28,000

Ms, piano short score & orchestral score for unfinished 1st movement of a piano concerto, [n.d.]. 36 pp, 330mm by 250mm. In the hand of Amadeus Eduard Anton Henschke; in brown ink on ruled staff paper. With related material. CNY Dec 19 (149) $1,800

ALs, 6 May 1824. 11 pp, 8vo. To [F. Voigts]. Criticizing the libretto of his opera Die Hochzeit des Camacho. JG Oct 2 (334) DM7,000

— 2 Mar [18]30. To the pbr Adolph Martin Schlesinger. Complaining about delay in the publication of his Lieder, Op.8 & Op.9, & stating his terms. S May 22 (623) £1,800 [Johnson]

— 2 July 1832. 2 pp, 8vo. To [John Pyke] Hullah. Declining an invitation. Framed. Altman collection. pnNY Sept 13 (172) $900

— 5 Sept 1832. 3 pp, 4to. To Heinrich

MENDELSSOHN-BARTHOLDY

Barmann. Complaining about his health. Repaired. P Dec 15 (68) $1,300

— 17 June [1833]. 2 pp, 8vo. To Mrs. Taylor. Regretting that his father's injury prevents his going out to dine. In English. S Nov 28 (587) £750 [Wilson]

— 9 Aug 1837. 1 p, 4to. To Karl Klingemann. Making arrangements for his visit to London. P Sept 24 (32) $900

— 28 Dec 1839. 1 p, 8vo. To Carl Stoer. Setting the date for a concert to be given by Stoer at Leipzig. star Apr 9 (732) DM2,200

— 2 Mar 1841. 2 pp, 8vo. To Johann Wilhelm Schirmer. Covering letter for the full score of a psalm, & chatting about Schirmer's wedding. star Apr 9 (733) DM6,100

— 8 Aug 1841. 2 pp, 4to. To an unnamed Professor. Discussing works by Beethoven & Bach; with a musical quotation. S Nov 28 (586) £2,600 [McGwynn]

— 20 Dec 1841. 1 p, 8vo. To Elisa Meerti. Apologizing for not playing in her concert. In French. star Apr 9 (734) DM2,400

— 20 Nov 1843. 4 pp, 8vo. To Karl Klingemann. Confidential letter regarding his move to Berlin & an offer to direct concerts in London. star Apr 9 (735) DM7,500

— 15 June [18]44. 1 p, 8vo. To Mrs. Grote. Regretting he cannot accept her invitations. In English. S Nov 28 (588) £1,050 [Haas]

— 29 May 1847. 1 p, 8vo. To Franz Messer. Thanking for a visit & saying he cannot play music now [after his sister's death]. With related material. star Apr 9 (737) DM3,500

Ls, 18 Aug 1817. 1 p, 4to. To Karl von Stein. Thanking for an invitation, but saying he cannot come. In French. star Apr 9 (731) DM8,500

Menzel, Adolph von, 1815-1905

ALs, 14 Sept 1861. 1 p, 8vo. Recipient unnamed. Expressing thanks. star Apr 8 (511) DM380

— [30 May 1870?]. 4 pp, 8vo. To [Spitta]. Requesting him to inquire about 4 watercolors sent to Ghent for an exhibition. With autograph envelope. HN May 22 (3117) DM380

— 14 Jan 1885. 4 pp, 8vo. To Karl Helmerding. Explaining his unfriendly behavior towards Helmerding's daughter. star Apr 8 (512) DM1,500

— 7 Nov 1896. 3 pp, 8vo. To an unnamed lady. Saying he has a meeting on Tuesday evening. star Apr 8 (513) DM400

Mercadante, Saverio, 1795-1870

Collection of 4 A Ls s, 1831 to 1860, & autograph musical quotation, sgd, [n.d.]. 5 pp, 4to & folio. Recipients unnamed. About musical matters. Aria, Il di sorge; 18 bars on 3 systems of 3 staves each. S May 22 (454) £250 [McCann]

Merchants' Guild

Ms, certificate confirming completion of apprenticeship for Johann Heinrich Grabenhorst, 24 June 1777. 1 p, 59cm by 71cm. Sgd by Peter Grabenhorst & 3 other members of the Braunschweig Merchants' Guild. In calligraphic script, accomplished in anr hand. With engraved vignettes. HN May 22 (2958a) DM700

Meredith, George, 1828-1909

ALs, 5 June 1895. 1 p, 8vo. To Miss MacPherson. Invitiation. sg Apr 9 (121) $70

Mesens, E. L. T.

Series of 3 A Ls s, 1931 to 1965. 5 pp, folio & 8vo (1 on postcard). To Rene Magritte. Suggesting an improvement to a painting, requesting contributions to magazines, & about an exhibition in Milan. With related material. S July 2 (979) £380 [Communaute de Francais de Belgique]

Messer, Franz Joseph, 1811-60

[A collection of 31 letters addressed to him, 1842 to 1859, mostly relating to music in Frankfurt, with related material, sold at star on 9 Apr 1987, lot 739, for DM3,200]

Messiaen, Olivier

A Ls s (2), 12 Jan 1949 & 1 July 1970. 2 pp, 8vo. To Mde. & M. Wischnegradsky. Regretting that Wischnegradsky has not found a suitable post. About the "carre magique" & his plan to deal with this in Traite de Rhythme. S Nov 28 (589) £300 [Billington]

Methodist Church

[A collection of more than 225 items, mostly Ls s, addressed to Bishops Frederick B. Leete & Herbert Welch, & other Methodist clergymen, by political, religious & literary figures, including 9 Presidents of the US, c.1890s to 1940s, sold at P on 29 Oct 1986, lot 26, for $ 5,000.]

Metternich, Klemens Wenzel Nepomuk Lothar von, 1773-1859

ALs, 21 Apr 1829. 2 pp, 4to. To the manager of an estate. Regarding the new miller & the distribution of living quarters. star Apr 9 (1056) DM650

— 12 Jan 1855. 2 pp, 4to. To Alexander von Humboldt. Reflecting about his life. In French. Margins repaired. star Apr 9 (1057) DM1,800

— 5 Sept 1855. 3 pp, to. To Alexander von Humboldt. Announcing the shipment of a paper cast of an Egyptian stela. In French. star Apr 9 (1058) DM1,000

Ls, 9 June 1844. 7 pp, folio. To Sir Robert Gordon. In 3d person, concerning the lawsuit of John Rayson pending at Constantinople. C Dec 3 (304) £110 [Des Pabilades]

Mexico

Ms, Manuale Monialium [c.1630]. 28 leaves, vellum, 215mm by 155m. Written in a roman minuscule hand. With double-ruled red borders, about 40 illuminated initials & hand-painted tp showing coat-of-arms of Cristobal Millan. In orig black shagreen bdg, gilt-stamped. Some 18th cent annotations. Modern folding case. Joaquin Garcia Icazbalceta collection. sg Sept 18 (177) $2,600

Meyer, C. W.

Ms, Statistics of the Department of the Gironde, [1846]. 272 pp, 4to. Full red mor gilt. Presentation copy to President Polk. wa May 30 (384) $85

Meyer, Conrad Ferdinand, 1825-98

Autograph postcard, sgd, 17 May 1884. To Hermann Sorgenfrey. Inquiring about Hermann Haessel's health & asking him to send books to G. A. Ressel. star Apr 8 (218) DM1,100

Meyerbeer, Giacomo, 1791-1864

[An important archive of more than 2,600 letters written by or to Meyerbeer, with diaries, drafts, contracts, autograph Mss, working papers for his operas, & other material relating to Meyerbeer & his family sold at S on 22 May 1987, lot 455, for £160,000 to Preussische Staatsbibliothek.]

Collection of ALs & autograph musical quotation; [n.d., "Monday"]. 2 pp, 8vo & 4to. To Ernestine von Hofmansthal. Covering letter, & scherzo, 8 bars in C, presto con fuoco; for piano. FD Dec 2 (3248) DM1,050

ALs, 19 Jan 1840. 2 pp, 8vo. Recipient unnamed. Reminding him of his promise to report about the opening of the theater & the performance of an opera at Gotha. star Apr 9 (740) DM320

ANs, [n.d.]. 1 p, 8vo. Recipient unnamed. Ordering scores for a concert. With ALs, [n.d.], 1 p, 8vo, ordering tickets for a performance. star Apr 9 (741) DM340

Meysenbug, Malvida von, 1816-1903

Series of 20 A Ls s, July 1887 to Sept 1902. 82 pp, 8vo & 12mo. To Cosima Wagner. About the Wagner family, her own situation, the Paris premiere of Lohengrin, etc. With anr 7 items, relating to Meysenbug & the Wagner family. P Sept 24 (54) $950

Michelangelo Buonarroti, 1475-1564

ADs, 31 July 1525. 1 p, 8vo, cut from a larger sheet. Receipt for 10 lire paid by Marco di Guadagnio toward the rent for the house in the via Ghibellina. Tipped into 2d Ed of Emile Ollivier's Michel-Ange. 1892; with material pertaining to Ollivier & small pen & ink sketch [16th cent Florentine] ascribed to Michelangelo. Red mor; in slipcase. S May 21 (277) £8,000 [Dreesman]

Middleton, Conyers

ALs, 31 May 1736. 2 pp, 4to. To Beaupre Bell, Jr. Discussing medals. S Jan 27 (945) £70 [Drury]

Miegel, Agnes, 1879-1964

Collection of 5 A Ls s, Ls & autograph postcard, sgd, 26 July 1944 to 12 Dec 1953. 16 pp, 4to & 8vo, & card. To Hanns Arens. About literary contributions & reminiscing about home. star Apr 8 (219) DM1,100

Mifflin, Thomas, 1744-1800

Ds, 1 Nov 1796. 1 p, folio. Land grant to John Nicholson. wa May 30 (152) $170

Milan

Ms, Historia Ducatus Mediolanensis sub Dominio Familie Vicecomitum, [19th cent]. 202 pp, 8vo. Vellum bdg. bba Nov 13 (181) £120 [Lanfranchi]

Milhaud, Darius, 1892-1974

Autograph music, Le Printemps (6), Calme, for piano; complete composition, 28 Mar 1920. Tp & 2 pp, 16 staves each. Inscr to Celine Laguarde on tp & at end. Some corrections. star Apr 9 (744) DM1,500

— Autograph music, Mazurka; 37 bars, complete composition; 1916. Tp & 5 pp, 8vo, on rectos only; 5 staves each. Inscr to Celine Laguarde on tp, in pencil. star Apr 9 (743) DM1,400

— Autograph music, song, Priere pour etre simple, to a text by Francis Jammes; sgd twice & dated May 1910. 3 pp, 16 staves each. star Apr 9 (742) DM2,000

Series of 13 A Ls s, c.1947 to 1949. 16 pp, various sizes. To Eugene Weintraub. Dealing with questions relating to the publication of his works. 1 ALs on a postcard, 1 on a Ls by Weintraub to Milhaud. S Nov 28 (591) £700 [MacNutt]

Photograph, sgd & inscr, Jan 1946. 25cm by 20cm. Inscr to Eugene Weintraub. S Nov

MILITARY MANUSCRIPTS

28 (590) £280 [Riskin]

Military Manuscripts

Ms, Reglement Vor die Koenigliche Preusische Infanterie..., 1743. 751 pp, 215mm by 158mm. Contemp vellum. Army manual. HK Nov 4 (453) DM600

— BAVARIA. - Ms, Ordnung vber ain Lanndt gewaligen hoerr Zug, [Bavaria or Palatinate,] 1536. 34 leaves, 307mm by 220mm. Extra contemp blindstamped brown lea with iron bolt. Suggestions for the organization of the army, probably addressed to Ludwig I, Kurfuerst von der Pfalz. In a neat cursive script in black ink. Ownership inscr of Joachim Graf von Ortenburg, 1591. HK Nov 4 (405) DM19,000

Mill, John Stuart, 1806-73

ALs, 24 Feb 1866. 2 pp, 8vo. To A. Burgess [?]. Thanking for a letter on the tenant right question. S Jan 27 (799) £280 [Boyle]

— 9 Aug 1867. 3 pp, 8vo. To Miss Carpenter. Inviting her to join a society to promote women's suffrage. C Dec 3 (306) £550 [Quaritch]

— 7 Aug [n.y.]. 1 p, 16mo. To W. F. Rae. Dinner invitation. sg Apr 9 (122) $150

Miller, Cincinnatus Hiner, 1839-1913. See: Miller, Joaquin

Miller, Henry, 1891-1980

Autograph Ms, comments about Germany, [c.1961]. 2 pp, 4to. Used for cover illus of W. Schmiele's biography of Miller. Hamburg, 1961. HN May 22 (3122) DM440

Typescript, working papers for the play Just Wild about Harry, 1962. About 185 pp, folio. With extensive corrections. Some carbon copies. S July 23 (165) £15,000 [Kenyusha Books]

Collection of 11 A Ls s, 6 autograph postcards, sgd, & 2 photographs, sgd, 1940 to 1945. Mostly to Rudolph Gilbert. About literary matters & contents not stated. wa May 30 (54) $750

ALs, 15 Apr 1936. 2 pp, 4to. To W. G. Campbell. Concerning Campbell's efforts to obtain a copy of The Tropic of Cancer in England, & hoping his new book Black Spring "will get by the Censors". S July 23 (166) £300 [Joseph & Sawyer]

Miller, Joaquin, 1839-1913

Series of 9 A Ls s, 1863 to 1902. Length, size, recipients & contents not stated. With related material. rf Mar 14 (42) $190

AMERICAN BOOK PRICES CURRENT

Millet, Jean Francois, 1814-75

ALs, 12 June 1874. 1 p, 8vo. To Theophile Silvestre. Announcing his visit. Was mtd. star Apr 8 (515) DM440

Milne, Alan Alexander, 1882-1956

Autograph Ms, play, Mr Pim Passes By, 1920. 82 pp, on rectos only; 4to. Green mor bdg. Working Ms. Inscr by Milne to Irene Vanbrugh, Christmas 1922. Carl H. Pforzheimer Library S Dec 18 (168) £3,200 [Joseph & Sawyer]

— Autograph Ms, play, The Ivory Door, June to Dec 1925. With autograph revisions, autograph foreword, & material concerning genesis of the work & sale of the Ms. In all c.115 pp, 4to, in 4 notebooks. With typescript of the play, 114 pp, 4to. Carl H. Pforzheimer Library S Dec 18 (169) £4,500 [Joseph & Sawyer]

Typescript, When We Were Very Young, draft; [late 1923 or early 1924]. 33 leaves, 4to; 7 leaves carbon copy. Containing 23 poems; with autograph corrections & unpbd prefatory poem. In 2 paper folders. With ALs, [c.early 1925], 2 pp, by Milne to E. H. Shepard, requesting him to illustrate One on a Time, & further material. P Dec 15 (69) $3,500

— MILNE, DAPHNE. - ALs, 28 Aug [n.y., c.1933]. 4 pp, 8vo. To Miss Salway. About Christopher Robin & Pooh. With related material. S July 23 (164) £900 [Joseph & Sawyer]

Milshtein, Zwy

ALs, [n.d.]. 1 p, folio. To Philippe. Describing the scene in a nightclub. With numerous pen-&-ink & watercolor sketches of waitresses & clients. S Nov 27 (411) £300 [Kent]

Mining Manuscript

Ms, Les Mines de Fer de Dannemora dans le Province Upland en Suede. [c.1788] 13 leaves, oblong folio, in contemp half russia With finely executed sketches & diagrams in pen, ink & watercolor, including a watercolor frontis sgd & dated M. R. Heland, 1788, 10 leaves with detailed sectional drawings, leaf with explanatory key, folding leaf with profile diagrams of the mine & 2 mtd hand-colored engravings of the copper mines at Catherineberg C Dec 3 (154) £7,000 [Henderson]

Mirabeau Family

[A collection of 4 letters by various members of the Mirabeau family, 1780 to 1785, 6 pp, sold at CNY on 19 Dec 1986, lot 176, for $400.]

1986 - 1987 • AUTOGRAPHS & MANUSCRIPTS

Mirabeau, Honore Gabriel Victor Riqueti, Comte de, 1749-91
ALs, 23 Apr 1784. 4 pp, 8vo. To an unknown count. About the legal battle over the suppression of a memoir. Some contemp corrections. C Dec 3 (307) £100 [L'Autographe]
— 18 Feb 1786. 1 p, 8vo. To G. J. Decker. About publication of a journal. sg Nov 6 (140) $250

Miro, Joan, 1893-1983
ALs, 31 Mar 1963. 1 p, 4to. Recipient unnamed. Encouraging him to consult a specialist about his illness. HN May 22 (3123) DM420
— 2 Jan 1972. 2 pp, 4to. Recipient unknown. Letter of introduction for Jose Pina. In French. On personal letterhead. sg Apr 9 (125) $225

Modersohn, Otto, 1865-1943
Collection of 5 A Ls s & 2 autograph postcards, sgd, 26 Feb 1916 to 8 Feb 1942. 8 pp, 4to & 8vo, & cards. To Frido Witte. About a variety of subjects. HN May 22 (3124) DM1,200
— Collection of 3 A Ls s & 3 autograph postcards, sgd, 14 Dec 1926 to 17 Feb 1927. 4 pp, 4to & 8vo, & cards. To an unnamed art collector. Concerning the sale of Modersohn's works, a consignment sent for inspection, etc. star Apr 8 (517) DM1,100
Series of 4 autograph postcards, sgd, 18 Dec 1894 to 1 Mar 1935. To Hans Mueller-Brauel. Asking him not to publish an article about Worpswede painters; thanking for congratulations on his birthday, etc. star Apr 8 (516) DM900

Modersohn-Becker, Paula, 1876-1907
ALs, 17 Jan 1906. 3 pp, 8vo. To Wilhelm Thiele. Chatting about a journey & thanking for a box of amethysts. HN May 22 (3125) DM2,200

Moellendorff, Wichard Joachim Heinrich von, 1724-1816
Ls, 23 Mar 1794. 1 p, folio. To Gen. Michaud. Regarding negotiations for an exchange of prisoners. star Apr 9 (1061) DM520

Moerike, Eduard, 1804-75
Autograph Ms, 2 poems, Frueh, im Wagen; & Abreise, [c.1846]. 2 pp, 8vo. Six 4-line stanzas & 29 lines. JG Oct 2 (106) DM10,000
— Autograph Ms, poem, Auf eine Christblume, [c.1846]. 1 p, 8vo. Two 4-line stanzas, sgd. JG Oct 2 (105) DM7,500
ANs, [n.d.]. 1 p, 45mm by 77mm; on verso of ptd visiting card. Recipient unnamed. Regarding a port of Georg Philipp von Greiffenclau. HK Nov 7 (2322) DM1,300
See also: Hoelderlin, Friedrich

Moholy-Nagy, Laszlo, 1895-1946
ALs, [n.d.]. 2 pp, folio. To his wife Lucia. Mentioning a film. Sgd Laci. star Apr 8 (518) DM420

Moltke, Helmuth, Graf von, 1800-91
Collection of 29 A Ls s & Ls, 21 Mar 1864 to 2 Dec 1890. 34 pp, mostly 8vo. To his cousin Eduard Ballhorn & members of his family. Discussing military affairs & family news. With related material. star Apr 9 (1062) DM4,500
ALs, 19 & 26 Aug 1868. 3 pp, 8vo. To his wife. Reporting about an inspection tour. Sgd H. star Apr 9 (1063) DM1,300
— 8 Nov 1870. 1 p, 8vo. Recipient unnamed. Commenting about French delusions & unsuccessful peace efforts. star Apr 9 (1064) DM900
Ls s (2), 5 Feb & 17 Nov 1879. 2 pp, folio. To the publishing firm Pierer at Altenburg. As Chief of the General Staff, concerning the ptg of catalogues of the General Staff's library. With related material. star Apr 9 (1065) DM520
Ls, 21 Jan [18]90. 1 p, 8vo. To bookseller C. L. Hirschfeld. Thanking for a book. sg Apr 9 (126) $80

Mommsen, Theodor, 1817-1903
ALs, 14 Sept 1866. 1 p, 8vo. To [Heinrich Abeken] of the Foreign Ministry. Regarding Eugen Borsmann's projected research in Italy. star Apr 8 (388) DM220

Monet, Claude, 1840-1926
ALs, [July/Aug 1865]. 2 pp, 8vo. To Frederic Bazille. Asking him to pose for some figures for his Dejeuner sur l'herbe. Fold split. S May 21 (279) £550 [Johnson]
— 1 Dec [1866]. 3 pp, 8vo. To Frederic Bazille. Requesting him to send some paintings, & about financial problems. S May 21 (280) £750 [Johnson]
— 25 June [1867]. 4 pp, 8vo. To Frederic Bazille. Describing his work & requesting financial help. S Nov 27 (414) £1,000 [Kent]
— 9 July [1867]. 3 pp, 8vo. To Frederic Bazille. Expressing anxiety about Camille who is expecting his child & requesting financial assistance. S May 21 (281) £700 [Smit]
— 29 June [1868]. 2 pp, 8vo. To Frederic Bazille. Announcing that he has been contemplating suicide & requesting money. S Nov 27 (416) £1,080 [Stein]
— [Dec 1868]. 6 pp, 8vo. To Frederic Bazille. Talking about family life with his small son & about his plans. S May 21 (282) £900 [Sakmyster]
— 11 Jan 1869. 4 pp, 8vo. To Frederic Bazille.

155

Asking him to purchase colors for him & saying he may be able to sell some pictures in Le Havre. S Nov 27 (417) £900 [Quaritch]
— 9 Aug [1869]. 1 p, 8vo. To Frederic Bazille. Urgently requesting money as they are now begging bread from Renoir. S Nov 27 (418) £800 [DuPont]
— 20 Feb 1890. 2 pp, 8vo. Recipient unnamed. About an article on Manet & the necessity to procure money. Framed. Altman collection. pnNY Sept 13 (89) $900

Monroe, James, 1758-1831
Autograph Ms, part of his A View of the Conduct of the Executive, in the Foreign Affairs of the United States, draft, [1797?]. 2 pp, 4to. Referring to difficulties after his arrival in Paris. Repaired. With 2 Ds s, 7 Nov 1812 & 12 Mar 1818. 2 pp, 4to & folio. "Additional Instructions" to US vessels not to stop British unarmed vessels bound for Sable Island. Sgd as Sec of State. Grant for military bounty lands to Isaac Ludlow, sgd as President. P Oct 29 (99) $1,600
ALs, 12 July 1802. 1 p, 4to. Recipient unnamed. About the testimony of some persons in London required for a legal case. Framed. Altman collection. pnNY Sept 13 (16) $650
— 13 July 1807. 2 pp, 8vo. To Lord Holland. In 3d person, reporting that his colleague has not arrived & saying he intends to present 2 countrymen to him. Framed. Altman collection. pnNY Sept 13 (17) $450
— [Mar 1808]. 3 pp, 4to. Recipient unknown. Enclosing letters [not included] for examination by his correspondent & disclaiming the intention to "disturb the feelings of either Mr. Jefferson or Mr. Madison". Repaired. P Oct 29 (100) $1,600
— 6 July 1812. 1 p, 12mo. To Joseph Gales. Requesting him not to publish a report until sent a correct copy. Ink erosion affecting several words. wa May 30 (295) $375
— 22 June 1821. 1 p, 4to. Recipient unnamed. Discussing the transfer of land from a member of his family to himself. With autograph address. wa May 30 (115) $1,400
— 20 Jan 1826. 4 pp, 4to. Recipient unknown. About his correspondent's & his own claims against the government. Sang collection. P Oct 29 (104) $4,250
AL, [n.d.]. 2 pp, 4to. To Henry Richard Fox, Lord Holland. Draft, letter of introduction for James Barbour. On integral leaf torn from a letter addressed to Monroe. pnNY June 11 (38) $200
Ls, 13 July 1815. 2 pp, folio. To David Gelston. As Sec of State, making arrangements for the shipment & distribution of the ptd Laws of the US to the governors of the Northern States. CNY Dec 19 (34) $750
— [3 May 1822]. 1 p, folio. To Tao Kwang, Emperor of China. Concerning the ship President Adams, plundered by Chinese subjects after being wrecked near Canton. Countersgd by Sec of State John Q. Adams. With elaborate headings, mimicking engraved type. Framed. P Oct 29 (103) $7,500
Series of Ds s, 4 Ds s, 11 Aug 1817 to 4 Dec 1822. 4 pp, folio. Land grants. Somewhat def. P Oct 29 (102) $1,000
Ds s (2) 11 July & 10 Dec 1823. 2 pp, folio. Land grants to Michael Kine & Thomas Sloo. pnNY June 11 (37) $425
Ds, 25 Feb 1802. 1 p, folio. Land grant, sgd as Gov. of Virginia. rf Nov 15 (12) $290
— [after 26 June 1812]. 1 p, folio. Ptd instructions for private armed vessels of the U.S.A.; unaccomplished. Following ptd text of act of Congress, 26 June 1812, concerning letters of marque, etc; 2 pp. P May 13 (106) $800
— 28 Aug 1812. 1 p, 4to. "Additional Instruction to the public and private armed vessels of the United States"; ptd. Sgd as Sec of State. wa May 30 (313) $700
— 29 Oct 1818. 1 p, 4to. Land grant. Countersgd by Josiah Meigs. rf Mar 14 (44) $220
— 6 Mar 1819. 1 p, folio. Appointment of Morris Miller as agent to treat with the Seneca Nation in New York. Countersgd by J. C. Calhoun. rf Mar 14 (43) $550
— 28 May 1823. 1 p, folio. Ship's passport for the brig Mars of Newburyport. Countersgd by John Q. Adams. wa May 30 (294) $700
— 6 Apr 1824. 1 p, folio. Patent issued to Bernard J. Malfeson. Countersgd by John Q. Adams. Attached to a copy of description of invention, 2 pp, folio. P May 13 (107) $1,200
Franking signature, [14 Jan 1812]. As Sec of State. rf Mar 14 (96) $250
— Anr, [27 June n.y.]. rf May 30 (23) $325
See also: United States

Montagu, Edward, 1st Earl of Sandwich, 1625-72
Ls, 25 July 1657. 1 p, 4to. To John Culmer. About an appointment as boatswain. sg Nov 6 (143) $150

Montesquieu, Charles de Secondat, 1689-1755
Autograph Ms, Plaisir fonde sur la raison; [c.1756]. 2 pp, folio. Part of his unfinished Essai sur le gout dans les choses de La nature et de L'art; pbd in the Encyclopedie under the rubric "Gout". Margin cut; 2 stamps of Collection Mony. S Nov 27 (421) £1,000 [Faure]

Montgomery, Bernard Law, 1st Viscount Montgomery of Alamein, 1887-1976
Collection of c.140 A Ls s & Ls s, 5 Mar 1942 to 4 Sept 1959. About 250 pp, 4to & 8vo. To Sir Edward Crowe. Letters to a friend, about the war & his later activities. With c.130 pp of enclosures, c.27 photographs, & some pamphlets. S July 24 (338) £8,500 [Caldur]

ALs, 7 Aug 1944. 2 pp, 4to. To Major Coulet. Requesting information about looting troops. With draft of reply, 8 Aug 1944. star Apr 9 (1286) DM1,700

— 11 May 1945. 1 p, 4to. To Lady Anderson. Thanking for her care of his son & on closing [present] 2 photographs, & his Victory Message, sgd & dated 8 May 1945. On captured German army writing-paper. S Dec 18 (291) £1,300 [Joseph & Sawyer]

Collection of ANs, Ls, 2 photographs, sgd, & signature on broadside, 1943 to 1950. Sizes not stated. Bet with Gen Sibert regarding the end of the war; asking Lloyd Jacob to a fund-raising dinner; encouraging the 8th Army to battle. With related material. C June 24 (57) £380 [Schulson]

Moore, Henry, 1898-1986
Collection of Ls & photograph, sgd & inscr, 27 Sept 1978. 1 p, 8vo, & 4 by 5 inches. Recipient unnamed. Thanking for praise of his work. Photograph inscr to Robert Lawing. wa May 30 (408) $130

Moore, Stanford, 1913-82
Ls, 26 Mar 1979. 1 p, folio. Recipient unnamed. Stating that the solving of the genetic code is "one of the most important discoveries of the present century". star Apr 8 (389) DM480

Moore, Thomas, 1779-1852
Autograph Ms, song, O thou who dry'st the mourner's tear, 1815. 3 pp, 4to. Text in Moore's handwriting, music in scribal hand. Engraver's copy. Trimmed & repaired. S Nov 28 (592) £200 [Wise]

Series of 9 A Ls s, 12 Jan 1828 to 6 Mar 1840. 12 pp, 4to & 8vo. To Col. Thomas Wildman. Mostly concerning his biography of Byron. S July 23 (81) £2,100 [Quaritch]

ALs, 4 Jan 1804. 4 pp, 4to. To Mr. Carpenter. Reporting about his stay in Virginia. C June 24 (124) £700 [Quaritch]

Moraes Soares, Manoel de. See: Medical Manuscripts

Morgan, Charles Langbridge, 1894-1958
Series of 5 A Ls s, 23 May to 17 Aug 1933. 26 pp, various sizes. To Edith Koch in Berlin. About Hitlerism. sg Mar 5 (184) $500

Morgan, Helen, 1900-41
Photograph, sgd & inscr, [n.d.]. 8 by 10 inches. Inscr to J. Walter Perron. wa May 30 (476) $65

Morgan, John Pierpont, 1837-1913
Ds, 1886. Size not stated. Bond for New Jersey Junction Railroad Company. Sgd on verso. wa May 30 (491) $350

Morgenstern, Christian, 1871-1914
ALs, 28 Dec 1898. 2 pp, 4to. To Eugen Diederichs. Offering his anthology Ein Sommer for publication. star Apr 8 (220) DM650

Morin, Jean Baptiste, 1583-1656
Ms, La Chasse du cerf. Mis en musique. [c.1750] Title & 28 leaves, 280mm by 218mm, in modern half calf. Copy of the 1709 Ed. Jeanson Ms 145 SM Mar 1 (417) FF4,000

Moritz, Kurfuerst von Sachsen, 1521-53
Ls, 16 Jan 1552. 1 p, folio. To the magistrate of the city of Erfurt. Letter of safe-conduct for "Cammer Secretarien Rath" von Sebottendort. star Apr 9 (1231) DM360

Morley, Christopher, 1890-1957
Collection of Ls & autograph Ms, sgd; 24 Mar [1919] & [c.June 1930]. 10 pp, 4to. To Horace Traubel, apologizing for not writing a poem for The Conservator. Essay, "Two Anniversaries", pbd in Saturday Review of Literature, 14 June 1930; about a visit to Walt Whitman's birthplace, etc. In pen & pencil; marked for the printer. With offprint of essay. Charles E. Feinberg collection. P Dec 15 (99) $600

Morning Chronicle
Document, 23 Oct 1769. 2 leaves, 620mm by 720mm. Agreement between the 20 proprietors of the Morning Chronicle and London Advertiser, including John Murray & James Christie; sgd by each. Cloth portfolio. C Dec 3 (308) £400 [Smith]

Morris, Gouverneur, 1752-1816
Ls, 1 May 1778. 1 p, folio. To Gov. [Clinton?]. As Member of the Continental Congress, about a meeting of the Legislature & the treaty with France. S July 24 (403) £500 [Maggs]

Morris, Lewis, Signer from New York
ALs, [n.d.]. 1 p, 12mo. To Messrs. Jones & Stuart. Ordering supplies. Inlaid. Charlotte Parker Milne collection. wd Nov 12 (54) $275

Morris, Robert, Signer from Pennsylvania
ALs, 14 Aug 1794. 3 pp, 4to. To James Carey. About legal counsel for a suit regarding public certificates. rf Mar 14 (45) $270
— 23 Nov 1799. 1 p, 4to. To Mr. Cranch. Ordering him to surrender property in Washington to new owners. Mtd. wa May 30 (140) $475
Ls, 27 Mar 1783. 1 p, 4to. To Gen. Nathanael Greene. Transmitting a bill of exchange (not present). Silked & framed with a port. P May 13 (109) $300
Ds, 4 May 1792. 1 p, 4to. Sight draft to Messrs. Donald & Burton for £150 payable to James Brown. Charlotte Parker Milne collection. wd Nov 12 (56) $150
— 28 May 1795. 1 p, 4to. Certificate for 10 shares in the North American Land Company, sgd as President of the Company. Countersgd by James Marshall. Partly ptd. sg Nov 6 (298) $200
— 10 Mar 1796. 1 p, 32mo. Promissory note of Samuel Meredith for $2,000 payable to Morris. Endorsed by Morris on verso. wa May 30 (427) $280
Franking signature, [n.d.]. 3.25 by 5 inches. Addressed to John Hancock. Charlotte Parker Milne collection. wd Nov 12 (55) $100

Morris, William, 1834-96
ALs, 16 Feb [1878]. 2 pp, 8vo. To Oakley. About a Working Men's meeting at which Gladstone is to speak. S Jan 27 (952) £130 [Bristow]
— 15 Jan [c.1893]. 2 pp, 8vo. To his friend [Rowley]. Referring to a pamphlet by Yves Guyot. star Apr 8 (519) DM320
— CRANE, WALTER. - Autograph Ms, essay entitled "William Morris: poet, artist & craftsman, & social reconstructor"; Oct 1896. 10 pp, folio. Working Ms. With printer's marks. S July 24 (482) £750 [Elliott]

Morse, Samuel F. B., 1791-1872
Series of 3 A Ls s, 30 Mar 1826 to 8 Aug 1868. 1 & 3 pp, 4to. To Charles R. Leslie, introducing J. B. Van Schaick. To Alexander J. Davis, informing him of his coming to New York. To Robert Sabine, protesting against "Hamel's calumnious paper read before the Society of Arts." P Oct 29 (105) $850

Morton, John, Signer from Pennsylvania
Ds, 3 Apr 1772. 1 p, size not stated. 18 pence colonial note, also sgd by John Sellers & C. Humphreys. Repaired. Tipped to larger sheet. Charlotte Parker Milne collection. wd Nov 12 (57) $100

Mosby, John Singleton, 1833-1916
ALs, 22 Oct [1896]. 1 p, 4to. To Chinn. Concerning a typographical error in his letter published in the Post & the silver issue. wa Oct 18 (132) $275
— 17 Oct 1897. 2 pp, 4to. To Chinn. Sending a newspaper & talking about his problems with McKinley. wa May 30 (243) $250
— 30 Nov 1902. 4 pp, 4to. To McGee. Regarding the controversy about fencing public land in Western Nebraska. wa May 30 (241) $600
— 20 Nov 1908. 1 p, 4to. To Alice Chinn. Announcing his visit on Friday. wa May 30 (244) $250
— 29 Mar 1909. 1 p, 8vo. To Mr. Chinn. Discussing the Civil War record of John A. Binns. On Department of Justice letterhead. sg Nov 6 (144) $300

Moscheles, Ignaz, 1794-1870
Autograph music, 2 short Mss, "Capriccio", 16 bars for piano, 11 May 1833, sgd & inscr to H. Phillips, 108mm by 244mm. Mtd. "Impromptu", 10 bars for piano, 14 Dec 1847, sgd & inscr to J. A. Baker. 199 mm by 164mm. C Dec 3 (419) £160 [McCann]

Mott, Sir Nevill Francis
Autograph Ms, article, The Cavendish 1932 / Theory and experiments; [n.d.]. 25 pp, mostly folio. Sgd at head. With covering ALs. star Apr 8 (390) DM350
ALs, 1 Nov [n.y.]. 1 p, 4to. Recipient unnamed. Responding to a question & saying he believes in God. star Apr 8 (391) DM300

Mottl, Felix, 1856-1911
Photograph, sgd & inscr, 1896. Cabinet size. Inscr to Oskar Brueckner, with musical quotation. star Apr 9 (746b) DM360

Motz, Friedrich von, 1775-1830
ALs, 8 Sept 1826. 1 p, 4to. To councillor of the Treasury Kessler. Concerning a failure of the crops. star Apr 9 (1066) DM220

Moxon, Edward, 1801-58. See: Lamb, Charles

Mozart, Wolfgang Amadeus, 1756-91
Autograph music, 9 symphonies, nos 22 to 30, K.162, 181-184, 199-202; c.1773 to 1774. 508 pp, 16.5cm by 22cm; wraps. Full score; 10 staves per page. Some revisions. Table of contents, 1 movement & a number of annotations in the hand of Leopold Mozart. S May 22 (457) £2,350,000 [Kirkman]
— Autograph music, aria, Ah piu tremar non voglio, K.71; [late 1769 or 1770]. 8 pp, 17cm by 22cm; in modern fitted case. Working Ms, 1st 48 bars only, notated in brown ink on up to 9 staves per p. S Nov 28 (594) £30,000 [Haas]
— Autograph music, sketch-leaf for Mass in C

minor, K.417A, & other works, including a canon or fugue subject in B flat with autograph title Von Pimberl und von Stanzerl; [c.1783]. 1 p, c.21cm by 27cm; in brown ink on 12 staves. 19th cent wraps. With a number of revisions. Lower right hand corner removed. With note of certification by Aloys Fuchs. S May 22 (457a) £16,000 [Schneider]
See also: Streicher, Johann Andreas

Muckley, L. Fairfax

[An extensive collection of ink drawings for Spenser's The Faerie Queene, 1897, some sgd, various sizes, sold at S on 19 June, lot 811, for £3,800 to Edberg.]

Mudd, James

Original drawings, 21 drawings in pencil, chalk & wash to illus The Rime of the Ancient Mariner. 20 sgd. 379mm by 541mm; mtd. In def portfolio. S June 19 (682) £550 [Sackin]

Mueller, Adam, 1779-1829

ADs, 16 Sept 1815. 1 p, folio. Receipt for a moving allowance of 1,000 guilders from Metternich's funds. star Apr 8 (392) DM240

Mueller, Johannes von, 1752-1809

ALs, 2 July 1782. 1 p, size not given. To Herrn de Kniegge. Offering his services. JG Oct 2 (249) DM720

Mueller, Otto, 1874-1930

ALs, 23 Apr 1929. 1 p, 4to. To Paul Westheim. Agreeing to do a lithograph, but saying he will need more time. star Apr 8 (520) DM850

Mulcaster, Richard, 1530?-1611

ALs, 24 Apr 1581. 3 pp, folio. To Abraham Ortelius. Asking questions about elementary drawing, talking about the publication of his Elementarie & including copy of poem, Ad librum suum Autor ipse, 36 lines. In Latin. S Dec 18 (6) £5,200 [Quaritch]

Mulliken, Robert Sanderson

ALs, 17 Oct 1978. 1 p, 4to. To an unnamed lady. Stating, upon request, that he does not believe in life after death. star Apr 8 (394) DM380

Munch, Edvard, 1863-1944

ALs, [n.d.]. 2 pp, 8vo. To Mr. Struck. Regarding an old cold needle plate. In German. Framed with a picture of Munch. P June 18 (140) $800

Munnings, Sir Alfred, 1878-1959

ALs, 10 Apr 1921. 4 pp, 8vo. Recipient unnamed. Discussing the mechanics of a horse's action; illus with 5 pen-&-ink sketches. Annotated in pencil by recipient. pn Dec 11 (111) £340 [Sullivan]

Murat, Joachim, 1767?-1815

ALs, 22 Oct 1800. 2 pp, folio. To Napoleon Bonaparte. Regarding military uniforms & pay. Tipped to larger sheet. Bullock collection. CNY Dec 19 (177) $220

— 27 Mar 1811. 1 p, 4to. To an unnamed minister. Reporting that he has received Durand's credentials & mentioning problems with Napoleon's plans. Sgd j napoleon. With 4 documents, sgd. S Nov 27 (422) £380 [Laws]

Musical Manuscripts

Ms, collection of c.60 services & anthems, [c.1740]. 278 pp, folio. Contemp dark red mor gilt. Ownership inscr of Charles Lord, Bishop of Kildare & Dean of Christ Church, Dublin, 1741. C June 24 (198) £100 [Lim]

— Ms, collection of arias by Felice Giardini & others [Italy, c.1800]. Over 300 pp, size not stated. Contemp bds; vellum spine. Mostly in full score. In several hands. S Nov 28 (542) £300 [MacNutt]

— Ms, Collection of cantatas for voice & continuo by Gasparini, Astorga, Mancini, Zipoli & Bononchini. [Italy?, 18th cent]; c. 245 pp, folio. Contemp calf. Ownership inscr by Maria Ducarel, 8 Oct 1768. S May 22 (365) £400 [MacNutt]

Musil, Robert, 1880-1942

Ls, 27 Dec 1932. 1 p, 4to. To H. Draws-Tychsen. Thanking for material received & asking him to give a message to [Marieluise Fleisser]. HN May 22 (3130) DM860

Mussolini, Benito, 1883-1945

[Mussolini's & Clara Petacci's death certificates, issued at Milan, 29 Apr 1945, 4 pp, folio, ptd with Ms insertions, sold at S on 27 Nov 1986, lot 424, for £2,400 to Joseph & Sawyer.]

[Residence certificates of Mussolini & Clara Petacci, issued after their deaths, with related material, May to July 1945, 7 pp, 8vo, sold at S on 27 Nov 1986, lot 425, for £300 to Joseph & Sawyer.]

Autograph Ms, speech about Luigi Luzzatti, 30 Mar 1927. 10 pp, folio, on headed paper of the Capo di Gabinetto. With autograph revisions. Sgd M. S May 21 (283) £850 [Lucas]

ALs, 29 June 1917. 1 p, 4to. Recipient unnamed. Requesting information about French opinion on the Austrian question.

MUSSOLINI

On Il Popolo d'Italia letterhead. In French. Torn. star Apr 9 (1067) DM1,100
— 3 Oct [1933]. 1 p, 4to. To Biagi. Suggesting that they discuss a problem at their next meeting. Framed. Altman collection. pnNY Sept 13 (150) $400

Ls, 19 Apr 1925. 2 pp, folio. To the royal secretary for the grand mastership of equestrian orders. As President of the Council of Ministers, recommending Enea Vigevani for a decoration. C Dec 3 (309) £110 [Huesken]

See also: Vittorio Emanuele III, 1869-1947

N

Nagel, Hanna, 1907-75
Collection of ALs, 3 Ls s & 4 autograph postcards, sgd, 20 Feb 1960 to 21 Mar 1961. 7 pp, folio, & cards. To Hein Kohn. Regarding efforts to sell her drawings. Including colored pen-&-ink sketch. star Apr 8 (521) DM330

Nansen, Fridtjof, 1861-1930
ALs, 17 Nov 1892. 2 pp, 8vo. To Mr. Hunter. Declining an invitation. Framed. Altman collection. pnNY Sept 13 (151) $170

Napoleon I, 1769-1821
[A collection of 18 items, documents, sgd, autograph corrections by Napoleon or letters sent to him, with broadside of the Peace of Luneville, sold at CNY on 19 Dec 1986, lot 191, for $350.]
[A collection of 3 documents, 1800 to 1804, 3 pp, folio, military promotions with secretarial signature by Hugues Maret, countersgd by Berthier & Carnot, sold at sg on 9 Apr 1987, lot 128, for $130.]
[A collection of 5 autograph endorsements, sgd, 24 May 1805 to 12 Dec 1811, on letters from Lieut. Floquerelle, the Duc de Feltre (2) & Marshall Berthier (2), sold at CNY on 19 Dec 1986, lot 189, for $950.]
[A collection of 5 autograph endorsements, sgd, 7 Feb to 6 Mar 1808, on letters from Major Gen. Abronde (?), mostly concerning leave, sold at CNY on 19 Dec 1986, lot 190, for $900.]
[A collection of 14 items relating to Napoleon's exile sold at CNY on 19 Dec 1986, lot 195, for $400.]

Ms, Manuscrit Venu de l'Ile Ste Helene, 1816; [c.1821]. 243 pp, 4to, in notebook. Mistakenly attributed to Napoleon. Including copies of 3 poems & essay about Napoleon. 2 engravings tipped in. C June 24 (59) £70 [Shutter]

Series of 3 Ls s, 11 to 15 May 1811. 4 pp, 4to. To Clarke. About measures relating to a regiment of Cuirassiers & ordering a commander to be reprimanded. Sgd Np. Clarke's annotations at foot. S Nov 27 (434) £600 [Wilson]

Ls, 3 Nov 1791. 1 p, folio. To Gen. Dallemagne. Requesting him to help Citoyen Perree to recruit sailors. Engraved vignette at head. Velvet mount set with 7 medallions of Napoleon. Framed. C June 18 (232) £1,400
— 26 pluviose an II [15 Feb 1794]. 1 p, folio. To the municipal officials at Cassis. As General of Artillery, asking them to requisition a company of gunners. With 13-word autograph addition. Sgd Buonaparte. S Nov 27 (426) £550 [Dr. Sam]
— 16 [Apr?] 1796. 2 pp, folio. To Philippe Aubernon. As General in chief of the Army of Italy, complaining about the lack of provisions. Bullock collection. CNY Dec 19 (178) $700
— 15 floreal an IV [4 May 1796]. 1 p, 4to. To the chief of staff. As Commander-in-Chief of the Army of Italy, giving instructions for the distribution of shoes. S Nov 27 (427) £580 [Edmond]
— 30 messidor an IV [18 July 1796]. 1 p, folio. To the commander at Milan. As Commander-in-Chief of the Army of Italy, informing him of casualties in the action at Mantua. With related material. S Nov 27 (428) £380 [Maggs]
— [18 Aug 1796]. 1 p, folio. To Gen. Kellermann. As General in chief of the Army of Italy, requesting him to send support troops. Bullock collection. CNY Dec 19 (179) $550
— 24 Oct 1796. 1 p, folio. To the commanding General at Brescia [Francois Macquart]. As General in chief of the Army of Italy, ordering him to ensure proper care for wounded soldiers. Probably in the hand of Leclerc. HN Nov 27 (2343) DM2,500
— 15 Aug 1798. 1 p, 4to. To Admiral Ganteaume. Regarding money to be distributed to naval officers. With autograph subscription, 3 words. Crawford collection. HN May 22 (3132) DM3,400
— [26 Nov 1798]. 1 p, 4to. To an unnamed general. Requesting him to name 60 Turks for service at the Cairo palace. Sgd Bonaparte. FD June 11 (3648) DM1,350
— 25 frimaire an 9 [18 Dec 1800]. 1 p, 4to. To the Minister of War. Notifying him of arrangements to transport guns to the army in Italy. Sgd Bonaparte. Framed. Altman collection. pnNY Sept 13 (68) $800
— 13 Sept 1801. 1 p, 4to. To Admiral Ganteaume. Mostly concerning payment for the navy. Engraved vignette at head. Velvet mount set with 6 medallions. Framed. C June 18 (234) £1,400
— 11 Sept 1802. 1 p, 4to. To [Gen. Berthier].

1986 - 1987 · AUTOGRAPHS & MANUSCRIPTS   NAPOLEON I

Requesting a list of officers to fill posts in French India. Engraved vignette at head. Velvet mount set with 6 medallions of Napoleon. Framed. C June 18 (235) £1,400
— 10 Jan 1803. 1 p, 4to. To [Gen. Dejean]. Regarding financial affairs of the 33d demi-Brigade. Engraved vignette at head. Velvet mount set with 6 medallions. Framed. Ingraham collection. C June 18 (236) £1,500
— 30 frimaire an XII [22 Nov 1803]. 1 p, 4to. To Admiral Verhuell. Requesting information concerning preparations for the invasion of England. S Nov 27 (431) £520 [Edmond]
— 1 prairial an 12 [21 May 1804]. 2 pp, folio. To the Bishop of Versailles. Referring to his call to Imperial power & ordering the Te Deum & Veni Creator to be sung in all churches in his diocese. Countersgd by Portalis & Maret. Framed. Altman collection. pnNY Sept 13 (69) $2,400
— 4 Jan 1805. 1 p, 4to. To Admiral Jean Raymond. Instructing him about the delivery of a letter to the King of England. P Dec 15 (72) $3,500
— 23 July 1805. 1 p, 8vo. To [Alexandre Berthier]. About the possibility of war & the execution of his plans for Italy. Framed. Altman collection. pnNY Sept 13 (71) $1,500
— 27 Aug 1806. 2 pp, 4to. To Eugene Beauharnais. Informing him about negotiations for peace with Austria. Sgd Nap. Inkstained. star Apr 9 (1069) DM3,000
— 3 Dec 1806. 2 pp, 4to. To Gen. Bertrand. Ordering him to occupy & defend Glogau. Sgd Nap. star Apr 9 (1070) DM1,700
— 7 Dec 1806. 2 pp, 4to. To Bertrand. Discussing supplies. S May 21 (289) £260 [Lucas]
— 11 Sept 1808. 1 p, 4to. To Monsieur Mollien. Ordering payment to King Charles & the Queen of Etruria. Framed. Altman collection. pnNY Sept 13 (72) $700
— 29 Oct 1808. 1 p, 4to. To Clarke. Discussing the forts of Montbach & Hartenberg near Mainz. Sgd N. S Nov 27 (433) £280 [Haas]
— 3 Mar 1809. 2 pp, 4to. To Gen. Clarke. Ordering that troops within the empire should be listed in the military Divisional record. Sgd Np. C Dec 3 (310) £240 [Huesken]
— 24 Mar 1810. 1 p, 4to. To [Archduke Charles]. Notifying him that he will meet Marie Louise at Compiegne. Mtd with a port. Framed. Ingraham collection. C June 18 (241) £1,900
— 15 July 1810. 1 p, 4to. To Gen. Clarke. Approving of his suggestions concerning troops in Germany. Sgd Np. With related

material. star Apr 9 (1071) DM1,050
— 19 July 1810. 1 p, 4to. To Gen. Clarke. Giving orders concerning the conduct of the war in Spain. Sgd Nap. With autograph correction. star Apr 9 (1072) DM1,200
— 23 Aug 1810. 1 p, 8vo. To the Duc de Feltre. Complaining about the escape of English prisoners of war at Auxonne. Sgd Nap. Velvet mount set with gilt medallion of Napoleon. Framed. C June 18 (242) £1,600
— 28 Sept 1810. 1 p, 4to. To [Eugene de Beauharnais]. Informing him of the armaments he will need at Corfu. Framed. Altman collection. pnNY Sept 13 (74) $650
— 25 May 1811. 1 p, 4to. To Marshal Berthier. Requesting information about troops marching to Bayonne. Torn from a vol. Bullock collection. CNY Dec 19 (182) $320
— 14 July 1811. 1 p, 4to. To the Duc de Feltre. Giving instructions concerning movements of troops & armaments. Framed. Altman collection. pnNY Sept 13 (75) $800
— 21 Oct 1812. 4 pp, 4to. To [Marshal Berthier]. Giving orders for the evacuation of Moscow. Sgd Np. C Dec 3 (312) £3,000 [Joseph]
— 26 Feb 1813. 1 p, 4to. To Gen. Lauriston. Giving orders regarding a depot for the army at Magdeburg. Sgd Np. star Apr 9 (1074) DM1,000
— 9 Apr 1813. 1 p, 4to. To Marshal Marmont. Giving instructions for troop movements preceding the battles of Luetzen & Bautzen. Bullock collection. CNY Dec 19 (184) $400
— 16 May 1813. 1 p, 4to. To [Marshal Berthier]. About an exchange [of prisoners?] with Austria. Sgd Nap. English trans on verso, in pencil. C Dec 3 (313) £240 [Huesken]
— 9 July 1813. 3 pp, 4to. To Comte de Cessac. Pointedly stating that his brother Joseph, King of Spain, has no right to issue declarations or orders in France. Sgd N. Bullock collection. CNY Dec 19 (185) $1,900
— 26 Aug 1814. 1 p, 4to. To Bertrand. Requesting information about a batallion of Chasseurs at Porto Longone. Sgd Np. S May 21 (290) £550 [Haas]
— 9 Sept 1814. 1 p, 4to. To Monsieur Taillade. Regarding arrangements for the manning of the brig [Inconstant]. Sgd Np. C June 24 (58) £500 [Turner]

Letter, [26 Oct 1804]. 1 p, folio. To the president of the canton Rolduc, Cornely. Inviting him to his coronation. With secretarial signature. Countersgd by Hugues Bernard Maret. star Apr 9 (1068) DM440

ANs, 29 floreal an VI [19 May 1798]. 1 p, folio. 12 words, at foot of order by Berthier instructing Menart about his embarkation;

altering order to suit Menart. Armee d'Angleterre letterhead. S Nov 27 (429) £620 [Edmond]

Collection of 4 Ds s & endorsement, sgd, 4 Sept 1798 to 17 Feb 1807. 5 pp, various sizes. Appointment, pardon, articles of assembly, etc. Bullock collection. CNY Dec 19 (186) $1,200

Ds, [1793; 30 fructidor an II]. 1 p, folio. As 1st Consul, military appointment for Andre Francois Le Nomme. Margins cut. wa May 30 (56) $850

— 16 June 1796. 1 p, folio. Order to the Captain of a frigate to surrender the services of Citoyen Charteau. Countersgd by Berthier. Framed. C June 18 (231) £400

— [4 Nov 1796]. 2 pp, folio. As General in Chief of the Army of Italy; proclamation addressed to his troops at the siege of Mantua. A few corrections. Bullock collection. CNY Dec 19 (180) $2,200

— 3 Sept 1798. 1 p, folio. Pay order in favor of his secretary Bourrienne. Countersgd by Bourrienne, acknowledging receipt. With ptd vignette & heading. Framed. C June 18 (233) £800

— 26 Apr 1801. 1 p, 445mm by 600mm. Grant of arms for Comte Davout. In ink on vellum, with calligraphic heading & small illuminated coat of arms. Framed. Ingraham collection. C June 18 (240) £3,000

— 6 July 1802. 1 p, 340mm by 360mm. Commission for Michel Duroc as Grand Marechal. Mtd with quill pen. Framed. C June 18 (238) £1,500

— 19 Apr 1803. 1 p, 335mm by 415mm. Award of a rifle of honor to Pierre Denain; partly ptd. Framed. C June 18 (237) £750

— 17 Feb 1807. 1 p, 395mm by 505mm. Pardon for Jean-Marie Merle; partly ptd. Sgd Nap. Countersgd by Maret & Reynier. Framed. Ingraham collection. C June 18 (239) £1,100

— 20 Sept 1812. 1 p, 425mm by 545mm. Appointment of Noel Varin to the service of the King of Spain; partly ptd. Framed. C June 18 (243) £450

— 20 Sept 1812. 1 p, 440mm by 580mm. Letters patent for the naturalization of Jean Baptiste Rouault de la Bonnerie as Austrian subject; sgd during burning of Moscow. Bullock collection. CNY Dec 19 (183) $550

— 12 Oct 1812. 1 p, folio. Authorization for the ship Hirondelle to export a cargo of silk, lace, etc., to England. Sgd Napol. Ptd heading with crest. Framed. C June 18 (244) £750

Autograph endorsement, 27 pluviose an IX [16 Feb 1801]. 1 p, folio. Note of approval, sgd Bonaparte, in margin of a document concerning non-payment of highway tax. S Nov 27 (430) £280 [Wilson]

— Anr, 22 words on a Ds by Alexandre Bertier, [n.d.], 1 p, folio, recommending Citizen Porta as 2d Lieut. Recommending a different person. Sgd N. Framed. Altman collection. pnNY Sept 13 (70) $800

— Anr, 4 Mar 1810; Np, returning a letter from the Duc de Feltre regarding reports from the Superintendent of Customs. With 2 further endorsements. Framed. Altman collection. pnNY Sept 13 (73) $450

— Anr, "NP". On ALs, 27 Aug 1811, 6 pp, folio, by Collin de Sussy to Napoleon; report concerning troop transportation, etc. sg Nov 6 (150) $650

— Anr, 4 Dec 1811. Note of approval, sgd N, in the margin of a report by Clarke, Minister of War, concerning recall of officers from Spain; 2 pp, folio. With engraved port. S Jan 27 (979) £200 [Libris]

— Anr, sgd, 6 May 1812, on "Ordres de Passe" 8 Apr 1812, submitted by the Ministry of War. 2 pp, folio. Cancelling a proposed transfer. With a note of approval, sgd Np, on 2d p. Also sgd by the Duc de Feltre. C Dec 3 (311) £240 [Wilson]

— Anr, 4 Aug 1812. Note of approval, sgd Np, on Ls by Alexandre [Berthier] requesting prolongation of leave for Cesar de Choiseul. 1 p, folio. Framed. Altman collection. pnNY Sept 13 (76) $500

— Anr, note of approval, sgd Np, on memorial by Bertrand, 20 Aug 1814, 1 p, folio, concerning the appointment of Capt. Messina as judge. star Apr 9 (1075) DM1,200

— Anr, 12 Jan 1815. 1 p, folio. Note of approval, initialled, on a report by Bertrand about musicians' salaries. S Nov 27 (437) £320 [Maggs]

Caricature, Die Fechtstunde; [1814]. Aquatint by Buchhorn after Schadow, c.23.5cm by 41.5cm. Showing Napoleon & Bluecher in a fencing match, with members of other nations watching. star Apr 9 (1076a) DM1,200

Endorsement, sgd, on a letter from Gen. Cavois, 3 July 1801; 1 p, folio. With anr endorsement, sgd, on a letter from the Council of Administration of a Regiment of Dragoons, 7 Aug 1797; 2 pp, folio. Bullock collection. CNY Dec 19 (187) $650

— Anr, 3 brumaire an XII [26 Oct 1803]. In margin of a memorandum by Lord Drummond-Melford, 3 pp, folio, offering his services as an intelligence officer. Forwarding memorandum to the Minister of War. Sgd Bonaparte. S Nov 27 (432) £280 [Maggs]

— Anr, 21 Feb 1805. Signature in the margin of a report by Berthier, 19 Feb 1805, 1 p,

folio, concerning guards for ships. P June 18 (142) $500
— Anr, 26 May 1813. In margin of a report by the Duc de Feltre, 12 May 1813, 1 p, folio, concerning the 16th Legion de Gendarmerie. Sgd N. Framed. C June 18 (245) £350
— Anr, 28 June 1813. Note of approval, sgd Np, on a report by the Duc de Feltre recommending that Baron de Heideck be allowed to serve in Bavaria & be awarded a decoration, 19 May 1813. 2 pp, folio. HN Nov 27 (2344) DM1,760
Signature, in the margin of a report by Alexandre Berthier, 8 Sept 1810, 1 p, folio, concerning leave for M. Maltzen. Allen collection. P Sept 24 (35) $600
Single sheet ptg, broadside announcing his abdication, ptd at Quimper, Brittany, c.25 June 1815; 490mm by 405mm. Marbled wraps. Bullock collection. CNY Dec 19 (192) $130
— IMPERIAL HOUSEHOLD. - Mss, salary lists for members of the Imperial household, all listed by name, 1807 to 1813; c.150 pp, folio. Mostly ptd forms with Ms insertions. S May 21 (238) £600 [Bouvier]
— MILLS, NELSON. - Autograph Ms, Private Journal, 7 to 20 Aug 1815. 56 pp [& blanks], 8vo. Sheepskin bdg. Account of Napoleon's 1st fortnight aboard the H. M. S. Northumberland. Bullock collection. CNY Dec 19 (193) $850
— MILLS, NELSON. - Series of 5 A Ls s, 3 Aug 1815 to 19 Apr 1816. 12 pp, 4to & folio. To Henrietta Moore. Reporting about Napoleon aboard H. M. S. Northumberland & on St. Helena. With a contemp copy of his Private Journal & further material relating to Napoleon. Bullock collection. CNY Dec 19 (194) $1,200

Napoleon I, 1769-1821 —& Others

Engraving, oval aquatint engraved group port of Napoleon, Cambaceres & Lebrun, by Bertaux after Vengorpe, [n.d.]. Hand-colored. Mtd above cut signatures of each consul, Napoleon's with 3 autograph lines. Framed. C June 18 (246) £3,000

Napoleon III, 1808-73

ALs, 29 Nov [1860]. 1 p, 8vo. To his Foreign Minister Edouard Thouvenel. Ordering measures for the protection of the city of Rome. star Apr 9 (1086) DM420
Ls, 2 Sept 1850. 1 p, folio. To the King of the Two Sicilies. As President, thanking for the award of an order. S May 21 (292) £250 [Maggs]
Autograph endorsement, on a memorial, 8 Feb 1854, requesting permission to give his name to a ship; 3 lines in pencil, declining request. Sgd N. star Apr 9 (1085) DM200

Napoleon III, 1808-73 —& Eugenie, Empress of the French, 1826-1920

Ls s (2), [1 by each], 29 Feb 1856 & 15 Feb 1860. 2 pp, folio. To an unnamed prince. Thanking for New Year's wishes. With portraits. sg Apr 9 (129) $475

Napoleonic Wars

[A collection of 5 A Ls s & 1 autograph endorsement, sgd, 1797 to 1813, 6 pp, various sizes, by Napoleonic generals who also served in the American War of Independence, sold at sg on 6 Nov, lot 154, for $100.]

[A collection of 76 items, mostly A Ls s & Ls s, by marshals & generals of Napoleon, sold at CNY on 19 Dec 1986, lot 175, for $4,450.]

[A collection of 24 letters, documents & transcripts, mostly by British officers, relating to various campaigns, especially the Battle of Waterloo, sold at CNY on 19 Dec 1986, lot 196, for$150.]

Naundorf, Karl Wilhelm, 1785?-1845. See: Louis XVII, 1785-95

Naval Manuscripts

Ms, copy book of letters from the captain of La Bordelaise off Spain & La Lilloise off Iceland to French officials, 21 Nov 1833 to 24 May 1836. 75 pp, folio. Half vellum bdg. C June 24 (60) £250 [Bush]
— Ms, Signal book, [c.1789]. 118 leaves, 8vo; orig black calf gilt. Over 500 hand-colored flag-signals; engraved borders. Some waterstains. bba Nov 13 (172) £420 [Hay]
— GEISSLER, MRS. - Ms, diary of an expedition of German warships to East Asia, 1902 & 1903. 267 pp (& several loose pp), in half lea vol, 4to, also containing Admiral Geissler's guestbook, 1895 to 1903, 13 pp. star Apr 9 (1281) DM1,800
— HOLLINSWORTH, JOHN. - Ms, Signal Book in the Channel Fleet in 1803. Also in the West Indies in 1804-5&6, c.40 pp, with hand colored illusts. Red lea gilt; contemp slip case. pn Dec 11 (97) £420 [Buckell & Ballard]
— KENNEDY, WILLIAM ROBERT, R. N. - Series of c.25 A Ls s, c.1850 to 1860; 70 pp. Chronicling his voyages aboard various ships. pn Dec 11 (98) £90 [Buckell & Ballard]

Nazi Leaders

Ms, 5 Apr 1946. 1 p, size not stated. Containing signatures of 20 Nazi leaders while on trial at Nuremberg. With related material. sg Apr 9 (130) $2,200

Neher, Caspar, 1897-1962
A Ls s (2), 25 Sept 1946. 2 pp, folio. To the pbr Reiss at Basel. Drafts, concerning a request to design costumes for Brecht's plays. With autograph telegram, sgd; draft. star Apr 9 (872) DM320

Nehru, Jawaharlal, 1889-1964
Signature, on a souvenir ptg of the Nuclear Test Ban Treaty; postmarked 7 Oct 1963. Size not given. wa Oct 18 (32) $50

Nelson, Horatio Nelson, Viscount, 1758-1805
Autograph Ms, log-book kept on board the Victory, 24 Oct 1803 to 31 Aug 1804. 44 pp, 4to. Daily entries recording the weather. Contemp wraps; cloth case. S Dec 18 (298) £11,000 [Joseph & Sawyer]

ALs, 7 Sept 1780. 1 p, 4to. To Hercules Ross. Expressing confidence that the home leave now granted to him will restore his health. Bullock collection. CNY Dec 19 (197) $3,500

— 28 Oct 1794. 1 p, folio. To Messrs. Marsh & Creed. Concerning money to be paid to Capt. Wolseley & Mrs. Nelson. Written with his right hand. Framed. S Dec 18 (300) £700 [Bonsor]

— 24 May 1799. 1 p, 4to. To his wife Fanny. Forwarding a letter from Josian. S Dec 18 (297) £2,000 [Wheal]

— 19 Aug 1801. 1 p, 4to. To Emma Hamilton. Asking her to visit him & saying he could come to the shore at short notice. C Dec 3 (315) £2,600 [Maggs]

— 6 Apr 1802. 1 p, 4to. To Messrs. Brown & Whitford. Ordering wine. C Dec 3 (318) £1,250 [Bristow]

— 11 Jan 1804. 2 pp, 4to. To his uncle William Suckling. Reporting about his son & saying he will hand him his letter. Sgd Nelson & Bronte. Somewhat def. Bullock collection. CNY Dec 19 (198) $700

— 17 Mar 1804. 3 pp, 4to. To Mrs. Denis. Hoping that "dear Ireland will yet be tranquillized". Slightly repaired. star Apr 9 (1087) DM10,500

— 17 Sept 1805. 5 pp, 4to. To Sir Andrew Snape Hamond. Saying that placing Hamond on the list of admirals after long years of civil employment would set a dangerous precedent. Seal tear. With note of authentication by Sir Graham Hamond. C Dec 3 (317) £1,500 [Huesken]

— 29 Jan to [23 Feb n.y.]. 3 pp, 4to. To Lady Hamilton. Love letter written at sea. Sgd 3 times in text. Was mtd. Bullock collection. CNY Dec 19 (200) $17,000

AL, 24 Sept 1801. 10 pp, 4to. To Lady Hamilton. About his affairs after the separation from his wife. Incomplete. C June 24 (62) £320 [L'Autographe]

ANs, 7 Jan 1802. 1 p, 12.5cm by 16cm. Recipient unnamed. In 3d person, ordering periodicals. Foxed. C Dec 3 (316) £420 [Pocock]

ADs, retained copy of his will of 5 Mar 1801 & copies of 2 codicils, sgd; 16 Mar 1801. 6 pp, folio. With autograph codicil, sgd, to an unspecified will, 25 Mar 1799, & 2 A Ls s by Emma Hamilton to John Scott, [1803]. Tipped into an extra-illus copy of E. Barrington. The Divine Lady. 1926. C June 24 (61) £22,000 [May]

Series of Ds s, 3 Ds s, 13 Feb to 25 Feb 1804. 3 pp, 4to. Fleet rendezvous orders to Capt. Stuart of H. M. S. Kent & Capt. White of H. M. S. Renown. Bullock collection. CNY Dec 19 (199) $2,800

Ds, 19 June 1779. 2 pp, folio; on bifolium from ship's register. List of 4 deserters from H. M. S. Badger, & declaring that "they deserve no Relief". On verso part of statement concerning provisions. C Dec 3 (314) £3,500 [May]

— 21 Mar 1784. 1 p, folio. Last will & testament of John Gore; partly ptd. Sgd by Nelson as witness, with his right hand. S Dec 18 (299) £1,500 [May]

— 22 Mar 1804. 1 p, folio. Enlistment paper for Michele Berlingieri of Naples. Sgd Nelson & Bronte. Countersgd by the Surgeon of H. M. S. Victory. Framed. Altman collection. pnNY Sept 13 (62) $1,200

— 24 Nov 1804. 2 pp, folio. Order to take an inventory of supplies on the ship Superb, addressed to the boatswains of 3 ships. Countersgd by John Scott. sg Apr 9 (131) $1,100

— BECKWITH, SIR THOMAS SIDNEY. - ALs, 3 Apr 1801. 3 pp, 4to. To Andrew Strahan. Reporting about Nelson & the Battle of Copenhagen. Bullock collection. CNY Dec 19 (204) $50

— SAUMAREZ, JAMES. - Ds, [n.d.]. 1 p, folio. Confirming Nelson's orders respecting the blockade of Cadiz; 24 hand-colored flags underneath. With contemp map & hand-colored engraving of the Battle of Trafalgar. Bullock collection. CNY Dec 19 (203) $150

Nelson, Thomas, Signer from Virginia
Autograph endorsement, [n.d.]. 1 p, 3 by 3.25 inches. "Letters and Receipts to Thos Nelson jr of Recent"[?]. Inlaid. Charlotte Parker Milne collection. wd Nov 12 (58) $150

Nesselrode, Karl Robert, Graf von, 1780-62
ALs, 30 July 1830. 2 pp, folio. To Ludwig I von Bayern. Thanking for a decoration. star Apr 9 (1088) DM360

New Jersey

— Parker, Joel, Gov. - Ds, 25 Mar 1883. 10 pp, folio; tied with silk ribbon. Supplement to Relief Act for the militia of 11 May 1861. With note of approval. wa May 30 (245) $65

New Plymouth

— Baylis, Francis. - Autograph Ms, Memoir of the Colony of New Plymouth, [c.1830]. 128 pp, 4to. Historical account up to c.1645. pnNY June 11 (39) $100

New York

[A collection of 2 Ds s by New York City mayors, 1790 & 1845, & Ms, report about harbor fortifications, 1807, 14 pp, sgd by Alderman [Nicholas] Fish, sold at sg on 9 Apr, lot 136, for $110.]

Document, 4 June 1706. 1 p, folio. Conveyance of land by William Traphagen to Jacob Kip; several signatures. Docketed on verso. sg Apr 9 (132) $225

— 4 June 1746. 1 p, folio. Conveyance by Rachel Kip to J. Hendricks Kip of land in Dutchess County near Rynbeck; several signatures. sg Apr 9 (135) $70

Newfoundland

Ms, memorandum, Reasons offered for opposeinge ye Settlem[en]t of a Governor in the New-found Land and removeall of ye Inhabitants there, [1664?]. 3 pp, folio. In a professional hand. Clifford of Chudleigh collection. S July 24 (253) £650 [Quaritch]

Newman, John Henry, Cardinal, 1801-90

ALs, 10 Feb 1839. 2 pp, 8vo. To the Rev. Robert Wilberforce. Stating he cannot decide immediately whether to accept a review by Wilberforce. With newspaper photograph tipped into margin. C Dec 3 (373) £160 [Tracey]

— [n.d.]. 1 p, 8vo. To James Mozley & John Bloxam of Magdalen College. "I will not trouble you to come this wet night..." star Apr 8 (398) DM550

Ney, Michel, Prince de la Moskowa, 1769-1815

Series of 3 Ls s, 14 thermidor an XIII [3 Aug 1805] to 3 Mar 1815. 6 pp, 4to. To various recipients. Relating to military affairs. S Nov 27 (441) £200 [Haas]

Ls, 28 Sept 1798. 1 p, folio. To [Gen.] Debilly. Covering letter for a report. With autograph addition. Repaired. star Apr 9 (1089) DM500

Ls, [24 July 1805]. 2 pp, 4to. To Gen. Dutailler. Informing him about the placing of troops at Etaples. C June 24 (64) £100 [Lowe]

Nicholas I, Emperor of Russia, 1796-1855

ALs, [n.d.]. 1 p, 8vo. Recipient unnamed. Discussing a political crisis. Sgd N. In French. star Apr 9 (1227) DM600

Ls s (2), 10 Sept 1827 & 5 Feb 1850. 5 pp, folio. To Francis I & Ferdinand II of the Two Sicilies. Sending congratulations on the birth of a son. Notifying him of the birth of a prince. wa May 30 (414) $550

Nicholas II, Emperor of Russia, 1868-1918

Ls, 14 July 1897. 1 p, folio. To Nicholas I of Montenegro. Credentials for his envoy Konstantin de Gubastov. In Russian, with official French trans. star Apr 9 (1229) DM1,300

ANs, 1 [June?] 1899. 1 p, 4to. To an unnamed aide. Requesting return of a file after reading. Sgd N. In Cyrillic. sg Apr 9 (138) $450

Nicholas V, Pope, 1397-1455

Document, 7 Mar 1449. 1 p, folio. Papal Bull, admonishing brothers to observe institutions of their order. Corner cut. wa May 30 (64) $240

Nicholson, Ben, 1894-1982

Collection of 24 A Ls s & postcards, sgd, c.1935 to 1954; c.50 pp, 4to & 8vo. To Eduardo Westerdahl. Relating to his own work & the state of British art. With c.50 photographs of his work. S Dec 18 (310) £5,200 [Marks]

Nicholson, William, 1872-1949

Original drawings, 23 illusts for Siegfried Sassoon's Memoirs of a Fox-Hunting Man, 1929; ink. In card mounts; various sizes. With Sassoon's ink drawing of a group around a camp-fire, sgd with monogram; & proof copy of book containing Nicholson's preliminary drawings & proofs for 20 vignettes; in pencil & ink. Orig wraps, 8vo. In fitted case, folio. S Dec 5 (501) £5,500 [Joseph & Sawyer]

Nicolai, Friedrich, 1733-1811

ALs, 14 Feb 1798. 3 pp, 8vo. To Abraham G. Kaestner. Thanking for a book about mathematics & about his latest work. JG Oct 2 (118) DM1,400

Nicolai, Otto, 1810-49

Autograph music, opera, Rosmonda d'Inghilterra, (1838), 1 leaf ("9") of full score; size not stated. Presentation inscr by Oswald Schrenk to Johannes Schueler, Dec 1938, pasted on. star Apr 9 (756) DM520

Nicolaus de Bruxella, c.1470-1532. See: Heems, Nicolas

Nicolaus de Lyra

Ms, Postilla super Evangelias et Epistolas Pauli, [Low Countries, 1st half of 15th cent]. 2 vols, 196 & 164 leaves, vellum & paper, 291mm by 205mm. Def contemp bdg of wooden bds with metal catches. In brown ink in a gothic cursive bookhand. With painted initials throughout in red. Some leaves def. S Dec 2 (43) £3,500 [McKittrick]

Nielsen, Carl, 1865-1931
ANs, 18 Nov 1922. 1 p, 8vo (card). To Dr. Fischer. Thanking for a book about coins. S May 22 (626) £150 [Lionheart]

Niembsch, Nikolaus, Edler von Strehlenau, 1802-50. See: Lenau, Nikolaus

Nightingale, Florence, 1820-1910
Series of 13 A Ls s, 1830 to 1900. Over 40 pp, 4to & 8vo. To various recipients, including her sister. Some unsgd retained drafts. With a letter of appointment, sgd, & some family photographs. S July 24 (293) £1,900 [Gotlieb]

A Ls s (2), 24 & 31 Aug 1858. 6 pp, 8vo. To Arthur Hugh Clough. About the publication of her Notes on Matters affecting the Health... of the British Army. Mentioning the Indian Sanitary Commission. S Dec 18 (336) £340 [Joseph & Sawyer]

ALs, 12 Mar 1855. 4 pp, 8vo. To Mrs. Sawtell. Asking her to superintend a hospital in the Crimea. With envelope, postmarked 24 Mar 1855. Sang collection. P Sept 24 (36) $750

— 22 Nov 1855. 4 pp, 8vo. To an unnamed lady. Mentioning articles required by soldiers on the Crimea. Repaired. Bullock collection. CNY Dec 19 (212) $650

— 21 June 1865. 2 pp, 12mo. To Mr. Rawlinson. Enclosing a note (not included) & requesting information about "Model dwellings". C June 24 (65) £240 [Wilson]

— 6 July 1886. 4 pp, 8vo. To [Dr. John] Murdoch. About his work in India. S Jan 27 (909) £220 [Maggs]

— 3 - 8 Jan 1889. 2 pp, 4to. To Fanny Dowding. About the illnesses of several acquaintances & her own health. Partly typed. C Dec 3 (319) £220 [Wilson]

Ls, 28 Dec 1888. 1 p, 4to. To Rebecca Smith. Thanking for pressed leaves. With autograph addition, 6 words. wa May 30 (59) $230

Ds, receipt for £ 200 for Sir John Kirkland, 11 Jan 1855. Size not stated. Initialled One Penny receipt stamp, F.N. pn Dec 11 (93) £300 [Maggs]

— RAGLAN, FITZROY JAMES HENRY SOMERSET, 1ST BARON. - ALs, 13 Nov 1854. 2 pp, 4to. To Florence Nightingale. Welcoming her to the Crimea. S July 24 (295) £1,600 [Joseph & Sawyer]

Nightingale, Frances Parthenope
Ms, Life and Death of Athena, An Owlet from the Parthenon, [n.d.]. Length not stated. Blue paper; half roan. Early draft version, written in a youthful hand. With orig pencil or pen-&-ink sketches. Dedicated to [Florence Nightingale]. With a copy of the 1st Ed, 7 other books or pamphlets & various letters & photographs of the Nightingale family. S July 24 (298) £2,200 [Franklin]

Nijinsky, Vaslav, 1890-1950
Ptd photograph, 1916. 5.5 by 3.5 inches. Sgd. Shown in La Spectre de la Rose. Faded. wa May 30 (24) $650

Nixon, Richard M.
Ls, 9 Nov 1967. 1 p, 4to. Recipient unnamed. Thanking for comments about his article in Reader's Digest. Personal letterhead. wa Oct 18 (34) $60

Photograph, sgd & inscr, [n.d.]. 10 by 8 inches. Inscr to Mildred Dayton. With related material. wa Oct 18 (33) $50

Signature, on reproduced color sketch from Life Magazine; 4to. Matted. wa May 30 (296) $70

Noble, Mark, 1754-1827
Autograph Ms, The Lives of the Fellows of the Society of Antiquaries in London, [n.d.]. 2 vols, 352 & 371 pp, 8vo. Sgd. With 13 folding genealogical tables. Some corrections. Cloth-backed bds. C June 24 (66) £1,200 [Pickering & Chatto]

Noe, Amedee de, 1819-79. See: Cham, 1819-79

Nolde, Emil, 1867-1956
Series of 11 A Ls s, 1930 to 1950; c.25 pp, mostly 4to. To Hans Fehr. Interesting letters to a friend regarding his work, exhibitions, & politics. FD Dec 2 (3208) DM16,500

ALs, 16 Oct 1944. 1 p, 8vo. To Dr. M. Klafkowski. Informing him of his move to the Schleswig area. VH Sept 12 (969) DM370

Ls, 4 June 1949. 1 p, 8vo. To O. Ralfs. Confirming receipt of pictures from an exhibition. VH Sept 12 (972) DM220

— 14 Jan 1954. 1 p, 4to. To Otto Ralfs. About an exhibition, his age & health. VH Sept 12 (970) DM240

Autograph postcard, sgd, 13 July 1917. To C. G. Heise. Asking for an address. star Apr 8 (522) DM300

Nordau, Max, 1849-1923

ALs, 17 Mar 1882. 4 pp, 8vo. To Sara Hutzler. Giving advice about an unwanted pregnancy among her friends. star Apr 9 (1094) DM500

Nouge, Paul

Series of 8 A Ls s, [1931 to 1938]. 9 pp, folio & 8vo (7 on postcards). To Rene & Georgette Magritte. About publication plans, holidays, apologizing after a discussion, etc. Including autograph poem, L'incantation supreme, dedicated to Georgette Magritte. S July 2 (980) £600 [Brachot]

Nuremberg

Ms, Nuernbergische Chronickh, [c.1585]. 2 parts in 1 vol, c. 300 pp, 310mm by 190mm. Contemp vellum bdg, using 15th cent Ms. Lacking some leaves. HK Nov 4 (436) DM1,300

— Ms, Zeit- und Geschichts-Beschreibung der Statt Nuernberg..., [c.1550-65]. About 380 pp, 288mm by 196mm. 18th cent bds; back covered with 15th cent vellum Ms. In black ink in several hands; some headings in red. Tp & index added in 18th cent. HK Nov 4 (435) DM1,500

O

Obstfelder, Sigbjoern, 1866-1900

Autograph Ms, play, Om varen. Proverbe. Herr Winge; [n.d.]. 4 pp, 4to. With related material. HN May 22 (3140) DM1,300

O'Casey, Sean, 1880-1964

Autograph Ms, play, Juno and the Peacock [sic], 1st draft, [1923]. 72 pp, including 8 blanks, written in 2 directions in school exercise book, 4to. In ink; some pencil notations & 2 small sketches of Capt. Boyle's head. Newspaper cutting, 8 May 1923, pinned inside cover. With near-final typescript of the play, [1923], 90 pp, 4to; some autograph revisions. C Dec 3 (374) £58,000 [Quaritch]

O'Connell, Daniel, 1775-1847

Autograph Ms, address to the people of Ireland after his indictment for conspiracy, draft; 14 Oct 1843. 2 pp, 4to. Sgd at end. S Dec 18 (265) £1,000 [Higgins]

L s, 15 Apr 1844. 3 pp, 4to. To Joseph Sturge. About an Anti-Slavery meeting, the Brazilian sugar question & slavery, & the possible execution of Brown. With autograph subscription. pn Dec 11 (94) £100 [Black]

Oesterreichischer Werkbund

Ms, minutes of plenary meeting, 8 Feb 1934. 3 pp, folio. Sgd by Walter Sobotka & Alois Welzenbacher. Mostly regarding the break-up of the group. With related material, including notice of withdrawal, 13 Nov 1933, sgd by 19 members. star Apr 8 (525) DM1,700

Offenbach, Jacques, 1819-80

ALs, 12 Sept 1863. 4 pp, 8vo. To Madame Porcher. Requesting a loan & reporting about performances of his operas. star Apr 9 (758) DM800

— 18 Mar 1878. 1 p, 8vo. To M. de Saint Victor. Complimenting him on his articles on music. S May 22 (627) £200 [Haas]

Collection of ADs & ALs, 17 Mar 1878 & 4 Mar [n.y.]. 2 pp, 8vo & 16mo. Receipt for 1,250 francs from M. Meyer for his operetta Maitre Peronilla. To the pbr Brandus, promising to send the finale of a work the next day. S May 22 (469) £320 [Haas]

Officium

Ms, Officium Sancti Nicolai Mirensis episcfopil, Paris, 1691. 20 leaves plus 2 orig flyleaves, vellum, 595mm by 410mm, in contemp calf over wooden bds. In a calligraphic roman hand in imitation of ptd type & music in black neums on a 4-line red stave, by D. Claudius Tissu, a Carthusian of Paris. With 13 miniatures, historiated initials & illuminated head- & tailpieces in full color & burnished gold. FD June 11 (8) DM32,000

O'Flaherty, Liam, 1896-1984

Collection of ALs & 7 Ls s & letters, 1928 to 1929. 19 pp, 4to. To Iris Barry. Concerning the completion of his 4th novel & a variety of other matters. S July 23 (168) £520 [Maggs]

Oken, Lorenz, 1779-1851

ALs, 7 Aug 1833. 3 pp, 8vo. To Adolph Wilhelm Otto. Regarding the next meeting of a medical society & describing his situation at Zurich. star Apr 8 (399) DM1,200

O'Neill, Eugene, 1888-1953

ALs, 23 June 1921. 2 pp, 8vo. To St. John Ervine. Discussing the production of various of his plays. wd June 19 (34) $2,400

Onslow, Georges

Autograph music, corrections to quintets Op. 72 & Op. 75; [n.d.]. 1 p, 8vo. In brown ink on 12 staves; presumably sent to pbr. S Nov 28 (598) £320 [Wurlitzer-Bruck]

Ophuels, Max, 1902-57
Ls, 17 Apr & 5 May 1956. 2 pp, 4to. To H. E. Mutzenbecher. Declining an invitation to Saarbruecken. With carbon copies of recipient's letters. star Apr 9 (873) DM220

Organists
[A collection of 8 items, letters, contracts & receipts, by German & Austrian organists, 17th to 19th cent, with related material, sold at FD on 2 Dec 1986, lot 3250, for DM1,100.]

Origen, c.185-c.254. See: Sermons

Orleans, Charles, Duc d', 1391-1465
Ls, 21 Feb 1448. 1 p, vellum, 130mm by 365mm. To Jehan Le Prestre. Informing him about a payment to Pierre Varmier. C June 24 (67) £400 [Castaing]

Orleans, Ferdinand Philippe Louis Charles Henri, Duc d', 1810-42
Ms, Chasses a courre faites par S. A. R. Monseigneur le Duc d'Orleans, pour les annees 1836-1848. 194 pp, 332mm by 226mm, in half shagreen. Jeanson Ms 176 SM Mar 1 (439) FF18,000

Orleans, Louis Philippe, Duc d', 1725-85
Ms, Chasses du cerf faites par l'equipage de Monseigneur le duc de Chartres pendant l'annee 1751. 58 pp, 139mm by 84mm, in contemp red mor gilt with arms of Louis Philippe I, Duc d'Orleans. Jeanson Ms 147 SM Mar 1 (438) FF38,000

Orlik, Emil, 1870-1932
Collection of c.50 A Ls s & postcards, sgd, 1910 to 1921. About 100 pp, various sizes. To Anny Schindler. Discussing theatrical productions, reporting about his paintings, etc; with a number of sketches. Some sgd Baer or B. With 3 copies of Orlik's port of Schindler, sgd in pencil, & related material. S Nov 27 (443) £1,300

ALs, 22 Jan 1920. 2 pp, 4to. To Mr. & Mrs. Leo Lewin. About Slevogt, a new kind of canvas, etc. Including watercolor, 9cm by 17cm, showing a bunch of flowers. HN May 22 (3142) DM640

— 5 Oct 1926. 3 pp, 8vo. To "Liebe Lolo". About the death of her dog. With drawing of dog at head. star Apr 8 (524) DM430

Series of 4 autograph postcards, sgd, 1898 to 1909. To Hugo Salus. 3 cards with pen-&-ink sketches, 1 with colored woodcut. With ALs, 1920, with lithograph, & drawing, 1907, in pencil. With 3 autographs by Walter Reimann. star Apr 9 (523) DM1,400
See also: Strauss, Richard

Orpen, Sir William, 1878-1931
Series of 20 A Ls s, 1917 to 1928. 29 pp, various sizes. To G. B. Alexander. About his work, his military service, etc. Including pen-&-ink drawing, a fly on a sleeping man's nose. sg Apr 9 (146) $300

— Series of 5 A Ls s, various dates. 6 pp, various sizes. Recipients & contents not stated. With photograph, 1929, 5.75 by 8 inches, sgd & inscr on mount; & pen-&-ink-&-wash self port, 1926, 5.5 by 4 inches, mtd. sg Apr 9 (147) $250

Series of 8 A Ns s, [1920s]. 8 pp, various sizes. Mostly to Reginald Scott. Contents not stated & about the price of a port. sg Apr 9 (145) $150

ANs, 15 Apr [19]25. 1 p, 4to. To "Master Piller". Responding to a request for his autograph. With pen-&-ink sketch, self port with a bottle of wine, at bottom of page. sg Apr 9 (144) $250

Orth, Johann, 1852-90?. See: Johann Salvator, 1852-90?

Osiander, Andreas, 1498-1552
Transcript, copy of 3 different items, in Latin; [n.d.], 1 p, folio. Letters from Osiander and Melanchthon to Friedrich, Abbot of St. Aegidien; commentary on the 2nd Epistle to the Thessalonians by Michael Rotting. Possibly in Osiander's hand. With a letter of authentication by a previous owner. JG Oct 2 (256) DM1,000

Otis, Harrison Gray, 1765-1848
Autograph Ms, speech in the Massachusetts Senate, 13 Jan 1811. 6 pp, size not stated. Answer to a speech by Gov. Gerry; sgd. Sang collection. pnNY June 11 (89) $90

Otto, King of Greece, 1815-67
ALs, 29 May 1853. 1 p, folio. To Major Gen. A. von der Mark. Draft, expressing thanks for maps of Bavaria. With a port. star Apr 9 (994) DM750

Otto I, Emperor, 912-73
Ds, [10 Sept] 960. 1 p, c.47cm by 54cm. Vellum. Deed, conveying 2 thirds of Diotmar's property in the Rednitz district to the nunnery at Druebeck. Sgd with monogramm, accomplished by the emperor. With wax seal of Otto III. star Apr 9 (1191) DM280,000

Ottobon, Jean Baptist. See: Charles I, 1600-49

Overbeck, Johann Friedrich, 1789-1869
ALs, 22 Oct 1856. 4 pp, 8vo. To Joseph Sutter. About financial help for Sutter & his health problems. HN Nov 27 (2356) DM850

Ovid

Ms, De Arte Amandi, De Remedia Amoris, Amores, & other love poems. [Rome or Naples, c.1470-80]. 110 leaves, vellum, 183mm by 120mm. Modern vellum over pastebds. In brown ink in a skilful humanistic cursive minuscule. With large initial & full illuminated border in white-vine style on tp, & 11 other large illuminated initials. S June 23 (92) £16,000 [Brown]

Oxenstierna, Johan, Count, 1611-57

Ls, 27 May 1647. 3 pp, folio. To Friedrich Wilhelm, Kurfuerst von Brandenburg. Letter of recommendation for Bernhard von Gehnard. star Apr 9 (1108) DM340

P

Paca, William, Signer from Maryland

Autograph Ms, [n.d.]. 2 pp, 4to. Fragment; contents not stated. Charlotte Parker Milne collection. wd Nov 12 (59) $125

Autograph endorsement, 26 Nov 1783. Signature on verso of a pay order; oblong 8vo. wa Oct 18 (135) $300

Pacific Rulers

[A collection of 7 autographs by Kings & Queens of the Pacific Islands, [19th cent], sold at CNY on 19 Dec 1986, lot 213, for $550.] Bullock collection. CNY Dec 19 (213) $550

Paderewski, Ignace Jan, 1860-1941

ALs, 5 Oct 1888. 1 p, 8vo. To [a news agency?]. Protesting against the price of newspaper clippings. In French. star Apr 9 (759) DM320

Autograph telegram, 15 May 1890. 1 p, 16mo. To Edouard Colonne. Declining an invitation. In French. sg Nov 6 (159) $90

Photograph, sgd & inscr, 13 Jan 1933. Framed; overall size 30cm by 23cm. Inscr to Frank Usher. With 6 others. S Nov 28 (599) £240 [Reuter]

Paer, Ferdinando, 1771-1839. See: Le Sueur, Jean Francois & Paer

Paganini, Nicolo, 1782-1840

ALs, [1818]. 2 pp, size not stated. To Luigi Germi. About the prospect of marriage, operas in Rome, Canova, his Rondo, etc. Without salutation. S May 22 (473) £2,000 [Sainati]

Paine, Robert Treat, Signer from Massachusetts

Document, 8 July 1777. 1 p, folio. Copy, approval of a petition for a private schooner of war owned by Robert Morris & others. Attestation by John Avery. Charlotte Parker Milne collection. wd Nov 12 (60) $100

Paisiello, Giovanni, 1740-1816

Ds, 31 Mar 1802. 1 p, 8vo. Receipt for 580 lire from Claudio Labaume. S May 22 (477) £250 [Riskin]

Palloy, Pierre Francois, 1754-1835

ALs, [1795/96]. 4 pp, folio. To J. B. Drouet. Congratulating him on his exchange as prisoner of war. Possibly draft. Sgd with paraph. star Apr 9 (1109) DM850

Pankhurst, Emmeline, 1858-1928

Series of 3 A Ls s, 30 Jan 1913 & [n.d.]. To Henry Harben & Mrs. Harben (2). About various subjects, mostly related to the movement for women's suffrage. C Dec 3 (320) £300 [Lawson]

Pannwitz, Rudolf, 1881-1969

Collection of 36 A Ls s & Ls s, 27 July 1904 to 22 Nov 1909. 153 pp, various sizes. To Ludwig Gurlitt. Confidential letters regarding his work as author & educator. With 7 letters to Gurlitt, Jan & Feb 1910, mostly regarding his illness. star Apr 8 (400) DM8,000

— Collection of 94 A Ls s & Ls s & 24 postcards, 1 July 1927 to 8 July 1931. Over 150 pp, various sizes, & cards. To Ludwig Gurlitt, some to Helene Gurlitt. Chronicling his life & work. Some letters with postscripts by his wife Charlotte. With related material. star Apr 8 (401) DM17,000

Panofsky, Erwin, 1892-1968

Collection of 15 A Ls s & postcards, sgd, c.1914 to 1921; c.30 pp, 4to & 8vo. To Franz Schoenberner. About a variety of subjects. With poem, Berliner Fruehlings-Sonnett. 1 ALs in Latin. S May 21 (293) £420 [Sotheran]

Pape, Frank C.

Original drawing, a giant in his lair, to illus Bunyan's The Pilgrim's Progress, 1910. In ink & watercolor. Sgd. 414mm by 310mm. Was mtd. Archives of J. M. Dent & Son. S June 19 (812) £1,400 [Sawyer]

Pappenheim, Jenny von, 1811-90

ALs, 11 Aug 1834. 4 pp, 8vo. To her half-sister Cecile von Gersdorff. Family news. In French. With related material. star Apr 8 (107) DM1,100

Parker, Bonnie —& Barrow, Clyde

Single sheet ptg, handbill for their arrest issued by the US Department of Justice, 21 May 1934. 2 pp, 4to. Including 2 photographs, descriptions, & criminal records. pnNY June 11 (89A) $200

Parmentier, Antoine Augustin
Autograph Ms, Rapport a l'Institut National sur le Pain des Troupes. [11 Nov 1796] 42 p, folio, loose in cardbd folder. Sgd & dated. S June 25 (122) £2,800

Parry, Sir William Edward, 1790-1855
Series of 5 A Ls s, 1838 to 1852. 13 pp, 8vo. To Vaugham Davis & his wife. Private letters. star Apr 8 (402) DM260

ALs, 16 Mar 1849. 4 pp, 8vo. To his son Charles. Regarding the anxiety about Franklin's expedition. S Jan 27 (890) £130 [Roberts]

Passionei, Domenico, Cardinal, 1682-1761
Ls, 12 Aug 1741. 3 pp, 4to. To A. Radetti, Bishop of Bergamo. Contents not stated. With autograph subscription. HN May 22 (3146) DM650

Passy, Frederic, 1822-1912
ALs, 7 Nov 1862. 6 pp, 8vo. To Louis-Francois Wolowski. Requesting his help in finding a teacher for Polish & Russian & a Polish chambermaid. star Apr 8 (403) DM400

Pasteur, Louis, 1822-95
A Ls s (2), 11 Nov 1856 & 9 June 1883. 2 pp, 4to & 8vo. To the Secretary of the Royal Society in London; regretting he cannot accept the Rumford medal personally. To the Vice-Chancellor of Cambridge University; regretting he cannot return to Cambridge. P Dec 15 (73) $1,800

ALs, 4 July 1877. 1 p, 8vo. To Dr. Bartian. Offering him his laboratory to use while in Paris. S Nov 27 (444) £480 [Lucas]

ANs, 19 Aug [c.1855]. On note card, 2.5 by 4.5 inches. Recipient unnamed. Giving instructions about a potentially rabid dog. P June 18 (150) $1,400

Autograph quotation, 7 Feb 1885. 1 p, 12mo. Sgd. Patriotic remark about France. Framed. Altman collection. pnNY Sept 13 (152) $550

Patti, Adelina, 1843-1919
[An album containing 25 cabinet & carte-de-visite photographs of Patti, some hand-colored, mostly by Bergamasco, sold at S on 28 Nov, lot 601, for £250 to MacNutt.]

ALs, 1 May 1868. 1 p, 8vo. To an unnamed author. Regarding publication of her port. star Apr 9 (761) DM240

Patton, George S., Jr., 1885-1945
ALs, [n.d.]. 1 p, 10 by 8 inches. To "Ollie". Over 50 words, on verso of port photograph, sgd & inscr; taken in Sicily, 11 July 1944. Def. With port photograph of "Ollie", [1939]. sg Nov 6 (160) $1,300

Paul I, Emperor of Russia, 1754-1801
Ls, 14 Aug 1789. 1 p, 4to. To Friedrich Nicolai. Thanking for the 2d vol of anecdotes of Friedrich II of Prussia. In French. star Apr 9 (1226) DM550

Ds, 12 Jan 1799. 1 p, folio. Award of the Order of St. Anne to "Secret Councillor" Mijulin. sg Apr 9 (150) $300

Paul III, Pope, 1468-1549
Document, 9 Dec 1546. 1 p, folio. Vellum. Papal Bull; recognizance of a cardinal. Lead seal. sg Nov 6 (161) $250

Paul VI, Pope, 1897-1978
Ls, 2 Oct 1942. 1 p, 4to. To Dr. Boggiano-Pico. Thanking for a donation of medical supplies. star Apr 9 (1123) DM650

Payne, Edward R. —& Others
[A calligraphic Ms, Let men do these things, compiled for Gwilym Jones with his favorite poems & illus by fellow artists, 1952, red mor bdg, 4to, sold at S on 5 Dec, lot 506, for £240 to Smallwood & Randall.]

Pedro II, Emperor of Brazil, 1825-91
Ls, 5 Feb 1843. 1 p, folio. To the Queen of the Two Sicilies. Letter of recommendation for his Envoy. Sgd Imperador. S Nov 27 (445) £200 [Lucas]

— 22 June 1869. 1 p, folio. To Emile Guillaume de la Roquette. Notifying him of the conferral of a decoration. star Apr 9 (922) DM360

Peiresc, Nicolas-Claude Fabri de, 1580-1637.
See: Rubens, Peter Paul

Penn, John, Signer from North Carolina
Ds, 10 Apr 1772. 1 p, 12mo. Rent statement, cut from larger document. Mtd. Charlotte Parker Milne collection. wd Nov 12 (61) $325

Penn, Thomas, 1702-75
Ds, 24 Mar 1735. 1 p, folio. Transferrance of land in West New Jersey once belonging to William Penn. Also sgd by attorneys for John & Richard Penn, & 2 witnesses. sg Apr 9 (151) $175

Penn, William, 1644-1718
ALs, 8 Oct 1689. 1 p, size not stated. Recipient unnamed. Desiring 500 acres to be laid out for John Day on the Schuykill or Delaware. With franking signature. rf Nov 15 (32) $2,800

Ds, 20 Sept 1681. 1 p, folio. Indenture, granting Enoch Flowers 2,000 acres in Pennsylvania. Engraved. P May 13 (112) $1,600

Autograph endorsement, sgd, 27 Aug 1683. 4 lines at foot of ALs by Enoch Flower to Penn, 25 Aug 1683, 1 p, folio. Ordering that Flower's 2,000 acres be laid out in Philadelphia. P May 13 (113) $2,100

Pennell, Joseph, 1857-1926
ALs, "5.7.9"[1909]. 2 pp, 8vo. To Way. About signing some prints. wa Oct 18 (136) $50

Pennsylvania
Document, 20 June 1768. 1 p, 267mm by 610mm, vellum. Conveyance by Patrick Hays & his wife to David Hays of 192 acres in Derry Township, Lancaster County; 5 signatures. Registered on verso by Edward Shippen. sg Apr 9 (45) $130

Pepys, Samuel, 1633-1703
Ds, 12 Apr 1661. 1 p, folio. Order from James Duke of York assigning Edward Eliot boatswain aboard the ship Mary. Repaired. sg Nov 6 (162) $250
— 17 May 1661. 1 p, folio. To the Clerk of the Cheque of His Majesty's Yard at Woolwich. Order "to enter" John Rudd & his servant with allowances for victuals. Countersgd by Peter Pett. Framed. Altman collection. pnNY Sept 13 (128) $850
— 24 Apr 1665. 1 p, folio. Discharge for the boatswain from the Little Unicorne. Torn. sg Nov 6 (163) $175
— 11 June 1672. 1 p, 8vo. Order to release material from Naval Stores to repair a ship. Also sgd by Brounker & Ernle. Framed with a port. S July 24 (346) £700 [Quaritch]
— 12 Dec 1672[?]. 1 p, folio. Order from the Navy Office to Charles Smith concerning payment to Mr. Maplesden. Repaired. sg Nov 6 (164) $300
See also: Charles II, 1630-85

Percy, Thomas, 1729-1811
ALs, 8 Dec [1774?]. 1 p, folio. To the Rev. George Ashby. Requesting further suggestions for a new Ed of his Reliques of Ancient English Poetry. pn Dec 11 (53) £280

Pergolesi, Giovanni Battista, 1710-36
Ms, Stabat Mater; vocal score, [after 1736]. 47 pp, folio. In contemp Italian hand. S May 22 (478) £250

Peron, Juan Domingo, 1895-1974
Series of 8 Ls s, 15 Feb to 3 Apr 1944. 9 pp, 8vo. To Jose C. Gregores. As Sec of Labor and Provision, regarding official business. With Ls, 21 Mar 1974, to Emilio Nogues. S May 21 (296) £400 [Pervanas]

Peron, Maria Eva Duarte ("Evita"), 1919-52
Photograph, sgd, [c.1945]; 5.25 by 3.75 inches. Sgd Eva Duarte. Was mtd. sg Nov 6 (168) $175

Perry, Matthew Calbraith, 1794-1858
Ls, 7 Sept 1847. 1 p, size not stated. Recipient unnamed. At Vera Cruz, ordering a sailor to report to U. S. S. Petrel. Endorsed on verso by Franklin Buchanan. rf Mar 14 (41) $210

Perry, Oliver H., 1785-1819
Ds, 31 Mar 1819. 1 p, 2.75 by 6.5 inches. Receipt for $295 "on account of my pay and subsistence". wa May 30 (486) $450

Pershing, John J., 1860-1948
Collection of 2 A Ls s, Ls & photograph, sgd & inscr, 1920 to 1940. 4 pp, 8vo & 4to, & 9 by 6 inches. Recipient & contents not stated: thanking for congratulations on his birthday. Photograph inscr to Daisy Harriman. wa May 30 (487) $180
ALs, 31 Oct [1930]. 2 pp, 8vo. To Mrs. Ellis. Accepting an invitation. wa May 30 (60) $130
Photograph, sgd & inscr, [5 Jan] 1923. 10 by 13 inches. Inscr to Roy Carruthers. With Ls, 1 p, 8vo, from Pershing to Carruthers; covering letter. Matted. sg Nov 6 (169) $90

Persian Manuscripts
Ms, Anthology of Persian poems. [Isfahan, A.H.1225/A.D.1810]. 176 leaves, 273mm by 172mm. Floral lacquer bdg. In nasta'liq script by Muhammad Shafii al-Najafi. With illuminated headpiece. S June 1 (159) £260 [Rastegar]
— Ms, Anthology. [Qajar, early 19th cent]. 269 leaves, 294mm by 190mm. Black lea gilt. In shikasteh script. With double page of illumination, upper corner torn. Some repairs. S Nov 20 (402) £300
— Ms, Firman of Abu'l-Nasr Mu'in al-Din Muhammad Akbar Shah. [Delhi, 4 Sept 1837]. 1 p, 105.4cm by 61cm. In elegant black nasta'liq within gold cloud-bands; finely illuminated. Framed. C June 16 (71) £4,200
— Ms, Guide to Mecca & Medina. [Persia, early 17th cent]. 42 leaves, 235mm by 140mm. Brown mor with stamped medallions. In nasta'liq script. With 14 colored drawings & illuminated headpiece. Repaired. S Nov 20 (387) £2,200
— Ms, Yahya Ibn Mirza Abu'l-Qasim Kankarani Bahram Nama. [Kashmir, A.H.1195/A.D.1780-81]. 27 leaves & 4 flyleaves, 222mm by 140mm. Brown mor bdg. In nasta'liq script. With 23 miniatures set within text & illuminated heading. C June 16 (70) £500
— ALI ABADI. - Diwan. [Qajar, 2d half of 19th cent]. 109 leaves, 276mm by 170mm. Lacquer bdg. In nasta'liq script. With double intercolumnar rules in gold & 5 illuminated headpieces. S Nov 20 (410) £500

PERSIAN MANUSCRIPTS

— Allah-Yar Ibn Allah-Quli al-Bukhari. - Maslak al Muttaqin, [Persia, A.H. 1232 / A.D. 1816]. 218 leaves & 25 blanks, 253mm by 147mm, in Asiatic bdg with wooden bds. In nasta'liq script by Mitza Sayyid Ahmed Khoquandi; with rules in gold, red & blue throughout, 1st 2 pp with ornamental borders, & Chinese colored woodcut. FD June 11 (18) DM1,800

— Bedhil (Mirza Muhammad Rafi'). - Hamlah-i Haydari. [Shiraz, A.H.1233/A.D.1817]. 326 leaves, 302mm by 205mm. Contemp lacquer bdg with battle scenes. In nasta'liq script by Ibn Murtaza Quli Khan Abarquhi Muhammad Ali. With 36 miniatures & 2 illuminated headpieces. S June 1 (160) £2,400

— Firdausi. - Shahnama. [Persia, A.H.1040/A.D.1640]. 525 leaves plus 3 flyleaves, 37.2cm by 24.2cm. Brown mor bdg, gilt stamped. In nasta'liq script by Saiyyid Riza bin Mir Abu Talib al-Husaini. With 55 miniatures & 2 half-page illuminated headings. C Nov 21 (63) £2,800

— Firdausi. - Shahnama. [Persia, early 17th cent]. 1 bifolium only, 260mm by 165mm. In nasta'liq script. With full-page miniature in gold & colors & elaborate foliate borders. Separated at fold. HK Nov 4 (442) DM1,900

— Firdausi. - Shahmana, 2d part only. [Turkman, Shiraz, c.1500]. 310 leaves, 310mm by 195mm. In 4 columns of nasta'liq script. With intercolumnar rules in gold, 21 miniatures & illuminated headpiece. Some repairs. S Nov 20 (377) £11,000

— Hafiz. - Diwan. [Khurasan, perhaps Mashhad, A.H.995/A.D.1586]. 438 leaves, 243mm by 150mm. 17th cent black mor with sunken medallions. In nasta'liq script by Ibn Abul-Makaram Adbul-Wahhab al-Hijazi. With 11 miniatures & illuminated headpiece. S Nov 20 (386) £4,000

— Hafiz. - Diwan. [Qajar, 19th cent]. 213 leaves, 153mm by 95mm. Contemp lacquer bdg. In shikasteh script. With illuminated headpiece. S June 1 (156) £300 [Lari]

— Ja'far bin Muhammad Jaffar. - Kitab al-Jaffar. [Persia, A.H.1283/A.D.1866-67]. 395 leaves & 2 flyleaves, 362mm by 235mm. Brown mor bdg. In naskhi script. With half-page illuminated heading. Introductory note by Ghulam Riza Hairan. C June 16 (101) £180

— Jami. - Shawahid al-Nubuwa. [Persia, A.H.964/A.D.1556]. 166 leaves, 270mm by 170mm. Brown mor with patterned paper covers. In nasta'liq script by Muhammad. With illuminated headpiece. S June 1 (139) £300 [Lari]

— Nizami. - Khamsa. [Shiraz, 2d quarter of 16th cent]. 298 leaves, 243mm by 160mm.

AMERICAN BOOK PRICES CURRENT

19th cent red lea decorated with animals. With headings on decorated panels, 8 miniatures & 4 illuminated headpieces. Waterstained. S Nov 20 (384) £1,200

— Sa'di. - Gulistan. [Persia, A.H.1206/A.D.1791]. 40 leaves & 3 flyleaves, 184mm by 114mm. Contemp floral lacquer bdg. In very fine black shafia script by Muhammad Qasim, written at various angles within gold cloud-bands. With miniature of a dervish. C June 16 (66) £1,600

— Sa'di. - Gulistan. [Persia, c.1500]. 155 leaves, 215mm by 137mm. Modern brown lea tooled in blind. In nasta'liq script by Sultan Ali al-Mashhadi. With later 16th cent illuminated headpiece; ff.81-82 later replacements. S Nov 20 (378) £800

— Sa'di. - Kulliyat. [Persia, A.H.705/A.D.1305]. 106 leaves, 228mm by 155mm. Brown mor stamped in blind. In naskhi script. With headings in gold on illuminated panels. Waterstained; repaired. S Nov 20 (364) £2,200

— Sayyid Zain al-Abidin. - Qasida. [Hyderabad, c.1915]. 6 leaves & 4 flyleaves, 285mm by 184mm. Bds. In nasta'liq within gold cloud-bands. With illuminated opening half-page. C June 16 (69) £300

Pestalozzi, Johann Heinrich, 1746-1827
Ms, defense of his method, beginning "Man hat der Methode lange den Vorwurf gemacht...", [n.d.]. 4 pp, folio. Dictation, with extensive autograph corrections, revisions & additions. star Apr 8 (404) DM4,200

Peter I, Emperor of Russia, 1672-1725
Ls, 15 Sept 1715. 1 p, 8vo. To Lieut. Col. Gennin. Regarding the supply of canon to ships of his fleet. Autograph addition of 2 words. C June 24 (68) £1,300 [L'Autographe]

— 25 July/5 Aug 1716. 1 p, 4to. To a duke of Holstein. Notifying him of the death of his sister Natalie. Henry Fatio collection. HN May 22 (3149) DM5,400

— 14 Feb 1721. 1 p, 4to. To Hetman Koronnyi. Consenting to the marriage of Prince Menshikov's daughter with Sapjeha's son. With related material. Unrelated French letter on verso of mount. HN May 22 (3150) DM3,600

ADs, [after 1697?]. 1 p, 8vo. Ordering punishments to deal with robbery in towns. Sgd Piter. Was mtd. S Nov 27 (446) £2,000 [Dr. Sam]

Document, 30 Nov 1713. 1 p, folio. Full powers for an unnamed Russian official to settle border problems with Turkey. In Russian, with official Latin trans. star Apr 9 (1224) DM650

Petermann, August, 1822-78
Collection of 5 A Ls s & 5 Ls s, 1 Apr 1870 to 12 Mar 1872. 10 pp, 8vo. To an unnamed contributor to the Mitteilungen aus Justus Perthes geographischer Anstalt. Regarding African maps. star Apr 8 (405) DM440

Peters, Richard, 1744-1828
ALs, 29 Aug 1777. 2 pp, 4to. To Gen. Edward Hand. As secretary to the Poard of War, informing him about the military situation. Seal tear; repaired. P May 13 (114) $500

Petrarca, Francesco, 1304-74
Ms, Canzoniere e Trionfi. [Florence, c.1460]. 190 leaves, vellum, 260mm by 168mm. Contemp blindstamped Florentine bdg of goatskin over wooden bds. In dark brown ink in a rounded humanistic minuscule, possibly by Antonio Sinibaldi. With painted initials throughout, 5 small illuminated initials & historiated initial with full lenth whitevine border, attributed to the Master of the Riccardina Lactantius. S June 23 (90) £16,000 [Brown]

Pfitzner, Hans, 1869-1949
ALs, [1906/07]. 2 pp, 8vo. To Ernst von Schuch. About a meeting concerning a perfomance of the overture of Das Christ-Elflein. star Apr 9 (764) DM400

— 31 Oct 1917. 2 pp, 8vo. To Willy Levin. Regarding the score [of his opera Palestrina] & rehearsals for a performance in Dresden. star Apr 9 (766) DM800

Photograph, sgd & inscr, 20 Sept 1917. Postcard size. On verso musical quotation, 2 bars from his Palestrina. star Apr 9 (765) DM260

Phebus, Gaston, Comte de Foix, 1331-91
Ms, Le Bon Varlet de chiens. [Northern France, perhaps Paris, 3nd of 15th cent] 67 leaves, vellum, 162mm by 92mm, in 18th-cent mor gilt. With 18 small miniatures in colors & liquid gold. Jeanson Ms 106 SM Mar 1 (464) FF950,000

— Ms, Livre de Chasse. [Bretagne, c.1430] 118 leaves, vellum, 261mm by 185mm, in 17th-cent red mor gilt. With 86 miniatures in rectangular compartments in colors & liquid gold & with 87 large illuminated initials. Jeanson Ms 101 SM Mar 1 (459) FF6,200,000

— Ms, Livre de chasse. [Flanders, perhaps Brussels, c.1480] 139 leaves, vellum, 317mm by 230mm, in 18th-cent calf gilt, armorial bdg. With 24 half-page miniatures & c.90 illuminated initials. Jeanson Ms 102 SM Mar 1 (460) FF700,000

— Ms, Livre de chasse. [Paris, c.1400-14] 52 leaves, vellum, 317mm by 238mm, in mor gilt with title on vellum. With grisaille miniature & 85 large illuminated initials. Jeanson Ms 103 SM Mar 1 (461) FF220,000

— Ms, Livre de Chasse. With Jean de Francieres. Livre de medecine d'oyseaulx. [France, 1480] 138 leaves, vellum, 313mm by 221mm, in 18th-cent red mor gilt. With 2 large & 81 small miniatures in the style of Jean Colombe or the Mamerot Master & 275 illuminated initials. Jeanson Ms 104 SM Mar 1 (462) FF2,600,000

— Ms, Livre de chasse. [France, 2d half of 15th cent] 125 leaves only, 268mm by 202mm, in blind-stamped mor in a medieval style. With 56 large decorated initials. Jeanson Ms 105 SM Mar 1 (463) FF95,000

Philip II, King of Spain, 1527-98
ALs, 17 Nov 1579. 2 pp, folio. To [King Henry of Portugal]. Suggesting that the position of the late Conde de Portalegre be given to Don M. de Silva. C June 24 (69) £850 [American Museum of Hist. Docs.]

Ls, 11 Aug 1557. 1 p, folio. To Ottavio Farnese, Duke of Parma. Informing him of the Spanish victory at Saint Quentin. Dispatch slits. S Nov 27 (447) £1,300 [Quaritch]

— 7 Oct 1557. 2 pp, folio. To Ottavio Farnese, Duke of Parma. About war with the Duke of Ferrara & his victory at St. Quentin. S May 21 (297) £420 [Maggs]

— 23 Jan 1568. 2 pp, folio. To Diego de Guzman de Silva. Instructing him to inform Queen Elizabeth of the imprisonment of his son Don Carlos. S Nov 27 (448) £1,850 [Haas]

Philip VI, King of France, 1293-1350
Document, 23 Mar 1346. 1 p, vellum, 275mm by 390mm. Grant to Marguerite, Countess of Flanders, & her son Louis of a daily rent of 50 livres tournois during their exile on account of the war with England. C June 24 (70) £350 [Joseph]

Philipp I, Landgraf von Hessen, 1504-67
Ls, 16 Apr 1559. 1 p, folio. To Kurfuerst August von Sachsen. Worrying about efforts to recruit soldiers for the Spanish service. star Apr 9 (1010) DM1,100

Ds, 8 Mar 1557. 4 pp, folio. Letter of protection. JG Oct 2 (448) DM700

Philipp II, King of Spain, 1527-98
Ls, 4 Jan 1585. 1 p, folio. To Don Diego de Orellana. Concerning redemption of a lease. star Apr 9 (1246) DM1,200

Piaf, Edith, 1915-63
Photograph, sgd & inscr, [n.d.]. 9.5 by 7 inches. Inscr to Diane Perron. wa May 30 (419) $270

Picasso, Pablo, 1881-1973
ALs, 13 Feb 1957. 1 p, 4to. To Andre. Sending a check. In red crayon, 2 lines underlined in blue. HN May 22 (3152) DM1,200

Piccolomini, Ottavio, 1599-1956
Ls, 15/5 June 1641. 1 p, folio. To the Princes of Anhalt. About negotiations with their envoy. star Apr 9 (1124) DM850
— FRANKFURT AM MAIN. - 2 Letters, sgd by B. von Hoeswick, 27 & 30 June 1648, 2 pp, folio, to Piccolomini. About rumors regarding Archduke Leopold's capture, & contents not stated. In French. star Apr 9 (1125) DM230

Pickering, Timothy, 1745-1829
[A collection of 22 items relating to his financial affairs, including 7 A Ls s by Pickering, sold at rf on 14 Mar, lot 47, for $425.]
ALs, 26 Sept 1782. 3 pp, 4to. To David Wolfe. Ordering him to procure horses for the Army in Massachusetts, paying with promissory notes. Herman Herst collection. rf Mar 14 (51) $210
— 17 Mar 1783. 2 pp, 4to. To David Wolfe. As Quartermaster Gen., concerning payment for a sergeant. Herman Herst collection. rf Mar 14 (53) $130
— 17 Apr 1784. 4 pp, 4to. To Peter Anspach. About arrangements for Washington's entry into Philadelphia. Herman Herst collection. rf Mar 14 (48) $210
— [29 Mar 1785]. 1 p, 4to. To David Wolfe. Contents not stated. With franking signature. rf Mar 14 (97) $260
— 18 Oct 1785. 1 p, 4to. To David Wolfe. Regarding the monument to Gen. Montgomery. Address leaf def. Herman Herst collection. rf Mar 14 (54) $220
— 6 June 1786. 2 pp, 4to. Recipient unknown. Regarding problems at an Episcopal academy. Trimmed. wa May 30 (62) $70
— 26 Feb 1788. 1 p, 4to. To David Wolfe. Stating that Mr. Hodgdon will take charge of official papers in order to settle accounts. Herman Herst collection. rf Mar 14 (52) $170
— 2 Apr 1794. 2 pp. 4to. To William Judd. About a court date regarding land claimed by Connecticut in northeastern Pennsylvania. Repaired. Herman Herst collection. rf Mar 14 (50) $65
— 11 Jan 1798. 1 p, 4to. To Richard Varick, Mayor of NY. As Sec of State, requesting information on a suit against a British commander regarding impressment of seamen. Herman Herst collection. rf Mar 14 (49) $130
— 27 June 1798. 2 pp, 4to. To Jacob Mayer. About problems with France & the division in Congress. wa May 30 (61) $350
See also: Adams, John

Pierce, Franklin, 1804-69
ALs, 7 Oct 1855. 2 pp, 4to. To the Rev. Henry A. Boardman. Thanking for a sermon & inviting him to the White House. P May 13 (115) $2,000
Ds, 1 Apr 1854. 1 p, c.9.75 by 15.75 inches. Grant of bounty land to William A. Pratt & Alfred N. Laurence. S Jan 27 (935) £180 [Faupel]
— 15 July 1854. 1 p, folio. Land grant. pnNY June 11 (41) $100
— 13 Oct 1855. 1 p, folio. Commission for Leonard Paulding as naval Lieut. With Ds, 1 May 1866, by Andrew Johnson; anr naval commission for Paulding. Both framed. P Oct 29 (115) $550
— 12 Feb 1856. 1 p, folio. Commission; partly ptd. Countersgd by Sec of the Navy J. D. Dobbin. wa Oct 18 (37) $160
— ptd ship's papers in 4 languages, not accomplished. 1 p, folio. Also sgd by Sec of State Marcy. Framed. Altman collection. pnNY Sept 13 (18) $500
— [n.d.]. 1 p, folio. Ship's papers in 4 languages; unaccomplished. Countersgd by William L. Marcy. Split in half. wa May 30 (297) $210

Franking signature, [3 Feb 1843]. rf May 30 (24) $400
— Anr, [1859]. With autograph address. rf Mar 14 (98) $190
— Anr, [15 Nov 1860]. rf Mar 14 (99) $190

Pinckney, Charles Cotesworth, 1746-1825. See: Heyward, Thomas & Others

Pinter, Harold
Autograph Ms, notebook containing stage directions etc. for a production of The Homecoming, [c.Sept 1965]. 33 pp, 12mo. Black cloth. With a program of the Berlin production, 11 Oct 1965. C June 24 (125) £550 [Maggs]

Piozzi, Gabriele. See: Piozzi, Hester Lynch Thrale & Piozzi

Piozzi, Hester Lynch Thrale, 1741-1821 —& Piozzi, Gabriele
Ds, 1 Apr 1786. 3 pp, folio. Power of attorney to John Cator, Jeremiah Crutchley & Henry Smith to sell property of her late husband Henry Thrale. With a letter by Messrs Barclay & Perkins, 12 Sept 1797, relating to the sale. S July 23 (24) £4,200 [Quaritch]

Pisani, Luigi, Doge of Venice, 1663-1741
Document, 1737. 1 p, folio. Vellum. Contents not stated. Lead seal. star Apr 9 (1273) DM320

Pissarro, Camille —& Pissarro, Lucien
ALs, 22 May 1890. 4 pp, 8vo. To Julie Pissarro. Describing their impressions of England. S Jan 27 (982) £140 [Blumberg]

Pissarro, Camille, 1830-1903
ALs, 9 May 1887. 3 pp, 8vo. To "Mon cher Heymann". Pleading for a cash advance. With ANs sgd Lucien Pissarro, 1911, acknowledging receipt of a medal & a diploma from delegates for the Barcelona International Exhibition. P Sept 24 (37) $1,300

— 28 May 1894. 1 p, 8vo. To Monsieur Lecomte. Inviting him. Framed. Altman collection. pnNY Sept 13 (90) $325

— 29 Dec 1902. 1 p, 8vo. To "Mon cher Rodo". Saying his mother is leaving & he has sent him money. Framed. Altman collection. pnNY Sept 13 (91) $1,300

ADs, 15 June 1892. 1 p, folio. Power of attorney for his wife Julie during his absence. S Jan 27 (983) £220 [Maggs]

Pissarro, Lucien. See: Pissarro, Camille & Pissarro

Pius IX, Pope, 1792-1878
ALs, 4 Jan 1831. 2 pp, folio. To Monsignore Uditore. About church matters. sg Nov 6 (170) $250

Pius V, Pope, 1504-72
Document, [30 Oct 1571]. 1 p, 505mm by 668mm. Vellum. Papal Bull "Unigeniti Dei" concerning the propagation of Christianity in Latin America. Orig copy sent to New Grenada. S June 23 (36) £3,500 [Brinton]

Pius VI, Pope, 1717-99
Document, 12 Sept 1797. 1 p, folio. Vellum. License for ordination as priest for Michael Angelus Pacelli. Holed. star Apr 9 (1117) DM420

Pius VII, Pope
Document, 31 Jan 1823. 1 p, folio. Vellum. Letter of indulgence. Countersgd by Cardinal Consalvi. star Apr 9 (1118) DM460

Pius XI, Pope, 1857-1939
Ls, 27 July 1926. 4 pp, folio. To Cardinal Lualdi. Appointing him legate. In Latin. star Apr 9 (1120) DM1,150

Pius XII, Pope, 1876-1958
Photograph, sgd, 11 June 1943; folio. Sgd under a request by a Hungarian lady for his blessing. star Apr 9 (1122) DM900

Planck, Max, 1858-1947
ALs, 21 Nov 1909. 2 pp, 8vo (lettercard). To Pastor Priebe. Thanking for his attempt to visit him & saying he would like to talk to him. star Apr 8 (406) DM1,100

— 11 Jan 1942. 2 pp, 4to. To Pastor Priebe. Recommending a lady for admission to a charitable foundation & talking about his family's situation. star Apr 8 (409) DM2,100

Plymouth Colony
Ds, 18 Dec 1689. 1 p, 310mm by 195mm. Deed for tract of land on the Narnassakett River. Sgd by Thomas Cushman, William Bradford, & John & Ro. Cotton. Somewhat def. sg Nov 6 (171) $350

Pocci, Franz, Graf von, 1807-76
ALs, 6 Nov 1859. 1 p, 8vo. To "Lieber Caspar". Sending tickets for a performance. star Apr 8 (526) DM300

Pole, Sir William, 1561-1635
Transcript, Survey of Devon, [c.1725]. 119 leaves, folio. Panelled calf. bba Nov 13 (164) £120 [Bennett]

Polk, James K., 1795-1849
ALs, 30 Apr 1841. 1 p, folio. To John W. Ford. Postponing a political meeting at Woodbury. P May 13 (116) $2,000

— 25 Apr 1845. 1 p, 4to. To Hon. Secretary Mason. Hoping he will help in the case of Mr. Robertson. Framed. Altman collection. pnNY Sept 13 (19) $1,400

Ds, 11 Mar 1841. 1 p, 4to. As Gov. of Tennessee, appointment for a Justice of the Peace. wa May 30 (298) $650

— 1 Nov 1845. 1 p, 13.25 by 15.75 inches. Recognizing Robert Grigg as British Consul for Alabama & Florida. Partly ptd. S Dec 18 (348) £420 [Wilson]

— 24 Mar 1847. 1 p, 17 by 14 inches. Commission for George H. Crosman as Major & Quartermaster. Countersgd by Sec of War Marcy. S Jan 27 (936) £360 [Wilson]

— 25 Nov 1848. 1 p, folio. Certificate of Merit for Private Daniel Mahoney; partly ptd. Countersgd by Sec of War Marcy. P Oct 29 (107) $1,100

Polk, James K., 1795-1849 —& Buchanan, James, 1791-1868
Ds, fragment; [n.d.], size not given. Sgd by Polk as President & Buchanan as Sec of State. With engraved port of each, 4.25 by 3.5 inches. wa Oct 18 (38) $230

Pompadour, Jeanne Antoinette, Marquise de, 1721-64

[A collection of documents, c.10 items, 1709 to 1747, relating to the affairs of Madame de Pompadour & her family, sold at S on 27 Nov, lot 451, for £240 to Dr. Sam.]

Ls, 11 Mar [n.y.]. 1 p, 8vo. Recipient unnamed. About the marriage of the Duc de Gramont. sg Apr 9 (154) $800

Ponchielli, Amilcare, 1834-86

Series of 8 A Ls s, 1874 to 1885. 29 pp, 8vo. To Antonio Ghislanzoni. Regarding libretti & other musical matters. S May 22 (480) £1,800 [MacNutt]

Ponten, Josef, 1883-1940

Collection of 6 A Ls s, 3 Ls s & 18 postcards, sgd (7 autograph), 25 Feb 1919 to 24 Aug 1937. Length not stated, 4to & 8vo. To the pbr Adolf Spemann. Discussing the relationship between author & pbr, Thomas Mann, other writers, & his own work. With related material. HN May 22 (3157) DM600

Pontifical

Ms, in Latin, [Brescia, 3d quarter of 15th cent]. 250 leaves (3 blanks), vellum, 320mm by 235mm. Lacking 1 leaf. Late 18th cent dark blue mor gilt bdg. In black & red ink in semi-rounded gothic liturgical hand. Many pp with music on a 4-line red stave. With illuminated initials throughout, 75 large illuminated initials & 36 historiated initials with illuminated borders. S Dec 2 (47) £58,000 [Johnson]

— **Ms,** in Latin, [Western France, c.1530]. 114 leaves & 2 flyleaves, vellum, 182mm by 124mm. Early 19th cent blue mor gilt bdg. In black ink in a fine roman hand in imitation of ptd type. With c.820 illuminated initials in green or blue on liquid gold panels & 3 large miniatures in full colors & gold with full borders formed of ropework designs. Probably illuminated for Yves de Mayeuc, Bishop of Rennes. S Dec 2 (48) £10,500 [Bibliotheque Municipale]

Pope, Alexander, 1688-1744

ALs, 14 Oct [1742]. 2 pp, 4to. To the Countess of Orrery. About a pair of guinea fowl Mr. & Mrs. Allen could send her. S Dec 18 (26) £1,400 [Quaritch]

Porter, Cole, 1893-1964

Playbill, [1940]. Program for New York performance of Panama Hattie. Sgd by Porter & Otis Bigelow's name added. Mtd. sg Nov 6 (172) $175

Porter, David, 1780-1843

ADs, 17 Apr 1821. 1 p, 4to. Promissory note for $1,000 to John Rodgers. Endorsed by Rodgers on verso. wa May 30 (66) $110
See also: Hamilton, Paul

Porter, David Dixon, 1813-91

Ds, 16 Nov 1876. 2 pp, folio. Recommending Dr. William Grier for the position as Chief of the Bureau of Medicine & Surgery. Also sgd by 3 other admirals. wa May 30 (249) $50

Porter, Endymion, 1587-1649

ALs, [n.d.]; 1 p, folio. To his "dear wife Olife Porter". Expressing his wish to be with her. Repaired. In cloth case. Alfred Morrison collection. S Dec 18 (7) £300 [Maggs]

Porter, Gene Stratton, 1868-1924

Ls, 30 Mar 1921. 2 pp, 4to. Recipient unnamed. About a catalpa tree, birds, lice, & the natural order of things. wa May 30 (420) $100

Portugal

Document, grant of trading privileges by Sebastian, King of Portugal to Jan van Pelcken. [Lisbon, 8 Dec 1570]. 19 leaves, 255mm by 190mm, vellum,255mm by 190mm, in mor gilt with silver bosses & with applied central plaques with van Pelcken arms in niello & silver. S Oct 23 (266) £4,800 [Israel]

Postal Service

— CLIFFORD, THOMAS, 1ST BARON CLIFFORD OF CHUDLEIGH. - 2 autograph Mss, memorandum on "The state of [the] post office as now managed", & notes on proposals & changes; with accounts & calculations of Post office profits, [1660s to 1673]. Together 4 documents, 7 pp, folio. S July 24 (254) £3,600 [Jackson]

Potier de Morais

Ms, Dom Castagne, chasseur errant, comedie. [early 18th cent] About 150 pp, 260mm by 183mm, in contemp mor gilt. Jeanson Ms 143 SM Mar 1 (471) FF3,500

Potter, Beatrix, 1866-1943

Original drawing, Mrs. Rabbit buttoning Peter's coat, [c.1901-1905]. Watercolor on silk, c.156mm by 161mm. Matted. After illustration in The Tale of Peter Rabbit. With authentication by Justin Schiller. P June 18 (155) $11,500

— Original drawing, Mrs. Rabbit with basket & umbrella, [c.1901-1905]. Watercolor on silk, c.156mm by 161mm. Matted. After illustration in The Tale of Peter Rabbit. With authentication by Justin Schiller. P June 18 (156) $11,500

— Original drawing, Old Mr. Benjamin Bunny walking, smoking a pipe, [c.1901-1905]. Watercolor on silk, c.156mm by 161mm. Matted. After illustration in The Tale of Benjamin Bunny. With authentication by Justin Schiller. P June 18 (158) $7,000
— Original drawing, Peter Rabbit in the garden, dropping onions, [c.1901-1905]. Watercolor on silk, c.156mm by 161mm. Matted. After illustration in The Tale of Benjamin Bunny. With authentication by Justin Schiller. P June 18 (157) $7,000
ALs, 2 Oct 1940. 1 p, 4to; torn from larger sheet. To Mr. Macdonald. About his renting her cottage. Sgd H. B. Heelis. C Dec 3 (375) £220 [MacNutt]
— 26 June 1942. 1 p, 8vo. To Mrs. Macdonald. Concerning a tenant's leaking roof & a visit to Low Yewdale. Sgd Beatrix Heelis. Tipped into a copy of Margaret Lane's The Tale of Beatrix Potter. 1946. 1st Ed. C June 24 (126) £210 [Joseph]

Pougny, Jean, 1892-1956
Autograph Ms, article about the theory of art, [1925]. 2 pp, 4to. In Russian. Trans by R. von Walter ptd in Paul Westheim, Ed., Kuenstlerbekenntnisse. Berlin, 1925, 345. star Apr 8 (527) DM3,500

Poulenc, Francis, 1899-1963
ALs, 15 May 1919. 1 p, folio. Recipient unnamed. Regarding invitations for the Apollinaire evening. S May 22 (629) £350 [Shapiro]
— 12 Jan 1932. 6 pp, 4to. To Nora Auric. About music & artists in Paris & his Concerto for 2 Pianos & Orchestra. Sgd Fr. S May 22 (482) £900 [Boys]
— [23 Jan 1933]. 8 pp, folio. To Nora Auric. About the success of his Bal masque & other matters. Sgd Fr. S May 22 (483) £700 [Boys]
— [1936]. 4 pp, 4to. To Nora Auric. Talking about his Litanies a la vierge noire. Sgd Fr. S May 22 (485) £450 [Boys]
— [17 Aug 1937]. 2 pp, 4to. To Nora Auric. Reporting that he now has a complete draft of his Mass. S May 22 (484) £350 [Boys]
— 1 Jan [1941]. 2 pp, 8vo. To Nora Auric. Complaining about the military occupation & offering condolences on the death of her mother. Sgd Fr. S Nov 28 (604) £550 [Harris]
— [1943]. 4 pp, 4to. To Georges Auric. Commenting on Honegger & Diaghilev, & reporting about a proposed Schumann-Poulenc festival. Sgd Fr. With a notebook by Auric. S Nov 28 (605) £900 [Harris]
— ["Dimanche", 1949 or 1950]. 4 pp, 4to. To Nora Auric. Praising Toscanini & reporting about the reception of Georges Auric's work in Italy. Sgd Francis. S May 22 (486) £800 [Boys]
— [n.d. "samedi saint"]. 4 pp, 8vo. To Nora Auric. Reporting about concerts with Pierre Bernac, his change of pbr, meetings with friends. S Nov 28 (606) £550 [Harris]
Concert program, [n.d.]. 1 p, folio. Typed; sgd & inscr with autograph musical quotation, 2 bars from his Mouvement perpetuel. In pencil. Also sgd by Pierre Bernac. S May 22 (630) £350 [Shapiro]

Pound, Ezra, 1885-1972
[An important collection of c.100 A Ls s & Ls s, 3 Jan 1935 to 30 July 1946, by Pound to John Hargrave, with annotated typescript of Pound's Rome broadcast of Jan 1935, & further related material, sold at S on 23 July, lot 173, for £18,000 to Maggs.]
Typescript, Song for the Plain Men of England, 43 lines with autograph insertions. With 2 Ls to Stanley Dixon, commenting on the song; with autograph insertions. 24 Jan to 6 Mar 1935; 4 pp, folio. S Dec 18 (175) £400 [Rota]
Ls, 8 Dec [c.1928]. 1 p, 4to. To Bernard Ragner of the Chicago Tribune. Commenting about recent articles. Some autograph annotations. Initialled. S Jan 27 (738) £120 [Zayas]
— [received 10 May 1933]. 3 pp, 4to. To D[ouglas] H[owell]. Grumbling about American publishers & suggesting a Ms should go to Farrar. Encapsulated. sg Apr 9 (155) $350

Powys, Llewelyn, 1884-1939
Autograph Ms, notebook containing 1st drafts of Omar Khayyam & Lodmoor, [n.d.]. 56 pp, 4to. Bds. Heavily revised. C June 24 (127) £450 [Bush]
Collection of 8 A Ls s, 1 autograph postcard, initialled, & bank check, endorsed. 21 Sept 1923 to 20 Mar 1928. 10 pp, various sizes. To Ada McVickar. Routine & literary matters. With related material. sg Nov 6 (173) $400

Prayer Books
Ms, Ausserloesener Kern Andaechtiger Gebetter..., [Germany, c.1730]. 752 leaves, vellum, 190mm by 135mm. In 4 vols; contemp black lea gilt. With 4 calligraphic title-pages, 24 full-page pen-&-ink illusts with colors, c.100 vignettes & numerous initials. HK Nov 4 (416) DM7,000
— Ms, collection of prayers in Latin. [France, 13th cent]. 14 leaves (1 blank), vellum 150mm by 110mm. In black ink in various scripts. Part of a vol possibly compiled by a divinity student in Paris, early 14th cent. HK Nov 4 (415) DM1,000
— Ms, in German, [Augsburg?, early 16th

PRAYER BOOKS

cent]. 175 leaves & 3 blanks, vellum, 135mm by 104mm. Lacking 2 leaves. Late 18th cent black mor gilt bdg. In very handsome calligraphic gothic script with elaborate flourished cadels in margins. With 40 illuminated initials in colors & liquid gold & 71 large historiated initials with elaborate borders in a variety of designs. Script close to the work of Leonhard Wagner; miniatures possibly by Leonhard Beck. S Dec 2 (52) £75,000 [Axel]

— Ms, in German, [Nuremberg?, c.1500]. 363 leaves (2 blank), vellum, 100mm by 75mm. 19th cent black pigskin over wooden bds. In brown ink in a rounded lettre batarde. With 5 large illuminated initials & 28 full-page miniatures within golden borders. Lacking at least 2 leaves. C June 24 (263) £28,000 [Tenschert]

— Ms, in Latin & German. [Southwestern Germany, 14th cent]. 127 leaves, vellum, 100mm by 70mm. 16th cent lea over wooden bds, worn; lacking clasps. In black ink in more than 1 gothic hand. With red & blue initials. Some leaves torn. HK Nov 4 (414) DM1,800

— Ms, in Latin, [Hungary, c.1425]. 299 leaves, vellum, 140mm by 103mm; lacking 1 leaf. Modern purple velvet over old thin wooden bds, def. In black ink in a small calligraphic gothic hand. With decorated initials throughout in red, blue or burnished gold, 19 large illuminated initials with partial borders & 19 very large historiated initials, probably by the Master of Koermoecbanya. Prayer added on f.108v in early 16th cent hand. S Dec 2 (45) £80,000 [Kraus]

— Ms, Kern aller Gebetter, [Germany, 1793]. 236 pp, 170mm by 105mm. Contemp red mor. Written for Martha Metternich in a fine calligraphic hand. With initials, floral vignettes & ornamental headings. HK Nov 4 (418) DM750

— Ms, Meess-Buech, Geistliches... mit andaechtig u. anmethigen Gebettern..., [Germany, 1757]. 497 pp, & blanks, 150mm by 100mm. Contemp dark brown lea; with silver clasp. In dark brown ink by Catharina Asam. With 12 engravings of saints, mostly by J. Oefele, pasted in. HK Nov 4 (419) DM800

— Ms, Pater Noster & other devotional offices, in Latin & French. [Tournai, c.1475-90]. 71 leaves & 2 flyleaves, vellum, 177mm by 117mm. Lacking 5 leaves. 19th cent red mor gilt bdg. In dark brown ink in a gothic liturgical hand. With small initials throughout in burnished gold on red & blue grounds with white tracery & 37 large miniatures within full borders of colored leaves & flowers, partly on liquid gold

AMERICAN BOOK PRICES CURRENT

grounds. S Dec 2 (55) £22,000 [Schoyen]

— Ms, Prayer Book in Latin, with some rubrics in German. [Nuremberg, c.1460-90]. 294 leaves, vellum, 108mm by 80mm, in 16th-cent blindstamped pigskin with clasps & catches. From the Dominican nunnery of St. Katherine in Nuremberg. S June 23 (98) £2,000 [Thomas]

— Ms, prayers apparently written for a soldier to supplement a Book of Hours. [Southern France, probably Provence, early 16th cent] 156 leaves, vellum, 205mm by 145mm, in 16th-cent mor gilt with oval plaques of the Crucifixion & of the Annunciation. Illuminated initials throughout in colors & gold. sg Dec 4 (163) $3,400

— Ms, Prayers in Dutch. [Flanders, late 15th cent]. 81 leaves, 120mm by 80mm. Vellum. Modern bds covered with ptd 16th cent missal leaf. In dark brown ink in gothic bookhand. With 3 painted calendar leaves, 4 pp of floral designs with ornamental & foliate borders, & 2 miniatures, 1 by a different artist. VH Sept 12 (912) DM6,800

Prendergast, Maurice, 1859-1924

ALs, [29 Mar 1916]. 2 pp, 4to. To Horace Traubel. Saying he wants to paint him again. Charles E. Feinberg collection. P Dec 15 (100) $200

Presidents of the United States

[A collection of 32 Presidential signatures, from John Adams to Eisenhower, mostly clippings, each mtd with an engraved port preceding the autograph, in 4to gilt-stamped lea album, sold at sg on 9 Apr, lot 157, for $5,500.]

[A group of 6 signatures on cards by William H. Taft, Calvin & Grace Coolidge, & Herbert & Lou Henry Hoover sold at sg on 9 Apr 1987, lot 156, for $325.]

Collection of 30 Presidential signatures, from Washington to Hoover. Comprising Als, Ls s, Ds s, etc. In gilt wine mor bdg with a port of each President preceding his autograph. P Oct 29 (108) $21,000

Group photograph, 8 Oct 1981; 4to. Ronald Reagan, Gerald Ford, Jimmy Carter & Richard Nixon; in the White House before Sadat's funeral. Sgd by all 4. P Dec 15 (75) $5,250.

Price, Vincent

ALs, [n.d.]. 1 p, 4to. To Kimmis Hendrick. Commenting on an article. With presentation copy of his I Like What I Know. Garden City, 1959. 8vo. 1st Ed, sgd on endpaper. wa May 30 (191) $80

Pridden, John, 1758-1825

[An album, 4to, containing Ms, "Collections for the History of St. Paul's Cathedral, London", ptd notes & engravings, as well as autograph drafts of letters to his Bishop, sold at bba on 13 Nov 1986, lot 165, for £240 to Maggs.]

Priestley, John Boynton

Typescript, article, "Are Authors Human Beings?" Corrected, with printer's proofs; 1931. 18 pp, folio. Bds. S Jan 27 (739) £190 [Ferret]

Pritchett, Victor Sawdon

[A collection of 2 autograph Mss & 5 typescripts, revised, with revisions of review articles, c.1973 to 1974, c.60 pp, 4to, sold at S on 23 July 1987, lot 171, for £300 to Apelbaum.]

Processional

— [Louvain, 1525]. 200 numbered & 17 unnumbered leaves, vellum (1 paper), 172mm by 124mm. 18th cent calf over wooden bds, richly gilt. Written by Franciscus Weert for the Premonstratensian monastery at Parc. In calligraphic textura with music on a 4-line red stave. With red & blue initials throughout, 11 large illuminated initials, 7 double-page illuminated borders, & miniature of donor (Servatius audiaens). FD June 11 (9) DM52,000

— [Southern France, c.1602]. Of Augustinian Use. 129 leaves, vellum, 100mm by 74mm, in old brown velvet over pastebds, rebacked. In brown ink in several suites of roman hands. With music throughout on a 4-line red stave, decorated & illuminated initials & 3 illuminated title pages. S June 23 (102) £300 [Marcus]

Prokofiev, Sergei Sergeevich, 1891-1953

ALs, 16 Mar 1930. 1 p, 4to. To Ivan Wischnegradsky. Inquiring about a cheque. In Russian. S Nov 28 (608) £500 [Harris]

— 2 Feb 1938. 2 pp, on headed postcard of the S.S. Normandie. Recipient unnamed. Describing life on board. In Russian. With French trans. S May 22 (631) £600 [MacNutt]

Proudhon, Pierre-Joseph, 1809-65

ALs, 4 Mar [Apr] 1862. 2 pp, 8vo. To P. Ch. A. Rolland. Sending part of his La propriete litteraire & commenting about French politics. Repaired. star Apr 9 (1185) DM850

Proust, Marcel, 1871-1922

ALs, [1907]. 2 pp, 8vo. To Marquis Illan de Casa-Fuerte. Comparing him to a Titian port. S May 21 (299) £580 [Maggs]

— [Feb 1915 or 1916]. 12 pp, 8vo & folio. To [Mme Anatole Catusse]. Regarding advice for his income tax declaration, his health, the War, & family news. C June 24 (151) £1,500 [Bush]

— [29 May 1918]. 8 pp, 8vo. To Marie Scheikevitch. Personal letter, saying his health will not allow him to see her & the Princess Soutzo, & describing his quarrel with the publishing firm of Calmann Levy. star Apr 8 (222) DM4,000

Proverbs

Ms, collection of c.670 proverbs & classical quotations, in English, Latin & Greek, mostly derived from Erasmus' Adagia; & fragmentary Socratic dialogue, [early 17th cent]. 37 leaves, 185mm by 145mm. 19th cent cloth bdg. Lacking some leaves. With notes by Spencer Savage proposing an identification with a lost work of Sir Francis Bacon. C June 24 (128) £1,900 [Maggs]

Prussia

[A collection of 13 files relating to military trials at Berlin & Potsdam, 1846 to 1860, sold at star on 9 Apr, lot 1184, for DM320.]

Psalm & Psalters

Ms, in Latin with a few additions in German, Psalter, with Canticles, Litany, Hours of the Virgin, & Office of the Dead. [Cologne or Trier, c.1200-1220]. 151 leaves, vellum, 192mm by 128mm. 19th-cent russia over old wooden bds, rebacked. In brown ink in an early gothic hand. With c.160 illuminated initials, full-page Beatus initial & fully illuminated facing page, 12 illuminated calendar pages in gold or silver & 3 full-page miniatures. Many early additions to the text. Ownership inscr of the Abbey of St. Matthias, Trier. S June 23 (76) £40,000 [Guyot]

Psalms & Psalters

Ms, in Amharic, Psalter. [Ethiopia, 17th/18th cent]. 202 leaves, 118mm by 88mm, in goatskin over wooden bds, blindstamped. In red & black ink. FD June 11 (23) DM1,200

— Ms, in Coptic, Psalter. [Upper Egypt, 9th cent]. 2 conjoint leaves only, vellum, 217mm by 240mm. In dark brown ink in Coptic uncial script. With 3 large painted initials in leafy designs infilled with green & red. Recovered from a bdg. S June 23 (130) £3,200 [Quaritch]

— Ms, in Latin, Psalter. [Cologne, 15th cent]

PSALMS & PSALTERS

217 leaves, vellum, 17cm by 12.5cm, in 16th cent brown lea over wooden bds. With Calendar, Litany & Hymns. Decorated initials in blue & red; some larger initials. Some musical notations in margins on 4-line staves. Last 14 leaves paper with 17th cent addenda. Margins cropped with some text loss. HN Nov 27 (2195) DM1,800

— Ms, in Latin, Psalter. [Eastern France or Rhineland, late 13th cent]. 1 leaf only, vellum, 177mm by 134mm. Parts of Psalms 78 & 79. In large gothic hand in brown ink. With large historiated initial in orange & green on highly burnished gold & decorative line-fillers. S Dec 2 (8) £1,000 [Maggs]

— Ms, in Latin, Psalter, with Canticles. [Lower Rhineland or Liege, 3d quarter of 12th cent]. 106 leaves only, vellum, 202mm by 142mm. Wooden bds covered with tawed lea, somewhat def. In brown ink in late romanesque bookhand. With full-page frontis, illuminated initials at beginning of every psalm & 9 very large illuminated initals. S Dec 2 (33) £30,000 [Pairvel]

— Ms, in Latin, Psalter, with Prayers, Canticles & Litany. [Central or Southwest Italy, late 12th cent]. 152 leaves only, vellum, 155 mm by 105mm. In paper wraps, detached. In dark brown ink in a small round late romanesque minuscule. With c.250 large painted initials & 2 illuminated initials. 2 initials cut out. S June 23 (75) £3,800 [Maggs]

— Ms, in Latin with a few rubrics in Dutch, Ferial Psalter. [Netherlands, 2d half of 15th cent]. 274 leaves, vellum, 107mm by 73mm. 18th-cent half red lea & marbled paper bds. In dark brown ink in a small gothic hand. With 12 very large illuminated initials with illuminated borders. S June 23 (99) £3,500 [Schoyen]

— Ms, in Latin with additions in French, Psalter & Prayerbook. [North Germany, Hildesheim?, c.1524]. 183 leaves, vellum, 164mm by 130mm. Modern blindstamped diced calf by Gruel. In brown ink in an angular calligraphic lettre batarde with gothic features. With 25 very large illuminated initials, full illuminated borders throughout in elaborate designs including over 100 miniatures, 12 historiated initials & 28 miniatures. S June 23 (100) £60,000 [Pairvel]

— Ms, Psalter, with Canticles, Song of Solomon, hyms in praise of the Virgin & prayer for the scribe or patron, Absalom, [Ethiopia, 19th cent]. 134 leaves, vellum, 236mm by 172mm. Contemp brown calf over wooden bds. In black ink in a regular square hand; headings in red. S Dec 2 (73) £300 [Thomas]

AMERICAN BOOK PRICES CURRENT

— Ms, Psalter, with prayers of the Prophets, Song of Songs & prayers to the Virgin, [Ethiopia, early 20th cent]. 113 leaves, vellum, 138mm by 105mm. Contemp blimdstamped brown calf over bds; spine def. In black ink in a regular square hand; headings in red. Decorated headpieces; post-war miniature of Virgin & Child added. S Dec 2 (74) £130 [Thomas]

Puccini, Giacomo, 1858-1924
Series of 3 A Ls s, 1923. 3 pp, 4to & 8vo. To Alessandro Varaldo. Recommendations for posts in the Society of Authors, & information about Maestro Vandini. S Nov 28 (614) £480 [Wurlitzer-Bruck]

A Ls s (2), 21 May [19]10 & 16 Mar [1]915. 2 pp, 8vo. To Alfredo Colombo & Antonio Bettolacci. About the success of Madama Butterfly in London & motor-cars. S May 22 (492) £400 [L. I. M.]

ALs, 22 July 1884. 2 pp, 8vo. To "Monsieur Herlik" [Alfred Ehrlich?]. Asking for a copy of his article about Puccini's opera Le Villi. In French. star Apr 9 (771) DM1,100

— 11 Aug 1884. 4 pp, 8vo. To Tornaghi. Requesting anr advance on his opera Edgar because of debts related to his mother's death. S May 22 (632) £380 [MacNutt]

— 19 Mar 1897. 3 pp, size not stated. To Signor Conte. About his interest in La Boheme & saying he will give the letter to Signor Ricordi. Framed. Altman collection. pnNY Sept 13 (173) $950

— 15 June 1898. 1 p, 8vo. To Monsieur Arene. Thanking for an article about La Boheme. In French. Framed. Altman collection. pnNY Sept 13 (174) $1,100

— [20 Feb 1902]. 3 pp, 4to. To Elvira Gemignani. Chatting about his day; with postscript. star Apr 9 (773) DM1,000

— 25 May 1905. 1 p, 4to. To [Eduardo] Vitale. About negotiations concerning Madame Butterfly. Framed with autograph envelope. Altman collection. pnNY Sept 13 (175) $1,200

— 13 Sept [1]905. 1 p, 8vo. To some unnamed ladies. About the success of Madama Butterfly in London. Framed with a postcard photograph. S Nov 28 (610) £280 [Maggs]

— 31 Jan [19]09. 4 pp, 8vo. Concerning the suicide of Doria Manfredi & the consequences for his wife & himself. On hotel letterhead. S Nov 28 (611) £1,800 [Kent]

— [n.d.]. 1 p, 8vo. To Antonio Bettolacci. About refurbishing his boat. S May 22 (497) £300 [L. I. M.]

— 1912. 1 p, 16mo. To Alexandra Signorini. Asking for an address. S Jan 27 (1059) £140 [MacNutt]

— [7 Apr 1914?]. 1 p, folio. To Carlo Gragnani.

Announcing 2 visitors from Lucca. star Apr 9 (774) DM520

— 12 Nov [1]914. 1 p, 8vo. To Alfredo Colombo. About the war. S May 22 (494) £350 [Sakmyster]

— 20 Feb [19]24. 2 pp, 4to. To Alessandro Varaldo. Regarding the behavior of his friend Vandini. S Nov 28 (615) £220 [Barnes]

Autograph postcard, sgd, 6 June [18]94. To Giovanni Verga. About the progress of his operatic setting of Verga's La lupa. With 2 postcards, sgd, 1901 & [n.d.]; one to Caruso, the other with a scene from Tosca on recto. S May 22 (488) £500 [MacNutt]

— 3 Mar [19]10. To G. Albinati. Referring to Boito. In pencil. With related material. S May 22 (491) £300 [McCann]

Autograph quotation, 2 bars from Un bel di, from Madama Butterfly, 30 Oct 1907. 1 p, folio. Sgd & inscr to Signor Sauerwein. S Nov 28 (612) £1,050 [Billington]

Photograph, sgd, [c.1900]. Postcard size. star Apr 9 (772) DM1,150

Photograph, sgd & inscr, 6 Mar [18]99. Overall size 28.5cm by 18cm. Inscr Al circolo universitario Bolognese "La Boheme". Mtd. S May 22 (490) £800 [MacNutt]

— Anr, 14 May [19]05. 190mm by 100mm. Full length; by Adolfo Ermini. FD Dec 2 (3252) DM1,100

— Anr, May [1]905; c.16cm by 10.5cm. Inscr to Mme Ferdinand Kohn. S Nov 28 (609) £720 [Wurlitzer-Bruck]

— Anr, 1913; c.14cm by 9cm. Inscr with musical quotation from La Boheme. S May 22 (495) £750 [Maggs]

— Anr, Oct 1920. 22.4cm by 16.8cm. Full length, sitting. Inscr to Franz Schalk. Photograph by Atelier Foka, Vienna. star Apr 9 (775) DM4,500

Ptd photograph, 10 June 1912. 24cm by 19cm. Sgd & inscr to Luigi Brignani. Framed. Altman collection. pnNY Sept 13 (176) $400

Pueckler-Muskau, Hermann, Fuerst von, 1785-1871

ALs, [n.d.]. 2 pp, 8vo. Recipient unnamed. About joining Fraeulein von Mengersen & the Grand Duchess for a ride. 2d leaf mtd. star Apr 8 (223) DM260

Pulgar, Fernando del

Ms, Cronica de los Reyes catholicos d. Fernando y D. Isabel, [1534-51]. 353 leaves (1 blank), & 3 flyleaves. 18th cent lea bdg. Margins wormed. FD June 11 (15) DM3,200

Purvis, Melvin H.

[An important archive of 50 A Ls s & 5 Ls s from Purvis to his wife Rosanne, 24 May 1927 to 28 Aug 1944, with many related items, documents, etc., was sold at sg on 6 Nov 1986, lot 174, for $2,200.]

Putnam, Israel, 1718-90

Ls, 12 Jan 1779. 2 pp, 4to. To George Clinton. Requesting flour for his troops. S July 24 (405) £380 [Block]

Pyle, Howard, 1853-1911

ALs, 9 Dec 1881. 1 p, 8vo. To Miss Sartain. Sending an illustration. Additional holograph notes at top of p & on integral leaf. wa Oct 18 (39) $110

Q

Quaritch, Bernard

Series of 13 A Ls s, 13 Sept 1883 to 4 Dec 1884. 18 pp, 4to. To George C. Haite. About the publication of Haite's Plant Studies for Artists. S Jan 27 (804) £85 [Rota]

Quiller-Couch, Sir Arthur, 1863-1944

Collection of 28 A Ls s & 5 Ls s, 4 May 1900 to 24 July 1939. 66 pp, 8vo & 4to. To Sir Henry Newbolt & Lady Newbolt (1). Lively letters mostly about literary matters. With draft reply from Henry Newbolt to Quiller-Couch, 3 Nov 1907, 2 pp, 4to. C Dec 3 (376) £380 [Joseph]

Series of c.50 A Ls s, 1919 to 1944, c.100 pp, 4to & 8vo. To members of the staff of J. M. Dent & Sons. About publishing projects. With c.60 file copies of letters from Dent's to Quiller-Couch & further rlated material. S July 23 (174) £400 [Joseph & Sawyer]

Quincy, Henry, 1726-80

ALs, 13 Apr 1775. 1 p, 4to. To his son-in-law Dr. Nathaniel Greene. Family news, & reporting that his sister Dolly is expected to have married John Hancock. P May 13 (122) $1,000

R

Raabe, Wilhelm, 1831-1910

ALs, 3 Apr 1883. 1 p, 8vo. To his pbr Westermann. Expressing the hope that his story Villa Schoenow may be a popular success. HK Nov 7 (2330) DM550

— 4 Jan 1893. 2 pp, 8vo. To Georg Boetticher. Declining to read from his works. star Apr 8 (224) DM700

RACHMANINOFF

Rachmaninoff, Sergei, 1873-1943
Series of 4 Ls s, July & Aug 1939, & 22 Apr 1940. Length & size not stated. To Ivan Wischnegradsky & his wife. Concerning financial assistance for recipient, making appointments, etc. S May 22 (499) £400 [Lionheart]
Photograph, sgd, [n.d.]; c.26cm by 21cm. Framed. S May 22 (498) £650 [MacNutt]
Photograph, sgd & inscr, 28 Oct [19]18; c.14cm by 9cm. Inscr to Dr. Andersen, in German. Creased; was mtd. S Nov 28 (617) £600 [Pulido]
— Anr, 4 Nov 1929. Framed, overall size 38cm by 28.5cm. Inscr to Frank Usher, in English. S Nov 28 (618) £480 [Reuter]

Racine, Jean Baptiste, 1639-99
ALs, 16 Aug [1685]. 2 pp, 8vo. To his sister-in-law Mademoiselle Riviere. Asking her to give the money due for Mr. Riviere's overcoat to a needy woman. Repaired. S Nov 27 (454) £6,500 [Chaponniere]

Rackham, Arthur, 1867-1939
Original drawings, (10), to illus S. J. Adair Fitz-Gerald's The Zankiwank and the Bletherwitch, 1896. In ink. Mostly sgd or initialled. Average size 315mm by 240mm. Archives of J. M. Dent & Son. S June 19 (817) £6,500 [Edberg]
— Original drawings, (11), headpieces & vignettes to illus S. Reynolds Hole's Our Gardens, 1899. In ink. Mostly sgd or initialled & dated 1899. Various sizes. Archives of J. M. Dent & Son. S June 19 (819) £280 [Beetles]
— Original drawings, (12), to illus Edward Grey's Fly Fishing, 1899. In ink. Mostly sgd & dated 1899. Various sizes. Archives of J. M. Dent & Son. S June 19 (820) £750 [Beetles]
— Original drawings, (40), illusts & designs for the Ingoldsby Legends, 1898. In ink. A number sgd or initialled. Various sizes. 1 def. Archives of J. M. Dent & Son. S June 19 (822) £17,000 [Edberg]
— Original drawings, (7), headpieces for R. H. Littleton's Out-Door Games, 1901. In ink. Mostly sgd & dated 1900. Various sizes. Archives of J. M. Dent & Son. S June 19 (821) £1,100 [Beetles]
Original drawing, 2 children in the basket of a balloon, to illus S. J. Adair Fitz-Gerald's The Zankiwank and the Bletherwitch, 1896. In ink & watercolor. Sgd & dated 1896. 329mm by 262mm. Archives of J. M. Dent & Son. S June 19 (814) £4,000 [Edberg]
— Original drawing, a giant in a clearing, ptd in Edward Lear's Book of Nonsense, 1980. In ink & watercolor. Sgd & dated 1901. 389mm by 266mm. Archives of J. M. Dent

AMERICAN BOOK PRICES CURRENT

& Son. S June 19 (828) £3,000 [Beetles]
— Original drawing, for Don Quixote. Of Don Quixote and Sancho Panza mtd on horse- & mule-back & near some windmills. 236mm by 316mm, in ink & watercolor. Sgd, 1904. Some abrasion. sg Oct 30 (52) $7,500
— Original drawing, for John Milton's Comus. 134mm by 132mm, in ink. Initialled beneath design. sg Oct 30 (147) $1,600
— Original drawing, for Peter Pan in Kensington Gardens, of a kite with Peter clingint to the tail. 211mm by 245mm, in ink & watercolor. Sgd, 1906. sg Oct 30 (19) $18,500
— Original drawing, "Get Secretly behind the Tree," for Izaak Walton's Compleat Angler. 245mm by 175mm, in watercolor. Sgd in full, 1931. sg Oct 30 (225) $6,000
— Original drawing, "Laura would call the little ones," the final illust for Christina Rossetti's Goblin Market. 240mm by 160mm, watercolor. Sgd in full. sg Oct 30 (179) $8,000
— Original drawing, The Two Pots. 213mm by 177mm, ink & watercolor, sgd, 1912. For Aesop's Fables. sg Oct 30 (1) $5,500
— Original drawing, the Zankiwank with 2 children in a railway station, to illus S. J. Adair Fitz-Gerald's The Zankiwank and the Bletherwitch, 1896. In ink & watercolor. Sgd & dated 1896. 254mm by 210mm. Archives of J. M. Dent & Son. S June 19 (813) £2,500 [Droller]
— Original drawing, the Zankiwank rushing towards the door of a post office, to illus S. J. Adair Fitz-Gerald's The Zankiwank and the Bletherwitch, 1896. In ink & watercolor. Sgd & dated 1896. 291mm by 241mm. Archives of J. M. Dent & Son. S June 19 (815) £2,500 [Drower]
— Original drawing, the Zankiwank leaping in the air, to illus S. J. Adair Fitz-Gerald's The Zankiwank and the Bletherwitch, 1896. In ink & watercolor. Sgd & dated 1896. 229mm by 183mm. Archives of J. M. Dent & Son. S June 19 (816) £2,500 [Drower]
— Original drawing, tp of T. T. Greg's Through a Glass Lightly, 1897. In ink; sgd. 286mm by 201mm. Archives of J. M. Dent & Son. S June 19 (818) £550 [Sawyer]
— Original drawing, watercolor illus for As I was going to St. Ives, incorporating self-port. Sgd & dated 1912. 266mm by 190mm. Verse written below; artist's address on verso. Reproduced in Mother Goose, 1913. S Dec 5 (513) £8,500 [Joseph & Sawyer]

Radetzky, Joseph, Graf von, 1766-1858
Ls, 26 June 1832. 2 pp, 4to. To an unnamed Lieut. Col. Regarding troops stationed in the Papal States. With autograph suscription. star Apr 9 (1186) DM280

Radziwill, Luise, Princess, 1770-1836
ALs, 19 May [1807]. 2 pp, 8vo. To Hofrat [Hahn]. Notifying him of her financial problems. With related material. star Apr 9 (1169) DM200

Raglan, Fitzroy James Henry Somerset, 1st Baron, 1788-1855. See: Nightingale, Florence

Railroads
[2 documents, subscription lists for ptd copies of Congressional speeches regarding the transcontinental railroad, by Representative Charles Lewis Scott, [11 July 1857], & Senator John B. Weller, [18 Apr 1856], 2 pp, 4to & folio, sold at P on 13 May 1987, lot 123, for $450.]

Railways & Engineering
[A collection of c.80 letters to George Ireland & his son James, c.1836 to 1860, over 200 pp, by members of his family & other workers in engineering, describing new engines & techniques, sold at C on 3 Dec 1986, lot 404, for £350 to Quaritch.]

Raleigh, Lady Elizabeth, 1565-1647
ALs, [c.Sept - Dec 1592]. 1 p, folio. To Sir Moyle Finch. From the Tower; thanking for his kindness & saying she would not risk her husband's safety for her own freedom. Sgd ER. C Dec 3 (324) £1,600 [Quaritch]

Raleigh, Sir Walter, 1552?-1618
Ms, A Discourse touching the consultation concerning the Peace with Spayne and the retayning of the Netherlands in society and protection. With A Counsell of Warr 27. Novembris 1587, & A Millitary discourse whether it be better for England to give an Invader present battaile or to temporize... [c.1625]; c.100 pp, modern mor-backed bds, folio. S Dec 18 (9) £700 [Finch]

Raleigh, Sir Walter, 1552?-1618 —& Others
Ds, 16 Feb 1616 [1617]. Receipt for £600, part payment for property in Surrey sold to Thomas Plummer. Also sgd by Lady Elizabeth Raleigh & their son Walter. C Dec 3 (325) £5,200 [Joseph]

Ramberg, Johann Heinrich, 1763-1840
ALs, 21 Apr 1817. 1 p, 8vo. To the pbr [Schmidt]. Regarding a frontis for Knigge's Ueber den Umgang mit Menschen. Mtd. star Apr 8 (528) DM1,200

Ramler, Karl Wilhelm, 1725-98
ALs, 15 Apr 1775. 2 pp, 8vo. To [H. C. Boie?]. Concerning the magazine Musenalmanach. With port. JG Oct 2 (130) DM530

Rance, Armand Jean Le Bouthillier de, 1626-1700
ALs, 22 Sept 1692. 3 pp, 4to. To Bernardin Gigault, Marquis de Bellefond. Sending condolences on the death of his son. star Apr 9 (1187) DM750

Rank, Otto, 1884-1939
ALs, 14 Sept 1927. 1 p, size not stated. To Dr. [George] Wilbur. Announcing his intention to sail for America in October. With related material. wa May 30 (67) $190

Raspail, Francois Vincent, 1794-1878
ALs, 30 Apr 1852. 3 pp, 8vo. To the Ed of L'Estafette. Regarding mandragore as a sleep inducer. Matted with a caricature. sg Nov 6 (175) $110

Rasputin, Grigory Efimovich
ALs, [n.d.]. 1 p, 8vo. To the manager of Mertens, international furriers. Asking about a job for a female relative of his. S Nov 27 (453) £4,000 [Dr. Sam]

Rauch, Christian Daniel, 1777-1857
ALs, 25 Oct 1828. 1 p, 8vo. To an unnamed banker. Requesting payment of 141 thalers from various funds. star Apr 8 (529) DM380

— 24 Apr 1855. 1 p, 8vo. To Heinrich Abeken. Regarding shipment of the King's present to the architect Canina in Rome. star Apr 8 (531) DM360

ANs, 22 Nov 1835. 1 p, 8vo. To [Karl Friedrich] Schinkel. Asking for "den versprochnen aeltern Carbonarimantel". With ALs, 1839, to Wilhelm Hensel, regarding a date. star Apr 8 (530) DM440

Ravara, Joseph. See: Washington, George

Ravel, Maurice, 1875-1937
ALs, [n.d.]. 2 pp, 8vo. To "Mon cher Calvo". Requesting him to give some information concerning Glinka's Rusian and Lyudmila to a lady. Framed. Altman collection. pnNY Sept 13 (178) $650

— 12 Apr [19]29. 1 p, 8vo. To Edwin Evans. Concerning 2 projected concertos & his Jeanne d'Arc project. S Nov 28 (624) £900 [Lee]

— 4 Nov 1929. 1 p, 8vo. To Marya Freund. Explaining that he cannot attend a social affair. star Apr 9 (777) DM1,300

— [n.d.]. 1 p, 8vo. To Fernand Ochse. Asking for Honegger's telephone no. S May 22 (633) £700 [Sims]

Ls, 18 Sept 1925. 1 p, 4to. To Franz Josef Hirt.

Regarding the revision of an opera score. Framed. Altman collection. pnNY Sept 13 (177) $500
— 4 Oct 1926. 1 p, 4to. To Franz Hirt. About a joint concert & saying his sonata is not finished yet. star Apr 9 (776) DM1,300
— 7 May 1929. 1 p, 4to. To [La direction des douanes]. As Vice President of the Societe Musicale Independante, requesting permission for a new piano constructed by Ivan Wischnegradsky to be imported into France. S Nov 28 (625) £550 [Wurlitzer-Bruck]

Read, George, Signer from Delaware
ADs, [n.d.]. 2 pp, folio. Legal document, contents not stated; draft. Was mtd. Charlotte Parker Milne collection. wd Nov 12 (62) $75

Reagan, Nancy. See: Reagan, Ronald & Reagan

Reagan, Ronald
Collection of 2 A Ls s, drafts, & autograph endorsement, sgd, Feb & 8 June 1967 & [n.d.]. To Gov. Walter J. Hickel of Alaska; routine exchange of good wishes. To Gov. Raymond Shafer of Pennsylvania; joking about basketball competition. Endorsement, 3 lines on top margin of carbon copy of his letter to Richard Nixon, 7 May 1965, in which he discusses campaign strategy. With related material. P Oct 29 (118) $650
ALs, 2 June 1967. Size not stated. Recipient unnamed. Draft, concerning a bill for school exercise programs. Sgd Ron. rf Nov 15 (14) $260
— 13 June 1967. 1 p, 4to. To Mr. Kalfain. Thanking for his "generous comments about my present job" & for saying he would make a good President. Sgd R R. On yellow ruled paper. sg Nov 6 (178) $550
— [12 July 1967]. 1 p, 4to. To Dan Sawhorn. Draft, giving advice on entering Eureka college. Sgd RR. With related material. P Oct 29 (119) $750
— [20 Nov 1967]. 1 p, 4to. To Hugh Flournoy. Draft, expressing his conviction that "academic freedom can be destroyed by those who deliberately provoke confrontation for causes having nothing to do with education." Sgd Ron. P Oct 29 (120) $2,700
— 20 Dec 1967. 1 p, 4to. To "Dear Myrt". Expressing his opinion about "all those writer types". Sgd Dutch. On yellow ruled paper; red line through text. sg Nov 6 (179) $425
Collection of Ls & photograph, sgd, 28 Jan 1972 & [c.1950]. 1 p, 4to, & 8 by 10 inches. To Kenneth Hubbs; acknowledging a letter commending performance of state employees. Photograph, seated next to a man

in suit. wa May 30 (300) $300
ANs, 15 June 1967. 11 lines. Recipient unnamed. Draft, declining an invitation. Sgd RR. rf Nov 15 (15) $210
— [30 June 1967]. Size not stated. To Walter Pidgeon. Draft, regretting his "inability to be at the Country Home Sunday." Sgd RR. 4 lines crossed out; address in anr hand. wa May 30 (301) $160
— 19 July 1967. Recipient unnamed. Draft, 4 lines. Referring to a postcard of Governor's Mansion, Charleston, W.Va. (present); wondering "what they did with the money in the Appalachia program." Sgd RR. rf Nov 15 (13) $300
— 7 Nov 1967. 3 lines. Recipient unnamed. Draft, thanking for a tie tack. Sgd RR. rf Nov 15 (16) $200
Photograph, sgd, [c.1960]; 8 by 10 inches. Chest-length pose. sg Nov 6 (176) $100

Reagan, Ronald —& Reagan, Nancy
Photograph, sgd & inscr, [n.d.], 10 by 8 inches. Inscr to Jackie & Bob [McBride] by [then Governor] Reagan; sgd by both. Framed. wa Oct 18 (42) $160

Reaumur, Rene Antoine Ferchault de, 1683-1757
Autograph endorsement, on ALs, 11 May 1740, 3 pp, 4to, from Gilles Augustin Bazin to Reaumur, regarding death of swallows due to cold weather. 5 lines, confirming Bazin's observations. Collector's stamp. star Apr 8 (410) DM250

Redi, Francesco, 1626-97
ALs, [n.d.]. 2 pp, folio. To Giulio Giannaro. Advising him to take a hot bath each day. C June 24 (177) £220 [Lim]

Reed, Joseph, 1741-85
Ds, 14 July 1781. 1 p, folio. Proclamation, concerning depreciated half pence. Sgd as President of the Supreme Executive Council of Pennsylvania. Countersgd by Timothy Matlack. Repaired. sg Nov 6 (311) $375

Regensburg
Ms, Extract der Statt Regenspurg Bauordnung, 1627. 33 leaves, 195mm by 155mm. Contemp vellum bdg using 12th cent theological Ms. Building regulations. HK Nov 4 (452) DM900

Reger, Max, 1873-1916
Autograph music, song, Gottes Segen, Op. 76, no 31; c.1907. 1 p, folio. Notated on 4 systems, each of 3 staves. In black & red ink; some corrections. Annotated for the printerr. Inscr on verso by Elsa Reger to Gretel Stein. S Nov 28 (629) £1,100 [Haas]
ALs, 28 Jan 1912. 5 pp, 8vo. To an unnamed

concert agent. Stating his conditions for concerts. star Apr 9 (780) DM1,100

Autograph postcard, sgd, 14 Sept 1903. To the pbr Augener. Concerning an Ed of his compositions. star Apr 9 (778) DM480

Photograph, sgd & inscr, 1907. 19.5cm by 14.5cm. Sitting at a table. Sgd & inscr to [Willy] von Beckerath on mount, 34cm by 22cm. star Apr 9 (779) DM900

Reibey, Mary, 1777-1855

[A collection of 5 A Ls s by Mary Reibey & 10 family letters mostly by her sons, to David Hope, 1821 to 1846, 77 pp, folio & 4to, about family & business news, with related material, sold at S on 24 July 1987, lot 328, for £11,000 to Burgess & Browning.]

ALs, 8 Oct 1792. 1 p, folio. To her aunt Mrs Hope. About her arrival in Botany Bay as a convict. Sgd Mary Haydock. S July 24 (327) £18,000 [Burgess & Browning]

Reichstein, Tadeusz

Autograph Ms, scientific paper by Reichstein & H. & K. Rasbach, Grammitis jungermannio[i]des (Klotsch) Ching auf den Azoren; [n.d.]. 6 pp, folio. With ALs, 10 Aug 1977; 1 p, 8vo. star Apr 8 (411) DM250

Reinecke, Carl, 1824-1910

Autograph music, "Symphonie angefangen 21. Mai 1874", 1st movement. 8 pp, folio. In pencil & ink. JG Oct 2 (340) DM530

Rembert, Ferdinand

Ms, Les Fleurs; Feb 1858 to 3 Apr 1862. 4 vols, 138mm by 110mm. Illuminated calligraphic Ms with 129 watercolor drawings by Rembert of floral subjects, mostly drawn after nature. 294 pp of text, written by Delvoye & Baudet; poetical verses in brown ink; captions & initials in gold & colors; index pp at end of vols in neo-Gothic style in red, blue & gold. Botanical information by Joseph de Caisne. Red crushed mor, gilt; coat-of-arms of Henri Leon Curmer. In red mor cases. Hunt collection. CNY Nov 21 (247) $36,000

Renault, Mary, Pseud. of Mary Challens

Series of c.50 Ls s, c.1956 to 1964. About 300 pp, mostly folio. To Julian Orde (Mrs. Abercrombie). On literary & artistic subjects. Some letters with autograph additions (1 entirely autograph), some with enclosed snapshots. S July 23 (175) £1,200 [Caldur]

Renoir, Pierre Auguste, 1841-1919

ALs, [Jan 1893]. 1 p, 8vo. To Paul Berard. Confirming Monsieur d'Hibouville is a good patriot. Framed with envelope. Altman collection. pnNY Sept 13 (93) $275

— [June 1898]. 1 p, 8vo. To Gustave Geffroy. Confirming a date. Framed with envelope. Altman collection. pnNY Sept 13 (95) $375

— 5 Apr 1899. 1 p, 8vo. To "Cher petits amies". Cancelling appointments because of his family's illnesses. Framed. Altman collection. pnNY Sept 13 (96) $425

— 23 June 1910. 1 p, 8vo. Recipient unnamed. Inviting him to lunch or dinner. Framed. Altman collection. pnNY Sept 13 (97) $400

— 14 Dec 1911. 1 p, 8vo. Recipient unnamed. Complaining about his health. Framed. Altman collection. pnNY Sept 13 (98) $500

— 3 July 1912. 1 p, 8vo. Recipient unnamed. Looking forward to meeting him in Paris. Framed. Altman collection. pnNY Sept 13 (99) $375

— 5 Feb [n.y.]. 1 p, 8vo. To "Mon cher Berard". About his visit with Deudon & saying it makes no difference to him who has the canvasses. Framed. Altman collection. pnNY Sept 13 (92) $900

— 5 Feb [n.y]. 1 p, 8vo. To Gustave Geffroy. Explaining why he failed to keep an appointment. S Nov 27 (455) £350 [Lucas]

— 12 June [n.y.]. 1 p, 8vo. To an unnamed lady. About an appointment with Durand-Ruel. In pencil. Framed. Altman collection. pnNY Sept 13 (101) $450

ANs, [Jan 1898]. 1 p, 8vo. To Theodor de Wyzenea. Concerning his season's plans. Framed. Altman collection. pnNY Sept 13 (94) $375

— [29 July 1914]. 1 p, 8vo. To Gustave Geffroy. Informing him that he is going to Fontainebleau. Framed with part of autograph envelope. Altman collection. pnNY Sept 13 (100) $350

Renouard, Johann Jeremias von, 1741-1810

[A collection of 7 Ds s by Friedrich II, Friedrich Wilhelm II, & Friedrich Wilhelm III, Kings of Prussia, 20 June 1775 to 24 May 1800, chronicling his military career, sold at auction on 9 Apr 1987, lot 1183, for DM3,200.]

Resnick, Judith A., 1949-1986

Photograph, sgd, [n.d.]. 4to. NASA color photograph; in space jacket. wa May 30 (454) $110

Reuter, Fritz, 1810-74

Series of 6 A Ls s, 20 May 1853 to 21 Oct 1854. 7 pp, folio. To Bernhard Ahrendt. Regarding the publication of his 1st books. star Apr 8 (225) DM5,800

REUTER

ALs, 1 Dec 1869. 3 pp, 8vo. To [Karl Helmerding]. Thanking for a present & reminiscing about their 1st meeting. 2d leaf mtd; with letter by Anton Ascher to Helmerding, 1872, on verso of mount. star Apr 8 (226) DM750

Reutter, Otto, 1870-1931

Collection of 16 A Ls s, 1 lettercard & 4 postcards, sgd, 1903-24. 36 pp, mostly 4to & 8vo, & cards. Mostly to Adolf Neuberger. Personal letters reporting about his work, his health, friends, etc. FD June 11 (3528) DM1,800

Series of 49 A Ls s, 1903 to 1921. 4to & 8vo. To Adolf Neuberger. Contents not stated. With related material. FD June 11 (3529) DM1,300

Series of 25 autograph postcards, sgd, 1907 to 1921. Mostly to Adolf Neuberger. With related material. FD June 11 (3530) DM1,200

Reverdy, Pierre, 1889-1960

Autograph Ms, essay, Poesie a part echec au poete, draft; [pbd 1935]. 24 pp, folio. With autograph revisions, sgd. With ALs, [n.d.], 4 pp, 8vo, by Reverdy to Maurice Sachs, on the suffering required for creative writing. S Nov 27 (456) £650 [Rota]

Revere, Paul, 1735-1818

Ds, 6 Jan 1790 [1795?]. 3 pp, 8vo. Petition of George French to open a tavern in Boston. Also sgd by 12 other subscribers. Repaired. sg Nov 6 (312) $2,500

Reynolds, Elizabeth

Original drawings, The twenty-four Classes of the Linnaean System of Botany, illus by Select Specimens of Indigenous Plants; 1833. 4to. Calf. 25 watercolors, 15 acccompanied by lines of verse. pn Dec 11 (10) £190 [Buckell & Ballard]

Reynolds, Sir Joshua, 1723-92

ALs, 25 May 1791. 3 pp, 4to. Recipient unnamed. Reporting that he lost the sight of one eye & about the delay in the publication of his Discourses. Framed. Altman collection. pnNY Sept 13 (102) $1,300
See also: Johnson, Samuel

Reynolds, Nicholas

ALs, [c.1573-1575]. 1 p, folio. To Abraham Ortelius. Sending copies of a map of Muscovy & ordering Mercator maps. In Latin. Repaired. S Dec 18 (270) £2,100

Richelieu, Armand-Jean du Plessis, Cardinal de, 1585-1642

[A collection of 4 Ms notebooks, in all 261 pp, 8vo; notes on the life & letters of Cardinal Richelieu, each stamped "From the Library of Le Duc de Richelieu 1875-1952", was sold at sg on 6 Nov, lot 182, for $50.]

Ls, 7 Sept 1624. 1 p, folio. To an unnamed prince. Expressing sympathy. With autograph subscription. star Apr 9 (1189) DM1,100

Ds, 24 Dec 1629. 6 pp, folio. Statement giving names, tonnages, etc. of ships of the French navy. 4 other signatures. C Dec 3 (326) £400 [L'Echiquier]

Richter, Hans, 1843-1916

Photograph, sgd & inscr, 1896. Cabinet size. Inscr to [Oskar Brueckner], with musical quotation from Wagner's Walkuere. star Apr 9 (781) DM650

Richter, Jean Paul, 1763-1825

ALs, 4 May 1824. 2 pp, 4to. To Luise Foerster. Asking her to send a medicine for his eyes. Green paper; seal tear. HK Nov 7 (2258) DM1,700

Rilke, Rainer Maria, 1875-1926

Autograph Ms, poem, A Marie Laurencin, sgd R & dated 1 Mar 1925. On recto & verso of tp of 1st ptg of his poem La Dormeuse, offprint of the magazine Commerce. Cahier trimestriels, no 2. Paris, 1924, pp 165 - 169; 8vo. Brocade bdg. HN Nov 27 (2367) DM3,800

Collection of ALs & autograph transcript, 11 Apr 1907 & winter 1907. 5 pp, 8vo. To "Frau Nonna" [Julie von Nordeck zu Rabenau]. Reporting about the finishing of his trans of Barrett-Browning's sonnets. Poem, Die Spitze, 12 lines. Sgd R.M.R. & inscr to Frau Nonna. star Apr 8 (228) DM4,500

Series of 4 A Ls s, 3 & 14 May 1926 & [n.d.]. 8 pp, 4to & 8vo. To Madame Henraux & [Lucien Henraux?]. Describing his life in Paris, & about "le changement terrible donc a ete frappe votre vie". C June 24 (154) £1,500 [Bush]

ALs, 22 Feb 1902. 4 pp, 4to. To Eugen Diederichs. Reporting about the ceremonies at the opening of the Bremen Hall of Art. With vignette by Heinrich Vogeler. Including copy of Rilke's "Festspielscene" read at the Bremen festivities, sgd, dated Feb 1902 & inscr to Diederich. star Apr 8 (227) DM4,400

— NOSTIZ-WALLWITZ, HELENE VON. - Autograph Ms, [fragment?], description of her first meeting with Rilke; [n.d.]. 2 pp, folio. With autograph envelope by Rilke to

Nostiz-Wallwitz, June 1916. star Apr 8 (229) DM500

Ringelnatz, Joachim, 1883-1934
Ls s (2), 24 Feb & 22 Mar 1926. 2 pp, 4to. To the editors of a magazine. Concerning a poem & complaining about the honorarium. With related material. star Apr 8 (230) DM360

Roberts, John Henry
Original drawings, The Ten Little Niggers; pictorial tp & 6 pp with 2 illusts; watercolor, [c.1895]. 294mm by 221mm. Each sgd with initials. Text pasted below each drawing; 2 more verses at end than usual. S Dec 5 (515) £400 [Marks]

Robespierre, Maximilien, 1758-94
ALs, 22 Feb 1787. 3 pp, 4to. To [Abbe Toques]. Discussing the problems of a lawsuit. Repaired. star Apr 9 (1190) DM10,000

Robinson, Charles
Original drawings, (11), to illus George Sand's The Master Mosaic Workers, 1900. In ink. Mostly captioned. Average size 280mm by 170mm. Archives of J. M. Dent & Son. S June 19 (837) £1,800 [Edberg]
— Original drawings, (11), to illus La Motte Fouque's Sintram and his Companions, 1900. In ink. Mostly captioned. Average size 380mm by 250mm. Archives of J. M. Dent & Son. S June 19 (834) £450 [A & H]
— Original drawings, (148), illusts & designs for The Reign of King Oberon, 1902. In ink; 1 watercolor. Mostly c.285mm by 195mm. 2 def. With related material. Archives of J. M. Dent & Son. S June 19 (841) £10,000 [Edberg]
— Original drawings, (2), angels singing, within ornamental borders, to illus Annie Matheson's Songs of Love and Praise, 1906. In ink. 206mm by 152mm & 210mm by 168mm. Archives of J. M. Dent & Son. S June 19 (843) £700 [Edberg]
— Original drawings, (28), illusts & designs for The Adventures of Odysseus, 1900. In ink. Various sizes. Archives of J. M. Dent & Son. S June 19 (836) £1,600 [Solo]
— Original drawings, (4), each depicting a child carried by an angel, pictorial endpapers for Andersen's Fairy Tales, 1899. In ink; sgd. 520mm by 419mm. Archives of J. M. Dent & Son. S June 19 (833) £1,300 [Beetles]
— Original drawings, (c.73), illusts & designs for Annie Matheson's Songs of Love and Praise, 1906. In ink. About 20 pp, various sizes. Archives of J. M. Dent & Son. S June 19 (842) £1,000 [Yablon]
Original drawing, 3 goblins beside a sleeping child, frontis for Reed Moorhouse's The Golden World, 1902. In ink. 367mm by 265mm. Archives of J. M. Dent & Son. S June 19 (838) £1,800 [Edberg]
— Original drawing, a man opening a door for a woman at night, to illus A Real Princess, in Andersen's Fairy Tales, 1899. In ink. Initialled. 520mm by 419mm. Archives of J. M. Dent & Son. S June 19 (831) £300 [Seeborg]
— Original drawing, girl & lamb on a hillside, to illus Little Lamb who made thee? in Blake's Songs of Innocence, 1912. In ink & watercolor. Sgd. 432mm by 266mm. Mtd on wooden board. Archives of J. M. Dent & Son. S June 19 (839) £3,000 [Solo]
— Original drawing, moon looking at an angel carrying a child, to illus What the Moon Saw, in Andersen's Fairy Tales, 1899. In ink. Initialled. 520mm by 419mm. Archives of J. M. Dent & Son. S June 19 (830) £1,700 [Bufano]
— Original drawing, Odysseus strapped to the mast, to illus The Adventures of Odysseus, 1900. In ink & watercolor. Sgd & dated 1900. 474mm by 351mm. Archives of J. M. Dent & Son. S June 19 (835) £1,700 [Vincent]
— Original drawing, pictorial headpiece to The Mermaid, in Andersen's Fairy Tales, 1899. In ink. Sgd & dated 1899. 520mm by 419mm. Archives of J. M. Dent & Son. S June 19 (832) £1,100 [Seeborg]

Robinson, Thomas Heath
Original drawings, (11), to illus Charles Kingsley's The Heroes, 1899. In ink; 1 watercolor. Captioned. Average size 355mm by 265mm. 5 mtd. Archives of J. M. Dent & Son. S June 19 (844) £5,000 [Edberg]
— Original drawings, (11), to illus Fairy Tales from the Arabian Nights, 1899. In ink; 1 watercolor. Captioned. Average size 340mm by 215mm. 3 mtd. Archives of J. M. Dent & Son. S June 19 (845) £6,500 [Edberg]
— Original drawings, (3), to illus Julius Caesar in Alice Hoffmann's adaptation for children, 1904. In ink & in watercolor. Sgd. 265mm by 170mm. Mtd. Archives of J. M. Dent & Son. S June 19 (849) £300 [Sawyer]
— Original drawings, (3), to illus The King with the Ugly Face in E. Hutton's A Children's Christmas Treasury, 1905. In ink. Sgd. 353mm by 270mm & 255mm by 311mm. Archives of J. M. Dent & Son. S June 19 (851) £1,200 [Klugerman]
— Original drawings, (54), illusts & designs for N. G. Royde-Smith's Una and the Knight and other Tales, 1905. In ink, 3 watercolors. Mostly sgd. Various sizes. 1 def. Archives of J. M. Dent & Son. S June 19 (852) £5,500

ROBINSON

[Solo]
— Original drawings, (6), to illus Katherine F. Boult's Heroes of the Norselands, 1903. In ink. Sgd. Average size 315mm by 210mm. Archives of J. M. Dent & Son. S June 19 (846) £650 [Ryder]
— Original drawings, (6), to illus Macbeth in Alice Hoffmann's adaptation for children, 1905. 1n ink. Sgd. Average size 350mm by 250mm. Archives of J. M. Dent & Son. S June 19 (850) £800 [Sawyer]
— Original drawings, (7), to illus Thomas Browne's Tom Brown's Schooldays, 1903. In ink. Sgd. Average size 285mm by 185mm. Archives of J. M. Dent & Son. S June 19 (847) £1,800 [Yablon]
— Original drawings, (8), to illus King Lear in Alice Hoffmann's adaptation for children, 1904. In ink. Sgd. Various sizes. Archives of J. M. Dent & Son. S June 19 (848) £1,200 [Sawyer]

Robinson, William Heath, 1872-1944
Original drawings, (10), to illus Don Quixote, 1929. In ink. Captioned; 3 sgd. Average size 360mm by 270mm. Archives of J. M. Dent & Son. S June 19 (855) £8,500 [Beetles]
— Original drawings, (2), Father Christmas entering & leaving a room through the chimney, possibly produced for E. Hutton's A Children's Christmas Treasury, 1905. In ink & watercolor. Sgd. 314mm by 254mm. Archives of J. M. Dent & Son. S June 19 (853) £4,000 [Beetles]
— Original drawings, (6), to illus Geraldine Hodgson's Rama and the Monkeys, 1903. In ink. 3 initialled. 299mm by 241mm. Archives of J. M. Dent & Son. S June 19 (854) £1,800 [Beetles]
Original drawing, dancing child; endpaper design for Uncle Lubin, 1902. Ink & watercolor, 280mm by 222mm. Sgd. Mtd. S Dec 5 (522) £500 [Beetles]
— Original drawing, Don Quixote & Sancho Pansa on a wooden Pegasus, to illus Don Quixote, 1929. In watercolor. Captioned & sgd. 372mm by 269mm. Archives of J. M. Dent & Son. S June 19 (862) £4,800 [Edberg]
— Original drawing, Don Quixote & Sancho Pansa with 2 shepherdesses, to illus Don Quixote, 1929. In watercolor. Captioned & sgd. 380mm by 270mm. Archives of J. M. Dent & Son. S June 19 (863) £1,800 [Beetles]
— Original drawing, Don Quixote on a donkey, to illus Don Quixote, 1929. In watercolor. Captioned & sgd. 380mm by 267mm. Archives of J. M. Dent & Son. S June 19 (856) £1,800 [Beetles]
— Original drawing, Don Quixote on his horse, responding to a barrage of stones, to illus Don Quixote, 1929. In watercolor. Captioned & sgd. 380mm by 269mm. Archives of J. M. Dent & Son. S June 19 (857) £1,700 [Droller]
— Original drawing, Don Quixote on his horse, looking across a river, to illus Don Quixote, 1929. In watercolor. Captioned & sgd. 380mm by 269mm. Archives of J. M. Dent & Son. S June 19 (858) £1,800 [Beetles]
— Original drawing, Don Quixote with a knight lying on a tomb, to illus Don Quixote, 1929. In watercolor. Captioned & sgd. 328mm by 226mm. Archives of J. M. Dent & Son. S June 19 (861) £2,200 [Edberg]
— Original drawing, Dorothea seated by a stream, to illus Don Quixote, 1929. In watercolor. Captioned & sgd. 380mm by 270mm. Archives of J. M. Dent & Son. S June 19 (859) £1,800 [Beetles]
— Original drawing, entitled "and fainted right away"; ink. 396mm by 298mm, initialled. Mtd. Reproduced in The Water Babies, 1914. S Dec 5 (524) £360 [Beetles]
— Original drawing, entitled "But Epimethus was a very slow fellow..."; ink. 392mm by 298mm; sgd. Mtd. Reproduced in The Water Babies, 1914. S Dec 5 (529) £400 [Beetles]
— Original drawing, entitled "He had a great pair of spectacles on his nose"; ink. 395mm by 298mm, sgd. Reproduced in The Water Babies, 1914. S Dec 5 (525) £850 [Beetles]
— Original drawing, entitled "Heading to Merchant's Wife"; reproduced in outline in Bill the Minder, 1912. Ink & watercolor; 230mm by 288mm. Initialled. Mtd. S Dec 5 (522) £950 [Beetles]
— Original drawing, entitled "Peter Quince"; ink. 445mm by 288mm, sgd. Mtd. Reproduced in A Midsummer Night's Dream, 1914 (included). S Dec 5 (523) £900 [Beetles]
— Original drawing, entitled "The Perfect Peace Pageant"; ink & wash. 344mm by 266mm; sgd. Mtd. Showing 6 men with different national flags seated in tub on carriage representing freedom of the seas; for Pearson's Magazine. S Dec 5 (530) £2,000 [Beetles]
— Original drawing, entitled "Ye are better than all the ballads"; ink. 423mm by 288mm, initialled. Mtd. Reproduced in The Water Babies, 1914. S Dec 5 (526) £1,100 [Greer]
— Original drawing, people in a park wearing animal head-dress; ink & wash. 410mm by 283mm, sgd. Mtd. Reproduced in The Sketch, 21 May 1941. S Dec 5 (534) £1,000 [Haghery]
— Original drawing, Sancho Panza as a jester on his donkey, to illus Don Quixote, 1929.

In watercolor. Captioned & sgd. 380mm by 270mm. Archives of J. M. Dent & Son. S June 19 (860) £1,400 [Beetles]
— Original drawing, "The End", young child diving into the sea; ink. 383mm by 298mm; initialled. Mtd. Reproduced in The Water Babies, 1914. S Dec 5 (528) £850 [Beetles]
— Original drawing, young child in the sea; ink. 387mm by 298mm; initialled. Mtd. Reproduced in The Water Babies, 1914 S Dec 5 (527) £400 [Beetles]

Rochambeau, Jean Baptiste Donatien de Vimeur, Comte de, 1725-1807
ALs, 11 Aug 1759. 2 pp, 4to. To [Louis de Bourbon-Conde, Comte de Clermont?]. Describing the previous day's victory "a l'entree de la gorge de Munden". C Dec 3 (327) £120 [L'Echiquier]

Rockefeller, John D., 1839-1937
Ds, [n.d.]. 2 pp, 8vo. Stock certificate in Missouri, Kansas & Texas Railway Company; partly ptd. Cancellation punches affecting signature. wd Nov 12 (15) $275

Rockwell, Norman, 1894-1978
Ls, 20 July 1976. 1 p, 8vo. Recipient unnamed. About requests for autographs. wa May 30 (70) $110
Signature, [8 Feb 1960]. On 1st Day Cover, 50th Anniversary Boy Scouts of America, with 4 cent stamp. wa May 30 (69) $100

Rodin, Auguste, 1840-1917
ALs, [6 Mar 1873]. 1 p, 8vo. To Dr. Camuset. Saying he will see him on Monday. star Apr 8 (532) DM260

Rodney, Caesar, Signer from Delaware
ALs, 10 Mar 1780. 1 p, 4to. To Samuel Patterson. Requesting him to pay Col. French Batell "for the Expences of the Privy Council". Charlotte Parker Milne collection. wd Nov 12 (63) $225

Rodney, George Brydges, 1718-92
ALs, 31 Mar 1762. 3 pp, 4to. To William Henry Lyttelton. About the naval war in the Caribbean after the fall of Martinique & announcing that aid will be sent to Jamaica. S Dec 18 (303) £1,050 [Palmer]

Rogers, Robert, 1731-95
ALs, 23 Feb 1760. 1 p, folio. To Paul Burbeen. Reporting about his losses in a recent attack near Ticonderoga. Repaired. Tipped into folder with transcript & a port. Bullock collection. CNY Dec 19 (218) $5,500

Rohan, Henry, Duc de, 1579-1638
Ms, Memoires, [c.1640?]. About 1,000 pp, in scribal hand. Calf with gilt panelling, stamped with A C monogram. S Jan 27 (985) £250 [Maggs]

Rolland, Romain, 1866-1944
Series of 3 A Ls s, 29 Oct 1913 to 26 Feb 1926. 10 pp, 8vo. To his publisher, discussing his novel Jean Christophe & his dramas. Recipients unnamed, about Stendhal's pillaging Carpani's life of Haydn, & requesting information about the papers of Baron de Breteuil. S Nov 27 (457) £420 [Lucas]
ALs, 26 Jan 1930. 4 pp, 8vo. To Camille Drevet. Explaining that he would like to defend the rights of man in general, not the rights of particular groups. star Apr 8 (231) DM250

Rollins, Edward Henry, 1824-89
ALs, 13 Feb 1871. 3 pp, 4to. Recipient unnamed. As Chairman of the New Hampshire Republican State Committee; discussing strategy for the March elections. sg Nov 6 (300) $80

Romania
— DOSITHEOS, PATRIARCH OF JERUSALEM. - Ls, June 1677. 1 p, folio. Deciding a dispute about ownership of 2 villages in Moldavia. In Greek; signature c.8cm by 24cm. With Romanian trans & English abstract. S May 21 (301) £300 [Pervanas]

Rommel, Erwin, 1891-1944
Photograph, sgd, [n.d.]. Postcard size. Sgd in pencil. star Apr 9 (1287) DM860

Roon, Albrecht, Graf von, 1803-79
ALs, 16 Dec 1877. 1 p, 4to. To Kammerherr von Huelsen. Notifying him of his son's enlistment as ensign. star Apr 9 (1220) DM500

Roosevelt, Eleanor, 1884-1962
ALs, 13 Aug 1958. 2 pp, 8vo. Recipient & contents not stated. wa May 30 (302) $100
Ls, 24 Feb 1945. 2 pp, 8vo. To Major Gubin. Expressing her opinion that more must be done to help the veterans. On White House letterhead. wa Oct 18 (138) $100

Roosevelt, Franklin D., 1882-1945
ALs, 20 Mar [1927]. 2 pp, 8vo. To Basil [O'Connor]. Enclosing a telegram from Tracy Daws (not present). Sgd FDR. wa May 30 (303) $700
Collection of 7 Ls s & Ds, 5 Sept 1919 to 18 Feb 1932. 8 pp, 4to. To various recipients; & extradition papers for a fugitive sought by New Jersey. P Oct 29 (122) $800
Series of 3 Ls s, 14 Dec 1917 to 6 Oct 1930. 3 pp, size not stated. To W. Schuyler Johnson

& Edwin Bjorkman, thanking for donations to the Navy. To Gov. Case, thanking for a book. pnNY June 11 (43) $375

Ls s (2), 29 Aug & 21 Nov 1932. 2 pp, 4to. To Joseph F. Simmons. Contents not stated. Worn. wd Nov 12 (17) $100

Ls, 1 Feb 1918. 1 p, 4to. To J. A. L. Moller. As Assistant Sec of the Navy, thanking for a present of binoculars for the Navy. With additional official documentation. sg Apr 9 (163) $250

— 12 Feb 1918. 1 p, 4to. Recipient unnamed. As Assistant Sec of the Navy, about a report on the Portsmouth Navy Yard. wa Oct 18 (141) $100

— 8 May 1918. 1 p, 4to. To Mrs. Wainwright. As Assistant Sec of the Navy, thanking for a present of binoculars for the Navy. With additional official documentation. sg Apr 9 (162) $175

— 12 June 1918. 1 p, 4to. As Acting Sec of the Navy; re-assignment of duty & location. File holes. wa Oct 18 (46) $80

— 29 May 1926. 1 p, 4to. To Glen W. Blodgett. Responding to a request for his autograph. With autograph subscription. P May 13 (125) $450

— 18 Jan 1932. 1 p, 4to. To Fanny Levenson. Thanking for photographs & news clippings. S Jan 27 (938) £80 [Sam]

— 21 May 1932. 1 p, 4to. To Mr. Hawkins. Thanking for support. wa May 30 (315) $110

— 15 Dec 1933. 1 p, 8vo. To Mrs. J. B. Harriman. Thanking for a letter of appreciation. With related material. wa May 30 (304) $250

— 8 July 1935. 1 p, 4to. To Edwin D. Bloom. Thanking for an autograph for his collection. P May 13 (126) $600

— 28 Oct 1935. 1 p, 8vo. To Thomas E. Winston. Sending wishes for his speedy recovery. Framed. Altman collection. pnNY Sept 13 (20) $375

— 30 Jan 1936. 4 pp, 4to. To Alfonso Lopez, President of Colombia. Suggesting an inter-American conference at Buenos Aires. P Oct 29 (123) $4,000

— 23 Apr 1936. 1 p, 4to. To Francis Skinner. Wishing him a speedy recovery. On White House letterhead. With White House envelope to Skinner dated 1934. sg Sept 18 (256) $175

— 27 July 1940. 1 p, 4to. Recipient unnamed. Thanking for a message. Mtd. wa May 30 (314) $170

— 29 Sept 1942. 1 p, 4to. To Sen. Josiah W. Bailey. Thanking for supporting his veto of a bill. With autograph correction. With ptd bill. wa May 30 (117) $375

— 18 May 1944. 2 pp, 4to. To Harry L. Hopkins. Expressing his relief at Hopkins's recovery & urging him not to return to Washington too soon. Sgd FDR. Robert Hopkins collection. P Oct 29 (65) $5,000

Letter, 5 June 1935. Size not stated. Typed draft, with holograph corrections, in pencil. Responding to a letter by Senator Henry Parkman, Jr., concerning a resolution of the Interstate Conference on Labor Compacts. With related ANs by Frances Perkins, & Ls from Parkman to Roosevelt. wa Oct 18 (139) $1,000

Collection of Ns & sgd envelope. Ns, fragment, [n:d., as President?], about preparing the "Potomac" for his use. Signature on envelope above ptd address; 27 Jan 1932. With related material. wa Oct 18 (47) $85

Ds, 1916. 1 p, oblong 4to.As Acting Sec of the Navy; certificate of service for Lawrence Johnson. Partly ptd. wa Oct 18 (140) $90

Autograph sentiment, [Dec 1937]. On tp of mimeographed typescript, Log of the Cruise of President Franklin D. Roosevelt to Dry Tortugas Florida 29 Nov 1937 - 6 Dec 1937. 21 pp, 4to, in cardboard binder. Sgd & inscr to Harry Hopkins. Robert Hopkins collection. P Oct 29 (64) $2,600

Roosevelt, Theodore, 1858-1919

Collection of ALs, 19 Ls s & 7 letters with stamped signatures, 1899 to 1904. About 30 pp, 4to & 8vo. To Eugene A. Philbin. About a variety of administrative matters. In an album containing c.400 other letters, telegrams, etc. addressed to Philbin, & further material related to Roosevelt. S July 24 (407) £4,000 [Richards]

— Collection of ALs & 4 Ls s, 10 May 1911 to 26 June 1913. 1 & 3 pp, various sizes. To William A. Prendergast. Mostly relating to New York politics. P Oct 29 (127) $3,250

Collection of 11 Ls s & typescript, sgd. 21 May 1894 to 27 Apr 1901. 12 pp, various sizes. To various recipients. Memorandum concerning guns on the U.S.S. Chicago. P Oct 29 (125) $1,000

— Collection of Ls & White House card, sgd, 26 Aug 1898 & [n.d.]. 1 p, 4to, & card. To H. L. Nelson. Apologizing for being unable to write an article. Card mtd. pnNY June 11 (45) $425

Series of 4 Ls s, 1896 to 1901. 4 pp, 4to. Recipients & contents not stated. pnNY June 11 (44) $650

— Series of 9 Ls s, 15 Apr 1910 to 4 Nov 1918. 9 pp, various sizes. To various recipients. With card, sgd, & 2 White House envelopes. P Oct 29 (126) $1,400

— Series of 5 Ls s, 4 Mar 1913 to 21 May 1914 & 3 July 1918. 5 pp, 8vo & 4to. To Ernest Harvier (4); discussing politics & a libel trial. To J. H. Snodgrass; short letter agreeing with a letter by recipient about the conduct of the war, with holograph revisions totalling 9 words. Bullock collection. CNY Dec 19 (220) $1,600

— Series of 4 Ls s, 7 Apr 1916 to 26 May 1917. 4 pp, 4to. To William Wingate Sewall. Letters to an old friend, also commenting on the political situation. P Oct 29 (128) $1,500

Ls, 7 Apr 1892. 1 p, size not stated. To Bernard Rowe. About his hunt in Texas. Mtd. pnNY June 11 (46) $550

— 8 Oct 1905. 1 p, 4to. To Charles Hughes. Thanking for a book & commenting on motorcars. S July 24 (406) £900 [Maddalena]

— 24 Jan 1906. 4 pp, 4to. To the Rev. Franklin C. Smith. Strongly denouncing birth control. Some autograph emendations. P May 13 (127) $6,500

— 20 Aug 1907. 1 p, 350mm by 280mm. "Remarks of President Roosevelt to the Gloucester Fishermen at Provincetown, Mass."; ptd on a board. Sgd in gray ink. sg Nov 6 (183) $350

— 26 June 1908. 1 p, 4to. To Adolph Roeder. Thanking for a book. Framed. Altman collection. pnNY Sept 13 (21) $375

— 9 Dec 1908. 1 p, 4to. To Frank S. Johnson. "Give both the Grotonian and the Harvard Man, or either of them, this note..." On White House letterhead. Signature faded. sg Sept 18 (257) $200

— 20 May 1916. 1 p, 4to. To Frank Annis. Thanking for a letter. Worn. With Ls by Frank Harper, 12 Feb 1912, 1 p 8vo, on Roosevelt's behalf. wa May 30 (119) $160

Ds, 27 June 1902. 1 p, folio. Appointment for Fred A. Field as U. S. Marshal in Vermont. Attached to frame. wa May 30 (316) $130

— 15 Dec 1904. 1 p, folio. Commission for Francis M. Dickens as Rear Admiral. pnNY June 11 (47) $275

Engraving, port, sgd & dated 24 Dec 1908. 11 by 7.75 inches. Framed; overall size 16.5 by 13 inches. S Jan 27 (939) £70 [Morris]

Group photograph, 17 June 1910. 12.6cm by 17.7cm. Sgd. Sitting on deck of a ship with officers of the merchant marine. star Apr 9 (1221) DM440

Photograph, sgd & inscr, 5 Dec 1905. 8.75 by 5.6 inches. In Rough Rider uniform. Inscr to his "Comrades of the Manila War". Torn; mtd. wa May 30 (305) $600

— Anr, 16 May 1906. 7.5 by 6.25 inches. Inscr on mount. wd Nov 12 (16) $425

White House card, [c.1905]; 1 p, 16mo. Sgd. sg Nov 6 (184) $175

— Anr, [n.d.]. Sgd. wa May 30 (118) $260

Roosevelt, Theodore, 1887-1944

Ls s (2), 12 Mar & 18 July 1932. 2 pp, 4to. To Mr. Tracy. As Gov. Gen. of the Philippines; letters of transmittal. wa May 30 (120) $60

Root, Elihu, 1845-1937

Collection of ALs & 2 Ls s, 15 May 1898 to 14 Jan 1937. 6 pp, 8vo & 4to. To Bronson Winthrop. About Winthrop joining the Army & running for Judge of the New York State Court of Appeals; thanking him. sg Nov 6 (186) $60

Rosegger, Peter, 1843-1918

ALs, [n.d.]. 1 p, 8vo. To an unnamed colleague. Declining to join a panel of judges for a literary prize. star Apr 8 (233) DM350

Rosenberg, Alfred, 1893-1946

Typescript carbon copy, file memorandum to Hitler about a telephone conversation with Dr. Koeppen regarding Rosenberg's plan to establish an office for Eastern European research, 23 Mar 1942. 4 pp, folio. Sgd R, in pencil. Some holograph corrections. sg Apr 9 (166) $200

Ross, George, Signer from Pennsylvania

Ds, 29 July 1752. 1 p, 8vo. Receipt for ledger & journal of Andrew Elliott & M. Groves; with 5-line endorsement. Inlaid. Charlotte Parker Milne collection. wd Nov 12 (64) $100

Rossetti, Christina Georgina, 1830-94

ALs, 12 Oct 1881. 4 pp, 8vo. To her brother D. G. Rossetti. Discussing his poems & her own works. S July 23 (89) £520 [Joseph & Sawyer]

ANs, 22 Apr 1880. 1 p, 8vo. Recipient unknown. Mentioning 7 sonnets. sg Apr 9 (167) $130

Rossetti, Dante Gabriel, 1828-82

A Ls s (2), [Nov 1878 to early 1879]. 4 pp, 8vo. To Theodore Watts. About his correspondence with "the Boulogne Lady", & reporting about rumors concerning items to be auctioned off at Whistler's house. Initialled. Bullock collection. CNY Dec 19 (222) $1,100

ALs, 2 Mar [1867?]. 3 pp, 8vo. Recipient unnamed. Apologizing for failing to keep an appointment. bba Nov 13 (151) £110 [Wilson]

— [n.d.]. 2 pp, 8vo. To Miss Heaton. Concerning a damaged picture. star Apr 8 (534) DM580

Rossini, Gioacchino, 1792-1868
[A collection of 4 checks, sgd, payable to M. Francesco Baccani, 1857 to 1861, sold at S on 22 May 1987, lot 505, for £850 to Wilson.]

Autograph music, "Laus Deo", for mezzo-soprano & piano, 1861. 3 pp, 8vo, with green ornamental border. Sgd at end & inscr "al Piovano Arlotto'. Supposedly unptd. star Apr 9 (783) DM4,600

— Autograph music, song in F major, for voice, violin & violoncello, beginning "Apprendete, o cari amanti"; c.1820. 23 bars on 3 pp, 230mm by 310mm. In black ink on 2 systems of 4 staves per p. Supposedly unpbd. Authentication by Francesco Caffi on 2d leaf. C Dec 3 (421) £2,500 [Haas]

ALs, 1 June 1822. 2 pp, 4to. To Luigi Prividali. Notifying him of his marriage, & about the mediocrity of La Maruzzi. S May 22 (503) £2,000 [Haas]

— [n.d.]. 1 p, 4to. To Graf Wenzel Robert Gallenberg. Concerning debts of a joint acquaintance. Lower margin cut. star Apr 9 (784) DM860

— 28 Nov 1841. 3 pp, 4to. To Aguado Marquis de las Marismas. Regarding the publication of his Stabat mater. P June 18 (174) $1,100

— 21 Mar 1844. 1 p, 4to. To Filippo Santocanale. Concerning financial matters. S May 22 (504) £350 [Wilson]

— 22 July 1859. 1 p, 4to. To Filippo Santocanale. Regarding financial arrangements. S May 22 (506) £350 [Wilson]

— 4 Dec 1859. 1 p, 4to. To the painter Chenavard. About Mozart & Palestrina designs for Besteghi. S May 22 (634) £300 [Dr. Sam]

Photograph, sgd & inscr, 1861; c.11cm by 6cm. Inscr to A. Farrenc, in French. S Nov 28 (630) £750 [Dr. Sam]

Rostand, Edmond, 1868-1918

Autograph transcript, poem, beginning "Je jette avec grace mon feutre", [n.d.]. 28 lines; sgd. 1 p, 4to. Mtd. star Apr 8 (234) DM800

Rothko, Mark, 1903-70

Series of 5 A L s, 1950. 7 pp, 8vo & 4to. To George Reavey. Regarding European travel plans & mutual friends. sg Apr 9 (168) $425

Rothschild, Albert, Freiherr von, 1844-1911

ALs, [n.d.]. 2 pp, 8vo. To Amalie Materna. Sending money for a poor person. With related material. star Apr 9 (1223) DM460

Rothschild, Karl, Freiherr von, 1788-1855

Ls, 18 Mar 1842. 4 pp, 4to. To the bankers M. A. von Rothschild at Frankfurt. Discussing the acquisition of an estate. With autograph postscript. star Apr 9 (1222) DM480

Rountree, Harry

Original drawings, (42), to illus Peter Lawless' The Golfer's Companion, 1937. In ink. Captioned; 8 sgd, 2 initialled. Various sizes. Archives of J. M. Dent & Son. S June 19 (865) £2,800 [Beetles]

— Original drawings, (7), oil painting of a Maori chieftain & 6 ink drawings, to illus The New Zealanders, 1928. Sgd. 459mm by 293mm & 506mm by 320mm. Archives of J. M. Dent & Son. S June 19 (864) £1,050 [Beetles]

Rowohlt, Ernst, 1887-1960

Collection of ALs, 11 Ls s, & autograph postcard, sgd, 4 Feb 1939 to 9 July 1947. 35 pp, folio & 8vo, & card. To Peter Zingler. Confidential letters to a friend regarding his life in South America, his return to Germany & the new beginning of his publishing firm after the war. With related material. star Apr 8 (274) DM3,200

Royal Academy

[A collection of over 700 letters, receipts & further material relating to the Winter Exhibition of Old Masters, 1871-1872, sold at S on 18 Dec 1986, lot 312, for £ 3,200 to Wilson.]

Ms, 1st General Assembly, 11 Jan 1830; signatures of 26 artists attending. 1 p, folio. Bullock collection. CNY Dec 19 (19) $800

Rubens, Peter Paul, 1577-1640

— PEIRESC, NICHOLAS-CLAUDE FABRI DE. - AL, 16 Oct 1620. 4 pp, folio. To Rubens. Draft, discussing his discovery of an ancient Ms of the Roman calendar of Constantine. With revisions. S May 21 (304) £5,000 [Bibliotheque de Carpentras]

Rubinstein, Anton, 1829-94

Autograph music, songs for voice & piano, Op. 8, [c.1858]. 17 pp, 4to. In Russian, inscr to Alexandrine Sokoloff. Marked for the ptr. With material relating to the German Ed. W. Heyer collection. HN May 22 (3163a) DM2,600

Rudolf, Archduke, 1858-89

[A half-length port of Rudolf, pencil & watercolors, size not stated, sgd, inscr & dated by him on mount, 15 Dec 1882, sold at HK on 7 Nov 1986, lot 2337, for DM1,300.]

ALs, 20 Oct 1881. 2 pp, 8vo. To Dr. Wiederhofer. Sending a copy of his "Orient-Reise". Repaired. star Apr 9 (1105)

DM900
— 11 Dec 1886. 2 pp, 8vo. To Baron Brunicki. Invitation to a hunt. star Apr 9 (1106) DM540
— 1 Jan 1888. Size not stated. To his brother-in-law Phillip. Thanking for good wishes. Tipped into 1st English Ed of his Sport and Ornitology. L, 1889. 8vo. wa May 30 (195) $250
— WEBER, TH. - ALs, 12 Feb 1889. 8 pp, 8vo. To Georg Umthammer. Describing the return of Rudolf's body to Vienna after his suicide at Mayerling & the situation at the court. With a letter by Weber to Umthammer, 1916, decribing the death of the Emperor. S Nov 27 (459) £650 [Haas]

Rudolf August, Herzog von Braunschweig, 1627-1704
Ds, 23 June 1680. 1 p, 4to. Ptd order regarding examination of travellers & prohibition of imports from areas infected with the plague. star Apr 9 (924) DM420

Rudolf II, Emperor, 1552-1612
Ls, 7 Jan 1577. 2 pp, folio. To the knights in Franconia. Ordering them to convoke a meeting. star Apr 9 (1197) DM750

Rueckert, Friedrich, 1788-1866
Autograph transcript, poem, Der gute Abend, [n.d.]. 1 p, size not stated. 2 four-line stanzas, sgd. HK Nov 7 (2341) DM750
ALs, 18 Aug [18]55. 1 p, 8vo. To Dr. H. Dieckmann, principal of a school at Hannover. Commenting about a school festival & promising a contribution to the school album. JG Oct 2 (132) DM500
Ds, [n.d.]. 1 p, 4to. Power of attorney for the sale of his house at Erlangen. star Apr 8 (235) DM580

Ruggles, Daniel, 1810-97
ALs, 16 June [n.y.]. 1 p, 8vo. To Gen. Beauregard. Indicating the dates that he reported the location of Gen. Villepique. Was mtd. wa Oct 18 (142) $200

Rush, Benjamin, Signer from Pennsylvania
Ds, 17 Apr 1786. 1 p, 8vo. Stating that certificate for $80 is the property of Dickinson College. Partly ptd. Charlotte Parker Milne collection. wd Nov 12 (65) $250
— 25 Dec 1792. 1 p, 12mo. Bill to Enoch Hubbard for medical services; sgd & endorsed. sg Nov 6 (190) $550

Ruskin, John, 1819-1900
[Ruskin's copy of Thomas Moore's Letters and Journals of Lord Byron, 1833, 3 vols, 8vo, copiously annotated in margins & on blank leaves, [1886 to 1887], sold at S on 18 Dec 1986, lot 79, for £800 to McDowell.]
Series of 61 A Ls s, 29 June 1865 to [25 Dec] 1886. 80 pp, 8vo. To Lily Armstrong. Chatty & playful letters, mentioning his & her activities. 2 signatures cut away. Bullock collection. CNY Dec 19 (223) $3,800
A Ls s (2), 22 Jan [18]65 & [n.d.]. 4 pp, 8vo. To [Frederic James] Shields, about drawing lessons at a girls school. To Crawley, asking for account of his expenses. pn Dec 11 (109) £80 [Wilson]
ALs, 20 June [1841]. 4 pp, 4to. To Henry Wentworth Acland. Commenting on his travels in Italy & the Alps, the art of Turner, Raphael & Michelangelo, & musing about the nature of beauty. S Dec 18 (313) £1,150 [Wilson]
— [c.1850]. 4 pp, 8vo. mtd with 2 ports & a watercolor sketch of Ruskin's house, framed. Apparently to the engraver R. P. Cuff. Giving detailed instructions on reproducing the exact proportions of a balcony for Plate 5 of Examples of the Architecture of Venice.d C July 22 (187) £700

Russell, Bertrand, 3d Earl, 1872-1970
Typescript carbon copy, statement for the press concerning his pacifism & his views on World War II; 1 p, 4to. Sgd. With Ls by his wife Patricia, 27 June 1940, transmitting statement to Mr. Levy. sg Apr 9 (171) $425
ALs, 10 Apr 1950. 1 p, 8vo. Recipient unnamed. Giving permission to be quoted. With autograph envelope. wa Oct 18 (48) $130
Ls, 25 Feb 1964. 1 p, 4to. To Jack Benjamin. Soliciting covenants for the Peace Foundations. Framed. Altman collection. pnNY Sept 13 (129) $300

Russian Imperial Family
[The signatures of 5 members of the Russian Imperial family, including Tsar Alexander II, his wife Maria, & their children [later Tsar] Nicholas, George & Xenia, on detached integral leaf of A L s, 18 Sept 1883, 1 p, 8vo, from Sir Donald Currie to his wife, sold at sg on 9 Apr 1987, lot 172, for $650.]
[A postcard, sgd by Grand Duchesses Olga, Tatiana, Maria & Anastasia, 1910, sending Easter greetings to an unnamed recipient, sold at S on 21 May 1987, lot 303, for £550 to Hoffman.]

Rutledge, Edward, Signer from South Carolina
Ds, 22 Mar 1793. 1 p, folio. Deposition of William Marshall & Alexander Inglis, sgd twice as attorney. Was mtd. Charlotte Parker Milne collection. wd Nov 12 (66) $125

S

Sacrobosco, Johannes
Ms, Algorismus, & Tractatus de Sphera; in Latin. [Italy, c.1349]. 30 leaves, vellum, 182mm by 130mm; 2 leaves 15th cent replacements. Vellum wrap. In black & dark brown ink in small scholastic bookhand. With 17 painted initials & 10 astronomical diagrams; many early glosses. Originally belonging to Brother Pietro di Santo Giovanni, a Franciscan of the province of Florence. S Dec 2 (35) £12,000 [Schoenberg]

Sadat, Anwar El, 1918-81
[A collection of 3 photographs of a book of signatures gathered by Braha Marcus-Ofseyer & presented to Sadat, [n.d.], 3.5 by 4.9 inches; each sgd by Sadat, was sold at wa on 18 Oct 1986, lot 50, for $100.]
Ls, June 1981. 1 p, 4to. To Braha Marcus-Ofseyer. As President of Egypt, thanking for her peace efforts. wa Oct 18 (49) $275
Photograph, sgd, [1981]; 7.25 by 5.75 inches. In military dress; sgd in Arabic. With covering letter, 10 June 1981, 1 p, 4to, by M.H.Raafat. sg Nov 6 (191) $150

Sade, Donatien Alphonse Francois, Marquis de, 1740-1814
AL, [1790s]. 2 pp, 356mm by 464mm. To his wife. In the margins around & on verso of an orig pencil drawing by de Sade of his wife's lover; bust sketch, with holes punched in face of port. Insulting letter full of satire & sexual references. With trans. sg Apr 9 (174) $1,600
— [11 Mar 1798]. 5 pp, 4to. To an unnamed lawyer. Describing his political fears & financial problems. star Apr 8 (236) DM2,400

Saint-Germain-en-Laye
Ms, Proces-verbal de visite et projects de coupes des bois du Roy de la Maistrise de sainct Germain en Laye, 1708. 138 pp with 3 colored plans, 315mm by 193mm, in mor gilt. Jeanson Ms 168 SM Mar 1 (497) FF40,500

Saint-Saens, Camille, 1835-1921
ALs, 23 Mar [1875]. 2 pp, 8vo. To [Victorin de Joncieres]. Commenting about critical reviews of his work. star Apr 9 (786) DM440
— [1882?]. 1 p, 8vo. Recipient unnamed. Saying he will not be able to go to Dieppe. Was mtd. wa May 30 (17) $90
— [n.d.] 3 pp, 8vo. To [Louis Gallet]. Concerning changes to the libretto of Ascanio. Sgd with twisted initials & sketch of a fly. star Apr 9 (788) DM440
— 27 Feb 1893. 2 pp, 8vo. Recipient unnamed. Accepting an honorary membership of a society at Florence. Illustrated letterhead; ship. star Apr 9 (787) DM250
— 30 July 1907. 6 pp, folio. To M. Honore Champion. Discussing an article by G. Jean-Aubry about French medieval music; with 13 autograph musical quotations. With anr letter by Saint-Saens, 2 Sept 1907. S May 22 (507) £850 [Haas]

Salieri, Antonio, 1750-1825
Autograph music, song, Lode alla Compagnia, for 3 voices; [n.d.]. 2 pp, 4to; each p mtd in paper folder. Sgd. Aloys Fuchs collection. P Dec 15 (77) $4,750

San Martin, Jose de, 1778-1850
ALs, 28 Dec 1838, 2 pp, 4to. To Mariano Alvarez. Commenting about the situation in Peru, & regarding payment of his pension. S May 21 (305) £700 [Lucas]
Ds, 2 May 1821. 1 p, folio. Order to Col. Zenteno to march on the area of Quinto which was supposed to be occupied by Columbian troops. pnNY Dec 10 (263) $950
— 13 Dec 1821. 1 p, folio. Passport for a sailor leaving from Callao with the English fleet. pnNY Dec 10 (264) $200

Sand, George, Pseud. of Amandine, Baronne Dudevant, 1804-76
Autograph Ms, Une promenade en Suisse; part of her Lettres d'un voyageur, dedicated to Charles Didier; [1836]. 61 numbered leaves, 4to (1 8vo). With autograph revisions; marked for press. S Nov 27 (460) £5,000 [Chaponniere]
ALs, 12 Feb 1860. 2 pp, 8vo. To Auguste Villemot. Thanking for defending her in the Figaro. star Apr 8 (237) DM1,100

Sand, George, Pseud. of Amandine, Baronne Dudevant, 1804-76
ALs, [n.d., "samedi 12"]. 4 pp, 8vo. Recipient unknown. Discussing the 5th act of her play Quintinie. Repaired. P Dec 15 (78) $400

Sandburg, Carl, 1878-1967
[A collection of 9 autographs, including 2 A Ls & typescript of his poem Grass, sgd & inscr, 1936 to 1963, sold at sg on 9 Apr 1987, lot 176, for $650.]

Sandringham
Ms, visitors' book of Sandringham, 1883 to 1901, c.33 pp & blanks, 4to. Mor bdg. Sgd by c.300 visitors, including Tsar Nicholas II, Queen Victoria, Edward VII, George V, Gladstone, & others, including members of European royal families. S July 24 (236) £1,250 [Maggs]

Sandwich, Edward Montagu, 1st Earl, 1625-72.
See: Montagu, Edward

Santander, Francisco de Paula, 1792-1840. See: Bolivar, Simon

Santo Domingo
— VELA, JUAN. - Ms, Carta de Hidalguia, 10 Mar 1529. Copy of orig issued in Spain in 1479, now presented to the alcalde & notary public at Santo Domingo; sgd by both. 8 leaves, folio. In later full limp vellum bdg. sg Sept 18 (265) $700

Sargent, John Singer, 1856-1925
Series of 4 A Ls s, 2 July 1914 to 17 June [1918]. 10 pp, 8vo. To Sir Charles Walston. About a request to paint Walston's port for Cambridge, & landscape paintings. wa May 30 (421) $475

ALs, [n.d.], "Jeudi". 3 pp, size not stated. To [Charles] Ephrussi. Complaining about the placement a painting. In French. Framed. Altman collection. pnNY Sept 13 (103) $450

Saroyan, William, 1908-81
Typescript, short story, The Story of the Young Man and the Mouse, [n.d.]. 5 pp, 4to. Sgd on 1st p. sg Nov 6 (193) $70

Ls, 5 Mar 1957. 1 p, 4to. To the Ed of Look Magazine. Explaining his views on death. Some corrections, autograph postscript & editorial markings. sg Nov 6 (192) $200

Sartre, Jean Paul, 1905-80
ALs, 29 May 1953. 1 p, 4to. Recipient unnamed. Concerning an article by Monsieur Asbron. Framed. Altman collection. pnNY Sept 13 (130) $300

Sassoon, Siegfried, 1886-1967
A Ls s (2), 27 Mar & 24 May [1917]. On postcard & lettercard. To an aunt. About The Old Huntsman & the war. S July 23 (176) £480 [Maggs]

Satie, Erik, 1866-1925
ALs, 16 Oct 1919. 2 pp, 8vo. To Leonce Rosenberg. Thanking for photographs of musical Mss. S May 22 (635) £650 [Amadeus]

— 10 May 1923. 1 p, 8vo. To Monsieur W. Mayr. "Merci des 'cent francs' recus par moi-meme." Sgd with calligraphic initials. star Apr 9 (790) DM2,400

Sauckel, Fritz, 1894-1946
Autograph Ms, [legal brief for his defense(?), n.d.]. 1 p, folio. Denying responsibility for actions initiated by others. With trans. wa May 30 (412) $425

Saunders, Henry S.
Autograph Ms, account of boyhood meeting with Walt Whitman, draft; 10 Jan 1915, 1 p, 4to. Sgd HSS. 2 leaves glued together; on verso 6 deleted lines. With ANs, May 1916, 1 p, 8vo; description of Ms. Sgd H.S.S. With a copy of Saunders's Whitman Portraits. Toronto, 1922; ALs by Saunders to Edwin O. Grover, 14 May 1934, tipped to endpaper. Charles E. Feinberg collection. P Dec 15 (102) $750

Savigny, Friedrich Karl von, 1779-1861
Autograph Ms, Homoeopathisches Tagebuch, [1828] to 16 July [1832]. 24 pp, folio. In autograph envelope. Listing medicine taken & describing his health & state of mind. With separate autograph leaf listing medicines. star Apr 8 (415) DM950

Collection of 53 A Ls s & 24 drafts or copies of letters, partly autograph, 18 Apr 1842 to 15 Mar 1861. About 160 pp, various sizes. To Friedrich Kroeber. Regarding the management of his estates & commenting about his personal affairs & the political situation. With c.200 letters by Kroeber to Savigny & further related material. star Apr 8 (417) DM38,000

Series of 271 A Ls s, 1792 to 1823. About 500 pp, mostly 4to. To his guardian Ludwig Friedrich Kroeber (2 to Friedrich Kroeber). Reporting about his studies, his career, etc., & discussing the management of his estates. With related material. star Apr 8 (414) DM100,000

ALs, 2 Dec 1833. 1 p, 4to. To Eduard Boecking. Thanking for contributions to a legal compilation. Repaired. star Apr 8 (416) DM950

Sayers, Dorothy L., 1893-1957
Collection of 8 Ls s & letter, Feb to Nov 1936. 12 pp, 4to & 8vo. To J. Hadfield of J. M. Dent & Sons. Concerning the publication of Tales of Mystery and Detection & proofs of The Image in the Mirror. With related material. S July 23 (179) £900 [Apelbaum]

Schaeffer, Albrecht, 1885-1950
ALs, 11 Mar 1929. 3 pp, 8vo. To Hans Wolffheim. Telling him that he has not been able to detect any poetical talent in the pages submitted to him. star Apr 8 (240) DM250

Schardt, Sophie von, 1755-1819
Autograph Ms, collection of poetry & prose by various authors, [n.d.], 160 pp, 8vo. On unused pp of an album originally belonging to her father-in-law C. W. C. von Schardt. Green mor gilt. star Apr 8 (109) DM820

Scharnhorst, Gerhard von, 1755-1813
ALs, 2 July [18]06. 1 p, 4to. To an unnamed colonel. As officer on the general staff, summoning him to Brunswick. sg Apr 9 (177) $130

Series of 3 Ls s, 14 Mar 1808 & 16 & 28 Mar 1809. 6 pp, 8vo. To von Buelow. Orders for the troops in the Main valley. Discussing equipment for the infantry. Granting leave of absence to Lieut. Sarkowsky. JG Oct 2 (457) DM1,700

Ls, 5 June 1808. 1 p, 4to. To Lieut. Baersch. Thanking for the 1st sheets of his Volksfreund. star Apr 9 (1237) DM550

Schaumann, Ruth, 1899-1975
Autograph Ms, poem, Johannes der Juenger, [n.d.]. 1 p, 8vo. Four 4-line stanzas. With ownership inscr. star Apr 8 (241) DM250

Schelling, Friedrich Wilhelm Joseph von, 1775-1854
ALs, 29 July 1827. 4 pp, 4to. To [Georg von Schenk]. Concerning ceremonies for the inauguration of the new Academy of Science in Munich. star Apr 8 (418) DM3,400

— 29 May [1848]. 1 p, 4to. Recipient unnamed. Covering letter for a magazine with a speech by Stueve. JG Oct 2 (271) DM520

— [n.d.]; 2 pp, 4to. Recipient unnamed. Concerning postponement of a meeting. JG Oct 2 (272) DM1,000

Schiele, Egon, 1890-1918
[Autograph corrections on the 1st page of the biographical material in a cat for his 1913 exhibition in Munich sold at S on 21 May 1987, lot 306, for £480 to Leopold.]

Autograph postcard, sgd, [Dec 1908]. To his mother Marie Schiele. New Year's wishes. In pencil. star Apr 8 (536) DM500

Schiller, Friedrich von, 1759-1805
Ms, suggestions for festivities to celebrate the advent of the new century at Weimar, sgd by Schiller & 6 others, 8 Dec 1800. 4 pp, folio. List of subscribers attached, 2 pp, folio, sgd by Goethe, Herder, & others. In 19th cent red half cloth bdg. star Apr 8 (243) DM20,000

ALs, 26 Jan 1798. 2 pp, 4to. To J. F. G. Unger. Promising to edit an almanac for ladies for the year 1800, saying Cotta will publish his Wallenstein, & recommending Madame Mereau. Probably unptd. star Apr 8 (242) DM32,000

Schlegel, August Wilhelm von, 1767-1845
ALs, 8 Dec 1830. 1 p, 4to. To Guillaume Guizot. Letter of recommendation for M. de Ribbentrop. In French. star Apr 8 (244) DM1,500

Schlegel, Friedrich von, 1772-1829
ALs, [n.d.]. 1 p, 8vo. Recipient unnamed. Expressing his thanks for the previous evening. star Apr 8 (245) DM260

Schleiermacher, Friedrich, 1768-1834
Ds, 1 Jan 1820, 1821 & 1822. 1 p, folio. Receipt for dues for 2 seats in Trinity Church, Berlin, issued to the bookseller Enslin. Sgd 3 times. Partly ptd. star Apr 8 (419) DM230

Schlemmer, Oskar, 1888-1943
ALs, 29 Nov 1919. 2 pp, 4to. To the newspaper Muenchener Neueste Nachrichten. Regarding the controversy about hiring Klee for the Stuttgart academy of arts. With related material. star Apr 8 (538) DM3,800

Schlesinger, Adolph Martin
[A collection of 46 letters & documents, 1795 to 1860, by various composers & others, to the publishing firm of Schlesinger, sold at star on 9 Apr 1987, lot 794, for DM4,400]

Schlesinger, Adolph Martin —& Schlesinger, Heinrich
[A collection of 33 letters & documents, partly autograph, relating to their publishing business, c.1800 to 1869, sold at HN on 22 May 1987, lot 3167, for DM1,200]

[A collection of 6 letters & documents relating to their contracts with musicians & composers, 1834 to 1852, sold at HN on 22 May 1987, lot 3168, for DM550.]

[A collection of 8 letters & documents relating to their contracts with musicians & composers, 1837 to 1850, sold at HN on 22 May 1987, lot 3169, for DM1,150.]

Schlesinger, Heinrich. See: Schlesinger, Adolph Martin & Schlesinger

Schmettau, Johann Ernst von, 1703-64
Ls, 24 Jan 1763. 1 p, 4to. To a military commander. Assigning quarters. star Apr 9 (1238) DM320

Schmidt, Arno, 1914-79
ANs, 25 Jan 1974, on Ls, 1 p, 4to, by his wife Alice Schmidt to an unnamed young author. Saying he does not have the time to read his Ms. File holes. FD Dec 2 (3215) DM900

Schmidt, Franz, 1874-1939
Autograph music, "Symphonisches Zwischenspiel" [for his opera Notre Dame], 1903. 2 titles & 100 pp, 33cm by 26cm. Cloth bdg. Fair copy of full score, sgd & inscr to Dr. Karl Werner. star Apr 9 (795) DM11,000

SCHUBERT

Schmidt-Rottluff, Karl, 1884-1976
ALs, 21 June 1936. 1 p, 4to. To Alexej von Jawlensky. Commenting about Jawlensky's journey to Hofheim. HN May 22 (3171) DM800

Schneider, Reinhold, 1903-58
Collection of ALs, 17 Ls s, 1 autograph postcard, sgd, & 14 postcards, sgd, 15 Jan 1949 to 24 July 1956. 27 pp, 8vo, & cards. To Karl Borromaeus Glock. Regarding his literary work & religious questions. 1 letter mtd; on verso of 3 letters carbon copy of Glock's replies. With related material. star Apr 8 (246) DM1,700

Schnitzler, Arthur, 1862-1931
Ls, 17 July 1924. 2 pp, 8vo. To Nathan Ausubel. Stating that he does not believe his work can influence young people in America. HN May 22 (3173) DM580

Schoenberg, Arnold, 1874-1951
[2 ptd notes by Schoenberg, thanks for congratulations on his birthday, Oct 1924, & announcement of his marriage, 1 Dec 1824, with autograph envelopes to Karl Kraus, & related material, sold at star on 9 Apr 1987, lot 799, for DM1,100.]
Autograph music, song, beginning "In hellen Traeumen hab ich Dich oft geschaut", [summer 1893]. 4 pp, 12 staves each, on rectos only. Sgd at end. Margins slightly def. Supposedly unpbd. star Apr 9 (796) DM20,000
ALs, 18 Nov 1910. 2 pp, 4to. To Alfred Guttmann. Discussing concert programs. star Apr 9 (797) DM4,600
— 9 June 1922. 2 pp, 8vo. To Otto Freund. About Anton von Webern's financial problems. star Apr 9 (798) DM4,000
— [5 Aug 1927]. 1 p, 4to. To Alban Berg & his wife. About his current project, & rejoicing about Berg's success in Russia. On 2d page of ALs by his wife Gertrud. star Apr 9 (800) DM7,500
— 22 Oct 1929. 1 p, folio. To Georg Wolfsohn. Reporting about his health & inviting him to a concert. star Apr 9 (801) DM2,200
— 12 Feb 1936. 1 p, 8vo. To the pbr Dr. Kalmus. Discussing exchange rates between pound & dollar. S May 22 (637) £550 [Kruyfhooft]
— 17 Feb 1937. 1 p, 8vo. To Georg Wolfsohn & his family. About his teaching & recent compositions. On verso of group photograph, Schoenberg, his wife & daughter, inscr & dated Dec 1936. Also inscr by his wife & daughter. star Apr 9 (803) DM3,800
— [Sept 1949]. 2 pp, 4to. To Professor Wilde at Goettingen. Expressing his appreciation of Wilde's research regarding Schoenberg's compositions, & about his music. On verso of letter in facsimile, 16 Sept 1949, thanking for congratulations on his birthday. HK Nov 7 (2345) DM2,050

Ls, 27 Sept 1924. 1 p, 8vo. To Louis Fleury. Informing him of the completion of his Wind Quintet. Framed. Altman collection. pnNY Sept 13 (179) $400
— Nov 1934. 2 pp, folio. To Georg Wolfsohn. Mimeographed letter of thanks for congratulations on his birthday; with autograph addition, 2 words. With ALs, [13 Dec 1933], & ptd announcement of his son's birth, [26 May 1937]. star Apr 9 (802) DM900
— 16 Jan 1946. 1 p, 8vo. To Peter Salm, Counter Intelligence Corps. Asking him to forward some letters to his relatives in Austria. Framed. Altman collection. pnNY Sept 13 (180) $375

ANs, 20 Apr 1951. 2 pp, size not stated. To Georg Wolfsohn. Birthday congratulations & inscription on recto & verso of tp of a presentation copy of his book Style and Idea. L: 1951. Orig cloth. star Apr 9 (804) DM15,000

Schreker, Franz, 1878-1934
ALs, 30 July 1919. 1 p, folio. To [Dr. Zeiss]. Saying he will come to Frankfurt & inquiring whether he can direct a performance of his Die Gezeichneten. star Apr 9 (806) DM540

Schroeder, Rudolf Alexander, 1878-1962
Collection of 2 A Ls s & autograph transcript, 30 Apr 1947 & 27 Aug 1958. 7 pp, folio. To Hans Wolffheim. Sending poems for a publication & comparing his own literary form with George's & Hofmannsthals's. Musing about his earlier poems & including a recent one. Poem, beginning "Ah, stumpfes Herz und Sinne, die nicht taugen!" Sgd R. A. S. star Apr 8 (250) DM1,800

Schubert, Ferdinand, 1794-1859
ALs, 16 Jan 1848. 2 pp, folio. To the Verein zur Verbreitung echter Kirchenmusik at Vienna. Requesting permission to perform a new Mass by Joh. Richter. On verso of 2d p refusal of permission, with 2 signatures; endorsed & sgd by Schubert. With related material. FD Dec 2 (3260) DM1,150

Schubert, Gotthilf Heinrich von, 1780-1860
ALs, 5 Nov 1856. 1 p, 4to. To the publishing firm Cotta. Reminding them that the last proof of his Geschichte der Seele is incomplete. star Apr 8 (420) DM320

Schuecking, Levin, 1814-83
Series of 4 A Ls s, 1848, 1853 & [n.d.]. To the editors of the magazine Morgenblatt. Offering contributions. JG Oct 2 (142) DM1,600

Schumann, Clara, 1819-96
Autograph Ms, draft of a concert program, [n.d.]. 1 p, 8vo. Sgd Clara Sch / K.K. oesterreichische Kammervirtuosin. star Apr 9 (809) DM380

Series of 3 A Ls s, 10 June 1858 to 27 Mar 1879. 8 pp, 8vo. Recipients unnamed. About her arrival at Wiesbaden. Regretting she did not hear "Genoveva" again. Inquiring about the health of the Landgraefin von Hessen. JG Oct 2 (346) DM1,200

ALs, 7 May 1854. 2 pp, 8vo. To Henriette [Reichmann]. Describing her distress about the illness of her husband. star Apr 9 (808) DM5,000

Schumann, Elisabeth
Photograph, sgd & inscr, [25 Dec] 1942. Overall size 33cm by 25.5cm. Inscr to Hugo Burghauser, in pencil. Mtd. S Jan 27 (1063) £100 [Owen]

Schumann, Robert, 1810-56
Autograph Ms, love poem to his wife Clara, 40 lines beginning "Egmonts Geliebte Klaerchen hiess"; c.1840. 3 pp, 8vo. Design of leaves & troubadour on 1st p. S Nov 28 (638) £2,000 [Haas]

ALs, May 1846. 1 p, 8vo. To Edward Hansick. Thanking him & mentioning his illness. Framed. P Sept 24 (41) $1,100

Schuyler, Philip, 1733-1804
Ls, 5 Jan 1779. 2 pp, folio. To George Clinton. About his court martial & Washington's wish that Schuyler & Clinton should converse. S July 24 (409) £350 [Block]

Schweitzer, Albert, 1875-1965
ALs, 18 Jan 1956. 1 p, folio. To William Hemmick. Thanking for birthday wishes. In French. With 3 photographs, 2 inscr. S Jan 27 (911) £240 [Gekoski]

— 14 Feb 1965. 2 pp, 8vo. To Anna Martina Gottschick. Declining to participate in the movement for the preservation of a church in Leipzig. With related material. HN May 22 (3182) DM520

ANs, 1 Dec 1932. 1 p, 8vo. To an unnamed donor. Postscript below Ls by his secretary Emmy Martin; regretting he was not able to see him in Paris. In French. star Apr 8 (422) DM240

— 24 Mar 1947. 1 p, 4to. To an unnamed pastor at Hamburg. Postscript to a letter by a nurse at Lambarene, 9 lines, responding to recipient's letter (carbon copy present) about Germans during the Nazi period. star Apr 8 (423) DM520

Schwind, Moritz von, 1804-71
ALs, [c.1824]. 1 p, 4to. To [Eduard Bauernfeld]. About seeing Anna Page & thanking for a poem. star Apr 8 (539) DM1,300

Scotland
[A group of 2 documents, 2 & 20 Mar 1688, concerning the lands of Torhouse McCullock, 2 pp, folio, sgd by 7 Scottish statesmen, sold at sg on 9 Apr 1987, lot 181, for $100.]

— CIVIL WAR. - 2 Mss, [c.1640]. 3 pp, folio & 4to, 3 satirical poems about the Civil War, & list of Scottish commissioners attending Parliament in 1640. C June 24 (103) £380 [Quaritch]

Scott, Robert Falcon, 1868-1812
Ls, 18 Nov 1909. 1 p, 8vo. To Ernest Hopwood of Wolseley Tool & Motor Car Co. Regarding a design for a new motor sledge. Fragment, last page only. Partly autograph; sgd twice. Was mtd. S Jan 27 (831) £250 [Norrie]

Scott, Sir Walter, 1771-1832
Collection of ALs, ANs, & autograph Ms, 3 Aug [n.y.], 23 Apr [n.y.], & [n.d.]. 3 pp, various sizes. To W. M. Tartt, declining a request. To Mr. McAllister, asking him to call the following day. 13 lines from his History of Scotland. pnNY June 11 (48) $450

Series of 4 A Ls s, 7 May 1824 & [n.d.]. 4 pp, 4to & 8vo. To George Cray, Robert Rutherford, Sir William Knighton & an unnamed recipient. About a variety of matters. C June 24 (129) £550 [Wilson]

ALs, 24 Feb 1831. 3 pp, 4to. To William Godwin. Explaining his financial problems. S July 23 (92) £580 [Jarndyce]

— 15 Mar [1831]. 1 p, 4to. To [Sir John Robison]. About his health, & informing him that he has received a framed print instead of books he was expecting. C June 24 (130) £250 [Wilson]

— 5 Feb [n.y.]. 1 p, 4to. To an unidentified artist. About proofs presented to the Royal Society. sg Apr 9 (179) $300

— 10 Mar [n.y.]. 1 p, 4to. To [Sir John Robison?]. Regarding the Edinburgh Oil Gas Light Company. C June 24 (131) £280 [Lucas]

— [n.d., "Monday 22"]. 1 p, 4to. To Sir James. About a date for a visit. Mtd. sg Apr 9 (180) $200

Ds, 2 Feb 1819; c.16.5 by 13.5 inches. Bond for loan of £1,800 to Archibald Constable & Co. by George Home Falconer & James Hay, trustees for Mrs. Alexander Falconer.

Sgd by Scott, Archibald Constable, & others. Repaired. S Dec 18 (80) £500 [Quaritch]

Scott, Winfield, 1786-1866
Collection of ALs & Ms, sgd, 30 & 29 Oct 1860, 3 pp, 8vo & 6 pp, 4to. To Sec of War John Buchanan Floyd. Covering letter. Memorial, expressing his views concerning the possibility of a disruption of the Union & giving military advice. P May 13 (129) $6,000
Franking signature, [3 May n.y.]. As Lieut. Gen. rf Mar 14 (100) $55
Signature, on ptd document, Gen. Orders No. 53; management of insubordination & mutiny. 20 Aug 1842; 3 pp, extracted from bound vol. Article 2 canceled in pen. sg Nov 6 (329) $80

Scriabin, Alexander, 1872-1915
ALs, [received 12 Jan 1911]. 2 pp, 16mo (card). To his pbr Nicolai Gustavovich. Discussing the ptg of his [Prometheus]. In Russian. S May 22 (638) £2,500 [Johnson]

Scutenaire, Louis
Collection of 14 A Ls s & postcards, sgd, c.1937 to 1950. 16 pp, folio & 8vo. To Rene Magritte. Commenting on Magritte's stay in London, about their holidays, etc. Some written jointly with his wife Irene Hamoir, some sgd without message. S July 2 (981) £600 [Brachot]

Seaborg, Glenn Theodore
Autograph Ms, essay, Recent Advances in the Chemistry of Organometallic Compounds of Actinide Elements, summary; [n.d.]. 2 pp, 4to. Sgd; with corrections. star Apr 8 (424) DM240

Searle, George. See: Almanacs

Searle, Ronald
Original drawings, 9 large ink sketches for BOAC advertisements, five captioned; [n.d.]. Various sizes. S June 19 (691) £1,000 [Beetles]
Original drawing, Those Magnificent Men in their Flying Machines; pictorial title, model for plane & pilot, & 11 illusts for animated title & intermission sequences; ink, watercolor & gouache. Mtd or drawn directly in sketchbook, 252mm by 355mm; dated June/July [19]64. S Dec 5 (544) £4,000 [Baillie]

Selby, Prideaux John
Autograph Ms, notebook with detailed descriptions of different species of birds in the writer's own collection & of those sent to him by other collectors. [c.1830-35] 26 pp plus blanks, oblong 4to, in contemp half lea gilt. S Oct 23 (754) £1,300 [Quaritch]

Selden, John, 1584-1654
Ms, The Discourse of John Selden Esq. or his sence of various matters Of weight and high Consequences Relating especially to Religion and State [before 1689]. 339 pp, folio. Contemp calf. In brown ink. Selden's Table Talk. C Dec 3 (377) £240 [Levy]

Semmes, Raphael, 1809-77
Cut signature, [n.d.]. With autograph subscription. wa May 30 (251) $150

Semper, Gottfried, 1803-79
ALs, 31 Aug 1838. 1 p, 8vo. To Karl Vogel von Vogelstein. Declining an invitation because of his wedding. star Apr 8 (540) DM420

Sermons
Ms, Homiliary, in Latin. [Spain, c.1175]. 125 leaves only, vellum, 243mm by 170mm. Modern vellum bdg. In brown ink by 2 scribes in a large late romanesque hand. With over 50 very large painted initials in red. S June 23 (73) £5,500 [Thomas]

— ORIGEN. - Ms, Homilies on Genesis & Exodus, in the Latin trans of Rufinus. [Lambach Abbey, Austria, 2d half of 12th cent]. 126 leaves, vellum, 255mm by 165mm. Medieval bdg of wooden bds covered with white tawed lea. In dark brown ink in a square late romanesque bookhand using punctus flexus punctuation. With 9 large initials in red, 17 large decorated initials in red & black, 2 sketches of romanesque ornament, & full-page drawing. S June 23 (74) £26,000 [Schoyen]

Sevier, John, 1745-1815
Ds, 1782. 1 p, 16mo. Writ for the arrest of James Stephenson, sgd as court clerk. wa May 30 (423) $350

Sevigne, Marie de Rabutin-Chantal, Marquise de, 1626-96
ALs, 1 May 1691. 4 pp, 8vo. To du Plessis. Promising to support his application as tutor in the household of the Duchesse de Lesdiguieres. Lacking part of postscript Pleiade Ed, no 1245. S Nov 27 (467) £900 [Charavay]
AL, [4 Nov 1671]. 1 p, 4to. To her son-in-law Monsieur de Grignan. Worrying about the health of her pregnant daughter. S Nov 27 (465) £750 [Jeffery]

— [4 Feb 1685]. 2 pp, 4to. To her daughter Madame de Grignan. About the Marquis de Rhodes having sold his position as Grand Master of Ceremonies, a forthcoming visit of the Doge of Genoa, etc. Incomplete. Pleiade Ed, no 903. S Nov 27 (466) £600 [Henry]

Sewall, Samuel, 1652-1730
Ds, 23 June 1718. 1 p, folio. Appointment of Dorothy Farnum as executor of the estate of her father; partly ptd. Sgd as Commmissioner for Governor Shute. sg Nov 6 (330) $350

Seward, William Henry, 1801-72
Franking signature, [14 Dec n.y.]. rf Mar 14 (101) $160

Shackleton, Sir Ernest, 1874-1922
— SHACKLETON, LADY E. - ALs, 1 Feb 1922. 1 p, 4to. To John [Quiller Rowett?]. Expressing her wishes for the disposal of her husband's body. Sgd Emmie. S Jan 27 (832) £220 [Norrie]

Shakespeare, William, 1564-1616
Ms, memorial extracts from Henry IV Part I, c.1594-1603. 58 lines on 3 pp. Mostly recast into indirect speech; differing from ptd version. In Elizabethan Ms notebook, also containing philosophical & theological notes, in Latin, 19 pp. Contemp vellum wraps; some later inscr. S Dec 18 (14) £150,000 [Quaritch]
— IRELAND, WILLIAM HENRY. - A collection of 10 forged Shakespearian documents. C June 24 (117) £1,700 [Ximenes]
— IRELAND, WILLIAM HENRY. - 3 forgeries, a cut signature on vellum, "introduction" to King Lear, & part of a scene between Kent, Gloucester & Edmund; [18th cent]. 2 pp, 4to, & vellum strip. Mtd. S July 23 (17) £850 [Leinweber]

Shaw, George Bernard, 1856-1950
[A series of 8 typed questionnaires with autograph answers by Shaw, about World War II & a number of other subjects, 1940 to 1950, 20 pp, folio & 8vo, sold at S on 23 July, lot 182, for £4,800 to Hyde.]
Original drawings, 2 stage designs for Acts III & IV of John Bull's Other Island, with autograph commentary, [1920s]. 2 pp, 16mo. With ANs, 14 Feb 1941, to his dentist Dr. Hugh Westoby. sg Apr 9 (184) $1,200
Typescript, working theatrical script of Pygmalion. Typed 25 Feb 1914; probably used at Aldwych Theatre for revival of the play, 10 Feb 1920. With typescript of the part of Mrs. Pearce, marked up & sgd by Agnes Thomas. In all c.100 pp; lacking tp, worn. S Dec 18 (180) £2,400 [Rota]
Collection of 11 A Ls s & autograph cards, sgd, 4 Ls s & cards, sgd, & 5 Ls & cards written on his behalf, 1908 to 1922. c.25 pp, 4to & 8vo, & cards. To W. H. Hoather. Relating to the developing & ptg of his photographs. S Dec 18 (178) £1,000 [Dupre]
Series of 3 A Ls s, 20 Aug 1910 to 16 Oct 1913. 4to. To "Sylvia". Discussing issues concerning women; about her pregnancy & child. P Dec 15 (79) $2,100
ALs, 8 Dec 1902. 2 pp, 16mo, on letter card. To W. Aubrey Smith. Declining a conference chairmanship. sg Nov 6 (194) $500
— 5 June 1903. 2 pp, 8vo. To William Wyes. Giving advice on his performance of Mellish in Cashel Byron's Profession. S Dec 18 (179) £500 [Dupre]
— 7 Dec 1904. 2 pp, 8vo. To W. S. Sonnenschein. Declining to agree to a new Ed of his early writings. star Apr 8 (252) DM680
— 22 Oct 1911. 2 pp, 4to. To Henry D. Harben. Proposing a plan of action concerning national insurance. Torn. C Dec 3 (378) £300 [Dupre]
— 16 Sept 1913. 2 pp, 8vo. To Granville Bantock. About Bantock's plan to write an overture entitled Man and Superman. With related material. S July 23 (180) £800 [Dupre]
— 18 Aug 1916. 2 pp, folio. To Milton Rosmer. Comparing service in the infantry & the Royal Horse Artillery & warning him not to touch The Man of Destiny. pn Dec 11 (31) £340 [Dupre]
— 12 A Ls s, 1921 to 1941. About 12 pp, various sizes (7 lettercards). To Hoppe & Dent of J. M. Dent & Sons. Regarding publishing projects. With related material. S July 23 (183) £1,900 [Dupre]
— 10 Sept 1924. 1 p, 4to. To H. Adair Marquand. Suggesting that students should be "having a good time until Germany, putting on muscle whilst we are putting on fat, turns the tables on us". On verso of Ls from Marquand to Shaw. C Dec 3 (379) £340 [Dupre]
— 4 Oct 1924. 2 pp, 8vo. To John A. Lincoln. Discouraging his efforts as a playwright. With related material by Shaw & Lincoln. P June 18 (179) $6,000
— 31 Dec 1928. 1 p, 8vo. To Mrs. Bennett. About the production of a play. Framed. Altman collection. pnNY Sept 13 (131) $650
— 26 Feb 1940. 2 pp, 8vo. To Ethel Davis. Saying he has paid her bill. S Jan 27 (740) £240 [Dupre]
— 15 Dec 1943. 1 p, 8vo. To Louis L. Appleton. Objecting angrily to the text of an interview. With copy of The Firefighter, Feb 1944, containing the interview. C Dec 3 (381) £250 [Dupre]
Series of 4 Ls s, 30 May to 11 July 1914. 4 pp, 4to. To Perriton Maxwell. Concerning the publication of his Pygmalion by Nash's Magazine. Sang collection. P Sept 24 (46) $1,600

Ls s (2), 7 Sept 1914 & 24 Feb 1916. 3 pp, 4to. To Clifford Sharp. Discussing revisions & a potential reprint of his Common Sense about the War. Sang collection. P Sept 24 (44) $1,400

Ls, 24 June 1915. 1 p, 4to. To Milton Rosmer. Commenting on a play he dislikes & on Rosmer's part in it. pn Dec 11 (30) £190 [Dupre]

— 7 Oct 1924. 2 pp, 4to. To T. E. Lawrence ["My dear Luruns"]. About correcting the proofs of Seven Pillars of Wisdom & correct punctuation. S Dec 18 (177) £1,600 [Joseph & Sawyer]

— 15 Dec 1945. 2 pp, 8vo. To Elisabeth Bergner. Saying she cannot play St. Joan any more. With autograph corrections. C June 24 (133) £650 [Wilson]

— 19 May 1948. 1 p, 8vo. To the National Institute for the Blind. Granting permission to "make talking films for the blind" of his works. With autograph corrections. With related material. C June 24 (134) £220 [Lucas]

Autograph postcards (2), sgd, 24 Nov 1940 & 16 Dec 1941. To Charles A. Smith. Declining to write an article about Stalin & anr proposal. S Jan 27 (742) £220 [Dupre]

Autograph postcard, sgd, 7 Jan 1916. To Madge McIntosh. Concerning an appointment. Initialled. Framed & double-glazed. Altman collection. pnNY Sept 13 (132) $200

— [n.d.]. To Lilian Simpson. Apologizing for delay in returning the proofs of Dying Image. Framed. Altman collection. pnNY Sept 13 (133) $100

ANs, 15 Jan 1902. 2 pp, 12mo (card). To Mr. Herty. Suggesting that he wait "until Miss Halston is free". C June 24 (132) £160 [Solomon]

— 5 Apr 1925, 1 p, 4to. To H. Robinson Shepherd. Nine lines, responding to Shepherd's query about skillful use of language. At the bottom of Shepherd's letter to Shaw, 31 Dec 1924. Sang collection. P Sept 24 (45) $850

Corrected galley proof, entry about Shaw in Dent's Everyman's Encyclopedia, [n.d.]. 2 sheets. With autograph revisions & corrections by Shaw & other corrections by Donald Ross. Tipped into made-up vol about the Encyclopedia including material by other authors. S July 23 (181) £380 [Dupre]

Cut signature, 2 Oct 1908. Mtd. pnNY June 11 (49) $90

Shaw, John Byam

Original drawing, "Reverie of Ormuz the Persian", in ink & watercolor, possibly to illus Laurence Hope's The Garden of Kama, 1914. 287mm by 317mm. S June 19 (692) £260 [Vincent]

Sheffield, Edmund, 1st Earl of Mulgrave, 1564?-1646

Ds, 1595. 1 p, 304mm by 472mm. Vellum. Sale of property. sg Apr 9 (185) $600

Shelley, Mary Wollstonecraft, 1797-1851

ALs, "Sunday" [29 Apr 1829 or 1835?]. 3 pp, 8vo. To [Cyrus Redding]. About an oil port of Shelley. Matted with a postcard port of Shelley. P Dec 15 (81) $1,500

— 20 Dec [n.y.]. 3 pp, 8vo. To Abraham Hayward. Dinner invitation. With material related to Hayward. S July 23 (93) £450 [Quaritch]

Shelley, Percy Bysshe, 1792-1822

[A copy of Seneca's Philosophi opera, Antwerp: Plantin, 1615, read by Shelley Apr to May 1815, with his autograph inscr & annotations in pencil on flyleaf & in the margin of 10 pp, sold at S on 18 Dec 1986, lot 82, for £9,500 to Quaritch.]

Autograph Ms, poems, The Sunset, & Song On a Faded Violet, 1818. 4 pp, 8vo. With corrections. S Dec 18 (88) £9,500 [Quaritch]

Autograph check, sgd, 13 Jan 1815; c.4.5 by 7 inches. £20 drawn on Brooker & Co., payable to "Hunt Esq. or bearer". Framed. S Dec 18 (82) £900 [Maggs]

— Anr, sgd, 24 Nov 1817. Drawn on Messrs. Brookes & Co. in favor of Mr. Calvert. On verso of ptd letter heading for John Calvert. S July 23 (95) £800 [L'Autographe]

Shepard, E. H.

Original drawing, pen-&-ink sketch with 3 illusts of a fisherman & his dreams around the poem Nothing Doing, reproduced in Punch, 27 Dec 1950. Sgd. 352mm by 507mm. Framed. S June 19 (702) £480 [Sawyer]

Sheridan, Philip Henry, 1831-88

ALs, 20 Apr [18]76. 3 pp, 8vo. To [Gen.] Ord. Inquiring about some documents. Stained. wa May 30 (252) $70

Sheringham, George

Original drawings, tp, 24 pencil & crayon sketches, & a map to illus The Redhead Twins. Tipped into cloth-backed album, 230mm by 310mm, with 24 pp of typed text. C June 24 (135) £120 [Bristow]

SHERMAN

Sherman, Roger, Signer from Connecticut

Ds, April 1757. 1 p, 8vo. Statement concerning payment of debt. Partly autograph; sgd Pettibone & Sherman. Charlotte Parker Milne collection. wd Nov 12 (67) $100

— 19 Aug 1771. 1 p, folio. Land sale. Sgd twice. Seal hole. wa May 30 (141) $140

Sherman, William Tecumseh, 1820-91

Series of 8 A Ls s, July 1883 to 4 Jan 1889. Various lengths & sizes. To John E. Tourtelotte. Chatting about his activities in retirement. With 2 A Ls s by Ellen Ewing Sherman to Tourtelotte. P Oct 29 (130) $1,000

ALs, 28 May 1863. 3 pp, 4to. To Admiral David D. Porter. Reporting about a battle resulting in the sinking of the gunboat Cincinnati. P Oct 29 (129) $2,300

— 1 Sept 1863. 3 pp, 4to. To Gen. James Birdseye McPherson. Discussing the problem of restraining "the violence & passion of the negroes" on abandoned plantations. Bullock collection. CNY Dec 19 (227) $1,600

— 29 Apr 1875. 2 pp, 8vo. To Mrs. Belknap. Regretting her cancellation of their appointment to attend a performance. On US Army Headquarters letterhead. sg Nov 6 (333) $60

— 1 June 1889. 3 pp, 4to. To R. W. Woodbury. Concerning a speech at a Fourth of July celebration. Framed. Altman collection. pnNY Sept 13 (22) $275

— 29 Oct [1890]. 3 pp, 8vo. To Andrew Carnegie. Thanking for a present of whiskey & saying he will meet "some of your Iron and Steel friends". With ANs, 31 Oct 1890, below Sherman's letter, from Carnegie to Mr. Bell; note of transmittal. Bullock collection. CNY Dec 19 (228) $420

— [n.d.]; 2 pp, 8vo. To W. C. Church. About a forthcoming speech. On US Army Headquarters letterhead. Affixed to front endpaper of The Sherman Letters. NY, 1894; 1st Ed. sg Nov 6 (334) $110

ANs, [c.1870]; 1p, 24mo, on verso of engraved calling card. To Sec of War Belknap. Letter of introduction for Col. Ward. sg Nov 6 (332) $60

Document, 26 Apr 1865. 2 pp, 4to. Terms of Gen. Joseph E. Johnston's surrender at Bonnett's House. Copy; with proxy signatures. wa May 30 (253) $1,300

Shostakovich, Dimitri, 1906-75

Photograph, sgd, [n.d.]. Postcard size. Half length. With envelope. star Apr 9 (805) DM900

Shovell, Sir Clowdisley, 1650-1707

Ds, 27 Dec 1701. 1 p, folio. Certificate confirming Edward Mann's service as pilot, 1689. Repaired. With later ptd material. C Dec 3 (328) £220 [Harris]

Sibelius, Jean, 1865-1957

Ms, music to the play Oedlan by M. Lybeck, full score. 1909; c.90 pp, folio. In a scribal hand, notated in black & red ink on up to 14 staves per p. Marked for performance in pencil. Autograph tp, sgd. Presumably unpbd. S Nov 28 (641) £500 [MacNutt]

Collection of 12 A Ls s & Ls, 1905 to 1932. 13 pp, 4to & 8vo. To Sir Granville Bantock. About his symphonies, concert programs, etc. In English & German. S May 22 (518) £4,200 [MacNutt]

ALs, 3 Oct 1905. 1 p, 4to. To Paul Juon. Looking forward to meeting him & to hear his new works. FD June 11 (3587) DM2,000

— 1 Aug 1925. 1 p, 4to. To Johannes Poulsen. Concerning his music for The Tempest. In Swedish. S May 22 (517) £550 [Kruyfhooft]

— 26 Apr 1930. 2 pp, 4to. Recipient unnamed. Regarding his music for The Tempest. In German; subscription in English. S Nov 28 (640) £580 [Wurlitzer-Bruck]

ADs, 15 May 1906. 1 p, 8vo. Receipt. HN May 22 (3187) DM420

Photograph, sgd & inscr, [n.d.]. 16.5cm by 10.5cm. Inscr to Sir Granville Bantock. With ANs on ptd visiting-card. S May 22 (516) £950 [MacNutt]

Sidney, Algernon, 1622-83. See: Fairfax, Thomas

Siegfried III von Eppstein, Archbishop of Mainz, d.1249

Document, 12 June 1247. 1 p, folio. Vellum. Confirmation of privileges granted the monastery of St. Michael's at Hildesheim by Pope Innocent IV. Fragment of wax seal. star Apr 9 (986) DM3,400

Sienkiewicz, Henryk, 1846-1916

Ds, 16 June 1906. 2 pp, folio. Proposal for the foundation of teachers' colleges. Also sgd by Krasinski & Osuchowski. With ptd leaflet. S Jan 27 (989) £150 [Niewod]

Signac, Paul, 1863-1935

ALs, 20 [Sept 1900]. 2 pp, 8vo. To Monsieur de Fletan. Thanking for an invitation & requesting him to send some music to a friend. Framed. Altman collection. pnNY Sept 13 (104) $400

Sikorsky, Igor I., 1889-1972

Collection of Ls & 2 photographs, sgd & incr. 16 Oct 1936, 1913, & [n.d.]. 1 p, 4to, & 5 by 8 inches. To R. B. Quick. About "propeller brakes on a multi-engine airplane". Photographs inscr to Quick; 1 showing Sikorsky with Emperor Nicholas II. With 1st Ed of Sikorsky's The Story of the Winged-S. NY, 1938. wa May 30 (337) $260

Sime, Sidney H.

Original drawing, entitled "John and the Ghosts"; ink & wash. 168mm by 263mm, sgd. Reproduced as pictorial heading to a story by Quiller-Couch in Pall Mall Magazine, 1901. S Dec 5 (551) £500 [Beetles]

— Original drawing, man at dinner with giants; ink, pencil & wash. 193mm by 281mm, sgd. Mtd. Reproduced in Pall Mall Magazine, 1899, to illus Housman's The Mountains of the Moon. S Dec 5 (550) £500 [Beetles]

Simmons, Paul

Original drawings, 12 paintings depicting scenes from Franklin W. Dixon's The Hardy Boys, each sgd & captioned; illusts for upper covers of the paperback Ed, [n.d.]. About 330mm by 280mm. S June 19 (703) £250 [Culpin]

Simms, William Gilmore, 1806-70

ALs, 4 Apr [1843?]. 1 p, folio. To Isaac K. Tefft. Commenting about William Hayne Simmons & Tefft's collection of autographs. On integral leaf of a letter from Simmons to Simms, 25 Mar 1843, 1 p, folio, regarding routes to St. Augustine. P May 13 (131) $600

Simons, Walter, 1861-1937

Ls, 17 Mar 1925. 1 p, 4to. To Edward Albert Filene. Thanking for the German Ed of Filene's book. star Apr 9 (1243) DM220

Simrock, Karl, 1802-76

ALs, 20 Apr 1874. 1 p, 8vo. To the publisher F. Vogel. Thanking for a fee & criticizing the bdg of Logaus Sinngedichte. star Apr 8 (425) DM320

Sinclair, Sir John, 1754-1835

A Ls s (2), 19 May 1797 & 6 Feb 1819. 3 pp, 4to. To William Adam, about a circular house. To R. Collins, about resumption of cash payments. With 2 A Ls s & related material. C June 24 (178) £240 [Hannas]

ALs, 26 May 1826. 3 pp, folio. To C. J. Stewart. Discussing a scheme to encourage emigration to Colombia. C June 24 (179) £50 [Hannas]

Sinclair, Upton, 1878-1968

Ls, 19 Aug 1940. 1 p, 4to. To Rene Taupin. About the occupation of France & saying culture cannot "exist under a totalitarian regime". star Apr 8 (253) DM340

Singer, Edmund, 1830-1912

Autograph music, "Cadenz zu Beethoven's Violin Conzert", 5 June 1859. 2 pp, size not stated. Sgd. star Apr 9 (810) DM260

Sinoviev, Alexander

Autograph Ms, response to journalists' questions about one of his works, [spring 1981]. 7 pp, folio. Sgd at head. In Russian. star Apr 8 (426) DM210

Sisley, Alfred, 1839-99

ALs, 13 Jan 1897. 1 p, 8vo. Recipient unnamed. Apologizing for giving him trouble & suggesting he may be able to find a frame for him. Framed. Altman collection. pnNY Sept 13 (105) $325

Sitgreaves, Lorenzo, 1811-88

Document, 4 July 1832. 1 p, 4to. His West point diploma; engraved vignettes. With cabinet photograph, in uniform. wa Oct 18 (145) $90

Sitwell, Dame Edith, 1887-1964

Autograph Ms, "Towards the end of the past about Hollywood P.283"; [n.d.]. 3 pp, folio, on endpapers of an old account book, sgd & entitled New Poems; in red & black ink. Further annotations on tp & last 2 leaves. Worn cloth bdg; in modern cloth box. Altman collection. pnNY Sept 13 (286) $375

Series of 70 A Ls s, 1 May 1952 to 17 Mar 1960. 286 pp, various sizes. To Gordon Watson. Interesting letters about her work, Watson's concerts, literary gossip. With autograph transcripts, sgd, of 7 poems, 14 pp, folio; 2 inscr to Watson. C Dec 3 (382) £4,500 [D'Arcy]

ALs, 7 Nov 1945. 8 pp, 8vo. To Norman Nicholson. Concerning Walton, Yeats, & her own works. S Jan 27 (743) £180 [Rankin]

Sitwell Family

[2 photographs by Cecil Beaton, 9.25 by 7.25 inches, showing Edith, Osbert, Sacheverell & Reresby in a drawing room, & Edith in a bed, both sgd by Beaton on mount, overall size 16.75 by 11.75 inches, framed, sold at S on 23 July, lot 185, for £650 to Bailey.]

Sixtus IV, Pope, 1414-84
Document, 1475. 1 p, folio. Vellum. Papal Bull. Contents not stated. wa May 30 (65) $450

Sixtus V, Pope, 1521-90
Ls, 1 May 1590. 1 p, 4to. To his treasurer Monsignore Cesi. Regarding a payment by Mario Montano. star Apr 9 (1113) DM1,000

Slavery
[The Ms record of judicial proceedings in Montgomery County, Texas, 27 Mar 1843, 10 pp, folio, concerning a judicial levy on "a Negro man named Moses" & a missing bill of sale for slaves, sold at sg on 9 Apr 1986, lot 208, for $200.]

Ms, act abolishing slavery in the territories of the U.S.A., passed 17 June 1862; 2 pp, blue paper; on ptd form. Draft of final version, endorsed on verso "H.R.374". wa May 30 (254) $750

ADs, 1818. 1 p, folio. Bill of sale for a slave named Peet. sg Nov 6 (336) $175

Ds, 9 Aug 1848. 1 p, 4to. Bill of sale for a slave named Hester to John Doon. Partly ptd. sg Nov 6 (337) $175

Slevogt, Max, 1868-1932
Autograph postcard, sgd, 21 Apr 1932. To "Herrn Jaegermeister Lewy". Accepting an invitation. On verso pen-&-ink sketch, 8.5cm by 12.5cm; 2 rabbits with human faces (1 self port) in front of hunter. star Apr 8 (541) DM900

Slitpacher, Johan, Monk of Melk
Ms, Fragmentum Biblie. [Austria, 1439?]. 134 leaves (15 blank) & 3 flyleaves, vellum & paper, 85mm by 62mm. Modern calf. In brown & red ink in a small cursive bookhand. With painted initials in red throughout & 3 pages with circular diagrams. Containing an alphabetical verse summary of the Bible & similar guides to astronomy, patristics, the Sentences of Peter Lombard, etc. S June 23 (83) £3,800 [Quaritch]

Sloan, John
Series of 3 A Ls s, 12 May 1909 to 20 May 1915. 3 pp, 4to & folio. To Horace Traubel. Sending a cheque [not included]; inviting him to his studio; declining to speak at a celebration of Walt Whitman's birth. Charles E. Feinberg collection. P Dec 15 (103) $500

Smetana, Friedrich, 1824-84
ALs, 7 Jan 1875. 3 pp, 8vo. To his daughters. About his unhappy situation, his loneliness & deafness. S May 22 (519) £2,200 [Haas]

— 1 Feb 1875. 3 pp, 8vo. To his daughters. Reporting about his daily routine, his pupils & friends. S May 22 (521) £6,200 [Henry]

— 20 June 1875. 4 pp, 8vo. To his daughters. Sending music, & complaining about his situation in Prague. S May 22 (522) £2,900 [Riskin]

Smith, James, Signer from Pennsylvania
Ds, 28 Oct 1789. 3 pp, folio. Petition of John M'Pherson asking pardon for a slave indicted for theft. Charlotte Parker Milne collection. wd Nov 12 (68) $275

Smith, Joseph, 1805-44
Ds, 7 Feb 1837. 1 p, 8vo. Engraved $5 bank note of the Kirtland Safety Society Bank; sgd by Smith as cashier & Sidney Rigdon as president. Tipped to larger sheet. Bullock collection. CNY Dec 19 (230) $550

— 10 Feb 1843. 1 p, 4to. Legal document affirming a debt due to the State of Illinois by Joseph Hadlock. Sgd by Smith as mayor of Nauvoo. sg Nov 6 (197) $1,000

Smith, Martin Luther, 1819-66
Autograph endorsement, 21 Jan 1865, sgd; on verso of ALs, 9 Jan 1865, 1 p, 4to, from Edward Willis to Gen. Beauregard. Concerning the rebuilding of railroads in Georgia. wa May 30 (257) $180

Smith, Samuel F., 1808-95
Autograph transcript, 2 verses of America; [n.d.]. 1 p, 8vo. In fine calligraphic hand; sgd. On card, in red cloth folder. CNY Dec 19 (231) $320

— Autograph transcript, 4 stanzas of America, sgd & dated May [18]94. 1 p, 4to. With autograph transcript of 1st stanza of America, [n.d.], 1 p, 18mo; ALs, 21 June 1888, 3 pp, 8vo, to Thomas W. Silloway, explaining the genesis of the hymn America; & ptd pamphlet, 1895. Bullock collection. CNY Dec 19 (232) $1,600

Smuts, Jan Christian, 1870-1950
Photograph, sgd, [n.d.]; 24cm by 20cm. Sgd on mount. Framed. pn Dec 11 (117) £45 [Reuter]

Sonnets sur la Passion de Jesus
Ms, [France, possibly Savoy, c.1630-40]. 112 leaves, 4 blanks, & 2 flyleaves, vellum, 194mm by 228mm. Contemp ruby mor gilt bdg. 109 poems, in French, with illuminated tp, 8 full-page miniatures & 86 large miniatures combined with texts to form visual poems. FD June 11 (11) DM75,000

Soong Mei-ling (Mme. Chiang Kai-shek)
Collection of Ls & photograph, sgd & inscr, 18 Aug 1941 & 1940. 1 p, 4to, & 8 by 10 inches. To Mrs. J. B. Harriman. Responding to a letter of encouragement. Photo-

graph inscr to Major McHugh. Waterstained; matted. wa May 30 (465) $100

Sophie, Kurfuerstin von Hannover, 1630-1714
ALs, 8/18 Nov [n.y., c.1655]. 3 pp, 8vo. To her mother [Elizabeth, Queen of Bohemia]. Discussing various princes, using cover names. In French. HN Nov 27 (2383) DM4,800

Sorge, Reinhard Johannes, 1892-1916
Autograph Ms, 1st 9 scenes of his "Franziskus-Mysterium", [1916]. 26 pp, folio. With 10th scene in the hand of Susanne Sorge & related material. star Apr 8 (254) DM1,900

Soubise, Charles de Rohan, Prince de, 1715-87
AL, 20 Oct [1758]. 2 pp, 4to. Recipient unnamed. Reporting about the military situation around Kassel. star Apr 9 (1244) DM360

Souideikine, Serge
Series of 6 A Ls s, dates not given. 6 pp, 8vo & 4to. To Kilbachich. On artistic & musical matters. With related material. sg Apr 9 (192) $120

Sousa, John Philip, 1854-1932
Autograph sentiment, 1931; 3.75 by 5.5 inches. On personal letterhead. wa Oct 18 (52) $60

Southey, Robert, 1774-1843
[An interleaved & annotated copy of the 1st Ed of his Letters From England, 3 vols, 8vo, 1807, with c.80 autograph annotations in the 1st 2 vols, sold at S on July 23, lot 99, for £3,200 to Quaritch.]
Collection of 3 A Ls s & autograph Ms, 1814 to 1837. 9 pp, 4to & 8vo. To Edward Thomas, William Taylor, & anr recipient. About a vol by Barre, his trip to the continent, his forthcoming Tale of Paraguay, etc. Ms, notes on "Sonnets". 1 letter with recipient's reply subscribed. S July 23 (98) £750 [Richards]
Series of 6 A Ls s, 1805 to 1814. 19 pp, 4to. To John May. Interesting letters on a variety of subjects. Tipped into his Life of Nelson, 1813. 2 vols in one, 8vo. 1st Ed. S Dec 18 (93) £1,900 [Quaritch]
— Series of 3 A Ls s, 3 Sept 1825 to 19 Jan 1832. 5 pp, 4to & 8vo. To Messrs. Longman, Hurst & Co, S. C. Hall, & the Rev. William Jackson. About a variety of matters. C June 24 (136) £220 [Ximenes]

Southwell, Sir Robert, 1635-1702
ALs, 22 May 1661. 2 pp, folio. To Robert Boyle. Retained draft, introducing Dr. Bacon & Dr. Walgrave. Initialled. S Jan 27 (912) £50 [Rota]

Sowerby, James, 1757-1822
Original drawing, William Curtis's Botanic Garden, Lambeth Marsh, ante 1787; watercolor, 279mm by 478mm. Sgd. Tipped to orig Whatman paper mount; matted. Hunt collection. CNY Nov 21 (260) $19,000 [Maggs]

Sowerby, John G. —& Crane, Thomas
Original drawings, 26 illusts for At Home, 1881; ink & watercolor. Various sizes. S Dec 5 (552) £4,500 [Whistler]

Spalatin, Georg, 1484-1545
ALs, [early Sept] 1528. 2 pp, folio. To Martin Luther. Discussing a case involving a promise of marriage. In Latin. With postscript, in German. star Apr 9 (1245) DM2,700

Spallanzani, Lazzaro, 1729-99
ALs, [n.d.]. 1 p, 4to. Recipient unnamed. Sending an engraving & hoping for the continuation of his patronage. Pasted down at corners. C June 24 (180) £130 [L'Autographe]

Sparr, Otto Christoph, Freiherr von, 1599?-1668
Ls, 14/4 Aug 1664. 1 p, folio. To Col. Graf von Sparr. Warning him about an application by Col. Marquese Pio for a post. With autograph subscription. With related material. star Apr 9 (1249) DM2,200

Speer, Albert, 1905-81
Series of 5 Ls s, & 1 letter with secretarial signature, 13 Nov 1970 to 2 July 1981. 6 pp, folio & 8vo. To Wing Commander John Peskett. Discussing German reaction to Hitler, the treatment of the Jews, the Nuremberg trial & his imprisonment at Spandau, etc. With related material. S May 21 (309) £560 [Pervanas]

Spinola, Ambrogio, Marchese, 1569-1630
Ls, 12 Dec 1620. 1 p, folio. To Marquese Francesco Stondrati. Thanking for a promotion. With autograph subscription. star Apr 9 (1250) DM550

Spohr, Louis, 1784-1854
Autograph music, fragment of his last quintet, [n.d.]. 2 pp, 4to. With ALs, 20 Oct 1839. 1 p, 8vo. To Anton Genast. Letter of recommendation for bearer. JG Oct 2 (347) DM1,300
ALs, 18 Jan 1855. 1 p, 4to. To Konopasek, conductor at Regensburg. Answering a question regarding the overture to Jessonda. star Apr 9 (813) DM950
Ds, [n.d.]. 1 p, folio. Certificate of honorary membership in the Deutscher Nationalverein fuer Musik und ihre Wissenschaft

for Andreas Hippolyt Chelard; sgd as president of the society. Countersgd by Gustav Schilling. Partly ptd. star Apr 9 (814) DM320

Spontini, Gaspare, 1774-1851
ALs, 26 Jan [n.y.]. 1 p, 4to. To Karl Adam Bader. Imploring him to sing in his opera on Sunday. Repaired. star Apr 9 (816) DM260

Series of Ds s, 3 Ds s, 5 Aug 1824 to 7 Nov 1844. 5 pp, folio. Contracts with A. M. Schlesinger. With autograph additions. HN May 22 (3194) DM450

Squire, Edward, d.1598. See: Elizabeth I, 1533-1603

Stanislas II Augustus, King of Poland, 1732-98
Ls, 1 Sept 1790. 2 pp, folio. To Ferdinand IV, King of Naples. Sending congratulations on the birth of a son & the marriage of 2 daughters. With autograph subscription. In Latin. star Apr 9 (1129) DM700

Stanley, Sir Henry Morton, 1841-1904
ALs, 12 Mar 1894. 4 pp, 8vo. To E. M. Parker. About Bishop Parker's spectacles. S July 24 (331) £350

Stanton, Edwin M., 1814-69
Ls, 27 Dec 1866. 2 pp, 4to. To Attorney Gen. Henry Stanbery. About the pardon of "one Smoot". wa May 30 (258) $80

Stark, John, 1728-1822
— STARK, ELIZABETH PAGE. - Signature, [n.d.]. 1 p, 16mo. sg Nov 6 (338) $150

Stefansson, Vilhjalmur, 1879-1962
Photograph, sgd & inscr, 22 May 1913. 12mo. Sgd & inscr to Henry Fairfield Osborn on mount; overall size 4to. sg Apr 9 (195) $90

Steibelt, Daniel, 1765?-1823
ALs, [received 28 Oct 1807]. 1 p, 4to. To the pbr Imbault. Promising to send his Rondo on Saturday. Repaired. S May 22 (639) £50 [Riskin]

Steichen, Edward, 1879-1972
Ls, 18 Aug 1965. 1 p, 4to. Recipient unnamed. Sending autographed copy of his book. wa May 30 (433) $70

Stein, Friedrich ("Fritz"), Freiherr von, 1772-1844
ALs, 27 June 1830. 4 pp, 8vo. To his niece Luise von Parry. About her husband's plans to settle in the Saale Valley, & describing the beauty of Breslau. With related material. star Apr 8 (111) DM640

Stein, Gertrude, 1874-1946
ALs, [n.d.]. 2 pp, 8vo. To "My dear Chitty". Saying "it does take time to do arithmetic". Framed. Altman collection. pnNY Sept 13 (134) $800
— 5 Dec 1945. 2 pp, folio. To [Bill] Walton. Introducing Lamont Johnson. Framed. Altman collection. pnNY Sept 13 (135) $700

Stein, Karl, Freiherr von und zum, 1757-1831
ALs, 7 Dec 1815. 3 pp, 4to. To Herzog Leopold Friedrich Franz von Anhalt-Dessau. Draft, explaining his reasons for declining the nomination as Prussian envoy to the Frankfurt diet. Sgd with paraph. In the margins & between the lines of Ls, 9 Oct 1815, from the Duke to Stein. star Apr 9 (1258) DM2,100
— 27 Nov 1823. 2 pp, 4to. To Miss Schroeder. Expressing his wish that she continue to work for his family. star Apr 9 (1259) DM1,850
Ls, 29 Apr 1815. 1 p, 4to. To Col. Ruehle von Lilienstern. Expressing his approval of Lilienstern's work. star Apr 9 (1257) DM700

Steinbeck, John, 1902-68
Autograph Ms, Autobiography: Making of a New Yorker, parts 2 & 3, pbd in New York Times Magazine, 1953. With 3 A Ls s, 1952, to his Ed Seymour Peck, concerning the essay. On rectos only of 12 sheets of yellow legal-size lined paper. CNY Dec 19 (233) $6,500
Series of 9 A Ls s, 24 Aug 1959 to 17 Feb 1962 & [n.d.]. 25 pp, folio & 4to. To Shirley Fisher. About his literary work, Dennis Murphy, American politics, etc. Fran Sammut Estate. wd Nov 12 (18) $7,000
Ls, 20 Feb 1963. 1 p, 4to. To Rockwell Kent's agent. Declining to comment on a work by Kent. sg Nov 6 (201) $325

Steiner, Rudolf, 1861-1925
ALs, 14 May 1904. 2 pp, 8vo. To [Eugen Diederichs]. Offering a work about mysticism [his Theosophie] for print. star Apr 8 (427) DM4,800

Steiner, Sigmund Anton, 1773-1838 —& Haslinger, Tobias, 1787-1842
[A collection of 28 letters & documents in Steiner's or Haslinger's hand, 1819 to 1835, relating to their publishing firm, sold at star on 9 Apr, lot 818, for DM5,000.]

Steinle, Edward, Ritter von, 1810-86
ALs, 26 June 1882. 3 pp, 8vo. To Alexander Linnemann. Notifying him that he has completed the designs for the Frankfurt cathedral windows. star Apr 8 (542) DM330

Steinmetz, Charles P., 1865-1923
Ls, 26 Oct 1909. 1 p, 4to. To J. S. Van Bylevelt. Commenting about university studies in Germany & America. wa May 30 (496) $190

Stendhal. See: Beyle, Marie Henri, ("Stendhal")

Stephan, Heinrich von, 1831-97
ALs, 24 Sept 1882. 3 pp, 4to. Recipient unnamed. About changes in his travel plans. star Apr 9 (1261) DM320
Collection of Ls & autograph Ms, sgd St., 2 Apr 1881. 4 pp, 4to. To Karl Helmerding. Apologizing officially for the late delivery of a letter. Autograph poem, 5 four-line stanzas, poetical apology with reference to Homer. With related material. star Apr 9 (1260) DM950

Stephens, Alexander H., 1812-83
Collection of ALS & photograph, sgd, 30 Nov 1875. 1 p, 8vo & carte size. To Ray De Lano. Complying with a request for his port. Photograph taken 1 Dec 1874; sgd on mount. wa May 30 (259) $475

Stephenson, George, 1781-1848
ALs, 28 Oct 1830. 2 pp, 4to. To Charles Tennant of H. Pollocks. Regretting that he is unable to inspect "your proposed line from Glasgow to Edinbro". C June 24 (181) £320 [Wilson]

Steuben, Friedrich Wilhelm von, 1730-94
Ls, 23 Aug 1783. 4 pp, 4to. To George Clinton. Reporting about the failure of his mission to Canada. S July 24 (408) £2,200 [Hoffman]

Stevenson, Carter L., 1817-88
ALs, 1 Sept 1861. 2 pp, 8vo. To Lieut. Andrews. About regulations concerning the signing of communications. wa May 30 (260) $95

Stevenson, Robert Louis, 1850-94
[2 autograph sentiments, sgd, 1 with pen-&-ink sketch of boat, 1 with watercolor of 3 ships, [n.d.], sold at pnNy on 11 June, lot 51, for $1,000.]
Autograph Ms, poems, The Celestial Surgeon, Ne sit Ancillae, draft verses of 14 lines, beginning "In April 'ere the day be here...", & rough drawing of a boat, [n.d.]. 2 pp, folio. In extra brown mor bdg by Sangorski & Sutcliffe, with related material. S July 23 (101) £3,000 [Dupre]
Collection of ALs & 2 Ls s, 4 Jan, 14 Aug & 4 Sept 1892. 18 pp, folio & 4to. To Adelaide Boodle & the "Children in the Cellar", her pupils. Describing Samoan life & the antics of Austin & Arick. S Dec 18 (96) £8,500

[Hofmann & Freeman]
ALs, Oct 1872. 12 pp, 8vo. To Charles Baxter. Whimsical letter to a friend, chatting about his health & the land of folly. Bullock collection. CNY Dec 19 (235) $8,000
— [18 July 1886?]. 1 p, 8vo. Recipient unknown. Recommending 2 books on Comedie Humaine. P Dec 15 (82) $600
— [n.d.; 1886 or after]. 4 pp, 12mo. To Theodore Watts-Dunton. Commenting on recipient's critique of Kidnapped. Tipped into a 1st Ed of Kidnapped. L, 1886; front hinge cracked. CNY Dec 19 (236) $5,500
— [n.d.]. 1 p, 8vo. To his agent [H. J.] Moors. Requesting him to forward letters. 3gd in full & with initials. In pencil. Mtd. S July 23 (105) £250 [Solomon]
— [n.d.]. 1 p, 8vo. To his lawyer Carruthers. Requesting an answer. S July 23 (110) £250 [L'Autographe]
— [n.d.]. 1 p, 8vo. To Mr. Hetherington. About sending a Samoan woman to him who is afraid to go to the German store. S July 23 (112) £350 [Maggs]
Collection of 25 A Ds s & 17 Ds s, 1890, 1891 & [n.d.]. 42 pp, mostly 8vo. Vouchers instructing his agent H. J. Moors to make payments to servants. S July 23 (106) £1,800
Series of Ds s, 4 Ds s, 1891. 4 pp, 8vo. 4 bills for various goods, sgd by Stevenson asking that they be paid. With fragment of an autograph letter to a neighbor, mtd. S July 23 (107) £400 [Solomon]
Ds, 10 Jan 1890. 3 pp, folio. Purchase deed for the Vailima estate in Samoa, sgd by Stevenson & the vendor William Johnston. With Johnston's receipt for the purchase money, 1 Aug 1890. S July 23 (102) £4,500 [Dupre]
Document, 20 Dec 1894, 7 pp, folio. Notarial copy of his last will & testament, Sept 1893. Certified by William Mitchell. Sewn with pink thread. S July 23 (114) £2,800 [Dupre]
Corrected page proofs, A Footnote to History, [1892]. 9 pp only, numbered 57-64 & 91. Sheet 91 in 3 portions, mtd. 8 sheets with autograph corrections. S July 23 (103) £1,400 [Hoffman & Freeman]
Photograph, [1893/94]. 7.75 by 5.5 inches. Last photograph of Stevenson, showing him & Chief Tuimalealiifano at Vailima; full length. S July 23 (115) £500 [Dupre]

Stieglitz, Alfred, 1864-1946
Collection of 2 A Ls s, 3 Ls s, autograph postcard, sgd, & ANs; 25 May 1915 to 25 Dec 1917. Various sizes. To Horace Traubel. About a variety of topics. Charles E. Feinberg collection. P Dec 15 (104) $1,500

Stifter, Adalbert, 1805-68
Autograph Ms, novella, Der Kuss von Sentze, [n.d.]. 1 p only, 4to. Heavily revised draft. HK Nov 7 (2349) DM3,400
Autograph transcript, poem, beginning "Du duerstend Herz!". 4 quatrains, sgd & dated Apr 1833. 2 pp, 8vo. S Nov 27 (471) £1,000 [Haas]
ALs, 14 Sept 1853. 1 p, folio. To Baron von Haan. About an administrative matter pending at Gmunden. HK Nov 7 (2350) DM5,000

Stimson, Henry Lewis, 1867-1950
Series of 8 A Ls s, 17 Nov 1911 to 17 Mar 1930. 28 pp, various sizes. To B[ronson] W[inthrop]. Mostly describing the war in France. sg Apr 9 (197) $550

Stockhausen, Karlheinz
Autograph Ms, "Text fuer Schallplatte (1973)"; 1 p, folio. Sgd. Written for a recording of his piece Aufwaerts. FD June 11 (3589) DM500
— Autograph Ms, "Text fuer Schallplatte (1973)"; 1 p, folio. Sgd. Written for a recording of his piece Aufwaerts. star Apr 9 (820) DM340

Stockton, Richard, Signer from New Jersey
ADs, [c.27 Feb 1765]. 1 p, folio. Deposition in the case of Vandike v. Van Arsdalon. Charlotte Parker Milne collection. wd Nov 12 (69) $275

Stokowski, Leopold, 1882-1977
Series of 5 Ls s, 1965 & 1968. 5 pp, 8vo. To Marty Wargo of London Records. Concerning recordings & concerts. wa May 30 (18) $250

Stolberg
— OLEARIUS, CARL JOSEPH. - Ms, Stolbergische Chronik seit 1800 bis 1861, 1834 to 1861. 416 & 66 pp, folio, in def files. Chronicles of the Counts Stolberg & their territory. With related material. HN May 22 (3197) DM1,600

Stolberg, Christian, Graf zu, 1748-1821
Autograph Ms, poem, Der achtzehnte Oktober, [n.d.]. 3 pp, 8vo. Eight 4-line stanzas, sgd. JG Oct 2 (149) DM2,800

Stolberg, Friedrich Leopold, Graf zu, 1750-1819
Autograph Ms, poem, Grabschrift meines Freundes Ahlemann, [n.d.]. 1 p, 8vo. 8 lines, sgd. JG Oct 2 (150) DM3,000

Storm, Theodor, 1817-88
Autograph Ms, fairy tale, Bulemanns Haus, 16 Jan 1864. 35 pp, 4to. Working Ms, sgd. VH Sept 12 (951) DM38,000
Autograph transcript, poem, beginning "Huete, huete den Fuss und die Haende", 4 lines. 1 p, 8vo [lettercard]. Fragment of autograph envelope by Storm, sender's signature, mtd on verso. star Apr 8 (255) DM1,100
Collection of ALs & autograph postcard, sgd, 7 Sept [18]76 & [n.d.]. 5 pp, 8vo. To Ursula Camenisch. Mentioning eye problems & inviting comments about his new work Aquis Submersus. Letter torn. JG Oct 2 (151) DM2,400
Series of 16 A Ls s, 25 Apr 1869 to 16 Mar 1884. About 65 pp, folio & 8vo. To A. J. Schindler. Mostly about his own & Schindler's work. With related material. S Nov 27 (472) £4,000 [Haas]
ALs, 16 Jan 1870. 1 p, 8vo. To Pauline Petersen. Asking for her visit to play music together. star Apr 8 (256) DM900
— 27 Jan 1881. 2 pp, 8vo. To Agathe Feldberg. Expressing good wishes for her marriage to Hermann Wegner. HN May 22 (3198) DM1,800
— 8 Oct 1884. 2 pp, 8vo. To his son Karl. Imploring him to write. With related ALs by Storm's daughter Gertrud, 9 Dec 1907. HK Nov 7 (2351) DM2,400

Stout, Rex, 1886-1975
Ls, 27 Oct 1969. 1 p, 8vo. To Hubbell Robinson. About television rights to his stories. sg Nov 6 (202) $130

Stowasser, Friedrich. See: Hundertwasser, Friedensreich

Stowe, Harriet Beecher, 1811-96
AN, [n.d.]. 1 p, 8vo. To Miss Mann. Mentioning the crisis about slavery. sg Apr 9 (198) $375

Strada, Ottavio
Ms, Simbola pontificum et imperatorum romanorum regumque, archiducum, cardinalium.... [c.1502] 2 vols, folio, in 16th-cent mor gilt. Length not given. SM Oct 20 (562) FF10,000

Stradanus. See: Straet, Jan vander

Straet, Jan vander, 1536-1605
Ms, A large & superb series of drawings, many of them preparatory drawings for plates in the Venationes, sold at SM on 1 Mar 1987, from the Jeanson collection, lots 515-539, at prices ranging from FF20,000 to FF300,000 Stradanus

Strauss, David Friedrich, 1808-74
ALs, 9 June 1858. 1 p, 4to. To Joseph Baer. Offering some of his books for sale. star Apr 8 (428) DM320

Strauss, Eduard, 1825-1916

ALs, 19 May 1876. 2 pp, folio. To the publishing firm [Schott]. Regarding the rights for the 1st performance of Wagner's Grosser Festmarsch at Vienna. With related material. star Apr 9 (822) DM400

Strauss, Johann, 1804-49

Series of Ds s, 4 Ds s, 15 Jan 1835 to 22 June 1843. Contracts with the publishing firm of Tobias & Carl Haslinger. With related material. star Apr 9 (823) DM3,600

— Series of 3 Ds s, 1835 to 1837. Length not stated. Contracts with the publishing firm of Tobias Haslinger. FD Dec 2 (3264) DM1,500

Ds, 13 Sept 1842. 3 pp, folio. Contract, Strauss & Tobias Haslinger ceding the English copyright to some waltzes to Robert Cocks. Also sgd by Haslinger, Cocks, Carl Czerny, & others. In German & English. With related material. HN May 22 (3200) DM850

Strauss, Johann, 1825-99

ALs, [n.d.]. 2 pp, 8vo. To his wife Adele. Making excuses for writing a flattering letter to Girardi. Sgd Jean auch Johannes. In pencil. star Apr 9 (825) DM650

— [n.d.]. 1 p, 8vo. To an unnamed musician. Notifying him of a change of program. star Apr 9 (826) DM750

Collection of Ls & 6 Ds s, Feb 1856 to 9 Jan 1864. 9 pp, folio & 4to. To Carl Haslinger, regarding fees. Contracts with Haslinger for 184 of his works. With related material. star Apr 9 (824) DM4,200

AN, [n.d.]. 6cm by 10cm. Recipient unnamed. On ptd visiting card, regretting that he is unable to find a book. With related material. S Jan 27 (1069) £160 [Dr. Sam]

Photograph, sgd & inscr, [n.d.]. Cabinet size. Inscr to Otto Pasch. FD Dec 2 (3265) DM780

Strauss, Richard, 1864-1949

Autograph music, "Kaiserhymne" for piano; 23 bars in C major, 20 Sept 1915. 1 p, 14 staves; size not stated. Some variants. With related material. star Apr 9 (827) DM5,500

— Autograph music, sketches for his opera Arabella, 3d act, [c.1930]. 48 pp, 13cm by 17.5cm; blue wraps. With anr 2 pp of text on inner cover. Inscr to Hugo Balzer, sgd & dated 16 July 1936. star Apr 9 (828) DM22,000

— Autograph music, song, Der Arbeitsmann, Op.39, no 3, sgd & dated 19 Dez 1918. 15 pp, folio. Presumably unpbd version for voice & orchestra; full score. In black ink on up to 30 staves per p; some alterations in pencil. Autograph tp, inscr to Fritz Stein. S Nov 28 (645) £22,000 [Maguire]

Collection of 4 A Ls s & Ls, 25 Sept 1937 to 11 Jan 1947. 11 pp, folio & 4to. To Erich von Prittwitz und Gaffron. Regarding performances of his works at Paris, Berlin & Vienna, & personal news. Including musical quotation, 2 bars. star Apr 9 (833) DM4,200

ALs, 7 Nov 1916. 1 p, 8vo. To Willy Levin. Mentioning his arrival at Garmisch & saying he is relaxing now. star Apr 9 (831) DM750

— 5 Sept 1894. 2 pp, 8vo. Recipient unnamed [Otto Singer?]. About the ptg of the piano score of Guntram & Freihild. HK Nov 7 (2354) DM650

— 17 May 1900. 2 pp, 8vo. To [Otto SInger?]. Offering him a position as conductor of a chorus. HK Nov 7 (2355) DM500

— 5 May 1905. 1 p, 8vo (lettercard). To a staff member of the publishing firm of Adolph Fuerstner. Notifying him of the completion of Salome & requesting an interview regarding business matters. star Apr 9 (829) DM600

— 13 Oct 1917. 1 p, 8vo. To Leo Slezak. Requesting him to forward some texts. Was mtd. star Apr 9 (832) DM700

— 25 May [19]24. 3 pp, 8vo. To his secretary in Vienna. Giving instructions & requesting help in a variety of matters. FD Dec 2 (3266) DM1,250

— 15 Oct [19]27. 4 pp, 8vo. To the director of La Scala. About alterations to a contract, proposed cuts in Rosenkavalier & the rehearsal schedule. S May 22 (526) £600 [Haas]

Ls, 5 Dec 1944. 1 p, 8vo. To "Herr Vicepraesident". Expressing his hope that peace may awaken German music to a new life, & pointing to the long tradition of opera in Germany. Carbon copy. Framed. Altman collection. pnNY Sept 13 (181) $800

ANs, 14 July 1911. 1 p, 8vo. To Vincenzo Sonzogno. Stating he is unable to provide a ticket for Bayreuth, & about perfomances in Munich. In French. S May 22 (641) £180 [Rankin]

— [n.d.]. 1 p, 12mo. To Frau Kapp. Concerning plants for his mother's grave. In pencil. Framed. Altman collection. pnNY Sept 13 (183) $300

Autograph quotation, 3 bars from Daphne, sgd & dated 1 Dec 1945. 1 p, 16mo. Framed. Altman collection. pnNY Sept 13 (182) $600

— Anr, 2 bars, sgd. [n.d.]. 1 p, 12mo. Framed. Altman collection. pnNY Sept 13 (184) $600

Photograph, sgd & inscr, 14 July 1914. 22cm by 15.7cm. Autograph musical quotation, 2

STRAUSS

bars, sgd, & inscr to Hans Hinrichsen, on mount; 30cm by 21cm. Faded; waterstained. star Apr 9 (830) DM1,400

— Anr, 11 Nov 1920. Mtd; overall size 24cm by 31cm. Inscr to Martucci Angelo, with musical quotation from Salome. S May 22 (528) £580 [Riskin]

— ORLIK, EMIL. - Orig drawing, group port of Strauss, his wife Pauline, son Franz & conductor Fritz Busch, at the dress rehearsal of Intermezzo; sgd, inscr & dated 3 Nov [19]24. Overall size 20.3cm by 26.5cm. In pencil. Framed. S May 22 (527) £650 [Simeone]

Stravinsky, Igor, 1882-1971

ALs, 1932. 3 pp, 4to. To Gavriil Ignatievich. About money for Vera Arturovna & a variety of matters. S May 22 (643) £180 [Dr. Sam]

Ls, 6 Aug 1924. 1 p, 8vo. To Vera Janocopulos. Inviting her to sing his suite Faun et Bergere. Framed. Altman collection. pnNY Sept 13 (186) $400

— 25 Aug 1928. 1 p, 4to. To S[am] Bottenheim. Regarding arrangements for concerts in Scheveningen & Dresden & a Paris hotel. Sgd in pencil. Framed. Altman collection. pnNY Sept 13 (187) $400

— 1 Apr 1930. 1 p, 4to. To Sam Bottenheim. Regarding concert arrangements in Brussels & Holland. Sgd in pencil. Framed. Altman collection. pnNY Sept 13 (188) $375

Autograph postcard, sgd, 7 Apr 1911. To Michel Dimitri Calvocoressi. Praising his translations. In French. star Apr 9 (834) DM1,300

Autograph quotation, Polka, 4 bars in treble & bass clef, sgd & dated 17 Apr 1917. 1 p, 12cm by 18cm. Framed. Altman collection. pnNY Sept 13 (185) $850

Corrected proof, 2 songs from Pribaoutki; 1917. 7 pp, 8vo. Full score, with markings in red & green ink, mauve & black pencil, & corrections. With autograph inscr to Lord Berners. S May 22 (529) £2,000 [Simeone]

Photograph, sgd & inscr, 17 May [19]36. 17cm by 23cm. Inscr to Ana Gastucci. S May 22 (530) £400 [Cox]

— Anr, 1945. 24cm by 19cm. Inscr to Eugene W[e]intraub, in English. Trimmed. S Nov 28 (649) £450 [Friedman]

— Anr, 1946. 8vo. Sgd & inscr to Kilbachich. In Russian. 1 corner def. sg Apr 9 (199) $110

Signature, [n.d.]. 1 p, 8vo (lettercard). Was mtd. star Apr 9 (836) DM260

AMERICAN BOOK PRICES CURRENT

Streicher, Johann Andreas, 1761-1833

[A collection of 30 A Ls s by various members of Beethoven's & Mozart's circle to Streicher, c.1790 to 1840, sold at S on 22 May, lot 324, for £8,000 to Johnson.]

Stresemann, Gustav, 1878-1929

Ls, 6 June 1928. 1 p, 4to. To Rudolf Hofmann. Thanking for birthday congratulations. star Apr 9 (1262) DM300

Strickland, Agnes, 1796-1874

Series of 36 A Ls s, 1843 to 1849; c.250 pp, various sizes. To Mrs. Craufurd. Describing her travels & her search for documents related to Mary, Queen of Scots. pn Dec 11 (54) £180 [Way]

Strindberg, August, 1849-1912

ALs, 1 May 1894. 6 pp, 8vo. To a French literary colleague. Discussing Emile Zola's importance for French literature. In French. S Nov 27 (473) £3,800 [Quaritch]

Struve, Gustav von, 1805-70

ALs, 30 Aug 1832. 3 pp, 4to. To the librarian Bernhardi. Saying he is not suited to be a journalist & about his problems with the censors. With related material. star Apr 9 (1263) DM1,200

Stuart, Charles Edward ("The Young Pretender"), 1720-88

ALs, 21 Dec 1779. 1 p, 4to. To Cantini. Giving permission for the Duncan brothers to stay at his palace in Rome. Sgd C. R. C Dec 3 (232) £250 [Maggs]

Stuart, James Ewell Brown, 1833-64

Autograph Ms, poem, beginning "Fill hight the goblet"; [n.d.]. 3 pp, 4to; written on rectos only. 14 couplets, parody of the drinking song Vive la compagnie; written for the wedding of "Ellen". Sgd in text. Cloth gilt folding case. CNY Dec 19 (238) $1,100

Original drawing, pencil sketch of hill with houses, 7.5 by 10 inches. Sgd J. E. B. wa May 30 (261) $425

ALs, 7 Mar 1862. 2 pp, 4to. To an unidentified Colonel. Giving detailed orders to prepare for troop movements the next day; marked "Private and Confidential". Repaired; red cloth gilt folding case. CNY Dec 19 (237) $3,400

Stuart, James Francis Edward ("The Old Pretender"), 1688-1766

Ls, 14 June 1718. 1 p, folio. To the Archbishop of Avignon. Thanking for condolences on the death of his mother. With autograph subscription; sgd Jacques R. C Dec 3 (287) £130 [Joseph]

Stuck, Franz von, 1863-1928
ALs, 29 Apr 1915. 1 p, 8vo. To Goldschmidt. Concerning his painting "Mary". star Apr 8 (543) DM220

Sucre, Antonio Jose de, 1795-1830
Ls, 13 Mar 1827, 1 p, 4to. To Col. Galvan. Concerning the advancement of Maj. Prudencio Jordan. With autograph subscription. File holes, stamped. In slipcase. sg Sept 18 (277) $650

— 2 Aug 1828. 1 p, 4to. To the President of the Bolivian Congress. Enclosing a Ds, his resignation message as President of Bolivia; 8 p, folio. Disbound. P Sept 24 (47) $3,500
See also: Bolivar, Simon & Sucre

Suffragettes
Ms, minute-book of the Central Committee of the Central National Society for Women's Suffrage, Jan 1896 to Feb 1898. 90 pp, 4to; limp roan, spine damaged. In a single hand; recording finances & activities. Several signatures. C Dec 3 (330) £700 [Quaritch]

Sullivan, Sir Arthur, 1842-1900
ALs, [n.d.]. 2 pp, 8vo. To Sir Edward Marsh. Arranging a dinner party. S Jan 27 (1072) £190 [Maggs]

Sullivan, Edmund Joseph, 1869-1933
Original drawings, The Kaiser's Garland; 50 pp, 4to, with 36 preliminary drawings & drafts for the text; in ink or pencil. Stitched. S Dec 5 (556) £200 [Wilson]

Sullivan, Louis, 1856-1924
ALs, 13 May 1912. 1 p, 4to. To Horace Traubel. Giving permission to print his letter to Walt Whitman, 3 Feb 1887. Charles E. Feinberg collection. P Dec 15 (105) $900

Sully, Thomas, 1783-1872
Collection of 2 A Ls s, 31 May 1809 & Nov 1842, 2 pp, 4to; & autograph Ms, sgd [1832?]; length not stated, 4to. Framed separately. Recipient unnamed; confirming receipt of money for a picture to be painted in London. To John Hill Wheeler, introducing [John Sartain]. Notes & pigment samples of "[Sir Thomas] Lawrences Palette in 1810". Robert E. Jones Estate. P Oct 29 (132) $900

Sumner, Charles, 1811-74
ALs, 4 Sept 1848. 2 pp, 4to. To Benjamin F. Butler. Inviting him to address a state convention in Boston. wa May 30 (78) $80

— 16 Jan [18]56. 3 pp, 8vo. To [Peleg Whitman] Chandler. Discussing pending elections & various candidates. With envelope. wa Oct 18 (148) $150

Sun Yat-sen, 1866-1925
ALs, 18 Nov 1896. 1 p, 8vo. Recipient unnamed. Accepting a dinner invitation. C June 24 (73) £400 [Chan]

Sutermeister, Heinrich
Autograph music, "Skizzen zum Te Deum 1976". 2 pp, 22cm by 29.5cm. In red & blue ballpoint pen, ink & pencil. With numerous revisons. Sgd & inscr. star Apr 9 (837) DM340

Swift, Jonathan, 1667-1745
Ds, 23 Dec 1719. 1 p, folio. As Dean of St. Patrick's, Dublin, convening a meeting of the Chapter. In Latin. S July 23 (27) £2,600 [Pickering & Chatto]

Swinburne, Algernon Charles, 1837-1909
Autograph Ms, "Six Years Old. / To H. W. M.", 30 Sept 1880. 2 pp, folio, on rectos only. With revisions. Mtd; in red mor bdg. S July 23 (118) £1,050 [Quaritch]

— Autograph Ms, The Earl of Mar's Daughter, [n.d.]. 2 pp, folio. Working Ms. On blue paper, mtd & in red mor bdg. S July 23 (117) £850 [Harck]

— Autograph Ms, "The Murder of Rizzio", notes for a dramatic work; [n.d.]. 12 pp, folio. In cloth portfolio. CNY May 11 (133) $3,500

— Autograph Ms, The Shelley Flower, [n.d.]. 1 p, 4to. On stiff paper; with related material. Crude repairs. S July 23 (119) £400 [Harck]

ALs, 26 Dec 1882. 7 pp, 8vo. To "Ned" [Edward Burne-Jones]. Ironical letter, explaining why he has declined to become Archbishop of Canterbury. S Dec 18 (97) £1,000 [Quaritch]

— 9 Sept 1903. 1 p, 8vo. To "Cousin Sermonda" [Mrs. Henniker Heaton]. Accepting an invitation. Framed with autograph envelope. Altman collection. pnNY Sept 13 (136) $275

Ds, 6 Dec 1875. 1 p, 8vo. Receipt for payment for copyright of Encyclopedia Britannica article; partly ptd. sg Apr 9 (202) $90

Sylva, Carmen, Pseud. of Elisabeth, Queen of Carol I of Romania, 1843-1916
Autograph Ms, story, Meister Manole, Jan 1885. 17 pp, 4to. Fair copy, sgd. star Apr 8 (30) DM680

Symeon Metaphrastes. See: Greek Manuscripts

Symonds, Arthur
Autograph Ms, A Note on Germany. 5 pp, 4to. Library markings. With typescript. sg Mar 5 (233) $250

— Autograph Ms, Cornwall. [N.d.]. 16 pp, 4to, sgd twice. Library markings. sg Mar 5 (251) $250

— Autograph Ms, Maupassant. [N.d.]. 50 pp,

4to. Library markings. sg Mar 5 (257) $950
— Autograph Ms, The East and the West. [N.d.]. 4 pp, 4to. Library markings. With typescript. sg Mar 5 (252) $325
— Autograph Ms, Two Stories by Villers de L'Isle Adam. [N.d.]. 53 pp, 4to, library stamps. sg Mar 5 (254) $650
— Autograph Ms, Villon. 41 pp, 4to. Library markings. Sgd twice. sg Mar 5 (255) $1,100

Symons, Julian
Autograph Ms, The Tell-Tale Heart: The LIfe and Works of Edgar Allan Poe. [c.1978] In 2 notebooks, c.260 pages. With carbon typescript & other related material. sg Mar 5 (216) $950

Syriac Manuscripts
Ms, calendar, [n.d.]. 1 leaf only, 23cm by 15.5cm. In black & red ink; colored ornamental border on recto. From the Convent of St. Catherine on Mount Sinai. FD June 11 (32) DM9,000
— Ms, Heirmologion. [Melchite, n.d.]. Fragment, 2 leaves, c.20cm by 13.5cm. In black & red ink, with circular & intertwined ornaments in borders. From the Convent of St. Catherine on Mount Sinai. FD June 11 (31) DM4,000
— Ms, homily, [9th cent]. 4 leaves, vellum, 25cm by 16cm. Fragment; written in dark brown ink in estrangelo script. From the Convent of St. Catherine on Mount Sinai. FD June 11 (28) DM18,000
— Ms, Melchite Gospel book, [n.d.]. Bifolium, 23.7cm by 15cm. Fragment of one of the oldest works of Melchite origin. In dark brown & red ink in estrangelo script. With full-page cross of Golgotha within colored ornamental borders & 2 full-page ornamental designs in colors. From the Convent of St. Catherine on Mount Sinai. FD June 11 (26) DM7,000
— Ms, Menaion. [13th cent?]. 1 leaf, 21.5cm by 14cm. Fragment, containing Melchite liturgical hymns for early Feb. In dark brown & red ink in estrangelo script. With ornamental borders. Ownership inscr of Germanus, Bishop of Sinai. From the Convent of St. Catherine on Mount Sinai. FD June 11 (27) DM13,000
— Ms, Parakletikon. [Antioch, 1190]. 5 leaves, 16cm by 25cm. Fragment, written in estrangelo script by the priest Michael. From the Convent of St. Catherine on Mount Sinai. FD June 11 (25) DM18,000
— Ms, Parakletikon. [Melchite, 10th cent]. 2 fragments, 9 leaves each, vellum, 22.5cm by 17cm. Palimpsest; older Armenian Ms, [6th cent], ownership on the Psalms by St. John Chrysostom, partly legible. From the Convent of St. Catherine on Mount Sinai.

FD June 11 (29) DM95,000
— Ms, Psalter, in the Peshitta version, [n.d.]. Fragment; bifolium, 13cm by 9cm. In black & red ink. With large ornamental border in black & red on f.1v. From the Convent of St. Catherine on Mount Sinai. FD June 11 (30) DM7,000
— Ms, Transitus Mariae. Fragment from Codex Arabicus (Atiya), 4 leaves, vellum, 15.5cm by 23.5cm. In very old estrangelo script. Palimpsest, with later Arabic text, [9th/10th cent]; in black ink. From the Convent of St. Catherine on Mount Sinai. FD June 11 (33) DM60,000

Szyk, Arthur
Original drawing, watercolor drawing of an oriental streetscene, to illus tales from the Arabian Nights. Sgd & dated 1948. 161mm by 122mm. S June 19 (708) £2,000 [Sawyer]

Szymanowski, Karol, 1883-1937
ALs, 28 Apr 1927. 2 pp, size not stated. To [Dr. Kalmus of Universal Edition]. Concerning the publication of his Stabat Mater & mentioning other works. In German. S May 22 (646) £580 [Niewodniczanski]

T

Taft, Helen H., 1861-1943
Franking signature, [13 Dec 1930]. rf Mar 14 (104) $85

Taft, William Howard, 1857-1930
Collection of ALs & Ls, [n.d.] & 12 Mar 1891. 2 pp, 8vo & 4to. To John Proctor Clarke. Asking that he recommend Taft to the President for an appointment as Circuit Judge. Thanking for his efforts on his behalf. P May 13 (133) $1,100
— Collection of ALs & 7 Ls s, 24 Apr 1908 to 21 Mar 1921. Various lengths & sizes. To Gen. Felix Agnus. Commenting on the political situation & enlisting the publisher's help. P Oct 29 (133) $3,500
Series of 4 Ls s, 1913 to 1922. 4 pp, 4to. To Ralph Easley. About Gompers, socialism, the Erdman Conciliation Act, etc. pnNY June 11 (55) $650
Ls, 1 Mar 1900. 2 pp, 4to. To his brother Harry. Recommending 2 stenographers. Mtd. pnNY June 11 (53) $100
— 30 Apr 1905. 1 p, 8vo. To the Periodical Publishers' Association. As Sec of War, declining the invitation to attend their annual dinner. wa Oct 18 (53) $65
— Aug 1907. 2 pp, 4to. To Richard Oulahan. Concerning an article written by Oulahan. With 2 Ls s, 1903 & 1908. pnNY June 11 (52) $425
— 4 Jan 1908. 1 p, 8vo. Recipient unnamed. As

Sec of War, thanking for information. Was mtd. wa Oct 18 (54) $65
— 23 Feb 1909. 1 p, 8vo. To Thomas Walsh. About the possibility of a visit on Tuesday. wa May 30 (122) $140
— 3 May 1913. 1 p, 4to. To R. U. Johnson. Expressing his intention to study socialism. Personal letterhead. wa Oct 18 (151) $65
— 19 Oct 1913. 1 p, 4to. To Julius Moritze. Thanking for his letter mentioning his book about the peace movement. With 4 Ls s, 1908 to 1916. pnNY June 11 (56) $225
— 11 Nov 1914. 1 p, 4to. To Miss Rebecca Smith. Family reminiscences. wa May 30 (121) $160
— [n.d.]. 1 p, 4to. To Mrs. John Walker. About her letter being passed on to the Council of the League & church property in Washington. Framed. Altman collection. pnNY Sept 13 (25) $225
ANs, 25 May 1919. 1 p, 12mo. Recipient unnamed. Sending best wishes. Framed. Altman collection. pnNY Sept 13 (24) $275
Ns s, 3 Apr 1915 & 20 July 1920. 2 pp, 4to. Recipient unnamed. Easter greetings; contents not stated. 2d signature smudged. rf Nov 15 (17) $130
Photograph, sgd & Inscr, 8 Mar 1910. Folio. Inscr to R. O. Moon. Framed. Altman collection. pnNY Sept 13 (23) $300
— Anr, 29 June 1915. 8.25 by 6.25 inches. Chest-length pose. Inscr to J. Y. B. Wood. Was mtd. sg Nov 6 (344) $120
Signature, [n.d.]. 1 p, 16mo. With other signatures, including his wife's & daughter's; possibly guest book list. With a port. wa May 30 (306) $80

Taft, William Howard, 1857-1930 —& Brandeis, Louis D., 1856-1941
Group photograph, [c.1920]. 8 by 10 inches. Portico with men in formal attire. Sgd by Taft & Brandeis. sg Nov 6 (203) $750

Taggart, Samuel, 1754-1825
Series of 7 A Ls s, 5 Mar 1814 to 22 Feb 1817. 26 pp, 4to. To Jedediah Morse. Commenting about his Congressional activities, wartime Washington, etc. Bullock collection. CNY Dec 19 (239) $380

Tailor's Guild of Toulouse
Document, statutes of the guild, in Latin & Langue d'Oc, 1509. 43 leaves (1 blank), vellum, 282mm by 215mm. Old red velvet bdg, detached from spine. In brown ink in a lettre batarde, opening words of chapters in gothic script. With nearly 100 small painted initials, 1 large & 2 small illuminated initials & 2 full-page miniatures. Including 26 pp of additions at end in various hands, [16th cent to 1732]. S June 23 (87) £8,500 [Bibliotheque de Toulouse]

Talbot, William Henry Fox, 1800-77
ALs, [n.d.], "Wednesday evening". 2 pp, 8vo. To C[harles] Wheatstone. About a scientific experiment. Framed with address leaf & double-glazed. Altman collection. pnNY Sept 13 (154) $900

Talleyrand-Perigord, Charles Maurice de, 1754-1838
Ls, [27 Nov 1797]. 2 pp, folio. To an unnamed German prince. As Foreign Minister, regarding territorial changes on the left bank of the Rhine. star Apr 9 (1264a) DM650
— [3 Aug 1802]. 2 pp, folio. To the French minister at Kassel, Rivals. Informing him about plans to evacuate French troops from Switzerland & French foreign policies. sg Apr 9 (205) $400
— 23 June 1806. 1 p, folio. To the French minister at Kassel, Dignon. Instructing him to request payment of a debt owed Madame de la Salle. star Apr 9 (1264b) DM350

Taney, Roger B., 1777-1864
Ds, 26 July 1811. Oblong 32mo. Frederick County summons; partly ptd. wa Oct 18 (55) $55
— 13 Feb 1813. 1 p, folio. Partly ptd; contents not stated. Sgd on verso. wa May 30 (79) $80
— 27 Sept 1833. 1 p, 4to. As Sec of the Treasury; contents not stated. wa May 30 (435) $50

Tarleton, Sir Banastre, 1754-1833
ALs, 16 Dec 1803. 1 p, folio. To Maj. Gen. Brownrigg. Notifying him of the lack of supplies for Col. Lundy's battalion. wa May 30 (327) $260

Tarrant, Margaret
Original drawings, (22), illusts & designs for Charles Kingsley's The Water-Babies, 1908. In watercolor & in ink. 10 sgd, 9 initialled. 180mm by 135mm (12) & various sizes. Archives of J. M. Dent & Son. S June 19 (866) £9,000 [Beetles]
— **Original drawings,** (25), illusts & designs for Robert Browning's The Pied Piper of Hamelin, 1912. In watercolor & in ink. 7 sgd, 9 initialled. 180mm by 135mm (8) & various sizes. Archives of J. M. Dent & Son. S June 19 (867) £9,000 [Beetles]

Tasso, Bernardo, 1493-1569
ALs, 29 Nov 1559. 2 pp, folio. To Sperone Speroni. Discussing revisions he is making to his L'Amadigi di Gaula. S Nov 27 (474) £2,800 [De Zayas]

TAUENTZIEN

Tauentzien, Friedrich Bogislaw von, 1710-91
Ls, 3 Jan 1777. 1 p, folio. Recipient unnamed. Returning New Year's wishes. star Apr 9 (1265) DM220

Taylor, George, Signer from Pennsylvania
Ds, 18 Mar 1772. 2 pp, folio. Examination of Mary Simpson concerning death of an infant, endorsed & sgd as Justice of the Peace. Some text loss. Charlotte Parker Milne collection. wd Nov 12 (70) $4,000

Taylor, Hamish
Autograph Ms, An account of our Voyage to New South Wales, 16 Sept 1839 - 26 Jan 1840. 41 pp, 8vo. Orig vellum. bba Nov 13 (178) £130 [Burgess Browning]

Taylor, Zachary, 1784-1850
Franking signature, [16 Oct n.y.]. rf May 30 (25) $850

Tchaikovsky, Peter Ilyich, 1840-93
Autograph music, song, Rondel; 12 bars, marked Allegretto grazioso, for voice & piano, [1888]. 1 p, 270mm by 174mm. In black ink on 3 systems of 3 staves each. Clefs & tempo in Tchaikovskys hand on verso. C Dec 3 (423) £5,000 [D'Arcy]
ALs, 5 June [1890]. 4 pp, 4to. To "Mania". Reporting about his work on The Queen of Spades & Souvenirs de Florence. In Russian. S Nov 28 (654) £2,200 [Haas]
— 2/14 June 1891. 1 p, 8vo. To [Wilhelm?] Berger. Answering a request for his photograph. star Apr 9 (841) DM5,800
— 30 Aug 1892. 1 p, 8vo. Recipient unknown. About purchasing a bicycle for his nephew. Sang collection. P Sept 24 (48) $1,700
— 24 Nov/6 Dec 1892. 3 pp, 8vo. To [Paul Collin]. Referring to his new opera & ballet & agreeing to a request. In French. C Dec 3 (425) £2,600 [Haas]
— [6/18 Aug 1893]. 2 pp, 8vo. To Ekaterina Laroche. Thanking for money & informing her that he will be in St. Petersburg earlier than expected. C June 24 (207) £1,300 [Schulson]
— 24 Sept 1893. 1 p, 8vo. To "Manitchka". Referring to LaRoche's overture Karomzina. Framed. P Sept 24 (49) $1,900
— 9 Nov [n.y.]. 1 p, 8vo. To "Katya". Concerning a dinner invitation. In green lea folding case. sg Apr 9 (207) $2,200
Ds, testimonial marking the retirement of Herr Lassmann from the Moscow Conservatoire, [n.d., c.1870]. 3 pp, folio. In German. Also sgd by 10 other members of his circle & fellow teachers at the Conservatoire. S Nov 28 (653) £1,250 [Haas]
Photograph, sgd & inscr, 20 Jan 1888. Cabinet size. Inscr in German. star Apr 9 (840) DM7,000

AMERICAN BOOK PRICES CURRENT

Tenniel, Sir John, 1820-1914
Proof copy, cartoon, Dropping the Pilot, 1901 [orig pbd 1890]. 250mm by 150mm. Inscr & sgd in margin. sg Nov 6 (204) $175
See also: Dodgson, Charles Lutwidge & Tenniel

Tennyson, Alfred, Lord, 1809-92
Collection of ALs & Ds, 15 Feb [1838] & 30 June 1872. 2 pp, 8vo & 4to. To Richard Bentley, declining an offer made earlier that day. Receipt for his pension from the Civil List. C Dec 3 (383) £170 [Wilson]
ALs, [1891]. 1 p, 8vo. To the Chancellor & Provost of Trinity College, Dublin. Declining an invitation to their tercentenary festivities. C Dec 3 (384) £95 [Bristow]
ANs, 8 Feb 1865. 1 p, 12mo. Recipient unnamed. Declining a request. Was mtd. Torn. wa May 30 (80) $110

Terry, Ellen, 1847-1928
Photograph, sgd & inscr, 17 July [18]88. Size not stated. Sgd on recto & verso; inscr to A. E. Allen. wa May 30 (430) $55

Thackeray, William Makepeace, 1811-63
ALs, 18 July 1831. 3 pp, 4to. To Edward FitzGerald. Reflecting on his life on his birthday. Fold tears. S Dec 18 (98) £1,700 [Collins]
— 19 Sept 1844. 2 pp, 8vo. To [the publishers Chapman & Hall?]. Commenting about his trip to the Levant & enclosing a Ms [not present]. Integral blank pasted to stiffer paper; with brief ANs by Charles Dickens, on envelope, pasted below. Bullock collection. CNY Dec 19 (241) $550

Thaer, Albrecht, 1752-1828
ALs, 10 Jan 1822. 7 pp, 4to. Recipient unnamed. About his sheep-breeding. In pencil. star Apr 8 (429) DM550

Thalberg, Sigismund, 1812-71
Ds, 29 Dec 1836. 1 p, folio. Contract with Tobias Haslinger regarding his Deux Notturnes pour le Pianoforte. With related material. star Apr 9 (838) DM460

Thayer, Sylvanus, 1785-1872
ALs, 3 May 1841. 1 p, 4to. Recipient unnamed. Ordering cement. wa May 30 (498) $180

Theological Manuscripts
Ms, collection of commentaries on religious texts, in various hands; one sgd Bernardus, Ratisbon [Regensburg], 1453. 167 leaves, 4to. Blind-stamped vellum over bds, def. In Latin; red & black ink. pn Dec 11 (12) £550 [Quaritch]
— Ms, Opuscula et Excerpta Varia Moralia. [Italy, mid-15th cent]. 245 leaves (36 blank) & 3 flyleaves, vellum, 117mm by 90mm.

214

18th-cent calf gilt. In brown ink in a very small gothic bookhand by several scribes. With initials throughout in red. Containing works by Antoninus Florentinus, Matthew of Cracow, Pseudo-Augustine, Bonaventura, & other Franciscan texts. S June 23 (82) £900 [Maggs]

Thiersch, Friedrich Wilhelm, 1784-1860
ALs, 29 Nov 1836. 3 pp, 8vo. To an unnamed printer. Sending a Ms & suggesting a reprint of his Ueber gelehrte Schulen. star Apr 8 (430) DM220

Thoma, Hans, 1839-1924
ALs, 3 Jan 1902. 2 pp, 8vo. To an unnamed painter. Saying he cannot buy recipient's painting "Pieta". star Apr 8 (544) DM220

Thoma, Ludwig, 1867-1921
ALs, 30 Aug 1894. 2 pp, 4to. To the Bavarian Department of Justice. Applying for admission as a lawyer to the district court at Dachau. HK Nov 7 (2358) DM900

Thomas, Dylan, 1914-53
Original drawing, "A Petition to the Government", [n.d.]. 346mm by 254mm. Watercolor & oil painting of giraffe-shaped creature being offered a petition. Ascribed to Dylan Thomas. S July 23 (187) £300 [Dylans Bookstore]
Collection of 7 A Ls s & Ls, 22 Feb to 24 Aug 1939. 10 pp, 4to & 8vo. Mostly to Richard Church of J. M. Dent & Sons. Concerning the publication of The Map of Love. With 14 carbon copies & memoranda of Dents's side of the correspondence. S July 23 (191) £1,700 [Dylans]
— Collection of 3 A Ls s & Ls, 8 Aug to 6 Nov 1945. 6 pp, 4to. To A. J. Hoppe & others of J. M. Dent & Sons. Concerning the publication of Deaths and Entrances. S July 23 (188) £700 [Wilson]
Series of 4 A Ls s, 30 Jan 1940 & 22 Nov 1952 to 16 Mar 1953. 9 pp, 4to. To E. F. Bozman & A. J. Hoppe of J. M. Dent & Sons. Concerning the publication of The Doctor and the Devils & A. Rolph's bibliography. S July 23 (192) £1,400 [Richards]
— Series of 5 A Ls s, 30 Jan 1940 to 6 Apr 1953. 9 pp, 4to & 8vo. To E. F. Bozman & anr staff member of J. M. Dent & Sons. About Quite Early One Morning. S July 23 (193) £1,500 [Wilson]
— Series of 3 A Ls s, 10 Sept to 28 Oct 1952. 5 pp, 4to & 8vo. To E. F. Bozman of J. M. Dent & Sons. Concerning the publication of Collected Poems, 1934-1952. S July 23 (189) £1,100 [Wilson]
ALs, 11 Sept 1953. 3 pp, 4to. To E. F. Bowman of J. M. Dent & Sons. About several of his works & discussing his financial crisis. S July 23 (194) £1,700 [Caldur]
Series of 8 Ls s & ALs, 8 Oct 1935 to 1 Sept 1936. 14 pp, mostly 4to. Mostly to Richard Church of J. M. Dent & Sons. About surrealism, Dylan's style of poetry, & the publication of Twenty-five Poems. With 11 letters, mostly carbon copies, from Church & Hadfield to Thomas. S July 23 (190) £4,000 [Caldur]

Thomas, Edward, 1878-1917
Series of 8 A Ls s, 1910 to 1913. 8 pp, 4to & 8vo. To J. M. Dent. Discussing publishing projects. S July 23 (196) £950 [Joseph & Sawyer]

Thomas, Isaiah, 1750-1831
ALs, 25 Aug 1806. 1 p, 4to. To M. W. T[imothy] Bigelow. Relating to the affairs of the Masonic Order. sg Nov 6 (205) $250

Thomson, Charles, 1729-1824
Autograph Ms, 8 [?] 1775. 1 p, folio. As Sec of the Continental Congress, list of committee to consider applications of persons "applying to be officers in the American Army". Sgd. Repaired. Charlotte Parker Milne collection. wd Nov 12 (71) $550

Thomson, Hugh, 1860-1920
Original drawing, elegant man at a woodworking bench; ink & watercolor. Sgd & dated [18]97. 284mm by 151mm. Framed. Reproduced in Jane Austen's Persuasion, 1897. S Dec 5 (560) £950 [White]
— Original drawing, eleven men around a dead horse; illus for the poem Widdecombe Fair, ink & watercolor. Sgd & dated [18]98. 310mm by 241mm. Framed. Presumably unpbd. S Dec 5 (557) £1,700 [White]
— Original drawing, girls with parasols & others leaving church; ink. 308mm by 215mm, sgd. Slightly spotted; framed. Reproduced in George Eliot's Scenes of Clerical Life, 1906. S Dec 5 (563) £700 [White]
— Original drawing, ink & watercolor drawing of a couple dancing in a ballroom, probably to illus Thackeray's The History of Samuel Titmarsh and the Great Hoggarty Diamond, 1902. Sgd. 307mm by 219mm. Framed. S June 19 (717) £1,900 [Edberg]
— Original drawing, ink sketch of a woman at a desk talking to a girl, to illus Fanny Burney's Evelina, 1903. Sgd. 312mm by 221mm. Framed. S June 19 (711) £600 [Vincent]
— Original drawing, ink sketch of a furious woman approaching a young lady, to illus Fanny Burney's Evelina, 1903. Sgd. 299mm by 220mm. Framed. S June 19 (712) £600 [White]
— Original drawing, ink sketch of a man

holding a letter away from a young lady, to illus Fanny Burney's Evelina, 1903. Sgd. 298mm by 212mm. Framed. S June 19 (713) £500 [Vincent]
— Original drawing, six ladies & young man around a table; ink. Sgd & dated 1906. 304mm by 239mm. Slightly discolored; framed. Reproduced in George Eliot's Scenes of Clerical Life, 1906. S Dec 5 (562) £700 [White]
— Original drawing, three women, one seated with baby; ink. 262mm by 205mm. Framed. Reproduced in Jane Austen's Sense and Sensibility, 1896. S Dec 5 (559) £700 [White]
— Original drawing, two women in confidential conversation; ink & watercolor. 293mm by 200mm, initialled. Framed. Reproduced in James Lane Allen's A Kentucky Cardinal, 1901. S Dec 5 (558) £1,700 [White]
— Original drawing, watercolor, "Miss Susan: They have Suspected for a Week," Act III of J. M. Barrie's Quality Street. 30.5cm by 25.5cm, sgd & dated 1913. Ck Dec 10 (83) £2,300
— Original drawing, watercolor, of Miss Henrietta & Miss Fanny for Barrie's Quality Street. 30.5cm by 25.5cm, sgd & dated 1913. Ck Dec 10 (82) £2,000

Thornton, Matthew, Signer from New Hampshire
Ds, 29 Oct 1756. 2 by 5 inches. As Justice of the Peace, fragment. Contents not stated. Mtd. Charlotte Parker Milne collection. wd Nov 12 (72) $175

Thornton, William, 1759-1828
Ds, 12 June 1824. 1 p, folio. Indenture between John Hoye & Julius Forrest for sale of a lot in Washington; sgd as witness. wa May 30 (438) $140
See also: Hoban, James & Thornton

Thurber, James, 1894-1961
Original drawing, Five-legged Rabbit about to Thump, 1946. Crayon drawing, 560mm by 520mm, laid down on rag board. Executed for his article What the Animals Were up To, ptd in Life Magazine, 21 Jan 1946. With a copy of the magazine. P June 18 (192) $2,250

Thurlow, Edward, 1st Baron, 1731-1806
Ds, 14 July 1773. 3 pp, folio. Report on James Fanyard's petition for a patent for a powder to stop bleeding, to be used by the British army. Sgd as Attorney Gen. sg Nov 6 (319) $90

Tieck, Ludwig, 1773-1853
ALs, 10 Aug 1794. 3 pp, 4to. To his sister Sophie. Apologizing for not writing, saying he will return to Berlin soon, & talking about his family. star Apr 8 (258) DM3,500
— 4 Dec 1830. 2 pp, 4to. To an unnamed theater manager. Letter of recommendation for Karl Blumauer. star Apr 8 (259) DM700
Ls, [early 1852]. 3 pp, 4to. To [Franz von Dingelstedt]. Wondering about his staging of Aristophanes in Munich. star Apr 8 (260) DM1,200

Tiffany, Charles Lewis, 1812-1902
ALs, 11 June 1895. 2 pp, 8vo. To George Wilson. Thanking for a photograph. wa May 30 (439) $170

Tilghman, Tench, 1744-86
ALs, 6 Apr 1778. 1 p, 4to. To Brig. Gen. John Lacey. Explaining Washington's order not to withdraw guards from the roads between Philadelphia & Newtown. sg Nov 6 (346) $350

Tiller, Terence
[A collection of autograph working Mss, in pencil, & working typescripts for his Notes for a Myth and Other Poems, c.1968, c.125 pp, various sizes, with a copy of the book, sold at S on 23 July 1987, lot 197, for £250 to John.]

Tinbergen, Jan
Autograph Ms, essay, Economic Growth and the Biosphere, 1977. 7 pp, 4to. Sgd at head. star Apr 8 (431) DM240

Tirpitz, Alfred von, 1849-1930
Ls, 27 May 1924. 1 p, folio. To a Royal Highness. Thanking for congratulations on his birthday. star Apr 9 (1283) DM450

Tischbein, Johann Heinrich Wilhelm, 1751-1829
ALs, Aug 1781. 1 p, 8vo. Recipient unknown. Announcing his visit. On verso text in a different hand. JG Oct 2 (314) DM500

Titanic Disaster
— ANGLE, F. - Account of disaster by a female survivor in lifeboat no 11, 15 Oct 1913. 2 pp, 8vo. Was mtd. S Jan 27 (891) £250 [Sayer]

Tobacco
Ms, draft of an act prohibiting the growing of tobacco in England in order to protect plantations in America, [1663]. 5 pp, folio. In a professional hand. Clifford of Chudleigh collection. S July 24 (252) £1,600 [Burgess & Browning]

Tocqueville, Alexis de, 1805-59
ALs, 15 Aug 1858. 2 pp, 8vo. To "Monsieur Grey". Requesting him not to postpone his visit. star Apr 9 (1266) DM220

Tod, John G., 1808-77
ALs, 14 Jan 1846. 2 pp, 4to. To Congressman George Sykes. Reporting about his journey to Texas to deliver Congress's joint resolution on the annexation of Texas. On integral blank of ptd copy of Anson Jones's proclamation, 12 Jan 1846, announcing Congressional resolution. P May 13 (134) $1,400

Tolkien, John Ronald Reuel, 1892-1973
ALs, 25 Sept 1954. 6 pp, 4to. To Naomi Mitchison. Commenting on her review of The Lord of the Rings & raising some points of interpretation. S Dec 18 (183) £1,500 [Collins]

Toller, Ernst, 1893-1939
ALs, 13 Feb [19]20. 2 pp, 4to. To his mother. From prison, sending a list of things needed, & reporting about his work. FD June 11 (3536) DM1,500
Collection of Ls, postcard, sgd, & postscript, sgd, to a letter by his secretary, 10 Oct 1928 to 4 Jan 1929. 2 pp, folio & card. To Alfred Guttmann of the Berlin Arbeiter-Saengerbund. About his new comedy & his inability to re-write songs at present. star Apr 8 (262) DM420

Tolstoy, Leo, 1828-1910
Autograph postcard, sgd, 22 Jan 1894. 1 p, 8vo. To Liubov Gurevitch. Requesting her to delete a passage about women in proofs of an article. Initialled. In Russian. S May 21 (313) £350 [Lucas]
Photograph, sgd, [n.d.]. Postcard size. star Apr 8 (263) DM1,000
— Anr, 17 Apr 1909. Postcard. P Dec 15 (83) $1,200

Toscanini, Arturo, 1867-1957
Collection of 6 A Ls s & 3 photographs, sgd, to Hugo Burghauser; mostly about concert programs. With an extensive series of A Ls s by Carla Toscanini. c.1936 to 1950; various sizes. S Nov 28 (656) £480 [Dr. Sam]
Christmas card, 1943. 3 ptd pp, 12mo. Sgd A.T. & inscr; in red ink. With port photograph mtd at left side. sg Nov 6 (208) $225

Tracy, Spencer, 1900-67
Photograph, sgd, [n.d.]. 7 by 5 inches. wa May 30 (378) $120
Photograph, sgd & inscr, [c.1940]. 7 by 5 inches. Was mtd. sg Nov 6 (209) $110

Trades
Document, Gesellenbrief, certificate of qualification as a journeyman gardener, issued to Andreas Urspringer by Friedrich Bader; 1 Mar 1762. 1 p, folio. Vellum. With elaborate floral, ornamental & heraldic illusts at head & in the margins. star Apr 9 (1005) DM500
— Gesellenbrief, certificate of qualification as a journeyman, issued by the linen weavers of Eichstaett to Johann Veit Schaeffer, 24 Oct 1762. 1 p, folio. Vellum. Sgd by 4 master weavers. With large initial. star Apr 9 (1004) DM220
— Gesellenbrief, certificate of qualification as a journeyman, issued by the Vienna shoemakers' guild to Friedrich Schueldi, 22 Apr 1811. 1 p, folio; partly ptd. With engraved ornamental border & view of the city. On verso endorsements by Austrian & Bavarian officials. star Apr 9 (1006) DM680

Traicte...de mariage
Ms, Traicte du sacrement de mariage... & Oraison a dieu pour luy demander lignee, [Paris?, after 1533]. 46 leaves, vellum, 210mm by 145mm; half vellum bdg in paper wraps. In brown & red ink in calligraphic bookhand, with gilt initials & double borders throughout. Leaves at beginning def. Dealing with marriage & child rearing from a catholic point of view. FD Dec 2 (11) DM12,000

Traite...
Ms, Traite de cavalerie contenant la connaissance des chevaux, les embouchures, la selle, la ferrure.... Paris, 1713. 66 pp plus 37 blanks, 12mo, in mor gilt. SM Oct 20 (441) FF6,500

Transatlantic Telegraph
Telegram, Aug 1858. Ptd on narrow strip of paper, in morse code. Sent from Newfoundland to Valentia Island. With contemp covering note, dated 24 Sept 1858. "One of the earliest, possibly the first, messages sent by cable across the Atlantic." S Dec 18 (340) £420 [Joseph & Sawyer]

Trimble, Robert, 1777-1828
Ls, 20 Aug 1815. 1 p, 4to. To Col. Jessup. Inviting him to dinner. Also sgd by J[esse] Bledsoe & B. Mills. Probably in Bledsoe's hand. Fold split. wa Oct 18 (153) $210

Tronchin, Francois, 1704-98
Autograph Ms, Catalogue de mes Livres & Manuscrits de Famille & autres, Oct 1796. 214 pp & 37 blanks, folio. Contemp boards. Some 1797 additions. With a Ms library cat, [2d half of 18th cent], 244 pp & 46 blanks, 4to. Contemp boards. Copious marginal comments in Tronchin's hand.

TRONCHIN

Both together listing c.8.000 items. C Dec 3 (385) £1,400 [Quaritch]

Truman, Harry S., 1884-1972
Collection of ALs & 38 Ls s, 16 Apr 1948 to 12 May 1972. 39 pp, various sizes. To Dwight Palmer & William R. Harris (1). Political & personal correspondence. With 2 Ls s by Bess Truman to Palmer & further related material. P May 13 (137) $7,500

ALs, 11 June 1953. 1 p, 4to. To Asley T. Cole. About his service in the 35th Division. Framed with a port. P May 13 (135) $1,700

Collection of 3 Ls s, 2 typescripts, sgd, & autograph endorsement, sgd, [c.2 June 1918] to 11 Apr 1946. Various lengths & sizes. To various recipients. Copies of farewell message & speech to Indiana Democratic Editorial Association. Approving a soldier's letter. P Oct 29 (134) $1,400

— Collection of 3 Ls s & group photograph, sgd, 20 July 1953 to 8 Nov 1963. 3 pp, 4to, & 4to photograph. To Charles Patrick Clark. Brief personal notes. Photograph showing Truman, Clark & John L. Lewis; sgd by Truman & Lewis. P May 13 (136) $550

Series of 11 Ls s, 1945 to 1967. 11 pp, size not stated. To Ralph F. or Lue C. Lozier. Contents not stated. With related material. Lue C. Lozier Estate. wd Nov 12 (20) $1,500

— Series of 4 Ls s, 1951 to 1954. 4 pp, 4to. To Dr. & Mrs. Miller. Expressing thanks. wa May 30 (308) $650

Ls, 6 Nov 1947. 1 p, 8vo. To Harry H. Woodring. Thanking for a letter. With autograph postscript, 11 words. On White House letterhead. wa May 30 (124) $375

— 17 Jan 1948. 1 p, 4to. To Carl Claudy. Thanking for a book. On White House letterhead. sg Apr 9 (211) $400

— 16 Feb 1949. 1 p, 8vo. To Dr. Albert R. Miller. Thanking for pictures. With port photograph, 13.25 by 10.25 inches. wa May 30 (125) $250

— 5 Jan 1953. 1 p, 4to. To Dr. & Mrs. Miller. Thanking for Christmas wishes. With hand colored Inauguration photograph by Miller, 3.75 by 2.75 inches; framed. wa May 30 (307) $300

— 22 Dec 1955. 1 p, 4to. To Carl Claudy. Thanking for a Christmas gift. sg Apr 9 (212) $175

— 30 Jan 1959. 1 p, 4to. To Mrs. Robert W. Hassselberg. Thanking her for her book. sg Nov 6 (211) $100

— 16 May 1962. 1 p, 4to. To J. Howard McGrath. Personal letter, about recipient's health & the death of Ralph Truman. wa May 30 (126) $170

— 21 Oct 1963. 1 p, 4to. To a magazine Ed. Concerning some World War I photographs. Encapsulated. sg Apr 9 (213) $450

— 6 Jan 1966. 1 p, 4to. To Paul F. Nachtmann. Thanking for Christmas greetings. Framed. Altman collection. pnNY Sept 13 (28) $200

Collection of 1 Ds & 1 Ls, [5] & 18 Sept 1945. 2 pp, 4to. Citation for Harry L. Hopkins's Distinguished Service Medal & related letter from Truman to Hopkins; expressing his wish that Hopkins may continue to advise him. Robert Hopkins collection. P Oct 29 (67) $2,500

Ds, 15 Oct 1946. 1 p, 4to. Warrant awarding a medal to Patrick H. Hodgson. Countersgd by Dean Acheson. Framed. Altman collection. pnNY Sept 13 (26) $475

Photograph, sgd & inscr, 15 Apr 1952. 9 by 7 inches. Inscr to Mrs. J. B. Harriman. Torn. wa May 30 (317) $120

— Anr, [n.d.], 8.5 by 6.5 inches. Sepia photo by Chase-Statler. Sgd as Senator, on mount. wa Oct 18 (56) $150

Signature, on Ls, 23 Oct 1965, from a young autograph collector. wa May 30 (309) $65

Trumbull, John, 1756-1843
Collection of ADs & autograph letter, 24 June 1790 & [n.d.]. 2 pp, 16mo & 12mo. Receipt for 3 Guineas from Richard Bache for prints. To G. Tait, about his selling the copperplate of the Declaration of Independence to Messrs Phelps. wa May 30 (330) $250

Trumbull, Jonathan, 1710-85
Ds, 9 Jan 1777. 1 p, 8vo. Pay order to Col. Elisha Shelton for £ 10,000, as requested by Washington. Countersgd by John Lawrence. sg Nov 6 (348) $250

Trumbull, Jonathan, 1740-1809
Ds, 10 May 1799. 1 p, folio. Appointment of Andrew Huntington as Judge of Probate; partly ptd. Sgd as Governor of Connecticut. sg Nov 6 (349) $175

— 15 Oct 1807. 1 p, 4to. Commission for Roderick Stanley as Ensign. Repaired. wa May 30 (447) $55

Turenne, Henri de la Tour d'Auvergne, Vicomte de, 1611-75
ALs, 9 Feb 1660. 3 pp, 4to. To Cardinal Mazarin. Reporting about the French troops in Flanders. Repaired. star Apr 9 (1270) DM1,100

Turgenev, Ivan, 1818-83
Collection of ALs, [n.d.], & autograph sentiment, 1873. 1 p; accepting an invitation to the house of Th. Charles. To Sophie de Gubernatz, on verso of calling card. Both stained; framed with a photograph. Altman collection. pnNY Sept 13 (137) $325

Photograph, sgd & inscr, 1879. Cabinet size. Inscr to William Little, on mount. In English. S May 21 (315) £400 [Hoffman]

Turkish Manuscripts
Ms, Berat of Sultan Ahmed III [Constantinople, A.H.1127/A.D.1715]. 132cm by 53cm. In diwani script in black, red & gold ink. Text scattered with powdered gold leaf. S June 1 (59) £6,500 [Ziai]
— **Ms,** Kitab-ser-i risale-i Brigevi Mehmed Efendi. [Ottoman, A.H. 1120 / A.D. 1708]. In naskhi script within gold bands. 272 leaves, 183mm by 122mm, in lea bdg, repaired. FD June 11 (20) DM2,400
— **Ms,** Ruznameh. [Ottoman, 19th cent]. Scroll vellum, length 122cm. Copied by Mustafa known as Hikmati Thani; script not stated. With headings in gold on maroon-painted panels & illuminated medallion & headpiece. S June 1 (154) £380 [Maggs]
— IBRAHIM HAKKI - Ma'rifat Nameh. [Ottoman, A.H.1184/A.D.1770]. 447 leaves & 3 flyleaves, 289mm by 190mm. Contemp brown mor gilt. In naskhi script by Umar bin Husain Erzerumi, at the instance of Sayyid Ahmad Ma'imi. With numerous colored diagrams & tables. C June 16 (58) £800

Turner, Joseph Mallord William, 1775-1851
A Ls s (2), [15 Dec 1827] & 11 Dec 1844. 5 pp, 4to. To J. P. Orde, about engravings from drawings. Seal tear. To Mr. [Wethorned?], concerning a commissioned painting. Holed. Bullock collection. CNY Dec 19 (242) $1,200

Twain, Mark. See: Clemens, Samuel Langhorne

Tweed, William Marcy, 1823-78
Series of 17 A Ls s, 9 Jan 1854 to 28 Oct 1857. Length not stated, 8vo & 4to. To James J. Murphy. About patronage & politics in NY & Washington. With 2 transcripts of telegraph messages from Tweed. P May 13 (138) $7,500
Ls, 13 Oct 1870. 1 p, 8vo. To James Grant Wilson. As Commissioner of Public Works, denying his request to lay gas mains. sg Nov 6 (213) $80

Tyler, John, 1790-1862
Collection of 2 A Ls s & autograph endorsement, sgd, 19 Mar 1832 to [c.1842]. 3 pp, 4to. To Mr. Smith, Cashier of the US Bank in Washington, about the discount of a note. To Sec of State Daniel Webster, recommending A.M. Green for the consulate at Galveston. Endorsement requesting a copy of a letter to Gov. Cass. P Oct 29 (135) $500

ALs, 20 Dec 1818. 2 pp, 4to. To his wife Letitia Christian Tyler. Family letter, & saying congressional duties prevent him from spending Christmas at home. Holed. P May 13 (139) $1,000
Ds, 16 Nov 1841. 1 p, 4to. Order to affix the US Seal to a commission for John S. Pendleton. sg Sept 18 (288) $275
— 19 July 1843. 1 p, folio. Ship's papers for the Persia of New Bedford. Also sgd in 3 other hands. Torn. Framed. Altman collection. pnNY Sept 13 (29) $700
— 17 July 1844. 1 p, folio. Surveyor's appointment in Salem & Beverly. rf Nov 15 (18) $375
Franking signature, [n.d.]. On cover addressed to the Acting Sec of the Treasury. rf May 30 (26) $150
— Anr, [n.d.]. rf Mar 14 (105) $260
— Anr, [n.d.]. Address panel of mourning envelope; Norfolk, Va. postmark. Mtd. wa Oct 18 (155) $95

Tyner, James Noble, 1826-1904
[An archive of c.50 items, mostly documents related to Tyner's career & letters addressed to him, c.1870s & later, sold at P on 13 May, lot 117, for $1,200.]

U

Ubbelohde, Otto, 1867-1922
ALs, 12 Feb 1913. 1 p, folio. To H. Hertling. About the ptg of an ornamental drawing. Mtd. star Apr 8 (547) DM500

Udet, Ernst, 1896-1941
Photograph, sgd, [c.1918]. Postcard size. In uniform. star Apr 9 (1042) DM400

Uhland, Ludwig, 1787-1862
ALs, 21 Nov 1853. 2 pp, folio. To the Royal notary at Pfullingen. Sending his final statement concerning his guardianship for his nephew Ludwig Meyer. star Apr 8 (266) DM700
ADs, 25 Sept 1830. 1 p, 4to. Receipt, sgd, for fees for articles ptd in the magazine Morgenblatt. On leaf with statement of fees due. star Apr 8 (265) DM510

Umlauff, Michael, 1781-1842. See: Gyrowetz, Adalbert & Umlauff

Unger, Johann Friedrich, 1753-1804
ALs, 5 July 1804. 1 p, 4to. To an unnamed author in Vienna. Looking forward to his new play & mentioning If[f]land. star Apr 8 (275) DM380

United States

— LOUISIANA PURCHASE. - Ds, [23 May 1803], 1 p, folio. Statement that the Louisiana Treaty & 2 related conventions, now ratified by Napoleon, have been delivered to the US envoys. Sgd by Francois de Barbe-Marbois, Robert R. Livington & James Monroe. With Ls, [28 May 1803], 1 p, 4to, from Barbe-Marbois to Livingston & Monroe. Requesting them to temporarily return the ratified treaties so that further copies can be made & to briefly delay the departure of Peter A. Jay for the US. Sang collection. P Oct 29 (94) $35,000

— SHAYS' REBELLION. - Ds, June 1786. 1 p, folio. Pay roll for men who "went to suppress the Mob at Northampton". Sgd by Capt. Gideon Stebbins. Frayed. sg Nov 6 (331) $350

— SUPREME COURT. - 6 engraved Supreme Court cards, 1966. 6 pp, 16mo. Sgd by Justices Tom C. Clark (inscr to Joseph R. Hovance), Abe Fortas, Hugo L. Black, W. O. Douglas, William J. Brennan, Jr., & John M. Harlan. sg Nov 6 (342) $225

— SUPREME COURT. - 5 engraved Supreme Court cards & 1 plain card, [n.d.]. 6 pp, 16mo & 12mo. Sgd by Justices Earl Warren, Potter Stewart, Byron R. White, Abe Fortas, Thurgood Marshall, & Hugo L. Black. sg Nov 6 (343) $225

— WAR OF 1812. PRIVATEERS' LOGBOOKS. - Ms, logs of 5 NY merchantmen, 1811 to 1815. More than 300 p, folio, def half lea bdg. Relating to the careers of Guy R. Champlin & Lewis Smith. With several pen-and-wash sketches of ships. P Oct 29 (136) $4,000

Utrillo, Maurice, 1883-1955
ALs, 19 Apr 1925. 1 p, 4to. To Nora Kars. Gallant verse letter. In pencil, with colored underlinings. S Nov 27 (476) £220 [Lee]

— 24 May 1941. 1 p, folio. Recipient unnamed. Suggesting he contact his agent Petrides. S Nov 27 (477) £340 [Lee]

V

Valerius Maximus
Ms, Factorum et Dictorum Memorabilium Libri IX, [North-East Italy, c.1350-80]. 145 leaves & 2 later flyleaves, vellum, 247mm by 174mm; lacking 1 leaf. 18th cent mottled calf bdg. In dark brown ink in a regular rounded Italian gothic bookhand. With c.135 decorated initials, 9 large painted initials in leafy & geometrical designs in full colors, & very large historiated initial on burnished gold ground, showing port of the author. S Dec 2 (40) £7,000 [Chiaramonte]

Vallandigham, Clement L., 1820-71
Franking signature, [21 Dec 1861]. rf Mar 14 (106) $150

Van Buren, Martin, 1782-1862
ALs, 16 Aug 1803. 1 p, size not stated. To William P. Van Ness. Asking him to come to Kinderhook. pnNY June 11 (61) $150

— 24 Nov 1817. 1 p, 8vo. As State Attorney Gen., announcing a rule "to each of the above defendants" requiring them to plead within 20 days. Framed. Altman collection. pnNY Sept 13 (33) $200

— 1 Nov 1826. 2 pp, 4to. To John L. Riker. About financial matters involving Peter Vosburgh & Mr. Van Schaack. Seal tear. With franking signature on integral address leaf. wa May 30 (310) $375

— 7 Mar 1834. 1 p, 8vo. Recipient unnamed. Dinner invitation. wa May 30 (127) $325

— 7 Oct 1843. 1 p, size not stated. To C. P. Van Ness. Sending him the requested letters, including "the one in respect to Quick-Silver". Framed with autograph envelope. Altman collection. pnNY Sept 13 (31) $375

— 14 Oct 1843. 2 pp, size not stated. To Russel[l] Jarvis. Saying he cannot take any part in the establishment of an intended publication due to the election campaign. Framed. Altman collection. pnNY Sept 13 (32) $300

Ds, 3 Oct 1838. 1 p, 4to. Order to affix the US Seal to "the Proclamation of the Convention with the Peru-Bolivian Confederation." P May 13 (140) $750

— [n.d.]. 1 p, 16 by 20.5 inches. Ship's papers in 4 languages; unaccomplished. Countersgd by Sec of State John Forsyth. S Jan 27 (941) £400 [Wilson]

Franking signature, [7 Aug 1843]. rf May 30 (27) $150

— Anr, [2 Sept n.y.]. rf Mar 14 (107) $190

Van de Velde, Henry, 1863-1957
ALs, [c.1910-1914). 1 p, 8vo. Recipient unnamed. About problems at the Weimar academy. Sgd v.d.V. star Apr 8 (549) DM500

Van Dorn, Earl, 1820-63
ADs, 12 Mar 1861. 1 p, 4to. Order requiring estimates of Army supplies. Inkstains. wa May 30 (261a) $600

Van Loo, Pieter, 1731-84 —& Van Noorde, Cornelis, 1731-95
Original drawings, Choix de jacintes, 13 water-color drawings of double hyacinths, sgd & dated 1765 (2, by Van Norde) & 1769; 1 unsgd. 31 leaves, drawings on rectos of 13, rest blank, 480mm by 293mm. Contemp red mor gilt with tooled floral border & hyacinth in centers; bound for Charles de

Rohan, Prince de Soubise. Hunt collection. CNY Nov 21 (185) $80,000

Van Noorde, Cornelis, 1731-95. See: Van Loo, Pieter & Van Noorde

Vanacker, Nicholas

Autograph check, 22 Apr 1659. 3 by 8 inches. Drawn on Clayton & Morris, ordering £10 to be paid to bearer. With receipt written underneath. "One of the very earliest recorded English cheques". S July 24 (431) £600 [Burgess & Browning]

Vanbrugh, Sir John, 1664-1726

Autograph Ms, proposals for rebuilding part of Hampton Court Palace, [c.1716?]. 3 pp, folio. With scribal copy of proposals, sgd by Vanbrugh. S Dec 18 (315) £3,000 [Curry]

Vandamme, Dominique Rene, Comte de Huencberg, 1770-1830

Ds, 27 May 1813. 1 p, 4to. Passport for Sr. Laroche. star Apr 9 (1271) DM320

Vanderbilt, Cornelius

Ds, 20 May 1868. 2 pp, 8vo. Stock certificate in the NY & Harlem Railroad Company. Also sgd by William H. Vanderbilt. Repaired with tape. wd Nov 12 (21) $400

Varnhagen von Ense, Karl August, 1785-1858

ALs, 18 Jan 1833. 3 pp, 4to. To [E. G. Gersdorf?]. Declining to work for his new magazine because of prior obligations. star Apr 8 (268) DM420

— 26 Jan 1838. 2 pp, 8vo. To an unnamed Ed of a magazine. Recommending a paper by August Boeckh about Frederick the Great for publication. star Apr 8 (269) DM540

— 24 May 1846. 1 p, 8vo. To Heinrich Heine. Letter of introduction for Herr Sougey-Avisard. With covering ALs, 26 May 1846, 1 p, 8vo, by Varnhagen to Sougey-Avisard. star Apr 8 (270) DM2,200

Vaudreuil, Louis Phillippe de Rigaud, Marquis de, 1724-1802

ALs, 25 Sept 1782. 2 pp, 4to. To Gov. Hancock. Regarding fortifications at Nantucket. wa May 30 (326) $450

Vauvenargues, Luc de Clapiers, Marquis de, 1715-47

Autograph Ms, Sur la morale et la physique; no 54 of his Reflexions sur divers sujets; [n.d.]. 4 pp, 4to. With autograph revisions. Traces of stitching. S Nov 27 (480) £350 [Charavay]

Vela, Juan. See: Santo Domingo

Venice

Ms, Serie di tutto che e occorso nel caso del Battesimo conferito...ad una figliolina ebrea d'un anno, invitis parentibus; c.1763. About 300 pp, contemp calf. Stamp of Paolo Saccoman. In Italian & Latin. Recording the facts of the case, depositions, etc. S Nov 27 (478) £750 [Quaritch]

Verdi, Giuseppe, 1813-1901

ALs, 12 Sept 1845. 2 pp, 8vo. To Andrea Maffei. About the beginning of his work on Attila, & comparing Naples & Busseto. Fold tear. S May 22 (542) £2,000 [Boys]

— [c.1847?]. 1 p, 16mo. To Andrea Maffei. Giving news of the Morosini family. Seal tear. S May 22 (543) £600 [Reuter]

— 7 Nov 1853. 2 pp, 8vo. To Tito Ricordi. Concerning singers for performances of Rigoletto & Il trovatore in Paris. S May 22 (647) £7,200 [Boys]

— 1 Apr 1857. 2 pp, 8vo. To Signor Monti. Chatting about a misunderstanding concerning flowers for Giuseppina Strepponi, dangerous props & the backwardness of Busseto. S Nov 28 (658) £900 [McCarthy-Ceeper]

— 8 Sept 1869. 1 p, 8vo. Recipient unnamed. Inviting him to visit. C June 24 (209) £420 [Wilson]

— [n.d.]. 1 p, 8vo. To Gen. Mengaldo. Thanking for good wishes & about his wife's health. With attestation by Perucchini. S May 22 (550) £600 [Rankin]

— 9 Sept 1879. 1 p, 8vo. To Signor Mola. About an old servant. Framed. Altman collection. pnNY Sept 13 (189) $900

— 14 Oct 1884. 1 p, 8vo. Recipient unnamed. Declining a libretto. In French. star Apr 9 (843) DM3,600

— 20 Dec 1894. 2 pp, 8vo. To Camille Du Locle. About Falstaff & Otello, & complaining about a Paris theater. Inscr by Du Locle on integral leaf. S May 22 (551) £2,400 [Boys]

— 5 Apr 1895. 2 pp, 8vo. To Emma Zilli. Acknowledging receipt of 2 letters & thanking for her good wishes. C Dec 3 (427) £700 [Benjamin]

AL, [c.1872]. 2 pp, size not stated. To [his pbr Ricordi?]. Draft, expressing his doubts that a performance of Aida in Germany or at Padua would be a success at this point. With many revisions. S Nov 28 (657) £2,800 [MacNutt]

Autograph telegram, 24 Feb 1897. To Domenico Cialdea. Sending congratulations & regretting he could not accept an honour. Sgd. pn Dec 11 (113) £360 [Wilson]

Verne, Jules, 1828-1905

ALs, 22 Sept 1889. 1 p, 12mo. To Nenie van der Gon Netscher. Answering her question by explaining that his writings are works of imagination, but that he tries to make them appear true. C Dec 3 (396A) £520 [L'Echiquier]

Autograph postcard, sgd, 4 Dec 1904. Recipient unnamed. Sending his autograph. Port postcard. star Apr 8 (276) DM780

ANs, June 1879. 1 p, 16mo. Recipient unnamed. Expressing his wish to visit all of North America. Framed. Altman collection. pnNY Sept 13 (138) $425

AN, Oct 1897. Recipient unnamed. On engraved visiting card, offering thanks & good wishes. S Jan 27 (991) £120 [Wilson]

Victoria, Queen of England, 1819-1901

Ds, 30 Nov 1852. 3 pp, 4to. Appointment of Charles Shapland Whitmore to the Office of Recorder at Gloucester. Countersgd by S. H. Walpole. Matted with a port. sg Nov 6 (215) $250

Victoria, Queen of England, 1819-1901

Collection of ALs & original drawing, 8 Nov 1895 & 21 Oct 1832. 3 pp, 8vo & 4to. Recipient unnamed. Forwarding a copy of a sermon; sgd VR. Pencil sketch, peasant girl with fruit basket leading a horse & rider down a hill; sgd PV. With related material. Bullock collection. CNY Dec 19 (243) $100

Series of 14 A Ls s, 1858 to 1874. 37 pp, 8vo. To Lady Caroline Barrington. About matters relating to her household, thanking for a gift, sending presents, & commenting about widowhood. With related material. S July 24 (238) £2,100 [Maggs]

ALs, 15 Oct 1856. 2 pp, 8vo. To "My dear George". Approving of appointments. Sgd VRg. C June 24 (74) £200 [Wilson]

— 11 Aug 1860. 2 pp, 8vo. To "My dear George". Approving of an appointment. Sgd VRg. C June 24 (75) £200 [Wilson]

— 2 Nov 1873. 6 pp, 8vo. To her son Prince Arthur, Duke of Connaught. Worrying about the health of her youngest son Prince Leopold. Repaired. C Dec 3 (336) £490 [Hardy]

— 28 May 1883. 3 pp, 8vo. To The Hon. Henry Byng. In 3d person, expressing her sorrow at the death of John Brown. S Dec 18 (219) £3,200 [F. A. S.]

— 22 Oct 1887. 4 pp, 8vo. To Lord & Lady Bray. In 3d person, sending photographs, referring to India, & saying she is learning Hindustani. S Jan 27 (761) £240 [Maggs]

Collection of 15 Sept 1848. 2 pp, 8vo. To her daughter Alice. In her own & Prince Albert's name, chatting about their activities at Balmoral. C Dec 3 (333) £450 [Hardy]

Series of 6 A Ls, 6 Nov 1896 to 13 Sept 1901. 20 pp, 8vo. To Lord George Hamilton. In 3d person, urging him to find a position for Rafiuddin Ahmed & recommending awards for people having served in India. S July 24 (237) £700 [Maggs]

Ls, 27 June 1837. 2 pp, 4to. To Marie Louise, Archduchess of Parma [previously Empress of the French]. Notifying her of her accession to the throne. With autograph subscription. S Dec 18 (218) £1,300 [F. A. S.]

— 24 Apr 1843. 1 p, 4to. To Ferdinand II, King of the Two Sicilies. Notifying him of the death of her uncle Augustus Frederick, Duke of Sussex. With autograph subscription. star Apr 9 (1001) DM310

— 9 Sept 1844. 1 p, 4to. To [Ferdinand II], King of the Two Sicilies. Notifying him of the birth of her son. With autograph subscription. pn Dec 11 (24) £280 [Maggs]

—' 28 June 1859. 4 pp, folio. To Prince Albert, Grand-Master of the Order of the Bath. Notifying him of the nomination of Dr. Adriano Dingli as member of the order. Sgd at head. With blue ribbon. star Apr 9 (1002) DM720

Ds s (2) 26 May & 22 June 1882. 1 p, 370mm by 540mm & 19 pp, folio. Commission & instructions for Robert Morier, Minister Plenipotentiary to the King of Spain. In green cloth box; seal in metal case. C Dec 3 (337) £400 [Maggs]

— Ds s (2) 27 Oct 1887 & 9 Mar 1897. 4 pp, folio. Commission for John Lowndes Gorst as 3d Secretary in the Diplomatic Service. Permission for Gorst to accept & wear an Egyptian decoration. Both partly ptd. C Dec 3 (338) £260 [Hardy]

Ds, 5 May 1838. 1 p, folio. Summons to the Duke of Cambridge to attend her coronation. S Jan 27 (763) £350 [Fas]

— 27 Feb 1867. 1 p, folio. Appointment for Edmund Campbell as Lieut. Col. in the Bombay Staff Corps. With 3 other commissions to Campbell. C June 24 (76) £130 [Solomon]

Document, 12 Nov 1872. Size not stated. Patent granted to Vitale Domenico de Michele, for improving process for manufacture of Portland Cement. pn Dec 11 (5) £85 [Heraldry]

Victoria, Empress of Friedrich III, 1840-1901

ALs, 1 Mar 1867. 3 pp, 8vo. To Grandduchess Sophie von Sachsen-Weimar. Requesting a contribution to a bazaar for disabled veterans. In French. star Apr 9 (1181) DM320

Victor-Perrin, Claude, Duc de Bellune, 1764-1841
Ls, 6 Sept 1807. 1 p, folio. To Villemanzy at Leipzig. Requesting that some troops be sent to Potsdam. star Apr 9 (1274) DM220

Villeneuve, Pierre Silvestre de, 1763-1806
ALs, 1 Nivoise an 6 [21 Dec 1797]. 2 pp, 4to. To Rear Admiral Vence. Contents not stated. sg Nov 6 (155) $200

Villiers, Barbara, Duchess of Cleveland, 1641-1709
A Ls s (2), [June 1673]. 3 pp, 4to. To Thomas Clifford, 1st Baron Clifford of Chudleigh. Requesting his help in obtaining money from the King & a warrant concerning revenues from the Forest of Dean. S July 24 (251) £1,500 [Quaritch]

Villiers, Joseph Coulon de, Sieur de Jumonville, 1718-54. See: Jumonville, Joseph Coulon de Villiers

Villiers, Louis Coulon de, 1710-57. See: Jumonville, Joseph Coulon de Villiers

Virchow, Rudolf, 1821-1902
ALs, 9 Dec 1893. 1 p, 8vo. Recipient unnamed. Dinner invitation. star Apr 8 (433) DM460
— 23 May 1894. 1 p, 8vo. To Jules Sachs. Saying he is not able to write an official letter of recommendation for him. star Apr 8 (434) DM440

Virginia
— WALLACE, WILLIAM. - 2 A Ls s, 8 June 1766 & 17 Apr 1767. 5 pp, folio. To David Mudie in Arbroath. Describing life as an employee in the tobacco trade. S Jan 27 (942) £240 [Blair]

Vittorio Emanuele III, King of Italy, 1869-1947
Ls, 15 May 1904. 1 p, folio. To Nicholas I of Montenegro. Notifying him of the birth of the Duke of Genoa's daughter. With autograph subscription. Countersgd by Foreign Minister Tittoni. star Apr 9 (1019) DM210
Ds, 7 Oct 1928. 1 p, folio. Military discharge. Countersgd by Mussolini. star Apr 9 (1020) DM450
— 1 Mar 1937. 1 p, folio. Appointment in the army. Countersgd by Mussolini. S Jan 27 (978) £220 [Bristow]

Vlaminck, Maurice de, 1876-1958
A Ls s (2), 9 Apr & 24 Sept 1956. 3 pp, 8vo. Recipient unnamed. Contents not stated. Saying he cannot provide a room for him at his house. star Apr 8 (551) DM480
ALs, 24 Oct 1935. 1 p, 8vo. To M. Delamain. Inquiring about the publication of a Ms. wa May 30 (3) $75
— 13 July 1954. 1 p, 4to. Recipient unnamed. About a consignment of lithographs & etchings. With related material. star Apr 8 (550) DM420

Vogeler, Heinrich, 1872-1942
A Ls s (2), 2 Dec 1904 & 31 Dec 1905. 3 pp, 8vo. To Anna Plate. Concerning a visit by Egon Petri. To Richard Graul, New Year's wishes. With bookplate for Franz Vogeler. FD June 11 (3537) DM750
ALs, 2 Dec 1904. 2 pp, 8vo. To Anna Plate. Concerning a visit by Egon Petri. With ALs, 31 Dec 1905, 1 p, 4to, to Richard Graul, & bookplate for Franz Vogeler. star Apr 8 (553) DM480
Series of 5 autograph postcards, 1897 to 1921. To Hans Mueller-Brauel. Regarding orders. About earlier designs for windows. With related material. star Apr 8 (552) DM1,200
— Series of 4 autograph postcards, initialled, 16 Aug 1911 to 7 Sept 1914. To Frido Witte. About an invitation, a visit, his new house, etc. One card with sketch of 3 soldiers. HN May 22 (3222) DM620

Voltaire, Francois Marie Arouet de, 1694-1778
ALs, 16 Mar 1751. 1 p, 8vo. To his publisher Georg Conrad Walther. Suggesting a text to advertise a new Ed of his works & ordering books. Sgd V. Bestermann no 3839. star Apr 8 (277) DM3,500
— 7 Oct [1762]. 2 pp, 4to. To Elie Bertrand. About the case of Jean Calas & mentioning Catherine the Great's intention to print the Encyclopedie. Sgd V. S Nov 27 (482) £2,800
— 3 June 1772. 1 p, 4to. To Charles Augustin Feriol, Comte d'Argental. Concerning the tragedy Asturie ou les loix de Minos. Sgd V. Written on final blank p of a letter to Voltaire by Marin, 3 pp, 4to. Bestermann Ed, nos 16713 & 16706. Tipped into a copy of Lettres secrettes. Geneva 1765 [1764]. 1st Ed[?]; Mortimer L. Schiff copy. S Nov 27 (483) £500 [Dr. Sam]
Ls, 15 Dec [1759] 4 pp, 8vo. To [Francois de Chennevieres]. Complimenting him on his stories & commenting on the news from France. C June 24 (157) £450 [Bush]

Von Kempis Family
[A collection of c.87 letters, mostly addressed to Johann Rainer von Kempis by members of his family, 1711 to 1773, mostly 8vo, relating to family matters & court news from Brussels, sold at VH on 12 Sept 1986, lot 931, for DM1,000.]

[A collection of 8 documents relating to property settlements of the von Kempis family at Bonn, 1732, 27 pp on 20 leaves, 4to, sold at VH on 12 Sept 1986, lot 929, for DM1,000.]

Voss, Johann Heinrich, 1751-1826
Autograph Ms, trans, Die Hirten. Theokrits vierte Idylle, [c.1808]. 4 pp, 8vo. 63 lines, sgd. JG Oct 2 (158) DM1,500
ALs, 10 June 1788. 2 pp, 8vo. To Klamer Schmidt. Requesting contributions to his Goettinger Musenalmanach. star Apr 8 (279) DM4,200

W

Wadsworth, Jeremiah, 1743-1804. See: Hancock, John

Wagner, Christian, 1835-1918. See: Wagner-Warmbronn, Christian

Wagner, Minna, 1809-66
ALs, 11 Sept [1858]. 4 pp, 8vo. To Cosima von Buelow [later Wagner]. About her husband, declining an invitation, & mentioning the breakup of their home at Asyl. With draft of part of the letter, 2 pp. S May 22 (559) £700 [Zurich Library]

Wagner, Richard, 1813-83
Autograph music, sketches for Lohengrin, act 2, scenes 3 & 4, [c.1847]. 2 pp, 38cm by 29cm. Some corrections in pencil; some differences in text from final version. star Apr 9 (844) DM26,000
— Autograph music, "Walkuere. No: 2. - Conductor", [Oct 1862]. 1 p, 8vo. Instructions to Wendelin Weissheimer for copying the beginning of Walkuere, act 3, (Walkuerenritt), to be played at a concert. star Apr 9 (845) DM7,000
Ms, conducting score of Beethoven's Egmont, Op. 84, [1852?]. 175 pp, folio. Contemp cloth-backed bds. With autograph annotations by Wagner & further annotations in anr hand. With note of authenticity by Dr. Max Fehr inside upper cover. C June 24 (211) £15,000 [Suita Trading]
Collection of ALs & ANs, 17 Nov 1859 & 15 Dec 1870. 2 p, 8vo. To Herr Frank. Covering letter for a paper. To [Schott & Co.?]. Covering letter for an expanded ending of a work. Bullock collection. CNY Dec 19 (153) $1,200
A Ls s (2), 30 Aug 1854 & 21 July 1868. 4 pp, 8vo. To Gottfried Semper; inviting him to Zurich. To "Herr Oberst", complaining about the delay in finishing a bath house. Bullock collection. CNY Dec 19 (155) $1,400
ALs, 28 May [18]51. 2 pp, 8vo. To Eduard Roeckel. Recommending the violinist Heimberger. S May 22 (560) £700 [Rankin]
— 27 Aug 1853. 1 p, 4to. To Musikdirektor Bohlen. Requesting an answer to an earlier inquiry. Holed. JG Oct 2 (349) DM2,400
— 24 June 1856. 4 pp, 16mo. To Julie Ritter. Informing her that he is taking the water cure at Mornex, & about his & Ritter's relatives. Initialled. With related material. P Sept 24 (58) $750
— 25 July 1861. 4 pp, 8vo. To Agnes Street-Klindworth. About his terrible time in Paris, the Flying Dutchman & Tristan, & hoping to go to Vienna soon. C June 24 (210) £1,700 [Bender]
— 22 Nov 1861. 1 p, 8vo. To Dr. Richard Faber. Postponing a dentist's appointment. star Apr 9 (846) DM1,700
— [1862?]. 1 p, 8vo. Recipient unknown. Concerning a rehearsal. With autograph music fragment, [n.d.], on strip of staff paper, 32mm by 172mm; correction to 2d horn part in Goetterdaemmerung. With related material. Bullock collection. CNY Dec 19 (154) $850
— 26 Jan 1869. 1 p, 8vo. To Anton Mitterwurzer. About the success of Die Meistersinger at Dresden & recipient's performance as Sachs & Wolfram. S May 22 (563) £1,000 [Schneider]
— 16 May 1869. 3 pp, 8vo. To Hans von Brousart. Concerning royalties for performances of Die Meistersinger at Hannover. CNY Dec 19 (150) $1,300
— 5 Oct 1870. 2 pp, 8vo. Recipient unknown. Ordering wine. Fold tear. Bullock collection. CNY Dec 19 (152) $700
— 4 June 1871. 1 p, 8vo. To the pbr Schott at Mainz. Asking that the score of Huldigungsmarsch be sent & discussing the title of Der Ring. S May 22 (564) £1,000 [Preussische Staatsbibliothek]
— 13 Aug 1871. 1 p, 16mo. To his pbr E. W. Fritzsch. Sending a table of contents for his Gesammelte Schriften und Dichtungen. S May 22 (648) £420 [West]
— 4 June 1872. 3 pp, 8vo. Recipient unnamed. Expressing his thanks to the members of the Berlin Koenigliche Kapelle for playing at Bayreuth. star Apr 9 (848a) DM2,200
— 19 Apr 1873. 1 p, 8vo. Recipient unnamed. Giving instructions for his hotel rooms in Cologne. star Apr 9 (848b) DM1,700
— [n.d.]. 1 p, size not stated. To "Cher ami". Inviting him & his wife to dinner. Framed. Altman collection. pnNY Sept 13 (190) $800
Ls, 18 May 1870. 3 pp, 8vo. Recipient unknown. Stating that he is not able to obtain a subsidy for his correspondent from the King of Bavaria. Bullock collection. CNY Dec 19 (151) $800
— 22 May 1875. 2 pp, 4to. To Court Musician Meyer in Berlin. Offering terms for participation in the Bayreuth orchestra; partly ptd. sg Apr 9 (215) $800

ANs, 31 Jan [n.y.]. 1 p, 8vo. To unnamed friends. Inviting them to Penzing. HK Nov 7 (2360) DM1,200
See also: Chamberlain, Eva Wagner

Wagner, Siegfried, 1869-1930
Collection of autograph postcard, sgd & ALs, [Sept 1919] & 5 June 1921. 3 pp, 4to & 8vo. Recipient unnamed. Announcing the birth of his son; on verso of photograph, postcard size, showing his elder children. To Georg Aleff, concerning a port photograph of Duehrkoop. star Apr 9 (849a) DM260

Wagner von Jauregg, Julius, 1857-1940
ALs, 21 Mar 1937. 3 pp, 4to. To Franz Theodor Csokor. Commenting on his drama "3. November 1918". star Apr 8 (435) DM420

Wagner, Winifred, 1897-1980
Series of 5 Ls s, 24 July 1956 to 18 Dec 1974. 5 pp, folio & 4to. To H. E. Mutzenbecher. Concerning the Richard Wagner Society & lectures by Mutzenbecher. star Apr 9 (849b) DM220

Wagner-Warmbronn, Christian, 1835-1918
ALs, 9 Dec 1893. 2 pp, 8vo. Recipient unnamed. Personal news. With autograph poem, Herbstgruende, sgd, on conjugate leaf. star Apr 8 (280) DM3,800

Wales
Ms, genealogical Ms arranged under family names, prefaced with tables of Popes, Bishops, & Kings down to Charles I, [early to mid-17th cent]. About 200 leaves, 4to. Contemp calf. Later part written in anr hand. Some later notes. Ownership inscr of J. B. Lloyd Philipps, 1859. S July 24 (269) £600 [Quaritch]

Wallace, Lew, 1827-1905
ALs, Christmas 1883. 4 pp, 8vo. To Mrs. Wyndham. Discussing the religious intentions of Ben Hur. Laid down on album leaf with signature of Mendelssohn on verso. S Dec 18 (349) £1,300 [Maggs]

Wallenstein, Albrecht von, Herzog von Friedland & Mecklenburg, 1583-1634
ALs, 6 Nov 1627. 1 p, folio. To [Hans Georg von Arnim]. Commenting about letters received from the King of Poland & the Duke of Pomerania. star Apr 9 (1277) DM6,500

— 23 Dec 1627. 1 p, folio. To Hans Georg von Arnim. Stating his intention to execute an officer if he should fail to appear after the 3d summons. Sgd HzF. C Dec 3 (339) £520 [Pollak]

— 7 Jan 1628. 1 p, folio. To an unnamed commander. About sending a secret letter from Schwarzenberg, the military situation, & the question of alliance with Sweden. Sgd AHzF. S Nov 27 (484) £2,600 [Henry]

Ls, 21 Apr 1622. 1 p, folio. To the magistrate of Nimburg. Instructing them to make payments only to soldiers & officers authorized by Heinrich von Waldstein. star Apr 9 (1275) DM1,800

— 23 Dec 1627. 1 p, folio. To the city of Stralsund. Requesting that Danish ships be prevented from leaving the Stralsund port. star Apr 9 (1278) DM2,400

Waller, Thomas ("Fats"), 1904-43
Autograph music, composition entitled "M. Ser", [n.d.]. Complete score for 11 instruments, 12 measures. 3 pp, 4to. In pencil. P June 18 (202) $1,000

— Autograph music, song, If it Ain't Love; 2 melodic sketches & bass line. 3 double folio sheets. In pencil & ink. With copy of ptd version, 1932. P June 18 (201) $1,100

— Autograph music, song, Strange as it Seems, [c.1932]. In 3 versions. 3 folio sheets. Partly in pencil. P June 18 (203) $1,000

— Autograph music, song, There's a Little Good in me, [n.d.]. Melodic sketch, on double folio sheet, in pencil; & typed lyrics, 2 pp, 4to. P June 18 (204) $650

Walpole, Horace, 4th Earl of Orford, 1717-97
[An important collection of correspondence, comprising c.257 A Ls s by Walpole & c.185 A Ls s by George Montagu, 1736 to 1770, with some related material, sold at S on 23 July, lot 29, for £45,000 to Burgess & Browning.]

ALs, 17 Feb 1769. 1 p, 4to. Recipient unnamed. Discussing some prints. Mtd. S July 23 (30) £400 [Wilson]

Walpole, Sir Robert, 1st Earl of Orford, 1676-1745
Ds, 29 Nov 1725. 2 pp, folio. Warrant for payment to Martin Bell. S Jan 27 (811) £70 [Weng]

Walser, Martin
Autograph Ms, Antaeische Musik, [n.d.]. 15 pp, folio; on verso of different leaves, some typescripts of a play. Essay for the magazine Weltwoche; sgd at head. star Apr 8 (281) DM1,800

ALs, 7 Mar 1979. 5 pp, folio. To a literary foundation. Draft, regarding grants for young authors. star Apr 8 (282) DM550

Walter, Bruno, 1876-1962
ALs, 31 Aug 1930. 2 pp, 4to. To Paul Hirsch. Announcing his visit. star Apr 9 (851) DM420

Walton, George, Signer from Georgia

Ds, [c.1782]. 1 p, folio. Summons, partly ptd. Charlotte Parker Milne collection. wd Nov 12 (73) $100

Cut signature, [n.d.]. wa May 30 (142) $70

Walton, Sir William, 1902-83

Autograph music, Foxtrot: Old Sir Faulk, from Facade, [1926?]. 7 pp, folio. Full score with vocal line; 2 systems of 7 staves per p. In pencil; traces of erasings. C Dec 3 (428) £5,500 [MacNutt]

War of 1812

— CLAUDE, JOHN. - Series of 10 A Ls s, Jan 1813 to Dec 1814. 27 pp, folio & 4to. To his brothers Dennis & Abram Claude. Soldier's letters written from Plattsburgh, NY. sg Apr 9 (217) $800

— MACKAY, AENEAS. - Autograph Ms, diary, 20 Oct 1810 to May 1815, trans & rewritten from the orig in 1818. 173 pp, folio. In French & English. Describing NY life & the war in NY State. pnNY June 11 (93) $1,700

— SHIPS' LOGS. - Mss, logs of the U.S. ships Alligator, Magnet, General Armstrong & Governor Tompkins, 22 Mar 1811 to 14 June 1813. About 140 pp, folio. Including entries recording encounters with British ships. With related material. S July 24 (410) £950 [Agnew]

Warhol, Andy, 1931-87

Typescript, thoughts about America, [n.d.]. 1 p, 8.5 by 11 inches. Sgd. wa May 30 (4) $500

Waring, Edward John. See: India

Warren, Gouverneur Kemble, 1830-82

ALs, 17 Apr 1864. 1 p, 8vo. To S. F. Baird. Inquiring about a work similar to Woodward's Manual of the Molluscs. wa May 30 (262) $170

Warren, John, 1753-1815

ALs, 15 Nov 1776. 2 pp, 4to. To Elbridge Gerry. Concerning the possibility of a reorganization of the Medical Department of the army. P May 13 (141) $1,500

Washington, Bushrod, 1762-1829

[A collection of Washington family papers, 14 items, 1694 to 1828, including letters addressed to him, sold at S on 24 July 1987, lot 413, for £700 to Apfelbaum.]

ALs, 25 Apr 1811. 1 p, 4to. To George Carter. Concerning payments on a debt due by Washington to Carter. Lacking lower right corner. wa Oct 18 (59) $150

Washington, George, 1732-99

Autograph Ms, "Compend of husbandry", fragment. 2 pp, 4 by 6.5 inches. 175 words, about the benefits of manure in farming. In lea folding case; with letters documenting provenance. rf Mar 14 (59) $4,000

Autograph transcript, copy of a letter to him from John Adams, 9 Oct 1798. 3 pp, 4to; regarding questions of rank among Major Generals Hamilton, Pinckney & Knox. Washington's name at foot of 3d p. Was mtd. P Oct 29 (146) $4,250

ALs, 10 Dec 1773. 2 pp, folio. To John Tayloe. Suggesting postponing the sale of George Mercer's lands till after the harvest. Separated at fold. P Dec 15 (85) $3,000

— 31 Oct 1774. 1 p, 4to. To John Tayloe. Asking him to be present at the sale of George Mercer's lands. P Dec 15 (86) $5,250

— 30 Nov 1774. 2 pp, 4to. To John Tayloe. Informing him about the sale of George Mercer's lands. P Dec 15 (87) $5,250

— 11 Dec 1775. 4 pp, folio. To John Tayloe. Expressing his opinion that James Mercer should not collect the debts arising from the sale of his brother's lands & reporting about the military situation in Boston. With postscript. Sgd twice. P Dec 15 (88) $9,000

— 12 Mar 1776. 4 pp, 4to. To John Tayloe. Answering questions concerning the Mercer estate & describing his offensive against the British in Boston. P Dec 15 (89) $24,000

— 17 June 1776. 1 p, 4to. To [Benjamin Franklin?]. Transmitting an earlier letter (not present). Mtd. P May 13 (143) $10,000

— 5 Aug 1777. 4 pp, 4to. To John Tayloe. Describing his efforts to meet with Howe's fleet & commenting on the loss of Ticonderoga. P Dec 15 (90) $22,000

— 11 Jan 1778. 2 pp, 4to. To Capt. George Lewis. Asking to have his baggage sent to Valley Forge. Repaired. Mtd. P May 13 (144) $9,000

— 20 Mar 1779. 4 pp, 4to. To Henry Laurens. About the suggestion to raise black troops. Badly stained. P May 13 (145) $15,000

— 20 June 1784. 17 pp, 4to. To Francis Lightfoot Lee & Ralph Wormeley, Jr. Summarizing his activities regarding the estate of George Mercer. Somewhat def. P Dec 15 (92) $16,000

— 15 Mar 1785. 2 pp, folio. To Col. Frederick Weissenfels. Requesting further information about his military service for a letter of recommendation. Framed. P Oct 29 (141) $6,250

— 25 Mar 1789. 2 pp, 4to. To Gov. George Clinton. Declining an invitation to stay with him, & wishing to enter NY without ceremony. CNY May 11 (137) $26,000

— 1 May 1792. 2 pp, 4to. To David Steuart, 11th Earl of Buchan. Regarding his port for Buchan's collection, executed by [Archibald] Robinson. Thanking for a gift. P Oct 29 (142) $8,000

— 29 Apr 1793. 2 pp, 4to. To his nephew Robert Lewis. Draft, regarding land which he intends to convey to Lewis & other landed property. Inlaid. P Oct 29 (143) $3,500

— 20 Oct 1795. 2 pp, 4to. To James Maury. Requesting him to send seeds. Retained copy, endorsed by Washington on verso. Hinged to anr leaf. P May 13 (150) $7,500

Ls, 6 Apr 1776. 1 p, 4to. To Maj. Gen. Artemas Ward. Concerning money wanted by Assistant Quarter Master Gen. Park & routine matters. Foxed, repaired; outer edge closely cropped. sg Nov 6 (216) $9,000

— 9 Aug 1776. 1 p, folio. To Gen. George Clinton. Enclosing a resolution of the New York Provincial Convention (not included) concerning Clinton's command. Fold splits. Fitzpatrick Ed, vol 5, p 396, misdated 8 Aug. P Oct 29 (137) $7,000

— [8 Sept 1776]. 1 p, folio. To Abraham Yates, Jr. Approving of the removal of the NY church bells to Newark. Silked. P Oct 29 (138) $10,000

— 8 Feb 1778. 1 p, folio. To Brig. Gen. John Lacey, Jr. Requesting him to stop communication between Philadelphia & the country, but to prevent plundering. Fold splits. Fitzpatrick Ed, vol 10, p 478, misdated 18 Feb. P Oct 29 (139) $14,000

— 12 Mar 1778. 2 pp, folio. To Gov. George Clinton. About problems of supply & the "mismanagement in the North River command". With contemp explanatory note in margin of 2d page. CNY May 11 (136) $10,000

— 26 Feb 1779. 1 p, folio. To Col. Wigglesworth. About officers from Gen. Glover's brigade meeting at Pickskill "to prefer claims", & regretting recipient's wish to resign. Written in James McHenry's hand. Framed. Altman collection. pnNY Sept 13 (34) $10,000

— 1 July 1781. 2 pp, 4to. To Col. Stewart. Concerning provisions & mentioning the possibility of moving further to the South. rf Mar 14 (58) $6,250

— 2 Aug 1783. 3 pp, folio. To Baron de Capellan du Sol. Thanking for a present sent by a Dutch patriotic society & commenting about Dutch-American relations. Was mtd. S July 24 (412) £4,600 [Joseph & Sawyer]

— 27 Sept 1788. 1 p, 4to. To Francis Adrian Van der Kemp. Congratulating him on his new home & asking for seeds. With franking signature on integral address leaf. P May 13 (146) $8,500

— 1 Mar 1797. 1 p, 4to. To Sen. John Rutherford. Requesting his presence in the Senate Chamber on 4 Mar [John Adams's inauguration]. Was mtd. P Oct 29 (145) $12,000

AN, [n.d.]; 4 lines at foot of a receipt sgd by Robert Mercer relating to the sale of George Mercer's lands, 11 Apr 1783. 2 pp, folio. P Dec 15 (91) $1,000

ADs, 18 Apr 1751. 1 p, folio. Survey of 375 acres on the Cacapon River belonging to Joseph Edwards. With small plat drawing of land. Framed. P May 13 (142) $9,000

Ds, 30 June 1783. 2 pp, 330mm by 210mm. Military discharge for Joseph Plomondon; partly ptd. Countersgd by J. Trumbull & 2 others. Silked. On verso acknowledgment of sale by Plomondon of 600 acres of land received for his services in the Continental Army, 1785. sg Nov 6 (355) $2,800

— [1783-1784]. 1 p, folio. Certificate of service & discharge from the army for Thomas Barron; partly ptd. Countersgd by Jonathan Trumbull. Framed. P Oct 29 (140) $2,500

— 10 May 1787. 1 p, folio. Membership certificate in the Society of the Cincinnati for John H. Buell; partly ptd. Torn; framed. wd Nov 12 (22) $2,900

— 15 June 1793. 1 p, folio. Sea letter for the brig Polly of Newburyport. Countersgd by Thomas Jefferson. Also sgd on verso by Washington & Jefferson. rf Nov 15 (19) $5,750

— [before 3 Aug 1793]. 9.75 by 9.25 inches. Fragment, upper portion of ship's papers for the Rising Sun. Countersgd by Jefferson. Framed with portraits of Washington & Jefferson. P May 13 (147) $4,000

— [before 3 Aug 1793]. 9.75 by 5.75 inches. Fragment, lower portion of ship's papers for the Rising Sun. Countersgd by Jefferson. Framed with portraits of Washington & Jefferson. P May 13 (148) $3,250

— [c.4 Jan 1794]. 1 p, folio. Ship's papers in 3 languages for the Betsy of Philadelphia. Countersgd by Jefferson. P May 13 (149) $8,000

— 1 Feb 1794. 1 p, folio. Ship's papers in 3 languages for the sloop Three Friends of Salem. Countersgd by Sec of State Thomas Jefferson. rf May 30 (13) $4,500

— 9 Apr 1795. 4 pp, 8vo. Fragment, appointment & salaries of inspectors of surveys & of port revenues, & list of auxiliary officers in 16 geographical districts. With a port. sg Apr 9 (219) $2,000

— 2 June 1796. 1 p, folio. Ship's papers in 3 languages for the brig The Drake, bound for Antigua; partly ptd. Countersgd by

WASHINGTON

Timothy Pickering & Joseph Whipple. Repaired. sg Nov 6 (354) $3,000
— 10 Dec 1796. 1 p, folio. Ship's passport for the Governor Bowdoin. Countersgd by Sec of State Pickering & Boston Collector Benjamin Lincoln. Faded. Framed. P Oct 29 (144) $3,250

Document, 1 Dec 1783. 1 p, folio. Testimonial of Maj. Caleb Gibbs; copy attested by Henry Knox. pnNY June 11 (64) $150

Check, 11 Sept 1799. 7 by 3.12 inches. Payable to William Thornton for $1,000. P May 13 (151) $5,000

Franking signature, [n.d.]. With autograph address to Gen. Woodford. rf May 30 (28) $3,250

Lottery ticket, 1768. 32mm by 63mm. For Mountain Road Lottery; no 286. Ptd; sgd by Washington. Margins cut; some text loss. Mtd with ptd silhouette, overall size 152mm by 215mm. sg Apr 9 (218) $2,800

— KITT, FRED. - Ds, 9 Mar 1795 & 17 Oct 1796. 1 p, 12mo. Receipt for money "to purchase sundries for the President's Household." Sgd twice. pnNY June 11 (65) $50

— RAVARA, JOSEPH. - 3 A Ls, 12 to 14 May 1793. 5 pp, folio & 4to. To Washington & the "English Ambassador". Extortionist letters; twice sgd Miranda Philad. 2 letters in English, 1 in French. With notes on Ravara's trial, Apr 1794, in the hand of Hilary Baker. 12 pp, folio. sg Nov 6 (217) $475

Washington, Martha Dandridge Custis

Address leaf, [c.1800]. 1 p, 4to. Addressed in her hand to her sister Anna Marie Dandridge Bassett; to be delivered by Capt. Possey. Repaired. sg Nov 6 (359) $700

Waters, Ethel, 1896-1977

Photograph, sgd & inscr, [n.d.]. 8 by 10 inches. Inscr to "Natlee" [Hammond]. With related material. wd Nov 12 (23) $250

Watt, James, 1736-1819

ALs, 25 July 1813. 1 p, 4to. Recipient unknown. Discussing personal matters & a particular razor. Matted with a port. sg Nov 6 (218) $550

Waugh, Evelyn, 1903-66

A Ls s (2), "Easter Tuesday" 1957 & 2 Jan 1958. 2 pp, 8vo. To Mrs. N. Verne. Thanking for a gift of children's books. With a copy of The Ordeal of Gilbert Pinfold. 1957. 1st Ed; inscr by Waugh to Mrs. Verne. S Dec 18 (184) £500 [Madelana]

ALs, [6 Jan] 1958. 2 pp, 4to. To Denis Verne. Regarding the Latin verse of Robert Knox. S Jan 27 (744) £200 [Brennan]

— 4 Sept [19]64. 2 pp, 8vo. To Peter Luke.

AMERICAN BOOK PRICES CURRENT

Apologizing for misrepresenting the manner of his grandfather's death. C Dec 3 (386) £180 [Stone Trough Books]

Wayne, Anthony, 1745-96

ALs, 3 Dec 1782. 2 pp, 4to. To Gen. Nathanael Greene. Complaining about lack of provisions for his troops. Seal hole in integral address leaf repaired. Bullock collection. CNY Dec 19 (246) $700

— 28 May 1787. 2 pp, 4to. To his son Isaac. Draft, about his return home & his son's education. With revisions. P May 13 (152) $2,400

— 17 Sept 1787. 2 pp, 4to. To Col. Francis Johnston. Requesting information about "certain bonds and a mortgage from one Pinkerton to Miss Penrose". With autograph draft reply on integral address leaf. Framed. Altman collection. pnNY Sept 13 (35) $700

Weber, Andreas Paul, 1893-1980

Series of 13 A Ls s, 6 May 1958 to 24 Aug 1974. 22 pp, 4to. To Anna Martina Gottschick. Mostly concerning his annual contributions to a calendar. HN May 22 (3225) DM650

Weber, Carl Maria von, 1786-1826

Autograph music, sketches or contrapuntal exercises, numbered 1 to 8; [n.d.]. 1 p, c.12cm by 18cm. In red ink. Removed from a notebook. With authentication by F. W. Jaehns. S Nov 28 (661) £620 [Haas]

ALs, 11 June 1822. 1 p, 4to. To the music pbr Eichhorn at Nuernberg. Stating his conditions for a performance of Freischuetz. With a port. star Apr 9 (853) DM5,500

— 6 May 1826. 1 p, 8vo. Recipient unnamed. Sending a march composed for the Royal Society of Musicians. In English. S May 22 (566) £950 [Schneider]

ADs, 3 June 1815. 1 p, 4to. Pay order in favor of Herr Ballabene et Comp., addressed to "Theater Cassier" Leiner for Weber's salary as director of the Prague Opera for 3 months. With endorsements by Leiner. star Apr 9 (852) DM1,400

Signature, [1815]. Engraved admission ticket for a concert, 6.5cm by 9.5cm. Sgd CMvWbr on verso. star Apr 9 (854) DM850

Weber, Friedrich Wilhelm, 1813-94

ALs, 28 Oct 1878. 4 pp, 8vo. To his friend Beggenberger. Personal news, & inviting his comments about his Dreizehnlinden. Initialled. JG Oct 2 (161) DM650

Webern, Anton von, 1883-1945

Autograph music, song, Wie bin ich froh!, to a text by Hildegard Jone. 6 pp & 2 blanks, size not stated. In green lea folder, gilt. Inscr to David Josef Bach, sgd & dated 13 Aug 1934, on tp. With related material. star Apr 9 (855) DM22,000

Collection of 2 A Ls s & 3 Ls s (2 with autograph postscripts), 16 Nov 1938 to 27 June 1939. 9 pp, 4to. To Erwin Stein. Regarding the publication of his String Quartet, Op. 28, talking about the importance of his music, & mentioning friends. star Apr 9 (856) DM10,000

A L s, 14 June 1929. 2 pp, size not stated. To Hermann Scherchen. Suggesting that he choose his revised 6 Orchesterstuecke Op. 6 & Schoenberg's Variations Op. 31 for a concert. S May 22 (649) £2,000 [Johnson]

— 6 Dec 1943. 1 p, 8vo. To an unnamed lady. Thanking for congratulations on his birth day. star Apr 9 (857) DM950

Webster, Daniel, 1782-1852

ALs, [22 June 1840]. 2 pp, 4to. To John Kerr. Regarding his schedule. With franking signature. rf Mar 14 (109) $170

— [n.d.]. 1 p, 4to. Recipient unnamed. Concerning finances & a visit to the Cape. Framed with a port. wd Nov 12 (24) $150

— 27 Apr 1843. 1 p, 4to. To John Gray. Declining a law case. sg Nov 6 (360) $100

Ls, 12 Apr 1842. 3 pp, 4to. To Messrs. J. H. Howland & Son Co., New York. As Sec of State, regretting the Department of State has no charge d'affaires in Central America to help recover a deceased agent's property. Was mtd. wa Oct 18 (157) $110

Ns, 22 May 1841. 1 p, 8vo. To George Rundle. As Sec of State, notifying him that his letter to Mr. Hunter has been transmitted. Mourning stationary. wa Oct 18 (158) $55

Ds, 22 May 1829. 1 p, 16mo. Promissory note. wa May 30 (441) $110

Webster, Noah, 1758-1843

Autograph Ms, definitions of the word "behind", part of the Ms for his American Dictionary of the English Language, pbd 1828. 1 p, 111mm by 201mm. With note of authentication by his daughter Elizabeth Jones on verso. Tipped to sheet with anr note of authenticity. CNY Dec 19 (247) $4,500

Weill, Kurt, 1900-50

ALs, 14 Feb 1935. 2 pp, 4to. Recipients unnamed. Criticizing a performance of The Three-Penny Opera relayed by the B.B.C. S May 22 (650) £450 [Simeone]

Weingartner, Felix, 1863-1942

A Ls s (2), 15 Mar & 2 Apr 1917. 2 pp, 4to. To Heinrich Braun. Regarding a textbook written by his wife Lilly Braun. With autograph musical quotation, sgd & dated 18 Feb 1902. star Apr 9 (859) DM220

Weiss, Emil Rudolf, 1875-1942

ALs, 22 Feb 1936. 2 pp, 4to. To the magazine Weltkunst. Responding to criticism. With related mateial. star Apr 8 (554) DM280

Weiss, Ernst, 1882-1940

A Ls s (2), 30 Apr 1936 & 26 Nov 1938. 6 pp, 4to & 8vo. To Paul Lester Wiener. Analyzing his relationship with Judith. Expressing his disapproval of dictatorial government. HN May 22 (3226a) DM720

Wellesz, Egon, 1885-1974

Series of 3 A Ls s, 1924 to 1929. 4 pp, folio. To Herr Mutzenbecher. Regarding his opera Alkestis & other works. S Jan 27 (1075) £100 [Simeone]

Wellington, Arthur Wellesley, 1st Duke, 1769-1852

Series of 3 A Ls s, 23 May to 10 Aug 1801. 5 pp, 4to & folio. To Lieut. Col. MacWhirter (1) & J. H. Piele. Relating to affairs at Seringapatam. Bullock collection. CNY Dec 19 (205) $550

— Series of 3 A Ls s, 4 Feb 1809 to 7 May 1819. 4 pp, 4to. To P. Rogers, Lieut. Col. West & Charles Stuart. About various subjects. With 4 A Ls s by Richard Colley Wellesley, 1812 to 1814. Bullock collection. CNY Dec 19 (207) $50

— Series of 12 A Ls s, 27 July 1819 to 14 Feb 1823. 13 pp, mostly 8vo. To George Hayter. Mainly concerning a painting ordered by Wellington. 2 A Ls s in 3d person; 10 stitched together. Bullock collection. CNY Dec 19 (210) $600

A Ls s (2), 12 Jan & 2 June 1819. 13 pp, 4to. To Baron Vincent. Discussing French policy. In French. S Jan 27 (814) £130 [Smith]

ALs, 11 Jan 1811. 4 pp, 4to. To Thomas Rowcroft. Assuring him that the troops in the Peninsular War "have suffered no Privations". Fold tears. Bullock collection. CNY Dec 19 (206) $200

— 16 Jan 1814. 1 p, 4to. To Mr. Weld. Ordering a pair of "white Worsted Web breeches". S Jan 27 (813) £130 [Bristow]

— 22 July 1814. 4 pp, 8vo. To the Earl of Westmeath. Saying it is not in his power to alleviate the misfortunes of Major Roberts. pn Dec 11 (93) £110 [Pedler]

— 7 Sept 1819. 3 pp, size not stated. To C. P. Leslie. Regarding preferments in the Irish church. Framed. Altman collection. pnNY Sept 13 (63) $200

WELLINGTON

— 9 Oct 1829. 3 pp, 8vo. To an Archbishop. Concerning "the selection of the Gentlemen to be preferred in the Church in Ireland". Nearly split in half. wa May 30 (442) $130

— 7 Dec 1839. 7 pp, 4to. To Henry Smart. Regarding the conduct of a Cinq Port pilot. S Jan 27 (812) £80 [Bristow] See also: George IV & Wellington

Wells, Henry, 1805-78 —& Fargo, William George, 1818-81

Ds, 11 Nov 1864. 1 p, 4to. Stock certificate no 2425 in the American Express Company. wa May 30 (82) $475

— 1865. Size not stated. American Express Company stock certificate. rf May 30 (14) $210

Wells, Herbert George, 1866-1946

Collection of 5 A Ls s & Ls, 1895 to 1917. 22 pp, 4to & 8vo. To J. M. Dent & Sons. Regarding the publication of various works. S July 23 (201) £850 [Ferret Fantasy]

Series of 4 A Ls s, [1913]. 8 pp, mostly 4to (1 card). To Mrs. Townshend. About his love for Rebecca West & her pregnancy by him. With ALs by Rebecca West to Mrs. Townshed. S July 23 (202) £2,800 [Gotlieb]

ALs, [n.d.]. Size not stated. Tongue-in cheek eulogy to Miss Boyle Bennett's chickens. With 1st Ed of The Time Machine. L, 1895; presentation copy inscr to Cosmo Rowe, & material relating to Rowe. S July 23 (122) £1,500 [Quaritch]

— 5 Nov 1926. 4 pp, 4to. To A. P. Watts Ltd. Paying tribute to Watts as a literary agent. With related material. In black deed box assigned for his papers. S July 23 (221) £260 [Minerva]

— 24 Aug 1939. 1p, 8vo. To Mr. Lakin. Requesting the last piece of an article. Framed. Altman collection. pnNY Sept 13 (139) $225

Werder, Dietrich von dem, 1584-1657

ALs, 30 May 1618. 1 p, folio. To Landgraf Moritz von Hessen-Kassel. About 2 ceremonial dresses ordered for him by the landgrave. star Apr 8 (284) DM1,050

Werefkin, Marianne von, 1870-1938

A Ls s (2), [1936]. 3 pp, folio. Recipient unnamed. About seizure of her property. Regarding an exhibition. star Apr 8 (555) DM700

Werfel, Alma, 1879-1964. See: Mahler-Werfel, Alma

AMERICAN BOOK PRICES CURRENT

Werfel, Franz, 1890-1945

Autograph Ms, sonnet, Eine Stunde nach dem Totentanz, [n.d.]. 1 p, 4to. In pencil. star Apr 8 (285) DM750

Collection of ALs & Ls, 9 Jan 1933 & 18 July 1939. 2 pp, 4to. To Alfredo Colombo. Regarding a request for a libretto; in Italian. Concerning fees; in German. With carbon copies of Colombo's replies. star Apr 8 (287) DM460

ALs, 2 July 1927. 2 pp, 4to. To Cornelius Czarniawski. Commenting about Bernhard Diebold & literary criticism. star Apr 8 (286) DM540

West Indies

— BOWYER, HENRY. - ALs, 10 June 1806, 3 pp, folio. To Major Luke Alen. Concerning plans for the reorganization of the West India Corps. With fair copy of Alen's Supplemental Observations on the local situation of The British West Indies, 1824. pn Dec 11 (126) £220 [Bodily]

Wetz, Richard, 1875-1935

Autograph Ms, libretto for his opera Das ewige Feuer, 1904. 21 leaves, in 8vo notebook. Sgd on tp. Fair copy with few corrections. With related material. FD Dec 2 (3272) DM650

Wheeler, Edward J.

Original drawings, 6 illusts for Mother Goose's Nursery Rhymes, pbd by Routledge; watercolor & gouache, c.180mm by 125mm. 4 initialled. With 1895 Ed, including companion book of fairy tales, in 1 vol. S Dec 5 (574) £500 [Abbott & Holder]

Whipple, William, Signer from New Hampshire

ALs, 10 July 1774. 1 p, 8vo. To his brother. About the price of cows & family news. Repaired & inlaid. Charlotte Parker Milne collection. wd Nov 12 (74) $225

Whistler, James Abbott McNeill, 1834-1903

Original drawing, 2 pen-&-ink sketches, both of 3 male heads (middle head self port); [n.d.], 255mm by 205mm. One of the sketches captioned, with butterfly signature. Tipped to stiffer sheet. Bullock collection. CNY Dec 19 (250) $1,600

Collection of 25 A Ls s & 18 A Ns s, c.1877 to 19 July 1890. 54 pp, 12mo & 8vo. To Theodore Watts [Watts-Dunton]. Mainly about invitations, social affairs, etc. Mostly with butterfly signature. With related material. Bullock collection. CNY Dec 19 (248) $7,000

Series of 3 A Ls s, [n.d.] & [16 Dec 1884]. 5 pp, 12mo & 8vo. To R. Caton Woodville; inviting him. To Mrs. Woodville, about a problem with a cistern. To Mrs. Alan Cole, concerning invitations. 2 with butterfly

signatures. Bullock collection. CNY Dec 19 (249) $700
ALs, [n.d.]; 1 pp, folio. To "Madame Carmen". Expressing concern about her health & asking her to write him in London. In French. On hotel letterhead. S Dec 18 (314) £300 [Quaritch]
— [n.d.]. 2 pp, 8vo. To "Mon cher Delatre". About colors he is interested in obtaining. C June 24 (212) £480 [Quaritch]

White, Edward Douglass, 1845-1921
Series of 5 A Ns, 1902. 5 pp, 32mo, on Supreme Court memorandum sheets. Answering questions put by Supreme Court Reporter Charles Henry Butler. 3 dated, 4 in pencil. wa May 30 (83) $80

White, Gilbert, 1720-93
ALs, [n.d., "Sunday even."]. 1 p, 4to. To Thomas Holt White. Giving instructions about a proposed journey. C Dec 3 (387) £450 [Bristow]

Whitgift, John, Archbishop of Canterbury, 1530?-1604
Collection of 2 A Ls s & Ls, 17 Sept 1583 to 2 Dec 1594. 3 pp, folio. To Matthew Hutton, Archbishop of York. About appointments & Hutton's problems at York. C Dec 3 (340) £700 [Quaritch]
— Collection of 3 A Ls s & 3 Ls s, 4 Nov 1594 to 17 May 1602. 8 pp, folio. To Matthew Hutton, Archbishop of York. About matters of Church & State, including the Essex trial. C June 24 (77) £3,000 [Joseph]

Whitman, Walt, 1819-92
Autograph Ms (2), fragments; [1871 or later]. On small oblong torn from larger leaf & on Department of Justice envelope. 3 unidentified lines, beginning "Charactered for..."; & label "After all.'&c." Both in pencil. Charles E. Feinberg collection. P Dec 15 (120) $700
Autograph Ms, beginning "Man's physiology complete I sing", [n.d.]. 1 p, size not stated. In ink with pencil revisions. Lower corner trimmed. Charles E. Feinberg collection. P Dec 15 (117) $1,200
— Autograph Ms, beginning "The main object henceforth"; [n.d.]. 1 p, 4to. In pencil & purple ink; stained. Charles E. Feinberg collection. P Dec 15 (116) $1,400
— Autograph Ms, draft, entitled "1861 and '62", [c.Jan 1886?]. 2 pp, 8vo. Introductory passage, in ink, with instructions to the printer. On verso pencil draft of self port in old age; crossed out. Stained. Charles E. Feinberg collection. P Dec 15 (119) $1,300
— Autograph Ms, fragment beginning "Departing Drops from a Passing Rain", [n.d.]. 1 p, size not stated. In pencil. Charles E. Feinberg collection. P Dec 15 (115) $550
— Autograph Ms, fragment, entitled "Morbid adhesiveness", [c.1865?]. 1 p, 8vo. 2 columns in red & black ink, written on verso of ptd tax form. Some paper loss; was mtd. Charles E. Feinberg collection. P Dec 15 (118) $1,500
AN, [after 7 May 1891]. 1 p, 8vo. To his printer [Henry Curtz]. Sending a clipping with a phrase from Epictetus [present] & requesting him to set it as letterhead. Lower part missing. Waterstained. Charles E. Feinberg collection. P Dec 15 (121) $1,300
Check, sgd, 30 Jan 1875. 6.25 by 2.6 inches. Drawn on National State Bank of Camden, N.J. Charles E. Feinberg collection. P Dec 15 (149) $400
— Anr, sgd, 6 Mar 1875. 7.1 by 2.9 inches. Drawn on National State Bank of Camden, N.J. Small paper loss. Charles E. Feinberg collection. P Dec 15 (150) $500
Corrected proof, Death's Valley, [n.d.]. 13.5 by 9.75 inches. Repaired. With autograph emendations, in ink. Charles E. Feinberg collection. P Dec 15 (129) $350
— Anr, Patroling Barnegat, [n.d.]. 1 p, 4.75 by 6.25 inches. Autograph ink inscr, sgd in text. Last 4 lines pasted to a piece of paper affixed to larger sheet. Charles E. Feinberg collection. P Dec 15 (144) $600
— Anr, Good-Bye My Fancy. Phila., 1891; tp only, 8vo. Prepared by Whitman as proof for section-title in 1891-92 Ed of Leaves of Grass. Ptd table of contents pasted to verso. Charles E. Feinberg collection. P Dec 15 (131) $250
— Anr, My 71st Year, [c.1891]. 1 p, 4.5 by 6 inches. With autograph emendations in pencil; partly differing from ptd version. Charles E. Feinberg collection. P Dec 15 (142) $350
Engraving, port used as frontispiece to 1860-61 Ed of Leaves of Grass; 8 by 5.25 inches. Sgd & inscr to "Dr. Rossa" [Daniel Bennett St. John Roosa]. Charles E. Feinberg collection. P Dec 15 (145) $950
Photograph, sgd, orig albumen print of G. F. E. Pearsall port used as frontis to 1876 Ed of Two Rivulets; size not stated. Framed with tp, sgd, from 1876 Ed of Leaves of Grass. Charles E. Feinberg collection. P Dec 15 (146) $1,000
Photograph, c.1879; size not stated. Inscr on verso by Horace Traubel. Framed. With wood-engraved port by W. J. Linton, 1872, framed with tp [proof?] of 1876 Ed of Leaves of Grass. Charles E. Feinberg collection. P Dec 15 (147) $400
Single sheet ptg, broadside prepared by Whitman advertising his books, [n.d.]. 630mm by 480mm, ptd on linen. Framed. Charles E. Feinberg collection. P Dec 15

WHITMAN

(110A) $800
— Anr, proof sheet of A Twilight song, [c.1890]. 8 by 7.25 inches. With autograph annotation at head, in pencil. Repaired. Charles E. Feinberg collection. P Dec 15 (152) $450
— BUCKE, RICHARD MAURICE. - Ls, 17 Dec 1897; 1 p, 4to. To Horace Traubel. About Ordway Partridge's bust of Whitman. With typescript carbon copy of Bucke's Last days [of Walt Whitman], [n.d.]; 32 pp, folio. With corrections. Charles E. Feinberg collection. P Dec 15 (95) $400
— ROME, THOMAS H. - Ls, 5 June 1898. 2 pp, 8vo. To Horace Traubel. Offering to sell Mss by Whitman & enclosing a ptd list of 70 items (present; 1 p, 8vo). Charles E. Feinberg collection. P Dec 15 (101) $750

Whitney, Eli, 1765-1825
ALs, 5 Jan 1813. 2 pp, 4to. To Decius Wadsworth. Recommending Roswell Lee for a commission in the army. P Oct 29 (148) $600

Whittier, John Greenleaf, 1807-92
Autograph Ms, poem, beginning "God pity them both, & pity us all"; [n.d.]. 1 p, 12mo. 4 couplets, sgd. Was mtd. sg Nov 6 (220) $200

ALs, "10th Mo. 3, 1876". 1 p, 8vo. To [Isaac W. Wood]. Mentioning his illness & his niece Mary Caldwell. wa Oct 18 (159) $110

Wiechert, Ernst, 1887-1950
Autograph sentiment, [n.d.]. 1 p, 8vo. Quatrain beginning "Mache den Leuten Spass..."; sgd. HK Nov 7 (2362) DM3,000

Wieland, Christoph Martin, 1733-1813
Autograph Ms, notes for a critical review of the epic poem Borussias [by D. Jenisch]; [end of July 1792]. 1 p, 4to, below bill by a craftsman for services rendered Wieland, 21 July 1792. star Apr 8 (291) DM1,700

ALs, 12 Aug 1772. 1 p, 8vo. Recipient unnamed. Confirming receipt of money for Agathon & sending his new address. JG Oct 2 (163) DM3,600

— 1 Dec 1787. 2 pp, 4to. To Professor Reinhold at Jena. Thanking for help, & about the marital prospects of his daughter. HK Nov 7 (2363) DM7,000

Autograph endorsement, 5 lines on verso of account with Weidmanns Erben & Reich, booksellers in Leipzig, 5 Mar 1785. 1 p, 4to. With related material. star Apr 8 (289) DM500

— Anr, 5 lines on verso of account with Weidmanns Erben & Reich, booksellers in Leipzig, 12 Oct 1791. 1 p, 4to. star Apr 8 (290) DM520

AMERICAN BOOK PRICES CURRENT

Wigman, Mary, 1886-1973
Series of 4 A Ls s, 1921/22 & [n.d.]. 13 pp, 4to & 8vo. To Eugen Diederichs. Reporting about the 1st performance of her Tanzdichtung & about her school. star Apr 9 (876) DM650

Wilde, Oscar, 1854-1900
Series of 3 A Ls s, 22 Nov 1889 to 20 May 1890. 16 pp, 8vo. To Herbert Vivian. Protesting strongly against the use of his name in Vivian's Reminiscences of a Short Life. With 4 A Ls s, 22 Nov 1889 to 21 May 1890, drafts of Vivian's answers to Wilde; & typescript of Vivian's article. In buckram folding case. P Dec 15 (93) $5,000

ALs, [Dec 1880]. 3 pp, 12mo. To Helena Modjeska. Requesting permission to introduce Mr. Benson & Mr. Rodd to her & praising her production of Adrienne Lecouvreur. CNY Dec 19 (251) $2,200

— 9 Dec 1887. 4 pp, 8vo. To an unnamed contributor to the magazine Women's World [Matilde Serao?]. Thanking her for a poem & asking her to write an article about Italy or Sicily. S Dec 18 (103) £1,300 [Maggs]

— 188[?]. 2 pp, 8vo. To [Richard D'Oyly] Carte. Requesting a box for tonight. S Jan 27 (723) £540 [Wilson]

— [n.d.]. 3 pp, 8vo. To Mr. Nutt. About a reading of one of his stories & discussing a new Ed. Waterstained. Framed & doubleglazed. Altman collection. pnNY Sept 13 (140) $850

— [n.d.]. 4 pp, 8vo. To Mr. [R. Cooke] Taylor. Hoping the book Taylor lent him has arrived safely & extending Lady Wilde's invitation to visit. S Dec 18 (104) £450 [Sims]

— [Nov or Dec 1891]. 4 pp, 4to. Recipient unknown. Declining the invitation of a Society & commenting about French art. CNY Dec 19 (252) $3,000

— [before June 1892]. 3 pp, 12mo. To John Coulson Kernahan. Giving permission to use a phrase of his in the title of a story. With postscript, requesting a proof of his preface. CNY Dec 19 (253) $950

— [3 May 1893]. 3 pp, 12mo. To Adrian Clifford. Accepting the post of Vice-President of [the Garrick Dramatic Society]. On hotel stationery. CNY Dec 19 (254) $850

— [n.d.]. 4 pp, 8vo. To Miss Richardson. Requesting her to write an article about the home life of Emperor Augustus. pn Dec 11 (56) £1,300

Autograph sentiment, Feb [18]82. 1 p, 8vo. Inscription, sgd, to Kenyon Fortescue, on leaf bearing reproduction of seal & signature of Henry VIII. Framed with a port photograph. P Sept 24 (59) $550

Wilder, Thornton, 1897-1976
Series of 3 A Ls s, 26 Sept to [21 Oct] 1975. 5 pp, size not given. To Mrs. Bettie Liddell. About using his title, The Bridge of San Luis Rey. Mentioning his operation & hoping he will be able to work again. wa Oct 18 (161) $300

Wilhelm I, King of Wuerttemberg, 1781-1864
Ds, 7 Dec 1842. 3 pp, folio. Confirmation of a sentence against the soldier G. F. Schaeufele. With related material. star Apr 9 (1300) DM520

Wilhelm I, Deutscher Kaiser, 1797-1888
Autograph Ms, brief note regarding Palmerston's decision not to enter the war between Prussia & Denmark, [Jan] 1864. 1 p, 8vo. In pencil. star Apr 9 (1175) DM360

ALs, 2 Dec 1847. 1 p, 8vo. To Graf Beust. As Prince of Prussia, thanking for a report about mines in Silesia. star Apr 9 (1173) DM260

— 27 June 1867. 2 pp, 8vo. Recipient unnamed. As King of Prussia, requesting information about discussions concerning assumption of the debts of the city of Frankfurt. star Apr 9 (1177) DM950

— 25 Dec 1871. 2 pp, 8vo. To [Heinrich von Abeken]. Proposing the conferral of dignities, & sending a bust of Bismarck. star Apr 9 (939) DM420

— 31 Jan 1881. 4 pp, 8vo. To Princess Amalie von Schleswig-Holstein. Regretting that she will be unable to attend the wedding of his grandson [Emperor Wilhelm II]. HK Nov 7 (2364) DM1,200

— 20 Aug 1883. 1 p, 8vo. To Frau von Renouard. Reminiscing about her deceased husband. With Ls by Wilhelm to Gen. von Renouard, 25 July 1882. star Apr 9 (940) DM340

Ls, 13 Mar 1887. 1 p, 4to. To the chancellor ot the Order of the Black Eagle. Requesting that the insignia be given to Nicolis de Robilant be sent to the Foreign Ministry. Countersgd by Bismarck. star Apr 9 (941) DM750

Ds, 23 June 1869. 1 p, folio. Commission for a councillor in the postal service, issued for the North German Union. Countersgd by Bismarck. star Apr 9 (1178) DM1,100

— 14 Nov 1870. 1 p, folio. Commission for R. von Borries. star Apr 9 (1179) DM440

— 19 Jan 1873, Size not stated. Conferral of the Iron Cross on Freiherr Rembert von Muenchhausen. With related material. VH Sept 12 (946) DM320

— 18 Jan 1878. 1 p, folio. Military appointment; partly ptd. Fold splits. wa Oct 18 (162) $90

See also: Hohenlohe-Schillingsfuerst, Chlodwig

Wilhelm II, Deutscher Kaiser, 1859-1941
[Hermine Princess Reuss. - A voluminous collection of A Ls s, Ls s, etc., 1925 to 1947, personal correspondence addressed to Marianne Geibel, documenting her husband's life in exile, with related material, sold at HN on 27 Nov, lot 2284, for DM4,200.]

[A collection of 15 telegrams, cards & photographs, some autograph, mostly sgd, correspondence with Marianne Geibel, 1925 to 1940, with some political comments, sold at HN on 27 Nov, lot 2401, for DM 2,400.]

[A collection of 5 signatures on weather reports, with 2 autograph additions, 1931 to 1936, 5 pp, 8vo, with related material, sold at star on 9 Apr, lot 953, for DM660.]

Autograph Ms, mathematical exercise, 10 Dec 1876. 2 pp, folio. Sgd. star Apr 9 (947) DM280

Collection of 2 A Ls s & autograph sketch. 13 & 14 June 1888. 5 pp, folio & 8vo. To the officer Gottberg. Giving orders to surround the palace in case of his father's death, with sketch of positions of troops. HN Nov 27 (2398) DM3,200

ALs, 31 Dec 1880. 3 pp, 8vo. To Princess Amalie von Schleswig-Holstein. About his wedding & the prospect of visiting her at Pau. HK Nov 7 (2366) DM1,100

Ls, [before 1914]. 1 p, folio. To Generaldirektor Ballin. Approving of work done. star Apr 9 (950) DM360

Ds, 16 June 1913. 1 p, folio. Appointment for Georg von Borries. Countersgd by von Dallwitz & Lentze. With material relating to von Borries's term as president of the Berlin police force, especially the workers' riots, 1908. star Apr 9 (949) DM1,800

Photograph, sgd, 1928. 39.1cm by 29.3cm. star Apr 9 (952) DM220

Signature, June 1927. On ptd port, after a painting; 59cm by 38.5cm. star Apr 9 (951) DM360

Wilhelm IV, Graf von Holland, c.1307-45
Document, [25] Feb 1343. 1 p, 4to. Vellum. Notification addressed to Jehan Maussard of feudal rights being transferred to "le signeur de baillnoel". star Apr 9 (1090) DM320

Wilhelmina, Queen of The Netherlands, 1880-1962
ALs, 23 Sept 1894. 4 pp, 8vo. To Julie Liotard. Reporting about her birthday. In French. star Apr 9 (1093) DM950

Wilhelmine, Markgraefin von Bayreuth, 1709-58

ALs, 12 June 1752. 3 pp, 4to. To Voltaire. About a visit by the Marquis d'Adhemar, Voltaire's stay at Potsdam, her brother Friedrich II, King of Prussia, etc. HN Nov 27 (2402) DM6,000

Ls, 21 Sept 1754. 2 pp, folio. To Markgraf Karl Alexander von Brandenburg-Ansbach. Sending congratulations on his engagement. With autograph subscription. In French. star Apr 9 (1157) DM1,050

Wilkes, Charles, 1798-1877

Ds, 1 July 1834. 4 pp, folio. Purchase of property in D. C. wa May 30 (470) $110

Wilkes, John, 1727-97

Series of 3 A Ls s, 10 to 12 Apr [n.y.]. 3 pp, 8vo. To Lord Massareene. Requesting a loan & about his failure to promptly repay his debt. S July 24 (271) £320 [Maggs]

William I, King of The Netherlands, 1772-1843

ALs, 29 Aug 1795. 1 p, 4to. To William Eden, 1st Baron Auckland. Accepting an invitation. Sgd G.Fr.PrHed d'Orange. In French. With related material. star Apr 9 (1091a) DM370

William I, King of Prussia, 1797-1888. See: Wilhelm I, 1797-1888

William II, King of England, 1650-1702

ALs, 5 July [n.y.]. 1 p, 4to. To the Conte de Waldec. As Prince of Orange, acknowledging receipt of his letters & informing him that he will continue his journey on horseback. With 2 engraved portraits. C June 24 (78) £180 [Maggs]

William III, King of England, 1650-1702

Ds, 18 Mar 1696. 1 p, folio. Money order to Paul Boyer for the relief of French Protestants in Ireland. Torn, laid down & framed. Altman collection. pnNY Sept 13 (40) $650

— 30 Mar 1700. 1 p, folio. Vellum. Warrant for the appointment of commissioners to discuss English & French claims in the Hudson Bay region. In Latin. Sgd Guliemus R. Matted. P Dec 15 (94) $1,000

William III, King of The Netherlands, 1817-90

ALs, 3 Feb 1848. 2 pp, 4to. To an unnamed opera director. As Crown Prince, recommending the work of the Dutch composer Van den Does. In French. star Apr 9 (1091b) DM260

William IV, King of England, 1765-1837

Series of 6 A Ls s, 12 Oct 1827 to 28 May 1830. 9 pp, 4to. To Sir William & Lady Harriet Hoste & a member of their household. About matters pertaining to the Navy, sending condolences, etc. With related material. C June 24 (79) £280 [Solomon]

Williams, William, Signer from Connecticut

ADs, 6 May 1772. 1 p, 16mo. Receipt for excise interest. wa May 30 (143) $140

— 25 Mar 1782. 1 p, 12mo. Pay order. wa May 30 (144) $110

Ds, 11 Mar 1775. 1 p, 12mo. Transfer of property from Abraham Bliss to Joseph White, sgd as witness. Fold splits repaired. wa May 30 (428) $80

Williamson, Henry, 1895-1977

Collection of 36 A Ls s, Ls s & postcards, sgd, 1939 to 1969. Over 50 pp, various sizes. To Anthony Gower. About Gower's & his own work. S July 23 (203) £600 [Joseph & Sawyer]

Wilson, Edward Adrian. See: Antarctica

Wilson, James, Signer from Pennsylvania

Ds, 14 Apr 1794. 3 pp, folio. Purchase of land from Aaron Levy & Joseph Fenwick. Fold tear. Charlotte Parker Milne collection. wd Nov 12 (76) $225

— 2 Jan 1796. 1 p, 12mo. Receipt for salary as Justice. wa May 30 (145) $250

Wilson, Woodrow, 1856-1924

Typescript, sgd, message to the Service Star Legion, [spring 1919]. 1 p, 4to. Praising the service of women to their country during the war. P Oct 29 (150) $1,600

Collection of ALs, Ls, & signature, 13 Mar 1901, 9 Nov 1904, & [n.d.]. 3 pp, 8vo. To Duffield Osborne, explaining he will not be able to attend a reception. To Bayard Stockton, about a memorial for Charles Woodruff Shields at Princeton. Signature with signatures of 8 members of his 2nd-term Cabinet. P Oct 29 (149) $850

Ls, 26 July 1910. 1 p, 8vo. To Mr. Alexander. Expressing his satisfaction that he is not dropping out of politics. On Princeton University letterhead. Framed. Altman collection. pnNY Sept 13 (36) $225

— 9 Dec 1910. 1 p, 8vo. Recipient unnamed. As President of Princeton, regretting he will not be able to come to Columbus, Ohio. Personal letterhead. wa Oct 18 (164) $50

— 9 Nov 1912. 1 p, 4to. To Edward A. Filene. As Governor of New Jersey, thanking for a message. sg Nov 6 (222) $110

— 23 Nov 1912. 1 p, 4to. Recipient unnamed. Letter of thanks. rf Nov 15 (20) $160

— 23 Dec 1912. 1 p, 4to. To Thomas B.

Mosher. As Governor of New Jersey, expressing his thanks for "a copy of the Memories of President Lincoln". wa Oct 18 (62) $100

— 6 Jan 1913. 1 p, 4to. To Norman Hapgood. Thanking for a copy of Congressman Kent's letter. star Apr 9 (1292) DM520

— 10 Feb 1913. 1 p, 4to. As Governor of New Jersey, sending his autograph. Was mtd. wa Oct 18 (163) $70

— 6 Apr 1914. 1 p, 4to. To Judge Robert Ludlow Fowler. Regretting he did not meet him. On White House letterhead. sg Nov 6 (223) $225

— 5 Sept 1917. 1 p, 8vo. To Henry Hall. About Hall's appointment as Washington correspondent of the London Times. Mtd. wa May 30 (128) $210

Ds, 1 Aug 1919. 1 p, folio. Appointment for Hilary P. Jones as Rear Admiral. Countersgd by Franklin D. Roosevelt. pnNY June 11 (94) $425

Photograph, sgd & inscr, [n.d.], c.6.75 by 10.5 inches. Sepia photograph by Harris & Ewing. Was mtd. sg Apr 9 (224) $350

— Anr, [n.d.], 9 by 6 inches, on sheet 13.4 by 9.75 inches. Framed. wa Oct 18 (61) $240

Signature, [n.d.]. On a Spalding No. 1 baseball, offered for sale at a Red Cross fund raising event during World War I. Also sgd by Thomas R. Marshall, Champ Clark, & 5 Representatives. P May 13 (153) $4,250

Winchilsea, Anne Finch,, Countess of, 1661-1720. See: Finch, Heneage

Winchilsea, Heneage Finch, 4th Earl, 1657-1726. See: Finch, Heneage

Windsor, Edward, Duke of, 1894-1972

Transcript, Instrument of Abdication, 10 Dec 1936. 1 p, 4to. Sgd Edward Duke of Windsor, [11 Feb 1966]. With covering letter by his secretary to Brendan T. Crowe. sg Apr 9 (56) $1,200

Photograph, sgd & inscr, 15.5cm by 19.5cm. Sgd Edward P & inscr "H. M. S. 'Hindoustan' 1911". Framed. Altman collection. pnNY Sept 13 (56) $275

Windsor, Edward, Duke of, 1894-1972 —& Windsor, Wallis Simpson, Duchess of

[A collection of 24 items by or concerning the Duke & Duchess of Windsor, mostly correspondence with Walter T. Prendergast, 1935 to 1946, was sold at P on 14 Sept, lot 60, for $3,750]

Windsor, Wallis Simpson, Duchess of

ALs, 12 July [c.1962]. 4 pp, 16mo. To unnamed friends. Complaining about problems with servants. sg Apr 9 (216) $400
See also: Windsor, Edward, Duke of &
Windsor

Witherspoon, John, Signer from New Jersey

ADs, 12 Sept 1778. 1 p, 8vo. Bill for expenses of John Pintard at Princeton. Charlotte Parker Milne collection. wd Nov 12 (77) $850

Witzleben, Erwin von, 1881-1944

Ptd photograph, [n.d.]. Postcard size. Sgd. star Apr 9 (1289) DM900

Wodehouse, Pelham Grenville, 1881-1975

Collection of 2 Ls s & autograph postcard, sgd, 1927 to 1971. 3 pp, 8vo. To Alastair Wallace. Thanking for fan mail; about A. A. Milne's Illness, etc. S Jan 27 (743) £280 [Usborne]

Woerth an der Donau

— STOCKHAMER, JOSUA. - Rechnung... vber alles Einnemen und Ausgeben, Bemelter verwaltung Des Schloss, Pauhofs, Preuhauss [etc.], [2 Feb 1563 to 2 Feb 1564]. 150 leaves, 313mm by 213mm. Contemp red vellum. Account book of a Bavarian castle & its appendages. With related material. HK Nov 4 (469) DM7,000

Wolcott, Oliver, Signer from Connecticut

Ls, 12 Jan 1793. 1 p, 4to. To John Kean, Cashier of the Bank of the U.S. Requesting payment for David Meade Randolph. Charlotte Parker Milne collection. wd Nov 12 (78) $125

Ds, 9 Sept 1774. 1 p, 12mo. Writ. Some tears. wa May 30 (146) $110

Wolcott, Oliver, 1760-1833

Ls, 19 Feb 1794. 1 p, 4to. To Nathaniel Appleton. As Comptroller of the Treasury; contents not stated. Was mtd. wa May 30 (85) $50

Wolf, Hugo, 1860-1903

Autograph music, song, Dereinst, dereinst, Gedanke mein; from Spanisches Liederbuch, [1890]. 2 pp, folio. In brown ink & blue pencil; some corrections. S Nov 28 (664) £6,500 [McGunn]

ALs, 3 Sept [1]890. 5 pp, 8vo. To Oskar Grohe. Mentioning his travel plans, his current projects, Liliencron, Peter Cornelius, etc. S Nov 28 (663) £1,300 [McGunn]

— 22 Jan 1894. 3 pp, 8vo. To Oskar Grohe. Talking about concerts & his itinerary. star Apr 9 (860) DM2,400

— 12 July 1895. 4 pp, 8vo. To an unnamed friend. Announcing the completion of Corregidor. star Apr 9 (861) DM3,000

Autograph postcard, sgd, 1 Nov 1895. To Heinrich Potpeschnigg. Asking about copies needed for Heckel. S May 22 (651) £300 [Schneider]

WOLFSKEHL

Wolfskehl, Karl, 1869-1948
Collection of 37 A Ls s, 4 Ls s & 4 autograph postcards, sgd, 24 Dec 1932 to 21 Jan 1936 & [n.d.]. 82 pp, mostly 4to, & cards. To an unnamed lady in Switzerland. Very personal letters, discussing ideas & feelings. Some long postscripts. With related material. star Apr 8 (292) DM5,500

Wolstein, Johann Gottlieb, 1738-1820
— WODOPIA, STEPHAN. - Materia Medica oder Artzneymittel Lehre. Vorgetragen von... Profesor Wohlstein... Director der practischen Viehartzney Schule zu Wien; 1790. 282 pp, 210mm by 140mm. Contemp lea gilt. HK Nov 4 (450a) DM1,500

Wood, L. Ashwell
Original drawings, (24), in ink & watercolor & in ink & wash, to illus the vols Racing Cars, & World Car Speed Records, in the Inside Information series. 2 sgd. Various sizes. With copies of the books. S June 19 (725) £480 [Mould]
— Original drawings, (38), in ink & watercolor & in ink & wash, to illus the vols Tanks and Armoured Cars; Civil Aircraft; Military Aircraft; & Space Travel, in the Inside Information series. 4 sgd. Various sizes. S June 19 (727) £500 [Mould]
— Original drawings, (38), in ink & watercolor, & in ink & wash, to illus the vols Trains Today; Famous Steam Trains; Exploring Under the Sea; & Hovercraft, in the Inside Information series. 3 sgd. Various sizes. S June 19 (728) £280 [Mould]

Woolf, Virginia, 1882-1941
ALs, [2 Apr 1922]. 1 p, 4to. To [Clive Bell]. Asking him to call on Wednesday & saying Miss Green is coming to collect the Ms of her novel. Sgd VW. C Dec 3 (388) £260 [Leinweber]

Woolman, John, 1720-72
ALs, 9 May 1754. 1 p, folio. To Johns Ely. Letter of condolence on the death of Mr. & Mrs. Ely's son. Sgd J.W.; repaired. sg Nov 6 (310) $150

Wordsworth, William, 1770-1850
ALs, [Nov 1845]. 1 p, 8vo. To a bookbinder [Fred. Westley]. Saying all he has previously written concerning the bdg of a book for Lady Rolfe "was but suggestion". Lower margin trimmed; mtd on album leaf. pn Dec 11 (57) £180 [Dupre]
Autograph quotation, 3 lines on poets, from Akenside. Sgd & dated 28 Oct 1834. 175mm by 115mm. Framed. pn Dec 11 (58) £110 [Dupre]

AMERICAN BOOK PRICES CURRENT

World War I
— NEWTON, CAPT. R. S. - Ms s, diaries, Aug 1914 to Jan 1919, c.800 pp in 10 field message books, describing his service in France, Gallipoli & Egypt. S Jan 27 (856) £320 [Trocchi]
— SPENCER, LIEUT. A. V. - Ms, diary, Aug to Nov 1914, length not stated. Describing service on the Western Front. With portions of diaries of Capt. G. K. Rose, 1915-17, & 4th Batallion War Diary, Apr to June 1918. S Jan 27 (857) £200 [Trocchi]
— WEBLIN, LIEUT. H. E. E. - Ms, war memoirs, Aug 1914 to Nov 1918; c.100 pp, 4to. Including account of service as midshipman at Gallipoli. With drawings. S Jan 27 (882) £200 [Imperial]

World War II
— ALLARD, LIEUT. GEOFFREY. - Ms, Flying Log Book, 1 June 1940 to 11 Mar 1941. 40 pp & blanks, 4to. Cloth. Sgd 8 times; with other signatures. With 3 photographs. Sydney Allard collection. S July 24 (347) £1,500 [Hoffman & Freeman]
— CHANGI JAIL, PRISONER OF WAR CAMP, SINGAPORE. - 2 typescripts, issues 1 & 3 of the clandestine magazine Here Today, [1944 & 1945]. About 95 pp, 4to. Rudimentary bdg in cloth bds. With pencil & watercolor illusts. S July 24 (332) £1,800
— YAMASHITA, TOMUYUKI, & AL. - 6 Ds s, 1945. 6 pp, 4to; carbon copies. Affidavits concerning US & Philippine currencies found in their hands after their capture. Sgd with Latin letters, 1 in Japanese. 2 sgd by Capt. Max D. Maule of the US Army. sg Nov 6 (225) $600

Wotruba, Fritz, 1907-75
[A collection of 5 autographs by Wotruba & further material, including letters by his wife, mostly concerning an exposition in Munich, 1951, was sold at JG on 2 Oct 1986, lot 316, for DM 700.]

Wrangel, Friedrich Ernst, Graf von, 1784-1877
Collection of ALs & Ls, 4 Feb 1850 & 17 Mar 1863. 2 pp, 8vo. To Graf Beust. About an invitation & a donation. With cut signature. star Apr 9 (1294) DM300

Wright, Orville, 1871-1948
Signature, on envelope dated 14 May 1938. Cachet for National Air Mail Week. wa Oct 18 (63) $210

Wright, Wilbur, 1867-1912
Photograph, sgd & inscr, [n.d.]. 6.25 by 4.25 inches. Inscr to Col. S. W. Roessler. Mtd. pnNY June 11 (95) $2,800

Wyndham, Sir Charles, 2nd Earl of Egremont, 1710-63

ALs, 9 July 1763. 3 pp, folio. To a Colonial Governor in America. As Sec of State, about relations between the colonies & the British Government, & the problem of smuggling on the high seas. sg Nov 6 (260) $425

Wythe, George, Signer from Virginia

ADs, 18 Mar 1767. 1 p, 8vo. Receipt for fees in a lawsuit. Fold splits. Charlotte Parker Milne collection. wd Nov 12 (79) $300

Y

Yamashita, Tomoyuki, 1885-1946. See: World War II

Yeats, William Butler, 1865-1939

Autograph Ms, seven poems, 6 presumably unpbd, presented by Yeats to Maud Gonne, 20 Oct 1891. 8 pp, pencil titles on 12 more, & c.80 blanks, 8vo. Thick vellum covered bds. S July 23 (127) £31,000 [Cohen]

Collection of 3 A Ls s & card, sgd, 1918 to 1919. 8 pp, 8vo & 16mo. To John & Miles Dillon. Discussing mediumship & evil spirits. With 5 Ls s by George Russell to Miles Dillon, 1923 to 1925, 7 pp, 4to; concerning articles for The Irish Statesman. S Dec 18 (187) £600 [Maggs]

— Collection of ALs & Ls, 20 Feb 1920 & 15 June [n.y.]. 3 pp, 8vo. To Gwen John. About a memento of Florence Farr & the casting of one of his plays. S Dec 18 (194) £220 [Maggs]

Series of 4 A Ls s, c.1894-1895. 9 pp, 8vo. To J. F. Bigger. Referring to his own works & Irish literature. S Dec 18 (186) £850 [Rota]

ALs, [9 May 1914]. Lettercard. To Walter Rummel. Arranging a meeting. S Jan 27 (746) £200 [Ronayne]

Ls, 3 Apr 1920. 1 p, 4to. To Miss Forbes. Concerning his anthologies & his agents. Framed. Altman collection. pnNY Sept 13 (141) $300

Young, Ann Eliza, b.1844

ALs, 20 May 1881. 13 pp, 8vo. To Mrs. Froiseth. About women's suffrage & her marriage to Brigham Young. Sang collection. P May 13 (108) $1,800

Young, Brigham, 1801-77

Ls, 12 Apr 1864. 1 p, 130mm by 120mm. To E. J. Mathews. Sending his autograph. Was mtd. sg Nov 6 (226) $250

Z

Zahn, Ernst, 1867-1952

Collection of 3 A Ls s & 17 autograph Mss, 1924 to 1935 & [n.d.]. 28 pp, 8vo. To "Mein liebes Schumettli". Chatting about his thoughts & activities. Poems, mostly sgd. HK Nov 7 (2369) DM900

Zapata, Emiliano

Typescript, sgd; Maniefiesto al Pueblo Mexicano, 25 Apr 1918. 2 pp, folio. About the need to overthrow Carranza & to establish a new government. Also sgd by Ayaquica & Marcelo Caraveo. P Oct 29 (152) $1,200

Collection of 1 Ls, 1 Ds & 7 typed Ds s [some carbon copies], 1909 to 1916. 24 pp, 4to & folio. On various matters pertaining to the Mexican revolution. With ALs, 15 May 1914, by Francis M. de Ellis to Zapata. P Sept 24 (61) $2,000

Zelter, Karl Friedrich, 1758-1832

Ns, 4 Oct 1821. 1 p, folio. To Freiherr von Altenstein. Submitting a new "constitution" for the Singakademie. With anr 9 signatures. star Apr 9 (862) DM750

Zenge, Luise von. See: Kleist, Heinrich von

Zenge, Wilhelmine von, 1780-1852. See: Kleist, Heinrich von

Zille, Heinrich, 1858-1929

ALs, 26 Apr 1917. 1 p, 4to. To the Ed of the magazine Ulk. Concerning his series Vadding in Frankreich. star Apr 8 (556) DM400

Zinoviev, Grigorii Avseevich, 1883-1936

ALs, 23 July [19]10. 3 pp. 8vo. Recipient unnamed. Discussing the composition of the delegation to the Copenhagen Congress of International Socialists & inquiring about an article. Fold tears. C Dec 3 (343) £740 [Quaritch]

Zoffany, John, 1733-1810

ALs, 16 May 1795. 1 p, 4to. To William & Thomas Raikes. Requesting them to send Gemelli to him, & about subjects of animals & prices. S July 24 (484) £250 [Maggs]

Zola, Emile, 1840-1902

Series of 3 A Ls s, 29 July to 10 Sept 1898. 8 pp, 8vo. To F. A. Vizetelly. Pertaining to his exile in England. Various signatures. S May 21 (319) £900 [Quaritch]

ALs, 5 July 1879. 1 p, 8vo. Recipient unnamed. Suggesting he visit Monsieur Desboutins who may provide him with a photograph of his painting. Framed. Altman collection. pnNY Sept 13 (142) $375

— 7 Nov [18]84. 1 p, 8vo. Recipient unnamed.

ZOLA

About the serialization of his novel La Joie de Vivre. C June 24 (158) £220 [Bush]
— 16 Jan 1894. 2 pp, 8vo. To [Ivan Halperine-Kaminski]. Sending some letters on Russia from Le Temps & making suggestions about an article. C Dec 3 (397) £160 [Dreyfus]

Autograph sentiment, 26 Nov 1894. 1 p, 8vo. Toast proposed at Naples; sgd. wa May 30 (444) $220

Zuckmayer, Carl, 1896-1977
Series of 3 Ls s, 2 July to 16 Dec 1971. 4 pp, folio. To Hans Esdras Mutzenbecher. About lectures at Baden-Baden. With carbon copies of 2 replies. star Apr 8 (294) DM350

Ls, 13 Nov 1928. 1 p, folio. To Alfred Guttmann of the Arbeiter-Saengerbund. Professing interest in his work, but saying he is preoccupied with his own projects. Sgd in pencil. star Apr 8 (293) DM260

Zweig, Stefan, 1881-1942
Autograph Ms, report about his experiences in the U. S. A., [1941]. 3 pp, folio. Written for an interview with the Jornal do Brasil; in French. star Apr 8 (295) DM4,800

Autograph transcript, poem, Maedchen vor der Bueste einer Bacchantin; [n.d.]. 2 pp, 4to. 7 quatrains, sgd. S Nov 27 (485) £280 [Lucas]

Series of 4 A Ls s, c.1901 to 1902. 10 pp [with enclosures], 8vo. To Karl Grosz. About the publication of one of his songs & enclosing 6 poems (present) to be set to music. With carte-de visite photograph, sgd & inscr. S Nov 27 (486) £750 [Jahns]

ALs, [winter 1941/42]. 1 p, 4to. To Paul Lester Wiener. Reporting about a conference & their life in Brasil. With 3 photographs. HN May 22 (3234) DM820

Ls s (2), 26 Dec 1936 & 12 Apr 1937. 4pp, 4to & 8vo. To Hans Wolffheim. Regretting that he is unable to help him find a publisher. With autograph subscriptions. star Apr 8 (296) DM560

Ls, 8 Apr 1940. 1 p, 4to. Recipient unnamed. Saying he will lecture in Paris & commenting about Otto Zarek. star Apr 8 (297) DM400

PART II

Books

ATLASES, BOOKS, BROADSIDES, AND MAPS & CHARTS ARE REPORTED IN THIS SECTION

A

Aa, Abraham Jacob van der, 1659-1733
— Aardrijkskundig woordenboek der Nederlanden. Gorinchem, 1839-51. 13 vols, including Supplement Cloth, some defs. B Oct 7 (1358) HF650

Abajian, James de T.
— Blacks in Selected Newspapers, Censuses and Other Sources: An Index to Names and Subjects. First Supplement. Bost.: G. K. Hall, 1985. 2 vols. Folio, cloth. cb Oct 9 (248) $65

Abbey Collection, John R.
— The Italian Manuscripts in the Library of Major J. R. Abbey. L, 1969. 4to, cloth, in d/j. pn Jan 22 (83) £45 [Forster]
— Life in England in Aquatint and Lithography. L., 1972. 4to, orig cloth, in d/j. Reprint of the 1953 Ed. bba Oct 16 (358) £130 [MacKay]
— Scenery of Great Britain and Ireland in Aquatint and Lithography. L, 1952. One of 500. 4to, cloth. S May 28 (826) £320
Anr Ed. L, 1972. 4to, orig cloth, in d/j. Reprint of 1952 Ed. bba Oct 16 (359) £220 [Shapero]
Anr copy. Cloth. Reprint of 1952 Ed. bba Oct 16 (360) £200 [Dawson]
— Travel in Aquatint and Lithography. L, 1956-57. One of 400. 2 vols. 4to, orig cloth; hinges wormed. sg Jan 22 (1) $600
Anr Ed. L, 1972. 2 vols. 4to, orig cloth, in d/js. Reprint of 1956-57 Ed. bba Oct 16 (361) £320 [Dawson]
Anr copy. Orig cloth. Reprint of 1956-57 Ed. bba Oct 16 (362) £300 [Dawson]

Abbot, Henry L. See: Humphreys & Abbot

Abbott, Berenice
— A Guide to Better Photography. NY, 1944. 4to, cloth, in d/j. wa Nov 6 (365) $52
— The World of Atget. NY, [1964]. 1st Ed. 4to, cloth, in d/j. ha Nov 7 (130) $60
Anr Ed. NY, 1981-82. Vols I & II. 4to, cloth, in d/j. wa Nov 6 (285) $50

Abbott, Berenice —& McCausland, Elizabeth
— Changing New York. NY, 1939. 4to, cloth. sg Nov 13 (1) $140

Abbott, George
— Views of the Forts of Bhurtpoore & Weire. L, 1827. Bound with: Views about Kurrah, Mannickpore. L, 1831. Folio, half mor. With litho title & 11 plates in 1st work & litho title & dedication & 8 plates in 2d work; on india paper throughout. S Apr 24 (330) £500 [Elte]

Abbott, John Stevens Cabot, 1805-77
— The History of the Civil War in America.... Springfield, 1863-65. 2 vols. 8vo, orig mor; rubbed. Some foxing. O Mar 24 (1) $60

A'Beckett, Gilbert Abbott, 1811-56
— The Comic Blackstone. L, 1844-46. 2 vols. 8vo, calf gilt by Zaehnsdorf, orig wraps bound in Vol I. Lacking half-title in Vol II. ag Feb 12 (49) $150
— The Comic History of England. L, 1847-48. Illus by John Leech. 2 vols in one. 8vo, orig cloth. With 20 hand-colored plates. sg Dec 18 (134) $80
Anr copy. 2 vols. 8vo, contemp half calf, worn. sg Dec 18 (135) $70
— The Comic History of Rome. [L, 1851]. 1st Ed, 1st Issue. Illus by John Leech. 10/9 orig parts. 8vo, orig wraps. sg June 11 (1) $250
Anr Ed. L, [1860s]. 8vo, orig cloth. With 10 hand-colored plates. ha May 22 (127)

$55

Abel, Clarke
— Narrative of a Journey in the Interior of China.... L, 1818. 1st Ed. 4to, contemp calf gilt; worn & broken. With 4 maps & 19 plates, 9 colored by hand. Some plates cropped. Inscr "From the author" on initial blank. S Nov 18 (1208) £460 [Maggs]

Anr copy. Contemp calf gilt; rebacked. With 19 plates, some hand-colored. Some cropping. S Feb 24 (485) £200 [Shapero]

Anr Ed. L, 1819. 4to, modern half syn. With 4 maps & 19 plates, including 8 colored aquatints. C Oct 15 (1) £400 [Thorp]

Abelin, Johann Philipp, d.c.1634
— Historische Chronica der Vier Monarchien von Erschassung der Welt. Frankfurt, 1642. Folio, disbound. Lacking engraved title, some prelims, some of the index, 9 text leaves & 2 plates. Sold w.a.f. ha Mar 13 (216) $200

Abelin, Johann Philipp, d.c.1634 —& Others
— Theatrum Europaeum, oder aussfuehrliche und warhafftige Beschreibung...aller und jeder denckwuerdiger Geschichten.... Frankfurt, 1635-1738. Vols I-XVIII (of 21). Folio, Vols I-XV in contemp calf, Vols XV-XVIII in contemp vellum. With engraved titles to each vol, 62 double-page or folding maps, 522 mostly double-page plates & c.635 ports, plates & other illusts. Minor worming & tears. Sold w.a.f. S Oct 23 (93) £21,000 [Bauer]

Abercrombie, Lascelles, 1881-1938. See: Gregynog Press

Abert, James W.
— Report and Map of the Examination of New Mexico. [Wash.], 1848. 1st Ed. 8vo, orig wraps, unopened; portion of rear wrap off at top, minor chipping. With folding map & 23 (of 24) plates. Senate Exec. Doc. 23, 30th Congress, 1st Session. sg Sept 18 (1) $275

Anr copy. Disbound. With folding map & 24 plates. Lacking tp; folding map with short tear. Senate Exec. Doc. 23, 30th Congress, 1st Session. wa Mar 5 (361) $150

Abraham a Sancta Clara, 1644-1709
— Etwas fuer Alle, das ist: Eine kurtze Beschreibung allerley Stands- Amkbts- und gewerbs-Persohnen.... Wuerzburg, 1711. Part 1 only. 8vo, contemp vellum; wormed. Some leaves wormed. HK Nov 4 (1692) DM4,600

Anr copy. Part 2. 8vo, HK Nov 4 (1693) DM2,600

Abrege...
— Abrege portatif de la chasse du cerf tire des meilleurs auteurs quo ont traite de cette matiere et d'apres la methode pratiquee a la cour du roi de Sardaigne. Turin: Honore Derossi, 1782. 12mo, mor gilt by Chambolle Duru. Jeanson copy. SM Feb 28 (1) FF4,000

Abrizzi, Isabella, Countess
— The Works of Antonio Canova in Sculpture and Modelling.... L, 1824. 2 vols. 4to, orig half mor; rubbed. bba Oct 30 (437) £60 [Hetherington]

Abul Hasan al Muchtar ibn Botlan. See: Elimithar, Elluchasem

Academia Medico-quirurgica. See: Puebla de Los Angeles

Academia Veneta
— Somma delle opera che ha da mandare in luce l'Academia Venetiana. Venice, 1558. 3 parts in 1 vol. 4to, late 18th-cent calf gilt extra. Old inscr washed out of 1st title. A. A. Renouard's copy. sg Oct 9 (75) $1,600

Acala, Jaime de
— Cavalleria christiana. Acala: Juan de Villanueva, 1570. 8vo, contemp vellum; loose in bdg. Margins trimmed; some stains; worming in gutters through half of vol. sg Oct 9 (1) $275

Accounts...
— An Account of the Municipal Celebration of the One Hundred and Fiftieth Anniversary of the Settlement of Baltimore.... Balt., 1881. 4to, cloth; worn & frayed, ring spot at rear cover. Ink underlinings & marginal markings. ha Sept 19 (148) $60

Accum, Friedrich Christian, 1769-1838
— A Practical Treatise on the Use and Application of Chemical Tests. L, 1818. 2d Ed. 12mo, contemp half sheep; worn, joints starting. Last few leaves partly dampstained. sg Jan 15 (270) $60

Acerbi, Giuseppe, 1773-1846
— Travels through Sweden, Finland, and Lapland, to the North Cape.... L, 1802. 1st Ed. 2 vols. 4to, later half calf; rubbed. With engraved port, folding map & 15 engraved plates. Plates cropped or stamped. Ck Dec 18 (95) £140 [Hannas]

Achterberg, Gerrit, 1905-62
— Huis. Ode. The Hague: Mansarde Pers, [1943]. One of 75. Folio, orig wraps; browned. B Feb 25 (1034) HF300
— Meisje. Groningen: In agris occupatis, 1944. One of 10. Orig wraps. B Feb 25 (1035) HF1,650

— Reiziger "doet" Golgotha. The Hague: Mansarde Pers, [1943]. One of 750. 4to, orig wraps; foxed & stained. B Feb 25 (1036) HF190

Ackerman, Forrest J.
— Lon of 1000 Faces. Beverly Hills, 1983. One of 52 with a piece from Chaney's make-up kit attached to a ribbon place mark. cb Sept 28 (3) $140

Ackerman, Phyllis. See: Pope & Ackerman

Ackermann Publications, Rudolph—London
— Cambridge. 1815. ("A History of the University of Cambridge.") 2 vols. 4to, contemp calf gilt with fore-edge paintings of King's College & Sion House. With 96 plates, including uncolored port, 60 colored views, 19 colored costume plates & 16 colored ports of the founders. C Oct 15 (119) £2,800 [Hall]

— The History of the Abbey Church of St. Peter's Westminster.... 1812. 1st Ed, 2d Issue. 2 vols. 4to, contemp calf; rebacked preserving orig spines, joints worn. bba Aug 20 (503) £130 [Wise]

Issue not specified. Contemp half mor gilt. With port, plan & 81 hand-colored plates. Some offsetting & staining, library stamps on titles & a few other leaves. bba Dec 18 (96) £150 [Scott]

Anr copy. Contemp calf gilt; rebacked. Some text leaves spotted & browned. C Oct 15 (3) £140 [Marshall]

Anr copy. Bdg not stated. With port, plan & 81 color plates Library markings. Sold w.a.f. Franklin Institute copy. F Sept 12 (3) $175

Anr copy. Old mor gilt; rebacked, rubbed. With port, plan & 80 hand-colored plates, some foxing & browning. pnNY Sept 13 (191) $415

— The Microcosm of London. 1808-10. 3 vols. 4to, half mor. With 104 hand-colored plates. pn Apr 30 (36) £4,000

Anr copy. Recent half calf. Some marginal dampstains. T Feb 19 (311) £110

Anr Ed. L, 1904. 3 vols. 4to, half vellum. Reprint of the 1808-10 Ed. ha Dec 19 (152) $70

— Oxford. 1814. ("A History of the University of Oxford.") 2 vols. 4to, contemp calf. With 82 hand-colored plates. Without the Founders' ports. Wormhole in 6 prelim pp of Vol II. SSA Feb 11 (426) R1,300

— Poetical Sketches of Scarborough. 1813. 1st Ed. Illus by Thomas Rowlandson. 8vo, contemp half calf; broken. With 20 (of 21) colored plates. T Feb 19 (439) £80

— Winchester, Eton & Westminster. L, 1816. ("The History of the Colleges of Winchester, Eton, and Westminster....") 4to, contemp russia gilt; rubbed. With 48 hand-colored plates. Lacking half-title. S June 25 (212) £1,000 [Grosvenor]

Anr copy. Contemp mor gilt; lower joint weak. S June 25 (239) £850 [Grosvenor]

Acosta, Cristoval de, 1597-1676?. See: Orta & Acosta

Acosta, Jose de, 1539?-1600
— Histoire naturelle et morralle des Indes.... Paris: Marc Orry, 1598. 8vo, old calf; worn. Library stamp & ownership inscr on tp; some spotting & early marginalia; lower portion of tp cut away. Crahan copy. P Nov 25 (3) $500

— The Naturall and Morall Historie of the East and West Indies.... L, 1604. 1st Ed in English. Trans by Edward Grimstone. 4to, later calf; rubbed, joints worn. Some browning & dampstains. O May 12 (1) $900

Anr copy. Contemp calf; rebacked preserving part of spine. Some headlines shaved; a few leaves with marginal tears or soiling. S Apr 24 (285) £1,000 [Quaritch]

Acton, Harold
— This Chaos. Paris: Hours Press, [1930]. Out-of-series copy. Bds. Minor dampstaining. Inscr. sg Dec 11 (146) $275

Acton, Roger
— The Abyssinian Expedition.... [L, 1868]. Folio, orig cloth; rebacked & covered in mor. Ck May 8 (331) £120

Acuna, Christoval, 1597-1676?
— Voyages and Discoveries in South America. L., 1698. 8vo, contemp calf; rebacked. With 2 folding maps. Some browning. S June 25 (428) £850 [Houle]

Anr copy. Later calf. Folding map to 1st part supplied in facsimile; 2d part has quarter-portion of orig folding map present with facsimile of entire map. sg Sept 18 (2) $200

Adam, Robert, 1728-92
— Ruins of the Palace of the Emperor Diocletian at Spalatro in Dalmatia. L, 1764. Folio, contemp calf; hinges split. With 61 plates on 54 sheets, 15 folding. Some soiling. C July 22 (3) £1,700

Anr copy. Contemp half calf; rubbed. With 61 plates on 54 sheets, some folding. Fore-margin of 1 plate shaved; some dust-soiling; waterstain at end. S Oct 23 (196) £1,500 [Felix]

Anr copy. Later half lea; worn, broken. With 61 plates; 1 plate frayed, a few soiled. wa Nov 6 (484) $1,400

ADAM

Adam, Victor
— Album de Ste. Pelagie. Paris, [c.1835]. 4to, orig half cloth; soiled. With 12 plates. bba Sept 25 (163) £60 [Grosvenor Prints]
— Les Chasses. Paris: Aumont, c.1845]. Oblong folio, contemp half lea gilt with monogram of Henri V of France. With 24 color plates. Jeanson copy. SM Feb 28 (4) FF45,000
— Musee du chasseur ou collection de toutes les especes de gibier de piol ou de plume.... Paris: Armand Robin, 1838. 2 parts in 1 vol. 8vo, contemp half lea; rubbed. Jeanson copy. SM Feb 28 (5) FF13,000
— Retour en France des depouilles mortelles de Napoleon. Paris, 1840. Oblong folio, half mor. With 16 plates. Some plates def; pictorial title cut down & mtd but def. Sold w.a.f. S Nov 10 (890) £100 [Grosvenor]
— Voyage d'un chasseur dans les differentes parties du monde...Ier partie. - Afrique. Paris: Lamy, 1839. 8vo, contemp half shagreen; rubbed. Jeanson copy. SM Feb 28 (6) FF3,500

Adams, Ansel Easton
— Images 1923-1974. NY, 1974. Folio, cloth, in d/j. wa Nov 6 (277) $70
— My Camera in Yosemite Valley. Yosemite National Park & Bost., 1949. 1st Ed. Folio, wraps; becoming detached. sg Nov 13 (3) $100
— Photographs of the Southwest. Bost.: NY Graphic Society, [1976]. Essay by Lawrence Clark Powell. Oblong 4to, cloth. Sgd. wa Nov 6 (278) $75
— Sierra Nevada: The John Muir Trail. Berkeley: Archetype Press, 1938. One of 500. Folio, cloth. sg May 7 (1) $300
— Yosemite and the Range of Light. Bost.: New York Graphic Society, 1979. Special Ed, with mtd ptd label sgd by Adams. Intro by Paul Brooks. Oblong 4to, cloth, in d/j. wa Nov 6 (281) $95; wa Nov 6 (282) $90

Adams, Ansel Easton —&
Joesting, Edward
— An Introduction to Hawaii. San Francisco: 5 Associates, [1964]. Folio, pictorial wraps; rubbed. cb Jan 8 (1) $55

Adams, Frederick B., Jr.
— Radical Literature in America. Stamford, Conn., 1939. One of 650. Worn. sg Jan 22 (2) $50

Adams, George, 1750-95
— An Essay on Electricity.... L, 1784. 12mo, contemp calf; spine rubbed. With 6 folding plates. S May 28 (607) £240
2d Ed. L, 1785. 8vo, modern pigskin. With 7 (of 8) plates. wa Nov 6 (199) $50
— Micrographia Illustrata, or, the Microscope

AMERICAN BOOK PRICES CURRENT

Explained.... L, 1746. 8vo, later half calf; rubbed, extremities worn. Some foxing, soiling or marginal staining. cb Feb 19 (187) $550

Adams, Henry, 1838-1918
— History of the United States during the Administration of Thomas Jefferson. NY, 1930. In soiled d/js with short tears. wa Sept 25 (291) $75

Adams, Herbert Mayow
— Catalogue of Books Printed on the Continent of Europe, 1501-1600, in Cambridge Libraries. Cambr., 1967. 2 vols. 4to, orig cloth; rubbed. bba Oct 16 (363) £280 [Frew Mackenzie]; HK Nov 4 (3113) DM750

Adams, James Truslow, 1878-1949
— History of the United States. NY, 1933. Federal Ed, One of 770, sgd. 4 vols. sg Mar 12 (1) $70

Adams, John, Topographer, fl. 1680
— Index Villaris: or an Alphabetical Table of all the Cities, Market Towns, Parishes.... L, 1680. Folio, later mor gilt; rubbed. First few leaves with small marginal wormholes. bba Mar 26 (35) £80 [Drury]

Adams, John, 1735-1826
— A Defence of the Constitutions of Government of the United States of America. NY & L, 1787. 2d American Ed. 12mo, contemp calf; front cover detached, rear cover loosening. sg Sept 18 (3) $350

Adams, John Quincy, 1767-1848
— Territory West of the Rocky Mountains. Message of the President of the United States. Wash., 1828. 8vo, sewn as issued; edges fraying. 20th Congress, 1st Session, H of R Exec. Doc. 199. cb Jan 8 (2) $50

Adams, Ramon F.
— The Rampaging Herd: a Bibliography. Norman, Okla., [1959]. 1st Ed. wa June 25 (2) $80

Adams, Richard, Novelist
— Watership Down. L, 1972. 1st Ed. In d/j. cb Sept 28 (7) $400; T Oct 15 (47) £240

Adams, Robert, Sailor
— The Narrative of Robert Adams, a Sailor, who was Wrecked on the Western Coast of Africa. L, 1816. 1st Ed. 4to, later half mor; worn, spine defective. Folding map stained & torn. bba Dec 18 (97) £40 [Hay]

Addison, Charles Greenstreet, d.1866
— Damascus and Palmyra. L, 1838. Illus by Wm. Makepeace Thackeray. 2 vols. 8vo, contemp half calf; rubbed. Some staining. bba Oct 30 (275) £120 [Wagner]

Addison, Joseph, 1672-1719
See also: Fore-Edge Paintings; Spectator...
— The Free-Holder. Or Political Essays. L, 1716. 12mo, contemp calf gilt; rebacked, rubbed. bba Nov 13 (210) £45 [Trocchi]
— Remarks on Several Parts of Italy. L, 1767. 8vo, lea gilt. sg Apr 23 (1) $100
— Works. Birm.: Baskerville, 1761. 4 vols. Folio, contemp calf gilt. Some staining affecting a few leaves in Vol IV. pnE Jan 28 (127) £480 [Joseph]
Anr copy. 4 vols. 4to, contemp calf gilt; spine ends chipped, joints cracked. sg Oct 9 (76) $225
Anr Ed. L, 1761. 4 vols. 4to, contemp calf; rebacked & recornered, old spines laid down. Title to Vol II soiled. Ck Nov 21 (32) £65

Addison, Thomas, 1793-1860
— On the Constitutional and Local Effects of Disease of the Supra-Renal Capsules. L, 1855. 1st Ed. 4to, orig cloth. With 11 colored plates. Some spotting, 2leaves & 1 plate loose. S Nov 27 (244) £5,000 [Quaritch]

Adelphi
— The Adelphi. L, 1923-33. Ed by John Middleton Murry. 98 Nos. Pictorial wraps; rubbed. bba Oct 30 (4) £100 [Moreton]

Adlum, John
— A Memoir on the Cultivation of the Vine in America and the Best Mode of Making Wine. Wash., 1828. 2d Ed. 12mo, contemp half mor. Browned. Crahan copy. P Nov 25 (5) $650

Adrianus Carthusiensis
— De remediis utriusque fortunae. [Cologne: Ulrich Zel, c.1470]. 4to, modern vellum bds. Gothic letter; 1st initial supplied in blue with red marginal extensions; rubricated throughout. Slight worming in 1st 3 leaves; early shelf-mark in fore-margin of f.1 recto; cancelled library stamp. 160 leaves. Goff A-54. S Nov 27 (1) £2,100 [Abrams]

Adrichomius, Christianus, 1533-85
— Theatrum terrae sanctae et biblicarum historiarum. Cologne, 1590. Folio, contemp vellum; soiled. With engraved title & 11 folding maps. Map of Jerusalem loose & linen-backed; engraved title damp-stained; lacking Universal Table. pn June 18 (169) £550 [Sperling]
Anr Ed. Cologne, 1600. Folio, contemp vellum bds. With engraved title & 12 folding maps. JG Mar 20 (1379) DM1,100

Adventurer...
— The Adventurer. L, [1753]-54. Ed by John Hawkesworth. 140 orig nos in 2 vols. Folio, contemp calf gilt, with signet arms; rubbed, rebacked, corners worn. One leaf torn in Vol I; 1 leaf holed in Vol II; some imprints cropped. C May 13 (161) £400 [Blackwell]

Adventures. See: Clemens, Samuel Langhorne

Ady, Thomas
— A Candle in the Dark. L, 1655. 1st Ed. 4to, contemp half calf; worn & loose. Lacking all before B2; Q2 torn at lower margin affecting a few words; rust hole in text of Q2 & V4. S May 29 (1135) £700

Aelian (Aelienus Tacitus)
— The Tactics of Aelian.... L, 1814. 4to, later half calf; 2 flyleaves torn. With 38 (of 39) plates. Lacking Plate 13; some foxing. cb Dec 18 (1) $180

Aelianus, Claudius
— A Registre of Hystories.... L: Thomas Woodcocke, 1576. 4to, later russia; broken, rubbed. First leaves stained; tp loose; some staining & soiling. S Sept 23 (286) £320 [New South Wales Government]
— Variae historiae libri XIII.... Rome, 1545. 4to, later mor gilt. Some Ms sidenotes; tp dust-soiled. bba Jan 15 (325) £220 [Poole]
Anr copy. Mor gilt. Huth copy. S Nov 27 (132) £600 [Maggs]
— Variae historiae libri XIIII.... Rome, 1545. 1st Ed in Greek. 4to, early calf. 1 leaf torn in margin, anr discolored. Herbert of Cherbury's copy with his arms in gilt on both covers & his cypher on the title. S Nov 27 (4) £1,000 [King]

Aemylius, Georg
— Biblicae Historiae magno artificio depictae.... Frankfurt: Christian Egenolph, [1539]. Illus by Hans Sebald Beham. 8vo, later calf over pastebd with repeating motif of Virgin & Child. Some marginal damp-stain. sg June 11 (32) $1,600

Aeneas Sylvius, Pope Pius II, 1405-64
— Asiae Europaeque elegantissima descriptio.... Paris: Galeotus a Prato, 1534. 8vo, modern half mor gilt. Lacking final blank; some browning. S July 14 (340) £180
— Historia rerum ubique gestarum. Venice: Johannes de Colonia & Johannes Manthen, 1477. Folio, 16th-cent vellum; endpapers from ptd binder's waste. 105 (of 106) leaves; lacking initial blank. S May 21 (13) £2,200 [Quaritch]

AESCHYLUS

Aeschylus, 525-456 B.C.
— Het treurspel van Agamemnoon. Amst., 1903. One of 40. Vellum. B Oct 7 (53) HF700
— Opera. Venice: Aldus, 1518. ("Tragoediae.") 8vo, 18th-cent calf with gilt coronets in spine compartments; rebacked with old spine laid down, lettering-piece lost. In Greek. Uzielli copy. P Sept 24 (99) $1,200
Anr Ed. Antwerp: Plantin, 1580. 16mo, later calf; joints split, rubbed. bba Nov 13 (3) £45 [Maggs]

Aesop, c.620-560 B.C.
See also: Golden Cockerel Press; Grabhorn Printing; Gregynog Press

Fables
— 1549. - Fabulae cum aliis quibusdam opusculis. Paris: widow of A. Birkmann. 16mo, contemp vellum; rubbed & warped, new endpapers. Some staining, mostly marginal. bba Apr 23 (95) £75 [Poole]
— 1578. - Receuil contenant le tirage a part des figures de L'Esbatiment moral des animaux. Anvers: Philippe galle. 4to, 17th-cent calf gilt with arms of de Thou & of his 2d wife (Olivier 216, fers 8 & 9). Jeanson copy. SM Feb 28 (7) FF50,000
— 1668. - The Fables. L. Bound with: Aesopics, or a Second Collection of Fables. L, 1668. 2 parts in 1 vol. 2d Ed of 1st part; 1st Ed of 2d part. Paraphrased in verse by John Ogilby. Folio, old sheep; broken. With engraved port & 81 plate. pn June 18 (213) £1,150 [Reisler]
— 1687. - Fables.... L: H. Hills for Francis Barlow. Folio, recent pigskin. Includes the suppressed plate 17, opposite p 22. Some soiling & ink splatters; final leaf inlaid; 1 illus cancelled with substitute laid on. cb July 30 (4) $500
— 1692. - Fables of Aesop and Other Eminent Mythologists. L: R. Sare, etc. Ed by Roger L'Estrange. Folio, contemp calf; rebacked. With frontis & 1 plate.. sg Oct 9 (77) $200
— 1793. - Fables. L: John Stockdale. 2 vols. 8vo, calf; rebacked. With engraved titles & 110 plates. sg Dec 18 (138) $175
— 1800. - Fabulae graecae, latine conversa. Parma: Bodoni. 4to, contemp calf gilt; worn. sg Oct 9 (130) $130
— 1823. - Fables Newcastle 8vo, 19th-cent calf; rubbed. A few leaves creased. S May 6 (86) £150 [Henderson]
— 1848. - Fables: a New Version.... L. Illus by John Tenniel. 8vo, contemp calf gilt; rubbed. bba Feb 5 (187) £55 [Jarndyce]
— 1909. - Fables. L. Illus by Detmold. 4to, orig cloth. S May 28 (859) £160

AMERICAN BOOK PRICES CURRENT

One of 750. Orig cloth; worn. With 25 colored plates. Ck Apr 24 (37) £190
— 1912. - L. One of 1,450. Illus by Arthur Rackham. 4to, orig cloth. With 13 colored plates. S May 6 (144) £170 [Hannas]
One of 1,450, sgd by the artist. Trans by V. S. Vernon Jones; illus by Arthur Rackham. Orig cloth; chipped. With 13 colored plates. K Oct 4 (373) $130
Anr copy. Half mor gilt. sg Oct 30 (2) $850
Anr copy. Half mor gilt; soiled & stained, backstrip darkened. sg Oct 30 (3) $150
— 1929. - Die schoensten Fabeln. Berlin Illus with 16 ink & watercolor drawings by Hedwig Jarke. Folio, mor gilt with onlaid monogram over a pictorial ground designed by K. Schulpig. Unique copy ptd for the children of Erna & Julius Goldschmidt. S June 17 (136) £3,200 [Uppstrom]
— 1936. - Fables. L. One of 525, sgd by the artist. Trans by Sir Roger L'Estrange; illus by Stephen Gooden. pn Mar 5 (89) £250 [Neubauer]
Anr copy. Vellum gilt. pnNY Sept 13 (192) $300
— 1973. - Le Favole di Esopo stampato in latino con la versione italiana di Accio Zucco.... Verona: Officina Bodoni One of 150. Orig mor gilt. With 66 woodcut illusts colored by hand. C May 13 (186) £650 [Marks]

Affecting...
— The Affecting History of the Children in the Wood Bost. [1798]. ("The Tragical History of the Children in the Wood.") 32mo, mor gilt. S June 18 (498) £260 [Nugee]

Affiches...
— Les Affiches etrangeres illustrees.... Paris, 1897. One of 1,000 on papier velin. 4to, modern cloth, orig wraps bound in; front cover badly torn & crudely mended. sg Feb 5 (277) $700

Africanus. See: Leo, Johannes

Agassiz, Alexander, 1835-1910
— Three Cruises of the United States Coast and Geodetic Survey Steamer 'Blake'. L 1888. 2 vols. Orig cloth; rubbed. Library markings. bba Mar 26 (341) £40 [Elliott]

Agassiz, Louis, 1807-73
— Contributions to the Natural History of the United States.... Bost., 1857-62. 1st Ed. 4 vols. 4to, orig cloth; worn, 1 spine torn. With 77 plates. pnNY Oct 16 (9) $80
Anr copy. Orig cloth; 3 spines torn. Lightly dampwrinkled. sg Jan 15 (128) $225

Agee, James, 1909-55
— Permit Me Voyage. New Haven, 1934. In d/j. O Jan 6 (2) $140

Aglio, Augustine. See: Kingsborough, Edward

Agocchie, Giovanni dall'
— Dell'arte di scrimia libri tre.... Venice: Giulio Tamborino, 1572. 4to, contemp vellum; spine def. Dampstained. S June 25 (1) £300

Agricola, Georgius, 1494-1555
— De ortu & causis subterraneorum.... Basel, 1558. Folio, 17th-cent mor gilt; foot of spine frayed, minor abrasions on lower cover. Waterstain on tp & a few leaves. C Dec 12 (3) £700 [Schwing]

— De re metallica. Basel: Froben, 1556. 1st Ed. Folio, contemp pigskin; both covers wormed & soiled. Woodcuts on p6 verso & q2 recto discolored; a few lower margins waterstained. S May 21 (20) £5,000 [Sims]

2d Ed. Basel, 1561. Folio, contemp sheep. With 1 wormhole affecting title & 1st 6 leaves; dampstain to lower margin of tp & 1st 6 leaves & upper corner of last 8 leaves. pn Apr 30 (117) £1,750 [Henderson]

2d Ed of 1st work. Bound with: De mensuris & ponderibus. Basel, 1550. Folio, later mor; 1 corner restored. Lacking 6 prelims in 1st work; lacking 3 prelims in 2d work & signature u not ptd. Sold w.a.f. C Dec 12 (4) £520 [Schwing]

Anr Ed. Basel, 1657. Folio, needs rebdg. Some browning & stains. sg Jan 15 (280) $650

Anr copy. Later vellum; soiled. T Mar 19 (324) £580

Anr Ed. L, 1912. Trans by Herbert C. & Lou Hoover. Folio, orig half vellum. Inscr. O May 12 (2) $350

Anr copy. Library stamp on tp. pn June 18 (128) £200 [Culpin]

Agricola, Johann Georg, 1558-1633
— Cervi cum integri et vivi, natura et proprietas.... Amberg: Michael Forstern, 1617. 4to, contemp vellum; worn. Schwerdt-Jeanson copy. SM Feb 28 (8) FF9,000

Agricola, P., Pseud.
— The New-York Gardener, or Twelve Letters from a Farmer to his Son.... White Creek NY, 1827. 8vo, mor by Grabau, orig front wrap & part of back wrap bound in, but front wrap dated 1828. Hunt copy. CNY Nov 21 (206) $350

Agricola, Rudolphus
— Inventione dialectica lib. III. Paris: S. Caluarini, 1558. 4to, contemp calf; rubbed. Bb3 & 4 misbound; some browning. bba Oct 16 (10) £150 [Maggs]

Agrippa, Camillo
— Trattato di scienza d'arme. Venice: Antonio Pinargenti, 1568. 4to, contemp vellum; soiled. With engraved title & 49 (on 37) plates. T Feb 19 (571) £480

Agrippa, Henricus Cornelius, 1486?-1535
— De incertitudine et vanitate scientiarum declamatio invectiva.... [Basle?], 1530. 8vo, Parisian calf gilt, c.1550. S Nov 27 (134) £1,800 [Pinter]

— De occulta philosophia libri tres. [Cologne: Johannes Soter], July 1533. Folio, modern half calf. Title repaired, slightly affecting woodcut. S Nov 27 (133) £400 [Pinter]

— Of the Vanitie and Uncertantie of Arts and Sciences. L, 1684. ("The Vanity of Arts and Sciences.") 8vo, 19th-cent half sheep; rear cover detached. sg Oct 9 (79) $225

— Paradoxe sur l'incertitude, vanite & abus des sciences.... L, 1603. 12mo, contemp vellum. Lacking prelim leaf 12. sg Jan 15 (281) $100

Agusti, Miguel, 1560-1630
— Libro de los secretos de agricultura.... Perpignan: Luis Roure, 1626. 4to, contemp vellum. Schwerdt-Jeanson copy. SM Feb 28 (9) FF11,000

Aikin, John, 1747-1822
— Biographical Memoirs of Medicine in Great Britain.... L, 1780. 8vo, contemp calf; rubbed, rebacked. bba Apr 9 (74) £75 [Wacker]

Anr copy. Contemp calf; worn. pnE Dec 17 (54) £150 [Phillips]

— A Description of the Country from Thirty to Forty Miles round Manchester. L, 1795. 4to, half vellum; soiled. With frontis, engraved title, folding map colored in outline, folding plan & 16 maps & plans. pn Mar 5 (264) £190 [Clark]

— England Delineated.... L, 1809. 6th Ed. 8vo, contemp calf; hinges cracked. With double-page map of England & Wales & 42 county maps. Some maps trimmed on outer edge. T Feb 19 (293) £95

Ainsworth, Edward
— The Cowboy in Art. NY: World, [1968]. One of 100. Foreword by John Wayne. Calf. cb July 30 (5) $130

Anr Ed. NY & Cleveland, 1968. Calf. cb Jan 8 (231) $140

AINSWORTH

Ainsworth, William Francis
— A Personal Narrative of the Euphrates Expedition. L, 1888. 1st Ed. 2 vols. 8vo, orig cloth; rubbed.   bba May 28 (219) £160 [Wagner]

Ainsworth, William Harrison, 1805-82
— Hilary St. Ives. L, 1870. 1st Ed. 3 vols. 8vo, later half mor; rubbed. Lacking half-titles. O Nov 18 (2) $110
— The Lord Mayor of London. L, 1862. 1st Ed. 3 vols. 8vo, later half mor; rubbed. O Nov 18 (3) $70
— The Miser's Daughter.... L, 1842. 1st Ed. Illus by George Cruikshank. 3 vols. 8vo, mor gilt by Riviere. Extra-illus with a duplicate set of the plates, hand-colored. sg Feb 12 (3) $450
— The Tower of London. L, 1840. 1st Ed in Book form. Illus by George Cruikshank. 8vo, half mor; rubbed. With 40 plates. sg Sept 11 (2) $80
Anr copy. Mor by the Guild of Women Binders with multi-colored mor inlays depicting characters from the book. Extra-illus with a duplicate sets of the plates, hand-colored & with a Cruikshank ALs. sg Feb 12 (50) $400
— Works. Phila.: Barrie, [c.1900]. ("Historical Romances.") One of 74 on japan vellum with plates in 2 states. 20 vols. 4to, mor gilt extra; spines faded, a few heads of spines chipped.   CNY Dec 19 (1) $500

Ainsworth, William Harrison, 1805-82 —& Aston, John Partington
— Sir John Chiverton, a Romance. L, 1826. 12mo, later half mor; rubbed. O Nov 18 (4) $80

Airy, Osmund, 1845-1928
— Charles II. L, 1901. One of 300 on japan with plates in 2 states, the port-frontis with 1 state in colors. 4to, mor gilt with royal arms. S July 13 (191) £160

Aitinger, Johann Conrad
— Kurtzer und einfaeltiger bericht vom Vogel-stellen jetzo auffs new mit Fleiss uebersehen und vemehret. Cassel: Salomon Schadewitz in Verlegung Johann Schuetzen, 1653. 4to, contemp vellum. Schwerdt-Jeanson copy. SM Feb 28 (10) FF30,000

Aitzema, Lieuwe van
— Herstelde leeuw, of discours over 't gepasseerde in de Vereenigde Nederlanden.... The Hague, 1652. 4to, calf; rubbed, new endpapers. Some stains & marginal wormholes. B Feb 25 (568) HF380
— Historie van het verhael van saken van staet en oorlogh.... The Hague, 1657-71. 14 vols in

AMERICAN BOOK PRICES CURRENT

15. 4to, vellum. Some stains & worming. B Feb 25 (566) HF4,500

Akenside, Mark, 1721-70
— The Pleasures of Imagination. L, 1744. 1st Issue, with footnote on p. 9. 4to, contemp calf; rubbed, rebacked, new endpapers. S Jan 13 (461) £50 [Smallwood]
3d Issue. 19th-cent mor gilt by F. Bedford. Minor stains.   pn Nov 20 (99) £55 [Hannas]
— The Poems. L, 1772. 1st Collected Ed, L.p. copy. 4to, contemp calf; rubbed & rebacked.   bba Nov 13 (227) £60 [Marvin]

Akurgal, Ekrem —& Others
— Treasures of Turkey. Geneva: Skira, [1966]. In d/j. Some stamps.   cb Mar 5 (194) $50

Alain-Fournier, Henri, 1886-1914
— Le Grand meaulnes. Paris, [1930]. One of 46 with a suite "en vero des bois" & an orig watercolor. Illus by Hermine David. 4to, mor with mor onlays by Paul Bonet. With a supplementary suite of 6 woodcuts & 3 proofs. SM Oct 20 (576) FF140,000

Alamanni, Luigi, 1495-1556
— La Coltivatione. Paris: Estienne, 1546. 4to, 17th-cent mor gilt; stain on lower cover, a few wormholes in spine. S Sept 23 (414) £220 [Maggs]
1st Ed. 8vo, early 17th-cent vellum; soiled & loose. Some dampstaining. S Jan 13 (336) £140 [Zayas]
— Gyrone il cortese Venice: Comin da Trino di Monferrato, 1549. ("Girone il cortese.") 4to, later half calf; spine worn. Ck Jan 16 (91) £50
— Opere Toscane. Venice: Peter Schoeffer for the heirs of Lucantonio Giunta, 1542. 8vo, 18th-cent vellum bds; soiled. Some browning; a few numerals cropped; tp slightly def, with a few small holes & loss of a few numerals of date. S Jan 13 (337) £80 [Zayas]

Alambert, Jean le Rond d', 1717?-83
— Sur la destruction des Jesuites en France.... Paris, 1765. Bound with: Lettre [Seconde Lettre; Addition] a Mr. *** conseiller du Parlement...Supplement a...sur la Destruction des Jesuites en France. Paris, 1767. 12mo, contemp mor gilt. With final errata leaf to 2d work. C Dec 3 (175) £320 [Quaritch]

Alastair. See: Voight, Hans Henning

Albanis de Beaumont, Jean Francois, Viscount, 1753?-1811?
— Select Views of the Antiquities and Harbours in the South of France. L, 1794. Folio, calf; rebacked. With hand-colored engraved title, 2 plans, 1 plain & 12 hand-colored plates.. SM Oct 20 (410)

FF5,000
— Voyage historique et pittoresque du Comte de Nice. Geneva, 1787. 1st Ed. Folio, calf. With engraved dedication, hand-colored map & 12 plates on 9 sheets, each hand-colored by Gabriel Lory the Elder. S Oct 23 (243) £350 [Lardanche]

Albert Victor, Prince —&
George, Prince of Wales
— The Cruise of her Majesty's Ship "Bacchante" 1879-1882. L, 1886. 2 vols. 8vo, cloth; rubbed. T Sept 18 (5) £38

Albertanus Causidicus Brixiensis
— Ars loquendi et tacendi. Cologne: [Heinrich Quentell], 1497. 4to, modern vellum. 12 leaves. Goff A-209. C Dec 12 (289) £750 [Israel]

Alberti, Leon Battista, 1404-72
— The Architecture...Painting...Statuary. L, 1755. Folio, bdg not indicated. Library markings. Sold w.a.f. Franklin Institute copy. F Sept 12 (47) $400
— L'Architettura. Venice, 1565. 4to, later vellum bds; soiled, upper joint slit. Tp wormed & with a tear repaired & 2 library stamps; some lower margins wormed. S Mar 10 (1009) £340 [Maggs]

Anr copy. 19th-cent calf gilt; rubbed. Some dampstaining; tp shaved. S July 14 (358) £280
— De re aedificatoria libri decem. Strassburg: Jacob Cammerlander, 1541. 4to, contemp vellum; spine def. R1-4 discolored. S June 25 (2) £500
— Della Architettura...Della Pittura...Della Statua. Londra: Tommaso Edkin, 1726. Folio, contemp half calf; broken. bba Apr 23 (53) £450 [Quaritch]

Albertinus, Franciscus
— Septem mirabilia orbis et urbis Romae et Florentinae civitas. Rome: Jacobum Mazochium, 7 Feb 1510. 4to, modern mor. Small patch of dampstaining throughout. 7 leaves; lacking final blank. S May 21 (21) £750 [Goldschmidt]

Albertus Magnus, 1193?-1280
— De animalibus. Venice: Joannes & Gregorius de Gregoriis de Forlivio, 21 May 1495. Folio, 18th-cent half vellum. 260 leaves. Goff A-225. Schwerdt-Jeanson copy. SM Feb 28 (12) FF12,000
— De secretis mulierum et virorum. [Leipzig: Melchior Lotter, 1502]. 4to, old vellum; rebacked. Early underscoring & marginalia. sg Dec 4 (2) $450
— De secretis mulierum [& other works]. Amst.: H. & T. Boom, 1669. 1st Collected Ed, Ferguson's 1st Issue. 12mo, contemp calf; worn,joints cracked. Hunt copy.

CNY Nov 21 (4) $80
— Liber aggregationis, seu liber secretorum.... [Cologne: Heinrich Quentell, c.1485]. 4to, modern vellum bds. Minor dampstains to a few margins. 24 leaves. Goff A-256. Hunt copy. CNY Nov 21 (2) $2,000

Anr Ed. Cologne: Cornelius von Zieriksie, [after 1500]. ("Liber aggregationis, seu liber de virtutibus herbarum....") 4to, modern mor. Washed. 24 leaves. Goff A-265. Hunt copy. CNY Nov 21 (3) $2,000

Albin, Eleazar, fl.1713-59
— Birds. L, 1731-34. ("A Natural History of Birds.") Vols I (of 3). 4to, contemp calf gilt; rubbed, spine def. Some plates cropped or cut down; Plate 99 torn along platemark; tear in Plate 10; small hole in R2 affecting text. S Feb 24 (542) £1,300 [Kiefer]

Anr Ed. L, 1738-40. Vols I-II. 4to, contemp calf; worn, repaired. With 205 hand-colored plates. Some tears repaired; several plates from anr copy. bba Jan 15 (399) £1,800 [Shapero]

Anr copy. 3 vols. 4to, contemp calf gilt. With 289 hand-colored plates only, some shaved, 1 with nick in lower margin. Sold w.a.f. C Oct 15 (208) £3,200 [Maggs]

Anr copy. With 284 hand-colored plates only.. C Apr 8 (163) £3,800 [Koromvokis]

Anr copy. Vols I-II. Contemp mor; worn. With 187 hand-colored plates only. Some stains & soiling. Sold w.a.f. S Oct 23 (656) £190 [Dennistoun]

Albinus, Bernard Siegfried, 1697-1770
— Explicatio tabularum anatomicarum Bartholomaei Eustachii.... Leiden, 1761. Folio, calf gilt. With 89 plates. B Feb 25 (1024) HF2,300

Anr copy. Contemp calf; rubbed, rebacked & recornered, new endpapers. With 39 plates having 46 accompanying outline plates & with 4 other plates, each with 2 illusts & 2 accompanying outline illusts. Library stamp on tp; some staining & spotting throughout. bba May 14 (270) £480 [Hildebrandt]

Anr copy. Contemp vellum bds; defective. With 47 plates accompanied by 54 outline plates. Some marginal dampstaining. S Nov 27 (245) £420 [Lane]
— Tables of the Skeleton and Muscles.... L, 1749. With 28 plates, plus 12 outline plates. Bound with: Albinus. Compleat System of the Blood-Vessels and Nerves. With 7 plates plus 4 outline plates. Folio, contemp half calf; worn & defective. Marginal dampstaining. S Nov 27 £1,700 [Lane]

Anr copy. With 28 plates, including 12 key plates, but lacks the 1st 12 plates of which

ALBINUS

the latter are outlines. Tp soiled; 2 leaves repaired; some stains. Sold w.a.f. S May 21 (175) £300 [Brandt]

Album...
— Album de la Galerie Contemporaine: Biographies & Portraits. Paris: Revue Illustree, [late 1870s]. Folio, orig cloth; worn. With 11 ports & 1 study of sculpture. sg Nov 13 (53) $700
— Album pintoresco de la Republica Mexicana. Mexico: Michaud y Thomas, [c.1850]. Oblong folio, contemp half lea; worn & soiled. With 45 plates, some colored. wa Mar 5 (393) $3,400
— Album Thijs Maris. Haarlem: Kleinmann, 1900. Illus by C. A. Lion Cachet. Folio, vellum gilt. B Oct 7 (47) HF550

Alcega, Juan de
— Libro de geometria, pratica, y traca, el qual trata de lo tocante al oficio de sastre.... Madrid: Guillermo Drouy, 1589. Folio, contemp vellum. Sig G, the separate folding sheet of patterns, has a small hole affecting 2 letters & small tear. C May 13 (135) £7,000 [Goldschmidt]

Alchabitius
— Libellus isagogicus. Venice: J. & G. de Gregoriis, de Forlivio, 18 Feb 1502. ("Alchabitius cum comento.") Trans by Joannes Hispalensis. 8vo, vellum bds. S Nov 27 (29) £550 [Philadelphia]

Alciatus, Andreas, 1492-1550
— Emblemata. Leiden: Plantin, 1591. 8vo, disbound. sg Oct 9 (186) $225
Anr copy. 16mo, 17th-cent vellum. sg Mar 26 (2) $175
— Les Emblemes. Paris: Chrestien Wechel, 1539. 8vo, mor gilt by Koehler. S June 25 (3) £2,400 [Lanfranchi]
— Paradoxorum ad Pratum, libri sex. Lyons, 1537. 8vo, old calf; rebacked, front cover detached. Last text leaf repaired; index bound at beginning. sg Oct 9 (80) $150

Alcock, Charles William
— Famous Cricketers and Cricket Grounds.... L, [1895]. 18 parts in 1 vol. Folio, cloth; marked. kh Mar 16 (3) A$200

Alcock, Sir Rutherford, 1809-97
— The Capital of the Tycoon. L, 1863. 1st Ed. 2 vols. 8vo, half mor gilt. With 2 folding hand-colored maps (linen-backed) & 16 plates. pn July 23 (101) £260
Anr copy. Orig cloth; chipped, spine torn & repaired. wa Nov 6 (198) $110

Alcott, Louisa May, 1832-88
— Little Women. Bost., 1868. 1st Ed. 8vo, orig cloth; joints split, foot of spine def. S May 6 (184) £50 [Burton-Garbett]

Aldam, W. H.
— A Quaint Treatise on "Flees...." L, 1876. 4to, half mor. With 2 colored plates & the series of 22 specimen flies on sunken mounts. sg Oct 23 (158) $800

Aldin, Cecil, 1870-1935
— An Artist's Models. L, 1930. One of 310. Orig vellum. Ck Sept 5 (104) £100
— Ratcatcher to Scarlet. L, [1926]. One of 100 with a sgd pencil sketch. 4to, orig half vellum gilt. With pictorial title & 15 plates. Ck Dec 10 (251) £160

Aldington, Richard, 1892-1962
— Balls. Westport CT: Pvtly ptd, 1932. "Ninety-nine Copies & a few others have been printed for fun by RWE at the Sign of the Ink Balls". Ptd wraps. sg Dec 11 (153) $300
— The Eaten Heart. Chapelle-Reanville, Eure: The Hours Press, 1929. 1st Ed, One of 200, sgd. 4to, orig half cloth; extremities worn. sg Dec 11 (154) $100
— Hark the Herald. [Paris: Hours Press, 1928]. Copy 8, ptd for Bob Brown. Wraps. sg Dec 11 (155) $425
— Images of War. L, 1919. 1st Ed, one of 120 on handmade paper. Illus by Paul Nash. Half cloth. sg Dec 11 (157) $175
— Last Straws. Paris: Hours Press, 1930. 1st Ed, One of 200 on Haut Vidalon paper, sgd. Worn. sg Dec 11 (158) $100
— Lawrence of Arabia: A Biographical Enquiry. L, 1954. Corrected page proofs. Inscr to Roy Campbell & with holograph corrections. sg Dec 11 (159) $1,200
— Roads to Glory. L, 1930. 1st Ed, one of 360, sgd. Orig half cloth. sg Dec 11 (160) $80

Aldrich, Thomas Bailey, 1836-1917
— Friar Jerome's Beautiful Book. Brooklyn: Valenti Angelo, 1952. One of 75. cb Dec 4 (301) $65

Aldrovandi, Ulisse, 1522-1605
— Monstrorum historia.... Bologna, 1642. Folio, contemp calf gilt; rebacked, corners worn. Lacking last blank in Part 2; engraved title shaved at top; tiny hole in Bb5; Ff2 & 3 misbound. S May 28 (608) £700

Alembert, Jean le Rond d', 1717?-83. See: Diderot & Alembert

Alexander, Conel Hugh O'Donel
[-] The Best Games of C. H. O'D Alexander. Oxford, 1976. Special Tournament Ed, one of 200. In d/j. pn Mar 26 (204) £65 [Pennig]

Alexander, George William
— Letters on the Slave-trade, Slavery, and Emancipation.... L, 1842. 8vo, mor. B Oct 7 (1255) HF500

Alexander, Sir James Edward, 1803-85
— An Expedition of Discovery into the Interior of Africa. L, 1838. 1st Ed. 2 vols. 8vo, modern half mor. With frontis & 6 plates. Inscr. EEA Oct 28 (389) R660
— Salmon-Fishing in Canada, by a Resident. L, 1860. Ed by Alexander. 8vo, half calf gilt. sg Oct 23 (159) $120

Alexander Trallianus
— Libri duodecim; Razae de pestilentia libellus. Venice: Haeredem Hieronymi Scoti, 1573. 16mo, old vellum; endleaves wormed. sg Jan 15 (62) $150

Alexander, William, Earl of Stirling, 1567?-1640
— Recreations with the Muses. L, 1637. 1st Ed. Folio, contemp calf, rebacked. Marginal worming; lacking initial & final blanks. sg June 11 (7) $60

Alexander, William, 1767-1816
— Austrians. L, 1813. ("Picturesque Representations of the Dress and Manners of the Austrians.") 4to, cloth. With 50 hand-colored plates. Some plates & leaves torn. bba Dec 18 (99) £75 [Smith]
Anr copy. Half mor gilt. pn Sept 18 (255) £240 [Bookroom]
— Chinese. L, 1814. ("Picturesque Representations of the Dress and Manners of the Chinese.") 4to, half lea; rubbed. With hand-colored additional title & 49 hand-colored plates.. pn Mar 5 (81A) £220 [Walford]
Anr copy. Half calf; lacking lower cover. With hand-colored title & 49 hand-colored plates. 1 plate torn; some text spotted. pn July 23 (71) £380 [Sweet]
Anr copy. Contemp half mor; worn. Lacking 1 plate. S July 14 (569) £260
Anr copy. Modern half mor gilt. With 50 hand-colored plates. S July 27 (568) £380
Anr copy. Old bds; broken, spine perished. wd June 19 (54) $250
— The Costume of China. L, 1805. 4to, contemp mor gilt by Macnair of Queen Street, with his ticket; rubbed. With 48 hand-colored plates. S Oct 23 (150) £650 [Tang]
Anr Ed. L, [plates dated 1814]. Folio, orig cloth. Text lacking. S Nov 18 (1209) £360 [Remington]

Alexandre, Aaron, c.1766-1850
— The Beauties of Chess, a Collection of the Finest Chess Problems.... L, 1846. Half calf; rubbed. pn Mar 26 (271) £45 [Courthey]
— Encyclopedie des Echecs, ou resume comparatif en tableaux synoptiques. Paris: D'Uturbie & Worms, 1837. 4to, half calf with Signet arms; rubbed. pn Mar 26 (121) £90 [Farmer]

Alexandre, Arsene
— The Decorative Art of Leon Bakst. L, 1913. Notes by Jean Cocteau. Folio, half vellum gilt; rubbed. bba June 18 (230) £360 [Hannan]

Algemeine. See: S., I. F.

Algemene...
— Algemene geschiedenis der Nederlanden. Utrecht, 1949-58. 12 vols. B June 2 (380) HF550

Alger, Horatio, 1832-99
— The Young Miner; or, Tom Nelson in California. San Francisco: Book Club of Calif., 1965. One of 450. Half cloth. cb Sept 11 (13) $50

Alger, William Rounseville. See: Whitman's copy, Walt

Ali Bey, 1766-1818
— Voyages d'Ali Bey el Abassi en Afrique et en Asie.... Paris, 1814. 4 vols, including Atlas. 8vo & 4to, contemp mor gilt, atlas in half mor. Phillipps copy. S June 25 (348) £900

Alicatus, Andreas, 1492-1550
— Emblemata. Leiden: Plantin, 1591. 8vo, old vellum; soiled. Marginal staining; some marginal tears. S Sept 23 (288) £170 [Poel]

Alison, Sir Archibald, 1792-1867
— History of Europe. L, 1860. 10th Ed. 14 vols. 8vo, calf gilt. pnE Oct 15 (53) £190

Aljechin, Aleksandr Aleksandrovich, 1892-1946
— Internationales und 37. Schweizerisches Schachturnier in Zurich 1934. Zurich, [1934]. Modern bds, orig upper wrap set in. pn Mar 26 (88) £50 [Levine]

Alken, Henry, 1784-1851
— A Collection of Sporting and Humourous Designs. L: Thomas M'Lean, 1824. 3 vols. Folio, orig mor gilt. With 314 hand-colored plates, cut round & mtd or inlaid, all within gilt borders, the colors exceptionally fresh. S Apr 23 (78) £25,000 [Craven]

ALKEN

- Ideas, Accidental and Incidental to Hunting, and other Sports.... L, [1826-30]. Folio, modern half mor. With 36 hand-colored plates only. Jeanson 1510. SM Feb 28 (13) FF45,000
- Illustrations to Popular Songs. L, 1823. Oblong folio, orig bds. With 40 (of 43) plates only. pnE Nov 12 (73) £130
- The National Sports of Great Britain. L, 1821. 1st Ed, 1st Issue, with colored title "British Sports" dated 1820. Folio, half mor gilt; worn. With 50 colored plates. Schwerdt-Jeanson copy. SM Feb 28 (14) FF55,000

  Anr Ed. L, 1825. Folio, mor gilt by Riviere. With 50 colored plates. sg Apr 2 (3) $1,600
- Notions. L: Thomas M'Lean, 1831-33. 4to, contemp half mor gilt. With 36 hand-colored plates. Jeanson copy. SM Feb 28 (15) FF14,000
- Scraps from the Sketch-Book. L, 1821. 4to, calf gilt; rebacked. With 42 hand-colored plates. sg June 11 (8) $750
- Some Do, and Some Do Not. L, [1821]. 1st Issue. Oblong folio, loose as issued in portfolio. With 7 hand-colored plates. SM Feb 18 (16) FF18,000
- Sporting Scrap Book. L, [1824]. 8vo, half mor gilt by Lloyd, Wallis & Lloyd. With 50 hand-colored plates. sg Apr 2 (2) $600

  Anr copy. Half mor gilt. With 49 hand-colored plates. Jeanson 1511. SM Feb 28 (18) FF11,000
- A Touch at the Fine Arts. L, 1824. 4to, contemp half mor; rubbed, joint cracking. With 12 hand-colored litho plates. Arms of Daniel Jarvis stamped on tp. C Oct 15 (4) £300 [Quaritch]

All...

- All the Memorials of the Courts of Great Britain and France.... The Hague, 1756. 4to, contemp calf. S Oct 23 (411) £850 [Quaritch]

Allan, John Harrison

- A Pictorial Tour in the Mediterranean. L, 1843. Folio, orig cloth; worn. With litho title heightened with gold & 40 plates. S Feb 23 (119) £400 [Mellon]

  Anr copy. Contemp half mor; worn & broken. With 39 plates. Some stains & foxing; lacking Pompey's Pillar plate. wa June 25 (476) $180

Allason, Thomas, 1790-1852

- Picturesque Views of the Antiquities of Pola, in Istria. L, 1819. 1st Ed. Folio, contemp half mor; worn. With frontis & 9 plates. S Jan 13 (338) £130 [Weinreb]

Allemagne, Henry Rene d'

- Les Accessoires du costume et du mobilier depuis le treizieme jusqu'au milieu du dixneuvieme siecle. Paris, 1928. 3 vols. Folio, orig half cloth; rubbed. bba Apr 23 (67) £180 [Fogg]; bba Apr 23 (67) £180 [Fogg]
- Les Cartes a jouer du XIVe au XXe siecle. Paris, 1906. 2 vols. 4to, half mor, orig wraps bound in. C Dec 3 (1) £850 [Henderson]
- Du Khorassan au pays des Backhtiaris. Paris, 1911. 4 vols. 4to, orig wraps; spines broken, most backstrips worn, loose or def. Inscr. S Jan 12 (310) £600 [Hosains]

Allen, Douglas

- Frederic Remington and the Spanish-American War. NY, [1971]. One of 150. 4to, half lea. Sgd. cb Jan 8 (232) $85

Allen, Ira

- The Natural and Political History of the State of Vermont. L, 1798. 8vo, contemp calf; rubbed & dried. With folding map having hand-colored boundaries. O Sept 23 (2) $700

Allen, James —&
Schoolcraft, Henry Rowe, 1793-1864

- Expedition to Northwest Indians. [Wash., 1834]. 8vo, disbound. With folding map. wa Sept 25 (390) $120

Allen, Jay. See: Quintanilla, Luis

Allen, John Fisk

- Victoria regia; or the Great Water Lily of America. Bost., 1854. Folio, orig bds. With 6 color plates. Horticultural Society of New York—de Belder copy. S Apr 27 (1) £15,000 [Hirsch & Adler]

Allen, Thomas, 1803-33

- A History of the Counties of Surrey and Sussex. L, 1831. 2 vols. 8vo, contemp half mor; worn. With engraved titles & 55 plates on india paper mtd. S May 28 (828) £190
- A New and Complete History of the County of York. L, 1828-31. 3 vols. 4to, later half calf. With frontises, titles & 145 plates, all on india paper, mtd. Ck Sept 26 (55) £120

  Anr Ed. L, 1829-31. 6 vols. 8vo, contemp calf gilt. With frontises & 139 plates only. Lacking ptd titles. S May 28 (827) £140
- The Picturesque Beauties of Great Britain: Kent. L: George Virtue, [c.1830]. 4to, contemp lea gilt; cuffed. With frontis, engraved title, folding map & 128 views on 64 plates. Folding map partially separated at fold. sg Nov 20 (145) $120

  Anr Ed. L: Virtue, 1833. 4to, half calf; rubbed. With engraved title, folding map &

124 views on 62 sheets. pn Dec 11 (88) £220 [Rankin]

Allen, William, 1793-1864
— Picturesque Views in the Island of Ascension. L, 1835. Folio, half calf. With 10 hand-colored plates & with small engraved map on tp. S June 25 (317) £480 [Traylen]
— Picturesque Views on the River Niger.... L, 1840. Oblong folio, contemp half mor; joints & corners rubbed. With 22 plates on 10 sheets, including folding panorama. C Dec 12 (226) £380 [Maggs]
  Anr copy. Orig cloth. Inscr. Ck May 8 (333) £440

Allerton, Reuben G.
— Brook Trout Fishing. NY, 1869. 8vo, orig cloth. With hand-colored folding plate of a brook trout. sg Oct 23 (160) $350

Allestree, Richard, 1619-81
— The Art of Contentment. Oxford, 1675. 1st Ed. 8vo, mor gilt with silvered floral stamps. Hoe copy. pn Nov 20 (56) £550 [Maggs]

Allgaier, Johann, 1763-1823
— Neue theoretisch-praktische Anweisung zum Schachspiel. Vienna, 1795-96. 2 vols. Half calf; rebacked. With 5 plates (3 folding, 2 colored). J. W. Rimington Wilson's signature on both vols. pn Mar 26 (349) £250 [Furstenberg]
— Neue theoretisch practische Anweisung zum Schachspiel. Vienna, 1802. 2 vols in 1. pn Mar 26 (350) £75 [Lewin]

Alliaco, Petrus de
— Concordantia astronomiae cum theologia.... Augsburg: Erhard Ratdolt, 2 Jan 1490. 4to, later vellum; hinges reinforced. Full-page device at end partly hand-colored. Some staining; margin of last leaf repaired. 56 leaves. Goff A-471. Broxborne copy. sg Dec 4 (4) $1,800

Allies'...
— The Allies' Fairy Book. L, [1916]. Illus by Arthur Rackham. Spine faded. With 12 color plates; endpapers stained. sg Oct 30 (6) $50
  1st Ed Deluxe. One of 525, sgd by Rackham. With 12 mtd color plates with lettered tissue guards. sg Oct 30 (5) $550

Allingham, Helen. See: Huish, Marcus Bourne

Allingham, William, 1824-89
— In Fairyland.... L, 1870 [1869]. 1st Ed. Illus by Richard Doyle. 4to, orig cloth; loose. pn Jan 22 (309) £290 [Henderson]
  2d Ed. L, 1875. Folio, orig cloth; worn, rebacked preserving spine. With 16 colored plates. Some stains. S Oct 6 (788) £100

[Thorp]
— The Music Master. L, 1855. 8vo, orig cloth. bba Aug 20 (78) £350 [Elton]

Allioni, Carlo, 1725-1804
— Flora Pedemontana. Turin, 1785. 3 vols in 2. Folio, contemp calf; 1 cover detached, spines & joints rubbed. With 92 hand-colored plates. Lacking port; hole in title to Vol II affecting vignette. de Belder copy. S Apr 27 (2) £4,000 [Boorlot]
  Anr copy. 3 vols. Folio, contemp half calf; rubbed. With port & 92 plates. Lacking 14 leaves from Vol II comprising the list & explanation of the plates & the index. Uncolored de Belder copy. S Apr 27 (2) £1,100 [Rainer]

Allison, Benjamin R.
— The Rockaway Hunting Club. [N.p]: Pvtly ptd, 1952. 4to, cloth. sg Oct 23 (450) $70

Allom, Thomas, 1804-72
— The Counties of Chester, Derby, Leicester, Lincoln, and Rutland, Illustrated. L, 1836. 4to, contemp half calf. With engraved title & 72 views on 36 plates. Engraved title browned. L Dec 11 (126) £120
— Itineraire pittoresque au nord de l'Angleterre.... L, 1835. 4to, orig cloth; soiled. With 72 views on 38 leaves. Ck Nov 21 (457) £45
— Views in the Tyrol. L, [1836]. 4to, orig cloth; broken, lacking spine. bba Dec 18 (100) £80 [Rainer]
  Anr copy. Orig cloth; rubbed. With engraved title, folding map & 45 plates. T May 21 (226) £105

Almack, Edward, 1852-1917
— Fine Old Bindings. L, 1913. One of 200, sgd by pbrs. Folio, orig cloth. bba Mar 12 (262) £240 [Forster]
  Anr copy. Contemp cloth; worn. sg Jan 22 (41) $300

Almagia, Roberto
— Monumenta Cartographica Vaticana. Vatican, 1944-52. 3 vols. Folio, orig half cloth; extremities worn. sg May 14 (184) $150

Almanacs
  See also: Miniature Books
— Agenda ou Almanach du Theatre Francois pour la preente annee. Paris, [1758]. 12mo, contemp mor gilt with arms of Denis-Pierre-Jean Papillon de la Ferte. With 10 pp of Ms notes on plays in a fine hand. C Dec 3 (52) £1,100 [Quaritch]
— Almanac pour les amis de la chasse....1/48. Nuremberg: G. W. Knorr, [1748]. 8vo, mor gilt janseniste by Trautz-Bauzonnet. With 12 plates. Jeanson copy. SM Feb 28 (20) FF28,000

ALMANACS

— Almanach de Versailles, annee 1779. Paris, [1779].. 12mo, contemp mor gilt, with port & arms of Louis XVI. S Nov 27 (30) £300 [Balsenc]

— Almanach des modes. Paris, 1814-22. Vols 1-9 (all pbd). 18mo, orig bds; minor defs. Some plates hand-colored. C Dec 3 (57) £1,850 [Sims]

— Almanach des spectacles, par K. Y. Z. Septieme annee. Paris, 1818-25. 8 vols. 32mo, contemp calf gilt. C Dec 3!158 £1,300 [Biobermuhle]

— Almanach du bon francois.... Paris: Desnos, [1789]. 2 parts in 1 vol. 18mo, contemp mor gilt. Jeanson copy. SM Feb 28 (21) FF8,000

— Almanach du comestibles, necessaire aux personnes de boun gout.... Paris: Desnos, [1778]. 3 parts in 1 vol. 16mo, contemp mor gilt by Riviere. C Dec 3 (79) £750 [Griffiths]

— Almanach iconologique.... Paris, 1765-81. For 1765-81 (all pbd). 17 vols. 18mo, contemp red mor gilt. C Dec 3 (60) £4,000 [Tulkens]

Anr copy. Later half mor by Zaehnsdorf. C Dec 3 (61) £550 [Tenschert]

— Almanach national de France. Paris, [1793]. 8vo, contemp mor gilt; rubbed. With folding map. bba Apr 23 (126) £100 [Frew Mackenzie]

Anr copy. Contemp calf. Last 2 leaves partly stained. pn Nov 20 (110) £95 [Coop]

— Almanach royal.... Paris: Laurent D'Houry, 1724. 8vo, contemp mor gilt. S Nov 27 (34) £250 [Chaponniere]

Anr Ed. Paris: la veuve D'Houry, 1742. 8vo, contemp mor gilt. S Nov 27 (33) £200 [Beoth]

Anr Ed. Paris, 1766. 12mo, contemp mor gilt with rococo plaque of leafy ornaments. S Mar 10 (893) £360 [Cain]

Anr Ed. Paris: Le Breton, [1772]. 8vo, contemp mor gilt with unidentified arms. S Nov 27 (31) £750 [Balsenc]

Anr Ed. Paris, [1783]. 8vo, contemp mor gilt with floral border & flower & fruit design. Sold as a bdg. Sold w.a.f. pn Jan 22 (37) £120 [Cavendish]

Anr Ed. Paris: D'Houry, [1784]. 8vo, contemp mor gilt by Larcher et Cie, with ticket. S Nov 27 (35) £350 [Chaponniere]

Anr Ed. Paris, [1792]. 8vo, contemp mor gilt. With folding map. pn nov 20 (112) £140 [Black]

— Cardanus Rider's British Merlin bedeckt with many Delightful Varieties.... L, 1737. 12mo, contemp mor gilt; upper hinge cracked. pn Nov 20 (115) £160 [King]

— Les Etrennes de Cupidon, Almanach nouveau pour l'annee 1786. Paris, [1786]. 24mo, contemp bds stitched with sequins & metal thread of a balloon carrying the Mongolfier brothers. C Dec 3 (69) £400 [Sourget]

— Etrennes mignonnes pour l'An...MDCCLXX. Strassburg, [1790]. 8vo, contemp mor gilt. HK Nov 4 (1727) DM800

— The Natal Almanac and Yearly Register.... Pietermaritzburg, 1865. ("The Natal Almanac and Yearly Register for 1866.") 8vo, cloth. SSA Oct 28 (760) R580

— Les Situations interessantes, almanach nouveau compose de douze jolies estampes dessinees et gravees par les plus celebres de l'art. Paris: Desnos, [n.d.]. 12mo, contemp mor gilt. With engraved title & 12 plates after Moreau le jeune. C Dec 3 (87) £300 [Beres]

— The Town and Country Almanack for the year 1777.... Edin., [1776]. 16mo, orig mor; rubbed. With folding map. T Sept 18 (516) £42

Almirante, Jose

— Bibliografia militar de Espana. Madrid, 1876. 4to, cloth. sg Oct 2 (220) $60

Alphabet...

— The Alphabet Book in Venezia. Venice, 1975. One of 300. 4to, half vellum. sg Jan 8 (4) $150

— Alphabet ou instruction chrestienne pour les petits enfans. Lyon: Robert Granjon, 1555. Bound with: Horae in Laudem beatissime Virginie Marie ad usum Romanum. Lyon: Robert Granjon, 1555-[58?] 8vo, contemp mor gilt. Lower portion of tp torn away affecting imprint. S June 17 (426) £250 [Dreyfus]

Alphand, Jean Charles Adolphe

— Les Promenades de Paris.... Paris, 1867-73. 2 vols. Folio, bdg not indicated. Library markings. Sold w.a.f. Franklin Institute copy. F Sept 12 (13) $900

Anr copy. 2 vols in 3. Folio, contemp mor gilt, armorial bdg; 1 spine repaired, the others slightly rubbed or torn. With frontis (mtd) & 126 plates & plans, 22 in color & hand-finished. Some marginal browning or staining to 1 text vol. de Belder copy. S Apr 27 (4) £2,000 [Walford]

Alpheraky, Sergius

— The Geese of Europe and Asia. L, 1905. 4to, cloth; dampstained. With frontis & 24 plates. Haverschmidt copy. B Feb 25 (144) HF600

Anr copy. Orig cloth. With colored frontis & 24 color plates. pn Apr 30 (346) £240 [Grahame]

Alting, Menso, the Younger
— Descriptio secundum antiquos agri Batavi & Frisii.... Amst., 1697-1701. 2 parts in 1 vol. Folio, vellum. With engraved title, 3 plates & 15 double-page maps. B Oct 7 (1399) HF500

Alva Ixtlilxuchitl, Fernando de
— Obras historicas. Mexico, 1891-92. 2 vols. 4to, half mor gilt by Jesus Calvillo; spines brittle. sg Sept 18 (4) $110

Alvares, Francisco, Asturian
— Noticia del establecimiento y poblacion de las colonias Inglesas en la America.... Madrid, 1778. 4to, contemp vellum; upper hinge cracked. Crahan copy. P Nov 25 (10) $300

Alvord, Thomas G. See: Derrydale Press

Amadis de Gaul
— Los Quatro libros de Amadis d'Gaula neuvamente impressos.... Venice: Giovanni Antonio de Nicolini da Sabbio for Giovanni Batista Pederzano, 7 Sept 1533. Folio, mor gilt c.1800. With b1 misbound after b7; 1st title remargined at top & fore-edge & soiled; some dampstains; marginal notes in an early hand. S May 21 (22) £2,500 [Israel]

Amadon, Dean. See: Brown & Amadon

Amat y Juniet, Manuel de
— Reglamento para el gobierno de la Adiana de esta ciudad.... Lima, 1773. 4to, contemp vellum. sg Sept 18 (5) $70

Amatus Lusitanus, Pseud. of Joao Rodriguez, de Castelo Branco
— In Dioscoridis Anazarbei de medica materia libros quinque. Strassburg: W. Ribelius, 1554. 4to, contemp pigskin over bds; stained & foxed. O Sept 23 (3) $450

Ambrosius, Saint, 340?-397
— Epistolae. Milan: Antonius Zarotus, 1 Feb 1491. Folio, half vellum. Initials supplied in pink & blue in a modern hand. Outer upper corners of a few leaves at the beginning & end wormed & repaired; 1 small wormhole in text of 1st 6 leaves; tear in fore-margin of k8 carefully repaired just touching but not obscuring the edge of the text on verso; some marginal dampstains. 192 leaves. Goff A-553. Pinelli-Wodhull copy, with notes in Wodhull's hand on flyleaf. S May 21 (2) £700 [Thomas]
— Opera. Basel: Johann Amerbach, 1492. Vol II only. Folio, 18th-cent half vellum; soiled, rear cover wormed. One wormhole in lower blank margins; "in excellent condition". 302 leaves. Goff A551. cb Oct 23 (7) $900
— Anr Ed. Basel, 1555. 5 vols in 3. Folio, old vellum. Erasmus's name inked out on Vol I title; lower portion of titles to Vols I & IV excised & restored. sg Oct 9 (86) $150

American...
— American Academy of Arts and Sciences: Memoirs. Bost., 1785. Vol I. 4to, orig bds; backstrip lacking, covers detached. Lacking plates; some browning. sg Sept 18 (6) $80
— American Archives. Wash., 1837-53. Ed by Peter Force. 4th Series, Vols I-VI & 5th Series, Vols I-III. Folio, disbound or becoming disbound. Series 4, Vols II & V partly waterstained; Series 5, Vol I partly dampstained & lacking front bd; library markings. wa Feb 19 (300) $150
— American Art Review. Bost., 1880-81. Vols I & II in 2 vols. Folio, half mor. sg June 11 (10) $200
Vol I. Bost., 1880. 4to, contemp cloth; front hinge split. ha Mar 14 (125) $250
— American Art by American Artists. NY: Collier, 1914. 4to, cloth; worn. Some fraying or creasing. O Oct 21 (4) $260
— American Book-Prices Current. NY, 1896-1972. Vols 1-75, annual vols for 1895-1969. 8vo, orig cloth, several in d/js; a few hinges cracked or weak. cba Feb 5 (6) $1,100
Indexes for 1941-45, 1945-50, 1950-55. NY, 1946-56. 3 vols. ha Dec 19 (23) $100
Vols 72-90. NY, 1966-84. K June 7 (6) $650
Vols 86-91 & Index for Vols 61-65. NY, 1971-86. Ck Nov 7 (11) £250
Vols 76-83. NY, 1973-78. cba Feb 5 (7) $500
Index vol for 1965-70. NY, 1974. 2 vols. Worn & soiled. wa Sept 25 (56) $80
Vols 85-86. NY, 1979-80. With the 1979 addendum.. cba Feb 5 (8) $225
Index for 1975-79. NY, 1980. 2 vols sg Jan 22 (4) $225
Index for 1975-79 & annual vols for 1980-83. NY, 1980-83. Together, 6 vols. sg Jan 22 (5) $350
Vols 86-87. NY, 1981-82. Worn & soiled. wa Sept 25 (56) $80
Index for 1979-83. NY, 1984. 2 vols. ha Dec 19 (25) $150
Vol 90. NY, 1985. ha Dec 19 (26) $55
Vol 91. NY, 1986. ha Dec 19 (27) $60
— American Etchers. NY, [1929-31]. 12 vols in 3 (complete set). 4to, cloth. sg June 11 (12) $110
— The American Review: a Whig Journal. NY, 1845. Vol I, Nos 2-6. 8vo, modern cloth. ha Dec 19 (244) $120
— American Statesmen: A Series of Biographies. Bost., 1898-1900. Ed by John T. Morse, Jr. 32 vols, 1st Series. 8vo, half mor

gilt. Sold w.a.f. O June 9 (4) $130

— American Turf Register and Sporting Magazine. Balt. & NY, 1829-44. Vols I-XII bound together. 8vo, lea; worn, hinges cracked. Some plates detached or torn. sg Oct 23 (161) $150

American Jewish Publication Society

— Constitution and By-Laws of the American Jewish Publication Society.... Phila.: C. Sherman, 1845. 8vo, orig wraps; chipped & soiled. Dropsie College copy. wa Mar 5 (198) $725

American Type Founders Company

— Specimens of Type, Ornaments and Borders.... [Jersey City, 1923]. 4to, cloth; shaken. sg Jan 22 (303) $50

Amery, Leopold C. M. S.

— The Times History of the War in South Africa. L, 1900-9. 2d Ed. 7 vols, including Index. 8vo, orig cloth; soiled, hinges of Vol V broken. S Nov 18 (936) £50 [Filbert]; SSA Oct 28 (392) R440

Anr copy. 6 vols; without Index. 8vo, orig cloth; rubbed & soiled. T Feb 19 (258) £60

Ames, Daniel T.

— Ames' Compendium of Practical and Ornamental Penmanship. NY, [1883]. Folio, orig cloth; rebacked, rubbed. Sold w.a.f. T Feb 19 (512) £55

Ames, Joseph, 1689-1759 —& Herbert, William, 1718-95

— Typographical Antiquities. L, 1785-90. 3 vols plus Vol IV of the 1819 Ed. 4to, orig wraps, unopened; soiled. With 2 ports & 8 plates. Stained. bba Jan 15 (258) £280 [White]

Anr Ed. L, 1810-19. 4 vols. 4to, mor gilt; rubbed. P Sept 24 (145) $550

Anr copy. Ed by Thomas Frognall Dibdin. Vols I-IV (all pbd). 4to, contemp calf gilt; Vol I rebacked preserving old spine. S July 28 (975) £250

Ames, Richard

— The Bacchanalian Sessions.... L, 1693. 4to, modern bds; soiled. Tp torn; some page numerals cropped; hole in corner of G1 not affecting text; 1st 2 leaves stained in upper margin. S Sept 23 (289) £130 [Knohl]

— The Last Search after Claret in Southwark.... L, 1691. ("The Search after Claret....") 4to, modern half mor by Crahan. Wing A-2989. Crahan copy. P Nov 25 (18) $550

Amhurst, Nicholas, 1697-1742

— Terrae-Filius; or, The Secret History of the University of Oxford. L, 1726. 8vo, contemp half calf; rubbed. Vol I lacks a12; Vol II lacks K5 (reproduced in Ms) & K6; Vol II with E6 torn & def, affecting text; other marginal tears & repairs; some spotting. bba Oct 16 (67) £40 [Martin]

Amic, Yolande

— L'Opaline francaise au XIXe siecle. Paris, 1952. 4to, cloth, in d/j; worn. O Jan 6 (5) $90

Amicis, Edmondo de, 1846-1908

— Holland and its People. NY, 1885. One of 325. 4to, orig cloth; corners frayed. sg Dec 18 (141) $150

Anr Ed. NY: Putnam's, 1885. One of 250 on linen with 2 sets of etchings, but lacking 1 set. 4to, half mor gilt; worn & soiled. wa Sept 25 (239) $170

Amiranashvili, Shalva

— Medieval Georgian Enamels of Russia. NY: Abrams, [c.1964]. In d/j. cb Mar 5 (76) $75

Amis...

— Amis et Amille. Paris: Le Nouveau Cercle Parisien du Livre, 1957. One of 30 for members of the family & those involved in the production. Illus by Andre Derain. 4to, unsewn in orig wraps. With 22 colored illusts. S June 17 (17) £300 [Marks]

Amman, Jost, 1539-91

— Geschlechter Buch: Darinn der loblichen Kaiserliche Reichs Statt Augspurg. Frankfurt: S. Feyrabend, 1580. 2d Ed. Folio, later vellum bds; soiled. With fullpage allegorical cut, 1 full woodcut border & 156 full-page woodcuts of knights in full armor, each with his coat-of-arms & family name. Lower outer corner of K3 repaired just touching the bottom of the coats-of-arms. S Nov 27 (137) £1,400 [Kraus]

— Habitus praecipuorum populorum, tam virorum quam foeminarum singulari arte depicti. Trachtenbuch.... Nuremberg: Hans Weigel, 1577. Folio, contemp blindstamped calf over wooden bds. With 220 full-page woodcuts. Some worming at end. FD June 11 (44) DM11,500

— Thierbuch, sehr kunstliche und wol gerissene Figuren, von allerley Thieren. Frankfurt: S. Feyerabend, 1579. 4to, mor gilt janseniste by Belz-Niedree. Jeanson copy. SM Feb 28 (22) FF68,000

— Venatus et aucupium. Frankfurt: Sigismund Feyerabend, 1582. 4to, 19th-cent mor gilt. With 40 wood-engraved plates. Jeanson copy. SM Mar 1 (369) FF78,000

Amos, William
— Minutes in Agriculture and Planting.... Bost., 1804. 4to, recent half calf gilt. With 7 plain & 2 hand-colored plates & 3 plates containing 10 specimens of dried grass. Strengthened on top fore-edge corner, not affecting text. T June 18 (71) £210

Amours...
— Amours des dames illustres de nostre siecle. Cologne, 1680. 12mo, contemp vellum; worn. Minor defs. sg Mar 26 (3) $50

Amsden, Charles Avery
— Navaho Weaving. Its Technic and History. Santa Ana, 1934. 8vo, cloth. Some foxing. sg Feb 5 (8) $200

Amsinck, Paul
— Tunbridge Wells, and its Neighbourhood. L, 1810. 4to, contemp sheep gilt; joints cracked. With 31 plates, some marginally dampstained. sg Nov 20 (3) $100

Amuchastegui, Axel
— Some Birds and Mammals of South America. L, 1966. One of 250, sgd. Text by Carlos Selva Andrade. Folio, orig half mor. Ck Jan 16 (29) £320; pn Oct 23 (163) £520 [Weldon & Wesley]

— Some Birds and Mammals of North America. L, 1971. Text by Les Line. Folio, orig cloth. With 16 colored plates. Ck June 19 (173) £130

Anr copy. Half mor gilt. pn Oct 23 (162) £280 [Weldon & Wesley]

One of 505. Orig half mor. With 16 colored plates. Ck Jan 16 (28) £240

Some Birds and Mammals of Africa. L, 1979. One of 505. Folio, half mor gilt. pn Dec 11 (226) £200 [Greyfriars]

Amundsen, Roald, 1872-1928
— The South Pole: an Account of the Norwegian Antarctic Expedition in the "Fram." L, 1912. 2 vols. Orig cloth; rubbed. kh Mar 16 (7) A$550

Amundsen, Roald, 1872-1928 —& Ellsworth, Lincoln
— Air Pioneering in the Arctic. NY, 1929. 4to, orig cloth; rubbed & soiled. Library stamps on title; ink stamps on plates. bba Dec 18 (105) £90 [Finch]

Amusemens...
— Les Amusemens de Spa: or, the Gallantries of the Spaw in Germany. L, 1737. 3d Ed. 2 vols. 8vo, contemp calf; worn. With 13 folding plates. Tape repairs to 2 pp in Vol II. cb Feb 19 (a24) $180

Anacreon, 572?-488? B.C.
See also: Nonesuch Press
— 1791. - Odaria.... Parma: Bodoni Press. 8vo, contemp sheep; rubbed. bba Jan 15 (364) £60 [Robertshaw]

Anatomy...
— Anatomy Epitomized and Illustrated.... L, 1737. 8vo, contemp calf; rubbed, rebacked. With 17 folding plates. Some tears & careless folding. bba Jan 15 (395) £130 [Phillips]

Anburey, Thomas
— Travels through the Interior Parts of America. L, 1789. 1st Ed. 2 vols. 8vo, contemp calf; joints cracked. With folding map (hand-colored in outline) & 6 plates. Small tear in fold. S Oct 23 (412) £300 [Traylen]

Anchieta, Joseph, 1533-97
— Sacra Rituum Congregation E mo & R mo D. Card. Imperiali Brasilien.... Rome, 1733. Folio, contemp vellum; def. S Oct 23 (434) £400 [Israel]

Ancient...
See also: Lockhart, John Gibson
— Ancient Cookery. From a Ms. in the Library of the Royal Society, Arundel Collection No 344. L: John Nichols for the Society of Antiquaries, [1790]. 4to, 19th-cent bds; rubbed. Hunt copy. CNY Nov 21 (61) $400

Andersen, Hans Christian, 1805-75
See also: Limited Editions Club
— Danish Fairy Legends and Tales. L, 1846. 8vo, contemp half calf; scuffed & worn, front cover detached. Marginal soiling. cb July 30 (8) $90

— Fairy Tales. L: Heinemann, 1900. Trans by H. L. Braekstad. 2 vols. 4to, orig cloth. cb Sept 11 (235) $60

Anr Ed. L, [1916]. Illus by Harry Clarke. 4to, cloth; soiled, spine chipped. With 27 plain & 13 colored plates. Inscr by Clarke. Ck Feb 13 (109) £150

Anr Ed. L, [1924]. Illus by Kay Nielsen. 4to, orig cloth; bumped. Ck Dec 10 (282) £150; S June 17 (259) £300 [Peters]

One of 500. Orig vellum gilt. cb June 18 (288) $550

Anr copy. Some browning to outer margins. Ck Feb 13 (11) £380

Anr Ed. NY, [1924]. 4to, cloth. With 12 color plates. S Dec 4 (207) £380 [Santin]

Anr copy. Cloth, in torn d/j. sg Jan 8 (175) $80

Anr Ed. L, [1932]. Illus by Arthur Rackham. 4to, orig cloth, in torn d/j. S Oct 6 (848) £120 [Santin]

Anr copy. Cloth; foot of spine dampstained. With 12 color plates. sg Oct 30 (8) $80

1st Ed Deluxe. L: Harrap, 1932. One of 525, sgd by the artist. 4to, orig vellum. With 12 color plates. sg Oct 30 (7) $1,100

Anr Ed. L, 1935. ("Fairy Tales and Legends.") One of 150. Illus by Rex Whistler. S Oct 6 (870) £240 [Thorp]

— Het leelijke jonge eendje. AMst., 1893. Illus by Theo van Hoytema. 4to, cloth, orig wraps pasted on; new endpapers. B Oct 7 (7a) HF500

— Stories. L, 1911. ("Stories from Hans Andersen.") One of 750. Illus by Edmund Dulac. 4to, orig vellum; stained. With 28 colored plates. Several leaves defaced by name stamp. Ck Apr 24 (89) £100

Anr copy. With 28 color plates. S Dec 4 (187) £380 [Thorp]

Anderson, Adam, 1692?-1765

— An Historical and Chronological Deduction of the Origin of Commerce.... L, 1764. 2 vols. 4to, contemp calf; lower joints cracked, small tears to 1 cover. With 3 folding maps. Small scorch mark to last 2 leaves of Vol I affecting a few letters. C Dec 12 (6) £400 [McCrow]

Anderson, Aeneas, fl.1802

— A Narrative of the British Embassy to China.... L, 1795. 1st Ed. 4to, half mor. S Nov 18 (1210) £190 [Sawyer]

Anr copy. Contemp calf gilt. sg Nov 20 (4) $200

Anderson, Andrew A.

— Twenty-Five Years in a Waggon in the Gold Regions of Africa. L, 1887. 2 vols. 8vo, orig cloth. With 14 plates. SSA Oct 28 (393) R210

Anderson, Gary J. —& Brimer, Ann E.

— Salar: The Story of the Atlantic Salmon. [Halifax: Atlantic Salmon Association, 1976]. One of 150. Oblong 4to, cloth. sg Oct 23 (1162) $50

Anderson, George William

— A New, Authentic, and Complete Collection of Voyages Round the World.... L: Alex. Hogg [1784-86). 2d Ed. Folio, contemp calf gilt; most joints split, worn. Lacking 1 map; some maps torn; some plates shaved or frayed; some stains. Sold w.a.f. bba Jan 15 (435) £120 [Grants]

Anr copy. Contemp calf; worn & repaired. Folding map def; some plates cropped, affecting platemark; prelims frayed; lacking list of subscribers & ads at end. bba Mar 26 (332) £280 [Franks]

2d Ed. Folio, contemp calf; worn & loose.

With port, folding map & 155 maps & plates. Some cropping, affecting platemark; some stains & tears, occasionally affecting text; lacking ads at end. bba Mar 26 (331) £300 [Franks]

Anr copy. Modern mor. Extreme corner of frontis torn away. S June 18 (305) £420 [Graton]

Anderson, James, 1662-1728

— Selectus diplomatum et numismatum Scotiae thesaurus. Edin., 1739. Folio, later mor; soiled, extremities rubbed. With engraved frontis, additional title & 181 plates. Ck Nov 21 (147) £180

Anderson, James, 1680?-1739

— Constitutions of the Antient Fraternity of Free and Accepted Masons. L, 1738. ("The New Book of Constitutions.") 4to, calfcontemp mor gilt; rebacked preserving orig spine, corners repaired. Some foxing & discoloration. S July 23 (283) £500 [Quaritch]

Anr Ed. L, 1756. 4to, modern half calf gilt. Some shaving & spotting. S July 23 (284) £300 [Ash]

Anr Ed. L, 1784. 4to, contemp half calf; rubbed. Frontis shaved; hand-colored plate cropped & frayed & stuck to front pastedown. bba Mar 12 (144) £55 [Elliott]

Anr copy. Modern half calf gilt. Some leaves discolored. S July 23 (284) £300 [Ash]

Anderson, James, 1739-1808

— The New Practical Gardener and Modern Horticulturist. L, [c.1875]. 4to, calf gilt; def. With 39 plates, 27 hand-colored. pn Dec 11 (159) £75 [Thomas]

Anr copy. Contemp half calf; rubbed. S Nov 10 (434) £90 [Traylen]

Anderson, John

— Political and Commercial Considerations Relative to the Malayan Peninsula.... Prince of Wales Island [Penang], 1824. 4to, cxontemp mor; rubbed. Watercolor port of the King of Kedah by A. T. Fransiz inserted. S Oct 23 (481) £5,800 [Orientum]

Anderson, John, b.1854

— The Unknown Turner. NY, 1926. One of 1,000. Folio, cloth. sg Feb 5 (319) $70

Anderson, Joseph, 1832-1916 —& Drummond, James, 1816-77

— Ancient Scottish Weapons. L, 1881. One of 500. 4to, orig half mor; spine rubbed, soiled. With 54 colored plates. S Jan 12 (5) £100 [McEwan]

Anderson, Martin
— The Satires of Cynicus. L, 1893. 4to, cloth; worn & soiled. Minor foxing. wa Sept 25 (275) $65

Anderson, Poul
— The Byworlder. L, 1972. 1st Hardcover Ed, Review copy. cb Sept 28 (23) $50
— Three Hearts and Three Lions. Garden City, 1961. In rubbed d/j. cb Sept 28 (37) $160
— Vault of the Ages. Phila., 1952. 1st Ed. In d/j by Paul Orban, stained at rear panel & flap. cb Sept 28 (40) $55

Anderson, Sherwood, 1876-1941
— Winesburg, Ohio.1st Ed, 1st ptg. Cloth; soiled. wa Dec 11 (2) $70

Andersson, Charles John, 1827-67
— Lake Ngami, or Explorations and Discoveries.... L, 1856. 8vo, later cloth. With 15 plates only. 1 plate stained. Ck Sept 26 (317) £40
Anr copy. Orig cloth; worn. With folding map (slightly torn) & 16 plates. S Nov 17 (631) £75 [Negro]

Andre, Albert —& Elder, Marc
— L'Atelier de Renoir. Paris, 1931. One of 500. 2 vols. Folio, cloth, orig wraps bound in. S June 17 (135) £3,200 [Uppstrom]

Andre, Peter. See: Chapman & Andre

Andreae Philopatri. See: Parsons, Robert

Andreini, Giovanni Batista
— L'Adamo, sacra rapresentatione. Milan: Geronimo Bordoni, 1617. 4to, orig vellum; lower cover def. Tear in lower margin of O4 repaired. S May 21 (88) pS480 [Lanfranchi]

Andrelinus, Publius Faustus
— De neapolitana victoria; De beata virgine.... Paris: Felix Baligault, [not before 1495]. 4to, 19th-cent mor gilt; spine end damaged. 6 leaves. Goff A-705. S Nov 27 (138) £900 [De Zayas]

Andreus, Hans, Pseud. See: Cobra

Andrews, James
— The Parterre, or Beauties of Flora. L, 1842. Folio, orig cloth. With 12 hand-colored plates. F Oct 30 (548) $250
Anr copy. Orig cloth; spine torn. pn Sept 18 (298) £550 [Heald]

Andrews, Henry C., fl.1799-1828
— The Botanist's Repository, for New, and Rare Plants. L, 1797-[1813?]. 10 vols. 4to, contemp mor. With 664 colored plates. Some plate captions & figures cut into bdg; lacking letter-press titles. de Belder copy. S Apr 27 (7) £13,000 [M Lan]
— Coloured Engravings of Heaths. L, [1794]-1802-9-[30]. 4 vols. Folio, contemp calf; worn, rebacked with later mor. With 288 hand-finished colored plates. de Belder copy. S Apr 27 (5) £6,500 [Traylen]
— Geraniums: or a Monograph of the Genus Geranium. L, 1805. 2 vols in 1. 4to, contemp mor gilt; rubbed, joints more severely so. With 124 hand-colored plates. de Belder copy. S Apr 27 (6) £12,000 [Minton]

Andrews, John —& Dury, Andrew
— A Map of the Country Sixty-Five Miles round London. L, 1807. Folio, contemp russia; worn & broken. With 20 double-page maps, hand-colored in outline. Ck May 15 (219) £320
— A Topographical Map of Wiltshire. L, 1773. Folio, contemp half calf; worn, joints cracked. With double page key map & 18 double-page sheets, hand-colored in outline. General map creased & margin browned; slight worming to upper blank margin of 1 map. C Apr 8 (1) £400 [Hatchwell]

Andrews, John, Geographer
— A Collection of Plans of the most Capital Cities of Every Empire...in Europe. L, 1772. 2 parts in 1 vol. 8vo, modern cloth. With double-page engraved title & 42 plates. FD June 11 (741) DM5,000
Anr copy. 4to, With double-page engraved title & 42 double-page plans. sg Nov 20 (5) $950

Andrews, Lorrin, 1795-1868
— A Dictionary of the Hawaiian Language.... Honolulu, 1865. 8vo, old half sheep; needs rebdg. Library copy. ha Sept 19 (156) $70

Andrews, Mottram
— A Series of Views in Turkey and the Crimea. L, 1856. Folio, orig half mor; soiled & rubbed, rebacked. With litho title & 17 plates. Some imprints cropped; several lower margins frayed. S Nov 17 (892) £170 [Hickmet]

Andrews, William Loring, 1837-1920
— An English XIX Century Sportsman, Bibliopole, and Binder of Angling Books. NY, 1906. One of 125. Bds. With 17 plates. sg Oct 23 (163) $300
— The Iconography of the Battery and Castle

Garden. NY, 1901. One of 135. O Mar 24 (6) $110

Androuet, du Cerceau, Jacques, fl.1549-84

— Le Premier Volume des plus excellents bastiments de France. Paris, 1576-79. 1st Ed. 2 vols. Folio, 18th-cent bds. With 149 engravings on 124 double leaves. Some spotting of text leaves; 2 plates in Vol I torn with loss. sg Apr 2 (6) $3,800

Angas, George French, 1822-86

— The Kafirs Illustrated.... L, 1849. Folio, contemp half mor; rubbed, joints cracked. With color port & 30 hand-finished colored plates. Some spotting; PLate 2 trimmed with loss of plate titles. Ck May 8 (356) £4,000

— Polynesia; a Popular Description of the Physical Features.... L, [1866]. 12mo, orig cloth; recased. With folding map. kh Mar 16 (8) A$110

— Savage Life and Scenes in Australia and New Zealand. L, 1847. 2 vols. 8vo, orig cloth; spines chipped. With 12 litho plates. C Apr 8 (2) £150 [Clapham]

Angeles, Juan de los. See: Juan de los Angeles

Angelio, Pietro, 1517-96

— Cynegetica. Lyon: Heirs of S. Gryphius, 1561. 4to, contemp Lyonnaise vellum Maioli bdg. Jeanson copy. SM Feb 28 (25) FF170,000

— De aucupio liber primus.... Florence: Giunta, 1566. 4to, 19th-cent shagreen with arms of J. Gomez. Jeanson copy. SM Feb 28 (24) FF5,000

Angelis, Paulus de

— Basilicae S. Mariae majoris.... Rome, 1621. Folio, contemp bds; worn, spine torn. With engraved title & 17 folding plates & plans. Some browning; some plates trimmed with slight loss. pnNY June 11 (108) $375

Angelo, Domenico, 1717?-1802

— The School of Fencing.... L, 1787. Oblong 8vo, contemp half sheep; joints split, worn. Lacking 1 plate; small stain in upper margin of most leaves, affecting some plates. bba Apr 9 (257) £200 [Hildebrandt]

Angelo, Henry

— Angelo's Pic Nic; or, Table Talk. L, 1834. Illus by George Cruikshank. 8vo, mor gilt. With a duplicate plate (uncolored) of the frontis supplied in proof. Bruton-Salomons copy. sg June 11 (135) $200

Angelo, Valenti

— A Battle in Washington Square. NY: Golden Cross Press, 1942. One of 200. cb Dec 4 (117) $65

— Valenti Angelo: Author, Illustrator, Printer. San Francisco: Book Club of Calif., 1976. One of 400. Folio, half cloth, in soiled d/j. cb Sept 6 (15) $300
Anr copy. Half cloth. sg Jan 8 (11) $375

Angelus de Clavasio, 1411-95?

— Summa angelica de casibus conscientiae. Chivasso: Jacobinus Suigus, de Suico, 13 May 1486. 1st Ed. 4to, modern calf. Small holes, repaired, in 2 final leaves; a few leaves soiled, some spotted & discolored. Some underlining of text. 385 (of 388) leaves. Goff A-718. S Nov 27 £2,000 [Fletcher]
Anr Ed. Nuremberg: Anton Koberger, 10 Feb 1492. Folio, old calf over wooden bds; worn, spine def. 310 (of 312) leaves; lacking 1st & last blank. Goff A-722. bba Jan 15 (320) £460 [Fletcher]

Angelus, Johannes

— Astrolabium planum. Venice: Johannes Emericus de Spira for Lucantonio Giunta, 9 June 1494. 4to, Vellum. 174 (of 176) leaves; lacking 2 blanks at end. Goff A-712. sg Apr 2 (7) $3,200

Anghiera, Pietro Martire d'. See: Martyr, Peter

Anglers' Club of New York

— The Anglers' Club Story. Our First Fifty Years, 1906-1956. NY: Pvtly ptd, 1956. One of 750. 4to, cloth. sg Oct 23 (164) $150

— The Best of the Anglers' Club Bulletin 1920-1972. NY, 1972. One of 1,000. sg Oct 23 (165) $80

Anglo-Saxon...

— The Anglo-Saxon Review. L, 1899-1901. Ed by Lady Randolph S. Churchill. Vols I & III-X. Together, 9 vols. Folio, lea, each vol a facsimile of a different early bdg. O Jan 6 (10) $160

Angus, William, 1752-1821

— The Seats of the Nobility and Gentry.... L, 1787. Oblong 4to, contemp half lea; rubbed. With engraved title & 63 plates. bba Apr 9 (258) £130 [Barker]
Anr copy. Contemp half mor; soiled. Ck Nov 21 (255) £280
Anr copy. Contemp calf; hinges cracked, rubbed. With 48 plates. pn Mar 5 (213) £140 [Leighfield]

Anker, Jean Thore Hojer Jensen
— Bird Books and Bird Art. Copenhagen, 1938. 4to, ptd wraps, unopened. With 14 plates. sg May 14 (567) $150

Anley, Charlotte
— The Prisoners of Australia. L, 1841. 12mo, orig cloth; spine chipped. CA Apr 12 (7) A$95

Annabel, Russell. See: Derrydale Press

Annals...
— Annals of Botany. Oxford, 1887-98. Vols 1-12. 8vo, half lea; worn. bba Oct 16 (268) £55 [C. Smith]
— The Annals of Sporting and Fancy Gazette. L, 1822-28. 13 vols. 8vo, contemp half calf gilt. Sold w.a.f. C Oct 15 (5) £2,200 [Blest]
Anr copy. Calf gilt; spines & extremities worn, joints weak. sg Apr 2 (8) $1,600

Annesley, George, Viscount Valentia & Earl of Mountmorris
— Voyages and Travels to India, Ceylon.... L, 1809. 3 vols. 4to, contemp mor gilt; broken. With 69 plates & maps. bba Mar 26 (338) £80 [Hay]
Anr copy. Contemp calf gilt; Vol I rebacked, orig spine laid down. With 69 maps & plates. A few fold breaks. C Oct 15 (109) £500 [Thorp]

Annesley, James
— Memoirs of an Unfortunate Young Nobleman, Return'd from a Thirteen Years Slavery in America where he had been sent by the Wicked Contrivances of his Cruel Uncle. L, 1743. 12mo, modern pigskin. Half mtd, title repaired. S Sept 22 (2) £50 [Cox]

Annual...
— The Annual Anthology. Bristol, 1799-1800. Ed by Robert Southey. 2 vols. 8vo, contemp calf gilt; rebacked. Lacking B8 in Vol I. S Jan 13 (485) £420 [Jarndyce]
— The Annual Register; or, a View of the History, Politics.... L, 1758-93. 33 vols 8vo, contemp calf gilt; joints cracked or starting. sg Mar 26 (4) $300

Another...
— Another Commonplace Book. San Francisco: Grace Hoper Press, 1956. One of 75. Half cloth; yawning slightly. cb Sept 11 (178) $70

Ansaldi, Arnaud. See: Arabian Nights

Anselm, Saint, 1033-1109
— Cantuariensis archiepiscopi, theologorum omnium sui temporis facile principis..... L, 1547. 4to, contemp calf; rebacked & rubbed. Ms notes on front free endpapers & tp; some stains. bba Oct 30 (6) £65 [Maggs]

Anselme de Sainte-Marie, Pere —& Du Fourney, Honore Caille, Sieur
— Histoire genealogique et chronologique de la maison royale de France.... Paris, 1726-33. 3d Ed. 9 vols. Folio, contemp calf gilt with arms of Francois Chartraire, comte de Montigny; worn. Some browning. sg Apr 2 (9) $700

Anselmo, Antonio, Jurist
— Tribonianus Belgicus, sive Dissertationes Forenses, ad Belgarum Principum Edicta. Brussels: B. Vivien, 1663. Folio, later half calf; worn. Some stains & soiling; minor tears & paper flaws. O Nov 18 (25) $50

Anson, George, 1697-1762
— A Voyage Round the World.... L, 1748. 1st Ed. 4to, early calf; rubbed & worn. kh Mar 16 (524B) A$150

Anr copy. Contemp calf; scuffed. With 42 folding maps, charts & plates. pnE Jan 28 (56) £300 [Thin]

Anr copy. Contemp calf; rebacked. Hole at lower margin of 1st few leaves. S Oct 23 (317) £420 [Crete]

Anr copy. Contemp calf; broken. With 42 plates & plans. Map opposite p 236 badly def; anr map cropped; some staining. 2d half of vol with single wormhole at inner lower margin. S Nov 18 (1002) £180 [Lewis]

Anr copy. Contemp calf; rebacked with sheep but broken. With 42 folding maps, charts & plates. sg Apr 23 215 $600

Anr copy. Later calf; worn, covers detached. Lacking 1 plate. wa June 25 (149) $350

Ed not given. 4to, calf; defective. With 42 folding maps, charts & plates. pn Jan 22 (34) £160 [Bookroom]

Anr Ed. L, 1749. 4to, contemp calf gilt; joints splitting, rubbed. With 42 plates & maps. A few plates with small tears. bba Aug 28 (291) £150 [Dailey]

9th Ed. L, 1756. 4to, contemp calf; worn. With folding frontis & 41 plates, maps & charts. C Dec 12 (7) £210 [Griffiths]

Anr copy. Contemp calf gilt; joints cracked. Ck May 15 (68) £140

15th Ed. L, 1780. 8vo, later cloth; tear in 1 chart repaired. With 3 folding maps. Tear in 1 chart repaired. CA Apr 12 (8) A$100

Ansrasy, Mano, Count —& Others
— Les chasses et le sport en Hongrie. Pest, [1857]. Folio, orig half lea, presentation bdg with upper cover gilt-lettered: "To Miss Augusta Warburton from Baron Andor Orczy". Lacking 6 color plates; 1

plate with marginal defs. Sold w.a.f. CNY May 11 (2) $500
Anr copy. Half shagreen. With 25 plates (13 full-page);. Jeanson 1565. SM Feb 28 (23) FF62,000

Ansted, David T.
— The Gold-Seeker's Manual. L, 1849. 12mo, orig cloth; spine chipped, front hinge racked. Tp stamped. sg Apr 2 (10) $850

Anstey, Christopher, 1724-1805
— The New Bath Guide. L, 1830. 8vo, mor gilt by Ramage. With 6 plates, 5 by Cruikshank, with later hand-coloring. sg Feb 12 (51) $110

Antigua
— Ansichten von Missions-Niederlassungen der evangelischen Brueder-Gemeinde. Basel: Birmann & Fils, [c.1830]. Folio, modern half mor. With 4 hand-colored views. Lacking text leaflet. S Apr 23 (286) £1,000 [Rosenkilde]

Antiquites...
— Antiquites mexicaines, relation des trois expeditions du Capitaine Dupaix. Paris, 1834-44. 12 parts in 1 vols. Folio, contemp half mor gilt; rubbed. With map, litho frontis & 166 plates on 161 leaves plus 10 duplicate plates colored by hand. S Apr 24 (288) £5,300 [Rainer]

Antoninus, Brother. See: Everson, William

Antoninus Florentinus, Saint, 1389-1459
— Chronicon. Nuremberg: Anton Koberger, 10 Jan 1491. Part 3 only. Contemp blind-stamped calf over wooden bds; torn, lacking clasps. Some marginal worming; tear in text of g7; some soiling. 340 leaves. Goff A-799. S Sept 23 (290) £260 [Scarre]
— Summa confessionum. Strassburg: Johann Grueninger, 17 Aug 1490. ("Confessionale. Defecerunt scrutantes scrutinio.") Vol II (of 4) only. Folio, contemp South German pigskin over wooden bds. Chained bdg with 6-link iron chain attached to ring at top of rear cover. 1st 40 leaves severely gnawed in outer margins with varying loss. 272 leaves. Goff A-877. sg Oct 9 (87) $1,400
Anr Ed. Toledo, 1511. ("Summa de confessione.") 4to, old vellum; worn & loose. Dampstained. sg Oct 9 (2) $500
— Summa theologica. Venice: Nicolaus Jenson, 1478-80. 2d Ed of Part 1; 5th Ed of Part 2. 2 vols. Folio, 18th-cent vellum; lower covers of both vols torn. Vol I with 1st & last leaves backed & with holes in 1st & last 3 leaves with minimal damage. Vol II with 2 small wormholes as far as b2 with slight loss of text & light waterstains in both vols. 254 leaves & 321 (of 323) leaves;

without the 1st leaf with the prefatory epistle & the last leaf with the register. Goff A-872. S May 21 (3) £800 [Mauss]

Antonio, Nicolas
— Bibliotheca Hispana vetus [Hispana nova]. Madrid, 1788. 2d Ed. 4 vols. Folio, modern cloth; worn, spine ends chipped, 1 cover partly detached. sg Oct 2 (32) $650
— Censura de Historias Fabulosas, Obra Posthuma. Valencia, 1742. Folio, contemp vellum. sg Mar 26 (5) $350

Antonius de Bitonto
— Sermones dominicales per totum annum. Strassburg: Johann Reinhard Grueninger, 25 Jan 1496. 8vo, old calf; front cover detached. Marginal stains; some headlines shaved; tp trimmed & mtd; lacking the 2 blanks. 254 (of 256) leaves. Goff A-892. sg Mar 26 (6) $500

Anville, Jean Baptiste Bourguignon d', 1697-1782
— Nouvel Atlas de la Chine.... The Hague, 1737. Folio, modern vellum. With 42 maps, the 1st 2 with contemp outline hand-coloring. Mtd on guards throughout. C Apr 8 (3) £2,600 [Blackwell]
Anr copy. Later half lea; endpapers renewed, orig stubs occasionally reinforced with modern paper. With 42 maps, the 1st 2 hand-colored in outline. sg Dec 4 (7) $1,700
— Proposition d'une mesure de la terre.... Paris, 1735. 12mo, contemp vellum; worn. With folding map. sg Mar 26 (7) $175

Anysius, Janus
— Varia poemata et satyrae. Naples: Johann Sultzbach, 1531. 4to, disbound. Some dampstains; stains on title; oxidized with resulting holes; last leaf soiled & frayed. sg Oct 9 (89) $130

Apianus, Petrus, 1495-1552
— Astronomicum Caesareum. Leipzig, [1967]. One of 750. Folio, mor gilt. sg Apr 2 (11) $1,400
— La Cosmographia. Antwerp: Jean Bellere, 1575. 4to, old vellum; worn, dampstaining in lower outer corners. With 1 volvelle & mtd folding map, lacking outer half. sg Jan 15 (282) $225
— Cosmographicus liber. Antwerp: I. Bellerus, 1594. ("Cosmographia, sive descriptio universi orbis....") Folio, contemp blind-tooled vellum; stained, 1 joint splitting at top. Waterstains; some wormholes; 2 leaves with volvelles on a stub & shorter at head & foot but not supplied from anr copy; some volvelles lacking. B Oct 7 (1339) HF3,200

Apicius Coelius,, fl.14-37 A.D.

— De opsoniis et condimentis.... L, 1705. 8vo, contemp calf; upper joint cracked. Minor repairs, affecting text of 1 preface leaf. Crahan copy. P Nov 25 (20) $550

— De re coquinaria libri decem. Milan: Guillermus Le Signerre (Johannes de Legnano), 20 Jan 1498. ("De re coquinaria.") 1st Ed, variant issue with title "Appicius Culinarius," device of the pbr & the letter to Merula. 4to, old half calf; worn. Tp rehinged; wormhole in margin through all but last gathering of book not affecting text. 42 leaves. Goff A-921. Simon-Crahan copy, P Nov 25 (22) $16,000

Anr Ed. Venice: Bernardinus Venetus, [c.1500]. 4to, 16th-cent mor gilt with blank shield in center; rebacked, rubbed. 32 leaves only. Goff A-922. Westbury copy. pn Sept 18 (84) £2,600 [Rota]

Anr Ed. Lyons: S. Gryphius, 1541. ("De re culinaria libri decem....") 8vo, mor. HN May 20 (1629) DM2,300

Apollonius Rhodius, 240-186 B.C.

— Argonauticorum libri quatuor. Oxford, 1777. 2 vols in 1. 8vo, contemp mor, armorial bdg; some wear. S Nov 10 (359) £80 [Mackenzie]

Apperley, Charles J., 1777?-1843

— The Life of a Sportsman; by Nimrod. L, 1842. 1st Ed, 1st Issue. 8vo, mor gilt by Riviere. With engraved title, port & 34 plates, all hand-colored. sg Apr 2 (15) $1,400

2d Issue. Half calf. With hand-colored title & 35 hand-colored plates. pn Mar 5 (5) £580 [Map House]

Anr copy. Orig cloth. With 36 hand-colored plates. pnE Jan 28 (283) £1,000 [Josephs]

Anr Ed. L, 1874. 8vo, cloth. With hand-colored engraved title & 38 hand-colored plates. sg May 21 (13) $500

Anr Ed. L, 1901. One of 60 L.p. copies. 2 vols. Folio, orig half cloth. With 36 plates, each in 2 states, plain & hand-colored. pn Mar 5 (299) £140

Anr Ed. L, 1905. 8vo, orig cloth; rubbed. T July 16 (97) £130

Anr Ed. L, 1914. pn Sept 18 (11) £130 [Goddard]

— Memoirs of the Life of the Late John Mytton, Esq. L, 1835. 1st Ed. Illus by Henry Alken. 8vo, orig cloth. With 12 hand-colored plates. pnE Jan 28 (280) £320 [Traylen]

Anr copy. Lev gilt by Riviere, orig cloth bound in. sg Apr 2 (13) $900

2d Ed. L, 1837. 8vo, mor gilt by Riviere. With engraved title & 18 hand-colored plates. pnE Jan 28 (281) £280 [Traylen]

Anr copy. Lev gilt by Riviere, orig covers bound in. sg Apr 2 (14) $850

3d Ed. L, 1851. 8vo, half calf gilt; rubbed. With engraved title & 18 hand-colored plates. Some leaves torn. pn Dec 11 (117) £150 [Plinke]

Anr copy. Orig cloth; discolored. S July 14 (285) £210

Anr copy. Mor gilt by Riviere; joints rubbed. With engraved title & 19 hand-colored plates. Some marginal stains. sg Feb 12 (8) $375

Anr copy. Orig cloth; worn. With engraved title & 18 hand-colored plates. sg June 11 (9) $130

4th Ed. L, 1869. ("The Life of John Mytton.") Orig cloth. With engraved title & 18 colored plates. pnE Jan 28 (282) £130 [Traylen]

5th Ed. L, 1870. 8vo, contemp mor gilt. With engraved title & 18 colored plates. HK Nov 4 (1880) DM900

Anr copy, Contemp mor gilt by Morrell. Some browning. HK Nov 4 (1881) DM800

Anr copy. Orig cloth; spine torn. With engraved title & 18 color plates. pn Jan 22 (99) £190 [Gibbs]

Anr copy. Orig cloth; lacking small portion of backstrip. With engraved title & 18 colored plates. sg May 21 (12) $175

Anr Ed. L, 1877. 8vo, orig cloth; worn. O June 9 (5) $250

— Nimrod Abroad. L, 1843. 2 vols. 8vo, mor gilt, orig cloth bound in. sg Feb 12 (7) $130

— Nimrod's Northern Tour. L, 1838. 8vo, contemp half calf; worn. Inscr to W. M. Thackeray & with folded broadside A Hunting Song inscr to Thackeray mtd to rear pastedown. sg June 11 (16) $550

— Sporting; Embellished by Large Engravings and Vignettes Illustrative of Field Sports.... L, 1838. 4to, contemp half mor; rubbed. With engraved title & 22 plates on india paper mtd. S Nov 10 (583) £90 [Way]

Anr copy. Contemp mor gilt; rubbed. With engraved title & 22 plates. S Nov 10 (584) £80 [Barker]

Appert, Nicholas, 1750-1841

— The Art of Preserving all Kinds of Animal and Vegetable Substances for Several Years.... L, 1811. 1st English Ed. 8vo, orig bds; spine worn, joints cracking. Westbury-Crahan copy. P Nov 25 (27) $450

Appian of Alexandria
— Historia Romana. Venice: Bernhard Maler, Erhard Ratdolt & Petrus Loeslein, 1477. 2 parts in one. Folio, 16th-cent calf rebacked with 18th-cent mor; scratched. Light staining in top margin of 2 leaves. A few marginal notes in various hands. 342 (of 344) leaves; lacking initial blank to each part. Goff A-928. S Nov 27 (5) £4,800 [Fletcher]
— Romaikon keltike...Romanarum historiarum. Paris: Charles Estienne, 1551. Folio, later half mor; rubbed. bba Jan 15 (327) £75 [Callea]

Appier, Jean (called Hanzelet) —& Thybourel, Francois
— Recueil de plusieurs machines militaires et feux artificiels pour la guerre, & recreation. Pont-a-Mousson, 1620. 1st Ed. 7 parts in 1 vol. 4to, half calf gilt; spine worn. FD June 11 (2665) DM3,600

Appleton & Co., Daniel
— Appleton's Cyclopaedia of American Biography. NY, 1887-89. Ed by J. G. Wilson & John Fiske. 7 vols, including 1902 Supplement. 4to, half mor, Supplement in cloth; rubbed & scuffed. Library markings in Supplement. sg Sept 18 (13) $275

Anr copy. 6 vols. 4to, half mor; corners rubbed. sg Feb 12 (9) $375

Anr copy. Modern cloth. sg June 11 (17) $275

Anr Ed. NY, 1888-89. 6 vols. 4to, half mor; rubbed. cb July 30 (10) $280

— Appleton's Dictionary of Machines, Mechanics, Engine-Work, and Engineering. NY, 1852. 4to, half lea; broken. wa Nov 6 (31) $70

Apponyi, A.
— Hungarica, Ungarn Betreffende im Auslande Gedruckte Buecher.... Munich, 1903-27. 4 vols. Half cloth, orig wraps bound in. sg May 14 (248) $350

Apuleius, Lucius
— Asinus aureus. Gouda, 1650. ("Metamorphoseos libri XI.") 2 parts in 1 vol. 8vo, vellum; back damaged, stained. With port. B Feb 25 (832) HF240
— Cupid & Psyche. L, 1935. One of 130. Trans by J. H. Mason; illus by Vivien Gribble. 4to, vellum. sg Jan 8 (6) $80

Aquaviva di Aragona, Belesarius
— De venatione et de aucupio.... Naples: J. Pasquet, 1 Aug 1519. Bound with: De instituendis liberis principum. Naples, 7 May 1519. And: Prefatio paraphrasis in economica Aristotelis. Naples, 5 June 1519. Folio, 19th-cent calf gilt. Jeanson copy.

SM Feb 28 (29) FF38,000

Aquila...
— Aquila. Annales Instituti Ornithologici Hungarici. Budapest, 1922-84. Vols 29-91. 63 vols in 33. B Feb 24 (2) HF650

Arabian Nights
— 1839-41. - The Thousand and One Nights. L. Edward William Lane's trans. 3 vols. 8vo, later half mor gilt. bba Oct 30 (169) £220 [Fogg]

Anr copy. Contemp lea; spine ends worn. sg Apr 23 (6) $100

— 1885-88. - The Book of the Thousand Nights and a Night, with Supplemental Nights. Benares: Kamashastra Society Sir Richard F. Burton's trans. 16 vols. 8vo, orig cloth; worn. A few leaves detached. Ck Oct 17 (67) £75
— 1900-1. - [Denver: Burton Society] One of 1,000. 16 vols. 8vo, orig cloth. ha May 22 (50) $80
— c.1905]. - [N.p.Medina Ed, one of 1,000. 17 vols, including Supplemental Nights. 8vo, half mor gilt. sg Sept 11 (3) $400
— 1920-21. - Le Livre des mille nuits et une nuit. Paris One of 100. Trans by J. C. Mardrus. 16mo, contemp half mor; rubbed. bba Sept 25 (264) £100 [Sambarth]

— The Adventure of Hunch-Back, and the Stories connected with it.... L, 1814. Illus by Wm. Daniell after Robt. Smirke. Folio, contemp half calf; rubbed. T July 16 (321) £120

Anr copy. Mor gilt; rubbed. L.p. copy. wa Mar 5 (17) $210
— The Arabian Nights: Tales from the Thousand and One Nights. L, [1924]. Illus by Edward J. Detmold. bba Jan 15 (209) £80 [Henderson]
— Sinbad der Seefahrer. Berlin, 1908. One of 300. Illus by Max Slevogt. Folio, orig vellum. HN Nov 26 (2126) DM1,200
— Sinbad the Sailor. L, [1911]. Illus by Edmund Dulac. 4to, orig cloth. With 23 colored plates. cb Sept 11 (244) $85; sg Jan 8 (66) $110
— Ansaldi, Arnaud. - Sinbad le Marin. Nice: Joseph Pardo, 1970. Unique copy on japon nacre with suite of illusts on japon nacre, 2 suites of the illusts in red & sepia outline on japon fantasie; watercolor drawings for 1 full-page illust & 1 border & 3 other large watercolor drawings. Folio, mor gilt with recessed panel containing a hand-painted illust on vellum. With large watercolor drawing for the double-page illust, large watercolor on vellum & large painting on wooden bd, all sgd & framed. S June 17 (66) £1,800 [Schoem]

Arago, Dominique Francois Jean, 1786-1853

— Le daguerrotype. Paris: Bachelier, 1839. 4to, modern wraps, unopened. In: Comptes rendus hebdomadaires des seances de l'Academie des Sciences. Tome Neuvieme (July-Dec 1839), pp 250-67. sg Nov 13 (40) $275

— Rapport de M. Arago sur le Daguerreotype... Paris, 1839. 8vo, orig wraps, unopened. bba May 14 (297) £380 [Phelps]

Arago, Jacques Etienne Victor, 1790-1855

— Promenade autour du monde.... Paris, 1822. 3 vols. 8vo & folio, contemp bds, Atlas not quite uniform. With map & 25 plates. S Oct 23 (509) £1,000 [Perrin]

Anr copy. 2 vols. 8vo & folio, mor. S Apr 24 (367) £500 [Saweres]

— Souvenirs d'un aveugle, voyage autour de monde. Paris, [1843]. 2 vols in 1 8vo, orig half mor; rubbed, upper joint with def. kh Mar 16 (10B) A$220

Aranda, Antonio de

— Verdadera Informacion de la Tierra Sancta.... Alcala, 1584. 8vo, old sheep; worn, front endpaper imperf. Browned & damp stained; corner off C5 with minimal loss. sg Oct 9 (3) $100

Aratus of Soli, c.315-c.245 B.C.

— Phaenomena.... Paris: Guil. Morelium, 1559. 4to, later calf; worn, joints starting. wa Sept 25 (528) $170

Arber, Agnes

— Herbals. Their Origin and Evolution. Cambr., 1938. sg May 14 (569) $175

Arber, Edward, 1836-1912

— The First Three English Books on America.... Birm., 1885. 4to, cloth, unopened. sg Oct 2 (33) $70

Arbuthnot, John, 1667-1735

— An Essay concerning the Effects of Air on Human Bodies. L, 1733. 1st Ed. 8vo, modern half calf. bba May 14 (298) £130 [Elliott]

— Tables of Ancient Coins, Weights and Measures.... L, 1727. 4to, contemp calf; worn, joints cracked. With 18 plates. sg Mar 26 (8) $120

Arcadian. See: Silesio, Mariano

Arch, John

— Memoir of...a Cherokee Young Man. Bost., 1832. 2 parts in 1 vol. 16mo, later half mor; rebacked. sg Mar 12 (51) $110

Archaeological...

— The Archaeological Journal. L, 1845-84. Vols 1-41. 8vo, orig cloth. C July 22 (4) £260

Archenholtz, Johann Wilhelm von, 1743-1812

— Memoires concernant Christine, Reine de Suede.... Amst., 1751-60. 4 vols. 4to, later 18th-cent mor gilt with arms of Paul I, Emperor of Russia. sg Oct 9 (152) $500

Archer, Sir Geoffrey Francis —& Godman, Eva M.

— The Birds of British Somaliland and the Gulf of Aden.... L, 1937-61. 4 vols. 4to, cloth. With 34 plates. Haverschmidt copy. B Feb 24 (242) HF1,200

Archimedes, 287?-212 B.C.

— Opera. Venice: Aldus, 1558. 2 parts in 1 vol. Folio, vellum bds; soiled. Spotted & stained. S Nov 27 (246) £420 [Quaritch]

Anr Ed. Oxford, 1792. Ed by Joseph Torelli. Folio, contemp calf. Library markings. Sold w.a.f. Franklin Institute copy. F Sept 12 (146) $450

Arctic...

— Arctic Bibliography. Wash. & Montreal, 1953-69. 12 vols. Some vols worn. ha Sept 19 (77) $55

Arctic Blue Books. See: England

Arcussia, Charles d', 1545-1617

— La Fauconnerie.... Aix: Jean Tholosan, 1598. 8vo, 18th-cent lea gilt; rubbed. Jeanson copy. SM Feb 28 (31) FF270,000

Anr Ed. Paris: Jean Houze, 1605. Bound with: Gommer, Pierre et Francois de. De l'autourserie et de ce qui appartient au vol des oiseaux. Paris, 1605. 8vo, contemp vellum. Jeanson copy. SM Feb 28 (32) FF38,000

Anr Ed. Rouen, 1643-44. 2 parts in 1 vol 4to, mor gilt. Jeanson 1278. SM Feb 28 (34) FF24,000

Ardeola...

— Ardeola. Revista Iberica de Ornitologia. Madrid, 1954-82. Vols 1-29. 29 vols plus the special number Homenaje al Fr. Bernis, 1971. B Feb 24 (5) HF450

Arena, Filippo

— La Natura e Coltura de'Fiori.... Palermo, 1767-68. 3 vols. 4to, contemp vellum. With 65 double-page plates. 13 plates slightly wormed in fold & with some loss. de Belder copy. S Apr 27 (9) £2,400 [Renard]

ARENAS

Arenas, Pedro de
— Vocabulario manual de las lenguas Castellana, y Mexicana. Los Angeles, 1793 8vo, 19th-cent half mor. Contents stained. cb Jan 8 (183) $130

Aretino, Pietro, 1492-1556
— De le lagrime d'angelica. [Venice?], 1555. 8vo, later calf gilt; spine rubbed. Some foxing. bba Aug 28 (88) £110 [Hesketh & Ward]

Argenti, Philip Panteles
— The Costumes of Chios. L, 1953. One of 500. 4to, orig cloth; worn. With 111 plates. sg June 4 (96) $150

Argote de Molina, Gonzalo, 1549-90
— Libro de la Monteria que mando escrivir...Rey Don Alonso de Castilla.... Seville: A. Pescioni, 1582. Folio, 19th-cent mor; joints rubbed. Small piece of upper outer corner of 1st 12 leaves repaired. Streeter-Crahan copy. P Nov 25 (29) $3,000

Anr copy. Mor gilt with arms of the Duc d'Olivares. Jeanson 1540. SM Feb 28 (36) FF72,000

Arias Montanus, Benedictus, 1527-98
— Naturae historia.... Antwerp: Plantin, 1601. 4to, contemp vellum; worn. Browned. T Sept 18 (330) £105

Aringhus, Paulus
— Roma subterranea novissima. Paris, 1659. 2 vols in 1. Folio, late 18th-cent russia gilt; spine worn. sg Oct 9 (91) $300

Ariosto, Ludovico, 1474-1533
— Orlando furioso. Venice: Gabriel Giolito, 1546. 8vo, 18th-cent vellum; recased, with later endpapers. cb Oct 23 (12) $75

Anr Ed. Venice, 1580. 4to, vellum. Stained, 1 leaf torn. B Oct 7 (1340) HF400

Anr copy. 18th-cent calf; scratched, joint worn. 1st corner torn within woodcut borders. S Nov 27 (136) £380 [DeZayas]

Anr Ed. Venice: Felice Valgrisi, 1603. 4to, contemp sheep; front free endpapers & upper cover detached. Worming to inner margin of 1st 40 leaves, affecting some text & illusts; 1 leaf with small tear; 1 small burn-hole slightly affecting text. bba Apr 23 (101) £75 [Rainer]

Anr Ed. Venice: Zatta, 1772-73. 4 vols. 4to, contemp half calf. With engraved titles, frontis, port & 57 plates. C Dec 12 (289) £650 [Spelmen]

AMERICAN BOOK PRICES CURRENT

Anr Ed. Birm.: Baskerville, 1773. 4 vols. 8vo, contemp calf; chipped, joints starting. sg Mar 26 (10) $275

Anr Ed. L, 1783. 5 vols. 8vo, contemp calf; soiled. wa Mar 5 (161) $130

Aristophanes, 448?-380? B.C.
See also: Limited Editions Club
— Comoediae undecim. Leiden: Raphelengius, 1600. 16mo, 18th-cent calf in a German silver bdg over red velvet, pierced & chased with a design of roses, thistles, etc.. Sold as a bdg w.a.f. J. H. Frere's copy. S June 25 (56) £480 [Symonds]
— The Eleven Comedies. NY, 1928. Illus by Jean de Bosschere. 2 vols. Half mor gilt by Sangorski & Sutcliffe. With 12 plain & 12 colored plates. cb Sept 11 (237) $300
— Komodiai ennea. Comoedia novem. Amst., 1670. 2 vols. 12mo, 18th-cent mor gilt. S May 21 (89) £300 [Bouvier]
— Lysistrata. L: Fanfrolico Press, 1926. One of 725. Trans by Jack Lindsay; illus by Norman Lindsay. 4to, half mor; worn. bba July 16 (358) £80 [Hannas]

Anr Ed. Sydney: Fanfrolico Press, 1926. One of 40. Folio, mor, in d/j. CA Apr 12 (167A) A$300
— Women in Parliament. L: Fanfrolico Press, 1929. One of 500. Trans by Jack Lindsay; illus by Norman Lindsay. Folio, orig half mor gilt. CA Apr 12 (168) A$380; pnE June 17 (175) £85

Aristotle, 384-322 B.C.
— De natura animalium.... Venice: Aldus, 1503-4. Folio, 18th-cent half calf. Inscr at foot of title partly deleted with damage to paper; a few small wormholes at beginning; several fore-margins repaired. S May 21 (24) £950 [Sokol]
— L'Ethica. Florence, 1550. 8vo, vellum bds. Some foxing. S Sept 23 (417) £190; S Mar 10 (1013) £190 [Maggs]
— Opera. Basel: J. Bebel & M. Isingrinius, 1550. Folio, later calf; worn. Later ink annotations; some worming. bba Mar 12 (97) £280 [Poole]
— Politiques, or Discourses of Government. L: Adam Islip, 1598. 1st Ed in English. Folio, old vellum; hinges cracked. First gathering with upper margins cropped; some browning; lacking initial & final blanks. sg June 11 (18) $425
— Problemata .... Frankfurt: Peter Brubach, 1548. Bound with: Cocles, Bartholomaeus. Physiognomiae & chiromantiae compendium. Strassburg: Johannes Albrecht, 1536. 8vo, contemp Louvain bdg by Jacob Baten,

stamped in blind on both covers with a panel of Hope; upper cover repaired, head of spine damaged. S Nov 27 (37) £1,250 [Forum Arts]
— Il Segreto de Segreti, le Moralita.... Venice: Giovanni Tacuino da Trino, 1538. 4to, old vellum. Dampstained at end. Sometimes attributed to Aristotle. sg Mar 26 (11) $60

Arkham...
— The Arkham Collector. Sauk City: Arkham House, 1967-71. Nos 1-10 Orig self-wraps. cb Sept 28 (47) $65

Anr copy. Nos 1-10. Orig Arkham cloth bdg with orig self-wraps bound in. cb May 7 (302) $00

— The Arkham Sampler. Sauk City: Arkham House, 1948-49. 8 issues from Spring 1948 to Winter 1949. Wraps; minor wear & tears. cb Sept 18 (48) $160

Anr copy. 7 Issues; lacking Vol I, No 3. Some tape repairs. cb May 7 (303) $110

Arkwright, William
— The Pointer and his Predecessors. L, 1902. Out-of-series copy. 4to, cloth, in d/j. sg Oct 23 (172) $200

Arland, Marcel
— Maternite. Paris, 1926. One of 960. Illus by Marc Chagall. HK Nov 4 (2936) DM1,700

Armaille, Louis Ambroise Henri d'
— Chasse a courre du chevreuil. Segre: Typographie Martin-Gueret, 1881. One of a few on papier verge & hors commerce. 8vo, mor gilt by Chambolle-Duru. Jeanson copy. SM Feb 28 (37) FF10,000

Armand-Dunaresq, Charles Edouard
— Uniformes de l'Armee Francaise en 1861. Paris: Lemercier, 1861. Folio, orig half cloth. With 56 plates. Some foxing. pn Jan 22 (259) £850 [Shapero]

Armitage, Albert Borlase
— Two Years in the Antarctic. L, 1905. 1st Ed. Cloth; rubbed & soiled. Inscr. bba Feb 5 (346) £80 [Morrell]

Armitage, John, 1807-56
— The History of Brazil.... L, 1836. 2 vols. 8vo, orig bds; damaged, spines partly perished. wd Nov 12 (88) $50

Armitage, Merle
— The Lithographs of Richard Day. NY, 1932. One of 500. Folio, bds. Sgd by Day. O Mar 24 (8) $80
— Rockwell Kent. NY, 1932. One of 550. 4to, half cloth, in tape-repaired d/j. cb Dec 4 (218) $70

Anr copy. Half cloth, in chipped d/j. cb June 18 (240) $75

— Warren Newcombe. NY, 1932. One of 500, with a sgd litho by Newcombe. 4to, wraps; soiled & rubbed. With frontis & 38 plates. cb July 30 (12) $70

Armstrong, Edmund Archibald
— Axel Herman Haig and his Work. L, 1905. 4to, cloth. sg June 4 (160) $80

Armstrong, John, of Minorca
— The History of the Island of Minorca. L, 1756. 2d Ed. 8vo, calf; rubbed. With folding map (with slight tear) & 4 plates. S Nov 17 (632) £80 [Scott]

Armstrong, John, 1758-1843
Notices of the War of 1812. NY, 1840. 2 vols. 8vo, orig cloth; front joint splitting. Marginal dampstains; some foxing. cb Dec 18 (6) $80

Armstrong, Mostyn John
— An Actual Survey of the Great Post-Roads between London and Edinburgh. L, 1776. 8vo, contemp calf; broken. With engraved title, general plan & 44 maps, with some boundaries hand-colored. S Jan 12 (68) £170 [George]
— A Scotch Atlas; or Description of the Kingdom of Scotland. L, 1794. 4to, contemp calf. With engraved title & contents page, & 30 hand-colored maps. S Nov 17 (758) £400 [Nicholson]

Anr copy. Contemp half calf; worn. With engraved title, index & 30 hand-colored maps. S May 29 (1138) £320

Armstrong, Terrence Ian Fytton. See: Gawsworth, John

Armstrong, Sir Walter, 1850-1918
— Gainsborough and his Place in English Art. L, 1898. 4to, half mor by Zaehnsdorf; rubbed. sg Feb 12 (159) $140

Arnaud, Francois, 1718-1805
— Les Epoux malheureux, ou histoire de Monsieur et Madame de [la Bedoyere]. Paris: la Veuve Ballard & Laporte, 1783. 2 vols in 1. 8vo, 19th-cent calf gilt. With 10 plates. S Nov 27 (38) £140 [Booth]

Arnauld, Antoine, 1612-94 —& Cambout de Ponchateau, Sebastien-Joseph
— La Morale Pratique des Jesuites. Cologne: 1583-95. 8 vols. 12mo, contemp mor gilt. With 2 plates in Vol II; half-titles to Vols IV, VI & VII only. Some discoloration to Vols IV & VIII; library mark. S Nov 27 (139) £350 [Wahlmuth]

Arnauld, Pierre
— Trois Traitez de la philosophie naturelle non encore imprimez.... Paris: Guillaume Marette, 1612. 4to, contemp calf. Dampstained. S May 6 (563) £350 [Rota]

Arnault, A. V.
— Vie politique et militaire de Napoleon. Paris: Librairie Historique, 1822-26. 2 vols. Folio, contemp half mor; worn, spine ends chipped. With 134 plates, most on india paper & mtd. Marginal discoloration; 1 plate margin torn. cb Dec 18 (7) $325

Arnault de Nobleville, Louis Daniel, 1701-78
— Aedonologie, ou traite du rossignol franc ou chanteur.... Paris, 1773. 12mo, 19th-cent half shagreen. Jeanson copy. SM Feb 28 (38) FF1,200

Arnold Arboretum
— Catalogue of the Library of.... Cambr., Mass., 1914-33. Compiled by Ethelyn Maria Tucker. 3 vols. 4to, disbound, unopened. sg May 14 (570) $275

Arnold, Edward Carleton
— British Waders. Cambr., 1924. 4to, orig cloth. pnE Dec 17 (258) £50 [McNaughton] One of 50. Orig half vellum. SSA Feb 11 (134) R350

Arnold, Matthew, 1822-88
— Poems. L, 1895. 3 vols. 8vo, mor gilt by the Doves Bindery. sg Feb 12 (11) $400
— Works. L, 1903-4. One of 775. 15 vols. Half mor gilt. pn Oct 23 (2) £320 [Traylen] Anr copy. Half calf gilt; scuffed. sg Feb 12 (12) $500

Arnold, Thomas, 1742-1816
— Observations on the Nature, Kinds, Causes, and Prevention of Insanity.... Leicester, 1782-86. 1st Ed. 2 vols. 8vo, half calf; shabby & loose. Lacking half-title in Vol II; titles dust-soiled & with library stamps; lower blank portion of half-title torn away; lower portion of last leaf of Vol II torn away with loss; 1 blank corner torn off. S May 28 (612) £420

Arnold, Sir Thomas Walker, 1864-1930 —& Grohmann, Adolf
— The Islamic Book. L, 1929. Out-of-series copy. 4to, orig mor gilt. With 104 plates. HN May 20 (34) DM750

Arnoldus de Villa Nova, 1235?-1312?
— De vinis. [Strassburg: Martin Schott, c.1484]. Folio, modern vellum. With colored three-quarter woodcut border & colored woodcut initials on A2r. Browned; some stains; A2 border shaved; A4 mended at top with some loss. 11 (of 12) leaves; lacking initial blank. Goff A-1082.

Schraemli-Crahan copy. P Nov 25 (30) $4,750
Anr Ed. [Leipzig: Melchoir Lotter, c.1500]. 4to, vellum by Marcus Crahan; bowed & loose. Browned; A5 torn without loss. 14 leaves. Goff A-1079. Crahan copy. P Nov 25 (31) $2,100

Arnot, David —& Orpen, Francis H. S.
— The Land Question of Griqualand West.... Cape Town, 1875. 8vo, orig cloth. With 4 folding maps. SSA Oct 28 (397) R440

Arnot, Hugo, 1749-86
— The History of Edinburgh. Edin., 1779. 1st Ed. 4to, contemp calf; rebacked, portion of orig spine preserved; rubbed. Map split & repaired. O Feb 24 (10) $50

Arnous de Riviere, J. See: Neumann & Arnous de Riviere

Arnoux, Charles Albert d'
— The Communists of Paris 1871. L, [1873]. 4to, orig cloth; spine chipped. With 40 hand-colored plates. sg Dec 18 (142) $90

Arp, Jean (or Hans), 1887-1966
— Auch das is nur eine Wolke. Basel, 1951. One of 130. 4to, orig wraps. S Sept 23 (611) £130 [Mytze]
— Weisst du schwarzt du. Zurich: Pra Verlag, 1930. One of 250. With 5 illusts by Max Ernst. Orig wraps. S June 29 (25) £1,000 [Negger]

Arpe, Petrus Fridericus
— De prodigiosis naturae et artis operibus Talismanes.... Hamburg, 1717. 8vo, modern calf. Library stamp on tp. bba Nov 13 (20) £90 [Poole]

Arrianus Flavius
— Ars tactica.... Amst., 1683. 8vo, 18th-cent mor gilt. With engraved title, folding plate & 2 folding maps. Jeanson 1381. SM Feb 28 (39) FF2,200
— Traite de la chasse.... Paris 1912. One of 150. 4to, half shagreen. Jeanson copy. SM Feb 28 (40) FF600

Arrianus, Flavius —& Oppianus
— Traitez de la chasse. Paris: Daniel Hortemels, 1690. 12mo, contemp red mor gilt with arms of the Dauphin, son of Louis XIV [Olivier 2522, fer 3]. Jeanson copy. SM Feb 28 (41) FF19,500

Arrow, Simon
— Count Fanny's Nuptials, being the Story of a Courtship. [L?]: G. G. Hope Johnstone, 1907. 4to, cloth. With 7 plates. L.p. copy. sg Dec 11 (288) $550

Art...

— L'Art d'archerie publie avec notes.... Paris: Philippe Renouard, 1901. One of 50. Jeanson copy. SM Mar 1 (324) FF2,200

— Art in Australia. Sydney, 1916-40. First Series Nos 1-11, Second Series Nos 1-2 & Third Series Nos 1-81. Together, 94 issues in 31 vols. Cloth, most retaining orig wraps. Some leaves waterstained; some foxing; some pages loose. CA Oct 7 (18) A$3,800

New Series, Vol I, Nos 1-2. Sydney, 1922. Wraps. CA Oct 7 (15) A$95

Third Series, Nos 1-42. Sydney, 1922-32. Wraps. CA Oct 7 (17) A$3,800

The Art of Margaret Preston. Sydney, 1927. One of 32 with an orig hand-colored woodcut. Half cloth. CA Oct 7 (141) A$2,400

— The Art Journal. L, 1849-53. Vols XI-XV. 4to, orig cloth. pn Jan 22 (57) £170 [Goulter]

Vols 9-16. L, 1857-64. 4to, orig half calf gilt. L Dec 11 (3) £240

— The Art of Confectionery. With Various Methods of Preserving Fruits.... Bost., 1866. 8vo, orig cloth. Some stains; library markings. sg Jan 15 (1) $50

— L'Art: Revue Hebdomadaire illustree. Paris & L, 1875-93. Vols 1-55. Folio, orig cloth; 1 spine torn. Includes 4 orig etchings by Goya. C July 22 (8) £4,000

— Art Work of Baltimore.... [N.p.]: Gravure Illustration Company, 1899. 1st Ed in orig 12 parts. Folio, orig wraps. With 72 plates. ha Nov 7 (137) $350

Artaud, Antonin

— Text und Briefe.... Cologne: Wolfgang Hake Verlag, 1967. One of 68 with the frontis. 4to, orig wraps. S June 29 (83) £1,300 [Rota]

Artemidorus

— Dell'Interpretatione de Sogni nuovamente di Greco.... Venice: Giolito, 1547. 8vo, contemp limp bds; shaken. Dampstained throughout; perforated stamps. sg Mar 26 (12) $80

Anr Ed. Venice: Gabriel Giolito de Ferrari, 1557. 4to, old vellum. Dampstained at end. sg Mar 26 (11) $60

Articulen...

— Articulen van Vrede Ende Confoederati...tusschen den Koning van Portugall.... The Hague, 1663. 4to, orig wraps; front wrap detached. Corner tip off final leaf. sg Sept 18 (37) $60

Artist...

— The Artist. L, 1931-42. Vols 1-22. Ck Sept 5 (98) £100

Arundale, Francis, 1807-53

— Illustrations of Jerusalem and Mount Sinai. L, 1837. 4to, orig cloth; spine torn. With frontis, map, plan & 19 views. pn Mar 5 (199) £190 [Walford]

Arundell, Francis Vyvyan. See: Condy & Arundell

Arvieux, Laurent d'

— Travels in Arabia the Desert. L, 1718. 8vo, contemp calf; worn. Lacking 1 plate; slightly stained at end. S Jan 12 (233) £65 [Burgess]

Asbjornsen, Peter Christen, 1812-85

— Norge Fremstillet i Tegninger. Christiania, 1848. Folio, disbound. With 82 plates, all with perforated stamps. bba Mar 12 (23) £150 [Bowers]

Asbjornsen, Peter Christen, 1812-85 —& Moe, Jorgen I, 1813-82

— East of the Sun and West of the Moon. L, [1914]. Illus by Kay Nielsen. 4to, orig cloth; rubbed, small stain to upper left of front cover. With 25 colored plates. cb Sept 11 (306) $90

Anr copy. Orig cloth; rubbed. With 25 color plates. S Dec 4 (205) £300 [Joseph & Sawyer]

Anr copy. With 25 colored plates. S June 17 (257) £380 [Hannah]

Anr copy. With 24 mtd color plates. sg Jan 8 (175) $80

Anr Ed. NY: Doran, [1927?]. Orig half cloth. With 25 colored plates. pn Mar 5 (332) £80 [Smith]

Anr copy. Orig cloth. S May 6 (137) £160 [Chandor]

Ascham, Roger, 1515-68

— Toxophilus. L: Edward Whitchurch, 1545. 4to, 19th-cent russia gilt. Ashburnham-Jeanson copy. SM Feb 28 (43) FF85,000

Anr Ed. L: Thomas Marshe, 1571. 4to, mor gilt. Lacking last leaf (blank). Jeanson 1747. SM Feb 28 (44) FF26,000

Aselli, Gaspare

— De lactibus sive de lacteis venis.... Leiden, 1640. 4to, contemp vellum; worn. S May 21 (176) £750 [Carey]

Ash, Edward C. See: Derrydale Press

ASHBEE

Ashbee, Charles Robert
— The Last Records of a Cotswold Community. L: Essex House Press, 1904. One of 75. wa Mar 5 (18) $160

Ashbee, Henry Spencer, 1834-1900
— Centuria librorum absconditorum.... L: Pvtly ptd, 1879. One of 250. 4to, modern half calf; hinge cracked. Small scratches through last 2 leaves. sg Jan 22 (18) $80
— An Iconography of Don Quixote, 1605-1895. L, 1895. 4to, contemp half lea, orig wraps bound in; scuffed. sg Jan 22 (108) $150

Ashendene Press—London
— A Chronological List, with Prices of the Forty Books... 1935. Orig wraps; backstrip faded. bba Oct 16 (364) £75 [Georges]
— A Descriptive Bibliography of the Books... 1935. One of 390. sg Dec 4 (9) $950; sg apr 2 (16) $2,200; sg June 11 (20) $1,200
— [Ecclesiasticus] The Wisdom of Jesus, the Son of Sirach... 1932. One of 328. P Sept 24 (102) $1,000
— A Hand-List of the Books Printed at the Ashendene Press MDCCCXCV-MCMXXV. 1925. O Nov 18 (14) $60
— BERNERS, DAME JULIANA. - A Treatyse of Fysshynge wyth an Angle. 1903. One of 150. sg Oct 23 (185) $325
— DANTE ALIGHIERI. - La Divina Commedia. 1902. (Lo Inferno only).. One of 135. S Dec 4 (98) £400 [Monk Bretton]
— DANTE ALIGHIERI. - La Vita Nuova. 1895. One of 45 on Japanese vellum. Inscr by St. John Hornby to Cicely Berkeley, his wife-to-be. sg Dec 4 (8) $1,100
— FRANCIS OF ASSISI. - I Fioretti.... 1922. One of 240. S June 18 (318) £250 [Maggs]
— FRANCIS OF ASSISI. - Un Mazzeto scelto dei fioretti... 1904. One of 25 on vellum. sg June 11 (19) $3,600
— SPENSER, EDMUND. - Minor Poems. 1925. One of 15 on vellum. CNY May 11 (3) $4,500
— THUCYDIDES. - The History of the Peloponnesian War. 1930. One of 260. cb Feb 19 (3) $1,300

Ashley, Clifford Warren
— Whaleships of New Bedford. Bost. & NY, 1929. One of 1,000. 4to, cloth; soiled & worn. With 60 plates. Inscr. wa Sept 25 (411) $120

Ashton, John
— Chap-Books of the Eighteenth Century. L, 1882. One of 100 L.p. copies. 8vo, half vellum; worn, inner joint broken, front endpaper torn. O Oct 21 (16) $70

AMERICAN BOOK PRICES CURRENT

Asiatic...
— The Asiatic Annual Register, or a View of the History of Hindustan.... L, 1800-12. 12 vols in 13 (complete set). 8vo, contemp half calf. C May 13 (209) £480 [Drury]

Asimov, Isaac
— The Caves of Steel. Garden City, 1954. Publisher's file copy. In d/j. cb Sept 18 (59) $130
— The Currents of Space. Garden City, 1952. In soiled d/j. cb Sept 18 (60) $60
— David Starr: Space Ranger. Garden City, 1952. In soiled d/j. cb Sept 28 (61) $85
— The End of Eternity. Garden City, 1955. In d/j. Inscr. cb Sept 18 (63) $140
— Foundation and Empire. NY: Gnome Press, [1952]. 1st Ed. 1st state bdg & 1st d/j. cb Sept 28 (66) $100
— Good Taste. Topeka: Apocalypse Press, 1976. One of 500. cb Sept 28 (70) $65
— I, Robot. NY: Gnome Press, 1950. In rubbed d/j; covers mildew-stained. cb Sept 28 (73) $130
— Nightfall and Other Stories. Garden City, 1969. 1st Ed, Review copy. In repaired d/j. cb Sept 28 (75) $70
— Pebble in the Sky. Garden City, 1950. In repaired d/j. cb Sept 28 (77) $100
Anr copy. In chipped & torn d/j; spine leaning & bumped at foot. cb Sept 28 (78) $65
— The Robots of Dawn. Huntington Woods MI: Phantasia Press, 1983. One of 35. Lea decorated with silver & plastic. cb Sept 28 (79) $400
— The Stars, Like Dust. Garden City, 1951. In lightly rubbed d/j; bdg spine ends bumped. cb Sept 28 (80) $75
— Three by Asimov. NY: Targ, 1981. One of 250. In d/j. cb Sept 28 (81) $50

Asser, Joannes
— Aelfredi regis res gestae. [L: John Day, 1574]. Bound with: Walsingham, Thomas. Ypodigma Neustriae vel Normanniae. L: John Day, 1574. And: Walsingham, Thomas. Historia brevis. L: H. Bynneman, 1574. Folio, contemp vellum; worn. Later leaves soiled; staining to lower margins. Ck Jan 30 (185) £320

Astle, Thomas, 1735-1803
— The Origin and Progress of Writing. L, 1803. 2d Ed. 4to, later calf. sg Jan 22 (19) $250

Astley, Thomas
— A New General Collection of Voyages and Travels.... L: Thomas Astley, 1745-47. 4 vols. 4to, old calf gilt; worn, 5 covers detached. With 4 frontises & 227 maps & plates. One leaf of plates list misbound in

Vol IV. L July 2 (111) £300
Anr copy. Contemp calf; chipped. A few short tears repaired. S Oct 23 (313) £900 [McKenzie]

Aston, John Partington. See: Ainsworth & Aston

Astruc, John, 1684-1766
— A Treatise of Venereal Diseases. L, 1754. 4to, contemp calf; rebacked. pnE Dec 17 (59) £160 [Thin]

Atget, Eugene
— A Vision of Paris. NY, 1963. Text by Marcel Proust. 4to, cloth, in d/j. sg Nov 13 (7) $100; sg May 7 (4) $150

Athanaeus. See: Jonson, Ben

Athenaeum, Liverpool
— A Catalogue of the Library of the Athenaeum, Liverpool. L, 1864. 8vo, mor gilt by Fazakerley. Presented to Alfred Booth on his retirement from the Presidency of the Athenaeum (so states mor onlay on inside upper cover). S Nov 10 (1) £50 [Quaritch]

Athenian...
— Athenian Letters or the Epistolary Correspondent of an Agent to the King of Persia.... L, 1798. 2 vols. 4to, recent half mor. With 2 frontises, folding map & 12 plates. T Apr 16 (293) £42

Athens
— Athenes moderne. Athens: M. P. Vreto, 1861. Folio, orig bds; worn. With 12 tinted lithos on laid india paper. S Feb 24 (409) £900 [Kalogeras]

Atherton, John
— The Fly and the Fish. NY, 1951. One of 220. sg Oct 23 (173) $140

Atkinson, Geoffroy
— La Litterature geographique francaise de la renaissance. Paris, 1927. One of 550. 4to, cloth, orig front wrap bound in. sg May 14 (658) $150
Anr copy. 2 vols, including 1936 supplement, in 1. 4to, cloth, orig wraps bound in. sg May 14 (659) $120

Atkinson, George Francklin
— The Campaign in India. L, 1859. Folio, orig cloth; def. With 26 plates on 20 sheets, including pictorial title. Foxed, some leaves loose. pn Apr 3021138 £220

Atkinson, Henry
— Expedition up the Missouri. Letter from the Secretary of War.... Wash., 1826. 8vo, removed from larger vol, with glue remains & stab-holes. cb Mar 19 (15) $110

Atkinson, James
— Medical Bibliography A & B [all pbd]. L, 1834. 8vo, orig cloth; rebacked. Inscr. S May 28 (815) £400

Atkinson, John Augustus, 1775-1831 —& Walker, James, 1748-1808
— A Picturesque Representation of the Manners...of the Russians. L, 1803-4. 3 vols in 1. Folio, 19th-cent half lea; hinges cracking, worn. With port & 100 hand-colored plates. Some waterspotting & browning. FD June 11 (854) DM2,850

Atkinson, Thomas Witlam, 1799-1861
— Oriental and Western Siberia. L, 1858. 8vo, orig cloth. With folding map & 20 plates. A few short tears in map neatly repaired. S Jan 12 (169) £140 [Grants]
— Travels in the Regions of the Upper and Lower Amoor. L, 1860. 1st Ed. 8vo, orig cloth; rubbed & repaired. bba May 28 (194) £40 [Ihler]

Atkinson, William
— Views of Picturesque Cottages with Plans. L, 1805. Folio, modern half mor. With engraved title & 19 plates, 12 hand-colored. Margins rubbed thin slightly, affecting lettering. bba Sept 25 (265) £300 [Demetzy]

Atkyns, Arabella, Pseud.
— The Family Magazine. L, 1747. 2 parts in 1 vol. 8vo, modern half calf. pn Nov 20 (173) £80 [Demetzy]

Atkyns, Sir Robert, 1647-1711
— The Ancient and Present State of Glocestershire. L, 1768. 2d Ed. Folio, contemp calf; rebacked, new endpapers. With double-page map & 73 plates. T Apr 1 (41) £1,600

Atlantic...
— Atlantic Tuna Club, Then and Now, 1914-1954. Pvtly ptd for Paul C. Nicholson, 1954. One of 175. Tp lightly foxed. sg Oct 23 (174) $140

Atlas
See also: Faden, William; Neptune...
— The American Military Pocket Atlas. L, [1776]. 8vo, half calf; scuffed, spine ends chipped, hinges cracked. With 6 folding maps, outlined in color. Tears at fold-lines of 4 maps. sg Nov 20 (195) $3,200
— Asher and Adams' New Statistical and Topographical Atlas of the United States. NY, [1872]. Folio, half lea; front cover nearly detached. With 28 double-page hand-colored maps. About half the maps foxed & browned from pressed flowers. sg Nov 20 (179) $200
— Atlas de toutes les parties connues du globe

terrestre. [Geneva, 1780?]. 4to, contemp calf; broken. With 49 double-page maps plus uncounted number of tables. T Oct 16 (293) £150
— Atlas maritimo de Espana. Madrid, 1789. Vol II only. Folio, contemp bds. With 15 double-page charts. Waterstained & creased; some margins frayed. S July 14 (595) £500
— Atlas national illustre des 86 Departements et des possessions de la France. Paris, 1852. 14^1/$_2$ by 20^1/$_2$ inches. Half lea. SM Oct 20 (407) FF1,600
— An Atlas of Ancient Egypt. L, 1894. 4to, orig cloth; worn, spine creased, hinges cracked. Blindstamp at bottom of tp. cb Nov 6 (92) $60
— The British Atlas. L, 1810. 4to, contemp calf; broken. With 57 maps hand-colored in outline & 21 (of 22) uncolored town plans. S May 29 (962) £450
— The California Water Atlas. Sacramento, 1979. Half lea. cb Oct 9 (38) $90
— Colton's Atlas of the World. NY, 1856. 2 vols. Folio, contemp cloth; worn, 1 cover detached. wa June 25 (211) $625
— Colton's General Atlas.... NY, 1857. Folio, half lea; loose. With 92 singlepage maps & 4 doublepage maps, fully hand-colored. Some maps split at centerfold; many margins chipped & soiled. sg Nov 20 (187) $475
— Johnson's New Illustrated Family Atlas. NY, 1866. Folio, orig half mor; worn. With engraved title, 6 plates & diagrams & 56 (of 57) hand-colored maps, 39 double-page. Many maps with small tears, fold-line separation or light dampstaining. sg Apr 23 (174) $175

Anr Ed. NY, 1867. Folio, orig half cloth; front cover detached. With 4 plates & 56 hand-colored maps, 39 double-page. Lacking double-page plate of national emblems; 8 maps torn or split at fold line; plate of mountains & rivers frayed & detached. sg Apr 23 (175) $250

Anr Ed. NY, 1872. Folio, half lea; needs rebdg. Initial leaves chipped & soiled; State of NY map split at centerfold, affecting image. sg Nov 20 (189) $400

Anr Ed. NY: Johnson & Ward, 1872. Folio, disbound. With 1 diagram, 3 world maps, 1 double-page plate of national emblems, 1 plate of mountains & rivers & 1 plate of coats-of-arms & 50 (of 51) double-page & 4 single-page maps, all hand-colored. Prelims torn; dampstaining in some margins, occasionally affecting maps. sg Apr 23 (176) $300

— Letts's Popular County Atlas. L, 1884. Folio, modern cloth. With 47 double-page color maps. S Nov 10 (763) £120 [Tooley]
— The London Modern Atlas. L, [c.1860]. Compiled by J. Betts. Folio, bds. With 26 hand-colored maps. S Nov 10 (978) £170 [Potter]
— Mitchell's New General Atlas.... Phila., 1869. 4to, disbound. With 58 maps, each fully hand-colored. Margins chipped & browned; several maps torn or chipped. sg Nov 20 (190) $275
— The National Atlas; Containing Elaborate Topographical Maps of the United States and the Dominion of Canada.... Phila., 1884-85. Folio, needs rebdg. With 40 (of 42) maps, some double-page, principal areas fully hand-colored. Lacking some text leaves. sg Nov 20 (191) $250

Anr copy. Half lea; front cover detached, needs rebdg. With 18 double-page & 22 single-page maps only, hand-colored. sg Apr 23 (187) $175

— New Topographical Atlas of the County of Hampden Massachusetts. Springfield, 1894. Folio, cloth; broken. Minor stains & fraying. O Nov 18 (136) $95
— Nieuwe Atlas, van de Voornaamste gebouwen en gezigten der stad Amsterdam. Amst.: D. J. Changuion & P. den Hengst, 1783. 2 vols. Folio, 19th-cent mor gilt by E. P. van Bommel. With map & 103 plates. S Oct 23 (242) £3,500 [Jonge]
— Ordnance Survey of Scotland. Edin.: A. K. Johnstone, [1856-57]. 131 sheets of maps, folio, all but 3 mtd on linen as unfolded sheets. Board of Agriculture blind stamps. S Jan 12 (54) £650 [Aberdeen]
— The Royal Illustrated Atlas of Modern Geography. L & Edin.: Fullarton, [c.1862]. Folio, orig half mor; broken. With engraved title & 76 maps colored in outline. Some tears & stains. bba May 14 (2) £340 [Diba]

Anr copy. Half mor gilt; worn, upper cover detached. With engraved title & 66 maps, partly colored, some double-page. Margins waterstained, as are final leaves & endpapers. L Dec 11 (202) £160

Anr copy. With 66 partly colored maps. Last 4 maps foxed. pn May 21 (422) £380 [Sweet]

Aubert du Petit-Thouars, Abel, 1758-1831
— Voyage autour du monde sur la Fregate la Venus.... Paris, 1840-44. Vols I-X in 2 boxes, without Atlas vol. Orig bds rebacked in mor. pn Dec 11 (179) £380 [Maggs]
— Voyage autour du monde sur la fregate La Venus: Atlas hydrographique. Paris, 1845. Folio, contemp bds; worn. With engraved title & 19 charts. Some waterstain on final plate. S Apr 24 (382) £1,100 [Quaritch]

Aubin, Nicolas
— Dictionnaire de marine contenant les termes de la navigation.... Amst.: Pierre Brunel, 1702. 4to, contemp calf with gilt cypher in center of both covers. With frontis, coat-of-arms & 29 hand-colored plates. Small hole in tp; 1 folding plate with 2 tears; hole in text of Dd4 affecting 1 letter only; some leaves wormed in fore-margin. S May 21 (134) £1,000 [Sims]

— Histoire des Diables de Loudun.... Amst., 1693. 12mo, contemp calf; rebacked, front free endpaper & blank loose. sg Oct 9 (173) $275

Aublet, Jean B. C. Fusee
— Histoire des plantes de la Guiane francoise.... L, 1775. 4 vols. 4to, contemp calf. With frontis & 392 plates. A few Ms annotations. Plesch—de Belder copy. S Apr 27 (10) £1,900 [Berg]

Aubrey, John, 1626-97
— Monumenta Britannica or a Miscellany of British Antiquities.... Bost., [1981]. 4to, half calf. O Nov 18 (15) $70

Aubry, Charles
— Chasses anciennes, d'apres les manuscrits des XIVe & XVe siecles. Paris: Charles Motte, 1837. Folio, half calf. With 12 hand-finished color plates. Jeanson copy. SM Feb 28 (45) FF8,500

Aucassin & Nicolette
— Aucassin & Nicolete.... L: David Nutt, 1887. One of 63. 8vo, lev gilt by Ruban. With frontis in 3 states, 1 sgd by Jacob Hood. wa Mar 5 (28) $450

One of 500 on Japanese paper. Trans by Andrew Lang. Mor extra in imitation of a Renaissance bdg, by Zaehnsdorf. sg Feb 12 (13) $1,200

Anr ed. [L: Harrap, 1917]. One of 125. Illus by Main R. Bocher. 4to, vellum with gilt design by Evelyn Paul. sg Dec 18 (206) $50

Auction. See: Livingston, Luther Samuel

Audebert, Jean Baptiste, 1759-1800 —& Vieillot, Louis Jean Pierre
— Oiseaux dores ou a reflets metalliques. Paris, An XI [1802]. Folio Ed, with plate captions ptd in gold. 2 vols. Contemp half mor gilt; rubbed. With 190 plates ptd in colors & with gold applied. Lacking the half-title & title to Vol II but those to Vol I repeated. S Oct 23 (657) £10,000 [Quaritch]

Auden, Wystan Hugh, 1907-73
— Look, Stranger! L, 1936. 8vo, cloth, in worn d/j. sg Dec 11 (171) $120

— Poems. L, 1930. 1st Trade Ed. 4to, orig wraps; soiled, upper cover scored. bba Apr 9 (194) £65 [Spencer]

Anr copy. Orig wraps; worn. Ck Dec 10 (341) £150

Edition A. L: Petersburg Press, 1974. one of 150 with separate impressions of 4 of the lithos sgd & numbered by the artist. Illus by Henry Moore. Folio, orig cloth. S Dec 4 (202) £800 [Joseph & Sawyer]

— Spain. [L, 1937]. Wraps. sg Mar 5 (9) $100

— Two Songs. NY, 1968. One of 100. Oblong 8vo, wraps. sg Mar 5 (10) $110

Audin, Marius
— Les Librets typographiques des fonderies francaises crees avant 1800.... Amst., 1964. 4to, cloth. sg Oct 2 (20) $60

Audsley, George Ashdown, 1838-1925
— The Ornamental Arts of Japan. L, 1882-[85]. 2 vols. 4to, cloth. Sold w.a.f. bba Mar 12 (288) £200 [Rainer]

Audsley, George Ashdown, 1838-1925 —& Bowes, James Lord, 1834-99
— Keramic Art of Japan. Liverpool & L, 1875-[80]. 2 vols. Folio, orig half mor. C July 22 (11) £460

Anr copy. Half lea. Lacking both titles; library markings but plates not stamped. Sold w.a.f. O Oct 21 (17) $100

Anr copy. Mor; lower covers detached. pn June 18 (29) £120 [Smith]

Anr copy. Orig mor gilt; rubbed. With 63 colored plates. pn June 18 (150) £200 [Arnold]

Audubon, John James, 1785-1851
— Audubon's America: The Narratives and Experiences of John James Audubon. Bost., 1940. Ed by D. C. Peattie. 4to, cloth. Sgd by Peattie. sg Sept 18 (22) $70

— The Birds of America. L, 1827-38. Fragment of Vol I only with 56 hand-colored plates. Bound in contemp half russia gilt with plates soiled & dampstained & torn, some with loss. This vol discovered by workmen in July 1970 during the renovations to the office of Joseph R. Young on Broad Street, Charleston, South Carolina. CNY May 11 (4) $32,000

1st 8vo Ed. NY & Phila., 1840-44. 7 vols. Mor gilt. With 500 hand-colored plates. C Apr 8 (165) £15,000 [Mitchell]

Anr copy. Contemp half mor; some joints cracking, rubbed. With half-title in each vol & 500 hand-finished color plates. CNY Nov 21 (11) $16,000

AUDUBON

Anr copy. Calf; needs rebdg. With 460 (of 500) color plates, many foxed & soiled, principally in margins. Text accompanying missing plates lacking. Vol VI lacking half-title, title & subscriber's list. sg Jan 15 (132) $6,000

Anr Ed. NY, 1859-60. 7 vols. 8vo, 19th-cent mor gilt; spines dampstained & discolored. With 499 (of 500) hand-colored plates; lacking Plate 171. Most plates with light browning or foxing; some dampstains; Plates 4, 52 & 488 inlaid; 1 leaf of text with corner restored. S May 13 (1) $4,250

2d Folio Ed. NY, 1860. Atlas of plates only. Contemp mor gilt; rebacked with orig backstrip laid down, edges renewed, scuffed. With engraved title on 140 plates on 98 sheets (of 150 plates on 105 sheets); lacking Plates 28, 28/239, 240/243, 253, 364, 395, 397/98. Tp with vertical crease, the crease also affecting the 1st 7 plates; 2 large repaired tears to sheet 98, 1 touching image; marginal repaired tear to sheet 88; Wild turkey with soiling to extreme marginal edges only & minute wear to corners; c.35 sheets foxed; 4 sheets darkened; single spot affecting margins of 4 sheets. Sold w.a.f. CNY Nov 21 (12) $28,000

Anr Ed. NY, [1870-71]. 8 vols. 8vo, orig mor. With 500 colored plates. Library stamps on titles. O May 12 (6) $5,100

Anr Ed. L, 1937. Text by Wm. Vogt. Folio, orig cloth. With port & 500 color plates. Haverschmidt copy. B Feb 24 (261) HF180

Anr Ed. NY, 1937. Folio, half cloth. With port & 500 colored plates. pn Oct 23 (165) £70

Anr copy. Half cloth; small stain on spine. sg Sept 18 (20) $50

Anr Ed. Amst., 1972-73. One of 250. Vol I only. Orig half cloth. C Oct 15 (210) £360 [Toscani]

— The Birds of America: A Selection of Plates.... L: Ariel Press, 1972-73. One of 1,000. 2 vols. Folio, orig half cloth. S Oct 23 (658) £1,000 [Lan]

— Birds of America. NY: Abbeville Press, [1981]. Folio, mor gilt. With 435 full-page color plates. ha Sept 19 (142) $200

Anr copy. Lea gilt. ha Dec 19 (107) $260

— The Original Water-Colour Paintings by John James Audubon for the Birds of America. NY & L, 1966. 2 vols. 4to, cloth. AVP Nov 20 (7) C$90 [Burns]; bba Oct 16 (312) £70 [Carothas]; bba Aug 28 (270) £65 [Blum]; bba Aug 28 (271) £80 [Elliott]

Anr copy. Orig cloth. pnE Dec 17 (259) £60 [Seeton]

Anr copy. Cloth. sg Sept 18 (21) $110; sg Jan 15 (133) $80; wa Nov 6 (128) $55

Anr copy. Cloth. With port & 431 plates. Haverschmidt copy. B Feb 24 (262) HF320

— Ornithological Biography.... Edin., 1831-39. 5 vols. 8vo, various bdgs; loose, damaged. Haverschmidt copy. B Feb 24 (260) HF950

Audubon, John James, 1785-1851 —& Bachman, John, 1790-1874

— The Viviparous Quadrupeds of North America. NY, 1845-48. 1st Ed. Plate vols I & III & 15 plates only of Vol III. Folio, disbound. With 115 hand-colored plates. Lacking text, Vol III title & contents leaf; titles & contents leaves to other vols frayed. C Oct 15 (202) £28,000 [Rice]

Anr Ed. NY, 1849-51-54. ("The Quadrupeds of North America.") 3 vols. 8vo, contemp half calf gilt over bds. With 155 hand-colored plates. Some plates with minor spotting; lacking half-title to Vol II. CNY Nov 21 (13) $2,800

Anr copy. Half mor; 1 cover loose. A few plates lightly soiled. sg Apr 2 (17) $2,400

Anr copy. Contemp mor gilt; repaired & worn. With 154 hand-colored plates. Lacking Plate 58, Orange-Bellied Squirrel. wa Mar 5 (238) $3,100

Anr copy. Old half calf; becoming disbound. With 155 hand-colored plates. Some browning & foxing. wd June 19 (59) $1,900

Anr Ed. L, 1851-53-[n.d.]. 3 vols. 8vo, disbound. With 155 hand-colored plates. Some plates thumbed. With ALs from V. G. Audubon to his aunt, informing her of his father's death. sg Dec 4 (10) $2,200

Anr Ed. NY, 1852-54-54. 3 vols. 8vo, contemp mor gilt. With 155 colored plates. Lacking half-titles; some foxing. cb June 4 (10) $4,000

Anr Ed. L, 1854-54-[n.d.]. Vol III only. Contemp mor; joints scuffed. With 55 hand-colored plates. Ck May 29 (191) £500

Anr Ed. NY: Lockwood, [c.1865]. 3 vols. 8vo, orig half mor; worn. With 155 colored plates. Library stamps on titles. O May 12 (5) $2,000

Audubon, John Woodhouse, 1819-62

— The Drawings of John Woodhouse Audubon Illustrating his Adventures Through Mexico.... San Francisco: Book Club of California, 1957. One of 400. cb Sept 11 (107) $150

Audubon, Maria R.
— Audubon and his Journals. NY, 1897. 2 vols. 8vo, orig cloth. cb Apr 2 (11) $950

Augustan...
— The Augustan Books of Modern Poetry: Edmund Blunden. L, [1925]. Ptd wraps; soiled. Inscr by Blunden. sg Dec 11 (189) $60

Augustine, Saint, 354-430
— De civitate Dei. Naples: Mathias Moravus, 1477. Folio, 18th-cent calf gilt. With 21 initials in red & blue with decorative penwork extending in to the margins. Foremargin of 1a2, 2a1 & 2a8 cut down but with no loss of text; last leaf becoming loose; bb8 misbound; a few lower margins waterstained. 296 (of 298) leaves. Goff A-1237. S May 21 (6) £1,300
— De la cita di Dio. [Venice: Antonio di Bartolommeo, not after 1483]. Folio, old vellum. Lacking 1 blank; scattered dampstains. Goff A-1248. P Dec 15 (156) $1,900
— Of the Citie of God.... L, 1610. Folio, modern half mor; spine varnished. Minor stains; lacking initial & final blanks. sg Oct 9 (93) $475
— Opera. Venice: Ad signum spei [i.e. Al segno della Speranza], 1550-52. 11 vols. 4to, later vellum. Some early markings on titles washed out; censor's inscr on Vol 11 title; some dampstains. sg Oct 9 (92) $325
— Opuscula... Venice: Octavianus Scotus, 28 May 1483. 4to, half calf; joints & spine wormed. A few leaves slightly damaged. 276 leaves; Goff A-1216. S Nov 27 (140) £1,100 [DeCayas]

Auldjo, John, d.1857
— Narrative of an Ascent to the Summit of Mont Blanc. L, 1828. 4to, later cloth. Perforated stamp on title & anr leaf. bba Feb 5 (364) £400 [Broseghini]

2d Ed. L, 1830. 8vo, half calf; rubbed. With 24 plates & maps. pn Mar 5 (6) £260 [Broseghini]

Aumale, Henri Eugene Philippe Louis d'Orleans, duc d', 1822-97
— Notes et documents relatifs a Jean, Roi de France, et a sa captivite en Angleterre. L: C. Whittingham, [1855]. One of 50 hors commerce. 4to, red mor gilt by the Veuve Niedree with the Aumale arms. SM Mar 1 (440) FF4,500

Aurora...
— Aurora Australis. Antarctica: Ptd at the Sign of the Penguins by Joyce & Wild, 1908. One of c.100 copies. Ed by Ernest Shackleton. 4to, Orig lea-backed packing case bds; rubbed, joint slightly split, loose

Inscr by the ptr Ernest E. Joyce, 1911. S Nov 18 (1223) £7,500 [Quaritch]

Austen, Jane, 1775-1817
— Emma. L, 1816. 1st Ed. 3 vols. 8vo, contemp half calf; rebacked preserving orig spines, rubbed. Lacking half-titles; a few leaves spotted & minor worming to inner blank margins of Vol I; blank corner of H2 in Vol II restored. C Dec 12 (316) £700 [Burmester]

Anr copy. Contemp half calf; corners worn. With half-titles. pnE Jan 28 (84) £4,100 [Steedman]

Anr copy. 19th cent half calf. Damp stained at beginning & end of each vol; Vol III lacking inserted ad; M12 apparently a cancel. sg Dec 4 (11) $750

— Northanger Abbey and Persuasion. L, 1818. 1st Ed. 4 vols. 12mo, 19th-cent calf gilt; joints repaired, lower cover of Vol I scratched; small tear repaired on upper cover, library blindstamp on binder's leaves. Lacking final blanks in Vol IV; some marginal holes; portion torn from corner of D9 & D10 in Vol III. S July 23 (35) £1,700 [Quaritch]

— Works. NY, 1906. ("Novels and Letters.") Chawton Ed, one of 1,250. 12 vols. 8vo, cloth. sg Feb 12 (14) $175

Hampshire Ed. NY, 1914. out-of-series copy. 12 vols. Half mor gilt. sg Dec 4 (12) $1,000

Austen, Ralph, d.1676
— A Treatise of Fruit-Trees.... Oxford, 1657. 2d Ed. 2 parts in 1 vol. 4to, contemp calf; rebacked, worn. 1 leaf torn affecting text; stained; edges cropped, loose. bba Aug 28 (139) £80 [Hippo]

Austin, Mary Hunter, 1868-1934
— Taos Pueblo. Bost., 1977. One of 950. Illus by Ansel Adams. cb Dec 4 (133) $350

Austin, Roland. See: Hyett & Austin

Austin, William, of Lincoln's Inn
— Haec Homo; Wherein the Excellency of the Creation of Woman is Described.... L, 1639. 12mo, contemp sheep; rubbed, worn, spine chipped. With engraved title & port. soiled, 2 final leaves fraying with loss of text. ha Oct 23 (15) $85

Austonius, Decimus Magnus
— Opera. Amst.: J. Blaeu, 1671. 8vo, contemp vellum; soiled. Tape repair to leaf of index. cb Oct 23 (14) $160

AUSTRALIA

Australia
— The Australian Irrigation Colonies on the River Murray. L, 1888. Folio, half mor gilt; worn. Ferguson 17976. T Sept 18 (67) £90
— The New South Wales Calendar and General Post Office Directory. Sydney, 1833. 8vo, orig bds; upper joint cracked, foot of spine torn. With folding frontis, folding colored plate of signals & folding plate of semaphore, plan, 2 engraved views, 11 plates including 3 ptd in blue & 2 folding tables. Title & 2 leaves repaired at corner with some loss; 1 ad shaved; 1 leaf holed affecting a few letters; some stains. C Oct 15 (167) £500 [Maggs]
— Port Essington...Copies or Extracts of any Correspondence relative to the Establishment of a Settlement at Port Essington. L, 27 Mar 1843. Folio, modern half mor. With folding hand-colored map. C Oct 15 (168) £320 [Scott Sandilands]
— Swan River Settlement...copies of the Correspondence of the Colonial Department with Certain Gentlemen proposing to form a Settlement in the Neighbourhood of the Swan River.... L, 13 May 1829. Folio, modern half mor. With folding hand-colored chart. C Oct 15 (176) £1,600 [Scott Sandilands]
— Victoria Illustrated. Second Series. Melbourne & Sydney: Sands, Kenny & Co., 1862. Oblong 4to, cloth. With engraved title & 43 plates. bba Dec 18 (231) £140 [Angle]

Authentic...
— An Authentic Narrative of the Proceedings of the Expedition under the Comand of Brigadier-Gen. Craufurd.... L, 1808. 8vo, 19th-cent calf; spine rubbed. Errata inked in but slip laid on verso of tp. cb Dec 18 (10) $150

Auzoles a La Peyre, Jacques d'
— Le Berger chronologique contre le pretendu geant de la science des temps.... Paris, 1663. 8vo, citron mor gilt with radiating suns. SM Oct 20 (470) FF75,000

Avedon, Richard
— Avedon Photographs 1947-1977. NY: Farrar, Straus & Giroux, [1978]. Intro by Harold Brodkey. Folio, bds. Inscr. wa Nov 6 (287) $75
— Nothing Personal. NY, 1964. Text by James Baldwin. Bds; scuffed, spine ends cracked. sg Nov 13 (10) $80
Anr copy. Bds; soiled. wa June 25 (80) $65
— Observations. NY, [1959]. Text by Truman Capote. Folio, bds; spine ends chipped. sg Nov 13 (11) $150
Anr copy. Bds; worn. sg Mar 5 (35) $100

AMERICAN BOOK PRICES CURRENT

Anr copy. Bds; spotted & bumped. sg May 7 (5) $120

Averani, Giuseppe
— Monumenta latina posthuma. Florence, 1769. 4to, old half calf; broken. Ck Mar 26 (13) $50

Averanus, Josephus. See: Averani, Giuseppe

Avermaete, Roger
— La Gravure sur bois moderne de l'Occident. Paris, 1928. One of 1,000. 4to, wraps. B Oct 7 (259) HF350

Aviler, Augustin Charles d', 1653-1700
— Cours d'architecture qui comprend les ordres de Vignole.... Paris, 1696-93. 2 vols in 1. 4to, contemp calf. With engraved title, frontis, 31 folding plates & 84 full-page plates. C May 13 (67) £320 [Maggs]
Anr Ed. Paris, 1699. 2 vols in 1. 4to, contemp calf; head of spine torn, spine cracked. With engraved title, frontis to Vol II & 31 folding plates. Some fold tears. Sgd by Edward Cresy on tp & with a small pencil sketch of a building on flyleaf. C July 22 (57) £320

Avity, Pierre d'
— The Estates, Empires, & Principallities of the World. L, 1615. 1st Ed in English. Folio, old calf; rebacked reaining old backstrip. sg Mar 26 (14) $325

Avril, Philippe, 1654-98
— Travels into divers parts of Europe and Asia.... L, 1693. 2 parts in 1 vol. 12mo, contemp calf; corners worn, rebacked. Short tear in A2. S Nov 10 (1211) £130 [Cavendish]
— Voyage en divers etats d'Europe et d'Asie.... Paris, 1692. 4to, contemp calf; rebacked retaining orig backstrip, worn. With port, 3 plates & folding map. Tp stamped. sg Apr 23 (9) $70

Ayala, Mariano d'
— Bibliografia Militare-Italiana Antica e Moderna. Turin, 1854. 8vo, half lea; spine ends & front joint chafed. Uzielli embossed stamp on tp. sg Oct 2 (221) $90

Ayer Collection, Edward Everett
— A Bibliographical Check List of North and Middle American Indian Linguistics in the Ayer Collection. Chicago, 1941. 2 vols. 4to, cloth. sg Oct 2 (10) $70

Ayer Collecton, Edward Everett
— Narratives of Captivity among the Indians of North America. Chicago, [1912]-28. 2 vols (including Supplement One). Wraps. sg June 11 (25) $80

Ayres, Philip, 1638-1712
— The Voyages and Adventures of Capt. Barth. Sharp...in the South Sea. L, 1684. 8vo, later calf gilt; joints weak. Old stamp on tp. sg Apr 23 (10) $750

Ayres Ramos Da Sylva De Eca, Matias
— Reflexoes sobre a Vaidade dos Homens.... Lisbon: Antonio V. da Silva, 1761. 4to, modern half cloth. Tp spotted & with small top edge repair; 1st 25 leaves dampstained in inner & top margins. sg Sept 18 (36) $60

Ayton, Richard, 1786-1823. See: Daniell & Ayton

Aytta, Viglius Zuichemus Ab
— Commentaria in decem titulos institutionum iuris civilis. Lyon, 1559. 8vo, contemp calf gilt; worn. Woodcut device on tp crudely colored; marginal dampstains. bba Oct 30 (170) £65 [Maggs]

Azara, Felix de, 1746-1811
— Voyages dans l'Amérique méridionale.... Paris, 1809. Atlas only. Orig bds; rebacked. Library stamp on title only. bba Mar 12 (12) £130 [Faupel]

Aznar de Polanco, Juan Claudio
— Arte nuevo de escribir.... Madrid, 1719. 1st Ed. Folio, contemp vellum; worn. With engraved title, frontis & 37 plates only. Inner margins wormed; some dampstains. S July 28 (1149) £360

B

B., H. See: Doyle, John

B., V.
— A Table of the 12 Astrologicall Houses.... L, 1654. 8vo, 19th-cent calf; rubbed. 1 leaf torn with loss of small portion of tables. pn Nov 20 (85) £95 [Buckell & Ballard]

Baardt, Pieter
— Deugden-spoor; in de ondeughden des werelts affgebeeldt.... Leeuw.: H. W. Coopman, 1645. Bound with: Baardt. Democratia corporis humani. Leeuw, 1640. 8vo, contemp vellum. With engraved title & 12 emblems. B Feb 25 (540) HF500

Babbage, Charles, 1792-1871
— On the Economy of Machinery and Manufactures. L, 1832. 1st Ed. 8vo, orig cloth. L.p. presentation copy, inscr. C Dec 12 (8) £850 [Quaritch]

Anr copy. Contemp half mor by Pelton, with gilt cypher on spine. Without ad leaf at end; B2 repaired; blindstamp on dedication & 3 other leaves. P Sept 24 (237) $250

Babbit, Edwin D.
— The Principles of Light and Color. NY, 1878. 8vo, orig cloth; corners frayed, soiled. sg Feb 5 (22) $275

Babcock, Philip H. See: Derrydale Press

Babington, John
— Tyrotechnia or, a Discourse of Artificiall Fire-Works. L 1635. Folio, contemp calf; worn. Lacking engraved title & 2 folding plates; tp torn in margins; a5 torn without loss; some dampstains. S Sept 23 (293) £180 [McNaul]

Bablet, Denis
— The Revolutions of Stage Design in the 20th Century. Paris: Leon Amiel, [1977]. In d/j cb Mar 5 (131) $100

Babson Collection, Grace K.
— A Descriptive Catalogue of the...Collection of the Works of Sir Isaac Newton. NY, 1950. One of 750. 2 vols. including Macomber's 1955 Supplement, one of 450. sg May 14 (572) $175

Bacci, Andrea, d.1600
— De naturali vinorum historia de vinis Italiae et de conviiviis antiquorum. Rome: N. Mutius, 1596. Folio, half lea; worn. SM Oct 20 (493) FF7,500

Variant issue with the superiorum permissu at end dated 1596. Old vellum; stained, with notes on endpapers & flyleaf. 1st 3 leaves restored at lower margins with some loss to engraved title; some worming at the front; waterstained. Crahan copy. P Nov 25 (34) $550

Bacher, Otto Henry
— With Whistler in Venice. NY, 1908. 4to, orig half cloth gilt; worn, hinges cracked. sg Feb 5 (327) $60

Bachman, John, 1790-1874. See: Audubon & Bachman

Bachman, Richard. See: King, Stephen

Back, Sir George, 1796-1878
— Narrative of the Arctic Land Expedition.... L, 1836. 8vo, half calf gilt. With folding map & 14 plates. pn Mar 5 (8) £150 [Maggs]

Anr copy. Half mor. With 16 plates on india paper. Lacking map; flaw in BB3. Manchester copy. S June 25 (374) £160 [Lake]

— Narrative of an Expedition in H.M.S. Terror. L, 1838. 1st Ed. 8vo, orig cloth; worn, lower cover detached. Folding map with short tear. bba May 28 (196) £200 [Bridge]

Backer, Augustin de & Alois de
— Bibliotheque des ecrivains de la Compagnie de Jesus. Liege, 1853-54. Vols I & II (of 7) only. 8vo, cloth; joints cracked, spines crudely reinforced. Library copy. sg Jan 22 (24) $90
— Bibliotheque de la Compagnie de Jesus.... Brussels & Paris, 1890-1909. 10 vols. 4to, half cloth; worn & shaken. sg Oct 2 (49) $800

Backhouse, James, 1794-1869
— A Narrative of a Visit to the Australian Colonies. L & York, 1843. 8vo, orig cloth; rebound. With 3 folding maps & 15 plates. CA Apr 12 (29) A$300

Bacon, Sir Francis, 1561-1626
See also: Cresset Press; Fore-Edge Paintings; Limited Editions Club
— Baconiana. L, 1679. 1st Ed, Issue with the imprimatur at A4 verso. 8vo, modern cloth. sg Mar 26 (16) $60
— Certaine Miscellany Works. L, 1629. 1st Ed. 4to, disbound. First & last few leaves frayed & dog-eared. sg Jan 15 (284) $100
— The Essayes or Counsels, Civill and Morall. L, 1680. 8vo, contemp mor gilt by Queens' Binder A. S June 25 (7) £ [Quaritch]
— The Historie of the Raigne of King Henry the Seventh. L, 1622. 1st Ed. Folio, contemp calf; repaired & rebacked, orig spine preserved. Small rust hole in lower margin of title. Gibson 116a; STC 1159. bba Apr 9 (4) £240 [Maggs]
Anr copy. Later half calf; rebacked. Ms alphabetical index bound in at end; Ms note tipped in at Ce; lower margin slightly holed. STC 1160. Ck Jan 26 (62) £130
Anr copy. Modern calf. Some soiling & browning. Gibson 116a; STC 1159. O May 12 (8) $225
Anr Ed. L, 1641. Folio, later half calf. Some stains & browning. bba Apr 9 (5) £80 [Maggs]
— Opera. Frankfurt, 1665. Folio, old vellum. Browned throughout. sg Mar 26 (15) $110
Anr Ed. L, 1730. 4 vols. Folio, contemp calf; broken, worn, rebacked. sg Jan 15 (286) $250
Anr copy. Contemp calf; rebacked, blistered, joints cracking. sg June 11 (26) $175
Anr copy. Old calf; front cover of Vol I detached but present, worn. wd June 19 (61) $125
— Sylva Sylvarum.... L, 1628. 2d Ed. Folio, old calf; rebacked, worn, spine brittle. With extra engraved title. Light dampstaining throughout. sg Jan 15 (135) $130
3d Ed. L, 1631. Folio, later half calf; rubbed. Margins of engraved title def & engraved title is laid down; some waterstains. Sold w.a.f. bba Jan 15 (10) £45 [Coupe]
Anr Ed. L, 1635. Bound with: Xenophon. The Historie. L, 1623. Folio, old calf; rebacked, edges worn. Port & additional title repaired & soiled; 2d work lacking final blank. L Dec 11 (370) £70
10th Ed. L: S. G. & B. Griffin, 1676. 8vo, contemp calf; worn, spine chipped & def, lifting. Leaf excised before engraved title; some signatures loosening. cb Feb 19 (26) $80
— The Twoo Bookes of Francis Bacon. Of the Proficience and Advancement of Learning.... L, 1605. 1st Ed. 8vo, contemp calf; rubbed. Lacking final blank & 2 errata leaves; some stains at beginning. Ck Jan 16 (60) £620
2d Ed. L, 1629. 4to, mor by Birdsall. Tp repaired; leaf 45/46 soiled & repaired in lower margin; other soiling. wd June 19 (62) $250
3d Ed. Oxford, 1633. 4to, needs rebdg. Soiled & dampstained. sg Oct 9 (94) $175
1st Ed in English of the Expanded Ed. Oxford, 1640. ("Of the Advancement and Proficience of Learning....") 2d Issue with Colophon dated 1640. Folio, early calf; free endpapers wrinkled & soiled. wa Mar 5 (240) $420
— Works. L, 1765. Ed by Thomas Birch. 5 vols. 4to, contemp calf; rubbed, joints worn. O Feb 24 (11) $100
Anr copy. Contemp calf; worn. S Feb 24 (512) £130 [Mackenzie]
Anr Ed. L, 1778. 5 vols. 4to, mor gilt. With 4 frontises & 2 folding tables. T Dec 18 (262) £380
Anr Ed. L: M. Jones, 1818. 12 vols. 12mo, contemp calf; joints weakening or repaired, upper cover of Vol I detached. cb Oct 23 (16) $110
Anr Ed. L, 1819. 10 vols. 8vo, contemp calf gilt; rubbed, joints cracking. S Jan 13 (340) £80 [Wade]
Anr Ed. L, 1825-36. 16 vols. 8vo, calf gilt, prize bdg; rubbed. S July 13 (210) £550
Anr copy. Calf gilt by Clark Bedford; some spines rubbed & worn. sg Sept 11 (5) $275
Anr copy. Contemp calf; spines rubbed. T Nov 20 (474) £200

Bacon, Mary Ann
— Flowers and their Kindred Thoughts. L, 1848. Illus by Owen Jones. 8vo, contemp calf; rebacked, rubbed. With pictorial title & 14 plates. bba Jan 15 (229) £70 [Barker]
— Winged Thoughts. L, 1851. Illus by Owen Jones. 8vo, orig blind-stamped calf; broken. With 12 plates. bba Sept 25 (165) £80

[Demetzy]

Bacon, Nathaniel, 1593-1660
— An Historicall Discourse of the Uniformity of the Government of England. L, 1647-51. 2 parts in 2 vols. 4to, contemp calf; rebacked. pn Mar 5 (276) £35 [Rix]

Bacon, Roger, 1214?-94
— The Cure of Old Age, and Preservation of Youth.... L, 1683. 1st Ed in English. 2 parts in 1 vol. 8vo, contemp calf; worn. Some dampstaining. S July 14 (288) £130

Bacon, Thomas, 1813-92. See: Fore-Edge Paintings

Badcock, Lovell
— Rough Leaves from a Journal kept in Spain and Portugal.... L, 1835. 8vo, 19th-cent half lea. sg Nov 20 (10) $90

Baddeley, John
The London Angler's Book, or Waltonian Chronicle.... L, 1834. 8vo, contemp half mor; rubbed. ALs bound in. bba Oct 30 (374) £170 [Hashimoto]

Baddeley, John Frederick
— Russia, Mongolia, China. L, 1919. One of 250. 2 vols. Folio, half cloth; spines stained. cb Feb 19 (27) $160

Anr copy. Orig half cloth. S Oct 23 (473) £900 [McManmon]

Badeau, Adam
— Military History of Ulysses S. Grant from April 1861 to April 1865. NY, 1885. 3 vols. 8vo, orig cloth; worn & soiled, hinge repaired. wa Sept 25 (304) $60

Badeslade, Thomas —&
Toms, William Henry
Chorographia Britanniae, or a Set of Maps of all the Counties in England and Wales.... L, 1742. 8vo, old calf; rebacked. With engraved title, dedication leaf, 5 (of 7) tables & 46 double-page maps. Some fold tears; Plate 3 torn with loss. Ck Sept 26 (38) £300

Anr copy. Contemp calf; broken. With engraved title, 7 engraved tables, 4 partly colored maps of England & Wales & 42 hand-colored county maps. Some tears or splits at centerfolds. pn Mar 5 (364) £440 [Burgess Browning]

Anr copy. With engraved title, dedication, 4 general maps & 42 hand-colored county maps. pn May 21 (322) £500 [Nicholson]

Anr copy. Old calf; rebacked. With engraved title & 40 maps. pn May 21 (323) £420 [Nicholson]

Anr copy. Contemp calf; worn. With engraved title, dedication leaf, 5 tables & 46 double-page maps. A few short splits without loss. S June 25 (233) £300 [Burgess]

Badger, Mrs. C. M.
— Floral Belles from the Green-House and Garden. NY, 1867. Folio, orig mor gilt; broken. With 16 hand-colored plates. 1 plate with marginal tear repaired. C Oct 15 (211) £350 [Burden]

Anr copy. Contemp mor gilt; rubbed. The last plate torn at inner blank margin. S Feb 24 (543) £550 [Wheldon]

Badger, George Percy, 1815-88
— The Nestorians and their Rituals. L, 1852. 1st Ed. 2 vols. 8vo, contemp calf gilt; joints rubbed. Lacking 2 plates. S May 6 (564) £200 [Alpha]

Baedeker, Friedrich Wilhelm Justus
— Die Eier der europaeische Voegel nach der Natur gemalt. Leipzig, 1855-63. 4 parts in 2 vols. 4to, orig bdg. With litho title & 80 color plates. B Feb 24 (118) HF750

Baer, Elizabeth
See also: Fowler & Baer
— Seventeenth Century Maryland: a Bibliography. Balt., 1949. One of 300. 4to, cloth, in d/j. sg Jan 22 (25) $110

Bage, Robert, 1728-1801
— Hermsprong; or Man as he is Not. L, 1796. 1st Ed. 3 vols. 12mo, contemp calf; worn, stained. sg Oct 9 (95) $500

Baglione, Giovanni
— Le Vite de' pittori, scultori.... Naples, 1733. 4to, old vellum; spine chipped. Some leaves soiled. S Nov 10 (44) £190 [Siruskan]

Baglivius, Georgius, 1669?-1707
— Opera omnia medico-practica et anatomica. Lyons, 1704. 1st Collected Ed. 4to, contemp calf; def. Tp & final leaf torn affecting text but without significant loss; margins stained. S Feb 24 (544) £240 [Bickersteth]

Bagrow, Leo
— History of Cartography. Cambr., Mass., 1964. Revised by R. A. Skelton. 4to, orig cloth, in d/j. sg Oct 2 (88) $120

Anr Ed. L, 1964. 4to, cloth. pn Jan 22 (78) £50 [Forster]

Baif, Lazare de, d.1547
— Annotationes in legem II de captivis, et postliminio reversis. Paris: R. Estienne, 1549. 4to, half lea. Lacking 1 leaf; some browning. HK Nov 4 (598) DM700

Baikie, Robert
— Observations on the Neilgherries. Calcutta, 1834. 8vo, disbound. With 3 folding maps hand-colored in outline (1 torn), 31 partially hand-colored maps, 1 plain & 10 hand-colored plates. bba Sept 25 (390) £1,000 [Ad Orientum]

Bailey, Henry
— Travel and Adventures in the Congo Free State.... L, 1894. 8vo, orig cloth; rubbed. cb Nov 6 (16) $110

Bailey, Liberty Hyde, 1858-1954
— Cyclopedia of American Horticulture. NY, 1906. 6 vols. 8vo, cloth; worn, some joints broken. O Nov 18 (18) $70

Anr copy. Orig half lea; extremities rubbed. sg Jan 15 (136) $175

Bailey, Samuel
— A Critical Dissertation on the Nature, Measures and Causes of Value. L, 1825. 8vo, later cloth; inner hinges cracked, spine frayed, 1 hinge previously repaired, some bubbling of cloth. Some soiling & browning, mainly marginal. P Sept 24 (238) $700
— Questions in Political Economy, Politics, Morals, Metaphysics, Polite Literature.... L, 1823. 8vo, calf gilt; rubbed, spine chipped. Library markings; some marginal staining & soiling. P Sept 24 (239) $300

Baillie, Matthew, 1761-1823
— The Morbid Anatomy of Some of the Most Important Parts of the Human Body. L, 1793. With: Baillie. A Series of Engravings Accompanied with Explanations ...Illustrate the Morbid Anatomy.... L, 1812. 2d Ed. 8vo & 4to, modern bds & half lea with arms of the Royal College of Physicians, respectively. pnE Dec 17 (61) £420 [Phillips]

Baillie-Grohman, William Adolph
— Fifteen Years' Sport and Life in the Hunting Grounds of Western American and British Columbia. L, 1900. 1st Ed. Soiled & rubbed, front hinge tender. With 3 folding maps; 1 plate detached & several foxed. cb Nov 6 (17) £100

Bailly, Jacques
— Devises pour les tapisseries du Roy. Paris: C. Blageart, 1668. 2 parts in 1 vol. Contemp calf over wooden bds. With 2 engraved titles & 12 double-page plates. Some worming & waterstaining. S Oct 23 (83) £480 [Shapero]

Baily, Nathan, d.1742. See: Worlidge, John

Bainbridge, George Cole
— The Fly Fisher's Guide.... Liverpool, 1816. 1st Ed. 8vo, half mor. pnE Dec 17 (298) £100 [Furniss]

Bainbridge, Henry Charles
— Peter Carl Faberge.... L, 1949. 4to, cloth, in d/j; worn. With port & 126 plates. O Jan 6 (16) $60

Anr copy. Half mor gilt. pn Oct 23 (121) £50 [Mannheim]

One of 350. Orig half mor. Ck May 29 (171) £120

One of 1,750. Orig cloth. bba Oct 30 (439) £35 [Hetherington]

Baines, Edward, Jr.
— History of the Cotton Manufacture in Great Britain. L, [1835]. 8vo, half calf. With 18 plates. pnE Oct 15 (189) £120

Baines, Thomas, 1806-81
— Yorkshire, Past and Present.... L, [1871-77]. 2 vols in 4. 4to, contemp calf; rubbed. Ck May 15 (163) £160

Anr copy. Cloth; spine heads worn. With folding map & 27 plates. Minor foxing to 7 plates. L Dec 11 (95) £50

Baines, Thomas, 1822-75
— The Birds of South Africa.... Johannesburg, 1975. One of 500. 4to, syn. bba Oct 30 (375) £70 [Greyfriars]
— The Gold Regions of South Eastern Africa. L, 1877. 8vo, orig cloth; rubbed & soiled. With folding map in back-cover pocket, folding facsimile & 3 (of 4) mtd photos. Ownership blindstamp on tp. S Nov 18 (1186) £70 [Negro]

Baionnette
— La Baionnette. Paris: L'Edition Francaise Illustree, 1915-16. Vols I-IV. 4to, half cloth; worn, soiled & stained. wa Sept 25 (188) $90

Baird, Joseph Armstrong. See: Grabhorn Printing

Baker, Charles H. Collins
— Lely and Stuart Portrait Painters. L, 1912. One of 375. 2 vols. 4to, cloth; rubbed. bba Dec 4 (195) £140 [Sims]

Baker, Charles Henry, Jr. See: Derrydale Press

Baker, Edward Charles Stuart
— The Indian Ducks and their Allies. L, 1908. 8vo, half mor gilt. With litho title & 30 colored plates. pn Oct 23 (168) £160 [Goddard]

Anr copy. Half mor; rubbed. S Feb 24 (545) £320 [Wellington]
— Indian Pigeons and Doves. L, 1913. Half mor. With 27 colored plates. pn Oct 23

(169) £95 [Greyfriars]

— The Nidification of Birds of the Indian Empire. L, 1932-35. 4 vols. Cloth; dampstain on cover of Vol IV. B Feb 24 (332) HF350

Baker, George, 1781-1851

— The History and Antiquities of the County of Northampton. L, 1822-41. Vol I only. Later half mor; rubbed. With frontis & 46 plates (33 on india paper, 1 hand-colored) plus 2 engraved plates (cropped & mtd, 1 hand-colored) & 1 hand-colored litho. Tp & dedication leaf torn & repaired. bba Sept 25 (437) £80 [Old Hall Bookshop]

Baker, Henry, 1698-1774

— An Attempt towards a Natural History of the Polype.... L, 1743. 8vo, contemp calf; upper cover detached. Lacking final blank. Ck June 19 (155) £110

— Employment for the Microscope. L, 1753. 8vo, contemp calf, rubbed. Plates affected by damp. Ck June 19 (153) £120

2d Ed. L, 1764. 8vo, later half calf; worn. cb Feb 19 (188) $150

Anr copy. Contemp calf; worn, 1 joint repaired. With 17 folding plates; 1 soiled in outer margin. S Nov 10 (436) £140 [Traylen]

— The Microscope Made Easy. L, 1743. 2d Ed. 8vo, contemp calf gilt. With folding table & 14 plates. S May 28 (617) £120

Anr Ed. L, 1769. 8vo, later half calf; rubbed. With 15 plates, 9 folding & 1 folding table. cb Feb 19 (189) $110

Baker, Sir Samuel White, 1821-93

— Ismailia. NY, 1875. 8vo, cloth; rubbed, spine ends frayed. Map with several tears. cb July 30 (15) $75

— The Nile Tributaries of Abyssinia. L, 1867. 1st Ed. 8vo, cloth; rubbed, corners worn. With 23 plates. cb Nov 6 (19) $75

— Wild Beasts and their Ways. L, 1890. 1st Ed. 2 vols. 8vo, orig cloth; rubbed. cb Nov 6 (20) $120

Anr copy. Calf; repaired. pn Sept 18 (39) £60 [Scott]

Baker, Thomas Turner

— The Recent Operations of the British Forces at Rangoon and Martaban. L, 1852. 8vo, modern cloth. With tinted frontis & 3 plates. Library markings but plates unstamped. sg Apr 23 (13) $70

Baker, Warren. See: John & Baker

Bakst, Leon, 1866?-1924. See: Levinson, Andre

Balbinus, Bohuslaus Aloysius, 1621-88

— Historia de ducibus, ac regibus Bohemiae. Prague, [1735]. Folio, contemp sheep. With frontis & 55 (of 56) plates. sg Mar 26 (17) $70

Balbus, Joannes

— Catholicon. Venice: Bonetus Locatellus for Octavianus Scotus, 20 Nov 1495. Folio, old vellum. Marginal dampstains at beginning & end; scattered stains elsewhere; tp soiled, with marginal repairs; last 2 leaves rehinged & remargined, with tear in lower inner corner. 312 leaves. Goff B-33. sg Apr 2 (18) $500

Baldemec

— A Week on the Jupiter River, Anticosti Island. Pvtly ptd, 1934. Bds; spine torn, extremities worn. sg Oct 23 (1171) $175

Baldner, Leonhard

— Vogel-, Fisch- und Thierbuch. Stuttgart, [1974]. 2 vols. Oblong 4to, bdg not stated. Facsimile of the Cassel copy. Haverschmidt copy. B Feb 24 (371) HF220

Baldry, Alfred Lys

— The Practice of Water-Colour Painting. L, 1911. Cloth; spine & rear cover damaged. With 38 color plates, 2 by Arthur Rackham. sg Oct 30 (15) $130

Baldwin, Edward. See: Godwin, William

Baldwin, James

— Go Tell It on the Mountain. NY, 1953. Wraps; worn & soiled. Advance proof copy. sg Mar 5 (11) $300

Baldwin, James, 1841-1925

— A Story of the Golden Age. NY, 1897. Orig cloth; rubbed. cb Sept 28 (94) $60

Baldwin, Thomas & Thomas J.

— A New and Complete Gazetteer of the United States.... Phila., 1854. 8vo, contemp sheep; worn. With folding hand-colored map. wa Sept 25 (499) $65

Baldwin, William Charles

— African Hunting from Natal to the Zambesi.... L, 1863. 2d Ed. 8vo, half calf, rubbed. With port & 16 plates. B Feb 25 (974) £160

Anr copy. Contemp calf. With folding map. SSA Oct 28 (405) R360

3d Ed. L, 1894. 8vo, cloth. SSA Oct 28 (406) R270

Bale, John, 1495-1563

— Illustrium maioris Britanniae scriptorum.... Basel: I. Oporinus, 1557-[59]. 2 parts in 1 vol. Folio, 18th-cent calf gilt; worn. Final imprimatur leaf in Vol II misbound, dampstaining. Ck Oct 31 (177) £170

Balen, Matthys
— Beschryvinge der Stad Dordrecht. Dordrecht, 1677. 4to, vellum; back damaged. With frontis, 11 ports & 4 folding plates; lacking 1 leaf of text. B Oct 7 (1377a) HF600

Balfour, James
— Reminiscences of Golf on St. Andrews Links. Edin., 1887. 8vo, bdg not described. pnC Jan 23 (22) £920

Ball, John, 1818-89
— Peakes, Passes, and Glaciers. L, 1859. 8vo, half calf; rubbed, edges worn. O Jan 6 (17) $75
— Series I-II. L, 1859-62. 3 vols. 8vo, orig cloth; soiled, 1 vol rebacked. Some spotting and marginal soiling 1 map torn. S Nov 17 (893) £150 [Henderson]

Ballantyne, Robert Michael, 1825-94
— Ungava; a Tale of Esquimaux-Land. Bost., 1859. 8vo, half lea gilt; worn. sg Oct 23 (175) $90

Ballard, J. G.
— News from the Sun. L: Interzone, 1982. One of 20. Pictorial wraps. cb Sept 28 (97) $60

Balsamo, Peolo
— A View of the Present State of Sicily. L, 1811. 4to, contemp calf gilt; rubbed. With folding map. Some stains. bba Oct 30 (280) £95 [Shapero]

Balston, Thomas
— The Cambridge University Press Collection of Private Press Types. Cambr., 1951. One of 350. Orig cloth. pn July 23 (43) £110 [Henderson]; S May 6 (40) £90 [Blackwell]
— Sitwelliana, 1915-1927; Being a Handlist of Works by Edith, Osbert, and Sacheverell Sitwell.... L, 1928. One of 70 with an extra suite of port plates sgd by the Sitwells. Inscr by Balston to Martin Secker. sg Dec 11 (442) $300

Baltimore
— Baltimore Book: A Christmas and New-Year's Present. Balt., 1838. 12mo, orig mor; loose. Contains the 1st Ptg of Poe's Siope: A Fable. ha Mar 13 (241) $80

Balzac, Honore de, 1799-1850
— Adieu. Paris, 1965. One of 200. Illus by Leonor Fini. 4to, unsewn in orig wraps. With 12 lithos. JG Mar 20 (1074) DM600
— Droll Stories. NY, 1928. One of 2,050. Illus by Ralph Barton. 2 vols. 4to, mor gilt by Sangorski & Sutcliffe. With 31 plates. cb Sept 11 (236) $400
— La Fille aux Yeux d'Or. Paris: Briffaut, [1923]. One of 40 on japon with the plates in 3 states, 2 with remarques, 1 of which is colored, & a sheet of pencil studies. Illus by Lobel-Riche. Folio, mor with onlays & gilt by Vermorel. With port & 12 plates. S Dec 4 (18) £220 [Gardimer]
— Die Frau Konnetable. Berlin, 1922. One of 380. Illus by Lovis Corinth. Folio, orig half vellum. S June 17 (94) £340 [Mosley]
— Le Peau de chagrin.... Paris, 1831. 1st Ed. 2 vols. 8vo, half mor gilt by L. Pouillet, 1871; rubbed. With 2 frontises by Tony Johannot on chine. FD June 11 (3909) DM2,000
— Les Proscrits. Paris, 1905. One of 80 on japan in 4to. Illus by Gaston Bussiere. Mor gilt with mor inlays by Affolter, orig wraps bound in. With 19 illusts in 2 states. S Sept 23 (619) £160 [Sayhoh]
— Scenes de la vie privee. Paris, 1830. 1st Ed. 2 vols. 8vo, modern half calf. S May 21 (132) £350 [Maggs]
— Works. Phila., [1895-1900]. Definitive Ed, One of 1,000. 53 vols. 8vo, mor gilt. With plates in 2 states. O May 12 (9) $850
— Caxton Ed. Phila., [1896-1900]. 52 vols. Orig cloth. Ck Nov 7 (71) £55
— Anr Ed. L, 1897-1900. 53 vols. Ck Nov 7 (60) £90
— Memorial Ed. Phila. [c.1899]. ("The Human Comedy.") One of 100. 52 vols. 8vo, mor gilt extra; rubbed. With pamphlet on Balzac by A. H. Tuttle tipped in. P Dec 15 (177) $5,500
— Anr Ed. NY: Bigelow, Brown, [c.1900]. 18 vols. 8vo, half mor gilt. sg Dec 4 (13) $750

Bampfield, Francis
— Paggnosia pantexia pansophia. All in One. L, 1677. 2 parts in 1 vol. Folio, contemp calf; rubbed, chipped, spine glue repaired. Lacking rear flyleaf, front free endpaper partially adhered to pastedown. cb Oct 23 (18) $70

Bancroft, Edward, 1744-1820
— Experimental Researches concerning the Philosophy of Permanent Colours.... L, 1794. Vol I (all pbd). 8vo, 19th-cent calf; upper joint split. Lacking initial blank. Matthew Boulton's signature, cropped, on tp. C Dec 12 (10) £600 [Bookpress]

Bancroft, Hubert Howe, 1832-1918
— History of Alaska. San Francisco, 1890. cb Oct 9 (4) $65
— Works. San Francisco, [1882]-1890. 39 vols. 8vo, calf; rubbed, some corners chipped, several joints starting. Library markings. cb Oct 9 (13) $500
— Anr Ed. San Francisco, 1883-90. 39 vols. 8vo, half cloth. Marginal dampstaining in several vols. Owner's stamp & accession number on some titles. sg Oct 2 (50) $325

Anr Ed. San Francisco, 1886-91. 39 vols. 8vo, orig calf gilt extra; light rubbing & scuffing. cb Jan 8 (8) $1,400

Bandelier, Adolph Francis, 1840-1914
— The Delight Makers. NY, [1890]. 12mo, orig cloth. sg Mar 12 (7) $50
— A Scientist on the Trail: Travel Letters.... Berkeley: Quivera Society, 1949. One of 500. cb Jan 8 (86) $80

Bandellus de Castronovo, Vincentius
— De singulari puritate et prerogative conceptionis salvatoris nostri Jesu Christi. Valladolid: Diego de Gumiel, 1502. 4to, later vellum; loose. Minor stains. Lacking prelims, errata leaf & final blank. sg Mar 26 (18) $225

Bandini, Angelo Maria, 1726-1803
— Vita e lettere di Amerigo Vespucci. Florence, 1745. 1st Ed. 4to, modern vellum. With frontis & folding table. sg Sept 18 (23) $200

Bandini, Ralph. See: Derrydale Press

Bankart, George Percy
— The Art of the Plasterer. L, 1908. 4to, orig cloth. bba July 16 (179) £40 [Fitzcamaldo]

Bankes, Thomas —& Others
— A New Royal Authentic and Complete System of Universal Geography. L, [c.1790]. 2 vols. Folio, contemp calf & modern half calf. Sold w.a.f. Ck May 15 (62) £480
Anr copy. 2 vols in 1. Folio, contemp calf; worn. With maps & 86 plates; some tears & dampstaining throughout. T Sept 18 (29) £440
Anr copy. 2 vols. Folio, contemp calf; broken. With 22 maps & 90 plates. Asia damaged along centerfold; marginal dampstains. T Nov 20 (32) £500

Banks Library, Sir Joseph
— DRYANDER, JOHN. - Catalogus bibliothecae historico-naturalis Josephi Banks. L, 1798-96-99. One of 250. Vols I-IV (of 5). 8vo, contemp half russia. C Dec 12 (11) £270 [Quaritch]

Bannerman, David Armitage
— Birds of the Atlantic Islands. Edin., 1963-68. 4 vols. Vols I & II stained. With 15 maps, 62 plain & 47 color plates. Haverschmidt copy. B Feb 24 (258) HF475
Anr Ed. L, 1963-68. 4 vols. Orig cloth, in d/js. pn Oct 23 (172) £220 [Weldon & Wesley]
— The Birds of Tropical West Africa. L, 1930-51. 8 vols. 6 vols inscr to George Carmichael Low. bba Sept 25 (199) £320 [Greyfriars]
Anr copy. Vols I-IV only. Cloth; soiled. pn Oct 23 (22) £170 [Graham]
Anr copy. 8 vols. pn Oct 23 (175) £300 [Palace]
— The Birds of West and Equatorial Africa. Edin., 1953. 2 vols. T May 21 (462) £150

Bannerman, David Armitage —& Bannerman, Winifred Mary
— Birds of Cyprus. L, 1958. Cloth, in d/j. pn Sept 18 (29) £70; pn Oct 23 (174) £80 [Richards]

Bannerman, David Armitage —& Lodge, George E.
— The Birds of the British Isles. Edin. & L, 1953-63. 12 vols. S Nov 10 (437) £220 [Head]
Anr copy. Cloth, in d/js. S May 28 (834) £204

Bannerman, Winifred Mary. See: Bannerman & Bannerman

Banville, Theodore de, 1823-91
— Les Poesies, 1841-1854. Paris, 1857. 1st Collected Ed, Ltd Ed on papier verge. 12mo, contemp half mor. ALs inserted. S July 28 (1152) £90

Baradere, H.
— Antiquites Mexicaines. Relation des trois expeditions du Capitaine Dupaix.... Paris, 1834-44. 2 vols in 1 of text & Atlas. Folio, half mor; rubbed. With map & 167 illusts on 162 sheets. Some spotting; short tear in 1st half-title & title. S Oct 23 (438) £5,000 [Perrin]

Baranano y Gutierrez, Policarpo
— La Insurreccion de Cuba pintada por si misma. Trinidad de Cuba, 1884. 8vo, orig wraps; frayed, lacking backstrip. sg Mar 12 (91) $110

Barba, Alvaro Alonso, fl.1640
— A Collection of Scarce and Valuable Treatises upon Metals, Mines and Minerals. L, 1738. Trans by the Earl of Sandwich. 12mo, contemp calf; rubbed. pn Mar 5 (293) £280 [Walford]

Barber, Joel D.
See also: Derrydale Press
— Wild Fowl Decoys. NY, [1934]. Cloth; spine ends & corners creased. cb May 21 (24) $95

Barber, John Warner, 1798-1885 —& Howe, Henry, 1816-93
— Historical Collections of the State of New York. NY, 1842. 8vo, contemp sheep; extremities worn. Folding map hand-colored in outline. Some foxing. sg Mar 12 (8)

Barber, Mary
— Poems on Several Occasions. L, 1734. 1st Ed. 4to, old calf; broken. O Mar 24 (13) $60

Barbey d'Aurevilly, Jules, 1808-89
— Les Diaboliques. Paris, 1874. 1st Ed. 12mo, mor gilt, orig wraps bound in. S June 17 (146) £320 [Roe]
— Du Dandysme et de G. Brummell. Paris, 1845. 16mo, contemp half lea. Inscr. sg Sept 11 (6) $325

Barbier, Antoine Alexandre
— Dictionnaire des ouvrages anonymes. Hildesheim, 1963. 4 vols. Titles stamped. bba Oct 16 (404) £150 [Hesketh & Ward]

Barbier, Antoine Alexandre, 1765-1825
— Dictionnaire des ouvrages anonymes et pseudonymes. Paris, 1822-27. 2d Ed. 4 vols. 8vo, contemp half lea. sg Jan 22 (27) $70

Barbier, Georges
— Designs on the Dances of Vaslav Nijinsky.... L, 1913. One of 400. 4to, orig wraps. FD Dec 2 (4202) DM1,400
— Dix-Sept Dessins sur le Cantique des Cantiques. Paris: La Belle Edition, 1914. One of 25 with an extra suite of illusts. 4to, orig wraps. S Dec 4 (3) £900 [Joseph & Sawyer]
— Falbalas et fanfreluches. Paris, 1922-26. Unsewn as issued in orig wraps. sg June 4 (24) $700

Barbon, Nicolas
— An Apology for the Builder.... L: for Cave Pullen, 1685. 4to, wraps. S July 24 (418) £1,100 [Riley-Smith]

Barbosa Machado, Diego
— Bibliotheca Lusitana Historica, Critica e Cronologica. Lisbon, 1741-59. 4 vols. Folio, 19th-cent half lea; worn. Some browning; Vol II dampstained, with small portion of title excised & restored. sg Oct 2 (51) $425

Barbut, Jacques
— The Genera Insectorum of Linnaeus. L, 1781. 4to, contemp calf gilt; rebacked. With frontis, 2 plain & 1 colored folding plates & 19 colored plates. Some browning; pen mark at foot of French title. S May 28 (578) £300

Barcia, Andres Gonzales de. See: Gonzales de Barcia, Andres

Barclay, James
— A Complete and Universal Dictionary of the English Language. Bungay, 1812. 4to, half calf; rubbed, hinges repaired. bba Dec 4 (113) £380 [Burgess Browning]
Anr copy. Contemp half mor; rubbed, joints split. Some maps cropped. S July 14 (894) £680
Anr Ed. L, [c.1840]. ("A Complete and Universal English Dictionary....") 4to, contemp calf; worn, upper joint broken. With engraved title, frontis & 49 county maps & town plans. Many leaves stained in lower portions; 1 map & 1 plate with small tear. Sold w.a.f. L July 2 (79) £420
Anr copy. Half mor; spine damaged. With 46 maps. pn Apr 30 (180) £480
Anr Ed. L, [1848?]. 4to, contemp calf; spine repaired with tape. With engraved title, 11 plates, 47 county maps & town plans. Some soiling; 3 plates torn; 4 maps with marginal defs; 7 maps with a short tear. Sold w.a.f. L Dec 11 (96) £440
Anr copy. Half mor; rubbed. Some maps hand-colored. pn May 21 (413) £500 [Map House]
Anr copy. Contemp half mor; worn, broken on front hinge. Some maps shaved with loss; dampstained. T May 21 (281) £480

Barclay, John, 1582-1621
See also: Golden Cockerel Press
— Argenis: or, the Loves of Poliarchus and Argenis. L, 1636. Trans by Kingsmill Long. 4to, mor gilt by Sangorski & Sutcliffe. With 24 plates. sg June 11 (27) $275

Barclay, Robert, 1648-90
— An Apology for the True Christian Divinity.... Birm.: Baskerville, 1765. 8th Ed. 4to, contemp calf; rubbed. bba Jan 15 (48) £40 [Grant's]

Barclay-Smith, Phyllis. See: Derrydale Press

Barere de Vieuzac, Bertrand, 1755-1841
— Rapport sur les chasses du roi.... Paris: Imprimerie Nationale, [1790]. 8vo, modern half vellum. Jeanson copy. SM Feb 28 (48) FF1,200

Barham, Richard Harris, 1788-1845
See also: Fore-Edge Paintings
— The Ingoldsby Legends. L, 1840-42-47. 1st Ed. 3 vols. 8vo, mor gilt by Larkins. sg Feb 12 (15) $425
Anr Ed. L, 1855. 3 vols. 8vo, mor by Bayntun with multi-colored mor inlays. sg Sept 11 (7) $425
Anr Ed. L, 1898. Illus by Arthur Rackham. Contemp mor gilt. sg Oct 30 (16) $80

Anr Ed. L & NY, 1907. 4to, cloth; soiled.
With 24 color plates. sg Oct 30 (18) $80
Anr copy. Cloth; worn. With 24 colored
plates. sg Jan 8 (226) $80
One of 560, sgd by Rackham. Orig vellum
gilt; warped. With 24 color plates. sg Oct
30 (17) $425
Anr copy. With 24 colored plates. wa Sept
25 (272) $230

Baring, Alexander, 1774-1848

— An Inquiry into the Causes and Consequences of the Orders in Council.... L,
1808. 2d Ed. 8vo, contemp half mor; spine
damaged, rubbed. bba Sept 25 (421) £70
[Cyclamen]

Barker, E. H.

— Literary Anecdotes and Contemporary
Reminiscences.... L, 1852. 2 vols. 8vo,
contemp half mor gilt; corners rubbed.
Titles & contents leaves inserted. sg Sept
11 (8) $140

Barker, Matthew Henry, 1790-1846

— Greenwich Hospital, a Series of Naval
Sketches.... L, 1826. Illus by George
Cruikshank. 4to, mor gilt by Root. With
12 colored plates. Marginal foxing. sg Apr
2 (19) $500
Anr copy. Mor gilt by Riviere; front cover
re-attached. With 12 hand-colored plates.
wa Mar 5 (110) $325
— Tough Yarns: A Series of Naval
Sketches...by the Old Sailor. L, 1835. 8vo,
orig cloth; piece chipped from head of
spine. With 8 plates. sg Feb 12 (52) $100

Barlaeus, Caspar, 1584-1648

Rerum per octennium in Brasilia et alibi
nuper gestarum.... Cleves, 1660. 2d Ed.
8vo, later vellum. With engraved title, port
& armorial plates, 3 maps & 5 views. sg
Mar 12 (9) $550

Barlow, Francis

— A Sett of Prints of Hunting, Hawking &
Fishing.... [L, after 1671]. Illus by
Wenceslas Hollar. 4to, half mor by
Saulnier. With engraved title & 11 plates.
Jeanson copy. SM Feb 28 (50) FF45,000
— Severall Wayes of Hunting, Hawking and
Fishing.... L: John Overton, 1671. Illus by
Wenceslas Hollar. 4to, half mor gilt by
Riviere. With 13 plates, most cut round &
mtd. Schwerdt-Jeanson copy. SM Feb 28
(49) FF60,000

Barnard, George, 1807-90

— The Theory and Practice of Landscape
Painting in Water-Colours. L & NY, 1871.
4to, orig cloth. sg Feb 5 (24) $70

Barnes, Joshua, 1654-1712

— The History of that most Victorious Monarch Edward IIId. Cambr., 1688. Folio,
contemp calf; rubbed, rebacked, new endpapers. Prelims misbound; tp soiled. bba
Mar 26 (39) £70 [Axe]; sg Mar 26 (20) $200

Barnes, Steven. See: Niven & Barnes

Barnett, Percy Neville

— Australian Book-Plates, and Book-Plates of
Interest to Australia. Sydney: Pvtly ptd,
1950. One of 200, sgd. 4to, bds, in d/j. kh
Mar 16 (32) A$250

Baron, Michel

Le Theatre. Paris: Pierre-Jacques Ribou,
1736. 12mo, 18th-cent calf gilt with arms
of the Marquise de Pompadour (Olivier
2399, fer 5). S Nov 27 (40) £200 [Booth]

Barozzi, Francesco, 1528-1612

— Cosmographia in quator libros distributa....
Venice: G. Perchacini, 1598. 8vo, contemp
vellum; soiled. Some text leaves loose;
occasional stains. S July 14 (682) £220

Barozzi, Giacomo, called Vignola, 1507-73

— Regles des cinq ordres d'architecture. Paris,
[c.1800]. 4to, modern half lea. With
engraved title & 58 plates. Some plates
soiled. S Nov 10 (45) £60 [Barker]
— Regola delli cinque ordini d'architettura.
Paris, [n.d.]. 8vo, modern calf. Engraved
throughout. With 58 plates (4 folding).
Fore-margin of 1st leaf repaired. S Nov 27
(41) £120 [Booth]
— Il Vignola illustrato proposto da Giambattista Spampani.... Rome, 1770. Folio,
half calf; def. With frontis, port & 55
plates. pn Oct 23 (44) £160
Anr copy. Contemp vellum; soiled & torn.
Some dampstains at beginning; 1 plate
bound upside-down. S Nov 10 (46) £130
[Elliott]

Barr, Louise Farrow

— Presses of Northern California and their
Books. Berkeley, 1934. One of 400. cb
Apr 2 (17) $80

Barratt, Thomas James

— The Annals of Hampstead. L, 1912. One
of 550, sgd. 3 vols. 4to, orig cloth; rubbed.
bba Aug 28 (318) £110 [Weinreb]
Anr copy. Orig cloth; scuffed. Folding
plan torn along folds. S Nov 17 (766) £160
[Brown]
Anr copy. Orig cloth; rubbed. T Oct 16
(330) £70

Barraud, Charles Decimus —& Travers, William T. L., 1819-1903
— New Zealand Graphic and Descriptive. L,1877. Folio, half mor gilt; loose. CA Apr 12 (36) A$950
Anr copy. Orig half mor; joints repaired. With colored title, map, 6 plain & 24 color plates. S Oct 23 (511) £800 [Turner]

Barre, Louis, 1799-1857
— Herculaneum et Pompei. Paris, 1862-63. 8 vols. 8vo, cloth; worn & soiled. wa Nov 6 (397) $90

Barrelier, Jacques, 1606-73
— Plantae per Galliam, Hispaniam et Italiam observatae. Paris, 1714. Folio, contemp calf; worn. With 3 engraved titles & 334 plates. With stamps of G. Cuvier & the Museum d'Histoire naturelle. S Apr 23 (21) £800 [Burden]

Barreme, Francois Bertrand de, 1640?-1703
— La Geometrie servant au mesurage et a l'arpentage. Paris: Denys Thierry, 1685. 12mo, contemp calf; rubbed. Small tear at fore-edge of engraved title. S Nov 27 (42) £140 [Booth]

Barres, Maurice, 1862-1923
— Un Jardin sur L'Oronte. Paris, 1927. One of 380. Illus by Sureda. 4to, unsewn in orig wraps. S June 17 (52) £250 [Perasi]

Barrett, Charles Golding
— The Lepidoptera of the British Islands. L, 1892-1907. 11 vols. 8vo, contemp half calf; 3 joints repaired. With 504 hand-colored plates. S Apr 23 (1) £900 [Wheldon]

Barrett, Ellen C.
— Baja California: A Bibliography.... Los Angeles, 1957-67. One of 550. 2 vols plus 1965-66 Supplement by Katharine M. Silvera, 1968. sg Jan 22 (28) $150

Barrie, James Matthew, 1860-1937
[-] The Allahakbarrie Book of Broadway for 1899. [N.p., Pvtly ptd for Barrie, 1899]. 1st Ed. 12mo, orig wraps; loose. Sgd by Barrie (as Captain) & by Mary Barrie, Bernard Partridge, Augustine Birrell, Daisy Partridge, E. H. Gilmour, A. de Navarro, Owen Seaman, A. E. W. Mason, Henry J. Ford, Herman G. Herkomer, Mary Anderson Navarro (the opposing captain), Blanche Griffin & Harry Plunket Greene. S Dec 18 (106) £750 [Laughton]
— Peter Pan in Kensington Gardens. L, [c.1920]. Illus by Arthur Rackham. 4to, orig bdg. B Oct 7 (290) HF220
Anr Ed. NY, 1930. Worn & soiled. sg Oct 30 (25) $90

Barrie, Sir James Matthew, 1860-1937
— The Little Minister. L, 1891. 1st Ed in Book form. 3 vols. 8vo, modern half mor. pnNY Sept 13 (194) $160
— Peter Pan in Kensington Gardens. L, 1906. Illus by Arthur Rackham. 4to, orig cloth. With 50 mtd color plates. sg Oct 30 (21) $110
One of 500. Orig vellum gilt; soiled & bowed; lacking ties. S Dec 4 (211) £300 [Joseph & Sawyer]
One of 500, sgd by Rackham. Orig vellum gilt. With 50 mtd color plates. sg Oct 30 (20) $1,300
Anr Ed. L, 1910. 4to, mor gilt. With 50 mtd color plates. sg Oct 30 (22) $150
Anr Ed. L, [1912]. 4to, orig cloth. With 50 mtd color plates. sg Oct 30 (24) $130
Deluxe issue with pictorial endpapers. Orig pictorial vellum gilt. With 50 mtd color plates. sg Oct 30 (23) $800
— Piter Pan. Paris: Hachette, 1911. One of 100. Folio, bds; rubbed, front cover dampstained. sg Oct 30 (26) $1,100
— Quality Street. [L, 1913]. Illus by Hugh Thomson. 4to, half mor. pn Mar 5 (327) £80 [Frazer]
One of 1,000. Vellum gilt. pnNY Sept 13 (195) $180
Anr copy. Orig vellum gilt; soiled. S May 6 (160) £140 [Hannas]
Anr copy. Paper clip stain on endpaper & limitation page. wa Dec 11 (593) $210
— Scotland's Lament. A Poem on the Death of Robert Louis Stevenson. L: Pvtly ptd for T. J. Wise, [1895]. One of 12. 8vo, sewn as issued. Wise piracy. Frank Hogan copy. bba July 2 (76) £420 [Quaritch]
— Works. NY, 1929-31. One of 1,030. 14 vols. Half cloth; some wear. O Sept 23 (16) $140

Barriere, Dominique, d.1678
— Villa Aldobrandina Tusculana.... Rome, 1647. Folio, contemp vellum; soiled. With engraved title & 19 plates. C May 13 (61) £1,300 [Weinreb]

Barrington, Daines, 1727-1800
— The Possibility of Approaching the North Pole Asserted. NY, 1818. 8vo, contemp calf; rubbed. sg Nov 20 (16) $250

Barrington, George, 1755-c.1840
— An Account of a Voyage to New South Wales. NY: J. Swain, [1796?]. ("A Voyage to New South Wales.") 8vo, contemp calf; rebacked, front hinge cracked. Margin of title and anr leaf torn & repaired. sg Nov 20 (17) $175
Anr Ed. L, 1810. 8vo, half calf; cracked, endpaper partly detached. With hand-

colored engraved title & 16 hand-colored plates. CA Apr 12 (38) A$360

Barros, Joao de, 1496-1570
— Da Asia. Lisbon, 1778-[88]. 24 vols. 12mo, 19th-cent half calf. C Apr 8 (4) £850 [Loman]

Barrough, Philip
— The Method of Physick.... L: R. Field, 1610. ("The Method of Phisick, Containing the Causes, Signes and Cures of Inward Diseases....") 4th Ed. 4to, contemp calf; worn. Tp mtd & def in blank margin; some headlines at end shaved or cut off; some worming affecting a few letters; stained & soiled in places. S May 28 (618) £100
6th Ed. L: R. Field, 1624. 4to, contemp calf; rebacked. pnE Dec 17 (65) £210 [Traylen]

Barrow, Isaac, 1630-77
— Lectiones Habitae in Scholis Publicis Academiae Cantabrigiensis: A. D. 1664 [...A.D. 1665]. L, 1683-84. 3 parts in 1 vol. Calf; rubbed. pn Jan 22 (44) £170 [Rotaoom]

Barrow, Sir John, 1764-1848
— An Account of Travels into the Interior of Southern Africa. L, 1801-4. 1st Ed. 2 vols. 4to, contemp calf gilt. With folding map, folding view & 8 maps & charts. Vol I lacking half-title, none called for in Vol II. C Oct 15 (7) £350 [Cavendish]
Anr copy. Contemp calf; loose, part of spine of Vol II missing. SSA Oct 28 (410) R500
2d Ed. L, 1806. ("Travels into the Interior of Southern Africa.") 2 vols. 4to, contemp half mor; worn, 1 vol broken. bba Dec 18 (107) £180 [Rainer]
Anr copy. Modern half calf. C Oct 15 (8) £190 [Bickersteth]
— Travels in China. L, 1804. 1st Ed. 4to, contemp calf gilt. 2 plates with adhesion marks at edge. S Feb 24 (486) £110 [Shapero]
1st American Ed. Phila., 1805. 8vo, contemp calf. wa Nov 6 (143) $55
— A Voyage to Cochinchina. L, 1806. 2 vols. 4to, contemp calf gilt, armorial bdg; upper joint repaired. With 19 colored plates & 2 folding maps. A few imprints & 1 caption of plate shaved. C Oct 15 (9) £550 [Brooke-Hitching]
Anr copy. 4to, 19th-cent calf gilt. With double-page map, double-page chart & 19 colored plates. FD June 11 (897) DM1,850
— Voyages of Discovery and Research within the Arctic Regions.... NY, 1846. 8vo, contemp half calf; worn & soiled, broken. With port & folding map. wa Nov 6 (115) $70

Barrows, John A. See: Waterman & Barrows

Barry, Sir Edward, 1696-1776
— Observations Historical, Critical, and Medical, on the Wines of the Ancients.... L, 1775. 1st Ed. 4to, contemp calf; front cover detached. First gathering coming loose. cb July 30 (206) $225
Anr copy. Half calf. Crahan copy. P Nov 25 (39) $400

Barry, George
— History of the Orkney Islands. Edin., 1805. 4to, later half calf; broken. T Sept 18 (75) £70

Bartell, Edmund
— Hints for Picturesque Improvements in Ornamental Cottages. L, 1804. 8vo, half lea; rubbed. With 6 plates. pn Jan 22 (201) £180 [Spelman]

Bartels, Max & Paul See: Ploss & Bartels

Barth, Heinrich, 1821-65
— Travels and Discoveries in North and Central Africa. Gotha, 1857-58. 5 vols. 8vo, contemp half calf. With 15 folding maps & 60 tinted plates. Ck May 8 (351) £360

Barth, John
— The Floating Opera. NY: Appleton, [1956]. 1st Ed. In d/j. Sgd. sg Mar 5 (13) $200
1st Issue. In frayed d/j. cb May 7 (3) $95
— Giles Goat-Boy. Garden City, 1966. One of 250. cb May 7 (4) $60; sg Dec 11 (3) $70

Barthelemy, Jean Jacques, 1716-95
— Voyage du jeune Anacharsis en Grece. Amst., 1799. 8 vols, including Atlas. 4to, text in wraps & Atlas in contemp calf; worn. With 39 double-page maps & plates, the maps hand-colored in outline. Lacking 1 general map but with Plate 19 bis, uncalled for.. S Feb 23 (63) £190 [Christodolou]

Barthelemy-Lapommeraye, Christophe Jerome. See: Jaubert & Barthelemy-Lapommeraye

Barthes, Roland
— Erte. Parma, 1972. 4to, silk. sg Jan 8 (69) $70

Barthez, Paul Joseph, 1734-1806
— Nouvelle mechanique des mouvements de l'homme et des animaux. Carcassonne, 1798. 4to, wraps, unopened; rebacked. Some leaves browned. S Nov 10 (438) £130 [Pickering]

BARTHOLINUS

Bartholinus, Thomas, 1616-80
— De angina puerorum Campaniae Siciliaeque epidemica exercitationes. Paris, 1646. 8vo, contemp vellum. Light stain on title. S May 21 (178) £450 [Pickering & Chatto]
— De cometa, consilium medicum, cum monstrorum nuper in Dania natorum historia. Copenhagen, 1665. 8vo, bds. Browned. S May 21 (179) £250 [Quaritch]
— De nivis usu medico.... Copenhagen, 1661. 8vo, cloth. British Museum duplicate with release stamps. S May 28 (619) £260
— De unicornu observationes novae. Amst., 1645. 2d Ed. 12mo, cloth. S May 28 (620) £150
Anr Ed. Amst., 1678. 12mo, contemp vellum. With engraved title & folding plate. FD June 11 (497) DM800

Bartholinus, Thoms, 1616-80
— De lacteis thoracis in homine brutisque nuperrime observatis.... Copenhagen: M. Marizan, 1652. 4to, old paper wraps; spine def. S May 21 (180) £2,600 [Quaritch]
— De medicina Danorum domestica dissertationes X. Copenhagen: Matthias Godicchenius for Petrus Haubold, 1666. 8vo, half calf gilt. Tears in last leaf mended. S May 21 (181) £200 [Pickering & Chatto]
— De pulmonum substantia & motu diatribe. Copenhagen: Henricus Goedianus, 1663. 8vo, old bds. S May 21 (182) £900 [Phillips]

Bartholomaeus Anglicus, fl.1230-50
— De proprietatibus rerum. L: T. Berthelet, 1535. Folio, contemp calf; rebacked. 1st leaf supplied in facsimile; some waterstaining, mostly to inner margins; some worming at end affecting letters. Crahan copy. P Nov 25 (40) $1,000

Bartholomew, Valentine
— A Selection of Flowers Adapted Principally for Students. L, [1821]-22. Folio, contemp half mor, orig wrap used as title. With 36 hand-colored plates. Tower—de Belder copy. S Apr 27 (13) £3,500 [Elliott]

Bartisch, Georg, 1535-1607?
— Ophthalmodouleia, das ist Augendienst. [Dresden: Matthes Stoeckel], 1583. Folio, disbound. Lacking some leaves. FD Dec 2 (511) DM5,000

Bartlett, Edward Everett
— The Typographic Treasures in Europe. NY & L, 1925. One of 585. Folio, orig half cloth; worn. O June 16 (18) $60
Out-of-series copy. Orig half cloth. bba Oct 16 (474) £60 [Check Books]

AMERICAN BOOK PRICES CURRENT

Bartlett, John Russell, 1805-86
— Personal Narrative of Explorations and Incidents in Texas.... NY, 1854. 1st Ed. 2 vols. 8vo, contemp calf; worn. With folding map & 16 plates. sg Mar 12 (10) $350

Bartlett, William Henry, 1809-54
See also: Finden, William; Willis & Coyne
— Forty Days in the Desert. L, [1849]. 8vo, orig cloth; worn. Inscr "J. Estelos Esq. from the Author". bba Oct 30 (283) £75 [Mandel]
— The History of the United States of North America. NY, [1856]. 3 vols. 8vo, contemp sheep; worn & soiled, Vol II spine shabby. Lacking pp 679-82 of Vol II & 2 plates in Vol II, but with 3 extra plates in Vol I. wa Feb 19 (291) $210
— The Nile Boat.... NY, 1851. 8vo, orig cloth. Some plates foxed. sg Apr 23 (16) $130
— Walks about the City and Environs of Jerusalem. L, [c.1845]. 2d Ed. 4to, orig cloth. With 27 maps & plates. pn Jan 22 (59) £45 [Trotter]

Bartoli, Daniello, 1608-85
— Del suono de' tremori armonici e dell' udito. Rome, 1679. 4to, contemp vellum bds. HK Nov 4 (907) DM1,000

Bartoli, Pietro Santi, c.1635-1700
— Colonna Traiana..... [Rome, 1673]. Oblong folio, old calf; worn, rebacked & recornered. With engraved title & 126 plates. With 1 marginal tear. S May 29 (1040) £160
— Columna cochlis M. Aurelio Antonino Augusto dicata.... Rome, 1704. Folio, contemp half lea; rebacked. With engraved title & dedication, & 77 plates only. HK Nov 4 (1647) DM500
— Museum Odescalchum, sive Thesaurus antiquarum gemmarum. Rome, 1751-52. 2 vols. Folio, later calf; rubbed. With 104 plates. Ck Nov 21 (140) £240
— Recueil de peintures antiques. Paris, 1783-87. Bound with: Rive, l'Abbe. Histoire critique de la pyramide de Caius Cestius. One of 10 l.p. copies. 2 works in 3 vols. Folio, contemp mor gilt. With 54 plates colored by hand in the style of the Comte de Caylus & 6 uncolored plates in Vol III. C May 13 (115) £6,000 [Marlborough]

Bartolus de Saxoferrato
— Codex: Super tribus ultimis libris codicis.... Venice: Nicolaus Jenson, 1477. Folio, vellum. Wormed. 84 (of 86) leaves; lacking 1st & last blanks. Goff B-205. S Nov 27 (141) £900 [Zeitlin]
— Digestum novum: Super prima parte digesti novi * Inforitatum: Super prima [secunda] parte Infortiati. Milan: Leonardus Pachel, 1491. 2 vols. Folio, modern calf. Accom-

panied by cover from previous bdg of the 1st vol bearing Royal Society bookplate & half of Pirckheimer bookplate designed by Duerer. 251 (of 252) leaves; 167 (of 168) leaves; 190 leaves. Goff B-236 & B-241; GKW 3623 & 3638. Pirckheimer set. sg Dec 4 (14) $2,200

Barton, Benjamin Smith, 1766-1815
— Fragments of the Natural History of Pennsylvania. Phila., 1799. Folio, bdg not indicated but orig wraps present. Library markings. Sold w.a.f. Franklin Institute copy. F Sept 12 (163) $650

Barton, Benjamin Smith, 1766-1815 —& Castle, Thomas, c.1804-38
— The British Flora Medica. L, 1877. 8vo, contemp half calf; rubbed. With 48 colored plates. pnE Dec 17 (179) £170 [Phelps]

Barton, Rose
Familiar London. L, 1904. One of 300. 4to, orig cloth; soiled. pn Nov 20 (208) £120 [Black]

Barton, William Paul Crillon, 1786-1856
— A Flora of North America. Phila., 1821-23. 1st Ed. 3 vols. 4to, contemp half calf; corners worn, rebacked. With 106 hand-colored plates. de Belder copy. S Apr 27 (14) £3,400 [Sourget]

Bartram, William, 1739-1823
— Travels through North and South Carolina, Georgia.... L, 1792. 8vo, contemp calf; rubbed, joints split. With folding map & 8 plates. Def in a2. S May 29 (1144) £340
Anr copy. Cloth. Each plate with perforated library stamp. sg Mar 12 (11) $200

Bartsch, J. Adam von, 1757-1821
Anleitung zur Kupferstichkunde. Vienna, 1821. 2 vols. 8vo, contemp half calf. With 11 folding plates. S Nov 10 (48) £60 [Vine]
— Le Peintre graveur. Vienna, 1803-21. 21 vols in 14 & Supplement of 1843. 8vo, half mor. C Dec 3 (2) £1,100 [Quaritch]
Anr Ed. Leipzig, 1854-70. 21 vols. 8vo, later half lea; worn & loose. sg May 14 (39) $150
Anr Ed. Leipzig, 1876. 21 vols in 16. 8vo, cloth. C July 22 (18) £300

Baruch, H. N.
— A Fisherman's Paradise. NY, 1910. Copy numbered 4.987.728. Inscr to Emlyn Gill. sg Oct 23 (176) $200

Basan, Pierre Francois, 1723-97
— Collection de cent-vingt estampes, gravees d'apres les tableaux & dessins...de M. Poullain. Paris, 1781. 4to, contemp calf gilt, armorial bdg; spine rubbed. With 119 (of 120) plates; lacking Plate 94. S Oct 23 (1) £550 [Schmidt]
— Receuil d'estampes gravees d'apres les tableaux du Cabinet de Monseigneur le Duc de Choiseul. Paris, 1771. 4to, orig bds; worn, spine lacking. With engraved title & 127 reproductions on 124 plates only. Plate 69 def; lacking port & plate 69×. S Feb 23 (3) £640 [L'Acquaforte]
— [Sale Catalogue] Catalogue des Tableaux du cabinet de feu M. Louis-Michel Vanloo.... Paris, 1772. Modern cloth. Priced throughout in a contemp hand. cb Feb 19 (5) $180
— [Sale Catalogue] Catalogue raisonne des differens objects de curiosites dans les sciences et arts.... Paris, 1775. Contemp calf. Priced throughout in a contemp hand. cb Feb 19 (6) $250

Basil the Great, Saint, c.330-379
— Opera. Basel: Froben, 1551. Folio, later blind-stamped cloth; worn. In Greek. bba Oct 30 (174) £190 [Sokol]

Basile, Giovanni Battista, c.1575-1632
— Il Pentamerone; or, the Tale of Tales. L, 1893. Ltd Ed. Trans by Sir Richard Burton. 2 vols. 8vo, half mor gilt. S Mar 9 (898) £55 [Owen]

Basket, Sir James
— History of the Island of St. Domingo.... L, 1818. 1st Ed. 8vo, modern bds; rubbed. O Nov 18 (21) $50

Baskin, Leonard
— Ars Anatomica: A Medical Fantasia. NY, [1972]. Folio, loose as issued in portfolio. With 13 plates. wa June 25 (528) $110

Basnage, Jacques, 1653-1725
— The History of the Jews.... L, 1708. Trans by Thomas Taylor. Folio, orig lea; broken. Some foxing & browning. S Feb 17 (13) £180 [Ben Alza]

Bason, Frederick T.
— A Bibliography of the Writings of William Somerset Maugham. L, 1931. One of 3 in red cloth & sgd by Maugham. With 5 Ls s from Bason to Duncan Cranford laid in. wd Nov 12 (178) $250

Bataille, Georges
— Le Mort. Paris, 1964. One of 20 with a plance refusee & a suite of the etchings sgd & numbered by the artist. Illus by Andre Masson. Oblong folio, unsewn in orig vellum. With 9 colored plates. S June 17 (127) £600 [Peeper]

Bates, Joseph D.
— Atlantic Salmon Flies and Fishing. Harrisburg: Stackpole, [1970]. One of 600. Half cloth. sg Oct 23 (177) $150
— The Atlantic Salmon Treasure. Montreal: Atlantic Salmon Association, 1975. One of

1,000. Mor gilt. sg Oct 23 (467) $70

Bates, Samuel P.
— History of Pennsylvania Volunteers, 1861-5.... Harrisburg, 1869-71. 5 vols. 4to, contemp half lea; worn, some joints splitting, 1 cover detached. wa June 25 (196) $140

Bathe, Greville & Oliver
— Oliver Evans: a Chronicle of Early American Engineering. Phila., 1935. One of 500. 4to, orig cloth; soiled & worn. wa Nov 6 (171) $110

Batsch, August Johann Georg Karl, 1761-1802
— Der Geoeffnete Blumengarten. Weimar, [1796]-98. 8vo, contemp half lea. With 99 (of 100) colored plates. Lacking Plate 37. HK Nov 4 (908) Dm1,800

Battara, Giovanni Antonio, 1714-89
— Fungorum agri ariminensis historia. Faenza, 1755. 4to, 19th-cent bds. With vignette title & 40 plates. Some browning. Crahan copy. P Nov 25 (41) $950

Anr copy. Bds; upper joint split. With 40 plates. C2-3 slightly creased; Plate 18 grazed. S May 28 (621) £320

Batty, Elizabeth Frances
— Italian Scenery. L, 1820. 4to, contemp half mor; worn. With engraved title & 60 plates. Library markings. bba Feb 5 (358) £75 [Barker]

Anr copy. Half mor; worn, rubbed. cb Oct 23 (20) $110

Anr copy. Calf, with arms of the Signet Library; def. pn July 23 (55) £270 [Thorp]

Anr copy. Half mor; joints repaired. Some plates foxed. sg Nov 20 (18) $200

Batty, Robert, d.1848
— French Scenery. L, 1822. 4to, contemp half mor; rubbed. With engraved title & 64 plates, all on india paper mtd. bba Apr 23 (347) £140 [Mandl]

Anr copy. Modern half mor. Lacking the cancelled half-title; some foxing; last few plates marginally dampstained. bba July 16 (136) £110 [Thorp]

Anr copy. Contemp mor gilt. With engraved title & 65 plates. Upper margins affected by dampstain. Ck Nov 21 (451) £130

Anr copy. Half mor gilt; rubbed. With engraved title & 64 plates. pn Dec 11 (23) £140 [Walford]

— German Scenery.... L, 1823. 4to, contemp mor. With engraved title & 61 plates. Ck Nov 21 (222) £1,200 [Quaritch]

Anr copy. Half calf gilt. S June 25 (301) £1,100 [Maliye]

— Hanoverian and Saxon Scenery. L, 1829. Folio, modern cloth. Ink stamps on plates; perforated stamp on title & 1 other leaf. bba Feb 5 (367) £750 [Elliott]

Anr copy. Contemp mor gilt; worn. HN May 20 (1217) DM3,700

Anr copy. Contemp half mor gilt. JG Mar 20 (454) DM5,600

Anr copy. Half mor gilt. With engraved title & 60 plates. Some plates foxed. sg Dec 4 (17) $1,700

— Scenery of the Rhine, Belgium and Holland. L, 1826. 4to, disbound. With engraved title, frontis & 60 plates. Ck Nov 21 (225) £650 [Walford]

— Select Views of Some of the Principal Cities of Europe. L, 1832. Folio, contemp calf; rubbed. With engraved title & dedication, 30 plates & 30 outline plates, each with small ink library stamps. bba Dec 18 (107) £180 [Rainer]

Anr copy. Contemp half calf; rubbed. With 5 plates at end with waterstained margins. C Oct 15 (10) £230 [Shapero]

Anr copy. Contemp half mor; joints rubbed. With engraved title, dedication & 30 plates, each in 3 states. Ck Nov 21 (224) £300

Anr copy. Contemp half mor; rubbed. With engraved title & dedication, 30 plates & 30 outline plates. S Feb 23 (4) £280 [Shapero]

— Welsh Scenery. L, 1825. 4to, contemp half mor; scuffed. With 35 plates. Ck Feb 27 (238) £90

Baudelaire, Charles, 1821-67
— Les Fleurs du mal. Paris, 1861. 2d Ed. 12mo, half mor. Some foxing. S May 21 (133) £600 [Shimoigusa-Shobo]

Anr Ed. Paris, 1910. One of 99 on japon with plates in 2 states. Illus by Georges Rochegrosse. 4to, mor extra by Charles Lanoe. With 27 plates. SM Oct 20 (587) FF7,000

Anr Ed. Paris, 1916. One of 200 on velin d'Arches. Illus by Emile Bernard. 4to, mor extra by Duryand-Pinard. FD Dec 2 (4210) DM2,200

Anr Ed. Paris, 1917. One of 50 on chine. Illus by Georges Rochegrosse. 8vo, mor extra by Blanchetiere. FD June 11 (4798) DM3,000

Anr Ed. Paris, 1920. One of 200 on verge d'Arches. Illus by Louise Hervieu. 8vo, mor extra, orig wraps preserved, by Georges Levitsky. SM Oct 20 (588) FF15,000

Anr Ed. Paris, 1940. One of 106. Illus by L. Lafnet. 4to, calf extra by G. Crette.

Extra illus with 3 orig designs by Lafnet & an extra suite of plates. SM Oct 20 (590) FF30,000
— Fleurs du mal in Pattern and Prose. L, 1929. One of 20, sgd by the artist. Illus by Beresford Egan. 4to, orig half vellum. bba May 14 (126) £210 [Oram]
— Oeuvres. Paris, 1922-37. One of 50 on japon imperial. Contemp half mor, orig wraps bound in; rubbed. With port in 2 states. Ck Sept 5 (190) £220
— Les Paradis artificiels.... Paris, 1861. Variant issue with title dated 1861 & wrap dated 1860, 12mo, half cloth, orig wraps bound in. S May 21 (134) £350 [Perrin]
  Anr Ed. Paris: Editions Vialetay, 1955. One of 16 on papier de Rives with an orig plate & 3 suites of plates. Illus by Mariette Lydis. 4to, sous chemise et etui. SM Oct 20 (589) FF3,500
— Petits Poemes en prose. Paris, 1926. One of 360. Illus by Marcel Gromaire. 4to, orig wraps; browned, backstrip broken. HN May 20 (2481) DM900

Baudelocque, Jean Louis, 1746-1810
— L'Art des accouchemens.... Paris, 1796. 2 vols. 8vo, contemp bds; rebacked with calf. With 17 folding plates. Some dampstaining, mostly in Vol II; small tear in Plate 6; last leaf in Vol I with tiny hole & small repair to margin; Vol II with small repair to blank portion of tp; short tear in E8; minor flaw in S5; marginal repair to Y8 affecting letters. S Nov 27 (249) £250 [Studd]

Baudement, Emile
— Les Races bovines au concours universel agricole de Paris en 1856.... Paris, 1861. 2 vols. Oblong folio, contemp half mor; rubbed. With 5 colored maps & 87 plates. S Apr 23 (22) £1,800 [Guller]

Baudry des Lozieres, Louis N.
— Voyage a la Louisiane. With: Second Voyage de la Louisiane. Paris, 1802-3. 3 vols. 8vo, contemp half calf; joints cracked, worn. With map. Robert R. Livingston's copy. sg Apr 23 (18) $650

Bauer, Franz Andreas, 1758-1840
— Illustrations of Orchidaceous Plants.... L, 1830-38. Folio, contemp mor gilt. With 15 plain & 20 hand-colored plates. A few plates foxed. Derby—de Belder copy. S Apr 27 (15) £3,800 [Asher]

Bauer, Louis Hopewell
— Aviation Medicine. Balt.: Williams & Wilkins, 1926. In torn d/j. wa Nov 6 (56) $60

Bauhaus
— Die Buhne im Bauhaus. Munich: Albert Langen, [1924]. Bauhausbucher 4. HN Nov 26 (1716) DM620

Bauhin, Jean —& Cherler, Jean Henri
— Historia plantarum universalis.... Yverdon, 1650-51-51. 3 vols. Folio, old vellum; rebacked with mor, edges & corners repaired. Collates as the Hunt copy except that Vol I has 9-page index not present in the latter; Vol II lacks 1 prelim; in Vols II & III index bound at end rather than beginning; & several blank leaves are lacking. Crahan copy. P Nov 25 (42) $1,300

Bauhin, Johann, 1541-1613
— Histoire notable de la rage des loups.... Montebeliard, 1591. 8vo, 18th-cent calf gilt. Lacking final blank. Jeanson copy. SM Feb 28 (52) FF16,000

Bauhinus, Caspar, 1560-1624
— Pinax theatri botanici.... Basel, 1623. 4to, contemp vellum. Tp stamped on verso. FD June 11 (532) DM2,600

Baum, Frank Joslyn
— The Laughing Dragon of Oz. Racine: Whitman, [1934]. Illus by Milt Youngren. Pictorial bds. Browned. cb Sept 28 (110) $325
  Anr copy. Bds; rubbed, front hinge cracked & repaired with glue, lacking front free endpaper. cb May 7 (108) $110

Baum, L. Frank, 1856-1919
— Once Upon a Time.... Chicago, [1917]. 1st Ed, 2d State. Worn & dusted. ha Dec 19 (156) $60
— Ozma of Oz. Chicago, [1907]. 1st Ed, 1st State. In 2dary bdg. K June 7 (41) $90
— The Scarecrow of Oz. Chicago, [1915]. 1st Ed, 1st State. Orig cloth; dampstain to rear cover, front cover yawning slightly. cb Sept 28 (107) $170
— Sky Island. Chicago, [1912]. 1st Ed. O Apr 28 (21) $130
— The Story of Jaglon. Chicago, [1953]. ("Jaglon and the Tiger Fairies.") Ed by Jack Snow. In rubbed d/j. cb Sept 28 (102) $85
  The Uplift of Lucifer. Los Angeles, 1963. One of 500. Wraps. cb Sept 28 (108) $70
— The Wonderful Wizard of Oz. Chicago & NY, 1900. 1st Ed, 1st State. 8vo, orig cloth, variant B spine imprint with pbr's name in plain type, stamped in red; lightly bumped, 1 plate detached but present, 2 plates just beginning to loosen from joint. cb Dec 4 (76) $900

Bauman, Hans F. S.
— 150 Years of Artists' Lithographs. L, 1953. One of 135. Illus by Graham Sutherland. 4to, orig vellum. With 13 colored illusts, & a sgd & numbered colored litho. S June 17 (287) £400 [Joseph]

Baumann, Gustave
— Frijoles Canyon Pictographs.... Sante Fe, [1939]. One of 500. Cloth. Minor stain affecting fore-edge of 1st 9 leaves. cb June 18 (11) $130

Baume, Antoine
— Chymie experimentale et raisonnee. Paris, 1773. 3 vols. 8vo, contemp calf. With port & 12 folding plates. C Dec 12 (12) £420 [Israel]

Bavaria
— Bairische Lanndsordnung. Ingolstadt: A. Weissenhorn, 1553. Bound with: Erclaerung der Landsfreiheit...widerumb verneut. Munich: A. Schobser, 1553. And: Declaration und erleuterung etlicher in Ieungst Bayrischer auffgerichter Policeyordnung begriffner Articul. [Munich: A. Schobser, 1557]. Folio, 19th-cent bds; worn. Each work with woodcut tp; 1st work with 3 folding woodcuts of fish. Marginal worming; some browning. Library stamps on 2d & last leaves. Crahan copy. P Nov 25 (43) $2,200

Baxter, Evelyn V. —& Rintoul, Leonora Jeffrey
— The Birds of Scotland. Their History, Distribution and Migration. L, 1953. 2 vols. pn Oct 23 (178) £85 [Old Hall]; pnE June 17 (130) £70

Anr copy. ALs sgd by both loosely inserted. pn Dec 11 (228) £120 [Graham]

Baxter, George
— The Pictorial Album; or, Cabinet of Paintings, for the Year 1837. L, [1837]. 4to, mor gilt; rubbed. With engraved title & 10 plates. pn Dec 11 (207) £350 [Thorp]

Baxter, Richard, 1615-91
— Reliquiae Baxterianae; or, Mr. Richard Baxter's Narrative.... L, 1696. Folio, 19th-cent mor. With engraved title, frontis & 9 plates. bba Aug 28 (178) £60 [P & P Books]

Baxter, William, 1787-1871
— British Phaenogamous Botany.... Oxford, 1834-43. Vols I-V (of 6). 8vo, contemp half calf. Sold w.a.f. C Apr 8 (207) £550 [Walford]

Anr copy. 6 vols. 8vo, mor gilt by Mackenzie. With 509 hand-colored plates. Plate 354 in Vol V spotted. S Apr 23 (2) £850 [Finer]

Anr copy. Half calf gilt. S May 6 (622) £750

Anr copy. Later half mor gilt. With 500 hand-colored plates. Some discoloration. S June 25 (146) £800 [Houle]

Bayardo, Matheo Maria. See: Boiardo, Matteo Maria

Bayer, Gottlieb Siegfried
— Museum sinicum in quo sinicae linguae et literaturae ratio explicatur. St. Petersburg, 1730. 2 vols in 1. 8vo, vellum bds. S Apr 23 (331) £280 [Ad Orientum]

Bayer, Johann, 1572-1625
— Uranometria: Omnium Asterismorum Continens Schemata. Ulm: Johann Goerlin, 1661. Folio, later vellum. With engraved title & 51 double-page charts, hand-colored in full throughout & with many star symbols painted with gold; each chart neatly titled in ink within a scroll on recto. Tp & margins a little browned. S Oct 23 (223) £1,500 [Martayan]

Bayle, Pierre, 1647-1706
— Dictionaire historique et critique. Rotterdam, 1720. 3d Ed. 4 vols. Folio, contemp calf; worn. bba Mar 12 (69) £40 [Bailey]

Anr copy. Contemp calf gilt; worn & repaired. HN Nov 26 (852) DM1,050

— The Dictionary. L, 1734-38. 5 vols. Folio, contemp calf; rubbed, some corners chipped. Half-title of Vol II torn. cb Oct 23 (21) $200

Anr copy. Bdg not indicated. Library markings. Sold w.a.f. Franklin Institute copy. F Sept 12 (114) $500

— Dictionnaire historique et critique. Amst. & Leiden, 1730. 4th Ed. 4 vols. Folio, half calf; rubbed, spines chipped. O Nov 18 (22) $80

— An Historical and Critical Dictionary. L, 1710. 4 vols. Folio, old calf; broken, joints tape-repaired. K Mar 22 (46) $110

— Oeuvres diverses. The Hague, 1727-31. 4 vols. Folio, contemp calf; worn. C May 13 (56A) £100 [Greenwood]

Anr copy. Contemp lea. Some browning. HK Nov 4 (1691) DM520

Bayley, Frank W., 1863-1932
— Five Colonial Artists of New England. Bost., 1929. One of 500. Folio, later cloth; worn. O Jan 6 (17) $75

Anr copy. Library markings. O Mar 24 (14) $50

Anr copy. Cloth. O May 12 (10) $150

Bayley, John Whitcomb, d.1869
— History and Antiquities of the Tower of London. L, 1821-25. 1st Ed. 2 vols. Folio, contemp half calf; rebacked with modern calf, rubbed, corners worn. With 30 plates, some soiled or marginally dampstained. cb Dec 18 (11) $85

Anr Ed. L, 1825. 2 vols. Folio, 19th-cent half mor by Mansell. With 27 plates & with 2 orig 17th-cent Tower warrants inserted. L.p. copy. S Nov 10 (767) £150 [Thorp]

Baylis, Edward
— A New and Compleat Body of Practical Botanic Physic.... L, 1791-93. Vol I (all pbd). 4to, contemp mor gilt; worn. With 48 hand-colored plates. Some plates trimmed; lacking ad slip. S Nov 10 (439) £280 [Way]

Anr copy. Modern half mor gilt, orig wraps preserved. de Belder copy. S Apr 27 (17) £1,500 [Elliott]

Bayliss, Marguerite F. See: Derrydale Press

Baylor, Armistead Keith
— Abdul, an Allegory. NY: Derrydale Press, 1930. One of 500. sg Oct 23 (13) $325

Bayros, Franz von
— Im Garten der Liebe. Pvtly ptd, [c.1915]. 4to, loose in bd portfolio; front hinge cracked. With 18 plates. sg Feb 12 (72) $200

Bazin, Gilles Augustin, d.1754
— Histoire naturelle des Abeilles. Paris, 1744. 2 vols. 8vo, contemp calf gilt; covers with minor surface damage. 4 plates supplied in duplicate; 1 plate discolored. sg Jan 15 (139) $250

Beach, Spencer Ambrose, 1860-1922
— Apples of New York. Albany, 1905. 2 vols. Cloth; worn. O Oct 21 (20) $100

Anr copy. Cloth; worn, 1 cover stained. O Nov 18 (23) $90

Beach, William Nicholas See: Derrydale Press

Beadle, John Hanson
— The Undeveloped West; or, Five Years in the Territories.... Phila.: National Publishing Co, [1873]. 8vo, orig mor; soiled. cb Jan 8 (10) $85

Beagle, Peter S.
— Lila the Werewolf. Santa Barbara: Capra Press, 1974. One of 75. Bds. cb May 7 (309) $55

Beall, Karen F.
— Cries and Itinerant Trades. Hamburg, [1975]. One of 750. Folio, cloth. Text in English & German. sg Oct 2 (54) $250

Bean, W. See: Watson & Bean

Beard, Charles R.
— A Catalogue of the Collection of Martinware formed by Mr. Frederick John Nettlefold. L, 1936. Folio, orig cloth. Library stamps on title & plates. S May 6 (363) £110 [Elliot]

Anr copy. Later cloth. Library markings. sg Feb 5 (78) $200

Beardsley, Aubrey, 1872-98
— A Book of Fifty Drawings. L, 1897. 4to, cloth; worn. sg Dec 11 (176) $70
— The Early Work. L, 1899. With: The Later Work. L, 1901. 2d ptg. Together, 2 vols. 4to, orig cloth; worn. sg June 4 (30) $250
— Letters from Aubrey Beardsley to Leonard Smithers. L, 1937. Orig cloth. cb May 7 (6) $50
— A Portfolio of Drawings Illustrating "Salome" by Oscar Wilde. [L: Lane, 1907]. Folio, loose as issued in half vellum folder; worn. With 17 plates on Japan vellum. S Oct 6 (758) £50 [Marks]
— A Portfolio of Aubrey Beardsley's Drawings Illustrating "Salome" by Oscar Wilde. [L: John Lane, 1920]. Folio, loose in portfolio. With 16 plates & cul de lampe. Ck Jan 30 (158) £170; sg June 18 (178) $150
— Reproductions of Eleven Designs Omitted from the First Edition of Le Morte Darthur. L, 1927. One of 300. 4to, orig calf-backed vellum bds. Ck Jan 16 (133) £170
— The Uncollected Work. L, 1925. Intro by C. Lewis Hind. 4to, cloth; rear cover blistered. sg Feb 5 (29) $80
— Under the Hill.... L, 1904. 4to, orig cloth; bumped, minor tape marks to free endpapers. With port & 16 plates. cb May 7 (7) $100

Beaton, Cecil
— The Best of Beaton. L, [1968]. 4to, cloth, in def d/j. Inscr. sg Nov 13 (12) $50

Beattie, James, 1735-1803. See: Fore-Edge Paintings

Beattie, William, 1793-1875
— The Castles and Abbeys of England. L, [c.1860]. 2 vols. Modern cloth. bba Dec 4 (335) £65 [Rainer]
— The Danube. L, [c.1840]. Illus by William H. Bartlett. 4to, orig cloth; worn. Lacking 2 ports & 1 map. Sold w.a.f. pn Sept 18 (242) £320 [Garwood]

Anr Ed. L, [1844]. Illus by W. H. Bartlett. 4to, contemp half calf; worn. With engraved title, map & 78 plates. S May 28 (838) £280
— Scotland Illustrated.... L, 1838. 2 vols. 4to,

BEATTIE

old lea; worn, Vol II bdg broken. With 2 engraved titles, folding map & 118 plates. K June 7 (332) $120

Anr copy. Half calf; worn. pn Nov 20 (231) £65

Anr copy. Calf; rebacked, rubbed. pn Mar 5 (187) £130 [Map House]

Anr copy. Mor gilt. With 2 engraved titles, folding map & 118 plates. Map torn; a few leaves with marginal tear. S Nov 17 (768) £85 [Arjomanc]

Anr copy. Mor gilt; worn. Map repaired. S Nov 17 (769) £130 [Boyd]

Anr copy. Contemp mor gilt; rubbed. Some spots & stains. S July 14 (291) £130

Anr copy. Calf gilt; rubbed, some wear to spines. Some foxing. T Apr 16 (70) £90

Anr Ed. L & NY, [1838]. ("Caledonia Illustrated....") 2 vols. 4to, calf gilt. With map & 145 plates. Sold w.a.f. pn Nov 20 (230) £140 [Goodall]

Anr Ed. L, 1842. 2 vols. 4to, orig cloth. Some foxing. pn Nov 20 (226) £90 [Kidd]

— Switzerland Illustrated.... L, 1834-36. Illus by William H. Bartlett. 2 vols. 4to, contemp half calf; worn. With 81 plates only. Text of Vol II incomplete. T Jan 22 (2) £180

Anr Ed. L, 1836. Illus by W. H. Bartlett. 2 vols. 4to, contemp lea; worn, lacking spines. With engraved titles, folding map & engraved plates. bba Dec 4 (301) £280 [Brailey]

Anr copy. Half mor; worn, 1 cover detached. With engraved titles, folding map & 106 plates. Perforated stamp on titles & a few leaves. bba Feb 5 (365) £260 [Walford]

Anr copy. 2 vols in 1. 4to, contemp mor gilt; rubbed. Some dampstaining & spotting; folding map torn. bba June 18 (332) £340 [Goulden]

Anr copy. 2 vols. 4to, contemp half mor; rubbed. Fold tear to map; minor spotting to engraved titles. C Oct 15 (11) £450 [Van Noord]

Anr copy. Contemp mor gilt. With engraved titles, folding map & 106 plates... C Dec 12 (268) £350 [Willan]

Anr copy. Contemp calf; rubbed. FD June 11 (857) DM1,500

Anr copy. Contemp half mor; rubbed. L Dec 11 (158) £100

Anr copy. Mor gilt; worn. pn May 21 (220) £340 [Brayley]

Anr copy. Contemp half mor; spines worn, 3 covers detached. 1 crudely hand-colored. sg Nov 20 (20) $350

Anr copy. Contemp half calf gilt. About

AMERICAN BOOK PRICES CURRENT

one-third of the plates foxed. sg Apr 23 (19) $475

Anr Ed. L, 1839. 2 vols. 4to, contemp mor gilt. With engraved titles, folding map & 106 plates. One imprint slightly cropped. S May 28 (837) £400

— The Waldenses. L, 1838. 4to, contemp half calf gilt; rubbed. With port, engraved title, folding map & 70 hand-colored plates. bba Oct 30 (284) £140 [Bailey]

Anr copy. Contemp half mor; rubbed. With port, engraved title, folding map & 20 plates. Ck Nov 21 (223) £110

Anr copy. Orig cloth. With port, engraved title & 70 hand-colored plates (map not mentioned). Ck Feb 27 (36) £120

Anr copy. Contemp calf gilt; rubbed. With port, engraved title, folding map & 70 hand-colored plates. L Dec 11 (158) £100

Anr copy. Contemp half calf; rubbed. With engraved title, port, folding map & 64 (of 70) plates. Some spotting & discoloration. S May 29 (1041) £110

Anr copy. Half mor gilt. With engraved title, port, folding map & 70 plates. Some stains. S July 14 (664) £120

Anr copy. Contemp half lea; worn, front cover detached. With port, engraved title, folding map & 70 hand-colored plates. sg Nov 20 (21) $140

Anr copy. Disbound. With 69 (of 70) plates. Sold as collection of plates. Sold w.a.f. sg Dec 18 (145) $100

Anr copy. Contemp mor; loose. Some foxing & marginal stains. SSA Feb 11 (451) R280

Anr copy. Contemp half mor; spine worn. With port, frontis, vignette title & 70 plates & folding map bound in at rear. Marginal dampstains. T May 21 (226) £105

Beatty Library, Sir A. Chester

— A Catalogue of the Turkish Manuscripts and Miniatures. Dublin, 1958. 1st Ed. Compiled by V. Minorsky. Folio, orig cloth. With frontis & 42 plates. C Nov 21 (32) £75

— A Handlist of the Arabic Manuscripts. Dublin, 1955-66. 8 vols. Ck Nov 7 (187) £300

Beaufort

— Le Grand Portefeuille Politique.... Paris, 1789. Folio, orig half calf; worn & rubbed. Light dampstain at foot of inner margins. S June 25 (62) £500

Beaufort, Daniel Augustus, 1739-1821
— Memoir of a Map of Ireland. Dublin, 1792. 2 parts in 1 vol. 4to, modern half lea. With folding map, colored in outline. bba Apr 9 (348) £60 [Emerald Isle]

Beaufort, Emily Anne, Viscountess Strangford
— The Eastern Shores of the Adriatic in 1863.... L., 1864. 8vo, orig cloth; rubbed. With port & 4 plates. Ck Feb 27 (234) £65

Beaufort, Henry Somerset, Duke of —& Watson, A. E. T.
— The Badminton Library of Sports and Pastimes. L, 1885-96. One of 250 L.p. copies. 29 vols, 4to, orig half mor; rubbed. Ck May 29 (1) £720

Anr copy. Half mor gilt, last vol in black rather than blue. S May 28 (832) £1,100

Beauharnois, Franciscus de
— Catalogus Bibliothecae Belharnosianae, quae vaenalis prostat in Aedibus Belharnosianis. Orleans: J. Boyer, 1683. 4to, contemp calf; joints split, worn. R2 marginally def. bba Aug 28 (2) £400 [Goldschmidt]

Beaulieu, Sebastien de, Sieur de la Pontault
— Les Glorieuses Conquestes de Louis le Grand.... Paris, 1694. 2 vols. Folio, contemp calf gilt; rebacked, 1 cover detached. With port & 193 plates, most double-page. With Some Ms description & contents lists. With an additional 21 ports & other plates. S June 25 (298) £15,000

Beaumarchais, Pierre Auguste Caron de, 1732-99
— La Folle Journee, ou Le Mariage de Figaro. Paris, 1785. 8vo, contemp wraps. With 5 plates. Several inner margins wormed. S Nov 27 (142) £500 [DeZayas]

Beaumont, Cyril William
— The History of Harlequin. L, 1926. One of 325. 4to, half vellum, in d/j. sg Feb 26 (126) $250

Beaumont, Cyril William —& Sitwell, Sacheverell
— The Romantic Ballet.... L, 1938. 4to, orig cloth. With 81 plates, some colored. Ck Oct 31 (8) £95

Beaumont de Perefixe, Hardouin de. See: Perefixe, Hardouin de Beaumont de

Beaumont, Francis, 1584-1616 —& Fletcher, John, 1579-1625
— The Wild-Goose Chase. L, 1652. 1st Ed. Folio, lev gilt by Riviere; front joint cracked, front cover warped. Without the correction slip on a1v. Washed; minor repair to tp fore-edge. Wilmerding copy. sg Apr 2 (20) $350

— Works. L, 1647. ("Comedies and Tragedies.") Bound with: Beaumont & Fletcher. The Wild-Goose Chase. L, 1652. 1st Ed. 1st Collected Ed, 2d state of the port. Folio, contemp calf; rebacked, preserving spine. C May 13 (156) £1,500 [Quaritch]

Anr copy. Later mor gilt; rubbed. Some tears & repairs, occasionally affecting text; margins somewhat stained, more severely at beginning. S Jan 13 (463) £160 [Rix]

Anr copy. Contep calf; rebacked, joints starting. Some close cutting at lower margin; some loss to lower margin of frontis. sg June 11 (29) $450

Anr Ed. Edin., 1812. 14 vols. 8vo, contemp calf; rebacked. sg Sept 11 (9) $275

Beaumont, John, d.1731
— Historisch-Physiologisch- und theologischer Tractat.... Frankfurt, etc., 1721. 4to, contemp vellum. Library stamp on tp & endpaper. S May 6 (565) £100 [Korn]

Beaumont, William, 1785-1853
— Experiments and Observations on the Gastric Juice.... Plattsburgh, 1833. 1st Ed. 8vo, orig half cloth; rubbed, stained & repaired. Waterstained at front & back. Crahan copy. P Nov 25 (45) $500

2d Ed. Burlington, Vt., 1847. ("The Physiology of Digestion....") 8vo, orig cloth; rebacked preserving portion of orig spine. Some stains & browning. O Oct 21 (22) $250

Anr copy. Orig cloth; rebacked, inner joints repaired. O Jan 6 (19) $160

Beaunier, Stanislas
— Traite-Pratique sur l'Education des Abeilles. Vendome, 1806. 8vo, orig wraps; worn & loose. Tp stamped. Inscr. sg Jan 15 (140) $100

Beaurain, Jean de, 1696-1771
— Histoire militaire de Flandre.... Paris, 1755. 1st Ed. 5 parts in 1 vol plus Atlas. Folio, contemp calf gilt; worn, joints cracked. With 84 (of 147) doublepage colored maps only. FD Dec 2 (2300) DM1,150

Anr copy. 5 parts in 2 vols. Folio, contemp calf gilt with arms of the family of Choiseul. Some plates creased; a few leaves discolored at margins. S July 14 (579) £700

Beauvilliers, Antoine, 1754-1817
— L'Art du cuisinier. Paris, 1814. 1st Ed. 2 vols. 8vo, contemp envelope bdg from old French vellum Ms leaves. Sgd as usual on tp of vol I. Crahan copy. P Nov 25 (46) $1,100

BEAVER

Beaver, Philip, 1766-1813
— African Memoranda.... L, 1805. 4to, modern half mor. Folding map repaired. Ck Nov 21 (210) £70

Beazley, Charles Raymond, 1868-1955
— The Dawn of Modern Geography.... L, 1906. 3 vols. Cloth; 1st 2 spines faded. sg Jan 22 (29) $130; sg May 14 (660) $200

Beccaria, Cesare Bonesana di, 1738-94
— An Essay on Crimes and Punishments.... L: for J. Almon, 1767. 8vo, contemp calf. sg Oct 9 (97) $300

Anr Ed. L: J. Almon, 1767. 8vo, contemp calf; broken. S Nov 10 (360) £220 [Traylen]

Beccaria, Giovanni Battista, 1716-81
— Dell' elettricismo artificiale e naturale.... Turin, 1772. ("Elettricismo artificiale.") 4to, contemp half calf; worn. With 11 folding plates. Lacking tp. bba Sept 25 (178) £140 [Gurney]

Beck, Lewis Calet, 1798-1853
— A Gazetteer of the States of Illinois and Missouri.... Albany, 1823. 1st Ed. 8vo, modern cloth; With fold-out map & 5 plates.. Some fold tears; scattered foxing. sg Mar 12 (13) $475

Becker, Joseph Ernest de. See: De Becker, Joseph Ernest

Becker, Robert H. See: Grabhorn Printing

Beckett, Samuel
— Echo's Bones. Paris: Europa Press, 1935. 1st Ed, One of 250. Orig wraps. bba May 28 (87) £300 [Redshaw]; sg Dec 11 (4) $200; sg Mar 5 (16) $150
— Ill Seen, Ill Said. Northridge CA, 1982. One of 299. sg June 11 (31) $150
— Murphy. L, 1938. 1st Ed. 1st bdg, in neatly repaired d/j. CNY May 11 (5) $2,500
— The North. L: Enitharmon Press, 1972. One of 12. Illus by Avigdor Arikha. Folio, unbound as issued in orig cloth portfolio. With 3 sgd etchings. Inscr to Miriam J. Benkovitz. sg Dec 11 (181) $650
— Poems in English. L, 1961. 1st Ed, One of 100. In glassine d/j. bba May 28 (88) £140 [Hosain]
[-] Reading University Library. Samuel Beckett: an Exhibition. [L, 1971]. One of 100. sg June 11 (30) $110
— Whoroscope. Paris: The Hours Press, 1930. 1st Ed, One of 100, sgd. Inscr to Brian Howard. S July 23 (130) £1,400 [Elliott]
One of 200 unsgd. T Oct 15 (69) £460

AMERICAN BOOK PRICES CURRENT

Beckford, Peter, 1740-1811
— Thoughts on Hunting. Salisbury, 1781. 1st Ed. 4to, contemp calf gilt. pnE Dec 17 (357) £180 [Traylen]

Anr copy. Calf gilt. Inscr "From the Author" on tp. S Nov 10 (587) £100 [Allen]

2d Ed. Salisbury, 1782. 4to, 19th-cent mor gilt. With frontis & 55 ports, plates & plans. Jeanson 1489. SM Feb 28 (53) FF2,600

Anr Ed. L, 1810. 8vo, contemp half calf by William Smith of Edinburgh; rubbed. With frontis, plan & 9 plates. Jeanson 1452. SM Feb 28 (54) FF800

Beckford, William, d.1799
— A Descriptive Account of the Island of Jamaica. L, 1790. 1st Ed. 2 vols in 1. 8vo, calf. Lacking initial blanks. S Nov 18 (1161) £170 [Burton-Garbett]

Anr copy. 2 vols. 8vo, contemp calf; worn, joints slit. Lacking half-titles. S May 29 (1145) £220

Beckford, William Thomas, 1760-1844
See also: Nonesuch Press
— Biographical Memoirs of Extraordinary Painters. L, 1780. 8vo, modern half mor. sg Oct 9 (98) $300
— Italy.... L, 1834. 1st Ed. 2 vols. 8vo, orig half mor; rubbed. bba Dec 4 (293) £420 [Barker]
— Recollections of an Excursion to the Monasteries of Alcobaca and Batalha. L, 1835. 8vo, calf gilt; rebacked. sg Apr 23 (20) $175
— Vathek. NY, 1928. Plates by Mahlon Blaine hand-colored by Esaye Rabkin. In chipped & torn d/j. cb Sept 28 (123) $120
— [Vathek] An Arabian Tale. L, 1786. 1st Ed. 8vo, contemp calf; broken. Lacking final blank; some holes & tears; tear in B5 repaired but just touching 1 word of text. Inscr. S Dec 18 (16) £500 [Quaritch]

Anr copy. 19th-cent calf gilt; rubbed, joints split. Inscr to Duff Cooper from Diana Cooper, 1917. S Mar 9 (174) £630 [Orpheus]

Anr copy. Early 19th-cent calf gilt; rubbed, covers detached. Inscr to Duff Cooper from Maurice Baring. S Mar 9 (773) £220 [Hannas]

Beckford Library, William Thomas
— [Sale Catalogue] The Hamilton Palace Libraries: Catalogue of the First-[Fourth] Portion of the Beckford Library. L, 1882-83. 4 vols in 1. 8vo, modern cloth. pn Oct 23 (84) £60 [Maggs]

Beckmann, John, 1739-1811
— A History of Inventions and Discoveries. L, 1814. 2d Ed. 4 vols. 8vo, contemp half calf by J. Winstanley of Manchester. bba Mar 26 (305) £150 [Goulden]

Becquerel, Antoine Henri, 1852-1908
— Recherches sur une propriete nouvelle de la matiere.... Paris, 1903. 4to, orig wraps, unopened. With 13 plates. Vol. 46 of Memoires de l'Academie des Sciences de l'Institute de France. sg Jan 15 (289) $225
— Sur les radiations emises par phosphorescene. Paris, 1896. In: Comptes rendus mensuels de travaux chimiques, CA11, No 8. wa Nov 6 (143) $330

Becqueret, Charles
— Heures Royales. Paris, 1666. 8vo, contemp lea gilt; rebacked preserving spine. With frontis & 2 plates. Sgd by Anne Wharton on front pastedown. bba Aug 28 (99) £190 [Bickersteth]

Bede, The Venerable, 673-735
— De natura rerum et tempore ratione libri duo. Basel: H. Petrus, Mar 1529. Folio, half vellum bds; rubbed. Some dampstaining. S July 28 (1049) £320
— The History of the Church of Englande. Oxford: Shakespeare Head Press, 1930. One of 475. Trans by Thomas Stapleton. Folio, half pigskin. CA Oct 7 (63) A$150

Bedloe, William
— The Excommunicated Prince: or, the False Relique. L, 1679. 1st Ed. Folio, modern half mor. sg Oct 9 (99) $175

Beebe, Charles William, 1877-1962
— Pheasants: Their Lives and Homes. Garden City, 1926. 2 vols. Bdg with minor waterstains. cb Nov 6 (26) $50
  Anr copy. Cloth; spotted. With 64 plates. wa Sept 25 (161) $65

Beechey, Frederick William, 1796-1856. See: Grabhorn Printing

Beerbohm, Sir Max, 1872-1956
— Fifty Caricatures. L, 1913. 4to, orig cloth. sg Dec 11 (183) $60
— Heroes and Heroines of Bitter Sweet. L, 1931. One of 100. Folio, loose as issued in orig portfolio. pn Sept 18 (235) £70 [Peters]
  Anr copy. Loose as issued. S Oct 6 (762) £120 [Rota]
  One of 900. Loose as issued. bba Sept 25 (120) £60 [Sumner Stillman]; T Feb 18 (131) £45
— A Peep into the Past. [NY]: Privately Printed, 1923. One of 300 on japan vellum. Half cloth; soiled, outer corners worn. sg Dec 11 (5) $100

— Rossetti and his Circle. L, 1922. One of 380. Orig cloth. S July 13 (136) £110
— A Survey. L, 1921. 1st Ed, One of 275. 4to, cloth, in d/j. With colored frontis & 51 plates. S Sept 22 (68) £120 [Martin]
  Anr copy. Orig cloth, in repaired d/j. S July 13 (134) £100
— Works. L, 1922-28. One of 780, sgd. 10 vols. O Nov 18 (24) $300; pnE Oct 15 (208) £300
— Zuleika Dobson. Oxford: Shakespeare Head Press, 1975. One of 750, sgd by Lancaster. Illus by Osbert Lancaster. 4to, half mor. S Sept 22 (69) £75 [Gorlin]

Beers, F. W.
— County Atlas of Washington Vermont. NY, 1873. Folio, cloth; spine backed with tape, loose in bdg. Plates brittle & with marginal tape-repairs. Sold w.a.f. O Sept 23 (17) $70
— State Atlas of New Jersey. NY, 1872. Folio, cloth; rebacked. Sold w.a.f. O Feb 24 (16) $250
  Anr copy. Orig cloth; rebacked, cracked. With 37 general maps & 67 city and village maps, all hand-colored. Some edges dampstained. wa Nov 6 (629) $220

Beeton, Isabella Mary
— The Book of Household Management. L, 1861. 1st Ed. 2 vols. 8vo, contemp half calf; rebacked. Lacking final leaf. T Mar 19 (442) £120

Beeverell, James
— Les Delices de la Grand Bretagne et de l'Irlande. Leiden, 1707. 8 vols in 9. 8vo, contemp calf gilt, armorial bdg; scuffed, small tear to lower cover of Vol I, joints weak. With engraved titles, dedication & 238 double page maps & plates. A few plates slightly discolored or just shaved; 1 plate from anr copy & detached. C Oct 15 (14) £420 [Scott]
  Anr Ed. Leiden: van der Aa, 1727. 8 vols. 8vo, contemp half calf; worn. With frontises & 237 plates & maps. Ck Nov 21 (439) £750 [Falapel]
  Anr copy. Contemp calf. Some titles torn without loss. S Apr 23 (124) £680 [Israel]

Beguillet, Edme
— Traite des subsistences et des grains.... Paris, 1780. 2 vols. 4to, contemp half calf. With 41 plates, most folding. Small stain to a few inner blank margins of Vol I plates. C Dec 12 (14) £280 [Israel]

Beham, Hans Sebald, 1500-50
— Biblisch Historien, figuerlich fuergebildet.... Frankfurt: Christian Egenolff, 1535. 8vo, 16th-cent lea. 2 illusts in facsimile. HK Nov 4 (599) DM9,000

BEHOURT

Behourt, Jean
— Esau ou le chasseur.... Rouen: Raphael du Petit Val, 1606. 12mo, 18th-cent calf gilt. Lacking final blank. Jeanson copy. SM Feb 28 (55) FF6,500

Beitraege...
— Beitraege zur Fortpflanzungsbiologie der Voegel m. Beruecks d. Oologie. Berlin, 1924-44. Vols 1-20. B Feb 24 (8) HF500
— Beitraege zur Vogelkunde. Leipzig, 1949-85. Vols 1-32. B Feb 24 (9) HF500

Bekker, Balthazar, 1634-98
— De Betoverde Wereld, zijnde een grondig onderzoek van 't gemeen gevoelen aangaande de Geeste.... Amst., 1691-93. 4 parts in 1 vol. 4to, vellum. Lacking port; blank lower corner waterstained. B Feb 25 (735) HF550

Belcher, Sir Edward, 1799-1877
— The Last of the Arctic Voyages. L, 1855. 2 vols in 1. 8vo, modern cloth; worn. With 2 folding maps bound in rather than in pocket. O Oct 21 (23) $410
— Narrative of a Voyage Round the World.... L, 1843. 1st Ed. 2 vols. 8vo, half lea. With 3 maps & 19 plates. pn Mar 5 (107) £240 [Belcher]
Anr copy. Orig cloth; spines faded. With 19 plates & 3 folding charts in end pocket. Library stamps. pn May 21 (264) £220 [Camberwell]
— Narrative of the Voyage of H.M.S. Samarang.... L, 1848. 1st Ed. 2 vols. 8vo, orig cloth. With 5 maps & 30 plates. "A fine set...free of the usual foxing". S Apr 24 (369) £1,150 [Quaritch]

Belgique...
— La Belgique horticole, journal des jardins des serres et des vergers. Liege, [1850]-51-85. Ed by C. & E. Morren. 35 vols in 32 (complete set). 8vo, contemp half mor, 4 vols in contemp cloth. With 31 ports, 14 other non-botanical plates & 667 litho plates, 613 colored, mostly by hand. de Belder set. S Apr 28 (247) £4,500 [Berg]

Belidor, Bernard Forest de, 1693?-1761
— Architecture hydraulique.... Paris, 1737-53. 4 vols. 4to, contemp calf; joints split. With 2 frontises & 219 folding plates. Lacking port; 1 plate margin & numeral shaved. C Dec 12 (16) £1,500 [Gilt Edge]
Anr copy. 19th-cent half lea; worn. With port, 2 frontises & 219 folding plates. Some waterspotting & browning. HN May 20 (1068a) DM1,000
— La Science des ingenieurs.... Paris, 1739. 4to, modern mor. With frontis & 53 plates. Marginal repairs. S Nov 18 (937) £75 [Dennistoun]

AMERICAN BOOK PRICES CURRENT

Belknap, Waldron P., Jr.
— American Colonial Painting. Cambr., Mass., 1959. 4to, cloth; worn. O Mar 24 (15) $60

Bell, Andrew
— Anatomia Britannica: A System of Anatomy. Edin., 1798. 3 parts in 2 vols. Folio, half cloth; worn & scuffed, joints reinforced. Some leaves detached & laid in; lacking 2 plates; library markings. sg Jan 15 (66) $700

Bell, Benjamin, 1749-1806
— A System of Surgery. Edin., 1791. 5th Ed. 6 vols. 8vo, contemp bds; worn. O Sept 23 (18) $380

Bell, Sir Charles, 1774-1842
— The Anatomy of the Brain. L, 1802. Bound with: A Series of Engravings, Explaining the Course of the Nerves. L, 1803. 4to, contemp calf gilt; short split at head of joints. With 1 plain & 11 colored plates in 1st work & with 9 plates in 2d work. C May 13 (198) £1,600 [Quaritch]
— Essays on the Anatomy of Expression in Painting. L, 1806. 1st Ed. 4to, half vellum. Lacking half-title & ad leaf. S May 28 (624) £220
— A Series of Engravings, Explaining the Course of the Nerves.... Phila., 1818. 1st American Ed. 4to, contemp calf; rubbed. With 9 plates. Some foxing. O Oct 21 (25) $200

Bell, Clive, 1881-1964
— The Legend of Monte Della Sibilla. L: Hogarth Press, 1923. 1st Ed. Orig bds, unopened, in d/j with 3 short tears. S Dec 18 (129) £300 [Sumner]
— Poems. L: Hogarth Press, 1921. 1st Ed. S Mar 9 (830) £60 [Sumner]

Bell, Ellis. See: Bronte, Emily

Bell, Gertrude, 1868-1926. See: Golden Cockerel Press

Bell, Harold Wilmerding
— Baker Street Studies. L, 1934. In chipped d/j. cb Apr 24 (1448) $90
— Sherlock Holmes and Dr. Watson: the Chronology of their Adventures. L, 1932. 1st Ed, One of 500. cb Apr 24 (1447) $95

Bell, J. Munro
— The Castles of the Lothians. Edin., 1893. One of 130 with proof impressions of the etchings. Folio, orig lea; rubbed. O Feb 24 (17) $110

Bell, James Stanislaus
— Journal of a Residence in Circassia.... L, 1840. 2 vols. 8vo, contemp calf gilt. With folding map & 12 plates, 3 colored. pn Mar 5 (297) £110 [Meynell]

Bell, John, 1691-1780
— Travels from St. Petersburg in Russia to Diverse Parts of Asia. Glasgow: Foulis, 1763. 1st Ed. 2 vols. 4to, half calf. pnE Jan 28 (57) £280 [Thin]

Bell, John, 1745-1831
— Bell's New Pantheon; or, Historical Dictionary. L, 1790. 2 vols in one. 4to, contemp calf gilt; rebacked, orig spine laid down; worn. sg Oct 9 (100) $80

Bell, John, 1763-1820
— Engravings Explaining the Anatomy of the Bones, Muscles and Joints. Phila., 1817-15. ("Engravings of the Bones, Muscles & Joints.") 3 books in 2 vols. 4to, contemp calf; rubbed. With 32 plates, including several duplicates. O Oct 21 (26) $170

Bell, Thomas, 1792-1880
— The Anatomy, Physiology, and Diseases of the Teeth. L, 1829. 1st Ed. 8vo, modern half mor; blistered. With 11 plates. sg Jan 15 (79) $350

Bell, William Abraham
— New Tracks in North America. L, 1869. 1st Ed. 2 vols. 8vo, orig cloth; worn, front hinge cracked. With folding map reaffixed with tape. cb July 16 (23) $225

Bell, William Dalrymple Maitland
— The Wanderings of an Elephant Hunter. L, 1923. 4to, orig bds; rubbed & soiled. T Sept 18 (10) $70

Bellamy, Joseph, 1719-90
— True Religion Delineated; or, Experimental Religion...in Two Discourses. Bost.: S. Kneeland, 1750. Preface by Jonathan Edwards. 8vo, contemp calf; worn. Foxed. sg Sept 18 (31) $50

Bellers, John, 1654-1725
— An Essay towards the Improvement of Physick.... L: Assigns of J. Sowle, 1714. 4to, wraps. Rule-border to title & a few page numerals shaved. S July 24 (420) £480 [Quaritch]

Bellet, Jose Brunet y. See: Brunet y Bellet, Jose

Bellew, Henry Walter, 1834-92
— Journal of a Political Mission in Afghanistan in 1857. L, 1862. 8vo, contemp half calf; worn, 1 cover detached. With 8 plates. Library stamp on flyleaf. bba May 28 (221) £170 [Hosains]

Bellial de Vertus, Le Sieur de, Pseud.
— Essai sur l'administration des terres. Paris, 1759. 8vo, calf. P Sept 24 (243) $450

Bellier de Villiers, A. C. E.
— Les Deduits de la chasse du chevreuil.... Paris: Victor Goupy, 1870. One of 10. 4to, mor gilt by Chambolle-Duru. Jeanson copy. SM Feb 28 (56) FF7,500

Bellin, Jacques Nicolas, 1703-72
— Description geographique de la Guyane.... Paris, 1763. 4to, contemp calf; worn. With engraved title, 20 maps & 10 plates. bba Dec 18 (109) £140 [Elliott]
Anr copy. Contemp mor gilt. C Oct 15 (12) £1,200 [Lyon]
— Le Petit Atlas maritime. Paris, 1764. Vol III only. Folio, contemp half calf; rubbed. With engraved titles & 124 maps, hand-colored in outline. bba Dec 4 (284) £1,200 [Parsons]
Anr copy. 6 parts in 5 vols. 4to, contemp mor gilt with arms of Pelet-Narbonne, of Languedoc; 1 cover marked. With engraved general & sectional titles & 575 maps, charts & plans, hand-colored in wash & outline throughout. Stamp of the Depot General de la Guerre on titles. s Oct 23 (20) £9,000 [Sourget]

Belloc, Hilaire, 1870-1953
— The Highway and its Vehicles. L, 1926. pn Mar 5 (242) £50 [Traylen]
Anr Ed. L: The Studio, 1926. Ltd Ed. 4to, orig cloth. bba Sept 25 (146) £50 [Goulden]

Bellori, Giovanni Pietro, 1636?-1700
— Le Pitture antiche delli grotte di Roma.... Rome, 1706. Folio, contemp calf gilt; hinges split. With 75 plates. C May 13 (62) £300 [Stern]
— Le Vite de pittori, scultori et architetti moderni.... Rome, 1728. 4to, old half sheep; spine rubbed, front joint partly cracked. With frontis & 14 plates. sg Mar 26 (21) $200

Belnos, Mrs. S. C.
— The Sundhya, or the Daily Prayers of the Brahmins. L, 1851. Folio, contemp half mor gilt. With hand-colored title & 24 hand-colored plates. S June 25 (187) £750 [Mansoor]

Belon du Mans, Pierre, 1517-64
— L'Histoire de la nature des oyseaux. Paris: G. Cavellat, 1555. Cavellat issue. Folio, mor gilt with arms of de Thou & of his first wife (Olivier 217, fer 4). Jeanson 1715. SM Feb 28 (57) FF75,000
— Les Observations de plusieurs singularitez et choses memorables, trouvees en Grece....

BELON DU MANS

Paris, 1588. 4to, 19th-cent half mor gilt; rubbed. Some dampstains throughout; some leaves closely shaved. T Mar 19 (402) £100

— Portraits d'oyseaux, animaux, serpens, herbes, arbres.... Paris, 1557. 4to, 18th-cent mor gilt. Minor repairs. Jeanson 7022. SM Feb 28 (58) FF44,000

Beltrami, Giacomo Constantino, 1779-1855

— A Pilgrimage in Europe and America. L, 1828. 1st Ed in English. 8vo, modern half mor gilt. With port & 2 engraved maps & plans. pnNY Sept 13 (196) $140

Belzoni, Giovanni Battista, 1778-1823

— Narrative of the Operations and Recent Discoveries...Egypt and Nubia. L, 1820. Plate vol only. Folio, half calf; worn. With 44 plates on 34 sheets, mostly hand-colored. pn Mar 5 (9) £1,100 [Weinreb]

3d Ed. L, 1822. 2 (of 3) vols; without Atlas vol. 8vo, disbound. With 2 plans. cb Nov 6 (28) $70

Bembo, Pietro, 1470-1547

— Gli Asolani. Venice: Aldus, 1505. 1st Ed, Issue with dedication to Lucrezia Borgia. 4to, old sheep; worn, spine wormed, crudely repaired at head; lowermost compartment off. Opening leaves soiled & dampstained; tp & following leaf frayed or torn & artlessly restored with some text supplied in Ms; lacking penultimate errata leaf & final blank, the errata supplied in Ms. sg Mar 26 (22) $175

Anr Ed. Venice: Aldus, 1515. 8vo, later vellum. First leaf dampstained. sg June 11 (2) $130

— Prose.... Venice: G. Tacuino, 1525. 1st Ed. Folio, early calf; worn. S May 21 (23) £280 [Thomas]

— Rime. Venice, 1547. 8vo, calf by Sangorski & Sutcliffe, armorial bdg. Hole in text of D5. S Sept 23 (296) £160 [Zyas]

Bendire, Charles Emil, 1836-97

— Life Histories of North American Birds. Wash., 1892-95. 2 vols. 4to, half calf gilt. Inscr. pn Oct 23 (181) £60 [Bles]

Benedictus

— Variations. Paris, [1928]. Folio, loose in ptd bds; worn, lacking backstrip. With 20 color plates. sg Dec 18 (143) $450

Benesch, Otto

— The Drawings of Rembrandt. L, 1973. 6 vols. 4to, orig cloth. HN May 20 (586) DM640

Benet, Stephen Vincent, 1898-1943

— James Shore's Daughter. Garden City, 1934. One of 307 L.p. copies, sgd. Hersholt copy. sg June 11 (34) $50

Benezet, Anthony, 1713-84

— Some Historical Account of Guinea.... Phila.: J. Crukshank, 1771. 8vo, later half calf. sg Mar 12 (14) $60

Benezit, Emmanuel, 1854-1920

— Dictionnaire critique.... Paris, 1948-55. 8 vols. Worn, some corners bumped. cb Oct 23 (27) $160

Anr Ed. Paris, 1960. 8 vols. S Oct 23 (316) £140; T May 21 (664) £230

Anr Ed. Paris, 1966. 8 vols. S Mar 9 (662) £190 [Thoma]

Anr Ed. Paris, 1976. 10 vols. Ck Oct 31 (84) £270; Ck Apr 24 (22) £280; HN Nov 26 (154) DM820; sg Feb 5 (33) $225; T Feb 19 (551) £175

Ben-Gurion, David

— Israel: a Personal History. NY & Tel Aviv, [1971]. One of 2,000, sgd. O Nov 18 (26) $100

Benjamin, Asher, 1773-1845

— The Practical House Carpenter.... Bost., 1830. 4to, old half calf; worn. Some stains & tears. O May 12 (11) $175

Benjamin, Israel Joseph, 1818-64

— Drei Jahre in Amerika.... Hanover, 1862. 3 parts in 2 vols. 8vo, orig wraps; Vol I lacking wraps; staining & small chips to Vol II. cb Jan 8 (11) $375

Benjamin, Samuel Green Wheeler, 1837-1914

— A Group of Etchers. NY: Dodd, Mead, [1882]. Folio, orig cloth; broken. With 18 (of 20) plates; lacking the Whistler & Dupont etchings. Sold w.a.f. O Jan 6 (20) $110

Benkovitz, Miriam Jeanette

— A Bibliography of Ronald Firbank. L, 1963. 2 vols, including 1980 supplement. In d/js. Sgd. sg Dec 11 (290) $50

Bennet, Abraham

— New Experiments on Electricity. Derby, 1789. 8vo, contemp half calf. With folding frontis & 3 folding plates. C Dec 12 (15) £600 [Maggs]

Bennet, Edward

— Shots and Snapshots in British East Africa. L, 1914. Cloth; joints rubbed, hinges weak. With 2 folding maps in cover pocket. cb Nov 6 (29) $65

Bennett, Arnold, 1867-1931

— Elsie and the Child. L: Curwen Press, 1929. One of 750. 4to, orig cloth; soiled. bba Nov 13 (304) £50 [Elliott]; bba Apr 23 (283) £35 [Elliott]
— The Old Wives' Tale.... L, 1908. 1st Ed. Orig cloth. Ls inserted. Beaverbrook copy. S May 6 (455) £85 [Horseman's]
— Venus Rising from the Sea. L, 1931. One of 350. Illus by E. McKnight Kauffer. 4to, orig cloth; soiled. pn Oct 23 (117) £75 [Mannheim]

Bennett, Frank Marion

— The Steam Navy...of the...United States. Pittsburgh. Warren, 1896. Orig cloth, worn. wa Nov 6 (218) $95

Bennett, George, 1804-93

— Gatherings of a Naturalist in Australasia.... L, 1860. 8vo, contemp calf gilt. With 1 plain & 7 colored plates. 1 leaf of contents misbound. C Oct 15 (144) £220 [d'Arcy]

Anr copy. Contemp calf; rebacked. C Oct 15 (146) £110 [Ebes]

Anr copy. Contemp calf gilt; worn. C Apr 8 (166) £260 [Graham]
— Wanderings in New South Wales.... L, 1834. 2 vols. 8vo, contemp calf gilt; rebacked. Lacking ad leaf, directions to binder leaf & Vol I half-title. C Oct 15 (145) £200 [Thorp]

Anr copy. Half mor gilt; rubbed. pn May 21 (263b) £160 [Hay Cinema]

Bennett, George W.

— An Illustrated History of British Guiana.... Georgetown, 1866. 1st Ed. 8vo, orig cloth. With 44 mtd photographs. Some foxing & small stains. S Oct 23 (435) £350 [Pulico]

Bennett, Ira E.

— History of the Panama Canal.... Wash., 1915. 8vo, mor gilt; worn, spine chipped. wa Nov 6 (223) $85

Bennett, Whitman

— A Practical Guide to American Nineteenth Century Color Plate Books. NY, 1949. O June 16 (19) $50

Bennett, William P.

— The First Baby in Camp. Salt Lake City, 1893. Orig wraps; rear wrap soiled, spine torn at foot. cb Jan 8 (12) $50

Benson, Arthur Christopher, 1862-1925

— The Book of the Queen's Dolls' House. [The Book of the Queen's Dolls' House Library]. L, 1924. One of 1,500. 2 vols. 4to, half cloth; hinges cracking. cb Apr 24 (654) $80

Anr copy. Half cloth; rebacked, orig spine laid on. cb Apr 24 (655) $55

Anr copy. Library vol only. Half cloth, in d/j. cb Apr 24 (656) $90

Anr copy. 2 vols. 4to, half cloth, in torn d/j; hinges starting. sg Oct 30 (28) $275

Benson, Frank Weston

— Etchings and Drypoints. Volume Two. Bost., 1919. One of 275 with sgd frontis etching. Compiled by Adam E. M. Paff. 4to, half cloth; soiled. sg Oct 23 (179) $800
— Etchings and Drypoints.... Bost., 1923. One of 525. Compiled by Adam E. M. Paff. Vol III (of 4) only. 4to, half cloth, in d/j. With orig sgd etching as frontis. sg Oct 23 (180) $400

Anr Ed. Bost., 1929. One of 600. Vol IV (of 4) only. 4to, half cloth, in d/j. With orig sgd etching as frontis. sg Oct 23 (181) $350

Anr Ed. Bost., 1959. One of 400. Vol V only. 4to, half cloth, in d/j. With orig sgd etching as frontis. sg Oct 23 (182) $800

Benson, Robert

— Sketches of Corsica, or a Journal.... L, 1825. 4to, orig bds; front joint starting. With 1 hand-colored & 5 plain plates. sg Nov 20 (59) $130

Benson, Thomas

— Vocabularium Anglo-Saxonicum. Oxford, 1701. 8vo, modern cloth. Marginal stains. sg Mar 26 (24) $175

Bent, Arthur Cleveland

— Life Histories of North American Birds. Wash., 1919-68. 21 vols in 23. Haverschmidt copy. B Feb 24 (264) HF500

Bentham, Jeremy, 1748-1832

— The Book of Fallacies: From Unfinished Papers.... L, 1824. 8vo, cloth; worn & stained. Tp stuck to free endpaper along inner margin resulting in a few short tears; shaken; remains of library labels on endpaper; smeared stamp on tp & p 5; waterstaining & buckling. P Sept 24 (244) $200

Anr copy. Contemp half mor, rubbed. Some stains. T July 16 (271) £160
— An Introduction to the Principles of Morals and Legislation. L, 1789. 4to, contemp calf. "Fine copy". S June 25 (63) £2,800 [Quaritch]
— Panopticon, or the Inspection-House. Dublin: Thomas Byrne, 1791. 3 parts in 1 vol. 8vo, orig wraps; broken. With folding table & 2 plates numbered I & III. Tear & marginal fraying in 1 plate, which is detached. C Dec 12 (274) £2,200 [Pickering & Chatto]

BENTIVOGLIO

Bentivoglio, Guido, Cardinal, 1579-1644
— Las Guerras de Flandes.... Amberes, 1687. Folio, contemp calf; rubbed, joints split. Library stamps on title & frontis; small stamps on plates. bba Dec 18 (111) £60 [Elliott]

Benton, Joseph Augustine, 1818-92
— The California Pilgrim.... Sacramento, 1853. 1st Ed. 8vo, orig cloth; rubbed, joints glue-repaired. With 6 plates. cb Jan 8 (131) $75

Beowulf
— Beowulf. NY, 1932. One of 950. Illus by Rockwell Kent; trans by W. E. Leonard. Folio, cloth. With 8 lithos. cb June 18 (201) $140; sg Jan 8 (144) $175

Berain, Jean
— Ornemens du peinture et de sculpture.... [Paris, c.1710]. Folio, contemp red mor gilt with arms of Louis XV. With 28 plates only. Leeds copy. C May 13 (108) £1,200 [Weinreb]
— Ornemens inventez par J. Berain. [Paris, 1688]. Bound with: Desseins de Cheminees & a further series of 39 plates of grotesques, wall decorations & ceiling designs. Folio, contemp calf over wooden bds; def. With 59 plates in all. Minor worming & waterstaining. S Oct 23 (87) £1,100 [Cumming]

Berain, Jean, 1640-1711
— Diverses pieces tres utiles pour les arquebuzieres. Paris, 1659. 4to, half shagreen. With 10 mtd plates. Jeanson copy. SM Feb 28 (59) FF27,000

Beraldi, Henri
See also: Portalis & Beraldi
— Les Graveurs du XIXe Siecle.... Paris, 1885-92. 12 vols. 8vo, contemp half mor, orig wraps bound in. With 38 plates. Extra-illus with 29 plates. C Dec 3 (4) £480 [Maggs]

Beregani, Niccola
— Historia delle guerra d'Europa.... Venice, 1698. 2 vols. 4to, contemp vellum. S Sept 23 (297) £290

Berenger, Jean Pierre, 1740-1807
— Collection de tous les voyages faits autour du monde.... Lausanne, 1788-89. 9 vols. 8vo, contemp calf; rubbed. Possibly lacking plates. Sold w.a.f. O Nov 18 (27) $50

Berenger, Richard, d.1782
— The History and Art of Horsemanship. L, 1771. 4to, contemp calf; rubbed, spine chipped. Small Persian stamp on titles; slight worming at beginning of Vol I & end of Vol II with small loss. S Jan 13 (342)

AMERICAN BOOK PRICES CURRENT

£160 [Cavendish]

Berenson, Bernard, 1865-1959
— The Drawings of the Florentine Painters. Chicago, 1938. 3 vols. 4to, cloth; soiled. Vol III with first 60 leaves stained in upper right corner. sg June 4 (36) $150
Anr Ed. Chicago, [1970]. 3 vols. cb Mar 5 (23) $110
— Italian Pictures of the Renaissance. L, 1957-68. 7 vols. 4to, orig cloth. HN May 20 (737) DM2,000

Berg, Otto Karl
— Darstellung und Beschreibung sammtlicher in der pharmacopoea Borussica aufgefuehrten offizinellen gewaechse. Leipzig, 1858-63. Illus by C. F. Schmidt. 4 vols. 4to, contemp half mor; not uniform. With 6 plain & 198 hand-colored plates. Plesch—de Belder copy. S Apr 27 (20) £1,800 [Rainer]

Berger, Christoph Heinrich von
— Commentatio de personis, vulgo larvis seu mascheris. Frankfurt & Leipzig: G. M. Knock, [1723]. 4to, orig bds; worn. With frontis & 84 plates. bba May 14 (330) £110 [Poole]

Bergeret, Jean Pierre
— Phytonomatotechnie universelle. Paris, 1783-84. 3 vols. Folio, orig bds & wraps; soiled, spines worn. With folding table & 320 hand-colored engraved & color-ptd plates. No half-title in Vol III. de Belder copy. S Apr 27 (21) £12,000 [Israel]

Berghaus, Heinrich
— Jordens Folkslag. Stockholm: Bonniers, [mid-19th cent]. 2 vols. in 1. 8vo, half mor; worn & soiled. With 32 hand-colored plates. wa Sept 25 (202) $130

Bergman, Ray
— Trout. Phila., 1938. One of 149. Lea. With extra suite of color plates, loose. Inscr twice. sg Oct 23 (186) $1,200

Bergman, Sir Torbern Olof, 1735-84
— Commentatio de tubo ferruminatorio.... Vienna, 1779. 8vo, contemp bds. With folding plate. C Dec 12 (275) £280 [Ronrells]
— Physical and Chemical Essays. L, 1788-91. Vols I-II. Contemp calf; 1 hinge split. C Dec 12 (17) £350 [Ronnells]

Bergomensis, Jacobus Philippus Foresti. See: Jacobus Philippus de Bergamo

Beristain y Souza, Jose Mariano, 1756-1817
— Biblioteca Hispano Americana Septentrional. Amecameca, 1883 & Santiago, 1897. 2d Ed. 4 vols. Sheep. sg Oct 2 (214) $100

Berlese, Laurent, 1784-1863
— Iconographie du genre Camellia. Paris: Cousin, [1839]-41-43. 3 vols. Folio, contemp half mor gilt. With 300 hand-finished colored plates. Some spotting & browning. de Belder copy. S Apr 27 (22) £30,000

Berliner, Abraham
— Targum Onkelos al Hatorah. Berlin, 1844. 2 vols. 8vo, contemp half lea, broken. Titles in German & Hebrew; text in German & Aramaic. Some marginalia. sg Sept 25 (37) $300

Berlyn, Annie
— Sunrise-Land ., 1894. 8vo, cloth. sg Oct 30 (29) $130

Bermudez, Joao
— Breve Relacao da embaixada...Icao Bermudez trouxe do Emperador da Ethiopia. Lisbon, 1565. 4to, half mor. Each leaf remargined; some wormholes repaired; A8 in pen facsimile. Azevedo-Samodaes copy. S Oct 23 (456) £750 [Maggs]

Bernard, Auguste Joseph
— Geofroy Tory: Painter and Engraver.... Bost. & NY, 1909. One of 370. Folio, bds. sg Jan 22 (301) $200; sg May 14 (405) $150

Anr copy. Half cloth; soiled, spine ends frayed. wa June 25 (41) $80

Bernard, Claude, 1813-78
— Memoire sur le pancreas.... Paris, 1856. 1st Ed. 4to, wraps. With 9 plates (4 hand-colored) on 5 sheets. S Nov 27 (250) £450 [Carey]

— L'Oeuvre. Paris, 1881. 8vo, modern half lea. sg Oct 2 (55) $60

— Sur une nouvelle fonction du foie.... Paris, 1850. 4to, bdg not given. In: Comptes Rendus de l'Academie des Sciences, Vol. XXXI, pp, 571-74.. wa Nov 6 (45) $120

Anr Ed. Paris: Bachelier, 1850. 4to, wraps. S Nov 10 (442) £200 [Giliard]

Bernard, Tristan, 1866-1947
— Tableau de la boxe. Paris, [1922] One of 318. Illus by A. D. de Segonzac. 4to, mor gilt by A. & J. Langrand, orig wraps bound in. FD Dec 2 (4231) DM2,500

Bernardus Trevisanus
— Le Texte d'alchymie, et le songe-verd. Paris: Laurent d'Houry, 1695. 12mo, calf. Lacking a leaf at end. S May 28 (626) £100

Bernath, Dezso
— Cleopatra. Her Life and Reign. L, 1907. Mor extra by Sangorski & Sutcliffe with inset miniature of Cleopatra in upper inner cover, bound for the J. W. Robinson Company. P Sept 24 (107) $1,900

Berners, Dame Juliana, b.1388?
See also: Ashendene Press

— Book of St. Albans. L: Wynkyn de Worde, [c.1518]. ("The Boke of Hawkynge and Huntynge, and Fysshynge.") 4to, 19th-cent mor gilt. Some repairs. Jeanson copy. SM Feb 28 (60) FF280,000

Anr Ed. L: William Powell, [c.1550]. 4to, 19th-cent calf gilt. Ashburnham-Jeanson copy. SM Feb 28 (61) FF140,000

Anr Ed. L: for Humfrey Lownes, 1595. ("The Gentlemans Academie. Or, the Book of S. Albans....") 4to, half cloth. Lacking the first & final blanks & Aa3-Dd1; tp remtd. Jeanson copy. SM Feb 28 (62) FF1,400

Anr Ed. L: Adam Islip, 1596. ("Hawking, Hunting, Fouling and Fishing....") 4to, mor gilt by Saulnier. Jeanson copy. SM Feb 28 (63) FF42,000

Anr Ed. L: Slliot, Stock, 1905. ("The Boke of Saint Albans....") 4to, half shagreen. Facsimile of the 1486 Ed. Jeanson copy. SM Feb 28 (64) FF1,000

— A Treatyse of Fysshynge wyth an Angle.... NY, 1875. 8vo, ptd wraps, in d/j. sg May 21 (19) $110

Anr copy. Orig wraps, unopened. wd Nov 12 (82) $100

Anr Ed. L, [1880]. 4to, orig vellum bds; worn, spine splitting. wa Nov 6 (102) $65

Anr Ed. NY, 1903. One of 160 on hand-made paper. Vellum. sg May 21 (20) $250

Bernier, Francois, 1620-88
— The History of the Late Revolution of the Empire of the Great Mogul. L., 1671-72. 1st Ed. 4 vols. 8vo, contemp calf; spine def, rubbed. Folding plate torn across; stamp on tp; lacking A2 & A3; a few headlines shaved. S Jan 12 (311) £130 [Diba]

— Suite des memoires...sur l'Empire du Grand Mogol. The Hague: Arnout Leers, 1671-72. 2 vols in 1. 12mo, contemp calf. Library bookplate. sg Nov 20 (22) $100

Bernoulli, Daniel, 1700-82
— Hydrodynamica, sive de viribus et motibus fluidorum commentarii. Strassburg, 1738. 1st Ed. 4to, contemp half lea. With engraved title & 12 folding plates. HK Nov 4 (920) Dm2,500

Anr copy. Vellum bds; inner joint broken. S June 25 (90) £1,700 [Phelps]

Bernoulli, Jacques, 1654-1705
— Dissertatio de gravitate aetheris. Amst., 1683. 8vo, contemp vellum. With frontis & 4 folding plates. Some worming. HK Nov 4 (921) pDM1,600

Bernoulli, Jean, 1667-1748. See: Leibnitz & Bernoulli

Bernsen, Paul S.
— The North American Waterfowler. Seattle, [1972]. One of 500. 4to, syn gilt, in d/j. sg Oct 23 (187) $50

Bernt, Walther
— Die Niederlaendischen Zeichner des 17. Jahrhunderts. Munich, 1957-60. 2 vols. 4to, orig cloth. bba Mar 12 (95) £75 [Bauers]

Beroalde de Verville, Francois, 1556-c.1612
— Le Moyen de parvenir. [Paris, 1757]. 2 vols. 16mo, old vellum; soiled. Lackig first & last blanks; tp torn at inner margin. S Mar 10 (1034) £75 [Hesketh]

Berry, William, 1774-1851
— Encyclopaedia Heraldica, or Complete Dictionary of County Maps.... L, [1828-30]. 3 vols. 4to, contemp calf gilt; rebacked retaining orig backstrips, broken. sg Feb 12 (174) $250
— The History of the Island of Guernsey. L, 1815. 4to, later half mor gilt; hinges tender. With folding map & 29 plates. T June 18 (31) £210

Bertall
See also: Arnoux, Charles Albert d'
— La Vigne. Voyage autour des vins de France. Paris: Plon, 1878. 2 vols. 8vo, orig ptd wraps, unopened; some wear. Deuzel-Crahan copy. P Nov 25 (52) $350

Berthelot, Claude Francois
— La Mecanique appliquee aux arts.... Paris, 1782. 2 vols. 4to, contemp half calf. With 132 plates. Plate 20 with upper margin shaved to plate frame & bound before Plate 26. C Dec 12 (19) £650 [Brooke-Hitching]

Berthelot, Marcelin Pierre Eugene, 1827-1907
— Collection des anciens alchemistes grecs. Paris, 1887-88. 4 vols. 4to, Vol I in orig wraps (def), the others in half mor. Franklin Institute copy. F Sept 12 (75) $325

Berthoud, Ferdinand, 1727-1807
— Essai sur l'horlogerie.... Paris, 1763. 1st Ed. 2 vols. 4to, contemp calf; rubbed, joints wormed. With 38 folding plates. Vol II with waterstain in corner of a few leaves & plates. C Dec 12 (20) £800 [Israel]
Anr copy. Contemp calf; worn, rebacked. S Nov 10 (195) £420 [Maronini]
— Memoire sur le travail des horloges et des montres a longitudes. Paris, 1792-97. 1st Ed. 3 parts in 1 vol. 4to, contemp half calf; joints split. With 7 folding plates. S May 21 (183) £650 [Gurney]

Bertin
— Album de chasseur ou recueil de nouvelles fanfares pour trois trompes. Paris, [c.1840]. 4to, calf. Lithographed throughout. SM Feb 28 (66) FF1,800

Bertin, Joseph
— The Noble Game of Chess. L, 1735. 8vo, modern half mor. pn Mar 26 (355) £700 [Kaminsky]

Bertin, Rene Joseph Hyacinthe
— Treatise on the Diseases of the Heart and Great Vessels. Phila., 1833. 8vo, calf. Library markings. pnE Dec 17 (70) £180 [Phillips]

Bertius, Petrus, 1565-1629
— Commentariorum rerum germanicarum, libri tres. Amst.: J. Jansen, 1616. Oblong 4to, contemp vellum; soiled. With engraved title, armorial plate, 23 maps & 101 plans & views, colored throughout in a contemp hand. Some browning throughout; duplicate of Weimar view at Uuuu3v pasted over the same; small piece torn from foot of Hhhh4 affecting letters. S Oct 23 (286) £8,500 [Schmidt]
Anr Ed. Amst.: Blaeu, 1635. 3 parts in 1 vol. 12mo, contemp vellum. With 16 double-page maps, 1 loose; lower inner corners dampstained in middle portion of vol. sg Oct 9 (101) $250
— Tabularum geographicarum contractarum libri septem.... Amst., 1606. 5 parts in 1 vol. Oblong 8vo, modern calf gilt. With engraved title & 174 maps & plate. Map of Cadiz at F5r pasted over a map of France, which is repeated correctly at G7v; some browning & rust-marks affecting letters. S Oct 23 (219) £2,500 [Maggs]
Anr Ed. Amst.: I. Hondius, 1616. 7 parts in 1 vol. Oblong 4to, 18th-cent calf; rubbed. Some browning & soiling; marginal tears. O May 12 (13) £2,700
— Theatrum geographiae veteris, duobus Tomis distinctum. Amst.: Elzevir for Hondius, 1618-19. 2 vols in 1. Folio, 19th-cent English bdg. With 2 engraved titles, port & 47 maps. FD Dec 2 (772) DM22,000

Bertoldo...
— Bertoldo, con Bertoldino e Cacasenno in ottava rima.... Bologna, 1736. Illus by J. M. Crespi under the name of Lodovico Mattioli. 4to, contemp vellum bds; soiled, spine worn. With 21 plates. Some spots & stains. S Jan 13 (361) £440 [Henderson]

Bertrand, Aloysius, 1807-41
— Dix contes de Gaspard de la Nuit. Paris, 1962. One of 140. Illus by Marcel Gromaire. 4to, orig wraps, unsewn as issued. SM Oct 20 (632) FF6,000

Bertrand, Jean —& Others
— Essays on the Spirit of Legislation, in the Encouragement of Agriculture, Population, Manufactures, and Commerce.... L, 1772. 1st Ed in English. 8vo, modern half calf. Marginal stains; tp spotted. S Nov 10 (361) £220 [Traylen]

Bertuch, Friedrich Johann Justin
— Bilderbuch fuer Kinder. Weimar, 1798-1813. Vols II & IV-VIII. 4to, half cloth. S Dec 5 (295) £1,200

Bertuch, Friedrich Johann Justin, 1747-1822
— Bilderbuch fuer Kinder. Weimar, 1798-1821. Vols 1-10, comprising 869 sections. 4to, half cloth. With 864 plates, many colored by hand & mtd on linen. S June 17 (429) £2,200 [Hough]

Berzelius, Jons Jacob von, 1779-1848
— Essai sur la theorie des proportions chimiques et sur l'influence chimique de l'electricite.... Paris, 1819. 8vo, contemp bds; worn. Old library stamps. sg Jan 15 (290) $375

Besant, Walter, 1836-1901 —& Others
— Survey of London. L, 1903-25. 10 vols. 4to, orig cloth. bba May 14 (46) £190 [Axe]

Beschreibung...
— Beschreibung der Feierlichkeiten welche bei Anwesenheit von ihre Majestaeten der Kaiser Alexander und Napoleon und mehrerer gekroenten Haeupter in Weimar und Jena am 6ten & 7ten October 1808. Weimar, 1809. Folio, contemp half calf. With 5 plates, 2 colored. Jeanson copy. SM Feb 28 (67) FF17,000

Besler, Basilius, 1561-1629
— Hortus Eystettensis sive diligens et accurata omnium plantarum.... Eichstatt & Nuremberg, 1613. 3 vols. 4to, 19th-cent half calf. With 361 plates only; some stains & spotting; other defs. HK Nov 4 (923) DM115,000

Anr copy. 2 vols. 4to, contemp blind-stamped pigskin over wooden bds; repaired. With 3 (of 4) engraved sectional titles & 367 plates of flowers & plants on 368 sheets, all in superb contemp coloring & with German nomenclature added in a contemp hand beneath the ptd Latin captions. Sectional titles backed; 3 prelim leaves repaired in outer & lower margins; several plates with outer and/or lower margins strengthened; other marginal tears

repaired; a number of plates trimmed to plate line at outer edge; slight paper creases in some plates. Earle—de Belder copy. S Apr 27 (23) £550,000 [Israel]

Anr copy. 4to, contemp blind-stamped pigskin over wooden bds with brass clasps & catches. With 4 sectional titles, port & 367 plates on 368 sheets. Some dampstaining; marginal tear repaired in port leaf; tear repaired in Spring sectional title. Uncolored de Belder copy. S Apr 27 (24) £130,000 [Israel]

Anr copy. 2 vols. 4to, half calf. With title, port & 367 plates "en coloris d'epoque". SM Oct 20 (413) FF600,000

3d Ed. Ingolstadt, 1713. 4to, contemp russia over wooden bds with blind-stamped borders & panel; restored, new endpapers. With engraved title & 367 plates. Tp & final leaf backed, the latter with 2 tears repaired; Martagon Imperiale slightly torn; a few small marginal tears mended. Horticultural Society of New York—de Belder copy. S Apr 27 (25) £52,000 [Burgess Browning]

— Icones sive: repraesentatio viva, florum et herbarum...noviter accutata diligentia promulgata. [Nuremberg, 1627?]. Folio, contemp vellum bds. With double-page engraved title, port (just trimmed) & 23 double-page plates. First plate with short split in centerfold; a few marginal stains. Horticultural Society of New York—de Belder copy. S Apr 27 (26) £22,000 [Israel]

Besson, Jacques
— Theatre des instrumens mathematiques & mechaniques.... Geneva, 1596. Folio, 19th-cent mor; rubbed. With 60 plates. Tp soiled, creased & lacking 1 corner; some stains & soiling throughout. P Sept 24 (106) $500

Best, Thomas
— A Concise Treatise on the Art of Angling.... L: C. Stalker, [1789?]. 2d Ed. 12mo, calf; worn, broken. sg Oct 23 (188) $175

Beste, John Richard Digby, 1806-85
— The Wabash. L, 1855. 1st Ed. 2 vols. 12mo, orig cloth; rubbed, becoming loose. Inscr. bba Mar 26 (342) £65 [Ginsberg]

Bester, Alfred
— The Demolished Man. Chicago: Shasta, [1953]. 1st Ed. In d/j. Sgd on front free endpaper for pre-publication purchasers of the book. cb Sept 28 (131) $140
— Tiger! Tiger! L: Sidgwick & Jackson, [1956]. In chipped & torn d/j. cb Sept 28 (134) $80

BESTERMAN

Besterman, Theodore
— A World Bibliography of Bibliographies. L, 1947-49. 2d Ed. 3 vols. 4to, cloth. bba Mar 12 (325) £75 [Rainer]; sg May 14 (261) $110
3d Ed. Geneva, [1955-56]. 2 vols. O June 16 (20) $70
Anr copy. 4 vols sg Oct 2 (56) $175

Betagh, William
— A Voyage Round the World. L, 1728. 8vo, contemp calf. With folding map. sg Apr 2 (21) $1,700

Bethune, George Amory
— The Uncertainties of Travel. A Plain Statement by a Certain Traveller. Bost.: Pvtly ptd, 1880. 8vo, cloth. sg Oct 23 (189) $200

Betins, Karlis —& Others
— Das Grosse Internationale Schachmeisterturnier zu Kemeri in Lettland 1937. Riga, 1938. Orig wraps. pn Mar 26 (96) £50 [Batsford]

Betjeman, Sir John
— Collected Poems. L, 1958. With 2 A Ls s & 1 autograph postcard, sgd to Martin Secker. bba July 2 (90) £120 [Maggs]
— Ghastly Good Taste. L, 1933. Ck Apr 24 (97) £35
1st Ed. Orig half cloth; lower corners bumped. sg June 4 (39) $140
Anr Ed. [L, 1970]. One of 200 specially-bound. Half mor. sg Mar 5 (20) £110
— Summoned by Bells. L, 1960. In d/j. Sgd. Ck Sept 5 (73) £40

Betts, Douglas A.
— Chess: An Annotated Bibliography of Works.... Bost., 1974. pn Mar 26 (356) £170 [Kits]

Beughem, Cornelis a, fl.1678-1710
— Incunabula typographiae; sive, catalogus librorum scriptorumque proximis ab inventione typographiae annis.... Amst., 1688. 12mo, contemp calf; spine ends chipped. sg Apr 2 (22) $1,000

Beveridge, Albert J., 1862-1927
— Abraham Lincoln. Bost., 1928. One of 1,000. Unopened. wa Feb 19 (65) $80

Beverley, Robert, c.1673-c.1722
— Histoire de la Virginie... Amst., 1707. 12mo, contemp calf; rubbed, corners bumped. With engraved title, folding table & 14 plates. O Oct 21 (27) $160
— The History of Virginia.... L, 1722. 8vo, calf gilt; rubbed. pn Mar 5 (277) £130
Anr copy. Modern half lea. With 15 plates, each with ink library stamp on recto, partly affecting image. Lacking ads. sg Mar 12 (257) $110

AMERICAN BOOK PRICES CURRENT

Bewick, Thomas, 1753-1828
[-] Bewick Gleanings.... Newcastle, 1886. 2 parts in 1 vol. 4to, orig pigskin; upper cover loose. Inscr by Julia Boyd. pn Oct 23 (139) £60 [Sanders]
Anr copy. Mor gilt by Waters. L.p. copy. S May 28 (627) £260
— A General History of Quadrupeds. Newcastle, 1790. 8vo, orig calf gilt. pn Oct 23 (135) £140 [Steedman]
3d Ed. Newcastle, 1792. 8vo, contemp mor gilt. Marginal foxing. sg Mar 26 (25) $200
Anr Ed. Newcastle, 1800. 8vo, contemp half calf gilt. Tp torn, with 1 corner def. L July 2 (38) £110
6th Ed. Newcastle, 1811. 8vo, contemp calf; worn, joints tender. ha Dec 19 (159) $65
7th Ed. Newcastle, 1820. 8vo, orig bds. pn Oct 23 (25) £50 [Smith]
8th Ed. Newcastle, 1824. 8vo, half calf; worn. pn Dec 11 (165) £60
— A History of British Birds. Newcastle, 1797-1804. 2 vols. 8vo, later half calf. bba Mar 12 (38) £90 [Camberwell]
Anr copy. 1st Ed. half mor; rubbed. Vol I lacking U1. Ck Oct 17 (22) £75
Anr Ed. Newcastle, 1797-1805. 2 vols. 8vo, modern cloth. sg Jan 15 (186) $100
1st Ed. Newcastle, 1797-1804. 2 vols. 8vo, contemp half calf; rubbed. S July 28 (1053) £170
Anr copy. Half calf; worn, Vol I needs rebdg. Sold as a collection of plates. Sold w.a.f. sg Dec 18 (147) $140
Mixed Ed. Newcastle, 1797-1804-21. 2 vols plus Supplements bound in 2 vols. 8vo, 19th-cent mor gilt with arms of the House of Commons library. Vol I lacking half-title; some spotting in Vol II. Roscoe 15c & 17c. bba Oct 30 (377) £150 [Claridge]
Anr Ed. Newcastle, 1804-5. 2 vols. 8vo, modern half mor. Roscoe 17d & 18c. bba May 14 (306) £110 [Waley]
Anr Ed. Newcastle, 1804. 2 vols. 8vo, calf gilt. Title to Vol I foxed. pn Sept 18 (310A) £85 [Scott]
Anr copy. 19th-cent lea; joints & extremities rubbed. sg Jan 15 (187) $200
Anr Ed. Newcastle, 1809. 2 vols in one. 8vo, calf; def, rebacked. Haverschmidt copy. B Feb 24 (387) HF250
Anr copy. 2 vols. 8vo, contemp calf; rebacked & rehinged. sg Jan 15 (188) $120
Anr Ed. Newcastle, 1821. 2 vols plus Supplement bound in. 8vo, contemp calf gilt; rubbed. pn Oct 23 (183) £55 [Bookroom]

Anr Ed. Newcastle, 1826. 2 vols. 8vo,
contemp calf; Vol I spine chipped at head.
sg Feb 12 (17) $150

Anr Ed. Newcastle, 1832. 2 vols. 8vo,
contemp calf; worn, upper bd detached.
pnE June 17 (60) £45

Anr copy. Contemp half calf; rubbed, label
coming loose. Vol II lacking 1 prelim leaf.
S Nov 10 (444) £65 [Head]

Anr Ed. Newcastle, 1847. 2 vols. 8vo,
contemp calf; rubbed. bba Oct 30 (378)
£90 [Cavendish]

Anr copy. Mor gilt by Riviere. Inscr by
Jane Bewick to William Harvey, 1860. C
Oct 15 (212) £260 [Thorp]

Anr copy. Contemp calf gilt. L Dec 11
(265) £90

— A Memoir of Thomas Bewick. Newcastle &
L, 1862. 8vo, orig cloth; rubbed. bba Apr
23 (207) £55 [Dawson]

Anr copy. With 17 plates. pnE Dec 17
(383) £70 [Steedman]

— A New Lottery Book of Birds and Beasts.
Newcastle, 1771. 32mo, orig floral bds;
backstrip repaired. Title & anr page discolored at fore-edge. S Dec 5 (296) £1,400
[J. Schiller]

— Select Fables. Newcastle, 1820. 7th Ed. 4to,
later cloth; affected by damp. Ck Feb 13
(111) £85

Anr Ed. Edin., 1879. One of 100. 4to, half
mor gilt. L July 2 (42) £160

— The Watercolors and Drawings of....
Cambr. MA: MIT Press, [1981]. 2 vols.
Oblong 8vo, orig cloth. O June 16 (21) $80

Anr Ed. L, [1981]. 2 vols. Oblong 4to, orig
cloth. O Mar 24 (17) $80

— Works. Newcastle, 1885-87. Memorial Ed,
One of 750. 5 vols. 8vo, orig half mor;
spines worn. S May 28 (628) £110

Beyer, August

— Memoriae historico-criticae librorum variorum, accedunt Evangeli Cosmopolitani....
Dresden, 1734. 8vo, 18th-cent half vellum;
worn. sg Mar 26 (26) $175

Beyle, Marie Henri ("Stendhal"), 1783-1842

— L'Abbesse de Castro. Paris, 1839. 1st Ed.
8vo, mor gilt extra, orig wraps bound in. S
Nov 27 (230) £350 [Rota]

— Memoires d'un touriste. Paris, 1838. 1st
Ed. 2 vols. 8vo, contemp calf; spines worn.
Minor foxing. sg Sept 11 (10) $400

— Promenades dans Rome. Paris, 1829. 1st
Ed. 2 vols. 8vo, contemp half calf; worn.
With frontises & folding plan. S May 29
(1147) £170

Bianco, Margery Williams, 1881-1944

— Poor Cecco. NY, 1925. Illus by Arthur
Rackham. 4to, orig cloth. With 7 mtd
color plates. Water-damaged; foxed &
soiled throughout. sg Oct 30 (31) $25

1st Ed Deluxe, One of 105, sgd by
Rackham. 4to, half vellum; front hinge
starting, front free endpaper tearing loose.
With 7 mtd color plates. sg Oct 30 (30)
$5,000

Bibiena, Ferdinand Galli

— L'Architettura civile preparata sulla
geometria.... Parma, 1711. Folio, bds;
worn, spine damaged. One gathering
sprung, some dampstaining at front &
back, a few leaves torn. CNY Dec 19 (9)
$1,300

Bible in Algonquian

— 1663-[61]. - The Holy Bible...Translated into
the Indian Language. Cambr., Mass.1st Ed
of John Eliot's Indian Bible. 4to, orig mor
gilt; worn, lacking ties, extremities rubbed
but "generally whole and sound". 3 leaves
with small holes, some leaves browned,
minor dampstain to upper inner margin of
New Testament. CNY Dec 19 (69)
$200,000

Bible in Arabic & Latin

— Sacrosancta quatuor Iesu Christi D. N.
Evangelia Arabice Scripta.... Rome: ex
typographia Medicea, 1619 [1591]. Folio,
modern vellum bds. Some marginal tears.
D & M 1643. S May 21 (17) £950
[Thomas]

Bible in Cherokee

— Exodus: or the Second Book of Moses.
Park Hill OK: Mission Press, 1853. 24mo,
loose as issued. One gathering dampstained. sg Mar 12 (62) $200

— Genesis or the First Book of Moses. Park
Hill OK: Mission Press, 1856. 24mo, loose
as issued. Upper margin of 2d gathering
dampstained. sg Mar 12 (63) $200

— Isaiah. Park Hill OK: Mission Press,
[c.1850]. 24mo, loose as issued. Margins
chipped. sg Mar 12 (64) $175

Bible in Chinese

— 1823. - New Testament. Malacca: AngloChinese Press. 8 parts. 8vo, each part in
orig wraps stitched in Chinese manner, the
whole in a contemp cover of blue silk over
paper with ivory pegs. Xylographic printing throughout. S Apr 23 (358) £1,900
[Fletcher]

Bible in Cree

- 1861-62. - L. 2 vols in 1. 8vo, orig lea gilt; worn & broken. AVP Nov 20 (20) C$350 [Woolmer]

Bible in Dutch
- 1562-61. - Biblia, dat is, de gantsche heylige Schrift.... Emden: Gilles van der Erve. Folio, 18th-cent calf. Stain on NT title; repair to inner blank margins of last leaves, not affecting text. D & M 3293. C May 13 (139) £1,200 [Wenner]
- 1676. - Amst.: J. V. Someren. 12mo, contemp tortoise-shell with white metal mounts & clasps. Section excised from lower left corner with slight loss of border; some dampstaining of lower margins. Ck Oct 31 (147) £260
- 1700. - Historie des ouden en nieuwen Testaments. Amst.: P. Mortier. 2 vols in 1. Folio, half calf. Some leaves repaired affecting text. Sold w.a.f. SSA Oct 28 (638) R440
- 1729. - Dordrecht 3 parts in 1 vol. Folio, russia over wooden bds; 1 clasp loose. With 6 folding maps & 25 plates; lower corner waterstained. B Feb 25 (741) HF2,000
- 1910. - Rembrandt Bibel. Amst. 2 vols. Folio, orig calf; rubbed. bba Oct 16 (406) £220 [Hay Cinema]

- Het Hooglied van Salomo. Amst., 1905. Ltd Ed. Illus by B. A. Van der Leck. Folio, orig half cloth. B Oct 7 (61) HF2,000; B Feb 25 (1046) HF1,800

Bible in English
- The Four Gospels. Verona: Officina Bodoni, 1962. One of 320. Folio, Orig mor gilt. S Dec 4 (152) £660 [Thomas]
- 1536. - [Tyndale's version]. Antwerp? "Mole" Ed. 4to, disbound. Lacking 3 leaves; 4 leaves def or torn across; signatures a-f damaged in lower margins or outer corners, affecting text in places; some worming in inner or lower margins, slightly affecting text. S July 23 (386) £1,800 [Smith]
- 1579. - [Geneva version]. Edin.: A. Arbuthnot & T. Bassadyne. 2 parts in 1 vol. Folio, contemp mor gilt; rubbed, joints cracked. Some browning. Herbert 158. bba Aug 20 (329) £280 [Hartly]
- 1582. - [1st Ed of the Douai New Testament] Rheims: John Fogny. 2 vols. 4to, later calf; rebacked, joints split. Titles soiled; OT marginally waterstained; NT slightly wormed in inner margin & lacking final blank. Herbert 300 & 177. bba Mar 26 (141A) £1,100 [Fletcher]
- 1583. - [Geneva version] L: Christopher Barker. Folio, late 17th-cent mor gilt; worn. Lacking initial blank & last leaf; some leaves def or repaired; some headlines shaved; slight dampstaining. Herbert 178. S July 14 (364) £900
- 1589. - The Text of the New Testament.... L: deputies of C. Barker. 8vo, later calf; worn, broken. Ck May 29 (201) £120
- 1598-1597. - L: Deputies of C. Barker. 4to, old calf gilt with brass fittings; rebacked. Margins trimmed close; some stains; several leaves torn at corner with varying loss; lacking 3A4 & 3S4. Herbert 243. sg Mar 26 (28) $225
- 1599. - [Geneva version] L: Deputies of C. Barker. 4to, contemp calf; rubbed, lacking clasps. pn Oct 23 (39) £130 [Brake]
- 1603. - L: Robert Barker. 4to, old half sheep; front joint restored, spine worn. Margins trimmed close; some headlines & sidenotes shaved; several leaves at beginning from anr copy. Herbert 273. sg Mar 26 (29) $200
- 1608. - L: R. Barker. 4to, contemp calf; rubbed, rebacked. 2d title laid down; A1 def; last leaf frayed & remargined; some stains. Herbert 293. bba Jan 15 (5) £100 [Brake]
- 1611. - [Authorized Version] L: Robert Barker With "he" reading in Ruth III, 15. Folio, contemp calf; rebacked & repaired. Tp to O.T., 1st leaf of dedication, map & table in photo-facsimile; lower part of O2-3 in N.T. & Aa3-4 plus Aa5-6 in old Ms facsimile, with Aa5-6 also supplied in photo-facsimile; marginal tears & repairs. Daphne du Maurier's copy. T Dec 18 (276) £540
- 1613-11. - L: Robert Barker With "she" reading in Ruth III,15. Folio, 18th-cent calf; broken, worn. Lacking map & some prelims; titles & many other leaves shaved, affecting headlines; many leaves soiled; some leaves with small holes or repairs; dampstaining to inner margin, sometimes affecting text. Sold w.a.f. Herbert 319. bba Sept 25 (3) £180 [Krown & Spellman]
- 1613-11. - [Authorized version] L: Robert Barker. Folio, contemp calf; spine worn. Lacking map & signature M in New Testament; Old Testament title soiled, frayed & relaid, first few leaves creased or frayed. T Sept 18 (291) £160

With "she" reading in Ruth III, 15. Early blind-stamped calf over wooden bds. Lacking 6 leaves & a few leaves at end; some margins worn affecting a few letters of text; 1 woodcut title torn & def. pn Sept 18 (204) £280 [Brake]

- 1615. - L: Robert Barker. 4to, old calf; worn & broken. Some stains & soiling; S8 & T1 from anr copy; piece torn from 3K1 with loss of text. Herbert 340. sg Mar 26 (31) $130

— 1616. - [Authorized version] L: Robert Barker. Folio, old calf gilt; repaired. Some staining. With 1615 Book of Common Prayer bound in. pn Nov 20 (57) £360 [Aspin]

— 1633. - The New Testament...Translated...by the English Colledge...in Rhemes. [Rouen?]: John Cousturier. 4to, contemp calf; rebacked & recornered, rubbed. With engraved title & 7 plates. Some waterstains. bba Mar 26 (142) £110 [Brake]

— 1635. - [Old Testament] [Rouen]: John Cousturier. 2d Ed of the Douai O.T. 2 vols, 4to, old calf; rebacked. Marginal tears not affecting text; errata leaf from anr copy; lacking engraved titles. Herbert 499. sg Mar 26 (32) $200

— 1637. - Cambr. 4to, calf gilt. pn Nov 20 (58) £360 [Maggs]

— 1653. - L: John Field. 24mo, mor extra. pn Nov 20 (59) £460 [Maggs]

— 1655. - L: E. T. for a Societie of Stationers. Bound with: The Psalms of David in Meeter. Edin., 1655. Wing B2463. 4to, contemp mor gilt with silver corner- & center-pieces, 2 silver clasps, initials A. U. on upper & A. R. on lower center-piece. Some cropping, tears & small defs. Herbert 644. bba Jan 15 (6) £170 [Bauman]

— 1660-59. - Cambr. 2 vols. Folio, later mor; worn. With 6 double-page plates, all cut down & 1 double-page map. Some leaves cleanly torn. Extra-illus with engraved title & 127 plates from 1718 Ed of Pierre de Hondt's "Figures de la Bible". Ck Oct 17 (89) £400

— 1660. - Cambr.: John Field. 3 vols. Folio, 18th-cent mor gilt by John Brindley. Lacking tp to Vol II; some spots & holes. D & M 668. Extra-illus with c.182 single & 36 double plates. S July 23 (385) £3,000 [Smith]

— 1672-79. - L. Folio, early mor gilt decorated with flowers, drawer handles, stars, dots, birds & rosettes. Sold w.a.f. pn Sept 18 (205) £2,000 [Toscani]

— 1679. - Amst.: Stephen Swart. Folio, 19th-cent mor; hinges rubbed. With 6 double-page engraved maps; final leaf strengthened, penultimate leaf torn & repaired. pnNY Sept 13 (247) £650

— 1679. - Oxford: at the Theater. 4to, Restoration bdg of mor gilt with pattern of drawer handle & pointille. sg Oct 9 (102) $300

— 1708. - [N.p.] Folio, 19th-cent calf over wooden bds; rubbed. With engraved title & 6 hand-colored maps & plans by Joseph Moxon. pnNY Sept 13 (248) $350

— 1717-16. - ["Vinegar" Bible]. Oxford: John Baskett. 2 vols. Folio, contemp mor gilt; rubbed, spine extremities worn. Herbert 942. C May 13 (151) £200 [Hamilton]

— 1723. - Oxford: John Baskett. 2 vols. 4to, old calf; worn. With engraved title & 6 folding maps & plans, all torn, a few with loss. Ck Oct 17 (71) £60

— 1739. - L: John Baskett. Folio, old calf; soiled. Some stains & soiling. D & M 796. Ck Sept 5 (83) £450

— 1747. - Oxford 4to, contemp mor gilt with the arms of George II & his cipher in compartments of spine, bound for one of the Chapels Royal; repaired. Stained. bba Oct 30 (13) £140 [Wagner]

— [c.1759]. - Oxford: Thomas Baskett. In 2 vols. 8vo, 18th-cent American sheep gilt by Taylor & Andrews of Wilmington. John Dickinson's copy, sgd by him on tp. F Oct 30 (512) $1,300

— 1763. - Cambr.: Baskerville With list of subscribers in 3d State. Folio, contemp mor gilt; lower outer corner of upper cover repaired. C Dec 12 (21) £3,400 [Temperley]
With list of subscribers in 2d State. Modern calf. Some dampstaining. S Nov 10 (362) £100 [Vine]

— 1767. - L: Mark Baskett & the Assigns of Robert Baskett. 4to, contemp mor gilt with mor inlays inscr Geo Heron Esq Daresbury Cheshire; corners bumped, spine rubbed. D & M 874. Ck Sept 5 (92) £950

— 1769-71. - Birm.: Baskerville. Folio, calf; rebacked. With 2 titles & 7 engraved plates; last few leaves repaired. pnNY Sept 13 (246) £325

— 1772. - Edin. 2 vols in 1. 12mo, mor gilt by James Scott of Edinburgh; rubbed. pn Nov 20 (62) £1,000 [Quaritch]

— 1791. - Worcester, Mass.: Isaiah Thomas. 2 vols. Folio, contemp calf. Lacking frontis & plates. Sold w.a.f. sg Sept 18 (284) $110

— 1795. - L. 4 vols. 4to, contemp mor gilt; rubbed. John Romney's copy. bba May 14 (75) £100 [Axe]

— 1798. - Phila. 2 vols. Folio, contemp calf; spine ends chipped. Some staining & browning. wa Mar 5 (253) $110

— 1800. - L: Thomas Macklin. 6 vols. Folio, contemp russia gilt by Staggemeier & Welcher. Some waterstaining. bba Mar 26 (143) £380 [Camberwell]
Anr copy. 6 vols in 14. Folio, later half lea. Extra-illus with 1,288 plates. C July 22 (20) £850
Anr copy. 6 vols. Folio, contemp mor gilt; extremities scuffed. Frontis to Vol I detached. Ck Apr 24 (210) £650

— 1812-14. - L. 6 vols. 4to, later mor gilt. Ck

BIBLE IN ENGLISH

Oct 17 (113) £280
— 1846. - The Illuminated Bible. NY 4to, orig mor; rebacked & with new endpapers. With 2 engraved titles & 1,600 plates. O June 16 (107) $120
— 1848. - New Testament. L: Wm. Pickering Trans by John Wycliffe. 4to, mor gilt with gros point dated 1849 inserted in upper cover, glazed with brass surround. pn Nov 20 (61) £780 [Joseph]
— 1974. - A Leaf from the First Edition of the First Complete Bible in English, the Coverdale Bible, 1535. San Francisco: Book Club of California One of 425. Intro by Allen P. Wikgren. 4to, cloth, in d/j. With orig leaf including part of Luke. cb Sept 11 (33) $200
Anr copy. With orig leaf. S May 6 (544) £80 [Maggs]

— The Book of Esther. NY: Golden Cross Press, 1935. One of 135. Designed & illuminated by Angelo Valenti. Mor. With 2 sets of proofs which were rejected by the pbr, each with different proposed hand-illuminated capitals. cb Dec 4 (119) $250
Anr copy. Pigskin. cb Dec 4 (120) $300
— The Book of Genesis. L: Riccardi Press, 1914. One of 500. Illus by E. Cayley Robinson. 4to, contemp vellum. With 10 color plates. pn Jan 22 (40) £45 [Reynard]
— The Book of Job.... Cummington MA: Cummington Press, 1944. One of 300. 4to, half mor; spine ends rubbed. sg Jan 8 (53) $250
Anr Ed. Leigh-on-Sea, 1948. One of 110. Illus by Frank Brangwyn. 4to, orig half vellum. With 33 plates. Ck Oct 31 (59) £200
— The Book of Jonah. N.p.: Hammer Creek Press, 1960. One of 40. Orig bds, in d/j. cb Dec 4 (186) $325
Anr Ed. Bronxville: Valenti Angelo, 1969. One of 35. cb Dec 4 (305) $95
Anr Ed. L: Clover Hill Editions, 1979. One of 10 ptd on vellum with extra sets of the illusts on vellum, japon & hand-made paper. Illus by David Jones. Orig mor gilt. S June 18 (343) £5,500 [Papermain]
— The Book of Ruth and Boaz.... NY: Press of Valenti Angelo, 1949. One of 150. cb Dec 4 (306) $225; cb Dec 4 (307) $100
— Ecclesiastes. L, [1902]. ("Ecclesiastes; or, The Preacher, and the Song of Solomon.") Ltd Ed. Designed by Charles Ricketts. Folio, orig half cloth. pn Mar 5 (291) £65 [Sotheran]
— Genesis. L: Riccardi Press, 1914. One of 500. Illus by F. Cayley Robinson. Vellum gilt. With 10 colored plates. pn Mar 5 (90)

AMERICAN BOOK PRICES CURRENT

£50 [Levine]
— The Holy Gospel According to Matthew, Mark, Luke and John. Verona: Officina Bodoni, 1962. One of 320. Folio, orig mor gilt. bba May 14 (147) £800 [Quaritch]
— Judith; reprinted from the Apocrypha. L, 1928. One of 100, sgd by W. Russell Flint. 4to, orig vellum. With frontis & 4 colored plates by Flint. Ck Sept 5 (109) £100
— The Second Chapter from the Gospel According to Saint Matthew. NY: Golden Cross Press, 1936. One of 100. cb Dec 4 (123) $85
Anr Ed. [NY, c.1960]. Wraps over flexible bds; small portion of spine rubbed. cb Dec 4 (327) $50
— The Sermon on the Mount. L, [1861]. Illus by W. & G. Audsley & Charles Rolt. 4to, cloth; rubbed. Foxed throughout. O Mar 24 (157) $80
Anr copy. Orig mor elaborately tooled in black & gilt; rubbed. O May 12 (175) $300
Anr copy. Orig cloth; rubbed. pn Dec 11 (112) £50 [Thorp]
Anr Ed. Bronxville: Press of Valenti Angelo, [1963]. One of 50. Half vellum. With additional gathering from the text, sgd by Angelo, laid in loose. cb Dec 4 (328) $150
— The Sixth Chapter of St. Matthew. N.p.: Hammer Creek Press, [n.d.]. One of 20 on Arches. cb Dec 4 (187) $275
One of 85. cb Dec 4 (188) $130
— The Song of Songs which is Solomon's. L, 1897. ("Song of Solomon.") Illus by H. Granville Fell. 4to, orig cloth. With 12 plates. Some foxing. B Oct 7 (279) HF300
Anr Ed. L, 1909. ("The Song of Songs.") One of 17 on vellum. Illus by W. Russell Flint. 4to, orig vellum, in d/j & portfolio in orig cloth. With 10 mtd colored plates & duplicate suite with paper caption leaves in portfolio. S June 17 (233) £700 [Joseph]
One of 500. Orig vellum. With 10 mtd colored plates. Ck Jan 16 (134) £50
Anr Ed. Phila.: Centaur Press, 1927. ("Song of Solomon.") One of 525, sgd by Wharton Esherick. Illus by Esherick. 4to, half cloth; stained. cb June 18 (71) $55
— The Story of the Exodus. Paris: Leon Amiel, 1966. One of 285. Illus by Marc Chagall. Folio, unbound as issued in wraps. sg Apr 2 (44) $16,000

Bible in French
— 1550. - [New Testament] Louvain 2 parts in 1 vol. Folio, contemp blindstamped calf over wooden bds; def, lacking 1 clasp. Final leaves repaired; some marginal repairs; dampstained; tp detached. S Sept 23 (298) £240 [Gilhofer & Ranschberg]

- 1567. - La Bible, qui est toute la saincte escriture. [Geneva]: F. Estienne. With: Calendrier historial. Geneva: F. Estienne, 1567. Title trimmed & mtd. 8vo, old calf; worn, spine chipped. Dampstained at beginning & end; some headlines shaved. sg Oct 9 (104) $175
- 1644. - Geneva Folio, old vellum; stained. Margins stained throughout. Ck Nov 21 (126) £80
- 1866. - Tours Illus by Gustave Dore. 2 vols. Folio, half lea; rubbed. Some foxing. O Oct 21 (56) $80

- Figures du Nouveau Testament Illustrees. Lyons: G. Rouille, 1570. 8vo, modern half mor. sg June 11 (38) $400
- Figures du Nouveau Testament declarees par Stanses * Actes des Apostres. Lyons: Estienne Michel, 1582. 2 vols in 1. 8vo, modern calf gilt. sg June 11 (39) $950

Bible in Gaelic
- 1685. - [1st Irish Old Testament] L. 4to, contemp calf; joints worn. Prelim leaf with the note about Irish type cut down & pasted onto verso of tp; some headlines cropped, holes with loss of text in 5N1 & 5O3; tear in 7C1. S Dec 18 (318) £450 [Traylen]

Bible in German
- 1483, 17 Feb. - Nuremberg: Anton Koberger. 2 vols. Folio, 16th-cent blind-stamped pigskin over wooden bds; rubbed. With 109 woodcuts colored by an early hand & 11 Ms initials in gold & silver & colors. Vol I wormed & repaired, affecting text on 2 leaves. 583 (of 586) leaves; lacking 3 blanks. Goff B-632. HK Nov 4 (604) DM80,000

 Anr copy. 18th-cent pigskin over wooden bds with monogram L.H.. With 109 woodcuts colored by an early hand. Some wear & defs. 583 (of 586) leaves; lacking 3 blanks. Goff B-632. HN May 20 (1632) DM47,000

 Anr copy. Part 2 (of 2) only. Folio, crude modern half lea. With woodcuts crudely hand-colored. Upper margins unevenly trimmed, lower margins dampstained; lacking initial & final blanks & 3 leaves, 2 leaves supplied from anr copy. 285 (of 290) leaves. Goff B-632. sg Oct 9 (105) $1,500
- 1527. - Das Neuw Testament. Strassburg: Johannis Grienigern. Folio, contemp pigskin over wooden bds; worn, a few wormholes. With a few woodcut initials supplied in Ms; 2 wormholes in fore-margin of initial leaves; wormhole in inner margin of endleaves just touching text of 2 leaves;

short in bottom margin of AA4-6; some soiling. S Nov 27 (6) £2,600 [Breslauer]
- 1540, Aug. - Biblia beider Allt und Newen Testementen.... Cologne: Hero Alopecius Fuchs. Folio, contemp blindstamped pigskin over wooden bds; rubbed, lacking clasps. Some leaves loose at beginning; small tear to upper margin of f4; woodcut on Cc4 cut out with loss of text on verso. S Mar 10 (1018) £600 [Kiefer]
- 1540. - Dat Nye Testament. Wittenberg 8vo, contemp blindstamped pigskin with port panel of Luther & 6 (of 8) cornerpieces. Imperf copy, sold w.a.f. sg Oct 9 (106) $375
- 1567. - Biblia; das ist, die gantze Heylige Schrifft.... Frankfurt: S. Feyerabent Rab & Weygand Hanen Erben. 2 vols. Folio, contemp lea over wooden bds; worn. JG Mar 20 (211) DM2,700
- 1677-76. - Lueneburg: Die Sternische Erben. 4 vols. 4to, 18th-cent calf gilt; upper cover of Vol III with 2 deep tears, spines worn at ends. Several plates in Vols II-IV with short tears (some repaired); small hole in Plate 29 & in the text of Yyy5 in Vol II affecting 2 letters; 1 leaf in Vol I torn touching headline; lower corner of Plate 13 of Vol II torn away. D & M 4220. S May 21 (92) £700 [Hildebrandt Rate Books]
- 1704. - Frankfurt Folio, later lea; worn, lacking clasps. Frontis laid down; edges cropped; a few leaves repaired with loss of text. Sold w.a.f. bba Aug 28 (104) £130 [Burmejo]
- 1720. - Nuremberg Folio, lea over wooden bds. Some browning & spotting. FD Dec 2 (21) DM1,000
- 1729. - [Luther's version] Basel: E. & J. R. Thurneysen. 2 vols. Folio, contemp lea. FD Dec 2 (22) DM1,300
- 1743. - Germantown, Pa.: Christoph Saur. 4to, contemp calf; worn, lacking clasps. Some browning. sg Apr 2 (24) $1,100
- 1747. - Nuremberg Folio, contemp pigskin over wooden bds. With 19 plates, including 12 ports. FD Dec 2 (24) DM2,200
- 1770. - Konstanz Bound in 4 vols. Folio, contemp calf; wormed. About 120 leaves in Vol II with small wormholes. HN Nov 26 (1093) DM540
- 1776. - ["Gun-Wad" Bible] Germantown, Pa.: Christoph Saur. 4to, calf. Some spotting & browning. HK Nov 4 (1703) DM1,100

 Anr copy. Contemp calf; rebacked with lea. K Dec 13 (210) $190

- Das Goldene Evangelienbuch von Echternach. Frankfurt, 1982. One of 250 specially bound. 2 vols. Folio, facsimile of

BIBLE IN GERMAN

text bound in reversed calf with elaborate additional cover in silk over bds with facsimile of orig bdg mtd on back, explanatory text in half vellum. S Sept 22 (231) £2,500 [Smith]

Bible in Greek

— 1546. - [New Testament] Paris: Robert Estienne. 2 parts in 1 vol. 8vo, early calf gilt; rubbed. Some browning. D & M 4616. S Sept 23 (421) £250 [Smith]

Anr copy. 18th-cent mor gilt. Lacking 1 prelim leaf. S May 21 (28) £250 [Koeppe]

Anr copy. Later mor gilt; rubbed. Ink notes erased from title of Vol I. T Feb 19 (574) £190

— 1549. - Paris: R. Estienne. 16mo, mor; worn, 2 covers loose. D & M 4620. bba Mar 26 (144) £150 [Brake]

— 1568-69. - Paris: Robert Estienne. 2 vols in 1. 16mo, 17th-cent mor gilt; joints weak. Margins trimmed close; tp soiled. D & M 4633; Schreiber 239. sg Mar 26 (33) $175

— 1601. - Frankfurt Folio, later half calf; rubbed. Some stains. S Mar 10 (1019) £85 [Edwards]

— 1633. - [New Testament]. He kaine diatheke. Leiden: Elzevir. 12mo, modern half mor. bba Apr 9 (9) £45 [Clarke]

— 1653. - [Old Testament] L: Roger Daniel. 8vo, early 18th-cent mor gilt; rebacked, orig backstrip laid down. With Apocrypha placed separately at end. sg Oct 9 (107) $90

— 1709. - Franeker 8vo, vellum; def, ties lacking. With 3 folding maps. B Feb 25 (745) HF260

— 1800. - Kaine diatheke. Wigorniae [Worcester], Mass.: Isaias Thomas, Jr.. 12mo, disbound. Some fraying. D & M 4775. K Oct 4 (427) $120

Anr copy. Contemp calf; worn. Old ink notations; lacking ad leaf. D & M 4775. K June 7 (249) $190

Anr copy. Lacking final ad leaf. sg Sept 18 (284) $150

Bible in Greek & Latin

— 1522. - Novum Testamentum omne. Basel: Joh. Frobenius Ed by Erasmus. Folio, modern pigskin. Lacking H2; marginal tears; last few leaves stained at outer margin; some soiling. S Feb 23 (64) £130 [Smith]

— 1589. - [New Testament] [Geneva: H. Estienne] Ed by Theodorus Beza. Folio, 19th-cent panelled calf; hinges rubbed. Tp torn & repaired with loss of text on verso; some ink annotations in margins. S Oct 23 (313) £75 [Edwards]

AMERICAN BOOK PRICES CURRENT

Bible in Hebrew

— 1517. - Magna Biblia Rabbinica; Mikraoth Gedoloth. Venice: Daniel Bomberg. 4 parts in 4 vols. Folio, modern syn. Vol I lacking all until Numbers 30:7 & some leaves are torn; Vol II with some stains & wormholes & last leaf soiled & remargined; Vol IV lacking Proverbs & with some worming restored & some remargining occasionally affecting headnotes. Some leaves supplied from anr copy. sg Sept 25 (39) $5,250

— 1544-46. - Paris: R. Estienne. 17 parts in 12 vols. 16mo, various bdgs. Some stains. S Feb 17 (16) £1,200 [Rosenfeld]

— 1546-48. - Magna Biblia Rabbinica. Venice: Daniel Bomberg. 4 vols. Folio, modern cloth. Vol III tp & 1st 5 leaves def & partly repaired with loss of text; Vol IV tp & 1st leaf def with loss & tp laid down. St. 125, col 24. bba Feb 19 (55) £2,600 [Ben Schmuel]

Anr copy. Modern half mor. Lacking the Targum Yerushalmi & last 4 leaves of index in Vol II; in Vol I the lower margin of title strengthened & a few other margins repaired & some cropping; Vol II has margin of tp repaired affecting border & 1 letter; in Vol III margins of title & 1st 4 leaves seriously def with loss. St. 125, col 24. bba Feb 19 (56) £2,000 [Thomas]

— 1565-66. - Antwerp: Plantin. 4to, later calf; rubbed. Stained & browned throughout. bba Mar 26 (148) £100 [Maggs]

— 1566-81. - Antwerp: Christopher Plantin. Hebrews & Latter Prophets only. Half lea; worn. D & M 5099. CAM Dec 3 (27) HF3,000

— 1573-74. - Antwerp: Plantin. 8vo, 18th-cent mor; rebacked retaining orig backstrip. Tp inlaid to size; some worming. D & M 5102; St. 227. sg Apr 30 (104) $1,000

— 1588. - Hamburg Folio, contemp wooden bds with lea backstrip; worn. Some stamps; lacking tp & 1st 5 leaves of preface. D & M 5108. T Sept 18 (297) £130

— 1618-19. - Basel: L. Koenig. 4 vols. Folio, modern mor. Some stains & fraying. St. 423, cols 69-70. S Feb 17 (18) £800 [Sol]

— 1635-36. - Amst.: Menasseh ben Israel & Hendrik Laurentius. 4to, modern mor. Some stains & browning. S Feb 17 (19) £700 [Mandanes]

Anr copy. Contemp calf over wooden bds; spine cr, hinge split. Marginal worming throughout. D & M 5124. sg Apr 30 (105) $1,500

— 1667. - Amst. 8vo, bds; worn. Tp soiled & partly detached; small hole in penultimate leaf; some stains & fraying. St. 553. CAM Dec 3 (38) HF1,100

— 1701. - Amst. 12mo, contemp vellum; upper joint split. Half-title soiled. St. 712. CAM Dec 3 (41) HF240
Anr copy. 8vo, syn. Lacking final leaf of preface; 1 cellotape repair. St. 712, col 113-14; D & M 5139. sg Apr 30 (108) $110
— 1705. - Amst. & Utrecht 8vo, old calf gilt; rubbed. With 4 engraved titles. Tears in last 4 leaves; some stains & minor defs. D & M 5141. CAM Dec 3 (42) HF750
Anr copy. Early half lea; rubbed. D & M 5141. CAM Dec 3 (43) HF400
Anr copy. Bound in 2 vols. 8vo, modern half lea. Interleaved & annotated; minor repair on outer margin of 1st title; some dampstains on top outer corners. D & M 5141. sg Sept 25 (40) $400
— 1711-10. - Berlin Oblong 16mo, contemp calf; rubbed. Small marginal wormhole at beginning. St. 791. CAM Dec 3 (44) HF1,200
— 1814. - Phila. 2 vols. 8vo, orig calf; rear cover of Vol II detached. Dampstained on front & closing blanks. sg Apr 30 (22) $1,000
— 1815. - The Hebrew Bible; from the Edition of Evarado van der Hooght. NY: Whiting & Watson. Nos 1 & 2 (of a projected 16, all pbd). 8vo, orig bds; backstrip torn. Stained. sg Apr 30 (23) $100

— Chamisha Chumshei Torah. Berlin: Soncino Gesellschaft, 1931-33. One of 850. Folio, half lea by Meink; rubbed. CAM Dec 3 (47) HF850
— [Torah & Haftorot] Amst., [1726]. 8vo, modern mor gilt. St. 865. bba Feb 19 (63) £350 [Loewy]
— [Torah, Chamesh Megillot & Haftorot] Amst., 1727. 3 vols. 8vo, old calf gilt; rubbed. A few leaves extended; tears in last leaves; shaken. St. 873; D & M 5146. CAM Dec 3 (45) HF900
— [Torah, Five Megillot & Haftarot]. Venice: Daniel Bomberg, 1548. Folio, old half calf; recased. Library stamp on title; marginal notes; some worming to lower margin, occasionally affecting single letters. St. 126, col 24. CAM Dec 3 (26) HF4,800

Bible in Hebrew & English
— 1774. - The Old Testament, English and Hebrew. L. 8vo, disbound. With 2 folding maps & 3 plates. Poor copy. D & M 3139. sg Sept 25 (42) $175
— 1845. - Phila.: C. Sherman. 5 vols. 4to, contemp calf; needs rebdg. Some repairs. sg Apr 30 (24) $750

Bible in Hebrew & French
— [1928]. - Paris: Les Textes Sacres One of 1,500. Folio, contemp half mor, orig wraps bound in. cb Oct 23 (25) $65

Bible in Hebrew & Greek
— 1584. - Antwerp: Christopher Plantin. 3 parts in 1 vol. Folio, orig calf; worn. Some stains. S Feb 17 (17) £400 [Thomas]
Anr copy. Contemp blind-tooled pigskin. Some worming & soiling. S Mar 10 (1021) £360 [Adampoulos]

Bible in Hebrew & Latin
— 1584. - Antwerp: Plantin. Folio, later calf; rubbed. Both titles relaid, outer margins of first few leaves of New Testament repaired & with marginal worming. T Sept 18 (298) £210
— 1618. - Geneva: P. de la Rouviere. Folio, contemp vellum; rubbed. St. 420, col 69. CAM Dec 3 (29) HF1,300
— 1699. - Berlin 4to, contemp vellum; rubbed. Some waterstaining. FD June 11 (53) DM1,500

Bible in Icelandic
— 1807. - That Nya Testamenta vors Drottins og Endurlausnara Jesu Christi. Copenhagen: Sebastian Popp. 8vo, modern cloth. Perforated stamp on title & anr leaf. D & M 5497. sg Mar 26 (34) $60

Bible in Italian
— 1556. - Il Nuovo ed Eterno Testamento di Giesu Christo. Lyons: J. de Tournes & G. Gazeau. 2 parts in 1 vol. 16mo, contemp vellum. Tp with small repair & small modern mtd blank label; some dampstaining. With spurious signatures of William Shakespeare & Queen Victoria. sg June 11 (41) $600
— 1961. - La Bibblia di Borso d'Este. Bergamo: Banco Popolare. 2 vols. Folio, syn gilt, with metal centerpieces in upper covers. With reproductions of the orig Ms leaves. sg Apr 2 (25) $375

— Figure del Vecchio Testamento. Figure del Nuovo Testamento. Venice: N. Bevilacqua, 1574. 2 parts in 1 vol. 8vo, old half calf; front joint cracked. sg June 11 (55) $400

Bible in Latin
— c.1450-55. - Mainz: Gutenberg. 1 leaf only, comprising Numbers xxxii.17-xxxiii.56 Framed. Marginal foxing; marginal slits & tears artlessly mended. P Sept 24 (164) $7,000
— 1480. - Venice: Franciscus Renner, de Heilbronn. 4to & 8vo, later blind-stamped calf. Tear in g5; 1st leaf def & remargined;

BIBLE IN LATIN

burnhole in some index leaves; repaired; heavy staining at beginning & near end. 458 (of 470) leaves; lacking last 11 leaves of index & last blank. bba Oct 16 (2) £650 [Mandl]

— 1484, 30 Apr. - Venice: Johannes Herbort de Seligenstadt. 4to, modern velvet over calf-covered bds; worn. With initials supplied in blue & red; initial on a2 recto with long extension into margin One small wormhole running through 1st half of text; some soiling & shaving of headlines; a few early annotations in margins. 408 leaves. Goff B-580. S June 25 (11) £950 [Symonds]

— 1486. - Biblia Latina. Basel: Johann Amerbach. Folio, contemp pigskin over wooden bds; upper joint split, both covers rubbed & wormed. Wormed throughout; some leaves soiled or dampstained. 537 (of 538) leaves; lacking final blank. Goff B-581. S Nov 27 (146) £1,800 [D. Smith]

— 1491, 27 June. - Basel: Johann Froben. 8vo, 18th-cent half sheep; worn. One leaf restored at top-edges with loss of headline; scattered marginal stains. Goff B-592. P Dec 15 (158) $6,000

— 1497, 26 Apr. - Strassburg: [Johann (Reinhard) Grueninger]. Folio, contemp blind-stamped calf; rubbed & wormed. Tp laid down & wormed & def; 1 leaf from a shorter copy; some leaves dampstained or wormed. 471 (of 492) leaves. Goff B-600. S Mar 10 (1022) £360 [Nosbusch]

— 1498, 8 May. - Venice: Simon Bevilaqua. 4to, old vellum Ms leaf over bds; worn, backed with later vellum. Marginal soiling & stains; leaves of 1st gatherings bound out of order; minor worming in upper margins at end. 278 leaves only (complete from B1 - beginning of Proverbs). Goff B-603. sg Mar 26 (35) $700

— 1512. - Lyons: J. Sacon. Folio, 18th-cent mor; spine wormed. Lacking 2 leaves. HK Nov 4 (602) DM1,500

— 1515, [20 Sept]. - Lyons: J. Sacon. 8vo, mor extra by M. Bueno. sg June 11 (43) $2,400

— 1518, 10 May. - Biblia cum concordantiis veteris & novi testamenti. Lyons: J. Sacon for A. Koberger. Folio, 18th-cent calf; rebacked, worn. Margin of tp & aa2 repaired; some dampstains. D & M 6101. S June 25 (9) £480

— 1520, 3 Dec. - Lyons: Stephan Guenard alias Pinetus. Folio, old calf; broken. Tp remargined & rehinged; minor marginal repairs at end; lacking 2a2-2b8, b1 & c8. sg Mar 26 (36) $350

— 1522. - Biblia cum concordantiis.... Lyons: Jacobus Sacon for Anton Koberger. Folio, contemp blind-tooled pigskin over wooden bds; worn, front cover partly detached. D

AMERICAN BOOK PRICES CURRENT

& M 6102. sg Oct 9 (110) $600

— 1526, 6 Nov. - Paris: Widow of T. Kerver. 2 parts in 1 vol. 8vo later calf; rubbed, joints split. Tp & last leaf soiled; some annotations. bba mar 26 (145) £160 [Bickersteth]

— 1527. - Nuremberg: J. Petreium. 8vo, later vellum; soiled. Tp repaired; some browning. bba Mar 26 (146) £180 [Hildebrandt]

— 1538. - Lyons: M. & G. Trechsel Illus by Hans Holbein. Folio, vellum; worn & loose. Minor worming, mainly marginal but affecting some headlines & c.14 letters of text. P Sept 24 (166A) $9,000

— 1541. - Venice: Peter Schoeffer. 2 vols. 8vo, early 17th-cent mor gilt, with monogram of Henri Monod; worn. sg Oct 9 (111) $325

— 1546. - Paris: R. Stephanus. 2 parts in 1 vol. Folio, old bds; worn. Wormed throughout; blank upper & lower margins of title excised. sg Oct 9 (112) $200

— 1563. - Lyons: Apud Guliel. Rouillium. 8vo, contemp calf; worn, upper cover def. T Jan 22 (326) £105

— 1563. - Lyons: G. Rouille. 8vo, mor gilt. Some dampstains. sg June 11 (49) $400

— 1570-69. - Biblia, ad vetustissima exemplaria nunc recens castigata. Antwerp: Christopher Plantin. 8vo, contemp vellum; rubbed. Tp holed & repaired; some soiling. Ck Jan 16 (96) £130

— 1580. - Testamenti Veteris Biblia Sacra.... L: Henry Middleton for W. Norton. 5 parts in 1 vol. 4to, contemp vellum; rubbed, inner hinges weak. Upper margins cropped; tp soiled; some stains. STC 2056.6. bba Sept 25 (1) £85 [Cox]

— 1588. - Venice: Gioliti. 4to, old vellum. Some stains at beginning & end; minor marginal repairs; general title trimmed & mtd; lacking front free endpaper. sg Mar 26 (37) $250

— 1593-92. - L: G. B[ishop], R. N[ewbery] & R. B[arker]. Folio, contemp calf gilt; rubbed & wormed. Tp cut out, laid down & def; some worming, affecting text. bba July 16 (210) £60 [Brake]

— 1603. - Hanover Folio, contemp calf; rebacked. Oval ink stamp to tp & contents. T Sept 18 (286) £75

— 1608. - Venice: E. Deuchinum & J. B. Pulciani. 4to, old vellum. Scattered dampstaining. sg June 11 (52) $150

— 1628. - Antwerp: Plantin. 8vo, old calf; worn. O Sept 23 (19) $70

— 1707-8. - L. Bound with: The Whole Book of Psalms Collected into English Meeter. L, 1702. Folio, contemp calf over wooden bds with brass corners; clasps deficient, some metal pieces lacking. Minor marginal tears. Herbert 897. T Sept 18 (292) £50

— 1740. - Louvain Folio, contemp calf gilt. With plate, port & 4 double-page maps. sg Oct 9 (113) $150
— 1740. - [Clementine Bible] Venice 3 vols. 8vo, vellum gilt, armorial bdg; rubbed, soiled. T Sept 18 (533) £100
— 1748. - Venice 2 vols. Folio, old vellum. With frontis in Vol I. sg Oct 9 (114) $80
— 1774. - Avignon 8vo, calf; rubbed, head of spine chipped. cb Oct 23 (24) $100
— 1913-14. - Leipzig: Insel-Verlag One of 290. 2 vols. Folio, orig pigskin. Facsimile of the Gutenberg Bible of c.1450-55. FD Dec 2 (33) DM9,200
— 1961. - Paterson & NY: Pageant Books One of 1,000. 2 vols. Folio, orig mor. Facsimile of the Gutenberg Bible of c.1450-55. C May 13 (138) £150 [Hamilton]

Anr copy. Mor gilt with Gutenberg monogram on covers. Facsimile of the Gutenberg Bible of c.1450-55. sg Apr 2 (26) $1,100

— 1968. - NY: Brussel & Brussel. 3 vols. Folio, orig cloth. Facsimile of the Gutenberg Bible. wa Feb 19 (239) $100

Bible in Malayan
— 1677. - Jang ampat Evangelia.... Oxford: H. Hall. 4to, contemp calf; rebacked, worn, loose. D & M 6492. sg Oct 9 (115) $450

Bible in Mongolian
— [St. Matthew's Gospel]. St. Petersburg, 1819. Bound with: [St. John's Gospel]. [St. Petersburg, 1819?]. Folio, contemp half sheep; rubbed. sg Oct 9 (116) $375

Bible in Mpongwe
— The Gospel of Matthew in the Mpongwe Language. Gaboon: Press of the A.B.C.F.M., 1850. 8vo, contemp half sheep; upper joint split. D & M 6878. S Nov 10 (1189) £320 [Quaritch]

Bible in Natick
— 1685-80. - Cambr.: Samuel Green. 2d Ed of John Eliot's Indian Bible. Trans by John Eliot. 4to, mor gilt. Lacking 5 leaves (supplied in facsimile). Title & 9 other leaves have losses supplied. Some margins renewed, many leaves repaired. I t2-4 and last 4 leaves cropped with loss of many ptd marginal notes. Some severe staining. Sold w.a.f. CNY Dec 19 (70) $6,500

Bible in Spanish
— 1661. - [Old Testament] Amst.: Joseph Athias. 8vo, later blind-stamped calf; rubbed. D & M 8481. bba Feb 19 (59) £550 [Rosenfeld]

Anr copy. Old lea; joints split. Tp extended, soiled & frayed; some browning; tears in last 3 leaves; last leaf mtd. D & M 8481. CAM Dec 3 (37) HF1,400

Bible in Syriac
— 1663-67. - Novum Testamentum Syriace.... Hamburg 3 parts in 1 vol. 8vo, contemp vellum. sg Oct 9 (117) $90

— The Rabbula Gospels: Facsimile Edition.... Olten, 1959. Ltd Ed. Folio, lea. With 20 plain & 29 color plates. sg Jan 22 (256) $225

Bible in Urdu
— [Gospel of St. John] [Probably Calcutta or Serampore, early 19th cent]. 64 leaves, 8vo, contemp calf. sg Nov 20 (23) $150

Bible in Yiddish
— 1687. - Amst.: Emanuel Atias. Folio, contemp calf over wooden bds; worn, clasp missing. Some stains; minor marginal defs. CAM Dec 3 (40) HF1,100

Bible, Polyglot

— Sanctus Matthaeus [in 12 languages]. Nuremberg, 1599. 4to, contemp vellum; rubbed. Some marginal dampstains; several leaves frayed, some repaired. T Sept 18 (353) £92

Biblia Pauperum
— [Block Book. Scenes from the life of Christ with Old Testament prefigurations & prophecies]. Schreiber's Ed I, though folios 12, 16-18, 22, 24, 29 & 37 exhibit minute variations. Folio, 279mm by 200mm, 19th-cent mor. Arranged in single sheets of 2 leaves each, ptd on 1 side only from a double woodblock, divided & mtd on thin guards, the blank sides not pasted together. Woodcuts colored sparingly in a contemp hand. Ff 1 & 40 def & laid down, f.1 with partial loss of text & woodcut at head & corners, f.40 (which apparently is from anr Ed & with different coloring) with lower right-hand quarter lacking & restored in places; several other leaves with minor tears, small wormholes or other imperfections repaired, affecting ptd surface slightly. 37 (of 40) leaves; lacking 32, 38 & 39 (m, s & t in 2d alphabet). John Gott —Dyson Perrins copy. S Nov 27 (148) £135,000 [Tenschert]

Biblicae...
— Biblicae historiae, arfiticiosissimis picturis effigiatae. [Frankfurt: Christian Egenolph, c.1536]. Illus by Hans Sebald Beham. 4to, mor gilt; front hinge cracked. With 37 (of 40) leaes & 74 woodcuts. sg June 11 (33) $1,200

BIBLIOGRAFIA...

Bibliografia...
— Bibliografia de arqueologia y ethnografia Mesoamerica y Norte de Mexico, 1514-1960. Mexico City, 1962. Folio, pictorial wraps, unopened. sg Sept 18 (18) $130

Bibliographica...
— Bibliographica: Papers on Books, their History and Art. L, 1895-97. 12 parts in 3 vols. 8vo, half mor gilt. sg June 11 (57) $275

Bibliotheque...
— Bibliotheque cynegetique d'un amateur avec notes bibliographiques. Paris, 1884. One of 300. 4to, half cloth. Jeanson copy. SM Mar 1 (586) FF1,400

Bicchierai, Allesandro
— Dei Bagni di Montecatini. Florence, 1788. 4to, contemp half sheep. Some worming to opening leaves. sg Apr 2 (27) $500

Bichat, Marie-Francois Xavier, 1771-1802
— A Treatise on the Membranes in General.... Bost., 1813. 8vo, contemp sheep; worn. Foxed. wa Mar 5 (285) $130

Bickham, George, the Younger, d.1758
— A Curious Antique Collection of Bird's-Eye Views.... L, 1796. 4to, half calf. With frontis & 46 plates. pn Apr 30 (118) £3,400 [Burgess]

Bickham, George, the Elder, d.1769
— The British Monarchy.... L, 1748. Folio, contemp calf; rebacked. With title, allegorical frontis & 48 maps. S Apr 23 (111) £3,800 [Burgess]
— The Universal Penman.... L, 1733-41. Folio, contemp half calf; rubbed. With frontis & 211 plates. Frontis & final plate laid down; some plates cropped close; marginal tears; most leaves soiled or spotted. bba Sept 24 (24) £150 [Vine]
Anr Ed. L, 1743. Folio, contemp calf; worn & rubbed at extremities. Engraved throughout. Lacking frontis & at least 1 prelim; some soiling & fraying; final plate torn. cb Feb 19 (23) $170

Bicknell, Clarence
— Flowering Plants and Ferns of the Riviera.... L, 1885. 1st Ed. 8vo, half mor; worn. Tear to 1 plate. S May 28 (630) £110

Bidloo, Govard, 1649-1713
— Anatomia humani corporis.... Amst., 1685. Folio, contemp vellum; soiled. With 97 (of 105) plates. HN Nov 26 (251) DM1,600

AMERICAN BOOK PRICES CURRENT

Bidwell, John, 1819-1900
— A Journey to California.... San Francisco: John Henry Nash, 1937. 4to, half cloth, in d/j. cb Oct 9 (16) $75

Bie, Oskar. See: Schnackenberg & Bie

Biechlin...
— Dises Biechlin sagt von baissen auch wie man den habich darzue gewene Sol.... Augsburg: Hans Schobsser, 1497. 4to, mor gilt by Bedford. Some repairs. 30 leaves. Copinger 2888. Jeanson copy. SM Feb 28 (68) FF240,000

Biel, Gabriel, 1425?-95
— Sacri canonis misse expositio. Basel: Jacobus Wolff of Pforzheim, 1510. Folio, old calf; rebacked, corners restored. Tp rehinged & remargined; lacking final blank; library stamp on tp & at end. sg Oct 9 (120) $150

Bierbaum, Otto Julius
— Das schoene Maedchen von Pao. Munich, 1910. One of 600. Illus by Franz von Bayros. Folio, orig bdg. With 7 lithos. HN Nov 26 (1720) DM800

Bierce, Ambrose, 1842?-1914. See: Limited Editions Club

Biermann, Georg
— Deutsches Barock und Rokoko. Leipzig, 1914. Ltd Ed. 2 vols. Folio, orig half calf; worn. Some waterstaining. HN May 20 (252) DM570

Bierstadt, Oscar Albert
— The Library of Robert Hoe. NY, 1895. One of 350. 8vo, cloth. O Nov 18 (28) $80

Bigelow, Francis Hill
— Historic Silver of the Colonies and its Makers. NY, 1917. Small tear at head of spine. O Mar 24 (18) $60

Bigelow, Horatio. See: Derrydale Press

Bigmore, Edward Clements —& Wyman, Charles William Henry
— A Bibliography of Printing. NY, 1945. 2 vols. Cloth; worn. Library markings. Facsimile of the 1880-86 Ed. O June 16 (25) $60

Bilder...
— Bilder zum Anschauungs-Unterricht fuer die Jugend. Esslingen, 1839. 2 vols. Folio, half cloth; worn & def. With 60 double-page hand-colored plates. Some spotting & browning. JG Oct 2 (1746) DM1,700

Bilderlexicon...
— Bilderlexicon der Erotik. Vienna & Leipzig, [1928-31]. 4 vols. 4to, half lea. sg Feb 12 (73) $275; sg Feb 12 (74) $275

Bilguer, Paul Rudolph, 1813-40
— Handbuch des Schachspiels. Leipzig, 1864. Modern cloth. pn Mar 26 (123) £50 [Von Morris]

Bilguer, Paul Rudolph von, 1815-40
— Handbuch des Schachspiels. Berlin: W. de Gruyter, [1916]. With the 1930 Supplement but without that of 1921. pn Mar 26 (124) £50 [Hoffman]

Billardon de Sauvigny, Louis Edme
— Les Apres-soupes de la societe.... Paris, 1783. 2d Ed of Vol I; other vols are 1st Eds. 23 parts in 6 vols. 12mo, mor gilt by Chambolle-Duru. With engraved titles & 22 plates. C May 13 (4) £420 [Zola]

Billings, Robert William, 1813-74
— The Baronial and Ecclesiastical Antiquities of Scotland. Edin. & L, [1848-52]. 4 vols. 4to, later half mor. With 240 plates. L.p. copy. C July 22 (22) £250

Anr copy. Half calf; worn & broken. O Feb 24 (18) $80

Anr copy. Mor gilt. sg Feb 12 (275) $400

Anr Ed. Edin., 1901. 4 vols. 4to, half mor. pnE May 20 (21) £100

Billot, C. P.
— Melbourne: An Annotated Bibliography.... [Geelong, 1970]. Cloth, in worn d/j. kh Mar 16 (41) A$130

Binet, Alfred, 1857-1911
— Psychologie des grands calculateurs et joueurs d'echecs. Paris, 1894. Modern cloth. Tear to tp & half-title without loss. pn Mar 26 (357) £60 [Levine]

Binet, Etienne, 1567-1639
— Essay des merveilles de nature, et de plus nobles artifices....par Rene Francois. 8vo,. contemp vellum Jeanson copy. SM Feb 28 (69) FF1,500

Binet, Etienne, 1569-1639
— Essai des merveilles de la nature.... Paris, 1638. 8vo, contemp vellum. bba Nov 13 (6) £110 [Poole]

— Essay des merveilles de nature et des plus nobles artifices. Paris, 1638. 8vo, contemp vellum; rubbed. bba Dec 4 (10) £75 [Poole]

Bing, Samuel, 1838-1905
— Artistic Japan.... L, [1888]-91. 6 vols. 4to, various bdgs, with wraps of the 36 monthly parts bound in; worn. Library markings. sg Feb 5 (178) $400

— Le Japon artistique. Paris, [1888]. 3 vols. Folio, orig half cloth; joints split. Some leaves loose. bba Aug 20 (316) £130 [Thorp]

Bingham, Joseph
— The French Churches Apology for the Church of England.... L, 1706. 8vo, contemp calf; broken. Dark stains on opening leaves; portion of blank outer margin off U3. sg Mar 26 (38) $100

Binyon, Laurence, 1869-1943
— The Drawings and Engravings of William Blake. L, 1922. Folio, half vellum; soiled. Ck Oct 17 (108) £40

One of 200. Vellum; worn. With 2 ports, 88 plain & 16 mtd colored plates. O Jan 6 (22) $140

Binyon, Laurence, 1869-1943 —& Sexton, J. J. O'Brien
— Japanese Colour Prints. L, 1923. 4to, cloth. With 16 colored plates. Marginal soiling; tp stamped. cb July 30 (22) $75

One of 100, but without the extra suite of plates. Orig pigskin; stained. With 16 colored & 30 plain plates. S Nov 10 (52) £80 [Samm]

Biographia...
— Biographia Britannica: or, the Lives of the most Eminent Persons.... L, 1747-66. 6 vols in 7. Folio, contemp calf gilt; rebacked, crudely rehinged. sg Oct 9 (121) $130

Bion, Nicolas, 1652?-1733
— Traite de la Construction et des Principaux Usages des Instrumens de Mathematique. The Hague, 1723. Folio, contemp vellum; loose. With 30 folding plates. Marginal dampstaining throughout, 1 leaf torn. sg Jan 15 (291) $500

Biondo, Michelangelo, 1497-1565
— Ad Christianissimum Regem Galliae. Rome: Antonio Blado, 1544. ("De canibus et venatione libellus....") 4to, bdg from a 14th-cent vellum Ms leaf. Jeanson copy. SM Feb 28 (70) FF8,000

Birago Avogadro, Giovanni Battista
— Delle Historie Memorabili che contiene le Sollevationi di Stato de Nostri Tempi. Venice, 1653. 4to, contemp calf gilt. Somw worming in upper outer corner of opening leaves. sg Oct 9 (122) $60

Birago, Francesco Mezzabarba, 1645-97
— Tratatto cinegetico, overo della caccia.... Milan: Gio. Battista Bidelli, 1626. 8vo, half mor gilt. Schwerdt-Jeanson copy. SM Feb 28 (71) FF2,200

BIRCH

Birch, Thomas, 1705-66
— The Heads of Illustrious Persons of Great Britain.... L, 1743-51. 1st Ed. Vol I only. Old half mor; worn, joints cracked, backstrip def. Marginal waterstaining. kh Mar 16 (42) A$220

Anr Ed. L, 1747-52. 2 vols in 1. Folio, half calf gilt. With 108 plates. pn Sept 18 (159) £220 [Ramsey]

Anr Ed. L, 1813. Folio, cloth; worn. Title soiled & torn along platemark. bba Dec 18 (112) £140 [Jeffrey]

Anr copy. Contemp half mor. C July 22 (25) £300

Anr copy. Contemp russia gilt; worn. S Sept 22 (208) £160 [Clark]

— The Life of the Honourable Robert Boyle. L, 1744. 1st Separate Ed. 8vo, contemp sheep; some wear, spine slightly def at base, joints split. bba Apr 9 (63) £75 [Weiner]

Bird, Henry Edward, 1830-1908
— Chess Masterpieces. L, 1875. Inscr. pn Mar 26 (359) £45 [Thompson]

Bird, John
— The Annals of Natal 1495 to 1845. Pietermaritzburg, 1888. 2 vols. 8vo, contemp calf. SSA Oct 28 (415) R220

Bird, William Wilberforce
— State of the Cape of Good Hope in 1822. L, 1823. 8vo, contemp half calf; rubbed. With 2 folding maps. SSA Oct 28 (416) R300

Birds...
— Birds of the World. L, 1969-71. 108 parts. 4to. B Feb 24 (64) HF260

Biringuccio, Vanuccio
— La Pyrotechnie.... Paris: Claude Fremy, 1566. 4to, old half sheep; joints cracked. Minor dampstains in lower margin. sg Jan 15 (292) $1,200

Biron, Sir Henry Chartres. See: Ragged, Hyder

Bisani, Alessandro
— A Picturesque Tour through Part of Europe, Asia, and Africa. L, 1793. 4to, contemp calf gilt; rubbed. With 6 folding plates. S Feb 23 (65) £220 [Maggs]

Bischoff, James, 1776-1845
— Sketch of the History of Van Diemen's Land. L, 1832. 8vo, modern cloth. With folding map hand-colored in outline & 2 plates. Tear to map repaired. bba Mar 12 (4) £150 [Bonham]

Bishop, Elizabeth
— North & South. Bost., 1946. In d/j; worn. sg Mar 5 (21) $200

Bishop, Isabella Lucy Bird, 1831-1904
— Journeys in Persia and Kurdistan. L, 1891. 2 vols. 8vo, orig cloth. bba May 28 (222) £110 [Loman]

Bishop, John George
— "A Peep in to the Past," Brighton in the Olden Time. Brighton, 1880. 4to, cloth; worn, orig spine laid down. Extra-illus & interleaved copy with many mtd cuttings & engravings. S Nov 10 (770) £140 [Grosvenor Park]

Bishop, Nathaniel Holmes, 1837-1902
— Four Months in a Sneak-Box: a Boat Voyage...down the Ohio and Mississippi Rivers. Bost., 1879. 1st Ed. 8vo, cloth; spine faded. sg Oct 23 (191) $90

Bishop, Richard Evett
— Bishop's Birds. L, 1936. One of 250. 4to, orig cloth. With 73 plates. Inscr. sg Oct 23 (193) $175

Anr Ed. Phila., 1936. One of 135. 4to, cloth; endpapers tape stained. With 73 plates & with frontis etching, sgd. sg Oct 23 (192) $400

One of 1,050. Orig lea. With 73 plates. K Oct 4 (59) $120

— Bishop's Wildfowl. St. Paul, 1948. 4to, lea. cb Nov 6 (36) $80; sg Oct 23 (194) $120

Bishop, Zealia Brown
— The Curse of Yig. Sauk City: Arkham House, 1953. One of 1,200. In d/j. cb Sept 28 (151) $55

Bissell, Alfred Elliott
— In Pursuit of Salar. Wilmington DE, 1966. One of 50. 4to, half cloth. Inscr. sg Oct 23 (195) $800

Bissell, Alfred Elliott —& Reese, Charles Lee
— Further Notes on the Pursuit of Salar. Wilmington DE, 1972. Half cloth. Inscr by Bissell to Charles Wood & with Ls from Reese to Wood & 2 Ls s from Bissell to Wood. sg Oct 23 (196) $900

Bisset, James, of Birmingham
— A Poetic Survey round Birmingham.... Birm., [1800]. 12mo, contemp mor gilt; head of spine chipped. With 28 hand-colored plates. C Dec 12 (22) £2,400 [Martin]

Bitting, Arvill Wayne
— Appertizing, or the Art of Canning.... San Francisco, 1937. sg Jan 15 (4) $100

Bitting, Katherine Golden
— Gastronomic Bibliography. San Francisco, 1939. Cloth. cb July 30 (253) $170; sg Jan 15 (5) $200
Anr copy. Cloth; shaken, front hinge crudely reinforced. sg Jan 15 (6) $200
Anr copy. Cloth; front hinge cracked. sg Jan 22 (40) $175
Anr copy. Cloth; shaken. sg May 14 (269) $600; SM Oct 20 (494) FF1,000

Bivero, Pedro de
— Sacrum oratorium piarum imaginum immaculatae Mariae et animae creatae.... Antwerp: Plantin, 1634. 4to, old calf with arms of the Austrian Emperor in gilt on both covers. S Sept 23 (422) £170 [Parikian]

Bivort, A.
— Album de Polologie. Brussels: Parent, 1847-50. Vols I-III in 1 vol. Oblong 4to, mor by Wigmore Bindery. With 137 colored plates, 1 double. de Belder copy. S Apr 27 (27) £4,000 [Arader]

Bizari, Pietro. See: Bizzari, Pietro

Bizzari, Pietro
— Persicarum rerum historia. Frankfurt: C. Marnium, 1601. ("Rerum Persicarum historia.") Folio, 18th-cent calf gilt, armorial bdg. Furstenberg copy. S June 25 (459) £450 [Diba]

Blaauw, Frans Ernst
— A Monograph of the Cranes. Leiden & L, 1897. One of 170. Folio, orig cloth. With 22 color plates. Haverschmidt copy. B Feb 24 (161) HF3,800

Blachford, M.
— Sailing Directions for the...St. Lawrence.... L, 1840. 8vo, recent cloth. AVP Nov 20 (23) C$1,100 [Memorial Univ. of New foundland]

Black, Joseph, 1728-99
— Experiments upon Magnesia Alba.... Edin., 1782. 12mo, wraps; torn. pnE Dec 17 (72) £920 [Aberdeen]
— Lectures on the Elements of Chemistry. Edin., 1803. 1st Ed. 3 vols. 4to, contemp calf; joints cracked, 1 cover detached. With port & 3 plates. C Dec 12 (23) £900 [Keating]

Black, Robert
— The Art of Jacob Epstein. Cleveland, [1942]. 4to, cloth, in torn d/j; bdg stained. CA Apr 12 (42) A$120

Blackburne, Joseph Henry, 1842-1924
— Games at Chess. L, 1899. Cloth. Sgd. pn Mar 26 (216) £110 [De Lucia]

Blacker, J. F. See: Gorer & Blacker

Blacker, William
— Art of Angling, and Complete System of Fly-Making. L, 1855. ("Art of Fly Making....") 12mo, orig cloth. pnE Dec 17 (341) £300 [Coleby]
— Catechism of Fly Making.... [L], 1843. 8vo, contemp calf gilt. With 6 plates & 18 (of 22) flies & fly-tying specimens mtd on 5 leaves. S Oct 23 (766) £900 [McKenzie]

Blackmore, John
— Views on the Newcastle and Carlisle Railway. Newcastle, 1837 [engraved title dated 1836]. 4to, contemp half calf; rebacked with orig backstrip relaid & new labels. With vignette title & 28 plates, some on india paper. One plate creased & relaid; 1 leaf of text creased & margins restored with archival tape. T May 21 (297) £210

Blackmore, Richard Doddridge, 1825-1900
— Lorna Doone. L, 1869. 1st Ed. 3 vols. 8vo, half mor gilt; spines faded. Lacking intial blank in Vol I & final blank & ads in Vol III. S Sept 22 (3) £180 [Jarndyce]

Blackstone, Sir William, 1723-80
— Commentaries on the Laws of England. Oxford, 1766-67-70-69. 2d Ed of Vols I & II; 4th Ed of Vol III; 1st Ed of Vol IV. 4 vols. 4to, contemp calf; hinges split, scuffed. C Dec 12 (25) £1,100 [Thorp]
2d Ed of Vols I & II, 1st Ed of Vols III & IV. Oxford, 1766-68. 4 vols. 4to, contemp calf; rubbed, joints cracked. pn July 23 (157) £460 [Frew]
Anr Ed. Oxford, 1766-69. 4 vols. 4to, old calf gilt; rebacked, rubbed. pnNY Sept 13 (202) $1,800
5th Ed. Oxford: Clarendon Press, 1773. 4 vols. 8vo, contemp calf; joints weak. sg Oct 9 (123) $275
7th Ed. Oxford, 1775. 4 vols. 8vo, calf gilt; corners bumped. L Dec 11 (374) £200
— The Great Charter and Charter of the Forest.... Oxford, 1759. 4to, needs rebdg. sg Oct 9 (124) $425
— Tracts, Chiefly Relating to the Antiquities and Laws of England. Oxford, 1771. 4to, contemp calf; joints splitting, rubbed. Some foxing. bba Aug 28 (204) £130 [Frognol Books]

BLACKWALL

Blackwall, John, 1790-1881

— A History of the Spiders of Great Britain and Ireland. L, 1859 (1860-64). 2 parts in 1 vol. Folio, half mor gilt. With 29 colored plates. Foxed. pn Mar 5 (189) £120 [Maggs]

Blackwell, Elizabeth, c.1700-58

— A Curious Herbal. L, 1737-39. 2 vols. Folio, 19th-cent half mor; spine of Vol I worn, Vol II rebacked with orig backstrip laid down. Engraved throughout. With 500 colored plates. Lacking tp & 2 index leaves in Vol I; Plate 464 in Vol II stained; 1st 2 leaves of Vol II torn & repaired. Hunt copy. CNY Nov 21 (29) $9,000
Anr copy. Contemp calf gilt; joints split, worn. Vol I dampstained at beginning & end & with last leaf of index creased; some spotting in 2d half of Vol II; tp to Vol II & some leaves of text dampstained; Plate 275 guarded. Sold w.a.f. S Oct 23 (662) £6,500 [Burden]
Anr copy. Contemp calf gilt; rebacked preserving orig spines. Dampstain in lower corner of a few plates. Horticultural Society of New York—de Belder copy. S Apr 27 (28) £6,000 [Minton]

— Herbarium Blackwellianum.... Nuremberg, 1750-66. Vol II. Contemp calf gilt with arms of the Academiae Caesareae; worn. With 100 hand-colored plates. Minor stain on blank margin of Plate 151; waterstain in margin of last plate; library stamp on tp. C Apr 8 (167) £2,000 [Ramsay]
Anr Ed. Nuremberg, 1750-65. 6 parts in 2 vols. Contemp calf gilt. With 6 color titles & 615 colored plates. FD June 11 (634) DM24,200
Anr Ed. Nuremberg, 1750-73. 6 parts in 3 vols. Folio, contemp vellum. With 3 (of 6) colored titles & 610 (of 615) color plates. Minor defs. HK Nov 4 (926) DM26,000
Anr Ed. Nuremberg, 1757-54-73. 6 vols in 4. Folio, contemp half calf; worn. With 6 hand-colored & gilded engraved titles & 615 hand-colored plates. Reichel—de Belder copy. S Apr 27 (29) £16,000 [Israel]
Anr copy. 6 vols. Folio, half cloth. With 6 hand-colored engraved titles & 615 hand-colored plates. Ms index inserted in Vol VI; some soiling & staining; repair to corner of Plate 45 of Vol I; engraved title to Vol II with tear repaired; Plate 337 torn & crudely repaired. S June 25 (143) £8,200 [Traylen]

Blackwood, Algernon

— The Fruit Stoners. L: Grayson & Grayson,

AMERICAN BOOK PRICES CURRENT

1934. In chipped & repaired d/j. cb Sept 28 (152) $50

Blackwood's...

— Blackwood's Edinburgh Magazine. Edin., 1831-49. Vols 29-66. 8vo, contemp half calf; rubbed & scuffed. Ck Nov 7 (85) £150

Blades, William F.

— Fishing Flies and Fly Tying. Harrisburg: Stackpole, 1951. One of 100. 4to, lea. sg Oct 23 (197) $300

Blaeu, Willem, 1571-1635 & Jan, 1596-1673

— Appendix Theatri A. Ortelii et Atlantis G. Mercatoris.... AMst., 1631. Folio, contemp vellum; worn & soiled. With engraved title & 97 (of 98) maps plus 24 inserted maps. Lacking Map 78, of Provence; several maps damaged by worming or tears with occasional loss of engraved surface; some stains. S Apr 23 (135) £14,000 [Niewodnic]

— Atlantis Appendix, sive pars altera, continens Tab: Geographicas diversarum Orbis regionum.... Amst., 1630. 475mm by 320mm, contemp vellum; foot of spine split. With engraved allegorical title & 60 double-page maps, richly colored throughout in a fine contemp hand. A few small wormholes in lower margin not affecting engraved surface; small waterstains at upper corners of 1 or 2 mapsheets; British Isles just shaved at lower neatline. "The finest coloured copy in existence". S Oct 23 (29) £46,000 [Israel]

— Atlas major, sive cosmographia Blaviana. Amst., 1662. Vol X only [Asia, China & Japan]. Folio, contemp vellum gilt. With 28 double-page maps colored in a contemp hand, with engraved titles heightened with gold. Browned throughout. S Oct 23 (472) £3,800 [Duchauflor]

— Le Grand Atlas, ou cosmographie Blaviane. Amst., 1667. 2d French text Ed. Vol VI [Scotland & Ireland]. Contemp vellum gilt; upper cover repaired at edges. With 55 maps finely colored in a contemp hand & heightened with gold. This copy almost entirely free of browning. S Oct 23 (160) £2,800 [Maggs]
Anr copy. 12 vols (complete set). Folio, orig vellum. With engraved titles & 599 maps, plans & plates, all colored by a contemp hand & heightened with gold. Added are 21 double-page maps by Nicolaes Visscher & Frederick de Wit. "A particularly fine copy". S Oct 23 (237) £100,000 [Jonge]

Anr Ed. Amst., 1967-68. One of 1,000. Vol XII only. sg Nov 20 (181) $250

— Grooten Atlas. Amst., [1648]-65. 13 parts in 9 vols. Folio, contemp vellum gilt. With 9 hand-colored titles heightened with gold, 7 ptd titles with colored vignettes & 605 maps & plates, all colored by a contemp hand. C Oct 15 (16) £52,000 [Tenschert]

— Nouveau Theatre d'Italie. Amst., 1704. 4 vols in 3. Folio, contemp calf gilt, armorial bdg; worn. With 270 maps & plates only, some hand-colored in outline. Plan of Rome shaved. Sold w.a.f. C Oct 15 (17) £14,000 [Broseghini]

— Novum Theatrum Pedemontii et Sabaudiae.... The Hague, 1726. 4 parts in 2 vols. Folio, contemp calf gilt; worn. S Apr 23 (156) £5,400 [Scheilk]

— Novus Atlas.... Amst., 1655. Vol VI only [China]. Folio, orig vellum gilt; wrinkled. Title & half-title fully hand-colored. With 17 double-page hand-colored maps with fully-colored cartouches. Minor offsetting; tear in margin of 1 map not affecting image; some dampstains & creases. Dutch text. Koeman I, B1 52. sg Dec 4 (19) $3,800

— Nuevo Atlas, o Teatro del Mundo [Atlas Major]. Amst., 1658-72. 10 vols in 11. Folio, orig vellum gilt. With 9 engraved titles with ptd overslips (none on Vols III & VIII) ptd titles in Vols III IV(i), VIII, & IX & with 544 maps & plates, all mostly double-page & hand-colored in a contemp hand, with 4 of the engraved titles heightened in gold. Some browning; some mostly marginal worming touching engraved surfaces of maps 7, 62, 63 & 65 in Vol I, maps 54-57 & 62 in Vol IV (ii) & map 2 in Vol V; some repairs; light adhesion damage to title of Vol V. S June 25 (279) £67,000 [Martinos]

— Le Theatre du monde ou nouvel atlas. Amst., 1638-48. Vols I & II in 2 parts & Vol III with the British Isles Supplement. Folio, contemp vellum gilt with arms of Amsterdam gilt; stained & worn. With 5 engraved titles & 279 maps, all but 5 double-page & mtd on guards. Some tears & splits; occasional creases & minor marginal dampstains. C Apr 8 (5) £15,000 [Burgess, Browning]

Anr copy. Parts 1-4 in 6 vols. Folio, contemp vellum gilt; Vol I rebacked, worn. With 6 engraved titles & 332 (of 337) maps. Some fingersoiling & other minor defs. FD June 11 (743) DM110,000

Anr Ed. Amst., 1640-50. Parts 1-4 in 4 vols. Folio, vellum gilt; worn & def. With 6 hand-colored engraved titles & 334 (of 336) hand-colored engraved plates. Some spotting & staining. VH Sept 12 (9) DM60,000

Anr Ed. Amst., 1654. Part 5 only. Folio, contemp calf; def. With engraved armorial title border (without ptd title overslip) & 55 maps. Waterstained but not browned; a few splits, generally without loss. S Nov 17 (759) £850 [Marshall]

— Theatrum orbis terrarum, sive Atlas novus. Amst., 1640. Vols I-III. 6 parts in 3 vols. Folio, contemp mor gilt; corners repaired. With 4 engraved titles, ptd divisional title in Vol III & 279 mostly double-page engraved maps colored in a contemp hand. Some browning; Lithuania in Vol I repaired at folds; some marginal waterstains & repairs without loss. S June 25 (278) £20,000 [Martinos]

Vol IV only: England & Wales. Amst.: Blaeu, 1640. Folio, half calf; worn. With 57 double-page maps. Lacking Hampshire; Wiltshire frayed & repaired; other defs. S July 28 (970) £4,800

Anr Ed. Amst., 1645. Folio, contemp vellum gilt; soiled. With engraved title & 60 mapsheets colored in a contemp hand. Port of William Camden inserted as frontis. Some creases or short splits; 2 maps (Koeman's Nos 1 & 13) def. S Oct 23 (162) £5,500 [Burden]

Anr Ed. Amst., 1649-55. 6 vols in 3. Folio, 18th-century calf; rubbed. With 402 colored maps. This set is Koemann I, 23B, 24C, 37C, 44, 49 & 53. Minor defs. FD Dec 2 (773) DM125,000

Vol V only: Scotland & Ireland. Amst., 1654. Folio, contemp vellum gilt. With 1 full-page & 54 double-page maps, colored in a contemp hand. Lacking engraved title; usual browning. S Nov 17 (750) £1,400 [Marshall]

Anr copy. Contemp bds; worn. With 53 double-page maps. Lacking general map & that of Rhum; lacking tp & several text leaves; dampstained throughout; some maps def. S July 28 (971) £800

Vol I only: Northern Europe. [Amst., 1655]. Folio, contemp vellum gilt; upper joint broken, head of spine torn. With 2 hand-colored engraved titles heightened with gold, title to 2d part with 2 pasted-on ptd slips & 115 (of 120) maps, 1 half page the others double page & 4 also folding, all hand-colored in outline with cartouches, coats-of-arms & compass roses fully colored. Mtd on guards throughout; 1st title crudely inserted on recent guard affecting the inner engraved area; map 25 from a smaller copy with margins extended; a few maps slightly discolored. C Oct 15 (15) £8,000 [Loose]

Vol VI only [China]. Folio, contemp vellum gilt; soiled. With engraved title & 16 (of 17) double-page maps, all fully hand-colored. Lacking Chekiang & pp

BLAEU

101-8 of text; waterstained. S Oct 23 (33) £950 [Shapero]

— Tooneel der Heerschappen van zyne Koninglyke Hooghaeid der Hartog von Savoye. Amst., 1693. 2 vols. Folio, half calf; worn. With engraved titles & 72 plates (of 140). S June 25 (213) £3,200

Blagdon, Francis William, 1778-1819
See also: Williamson & Blagdon

— Authentic Memoirs of the late George Morland. L, 1806 [but 1824 or later]. Folio, mor gilt by Morrell; spine & corners scuffed. With 19 (of 20) plates & etched facsimile plate mtd at end. C Apr 8 (172) £2,500 [Marks]

Blair, Eric Arthur. See: Orwell, George

Blair, Hugh, 1718-1800

— Lectures on Rhetoric and Belles Lettres. L: A. Strahan & T. Cadell, 1796. 3 vols. 8vo, contemp calf; spine ends chipped. cb Oct 23 (28) $55

Anr Ed. L, 1798. 3 vols. 8vo, contemp calf; worn. Some foxing. cb Oct 23 (29) $55

Blair, John, d.1782

— The Chronology and History of the World. L, 1754. 2 vols. Folio, contemp calf gilt; worn. With engraved title, 13 double-page folding engraved maps & 56 double-page engraved tables. Lacking E leaf after preface & with 1 text leaf torn & defective. Sold w.a.f. bba Nov 13 (221) £110 [Trotter]

Blair, Robert, 1699-1746

— The Grave.... L, 1808. 4to, old bds; rubbed. With engraved title & 11 plates after William Blake & port after T. Phillips, all engraved by Schiavonetti. Port silked on verso. O Jan 6 (24) $240

Anr copy. Orig cloth. Some dampstains to upper margins; tp def. pn Nov 20 (212) £95 [Collmann]

Anr copy. Half calf; worn. Some foxing. sg June 4 (41) $250

Anr Ed. L, 1813. 4to, orig bds. With engraved title & 11 plates after William Blake & port after T. Phillips, all engraved by Schiavonetti. Spotted. S Dec 4 (167) £200 [Davidson]

Blake, Robert

— A Letter Sent from his Excellency Generall Blake to the King of Denmark.... L: for D. G., 1652. 4to, modern wraps. Top edge trimmed, just touching 1 page numeral. S Dec 18 (294) £420 [Lawson]

AMERICAN BOOK PRICES CURRENT

Blake, William, 1757-1827
See also: Nonesuch Press

— All Religions are One. L: Trianon Press, 1970. One of 600. 4to, half mor; worn. O May 12 (16) $75

— America, a Prophecy. L: Trianon Press, 1963. Folio, half mor. With 18 plates. O May 12 (17) $300

One of 20 with a set of hand-colored plates showing progressive stages in the stencil work. Orig mor. With 18 color plates. S Dec 4 (178) £200 [Thorpe]

— The Book of Ahania. Paris: Trianon Press, 1973. One of 750. 4to, half mor. K Oct 4 (64) $130; O May 12 (18) $70

— The Book of Los. L, 1976. One of 480. 4to, orig half mor gilt. O May 12 (19) $100

— The Book of Thel. San Francisco: Book Club of California, 1930. One of 300. Illus by Julian Links. Vellum. Loosely laid in is Ls from Rockwell Kent to Oscar Lewis, commenting on alleged plagiarism of the illusts. cb Dec 4 (79) $250

— A Cradle Song; The Divine Image; A Dream; Night. NY, 1949. One of 125. cb Dec 4 (303) $100

— Designs for Gray's Poems. Clairvaux: Trianon Press, 1972. ("Water-Colour Designs for the Poems of Thomas Gray.") One of 518. Ed by Geoffrey Keynes. Orig half mor. S Dec 4 (179) £350 [Hirsch]

— Europe, a Prophecy. L, 1969. Ltd Ed. Folio, orig half mor. Wtih 18 colored plates. S Oct 6 (712) £70 [Martin]

— Illustrations of the Book of Job. L, 1825. Engraved title & 21 plates, all proof impressions. 4to, half mor. Margins of 1 plate badly spotted. S Dec 4 (165) £6,300 [Davidson]

— Illustrations to the Bible. L: Trianon Press, 1957. One of 506. Folio, orig half mor. With 9 colored plates. cb July 30 (24) $190; O May 12 (20) $250

Anr copy. Orig half mor; spines rubbed. With 9 color plates. S Dec 4 (177) £280 [Finch]

Anr copy. Orig half mor; endpaper marked. With 9 colored plates. S June 17 (210) £420 [Kemyusha]

Anr copy. Half mor. sg Feb 5 (37) $350

— Jerusalem. L: Trianon Press, [1951]. One of 516. Folio, orig wraps. S Dec 4 (175) £420 [Hirsch]

Anr copy. Orig cloth; some wear. S June 17 (209) £440 [Kemyush]

Anr Ed. L: Trianon Press, 1974. Half mor. K Oct 4 (62) $225; O May 12 (21) $100

— A Letter from William Blake...to Thomas Butts. [Northampton, Mass.: Gehenna Press, 1964]. One of 50 specially bound with an extra suite on japan vellum, each sgd. Illus by Leonard Baskin. 16mo, mor gilt. With 4 full-page woodcuts. sg Dec 4 (16) $600

— The Marriage of Heaven and Hell. [L: Trianon Press, 1960]. One of 480. Folio, half mor. Facsimile of the Rosenwald Ms. O May 12 (22) $150

Anr Ed. L, [1868]. 4to, orig half calf. Hand-colored. Facsimile of 1790 Ed. bba May 14 (150) £120 [Clark]

Anr Ed. L, Toronto & NY, 1927. With 27 colored plates. sg Jan 8 (30) $460

Out-of-series copy marked for presentation, With 27 colored plates. K Oct 4 (63) $170

Anr Ed. [L: Trianon Press, 1960]. Folio, half mor; spine discolored. With 27 colored plates. Facsimile of the Rosenwald Ms. sg Apr 2 (28) $350

— The Song of Los. Paris: Trianon Press, 1975. One of 400. 4to, half mor. O May 12 (23) $90

— There is no Natural Religion. L: Trianon Press, 1971. One of 616. 2 vols. 4to & 8vo, half mor. O May 12 (24) $80

— Works. L, 1893. Ed by Ellis & Yeats. 3 vols. 8vo, orig half mor; worn. L.p. copy. S May 6 (90) £180 [Mills]

One of 150 L.p. sets. Orig half lea; worn, endpapers dampstained. sg Feb 12 (25) $600

One of 500. Orig cloth. pn Oct 23 (349) £340 [Finch]

Blake, William Hume, 1809-70
— Brown Waters. Toronto, 1940. One of 1,000. Illus by Clarence A. Gagnon. Orig cloth, in torn d/j. With 8 colored plates. O June 9 (20) $130

Blakeney, Thomas S.
— Sherlock Holmes: Fact or Fiction? L, 1932. In d/j. cb Apr 24 (1443) $150

Anr copy. Foxed. cb Apr 24 (1444) $85

Blakey, Dorothy
— The Minerva Press 1790-1820. L, 1939. 4to, half cloth; spine stained. With 9 plates. sg May 14 (213) $60

Blakey, Robert, 1795-1878
— Historical Sketches of the Angling Literature of All Nations.... L, 1856. 12mo, half mor; worn, broken. sg Oct 23 (198) $100

Blakiston, John, 1785-1867
— Twelve Years' Military Adventure in Three Quarters of the Globe.... L, 1829. 2 vols. 8vo, contemp bds; worn. Author's copy with holograph notes & note on front pastedown reading "If another edition is called for it should be printed from this copy". Ck June 19 (143) £120

Blakston, W. A. —& & Others
— The Illustrated Book of Canaries and Cage-Birds.... L, [1877-80]. 4to, orig cloth; rubbed, inner hinge split. Ck May 29 (218) £95

Anr copy. Contemp half mor; worn. With 56 (of 60) colored plates. Ck June 19 (121) £95

Anr copy. Orig cloth; broken. With 49 color plates only. Outer margin of title torn away. S Jan 13 (629) £70 [Bailey]

Blanc, Mathieu
— La Bienfaisance de Louis XVI.... Marseilles: Antoine Favet, 1783. 8vo, contemp Marseillais mor gilt with arms of Marseille (Olivier 772, fer 8) in center. S Nov 27 (46) £200 [Booth]

Blancanus, Josephus
— Sphaera mundi seu cosmographia demonstrativa.... Modena: A. & H. Cassianus, 1653-54. 2 parts in 1 vol. Folio, 18th-cent bds; upper joint torn. A few small stains & spots. S June 25 (89) £460 [Quaritch]

Blanck, Jacob Nathaniel
— Bibliography of American Literature. New Haven, 1955-83. Vols I-VI only. cb Sept 11 (226) $475

Anr copy. 5 vols. Cloth. cba Feb 5 (37) $250

Anr copy. Vols I-VII. sg Jan 22 (37) $400

Blanco, Manuel
— Flora de Filipinas. Manila, 1877-80-[83]. L.p. Issue. 6 vols. Folio, orig half mor gilt; extremities of spines rubbed. With frontis, plate symbolising the death of Blanco, port, plate of Ms facsimile & 477 color plates. de Belder copy. S Apr 27 (30) £4,500 [Rainer]

Blanc-Saint-Bonnet, Joseph Marie, 1785-1841
— Manuel des chasseurs, ou code de la chasse. Paris, 1820. 8vo, contemp bdg. Jeanson copy. SM Feb 28 (72) FF500

Blancus, Guilielmus, Bishop of Grasse & Vence, 1551?-1601
— Discours de Mgr. Guillaume le Blanc... touchant l'affliction qu'ils endurent les loups.... Tournon: Claude Michel, 1598. 8vo, 18th-cent calf gilt. Jeanson copy. SM Mar 1 (333) FF8,000

Bland, John
— Trade Revived, or a Way Proposed.... L, 1659. 4to, wraps. Some shaving. S July 24 (423) £1,350 [Riley-Smith]

Blankaart, Steven
— Die neue heutiges Tages gebraeuchliche Scheide-Kunst.... Hannover & Braunschweig: Gottlieb Heinrich Grentz, 1689. 8vo, modern half mor. Upper inner corner of A8 torn & restored with slight text loss. sg Mar 26 (39) $375

Blarrorvio, Petrus de
— Insigne nanceidos opus de bello nanceiano. Saint Nicolas du Port: Petrus Jacobi, 5 Jan 1518 [1519]. 1st Issue, with privilege dated 4 Sept 1518. Folio, mor gilt with arms of Lorraine onlaid in yellow & red gilt in upper cover & the Lorraine cross onlaid in white on lower cover, by Cayon Liebault of Nancy, sgd at foot of spine. Foremargins of 1st 15 leaves & 20 leaves at end repaired mostly in lower corner; tp spotted. S May 21 (15) £1,700 [Kraus]

Blast...
— Blast: Review of the Great English Vortex. L, 1914-15. Nos 1-2 (all pbd). Mor with reproductions of orig wraps to No 1 mtd under transparent plastic on covers, orig wraps bound in. S July 13 (158) £480

Blatchford, Samuel, 1829-93
— Reports of Cases in Prize.... Wash.: Govt. Printing Office, 1866. 8vo, contemp calf; rubbed, spine ends chipped. cb Dec 18 (18) $55

Blaxland, Gregory
— A Journal of a Tour of Discovery across the Blue Mountains, New South Wales.... Sydney, 1893. One of 55. 8vo, contemp half mor. C Oct 15 (147) £450 [Quaritch]

Blaxton, John
— The English Usurer. Marlborough: ptd by John Norton for Thomas Ewen, 1634. Unrecorded Ed. 4to, wraps. Fore-margin of woodcut shaved. S July 23 (421) £1,250 [Institute of Actuaries]

2d Ed. Oxford, 1634. 4to, modern half mor. Wormhole in upper margin; frontis def with loss to woodcut & loss of 2 letters of text. STC 3129a. S Mar 10 (1025) £100 [Bennett]

Bleasdale, John Ignatius
— An Essay on the Wines Sent to the late Intercolonial Exhibition, by the Colonies of Victoria, New South Wales, and South Australia.... Melbourne, 1876. 8vo, orig ptd wraps. kh Mar 16 (45B) A$220

Blebelius, Thomas
— De sphaera.... Wittenberg, 1582. 8vo, new bds. Lacking last leaf; closely cut at outer margins affecting marginalia & some text. S July 28 (1055) £200

Blegny, Nicolas de
— Le Bon Usage du the, du caffe et du chocolat.... Lyons: T. Amaulry, 1687. 12mo, contemp calf; rebacked. Browned; corner of 1 leaf repaired. Crahan copy. P Nov 25 (61) $600

Blenerhasset, Thomas
— The Seconde Part of the Mirrour for Magistrates.... L, 1578. 4to, lev by Riviere. Washed; marginal repairs. STC 3131. sg Apr 2 (29) $750

Blew, William C. A.
— Brighton and its Coaches. L, 1894 [1893]. 1st Ed. 8vo, contemp half calf. With 10 colored plates only. Ck May 15 (165) £40

Anr copy. Half mor gilt. With 20 hand-colored plates. pn Mar 5 (61A) £45 [Druett]

Anr copy. Orig cloth. pn Mar 5 (66) £50 [Druett]

Anr copy. Orig cloth; spine ends & corners bumped. With 20 plates. sg Nov 20 (25) $150

Bligh, William, 1754-1817
See also: Golden Cockerel Press

— The Log of H.M.S. Bounty 1787-1789. [Guildford]: Genesis Publications, 1975. One of 500. Folio, half calf. S Nov 18 (1005) £170 [Meikle]

— Relation de l'enlevement du navire le Bounty. Paris, 1790. 8vo, modern half pigskin. With 3 folding maps. Scattered foxing. wa Sept 25 (129) $550

— A Voyage to the South Sea.... Dublin, 1792. 8vo, half calf; scuffed. pnE Jan 28 (63) £360 [Traylen]

Anr Ed. L, 1792. 4to, half calf. With port, 6 maps & plans & plate of bread-fruit. Some spotting; 1 folding plate browned. S Oct 23 (510) £1,500 [Quaritch]

1st Ed. 4to, mor gilt. Tp creased; some offsetting. CA Apr 12 (44) A$2,800

Blish, James Benjamin
— Earthman, Come Home. NY: Putnam, [1955]. In d/j. cb Sept 28 (155) $60

— The Triumph of Time. L, 1959. ("A Clash of Cymbals.") In d/j. cb Sept 28 (154) $70

Bliss, Carey S.
— A Leaf from the 1583 Rembert Dodoens Herbal Printed by Christopher Plantin. San Francisco: Book Club of Calif., 1977. One of 385. O June 16 (29) $60

Bliss, William R.
— Paradise in the Pacific. NY, 1873. 8vo, contemp half calf. Foxed. Inscr. cb Feb 19 (38) $140

Blith, Walter, fl.1649
— The English Improver.... L, 1649. 1st Ed. 4to, modern cloth. Margins cropped; holes in tp where name erased; perforated library stamp on tp & 2 other leaves. bba Aug 28 (173) £95 [Comben]

Anr copy. Modern calf by Lloyd; joints broken & reinforced with cloth tape. Stain to part of 1st 18 leaves. Hunt copy. CNY Nov 21 (30) $320

Anr Ed. L, 1653. ("The English Improver Improved....") 4to, contemp calf; rubbed. With engraved title & 2 plates with tears. S May 29 (1149) £120

Bloch, Marcus Elieser, 1723-99
— Ichthyologie, ou Histoire naturelle des poissons. Paris, 1786-88. Parts 3-6. Bound in 2 vols. Folio, contemp lea; worn & def. With 144 colored plates. FD June 11 (693) DM24,000

— Ichtyologie.... Berlin, 1785-97. Parts 1-8 (of 12) in 3 vols. Folio, contemp mor gilt. With 6 engraved title vignettes & 216 color plates heightened with gold & silver. HK Nov 4 (984) DM38,000

Bloch, Robert
— Psycho. NY, 1959. In worn d/j. cb May 7 (186) $95

One of 200. In d/j; spine cracked, shaken. sg Dec 11 (9) $80

Block, Laurie
— An Odd Bestiary; or, a Compendium of Instructive and Entertaining Descriptions.... [N.p.]: Cheloniidae Press, 1982. One of 300. Illus by Alan James Robinson. Folio, half mor. sg Jan 8 (45) $200

Blockler, Georg Andreas
— Theatrum Machinarum Novum. Nuremberg, 1662. Folio, bdg not described. Franklin Institute copy. F Sept 12 (313) $1,100

Bloemaert, Abraham, 1564-1651
— Oorspronkelyk en vermaard konstryk tekenboek.... Amst., 1740. 8 parts in 1 vol. Folio, half calf. With engraved title & dedication & 173 plates, title & 8 plates tinted. B Feb 25 (536) HF2,300

Blome, Richard, d.1705
See also: Cox & Blome; Cresset Press
— Britannia: or a Geographical Description.... L, 1673. 1st Ed. Folio, modern calf. With 49 maps & 24 plates of arms on 12 leaves. Lacking Buckinghamshire. With plate of London & additional folding map of England inserted on guard. Def margins of 2 maps repaired; Surrey torn. C Apr 8 (66) £1,300 [Redelmeier]

Anr copy. 19th-cent half mor with library blind-stamp on covers. With 48 (of 50) maps & 10 (of 12) leaves of coats-of-arms. Tp stamped on verso; some fraying, tears & holes; North Wales & Scotland torn & repaired; Ireland torn with slight loss; Isle of Wight cropped. S Feb 24 (502) £1,100 [Bueden]

— The Present State of His Majesties Isles and Territories in America.... L, 1687. 8vo, cloth. With plate & 6 (of 7) folding maps. Frontis torn; folding chart reinforced along fold; maps with perforated library stamps; some worming. sg Mar 12 (15) $325

Blondel, François, 1618-86
— Thermarum aquisgranensium et porcetanarum elucidatio & thaumaturgia.... Aachen, 1688. 8vo, modern cloth; worn. With folding plan & folding plate. Some spotting & soiling; corner of last few leaves affected by damp. S July 14 (371) £280

Blondel, Jacques Francois, 1705-74
— Cours d'architecture. Paris, 1771-77. 12 vols in 9. 8vo, later half mor gilt; rubbed. Vol I lacking a2; text leaves of plate vols laid down. bba Aug 20 (308) £650 [Maggs]

Blossfeldt, Karl
— Art Forms in Nature. NY: Weyhe, 1929. 4to, cloth; rubbed. With 120 photogravures. sg May 7 (8) $120

Blount, Edward
— Notes on the Cape of Good Hope, made during an Excursion in that Colony in the Year 1820.... L, 1821. 8vo, cloth. SSA Oct 28 (421) R320

Blum, Andre
— The Origin and Early History of Engraving in France. NY & Frankfurt, 1930. One of 200. Folio, needs rebdg. sg May 14 (41) $100

Blume, Karl Ludwig, 1796-1862
— Collection des orchidees les plus remarquables de l'Archipel Indien et du Japon. Amst., 1858-[59]. Vol I (all pbd). Folio, contemp half mor; rubbed, upper joint repaired. With litho title & 70 hand-colored plates. Tear at inner margin of half-title; some spotting. de Belder copy. S Apr 27 (32) £3,800 [Lyon]

— Flora Javae. Brussels, 1828-[51]. 3 vols. Folio, orig bds; soiled. With litho frontis & 261 plates, all but 14 hand-colored. Horticultural Society of New York—de Belder copy. S Apr 27 (31) £3,500 [Marshall]

— Rumphia.... Leiden & Amst., 1835-48. 4 vols. Folio, contemp half mor; marked. With 3 frontises & 210 plates, of which 159 are hand-colored. Drayton-de Belder copy. S Apr 27 (33) £7,000 [Chong]

Blunden, Edmund Charles
— The Bonadventure. A Random Journal.... L, [1922]. 1st Ed. Orig cloth. Inscr. sg Dec 11 (190) $90
— Fall In, Ghosts. L: White Owl Press, 1932. Ptd wraps, variant with title ptd "Fall, In Ghosts"; soiled. sg Dec 11 (192) $60
— To Nature. L: Beaumont Press, 1923. One of 310. Half cloth. Inscr to W. Gray, with 6 lines of verse. sg Dec 11 (194) $80
— Undertones of War. L, 1928. 1st Ed. Inscr on card mtd on front pastedown. sg Dec 11 (195) $60

Blunt, Lady Anne, 1837-1917. See: Gregynog Press

Blunt, Wilfrid Jasper Walter. See: Sitwell & Blunt

Blunt, Wilfrid Jasper Walter —& Jones, Paul
— Flora superba. L, 1971. One of 405. Illus by Paul Jones. Folio, half vellum. With 16 colored plates. pn Sept 18 (10) £240 [Way]

Blunt, Wilfrid Scawen, 1840-1922. See: Gregynog Press; Kelmscott Press

Boaden, James, 1762-1839
— Memoirs of Mrs. Siddons. L, 1893. 8vo, later half mor gilt by Bayntun. bba Apr 9 (145) £50 [Whatman]
One of 150 L.p. copies. Mor gilt by Birdsall. Extra-illus with c.240 plates & a few programs. S July 13 (192) £400

Boccaccio, Giovanni, 1313-73
See also: Limited Editions Club
— Amorosa visione.... Milan: Zannotti Castiglione, 1521. 4to, 19th-cent half calf; joints cracked. Minor defs. Without the Apologia of Geronimo Claricio. sg Mar 26 (40) $70
— De casibus virorum. L: Richard Tottel, 1554. ("A Treatise Excellent and Compendious, Shewing the Falles of Sondry Most Notable Princes....") Folio, early vellum bds. Small tear in Y3 recto repaired; some soiling. S Sept 23 (425) £200 [Pampolini]
— De las illustres mugeres. Seville, 1528. Folio, old calf; worn. Wormed in upper outer corners, occasionally entering text; some holes repaired; lacking tp. sg Oct 9 (6) $250
— La Genealogia de gli dei.... Venice: Giacomo Sansovino, 1569. 4to, later vellum. Occasional underscoring. sg Oct 9 (129) $90
Anr Ed. Venice, 1627. 4to, 17th-cent calf gilt bound for John Evelyn; some defs. Evelyn copy, inscr by Evelyn. S May 21 (94) £1,500 [Evelyn]
— The Nymphs of Fiesole. Verona: Bodoni, 1952. One of 225. 4to, orig half vellum. S June 18 (333) £500 [Hartnoll]; sg June 11 (63) $425
— Opera. [Venice, c.1530]. Trans by Nicolo Liburnio. 4to, vellum bds. Some worming; marginal annotations in an early hand. S Sept 23 (427) £150 [De Zayas]

Decameron in English
— 1620. - The Decameron.... L.1st Ed in English. 2 vols. Folio, contemp calf; joints worn, spine restored. Some soiling or dampstaining; errata leaf rehinged after first A6; first B6 fore-edge shaved; upper margin of 2d title cropped. sg Apr 2 (30) $2,800
— 1684. - L. Folio, contemp calf; rubbed & rebacked. Lacking tp & last leaf (supplied in pen facsimile); ink accession number on tp. Sold w.a.f. bba Aug 28 (180) £55 [Titles]
— 1925. - NY: Boni & Liveright Illus by Clara Tice. 2 vols. Some foxing; some leaves roughly opened. cb Sept 11 (320) $55
— 1934-35. - The Decameron. Oxford: Shakespeare Head Press Out-of-series copy. 2 vols. 4to, orig mor. S Oct 6 (713) £190 [Thorp]
— 1949. - Garden City One of 1,500. Illus by Rockwell Kent. 2 vols. 4to, orig bdg. With 32 colored plates. cb Dec 4 (221) $140
Anr copy. Cloth. cb June 18 (202) $80

Decameron in French
— An X [1801]. - Paris 11 vols. 8vo, calf gilt; rubbed. With 11 engraved titles & 110 plates. pn Apr 30 (276) £100

Decameron in German
— 1535. - Centum Novella. Strassburg: Camerlander for Albrecht. Folio, contemp blind-stamped pigskin; soiled & worn. Some browning & staining; some waterstains. FD June 11 (70) DM21,000

Decameron in Italian
— 1573. - Florence: Giunti. 4to, contemp vellum bds; joints split, rubbed. Part of date cut from title; repairs to title & upper margin of several leaves. bba Apr 23 (96) £55 [Wilfred]
Anr copy. Vellum bds. Title & 12 fore-edge margins repaired; some dampstains. S Sept 23 (302) £60 [Pampoloni]
— 1587. - Florence: Giunta. 4to, early calf; scraped. Minor dampstain to a few foreedge margins at end. S Mar 10 (1026) £130 [Maggs]
— 1665. - Amst.: Elzevier. 12mo, mor gilt by P. Kersten. JG Oct 2 (1544) DM500
— 1729. - Venice: Pasinello. 4to, contemp mor

gilt armorial bdg; spine wormed. Slight worming in inner margin, affecting text at end. Reprint of the 1527 Giunta Ed. S Sept 23 (426) £75 [Thomas]

Anr copy. 19th-cent vellum. Tp gutter reinforced on verso; marginalia in Italian throughout. sg Mar 26 (41) $80

Anr copy. Contemp vellum bds; soiled. wa Mar 5 (166) $180

— 1757. - L [but Paris] 5 vols in 2. 8vo, later half calf; rubbed. Sold w.a.f. bba July 16 (34) £120 [Fisher]

Anr copy. 5 vols. 8vo, contemp sheep gilt; worn, joints cracked. With 5 frontises, port & 110 plates; dampstaining of text leaves at end of Vol III. sg Oct 9 (128) $400

Anr copy. Half calf; extremities worn. With 115 plates. Dampstaining in upper margins of 20 plates, affecting several images. sg June 11 (62) $475

Boccamazza, Domenico

— Della caccia libri VIII. Rome: Gyronimo de Cartolari, 1548. vo, mor gilt by Chambolle-Duru. Lacking tp. Schwerdt-Jeanson copy. SM Feb 28 (76) FF28,000

Bock, Hieronymus, 1489? 1554

— De stirpium.... Strassburg: Richel, 1552. 4to, 17th-cent half calf; worn, hinges cracked, tp loose, last leaf detached. Minor dampstains; F7 with lower corner torn & repaired; some worming; lacking port of author. Hunt copy. CNY Nov 21 (31) $1,700

Anr Ed. Strassburg: Vendelinus Rihelius, 1552. 4to, 17th-cent vellum. Some worming; lacking 6 text leaves. HK Nov 4 (930) DM5,200

Bock, Paul Aloise de

— Paul Delvaux. NY: Rizzoli [1976]. 4to, cloth, in d/j. cba Mar 5 (54) $65

Bocquet de Chanterenne, Jean Joseph

— Plaisirs, varennes et capitaineries. Paris: Prault, 1744. 12mo, mor gilt by Cape. Lacking last leaf entitled Ici doivent estre placees treize cartes (they were never pbd). Jeanson copy. SM Feb 28 (77) FF1,300

Bode, Clement Augustus, Baron de. See: De Bode, Clement Augustus

Bodenehr, Johann Georg

— Teutschland.... Augsburg, [1682?]. 8vo, contemp calf with arms of Herberstein of Silesia; rubbed. With engraved title, scale plate, map, index map & 32 mapsheets, hand-colored in outline with the Imperial boundary colored in gold. S Nov 10 (842) £290 [Liepe]

Bodenschatz, Johann Christoph Georg

— Kirchliche Verfassung der heutigen Juden. Frankfurt, 1748-49. 2 vols in 1. 4to, contemp vellum; minor worming to upper cover, spine soiled. With frontis & 29 plates. Library stamps; marginal worming. CAM Dec 3 (49) HF2,800

Bodin, Jean, 1530-96

— De magorum daemonomania.... Basel: Thomas Guarinus, 1581. 4to, old vellum Ms leaves over pastebd; rebacked, front hinge cracked. Some dampstains. sg Dec 4 (140) $425

— Demonomania de gli Stregoni. Venice: Aldus, 1589. 4to, old vellum; dampwrinkled. Some stains. sg Mar 26 (42) $375

Bodio, Stephen

— Trout: Brook, Brown & Rainbow. Easthampton MA: Cheloniidae Press, 1986. One of 50. Illus & colored by Alan James Robinson. Folio, bds. sg Dec 4 (36) $425

Bodoni, Giovanni Battista, 1740-1813

— Serie de' caratteri greci di Giambatista Bodoni. Parma: Bodoni, 1788. 4to, bds; rubbed. S Nov 27 (149) £700 [Appleton]

Body, Albin

— Une Societe cynegetique en Condros au dix-huitieme siecle. Spa, 1883. 4to, half shagreen. Jeanson copy. SM Feb 28 (78) FF1,000

Boeckler, Georg Andreas

— Theatrum machinarum novum.... Cologne, 1662. Folio, contemp calf; worn. With engraved title & 154 plates. Plate 23 torn without loss. S June 25 (92) £1,050 [Sourget]

— Theatrum machinarum novum: das ist: Neu-vermehrter Schauplatz der mechanischen Kuensten. Nuremberg, 1673. Folio, 19th-cent half sheep; broken, worn. With engraved title & 154 plates. Text leaves browned, 1 plate torn. sg Jan 15 (293) $750

Boehme, Jacob, 1575-1624

— Des gottseeligen hocherleuchteten Jacob Boehmens...alle theosophische Wercken. Amst., 1682. 15 parts in 11 vols plus Index. 12mo, contemp half lea gilt; worn. JG Oct 2 (1545) DM6,500

— XL. Questions Concerning the Soule. L: M. Simmons, 1647. 4to, old half calf; rubbed, rebacked. With table & folding plate. Some stains & browning; lacking errata & privilege leaves. O May 12 (26) $250

Boehn, Max von, 1850-1921. See: Fischel & Boehn

Boek...

- Het Boek [incorporating Bibliographische Adversaria (1873-94); Tijdschrift voor Boek en Bibliotheekwezen (1903-11)]. Amst., 1873-1966. 52 vols, various bdgs. Lacking title & table of Vol XXXIV. B Oct 7 (470) HF4,000
- Het Boek van PTT. Leiden, 1938. Illus & designed by Piet Swart. Orig wraps. B Oct 7 (254) HF400

Boerhaave, Hermann, 1668-1738

- Elementa chemiae. Leiden, 1732. 2 vols. 4to, contemp calf; worn, 1 cover detached. With 17 folding plates. Lacking the 2 star leaves "Conspectus seriei chimicarum" in Vol II & 4C4 in Vol I & 3G4; Bodleian duplicate stamp. S Nov 10 (448) £200 [Rota]
- Index alter plantarum quae in horto Academico Lugduno Batavo aluntur. Leiden, 1727. Part 2 only. 4to, later half calf; corners worn. With 40 plates. C Apr 8 (169) £100 [Pilo]
- Institutiones medicae in usum annuae exercitationis domesticos. Leiden, 1708. 12mo, contemp half vellum; lower cover soiled. With addenda leaf. S Nov 27 (294) £700 [Gurney]
- Materia Medica, or a Series of Prescriptions.... L, 1741. 8vo, calf; rebacked. With a port loosely inserted. S Nov 10 (447) £85 [Libris]
- A Method of Studying Physick.... L, 1719. 8vo, contemp calf; rebacked. T Sept 18 (366) £105
- Praelectiones academicae de lue venerea. Franeker, 1751. 8vo, old half vellum. Rubber stamp on each side of title; some annotations. S Nov 10 (446) £50 [Poole]

Boethius, Anicius Manlius Torquatus Severinus, 480?-524?

- De consolatione philosophiae. Strassburg: Pruess, 1491. 4to, contemp blindstamped lea over wooden bds; worn. Some worming. 189 (of 190) leaves. Goff B-792. HK Nov 4 (608) DM1,200

  Anr Ed. Strassburg: Johann Pruess, before 6 Mar 1491. 4to, contemp blind-panelled calf over wooden bds; head & foot of spine restored, joints splitting, lacking clasps. Minor worming to a few leaves at front touching a few letters. 174 leaves. Goff B-794. C May 13 (116) £750 [Fletcher]

  Anr Ed. Lyon: Jean de Platea for Simon Vincent, [c.1521]. ("Cum Triplici Commento.") 2 parts in 1 vol. 4to, mor by L. Brocca. Short tear in f5; marginal waterstain to a few leaves at the front; small wormholes through text. FD Dec 2 (40) DM1,200

- De philosophico consolatu sive de consolatione philosophiae.... Strassburg: Johannes Grueninger, 1501. Folio, 19th-cent calf gilt. Hole in woodcut on C2; headline of 11 shaved; some leaves soiled; tp soiled & repaired. S May 21 (16) £900 [Thomas]
- Della consolatione de la filosofia. Florence: Lorenzo Torrentino, 1551. Trans by Cosimo Bartoli. 8vo, old vellum. Tp with old signature & stain along bottom edge. sg Mar 26 (43) $100

Boetticher, Jacob Gottlieb, 1754-92

- A Geographical, Historical, and Political Description of the Empire of Germany, Holland.... L, 1800. 4to, contemp calf; rubbed. With 27 maps & plans. S May 29 (1152) £190

Bogeng, Gustave Adolf Erich

- Geschichte der Buchdruckerkunst: der Fruehdruck. Hellerau bei Dresden, [1930]. Folio, orig half vellum. bba June 18 (13) £190 [Fogg]
- Die Grossen Bibliophilen. Leipzig, 1922. 3 vols. 4to, cloth; worn & shaken. sg May 14 (270) $120

Boggs, Mae Helene Bacon

- My Playhouse was a Concord Coach.... Oakland, Calif., [1942]. 4to, cloth. cb Oct 9 (21) $225

  Anr copy. Tp stamped. cb Apr 2 (33) $110

Bohatta, Hanns

- Bibliographie der livres d'heures horae B.M.V., officia...des XV. und XVI. Jahrhunderts. Vienna, 1909. Ltd Ed with text in German. 4to, half lea, orig wraps bound in; rebacked with cloth. sg May 14 (407) $70

  Anr Ed. Vienna, 1924. Cloth. sg May 14 (409) $150

- Katalog der Inkunabeln der Fuerstlich Liechtenstein'schen Fideikommissbibliothek und der Hauslabsammlung. Vienna, 1910. 4to, half vellum; soiled, orig vellum wraps bound in. sg May 14 (410) $90

Bohny, Nicholas

- The New Picture Book. Edin., 1865. Oblong 4to, orig half cloth; soiled, loose. With 36 hand-colored plates. pn Jan 22 (310) £190 [Quaritch]

Bohun, Edmund, 1645-99

- The Character of Queen Elizabeth.... L, 1693. 1st Ed. 8vo, contemp calf; joints starting. sg Oct 9 (185) $140

Boiardo, Matteo Maria, 1434-94
— Roland l'amoureux. Paris, 1619. Trans by Francois de Tosset. 8vo, contemp calf-backed vellum. Michael Wodhull's copy. S July 14 (373) £280

Boileau-Despreaux, Nicolas, 1636-1711
— Oeuvres. Amst., 1718. Illus by Bernard Picart. 2 vols. Folio, contemp red mor gilt; minor restoration to head & foot of spines. With vignette port of Erasmus, folding port, frontis with port of author, frontis to Le Lutrin, 6 plates, 2 vignettes & 27 culs-de-lampe. Lamoignon copy. C Dec 3 (172) £550 [Maggs]

Anr Ed. Paris, 1789. One of 250. 2 vols. 4to, contemp mor gilt. C May 13 (117) £260 [Marlborough]

Boillot, Joseph
— Nouveaux Pourtraitz et figures de termes pour user en l'architecture.... Langres: J. Des Preyz, [1592]. Folio, contemp vellum; some rubbing. With port & 55 plates. Jeanson copy. SM Feb 28 (79) FF45,000

Boinet, Amedee Charles Leon
— La Collection de Miniatures de M. Edouard Kann. Paris, 1926. Out-of-series copy Folio, modern bds with orig wraps bound in. With 48 plain plates & 2 color plates. Ck Nov 28 (199) £130

Boisgelin de Kerdu, P. M. Louis de, 1758-1816
— Ancient and Modern Malta. L, 1805. 2d Ed. 2 vols. 4to, disbound. Some plates stamped on rectos. Sold w.a.f. O Nov 18 (29) $170

Boissard, Jean Jacques, 1528-1602
— Romanae urbis topographiae. Frankfurt, 1597-1602. Parts 1-5 (of 6) in 1 vol. Folio, contemp lea; wormed. Some spotting & browning. HK Nov 4 (610) pDM2,800

Boissier, Edmond, 1810-85
— Voyage botanique dans le Midi de l'Espagne.... Paris, 1839-45. 2 vols. 4to, orig half cloth. With double-page colored synoptic chart & 205 (on 206) hand-colored plates. Library stamps removed from titles; some soiling. de Belder copy. S Apr 27 (34) £1,800 [Asher]

Boitard, Pierre, 1787-1859
— Traite de la composition et de l'ornement des jardins.... Paris, 1825. 3d Ed. Oblong 4to, recent half calf. With 97 plates. T July 16 (112) £260

Bol, Hans, 1534-93
— Venationis, piscationis, et aucupii typi. Antwerp: P. Galle, 1582. 8vo, contemp vellum. With frontis & 47 plates. Jeanson copy. SM Feb 28 (80) FF75,000

Bolton, Arthur T.
— The Architecture of Robert and James Adam. L, 1922. 2 vols. Folio, orig cloth. Ck Feb 13 (162) £160

Anr copy. Orig cloth; worn. S Feb 24 (639) £190 [Sims]; S May 6 (366) £190 [Sims]

Anr copy. Orig cloth; worn. Marginal dampwrinkling. sg Feb 5 (41) $200

Bolton, Herbert Eugene
— Fray Juan Crespi: Missionary Explorer.... Berkeley, 1927. cb Oct 9 (22) $65

Bolton, James, d. 1799
— Harmonia Ruralis, or, an Essay towards a Natural History of British Song Birds. L, 1824. 2d Ed. 2 vols. 4to, orig half mor gilt; rubbed. With 81 hand-colored plates, including frontis. pn June 18 (73) £1,400 [Walford]

Anr copy. Half lea; rubbed. With 81 hand-colored plates. Some leaves of text & 4 plates loose & frayed. pn July 23 (20) £650 [Walford]

Anr copy. Half calf gilt; top of 1 spine damaged. With 80 hand-colored plates. pn July 23 (150) £780 [Walford]

Anr Ed. L, 1830. 2 vols in 1. 4to, half calf. With frontis & 80 colored plates. JG Oct 2 (1349) DM2,600

Anr Ed. L, 1845. 2 vols in 1. 4to, cloth. With frontis & 80 hand-colored plates & with 4 extra plates pasted in at front. All plates stamped. bba Aug 28 (141) £170 [Elliott]

— A History of Fungusses, Growing about Halifax.... Halifax & Huddersfield, 1788-91. 3 vols plus supplement in 1 vol. 4to, half calf over bds; rebacked with orig spine laid down. Crahan copy. P Nov 25 (62) $900

Anr copy. 4 vols in 2, including Supplement. 4to, contemp calf gilt; rebacked. With engraved title & 182 hand-colored plates. Dedication copy, inscr to the Earl of Gainsborough noting that this is the only copy ptd on writing paper. de Belder copy. S Apr 27 (36) £5,000 [Fleming]

Bommier, Rene
— Notre Sauvagine et sa chasse. Chateau de Wardrecques, 1920. 4to, pigskin janseniste bdg by Stroobants. Jeanson copy. SM Feb 28 (81) FF1,800

Bonacini, Claudio
— Bibliografia delle arti scrittorie et della calligrafia. Florence, 1953. Orig wraps; loose. bba Oct 16 (459) £65 [Marlborough]

BONAFOUS

Bonafous, Louis Abel de. See: Fontenai, Abbe de

Bonafous, Matthieu, 1793-1852
— Histoire naturelle, agricole, et economique du mais. Paris & Turin, 1836. Folio, contemp half mor; rubbed. With 15 hand-finished color plates, 5 uncolored plates. Some spotting. L.p. copy. de Belder copy. S Apr 27 (38) £4,400 [Israel]

Bonanni, Filippo, 1638-1725
— Numismata summorum pontificum templi Vaticani fabricam indicantia.... Rome, 1715. Folio, contemp vellum; upper hinge split. With 91 plates. Tear in fold of Plate 15; dampstaining on some leaves; short marginal tear on title. S Sept 23 (537) £220 [Tosi]

Bonaparte, Charles Lucien, 1803-57
See also: Wilson & Bonaparte
— Iconographia della fauna italica. Rome, 1832-41. 3 vols. Folio, half cloth. With 182 hand-colored plates. HK Nov 4 (938) DM8,000

Bonaparte Collection, Lucien
— Choix de gravures a l'eau forte.... L, 1812. Folio, mor gilt. With 142 plates. pn Dec 11 (184) £55 [Barker]

Bonar, Alexander, 1810-92 —& McChyne, Robert Murray, 1813-43
— Narrative of a Mission of Inquiry to the Jews from the Church of Scotland in 1839. Phila.: Presbyterian Board of Publication, 1845. 8vo, contemp half lea; worn. With 3 maps & 4 plates. Dampwrinkled; foxed. sg Sept 25 (16) $300

Bonatus de Forlivio, Guido
— Decem Tractatus astronomiae. Augsburg: Erhard Ratdolt, 26 Mar 1491. 4to, 19th-cent vellum; rear joint starting, hinges reinforced. 2d title soiled; scattered wormholes towards end; lacking 1st 14 leaves. 408 (of 422) leaves. Goff B-845. Warwick-Pollock-Butler copy. sg Dec 4 (20) $1,100

Bonaventura, Saint, 1221-74
— Tractatus et libri quam plurimi. Strasbourg: Martin Flach, 1489. Folio, contemp calf over wooden bds. H-C 3465. HK Nov 4 (611) DM2,000

Bond, John Walpole
— A History of Sussex Birds. See: Walpole-Bond, John

Bone, Muirhead
— Glasgow. Fifty Drawings.... Glasgow, 1911. One of 200. Folio, bdg not described. With 50 plates & some duplicate color plates. pnE Nov 12 (68) £75

AMERICAN BOOK PRICES CURRENT

Bone, Muirhead & Gertrude
— Old Spain. L, 1936. One of 265. 2 vols, with portfolio with 2 sgd drypoints by Muirhead Bone. Folio, orig pigskin. Ck Jan 30 (191) £380
Anr copy. 2 vols & 2 portfolios with 2 drypoints in each. Folio, pigskin. S Nov 17 (894) £320 [Orssich]

Bonelli, Giorgio, b.1724
— Hortus Romanus. Rome, 1772-1784. Vols I-VII (of 8). Folio, contemp half vellum; rubbed. With 5 ports, double-page plate & 700 hand-colored plates with blue wash borders. 3 plates browned; Plates 61-100 in Vol VII waterstained, most plates only affected in margins; occasional staining, mainly in margins, in other vols; paper adhesion to Plate 100 in Vol IV. C Oct 15 (213) £20,000 [Baskett & Day]
Anr Ed. Rome, 1772-1793. 8 vols. Folio, contemp half vellum. With 8 colored titles, 5 ports, plan & 600 hand-colored plates. L.p. copy. Plesch—de Belder copy. S Apr 27 (39) £48,000 [Israel]

Bonfadini, Vita
— La Caccia dell'arcobugio.... Ferrara: G. Gironi, [1652]. 12mo, 19th-cent half shagreen. SM Feb 28 (83) FF3,200

Boniface VIII, Pope, 1235?-1303
— Liber sextus decretalium. Basel: Johann Froben & Johann Amerbach, 1 Dec 1500. 4to, early calf; lacking clasps; cover & 7 leaves detached. Small marginal restoration without loss. 288 leaves. Goff B-1015. P Dec 15 (162) $1,700
Anr Ed. Venice: Luc'Antonio Giunta, 1514. 5 parts in 1 vol. 4to, later blind-stamped calf; rubbed, rebacked, lacking clasps. Tp & prelims marginally frayed; small wormholes, affecting a few letters. bba Aug 20 (339) £240 [Bermejo]
— Liber Sextus decretalium. Venice: heirs of Octavianus Scotus, 1525. 4to, vellum. Some wormholes in lower margin of 1st few leaves. S Sept 23 (430) £110 [Poel]

Boniface VIII, Pope, 1235?-1303
— Liber sextus decretalium. Antwerp: C. Plantin, 1569. ("Sextus decretalium liber.") 8vo, contemp calf; worn. Marginal worming; some staining. bba Nov 13 (2) £45 [Bennett & Kerr]

Bonnard, Camille
— Costumes des XIIIe, XIVe, et XVe Siecles.... Paris, 1860. ("Costumes historiques des XIIIe, XIVe et XVe siecles.") Vols I-II (of 3), 4to, cloth. With 198 (of 200) hand-colored engraved plates, soiled, many leaves torn or marginally repaired. bba Dec 18 (113) £100 [Erlini]

Bonnaterre, Pierre Joseph
— Ichthyologie. Paris, 1788. 4to, contemp half calf; rebacked. With 102 plates. Outer margins dampstained. Ck Apr 24 (15) £160

Bonne, Rigobert, 1727-94
— Atlas de toutes les parties connues du globe terrestre. [Geneva: J. L. Pellet, 1780]. 4to, contemp vellum; warped. With 50 folding maps. Dampstains in margins of most plates; lacking tp, text & 23 tables. sg Apr 23 (162) $800
— Atlas moderne ou collection de cartes sur toutes les parties du globe terrestre. Paris, 1787. Folio, half cloth. With engraved title & 38 double-page maps colored in outline. pn Dec 11 (404) £520 [Nicholson]

Bonnemaison, Fereol
— Galerie de son Altesse Royale Madame la Duchesse de Berry. Ecole Francaise. Peintres modernes. Paris, 1822. 2 vols. Folio, contemp half lea; worn & def. With 97 plates only. JG Oct 2 (548) DM2,400

Bonner, James
— A New Plan for Speedily Increasing the Number of Bee-Hives in Scotland.... Edin., 1795. 8vo, contemp bds; rebacked. Johannson copy. g Jan 15 (142) $100
Anr copy. Contemp bds; spine ends chipped. sg Jan 15 (141) $175

Bonner, T. D.
— The Life and Adventures of James P. Beckwourth, Mountaineer.... NY, 1856. 1st Ed. 12mo, orig cloth; spine ends frayed. sg Sept 18 (29) $150

Bonnet, Charles, 1720-93
— Recherches sur l'usage des feuilles dans les plantes. Goettingen & Leiden, 1754. 1st Ed. 4to, contemp mor gilt with arms of Charles Savalette de Buchelet. With engraved title & 31 folding plates. FD June 11 (535) DM15,000

Bonney, Thomas George, 1833-1923
— The Peaks and Valleys of the Alps. L, 1868. Illus by Elijah Walton. Folio, loose in half mor; rubbed, spine torn. With engraved title & 21 color plates. Some spotting. S May 29 (1042) £850
— Vignettes. Alpine and Eastern-Alpine Series. L, 1873. Illus by Elijah Walton. 4to, orig cloth; rubbed. With 24 colored plates. S Feb 24 (412) £160 [Burgess]

Bonpland, Aime J. A., 1773-1858
See also: Humboldt & Bonpland
— Description des plantes rares cultivees a Malmaison et a Navarre. Paris, 1813. Vol I (all pbd). Folio, contemp half mor. With 64 hand-finished color plates. Light foxing on 1 plate & some light offsetting on a few others; some spotting. L.p. copy. de Belder copy. S Apr 27 (40) £24,000 [Brittain]

Bonsal, Stephen
— Edward Fitzgerald Beale: A Pioneer.... NY, 1912. Bdg rubbed. cb Oct 9 (23) $65

Bonser, Alfred E. —& Others
— The Land of Enchantment. L, 1907. Illus by Arthur Rackham. 4to, orig cloth. sg Oct 30 (131) $100

Bontekoe, Cornelis
— Tractat van het Excellenste Kuryd Thee.... The Hague: P. Hagen, 1679. 2d Ed. 3 parts in 1 vol. 8vo, bds. Crahan copy. P Nov 25 (63) $500

Bontius, Jacobus
— De medicina Indorum libri IV. Leiden: F. Hackius, 1642. 12mo, recent vellum bds. Engraved title repaired in lower margin; some dampstains. S Nov 10 (449) £320 [Phelps]

Bonwick, James, 1817-1906
— Discovery and Settlement of Port Philip. Melbourne, 1856. 12mo, orig cloth; new endpapers. Repair to folding map. kh Mar 16 (48) A$80
— Port Phillip Settlement. L, 1883. 8vo, orig cloth; spine soiled. With frontis, 29 plates, 1 map & 6 facsimile letters. Lacking "copy of old newspaper". Ck Sept 26 (216) £120

Boodt, Anselmus Boetius de, 1550?-1634
— Florum, herbarum, ac fructuum selectiorum icones.... Bruges: Kerchove, 1640. Oblong 4to, contemp vellum. With 31 plates. Small hole in text of O2. de Belder copy. S Apr 27 (42) £5,000 [Bjorck]

Book. See: Codex....

Book, Booke, or Boke
— Book Auction Records. L, 1942-81. Vols 39-77. Ck Nov 7 (24) £200
Vols 50-73 plus 3 indexes. L, 1954-76. pn Sept 18 (254) £80 [Weston Lewis]
Vols 54-71. L, 1956-74. T Apr 16 (349) £40
Vols 59-74. L, 1962-78. Ck Jan 16 (178) £90
Vols 61-71. L, 1965-75. bba Oct 30 (441) £80 [Garwood]
Vols 64-71. L, 1967-74. O June 16 (31) $50

Vols 67-73. L, 1967-76. T Oct 16 (595) £70
Vols 66-83 in 17 (lacking Vol 81). L, 1969-86. bba Aug 20 (277) £460 [Avon]
Vols 72-82. Folkestone, 1974-85. 11 vols. Orig cloth. pnE Jan 28 (324) £280 [Johnston]
Vols 75-82. L, 1978-85. bba Oct 16 (409) £260 [Mytze]
— The Book Collector. L, 1952-76. Vols 1-25 in 100 orig parts, plus Index for 1956-75 (lacking vol for 1961). With related ephemera & 1 odd vol. Orig wraps; several spines creased, bumped or damaged. cba Feb 5 (41) $700
Vol 1-35, No 3, plus General Index, 1952-61. L, 1952-86. pnE Jan 28 (325) £170 [McKenzie]
Vols 1-20. L, 1952-71. Some dampstains. Sold w.a.f. pn Oct 23 (86) £120 [Maggs]
Vols 1-32, lacking Vol 32, No 2. With: Book Handbook, Nos 1-6 & Vol 2, Nos 1-4, 1947-52. L, 1952-85. Wraps. O June 16 (32) $320
Vols 1-33, lacking Vol 27. With Index for 1952-61 & 8 loose issues. L, 1952-84. O May 12 (28) $375
— A Book of Fruits & Flowers.... L: Ptd by M.S. for Tho: Jenner, 1653. 4to, modern calf. Marginal tear in C1 mended. Hunt copy. CNY Nov 21 (63) $2,200
— Book of Nature, Embracing a Condensed Survey of the Animal Kingdom. Phila.: S. C. Atkinson, 1834. Ed by an Association of Scientific Gentlemen of Philadelphia. 2 vols. 4to, contemp half calf; not uniform. Some plates partially torn away. Sold w.a.f. O Oct 21 (33) $60
— The Book of the London International Chess Congress. L, 1900. One of 500. Orig cloth; lower hinge worn. pn Mar 26 (56) £60 [De Lucia]
Anr copy. Orig cloth; upper hinge worn. pn Mar 26 (57) £50 [Batsford]

Book of Common Prayer
— 1662. - Cambr. 8vo, contemp mor gilt & inlaid with geometric centerpieces & sidepieces in red & citron mor. C May 13 (153) £2,400 [Hedworth]
— 1681. - Oxford Folio, contemp Restoration bdg of black mor tooled in gilt with red & blue mor onlays to a panel design with stepped corners & stepped centerpiece surrounded by leafy sprays, flowers & circles; corners rubbed, upper joint weak, onlays chipped on upper cover, 2 wanting from spine & 3 from lower cover. C Dec 12 (314) £450 [Schwing]
— 1700. - Oxford Bound with: The Whole Book of Psalms. L, 1700. 8vo, later 18th-cent mor gilt; extremities worn. Some soiling; minor stains. sg Oct 9 (132) $140

— 1704. - L. 8vo, contemp mor to a cottage-roof pattern, inlaid with mor. Lacking 4 hand-colored plates. Sold w.a.f. C May 13 (154) £300 [Fletcher]
— 1717. - L: John Sturt. 8vo, contemp London bdg of mor; 1 corner chipped. Circular table with volvelle possibly from anr copy & wanting the 2 pointers. S July 23 (387) £550 [Lyon]
Anr copy. Contemp mor gilt. Volvelle supplied in facsimile. Engraved throughout. sg June 11 (66) $750
— 1739. - L: Basket. 4to, contemp mor gilt; rubbed. First few leaves def, affecting text. Sold w.a.f. bba Oct 30 (15) £40 [Francis]
— 1758. - Cambr.: Joseph Bentham. 4to, contemp mor gilt with arms of George II. F Jan 15 (357) $130
— 1760. - Cambr.: Baskerville. 1st 8vo Ed. Contemp mor extra; repair to small damage on lower back cover. pn Apr 30 (79A) £880 [Maggs]
Anr copy. Contemp mor; spine dulled, chipped at foot. sg Oct 9 (133) $150
— 1762. - Cambr.: Baskerville. 8vo, contemp mor gilt; rubbed. Gaskell 19. bba Aug 28 (202) £150 [Cavendish]
Anr copy. Contemp mor extra. pn Nov 20 (64) £450
Anr copy. Mor gilt. pnE Jan 28 (359) £220 [Steedman]
— 1772. - Oxford 12mo, contemp mor gilt with shaped centerpiece of white lea; worn & scuffed. bba June 18 (183) £130 [Wilson]
— 1849. - Oxford 32mo, mor gilt. P Sept 24 (109) $230
— 1904. - [NY: Plimpton Press]. American Ed. Folio, mor gilt extra by M. Walter Dunne; extremities rubbed. cb Feb 19 (39) $100

Bookman's...
— Bookman's Price Index. Detroit, [1964-73]. Vols 1-6. K June 7 (218) $160
Vols 7-19. Detroit, [1973-80]. K June 7 (219) $500

Bookworm...
— Bookworm: An Illustrated Treasury of Old Time Literature. NY, 1888-92. Vols I-IV only. 8vo. Vol I, contemp half vellum; others, orig cloth; rubbed & soiled. bba Oct 30 (443) £55 [Goldman]

Booth, Edward Thomas
— Rough Notes on the Birds.... L, 1881-87. 3 vols in orig 15 parts. Folio, orig bds; discolored. With 2 maps & 114 hand-colored plates. Some foxing affecting a number of plates. S Oct 23 (660) £2,500 [Holland]
Anr copy. 3 vols. Folio, orig half mor gilt; rubbed. S June 25 (147) £3,400 [Quaritch]

Booth, Edwin Carton
— Australia. L, [1873-76?]. 2 vols. 4to, cloth. Most plates foxed. CA Apr 12 (47) A$800
Anr copy. Contemp half mor; rubbed, not uniform. With 7 maps only. Ck May 15 (45) £520
Anr copy. Contemp half mor; rubbed. Minor marginal dampstaining. T Mar 19 (3) £420

Booth, Stephen
— The Book Called Holinshed's Chronicles.... San Francisco: Book Club of California, 1968. Ltd Ed. 4to, half cloth. With orig leaf from the 1587 Ed. cb Sept 11 (22) $120

Booth, William Beattie, 1804?-74. See: Chandler & Booth

Borba de Moraes, Rubens
— Bibliographia Brasiliana. Amst., 1958. 2 vols. In d/js. O June 16 (45) $60
Anr Ed. Los Angeles, 1983. 2 vols. 4to, cloth, in d/js. bba oct 16 (365) £85 [Georges]

Borden, William Cline
— The Use of the Roentgen Ray by the Medical Department of the United States Army in the War with Spain. Wash., 1900. 4to, cloth; soiled & worn. With 38 plates. wa Nov 6 (57) $100

Bordeneuve, J.
— Les Grandes Chasses en Indochine. Saigon: Albert Portail, 1925. 4to, half shagreen. Jeanson copy. SM Feb 28 (84) FF2,400

Bordley, John Beale, 1727-1804
— A Summary View of the Courses of Crops, in the Husbandry of England & Maryland.... Phila.: Charles Cist, 1784. 4to, sewn as issued. Marginal stain on tp. Hunt copy. CNY Nov 21 (32) $650

Bordona, Jesus Dominguez. See: Dominguez Bordona, Jesus

Bordone, Benedetto
— Isolario. Venice: Aldus for Federico Toresano, 1547. Folio, half vellum; rubbed. With 112 maps & plans (4 double-page, 4 double half-page, 2 full-page) & 1 woodcut diagram. Tp soiled; minor marginal stains; contemp marginalia on a few leaves. P Oct 29 (1) $3,250
— Libro de Benedetto Bordone nel qual si ragiona de tutte l'isole del mondo. Venice: Nicolo de Aristotile, detto Zoppino, June 1534. ("Isolario....") Folio, later vellum. With 2 full-page & 4 double-page maps. sg Dec 4 (23) $3,400

Borelli, Giovanni Alfonso, 1608-79
— De motu animalium. Rome, 1680-81. 1st Ed. 2 vols. 4to, contemp vellum bds. With 18 plates. Library stamp on title. O May 12 (30) $250
Anr Ed. Leiden, 1685. 2 parts in 1 vol. 4to, vellum; soiled. With engraved title & 18 folding plates. pn May 21 (254) £320
Anr Ed. Naples, 1734. 4to, later 18th-cent half lea gilt. With 19 folding plates. sg Jan 15 (295) $400
— De Vi Percussionis. Leiden, 1686. 4to, old calf; rubbed & rebacked. With 6 folding plates. Ck Nov 7 (104) £900

Borget, Auguste, b.1809
— La Chine et les chinois. Paris, [1842]. Folio, contemp half mor; rubbed. With engraved title, litho title, 2 engraved dedication leaves & 32 tinted lithos on 25 sheets. S Oct 23 (23) £6,000 [Browning]

Borghini, Vincenzo Maria
— Discorsi. Florence: Giunta, 1584-85. 4to, 18th-cent Italian vellum. S Sept 23 (305) £190 [Goldschmidt]

Borlase, William, 1695-1772
— The Natural History of Cornwall. Oxford, 1758. 1st Ed. Folio, mor gilt by Riviere. With folding map & 28 plates. pn Oct 23 (329) £130 [Quaritch]
— Observations of the Antiquities Historical and Monumental, of the County of Cornwall. Oxford, 1754. 1st Ed. Folio, contemp calf; rebacked. With 32 plates. With ALs from Borlase on matters of antiquarian interest. cb Dec 18 (23) $160
2d Ed. L, 1769. ("Antiquities Historical and Monumental of the County of Cornwall.") Folio, contemp calf; rubbed & rebacked with orig backstrip relaid. With 2 maps & 25 plates. T July 16 (69) £230
— Observations on the Ancient and Present State of the Islands of Scilly.... Oxford, 1756. 4to, contemp calf; joints rubbed. With 5 folding plates. Ck Nov 21 (342) £180

Born, Ignaz von; 1742-91
— New Process of Amalgamation of Gold and Silver Ores, and Other Metallic Mixtures.... L, 1791. 4to, contemp half calf; head of spine rubbed. With 22 plates. Hole in N4 affecting a few letters. C Dec 12 (27) £600 [Zechner]

Borrow, George Henry, 1803-81
See also: Limited Editions Club
— Romantic Ballads. Norwich, 1826. 1st Ed, 1st Issue. 8vo, contemp half calf; rubbed, new endpapers. bba Jan 15 (85) £260 [Johnson]
— Works. L & NY, 1923-24. One of 775. 16

vols. Half mor by Stikeman. sg Feb 12 (27) $425

Bosio, Giacomo
— Histoire des chevaliers de l'ordre de S. Jean de Hierusalem.... Paris, 1659. In 1 vol. Folio, contemp lea. With 2 engraved titles & 5 plates. FD June 11 (901) DM3,100

Bosqui, Edward. See: Grabhorn Printing

Bosse, Abraham
— Traite des manieres de graver en taille douce sur l'airin. Paris, 1701. 2d Ed. 8vo, calf gilt; rubbed. With engraved title & dedication & 16 plates. FD June 11 (2149) DM1,600

Bossert, Helmuth Theodor
— An Encyclopaedia of Colour Decoration.... L, 1928. 4to, orig cloth. S Mar 9 (656) £85 [Wise]
— Geschichte des Kunstgewerbes aller Zeiten und Voelker. Berlin, 1928-35. 6 vols. 4to, cloth; front hinge cracked, spine extremities chipped. sg June 18 (45) $70
— Ornament.... L, 1924. Folio, orig cloth. Ck Jan 30 (213) £65

Bossert, Helmuth Theodor —& Guttmann, Heinrich
— Aus der Fruehzeit der Photographie, 1840-70. Frankfurt, 1930. 1st Ed. sg May 7 (9) $90

Bossi, Benigno
— Mascarade a la grecque. Parma, 1771. Folio, contemp wraps. With 2 leaves of engraved text, engraved altariform dedication & 9 plates. A few light dampstains, mainly marginal. P Nov 25 (368) $2,600
— Opere. Milan: G. Bettalli, [c.1790]. This a collection of 177 etchings bound in contemp calf. sg Apr 2 (31) $7,000

Bossoli, Carlo, 1815-84
— The War in Italy, L, 1859-60. 4to, orig cloth; def. With tinted title, 2 maps & 37 plates. pn June 18 (221) £240 [L'Aquaforte] Anr Ed. L, [1860]. 8vo, orig cloth; gutta-percha perished. With litho title, 2 maps & 29 tinted litho plates. Lacking ptd title. C Dec 12 (28) £260 [Walford]

Bossom, Alfred Charles
— Building to the Skies. The Romance of the Skyscraper. L: Studio, 1934. 4to, cloth, in worn d/j; worn & soiled, hinge repaired. Inscr, 1948. wa Sept 25 (167) $50

Bossuet, Jacques Benigne, 1627-1704
— De Nova Quaestione Tractatus Tres. Paris: Johannem Anisson, 1698. 8vo, contemp calf; joints rubbed. S Sept 23 (306) £30 [William]

Bossuit, Francis
— Beeld-Synders Kunst-Kabinet. Amst., 1727. Illus by Mattys Pool. 4to, 18th-cent calf; upper cover scratched. S Sept 23 (540) £330 [Weinreb]

Boston Athenaeum
— A Catalogue of the Washington Collection in the Boston Athenaeum.... Bost., 1897. One of 55 on special paper. Compiled by Appleton P. C. Griffin. 8vo, cloth. sg Oct 2 (304) $60

Boston Museum of Fine Arts
— The Artist & the Book: 1860-1960. Bost., 1961. 4to, orig cloth; soiled. sg Feb 5 (21) $150

Boswell, Henry
— Historical Descriptions.... L, [1786]. Folio, contemp half calf. With frontis, 50 maps & 190 plates, views & plans. S Apr 23 (112) £850 [Traylen]

Boswell, James, 1740-95
See also: Limited Editions Club
— An Account of Corsica... Glasgow: Foulis for Dilly, 1768. 8vo, 19th-cent sheep; broken. sg Nov 20 (26) $100
Anr Ed. L, 1769. 8vo, 19th-cent half mor; rubbed. Port inserted on a stub & possibly from anr copy; map with tears along edges; inscr leaf waterstained. Inscr to Andrew Lumisden. P Sept 24 (132) $1,200
— The Journal of a Tour to the Hebrides.... Dublin, 1785. 8vo, calf. pn Dec 11 (168) £120
Anr copy. Calf gilt, oval reserve on lower cover with pen drawing of an abbey; rebacked, upper cover has lost its drawing. pnE Jan 28 (59) £160 [Traylen]
1st Ed. L, 1785. 8vo, mor gilt by Riviere. With 20 hand-colored plates, plus 2 extra ports. Extra-illus with 20 plates from Rowlandson's Picturesque Beauties of Boswell. sg June 11 (340) $3,800
Anr Ed. L, 1786. 8vo, later half calf; worn. pnE Nov 12 (90) £45
— The Life of Samuel Johnson.... L, 1791. 1st Ed, with the "gve" reading. 2 vols. 4to, contemp mor gilt with University of Oxford arms; rebacked. pnE Jan 28 (108) £1,500 [Thin]
Anr copy. Contemp calf gilt; rebacked. sg June 11 (72) $1,800
2d Ed. L, 1793. 3 vols. 8vo, contemp calf; joints splitting. With port & 1 plate only. Lacking half-titles. bba Feb 5 (171) £60 [Scott]
Anr Ed. Bost., 1807. 3 vols. 8vo, contemp calf; rubbed. O Feb 24 (22) $180
Anr Ed. L, 1831. 5 vols. 8vo, calf gilt. sg

Sept 11 (32) $225

Anr Ed. L, 1839. 10 vols. 8vo, half mor by Zaehnsdorf; some spine ends & raised bands scuffed, Vol I frontis loose. sg Sept 11 (33) $175

Anr Ed. L: H. G. Bohn, 1859. 10 vols. 8vo, half calf. Library markings; some soiling & staining. wa Sept 25 (1) $100

— The Live of Samuel Johnson. L, 1791. 1st Ed, With the "gve" reading. 2 vols. 4to, contemp calf gilt; Vol I rebound preserving orig covers, Vol II rebacked & repaired. Lacking initial blank in Vol II; additional port of Johnson tipped into Vol I; port frontis foxed; [A]? of Vol I torn & repaired slightly affecting text; title of Vol II guarded; some discoloration or spotting. Together with The Principal Corrections and Additions (lacking last leaf). S July 23 (20) £850 [Traylen]

— The Principal Corrections and Additions to the First Edition of Mr. Boswell's Life of Dr. Johnson. L, 1793. 1st Ed. 4to, modern calf; new endpapers. pnE Jan 28 (117) £1,300 [Traylen]

— Private Papers from Malahide Castle in the Collection of Ralph Heyward Isham. L, 1928-37. Ed by Geoffrey Scott. 21 vols, including Catalogue, Index & Journal of a Tour to the Hebrides. 4to & folio, orig bds. sg Apr 2 (32) $750

Bosworth, Newton, 1848

— A Treatise on the Rifle, Musket, Pistol, and Fowling-Piece.... NY, 1846. 12mo, orig cloth; spotted. O June 9 (27) $80

Botanic...

— The Botanic Garden.... L, 1825-[51]. Ed by Benjamin Maund. Vols I-XIII plus The Fruitist, The Floral Register & Part I of the Auctarium. 8vo, calf gilt. With 307 (of 312) hand-colored plates each with 4 figures of plants & 17 (of 72) hand-colored plates of fruits. Floral Register & Auctarium both incomplete. Sold with an extra set of Parts 11, 14 & 15. CNY May 11 (70) $5,500

Anr copy. Vols I-XIII (complete set), plus The Fruitist, The Floral Register & the Auctarium. 8vo, half mor. With 314 hand-colored plates. Fruitist lacking engraved title. pnE Dec 17 (216) £3,300 [Graham]

Anr copy. 18 vols in 16, including The Fruitist, The Floral Register & Auctarium. 8vo, contemp calf gilt. With 15 uncolored engraved titles, 312 plates & 72 illusts colored by hand. de Belder copy. S Apr 28 (234) £6,200 [Burgess Browning]

Anr copy. Vols I-XIII (complete) plus The Fruitist, The Floral Register & The Auctarium. 8vo, contemp mor gilt; rubbed. With 312 hand-colored plates. Some foxing.

Sold w.a.f. S June 25 (168) £4,200 [Traylen]

Vol I. Contemp half calf. HK Nov 4 (1066) DM1,600

Vol III. Contemp half calf. HK Nov 4 (1067) DM1,600

Vols II-V. Contemp half calf gilt. Sold w.a.f. C Oct 15 (245) £850 [Berg]

Anr copy. Contemp calf; rubbed, Vols III & IV lacking spines & broken. S Feb 24 (594) £1,100 [Dennistoun]

Vols I-VII. Contemp half calf; discolored. Stain on Plate 149. Sold w.a.f. S Oct 23 (731) £1,800 [Thomson]

Vols I-VIII. Contemp half calf; rubbed, 1 spine chipped at head. Sold w.a.f. S Apr 23 (48) £2,000 [Koch]

Botanical. See: Loddiges, Conrad & Sons

Botanist...

— The Botanist: Containing Accurately Coloured Figures of Tender and Hardy Ornamental Plants. L, [1837-46]. Ed by Benjamin Maund & J. S. Henslow. Vol I only. Contemp half mor. Last plates repaired with tape. bba Apr 23 (144) £340 [Russell]

Anr copy. 5 vols. 4to, orig half mor gilt. With engraved titles & 225 (of 250) hand-colored plates. Library blindstamps on each title & on 178 plates. Sold w.a.f. CNY May 11 (71) $850

Anr copy. Contemp half lea; 3 vols worn. FD June 11 (557) DM4,000

Bottomley, Gordon, 1874-1948

Frescoes from Buried Temples. L: The Pear Tree Press, 1928. Ltd Ed. Illus by James Guthrie. Folio, unbound as issued in orig wraps. S Dec 4 (94) £1,100 [Penny Chrim]

One of 55. Unbound as issued in orig wraps, endpapers & wraps ptd in silver & gold. With 35 intaglio plates of text, cover design, endpapers, 3 subtitles & 17 illusts ptd from blocks or woodcuts & 2 illusts ptd from plates. S June 17 (242) £1,250 [Wilsey]

Botvinnik, Mikhail Moiseevich

— Shakhmatnoe tvorchestvo Botvinnika. Moscow, 1965-68. 3 vols. In d/js. pn Mar 26 (217) £90 [Gorton]

Bouche, Henri. See: Dollfus & Bouche

Boucher, Anthony

— The Case of the Seven of Calvary. NY, 1937. In chipped d/j. cb May 7 (188) $65

Boucher, Francois
— 20,000 Years of Fashion. NY: Abrams, 1967. Folio, cloth, in d/j. Owner's stamp at foot of tp & other places. cb Mar 5 (45) $75

Boucher, Jonathan
— A View of the Causes and Consequences of the American Revolution.... L, 1797. 8vo, modern half mor by Stern & Dess; rubbed. Inscr "From the Author" on half-title. O May 12 (31) $300

Bouchette, Joseph, 1774-1841
— The British Dominions in North America. L, 1831. 1st Issue. 2 vols. 4to, cloth; joints cracked. With 29 plates & maps & 3 engraved tables, some marginal tears. Prospectus, sgd by author, bound in at end. bba Dec 18 (115) £140 [Elliott]
— A Topographical Description of the Province of Lower Canada.... L, 1815. 8vo, old calf; rebacked in mor. Library stamp on tp. O May 12 (32) $400
— A Topographical Dictionary of the Province of Lower Canada. L, 1832. 4to, modern half lea. AVP Nov 20 (26) C$150 [Fakoni]

Bouchot, Henri
— Catherine de Medicis. Paris, 1899. One of 1,000. 4to, half mor gilt by Canape. B Oct 7 (321) HF200

Bouchot, Henri Francois Xavier Marie, 1849-1906
— L'Epopee du Costume militaire francaise. Paris, [1898]. 4to, orig mor gilt; rubbed. With 10 color plates. bba Aug 28 (69) £54 [Lenton]

Boufflers, Stanislas Jean de
— Oeuvres. Paris: Didot jeune, 1813. 2 vols. 8vo, calf with lattice-work pattern by Thouvenin. S Nov 27 (49) £850 [Appleton]

Bougainville, Hyacinthe Yves Philippe Potentien, Baron de, 1781-1846
— Journal de la navigation autour du globe.... Paris, 1837. 2 text vols & Atlas, 4to & folio, half calf: rebacked preserving orig spines. Atlas with 56 plates & charts (some bound upside down), some colored. S Apr 24 (370) £6,000 [Perrin]

Bougainville, Louis Antoine de, 1729-1811
— Traite du calcul integral.... Paris, 1754-56. 2 vols in 1. 4to, contemp vellum bds; rubbed. With 3 folding plates. 2 leaves torn in Vol II; some margins stained in Vol I. Hunt copy. CNY Nov 21 (37) $350
— Voyage autour du monde.... Paris, 1771. 1st Ed. 4to, contemp calf. With 20 folding maps & 3 plates. LIbrary stamps on tp & half-title; 1 plate with short tear. S Oct 23 (19) $1,300 [Frers]

Anr copy. Contemp calf; joints worn. Library stamps on title & half-title; 1 plate with short tear. S Apr 24 (371) £800 [Perrin]
— A Voyage Round the World.... L, 1772. 8vo, contemp calf; lower joint wormed. With 5 folding maps & 1 folding plate. World chart shaved in lower margin. C Dec 12 (29) £850 [Traylen]

Anr copy. Contemp calf; rubbed, joints broken. 2 maps torn, 1 shaved. S Feb 24 (418) £380 [Shapero]

Bouguer, Pierre, 1698-1758
— Traite du navire, de sa construction.... Paris, 1746. 1st Ed. 4to, contemp calf; joints split, rubbed. With 12 folding plates. Lacking errata leaf. bba Sept 25 (181) £110 [Greenwood]

Boulainvilliers, Henri de, Comte
— Memoires presentes a Monseigneur le Duc d'Orleans.... The Hague, 1727. 2 vols. 12mo, contemp calf; rubbed. bba Oct 16 (23) £50 [Braunschweig]

Boulger, George S., 1853-1922 —& Perrin, Ida Southwell
— British Flowering Plants. L, 1914. Ltd Ed. 4 vols. 4to, orig cloth. With 300 colored plates. pn Oct 23 (27) £55 [Egee]

Anr copy. Orig cloth; soiled. T Oct 16 (418) £80

Boulle, Pierre, b.1912
— The Bridge over the River Kwai. NY, [1954]. Advance review copy. Wraps. sg Mar 5 (23) $50

Boulton, William B.
— The History of White's. L, [1892]. Ltd Ed. 2 vols. 4to, contemp half mor gilt; spines rubbed. bba Dec 18 (116) £30 [Scott]

Out-of-series copy. Orig cloth; affected by damp. Ck Oct 17 (37) £45

Bourchier, George
— Eight Months' Campaign against the Bengal Sepoy Army.... L, 1858. 8vo, recent half calf. Half-title with paper repair at top; tp & frontis with small dampstain to lower gutter corner. cb Dec 18 (24) $95

Bourgoin, Jules
— Les Elements de l'art arabe. Paris, 1879. 8vo, orig half cloth; rebacked preserving orig spine, rubbed. bba Aug 28 (41) £150 [Axe]

Bourgoing, Jean Francois de, 1748-1811
— Travels in Spain.... L, 1789. 3 vols. 8vo, contemp calf; rebacked. With 11 folding plates (1 with 2 subjects). Lacking half-titles. S July 14 (296) £160

Bourke-White, Margaret
— Eyes on Russia. NY, 1931. 4to, cloth; rubbed, front hinge cracked. With 40 plates. sg Nov 13 (14) $70

— Shooting the Russian War. NY: Simon & Schuster, 1942. 8vo, cloth; worn & soiled. Inscr to Dr. Henry Field. wa Nov 6 (291) $60

Bourne, John, Civil Engineer
— A Treatise on the Screw Propeller.... L, 1867. 4to, orig cloth; front hinge cracked. With 54 plates, some folding. Library copy. wa Nov 6 (22) $75

Bourne, John C. —& Britton, John, 1771-1857
— Drawings of the London and Birmingham Railway. L, 1839. 4 parts in 1 vol. Folio, orig half cloth; worn. With lithographed title, 30 plates on 26 sheets & 2 maps on 1 sheet. pn June 18 (176) £1,500 [Frew]

Bourniquel, Camille
— La Feerie et le royaume. Paris: Mourlot, 1972. One of 10. Illus by Marc Chagall. Orig sleeve & slipcase. With 10 colored lithographs. JG Oct 2 (1884) DM10,000

Boutcher, William
— A Treatise on Forest Trees. Edin., 1775. 4to, contemp calf gilt. pnE Dec 17 (180) £190 [McNaughton]

Anr copy. Contemp calf; worn & soiled, front joint splitting. wa Nov 6 (175) $75

Boutellier, Ernest
— Playsir de chasse et desduit. Metz: Rousseau Pallez, 1861. One of 60. 4to, mor janseniste by Chambolle-Duru, Jeanson copy. SM Feb 28 (87) FF1,800

Boutens, Petrus Cornelis, 1870-1943
— Reizang van burgers, terugkeerend uit de ballingschap. Heerenveen, 1944. One of 90. Orig wraps. B Oct 7 (237) HF650

Boutet, Henri
— Pointes sechès. Paris, 1898. One of 50 on japon imperial with orig drypoint, sgd, & with additional suite of the plates on chine. 4to, half mor, orig wraps bound in. 2 leaves slightly def. This copy also has the etched illusts for the cover & title-vignette, that for the cover in 2 states, & a drawing sgd. S June 17 (79) £300 [Sims]

Douton, Victor
— Quel est l'auteur du Livre du Roy Modus et de la Royne Ratio? Paris: Barthe, [1888]. One of 50. 4to, half shagreen. SM Mar 1 (585) FF800

Bova, Ben
— The Star Conquerors. Phila.: Winston, [1959]. 1st Ed. In chipped d/j. cb Sept 28 (184) $60

Bovet Collection, Alfred
— Lettres autographes.... Paris, 1887. One of 500. Catalogued by Etienne Charavay. 4to, cloth. 1st 2 pp stained. sg Jan 22 (75) $60

Bowdich, Thomas Edward, 1791-1824
— Excursions in Madeira and Porto Santo. L, 1825. 1st Ed. 4to, modern half calf. With 18 plain & 4 colored plates. Upper margins trimmed & repaired. Ck May 8 (310) £150

— Mission from Cape Coast Castle to Ashantee. L, 1819. 4to, contemp half calf; rubbed. With 3 maps, 10 illusts on 7 sheets, 5 pp of engraved music & folding engraved copy of the commission carried by Peddie, Campbell & Cowdry. S Oct 23 (460) £450 [Bonham]

Anr copy. Modern half calf. With 2 maps, 7 hand-colored plates, facsimile plate, 5 pp of engraved music & 1 plan. Half-title & title reinforced with gauze & with new margins. 1st leaf of intro repaired touching 1 letter of text. S Feb 24 (468) £140 [Huggel]

Bowen, Abel, 1790-1850
— The Naval Monument.... Bost., 1816. 1st Ed. 8vo, old calf; rubbed & worn, front cover detached. With 26 plates. Top inch of title torn off. cb Dec 18 (25) $75

Bowen, Emanuel, d.1767
See also: Owen & Bowen

— A Complete Atlas, or Distinct View of the Known World. L, 1752. Folio, half calf; spine def. With 69 maps hand-colored in outline. Some staining along centerfold of 10 maps. pn Dec 11 (405A) £2,900 [Sweet]

— The Maps and Charts to the Modern Part of the Universal History. L, 1766. Folio, sewn. With 37 maps plus 2 additional maps of Italy. Some soiling & browning; some torn, 1 with loss; tp lacking; contents leaf detached. Ck May 15 (330) £800

Bowen, Emanuel, d.1767 —& Bowen, Thomas
— Atlas Anglicanus, or a Complete Sett of Maps of the Counties of South Britain. L, [1767]. Oblong folio, modern calf with part of orig spine preserved. With 44 (of 45) double-page maps, hand-colored in outline. Engraved title repaired; 1st 3 maps with small repairs. pn May 21 (326) £920 [Map House]

Bowen, Emanuel, d.1767 —& Kitchin, Thomas, d.1784

— The Large English Atlas. L: Robert Sayer, [c.1760 or later]. Folio, contemp half calf; hinges cracked. With 47 double-page maps, handcolored in outline. pn May 21 (371) £3,100 [Magna]

Anr Ed. L, 1763. Folio, half calf. With 47 hand-colored maps. Dampstain throughout in upper margin, with general map of England seriously affected; 6 maps with vertical creases, including England; all maps mtd on guards. C Oct 15 (129) £2,600 [Burden]

Anr Ed. L: Robert Sayer, [c.1780]. Folio, contemp half calf; worn. With 45 (of 47) double-page or folding maps, hand-colored in outline. Small stain in upper margin just touching neatlines in a few instances. S Apr 24 (113) £3,000 [Burgess]

Bowen, Frank Charles

— The Sea, its History and Romance. L, 1924-26. 4 vols in 2. 4to, half mor gilt, orig wraps bound in; rubbed. sg Sept 11 (34) $110

Anr copy. 4 vols in 16 parts. 4to, wraps; worn. sg Nov 20 (27) $50

Bowen, Thomas. See: Bowen & Bowen

Bowers, Fredson

— Principles of Bibliographical Description. Princeton, 1949. In chipped & repaired d/j. cb Feb 5 (59) $55

Bowes, James Lord, 1834-99. See: Audsley & Bowes

Bowker, J. H. See: Trimen & Bowker

Bowler, Thomas William, d.1869

— The Kafir Wars and British Settlers in South Africa. L, 1865. 4to, orig cloth; worn. With frontis & 19 tinted views. Text & plates loose; some stain in lower margin of plates throughout. pn Mar 5 (215) £450 [Talbot]

Anr copy. Modern cloth; orig cloth front cover laid down. With 20 plates, last 10 dampstained in inner margin, affecting image. sg Nov 20 (28) $950

Anr copy. Orig cloth; rebacked. SSA Feb 11 (463) R2,400

— Pictorial Album of Cape Town. Cape Town, 1866. Oblong 4to, orig bds. With folding colored frontis & 11 colored plates. SSA Feb 11 (464) R4,000

Bowles, Carington, 1724-93

— Bowles's Florist. L, [1774]-77. 4to, 19th-cent calf; upper cover loose. With 60 hand-colored plates. Some discoloration; inner margin of tp & following leaf reparied; tp with part of imprint & price erased. de Belder copy. S Apr 27 (41) £2,800 [Ursus Books]

Anr Ed. L, 1777. 8vo, modern cloth. With 60 plates. Library stamp in corner of each plate & on tp; some plates soiled. S Nov 10 (450) £260 [Elliott]

— Bowles's New Medium English Atlas. L, 1785. 4to, old calf; rebacked. With 44 hand-colored double-page maps. pn May 21 (331) £920 [Intercol]

— Bowles's Post-Chaise Companion. L, 1782. 2 vols. 8vo, contemp mor; rubbed. With engraved general map & 100 double-page strip road maps. Ck Sept 26 (37) £260

Bowley, Sir Arthur Lyon

— The Mathematical Groundwork of Economics. Oxford, 1924. 8vo, orig cloth; worn. P Sept 24 (249) $300

Bowness, Alan

— The Complete Sculpture of Barbara Hepworth 1960-69. L, 1971. 1st Ed, One of 150, with an orig screenprint, sgd by Hepworth. 4to, orig cloth, in d/j. S Nov 10 (56) £110 [Fitton]

Bowring, Sir John, 1792-1872

— Minor Morals for Young People. L & Edin., 1834-39. 3 vols. 8vo, half mor gilt. With 12 plates by Cruikshank & 8 by Wm. Heath. However, 6 of the Heath plates are apparently in facsimile. sg Feb 12 (53) $100

Bowyer, Robert, 1758-1834

— The Campaign of Waterloo. L, 1816. Folio, contemp cloth; rebacked in calf. With map, 2 port plates & 6 (on 4) hand-colored plates. Folding plate torn & repaired. Ck Apr 24 (53) £130

Anr copy. Loose in orig bds; backstrip def. Lacking folding view of the battle. T Feb 19 (264) £92

— An Illustrated Record of Important Events in the Annals of Europe.... L, 1815. With map, 4 plain & 19 colored plates. Bound with: Bowyer, The Campaign of Waterloo. L, 1816. Folio, half mor gilt. With 2 plates of ports, 1 plate of facsimile signatures, 2 plans & 24 hand-colored plates on 22 sheets. Folding plates torn & repaired along folds; a few plates with light offset; minor tears in margins of text. pn Dec 11 (218) £650 [Davis]

Anr copy. With map, 4 plain & 19 colored plates. One leaf torn; some folding plates split. Bound with: Bowyer, The Campaign of Waterloo. L, 1816. With map & 6 (on 4) colored plates. half calf gilt; rubbed. pn Apr 30 (40) £900

Anr copy. With map, 4 plain & 19 colored plates. One leaf torn; some folding plates split. Bound with: Bowyer, The Campaign of Waterloo. L, 1816. With map & 6 (on 4) colored plates. And: Bowyer. The Triumphs of Europe. L, 1814. Lacking tp. half mor. S May 6 (486) £1,000 [Hill]

Anr Ed. L, 1816. Folio, contemp half lea; rubbed. One plate torn at fold. S Feb 24 (413) £220 [Hill]

Boyd, Julian Parks
— Indian Treaties Printed by Benjamin Franklin.... Phila., 1938. One of 500. Folio, orig cloth; soiled. sg Oct 2 (142) $110

Boydell, John & Josiah
— Graphic Illustrations of the Dramatic Works of Shakespeare. L, 1803. ("A Collection of Prints Illustrating the Dramatic Works of Shakespeare.") 2 vols. Folio, contemp half mor; rebacked, old spines laid down. With 2 ports & 96 plates. With 2 plates repaired. Ck Sept 5 (178) £400
— An History of the River Thames. L, 1794-96. 2 vols. Folio, contemp half calf; worn & rubbed. With frontis, 2 folding maps & 76 colored plates. Some foxing & browning. pnE Dec 17 (387) £2,100 [Marshall]

Boyer, Richard L.
— The Giant Rat of Sumatra. L, 1977. In d/j. cb Apr 24 (1301) $55

Boyle, Frederick
A Ride Across a Continent. L, 1868. 2 vols in 1. 8vo, orig cloth; rubbed. T Sept 18 (24) £46

Boyle, Robert, 1627-91
— Chymista scepticus, vel dubia et paradoxa chymico-physica.... Rotterdam, 1668. 12mo, contemp calf gilt. sg Jan 15 (298) $225

A Continuation of New Experiemnts Physico-Mechanical, Touching the Spring and Weight of the Air...The I. Part.... Oxford, 1682. 4to, contemp calf. With 7 (of 8) folding plates. HK Nov 4 (941) DM640
— Medicina Hydrostatica: or, Hydrostaticks applyed to the Materia Medica. L, 1690. 1st Ed. 8vo, contemp calf; rubbed. With 16-page catalogue of Boyle's works at end. Tp holed affecting 1 character; half-title holed. Ck June 19 (156) £400
— Medicinal Experiments.... L, 1696-98. 3 vols in 2. 12mo, contemp calf. Lacking port. sg Jan 15 (70) $80
— New Experiments Physico-Mechanicall, Touching the Spring of the Air and its Effects.... Oxford, 1662. 2d Ed. 3 parts in 2 vols. 4to, old calf; dampstained. sg Jan 15 (296) $1,300

3d Ed. L, 1682. 3 parts in 1 vol. 4to, contemp calf; rebacked, rubbed. S Nov 27 (252) £340 [Thomas]
— New Experiments and Observations Touching Cold.... L, 1683. 2d Ed. 4to, syn; title rehinged. With 1 (of 2) plates. Library stamps. sg Jan 15 (299) $60
— The Philosophical Works. L, 1725. 3 vols. 4to, later calf; spines rubbed. With 21 folding plates. Minor spotting. S Nov 10 (451) £450 [Mackenzie]
— Tracts...containing New Experiments, touching the Relation betwixt Flame & Air.... L, 1672. 8vo, contemp calf; rebacked. Lacking 1st blank, some browning & spotting, title repaired. S Nov 27 (251) £340 [Thomas]
— Works. L, 1744. 5 vols. Folio, contemp calf; rubbed, corners scuffed. With 24 plates on 15 folding sheets. C Dec 12 (30) £800 [MacKenzie]

Boyle, Roger, 1st Earl of Orrery, 1621-79
— A Treatise of the Art of War.... L, 1677. 1st Ed. Folio, contemp calf; rubbed, splits in upper joint. With port & 6 double-page plates. Lacking final blank. S July 14 (297) £280

Boylesve, Rene, 1867-1926
— Le Carrosse aux deux lezards verts. Paris, 1921. One of 300. Illus by Georges Barbier. Unsewn in orig wraps. S Dec 4 (4) £480 [Joseph & Sawyer]

Boynton, Charles Brandon, 1806-83
— The History of the Navy during the Rebellion. NY, 1867-69. 1st Ed. 2 vols. 4to, cloth; joints of Vol II starting. cb Dec 18 (26) $95

Boys, Thomas Shotter, 1803-74
— Original Views of London.... L, 1954-55. 2 vols. Folio, half mor; worn. Facsimile of the 1842 Ed. sg Apr 23 (23) $120
— Picturesque Architecture in Paris, Ghent, Antwerp, Rouen. L, 1839. Folio, mor gilt; rubbed, foot of spine worn, hinges strengthened. With title & 28 chromolithographed views on 26 leaves. Some waterstain to tp, dedication & a few plates. C Oct 15 (18) £1,500 [Heald]

Brackenbury, George
— The Campaign in the Crimea. L, 1855-56. 1st & 2d Series. 8vo, orig cloth. S Nov 18 (938) £80 [Alanen]
— Descriptive Sketches, illustrating William Simpson's Drawings of the Seat of the War in the East. First Series. L, 1855. 4to, 19th-cent half lea; worn. With 20 plates on 10 leaves. sg Nov 20 (29) $100

Brackenridge, Henry M., 1786-1871
— Views of Louisiana. Pittsburgh, 1814. 1st Ed. 8vo, cloth; needs rebdg. sg Mar 12 (17) $275
Anr Ed. Balt., 1817. 12mo, old calf. Heavily foxed. wd June 19 (69) $125

Bracton, Henricus de, d.1268
— De legibus et consuetudinibus, Angliae libri quinque. L, 1569. 1st Ed. Folio, calf by Riviere; broken. One leaf possibly from anr copy. sg Oct 9 (134) $1,600
Anr copy. Old calf; rejointed, spine ends worn, rear cover detached. Marginal soiling or stains; tear in last leaf mended. sg Apr 2 (33) $1,600
2d Ed. L, 1640. 4to, old calf; rebacked. Marginal browning; title & last leaf rehinged. sg Oct 9 (135) $375

Bradbury, Ray
See also: Limited Editions Club
— The Anthem Sprinters and Other Antics. NY, 1963. Review copy. In d/j. Inscr, 1978. cb Sept 28 (190) $300
— Dandelion Wine. Garden City, 1957. In d/j. Sgd. cb May 7 (315) $110
— Dark Carnival. Sauk City, Wisc., 1947. One of 300. In d/j. cb Sept 28 (193) $325
— Fahrenheit 451. NY: Ballantine Books, [1953]. One of 200. Orig Johns-Manville Quinterra asbestos. cb Sept 28 (194) $1,500
One of 451 bound in Johns-Manville quinterra asbestos. Inscr. cb May 7 (316) $800
— The Last Circus & the Electrocution. Northridge: Lord John Press, 1980. One of 100. Intro by W. F. Nolan; illus by Joe Mugnaini. Sgd by author, introducer & artist. cb Sept 28 (197) $50; cb May 7 (317) $80
Uncorrected proof. Wraps with taped spine, in d/j. cb Sept 28 (196) $70
— The Love Affair, a Short Story, and Two Poems. Northridge CA: Lord John Press, 1982. One of 100. cb Sept 28 (198) $60
— The Martian Chronicles. Garden City, 1950. 1st Ed. In d/j. Inscr. cb Sept 28 (199) $150
— The Mummies of Guanajuato. NY: Harry N. Abrams, [1978]. In d/j. cb Sept 28 (201) $55
— This Attic Where the Meadow Greens. Northridge: Lord John Press, 1979. One of 75. Half cloth. Sgd. cb Sept 28 (203) $65

Bradford, Duncan
— The Wonders of the Heavens.... Bost., 1837. Folio, half lea; worn, backstrip mostly lacking. With 6 plates & 6 hand-colored folding plates of the constellations. sg Apr 23 (166) $130

Bradford, Thomas Gamaliel, 1802-87
— A Comprehensive Atlas.... Bost. & NY, [1835]. 4to, disbound. With frontis, engraved title, 9 plates & 60 partly colored maps. pn Jan 22 (346) £280 [Whiteson]

Bradford, William, 1590-1657
— History of Plymouth Plantation 1620-1647. Bost.: Massachusetts Historical Society, 1912. 2 vols. 8vo, half cloth. sg Sept 18 (34) $100

Bradford, William, c.1779-1857
— Sketches of the Country, Character, and Costume in Portugal and Spain. L, 1809-10. 2 parts in 1 vol. 4to, orig cloth; worn. With frontis & 53 color plates. bba Dec 4 (293) £420 [Barker]
Anr copy. Modern cloth. With 52 hand-colored plates. Lacking frontis & French Dragoon plate. Blindstamps in corners of plates; tp & list of plates stamped "discards." Sold w.a.f. C Apr 8 (6) £400 [Armero]
Anr copy. Modern half mor. With frontis & 53 hand-colored plates. Separate title to supplement, with a loosely inserted pencil & gray wash sketch of Plate 20 inscr in pencil "Original." Some soiling; marginal tear in 1 leaf of text. Sold w.a.f. S June 25 (186) £700 [Colombo]
Anr Ed. L, 1809-10 [watermarked 1823-24]. 3 parts in 1 vol. 4to, contemp mor gilt; rubbed. With frontis & 53 hand-colored plates. Lacking 1 title; lacking 1 listed view but with 2 extra to list present. T Mar 19 (1) £400

Bradley, Edward, 1827-89
— Photographic Pleasures, Popularly Portrayed with Pen & Pencil. L, 1859. 8vo, loose in orig cloth; rubbed & frayed. With 70 caricatures. Minor marginal stains. T Feb 19 (455) £54

Bradley, John William, 1830-1916
— A Dictionary of Miniaturists, Illuminators, Calligraphers.... L, 1887-89. 3 vols. 8vo, half lea; scuffed, stain on Vol III. sg Feb 5 (47) $225

Bradley, Marion Zimmer
— The Brass Dragon. L: Methuen, [1978]. In d/j. cb Sept 28 (209) $50

Bradley, Martha
— The British Housewife. L, [c.1790]. 2 vols. 8vo, calf (Vol I) and half mor (Vol II); worn. sg Jan 15 (7) $250

Bradley, Omar N.
— A Soldier's Story. NY, [1951]. Inscr. wa May 30 (160) $70

Bradley, Richard, d.1732
— A Complete Body of Husbandry. L, 1727. 8vo, calf gilt. With 4 folding plates. pn Jan 22 (223) £80 [Fren]
— Dictionarium Botanicum. L, 1728. 2 vols. 8vo, contemp calf; rubbed. pn Jan 22 (224) £55 [Maggs]
— A General Treatise of Husbandry and Gardening. L, 1726. 2 vols. 8vo, contemp calf gilt; rubbed. With 17 plates. pn Jan 22 (225) £70 [Maggs]
— A Philosophical Account of the Works of Nature.... L, 1721. 4to, contemp calf; rebacked, worn, new endpapers. With 28 hand-colored plates. CNY Nov 21 (38) $350

Anr copy. Contemp calf gilt; joints cracked. pn Mar 5 (196) £180 [Maggs]
— Ten Practical Discourses Concerning Earth and Water, Fire and Air, as they Relate to the Growth of Plants. L, 1727. 1st Ed. 8vo, contemp calf. Some text browned. pn Jan 22 (226) £85 [Spelman]; pnE Dec 17 (181) £120 [Maggs]

Bradley, Will H.
[-] Boktryckeri Kalendern 1910. [Sweden, 1910]. 8vo, orig cloth; worn & shaken, spine torn. Inscr to Bradley by the Ed. O June 16 (46) $110

Bradshaw, Percy Venner
— The Art of the Illustrator. L, [1918]. 20 orig parts. Folio, unbound as issued in orig wraps. With mtd ports & plates. Ck Sept 5 (28) £65; Ck Apr 24 (183) £40

Bragg, Benjamin, Pseud.
— A Voyage to the North Pole. L, 1817. 12mo, contemp half calf; worn. O Sept 23 (86) $220

Bragg, Sir William Henry —& Bragg, Sir William Lawrence
X Rays and Crystal Structure. L, 1915. Spine faded, ends rubbed. sg Jan 15 (300) $150

Bragg, Sir William Lawrence. See: Bragg & Bragg

Braght, Tieleman Jans van
— Der blutige Schau-Platz.... Ephrata, 1748-49. 1st Ed. 2 vols in 1. Folio, contemp calf over bds; rebacked. With the 2 frontises. sg Mar 12 (18) $425

Brahe, Tycho, 1546-1601
— Astronomiae instauratae mechanica. Nuremberg, 1602. 2d Ed. Folio, contemp vellum; soiled. Some worming at beginning; tp worn. FD Dec 2 (433) DM2,500
— De mundi aetherei recentioribus phaenominis liber secundus. [Uraniborg, 1588] & Prague, 1603. 4to, contemp vellum; soiled, recased. Some browning & marginal dampstaining, minor marginal worming in some gatherings affecting c.6 characters; some ink corrosion to foot of tp from inscr. P Sept 24 (133) $6,700
— Historia coelestis. Augsburg, 1666. Folio, contemp vellum; spine damaged, cover & endleaves wormed. With 2 (of 3) plates; lacking port. sg Jan 15 (301) $850

Braine, John
— Room at the Top. L, 1957. 8vo, cloth, in d/j with chipped edges. sg Mar 5 (24) $50

Bramah, Ernest
— The Eyes of Max Carrados. L, 1923. In d/j. cb Nov 20 (11) $300
— Max Carrados Mysteries. L, [c.1927]. Bdg lightly soiled. Faint foxing to tp & prelims. cb Nov 20 (15) $50
— The Specimen Case. L, [1924]. In chipped d/j. cb Nov 20 (18) $70

Brancaccio, Lelio
— I Carichi Militari. Venice, 1620. 4to, old vellum. sg Mar 26 (47) $150

Brand...
— Brand Book II. [San Diego: San Diego Corral, 1971]. One of 500. Folio, cloth. cb Jan 8 (216) $60

Brand, Lieut. Charles
— Journal of a Voyage to Peru. L, 1828. 8vo, contemp half sheep; rebacked preserving contemp spine, rubbed. With 4 plates. Frontis repaired. bba Sept 25 (412) £95 [Morrell]

Brand, John, 1744-1806
— The History and Antiquities of the Town and County of Newcastle upon Tyne. L, 1789. 1st Ed. 2 vols. 4to, half calf gilt; rubbed. With port, 2 engraved titles, folding plan & 31 plates. pn Mar 5 (261) £130 [Minesen]
— Observations on Popular Antiquities.... L, 1813. 2 vols. 4to, contemp calf; joints worn, 1 cover loosening. Lacking half-titles. sg Sept 18 (35) $50

Brand Library, John

BRAND

— Bibliotheca Brandiana. A Catalogue of the...Library.... L, [1807]. 2 parts in 1 vol. 8vo, cloth. sg Jan 22 (38) $200

Brand, Max. See: Derrydale Press

Brandis, D. See: Stewart & Brandis

Brandt, Bill
— The English at Home. NY & L, 1936. 4to, bds; rubbed. S Mar 9 (727) £75 [Pack]
— Perspective of Nudes. NY, 1961. 4to, bds, in repaired d/j. sg Nov 13 (17) $100

Anr copy. Bds; in frayed d/j. sg May 7 (11) $130

Brandt, Herbert William
— Alaska Bird Trails. Adventures of an Expedition by Dog Sled.... Cleveland: Bird Research Foundation, 1943. Cloth, in torn, tape-repaired d/j. Inscr. wa Nov 6 (16) $70

Brandt, Johann Friedrich von, 1802-79 —& **Ratzeburg, J. T. C.**
— Medizinische Zoologie, oder Getreue Darstellung und Beschreibung der Thiere.... Berlin, 1829-33. 2 vols. 4to, contemp half lea; worn. Lacking 3 plates. HN May 20 (1064) DM1,200

Brangwyn, Frank, 1867-1956
— Ten Woodcuts. L, 1924. One of 270. 4to, half cloth; worn. wa Sept 25 (290) $170
— The Way of the Cross. L, [1935]. One of 250. With commentary by G. K. Chesterton. 4to, orig vellum gilt. With 14 plates. S Mar 9 (659) £120 [Thornton]

Brannon, George
— Vectis Scenery.... L, 1823. Oblong folio, later half calf. With 55 plates (26 called for), including a hand-colored aquatint. Tp soiled. S Nov 10 (771) £200 [Sampson]

Anr Ed. Wooton-Common, Isle of Wight, 1823. Oblong folio, bds; worn. With 26 plates. wd June 19 (70) $100

Anr Ed. L, [1837]. Oblong 8vo, contemp half lea; worn. With engraved title, map & 47 plates. S May 28 (843) £85

Brannon, Philip
— The Park and the Crystal Palace. L: Ackermann, 1851. Folio, old half mor gilt. With color title & 4 color plates heightened with hand-coloring One text leaf torn & repaired; 1 plate torn on lower margin; some soiling & slight staining. Extra-illus with 6 plates from McNevin's Souvenir of the Great Exhibition. pnNY Sept 13 (204) $550

Brant, Irving. See: Roosevelt's copy, Franklin D.

AMERICAN BOOK PRICES CURRENT

Brantome, Pierre de Bourdeille, Sieur de, 1535?-1614. See: Golden Cockerel Press

Braque, Georges, 1882-1963
— Carnets intimes. Paris, 1955. Folio, orig bds. Verve Nos 31/32. sg June 4 (340) $120
— The Intimate Sketchbooks. NY, 1955. Folio, orig bds; worn. Verve Nos 31/32. bba Oct 16 (329) £60 [Coultas]

Brasher, Rex, 1869-1960
— Birds and Trees of North America. Kent, Conn., 1929-32. Vol with Plates 289-348 only (of 12 vols). Pictorial Masonite with lea back & tips. sg Sept 18 (35) $225

Anr Ed. NY, 1961-62. 4 vols. Oblong folio, half mor. With 875 colored plates. pn Oct 23 (187) £170 [Greyfriars]

Brassai, Pseud. of Gyula Halsz
— Paris de nuit. Paris: Arts et Metiers Graphiques, 1933. Spiral bound pictorial wraps; rubbed. Some soiling of text. S May 6 (489) £85 [Fronlich]

Brassey, Annie, Baroness, 1839-87
— Tahiti: A Series of Photographs. L, 1882. 8vo, orig cloth. With 30 plates. S Apr 23 (372) £520 [Hitching]

Brassey, Thomas Allnutt Brassey, 2d Earl, 1863-1919
— Diary of a Hunting Trip, 1888. Battle, 1889. 8vo, ptd wraps; soiled. sg Oct 23 (199) $425

Brassington, William Salt
— Historic Bindings in the Bodleian Library. L, 1891. 4to, bdg not described. Perforated stamps on plates. bba Feb 5 (80) £60 [Zeitlin]
— A History of the Art of Bookbinding. L, 1894. 8vo, cloth. O June 16 (47) $200

Anr copy. Mor extra by J. H. Carrington. pn July 23 (106) £240 [Stone]

Brathwaite, Richard, 1588-1673
— The English Gentleman. L, 1630. 1st Ed. 4to, early vellum; soiled. With engraved title (frayed & soiled); folding explanation leaf bound in so that it cannot be unfolded. Lacking final leaf; small holes in margin of title; D2 torn without loss; rust-hole in Xx4 affecting only a few letters; some worming in inner margin; some marginal dampstaining. S Sept 23 (308) £180 [Vine]

2d Ed. L, 1633. 4to, contemp calf. Corner torn from engraved title slightly affecting plate. L July 2 (205) £200

3d Ed. L, 1641. Folio, contemp calf; worn. Contents leaf with 2 short tears; B4 torn without loss; a few small holes with little loss; some dampstains. S Sept 23 (307) £160 [McNaul]

Anr copy. Contemp calf; rebacked, knifescores to covers. Marginal dampstains & browning; some repairs; library markings. T Mar 19 (330) £200
— The English Gentlewoman Drawne Out to the Full Body.... L, 1631. 1st Ed. 4to, contemp vellum; some soiling. With engraved title & initial folding sheet. Small hole in engraved title & marginal tear; small tear in fold of leaf of explanation; some leaves dampstained. Evelyn copy. C Dec 12 (318) £550 [Thomas]
— A Survey of History: or, a Nursery for Gentry. L, 1638. 4to, contemp calf; rebacked. Engraved title lacking & supplied in facsimile; 1st & last 2 leaves holed or torn affecting borders. S Mar 10 (1031) £50 [Robertshaw]

Braun, A.
— Recueil de dessins servant de materiaux destines a l'usage des fabriques d'etoffes.... Paris, 1842. Folio, modern half mor. With 30 plates, 10 colored. Repaired; library stamp on title. S Feb 23 (660) £500 [Sims]

Braun, Johann
— Vestitus sacerdotum hebraeorum.... Amst., 1701. 2 vols in 1. 4to, contemp vellum. Marginal worming. CAM Dec 3 (50) HF480

Braun, Thomas
— L'An. Bruxelles, 1897. Illus by Frantz M. Melchers. 4to, vellum. With 16 color plates. B Oct 7 (26) HF580
Anr copy. Half lea. FD June 11 (5140) DM2,400

Braun-Ronsdorf, Margarete
— The History of the Handkerchief. Leigh-on-Sea, 1967. 4to, orig cloth, in d/j. Ck Oct 31 (35) £40

Braybrooke, Richard Griffin, Baron. See: Griffin, Richard

Braybroune, Wyndham W. Knatchbull-Hugesson, Baron —& Chubb, Charles
— The Birds of South America. L, 1913-17. Illus by H. Gronvold. 2 vols. 8vo & 4to, cloth & half-cloth portfolio. With 38 plates, hand-colored. B Feb 24 (289) HF1,300

Brayley, Edward Wedlake, 1773-1854
See also: Britton & Brayley
— Ancient Castles of England and Wales. L, 1825. 2 vols. 4to, half mor gilt. pn Jan 22 (167) £70 [Clegg]
Anr copy. Half calf; defective. With 2 engraved titles, 2 frontises & 104 plates. pn Jan 22 (171) £55
— The History and Antiquities of the Abbey Church of St. Peter, Westminster. L, 1818-23. L.p. copy. 2 vols. 4to, later half russia; rubbed. With engraved titles & 59 plates, most being proof impressions. L.p. copy. Ck May 15 (131) £60
— Londiniana; or Reminiscences of the British Metropolis. L, 1829. 4 vols. 8vo, contemp calf gilt; rebacked. cb June 4 (26) $140
— A Topographical History of Surrey. Dorking & L, 1850. 5 vols. 8vo, half calf gilt; 2 covers loose. pn Nov 20 (9) £110 [Traylen]
Anr copy. Orig cloth; worn, hinges reinforced. S May 28 (844) £180
Anr Ed. L, [1878-81]. ("History of Surrey ") 4 vols in 6. 4to. contemp half calf; rubbed. bba Apr 23 (357) £120 [Axe]

Brayley, Edward Wedlake, 1773-1854 —& Havell, Daniel
— Historical and Descriptive Accounts of the Theatres of London. L, 1826 [1827]. 4to, later half cloth; soiled & worn. Lacking 1 plate. wa Dec 11 (534) $650

Breasted, James Henry, 1865-1935
— The Edwin Smith Surgical Papyrus.... Chicago, 1930. 2 vols. 4to, bdg not given With 42 plates. cb Nov 6 (96) $170

Bree, Charles Robert, 1811-86
— A History of the Birds of Europe.... L, 1859-63. 4 vols. 8vo, half calf; restored. With 238 colored plates. pn Oct 23 (188) £220 [Paul]
Anr copy. Orig cloth; worn. With 237 (of 238) hand-colored plates. Marginal staining in Vol IV. Sold w.a.f. S Feb 24 (550) £170 [Elliott]
Anr copy. Vols I-III (of 4). 8vo, cloth. With 179 hand-colored plates. Some tears & repairs. S Feb 24 (551) £160 [Pavlov]
Anr Ed. L, 1863-67. 4 vols. 4to, modern cloth. With 238 hand-colored plates. S Nov 10 (452) £260 [Whittaker]
Anr copy. Orig cloth; marked. S May 28 (637) £250
Anr Ed. L, 1866-67. 2d Issue. 4 vols. 8vo, orig cloth; chipped. With 238 color plates, 1 detached. Ck Nov 21 (106) £300

Breen, Patrick, d.1868
— The Diary of.... San Francisco: Book Club of California, 1946. One of 300. Half cloth. cb Sept 11 (1) $140

Breeskin, Adelyn D.
— Mary Cassatt.... Wash., 1970. 4to, cloth, in d/j. S Nov 10 (229) £650 [Fontbrune]

BREHM

Brehm, Alfred Edmund, 1829-84
— Cassell's Book of Birds.... L, [1869-73]. 4 vols in 2. 4to, contemp half calf; rubbed. Ck June 5 (6) £140

Brehm, Alfred Edmund, 1829-84 —& Duemichen, Johannes
— Nilbilder...Naturaufnahmen Waehrend zweier Orientreisen 1862 und 1865. Wandsbeck, 1881. 4to, orig cloth; worn, spine def. With frontis map & 24 color plates mtd on card. Some staining & spotting; pp 37-40 with tears reparied with tape. S Oct 23 (371) £300 [Bonham]

Breitkopf, Johann Gottlob Immanuel
— Versuch den Ursprung der Spielkarten. Leipzig, 1784. Vol I. 4to, later bds; worn. With 12 folding plates. sg May 14 (517) $1,400

Breitner, George Hendrik
— Indrukken en biographische aanteekeningen van A. Pit, W. Steenhoff, J. Veth en W. Vogelsang. Amst., [1904-8]. One of 25. 4to, loose as issued in portfolio. B Feb 25 (1040) HF1,200

Bremer Press—Toelz, Munich, etc.
— Chansons d'Amour. 1921. One of 270. FD Dec 2 (4248) DM1,200
— Missale Romanum. 1928-32. In pigskin extra bdg by Ignatz Wiemeler. FD Dec 2 (4740a) DM26,000
— DANTE ALIGHIERI. - La Divinia commedia. 1921. One of 300. sg Dec 4 (25) $150
— EMERSON, RALPH WALDO. - Nature. [Munich: Bremer Press, 1929]. One of 250. Half vellum; soiled. sg Jan 8 (37) $70
— HOMER. - Ilias. Odysseia. 1923-24. One of 615. 2 vols. Orig vellum gilt. sg Dec 4 (26) $550
— SCHULTE-STRATHAUS, E. - Die echten Ausgaben von Goethes Faust. 1932. One of 85. sg May 14 (382) $175
— TIBULLUS ALBIUS. - Elegiae. 1920. One of 238. sg Jan 8 (38) $60

Brenchley, Julius L., 1816-73. See: Remy & Brenchley

Brennan, Joseph Payne
— Nightmare Need. Sauk City: Arkham House, 1964. One of 500. In d/j. cb Sept 28 (215) $65
— Nine Horrors and a Dream. Sauk City: Arkham House, 1958. One of 1,200. In d/j. cb Sept 28 (216) $80
— Scream at Midnight. New Haven: Macabre House, 1963. One of 250. cb Sept 28 (217) $180

AMERICAN BOOK PRICES CURRENT

Brerewood, Edward, 1565?-1613
— Enquiries touching the Diversity of Languages and Religions.... L, 1622. 4to, contemp vellum. Ck Jan 16 (150) £190

Breslauer, Bernard. See: Grolier Club

Bressani, Francesco Giuseppe, 1612-72
— Breve relatione d'alcune missioni.... Macerata, 1653. 4to, modern mor. Some browning & staining; wormed at beginning with slight loss of text & occasionally at lower blank margin elsewhere; B4 repaired. S Apr 24 (258) £2,500 [Maggs]

Breton, Andre, 1896-1966
— Le Chateau Etoile. Paris, [1936]. One of 55. Illus by Max Ernst. Folio, orig cloth. S June 29 (37) £4,800 [Bolligar]
— Le Surrealisme et la peinture. NY, 1945. 4to, orig cloth; rubbed. Inscr to Rene Magritte. S July 2 (992) £480 [Gekoski]

Breton, Andre, 1896-1966 —& Legrand, Gerard
— L'Art magique. Paris, 1957. 4to, orig cloth. With 64 plain & 16 colored plates. Inscr by both to Rene Magritte. S July 2 (993) £250 [Bowden]

Breton de la Martiniere, Jean Baptiste Joseph
— China: Its Costume, Arts, Manufactures.... L, 1812. 1st Ed in English. 4 vols in 2. 12mo, contemp mor gilt; rubbed. With 80 hand-colored plates. S July 14 (299) £280
Anr Ed. L, 1824. 4 vols in 2. 12mo, contemp mor gilt; rubbed. With 80 hand-colored plates. A few imprints shaved. S Nov 18 (930) £240 [Cavendish]
— La Chine en Miniature. Paris, 1811-12. 6 vols. 18mo, contemp mor gilt. With 108 hand-colored plates. Ck May 15 (33) £500
— Le Japon, ou moeurs, usages et costumes.... Paris, 1818. 4 vols. 12mo, contemp calf gilt. With 51 hand-colored plates. Ck May 15 (32) £400

Breton, Nicholas, 1545?-1626?
— The Twelve Monethes and Christmas Day. NY, 1951. Inscr by Bruce Rogers to Robert Gibbings & by Gibbings to Alex Hyman. bba Aug 20 (182) £110 [Deighton Bell]

342

1986 - 1987 · BOOKS

Breton, William Henry, d.1887
— Excursions in New South Wales, Western Australia, and Van Diemen's Land.... L, 1833. 8vo, orig cloth; rebacked. With hand-colored frontis & 1 plate; title & frontis browned. pnNY Sept 13 (205) $160
2d Ed. L, 1834. 8vo, modern half mor by Sangorski & Sutcliffe. Inscr erased from tp; marginal notes. kh Mar 16 (58) A$300

Brettschneider, R. von
— R. Franz von Bayros. Bibliographie s. Werke. Leipzig, 1926. 12mo, tape-rebacked bds. sg Jan 22 (76) $90

Breuil, Henri See: Cartailhac & Breuil

Breval, John Durant, 1680?-1738
— Remarks on Several Parts of Europe.... L, 1738. 2 vols in 1. Folio, contemp calf; worn & broken. T Jan 22 (271) £50

Breviarium
— 1608 [1606]. - Breviarium romanum. Paris 4to, contemp Parisian bdg a la fanfare of red mor gilt with central oval containing a coat-of-arms apparently replacing anr coat, the charges of which have been obliterated. S May 21 (96) £6,500 [Sourget]

Brevoort, James Carson, 1818-87
— Notes on Some Figures of Japanese Fish. [Wash.: Nicholson, 1856]. 4to, early half mor; worn. With 10 hand-colored lithos (1 stained). Extracted from Vol II of Perry's Narrative. wa Nov 6 (144) $70

Brewer, James Norris, fl.1799-1829
— The Beauties of Ireland. L, 1825-26. 2 vols. 8vo, modern cloth. With 24 plates, some stained. S Feb 24 (377) £100 [Beasly]

Breyn, Jakob
— Exoticarum aliarumque minus cognitarum plantarum centuria prima. Danzig, [1674]-78. Folio, contemp mor gilt by John Brindley. With engraved title & 101 plates. Some leaves including engraved title slightly discolored. Plesch—de Belder copy. S Apr 27 (43) £5,000 [Bjorck]
— Prodromi fasciculi rariorum plantarum primus et secundus.... Danzig, 1739. 4to, contemp half calf; worn. With port & 32 plates. Coward—de Belder copy. S Apr 27 (44) £1,300 [Robert]

Brice, Germain, 1652-1727
— Nouvelle description de la ville de Paris. Paris, 1725. 8th Ed. 4 vols, 12mo, contemp half mor; rubbed. With folding map & 37 folding views. Map torn without loss & repairs; 4 plates cropped with some loss of caption & plate-mark; some maps with tears or holes with slight loss. S July 14

BRIEFE...

(665) £120

Bricker, Charles
— Landmarks of Mapmaking. Amst., 1968. Folio, half cloth, in d/j. cba Feb 5 (169) $50
Anr copy. Cloth, in d/j. sg Jan 22 (97) $150
Anr copy. Cloth, in chipped d/j. sg Jan 22 (98) $70

Bridges, John, 1666-1724
— The History and Antiquities of Northamptonshire. Oxford, 1791 [i.e., 1762-91]. Compiled by Peter Whalley. 2 vols. Folio, contemp russia; Vol I rebacked, Vol II joints worn. Sold w a f Ck May 15 (139) £80

Bridges, Robert, 1844-1930. See: Gregynog Press

Bridges, Thomas, fl.1759-1775
— A Burlesque Translation of Homer. L, 1772. 8vo, contemp calf gilt; worn, joints cracked. cb Feb 19 (135) $75
4th Ed. L, 1797. 2 vols. 8vo, modern calf; backstrips brittle, joints rubbed. sg Sept 11 (36) $175

Bridgit, Saint, 1303?-73
— Revelations. [Luebeck]: Bartholomaeus Ghotan [for Wadstena Monastery, before 25 Nov], 1492. ("Epigramma libri presentis.") Folio, 18th-cent half calf. Long wormhole in 1st 6 leaves & round wormhole from 2g7 to the end affecting text; some wormholes in margins at the beginning & end, those at the beginning repaired; crude repairs in the lower margin of a1 & a12 with no damage to text; many lower or upper margins waterstained or dampstained; 2g10 wanting a blank portion of the upper margin. 422 leaves. Goff B-687. S May 21 (1) £1,800 [Dahlstorm]
Anr Ed. Nuremberg: F. Peypus for A. Koberger, 15 Nov 1517. ("Revelationes celestes.") Folio, contemp blindstamped lea. Some waterstaining. HK Nov 4 (607) DM2,600

Brief...
See also: Guatemala
— A Brief Description of the Province of Carolina.... L, 1666. 4to, half mor. Blank margin repaired; some stains. S June 25 (378) £12,000 [Robinson]

Briefe...
— A Briefe Relation of the Discovery and Plantation of New England. L, 1622. 4to, half mor. Imprint & fore-margin of tp cropped; 1 or 2 headlines shaved; short tear in D4 repaired without loss; small rust-hole in dedication leaves. S June 25 (400) £13,500 [Reese]

Brieger, Peter H. —& Others
— Illuminated Manuscripts of the Divine Comedy. L, 1970. 2 vols. 4to, cloth, in d/js. S Nov 10 (4) £60 [Green]

Brierly, Sir Oswald Walter, 1817-94
— The English & French Fleets in the Baltic, 1854. L: Day, 1854-55. Folio, contemp half mor, orig front wrap bound in as title. With 18 tinted & colored lithos on 15 plates, on thick paper. C Oct 15 (19) £4,000 [Marshall]

Briggs, Charles Frederick —& Maverick Augustus
— The Story of the Telegraph.... NY, 1858. 1st Ed. 8vo, orig cloth; soiled & worn. wa Nov 6 (91) $80

Briggs, L. Cabot. See: Derrydale Press

Brigham, Clarence Saunders
— History and Bibliography of American Newspapers, 1690-1820. Worcester, Mass., 1947. 2 vols. 4to, cloth. With Brigham's Additions & Corrections, 1961. sg Oct 2 (15) $150
— Paul Revere's Engravings. Worcester, Mass., 1954. 1st Ed. 4to, cloth, in worn d/j. With 77 plates. Pencil underscoring on several leaves. sg June 8 (51) $50

Brillat-Savarin, Jean Anthelme, 1755-1826
See also: Limited Editions Club
— Fisiologia del gusto. Mexico: Juan R. Navarro, 1852. 8vo, contemp half calf. Some foxing; 1 leaf of intro torn & repaired. Crahan copy. P Nov 25 (73) $450
— Physiologie du gout.... Paris, 1826. 1st Ed. 2 vols. 8vo, contemp half calf; joints repaired & rebreaking, spine heads renewed. Crahan copy. P Nov 25 (71) $1,700

Brimer, Ann E. See: Anderson & Brimer

Brincken, Juljusz, Baron, 1792-1846
— Memoire descriptif sur la Foret Imperiale de Bialowieza, en Lithuanie. Varsovie: N. Gluecksberg, 1828. 4to, mor gilt by Riviere. Jeanson copy. SM Feb 28 (92) FF11,000

Brinckman, Arthur
— The Rifle in Cashmere: A Narrative of Shooting Expeditions.... L, 1862. 8vo, orig cloth; worn, soiled & stained. wa Nov 6 (190) $160

Brinkley, Frank, 1841-1912
— Japan. Described and Illustrated by the Japanese. Bost. [1897-98]. Edition de Grand Luxe, One of 250. 10 vols. Folio, half cloth. With 60 hand-colored albumen photographs individually mtd on colored paper. Lacking 6 examples of orig Japanese artwork & 7 color reproductions of monuments of Japanese art. sg May 7 (49) $1,600
Memorial Ed. Bost. [1897]. One of 100. 10 vols. Folio, cloth over bds in Japanese manner. sg Nov 13 (66) $400
Anr Ed. Bost., [1897-98]. Orig 15 parts. Folio, pictorial wraps. sg May 7 (50) $350
— Oriental Series: Japan and China. L, 1903-4. Ltd Ed. 12 vols. Orig cloth. Ck Nov 7 (135) £200

Brinley, Francis
— Life of William T. Porter. NY, 1860. 12mo, cloth; worn. sg Oct 23 (434) $110

Brinley Library, George
— [Sale catalogue] Catalogue of the American Library.... Hartford, 1878-93. Parts I-V, plus Index. Together, 6 parts bound in 4 vols. 8vo, half mor, Index in wraps. sg May 14 (2) $325

Brion, Marcel
— Romantic Art. NY: McGraw-Hill, [1960]. Folio, cloth, in d/j. cb Mar 5 (31) $75

Briscoe, John
— A Discourse of Money. L, 1696. 8vo, 19th-cent half mor. C May 13 (119) £580 [Quaritch]

Brisson, Mathurin Jacques, 1723-1806
— Ornithologie.... Paris, 1760. 1st Ed. 7 vols in 6, including Supplement. 4to, contemp calf; rubbed, joints split. With engraved titles & 261 folding engraved plates, all but 7 hand-colored. Occasional light soiling. bba Dec 4 (253) £3,600 [Quaritch]

Bristol Chess Club
— Souvenir of the Bristol Chess Club. L, 1849. Compiled by Elijah Williams. Orig bds. pn Mar 26 (524) £45 [Caissa]

Britannicus, Probus. See: Johnson, Samuel

British...
— British Birds. An Illustrated Magazine Devoted to Birds on the British List. L, 1907-86. Vols 1-79. Lacking title & table to Vol 57. B Feb 24 (14) HF1,250
— British Chess Association: Transactions. L, 1868. Fol 1866 & 1867. Cloth. pn Mar 26 (33) £60 [Hoffman]
— The British Florist; or Lady's Journal of Horticulture. L, 1846. 6 vols. 8vo, orig cloth; rubbed. With 81 hand-colored plates. Titles foxed. CNY May 11 (7) $550
— British Hunts and Huntsmen.... L, 1908-11. 4 vols. Folio, orig half mor gilt; soiled. S Nov 10 (588) £90 [Head]
— The British Librarian: Exhibiting a Compendious Review.... L, 1738. Contemp

sheep; rubbed. cb Feb 5 (62) $110

British American Land Company
— Lands for Sale, in the Eastern Townships of Lower Canada.... [N.p., 1835]. 4 pp, with hand-colored map, 580mm by 430mm. S Apr 23 (253) £250 [Arader]

British Chess Magazine
— The British Chess Magazine. L, 1883. Vol 3. pn Mar 26 (144) £120 [Russell]

Vol 7. L, 1887. pn Mar 26 (145) £90 [Russell]

Vol 10. L, 1890. Half calf; scuffed. pn Mar 26 (147) £90 [Russell]

Vol 9. pn Mar 26 (148) £50 [Russell]

Vol 12. L, 1892. pn Mar 26 (149) £50 [Russell]

Vol 13. L, 1893. pn Mar 26 (150) £110 [Russell]

Vol 14. L, 1894. pn Mar 26 (151) £50 [Russell]

Vol 15. L, 1895. pn Mar 26 (152) £50 [Russell]

Vol 16. L, 1896. pn Mar 26 (153) £50 [Russell]

Vol 17. L, 1897. pn Mar 26 (154) £40 [Russell]

Vol 18. L, 1898. pn Mar 26 (155) £50 [Russell]

Vol 19. L, 1899. pn Mar 26 (156) £50 [Russell]

Vols 20-29 & Index for 1880-1930. L, 1900-9. pn Mar 26 (157) £280 [Russell]

Vols 30-39. L, 1910-19. pn Mar 26 (158) £280 [Russell]

Vols 40-49. L, 1920-29. pn Mar 26 (159) £140 [Russell]

Vols 50-59. L, 1930-39. pn Mar 26 (160) £160 [Russell]

Vols 60-69. L, 1940-49. pn Mar 26 (161) £240 [Russell]

Vols 70-79. L, 1950-59. pn Mar 26 (162) £100 [Russell]

Vols 80-103. L, 1960-83. pn Mar 26 (163) £180 [Russell]

British Museum—London
— The Book of the Dead. 1890. Ed by E. A. Wallis Budge. Folio, orig half mor; backstrip deficient. T Sept 18 (282) £50

Anr copy. Orig half mor; rubbed. With 37 colored double-page plates. Small ink stamp on tp. T Sept 18 (283) £45

Anr Ed. 1895. Folio, contemp half mor; worn. bba Sept 25 (361) £280 [Loman]

Anr copy. Contemp half mor; rubbed & scuffed at extremities; broken. cb Nov 6 (98) $55

Anr Ed. 1899. By E.A. Wallis Budge. Folio, contemp half mor; broken. bba Sept 25 (360) £45 [Museum Bookshop]

Anr Ed. 1913. Ed by E. A. Wallis Budge. 2 vols. With 37 colored double-page plates. pn Oct 23 (368c) £75 [Check]

— WARNER, SIR GEORGE FREDERIC. - Queen Mary's Psalter. 1912. 4to, orig half mor. bba Aug 28 (14) £90 [Fogg]

Catalogues
— Books, Manuscripts, Maps and Drawings...(Natural History). 1903-40. 8 vols, including the 3 vol Supplement. 4to, cloth, Supplement wraps bound in. sg Oct 2 (72) $850

Anr copy. 5 vols, without the 3 vol Supplement. 4to, cloth. sg May 14 (578) $200

Anr copy. 8 vols, including the 3 vol Supplement. 4to, orig cloth. sg May 14 (579) $900

— Books Printed in the XVth Century.... L, 1908-63. Vols I-IX. Folio, cloth & half cloth. sg May 14 (414) $1,100

— Collection of Birds' Eggs.... 1901-12. Compiled by E. W. Oates & S. G. Reid, with Vol V compiled by W. R. Ogilvie-Grant. 5 vols. B Feb 24 (225) HF425

— Engraved British Portraits.... 1908-25. Compiled by Freeman O'Donoghue & Henry M. Hake. 6 vols, including Supplements & Indexes. Orig cloth. bba Nov 13 (71) £320 [Howard]

— The Harleian Collection of Manuscripts. 1808-12. 4 vols. Folio, orig bds; worn. T Oct 16 (532) £95

— Irish Manuscripts.... 1926. Compiled by Standish Hayes O'Grady & Robin Flower. 2 vols. sg Jan 22 (79) $150

— Italian Drawings.... 1950. Compiled by A. W. Popham & P. Pouncey. 2 vols. HN May 20 (334) DM600

— Ivory Carvings of the Christian Era.... 1909. Compiled by O. M. Dalton. 4to, cloth. pn Sept 18 (248) £170 [Thorp]

— Lepidoptera Phalaenae. 1898-1914. Compiled by Sir George Francis Hampson. 14 vols, including Supplement. cb Nov 6 (193) $250

— Printed Books: 1881-1900, 1900-5. Ann Arbor, 1946-50. 68 vols. Cloth. Ck Nov 7 (2) £380

Anr copy. Library markings. O June 9 (30) $100

— Printing and the Mind of Man.... [1963]. wa Nov 6 (533) $140

— A Short Title Catalogue of French Books, 1601-1700.... Folkestone, 1973. Compiled by V. F. Goldsmith. 4to, cloth. sg Jan 22 (80) $110

Britton, John, 1771-1857
See also: Bourne & Britton
— The Architectural Antiquities of Great Britain. L, 1835. 5 vols. 4to, contemp half mor gilt; rubbed. Some stains. S May 28 (851) £170
— Bath and Bristol, with the Counties of Somerset and Gloucester.... L, 1829. Illus by T. H. Shepherd. 4to, contemp half calf; worn. With engraved title & 48 views on 24 plates, on india paper mtd. Some stains. S May 28 (849) £180
— The Beauties of Wiltshire.... L, 1801-25. 3 vols. 8vo, calf gilt; rubbed. With engraved titles, 27 plates & 1 folding map. S Nov 17 (774) £95 [Rankin]
— The Fine Arts of the English School.... L: Chiswick Press, 1812. 1st Ed. Folio, mor. With 23 plates. pn Dec 11 (183) £110 [Cavendish]
— The History and Antiquities of the Cathedral Church of Salisbury. L, 1814. 4to, old bds. O Oct 21 (34) $60
— The History and Description with Graphic Illustrations of Cassiobury Park. L, 1837. Ltd Ed. Folio, contemp half mor gilt; shaken & rubbed. With 21 views on 20 sheets. pn Jan 22 (56) £140 [Clegg]
— Picturesque Antiquities of the English Cities. L, 1830. 4to, contemp half calf. With 61 plates. C July 22 (33) £320

Anr copy. Contemp half calf. With 60 plates, some soiled. L.p. copy. Ck Nov 21 (347) £300

Anr copy. Contemp mor gilt; worn. With 60 plates, all but 1 in 2 states, on india paper, mtd. S May 28 (850) £300
— The Pleasures of Human Life. L, 1807. Illus by Thomas Rowlandson. 8vo, mor gilt by Riviere. With engraved title & 6 hand-colored plates. sg Feb 12 (261) $250

Britton, John, 1771-1857 —&
Brayley, Edward Wedlake, 1773-1854
— The Beauties of England and Wales.... L, 1801-18. 19 vols in 26, including Brewer's introductory vol. 8vo, contemp calf; covers detached, backstrips lacking, 1 vol in modern cloth. bba May 14 (39) £280 [Smith]

Anr copy. 18 vols in 25; without Brewer's Introduction. 8vo, calf gilt; worn, most spines detached, 1 lacking. Vol I, Part 1 without the plates; some plates wormed; many vols affected by damp causing staining & spotting. Sold w.a.f. L Dec 11 (100) £160

Anr copy. 19 vols in 26 including Barrer's Introduction. 8vo, contemp mor gilt; some bdgs rubbed. with 25 engraved titles, 59 hand-colored double-page maps, 1 folding map, 21 double-page plans & 713 plates. Marginal waterstaining to plates throughout. Sold w.a.f. S May 28 (848) £850
— Devonshire & Cornwall Illustrated. L, 1829-32. Orig parts 1-36. Orig wraps; soiled. With 2 engraved titles, 2 maps & 69 plates. Ck May 15 (130) £200

Anr Ed. L, 1832. 2 vols in 1. 4to, contemp half mor. With 2 engraved titles & 138 views on 69 leaves & 2 maps. Ck Nov 21 (454) £280

Anr copy. Half mor; rubbed. With 2 maps, 2 engraved titles & 138 engravings on 69 sheets. Some browning. pn Sept 18 (191) £190 [Walford]

Anr copy. 2 vols. 4to, mor gilt. With 2 engraved titles, 2 maps & 138 views on 69 sheets. pn Mar 5 (216) £190 [Nicholson]

Anr copy. 2 vols in 1. 4to, contemp russia gilt; worn. With engraved title, 2 maps & 133 views only (of 138) on 69 plates. With 1 plate repaired, anr with lower half missing. S May 28 (847) £160

Anr copy. Disbound. With engraved titles & 138 views on 69 leaves. Some dampstaining & foxing. T Feb 19 (323) £210

Britton, Nathaniel Lord, 1859-1934 —&
Brown, Addison
— An Illustrated Flora of the Northern United States.... NY, 1896-98. 1st Ed. 3 vols. 4to, cloth; shaken & shelf-worn, inner joints broken. O Oct 21 (35) $80

Britwell Court Library
— The Britwell Handlist, or Short-Title Catalogue.... L, 1933. 2 vols. 4to, cloth, unopened. sg Jan 22 (81) $100
— [Sale Catalogue] Catalogue...of the Renowned Library...the Property of S. R. Christie Miller. L, 1916-27. Parts 9-19 bound in 2 vols. Cloth. Sold w.a.f. pn Oct 23 (88) £75 [Forster]

Brivois, Jules, 1832-1920
— Bibliographie des ouvrages illustres du XIXe siecle.... Paris, 1883. One of 900. 8vo, half mor; front cover detached. sg May 14 (228) $50

Broadley, Alexander Meyrick
— Napoleon in Caricature 1795-1821. L, 1911. Ltd Ed. 2 vols. Folio, cloth; hinges cracked. sg Feb 10 (67) $100

Broadsides
— AMERICAN REVOLUTION. - Baltimore, December 30. Congress received the following Intelligence from the Council of Safety [1st ptd account of Washington's crossing of the Delaware]. Balt.: John Dunlap, 30 Dec 1776. Handbill, 231mm by 168mm. Margins unevenly trimmed. P May 13 (20)

$9,000
- AMERICAN REVOLUTION. - An Elegiac Poem Composed on the Never-to-be-Forgotten Terrible and Bloody Battle Fought at an Intrenchment on Bunker-Hill.... Salem: E. Russell, 1775. 495mm by 387mm. Framed. Some closed tears & small repairs at folds & elsewhere costing portions of c.20 words & several coffins. P May 13 (18) $11,000
- BATTLE OF PLATTSBURG. - 1814 - Noble Lads of Canada.... NY, 1814. 225mm by 230mm. With 15 satirical verses. S June 25 (375) £780
- CIVIL WAR, AMERICAN. - How the War Commenced, and How Near It Is Ended. NY, 1 Oct 1864. 17.75 by 11.75 inches. Frayed; some tears; several small holes in folds with loss of text. wa Sept 25 (431) $55
- DOUGLAS, STEPHEN A. 'Boy' Lost! Left Washington D.C., some time in July....Has an Idea that he is a Candidate for the Presidency.... [N.p., after July 1860]. Folio size. Repaired on verso. CNY Dec 19 (63) $1,700
- HOSMER, HEZEKIAH LORD. - Charge of Chief Justice Hosmer, to the Grand Jury of the First Judicial District, M.T., Delivered, December 5th, 1864. [Virginia, 1864]. 308mm by 193mm, folded & unbound as issued. sg Mar 12 (184) $400
- ITURBIDE, AGUSTIN. - Advertencia. Mexicanos. Hoy llegarah a la gran Mexico [announcing defeat of the Royalist forces that tried to overthrow him]. Mexico City: Imprenta Imperial, 6 Apr 1822. Folio. sg Sept 18 (138) $100

Brockedon, William, 1787-1854
- Illustrations of the Passes of the Alps.... L, 1828-29. 2 vols. 4to, modern cloth. Library stamps. bba Feb 5 (366) £160 [Mandell]
Anr copy. Old half mor gilt; 1 cover detached, hinges rubbed. With 109 plates & maps. 1 plate with tear on margin. pnNY Oct 16 (13) $300
Anr copy. Contemp mor gilt. With 96 plates & 13 maps. Blindstamps in lower margins. S May 28 (852) £430
Anr copy. Contemp half lea by A. Macomie; rubbed. With 109 plates, including 12 divisional titles with vignettes & 12 maps. S July 14 (666) £350
Anr copy. Contemp mor gilt. With 109 plates & maps. Embossed stamp in margin of plates. With 3 A Ls s laid in. sg Dec 4 (27) $1,100

Brodrick, William
See also: Salvin & Brodrick
- Falconers' Favourites. L, 1865. Folio, orig cloth. With 6 hand-finished colored plates. Schwerdt-Jeanson copy. SM Feb 28 (93) FF17,000

Broinowski, Gracius J.
- The Cockatoos and Nestors of Australia and New Zealand. L, 1888. Folio, mor gilt. With 13 colored plates. kh Mar 16 (61) A$100

Brome, James
- Travels over England, Scotland and Wales. L, 1707. 2d Ed. 8vo, modern half calf. bba Nov 13 (138) £60 [Hannas]

Bromhall, Thomas
- A Treatise of Specters.... L, 1658. Folio, later calf; loose, rubbed. Stained. S May 29 (1157) £140

Bromley, George W. —& Walter, S.
- Atlas of the City of New York.... Phila.: G. W. Bromley, 1911. Folio, half lea; worn & broken. With 50 double-page maps with principal areas fully hand-colored. Maps linen backed. og Nov 20 (184) $175

Bromley, Henry
- A Catalogue of Engraved British Portraits. L, 1793. 1st Ed. 4to, contemp half mor; rubbed, partially split at base of front hinge. T Oct 16 (570) £40

Bronte, Charlotte, 1816-55
- Jane Eyre. L, 1847. 1st Ed. 3 vols. 8vo, orig cloth; rubbed. Without the inset fly-title for catalogue and the inset ad leaf for the Calcutta Review; some gatherings loose. S Dec 18 (35) £3,800 [Quaritch]
- The Professor. L, 1857. 1st Ed. 2 vols. 8vo, orig half cloth; rubbed. O8 of Vol I torn & def in upper corner with slight loss of text. bba Oct 16 (129) £200 [Pickering & Chatto]
Anr copy. Contemp calf gilt; rebacked. pnNY Sept 13 (206) $150
- Shirley. L, 1849. 1st Ed. 3 vols. 8vo, modern mor; worn. With ads dated Oct 1849 in Vol I. O Nov 18 (34) $220
Anr copy. Orig cloth; chipped & torn. S July 13 (88) £160
- Villette. L, 1853. 1st Ed. 3 vols. 8vo, orig cloth gilt; spines faded, a few hinges shaky. pnNY Sept 13 (207) $600

Bronte, Charlotte, Emily & Anne
- Works. Edin., 1911. 12 vols. Orig cloth. T Apr 16 (276) £60
Thornton Ed. Edin., 1924. Ed by Temple Scott. 12 vols. Calf by Zaehnsdorf. sg Sept 11 (39) $475

BRONTE

Anr Ed. Oxford: Shakespeare Head Press, 1931-38. 19 (of 20) vols; lacking Bibliography vol. S June 18 (350) £60 [Kemyusha]

Bronte, Emily, 1818-48
— Wuthering Heights. NY, 1931. One of 450, sgd by the artist. Illus by Clare Leighton. 4to, cloth. cb Dec 4 (263) $80

Brooke, Sir Arthur de Capell
— A Winter in Lapland and Sweden.... L, 1827. 4to, cloth; soiled. With frontis, map & 21 plates; some spotting. bba Dec 18 (119) £100 [Damms]
— Winter Sketches in Lapland. L, 1826. 1st Ed. 4to, orig bds; rebacked, rubbed. With 24 plates on india paper. S Oct 23 (244) £850 [Germundson]

Brooke, Frances, 1724-89
— The History of Emily Montague. L, 1769. 4 vols. 12mo, contemp calf gilt. sg Sept 18 (186) $600

Brooke, Sir James, Rajah of Sarawak, 1803-68
— Narrative of Events in Borneo and Celebes.... L, 1848. 1st Ed. Ed by Capt. Rodney Mundy. 2 vols. 8vo, orig cloth. With port, 17 plates & 5 charts. pn Oct 23 (16) £240 [Cavendish]

Brooke, Ralph, 1553-1625
— A Catalogue and Succession of the Kings, Princes...of England.... L, 1619. Folio, contemp calf; spine worn. Marginal stains; tp border just shaved. bba Aug 28 (167) £85 [Bennett & Kerr]

Brooke, Sir Robert
— Le Liver des Assises & Plees del Corone. L: Richard Tottell, 1580. Folio, old calf; worn. Outer margins of tp & other leaves crumbled or affected by damp; last leaf torn with loss. Ck Sept 5 (173) £80

Brookes, Richard
See also: Fore-Edge Paintings
— A New and Accurate System of Natural History. L, 1763. 6 vols. 12mo, contemp calf. With 146 plates. Some tears. S Nov 10 (455) £160 [Shapero]
Anr copy. Contemp calf; spines rubbed. Some plates cropped. S Nov 10 (456) £150 [Scott]

Brookes, Samuel
— An Introduction to the Study of Conchology. L, 1815. Folio, bds; def. With 2 plain & 9 hand-colored plates. pn June 18 (42) £150 [Dixon]

AMERICAN BOOK PRICES CURRENT

Brooks, Catherine
— The Complete English Cook; or Prudent Housewife.... L: Ptd for the Authoress & sold by J. Cooke, [c.1770]. 12mo, disbound. Tp soiled. Hunt copy. CNY Nov 21 (64) $420

Brookshaw, George
— Pomona Britannica. L, [1804]-12. 1st Ed in Book form. Folio, contemp mor gilt; joints worn. With 90 colored plates, finished by hand. Linnean Society—de Belder copy. S Apr 27 (46) £62,000 [Heywood Hill]
Anr Ed. L, 1812. 4to, contemp mor gilt; edges rubbed, minor abrasions on sides. With 90 hand-finished colored plates, some watermarked 1810-16. A few plates unnumbered; 1 plate of strawberries splitting at plate mark & strengthened on verso. C Oct 15 (214) £58,000 [Ursus]

Brosses, Charles de, 1709-77
— Traite de la formation mecanique des langues.... Paris, 1765. 12mo, contemp calf gilt; rubbed. With 9 plates. S June 25 (91) £300

Brotherhead, William
— The Book of Signers.... Phila., [1872]. ("The Centennial Book of the Signers.") Folio, unbound in wraps; chipped. cb Dec 18 (222) $100
— The Book of the Signers.... Phila., 1861. 1st Ed. Folio, half mor. ha Dec 19 (117) $50

Brouaut, Jean
— Traite de l'eau de vie.... Paris: Jacques de Senlecque, 1646. 1st Ed. 4to, contemp vellum; soiled, upper hinge cracked. Some browning & marginal staining. Crahan copy. P Nov 25 (79) $500

Brough, Robert Barnabas, 1828-60
— The Life of Sir John Falstaff. L, 1858. Illus by George Cruikshank. 8vo, mor gilt by Sangorski & Sutcliffe. With 20 plates. sg Feb 12 (30) $275

Broughton, Hugh, 1549-1612
— A Concent of Scripture. L: G. Simpson & W. White, [1590]. 4to, calf. With engraved title & 5 engraved plates; lacking folding map. ha Dec 19 (290) $65

Broughton, William Robert, 1762-1821
— Voyage de decouvertes dans la partie septentrionale de l'ocean Pacifique. Paris, 1807. 2 vols. 8vo, contemp half mor, spines with gilt monogram of Napoleon I. Vol II with blue ink stain to margins of about half the leaves. cb Apr 2 (40) $450
— A Voyage of Discovery to the North Pacific Ocean. L, 1804. 1st Ed. 4to, contemp half cloth; broken & worn. Some fraying; small fold splits to 1 map. cb Mar 19 (39) $1,300

Anr copy. Contemp calf; rebacked. With 9 plates & maps, 2 misbound. S Apr 24 (373) £2,200 [Perrin]

Brown, Abbie Farwell, d.1927

— The Lonesomest Doll. Bost., [1928]. Illus by Arthur Rackham. 4to, cloth. With 3 plates. Library stamps. sg Oct 30 (35) $140

Brown, Addison. See: Britton & Brown

Brown, C.

— A Narrative of the Expedition to South America.... L, 1819. 8vo, later half calf; rubbed, upper joint split. Lacking half-title; some browning. bba Apr 9 (421) £280 [Maggs]

Brown, Edward, M. D.

— A Brief Account of Some Travels.... L, 1685. Folio, contemp calf; rebacked. Some foxing. pnE Jan 28 (60) £350 [Martin]

Anr copy. Contemp calf; rubbed, split in joint. A few plates with short tears; small rust-hole in O3 affecting a few letters; last few leaves dampstained. S Feb 23 (67) £200 [Kiefer]

Brown, Eleanor & Bob

— Culinary Americana. NY, [1961]. In d/j. sg Jan 15 (9) $100

Brown, Frederic

— Angels and Spaceships. NY, 1954. In d/j. cb Sept 28 (220) $90

— Martians, Go Home. NY, 1955. In repaired d/j. cb Sept 28 (223) $90; cb May 7 (322) $50

— Mitkey Astromouse. NY: Harlan Quist, [1971]. Illus by Helen Edelmann. Currey's B bdg, in bumped d/j. cb Sept 28 (222) $55

Brown, Henry Collins

— The Lordly Hudson. NY, [1937]. One of 920. Folio, cloth. sg Mar 12 (193) $130

Out-of-series copy, but sgd. Orig cloth; soiled & worn. wa Nov 6 (440) $85

Brown, James. See: Lizars & Brown

Brown, James S.

— California Gold...History of the First Find.... Oakland, 1894. 12mo, orig wraps; splitting along spine. cb Oct 9 (27) $170; sg Mar 12 (19) $150

Brown, John, 1827-63

— Chess Strategy: a Collection of the Most Beautiful Chess Problems. L, 1865. Cloth. With ALs of H. Staunton inserted. pn Mar 26 (279) £45 [Farmer]

Brown Library, John Carter

— Bibliotheca Americana. Providence, 1875-82. One of 100. 2 vols. 4to, cloth; Vol I, worn, rebacked retaining orig backstrip. Leaves loose. sg Oct 2 (173) $150

Anr Ed. Providence, 1919-31. 5 vols. 4to, cloth; spine ends frayed. sg May 14 (3) $225

Anr Ed. NY, 1975-63 & Providence, 1973. 7 vols. 4to, cloth. O June 16 (48) $310

Brown, John ("Estimate Brown"), 1715-66

— An Estimate of the Manners and Principles of the Times. L, 1757. 8vo, contemp calf gilt; rubbed. bba Apr 23 (187) £33 [Frost]

Brown, John J.

— The American Angler's Guide.... NY, 1845. 1st Ed. 12mo, cloth. sg Oct 23 (201) $475

2d Ed. NY, 1846. 12mo, cloth; spine worn. Title & a few pp foxed. sg Oct 23 (202) $90

Brown, Leslie —&
Amadon, Dean

— Eagles, Hawks and Falcons of the World. [NY, 1968]. 2 vols. 4to, orig cloth. sg Jan 15 (189) $100

Brown, Louise Norton

— Block Printing & Book Illustration in Japan. L & NY, 1924. Folio, orig half cloth; rubbed. bba Oct 16 (410) £220 [Robertshaw]

Brown, Margaret Read

— The Wild Flowers of Southern and Western India. Brussels, [1868]. Folio, later half mor. With 15 hand-finished color plates. Lacking 1 leaf of text; 1 text leaf torn & repaired; anr torn at outer blank margin; some spotting & browning. de Belder copy. S Apr 27 (48) £3,200 [Brittain]

Brown, Paul. See: Derrydale Press

Brown, Robert, 1773-1858

— A Brief Account of Microscopical Observations...Active Molecules in Organic and Inorganic Bodies* Additional Remarks on Active Molecules. L, [1828-29]. 2 vols. 8vo, contemp half russia; spines worn. In: The Philosophical Magazine, New Series, Vol IV, pp 161-73 & Vol VI, pp 161-66. S Nov 10 (457) £400 [Phillips]

— Vermischte Botanische Schriften. Schmalkalden or Nuremberg, 1825-34. 5 vols. 8vo, cloth. bba Oct 16 (271) £260 [Maggs]

Brown, Rosel George. See: Laumer & Brown

Brown, Samuel R., 1775-1817
— Views of the Campaigns of the North-Western Army.... Phila., 1815. 12mo, later half calf. Several leaves repaired, including frontis & tp; text dampstained. sg Sept 18 (300) $50
— The Western Gazetteer, or Emigrant's Directory.... Auburn, 1817. 8vo, recent cloth. ha Sept 19 (150) $55

Brown, Solyman, 1790-1876
— Dentologia: A Poem on the Diseases of the Teeth.... NY: Peabody & Co., 1833. 8vo, orig cloth; worn, front hinge cracked. sg Jan 15 (80) $200

Brown, Capt. Thomas
— Illustrations of the Fossil Conchology of Great Britain and Ireland. L, 1849. 4to, half mor; rubbed & scuffed. With 116 hand-colored plates. sg Jan 15 (190) $110

Brown, William Francis
— Retriever Gun Dogs. West Hartford VT: Countryman Press, 1945. Out-of-series copy. sg Oct 23 (204) $70

Brown, William Henry, 1808-83
— Portrait Gallery of Distinguished American Citizens.... NY, 1931. One of 600. Folio, cloth. Facsimile of the Hartford 1845 Ed. O Feb 24 (31) $130

Brown, William Henry, 1836-1910
— The History of the First Locomotives in America. NY, 1871. 8vo, cloth. Inscr. O Mar 24 (33) $80

Anr copy. Cloth; worn, soiled. With 10 plates (6 folding). Last few pp waterstained. wa Nov 6 (69) $180

Brown, William Robinson. See: Derrydale Press

Browne, Belmore
— The Conquest of Mount McKinley. NY & L, 1913. O Oct 21 (36) $90

Browne, Edward, 1644-1708
— An Account of Several Travels through a Great Part of Germany. L, 1677. 1st Ed. 4to, new cloth. With 6 plates, some double-page. Small tear in blank margin of plate of St. Stephen. S May 28 (640) £120
— A Brief Account of Some Travels in Hungaria, Austria.... L, 1673. 4to, contemp calf; rebacked. With 9 plates. Lacking 1st blank. S May 28 (639) £170
— A Brief Account of some Travels in Divers Parts of Europe. L, 1687. 2d Ed. Folio, new cloth. Hole in blank portion of tp mended; stain in inner upper corner of following leaf in K2 & T3. S May 28 (638) £240

Browne, Irving, 1835-99
— Ballads of a Book-Worm. East Aurora: Roycrofters, 1899. One of 850. 8vo, bds, unopened. sg Jan 8 (252) $60

Browne, J. Vincent. See: King & Browne

Browne, James, 1793-1841
— A History of the Highlands and of the Highland Clans. Edin.: Fullarton, [1851-52]. 4 vols. 8vo, orig cloth; worn, hole in 1 spine. O Feb 24 (32) $150

Browne, Maggie, Pseud. of Margaret Hamer Andrewes
— The Book of Betty Barber. L, [1910]. Illus by Arthur Rackham. 4to, orig cloth; worn. With 6 color plates. sg Oct 30 (37) $300
— The Surprising Adventures of Tuppy and Tue. L, 1904. Illus by Arthur Rackham. Half mor. With 4 color plates. sg Oct 30 (36) $475

Browne, Nina E. See: Lane & Browne

Browne, Richard, fl.1674-94
— Medicina musica; or, a Mechanical Essay on the Effects of Singing.... L, 1729. 8vo, contemp calf; rubbed, joints split. Ck Apr 24 (72) £260

Browne, Sir Thomas, 1605-82
— Certain Miscellany Tracts. L, 1684. 1st Ed. Issue not given. 8vo, contemp calf; worn. pn Jan 22 (2) £110 [Cavendish]
— Christian Morals.... L, 1756. 2d Ed. 8vo, contemp calf; broken. S Nov 10 (364) £40 [Burmester]
— Posthumous Works. L, 1712. 1st Ed. 8vo, orig calf. With port & 22 plates. pnE Jan 28 (86) £340 [Maggs]
— Pseudodoxia Epidemica.... L, 1646. 1st Ed. Folio, contemp calf; joints cracked, spine ends restored. Minor worming in upper inner covers. sg Mar 26 (49) $275

2d Ed. L, 1650. Folio, new calf. Hole in R4; marginal tears in L3 & O3. S Nov 10 (458) £90 [Bookroom]

4th Ed. L, 1658. Folio, later half calf. sg Oct 9 (136) $175

5th Ed. L, 1669. 4to, later half calf; worn, upper cover detached. With 2 plates. Lacking initial blank; 1 corner torn. S Sept 22 (163) £95 [Laws]

Anr copy. Bdg not described but loose & spine missing. SSA Feb 11 (470) R200
— Religio Medici.... L, 1669. 3 parts in 1 vol. 8vo, contemp sheep; spine worn, rubbed. Some headlines cropped close. bba Mar 26 (162) £50 [Parsons]
— Works. L, 1686. Folio, later half calf; worn. Port laid down. Ck Jan 30 (27) £110
Anr copy. Calf; rebacked. pnE Jan 28 (87) £280 [Thin]

Anr Ed. L, 1846. 4 vols. 8vo, later mor gilt; soiled. cb Feb 19 (43) $55

Browne, William George
— Travels in Africa, Egypt and Syria.... L, 1799. 1st Ed. 4to, contemp lea gilt. Some browning & spotting. FD Dec 2 (1029) DM1,200

2d Ed. L, 1806. 4to, half lea; worn. With frontis & 4 plates, 3 folding; some mildew & dampstaining affecting plates. sg Nov 20 (32) $60

Browning, Elizabeth Barrett, 1806-61
See also: Limited Editions Club
— Letters to Robert Browning and Other Correspondents. L: for Thomas J. Wise, 1916. One of 30. 8vo, half mor by Riviere, orig ptd wraps bound in. Clement Shorter's copy. S July 23 (39) £300 [Gotlieb]
— Poetical Works. L, 1889-90. 6 vols, 8vo, half mor by Bayntun. sg Sept 11 (40) $175
— Sonnets from the Portuguese. [Bost.: Copeland & Day], 1896. Ltd Ed with illusts hand-colored. Illuminated by Emilie Marthecia Whitten. 8vo, orig bds, in d/j. sg June 11 (76) $425

Anr Ed. San Francisco, 1927. One of 250. 2 vols, including facsimile. Folio & 8vo, half vellum & wraps. cb Sept 11 (190) $180

Browning, Robert, 1812-89
See also: Doves Press; Eragny Press; Limited Editions Club
— Bishop Blougram's Apology. L, 1931. Ltd Ed. Orig cloth, in d/j. cb Dec 4 (107) $60
— Dramatic Romances and Lyrics. L: Vale Press, 1899. One of 210. Illus by Charles Ricketts. 8vo, mor gilt with central medallion in red, yellow & orange inlays, vellum doublures. pn Nov 20 (80) £680 [George]
— Evelyn Hope. Phila.: Pvtly ptd, 1922. One of 12 hand-illuminated by J. S. & with 11 orig watercolor vignettes. 4to, cloth. ha Dec 19 (163) $500
— Last Ride, East Aurora, NY: Roycroft Shop, 1900. Ltd Ed. Vellum. sg Jan 8 (253) $225
— The Pied Piper of Hamelin. L, etc.: Routledge, [1888]. Illus by Kate Greenaway. 4to, orig half cloth; corners bumped. O Oct 21 (74) $90

Anr Ed. L, [1934]. Illus by Arthur Rackham. Wraps, in d/j. With 4 color plates. sg Oct 30 (39) $150

One of 410, sgd by Rackham. Vellum; soiled & rubbed. sg Oct 30 (38) $650

Anr Ed. Phila., [1934]. Cloth, in d/j. With 4 color plates. sg Oct 30 (40) $110
— Rabbi Ben Ezra. Hingham, Mass., 1904. One of 160. Bds; spine worn. sg Jan 8

(286) $60
— The Ring and the Book. L, 1868-69. 1st Ed. 4 vols. 8vo, orig cloth; rubbed. bba Oct 30 (21) £50 [Bickersteth]; pn Nov 20 (91) £85 [Jarndyce]
— Sordello. L, 1840. 1st Ed. 12mo, orig cloth; rubbed. bba Dec 4 (98) £170 [Hannas]
— Works. L, 1888-94. ("The Poetical Works.") 17 vols plus the 1914 New Poems by Robert & E. B. Browning. 8vo, mor gilt. sg Sept 11 (41) $400

Centenary Ed. L, 1912. one of 526. 10 vols. pnE Oct 15 (228) £150

Browning, Robert & Elizabeth Barrett
— Works. NY: Society of English & French Literature, [1898]. One of 1,000. Ed by Charlotte Porter & Helen Clarke. 18 vols. Half mor; some soiling. wa Sept 25 (2) $180

Bruccoli, Matthew J.
— First Printings of American Authors. Detroit: Gale, [1977-79]. 4 vols. 4to, cloth; worn. K June 7 (135) $250

Bruce, Sir James, 1730-94
— Travels to Discover the Source of the Nile. Edin., 1790. 1st Ed. 5 vols. 4to, contemp calf. Ck May 8 (355) £520

Anr copy. Contemp calf gilt. With 3 folding maps & 58 plates. Library markings; maps with a few short marginal tears; some plates with imprint or edge of image shaved. P Sept 24 (134) $750

Anr Ed. Dublin, 1790-91. 6 vols. 4to, contemp calf; rubbed. Ck May 8 (316) £700

Anr Ed. L, 1790. 8 vols. 12mo, contemp calf; worn, broken. With 3 folding maps & 58 plates. Some spotting. Ck Sept 26 (53) £240

Anr copy. Contemp calf gilt; spine worn, loose. With 3 folding maps & 59 plates. SSA Feb 11 (472) R800

2d Ed. Edin., 1804-5. 8 vols, including Atlas. 8vo & 4to, contemp half calf. With 3 folding maps & 79 engraved plates. Ck Nov 7 (142) £250

Anr copy. 8 vols. 8vo, contemp half russia gilt. With 3 frontises & with 3 folding maps & 79 plates in Atlas. C Dec 12 (33) £300 [Traylen]

3d Ed. Edin., 1813. Atlas only. 4to, contemp calf; worn. With 82 plates & maps. FD Dec 2 (1030) DM1,100

Bruce, Miner W.
— Alaska: Its History and Resources.... Seattle, 1895. Orig cloth; soiled. With large colored folding map inserted in rear pocket. Minor fold breaks. cb Jan 8 (3) $80

Bruehl, Anton
— Photographs of Mexico. NY, [1933]. One of 1,000. Folio, orig half mor. Ck Oct 31 (54) £60
   Anr copy. Half lea; worn. Sgd. O Jan 6 (34) $200

Bruel, Francois Louis
— Histoire aeronautique par les monuments.... Paris, 1909. One of 325. 4to, orig wraps; stitching def. C Dec 3 (8) £950 [Tunick]

Bruff, Joseph Goldsborough
— Gold Rush. NY, 1944. 4to, orig half cloth. wa Sept 25 (335) $180

Bruguiere, Francis
See also: Sieveking, Lancelot de Giberne
— Beyond This Point. L: Duckworth [c.1935]. 4to, cloth. With 23 plates. sg Nov 13 (19) $100
— San Francisco. San Francisco, 1918. Bds with mtd photographic reproduction; broken. sg May 7 (14) $80

Bruin, Cornelis de. See: Le Brun, Cornelius

Brunet, Gustave, 1807-96
— Imprimeurs imaginaires et libraires supposes. Paris, 1866. 8vo, half mor; head of spine chipped. sg May 14 (280) $225
— La Reliure ancienne et moderne. Paris, 1878. 8vo, contemp half lea; extremities worn. Old stamps on titles; light dampstaining in upper inner corners throughout. sg May 14 (96) $350

Brunet, Jacques Charles, 1780-1867
— Manuel du libraire et de l'amateur de livres. Paris, 1814. 2d Ed. 7 vols, including 1834 Supplement in 3 vols. 8vo, contemp half calf; joints split, Supplement crudely rebacked. bba Apr 23 (10) £110 [Cooper]
   3d Ed. Paris, 1820. 4 vols. 8vo, vellum; spines soiled. bba Sept 25 (359) £60 [Clark]
   Anr Ed. Paris, 1842-44. 5 vols. 8vo, contemp half lea. sg Jan 22 (82) $110
   Anr copy. Needs rebdg. sg Jan 22 (83) $50
   Anr Ed. Paris, 1860-65. 6 vols plus 2-vol Supplement of 1878-80. 8vo, orig half mor; rubbed. bba Oct 16 (368) £300 [Frew Mackenzie]
   Anr copy. 8 vols, including 1878-80 Supplement. 8vo, half mor. C Dec 3 (11) £450 [Maggs]
   Anr copy. Half mor; not uniform. C Dec 3 (11) £450 [Maggs]
   Anr copy. 6 vols plus Supplement of 1878. 8vo, bdg not indicated. Library markings. Sold w.a.f. Franklin Institute copy. F Sept 12 (57) $180
   Anr copy. 6 vols. Half lea; rebacked, retaining orig backstrips; worn. sg Oct 2 (74) $130
   Anr copy. 6 vols plus supplement in 2 vols & Deschamps, Dictionnaire de Geographie. Together, 9 vols. 8vo, half lea; not uniform. sg May 14 (281) $600
   Anr Ed. Berlin, 1922. 6 vols. 8vo, half mor; rubbed. Ms index by E. J. Dingwall inserted. bba Mar 12 (329) £260 [Orssich]
   Anr Ed. Copenhagen, 1966-68. 9 vols. Reprint of the Paris 1860-80 Ed. Ck Nov 7 (1) £300

Brunet y Bellet, Jose, 1818-1905
— El Ajedrez investigaciones sobre su Origen. Barcelona, 1890. Modern cloth. pn Mar 26 (367) £85 [Wild]

Bruni, Leonardo, Aretinus, 1369-1444
— Historia fiorentina. Florence: Bartolommeo di Libri, 5 June 1492. ("Le Historie Eiorentine.") Bound with: Poggius Florentinus. Historia Fiorentina. Florence: Bartolommeo di Libri, 1492. Folio, 18th-cent vellum. Bruni title & 1st index-leaf restored extensively with some text on the index-leaf in good facsimile; some stains; early marginalia; some worming costing parts of 1 or 2 letters per page. 222 & 116 leaves. Goff B-1248 & P-874. P Sept 24 (135) $1,300

Brunner, John
— Stand on Zanzibar. Garden City, 1968. In d/j. cb Sept 28 (235) $65

Bruns, Henry P.
— Angling Books of the Americas. Atlanta, 1975. One of 500. 4to, cloth. sg Oct 23 (205) $350

Brunschwig, Hieronymus, c.1450-c.1512
— Liber de arte distulandi simplicia et composita. Das new Buech d'rechten Kunst zu Distillieren. Strassburg: J. Grueninger, 1505. ("Medicinarius Das Buch der Gesundheit. Liber de arte distilandi....") Folio, contemp blind-stamped pigskin; worn, rebacked with orig spine preserved, lacking clasps. About a dozen leaves torn & repaired, affecting text; marginal tears & repairs; soiled throughout; contemp marginalia; 2 later leaves at beginning; 94-leaf-contemp German Ms bound in at end; ff. I & X supplied in facsimile; lacking the Ficino & the Konrad. Crahan copy. P Nov 25 (82) $1,600

Brunus Aretinus, Leonardus. See: Bruni, Leonardo·fAretinus

Brush, Charles Francis
— Collection of Original U. S. Patents, relating to Electrical Machinery.... Wash., 1878-94. Bound in 1 vol. Folio, bdg not described. Franklin Institute copy. F Sept 12 (334) $400

Brusselsche...
— Brusselsche Eer-Triumphen; das ist, eene waerachtighe beschrijvinghe van de Hertoghlijcke Huldinghen.... Brussels: Pieter de Dobbeleer, [n.d.]. Bound with: Petrus de Cafmeyer. Hooghweerdighe Historie van het Alder-Heylighste Sacrament van Mirakel. Brussels, 1735. Folio, contemp calf, worn, joints cracked. With engraved title & 10 plates in 1st work & frontis & 51 plates in 2d work. sg Apr 2 (34) $850

Bruto, Stephano Junio. See: Languet, Hubert

Brutus, Stephanus Junius (Pseud.). See: Languet, Hubert

Bruvoll, John
— Angling in the Laerdal River.... Oslo, [1970s]. One of 1,000. 4to, cloth. sg Oct 23 (414) $110

Bruyn, Cornelis de. See: Le Brun, Cornelius

Bry, Johann Theodor de, 1561-1623
— Anthologia magna, sive florilegium novum & absolutum. Frankfurt: Officina Bryana, 1626. Folio, contemp calf gilt; repaired at head & foot. With engraved title & 142 plates, some folding. Some browning; 1 folding plate torn & repaired; an early copy of an amaryllis in watercolor bound in at end. Horticultural Society of New York —de Belder copy. S Apr 27 (92) £3,500 [Shapero]
— Anthologia Meriana CXV continens plantarum.... Frankfurt: Fleischer, 1776. Folio, contemp bds. With 115 plates. Stain on Plates 103 & 107. Horticultural Society of New York—de Belder copy. S Apr 27 (95) £3,800 [Shuster]
— Florilegium novum, hoc est variorum maximeque rariorum florum.... Oppenheim, 1611. Trial proof issue. Folio, contemp calf gilt; rubbed. With engraved title & 60 plates, of which 7 are repeats. Plates are before numbers. Tp soiled; 1 plate torn; some stains. S Apr 27 (90) £6,500 [Junk]
  Anr Ed. Oppenheim, 1612-[14]. Folio, half calf. With engraved title & 137 plates, including 26 plates from the Florilegium renovatum, 1641, & 15 contemp watercolors of flowers on interleaves; "it is in fact a nonce assembly of the de Bry plates...." Some tears & repairs; 3 plates mtd; a few plates trimmed within platemark; lacking dedication, preface & Brevis Descriptio; Ms index inserted at end; interleaved. de Belder copy. S Apr 27 (91) £4,200 [Shapero]
  Anr Ed. Frankfurt: Merian, 1641-47. ("Florilegium renovatum et auctum: das ist...Blumenbuch....") Folio, contemp calf gilt; upper joint split. With engraved title, double-page plate of the garden of Johan Schwinden & 174 plates, all in contemp hand-coloring. Engraved title, vignette on ptd title, initials & garden plan heightened with gold. This copy without Plate 142 (pbd in 1644) but with a plate numbered 50a, Iris susiana major. Engraved title, B1-3 & 1 plate inlaid; minor worming to lower margins of last few plates. de Belder copy. S Apr 27 (93) £90,000 [Arader]
— Recueil de plantes desinees et gravees anciennement a Francfort par la celebre famille Merian. Frankfurt, 1770. Folio, contemp half calf; upper joint splitting, rubbed. With 384 plates. Horticultural Society of New York—de Belder copy. S Apr 27 (94) £10,000 [Elliott]

Bry, Johann Theodor de, 1561-1623, & Johann Israel de
— [Little Voyages] Indiae orientalis navigationes. Frankfurt, 1598-1613. 10 (of 12) parts in 2 vols. Folio, contemp vellum; spines chipped & with small repairs. With 9 engraved titles, 2 engraved title vignettes, dedication, 18 maps, 1 plate of coins & 232 half-page illusts. Lacking the last map for Part 10; 1 map in Part 2 torn & repaired at fold; Plate 8 in Part 7 torn at fold with small loss of text, 1 or 2 plates just shaved. C Dec 12 (230) £9,000 [Israel]

Bryan, Michael, 1757-1821
— Dictionary of Painters and Engravers. L, 1816. ("A Biographical and Critical Dictionary of Painters and Engravers.") In 17 vols. 4to, contemp mor gilt, Index vol in contemp half mor. Lacking Vol 17 after Watson. Extra-illus with c.2,000 plates. C July 22 (34) £6,000
  Anr Ed. L, 1893-95. 2 vols extended to 35. 8vo, mor gilt by Riviere. Sold w.a.f. Extra-illus with the addition of c.4,000 ports & engravings, some 88 ptd in colors. S July 23 (475) £10,000 [Henderson]
  Anr Ed. L, 1903-5. 5 vols. 4to, half lea; loose & rubbed. sg Feb 5 (59) $200
  Anr Ed. L, 1918-19. 5 vols. 4to, orig cloth. pn Jan 22 (26) £85 [Alexander]
  Anr Ed. L, 1920-21. 5 vols. 4to, orig cloth; worn & shaken. sg Feb 5 (160) $60
  Anr Ed. L, 1930-34. 5 vols. 4to, orig cloth. Library markings. bba Jan 15 (277) £60 [Zwemmer]; S Nov 17 (635) £75 [Ash]

Bryant, Gilbert Ernest
— The Chelsea Porcelain Toys. L, 1925. One of 650. S Nov 17 (636) £120 [Sims]

Bryant, William Cullen, 1794-1878. See: Picturesque...

Bryant, William Cullen, 1794-1878 —& Gay, Sydney H., 1814-88
— A Popular History of the United States. NY, 1878-80. 4 vols. Orig half lea; rubbed. Some foxing of plates. sg Sept 18 (46) $50

Bryden, Henry Anderson
— Gun and Camera in Southern Africa. L, 1893. 8vo, cloth; rubbed. Foxed. cb May 21 (39) $70

Brydges, Sir Samuel Egerton, 1762-1837
— Recollections of Foreign Travel.... L, 1825. 2 vols. 8vo, later calf gilt; rubbed, spines scuffed. cb Feb 19 (44) $60

Brydone, Patrick, 1743-1818
— A Tour through Sicily and Malta. L, 1775. 2 vols. 8vo, contemp calf gilt; rubbed. Folding map torn & frayed. bba Jan 15 (462) £40 [Axe]

Buchan, John, 1875-1940
— Scholar Gipsies. L & NY, 1896. 1st Ed. Illus by D. Y. Cameron. 8vo, orig cloth. bba July 2 (106) £110 [Maggs]; T Oct 15 (190) £105

Buchan, William, 1729-1805
— Domestic Medicine.... Edin., 1769. 1st Ed. 8vo, modern calf. pnE Dec 17 (78) £200 [Traylen]
  Anr Ed. Phila., 1799. 8vo, contemp calf; rubbed. Some soiling, foxing & stains. O Oct 21 (37) $90

Buchanan, Donald W.
— James Wilson Morrice. A Biography. Toronto, [1936]. With related material. AVP Nov 20 (31) C$125 [Woolmer]

Buchanan, Francis Hamilton, 1762-1829
— A Journey from Madras through the Countries of Mysore, Canara, and Malabar. L, 1807. 1st Ed. 3 vols. 4to, contemp russia gilt. With frontis, hand-colored folding map, 5 folding tables & 37 plates, 1 hand-colored. C Dec 12 (34) £520 [Old Hall]

Buchanan, George, 1506-82
— Opera. Edin., 1715. 2 vols. Folio, contemp calf; rebacked. With frontis. Browned. bba Sept 25 (16) £50 [Bennett & Kerr]

Buchanan, James, 1791-1868
— Message from the President...December 7, 1847. Wash.: Wendell & Van Benthuysen, 1847. 2 vols. 8vo, contemp half calf; chipped & torn. 30th Congress, Sen. Exec. Doc. 1. ha Sept 19 (172) $85

Buchanan, Robertson, 1770-1816
— Practical and Descriptive Essays on the Economy of Fuel, and Management of Heat. Glasgow, 1810. 4 parts in 1 vol. 8vo, half calf; rebacked, orig spine laid down, rubbed, some fraying along fore-edge. With 5 plates. P Sept 24 (250) $320

Buc'hoz, Pierre Joseph, 1731-1807
— Centuries de planches enluminees et non enluminees.... Paris & Amst., [1775?]-81. 2 vols. Folio, contemp half calf; worn, some bdgs broken. Engraved throughout. With 20 series of 10 plates each, all plates in 2 states, 1 uncolored, the other hand-colored; together, 400 plates. Each series with title & explanatory text leaf. Blank lower margin excised from title to Part 1; tp & Plate 1 (uncolored) rehinged in Part 2; Plate 9 with lower margin cropped to plate mark; Plate 10 (colored) & text leaf crudely rehinged in Part 20; with 19th-cent Dutch owner's explanatory text slips tipped to gutter of a number of the colored plates, in a few cases encroaching on plate mark but not affecting image. sg Dec 10 (28) $3,400

— Histoire universelle du regne vegetal. Paris, 1783. ("Herbier artificiel, representant plus de quinze cents plantes....") 12 parts in 4 vols. Folio, contemp calf. With frontis & 1,200 plates. Half-titles in Vols II-IV. de Belder copy. S Apr 27 (47) £5,500 [McCarthy]

Buck, Sir George, d.1623
— The History of the Life and Reigne of Richard the Third. L, 1646. 1st Ed. Folio, contemp calf; rubbed, joints split. bba Mar 26 (14) £120 [Smallwood & Randall]

Buck, Samuel & Nathaniel
— Antiquities; or Venerable Remains of Above Four Hundred Castles, Monasteries.... L, 1774. 3 vols. Folio, contemp calf gilt; rebacked & rubbed. With 2 engraved titles, port & 510 plates. Lacking index map & plate of Lambeth Palace; 1st 9 antiquity plates inserted from a smaller copy; view of Reading trimmed. Sold w.a.f. C Oct 15 (20) £14,000 [Weinreb]

Buck, Walter J. See: Chapman & Buck

Buckingham, James Silk, 1786-1855
— National Evils and Practical Remedies with the Plan of a Model Town. L: Peter Jackson, [c.1849]. 8vo, orig cloth; spine head torn, library markings. With the folding plate, supplementary sheet & folding plan. P Sept 24 (251) $225
— Travels among the Arab Tribes Inhabiting the Countries East of Syria and Palestine. L, 1825. 4to, later half calf; worn. Map foxed. Library copy. sg Nov 20 (34) $350

Buckingham, Nash
See also: Derrydale Press
— Game Bag. Tales of Shooting and Fishing. NY, [1945]. One of 1,250. Orig cloth. ag Oct 23 (206) $100

Buckland, William, 1784-1856
— Reliquiae diluvianae. L, 1824. 2d Ed. 4to, contemp half lea; worn. With 27 maps & plates, 3 hand-colored, 1 folding. One leaf torn in lower margin. S Jan 13 (347) £130 [Bickersteth]

Buckley, Charles Burton
— An Anecdotal History of Old Times in Singapore. Singapore, 1902. 2 vols. 8vo, orig wraps. Tp to Vol II & facing frontis repaired. Sgd. S Apr 23 (334) £380 [Maggs]

Buckley, Wilfred, 1878-1933
— The Art of Glass. L, 1939. Cloth, in d/j. CA Apr 12 (49) A$75
— Notes on Frans Greenwood and the Glasses that he Engraved.... L, 1930. 4to, orig half cloth, in torn d/j. S Nov 10 (57) £120 [McCarthy]

Bude, Guillaume, 1468-1540
— Commentarii linguae Graecae. Paris: R. Estienne, 1548. Folio, contemp calf; rebacked, orig spine preserved. Small tear in margins of y5 & Qq8; hole in margin of M7. S Sept 23 (310) £140 [Sokol]
— De Asse et partibus eius.... Cologne: J. Soter, 1528. Bound with: Macrobius, Ambrosius Theodosius. In Somnium Scipionis.... Cologne, 1527. 8vo, later calf with metal clasps; 1 clasp lacking, worn. Annotated throughout. cb Oct 23 (38) $180
— De philologia libri ii. Paris: Jodocus badius Ascensius, Nov 1532. Folio, 19th-cent half vellum. Schwerdt-Jeanson copy. SM Feb 28 (94) FF5,000
— Libri V. de asse, & partib. eius.... Venice: Aldus, Sept 1522. 4to, 18th-cent vellum. C May 13 (140) £360 [Maggs]
— Traitte de la venerie.... Paris: Auguste Aubry, 1861. One of 5 on vellum. 8vo, mor gilt by Smeers. Jeanson copy. SM Feb 28 (95) FF6,500

Budge, Sir Ernest Alfred Wallis, 1857-1934
— The Egyptian Sudan. L, 1907. 2 vols. cb Nov 6 (42) $120
See also: British Museum

Buechner, Georg, 1813-37
— Dantons Tod. Maastricht: Halcyon Press, 1930. One of 225. B Oct 7 (124) HF160

Buel, Clarence Clough. See: Johnson & Buel

Buenting, Heinrich, 1545-1606
— Itinerarium Sacrae Scripturae, Das ist, Ein Reisebuch.... [Wittenberg, 1588?]. Folio, contemp blindstamped pigskin over wooden bds; worn. With 9 woodcuts. Lacking tp & 1st few leaves; browned & slightly wormed throughout. S Nov 18 (1064) £550 [Sefer]

Buffet, Bernard
— Lithographs, 1952-1966. NY, [1968]. Text by Fernand Mourlot. 4to, orig wraps, in d/j. With 11 plates. sg Feb 5 (61) $60
Anr copy. Orig wraps, in mylar d/j. sg June 4 (54) $120
— Oeuvre grave. Paris, 1967. Text by Fernand Mourlot. 4to, orig wraps. With 11 lithos including cover. S Nov 10 (134) £110 [Fitton]

Buffon, Georges Louis Marie Leclerc, Comte de, 1707-88
— Les Chants de la foret. Geneva, 1968. Unique copy with 2 suites of the etchings on satin & 2 on Rives, the pencil drawing for a double-page illust, a double-page pencil drawing of a bull, and 5 other drawings, all sgd or inscr by the artist. Illus by Tavy Notton. 4to, unsewn in orig wraps. S June 17 (133) £1,300 [Schoeni]
— Histoire naturelle generale et particuliere. Paris, 1749-1804. 1st Ed. 38 vols in 39; lacking the 5 vols of Poissons & the 1 vol of Cetacees. Contemp calf gilt; worn. Sold w.a.f. S Apr 23 (25) £1,800 [Wheldon]
Anr Ed. Paris, 1750-78. Vols I-XXII, lacking Vol XVI. And with Vols II-V of the Supplement. Together, 25 vols. 4to, cloth; worn. Sold w.a.f. bba Dec 18 (121) £200 [Acquaforte]
Anr Ed. Paris, 1799. 18 vols. 8vo, half calf gilt. With 263 (of 283) plates; 7 vols dampstained. Haverschmidt copy. B Feb 24 (89) HF650
Anr Ed. Paris, 1799-1808. 127 vols. 8vo, contemp calf gilt; worn. With 1,100 colored plates. FD Dec 2 (737) DM34,000
— Histoire naturelle des oiseaux. Paris, 1770-86. 10 vols. Folio, contemp mor gilt with arms of Louis XV [Olivier 2495, fer 20]. With 966 hand-colored plates only. Lacking the 35 plates of insects & Plates 113, 138,

BUFFON

146, 291, 397, 476 & 480. L.p. copy. S June 25 (144) £50,000 [Sourget]

— Natural History.... L & York, 1812. 20 vols. 8vo, contemp calf gilt; worn. S Feb 24 (516) £300 [Vesley]

Anr copy. Contemp half calf; broken. Sold w.a.f. T Sept 18 (111) £125

Anr Ed. L, 1821. 2 vols. 8vo, contemp half calf. Ck Oct 17 (53) £55

— Oeuvres. Brussels, 1828-33. 20 vols in 11, including 6 plate vols in 4. 8vo, contemp half mor; rubbed. With 5 ports, 2 double-page maps, 1 double-page table & 730 (of 732) plates, many hand-colored. Library markings; some staining. bba Jan 15 (404) £320 [Elliott]

Buffum, Edward Gould

— Six Months in the Gold Mines.... Phila., 1850. 12mo, orig cloth. Square torn from upper corner of dedication page. sg Mar 12 (22) $225

Bugg, Francis

— News from Pensilvania: Or a Brief Narrative.... L, 1703. 8vo, wraps. S June 25 (376) £480

Bugler, Arthur

— H.M.S. Victory. Building, Restoration and Repair. L, 1966. 2 vols, including portfolio of drawings. 4to, orig cloth, in d/js. sg Nov 20 (160) $175

Builder's...

— The Builder's Practical Directory or Buildings for all Classes.... L, [1855-57]. 4to, contemp half calf gilt; rubbed. Some spotting. T Feb 19 (534) £95

Bujanda, Gaspar de

— Compendio de las leyes expedidas sobre la caza. Madrid, 1691. 4to, contemp vellum. Lower corner of 1 leaf lacking. Schwerdt-Jeanson copy. SM Feb 28 (96) FF6,500

Bula N'Zau, Pseud. See: Bailey, Henry

Bulkeley, John —& Cummins, John

— A Voyage to the South Seas.... L, 1743. 8vo, modern bds. Some dampstains. sg June 11 (78) $100

Bull, Henry Graves. See: Hogg & Bull

Bullandre, Simon de, 1544-1614

— Le Lievre. Paris: Pierre Chevillot, 1585. 4to, contemp vellum gilt. SM Feb 28 (97) FF30,000

AMERICAN BOOK PRICES CURRENT

Bullen, Frank Thomas, 1857-1915

— The Cruise of the "Cachalot". L, 1898. 1st Ed. 8vo, cloth; worn. O Nov 18 (35) $70

Bullen, Henry Lewis

— The Nuremberg Chronicle: a Monograph. San Francisco, 1930. One of 300. Folio, half lea. cb Sept 11 (25) $275

Bulliard, Pierre, 1742-93

— Flora Parisiensis, ou descriptions et figures des plantes qui croissent aux environs de Paris.... Paris: Didot le jeune, 1776-83. 6 vols in 7. 8vo, contemp calf gilt; joints worn. With engraved title, 2 plates in introduction & 620 hand-colored plates. Horticultural Society of New York—de Belder copy. S Apr 27 (50) £5,200 [Goodwin]

— Herbier de la France.... Paris, 1780-1809. 5 vols in 6, including the Dictionnaire elementaire de botanique & the Histoire des champignons. Folio, modern half mor gilt. With color title & 602 engraved plates mostly color-printed & a further 12 plates, 10 colored by hand. Lacking last index leaf from Herbier, the Histoire des champignons lacking pp 685-700. de Belder copy. S Apr 27 (51) £9,000 [Richardson]

Bullock, William, fl.1808-28

— Six Months' Residence and Travels in Mexico.... L, 1824. 1st Ed. 8vo, contemp half calf. With 2 folding maps, folding table & 16 plates, 4 hand-colored. Frontis soiled. S June 25 (430) £450 [Houle]

Bullot, Maximilien, d.1748. See: Helyot & Bullot

Bulwer, James

— Views in the Madeiras. L, 1827. Folio, half mor. Some stains. S Apr 23 (157) pS1,000 [Dupont]

Bump, Gardiner —& Others

— The Ruffed Grouse. [Albany], 1947. 4to, cloth. sg Oct 23 (207) $70

Bumstead, John

— On the Wing. A Book for Sportsmen. Bost., 1869. 12mo, cloth; worn. sg Oct 23 (208) $70

Bunbury, Sir Charles James Fox, 1809-86

— Journal of a Residence at the Cape of Good Hope.... L, 1848. 8vo, modern half calf. With frontis & 4 plates. Plates stained in margins. SSA Oct 28 (441) R230

Anr copy. Orig cloth. SSA Oct 28 (442) R340

Bunbury, Henry W., 1750-1811

— An Academy for Grown Horsemen. L, 1787. 1st Ed. Folio, old half lea; worn. Lacking B1. O Nov 18 (36) $120

3d Ed. L, 1808. 8vo, contemp calf gilt. With 29 hand-colored plates. Outer edge cut close; 1 plate frayed. T Oct 16 (492) £110

Anr Ed. L, 1809. Illus by Thomas Rowlandson. 8vo, mor gilt by Riviere; front joints weak. With 29 hand-colored plates. Marginal repairs. sg Feb 12 (32) $350

Anr copy. Bound with: Grose, Francis. Lexicon Balatronicum. L, 1811. contemp sheep gilt by Lubbock of Newcastle; joints worn. sg May 21 (33) $100

Anr copy. Modern lev gilt by Riviere. sg June 11 (341) $400

— Annals of Horsemanship.... L, 1791. 1st Ed. Folio, old half lea; worn. With 17 plates. Tp trimmed & remtd; 1st few leaves detached. O Nov 18 (37) $130

Bunce, Daniel

— Travels with Dr. Leichhardt in Australia. Melbourne, 1859. 12mo, modern half calf. kh Mar 16 (64) A$420

Bunch, Mother, Pseud.

— Mother Bunch's Fairy Tales.... L, 1817. ("The Celebrated Fairy Tales of....") 2 vols in 1. 12mo, orig half lea; worn. With 12 hand-colored plates.. S June 18 (467) £420 [Moon]

Bungener, Laurence Louis Felix. See: Fore-Edge Paintings

Bunyan, John, 1628-88

See also: Cresset Press

— The Pilgrim's Progress. Poneke [Wellington], 1854. ("He Moemoea. Otira, ko nga korero o te huarahi....") Trans into Maori by Henry Tacy Kemp. 8vo, modern calf. With 6 plates. S June 25 (498) £200

Anr Ed. L: Essex House Press, 1899. One of 750. 16mo, vellum. sg Jan 8 (70) $130

Buonaccorsi, Biaggio

— Diario de'successi piu importanti seguiti in Italia.... Florence: Giunta, 1568. 4to, 18th-cent vellum gilt. S Sept 23 (311) £160 [Maggs]

Buonaiuti, B. Serafino

— Italian Scenery. L, 1806. 1st Ed. Folio, contemp mor gilt; rubbed, lower cover stained. Ck Nov 21 (204) £350

Anr Ed. L, 1823. 4to, contemp half lea; worn, broken. With 32 hand-colored plates, lacking leaf of music. bba Dec 18 (123) £160 [Erlini]

Anr copy. Mor gilt; worn. With 32 hand-colored plates & 1 leaf of music. pn May 21 (128) £400 [Marinoni]

Buonanni, Filippo, 1638-1725

— Ricreatione dell'occhio e della mente nell'osservation' delle chiocciole.... Rome, 1681. 4to, old half vellum. With 3 frontises & 109 plates of sheels, some with Ms captions. Tear in tp. S June 25 (12) £420

Burbank, Luther, 1849-1926

— Luther Burbank: His Methods and Discoveries and their Practical Application. NY: Luther Burbank Press, 1914-15. 12 vols. O Sept 23 (28) $130

Burbidge, Frederick William Thomas, 1847-1905

— The Narcissus: its History and Culture. L, 1875. 8vo, orig cloth. With frontis & 47 hand-finished colored plates. S Nov 10 (460) £330 [Blest]

Anr copy. Bound at end is Ye Narcissus or Daffodyl Flowre, and hys Root, 1884, ed by Burbidge. Also: Barr & Son's Daffodyl Conference Supplementary Catalogue of Species and Varieties of Narcissus, 1884. cloth. Author's copy, sgd at foot of tp, with 2 small ink sketches. S Nov 10 (459) £420 [Maggs]

Burchardus, Probst von Ursperg, d.1230

— Chronicon abbatis Urspergen a Nino rege Assyriorum magno: usque ad Fridericum II Romanorum imperatorem. Augsburg: Joannes Miller, 1515. 1st Ed. Folio, vellum from musical Ms. FD June 11 (73) DM3,800

Anr Ed. Strassburg: Krafft Mueller, 1540. ("Chronicum abbatis Urspergensis....") Folio, contemp lea; worn & def. JG Mar 20 (220) DM700

Burchell, William John, 1782-1863

— Travels in the Interior of Southern Africa. L, 1822-24. Vol I only. 4to, orig bds; broken. Sold w.a.f. Ck May 15 (1) £160

Anr copy. Vol I only. Contemp calf; worn & loose. Lacking half-title. S Nov 17 (638) £220 [Negro]

Anr copy. 2 vols. 4to, contemp calf gilt; rebacked. With folding map & 20 hand-colored plates. Hints on Emigration to the Cape of Good Hope inserted in Vol I. Lacking half-titles. S Apr 24 (320) £1,250 [Chalmers]

Anr copy. Modern calf with all plates bound at the back of the text. With 20 hand-colored plates & folding map. SSA Oct 28 (444) R4,000

BURCHETT

Burchett, Josiah, 1666-1746
— A Complete History of the Most Remarkable Transactions at Sea. L, 1720. 1st Ed. Folio, contemp calf; brittle, spine worn. With frontis, port & 9 folding or double-page maps by Herman Moll. sg Nov 20 (35) $325

Burckhardt, John Lewis, 1784-1817
— Arabic Proverbs.... L, 1830. 1st Ed. 4to, modern cloth. sg Nov 20 (36) $300
— Travels in Arabia. L, 1829. 2 vols. 8vo, contemp calf; worn, rebacked & recornered. One map torn along fold. S July 14 (857) £260
— Travels in Nubia. L, 1819. 4to, orig bds, uncut, with paper label on spine. S June 25 (350) £380 [Kahn]

Burges, William, 1827-81
— Architectural Drawings. L, 1870. Folio, half lea. With 75 plates. C July 22 (36) £650

Burgess, Anthony
— Coaching Days of England. L, 1966. Oblong folio, cloth, in d/j. ha Mar 13 (260) $50; pn Jan 22 (105) £35 [Edrich]; pn Mar 5 (70) £35 [Sotheran]

Burgess, Gelett, 1866-1951
— Bayside Bohemia: Fin de siecle San Francisco & its Little Magazines. San Francisco: Book Club of California, 1954. One of 375. 4to, cloth. cb Sept 11 (26) $60; cb Jan 22 (9) $50
— The Purple Cow! [San Francisco, 1895]. 1st Pbd Ed, 1st State. 12mo, wraps. cb Oct 9 (28) $110
State not indicated. Wraps; chipped. sg Sept 11 (43) $60

Burgess, Henry W.
— Eidodendron. Views of the General Character & Appearance of Trees.... L, 1827. Folio, contemp half mor; worn. With 3 variant litho titles & 54 mtd plates. Some dampstaining & spotting. Ck Jan 16 (181) £190

Burges-Short, G. See: Chichester & Burges-Short

Burgoyne, Sir John, 1722-92
— A State of the Expedition from Canada.... L, 1780. 4to, modern half mor gilt; 1 laid down on cloth; title holed. With 6 maps & plans with hand-colored details. pnNY Sept 13 (209) $300
1st Ed. 4to, later half calf. With 6 maps & plans. With the Supplement bound in. sg Apr 2 (35) $1,400

AMERICAN BOOK PRICES CURRENT

Burgsdorf, Friedrich August Ludwig von
— Versuch einer voellstandigen Geschichte vorzueglicher Holzarten.... Berlin, 1783-1800. 3 vols in 2. 4to, contemp half calf. With engraved dedication, frontis, 44 folding plates & 4 folding tables, most colored by hand. de Belder copy. S Apr 27 (52) £2,600 [Arader]

Burke, Edgar
— American Dry Flies and How to Tie Them. NY, 1931. One of 500. 12mo, wraps. With 2 plates. sg Oct 23 (27) $200; wd Nov 12 (83) $200

Burke, Edmund, 1729-97
— An Account of the European Settlements in America. L, 1758. 2 vols. 8vo, contemp calf; broken. With 2 folding maps. sg Sept 18 (48) $225
6th Ed. L, 1777. 2 vols. 8vo, contemp calf; rubbed. With 2 folding maps. sg Sept 18 (49) $100
— An Appeal from the New to the Old Whigs.... L, 1791. Bound with: A Letter...from Mr. Burke...in Answer to Some Objections to his Book on French Affairs. L, 1791. 1st Ed. 8vo, contemp sheep; worn, front cover detached. Both works lacking half-titles. Todd 54E & 56B. sg Oct 9 (138) $150
— A Letter from the Rt. Honourable Edmund Burke to the Duke of Portland on the Conduct of the Minority in Parliament.... L, 1797. 1st Ed. 8vo, modern wraps. Lacking A2 & O2. bba Oct 16 (82) £40 [Cathach]
— Reflections on the Revolution in France. L, 1790. 1st Ed. 8vo, modern half mor. Lacking half-title. bba Feb 5 (170) £120 [Parsons]
Anr copy. Contemp calf; rebacked. FD Dec 2 (2281) DM2,700
Anr copy. Contemp half calf; broken. Lacking half-title. O Oct 21 (38) $60
Anr copy. Contemp calf gilt. pn Sept 18 (93) £220 [Lyons]
Anr copy. Contemp half calf; worn, front joint cracked. wa Dec 11 (689) $110
2d Ed, 2d impression. 8vo, half mor gilt by Stikeman. With port added. sg Feb 12 (34) $275
Anr copy. Contemp calf; rebacked & rehinged. Todd 53c. sg Mar 26 (50) $130
Anr copy. Orig wraps; green paper backing def. Todd 53c. sg June 11 (80) $175
— Two Letters on the Conduct of our Domestick Parties, with Regard to French Politics.... L, 1797. 8vo, sewn. bba Apr 9 (81) £120 [Spencer]
— Works. L, 1792-1827. 8 vols. 4to, contemp

half vellum; worn, joints split, 1 spine def. bba Apr 9 (80) £160 [Spencer]

Anr copy. Contemp calf. Lacking half-titles to Vols 4-8. C Dec 12 (35) £950 [Cavendish]

Anr Ed. L, 1803. 8 vols. 8vo, calf gilt; rebacked. pn Oct 23 (108) £60 [Bookroom]

Anr Ed. L, 1826-27. 16 vols. 8vo, calf gilt; spines rubbed. S Feb 23 (7) £140 [Traylen]

Burke, H. Farnham

— The Historical Record of the Coronation of their Most Excellent Majesties King Edward VII and Queen Alexandra. Pvtly ptd, 1901. Folio, orig half mor, rubbed & soiled. Ck Jan 30 (16) £50

Burke, Sir John Bernard, 1814-92

— A Visitation of the Seats and Arms of the Noblemen and Gentlemen of Great Britain. L, 1852-55. 1st & 2d Series, in 4 vols, 8vo, half mor by Worsfold; rubbed. Some dampstains in 1 vol. O June 9 (28) $100

Burn, Richard. See: Nicolson & Burn, Richard

Burn, Robert Scott

— Working Drawings and Designs in Architecture and Building. L & Edin., [c.1865]. Folio, contemp half calf; rubbed. With 57 plates, all but 1 double-page. Many plates dampstained in lower corner; some small tears or marginal defs. bba Apr 9 (430) £80 [Maggs]

Burnaby, Andrew, 1734-1812

— Travels through the Middle Settlements of North-America.... L, 1798. 4to, contemp calf; rebacked with modern calf. With folding map & 2 plates. sg Sept 18 (50) $450

Burnaby, Anthony

— Two Proposals, humbly offer'd.... L, 1696. 4to, wraps. Fore-margin of tp shaved. S July 24 (424) £280 [Lawson]

Burne-Jones, Sir Edward Coley, 1833-98

— The Beginning of the World. L, 1902. 4to, orig half cloth; soiled. With 25 plates. S Oct 6 (776) £60 [MPL]

— The Flower Book. L, 1905. One of 300. 4to, orig half mor; worn & dampstained. S Dec 4 (185) £1,500 [Haydon]

Anr copy. Mor gilt. S June 17 (217) £3,000 [Mr. K]

Burnell, John

— Bombay in the Days of Queen Anne.... L: Hakluyt Society, 1933. Intro by Samuel T. Sheppard. Inscr by Sheppard. sg Nov 20 (76) $50

Burnery, James, 1750-1821

— A Chronological History of the Discoveries in the South Sea.... L, 1803-17. Vol I (of 5) only. 4to, 19th-cent half calf; backstrip partly detached. Some foxing. sg Nov 20 (38) $80

Burnet, Gilbert, 1643-1715

— History of his Own Time. Dublin, 1724-34. 1st Dublin Ed. 2 vols. Folio, contemp calf; rebacked, rubbed. bba Dec 4 (60) £70 [Hay]

Anr Ed. Oxford, 1833. 6 vols. 8vo, mor; rubbed, 1 cover detached. Extra-illus with ports, views, etc.. O Feb 24 (31) $50

— Some Letters containing an Account of...Switzerland, Italy, &c. [N.p.], 1687. 12mo, contemp calf gilt; lacking backstrip, crudely tape-repaired. bba Nov 13 (133) £35 [Fisher]

— Some Passages of the Life and Death of...John, Earl of Rochester. L, 1680. 1st Ed. 8vo, late 17th-cent mor. sg Oct 9 (304) $60

Burnet, John, 1784-1868

— Practical Hints on Composition in Painting. L, 1837 [1839]. ("A Treatise on Painting....") 4 parts in 2 vols. 4to, 19th-cent mor by Tout. Extra-illus with c.170 plates & prints. S Nov 10 (58) £260 [Sanders]

— Practical Treatise on Paintings. L, 1827. 4to, contemp russia gilt; extremities rubbed. Minor foxing. sg Feb 5 (62) $200

Burnet, John, 1784-1868 —& Others

— Engravings from the Pictures of the National Gallery. L, 1840. Folio, contemp half lea gilt; worn, joints starting. Most plates foxed in margins. sg June 18 (220) $150

Burnett, Gilbert Thomas, 1800-35

— An Encyclopaedia of Useful and Ornamental Plants.... L, 1852. Vol II only. 4to, disbound. With 130 hand-colored plates. pn Nov 20 (225) £300 [Nicholson]

Burnett, M. A.

— Plantae Utiliores; or, Illustrations of Useful Plants Employed in the Arts and Medicine. L, [1839]-42-47-50. Vols I-II only. Contemp half calf; rubbed. With 238 hand-colored plates, including some from other vols & with the dedication leaf for Vol III rather than that for Vol II. Minor tears in text. Sold w.a.f. S Nov 10 (461) £850 [Burden]

Burnett, William. See: Dugdale & Burnett

BURNEY

Burney, Charles, 1726-1814
— An Account of Musical Performances in Westminster-Abbey.... L, 1785. 1st Ed. 4to, later calf gilt by Lubbock of Newcastle; front cover detached, shelf numbers on spine, endpapers & top edges stamped. sg Feb 26 (131) $110

Burney, Frances, 1752-1840
— Diary and Letters of Madame D'Arblay.... L, 1876. 4 vols. 8vo, cloth. sg Sept 11 (44) $70
— Evelina, Or, A Young Lady's Entrance into the World. L, 1898. Illus by Arthur Rackham. 8vo, modern calf. With 16 plates. sg Oct 30 (41) $175
— Memoirs of Doctor Burney, Arranged from his own Manuscripts.... L, 1832. 3 vols. 8vo, contemp half calf gilt by Bedford; some scratches. T Feb 19 (436) £100

Burney, James, 1750-1821
— A Chronological History of the Discoveries in the South Sea.... L, 1803-17. 5 vols. 4to, cloth; soiled. With 41 engraved maps & plates, 1 torn & repaired. bba Dec 18 (124) £2,000 [Remington]

Burns, John, 1774-1850. See: Fore-Edge Paintings

Burns, Robert, 1759-96
See also: Limited Editions Club
— The Cotter's Saturday Night. Bost.: Bibliophile Society, 1915. One of 475. Designed & engraved by Arthur Macdonald. Mor gilt. cb Sept 11 (238) $75
— Poems, Chiefly in the Scottish Dialect. Edin., 1787. 2d (1st Edin.) Ed, Issue not indicated. 8vo, mor gilt by Zaehnsdorf. Tp repaired. pnE June 17 (120) £170
Issue with "skinking" on p.263. Modern calf. pn Nov 20 (92) £100 [Traylen]
Anr copy. Mor gilt. pn Jan 22 (206) £420 [Johnson]
Anr copy. Calf gilt. S Sept 22 (7) £120 [Bennett]
Issue with "stinking" on p.263. Contemp calf; rebacked. Ck Sept 5 (216) £70
— Works. L, 1834. 8 vols. 8vo, calf; worn & soiled. wa Feb 19 (73) $140
Anr Ed. Edin., 1877. 6 vols. 8vo, half mor; scuffed. Extra-illus with plates. sg Feb 12 (35) $225

Burr, Mrs. A. W.
— Sketches. [N.p., c.1850]. Folio, loose as issued in orig portfolio; new calf spine & corners. With 14 hand-colored lithos mtd on 12 sheets. S June 25 (352) £2,800 [Martinos]

AMERICAN BOOK PRICES CURRENT

Burrard, Sir Gerald
— Big Game Hunting in the Himalayas and Tibet. L, 1925. Rubbed & soiled, corners bumped. cb Nov 6 (43) $85
— The Modern Shotgun. L & NY, 1931-32. 3 vols. Orig cloth; marked. S Nov 10 (589) £75 [Palace]
Anr copy. In frayed d/js. T Oct 16 (384) £50

Burroughs, Edgar Rice, 1875-1950
— Back to the Stone Age. Tarzana, Calif., [1937]. 1st Ed. In creased laminated jacket. cb Sept 28 (243) $200
— The Deputy Sheriff of Comanche County. Tarzana, [1940]. In d/j with tear at top rear joint. cb Sept 28 (246) $190
Anr copy. In chipped d/j. cb May 7 (325) $110
— Escape on Venus. Tarzana, [1946]. In chipped d/j. cb May 7 (326) $50
Anr copy. In soiled d/j. cb May 7 (327) $50
— John Carter of Mars. Racine: Whitman, [1940]. Pictorial bds. A "Better Little Book". cb Sept 28 (250) $100
— Jungle Tales of Tarzan. Chicago, 1919. Illus by J. Allen St. John. 1st bdg. cb May 7 (334) $65
— The Lad and the Lion. Tarzana, [1938]. In tape-repaired d/j. wa June 25 (306) $90
— Llana of Gathol. Tarzana, [1948]. In d/j. cb Sept 28 (251) $65
— The Master Mind of Mars. Chicago: McClurg, 1928. cb Sept 28 (252) $90
— The Oakdale Affair - The Rider. Tarzana, [1937]. cb Sept 28 (253) $100
— Synthetic Men of Mars. Tarzana, Calif., [1940]. 1st Ed. In d/j. wa Dec 11 (145) $120
Anr copy. In soiled & repaired d/j. wa June 25 (307) $140
— Tarzan and the Leopard Men. Tarzana, Calif., [1935]. 1st Ed. Illus by J. Allen St. John. In faded d/j. wa June 25 (308) $180
— The Warlord of Mars. Chicago, 1919. 1st Ed, 1st Issue. Cloth; spine leaning. Tape repair to frontis. cb May 7 (355) $65

Burroughs, John, 1837-1921
— Works. Bost., 1904-22. Autograph Ed, One of 750. 23 vols. Half mor gilt. sg Sept 11 (45) $500

Burrus, Ernest J.
— Kino and the Cartography of Northwestern New Spain. [Tucson], 1965. One of 750. Folio, cloth. Inscr. cb Oct 9 (29) $225

Burt, Struthers
— Powder River: Let 'er Buck. NY, [1938]. Illus by Ross Santee. With 15 of the illusts highlighted in watercolor by Santee & with his signature on tp & 1st chapter head. sg Sept 18 (264) $375

Burthogge, Richard
— An Essay upon Reason, and the Nature of Spirits. L, 1694. 1st Ed. 8vo, new bds with mor spine. S May 28 (642) £320

Burton, John, 1710-71
— Monasticon Eboracense: and the Ecclesiastical History of Yorkshire. York, 1758. Folio, contemp calf; rebacked. T June 16 (41) £65

Burton, Reginald George
— Sport & Wild Life in the Deccan. Phila.: Lippincott, [c.1925]. 8vo, cloth, in chipped d/j; soiled. With folding map & 20 plates. wa Sept 25 (131) $55

Burton, Sir Richard Francis, 1821-90
— The Book of the Sword. L, 1884. 8vo, orig cloth; worn. sg Nov 20 (110) $275; sg Apr 23 (29) $120

— First Footsteps in East Africa. L, 1856. 8vo, contemp calf; spine rubbed. With 2 maps & 4 colored plates. Ck May 8 (323) £320

Memorial Ed. L, 1894. 2 vols. 8vo, orig cloth; rubbed. With 2 maps & 4 color plates. cb Nov 6 (45) $110

— The Kasidah.... L, 1880. 1st Ed. 4to, orig wraps; spine restored. sg Apr 2 (37) $700

— The Lake Regions of Central Africa. L, 1860. 1st Ed. 2 vols. 8vo, orig cloth. B Oct 7 (1297) HF550

Anr copy. Orig cloth; soiled. S July 14 (819) £400

1st American Ed. NY, 1860. 2 vols. 8vo, cloth; rubbed, hinges weak. cb Nov 6 (45) $110

— The Land of Midian Revisited. L, 1879. 1st Ed. 2 vols. 8vo, orig cloth; rubbed & soiled. Some leaves torn. bba May 14 (351) £220 [Loman]

— Personal Narrative of a Pilgrimage to El-Medinah and Meccah. L, 1855-56. 1st Ed. 3 vols. 8vo, orig cloth. With 14 plates (5 colored) & 4 maps & plans. S Apr 24 (228) £1,400 [Brown]

Anr copy. Half mor gilt. With 14 plates & 4 maps & plans. Lacking ad leaves; titles stamped. S June 25 (351) £750 [Traylen]

Memorial Ed. L, 1893. 2 vols. 8vo, orig cloth; spine ends chipped, corners worn. sg Apr 23 (32) $80

— Two Trips to Gorilla Land. L, 1876. 1st Ed. 8vo, orig cloth; joints worn. With 2 folding maps & 4 plates. C Oct 15 (21) £650

[Cavendish]
— Vikram and the Vampire. L, 1893. One of 200. 8vo, orig cloth; spine ends torn, frontis detached. sg Apr 23 (33) $90

— Wanderings in West Africa. L, 1863. 2 vols. 8vo, orig cloth. pn Mar 5 (10) £360 [Scott]

— Zanzibar: City, Island and Coast. L, 1872. 1st Ed. 2 vols. 8vo, orig cloth; soiled, 1 spine chipped. Ck May 8 (319) £650

Burton, Sir Richard Francis, 1821-90 —& Smithers, Leonard
— Priapeia. Cosmopoli: pbd by the translators, 1890. One of 500. 4to, orig cloth, upper cover repaired. bba Jan 15 (116) £80 [Doak]

Burton, Robert, 1577-1640
See also: Nonesuch Press
— The Anatomy of Melancholy. Oxford, 1624. 2d Ed. Folio, contemp calf; worn, new endpapers. Tp soiled, def & remtd; some fraying. Sold w.a.f. bba Aug 28 (168) £95 [Hippo]

4th Ed. Oxford, 1632. Folio, modern sheep. Tp & leaves before dedication lacking; some repaired worming. Sold w.a.f. Ck Feb 13 (104) £50

Anr copy. Later calf; rubbed. Engraved title repaired at inner margin. S Sept 22 (164) £440 [Heurs Doff]

Anr copy. Contemp calf; rubbed, spine a little def. Tp shaved; fore-margin of dedication leaf repaired; a few tears & holes; L3 misbound before L2. S Mar 10 (1033) £260 [Bennett]

Anr copy. Contemp calf; rubbed, spine def. Tp shaved & foot cropped with loss of imprint; fore-margin of dedication-leaf repaired; a few tears & small holes, scarcely affecting text; L3 misbound before L2. Sold w.a.f. S July 14 (377) £170

Anr copy. Old calf; rejointed, broken. Lacking port & last leaf of Index. sg Jan 15 (71) $80

5th Ed. Oxford, 1638. Folio, contemp calf; 1 joint torn, rubbed & wormed. Engraved title wrinkled; some soiling. S May 29 (1159) £220

Anr copy. Contemp calf; worn, head of spine restored. Dampstaining in lower corners, lacking front free-endpaper. sg Mar 26 (51) $130

8th Ed. L, 1676. Folio, 19th-cent calf; rebacked preserving orig spine. Some foxing. O Sept 23 (29) $160

Anr copy. Later half calf; upper cover detached. S Mar 10 (1032) £160 [Harrington]

Burton, William, 1575-1645

— The Description of Leicester Shire.... L, [1622]. 1st Ed. Folio, early 19th-cent russia; rubbed, upper joint split. With engraved title, port & folding map. Lacking last leaf; map shaved; map torn. S July 14 (301) £140

Burton, William, 1609-57

— A Commentary on Antoninus his Itinerary.... L, 1658. Folio, contemp calf; worn. S May 29 (1158) £130

Bury, Lady Charlotte, 1775-1861

— Diary Illustrative of the Times of George the Fourth.... L, 1839. 4 vols. 8vo, half mor; worn & scuffed. sg Sept 11 (47) $50

Bury, Mrs. Edward

— A Selection of Hexandrian Plants.... L, 1831-34. Folio, contemp half mor; joints rubbed. With engraved title & 51 hand-colored aquatint plates. One text leaf loose. de Belder copy. S Apr 27 (53) £44,000 [Ursus]

Bury, Thomas Talbot, 1811-77

— Coloured Views of the Liverpool and Manchester Railway. L, 1831. 4to, half lea. With 16 hand-colored plates, including the view of the Tunnel in States 1 & 2, the Edgehill entrance in States 1 & 4 & entrance into Manchester at Bridge Street in States 1 & 2; margin of 1st state of the latter plate sgd Geo. Robt. Stephenson. Some margins soiled or stained. S Oct 23 (183) £1,600 [Hall]

One of 250. Half mor. WIth 13 hand-colored plates. Light stain affecting the plate showing the Northumbrian. S June 25 (241) £1,100 [Haut]

Facsimile Ed. Oldham, [1977]. 4to, orig mor gilt. Ck Sept 26 (236) £65

— Six Colored Views on the London and Birmingham Railway. L, 1833. Part 1 (all pbd). 4to, contemp half calf; rubbed. With 12 hand-colored plates; lacking Plate 7. Tp spotted; marginal soiling. S Apr 23 (85) £1,000 [Saville]

Busby, Thomas Lord

— Costume of the Lower Orders in Paris. [L, c.1820]. 12mo, modern half mor. With pictorial title & 27 hand-colored plates. C May 13 (64) £300 [Dailey]

— The Fishing Costume and Local Scenery of Hartlepool. L, 1819. 4to, contemp half mor. With 6 colored plates. pnE Jan 28 (232) £620 [Steedman]

Busch, Wilhelm

— Schnaken & Schnurren. Munich: Braun & Schneider, [c.1885]. 4to, cloth; worn. wa Sept 25 (193) $55

Bussato, Marco

— Giardino di agricoltura. Venice: G. Fiorina, 1592. 4to, half vellum. Lower outer corners of c.25 leaves at end repaired affecting a few catchwords & letters in the table. Crahan copy. P Nov 25 (85) $1,400

Anr copy. Vellum. G5 recto with space below text blank; upper outer blank corners of last 4 leaves mended. S Oct 23 (665) £650 [Frers]

Anr Ed. Venice: Sebastiano Combi, 1612. 4to, contemp vellum; worn, front joint cracking. Tp soiled; some browning. Hunt copy. CNY Nov 21 (45) $700

Bussus, Matthaeus, 1428-1502

— Familiares et secundae...Epistolae. Mantua: Vincentium Bertochum, 1498. Folio, later calf; worn, joints splitting, ink notations on front & rear blanks. 143 (of 144) leaves. wa Sept 25 (569) $450

Busti, Bernardino de

— Rosarium sermonum.... Hagenau: Heinrich Gran for Johannes Rynman, 1503. Folio, old vellum. Tp frayed at fore-edge; marginal dampstains at end. sg Oct 9 (139) $150

Busti, Bernardinus de

— Rosarium sermonum. Hagenau, 1503. Folio, old vellum. Tp rehinged & frayed; light marginal dampstaining at end. sg Mar 26 (52) $150

Butel-Dumont, Georges Marie

— Theorie du Luxe. [N.p.], 1771. 2 parts in 1 vol. 8vo, contemp calf gilt; front joint cracked. sg Mar 26 (53) $200

Butler, Arthur Gardiner, 1844-1925

— Birds of Great Britain and Ireland. L, [1907-8]. 2 vols. 4to, orig cloth. With 115 color plates. pn Jan 22 (113) £95 [Demetzy]

Anr copy. Half cloth. With 107 colored plates of birds & 8 colored plates of eggs. pnE Dec 17 (260) £85 [Greyfriars]

— Foreign Finches in Captivity. L, 1899. 2d Ed. 4to, orig cloth; rebacked. pn Mar 5 (11) £120 [Walford]

Anr copy. Half mor gilt; scuffed. With 60 color plates. pn Mar 5 (81B) £140 [Map House]

— Lepidoptera Exotica, or Descriptions and Illustrations of Exotic Lepidoptera. L, 1874. 4to, half mor, orig wraps for the 20 parts bound at end. With 64 colored plates. S May 28 (579) £280

Butler, Arthur Stanley George
— The Architecture of Sir Edward Lutyens. L, 1950. 3 vols. Folio, orig cloth, 2 vols in d/js. S July 13 (32) £650

Anr copy. With: Hussey, Christopher, E. C. The Life of Sir Edward Lutyens. L, 1950. Together, 4 vols. Folio & 4to, orig cloth, in d/js. T Dec 18 (295) £520

Butler, Charles, d.1647
— The Feminin Monarchi, or the Histori of Bees. L, 1623. 2d Ed. 4to, 19th-cent half mor; rubbed. Minor marginal tears; some browning; Ms notes on final blank. Crahan copy. P Nov 25 (86) $400

Anr Ed. Oxford, 1634. 4to, contemp calf; rubbed, rebacked. Minor fraying to tp; some browning & soiling; marginal worming from V3-Z1 just touching 2 letters of a shoulder-note. P Nov 25 (87) $400

Anr copy. Modern half calf; joints worn. Dampstained. sg Jan 15 (143) $375

Butler, Francis. See: Johns & Butler

Butler, Frank Hedges
— Wine and the Wine Lands of the World. L, 1926. 8vo, cloth. sg Jan 15 (10) $50

Butler, Henry
— South African Sketches. L, 1841. Folio, orig cloth; rebacked, old spine laid down. With frontis & 31 views on 15 plates, some hand-colored. Ck May 8 (301) £220

Anr copy. Orig cloth; worn & affected by damp. With 31 (on 15) colored plates. S Feb 24 (469) £140 [Robinson]

Butler, Joseph, 1692-1752
— The Analogy of Religion, Natural and Revealed.... L, 1736. 4to, 18th-cent calf; front joint cracked. sg Oct 9 (140) $110

Butler, Samuel, 1612-80
— Hudibras. L, 1810. Illus by Rowlandson after Hogarth. 2 vols. 8vo, orig bds; worn. Lacking 1 plate. sg Feb 12 (36) $90

Ed not specified. L, 1819. Bound in 3 vols 8vo, contemp mor gilt, rebacked. Extra-illus with ports & views. sg Feb 12 (37) $130

Anr Ed. L: M'Lean, 1819. Illus by J. Clark. 2 vols. 8vo, calf gilt; rebacked, some wear. With 11 colored plates; lacking frontis in Vol I. sg Sept 11 (48) $100

Anr Ed. L, 1835. 8vo, modern half mor; spine rubbed. cb Feb 19 (45) $60

Butler, Samuel, 1774-1839
— Atlas of Antient Geography. Phila., 1838. 8vo, orig half lea; scuffed, front hinge cracked. With engraved title & 22 double-page maps, all but 1 hand-colored in outline. sg Apr 23 (164) $100

Butler, Samuel, 1835-1902
See also: Gregynog Press; Limited Editions Club
— The Way of All Flesh. L, 1903. 1st Ed, issue not stated. wd Nov 12 (100) $200
— Works. L, 1923-26. Shrewsbury Ed, One of 750. 20 vols. Half vellum. pnE Oct 15 (226) £440

Butsch, Albert Fidelis
— Die Buecher-Ornamentik der Renaissance. Leipzig: G. Hirth, 1878. Folio, half mor. S Sept 23 (432) £170 [Kabbinet]

Butterworth, Benjamin
— The Growth of Industrial Art. Wash., 1892. Folio, orig cloth. Lacking pp 25-32. K Oct 4 (77) $275

Butterworth, Edwin —&
Tait, Arthur Fitzwilliam
— Views on the Manchester and Leeds Railway. L, 1845. Folio, loose in orig cloth; worn. With litho title & 19 plates. S Oct 23 (170) £660 [Lobard]

Buxton, Edward North
— Two African Trips. L, 1902. With folding map in endpocket. cb Nov 6 (48) $75

Buxtorf, Joannes, 1599-1664
— Synagoga Judaica. Basel: Koenig, 1661. 8vo, contemp vellum. Library stamp on tp. bba May 28 (343) £110 [Freedman]

Buy de Mornas, Claude, d.1783
— Atlas methodique et elementaire. Paris, 1761. Part 1 (of 4). Folio, contemp calf; def. With double-page allegorical title, dedication & 55 double-page plates, several hand-colored. Some staining & dust-soiling throughout. S July 14 (591) £340

Anr copy. Parts 1 & 2 (of 4). Folio, orig calf; worn & scuffed, joints cracked, spine ends lacking, joints & spine glue-mended. With 97 maps & historical scenes, of which 85 are hand-colored in outline or fully colored. sg Nov 20 (185) $900

Byam, Lydia
— A Collection of Exotics from the Island of Antigua. [L, 1797]. Folio, contemp bds; rebacked in calf & recornered. With 12 hand-colored plates. Tp slightly soiled. de Belder copy. S Apr 27 (56) £6,000 [Fleming]
— A Collection of Fruits from the West Indies. L, 1800. Folio, orig bds; worn, spine repaired. With 9 hand-colored plates. Last plate browned; tp soiled & with old inscr in upper margin. S Apr 23 (28) £3,000 [Quaritch]

Anr copy. Cloth portfolio. Slight marginal tears to title; margins slightly soiled. de Belder copy. S Apr 27 (55) £4,500 [Prince]

Byerly, Thomas. See: Percy, Sholto & Reuben

Byfield, Nathaniel, 1653-1733
— An Account of the Late Revolution in New-England. L, 1689. 1st Ed. 4to, half calf. S June 25 (405) £850 [Nebenzahl]

Bynner, Witter
See also: Ford & Bynner
— An Ode to Harvard and Other Poems. Bost., 1907. Inscr. sg Mar 5 (28) $50

Byrd, Cecil K.
— A Bibliography of Illinois Imprints, 1814-58. Chicago, [1966]. In d/j. sg Oct 2 (169) $40

Byrne, Arthur —&
Stapley, Mildred
— Majorcan Houses and Gardens. NY, 1928. Library markings. bba Feb 5 (123) £55 [Kamiliya]

Byrne, Muriel Saint Clare. See: Sayers & Byrne

Byron, George Anson, Baron Byron
— Voyage of H.M.S. Blonde to the Sandwich Islands. L, 1826. 1st Ed. 4to, half mor; rubbed. With 11 plates, plan & folding map. P Sept 24 (136) $900

Byron, George Gordon Noel, Lord, 1788-1824
— Beppo, a Venetian Story. [Kentfield, Calif.]: Allen Press, 1963. ("A Venetian Story.") One of 150. Oblong folio, loose as issued. With 35 plates. sg Dec 4 (3) $275
— Don Juan. Cantos I-XV. L, 1819-24. 1st Ed. 6 vols. 4to & 8vo, orig bds; some spines worn or repaired. Vols II-VI are L.p. copies. Samuel Rogers' set. S July 23 (43) £1,200 [Gekoski]
— English Bards and Scotch Reviewers. L, [1809]. 1st Ed, 1st Issue. 12mo, early calf gilt; worn & soiled. wa Sept 25 (645) $75
  3d Ed. L, 1810. Late 19th-cent mor gilt. Extra-illus with 176 ports & plates. sg Sept 11 (113) $100
  4th Ed. Modern half mor gilt; extremities worn. Extra-illus with 79 ports, some mtd India-proofs. sg Sept 11 (114) $70
  Anr copy. One vol extended to 3. 19th-cent half lea gilt; broken. Extra-illus with 51 plates. sg Sept 11 (115) $70
— Hebrew Melodies. L: I. Nathan, [1815]. ("A Selection of Hebrew Melodies...accompaniments by I. Braham & I. Nathan....") 2 parts in 1 vol. Folio, orig wraps; soiled. Last 3 leaves soiled. S Jan 13 (468) £360 [Joseph]
— Hours of Idleness. Newark, 1807. 1st Ed. 8vo, modern mor gilt by Riviere. bba May 14 (343) £500 [Wasserman]
  Anr copy. Half mor. Some spots & stains. S Jan 13 (469) £240 [Jarndyce]
— Manfred, a Dramatic Poem. L, 1817. 1st Ed, 2d Issue. 8vo, orig wraps; spine def. S Jan 13 (470) £110 [Bickersteth]
— Marino Faliero.... L, 1821. 1st Ed, 1st Issue. 8vo, orig bds; rubbed, joints split. S Jan 13 (471) £100 [Bickersteth]
— Mazeppa. L, 1819. 1st Ed. 8vo, orig wraps; spine torn. S Jan 13 (473) £170 [Bickersteth]
  2d Issue. Orig wraps; rubbed & soiled. S Jan 13 (472) £70 [Bauman]
— Ode to Napoleon Buonaparte. L, 1814. 1st Ed. 8vo, mor gilt. S Sept 22 (8) £160 [Burmeister]
— The Poetical Works. L, 1839. 8 vols. 8vo, contemp sheep gilt; spines rubbed, 1 cover detached. sg Sept 11 (49) $350
— The Prisoner of Chillon.... L, 1816. 1st Ed, 1st Issue. 8vo, mor gilt by Riviere, orig wraps preserved. S Jan 13 (475) £140 [George]
  Anr Ed. L: Day & Son, [1865]. Illus by W. & G. Audsley. 4to, cloth; some wear. O May 12 (36) $180
— The Siege of Corinth.... L, 1816. 1st Ed. 8vo, orig wraps; stained. S Jan 13 (476) £170 [Joseph]
— Werner, a Tragedy. L, 1823. 1st Ed, 1st Issue. 8vo, orig wraps; rubbed & soiled. S Jan 13 (477) £150 [Joseph]
— Works. L, 1842. 1 vol extended to 3. 8vo, late 19th-cent half mor gilt. Extra-illus with c.400 plates. sg Sept 11 (116) $250
  Anr Ed. Bost.: F. A. Niccolls, 1900. One of 1,000. 16 vols. Half mor. cb Dec 4 (88) $325

Byron, Robert, 1905-41 —&
Rice, David Talbot
— The Birth of Western Painting. L, 1930. 4to, orig cloth. Paul Nash's copy. S May 6 (133) £65 [Joseph]

Byvanck, Alexandre Willem
— La Miniature dans les Pays-Bas septentrionaux. Paris, 1937. 4to, contemp half mor, orig wraps preserved; rubbed. bba Oct 16 (460) £120 [Fogg]

C

C., Francis. See: Conscience, Francis Antoine

C., G. E. See: Cokayne, George Edward

C., J.
— Verstandige Huys-Houder...in Bestieren der Hof-steden.... Amst.: Cornelius Jansz, 1661. 4to, modern mor by Grabau; rubbed. Rust-hole affecting engraved title vignette. Hunt copy. CNY Nov 21 (46) $550

Cabala...

— Cabala, Mysteries of State, in Letters of the Great Ministers of K. James and K. Charles. L, 1654. 4to, contemp sheep; rubbed, rebacked, old spine preserved. Wing C183. bba Apr 9 (16) £45 [Robertshaw]

— Cabala, sive Scrinia sacra, Mysteries of State and Government.... L, 1691. 3d Ed. 2 parts in 1 vol. Folio, old calf; broken. Some soiling & fraying. O Nov 18 (38) $90

Cabell, James Branch, 1879-1958

— The Eagle's Shadow. NY, 1904. 1st Ed, 1st Issue. Inscr to a relative, Mrs. Thomas Branch. ha May 22 (138) $100
— Works. NY, 1927-30. One of 1,590. 18 vols. sg Sept 11 (50) $300
  Storisende Ed. cb Sept 28 (269) $550

Cabinet...

— Cabinet du Roi: Fetes de Versailles. Paris, 1679-76-73. 3 parts in 1 vol. Folio, contemp mor gilt with arms of Louis XIV; joint repaired. With 20 double-page plates plus a duplicate suite on thick paper of the 9 plates from Les Plaisirs de l'Isle Enchantee. C Dec 3 (174) £2,700 [Gilman]
  Anr copy. Les Divertissemens de Versailles & Relation de la Fete de Versailles only. Old half mor, armorial bdg; worn. CNY Nov 21 (47) $1,500
— The Cabinet of Genius. L, 1787. Vol I only. 4to, contemp half vellum; worn. bba May 28 (49) £170 [Shapero]
  Anr copy. 2 vols. 4to, old calf; rubbed. pn Sept 18 (170) £240 [Shapero]
— Cabinet of Natural History and American Rural Sports. Phila., 1830-33. 3 vols, 4to, mor gilt & half cloth. With 2 ports, 3 engraved titles, 54 color plates & 3 uncolored plates. sg Apr 2 (72) $3,600
  Anr Ed. Phila., 1830-32. Vols I-II (of 3). 4to, orig half cloth; Vol II loose, prelims started in Vol I. With 2 ports, 2 engraved titles & 48 plates, most colored by hand. Heavy foxing throughout. wd June 19 (71) $1,200
— The Cabinet-Maker's Assistant. Glasgow, 1853 [1851-53]. Folio, modern half mor gilt. With litho title & 101 plates. Marginal tears & repairs. S Mar 9 (655) £200 [Marsden]

Cadet de Gassicourt, Charles Louis

— Cours gastronomique, ou les diners de Manant-Ville.... Paris: Capelle et Renand, 1809. 8vo, silk over bds; joints worn. With folding map (stained). Lacking half-title; paper fault on tp affecting text. Crahan copy. P Nov 25 (89) $300

Caesar, Caius Julius, 100-44 B.C.

See also: Limited Editions Club

The Commentaries

— 1519. - Venice: Aldus. 8vo, 18th-cent half mor; worn. cb Oct 23 (4) $130
— 1635. - Leiden: Elzevir. 12mo, contemp mor gilt with arms of Antoine III, duc de Gramont [Olivier 660]. With engraved title & 3 folding maps & 5 woodcuts. S June 25 (13) £200 [Schwing]
— 1677-76. - L. Trans by Clement Edmonds. Folio, contemp calf; rebacked. With frontis & 14 plates. T Oct 16 (519) £48
— 1712. - L: Tonson. 2 vols. Folio, calf; rubbed, hinges cracked. With 2 double-page titles, port, 6 double-page maps & 78 plates. L.p. copy. pn Mar 5 (13) £380 [Bartlett]
— 1790. - L. 2 vols. 8vo, contemp mor; rebacked. Vol I frontis & tp foxed. sg Feb 12 (38) $120
  Anr copy. Contemp mor; rubbed. T Feb 19 (451) £70
— 1894. - Les Commentaires de la guerre gallique, reproduits en fac-simile d'apres le manuscrit originale.... Paris: Pour la Societe des Bibliophiles Francois. 3 vols. 8vo, mor extra by Chambolle-Duru. With 24 ports & 12 plates of machines of war & 3 double-page maps, all in colors or in grisaille with gold. Jeanson copy. SM Feb 28 (99) FF30,000
— 1914. - Commentarii rerum in Gallia gestarum VII. L. One of 12. Vellum. sg June 11 (331) $550

Cahiers...

— Cahiers G I M. Paris, 1936. Nos 1-9 (complete set). Orig wraps. S June 29 (34) £800 [Arginthan]

Caillet, Albert Louis

— Manuel bibliographique des sciences psychiques ou occultes. Paris, 1912-13. 3 vols. Half cloth, orig wraps bound in. sg May 14 (338) $150
  Anr copy. Cloth, orig wraps bound in; chafed. sg May 14 (339) $325
  Anr Ed. Nieuwkoop, 1964. One of 300. 3 vols. Reprint of Paris 1912 Ed. bba Oct 16 (369) £70 [Hesheth & Ward]

Caillie, Rene, 1799-1838

— Travels through Central Africa to Timbuctoo.... L, 1830. 2 vols. 8vo, contemp half calf; 1 vol disbound, the other becoming disbound. Map with tears; foxing to titles & frontises. cb Feb 19 (47) $85

CAILLIE

Anr copy. Orig half cloth; bumped, joints cracked. One of the 2 folding maps detached. Ck May 8 (294) £120

Cain, James
— Serenade. NY, 1937. In d/j; worn. sg Mar 5 (29) $200

Caius, Joannes, 1510-73
— De canibus Britannicis liber unus; De rariorum animalium et stirpium historia, liber unus; De libris propriis, liber unus. L: Gulielmum Seresium, 1570. 3 parts in 1 vol. 8vo, mor extra by Deseuil. Lower margin of tp repaired. Jeanson 1399. SM Feb 28 (100) FF180,000

Anr Ed. L: C. Davis, 1729. 3 parts in 1 vol. 8vo, 18th-cent mor gilt. Tp soiled. Jeanson 1313. SM Feb 28 (101) FF14,000
— Of Englishe Dogges.... L: Richard Johnes, 1576. 4to, mor gilt janseniste by Riviere. Some repairs. Schwerdt-Jeanson copy. SM Feb 28 (102) FF32,000

Calderwood, David
— The History of the Kirk of Scotland.... Edin.: Woodrow Society, 1842-49. 8 vols. 8vo, orig cloth; worn. O Mar 24 (36) $80

Caldicott, John William, Antique dealer
— The Values of Old English Silver.... L, 1906. 4to, cloth. sg Feb 5 (298) $100

Caldwell, Erskine
— We Are the Living.... NY, 1933. 1st Ed, one of 250. sg June 11 (83) $70

Calendario...
— Calendario per la real Corte per l'Anno Bisestile 1784. Turin, [1785]. 24mo, contemp calf gilt & hand-painted with floral sprays, inset with painted miniatures of hot-air balloons. C Dec 3 (65) £4,000 [Beres]

Calendrier...
— Calendrier de la cour, tire des ephemerides, pour l'annee 1777. Paris, 1777. 18mo, contemp mor with onlays enclosing 2 orig gouache paintings by Moreau le jeune (sgd), on the upper cover a young woman in pink with yellow underskirt wearing a black bonnet & on the lower cover a young man in a blue coat, pale undercoat, pink breeches & white stockings, wearing a tricorn, both within a floral border protected by mica. Carnarvon copy. C Dec 3 (66) £30,000 [Beres]
— Calendrier de la cour, tiree des ephemerides pour l'anne 1780.... Paris, 1780. Bound with: Le Tresor des Almanachs. Paris, 1780. 32mo, vellum with mor miniatures with hunting scenes. Rahir—Jeanson copy. SM Feb 28 (103) FF23,000

California
— The General Railroad Laws of California.... Sacramento, 1862. 8vo, orig ptd wraps; chipped & soiled. cb Jan 8 (153) $160
— History of Alameda County.... Oakland, 1883. 8vo, calf; needs rebdg. sg Mar 12 (26) $60
— In the Supreme Court of the State...The People...vs. George Washington, Respondent. Brief for the People. Jo Hamilton, Attorney-General. Sacramento, 1867. Orig wraps; stamp on front wrap. cb Oct 9 (263) $70
— Proceedings of a Public Meeting of the Democratic Members of the Legislature of California, Opposed to the Election of a United States Senator.... San Francisco, 1854. 8vo, disbound. cb Jan 8 (163) $55

Callander, John
— Terra Australis Cognita, or Voyages to the Terra Australis, or Southern Hemisphere. Edin., 1766-68. 3 vols. 8vo, calf. Piece cut from head of titles; ad leaf lacking in Vol I; map lacking in Vol II. CA Apr 12 (54) A$2,000

Anr copy. Contemp calf. With folding chart & folding maps of the Strait of Magellan & the coast of Australia. S June 25 (318) £2,600 [Traylen]

Callcott, Sir Augustus Wall
— Italian and English Landscapes. L, 1847. Folio, orig half mor gilt; broken. With litho title & 25 litho plates. pnNY Oct 11 (1) $600

Callieres, Jacques de
— Histoire du Mareschal de Matignon. Paris, 1661. Folio, contemp calf; bumped. Some stains. Ck Jan 30 (187) £65

Callimachus
— Opera. Glasgow: Foulis, 1755. Folio, recent half calf. Lacking the 3 plates; interleaved with blanks; some dampstains. T Feb 19 (484) £50

Callot, Jacques, 1592-1635
— Les Images des Saints. Paris: Israel Henriet, 1636. Folio, 19th-cent mor gilt armorial bdg by Charles Hering, with his ticket. With frontis & 122 plates in 2d state. S May 21 (98) £1,800 [Sourget]

Callotto...
— Il Callotto Resusciato, oder Neue eingerichtes Zwerchen Cabinet. [Augsburg: Baeck, c.1720]. Folio, half vellum. Minimal worming. HK Nov 4 (2437) DM5,000

Calvert, Albert Frederick
— My Fourth Tour in Western Australia. L, 1897. 1st Ed. 4to, contemp mor gilt by Zaehnsdorf. With folding map colored. Inscr to his son, June 1898. C Oct 15 (148) £240 [Maggs]
— South-West Africa during the German Occupation, 1884-1914. L, 1915. 8vo, cloth. Some foxing. sg Nov 20 (40) $175

Calvert, Frederick, 6th Baron Baltimore
— A Tour to the East.... L, 1767. 8vo, contemp calf; upper cover detached, worn. ha May 22 (115) $100
[-] The Trial of Frederick Calvert...for a Rape on the Body of Sarah Woodcock.... L: for William Owen & Joseph Gurney, 1768. Folio, modern mor. sg Oct 9 (141) $250

Calvin, John, 1509-64
— The Commentaries upon the Actes of the Apostles.... L, 1585. 8vo, calf gilt with guards from a 15th-cent Ms on vellum, a contemp L bdg decorated with large arabesque cornerpieces & a lozenge-shaped centerpiece, field seme with rosettes, flat spine tooled all over. Manchester copy. S July 24 (388) £850 [Maggs]
— The Commentaries upon the Actes.... L, 1585. 1st Ed in English. 8vo, contemp calf with arabesque center; rebacked, corners restored. Dampstaining at end; title possibly from anr copy. sg Oct 9 (142) $400

Calvino, Italo
— The Silent Mr. Palomar. NY: Targ, 1981. One of 250. Half cloth. cb Feb 5 (239) $70

Calvo, Marco Fabio
— Antiquae urbis Romae cum regionibus simulachrum. Rome: Valerio Dorico, Apr 1532. Folio, bdg not described. HK Nov 4 (615) DM2,500

Calvoer, Henning
— Acta historico-chronologico-mechanica circa metallurgiam. Braunschweig, 1763. 1st Ed. 2 parts in 1 vol. Folio, contemp calf; rubbed. With 47 plates. HN May 20 (973) DM1,200

Camargo, Diego
— Historia de Tlaxcala. Mexico, 1892. 8vo, modern mor by Lakeside Press. Inscr by Prospero Cahuantzi, Governor of the State of Tlaxcala. sg Sept 18 (51) $110

Cambout de Ponchateau, Sebastien-Joseph.
See: Arnauld & Cambout de Ponchateau

Cambridge...
— Cambridge Bibliography of English Literature. NY, 1941. Ed by F. W. Bateson. 4 vols. In d/js. cba Feb 5 (65) $110
Anr copy. In d/js; worn. sg Oct 2 (80)

$120; sg Jan 22 (87) $120; sg May 14 (215) $150
Anr Ed. Cambr., 1969-77. 5 vols, including Supplement. In d/js. bba Apr 23 (11) £85 [De Boer]; sg Jan 22 (88) $350
Ed by George Watson. Cambr., 1974-77. ("The New Cambridge Bibliography of English Literature.") 5 vols. S July 13 (78) £250
— The Cambridge History of English Literature. Cambr., 1932. Ed by A. W. Ward & A. R. Waller. 15 vols, including Index. T Apr 16 (364) £42
— Cambridge Medieval History. Cambr., 1911-1936. 8 vols text, 8 portfolios of maps. bba Mar 12 (367) £50 [Bennett & Kerr]
— Cambridge Modern History. Cambr., 1902-12. 14 vols, including Index & Atlas. bba Mar 12 (368) £45 [Hay Cinema]

Cambridge, Richard Owen, 1717-1802
— An Account of the War in India.... L, 1761. 2 parts in 1 vol. 4to, contemp calf; worn. With 18 maps & plates. Blank corner torn from 1 leaf towards end. S June 25 (463) £320 [Mediolanum]

Cambridge University
— Early English Printed Books.... Cambr., 1900-7. 4 vols. 8vo, orig cloth. With Appendix to Vol III. sg Oct 2 (81) $50

Camden, William, 1551-1623
— The Abridgment of Camden's Britannia.... L: John Bill, 1626. Oblong 8vo, contemp calf gilt. With engraved title & 52 maps. Some stains & marginal repairs to first few leaves; 3 maps misbound or transposed. S Apr 23 (109) £2,800 [Haggis]
Anr Ed. L, 1701. ("Britannia Abridg'd.") 2 vols. 8vo, old calf; rebacked. With 2 general hand-colored maps & 59 hand-colored county maps. pn May 21 (394) £900 [Intercol]
Anr copy. Contemp calf; hinges cracked, rubbed. With port & 59 folding maps. pn May 21 (425) £700 [Nicholson]
Anr copy. Vol II only. Contemp calf; joints split, rubbed. With port & 36 folding maps only. S May 28 (965) £340
— Anglica, Normanica, Hibernica, Cambrica, a veteribus scripta. Frankfurt, 1603. 1st Ed. Folio, contemp vellum; rubbed, front endpaper torn. Owner's stamp on tp & 3 other leaves, not affecting text. bba Aug 28 (94) £60 [Bennett & Kerr]
Anr copy. Old vellum, worn. Hole in title not affecting text; some stains. S Nov 17 (776) £50 [Elliott]
— Annales rerum Anglicarum et Hibernicarum regnante Elizabetha.... L, 1615-27.

CAMDEN

1st Ed. Folio, contemp calf gilt; joints cracked, rubbed. Ink library accession number on top of title; bookplate of Magdalene College Cambr on verso of tp. bba Oct 30 (24) £60 [Wall]
— Britannia: or a Chorographical Description.... L, 1637. ("Britain....") 2d Ed of Holland's trans. Folio, calf gilt by Waters of Newcastle. With plates of coins & 57 maps, all but 1 double-page. 1st 9 leaves inlaid, including tp & frontis; some marginal waterstaining. C Oct 15 (134) £2,000 [Hamlet]

1st Ed of Gibson's trans. L, 1695. ("Britannia....") Folio, modern half mor; rubbed. With port & 50 double-page or folding maps & 9 plates of coins & antiquities. P2 torn; DD1 with repairs; a few other marginal tears & repairs; corner torn from map of Scotland, affecting plate surface; library stamps & ink accession number on tp, port & plates; maps with perforated stamps. bba Aug 28 (311) £500 [Burgess Browning]

Anr copy. Contemp calf. North Wales lacking small portion of lower right corner; 4 maps with repairable tears. pn Oct 23 (411) £750 [Postaprint]

Anr copy. Contemp calf; rebacked. Margins trimmed & repaired. pn Apr 30 (470) £620 [Saville]

Anr copy. Old calf; rebacked, rubbed. With port, 9 plates & 50 folding maps. Wormed throughout, mainly on upper & lower margins; some paper repair on upper margins; worm holes affecting edges of some maps; library stamp on tp. pnNY Oct 11 (16) $850

Anr copy. Contemp calf; rebacked. Lacking Chubb's maps 2, 4-6, 8-9, 11-12; some leaves torn or repaired; occasional waterstains. S Jan 12 (66) £480 [Kidd]

Anr copy. Some dampstaining & a few short tears. S Feb 24 (378) £950 [Noble]

Anr copy. 19th-cent half calf; worn. Some soiling; tears & small holes affecting a few maps & leaves of text; port & tp mtd; margins of a few maps shaved. S May 29 (966) £500

Anr copy. Contemp calf; rebacked, worn. With port, 50 double-page or folding maps & 9 plates of coins or antiquities. Several maps cut close to or just within platemarks. S June 25 (232) £700 [Faupel]

2d Ed of Gibson's trans. L, 1722. 2 vols. Folio, contemp calf. pn Apr 30 (471) £920 [Postaprint]

Anr copy. 18th-cent calf gilt; joints weak. With port & 51 double-page or folding maps, hand-colored in outline, the embellishments fully so, & with 10 plates of coins.

A few faint stains & repairs; 1 folding map torn without loss. Colored copy. S Apr 23 (110) £2,200 [George]

Anr Ed. L, 1753. 2 vols. Folio, contemp calf. With port, 51 double-page or folding maps & 10 plates. pn Apr 30 (472) £920 [Postaprint]

1st Ed of Gough's trans. L, 1789. Vol I only. Disbound. Port, title & prelims def. Sold w.a.f. bba Jan 15 (477) £170 [Bailey]

2d Ed of Gough's trans. L, 1806. ("Britannia....") 4 vols. Folio, half calf gilt; hinges cracked. pn May 21 (336) £280 [Traylen]

Anr copy. Contemp russia gilt by Lubbock of Newcastle with his ticket. With port, 104 plates & 57 maps (the 50 general & county maps hand-colored in wash & outline). S June 25 (235) £700 [Traylen]
— Britannia, sive florentissimorum regnorum Angliae.... L: R. Newbery, 1587. 2d Ed. 2 parts in 1 vol. 8vo, old calf gilt; rebacked. Tp browned; Oo2 with small marginal tear; lacking final blank. L Dec 11 (101) £90

Anr Ed. L, 1607. Folio, contemp calf gilt, stamped IP; joints repaired. With engraved title, 57 maps & 8 plates of coins. Maps, plates, most illusts & initials colored in an early hand. Engraved title cut round & mtd; a few neatlines just shaved; lacking the dedication to King James; first few leaves lightly discolored. Colored copy. S Apr 23 (107) £3,000 [Traylen]

Anr Ed. Amst.: Jansson, 1617. 8vo, contemp vellum. With 2 folding maps & 44 other maps. Tear at margin of G7; marginal waterstain to map & a few leaves at front; 1 map with small hole. C Oct 15 (22) £800 [Franks]

Anr copy. Modern pigskin. With 44 maps. Small portion of 1 map margin lacking; some dampstains. With Erasmus Darwin's signature on 1st blank. pn May 21 (333) £600 [Green]

Anr copy. Contemp calf; rebacked. With 43 maps only. Some outer margins trimmed. pn May 21 (334) £440 [Map House]

Anr Ed. Amst.: Blaeu, 1639. 12mo, contemp vellum; worn. With 19 maps. pn May 21 (335) £180 [Burden]
— The Historie of the most Renowned and Victorious Princesse Elizabeth.... L: M. Flesher for J. Tonson, 1688. ("The History of the Life and Reign of the...Princess Elizabeth....") 4th Ed. Folio, contemp calf; hinges cracked. Wing C-363. pn Sept 18 (145) £70 [Finch]

Anr Ed. Oxford, 1692. ("Tomus Alter & Idem: or the Historie of the Life....") 4to, contemp calf with initials W. S. stamped on

368

covers; spine split. Ck Jan 30 (25) £140
— Remaines, Concerning Britaine. L, 1605. 1st Ed. 2 parts in 1 vol. 4to, later mor gilt, armorial bdg. wa Dec 11 (683) $110

5th Ed. L, 1637. 2d Issue. 4to, contemp calf gilt; joints split, rubbed. Last few leaves marginally def; ink stain to 1st few leaves; tp with small holes & soiled; some worming affecting text. bba Mar 26 (157) £50 [Ihler]

Anr Ed. L: Harper for Waterson, 1637. 4to, old calf; rebacked. Some stains & marginalia. STC 4526. O Sept 23 (30) $50

Anr Ed. L: for Simon Miller, 1657. 4to, contemp sheep, worn. Wing C-374C. David Barclay's copy. T Nov 20 (302) £220

Camera Work
— 1903. - NY No 4. Wraps. sg May 7 (15) $950
— 1904-5. - NY Nos 8-9. Orig wraps; chipped, portion of 1 spine lacking. sg Nov 13 (20) $350
— 1905. - NY No 12. sg Nov 13 (22) $1,100
— 1906. - NY No 15. sg Nov 13 (23) $300
— 1909. - NY No 27. sg May 7 (16) $1,100
— 1910. - NY No 30-32. sg May 7 (21) $1,400
Nos 30-81. sg May 7 (20) $275
— 1911. - NY No 33. sg May 7 (17) $800
No 36. Inscr by Stieglitz to Arthur Dove. sg Nov 13 (26) $4,500; sg May 7 (18) $6,200
— 1912. - NY No 40. sg Nov 13 (28) $650; sg May 7 (19) $1,200
— 1915. - NY No 47. Inscr by Stieglitz to Arthur Dove. sg Nov 13 (29) $800
— 1917. - NY No 49/50. sg Nov 13 (30) $9,500

Camerarius, Joachim, the Younger, 1534-98
— Hortus medicus et philosophicus.... Frankfurt: Joannes Feyrabend, 1588. 3 parts in 1 vol. 4to, 17th-cent calf; extremities worn. Lacking Hh4 in Part 3; tear in A2 of Part 1 repaired. Hunt copy. CNY Nov 21 (48) $1,800
— Symbolorum & emblematum ex re herbaria desumtorum centuria una collecta. Nuremberg, 1590. 4to, contemp calf gilt; rebacked, inner upper joint broken, new endpapers. With 4 engraved titles & 400 plates. Horticultural Society of New York —de Belder copy. S Apr 27 (57) £2,600 [Israel]
— Symbolorum et emblematum centuriae tres.... [Leipsig], 1605. 4to, contemp mor gilt, armorial bdg; broken. Browned. sg Oct 9 (187) $300
Anr Ed. Leipzig: Typis Voegelinianis, 1605. 4 parts in 1 vol. 4to, old vellum; soiled. Lacking final blank; some annotations. S Sept 23 (313) £340 [Leinweber]

Cameron, Julia Margaret, 1815-79
— Victorian Photographs of Famous Men and Fair Women. L, 1926. One of 450. 4to, orig half vellum. Some spotting to text. S Dec 18 (130) £250 [Blackwell]

Camoens, Luis de, 1524?-80
— The Lusiad, or, Portugal's Historicall Poem... L, 1655. 1st Ed in English. Trans by Richard Fanshaw. Folio, contemp calf; spine ends worn. With folding frontis (cut down & relaid) & 2 ports. T Oct 16 (517) £380

Camp, Charles L.
— James Clyman, American Frontiersman.... Portland OR: Champoeg Press, [1960]. One of 1,450. cb Oct 9 (46) $70

Campanella, Tommaso, 1568-1639
— Realis philosophiae epilogisticae partes quatuor.... Frankfurt, 1623. 4to, modern half mor. Marginal dampstaining; inner blank margin of tp restored & re-inserted. C Dec 12 (276) £5,000 [Quaritch]
— Thomas Campanella an Italian Friar...His Advice to the King of Spain.... L: for Philemon Stephens, [1660]. 4to, contemp calf; rebacked. Small piece torn from lower margin of title; lacking 2d A1; ink accession number. Sold w.a.f. bba Aug 28 (176) £40 [News Today]

Campbell, Alexander, 1764-1824
— Albyn's Anthology: or a Select Collection of the Melodies and Vocal Poetry Peculiar to Scotland and the Isles.... Edin., 1816-18. 2 vols. Folio, orig bds. pnE Nov 12 (215) £120
— A Journey from Edinburgh through Parts of North Britain. L, 1802. 1st Ed. 2 vols in 1. 4to, contemp half calf; soiled. With 44 plates. Ck Sept 26 (297) £90
2d Ed. L, 1811. 2 vols. 4to, disbound. With 44 plates. sg Nov 20 (41) $60

Campbell, Ambrose George, 1799-1884
— The Wrongs of the Caffre Nation.... L, 1837. 12mo, modern half mor. SSA Oct 28 (472) R480

Campbell, Archibald James
— Nests and Eggs of Australian Birds. Sheffield, 1900. 4to, cloth. pn Oct 23 (191) £240 [Bles]

Campbell, Colin, d.1720 —& Others
— Vitruvius Britannicus. L, [1715]-17-31-67-71. Vols I-II. contemp calf; worn. With engraved titles, dedication & 158 plates only, plus 3 extra plates inserted in Vol I. Some repairs. bba Apr 23 (54) £2,600 [Ramsay]

CAMPBELL

Anr Ed. L, 1717-31. Vols II & III (of 5) only. Folio, contemp calf; worn. With engraved title in Vol II only & 148 plates. Some cropping; 1 plate torn with loss. S July 13 (220) £1,600

Anr Ed. L, 1725-67-71. Vols I-III & a composite vol. Folio, contemp half calf; worn, joints cracked. With 281 plates. Sold w.a.f. C Oct 15 (23) £13,000 [Weinreb]

Anr Ed. L, 1767. Vol IV only. Folio, contemp half mor; joints rubbed. With engraved title, dedication & 79 plates. Some marginal staining. Ck Feb 27 (97) £1,500

Campbell, Donald, 1883-1949
— Arabian Medicine and its Influence on the Middle Ages. L, 1926. 2 vols. 8vo, cloth. sg May 14 (581) $150

Campbell, George, 1719-96
— The Philosophy of Rhetoric. L, 1776. 1st Ed. 2 vols. 8vo, contemp sheep. sg Oct 9 (143) $80

Campbell, John, 1708-75
— A Political Survey of Britain. L, 1774. 1st Ed. 3 vols, including Index. 4to, contemp calf gilt & half gilt; def at head of spines. S June 25 (64) £400 [Foster]

Anr copy. 2 vols. 4to, contemp half calf; rubbed. With 3 engraved titles, 2 folding maps & 25 (of 28) plates plus 3 hand-colored plates of arms. T Feb 19 (312) £85

Campbell, John, 1766-1840
— Travels in South Africa [2d Journey].... L, 1822. 2 vols. 8vo, bdg not described. With folding map, colored frontis & 10 colored plates. SSA Oct 28 (475) R1,600
— Voyages to and from the Cape of Good Hope. Phila., 1840. 1st American Ed. 12mo, contemp cloth; joints rubbed. cb Nov 6 (49) $55

Campbell, John W., 1910-71
— Cloak of Aesir. Chicago: Shasta, [1952]. In d/j. Sgd on half-title. cb Sept 28 (273) $50
— The Mightiest Machine. Providence: Hadley, [1947]. In 1st d/j (rubbed & chipped). cb Sept 28 (275) $50

Campbell, Thomas
See also: Fore-Edge Paintings
— Diary of a Visit to England in 1775.... Sydney, 1854. 8vo, orig cloth; badly dampstained. bba Nov 13 (103) £60 [Axe]

Campbell, Thomas, 1777-1844
— Gertrude of Wyoming.... L, 1809. 1st Ed. 4to, contemp half lea; corners & spine ends chipped. John Ruskin's copy, with his check, sgd, laid in. sg Feb 12 (39) $130
— Letters from the South. L, 1837. 2 vols. 8vo, half lea; worn, joints starting. With folding map & 5 plates, some stained. sg

AMERICAN BOOK PRICES CURRENT

Nov 20 (42) $60

Campbell, W. F.
— Life in Normandy: Sketches of French Fishing.... Edin., 1863. 2 vols. 8vo, orig cloth; rubbed, spines split. T Feb 19 (233) £50

Campe, Joachim Heinrich, 1746-1818
— Histoire de la decouverte de l'Amerique. Paris, 1836. 2 vols. 12mo, old calf; rubbed & dried. With 2 frontises & 2 folding maps. O Oct 21 (39) $60

Campelli, Giovanniti Ibex sive de capra montana carmen venatorium. —&
Venice: Andrea Poletti, 1697 8vo, 19th-cent mor with arms of Ferdinand, King of the Two Sicilies. Schwerdt-Jeanson copy. SM Feb 28 (104) FF12,000

Campen, Jacob van, 1595-1657
— Afbeelding van 't stadt huys van Amsterdam. Amst., 1661. 1st Ed. Folio, bdg not indicated. A few text leaves frayed; library markings. Sold w.a.f. Franklin Institute copy. F Sept 12 (6) $275

Camus, Albert
— Oeuvres. Paris, [1962]. One of 200 with a suite on japon nacre & an extra colored litho by each artist. 7 vols. 4to, unsewn as issued in orig wraps, unopened. With the intro volume with specimen pages. S June 17 (126) £400 [Peeper]
— September 15th, 1937. Bronxville: Valenti Angelo, 1963. One of 50. Bds. cb Dec 4 (309) $55
Unique copy on japan vellum, with supporting ANs. cb Dec 4 (308) $350

Canal, Antonio. See: Canaletto

Canaletto, 1697-1768
— Urbis Venetiarum prospectus celebriores. Venice: Theodor Viero, [n.d.]. 3 parts in 1 vol. Oblong folio, bds. With engraved divisional title to Part 1 (only), double port & 38 plates. S June 25 (214) £4,500 [Giunta]

Canard, Nicolas Francois, c.1750-1833
— Grundsaetze der Staatswirthschaft.... Vienna: B. B. Ph. Bauer, 1814. Bound with: Maitland, James, 8th Earl of Lauderdale. Ueber National-Wohlstand. Vienna: B. B. Ph. Bauer, 1814. 8vo, ptd wraps; lacking lower portion of spine. 4 folding tables in 1st work. Last few leaves creased. Neue Hand-Bibliothek fuer Staatswirthschaft National-Oekonomie und Finanz-Wissenschaft. Siebenter Band. P Sept 24 (253) $475
— Principes d'economie politique, ouvrage couronne par l'Institut National.... Paris: Buisson, 1801 [An X]. 8vo, later calf.

Half-titles repaired; some staining. P Sept 24 (254) $1,200

Candolle, Augustin Pyramus de, 1778-1841
See also: Delessert & Candolle
— Astragalogia, nempe astragali biserulae et oxtropidis.... Paris, 1802. Folio, contemp half mor. With 50 plates. L.p. copy. Derby—de Belder copy. S Apr 27 (59) £1,600 [Solomon]
— Plantarum succulentarum historia, ou Histoire naturelle des plantes.... Paris, [1799-1805]. Parts 1-26 in 2 vols. Folio, late 19th-cent half mor; rubbed. With 158 hand-finished color plates after Redoute. Marginal dampstaining, lacking titles but with index to Fascicules 1-2 at end of Vol II & the ptd wraps for fascicule 26 inserted in Vol I. Horticultural Society of New York —de Belder copy. S Apr 27 (60) £4,800 [C. Van Loock]
Didot issue. Parts 1-24 in 1 vol. Folio, contemp mor gilt; broken. With 144 hand-finished color plates after Redoute. This copy with 2 title-pages & an index leaf to each vol but without preface or half-titles. L.p. copy. Loch—de Belder copy. S Apr 27 (58) £9,200 [Minton]
— Plantes rares du Jardin de Geneve. Geneva, 1829. 4to, half mor by Jeanne Gazel of Nice, orig wrap of 1st livraison bound in. With 24 hand-finished colored plates. Plesch—de Belder copy. S Apr 27 (61) £1,600 [Junk]

Canini, Giovanni Angelo
— Iconografia. Cioe Disegni d'imagini de famosissimi monarchi.... Rome, 1669. 1st Ed. Folio, contemp calf; rebacked. With engraved title & 114 plates. T Sept 18 (326) £64

Canisius, Petrus, 1521-97
— Authoritatum sacrae scripturae.... Venice: Aldus, 1571. 3 parts in 1 vol. 4to, contemp pigskin. sg Oct 9 (81) $200

Canova, Antonio, 1757-1822
— Works. L, 1824. 2 vols. 4to, mor gilt. With 98 plates. pn Jan 22 (256) £45

Cantillon, Richard
— Essai sur la nature du commerce general. L [but probably Paris or Holland], 1755. 12mo, contemp calf gilt; joints rubbed. Stain on leaves P7-Q5. P Sept 24 (255) $14,000

Cantone, Oberto
— L'Uso prattico dell' aritmetica.... Naples: Tarquinio Longho, 1599. 1st Ed. 4to, modern vellum bds. Prelims wormed; some browning & staining. S Nov 27 (253) £800 [Martin]

Capek, Karel
— War with the Newts. L: Allen & Unwin, [1937]. In chipped d/j. cb Sept 28 (281) $190

Capel, Arthur, Baron Capel
— Excellent Contemplations, Divine and Moral. L, 1683. 12mo, contemp sheep; rubbed & rebacked. Some worming affecting text. S Mar 10 (1037) £50 [Robertshaw]

Capel, Rudolf
— Lectionum bibliothecariarum memorabilium syntagma.... Hamburg: Georg Wolf, 1682. 12mo, old calf. Margins trimmed; lacking engraved title & A1. sg Mar 26 (55) $50

Capilli, Giovanni Battista. See: Egnatius, Johannes Baptista

Capitaine, L. &
Chanlaire, Pierre Gregoire
— Carte chorographique de la Belgique.... Paris, 1796 [An IV]. 4to, contemp half cloth; worn, spine lacking. With key-map & large-scale map on 64 sheets, all doublepage & mtd on stubs. Engraved throughout. Perforated stamps on maps; tp soiled, some maps stained. bba Dec 18 (125) £120 [Robertshaw]
Anr copy. 19th-cent bds. With 62 full-page mapsheets. S Oct 23 (22) £650 [Niew]

Capote, Truman
— A Christmas Memory. NY, [1956]. One of 600. sg Mar 5 (30) $150
— In Cold Blood. NY, [1965]. In tape-repaired d/j. Sgd. sg Dec 11 (10) $130
One of 500. sg Mar 5 (31) $225
— Music for Chameleons. NY, 1980. One of 350. sg Mar 5 (32) $110
— Other Voices, Other Rooms. NY, [1948]. 1st Ed. In rubbed d/j. cb May 7 (11) $110
Anr copy. In d/j. sg Mar 5 (33) $225
— A Tree of Night. NY, [1949]. In rubbed d/j. cb May 7 (12) $70

Capparoni, Giuseppe
— Raccolta degli ordini religiosi che esistono nella citta di Roma.... Rome, 1826. 4to, half mor. With engraved title & c.178 hand-colored plates. A few plates with foxing. S Nov 27 (51) £280 [Bifolco]

Capper, James, 1743-1825
— Observations on the Passage to India, through Egypt.... L, 1785. 3d Ed. 8vo, contemp calf; corners & joints worn. Dampstain on outer corners of text; 1 map paper-repaired on verso. sg Nov 20 (43) $150

CARACCIOLUS

Caracciolus, Robertus, 1425-95
— Sermones de timore divinorum iudiciorum. Venice: Johannes de Colonia & Johannes Manthen, 1475. 4to, contemp calf over wooden bds; spine repaired. Some worming at beginning & end. 94 leaves. Goff C-184. S Nov 27 (9) £1,600 [Pirages]

Carafa, Giuseppe. See: Notizia...

Carbonelli, Giovanni
— Bibliographia medica typographica pedemontana.... Rome, 1914-[19]. Folio, orig wraps; chipped. sg May 14 (582) $225

Carcano, Francesco, called Sforzino
— Tre Libri degli uccelli da Preda. Venice: Giolito, 1585. 8vo, later half vellum. sg Jan 15 (191) $175

Anr copy. Contemp vellum gilt. Jeanson 1042. SM Feb 28 (107) FF5,000

Carcano, Michael de
— Sermonarium de peccatis.... Basel: Michael Wenssler, 29 May 1479. Folio, contemp South German calf over wooden bds, richly tooled in blind & with chased & embossed metal center and corner pieces of Nuremberg type. Lacking 2 clasps. 272 (of 274) leaves; leaves 102 & 112 supplied in contemp Ms. Goff C-195. S Nov 27 (11) £6,000 [Scheyer]

Carco, Francis, Pseud, 1886-1958
— Montmartre vecu par Utrillo. Paris, 1947. One of 15 with cancelled suite of the illusts on japon, the decomposition of 1 illust & a suite of 7 unused illusts. 4to, unsewn in orig wraps. S June 17 (56) £3,200 [Marks]

Cardim, Antonio Francisco
— Relacam da viagem do Galeam Sao Lourenco.... Lisbon: Domingos Lopes Roza, 1651. 4to, modern mor. Small wormhole through blank mmargins; minor worming repairs in margins of last 2 leaves affecting 1 letter of catchword. C Apr 8 (7) £260 [Quaritch]

Careless, John, Pseud.
— The Old English Squire.... L, 1821. 8vo, lev gilt by Riviere. With 24 hand-colored plates. Small stain on 1 text leaf. sg Apr 2 (46) $175

Anr copy. Modern mor gilt. sg June 11 (99) $325

Careme, Marie Antonin, 1784-1833
— Le Patissier pittoresque. Paris: Firmin Didot, 1828. 8vo, contemp half mor gilt; rubbed. Some spotting & soiling; several plates with short tears in blank margins; 1 plate with margin restored; 2 plates with closed tears, 1 into image. P Nov 25 (100) $700

AMERICAN BOOK PRICES CURRENT

Anr copy. Orig wraps; frayed & soiled. With engraved title, dedication leaf & 125 plates. Foxed; some holes in blank margin of half-title; single wormhole through rear wrap & final 26 plates. P Nov 25 (101) $650

Anr Ed. Paris, 1842. 8vo, half calf. S May 21 (139) £400 [Weiss]

— Le Patissier royal parisien. Paris, 1841. 2 vols. 8vo, 19th-cent half calf. With engraved title & 41 plates. Some foxing. S May 21 (140) £450 [Weiss]

Carew, George
— A Retrospect into the Kings Certain Revenue.... L, 1661. Folio, contemp calf; worn. Some worming in lower margin affecting rules only. P Sept 24 (256) $600

Carey, David, 1782-1824
— Life in Paris. L, 1822. Illus by George Cruikshank. 8vo, lev gilt by Root. With 21 colored plates. Inscr washed out of half-title. sg Feb 12 (55) $325

Anr copy. Mor gilt by Sangorski & Sutcliffe. With 21 hand-colored plates & with the half-title & Binder's leaf. sg June 11 (137) $475

Anr copy. 1st Ed. 8vo, mor. With 21 hand-colored plates; half-title stained & repaired. wd Nov 12 (107) $400

Carey, Henry, d.1743. See: Golden Cockerel Press

Carey, Mathew, 1760-1839
— A Short Account of the Malignant Fever.... Phila., 1793. 3d Ed. 8vo, modern half mor gilt. pn Mar 5 (12) £75 [Knowles]

Carey, Robert, Earl of Monmouth
— Memoirs of Robert Carey written by Himself.... L: J. Hughes for R. & J. Dodsley, 1759. 8vo, later 19th-cent mor. sg Oct 9 (144) $80

Carion, Johannes, 1499-1537
— The Thre Bokes of Cronicles.... L: [J. Day] for Gwalter Lynne, 1550. 4to, 19th-cent russia, armorial bdg; rejointed, preserving spine. Corners torn or cut out on tp, C4 (affecting sidenote) & C8; minor flaws in Z4 & 2O8 with slight damage to text; some tears & rust marks; early 17th-cent marginalia. Roxburghe—Signet Library copy. S Dec 18 (224) £950 [Finch]

Carleton, George Washington
— Our Artist in Cuba. NY, 1865. 8vo, cloth. sg Sept 18 (70) $110

Carleton, William, 1794-1869

— Tales and Sketches...of the Irish Peasantry. Dublin, 1851. 8vo, half mor gilt; spine chipped at head. sg Feb 12 (40) $140

— Traits and Stories of the Irish Peasantry. Second Series. Dublin, 1833. 3 vols. 12mo, half calf gilt; worn. sg Sept 11 (52) $175

Carlevariis, Luca, 1663-1730

— Le Fabriche, e vedute di Venetia. Venice, [1703]. Oblong folio, half mor gilt; rubbed. With 91 (of 103) plates. Lacking tp & dedication; stain in upper margin of 1st few plates; 6 additional photographic plates inserted. pn June 18 (164) £3,800 [Shapero]

Carli, Gian Rinaldo

— Delle lettere Americane. Cremona, 1781-83. 3 vols in 1. 8vo, contemp calf; extremities worn. With folding map. sg Sept 18 (52) £80

Carls, F. H.

— Album de Pernambuco e seus arrabaldes. [Pernambuco, c.1878]. Folio, loose in fold-over cloth box. With 40 hand-colored views only. Tp & prospectus in facsimile; plates browned; margins of the view of Olinda def & repaired. S Oct 23 (441) £1,400 [Girou]

Carlyle, Thomas, 1795-1881

See also: Doves Press; German...

— The French Revolution. L, 1837. 1st Ed. 3 vols. 8vo, contemp half mor; rubbed. Lacking half-titles. S Sept 22 (9) £160 [Steedman]

Anr copy. Orig half cloth. sg June 11 (90) $1,400

Anr copy. Calf gilt by Morrell; worn & soiled. Lacking half-titles. wa Sept 25 (646) $375

— Past and Present. L, 1843. 1st Ed. 8vo, contemp half calf; worn. Ck Sept 5 (14) £90

— Works. L, 1896-99. Centenary Ed. One of 300. 30 vols plus 4 vols of index & supplementary translations. 8vo, cloth. ha May 22 (51) $175

Anr copy. 30 vols. 8vo, orig cloth; rubbed. pn Mar 5 (325) £70 [Martin]

Carlyle's copy, Thomas

— HARDY, SIR THOMAS DUFFUS. - General Introduction to the Materials for the History of Britain. L, 1848. Folio, contemp bds; broken. With numerous holograph annotations in pencil & sgd by Carlyle. S Dec 18 (42) £1,000 [Serendipity]

Carman, Bliss, 1861-1929

— Poems. NY & L, 1904. One of 500. 2 vols. Folio, mor by Chivers, each vol with hand-painted center panel; Vol I bdg bowed from exposure to damp. Library markings. Sold w.a.f. With Autograph Ms poem, sgd, inserted as frontis. O June 9 (29) $170

Carmena y Millan, Luis

— Catalogo de la Biblioteca Taurina. Madrid, 1903. One of 50. Half lea, orig wraps bound in. sg Oct 2 (75) $175

Carmichael, Hoagy B. See: Garrison & Carmichael

Carmody, Francis

— Physiologus: The Very Ancient Book of Beasts, Plants and Stones.... San Francisco: Book Club of California, 1953. One of 325. Illus by Mallette Dean. With ALs of Dean laid in. cb Sept 11 (240) $180

Carnarvon Library, George Edward S. M. Herbert, 5th Earl of, 1866-1923

— Catalogue of Books Selected from the Library of an English Amateur. L: Pvtly ptd, 1893-97. One of 3 on vellum. 2 parts in 1 vol. Folio, half mor. With 2 colored & 19 plates. Inscr. C Dec 3 (13) £1,600 [Maggs]

Carne, John, 1789-1844

— Syria, the Holy Land, Asia Minor. L, [1836-38]. 3 vols in 1. 4to, contemp mor. With 3 engraved titles, 2 maps & 117 plates. Port not mentioned. bba May 28 (277) £160 [Backus]

Anr copy. 3 vols. 4to, cloth; def. With port, 2 (of 3) engraved titles, 2 maps & 117 plates. Some spotting. pn Dec 11 (27) £70 [Dupont]

Anr copy. Contemp mor gilt; rubbed. With engraved titles, 3 maps, port & 117 plates. Some stains; 1 plate with marginal tear. S Nov 10 (1067) £180 [De Visser]

Anr copy. 3 vols in 1. 4to, contemp mor gilt; broken. With port, 3 engraved titles, 2 maps & 114 (of 117) plates. Plates at end stained. S Nov 18 (1065) £110 [Halperin]

Anr copy. 3 vols. 4to, contemp half calf. With engraved titles, 2 maps & 117 plates. S May 28 (854) £110

Anr copy. 3 vols in 2. 4to, half mor gilt; worn. With port, 3 engraved titles, 2 maps & 117 plates. Some foxing. S July 14 (737) £130

Anr Ed. L, [1842]. Illus by W. H. Bartlett. Vols II & III only. Disbound. sg Sept 25 (295) $200

Carnegie, George Fullerton
— Golfiana or Niceties Connected with the Game of Golf. Edin., 1833. 2d Ed. pnC Jan 23 (45) £9,800
Anr Ed. Edin., 1842. pnC July 16 (39) £5,600

Carneiro, Antonio de Maris. See: Mariz Carneiro, Antonio de

Caro, Varro, Columella & Palladius
— Scriptores rei rusticae. Paris: Estienne, 1543. ("Libri de re rustica.") 4 (of 5) parts in 1 vol (lacking Columella). 8vo, early vellum. Minor dampstains at beginning & end. sg Oct 9 (197) $225

Carolinas
— The Two Charters Granted by King Charles IId to the Proprietors of Carolina.... L: Richard Parker, [1705?]. 4to, half calf. Minor stains; last leaf dust-soiled. S June 25 (380) £1,300

Carossa, Hans
— Eine Kindheit. Leipzig, 1923. One of 100. Mor. HK Nov 4 (2991) DM750

Carpenter, Robert Ruliph Morgan
— Game Trails in Idaho and Alaska. Pvtly ptd, [1940]. One of 400. 4to, cloth. sg Oct 23 (212) $150

Carpue, Joseph Constantine, 1764-1846
— A History of the High Operation for the Stone by Incision above the Pubis.... L, 1819. 8vo, contemp mor extra. Inscr to the Duke of York. Ck Nov 21 (9) £430 [Phillips]

Carr, Sir John, 1772-1832
— Caledonian Sketches, or a Tour through Scotland.... L, 1809. 1st Ed. 4to, modern half lea. With folding frontis & 11 plates. K Oct 4 (85) £140
Anr copy. Contemp calf gilt. pnE Nov 12 (270) £85
Anr copy. Modern half mor. With folding frontis & 11 hand-colored plates. wa Mar 5 (221) $120
— Descriptive Travels in the Southern and Eastern Parts of Spain.... L, 1811. 4to, contemp calf; rubbed. With folding frontis & 5 views. Some spotting & slight marginal worming. T Nov 20 (19) £135
Anr copy. Orig bds; spine & corners worn, becoming disbound. wa Dec 11 (700) $170
— A Northern Summer or Travels Round the Baltic.... L, 1805. 4to, later half calf; soiled. With 11 plates, 1 folding & torn. Some fraying. S Nov 17 (896) £70 [Elliott]
Anr copy. Contemp calf; rebacked. With 11 plates. T Oct 16 (267) £135
Anr copy. Contemp calf; rubbed. Some spotting & marginal worming. T Nov 20 (18) £100
— The Stranger in France. L, 1803. 4to, contemp half calf; broken. With 12 plates (frontis not mentioned). T Oct 16 (268) £55
— The Stranger in Ireland. L, 1806. 1st Ed. 4to, contemp calf; rubbed, rebacked. Lacking Killarney; 1 plate cropped. bba Apr 9 (350) £160 [Fisher]
Anr copy. Modern half mor gilt by Bayntun. With hand-colored map & 16 plates, 5 folding. C Oct 15 (24) £300 [Sotheran]
— A Tour through Holland.... L, 1807. 1st Ed. 4to, contemp half calf; rubbed & broken, some leaves detached. With map & 20 plates. S Nov 17 (897) £280 [Maliye]
Anr copy. Contemp half calf; broken. Some plates offset; 1st 4 leaves badly spotted. S Nov 17 (898) £220 [Maliye]
— A Tour through Holland, along the Right and Left Banks of the Rhine, to the South of Germany.... Phila., 1807. 4to, calf gilt. sg Nov 20 (44) $150

Carr, John Dickson, 1906-77
— The Department of Queer Complaints. NY, 1940. Bdg with some waterstaining. cb May 7 (204) $65
— It Walks by Night. NY, 1930. Owner's rubberstamp to front free endpaper. cb May 7 (212) $55
— The Mad Hatter Mystery. NY, 1933. Bdg worn, with 1 corner showing. Seal broken. cb May 7 (217) $60

Carracci, Annibale, 1560-1602
— Galeria nel Palazzo Farnese in Roma.... Rome: Fran. Collignon, [17th cent]. Folio, half vellum; worn & scuffed. With 40 plates trimmed & mtd on 29 leaves of irregular size. ha Sept 19 (3) $450

Carrasco del Saz, Francisco
— Opera. Madrid, 1648. Bound with: Tractatus de casibus curiae. Madrid, 1630. Folio, 19th-cent half lea; loose. Some browning & dampstaining. sg Mar 12 (44) $70

Carrera, Pietro
— Il Gioco de gli scacchi.... Militello, 1617. 4to, modern mor. Tp washed & remargined. sg Apr 2 (40) $750

Carrera, Pietro, 1571-1647
— A Treatise on the Game of Chess. L, 1822. Modern cloth. pn Mar 26 (373) £60 [Caissa]

Carriage...
— The Carriage Builders' and Harness Makers' Art Journal. L, [1859]. Vol I. 4to, contemp half calf; rubbed. With 59 plates, 14 hand-colored under varnish. Spotted. bba May 28 (61) £480 [Ward]

Carrington, Leonora
— La Dame Ovale. Paris: Guy Levis Mano, 1939. One of 535. Illus by Max Ernst. Orig wraps. S June 29 (45) £500 [Neggar]

Carrington, Nicholas Toms
— Dartmoor: a Descriptive Poem. L, 1826. 1st Ed. 8vo, recent bds with linen backstrip. T Mar 19 (91) £50

Anr copy. Orig bds; backstrip def. With 12 plates. T June 16 (60) £40

Carroll, John M.
— The Black Military Experience in the American West. NY, [1971]. One of 300. In d/j. Sgd. cb Jan 8 (239) $55

Carroll, Jonathan
— The Land of Laughs. NY: Viking, [1980]. Uncorrected Proof. Wraps. cb Sept 28 (285) $70

Carroll, Lewis. See: Dodgson, Charles Lutwidge

Cartailhac, Emile —& Breuil, Henri
— Peintures et gravures murales des cavernes paleolithiques. Monaco, 1906-15. Folio, recent cloth. T Oct 16 (563) £50

Cartari, Vincenzo
— Imagines deorum.... Lyons: Guichard Juleron for B. Honorat, 1581. 4to, limp vellum; soiled. Lacking final gathering; top portion of Eee3-4 torn away; short tear at top of Ll4 just touching woodcut. S Mar 10 (1039) £70 [Clarke]

Carte...
— La Carte Surréaliste. [Paris, 1937]. Nos 1 21 (complete set). Ptd on pale green card S June 29 (38) £350 [Bolligar]

Carte, Thomas, 1686-1754
— An History of the Life of James, Duke of Ormond. L, 1736-36-35. 3 vols. Folio, contemp calf; rebacked. bba Apr 9 (316) £110 [Emerald Isle]

Carter, Charles
— The Complete Practical Cook.... L, 1730. 1st Ed. 4to, contemp calf; worn, rebacked, endpapers stained. With 60 plates. Plate 13 soiled & repaired along fold with loss; Plate 60 soiled along fold & chipped; marginal tear in F3; some staining & browning, mostly marginal. P Nov 25 (102) $500

Carter, E. S.
— The Life and Adventures of E. S. Carter.... St. Joseph, Mo., 1896. 1st Ed. 8vo, orig wraps; creased, chipped & torn. cb Jan 8 (20) $550

Carter, Harry. See: Morison & Carter

Carter, John, 1748-1817
— The Ancient Architecture of England. L, 1806. 2 parts in 1 vol. Folio, contemp half calf; worn, joints split. bba May 14 (236) £180 [Blake]

Anr Ed. L, 1806-7. 2 parts in 1 vol. Folio, half calf; worn & broken. T Jan 22 (290) £80

— Specimens of the Ancient Sculpture and Painting.... L, 1780-87 [1780-94]. 1st Ed. 2 vols. Folio, contemp calf; broken, worn. T Jan 22 (291) £100

Carter, John Waynflete, 1905 75 & Muir, Percy H.
— Printing and the Mind of Man. L, 1967. 4to, orig cloth, in d/j. bba Oct 16 (411) £80 [Marks]; bba Mar 26 (5) £90 [Parsons]; cb Feb 5 (66) $110

Anr copy. Library markings. O June 16 (155) $80

Anr Ed. NY, 1967. 4to, cloth; in d/j. cb Sept 11 (228) $150

Anr copy. Cloth; in soiled d/j. cb Feb 19 (53) $55

Anr copy. Cloth; backstrip bumped, 1 small tear. ha Dec 19 (34) $85

Anr copy. Cloth; in d/j. sg Jan 22 (89) $130

Anr copy. In chipped d/j. wa June 25 (56) $120

2d Ed. Munich, 1983. 4to, orig cloth, in d/j. cb Feb 5 (67) $85

Carter, John Waynflete, 1905-75 —& Pollard, Graham
— An Enquiry into the Nature of Certain Nineteenth Century Pamphlets. L & NY, 1934. sg Jan 22 (90) $100; sg June 11 (94) $60

Anr copy. Cloth, in d/j; rubbed, hinges stained. Inscr by Carter. ha Dec 19 (35) $65

Carter, Matthew
— Honour Redivivus or an Analysis of Honor and Armory. L, 1655. 8vo, later half sheep; joints split, rubbed. Lacking frontis; engraved title cropped at outer edge. bba Apr 23 (175) £45 [Knohl]

Anr Ed. L, 1673. 8vo, 19th-cent mor. With frontis, engraved title & 9 plates. bba Aug 28 (178) £60 [P & P Books]

CARTER

Carter, Thomas, d.1867
— War Medals of the British Army.... L, 1893. 8vo, orig cloth; spine ends & corners bumped, hinge cracking. cb Dec 18 (32) $110

Carter, Thomas Francis, 1882-1925
— The Invention of Printing in China.... NY, 1931. wa Feb 19 (247) $55

Carteret, Leopold
— Le tresor du bibliophile.... Paris, 1924-28. 4 vols. Half mor, orig wraps bound in. S Nov 27 (52) £300 [Quaritch]

Cartier-Bresson, Henri
— Beautiful Jaipur. Jaipur, 1948. Cloth, in d/j; worn. O Jan 6 (36) $110
— The Decisive Moment. NY, [1952]. Folio, bds, in worn d/j. With separate pamphlet of captions laid in. sg Nov 13 (31) $200
Anr copy. Bds. sg May 7 (27) $425
— The Europeans. NY, [1955]. Folio, pictorial bds; rubbed, spine ends chipped. sg Nov 13 (32) $100
Anr copy. Bds, remnants of plastic d/j. With the pamphlet of captions laid in. sg May 7 (28) $175
— From One China to the Other. NY: Universe Books, [1956]. Text by Han Suyin. 4to, cloth, in d/j. wa Nov 6 (295) $55
— The World of Henri Cartier-Bresson. NY, 1968. Oblong folio, cloth, in d/j. sg Nov 13 (33) $80

Cartwright, George, 1739-1819
— A Journal of Transactions and Events during a Residence of Nearly Sixteen Years on the Coast of Labrador. Newark, 1792. 3 vols. 4to, contemp calf gilt; head of 1 spine worn. With port & 2 folding maps on 3 sheets. Lacking initial blank in each vol; 2 small fold tears. C Oct 15 (25) £1,500 [Marshall]
Anr copy. Contemp calf; rebacked. Some foxing; lacking 3 maps. sg Mar 12 (34) $250

Cartwright, William, 1611-43
— Comedies, Tragi-Comedies, with Other Poems. L, 1651. 2 parts in 1 vol. 8vo, modern calf; soiled. Port, title & dedication leaves cropped, slightly affecting text; other margins cut close; lacking last 2 leaves. bba Jan 15 (18) £120 [Korn]

Carvalho, Joao Jorge de
— Gaticanea, ou cruelissima guerra entre os canes e os gatos.... Lisbon: Francisco Luiz Ameno, 1781. 8vo, calf; worn. With 2 folding plates. S Nov 27 (53) £480 [Goldschmidt]

AMERICAN BOOK PRICES CURRENT

Carver, Jonathan, 1732-80
— Voyage dans les parties interieures de l'Amerique septentrionale.... Paris, 1784. 8vo, bds; worn & soiled. With folding map. wa Mar 5 (370) $210

Cary, Henry, Viscount Falkland
— The History of the Life, Reign, and Death of Edward II.... L, 1680. Folio, contemp calf; joints cracked, blistered, hinges cracked. sg June 11 (95) $100

Cary, John, d.1720
— A Discourse Concerning the Trade of Ireland and Scotland.... L, 1696. 4to, wraps. S July 23 (427) £650 [Drury]

Cary, John, c.1754-1835
— Actual Survey of the Country Fifteen Miles Round London. L, 1786. 8vo, contemp half calf; rubbed. With 50 maps, hand-colored in outline. Ck Sept 26 (36) £190
— New and Correct English Atlas. L, 1787. 4to, half lea; very worn. Soiled. bba Apr 9 (404) £200 [Crossley]
Anr copy. Modern calf. With 47 maps, hand-colored in outline. Lacking list of subscribers. C Apr 8 (67) £320 [Leicester]
Anr copy. Orig lea gilt; spine worn, flap detached. With engraved title, dedication, general map & 45 county maps, hand-colored in outline. With 2 maps of Yorkshire browned. L Dec 11 (194) £220
Anr copy. Cloth; soiled. With 46 maps, hand-colored in outline; lacking general map. pn May 21 (338) £320 [Hughes]
Anr copy. Bds; def. With 47 maps, hand-colored in outline. pn May 21 (339) £360 [Stabik]
Anr copy. Modern half calf preserving contemp bds. Minor spotting. S Nov 17 (755) £320 [Hughes]
Anr copy. Contemp calf; rubbed & rebacked. Minor marginal tears. S Nov 17 (756) £320 [Hughes]
Anr copy. Contemp half calf; worn. S Nov 17 (757) £300 [Shapero]
Anr copy. Modern half mor. With engraved title, general map hand-colored in outline & 45 uncolored county maps. S May 28 (967) £300
Anr Ed. L, 1793. 4to, modern calf gilt. With engraved title & 47 maps, hand-colored in outline. Lacking dedication & list of subscribers. C Apr 8 (68) £340 [Gaston]
Anr copy. Cloth. pn May 21 (337) £320 [Postaprint]
Anr copy. Later half cloth; worn. Lacking 1 map; tp soiled & repaired; some leaves detached. T Feb 19 (336) £420

Anr Ed. L, 1809. Folio, bds. With 47 maps hand-colored in outline. Lacking tp. pn May 21 (340) £360 [Magna]

Anr copy. Half calf. With 44 hand-colored maps; lacking Cornwall. pn May 21 (341) £550 [Burden]

Anr Ed. L, 1818. 4to, contemp lea; rebacked. With engraved title & 47 maps, hand-colored in outline. S Nov 17 (759) £360 [Tooley]

Anr copy. Contemp half mor; rubbed. Hampshire torn at fold. S Jan 13 (351) £480 [George]

Anr Ed. L, 1823. 4to, contemp calf gilt; spline repaired at foot, upper cover abraded. With engraved title & 47 maps, hand-colored in outline. C Oct 15 (26) £500 [Quaritch]

Anr copy. Half calf; rubbed. pn Nov 20 (269) £400 [Leadley]

— New Itinerary.... L, 1815. 6th Ed. 8vo, modern half calf. bba Apr 9 (405) £50 [Rainbow]

— New Map of England and Wales.... L, 1794. 4to, disbound. With dedication, hand-colored general map & map in 77 sections, numbered to 81, hand-colored in outline. Lacking engraved title; some stains; dedication leaf soiled & frayed. bba Mar 26 (327) £45 [Jeffery]

Anr copy. Contemp half calf; worn. With engraved title & dedication, hand-colored general map & map in 77 sections, numbered to 81, hand-colored in outline. Some spotting. Ck May 15 (302) £95

Anr copy. Half calf; rubbed. Sold w.a.f. pn May 21 (343) £130 [Nicholson]

Anr copy. Orig half calf; rebacked & corners restored. T Nov 20 (82) £110

Anr Ed. L, 1832. ("Improved Map of England & Wales.") Folio, contemp half lea; rubbed. With engraved title, index map & hand-colored maps on 65 sheets. pn Dec 11 (407) £450 [Nicholson]

Anr Ed. L, 1842. ("Improved Map of England and Wales....") Oblong folio, half calf; spine def. pn Oct 23 (413A) £90 [Jeffreys]

— New Universal Atlas. L, 1808. Folio, contemp half russia; lower cover lacking. With 47 hand-colored maps only; the 1st & last maps soiled & torn; 1 map detached & torn in half; some maps torn in fold; lacking text. Ck May 15 (319) £480

— Survey of the High Roads from London. L, 1790. 4to, contemp calf; rubbed. With engraved title, hand-colored general plan, general map & 80 strip maps on 40 sheets, all hand-colored. Some stains & spotting. pn Mar 5 (365) £220 [Postaprint]

Anr copy. Calf gilt. pn May 21 (344) £320 [Falke]

Anr Ed. L, 1799. 4to, later sheep; rubbed. bba Aug 20 (456) £240 [Henly]

Anr Ed. L, 1801. 4to, later mor folder; rubbed. With engraved title, general plan & 80 hand-colored strip maps on 40 leaves. Ck Sept 26 (281) £210

— Traveller's Companion, or a Delineation of the Turnpike Roads of England and Wales. L, 1790. 8vo, calf gilt; worn. Lacking Yorkshire. pn May 21 (345) £130 [Nicholson]

Anr Ed. L, 1791. 8vo, calf. With 43 maps on 23 plates (including map in end pocket), hand-colored in outline. Tear in folding map. L Dec 11 (195) £80

Anr copy. Contemp half calf; broken. Yorkshire torn along folds. T Feb 19 (295) £95

Anr Ed. L, 1810. 8vo, calf gilt; rebacked. With 43 maps, hand-colored in outline. pn May 21 (347) £130 [Nicholson]

Anr Ed. L, 1817. 8vo, contemp calf; rebacked. With 43 maps on 23 plates (including map in end pocket), hand-colored in outline. pn Sept 18 (349a) £90 [Postaprint]

Anr Ed. L, 1821. 8vo, mor. With 43 maps on 23 plates (including map in end pocket), hand-colored in outline. Folding map slightly torn & repaired. pn May 21 (349) £110 [Saville]

Anr Ed. L, 1828. 8vo, half calf. With 43 maps colored in outline. pn May 21 (350) £140 [Clarke]

Cary, John, c.1754-1835 —&
Stockdale, John

— New British Atlas.... L, 1805. Folio, half mor; spine torn. With 50 maps hand-colored in outline. New Jersey def. pn Dec 11 (406) £600 [Nicholson]

Anr copy. Half calf. With engraved title & 49 double-page maps, hand-colored in outline. pn May 21 (351) £520 [Postaprint]

Cary, Thomas G.

— Gold from California, and its Effects on Prices. NY, 1856. Orig wraps; soiled, stained & foxed. Inscr. cb Jan 8 (21) $55

Casa, Giovanni della

— Le Galatee. [Geneva: J. de Tournes, 1609]. 16mo, vellum bds. S Sept 23 (434) £260 [Maggs]

Casanova de Seingalt, Giacomo Girolamo
See also: Limited Editions Club
— Memoirs. [N.p.]: Aventuros, 1925. One of 1,000. Trans by Machen; illus by Rockwell Kent. 12 vols. 4to, mor preserving orig endpapers. O May 12 (37) $375

Casas, Bartolome de las, 1474-1566
— Istoria o brevissima relatione della distruttione dell' Indie occidentali.... Venice, 1626. 4to, contemp vellum. sg Mar 12 (45) $350
Anr Ed. Venice, 1630. 4to, old vellum. Dampstaining to outer margin, occasionally affecting text; library markings. Text in Spanish & Italian. sg Mar 12 (46) $150
— Obras. Barcelona, 1646. 4to, 19th-cent sheep gilt; worn, front cover detached. Marginal worming throughout; many leaves remargined; some dampstains; last leaf backed; lacking 1st 2 leaves. sg Sept 18 (54) $120

Casati, Gaetano, 1838-1902
— Ten Years in Equatoria. L, 1891. 2 vols. 8vo, orig cloth; worn. pn Apr 30 (10) £110

Case...
— The Case and Claim of the American Loyalists.... L, 1783. Issue having imprint. 8vo, sewn as issued; 1st & last page soiled. P Sept 24 (234) $175

Case, Arthur Ellicott
— A Bibliography of English Poetical Miscellanies 1521-1750. L, 1935. 4to, half cloth, unopened. sg May 14 (216) $50

Casley, David
— A Catalogue of the Manuscripts of the King's Library.... L, 1734. 4to, contemp calf; rebacked. With 16 plates. Perforated stamp on tp & anr leaf. sg Mar 26 (57) $225

Caslon, William & Son
— A Specimen of Printing Types. L, 1764. 4to, contemp calf gilt. 38 leaves ptd on 1 side only. C Dec 12 (40) £2,500 [Bookpress]
Anr Ed. L, [c.1785]. 4 leaves. Folio. bba Oct 16 (477) £65 [Forster]

Caspar, Max
— Bibliographia Kepleriana. Munich, 1936. Folio, cloth. bba Feb 5 (72) £60 [Dawson]; sg May 14 (583) $150

Cassas, Louis Francois
— Voyage pittoresque de la Syrie.... Paris, 1791-99 [An VII]. Folio, unbound. With 40 leaves of text & 155 (of 180?) plates. Some marginal dampstains. S Oct 23 (26) £1,700 [Kay]

Cassell's...
— Cassell's Old and New Edinburgh.... Edin., [n.d.]. 6 vols. 8vo, orig cloth. pnE Nov 12 (250) £42
— Cassell's Picturesque Australia.... L, 1889-90 [1888-92]. Ed by Edward Ellis Morris. 4 vols. 8vo, orig cloth; back cover of Vol I stained. bba Oct 30 (339) £80 [Nosbuesch]

Casserius, Julio, d.1616
— De vocis auditusque organis historia anatomica.... Ferrara, 1600-1. Folio, contemp calf, with Northumberland arms; rebacked. S May 21 (188) £3,000 [Brett]

Cassianus, Joannes, 360?-435?
— De institutis coenobiorum. Lyons: Simon Bevilacqua, 19 Sept 1516. 8vo, old lea; front cover imperf, hinges cracked. Some dampstains. sg Oct 9 (145) $175

Cassin, John, 1813-69
— Illustrations of the Birds of California.... Phila., 1862. 4to, half mor. With 50 color plates. sg Apr 2 (41) $1,200

Cassini de Thury, Cesar Francois, 1714-84
— Carte de France. Paris, [1789]. 2 vols. Folio, contemp half calf; def. With 182 engraved sheets & 4 index sheets. Lacking the triangulation diagram; some staining. S Oct 23 (54) £1,200 [Niew]
— La Meridienne de l'observatoire Royale de Paris, verifiee.... Paris, 1744. 4to, contemp calf; worn. With 14 plates. HN May 20 (966a) DM1,100

Cassini, Giovanni Domenico, 1625-1712
— La Meridiana del tempio di S. Petronio tirata, e preparata per le osservazioni astromomiche l'anno 1655.... Bologna, 1695. 4to, bds. With 2 folding plates; minor tears. S Nov 27 (254) £600 [Fame]

Cassini, Jacques, 1677-1756
— Tables astronomiques du soleil, de la lune.... Paris, 1740. 2 parts in 1 vol. 4to, mor. With 5 folding plates.. SM Oct 20 (424) FF38,000

Castell, Edmund, 1606-85
— Lexicon heptaglotton.... L, 1669. 2 vols. Folio, early 19th-cent russia; spines chipped, joints split, 1 cover detached. Ck Apr 24 (211) £110

Castell, Robert
— The Villas of the Ancients Illustrated. L, 1728. 2 parts in 1 vol. Folio, modern calf; rubbed. Marginal tears. S July 14 (586) £350

Castellamonte, Amedeo di
— Venaria reale. Palazzo di piacere.... Turin, 1674. Folio, mor janseniste by Pouillet. With 4 plates repaired, 1 affecting caption. Jeanson 1078. SM Feb 28 (108) FF35,000

Castellan, Antoine Laurent, 1772-1838
— Moeurs, usages, costumes des Othomans. Paris, 1812. 6 vols. 18mo, contemp blind-stamped calf. With 72 hand-colored plates. Ck May 15 (34) £280

Castellense, Adriano, Cardinal, b. c.1458
— De sermone latino, et modis latinae loquendi iam denvo restitutus. Venice: Melchior Sessa, Feb 1534. 8vo, mor gilt by Hardy, with arms of Baron Seilliere. Jeanson copy. SM Feb 28 (110) FF2,200
— Venatio. Strasbourg: Matthias Schurer, Aug 1512. 4to, half cloth. Jeanson copy. SM Feb 28 (109) FF2,500

Castellesi, Adriano, Cardinal, b. c.1458. See: Castellense, Adriano

Castelli, Pietro, d.c.1657
— Exactissima descriptio rariorum quarundam plantarum...in horto Farnesiano. Rome, 1625. Folio, bds, uncut. Some damp-stains; tp repaired in lower inner margin; small repair to f.4. S Oct 23 (667) £300 [Segal]

Castelnau, Michel de, 1526?-92
— Memoirs of the Reigns of Francis II and Charles IX of France.... L, 1724. Folio, modern bds. Tear to R1; severe damp-stains at end; imperf margins of last leaf reinforced. sg Oct 9 (146) $90

Castiglione, Baldassare, 1478-1529

Il Cortegiano
— 1727. - Il Cortegiano; or The Courtier.... L. 4to, modern half calf. sg Oct 9 (147) $150
— 1900. - L: Essex House Press One of 200. Trans into English by Thomas Hoby. sg June 11 (188) $275

Castillon, A.
— Chasses aux Indes. Paris: A Courcier, [c.1860]. 4to, orig bdg. Jeanson copy. SM Feb 28 (111) FF800
— Chasses en Afrique. Paris: A. Ghio, [1858]. 4to, orig bdg. Schwerdt-Jeanson copy. SM Feb 28 (112) FF3,200

Castle, Thomas, c.1804-38. See: Barton & Castle

Castlman, Riva
— Technics and Creativity. II. Gemini Gel. NY: Museum of Modern Art, [1971]. Illus by Jasper Johns. 4to, wraps. Sgd by Johns. sg Feb 5 (196) $175

Castro, Casimiro
— Album of the Mexican Railway. Mexico, 1877. Oblong folio, loose in orig cloth; worn. With colored frontis, double-page map & 24 colored plates. Marginal soiling to some plates; 3 plates with tears in blank margin; 1 plate & map torn into image; 1 plate loose. P Sept 24 (137) $1,500

Anr copy. Orig cloth; rubbed. With colored title & 24 color views. Some spotting in margins; marginal tears to tp; minor tears at lower blank margin. S Apr 24 (295) £2,000 [Dailey]

Castronius, Benedictus Maria
— Horographia universalis.... Palermo, 1728. Folio, old calf; rebacked. With 19 double-page or folding plates, 1 with additional engraved section tipped onto plate surface. Lacking final index leaf; section of tp excised; 1 plate with soiled margins. Ck Jan 30 (47) £160

Catalogue...
— Catalogue of a Collection of Pictures; formed with the greatest care...and consigned to Mr. Samuel Pawson. L, [n.d.]. 8vo, contemp calf. C Dec 12 (41) £420 [Weinreb]

Cataneo, Pietro
— Le Pratiche delle due prime mathematiche.... Venice: Giovanni Griffio, 1559. 4to, vellum. Lacking last blank. S Sept 23 (515) £120 [Vine]

Catesby, Mark, 1679?-1749
— The Natural History of Carolina, Florida, and the Bahama Islands.... L, 1731-[43]. 1st Ed. 2 vols. Folio, contemp calf gilt with onlaid mor gilt cornerpiece ornaments; rebacked & regilt with orig mor labels laid down. With double-page map & 219 (of 220) plates, all hand-colored. Lacking Plate 62 in Vol II. CNY May 11 (9) $120,000

Anr copy. Contemp russia; rebacked. With hand-colored map & 220 hand-colored plates. Horticultural Society of New York —de Belder copy. S Apr 27 (62) £150,000 [Ursus]

2d Ed. L, 1754. 2 vols. Folio, half calf. With 220 hand-colored plates. Some discoloration throughout; some spotting. Horticultural Society of New York—de Belder copy. S Apr 27 (63) £28,000 [Schrire]

3d Ed. L, 1771. 2 vols. Folio, old half mor; worn. With folding colored map & 220 hand-colored plates. Without List of Encouragers; Plate 75 torn into plate; 10 other plates with marginal tears, some repaired; other minor defs. Arthur Cleveland Bent's copy. CNY Nov 21 (51) $24,000

Catesby

Anr Ed. L, 1771 [but most plates watermarked 1815-16]. 2 vols. Folio, recent half calf. With folding hand-colored map & 220 hand-colored plates. Marginal soiling; marginal tears repaired. S June 25 (149) £34,000 [Quaritch]

— Piscium, serpenteum, insectorum... Carolinae, Floridae et Bahamensium.... Nuremberg, 1750. Bound with: Trew, Christoph Jakob. Hortus Nitidissimis....Nuremberg, 1750. Folio, late 18th-cent calf gilt, upper cover dated 1790 & lettered J. L. G. Z. S. W. u H. 1st work with 66 (of 100) hand-colored plates & 1ith 1 of these torn & tp torn & repaired. 2d work with 43 (of 180) hand-colored plates, with tears in 9 & several trimmed & a stain on Plate 34. S Oct 23 (683) £13,500 [Browning]

Cather, Willa, 1873-1947

— Death Comes for the Archbishop. NY, 1927. 1st Ed. In d/j. Inscr to Carl Pforzheimer. sg Mar 5 (37) $700

Anr Ed. NY, 1929. One of 170 L.p. copies. 4to, in d/j. sg Mar 5 (38) $275

— Lucy Gayheart. NY, 1935. 1st Ed, one of 749, sgd. L. p. copy. sg Mar 5 (40) $100

Anr copy. In chipped d/j. wa Sept 25 (647) $140

— Not Under Forty. NY, 1936. 1st Ed, One of 333 on Japan vellum, sgd. In d/j. L. p. copy. sg Mar 5 (51) $225

— Sapphira and the Slave Girl. NY, 1940. 1st Ed, One of 520, sgd. In d/j. L. p. copy. sg Mar 5 (42) $225

Anr copy. In d/j; soiled. sg Mar 5 (43) $130

— Shadows on the Rock. NY, 1931. 1st Ed, One of 619. In d/j; edges worn. L. p. copy. sg Mar 5 (44) $200

Catherine of Siena

— Obra de las epistolas y oraciones.... Alcala: Arnaldo Guillermo de Brocar, 22 Nov 1512. Folio, disbound. Dampstained; wormed, affecting text; tp & following leaf torn in blank outer margin; lacking final blank. sg Oct 9 (8) $750

Catholic...

— The Catholic Encyclopedia. NY, 1907-22. 17 vols. 4to, half lea, Index in cloth. sg Jan 22 (105) $150

Anr Ed. NY, 1913-14. 16 vols. 4to, later cloth, orig covers & backstrips laid down; worn & shaken. sg Oct 2 (100) $60

Catich, Edward M.

— Letters Redrawn from the Trajan Inscription in Rome. Davenport, Iowa: Catfish Press, [1961]. Oblong 4to, loose in folder, as issued. With 93 plates. sg Jan 8 (40) $110

Catlin, George, 1796-1872

— Letters and Notes on the Manners, Customs, and Condition of the North American Indians. L, 1841. 1st Ed. 2 vols. 8vo, orig cloth; rubbed, top of spine of Vol II torn & def & bdg broken. With 3 maps & 175 plates only; lacking plates 28/31, 62 & 77/78. Some staining. bba Mar 12 (14) £100 [Sanders]

Anr copy. Contemp mor gilt; joints rubbed. With 3 maps. Inscr to C. A. Murray. P May 13 (2) $2,200

Anr copy. Orig cloth; worn, hinges broken in Vol I, Vol II rebacked. Some spotting & marginal browning; pencil annotations in Vol I. S Nov 18 (1104) £110 [Noshuch]

2d Ed of Vol II, 1st Ed of Vol I. 2 vols. 8vo, orig cloth; 1 bdg detached & worn, the other rubbed, lacking back endpaper of Vol I. With frontis, 3 maps & 176 plates & with errata slip tipped into Vol I. bba Oct 30 (292) £130 [Angle]

1st American Ed. NY, 1841. 2 vols. 8vo, half mor; joints & extremities worn. Some foxing; some plates repaired. sg Mar 12 (47) $325

Anr copy. Orig cloth; joints starting, Vol II loose in bdg. Lacking 1 plate. sg Mar 12 (48) $140

Anr Ed. L, 1844. 2 vols. 8vo, half mor gilt; rubbed. Dampstained. pn Apr 30 (128) £120 [Bookroom]

Anr copy. Contemp half mor; joints & corners rubbed. S Nov 18 (1103) £140 [Sephlen]

Anr Ed. L, 1876. ("Illustrations of the Manners, Customs, and Condition of the North American Indians.") 2 vols. 8vo, orig cloth; worn. With 177 color plates. S Nov 18 (1102) £280 [Toms]

Anr copy. Orig cloth; spine ends frayed. With 180 colored plates. sg Mar 12 (49) $950

Anr copy. Contemp half mor; worn, front hinge of both vols broken. wa Nov 6 (550) $300

Anr Ed. L, 1841 [but c.1892]. ("The Manners, Customs, and Condition of the North American Indians.") 2 vols. 8vo, orig cloth. pn Mar 5 (133) £160 [Levine]

Anr Ed. Edin., 1903. ("North American Indians.") 2 vols. 4to, cloth; spotted. wd June 19 (73) $125

Anr Ed. Edin., 1926. 2 vols. 4to, orig cloth. Ck Nov 21 (207) £220

Anr copy. Cloth. sg Mar 12 (50) $250

— North American Indian Portfolio. L, 1844. 1st Ed. Folio, text in modern wraps, plates in later mats or later card mounts. With 25 plates with modern coloring & captions in ink. Some foxing under the color. Sold w.a.f. CNY Nov 21 (53) $12,000

Anr copy. Contemp half mor gilt; spine & corners worn, recent endpapers & blank interleaves. With 25 uncolored plates. P Nov 21 (52) $13,000

Anr copy. Contemp half mor; rubbed, hinges reinforced. With 25 colored plates. Plate 13 with marginal chip, tear & closed tear into image; 4 other plates with short tears or closed tears in blank margins; several plates spotted or with creases; pinholes to corners of most images. P May 13 (3) $35,000

Anr copy. Orig half mor gilt; upper cover waterstained, inner bdg broken. With 25 hand-finished color plates mtd on card, several heightened with gum arabic. Some mounts & a few plates faintly spotted. S Nov 18 (1101) £19,000 [Rows]

Anr copy. Half shagreen gilt by A. Tarrant. With 25 hand-finished color plates. Jeanson 1561. SM Feb 28 (113) FF170,000

Anr Ed. L: Geo. Catlin, [c.1845]. Folio, half lev gilt; extremities worn. With 2 complete sets of the 31-plate issue, plain & hand-colored. With ptd title & 8 leaves of descriptions of 1st 25 plates supplied from 1st Ed. Text leaves creased at gutter margins; 1 color plate repaired; plain plates foxed. CNY Dec 19 (42) $30,000

Catlow, Agnes, 1807?-89 and Maria E.
— Sketching Rambles; or Nature in the Alps.... L, [1861]. 2 vols. 8vo, orig cloth; joints rubbed. With 20 tinted litho plates. Ck Nov 21 (239) £130

Cato, Marcus Porcius, 234-149 B.C.
— Cato's Moral Distichs. San Francisco: Book Club of California, 1939. One of 250. Facsimile of the Benjamin Franklin Ed of 1735, with an orig leaf from a Franklin-ptd work tipped in. cb Sept 11 (29) $80

Cato, Varro, Columella & Palladius
— Scriptores rei rusticae. Venice: Aldus & Andreas [d'Asola], May 1514. ("Libri de re rustica.") 4to, contemp blind-stamped calf; rebacked retaining orig spine, repaired. A few margins lightly stained; some margins with early Ms notes. S May 21 (30) £350 [Thomas]

Anr copy. 19th-cent mor gilt. sg June 11 (4) $450

Anr Ed. Florence: Junta, July 1515. 8vo, 18th-cent yapp-edged vellum. Hunt copy. CNY Nov 21 (251) $240

Anr Ed. Florence: Heirs of P. Giunta, 1521. 8vo, limp vellum. Some worming in margins, occasionally touching text. S Sept 23 (489) £130 [Roberts]

Anr Ed. Venice: Aldus, Dec 1533. 4to, mor gilt. Some browning. Jeanson 1492. SM Mar 1 (348) FF3,000

Anr Ed. Basel: J. Hervagius, 1535. 8vo, contemp blindstamped calf; rubbed, rebacked. Tp cut out & remtd; EE2 repaired in margin. bba Aug 20 (342) £110 [C. Smith]

Caton, John Dean, 1812-95
— The Antelope and Deer of America.... NY, 1877. 8vo, orig cloth. Some foxing. sg Jan 15 (192) $70

Cats, Jacob, 1577-1660
— Houwelyck, dat is de gantsche gelegentheyt des echten staets. [Haarlem, 1642?]. ("Houwelick, dat is het gansch Beleyt des Echten-Staets....") 4to, later mor; rubbed. Minor soiling. T Apr 16 (290) £190

Catullus, Caius Valerius, 84?-54 B.C.
— Carmina. Venice: Joannes Tacuinus de Tridino, 28 Apr 1496. Folio, later vellum bds. Minor spotting & discoloration. 36 leaves. Goff C-325. S Nov 27 (151) £480 [Themis]

Catullus, Tibullus & Propertius
— Opera. Paris: S. Colines, 1529. 8vo, 17th-cent mor gilt, with arms of Charles de Castellan. Inscr by Charles de Castellan as his gift to the Abbaye de Sauve-Majeure in 1678. C May 13 (141) £350 [Rota]

Anr Ed. Birm.: Baskerville, 1772. 4to, contemp calf gilt; rebacked, rubbed. Tp stained & some other leaves spotted. bba Jan 15 (56) £40 [Karlou & Crouch]

Mixed state, A2 a cancel, H3 with "Charbydis". Old bds; worn, some staining. Text lightly rippled. ha Dec 19 (155) $50

Cau, Cornelis —& Others
— Groot Placaat-Boeck, vervattende de edicten van de Heeren Staten Generael der Vereen. The Hague, 1658-1797. 9 (of 10) vols; lacking General Index. Folio, calf gilt. Some defs. B Feb 25 (710) HF6,000

Cauchy, Augustin Louis
— Lecons de calcul differentiel et de calcul integral.... Paris, 1840-44. Vols I-II (of 4). 8vo, Half calf by H. H. Hayes at the Ohio Observer Office. Foxed. bba Aug 28 (124) £90 [Camille-Bernard]

Caulfield, James, 1754-1826
— Calcographiana: the Printsellers Chronicle and Collector's Guide.... L, 1814. 8vo, mor by C. Smith, with ticket; worn. O May 12 (38) $220
— The High Court of Justice. L, 1820. 4to, old bds; rebacked. O Feb 24 (37) $75

Caulin, Antonio, b.1718
— Historia coro-graphica natural y evangelica de la Nueva Andalucia.... Madrid, 1779. Folio, vellum bds. With engraved title, folding map & 3 plates. Some stains. S Oct 23 (437) £900 [Pulico]

Caunter, John Hobart, 1794-1851. See: Daniell & Caunter

Cause, Hendrik
— De Koninglycke Hovenier, aanwyzende de middelen om Boomen.... Amst., [1676]. With engraved title & 31 plates. Bound with: Commelin, Jan. Nederlantze Hesperides. Amst., 1676. With engraved title & 26 plates. Folio, contemp vellum; soiled, lower joint broken. de Belder copy. S Apr 27 (66) £2,000 [Bjork]

Cavafy, Constantine P.
— Fourteen Poems. Lond.: Editions Alecto, 1966. Ed not indicated, One of 500. Illus by David Hockney. With 12 plates. S June 17 (245) £600 [Sims]
— Poiemata. Alexandria, 1935. 4to, contemp half mor, orig wraps bound in. Autograph Ms poem tipped in. Kh. A. Nomikos's copy. S May 21 (142) £1,300 [Pervanas]

Cavalcanti, Guido, c.1250-1300
— Rime. Genoa, 1932. Ed by Ezra Pound. 4to, wraps. Foxed at beginning. sg Dec 11 (97) $275

Cavalieri, Bonaventura, 1598-1647
— Nuova prattica astrologica.... Bologna: Ferroni, 1639. 12mo, 17th-cent vellum gilt. S May 21 (97) £650 [Pervanas]
— Trigonometria plana, et sphaerica, linearis, & logarithmica. Bologna, 1643. 4to, old calf. With engraved title & folding plate. pn Jan 5 (14) £160 [Erlini]

Cavalieri, Giovanni Battista, 1525-97
— Pontificum Romanorum Effigies. Rome, [1580]. 8vo, later vellum. With 2 engraved titles, frontis & 230 (of 231) ports; scattered marginal foxing & early marginalia. sg Oct 9 (149) $175

Cavallo, Tiberius, 1749-1809
— A Treatise on the Nature and Properties of Air. L, 1781. 1st Ed. 4to, contemp half calf; spine rubbed. With 3 plates. Some pencil corrections & annotations. C Dec 12 (42) £420 [Quaritch]

Cavanilles, Antonio Jose
— Icones et descriptiones plantarum.... Madrid, 1791-1801. 6 vols. Folio, contemp half mor; rubbed. With 601 plates. V2 in Vol II torn not affecting text; some browning. Horticultural Society of New York —de Belder copy. S Apr 27 (64) £4,000 [Tan]

Cave, Jane. See: Goldsmith, Oliver

Cave, Roderick
— The Private Press. L, [1971]. bba July 2 (12) £60 [Thomson]

Cavendish, George, 1500-62?. See: Kelmscott Press

Cawood, Francis
— Navigation Compleated: being a New Method Never before attain'd to by Any. L: for A. Bettesworth, 1710. 4to, contemp sheep; worn. Foot of dedication shaved just touching letters. S Apr 23 (74) £2,400 [Quaritch]

Caxton Club—Chicago
— DAVENPORT, CYRIL. - Roger Payne: English Bookbinder of the Eighteenth Century. 1929. 1st Ed, One of 250. Library markings. bba Feb 5 (83) £140 [Zeitlin]
— DAVENPORT, CYRIL. - Samuel Mearne, Binder to King Charles II. 1906. One of 252. Perforated stamps on plates. bba Feb 5 (82) £150 [Kuyper]; sg Apr 2 (69) $325
— DAVENPORT, CYRIL. - Thomas Berthelet, Royal Printer and Bookbinder to Henry VIII. 1901. One of 252. 4to, half cloth; rubbed, library number on base of spine. With 18 plates in colors & gold Perforated library stamps on title & plates. bba Feb 5 (81) £110 [Zeitlin]
— OWENS, HARRY J. - Doctor Faust. 1953. One of 350. sg Jan 8 (130) $175
— POLLARD, ALFRED WILLIAM. - An Essay on Colophons. Chicago, 1905. One of 252. O June 16 (150) £130
— UZANNE, OCTAVE. - The French Bookbinders of the Eighteenth Century. 1904. One of 252. Folio, disbound. With 20 plates. Library markings. bba Feb 5 (84) £55 [Zeitlin]
— WILKINS, ERNEST HATCH. - The Trees of the Genealogia Deorum of Boccaccio. 1923. One of 160. cb Dec 4 (90) $95

Caxton, William, 1422?-91
— The Game and Playe of the Chesse.... L, 1883. Recent pigskin. Reprint of 1474 Ed. cb Dec 4 (91) $100
— The Life of St. George.... New Fairfield, CT, 1957. One of 300. Designed by Bruce Rogers. cb Dec 4 (339) $80

Caylus, Anne Claude Philippe, Comte de, 1692-1765
— Receuil d'antiquites egyptiennes.... Paris, 1761-56-67. 7 vols. 4to, contemp calf; rubbed. With frontises & 830 plates, 12 folding. C Dec 12 (43) £700 [Johnson]
— [Receuil des pierres gravees du cabinet du Roi.] [N.p., c.1750]. 4to, contemp mor gilt. With 306 plates before numbers a l'eauforte. First plate with title in Ms. With 2

Cecil, William, Baron Burghley, 1520-98
— The Copy of a Letter Sent Out of England.... L: R. Field, 1588. ("Certaine Advertisements Out of Ireland....") Part 2 (of 2) only. Bound with: Cosin, Richard. Conspiracie for Pretended Reformation. L: Deputies of Christopher Barker, 1592. Tp def & restored; small rust-hole in margin of A4. 4to, 19th-cent half calf. First work with hole in 1 leaf not affecting text; note on last page in contemp secretary hand "This is Mr. Richard ffoxes boke.". S Dec 18 (225) £800 [Finch]

Cellarius, Andreas
— Architectura militaris oder gruendtliche Underweissung der...gebraeuchlichen Fortificationen.... Amst.: J. Jansson, 1656. Folio, half vellum. With engraved title, 90 plates & 13 double page tables. 2 plates torn in fold, anr torn & repaired; some waterstaining at beginning. C Oct 15 (27) £280 [Yamanaka]

— [Atlas coelestis]. Harmonia macrocosmica; seu, Atlas universalis et novus.... Amst., 1708. Folio, old calf. With frontis & 29 double-page hand-colored maps. C Apr 8 (9) £5,500 [Mediolanum]

Anr copy. Contemp bds; rubbed. FD Dec 2 (775) DM15,000

Anr copy. Contemp calf. With frontis & 29 double-page maps with contemp hand-coloring. Without text; some marks at centerfolds. S Oct 23 (226) £5,200 [Browning]

— Harmonia macrocosmica seu Atlas universalis et novus.... Amst., 1708. Folio, half lea; worn & loose. With engraved title & 29 double-page hand-colored maps. One map soiled. HN May 22 (1070) DM9,000

Cellarius, Christoph, 1638-1707
Geographia antiqua.... L, 1755. 8vo, contemp sheep; worn, front cover detached. With plate & 26 folding maps. sg Apr 23 (168) $100

Anr Ed. L, 1775. Contemp calf; joints & corners rubbed, hinges reinforced. With 1 plate & 26 folding maps. cb Feb 19 (55) $200

— Notitia orbis antiqui sive Geographia Plenior.... Leipzig, 1701-6. Vol II (of 3) only. 4to, later half pigskin; hinge broken, most pp loose. With 13 double-page maps. Title repaired. wa Sept 25 (492) $60

Anr Ed. L, 1703. Vol I (of 2). 4to, contemp calf; broken. With engraved title, port, plate & 20 maps. T May 21 (264) £110

Cellini, Benvenuto, 1500-71
See also: Limited Editions Club
— The Life of Benvenuto Cellini.... L, 1771. 1st Ed in English. Trans by Thomas Nugent. 2 vols. 8vo, contemp calf. sg Mar 26 (59) $80

Anr Ed. L: Vale Press, 1900. One of 300. Trans by J. A. Symonds. 2 vols. Folio, half vellum; soiled. cb Sept 11 (220) $225

— The Treatises of Benvenuto Cellini on Goldsmithing and Sculpture. L: Essex House Press, 1898. One of 600. 4to, orig cloth; rubbed & faded. bba Dec 4 (156) £65 [Elliott]

— Vita.... Cologne. P. Martello [Naples, 1728]. 1st Ed. 4to, contemp mor gilt; rubbed. Some spots & stains. S Jan 13 (352) £420 [Marlborough]

Celsus, Aurelius Cornelius
— De re medica, libri octo.... Lyons: Tornaesium & Gazeium, 1549. 32mo, old calf. Partial dampstaining throughout. sg Jan 15 (74) $200

Celtis, Conrad
— Ludus Diane in modum comedie.... Nuremberg: Hieronymus Hoelzel, 15 May 1500. 4to, mor janseniste by Sangorski & Sutcliffe. Schwerdt-Jeanson copy. SM Feb 28 (114) FF40,000

Cendrars, Blaise, 1887-1961
— La Fin du monde.... Paris, 1919. One of 1,200. Illus by Fernand Leger. 4to, half mor gilt, orig wraps bound in. FD June 11 (5093) DM3,200

Cennini, Cennino
— A Treatise on Painting.... L, 1844. 8vo, orig cloth by Remnant & Edmonds; worn. O Mar 24 (39) $60

Certain or Certaine...
— Certain Necessary Directions, as well for the Cure of the Plague.... L, 1665. 4to, new vellum bds; soiled. Inner blank margin of tp & 1st 3 leaves mended with new paper; headlines cut into or cut off; some stains. S May 28 (646) £100

Certain Traveller. See: Bethune, George Amory

Cervantes Saavedra, Miguel de, 1547-1616
— Novelas.... The Hague: Jean Neulme, 1739. 2 vols. 8vo, contemp calf; extremities worn. sg Mar 26 (61) $110

— Novelas exemplares. Brussels, 1625. 8vo, 18th-cent calf. S June 25 (15) £500 [Quaritch]

— Los Seys Libros de la Galatea. Barcelona: Sebastian de Cormellas, 1618. 8vo, old calf; backstrip def. Margins trimmed; some dampstains. sg Mar 26 (60) $950

CERVANTES SAAVEDRA

— Los Trabaios de Persiles y Sigismunda. Madrid: for Juan de la Cuesta, 1617 [but Melchor Sanchez, c.1660]. 4to, contemp vellum; loose. Browned; scattered stains. sg Mar 26 (63) $225

Don Quixote in Portuguese

— 1617. - Lisbon 8vo, modern calf. Lacking 1st 4 leaves & last 5 leaves (all supplied in photocopy). S Nov 27 (153) £650 [Quaritch]

Anr copy. 4to, old calf, with gilt initials HT surmounted by a ram's head in center of covers; worn, front cover loose. Margins trimmed close. sg Mar 26 (62) $1,100

Don Quixote in Spanish

— 1662. - Brussels 2 vols. 8vo, old sheep; scuffed. With 2 frontises & 16 plates Dampstained, not affecting plates; K1 & K5 in Vol I torn & repaired. sg Oct 9 (10) $700

— 1777. - Madrid 4 vols. 8vo, contemp calf; rubbed, rebacked. S Sept 23 (549) £50 [Duran]

— 1780. - Madrid: Joaquin Ibarra. 4 vols. 4to, contemp mor gilt; spines scuffed. With engraved titles, port & 31 plates, all proofs before letters, & map. C May 13 (120) £2,600 [Chaponniere]

Anr copy. 18th-cent russia; joints worn. With 4 engraved titles, map, port & 31 plates. About 15 leaves at start of Vol I stained; Vol II wormed. S Nov 27 (152) £800 [Soley]

Anr copy. Contemp mor; spine ends rubbed. With 4 engraved titles, port, double-page map & 31 plates; foxing affecting margin of some plates. sg Oct 9 (11) $1,800

— 1781. - L & Salisbury 6 vols in 3. 4to, contemp calf; joints weak or starting. sg Oct 9 (12) $250

— 1804-05. - Berlin 6 vols. 8vo, orig bds; hinges cracked. sg Oct 9 (13) $50

— 1814. - Paris & L. 7 vols. 12mo, contemp sheep; badly worn. With 39 plates, occasional dampstaining affecting some; minor worming in last vol. sg Oct 9 (14) $60

— 1854. - Madrid 4 vols in 2. 4to, contemp lea; scuffed. With 33 plates. sg Sept 11 (60) $130

— 1916-17. - Madrid One of 125. Illus by Ricardo Marin. 4 vols. Folio, orig wraps, unopened. sg Sept 11 (61) $110

Dutch Versions

— 1746. - De voornaamste gevallen van den wonderlyken Don Quichot.... The Hague 4to, old half cloth. With 30 (of 31) plates; lacking plate 16. sg Oct 9 (41) $90

AMERICAN BOOK PRICES CURRENT

English Versions

— 1620. - L.2d Ed in English of Part 1; 1st Ed in English of Part 2. 2 vols. 4to, Mor gilt by Riviere. Washed; lacking Vol I initial blank & Vol II final blank. sg Oct 9 (15) $2,200

— 1652. - L. Folio, early 19th-cent sheep; crudely rebacked & rehinged, orig backstrip laid down. sg Jan 22 (16) $375

— 1675. - L. Folio, modern half lea; extremities rubbed. Browned; 2F3 may be from anr copy. sg Oct 9 (17) $110

— 1687. - L. Trans by John Phillips. Folio, old calf; rebacked & crudely rehinged. With 8 plates; c.40 leaves dampstained in upper corner. sg Oct 9 (18) $350

— 1742. - L. Trans by Charles Jarvis. 2 vols. 4to, contemp sheep; rebacked, corners restored, hinges reinforced. With 69 plates. sg Oct 9 (9) $350

Anr copy. Modern calf gilt. Vol II tp repaired with cellotape. sg Feb 12 (42) $350

Anr copy. Modern mor gilt; extremities rubbed, Vol I front cover detached. sg Mar 26 (65) $275

— 1755. - L. Trans by Tobias Smollett. 2 vols. 4to, contemp calf; rebacked & rehinged. sg Oct 9 (22) $110

— 1782. - L. Trans by Tobias Smollett. 4 vols. 12mo, contemp calf; joints weak. Opening leaves of Vol III stained. sg Oct 9 (23) $60

— 1796. - Dublin Trans by Tobias Smollett. 4 vols. 8vo, contemp calf; rebacked, rehinged. With 22 plates. sg Oct 9 (23) $60

— 1801. - The Life and Exploits of.... L. 4 vols. 8vo, contemp calf gilt; Vol I joints cracked. sg Oct 9 (24) $60

Anr copy. Later sheep gilt; broken. With port of Cervantes, folding map & 19 (of 20) plates. sg Oct 9 (25) $40

— 1811. - L. 4 vols. 8vo, modern calf gilt. sg Oct 9 (26) $80

— 1818. - L. Trans by Mary Smirke; illus by Robert Smirke. 4 vols. 8vo, half lea; spines worn. sg Oct 9 (27) $110

— 1819. - L. Illus by C. Jarvis. 4 vols. 8vo, contemp half lea; rubbed, some spines def. With 24 colored plates. bba Jan 15 (233) £100 [Fisher]

Anr copy. Calf gilt. Lacking half-titles. S July 28 (1163) £175

Anr copy. Contemp lea gilt; rebacked in calf. wa Mar 5 (172) $220

Anr copy. Trans by C. Jarvis. Contemp calf; joints worn, inner hinge of Vol I broken. With 24 plates by J. H. Clark. A few leaves stained; library stamps on titles. bba Aug 28 (215) £50 [Archdale]

— 1820. - L: Hurst, Robinson Illus by Richard

Westall. 4 vols. 8vo, mor gilt; worn. With 24 plates, including engraved titles. Foxed. sg Oct 9 (28) $140
— 1820. - The Spirit of Cervantes; or, Don Quixote Abridged. L. 4to, orig cloth; backstrip partly detached. With 4 color plates. Some foxing of text. sg Oct 9 (29) $140
Anr copy. Contemp half lea gilt. Some foxing at beginning. sg Oct 9 (30) $150
— 1840. - L. Trans by Charles Jarvis; illus by Tony Johannot. 3 vols. 8vo, half mor gilt; 1 spine worn at head. sg Sept 11 (59) $60
— 1879-84. - Edin. One of 50 L.p. copies. Illus by Ad. Lalauze. 4 vols. 8vo, orig cloth; Vol IV front hinge cracked. With 37 plates in 2 states, on hollande & as mtd india-proofs. sg Apr 2 (42) $275
— 1885. - L. 4 vols. 8vo, mor gilt. Extra-illus with c.75 plates. S July 13 (193) $200
— 1900. - Don Quixote of the Mancha, retold by Judge Parry. L. One of 100 on Japanese vellum. Illus by Walter Crane. 8vo, orig bds; front joint cracked. With colored frontis, pictorial title & 10 plates. sg Sept 11 (73) $130
— 1906-7. - NY One of 140. 5 vols. 4to, orig half vellum. Library markings. bba Aug 28 (273) £120 [Clark]

French Versions

— 1768. - Histoire de l'admirable Don Quichotte de la Manche. Amst. & Leipzig 6 vols. 12mo, early half calf. sg Oct 9 (33) $225
— 1776. - Les Principales aventures de l'admirable Don Quichotte. Liege 4to, calf gilt. With 31 plates. Tp repaired in margin; P4 repaired affecting text; soiled. S July 28 (1165) £320
Anr copy. Orig bds; loose, lacking backstrip. sg Oct 9 (34) $275
— 1781. - Lyons 6 vols. 12mo, contemp calf; spines worn. With 28 plates. sg Oct 9 (35) $60
— 1795. - Brussels 4to, contemp half sheep; worn, front joint starting. With 4 (of 8) prelims. sg Oct 9 (36) $60
— 1836-37. - L'Ingenieux Hidalgo Don Quichotte. Paris Trans by Louis Viardot; illus by Tony Johannot. 2 vols. 8vo, contemp half calf gilt; hinges cracked, joints weak. Several leaves of Vol I heavily foxed. sg Oct 9 (37) $90

German Versions

— 1683. - Don Quixote von Mancha, Abenteurliche Geschichte.... Basel & Frankfurt: Johann Ludwig du Four 2d Issue. 2 vols. 8vo, 19th-cent bds; spine ends worn. Margins trimmed; some foxing & stains; minor marginal tears; Vol I lacking final blank. sg Oct 9 (38) $850

Italian Versions

— 1677. - L'Ingegnoso cittadino Don Chisciotte della Mancia. Rome 2 vols. 8vo, 18th-cent Italian half vellum; spines wormed, hinges cracked. With engraved title & 12 (of 16) plates; margins trimmed, marginal worming in both vols, occasionally affecting text. sg Oct 9 (40) $80

Swedish Versions

— 1818. - Den Tappre och Snillrike Riddaren Don Quixote af Mancha.... Stockholm 4 vols. 8vo, contemp half lea; spines rubbed. Some foxing. sg Oct 9 (42) $200

Cescinsky, Herbert

— Chinese Furniture. L, 1922. 4to, orig half mor. Ck Sept 5 (105) £70

— English Furniture of the Eighteenth Century. L, [1909-11 & n.d.]. 3 vols. 4to, orig half mor; rubbed, hinges repaired. bba Dec 4 (220) £90 [Bowers]
Anr copy. Orig half mor; rubbed. L July 2 (15) £120
Anr copy. Orig half mor gilt. pn Sept 18 (203) £120 [Demetzy]
Anr copy. Orig half mor. pn Nov 20 (29) £110 [Traylen]
Anr copy. Orig half mor; rubbed. pn Jan 22 (161) £90 [Macfarlane]
Anr copy. Half mor gilt. S Oct 23 (311) £65 [Elliott]
Anr copy. Orig half mor; rubbed. S Nov 10 (59) £100 [McCarthy]; S Mar 9 (640) £110 [Stodart]; S Mar 9 (663) £55 [Haramundanis]; S May 6 (370) £85 [Stodart]

— The Gentle Art of Faking Furniture. L, 1931. 4to, cloth. L Dec 11 (11) £50

— The Old English Master Clockmakers. L, 1938. 4to, cloth, in d/j. kh Mar 16 (80) A$110

Cescinsky, Herbert —& Gribble, Ernest

— Early English Furniture and Woodwork. L, 1922. 2 vols in 1. Folio, cloth. pn Sept 18 (3) £60 [Potterton]
Anr copy. Cloth; dampstained. pn Jan 22 (170) £40 [Elliott]
Anr copy. Cloth; rubbed. T Oct 16 (562) £62
Anr copy. 2 vols. Folio, orig mor gilt; spines worn. T Feb 19 (501) £40

Cesio, Carlo
— Cognitione de muscoli del corpo humano per il disegno. Rome: Francesco Collignon, 1679. Folio, contemp vellum. With 16 plates. Wormholes in inner margin of last few plates. S May 21 (189) £1,800 [Quaritch]

Chabert, Joseph Bernard, Marquis de
— Voyage fait par ordre du roi en 1750 et 1751, dans l'Amerique septentrionale. Paris, 1753. 1st Ed. 4to, contemp calf. With folding table & 6 folding maps & plans. S June 24 (377) £380 [Houle]

Chabot, Auguste Jean Francois de
— La Chasse a travers les ages. Paris, 1898. One of 50 on japon imperial. 4to, half mor gilt by Champs. Jeanson 1552. SM Feb 28 (115) FF6,500
— La Chasse du chevreuil.... Paris, 1879. 4to, mor gilt, armorial bdg by Smeers. Inscr to the King. Jeanson copy. SM Feb 28 (116) FF22,000

Chacon, Gonzalo, the Elder. See: Luna, Alvaro de

Chagall, Marc
See also: Bible in English; Meyer, Franz
— Chagall lithographe. Monte Carlo: Andre Sauret, 1960-63-69-74. 5 vols including 1984 supplement. 4to,. Cloth, in d/js. With 28 lithos. B Oct 7 (946a) HF4,400
Vol I only.. Orig cloth, in d/j. HN May 20 (2385) DM2,700
Vols I-III. HK Nov 4 (2937) DM1,100
— Dessins pour la Bible. Paris, 1960. Folio, bds. Verve No 37/38. FD Dec 2 (4265) DM4,500; HN Nov 26 (1758) DM4,000; HN May 20 (2381) DM5,200
Anr copy. Bds; rubbed, frayed. Verve No 37/38. P Dec 15 (183) $1,900
Anr copy. Bds; spine bumped. Verve No 37/38. sg Apr 2 (43) $3,400
— Drawings for the Bible. NY, 1960. Folio, bds. Verve No 37/38. FD Dec 2 (4266) DM5,000; HN May 20 (2382) DM4,800
Anr copy. Bds, in d/j. Verve No 37/38. P Dec 15 (184) $1,900; sg Jan 8 (41) $2,000
— Eaux-fortes pour la Bible. Paris, 1956. 4to, orig bds; soiled, rubbed. Verve No 33/34. P Dec 15 (182) $2,200
— Illustrations for the Bible. NY, 1956. Folio, orig bds. Verve No 33/34. HK Nov 4 (2935) DM6,500
— The Jerusalem Windows. NY, 1962. Text by Jean Leymarie. Folio, cloth, in d/j. sg Feb 5 (84) $300
Anr copy. Cloth, in chipped d/j. sg June 8 (77) $200
— The Lithographs of Chagall. Monte Carlo & NY or Bost., 1960-74. Vol II only. Cloth, in d/j. B June 2 (982) HF1,500; sg June 4 (81) $225
American Ed of Vols I-II; French Ed of Vols III-IV. In d/js. sg Dec 4 (35) $2,000
Vol IV only. Text by Fernand Mourlot. Orig cloth, in d/j. sg Feb 5 (85) $300
— Vitraux pour Jerusalem. Monte Carlo, 1962. 4to, cloth. B June 2 (981) HF800; JG Mar 20 (1401) DM800

Chalcondylas, Laonicus
— Historie generale des Turcs.... Paris, 1662. 2 vols. Folio, contemp calf; stitching def. Wormed throughout with loss. Sold w.a.f. S Feb 23 (72) £160 [Hantzis]

Chalmers, George, 1742-1825
— A Supplemental Apology for the Believers in the Shakspeare-Papers.... L, 1799. 8vo, later half mor; corners rubbed. sg Jan 22 (206) $90

Chalmers, Patrick Reginald
— Birds Ashore and A-Foreshore. L, [1935]. One of 150. Illus by Winifred Austen. 4to, orig half mor; rubbed. With 16 colored plates. T Mar 19 (119) £100

Chalmers, Thomas, 1780-1847
— On Political Economy, in Connexion with the Moral State.... Glasgow: Collins, 1832. 8vo, modern half calf. Some spotting; library markings on 1 leaf. P Sept 24 (258) $400
— The Supreme Importance of a Right Moral to a Right Economical State of the Community.... Glasgow: William Collins, 1832. 8vo, orig wraps; spine & edges chipped, soiled, tear in outer margin of upper wrap. Marginal soiling. P Sept 24 (259) $280

Chalupetzky, Ferenc
— A Gyori Sakk-Kongresszus.... Gyori, [1925]. One of 40. Cloth; hinges repaired. pn Mar 26 (74) £65 [Hoffman]

Chamberlain, Henry
— A New and Compleat History and Survey of London.... L, [1770]. Folio, contemp calf; hinges broken. Folding plan & folding map torn without loss. T Jan 22 (42) £60

Chamberlain, Lieut. Henry
— Views and Costumes of the City and Neighbourhood of Rio De Janeiro. L, 1822. 4to, contemp half mor gilt; rubbed. With 36 hand-colored plates. "A fine tall copy". S July 25 (447) £44,000 [Quaritch]

Chamberlaine, John, 1745-1812. See: Holbein, Hans

Chamberlayne, John, 1666-1723

— The Natural History of Coffee, Thee, Chocolate, and Tobacco. L, 1682. 1st Ed. 4to, wraps. Rule border to tp shaved at foot. S July 23 (428) £700 [Drury]

Chamberlin, A. N.

— Cherokee Pictorial Book with Catechism and Hymns. Tahlequah: T. W. Foreman, 1888. 12mo, modern cloth. sg Mar 12 (58) $325

Chambers, Amelia

— The Ladies Best Companion: or a Golden Treasure for the Fair Sex.... L: J. Cooke, [c.1775]. 12mo, disbound. Frontis detached; hole in last leaf affecting 1 letter. Hunt copy. CNY Nov 21 (65) $550

Chambers, Andrew Jackson

— Recollections. [N.p., 1947]. 1st Ed. Recent half mor. cb Jan 8 (23) $55

Chambers, Ephraim, d.1740

— Cyclopaedia: or, an Universal Dictionary of Arts and Sciences. L, 1738. 2d Ed. 2 vols. Folio, contemp calf; spine & extremities worn. With double-page frontis & 20 plates, 8 folding. With 2 plates torn; some marginal worming. Ck Apr 24 (212) £110

Anr Ed. L, 1747. 4 vols, including 2 supplements. Contemp calf; 2 vols rebacked. pn Nov 20 (36) £90 [Weiner]

Anr Ed. L, 1783-86. 4 vols. Folio, modern cloth; loose, rubbed. bba Oct 30 (30) £60 [Axe]

Anr Ed. L, 1786-91. 4 vols in 6. Folio, contemp half calf; worn. With engraved title & 152 plates. Ck Sept 5 (175) £110

Chambers, Robert

— A Biographical Dictionary of Eminent Scotsmen. Glasgow: Blackie, 1840. 4 vols. 8vo, contemp half mor; rubbed. Library stamps. O Feb 24 (38) $80

— Domestic Annals of Scotland.... Edin., 1848. 2 vols in 3. 8vo, half mor by Bayntun; rubbed. O Feb 24 (39) $110

Chambers, Robert, 1802-71

— Vestiges of the Natural History of Creation. L, 1844. 2d Ed. 8vo, contemp calf gilt; rubbed. S Nov 10 (464) £180 [Quaritch]

Chambers, Robert William, 1865-1933

— The King in Yellow. Chicago, 1895. Bdg soiled, rubbed, corners & spine foot bumped. A few pp roughly opened. cb Sept 28 (297) $60

Chambers, Sir William, 1726-96

— Plans, Elevations, Sections and Perspective Views of the Gardens and Buildings at Kew.... L, 1763. Lacking 4 plates; title & dedication leaves loose & creased. Bound with: Chambers. Designs of Chinese Buildings, Furniture.... L, 1757. With 21 plates. 1st Eds. Folio, contemp calf with the Chambers crest on sides; worn & broken. Wormhole in extreme inner blank margin of a few leaves of text. S Apr 23 (89) £2,900 [Henderson]

— A Treatise on Civil Architecture. L, 1759. 1st Ed. Folio, bdg not indicated. Library markings. Sold w.a.f. Franklin Institute copy. F Sept 12 (14) $400

Anr Ed. L, 1825. ("A Treatise on the Decorative Part of Civil Architecture.") 2 vols. 8vo, half calf; worn, 1 spine restored. HN May 20 (154) DM600

Chameleon...

— The Chameleon: a Bazaar of Dangerous and Smiling Chances. L: Gay & Bird, [1894]. Vol I, No 1 (all pbd). 4to, wraps, unopened; worn. Margins torn, 1 tear repaired with tape. With contributions by Oscar Wilde & Lord Alfred Douglas. S July 23 (123) £2,300 [Manyon]

Chamisso, Adelbert von, 1781-1838

— Peter Schlemiels Schicksale. Leipzig: Insel-Verlag for Janus-Presse, 1922. One of 315. 4to, mor gilt. HK Nov 4 (2994) DM520

— Werke. Leipzig, 1836-39. 6 vols. 12mo, contemp cloth. With 2 maps, 2 ports, 5 plates & folding table. HK Nov 4 (2440) DM600

Anr copy. 6 vols in 3. 12mo, contemp half calf; worn. With 2 maps, 2 ports, 4 plates & folding table. JG Oct 2 (1551) DM1,200

Chamouin, J. B. M.

— Collection de vues de Paris prises au daguerreotype. Paris, [c.1850]. Oblong folio, orig half calf; worn. With engraved title & 26 plates. O Jan 6 (38) $90

Anr copy. Orig cloth; hinges cracked, soiled. With 24 plates only. pn June 18 (204) £100 [Reynold]

Anr copy. Orig half calf; worn. With engraved title & 26 plates. S Nov 17 (900) £160 [Marshall]

Champfleury, Pseud. of Jules Francois Felix Husson

— Les Chats. Paris, 1870. Edition de Luxe. 8vo, half mor. S May 6 (171) £480 [Platemark]

CHAMPLAIN

Champlain, Samuel de, 1567-1635
— Voyages et descouvertures faites en la Nouvelle France.... Paris, 1619. 8vo, later mor gilt; rubbed, front joint cracked at head. Engraved title with 2 short marginal tears; a few marginal wormholes at beginning just touching 2 letters of shoulder notes; M6 & M7 creased. P May 13 (4) $12,000

Chandler, Alfred, 1804-96 —& Booth, William Beattie, 1804?-74
— Illustrations and Descriptions of the Plants which Compose the Natural Order Camellieae.... L, 1831. Vol I (all pbd). Folio, recent mor gilt. With 40 hand-colored plates. Without the 4 unpbd plates & their accompanying letterpress. Bits of paint flaked from foliage of a few plates. S Oct 23 (674) £8,500 [Sourget]

Anr copy. Contemp mor extra. With 39 (of 40) hand-colored plates on large paper. de Belder copy. S Apr 27 (45) £7,500 [Jackson]

Chandler, Raymond, 1888-1959
— The Big Sleep. NY, 1939. Minor foxing; tape stains to rear endpapers. cb May 7 (236) $85
— Farewell, My Lovely. NY, 1940. In lightly chipped d/j. cb Nov 20 (35) $600
— Five Murders. NY, [1944]. 1st Ed. Wraps. No 19 of the Murder Mystery Monthly. cb Nov 20 (37) $190
— Five Sinister Characters. NY, [1945]. Wraps. cb Nov 20 (36) $140
— The Lady in the Lake. NY, 1943. In chipped d/j. cb Nov 20 (38) $375
— The Long Good-Bye. L, [1953]. In frayed d/j. cb May 7 (237) $200
— Playback. L, [1958]. In chipped d/j. cb Nov 20 (40) $50
— Raymond Chandler Speaking. L, [1962]. Proof copy. Orig wraps. T Feb 18 (84) £55

Chandler, Raymond, 1888-1959 —& Silliphant, Sterling
— The Little Sister. Culver City: Katzka-Berne, 15 May 1968. Folio, studio wraps. Screenplay filmed under the title Marlowe. cb Nov 20 (39) $65

Chandler, Richard —& Others
— Ionian Antiquities. L, 1769. Folio, contemp mor gilt. S Feb 23 (74) £420 [Weinreb]

Chandler, Richard, 1738-1810
— Travels in Asia Minor.... Oxford, 1775. 1st Ed. 4to, contemp calf; rubbed, lower joint broken, upper cover detached. With folding map, slightly torn. S Jan 13 (353) £130 [MacKenzie]

2d Ed. L, 1776. 4to, contemp calf; worn, joints broken. With folding map & 6 plans. Map repaired at fold. S Jan 13 (354) £190 [McKenzie]

Chandler, Samuel, 1693-1766
— The History of Persecution.... L, 1736. 8vo, modern half calf. Some plates laid down; some foxing & stains. bba Jan 15 (38) £40 [Grant's]

Chanlaire, Pierre Gregoire. See: Capitaine & Chanlaire

Channell, Leonard Stewart
— History of Compton County and Sketches of the Eastern Townships.... Cookshire, Quebec, 1896. Folio, orig cloth; recased, backstrip frayed. Library stamp on tp. AVP Nov 20 (59) C$120 [Woolmer]

Channing, William Ellery, 1780-1842
— Slavery. Bost.: James Munroe, 1835. 12mo, contemp cloth; stained, joints split. Some foxing. wa Nov 6 (608) $50

Chapelain, Jean, 1595-1674
— La Pucelle ou la France delivree. Paris, 1656. Folio, 19th-cent half sheep gilt; spine def. Some browning, stains & repairs. sg Mar 26 (67) $60

Chapelle, Howard Irving
— The History of American Sailing Ships. NY: Norton, 1935. One of 121. 4to, orig cloth. Frontis etching by George C. Wales sgd in pencil. wa Nov 6 (141) $400

Chaplin, Charles
— My Trip Abroad. NY: Harper, [1922]. Bds; worn, shaken. sg Nov 20 (45) $50

Chapman, Abel, 1851-1929
— On Safari: Big-Game Hunting in British East Africa. L, 1908. 1st Ed. Orig cloth; corners rubbed; lacking front free endpaper. b Nov 6 (59) $70

Anr copy. Orig cloth; rubbed. cb May 21 (46) $120

Anr copy. Orig cloth; extremities worn. cb May 21 (47) $95

— Savage Sudan. NY, 1922. Corners & spine ends bumped & rubbed, a few tears in spine ends. cb Nov 6 (60) $95

Chapman, Abel, 1851-1929 —& Buck, Walter J.
— Wild Spain (Espana Agreste): Records of Sport with Rifle.... L, 1893. Later half mor; rubbed. cb Nov 6 (62) $70

Chapman, Frederik Henrik af
— A Treatise on Ship-Building. Cambr., 1820. 4to, half mor. With 2 folding tables & 23 plates. Stamps of Franklin Institute. S Oct 23 (187) £600 [Kungliga]

Chapman, George, 1559?-1634
See also: Marlowe & Chapman
— The Warres of Pompey and Caesar. L, 1631. ("Caesar and Pompey: a Roman Tragedy....") 4to, half lea. Lacking initial blank; margins trimmed; some cropping. STC 4993. sg Mar 26 (68) $750

Chapman, James
— Travels in the Interior of South Africa. L, 1868. 2 vols. 8vo, orig cloth; marked. With frontis, 6 engraved plates & 2 folding maps (1 in need of restoration). SSA Oct 28 (494) R1,750

Chapman, John —&
Andre, Peter
— Map of the County of Essex. L, 1777. Folio, contemp calf; rebacked, rubbed. With hand-colored general map & 23 hand-colored maps (3 with small tears at lower centerfold). pn May 21 (352) £430 [Hadland]
Anr copy. Half calf; def. With 26 double-page sheets, including title, list of subscribers & key map. Maps hand-colored in outline. Some creases & splits without apparent loss. S Nov 17 (714) £420 [Ash]
Anr copy. Contemp half calf; worn. Minor marginal repairs. S Apr 23 (117) £450 [Campbell]

Chappe d'Auteroche, Jean, 1728-69
— A Journey into Siberia. L, 1770. 4to, contemp calf; joints cracked. With folding map & 9 plates. Ck Sept 26 (78) £200
— Voyage en Californie. Paris, 1772. 1st Ed. 4to, contemp half calf gilt. With folding plan & 3 plates. With bookplate of J. C. Dezauche. S Apr 24 (259) £600 [Perrin]
— Voyage en Siberie. Paris, 1768. 2 vols in 3 plus Atlas vol. Contemp calf, Atlas in contemp half calf; worn. Lacking the frontis in the Atlas. FD Dec 2 (977) DM3,500
Anr copy. 2 vols in 3 plus Atlas. 4to & folio, russia gilt, Atlas in contemp vellum. With engraved frontis, 53 plates, 3 maps & 57 tables; Atlas with frontis index map & 30 large maps. Some marginal staining. J July 14 (839) £850
— A Voyage to California. L, 1778. 8vo, contemp calf. With folding map. S June 25 (383) £700 [Houle]

Chappee, Julien
— La Tenue de chasse du roi Rene.... Paris, 1912. 4to, half shagreen. Jeanson copy. SM Feb 28 (119) FF600

Chappell, H. W. See: Frank & Chappell

Chaptal, Jean Antoine Claude, 1756-1832
— Chimie appliquee aux arts. Paris, 1807. 4 vols. 8vo, contemp half russia. With 12 folding plates. C Dec 12 (45) £280 [Bookpress]
— Elements of Chemistry. Phila.: Lang & Ustick, 1796. 1st American Ed. 3 vols in 1. 8vo, contemp sheep; spine torn, crudely restored. Title soiled, rehinged, corner off. sg Jan 15 (303) $50

Chapuis, Alfred —&
Droz, Edmond
— Automata. A Historical and Technological Study. Neuchatel & L, 1958. 4to, orig cloth, in d/j. pn Dec 11 (312) £80 [Walford]
Anr copy. Cloth. sg Jan 15 (304) $120

Chapuis, Alfred —&
Jaquet, Eugene
— Technique and History of the Swiss Watch. Olten [1953]. 4to, orig cloth, in d/j. sg Jan 15 (321) $50

Chardin, Sir John, 1643-1713
— Journal du voyage du Chevalier Chardin en Perse et aux Indes Orientales. Amst., 1686. 2d Ed. Vol I (all pbd). 12mo, contemp calf. With port, engraved title, folding map & 11 plates. Ck May 15 (30) £70
— The Travels.... L, 1686. Vol I (all pbd). Folio, contemp calf; rubbed, joints cracked & frayed. With engraved title, frontis, folding map & 16 plates. 2E2 with small rust-hole; a few plates shaved; 1 plate torn, anr plate repaired. C Apr 8 (76) £320 [Knirck]
Anr copy. Contemp calf; worn. With port, engraved title, map (repaired) & 16 plates. Some marginal tears; 2 plates repaired & a few cropped; Oooo torn with loss to running title. S Feb 23 (9) £220 [Shapero]
Anr Ed. L: Argonaut Press, 1927. One of 975. 4to, orig half vellum, unopened. cb Feb 19 (56) $150

Charles'...
— Charles' Wain: A Miscellany of Short Stories. L, [1933]. One of 95, sgd by all 18 contributors. Unopened. pn May 21 (205) £85 [Ferret Fantasy]; sg Dec 11 (205) $150

Charles, C. J. See: Duveen, Charles Joel

CHARLES EDWARD

Charles Edward, Prince, 1720-88
— [-] James R....We hereby nominate...Our dearest Son Charles, Prince of Wales, to be sole Regent.... [N.p., 1745]. 4 pp, half-sheet 4to, unbound as issued. Soiled & worn, creased with fold breaks; small portion torn from blank inner margin. sg Oct 9 (150) $130

Charles I, King of England
— Eikon Basilike. The Pourtraicture of His Sacred Majestie.... L, 1649. 8vo, contemp calf gilt; rubbed. Minor defs. bba Apr 23 (174) £70 [Francis]
— A Large Declaration Concerning the Late Tumults in Scotland. L, 1639. Folio, contemp calf; rubbed. John Rushworth's copy, with his marginalia. O May 12 (39) $175

Anr copy. Old calf; broken. Hole in tp not affecting text; some dampstains to 1st 30 leaves. pn Sept 18 (304) £50 [Rix]

Charles II, King of England
— An Account of the Preservation of King Charles II after the Battle of Worcester...by himself. Glasgow: Foulis, 1766. 1st Ed. 8vo, later half calf; rubbed. O Feb 24 (42) $65
— A Collection of His Majestie's Gracious Letters, Speeches, Messages and Declarations. L, 1660. 4to, contemp mor gilt with Royal arms on cover; top of backstrip damaged. bba July 16 (224) £80 [Wise]

Charles IX, King of France
— La Chasse Royale.... Paris: Nicolas Rousset et Gervais Alliot, 1625. This copy with both variants of the tp. 8vo, mor gilt by Trautz-Bauzonnet. Jeanson copy. SM Feb 28 (120) FF50,000

With the stag hunt vignette on the title & with Charles spelled correctly. 18th-cent mor gilt. De la Valliere—Heber-Pichon-Gallice-Jeanson copy. SM Feb 28 (121) FF60,000

Anr Ed. Paris: Auguste Aubry, 1858. One of 250. 8vo, contemp half shagreen; worn. Jeanson copy. SM Feb 28 (122) FF1,500

Charleton, Walter, 1619-1707
— Two Discourses. I. Concerning the Different Wits of Men: II. Of the Mysterie of Vintners. L, 1669. 8vo, modern mor by Crahan. Lacking initial blank; 2 leaves def from faulty printing; marginal repair on I7 & P7; corner of tp cut away & repaired affecting rule. Crahan copy. P Nov 25 (109) $450

AMERICAN BOOK PRICES CURRENT

Charlevoix, Pierre Francois Xavier de, 1682-1761
— Histoire et description generale du Japon. Paris, 1736. 1st Ed. 2 vols, including Supplement. 4to, contemp calf. S June 25 (464) £1,800 [Bjorck]
— Histoire et description generale de la Nouvelle France.... Paris, 1744. 3 vols. 4to, contemp calf. With 28 folding maps & 44 botanical plates on 22 sheets. Some tears at folds. S June 25 (384) £1,000 [Arader]

2d Ed. 6 vols. 12mo, contemp sheep; rubbed, joints cracking. With 44 folding plates & 28 folding maps. Library & duplicate stamps on title & final pages. P Dec 15 (185) $1,100

Charnois, Jean Charles Le Vacher de
— Costumes et annales des grands theatres de Paris.... Paris: Janinet, 1786-89-[90]. Issues 1-48 bound in 2 vols. Contemp calf gilt. With 47 (of 48) plates, 37 ptd in color & finished by hand. Most issues bound without titles; Nos 12 & 43 have no plates. Sold w.a.f. C Apr 8 (12) £1,150 [Weinreb]

Charpentier, Francois, 1620-1702
— Discours d'un fidele sujet du Roy.... Paris, 1664. 8vo, modern half calf. Tp soiled. S Apr 23 (336) £400 [Lake]

Charrier, ——
— Discours traittant de l'antiquite, utilite, excellences & prerogatives de la pelleterie.... Paris: Pierre Billaine, 1634. 8vo, mor janseniste by Chambolle-Duru, 1869. SM Feb 28 (124) FF7,000

Charsley, Fanny Anne
— The Wild Flowers Around Melbourne. L, 1867. Folio, mor gilt; cracked. With 14 colored plates. Some foxing. CA Apr 12 (61) A$2,000

Chase, Owen. See: Golden Cockerel Press

Chasse...
— La Chasse du cerf en rime francoise. Paris: Techener, 1840. One of 50 on hollande. 8vo, mor gilt by Bauzonnet-Trautz. Jeanson copy. SM Feb 28 (127) FF2,200

Chasses...
— Chasses dan la Foret de Bialowieza. St. Petersburg: Imprimerie de l'Academie Imperiale des Sciences, [1861]. 4to, contemp shagreen. With 4 plain & 5 color plates. Jeanson 1624. SM Feb 28 (128) FF14,000

Chastenet, Armand Marie Jacques de
— Du Magnetisme Animal, considere dans ses rapports avec diverses branches de la physique generale.... Paris, 1820. 8vo, contemp half lea, with gilt cipher of the Empress Marie Louise; spine ends & cor-

ners worn. sg Jan 15 (305) $100

Chatelain, Henri Abraham
— Atlas historique, ou nouvelle introduction a l'histoire.... Amst., 1708-19. Vols I-II (of 7). Folio, contemp calf; worn. With engraved title & 66 double-page or folding maps & genealogical tables. S Nov 10 (844) £280 [Nicholson]
4th Ed of Vol I, 2d Ed of Vols II & III, 3d Ed of Vol IV & 2d Ed of Vols V-VII. Amst., 1720-39. 7 vols. Folio, contemp calf gilt; rubbed. With 250 plates. Lacking engraved titles. S Oct 23 (227) £5,000 [Tooley]

Chater Collection, Sir Catchick P.
— The Chater Collection, Pictures Relating to China, Hongkong, Macao.... L, 1924. One of 750. Ed by James Orange. 4to, orig cloth, in d/j. L July 2 (25) £600
Anr copy. Orig cloth. pn Apr 30 (355) £450 [Yablon]; pnE Oct 15 (118) £300

Chatterton, Edward Keble, 1878-1944
— Ship-Models. L, 1923. One of 1,000. 4to, orig cloth; scuffed. S Jan 13 (634) £35 [Trocchi]
— Steamship Models. L, 1924. One of 1,000. 4to, orig cloth; soiled & worn. wa Nov 6 (142) $95

Chatterton, Thomas, 1752-70
— Miscellanies in Prose and Verse. L, 1778. 1st Ed. 8vo, later calf; rebacked. Dampstaining in lower outer corner throughout. sg Mar 26 (72) $50
— Poems, Supposed to have been Written at Bristol, by Thomas Rowley.... L, 1898. ("The Rowley Poems.") One of 210. Illus by Charles Ricketts. 2 vols. 8vo, orig bds. S May 6 (46) £50 [Cox]

Chatto, William Andrew, 1779-1864
— The Angler's Souvenir. L, 1835. 8vo, mor gilt. sg May 21 (38) $150
— A Treatise on Wood Engraving. L, [1861]. 8vo, orig cloth. sg Feb 5 (86) $80

Chaucer, Geoffrey, 1340?-1400
See also: Kelmscott Press; Limited Editions Club
— Canterbury Tales. L, 1830. 5 vols. 8vo, mor gilt. pn Apr 30 (29) £210 [Frew]
Anr Ed. L: Riccardi Press for the Medici Society, 1913. One of 500. Illus by W. Russell Flint. 3 vols. 4to, orig half cloth; soiled. S June 17 (234) £260 [Marzam]
Anr Ed. NY, 1930. One of 75. Illus by Rockwell Kent. 2 vols. Folio, orig blindstamped pigskin; spines darkened & brittle. With suite of 5 large orig panel prints, each sgd by Kent. sg Jan 8 (145) $850
One of 75 with extra suite of sepia prints, each sgd. Pigskin gilt; soiled, rubbed. wa June 25 (466) $950
Out-of-series copy. Cloth; dust-soiled. cb Dec 4 (224) $180
— The Romaunt of the Rose. L, 1908. One of 500. Orig vellum. S Oct 6 (816) £50 [Santin]
— Works. L: Jhon Kyngston for Jhon Wight, 1561. 5th Ed, 2d Issue. Folio, modern blind-panelled calf; scratched. A few titles shaved; several leaves strengthened or repaired; some browning & marginal dampstaining; hole at the foot of leaves 2g3-3U8 not affecting text. STC 5076. S July 23 (1) £700 [Spedding]
Anr Ed. L: Adam Islip, 1598. Folio, 18th-cent calf gilt; rubbed, upper joint cracked. Some worming; lacking Corrections and Annotations; lacking 1st & final blanks. C May 13 (157) £620 [Bennett & Kerr]
Anr Ed. L, 1687. Ed by Thomas Speght. Folio, calf; broken, worn. Marginal tears & repairs. S Mar 10 (1043) £220 [Bennett]
Anr copy. Calf; worn & broken. Some stains & soiling; hole in B1 with loss. Sold w.a.f. S July 14 (381) £150
Anr Ed. L, 1721. Folio, contemp calf; worn. Lower blank margin wormed at end. S Jan 13 (481) £90 [McKenzie]
Anr copy. Early 19th-cent half lea; worn. S Jan 13 (482) £200 [Stern]
Anr Ed. Oxford, 1894-97. Ed by W. W. Skeat. 6 vols. 8vo, cloth; soiled. Ck Nov 7 (35) £40
Anr Ed. Oxford: Shakespeare Head Press, 1928-29. One of 375. 8 vols. 4to, half mor; corners bumped. sg Dec 4 (79) $3,400
Anr Ed. Cleveland: World Publishing Co., [1958]. Folio, orig cloth, in d/j. Facsimile of the Kelmscott Chaucer. pn Mar 5 (170) £50 [Walford]

Chauchard, Jean Baptiste Hippolyte
A General Map of the Empire of Germany.... L, 1800. Folio, contemp half russia. With index map & map on 25 sheets. C Dec 12 (46) £170 [Rivara]

Chauffourt, Jacques de, fl.1575-1642
— Instruction sur le faict des eaues et forests.... Rouen: David du Petit Val, 1618. 8vo, contemp vellum. Jeanson copy. SM Feb 28 (129) FF1,000

Chaumeton, Francois Pierre, 1775-1819
— Flore médicale. Paris, 1814-20. Illus by Lambert, chiefly after Turpin. 7 vols in 8. 8vo, contemp half calf gilt. With 424 plates. FD Dec 2 (452) DM6,000
Anr copy. Contemp calf gilt. With 2

CHAUMETON

folding tables & 424 hand-finished color plates. de Belder copy. S Apr 27 (65) £5,000 [Heuer]

Chauncy, Sir Henry, 1632-1719
— The Historical Antiquities of Hertfordshire. L, 1700. Folio, later calf gilt; rebacked, rubbed & torn. Folding map shaved & with short tear along fold; 1 plate with rust-hole; dampstained along lower margin throughout. S May 28 (990) £600

Chayt, Steven & Meryl
— Collotype: being a History-Practicum-Bibliography. Winter Haven FL: Anachronic Editions, 1983. One of 85. 4to, cloth, unopened. sg Jan 22 (124) $225

Cheadle, Walter Butler. See: Fitzwilliam & Cheadle

Chelminski, Jan V.
— L'Armee du Duche de Varsovie. Paris, 1913. Out-of-series copy. Folio, wraps. With 48 mtd color plates & 10 plain plates. pn July 23 (116) £110 [Mier]

Chemnitz, Martin
— Lororum theologicorum, reverendi et clarissimi theologi.... Frankfurt: Joannes Spies, 1592. 4to, later half sheep. Some underlining & marginal staining. ha Dec 19 (293) $50

Chenavard, Antoine Marie
— Six Vues et details dessines a Athenes.... Lyon, 1857. Folio, orig bds. S Oct 23 (327) £320 [Martinos]
— Voyage en Grece et dans le Levant.... Lyon, 1858. Folio, orig half mor; upper joint split. With 79 plates & maps. S Oct 23 (328) £900 [Wood]
Anr copy. 2 vols in 1. Folio, contemp half cloth. With 55 maps & plates. S Feb 23 (414) £900 [Martinos]

Cheney, A. Nelson. See: Orvis & Cheney

Cherbuin, L. See: Falkeisen & Cherbuin

Cherler, Jean Henri. See: Bauhin & Cherler

Cherokees. See: Indians, North American

Cherry-Garrard, Apsley
— The Worst Journey in the World. L, 1922-23. 1st Ed, 1st Issue. 2 vols. Orig bds. With the private offprint with special preface, 64 pp, 1923. CA Apr 12 (63) A$1,400
Later Issue. 2 vols. Without Supplement. kh Mar 16 (83) A$350

AMERICAN BOOK PRICES CURRENT

Cherville, Gaspard Georges de
— Les Chiens et les chats d'Eugene Lambert. Paris, 1888. One of 100. 4to, mor; marked. With 6 plates. S May 6 (166) £130 [Hildebrandt]

Cheselden, William, 1688-1752
— Osteographia, or the Anatomy of the Bones. L, 1733. 1st Ed. Folio, contemp half sheep; worn, joints split, new endpapers. With 2 series of 56 plates, one with text on verso & the other without. Stamp on front free endpaper. bba May 14 (274) £1,800 [Phelps]
— A Treatise on the High Operation for the Stone. L, 1723. 8vo, new half calf. With 17 plates. Top of Plate IX cut away. S May 21 (191) £450 [Phillips]

Cheshire, Horace F.
— The Hastings Chess Tournament 1895. NY, 1896. 8vo, orig cloth. Inscr by Emanuel Lasker. pn Mar 26 (51) £140 [Furstenberg] Anr copy. Orig cloth; rubbed. pn Mar 26 (52) £65 [Dennis]

Chess...
— Chess. Sutton Colfield, 1935-83. Ed by Baruch H. Wood. Vols 1-47; lacking Vol 30. pn Mar 26 (170) £240 [Kuiper]
— The Chess MOnthly. L, 1879-96. Vols 1-17 (all pbd). Half calf; not uniform. Library stamps. pn Mar 26 (174) £320 [Chandler]

Chesterfield...
— Chesterfield Travestie; or School for Modern Manners. L: Tegg, 1808. Illus by Thomas Rowlandson. 8vo, mor gilt by Riviere. With 10 plates. sg Feb 12 (263) $300

Chesterfield, Philip Dormer Stanhope, 4th Earl of, 1694-1773
— Letters written by the Late Right Honourable Philip Dormer Stanhope, Earl of Chesterfield, to his Son.... L, 1774. 1st Ed. 2 vols. 4to, contemp calf; upper joints weak. pnE Jan 28 (128) £160 [Thin]
Anr copy. Contemp calf; joints reinforced. sg June 11 (100) $500
— Miscellaneous Works. L, 1777-78. 2 vols. 4to, contemp calf; rejointed but broken. sg Oct 9 (151) $150

Chesterton, Gilbert Keith, 1874-1936
— Gloria in Profundis. [L: Faber & Gwyer, 1927]. One of 350. Illus by Eric Gill. Bds. No 5 of the Ariel Poems Series. cb Dec 4 (108) $50
— The Scandal of Father Brown. L, 1935. In chipped d/j. cb Nov 20 (46) $110

Chetwood, William Rufus, d.1766
— The Voyages, Dangerous Adventures and Imminent Escapes of Capt. Rich. Falconer. L, 1724. 2d Ed. 12mo, contemp calf; rubbed, joints splitting. Tp & 1st leaf of text torn; many leaves shaved at upper margin, affecting headlines; some dampstaining. bba Oct 16 (66) £70 [Bickersteth]

Chevalier, Michel, 1806-79
— Lettres sur l'Amerique du Nord. Brussels, 1844. 2 vols. 8vo, orig wraps; worn. With folding map. O Sept 23 (34) $70

Chevalier, Ulysse, 1841-1923
— Repertoire des sorces historiques du moyen age. Montbeliard, 1894-1903; Paris, 1905-7. Topographie, 2 vols in one; Bio-bibliographie, 2 vols. Together, 4 vols. 8vo, needs rebdg. sg May 14 (201) $175

Chevallier, Gabriel
— Clochemerle. Paris, 1934. Orig wraps; rubbed. bba Oct 16 (200) £55 [Leichti]

Chevallier, Guillaume Sulpice. See: Gavarni

Chevigne, Louis M. J. Le Riche, Comte de
— La Chasse et la peche suivies de poesies diverses. Reims, 1832. 12mo, contemp mor. Jeanson copy. SM Feb 28 (131) FF2,500
— La Chasse, poeme en deux chants. Paris, 1828. 8vo, mor gilt by Chambolle-Duru. Jeanson copy. SM Feb 28 (130) FF4,200

Chevreul, Henri, 1819-89
— Bombonnel le tueur de pantheres. Paris: Auguste Aubry, 1860. 8vo, mor janseniste by Gruel. Jeanson copy. SM Feb 28 (133) FF2,800

Chevy Chase. See: Famous...

Cheyne, George, 1671-1743
— The English Malady: or, a Treatise of Nervous Diseases.... L, 1733. 1st Ed. 8vo, contemp calf. pnE Dec 17 (80) £320 [Phelps]
— An Essay of Health and Long Life. L, 1724. 8vo, contemp calf, top half of front free endpaper missing. Narrow strip cut from tail of title. pnE Dec 17 (81) £320 [McCormack]; sg Jan 15 (76) $150
— An Essay on Regimen.... L, 1740. 8vo, contemp calf; rebacked. sg Jan 15 (76) $150

Cheyne, John, 1777-1836
— An Essay on Hydrocephalus Acutus, or Dropsy in the Brain. Phila., 1814. 12mo, new cloth. Inner blank margin of tp, following leaf & last leaf strengthened. S May 28 (647) £200

Chicago
— Chicago As It Is. A Strangers' and Tourists' Guide.... Chicago, 1866. 16mo, orig cloth; worn. Small tear in folding map. O Oct 21 (42) $65

Chichester, H. M. — & Burges-Short, G.
— The Records and Badges of Every Regiment and Corps in the British Army. L, 1900. pn Oct 23 (4) £60 [Neale]

Chifflet, Jean Jacques
— Lilium Francicum, veritate historica, botanica et heraldica illustratum.... Antwerp: Plantin, 1658. Folio, later vellum bds; tear in lower cover. Minor browning. de Belder copy. S Apr 27 (67) £1,600 [Macdougall]

Chigorin, Mikhail I.
— M. I. Chigorin [White Russian Chess Player (350 Selected Games)]. Moscow, 1949. Orig half cloth. pn Mar 26 (261) £40 [Chen]
— Michail I. Tschigorin: 400 Partien.... Hamburg: E. Wildhagen, [1960]. pn Mar 26 (263) £45 [Chen]
— [Selected Games]. Leningrad, 1926. Wraps. pn Mar 26 (262) £45 [Hoffman]

Child, Sir Josiah, 1630-99
— Brief Observations concerning Trade, and Interest of Money. L: for Elizabeth Calvert, 1668. 4to, wraps. S July 24 (432) £620 [Pickering]
— Traites sur le commerce et sur les avantages qui resultent de la reduction de l'interest de l'argent.... Amst. & Berlin, 1754. Trans by Vincent de Gournay. 16mo, contemp calf; rubbed. Some spotting & browning. P Sept 24 (297) $200

Child, Lydia Maria, 1802-80
— An Appeal in Favor of that Class of Americans called Africans. Bost., 1833. 8vo, orig cloth; spine-tips frayed. Minor stains & foxing. O Nov 18 (40) $110

Childers, Erskine
— The Riddle of the Sands: A Record of Secret Service.... L, 1903. Orig cloth; small tear on spine. Some soiling. S Jan 13 (540) £170 [Cavendish]

Chilton, Charles, 1860-1929
— The Subantarctic Islands of New Zealand. Wellington, 1909. 2 vols. 4to, cloth; rubbed. A few leaves in Vol I damaged & def. bba Mar 26 (356) £75 [Hay]

Chinese...
— The Chinese Repository. Canton, 1833-51. 2d Ed of Vols I-II, the others 1st Ed. 20 vols in 11. 8vo, half calf. A few leaves def; lacking the 1st number in Vol XX. Sold

w.a.f. S Oct 23 (474) £2,400 [Orientum]

Chippendale, Thomas, 1718?-79
— The Gentleman and Cabinet-Maker's Director. L, 1754. 1st Ed. Folio, modern half mor gilt; soiled. With engraved dedication & 160 (of 161) plates. Lacking half-title, title & list of subscribers; first few leaves rehinged; several plates torn & repaired or remargined with minimal loss; soiled. S July 13 (13) £500

2d Ed. L, 1755. Folio, bdg not described but worn & crudely repaired. Lacking 10 plates; tp & dedication crudely repaired with loss; some tears. S May 6 (373) £520 [Shapero]

3d Ed. L, 1762. Folio, bdg not indicated. Library markings. Sold w.a.f. Franklin Institute copy. F Sept 12 (110) $1,600

Anr copy. Modern half mor; rubbed. With 200 plates; some misbound. Sold w.a.f. S Apr 23 (90) £1,600 [Heneage]

Anr Ed. NY, 1938. Folio, cloth, in d/j. Facsimile of the 1762 Ed. pnE Nov 12 (58) £55

Anr copy. Cloth; worn. Facsimile of the 1762 Ed. sg June 4 (90) $140

— Sketches of Ornament. L, 1779. Bound with: The Principles of Drawing Ornaments Made Easy....L, 1780. And: The Young Painter's Assistant in the Art of Drawing. L, 1753. And: A New Book of Vases. L, 1773. 4to, half calf; def. Sold w.a.f. S Oct 23 (197) £2,200 [Quaritch]

Chiu-Shin
— Chiushingura: or, the Loyal League. A Japanese Romance. L, 1880. Trans by Frederick V. Dickins. Orig cloth. cb Mar 5 (233) $100

Choderlos de Laclos, Pierre A. F. See: Laclos, Pierre A. F. Choderlos de

Choiseul-Gouffier, Marie Gabriel F. A., Comte de, 1752-1817
— Voyage pittoresque de la Grece. Paris, 1782-1809-22. 2 vols in 3. Folio, half mor; worn. With port, 2 folding maps & 283 maps & plates on 168 sheets, including the double-page plate "76 bis" in Vol II. S Apr 24 (213) £3,400 [Tsigaras]

Anr Ed. Paris, 1782-1822. 3 parts in 2 vols. Folio, contemp calf gilt; repaired. With engraved titles, port, 2 large folding maps & 280 maps & plates on 167 sheets, including the double-page Plate 76 bis in Vol II. Lacking 1 sheet in Vol II with 4 Turkish costume plates. S June 25 (342) £1,500 [Leinweber]

Chomel, Noel, 1632-1712
— Dictionarie Oeconomique: or, the Family Dictionary. L, 1727. 2 vols. Folio, contemp half calf; paper sides worn. S May 28 (817) £220

Chorier, Nicolas, 1612-92
— Joannis Meursii elegantiae Latini sermonis.... Leipzig, 1913. One of 10 on vellum. 2 vols in 1. 12mo, orig mor gilt; spine worn. FD June 11 (4860) DM6,000

Choris, Louis, 1795-1828
— Voyage pittoresque autour du monde.... Paris: Firmin Didot, 1822. Folio, contemp calf gilt; worn, spine def. With 103 (of 104) hand-colored plates & 2 maps. HN Nov 26 (335) DM5,400

— Vues et paysages des regions equinoxiales.... Paris, 1826. One of 50 L.p. copies. Folio, orig bds; joints worn, loose. With 24 hand-colored plates. Half-title bound after title. S Oct 23 (315) £4,500 [Quaritch]

Anr copy. Contemp half lea; joints worn, contents slightly loose. Lacking dedication leaf & with half-title bound after title in place of dedication leaf. S Apr 24 (374) £2,200 [Perrin]

Choulant, Ludwig Johann, 1791-1861
— History and Bibliography of Anatomic Illustration. Chicago, [1920]. sg May 14 (586) $175

Christ, Johann Friedrich
— Anzeige und Auslegung der Monogrammatum. Leipzig, 1747. 8vo, contemp calf; rubbed, joints split. bba Jan 15 (351) £70 [Robertshaw]

— Dictionnaire des monogrammes, chiffres, lettres initiales.... Paris, 1750. 8vo, contemp calf; worn. With 6 folding plates. S Jan 13 (356) £65 [Weinreb]

Christian, M. A.
— Debuts de l'Imprimerie en France. Paris, 1905. 4to, half mor gilt, orig wraps bound in. sg Jan 22 (117) $140

— Origines de l'Imprimerie en France. Paris, 1900. Folio, half mor, orig wraps bound in; corners & joints worn. L.p. copy. sg Jan 22 (116) $50

Christie, Agatha
— Cards on the Table. L: Collins, [1936]. Bdg bumped. cb Nov 20 (51) $80

— The Hound of Death and Other Stories. L: Odhams Press, [1933]. In chipped & repaired d/j. cb Nov 20 (55) $60

— Murder in Mesopotamia. L: Collins, [1936]. Bdg rubbed & soiled. Some dampstaining. Inscr. cb Nov 20 (57) $500

— The Mysterious Mr. Quin. L: Collins, 1930. Spine ends bumped. cb Nov 20 (58) $55

— Partners in Crime. L: W. Collins, [1929]. cb Apr 24 (1172) $150
— Poirot Investigates. NY, 1925. Covers soiled, spine rippling. cb Nov 20 (59) $100

Chronicles
— Croneken der Sassen. Mainz: Peter Schoeffer, 6 Mar 1492. Folio, 16th-cent blindstamped pigskin over wooden bds. Some tears, repaired; wormed; stained. 283 leaves; lacking final leaf. Goff C-488. FD Dec 2 (41) DM40,000
— Die Cronica van der hilliger Stat van Coellen. [Cologne]: Johann Koelhoff the Younger, 23 Aug 1499. Folio, 19th-cent half calf; worn & def. Worn & repaired; browned. 348 (of 368) leaves. Goff C-476. VH Sept 12 (818) DM7,000

Chubb, Charles. See: Braybroune & Chubb

Chubb, Ralph Nicholas
— The Secret Country. Kingsclere Woodlands, 1939. One of 30. Folio, half mor; soiled. pn Mar 5 (91) £340 [Henderson]
— The Secret Country, Tales of Vision. Kingsclere Woodlands, 1939. One of 37. Folio, orig half mor; rubbed. Lithographed throughout. S June 17 (220) £500 [Christopher]
— The Sun Spirit, a Visionary Fantasy. Fair Oak, near Kingsclere, 1931. One of 6 with 10 illusts colored by hand. Folio, orig half mor; upper joint repaired. Lithographed throughout. S June 17 (221) £900 [Randolph]

Church Library, Elihu Dwight
— A Catalogue of Books Consisting of English Literature and Miscellanea.... NY, 1907-9. One of 150. Compiled by George W. Cole. 2 vols. Worn. sg Oct 2 (104) $225
— A Catalogue of Books Relating to the Discovery and Early History of North and South America.... NY, 1907. One of 150. Compiled by George W. Cole. 5 vols. 4to, cloth; worn & shaken. sg May 14 (4) $600
Anr Ed. NY, 1951. Compiled by George Watson Cole. 5 vols. 4to, cloth; soiled. bba Jan 15 (261) £210 [Baumann]; bba Mar 26 (7) £160 [Shapero]
Anr copy. Cloth; worn. Library markings. O June 16 (58) $160

Church, John
— A Cabinet of Quadrupeds. L, [1794]-1805. 2 vols. Folio, contemp mor gilt; rubbed. With 84 plates. Marginal stains in Vol I. O May 12 (42) $350

Church, Thomas
— Entertaining Passages Relating to Philip's War.... Bost.: B. Green, 1716. 4to, half mor. Some shaving. S June 25 (410) £6,800
— Entertaining History of King Philip's War.... Newport, 1772. 2d Ed. 8vo, disbound. With 2 ports by Paul Revere. Foxed; 3 letters offset from tp to frontis traced in ink; A4 creased & ptd so as to cause short tear into text; D1 & G8 with marginal tears into text; F2 with short tear in blank margin. P Oct 29 (17) $1,300

Churchill, Awnsham & John
A Collection of Voyages and Travels. L, 1704-32. 1st Ed. 6 vols. Folio, contemp calf; some covers detached, joints split, worn. With 2 engraved titles & 169 maps & plates. Vol II lacking all between Ss1 & Zz2; marginal tears & defs; some worming to first few leaves of Vol II. Sold w.a.f. bba June 18 (304) £1,000 [Shapero]
Anr Ed. L, 1732. 6 vols. Folio, cloth; soiled. One or 2 plates torn & def; 1 plate repaired; a few leaves stained; ink or perforated library stamps on titles & plates. bba Jan 15 (436) £600 [Shapero]
Anr Ed. L, 1732. 8 vols. Folio, contemp calf; joints weak. With 4 ports & 273 maps & plates. Some tears & small wormholes touching a few letters. S June 25 (323) £2,000 [Traylen]

Churchill, Charles, 1731-64
See also: Goldsmith, Oliver
— Poems. L, 1763-65. 2 vols. 4to, contemp calf; joints cracked. Ck June 5 (96) £45

Churchill, G.C. See: Gilbert & Churchill

Churchill, James Morss. See: Stephenson & Churchill

Churchill, Sir Winston L. S., 1874-1965
— A History of the English-Speaking Peoples. L, 1956-58. 1st Ed. Vols I & II (of 4) only. Orig cloth, in d/js. Presentation copies, each vol with a sheet of paper inscr by Churchill laid in. S Sept 22 (166) £400 [Rothman]
3d Ed of Vol I; 2d Ed of Vols II & III. Vols I-III. Orig cloth in d/js. Inscr to Tom O'Brien. S Dec 18 (252) £1,550 [F.A.S.]
— Into Battle. L, 1941. Mor. Inscr to John Peck. S July 24 (309) £700 [Rothman]
— London to Ladysmith via Pretoria. L, 1900. 1st Ed. 8vo, orig cloth; soiled. pn Mar 5 (184) £50 [Levine]
Anr copy. With 3 folding maps (1 colored). S Sept 22 (76) £240 [Rothman]
Anr copy. Modern mor. 3 folding maps slightly torn. S Jan 13 (542) £130 [Perrin]

CHURCHILL

— Marlborough, his Life and Times. L, 1934-36. 1st Ed. 3 (of 4) vols. Orig cloth. Inscr to Dr. Meilijink & with an ALs to him thanking him for his assistance, 16 June 1937. S Sept 22 (72) £1,000 [Sotheran]
— My African Journey. L, 1908. 1st Ed. pn Mar 5 (72) £110 [Joseph]

Anr copy. Orig cloth; lower hinge torn. pn Mar 5 (238) £50

Anr copy. Part of rear endpaper cut away. T Mar 19 (18) £70

— My Early Life. A Roving Commission. L, 1948. Mor gilt by Bumpus. Inscr. S July 13 (143) £580
— Painting as a Pastime. L, 1949. 3d Impression. Inscr to Kathleen Duncanson. With Ls. S July 13 (144) £700
— The River War. L, 1899. 1st Ed. 2 vols. 8vo, cloth; worn. pn Mar 5 (71) £720 [Meyer]

Anr copy. Later mor gilt. S Sept 22 (77) £460 [Smith]

— Savrola. L, 1900. 1st English Ed. 8vo, orig cloth; worn. S Sept 22 (74) £130 [Smith]

Anr copy. Orig cloth; spine torn. S Sept 22 (75) £110 [Smith]

Anr copy. Orig cloth; worn. S Jan 13 (544) £85 [Lord]

Anr Ed. NY, 1900. 8vo, orig cloth; slightly rubbed. Prelims slightly spotted. bba May 14 (109) £180 [Mayow]

— The Second World War. Bost., 1948-53. 1st American Ed. 6 vols. In frayed d/js. O Oct 21 (44) $50

1st English Ed. L, 1948-54. 6 vols. In soiled d/js. wa Sept 25 (543) $80

Anr copy. Half mor gilt by Asprey. wd June 19 (75) $550

— The Unknown War: the Eastern Front. NY, 1931. 1st American Ed. pn Jan 22 (213) £35 [Joseph]
— Works. L, 1974-75. Centenary Ltd Ed. 34 vols. S Dec 18 (254) £1,100 [Kronos]

Churton, Edward, 1800-74. See: Richardson & Churton

Chytraeus, Nathan

— Variorum in Europa itinerum delicaciae.... Herbornae Nassouiorum [Herborn, Prussia], 1594. 8vo, vellum; soiled. Ms annotations; marginal stains at beginning & end of volume; browned throughout. L Dec 11 (385) £260

Ciaccone, Alfonso

— Vitae, et res gestae Ponticium Romanorum et S. R. E. Cardinalium. Rome, 1677. 4 vols. Folio, contemp vellum gilt; marked & rubbed. bba Oct 16 (16) £320 [Erlini]

AMERICAN BOOK PRICES CURRENT

Ciacconius, Petrus Toletanus

— De Triclinio sive de modo convivandi apud priscos Romanos.... Heidelberg: Sanctandreana, 1590. 8vo, old vellum; loose. Dampstained throughout, front flyleaves with portions missing. sg Jan 15 (11) $150

Cibber, Colley, 1671-1757

See also: Golden Cockerel Press
— An Apology for the Life of Mr. Colley Cibber...Written by himself. L, 1740. 1st Ed. 4to, contemp calf. With port having outer corner torn. C Dec 12 (320A) £90 [Vine]

Anr copy. Contemp calf gilt; worn. pnE Jan 28 (129) £150 [Thin]

Anr copy. Contemp calf; worn & rebacked. Frontis repaired; some soiling; title more severely soiled & repaired at outer corners. S Sept 22 (217) £55 [Cox]

Cibot, Pierre Martial

— Lettre de Pekin, sur le genie de la langue chinoise.... Brussels: de Boubers, 1773. 4to, contemp half calf; broken. With 29 plates. S Nov 27 (154) £200 [Quaritch]

Cicero, Marcus Tullius, 106-43 B.C.

See also: Franklin Printing, Benjamin
— De amicitia, sive Laelius de amicitia. Paris, 1750. ("De amicitia....") 16mo, contemp calf; repaired. Houghton copy. CNY May 11 (84) $100
— De officiis.... Venice: Joannus Tacuinus, 28 Nov 1514. Bound with: Apuleius, Lucius. Asinus aureus. Venice: Joannus Tacuinus, 21 May 1516. Folio, contemp German wooden bds with blind-tooled pigskin spine; clasps repaired. Short tear at top of E1 in 2d work. S Nov 27 (57) £780 [Abramshmidt]
— Epistolae ad Brutum, ad Quintum fratrem, ad Atticum. Venice: Aldus, Nov 1544. ("Epistolae ad Atticum....") 8vo, contemp calf; worn & wormed, rebacked. Marginal staining. bba Apr 23 (94) £45 [Bennett & Kerr]
— Epistolarum familiarum. Paris: Michael Vascosanus, 1534. ("Epistolae familiares.") Folio, old half sheep; joints starting. Partial dampstaining at beginning & elsewhere; tp rehinged & remargined; lacking last leaf. sg Mar 26 (73) $130

Anr Ed. Amst. & Leiden: Elzevir & Hackios, 1677-76. ("Epistolarum libri XVI ad familiares....") 2 vols. 8vo, later half vellum; darkened, 1 spine label rubbed away, worn. With added engraved title. cb Oct 23 (65) $55

— The Familiar Epistles.... L, [1620]. Trans by J. Webbe. 12mo, contemp calf; worn. Some worming affecting text; a few spots &

stains. S July 14 (304) £170

— Opera. Paris: B. Turresanus, 1566-65. 4 vols in 2. Folio, contemp calf, armorial bdg; rebacked. pn Oct 23 (334) £100 [Sokol]

Anr Ed. Leiden: Elzevir, 1642. 10 vols. 12mo, 18th-cent mor gilt. S Nov 27 (58) £1,300 [Bourget]

Anr Ed. Biponti, 1780-87. 13 vols, including Index. 8vo, half calf; spine ends damaged. B Feb 25 (837) HF250

— The Orations. L, 1741. 3 vols. 8vo, contemp calf; joints starting. sg Mar 26 (74) $110

Cicognara, Leopoldo, 1767-1834 —& Others

— Le Fabbriche e i monumenti cospicuidi Venezia. Venice, 1838-40. 2 vols. Folio, later half mor. With frontises with vignettes, engraved title vignettes & 259 plates. C July 22 (42) £600

Cieca di Lione, Pietro de. See: Cieza de Leon, Pedro de

Cieza de Leon, Pedro de

— La Prima Parte dell' historia del Peru.... Venice: G. Ziletti, 1560-65. 2 vols. 8vo, later vellum; hinges cracked. sg Sept 18 (59) $300

Cipelli, Giovanni Battista. See: Egnatius, Johannes Baptista

Cippico, Coriolano. See: Ingresso

Cipriani, Giovanni Battista, 1727-85

— A Collection of Prints after the Sketches and Drawings.... L, 1789. Folio, contemp half russia; worn, broken. With engraved title, port & 49 illusts on 48 plates, some ptd in colors. Some soiling. C July 22 (43) £1,500

Circinianus, Nicolaus

— Ecclesiae, Anglicanae trophaea.... Rome: Grassi, [1584]. Part 1 only. 4to, old vellum; endpapers renewed. With engraved title & 35 plates. Some plates dampstained in lower outer corners; small ink stains on last plate. sg Oct 9 (155) $350

Cisneros, Jose, b.1597

— Discurso que en el insigne Auto de la Fe, celebrado en...Lima...1639. Lima: Geronymo de Contreras, 1639. 4to, modern calf gilt; rubbed. Stamp removed from tp & 2 other leaves; inner margins of 1st gathering reinforced; some stains. P Oct 29 (2) $1,700

Citizen...

— The Citizen Soldier, a Military Paper.... Windsor VT, 1840-41. Ed by Major S. Swett, Jr. Vol I, Nos 1-52, bound in 1 vol. 4to, half lea; worn. Some foxing. O Nov 18 (41) $120

Civil War, American

— Military Maps Illustrating the Operations of the Armies of the Potomac & James.... Wash., [1869]. Folio, contemp half mor; upper cover detached. With litho title & 16 maps on 17 mapsheets, all backed with linen. Embossed stamp on tp. S June 25 (361) £650 [Voorhees]

Civinini, Giovanni Domenica

— Della storia e natura del caffe. Florence, 1731. 4to, contemp vellum; foot of spine frayed. With folding plate. C Oct 15 (215) £320 [Quaritch]

Clacy, Ellen

— A Lady's Visit to the Gold Diggings of Australia, in 1852-53. L, 1853. 8vo, half calf; rubbed. Frontis foxed & detached; tp & some leaves foxed. CA Apr 12 (64) A$190

Claflin, William Henry

— Partridge Adventures. Belmont MA: Pvtly ptd, 1951. sg Oct 23 (216) $225

— Partridge Rambles. Pvtly ptd, 1937. sg Oct 23 (217) $225

Clairville, Joseph Philippe de, 1742-1830

— Auswahl von Pflanzen und Gestraeuchen. Zurich, 1796. Vol I (all pbd). 4to, orig bds. With 27 hand-colored plates. de Belder copy. S Apr 27 (79) £1,600 [Junk]

Clamorgan, Jean de

— La Chasse du loup.... Paris: Jacques Du Puis, 1566. 4to, mor gilt by Chambolle-Duru. Grandjean D'Alteville-Pichon-Gallice-Jeanson copy. SM Feb 28 (135) FF110,000

Anr Ed. Paris: G. Buon for Jacques Du Puis, 1572. 4to, mor gilt by Cape. Jeanson copy. SM Feb 28 (136) FF20,000

Anr Ed. Lyon: Gabriel Cartier, 1584. 4to, mor by Lortic. Some repairs. Jeanson copy. SM Feb 28 (137) FF8,500

Anr Ed. Lyon: Gabriel Cartier, 1597. 8vo, mor gilt by Chambolle-Duru. Jeanson copy. SM Feb 28 (138) FF11,000

Clapham, Richard. See: Derrydale Press

Clapp, Frederick Mortimer, 1879-1969

— An History of the 17th Aero Squadron. [N.p.], Dec 1918. K June 7 (35) $180

Clappe, Louise Amelia Knapp Smith
— The Shirley Letters from California Mines.... San Francisco, 1922. One of 450. Half cloth, in d/j. With 8 colored plates. cb Oct 9 (45) $120

Clapperton, Capt Hugh. See: Denham & Clapperton

Clapperton, Robert H.
— Paper. Oxford: Shakespeare Head Press, 1934. One of 250. Folio, half mor gilt. pn Mar 5 (15) £480 [Henderson]

Clare, John, 1793-1864
— Poems Descriptive of Rural Life and Scenery. L, 1820. 1st Ed. 12mo, contemp half calf; rubbed, rebacked, old spine preserved. bba Dec 4 (93) £200 [Hannas]

Clarendon, Edward Hyde, 1st Earl of, 1609-74
— The History of the Rebellion and Civil Wars in England.... L, 1705-6. 3 vols in 7. 8vo, contemp calf; rubbed, a few joints split. bba Apr 9 (49) £75 [Francis]
  Anr Ed. Oxford, 1707. 3 vols. Folio, contemp blind-stamped vellum; soiled. Some leaves in Vol III browned & spotted. S Sept 22 (218) £110 [Kreigstein]
— State Papers Collected by.... Oxford, 1767-73-86. 3 vols. Folio, later calf; rebacked. Vol I dampstained in lower outer corner throughout, with occasional traces of mold. sg Oct 9 (156) $90
— State Papers...containing the Materials from which The History of the Great Rebellion was Composed. Oxford, 1767-73-86. 3 vols. Folio, contemp calf gilt; some joints split, rubbed. bba Aug 28 (203) £130 [Titles]

Claret de Fleurieu, Charles Pierre, 1738-1810
— Decouvertes des Francois en 1768 & 1769 dans le Sud-Est de la Nouvelle Guinee. Paris, 1790. 4to, contemp calf; rubbed, head of spine chipped. With 12 folding maps & plans. A few plates creased. C Apr 8 (10) £550 [Perrin Thomas]

Clark, Daniel
— Deposition of...in Relation to the Conduct of General James Wlkinson.... Wash., 1808. Recent half mor. cb Jan 8 (25) $300
— Proofs of the Corruption of Gen. James Wilkinson.... Phila., 1809. 8vo, 19th-cent half mor; rubbed, front cover & free endpaper detached. cb Jan 8 (26) $350
  Anr copy. Disbound. K June 7 (78) $85

Clark, Edwin
— The Britannia and Conway Tubular Bridges. L, 1850. 3 vols, including atlas of plates. 8vo & folio, bdg not indicated. Library markings. Sold w.a.f. Franklin Institute copy. F Sept 12 (319) $750

Clark, George Thomas, 1809-98
— Mediaeval Military Architecture in England. L, 1884. 2 vols. 8vo, orig cloth; recased. Library markings. cb Dec 18 (43) $55

Clark, Hugh
— A Concise History of Knighthood. L, 1784. 1st Ed. 2 vols. 8vo, orig bds; broken, backstrips lacking. Marginal staining. bba Oct 16 (92) £40 [Fiske]

Clark, J. O. M. See: Noel & Clark

Clark, John, 1744-1805
— Observations on the Diseases which Prevail in Long Voyages to Hot Countries.... L, 1775. 8vo, contemp calf. pnE Dec 17 (83) £330 [Harding-Brookes]

Clark, John Heaviside, 1770-1863
— A Practical Illustration of Gilpin's Day.... L, 1811. Folio, contemp half lea; worn, spine def, 1 orig wrap loosely inserted. With 30 hand-colored plates. S Nov 17 (645) £1,700 [Henderson]

Clark, John Paterson
— A Practical and Familiar Treatise on the Teeth and Dentism. L, 1836. 8vo, orig cloth. With 4 plates. Lightly foxed or dampstained. sg Jan 15 (81) $130

Clark, Kenneth —& Others
— Sidney Nolan. L, 1961. 4to, orig cloth, in d/j. Ck Oct 17 (182) £20

Clark, Kenneth MacKenzie
— The Drawings of Leonardo da Vinci in the Collection...at Windsor Castle. L, [1968-69]. 2d Ed. 3 vols. sg Feb 5 (97) $100
  Anr Ed. NY: Phaidon, [1969-70]. 3 vols. In d/js. sg June 11 (275) $100

Clark, Robert, 1825-94
— Golf; a Royal and Ancient Game. L, 1875. 8vo, cloth. pnC Jan 23 (56) £480; pnC Jan 23 (57) £420
  Anr copy. Later lea. pnC Jan 23 (58) £400
  Anr copy. Orig cloth; worn & coiled. Library markings. wa Mar 5 (262) $450
  Anr Ed. L, 1893. 8vo, orig cloth. pnC Jan 23 (51) £200; pnC Jan 23 (52) £260; pnC Jan 23 (53) £180; pnC Jan 23 (55) £400
  Anr Ed. L, 1899. 8vo, cloth. pnC Jan 23 (54) £180

Clark, Roland
See also: Derrydale Press
— Pot Luck. West Hartford, VT, [1945]. One of 460. Worn. Inscr to John Holman, thanking him for writing the Intro. sg Oct 23 (218) $150

Clark, Samuel, Teacher of Mathematics
— The Laws of Chance.... L, 1758. 8vo, orig lea; spine worn. FD June 11 (580) DM1,000

Clark, Thomas Dionysius
— Travels in the Old South: a Bibliography. Norman, Oklahoma, [1956-59]. 3 vols. Cloth, in d/js. sg Oct 2 (105) $175
— Travels in the New South. A Bibliography. Norman, OK, [1962]. 2 vols. In d/j. sg Jan 22 (118) $120

Clark, William, 1770-1838. See: Lewis & Clark; Limited Editions Club

Clarke, Arthur C.
— 2001: A Space Odyssey. NY: New American Library, [1968]. In d/j. Sgd. cb Sept 28 (328) $120
— 2010: Odyssey Two. Huntington Woods: Phantasia Press, 1982. One of 26. Lea gilt. cb Sept 28 (330) $600
One of 650. In d/j. cb Sept 28 (331) $65
Anr Ed. NY: Ballantine Books, [1982]. In d/j; Inscr by Clark & by jacket artist Michael Whelan. cb May 7 (339) $75
— Against the Fall of Night. NY: Gnome Press, [1953]. In worn & chipped d/j; bdg bumped. cb Sept 28 (318) $50
Anr Ed. NY: Harcourt Brace, [1956]. ("The City and the Stars.") In rubbed d/j. cb Sept 28 (320) $75
— The Fountains of Paradise. L, 1979. In d/j. cb Sept 28 (322) $70
— Imperial Earth. L, 1975. Bds (1st bdg), in d/j. cb Sept 28 (325) $80
— Rendezvous with Rama. L, 1973. In d/j. cb Sept 28 (327) $80

Clarke, Asa B.
— Travels in Mexico and California.... Bost., 1852. 1st Ed. 12mo, orig wraps. Inscr by Clarke's daughter to George W. Beattie. cb Apr 2 (57) $500

Clarke, Brian. See: Goddard & Clarke

Clarke, Edward Daniel, 1769-1822
— Travels in Various Countries of Europe, Asia and Africa. L, 1816-24. ("Travels in Europe, Asia, Africa.") 11 vols. 8vo, contemp calf; some bdgs rebacked preserving orig spines. With 41 plates & maps, most folding, 1 partly hand-colored. Some staining. bba Oct 30 (294) £180 [Shapero]
Anr copy. Orig bds; worn, a few covers detached. T Mar 19 (16) £110

Clarke, J.
— A Series of Twenty-Four Views Illustrative of the Holy Scriptures.... L, 1833. 4to, contemp wraps; soiled. Ck Sept 26 (99) £55

Clarke, Mrs. J. Stirling
— The Habit and the Horse; A Treatise on Female Equitation. L, 1860. 4to, orig cloth; worn. With 9 plates, 6 finished by hand. Some spotting. pn Mar 5 (217) £110 [Demetzy]

Clarke, James Stanier, 1765?-1834
— The Life of James the Second.... L, 1816. 2 vols. 4to, half mor. Some foxing. O Feb 24 (47) $50

Clarke, Samuel, 1599-1683
— A General Martyrologie. Containing a Collection of all the Greatest Persecutions.... L, 1677. 3d Ed. 2 parts in 1 vol. Folio, old half cloth; worn. With 10 plates, trimmed & mtd; lower margin of last 19 leaves crudely restored. sg Oct 9 (157) $110

Clarke, Samuel, 1675-1729. See: Leibnitz & Clarke

Classiques...
— Les Classiques de la table.... Paris, 1846. 8vo, 19th-cent half sheep gilt; scuffed, backstrip loose, broken. sg Jan 15 (12) $100

Claude Lorrain (Claude Gelee), 1600-82
— Liber Veritatis, or a Collection of Prints.... L, 1777-1819. 3 vols. Folio, contemp half mor gilt. With 3 ports & 300 plates. C Oct 15 (28) £3,200 [Armiro]
Anr copy. Contemp calf gilt, armorial bdg; joints weak or broken. With 2 (of 3) ports & 300 plates. S Oct 23 (5) £5,000 [Yamanaka]
Anr copy. Contemp half mor gilt; rubbed. With 3 ports & 300 plates. Blindstamps on plates. S Feb 24 (503) £2,900 [Kiefer]

Claudel, Paul, 1868-1955
— Cent phrases pour eventails. Tokyo, 1927. One of 200. 3 vols. Oblong 8vo, orig silk over bds. S Nov 10 (63) £80 [Vine]
— Jeanne d'Arc au Bucher. Paris, 1954. One of 35 with an extra suite of the plates with remarques. Illus by Albert Decaris. 4to, unsewn in orig wraps. S Sept 23 (623) £150 [Vendler]

CLAUDIANUS

Claudianus, Claudius
— Opera. Venice: Aldus, Mar 1523. 8vo, later mor. F Jan 15 (229) $350
Anr Ed. Amst., 1760. 4to, mor gilt. pnE Dec 17 (13) £75 [McKenzie]

Claudin, Anatole, 1833-1906
— Histoire de l'imprimerie en France au XVe et au XVIe siecle. Paris, 1900-14. Vols I-IV (without index). 4to, orig lea, Vol III unbound. sg May 14 (424) $850

Clavius, Christophus, 1537-1612
— Astrolabium. Rome, 1593. 1st Ed. 4to, old vellum. Lacking last 3 leaves; tp repaired. O May 12 (43) $475
— Commentaria in Euclidis elementa geometrica & in sphaerica Theodosii.... Mainz, 1612. Folio, contemp calf; worn, joints split. Some leaves browned. Sold w.a.f. S Nov 10 (466) £40 [Faure]
— Epitome arithmeticae practicae. Rome: Dominicus Basa, 1585. 8vo, old vellum; upper cover wormed. Tp soiled; some browning. Ck Jan 30 (32) £120
— Fabrica et usus instrumenti ad horologiorum descriptionem. Rome: Dominicus Basa, 1586. 1st Ed. 4to, old vellum; spine worn. Some spotting; partly misbound. Ck Jan 30 (31) £420
— Horologiorum nova descriptio. Rome: A. Zannetti, 1599. 4to, old vellum; head of spine torn with loss, front inner hinge split. L4 torn with loss to upper blank margin; some blank margins wormed. Ck Jan 30 (34) £240

Clay, Enid. See: Golden Cockerel Press

Cleaveland, Henry —& Others
— Village and Farm Cottages.... NY, 1856. 8vo, orig cloth. bba Sept 25 (266) £45 [Weinreb]

Cleland, Thomas Maitland
[-] The Decorative Work of T. M. Cleland. A Record and Review. NY, 1929. One of 1,200. 4to, cloth. cb Dec 4 (227) $50
Anr copy. Cloth; rubbed. ha Dec 19 (168) $110; sg Jan 22 (119) $50

Clemenceau, Georges
— Figures de Vendee. Paris: Maurice Mery, 1903. Illus by Charles Huard. 8vo, contemp vellum with illusts on covers by Charles Huard, bound by G. Maravon. With 52 etchings; orig watercolor laid on as frontis. cb Feb 19 (59) $120

Clemens, Samuel Langhorne, 1835-1910
— The £1,000,000 Bank-Note and Other Stories. NY, 1893. 1st Ed. 8vo, cloth; worn. O Jan 6 (188) $70
— The American Claimant. NY, 1892. 1st Ed. 8vo, orig cloth; worn. sg Feb 12 (319) $70
Anr copy. Orig cloth; backstrip darkened, bookplate. sg Feb 12 (320) $50
Anr copy. Orig cloth; extremities rubbed, front hinge starting. sg June 11 (414) $100
Anr copy. Cloth; bookplate clumsily removed. wd June 19 (78) $125
— The Celebrated Jumping Frog of Calaveras County.... NY, 1867. 1st Ed, 1st Ptg. 12mo, orig cloth, position of frog not indicated; spine & corners frayed, foreedges dampstained at end. sg Feb 12 (315) $1,000
Anr copy. Orig green cloth, with frog in lower left corner; light stain on back cover. Clemens Library bookplate, sgd by A. B. Paine. wd June 19 (79) $2,600
2d Ptg. Cloth, with frog in lower left corner; hinge cracked, backstrip faded. ha Dec 19 (167) $200
— Concerning Cats. Two Tales by Mark Twain. San Francisco: Grabhorn Press for the Book Club of California, 1959. One of 450. 4to, half cloth, in d/j which has been clipped to show spine label. cb Sept 11 (169) $65
— A Connecticut Yankee in King Arthur's Court. NY, 1889. 1st Ed. 8vo, orig cloth. With orig ink drawing by Dan Beard (reproduced on p 63) mtd in cloth book box with lea label. F Jan 15 (239) $1,800
Anr copy. Cloth; worn. O Jan 6 (187) $80
Anr copy. Half mor; Rubbed. One leaf torn. wa Nov 6 (658) $95
— The Curious Republic of Gondour.... NY, 1919. 1st Ed. 12mo, bds, in worn & chipped d/j. wd June 19 (80) $150
— A Double Barrelled Detective Story. NY & L, 1902. 1st Ed. Illus by Lucius Hitchcock. cb Apr 24 (1123) $160
Anr copy. Some wear. cb Apr 24 (1124) $55
— Following the Equator. Hartford, 1897. 1st Ed, Salesman's sample copy. 8vo, cloth; alternate spines for 2 dif lea bdgs laid onto front pastedown. O May 12 (189) $700
— Huckleberry Finn. NY, 1885. 1st American Ed, 1st Issue. 8vo, orig cloth; extremities worn, rear hinge starting. Tear to 1 text leaf; some foxing. sg June 11 (413) $325
Anr copy. Orig cloth. "An unusually fine, bright copy". wd June 19 (76) $1,500
Early Issue. Orig cloth; worn, frayed, spine ends chipped. ha Mar 13 (254) $75

1986 - 1987 · BOOKS — CLEMENS

Anr copy. ("The Adventures of Huckleberry Finn.") Orig cloth. Slip affixed to front free endpaper reading "Truly yours, Mark Twain. Apl./94". sg Apr 2 (201) $2,200

Issue not indicated. Cloth; worn & stained, front cover bubbled. Prelims stained; some dampstaining. wd June 19 (77) $200

Mixed Issue. Orig cloth; spine ends worn. Some spotting. sg Feb 12 (318) $275

— The Innocents Abroad. Hartford, 1869. 1st Ed, 1st Issue. 8vo, orig cloth; joints repaired. cb Jan 22 (210) $110

Anr Ed. Hartford: American Publishing Co, 1872. 8vo, half calf by Zaehnsdorft slightly worn. wa Sept 25 (51) $70

— Life on the Mississippi. Bost., 1883. 1st American Ed, 1st State. 8vo, orig cloth; a few hinges cracked or cracking. cb Jan 22 (211) $75

Anr copy. Orig calf, hinge cracked, rubberstamp to verso of front free endpaper. cb May 7 (155) $130

Anr copy. Sheep; rubbed. O Nov 18 (188) $130

Anr copy. Later half mor by R. R. Donnelly, orig front cover & spine bound in. O June 9 (187) $160

Anr copy. Cloth; soiled. wa Dec 11 (298) $170

Anr copy. Orig cloth; front hinge weak, spine & hinges frayed, head of spine worn & partly perished. wd June 19 (85) $100

State Intermediate A. Orig cloth; worn. wa Nov 6 (660) $100

1st Ed. L, 1883. 8vo, orig cloth; head & foot of spine soiled. wd Nov 12 (102) $150

— The Love Letters of Mark Twain. NY, 1949. 1st Ed, one of 155. In d/j. With leaf at front with signatures as Clemens & Twain. With presentation inscr by Clara Clemens Samossoud, 1949. CNY May 11 (16) $700

— Mark Twain: San Francisco Correspondent. Selections from his Letters... San Francisco: Book Club of Calif., 1957. One of 400. Half cloth. cb Sept 11 (8) $160

— Mark Twain's Autobiography. NY, 1924. 1st Ed. 2 vols. sg Sept 11 (277) $90

— Mark Twain's Sketches, New and Old. Hartford & Chicago, 1875. 1st Ed, 1st State. 8vo, cloth; spine tips frayed, inner joint broken. Some marginal stains towards end. O Nov 18 (189) $50

Anr copy. Orig cloth; spine ends chipped. sg June 11 (415) $175

— The Mysterious Stranger. NY, [1916]. 1st Issue, with the code K-Q on copyright page. Illus by N. C. Wyeth. O Oct 21 (184) $90

— Personal Recollections of Joan of Arc. NY, 1896. 1st Ed, 1st State. 8vo, cloth. wd June 19 (86) $125

— The Prince and the Pauper. Bost., 1882. 1st American Ed. 8vo, cloth; corners bumped, front joint cracked. Inscr, 1891. CNY May 11 (12) $600

One of a very few copies ptd on china paper & in special bdg, this being the dedication copy to his daughter Clara. Orig cloth; spine ends frayed. Inscr. CNY May 11 (11) $32,000

— Pudd'nhead Wilson. Hartford, 1894. 1st American Ed in Book form. 8vo, cloth. F Jan 15 (238) $150

Anr copy. Contemp sheepskin worn, front joint broken. wa Nov 6 (667) $130

Anr copy. Cloth. wa Dec 11 (299) $130

Anr copy. Orig cloth; rubbed. wd June 19 (89) $150; wd June 19 (90) $150

1st English Ed. L: Chatto & Windus, 1894. 8vo, orig cloth; front joint cracked. Sgd as Twain on front pastedown. CNY May 11 (14) $900

— Punch, Brothers, Punch! and other Sketches. NY, [1878]. 1st Ed in Book form, 1st Issue. 16mo, orig cloth; rubbed. wd June 19 (87) $300

— Roughing It. Hartford, etc., 1872. 1st American Ed. 8vo, orig mor gilt presentation bdg reading Mrs. S. L. Clemens/December 26th. 1872; loose, front cover nearly detached. Inscr to his wife. CNY May 11 (10) $11,000

Anr copy. Orig sheep; rubbed, joints broken. With p 592 a blank & p 242 in Blanck's state A. O Nov 18 (190) $70

Anr copy. Cloth; worn. O Apr 28 (194) $60

Anr copy. Orig cloth; spine ends worn. Minor foxing on title. sg Feb 12 (316) $120

Anr Ed. Kentfield, Calif., 1953. One of 200. Half bds. cb July 16 (6) $120

— The Stolen White Elephant, etc. Bost., 1882. 1st American Ed. 16mo, orig cloth; soiled. With pencilled revisions & annotations by Twain totalling 24 words. CNY May 11 (13) $3,200

— Tom Sawyer. Hartford, 1876. 1st American Ed, 2d Issue. 8vo, cloth; ends worn. sg Feb 12 (317) $150

Blanck's 3d Ptg. Orig cloth; worn. Some soiling & minor stains. O Oct 21 (183) $110

— Tom Sawyer Abroad, Tom Sawyer Detective.... NY, 1896. 8vo, cloth. wd June 19 (88) $300

— A Tramp Abroad. Hartford & L, 1880. 1st Ed. 8vo, orig cloth; worn & faded, front hinge cracked. wd June 19 (91) $125

— Works. Hartford, 1899-1907. Autograph

Ed, one of—512. 25 vols. 8vo, half mor; hinges cracking, some spines faded. wd June 19 (97) $750

Definitive Ed, one of—1,024. NY, 1922-25. 35 vols. Mor gilt; rubbed. P Sept 24 (139) $2,800

Memorial Ed. NY, 1929. One of 90 with leaf of Ms by Twain bound in Vol I. 37 vols. Calf gilt by Riviere. sg Dec 4 (199) $3,400

Stormfield Ed, one of—1,024. 37 vols. Half mor gilt by Bayntun; rubbed. S July 23 (135) £850 [Joseph]

Clemens's copy, Samuel Langhorne
— PAINE, ALBERT BIGELOW. - Thomas Nast: his Period and his Pictures. NY, 1904. 8vo, orig cloth; soiled. sg Feb 5 (233) $80

Clemens, Samuel Langhorne, 1835-1910 —& Harte, Bret, 1836-1902
— Ah Sin: A Dramatic Work. San Francisco: Book Club of Calif., 1961. One of 450. cb Dec 4 (83) $50
— Sketches of the Sixties.... San Francisco, 1926. 1st Ed, One of 2,000. Half cloth, in d/j. Inscr by the pbr. cb Jan 22 (218) $65
2d Ed. San Francisco, 1927. Half cloth; worn. O Sept 23 (78) $110

Clemens, Samuel Langhorne, 1835-1910 —& Warner, Charles Dudley
— The Gilded Age. Melbourne, 1874. 1st Australian Ed. 8vo, orig cloth; rubbed, hinge cracking. cb Jan 22 (209) $55

Clement, of Alexandria
— Opera. Florence: Laurentius Torrentinus, 1550. 1st Ed. Folio, contemp calf gilt by the Medallion Binder for King Edward VI of England. Manchester copy. S July 23 (225) £65,000 [Quaritch]

Clement, Hal, Pseud.
— Close to Critical. L, 1966. In d/j. cb Sept 28 (333) $140
— Mission of Gravity. Garden City, 1954. In d/j, rubbed; spine ends bumped. cb Sept 28 (334) $80

Clement I, Pope, Saint
— Recognitionum libri X. Basel: J. Bebelius, 1526. Folio, modern half calf; rubbed. Small holes in title & 1st leaf; outer margin of title shaved; waterstains. bba Jan 15 (322) £60 [Karlov & Crouch]

Clement V, Pope, 1264-1314
— Constitutiones.... Mainz: Peter Schoeffer, 10 Sept 1476. Folio, contemp blind-tooled pigskin over wooden bds; the two covers differently decorated; wormed; damaged. Wormed; some marginal waterstaining. 76 leaves. Goff C-721. Laurence Hodson's copy. S Nov 27 (12) £7,000 [Fletcher]

Anr Ed. Nuremberg: Anton Koberger, 15 Jan 1482. Folio, later bds; worn. With color-wash miniature at head of text on A2r. B3-4 & G7-H2 mended in margins without loss; thumbed; some dampstains. 59 (of 60) leaves; lacking initial blank. Goff C-725. P Sept 24 (140) $1,100

Clenardus, Nicolaus
— Institutiones absolutissimae in Graecam linguam.... Turin: Giovanni Domenico Tarino, 1589. 3 parts in 1 vol. 8vo, modern vellum. Some dampstains & browning. sg Oct 9 (158) £110

Clere, W. G. See: Le Clerc, Nicolas Gabriel

Clerk, John, 1728-1812
— A Series of Etchings, Chiefly of Views in Scotland. Edin., 1855. Folio, contemp half lea. With 55 numbered plates, 1 unnumbered plate & port. S July 28 (981) £200

Clery, Jean Baptiste Cant Hanet, 1759-1809
— A Journal of Occurrences at the Temple, during the Confinement of Louis XVI.... L, 1798. 8vo, contemp calf; rubbed. bba Apr 9 (83) £40 [Maguire]

Cleveland Public Library
— Catalog of the Chess Collection [John G. White Dept]. Bost., 1964. 2 vols. 4to, cloth. pn Mar 26 (383) £320 [Levine]
— Catalogue of Folklore, Folklife and Folk Songs. Bost., 1978. 3 vols. Folio, cloth; some wear. O Mar 24 (43) $60

Clifton, Mark —& Riley, Frank
— They'd Rather Be Right. NY: Gnome Press, 1957. In rubbed d/j. cb Sept 28 (337) $50

Clinton, De Witt, 1769-1828
— Remarks on the Fishes of the Western Waters of the State of New-York.... NY, 1 Feb 1815. 8vo, modern wraps; foxed. sg Oct 23 (219) $150

Clouzot, Henri
— Painted and Printed Fabrics. NY, 1927. 4to, cloth. With colored frontis & 42 plates. sg Feb 5 (314) $140

Clouzot, Henri —& Follot, Charles
— Histoire du papier peint en France. Paris, 1935. 4to, later cloth. With 27 colored mtd plates Library markings. O Sept 23 (36) $130

Anr copy. Wraps. O June 16 (61) $210

Clowes, Sir William Laird, 1856-1905
— The Royal Navy. L, 1897-1903. 7 vols. 4to, orig cloth; loose. L Dec 11 (340) £320

Clusius, Carolus. See: Lecluse, Charles de

Clute, John Jacob
— Annals of Staten Island.... NY, 1877. One of 500. 8vo, orig cloth; spine ends worn. Small portion of title abraded. sg Sept 18 (207) $100

Clutterbuck, Robert, 1772-1831
— The History and Antiquities of the County of Hertford. L, 1815-27. 1st Ed. 3 vols. Folio, contemp mor gilt; lower edge dampstained. With folding map & 53 plates & plans, 3 hand-colored. Lower margin dampstained throughout. S May 29 (991) £360

Anr copy. Orig bds; Vol I with covers & backstrip loose, anr backstrip torn. With folding map, 53 plates & plans (most marked "proof" in margin), 3 hand-colored. A few leaves in Vol I loose. S May 29 (992) £500

Cluverius, Philippus, 1580-1622
— Introductionis in Universam Geographiam.... Venice: Turrinum, 1616. 12mo, contemp vellum; worn. Some worming, affecting index. O Nov 18 (42) $80

Anr Ed. Amst.: Elzevir, 1661. 12mo, needs rebdg. With engraved title, folding chart & 38 double-page maps. sg Nov 20 (52) $225

Anr Ed. Amst.: Elzevir, 1662. 12mo, old calf; rubbed, rebacked. With engraved title, 2 folding charts & 31 (of 38) double-page maps, hand-colored in outline; maps loose. pnNY Sept 13 (503) $400

Anr Ed. Leiden: Elzevir, 1672. 12mo, contemp calf; def. With engraved title, 2 tables & 33 maps. A few small tears & neatlines shaved. Sold w.a.f. S Jan 12 (93) £220 [Nicolas]

Anr Ed. L, 1711. 4to, contemp calf gilt; worn. With engraved title, 46 maps & 10 plates. Some dust-soiling, a few leaves of text repaired without loss. S Oct 23 (24) £400 [Biba]

Clymer, W. B. Shubrick —&
Green, Charles R.
— Robert Frost: A Bibliography. Amherst, 1937. One of 150, sgd by Frost. Half mor. O Mar 24 (44) $90

Coates, Charles, 1746?-1813
— The History and Antiquities of Reading. L, 1802-[10]. 2 parts in 1 vol. 4to, contemp calf; rubbed, rebacked preserving old spine. With folding map (slight tears at folds), 1 plan & 6 hand-colored plates. S Nov 17 (778) £100 [Young]

Anr copy. Vol II only. Contemp half mor; worn & broken. Text incomplete; lacking 5 plates; 2 plates torn without loss; 2 plates detached & frayed. Sold w.a.f. T Feb 19 (310) £560

Cobarrubias, Pietro di. See: Covarrubias, Pedro de

Cobbett, William, 1763-1835
— The American Gardener. L, 1821. 12mo, old half mor gilt. 1 index leaf torn & repaired. Hunt copy. CNY Nov 21 (58) $110

— The English Gardener.... L, 1838. 8vo, contemp half calf; worn. O Sept 23 (37) $70

— Paper against Gold and Glory against Prosperity.... L, [1817]. Nos 1-15 in 1 vol. 8vo, bds; chipped & rubbed. P Sept 24 (261) $150

— The Pride of Britannia Humbled. Phila., 1815. 2d Ed. 12mo, orig paper over wooden bds; recased. sg Mar 12 (262) $60

— Rural Rides in the Counties of Surrey, Kent, Sussex.... L, 1930. One of 1,000. Illus by John Nash. 3 vols. Orig half cloth; spines soiled. S Mar 9 (730) £80 [Archdale]

Out-of-series copy. Half cloth. pnE Jan 28 (64) £110 [Josephs]

— The Woodlands. L, 1825 [but 1828]. 1st Ed. 8vo, cloth, unopened; rubbed & soiled. bba Aug 20 (65) £110 [Dawson]

— A Year's Residence in the United States of America. L, 1822. 12mo, orig half cloth; spine worn, rubbed. Frontis torn & offset onto title. bba Oct 16 (233) £50 [Hawkins]

Cobden-Sanderson, Thomas James, 1840-1922
See also: Doves Press
— Cosmic Vision. L, 1922. 1st Ed. cb Feb 19 (60) $55

— Four Lectures. San Francisco: Book Club of California, 1974. One of 450. Half cloth. cb Sept 11 (30) $70; sg Jan 8 (31) $70; sg Jan 22 (121) $150

— Journals. L, 1926. One of 1,000. 2 vols. sg Jan 22 (120) $175

One of 1,050. Unopened, in d/js. sg June 11 (109) $150

Cobra
— Cobra. Paris, 1952. One of 100. Illus by Karel Appel. 4to, orig wraps. Issue devoted to Hans Andreus's De ronde kant van de aarde. B Oct 7 (437) HF42500

Coburn, Alvin Langdon
— New York. L & NY, [1910]. Folio, half calf gilt; scuffed. sg Nov 13 (36) $2,200

Coburn, Wallace David
— Rhymes from a Round-Up Camp. Great Falls, Montana, 1899. 1st Ed, 2d Issue. Illus by Charles M. Russell. 8vo, orig fawn lea over bds. With 8 plates. sg Sept 18 (261) $400

Coccejus, Johannes
— Lexicon et commentarius sermonis Hebraici et Chaldaici. Amst.: J. a Someren, 1669. Folio, half calf; rubbed. Lacking port, upper margin stained, lower margin wormed. B Feb 25 (746) £360

Cocchi, Antonio Celestino, 1695-1758
— The Pythagorean Diet of Vegetables Only.... L, 1745. 8vo, modern half mor. Crahan copy. P Nov 25 (461) $350

Cochrane, Charles Stuart
— Journal of a Residence and Travels in Colombia.... L, 1825. 2 vols. 8vo, modern mor by Bayntun. With 2 colored frontises & map. Short tear in map repaired. S July 14 (306) £250

Cochrane, Thomas, Earl of Dundonald. See: Dundonald, Thomas Cochrane

Cochran-Patrick, Robert William
— Catalogue of the Medals of Scotland. Edin., 1884. One of 350. 4to, half mor. pnE June 17 (156) £80

Cock, Thomas
— Kitchin-Physick.... L, 1676. Bound with: Miscelanea Medica; or a Supplement to Kitchin-Physick. L, 1675. 8vo, modern half calf; joints rubbed. Some trimming; a few headlines shaved; 11 leaves probably from a shorter copy. Crahan copy. P Nov 25 (117) $750

Cockburn, James Pattison, 1779?-1847
— Swiss Scenery. L, 1820. 4to, contemp half mor; rubbed. With engraved title & 60 plates. Library markings. bba Apr 23 (348) £420 [Fisher]

Anr copy. Contemp mor gilt by Simier, with arms of the Duchesse de Berry. With engraved title & 61 plates. S Apr 23 (160) £900 [Castle]

Anr copy. 19th-cent mor gilt by Simier, with arms of the Duchesse de Berry. With engraved title, 62 plates & text vignette at end, all mtd india-proofs. sg Dec 4 (40) $550

— Views to Illustrate the Route of the Simplon. L, 1822. Folio, contemp half lea; worn. With 50 plates. S Apr 23 (159) £1,350 [King]

— Views to Illustrate the Route of Mont Cenis. L, 1822. Folio, contemp half calf; worn. With 49 (of 50) plates. T Mar 19 (25) £640

Cockerell, Charles Robert, 1788-1863
— The Temples of Jupiter Panhellenius at Aegina.... L, 1860. Folio, contemp half mor. With 2 engraved dedications, 37 plates & 1 mtd photo. C July 22 (46) £700

Anr copy. Contemp half calf; worn. Lacking 1 plate. JG Mar 20 (1357) DM900

Cockerell, Sir Sydney C.
— Old Testament Miniatures: a Medieval Picture Book.... NY, [1969]. Folio, cloth. sg Feb 5 (236) $70

Cockle, Maurice J. D.
— A Bibliography of English Military Books up to 1642.... L, 1900. One of 250. 4to, orig cloth. sg May 14 (286) $250

Cockx-Indestege, Elly —& Glorieux, Genevieve
— Belgica Typographica 1541-1600. Nieuwkoop, 1968-80. 2 vols (Vol II in 6 parts). 4to, Vol I in orig cloth, Vol II loose as issued in orig wraps. bba Oct 16 (478) £70 [Heiztingugh]

Cocteau, Jean, 1889-1963
— Dessins. Paris, 1923. One of 400. 4to, orig wraps. pn June 18 (79) £280 [Shapero]

— Dessins en marge du text des Chevaliers de la Table Ronde. Paris, 1941. 4to, orig wraps. Inscr with a full-page drawing to Rodolpho Nicoletti, 1947. S Sept 23 (621) £240 [Falk]

— Vaslav Nijinsky, six vers.... Paris, [1910]. One of 934. Illus by Paul Iribe. 4to, half mor; hinges cracking. Inscr. wd June 19 (100) $600

Codex...
— Der Codex Aureus der Bayerischen Staatsbibliothek in Muenchen. Munich, 1921-25. One vol text; 5 vols colored facsimiles: together, 6 vols. Folio, orig wraps. HK Nov 4 (3126) DM1,800

— Codex Cenannensis. Berne, 1950-51. ("Evangeliorum quattuor Codex Cenannensis.") One of 500. 3 vols. Folio, orig vellum gilt & half vellum. C Dec 12 (365) £1,500 [Finer]; sg Dec 4 (222) $1,800

— Codex Durmachensis. Lausanne & Freiburg, 1960. ("Evangeliorum quattuor Codex Durmachensis.") One of 650. 2 vols. Folio, orig mor & half mor, in d/js. C Dec 12 (364) £380 [Thomas]

Anr copy. Lea & half lea. sg Dec 4 (21) $400

— Codex Lindisfarnensis. Evangeliorum quattuor. Oltun & Lausanne, 1956-60. One of 680. 2 vols. Folio, orig half vellum & vellum. S Nov 10 (367) £620 [Fogg]

— Codex Vindobonensis Mexic. I. Vienna, 1929. Oblong 4to, wooden bds; warped.

52 pp in facsimile, accordion-folded & 24-page descriptive folder. sg Mar 12 (181) $300
— Corpus Codicum Americanorum Medii Aevi. Copenhagen, 1942-52. 4 vols in 6. Folio, half vellum. Library markings. sg Mar 12 (183) $550
— Troano codex. Madrid, 1930. 70 pp on 35 accordion-folded sheets, 220mm by 115mm. sg Mar 12 (182) $200

Codroipo, Francesco
— Dialogo de la caccia de' falconi.... Udine: Giovanbattista Natolini, 1600. 4to, 18th-cent vellum. Some stamps. Jeanson 1290. CM Feb 28 (110) FF3,200

Cody, William F., 1846-97. See: Inman & Cody

Coggiatti, Stelvio. See: Trechslin & Coggiatti

Cohen, Henry, 1808-80
— Guide de l'amateur de livres a vignettes du XVIIIe siecle. Paris, 1912. 6th Ed. 2 vols in 1. 8vo, orig wraps. bba Oct 16 (370) £100 [Frew Mackenzie]
  One of 50 on hollande with a duplicate set of the plates before letters. 2 vols. 8vo, mor gilt by Riviere; needs rebdg. C Dec 3 (16) F550 [Tenschert]
  One of 1,000. 4to, half lea. sg May 14 (287) $250

Cohn, Albert Mayer
— George Cruikshank: a Catalogue Raisonne. L, 1924. One of 500. 4to, cloth; hinges reinforced. sg Oct 2 (112) $275

Cohn, Louis Henry
— Bibliography of the Works of Ernest Hemingway. NY, 1931. One of 500. cb May 7 (106) $120; sg Mar 5 (99) $120

Coissac, G. Michel
— Histoire du cinematographe, de ses origines a nos jours. Paris, 1925. Wraps; broken. sg Nov 13 (37) $100

Coit, Daniel Wadsworth, 1787-1876. See: Grabhorn Printing

Cokayne, George Edward, 1825-1911
— Complete Peerage of England, Scotland, Ireland.... L, 1910-59. 13 vols in 14. 4to, orig cloth. bba Aug 20 (101) £1,800 [Duffy]
— The Complete Peerage of England, Scotland, Ireland.... L, 1910-59. New Ed by Vicary Gibbs. 14 vols. Ck Sept 5 (74) £450

Coke, Sir Edward, 1552-1634
— Epitome undecim librorum relationum.... L, 1640. 8vo, old sheep; rebacked. Minor stains. sg Oct 9 (164) $90
— An Exact Abridgement in English of the Eleven Books of Reports. L, 1651. 2d Ed. 12mo, old calf; rubbed. Lacking leaf A1. O Oct 21 (94) $100
— The First [-Fourth] Part of the Institutes of the Laws of England. L, 1639-42-60-69. 4th Ed of Vols 1 & 4, 1st Ed of Vol 2 & 3d Ed of Vol 3. Folio, contemp calf; 2 bdgs rebacked. sg Mar 26 (76) $750
— The First Part of the Institutes of the Lawes of England.... L, 1639. 4th Ed. Folio, old calf; worn. Lacking initial blank; 1st few leaves with small marginal holes & a few other slight tears not affecting text; Pp4 torn in margin with loss; only 1 port. S Sept 23 (320) £120 [Tunkel]
— The First [-Second] Part of the Institutes of the Laws of England. L, 1629-42. 2 vols. Folio, contemp calf; not uniform. First part with B1 supplied from anr copy. sg apr 2 (51) $900
— Institutes of the Laws of England. L, 1656-69. 4 parts in 3 vols. Folio, contemp half calf; rebacked preserving calf spine. Some foxing & marginalia. Wing C4924, 50, 63, 31. bba Oct 16 (60) £600 [Maggs]
— The Reports. L, 1727. 13 vols in 6, plus Index. Together, 7 vols. 8vo, contemp calf; rebacked, endpapers renewed. Titles stamped. sg Oct 9 (165) $350
— The Second Part of the Institutes.... L, 1642. Folio, contemp calf; becoming disbound. Some old marginalia & occasional underlining. K Mar 22 (166) $225

Coke, Roger
— A Detection of the Court and State of England.... L, 1719. 3 vols. 8vo, contemp calf; rubbed. O Feb 24 (48) $70

Coke, Zachary
— The Art of Logick.... L, 1654. 8vo, contemp calf; broken. Some dampstaining in lower margins. sg Mar 26 (77) $80

Coker, John, d.1635?
— A Survey of Dorsetshire. Containing the Antiquities and Natural History.... L, 1732. Folio, modern mor gilt. With folding map & 6 plates. L Dec 11 (102) £150
  Anr copy. Contemp calf; rebacked & repaired. With folding map & 6 plates, 1 in facsimile. Map laid down; some stains. L July 2 (84) £60

Colange, Leo de
— Voyages and Travels or Scenes in Many Lands. Bost.: Walker, [1887]. 4 vols. 4to, half lea; rubbed. O Nov 18 (44) $190

Colardeau, Charles Pierre
— Le Temple de Gnide. Paris, [1772?]. 8vo, mor gilt by Cuzin. Eugene Paillet's copy. Extra-illus with a duplicate proof set of the title-vignette & plates before letters, loosely inserted eaux-forte of 3 plates; 3 loosely

inserted copies of a port in bistre of Colardeau, including 1 before letters. C Dec 3 (104) £360 [Tulkens]

Colas, Rene
— Bibliographie generale du costume et de la mode. Paris, 1933. 2 vols in 1. Contemp half mor, orig wraps bound in; rubbed & soiled. bba Oct 16 (371) £200 [Diba]

Anr copy. 2 vols. Half calf gilt. pn July 23 (273) £80 [Koch]

Anr copy. Orig wraps; worn. sg Jan 22 (122) $150

Colburn, Frona Eunice Wait
— Wines and Vines of California. San Francisco, 1889. 8vo, front wrap only present. Some foxing, staining & worming. cb July 30 (213) $160

Colburn, Warren, 1793-1833
— Ka hope no ka helunaau.... Oahu: Mission Press, 1835. 12mo, contemp half lea; extremities worn, front joint reinforced with cellotape. sg Sept 18 (125) $120

Cole, G. —&
Roper, J.
— The British Atlas. L, 1810. Folio, contemp half calf; rubbed. With 58 maps, colored in outline & 21 city plans. pn May 21 (353) £750 [Nicholson]

Cole, George
— The Contractor's Book of Working Drawings of Tools & Machines.... Buffalo, 1855. Oblong folio, orig cloth. Franklin Institute copy. F Sept 12 (339) $1,500

Cole, George Watson, 1850-1939. See: Church Library, Elihu Dwight

Cole, Ralph
— The Young Angler's Pocket Companion. L, 1795. 12mo, half calf; worn. With frontis & 2 plates. Cellotape repair on right margin of frontis & left margin of tp. sg May 21 (40) $150

Cole, Sylvan, Jr. See: Soyer, Raphael

Cole, William
— Select Views of the Remains of Ancient Monuments of Greece. L, 1835. Folio, orig cloth; rebacked. With 12 hand-colored plates. S Oct 23 (329) £2,000 [Martinos]

Colebrook, Robert H.
— Twelve Views of Places in the Kingdom of Mysore. L, 1805. 2d Ed. Folio, contemp bds; rebacked with cloth. With 12 hand-colored plates. Lacking dedication; very faint fold mark to some plates; short tear to 1 leaf; some minor marginal stains. C Apr 8 (77) £700 [Ponterlovitale]

Colebrooke, Henry Thomas
— A Grammar of the Sanscrit Language. Calbutta, 1805. Folo, half mor. Minor worming at beginning & end. S Apr 23 (338) £1,900 [Ad Orientum]

Coleman, Charles, Artist
— A Series of Subjects Peculiar to the Campagna of Rome and Pontine Marches. Rome, 1850. Folio, half mor; rubbed. With engraved title & 53 plates, some mtd 2 to a page. Tp spotted & with library stamp on verso; library markings. S May 29 (1043) £400

Coleman, J. Winston, Jr.
— A Bibliography of Kentucky History. Lexington, 1949. 8vo, cloth, in rubbed d/j. Inscr. ha Dec 19 (38) $55

Coleman, William, 1766-1829
— A Collection of the Facts and Documents, relative to the Death of...Alexander Hamilton. NY, 1804. 8vo, contemp bds; rebacked in calf. O Nov 18 (45) $90

Anr Ed. Bost., 1904. One of 430. ha May 22 (287) $60

Coleman's...
— Coleman's Pattern Book. Phila., [c.1870]. 4to, bdg not described. Lacking tp. Franklin Institute copy. F Sept 12 (33) $1,100

Coleridge, Hartley
— Poems. Leeds, [1833]. Vol I (all pbd). 8vo, contemp mor. Tp spotted; book label pasted to verso of errata-leaf at end. bba Oct 30 (38) £75 [Axe]

Coleridge, Samuel Taylor, 1772-1834
Fore-Edge Paintings; Kelmscott Press; Nonesuch Press; Wordsworth & Coleridge
— Biographia Literaria; or, Biographical Sketches.... L, 1817. 1st Ed. 2 vols in 1. 8vo, orig bds; soiled & rebacked. K June 7 (83) $130

Anr copy. 2 vols. 8vo, orig bds; worn. S Nov 17 (646) £220 [Finch]

Anr copy. Orig bds; joints starting, spine ends chipped, corner torn out of Vol I front free endpaper. R. P. Gillies' copy. sg Apr 2 (52) $550

— Biographia Literaria; or Biographical Sketches.... L, 1817. 1st Ed. 2 vols. 8vo, orig bds; joints starting. sg June 11 (110) $325

Coleridge, Samuel Taylor, 1772-1834
— Christabel; Kubla Khan, a Vision; the Pains of Sleep. L, 1816. 1st Ed. 8vo, modern mor gilt. Title & 2 other leaves repaired; lacking ads. pnNY Sept 13 (211) $425

Anr copy. Orig wraps; soiled, spine torn at head & foot. Some dampstains. S Jan 13 (484) £520 [Zayas]

Anr copy. Sheep gilt by Riviere. sg Sept 11 (64) $550

— Poems on Various Subjects. Bristol & L, 1797. ("Poems by S. T. Coleridge...to which are now Added Poems by Charles Lamb and Charles Lloyd.") 2d Ed. 8vo, contemp calf gilt. S Jan 13 (483) £240 [Jarndyce]

Anr copy. Contemp calf; joints worn. Prelims browned. sg June 11 (111) $80

— The Rime of the Ancient Mariner. Edin., 1837. Illus by David Scott. Folio, mor by Henderson & Bisset, orig wraps bound in. With 25 plates on mtd india paper. O Oct 21 (45) $180

Anr Ed. L, [1910]. Illus by Willy Pogany. 4to, orig cloth; upper hinge split. With 20 colored plates. One leaf torn. bba Feb 5 (289) £50 [Bailey]

One of 525. Orig mor gilt; rubbed. S Oct 6 (841) £80 [Frazer]

Anr Ed. L, 1945. One of 700. Illus by Duncan Grant. Orig mor gilt. With 5 colored plates. S Oct 6 (812) £110 [Lee]

Anr Ed. NY: Chilmark Press, 1964. Ltd Ed. Illus by David Jones. 4to, orig cloth. With 10 engravings. bba Mar 26 (260) £95 [Henderson]

Anr Ed. Will Carter for Editions Alecto, 1976. One of 140. Illus by Patrick Procktor. 4to, orig half cloth. S June 17 (345) £850 [Hartnoll]

— Sibylline Leaves. L, 1817. 1st Ed. 8vo, calf gilt. sg June 11 (112) $250

Coles, Charles
— Game Birds. NY: Dodd, Mead, [1983]. Folio, cloth, in d/j. ha Sept 19 (247) $60

Coles, Elisha, d.1715?
— An English Dictionary, Explaining the Difficult Terms.... L, 1692. 8vo, contemp calf; worn. Some catchwords cropped; tp frayed; final leaf torn at corner with loss. S Nov 10 (368) £110 [Quaritch]

Coles, William, 1626-62
— Adam in Eden. L, 1657. Folio, later calf; rubbed. Tp torn & mtd; marginal worming; incomplete at end. Sold w.a.f. bba Aug 28 (175) £60 [Elliott]

Anr copy. Contemp calf; rebacked, lacking lower endpaper. Browned; tears to 3E2, 4G1 & 4G4 affecting text; lacking 1 leaf. Crahan copy. P Nov 25 (122) $600

Anr copy. Half calf; worn, corners trimmed. Lacking ad leaf at end; outer blank corners cropped throughout; some browning & staining; tears in Y3 & 2G3; outer margin of H2 trimmed; some leaves wormed; rusthole in 3K4; tp soiled & with deleted ownership inscr at head. S Nov 10 (467) £130 [Wheldon]

Colette, Sidonie garielle, 1873-1954
— Chats. Paris, [n.d.]. One of 300. Illus by Jacques Nam. 4to, loose as issued in orig half cloth. S May 6 (167) £650 [Maurer]

Collaert, Adrianus, d.1618
— Piscium vivae icones factae ab Adriano Collardo.... [Antwerp, 1610?]. 4to, half vellum. With 24 (of 26) plates. Tp cut rount & mtd; an engraving of fish by Nicolaes de Bruyn from anr work bound at end. S Apr 23 (31) £480 [Segag]

Colle, Charles, 1709-83
— La Partie de chasse de Henri IV, comedie. Paris, 1766. 8vo, mor gilt by Cuzin. With frontis & 3 plates & with Gravelot's 4 original drawings. Lacking the half-title. Jeanson copy. SM Feb 28 (141) FF75,000

Anr copy. Mor janseniste by Zucker. With frontis & 3 plates.. Hoe-Jeanson copy. SM Feb 28 (142) FF1,000

— Theatre de societe. Ou recueil de differentes pieces.... The Hague & Paris: P. F. Gueffier, 1768. 2 vols. 8vo, contemp mor gilt. With 5 leaves of autograph Ms inserted to restore censored scenes & with corrections on several pages in Colle's hand. Jeanson copy. SM Feb 28 (143) FF30,000

Collectanea...
— Collectanea Adamantea XV; the Un-Natural History, or Myths of Ancient Science. Edin.: Pvtly ptd, 1886. One of 75 L.p. copies. Trans & Ed by Edmund Goldsmid. 4 vols. 8vo, ptd vellum; worn. sg Sept 11 (240) $110

Collection....
See also: Byam, Lydia

— Collection complete des tableaux historiques de la Revolution Francaise. Paris, 1802. Folio, mor gilt; spine def. With 2 frontises & 213 plates. HN Nov 26 (951) DM4,000

— Collection de vues des principaux palais, eglises, batimens publies, campagnes & jardins tant de Vienne que de ses environs.... Vienna: Maria Geissler, [1812?]. Oblong 4to, contemp russia extra. With engraved title, 2 folding & 72 hand-colored plates. Folding plates a little def in folds; some light stains. P June 18 (71) $900

— Collection de costumes nationaux

COLLECTION...

d'Allemagne. Frankfurt: C. Juegel, [1832?]. 4to, contemp mor gilt; gutta-percha perished & plates detached. With 15 hand-colored plates. Lacking tp. Sold w.a.f. C Apr 8 (34) £750 [Marcus]

— A Collection of Anthems Used in His Majesty's Chapel Royal. L, 1795. 8vo, contemp red mor Chapel Royal bdg. pn Nov 20 (65) £380 [Stevens]

— A Collection of Engravings...by the Most Celebrated Masters. L: W. T. Gilling, [c.1810]. 2 vols. Folio, half calf; worn. S Feb 23 (665) £1,300 [Collmann]

Colley, Richard, 1690?-1758

— An Account...of the Royal Hospital of King Charles II...near Dublin. Dublin, 1725. 12mo, contemp calf gilt. pn Nov 20 (137) £180 [Lyon]

Collie, James

— The Royal Palace of Linlithgow. L: Weale, [c.1840]. 4to, cloth; broken. Some foxing & soiling. O Feb 24 (49) $50

Collie, John Norman. See: Stutfield & Collie

Collier, Jane

— An Essay on the Art of Ingeniously Tormenting.... L, 1809. 12mo, orig bds. With 5 hand-colored plates. sg Feb 12 (264) $250

Collier, Jeremy, 1650-1726

— The Great Historical, Geographical, Genealogical and Poetical Dictionary.... L, 1701-27. 4 vols, including Appendix & Supplement. Folio, contemp calf gilt; rubbed. Title of Vol IV chipped. cb Oct 23 (45) $190
Anr Ed. L, 1701. 2 vols. Folio, calf gilt; rubbed. pn Jan 22 (59) £45 [Trotter]

— A Short View of the Immorality and Profaneness of the English Stage. L, 1698. 1st Ed. 8vo, contemp calf; rubbed, upper joints cracked. Tp soiled; some creasing. Ck Jan 30 (130) £80

Collier, John
See also: Nonesuch Press

— Green Thoughts. L, 1932. One of 550. Furnival Book No 12. cb Sept 28 (341) $140

— No Traveller Returns. L, 1931. One of 210. 8vo, orig velveteen gilt; extremities rubbed, 1 hinge cracking. cb Sept 28 (342) $110

Collier, V. W. F.

— Dogs of China & Japan in Nature and Art. L, 1921. 4to, orig cloth; soiled, rebacked. bba May 14 (246) £40 [Robertshaw]

AMERICAN BOOK PRICES CURRENT

Collingridge, George

— The Discovery of Australia. Sydney, 1895. 4to, cloth; soiled. bba Dec 18 (127) £60 [Angle]

Collingwood, Adam

— Anecdotes of the Late Lord Viscount Nelson.... L, 1806. 8vo, contemp half calf; rubbed. Frontis torn & def; outer margin cropped close. bba Oct 16 (108) £60 [Fiske]

Collins, Anthony, 1676-1729

— A Discourse of Free-Thinking.... L, 1713. Bound with: Phileutherus Lipsiensus [Richard Bentley]. Remarks upon a late Discourse of Free-Thinking.... L, 1716. 8vo, contemp calf; rebacked. cb Oct 23 (46) $80

Collins, Arthur, 1690?-1760

— Historical Collections of the Noble Families of Cavendishe, Holles, Vere, Harley and Ogle. L, 1752. Folio, contemp calf; rubbed. With 12 engraved plates. bba Nov 13 (219) £110 [Maggs]

— The Peerage of England. L, 1756. 5 vols in 6. 8vo, contemp calf; worn, joints starting. With 179 plates only. sg Mar 26 (78) $130

Collins, David, 1756-1810

— An Account of the English Colony in New South Wales. L, 1798-1802. 2 vols. 4to, calf gilt; Vol II rebacked & worn. Marginal notes; some plates foxed. CA Apr 12 (69) A$5,500
Anr copy. Vol I only. Contemp half russia. With 20 plates. Lacking half-titles. S Oct 23 (512) £700 [Dosz]
2d Ed. L, 1804. 4to, cloth; soiled. With 2 maps & 23 plates. Frontis repaired & with small tear in outer margin. bba Dec 128 £170 [Elliott]
Facsimile Ed. Adelaide, 1971. 2 vols. 4to, cloth. CA Apr 12 (70) A$75

Collins, Capt. Greenville

— Great Britain's Coasting Pilot. L, 1693. 1st Ed. Parts 1 & 2 in 1 vol. Folio, contemp calf; spine lacking, worn & stained. With engraved title & 48 charts. Waterstained; some discoloration. Additional map of the Sea Coast from Arundel in Sussex, to St. Albans, by Emanuel Bowen, 1731, inserted. C Apr 8 (11) £1,800 [Kidd]
Anr Ed. L, 1745. Folio, contemp half calf; worn. With engraved title & 49 plates. Lacking Isles of Scilly but with Joseph Avery's 1731 South Coast chart inserted; worming in inner margins, affecting title & 1st few leaves; a few fold tears & stains. S Oct 23 (163) £2,000 [Lyster]
Anr copy. Contemp calf; worn. With engraved title & 50 plates (41 double-page,

5 folding, 3 full-page & 1 in text). Some browning & waterstaining. S Oct 23 (164) £1,900 [Nicholson]

Anr Ed. L, 1753. Folio, contemp calf; worn. With frontis & 49 plates & charts. One map torn; some stains & soiling. C Apr 8 (11A) £900 [Burgess Browning]

Anr Ed. L, 1767. Folio, contemp calf; def. With 44 double-page or folding charts & 4 full-page charts. S Nov 17 (753) £1,400 [Postaprint]

Collins, Henry George
— The New British Atlas.... L, [c.1848]. Folio, contemp half mor; worn. With 43 mostly double-page hand-colored maps. Lacking the general map of England. S Oct 23 (166) £600 [Burden]

Collins, John, 1625-83
— Salt and Fishery. L, 1682. 4to, half calf. Several headlines shaved; rule border at foot of title cropped. S July 23 (433) £350 [Lawson]

Collins, Samuel, 1618-70
— Relation curieuse de l'estat present de la Russie. Paris, 1679. 12mo, early calf gilt, armorial bdg; rebacked, orig backstrip laid down, bowed. sg Nov 20 (53) $100

Collins, Wilkie, 1824-89
See also: Dickens & Collins
— The Haunted Hotel: A Mystery of Modern Venice. L, 1879 [1878]. Illus by Arthur Hopkins. 2 vols. 8vo, contemp half mor; rubbed & scuffed, joints cracking, 1 plate detached. cb Nov 20 (70) $60
— Man and Wife. NY: Harper, 1870 [1873?]. Orig cloth; ink name on front free endpaper, hinges cracking. cb Nov 20 (71) $50
— The Moonstone. L, 1868. 1st Ed. 3 vols. 8vo, orig cloth; worn, corners bumped, spine ends chipped. Some soiling. cb Sept 28 (343) $140
— Rambles Beyond Railways. L, 1851. 1st Ed. 8vo, orig cloth; frayed. With 12 plates. Top margin of last 2 plates dampstained. T Feb 19 (456) £42

Collinson, John, 1757?-93
— The History and Antiquities of the County of Somerset.... Bath, 1791. 3 vols. 4to, contemp half mor; rebacked preserving orig spine. With 41 plates. Folding map torn away. bba Aug 28 (312) £160 [Blake]

Anr copy. Contemp half calf; worn. With folding map & 40 plates. Map badly torn along folds; most plates with tears. S Jan 12 (74) £55 [Smith]

Anr copy. Later half mor gilt; rubbed. Folding map with small tear. T Mar 19 (63) £150

Collinwood, Francis —& Woollams, John
— The Universal Cook, and City and Country Housekeeper. L, 1792. 8vo, half mor; rubbed. With frontis, 12 plates of Bills of Fare & 1 plate of carving. Some leaves soiled. Crahan copy. P Nov 25 (123) $220

Anr Ed. L, 1797. 8vo, contemp calf; worn, upper cover def. With frontis & 12 plates. Contents partly dampstained. T Feb 19 (411) £75

Collis, Maurice Stewart
— The First Holy One. L, 1948. Inscr to his brother. Sold with Autograph Ms, typescript carbon & other related material. bba Dec 4 (136) £70 [Burgess Browning]
— The Grant Peregrination. L, 1949. Sold with Autograph Ms draft, typescript carbon copy & other related material. bba Dec 4 (137) £70 [Burgess Browning]
— Quest for Sita. L, 1946. One of 500. Illus by Mervyn Peake. 4to, orig cloth. T Oct 15 (114) £50
— Siamese White. L, 1936. Sold with the Autograph Ms of 1st & 2d drafts & the page proofs of the 1936 & 1951 Eds. bba Dec 4 (134) £170 [Burgess Browning]

Collodi, Carlo, 1826-90
— The Story of a Puppet, or the Adventures of Pinocchio. L, 1892. 8vo, orig cloth; backstrip discolored. bba Aug 20 (85) £320 [Stone]

Colomb, Philip Howard
— The Great War of 189-; A Forecast. L, 1893 [1892]. Illus by F. Villiers. Bdg bumped. cb Sept 28 (344) $75

Colombo, Fernando, 1488-1539
— Historie del S. D. Fernando Colombo.... Venice: Giuseppe Tramontin, 1685. 12mo, contemp bds. Dampstains on tp & some other prelims. sg Sept 18 (62) $130

Colomboni, Angelo Maria
— Prattica gnomonica.... Bologna, 1669. 4to, contemp vellum; spine repaired. Tp soiled & wormed; light dampstaining throughout; some worming in the text from 4E3 to the end. S May 21 (99) £260 [Lanfranchi]

Colonna, Fabio, 1567-1650?
— Minus cognitarum rariorumque nostro coelo orientium stirpium.... Rome, 1616. 4 parts in 1 vol. 4to, later half calf; rebacked preserving orig spine. With port & 3 engraved titles & 131 large illusts. Single wormhole to inner margin of quires A through X; lacking last leaf. Hunt copy. CNY Nov 21 (60) $1,100

Anr copy. Contemp bds; rebacked in vellum. Lacking 1 engraved title. FD Dec

COLONNA

2 (454) DM2,100

Colonna, Francesco, d.1527

— Hypnerotomachie, ou discours du songe de Poliphile.... Paris: Matthieu Guillemot, 1600 [but after 1610]. ("Le Tableau des riches inventions couvertes du vvoile de feintes amoureuses....") 4to, 18th-cent mor; corners restored, lower hinge split. Small wormholes throughout, mostly marginal; last leaf torn & repaired. C May 13 (121) £800 [Bifolco]

— Hypnerotomachia Poliphili. L, 1904. ("Poliphili Hypnerotomachia.") Folio, later calf gilt by Bremer Binderei. Facsimile of 1499 Aldine Ed. JG Oct 2 (1431) DM1,200

Colonna, Vittoria, 1492-1547

— Rime. Venice: N. Zoppino, 1540. Bound with: Ariosto, Ludovico. Le Satire. Venice: Zoppino, 1535. And: Ariosto. Le Rime. Venice: Iacopo MOdanese, 1546. And: Politanus, Angelus. Stanze cominciate per la giostra del magnifico Giuliano di Piero de Medici. 8vo, contemp calf Grolieresque bdg; heavily restored, coloring renewed, rebacked, both covers laid down. S Sept 23 (321) £1,400 [Maggs]

Colophon...

— The Colophon: A Book Collector's Quarterly. NY, 1930-50. Complete set: First Series, 20 parts* New Series, 12 parts* New Graphic Series, 4 parts* The New Colophon, Vols I-III in 9 parts* Index, 1930-35* Annual of Bookmaking, 1938* Keller's Index. 1968. Together, 48 vols. 4to & 8vo, bds & cloth. With c.40 ephemeral items. cba Feb 5 (73) $600

Anr copy. First Series, lacking only Parts 5 & 17; New Series, 12 parts; New Graphic Series, lacking only Part 3; The New Colophon, lacking only Vol III. With: identical duplicate set of Vol I & II of The New Colophon. Together, 47 vols. 4to & 8vo, bds & cloth. ha Dec 19 (39) $210

Anr copy. Parts 1-16 only. O Sept 23 (38) $280

Anr copy. Complete set: First Series, 20 parts* New Series, 12 parts* New Graphic Series, 4 parts* The New Colophon, Vols I & II in 8 parts & Vol III* Index, 1930-35* Annual of Bookmaking, 1938. Together, 47 vols. 4to & 8vo, bds & cloth. O May 12 (45) $350

Color. See: Earhart, John F.

Colored. See: Smith, Sir James Edward

AMERICAN BOOK PRICES CURRENT

Colquhoun, Patrick, 1745-1820

— A Treatise on the Police of the Metropolis.... L, 1796. 8vo, contemp calf; rubbed, upper joint split. Lacking half-title. bba Apr 23 (196) £35 [Bookroom]

Anr Ed. L, 1806. 8vo, contemp half mor; rubbed. bba Sept 25 (103) £45 [Cameron]

Columella, Lucius Junius Moderatus

— De cultu hortorum. De re rustica liber X. Venice: D. S., [1481-82]. Folio, half calf; old wraps bound in, rubbed. Repairs to lower margins of 1st 5 leaves affecting text. 12 leaves. Goff C-764. Crahan copy. P Nov 25 (124) $1,300

— Les Douze Livres...des choses rustiques.... Paris: Jacques Kerver, 1555. 4to, contemp calf gilt; spine with 18th-cent labels, rubbed, 3 corners with lea renewed, chip in head of spine. Hunt copy. CNY Nov 21 (61) $500

Colville, Samuel

— Colville's San Francisco Directory Volume I.... San Francisco: Commercial Steam Press, 1856. Orig bds; later lea spine, scuffed. Minor foxing. cb Oct 9 (176) $275

Colvin, Sir Sidney, 1845-1927

— Early Engraving & Engravers in England. L, 1905. Folio, contemp half mor; rubbed. Ck Feb 13 (5) £85

Colynet, Antony

— The True History of the Civill Warres of France.... L: T. Woodcock, 1591. 4to, contemp sheep; broken. Lacking tp; some headlines cropped close; some stains. bba Mar 26 (151) £45 [News Today]

Combe, George, 1788-1858

— Elements of Phrenology. Phila.: E. Littell, 1826. 8vo, orig bds; joint cracked. Frontis chipped; library markings. ha Dec 19 (88) $75

Combe, William, 1741-1823

See also: Hanger, George

— The Dance of Life. L: R. Ackermann, 1817. Illus by Thomas Rowlandson. 8vo, orig cloth. sg June 11 (345) $750

Anr copy. Calf gilt. sg June 11 (346) $325

— The Diabo-Lady; or, a Match in Hell. L, 1777. 4to, modern half mor. sg Mar 26 (79) $80

— The English Dance of Death. L, 1815-16. 1st Ed in Book form. Illus by Thomas Rowlandson. 2 vols. 8vo, half calf; worn, backstrips missing or def. With frontis, engraved title & 66 plates only. Lacking tp. Sold w.a.f. bba June 18 (298) £190 [Pirages]

Anr copy. 8vo, contemp half calf; rebacked, old spines laid down. With 72 hand-colored plates. One plate torn with slight loss & repaired; several margins torn & repaired. Ck June 5 (98) £400

Anr copy. 2 vols. 8vo, orig cloth. With 74 hand-colored plates. sg June 11 (343) $1,600

— The English Dance of Death * The Dance of Life. L, 1815-17. 1st Eds. Illus by Thomas Rowlandson. 3 vols. 8vo, orig bds; 2 spines def, joints split. bba Aug 28 (275) £500 [Hildebrand]

Anr copy. Mor gilt by Whitman Bennett. With 2 unsgd autograph specimens in Combe's hand tipped in Vol I of the Dance of Death. sg Apr 2 (55) $1,900

Anr copy. Mor gilt by Riviere. With 100 hand-colored plates. sg June 11 (344) $1,500

— The History of Johnny Quae Genus. L: R. Ackermann, 1822. Illus by Thomas Rowlandson. 8vo, later mor gilt by Riviere; joints rubbed. S Sept 22 (221) £120 [Burman]

Anr copy. Orig cloth; spine holed. Some soiling. S July 14 (483) £100

Anr copy. Mor gilt; broken. sg Sept 11 (255) $225

Anr copy. Lev gilt by Riviere. With unsgd autograph Ms leaf by Combe. sg Apr 2 (57) $300

Anr copy. Mor gilt by Bumpus. Some foxing. sg June 11 (348) $300

— Journal of Sentimental Travels in the Southern Provinces of France. L: Ackermann, 1821. Illus by T. Rowlandson. 8vo, mor gilt by Zaehnsdorf. With 18 colored plates. With the 4-page ad for the parts issue of Johnny Quae Genus. C Apr 8 (12A) £500 [Old Hall]

Anr copy. Lev gilt. With 18 colored plates. sg apr 2 (56) $450

Anr copy. Mor gilt, orig cloth bound in. sg June 11 (347) $1,200

— The Tour[s] of Doctor Syntax in Search of [1] the Picturesque; [2] Consolation; [3] a Wife. L: Ackermann, [1812]-20-[21]. Illus by Thomas Rowlandson. 3 vols. 8vo, mor gilt by Riviere; joints rubbed. With 2 engraved titles & 78 hand-colored plates. Some marginal tears; 1 hole. S Dec 18 (46) £550 [Woods]; sg Apr 2 (53) $850

1st Ed of Vols I & III; 2d Ed of Vol II. 3 vols. 8vo, half mor gilt by Birdsall; a few joints starting. With 2 engraved titles & 78 hand-colored plates. Small stain on Vol I frontis & tp. sg Sept 11 (65) $550

Anr copy. Mor gilt by Riviere; 1 cover starting, several joints slightly worn. sg June 11 (342) $1,200

Anr copy. Contemp half calf gilt; worn. With 79 hand-colored plates. T Oct 16 (490) £260

9th Ed of 1st Tour; 3d Ed of 2d Tour; 1st Ed of 3d Tour. L, 1819-20-21. 3 vols. 8vo, later mor gilt; joints & 1 lower cover rubbed. Minor cropping to 3d Tour. S Sept 22 (222) £200 [Hethering]

Miniature Ed. L: Ackermann, 1823. Illus by Thomas Rowlandson. 3 vols. 12mo, contemp half calf; rubbed. With 78 hand-colored plates. Vol II has no engraved title; Vols I & II lack ads; Vol III lacks leaf of directions. Duff Cooper's copy. S Mar 9 (776) £200 [Smith]

Anr copy. Orig bds; joints rubbed. With 3 engraved titles & 71 hand-colored plates. Lacking ads in Vol I. sg June 11 (349) $650

"9th" Ed. L, 1855. 3 vols. 8vo, orig cloth, unopened. pn Nov 20 (222) £120 [Bookroom]

Anr copy. Half mor. With 81 hand-colored plates. sg June 11 (350) $375

1st Tour

— [1812]. - L: Ackermann. 1st Ed. Illus by Thomas Rowlandson. 8vo, contemp calf gilt. With engraved title & 30 hand-colored plates. L July 2 (51) £140

2d Ed. 8vo, half calf; rubbed. With engraved title & 30 hand-colored plates. pn July 23 (58) £110 [Goddard]

— 1813. - L.5th Ed. 8vo, mor gilt by Sangorski & Sutcliffe. With colored title & 30 colored plates. sg Feb 12 (265) $225

Syntax Imitations, not by Combe

— Doctor Syntax in Paris. L, 1820. 1st Ed. 8vo, contemp calf gilt. With hand-colored engraved title & 17 hand-colored plates. sg Apr 2 (59) $300

— The Grand Master or Adventures of Qui Hi in Hindostan. L, 1816. Illus by Thomas Rowlandson. 8vo, mor gilt by Zaehnsdorf. With 1 tinted & 28 hand-colored plates. S July 13 (194) £340

Anr copy. Lev extra. With 28 colored plates, including title & folding map. sg Apr 2 (58) $375

Anr copy. Orig bds; covers detached but present. In half mor slipcase. With engraved title & 27 hand-colored plates. wd Nov 12 (186) $225

— The Life of Napoleon. L, 1815. 1st Ed. Illus by George Cruikshank. 8vo, contemp calf gilt; rebacked, orig spine laid down. With hand-colored title vignette & 29 hand-colored plates. C June 18 (222) £160

Anr copy. Half mor by Sangorski & Sutcliffe. With 30 colored plates, including

COMBE

title. Several leaves lightly soiled; lower margins of a few plates shaved close. Ck Nov 21 (363) £150

Anr copy. Contemp mor gilt; spotted. With 30 colored plates. JG Oct 2 (1554) DM900

Anr copy. Lev gilt by Bickers. sg Apr 2 (54) $450

2d Ed. L, 1817. 8vo, half russia; rubbed. With 30 hand-colored plates. Marginal tear. S July 14 (561) £160

— The Tour of Doctor Syntax through London. L, 1820. 8vo, orig bds; rebacked, rubbed. With 19 hand-colored plates. Frontises & titles soiled & laid down. bba July 16 (385) £70 [Mandel]

Anr copy. Contemp half calf; rubbed. With hand-colored title & 19 plates. Ck Nov 21 (356) £85

Anr copy. Mor gilt by Riviere. With 20 hand-colored plates. sg Apr 2 (61) $250

Combles, ——, de, d.1770?
— L'Ecole du jardin potager.... Paris: A. Boudet, 1749. 2 vols. 12mo, contemp calf gilt; rubbed. Some worming in Vol I, affecting some text. Crahan copy. P Nov 25 (125) $250

Comenius, John Amos, 1592-1610
— Janua linguarum reserata aurea. Prague, 1694. 8vo, old vellum; loose in bdg. Browned & dampstained; old stamp on title; lacking h5. sg Mar 26 (80) $80

Comines, Philippe de, Seigneur d'Argenton
— The Historie.... L, 1614. Folio, contemp calf; rubbed, rebacked but broken. Tp cropped. bba Aug 20 (2) £55 [Bennett & Kerr]

Anr Ed. L, 1674. ("The Memoirs....") 8vo, contemp calf; worn. First few leaves marginally torn. bba July 16 (229) £45 [Shankland]

Commelin, Caspar, 1636-93
— Beschryvinge van Amsterdam.... Amst., 1694-93. 2 vols. Folio, calf; worn. With engraved title & 52 plates, plans & maps. Some stains. B June 2 (454) HF2,900

Anr copy. Vellum; soiled, front cover of Vol II damaged. Marginal dampstain in Vol II. B June 2 (455) HF1,550

Commelin, Caspar, 1667-1731
— Horti medici Amstelaedamensis plantae rariores et exoticae. Leiden, 1715. Bound with: Praeludia Botanica....Leiden, 1715. 4to, contemp calf; lightly scraped. With 43 plates in 1st work & 33 plates in 2d work. A few leaves lightly discolored. Horticultural Society of New York—de Belder copy. S Apr 27 (81) £1,200 [Macdougall]

Commelin, Isaac, 1598-1676
— Begin ende Voortgang vande Vereenigde Neederlantsche Geoctroyeerde oost-Indische Compagnie. [Amst.], 1646. In 2 vols. Oblong 4to, 19th-cent vellum. With 2 engraved titles, 2 folding maps & 230 plates & maps. A few headlines & plates shaved; 2 plates & 1 text leaf torn & neatly repaired with small losses. C Dec 12 (228) £3,200 [Bjork & Borjesson]

— Histoire de la vie & actes memorables de Frederic Henry de Nassau Prince d'Orange. Amst., 1656. 2 parts in 1 vol. Folio, 18th-cent calf gilt; broken. With frontis, port & 34 plates & plans, all but the last colored in a contemp hand. Some plates just shaved at neatlines. Colored copy. S Oct 23 (440) £10,000 [Israel]

— Tweede deel van het Begin ende Voortgangh der Vereenighde Nederlandtsche Geoctroyeerde Oost-Indische Compagnie. Amst., 1646. Vol II only in 10 parts. 4to, contemp vellum; soiled. With 68 (of 70) maps & plates. Some tears & errors in foliation. S June 25 (484) £850

Commelin, Jan, 1629-92
See also: Cause, Hendrik
— Horti medici Amstelodamensis rariorum plantarum historia. Amst., 1697-1701. 2 vols in 1. Folio, contemp calf; joints worn, tears on both covers of Vol II. With 2 frontises, 5 engraved coats-of-arms & 223 plates. Some leaves soiled in the margins. Vilmorin—de Belder copy. S Apr 27 (80) £4,500 [Joseph]

— Nederlantze Hesperides. Amst., 1676. Bound with: Cause, Hendrik. De Koninglucke Hovenier. Amst., 1676. Folio, half mor; rubbed. Lacking 6 plates (of 62); portions restored on a few leaves; some stains & browning. Sold w.a.f. Crahan copy. P Nov 25 (126) $450

Commercial...
— Commercial Directory; Containing a Topographical Description.... Phila., 1823. 4to, calf; def. With folding map hand-colored in outline, vignette title, folding plan (loose) & 6 plates. Some browning. pn Mar 5 (267) £130 [Demetzy]

Common...
— Common PlaceBook Three. San Francisco: Grace Hoper Press, 1960. One of 75. Half cloth; spine leaning. cb Sept 11 (179) $60

Commoner, A. See: Extraordinary...

Communications...
— Communications to the Boards of Agriculture; on Subjects Relative to the Husbandry, and Internal Improvement of the Country. L, 1797-1800. Vols I & II (of 7)

only. 4to, contemp calf; rubbed, joints cracked, 1 front cover loose. sg June 4 (173) $150

Compagnie Belge de Colonisation
— Amerique Centrale. Colonisation du district de Santo-Thomas de Guatemala.... Paris, 1844. 8vo, contemp half vellum. With 5 hand-colored maps & 4 plates, all dampstained in upper inner corner. sg Sept 18 (115) $60

Company of Clothworkers
— The Charter of the Company of Clothworkers of London. L, 1648. 4to, wraps. Some discoloration; page numerals cropped. S July 24 (430) £650 [Wickhem]

Compleat. See: Nobbes, Robert

Complete...
— The Complete Farmer: or a General Dictionary of Husbandry.... L, 1766. 1st Ed. Folio, contemp calf; joints split, rubbed. With frontis & 27 plates, 8P1 almost completely torn; 3 other leaves with tears; 1 plate with small hole affecting surface. bba Oct 16 (314) £150 [Rainer]
Anr copy. Blindstamped calf. With 28 plates. Crahan copy. P Nov 25 (128) $250

Composing...
— Composing Room Memories. Letters from Eminent Americans Concerning the Advantages & Satisfactions Gained from an Acquaintance with Type.Mor gilt by Peter Fahey. cb Sept 11 (247) $170

Comstock, Francis Adams
— A Gothic Vision: F. L. Griggs and his Work. Bost., 1966. One of 600. 4to, cloth; worn. O Jan 6 (42) $70

Conder, Josiah, b.1852
— The Floral Art of Japan. Yokohama, 1899. Folio, orig cloth; rubbed. Library markings. bba Feb 5 (149) £60 [Lloyds]
— The Flowers of Japan and the Art of Floral Arrangement. Tokyo, 1891. Folio, cloth backed pictorial wraps; laced. sg Feb 5 (180) $600
— The Modern Traveller. L, 1825-31. 30 vols. 12mo, contemp half mor; spines chipped. Sold w.a.f. Ck May 15 (24) £70
Anr copy. 32 vols. 12mo, contemp half mor; rubbed. S July 14 (870) £230

Condillac, Etienne Bonnot de, 1715-80
— Le Commerce et le Gouvernement.... Paris, 1776. 12mo, contemp sheep; upper joint cracked. Margins trimmed close. P Sept 24 (263) $550
— La Logique ou les premiers developpemens de l'art de penser. Paris, 1789. 8vo, contemp half calf; worn. Some foxing. sg Oct 9 (166) $425
— Oeuvres. Paris, 1798. 23 vols. 8vo, calf gilt. B Feb 25 (915) HF2,300

Condy, Nicholas —&
Arundell, Francis Vyvyan
— Cothele, on the Banks of the Tamar.... [L, c.1830]. Folio, loose in half mor. With litho title, dedication, plan & 13 plates only. Marginal tears. S May 29 (993) £110
Anr Ed. [L, 1840]. Folio, modern half mor by S. Franks, retaining orig coat-of-arms inside upper cover. With litho title, dedication, plan & 16 plates. Plates & text have been washed & re-colored. T Nov 20 (72) £430

Conestaggio, Girolamo Franchi di, d.1635
— Historien der Koenigreich, Hispannien, Portugal und Aphrica.... Munich: A. Berg, 1589. Folio, contemp blindstamped pigskin over wooden bds. FD June 11 (128) DM2,800

Coney, John, 1786-1833
— Beauties of Continental Architecture, in a Series of Views.... L, 1843. Folio, contemp half mor gilt; rubbed. With 28 plates and mounted engraved vignette on each page of text. Tp stained on top margin. T Jan 22 (288) £100

Confederate States of America
— Army Regulations, adopted for the Use of the Army of the Confederate States.... Richmond: West & Johnson, 1861. 8vo, orig half sheep; worn & scuffed. One leaf torn. ha Nov 7 (3) $200
— Regulations for the Army of the Confederate States. Richmond, 1862. 12mo, contemp cloth from a book entitled Philosophy and Practice of Slavery; front hinge broken, soiled & worn. Rear blank leaves partly torn away. sg Sept 18 (64) $200

Confiturier...
Le Confiturier royal, ou nouvelle instruction pour les confitures.... Paris, 1776. 12mo, calf; edges rubbed. With 3 folding plates. S Nov 27 (97) £170 [Greenwood]

Confucius. See: Limited Editions Club

Congregation Kaal Kadosh Mickve Israel. See: Philadelphia

Congreve, William, 1670-1729
See also: Nonesuch Press
— The Way of the World. L, 1928. One of 875 on japan vellum. Illus by A. R. Middleton. sg Jan 8 (281) $50
— Works. Birm.: Baskerville, 1761. 3 vols. 8vo, contemp calf; rebacked. Some spotting & browning. bba Jan 15 (47) £50

[Bookroom]
Anr copy. Contemp calf gilt; spine ends chipped, joints cracked or starting. Old German library stamps on titles; opening leaves of Vol I browned. sg Mar 26 (82) $150

Connecticut
— Acts and Laws of his Majesty's English Colony of Connecticut. New London, 1750. Folio, contemp calf; rebacked. First 15 leaves stained & soiled. sg Mar 12 (88) $140

Connett, Eugene V.
See also: Derrydale Press
— American Sporting Dogs. NY, [1948]. In torn d/j. sg Oct 23 (220) $60
— Duck Shooting Along the Atlantic Tidewater. NY, 1947. 4to. In chipped & stained d/j. cb may 21 (51) $90

Anr copy. Cloth; lower cover dampstained. cb May 21 (52) $50

One of 149. Mor gilt; worn. With an extra set of 13 colored plates laid in. sg Oct 23 (222) $750
— Wildfowling in the Mississippi Flyway. NY, [1949]. 4to, cloth, in d/j; worn. sg Oct 23 (223) $110; sg May 21 (43) $120

Anr copy. Cloth. sg May 21 (44) $120

Connoisseur...
— Connoisseur: An Illustrated Magazine for Collectors. L, 1901-14. Vols 1-39 plus Index to Vols 1-2, in 2 vol. 4to, half lea; rubbed & a bit corroded. O Nov 18 (47) $160

Connolly, Cyril V.
— The Rock Pool. Paris: Obelisk Press, 1936. 1st Ed. Orig wraps. bba Oct 30 (244) £110 [Bologna]

Anr copy. Orig wraps; worn. T Feb 18 (112) £80

Conquest, John Tricker, 1789-1866
— Outlines of Midwifery. L, 1820. 8vo, orig bds; worn, hinges split. With 12 plates. 1 leaf torn. pnNY Sept 13 (212) $120

Conrad, Joseph, 1857-1924
— Conrad's Manifesto: Preface to a Career. Phila., 1966. One of 1,100 on Fabriano paper. sg June 4 (26) $70
— The Dover Patrol. Canterbury: Pvtly ptd, 1922. 1st Ed, One of 75. Later mor gilt, orig wraps bound in; soiled. Inscr. bba Jan 15 (172) £170 [Rota]
— The First News. Pvtly ptd by Clement Shorter, 1918. One of 25. 4to, orig wraps. S Dec 18 (115) £320 [Quaritch]
— John Galsworthy. An Appreciation. Canterbury, 1922. One of 75. Orig wraps. sg Dec 11 (11) $175
— Laughing Anne. L, 1923. One of 200. Sgd & with related material. S Dec 18 (113) £220 [Gekoski]
— The Nigger of the "Narcissus". L, 1898. 1st English Ed. 8vo, cloth; rubbed. A. Edward Newton copy. O May 12 (47) $275
— Notes on my Books. L, 1921. One of 250. O Nov 18 (48) $100
— One Day More. L, 1917. 1st Ed, one of 25. Orig wraps, unopened. Sgd by Clement Shorter. S Dec 18 (114) £380 [Quaritch]
— The Polish Question. A Note on the Joint Protectorate.... Pvtly ptd by Clement Shorter, 1919. Out-of-series copy. 4to, orig wraps; dust-soiled. Inscr to A. T. S Dec 18 (116) £480 [Quaritch]
— The Secret Agent: A Drama in Three Acts. L, 1923. One of 1,000. 4to, orig bds; worn. S Jan 13 (550) £50 [Alldoc]
— The Tale. Pvtly ptd by Clement Shorter, 1919. One of 25. 4to, orig wraps. Inscr to A. T. S Dec 18 (117) £600 [Blackwell]
— Works. L, 1921-27. One of 780. 20 vols. Mor gilt. sg Dec 4 (41) $2,000

Anr copy. Orig half cloth; rubbed. sg Dec 4 (42) $750

Medallion Ed. L, 1925. 20 vols. With 19 vols in d/js. Ck Sept 5 (96) £100
— Youth. Edin. & L, 1902. 1st Ed. Orig cloth. bba July 2 (123) £100 [Joseph]

Conrad, Joseph, 1857-1924 —& Ford, Ford Madox, 1873-1939
— The Nature of a Crime. L, 1924. In d/j. sg June 11 (114) $50

Conscience, Francis Antoine, 1795-1840
— Suite de differentes races de chiens. Paris: Bulla, [1832-33]. Folio, half shagreen. SM Feb 28 (98) FF7,000

Conscience, Hendrik, 1812-83
— De Leeuw van Vlaanderen. Antwerp, 1912. Ltd Ed. Illus by A. van Neste. 4to, cloth. B Oct 7 (71) HF340

Constable, John, 1776-1837
— English Landscape Scenery. L, 1855. Folio, half mor; rubbed. pn Jan 22 (195) £200 [Shapero]

Anr copy. Contemp half mor; rubbed. With 40 plates. S Nov 10 (65) £300 [Soncini]

Constant de Rebecque, Benjamin Henri
— Adolphe, anecdote trouvee dans les papiers d'un inconnu. Paris & L, 1816. 1st Ed. 12mo, 19th-cent bds; backed in calf, repaired. Lacking ad leaf; pp 157-64 stained; extreme lower blank corner of C12 torn off. S Mar 9 (920) £160 [Museion]

Anr Ed. Paris: La Societe d'Edition Le Livre, 1930. One of 20 on japon, with 2 extra suites of the illusts. Illus by Pierre Gandon. Orig wraps. sg Jan 8 (49) $50

Constant, Samuel Victor
— Calls, Sounds and Merchandise of the Peking Street Peddlers. Peking, [1937]. Silk. With 62 color plates. sg Nov 20 (47) $140

Constitution...
— The Constitution of the State of Massachusetts...with President Washington's Farewell Address. Bost.: Manning & Loring, 1805. Some stains & browning. bba Dec 4 (283) £30 [Goldman]

Constitution of the United States of America
— Acts Passed at a Congress of the United States of America.... NY: Francis Childs & John Swaine, [1791]. Folio, contemp calf. Reissue of 1st Ptg of the Constitution, with Acts Passed at the 2d & 3d Sessions. wa Sept 23 (438) $190
— We, the People of the United States.... Phila.: Dunlap & Claypoole, 19 Sept 1787. 466mm by 291mm, 4 pp. Disbound. In: The Pennsylvania Packet and Daily Advertise, No 2690. P May 13 (5) $100,000

Conti, Natale, 1520?-80?
— De Venatione, libri IIII. Venice: Aldus, 1551. 8vo, mor gilt by Thouvenin. 2 leaves with drawings of animals in the lower margins; 2 leaves stamped. Jeanson copy. SM Feb 28 (144) FF3,400

Continental...
— The Continental Tourist: Belgium and Nassau. L: Black & Armstrong, [1883-84]. 8vo, orig cloth; soiled. With frontis, engraved title, 2 folding plans (stained) & 60 plates. pn May 21 (29) £120 [Garwood]

Continental Congress
— Journal of the Proceedings of Congress, Held at Philadelphia, From September 5, 1773, to April 30, 1776. L, 1778. 8vo, modern cloth. Library markings. sg Mar 12 (86) $120

Conway, Sir William Martin, 1856-1937
— Climbing and Exploration in the Karakoram Himalayas. L, 1894. 8vo, cloth; worn. With folding maps in front & rear pockets. sg Nov 20 (54) $150

Cook, Frederick Albert
— Through the First Antarctic Night.... NY, 1900. 8vo, cloth. sg Nov 20 (7) $200

Cook, Capt. James, 1728-79
— Le Pilote de Terre-Neuve.... [Paris: Depot General de la Marine, 1784]. Folio, modern half cloth. With 11 large coastal survey charts. Lacking tp; several margins repaired. S Apr 23 (254) £2,000 [Fisher]

First Voyage
— HAWKESWORTH, JOHN. - An Account of the Voyages.... Dublin, 1773. 1st Pirated Ed. 3 vols. 8vo, cloth. With 52 engraved maps & plates. bba Dec 18 (156) £380 [Rainer]
1st Ed. L, 1773. 3 vols. 4to, half calf; joints broken, stained. Lacking 2 plates; some charts torn at fold; some leaves stained or foxed; 1 leaf with scribble; piece torn from contents leaf of Vol III. CA Apr 12 (72) A$1,200

Anr copy. Atlas only. Orig bds; broken, worn. With 52 maps & plates. Charts 1 & 2 torn; 2 plates & 1 map dust-soiled. Loosely inserted are 3 folding maps by Thomas Kitchin. Sold w a f. L, July 2 (117) £580

Anr copy. 3 vols. 8vo, half calf; worn, hinges cracked. Lacking Plate 11; 1 chart torn; some browning. pn Oct 23 (30) £470 [Hinchcliffe]

Anr copy. 3 vols. 4to, modern calf, marked. S Nov 18 (1239) £800 [Quaritch]

Anr copy. Modern calf; spines marked. With 43 (of 52) plates & charts. S May 29 (1132) £180

2d Ed. 3 vols. 4to, contemp half calf gilt; corners rubbed, joints cracking. With 52 plates & maps. Small wormhole in blank margins of a few plates, not affecting ptd area. C Oct 15 (185A) £900 [Ebes]

Anr copy. 3 vols. 8vo, contemp calf; rebacked. With 52 charts & views. A few tears without loss; 1 or 2 neatlines just shaved. S Apr 24 (375) £1,200 [Saweres]
"3d" Ed. L, 1785. 4 vols. 8vo, later mor. With 2 folding maps & 9 folding plates. Some leaves stained; 3 plates torn at fold; some early leaves of Vol IV wormed. CA Apr 12 (74) A$350

— HAWKESWORTH, JOHN. - Relation des voyages.... Paris, 1774. 8 vols in 4; without 4to Atlas vol. Bdg not described. Plate 10 in Vol II torn; Plate 7 in Vol III torn; 3 leaves in Vol III scribbled on; Map 25 in Vol IV torn. CA Apr 12 (75) A$1,000

Anr copy. 8 vols in 4 plus the 4to Atlas vol. Contemp calf; minor wear. kh Mar 16 (100) A$750

Anr copy. 8 vols in 4; without 4to Atlas vol. Old calf gilt; rubbed. pnNY Sept 13 (244) $225

— PARKINSON, SYDNEY. - A Journal of a Voyage to the South Seas.... L, 1773. 1st Ed. 4to, later half mor; worn. With port &

COOK

27 plates. Errata leaf at end. L.p. copy. S Oct 23 (523) £1,400 [Perrin]

Anr copy. Contemp half calf; upper joint weak. With port & 27 plates. S June 25 (503) £1,500 [Maggs]

2d Ed. L, 1784. 4to, later half calf; rubbed. With port, double-page map & 27 plates. Minor spotting & discoloration. C Apr 8 (48) £1,300 [Waterfield]

Second Voyage

— A Second Voyage Round the World.... L, 1776. 4to, orig bds, uncut; worn, spine def. S Oct 23 (513) £3,200 [Huber]

— A Voyage towards the South Pole and Round the World. L, 1777. 1st Ed. 2 vols. 4to, cloth. With port & 63 plates & charts. Some cropping; some maps repaired with tape; library stamps; Vol I lacking final blank; 1 leaf misbound.   bba Feb 5 (339) £320 [Elliott]

Anr copy. Early calf; rebacked & repaired. kh Mar 16 (97) A$2,000

Anr copy. Atlas only. Orig bds; worn & stained, upper cover detached. With 63 charts & plates. Chart 1 loose with 2 small tears & frayed at edge; Plates 53, 55 & 59-61 stained in 1 corner. Sold w.a.f. L July 2 (113) £650

Anr copy. Half calf; worn & broken. With port & 63 plates & charts. Last plate stained at head. S Jan 12 (179) £650 [Shapero]

Anr copy. 2 vols. 4to, contemp calf; rebacked. With port, 13 maps & charts & 50 plates & folding table. Small tears in charts & 2 leaves; a few plate imprints shaved or cut away; some foxing. S Apr 24 (363) £1,800 [Saweres]

3d Ed. L, 1779. 2 vols. 4to, contemp calf; rubbed & broken, spines lacking. With port & 63 plates & charts. Ck May 15 (52) £480

4th Ed. L, 1784. 3 vols. 4to & folio, calf & half calf. With port & 63 plates & maps. Some plates with marginal stains; some plates frayed; partially misbound. CA Apr 12 (74) A$350

Anr copy. Atlas vol only. Contemp calf; broken, spine lacking. With 2 double-page charts & 61 plates. Ck May 15 (53) £1,600

Third Voyage

— A Voyage to the Pacific Ocean.... L, 1784. Atlas vol only. 8vo, contemp bds; worn, spine def. With 2 folding charts & 61 plates. Some dampstaining. C Dec 12 (48) £850 [Traylen]

1st Ed. 3 vols (lacking Atlas). 4to, contemp calf; rebacked & rehinged, joints cracked or starting. With 24 maps & plates. sg Nov 20 (55) $375

2d Ed. L, 1785. 3 vols; lacking Atlas vol. 4to, old calf; rehinged. Repairs to 1st title & following leaf. kh Mar 16 (98) A$1,600

— ELLIS, WILLIAM. - An Authentic Narrative of a Voyage Performed by Captain Cook...in Search of a North-West Passage. L, 1782. 1st Ed. 2 vols. 8vo, contemp half calf; top half of spine of Vol I missing. With folding chart & 21 plates. SSA Feb 11 (486) R160

— LEDYARD, JOHN. - A Journal of Captain Cook's Last Voyage.... Hartford: Nathaniel Patten, 1783. 1st Ed. 8vo, contemp calf; front cover detached. Lacking map. sg Nov 20 (98) $130

— RICKMAN, JOHN. - Journal of Captain Cook's Last Voyage.... L, 1785. 8vo, contemp calf; rebacked. S Jan 12 (332) £900 [Mowbray]

Three Voyages

— [Set of Hawkesworth, South Pole & Pacific Ocean]. L, 1773-77-84. 1st Eds. 8 vols. 4to & folio, modern half vellum. 1st work with 1 plate having small tear repaired; 2d work with chart of Southern Hemisphere repaired & laid down with slight loss; 3d work with the 2 charts laid down. S Oct 23 (514) £3,000 [Walford]

Anr copy. 10 vols including the 1888 Kippis. 8vo, contemp calf with Prince Regent's arms. Prince-Regent's copy. S Apr 23 (182) £8,200 [Mitchell]

Anr copy. 9 vols. 4to & folio, contemp calf; not uniform. Some cropping & spotting. S June 25 (322) £4,300 [Arader]

Anr copy. 9 vols. 4to & foli, contemp calf (not uniform), Atlas in modern half calf. S June 25 (495) £5,000 [Helm]

2d Ed of 2d Voyage, 1st Eds of others. L, 1773-84-85. 8 vols including Atlas. 8vo & 4to, rebound in calf. Some plates creased & some hinged in. CA Apr 12 (71) A$5,500

2d Eds. L, 1773-77-85. 9 vols. 4to & folio, contemp calf. With 52 maps in 1st voyage, frontis (shaved) & 63 maps & plates in 2d voyage & 87 maps & plates in Atlas vol. C Oct 15 (185) £3,200 [Remington]

Three Voyages Abridged

— Captain Cook's Three Voyages to the Pacific Ocean.... Bost, Jan 1797. 2 vols in 1. 12mo, modern half lea; rebacked. Some stains; marginal restoration of a few plates & some text leaves; some cropping. sg Nov 20 (57) $325

Cook, Orator Fuller —& Underwood, L. M.

— A Century of Illustrative Fungi.... Syracuse, 1889. 8vo, cloth; worn, front hinge cracked. With specimens of 100 species of fungi in small paper envelopes, generally mtd 3 to the leaf. Some marginalia. sg Jan 15 (193) $150

Cooke, Alexander, 1564-1632
— Pope Joane. A Dialogue betweene a Protestant and Papist. L, 1610. 1st Ed. 4to, contemp calf; rubbed, rebacked. Tp & last leaf soiled; some page-numerals shaved. S July 14 (308) £300

Cooke, Capt. Edward
— A Voyage to the South Sea, and Round the World.... L, 1712. 1st Ed. 2 vols. 8vo, modern half calf. With 1 map repaired in center, anr dampstained & repaired; 1 plate slightly wormed; titles repaired; 1 leaf holed in lower margin; 1 leaf torn affecting text; first few leaves in Vol II with wormhole & most leaves dampstained. bba Aug 20 (460) £200

Anr copy. Old calf; rebacked, worn. Lacking the map of the Amazons, but with a 1744 French map of the same region inserted. O May 12 (48) $550

Anr copy. Contemp calf; rebacked. With 20 maps & plates. Marginal stains; margins of plates soiled. S Oct 23 (318) £600 [Walford]

Cooke, Edward William, 1811-80
— Fifty Plates of Shipping and Craft. L, 1829. 4to, later half calf; rubbed. Tp with tear in margin. bba Apr 23 (301) £400 [Frew Mackenzie]

Anr copy. Half mor; worn. With title & 48 plates on India paper; 2 plates affected by spotting. T Sept 18 (68) £400

— Sixty-Five Plates of Shipping and Craft. L, 1829. 4to, orig cloth; spine with small tear at head. C Dec 12 (49) £600 [Cavendish]

Cooke, Edward William, 1811-80 —& Rennie, George, 1791-1866
— Views of the Old and New London Bridges. L, 1833. Folio, contemp half calf; rubbed. With 12 plates, most waterstained or spotted. bba June 18 (372) £140 [Elliott]

Cooke, George, 1781-1834
— Views in London and its Vicinity. L, [1834]. 8vo, contemp half calf gilt; top of spine torn. With 48 plates. Some spotting & waterstaining. bba May 14 (416) £110 [Clare]

Cooke, Philip St. George, 1809-95
— Report from the Secretary of War Communicating...Official Journal of Cooke, from Santa Fe to San Diego.... [Wash., 1849]. 8vo, modern calf gilt. sg Mar 12 (89) $140

Cooke, William, Rector of Oldbury
— The Medallic History of Imperial Rome.... L, 1781. 1st Ed. 2 vols. 4to, contemp calf gilt; rubbed, joints cracked. bba Oct 30 (455) £40 [Axe]

Cooke, William B. See: Humphreys & Cooke

Cooke, William Bernard, 1788-1855 —& Owen, Samuel
— The Thames. L, 1811. 2 vols. 8vo, contemp calf; rebacked, bumped. With 84 plates. Ck Sept 26 (150) £150

Cookson, James. See: Fore-Edge Paintings

Cookson, Mrs. James
— Flowers Drawn and Painted After Nature, in India. L, [1835]. Folio, loose in contemp half calf; rubbed. With 31 hand-colored plates. Slight marginal soiling. de Belder copy. S Apr 27 (82) £5,500 [Ursus Books]

Coolidge, Calvin, 1872-1933
— Autobiography. NY, 1929. 1st Ed, one of 1,000 L.p. copies. sg Sept 18 (68) $60

Coomaraswamy, Ananda Kentish
— Mediaeval Sinhalese Art. L: [Essex House Press, 1907-8]. One of 400. Folio, half cloth; rebacked, soiled. With 53 plates. Inscr. sg Feb 5 (101) $200

Cooper, A.
— The Complete Distiller.... L, 1757. 8vo, contemp calf; joints broken & reinforced with cloth tape, corners worn. CNY Nov 21 (66) $150

Cooper, Abraham
— Impressions of a Series of Animals, Birds.... L, 1821. 8vo, bds; worn. With 16 mtd india-proof plates. Some foxing. sg Oct 23 (224) $325

Cooper, Sir Astley Paston, 1768-1841 —& Travers, Benjamin, 1783-1858
— Surgical Essays. Part I. & II. Phila., 1821. 4to, contemp sheep. With 21 plates. sg Jan 15 (77) $200

Cooper, Charles Henry
— Memorials of Cambridge. Cambr., 1860-61-66. 3 vols. 4to, cloth; worn. sg Dec 18 (155A) $175

Cooper, Douglas
— Picasso Theatre. NY, [1968]. 4to, cloth, in d/j. sg Jan 8 (205) $175

— The Work of Graham Sutherland. L, 1961. 4to, orig bds. Presentation copy, inscr by Sutherland. bba Dec 4 (197) £65 [Bowers]

Anr copy. Orig bds. Inscr to Somerset Maugham by both Cooper & Sutherland & with orig crayon drawing in 10 colors by

Sutherland on half-title. S June 17 (286) £950 [Maggs]

Cooper, James Fenimore, 1789-1851
— The History of the Navy of the United States of America. Phila., 1840. 2d Ed. 2 vols. 8vo, orig cloth; worn, slight tearing at tops & edges of spine. With 2 frontis maps. O Oct 21 (46) $60
— The Last of the Mohicans. Paris, 1826. 2 vols. 12mo, modern half mor. Some foxing. sg Sept 11 (66) $130
— The Prairie. L, 1827. 1st Ed. 3 vols. 12mo, contemp half mor; spine & extremities worn. cb May 21 (66) $130

Cooper, John
— A Report on the Proceedings against Abraham Thornton...Murder of Mary Ashford.... Warwick, 1818. 8vo, modern cloth. With folding frontis map. pnE Nov 12 (24) £42

Cooper, Thomas, 1517-94
— Thesaurus Linguae Romanae et Britannicae. L, 1584. Folio, contemp blind-stamped calf; upper cover & 1st few leaves detached. Tp laid down; some other leaves repaired. bba Mar 12 (150) £55 [Wise]

Copernicus, Nicolaus
— De revolutionibus orbium coelestium. Basel: Henricpetrina, 1566. 2d Ed. Folio, later half vellum. Library markings. Sold w.a.f. Franklin Institute copy. F Sept 12 (49) $5,750

Cope's..
— Cope's Smoke Room Booklets. Liverpool, 1889-96. Nos 1-14 in 1 vol. 8vo, contemp cloth, orig wraps bound in. Some soiling. Ck Oct 31 (176) £120

Coppard, Alfred Edgar, 1878-1957
See also: Golden Cockerel Press
— The Higgler. NY, [1930]. One of 39. bba July 2 (132) £100 [Cox]

Copper-plate...
— The Copper-plate Magazine.... L, 1778. 3 vols in 1. 4to, contemp calf; crudely rebacked. Lacking engraved title. Sold w.a.f. S July 14 (486) £100
Vols I-V. L, 1792-1802. Oblong 4to, half mor. With 5 engraved titles & 250 plates. S Oct 23 (171) £850 [Nicholson]

Coquiot, Gustave, 1865-1926
— La Terre frottee d'ail. Paris, 1925. One of 15 with a suite of illusts on rosa velin. Illus by Dufy. 4to, mor extra by Creuzevault, orig wraps bound in. Inscr to Fernand Fleuret by Dufy. FD Dec 2 (4328) DM3,200

Corbett, Col. Edward
— An Old Coachman's Chatter. With some Practical Remarks on Driving.... L, 1890. Illus by John Sturgess. 8vo, half mor gilt. pn Mar 5 (61B) £100

Cordell, Eugene Fauntleroy, 1843-1913
— The Medical Annals of Maryland, 1799-1899. Balt., 1903. Library markings. ha Mar 13 (187) $140

Cordiner, Charles, 1746?-94
— Remarkable Ruins and Romantic Prospects of North Britain. L: P. Mazell, 1788-95. 2 vols in 3. 4to, contemp calf; worn. Library stamps on tp; ink stamps on plates; some plates stained; lacking 2d engraved title & 1 plate. bba Dec 18 (130) £60 [Laycock]

Cordiner, James
— A Description of Ceylon. L, 1807. 2 vols. 4to, cloth; soiled. With 25 maps & plates. bba Dec 18 (131) £160 [Elliott]

Cordus, Valerius, 1515-44
— Annotationes in Pedacii Dioscoridis anazarbei de medica materia libros V.... Strassburg: J. Rehelius, 1561. Folio, contemp blindstamped pigskin over wooden bds with outer border of floral lozenges & other ornamental stamps, enclosing Savior/Annunciation/Baptism/Resurrection roll, Crucifixion panel-stamp on front cover with legend "Ach Got Sei Mir Armen Sunder Gnedig," initials T.B. & stamped Iacob above Melis; lacking clasps & catches, front cover paint-spattered. sg Dec 4 (43) $3,600

Corelli, Marie
— The Devil's Motor. L, [1910]. One of 100. Illus by Arthur Severn. 4to, orig mor gilt; lower cover dampstained. pnNY Sept 13 (213) $100

Corinth, Lovis, 1858-1925
— Das hohe Lied. Berlin, 1911. One of 60 on japon. Folio, orig lea. FD June 11 (4863) DM5,000
One of 60 on japan with each full-page illust sgd. Orig calf gilt; stained. With 26 color lithos. S Dec 4 (8) $800 [Percrual]
— Das Leben Walter Leistikows. Berlin, 1910. 4to, orig bds. B Oct 7 (371) HF360

Corneille, Pierre, 1606-84
See also: Thomas a Kempis
— Le Theatre. [Geneva], 1764. 8vo, contemp calf gilt. With 33 (of 34) plates. S Nov 27 (62) £380 [Booth]
Anr Ed. Geneva [Berlin], 1774. Ed by Voltaire. 8 vols. 4to, contemp calf; rubbed, spines darkened. With 34 plates. O May 12 (49) $200
Anr copy. Calf. Some leaves discolored. S

Nov 27 (63) £550 [Teuschart]
Anr Ed. Paris, 1797. 12 vols. 8vo, contemp calf; rubbed. bba Dec 4 (22) £100 [Archdale]

Cornelius, Brother, (Herman Emanuel Braeg)
— Keith: Old Master of California. [Fresno, 1956]. Vol II (Supplement) only. In d/j. cb Jan 8 (103) $70

Cornelius, Wilhelm. See: Kobbe & Cornelius

Corney, Bolton, 1784-1870
— Curiosities of Literature, By I. D'Israeli, Esq.... Greenwich, [1837]. 1st Ed. 12mo, modern half mor gilt. Inscr. bba Mar 20 (206) £100 [Burmester]

Corney, Peter
— Voyages in the Northern Pacific.... Honolulu, 1896. 8vo, later half calf; joints cracked. sg Apr 23 (37) $250

Cornut, Jacques Philippe, 1606-51
— Canadensium plantarum aliarumque nodum editarum historia. Paris: Simon le Moyne, 1635. 4to, later sheep; head of spine repaired. With 68 plates. Lower margin of title & lower outer corner of Dii restored; small tear or hole in outer blank margin of Ci & Bbii. S Apr 27 (83) £1,600 [Asher]

Coronado, Francisco Vasquez de, 1510-54. See: Grabhorn Printing

Coronelli, Vincenzo Maria, 1650-1718
See also: Levanto, Francesco Maria
— Atlante veneto. Venice: Domenico Padovani, [1691-97]. ("Isolario descrittione geografico-historia....") 2 vols in 1. Folio, contemp half calf. With engraved title, 2 frontises, 36 double-page & 36 full-page plates in Vol I & 30 double-page & 3 full-page plates in Vol II; 150 engraved text illusts. Some dampstaining at beginning of Vol I & at end of Vol II; some tears & stains. Sold w.a.f. puNY Sept 13 (333) $500

Memorie istoriografiche delli regni della Morea. [Venice:] Libraria del Colosso, [1686]. 8vo, contemp vellum bds; soiled. With engraved half-title, engraved arms of Maximilian, vignette of Neptune & 34 maps, plans & views on 30 plates on thick paper throughout. S Oct 23 (330) £600 [Wood]

Corrado, Vincenzo
— Il Cuoco Galante. Naples: Stamperia Raimondiana, 1773. 4to, 19th-cent half calf; joints rubbed. Some spotting. Crahan copy. P Nov 25 (138) $1,200

Corradus, Sebastianus
— Commentarius in quo M. T. Ciceronis de claris oratoribus liber...explicantur. Florence: Laurentius Torrentinus, 1552. Folio, modern half sheep. sg Oct 9 (154) $130

Correspondence...
— Correspondence Relating to Fortification of Morris Island and Operations of Engineers. Charleston, 1864. 12mo, cloth. sg Mar 12 (85) $400

Corrozet, Gilles, 1510-68
— Hecatomgraphie. Paris: D. Janot, 1543. 8vo, old calf; rubbed, spine def. Lacking all after N8, small marginal wormholes. bba Oct 16 (7) £120 [Braunschweig]

Corry, John, fl.1825
— The Life of George Washington. NY: Low, 1807. 12mo, mor by Sangorski & Sutcliffe. With port. sg Sept 18 (304) $175

Corsini, Accursio, 1549-1630
— Apologetico della caccia. Bergamo: Comin ventura, 1626. 4to, contemp vellum. Jeanson copy. SM Feb 28 (145) FF5,000

Corte Real, Jeronimo
— Naufragio e lastimoso sucesso da perdicam de Manoel de Sousa de Sepulveda.... Lisbon: Simao Lopez, 1594. 4to, modern half mor. Small repair to licence leaf affecting a few letters on verso. C Apr 8 (13) £520 [Ramer]

Cortes, Hernando, 1485-1547
— Praeclara Ferdinandi Cortesii de nova maris oceani Hyspania narratio. Nuremberg: F. Peypus, 1524. 1st Latin Ed. Bound with: Cortes. Tertia Ferdinandi Cortesii...in nova maris oceani Hyspania generalis preaefecti preclara narratio. Nuremberg, 1524. Folio, later vellum bds; soiled, portions of spine loose & repaired. With woodcut plan of Mexico & woodcut map of the Gulf of Mexico on a single sheet; final prelim with woodcut port of Pope Clement VII on verso; H8 blank & genuine. Stamps on title; half of the leaves in 1st work with minor worming in lower blank margins & map partly rebacked & with wormholes repaired affecting surface of map. 2d work with stamps on recto of final leaf; Dd5 with tears in margins repaired; Hh2-Hh3 with small portion of lower blank margin lost; minor worming in outer margins. S Apr 24 (298) £12,000 [Clavreuil]

Cortesao, Armando
— Portugaliae Monumenta Cartographica. Lisbon, 1960. 5 vols plus Index. Half vellum; covers of Index vol warped. sg Apr 23 (38) $900

419

Cortesao, Armandus —& Teixeira da Mota, Avellinus
— Portugallieae Monumenta Cartographica. Lisbon, 1960. 6 vols. Folio, syn. S Oct 23 (43) £700 [Tooley]

Cortese, Ferdinando. See: Cortes, Hernando

Cosgrove, Rachel R.
— The Hidden Valley of Oz. Chicago: Reilly & Lee, [1951]. In d/j with small tears. cb Dec 4 (40) $110

Cosmos
— Cosmos. [Jamaica, NY, 1933-35]. Unique copy for the Ed, Ray Palmer, sgd by all 18 authors & inscr by 17 of them. Syn. A collaborative effort of 18 authors, pbd in 17 parts as supplements to Science Fiction Digest. cb Sept 28 (357) $2,500

Costa, Emanuel Mendes da
— Historia naturalis testaceorum Britanniae, or the British Conchology. L, 1778. 4to, contemp calf; loose. With 17 plates. In English & French. C Dec 12 (51) £550 [Quaritch]

Costalius, Petrus. See: Coustau, Pierre

Coste, Pascal
— Monuments modernes de la Perse. Paris, 1867. Folio, contemp half mor gilt. With 71 plates on 56 sheets. One plate foxed. S Oct 23 (373) £3,000 [Markavian]

Costello, Dudley
— Holidays with Hobgoblins and Talk of Strange Things. L, 1861. 8vo, cloth. With 4 plates. sg Feb 12 (59) $90
— Piedmont and Italy.... L, 1859-61. 2 vols in 6 parts. 4to, orig cloth. With engraved titles, 6 ports & 124 plates. pn Mar 5 (16) £290 [Traylen]
Anr Ed. L, 1861. 2 vols in one. 4to, contemp mor gilt; worn. bba Dec 18 (132) £150 [Elliott]

Coster, Charles de, 1827-79
— Die Geschichte von Ulenspiegel und Lamme Goedzak. Munich, 1926. Illus by Frans Masereel. 2 vols. 4to, orig cloth. B Oct 7 (190) HF380

Costume...
— The Costume of the Russian Empire. L, 1803. Folio, mor gilt. With 73 hand-colored plates, including title. HN Nov 26 (837) DM1,600
Anr copy. Bdg not described but spine worn. pn Apr 30 (42) £190 [Walford]
Anr copy. Contemp mor gilt. S Apr 23 (71) £550 [Rainer]
Anr copy. Contemp mor gilt; rubbed. Some discoloration. S June 25 (185) £650 [Houle]
Anr Ed. L, 1804. Folio, mor gilt; def. With 73 hand-colored plates, including title. pn Dec 11 (43) £180 [Srafino]
Anr Ed. L, 1804 [plates watermarked 1818-20]. Folio, contemp mor gilt; rubbed. With 73 hand-colored plates, including title. C Apr 8 (156) £280 [Gaston]
— The Costume of Yorkshire. L, 1814. 4to, contemp calf; worn & broken. With frontis & 40 hand-colored plates. Tp soiled. bba Mar 26 (283) £750 [Peel]
Anr copy. Mor gilt; rubbed. Small stain in margin of Plate 18. pn Apr 30 (70) £1,500 [Traylen]
Anr copy. Illus by George Walker. Folio, half mor. With 40 colored plates. Tear in 1 plate repaired; 1 text leaf with margin repaired; some soiling. S Oct 23 (157) £750 [Robinson]
Anr copy. Contemp mor. With 40 hand-colored plates. Small tears just touching engraved surface of 1 or 2 plates; 1st few leaves detached & slightly frayed at margins. S June 25 (192) £825 [Haut]
Anr Ed. Leeds, 1885. One of 600. 4to, half mor; worn, lose in bdg. With frontis & 40 colored plates. Library copy. sg Dec 18 (232) $80

Costumes...
See also: Sardou, Victorien
— Costumes populaires et villageois de la Hollande. Amst., [c.1830]. 8vo, contemp bds; joints def. With 20 hand-colored plates. sg June 11 (115) $325

Coterie....
— Coterie. L, 1919-21. Nos 1-6/7 (all pbd) in 6 vols. wa Mar 5 (69) $130

Cotgrave, Randle, d.1634?
— A Dictionarie of the French and English Tongues. L, 1611. 1st Ed. Folio, contemp calf gilt; spine repaired, rubbed. bba Feb 5 (159) £100 [Cox]

Cotman, John Sell, 1782-1842
— Architectural Antiquities of Normandy. L, 1822. 2 vols in 1. Folio, contemp half mor. With 96 plates. C July 22 (52) £400
— Architectural Antiquities of Norfolk; Specimens of Architectural Remains...in Norfolk. L, 1838. 2 vols. Folio, contemp half mor. Ck Sept 26 (65) £90
— Engravings of Sepulchral Brasses in Norfolk and Suffolk. L, 1839. 2 vols. Folio, contemp half mor; rubbed. Ck Nov 21 (288) £160
— A Series of Etchings Illustrative of the Architectural Antiquities of Norfolk. L, 1818. Folio, contemp half russia gilt. With 60 plates. Some spotting & discoloration.

C July 22 (51) £460

Cotovicus, Joannes
— Itinerarium Hierosolymitanum et Syriacum. Antwerp, 1619. 4to, vellum. Sold w.a.f. pn May 21 (263) £340 [Cosiaris]

Cottafavi, Gaetano
— Raccolta delle principali vedute di Roma e suoi contorni. Rome, [1837]. Bound with: Amici, Domenico. Raccolta di trenta vedute degli obelischi.... Roma, 1839. Oblong folio, contemp half calf; rubbed. With engraved title & 69 plates in 1st work & engraved title & 14 plates in 2d work. S Oct 23 (15) £500 [Cippiello]

Anr Ed. L, [1843]. Oblong folio, contemp half mor; broken. With engraved title & 80 plates. Library markings; some stains. bba Feb 5 (359) £140 [Rainer]

Anr copy. Contemp mor gilt; head of spine def. With engraved title & 49 plates. S Feb 24 (415) £190 [Bifolco]

Anr copy. Half mor; rubbed. S May 29 (1044) £190

Cottingham, Lewis Nockalls, 1787-1847
— Plans, Elevations, Sections, Details, and Views...Chapel of King Henry the Seventh, at Westminster Abbey Church.... L, 1822-29. 1st Ed. 2 vols in 1. Folio, orig bds; rebacked. With 72 (of 73) plates. Many plates dampstained on lower margin affecting surface; a few plates torn; stained & frayed at beginning & end. Sold w.a.f. bba Aug 28 (31) £110 [Weinreb]

Cotton, Charles, 1603-87. See: Walton & Cotton

Cotton, Charles, 1630-87
See also: Fore-Edge Paintings; Walton & Cotton
— Poems on Several Occasions. L, 1689. 1st Ed. 8vo, contemp sheep. Ck Jan 30 (12) £160
— The Wonders of the Peake. L, 1681. 8vo, contemp calf; rebacked. Lacking final blank. C Dec 14 (322) £170 [Hannas]

Cotton, H. S.
[-] [Sale Catalogue] Catalogue of the Very Interesting and Singularly Curious Collection of Books on Angling, the Property of the Rev. H. S. Cotton.... L: S. Leigh Sotheby, 1838. 8vo, half calf gilt. Thomas Westwood's annotated copy. With ALs of Cotton. sg Oct 23 (225) $850

Cotton, Henry
— A List of Editions of the Bible.... Oxford, 1821. 8vo, calf; rebacked. sg Jan 22 (126) $80

Cotton, John, 1584-1652
— The Way of the Churches of Christ in New-England. L, 1645. 4to, mor gilt by Zaehnsdorf. Outer corners of tp restored. sg Dec 4 (44) $550

Cotton, Sir Robert Bruce, 1571-1631
— A Short View of the Long Life and Raigne of Henry the Third. [L], 1627. Bound with: Hayward, John. The Life and Raigne of King Edward the Sixt. L, 1630. 4to, old bds; rebacked. bba May 14 (53) £100 [Axe]

Cotugno, Domenico, 1736-1822
— De sedibus variolarum syntagma. Vienna, 1771. 8vo, half calf. S Nov 10 (469) £70 [Phelps]

Cotwyck, Jan van. See: Cotovicus, Joannes

Couch, Jonathan, 1789-1870
— A History of the Fishes of the British Islands. L, 1862-65. 4 vols. 8vo, mor gilt. With 252 hand-colored plates. pnF Dec 17 (351) £500 [Graham]

Anr Ed. L, 1867-66-67. 4 vols. 8vo, orig cloth; marked. With 252 colored plates. S Nov 17 (648) £200 [Smith]

Anr Ed. L, 1868-69. 4 vols. 8vo, contemp calf gilt. With 252 colored plates. S Nov 10 (470) £380 [Spelman]

Anr Ed. L, 1877-78. 4 vols. 8vo, orig cloth. With 252 plates. C Apr 8 (174) £300 [Pontario Vitale]

Anr Ed. L, [c.1880?]. 4 vols. 8vo, orig half lea; spines damaged. With 253 color plates, stamped on recto. sg Jan 15 (194) $325

Country...
— The Country Gentleman's Vade Mecum: or his Companion for the Town. L, 1699. 8vo, contemp sheep; rebacked, worn. Many leaves repaired in lower margin. bba Aug 28 (186) £85 [Hippo]
— Country Life.... L, 1897. pnC Jan 23 (59) £360

Couperus, Louis Marie Anne, 1863-1923
— De stille kracht. Amst., [1900]. 2 parts in 1 vol. B Oct 7 (37) HF450

Couplet, Philippe
— Histoire d'une Dame Chretienne de la Chine. Paris, 1688. 12mo, contemp calf; early scrawls on front endpaper. Contemp Parisian monastic library marking on p 1. sg Nov 20 (60) $100

Courieres, Edouard des
— Physiologie de la Boxe. Paris, 1929. One of 60 on japon with 2 extra suites of lithos, 1 on japon & 1 on montval. Illus by Luc-Albert Moreau. Folio, unsewn in orig wraps. S Dec 4 (23) £200 [Trimits]

Cournot, Antoine Augustin, 1801-77
— Exposition de la Theorie des Chances et des Probabilites. Paris, 1843. 8vo, contemp half mor; rubbed. With folding plate & errata. Library stamps on tp, half-title & at end; marginal tear on tp; some foxing. P Sept 24 (265) $350
— Recherches sur les principes mathematiques de la theorie des richesses. Paris, 1838. 8vo, half mor; rebacked, front free endpaper broken, repaired. Library markings. P Sept 24 (267) $4,000
— Revue sommaire des doctrines economiques. Paris, 1877. 12mo, contemp half cloth. Library stamp on tp verso; endpapers & last leaf of text browned. P Sept 24 (268) $950

Courte de la Blanchardiere, Rene
— A Voyage to Peru. L, 1753. 12mo, contemp calf; lower joint splitting, rubbed. 3 leaves holed at top outer corner, affecting text. bba Sept 25 (413) £230 [Way]

Cousin, Jean, the Younger
— L'Art de dessiner. Paris, 1750. 4to, contemp half mor; hinges weak. Most leaves soiled. sg June 11 (116) $225

Cousinery, Esprit Marie
— Voyage dans La Macedoine. Paris, 1831. 2 vols in 1. 4to, contemp half calf; worn, spine torn. Lacking several plates. S Feb 23 (120) £120 [Dima]

Coustau, Pierre
— Pegma. Lyons: Matthiam Bonhomme, 1555. 8vo, 18th-cent mor; rebacked. Foxed & soiled; tp & 2 other leaves remargined. cb July 30 (49) $600

Coutepoff, Nicolas
— La Chasse Grand-Ducale et Tsarienne en Russie. St. Petersburg, 1896-1902. Vol I only. Orig calf with arms of Russia. Jeanson 1713. SM Feb 28 (147) FF7,500

Couts, Joseph
— A Practical Guide for the Tailor's Cutting-Room.... Glasgow, [1848]. 4to, contemp half calf; worn. With 4 plain & 13 hand-colored fashion plates & 18 diagrammatic plates. Ck Apr 24 (207) £150

Covarrubias, Pedro de, 1530
— Remedio de jugadores. Salamanca: Juan de Junta, 20 June 1543. 4to, contemp calf; rebacked. Schwerdt-Jeanson copy. SM Feb 28 (139) FF17,000

Covens, Johannes —&
Mortier, Cornelis
— Atlas nouveau. Amst., 1733-[48]. Folio, contemp half calf; worn. With Sansons Inleiding tot de Geographie on 20 leaves & 136 double-page or folding mapsheets, hand-colored in outline.. S Apr 23 (142) £4,000 [George]

Cowan, Robert Ernest
— A Bibliography of the History of California and the Pacific West 1510-1906. San Francisco, 1914. One of 250. Half cloth; rubbed & soiled. sg Oct 2 (76) $200
Anr Ed. Columbus, 1952. 4to, cloth. Dampstained. cb Oct 9 (51) $50

Cowan, Robert Ernest & Robert G.
— A Bibliography of the History of California, 1510-1930. San Francisco, 1933. 1st Ed. 3 vols. 4to, half cloth. cb July 16 (68) $160
Anr Ed. San Francisco, 1964. 4 vols in 1. 4to, cloth. cb Oct 9 (51) $110
2d Ed. 4 vols. 4to, half cloth; rubbed & soiled. sg Oct 2 (77) $200

Coward, Noel
— A Withered Nosegay. L, 1922. Cloth; spine ends frayed, tear on spine repaired. Inscr to Gladys Cooper. sg Dec 11 (207) $275

Cowart, Jack
— Roy Lichtenstein 1970-1980. NY, [1981]. Folio, cloth. Sgd by Lichtenstein. wa Sept 25 (244) $80

Cowell, John, 1554-1611
— The Interpreter. Cambr., 1637. 1st Ed. 4to, contemp calf; rubbed. Light stain to tp & 1st few leaves. pn May 21 (164) £150 [Sayer]

Cowie, George
— The Bookbinder's Manual: Containing a Full Description of Leather and Vellum Binding.... L, 1829. 12mo, old half lea; rubbed. Some leaves loose. bba Sept 25 (373) £650 [Maggs]
Anr copy. Orig bds. S July 14 (455) £700

Cowley, Abraham, 1618-67
— Poems. L, 1656. 1st Ed. Folio, contemp calf; rebacked. Lacking frontis; Part 2 wormed with loss; some dampstaining of upper margins. Ck Apr 24 (7) £70
— Works. L, 1668. 8vo, contemp calf; repaired. Some stains. S May 6 (422) £75 [Camberwell]
Anr copy. Contemp calf; rebacked, rehinged. Opening leaves wormed in upper margin. sg Mar 26 (84) $80

Cowley, John. See: Dodsley & Cowley

Cowper, Charles —&
Downes, Charles
— The Building Erected in Hyde Park for the Great Exhibition. L, 1851-52. 4to, bdg not indicated. Library markings. Sold w.a.f. Franklin Institute copy. F Sept 12 (7) $1,300

Cowper, William, 1666-1709
See also: Fore-Edge Paintings
— Anatomia corporum humanorum centum et quatuordecim tabulis.... Leiden, 1739. Folio, contemp calf gilt. With engraved title & 114 (of 115) plates. Some wear & defs. HK Nov 4 (925) DM4,500

Anr copy. Lea gilt; worn & def. With frontis, engraved title & 114 plates. VH Sept 12 (2859) DM5,600

— Anatomia corporum humanorum centum et viginti tabulis.... Utrecht: Nicolaus Muntenda, 1750. Folio, modern half calf. With frontis & 119 plates, 2 hand-colored. Repaired tears to folding plates. S June 25 (94) £900 [Hildebradt]

— The Anatomy of Humane Bodies.... [Oxford & L, 1698]. Folio, contemp blind-stamped calf; rebacked in mor. With port (torn & laid down), engraved title & 114 plates, all mtd on stubs. Some plates shaved; 1 plate badly torn & slightly def; dedication leaves torn; some stains. bba May 14 (275) £1,100 [Phillips]

Anr copy. Contemp calf gilt; worn, upper joint cracked. With engraved title, port & 114 plates. Tear at fold of 1 plate, anr creased. C May 13 (122) £1,500 [Phillips]

Anr copy. Contemp calf; worn, joints cracked. With port (trimmed & mtd), engraved title & 114 plates (2 torn). Ck Jan 16 (58) £950

Anr copy. Disbound. With port (cut down & mtd), engraved title & 113 (of 114) plates. Some plates folding or with tears & repairs. Sold w.a.f. S Nov 10 (471) £450 [Phelps]

2d Ed. Leiden, 1737. Folio, later half sheep; rubbed, joints split, new endpapers. Lacking Plates 2 & 12; lower margin stained, affecting text & some plates, a few text leaves torn in margin. bba May 14 (276) £650 [Phelps]

Cowper, William, 1731-1800
— Works. L, 1836-37. Ed by Robert Southey. 15 vols. 8vo, mor gilt by Zaehnsdorf; some corners worn. sg Sept 11 (69) $375

Cox, Charles E., Jr. See: Derrydale Press

Cox, David, 1783-1859
— A Treatise on Landscape Painting.... L, 1813-14. 12 parts in 1 vol. Oblong folio, modern half mor. Lacking 2 plates & tp; marginal tears; dedication, advertisement & last plate mtd. S Feb 24 (517) £280 [Russell]

2d Issue with Plate 16 of haymaking. Contemp half calf; rubbed. With 24 etched & 32 aquatint plates, 16 colored by hand. Somewhat soiled, 1 plate creased. C July 22 (53) £850

Cox, Euan Hillhouse Mettiven
— The Plant Introductions of Reginald Farrer. L, 1930. One of 500. 4to, orig cloth. bba Mar 26 (293) £60 [Check]

Cox, Morris
— Blind Drawings: Examples of an Exercise.... L: Gogmagog Private Press, 1978. One of 30 with orig drawing & with facsimiles ptd on handmade Japanese papers from transferred hand-engraved intaglios. Intro by Colin Franklin. Half vellum. cb Sept 11 (99) $150

Cox, Nicolas. See: Cresset Press

Cox, Nicolas —&
Blome, Richard, d.1705
— The Gentlemans Recreation. L, 1674. 8vo, mor gilt janseniste by Saulnier. Wing C-6702. Schwerdt-Jeanson copy. SM Feb 28 (148) FF10,000

Anr Ed. L, 1686. 2 parts in 1 vol. Folio, 19th-cent calf gilt. Lacking 1 plate; some repairs. Wing B-3213. Jeanson 1577. SM Feb 28 (75) FF17,000

— The Gentleman's Recreation.... L, 1697. 8vo, contemp calf; backstrip worn. With engraved title, folding frontis & 4 folding plates. sg Dec 4 (45) $400

— The Gentlemans Recreation. L, 1721. 8vo, calf; rebacked. pnE Dec 17 (317) £160 [McKenzie]

Cox, Palmer, 1840-1924
— The Brownies at Home. L & NY, 1893. 8vo, bds; light wear. O Apr 28 (54) $110

Cox, Thomas, d.1734
— Magna Britannia et Hibernia antiqua & nova. L, 1720-31. 6 vols. 4to, contemp calf; worn. With 45 maps only. Some stains. Sold w.a.f. Ck Nov 21 (440) £640

Coxe, John Redman, 1773-1864
— The American Dispensatory, Containing the Operations of Pharmacy.... Phila., 1810. 2d Ed. 8vo, contemp calf; rubbed, endpapers stained. Signature torn from blank margin of title. O Sept 23 (42) $80

Coxe, Peter, d.1844
— The Social Day. L, 1823. 1st Ed. 8vo, later half mor gilt. With 32 plates in mtd india-proof state. sg Sept 11 (70) $250

Coxe, William, 1747-1828
— Account of the Russian Discoveries between Asia and America. L, 1780. 1st Ed. 4to, contemp calf gilt; joints cracked. With folding charts & view. Some fold breaks. S Oct 23 (502) £300 [Marshall]

Anr copy. Contemp calf; rebacked. With plate & 4 folding maps. sg Dec 4 (46) $800

— An Historical Tour in Monmouthshire.... L,

1801. 2 vols in 1. 4to, contemp half calf, spine worn. Lacking Plate 5 lired. T Jan 22 (73) £220
— Memoirs of the Life and Administration of Sir Robert Walpole. L, 1798. 3 vols. 4to, modern half calf. With port & 4 facsimiles. bba Jan 15 (68) £50 [Bookroom]
— Nouvelles Decouvertes des Russes entre l'Asie et l'Amerique.... Neuchatel, 1781. 8vo, contemp calf; becoming disbound. Lacking folding view plate; 1 map torn & mended; notations on tp. sg Apr 23 (39) $60
— Travels in Switzerland. L, 1791. 2d Ed. 3 vols. 8vo, contemp calf; rebacked, rubbed. Folding map partly torn along folds. T Apr 16 (11) £45
— Travels into Poland, Russia, Sweden, and Denmark. L, 1784-90. 3 vols. 4to, contemp calf; worn. Some spotting & browning. bba Feb 5 (368) £55 [Scott]
Anr Ed. L, 1784. 2 vols. 4to, contemp calf. With an additional vol containing an account of a 2d journey, not further identified. C Dec 12 (54) £480 [Hannas]
Anr Ed. L, 1784-90. 3 vols. 4to, calf gilt; 2 bdgs broken, hinges of Vol III breaking. With 12 plates & 14 maps & plans. 1 map creased; 1 leaf torn & repaired on outer margin. pnNY Oct 16 (17) $250
2d Ed. L, 1785. 2 vols. 4to, contemp calf; rubbed, joints split. With 1 map torn. bba Aug 20 (491) £200 [Scott]
Anr copy. Modern half mor; rubbed. One map cleanly torn. Ck Feb 27 (156) £170
Anr Ed. L, 1792. 8vo, contemp calf; rebacked, rubbed. Library stamps. bba Mar 12 (26) £65 [Hannas]
Anr Ed. L, 1802. 5 vols. 8vo, contemp calf; rubbed. bba Oct 30 (297) £120 [Mandl]

Coykendall, Frederick
— Arthur Rackham: A List of Books Illustrated by Him. NY, 1922. One of 175. Orig bds; stained. sg Oct 30 (55) $425; sg Jan 8 (242) $400

Coyne, Joseph Stirling, 1803-68. See: Willis & Coyne

Coyner, David H.
— The Lost Trappers; a Collection of Interesting Scenes and Events in the Rocky Mountains. Cincinnati, 1850. 12mo, orig cloth; worn & soiled. Some soiling & foxing. wa June 25 (219) $110

Cozzens, Frederic S. —&
Kelley, J. D. Jerrold, 1847-1922
— American Yachts. NY: Scribner's [1884-85]. Text vol & 2 folders, Folio, text in orig half mor & contained in a recess in 1 of the 2 boxes containing the folders. With 27 color plates heightened with varnish, mtd. S Apr 23 (82) £30,000 [Cape]

Cozzens, Frederic Schiller
— Yachts and Yachting. NY: Cassell, [1887]. 4to, cloth. Library markings. wa Nov 6 (30) $70

Crabbe, George, 1754-1832
See also: Fore-Edge Paintings
— The Poetical Works.... L, 1834. 8 vols. 8vo, half calf gilt. Foxed, affecting plates. sg Sept 11 (71) $130

Crachet, Pierre Marie
— Dissertatiuncula inauguralis, circa hanc quaestionem diaeteticam.... Montpelier: Picot, 1688. 8vo, 18th-cent half vellum. S June 25 (16) £250

Craddock, Harry
— The Savoy Cocktail Book. NY, 1930. Half cloth. sg June 4 (21) $225

Craig, Clifford
— The Engravers of Van Diemen's Land. [Hobart], 1961. Ltd Ed, sgd. CA Oct 7 (44) A$260; kh Mar 16 (130) A$350
— Old Tasmanian Prints. Launceston, 1964. One of 1,000. CA Oct 7 (45) A$260

Craig, Clifford —& Others
— Early Colonial Furniture in New South Wales and Van Diemen's Land. Melbourne, 1972. 4to, cloth, in d/j. kh Mar 16 (132) A$190

Craig, Edith N. See: Robertson & Craig

Craig, Edward Gordon, 1872-1966
— The Art of the Theatre. L, 1905. 1st Ed, One of 150. Preface by R. Graham Robertson. 4to, cloth. ANs of presentation laid in. sg Feb 26 (71) $200
— Books and Theatres. L & Toronto, 1925. Orig half cloth, in d/j. sg Feb 26 (82) $80
— Gordon Craig's Book of Penny Toys. Hackbridge, 1899. One of 550. 4to, half cloth; back cover stained, front hinge cracked. With Ls regarding publication of the book. sg Feb 26 (69) $2,000
— Henry Irving. Ellen Terry. A Book of Portraits. Chicago, 1899. Cloth; stained, front hinge cracked. sg Feb 26 (91) $225
Anr copy. Orig bds; rebacked. sg June 11 (118) $100
Anr copy. Orig bds; spine perished, corners bumped. With Ellen Terry's bookplate designed by Gordon Craig. wd June 19 (103) $175
— Nothing; or, the Bookplate. L, 1924. 1st Ed, one of 280 L.p. copies. pn June 18 (256) £100 [Uchida]
Anr copy. Lacking the bookplate of Jan C. de Vos. S Jan 13 (636) £40 [Thornton]

Anr copy. With a sgd woodblock bookplate. sg Feb 26 (81) $225
— On the Art of the Theatre. L, 1911. One of 150. 4to, cloth. sg Feb 26 (72) $300
— Paris Diary, 1932-1933. North Hills: Bird & Bull Press, 1982. One of 350. Half cloth. sg Jan 8 (19) $70

Anr copy. Orig half mor. sg Feb 26 (139) $120

— A Production, being Thirty-two Collotype Plates of Designs...for The Pretenders of Henrik Ibsen. L, 1930. One of 105 on handmade paper, sgd. Folio, orig half vellum gilt, in orig paper wrap; lower corners bumped. sg Feb 26 (85) $900

One of 650. Orig cloth; worn. sg Feb 26 (86) $250

Anr copy. Orig cloth; spine ends torn, corners bumped, stain on front cover. sg Feb 26 (87) $150

— Scene. L, 1923. 4to, orig bds. sg Feb 26 (78) $60

One of 100. Cloth, in d/j. sg Feb 26 (77) $350

— Towards a New Theatre.... L, 1913. 1st Ed. 4to, orig cloth; rebacked preserving orig spine. Some foxing. bba Feb 5 (225) £65 [Hetherington]

1st American Ed. NY, 1913. 4to, cloth; front free endpaper browned. sg Feb 26 (75) $60

— Woodcuts and Some Words. L, 1924. One of 160, sgd. 4to, contemp cloth, in d/j. pn Oct 23 (143) £75 [Cox]

Anr copy. Cloth. Sgd proof of woodcut inserted. sg Feb 26 (79) $325

Craig, Maurice James
— Irish Book Bindings, 1600-1800. L, 1954. Folio, orig cloth. With colored frontis & 58 plates. cba Feb 5 (76) $75

Anr copy. Orig cloth, in d/j. pn Nov 20 (136) £160 [Hannas]

One of 750. Orig cloth, in soiled d/j. cb June 18 (76) $160

Cramer, Johann Andreas, 1710-77
— Anfangsgruende der Metallurgie. Blankenburg & Quedlinburg, 1774-77. Vols I-III, Part 1 (all pbd) in 1 vol. Folio, later half calf. With 41 plates & 32 folding sheets. C Dec 12 (55) £350 [Demetzy]

Anr copy. Vols I-III, Part 1 (all pbd) in 2 vols. Folio, bdg not indicated. Library markings. Sold w.a.f. Franklin Institute copy. F Sept 12 (368) $800

— Elements of the Art of Assaying Metals.... L, 1741. 8vo, modern half calf. With 6 folding plates. Some staining or browning; 1 plate repaired in margin; errata corrected in ink. bba May 14 (299) £260

[Bickersteth]

Cranach Press—Weimar
— Das Hohe Lied Salomo. 1931. One of 50 on japon. Illus by Eric Gill. HN Nov 26 (1525) DM4,600
— RILKE, RAINER MARIA. - Duineser Elgien: Elegies from the Castle of Duino. 1931. One of 200. Trans by V. & E. Sackville-West. Orig half vellum. S Dec 18 (141) £650 [Thorp]; S June 17 (371) £500 [Maggs]
— SHAKESPEARE, WILLIAM. - Hamlet. 1928. One of 230. Mor extra by Rudolf Lang. FD Dec 2 (4303a) DM9,000; sg Feb 26 (94) $2,800

Am Ed. 1930. One of 300. HN Nov 26 (1526) DM4,600; P June 18 (31) $3,000; sg Feb 26 (95) $2,400

Crane, Hart, 1899-1932
— Voyages: Six Poems from White Buildings. NY, 1957. One of 975. Illus by Leonard Baskin. Oblong folio, wraps. K June 7 (39) $150
— White Buildings. NY: Boni & Liveright, 1926. 1st Ed, 2d Issue. sg Mar 5 (46) $120

Crane, Stephen, 1871-1900
See also: Grabhorn Printing
— Maggie, a Girl of the Streets. NY, 1896. 1st Pbd Ed. 12mo, orig cloth; spine rubbed. cb Feb 19 (65) $180
— The Open Boat.... L, 1898. 1st English Ed. 8vo, orig cloth. F Jan 15 (105) $110
— The Red Badge of Courage. NY, 1895. 1st Ed, 1st Issue. 8vo, orig cloth; rubbed, shaken. Corner excised from initial blank. sg Feb 12 (44) $450
— Works. NY, [1925-26]. One of 750. Ed by Wilson Follett. 12 vols. bba Mar 26 (237) £80 [Elliott]; ha May 22 (55) $150; sg Sept 11 (72) $80

Anr copy. Unopened. O Jan 6 (46) $160

Crane, Walter, 1845-1915
— The First of May, a Fairy Masque. L, 1881. One of 200, sgd. Oblong folio, loose as issued in orig cloth portfolio. With 57 proof plates on india paper. Marginal stains. S Oct 6 (781) £70 [Luia]
— Flowers from Shakespeare's Garden. L, 1906. Orig half cloth; rubbed. With 40 colored litho plates including title. bba Sept 25 (167) £50 [Oram]; L Dec 11 (58) £50
— Kunst en samenleving. Amst., 1903. Designed by G. W. Dijsselhof. 4to, half calf gilt. B Oct 7 (55) HF400
— Renascence: A Book of Verse. L, 1891. One of 100. 8vo, half vellum; soiled, spine ends creased & corners rubbed. cb Feb 19 (66) $80
— Triplets. Comprising the Baby's Opera, The Baby's Bouquet, and the Baby's Own

Aesop. L, 1899. 4to, half vellum; back damaged. B Oct 7 (268) HF600

Crantz, David, 1723-77
— The Ancient and Modern History of the Brethren.... L, 1780. 8vo, modern half calf; rubbed. Library stamp on tp verso & on ad leaf. bba Nov 13 (233) £75 [Armstrong]
— The History of Greenland. L, 1820. 2 vols. 8vo, half lea; front bds detached. With folding map & 7 plates. sg Nov 20 (61) $90

Crapsey, Edward
— The Nether Side of New York. NY, 1872. 8vo, orig cloth. sg Sept 18 (208) $150

Crashaw, Richard, 1613?-49
— Steps to the Temple.... L, 1646. 1st Ed. 12mo, mor gilt by Riviere. With leaf of author's motto & "Reader, there was a sudden mistake" bound after A4. C Dec 12 (323) £700 [Bennett]

Crasso, Lorenzo
— Elogii di capitani illustri. Venice, 1683. 4to, orig bds; soiled, shaken. Old stamps on title of the Deutsche Heeresbuecherei of Berlin & the Koenigliche Kriegs-Akademie Bibliothek. sg Mar 26 (85) $140

Crauzat, Ernest de
— L'Oeuvre grave et lithographie de Steinlen. Paris, 1913. One of 20 on chine for Les XX. 4to, bds. With 11 orig graphics, 4 in 2 states & 7 in 3 states. HK Nov 4 (3084) DM3,400

Craven, Lady Elizabeth, 1750-1828
— A Journey through the Crimea to Constantinople. L, 1789. 4to, 19th-cent half sheep; joints starting. With folding map & 6 plates. sg Nov 20 (62) $225

Crawfurd, John, 1783-1868
— Journal of an Embassy from the Governor General of India to the Court of Ava.... L, 1834. 2d Ed. 2 vols. 8vo, orig cloth; rubbed, joints split. bba May 28 (195) £130 [Ad Orientem]

Crawhall, Joseph, the Elder
— Grouse Shooting Made Quite Easy.... L, 1827. 4to, later half lea; extremities worn. With 29 plates. Interleaved with blank pages. sg Oct 23 (228) $2,600

Crawhall, Joseph, b.1821
— Chap-book Chaplets. L, 1883. 4to, orig bds; rebacked, preserving orig spine. T Oct 15 (92) £42
— Chorographia, or a Survey of Newcastle upon Tyne: 1649. Newcastle, 1884. 4to, orig half vellum; soiled. cb Feb 19 (66) $80
— A Collection of Right Merrie Garlands for North Country Anglers. Newcastle, 1864. 8vo, contemp half lev; joints rubbed, front free endpaper splitting at gutter. cb May 21 (53) $55
One of 50 L.p. copies. Half mor. sg May 21 (45) $450
— The Compleatest Angling Booke that ever was writ.... Newcastle, 1859. One of 40. 4to, lea. Inscr by Crawhall to his wife & with a note on the flyleaf by Crawhall's nephew & an autograph postcard from Crawhall to his nephew. sg Oct 23 (227) $3,200
Anr Ed. Newcastle, 1881. One of 100. 4to, orig cloth; spine faded. S July 28 (1016) £200

Crawshay, Richard
— The Birds of Tierra del Fuego. L, 1907. One of 300. Folio, half mor gilt. With colored map, 21 hand-colored lithos & 23 photographic plates. S Oct 23 (668) £500 [Frers]

Crebillon, Claude Prosper Jolyot de, 1707-77
— Tanzai et Neadarne. Histoire Japonoise. Pekin [i.e., Paris], 1734. 1st Ed. 2 vols. 12mo, contemp mor gilt; 1 joint starting. Pollard copy. sg Oct 9 (168) $250

Crebillon, Prosper Jolyot de, 1675-1762
— Oeuvres. Paris, 1797. 2 vols. 8vo, mor gilt by Hardy-Mennil. L.p. copy on papier velin, extra-illus with 4 ports & 17 proof plates. C Dec 3 (106) £550 [Heyward]
Anr Ed. Paris, 1818. 2 vols. 8vo, contemp mor by Simier. With port & 9 plates before letters. L.p. copy on papier velin. C Dec 3 (107) £600 [Sourget]

Creeley, Robert
— The Charm: Early and Uncollected Poems. Mount Horeb: Perishable Press, 1967. One of 250. Half mor, unopened. sg Jan 8 (199) $100

Crescentiis, Petrus de, 1230?-1310?
— Le Bon Mesnaiger. Paris: Estienne Caveillet, 16 Apr 1540. Folio, modern mor gilt by Rene Aussourd. Rusthole & patch to lower margin of f.xx8v; f.lxix with repaired tears; corners of 1 index leaf & of last 5 leaves repaired; minor stains. Hunt copy. CNY Nov 21 (83) $2,500
Anr Ed. Paris: Estienne Caveiller for Vincent Sertenas, 16 Apr 1540. Folio, contempcalf; repaired. Jeanson copy. SM Feb 28 (154) FF40,000
— Commodorum ruralium. Augsburg: Johann Schuessler, c.16 Feb 1471. ("Ruralia commoda.") Folio, contemp blind-stamped red sheep over wooden bds with metal fittings (some lacking); rubbed. F1 with large decorated initial extending into inner margin & lower margin illuminated with

foliage & roses in green & red heightened with gold; coat-of-arms in right margin; large initials throughout in blue or green with red penwork. Some wear to lower margin of 1st leaf; tear to f.86; some stains. 211 (of 212) leaves; lacking blank at end. Goff C-965. Simon-Crahan copy. P Nov 25 (140) $25,000

Anr copy. Remboitage of a contemp English bdg. With a contemp Ms index tipped in. 210 (of 212) leaves; lacking 2 blanks at end. Goff C-965. Jeanson 1697. SM Feb 28 (149) FF170,000

Anr Ed. [Speier: Peter Drach, c.1490-95]. ("Opus ruralium commodorum.") Folio, mor gilt by Riviere. 138 leaves. Goff C-969. Schwerdt-Jeanson copy. SM Feb 28 (150) FF160,000

Anr Ed. Venice: F. Sansovino, 1561. ("Pietro Crescentio Bolognese tradotto nuovamente....") 4to, contemp vellum; wrinkled & soiled. Minor dampstain to fore-margin of last several quires. Hunt copy. CNY Nov 21 (84) $900

Anr copy. Vellum. Crahan copy. P Nov 25 (139) $350

Anr Ed. Florence: Cosimo Giunti, 1605. ("Trattato dell' agricoltura....,") 4to, later vellum. Tp soiled. Hunt copy. CNY Nov 21 (85) $200

— De agricultura vulgari. Venice, 1519. 4to, contemp mor; rubbed, with 4 clasps & catches (def). Quires t & u browned. Hunt copy. CNY Nov 21 (82) $4,000

— De agricultura. Florence: Nicolaus Laurentii Alemanus, 15 July 1578. Folio, 18th-cent half calf. Lower corners of 1st 8 leaves patched or repaired; 1st leaf with patch to fore-margin just affecting 3 letters of text on a1v; dampstains & traces of old mildew to corners & fore-margins of some leaves at front & back; wormhole to margins of last 15 leaves; some marginalia. 201 (of 202) leaves; lacking final blank. Goff C-973. Hunt copy. CNY Nov 21 (81) $4,000

— De omnibus agriculturae partibus.... Basel: Henricus Petri, 1548. Bound with: Agricola, Georgius. De Ortu & Causis subterraneorum.... Basel: Froben, 1546. Folio, contemp blindstamped lea over wooden bds; 1 clasp detached. Jeanson 1705. SM Feb 28 (151) FF40,000

— Le Livre de prouffitz champestres et ruraulx touchat le labour des champs vignes et iardins.... Paris: Philippe Le Noir for Jean Petit, 15 Feb 1529. Folio, mor with arms of Baron Seilliere, by Chambolle-Duru, 1868. Jeanson Ms. SM Feb 28 (153) FF85,000

— Le Livre des ruraulx prouffitz du labour des chaps. Paris: Jean Bonhomme, 15 Oct 1486. Folio, 16th-cent calf gilt; rebacked. Some tears & faults. 244 (of 246) leaves; lacking initial & final blanks. Goff C-970. SM Feb 28 (152) FF220,000

— La Maniere denter et planter en iardins. [N.p., c.1860]. One of a few on vellum. 8vo, mor janseniste by Masson-Debonnelle. Jeanson copy. SM Feb 28 (155) FF6,500

— New Feldt und Ackerbaw. Frankfurt, 1583. Folio, disbound. Imperf copy, also with scattered stains, fraying, tears & repairs affecting text; index leaves def. Sold w.a.f. sg Jan 15 (196) $325

— Von dem Nutz der Ding die in Aeckeren gebauwt Werdt. Strasbourg. Johann Schott for Johann Knobloch & Paul Goetz, 1518. Folio, mor janseniste by Huser. Jeanson copy. SM Feb 28 (156) FF78,000

Cresset Press—London
— The Apocrypha. 1929. One of 450. cb Sept 11 (86) $140
— BACON, SIR FRANCIS. - The Essayes or Counsels Civill and Morall. 1928. One of 250. Syn. sg Jan 8 (50) $100
— BLOME, RICHARD. - Hawking or Falconry. 1929. One of 650. Ck Apr 24 (67) £75
— BUNYAN, JOHN. - The Pilgrim's Progress. 1928. One of 195. 2 vols. Orig bds; worn. CA Oct 7 (40) A$400
One of 1,600. sg Jan 8 (179) $50
— COX, NICOLAS & BLOME, RICHARD. - The Gentleman's Recreation. 1928. One of 50. sg Oct 23 (226) $200
— HERRICK, ROBERT. - The Poetical Works of Robert Herrick. 1928. One of 750. 4 vols. sg June 11 (119) $80
— JOHNSON, ALFRED FORBES. - Decorative Initial Letters. 1931. One of 500. pn Nov 20 (153) £65 [Brayley]
— LAWRENCE, D. H. - Birds, Beasts, and Flowers. 1930. One of 500. cb May 7 (116) $85
— LAWSON, WILLIAM. - A New Orchard and Garden.... 1927. One of 650. T Oct 15 (172) £55
— MILTON, JOHN. - Paradise Lost; Paradise Regain'd. 1931. One of 195. 2 vols in 1. S Oct 6 (731) £160 [Thorp]
Anr copy. 2 vols. S May 6 (70) £80 [Henderson]
— PAINTER, WILLIAM. - The Palace of Pleasure. 1929. One of 500. 4 vols. Half cloth. Each vol with a bookplate designed by Eric Gill; one sgd. sg Jan 8 (151) $120
— SPENSER, EDMUND. - The Shepheards Calendar. 1930. One of 350. sg Sept 11 (265) $400
— SWIFT, JONATHAN. - Gulliver's Travels. 1930. One of 195. 2 vols. sg Dec 4 (193) $700
One of 205. Orig half mor. With 17 hand-colored plates & 5 maps. S Dec 4

(220) £1,750 [Mitchell]

Cresswell, Samuel Gurney
— A Series of Eight Sketches in Colour...of the Voyage of H.M.S. Investigator. L, 1854. Folio, contemp half calf. With map & 6 colored plates. Some foxing. pnE Jan 28 (80) £970 [Traylen]

Creswell, Keppel A.
— A Bibliography of the Architecture, Arts and Crafts of Islam.... [Cairo], 1978. One of 500. Folio, cloth. sg Feb 5 (171) $275

Creswell, Keppel A. —& Others
— The Mosques of Egypt. Giza, 1949. 2 vols. Folio, orig cloth. bba Oct 30 (456) £260 [Check Books]; bba May 14 (261) £280 [Fogg]

Creswicke, Louis
— South Africa and the Transvaal War. L, 1900-[02]. 8 vols, including 2 Supplements. Worn, spine leaning. cb Dec 18 (47) $85

Cresy, Edward
— A Practical Treatise on Bridge-Building.... L, 1839. Folio, bdg not described. F Sept 12 (320) $300

Cretin, Guillaume
— Chantz royaulx oraisons, et aultres petitz traictez.... Paris: Galiot du Pre, 25 Apr 1527. 8vo, mor gilt by Trautz-Bauzonnet. SM Feb 28 (158) FF45,000

Anr Ed. Paris: for Jehan Saint-Denys, [c.1529]. 8vo, mor gilt by Cape. Jeanson copy. SM Feb 28 (159) FF62,000

— Le Debat de deux dames sur le passetemps de la chasse.... Paris: Anthoine Couteau pour Jehan Longis, 1 Apr 1526. 8vo, mor gilt by Magnin with the letters CR (Couturier de Royas) interlaced in center panel. Jeanson Ms. SM Feb 28 (160) FF40,000

Crevaux, Jules Nicolas
— Voyages dans l'Amerique du Sud. Paris, 1883. 4to, half cloth. B Feb 25 (784) HF400

Crevecoeur, Michel Guillaume St. Jean de, 1735-1813
— Letters from an American Farmer.... L, 1782. 8vo, orig bds; backstrip chipped with loss, upper cover detached. With 2 folding maps. Hunt copy. CNY Nov 21 (86) $800

Anr copy. Modern cloth. With 2 folding maps, each with 2 perforated library stamps. sg Mar 12 (90) $300

Anr Ed. L, 1783. 8vo, old half calf; spine cracked, upper cover detached. With 2 folding maps. Hunt copy. CNY Nov 21 (87) $180

Anr Ed. Phila.: Mathew Carey, Mar 4 1793.

12mo, contemp calf; worn, upper cover crudely reattached. Foxed throughout. Hunt copy. CNY Nov 21 (88) $220

— Lettres d'un Cultivateur Americain.... Paris, 1784. 2 vols. 8vo, modern half calf. CNY Nov 21 (89) $250

Anr Ed. Paris, 1787. 3 vols. 8vo, calf gilt. With engraved titles, 6 folding maps & 3 plates. A few leaves in Vol II discolored. S Sept 23 (507) £370 [Quaritch]

— Voyage dans la haute Pensylvanie et dans l'etat de New York. Paris, 1801, [An IX]. 3 vols. 8vo, bds. With 7 plates, 3 maps & 3 tables. S Sept 23 (508) £200 [Schdeni]

Anr Ed. Paris, 1801. 3 vols. 8vo, contemp half calf by Grosclaude, with his ticket; outer joints repaired. Hunt copy. CNY Nov 21 (90) $450

Cries...
— The Cryes of the City of London drawn after the Life. L: H. Overton, 1711. Illus by Pierce Tempest. Folio, later half calf. With engraved title & 73 plates. Fore-edges of tp & of Plates 11, 16 & 24 repaired; other repairs. Sold w.a.f. Crahan copy. P Nov 25 (447) $1,200

Cripps-Day, Francis Henry
— A Record of Armour Sales, 1881-1924. L, 1925. Folio, cloth. pnE June 17 (155) £50

Crisp, Sir Frank, 1843-1919
— Mediaeval Gardens. L, 1924. One of 1,000. 2 vols. 4to, orig cloth; soiled. bba Sept 25 (339) £200 [Goldstone]

One of 1,000. Orig cloth, in d/j. Ck Nov 7 (136) £45

Crisp, Frederick Arthur, 1851-1922
— Memorial Rings. L, 1908. One of 150. 4to, half vellum gilt; worn. Library stamp on title. sg Feb 5 (103) $50

Croall, Alexander. See: Johnstone & Croall

Crofton, Helen Rose Anne Milman. See: Milman, Helen Rose Anne

Crofutt, George A.
— Crofutt's New Overland Tourist and Pacific Coast Guide.... Chicago: Overland Publishing, 1878. Vol I. Orig cloth wraps; rubbed. Some rubberstamps to prelims. cb Jan 8 (33) $60

Croke, Sir George
— An Abridgement of the Three Volumes of Reports.... L: for John Starkey et al, 1665. 8vo, modern calf. Imprimatur leaf torn in inner margin; lacking last leaf of table. bba Sept 25 (7) £75 [P & P Books]

Crombie, Benjamin William
— Modern Athenians. A Series of Original Portraits. L, 1882. 4to, half mor gilt; split. pnE Nov 12 (100) £50
Anr copy. Half mor. pnE Nov 12 (241) £100

Crombie, Charles
— The Rules of Golf Illustrated. L, 1905. pn June 18 (80) £350 [Hildebrandt]; pnC July 16 (37) £340; pnC July 16 (38) £340
Anr Ed. L, [n.d.]. Oblong 4to, orig half cloth. pnC Jan 23 (41) £340; pnC Jan 23 (42) £340; pnC Jan 23 (43) £320; pnC Jan 23 (44) £300

Cronau, Rudolf
— Von Wunderland zu Wunderland. Leipzig, 1886. Folio, orig cloth. With 25 mtd plates. S Oct 23 (415) £1,000 [Monckton]

Cronin, William Vine. See: Graves & Cronin

Crooke, Helkiah, 1576-1635
— Microcosmographia, a Description of the Body of Man. [L: W. Jaggard, 1615]. ("Mikrokosmographia: a Description of the Body of Man.") 1st Ed. Folio, contemp calf; worn. Lacking tp; prelims frayed. T Nov 20 (443) £100

Cross, Gorham Lamont
— Partridge Shortenin', being an Instructive and Irreverent Sketch.... Wellesley Hills MA: Pvtly ptd, [1949]. One of 100. Inscr. sg Oct 23 (230) $275

Cross, Thomas
— The Autobiography of a Stage Coachman. L, 1904. One of 500. 2 vols. 4to, orig cloth. With 43 hand-colored plates. pn Apr 30 (134) £170 [Sheppard]

Crow, Gerald Henry
William Morris, Designer.... L: The Studio, 1934. 4to, orig cloth; soiled. Sgd. bba Feb 5 (199) £70 [Burmester]

Crow, Hugh
— Memoirs.... L, 1830. 8vo, modern half mor. With folding map, port, 3 plates & a leaf of music. Marginal tear to e2 not affecting text. S Nov 18 (1187) £80 [Cavendish]

Crowell, Benedict —& Wilson, Robert Forrest
— How America Went to War. New Haven, 1921. One of 500. 6 vols. sg Sept 18 (312) $50

Crowley, Aleister
— The Diary of a Drug Fiend. L, [1922]. 1st Ed. Orig cloth; rubbed. bba May 14 (438) £50 [Quaritch]
Anr copy. Orig cloth, in d/j. First few leaves spotted. S Jan 13 (552) £140 [Burwood]
— Moonchild. L: Mandrake Press, 1929. In rubbed & chipped d/j. cb Sept 28 (363) $250
— The Spirit of Solitude...The Confessions. L: Mandrake Press, 1929. 1st Ed. 2 vols. 4to, orig cloth. bba May 14 (439) £180 [Bishop-Culpeper]

Crowley, John
— Little Big. L, 1982. In d/j. cb Sept 28 (366) $85

Crowne, John, 1640?-1703?
— The Married Beau.... L, 1694. 1st Ed. 4to, 19th-cent half calf. Library stamps; upper margin closely trimmed. O Feb 24 (51) $70

Crowquill, Albert. See: Forrester, Alfred Henry

Crozat, Joseph Antoine, Marquis de Tugny
— Recueil d'estampes d'apres les plus beaux tableaux...qui sont en France. Paris, 1729-42. 2 vols. Folio, contemp calf; rubbed. With 175 plates only, some tinted. A few plates with marginal tears; marginal staining to Vol I. S Nov 10 (209) £1,300 [Russell]

Crozet, Julien Marie
— Nouveau voyage a la mer du sud.... Paris, 1783. 8vo, contemp calf; worn. With 2 maps & 5 plates. S Oct 23 (515) £2,000 [Perrin]

Cruden, Alexander, 1701-70
— A Complete Concordance to the Holy Scriptures.... L, 1738. 4to, contemp sheep; worn, rebacked. sg Mar 26 (87) $70

Cruikshank, George, 1792-1878
— The Bottle. L, etc., [1847]. Folio, later half mor, orig wraps bound in. With 8 colored plates. Title & plates backed with linen. ha May 22 (148) $120
— The Comic Almanack. L, 1835-53. 19 issues in 5 vols [complete]. 8vo & 12mo, mor gilt by Riviere, orig wraps & ads bound in. sg June 11 (126) $1,600
Anr copy. Half mor gilt. Lacking orig wraps & ads. sg June 11 (127) $200
Anr copy. 19 vols (all pbd). 8vo or 12mo, orig wraps or cloth; 1 cover torn & repaired, some spines chipped. Some ads & prelims lacking. sg June 18 (191) $325
Anr Ed. L: John Camden Hotten, [n.d.]. 2 vols. 8vo, half calf gilt, orig cloth bound in. sg June 11 (128) $200

CRUIKSHANK

— The Comic Alphabet.... [L], 1836. 1st Ed. 12mo, mor by the Guild of Women Binders with multi-colored mor inlays depicting figures from the alphabet. With 24 hand-colored plates. sg Feb 12 (47) $475
Later Issue, with ad on back cover dated 1837. Orig bds. With 24 hand-colored plates. sg June 11 (130) $175
Anr Ed. L: Tilt, [1837]. 128mm by 2,040mm, folded into bds. With 24 illusts colored by hand. S June 17 (431) £450 [Joseph & Sawyer]
— Cruikshankiana. L: F. Bentley, [183?]. Folio, half lea; worn, broken. Dampstaining, not affecting plates. sg Dec 18 (160) $250
— A Discovery concerning Ghosts.... L, 1863. 8vo, orig wraps; spine worn at foot. sg Sept 11 (76) $110
— Fairy Library. L, [1853-64]. Hop-O'-My-Thumb a variant or later issue. 4 vols. 4to, orig wraps. Includes: Hop-o'-My-Thumb; Jack and the Bean-Stalk; Cinderella; Puss in Boots. sg June 11 (131) $700
1st Ed, Mixed issues. 4 vols (complete set) in 1 vol. 4to, mor. With 24 plates, all mtd india-proofs. Some text leaves stained. sg Apr 2 (64) $275
— The Humourist: A Collection of Entertaining Tales. L, 1819-20. 2d Issue with Vol I on ptd title. 4 vols. 8vo, calf gilt. With engraved titles & 36 hand-colored plates. sg June 11 (143) $1,800
— Illustrations of Popular Works. L, 1830. Part 1 (all pbd). 4to, calf gilt by Worsfold, orig wraps bound in. With 6 plates on India paper. sg June 11 (125) $110
— London Characters. L, 1829. 12mo, orig bds. With reprint title & 24 hand-colored plates. S June 17 (223) £250 [Joseph & Sawyer]
— Omnibus. L, 1842. 1st Ed in Book form. 8vo, calf by Zaehnsdorf; rubbed. S Jan 13 (637) £80 [Cavendish]
Anr Ed. L, 1885. One of 300. 4to, half mor gilt by Bennet. Cruikshank signature pasted down on front free endpaper. sg Sept 11 (78) $150
— Points of Humour. L, 1820. 2 parts in 1 vol. 8vo, lev gilt by Riviere. ALs laid in. sg Apr 2 (63) $400
— Scraps and Sketches. L, 1828-32. Oblong folio, contemp half calf; extremities worn. Plates in Part 1 foxed; lacking ads. sg June 11 (123) $275
— Sunday in London.... L, 1833. 8vo, calf; worn, bottom edge of spine chipped. sg Sept 11 (80) $80
— Table-Book. L, 1845. Ed by G. A. a Beckett. 8vo, later calf gilt, orig cloth bound in, by Stikeman; front cover stained.

AMERICAN BOOK PRICES CURRENT

With 12 plates. Marginal stains. cb Feb 19 (70) $75
Anr copy. Half mor gilt. With 11 (of 12) plates. sg Feb 12 (48) $225
Anr Ed. L, 1885. 4to, half mor; soiled. With 12 plates. wd June 19 (104) $300

Cruikshank, George, 1792-1878 —& Others

— The Attorney-General's Charges against the late Queen.... L, [1821]. Folio, half mor; rubbed. Lacking 1 plate & with additional plate inserted, The Armorial Bearings of the White Cat. S June 17 (222) £1,400 [Joseph & Sawyer]

Cruikshank, Isaac Robert & George

— The Cruikshankian Momus. L, 1892. One of 520. 4to, orig cloth; rubbed. With 52 hand-colored plates. pn Dec 11 (17) £65 [Robertshaw]

Cruikshank, Isaac Robert, 1789-1856

— The Devil among the Fancy.... L, 1822. 8vo, calf gilt by Riviere. With hand-colored frontis & 2 ports. C Apr 8 (15) £240 [Chelsea Rare Books]

Crunden, John

— Convenient and Ornamental Architecture.... L, 1767. 1st Ed. Folio, modern bds. With 56 plates. Some tears at folds; some plates strengthened at inner margin. Sold w.a.f. S Nov 10 (69) £140 [Barker]

Cruttwell, Clement

— Atlas to Cruttwell's Gazetteer. L: for G. C. & J. Robinson, [1799]. 8vo, old bds; worn, disbound. With 24 (of 26) double-page maps, hand-colored in outline. Tp lacking. Ck May 15 (318) £180
Anr Ed. L: for G. C. & J. Robinson, [1808]. 8vo, contemp half calf; rubbed. With 28 double-page maps, hand-colored in outline. Many maps with tears, mostly in lower blank margin. S Jan 12 (91) £180 [Marsham]

Cruz Cano y Holmedilla, Juan de la

— Coleccion de trajes de Espana.... Madrid, 1777. Vol I (all pbd). Folio, 19th-cent half lea; spine torn. With engraved title within hand-colored border & 45 (of 80) hand-colored plates. Lower fore-corner of tp torn away with loss of a few words of Advertencia. Sold w.a.f. C Oct 15 (29) £950 [Armiro]

Cruz Lima, Eladio de

— Mammals of Amazonia. Rio de Janeiro, 1945. One of 975. Vol I: General Introduction and Primates. Folio, wraps; worn. With 42 colored plates. cb Nov 6 (68) $75

Cuala Press—Churchtown & Dublin
— FENOLLOSA, ERNEST F. - Certain Noble Plays of Japan.... 1916. One of 350. bba May 28 (115) £60 [Maggs]
— GOGARTY, OLIVER ST. JOHN. - Elbow Room. 1939. One of 450. Unopened. sg Dec 11 (12) $150
— HIGGINS, F. R. - Arable Holdings. Dublin, 1933. One of 300. Unopened copy. sg Dec 11 (13) $50
— O'CONNOR, FRANK. - A Lament for Art O'Leary. 1940. One of 130. Ck Apr 24 (43) £70
— SYNGE, JOHN MILLINGTON. - Deirdre of the Sorrows. 1910. One of 250. bba May 28 (119) £80 [Maggs]
— SYNGE, JOHN MILLINGTON. - Poems and Translations. 1909. One of 250. bba May 28 (118) £60 [Maggs]
— YEATS, WILLIAM BUTLER. - The Bounty of Sweden. 1925. One of 400. bba May 28 (136) £70 [Catnach]; sg Dec 11 (142) $130
Anr copy. Unopened. sg Dec 11 (143) $80
— YEATS, WILLIAM BUTLER. - The Cat and the Moon.... 1924. One of 500. Unopened. bba May 28 (135) £55 [Sumner]
— YEATS, WILLIAM BUTLER. - Dramatis Personae. 1935. One of 400. bba May 28 (150) £40 [Martin]
— YEATS, WILLIAM BUTLER. - Estrangement. 1926. One of 300. Unopened. bba May 28 (138) £40 [Martin]
— YEATS, WILLIAM BUTLER. - If I Were Four-and-Twenty. 1940. One of 450. Unopened. sg Dec 11 (145) $60
— YEATS, WILLIAM BUTLER. - In the Seven Woods. 1903. One of 325. S Jan 13 (619) £160 [Catnach]
— YEATS, WILLIAM BUTLER. - The King of the Great Clock Tower. 1934. One of 400. bba May 28 (148) £40 [Clark]
— YEATS, WILLIAM BUTLER. - Michael Robartes and the Dancer. 1920. One of 400. bba May 28 (132) £60 [Clark]
— YEATS, WILLIAM BUTLER. - October Blast. 1927. One of 350. Unopened. bba May 28 (139) £45 [Clark]
— YEATS, WILLIAM BUTLER. - On the Boiler. [1939]. Orig wraps. bba May 28 (152) £55 [Somebet]
Anr copy. Orig wraps. Forrest Reid's copy. With ALs from E. C. Yeats. T Nov 20 (271) £100
Anr copy. Orig wraps. Forrest Reid's copy, with ALs from E. C. Yeats on the production of this work. T Feb 18 (2) £230
— YEATS, WILLIAM BUTLER. - A Packet for Ezra Pound. 1929. One of 425. bba May 28 (143) £40 [Maggs]
— YEATS, WILLIAM BUTLER. - Reveries over Childhood and Youth. 1915. One of 425. Text plus portfolio of plates. T Feb 18 (10) £115
— YEATS, WILLIAM BUTLER. - A Selection from the Love Poetry. 1913. One of 300. Orig half cloth; soiled, lacking most of spine label. bba Sept 25 (139) £35 [Cox]
— YEATS, WILLIAM BUTLER. - Seven Poems and a Fragment. 1922. One of 500. Unopened. bba May 28 (133) £45 [Sumner]
— YEATS, WILLIAM BUTLER. - Stories of Michael Robartes and his Friends. 1931. One of 450. bba May 28 (146) £45 [Clark]
— YEATS, WILLIAM BUTLER. - Stories of Red Hanrahan. 1904 [1905]. One of 500. bba May 28 (128) £60 [Maggs]
— YEATS, WILLIAM BUTLER. - Two Plays for Dancers. 1919. One of 400. bba May 28 (131) £60 [Redshaw]
— YEATS, WILLIAM BUTLER & OTHERS. - Broadsides. A Collection of Old and New Songs. 1935. One of 100. Ed by W. B. Yeats & F. R. Higgins. [New Series]: Nos 1-12 in 1 vol. bba May 28 (123) £250 [Catnach]; T Feb 18 (13) £190

Cubero Sebastian, Pedro
— Descripcion general del mundo y notables sucessos que has sucedido en el. Valencia, 1697. 4to, old vellum; loose. Damp-stained; minor marginal worming; last few leaves frayed with loss. sg Nov 20 (64) $175

Cuccioni, T.
— Cento Vedute di Roma e sue vicinanze.... Rome, [c.1840]. Oblong 4to, later half mor; rubbed. With engraved title & 98 plates. Ck May 15 (100) £60

Cudworth, Ralph, 1617-88
— The True Intellectual System of the Universe. L, 1678. 1st Ed. Part 1 (all pbd). Folio, contemp calf; broken. Marginal repairs. pn Sept 18 (4) £140 [Waterfield]

Cuitt, George, 1779-1854
— Wanderings and Pencillings amongst Ruins of the Olden Time. L, 1855. Folio, half mor; rubbed. T Jan 22 (38) £110

Culin, Robert Stewart, 1858-1929
— Games of the North American Indians. Wash., 1907. 4to, contemp half lea; spine worn. Bureau of American Ethnology, Vol XXIV. sg Sept 18 (10) $100

Cullen, William, 1710-90
— Lectures on the Materia Medica. L, 1772. 1st Ed. 4to, modern calf gilt. pnE Dec 17 (89) £360 [Harding-Brookes]

Culmann, Leonhard
— Sententiae Pueriles Anglo-Latinae pro Primus Latinae Linguae....Sentences for Children.... L, 1680. 12mo, contemp vellum, orig wraps bound in. S June 18 (432) £680 [Russell]

Culpeper, Nicholas, 1616-54
— The English Physician Enlarged.... L, 1652. Folio, modern lea. Lacking 1 leaf, anr torn affecting text; sold w.a.f. bba Nov 13 (37) £100 [Phelps]
  Anr Ed. L, 1656. 8vo, needs rebdg. Some stains & browning. O Feb 24 (52) $120
  Anr copy. Calf. Some stains. sg Jan 15 (78) $300
  Anr Ed. L, [1798?]. ("Culpeper's English Physician and Complete Herbal.") 4to, contemp calf; worn, covers detached. T Feb 19 (374) £60
  Anr Ed. L, 1814. ("Culpeper's Complete Herbal....") 4to, contemp calf; worn & broken. With port & 11 hand-colored plates only. Some plates frayed & def. bba Jan 16 (77) £40 [Wise]
  Anr Ed. L, 1815. 4to, contemp calf; rebacked, orig backstrip laid down, corners repaired. With port & 40 colored plates. Port repaired; some dustsoiling, mostly to outer blank margins of plates; Plate 18 with small hole, tear & 1 blank corner torn away; Plate 7 with corner cut off; text leaf EE1 torn; FF1 torn & 1 corner def with loss of a few words; 2 leaves repaired at end. L Dec 11 (273) £50
  Anr Ed. L, 1824. 4to, old calf; rebacked preserving orig spine, which is a bit corroded. With port & 40 colored plates. Some foxing. O Oct 21 (47) $180
— Mr. Culpeper's Treatise of Aurum Potabile.... L: G. Eversden, 1656. 2 parts in 1 vol. 8vo, calf. Lacking A1; margins trimmed, affecting some text; some browning. Crahan copy. P Nov 25 (141) $450

Culpeper, Sir Thomas, the Younger, 1626-97
— A Discourse, Shewing the Many Advantages which will Accrue to this Kingdom by the Abatement of Usury.... L, 1668. 4to, wraps. S July 23 (435) £480 [Institute of Actuaries]

Culver, Henry Brundage
— Contemporary Scale Models of Vessels of the Seventeenth Century. NY, 1926. 1st Ed, One of 1,000. Folio, half vellum; marked & rubbed. Library stamps. bba Mar 12 (292) £35 [Elliott]

Cumming, Alexander, 1733-1814
— The Elements of Clock and Watch-work.... L, 1766. 4to, contemp half calf; foot of spine frayed. With 16 plates. Small hole in frame of 1 plate. C Dec 12 (57) £1,500 [Bookpress]
  Anr copy. Later half calf; rubbed. With 16 folding plates. With errata leaf. S Nov 10 (196) £320 [Traylen]

Cumming, T. G.
— Illustrations of the Origin and Progress of Rail and Tram Roads, and Steam Carriages.... Denbigh, 1824. 8vo, modern half calf. S May 28 (942) £190

Cummings, Edward Estlin, 1894-1962
— 95 Poems. NY: Harcourt, Brace, [1958]. One of 300. wa Sept 25 (649) $750
— Eimi. NY, 1933. One of 1,381, sgd. Cloth, in d/j. Inscr. sg Dec 11 (16) $150
— The Enormous Room. NY, [1922]. 1st Ed, p 219 censored. Orig cloth. sg June 11 (155) $130

Cummins, John. See: Bulkeley & Cummins

Cunard, Nancy
— Outlaws. L, 1921. 1st Ed. Bds; spine worn. T Oct 15 (75) £52
— Parallax. L: Hogarth Press, 1925. Orig bds. S Mar 9 (831) £170 [Whiteson]
  Anr copy. Orig bds; worn & soiled. sg Dec 11 (218) $100

Cunard, Nancy —& Padmore, George
— The White Man's Duty. L, [1943]. Wraps; 2 small creases on front cover. sg Dec 11 (221) $110

Cundell, James
— Rules of the Thistle Golf Club. Edin., 1824. Rebound within card covers. pnC Jan 23 (60) £4,000

Cunha, Rodrigo da
— Catalogo dos Bispos do Porto.... Oporto, 1742. Folio, contemp sheep. Last few leaves marginally dampstained. bba Nov 13 (24) £35 [Baldwin]

Cuningham, William
— The Cosmographical Glasse, Conteinyng the Pleasant Principles of Cosmographie.... L, 1559. 1st Ed. Folio, calf gilt with arms of Rubert Dudley, Earl of Leicester. Lacking blank T4, title inlaid, view of Norwich partly in pen facsimile, other defs. S Nov 27 (257) £2,400 [Quaritch]

Cunitia, Maria
— Urania propitia sive tabulae astronomicae mire faciles. Bicini Silesiorum [Pitschen], 1650. 1st Ed. Folio, contemp vellum. Some browning. S June 25 (95) £1,600 [Quaritch]

Cunn, Samuel
— A New Treatise of the Construction and Use of the Sector.... L, 1729. 8vo, later sheep; worn. Folding plate with small tears. ha Sept 19 (267) $80

Cunningham, Peter Miller, 1789-1864
— Two Years in New South Wales.... L, 1827. 1st Ed. 2 vols. 8vo, modern calf. Some foxing. kh Mar 16 (140) A$250

Curious...
— The Curious Adventures of a Little Mouse, or a Bad Boy Changed in a very Comical Manner into a Good Boy. L: W. Lane, [c.1790]. 16mo, orig Dutch floral bds. S Dec 5 (278) £250 [Hirsch]

Curnonsky, M. Ed., Pseud.
— France paradis du vin et de la bonne chere. [Paris, 1933]. 4to, half cloth, orig wraps bound in. sg Jan 15 (14) $50

Curr, Edward Micklethwaite
— An Account of the Colony of Van Diemen's Land.... L, 1824. 12mo, orig bds; head of spine torn. Signature cut from head of title. C Oct 15 (151) £220 [Maggs]
— The Australian Race, its Origin, Languages, Customs.... Melbourne & L, 1886. 4 vols, including "Vocabulary." 8vo & follo, contemp mor gilt; corners rubbed. Ck Sept 26 (219) £380

Currier. See: Peters, Harry Twyford

Curson, Henry
— The Theory of Sciences Illustrated. L: Richard Smith, 1702. 8vo, contemp calf; spine ends chipped, spine glazed & secured to front covers with glue. Tp foxed. cb Oct 23 (51) $75

Curtis, Atherton
— Catalogue de l'oeuvre et grave de R. P. Bonington. Paris, 1939. 4to, orig wraps; worn. Inscr. pn Sept 18 (294) £120 [Sims]

Curtis, Edward S., 1868-1952
— The North American Indian. Cambr., Mass., 1907-30. Ed by F. W. Hodge; foreword by Theodore Roosevelt. Vols I-II only. Orig half mor; rubbed. With 153 (of 154) plates. P May 13 (7) $2,300

Curtis, Henry, 1819-89
— The Beauties of the Rose. Bristol, 1850-53. 1st Ed. 2 vols in 1. 4to, half mor. With 38 hand-colored plates. A few leaves foxed. Howard—de Belder copy. S Apr 27 (84) £2,200 [van Look]

Curtis, John, 1791-1862
— British Entomology. L, 1824-39 [1823-40]. Vols I & III in 1 vol only. Contemp half mor; rubbed. With 98 hand-colored plates. bba May 14 (306) £110 [Waley]

Anr copy. 16 vols. 8vo, With 770 hand-colored plates & with errata uncorrected. C Oct 15 (217) £3,800 [Niedhardt]

Anr copy. 8 vols. 8vo, calf gilt by Hayday. With 770 hand-colored plates. S Apr 23 (3) £2,600 [Ganske]

Anr copy. Contemp calf gilt; slight wear. de Belder copy. S Apr 27 (85) £4,000 [Hamilton]

Anr Ed. L, 1862. 8 vols. 8vo, orig cloth; 3 spines broken. With 770 colored plates. Lacking Plate 88, 122 & 770 but with 3 duplicates. pn Apr 30 (302) £1,200 [Greyfriars]

Anr copy. Modern half mor gilt. With 770 hand-colored plates. S Apr 23 (4) £1,950 [Schreider]

Anr copy. Lepidoptera: Parts 1 & 2. Contemp half calf gilt; scuffed. With 194 plates, 12 duplicated. T Nov 20 (127) £700

Anr copy. Coleoptera: Parts 1 & 2. Contemp half calf gilt; loose. With 257 hand-colored plates, including Plate 560 not called for. T Nov 20 (128) £500

— Farm Insects: Being the Natural History.... Glasgow, 1860. 8vo, orig cloth; split on hinges. With 16 hand-colored plates. T Oct 16 (389) $65

— The Genera of British Lepidoptera. L, 1858. 4to, orig cloth. With 35 hand-colored plates. pn Sept 18 (308) £55 [Culpin]

Curtis, Paul A. See: Derrydale Press

Curtis, William, 1746-99
— The Botanical Magazine; or, Flower Garden Displayed. Vols 1-6. Bound in 2 vols. 8vo, contemp calf; extremities worn. With 1 plain & 215 colored plates. sg June 18 (194) $4,200

Vols 1-184. L, 1787-1983. Bound in 163 vols, plus 1 vol of Dedications & ports, 2 index vols & 1 vol containing 17 plates missing from Vol 53. Together, 167 vols. Half mor gilt. With 10,558 plates, most colored by hand. Lacking 16 plates & 1 text leaf. Sold w.a.f. C Oct 15 (218) £52,000 [Mitchell]

Vols 1-30. L, 1787-1809. Bound in 15 vols. 8vo, contemp calf. With 1,230 hand-colored plates, many folding. Sold w.a.f. pnE Dec 17 (189) £6,000 [Bless]

Vols 1-4. L, 1787-91. Bound in 2 vols. Contemp calf, spines chipped, joints cracked. With 144 hand-colored plates & 1 uncolored plate. Some plate-marks shaved; 1 plate loose. S Nov 10 (472) £1,250 [Blest]

Vols 1-9. L, 1792-96. Bound in 3 vols. 8vo, 19th-cent half calf; rubbed. With 1 plain & 323 hand-colored plates. Plate 119 torn; some plates trimmed; some dampstaining in Vol IX. Sold w.a.f. S June 25 (151) £1,650 [Robinson]

Vols 1-14. L, 1793-1800. 8vo, contemp half calf; worn, most joints cracked. With 498 plates only, all but 1 hand-colored. Some soiling; Plate 181 def. Sold w.a.f. P

CURTIS

June 18 (34) $7,500

Vols 1-3. L, 1793-97. Bound in 1 vol. Contemp calf; worn, upper cover loose. With 108 hand-colored plates. Some soiling; 1 text leaf repaired. S Nov 10 (473) £600 [Garrett]

Vols 6-9. L, 1793-96. 8vo, contemp half calf; worn. pnE June 17 (51) £740

Vol 71 (Third Series, Vol I) only. L, 1845. Contemp half mor; rubbed. bba Aug 20 (434) £420 [Rainbow]

Third Series, Vol 9. L, 1853. Contemp calf. Sold w.a.f. C Oct 15 (219) £220 [Koromoukis]

— Flora Londinensis. L, [1775]-77-98. 6 parts in 2 vols. Folio, contemp calf; rebacked. With 435 hand-colored plates on 432 leaves. pnE Dec 17 (190) £5,700 [Traylen]

Anr copy. Contemp russia; worn, rebacked with mor. With 432 hand-colored plates. A few dampstains at end of Part 2; a few plates just trimmed; marginal repair to 1 plate in Part 5; lacking tp & dedication leaf to Vol II; lacking 1 list of subscribers & the individual indexes to Parts 1-3. S Oct 23 (666) £5,500 [Ramsay]

Anr copy. Parts 1-5 (of 6). Folio, contemp half mor with blindstamps on covers. With 360 hand-colored plates. All plates stamped; some plates trimmed. S Feb 24 (504) £2,300 [Burgess]

Anr copy. 6 parts in 2 vols. Folio, contemp calf; corners rubbed. With 435 hand-colored plates on 432 leaves. This copy contains the Catalogue of certain plants, the General Observations & the general indexes & indexes to fascicles 1-3 & 5-6. Braybrooke—de Belder copy. S Apr 27 (86) £8,000 [Westhoff]

Anr copy. Contemp russia; rebacked, worn. With 432 hand-colored plates. Some plates trimmed to plate-mark; small hole in Plate 334 of Vol II; without the 6 fascicle indexes; Curtis's Catalogue of plants in the environs of Settle and general Observations on Grasses bound at end. S June 25 (150) £6,500 [Hail]

Anr copy. Vol II only. Contemp calf. With c.177 hand-colored plates only. Lacking tp; some discoloration. Sold w.a.f. S July 28 (1063) £1,900

Anr Ed. L: Bohn, 1835. 5 vols. Folio, contemp half mor by MacKenzie; foot of spine of Vol V missing. With 659 hand-colored plates on 647 leaves. de Belder copy. S Apr 27 (87) £10,500 [Israel]

— Lectures on Botany. L, 1805. 3 vols in 2. 8vo, half calf; def. With port & 119 hand-colored plates. pn Mar 5 (81C) £480 [Levine]

Curtis, Winifred. See: Stones & Curtis

Curtius (Quintus Curtius Rufus)

— De la vie et des actions d'Alexandre le Grand. Lyon: Pierre Thened, 1705. 2 vols. Contemp calf; worn, 1 spine head chipped. With engraved title, folding map & 1 folding plate. cb Oct 23 (187) $80

Curwen Press—London

— The Curwen Press Miscellany. L, 1931. One of 275. S May 6 (77) £160 [Mills]

Curzon, George Nathaniel

— Tales of Travel. L, 1923. sg Apr 23 (42) $50

Curzon, Robert

— Visits to Monasteries in the Levant. L, 1865. 5th Ed. 8vo, calf gilt; worn. sg Nov 20 (66) $80

Cushing, Frank Hamilton, 1857-1900

— My Adventures in Zuni. Santa Fe: Peripatetic Press, [1941]. One of 400. In d/j. sg Sept 18 (72) $225

Cushing, Harvey, 1869-1939

— A Bio-Bibliography of Andreas Vesalius. NY, 1943. Ltd Ed. 4to, half mor. sg May 14 (588) $200

— Studies in Intracranial Physiology & Surgery. L, 1926. 1st Ed. S May 28 (656) £100; wa Mar 5 (287) $160

Cushing, Luther S.

— Rules of Proceeding and Debate in Deliberative Assemblies. Bost., 1845. 12mo, orig sheep; rubbed, joints starting. P May 13 (8) $600

Cussans, John Edwin, 1837-89

— History of Hertfordshire. L, 1870-81. 3 vols. Folio, later half mor gilt; rubbed. Ck May 15 (132) £220

Anr copy. Half mor gilt by Riviere; rubbed. With 24 plates only, some colored. Lacking map. S May 29 (994) £140

Custer, Elizabeth Bacon

— Tenting on the Plains.... NY: Charles L. Webster, 1887. Orig half cloth. Inscr to Kern Dodge. cb Jan 8 (37) $160

Custos, Dominic

— Fuggerorum et fuggerarum, quae in familia natae.... Augsburg, 1618. Folio, vellum bds; new endpapers. With engraved title, plate & 127 ports. Some margins repaired; some light staining. S May 21 (100) £700 [Marlborough]

Cutler, Nathaniel —& Halley, Edmund

— Atlas Maritimus & Commercialis: or, a General View of the World. L, 1728. 2 parts in 1 vol. Folio, old calf; upper cover torn & def. With 54 maritime charts & 5 charts mtd in tex. First chart with tear at fold; 1 chart of South America slightly def; lacking small area of title; small area chewed away on both plates of hemispheres. C Oct 15 (131) £1,900 [Burden]

Cuvier, Frederic Georges, 1773-1838. See: Geoffroy Saint-Hilaire & Cuvier

Cuvier, Georges L. C., Baron, 1769-1832
See also: Lacepede & Cuvier

— The Animal Kingdom. L, 1834-37. Trans by Henry MacMurtrie. 8 vols. Half calf. bba Apr 23 (145) £260 [Greyfriars]

Anr Ed. L, 1834. 4 vols. contemp half calf; rubbed. Ck Sept 5 (159) £170

Anr Ed. L & Edin., 1839. 4to, contemp half mor; rubbed, covers detaching. cb Nov 6 (71) $140

Cuvillies, Francois de

— Morceaux de caprice a divers usages. Munich & Paris, [n.d.]. 26 parts only (A-L, N-V, 22-28) in 1 vol. Folio, mor gilt by Chambolle-Duru. With 150 plates (whole work has 205). Sold w.a.f. C Dec 3 (108) £7,500 [Sourget]

Cyclopaedia...

— Cyclopaedia of Architectural Illustration. Bost., [n.d.]. 5 vols in 10. Folio, half mor gilt; rubbed, 1 spine strengthened with tape. Some tears. pnNY Oct 11 (11) $375

Cynicus. See: Anderson, Martin

Cyril of Alexandria, Saint

— Opera. Cologne: Melchioris Nouesiani, 1546. 2 vols. Folio, contemp vellum. Some browning & old waterstains. T Sept 18 (341) $75

D

D., C.

— New England's Faction Discovered; Or, a Brief and True Account of their Persecution of the Church of England.... L, 1690. 4to, wraps. S June 25 (407) £1,300

D., C. A. See: Tarpon...

D., H. See: Doolittle, Hilda

Dacier, Emile —& Others

— Jean de Jullienne et les graveurs de Watteau au XVIIIe siecle. Paris, 1929-21-22. 4 vols, including portfolio of plates. Folio, orig wraps. Some browning & waterstains. HN May 20 (647) DM820

Dada...

— Dada Austellung Dada-Vorfruehling. [Cologne, 1920]. Text by Max Ernst & J. T. Baargeld. 4to, unbound as issued. S June 29 (7) £700 [Arginthan]

— Dada Souleve Tout. Paris, 1921. 2 pp, 4to, unbound as issued. S June 29 (9) £900 [Linsson]

Anr copy. Small portions torn away at 3 corners. S June 29 (10) £200 [Arginthan]

Dagley, Richard, d.1841

— Takings, or the Life of a Collegian.... L, 1821. 8vo, half calf gilt by Zaehnsdorf. With 26 hand-colored plates. pn July 23 (170) £170 [Thorp]

Dahl, Roald

— The Gremlins.... NY, 1943. Illus by Walt Disney Studios. 4to, orig half cloth, in torn d/j. S June 18 (434) £240 [Peters]

Anr Ed. L: Collins, [1944]. 4to, orig half cloth, in torn d/j. bba Oct 30 (248) £220 [Clute]

Anr copy. Orig half cloth; upper joint split. bba Aug 20 (152) £75 [Elliott]

Anr copy. Orig half cloth; chipped. T Feb 18 (86) £50

Dahlberg, Erik Johnsson, Count, 1625-1703

— Suecia antiqua et hodierna. Stockholm, 1690-1714. 3 vols in 1. Folio, contemp calf; rebacked preserving orig spine. With 3 engraved titles, 4 ports & 211 plates only. Some tears affecting surface. Sold w.a.f. C May 13 (65) £750 [Bifolco]

Anr Ed. [Stockholm, 1693-1713]. 3 vols in 1. Oblong folio, 18th-cent calf gilt; rubbed, upper joint weak. With 3 engraved titles & 340 plates. Several plates mtd in or with margins extended. Sold w.a.f. S Oct 23 (249) £1,300 [Marshall]

Dainty...

— Dainty Dishes for Indian Tables. Calcutta, 1881. 8vo, cloth; extremities frayed. sg Jan 15 (15) $225

Dale, Edward Everett

— The Range Cattle Industry. Norman: U of Oklahoma Press, 1930. Some wear to cloth bdg; worn, slight tearing at tops & edges of spine. With 2 frontis maps. O Oct 21 (50) $120

Dale, Harrison Clifford
— The Ashley-Smith Explorations, and the Discovery of a Central Route to the Pacific. Glendale: Arthur H. Clark, 1941. cb Oct 9 (55) $75

Dalgarno, George
— Works. Edin.: Maitland Club, 1834. One of 12 L.p. copies. 4to, half mor; rubbed. O Feb 24 (53) $80

Dali, Salvador
— La Conquete de l'irrationnel. Paris, [1935]. Orig wraps; loose. Inscr to Rene Magritte. S July 2 (999) £600 [Quaritch]

Dalla Torre, Karl Wilhelm von. See: Hartinger & Dalla Torre

Dalliere, Alexis
— Les Plantes ornementales a feuillage panache et colore. Gand, 1873-74. Vol I only. Oblong 4to, cloth; worn. With 5 plain & 25 color litho plates. sg Dec 18 (154) $300

Dallington, Sir Robert, 1561-1637
— Aphorismes Civill and Militarie: Amplified with Authorities.... L, 1613. 2 parts in 1 vol. Folio, 19th-cent half mor; rubbed. Title soiled & chipped. cb Oct 13 (52) $65

Dalrymple, Alexander, 1737-1808
— A Collection of Charts and Memoirs. L, 1771-72. 4to, contemp half calf. With 11 double-page folding charts & coastal profiles, 1 with overslip. With a 7th tract entitled Memoir of a Chart of the Southern Ocean, not called for in contents. Inscr to Mathew Boulton. C Dec 12 (58) £5,200 [Quaritch]

Dalrymple, Sir John, 1726-1810
— Memoirs of Great Britain & Ireland. Edin & L, 1771-73-88. 3 vols. 4to, contemp calf; recently rebacked. T Sept 18 (350) £86

Dalton, John, 1766-1844
— A New System of Chemical Philosophy. Manchester, 1808-27. Part 1 in 2 vols & Vol II, Part 1, in 3 vols. 8vo, modern half calf. Last vol lacking Sig. U. bba May 14 (300) £500 [Phelps]

Anr copy. Parts 1 & 2 of Vol I only. Later half calf. With 8 plates. C Dec 12 (59) £500 [Phelps]

Dalton, Michael, d.1648?
— The Countrey Justice. L: Society of Stationers, 1618. 1st Ed. Folio, contemp vellum; stained & wrinkled, small hole in front cover. Some soiling & staining; G1 with 2 small internal tears; K6 with tear in blank margin; 2E5 with rust hole touching 5 letters; 2K5 with hole & closed tear affecting a few characters; errata leaf laid down with loss. P Sept 24 (271) $950

Dalvimart, Octavien
— The Costume of Turkey. L, 1802. Folio, contemp mor gilt; rubbed. With hand-colored vignette on English title & 61 hand-colored plates. S June 25 (189) £500 [Houle]

Anr Ed. L, 1804. Folio, contemp mor gilt; rubbed. With 60 colored plates. Some margins frayed. S July 29 (935) £550

Anr Ed. L, 1802 [plates watermarked 1817]. Folio, contemp mor gilt; spine frayed. With 60 hand-colored plates. C Apr 8 (157) £750 [Gaston]

Daly, Augustin, 1838-99
— Woffington. A Tribute to the Actress and the Woman. [N.p.], 1888. One of 150. Folio, orig cloth; worn. Inscr to F. Hopkinson Smith. sg Feb 26 (243) $80

Daly, Cesar, 1811-94
— L'Architecture privee au XIXme siecle sous Napoleon III... Paris, 1872. Series I-III (all pbd). 8 vols. Folio, contemp half mor gilt; Series III not uniform. With 368 plates, some ptd in colors & heightened with gold. C July 22 (55) £1,600

— Motifs historiques d'architecture et de sculpture d'ornement.... Paris, 1869-80. 4 vols. Folio, half mor; the 2 series not uniform. ALs inserted. C July 22 (56) £850

Dalyell, Sir John Graham, 1775-1851
— Rare and Remarkable Animals of Scotland.... L, 1847-48. 2 vols. 4to, orig half cloth; worn. With 110 color plates. sg Jan 15 (198) $300

Dalzel, Archibald
— The History of Dahomy, an Inland Kingdom of Africa.... L, 1793. 1st Ed. 4to, modern cloth. Folding map slightly torn. bba Dec 18 (134) £75 [Hay]

Dalziel, George & Edward
— The Brothers Dalziel, a Record of Fifty Years Work 1840-1890. L, 1901. 1st Ed. 4to, orig cloth; rubbed. Presentation copy, inscr by Edward Dalziel. bba Dec 4 (179) £55 [Pyke]

Dame..
— Dame Wiggins of Lee and her Seven Wonderful Cats. NY: Solomon King, [c.1825]. 12mo, wraps. With frontis, vignette title & 16 pp each with illust & accompanying verses; engraved throughout & colored by hand. Restored at inner margins. S Dec 5 (300) £600 [Schiller]

Damer, Eyre
— When the Ku Klux Rode. NY: Neale, 1912. cb Oct 9 (266) $85

Dami, Luigi
— The Italian Garden. NY, [1925]. Folio, orig cloth; worn. With 351 plates. wa Mar 5 (100) $160

Damiano da Odemira
— Libro da imparare giochare a scachi. [Rome, c.1528]. 8vo, contemp vellum. pn Mar 26 (387) £1,300 [De Lucia]

Damianus, Janus
— Ad Leonem X Pont. Max. de expedition in Turcas elegeia. Basel: Froben, 1515. 4to, modern mor; new endpapers. B2v stained; 1 small wormhole in text; some headlines shaved. S July 14 (385) £240

Damier, Paul Eduard
— Wappen-Buch saemmtlicher zur Ehstlaend-ischen Adelsmatrikel gehoeriger Familien.... Reval, 1837. 4to, mid-19th-cent half lea, orig wraps bound in; joints & extremities worn. With frontis, title, dedication, 182 plates & 9-page subscribers' list. Lithographed throughout. sg Dec 4 (83) $110

Damon, Samuel Chenery, 1814-85
— A Journey to Lower Oregon and Upper California.... San Francisco, 1927. One of 250. cb Dec 4 (143) $140

Dampier, William, 1652-1715
— A New Voyage Round the World. L, 1697. 2d Ed. 8vo, contemp calf; inexpertly rebacked, endpapers renewed. With 5 maps. One map with fold-out portion lacking; anr remtd & reinforced along folds. sg Mar 12 (92) $300
— A Voyage to New Holland.... L, 1703. 8vo, later calf gilt; worn. With folding map & 14 plates, including 4 of land-profiles. Vol III of Dampier's Voyages. sg Dec 4 (47) $300

Dampierre, Marc Antoin, Marquis de, 1676-1756
— Recueil de fanfares pour la chasse.... Paris: Le Clerc, [c.1778]. Folio, contemp bdg. Jeanson copy. SM Feb 28 (161) FF48,000

Dana, Richard Henry, Jr., 1815-82
See also: Limited Editions Club
— To Cuba and Back. Bost., 1859. 1st Ed. 12mo, cloth; worn. O Jan (49) $50

Danckwerth, Caspar —&
Mejer, Johannes
— Newe Landesbeschreibung der zweye hertzogthuemer Schleswich und Holstein. [Husum], 1652. Folio, contemp vellum. With 40 double-page or folding plates.

Some browning & spotting; other minor defs. FD Dec 2 (777) DM11,800

Daniel, of Istanbul, Protosyngelos of Sinai
— [A Short Description of the Holy Mountain of Sinai founded by God.] Venice, 1784. 4to, contemp paper bds. Ptd in karamanlidika, or Turkish translaterated into Greek characters. S Oct 23 (332) £700 [Quaritch]

Daniel, William Barker, 1753?-1833
— Rural Sports. L, 1801-2. 3 vols in 4. 4to, half mor gilt; front cover of last vol detached. sg May 21 (47) $130

Anr Ed. L, 1805-13. 4 vols, 4to, contemp mor & later mor-backed cloth. With 70 plates & port. pnE Dec 17 (356) £1,750 [Graham]

Anr Ed. L, [1805]. 3 vols. 4to, mor gilt. Some wear & staining. sg May 21 (48) $1,300

Anr Ed. L, 1812-13. 4 vols, including Supplement. 4to, half mor; spines worn. With 3 additional titles & 68 plates. sg Oct 23 (234) $250

Daniell, Samuel, 1755-1811
— Sketches Representing the Native Tribes.... L, 1820. Oblong 4to, orig half cloth; rubbed. With 48 plates & 1 extra plate loosely inserted. Some stains. bba Aug 28 (299) £120 [Kelly]

Anr copy. Contemp bds. With 46 (of 48) plates. SSA Feb 17 (190) R1,900

Daniell, Thomas, 1749-1840 & William, 1769-1837
— Oriental Scenery. L, 1812-16. 6 parts in 3 vols. Folio, later half mor; worn, broken, lacking 1 spine. With 6 engraved titles & 144 plates. Part 6 lacking plans. bba Dec 18 (135) £340 [Parsons]

Anr copy. 6 vols in 3. 4to, later half mor; worn, top of 1 spine def, some covers detached. With 6 engraved titles & 144 plates. Lacking plans in Part 6; library stamp on tp & 1st engraved titles in each vol; inkstamps on plates. bba Jan 15 (454) £460 [Ranier]

Anr copy. Contemp half mor; worn. Lacking 1 plate (No 18 in Vol III); lacking text leaf for Plate 17; 1 title detached. S Jan 12 (312) £1,100 [Mansoor]

Anr Ed. L, 1816 [but later remainder issue]. 6 vols. 4to, contemp half mor; rubbed. Each vol with 24 uncolored plates; Vol 6 with an additional 8 plans. Together, 152 plates. Some spotting. C Apr 8 (79) £1,300 [Hosains]

Anr copy. 6 vols in 1. 4to, orig cloth; spine faded. Each vol with 24 uncolored plates. Lacking the 8 engraved plans. C Apr 8

(80) £1,300 [Hosains]
- A Picturesque Voyage to India.... L, 1810. Oblong folio, contemp calf. With 50 colored plates. Madeira with stain in margin; plates mtd on guards. C Oct 15 (122) £1,500 [Mackenzie]

Anr copy. Later mor; repaired & restored. On guards throughout; a few plates & leaves at front with 2 minor holes; some marginal worming. C Apr 8 (81) £800 [Mansoor]

Anr copy. Modern half mor gilt. Occasional discoloration. S Oct 23 (482) £2,800 [Mrs. Sneyd]

Daniell, William, 1769-1837 —&
Ayton, Richard, 1786-1823
- A Voyage Round Great Britain.... L, 1814-25. 8 vols in 4. 4to, contemp mor gilt; rebacked, preserving orig backstrips. With uncolored aquatint dedication, large folding map, 1 uncolored plate & 308 hand-colored plates. Former Morgan Library copy. C Apr 8 (17) £16,000 [Marlborough]

Anr copy. Half mor. With 308 hand-colored plates. Without the uncolored plate of Kemaes Head & without the folding map. S Oct 23 (182) £13,000 [Scotish]

Daniell, William, 1769-1837 —&
Caunter, John Hobart, 1794-1851
- Scenes in India. L, 1846. 8vo, mor; front hinge worn. sg Nov 20 (77) $80

Danielson, Richard Ely. See: Derrydale Press

Dante Alighieri, 1265-1321
See also: Ashendene Press; Bremer Press; Limited Editions Club; Nonesuch Press
- Dante con l'espositioni di Christoforo Landino et d'Alessandro Vellutello. Venice: G. B. Sessa, 1596. Folio, old calf; rubbed, hinges split. pnNY June 11 (107) $275

Anr copy. 19th-cent half calf. Some leaves foxed towards end. sg Apr 2 (68) $350
- Opere. Venice: B. Stagnino, 1536. 4to, later 19th-cent sheep; rebacked, orig backstrip laid down. Opening leaves wormed in gutters, slightly affecting text; light dampstaining in upper inner corner. sg Oct 9 (171) $400
- La Vita nova. Paris, 1907. One of 130. Illus by Maurice Denis; trans by Henry Cochin. 4to, mor extra by Marius Michel with large fleur de lys mor onlay. With an orig aquarelle. SM Oct 20 (607) FF115,000

Divina Commedia in Italian
- 1481, 30 Aug. - Florence: Nicolaus Laurentii Alamanus. Folio, old vellum bds. Sold w.a.f. 330 (of 373) leaves only. Goff D-29. sg Mar 26 (94) $750

- 1493, 29 Nov. - Venice: Matteo Capcasa. Folio, modern half mor gilt by Michel. Tiny hole in border of 2a1; short tear in lower margin of k6 slightly affecting text; O5 re-margined; some dampstaining & soiling at beginning & end. 310 (of 311) leaves; lacking final leaf with register. Goff D-34. S May 21 (7) £1,200 [Koeppe]
- 1502. - Le Terze Rime. Venice: Aldus Issue not stated. 8vo, mor by Bozerian. FD Dec 2 (48) DM6,000

Variant Issue with a different title & inverted initial V instead of an A at the beginning of Aedib. in the colophon. Contemp mor gilt; wormed, spine def. Blank 12 & final leaf supplied from a shorter copy. S Mar 10 (1049) £600 [King]
- 1552. - Lyons: Guglielmo Rovillio. 16mo, later calf gilt; worn. Last leaf holed, affecting text. bba Nov 13 (1) £55 [Kunkler]
- 1808. - L. 3 vols. 16mo, mor gilt. sg Sept 11 (87) $60
- 1861. - L'Inferno. Paris: Hachette Illus by Gustave Dore. Folio, half mor gilt; rubbed, soiled. Title & first few leaves waterstained. T Sept 28 (183) £59
- 1911. - Divina Commedia. Facsimile della Edizione Principe de Foligno. Turin One of 200. 4to, vellum. cb Feb 19 (74) $160

Divina Commedia in Italian & German
- 1921. - Vienna, etc. One of 1,100. Illus by F. von Bayros. 3 vols. 4to, contemp half calf gilt. HK Nov 4 (2924a) DM950

Divina Commedia in Italian
- 1925. - [Berlin] One of 200. Illus by Botticelli. 3 vols. Folio, orig bds; spine worn, 1 spine def. HN Nov 26 (1617) DM520

English Versions
- 1866. - L. Trans by Henry Francis Cary; illus by Gustave Dore. 4to, mor gilt; worn & soiled. wa Feb 19 (379) $60
- 1906. - Bost. & NY One of 650 L.p. copies. Trans by Henry Wadsworth Longfellow; illus by Flaxman. 6 vols. Mor gilt; 1 hinge cracked. With frontises in 2 states, colored & uncolored. cb Feb 19 (73) $850
- 1931. - The Inferno. NY One of 1,200. Illus by William Blake. Folio, calf. With 7 plates. cb Sept 11 (80) $140
- 1969. - NY Trans by Thomas G. Bergin; illus by Leonard Baskin. 3 vols. Folio, half cloth. sg June 4 (27) $60

French Versions
- 1959-63. - La Divine Comedie. ParisLtd Ed. Illus by Salvador Dali. 6 vols. Folio, loose as issued in wraps & board folders. With

100 colored plates. S June 17 (97) £460 [Festeman]

Dapper, Olfert, d.1690
— Asia.... Nuremberg, 1681. 2 parts in 1 vol. Folio, contemp vellum; warped. Some tears repaired; some plates with marginal portions torn away. Sold w.a.f. S Nov 18 (1212) £190 [Clarke]
— Description de l'Afrique. Amst., 1686. 1st Ed in French. Folio, contemp calf; joints split, head of spine worn. With engraved title, folding map & 39 (of 42) double-page maps & plates. Lacking also 5 text leaves; 1 leaf with tear; 1 plate torn at foot. Sold w.a.f. C Dec 12 (229) £330 [Strasser]

Anr copy. Contemp calf; rubbed. With engraved title, folding map of Africa, 13 double-page maps & plans & 29 plates. S Oct 23 (144) £1,000 [Strasser]

— Description exacte des isles de l'archipel.... Amst., 1703. Folio, contemp calf gilt. With engraved title, 5 plates of medallions & 25 full-page & double-page plates. Sold w.a.f. pn Mar 5 (305) £650 [Nicholson]

Anr copy. Contemp calf. With 5 plates of medals & 29 maps & plates. Lacking the engraved title. S Apr 24 (214) £950 [Tsigaras]

— Historische beschrijving der stadt Amsterdam. Amst., 1663. Folio, half mor; hinges broken. With title, 65 double-page plates, folding prospectus & 3 double-page plans. T Sept 18 (42) £620

— Naukeurige beschryving van gantsch Syrie.... Amst., 1677-78. Folio, contemp calf; rebacked preserving orig spine. With folding map after Visscher, 6 folding maps after van Adrichom, 18 folding plates, plan of Jerusalem after Villalpando & panorama after Hollar. Some browning. Large, thick paper copy. S Oct 23 (374) £1,300 [McKenzie]

Anr copy. Contemp blindstamped vellum; covers bowed, hinges starting at either end. With engraved title & 38 plates & maps. Several plates cropped at fore-edges, some with repairs. sg Apr 30 (153) $1,200

— Naukeurige beschryving der Eilanden, in de Archipel der Middelantische Zee.... Amst., 1688. Folio, old calf; def. Sold w.a.f. pn June 18 (217) £780

— Naukeurige, beschryving van Morea.... Amst., 1688. Folio, contemp calf; spines def. With engraved title & 16 plates. A few neatlines just shaved; inner marginal worming from time to time; faint waterstains. S Apr 24 (215) £900 [Tsigaras]

— Umbstaendliche und eigentliche Beschreibung von Asia. Nuremberg, 1681. 2 parts in 1 vol. Folio, contemp vellum bds. With half-title, frontis & 31 illusts & maps on 24 sheets. Some discoloration. S Oct 23 (483) £1,150 [Maggs]

Darbee, Harry
— Catskill Flytier. My Life, Times and Technique. Phila., [1977]. One of 125. 4to, lea. With a salmon fly, "Little Inky Boy," tipped to limitation leaf. sg Oct 23 (235) $225

Darby, William, 1775-1854
— The Emigrant's Guide to the Western and South-Western States and Territories. NY, 1818. 8vo, modern half mor; worn. With 3 maps, 1 colored in outline. Several tears along folds, each with perforated library stamp. sg Mar 12 (93) $100
— A Tour from the City of New-York, to Detroit, in the Michigan Territory.... NY, 1819. 1st Ed. 8vo, modern cloth. With 3 folding maps, 2 hand-colored in outline. Small hole in title, not affecting text; last few leaves dampstained. sg Mar 12 (94) $150

Darcel, Alfred
— L'Art architectural en France.... Paris, 1866. Vol II only. 4to, loose in ptd portfolios as issued. Sold w.a.f. O Jan 6 (50) $100
— Les Tapisseries decoratives du garde-meuble. Paris: J. Baudry, [c.1880]. Ed by Edouard Guichard. 1 vol in 2. Folio, half mor; worn. S Nov 10 (71) £70 [Heneage]

D'Arces, Jean. See: Darcio, Giovanni

Darcio, Giovanni, d.1543
— Venusini canes, recens in lucem aediti. Paris: Simon de Colines, 1543. 8vo, 19th-cent mor gilt. Jeanson 1179. SM Feb 28 (163) FF12,000

Anr copy. Mor janseniste by Mouchon. Jeanson 1939. SM Feb 28 (164) FF4,000

Darlow, Thomas Herbert —&
Moule, Horace Frederick
— Historical Catalogue of the Printed Editions of the Holy Scripture.... L, 1903-11. One of 50 for presentation. 2 vols in 4. sg May 14 (262) $850

Darrah, Henry Zouch
— Sport in the Highlands of Kashmir. L, 1898. 8vo, cloth; hinge cracked. With 2 folding maps in rear cover pocket. Library markings. cb Nov 6 (72) $160

Anr copy. Orig cloth; rubbed. Lacking map in rear pocket. T Oct 16 (301) £46

Dart, John, d.1730
— The History and Antiquities of the Cathedral Church of Canterbury. L, 1726. Folio, contemp calf; worn, upper joint broken. Marginal tear to R1. L Dec 11 (106) £60

Anr copy. Contemp calf; rebacked, corner repaired. With 41 plates. pn Jan 22 (92) £80 [Clegg]

Dart, Robert Paul. See: Hoyt Collection, Charles B.

Darton, F. J. Harvey. See: Sawyer & Darton

Darton, William, 1747-1819
— New Miniature Atlas. L, 1820. 12mo, modern half mor gilt. With engraved title & 56 hand-colored maps. pn May 21 (379) £240 [Way]

Darwin, Bernard
— The Golf Courses of the British Isles. L, 1910. pnC Jan 23 (72) £260; pnC Jan 23 (73) £420
— A Golfer's Gallery by Old Master. L: Country Life, [1927]. One of 500. Folio, orig cloth. pnC July 16 (45) £260
  Anr copy. Lacking 2 plates. pnC July 16 (46) £130; pnC July 16 (47) £240

Darwin, Charles, 1809-82
— The Descent of Man and Selection in Relation to Sex. L, 1871. 1st Ed, 1st Issue. 2 vols. 8vo, orig cloth; rubbed, broken. bba Sept 25 (203) £280 [19th-cent Shop]
  2d Issue. Orig cloth; rubbed, holes in rear cover of Vol I. Some spotting. T Apr 16 (167) £80
  1st American Ed. NY, 1871. 2 vols. 8vo, orig cloth; spine ends frayed. sg Jan 15 (200) $80
— The Different Forms of Flowers on Plants of the Same Species. L, 1877. 1st Ed. 8vo, orig cloth; rubbed. Pencilled underlining & marginalia. bba Sept 25 (208) £130 [Bickersteth]; pnNY Sept 13 (218) $225
— The Effects of Cross and Self Fertilisation in the Vegetable Kingdom. L, 1876. 1st Ed. 8vo, orig cloth; rubbed. Pencilled underlining & marginalia. bba Sept 25 (207) £130 [Bickersteth]
  Anr copy. Orig cloth; slight wear. pnNY Sept 13 (215) $170
— The Expression of the Emotions in Man and Animals. L, 1872. 1st Ed. 8vo, orig cloth. Haverschmidt copy. B Feb 24 (476) HF420; pnE Dec 17 (363) £100 [Bickerstaff]
  Anr copy. Orig cloth; worn. With 7 plates. pnNY Sept 13 (217) $350
  1st American Ed. NY: D. Appleton, 1873 [1872]. 8vo, orig cloth; spine ends chipped. sg Jan 15 (201) $80
  Anr Ed. NY, 1873. 8vo, orig cloth; rubbed, covers spotted. With 7 heliotype plates. K June 7 (97) $90
— The Formation of Vegetable Mould through the Action of Worms. L, 1881. 1st Ed. 8vo, orig cloth. pnNY Sept 13 (216) $130
— Journal of Researches into the Geology and Natural History of the Various Countries.... L: J. Murray, 1852. New Ed. 8vo, orig cloth; spine worn. Inscr to W. B. Tegetmeier. S Dec 18 (331) £700 [Korn]
— On the Origin of Species.... L, 1859. 1st Ed. 8vo, orig cloth; worn & def. HN May 20 (979) DM5,400
  Anr copy. Orig cloth; extremities worn, upper hinge tender. B1 detached, corner of F6 broken away without loss. P Dec 15 (188) $2,500; pnE Dec 17 (361) £4,000 [Phelps]
  Anr copy. Orig cloth; recased. Searles Wood's copy. S Nov 27 (256) £4,000 [Quaritch]
  Anr copy. Orig cloth; upper cover stained. With ad leaves at end & with tipped-in transcript of the passage on p 184 suppressed in later Eds. Inscr to William Bernhard Tegetmeier, with ALs about the work. S Dec 18 (333) £7,800 [Kohler]
  3d Issue. Orig cloth, variant b; inner hinges broken. Some pencil annotations in margins. S May 21 (193) £3,200 [Marshall]
  Anr copy. Orig cloth, variant a; recased, soiled. Some leaves torn; a few leaves loose. S June 25 (96) £1,500 [Moore]
  3d Issue, with ads dated June 1859. Orig cloth; spine worn at head & foot, inner hinges weak. S Oct 23 (669) £3,000 [Quaritch]
  2d Ed. L, 1860. 2d Issue. 8vo, orig cloth; upper hinge broken. With 32 pp of ads at end. S Nov 10 (474) £280 [Louas]
  1st American Ed. NY, 1860. 8vo, orig cloth; backstrip rubbed, lower joint torn & cracked. Text slightly rippled. ha Sept 19 (253) $85
— On the Various Contrivances by which British and Foreign Orchids are Fertilised by Insects. L, 1862. 1st Ed. 12mo, orig cloth; upper joint cracked, extremities rubbed. Hunt copy. CNY Nov 21 (97) $220
— The Variation of Animals and Plants under Domestication.... L, 1868. 1st Ed, 1st Issue. 2 vols. 8vo, orig cloth; rubbed. Portions cut from 2 ad leaves at end of Vol II. bba June 18 (141) £140 [Fenelon]; pnNY Sept 13 (214) $250
— La Vie et la correspondance.... Paris, 1888. 2 vols. 8vo, orig cloth; rubbed. bba Oct 30 (381) £40 [Kohler]
— The Zoology of the Voyage of H.M.S. Beagle. L, 1840-43. 5 orig parts in 18 (of 19; lacking the 4th section of Part 1 "Fossil Mammalia"). 4to, orig cloth-backed ptd wraps. C Oct 15 (137) £8,500 [Lenon]

Darwin, Charles, 1809-82 —& Others
— Narrative of the Surveying Voyages of his Majesty's Ships Adventure and Beagle.... L, 1839. 1st Ed. 4 vols. 8vo, orig cloth. Lacking the 9 loose folding charts from the pockets provided. C Oct 15 (136) £2,000 [Maggs]

Anr copy. 4 vols, including Appendix to Vol II. 8vo, half mor gilt by Morrell. With 47 plates & charts & 9 folding maps. Maps refolded & 1 with short tear at old fold. CNY Nov 21 (98) $3,500

Anr copy. Old calf gilt. Maps refolded. CNY Dec 19 (55) $3,000

Anr copy. Orig cloth, spines chipped or torn & repaired. Library markings. P Sept 24 (141) $2,000

Anr copy. With 47 plates & 9 folding maps & charts. The 2 maps to Vol III in facsimile; some foxing. S June 25 (497) £4,000 [Becker]

Darwin, Erasmus, 1731-1802
— The Botanic Garden. L, 1791. 2 vols in 1. 4to, contemp half calf. With 19 plates. pn Jan 22 (228) £70 [Greyfriars]

1st Ed of Part 1; 3d Ed of Part 3. 2 vols. 4to, contemp half calf; rubbed. With 20 plates. Without errata leaf at end of Vol I. S Oct 6 (767) £60 [Bookroom]

Dashwood, Richard Lewes
— Chiploquorgan; or, Life by the Camp Fire.... Dublin, 1871. 8vo, half mor; rubbed. O Oct 21 (51) $70

Daudet, Alphonse, 1840-97
— Oeuvres. Paris, 1899-1901. Edition Definitive. 18 vols. 8vo, contemp half mor; rubbed. bba Mar 12 (123) £80 [Nolan]

— Sapho. Paris: Collection Charpentier Maison Quantin, 1888. One of 50 L.p. copies on Japon with plates in 2 states. 8vo, mor gilt by Bretault, orig wraps bound in. Some plates spotted. S Oct 6 (691) £60 [Luia]

— Works. Bost., 1898-1900. Champrosay Ed, one of 100. 24 vols. 8vo, half mor gilt by Stikeman; bookplates removed. sg Sept 11 (88) $650

Davenant, Charles, 1656-1714
— A Discourse upon Grants and Resumptions. L, 1700. 1st Ed. 8vo, sheep; rubbed, joints cracked, spine chipped at tail. P Sept 24 (273) $275

Davenant, Sir William, 1606-68
— Works. L, 1673. 1st Collected Ed. Folio, lev gilt by Roger de Coverley. sg Dec 4 (48) $800

Davenport, Cyril
See also: Caxton Club
— English Embroidered Bookbindings. L, 1899. 4to, orig cloth; rubbed. T Apr 16 (330) £88
— English Heraldic Book-Stamps. L, 1909. 4to, orig cloth. sg May 14 (98) $110
— Royal English Bookbindings. L, 1896. 8vo, orig cloth. With 8 colored plates. bba Mar 12 (335) £55 [Wood]

Anr copy. Library cloth. Library stamp on verso of title. bba July 16 (195) £40 [Hannan]

Anr copy. Orig cloth; worn, covers bowed, spine-tips stained & frayed. With 8 colored plates. O June 16 (68) $70

Davidov, V. P.
— Atlas k putevym zapiskam Davidova.... Paris & St. Petersburg, 1840. Part 1 only. Folio, contemp half lea. With 13 hand-colored lithos heightened with gum arabic (1 double-page with short split in fold) & 10 plans, 1 with details hand-colored. General title loosely inserted. Foxed. S June 25 (343) £1,800 [Hantzis]

Davidson, Donald
— Lee in the Mountains. NY, 1949. In torn d/j. Inscr. sg Dec 11 (17) $60

Davidson, James, 1793-1864
— Bibliotheca Devoniensis: A Catalogue of the Printed Books Relating to the County of Devon. Exeter, 1852. 4to, orig cloth; spine browned. L July 2 (16) £80

Davidson, John
— In a Music-Hall and Other Poems. L, 1891. 8vo, orig cloth. Tipped in is ALs to Edmund Gosse, sending the book & requesting an opinion of its merits. sg Sept 11 (89) $225

Davidson, Rodney
— A Book Collector's Notes. Melbourne, 1970. One of 250. Cloth flecked. kh Mar 16 (149) A$60

Davies, Arthur B.
[-] Arthur B. Davies: Essays on the Man and his Art. Wash.: Phillips Memorial Gallery, [1924]. 4to, half vellum. cba Mar 5 (52) $65

One of 50 with orig drawing. Folio, lev gilt. sg Dec 4 (49) $1,100

Davies, Edwin. See: Fore-Edge Paintings

Davies, G. Christopher, 1849-1922
— On Dutch Waterways: The Cruise of the S.S. Atalanta.... L: Jarrold & Sons, [1887]. 4to, orig cloth; worn, front hinge cracked. sg Nov 13 (41) $80

Davies, Hugh William
— Bernhard von Breydenbach and his Journey to the Holy Land.... L, 1911. One of 200. 4to, cloth. S Nov 10 (8) £110 [Traylen]
Anr copy. Orig half calf; joints rubbed. sg May 14 (427) $110
— Catalogue of Early German Books in the Library of C. Fairfax Murray. L, 1962. 2 vols. 4to, orig cloth. bba Oct 16 (372) £130 [Frew Mackenzie]

Davies, John, 1569-1626
— Historical Relations: or, a Discovery of...Why Ireland was Never entirely Subdued.... Dublin, 1664. 8vo, contemp calf; rubbed. Dedication leaf misbound; some leaves marginally def, affecting sidenotes. bba Apr 9 (304) £70 [Emerald Isle]

Davis, Charles Henry, 1807-77
— Narrative of the North Polar Expedition. Wash., 1876. 4to, orig cloth; worn & rubbed, lacking front free endpaper. Blindstamp to title. cb June 4 (95) $850
Anr copy. Contemp mor; worn. With 34 plates & 6 maps. Some foxing. wa Nov 6 (118) $60
— Report on Interoceanic Canals and Railroads between the Atlantic and Pacific Oceans. Wash., 1867. 8vo, orig cloth; worn. With 14 maps & plans. Rear endpapers stained. wa Nov 6 (224) $120

Davis, Edmund Walstein
— Salmon-Fishing on the Grand Cascapedia. [NY], 1904. One of 100. 8vo, half vellum. sg Oct 23 (237) $550
— Woodcock Shooting. Pvtly ptd by the De Vinne Press, 1908. One of 100 on japan vellum. 4to, half vellum. With 39 plates. sg Oct 23 (238) $1,100

Davis, Jefferson, 1808-89
— The Rise and Fall of the Confederate Government. NY, 1881. 1st Ed. 2 vols. 8vo, cloth; worn. With 19 plates & 14 maps. O Sept 23 (43) $95
Anr copy. Contemp sheep; worn, 2 joints split. Some maps poorly folded & soiled. wa Feb 19 (38) $65

Davis, Sonia H. See: Lovecraft, Howard Phillips

Davis, Winfield J. See: Illustrated...

Davy, Sir Humphry, 1778-1829
— Elements of Chemical Philosophy. L, 1812. Vol I, Part I (all pbd). 8vo, contemp calf. With 12 plates. H6-7 detached. C Dec 12 (62) £420 [Phelps]
Anr copy. Syn; browned & dampstained. sg Jan 15 (306) $80
— Researches, Chemical and Philosophical, chiefly concerning Nitrous Oxide. L, 1800. 1st Ed. 8vo, contemp half russia. C Dec 12 (61) £2,300 [Georges]
— Six Discourses Delivered before the Royal Society.... L, 1827. 4to, old wraps; spotted & frayed, backstrip def. S Feb 24 (560) £75 [Shindler]
Anr copy. Contemp half mor; soiled & worn. wa Nov 6 (162) $230

Davy, John, 1790-1868
— An Account of the Interior of Ceylon. L, 1821. 4to, modern half calf. Map repaired along folds; some worming, occasionally affecting text & plate margins. bba Oct 30 (298) £100 [Shapero]

Dawdy, Doris Ostrander
— Artists of the American West. Chicago: Swallow Press, [1980]-81-85. 2d Ptg of Vol II. 3 vols. cb Oct 9 (9) $55

Dawson, George, 1813-83
— Pleasures of Angling with Rod and Reel for Trout and Salmon. NY, 1876. 1st Ed. 8vo, cloth. First few pp dampstained. sg Oct 23 (242) $130

Dawson, Henry B., 1821-89
— Battles of the United States, by Sea and Land.... NY, [1858]. 2 vols. 4to, later half mor; joints rubbed & starting. With 41 plates. cb Dec 18 (52) $50
Anr copy. Orig half mor; worn. O Mar 24 (50) $70

Dawson, Robert
— The Present State of Australia. L, 1831. 2d Ed. 8vo, contemp half calf; rubbed. Ck Feb 27 (33) £130

Dawson, Simon James, 1820-1902
— Report on the Exploration of the Country between Lake Superior and the Red River Settlement. Toronto, 1859. 4to, half mor; broken. With 3 folding maps. bba Dec 18 (259) £240 [Burgess Browning]

Dawson, Thomas Rayner, 1889-1951
— Retrograde Analysis. Leeds, 1915. Half mor gilt by Zaehnsdorf. pn Mar 26 (287) £130 [Poole]

Dawson, William Leon
— The Birds of California. San Diego, 1923. One of 100, sgd. 4 vols. 4to, syn. cb Mar 19 (72) $140
Anr copy. Pictorially embossed syn; rubbed. cb Apr 2 (75) $325
Anr copy. Cloth; worn. O Mar 24 (51) $90
Student's Ed. 3 vols. 4to, cloth; rubbed. cb Nov 6 (74) $100

Day, Angel
— The English Secretorie, or Methode of Writing.... L, 1635. 8vo, contemp sheep; worn. Some dampstaining; worming affecting some text. bba Aug 28 (169) £60 [Elliot]

Day, Francis, 1829-89
— British and Irish Salmonidae. L & Edin., 1887. 8vo, orig cloth. pnE Dec 17 (290) £60 [Maggs]

Day Lewis, Cecil. See: Lewis, Cecil Day

Days...
— Days of the Dandies. L: Grolier Society, [after 1900]. One of 1,000. 15 vols. 8vo, half mor gilt. cb Dec 4 (100) $225

De Becker, Joseph Ernest, 1863-1929
— The Nightless City, or, the History of the Yoshiwara Yukwaku. Yokohama: Max Nossler, [c.1905]. cb Mar 5 (224) $150

De Bode, Clement Augustus, Baron
— Travels in Luristan and Arabistan. L, 1845. 1st Ed. 2 vols. 8vo, orig cloth; spine frayed. pn Mar 3 (298) £190 [Morrell]

De Bry, Johann Theodor
— Florilegium novum, hoc est variorum maximeque rariorum florum.... See: Bry, Johann Theodor de

De Bure, Guillaume Francois, 1731-82
— [Sale catalogue] Catalogue des livres de la bibliotheque de feu M. de Duc de La Valliere. Paris, 1783. 3 vols. 8vo, half calf. FD June 11 (387) DM1,350
— Supplement a la bibliographie instructive...cabinet de feu M. Louis Jean Gaignat. Paris, 1769. 2 vols. 8vo, contemp calf gilt; rebacked, rubbed. Priced throughout in a contemporary hand. cb Feb 5 (95) $80

De Camp, L. Sprague
— Demons and Dinosaurs. Sauk City: Arkham House, 1970. In d/j. cb Sept 28 (379) $75
  Anr copy. In stained d/j. Inscr to Lois Newman. cb Sept 28 (380) $55
— The Wheels of If. Chicago, 1948. Review copy. In soiled d/j. cb Sept 28 (400) $65

De Camp, L. Sprague —& Miller, P. Schuyler
— Genus Homo. Reading: Fantasy Press, 1950. One of 500. In d/j. Inscr by Miller & sgd by De Camp on inserted nebula leaf. cb Sept 28 (381) $110

De Camp, L. Sprague —& Pratt, Fletcher
— The Incomplete Enchanter. NY: Holt, [1941]. In creased d/j. cb Sept 28 (385) $90
— Walls of Serpents. Huntington Woods, Michigan: Phantasia Press, 1978. One of 200. In d/j. cb Sept 28 (399) $60

De Chair, Somerset. See: Golden Cockerel Press

De Cloet, ——
— Voyage pittoresque dans le Royaume des Pays Bas. Brussels, 1825. 2 vols in 3. Oblong 4to, half sheep; extremities rubbed. With folding colored map & 201 plates only. Sold w.a.f. P Sept 24 (143) $800

De Gouy, Louis Pullig. See: Derrydale Press

De Graff, Simon
— The Modern Geometrical Stair-Builder's Guide.... NY, 1845. 8vo, orig cloth; spine worn. With 22 plates. K Dec 13 (65) $110

De Grey, Thomas
— The Compleat Horse-Man, and Expert Ferrier. L, 1651. 2d Ed. 4to, contemp calf; rubbed. Some stains & foxing. O May 12 (52) $400

De Kock, Charles Paul, 1794-1850. See: Kock, Charles Paul de

De la Escosura, Patricio. See: Escosura, Patricio de la

De la Mare, Walter, 1873-1956
— Desert Islands and Robinson Crusoe. L, 1930. One of 650. cb June 18 (78) $55

De La Pilorgerie, Jules
— Histoire de Botany-Bay, etat present des colonies penales de l'Angleterre.... Paris, 1836. 8vo, contemp half mor; rubbed. T July 16 (12) $125

De Larrey, Isaac. See: Larrey, Isaac de

De Laune, Thomas, d.1685
— Angliae Metropolis, or, the Present State of London. L, 1690. 8vo, 19th-cent mor gilt. With frontis & 13 plates (with an additional folding plate of the Royal Exchange). Ck Sept 26 (40) £200

De l'Isle, Jacques Nicolas —& Others
— Russischer Atlas, welcher in einer General Charte und Neunzehn Special Charten das gesamte Russische Reich.... St. Petersburg, 1745. Folio, orig half lea; worn & scuffed. Institutional stamp & some minor soiling on tp; margin of 1 map soiled. sg Dec 4 (110) $3,000

De Moivre, Abraham, 1667-1754
— The Doctrine of Chances. L, 1718. 1st Ed. 4to, contemp calf; worn & loose. Stamps on tp. bba June 18 (178) £230 [Fenelon]

De Mole, F. E.
— Wild Flowers of South Australia. L, 1861. Folio, mor gilt; rubbed & loose. With hand-colored litho title & 20 hand-colored plates. Inscr. Dedication copy, with ALs. pn Mar 5 (320) £1,050 [Quaritch]

De Morgan, August
— Arithmetical Books from the Invention of Printing to the Present Time.... L, 1847. 8vo, cloth; spine worn, joints torn. sg Oct 2 (118) $70

De Muncq, Alexander, 1655-1719. See: Muncq, Alexander de

De Puy, Henry Farr, 1859-1924
— A Bibliography of the English Colonial Treaties with the American Indians.... NY, 1917. One of 125. 8vo, half cloth; worn, prelims loose & torn. sg Sept 18 (75) $70

De Quincey, Thomas, 1785-1859
— Confessions of an English Opium-Eater. L, 1822. 1st Ed. 12mo, orig bds. Lacking ad leaf. S Jan 13 (487) £220 [Blackwell]

Anr copy. Orig bds; joints split. S May 6 (423) £620 [Joseph]

— Klosterheim; or, the Masque. By the English Opium-Eater. Edin. & L, 1832. 8vo, orig half cloth. sg Sept 11 (90) $175

— The Logic of Political Economy. Edin. & L, 1844. 1st Ed. 8vo, later half lea; worn, joints cracked. Marginal soiling. P Sept 24 (274) $540

— Works. Bost., 1851-59. 23 vols. 12mo, orig cloth; some corners worn, some spines chipped, Opium Eater separated from bdg with pastedowns still attached to text. ha Dec 19 (177) $120

Anr Ed. Bost., 1854-60. 21 vols. 8vo, half calf; 1 spine chipped at head. sg Feb 12 (115) $500

Anr Ed. Edin., 1862-71. 16 vols. 8vo, half mor gilt. pn Apr 30 (304) £170 [Demetzy]

Anr copy. Calf gilt. sg Feb 12 (116) $550

De Renne Library, Wymberley Jones
— Catalogue of the Wymberley Jones de Renne Georgia Library at Wormsloe. Wormsloe: Pvtly ptd, 1931. One of 300. 3 vols. 4to, orig cloth. sg Oct 2 (149) $475

De Ricci, Seymour —& Wilson, W. J.
— Census of Medieval and Renaissance Manuscripts in the United States and Canada. NY, 1935-40-62. 3 vols. 4to, orig cloth; rubbed, hinges cracked or starting. sg May 14 (292) $350

De Roos, Frederick Fitzgerald, 1804-61
— Personal Narrative of Travels in the United States and Canada.... L, 1827. 1st Ed. 8vo, contemp half calf; worn, backstrip def at top. With folding frontis & 12 plates. Frontis foxed & rebacked with linen. ha May 22 (284) $80

De Rossi, Giovanni. See: Rossi, Giovanni Bernardo de

De Rossi, Giovanni Gherardo. See: Rossi, Giovanni Gherardo de

De Rousiers, Paul
— La Vie Americaine. Paris, 1892. 4to, later half calf, orig wraps bound in. With frontis, 320 plates & 17 maps & plans. sg Mar 12 (98) $140

De Smet, Pierre Jean, 1804-73
— Life, Letters, and Travels. NY, 1905. Ed by Hiram M. Chittenden & A. T. Richardson. 4 vols. Half mor; scuffed, spines faded. cb Jan 8 (24) $275

De Sola, Abraham. See: Lyons & De Sola

De Soto, Hernando
See also: Grabhorn Printing
— Virginia Richly Valued.... L, 1609. 1st Ed in English. Trans by Richard Hakluyt. 4to, half mor. Tp soiled; stains throughout; some headlines shaved; final leaf with repair affecting a few letters. S June 25 (417) £10,500 [Robinson]

De Vinne, Theodore Low, 1828-1914
See also: Grolier Club
— The First Editor: Aldus Pius Manutius. NY: Targ Editions, [1983]. One of 250. Illus by Antonio Frasconi. Half cloth. cb Feb 5 (81) $110

De Vries, Hugo, 1848-1935
— Die Mutationstheorie. Versuche und Beobachtungen ueber die Entstehung von Arten im Pflanzenreich. Leipzig, 1901-3. 2 vols. 8vo, half sheep; worn. With 12 colored plates. sg Jan 15 (264) $110

De Wint, Peter, 1784-1849. See: Light & De Wint

De Wit, Frederick
— Atlas. [Amst.?, 1680]. Folio, modern half mor gilt. With 10 engraved maps only, early hand-coloring; most torn & strengthened, 2 detached, some browning. pnNY Sept 13 (505) $300

— Germania Inferior sive XVII Provinciarum.... Amst., [1690?]. Folio, half vellum. With engraved title & 25 double-page maps. Fold breaks repaired affecting surface. S June 25 (268) £1,100

Dean, Bashford, 1867-1928
— A Bibliography of Fishes. Koenigstein, 1972. Vols I-II (of 3). Reprint of 1916 Ed. sg Oct 23 (243) $60

Dean, George Alfred
— Essays on the Construction of Farm Buildings and Labourers' Cottages. Stratford, 1849. 4to, orig cloth; rubbed. With 16 plates, some torn. bba Sept 25 (268) £220 [Weinreb]

Dean, Henry
— Dean's Recently Improved Analytical Guide to the Art of Penmanship. NY, [1808]. 4to, modern half cloth; worn. Some browning; minor tears & stains; lacking frontis & 1 plate. Sold w.a.f. O Mar 24 (52) $140

Dearden, Robert R., Jr. See: Grabhorn Printing

Deasy, Henry Hugh Peter
— In Tibet and Chinese Turkestan. NY, 1901. Library markings. cb Nov 6 (74) $100

Debeaumont, M.
— Jurisprudence des rentes, ou code des rentiers. Paris, 1784. 12mo, contemp mor gilt, armorial bdg. S June 25 (66) £220

Decaisne, Joseph, 1807-82
— Le Jardin fruitier du museum, ou iconographie.... Paris, [1858]-62-75. 9 vols. 4to, contemp half mor. With 508 hand-finished color plates. Peltereau—de Belder copy. S Apr 27 (96) £3,200 [Asher]
— Recherches anatomiques et physiologiques sur la Garance.... Brussels, 1837. 4to, modern half mor, orig front wrap bound in. With 1 plain & 9 hand-colored plates. Plesch copy. S Nov 10 (478) £150 [Windham]

Decker, Malcolm. See: Decker, Peter

Decker, Peter
— A Descriptive Check List...of Western Americana.... NY, 1960. 4to, cloth. Interleaved. sg Mar 12 (233) $80

Defence. See: Foyer, Archibald

Defense...
— A Defense of the Ecclesiasticall Regiment in England. L, 1574. 8vo, 18th-cent half mor. Headlines shaved with loss. Ck Apr 24 (197) £170

Defoe, Daniel, 1659?-1731
See also: Limited Editions Club
— The Consolidator: or, Memoirs of Sundry Transactions from the World in the Moon. L, 1705. 1st Ed. 8vo, contemp calf; front joint cracking. cb Sept 28 (403) $300

Anr copy. Contemp calf; joints restored. Some browning; paper crack in lower inner margin of 1st 3 leaves. sg Dec 4 (50) $225
— An Essay on the History and Reality of Apparitions. L, 1729. ("The Secrets of the Invisible World Disclos'd....") 1st Ed, 2d Issue. 8vo, contemp calf; rebacked, rubbed. bba Aug 20 (29) £90 [Rhys Jones]
— The History of the Most Remarkable Life and Extraordinary Adventures of...Colonel Jaque.... L, 1738. 4th Ed. 8vo, modern half calf. Frontis & tp repaired, affecting letters on tp; some marginal worming. bba Nov 13 (207) £65 [Hannas]
— The Judgment of the Whole Kingdoms and Nations.... L, 1710. 8vo, contemp calf gilt; rubbed, upper hinge split. bba Nov 13 (205) £35 [P & P]
— Jure Divino: a Satyr. L, 1706. Folio, 19th-cent half calf; rubbed. F Jan 15 (222) $110
— A Letter from Captain Tom to the Mobb.... L, 1710. 8vo, disbound. In book-box. T Sept 18 (511) £170
— Moll Flanders. L, 1929. Illus by John Austen. Mor by Sangorski & Sutcliffe. cb Dec 4 (35) $80
— Robinson Crusoe. L, 1719-20. ("The Life and Strange Surprizing Adventures of Robinson Crusoe....* The Farther Adventures....* Serious Reflections....") 1st Ed. Part 1 only. Contemp calf. Text browned; tp, frontis & leaf of preface stained; 2 small tears to C2 & R2. L Dec 11 (390) £280

Anr copy. 3 vols. 8vo, mor gilt by Riviere. Tear in 1 fold & 1 leaf repaired; margin of Vol I cut short. Houghton copy. P June 18 (36) $14,000

Anr copy. First & 3d works, later calf gilt. 2d work, contemp calf; 1st work, broken; 2d work, rubbed joints cracking; 3d work, 1 cover detached. S Sept 22 (12) £300 [Leinweger]

Anr Ed. L, 1719. ("The Life and Strange Surprizing Adventures of Robinson Crusoe....* The Farther Adventures....") 2 vols. 8vo, 19th-cent russia gilt by Clarke & Bedford; 3 joints repaired. Gosford-Rosebery copy, with Gosford stamp. S Dec 18 (19) £2,300 [Quaritch]

3d Ed of Vol I; 1st Eds of Vols II & III. L, 1719-20. ("The Life and Strange Surprizing Adventures of Robinson Crusoe....* The Farther Adventures....* Serious Reflections....") 3 vols. 8vo, contemp calf gilt; broken. sg Mar 26 (96) $600

Anr Ed. Amst., 1720-21. ("La Vie et les avantures surprenantes de Robinson Crusoe....") 3 vols. 12mo, mor gilt by Pougetoux. Lacking 3 plates & with 4 duplicate plates bound in. C May 13 (8) £110 [Bennett]

Anr Ed. L: John Stockdale, 1790. ("The

DEFOE

Life and Strange Surprising Adventures of Robinson Crusoe.") 2 vols. 8vo, contemp calf gilt. With engraved titles, port & 14 plates. sg Apr 23 (43) $400

Anr Ed. L, 1929. ("The Life and Strange Surprizing Adventures of Robinson Crusoe.") One of 535. Illus by E. McKnight Kauffer. 4to, orig cloth; unopened. bba Nov 13 (308) £85 [Marks]

Anr copy. Cloth. cb June 18 (166) $80

Anr Ed. L: Basilisk Press, 1979. ("The Life and Surprising Adventures of Robinson Crusoe.") One of 25. Illus by Edward Gordon Craig. 4to, orig mor gilt by Tony Miles. With 10 wood-engraved plates, initialled & dated in pencil by Craig. S May 6 (41) £300 [Hannas]

Anr copy. Orig mor gilt. S June 18 (354) £420 [Hartnoll]

— The Storm. L, 1704. 1st Ed. 8vo, later calf gilt. F Jan 15 (223) $225

— A Tour Thro' the Whole Island of Great Britain.... L, 1724-27. 3 vols. 8vo, old calf gilt; rebacked. With 2 folding maps & folding plan. pn Sept 18 (95) £600 [Quaritch]

8th Ed. L, 1778. 4 vols. 12mo, old calf; worn, some joints cracked. With 2 folding maps. ha Dec 19 (89) $100

— Works. Oxford [ptd] & L, 1840-41. ("The Novels and Miscellaneous Works.") 20 vols. 8vo, orig cloth; rubbed. bba Oct 16 (88) £170 [Duncan]

Anr copy. Half mor; scuffed. pnE Jan 28 (90) £360 [Traylen]

Anr copy. Half vellum gilt. sg Sept 11 (91) $225

Anr Ed. L, 1923-27. One of 775. bba Nov 13 (280) £50 [Joseph]

Anr Ed. Oxford: Shakespeare Head Press, 1927-28. ("Novels and Selected Writings.") One of 750. 14 vols. Orig cloth; 2 spines damaged, 1 lower cover dented. Ck Apr 24 (228) £60

Degas, Edgar

— Catalogue des tableaux, pastels et dessins par Edgar Degas a Galerie Georges Petit. Paris, 1918-19. 4 vols. 4to, half cloth, orig upper wraps bound in. S June 17 (14) £700 [Uppstromm]

Degenhart, Bernhard —& Schmitt, Annegrit

— Corpus der Italienischen Zeichnungen, 1300-1450. Berlin, 1968. 4 vols. Folio, orig cloth. sg June 4 (109) $500

AMERICAN BOOK PRICES CURRENT

Deidier,——, Abbe, 1696-1740

— Manuel de l'artificier. Paris, 1757. 12mo, orig wraps; spine chipped, loose in bdg. With 12 folding plates. sg Jan 15 (345) $250

Deighton, Len

— The Ipcress File. L, 1962. In d/j. cb Nov 20 (79) $55

Dejean, Ferdinand. See: Hornot, Antoine

Dekker, Eduard Douwes, the Elder. See: Multatuli

DeKock, Charles Paul, 1794-1850. See: Kock, Charles Paul de

Del Rio, Martin Antonio

— In Canticum canticorum Salomonis commentarius.... Lyons: Horatius Cardon, 1604. 4to, old half vellum; spine imperf. Old signature in lower margin of tp with small piece chipped away. sg Oct 9 (47) $140

— Disquisitionum magicarum, libri sex.... Lyons, 1612. 4to, 17th-cent calf; front cover partly detached. Minor repair on title verso. sg Mar 26 (97) $225

Delacour, Alfred

— Gibier de France. Paris: Editions Argo, 1929. One of 45 on japon imperial. 4to, half mor by Saulnier. Jeanson copy. SM Feb 28 (167) FF1,800

Delacour, Jean Theodore

— The Waterfowl of the World. L, 1954-64. 4 vols. 4to, cloth. With 66 color plates & 108 maps. B Feb 25 (145) HF300

Delafield, Richard, 1798-1873

— Report on the Art of War in Europe.... Wash.: George W. Bowman, 1860. 4to, recent cloth. Extra title chipped & laid down; some folding plates with minor tears. 36th Congress, 1st Session, Sen Exec Doc 59. ha Nov 7 (10) $65

Anr Ed. Wash., 1861. 4to, orig; worn. With frontis & 54 plates, mostly folding. 36th Congress, 2d Session, House Executive Document. wa Sept 25 (457) $60

Delafleur, Nicolas Guillaume

— Nicolaus Guillelmus a florae Lotharingus. Rome, 1638. Folio, unbound in cloth-backed box. With port & 12 plates. 2 holes in 1 upper blank margin; a few spots on plates. This copy without engraved numbers. de Belder copy. S Apr 27 (97) £5,500 [Macdougall]

Delano, Alonzo, 1806-74
— The Miner's Progress; or, Scenes in the Life of a California Miner.... Sacramento, 1853. 12mo, orig wraps; stained. sg Mar 12 (96) $325

Delano, Amasa, 1763-1823
— A Narrative of Voyages and Travels in the Northern and Southern Hemispheres.... Bost., 1817. 8vo, cloth. With frontis (stamped), folding map & plate. Some library markings. sg Apr 23 (46) $200

Delaporte, Yves
— Les Vitraux de la Cathédrale de Chartres.... Chartres, 1926 [1927]. 1 vol text & 10 portfolios of plates. 4to, wraps & portfolios. With 951 plates, 29 colored, 18 by hand. B Oct 7 (928) HF1,000

Delaval, E. H.
— An Experimental Inquiry into the Causes of the Changes of Colours. L, 1777. 4to, modern half calf; worn. Lacking blank G4. C Dec 4 (277) £220 [Phelps]

Delegorgue, Adulphe
— Voyage dans l'Afrique australe notamment dans...Natal.... Paris, 1847. 2 vols. 8vo, contemp half mor. With port, 2 folding maps & 8 plates. SSA Oct 28 (511) R320

Delegorgue-Cordier, John, b.1782
— La Chasse au tir. Paris, 1827. 8vo, 19th-cent half calf gilt. Jeanson copy. SM Feb 28 (168) FF2,800

Delessert, Adolphe
— Souvenirs d'un voyage dans l'Inde. Paris, 1843. 4to, modern half mor. With folding map, 8 views, 3 uncolored & 24 hand-colored plates. Some stains. Ck May 21 (119A) £300

Delessert, Benjamin, 1773-1847 —& Candolle, Augustin Pyramus de, 1778-1841
— Icones selectae plantarum.... Paris, 1820-46. L.p. Issue. 5 vols. Folio, contemp bds; rubbed. With engraved titles & 501 plates. Some spotting, almost entirely marginal. Horticultural Society of New York—de Belder copy. S Apr 27 (98) £2,600 [Rainer]

Delille, Jacques Montanier, 1738-1813
— L'Homme des champs, ou les georgiques françoises. Strassburg, 1800. 8vo, orig bds; rubbed. bba Oct 16 (40) £50 [Mills] Anr Ed. Paris, 1805. 8vo, contemp mor gilt. Schiff copy. S Mar 10 (924) £190 [Museion]

Delisle de Moncel
— Methodes et projets pour parvenir a la destruction des loups dans le royaume. Paris, 1768. 12mo, mor with arms of the Prince de Conde. Dedication copy. Jeanson copy. SM Mar 1 (358) FF3,400

Delisle, Guillaume, 1675-1726
— Atlante novissimo che contiene tutte le parti del mondo. Venice, 1740-50. 2 vols. Folio, old mor & calf gilt; rubbed. With engraved titles & 28 maps only, partly hand-colored; 2 torn down center-fold; 1 vol waterstained. pnNY Sept 13 (504) $950

Delisle, Joseph Nicolas, 1688-1768 —& Others
— Russischer Atlas, welcher in einer General-Charte und neunzehen Special-Charten.... St. Petersburg, 1745. Folio, contemp calf. With large folding general map & 19 double-page maps. Folding map repaired without loss; tp a little soiled & mtd; text leaves strengthened at outer margins. S Oct 23 (277) £1,900 [Heckrotte]

Della Bella, Stefanino
— A Collection of Etchings. L, 1818. Ed by Thomas Dodd. Folio, contemp mor gilt; rubbed. bba July 16 (387) £500 [Crisp] Anr copy. Contemp half lea, rubbed, upper joint cracked. With frontis & 159 engravings on 87 leaves. Some foxing & soiling. C July 22 (58) £650

Della Strada, Giovanni. See: Straet, Jan van der

Delmet, Paul
— Chansons de Montmartre. Paris, [1896]. Illus by Steinlen. 8vo, half calf gilt. HK Nov 4 (3084a) DM850

Delord, Taxile, 1815-77
— Un Autre monde. Paris, 1844. Illus by J. J. Grandville. 4to, half mor; corners worn. With frontis & 32 (of 36) hand-colored plates. Some repairs & staining. bba Dec 4 (181) £65 [Laffont]

Delphika...
Delphika Grammata/ The Sayings of the Seven Sages of Greece. Verona, 1976. One of 160. 8vo, half vellum. bba Apr 9 (244) £150 [Cox]

Delteil, Joseph
— Jeanne d'Arc. Paris, 1926. One of 425. Illus by Touchagues. 4to, pictorial half mor gilt. S Oct 6 (704) £75 [Thorp]

Delteil, Loys, 1869-1927
— Le Peintre-graveur illustre. Paris, 1920. Vols X & XI. H. de Toulouse-Lautrec. 2 vols. 4to, half lea; loose. HN Nov 26 (2155) DM1,400
Vols I-XXXII (complete set). NY & Paris, 1969-70. 32 vols, including Index. Reprint

DELTEIL / AMERICAN BOOK PRICES CURRENT

of 1906-26 Ed. S Nov 10 (73) £1,300 [Shrubman]; S July 13 (19) £1,400; sg June 4 (110) $2,400

Demachy, Jacques Francois de
— L'Art du distillateur liquoriste. Paris, 1775. Folio, modern half mor. Some leaves dampstained; last leaf torn. Crahan copy. P Nov 25 (148) $300

Demands...
— The Demands of the Rebels in Ireland, unto the...Councell of Dublin. L, 1641. 4to, modern bds. bba Apr 9 (297) £75 [Catnach]

Dement'ev, Georgii Petrovich —& Others
— Birds of the Soviet Union. Jerusalem, 1966-70. 6 vols. Vol IV is a 4to photocopy. B Feb 24 (454) HF65000

Demetrius Pepagomenus
— Kynosophion ac opusculum Phemonis.... Vienna: J. Singrenius, 1535. 2 parts in 2 vols. 4to, calf with arms of the comte de Beaufort, Part 2 in modern half cloth. Jeanson copy. SM Feb 28 (170) FF5,000

Demidoff, Anatole de, 1813-70
— Album du voyage dans la Russie meridionale et la Crimee. Paris, [c.1850]. Folio, contemp calf gilt with arms of John Frederick, Earl Cawdor; joints cracked. With 100 plates, including title. S Feb 23 (77) £480 [Martinos]

Demosthenes, 385?-322 B.C.
See also: Fore-Edge Paintings
— Opera. Paris: Joannes Benenatus, 1570. ("Demosthenous Logoi, kai prooimia demegorika, kai epistolai.") Folio, contemp calf; rebacked, corners restored. sg Oct 9 (172) $350
— Oratione di Demostene contra la legge de Lettine. Venice: Aldus, 1504. Folio, 19th-cent blind-tooled calf over bds. Small tear along gutter of tp; inked stamp of Royal Society. sg June 11 (5) $2,400
— Orationes duae & sexaginta.... Venice: Aldus, Nov 1504. Folio, 19th-cent calf gilt. Final 12 lower blank margins repaired; some dampstains. S May 21 (33) £650 [Hesketh & Ward]
— The Three Orations of Demosthenes Chiefe Orator among the Grecians in Favour of the Olynthians...with those his Fower Orations...against King Philip of Macedonia. L: Henrie Denham, 1570. 1st Ed in English. 4to, 19th-cent blind-stamped panelled mor; joints & edges rubbed. Possibly lacking a final blank; some discoloration or waterstaining in margins; small wormhole in 1st few gatherings affecting text; a few sidenotes just shaved; rust-hole in R2 affecting 1 word. S July 23 (2) £900 [Poole]

Demours, Antoine Pierre
— Observation sur une pupille artificielle ouverte aupres de la sclerotique. Paris, 1800. 8vo, bds. Extracted from: Journal de Medecine. S Nov 10 (479) £60 [Phelps]

Demoustier, Charles Albert, 1760-1801
— Lettres a Emilie, sur la Mythologie. Paris, 1803. 6 parts in 3 vols. 8vo, mor gilt; corners crushed. With 36 plates. sg Sept 11 (92) $80

Denecke, C. L.
— Vollstaendiges Lehrgebaeude der ganzen Optik.... Altona, 1757. 4to, contemp calf. With frontis, 4 tables & 89 plates; 1 table in facsimile. Tp library stamped; some spotting. FD June 11 (678) DM1,200

Anr copy. Contemp half calf; worn. Lacking 2 leaves at end; Plates 65 & 86 frayed; small hole in Plate 78. S June 25 (97) £1,600 [Moore]

Denham, Maj. Dixon —& Clapperton, Capt. Hugh
— Journal of a Second Expedition into the Interior of Africa.... L, 1829. 1st Ed. 4to, contemp half mor; rubbed. Short tears in folds. bba Aug 20 (479) £140 [Henderson]

Anr copy. Contemp calf; worn. Lacking leaves before frontis map; also lacking rear flyleaf; map with a 3-inch tear. cb Feb 19 (58) $70

Denham, Sir James Steuart, 1712-80
— An Inquiry into the Principles of Political Oeconomy.... L, 1767. 2 vols. 4to, contemp calf gilt; rubbed, joints weak. Vol I lacking the 1st leaf; some spotting; a few leaves with fold marks. S July 23 (460) £1,800 [Pickering]

Anr copy. Disbound. With 2 tables & with errata leaf in Vol II. sg Dec 4 (51) $800

1st Ed. 2 vols. 4to, calf; rubbed, lacking label in Vol I, heads & tails of spines chipped, joints cracking, endpapers stuck together in Vol II, surface worming. Lacking half-title in Vol I; Vol II with portion of a leaf remaining following text; some worming in corners & margins. P Sept 24 (407) $1,500

Anr copy. Contemp calf; rebacked retaining orig spines. Lacking folding table in Vol II; small wormhole in upper margin of final leaves of Vol II. S June 25 (82) £1,000 [Perceval]

Denicke, C. L. See: Denecke, C. L.

448

Denis, Johann Nepomuk Cosmas Michael
— Wiens Buchdruckergeschicht bis M.D.L.X. Vienna, 1782. 4to, 19th-cent half cloth; backstrip partly detached. sg Oct 2 (119) $140

Denis, Michael
— Einleitung in die Buecherkunde. Vienna, 1795-96. 2 vols in 1. 4to, contemp half russia; small tear at head of spine. C Dec 12 (64) £280 [Maggs]

Dennis, Nigel
— Cards of Identity. L, 1955. In d/j by Lucien Freud. Inscr to Theodore Bosanquet. sg Dec 11 (222) $500

Denny, Henry
— Monographia Anoplurorum Britanniae; or an Essay...Parasitic Insects.... L, 1842. 8vo, orig cloth; rebacked retaining orig backstrip, rehinged. sg Jan 15 (203) $110
— Monographia Anopluborum Britanniae; or an Essay...Parasitic Insects.... London, 1842. 8vo, later half calf; rubbed, spine dry. With 26 hand-colored plates. Some soiling & staining at beginning, including tp; half-title chipped; some adhesion damage. cb Feb 19 (78) $650

Dennys, John
— The Secrets of Angling. L: Robert Triphook, 1811. One of 100. 8vo, calf gilt; worn. Wormholes on last few pages. sg May 21 (51) $100

Denon, Dominique Vivant, 1747-1825
— Voyages dans la basse et haute Egypte. L, 1809. 3 vols, including Atlas. 4to & Folio, contemp cloth & half calf. With frontis & 109 plates. Caption to 1 plate shaved, a few short tears repaired in folding plates. S Oct 23 (376) £850 [Perrin]

Denon, Dominique Vivant, Baron, 1747-1825
— L'Oeuvre originale. Paris, 1873. One of 500. 2 vols. Folio, half mor. C Dec 3 (19) £400 [Quaritch]
— Travels in Upper and Lower Egypt. L, 1803. 3 vols in 2. 8vo, 10th-cent half cloth; rubbed & worn, joints tender. With 53 (of 61) plates; plates bound throughout the vols, many trimmed at margins. cb Nov 6 (77) $225
Anr copy. 3 vols, including Atlas vol. 4to & 8vo, contemp calf. With 60 folding maps & plates. S Oct 23 (375) £450 [Schober]
— Voyage dans la basse et la haute Egypte.... Paris: Didot l'aine, 1802 [An X]. 2 vols. Folio, contemp lea gilt. With 141 plates & map plus 1 extra plate. FD Dec 2 (1032) DM8,800

Densmore, Marianne
— Les Estampes erotiques japonaises. Paris, 1961. Folio, loose as issued in orig cloth. With 40 plain & 20 colored plates. sg Apr 2 (119) $375

Denton, Daniel
— A Brief Description of New-York. L, 1670. 4to, half mor. Lacking the initial blank; imprint cut close but intact. S June 25 (382) £10,000 [Quaritch]

Deperthes, Jean Louis Hubert Simon, 1730-92
— Histoire des Naufrages.... Paris, 1794 [An III]. 3 vols. 8vo, contemp calf gilt; worn. With 6 plates. sg Dec 4 (52) $300

D'Epinay, Louise Florence Petronille, 1726-83
— Les Conversations d'Emilie. Leipzig, 1774. 8vo, mor gilt, orig calf covers bound in at end. With signature "C. Louis Napoleon" & with stamp of Queen Hortense at head of title & 1st leaf. Extra-illus with 2 plates. C May 13 (25) £280 [Chaponniere]

Depons, Francois
— A Voyage to the Eastern Part of Terra Firma.... NY, 1806. 1st Ed in English. 3 vols. 8vo, modern half lea. With folding map having tear at hinge & perforated & ink library stamps. sg Mar 12 (97) $60

Depping, George Bernhard. See: Rechberg & Depping

Der Sturm
— Erster Deutscher Herbstsalon. Berlin, 1913. 4to, orig wraps. S June 29 (1) £280 [Reiningheus]
— Siebenundreissigst Ausstellung: Max Ernst, George Muche.... Berlin, [1916]. S June 29 (2) £300 [Arsintnan]

Derby, George H.
See also: Grabhorn Printing
— Report of the Secretary of War, Communicating, in Compliance with a Resolution of the Senate, a Reconnoissance of the Gulf of California and the Colorado River. [Wash., 1852]. 8vo, glued into plain paper wrap. 32d Congress, 1st Session, Senate Ex. Doc. No 81. cb Mar 19 (77) $100

Derham, Robert
— A Manuell or, Brief Treatise of Some Particular Rights and Privileges belonging to the High Court of Parliament. L; for Mathew Walbancke, 1647. 8vo, old calf; worn. Minor stains & soiling. O Feb 24 (54) $70

Derleth, August. See: Lovecraft & Derleth

Derleth, August William
— Arkham House: The First 20 Years.... Sauk City, 1959. Wraps. cb Sept 28 (417) $65
— The Casebook of Solar Pons. Sauk City, 1965. In d/j. cb May 7 (259) $65
  Anr copy. In d/j. Michael Harrison's copy. cb Apr 24 (1223) $50
— The Memoirs of Solar Pons. Sauk City, 1951. In d/j. cb May 7 (260) $110
— Not Long for this World. Sauk City, 1948. In rubbed d/j. Inscr. cb Sept 28 (420) $75
— The Return of Solar Pons. Sauk City: Mycroft & Moran, 1958. In d/j. cb Apr 24 (1220) $95
— The Solar Pons Omnibus. Sauk City: Arkham House, [1982]. 2 vols. As new in orig shrink wrap. cb Sept 28 (422) $50
— Thirty Years of Writing, 1926-1956. [Sauk City: Arkham House, n.y.]. Wraps; creased. cb Sept 28 (427) $225

Derriere le Miroir—Paris
— Hommage a Aime et Marguerite Maeght. 1982. Folio. B Oct 7 (952) HF1,000

Derriery, Charles
— Gravure et Fonderie de C. Derriery, Specimen Album. Paris, 1862. Folio, mor gilt. About 15 leaves soiled or mended with tape. sg Dec 4 (200) $500

Derrydale Press—New York
— The American Shooter's Manual... 1928. One of 375. Unopened. sg Oct 23 (3) $70
— A Decade of American Sporting Books & Prints by the Derrydale Press 1927-1937. 1937. One of 950. Inscr by Eugene V. Connett. sg Oct 23 (45) $100; sg May 21 (61) $80
— Hell for Leather! 1928. One of 350. Unopened. sg Oct 23 (68) $50
— Some Early American Hunters. 1928. One of 375. Unopened. sg Oct 23 (127) $110
— The Sportsman's Companion, or an Essay on Shooting. 1930. One of 200. Inscr. cb May 21 (83) $200
  Anr copy. Rebound in half mor. Inscr. sg Oct 23 (133) $90
  Anr copy. Unopened. Inscr. sg Oct 23 (134) $80
  Anr copy. Unopened. sg May 21 (90) $80
— The Sportsman's Portfolio of American Field Sports. 1929. Facsimile of the Boston 1855 Ed, One of 400. sg Oct 23 (135) $175
— The Westminster Kennel Club. 1929. One of 100. Facsimile of the 1886 Ed. sg Oct 23 (149) $700
— Yacht Racing Log. 1933. Intro by Herbert L. Stone. sg Oct 23 (1153) $400
— ALVORD, THOMAS G. - Paul Bunyan, and Resinous Rhymes of the North Woods.

1934. One of 332. Inscr to Paul Mellon. sg Oct 23 (1) $110
— ANNABEL, RUSSELL. - Tales of a Big Game Guide. 1938. One of 950. Two prelim leaves detached. cb May 21 (57) $225; sg Oct 23 (4) $350
— ASH, EDWARD C. - The Practical Dog Book. 1931. One of 500. sg Oct 23 (5) $50
— BABCOCK, PHILIP H. - Falling Leaves: Tales from a Gun Room. [1937]. One of 950. cb May 21 (58) $90
  Anr copy. Worn; inner joints broken. O Feb 24 (51) $70
  Anr copy. Inscr. sg Oct 23 (6) $100; sg Oct 23 (6) $100
— BAKER, CHARLES HENRY, JR. - The Gentleman's Companion. 1939. One of 1,250. 2 vols. cb Nov 6 (78) $65; sg Oct 23W17 $90
  Anr copy. Inscr. sg May 21 (53) $130
— BANDINI, RALPH. - Veiled Horizons... [1939]. One of 950. Unopened. sg Oct 23 (9) $90
— BARBER, JOEL D. - 'Long Shore. [1939]. One of 750, sgd.. cb May 21 (59) $80
  Anr copy. Unopened. sg Oct 23 (10) $450
— BAYLISS, MARGUERITE F. - Bolinvar. 1937. One of 950. 2 vols. Inscr mtd. sg Oct 23 (12) $50
— BEACH, WILLIAM NICHOLAS. - In the Shadow of Mount McKinley. 1931. One of 750. sg Oct 23 (14) $250
— BIGELOW, HORATIO. - Gunnerman. [1939]. One of 950. cb May 21 (60) $140
  Anr copy. Inscr. sg Oct 23 (15) $140
— BRAND, MAX. - The Thunderer. 1933. One of 950. sg Oct 23 (17) $60
— BRIGGS, L. CABOT. - Bullterriers: the Biography of a Breed. [1940]. One of 500. sg Oct 23 (18) $325
— BROWN, PAUL. - Aintree: Grand Nationals —Past and Present. 1930. One of 850. sg Oct 23 (20) $90; sg May 21 (54) $150
— BROWN, PAUL. - Hits and Misses. 1935. One of 950. sg Oct 23 (21) $225; sg May 21 (55) $225
— BROWN, WILLIAM ROBINSON. - The Horse of the Desert. 1929. One of 750. Folio, orig cloth; rubbed. bba Dec 18 (120) £130 [Ched]; sg Oct 23 (22) $200
— BUCKINGHAM, NASH. - Blood Lines... [1938]. One of 1,250. cb May 21 (61) $80; sg Oct 23 (23) $140
— BUCKINGHAM, NASH. - De Shootinest Gent'man and Other Tales. [1934]. One of 950. sg Oct 23 (24) $300
— BUCKINGHAM, NASH. - Mark Right! [1936]. One of 1,250. sg Oct 23 (25) $175
— BUCKINGHAM, NASH. - Ole Miss'. 1937. One of 1,250. sg Oct 23 (26) $175
— CLAPHAM, RICHARD. - The Book of the Fox. 1931. One of 750. sg Oct 23 (31) $90
— CLARK, ROLAND. - Etchings. 1938. One of

800. Corners broken & tape repaired. sg Oct 23 (32) $475; sg May 21 (56) $275
— CLARK, ROLAND. - Gunner's Dawn. 1937. One of 50, with an orig color etching, sgd. cb May 21 (62) $1,600
Anr copy. Inscr. sg Oct 23 (33) $1,000
One of 950, with orig sgd etching. cb May 21 (63) $500; sg Oct 23 (34) $500
— CLARK, ROLAND. - Stray Shots. 1931. One of 500, sgd. sg Oct 23 (36) $1,500
One of 35, sgd, & with each of the 13 etchings sgd. sg Oct 23 (35) $3,000
— CONNETT, EUGENE V. - American Big Game Fishing. [1935]. One of 850. sg Oct 23 (2) $250; sg May 21 (57) $275
One of 950. Inscr by Kip Farrington to Fred Hardy. S July 28 (1022) £140; wa Nov 6 (163) $65
— CONNETT, EUGENE V. - Feathered Game. 1929. One of 50 L.p. copies. Unopened. sg Oct 23 (37) $2,000
— CONNETT, EUGENE V. - Fishing a Trout Stream. [1934]. One of 950. Rubbed. sg Oct 23 (38) $150
— CONNETT, EUGENE V. - Magic Hours, Wherein We Cast a Fly Here & There.... 1927. One of 100. sg Oct 23 (39) $7,500
— CONNETT, EUGENE V. - Random Casts. 1939. One of 1,075. Inscr. sg Oct 23 (40) $150
— CONNETT, EUGENE V. - Upland Game Bird Shooting in America. 1930. One of 75, with 6 orig sgd etchings. With frontis inscr by artist & title inscr by author. sg Oct 23 (41) $3,600
One of 850. cb May 21 (64) $325; sg Oct 23 (141) $275; wd June 19 (110) $150
— COX, CHARLES E.,. - John Tobias, Sportsman. [1937]. One of 950. sg Oct 23 (42) $90; sg May 27 (58) $70
— CURTIS, PAUL A. - Sportsmen All. [1938]. One of 950. cb Nov 6 (79) $55; sg Oct 23 (43) $80; sg May 21 (59) $50
— DANIELSON, RICHARD ELY. - Martha Doyle and other Sporting Memories. [1938]. One of 1250. Unopened. sg Oct 23 (43) $80
— DE GOUY, LOUIS PULLIG. - The Derrydale Cook Book of Fish and Game. 1937. One of 1,250. 2 vols. cb May 21 (67) $170
— FERGUSON, HENRY LEE. - The English Springer Spaniel in America. 1932. One of 850. O Feb 24 (60) $60
— FOOTE, JOHN TAINTOR. - Jing. [1936]. One of 950. Unopened. sg Oct 23 (48) $70
— GAMBRILL, R. V. N. & MACKENZIE, JAMES C. - Sporting Stables and Kennels. 1935. One of 950. Worn & soiled. sg Oct 23 (50) $80
— GAMBRILL, RICHARD V. N. & MACKENZIE, JAMES C sg May 21 (62) $150
— GEE, ERNEST RICHARD. - Early American Sporting Books.... 1928. One of 500. K Oct 4 (131) $110; O Nov 18 (72) $80; sg May 21 (63) $90
One of 100 with date "December 1928". sg Oct 23 (51) $175
— GOSNELL, HARPUR A. - Before the Mast in the Clippers.... 1937. One of 950. sg Oct 23 (54) $100
— GRAND, GORDON. - Colonel Weatherford and his Friends. 1933. One of 1,450. sg Oct 23 (55) $70
— GRAND, GORDON. - The Southborough Fox, and Other Colonel Weatherford Stories. 1939. One of 1,450. O Nov 18 (52) $50
— GRAY, DAVID. - Sporting Works. 1929. One of 750. 3 vols. sg May 21 (67) $90
— GRAY, PRENTISS N. - Records of North American Big Game. 1932. One of 500. Inscr. sg Oct 23 (60) $1,100; sg May 21 (66) $800; wa Mar 5 (256) $450
— GRINNELL, GEORGE BIRD. - Hunting Trails on Three Continents. 1933. One of 250. Tape repaired. sg Oct 23 (61) $750
— HAIG-BROWN, RODERICK L. - The Western Angler.... 1939. One of 950. 2 vols. sg Oct 23 (62) $475
Anr copy. Unopened. sg May 21 (68) $500
— HATCH, ALDEN & KEENE, FOXHALL. - Full Tilt.... 1938. One of 950. sg Oct 23 (65) $50
— HENRY, SAMUEL J. - Foxhunting is Different. 1938. One of 950. sg Oct 23 (68) $50
— HERBERT, HENRY WILLIAM. - My Shooting Box. 1941. One of 250. sg Oct 23 (70) $100
— HERBERT, HENRY WILLIAM. - Sporting Novels. 1930. One of 750. 4 vols. Unopened. sg Oct 23 (69) $80
— HERBERT, HENRY WILLIAM. - Trouting Along the Catasauqua. NY, 1927. One of 423. Unopened. sg Oct 23 (71) $200
— HERBERT, HENRY WILLIAM. - The Warwick Woodlands. 1934. One of 250. sg Oct 23 (72) $200
— HERVEY, JOHN. - Lady Suffolk, the Old Grey Mare of Long Island. 1936. One of 500. Unopened. sg May 21 (69) $60
— HUNT, LYNN BOGUE - An Artist's Game Bag. 1936. One of 1,250. cb May 21 (70) $170
Anr copy. Rubbed, small tears & tape stains on d/j. sg Oct 23 (77) $250
De Luxe Ed. sg May 21 (71) $225
— HUNTER, ANOLE. - Let's Ride to Hounds. 1929. One of 850. Unopened. sg Oct 23 (78) $40
— JENNINGS, PRESTON J. - A Book of Trout Flies. [1935]. One of 850. sg Oct 23 (80) $225
— KENDALL, PAUL GREEN. - Polo Ponies: their Training and Schooling. 1933. One of 850. sg Oct 23 (110) $110
— KIRMSE, MARGUERITE. - Dogs. 1930. One

of 750. With sgd etching as frontis. sg Oct 23 (84) $400; sg May 21 (73) $450
— KIRMSE, MARGUERITE. - Dogs in the Field. 1935. One of 685. With sgd etching as frontis. sg Oct 23 (85) $275
— LANIER, HENRY W. - A.B. Frost: the American Sportsman's Artist. [1933]. One of 950. Tp stamped. cb May 21 (71) $200; sg Oct 23 (86) $250; sg May 21 (74) $350; wd June 19 (111) $250
— LEE, AMY FREEMAN. - Hobby Horses. 1940. One of 200. sg Oct 23 (87) $100
— LITTAUER, VLADIMIR S. - Be a Better Horseman: an Illustrated Guide to the Enjoyment of Modern Riding. 1941. One of 1,500. sg Oct 23 (90) $70
— LUARD, LOWES DALBIAC. - The Horse: Its Action and Anatomy. 1936. One of 150. sg Oct 23 (93) $250
— MANCHESTER, HERBERT. - Four Centuries of Sport in America, 1490-1890. 1931. One of 850. sg Oct 23 (96) $100
— MARKLAND, GEORGE. - Pteryplegia: The Art of Shooting-Flying. 1931. One of 200 colored by hand. Soiled. sg Oct 23 (97) $140

One of 300. cb may 21 (72) $150; cb May 21 (73) $55
— MONTGOMERY, RUTHERFORD G. - High Country. 1938. One of 950. cb May 21 (74) $90

Anr copy. Unopened. S Oct 23 (98) $40
— NEWMAN, NEIL. - Famous Horses of the American Turf. 1931-32-33. One of 750. 3 vols. sg Oct 23 (101) $200

Anr Ed. 1931-33. sg May 21 (76) $110
— O'CONNOR, JACK. - Game in the Desert. [1939]. One of 950. cb Nov 6 (81) $375

Anr copy. Inscr. cb May 21 (75) $400

Anr copy. Unopened. sg Oct 23 (102) $475
— PALMEDO, ROLAND. - Skiing: The International Sport. 1937. One of 950. O Sept 23 (44) $90

Anr copy. Inscr. sg Oct 23 (104) $175; sg May 21 (78) $70
— PHAIR, CHARLES. - Atlantic Salmon Fishing. 1937. One of 950. Bdg soiled & rubbed. S Nov 10 (548) £90 [Cheeseborough]; sg Oct 23 (105) $450; sg May 21 (79) $400
— PICKERING, HAROLD G. - Angling of the Test, or True Love under Stress. 1936. One of 297. sg Oct 23 (106) $150; sg May 21 (80) $140
— PICKERING, HAROLD G. - Dog-Days on Trout Waters. 1933. One of 199. sg Oct 23 (107) $300
— PICKERING, HAROLD G. - Merry Xmas. Mr. Williams. 20 Pine St. N.Y. 1940. Out-of-series copy. sg Oct 23 (108) $300
— PICKERING, HAROLD G. - Neighbors Have My Ducks. 1937. One of 227. sg Oct 23 (109) $400
— PICKERING, HAROLD G. - Trout Fishing in Secret. 1931. One of 99, sgd. With typed note, sgd, from Pickering to Charles B. Wood laid in. sg Oct 23 (110) $750
— POLLARD, HUGH BERTIE CAMPBELL & BARCLAY-SMITH, PHYLLIS. - British & American Game-Birds. 1939. One of 125 on handmade paper. With an orig pencil drawing by Philip Rickman. sg Oct 23 (111) $600
— POOR, CHARLES LANE. - Men against the Rule. 1937. One of 950. sg Oct 23 (112) $60; sg May 21 (81) $70; wa Nov 6 (166) $60
— REEVE, J. STANLEY. - Foxhunting Formalities. 1930. One of 990. sg Oct 23 (113) $90; sg May 21 (82) $90; sg May 21 (83) $70
— REEVE, J. STANLEY. - Red Coats in Chester County. 1940. One of 570. K June 7 (312) $100

Anr copy. Inscr. sg Oct 23 (114) $150; sg May 21 (84) $130
— RIVES, REGINALD W. - The Coaching Club.... 1935. One of 300. sg Oct 23 (115) $300
— SANTINI, PIERO. - Riding Reflections. 1932. One of 850. sg Oct 23 (116) $60
— SHELDON, HAROLD P. - Tranquillity. 1936. One of 950. cb May 21 (76) $160

Anr copy. Endpapers tape-stained. sg Oct 23 (119) $350

Unnumbered copy for review purposes, so stamped. cb May 21 (77) $80
— SHELDON, HAROLD P. - Tranquillity Revisited. 1940. One of 485. sg Oct 23 (119) $350; sg May 21 (85) $400; wd June 19 (112) $175
— SHEPPERD, TAD. - Pack & Paddock. [1938]. One of 950. sg May 21 (86) $100

Anr copy. Inscr. wa Feb 19 (24) $60
— SIMMONS, ALBERT DIXON. - Wing Shots. [1936]. One of 950. cb May 21 (78) $70
— SMITH, EDMUND WARE. - The One-Eyed Poacher of Privilege. [1941]. One of 750. sg Oct 23 (122) $200
— SMITH, EDMUND WARE. - Tall Tales and Short. [1938]. One of 950. Inscr. sg Oct 23 (123) $225
— SMITH, EDMUND WARE. - A Tomato Can Chronicle.... [1937]. One of 950. sg Oct 23 (124) $90
— SMITH, HARRY WORCESTER. - Life and Sport in Aiken.... 1935. One of 950. sg Oct 23 (125) $90
— SMITH, JEROME V.C. - Trout and Angling. 1929. One of 325. sg Oct 23 (126) $70; sg May 21 (87) $100; wd June 19 (113) $850
— SOMERVILLE, EDITH & MARTIN, VIOLET. - Sporting Works. 1927. One of 500. 7 vols. sg Oct 23 (128) $325; wd Nov 12 (109) $175

- SPILLER, BURTON L. - Firelight. [1937]. One of 950. cb May 21 (79) $130; sg Oct 23 (129) $100
- SPILLER, BURTON L. - Grouse Feathers. 1935. cb May 21 (80) $130; K Dec 13 (86) $120
- SPILLER, BURTON L. - More Grouse Feathers. [1938]. One of 950. cb May 21 (81) $130

  Anr copy. Inscr. sg Oct 23 (131) $130; sg May 21 (89) $130
- SPILLER, BURTON L. - Thoroughbred. 1936. One of 950. cb May 21 (82) $110

  Anr copy. Inscr. sg Oct 23 (132) $200
- STONE, HERBERT L. & LOOMIS, ALFRED F. - Millions for Defense. [1934]. One of 950. sg Oct 23 (136) $60
- STREETT, WILLIAM B. - Gentlemen Up. 1930. One of 850. Front cover stained. sg Oct 23 (137) $130
- STURGIS, WILLIAM B. - New Lines for Flyfishers. [1936]. One of 950. cb May 21 (84) $80
- THOMAS, JOSEPH B. - Hounds and Hunting through the Ages. 1928. One of 750. Spine faded & blistered. Owner's name rubberstamped on endpaper. sg Oct 23 (139) $70

  2d Ed. 1929. One of 250. sg Oct 23 (140) $70
- VAN URK, JOHN BLAN. - The Story of American Foxhunting.... 1940-41. One of 950. 2 vols. sg Oct 23 (143) $80
- VOSBURGH, W.S. - Cherished Portraits of Thoroughbred Horses from the Collection of William Woodward. 1929. One of 200. Mor gilt by Sangorski & Sutcliffe. Inscr by Woodward. sg Oct 23 (144) $1,100; sg May 21 (91) $1,000
- WALDEN, HOWARD T. - Big Stony. 1940. One of 550. Unopened. sg Oct 23 (145) $100; sg May 21 (92) $225
- WALDEN, HOWARD T. - Upstream & Down. 1938. One of 950. sg Oct 23 (146) $90
- WATSON, FREDERICK. - Hunting Ple. 1931. One of 750. Unopened. sg Oct 23 (148) $70; sg May 21 (93) $90
- WHITE, FREDERICK. - The Spicklefisherman and Others. 1928. One of 740. sg May 21 (94) $120

  One of 775. sg Oct 23 (150) $120
- WHITMAN, MALCOLM D. - Tennis: Origins and Mysteries. 1932. One of 450. Unopened. sg Oct 23 (151) $400; sg May 21 (95) $300
- WILLIAMS, BEN AMES. - The Happy End. [1939]. One of 1,250. sg Oct 23 (152) $80
- WISE, CAPT. HUGH D. - Tigers of the Sea. 1937. One of 950. ha Dec 19 (179) $75

Derys, Gaston, Pseud. of Gaston Collomb
- Mon Docteur le vin. Paris, [1936]. Illus by Raoul Dufy. 4to, orig wraps. pn Nov 25 (166) $600

Des Courieres, Edouard
- Physiologie de la Boxe. Paris, [1929]. One of 20 lettered copies with additional suite of plates on Annam paper. Folio, wraps; backstrip torn, gatherings loose as issued. sg May 21 (28) $120

Des Murs, Marc Athanase Paarfait Oeillet, 1804-78?
- Animaux nouveaux ou rares.... Paris, 1855. 4to. With 20 color plates. B Feb 24 (300) HF750

Desaguliers, John Theophilus, 1683-1744
- A Course of Experimental Philosophy. L, 1734-44. 2 vols. 4to, contemp calf; rubbed, joints worn. With 2 letters affected on 3Hv of Vol I, plate with corner tear in Vol II. C Dec 12 (65) £550 [Keating]

  Anr copy. Calf. With 78 folding plates. Some spotting; 1 plate cropped, anr torn. S May 28 (659) £360
- A System of Experimental Philosopy, prov'd by Mechanicks.... L, 1719. 4to, contemp calf; worn. With 10 plates; some staining. bba Dec 4 (273) £170 [Phillips]

Descamps-Scrive, Rene
- Bibliotheque.... Paris, 1925. 3 vols. 4to, half mor, ptd wraps preserved. bba Sept 25 (362) £160 [Hay Cinema Book Shop]

Descartes, Rene, 1596-1650
- De homine. Leiden, 1662. 1st Ed, 2d Issue. 4to, contemp vellum. With 10 plates, 1 with 2 overlays. S June 25 (98) £520 [Quaritch]
- Discours de la methode.... Paris, 1668. 4to, contemp calf gilt; worn. Some browning & waterstaining; some worming. HN Nov 26 (1125) DM600
- A Discourse of the Method for the Well Guiding of Reason.... L: ptd by Thomas Newcombe, and are to be sold at his house over against Bay-nards Castle, 1649. 1st English Ed, variant imprint. 8vo, later sheep; upper joint weak. S Dec 18 (324) £1,700 [Quaritch]
- Epistolae.... Amst., 1668. 1st Ed in Latin. 2 parts in 1 vol. 4to, contemp vellum; soiled. T Mar 19 (403) £130
- Principia philosophiae. Amst.: Elzevir, 1644. 4to, contemp vellum; worn. Lacking 1 leaf. HN Nov 26 (1127) DM2,500

Deschamps, John
— Scenery and Reminiscences of Ceylon. L, 1845. Folio, orig cloth gilt; rebacked in calf. With hand-colored title & 12 hand-colored plates. Some outer margins repaired with tape. S June 25 (462) £1,900 [Lennox]

D'Esclands, Alphonse Fery, Duc. See: Fery d'Esclands & Others

Descourtilz, Jean Theodore
— Beija-flores do Brasil. Rio de Janeiro, 1960. Ltd Ed. Folio, cloth. B Feb 24 (291) HF200

Descourtilz, M. E.
— Flore (pittoresque et) medicale des Antilles, ou traite des plantes usuelles des colonies francaises.... Paris, 1821-29. 8 vols. Folio, contemp half mor; rubbed, 1 bdg broken. With 600 hand-finished color plates. Some foxing, mainly in text; 1st 20 pp in Vol III stained. Horticultural Society of New York—de Belder copy. S Apr 27 (99) £4,200 [Berg]

Description...
See also: Knight, Cornelia
— Description de toutes les nations de l'Empire de Russie...Premiere Collection Nations d'origine Finnoise & Seconde Collection Les Nations Tartares. St. Petersburg, 1776. 3 parts in 1 vol. 4to, half calf; hinges cracked, rubbed. With 75 hand-colored plates, a few with outer margin trimmed; 3 leaves of text torn. Titles in French, German & Russian. pn Jan 22 (96) £300 [Cavendish]
— Description de l'Egypte ou recueil des observations et des recherches pendant l'Expedition de l'Armee Francaise. Paris: Imprimerie Imperiale [Royale], 1809-[30]. Histoire Naturelle, Planches, Tome Premier only. Folio, orig bds; scuffed, lacking backstrip. With 62 plates, 14 ptd in color & finished by hand. Some spotting. Sold w.a.f. C Oct 15 (220) £2,300 [Al Saud]
1st Ed. Paris, 1817-[30]. Bound in 23 vols. Folio, later half mor gilt. With 33 ports & plates in text vols. Plate vols with half-titles in all but the 3 grande Monde vols & Histoire Naturelle Vol II & with 840 plates of which 44 are ptd in colors (some finished by hand). Atlas with engraved title, 2 key plates on 1 sheet, engraved general map on 3 sheets & detailed map engraved on 47 plates & ptd on 44 sheets. Minor spotting. Antiquities I with dampstain to a few corners & minor worming to a few inner blank margins; a few plates with minor corner tear; lacking port of Napoleon. C Apr 8 (18) £17,000 [Carlton Hobbs]
Anr copy. Half mor. Text vols with 4 ports, 3 folding maps & 28 plates. Plate vols with frontis, 2 maps, 833 plates & a further 6 duplicate impressions (on 5 sheets); of these plates 42 are ptd entirely or partly in colors & some of these are finished by hand. Atlas with engraved title, engraved index leaf, general map in 3 sheets & the detailed map engraved on 47 plates. Some foxing. S Oct 23 (48) £15,000 [Raban]
— A Description of Bartholomew Fair and the Droll Folks that are There. L: J. Fairburn, [19th cent]. 16mo, orig ptd wraps; rebacked. S Dec 5 (301) £1,700 [Hackhofer]
— A Description of Candia, in its Ancient & Modern State. L: J. C. for W. Crook, 1670. 8vo, early calf; rebacked, worn. Margins trimmed; some foxing at end. sg Nov 20 (63) $250
— A Description of England and Wales. L: Newbery, 1769-70. 10 vols. 8vo, half calf; spines worn, hinges broken. T Sept 18 (82) £70
— A Description of the Westminster Tobacco Box, the Property of the Past Overseers' Society, of St. Margaret and St. John the Evangelist Westminster.... L, 1887. 4to, orig mor; rubbed. O Oct 21 (53) $60

Descriptive...
— A Descriptive Poem of Bartholomew-Fair, for the Instruction and Amusement of the Young of Both Sexes.... L: H. Turpin, [c.1780]. 24mo, orig Dutch floral bds; rebacked. Some headlines & the edge of 1 plate shaved. S Dec 5 (302) £900 [Schiller]

Descrizione...
— Descrizione delle feste celebrate in Parma l'anno MDCCLXIX per...nozze di...Don Ferdinando colla Reale Arciduchessa Maria Amalia. Parma, [1769]. Folio, contemp green mor gilt, with arms of Ferdinand I, Duke of Parma; repaired. With frontis & 36 plates. Abdy copy. FD Dec 2 (3805) DM15,000

Deseine, Francois Jacques, d.1715
— Beschryving an oud en nieuw Rome. Amst., 1704. With 3 engraved titles & 102 maps, plans & plates. Bound with: Kennett, Basil. De Aaloudheden van Rome. Amst., 1704. With engraved title & 18 maps, plans & views. Folio, contemp calf gilt; spine ends worn. Some stains. B Feb 25 (816) HF1,800

Desfontaines, Rene Louiche, 1750-1833
— Choix des plantes du Corollaire des instituts de Tournefort. Paris, 1808. 4to, early 20th-cent half mor; spine rubbed. With 70 hand-colored plates. Horticultural Society of New York—de Belder copy. S Apr 27 (101) £1,400 [Junk]
— Flora atlantica, sive historia plantarum....

Paris, [1798]-1800 [An VI-VIII]. 3 vols. 4to, orig bds; rubbed. With 263 plates. Some spotting. Balfour—de Belder copy. S Apr 27 (100) £1,000 [Robinson]

Desgodetz, Antoine, 1653-1728
— The Ancient Buildings of Rome. L, 1771-95. 2 vols. Folio, bdg not indicated. Library markings. Sold w.a.f. Franklin Institute copy. F Sept 12 (15) $600
— Les Edifices antiques de Rome. Paris, 1682. Folio, contemp calf; rebacked, corners worn. Some leaves soiled. C May 13 (68) £550 [Thomas]

Desgraviers, Auguste Claude Leconte, 1749-1822
— L'Art du valet de limier.... Paris: Prault, 1784. 2 parts in 1 vol. 12mo, contemp mor gilt with arms of de Piis (restored). Jeanson copy. SM Feb 28 (171) FF9,000

Anr Ed. [N.p.]. 1810. ("Essai de venerie, ou l'art du velet de limier.") Unique copy on vellum. 8vo, contemp red mor gilt with arms of Louis XVIII. Jeanson copy. SM Feb 28 (173) FF9,500

Anr Ed. Paris: Levrault, 1810. 8vo, contemp half calf; worn. Jeanson copy. SM Feb 28 (172) FF2,400

Desmarest, Anselme Gaetan, 1784-1838
— Histoire naturelle des tangaras, des manakins et des todiers. Paris, 1805-[7]. 2 parts in 1 vol. Folio, contemp half mor gilt. With 72 plates in 2 states, uncolored & ptd in colors & finished by hand. S Oct 23 (670) £2,500 [Quaritch]

Desnos, Louis C.
— L'Indicateur fidele ou guide des voyageurs. Paris, 1765. 8vo, contemp calf. With engraved title, dedication, general map, plan & 17 double-page road maps, hand-colored in outline. Some fold breaks; upper outer corner of last leaf torn with loss; some spotting throughout. C Oct 15 (51) £230 [Cavendish]

Detaille, Edouard —& Richard, Jules, 1825-99
— Types et uniformes. L'Armee Francaise. Paris, [1885-89]. 16 orig parts in 2 vols. Folio, wraps, in loose orig cloth folder; worn. With 2 engraved titles & 60 colored plates. HN Nov 26 (1031) DM900

Deuchar, David
— A Collection of Etchings after the most Eminent Masters of the Dutch and Flemish Schools. [Edin.], 1803. 2 vols. Folio, disbound. With 321 mtd etchings on 123 pp. Sold w.a.f. L July 2 (17) £500

Anr copy. Contemp mor gilt; extremities worn, 1st signature of Vol II nearly detached. sg Dec 18 (164) $800

Anr copy. Folio, loose as issued in portfolio. With dedication & 351 (of 370) etchings only. Lacking tp. With small watercolor drawing. sg June 18 (197) $700

Devauchelle, Roger
— La Reliure en France. Paris, 1959-61. 3 vols. 4to, half mor, Vol II unbound. sg May 14 (99) $1,800

Deventer, Hendrik van, 1651-1724
— Observations importantes sur le manuel des accouchemens. Paris, 1734. 2 parts in 1 vol. 4to, old calf; worn, rebacked. With 37 plates, 1 folding & torn. bba Jan 15 (390) £320 [Phelps]

Dewar, George Albemarle Bertie, 1862-1934
— Wild Life in Hampshire Highlands. L, 1899. 8vo, cloth. With 7 plates. sg Oct 30 (57) $110

D'Ewes, Sir Simonds, 1602-50
— The Journal of all the Parliaments during the Reign of Queen Elizabeth.... L, 1682. Folio, later sheep; rebacked. sg Oct 9 (174) $130

Deyeux, Theophile
— Le Vieux Chasseur. Paris: Houdaille, [1835]. 8vo, mor gilt by Chambolle-Duru. Jeanson copy. SM Feb 28 (174) FF13,000

Dezallier d'Argenville, Antoine Joseph, 1680-1765
— Abrege de la vie des plus fameux peinteures. Paris, 1745-52. 1st Ed. 3 vols. 4to, contemp lev gilt. With 221 ports & 13 frames of the 1st Ed, 13 ports & 6 frames of the 1762 Ed & 2 ports in 2 states, 1 cut out, 2 remtd. Lacking tp & text but with 4 leaves of text with engraved vignettes loosely inserted. Hoe copy. bba Sept 25 (169A) £160 [Archdale]

Anr copy. 2 (of 3) vols. 4to, contemp calf; rubbed, joints cracked. bba July 16 (161) £50 [Archdale]

Anr copy. 2 vols. 4to, later half calf; worn. With hand-colored frontis. First gathering in Vol I detached (but present). cb Oct 23 (13) $350

Anr copy. 3 vols. 4to, contemp calf gilt; rubbed, joints cracking. S Nov 10 (74) £120 [Erlini]

— L'Histoire naturelle eclaircie dans deux de ses parties principales. La Lithologie et la conchyliologie. Paris, 1757. 4to, contemp calf; worn & def. With 41 plates. FD June 11 (701) DM1,600

455

DIALOGO...

Dialogo...
— Dialogo facetissimo et ridiculosissimo di Ruzzante. Venice: Stefano di Alessi, 1554. 8vo, 18th-cent wraps. Some dampstains; old notes on last page. Schwerdt-Jeanson copy. SM Feb 28 (175) FF3,000

Dialogues. See: Lyttelton, George Lyttelton

Dialogus...
— Dialogus inter clericum et militem.... [Cologne: Printer of Augustine De fide, c.1473]. 4to, later vellum; remboitee with new endpapers, soiled. Some stains & smudges; some gutters strengthened without loss. 16 leaves. Goff D-147. P Sept 24 (144) $6,750

Diaz del Castillo, Bernal, c.1492-1581?
— The True History of the Conquest of Mexico.... L, 1800. 1st Ed in English. 4to, modern calf with mor spine, arms of John Philip Kemble laid on from orig bdg; worn. Frontis dampstained. O Mar 24 (55) $150
Anr copy. Calf; worn, lacking back. Plan and a few pp dampstained. John Philip Kemble's copy. wa Sept 25 (440) $230

Dibdin, Thomas Frognall, 1776-1847
— Aedes Althorpianae.... L, 1822. 2 vols. 8vo, later cloth; later endpapers. Titles stamped. cb June 18 (80) $65
Anr copy. 2 vols in one. 8vo, later mor; foot of spine dampstained, front hinge starting. L.p. copy. sg Jan 22 (136) $175
— The Bibliographical Decameron. L, 1817. 3 vols. 4to, orig bds; scuffed, spines worn or def. S Feb 23 (13) £130 [Dinton]
— A Bibliographical, Antiquarian, and Picturesque Tour in France and Germany. L, 1821. 1st Ed. 3 vols. 4to, later half mor; joints rubbed. bba Dec 18 (139) £160 [Hannas]
Anr copy. Contemp mor gilt; worn. Library markings; ink stamps on plates. bba Feb 5 (47) $100 [Hildebrandt]
Anr copy. Mor gilt by Riviere; minor wear. HN May 20 (1742) DM1,800
Anr copy. Orig bds; scuffed, spines worn or def. L.p. copy. S Feb 23 (12) £250 [Tiger]
Anr copy. Contemp half lea; Vols II & III lacking backstrips. sg Jan 22 (133) $150
Anr copy. Contemp calf; rebacked, orig backstrips laid down; 1 vol broken. sg Jan 22 (134) $150
2d Ed. L, 1829. 3 vols. 8vo, contemp mor gilt; rubbed. HN Nov 26 (1131) DM500
Anr copy. Modern half mor. With 12 plates; several dampstained in upper corner. sg Jan 22 (135) $110
— A Bibliographical, Antiquarian and Picturesque Tour in the Northern Counties of England and in Scotland. L, 1838. 1st Ed. 2 vols. 8vo, mor gilt. pnE Jan 28 (329) £220 [Smith]
— The Bibliomania.... L, 1811. 2d Ed. 8vo, contemp sheep; joints worn. sg Jan 22 (131) $130
Anr Ed. L, 1842. 2 vols in 1. 8vo, contemp bds; worn & soiled. O Feb 24 (64) $100
Anr copy. Half mor; rubbed. O May 12 (54) $175
Anr Ed. Bost., 1903. One of 483 with plates in 2 states. 4 vols. 4to, bds; spine ends frayed. sg Jan 22 (32) $80
— Bibliotheca Spenceriana. L, 1814-22. Vols I-IV. 4to, contemp calf; worn, covers detached or starting. Marginal dampstains in Vol III with traces of mold. sg May 14 (293) $225
— An Introduction to the Knowledge of Rare and Valuable Editions of the Greek and Latin Classics. L, 1808. 3d Ed. 2 vols. 8vo, contemp calf gilt; joints rubbed. Lacking 1st & last leaf in Vol I. bba Oct 30 (459) £65 [Goldman]
4th Ed. L, 1827. 2 vols. 8vo, later calf; recased. cb June 18 (81) $65
Anr copy. Needs rebdg. sg Oct 2 (120) $175
Anr copy. Modern half mor. Lacking half-titles. sg Jan 22 (137) $150
Anr copy. Contemp calf; rubbed, rebacked, endpapers renewed. sg May 14 (202) $225
Anr copy. Contemp half lea gilt; backstrips def. sg May 14 (203) $200
— The Library Companion. L, 1824. 1st Ed. 2 vols. 8vo, 19th-cent calf. Some foxing. O May 12 (55) $80
Anr copy. Half calf; worn. ALs to Pickering loosely inserted. pn Dec 11 (104) £70 [Maggs]
— Reminiscences of a Literary Life. L, 1836. 1st Ed. 2 vols. 8vo, modern mor. Vol II lacking final blank. bba Oct 30 (458) £100 [Clark]
Anr copy. Half lea; worn. sg Jan 22 (138) $50

Dichter, Harry —& Shapiro, Elliott
— Early American Sheet Music, its Lure and its Lore. NY, 1941. 4to, cloth; rubbed. cb Feb 5 (82) $60

Dick, Joseph von Salm-Reiffescheidt. See: Salm-Reiffescheidt-Dick, Joseph von

Dick, Philip K.
— The Man in the High Castle. NY: Putnam, [1962]. 1st Ed, with code D36 at base of p 239. In rubbed d/j. cb Sept 28 (437) $75
— Martian Time-Slip. L: New English Library, [1976]. In d/j. cb Sept 28 (438) $50

Dickens, Charles, 1812-70
See also: Limited Editions Club; Nonesuch Press
— Barnaby Rudge. L, 1841. 1st Ed in Book form. 8vo, orig cloth; rubbed & loose. bba Jan 15 (91) £150 [Sumner & Stillman]
— The Battle of Life. L, 1846. 1st Ed, 4th Issue. 8vo, orig cloth. pn Dec 11 (316) £90 [Pederson]
— Bleak House. L, 1852-53. 1st Ed in orig 20/19 parts. 8vo, wraps; some detached, 1 stained. Some plates waterstained; lacking some ads. wa Mar 5 (71) $210

Anr copy. Wraps; spines chipped & partly perished, several rebacked. wd June 19 (115) $400

1st Ed in Book form. L, 1853. 8vo, contemp half mor; rubbed. Lacking half-title. bba Oct 16 (125) £50 [Scott]

Anr copy. Orig cloth; rubbed, upper joint split. Some waterstaining to margins of plates. bba Jan 15 (97) £90 [Summer & Stillman]

Anr copy. Later half mor. F Jan 15 (212) $150

Anr copy. Contemp half lea; rubbed. Some foxing. O Oct 21 (54) $50

Anr copy. Contemp half calf; rubbed. Plates foxed. O Nov 18 (53) $110

Anr copy. Contemp half lea gilt; minor surface damage on front cover. Lacking half-title. sg Feb 12 (122) $60

— [Christmas Books]. L, 1843-48. 1st Eds. 5 vols. 12mo, presentations by Sangorski & Sutcliffe for "Irene," with 3 of the vols inscr by the binders. All with additional Ms presentation leaves inserted, 8 in all, all illuminated & gilt, 3 with a carol & 1 fully illus with a street-scene in pen & watercolor. S July 23 (63) £3,400 [Cooleman]

4th Issue of The Battle of Life; 2d issue of others. Mor gilt by Sangorski & Sutcliffe; some covers detached, orig cloth bound in. sg Feb 12 (127) $400

Issues not indicated. Calf, orig cloth bound in. wd June 19 (116) $800

Anr Ed. L, 1886-[88]. 5 vols. 12mo, contemp calf gilt, orig cloth bound in. Ck Dec 10 (366) £320

— A Christmas Carol. L, 1843. 1st Ed, 1st Issue. 8vo, orig cloth; rebacked with orig backstrip relaid. With 4 hand-colored plates. T Feb 19 (592) £780

1st American Ed. Phila., 1844. 8vo, orig cloth; worn. With 4 plain & 3 hand-colored plates after John Leech. S Sept 22 (14) £100 [Studd]

Anr Ed. L, 1915. One of 525, sgd by Rackham. Illus by Arthur Rackham. 4to, orig cloth; slightly warped, lacking ties. With 12 mtd color plates. sg Oct 30 (58) $900

Anr Ed. Phila., 1915. 4to, orig cloth; spine faded. sg Oct 30 (59) $60

— David Copperfield. L, 1849-50. 1st Ed in orig 20/19 parts. 8vo, orig wraps; spines repaired or rebacked. With all the inserted ads & slips including the 8 Lett's Diaries specimens (1 def) & a portion of the folding sheet, with the Household Words slip from part 16 also in part 17. S Dec 18 (50) £1,500 [Kenyusha]

1st Ed in Book form. L, 1850. 8vo, contemp half mor; rubbed. bba Sept 25 (71) £85 [Jarndyce]

Anr copy. Orig cloth; rubbed, upper cover & spine loose. bba Jan 15 (96) £75 [Frew Mackenzie]

Anr copy. Modern mor gilt. With 40 plates. pn Nov 20 (45) £190 [Jarndyce]

Anr copy. Contemp half calf. Lacking half-title. sg Sept 11 (98) $100

Anr copy. Contemp half mor; soiled & worn, front joint starting. Plates spotted & dampstained. wa Sept 25 (655) $70

— Dombey and Son. L, 1846-48. 1st Ed in orig 20/19 parts. 8vo, orig wraps, in half mor slipcase; soiled. Lacking 1 ad from Part 2. With 1 other supplement part. pnNY Sept 13 (223) $900

1st Ed in Book form. L, 1848. 8vo, orig cloth; rubbed. Some waterstaining, mostly marginal. bba Jan 15 (95) £55 [Frew Mackenzie]

Anr copy. Contemp half calf; worn. cb Feb 19 (80) $55

Anr copy. Modern mor gilt. With engraved title & 38 plates. pn Nov 20 (46) £170 [Joseph]

Anr copy. Modern calf gilt. S Oct 23 (320) £65 [Trocchi]

Anr copy. Contemp half calf. One plate & adjacent text leaf torn in upper margin without loss. sg Sept 11 (93) $70

Anr copy. Contemp half calf; joints cracked. sg Feb 12 (120) $60

Anr copy. Half calf; soiled & worn. Lacking half-title & errata leaf. wa Sept 25 (653) $65

Anr Ed. L, 1858. ("The Story of Little Dombey.") 16mo, mor by Ramage, orig wraps bound in. sg Feb 12 (124) $90

DICKENS

— George Silverman's Explanation. Bost., Jan-Mar 1868. 1st Ed. 8vo, orig wraps. In: The Atlantic Monthly, Nos 123-125. pn Dec 11 (110) £380 [Jarndyce]
— Great Expectations. L, 1861. 1st Ed in Book form. 3 vols. 8vo, orig cloth; tailpiece of Vol I torn. pn Nov 20 (43) £12,000 [Quaritch]
— Hard Times. L, 1854. 1st Ed in Book form. 8vo, orig cloth. S Sept 22 (16) £300 [Valentine Books]
— The Haunted Man and the Ghost's Bargain. L, 1848. 1st Ed. 12mo, orig cloth; spine frayed. O Nov 18 (54) £60
[-] The Library of Fiction. L, 1836-37. 2 vols. 8vo, mor gilt. Includes 2 Dickens' stories. sg Feb 12 (128) £60
— Little Dorrit. L, 1855-57. 1st Ed in orig 20/19 parts, 1st Issue. 8vo, orig wraps, in later mor gilt box; worn. pnNY Sept 13 (222) $1,400
Anr copy. Orig wraps; front wrap to Part 4 detached but present, the others rebacked neatly. Lacking 1st leaf of "Advertiser" in last No. wd June 19 (118) $400
1st Ed in Book form. L, 1857. 8vo, contemp half lea; rubbed. Some foxing. O Oct 21 (55) $50
Anr copy. Half calf gilt. pn Sept 18 (122) £55 [Bookroom]
Anr copy. Modern mor. Lacking errata slip on p.481. pn Nov 20 (48) £140 [Jarndyce]
Anr copy. Contemp half calf; soiled & worn. wa Sept 25 (654) $80
— Martin Chuzzlewit. L, 1844. 1st Ed in Book form, 2d Issue. 8vo, modern mor gilt. pn Nov 20 (49) £320 [Jarndyce]
— Master Humphrey's Clock. L, 1840-41. 1st Ed in Book form. 3 vols. 4to, orig cloth; bumped, some signatures partially sprung. Some spotting. cb Feb 19 (81) £170
Anr copy. 3 vols in 1. 4to, old cloth; worn & shaken. O June 9 (53) £80
Anr copy. 3 vols in 2. 4to, modern cloth. Vol II prelims misbound. sg Feb 12 (117) $50
Anr copy. 3 vols. 8vo, orig cloth; recased. Some stains. wa Dec 11 (244) £130
Anr copy. Orig cloth; worn & soiled, a few black stains on Vol II. wa Mar 5 (72) $180
[-] Memoirs of Joseph Grimaldi. L, 1838. 1st Ed, 1st Issue. Ed by Dickens; illus by George Cruikshank. 2 vols. 8vo, calf gilt. With port & 12 plates. pn Nov 20 (50) £280 [Jarndyce]
— The Mystery of Edwin Drood. L, 1870. 1st Ed in Book form. 8vo, orig cloth; tail of spine rubbed. Flyleaf inscr "Catherine Dickens, 70 Gloucester Crescent August 1870". L Dec 11 (398) £320

AMERICAN BOOK PRICES CURRENT

Anr copy. Mor gilt, ads & lower wrap bound in. Foxed. pn Nov 20 (51) £75 [Joseph]
1st Ed, in orig 6 parts. 8vo, orig wraps; spines chipped & repaired. Complete with cork ad at rear of No 2. cb May 7 (261) $300; pn June 18 (235) £200 [Campbell]
Anr copy. Orig wraps; rebacked, spines chipped. sg Sept 11 (94) $120
— Nicholas Nickleby. L, 1839. 1st Ed in Book form, 1st Issue. 8vo, mor gilt. Lacking half-title. pn Oct 23 (47) £150 [Jarndyce]
Issue not stated. Half mor gilt. Lacking half-title. pn Nov 20 (95) £110 [Jarndyce]
— The Old Curiosity Shop. L, 1841. 8vo, orig cloth; rubbed. Some leaves torn in margins. bba Jan 15 (93) £140 [Summer & Stillman]
Anr copy. Contemp half calf. sg Feb 12 (118) $70
— Oliver Twist. L, 1838. 1st Ed in Book form, Issue not indicated. Illus by George Cruikshank. 3 vols. 12mo, contemp half calf; extremities worn. Lacking half-titles. sg Sept 11 (97) $90
2d Ed in Book form. 3 vols. 12mo, half mor. Lacking half-titles. pn Dec 11 (263) £85 [Valentine]
Anr Ed. L, 1839. 3 vols. 12mo, half calf gilt. Small repair to last leaf of Vol II. T Oct 16 (488) £125
— Our Mutual Friend. L, 1864-65. 1st Ed, in orig 20/19 parts. 8vo, orig wraps; rebacked. sg June 11 (159) $800
1st Ed in Book form. L, 1865. 2 vols. 8vo, contemp half mor gilt; joints & extremities rubbed. Prelims foxed. cb Feb 19 (82) $140
Anr copy. Later half mor. F Jan 15 (213) $130
Anr copy. Modern mor, upper wrap of No 8 bound in; lower corner of upper cover scuffed. pn Nov 20 (52) £90 [Joseph]
Anr copy. Half mor gilt; rubbed. pn Mar 5 (153) £50 [Ross]
— [Pickwick Papers]. L, 1837. 1st English Ed in Book form, 1st Issue. 8vo, mor by Root. Tear repaired at foot of pictorial title. O Sept 23 (45) $370
Early Issue. Mor gilt; upper cover of Part 4 & 4 ad leaves bound in. Engraved title repaired. pn Nov 20 (53) £70 [Joseph]
Anr copy. Modern half calf gilt. Half-title repaired. Extra-illus with plates, many in 2 states. S Jan 13 (489) £100 [Demetzy]
Anr copy. Mor extra with miniature of Dickens painted on ivory set into inside upper covers of each vol & with a cut signature inserted in Vol I, bdg by Bayntun. With 43 plates, each in 3 or 4 states, 1

colored by hand. And with 12 plates by C. E. Brock colored by hand with Ms captions, 1921. S July 23 (50) £1,600 [Greer] Issue not specified. Half sheep; 1 joint repaired, the other starting, worn. Plates heavily stained. sg Sept 11 (99) $100
Late Issue. Early calf; worn & soiled, front joint partly split. wa Mar 5 (73) $120
Anr Ed. L, 1910. Illus by Cecil Aldin. 2 vols. Folio, orig cloth; soiled. With 24 colored plates. AL (in 3d person) to Edward Whymper pasted to verso of upper cover of Vol I. L July 2 (56) £130
— Mr. Pickwick. One of 350. Illus by Frank Reynolds. 4to, orig vellum gilt. pn Jan 22 (316) £60 [Fraser]
Anr copy. Contemp vellum. SSA Feb 11 (501) R300
— Sketches by "Boz." L, 1836. First Series only. 2 vols. 12mo, half calf gilt. L Dec 11 (391) £160
1st Ed in Book form of 1st Series; 1st Ed of 2d Series. 3 vols. 12mo, orig cloth; slightly rubbed. pn Nov 20 (44) £1,700 [Joseph]
Anr Ed. L, 1836-37. 3 vols. 12mo, mor gilt by Robertson of Edinburgh, orig cloth bound in. Plates a little discolored; 2 small holes in Vol II. S July 23 (18) £1,150 [Ball]
Anr Ed. L, 1839. 8vo, mor gilt by Zaehnsdorf. With duplicate set of plates hand-colored & with title & 12 plates on india paper done for 2d series inlaid to 8vo. pn Nov 20 (54) £400 [McKenzie]
— The Strange Gentleman; a Comic Burletta, in Two Acts. L, 1837 [1871]. 8vo, modern half mor, orig wraps bound in. sg June 11 (160) $80
— A Tale of Two Cities. L, 1859. 1st Ed in Book form, 1st Issue. 8vo, half calf; head of spine def, rubbed. L Dec 11 (397) £120
Anr copy. Later half lea. O June 9 (54) $120
Anr copy. Orig cloth; worn. pn Nov 20 (38) £360 [Jarndyce]
Anr copy. Half calf; rubbed. S Sept 22 (15) £200 [Valentine Books]
Anr copy. Contemp half mor gilt. Inscr to Mary Cowden Clarke & with an exchange of A Ls s between them. S July 23 (61) £18,000 [Maggs]
Issue not indicated. Half calf. pnE June 17 (160) £70
— The Village Coquettes: A Comic Opera. L, 1836. 1st Ed. 8vo, unbound. sg June 11 (160) $80
— Die Weihnachtsabend. Zurich, 1910. Illus by Arthur Rackham. Cloth; rubbed. With 12 mtd color plates. sg Oct 30 (61) £120
— Works. L: Chapman & Hall, [1880s]. Illustrated Library Edition. 30 vols. 8vo, half

mor gilt by Tout. sg Dec 4 (56) $3,400
Anr Ed. L, 1890-93. 17 vols. 8vo, contemp half calf; worn. bba Aug 28 (232) £150 [Lyon]
Anr Ed. L, 1892. 17 vols. 8vo, half mor gilt. pn May 21 (83) £220 [Joseph]
Anr Ed. L, 1894-96. 16 vols. 8vo, half calf. S Sept 22 (17) £320 [T. Symonds]
Gadshill Ed. L, 1897-1903. 36 vols only; lacking Miscellaneous Papers. Orig cloth. bba Oct 30 (52) £130 [Whatman]
Authentic Ed. L, 1901-[6]. 21 vols. Cloth; lower cover of Vol 13 soiled; outer margin dust spotted. L Dec 11 (399) £50
Anr Ed. L, 1905-11. 22 vols. Contemp half mor by Riviere. Presented by the staff of the Northern Ed of the Daily News to Mr. Henry T. Cadbury, Managing Director, on the occasion of his marriage in the Dickens Centenary Year, 1912. T Apr 16 (261) £460
Anr Ed. L, 1929. Ltd Ed. 40 vols. Calf gilt by Riviere with facsimile Dickens signature stamped on front covers. sg Dec 4 (57) $3,000

Dickens Association copy, Charles
Anr Ed.
— JONSON, BEN. Works, L, 1838. 8vo, presentation red mor gilt. Inscr by Dickens: "Miss Fortescue, In remembrance of the amateur performance of Every Man in his Humor, on the [ ] September 1845, and with the best wishes of the Company: to wit Charles Dickens otherwise Bobadil." Sgd beneath by the other members of the cast, John Forster, Mark Lemon, Douglas Jerrold & John Leech. P June 18 (39) $9,000

Dickens, Charles, 1812-70 — & Collins, Wilkie, 1824-89

— The Wreck of the Golden Mary.... Kentfield, Calif.: Allen Press, 1956. One of 200. sg Jan 8 (2) $150

Dickes, William Frederick

— The Norwich School of Painting. L & Norwich, [1906]. One of 100. 4to, orig mor gilt; soiled. pn Oct 23 (342) £120 [Walford]

Dickey, James

— Jericho. The South Beheld. Birmingham AL, [1974]. Illus by Hubert Shuptrine. Oblong folio, cloth, in d/j with a few small tears. Sgd by Dickey & Shuptrine. O Feb 24 (172) $50

DICKINSON

Dickinson, Emily, 1830-86
See also: Masque...
— Letters of.... Bost., 1894. Ed by Mabel Loomis Todd. 2 vols. 16mo, orig cloth with Roberts Bros imprint on spine; worn. O Nov 18 (57) $60
— Poems by Emily Dickinson Edited by Two of her Friends.... Bost., 1890. 1st Ed. Ed by Mabel Loomis Todd & T. W. Higginson. 12mo, cloth; soiled. wa Dec 11 (28) $375
— Poems by Emily Dickinson...Second Series. Bost., 1891. 8vo, orig half cloth; worn & soiled. wa June 25 (330) $120

Dickinson, Francis Arthur
— Lake Victoria to Khartoum. L, 1910 [1909]. Intro by Winston Churchill. 8vo, half mor; rubbed. cb Nov 6 (82) $55

Dickinson, Henry Winram —&
Jenkins, Rhys
— James Watt and the Steam Engine. L, 1927. 4to, cloth; worn, soiled, 1 corner chipped. With port, 2 maps & 104 plates. wa Nov 6 (83) $150

Dickinson, John, 1732-1808
— Letters from a Farmer in Pennsylvania. L, 1768. 8vo, contemp sheep. Library markings. Theodore Foster's copy. F Jan 15 (510) $375

Dickson, Albert Jerome
— Covered Wagon Days. Cleveland, 1929. 1st Ed. cb Oct 9 (62) $50

Dickson, Carter. See: Carr, John Dickson

Dickson, Gordon R.
— Necromancer. Garden City, 1962. 1st Ed. In d/j. cb Sept 28 (444) $55

Dickson, R. W.
— A Complete Dictionary of Practical Gardening. L, [1805]-7. 2 vols. 4to, contemp mor gilt; rubbed. With 61 hand-colored plates & 13 plain plates. Short tear in 2U3 of Vol II; some foxing. S Oct 23 (672) £1,600 [Schire]

Anr copy. Contemp calf gilt; upper joint of Vol I weak. With 13 plain & 61 hand-colored plates. Monypenny—de Belder copy. S Apr 27 (102) £2,200 [Krohn]

Anr Ed. L, 1812. ("The New Flora Britannica.") Illus by Sydenham Edwards. 2 vols. 4to, contemp mor gilt; spine & corners rubbed. With 61 hand-colored plates. C Apr 8 (176) £3,500 [Kaye]

Anr copy. ("The New Botanic Garden.") Contemp calf. With 61 hand-colored plates & additional plate 19a. pnE Dec 17 (193) £1,600 [Graham]

Dickson, Robert, 1828-93
— Introduction of the Art of Printing into Scotland. Aberdeen: Edmond & Spark, 1885. One of 500. 8vo, pictorial cloth; worn. O Feb 24 (65) $50

Dictionarium. See: Worlidge, John

Dictionary...
— Dictionary of American Biography. NY, 1928-44. 22 vols, including Index. 4to, cloth. bba Dec 4 (129) £150 [Monckton]

Anr copy. 22 vols, including Index & Supplement I. 4to, orig cloth, Vol I rebound in cloth. Library markings. sg Sept 18 (78) $750

Anr copy. Cloth. sg Dec 4 (59) $550

Anr Ed. NY, 1946. 22 vols in 11 sg Oct 2 (121) $600

Anr Ed. NY, 1957-61. 12 vols, including Supplements & Index. 4to, cloth. sg Apr 2 (70) $400

Anr Ed. NY, [1958]. 22 parts in 11 vols. 4to, cloth. sg Jan 22 (139) $550

— Dictionary of Scientific Biography. NY, [1970-80]. 16 vols in 8. 4to, orig cloth. FD Dec 2 (214) DM1,800

— Dictionary of American History. NY, 1942. 5 vols plus Supplement One & Index. 4to, cloth. sg June 11 (165) $225

— The Dictionary of National Biography. L, 1885-1981. 74 vols, including 11 supplements & the Concise Dictionary. S July 13 (59) £550

Anr Ed. L, 1908-30. 24 vols, including indexes & supplement. Half mor; 1 cover detached, rubbed. pn Sept 18 (276) £160 [Shapero]

Anr Ed. L, [1921]-49. 25 vols, including Supplement & "Twentieth Century" to 1930. Orig cloth; rubbed. Ck Sept 5 (198) £250

— The Dictionary of National Biography...Concise Dictionary. L, 1948-71. 3 vols, including Supplements covering 1931-40 & 1951-60 sg Jan 2 (141) $175

— The Dictionary of National Biography. L, 1975. Compact Ed. 2 vols. Folio, cloth, boxed with magnifying glass. cb Feb 5 (83) $225

— Dictionary of Scientific Biography. NY, [1970-80]. 16 vols in 8. 4to, orig cloth. Ck Nov 7 (21) £550

Dictionnaire...
— Dictionnaire theorique et pratique de chasse et de peche. Paris, 1769. 8vo, contemp calf gilt. Sometimes attributed to Jean-Baptiste Claude Izouard, called Delisle de Sales, or to Delisle de Moncel. Jeanson copy. SM Feb 28 (169) FF4,200

— Dictionnaire des sciences naturelles. Paris & Strassburg, 1816-30. Plate vols 1-12 only. 4to, cloth. Sold w.a.f. bba Dec 18 (138) £750 [Elliott]

— Dictionnaire des sciences occultes. Paris, 1848. 2 vols. 4to, modern half calf. Vol I lacking tp; some foxing. sg Sept 11 (101) $80

— Dictionnaire abrege du Surrealisme. Paris, 1938. Orig wraps; worn. S June 29 (43) £250 [Nogemi]

Diderot, Denis, 1713-84

— Principes de la philosophie morale.... Amst. [but Paris]. chez Zachariae Chatelain, 1745. 8vo, contemp calf. Inscr to Mme de Sainte Croix. C Dec 3 (177) £3,200 [Perrin Thomas]

Diderot, Denis, 1713-84 —& Alembert, Jean le Rond d', 1717?-83

— Encyclopedie. Lucques & Paris, 1758-76. Set consisting of: Encyclopedie, ou dictionnaire raisonne des sciences et des arts. 17 vols. Lucques & [no imprint], 1758-71. And: Recueil de planches. 11 vols. Lucques & Paris, 1765-76. Together, 28 (of 35) vols. Folio, contemp calf; broken. Soiled & foxed throughout. sg Apr 2 (71) $6,500

Anr Ed. Paris, Neuchatel & Geneva, 1765-72. 17 vols plus the 11 vols of Recueil de planches only. Together, 28 (of 35) vols. Folio, contemp calf; rubbed. Sold w.a.f. S June 25 (99) £4,400 [Burgess]

— Recueil de planches. Paris, 1762-72. Vol VIII. Contemp bds; worn. HK Nov 4 (1741) DM600

Diehl, Edith

— Bookbinding: its Background and Technique. L & NY, 1946. 2 vols. cb Feb 5 (84) $65; O Sept 23 (46) $50; O June 16 (71) $50

Anr copy. 2 leaves loose in Vol I. sg Jan 22 (12) $150; wa June 25 (15) $90

Diemerbroeck, Isbrandus de, 1609-74

— Anatome corporis humani. Lyons, 1679. 4to, contemp calf; brittle, spine ends worn. With extra title & 13 plates. Stained; worming affecting c.15 text leaves & 1 plate. sg Jan 15 (93) $275

Diesel, Rudolf, 1857-1913

— Theory and Construction of a Rational Heat Motor. L & NY, 1894. 8vo, cloth; worn. With 3 folding plates. wa Nov 6 (34) $160

Dietrich, Albert Gottfried

— Flora Regni Borussici. Flora des Koenigreichs Preussen.... Berlin, 1833-44. 12 vols. 8vo, contemp half mor gilt; rubbed. With 864 hand-colored plates. Plesch—de Belder copy. S Apr 27 (103) £4,200 [Sourget]

Dietrich, Friedrich Gottlieb

— Die linneischen Geranien fuer Botaniker und Blumenliebhaber, Parts 1-5. Weimar, 1801-3. Bound with: Darstellung vorzueglicher Zierpflanzen...fuer Botaniker und Blumenliebhaber, Part 1. Weimar, 1803. 4to, contemp bds. With 20 hand colored plates in 1st work & 4 hand-colored plates in 2d work. Some spotting. Horticultural Society of New York—de Belder copy. S Apr 27 (104) £1,000 [Luzarraga]

Dietrich, Philippe-Frederick, Baron de

— Description des gites de mineral, des forges et des salines des Pyrenees. Paris, 1786. 2 (of 6) parts in 2 vols. 4to, contemp half calf. With 2 plain & 4 folding hand-colored plates. Lacking half-title. C Dec 12 (70) £300 [Birmingham Assay Office]

Digges, Sir Dudley, 1583-1639

— The Compleat Ambassador, or Two Treaties.... L, 1655. 1st Ed. Folio, contemp calf; broken, cracked. Title soiled, frayed & nearly detached; lower edges dampstained. cb Oct 23 (57) $55

— The Defence of Trade. L, 1615. 4to, half calf. S July 23 (436) £3,000 [Riley-Smith]

Dighton, Basil L. See: Lawrence & Dighton

Dighton, Phoebe

— Relics of Shakespeare. L: Ackermann, 1835. 4to, cloth; spine repaired. With 10 plates, all hand-colored except that of Ann Hathaway's bdg. Introductory leaf soiled. S Apr 23 (121) £600 [19th-century]

Dilich, Wilhelm

— Beschreibung und Abriss dero Ritterspiel.... Cassel: Wilhelm Wessel, 1601. Folio, contemp blind-stamped calf over wooden bds. Lacking port & address to the reader; tp at outer margin & repaired; some foxing & spotting. S May 21 (101) £1,000 [Maggs]

Dilke, Emilia Francis Strong Pattison, Lady

— French Engravers and Draughtsmen of the XVIIIth Century. L, 1902. One of 150. 4to, cloth. With 50 plates. O June 16 (71) $50

Dillenius, Johann Jakob, 1687-1747

— Hortus Elthamensis seu plantarum rariorum.... L, 1732. One of 250. 2 vols. Folio, contemp vellum bds. With 322 (of 325) plates. Lacking Plates 168, 211 & 224; neat repair to Plate 125; some stains to margins. S Oct 23 (678) £1,700 [Burden]
Anr copy. Contemp vellum bds; soiled. With 325 plates. Horticultural Society of New York—de Belder copy. S Apr 27 (105) £4,000 [Junk]
Anr Ed. Leiden, 1774. ("Horti Elthamensis plantarum rariorum icones....") 2 vols in 1. Folio, orig bds; rubbed. With 325 plates. Some worming in upper margin occasionally affecting plate numbers. Horticultural Society of New York—de Belder copy. S Apr 27 (107) £31,000 [Israel]

Dillon, Peter, 1785?-1847

— Narrative and Successful Result of a Voyage in the South Seas.... L, 1829. 2 vols. 8vo, modern half calf. Some foxing; repair to 1 folding frontis. kh Mar 16 (152B) A$700

Dillon, Richard

— Images of Chinatown: Louis J. Stellman's Chinatown Photographs. San Francisco: Book Club of Calif., 1976. One of 450. cb Sept 11 (34) $65

Dimand, Maurice S.

— The Ballard Collection of Oriental Rugs in the City Art Museum of St. Louis. St. Louis, 1935. One of 1,000. sg Feb 5 (245) $200

Dinet, Etienne, 1861-1929 —& Suliman Ben Ibrahaim Baemer

— La Vie de Mohammed, Prophete d'Allah. Paris, 1918. One of 925. 4to, orig mor gilt by Sangorski & Sutcliffe. Ptd in colors & gold. S Mar 9 (735) £250 [Harrington]

Dingley, Robert

— Vox Coeli; or, Philosophical...Observations of Thunder. L, 1658. 8vo, modern half calf. Some spotting. bba Nov 13 (191) £45 [Elliott]

Dio Chrysostomus

— De Regno. Bologna: Franciscus (Plato) de Benedictis, 1493. 4to, modern half calf. 1st leaf stained & repaired at margins shaving 1 letter; marginal repair to final leaf affecting 1 letter; minor worming to inner blank margin of last few leaves; a few leaves stained. 44 leaves. Goff D-205. C Dec 12 (290) £420 [Maggs]

Diodorus Siculus

— The Historical Library of Diodorus the Sicilian. L, 1700. Folio, contemp calf; worn, joints split. bba Jan 15 (28) £60 [Quaritch]

Diogenes Laertius

— The Lives, Opinions, and Remarkable Sayings of the Most Famous Ancient Philosophers. L, 1688. Vol I (all pbd). 8vo, contemp calf; covers partly detached. sg Mar 26 (100) $110

— Vitae et sententiae philosophorum. Venice: [Bonetus Locatellus] for Octavianus Scotus, 18 Dec 1490. ("De Vita & moribus philosophorum.") 4to, later bds. Some dampstaining & soiling throughout; a1 refaced conserving the 2 lines of title on the recto; o7 rebacked; worming in the text of a1-5 & o4-8; some dampstaining & soiling throughout. 111 (of 112) leaves; lacking final blank. Goff D-222. S Mar 10 (1052) £340 [Poole]
Anr Ed. Venice: Philippus Pincius for Benedictus Fontana, 22 June 1497. ("Vitae & Sententiae eorum qui in philosophia....") Folio, later half vellum. Dampstained; final leaf torn & repaired; some worming of outer margins. 96 leaves. Goff D-225. Ck June 5 (74) £200
Anr Ed. Amst.: H. Wetsten, 1692. ("De vitis, dogmatibus et apophthegmatibus clarorum philosophorum.") 2 vols. 4to, contemp vellum. Library markings. O June 9 (55) $90

Dionis du Sejour, ——, Mlle

— Origine des graces.... Paris, 1777. Illus by Cochin. 8vo, mor extra by Chambolle-Duru. Repair at A4 & E8 with a few letters supplied in Ms. C May 13 (12) £400 [Maggs]

Dionysius Areopagiticus

— Opera. Acala, 1541. 8vo, old vellum; loose. Marginal dampstains at beginning & end; some worming. sg Oct 9 (48) $175

Dionysius Halicarnassus

See also: Jefferson's copy, Thomas

— Antiquitates Romanae. Paris: R. Stephanus, 1546-47. ("Antiquitatum Romanarum lib. X.") 2 parts in 1 vol. Folio, 19th-cent calf gilt; joints worn. S Sept 23 (443) £400 [Maggs]
Anr copy. Early 19th-cent calf gilt. First part lacking all after 2t6 at end; some rust-holes. S July 14 (387) £100

Dioscorides, Pedacius
— De medica materia libri sex. Florence: Giunta, 1518. Folio, vellum bds; inner hinges broken. Tp cut out & mtd; piece torn from e8 affecting text; some tears & staining. S Nov 10 (480) £200 [Wheldon]
— The Greek Herbal. Oxford, 1934. 4to, cloth. sg Jan 15 (94) $175

Diplomatic...
— Diplomatic Correspondence of the American Revolution. Bost., 1829-30. Ed by Jared Sparks. 12 vols. 8vo, contemp sheep; soiled & stained, worn. wa Mar 5 (409) $125

Directory...
— Directory of Pittsburgh and Allegheny Cities.... Pittsburgh: Geo. H. Thurston, 1863. 8vo, half lea; spine worn away, covers stained at edges. Some stain to text at outer corners. sg Sept 18 (235) $120

Dirom, Alexander
— A Narrative of the Campaign in India.... L, 1794. 2d Ed. 4to, modern half calf; rubbed & worn. With 9 maps & plates. cb Dec 18 (53) $160

Discourse...
— A Discourse concerning the Fishery within the British Seas. L, 1695. 16 leaves. 4to, wraps. S July 23 (437) £350 [Lawson]

Disney, John
— Museum Disneianum, being a Collection of Ancient Marbles.... L, 1849. 4to, contemp half mor; rubbed, front inner joint cracked. Tears in text repaired. K Mar 22 (20) $150

Disney Studios, Walt
— The Adventures of Mickey Mouse. L, 1931. Orig bds, in d/j. wa Dec 11 (621) $160
— Three Little Pigs. L, 1934. 4to, orig bds, in d/j. With stand-up cardboard cut-outs of the pigs. wa Nov 6 (521) $150

Disraeli, Benjamin, 1st Earl of Beaconsfield, 1804-81
— Endymion. L, 1880. 1st Ed. 3 vols. 8vo, mor by Riviere; joints rubbed. Lacking Z2 in Vol II & Z6 in Vol III. Inscr to his pbr, Norton Longman. S Dec 18 (62) £600 [Woods]
— Vindication of the English Constitution.... L, 1835. 1st Ed. 8vo, bds; worn. S July 13 (226) £160
— Works. NY, [1904-5]. Empire Ed, One of 1,244. 20 vols. ha May 22 (56) $100
 Anr copy. Lea gilt; spines dried. O Mar 24 (57) $130

D'Israeli, Isaac, 1766-1848
— Flim-Flams!; or, the Life and Errors of my Uncle.... L, 1805. 3 vols. 16mo, contemp half calf; broken. sg Sept 11 (86) $50

Distant, William Lucas
— Rhopalocera Malayana: a Description of the Butterflies of the Malay Peninsula. L, 1882-86. 4to, mor. With 46 colored plates. S Apr 23 (5) £900 [Orient]
 Anr copy. Contemp half mor gilt, orig part wraps bound in; rubbed. S May 28 (662) £650
 Anr copy. Contemp half mor gilt; upper cover detached. Text & title spotted. S May 28 (663) £500

Ditz...
— Les Ditz des bestes. [Lyon: Martin Havard, c.1499]. 4to, calf gilt by C. Lewis. 4 leaves. GKW 8484. Jeanson copy. SM Feb 28 (181) FF45,000
 Les Ditz joyeux des oiseaulx. [Lyon: Imprimeur du Champion des Dames, c.1485-90]. 4to, mor janseniste by Duru. 6 leaves. GKW 8485. Jeanson copy. SM Feb 28 (182) FF130,000

Divertissemens. See: Cabinet...

Dix, John Ross
— Amusing and Thrilling Adventures of a California Artist.... Bost., 1854. 12mo, ptd wraps crudely sewn & pinned, stained & yellowed; corners creased & chipped. sg Nov 13 (68) $3,200

Dixon, Charles, 1858-1926
— The Game Birds and Wild Fowl of the British Islands. Sheffield, 1900. 2d Ed. 4to, orig cloth; worn. With 41 plates. pn Sept 18 (14) £65 [Goddard]; pn May 21 (206) £130 [Shapero]

Dixon, Capt. George, 1755?-1800
— Voyage autour du monde.... Paris, 1789. 4to, 19th-cent half mor; rubbed. With 22 plates & maps. O May 12 (57) $400
 Anr copy. Half mor, with Wharncliffe arms. With folding map & 21 charts & plates. Some foxing. S Oct 23 (516) £500 [Perrin]
— A Voyage Round the World.... L, 1789. 1st Ed, Issue not stated. 4to, later half vellum. Tp repaired; lacking half-title; lacking Falkland Islands shells plate but the Cancer Raninus crab plate repeated. S June 25 (385) £500 [Sellers]
 2d Ed. 4to, contemp calf; broken & detached along with endpaper, half-title & frontis chart (which is laid down on linen). Some stains. cb Mar 19 (78) $375

Dobie, James Frank, 1888-1964
— Mustangs and Cow Horses. Austin: Texas Folk-lore Society, 1940. In d/j. Inscr by Dobie & with 4 Ross Santee inscrs. sg Sept 18 (79) $225

Dobson, Austin, 1840-1921
— The Ballad of Beau Brocade, and other Poems. L, 1892. One of 450 L.p. copies. Illus by Hugh Thomson. 4to, cloth; corners worn. wa Sept 25 (281) $70
— Eighteenth Century Vignettes. L, 1892-94. 1st & 2d Series. 4to, contemp half mor gilt; rubbed. Extra-illus with c.175 plates. bba Sept 25 (170) £85 [Burwood]
— Thomas Bewick and his Pupils. L & Bost., 1884. One of 200. 4to, half vellum; rubbed, spine ends chipped. cb Feb 19 (85) $50

Anr copy. Modern half mor gilt. L July 2 (43) £90

Dodart, Denis
— Memoires pour servir a l'histoire des plantes. Paris: Imprimerie Royale, 1676. Folio, contemp mor gilt with arms of Louis XIV. With frontis & 39 plates. Minor foxing. Plesch—de Belder copy. S Apr 27 (107) £31,000 [Israel]

Dodd, Charles. See: Tootell, Hugh

Dodd, William, 1729-77. See: Johson & Dodd

Dodge, Grenville Mellen
— Letter from the Secretary of the Interior.... Wash., 1868. 8vo, modern half calf. cb Jan 8 (47) $65

Dodge, Richard Irving, 1827-95
— Our Wild Indians.... Hartford, 1883. Orig cloth; new endpapers. Some foxing. cb Jan 8 (48) $55

Dodgson, Campbell
— A Complete Catalogue of the Etchings and Dry-Points of Edmund Blampied. L, 1926. One of 350. 4to, orig cloth. With sgd frontis & 60 plates. S Nov 10 (75) £380 [Marks]

Anr copy. Orig cloth; front hinge starting. sg June 4 (42) $700
— Old French Colour-Prints. L, 1924. One of 1,250. 4to, half vellum. O June 16 (74) $60

Out-of-series copy. Orig half vellum gilt; spine worn. L July 2 (18) £50

Dodgson, Charles Lutwidge, 1832-98
See also: Limited Editions Club
— Alice's Adventures in Wonderland. L, 1865. 1st Ed. 2 vols. 8vo, mor gilt by Bayntun with white rabbit & red queen on upper covers. Vol I, short tears in margin of last gathering repaired; Vol II, surface of 1 p rubbed. With copies of Warren Weaver's report certifying all signatures are of the 1865 Ed and with photos of the disbound vol & related correspondence. S Dec 5 (304) £45,000 [J. Schiller]

2d (1st Pbd) Ed. L, 1866 [1865]. 8vo, mor gilt by Riviere, orig cloth bound in; upper hinge cracked. pn Nov 20 (251) £450 [Traylen]

Anr copy. Cloth; worn, rebacked, orig spine preserved. S Dec 5 (305) £200 [Hirsch]

1st American Ed, comprising the sheets of the 1st (suppressed) English Ed with a cancel title. NY: D. Appleton & Co., 1866. 8vo, mor gilt with orig covers bound as doublures. E8, F3 &F6 on thicker, creamier stock & may be in facsimile. With ALs 12 Feb 1890. Gribbel copy. P Sept 24 (147) $1,100

Anr copy. Orig cloth; spine def. S June 18 (436) £2,000 [Shobo]

Anr Ed. NY, 1872. Illus by Sir John Tenniel. 8vo, half calf gilt. pnNY June 11 (110) $225

Anr Ed. L, 1886. ("Alice's Adventures Under Ground.") 8vo, orig cloth; front hinge starting. Facsimile of Dodgson's 1st Ms draft of "Alice". sg June 11 (91) $325

Anr Ed. L, 1889. ("The Nursery Alice.") 4to, orig half cloth. S June 18 (441) £700 [Randolph]

Anr Ed. L, 1890. 4to, orig half cloth; worn. S Oct 7 (956) £50 [Lovett]

Anr Ed. L, [1907]. Illus by Arthur Rackham. 8vo, orig cloth. With 13 color plates. sg Oct 30 (45) $110

One of 1,130. 4to, orig cloth. pn May 21 (284) £320 [Joseph]

1st Ed Deluxe, One of 1,130, sgd by Rackham. 4to, orig cloth in half mor gilt folding case. With 13 mtd color plates. With an orig pen & wash sketch of Alice. sg Oct 30 (43) $5,500

Anr copy. Cloth. Endpapers stained. sg Oct 30 (44) $550

Anr Ed. NY, [1907]. 8vo, cloth. With 13 color plates. sg Oct 30 (46) $175

Anr copy. 4to, orig cloth; rubbed. With 13 colored plates. sg Jan 8 (227) $100

Anr Ed. NY, 1927. Calf gilt by Riviere. Facsimile of Appleton's 1866 Ed. cb Feb 19 (51) $100

Anr Ed. Paris: Black Sun Press, 1930. ("Alice in Wonderland.") One of 20. Illus by Marie Laurencin. Oblong 4to, orig bdg; soiled & rubbed. JG Oct 2 (2118a) DM6,500

One of 790. Loose as issued in wraps & portfolio. wd June 19 (66) $2,200

Anr Ed. L, 1932. Bound with: Dodgson. Through the Looking Glass. L, 1933. Mor gilt by Riviere inlaid with pictures of Alice. sg Sept 11 (56) $425

Anr Ed. NY, 1969. One of 200 with extra suite on japon nacre. Illus by Dali. Folio, unsewn in orig wraps. sg Dec 4 (31) $1,000

— Aventures d'Alice au pays des merveilles. L, 1869. Illus by Sir John Tenniel. 8vo, orig cloth; hinges tender. Inscr to Lorina Charlotte Liddell. P June 18 (43) $5,000

Anr Ed. Paris, [1907]. Illus by Arthur Rackham. 8vo, cloth; worn. With 13 color plates. With bookplate of Harry & Caresse Crosby. sg Oct 30 (47) $275

— La Chasse au Snark. Paris, 1950. One of 25 with etched plates. Illus by Max Ernst. Orig wraps. S June 29 (59) £4,800 [Rota]

— Elementary Treatise on Determinants. L, 1867. 4to, calf, orig covers bound in. Library stamp on tp. O May 12 (58) $500

— Feeding the Mind. L, 1907. 8vo, ptd wraps; worn. O Nov 18 (39) $50

— The Game of Logic. L, 1886. 8vo, orig cloth. With the card board & 9 counters in orig loosely inserted envelope. Chew copy. S june 18 (440) £700 [Joseph]

2d Ed. L, 1887. 12mo, orig cloth. With card & 9 counters in envelope. Inscr. S June 18 (439) £1,800 [Randolph]

— The Hunting of the Snark. L, 1876. 1st Ed. 12mo, orig cloth; rubbed & soiled. bba Dec 4 (109) £60 [Wise]

Anr copy. Orig cloth; shaken, inner joints broken. O Apr 28 (36) $60

— Sylvie and Bruno Concluded. L: Macmillan, 1893. 1st Ed. 8vo, orig cloth, in frayed d/j. T Feb 18 (182) £110

— Through the Looking-Glass. L, 1872 [1871]. 1st Ed, 1st Issue, with "wade" on p. 21. 8vo, lev gilt by Riviere, orig cloth bound in. pn Nov 20 (252) £400 [Traylen]

Anr copy. Orig cloth; rubbed & shaken. pn Nov 20 (253) £90 [Demetzy]

Anr Ed. L, 1872. 8vo, orig cloth; soiled, hinges broken. Some internal soiling, 1st 3 gatherings loose. S Oct 7 (957) £70 [Sotheran]

2d Issue. Orig cloth by Burn, with their ticket; rubbed & soiled, inner hinges split. S May 6 (193) £200 [Shimogosa Shobo]

Dodgson, D. S.

— General Views and Special Points of Interest of the City of Lucknow. L, 1860. Folio, cloth. With engraved title, map & 27 views on 11 sheets. Some plates loose or frayed. S July 14 (841) £80

Dodoens, Rembert, 1518-85

— Cruydeboeck. Leiden: Plantin, 1618. ("Cruydt-Boeck....") Folio, contemp vellum over wooden bds; stained, lacking 1 tie. Upper margin of tp just shaved; 2 leaves torn & repaired; a few margins strengthened; occasional minor staining mainly in margins. Sold w.a.f. C Oct 15 (221) £700 [Marshall]

Anr Ed. Antwerp: Plantin, 1644. Folio, old calf; rebacked with most of old gilt backstrip laid down, corners renewed. Lacking last leaf; small wormhole affecting text & illusts from the front to O4; minor wormhole to blank foremargin from front to Ii4; worming affecting upper blank margin from Rrrr2 to end; 2 index leaves with minor tears; some stains & browning. Hunt copy. CNY Nov 21 (101) $350

— De sphaera.... Antwerp: C. Plantin, 1584. 8vo, 19th-cent half lea. FD Dec 2 (434) DM5,000

— Florum, et coronariarum odoratarumque. Antwerp: Plantin, 1568. 8vo, contemp calf; lea at corners & at head & tail of spine renewed, orig Ms endleaves removed; some soiling or staining, affecting a few lines of text on last 20 leaves. With 107 woodcuts of flowers & herbs, many full-page & those to p 232 touched with color. Some marginal soiling or staining. CNY Nov 21 (100) $1,200

— Historia vitis vinique: et stirpium nonnullarum aliarum. Cologne: Maternus Cholinus, 1580. Bound with: Rousset, Francois. Hysterotomotokia. Basel: C. Valdkirch, 1588. 8vo, vellum. 1st work with old library stamps on tp; browned. Simon-Crahan copy. P Nov 25 (155) $1,200

— A Niewe Herball. L [Antwerp ptd], 1578. ("A Niewe Herball, or Historie of Plantes.") Folio, contemp calf. Small repair to lower inner margins of tp & 1st few leaves; marginal repairs to 3 leaves of index & 1st leaf of table repaired with some loss; wormed at beginning. T July 16 (75) £1,650

— Stirpium historia commentariorum. Antwerp: Plantin, 1616. ("Stirpium historia pemptades sex.") Folio, vellum; upper joint cracking. Marginal tears. Crahan copy. P Nov 25 (156) $1,100

Dodsley, Robert

— The Oeconomy of Human Life. See: Oeconomy...

Dodsley, Robert, 1703-64
— A Compendium of Authentic and Entertaining Voyages. L, 1766. 2d Ed. 7 vols. 12mo, contemp sheep; worn & brittle. Library markings on titles. sg Apr 23 (136) $225

Dodsley, Robert, 1703-64 —& Cowley, John
— The Geography of England.... L, 1744. 8vo, contemp bdg; upper cover detached. With 56 maps. Some tears. pn May 21 (415) £520 [Nicholson]

Dodsworth, Roger, 1585-1654. See: Dugdale & Dodsworth

Dodwell, Charles Reginald
— The Canterbury School of Illuminations.... Cambr., 1954. 4to, cloth, in d/j. pn Jan 22 (86) £100 [Fogg]

Dodwell, Edward, 1767-1832
— A Classical and Topographical Tour through Greece.... L, 1819. 2 vols. 4to, calf gilt with arms of Cawdor. With 2 folding maps & 64 plates. pn May 21 (230) £400 [Nichols]
Anr copy. Cloth & half cloth; 1 cover detached. With 1 folding map & 66 plates. Library stamps on plates & titles; folding map repaired; hole in 1 plate; possibly lacking last leaf in Vol II. S Feb 23 (79) £280 [Camp]
Anr copy. Contemp half calf; rubbed, broken. Head cut from title of Vol I; lacking ads; some dampstains. S May 29 (1179) £250
— Views and Descriptions of Cyclopian or Pelasgic Remains in Greece and Italy. L, 1834. Folio, half calf. With 131 plates. Some discoloration; library stamp on tp verso. S Apr 24 (216) £1,100 [Camp]
— Views in Greece, from Drawings by... L, 1821. Folio, half mor gilt; broken. With 30 hand-colored plates mtd on card. S Apr 24 (217) £3,800 [Tsigaras]
Anr copy. Half mor; rebacked. Some offsetting from plates onto facing text. S June 25 (344) £4,200 [Marshall]

Doebel, Heinrich Wilhelm
— Neueroeffnete Jager-Practica.... Leipzig: J. S. Heinsius, 1746. ("Eroeffnete Jaeger-Practica....") Folio, contemp vellum; worn. Jeanson copy. SM Feb 28 (183) FF17,000

Dolbear, Amos Emerson
— The Telephone.... L, 1878. 8vo, orig bds; soiled. C May 13 (200) £90 [Mackenzie]

Dolce, Lodovico, 1508-68
— Le Trasformationi. Venice: Francesco Sansovino, 1568. 4to, 19th-cent half calf; backstrip loose. Lacking last prelim leaf & final leaf; some stains. S Sept 23 (324) £120 [McNaul]

Dolce, Ludovico, 1508-68
— Aretin: A Dialogue on Painting. L, 1770. 8vo, contemp calf. Ck Jan 30 (6) £120

Dollfus, Charles —& Bouche, Henri
— Histoire de l'aeronautique. Paris, 1942. Folio, half calf; rubbed & marked. Stamp at end. bba Feb 5 (307) £60 [Weiner]

Dolphin...
— The Dolphin: A Journal of the Making of Books. NY, 1933-41. Nos 1-4, in 6 vols. 4to, cloth. O May 12 (59) $200
Anr Ed. NY, 1935. No II, only. O Sept 23 (47) $50; O Mar 24 (58) $50

Domat, Jean
— Les Loix civiles dans leur ordre naturel.... The Hague, 1703. 2 vols in 1. Folio, old bds; rebacked with pigskin. sg Oct 9 (180) $175
Anr Ed. Paris, 1777. 2 vols in 1. Folio, calf. B Feb 25 (1001) HF950

Dome
— The Dome. L, 1897-1900. 1st Series, Nos 1-5, 2d Series, Nos 1-7 (all pbd). 4to, orig bds & cloth; rubbed. Lacking 1 port in N.S. 3 & tables of contents to N.S. 1-3 & 7; fold of 1 plate repaired. B Oct 7 (276) HF1,300
Anr copy. 1st Series, Nos 1-5 (complete), 2d Series, Nos 1-4 (of 7). 4to, orig bds; rubbed. Lacking tp & 1 plate of the new series. B June 2 (1193) HF700

Domesday-Book...
— Domesday Book, seu Liber censualis.... L, 1783-1816. 4 vols. Folio, 19th-cent half mor. sg Oct 9 (181) $650

Dominguez Bordona, Jesus
— Spanish Illumination. Florence & Paris, [1930]. 2 vols. 4to, orig cloth; worn. Perforated stamp on titles & 4 leaves. bba Feb 5 (96) £55 [Bennett & Kerr]

Dominicus de Flandria
— Quaestiones in commentaria Thomaë de Aquino super Metaphysicis Aristotelis. Venice: Petrus de Quarengiis for Alexander Calcedonius, 20 Aug 1499. Folio, 19th-cent half sheep; shaken. Some browning & staining; some headlines shaved; some worming in lower inner corners occasionally affecting text; artlessly repaired. 350 leaves. Goff D-306. sg Dec 4 (60) $650

Dominis, Marco Antonio de
— Assertor Gallicus.... Paris: Typographia Regia, 1646. 4to, contemp calf gilt; joints split, rubbed, front free endpaper creased & with tear. bba Sept 25 (245) £130 [Frew Mackenzie]

Donaldson, Stephen R.
— Gilden-Fire. San Francisco, 1981. One of 270. In d/j. cb Sept 28 (451) $65

Donaldson, Thomas C., 1843-98
— The George Catlin Indian Gallery in the U. S. National Museum. Wash., 1886. One vol in 2. 8vo, cloth. With 5 folding maps & 142 plates. Some tears & soiling. wa Sept 25 (430) $75

Donn, Benjamin, 1729-98
— A Map of the County of Devon, wtih the City and County of Exeter. L, 1765. Folio, contemp half calf; worn & loose. With general map & 9 sectional maps only. L July 2 (132) £320

Donne, John, 1573-1631
See also: Nonesuch Press
— Ignatius his Conclave, or his Inthronisation in a late Election in Hell. L, 1635. Bound with. Walter of Henley. The Booke of Thrift. L: John Wolfe, 1589. 12mo, 18th-cent calf. Outer portion of title of 2d work torn off with partial loss of text but without loss of imprint; minor paper fault in C7. C May 13 (160) £3,500 [Lawson]
— Letters to Severall Persons of Honour.... L, 1651. 1st Ed, 1st Issue. 4to, 17th-cent sheep; rubbed. Lacking port, 1st few leaves soiled, slight worming in upper margin throughout. S Sept 22 (167) £340 [Zayas]
— LXXX Sermons. L, 1640. 1st Ed. Folio, contemp calf; rebacked, rubbed. With engraved title with port of Donne. Some dampstaining; 1 or 2 rust-holes; a few short tears; lacking 1st & last blanks. S Mar 10 (1053) £300 [Harrington]
— Poems. L, 1669. 7th Ed. 8vo, later calf. Lacking 1st & final blanks; some cropping. S Jan 13 (365) £180 [Bennett]
Anr copy. Later 19th-cent calf. Tears in 3 leaves repaired affecting text; a few head-lines shaved; lacking first & last blanks. Inscr to Diana Manners Cooper by Maurice Baring, 1914. S Mar 9 (777) £360 [Hannas]
Anr Ed. Oxford, 1912. 2 vols. Modern half mor. sg Sept 11 (104) $200
— Poems, by J. D..... L, 1633. 1st Ed. 4to, calf gilt; lower joint worn; upper joint cracked. With "The Printer to the Understanders" and "Hexastichon Bibliopolae" leaves. P Dec 15 (190) $1,200
3d Ed. L, 1639. 8vo, lev gilt extra. sg Oct 9 (182) $800
Anr Ed. L, 1719. ("Poems on Several Occasions....") 12mo, contemp calf; rubbed, upper cover almost detached. bba Mar 26 (54) £55 [Francis]

Donovan, Edward, 1768-1837
— An Epitome of the Natural History of the Insects of China. L, 1798. 4to, modern half calf gilt. With 50 hand-colored plates. pn Apr 30 (119) £2,100 [Wheldon & Wesley]
— The Natural History of British Insects. L, 1792-1813. Vols I-VIII only. Later cloth. Sold w.a.f. C Apr 8 (208) £650 [Wellesley]
— The Naturalist's Repository, or Monthly Miscellany of Exotic Natural History.... L, 1823-27. Vols I-II. Orig cloth. Lacking 4 plates. pn Dec 11 (29) £420 [Thomas]
Anr Ed. L, [c.1835]. ("The Naturalist's Repository of Exotic Natural History.") 2 vols. 8vo, orig cloth; lower covers spotted, gutta percha perishing. With 72 hand-colored plates. Reissue of Vols I-II. C Oct 15 (223) £700 [Thompson]
— Quadrupeds. L, [1810]-1820. ("The Natural History of British Quadrupeds.") 3 vols. 8vo, half vellum gilt by Birdsall. With 72 hand-colored plates. C Oct 15 (222) £900 [Clubley]

Doolittle, Hilda, 1886-1961
— The Hedgehog. L, 1936. One of 300. In d/j. sg Dec 11 (223) $175
— Heliodora and Other Poems. L, 1924. Inscr. sg Mar 5 (50) $175

Doorly, Eleanor
— The Insect Man. Cambr., [1936]. 1st Ed, one of 6. Intro by Walter de la Mare. In def d/j. Inscr to Robert Gibbings & by him to Alex Hyman. bba Aug 20 (185) £220 [Stone]

Doppelmayr, Johann Gabriel
— Atlas novus coelestis.... Nuremberg, 1742. Folio, contemp half vellum; rubbed, spine torn. With engraved title & 30 double-page engraved chart, partly hand-colored, some within pink, yellow or blue wash borders, mtd on guards. C Apr 8 (19) £2,300 [Phelps]
Anr copy. Bds. With engraved title & 29 (of 30) double-page engraved charts, some with outlines & details colored. One map loose, anr def. FD June 11 (744) DM6,000

Doran, John, 1807-78
— "Their Majesties' Servants." Annals of the English Stage. L, 1888 [1887]. 3 vols in 6. 8vo, lea by James Forbes; rubbed. With 50 ports. ALs inserted. Extra-illus with ports & plates. O June 16 (75) $260

Dorat, Claude Joseph, 1734-80
— Les Baisers.... The Hague & Paris, 1770. 8vo, mor gilt by Trautz-Bauzonnet. L.p. copy on hollande. C Dec 3 (111) £4,000 [Beres]

Anr copy. Mor gilt by Cuzin. With engraved title & frontis. L.p. copy on hollande. C Dec 3 (112) £1,600 [Tenschert]

Anr copy. Mor gilt by Lortic a la janseniste. FD Dec 2 (3711) DM1,600

2d Issue. Mor by Riviere. With engraved title & frontis. With a vol containing proof impressions of 16 head- & tail-pieces. C Dec 3 (113) £350 [Sourget]

— Fables nouvelles. The Hague, 1773-[75]. 8vo, mor gilt by Trautz-Bauzonnet. Extra-illus with port of Dorat & duplicate 1 vignette. C Dec 3 (114) £1,500 [Sourget]

Dore, Gustave, 1833-83
— The Dore Gift Book of Illustrations to Tennyson's "Idylls of the King." L, [1870]. 4to, contemp mor gilt extra; rubbed, rehinged. Endpapers heavily foxed, plates slightly so. cb Oct 23 (59) $50

Dore, Gustave, 1833-83 — & Jerrold, William Blanchard, 1826-84
— London. L, 1872. Folio, orig cloth; spine def. pn Mar 5 (85) £90 [Trochi]

Dore, Henri
— Recherches sur les superstitions en Chine. Shanghai, 1911-38. 18 vols. 8vo, orig half cloth; soiled. bba Aug 28 (295) £650 [Cavendish]

Doring, Ernest
— The Guadagnini Family of Violin Makers. Chicago, 1949. One of 1,500. Cloth. Stained in lower right corner, occasionally affecting text. sg Feb 26 (227) $110

— How Many Strads? Our Heritage from the Master. Chicago, 1945. One of 1,400. Pictorial cloth. Inscr. sg Feb 26 (228) $400

Dorlandus, Petrus
— Viola animae, sive de natura hominus. Cologne: Heinrich Quentell, 16 July 1501. 4to, early 19th-cent russia; rebacked, worn. Foxed at beginning; some early underscoring; some worming throughout; lacking final blank. sg Oct 9 (49) $225

Dorset...
— Dorset Natural History and Archaeological Society: Proceedings. Sherborne, 1877-1984. Vols 1-106. Cloth or wraps. With 3 indices & photocopy of anr. Sold w.a.f. Sgd by J. C. M. Mansel-Pleydell (1st president of the Society) on tp of Vol I. L Dec 11 (109) £160

Dortu, M. G.
— Toulouse-Lautrec et son oeuvre. NY, 1971. One of 1,450. 6 vols. 4to, orig cloth. Ck Nov 28 (336) £160; Ck Nov 28 (337) £160

Dos Passos, John
— Three Soldiers. NY, [1921]. 1st Ed, 1st State. In d/j. sg Mar 5 (51) $275

Dossie, Robert, d.1777
— The Handmaid to the Arts. L, 1764. 2d Ed. 2 vols. 8vo, orig bds. sg Feb 5 (109) $225

Doughty, Charles Montagu, 1843-1926
— Travels in Arabia Deserta. Cambr., 1888. 1st Ed. 2 vols. 8vo, orig cloth; rubbed, rebacked, old spines preserved, new endpapers. Folding map in pocket mtd on linen; library stamps on titles & half-titles. bba Aug 20 (483) £120 [Hay]

Anr Ed. L, [1926]. 2 vols. Calf gilt by Brian Frost. cb Sept 11 (241) $275

Doughty, John & Thomas
— The Cabinet of Natural History and American Rural Sports. Phila.: J. & T. Doughty, 1830-32. Vols I-II (of 3). 4to, old half mor, with orig wraps in half mor case; Vol I worn. sg Oct 23 (249) $2,400

Douglas, John, Bishop of Salisbury
— A Letter Addressed to Two Great Men.... L: A. Millar, 1760. 8vo, disbound. sg Sept 18 (234) $80

Douglas, Norman, 1868-1952
— Alone. L, 1921. 1st Ed. Lytton Strachey's copy. sg Dec 11 (226) $50

— Birds and Beasts of the Greek Anthology. L, 1928. Corrected page proofs. Wraps; broken, lacking backstrip. sg Dec 11 (227) $300

— Fabio Giordano's Relation of Capri. Naples, 1906. One of 250. Orig wraps. Inscr. bba July 2 (151) £120 [Ritchie]

— Fountains in the Sand. L, 1912. 1st Ed. ALs inserted. bba July 2 (153) £450 [Updike]

— In the Beginning. [Florence], 1927. 1st Ed, one of 700. Bds. ALs inserted. bba July 2 (161) £55 [Vanderos]

One of 700, sgd. Bds. Inscr. sg Dec 11 (228) $50

— London Street Games. L, [1916]. 1st Ed, One of 500. Inscr. bba July 2 (156) £70 [Sumner]

— Looking Back.... L, 1933. 1st Ed, One of 500. In d/js. sg Dec 11 (19) $50

Uncorrected page proofs. Unbound. sg Dec 11 (229) $50

— Nerinda. Florence: G. Orioli, 1929. 1st Ed, One of 475, sgd. sg Dec 11 (20) $50

— On the Herpetology of the Grand Duchy of Baden. L, 1894. 8vo, orig wraps. bba July

2 (150) £420 [Maggs]
— One Day. Chapelle-Reanville: The Hours Press, 1929. 1st Ed, Out-of-series copy, sgd. Lea; spine faded. Inscr. sg Dec 11 (230) $250
— Report on the Pumice Stone Industry of the Lipari Islands. L, 1895. One of 80. 8vo, sewn. Inscr. sg Dec 11 (231) $350
— Siren Land. L & NY, 1911. Orig cloth, in torn & def d/j. bba July 2 (152) £110 [Scott]
— Some Antiquarian Notes. Naples, 1907. One of 250. Orig wraps; rebacked & repaired. Last 4 leaves holed & def, affecting text. Sold w,a,f. Inscr. bba July 16 (325) £50 [Clark]
— Some Limericks. [Florence]: Pvtly ptd, 1928. ("Some Limericks Collected for the Use of Students....") Out-of-series copy. Inscr. S May 6 (459) £75 [Scott]
— Summer Islands. [L]: Corvinus Press, 1942. One of 7 lettered copied on handmade paper, sgd. 4to, bds. Inscr & with ANs to John Mavrogordato laid in. sg Dec 11 (233) $700
— Together. L, 1923. 1st Ed, One of 275 L.p. copies, sgd. Inscr. sg Dec 11 (234) $50

Douglas, Sir Robert, 1694-1770
— The Peerage of Scotland. Edin., 1764. Folio, contemp half calf; rubbed. With 10 plates. O Feb 24 (69) $85

Douglass, Frederick, 1817?-95
— My Bondage and My Freedom. NY & Auburn, 1855. 1st Ed. 8vo, orig cloth; worn. Some stains. wa Feb 19 (174) $100

Douglass, William, c.1691-1752
— Summary, Historical and Political, of...British Settlements in North-America. L, 1755. 2 vols. 8vo, contemp calf; loose, lacking front free endpaper. sg Mar 12 (100) $250

Doves Press—London
— The English Bible. 1903-5. One of 500. 5 vols. sg Apr 2 (23) $1,900
— Pervigilium Veneris. 1910. One of 150. sg June 11 (167) $250
— BROWNING, ROBERT. - Men and Women. 1908. One of 250. 2 vols. Hand-flourished copy. sg Apr 2 (73) $475
— CARLYLE, THOMAS. - Sartor Resartus. 1907. One of 300. CNY May 11 (40) £1,000
— COBDEN-SANDERSON, THOMAS JAMES. - Amantium Irae. Letters to Two Friends 1914. One of 150. In lev gilt by the Doves Bindery dated 1919. sg Apr 2 (50) $375
— COBDEN-SANDERSON, THOMAS JAMES. - Credo. 1908. One of 12 on vellum. Mor gilt by the Doves Bindery. FD June 11 (4884) DM3,700
— COBDEN-SANDERSON, THOMAS JAMES. - The Ideal Book or Book Beautiful. 1900. One of 300. Mor gilt by the Doves Bindery. sg Apr 2 (49) $800
— EMERSON, RALPH WALDO. - Essays. 1906. One of 300. Orig vellum. sg Apr 2 (74) $300
— GOETHE, JOHANN WOLFGANG VON. - Torquato Tasso ein Schauspiel.... 1913. One of 12 on vellum & with initials in gold by Graily Hewitt. Mor gilt. FD June 11 (4945) DM8,400
— MACKAIL, JOHN WILLIAM. - William Morris: an Address.... 1901. One of 300. bba Apr 9 (241) £95 [Axe]
— RUSKIN, JOHN. - Unto this Last. 1907. One of 300. Inscr by Emery Walker. og Jan 8 (62) $325; sg Jan 8 (63) $150
— TENNYSON, ALFRED. - Seven Poems and Two Translations. 1902. One of 325. cb Sept 11 (88) $110

Anr copy. Mor gilt with garland of roses, by Cobden-Sanderson, sgd & dated 1903. pn Nov 20 (75) £800 [Georges]; sg Jan 8 (64) $110

Dow, Alexander
— The History of Hindostan. L, 1803. 3 vols. 8vo, sheep; rebacked. With folding map & 4 plates. sg Apr 23 (40) $130

Dow, George Francis, 1868-1936
— Slave Ships and Slaving. Salem, Mass.: Marine Research Society, 1927. Orig half cloth; worn. Library stamps on front endpapers. O Jan 6 (53) $90

Anr copy. Cloth; corners worn. wa Sept 25 (392) $50

Downes, Charles. See: Cowper & Downes

Downie, William
— Hunting for Gold: Reminiscences.... San Francisco, 1893. 8vo, orig cloth; newly rebacked & recornered. cb Oct 9 (67) $70; sg Mar 12 (101) $150

Downing, Andrew Jackson, 1815-52
— A Treatise on the Theory and Practice of Landscape Gardening.... NY, 1853. 5th Ed. 8vo, orig cloth; rubbed. Frontis stained. bba Sept 25 (270) £75 [Weinreb]

Downs, Joseph
— American Furniture. NY, 1952. 1st Ed. 4to, cloth, in d/j. With 10 color plates. O Feb 24 (7) $60

Downs, T. Nelson
— The Art of Magic. Buffalo, 1909. Ed by J. N. Hilliard. 8vo, cloth; worn. sg Feb 26 (144) $80

Anr copy. Cloth; hinges starting. sg Feb 26 (176) $100

Doyle, Sir Arthur Conan, 1859-1930
— The Adventure of the Speckled Band. L, 1892. Wraps. In: The Strand Magazine, Issue 14 of Vol III, Feb 1892, pp 142-57. cb Apr 24 (161) $95
— The Adventure of the Engineer's Thumb. L, 1892. Wraps. In: The Strand Magazine, Issue 15 of Vol III, Feb 1892, pp 276-88. cb Apr 24 (164) $55
— The Adventure of the Noble Bachelor. L, 1892. Wraps. In: The Strand Magazine, Issue 16 of Vol III, Apr 1892, pp 386-89. cb Apr 24 (168) $80
— The Adventure of the Copper Beeches. L, 1892. Wraps. In: The Strand Magazine, Issue 18 of Vol III, June 1892, pp 613-28. cb Apr 24 (174) $130
— The Adventure of the Silver Blaze. [L: George Newnes, 1892]. Silk over bds, stamped with gilt crown. In: The Strand Magazine, Issue 24, Vol IV, Dec 1892, the Royal Edition. cb Apr 24 (177) $55
— The Adventure of the Musgrave Ritual. L, 1893. Wraps. In: The Strand Magazine, Issue 19 of Vol V, May 1893, pp 479-89. cb Apr 24 (193) $80
— The Adventure of the Reigate Squire. L, 1893. Wraps. In: The Strand Magazine, Issue 30 of Vol V, June 1893, pp 601-12. cb Apr 24 (195) $80
— The Adventure of the Crooked Man. L, 1893. Wraps. In: The Strand Magazine, Issue 31 of Vol VI, July 1893, pp 22-32. cb Apr 24 (199) $55
— The Adventure of the Resident Patient. L, 1893. Wraps. In: The Strand Magazine, Issue 32 of Vol VI, July 1893, pp 128-38. cb Apr 24 (202) $75
— The Adventure of the Greek Interpreter. L, 1893. Wraps. In: The Strand Magazine, Issue 33 of Vol VI, Sept 1893, pp 296-307. cb Apr 24 (204) $75
— The Adventure of the Final Problem. L, 1893. Wraps. In: The Strand Magazine, Issue 36 of Vol VI, Dec 1893, pp 559-70. cb Apr 24 (211) $150
— The Adventure of the Priory School. L, 1904. Wraps. In: The Strand Magazine, Issue 158 of Vol XVII, Feb 1904, pp 123-40. cb Apr 24 (273) $85
— The Adventure of the Abbey Grange. L, 1904. Wraps. In: The Strand Magazine, Issue 165 of Vol XVIII, Dec 1904, pp 603-17. cb Apr 24 (281) $65
— The Adventure of the Second Stain. L, 1904. Wraps. In: The Strand Magazine, Issue 168 of Vol XVIII, Dec 1904, pp 603-17. cb Apr 24 (282) $65
— The Adventure of Wisteria Lodge. L, 1908. 2 Issues. Wraps. In: The Strand Magazine, Issues 213 & 214 of Vol XXXVI, Sept & Oct 1908. cb Apr 24 (286) $120
— The Adventure of the Red Circle. L, 1911. 2 Issues. Wraps. In: The Strand Magazine, Issues 243 & 244 of Vol LXI, Mar & Apr 1911. cb Apr 24 (291) $85
— The Adventure of the Creeping Man. L, 1923. Wraps. In: The Strand Magazine, Issue 387, Vol LXV, Mar 1923, pp 211-24. cb Apr 24 (324) $65
— The Adventure of the Three Garridebs. L, 1925. Wraps. In: The Strand Magazine, Issue 409 of Vol LXIX, Jan 1925, pp 2-14. cb Apr 24 (330) $85
— The Adventure of the Blanched Soldier. L, 1926. Wraps. In: The Strand Magazine, Issue 431 of Vol LXXII, Nov 1926, pp 422-34. cb Apr 24 (335) $60
— The Adventure of the Retired Colourman. L, 1927. Wraps. In: The Strand Magazine, Issue 433 of Vol LXXIII, Feb 1927, pp 108-16. cb Apr 24 (336) $65
— The Adventure of the Veiled Lodger. L, 1927. Wraps. In: The Strand Magazine, Issue 434 of Vol LXXIII, Feb 1927, pp 108-16. cb Apr 24 (337) $70
— The Adventures of the Beryl Coronet. L, 1892. Wraps. In: The Strand Magazine, Issue 17 of Vol III, May 1892, pp 511-25. cb Apr 24 (170) $75
— The Adventures of Sherlock Holmes. L, 1892. 1st Ed in Book form. 8vo, orig cloth. With piece of paper inscr "Yours Affectionately, ACD". cb Apr 24 (375) $550
Anr copy. With: The Memoirs of Sherlock Holmes. L, 1894. Illus by Sidney Paget. 2 vols. 8vo, Minor foxing. S July 23 (77) £600 [Minerva]
Anr copy. With: The Memoirs of Sherlock Holmes. L, 1894. Illus by Signey Paget. cb Apr 24 (373) $1,100
Anr copy. With: The Memoirs of Sherlock Holmes. L, 1894. cb Apr 24 (374) $650
— Adventures of Gerard. L: George Newnes, [1903]. cb Apr 24 (530) $90
— The Annotated Sherlock Holmes. L: John Murray, [1968]. Ed by W. S. Baring-Gould. 2 vols. In d/js. cb Apr 24 (770) $55; cb Apr 24 (771) $65
2d Ed, 2d ptg. 2 vols. In d/js. cb Apr 24 (771) $65; cb Apr 24 (773) $55
— Beyond the City. L, 1891. Orig wraps. In: the Csristmas 1891 issue of Good Words. cb Apr 24 (360) $80
— The Black Ear (J. Habakuk Jephson's Statement). Chicago: Max Stein, [n.d.]. Orig wraps. cb Apr 24 (24) $55
— The Boscombe Valley Mystery. L, 1891. Wraps. In: The Strand Magazine, Issue 10 of Vol II, Oct 1891, pp 401-16. cb Apr 24 (150) $70

— The British Campaign in France and Flanders. L, 1916-19. 1st Ed. 6 vols. Cloth. cb Apr 24 (597) $55
1st Ed, except Vol I, which is 4th impression. 6 vols. Cloth. Inscr. cb Apr 24 (595) $140
— The British Campaigns in Europe 1914-1918. L, 1928. Inscr. cb Apr 24 (689) $200
— The British Campaign in France and Flanders. L, 1916-19. 1st Ed. 6 vols. Cloth. Inscr. cb Apr 24 (596) $140
— The Captain of the Polestar and Other Tales. L, 1890. 8vo, cloth over bds. cb Apr 24 (83) $170
— The Case for Spirit Photography. L: Hutchinson, [1922]. Wraps; worn & chipped. Some creases. cb Apr 24 (623) $80; cb Apr 24 (1986) $55
Anr Ed. NY: Doran, 1923. Cloth. cb Apr 24 (624) $55
— A Case of Identity. L, 1891. Wraps. In: The Strand Magazine, Issue 9 of Vol II, Sept 1891, pp 248-59. cb Apr 24 (149) $85
— The Case of Oscar Slater. L: Hodder & Stoughton, [1912]. Orig wraps. cb Apr 24 (566) $75
— The Case-Book of Sherlock Holmes. L, [1927]. 1st Ed. Light foxing to half-title & title. cb Nov 20 (98) $225; cb Apr 24 (683) $100
Anr copy. In chipped d/j. cb Apr 24 (685) $200
Murray's Imperial Library Ed. L: John Murray, 1927. In chipped d/j. cb Apr 24 (685) $200
— Collected Poems. L, 1928. 2d Issue. In d/j. Jean Conan Doyle's annotated copy. cb Apr 24 (630) $85; cb Apr 24 (632) $110
— The Coming of the Fairies. L: The Psychic Press, [1928]. 2d Issue. cb Apr 24 (627) $65
— Coup d'oeil sur la guerre. L, 1915. Wraps. Some stains & library stamps. cb Apr 24 (593) $65
— Le Crime du Congo. Paris, [1910]. Orig wraps; chipped & worn. cb Apr 24 (558) $65
— Danger! And Other Stories. L, 1918. 1st Ed. In d/j. cb Apr 24 (607) $90
Anr copy. In torn d/j. T Feb 18 (94) £48
— The Doings of Raffles Haw. L, 1892. 8vo, cloth. cb Apr 24 (366) $110; cb Apr 24 (367) $65
— The Exploits of Brigadier Gerard. L, 1896. 1st Ed. 8vo, cloth. cb Apr 24 (445) $80
Anr copy. Orig cloth; spine ends worn. cb Apr 24 (450) $50
— The Firm of Girdlestone, a Romance of the Unromantic. L, 1890. 1st Ed. 8vo, cloth.

cb Apr 24 (86) $70
— The Five Orange Pips. L, 1891. Wraps. In: The Strand Magazine, Issue 11 of Vol II, Nov 1891, pp 481-91. cb Apr 24 (155) $55
— The Great Boer War. L, 1900. 8vo, cloth. With the armorial bookplate of the dedicatee, Sir John L. Langman. cb Apr 24 (496) $130
Anr copy. Cloth. With armorial bookplate of the dedicatee, Sir John L. Langman. cb Apr 24 (496) $130
Anr copy. Cloth; inner hinges weak. cb Apr 24 (497) $65
Anr copy. Cloth. Inscr. cb Apr 24 (498) $140
Complete Ed. L, 1902. cb Apr 24 (500) $75
Suppressed Ed. L: Thomas Nelson, [n.d.]. cb Apr 24 (503) $100
— The Great Shadow. Bristol & L, [1892]. 8vo, cloth; upper inner hinge breaking. bba Oct 16 (166) £40 [Gibson]
— The Green Flag, and Other Stories.... L, 1900. 8vo, cloth. cb Apr 24 (1974) $65
— The Grey Dress. L: The Daily Mail for The Union Jack Club, [1908]. In: The Flag: The Book of the Union Jack Club, pp 66-67. cb Apr 24 (552) $55
— The Gully of Bluemansdyke. L, 1893. 8vo, orig cloth. cb Apr 24 (301) $180
— His Last Bow. L, 1917. Wraps. In: The Strand Magazine, Issue 321 of Vol LIV, Sept 1917, pp 226-36. cb Apr 24 (314) $95
1st Ed. Bdg marked & spine creased. cb Apr 24 (1980) $95
— The History of Spiritualism. L, 1926. 2 vols. In d/js. bba Mar 12 (496) £95 [Hackhofer]
Anr copy. In d/j. cb Apr 24 (660) $130; cb Apr 24 (661) $130; cb Apr 24 (662) $60
— The Hound of the Baskervilles. L, 1901. 1st installment. Wraps. In: The Strand Magazine, Issue 128 of Vol XXII, Aug 1901, pp 122-32. cb Apr 24 (258) $110
Complete serialization. L, 1901-2. 2 vols. Cloth. In: The Strand Magazine, Vols XXII & XXIII, Aug 1902-Apr 1902. cb Apr 24 (518) $355
1st Ed. L, 1902. In forged d/j. 2 plates misbound. bba Aug 20 (154) £250 [Hunt]; cb Apr 24 (528) $600
Anr copy. A number of plates loose; 1 or 2 torn in margins. S Sept 22 (80) £280 [Laws]
Anr copy. Orig cloth; spine slightly soiled. S Dec 18 (112) £500 [Joseph & Sawyer]
Anr copy. Orig cloth; worn. S May 6 (460) £220 [Hannas]
2d Installment. Wraps. In: The Strand Magazine, Issue 134 of Vol XXIII, Feb

1902, pp 122-30. cb Apr 24 (259) $80
Anr Ed. San Francisco: Arion Press, 1985. One of 400. sg Jan 8 (7) $200
— How Brigadier Gerard Lost his Ear. L, 1902. Wraps. In: The Strand Magazine, Issue 140 of Vol XIV, Aug 1902, pp 123-35. cb Apr 24 (262) $50
— How the Brigadier Played for a Kingdom. L, 1895. Wraps. In: The Strand Magazine, Issue 60 of Vol X, Dec 1895, pp 603-15. cb Apr 24 (228) $50
— The Last Adventures of Sherlock Holmes. L, 1901. Souvenir Ed. Inscr, 2 Oct 1901. cb Apr 24 (708) $355
— The Last Resource. L, 1930. Wraps. In: The Strand Magazine, Issue 480 of Vol LXXX, Dec 1930, pp 605-12. cb Apr 24 (349) $100
— The Lost World. L, 1912. Wraps. In: The Strand Magazine, Issue 262 of Vol LXIV, Oct 1912, pp 362-75. cb Apr 24 (294) $50
1st Ed. Orig cloth; extremities rubbed. cb Sept 28 (462) $180
Anr copy. Cloth. cb Apr 24 (569) $250
Anr copy. Cloth; some wear. cb Apr 24 (570) $140
Anr copy. Cloth, variant bdg. cb Apr 24 (573) $110
Anr copy. Cloth. cb Apr 24 (1978) $65
1st English Ed, L.p. Issue, one of 190 in light blue cloth. cb Apr 24 (1977) $1,500
Anr Ed. L, [1914]. One of 1,000 L.p. copies. Tan cloth. Plate to p. 276 supplied in facsimile. cb Apr 24 (572) $110
— Lot No. 249. L, 1892. Orig cloth. In: Harper's Monthly Magazine for Sept 1892. cb Apr 24 (353) $75
— The Love Affair of George Vincent Parker. L, 1901. Wraps. In: The Strand Magazine, Issue 124 of Vol XXI, Apr 1901. cb Apr 24 (254) $55
— The Maracot Deep: The Lost World Under the Sea. I. L, 1927. Wraps. In: The Strand Magazine, Issue 442 of Vol LXXIV, Oct 1927, pp 320-31. cb Apr 24 (343) $55
— The Memoirs of Sherlock Holmes. L, 1894 [1893]. Illus by Sidney Paget. 8vo, orig cloth; worn, hinges reinforced. S Sept 22 (81) £180 [Smith]
Anr Ed. L, 1894. 12mo, orig cloth; prize copy, a few leaves loose. bba Sept 25 (123) £80 [Pordes]
— Memories and Adventures. Bost., 1924. 1st American Ed. Rear inner hinge split. cb Apr 24 (645) $55
Anr Ed. L: Hodder & Stoughton, [1924]. cb Apr 24 (639) $120
Anr copy. Inscr. cb Apr 24 (641) $225; cb Apr 24 (642) $100

Anr copy. Rubbed, rear hinge split. Inscr. cb Apr 24 (643) $130; O June 9 (57) $145
2d Ed. L, 1930. cb Apr 24 (647) $95
— Micah Clarke his Statement. L, 1889. 1st Ed. 8vo, orig cloth. cb Apr 24 (62) $150
Anr copy. Orig cloth; inner joints starting. cb Apr 24 (64) $50
— The Mystery of Cloomber. L, 1889. 8vo, contemp cloth. Rebound without ads. cb Apr 24 (71) $250
Anr Ed. L: Hodder & Stoughton, [1913]. 8vo, cloth. Sgd. cb Apr 24 (78) $80
— The New Revelation. L, 1918. In chipped d/j. Inscr. cb Apr 24 (611) $160; cb Apr 24 (612) $60
— A Night Among the Nihilists. L, 1881. Orig cloth. In: London Society Vol 39, Apr 1881. cb Apr 24 (3) $60
— Our Second American Adventure. L: Hodder & Stoughton, [1924]. In d/j. cb Apr 24 (648) $50
— Out of the Running. L, 1892. Folio, bds. In: Black & White for 2 Jan 1892. cb Apr 24 (125) $90
— The Parasite. L, 1894. 1st Ed. 8vo, orig wraps; rubbed & soiled, spine def. bba Jan 15 (175) £80 [Gibson]
Anr copy. Orig cloth; joints & extremities rubbed. cb Nov 20 (122) $55; cb Apr 24 (418) $110
Anr copy. Orig cloth; worn. cb Apr 24 (419) $55
— Pheneas Speaks: Direct Spirit Communications in the Family Circle. L: The Psychic Press, [1927]. Wraps. cb Apr 24 (669) $50
— The Poison Belt. L: Hodder & Stoughton, 1913. cb Apr 24 (583) $80
— The Poison Belt. Being an Account of Another Adventure.... L, [1913]. Illus by Harry Rountree. With 16 plates. cb Nov 20 (126) $55
— The Red-Headed League. L, 1891. Wraps. In: The Strand Magazine, Issue 8 of Vol II, Aug 1891, pp 190-204. cb Apr 24 (145) $85
— The Refugees. L, 1893. 3 vols. 8vo, later half calf. Some foxing. cb Apr 24 (396) $200
1st Ed in Book form. 3 vols. 8vo, calf gilt by Bayntun. cb Apr 24 (395) $350
— The Return of Sherlock Holmes. L, 1905. 1st Ed. Fine copy. cb Apr 24 (538) $550
Anr copy. Cloth; scuffed. Minor foxing. cb Apr 24 (539) $65; cb Apr 24 (588) $550
Anr copy. Cloth; worn, hinges broken. S Sept 22 (82) £190 [Gibson]
Anr copy. Cloth; backstrip def. T Feb 18 (93) £60
— Rodney Stone. L, 1896. 12 Issues. Wraps.

In: The Strand Magazine, Issues 61-72 of Vols XI-XII, Jan-Dec 1896. cb Apr 24 (229) $160
— Round the Fire Stories. L: Smith, Elder, 1908. cb Apr 24 (553) $130; cb Apr 24 (1976) $95
— Round the Red Lamp. L, 1894. 1st Ed. 8vo, orig cloth. cb Apr 24 (428) $100
— A Scandal in Bohemia. L, 1891. Wraps. In: The Strand Magazine, Issue 7 of Vol II, July 1891, pp 61-75. cb Apr 24 (143) $170
— The Second Sherlock Holmes Illustrated Omnibus. L, 1979. In d/j. cb Apr 24 (797) $55

A Sherlock Holmes Competition. L, 1927. Wraps. In: The Strand Magazine, Issue 435 of Vol LXXIII, Mar 1927, pp 281-84. cb Apr 24 (339) $80

— The Sherlock Holmes Collected Edition. L, 1974. 9 vols. In d/js. cb Apr 24 (786) $450
— The Sign of Four. L, 1890. ("The Sign of the Four; or, the Problem of the Sholtos.") Cloth, lacking front free endpaper. In: Lippincott's Monthly Magazine 45, No 266. De Waal 271. cb Apr 24 (98) $150
1st Separate Ed in Book form. 8vo, orig cloth; spine rebuilt with a Spencer Blackett spine laid on (however, the covers & contents are of 2d issue). cb Apr 24 (99) $180
2d Issue. Orig cloth. cb Apr 24 (100) $355
2d Ed. L, 1892. 8vo, cloth; worn & shaken, inner joint broken. O Oct 21 (59) $100

— The Stark Munro Letters. L, 1895. 1st Ed. 8vo, cloth. cb Apr 24 (436) $90
Anr copy. Cloth; shaken. cb Apr 24 (437) $65

— The Stark Munro Letters & Round the Red Lamp. L, 1903. Inscr to Edward Sackville-West. cb Apr 24 (439) $160

— A Straggler of '15. L, 1891. Folio, bds. In: Black & White for 21 Mar 1891. cb Apr 24 (124) $80

— A Study in Scarlet. L, 1891. 8vo, cloth. cb Apr 24 (39) $355
2d Ed. L, 1892. 2d Impression. 8vo, cloth. cb Apr 24 (41) $225
Anr copy. Cloth; faded. cb Apr 24 (42) $100
Anr Ed. L, 1893. 5th Impression. 8vo, cloth; rear cover marked. cb Apr 24 (44) $65; cb Apr 24 (45) $120
Colonial Ed. L, 1895. Illus by Geo. Hutchinson. 8vo, cloth; rubbed. cb Apr 24 (47) $50
Anr Ed. [Morristown, 1960]. One of 500. Wraps. Facsimile of Beeton's Christmas Annual, 1887. cb Apr 24 (38) $500

— The Three Correspondents. L, 1896. Wraps. In: The Windsor Magazine, Oct 1896, pp 373-86. cb Apr 24 (441) $50

— Three of Them: A Reminiscence. L, 1923. Inscr by Jean Conan Doyle. cb Apr 24 (634) $255

— Through the Magic Door. L, 1906-7. In: Cassell's Magazine, Nov 1906-Nov 1907, 13 issues in 2 vols. cb Apr 24 (548) $80
Anr Ed. L, 1907. cb Apr 24 (549) $65

— The Tragedy of the Korosko. L, 1897. 8 Issues. Wraps. In: The Strand Magazine, Issues 77-84 of Vols XIII-XIV, May-Dec 1897. cb Apr 24 (234) $110
Colonial Ed. L, 1898. 8vo, cloth. cb Apr 24 (470) $63
Anr Ed. Phila., 1898. ("A Desert Drama: Being the Tragedy of the Korosko.") 8vo, cloth. cb Apr 24 (469) $50

— Uncle Bernac: A Memory of the Empire. L, 1897. 12mo, orig cloth. cb Apr 24 (454) $80

— Uncle Jeremy's Household. L, 1886-87. Orig cloth. In: The Boy's Own Paper, Vol 9, Nos 417-23. cb Apr 24 (26) $65

— The Unknown Conan Doyle. L, 1982-86. Ed by John Michael Gibson & Richard Lancelyn Green. 3 vols. Inscr by Gibson & Green. cb Apr 24 (793) $70

— The Valley of Fear. L, 1914-15. 9 Issues. Wraps. In: The Strand Magazine, Issues 285-93 of Vols LXVIII & LXIX. cb Apr 24 (303) $400
Anr copy. 2 vols. New cloth. In: The Strand Magazine, Vols 48-49, July-Dec 1914 & Jan-June 1915. cb Apr 24 (586) $55
1st Ed in Book form. L, 1915. Cloth,. Minor foxing. cb Apr 24 (589) $160
Anr copy. Some foxing. cb Apr 24 (589) $160

— Verbatim Report of a Public Debate on "The Truth of Spiritualism" between Sir Arthur Conan Doyle...and Joseph McCabe.... L, 1920. Orange cloth. cb Apr 24 (814) $110
Anr copy. Green paper wraps; soiled. cb Apr 24 (815) $50

— The Vital Message. L: Hodder & Stoughton, [1919]. Inscr to Ernest Wild. cb Apr 24 (619) $130

— The Voice of Science. L, 1891. Wraps. In: The Strand Magazine, Issue 3 of Vol I, Mar 1891, pp 312-17. cb Apr 24 (142) $50
Royal Ed. Silk over bds. In: The Strand Magazine, Issue 3 of Vol I, Mar 1891, pp 312-17. cb Apr 24 (140) $80

— The War in South Africa. L, 1902. 1st Ed, 2d Issue. Wraps. cb Apr 24 (509) $70

— The White Company. L, 1891. 2 vols, half lea; not quite uniform. In Vols 16 & 17

DOYLE

(New Series) of The Cornhill Magazine. cb Apr 24 (126) $225

2d Ed. L, 1892. 8vo, orig cloth. cb Apr 24 (127) $80

— Works. L, 1903. Author's Ed, One of 1,000, sgd. 12 vols. cb Apr 24 (734) $900

Anr copy. Minor wear. cb Apr 24 (735) $325

Anr copy. Portion of tp to Memoirs supplied from anr copy. cb Apr 24 (736) $225

Doyle, James W. E., 1822-92

— A Chronicle of England.... L, 1864. 1st Ed. 4to, mor by Riviere; worn. O Mar 24 (59) $100

Anr copy. Syn; worn. wa Sept 25 (550) $200

Doyle, John
See also: Graves, Robert

— Political Sketches &c. By H. B. L, 1829-37. Vols I-IV only. Oblong folio, half mor; upper covers worn. With c.240 plates, some hand-colored. pnE Dec 17 (4) £520 [Marshall]

D'Oyly, Sir Charles, 1781-1845

— Views of Calcutta and its Environs. L, 1848. Folio, half mor. With 27 hand-colored views on 25 sheets. Folding view with short tears repaired. S Apr 23 (327) £2,000 [Shapero]

Drake, Edward Cavendish

— A New Universal Collection of Authentic and Entertaining Voyages and Travels. L, 1771. Folio, later half mor; def. Repair to 1 text leaf; 1 map creased & torn; some stains. kh Mar 16 (155B) A$450

Anr copy. Contemp calf; hinges cracked, rubbed. With 56 plates. pn July 23 (173) £170 [Sweet]

Drake, Francis, 1696-1771

— Eboracum: or the History and Antiquities of the City of York. L, 1736. 2 vols. Folio, contemp calf; joints cracked. Ck Sept 26 (186) £75

Anr copy. 2 vols in one. Folio, contemp calf; rubbed, joints broken. With 59 plates & maps. O Feb 24 (71) $300

Drake, Francis Samuel, 1828-85

— The Indian Tribes of the United States.... Phila., 1891-84. 2 vols. 4to, orig cloth. With 100 plates, some hand-colored. pnNY Oct 11 (18) $300

Drake, Maurice & Wilfred

— Saints and their Emblems. L, 1916. Folio, half cloth. With 10 plates. sg May 14 (294) $80

Drake, Samuel Adams

— The Heart of the White Mountains. NY, 1882. 4to, orig cloth. Inscr. O June 9 (58) $130

Drayson, Alfred Wilks, 1827-1901

— Sporting Scenes amongst the Kaffirs of South Africa. L, 1858. 8vo, bdg not described. With frontis & 7 litho plates. SSA Oct 28 (531) R540

Drayton, Michael, 1563-1631

— Poems. L, 1637. 12mo, old vellum; rebacked. Lacking A2; engraved title relaid; top corner of A3 torn away without loss; some old marginalia. T Mar 19 (396) £75

— Poly-Olbion. L, 1622. ("A Chorographicall Description....") 1st Ed, 3d Issue. Lacking general ptd title. Bound with: The Second Part. L, 1622. 1st Ed. Folio, 19th-cent russia gilt. With engraved title, plate of Prince Henry & 30 double-page mapsheets. Title to Part 2 bound in as general ptd title; 7 plates with repairs; a few leaves of text repaired at inner margin. S Apr 23 (106) £2,800 [Burgess]

Dreams...

— Dreams and Derisions. NY, 1927. One of 200. 4to, half mor; spine ends rubbed. cb Dec 4 (223) $200

Anr copy. Later half mor. Lacking colophon leaf but with the clipped portion bearing device & limitation statement laid in loose. cb June 18 (204) $110

Anr copy. Later half mor; new endpapers. cb June 18 (204) $110

Anr copy. Half lea. sg Jan 8 (146) $225

— Dreams that Money Can Buy. NY: Films International of America, 1947. Cover design based on an illust by Max Ernst (who appeared in the film). Orig wraps. S June 29 (52) £180 [Rota]

Dreiser, Theodore, 1871-1945

— Epitaph: a Poem. NY, [1929]. One of 800, sgd. Unopened. sg June 11 (169) $80

Dresden Royal Gallery

— Recueil d'estampes d'apres les plus celebres tableaux de la Galerie Royale de Dresde. Dresden, 1753-57. 2 vols. Folio, orig bds; badly worn. With 2 frontises, 2 plans & 100 plates. Waterstain on titles & outer margins of some plates. pnE Dec 17 (1) £1,100 [L'Acquaforte]

Dresser, Henry Eeles, 1838-1915
— Eggs of the Birds of Europe. L, [1905]-10. 2 vols. 4to, contemp half mor, orig 13 wraps to Parts 1-24 bound in at end. With 106 colored plates. C Apr 8 (145) £750 [Mitchell]
— A History of the Birds of Europe. L, 1871-81. Vol VIII only. 4to, contemp half mor; rubbed. With 80 hand-colored plates.. bba Dec 4 (256) £700 [Rainer]
Anr Ed. L, 1871-96. 9 vols, including Supplement. 4to, contemp half mor gilt; rubbed. With 2 plain & 721 hand-colored plates. One leaf with small repair; titles & a few plates with minor spotting. H. M. Upcher's subscriber's copy. C Apr 8 (144) £9,000 [Mitchell]
Anr copy. Half mor gilt. With 721 hand-colored plates, 2 plain plates & 9 engraved titles. pn Apr 30 (224) £5,200 [Russell]
— A Manual of Palaearctic Birds. L, 1902-3. 2 vols. Half mor, orig wraps bound in at end. S Feb 24 (563) £75 [Maggs]

Drexel, Jeremy, 1581-1638
— The Christians Zodiake of Twelve Signes of Predestination unto Life Everlasting. L; for Samuel Browne, 1647. 24mo, modern calf gilt. With engraved title & 12 full-page illusts. Some soiling & cropping; a few tears repaired. S Mar 10 (1054) £190 [McKenzie]

Drexler, Arthur
— The Drawings of Frank Lloyd Wright. NY: Horizon Press, [1962]. In worn & chipped d/j. cb Mar 5 (214) $55

Drey, O. Raymond
— Edward Wadsworth. [N.p.]: Morland Press, 1921. One of 30. Orig half cloth. With 14 mtd wood-engravings. S June 17 (291) £5,200 [Garton]

Dreyfus, John. See: Nonesuch Press

Dring, Thomas, 1758-1825
— Recollections of the Jersey Prison-Ship.... Morrisania, 1865. One of 50 L.p. copies. 8vo, half mor; worn. sg Sept 18 (113) $60

Drinkwater, John, 1762-1844
— A History of the Late Siege of Gibraltar. L, 1785. 1st Ed. 4to, contemp calf. With 10 folding plates & plans. One plate torn. Ck May 15 (59) £65
2d Ed. L, 1786. 4to, orig bds; soiled. Sold w.a.f. Ck Sept 26 (238) £60
Anr copy. Contemp half calf; rebacked & cornered. With 10 folding maps & plates (some soiled). Ck Feb 27 (78) £160

Dronckers, Emily
— Verzameling F. G. Waller: Catalogus van nederlandsche en vlaamsche populaire Boecken. The Hague, 1936. 4to, cloth. bba Oct 16 (374) £54 [Hay Cinema]

Droz, Edmond. See: Chapuis & Droz

Drujon, Fernand
— Les Livres a clef. Paris, 1888. One of 650. 8vo, contemp half mor; rubbed. bba June 18 (3) £55 [Trocchi]

Drukkers...
— Het Drukkers Jaarboek. Amst., 1906-11. 4 vols. Orig bdgs. B Oct 7 (1) HF800

Drummond, Alexander, d.1769
— Travels through Different Cities of Germany, Italy, Greece.... L, 1754. 1st Ed. Folio, 18th-cent calf gilt; worn. With frontis & 34 plates & maps. S July 14 (738) £450

Drummond, James, 1816-77. See: Anderson & Drummond

Drummond, William Henry, 1845-79
— The Large Game and Natural History of South and South-East Africa. Edin., 1875. 8vo, orig cloth; def. With color frontis, map & 12 plates. 2 leaves torn. B Feb 25 (976) HF180
Anr copy. Orig cloth; recased with new endpapers. With colored frontis & 12 color plates. cb May 21 (91) $110

Drury, Dru, 1725-1803
— Illustrations of Natural History. L, 1770-82. 3 vols. 4to, half calf. With 150 color plates. FD june 11 (702) DM4,600
Anr copy. Modern half mor. With 150 hand-colored plates & 1 uncolored schematic plate. Plate 1 in Vol II soiled & frayed in extreme upper margin; small smudge on Plate 37 of Vol III. S Apr 23 (7) £1,600 [Antik]
Anr copy. Modern half calf. Plate 11 in Vol III short in margins; some spotting. S June 25 (152) £1,450 [Gilbert]
Anr Ed. L, 1837. ("Illustrations of Exotic Entomology.") 3 vols. 4to, 19th-cent half mor; soiled & scuffed. With 1 plain & 150 colored plates. cb June 4 (50) $1,100
Anr copy. Half lea. With 1 plain & 149 colored plates. Titles stamped. pn Oct 23 (6) £760 [Weldon & Wesley]

Drury, Maj. W. P.
— The Peradventures of Private Pagett. L, 1904. Illus by Arthur Rackham. With 8 plates. sg Oct 30 (65) $150

Dry, Camille N.
— Pictorial St. Louis. The Great Metropolis of the Mississippi Valley. St. Louis: Compton & Co., 1876. Oblong folio, half lea; joints starting, endpapers & a few leaves soiled. With litho title, 2 frontis views, & 110 plates. Each leaf silked with translucent rice paper; some tears affecting images. sg Dec 18 (223) $1,700

Dryander, John. See: Banks Library, Sir Joseph

Dryden, John, 1631-1700
— Absalom and Achitophel. L, 1681. 1st Ed, 1st Issue. Parts 1-2 in 1 vol. Folio, calf; joints rubbed. Some dampstains. sg Apr 2 (75) $1,100
— Fables Ancient and Modern.... L, 1713. 8vo, contemp calf; rubbed. O Nov 18 (58) $80

Anr Ed. L, 1797. Folio, contemp calf; rebacked. With 9 plates. Lacking half-title. T Mar 19 (314) £130
— Of Dramatick Poesie.... L, 1928. One of 580. With prefatory essay by T. S. Eliot. 4to, half cloth, unopened; rubbed. sg Dec 11 (24) $80
— Troilus and Cressida.... L, 1679. 1st Ed of Dryden's adaptation. 4to, modern half mor gilt. Kern copy. sg June 11 (171) $375
— Works. L, 1808. Ed by Sir Walter Scott. 18 vols. 8vo, contemp calf gilt; marked, some spines cracking. S Jan 13 (366) £320 [Weinreb]

Du Bartas, Guillaume de Saluste, 1544-90
— Bartas his Devine Weekes and Workes. L, 1633. Folio, bdg not described. Engraved title & frontis torn & repaired in margin; some spotting & soiling. S Nov 10 (650) £70 [Rix]
— His Devine Weekes and Workes. L, 1621. ("His Divine Weekes and Workes") Folio, contemp calf; rebacked. With engraved title & port; Oo2 present; short tear in inner margin of A2; small rust hole; a few margins repaired or strengthened; waterstains. STC 21654. bba Jan 15 (11) £180 [P & P Books]

Du Bec, Jean, 1540-1610
— Discours de l'antagonie du chien.... [Paris: Crapelet, 1850]. 8vo, half mor. Jeanson copy. SM Feb 28 (185) FF1,100

One of 2 on vellum. Mor janseniste by Duru, 1857. Jeanson copy. SM Feb 28 (184) FF9,500

Du Cange, Charles du Fresne, Sieur, 1610-88
— Glossarium ad scriptores mediae et infimae latinitatis. Paris, 1733-36. 6 vols. Folio, calf gilt. B Oct 7 (1118) HF1,200

Du Choul, Guillaume
— Discours de la religion des anciens romains. Lyon, 1556. Folio, contemp half vellum. Tp soiled; lacking last 2 leaves. bba Dec 4 (1) £65 [Laffont]

Anr Ed. Lyons: Guillaume Rouille, 1567. 2 parts in 1 vol. 4to, 18th-cent calf; some wear. S Nov 27 (158) £200 [Williams]

Du Fouilloux, Jacques, 1521?-80
— La Caccia.... Milan, 1615. 8vo, 18th-cent calf gilt in the style of Padeloup. Jeanson copy. SM Feb 28 (197) FF5,500
— Neuw Jag unnd Weydwerck Buch.... Frankfurt: Feyerabendt, 1582. 2 parts in 1 vol. Folio, contemp blind-stamped calf over wooden bds with remains of clasps. Jeanson copy. SM Feb 28 (198) FF88,000

Anr Ed. Strasbourg: Bernhart Jobin, 1590. ("New Jaegerbuch.") Folio, mor extra by Chambolle-Duru. Jeanson copy. SM Feb 28 (199) FF95,000
— La Venerie.... Poitiers: les de Marnefz & Bouchetz freres, 1561. Folio, mor gilt by Trautz-Bauzonnet. Jeanson copy. SM Feb 28 (186) FF290,000

Issue without date on tp. Mor extra by Chambolle-Duru. Jeanson copy. SM Feb 28 (187) FF270,000

Anr Ed. Poitiers: les de Marnefz & Bouchetz freres, 1562. 4to, mor gilt by Trautz-Bauzonnet. Jeanson copy. SM Feb 28 (188) FF90,000

Anr Ed. Poitiers: les de Marnefz & Bouchetz freres, 1568. 4to, blind-stamped mor by Thompson. Jeanson copy. SM Feb 28 (189) FF52,000

Anr Ed. Paris: Galiot du Pre, 1573. 4to, contemp vellum with arms of Baron Pichon. Jeanson copy. SM Feb 28 (190) FF80,000

Anr Ed. Paris: F. le Mangier, 1585. 2 parts in 1 vol. 4to, 18th-cent calf gilt. Jeanson 1270. SM Feb 28 (191) FF45,000

Anr Ed. Paris: Abel l'Angelier, 1606-7. 2 parts in 1 vol. 4to, mor janseniste by Trautz-Bauzonnet. Jeanson copy. SM Feb 28 (192) FF30,000

Anr Ed. Paris: Claude Cramoisy, 1628. 2 parts in 1 vol. 4to, mor gilt with the symbol of the Bibliotheque de Mello in the center, by Hardy. Jeanson copy. SM Feb 28 (193) FF17,000

Anr Ed. Rouen, 1650. 2 parts in 1 vol. 4to, mor gilt by Chambolle-Duru. Jeanson 1440. SM Feb 28 (194) FF20,000

Anr Ed. Bayreuth, 1754. 4to, mor janseniste by Duru. Reprint of the Poitiers 1568 Ed. Jeanson copy. SM Feb 28 (195) FF190,000

Anr Ed. Niort: Chez Robin & L. Favre, 1864. One of 50. 4to, later half shagreen. Jeanson copy. SM Feb 28 (196) FF3,000

Du Fourney, Honore Caille, Sieur. See: Anselme de Sainte-Marie & Du Fourney

Du Fresnoy, Charles Alphonse, 1611-65
— De Arte Graphica. The Art of Painting.... L, 1695. 1st Ed of John Dryden's trans. 4to, contemp calf; rebacked, broken. sg Feb 5 (111) $120

Anr copy. Contemp calf; rebacked. sg June 4 (119) $100

Du Halde, Jean Baptiste, 1674-1743
— A Description of the Empire of China.... L, 1738-41. 2 vols. Folio, bdg not indicated. Library markings. Sold w.a.f. Franklin Institute copy. F Sept 12 (138) $950
— The General History of China.... L, 1736. 4 vols. 8vo, contemp calf; spines worn. With 4 folding maps & 18 plates, 1 loose, anr torn. sg Nov 20 (49) $300

Du Maurier, George, 1834-96
— Trilby. NY, 1894. Extracted from Harper's New Monthly Magazine. 8vo, lev gilt by Rowfant Bindery; hinges rubbed. wd Nov 12 (91) $100

Anr Ed. L, 1895. One of 250 L.p. copies, sgd. 4to, orig half vellum. With frontis & 6 plates. cb July 30 (60) $100

Du Passage, Edouard Guy, Comte, 1872-1925
— Un Siecle de venerie dans le nord de la France. Paris, 1912. One of 500. 4to, half shagreen. Jeanson copy. SM Feb 28 (200) FF1,800

Du Sable, Guillaume
— La Muse Chasseresse. Paris, 1611. 12mo, 18th-cent mor gilt; rubbed. Jeanson copy. SM Feb 28 (204) FF7,000

Du Verdier, Antoine, 1544-1600
— La Prosopographie ou description des personnes insignes.... Lyons: Gryphius, 1573. Bound with: Du Verdier, Les Omonimes, satire des moeurs corrompues de ce siecle. Lyons, 1572. 4to, half calf. Lacking leaf before title; small corner torn from blank margin of 1 leaf. S June 25 (18) £400 [Schmidt]

Du Verney, Guichard Joseph, 1648-1730
— Traite de l'organe de l'ouie.... Paris, 1683. 12mo, contemp calf gilt; worn. S Nov 27 (258) £850 [Pelckschmidt]
— Traite de l'organe de l'ouie, contenant la structure, les usages & les maladies de toutes les parties de l'oreille. Paris, 1683. 1st Ed. 12mo, contemp sheep; worn, broken. With 16 colored plates. sg Jan 15 (95) $1,200

Duane, James Chatham, 1824-97
— Report to the Aqueduct Commissioners. [N.p.], 1895. Folio, orig cloth; worn, front cover nearly detached. sg Nov 20 (135) $70

Dubois, Alphonse Joseph Charles
— Synopsis avium. Nouveau manuel d'ornithologie. Brussels, 1902-[4]. 2 vols. 8vo, half shagreen; rubbed. With 16 color plates. B Feb 24 (69) HF280

Dubois Duperay, R.
— Papillons d'Europe. L, 1784-86-94. 3 parts in 2 vols. 4to, contemp calf gilt; worn. With 3 watercolor titles & 299 plates, of which 191 are orig watercolors by Dubois & 108 are hand-colored engravings. A further 48 orig watercolor plates of beetles are bound at end of 2d vol. Tear in Plate 110 of Part 2. S Apr 23 (33) £3,500 [Sims]

Dubois, Guillaume, called Cretin, d. c.1525. See: Cretin, Guillaume

Dubois, Urbain
— Artistic Cookery. L 1870. 4to, contemp half lea; spine ends worn, front joint starting. With 80 plates, some foxed. sg Jan 15 (17) $400

Dubourg, Matthew
— Views of the Remains of Ancient Buildings in Rome and its Vicinity. L, 1820. Folio, bdg not indicated. With 26 color plates. Library markings. Sold w.a.f. Franklin Institute copy. F Sept 12 (8) $550

Anr Ed. L, 1844. Folio, contemp half lea; spine worn & repaired with adhesive tape. With 26 hand-colored plates. C Oct 15 (31) £600 [Valcke]

Dubreuil, Jean, 1602-70
— La Perspective pratique. Paris, 1642-47-49. Vol I only. Contemp calf; joints cracked. Ptd title from anr part; 1 leaf torn & repaired. sg Feb 5 (110) $300

2d Ed of Vol I; 1st Ed of Vols II & III. Paris, 1651-47-49. 3 vols. 4to, contemp calf; rubbed, joints weak. C July 22 (64) £580

Dubuisson, ——
— L'Art du distillateur et marchand de liqueurs.... Paris, 1779. 1st Ed. 2 parts in 1 vol. 8vo, contemp calf; spine worn, rubbed. Crahan copy. P Nov 25 (162) $650

Ducarel, Andrew Coltee, 1713-85
— Anglo-Norman Antiquities Considered in a Tour through Part of Normandy. L, 1767. Folio, contemp half calf; upper cover detached. With port (cropped) & 20 plates. bba Oct 30 (300) £85 [Shapero]

**Duchamp, Marcel —&
Halberstadt, P.**
— Opposition et cases Conjugees-Opposition und Schwesterfelder-Opposition.... [Paris: L'Echiquier, 1932]. 4to, orig wraps. Lacking 1 leaf. pn Mar 26 (288) £1,900 [Galerie]

Duchesne, Jean, 1779-1855
— Musee francais, ou recueil des plus beaux Tableaux....qui existaient au Louvre avant 1815. Paris & L, 1829-30. 4 vols. Folio, modern cloth or half mor; some covers detached. Some spotting; 1 title repaired. Sold w.a.f. S Nov 10 (211) £2,100 [Scheick]

Dudley, Robert. See: Russell & Dudley

Duemichen, Johannes. See: Brehm & Duemichen

Duerer, Albrecht, 1471-1528
— Albrecht Duerers Randzeichungen aus dem Gebetbuche des Kaisers Maximilian I. Munich: G. Franz, [c.1845]. Folio, contemp calf with remains of clasps; rebacked & repaired. Some foxing. cb Oct 23 (62) $85
— De urbibus, arcibus, castellisque, condendis.... Paris: C. Wechel, 1535. Folio, modern vellum bds. Some fraying. S May 21 (35) £650 [Laget]
— The Little Passion. Verona: Officina Bodoni, 1971. One of 140. Half mor gilt. pnNY Mar 12 (103) $325
— Passio Christi.... Nuremberg: H. Hoelzel, 1511. 4to, mor stamped with Duerer's monogram by Riviere. With woodcut of the Man of Sorrows on tp & 36 woodcuts depicting the Fall of Man, all with monogram. Short slit in lower blank margin of tp & C1; upper margin of title & part of C1-C3 strengthened without loss. S June 25 (20) £12,500
— Underweysung der messung mit dem zirckel unnd richtscheyt in Linien ebnen unnd gantzen corporen. Arnham: Johan Janssen, 1603. Folio, contemp blindstamped pigskin; rebacked, new endpapers. Some repairs with minimal loss of text; short tear in text of last 3 leaves; most leaves discolored. S May 21 (102) £500 [Hasbach]

Duff, Edward Gordon, 1863-1924
— A Century of the English Book Trade.... L, 1905. Half mor. Perforated or ink stamps on plates. bba Feb 5 (45) £50 [Rix]

Dufief, Nicolas Gouin, 1776?-1834
— Dufief's Nature Displayed in her Mode of Teaching Language to Man.... Phila., 1811. 2 vols. 8vo, orig bds; broken. sg Mar 26 (103) $120

Dufour, John James
— The American Vine-Dresser's Guide.... Cincinnati, 1826. 12mo, contemp sheep; rubbed. Marginal tears, 1 affecting a numeral. Crahan copy. P Nov 25 (163) $500

Dufour, Philippe Sylvestre, 1622-87?
— The Manner of Making of Coffee, Tea and Chocolate.... L: Wm. Crook, 1685. 12mo, contemp sheep; joints cracked, rubbed. Browning & soiling; A3 with tear affecting text. Crahan copy. P Nov 25 (165) $900

Dufour, Pierre. See: Lacroix, Paul

Dufresne de Saint-Leon, A. See: Marais & Dufresne de Saint-Leon

Dufresne, Frank
— Alaska's Animals & Fishes. West Hartford, Vermont, [1946]. One of 475. Illus by Bob Hines. Inscr by Dufresne. sg May 21 (97) $100

Dufy, Raoul
— Dessins et Croquis. Paris, 1944. One of 199 on velin de Vidalon. 4to, loose as issued in orig wraps. S Nov 10 (236) £70 [Roe]

Dugdale, James
— The New British Traveller. L, 1819. 4 vols. 4to, calf; hinges worn. Some stains. pn May 21 (180) £170 [Camberwell]

**Dugdale, Thomas —&
Burnett, William**
— England and Wales Delineated. L, [1845?]. ("Curiosities of Great Britain.") Vols 1-9 only. Orig cloth; worn. pn Dec 11 (69) £180 [Bowdage]
Anr copy. 10 vols in 5. Half calf; rubbed. pn Mar 5 (79) £190 [Map House]

Dugdale, Sir William, 1605-86
— The Antiquities of Warwickshire.... L, 1656. 1st Ed. Folio, old calf; rebacked at an early date. Port trimmed & remtd; minor tears; marginal repairs. Sold w.a.f. O Oct 21 (60) $130
Anr copy. Russia gilt. Prospect of Warwick slightly cropped at head. S Nov 17 (652) £290 [Mace]
Anr Ed. Coventry, 1765. Folio, contemp calf; worn, rear cover def, upper cover detached. Frontis torn without loss. T July 30 (56) £190
— The Baronage of England. L, 1675-76. 2 vols in 1. Folio, contemp calf; rebacked, front joint cracked, extremities worn. sg June 11 (173) $80
— The History of Imbanking and Drayning of Divers Fenns and Marshes.... L, 1772. Folio, contemp calf; rebacked. With 11 folding maps. pn Jan 22 (21) £190 [Axe]

— The History of St. Paul's Cathedral.... L, 1658. 1st Ed. Folio, contemp mor-rebacked russia gilt; rubbed. With port & 44 plates, 14 double-page or folding. Lacking final blank; hole in B1 affecting text; 1 plate torn; marginal repair to Zzz2. S July 14 (588) £240

Dugdale, Sir William, 1605-86 —& Dodsworth, Roger, 1585-1654
— Monasticon Anglicanum. L, 1655-73. 3 vols. Folio, contemp calf; 1 cover detached, worn, Vol III rebacked, now uniform. With engraved title & 98 plates only. Vol III tp repaired; some fold tears; 2 plate corners torn away; dampstains in Vols II-III. bba Oct 16 (59) £150 [Bennett & Kerr]

Anr copy. Old calf gilt; rubbed, some wormholes in spines. With engraved title & 102 plates only. Sole w.a.f. bba Aug 20 (12) £160 [Robertshaw]

Anr Ed. L, 1682-61-73. 3 vols. Folio, calf gilt; most covers detached. Some cropping; all after 7G1 in Vol I torn or def; Vols II & III lacking initial blank. Sold w.a.f. S Nov 17 (651) £250 [Elliott]

2d Ed of Vol I, 1st Ed of Vols II-III. L, 1682-71-63. 3 vols. Folio, calf; hinges worn. pn Dec 11 (196) £260 [Clegg]

Anr Ed. L, 1693. ("Monasticon Anglicanum, or the History of the Ancient Abbeys....") 3 vols in 1. Folio, calf; re-backed. pnE nov 12 (203) £75

Anr Ed. L, 1718. 3 parts in 1 vol. Folio, contemp calf; worn. S Feb 24 (381) £130 [Seibu]

Anr Ed. L, 1817-30. 6 vols in 8. Folio, half calf, cloth or disbound. Some staining. bba Jan 15 (478) £160 [Jeffery]

Anr copy. 6 vols in 8 plus 1 vol of John Steven's supplement. Folio, contemp half calf; rebacked preserving spines. bba Apr 23 (202) £320 [Shapero]

— Monasticum Anglicanum. L, 1849. 6 vols in 8. Folio, contemp half mor. C July 22 (65) £300

Duhamel du Monceau, Henri Louis, 1700-81?
— De l'exploitation des bois, ou moyens de tirer un parti avantageux.... Paris, 1764. 2 parts in 2 vols. 4to, contemp calf with crest of the Duke of Buccleuch; Vol I rebacked. With 36 folding plates. C Apr 8 (125) £300 [Gaston]

— Des Semis et plantations des arbres.... Paris, 1760. 4to, contemp calf with crest of the Duke of Buccleuch; joints & corners rubbed. With 17 folding plates. C Apr 8 (124) £220 [Perrin Thomas]

— Du transport, de la conservation et de la force des bois.... Paris, 1767. 1st Ed. 4to, contemp calf gilt with crest of the Duke of Buccleuch. With 27 folding plates. C Apr 8 (126) £170 [Perrin Thomas]

— La Physique des arbres.... Paris, 1758. 2 vols. 4to, contemp calf with crest of the Duke of Buccleuch. With 50 folding plates. C Apr 8 (123) £260 [Perrin Thomas]

Anr copy. Modern half mor by Crahan. Crahan copy. P Nov 25 (167) $250

— A Practical Treatise of Husbandry. L, 1759. 4to, old calf gilt; rebacked in mor, hinges reinforced. With 6 plates by J. Mynde & folding table. Hunt copy. CNY Nov 21 (103) $220

Anr Ed. L, 1762. 4to, contemp calf; rubbed. Heertje copy. P Nov 25 (168) $200

— Traite de la fabrique des manoeuvres pour les vaisseaux.... Paris, 1747-69. 2 parts in 1 vol. 4to, contemp sheep; worn. With 13 folding plates. Some stains & browning. Ck Apr 24 (18) £240

— Traite des arbres et arbustes. Paris, 1755. 1st Ed. 2 vols. 4to, contemp calf gilt with Buccleuch arms; joints weak, spines & corners scuffed. With 250 woodcut plates & 4 engraved plates. C Apr 8 (122) £1,700 [Ramsay]

Anr copy. 2 vols in 1. 4to, contemp calf gilt; rubbed, joints repaired. With 250 woodcut plates & 4 folding engraved plates. Marginal stains in the text. S Oct 23 (673) £950 [Schire]

2d Ed. Paris, 1800-15. Vols I-V (of 7) only. Folio, contemp bds; 1 spine lacking. With 423 hand-finished colored plates & 2 uncolored plates of olive presses. Occasional discoloration of some plates; 1 text leaf torn in Vol I; piece torn from margin of 1 leaf in Vol IV. S Apr 23 (26) £8,000 [Cape]

Anr Ed. Paris, 1800-19 [title dated 1825]. 7 vols. Folio, contemp half calf with crowned monogram gilt of Louis Philippe on spine. With 2 plain & 496 hand-finished color plates. Rubberstamped on titles or half titles is "Conservation des forets de la couronne". de Belder copy. S Apr 27 (111) £20,000 [Junk]

Anr Ed. Paris, 1825. 7 vols. Folio, 19th-cent half mor; rubbed. With engraved title & 496 color plates, some hand-finished, & 2 plain plates. Lacking the engraved title in Vol I; some discoloration; tp to Vol I creased & repaired at upper inner corner; half-title soiled in Vol I; 3 plates at end of Vol III with small pieces torn from outer margins. S Oct 23 (684) £13,500 [Walford]

— Traite des arbres fruitiers. Paris, 1768. 2 vols. 4to, contemp calf, not uniform; Vol I sides def. With 162 (of 180) plates only.

DUHAMEL DU MONCEAU

Minor discoloration. Sold w.a.f. C Oct 15 (224) £1,800 [Schrire]
Anr copy. Contemp half calf gilt with Garter crest of the 3d Duke of Buccleuch, unopened; joints cracked. With frontis & 180 plates. C Apr 8 (127) £2,000 [Erlini]
Anr copy. Contemp calf gilt. de Belder copy. S Apr 27 (109) £2,500 [McCarthy]
Anr copy. Contemp half calf; rubbed. With frontis & 181 plates. Some browning & marginal staining, affecting some plates in Vol II. S June 25 (153) £2,600 [Schrire]
Anr Ed. Paris, [1807]-35. 6 vols in 5. Folio, contemp half mor; rubbed, 1 cover detached. With 2 plain & 420 hand-finished color plates. Some spotting & browning. L.p. copy. de Belder copy. S Apr 27 (110) £50,000 [Israel]

Duhamel du Monceau, Henri Louis, 1700-81? —& Others

— Description des arts et metiers, faite ou approuvee par Mm. de l'Academie des Sciences. Paris, 1762-83. 46 works in 7 vols. Folio, contemp half calf. Sold w.a.f. C Dec 12 (66) £8,000 [Pickering & Chatto]

Duhamel du Monceau, Henri Louis, 1700-81? —& La Marre, L. H. de

— Traite general des pesches, et histoire des poissons. Paris, 1769. 4 vols in 3. Folio, half mor gilt. With 250 plates. FD Dec 2 (2823) DM9,000

Duhamel, Georges, 1884-1966

— Lapointe et Ropiteau. Geneva, 1919. One of 35. Illus by Frans Masereel. B Oct 7 (187) HF200
— Maurice de Vlaminck. Paris, 1927. One of 875. 4to, modern half mor. With 28 plates, including 4 etchings. S Nov 10 (237) £85 [Roe]

Duhaut-Cilly, Auguste Bernard

— Viaggio Intorno al Globo Principalmente alla California.... Turin: Tipografico Fontana, 1841. 2 vols. 8vo, modern cloth. With 2 frontises & 2 plates. Foxing throughout; library markings. sg Apr 23 (49) $110

Duke, J.

— The Compleat Florist. L, 1747. 8vo, contemp calf; joints split, worn. Lacking engraved title & Plate 67; some stains; some plates trimmed to plate-mark. Sold w.a.f. S June 25 (154) £1,600 [Gilbert]

AMERICAN BOOK PRICES CURRENT

Dulac, Edmund, 1882-1953

— Fairy Book: Fairy Tales of the Allied Nations. L, [1916]. 4to, orig cloth; rear cover faintly waterstained. With 15 colored plates. cb Sept 11 (243) $70
— Picture Book for the French Red Cross. L, [1915]. 4to, orig cloth; worn. With port & 19 colored plates. O Apr 28 (59) $60

Duller, Eduard, 1809-53

— Das Deutsche Volk in seinen Mundarten, Sitten, Gebraeuchen.... Leipzig, 1847. 8vo, later half sheep. With 49 of (50) hand-colored plates. Pages 63-64 of text misbound, a few pp torn, 1 plate with adhesions. ha Sept 19 (210) $950
— Die malerischen und romantischen Donaulaender. Leipzig: Wigand, [c.1840]. 8vo, contemp bds; rubbed. With 56 (of 60) plates. JG Oct 2 (1042) DM1,000

Dulletin...

— Bulletin D. Cologne, [1919]. Ed by Alfred Gruenewald (as J. T. Baargeld) & by Max Ernst. 4to, orig wraps. S June 29 (4) £5,400 [Shilton]

Dumas, Alexandre, 1802-70, pere

— Grand Dictionnaire de cuisine. Paris, 1873. 1st Ed. 8vo, later half mor; extremities worn, shaken; orig front wrap bound in. sg Jan 15 (18) $225
— The Three Musketeers. NY, 1894. One of 775. Illus by Maurice Leloir. 2 vols. Cloth. cb Sept 11 (245) $55
— Les Trois Mousquetaires. Paris, 1894. Illus by Maurice Leloir. 2 vols. Folio, half mor; rubbed. O Feb 24 (72) $70

Dumas, Alexandre, 1824-95, fils. See: Limited Editions Club

Dummer, Jeremiah, 1645-1718

— A Letter to a Friend in the Country.... L, 1712. 8vo, wraps. S June 25 (386) £450

Dumont, Jean, Baron de Carlscroon —& Rousset de Missy, Jean

— The Military History of the late Prince Eugene of Savoy and of the late John, Duke of Marlborough. L, 1736-37. 2 vols. Folio, contemp calf; rubbed. With frontis & 84 plates & maps. Ck Feb 27 (79) £400

Dumont, Jules Sebastien Cesar, 1790-1842

— Voyage autour du monde. Paris, 1863-69. 4 vols. Folio, half mor. kh Mar 16 (158) A$280

Dunbar, Seymour

— A History of Travel in America. Indianapolis, [1915]. One of 250. 4 vols. Half cloth. With 12 color plates. cb Mar 19 (82) $200

Duncan, David Douglas
— Goodbye Picasso. [N.p.], 1974. 4to, cloth, in d/j. Inscr. sg Jan 8 (206) $80

Duncan, Francis
— Our Garrisons in the West.... L, 1864. 8vo, cloth. With folding map. AVP Nov 20 (98) C$85 [McGill]

Duncan, Isadora, 1878-1927
— The Art of the Dance. NY, 1928. 4to, half cloth; top of spine torn. sg Feb 26 (146) $80

Anr copy. Half cloth. Sgd. wd June 19 (119) $175

Duncan, William
— The Elements of Logick.... L: R. & J. Dodsley, 1764. 12mo, contemp calf; rubbed. cb Oct 23 (63) $60

Dundas, Henry, 1st Viscount Melville
[-] An Abstract of the Trial of Henry Lord Viscount Melville. L, 1806. Oblong folio, sewn as issued in wraps; margins of upper wrap torn. Margins dust-soiled or creased. S Oct 23 (174) £400 [Maggs]

Dundonald, Thomas Cochrane, 10th Earl of, 1775-1860
— The Autobiography of a Seaman. L, 1860. 2d Ed. In 2 vols. 8vo, contemp half calf by Maclaren & Macniven; rubbed. With 4 charts, 3 folding. A few leaves lightly soiled or spotted. bba Mar 26 (217) £85 [Check]

— Narrative of Services in the Liberation of Chili, Peru, and Brazil, from Spanish and Portuguese Domination. L, 1859. 2 vols. 8vo, orig cloth; worn, bookplates removed & later bookplates added. sg Sept 18 (81) $130

Dunham, Cecily
— Greetings from Atlantic City. [N.p.], 1977. One of 25. Folio, loose in cloth folder as issued. With 6 plates. sg Jan 8 (67) $100

Dunham, Curtis
— The Amazing Adventures of Bobbie in Bugabooland.... Indianapolis: Bobbs-Merrill, [1907]. Pictorial bds; rubbed, spine chipped. cb Dec 4 (104) $55

Dunkerley, William Arthur
— The Book of Sark. L, 1908. One of 500. Illus by William A. Toplis. Folio, orig vellum gilt; rubbed & soiled. bba Feb 5 (386) £90 [Thesaurus]

Anr copy. Orig vellum; warped. Inscr to Nurse Toplis. Ck May 15 (174) £90

Anr copy. Orig half cloth; soiled. L Dec 11 (75) £60

Dunlap, William, 1766-1839
— History of the New Netherlands.... NY, 1839-40. 2 vols. 8vo, half cloth. With port & 3 maps. Port loose; several small library stamps; foxed throughout. sg Mar 12 (194) $60

Dunlop, John, M.D.
— Mooltan during and after the Siege. L, 1849. Folio, orig cloth; repaired. With litho title & 21 plates. Tear to 1 plate; some margins frayed. pn Sept 18 (289) £140 [Trocchi]

Dunlop, Robert Glasgow
— Travels in Central America. L, 1847. 8vo, orig cloth; worn & loose. sg Mar 6 (102) $200

Dunn, Samuel, d.1794
— A New Atlas of the Mundane System.... L, 1788. Folio, old half calf; worn, spine crudely repaired. With 30 double-page maps, hand-colored in outline. Several maps detached. Ck Feb 27 (129) £540

5th Ed. L: Laurie & Whittle, 1800. Folio, contemp calf; def. With 6 double-page plates & 45 double-page maps, hand-colored in outline. Some margins frayed & some tears with slight loss. S Jan 12 (95) £650 [Grants]

Duns Scotus, Joannes, 1265?-1308?
— Scriptum super sententias. [Lyons: J. Myt, 1520]. Vol II only. 8vo, mor gilt by Roger de Coverly. sg June 11 (174) $200

Dunsany, Edward Plunkett, 18th Baron
— The Chronicles of Rodriguez. L & NY, 1922. One of 500. Illus by S. H. Sime. 4to, half vellum, in d/j with tear to spine head. Sgd twice by Dunsany. cb May 7 (364) $110

Dunthorne, Gordon
— Flower and Fruit Prints of the 18th and Early 19th Centuries. L, 1938. Anr Issue. 4to, orig cloth. pnE Dec 17 (192) £190 [Greyfriars]

Anr Ed. Wash., 1938. 4to, cloth; head of spine worn. With ALs from Dunthorne to Raymond Leopold laid in. sg Oct 2 (122) $275

Anr Ed. NY, 1970. 4to, cloth. sg Jan 15 (204) $200

Dunton, John, 1659-1733
— Athenian Sport. L, 1707. 8vo, contemp calf; rubbed & stained. bba May 14 (56) £100 [Bickersteth]

— The Phenix: Or, a Revival of Scarce and Valuable Pieces.... L, 1707-8. 2 vols. 8vo, old calf; rebacked & worn. O Nov 18 (144) $90

Dupaix, Guillelmo. See: Baradere, H.

Dupetit-Thouars, Abel Aubert. See: Aubert Dupetit-Thouars, Abel

Duplan, Jean Leopold
— Tableau de la venerie. Paris: Nouvelle Revue Francaise, 1923. One of 300. 4to, half mor gilt by Saulnier. Jeanson copy. SM Feb 28 (202) FF1,000

Dupont de Nemours, Pierre Samuel, 1739-1817
— Lettre a la Chambre du Commerce de Normandie sur le memoire qu'elle a publie relativement au traite de commerce avec l'Angleterre.... Rouen & Paris: Moutard, 1788. 8vo, wraps; rubbed, frayed, torn along joints & edges. R gathering lightly browned. P Sept 24 (276) $500

Duppa, Richard, 1770-1831
— Illustrations of the Lotus of Antiquity. L, 1813. 4to, contemp half mor; worn. With 5 wholly or partly hand-colored plates (1 loose). Plesch—de Belder copy. S Apr 27 (113) £700 [Asher]
— Illustrations of the Lotus of the Ancients.... L, 1816. One of 25. Folio, later half mor; spine discolored. With 12 hand-colored plates. 1 platemark cropped. Plesch—de Belder copy. S Apr 27 (112) £2,000 [Kristina]
— The Life of Michel Angelo Buonarroti.... L, 1807. 2d Ed, L.p. copy. 4to, contemp calf gilt; upper joint split; rubbed. bba Oct 30 (464) £40 [Barker]

Dupre, August. See: Thudichum & Dupre

Dupre de Saint-Maur, Nicolas Francois
— Essai sur les monnoies.... Paris, 1746. 2 parts in 1 vol. 4to, calf; worn. Browned. P Sept 24 (277) $325
— Recherches sur la valeur des monnoies.... Paris, 1762. 12mo, contemp calf gilt; rubbed. Some browning; tear into text on A2. P Sept 24 (278) $350

Dupuis, Joseph
— Journal of a Residence in Ashantee. L, 1824. 4to, contemp half calf; rubbed, rebacked. With folding map & 15 plates. Some plates torn along folds. bba Oct 30 (301) £180 [Graves-Johnson]

Anr copy. Orig bds; worn, upper cover detached. With 16 plates; 1 torn at folds, anr imperf. S May 29 (1115) £160

Dupuit, Jules
— La Liberte commerciale, son principe et ses consequences. Paris: Guillaumin, 1861. 8vo, modern half cloth, orig wraps bound in. Some spotting. P Sept 24 (279) $480

Durand, Jean Nicolas Louis, 1760-1834
— Receuil et parallele des edifices de tout genre, anciens et modernes, remarquables par leur beaute. Venice, 1833. 3 vols, including Atlas. Folio, old half vellum; worn. With 266 plates. Some stains at beginning of 1 vol. S Nov 10 (212) £150 [Maronini]

Durand-Brager, Jean Baptiste Henri, 1814-79
— Sainte-Helene. Translation du cercueil de l'Empereur Napoleon a bord de la Fregate La Belle-Poule. Paris, 1844. Folio, contemp half calf; worn. With 5 ports & 24 views. Wormholes affecting 10 plates. S Oct 23 (458) £800 [Marshall]

Durante, Castore, 1520-90
— Il Tesoro della sanita. Rome: F. Zannetti for I. Tornieri & I. Biricchia, 1586. 4to, vellum. With port. Foxed; last few leaves with marginal worming; signatures to tp. Crahan copy. P Nov 25 (171) $450

Duranti, Guillelmus, 1237?-96
— Rationale divinorum officiorum. Strassburg: [Ptr of the 1483 Jordanus de Quedlinburg (Georg Husner)], 1484. Folio, contemp calf over wooden bds tooled in blind. 2 burnholes; piece clipped from margin of 2d leaf; some leaves frayed. 276 leaves. Goff D-428. HN May 20 (1640) DM1,400
— Speculum judiciale. Padua: Johannes Herbort de Seligenstadt, 1479-78. 4 parts (of 5); lacking the Inventarium, bound in 3 vols. Disparate contemp red sheep & brown calf over wooden bds; worn, clasps lost, rebacked. Marginal stains; some worming, mainly in margins; a few leaves frayed. 724 (of 728) leaves; lacking initial & final blanks. Goff D-448. P Sept 24 (151) $1,600

Durenceau, Andre
— Inspirations. Woodstock, [1928]. Folio, bds; extremities worn. With 22 (of 24) pochoir plates. Some plates foxed or soiled. sg June 18 (199A) $600

Duret, Claude, d.1611
— Histoire admirable des plantes et herbes.... Paris: Nicolas Buon, 1605. 8vo, contemp calf; 1 corner restored. Margins trimmed close; some cropping, affecting some sidenotes & several woodcuts. sg Dec 4 (63) $550

Duret, Theodore, 1838-1927
— Histoire des peintres impressionistes. Paris, [1923]. Orig wraps. Some dampstains. S Nov 10 (239) £160 [Eliopoulos]
— Die Impressionisten. Berlin, 1914. 4to, half vellum; worn. HN May 20 (2409) DM600
— Manet and the French Impressionists. L & Phila., 1910. With 4 etchings by Manet,

Morisot & Renoir (2). Light foxing to text. sg Dec 4 (64) $800; sg June 11 (175) $550

Durieux, Tilla
— Spielen und Traeumen. Berlin, 1922. One of 25. Illus by E. Orlik. 4to, orig bdg. With 6 plates. HN Nov 26 (2023) DM1,200

Durling, Richard J.
— A Catalogue of Sixteenth Century Printed Books in the National Library of Medicine. Bethesda, 1967. 4to, orig cloth. bba Oct 16 (375) £60 [Sokol]

Anr copy. 2 vols, including Kritatsy's 1971 Supplement. 4to, sg May 14 (612) $250

Durrell, Lawrence
— The Alexandria Quartet. L, 1957-60. ("Justine; Balthazar; Mountolive; Clea.") 4 vols. In d/js. sg Mar 5 (55) $325

1st Collected Ed. L, 1962. one of 500. cb May 7 (19) $225

Anr copy. Corners rubbed. sg Dec 11 (21) $110

— The Black Book. Paris: Obelisk Press, 1938. 1st Ed. Orig wraps; spine frayed at top. T Feb 18 (110) £260

Durrieu, Paul, 1855-1922
— La Miniature flamande au temps de la cour de Bourgogne.... Brussels, 1921. Folio, contemp mor; rubbed, foot of spine chipped. cb Feb 5 (87) $80

Durrieu, Paul, Comte, 1855-1922
— Le Terrier de Marcoussis.... Paris: Pour la Societe des Bibliophiles Francois, 1926. One of 245. 4to, half shagreen. Jeanson copy. SM Feb 28 (203) FF1,800

Durrow, Book of. See: Codex...

Dury, Andrew
See also: Andrews & Dury
— A Collection of Plans of the Principal Cities of Great Britain and Ireland. L, [1764]. Oblong 8vo, contemp calf; rebacked. With engraved title, dedication & contents leaf, 22 hand colored maps & 19 hand colored plans. pn May 21 (359) £720 [Burgess Browning]

— A New General and Universal Atlas. L, [c.1763]. Oblong 8vo, contemp sheep; extremities rubbed. With engraved title & 39 maps, colored in outline. Some tears at folds. Ck May 15 (301) £190

Dushesne, Andre, 1584-1640
— Histoire de la Maison de Chastillon sur Marne.... Paris, 1621. Folio, needs rebdg. Marginal dampstains at end; minor tears; tp stamped. sg Mar 26 (102) $250

Dutton, Capt. Clarence Edward
— Atlas to Accompany the Monograph on the Tertiary History of the Grand Canyon District. Wash., 1882. Folio, orig cloth. With 23 plates & maps. Sheet XV removed & mtd on bd; Sheet XVIII abraded & with a repaired tear. cb Apr 2 (79) $425

Anr copy. Orig cloth; worn. With 22 plates & maps, a few small tears along lower margin. pn Jan 22 (341) £560 [Burgess]

— Tertiary History of the Grand Canyon District. Santa Barbara, 1977. 2 vols. 4to & folio, half syn. sg Mar 12 (103) $100

Dutton, Eric A.T.
— Kenya Mountain. L, 1929. 1st Ed. With folding map bound in. T Sept 18 (16) £50

Dutton, Francis, 1816-77
— South Australia and its Mines.... L, 1846. 8vo, orig cloth. Library copy. wa Nov 6 (130) $120

Dutton, Geoffrey
— Russell Drysdale. L, [1964]. 4to, cloth, in d/j. kh Mar 16 (161) A$130

Dutuit, Auguste
— La Collection Dutuit, Livres et Manuscrits. Paris, 1899. One of 350. Folio, orig half pigskin; rubbed. bba Oct 30 (465) £180 [Fogg]

Dutuit, Eugene
— L'Oeuvre complete de Rembrandt. Paris, 1883-85. 3 vols, including Supplement. 4to, half mor by Pagnant; 2 spines rubbed. Plates 213, 281 & 342 not present, as explained by inserted leaves. Without the extra album of 8 plates. C Dec 3 (20) £200 [Stogdon]

Duval de la Lissandriere, Pierre Neel
— Traite universel des eaux et forests de France.... Paris: Estienne Michallet, 1699. 8vo, contemp red mor with arms of Michel de Chamillart. Jeanson copy. SM Feb 28 (205) FF5,000

Duval, Neel, Sieur de la Lissandriere. See: Duval de la Lissandriere, Pierre Neel

Duveen, Charles Joel
— Elizabethan Interiors, by C. J. Charles. NY: F. Greenfield, [c.1919]. One of 500. Folio, half vellum; soiled. Inscr. wa Sept 25 (168) $130

Duveen, Denis Ian
— Bibliotheca alchemica et chemica: an Annotated Catalogue of Printed Books. L, 1949. One of 200. 4to, orig cloth. sg May 14 (591) $350

Anr copy. Orig cloth; rubbed. Library markings. With 16 plates bound in at end. T Mar 19 (370) £135

Duyckinck, Evert Augustus, 1816-78

— National Portrait Gallery of Eminent Americans. NY, [c.1870]. 2 vols. 4to, half mor; rubbed. sg June 4 (121) $70

— Portrait Gallery of Eminent Men and Women of Europe and America. NY, [c.1873]. 2 vols. 4to, half sheep; worn. With extra engraved title. ha Sept 19 (152) $50

Dyer, Sir James, 1512-82

— Ascuns novel cases. L: R. Tottell, 1585. Folio, contemp calf gilt, with ovals on covers flanked by initials I.L.; spine worn. Worming to blank margins of 1st few leaves; lacking J3 & 4. Ck Apr 24 (209) £110

Dykes, Jeff

— Fifty Great Western Illustrators: A Bibliographic Checklist. Flagstaff, [1975]. One of 200. 4to, half lea. Sgd. cb Jan 8 (253) $80

E

E., J. See: Elsum, John

E., W. T. See: Emmet, William Temple

Eales, Mary

— The Compleat Confectioner. L, 1733. 8vo, contemp sheep gilt; broken, extremities worn. P Nov 25 (172) $500

Anr copy. Contemp calf; rubbed. Minor discoloration of a few leaves. P Nov 25 (173) $600

Earhart, John F.

— The Color Printer.... Cincinnati, 1892. 4to, orig cloth; recased & rebacked, preserving orig spine. With 90 plates. Small piece torn from blank corner of title. O May 12 (62) $250

Earle, Alice Morse, 1853-1911

— Two Centuries of Costume in America.... NY, 1903. 2 vols. Orig half calf; rubbed. O Mar 24 (65) $55

Earle, Augustus

— A Narrative of a Nine Months' Residence in New Zealand.... L, 1832. 8vo, modern half mor gilt. With 7 plates. Some dampstaining & foxing. sg Apr 23 (50) $225

Earle Collection, Cyril

— The Earle Collection of Early Staffordshire Pottery. L, [1915]. One of 250. Folio, mor gilt. S Nov 10 (77) £80 [Heneage]

Earnest, Adele

— The Art of the Decoy: American Bird Carvings. NY, [1965]. 4to, cloth, in d/j; rear cover torn. sg Oct 23 (244) $50

Earwaker, John Parsons

— East Cheshire: Past and Present. L, 1877-80. 2 vols. 4to, orig cloth; spines worn & tape-repaired. T Sept 18 (74) £105

East India Company

— Recueil des voyages qui ont servi a l'etablissement et aux progrez de la compagnie des Indes Orientales, formee dans les Provinces Unies des Pais-Bas. Rouen: J. B. Machuel, 1725. 12 vols, including 2 Supplements. 12mo, contemp calf gilt; rubbed. With 2 engraved titles & 74 plates & maps. A few marginal tears. S Apr 23 (190) £900 [Perrin]

— Recueil des voyages qui ont servia l'etablissement et aux progres de la Compagnie des Indes Orientales, formee dans les Provinces Unies des Pais-Bas. Rouen: Pierre le Boucher, 1725. 10 vols. 12mo, contemp calf; rubbed. Some cropping & repairs. Sold w.a.f. S June 25 (476) £400

East India Company, Dutch

— RENNEVILLE, RENE AUGUSTIN CONSTANTIN DE. - Recueil des voiages qui ont servi a l'etablissement & au progres de la Compagnie des Indes Orientales.... Amst., 1725. 7 vols in 6. 8vo, contemp vellum; 2 spines flaked. With 3 frontises & 55 maps & plates, most folding. A few plates frayed at margin; 2 plates detached; 1 folding section severed, anr slit. C Dec 12 (257) £400 [Sweet]

East Jersey

— A Brief Accout of the Province of East-Jersey in America.... L, 1682. Bound with: Proposals by the Proprietors of East-Jersey in America, for the Building of a Town on Ambo-Point. L, 1682. 4to, half mor. S June 25 (387) £9,500

Eastlake, Charles Locke, 1836-1906

— A History of the Gothic Revival in England. L, 1872. 4to, orig cloth; worn & soiled, tear along rear joint. wa Nov 6 (431) $75

Eastman, Mary Henderson, b.1818

— American Aboriginal Portfolio. Phila., [1853]. 4to, orig cloth gilt. With engraved title & 26 plates. S Oct 23 (416) £500 [Strausbaugh]

Anr copy. Orig cloth gilt; worn. wd June 19 (121) $450

Eaton, Daniel Cady, 1834-95
— Ferns of North America. Salem & Bost., 1878-80. Parts 2 & 6-27 only. 4to, orig wraps, unopened. Library markings. ha Sept 19 (255) $100

— The Ferns of North America. Salem & Bost., 1879-80. 2 vols. 4to, half mor; worn. With 81 color plates. O May 12 (64) $400

Anr copy. Modern cloth. pnNY Oct 11 (20) $160

Eaton, Elon Howard
— Birds of New York. Albany, 1910-14. 1st Ed. 2 vols. 4to, cloth; worn. With 106 colored plates. sg Sept 18 (82) $80

Ebel, Johann Gottfried, 1764-1830
— Voyage pittoresque dans le Canton des Grisons en Suisse. Zurich, 1827. Oblong 8vo, contemp bds; spine def. With engraved title, folding map, 5 key plates & 32 views. S Apr 23 (162) £7,000 [Chapponiere]

Ebel, Johann Gottfried, 1764-1830 —& Meyer, Johann Jacob
— Voyage pittoresque dans le Canton des Grisons en Suisse.... Zurich: J. J. Meyer, 1827. 8vo, contemp bds. With engraved title, folding map & 31 (of 32) plates, with the 5 key plates each containing 6 views & the separate key plate to Plate 7b. A few leaves with vertical creases. C May 13 (114) £3,200 [Faber]

Ebers, Georg
— Egypt: Descriptive, Historical and Picturesque.... L, [1880-83]. 2 vols. 4to, contemp calf gilt; crudely rebacked, worn. bba Oct 30 (302) £55 [P & P]

Ebers, Georg —& Guthe, Hermann
— Palaestina in Bild und Wort. Stuttgart & Leipzig, 1883-84. 2 vols. Folio, half calf gilt. With 1 plan, 2 maps & 39 plates including engraved title. JG Oct 2 (841) DM700

Eberstadt, Edward
— The Annotated Eberstadt Catalogues of Americana. NY, 1965. One of 750. Nos 103-138 (1935-1956). 4 vols. cb Feb 5 (89) $140; sg Oct 2 (124) $275

Ebert, Friedrich Adolf, 1791-1834
— A General Bibliographical Dictionary. Oxford, 1837. 4 vols. 8vo, cloth. sg May 14 (296) $70

Ecke, Gustav
— Chinese Painting in Hawaii. [Honolulu, 1965]. One of 550. 3 vols. 4to, cloth. cb July 30 (61) $350

Eckel, John C.
— The First Editions of the Writings of Charles Dickens. L, 1913. One of 750. 4to, cloth, in d/j. sg Jan 22 (146) $150

Economisch...
— Economisch-Historisch Jaarboek. Bijdragen tot de economische geschiedenis van Nederland. The Hague, 1915-80. Vols 1-43. B June 2 (745) HFl,000

Edda
— Edda of Saemund. Bristol, 1797. ("Icelandic Poetry, or the Edda of Saemund.") Trans by Amos Simon Cottle. 8vo, later cloth. sg Sept 11 (209) $130

Eddis, William, b.1745?
— Letters from America, Historical and Descriptive.... L, 1792. 1st Ed. 8vo, modern half calf gilt. pn Mar 5 (21) £90 [Maggs]

Eddy, John W.
— Hunting on Kenai Peninsula.... Seattle, Wash., 1924. Sgd. cb May 21 (98) $80

Ede, Harold Stanley
— A Life of Gaudier-Brzeska. L, 1930. One of 350. Folio, cloth; spine stained. Ck Oct 31 (186) £90

Anr copy. Cloth; worn. pn Sept 18 (212) £80 [Henderson]

Eder, Joseph Maria
— History of Photography. NY, 1945. sg Nov 13 (45) $90

Edgerton, Harold E. —& Killian, James R.
— Moments of Vision. The Stroboscopic Revolution in Photography. Cambr. MA: MIT Press, [1979]. Special Issue, with mtd color photos by Edgerton sgd by him. In d/j. Sgd by both on tp. wa Nov 6 (307) $110

Edgeworth, Maria, 1767-1849
— Castle Rackrent, an Hibernian Tale. L, 1800. 8vo, contemp calf; joints starting. sg Feb 12 (134) $50

— Tales and Miscellaneous Pieces. L, 1825. 14 vols. 8vo, calf; spine ends rubbed. cb July 30 (62) $300

— Tales and Novels. L, 1832-33. 18 vols. 8vo, half calf. S Sept 22 (20) £300 [Lyon]

Edgeworth, Maria, 1767-1849 —& Edgeworth, Richard Lovell, 1744-1817
— Practical Education. L, 1798. 2 vols. 4to, contemp half calf; broken. T Oct 10 (498) £270

2d Ed. L, 1801. 3 vols. 8vo, contemp calf; repaired. bba May 14 (175) £100 [Subunso]

EDGEWORTH

Edgeworth, Richard Lovell, 1744-1817
See also: Edgeworth & Edgeworth
— Essays on Professional Education. L, 1809. 1st Ed. 4to, contemp half calf; upper cover detached. T Oct 16 (499) £270

Edinburgh...
— The Edinburgh Journal of Natural History and of the Physical Sciences. Edin., 1839-40. Vols I & II bound in one. Folio, half calf; defective. With 128 hand-colored plates. pn Jan 22 (15) £380 [Ramsey]
— The Edinburgh Practice of Physic, Surgery and Midwifery.... L, 1803. 5 vols. 8vo, orig bds; hinges def, worn, some spines torn. Some worming in inner margin of some leaves at end of Vol II; lacking some text & index at end of Vol III. Sold w.a.f. S Nov 10 (482) £70 [Phelps]

Edinburgh Chess Club
— The Games of the Match...between the London and the Edinburgh Chess Clubs.... Edin.: W. Blackwood, 1929. Disbound. pn Mar 26 (111) £70 [Farmer]

Edmondes, Sir Clement, 1564?-1622
— Observations upon the Five First Bookes of Caesars Commentaries. L, 1609 [engraved title dated 1604]. Issue without the 2 dedicatory leaves. Folio, contemp vellum gilt. With port, engraved title & 6 plates only, some hand-colored. Ck Jan 16 (152) £150

Edmondson, John Ludlam. See: Sugden & Edmondson

Edo...
— Edo Ryoku Ryori Taizen. [N.p., 1835]. 4 vols in 2, 184mm by 129mm, wraps. Menus & recipes from the Tokyo tea-house The Yaozen. Crahan copy. P Nov 25 (174) $600

Edschmid, Kasimir, Pseud. of Eduard Schmid
— Die Furstin. Weimar, 1918. One of 130. Illus by Max Beckmann. 4to, mor by Enders. C May 13 (188) £2,100 [Koch]

Edward of Norwich, 2d Duke of York, 1373?-1415
— The Master of Game. L, 1904. One of 600. Folio, orig calf. Jeanson 1251. SM Feb 28 (47) FF4,000

Edward VI, King of England. See: Clement

Edward VIII, King of England. See: Windsor, Edward

Edwards, Arthur Cecil
— The Persian Carpet. L, 1953. 4to, cloth, in d/j. sg Feb 5 (240) $150

AMERICAN BOOK PRICES CURRENT

Edwards, Bryan, 1743-1800
— The History, Civil and Commercial, of the British Colonies in the West Indies. L, 1801. 3 vols. 8vo, contemp half vellum; rebacked, orig spines preserved, 2 covers detached. With port & 20 folding maps & plates, including hand-colored map of Jamaica with annotations & emendations in red & black ink. Lacking St. Domingo; 1 plate creased & slightly frayed; a few tears & stains. C Apr 8 (85) £190 [Joseph]

Anr copy. Contemp calf. Embossed library stamp on titles; several plates with minor tears along folds, 1 with tear affecting image. sg Mar 12 (104) $250

Edwards, George, 1694-1773
— A Natural History of Uncommon Birds. L, [1739]-43-64. ("A Natural History of Birds × Gleanings of Natural History.") 7 vols. 4to, contemp mor gilt; rubbed, call numbers on spines. With 293 (of 362) hand-colored plates. First 4 vols with the French trans bound at end. Gleanings lacking frontis & port. Library markings. P June 18 (48) $8,500

— Verzameling van uitlandsche en zeldsaame Vogelen. Amst.: J. C. Sepp, 1772-81. Ed by Johann M. Seligmann. 5 vols. Folio, contemp half vellum gilt; worn. With 473 hand-colored plates. Vol I lacking the 2 leaves of index. S Oct 23 (739) £15,500 [Schire]

Edwards, John, fl.1768-95
— The British Herbal. L, [1769]-70. 1st Ed. Folio, half russia. With 99 (of 100) hand-colored plates. Marginal tears repaired on tp & final index leaf; lacking Plate 39. C Oct 15 (189) £9,500 [Marshall]

Anr copy. Contemp calf; worn & def. With 72 hand-colored plates only. Some dampstains & discoloration. Sold w.a.f. S Apr 23 (34) £3,000 [Wellbeck]

Anr Ed. L, 1775. ("A Select Collection of One Hundred Plates....") Folio, contemp russia gilt; repaired, rubbed. With 100 hand-colored plates. A few spots; 1 plate slightly browned. Linnean Society—de Belder copy. S Apr 27 (114) £19,000 [Hill]

— A Collection of Flowers, Drawn after Nature.... L, [1783-95]. Folio, old mor; def. With engraved title & 71 hand-colored plates only. Worn & waterstained with paper brittle & margins chipped; tp badly torn & stained. Sold w.a.f. CNY Nov 21 (104) $16,000

Edwards, Jonathan, 1703-58
— A Careful and Strict Enquiry into the Modern Prevailing Notions of that Freedom of Will.... Bost.: S. Kneeland, 1754. 1st Ed. 8vo, contemp calf; rebacked. Tp tender & thin in spots. sg Mar 12 (105) $375

Edwards, Lionel
— My Hunting Sketch Book. L, 1928. Vol I (of 2) only. 4to, half vellum; worn & soiled. sg May 21 (99) $175

Anr copy. Cloth. With 15 color plates & with 15 orig color drawings. Jeanson 1707. SM Mar 1 (207) FF3,800

— The Passing Seasons. L, [1927]. One of 250. Oblong folio, orig bds, in torn d/j; soiled. With 18 colored plates. S June 17 (231) £500 [Way]

— A Sportsman's Bag. L, [1926]. One of 100, with the plates sgd. Folio, orig bds, in def d/j; soiled. S June 17 (230) £260 [Way]

Edwards, Ralph. See: Macquoid & Edwards

Edwards, Sydenham Teak, 1769?-1819
— The Botanical Register. L, 1815-47. Vols 1-21 only. Half mor, not quite uniform; some rubbed. With 1,759 hand-colored plates only. Vol 19 lacking title & indexes. Sold w.a.f. S Oct 23 (680) £7,800 [Walford]

Anr copy. John Lindley's Appendix only, in 3 parts. 8vo, orig wraps. With 9 colored plates. S Apr 23 (46) £700 [Antipodean]

Anr copy. 33 vols plus Appendix which is bound into Vol 26 of this set (complete). Contemp half calf; rebacked & repaired, old spines preserved, a few joints split, 1 cover detached. Sold w.a.f. Plesch—de Belder copy. S Apr 27 (115) £16,000 [Antipodian]

Anr copy. Vols 1-2 only. Bds; not uniform. With 177 hand-colored plates. Lacking tp & 1st leaf of the catalogue of books in Vol I. Sold w.a.f. S July 28 (1066) £1,400

Anr Ed. L, 1815. Vol I only. 8vo, contemp mor gilt; worn & soiled. With 76 (of 90) hand-colored plates. wa Nov 6 (18) $210

Nos 130 & 131. L, 1825-26. Wraps as issued; worn, 1 missing. With 16 hand-colored plates. Slight stains to 2 plates. L Dec 11 (276) £70

New Series 1-10 (all pbd) in 10 vols. L, 1836-47. 8vo, later cloth. With 688 hand-colored plates, a few folding. Library markings, including perforated stamps on titles & on 5 frontises. bba Jan 15 (406) £2,800 [Walford]

Vol 24. L, 1838. Half lea gilt. pn Sept 18 (241) £620 [Richards]

Edwards, William B.
— The Story of Colt's Revolver. Harrisburg: Stackpole, [1953]. Ltd Ed. Mor gilt. cb Oct 9 (50) $80

Eeden, Frederik Willem van, 1860-1932
— De kleine Johannes. The Hague: Mouton, 1887. Orig cloth. B Oct 7 (5) HF320

Anr Ed. The Hague, 1898. One of 40. Illus by Edzard Koning. 4to, vellum gilt. B Oct 7 (39) HF750

Egan, Pierce, 1772-1849
— Anecdotes of the Turf, the Chase.... L, 1827. 8vo, modern half mor. With hand-colored frontis & 12 plates. Ck Sept 5 (130) £140

Anr copy. Shagreen gilt by Riviere. With 13 hand-colored plates. Schwerdt-Jeanson copy. SM Mar 1 (208) FF4,000

— Book of Sports, and Mirror of Life.... L, 1832. 1st Ed. 8vo, contemp half calf, orig wraps bound in; lacking front cover to Part 1. Tp stained. bba Mar 26 (204) £70 [Valentine]

— Every Gentleman's Manual——A Lecture on the Art of Self-Defence.... L: Sherwood & Bowyer, 1845. 8vo, orig cloth; lacking backstrip, cover panels reattached with glue visible at joints. ha Sept 19 (249) $50

— Finish to the Adventures of Tom, Jerry and Logic.... L, 1830. 1st Ed, Issue not indicated. Illus by Robert Cruikshank. 8vo, mor gilt by Bedford. With 36 hand-colored plates. sg Feb 12 (137) $425

Later Issue. Lev. With 36 hand-colored plates. sg June 11 (154) $650

— Life in London. L, 1821. 1st Ed, 1st Issue, with no footnote on p. 9. Illus by I. R. & George Cruikshank. 8vo, mor gilt; front cover detached, spine chipped at head. With 36 hand-colored plates & 3 folding leaves of engraved music. Lacking half-title & inserted ad. sg Feb 12 (135) $130

Anr copy. Mor by Zaehnsdorf. Some browning & foxing. L.p. copy. wd Nov 12 (108) $500

Anr Ed. L, 1830. 8vo, contemp bds; rebacked. With 36 hand-colored plates & 3 folding sheets of music. Marginal tears not affecting text; most plate imprints cropped. S Nov 10 (371) £100 [Seibu]

— The Life of an Actor. L, 1825. 1st Ed. 8vo, calf gilt by Dayntun. bba Oct 30 (61) £180 [Cavendish]

Anr copy. Later mor; rubbed. With 27 color plates. Some foxing. O May 12 (65) $295

Anr copy. Mor gilt by Zaehnsdorf. With 27 colored plates. sg Feb 12 (136) $300

— Sporting Anecdotes. L, 1825. 8vo, mor gilt

by Riviere; spine head rubbed. Tp soiled & frayed with 2 repaired corners & repaired tears; blank inner corner of frontis repaired. cb May 21 (100) $120

Egan Imitations not by Egan

— Real Life in Ireland. L, 1821. 1st Ed. 8vo, lev gilt. With colored frontis & 18 hand-colored plates. Minor foxing; 4 plates trimmed & inlaid. sg Feb 12 (138) $325
— Real Life in London. L, 1824. 2 vols. 8vo, lea gilt. HK Nov 4 (2837) DM650
— Real Life in Ireland. L, [1829]. 8vo, modern half mor gilt. With hand-colored frontis & 18 plates; frontis torn on margin. pnNY Sept 13 (226) $250
— Real Life in London. L, 1821-22. 1st Ed. 2 vols. 8vo, contemp half calf; worn. S July 14 (496) £85
   Anr copy. Mor gilt by Wood. sg Feb 12 (139) $200

Egbert, Donald Drew
— The Tickhill Psalter and Related Manuscripts. NY, 1940. 4to, cloth, in d/j. Library markings. bba Feb 5 (97) £110 [Fogg]

Ege, Otto F.
— Original Leaves from Famous Books.... [Cleveland, c.1950]. One of 50. Folio, matted with ptd annotations tipped onto each mat, loose as issued in cloth folding case. Includes 6 Ms leaves (from 12th to 14th century) & 34 ptd leaves (from 15th to 20th century). P Dec 15 (192) $1,600

Egerton, Daniel Thomas
— Fashionable Bores or Coolers in High Life by Peter Quiz. L, 1824. Oblong 4to, mor gilt by Riviere; joints rubbed, corners bumped, front wrap bound in at rear. Lacking 2 plates. sg June 11 (179) $650

Egerton, Michael
— Collinso furioso or Matters to Tatters. L, July 1825. 4to, later mor gilt extra by Bayntun; rubbed, front cover nearly detached. cb Oct 23 (64) $90

Egnatius, Johannes Baptista, Pseud. of G. B. Capilli
— Summaire chronique contenans les vies, gestes et cas fortuitz de tous les Empereurs.... Paris: Geoffroy Tory, 13 Apr 1529. Trans by Geoffroy Tory. 8vo, contemp calf; spine wormed. Very small wormhole in final 28 leaves affecting a few letters. S Nov 27 (161) £5,000 [Abrams]

Eguia, Jose Joaquin de
— Memoria sobre la utilidad e influjo de la mineria.... Mexico, 1819. 4to, contemp sheep. sg Sept 18 (83) $325

Eichendorff, Joseph Carl Benedict von
— Gedichte. Berlin, 1837. 8vo, contemp half cloth. Some spotting. HK Nov 4 (2462) DM1,500

Eichhorn, Johann
— Die Geistliche Ruest und Schatskammer. Nuremberg, 1693. 12mo, contemp German silver bdg with maker's mark of Joseph Herterich. P Sept 24 (115) $3,000

Einstein, Albert, 1879-1955
— Die Grundlage der allgemeinen Relativitaetstheorie. Leipzig, 1916. Contemp half lea. With port & 10 plates. HN May 20 (1051) DM600
— The Meaning of Relativity. Princeton, 1950. 3d Ed. sg Jan 15 (309) $800
— Relativity.... NY, 1920. Soiled & worn. wa Nov 6 (169) $55

Einstein, Albert, 1879-1955 —& Infeld, Leopold
— The Evolution of Physics. NY, 1942. In d/j. Inscr by Einstein. O Jan 6 (54) $650

Einstein, Carl
— Georges Braque. Paris & NY, [1934]. One of 200 with an orig etching. Illus by Georges Braque. 4to, wraps. pnNY Sept 13 (227) $275

Eisen, Gustav, 1847-1940 —& Kouchakji, Fahim
— Glass: its Origin, History.... NY, 1927. 2 vols. 4to, orig half cloth. S Mar 9 (669) £110 [Laget]
   One of 525. Orig half cloth. O May 12 (66) $210; sg June 4 (146) $225

Eisenberg,——, Baron d'
— La Perfezione e i difetti del cavallo. Florence, 1753. Folio, contemp vellum; spine worn. With engraved title & 23 plates. HN Nov 26 (266) DM540

Eisenhower, Dwight David, 1890-1969
— Crusade in Europe. Garden City, 1948. In frayed d/j. Sgd. wa May 30 (166) $180
   One of 1,426. Inscr to Bob Lovett. wd Nov 12 (110) $800

Eisenloeffel, Nico. See: Nescio

Eisenmenger, Johann Andreas
— Des bey 40 Jahr der Judenschafft mit Arrest bestrickt gewesene...Entdecktes Judenthum.... [Frankfurt], 1700. 2 parts in 1 vol. 4to, contemp half vellum; spine torn. Lacking 1st & last leaf in Vol I; Tt2 in Vol II torn & repaired in margin. S Mar 10

(1058) £300 [Nosbusch]
— Entdecktes Judenthum, oder Gruendlicher und Wahrhaffter Bericht.... Koenigsberg, 1711. 2 vols. 4to, orig vellum. S Feb 17 (41) £350 [Wyler]

Ekelof, Adolf
— Ett ar i Stilla Hafvet. Reseminnen fran Patagonien, Chili, Peru, Californien.... Stockholm, 1872. 4to, orig cloth; rubbed. With 12 plates. cb Jan 8 (51) $350

Anr copy. Bds; badly worn, spine crudely repaired. 1 detached. sg Nov 20 (67) $200

Elder, Marc. See: Andre & Elder

Eldershaw, M. Barnard, Pseud. of Marjorie F. Barnard & Flora S. Eldershaw
— The Life and Times of Captain John Piper. Sydney: Australia Limited Editions Society, 1939. One of 350. Orig calf gilt. CA Oct 7 (59) A$240

Elements...
— The Elements of Chess. Bost.: Ptd for W. Pelham, 1805. Disbound. Some stains; last leaf repaired with small tear. pn Mar 26 (362) £200 [De Lucia]

Elettricismo...
— Dell'Elettricismo, o sia delle forze elettriche de' corpi, svelate dalls fiscia sperimentale, con un'ampia dichiarazione della luce elettrica.... Venice: Recruti, 1746. 8vo, later half calf. A few leaves soiled. S Nov 10 (483) £160 [Phelps]

Eleventh...
— An Eleventh Century Anglo-Saxon Illustrated Miscellany, British Library Cotton Tiberius B V Part I.... Copenhagen: Rosenkilde & Bagger, 1983. Folio, wraps. Vol XXI of Early English Manuscripts in Facsimile. ha Dec 19 (46) $130

Elexpuru, Antonio de
— Compendio de las prevenciones que...Manuel de Amat y Junient...hizo para la Difensa de la Guerra contra Portugal e Inglaterra. Lima, 1763. Folio, disbound. Glue stain at top inner edge; bottom inner edge frayed on 1st leaf; some shaving, affecting italicized marginalia on 2 leaves. sg Sept 18 (84) $200

Elias, Julius
— Die Handzeichnungen Max Liebermanns. Berlin, 1922. One of 480. Folio, orig half cloth. With 93 plates & 2 etchings. HK Nov 4 (3028) DM1,260
— Max Liebermann zu Hause. Berlin, 1918. Ltd Ed. Folio, mor by Maria Luehr; worn. HN May 20 (2642) DM2,400

Elimithar, Elluchasem
— Tacuini sex rerum non naturalium.... Strassburg: J. Schott, 1533. 2d Ed. Folio, sheep. Woodcut on K1 shaved; marginal stains. Westbury-Crahan copy. P Nov 25 (175) $2,000
— Tacuinis sanitatis Elluchasem Elimithar medici de Baldath, de sex rebus non naturalibus.... Strassburg: J. Schottus, 1531. Folio, modern vellum. With 40 woodcuts by Hans Weiditz. Lower inner corners of many leaves repaired with some words in pen facsimile. S Nov 27 (276) £3,000 [Israel]

Eliot, George, 1819-80
— Adam Bede. Edin. & L, 1859. 1st Ed. 3 vols. 8vo, orig cloth, Carter's variant B. sg June 11 (180) $800
— Daniel Deronda. Edin. & L, 1876. 1st Ed, in 8 orig parts, 1st Issue. 8vo, orig wraps; spines soiled & rubbed. Lacking errata leaf. bba Oct 30 (64) £160 [Maggs]

1st Ed in Book form. 4 vols. 8vo, half calf gilt. pn Jan 22 (265) £90 [Scott]
— Felix Holt the Radical. Edin. & L, 1866. 1st Ed. 3 vols. 8vo, orig cloth, unopened; spines rubbed. S July 13 (98) £90
— Middlemarch. Edin. & L, 1871. 1st Ed in Book form. 4 vols. 8vo, contemp mor; rubbed. bba July 16 (301) £170 [Pordes]

Anr copy. Half calf gilt. pn Jan 22 (264) £90 [Scott]
— The Mill on the Floss. Edin. & L, 1860. 1st Ed. 3 vols. 8vo, orig cloth. F Oct 30 (202) $150
— Silas Marner. Edin. & L, 1861. 1st Ed. 8vo, 19th-cent half mor. Lacking half-title & pbr's cat. sg Feb 12 (140) $100
— The Spanish Gypsy. Edin & L, 1868. 1st Ed. 8vo, orig cloth; soiled. Inscr & with holograph corrections. Kern copy. Sold with a copy of Bronte's The Professor. P June 18 (52) $9,250
— Works. Edin., 1878-85. Cabinet Ed. 24 vols. 8vo, half mor. S May 6 (429) £420 [Goldstein]

Library Ed. L, 1901. 10 vols. Calf gilt. S July 13 (100) £350

Eliot, John, 1604-90
See also: Eliot, John; Whitefield, Henry; Winslow, Edward
— A Brief Narrative of the Progress of the Gospel amongst the Indians.... L: for John Allen, 1671. 4to, mor gilt by W. Pratt for Henry Stevens, 1884. Headline of title & 4 headline page numerals shaved. Eliot's Indian Tract No 11. Hoe copy. CNY Dec 19 (80) $6,500
— A Further Accompt of the Progresse of the Gospel amongst the Indians.... L: M.

Simmons for the Corporation of New-England, 1659. 4to, mor gilt by Bedford. Title rules just cropped at top; 1 headline shaved; 10 page numerals shaved. Eliot's Indian Tract No 9. Bibliotheca Lindesiana—Hoe copy. CNY Dec 19 (79) $9,000

— A late and further Manifestation of the Progress of the Gospel amongst the Indians in New-England.... L: M.S., 1655. 1st Ed. 4to, lev gilt by Bedford. Eliot's Indian Tract No 8. Bibliotheca Lindesiana—Hoe copy. CNY Dec 19 (78) $2,500

— New England's First Fruits. L: for Henry Overton, 1643. 4to, mor gilt. Lacking errata & final blank leaf; title soiled. Eliot's Indian Tract No 1. Hoe Copy. CNY Dec 19 (71) $6,000

Anr copy. Half calf. Tp dust-soiled; 1st word of title & some page numerals shaved; fore-margins of final 2 leaves slightly def with loss of 1 or 2 letters. S June 25 (403) £2,200 [Reese]

Eliot, John, 1604-90 —& Mayhew, Thomas

— Tears of Repentance: Or, a Further Narrative of the Progress of the Gospel Amongst the Indians.... L: Peter Cole, 1653. 1st Ed. 4to, half mor. Tp, C3, A2, B1-C4 & K4 all with upper margin renewed with facsimile to headlines or page numerals; blank foremargin of A2 renewed; a further 20 leaves with page numerals cropped but legible; final leaf supplied from Church's "Third Edition". Eliot's Indian Tract No 7. CNY Dec 19 (77) $1,000

Eliot, Thomas Stearns, 1888-1965

— Ash Wednesday. L & NY, 1930. One of 600. S July 13 (147) £150; sg Dec 11 (22) $250; wa Dec 11 (154) $280

— The Cultivation of Christmas Trees. L, [1954]. 1st Ed. Orig ptd wraps; soiled & worn. Inscr & dated. wa Sept 25 (660) $100

— Ezra Pound: His Metric and his Poetry. NY, 1917 [pbd Jan 1918]. 1st Ed. Orig bds; worn. S May 6 (461) £100 [Korn]

— For Lancelot Andrewes. L, [1928]. 1st Ed. Orig cloth; rubbed. Inscr. bba Sept 25 (125) £100 [Heritage]

— Geoffrey Faber, 1889-1961. L, 1961. One of 100. Orig bds. Inscr to Frank Morley. sg Mar 5 (58) $1,700

— Old Possum's Book of Practical Cats. L, 1939. 1st Ed. In d/j. pn Mar 5 (22) £55 [Demetzy]

Anr Ed. NY: Harcourt, Brace, [1946]. In d/j. Inscr. O May 12 (67) $375

— Poems. L: Hogarth Press, 1919. 1st Ed, 1st State, with "capitaux" on p. 13. Orig wraps; worn. T Nov 20 (273) £300

— Prufrock and Other Observations. L: The Egoist, 1917. 1st Ed, one of 500. Orig wraps; soiled, creased. Some leaves loose; last leaf glued to lower wrap. P June 18 (54) $1,000

Anr copy. Orig wraps bound in. Inscr by Desmond McCarthy. sg Mar 5 (59) $550

— Triumphal March. [L, 1931]. 1st Ed, one of 300. Orig wraps. kh Mar 16 (168) A$140

— The Waste Land. NY, 1922. 1st Ed in Book form, 1st State. One of 1,000. Orig flexible cloth, in d/j with inner glassine jacket. P June 18 (55) $3,500

2d State. Orig flexible cloth, in d/j with inner jacket of glassine. P June 18 (56) $1,500

1st English Ed in Book form. L: Hogarth Press, 1923. Orig bds, label state not mentioned, unopened; rubbed. P June 18 (58) $500

Anr copy. Orig bds. Some spotting. pn Sept 18 (287) £260 [Bell, Book]

Elkus, Richard J. See: Grabhorn Printing

Ellendigh...

— Het Ellendigh leven der Turcken, Moscoviters en Chinesen, aende Christenheyt vertoont.... The Hague, 1664. 4to, 19th-cent half calf. With plate & 3 text illusts hand-colored, probably later. Some stains & soiling. sg Nov 20 (168) $120

Ellicott, Andrew, 1754-1820

— The Journal.... Phila., 1803. 4to, contemp calf; recased, worn. With 14 maps & charts. Some repairs & offset; tp & preface repaired. wa Mar 5 (377) $800

Anr Ed. Phila., 1814. 4to, half lea; needs rebdg. With 13 (of 14) maps & plates. Most plates with perforated library stamps; several with tears near hinge. sg Mar 12 (106) $250

Elliot, Daniel Giraud, 1835-1915

— Bucerotidae. L, 1877-82. ("A Monograph of the Bucerotidae, or Family of the Hornbills.") Folio, contemp half mor; rubbed. With 2 plain & 57 hand-finished colored plates. Minor spotting to title & 2 blank plate margins. C Apr 8 (146) £3,500 [Helianthus]

— Felidae. [NY], 1878-83. ("A Monograph of the Felidae or Family of the Cats.") 1st Ed. Fragment only. Folio, disbound. Comprises 34 hand-colored plates (some with later coloring) & most of accompanying letterpress. Sold w.a.f. CNY May 11 (139) $9,500

— The Life and Habits of Wild Animals. NY, 1874. 1st American Ed, L.p. copy. Folio, orig cloth; rubbed. bba Nov 13 (55) £50

[Rainer]
— The New and heretofore Unfigured Species of the Birds of North America. NY, [1866]-69. 2 vols in orig 15/14 parts. Folio, orig bds; rebacked with lea. With 72 hand-colored plates. Stain in margin of 1 plate; some plates chipped in outer margins in Part 1; a few text leaves brittle at edges. S Oct 23 (681) £5,000 [Wesley]
— North American Shore Birds. L, 1895. One of 100. 4to, cloth; soiled. sg Oct 23 (255) $100
— A Review of the Primates. NY, 1912 [1913]. 3 vols. 4to, orig wraps; worn, corners bumped. Library markings. cb June 4 (55) $350
— Tetraoninae. NY, [1864]-65. ("A Monograph of the Tetraoninae, or Family of Grouse.") Orig 4/5 parts. Folio, orig ptd bds; rebacked. With 27 hand-finished colored plates. Tp & prelims bound at end of Part 4/5; 1st plate in Part 4/5 with margins chipped; 1 plate detached; some other marginal tears. S Apr 23 (35) £6,000 [Mitchell]
— The Wild Fowl of the United States.... NY, 1898. One of 100. 4to, cloth; soiled. sg Oct 23 (256) $100

Elliot, Capt. Robert
— Views in the East Comprising India, Canton, and the Shores of the Red Sea. L, 1835. ("Views in India, China, and on the Shores of the Red Sea.") 2 vols. 4to, contemp half mor; worn, upper cover of Vol I detached. With colored frontis, engraved title & 61 plates. T Dec 18 (5) £85

Ellis, Frederick Startridge
— The History of Reynard the Fox. L, 1897. One of 50. Illus by Walter Crane. 8vo, mor extra by the Hampstead Bindery. C Dec 12 (369) £1,400 [Joseph]

Ellis, G.
— New and Correct Atlas of England and Wales. L, [1819]. 4to, half lea; rubbed. With 55 hand-colored maps. pn May 21 (416) £320 [Quaritch]

Ellis, George Viner —& Ford, G. H.
— Illustrations of Dissections...of the Human Body. L, 1867. Folio, contemp half mor; rubbed. With 58 colored plates. 1 plate with short tear in lower margin. bba May 14 (227) £170 [Phillips]

Anr copy. Loose in half mor; worn & def. With 57 colored plates, all with Ms notes. Some plates soiled or torn. Sold w.a.f. S Nov 10 (484) £100 [Tucker]

2d Ed. L, 1876. Folio, contemp half mor; rubbed. With 58 colored plates. bba May 14 (278) £80 [Hildebrandt]

Ellis, Henry, 1721-1806
— Reise nach Hudsons Meerbusen.... Goettingen, 1750. 8vo, contemp calf; worn. With 2 maps & 9 plates. FD June 11 (1096) DM670
— A Voyage to Hudson's Bay.... L, 1748. 1st Ed. 8vo, contemp calf; rubbed. With folding map & 9 plates. Ck Sept 26 (77) £300; Ck May 21 (57) £190

Anr copy. Modern half calf. One map only partly present. sg Mar 12 (35) $130

Ellis, Sir Henry, 1777-1855
— Journal of the Proceedings of the late Embassy to China. L, 1817. 1st Ed. 4to, orig half calf; worn. Lacking folding map; 1 plate torn in margin. Sold w.a.f. bba Aug 20 (474) £120 [Fisher]

Anr copy. Modern half calf. With port, 3 charts & 7 colored plates. Port & charts spotted & browned. C Oct 15 (33) £170 [Sweet]

Ellis, John, Cartographer
— English Atlas, or a Complete Choreography of England and Wales. L, 1766. Oblong 4to, contemp calf; rubbed. With 54 double-page maps hand-colored in outline with yellow wash borders. Cornwall with short tear; some fold breaks. C Dec 12 (72) £850 [Burgess Browning]

Anr copy. Calf; rubbed. With 48 maps on 24 sheets; lacking Maps 1 & 2. pn Nov 20 (273) £320 [Nicholson]

Anr copy. Half vellum; worn. With 50 uncolored maps, 2 folding. pn May 21 (360) £500 [Nicholson]

— English Atlas, or a Compleat Choreography of England and Wales. L, 1768. Oblong 4to, orig half calf; worn. With 50 double-page maps. pn May 21 (361) £550 [Nicholson]

Anr Ed. L, [c.1780]. 4to, old bds; worn. With 49 hand-colored maps. Affected by damp throughout. Ck Jan 16 (224) £250

Ellis, John, 1710-76
— An Historical Account of Coffee. L, 1774. 4to, 19th-cent half lea; upper cover detached, rubbed. With hand-colored folding plate (blank corner spotted) & with uncolored copy of the plate inserted at the front. C Oct 15 (226) £650 [Baskett & Day]
— The Natural History of Many Curious and Uncommon Zoophytes.... L, 1786. 4to, contemp calf. With 63 plates. Some waterspotting. FD June 11 (704) DM550

Anr copy. Contemp half calf gilt; rubbed, joints cracked. S Jan 13 (368) £90 [Wesley]

Ellis, Tristram James

— On a Raft, and Through the Desert. L, 1881. One of 25. 2 vols. 4to, orig vellum; soiled. Ck Jan 16 (57) £180

— Twelve Etchings of the Principal Views and Places of Interest in Cyprus. L, 1879. One of 5 of remarque proofs with the plates on Japanese silk paper. Oblong folio, loose as issued in orig half mor folder. Lacking 3 text leaves. S Oct 23 (334) £2,100 [Habibis]

Ellis, William, Surgeon. See: Cook, Capt. James

Ellis, William, d.1758

— The Compleat Planter and Cyderist.... L, 1756. 8vo, mor gilt by Crahan. Lacking H4; tp soiled; tear in upper margin touching text. Crahan copy. P Nov 25 (176) $350

— A Compleat System of Experienced Improvements Made on Sheep, Grass-Lambs and House-Lambs. L, 1749. 3 parts in 1 vol. 8vo, contemp calf; worn. bba Sept 25 (227) £190 [Burmester]

Ellis, William, 1794-1872

— Narrative of a Tour through Hawaii. L, 1826. 1st Ed. 8vo, orig bds; rebacked, new endpapers. With folding map & 7 plates. cb June 4 (56) $375

Ellison, Harlan

— All the Lies that are my Life. San Francisco, 1980. One of 200. In d/j. cb Sept 28 (482) $190

— Dangerous Visions. Garden City, 1967. In rubbed d/j. cb Sept 28 (489) $225

— Shatterday. Bost., 1980. In d/j. cb Sept 28 (486) $50

— Stalking the Nightmare. Huntington Woods: Phantasia Press, 1982. One of 50 bound in mor & in a "Witch's Grimoire Box". cb Sept 28 (487) $650

One of 700. In d/j. cb Sept 28 (488) $110

Ellms, Charles

— The Tragedy of the Seas.... NY, 1841. 8vo, later cloth. FDR sgd copy. pnNY Sept 13 (284) $325

Ellsworth, Lincoln. See: Amundsen & Ellsworth

Elman, Robert

— The Great American Shooting Prints. NY, 1972. Oblong folio, cloth, in d/j. With 72 colored plates. sg Oct 23 (509) $70

Elmes, James, 1782-1862. See: Shepherd & Elmes

Elphinstone, Mountstuart, 1779-1859

— An Account of the Kingdom of Caubul.... L, 1815. 1st Ed. 4to, contemp calf; rebacked, corners restored. With 2 hand-colored maps, 1 uncolored plate & 13 hand-colored plates. Fold tears to map; uncolored plate spotted. C Apr 8 (87) £400 [Gaston]

Anr copy. Contemp half calf; worn. With 15 plates, most hand-colored. sg Nov 20 (68) $450

2d Ed. L, 1819. 2 vols. 8vo, orig cloth; rubbed, 1 vol rebacked with old spine preserved. With folding map & plate & 13 hand-colored plates. Some spotting & soiling. bba Oct 30 (303) £140 [Check]

Elsholtz, Johann Sigismund, 1623-88

— The Curious Distillatory.... L: J. D. for Robert Boulter, 1677. 8vo, contemp half calf; worn. T Dec 18 (338) £320

Elsum, John

— Epigrams upon the Paintings of the Most Eminent Masters, Antient and Modern. L, 1700. 1st Ed. 8vo, contemp calf; rebacked. Some browning; clean tear to title. sg Mar 26 (104) $50

Eluard, Paul, 1895-1952

— Les Animaux et leurs hommes. Paris, 1920. One of 575. Orig wraps. Inscr to Rene Magritte, 1929. S July 2 (1002) £400 [Uhlmann]

— Le Dur Desir de Durer. Paris, 1946. One of 330. Illus by Marc Chagall. Folio, unsewn in orig wraps. With colored frontis & 25 illusts. sg Apr 2 (45) $900

— A L'Interieur de la vue. [Paris, 1947]. Unbound sheets. Inscr to Rene Magritte. S July 2 (1007) £450 [Ex Libris]

— Les Malheurs des immortels. Paris, 1945. Hors commerce copy. Illus by Max Ernst. Orig wraps. Inscr to Rene Magritte. S July 2 (1006) £420 [19th-cent Shop]

Anr Ed. Cologne: Galerie der Spiegel, [1960]. One of 85 on Zerkall buetten with the frontis sgd & numbered. Folio, orig wraps. Inscr with a drawing by Ernst on flyleaf. S June 29 (69) £2,400 [Ducesse]

— Poesie et verite 1942. L: Gallery Editions, 1942. One of 500. Wraps, in soiled d/j. bba Oct 30 (183) £65 [Clark]

— Repetitions. Paris: Au Sans Pareil, 1922. One of 350. Illus by Max Ernst. Orig wraps. S June 29 (14) £1,000 [Trinity Fine Arts]

Anr Ed. Cologne: Galerie der Spiegel, 1962. Orig wraps. Inscr by Ernst to Rene Magritte. S July 2 (1013) £400 [Takahata]

— Thorns of Thunder. L, [1936]. 1st Ed, one of 600. Frontis by Picasso. bba Oct 30

(182) £45 [Clark]
— Voir. Geneva & Paris, 1948. Folio, wraps; spine chipped. Inscr to Rene Magritte. S July 2 (1008) £150 [Pradene]

Elwes, Henry John, 1846-1922
— A Monograph of the Genus Lilium. L, [1877]-80. With: Grove, Arthur & Cotton, A. D. A Supplement to Elwes' Monograph of the Genus Lilium. L, 1933-40. And: Turrill, W. B. Supplement.... 1960-62. All 9 parts of the supplements present. 2 vols in 4. Folio, contemp half mor, orig wraps bound in, Supplement in orig wraps. With 78 hand-colored plates & 10 chromolithographed plates, 1 photograph & 1 colored map. Some spotting in Vol I. S Apr 27 (118) £8,000 [Sotheran]

Elwes, Henry John, 1846-1922 —& Henry, Augustine
The Trees of Great Britain and Ireland. Edin., 1906-13. 7 vols in 15 orig parts. 4to, orig wraps. C Oct 15 (190) £950 [Daskett & Day]

Anr copy. 7 vols. 4to, wraps. S Feb 24 (521) £360 [Hunersdorf]

Flyot, Sir Thomas, 1490?-1546
— The Castell of Helth Corrected.... L: Thomas Berthelet, 1541 [but 1548-49?]. 8vo, 19th-cent calf; rubbed. Lacking final blank; some dampstains; 2 wormholes through half the text; some marginal worming; tp frayed; A5 & A8 mended; marginalia & underscores. Crahan copy. P Nov 25 (178) $600

Anr Ed. L: Thomas Marsh, 1587. 8vo, old calf; rebacked, upper cover detached, worn. Tp stained & upper corner frayed & with woodcut border cropped; fore edges of 1st gathering stained; some cropping; lacking last leaf. Hunt copy. CNY Nov 21 (109) $600

Embury, Emma C.
— American Wild Flowers in Their Native Haunts. NY, 1845. 4to, orig cloth; worn, spine torn. With 20 colored plates. O Nov 18 (62) $225

Emerson, George Barrell, 1797-1881
— A Report on the Trees and Shrubs...Massachusetts. Bost., 1875-79. 2 vols. 8vo, orig cloth; spine ends torn. sg Jan 15 (205) $110

Emerson, Peter Henry
— Wild Life on a Tidal Water. L, 1890. One of 500 [but 300]. 4to, orig half lea; worn, upper cover detached. With 30 photoetchings. Perforated stamps throughout. bba Mar 12 (41) £70 [Rainer]

Anr copy. Orig pictorial cloth backed in lea. With 30 plates. Without the port. Mtd to half-title is a platinum print initialed in pencil. sg May 7 (35) $2,000

Emerson, Peter Henry —& Goodall, T. F.
— Life and Landscape on the Norfolk Broads. L, [1886]. Oblong folio, orig cloth; disbound. With 39 (of 40) mtd platinum prints. Some foxing to text leaves; 1st & last leaves scuffed & chipped. sg Nov 13 (46) $18,000

Emerson, Ralph Waldo, 1803-82
See also: Bremer Press; Doves Press
The Essay on Friendship. East Aurora, [1899]. One of 50. 8vo, ptd bds; spine worn. sg Jan 8 (254) $60
— Works. Cambr., Mass., 1903-4. Autograph Centenary Ed, One of 600 with leaf of autograph Ms. 12 vols. Half mor gilt. P June 18 (60) $1,600

Emigrant...
— The Emigrant in Australia or Gleanings from the Gold-Fields. L, 1852. 1st Ed. 8vo, orig wraps. With 4 folding maps, 4 wood-engraved illusts & 4 leaves of ads. S Nov 18 (1240) £320 [Quaritch]

Emmet, William Temple
— Good Hunting! A Record of Certain Occurrances in British Columbia.... NY, 1901. One of 100. Bds. Some wear & dampstaining. sg Oct 23 (258) $650

Emory, William Hemsley
— Notes of a Military Reconnoissance, from Fort Leavenworth...to San Diego.... Wash., 1848. 8vo, orig mor presentation bdg. With 43 plates. Lacking folding map. Inscr to Jefferson Davis. cb Oct 9 (73) $900

Anr copy. Modern half mor. With folding map & 40 (of 43) plates. cb Jan 8 (53) $250
— Report on the United States and Mexican Boundary Survey.... Wash., 1857-59. House Issue. Vol I. Cloth; spine gone. Library markings; plates stamped on versos. Sold w.a.f. O June 9 (61) $50

Emy, ——
— L'Art de bien faire les glaces d'office ou les vrais principes pour congeler tous les rafraichissemens.... Paris: Chez Le Clerc, 1768. 12mo, contemp sheep gilt. With frontis. Crahan copy. P Nov 25 (179) $900

Enault, Louis, 1824-1900
— L'Amerique centrale et meridionale. Paris, 1867. 8vo, orig wraps, unopened; soiled, spine chipped. With 20 plates, 2 hand-colored. sg Sept 18 (86) $150
— Londres. Paris, 1876. Illus by Gustave Dore. 4to, half mor gilt. Spotted. pn Sept 18 (148) £70

ENCOUNTER

Encounter
— Encounter. L, 1953-84. Nos 1-364, lacking only No 291 (but with a duplicate of No 272). With some indexes. Sold w.a.f. S Sept 22 (84) £100 [Quaritch]

Encyclopaedia...
— Encyclopaedia Londinensis; or, Universal Dictionary of Arts, Sciences, and Literature. L, 1810-29. Ed by John Wilkes. Map vol only. Half mor gilt. With 1 hand-colored double-page town plan & 44 hand-colored maps. pn May 21 (362) £460 [Burden]
— Encyclopaedia of Sport. L, 1897-98. 2 vols. 8vo, contemp half mor; rubbed at joints. cb Nov 6 (128) $95

Encyclopaedia Britannica
— Encyclopaedia Britannica. Edin., 1778-84. 2d Ed. 10 vols. 4to, contemp calf gilt; rebacked & corners rubbed. bba Dec 4 (73) £240 [Kohler]
3d Ed. Edin., 1797-1803. 18 vols. 4to, contemp half calf; some joints cracked, some bdgs broken. T Oct 16 (528) £55
Anr Ed. Edin., 1810-24. 4th Ed. 26 vols, including Supplement. contemp calf gilt; joints rubbed or split. bba Dec 4 (74) £320 [Landry]
4th Ed. L, 1815. 20 vols. 4to, contemp calf gilt; rubbed, a few joints cracked. Some small defs. S Jan 13 (369) £420 [Zayas]
Anr Ed. Edin., 1823. 20 vols. 4to, contemp calf gilt; rebacked preserving orig spines. Some staining. bba Dec 4 (75) £340 [Kohler]
7th Ed. Edin., 1842. 21 vols. 4to, contemp half calf; joints cracked, rubbed. Some staining. bba Dec 4 (76) £220 [Kohler]
9th Ed. L, 1875-1903. 35 vols. 4to, contemp half mor; rubbed. bba Mar 12 (170) £75 [Nosbuesch]
11th Ed. L, 1910-11. 29 vols, including Index. Orig lea; top of 1 spine def. bba Mar 26 (236) £95 [Fletcher]
Anr copy. 32 vols in 16. Contemp half mor; rubbed. bba July 16 (317) £130 [Quaritch]
Anr Ed. L, 1910-22. 32 vols. Half sheep. ha May 22 (338) $90
11th Ed (1 Supplement to 12th Ed). 32 vols, including 3 Supplements. Half mor; rubbed. cb Oct 23 (72) $150
11th (handy) Ed. L, 1910-11. 32 vols Orig half mor; rubbed. Ck Sept 5 (115) £110
12th Ed. L, 1910-11 & 1922. 32 vols in 16. Orig half mor; worn, in fitted oak bookcase. bba Mar 26 (235) £45 [Goulden]
Anr copy. 32 vols. Orig half mor; rubbed. bba Apr 9 (150) £90 [Fletcher]

AMERICAN BOOK PRICES CURRENT

Anr Ed. L, 1910-22. 32 vols. Mor gilt in wooden cabinet. cb June 18 (91) $250
11th Ed. L, 1911-22. 29 vols. Folio, half calf; spine ends scuffed. ha Dec 19 (296) $120
Anr Ed. L, 1922. 32 vols in 16. 4to, orig half mor; 1 spine torn, rubbed. bba Dec 18 (19) £75 [Coombs]
Anr Ed. L, 1956. 24 vols plus Yearbooks for 1956 & 1957. T Apr 16 (191) £55
Anr copy. 24 vols. T Apr 16 (192) £55

Enderbie, Percy, d.1670
— Cambria Triumphans, or Brittain in its Perfect Lustre. L, 1810. Folio, contemp calf; rebacked. T Mar 19 (88) £90

Enders, John Ostrom
— Random Notes on Hunting. Hartford: Pvtly ptd, 1955. One of 300. Inscr. sg Oct 23 (259) $600

Enemy...
— The Enemy: A Review of Art and Literature. L, 1927-29. Ed by Wyndham Lewis. Nos 1-3 (all pbd), orig wraps; Nos 1 & 2 rebacked and repaired. bba Dec 4 (140) £90 [Marten]
Anr copy. Orig wraps; soiled. No 2 sgd by Lewis on title. S July 13 (159) £220

Enfield, William, 1741-97
— An Essay towards the History of Liverpool.... L, 1774. Folio, later half mor with contemp bds. With 3 folding maps & plans & 9 plates. bba Apr 9 (382) £80 [RIBA]
— Institutes of Natural Philosophy.... L, 1785. 4to, contemp calf; rebacked, lower joint split. With 11 folding plates. Some foxing. S Nov 10 (485) £250 [Traylen]

Engel, Johann. See: Angelus, Johannes

Engelbach, Lewis
— Naples and the Campagna Felice. L: Ackermann, 1815. 8vo, later calf gilt. With 2 maps & 16 colored plates. 1st plate & tp repaired & mtd; some plate numbers cropped. S Nov 17 (903) £150 [Vine]
Anr copy. Calf gilt. With aquatint title, 2 maps & 15 hand-colored plates. Some plate numerals cropped. S July 14 (668) £300
Anr copy. Mor gilt; head of spine chipped, front cover detached. With 2 maps & 16 colored plates. sg Apr 23 (51) $175
Anr copy. Modern lev gilt by Riviere. With 2 maps & 15 colored plates. sg June 11 (351) $325

Engelhard, Maurice, 1820-91
— La Chasse dans la Vallee du Rhin.... Strasbourg [Paris: Auguste Aubry], 1864. One of 310. 12mo, mor janseniste by Gruel. Jeanson copy. SM Mar 1 (209) FF1,700

Engelhardt, Zephyrin, 1851-1934
— The Missions and Missionaries of California. San Francisco, 1908-15. 5 vols, including index. 8vo, orig cloth; worn, hinges weak. Titles stamped in 1st 2 vols. cb July 16 (90) $190

Engels, Friedrich
— Die Lage der arbeitenden Klasse in England. Leipzig, 1848. 8vo, half cloth; spine ends worn. With folding map. Short tear in several inner margins neatly repaired. Inscr to Jenny Marx. S Nov 27 (223) £1,600 [Heertje]

Engineer...
— The Engineer and Machinist's Assistant. Glasgow, 1854. Folio, half lea; worn, hinges broken. Library markings; some tears & stains. wa Nov 6 (206) $120

England
— England Illustrated.... L, 1764. 2 vols. 4to, contemp calf; rebacked. With 2 folding maps, 53 county maps & 134 plates. pn May 21 (183) £600 [Eisler]

Admiralty
— ARCTIC BLUE BOOKS. - Report of the Committee Appointed by the Lords Commissioners of the Admiralty to Inquire into and Report on the Recent Arctic Expeditions in Search of Sir John Franklin.... L, 1852. With: Additional Papers, 1852; Further Correspondence, 1852; Papers Relative, 1854; Further Papers, 1855; Tea Coloured Views, 1850. Together, 6 vols in 5. Folio, cloth. Library markings. bba Feb 5 (345) £1,300 [Remington]

Laws & Statutes
— An Act Declaring the Rights and Liberties of the Subject, and Settling the Succession of the Crown. L, 1689. Folio, contemp sheep gilt; broken. 1 William & Mary sess. 2, cap. 5. sg Oct 9 (189) $1,800
— A Collection of the Several Statutes and Parts of Statutes, Now in Force, Relating to High Treason, and Misprison of High Treason. L, 1709. Bound with: A Form and Method of Trial of Commoners, in Cases of High Treason.... L, 1709 8vo, contemp mor gilt, armorial bdg. sg Oct 9 (332) $140
— The Statutes at Large.... L, 1763-1826. Ed by W. Hawkins. 28 vols. 4to, contemp calf gilt. pn July 23 (91) £260 [Wade]
Anr Ed. L, 1786. 10 vols. 4to, contemp calf. sg Oct 9 (188) $400
— The Statutes of Henry VII. L, 1869. Ed by John Rae. Folio, orig half mor; rubbed. Facsimile of the Caxton 1489 Ed. bba Apr 9 (141) £55 [Skoob]

Parliament
— An Exact Collection of All Remonstrances, Declarations...betweene the Kings most Excellent Majesty and...Parliament. L: E. Husbands, 1643. 4to, half mor; worn. O Feb 24 (111) $160
2d Ed. L: Husbands, 1643. 4to, old calf. Frontis & tp cut down & relaid. T Mar 19 (278) £55
— House of Commons. The Evidence at large, as laid before the Committee of the House of Commons, Respecting Dr. Jenner's Discovery of Vaccine Inoculation.... L, 1805. 8vo, new half calf. S May 28 (703) £460
— Port Essington...Copies or Extracts of any Correspondence relative to the Establishment of a Settlement at Port Essington. L, 27 Mar 1843. Folio, modern half mor. With folding hand-colored map. C Oct 15 (168) £320 [Scott Sandilands]
— Report from the Select Committee on the House of Commons' Buildings. Westminster, 13 May 1833. Folio, early half sheep; worn. Some plates misfolded with dusting & a few edge chips; library markings. ha Sept 19 (131) $250
— Swan River Settlement...Copies of the Correspondence of the Colonial Department with Certain Gentlemen proposing to form a Settlement in the Neighbourhood of the Swan River.... L, 13 May 1829. With folding hand-colored chart. C Oct 15 (176) £1,600 [Scott Sandilands]

Proclamations
— [Elizabeth I] Against the use of hand-guns. L: Richard Jugge & John Cawood, [1559]. Folio. Short marginal tears neatly repaired; 2 stamps on margins. S Dec 18 (231) £500 [Sanderson]

Englefield, Sir Henry Charles, 1752-1822
— A Description of the Principal Picturesque Beauties...of the Isle of Wight. L, 1816. 1st Ed. 4to, half mor gilt. With half title & 47 plates (1 hand-colored) & 3 folding maps (1 colored). pn Dec 11 (70) £220 [1 horp]
Anr copy. Half mor gilt; rubbed. With 50 maps & plates, 2 hand-colored. pn Apr 30 (192) £240 [Smith]

Englefield Collection, Sir Henry Charles
— Vases from the Collection.... L, 1819. By Henry Moses. 4to, orig cloth; lower cover stained. Some stain in upper margin. L.p.

English...

copy. pn Dec 11 (189) £60 [Garrett]

— English Chartist Circular and Temperance Record for England and Wales. L, [1841-42]. Nos 1-114. Bound in 1 vol. Folio, modern half cloth. Some tears. bba May 14 (214) £110 [Biblio Archive]
— The English Midwife Enlarged.... L, 1682. 8vo, contemp calf; rubbed. With frontis & 5 (of 7) folding plates, 1 def. Sold w.a.f. bba Sept 25 (196) £50 [Phelps]
— The English Pilot. L, 1758. ("The English Pilot. The Fourth Book...Describing the West-India Navigation from Hudson's-Bay to the River Amazones.") Folio, contemp calf; worn. With 25 double-page or folding coastal charts. Some waterstains & browning. S Oct 23 (51) $3,600 [Burden]

Anr Ed. L, 1786-88. ("The English Pilot, describing the...whole Mediterranian Sea. Part III.") Folio, contemp sheep; worn. With folding general chart & 17 double-page charts. S Oct 23 (241) £800 [Traylen]

English Opium-Eater. See: De Quincey, Thomas

English, Thomas Harks

— An Introduction To the Collecting...of Whitby Prints. L, 1931. One of 210. 2 vols. 4to, cloth. pnE June 17 (126) £75

Engravings. See: Burnet & Others

Enquiry...

— An Enquiry into the Causes of the Encrease and Miseries of the Poor of England. L, 1738. 8vo, half mor. Last leaves stained; tp & last leaf soiled. sg Mar 26 (108) $130

Enschede, Charles, 1855-1919

— Fonderies de caracteres et leur materiel dans les Pays-Bas du XVe au XIXe siecle. Haarlem, 1908. Folio, cloth. B Oct 7 (481) HF900

Anr copy. Cloth, unopened. "Fine copy". sg Dec 4 (67) $200
— Typefoundries in the Netherlands.... Haarlem, 1978. Folio, orig half pigskin. bba Oct 16 (482) £160 [Morrison]

Enschede, Jan Willem, 1865-1926

— De boekletter in Nederland. Amst., 1902. Orig wraps; back damaged. Mededeelingen over Boekkunst No 1. B Oct 7 (2) HF140

Entire. See: Oldfield, Thomas Hinton Burley

Entomologist

— The Entomologist. L, 1864-1967. Vols 2-100, Part 2. 51 vols. 8vo, half mor, last 14 parts in orig ptd wraps. Sold w.a.f. S Apr 23 (8) £700 [Papworth]

Entomologist's Record...

— The Entomologist's Record and Journal of Variation. L, 1890-1972. Vols 1-84 & Supplement to Vol 35-63. 34 vols plus from Vol 80 on in parts. 8vo, half mor & orig wraps. Sold w.a.f. S Apr 23 (9) £700 [Rigout]

Entrecasteaux, Antoine R. J. de B., 1737-93

— Voyage de Dentrecasteaux, envoye a la recherche de La Perouse. Paris, 1807-8. 3 vols, including Atlas. 4to & folio, text in half calf, Atlas in orig bds. With 33 plates in text vols & Atlas with engraved title, engraved list of plates & 39 charts & coastal profiles. S Oct 23 (46) £2,500 [Maggs]

Ephrussi, Charles

— Albert Duerer et ses dessins. Paris, 1882. One of 100 on hollande with plates in 2 states. Folio, contemp half mor; rubbed & soiled. Ck Nov 21 (170) £40

Epictetus

— The Discourses. L, 1877. 8vo, calf by Sangorski & Sutcliffe; rubberstamp on front flyleaf. sg Sept 11 (111) $110
— Morals. L, 1704. ("Epictetus: His Morals, with Simplicius: His Comment.") 8vo, contemp calf; rubbed, joints cracking, spine chipped & repaired. Tp dusty. cb Oct 23 (74) $50

Epicurus, 342?-270 B.C. See: Limited Editions Club

Epinay, Louise Florence Petronille d'. See: D'Epinay, Louise Florence Petronille

Epistolae...

— Epistolae diversorum philosophorum, oratorum, rhetorum. Venice: Aldus, 1499. 2 parts in 1 vol. 4to, calf gilt by G. Huser; the 2 parts bound in reverse. Washed copy; some marginal defs repaired. 404 leaves. Goff E-64. S Nov 27 (158) £200 [Williams]

Epitome...

— Epitome Gestorum LVIII Regum Franciae. Lyon: B. Arnoullet, 1546. 8vo, contemp calf; joints split. One of the vignettes crudely hand-colored; some spots & stains; lacking vi. bba Oct 16 (8) £80 [Rix]
— Epitome of the Aeronautical Annual. Bost., 1910. 8vo, orig wraps; worn & soiled. wa Nov 6 (135) $100

Epstein, Jacob, 1880-1959

— Let There be Sculpture. L, 1955. ("Epstein. An Autobiography.") One of 195, sgd. Lea. sg Dec 11 (245) $100
— Seventy-Five Drawings. L, 1929. One of 220. Oblong 4to, vellum gilt. pn June 18 (48) £150 [Heatherington]

Equicola d'Alveto, Mario, 1470-1525
— Dell'Istoria di Mantova libri cinque. Mantua: F. Osanna, 1607. 4to, 17th-cent calf gilt, with monogram. Chatsworth copy. S Sept 23 (328) £160 [Erlini]

Equinox...
— The Equinox...Review of Scientific Illuminism. L, 1909-19. Vol I, Nos 1-4 only. Ed by Aleister Crowley. 4to, orig half cloth; rubbed & stained. bba May 14 (442) £90 [Grantis]

Eragny Press—London
— The Book of Ruth and the Book of Esther. 1896. One of 115. S June 18 (313) £800 [Papemain]; S June 18 (314) £250 [Hoffman]
— BROWNING, ROBERT. - Some Poems by Robert Browning. 1904. One of 215. pn Nov 20 (76) £600 [Pirages]
— FLAUBERT, GUSTAVE. - La Legende de Saint Julien l'Hospitalier. 1900. One of 226. Lev gilt by E. Dreyfoos with a center oval surrounded by swirls and tendrils in a lozenge shape with elaborate border onlay with stylized bouquets in corners; hinges starting. sg Sept 11 (112) $375
— KEATS, JOHN. - La Belle Dame sans Merci. 1906. One of 200. Mor gilt by Colin McLeish, 1913. S June 18 (315) £700 [Hartnoll]
— PERRAULT, CHARLES. - Deux Contes de ma Mere L'Oye. 1899. One of 220. B Oct 7 (294) HF1,050
— VILLON, FRANCOIS. - Les Ballades. 1900. One of 222. sg June 4 (258) $350; sg June 11 (186) $100

Erasmus, Desiderius, 1466?-1536
— Adagia. Paris, 1579. ("Adagiorum chiliades quatuor.....") Folio, modern half mor. Some soiling. S Sept 23 (329) £120 [Marlborough]
— Colloquia. Leiden: Elzevir, 1643. 12mo, contemp vellum bds. bba Mar 26 (111) £40 [Frew Mackenzie]
— L'Eloge de la folie. [Paris], 1751. Illus by Charles Eisen. 4to, 18th-cent calf gilt; worn, corners repaired. With 13 plates. S Mar 10 (929) £240 [Maggs]
— Moriae Encomium; or, the Praise of Folly. L, 1668. 8vo, contemp calf; spine ends chipped, front covers detached. sg Mar 26 (110) $70
— The Praise of Folie.... L, 1668. ("Moriae Encomium; or, the Praise of Folly....") 1st Ed of John Wilson's trans. 8vo, contemp calf; spine ends chipped, front cover detached. sg Mar 6 (110) $90
Anr Ed. NY: Heritage Press, [c.1944]. Illus by Frans Masereel. B Oct 7 (92) HF250

Ercker, Lazarus, d.1593
— Beschreibung allerfurnemisten mineralischen Ertz unnd Bergkwercks Arten. Frankfurt: J. Feyerabend, 1598. Folio, 19th-cent half lea. Lacking 2 numbered & 1 unnumbered leaves. FD Dec 2 (62) DM1,000

Ercolani, Giuseppe Maria. See: Neralco, Pastore Arcade

Erens, Frans, 1857-1935
— Dansen en rhytmen. Amst., [1893]. Orig wraps. B Oct 7 (13) HF200

Erixon, Sigurd Emanuel
— Folkig moebelkultur i svenska Bygder. Stockholm, 1938. 4to, half calf. cb July 30 (66) $75

Erizzo, Sebastiano, 1525-85
— Le Sei Giornate.... Venice: Giovan Varisco, 1567. 1st Ed. 4to, 18th-cent bds; spine rubbed. S Sept 23 (330) £65 [Vine]

Erni, Hans
— Weg und Zielsetzung des Kuenstlers. Zurich, 1943. One of 62. Orig half calf. S Dec 4 (9) £110 [Sims & Reed]

Ernst, Max
[-] Exposition Max Ernst. Paris: galerie Van Cleer, 1926. 4to, unbound as issued. S June 29 (18) £180 [Arginthan]
— Histoire Naturelle. Paris, 1926. One of 306. Folio, unsewn as issued in orig protfolio. S June 29 (17) £3,500 [Ursus]
Anr Ed. Cologne: galerie Der Spiegel, 1965. One of 700. Folio, orig wraps. S June 29 (79) £220 [Arginthan]
— A L'Interieur de la Vue. Paris, 1947. One of 610. Orig wraps. S June 29 (53) £320 [Naggar]
[-] Max Ernst. Berlin: Galerie Alfred Flechtheim, 1929. 4to, orig wraps; rebacked. S June 29 (23) £200 [Beum]
— Maximiliana, ou l'Exercise Illegal de l'Astronomie.... Paris, 1964. One of 75. Folio, unsewn in orig vellum. S June 29 (75) £18,000 [Ursus]
— Oeuvres de 1919 a 1936. Paris. Cahiers d'Art, [1937]. 4to, orig wraps; loose, stitching def. Inscr to Rene Magritte. S July 2 (1012) £400 [Takahata]
— Paramythen: Gedichte und Collagen. Cologne: Galerie Der Spiegel, 1955. One of 60 with the colored etching. Orig wraps. S June 29 (62) £1,300 [Beres]
— Paramythes. [Paris] 1967. One of 1,000. Folio, wraps. Inscr to Rene Magritte. S July 2 (1014) £450 [Randku]
— Reve d'une petite fille qui volut entrer au Carmel. Paris, 1930. One of 950. 4to, half lea gilt by A. Vatant. FD June 11 (4897)

DM1,750
— Reve d'une petite Fille qui volut entrer au Carme. Paris, 1930. One of 1,000. 4to, orig wraps. S June 29 (24) £1,050 [Trinity]
— Une Semaine de Bonte.... One of 800. 5 vols. 4to, orig wraps. S June 29 (31) £2,300 [Mulon]
— Sept Microbes vues a travers un Temperament.... Cologne: Galerie der Spiegel, 1959. One of 150. Folio, orig wraps. S June 29 (66) £250 [Beres]
[-] BRETON, ANDRE. - Exposition Dada Max Ernst. Paris: Au Sans Pareil, [1921]. Folding sheet, 8vo, unbound as issued. S June 29 (11) £650 [Arginthan]

Escher, A. von
— Die Schweizer Regimenter in fremden Diensten, 1515-1860. [Zurich: K. Hiersemann, 1903]. 1st & 2d Series. Folio, mtd on card as issued, in cloth portfolio. With 50 hand-colored plates, each sgd. S Oct 23 (192) £2,800 [Swiss]

Eschinardi, Francesco
— Espositione della Carta Topografica Cingolana dell'Agro Romano.... Rome, 1696. 12mo, contemp vellum. Marginal stains; lacking front free endpaper. sg Mar 26 (111) $110

Escholier, Raymond
— Delacroix.... Paris, 1926-29. One of 200. 3 vols. 4to, orig wraps. S July 13 (24) £80

Escoffier, August, 1847-1935
— Le Guide Culinaire. Aide Memoire de Cuisine Pratique.... Paris, 1903. 1st Ed. 8vo, orig cloth; rubbed. Some creasing & browning; a few leaves cracking along inner margin. Crahan copy. P Nov 25 (187) $450

Escosura, Patricio de la, 1807-78
— Espana artistica y monumental. Paris, 1842-44. 3 vols. Folio, later half mor. With 144 plates. C July 22 (68) £2,800

Esdaile, James
— Mesmerism in India and its Practical Application.... L, 1846. 8vo, orig cloth. T Mar 19 (284) £100

Esmerian Library, Raphael
— [Sale Catalogue] Bibliotheque Raphael Esmerian. Paris, 1972-74. 5 vols plus Supplement to Part 2. 4to, cloth. bba Oct 16 (455) £260 [Quaritch]
Anr copy. 5 vols. 4to, Without the Part 2 supplement. sg May 14 (104) $500
Anr copy. Without the Supplement to Part 2. sg June 11 (187) $300

Esnault-Pelterie, Robert A. C.
— L'Astronautique. Paris, 1930. 1st Ed. Orig wraps, unopened. sg Jan 15 (356) $200

Essay...
See also: Temple, Sir William
— An Essay for Discharging the Debts of the Nation, by Equivalents, in a Letter to...Charles, Earl of Sunderland. L, 1720. 8vo, disbound. sg Oct 9 (320) $325

Essayes...
— Essayes of Natural Experiments made in the Academie del Cimento.... L, 1684. 1st Ed in English. 4to, contemp calf; rubbed, joints split. With engraved title & 19 plates. Plate 7 misbound; tp soiled. bba Jan 15 (375) £500 [Phelps]

Essling, Victor Massena, Prince d', 1836-1910
— Les Livres a figures venetiens de la fin du XVe siecle.... Paris & Florence, 1907-14. 3 parts in 6 vols. 4to, half vellum, orig wraps bound in; some joints cracked. sg May 14 (434) $1,100

Estampes
— Estampes. Paris, 1950. One of 250. Ed by Robert Rey. Folio, ptd wraps; upper cover torn. With 12 wood-engraved plates ptd in colors & 42 color-proofs decomposition of the Braque plate. P Sept 24 (208) $1,400

Estancelin
— Collection de cartes concernant les forets, triages et bois taillis du Comte-Pairie d'Eu.... [N.p.], 1768. 4to, contemp mor gilt with arms of Louis-Charles de Bourbon, comte d'Eu. Jeanson copy. SM Mar 1 (210) FF155,000

Estienne, Charles, 1504-64
— L'Agriculture et maison rustique.... Paris: Jacques Du-Puis, 1564. 4to, mor gilt janseniste by Huser. Jeanson copy. SM Mar 1 (211) FF55,000
— De dissectione partium corporis humani libri tres. Paris, 1545. Folio, half vellum bds. Some worming affecting text; some leaves spotted or marginaly stained; tp soiled at outer blank corners. Unpressed copy. S June 25 (102) £6,500 [Koch]
— De re hortensi libellus.... Paris: R. Estienne, 1536. 8vo, modern wraps. Small portion of bottom of tp torn away; 2 wormholes to margin of title & following 3 leaves; dampstain to lower edges. CNY Nov 21 (113) $60
Anr Ed. Lyons: Sebastian Gryphius, 1539. 8vo, modern calf. Tp margin repaired. Hunt copy. CNY Nov 21 (115) $120
Anr Ed. Paris: R. Estienne, 1539. 8vo, modern vellum. CNY Nov 21 (114) $320
Anr Ed. Paris: R. Estienne, 1545. 8vo,

modern vellum by L. Juillet. Minor marginal soiling. CNY Nov 21 (116) $85
— Latinae linguae cum graeca collatio ex Prisciano. Paris, 1554. Bound with: Hegendorf, Christoph. Dialecticae legalis quinque. Paris, 1535. And: Estienne. De latinis et graecibus nominibus arborum, fruticum.... Paris, 1554. 8vo, early vellum bds. S May 21 (36) £450 [Hesketh & Ward]

Estienne, Charles, 1504-64 —& Liebault, Jean, d.1596

— L'Agriculture et maison rustique.... Paris: Jacques du Puys, 1574. 4to, contemp vellum; spine with repaired wormhole. Ink armorial stamp on tp margin. Fugger-Hunt copy. CNY Nov 21 (119) $3,500
— L'Agriculture et maison rustique.... Luneville: Charles de la Fontaine, 1577. 2 parts in 1 vol. 4to, contemp vellum. Jeanson copy. SM Mar 1 (212) FF18,000
— L'Agriculture et maison rustique.... Lyon: Pierre Rigaud, 1622. 4to, modern half mor; hinges rubbed, dampstain to upper corner of 1st few quires. Tp soiled. CNY Nov 21 (120) $320
— XV Buecher vom dem Feldbaw und recht volkommener Wolbestellung eines bekoemmlichen Landsitzes.... Strassburg: Bernhard Jobin, 1592. Folio, half mor by Lortic, armorial bdg. Some browning & spotting; tp wormed. FD June 11 (87) DM8,500
Anr Ed. Strassburg: Bernhard Jobins Erben, 1598. Folio, contemp blindstamped pigskin; clasps & catches lacking. Some spotting & dampstains; corner of final blank leaf torn away; some leaves stained where index tabs were pasted to foremargin; tp shaved by binder along foreedge. Hunt copy. CNY Nov 21 (117) $900

Estienne, Henri, 1528?-98

— Conciones sive orationes ex Graecis latinisque historicis excerptae. [Geneva], 1570. 2 parts in 1 vol. Folio, contemp vellum. Ck Sept 5 (211) £150
— L'Introduction au traite de la conformite des merveilles anciennes avec les modernes. [Geneva], 1566. 8vo, 19th-cent mor gilt; cover detached. Library stamps on tp & some other leaves. bba Oct 30 (184) £130 [Braunschweig]
— Paralipomena grammaticarum Gr. linguae inst. [Geneva]. H. Estienne, 1581. Bound with: Enocus, Lodicus. De puerili Graecarum literarum doctrina. Geneva, 1555. 8vo, contemp blindstamped pigskin, with the initials ICL & the date 1604 on upper cover. S Sept 23 (399) £300 [Sokol]

Etherton, Percy Thomas

— Across the Roof of the World. NY, [1911]. 1st American Ed. 8vo, cloth; stained, extremities worn. Frontis detached. cb Nov 6 (129) $130

Etrennes...

— Etrennes geographiques 1760. Paris, 1760. 16mo, contemp red mor gilt with arms of Louise-Honorine Crozat de Chatel, Duchesse de Choiseul-Stainville. With 26 double-page maps colored in outline. Some fold breaks. C Dec 3 (70) £2,200 [Quaritch]

Ettingshausen, Constantin, Freiherr von

— Physiotypia plantarum Austriacarum.... Vienna, 1873. 2 vols in 12. 4to & folio, orig wraps; worn. Text vols with 30 nature-ptd plates & 10 vols with 1,000 nature-ptd plates. A few plates slightly stained. de Belder copy. S Apr 27 (119) £8,500 [Rainer]

Euclid

— Optica & catoptrica Florence: Giunta, 1573. ("La Prospettiva....") 2 parts in 1 vol. 4to, vellum. Wormed throughout. sg Jan 15 (310) $120

Elementa

— 1482, 25 May. - Venice: Erhard Ratdolt. 1st Ed, 2d State. Folio, 17th-cent vellum; rebacked. Some worming, affecting a few diagrams; tear repaired in D6 & M7 affecting text; a few leaves at end faded possibly due to having been washed; a few inner margins repaired, some with loss of border on a2. 137 leaves; lacking final blank. Goff E-113. C Dec 12 (279) £2,700 [Thomas]
— 1705. - Oxford Folio, contemp calf; rebacked, rubbed. bba Mar 26 (318) £120 [Phelps]
— 1847. - L. 4to, half mor gilt; worn. Last few leaves dampstained. sg Apr 2 (38) $550

Opera

— 1510, 26 Mar. - Venice: Joannes Tacuinus. Folio, contemp blind-stamped mor; spine repaired. Tear in tp repaired slightly affecting woodcut & a few letters; some stains; early Ms notes on endleaves & in margins. Thomas-Stanford 5. S June 25 (101) £1,250 [Leget]

Euler, Leonhard, 1707-83
— Institutiones calculi differentialis.... St. Petersburg, 1755. 4to, modern cloth. Pencil accession numbers. bba Aug 28 (126) £320 [Camille-Bernard]
— Introductio in analysin infinitorum. Lausanne, 1748. 1st Ed. 2 vols. 4to, contemp calf; rubbed, joints cracked. With additional engraved title, port & 40 plates.. Ck Nov 7 (117) £750
— Scientia navalis. St. Petersburg, 1749. 1st Ed. 2 vols. 4to, contemp calf gilt; rubbed. With 65 folding plates. Occasional browning or staining. S June 25 (103) £600 [Koch]
— Theoria motus corporum solidorum seu rigidorum. Rostock, 1765. 1st Ed. 4to, contemp half calf; rubbed. With 15 folding plates. Some browning. S July 25 (104) £750
— Theoria motuum planetarum et cometarum.... Berlin, [1744]. Bound with: Euler. Theoria motus lunae....St. Petersburg, 1753. 1st Eds. 4to, contemp vellum. S June 25 (105) £1,700 [Landenchet]

Eumorfopoulos Collection, George
— HOBSON, ROBERT LOCKHART. - Catalogue of the Chinese, Corean and Persian Pottery and Porcelain.... L, 1925-28. 6 vols. Folio, orig cloth. S Nov 10 (79) £1,300 [Heneage] Anr copy. Cloth; 1 bdg rebacked. sg June 11 (190) $900

Eunapius, Sardianus
— De vitis philosophorum et sophistarum.... Antwerp: Plantin, 1568. 8vo, 18th-cent calf. A few early notes on 1st title. S Nov 27 (163) £220 [De Zayas]

Eusebius Pamphili, 260?-340?
— Evangelica praeparatio libri XV. Paris: Estienne, 1544. 1st Ed in Greek. Folio, contemp tooled calf; rebacked, scratched. Corner of title repaired; 4 leaves of text heavily annotated in an early hand. S Nov 27 (13) £1,050 [Thomas]
— Historia ecclesiastica. Mantua: Johannes Schallus, [not before 15] July 1479. Folio, vellum; soiled, spine def. Very short copy; many leaves loose; some worming in margins; early Ms annotations; fore-margins of f.171 damaged, affecting text. S Sept 23 (331) £310 [Zyas]
Anr Ed. Paris: R. Stephanus, 1544. ("Ecclesiasticae historiae.") Folio, later mor gilt; rubbed. Tp & 1st few leaves marginally stained. bba Oct 30 (185) £580 [Maggs]

Eustachius, Bartolomaeus, 1524?-74
See also: Albinus, Bernard Siegfried
— Tabulae anatomicae. Amst., 1722. Folio, modern half mor. With engraved title & 47 plates. pn Nov 20 (209) £600 [Serafino]

Eustathius Macrembolites
— De Ismeniae et Ismenes amoribus, libri XI. Paris, 1618. 1st Ed. 8vo, old vellum. Prelim leaves misbound; front pastedown & flyleaf covered in notes in an early French hand. S Sept 23 (332) £200 [Thotias]

Eustis, Celestine
— Cooking in Old Creole Days.... NY, 1904. 8vo half cloth. sg Jan 15 (21) $110

Euwe, Machgielis
— Wereldkampionschap Schaken 1948. Lochem: De Tijdstroom, [1948]. One of 20 with signatures of the participants. pn Mar 26 (101) £650 [De Lucia]
— Wereldschaaktoernooi, 1950. Lochem: De Tijdstroom, 1951. Ltd Ed, sgd by all 20 players. pn Mar 26 (102) £220 [Furstenberg]

Evans, Arthur Humble. See: Wilson & Evans

Evans, Charles, 1850-1935
— American Bibliography. NY, 1941-67. 15 vols, including Index. sg Jan 22 (152) $600

Evans, Charles Seddon
— Cinderella. Phila. & L, 1919. Illus by Arthur Rackham. 4to, orig half cloth, in torn d/j. cb Feb 19 (223) $95
Anr copy. Orig half cloth. pnE June 17 (55) £42
One of 325 on japan. Orig half vellum; minor dampstaining. Lacking the accompanying color plate. sg Oct 30 (66) $400
One of 850. Orig half cloth, in d/j; extremities rubbed. Ck Jan 30 (161) £110
— The Sleeping Beauty. L, [1920]. One of 625. Illus by Arthur Rackham. 4to, half vellum. sg Oct 30 (68) $600

Evans, David. See: Harrison & Evans

Evans, Elwood, 1828-98
— Washington Territory, her Past, her Present, and the Elements of Wealth which Ensure her Future. Olympia, 1877. 1st Ed. 8vo, half cloth with orig wraps taped in; rear wraps torn, adhered to last page. cb Jan 8 (55) $75

Evans, George Bird
— An Affair with Grouse. [N.p.]: Old Hemlock, 1982. One of 1,000. 4to, syn. sg Oct 23 (260) $70
— The Bird Dog Book. Clinton NJ: Amwell Press, [1979]. One of 1,000. 4to, syn. Inscr to Charles Wood. sg Oct 23 (261)

$130
— Recollections of a Shooting Guest. Clinton NJ: Amwell Press, [1978]. One of 1,000. 4to, syn. Inscr. sg Oct 23 (262) $70
— The Upland Gunner's Book. Clinton NJ: Amwell Press, [1979]. One of 1,000. 4to, syn. Inscr. sg Oct 23 (263) $100
— The Woodcock Book. Clinton NJ: Amwell Press, [1977]. One of 1,000. 4to, cloth. Inscr. sg Oct 23 (264) $175

Evans, George William
— Voyage a la terre de Van Diemen.... Paris, 1823. 8vo, later calf. With folding plate & folding map. Piece torn from title; some stains; lacking all before title. CA Apr 12 (89) A$250

Evans, Henry Ridgely
— Adventures in Magic. NY, 1927. Spine chipped & torn. Faint vertical fold to entire vol. Inscr. ha Dec 19 (300) $60
— Cagliostro: a Sorcerer of the Eighteenth Century. NY, 1931. Inscr. ha Dec 19 (301) $65
— Some Rare Old Books on Conjuring and Magic.... Kenton, Ohio, 1943. ha Dec 19 (303) $225

Evans, Joan
— English Jewellery from the Fifth Century A.D. to 1800. L, [1921]. Folio, cloth; soiled. Ck Jan 30 (94) £95

Evans, Lewis, 1700?-56. See: Franklin Printing, Benjamin

Evans, Oliver, 1755-1819
— The Young Mill-Wright and Miller's Guide. Phila., 1829. 8vo, contemp calf; spine head repaired. With 27 plates, some folding. wa Nov 6 (213) $90

Evans, Walker
— American Photographs. NY, [1938]. Text by Lincoln Kirstein. 4to, cloth. cb July 30 (68) $70
Anr copy. Cloth, in d/j. sg May 7 (36) $100

Evans, William
— A New English-Welsh Dictionary.... Carmarthen, 1771. 8vo, contemp calf gilt; joints split. Some soiling. Mostyn copy. Ck Oct 17 (165) £100

Evelyn, John, 1620-1706
See also: Nonesuch Press
— Acetaria. A Discourse of Sallets. L, 1699. 1st Ed. 8vo, contemp calf gilt; worn, inner hinges reinforced. Tp browned; rust-hole to last 3 leaves; folding table with clean tear at fold. Fine-paper copy. Hunt copy. CNY Nov 21 (67) $600
Anr copy. Calf; joints cracking, corners knocked. Lacking initial blank; browned & spotted. Crahan copy. P Nov 25 (190) $250
— Memoirs.... L, 1819. 2d Ed. 2 vols. 4to, contemp calf gilt; rebacked, rubbed. L July 2 (221) £140
Anr Ed. L, 1906. ("The Diary of John Evelyn....") 4 vols. mor gilt with onlays by Jean Eschmann. ALs from Eschmann inserted. S July 14 (471) £160
— Navigation and Commerce, their Origin and Progress. L, 1674. 1st Ed. 8vo, calf; rebacked & repaired along inner hinge of upper cover. Marginal browning & staining; some edges & corners with tears. P Sept 24 (201) $450
— Numismata, a Discourse of Medals.... L, 1697. 1st Ed. Folio, contemp calf; rebacked. Gutters dampstained at end. sg Mar 26 (113) $175
— Publick Employment and an Active Life Prefer'd to Solitude.... L, 1667. 1st Ed, 2d Issue. 8vo, contemp sheep; rubbed. Lacking 1st blank; many upper margins frayed, affecting page numerals. bba May 28 (36) £250 [Martin]
Anr copy. Calf; rebacked with mor, rubbed. Imprimatur leaf torn along inner margin & shorter along the fore-edge; stamp partially erased from tp; some soiling & spotting; light waterstains. P Sept 24 (282) $600
— Sculptura. L, 1769. 8vo, contemp calf; rebacked; gatherings H & I transposed. sg Mar 26 (114) $100
— Sylva.... L, 1664. 1st Ed. 3 parts in 1 vol. Folio, old calf; worn. pn Sept 18 (168) £130 [Finch]
Anr copy. Contemp calf; spine worn. pn Jan 22 (221) £170 [Maggs]
Anr copy. Contemp calf gilt. Lacking 1 leaf. pnE Dec 17 (194) £260 [Maggs]
2d Ed. L, 1670. 3 parts in 1 vol. Folio, modern cloth. Some stains; inner margins affected by worm; lacking errata. T Mar 19 (329) £65
4th Ed. L, 1706. Folio, contemp calf; broken & worn. Port detached. bba Sept 25 (212) £50 [Comben]
Anr Ed. York, 1776. 4to, calf; upper cover renewed & rebacked. With port & 39 plates only (of 40). Folding table slightly torn; prelims stained; port & tp laid down, frayed & repaired. L Dec 11 (278) £50
Anr copy. Calf; worn & broken. With port & 40 plates, most with hand-coloring. S Jan 13 (372) £220 [Demetzy]
Anr copy. 19th-cent half calf; rubbed. With port & 41 plates, all but 1 hand-colored. Some contemp Ms notes in text & at foot of a few plates. Inscr to Dr. White.

Tuke—de Belder copy. S Apr 27 (122) £2,200 [Heywood Hill]

Anr Ed. York, 1786. 2 vols. 4to, contemp russia gilt; rebacked & repaired at corners. With port, 1 plain & 41 hand-colored plates & 2 tables. Lacking a folding table in Vol II; some foxing; plate at p 164 & 2 following leaves detached in Vol I. S Oct 23 (682) £420 [Hindmarch]

Everard, Anne
— Flowers from Nature. L, 1835. Folio, orig cloth. With hand-colored frontis & 12 plates. pn Apr 30 (223) £550 [Burgess]

Everard, Harry Stirling Crawfurd
— A History of the Royal & Ancient Golf Club St. Andrews from 1754-1900. Edin., 1907. 4to, cloth. pnC July 16 (55) £290

Anr copy. Orig cloth; soiled. S Feb 24 (630) £400 [McEvan]

Anr copy. Orig cloth; rubbed & soiled. Lacking 1 leaf; several leaves detached. T Feb 19 (416) £300

Everett, George
— The Path-way to Peace and Profit. L, 1694. 4to, wraps. Some shaving; light stains. S July 24 (441) £280 [Quaritch]

Everett, Horace, 1780-1851
— Regulating the Indian Department: Report. [Wash.], 1834. 8vo, recent half mor. With folding map. 23rd Congress, 1st Session, House Report 474. cb Jan 8 (56) $100

Anr copy. Disbound. With folding outline-color map. 23rd Congress, 1st Session, House Report 474. wa Sept 25 (449) $120

Everitt, Nicholas
— Broadland Sport. L, 1902. De Luxe Ed, One of 100. 4to half lea; worn. sg Oct 23 (266) $80

Everson, William
— Eastward the Armies. [Torrance, Calif.]: Labyrinth Editions, [1980]. One of 200, sgd. Illus by Tom Killion. Folio, half cloth. With 3 linocuts, 1 sgd. sg Dec 11 (25) $150

— In the Fictive Wish. [Berkeley]: Oyez Press, [1967]. One of 200. Inscr. sg Mar 5 (61) $150

— Renegade Christmas. Northridge CA: Lord John Press, 1984. One of 26. 4to, half lea; worn. sg Mar 5 (62) $70

— These Are the Ravens. San Leandro, 1935. 8vo, self-wraps. Inscr. sg Mar 5 (61) $300

— Triptych for the Living. Oakland, 1951. 1st Ed, One of 200. 4to, goat, but not bound by author. Inscr. sg Dec 11 (26) $300

Every...
— Every Lady her own Shoemaker: or a Complete Self-Instructor.... NY: DeWitt & Davenport, [1856]. 16mo, cloth. With 5 folding pattern plates. O Sept 23 (53) $300

Anr copy. Cloth; worn. With 5 (of 6) folding diagrams. O Jan 6 (58) $220

Ewald, Mrs. ——
— Jerusalem and the Holy Land. L, 1854. Oblong folio, orig cloth; worn. bba May 28 (285) £200 [Steinberg]

Ewart, Alfred James
— Flora of Victoria. Melbourne, 1930. kh Mar 16 (172) A$130

Exposition Internationale des Arts decoratifs et industriels modernes. See: Paris

Exquemelin, Alexandre Olivier, 1645?-1707
— Bucaniers of America.... L, 1684-85. 1st Ed in English. Vol I only (Parts 1-3). 4to, contemp calf; worn. One port torn & adhering to Q2v. S June 25 (436) £550 [Perceval]

Anr Ed. L, 1704. ("The History of the Bucaniers of America.") 4to, contemp calf; rubbed, rebacked. With 15 maps & plates. Some plates with tears. O May 12 (68) $400

— Histoire des avanturiers.... Paris, 1688. 2 vols in one. 12mo, old calf; crudely repaired. With 3 folding maps, some with separations at fold-lines. Some tears, not affecting text. sg Nov 20 (70) $175

Exsteens, Maurice
— L'Oeuvre grave et lithographie de Felicien Rops. Paris, 1928. One of 500. 5 vols, including portfolio of plates. 4to, orig wraps. With a copy of the Rops number of La Plume, 1896. S June 17 (48) £440 [Sims]

Anr copy. Bound in 4 vols. 4to, cloth. sg Feb 5 (288) $650

Extraordinary...
— Extraordinary Red Book. A List of all Places, Pensions, Sinecures...exhibiting also a complete view of the National Debt....By a Commoner. L, 1816. 12mo, bds; rebacked, orig label laid down. Lower portion of T3 torn away with loss; endpapers stamped. P Sept 24 (284) $150

Eyre, Edward John, 1815-1901
— Journals of the Expeditions of Discovery into Central Australia. L, 1845. 2 vols. 8vo, half calf; rubbed. Library markings; lacking the 2 detached folding maps; bound without ads. kh Mar 16 (173) A$850

Eyries, Gustave —& Perret, P.

— les Chateaux historiques de la France. Paris & Poitiers, 1877-81. De Luxe Ed, one of 50 on Whatman. 3 vols. Folio. Vol III lacking list of plates at end; ink accession number on titles. bba Dec 18 (141) £180 [Rainer]

Eyton, Robert William, 1815-81

— Antiquities of Shropshire. L, 1854-60. Ltd Ed. 12 vols in 6. 8vo, contemp calf gilt; worn & loose. Perforated stamps & accession numbers on titles. bba Mar 12 (17) £110 [Axe]

Eyton, Thomas Campbell, 1809-80

— A History of the Rarer British Birds.... L, 1836. 2 parts in 1 vol. 8vo, cloth. pn Dec 11 (166) £65 [Wood]

Anr copy. Half cloth. With both versions of pp 25/26. pnE Dec 17 (379) £65 [Seeton]

Eytzinger, Michael von

— Iconographia Regum Francorum.... Cologne: J. Bueschschmacher, 1598. Illus by Jost Amman & Virgil Solis. 4to, contemp vellum; worn. With 63 ports. O Sept 23 (6) $325

F

F., J. See: Falconer, John

F., M. T.

— My Chinese Marriage. NY, 1921. Stamp on front free endpaper. Ghostwritten by Katherine Anne Porter. sg Mar 5 (218) $200

Faber du Faur, Christian Wilhelm von

— Blaetter aus meinem Portefeuille, im Laufe des Feldzugs 1812.... Stuttgart, [1831-43]. Folio, contemp half mor; broken, lacking backstrip, corners rubbed. With litho title (slightly soiled) & 100 hand-colored plates. Plate 2 with vertical crease just touching plate at inner margin; 2 plates with tears repaired. C Oct 15 (35) £4,500 [Maggs]

Faber, Petrus, 1540-1600

— Agonisticon. Lyons: F. Faber, 1592. 4to, vellum bds. Some discoloration. S Mar 10 (1060) £170 [Maggs]

Fabre, Jean Antoine, 1748-1839

— Essai sur la maniere la plus avantageuse de construire les machines hydrauliques.... Paris, 1783. 4to, contemp half calf. With 6 folding plates. C Dec 12 (75) £500 [Spelman]

Fabri, Jean. See: Siestrunck & Fabri

Fabricius, Johann Albert, 1668-1736

— Bibliographia antiquaria.... Hamburg, 1760. 3d Ed. 2 vols in 1. 4to, contemp calf; rubbed, joints weak. Small hole in 1 leaf. bba Mar 12 (336) £45 [Poole]

— Biblioteca latina sive notitia auctorum veterum latinorum.... Hamburg: Benjamin Schiller, 1708. Bound with: Morhof, Daniel Georg. De ratione conscribendarum epistolarum libellus.... Luebeck: Peter Boeckmann, 1716. 8vo, contemp vellum; soiled, rear cover stained & with 1 small gouge. cb Oct 23 (78) $130

Fabrizzi, Girolamo, 1537-1619

— Opera anatomica.... Padua: R. Meglietti, 1625. 1st Collected Ed. Folio, contemp calf; rubbed, rebacked & recornered. With 38 plates only. Part 1 lacking 3 gatherings; lacking some leaves in other parts; library stamps on engraved title & a few plates; small tear to engraved title repaired. bba May 14 (281) £550 [Rainer]

— Pentateuchos cheirurgicum.... Frankfurt: Petrus Fischer, 1592. 8vo, vellum; worn. Tp soiled; marginal dampstains. S Nov 27 (295) £400 [Van Hee]

Fabyan, Robert, d.1513

— The Chronicle.... L: John Kynston, 1559. 2 vols in 1. Folio, contemp calf; worn, upper joint split, lower joint crudely repaired. Lacking BBB5 & final blank; small wormholes in 1st few leaves, affecting text. STC 10664. bba Feb 5 (158) £450 [Stewart]

Anr copy. Folio, later mor gilt; rebacked preserving spine, rubbed. Lacking final blank; some worming throughout, affecting titles & text; 2 leaves marginally def; library stamp on tp. STC 10663. bba Apr 23 (169) £600 [Rix]

Anr Ed. L: John Kyngston, 1559. 2 vols in 1. Folio, mor by Bedford; joints rubbed. Lacking final blank; 3 leaves inlaid; some 30 leaves restored or repaired, affecting text of c.10 leaves. S Dec 18 (233) £1,100 [Rix]

Faden, William

— A New General Atlas. L, [1801 or later]. Folio, half calf; rebacked. With 54 maps including 1 extra, hand-colored in wash & outline throughout. S Oct 23 (232) £1,900 [Walford]

— The North American Atlas, Selected from the Most Authentic Maps.... L, 1777. Folio, bdg not described. With 42 maps with contemp hand-coloring. Some maps with library stamps. Franklin Institute copy. F Sept 12 (133) $26,000

Fahey, Herbert. See: Grabhorn Printing

FAHNDRICH

Fahndrich, H. —& Others

— Internationales Kaiser-Jubilaeums-Schachturner Wien 1898. Vienna, 1898. 8vo, cloth. pn Mar 26 (55) £70 [Bass]

Faider, Amedee

— Histoire du droit de chasse.... [Brussels, 1877]. 8vo, calf gilt with arms. Schwerdt-Jeanson copy. SM Mar 1 (217) FF1,150

Fainlight, Ruth. See: Sillitoe & Fainlight

Fairbairn, James

— Crests of the Families of Great Britain and Ireland. Edin. & L, [1860]. 2 vols. 8vo, half calf; rubbed, spine-tips worn. O June 9 (62) $50

Anr Ed. Edin., 1892. ("Fairbairn's Book of Crests of the Families of Great Britain and Ireland.") 2 vols. 4to, orig cloth; spines worn. With 229 plates. T Mar 19 (366) £60

Anr Ed. L, 1905. 2 vols. 4to, orig cloth, in chipped d/js; corners bumped. wa Sept 25 (236) $160

Fairburn, John

— Fairburn's Description of the Popular and Comic New Pantomime, called Harlequin and Mother Goose. L, [1806]. Frontis by George Cruikshank. 12mo, lev gilt by Riviere, orig wraps bound in. sg June 11 (139) $700

Fairfield, Asa Merrill

— Fairfield's Pioneer History of Lassen County, California.... San Francisco, [1916]. Cloth. With folding map & 4 plates. Red pencil underlining through first few chapters. cb Jan 8 (57) $50

Fairy...

— A Fairy Garland. L, [1928]. One of 1,000. Illus by Edmund Dulac. 4to, half vellum; soiled. With 12 color plates. cb June 18 (85) $100

Anr copy. Orig half vellum. S Dec 4 (190) £200 [Mill-Studln]; S Dec 4 (191) £200 [Thorp]

Faithful...

— Faithful Friends: Pictures and Stories for Little Folk. L, [1913?]. 4to, cloth; soiled & spotted, front free endpaper with small square cut out. Several leaves clumsily reinforced with brown paper tape; several plates & pages torn, affecting some image or text; foxed & soiled throughout. sg Oct 30 (70) $140

AMERICAN BOOK PRICES CURRENT

Falco, Benedetto di

— Descrittione de i luoghi antiqui di Napoli.... Naples, 1568. 8vo, 18th-cent vellum; soiled. Dampstains. S Jan 13 (373) £150 [Zayas]

Falconer, John

— Cryptomenysis Patefacta: or, the Art of Secret Information Disclosed without a Key. L, 1685. 1st Ed. 8vo, contemp calf; joints split, rubbed. Lacking 1st & last blanks; some numerals shaved. S July 14 (392) £130

Anr copy. Contemp calf; loose, spine worn. Lacking initial leaf; slight gnawing along fore-edges. sg Oct 9 (202) $300

Falconer, William, 1732-69
See also: Fore-Edge Paintings

— The Shipwreck, a Poem. L, 1804. 8vo, contemp calf; rubbed. S Sept 22 (24) £50 [Cox]

— A Universal Dictionary of the Marine. L, 1769. 1st Ed. 4to, contempd half mor; rebacked preserving orig backstrip. With 12 folding plates. Small tears to 4 plates. C Dec 12 (230) £9,000 [Israel]

Anr copy. Old calf. Several plates browned & foxed; a few small tears. wd June 19 (123) $325

— An Universal Dictionary of the Marine. L, 1815. 4to, modern cloth. With 36 plates. sg Nov 20 (71) $120

Falda, Giovanni Battista
See also: Rossi & Falda

— Le Fontane di Roma, nelle piazze e luoghi publici della citta. Rome: Giovanni Giacomo di Rossi, [1691]. 4 parts in 1 vol. Oblong 4to, mor gilt by Sizer. With 107 plates, including titles & dedications. Last 2 plates laid down. C Oct 15 (36) £2,200 [Mackenzie]

Anr copy. Lea. With 4 frontises & 99 plates (3 folding). SM Oct 20 (447) FF15,000

— Li Giardini di Roma. Rome, 1683. Oblong folio, contemp calf, with arms of Sir Hugh Wyndham. With engraved title, engraved dedication & 19 (of 21) plates, before numbers. C May 13 (70) £750 [Thomas]

Anr copy. Bdg not given. With 20 plates, including title. S Oct 23 (53) £800 [Lyon]

Anr Ed. Rome: G. G. Rossi, [c.1683?]. Oblong folio, wraps. With 20 plates. Lacking the Odescalchi Palazzo plate; small stamp on title. S June 25 (215) £550 [550] [Lake]

Fale, Thomas
— Horologiographia. The Art of Dialling. L: T. Orwin, 1593. 1st Ed. 4to, old vellum; soiled, modern endpapers. Some leaves shaved with loss; lacking tables at end; H1-2 cleanly torn; stained. Ck Jan 30 (33) £220

Anr Ed. L, 1652. 4to, half calf; worn. pn Jan 22 (186) £280 [Cavendish]

Falke, Otto von
— Decorative Silks. NY, 1922. Folio, cloth; rubbed, upper joint split, broken. bba Dec 18 (142) £50 [Elliott]

Falkeisen, J. J. —& Cherbuin, L.
— Recueil des vues principales de Milan et ses environs. Milan: Ferd. Artaria & fils, [c.1850]. Oblong folio, orig bds; worn, spine defective. With 57 plates, with small ink stamps on plates. bba Dec 18 (143) £750 [L'Acquaforte]

Falkner, Thomas, 1707-84
— A Description of Patagonia.... Hereford, 1774. 1st Ed. 4to, half mor by Lloyd. With folding map in 2 sections; 1 with small tear. C Dec 12 (232) £600 [Maggs]

Falstaff, Sir John
— Original Letters &c. of Sir John Falstaff.... L, 1796. 12mo, flowered cloth by Mrs. Southey. Robert Southey's copy. S Jan 13 (524) £300 [Quaritch]

Family...
See also: Atkyns, Arabella

— Family Circle and Parlor Annual. NY, [c.1840]. Vol not specified. 8vo, orig mor gilt; rubbed. FDR sgd copy. pnNY Sept 13 (283) $270

Famous...
— The Famous and Renowned History of the Memorable, but Unhappy Hunting on Chevy-Chase.... L: Thomas Norris, [c.1720]. 4to, modern half vellum. Several words lacking at the bottom of the first page because of an error in printing. Schwerdt-Jeanson copy. SM Feb 28 (134) FF8,000

— Famous Curiosities Lodged in the Tower of London. L, [c.1771]. 2 vols. 32mo, orig wraps; those of Vol II loose. S June 17 (455) £400 [Quaritch]

Fane, John, 11th Earl of Westmorland
— Memoir of the Early Campaigns of the Duke of Wellington in Portugal and Spain. L, 1820. 8vo, contemp half mor; rubbed. Some foxing. bba Aug 28 (218) £80 [Trotman]

Fanin, Colonel ——
— The Royal Museum at Naples; being Some Account of the Erotic Paintings, Bronzes, and Statues.... L, 1871. 4to, contemp half mor; lower cover worn. With 60 plates. S Mar 9 (741) £140 [Quaritch]

Fanning, Edmund, 1769-1841
— Voyages & Discoveries in the South Seas. Salem MA; Marine Research Society, 1924. With 32 plates. cb Jan 8 (58) $70

— Voyages Round the World. NY, 1833. 1st Ed. 8vo, orig half calf; joints cracked. With 5 plates (2 folding). Both folding plates torn along fold with minor loss of image. sg Apr 23 (54) $300

Fantin-Latour, Henri, 1836-1904
— L'Oeuvre de Fantin-Latour. Paris, 1906. One of 25 on japon with a separate folder of 4 lithos. Ed by M. Leonce Benedite. Folio, unsewn as issued. Loosely inserted is an ALs, & other related material. S June 17 (23) £650 [Fogg]

Faraday, Michael, 1791-1867
— Chemical Manipulation.... Phila., 1831. 1st American Ed. 8vo, needs rebdg. Scattered foxing. sg Jan 15 (311) $140

— Experimental Researches in Chemistry and Physics. L, 1859. 1st Ed. 8vo, orig cloth; worn, joints repaired. With 3 plates. wa Nov 6 (172) $210

— Faraday's Diary. L, 1932-36. 8 vols, including Index. Ck Nov 7 (101) £160

Faria y Sousa, Manuel de, 1590-1649
— Africa Portuguesa. Lisbon, 1681. Folio, contemp calf; rubbed, short splits to joints. Tp & a few leaves wormed. C Apr 8 (20) £380 [Witwaterstrand University]

Faringdon, John
— Views and Scenery on the River Thames.... L: W. Bulmer, [plates watermarked 1808]. Folio, contemp russia; worn, lower cover detached. With frontis, folding map & 75 (of 76) hand-colored plates. Lacking Plate 62 of London Bridge; double-page plates torn in folds; 1st 50 plates with small hole affecting surface. C July 22 (69) £1,800

Farley, John
— The London Art of Cookery.... L, 1783. 8vo, contemp sheep; worn, joints cracked. With port & 12 plates. Some browning & soiling; notes on endpapers. Crahan copy. P Nov 25 (192) $300

Anr Ed. L, 1789. 8vo, modern half calf. With port & 12 plates. Some slight stains. pn Nov 20 (174) £55 [Brown]

Anr Ed. L, 1796. 8vo, half lea; rubbed. Lacking 1 plate; port & plates stained; port detached. bba Apr 23 (229) £70 [Aris]

Farley, Robert
— Lychnocausia. L: Thomas Cotes, 1638. 8vo, later calf; broken. With 58 full-page emblems. wa Mar 5 (188) $260

Farm...
— The Farm, or a Picture of Industry. Phila.: B. & T. Kite, 1812. Orig wraps. 10 pp each with illust & accompanying verse; engraved throughout. S Dec 5 (307) £500 [Schiller]

Farmain de Rosoi, Barnabe
— Les Sens, poeme en six chants. L [but Paris], 1766. 8vo, mor extra by Zaehnsdorf. With 7 plates & 2 leaves of music. Extra-illus with 1 plate & a duplicate set of the vignettes & culs-de-lampe before text. C May 13 (15) £220 [Greenwood]

Farmer, John Stephen
— Merry Songs and Ballads. L, 1897. 5 vols. 8vo, half mor gilt by Zaehnsdorf; minor rubbing. bba Sept 25 (28) £160 [Thorp]

Farmer, Philip Jose
— A Barnstormer in Oz. Huntington Woods: Phantasia Press, 1982. One of 600. In d/j. cb Sept 28 (499) $50
— The Fabulous Riverboat. NY: Putnam, [1971]. In creased d/j. cb May 7 (367) $65
— A Feast Unknown.... Kansas City: Fokker D-LXIX Press, [1975]. One of 200. cb May 7 (368) $120
— Flesh. Garden City, 1968. In d/j. cb May 7 (369) $65
— Gods of Riverworld. NY, 1983. 1st Trade Ed, Uncorrected Proof. Wraps. cb Sept 28 (511) $50
— The Green Odyssey. NY: Ballantine, [1957]. In chipped d/j. cb May 7 (370) $85
— The Image of the Beast. North Hollywood: Essex House, 1968. Wraps. Sgd on half-title. cb Sept 28 (513) $60
— The Magic Labyrinth. Huntington Woods: Phantasia Press, 1980. One of 500. In d/j. cb Sept 28 (515) $80
— The Maker of Universes. Huntington Woods, Michigan: Phantasia Press, 1980. One of 200. In d/j. cb Sept 28 (517) $200

Farmer's...
— The Farmer's Wife; or the Complete Country Housewife.... L: Alexander Hogg, [1780]. 12mo, disbound. Tp & frontis detached; 1st leaf of preface with clean marginal tear. Hunt copy. CNY Nov 21 (69) $260

Farnham, Thomas Jefferson, 1804-48
— Travels in the Californias.... NY, 1849. ("Life, Adventures, and Travels in California....") 8vo, orig calf; rubbed, joints starting. cb Jan 8 (59) $120

Farnie, Henry Brougham
— The Golfer's Manual. Cupar, 1857. pnC Jan 23 (83) £2,300

Farquhar, George, 1678-1707
— The Recruiting Officer. L, 1926. Folio, half vellum. cb Sept 11 (250) $50

Farrell, James T.
— Studs Lonigan. NY, 1935. In d/j. Inscr. sg Mar 5 (64) $150

Fassam, Thomas
— An Herbarium for the Fair. L, 1949. One of 250, sgd. 4to, orig half mor. pnE Dec 17 (195) £70 [Traylen]

Fasson, Stewart M. See: Hamilton & Fasson

Father's...
— The Father's Gift, or the Way to be Wise and Happy. L: E. Newbery, 1794. 32mo, orig Dutch floral wraps; worn. Small hole in tp repaired. S Dec 5 (309) £220 [Quaritch]

Fauchard, Pierre
— Le Chirurgien dentiste.... Paris, 1786. 2 vols. 12mo, contemp sheep; worn. With port & 42 plates. sg Jan 15 (82) $1,800

Faujas de Saint-Fond, Barthelemi, 1741-1819
— Description des experiences de la machine aerostatique de M. de Montgolfier.... Paris, 1783. 1st Ed. 2 vols, including the Premiere Suite de la Description, 1784. 8vo, contemp half lea; worn. With 9 plates & folding table plus 5 plates in the Premiere Suite.. With 2 extra plates tipped into Vol II. C Dec 12 (76) £800 [Pickering & Chatto]
  Anr copy. 8vo, old bds. With 9 plates & the 4-page Supplement. Minor soiling & foxing. O May 12 (71) $500

Faulkner, Thomas, 1777-1855
— An Historical and Topographical Description of Chelsea.... L, 1810. 8vo, calf gilt. pn Sept 18 (165) £55 [Galloway]
  Anr copy. Contemp half mor; rubbed. With folding map & 11 plates. Map offset & with short tear. S Nov 17 (783) £120 [Boyd]
— An Historical and Topographical Account of Fulham.... L, 1813. 8vo, half cloth; rubbed, new endpapers. Most plates stained. bba Oct 30 (305) £45 [Wise]
  Anr copy. Contemp half calf. With frontis, folding map (short tear repaired), 7 plates & folding table. S Nov 17 (782) £90 [Boyd]
— History and Antiquities of Kensington. L, 1820. 4to, contemp half lea; rubbed, upper joint split. Lower margin cut from title. bba Mar 26 (368) £110 [Woodruff]

Faulkner, William, 1897-1962

— Absalom, Absalom! NY, 1936. In d/j. sg Dec 11 (27) $175; sg Mar 5 (66) $130

   One of 300, sgd. Half cloth. sg Mar 5 (65) $900

— A Fable. NY, [1954]. 1st Ed, one of 1,000. S July 13 (148) £150

— Go Down, Moses. NY, [1942]. One of 100, sgd. New half lev; Rubbed. Number on title & dedication leaf professionally removed. wa Sept 25 (661) $2,700

— A Green Bough. NY, 1933. One of 360, sgd. sg Mar 5 (67) $325

— Idyll in the Desert. NY, 1931. 1st Ed, one of 400, sgd. Orig bds, unopened; worn. pnNY Sept 13 (228) $450

— Light in August. [NY, 1931]. 1st Ed, Issue not given. sg Mar 5 (68) $150

   Anr Ed. [NY, 1932]. Issue not specified. In chipped d/j. cb May 7 (23) $250

— The Mansion. NY, [1959]. 1st Ed. In d/j. sg Dec 11 (29) $60

— Pylon. NY, 1935. Cloth, in def d/j. wa Dec 11 (252) $120

   1st Ptg. In soiled d/j. wa Sept 25 (662) $70

— The Reivers. NY, [1962]. 1st Ed, one of 500, sgd. wd June 19 (124) $275

— Requiem for a Nun. NY, 1951. In d/j. cb May 7 (24) $65

— Sanctuary. NY, [1931]. 1st Ed, 1st Ptg. In stained & chipped d/j. wa Dec 11 (253) $130

— Sartoris. L: Chatto & Windus, 1932. 1st English Ed. Half mor. Title & 2 leaves stained. wa Sept 25 (13) $70

— The Unvanquished. One of 250, sgd. Half cloth; dampstained. sg Mar 5 (69) $400

Faure, Felix

— Les Chasses de Rambouillet depuis les temps primitifs de la Gaule jusqu'a nos jours. Paris, 1898. One of 150 on japon. 8vo, mor extra by Marius Michel. Jeanson copy. SM Mar 1 (219) FF14,000

Fauriel, Claude Charles

— Chants populaires de la Grece moderne.... Paris, 1824-25. 2 vols. 8vo, contemp half calf; marked. First 3 leaves in Vol II soiled in corner. S Feb 23 (81) £280 [Martinos]

Favier, Alphonse

— Peking. Histoire et description. Peking, 1897. 4to, half mor; corners bumped & rubbed. sg Apr 23 (55) $100

Fay, Bernard. See: Grolier Club

Fearing, Daniel Butler

— A Catalogue of an Exhibition of Angling Book Plates.... NY: Pvtly ptd, 1918. One of 500. 4to, ptd bds; soiled. sg Oct 23 (267) $80

— Some Early Notes on Striped Bass. Newport: Pvtly ptd, 1917. One of 25. Ptd wraps; some stains & wear. Library markings. Inscr. sg Oct 23 (268) $700

Fearnside, William Gray. See: Tombleson & Fearnside

Fearnside, William Gray —& Harral, Thomas, d.1853

— The History of London. L, 1838. With frontis, vignette title & 27 plates. Bound with: Trotter, William Edward. Select Illustrated Topography of Thirty Miles Around London. L, 1839. With engraved title & 32 plates only. pn Sept 18 (158) £150 [Map House]

   Anr copy. With engraved title & 30 plates. Bound with: Trotter, William Edward. Select Illustrated Topography of Thirty Miles Around London. L, 1839. With engraved title, map & 34 plates; 2 plates loose. 8vo, orig cloth; worn. pn Dec 11 (31) £200 [Nicholson]

— Holmes's Great Metropolis. L, [1851]. Ed by Fearnside & Harral. 8vo, orig cloth. With 50 plates. pn Mar 5 (81D) £120 [Whiteson]

Fearon, Henry Bradshaw

— Sketches of America. A Narrative of a Journey.... L, 1818. 1st Ed. 8vo, later half vellum. sg Mar 12 (107) $110

Feather, John

— English Book Prospectuses: An Illustrated History. Newton PA: Bird & Bull Press, 1984. One of 300. Bds. With 14 folding facsimiles loose in paper folder as issued. sg Jan 8 (20) $120

Featon, E. H. & S.

— The Art Album of New Zealand Flora. Wellington & L, 1889. Vol I (all pbd). 4to, modern half mor. With frontis & 39 colored plates. S July 28 (1070) £200

Federalist...

— Le Federalist; ou collection de quelques ecrits en faveur de la Constitution proposee aux Etats Unis.... Paris, 1792. 1st Ed in French. 2 vols. 8vo, later half vellum. Library markings. sg Mar 12 (108) $175

Feith, Jan, 1874-1944

— Herinnering aan het bloemen-corso. Haarlem, 1896. 4to, half cloth. Some waterstains; strip of paper glued over tp. B Oct 7 (23) HF200

Felibien, Andre, 1619-95
See also: Cabinet...
— Les Divertissemens de Versailles donnez par le Roy a toute sa cour au retour de la conqueste de la Franche-Comte en l'annee 1674. Paris, 1676. Folio, contemp vellum bds gilt; soiled, splits in upper hinge. With 6 double-page plates. C May 13 (71) £1,600 [Lanfranchi]

Felixmueller, Conrad & Londa
— ABC. Ein geschuetteltes geknuetteltes Alphabet in Bildern mit Versen. Dresden, 1925. One of 100. Oblong 4to, orig wraps with orig silk stitching. With 15 hand-colored woodcuts. C Dec 12 (377) £1,100 [Quaritch]

Fellowes, Robert, 1771-1847
— The History of Ceylon from the Earliest Period...by Philalethes. L, 1817. 2 parts in 1 vol. 4to, contemp calf gilt; rebacked. With port, folding map & 14 plates. FD Dec 2 (1096) DM2,200

Fellowes, William Dorset
— A Visit to the Monastery of La Trappe. L, 1818. 1st Ed. 8vo, modern half calf. With 2 plain & 12 hand-colored plates. bba Oct 16 (216) £80 [Guenter]

Fellows, Sir Charles, 1799-1860
— An Account of Discoveries in Lycia. L, 1841. Orig cloth; rubbed, backstrip almost detached. Some spotting. T Apr 16 (8) £60
— A Journal Written During an Excursion in Asia Minor. L, 1839. 4to, later half mor. S Feb 24 (488) £80 [Bonham]

Feltham, John
— A Guide to all the Watering and Sea Bathing Places. L, [1803]. 12mo, old calf; worn. Stained. bba Dec 4 (338) £50 [Clay]
— A Tour through the Island of Man.... Bath, 1798. 8vo, contemp calf; rebacked. With folding map, folding table & 2 plates. pn Dec 11 (214) £60 [Books]

Felton, William, Coachmaker
— A Treatise on Carriages, Comprehending Coaches, Chariots.... L, 1794-95. 1st Ed. 2 vols in 1. 8vo, later half mor; rubbed. With 53 plates. Some plates cropped, affecting platemark; a few plates with marginal tears; library stamp on verso of tp & 1 other leaf. bba Aug 20 (313) £380 [Henderson]

Female...
— Female Triumph!!, or the Defeat of the Orange. L: G. Blackman, 1816. 16mo, orig ptd wraps. With engraved title & 7 plates colored by hand. S Dec 5 (279) £300 [Hirsch]

Fen...
— The Fen and Marshland Churches. Wisbech, 1867-69]. Photographs by Edward Johnson. 3 vols. 4to, orig cloth; soiled. Lacking 1 albumen print. Sold w.a.f. bba Aug 28 (314) £80 [British Architectural Lib.]

Fenelon, Francois de Salignac de la Mothe, 1651-1715
— Les Avantures de Telemaque.... L: R. Dodsley, 1738. 2 vols. 8vo, late 18th-cent mor gilt. With frontis & port & 24 plates. Minor discoloration. S Nov 27 (69) £280 [Teuschart]
Anr Ed. Leiden & Amst., 1761. Folio, later half mor; joints rubbed. With frontis, port & 24 plates. cb Oct 23 (81) $250
Anr Ed. Paris: [Didot], 1790. 2 vols. 8vo, contemp mor gilt extra; ends worn, hinges reinforced. Lacking the frontis & 6 plates but with the port after Vivien & the 24 plates after Marillier. sg Oct 9 (203) $110
— Les Aventures de Telemaque. Paris: Didot l'Aine, 1784. One of 350. 2 vols. 8vo, contemp mor gilt. S July 28 (1178) £450
Anr Ed. Paris: [Didot], 1790. 2 vols. 8vo, contemp calf gilt; joints starting. With port. Lacking the 6 plates, but with a suite of 24 unsgd plates. sg Mar 26 (115) $50
— Oeuvres. Paris, 1787. 5 vols. 4to, early 19th-cent russia gilt; rubbed. S Jan 13 (376) £80 [Duran]

Fenn, Eleanor, 1743-1813
— Fables in Monosyllables; Morals to a Set of Fables. L: John Marshall, [c.1783]. 2 parts in 1 vol. 8vo, orig half sheep. S June 17 (417) £320 [Peters]
— Fables in Monosyllables, by Mrs. Teachwell.... L, [c.1790?]. 2 parts in 1 vol. 12mo, orig half sheep; spine & stitching defective. S Dec 5 (280) £280 [Wakefield]

Fennell, James Hamilton. See: Fore-Edge Paintings

Fenollosa, Ernest F., 1853-1908
See also: Cuala Press
— Epochs of Chinese & Japanese Art. NY, [1913]. 2 vols. 4to, half cloth. With 15 colored plates. cb July 30 (70) $110

Fenton, Richard, 1746-1821
— A Historical Tour through Pembrokeshire. L, 1811. 4to, contemp half mor; rubbed. S Jan 12 (77) £120 [Palace]

Feo Cardozo de Castello Branco e Torres, Joao Carlos
— Memorias contendo a biographia do Vice Almirante Luiz da Motta Feo e Torres.... Paris, 1825. 8vo, bdg not described. Lacking the plan of Luanda. S Nov 18

(1188) £90 [Maggs]

Fer, Nicolas de, 1646-1720
— Atlas curieux, ou le monde represente dans les cartes. Paris, 1717. Fragment of 43 engraved leaves only. Oblong folio. Dampstained, 2 leaves flawed. B Feb 25 (791) HF1,100
— Introduction a la fortification. Paris, 1692 [but c.1705]. Oblong folio, contemp calf; rebacked & repaired, new endpapers. With engraved title & 183 plates & maps. 1st title soiled; 4 plates shaved at fore-margin; rust-hole in 1 other. S Oct 23 (191) £1,050 [Orssich]

Ferber, Edna
— Giant. Garden City, 1952. In d/j. Sgd. sg Mar 5 (71) $50
— Saratoga Trunk. Garden City, 1941. One of 562. sg Mar 5 (72) $120

Ferguson, Henry Lee. See: Derrydale Press

Ferguson, James, 1710-76
— Lectures on Select Subjects in Mechanics.... L, 1764. 4to, contemp calf; joints split. With 23 folding plates, 1 dampstained. bba Oct 16 (300) £220 [Phillips]
  Select Mechanical Exercises. L, 1773. 1st Ed. 8vo, contemp calf; rebacked. With 9 folding plates. Some soiling; 2 plates cropped; 1 plate repaired at outer margin. S May 28 (664) £120

Ferguson, John, 1837-1916
— Bibliotheca Chemica: a Catalogue of...the Collection of the late James Young. Glasgow, 1906. 2 vols. 4to, orig cloth. Library markings. S Mar 9 (717) £140 [Quaritch]
  Anr copy. Cloth; rebacked. sg May 14 (593) $70
  Anr Ed. L, 1954. ("Bibliotheca Chemica. A Bibliography of Books on Alchemy, Chemistry and Pharmaceutics.") 2 vols. Reprint of the Glasgow 1906 Ed. bba Oct 16 (376) £65 [Hay Cinema]; bba Nov 13 (87) £65 [Lanfranchi]; Ck Nov 7 (4) £100
  Anr copy. With 1 d/j. Reprint of the Glasgow 1906 Ed. Ck Nov 7 (99) £110; sg Jan 22 (153) $90; 1 Oct 16 (560) £66

Ferguson, John Alexander, 1881-1969
— A Bibliography of Australia. Sydney, 1941-69. 7 vols. 8vo, cloth. CA Apr 12 (92) A$500
  Anr Ed. Sydney & L, 1941-55. Vols I-IV (of 7) sg Oct 2 (138) $130
  Anr Ed. Sydney & L, 1941-69. Vols I-IV (of 7) sg Jan 22 (154) $80
— Bibliography of Australia, 1784-1850. Canberra, 1975-77. Facsimile Ed. Vols I-IV only. In d/js. kh Mar 16 (182) A$150

Mixed Ed. Canberra, 1975-51-69. 7 vols. bba Jan 15 (263) £190 [Finer]

Fergusson, James, 1808-86
— Illustrations of the Rock Cut Temples of India. L, 1845. Atlas only. Folio, loose in half calf. With litho title & 18 plates. Soiled, stained & wormed in margins. S Feb 24 (489) £140 [Ollia]

Ferishta, Muhammad Kasim ibn Hindu Shah, Astrarabadi
— History of Dekkan. Shrewsbury, 1794. 6 parts in 2 vols. 4to, contemp calf; rubbed. S Jan 13 (374) £200 [Daley]

Fernandez de Navarrete, Martin
— Biblioteca Maritime Espanola.... Madrid, 1851. 2 vols. 8vo, modern half mor. sg Oct 2 (140) $60
— Coleccion de los viages y descubrimentos qui hicieron por mar los Espanoles desde fines del Siglo XV. Madrid, 1837-80. Mixed Ed. 5 vols. 8vo, sheep gilt. sg Oct 2 (139) $375

Fernandez Ferreira, Diogo
— Arte de caca da altaneria. Lisbon, 1616. 4to, 19th-cent vellum. Upper margin of frontis rubbed. Jeanson 1649. SM Mar 1 (220) FF30,000

Ferne, Sir John
— The Blazon of Gentrie. L: J. Windet for A. Maunsell, 1586. 4to, contemp vellum; soiled, lower edge of lower cover torn away. S July 23 (276) £250 [Lawson]

Fernel, Jean, 1497-1558
— Universa medicina primum studio.... Geneva: Samuel de Tournes, 1680. Folio, contemp calf gilt; wormed. Marginal stains at beginning & end; some browning; lower forecorners of Rr4-6 repaired with loss of a few letters; lacking final blank. S Nov 10 (486) £80 [Elliott]

Ferrari, Enrique Lafuente. See: Lafuente Ferrari, Enrique

Ferrari, Giovanni Battista, 1584-1655
— De florum cultura. Rome, 1633. 1st Ed. 4to, contemp vellum. With 2 engraved titles & 45 plates. Waterstained; last leaf holed. FD June 11 (541) DM2,150
  Anr copy. Contemp calf; rubbed. With frontis, 6 plates of parterres & 39 plates of plants, etc. Some stains. Horticultural Society of New York—de Belder copy. S Apr 27 (123) £900 [Macdougall]
  Flora, overo cultura di fiori. Rome, 1638. 1st Ed in Italian. 4to, modern calf. With engraved title, frontis & 45 plates. Some discoloration. C Oct 15 (191) £450 [Thorp]
— Hesperides, sive de malorum aureorum

FERRARI

cultura et usu.... Rome, 1646. 4to, contemp mor gilt with initials DE & a lion & star from orig owner's arms in the compartments of the spine. With frontis & 100 plates. Frontis cut down with 1 tear & a repair; some dampstains in upper portion of 1st few leaves. de Belder copy. S Apr 27 (124) £5,000 [Baskett]
1st Ed. Folio, contemp half vellum. With frontis & 100 plates, all hand-colored. Corner torn from 1 plate, anr loose & torn, a few cropped. bba Dec 4 (257) £3,400 [Israel]
Anr copy. Modern half calf; worn. With engraved title & 100 plates. HN May 20 (1039) DM3,400

Ferrario, Giulio
— Le Costume ancien et moderne ou histoire.... Milan, 1815-29. L.p. subscriber's copy. 15 vols in 18. Folio, cloth. With 1,437 (of 1,441) engraved maps & plates, all but a few hand-colored. bba Dec 18 (144) £3,000 [Crossley]
Anr Ed. Milan, 1827. Afrique, only. 2 vols. Folio, cloth; soiled. With 154 plates. Sold w.a.f. pn Jan 22 (245) £160
— Il Costume antico e moderno o Storia del Governo.... Florence, 1827-28. America. Vols II & IV only. Folio, orig half vellum; worn, backstrips torn. With folding map &36 plates in Vol I and 47 plates in Vol IV. sg Dec 18 (170) $110

Ferrerio, Pietro
— Palazzi di Roma.... [Rome, 1655]. Oblong folio, contemp calf; worn, broken. With engraved title & 41 plates. Marginal dampstains. C Apr 8 (128) £650 [Forcade]
Anr copy. 2 parts in 2 vols. Oblong folio, 18th-cent calf gilt; rebacked. With engraved titles & 101 plates before numbers. C May 13 (72) £1,300 [London]
Anr Ed. [Rome, c.1675]. 2 parts in 1 vol. Oblong folio, old calf; joints cracked. With 2 engraved titles & 129 plates. Ck Sept 26 (88) £1,100

Ferriar, John, 1764-1815
— An Essay Towards a Theory of Apparitions. L, 1813. 8vo, contemp calf; front joint cracked. sg Jan 15 (312) $80

Ferrieres, Henri de
— Livre du roi Modus.... Chambery: Antoine Neyret, 1486. Folio, mor gilt by Bauzonnet-Trautz. Gothic letter. With 57 woodcuts in the text. 104 leaves. Goff M-739. Jeanson copy. SM Mar 1 (222) FF2,200,000
Anr Ed. Paris: Jehan Janot, [1521]. ("Sensuyt le liure du roy Modus....") 4to, mor gilt janseniste by Trautz-Bauzonnet.

With the arms on Charles Henri de Lorraint Vaudemont on papier de chine at beginning. Jeanson copy. SM Mar 1 (223) FF200,000
Anr Ed. Paris: Jehan Trepperel, [c.1525]. 4to, mor gilt janseniste by Trautz-Bauzonnet. Jeanson copy. SM Mar 1 (224) FF320,000
Anr Ed. Paris: Gilles Corrozet, 1560. ("Le Roy Modus des deduitz de la chace....") 8vo, mor gilt by Bauzonnet-Trautz with arms of Baron Pichon. Jeanson copy. SM Mar 1 (225) FF36,000
Anr Ed. Paris: Elzear Blaze, 1839. ("Le Livre du roy Modus....") One of 2 on peau de velin. 8vo, red mor a la fanfare by Lebrun. Jeanson copy. SM Mar 1 (226) FF88,000

Ferris, Benjamin G.
— Utah and the Mormons. NY, 1854. 12mo, orig cloth; spine frayed. Holograph marginal notes. sg Sept 18 (188) $50

Ferris, Warren Angus, 1810-73
— Life in the Rocky Mountains.... Denver, 1910. 4to, cloth; worn. O June 9 (63) $110

Fery d'Esclands, Alphonse, Duc —& Others
— Congres International des Echecs, compte rendu du Congres de 1867. Paris, 1868. 8vo, modern cloth, orig wraps bound in. pn Mar 26 (34) £95 [Hoffman]
Anr copy. Contemp calf gilt. Some stains. pn Mar 26 (35) £50 [Farmer]

Feuerlein, Johann Conrad
— Nuernbergisches Schoenbart-Buch und Gesellen-Stechen. [Schwabach, 1765]. Bound with: Mueller, Johann. Discurs ob Georgen Rixners thurnier-Buch..... 1766. 4to, half calf; def. S Sept 23 (449) £340 [Goldschmidt]

Feuillee, Louis
— Journal des observations physiques, mathematiques et botaniques faites...sur les cotes orientales de l'Amerique meridionale.... Paris, 1714. Vols I & II (of 3) in 1. 4to, contemp calf. With 73 plates & maps. S Feb 23 (176) £130 [Shapero]

Feuillets...
— Feuillets d'art. Paris, 1919-22. Ed by Edmond Moussie & Michel Dufet. Nos 1-6 (all pbd). 4to, broche; torn or missing. SM Oct 20 (617) FF12,000

Feulner, Adolf, 1884-1945
— Bayerisches Rokoko. Munich, [1923]. Folio, cloth. bba Aug 28 (74) £50 [Mytze]

Feyjoo y Montenegro, Benito Geronimo

— Cartas Eruditas y Curiosas. Madrid: Gabriel Ramirez, 1765. 5 vols. Contemp calf; rubbed, joints cracked. Ck Nov 7 (93) £100

Fezensac, Jean de Montesquiou

— Siroco ou le recit nocturne. Paris, 1933. One of 20 on japon ancien with 2 extra suites of the plates in uncolored state & with remarques. Illus by Edouard Chimot. 4to, calf. S June 17 (87) £310 [Marks]

Fiammelli, Giovanni Francesco

— La Riga matematica.... Rome: C. Vullietti, 1605. 4to, contemp vellum. Worming in lower margins throughout, occasionally affecting text; tear in penultimate leaf; 2 small holes in tp caused by deletion of an ownership inscr. S May 21 (104) £420 [Lanfranchi]

Ficino, Marsilio, 1433-99

— Epistolae. Nuremberg: Anton Koberger, 24 Feb 1497. 4to, contemp pigskin tooled in blind, with brass clasps; soiled, wormed, spine def at top. Worming restored throughout, costing a few letters on each leaf, some dampstains, chiefly marginal, marginal tear in I6 mended; some early marginalia. 254 leaves. Goff F-155. P Dec 15 (161) $2,600

Field, Barron, 1786-1846

— Geographical Memoirs on New South Wales.... L, 1825. 8vo, later cloth. Tp & plates stained. CA Oct 7 (65) A$650

Field, Eugene, 1850-95

— With Trumpet and Drum. NY, 1892. 8vo, cloth. Inscr & with drawing by Field captioned with a 6-line poem. sg Sept 11 (125) $150

— Works. NY, 1896-97. 10 vols. 8vo, half mor. sg Sept 11 (127) $100

Anr Ed. NY, 1896-1901. One of 100. 12 vols. 12mo, half lev gilt by Stikeman. sg Feb 12 (146) $350

Anr Ed. NY, 1903-4. 12 vols. Half mor; 1 bdg broken. sg Sept 11 (128) $100

Field, Richard, 1561-1616

— Of the Church. L: N. Okes for S. Waterson, 1606. Book 5 only. Contemp vellum; soiled. STC 10856. Ck Jan 21 (157) £65

Field, Thomas W., 1820-81

— An Essay towards an Indian Bibliography.... NY, 1873. 1st Ed. 8vo, cloth. sg Oct 2 (141) $100

Anr Ed. Columbus, 1951. Reprint of 1873 Ed. wa June 25 (55) $80

Fielding, Henry, 1707-54

— An Apology for the Life of Mrs. Shamela Andrews. L, 1741. 8vo, 19th-cent half lea; extremities worn. Margins trimmed; half-title soiled; some stains. sg Oct 9 (205) $70

— Examples of the Expositon of Providence in the Detection and Punishment of Murder.... L: for A. Millar, 1752. 12mo, contemp sheep; rebacked. C Dec 12 (324) £600 [Pressler]

— The History of the Adventures of Joseph Andrews.... L, 1742. 1st Ed. 2 vols. 12mo, modern calf gilt; upper cover scratched. Lacking ads. S May 6 (431) £320 [Hannas]

— The History of Tom Jones.... L, 1749. 1st Ed. 6 vols. 8vo, contemp calf; not quite uniform; 1 cover detached; worn. Two leaves torn in Vol V with loss of a few letters; some spotting & soiling. S Sept 22 (25) £200 [Pickering & Chatto]

Anr copy. 6 vols. 12mo, contemp calf onlaid with mor gilt; rubbed. A few marks & tears; tear in I16 of Vol I affecting press figure; small portion of upper margin of D2 in Vol I torn away, just touching headline. S Dec 18 (20) £1,600 [Quaritch]

Anr copy. New half calf simulating contemp bdg. Lacking blanks at end of Vols I & III. Larry McMurtry's copy. wa Sept 25 (664) $850

2d Ed. 6 vols. 12mo, contemp calf; joints weak or starting, 1 cover detached. Some foxing. sg Oct 9 (206) $130

— The Journal of a Voyage to Lisbon. L, 1755. 2d Ptd ed (1st Pbd Ed). 12mo, modern calf gilt. pnNY Sept 13 (229) $170

Anr copy. Contemp calf; rebacked. Duff Cooper's copy. S Mar 9 (778) £240 [Quaritch]

— Pasquin: A Dramatick Satire of the Times. L, 1736. 1st Ed. 8vo, modern half calf. C Dec 12 (325) £130 [Pressler]

Anr copy. 19th-cent sheep; spine ends worn. sg Oct 9 (204) $175

— A Proposal for Making an Effectual Provision for the Poor.... L, 1753. Bound with: Fielding, John. A Plan for a Preservatory and Reformatory for the Benefit of Deserted Girls, and Penitent Prostitutes. L, 1758. And: Fielding, Henry. An Enquiry in to the Causes of the late Increase of Robbers.... L, 1751. 8vo, half calf. pnE Jan 28 (156) £1,500 [Maggs]

— Works. L, 1806. 10 vols. 8vo, later calf; rubbed & worn. wa Feb 19 (79) $120

Anr Ed. L, 1871-72. 11 vols, including Miscellanies and Poems. 8vo, contemp calf. C July 22 (71) £420

Anr Ed. L, 1898-99. One of 750. 12 vols. 8vo, half calf gilt. pnE Jan 28 (92) £320

FIELDING

[Pederson]
Anr Ed. Oxford: Shakespeare Head Press, 1926. One of 520 L.p. copies. 10 vols. Half cloth. cba Feb 5 (236) $75
One of 1,030. Orig cloth. "A mint set". bba Dec 4 (161) £230 [F. Mackenzie]

Fielding, Mantle. See: Morgan & Fielding

Fielding, Newton Smith, 1799-1856
— Chiens de chasse. Paris: Rittner, 1828. 4to, half vellum. Jeanson copy. SM Mar 1 (227) FF7,800

Fielding, Theodore Henry, 1781-1851
— British Castles. L, 1825. Oblong 4to, contemp half mor; rebacked, rubbed. With 25 colored plates. S Oct 23 (173) £250 [Marshall]
— Picturesque Description of the River Wye. L, 1841. Folio, orig cloth; worn. With 12 hand-colored plates. C Dec 12 (233) £500 [Rostron]

Fielding, Theodore Henry, 1781-1851 —& Walton, J.
— A Picturesque Tour of the English Lakes. L: Ackermann, 1821. 4to half calf gilt. With hand-colored title & 48 plates. pnE Jan 28 (239) £520 [Thin]
Anr copy. Contemp half calf; spine rubbed. With 48 hand-colored plates. Half-title bound after title. S Oct 23 (172) £550 [Breen]
Anr copy. Orig cloth; rebacked preserving orig spine. With pictorial title & 48 hand-colored plates. S May 29 £998 £440
Anr copy. Contemp lea gilt; extremities worn. sg Apr 2 (80) $700

Fields, James T.
— Yesterdays with Authors. Bost., 1900. 8vo, mor by Root. Extra-illus with c.100 plates. wa Dec 11 (320) $290

Fifaddy, Frederick Augustus
— The Adventures of Uncle Sam, in Search of his Lost Honor. Middletown, CT, 1816. 12mo, orig bds; backstrip chipped away, front cover loose. Foxed. sg Mar 12 (109) $60

Figueiredo e Silva, Antonio Joaquim de
— Estudos sobre o Linho da Nova Zelandia. Lisbon, 1855. 4to, modern half calf. sg Nov 20 (138) $50

Filatro, Euonomo. See: Gesner, Conrad

Filhol, Antoine Michel
See also: Lavalee & Filhol
— Galerie du Musee Napoleon.... Paris, 1804-15. 10 vols. 8vo, contemp mor gilt with central Imperial coat-of-arms with eagle on front & back covers. C June 18 (223) £500

AMERICAN BOOK PRICES CURRENT

Anr copy. Later half mor. Lacking 2 plates in final vol. Ck June 19 (182) £240

Filial...
— Filial Duty Recommended and Enforced, by a Variety of Instructive and Entertaining Stories. L: E. Newbery, [c.1790]. 24mo, orig Dutch floral bds. S Dec 5 (310) £200 [Hirsch]

Filicaia, Vincenzio da, 1642-1707. See: Fore-Edge Paintings

Filippi, Filippo de, 1869-1938
— Karakoram and Western Himalaya. L, 1912. 4to, cloth; soiled, shaken. Lacking the Atlas vol. cb Nov 6 (133) $275

Filson, John, 1747?-88
— Histoire de Kentucke.... Paris, 1785. 1st Ed in French. 8vo, disbound. With folding map. Several library stamps on half-title & title. sg Mar 12 (110) $550
Anr copy. Contemp calf. Library stamps on title. sg Apr 2 (81) $750

Fincham, John, d.1859
— On Masting Ships, and Mast Making. L, 1829. 8vo, orig cloth; rubbed, spine repaired. Inscr. bba Nov 13 (38) £70 [Hay Cinema Bookshop]

Finden, William, 1787-1852 & Edward Francis, 1791-1857
— Findens' Tableaux of National Character.... L, 1843. 2 vols. Folio, contemp mor gift bdgs. sg Feb 12 (147) $200
— Illustrations to the Life and Works of Lord Byron. L, 1833-34. 3 vols. 4to, half mor. pn Dec 11 (32) £140 [Athens]
Anr copy. Mor gilt. pn Dec 11 (33) £130 [Athens Books]
— Landscape Illustrations of the Waverley Novels. L, 1834. 3 vols. 8vo, mor gilt; rubbed. With 122 plates. pn Jan 22 (53) £75 [Cavendish]
— Views of Ports and Harbours, Watering Places, Fishing Villages...on the English Coast. L, 1842. ("The Ports, Harbours, Watering Places and Coast Scenery of Great Britain.") Illus by W. H. Bartlett. 2 vols in 1. 4to, orig cloth. bba Jan 15 (479) £280 [Henderson]
Anr copy. 2 vols. 4to, half mor gilt. With 2 engraved titles & 123 plates. Some foxing. pn Dec 11 (71) £280 [Mizon]
Anr copy. Calf gilt. With engraved titles & 122 plates. Some spotting. pn Dec 11 (72) £280 [Croft]
Anr copy. Contemp half mor; worn. T Nov 20 (45) £300
Anr Ed. L, 1844. 2 vols in one. 4to, library cloth. With engraved titles & 141 plates.

With ink and perforated library stamps on 1st ptd title & final leaf. bba Dec 4 (334) £250 [Schuetzer]

Anr copy. 2 vols in 1. 4to, contemp calf; rubbed, upper joint split. With 2 engraved titles, port & 123 plates. Ptd title in Vol I only. S May 29 (999) £300

Anr Ed. L, [n.d.]. 2 vols. 4to, contemp pictorial mor gilt. With engraved titles & 108 plates. S May 28 (867) £380

Finden, William, 1787-1852 & Edward Francis, 1791-1857 —&
Horne, Thomas Hartwell, 1780-1862
— Landscape Illustrations of the Bible.... L, 1836. Bound in 3 vols. 4to, mor gilt; rubbed. With 2 engraved titles & 94 plates on india paper. pn Sept 18 (133) £80 [Cohen]

Findlay, Frederick Roderick Noble
— Big Game Shooting and Travel in South-East Africa. L, 1903. Frontis detached but present. cb Nov 6 (134) $120

Fine, Oronce, 1494-1555
— De geometrica practica. Strassburg, 1544. Folio, modern half vellum. Stains on I1-2 & I6; marginal dampstains; library stamp on title. S June 25 (106) £250 [Chatto]
— De solaribus horologiis, & quadrantibus.... Paris: [B. Praevost?] apud Gulielmum Cavellat, [1560]. 4to, old limp vellum. Folding diagram & V1 supplied in facsimile & loosely inserted; last 2 leaves holed with loss. Ck Jan 30 (29) £180

Finlayson, George, 1790-1828
— The Mission to Siam, and Hue.... L, 1826. 8vo, contemp half calf; spine rubbed. T Feb 19 (235) £125

Finney, Jack
— Time and Again. NY: Simon & Schuster, [1970]. Review copy. In d/j. cb Sept 28 (529) $60

Finsch, Otto, 1839-1917
— Die Papageiu. Leiden, 1867-68. 2 vols in 3. 8vo, orig bdg; worn. B Feb 24 (173) HF650

Firbank, Ronald, 1886-1926
— Caprice. L, 1917. 1st Ed. Vellum; soiled. Firbank's copy. sg Dec 11 (264) $500
Anr copy. Worn. Inscr. sg Dec 11 (265) $375
— Concerning the Eccentricities of Cardinal Pirelli. L, 1925. Page proofs, with a few minor corrections. Unbound. sg Dec 11 (266) $400
— Inclinations. L, 1916. 1st Ed. Vellum; some soiling & warping. Firbank's copy. sg Dec 11 (268) $650

— A Letter from Arthur Ronald Firbank to Madame Albani. L: Centaur Press, [1934]. One of 50. In ptd envelope. Photographic postcard of Mme Albani, sgd, laid in. sg Dec 11 (269) $110
— Odette: a Fairy Tale for Weary People. L, 1916. Illus by Albert Buhrer. 4to, wraps; spine frayed. With ALs to Firbank's manager laid in. sg Dec 11 (273) $375
Anr copy. Orig wraps; frayed. T May 20 (28) £200
— Odette D'Antrevernes. L, 1905. 1st Ed. Wraps. With Firbank's Ms revisions. sg Dec 11 (271) $1,700
One of 10 on Japan vellum. Vellum; warped & soiled. Presentation copy for Queen Alexandra. sg Dec 11 (270) $3,000
— Vainglory. L, 1915. Inscr. sg Dec 11 (281) $175
— Valmouth. L, 1919. 1st Ed. With frontis by Augustus John. Vellum; soiled. sg Dec 11 (282) $2,000
— Works. L, 1929. One of 235. 5 vols. In d/js. sg Dec 11 (286) $250

Firmin, Giles
— The Real Christian; or, a Treatise of Effectual Calling. Bost.: Rogers & Fowle for J. Edwards, 1742. 12mo, contemp calf; worn. Some foxing & soiling; marginal annotations. sg Sept 18 (32) $130

Firmin-Didot, Ambroise, 1790-1876
— Nouvelle Biographie Generale.... Copenhagen, 1963-69. 46 vols in 23. Reprint of 1855-67 Ed. bba Oct 16 (63) £350 [N. Phillips]

Firmin-Didot Library, Ambroise
— [Sale catalogue] Catalogue illustre des livres precieux, manuscrits et imprimes.... Paris, 1878-84. One of 500. 6 vols. 4to, contemp half cloth, orig wraps bound in. bba Mar 12 (270) £80 [Maggs]
Anr copy. Parts 1-5 (of 6). Cloth, orig wraps bound in. With index booklet for Part 2 only. sg May 14 (62) $120

Fischel, Oscar —&
Boehn, Max von, 1850-1921
— Modes and Manners of the Nineteenth Century. L, 1927. 4 vols. Half calf gilt. sg Sept 11 (130) $110

Fischer, Carlos
— Les Costumes de l'opera. Paris, 1931. 4to, orig half cloth; soiled & stained. cba Mar 5 (63) $65

Fischer von Waldheim, Gotthelf, 1771-1853
— Entomographia Imperii Russici. Moscow, 1820-22. Vol I (of 5). 4to, later half mor gilt. S Nov 10 (487) £240 [Quaritch]

Fish, Robert L.
— The Incredible Schlock Homes. NY, [1966]. In creased d/j with a few tiny tears. cb Nov 20 (166) $55

Fisher, Albert Kenrick, 1856-1948
— The Hawks and Owls of the United States.... Wash., 1893. 8vo, orig cloth. With 16 plates. Haverschmidt copy. B Feb 24 (266) HF220

Anr copy. Orig cloth; rubbed. cb Apr 2 (89) $95

Fisher, George Thomas
— Photogenic Manipulation: Containing the Theory and Plain Instructions in the Art of Photography.... Phila.: Carey & Hart, 1845. 16mo, orig cloth; spine ends frayed, free endpapers def. Library markings. ha Nov 7 (165) $240

Fisher, Harrison
— Bachelor Belles. NY, 1908. Cloth; rubbed. K June 7 (136) $120

Fisher, Irving, 1867-1947
— Mathematical Investigations in the Theory of Value and Prices. New Haven, 1926. 8vo, orig cloth; rubbed. Marginal browning. Inscr, 1927. P Sept 24 (286) $475

Fisher, John, 1459-1535
— Assertiones Lutheranae confutatio. Antwerp: M. Hillenius, 1523. Folio, half mor gilt by Birdsall. Woodcut border of tp shaved; some waterstains. Chatsworth copy. C Dec 12 (291) £500 [Thomas]
— De veritate corporis et sanguinis Christi in Eucharistia. Cologne, 1527. 4to, 18th-cent calf; both covers torn, upper joint repaired. Lower blank margin of initial leaves wormed. S Mar 10 (1061) £280 [Maggs]

Fisher, P. See: Chatto, William Andrew

Fiske, Willard, 1831-1904
— The Book of the First American Chess Congress. NY, 1859. 8vo, orig cloth. pn Mar 26 (30) $160 [De Lucia]
— Chess in Iceland and in Icelandic Literature. Florence, 1905. Modern cloth. pn Mar 26 (394) £80 [Hannas]

Fitch, John
— The Original Steam-Boat Supported. Phila., 1788. Bound with: Rumsey. A Plan Wherein the Power of Steam is...Shewn. [N.p., n.d.]. 8vo, bdg not described. Franklin Institute copy. F Sept 12 (354) $2,250

**Fite, Emerson D. —&
Freeman, Archibald**
— A Book of Old Maps, Delineating American History.... Cambr., Mass., 1926. 1st Ed. Folio, cloth. sg May 14 (188) $130

Fitton, William Henry, 1780-1861
— An Account of Some Geological Specimens from the Coasts of Australia. L, 1826. 8vo, modern half calf. Minor spotting to margins of 2 plates. C Oct 15 (153) £220 [Bonham]

Fitzclarence, George Augustus, Earl of Munster
— Journal of a Route Across India.... L, 1819. 4to, half calf gilt. Folding map torn. pn June 18 (105) £250 [Turner]

Fitzgerald, F. Scott, 1896-1940
— All the Sad Young Men. NY, 1926. 1st Ed. cb May 7 (27) $80

2d or 3d printing. In torn & creased d/j. cb May 7 (28) $250
— The Beautiful and Damned. NY, 1922. 1st Ed, 1st Ptg. Bdg rubbed. T Oct 15 (157) £50

Anr copy. In chipped & soiled d/j. A few leaves poorly opened. wa Dec 11 (34) $230
— The Crack-up, with other Uncollected Pieces.... NY, [1954]. Issue for distribution in England. Ed by Edmund Wilson. In d/j with tears at spine ends. cb May 7 (34) $50
— Fie! Fie! Fi-Fi! [Cincinnati, NY & L]: John Church Co., [1914]. 1st Ed. 4to, orig half cloth; soiled & bumped. cb May 7 (40) $650
— The Great Gatsby. NY, 1925. 1st Ed, 1st Ptg. Orig cloth; spine leaning & varnished. cb May 7 (41) $80; wa Dec 11 (35) $80
— John Jackson's Arcady. Bost., [1928]. 1st Ed. Orig wraps; blindstamp to bottom of rear wrap. cb May 7 (44) $475
— The Mystery of the Raymond Mortgage. NY, 1960. One of 750. Wraps. cb May 7 (48) $130
— Tender is the Night. NY, 1934. 1st Ed. In d/j. sg Mar 5 (74) $750
— This Side of Paradise. NY, 1920. 1st Ed, 1st Ptg. cb May 7 (55) $225
— The Vegetable. NY, 1923. 1st Ed. In d/j with some dampstains & rubbing. cb May 7 (57) $200

Anr copy. Cloth. Sgd on front free endpaper. wa Sept 25 (665) $375

Fitzgerald, Robert
— Salt-Water Sweetned.... L: W. Cademan, 1683. 4to, loose in later wraps. Lacking 1st & last blanks. C May 13 (123) £700 [laget]

Fitzgerald, Robert D., 1830?-92
— Australian Orchids. [East Melbourne]: Lansdowne Eds, 1977. Facsimile Ed, One of 350. 2 vols. Folio, orig half mor. Facsimile of the Sydney, [1875]-1882-[1893] Ed. kh Mar 16 (187) A$420

Fitzgerald, S. J. Adair
— The Zankiwank and the Bletherwitch. L, 1896. Illus by Arthur Rackham. 8vo, cloth. sg Oct 30 (73) $600

Fitzherbert, Sir Anthony
— La Graund Abregement de le Lay. L: Richard Tottell, 1577. ("La Graunde Abridgement") 2 parts in 1 vol. Folio, contemp calf; artlessly rebacked. Tear in 1st 2V8. sg Oct 9 (209) $225

Fitzherbert, Sir Anthony, 1470-1538
— La Table conteynant en sommaire les choses notables en la graunde abridgement. L: Richard Tottel, 1565. Folio. modern half mor. Dampstained in upper portion of 2d half. sg Oct 9 (208) $900

Fitzherbert, Sir John
— The Boke of Husbandry. L: Thomas Berthelet, 1534 [1535?]. 8vo, early 19th-cent mor gilt. Minor dampstains to C6-8; C8 with small hole in lower margin repaired. Hunt copy. CNY Nov 21 (121) $4,500

Fitzpatrick, T. J.
— Rafinesque. A Sketch of his Life. Des Moines, 1911. sg May 14 (594) $140

Fitzwilliam, William Wentworth, Viscount Milton —& Cheadle, Walter Butler
— Voyage de l'Atlantique au Pacifique. Paris, 1866. 8vo, orig half lea. cb Jan 8 (124) $65

Five...
— Five on Paper. North Hills: Bird & Bull Press, 1963. One of 169. 4to, mor. Hunt copy. CNY Nov 21 (211) $160

Flacius, Matthias, 1520-75
— Catalogus testium veritatis. Strasbourg & Basel: Oporinus, 1562. 4to, 18th-cent calf with Signet arms; rebacked. Ms notes in a later hand bound in. Ck Jan 30 (182) £90

Flaherty, Robert J.
— My Eskimo Friends. Nanook of the North. NY, 1924. 4to, bds. Inscr. sg Nov 13 (50) $100

Flake, Chad J.
— Mormon Bibliography, 1830-1930. Salt Lake City, 1978. 4to, cloth. sg Jan 22 (156) $100

Flament-Hennebique, Robert
— En suivant mon fusil. Paris, 1938. One of 4 on japon with an orig drawing as frontis. 4to, half mor by Gauche. Jeanson copy. SM Mar 1 (228) FF2,200

Flamsteed, John, 1646-1719
— Atlas coelestis. L, 1729. 1st Ed. Folio, modern half calf. With port & 27 double star charts. Discoloration to 4 maps. Ck Feb 27 (80) £1,250

Flatman, Thomas, 1637-88
— Poems and Songs. L, 1674. 1st Ed. 8vo, contemp sheep. Unpressed copy. Lacking A1 & A2. C Dec 12 (320) £200 [Maggs]

Flaubert, Gustave, 1821-80
See also: Eragny Press; Golden Cockerel Press
— Herodias. Berlin, 1919. One of 200. Illus by M. Slevogt. 4to, orig half vellum. With 6 lithos. HN Nov 26 (2010) DM550
— Novembre. [Paris, 1928]. One of 25 on japon imperial with plates in 3 states, 2 sgd sketches & 5 sgd proofs. Illus by Edgar Chahine. 4to, mor gilt extra by Maylander with floral mor onlays. With 21 plates. Abdy copy. SM Oct 20 (620) FF25,000
— Oeuvres. Paris, 1921-25. 12 vols. 4to, contemp half mor, orig wraps bound in; rubbed. bba Oct 30 (187) £80 [Nosbuesch]; bba Oct 30 (188) £50 [Nosbuesch]

Flaxman, John, 1755-1826
— Compositions from the Works, Days and Theogony of Hesiod. L, 1817. Illus by William Blake. Oblong folio, half mor. With engraved title & 36 plates. Last few plates dampstained in margins. S Oct 6 (768) £65 [Bickersteth]

Flechier, Esprit, Bishop of Nimes, 1632-1710
— Histoire du Cardinal Ximenes. Amst.: Henry Desbordes, 1693. 2 vols in 1. 12mo, contemp calf. Contemp inscr of the Jesuit College of Louvain on tp. sg Mar 26 (292) $700

Fleetwood, Bishop William, 1656-1725
— Chronicon Preciosum: or an Account of English Money.... L, 1707. 1st Ed. 8vo, contemp calf. Marginal worming at beginning. S Sept 22 (234) £130 [Mystery]
— Chronicon Preciosum, or an Account of English Gold and Silver Money. L, 1745. 2d Ed. 8vo, contemp calf; joints split, rubbed. With 12 plates. bba Aug 28 (196) £60 [Northcote]

Anr copy. Calf; broken. With 12 plates. Bound with the appendix. pn June 18 (64) £95 [Campbell]

Fleming, Ian
— Casino Royale. L, 1953. 1st Ed. In d/j; lower cover of bdg soiled. S July 23 (141) £680 [Quaritch]
  1st American Ed. NY, 1954. In d/j with a few tiny tears. cb Nov 20 (167) $275
— Diamonds Are Forever. L, 1956. Bds, in d/j. sg Dec 11 (32) $110
— From Russia, With Love. L, [1957]. 1st Ed. In soiled & chipped d/j. cb Nov 20 (172) $55
— Goldfinger. L, 1959. 1st Ed. Orig cloth, in d/j. cb Nov 20 (173) $60
  Anr copy. Orig cloth; soiled. Inscr. S Jan 13 (563) £550 [Berryman]
  Anr copy. Worn. Inscr. sg Mar 5 (75) $1,500
— Live and Let Die. NY: Macmillan, 1955. 1st American Ed. In soiled d/j. Inscr. wa Sept 25 (666) $100
— On Her Majesty's Secret Service. L, [1963]. 1st Ed, one of 250, sgd. Ck Dec 10 (345) £550
  One of 250. S Dec 18 (124) £725 [de Freitas]
  Anr copy. Half vellum. sg Dec 11 (33) $1,300
— Thunderball. L, [1961]. Orig cloth; soiled. Some leaves with stain in upper outer corner. Inscr. S Jan 13 (564) £280 [Berryman]

Fleming, John F. See: Wolf & Fleming

Flers, Robert de, 1872-1927
— Ilsee, Princesse de Tripoli. Paris, 1897. One of 252. Illus by Alphonse Mucha. 4to, orig wraps. S Dec 4 (26) £1,700 [Sims, Reed]

Fletcher, Cora C., Pseud.
— The Emperor's Lion. Verona: Plain Wrapper Press, [1976]. One of 71. Illus by Fulvio Testa. Bds. cb Sept 11 (207) $50

Fletcher, John, 1579-1625. See: Beaumont & Fletcher

Fletcher, John Gould
— Fire and Wine. L, 1913. sg Mar 5 (76) $70

Fletcher, Phineas, 1582-1650
— The Purple Island, or the Isle of Man.... Cambr., 1633. 1st Ed. 4to, 19th-cent calf; rebacked, preserving orig spine. Lacking blanks before 1st & 2d parts; small wormhole through most of 1st part & sprinkled worming at foot of others, affecting some text. C Dec 12 (327) £150 [Rix]
  Anr copy. Lev gilt by The Club Bindery. Lacking 2 blanks before the Piscatorie Eclogs, these replaced with blanks that are not genuine. Clawson copy. F Jan 15 (225) $325

Fletcher, William Younger, 1830-1913
— English Bookbindings in the British Museum. L, 1895. One of 500. Folio, cloth; worn, shaken. O May 12 (74) $175

Fleuron...
— The Fleuron: A Journal of Typography. L & Cambr., 1923-30. Ed by Oliver Simon & Stanley Morison. Nos 1-7 (all pbd). 4to, orig half cloth; rubbed. bba Oct 16 (483) £380 [Quevedo]

Flight, Edward
— The True Legend of St. Dunstan and the Devil. L, [n.d.]. Illus by George Cruikshank. 8vo, half calf. This copy with 8 india-proofs mtd & bound to face matching book illusts. sg June 11 (141) $275

Flinders, Matthew, 1774-1814
See also: Golden Cockerel Press
— A Voyage to Terra Australis. Adelaide, 1966. 2 vols plus Atlas in portfolio; together 3 vols. 4to, orig cloth. Australiana Facsimile Eds No 37. kh Mar 16 (194) A$420

Flint, Ralph
— Contemporary American Etching. NY, [1930-31]. Bds; worn. O Jan 6 (60) $90

Flint, Sir William Russell
— Etchings and Drypoints. Catalogue raisonne. L: Colnaghi, 1957. One of 135, sgd. 4to, orig cloth. S May 6 (115) £140 [Marks]
— In Pursuit. L, 1970. One of 900, sgd. 4to, half mor gilt. pn Sept 18 (118) £70 [Way]
— The Lisping Goddess. L, 1968. One of 275. Folio, orig half mor. S May 6 (120) £50 [Elkin Matthews]
— Models of Propriety. L, 1951. One of 500. 4to, bba Apr 23 (285) £90 [Lydian Bookstore]
  Anr copy. Cloth. S May 6 (118) £90 [Peters]
— Shadows in Arcady. L, 1965. One of 500, sgd. 4to, orig cloth. S May 6 (113) £85 [Peters]

Flinter, George Dawson
— A History of the Revolution of Caracas.... L, 1819. 8vo, modern half calf. Some leaves soiled. bba Sept 25 (414) £260 [Burton-Garbett]

Flitnerus, Joannes
— Nebulo nebulonum, hoc est, jocoseria nequitiae censura.... Frankfurt, 1663. 8vo, 18th-cent lea gilt. FD Dec 2 (58) DM1,600

Flora...
— Flora and Sylva: A Monthly Review. L, 1903-5. 3 vols (all pbd). Orig cloth; rubbed & soiled. bba Jan 15 (407) £110 [Elliott]
Anr copy. Library stamps on flyleaves. L July 2 (159) £120
Anr copy. Orig cloth; damage to spine of Vol III. pn Mar 5 (311) £170 [Walford]

Floral...
— The Floral Magazine: Comprising Figures and Descriptions of Popular Garden Flowers. L, 1861-62. Ed by Thomas Moore. Vols I & II in 2 vols plus Companion to the Floral Magazine. 8vo, contemp calf, not uniform. Sold w.a.f. C Oct 15 (227) £1,500 [Scott Sandilands]
Anr copy. Vols I & II in 1 vol. 8vo, contemp mor; rubbed. With 128 hand-colored plates. Ck June 19 (123) £850

Florencia, Francisco de —& Oviedo, Juan Antonio de
— Menologio de los varones mas senalados en perfeccion Religiosa de la Compania de Jesus de nueva-Espana. [Mexico, 1747]. 4to, contemp vellum. Lacking port. S Oct 23 (417) £1,000 [Quaritch]

Floriani, Pietro Paolo
— Difesa et offesa delle piazze.... Venice, 1654. 2d Ed. Folio, contemp half calf; rubbed. With engraved title, port & 44 plates only. Sold w.a.f. Ck Nov 21 (371) £100

Florilegium. See: Greek Anthology

Florinus, Franciscus Philippus
— Oeconomus prodens et legalis.... Nuremberg, 1705. Folio, contemp calf; repaired. Lacking frontis, 1 plate & several text leaves. HK Nov 4 (1852) DM1,800
— Oeconomus prudens et legalis. Oder Allgemeiner Kluger und Rechtsverstaendiger Haus-Vatter.... Nuremberg, [c.1750?]. 9 parts in 1 vol. Folio, contemp vellum. HK Nov 4 (1853) DM750

Florio, John, 1553?-1625
— Florios Second Frutes. L: Thos. Woodcock, 1591. 1st Ed. 2 parts in 1 vol. 4to, old calf. Lacking 2A4 of Gardine; some waterstaining; slight worming in upper inner margin; some tears & holes, that in G2 affecting text. S Dec 18 (4) £700 [Quaritch]
Anr copy. Bound with: Giardino di Ricreatione nel quale crescono fronde, fiori e frutti... L, 1591 4to, later mor; rubbed. First title & final leaf soiled & frayed, dampstaining throughout. T Sept 18 (106) £240
— Vocabulario Italiano & Inglese. A Dictionary.... L, 1688-87. 2d Ed. 2 parts in 1 vol. Folio, contemp calf; worn, spine frayed. Last leaf browned; lacking final blank. C Dec 12 (79) £200 [Maggs]

Flosculi...
— Flosculi Sententiarum: Printers Flowers Moralised. [Northampton: Gehenna Press, 1967]. One of 250. Folio, mor. sg Jan 8 (79) $450

Flower, John
— Views of Antient Buildings in the Town and Country of Leicester. L, [c.1830]. Folio, orig cloth. With pictorial title & 24 plates. pn June 18 (138) £120 [Marlborough]

Fludd, Robert, 1547-1637
— Tractatus secundus de naturae simia seu technica macrocosmi historia in partes undecim divisa. Oppenheim, 1618. Vol II only. Folio, early calf; upper cover detached, lower joint def. Xx4 from a shorter copy; 1 leaf misbound. S May 21 (195) £1,100 [Verlag]
— Utriusque cosmi majoris et minoris.... Oppenheim, 1617-19. Vol I (2 parts) only. Folio, 18th-cent calf. With 7 (6 folding) plates. First engraved title trimmed; Part 1 lacking w leaves at end; Part 2 lacking 1 military plate & with 1 folding plate repaired. S Nov 27 (262) £1,700 [DeZayas]

Foesius, Anutius, 1528-95
— Oeconomia Hippocratis, alphabeti serie distincta.... Frankfurt: A. Wecheli heredes, 1588. Folio, old calf; rebacked. Bodleian duplicate stamp. S Nov 10 (488) £220 [Phillips]

Fogazzaro, Antonio. See: Grabhorn Printing

Foley, Edwin
The Book of Decorative Furniture. L, 1910-11. 2 vols. 4to, cloth; spine ends torn. sg June 4 (139) $80

Folkard, Henry Coleman
— The Wild-Fowler; a Treatise on Ancient and Modern Wild-Fowling.... L, 1859. 1st Ed. 8vo, orig bdg; spine repaired, new endpapers. Some plates with stains. pnE Dec 17 (365) £70 [Furniss]

Follot, Charles. See: Clouzot & Follot

Folter, Roland. See: Grolier Club

Fontaine, G., Mlle.
— Collection de cent especes ou varietes du genre camellia. Brussels, 1840. Folio, contemp half mor, rubbed. With 90 (of 100) hand-colored plates. Large piece torn from title without loss; faint stamp on 1 plate. Vilmorin—de Belder copy. S Apr 27 (125) £7,500 [Elliott]

Fontaine, Nicolas, Sieur de Royaumont
— The History of the Old and New Testament. L, 1690-88. 2 vols in 1. Folio, lea; worn. One map laid down. pn May 21 (184) £75 [Cohen]

Fontaine, Pierre Francois Leonard, 1762-1853.
See: Percier & Fontaine

Fontaines-Guerin, Hardouin de. See: Hardouin

Fontana, Carlo, 1634-1714
— Templum Vaticanum et ipsius origo.... Rome, 1694. Folio, contemp calf; worn. With 79 plates, 9 folding, 1 double-page. Small hole in 1 part title affecting 1 letter. C July 22 (72) £1,500
— Utilissimo trattato dell'acque correnti.... Rome, 1696. Folio, contemp vellum. Some worming. HK Nov 4 (986) DM1,900

Fontana, Fulvio, 1649-1723
— I pregi della Toscana nell'impresse piu' segnalate de' cavalieri di Santo Stefano. Florence, 1701. Folio, contemp vellum. With port, frontis & 37 plates. C Dec 12 (235) £950 [Maggs]

Fontani, Francesco, 1748-1818
— Viaggio pittorico della Toscana. Florence 1801-3. 1st Ed. 3 vols. Folio, contemp half mor; extremities rubbed, spine of Vol III torn with loss. With 5 double-page maps & plans & 204 plates. Ck Sept 26 (52) £500
Anr Ed. Florence, 1802. Vol I (of 3) only. Folio, contemp half russia; worn, joints broken. With 2 folding plans, 5 other plans & 72 plates. C July 22 (74) £1,800

Fontenai, Abbe de
— Galerie du Palais Royal. Paris, 1786-1808. Illus by J. Couche. Vol I only. Contemp half mor. With engraved title & 101 plates only. FD June 11 (768) DM1,050

Fontenelle, Bernard le Bovier de, 1657-1757
See also: Nonesuch Press
— A Discourse of the Plurality of Worlds.... L, 1688. ("A Plurality of Worlds....") 8vo, contemp calf; upper cover almost detached. T Sept 18 (500) £76

Foote, John Taintor. See: Derrydale Press

Foras, Elio Amedee Jacques Francois, comte de, 1830-99
— Armorial et nobiliaire de Savoie. Grenoble, 1878. 4 vols. Folio, half mor. SM Oct 20 (448) FF22,000

Forbes, Duncan, 1798-1868
— The History of Chess. L, 1860. Orig cloth; rebacked. pn Mar 26 (398) £80 [Wolmark]
— Observations on the Origin and Progress of Chess.... L, 1855. Disbound. pn Mar 26 (397) £80 [Quaritch]

Forbes, Edward, 1815-54 —&
Hanley, Sylvanus, 1819-99
— A History of British Mollusca. L, 1853. 4 vols. 8vo, orig cloth; dampstained, covers warped. With 203 plates. cb June 4 (67) $160

Forbes, Edwin, 1839-95
— Life Studies of the Great Army. NY, [1876]. In portfolio; broken & worn. With 40 plates. Plate 17 very worn; some others are also worn or browned. K Mar 22 (81) $325

Forbes, James, 1773-1861
— Pinetum Woburnense: or, a Catalogue of Coniferous Plants.... L, 1839. One of 100. 8vo, contemp calf; rebacked. With 68 hand-colored plates. Inscr by the Duke of Bedford. de Belder copy. S Apr 27 (18) £2,500 [Heuer]
— Salictum Woburnense: or, a Catalogue of Willows Indigenous and Foreign in the Collection...at Woburn Abbey. L, 1829. One of 50. 4to, orig bds; rebacked with mor, rubbed. With folding frontis & 140 colored plates. Inscr. de Belder copy. S Apr 27 (19) £2,500 [Maggs]

Forbes, James David, 1809-68
— Norway and its Glaciers.... Edin., 1853. 8vo, orig cloth; rubbed, rebacked, old spine preserved. bba Nov 13 (125) £85 [Bowers]
Anr copy. Contemp half calf; rubbed. With 2 maps & 10 colored plates. Lacking half-title; some leaves at beginning misbound. S July 14 (669) £70

Forbes, Sir John
— Original Cases with Dissections and Observations Illustrating the Use of the Stethoscope and Percussion in the Diagnosis of Diseases of the Chest.... L, 1824. 1st Ed. 8vo, contemp half calf gilt. With 3 plates. Lacking half-title. pnE Dec 17 (93) £920 [Phelps]

Forbin, Louis, Comte de, 1777-1841
— Voyage dans le Levant en 1817 et 1818. Paris, 1819. Folio, half mor, uncut. With 2 plans & 78 plates. Some stains to lower margins. S Oct 23 (377) £2,000 [Lewis]

Forbush, Edward Howe, 1858-1929
— Birds of Massachusetts.... [Bost.], 1925-29. 3 vols. sg Sept 18 (94) $110
Anr copy. Small patch of adhesion damage to Plate 10, Vol I. sg Apr (94) $110
2d Ed of Vol I, 1st Ed of Vols II-III. [Bost.], 1928-27-29. 3 vols. O Mar 24 (73) $80
— Important American Game Birds.... Wilmington DE, [1917]. Pictorial wraps; faint library stamp on front cover. Inscr. sg Oct 23 (352) $60

Force, Peter, 1790-1868
— American Archives. Fourth and Fifth Series. Wash., 1837-53. 9 vols (all pbd). Folio, contemp bds; shabby & becoming disbound, 1 rear cover lacking. wa Mar 5 (379) $130

Ford, Charles Henri
— Secret Haiku. NY: Red Ozier Press, [1982]. One of 155. Illus by Isamu Noguchi. Cloth. sg Jan 8 (176) $110

Ford, Ford Madox, 1873-1939
See also: Conrad & Ford
— The Brown Owl. L, 1892. 2d Ed. 12mo, orig cloth; rubbed & soiled. Sgd. bba Oct 30 (93) £100 [Pioneer]
— Great Trade Route. NY, 1937. 1st Ed. In creased d/j. cb May 7 (66) $50
— Mister Bosphorus and the Muses. L, 1923. 1st Ed. 4to, orig half cloth; rubbed. bba Apr 9 (254) £70 [Lobo]

Ford, G. H. See: Ellis & Ford

Ford, Henry, 1863-1947
— Today and Tomorrow. L, 1926. S Sept 22 (235) £80 [Drury]

Ford, Julia Ellsworth
— Imagina. NY, 1914. 4to, cloth; worn. sg Oct 30 (74) $40
— Snickerty Nick & the Giant. Los Angeles: Suttonhouse, [1935]. 3d ptg. Rhymes by Witter Bynner; music by Charles Arthur Ridgway; illusts by Arthur Rackham. 4to, cloth, in torn d/j. sg Oct 30 (77) $500

Ford, Julia Ellsworth —& Bynner, Witter
— Snickerty Nick and the Giant. NY, 1919. Illus by Arthur Rackham. 4to, mor by Zaehnsdorf. With 3 color plates. Owner's markings on title. sg Oct 30 (76) $250

Ford, Paul Leicester, 1865-1902
— Mason Locke Weems, his Works and Ways.... NY, 1929. One of 200. 3 vols. Half cloth; worn. Library markings. O Oct 21 (63) $110

Forde, Edward
— Experimented Proposals how the King may have Money to Pay and Maintain His Fleets. L: W. Godbid, 1666. 4to, wraps. Shaved at foot with loss of signatures & some text. S July 24 (438) £380 [Lawson]

Fordyce, William
— The History and Antiquities of the County Palatine of Durham. Newcastle & Edin., 1857. 2 vols. 4to, half calf; rubbed; upper covers detached. O Feb 24 (181) $60

FORE-EDGE PAINTINGS

Fore-Edge Paintings
— Bible in English. Glasgow, 1857. ("The Portable Folio Family Bible.") Folio, lea gilt with painting of a hunting scene. sg Sept 11 (164) $500
— [Bible in Greek] He Kaine Diatheke.... L, 1820. 8vo, mor gilt prize bdg with painting of 4 Greeks in national dress standing before the Acropolis. sg Sept 11 (153) $175
— [Bible] Nuevo Testamento. Paris, 1823. 12mo, contemp mor gilt with divided paintings of Richmond & Lambeth Palace. Sold w.a.f. P Sept 24 (157) $550
— The Book of Common Prayer. L, 1713. 8vo, contemp mor with view of the shipwreck of St. Paul on Malta; rebacked. sg Sept 11 (135) $250

Anr Ed. Cambr., 1764. 4to, contemp mor gilt with painting of the ruins of Fountains Abbey. O Sept 23 (55) $390

Anr Ed. L, 1861. 12mo, orig lea with painting of Anne Hathaway's cottage. O Jan 6 (61) $90

— Compendium of Christian Instruction. L, 1822. 3 vols. 12mo, mor gilt with painting of cityscape with people and horses. sg Sept 11 (141) $400
— Elegant Epistles, being a Copious Selection.... L: for John Sharpe, [c.1820?]. 24mo, contemp mor gilt with painting of a country road with pedestrians, horseman & carriage. sg Sept 11 (147) $80
— Elements of Christian Theology. L, 1837. 8vo, contemp lea with painting of a view of Winchester. O Sept 23 (58) $210
— The Gem: A Christmas and New Year's Present. For 1842. Phila., [1842]. 8vo, orig lea with painting of a fox-hunting scene; rubbed. O Jan 6 (64) $110
— The Gift of Friendship: A Token of Remembrance for 1849. Phila.: Henry F. Anners, [1848]. 12mo, contemp lea gift bdg with view of a sailing ship & portrait of a naval officer. sg Sept 11 (150) $200
— The Holy Bible, Containing the Old and New Testaments. NY, 1870. 8vo, contemp mor with painting of Battery Park in New York. O Jan 6 (65) $110
— A List of the Officers of the Army and Royal Marines on Full and Half-Pay.... [L], 1818. 8vo, contemp lea gilt with views of Whitehall & horse guards. sg Sept 11 (156) $300
— Recreations in Natural History.... L, 1815. 8vo, contemp mor with painting of a horse-drawn cart passing in front of Guilford Castle. O Sept 23 (61) $240
— The Royal Kalender; and Court and City Register.... L, [1817]. 12mo, contemp mor gilt with painting of Blenheim Palace. sg Sept 11 (166) $325

FORE-EDGE PAINTINGS

— The Town and Country Almanack for 1798. Edin., [1798]. 12mo, contemp mor gilt with painting of a horse-racing scene (slightly marred by loose gathering in center of book). sg Sept 11 (176) $150

— Yu Hai [volume for Catalog of Chinese Classics Yi King, with commentaries]. [N.p., n.d.]. 8vo, wraps, with painting by Lu Hongnian of a Chinese Christian Scene. Some repairs. Sold w.a.f. P Sept 24 (162) $400

— ADDISON, JOSEPH. - Poetical Works. L, 1807. 24mo, contemp calf with painting of a reclining woman in garter belt & stockings masturbating a man standing over her; rebacked. sg Feb 12 (148) $375

— BACON, SIR FRANCIS. - Verulamiana; or Opinions on Men, Manners, Literature.... L, 1803. 8vo, vellum gilt with paintings of St. Albans & Giddy Hall. Sold w.a.f. P Sept 24 (152) $400

— BACON, THOMAS. - First Impressions and Studies from Nature in Hindostan. L, 1837. 2 vols. 8vo, 19th-cent sheep gilt with views of Whitehall & of Tilbury Fort. sg Sept 11 (131) $375

— BARHAM, RICHARD HARRIS. - The Ingoldsby Legends. L, 1870. 4to, contemp lea gilt with fore-edge of 2 turbaned men in landscape with ocelot. sg Sept 11 (132) $375

Anr Ed. L, 1874. 4to, contemp lea gilt with London view looking across the Thames. sg Sept 11 (133) $350

— BEATTIE, JAMES. - The Minstrel.... L, 1801-3. 2 vols. 12mo, contemp mor gilt with view of Fishmongers' Hall & of horse guards parading. sg Sept 11 (134) $225

— BROOKES, RICHARD. - The Art of Angling, Rock and Sea-Fishing. L, 1740. 1st Ed. 12mo, mor gilt by Zaehnsdorf with painting of an angling scene. S July 23 (279) £350 [Figgis]

— BUNGENER, LAURENCE LOUIS FELIX. - The Preacher and the King. L, 1853. 8vo, contemp lea extra with painting of Sun King emblem flanked by man & woman in 17th-cent dress. sg Sept 11 (136) $130

— BURNS, JOHN. - The Principles of Christian Philosophy. L, 1832. 12mo, contemp mor gilt with view of St. Paul's Cathedral. sg Sept 11 (137) $110

— CAMPBELL, THOMAS. - Poetical Works. Edin., 1837. 4mo, contemp lea gilt with angling scene. sg Sept 11 (138) $140

— CAMPBELL, THOMAS. - The Poetical Works. L, 1846. 8vo, contemp mor gilt with double painting of 2 views at Eton. O Sept 23 (56) $410

— CAMPBELL, THOMAS. - Poetical Works. L, 1851. 8vo, contemp mor gilt with view of Glasgow University. sg Sept 11 (139) $300

— CAMPBELL, THOMAS. - The Poetical Works. L, [c.1870]. 8vo, contemp mor with painting of Bush Hill, near Philadelphia. O Jan 6 (62) $90

— CAMPBELL, THOMAS & COLERIDGE, SAMUEL TAYLOR. - Poetical Works. Edin.: Gall & Inglis, [c.1860]. 12mo, contemp lea gilt with view of coach and horses passing through rugged landscape. sg Sept 11 (140) $250

— COOKSON, JAMES. - A New Family Prayer-Book.... Winchester, 1784. 8vo, contemp mor with early painting of Durham Cathedral. ha Sept 19 (251) $450

— COWPER, WILLIAM. - Poems. L, 1810. 2 vols. 8vo, contemp mor gilt by Taylor & Hessey with painting of a castle with cows & anr of a castle near a village. C Apr 8 (22A) £450 [Weber]

Anr Ed. L, 1840. 8vo, contemp lea gilt with painting of walnut gathering near Newbury, Berkshire; extremities scuffed. sg Sept 11 (143) $120

— COWPER, WILLIAM. - Poetical Works. Edin.: Gall & Inglis, [c.1860]. 12mo, contemp lea gilt with longitudinally-painted view of man standing under tree beside stream while his dog romps in water. sg Sept 11 (142) $325

— COWPER, WILLIAM. - The Task. L, 1825. 24mo, contemp lea gilt with painting of Ross, Herefordshire. sg Sept 11 (144) $200

— CRABBE, GEORGE. - Poetical Works. L, 1851. 8vo, contemp lea extra with painting of a hunting scene. sg Sept 11 (145) $375

Anr Ed. L, [c.1855]. 8vo, contemp mor gilt with painting of 3 English folk outside a cottage; rubbed. O Jan 6 (63) $90

— DAVIES, EDWIN. - Other Men's Minds.... L: Frederick Warne, [1874]. 8vo, mor gilt with painting of a river bank with city scene in background; rubbed. cb Oct 23 (86) $275

— DEMOSTHENES. - The Orations. L, 1872. 12mo, contemp bds with double painting of train crossing bridge at King's Landry & of anr train crossing the bridge over River Amber, Ambergate, Derbyshire; hinge cracked. sg Sept 11 (146) $375

— FALCONER, WILLIAM. - The Shipwreck, a Poem. L, 1804. 8vo, contemp mor gilt with painting of a marine view with frigate under shortened sail; joints weak. sg Sept 11 (149) $275

— FENNELL, JAMES HAMILTON. - A Natural History of British and Foreign Quadrupeds. L, 1843. 8vo, mor gilt with painting of an early scene at the Regents' Park Zoo, including an elephant & a camel. cb Oct 23 (87) $500

— FILICAIA, VINCENZIO DA. - Poesie Toscane. Florence, 1827. 2 vols in 1, 8vo, 19th-cent mor with divided fore-edge paintings of Venice & Florence. Sold w.a.f. P Sept 24

(155) $400
— GORDON, ADAM LINDSAY. - Poems. L, [c.1891]. 8vo, contemp calf gilt with painting of the arrival of the Geelong Mail at Ballarat. sg Sept 11 (151) $200
— HEAD, SIR FRANCIS BOND. - Bubbles from the Brunnens of Nassau. L, 1834. 8vo, contemp mor with painting of a scene in Oxford Street. bba Sept 25 (66) £110 [Hay Cinema]
— HOLLOWAY, WILLIAM. - The Peasants Fate: A Rural Poem.... L, 1802. 8vo, 19th-cent half lea with view of the Thames. sg Sept 11 (152) $200
— HOMER. - The Iliad. L, 1854. 8vo, contemp mor with painting of a lively street scene in Charing Cross. O Sept 23 (59) $220
— IRELAND, SAMUEL. - A Picturesque Tour through Holland, Brabant and part of France. L, 1790. 1st Ed. 2 vols. 4to, mor gilt with painting of Haarlem & cityscape of Amsterdam. With engraved titles & 44 plates, all hand-colored. L.p. copies. sg Dec 4 (72) $950
— KING, EDWARD. - Hymns to the Supreme Being. L, 1798. 8vo, mor by Kalthoeber with painting of a rural scene with a sailboat. Sold w.a.f. P Sept 24 (156) $350
— LAMB, CHARLES. Specimens of English Dramatic Poets.... L, 1849. 8vo, contemp lea with painting of an English seaside village. sg Feb 12 (150) $250
— LANGLAND, WILLIAM. - The Vision and the Creed of Piers Plowman. L, 1832. 2 vols. 12mo, contemp lea gilt with paintings of Shrewsbury, Winchester, Hereford & Ross-on-Wye. sg Sept 11 (154) $600
— LE SAGE, ALAIN RENE. - The Adventures of Gil Blas of Santillane. L, 1836. 2 vols. 8vo, contemp lea gilt with paintings of men dueling & of man on horseback accompanied by anr man on foot; Vol I front hinge cracked. sg Sept 11 (155) $325
— LITTLE, THOMAS. - Works. L, 1819. 12mo, contemp russia with painting of horseman in landscape; broken. sg Sept 11 (157) $110
— LONGFELLOW, HENRY WADSWORTH. - The Poetical Works. Edin., [c.1850]. 8vo, contemp mor with painting of a waterfront scene in Philadelphia. O Sept 23 (60) $200 Anr Ed. L: Warne, [1880]. 8vo, contemp lea with painting of Times Square in New York; rubbed. O Jan 6 (66) $250
— LYTTON, EDWARD GEORGE EARLE BULWER, - Lucile. L, 1867. 12mo, later mor gilt with "action-packed nautical scene with huge whale chomping on whaleboat as crew dives for safety". sg Sept 11 (159) $350
— MACPHERSON, JAMES. - The Poems of Ossian. Glasgow, 1824. 2 vols. 12mo, mor gilt with painting of the Forum of Nerva & of the Temple of Pallas. sg Sept 11 (158)

$300
— MERLE D'AUBIGNE, JEAN HENRI. - History of the Reformation of the Sixteenth Century. Edin., 1847. Vol I. 8vo, contemp lea gilt with centerpiece port of Luther & painting of Gurney's Steam Carriage passing through a town.. sg Sept 11 (160) $225
— MILTON, JOHN. - Poetical Works. L, [later 19th cent]. 8vo, contemp lea with painting of an 18th-cent court tennis scene. sg Sept 11 (161) $130
— MILTON, JOHN. - The Poetical Works. L, 1861. 8vo, contemp mor with painting of an English village scene; rubbed. O Jan 6 (67) $90
Anr Ed. L: Ward, Lock, [c.1870s]. 8vo, contemp lea with painting of a city view; scuffed. sg Feb 12 (151) $100
— MOIR, DAVID MACBETH. - Works. Edin., 1852. Vol II. 12mo, contemp lea gilt with view of Whitehall. sg Sept 11 (162) $100
— NORTON, MRS. _____. The Dream, and Other Poems. L, 1841. 8vo, contemp mor with painting of 2 children playing with a dog-cart. O Jan 6 (68) $130
— OSBORNE, EDWARD. - The Colloquies. L, [1853]. 8vo, contemp mor with double-paintings of scenes of London. Sold w.a.f. P Sept 24 (158) $750
— PLUTARCH. - Lives. Balt.: Neal, 1831. 8vo, mor gilt with view of the Acropolis. sg Sept 11 (163) $140
— POPE, ALEXANDER. - The Poetical Works. Edin.: Gall & Inglin, [c.1860?]. 12mo, contemp lea gilt with painting of an English village. sg Feb 12 (153) $250
— POPE, ALEXANDER. - Works. L: Charles Daly, [c.1840?]. 12mo, contemp lea gilt with painting of Broad Street, Oxford. sg Feb 12 (152) $200
— ROGERS, SAMUEL. - Italy A Poem. L, 1836. 8vo, contemp mor gilt with double paintings of a scenic view of Italy & a view of the Palazzo Guissini in Venice. Sold w.a.f. P Sept 24 (159) $400
— ROGERS, SAMUEL. - The Pleasures of Memory. L, 1796. 12mo, old calf with painting of a stone bridge in a rural setting. Yet anr bdg attributed by pencilled note to Edwards of Halifax. O Sept 23 (62) $300
— ROLLAND, ROMAIN. - Vie de Beethoven. Paris, 1913. 8vo, mor with modern painting of a European city; scuffed. sg Sept 11 (165) $175
— RUSKIN, JOHN. - Selections from the Writings. L, 1894. 2 vols. 8vo, contemp vellum bds gilt with paintings of a seascape with mountain. bba Aug 28 (224) £180 [Subun-So]
— SCOTT, SIR WALTER. - Marmion. Edin., 1808. 8vo, contemp lea with painting of John Knox's house; joints rubbed. sg Sept 11 (167) $225

FORE-EDGE PAINTINGS

Anr Ed. L, 1809. 8vo, contemp mor gilt with painting of Tantallon Castle. sg Sept 11 (168) $150

Anr Ed. L, 1810. 8vo, contemp mor with painting of Hever Castle. O Sept 23 (63) $300

Anr Ed. Edin., 1811. 8vo, mor with painting of London seen from the Thames, by Taylor & Hessey. sg Sept 11 (170) $450

— SCOTT, SIR WALTER. - Marmion; a Tale of Flodden Field. Edin., 1808. 8vo, mor with painting of hunters on horseback. cb Oct 23 (88) $400

— SCOTT, SIR WALTER. - Poetical Works. Edin., 1868. 8vo, contemp lea with painting of men playing golf at Bruntsfield Links. sg Sept 11 (169) $175

— SHELLEY, PERCY BYSSHE. - The Minor Poems. L, 18155. 8vo, modern mor gilt with painting of the Thames & Houses of Parliament. sg Feb 12 (154) $300

— SHEPARD, E. CLARENCE. - Francia, a Tale of the Revolution of Paraguay. L, 1851. 8vo, contemp mor gilt with painting of a street scene in Asuncion; rubbed. bba Sept 25 (67) £110 [Hay Cinema Bookshop]

— SMILES, SAMUEL. - Thrift. L, 11882. 8vo, contemp lea gilt with painting of Oxford. sg Feb 12 (155) $175

— SMITH, ELIZABETH. - Fragments in Prose and Verse. L, 1814. 8vo, contemp mor by Taylor & Hessey with painting (not described). Sold w.a.f. P Sept 24 (161) $1,100

— SOMERVILE, WILLIAM. - The Chase. L, 1796. Bound with: Goldsmith & Parnell. Poems. L, 1795. Illus by Thomas Bewick. 8vo, contemp mor by Henry Walther, with painting of mtd foxhunters & their hounds. sg Dec 4 (183) $750

— STENNETT, SAMUEL. - Discourses on Personal Religion. L, 1796. 8vo, later mor with double painting of scenes in Canterbury & Wells. O Sept 23 (64) $575

— STRUTT, JOSEPH. - The Sports and Pastimes of the People of England. L, 1810. 4to, contemp calf with painting of a fox-hunting scene; rebacked preserving orig spine. O Sept 23 (65) $290

— TASSO, TORQUATO. - La Gerusalemme Liberata. L, 1796. 2 vols. 12mo, mor gilt with paintings of the Rialto at Venice & of the Ponti Sesto in Rome. sg Sept 11 (171) $450

— TAYLOR, JEREMY. - The Rule and Exercises of Holy Dying. L, 1845. 12mo, later lea with painting of a graveyard scene with bone brandisher. sg Sept 11 (172) $200

— TENNYSON, ALFRED. - Enoch Arden. L, 1864. 8vo, mor gilt by Zaehnsdorf dated 1897 with double painting of Thames with St. Paul's in background & with Tower of London & Tower Bridge. sg Sept 11 (173) $475

— TENNYSON, ALFRED. - Idylls of the King. L, 1859. 8vo, contemp mor with scene in Knowles Park. O Sept 23 (66) $190

— TENNYSON, ALFRED. - Works. L, 1884. 8vo, contemp prize bdg of lea gilt with painting of Whitehall. sg Feb 12 (156) $120

Anr Ed. L, 1898. 8vo, contemp lea with painting of topless woman whose streaming hair blends into an abstract pattern behind her. sg Sept 11 (174) $200

— TERENTIUS AFER, PUBLIUS. - Comoediae sex. L, 1825. 12mo contemp calf gilt with painting of a view of Venice across the lagoon. sg Sept 11 (175) $100

— THOMAS A KEMPIS. - On the Imitation of Christ. L, 1865. 12mo, contemp lea with view of St. Paul's. sg Feb 12 (158) $275

— THOMSON, JAMES. - Poetical Works. L, 1805. 12mo, contemp vellum gilt in the style of Edwards of Halifax with painting of a castle, river & bridge. C Apr 8 (22) £220 [Weber]

— TRENCH, RICHARD CHENEVIX. - The Story of Justin Martyr.... L, 1857. 8vo, contemp mor with painting of 2 comical figures duelling with swords. O Jan 6 (70) $140

— WALTON, IZAAK & COTTON, CHARLES. - The Complete Angler, or Contemplative Man's Recreation. L, 1784. 4th Hawkins Ed. 8vo, modern calf with vertical painting of 2 men fishing & a large fish in the water. sg Dec 4 (201) $400

— WINTERBOTHAM, WILLIAM. - An Historical, Geographical, Commercial and Philosophical View of the American United States.... L, 1795. 1st Ed. 4 vols. 8vo, early 19th-cent calf with paintings of Washington, Pyramid of Cholula, New York & Philadelphia; rebacked, corners worn. With 19 (of 22) plates & 2 (of 3) plans; lacking maps & folding tables. sg Dec 4 (73) $475

— WORDSWORTH, WILLIAM. - Poetical Works. L: Frederick Warne, [c.1880]. 8vo, contemp lea with painting of a harbor view; scuffed. sg Feb 12 (158) $275

— YOUNG, EDWARD. - The Complaint: or, Night-Thoughts. L, 1821. 8vo, contemp mor with painting of a Welsh farm scene. O Jan 6 (71) $140

— ZOLLIKOFER, GEORGIUS JOACHIMUS DE. - Exercises of Piety for the Use of Enlightened and Virtuous Christians. L, 1805. 8vo, contemp lea gilt with painting of a landscape view near Abingdon, Berkshire. sg Sept 11 (178) $100

Foreign...

— Foreign Field Sports: Fisheries, Sporting Anecdotes.... L, 1814-13. 1st Ed. 4to, half calf; hinges split. With 110 hand-colored plates. Tear to margin of 1 plate. pn June 18 (31) £720

Anr copy. Contemp mor gilt. Jeanson 1698. SM Mar 1 (231) FF16,000
Anr Ed. L: Edward Orme [c.1823]. Folio, contemp mor gilt; rubbed. With 110 hand-colored plates. S Oct 23 (519) £1,750 [Holland]

Foresi, Bastiano
— Libro chiamato ambizione. [Florence: Antonio di Bartolommeo Miscomini, c.1485]. 4to, 19th-cent mor gilt. 85 (of 90) leaves; lacking first & final blanks, title & 2 leaves of contents. Goff F-243. S Mar 10 (1064) £240 [Callea]

Forester, Johann Georg Adam. See: Forster, Georg

Forester, Thomas
— Rambles in the Islands of Corsica and Sardinia. L, 1858. 8vo, contemp calf gilt; rubbed. With map, hand-colored in outline, & 8 plates. One folding plate torn; tp cropped at lower margin. S May 29 (1045) £140

Foresti, Jacobus Philippus
— Novissime hystoriarum omnium repercussiones. See: Jacobus Philippus de Bergamo

Form...
— Form, a Quarterly of the Arts. L & NY, 1916-17. Vol I, Nos 1 & 2. Folio, orig wraps; worn & slightly def. bba Apr 23 (62) £60 [Fogg]
Anr copy. Orig wraps; No 1 soiled & torn. Ck Oct 31 (159) £200

Forman, Henry Chandler
— Early Manor and Plantation Houses of Maryland.... Easton, [1934]. 4to, cloth. ha May 22 (235) $140

Fornari, Hieronymus de
— De anime humane immortalitate. Bologna: Giustiniano da Rubiera, 22 Dec 1519. 4to, modern bds. Minor marginal dampstains at end. sg Oct 9 (294) $250

Forney, Matthias Nace, 1835-1908
— Locomotives and Locomotive Building.... NY, 1886. 4to, cloth. bba June 18 (96) £55 [Humm]
Anr copy. Orig cloth; soiled & faded. With 34 plates. wa Nov 6 (72) $150

Forrest, Charles Ramus
— A Picturesque Tour along the Rivers Ganges and Jumna. L, 1824. 4to, contemp half calf. With folding map & 24 hand-colored plates. bba Jan 15 (455) £1,300 [Henderson]
Anr copy. Contemp half cloth; worn. With folding map & 24 plates, all hand-colored. Minor soiling to some plates. C Dec 12 (236) £1,400 [Maggs]

Forrest, Earle Robert
— Arizona's Dark and Bloody Ground. Caldwell, Idaho, 1936. 1st Ed. With 23 plates. sg Mar 12 (5) $60

Forrest, Capt. Thomas, 1729?-1802?
— Voyage aux Moluques et a la Nouvelle Guinee.... Paris, 1780. 4to, contemp calf; rubbed, joints split. With 29 (of 30) plates & charts. First few leaves waterstained; some plates cropped. bba Oct 30 (306) £240 [Shapero]

Forrester, Alfred Henry, 1804-72
— A Goodnatured Hint About California. L. D. Bogue, [1849]. 8vo, orig wraps. Several tape repairs & reinforcements to versos. cb Oct 9 (77) $650

Forshaw, J. M.
— Australian Parrots. Melbourne: Lansdowne Editions, 1980. One of 1,000. 2 vols. Folio, orig mor. kh Mar 16 (195) A$480
Anr copy. Mor extra. pn Oct 23 (207) £700 [Graham]
— Parrots of the World. Garden City, 1973. Folio, cloth, in d/j. O Jan 6 (72) $80
Anr Ed. Melbourne, 1973. Folio, orig cloth. With 158 plates. Haverschmidt copy. B Feb 24 (174) HF360
Anr copy. Orig cloth, in d/j. pn Oct 23 (208) £160 [Tryon]

Forssell, Christian Didrik
— Une Annee en Suede.... Stockholm, 1836. 4to, orig cloth. With hand-colored engraved title & 47 hand-colored plates. S May 29 (1046) £260

Forster, Edward Morgan, 1879-1970
— Alexandria: A History and a Guide. Alexandria, 1938. 2d Ed, One of 250, sgd. Orig bds; faded, worn. pnNY Sept 13 (230) $175
— A Passage to India. L, 1924. Cloth; rubbed. cb May 7 (72) $80
Anr copy. Worn. sg Dec 11 (34) $110
— A Room with a View. L, 1908. 1st Ed. Orig cloth, rubbed & bumped. Dampstain affecting lower corner of upper cover & 1st part of text. cb May 7 (73) $75
— The Story of the Siren. Richmond: Hogarth Press, 1920. One of 550. Orig wraps. S Dec 18 (133) £240 [Somner]

Forster, Georg, 1754-94
— A Voyage Round the World.... L, 1777. 2 vols. 4to, contemp russia gilt. C Dec 12 (81) £2,500 [Traylen]
Anr copy. Later half calf. CA Apr 12 (94) A$1,800
Anr copy. Contemp calf; rebacked. With

FORSTER

folding map. S Oct 23 (319) £1,500 [Branners]

Anr copy. Contemp calf gilt. S Apr 24 (377) £2,100 [Perrin]

Forster, George, d.1792
— A Journey from Bengal to England. L, 1798. 2 vols in 1. 4to, calf; rebacked. pn Sept 18 (272) £90 [Shapero]

Forster, Johann Reinhold, 1729-98
— History of the Voyages and Discoveries made in the North. L, 1786. 4to, contemp russia gilt. With 3 folding maps. C Dec 12 (83) £1,600 [Brooke-Hitching]

Anr copy. Contemp russia; rebacked. S Oct 23 (504) £350 [Quaritch]

Anr copy. Contemp calf; rebacked, stamp removed from front cover. With 1 map only (of 3). sg Apr 23 (56) $100

— Observations Made during a Voyage Round the World.... L, 1778. 1st Ed. 4to, contemp russia gilt. With folding map & folding table. C Dec 12 (82) £1,300 [Traylen]

Forster, John, 1812-76
— The Life and Adventures of Oliver Goldsmith. L, 1848. One vol extended to 3. 8vo, modern mor gilt. Extra-illus with c.150 plates. sg Sept 11 (117) $175

— The Life of Charles Dickens. L, 1872-74. 3 vols. 8vo, contemp half calf gilt. With 2 A Ls s laid in. sg Sept 11 (188) $475

Forsyth, James William, 1836-1906 —& Grant, Frederick Dent
— Report of an Expedition up the Yellowstone River. L, 1875. 8vo, orig wraps; soiled. Map with some tears. cb Apr 2 (99) $70

Forsyth, Robert, 1766-1846
— The Principles and Practice of Agriculture. Edin., 1804. 2 vols. 8vo, contemp half mor; rubbed. With frontises & 21 plates. Lacking half-titles; some leaves in Vol I creased at fore-edge. P Nov 25 (198) $100

Forsyth, William, 1737-1804
— A Treatise on the Culture and Management of Fruit-Trees. L, 1802. 1st Ed. 4to, orig bds; backstrip def, worn, spine treated with a clear preservative. With 13 plates. Hunt copy. CNY Nov 21 (123) $130

Anr copy. Contemp sheep; spine ends chipped. sg Jan 15 (211) $70

Anr Ed. Phila., 1802. 8vo, contemp calf; rebacked, worn. With 13 plates. CNY Nov 21 (124) $110

Anr Ed. Albany, 1803. 8vo, contemp calf; rebacked, scuffed & wormed. With 13 plates. sg Jan 15 (212) $70

AMERICAN BOOK PRICES CURRENT

Fort, Paul, 1872-1960
— Les Ballades francaises. Lyons, 1927. One of 120 exemplaires nominatifs, this copy for M. C. Tournier. Illus by Francois Louis Schmied. 4to, unsewn as issued in orig wraps. S Dec 4 (29) £880 [Marks]

Fortescue, Sir John, 1394?-1476
— De laudibus legum Angliae. L, 1660. 8vo, calf; worn, joints split. bba Nov 13 (192) £70 [Bennett & Kerr]

Fortescue, Sir John William, 1858-1933
— A History of the British Army. L, 1910-30. 13 vols in 14, plus 6 map vols. Together, 20 vols. pn Oct 23 (74) £480 [Cavendish]

Fortin, Francois
— Les Ruses innocentes.... Paris, 1660. 4to, contemp mor gilt. With 66 woodcut plates, 9 folding. With the author's name on the title. Jeanson 1546. SM Mar 1 (232) FF50,000

— Les Ruses innocentes, dans lesquelles se voit comment on prend les Oyseaux passagers.... Paris: Charles de Sercy, 1688. 4to, contemp calf. With 66 plates. Jeanson 1091. SM Mar 1 (233) FF17,000

Fortune, Robert, 1813-80
— A Residence among the Chinese. L, 1857. 8vo, orig cloth; worn. pn July 23 (174) £95 [Hay]

Fosbroke, Thomas Dudley, 1770-1842
— Abstracts of Records and Manuscripts respecting the County of Gloucester. Gloucester, 1807. 2 vols. 4to, contemp calf gilt; rubbed, rebacked & repaired, old spines preserved. Extra-illus. bba June 28 (205) £280 [Shapero]

Foskett, Daphne
— A Dictionary of British Miniature Painters. L, 1972. 2 vols. 4to, cloth, in d/js. pn July 23 (139) £130 [Limner]

Fossati, Gaspard, 1809-83
— Aya Sophia, Constantinople, as Recently Restored.... L, [1852]. Folio, orig half mor; def. With litho title & 15 (of 25) colored plates. A few mounts cut down; some marginal discoloration. S Nov 18 (1068) £600 [Shalabi]

Fosse, ——
— Idees d'un militaire pour la disposition des troupes.... Paris, 1783. Illus by L. M. Bonnet. 4to, later half calf. With 11 hand-colored maps. Some soiling & trimming. C May 13 (18) £420 [Dennistoun]

Foster, Alan Dean
— Spellsinger at the Gate. Huntington Woods: Phantasia Press, 1983. One of 450. In d/j. cb Sept 28 (537) $60

Foster, Frank. See: Puseley, Daniel

Foster, George G., d.1850
— The Gold Mines of California. NY, 1848. ("The Gold Regions of California.") 2d Issue. 8vo, disbound. Some foxing. sg Mar 12 (113) $150

2d Ed. 8vo, ptd wraps; torn & chipped, front wrap with small portion missing. sg Mar 12 (114) $150

Foster, Joshua James, 1847-1923
— Miniature Painters British and Foreign. L & NY, 1903. One of 175 de luxe copies. 2 vols. 4to, orig vellum bds; soiled. bba Aug 28 (17) £65 [Blum]

Foster, Samuel, d.1652
— The Art of Dialling.... L: J. R. for Francis Eglesfield, 1675. 4to, modern half calf. Folding plate repaired at lower margin; tp torn with loss to lower margin affecting imprint; most lower blank margins affected by damp, the majority repaired. Ck Jan 30 (39) £260
— Miscellanies: or, Mathematical Lucubrations.... L, 1659. Folio, recent mor. Some dampstains; tp & several leaves strengthened with archival tissue. T Sept 18 (336) $300

Foster, William Harnden
— New England Grouse Shooting. NY, 1942. 4to, orig cloth; front hinge tender. cb May 21 (106) $80

Anr copy. Orig cloth, in d/j; soiled. Inscr. sg Oct 23 (273) $70

Fothergill, George Algernon
— An Old Raby Hunt Album, 1786-1899. Edin., 1899. Ltd Ed. Folio, orig half cloth; worn. cb May 21 (107) $160

Foudras, Theodore Louis Auguste, Marquis de, 1800-72
— Un Capitaine de Beauvoisis. Paris. CAdot, 1849 [but 1852-51]. 4 vols. 8vo, orig bdgs. Schwerdt-Jeanson copy. SM Mar 1 (234) FF4,400
— Les Gentilshommes chasseurs. Paris: Alexandre Cadot, 1850-51. 2 vols. 8vo, contemp calf calf. Jeanson copy. SM Mar 1 (235) FF2,000

Fougasses, Thomas de
— The General Historie of the Magnificent State of Venice.... L, 1612. 2 vols. Folio, 18th-cent calf gilt; spine worn. Lacking final blank. Ck Jan 30 (17) £170

Fouilloux, Jacques du. See: Du Fouilloux, Jacques

Fouquier, Marcel
— Les Grands Chateaux de France. Paris, 1907. 2 vols. Folio, contemp half mor; extremities worn. Fore-edges foxed. cb Mar 5 (68) $80

Fourcroy, Antoine Francois de, 1755-1809
— Synoptic Tables of Chemistry. L, 1801. Folio, orig wraps; upper cover torn at outer margin & extreme upper corner torn off, spine def. With 12 double-page tables. Outer blank margins creased. S May 21 (196) £500 [Phelps]

Anr copy. Contemp half calf; worn. Detached from guards throughout; some stains. S July 28 (1073) £350
— Tableaux synoptiques de chimie. Paris, 1800 [An VIII]. Folio, contemp half sheep; rubbed. C Dec 12 (85) £1,200 [Rota]

Fourier, Jean Baptiste Joseph, 1768-1830
— Oeuvres. Paris, 1888-90. 2 vols. 4to, orig wraps, unopened. cb June 4 (71) $90

Fourmont, Etienne
— Linguae sinarum mandarinicae hieroglyphicae grammatica.... Paris, 1742. Folio, contemp calf; joints def. S Apr 23 (340) £700 [Ad Orientum]

Fourreau, Jules. See: Jordan & Fourreau

Fovargue, Stephen
— A New Catalogue of Vulgar Errors. Cambr., 1767. 8vo, modern half calf. Lacking final blank; some stains. bba Nov 13 (225) £60 [Axe]

Fowler, Arthur Anderson
— The Ballad of Myra Gray and other Sporting Verse. By Somerset. NY: Pvtly ptd, 1927. One of 250. Half cloth; worn. Inscr. sg Oct 23 (274) $50

Fowler, Laurence Hall —& Baer, Elizabeth
— The Fowler Architectural Collection of the Johns Hopkins University: Catalogue. Balt, 1961. One of a few copies with Fowler's name spelled Lawrence. 4to, orig cloth. With cancel title laid in. ha Mar 13 (227) $675

Fowles, John
— The Collector. Bost., [1963]. Advance copy. Wraps. wa June 25 (355) $100

Anr Ed. L, [1963]. In d/j. bba Nov 13 (293) £00 [Hay]

Anr copy. In soiled & chipped d/j. Burn mark affecting 2 prelim leaves. cb May 7 (74) $110

Anr copy. In torn & soiled d/j. S Jan 13

FOWLES

(566) £70 [Conway]
Anr copy. Bds in d/j. T May 20 (31) £140
— The French Lieutenant's Woman. L, 1969. In d/j. Literary Guild rubberstamp at foot of title page. Sgd. cb May 7 (75) $110
Anr copy. Orig wraps, in d/j. kh Mar 16 (196B) A$90
Anr copy. In d/j. sg Mar 5 (79) $90
Uncorrected proofs. Orig wraps. bba Oct 30 (249) £95 [Maggs]
— The Magus. L: Jonathan Cape, [1966]. 1st Ed. In d/j. cb May 7 (76) $130
1st English Ed. sg Dec 11 (35) $90

Fox, Augustus Henry Lane. See: Pitt-Rivers, Augustus Henry Lane Fox

Fox, George, 1624-91
— A Journal, or Historical Account of the Life, Travels.... L, 1765. 3d Ed. Folio, old calf; worn & scuffed with some peeling. Title tape-repaired, a few leaves attached but separated. ha Sept 192 (260) $70

Fox, George Henry
— Photographic Illustrations of Skin Diseases. NY, 1881. 4to, half mor; worn. With 48 plates by Edward Bierstadt, colored by Dr. Joseph Gaertner. Browned & foxed throughout. wa Sept 25 (249) $110

Fox, Lady Mary
— Account of an Expedition to the Interior of New Holland. L, 1837. 8vo, contemp cloth; rubbed, dampstained. bba Nov 13 (104) £95 [Bonham]

Foxon, D. F.
— English Verse 1701-1750. Cambr., 1975. 2 vols. 4to, cloth, in d/js. sg Jan 22 (159) $80

Fox's...
— The Fox's Prophecy. NY: Sporting Gallery & Bookshop, 1939. Bds. Inscr by Melville E. Stone of the gallery. sg Oct 23 (277) $90

Foyer, Archibald
— A Defence of the Scots Settlement at Darien. L, 1699. 8vo, mor. C Dec 12 (328) £240 [Drury]

Foy-Vaillant, Jean
— Numismata aerea imperatorum, Augustarum, et Caesarum.... Paris, 1697. 2 parts in 1 vol. Folio, contemp vellum. sg Oct 9 (281) $140

Fracastoro, Girolamo, 1483-1553
— Syphilis, sive morbus gallicus. Verona, 1530. 1st Ed. 4to, recent vellum. Marginal dampstains; tp cleaned & with stamp removed; lacking 1 blank. S May 21 (197) £2,000 [Thomas]

AMERICAN BOOK PRICES CURRENT

Fraccus, Ambrosius Novidius
— Sacrorum fastorum libri XII. Rome: Ant. Bladus Asulanus, 1547. 4to, contemp calf. Minor worming to upper margins. sg Mar 26 (120) $700

Fragmenta...
— Fragmenta poetarum veterum latinorum quorum opera.... Geneva: Henricus Stephanus, 1564. 8vo, mor gilt by Roger Payne. Hoe copy. S Sept 23 (451) £280 [Busck]

Francais...
— Les Francais peints par eux-memes. Paris, 1840-42. 9 vols. 8vo, contemp half lea. With 9 frontises, double-page map & 404 (of 407) plates. B Feb 25 (936) HF1,100
Anr copy. Half calf. SM Oct 20 (452) FF4,500

France

Laws & Statutes

— De C. IX. Mandement expres du roy, sur peine de la vie a toutes personnes.... Lyon 1562. 8vo, half mor by Prat. SM Mar 1 (435) FF2,000
— Ensuyt le pris que les pouailliers, regratiers, rotisseurs & tout autres vedront chascune piece de volaille.... [Paris: Jacques Niverd, 1546]. 4to, mor janseniste by Cuzin. Jeanson copy. SM Mar 1 (475) FF14,000
— Les Loix statutz et ordonnances du royaulme de France.... [Paris: Alain Lotrian pour Jean Petit, 1519 or 1520]. 4to, mor gilt by Trautz-Bauzonnet. Jeanson copy. SM Mar 1 (432) FF36,000
— Ordonnance du Roy...sur le faict de la Chasse.... Paris: Veuve Jacques Nyverd, 1549. 8vo, mor janseniste by Duru 1849. Jeanson copy. SM Mar 1 (434) FF5,500
— Ordonnances faictes par le Roy...sur le Faict des chasses eaues.... Paris: Richard Gonault, [1548]. 8vo, vellum. Jeanson copy. SM Mar 1 (433) FF5,800
— Le Taux & Pris aquoy les vollaiges & givier doibuent estre venduz par les poullailliers de ceste ville & faulxbourgs de Paris. Paris: Jacques Niverd, [1546]. 4to, mor janseniste by Cuzin. Jeanson copy. SM Mar 1 (476) FF28,000

France, Anatole, 1844-1924
See also: Limited Editions Club
— Clio. Paris, 1900. Illus by Alphonse Mucha. 8vo, bds, orig wraps bound in. S Oct 6 (682) £70 [Marks]
Anr copy. Orig wraps. S Nov 27 (68) £90 [Crete]
Anr copy. Half cloth, orig wraps bound in. sg June 4 (221) $80

— Les Dieux ont soif. Brussels, 1938. One of 124 on velin. Illus by Sylvain Sauvage. 4to, half calf gilt by Rene Assourd, orig wraps bound in. HN May 20 (2430) DM1200

— Histoire comique. Paris, 1926. One of 20 with 2 extra suites of illusts on chine & japon. Illus by Llano-Florez. Mor gilt by Crette, orig wraps bound in. With a 3d extra copy of the frontis, sgd, bound in & with ALs of France tipped in & 4-page holograph assessment of the book by Claude Areline. P Sept 24 (109A) $500

— La Leçon bien apprise.... Paris, 1898. Illus by Leon Lebegue. 4to, mor gilt by Carayon, orig wraps bound in. With 25 colored illusts; bound in is anr set of the illusts without the text & in uncolored state. S Sept 23 (664) £160 [Thorpns]

The Life of Joan of Arc. L: John Lane, 1909. One of 500. 2 vols. Mor extra with vignette of Joan on steed on both covers, by Riviere. cb Sept 11 (251) $275

— Thais. Paris, 1900. One of 300. Illus by Paul-Albert Laurens. 8vo, mor extra with inlays by Affolter, orig wraps bound in. With 7 plates in 4 states, 2 title vignettes & 51 illusts in the text in 3 states. Opening lines of the work copied in ink & sgd by Anatole France. With 5 A Ls s from Affolter to Elie M. Cattavi inserted. S Sept 23 (662) £260 [Anciens]

Anr Ed. Paris, 1909. One of 150 on japon with plates in 3 states. Illus by E. Decisy after Georges Rochegrosse. Mor gilt by Bernascon, orig wraps bound in. S Oct 6 (694) £100 [Saynof]

— Vie de Jeanne d'Arc. Paris, [1909-10]. One of 300. 4 vols. 4to, half mor by Pagnant, orig wraps bound in. B Oct 7 (337) HF400

— Works. NY, 1924. Autograph Ed, one of 1,075. 30 vols. half cloth; rubbed. ha May 22 (56) $100

Anr copy. Half mor gilt by Stikeman. sg Sept 11 (189) $650

Francesco III, Duke of Modena
— Della storia e della ragione d'ogni poesia. Bologna, 1739-52. 5 vols in 7. 4to, contemp calf; joints split. bba Oct 30 (190) £70 [Erlini]

Franchere, Gabriel, 1786-1863
— Narrative of a Voyage to the Northwest Coast of America.... NY, 1854. 1st American Ed. 8vo, orig cloth; chipped, worn & soiled, front hinge broken. With 3 plates. wa June 25 (231) $150

Franchi, Diego de
— Historia del patriarcha S. Giovangualberto primo abbate & institutore del monastico ordine di Vallombrosa. Florence: Gio. Batista landini, 1640. 4to, 18th-cent half calf; spine wormed. Tear in fore-margin just touching a ptd margin note & in the inner blank margin of Xx1. S May 21 (105) £220 [Parikian]

Franchieres, Jean de
— La Fauconnerie.... Poitiers: Enguilbert de Marnef et les Bouchetz freres, 1567. 4to, 17th-cent calf; worn. Heber-Offremont-Pichon-Jeanson copy. SM Mar 1 (238) FF52,000

Francis, Charles Richard
— Sketches of Native Life in India.... L, 1848. 4to, contemp cloth; rebacked in calf. With 22 plates. S May 29 (1127) £260

Francis, Dick
— Bonecrack. L, 1971. In d/j. Inscr. cb Nov 20 (184) $110
— Dead Cert. L.: Michael Joseph, 1962. Uncorrected proof copy. Orig ptd wraps. T Oct 15 (59) £310
— For Kicks. L, 1965. In d/j with small tear to upper right corner. cb Nov 20 (186) $100
— Odds Against. L, 1965. In d/j. cb Nov 20 (188) $100

Francis, Francis
— A Book on Angling: a Complete Treatise.... L, 1867. 1st Ed. 8vo, half calf; rubbed. pn Nov 20 (192) £55 [Brown]

Francis of Assisi, Saint, 1182-1226
See also: Ashendene Press; Limited Editions Club
— The Canticle of the Sun. NY: Press of Valenti Angelo, [1951]. One of 100. cb Dec 4 (310) $85

Franciscans
— Monumenta ordinis minorum. Salamanca: Juan de Porras et industria fratrum minorum, 1511. 4to, modern mor gilt. Lower outer corner of margin of AA2 torn away; hole in lower margin running through 2d section of the work; a few small wormholes at beginning & end repaired. S Nov 27 (14) £900 [Thomas]

Francisci, Erasmus
— Ost- und West-Indischer wie auch Sinesischer Lust- und Stats-Garten.... Nuremberg, 1668. Folio, contemp lea gilt. With engraved title & 66 plates. FD Dec 2 (912) DM2,600

Anr copy. Contemp pigskin; worn. Marginal tears; p 1503 def; some waterstains & foxing. Crahan copy. P Nov 25 (200) $750

Franck, Richard
— Northern Memoirs.... Edin., 1821. Ltd Ed. Preface & notes by Sir Walter Scott. 8vo, calf gilt. pnE Dec 17 (319) £180 [Steedman] Anr copy. Modern mor. sg Oct 23 (278) $175

Franck, Sebastian, 1499-1543?
— Weltbuech. Tuebingen: Ulrich Morhart, 1534. Folio, 19th-cent half lea. Some browning & waterstaining. HK Nov 4 (634) Dm1,050

Francklin, William
— Military Memoirs of G. Thomas. Calcutta, 1803. 1st Ed. 4to, contemp half calf; rubbed, upper joint split. With frontis, folding plate & map (both slightly torn). S May 29 (1191) £550

Franco, Francisco Soares
— Ensaio sobre os melhoramentos de Portugal.... Lisbon, 1820-21. 4 orig parts. 4to, disbound & laid in early bd portfolio. P Sept 24 (288) $370

Francois, Rene. See: Binet, Etienne; Binet, Etienne

Francucci, Scipione
— La Caccia etrusca, poema. Florence: I. Giunti, 1624. 4to, contemp calf. Some browning. Jeanson copy. SM Mar 1 (239) FF1,900

Frane, Jeff —&
Rems, Jack
— A Fantasy Reader: The Seventh World Fantasy Convention Book. Berkeley, [1981]. One of 1,000. In d/j. cb Sept 28 (540) $50

Frank, B. F. —&
Chappell, H. W.
— The History and Business Directory of Shasta County. Redding CA: Redding Independent Book & Job Printing, [1881]. 8vo, contemp bds with syn spine, orig front wrap bound in after p 4 & orig back wrap bound in after p 36. cb Oct 9 (218) $180

Frank Leslie's...
— Frank Leslie's Illustrated Newspaper. NY, 1861-65. Vols XI-XIX. Folio, contemp half mor; rubbed, 1 vol broken. bba Dec 18 (150) £900 [Jeffrey]

Frank, Robert
— The Americans. NY, [1959]. Intro by Jack Kerouac. In repaired d/j. Sgd on half-title. sg May 7 (38) $750

Frankau, Julia, 1864-1916
— Eighteenth Century Artists. William Ward...James Ward.... L, 1904. Portfolio only. Folio, loose as issued in orig cloth; lacking ties. With 40 plates, 19 colored. bba Mar 26 (45) £650 [Sanders]

— The Story of Emma, Lady Hamilton. L, 1911. 2 vols. Folio, orig vellum gilt; 1 cover waterstained. bba Jan 15 (130) £50 [Erlini]

Frankfurter...
— Frankfurter Mess-Relation; das ist, Halbjaehrliche Erzhelungen der neusten Staats- und Welt-Geschichten.... Frankfurt, [1765-70]. For the years 1764-70. 12 parts in 1 vol. 4to, old half lea. Minor stains; worming in inner corners. sg Oct 9 (210) $275

Franklin, Alfred
— Dictionnnaire des noms, surnoms, et pseydonymes latins de l'histoire litteraire du Moyen Age.... Paris, 1875. 8vo, contemp half lea. sg Jan 22 (160) $70

Franklin, Benjamin, 1706-90
See also: Limited Editions Club

— Autobiography. L, 1818-19. ("Memoirs of the Life and Writings....") 6 vols. 8vo, contemp calf; spines worn. Ck Jan 16 (6) £75

— Political, Miscellaneous, and Philosophical Pieces.... L, 1779. 8vo, contemp calf; rebacked. pnE Jan 28 (25) £320 [Maggs] Anr copy. Contemp calf; rebacked, several leaves loose at ends. Library markings. sg Sept 18 (95) $200 Anr copy. Modern cloth. Upper margins of 1st 4 leaves dampstained. sg Mar 12 (115) $250

— The Way to Wealth, or Poor Richard Improved. Paris, 1795. One of 6 L.p. copies. 8vo, mor extra by Bozerian. Nodier-Hoe-Bishop copy. FD June 11 (3981) DM13,500

Franklin Printing, Benjamin
— CICERO, MARCUS TULLIUS. - Cato Major. Phila., 1744. 1st Ed, 2d State, with "only" on p. 27. 8vo, contemp calf gilt; joints cracked. Small hole & minute tear to blank margin of title; some foxing & soiling. P May 13 (9) $2,200

— EVANS, LEWIS. - Geographical, Historical, Political, Philosophical and Mechanical Essays. Phila., 1755. 1st Ed, 1st Issue of text, 1st Issue of map. 4to, orig wraps. Map with contemp coloring. C Oct 15 (34) £11,000 [Arader]

Franklin, Jean Dwight
— Why. NY: Derrydale Press, 1929. One of 900. sg Oct 23 (49) $200

Franklin, Sir John, 1786-1847
— Narrative of a Journey to the Shores of the Polar Sea.... L, 1823. 1st Ed. 4to, half mor; upper cover detached. With 4 maps & 30 plates, 10 hand-colored. Perforated library stamp on tp & maps; ink stamp on plates. bba Mar 26 (339) £100 [Rainer]
Anr copy. Old calf gilt; rebacked. With 30 plates (26 hand-colored), the 1st a later copy. pnNY Sept 13 (231) $325
— Narrative of Journey to the Shores of the Polar Sea.... L, 1823. 1st Ed. 4to, contemp calf; rebacked preserving orig spine. With 30 plates (11 hand-colored) & 4 folding maps. Small hole affecting 1 letter on b3. S Nov 10 (1224) £380 [Bonham]
— Narrative of a Journey to the Shores of the Polar Sea.... L, 1824. 2d Ed. 2 vols. 8vo, modern half lea; worn. Library stamps on plates, map with additional perforated stamp. sg Mar 12 (116) $80

Franks, David
— The New York Directory...for...1786. NY, 1786. 12mo, mor gilt. Scorched, occasionally obscuring legibility; each leaf separately encapsulated; 12 of the 41 leaves remargined on at least 1 side; lacking final blank; other defs. Sold w.a.f. P May 13 (10) $2,600

Franzini, Federico
— Roma antica e moderna. Rome, 1678. 8vo, vellum. S Nov 10 (905) £95 [Henderson]

Fraser, James Baillie, 1783-1856
— Journal of a Tour through Part of the Snowy Range of the Himala Mountains.... L, 1820. 1st Ed. 4to, contemp calf gilt. With folding map. Lacking half-title. C Apr 8 (88) £700 [Gaston]
— Narrative of a Journey into Khorasan.... L, 1825. 1st Ed. 4to, modern calf; orig cover preserved. pn Dec 11 (98) £360 [Lomax]
— Views in the Himala Mountains. L, 1820. Folio, contemp half calf; worn, spine chipped. With hand-colored title & 20 hand-colored plates, all on guards. Some plates soiled or stained. Ck Nov 21 (230A) £5,000 [Rostron]

Fraser, Sir William, 1816-98
— The Chiefs of Grant. Edin., 1883. One of 150. 3 vols. 4to, orig lea gilt. sg Feb 12 (276) $50

Frasier, Isaac
— A Brife Account of the Life, and Abominable Thefts, of the Notorious Isaac Frasier...penned from his own Mouth.... [New Haven: T. & S. Green, 1768]. 8vo, later wraps. Lacking final leaf with the conclusion of his death speech; tp present in part only. Some tears & chips. sg Mar 12 (117) $650

Frazer, Sir James George, 1854-1941
— The Golden Bough. 1936-37. 3d Ed. 12 vols, including Bibliography & General Index all but 2 with d/js. pn Jan 22 (254A) £85 [Grant]
Anr Ed. L, 1936-37. 12 vols plus Supplement. Ck Oct 17 (158) £150
Anr Ed. NY, 1951. 13 vols. Cloth. s Nov 10 (376) £110 [Traylen]

Frazier, Don
— Recognizing Derrydale Press Books. Long Valley, NJ: Pvtly ptd, 1983. One of 347. Lea. Inscr. sg Oct 23 (154) $70

Freart, Roland, Sieur de Chambray
— A Parallel of the Antient Architecture with the Modern.... L, 1723. 3d Ed. Trans by John Evelyn. 2 parts in 1 vol. Folio, contemp calf; hinges split. With engraved frontis, port & 40 plates; title frayed. T Sept 18 (483) £95

Frederick II, Emperor
— The Art of Falconry.... Stanford CA, 1961. 4to, cloth. With 188 plates. B Feb 24 (134) HF350
— Reliqua librorum Friderici II, Imperatoris, De arte venandi cum avibus. Augsburg: J. Praetor, 1596. 8vo, mor gilt by Trautz-Bauzonnet. Jeanson 1485. SM Mar 1 (242) FF18,000
Anr Ed. Graz, 1969. ("De arte venandi cum avibus.") Ltd Ed. 2 vols. Folio, orig calf & half calf. HN Nov 26 (66) DM1,600

Frederick II, King of Prussia
See also: Washington's copy, George
— Oeuvres posthumes. Berlin, [Strasbourg] 1788. 1st Ed. 15 vols. 8vo, contemp calf gilt; spines rubbed. bba Jan 15 (361) £110 [Nosbuesch]
Anr Ed. Berlin, 1789. 15 vols. 8vo, contemp calf. pnE Jan 28 (31) £210 [Josephs]

Frederiks, Johan Willem
— Dutch Silver. The Hague, 1952-61. 4 vols. 4to, cloth, in d/js. S Nov 10 (83) £420 [Tulkens]

Free Society of Traders in Pennsylvania. See: Pennsylvania

Freeman, Archibald. See: Fite & Freeman

Freeman, Douglas Southall, 1886-1953
— R. E. Lee: A Biography. NY, 1936. 4 vols. Half mor. sg Sept 11 (225) $425
Anr Ed. NY, 1937. 4 vols. sg Sept 18 (159) $60

Freeman, Richard Austin, 1862-1943
— A Certain Dr. Thorndyke. L, 1927. In chipped & repaired d/j. Goldstone copy. cb Nov 20 (192) $100
— The Eye of Osiris. L, [c.1911]. Bdg rubbed, spine creased. cb Nov 20 (195) $110

Fregoso, Antonio, d.1515
— Cerva biancha. Milan: J. A. Scinzenzeler, 23 Jan 1517. 8vo, 18th-cent vellum. Schwerdt-Jeanson copy. SM Mar 1 (243) FF3,200
Anr Ed. Venice: Nicolo Zopino de Aristotile, 22 Mar 1525. 8vo, contemp blindstamped mor with figure of blind Love in center. Jeanson copy. SM Mar 1 (244) FF10,800

Freiligrath, Ferdinand —&
Schuecking, Christoph Bernhard Levin
— Das Malerische und romantische Westfalen. Barmen, [1842]. 8vo, contemp half calf; rubbed. With engraved title & 29 plates. A few leaves loose; some spotting. JG Oct 2 (1180) DM1,700
2d Ed. Paderborn, 1872. 8vo, orig cloth; worn, spine def. With 28 plates. Some spotting. HN Nov 26 (474) DM1,800
Anr copy. Contemp half lea. sg Nov 20 (157) $260

Freind, John, 1675-1728
— The History of Physick. L, 1725-26. 1st Ed. 2 vols. 8vo, contemp calf. pnE Dec 17 (94) £180 [Maggs]

Fremont, John Charles, 1813-90
— Geographical Memoir upon Upper California.... San Francisco: Book Club of Calif., 1964. One of 425. cb June 18 (22) $50
— Memoirs of my Life. Chicago, 1887. Vol I (all pbd). 4to, mor gilt extra; rubbed & scuffed. With 7 maps & 81 (of 82) plates. cb Oct 9 (78) $225
Anr copy. 4to, cloth. With 7 maps & 82 plates. cb July 16 (99) $130
— Report of the Exploring Expedition to the Rocky Mountains.... Wash., 1845. 1st Ed, House Issue. 8vo, recent cloth. With 27 maps & plates; folding map splitting along central crease. cb Jan 8 (63) $250
Anr copy. Contemp half calf. Lacking 1 plate & 2 folding maps. cb Apr 2 (101) $110

Anr copy. Half lea; worn, joints broken. Lacking folding map. Sold w.a.f. Clipped signature tipped to front pastedown. O Oct 21 (65) $50
Senate Issue. Orig cloth; rebacked, orig spine preserved. Folding map with slight wear at some folds. cb Mar 19 (95) $400
Anr copy. Cloth; bound upside down. Some edge tears, minor stains & fold breaks to folding map. O Nov 18 (69) $250
Anr copy. Orig cloth; worn. With 22 plates & 4 (of 5) maps, lacking that in pocket. Foxed. sg Sept 18 (97) $200

Frenaud, Andre
— Poemes de Brandebourg. Paris, 1947. One of 150 on vellum. Illus by Jacques Villon. 4to, orig wraps. With 6 colored etchings. SM Oct 20 (676) FF5,500

French, John, 1616?-57
— The Art of Distillation.... L, 1651. 1st Ed. 4to, modern calf. Soiled; frayed. Crahan copy. P Nov 25 (202) $500
2d Ed. L, 1653-52. 2 parts in 1 vol. 4to, later calf; rubbed. Marginal tears; some soiling & spotting. S Nov 10 (489) £200 [Spelman]

French, Paul. See: Asimov, Isaac

Frere, Benjamin
— The Adventures of a Dramatist on a Journey to the London Managers. L, 1813. 2 vols. 12mo, contemp calf. Minor waterstaining. C Dec 12 (86) £260 [Hannas]

Freshfield, Douglas W., 1845-1934
— The Exploration of the Caucasus. L, 1896. 1st Ed. 2 vols. 4to, orig cloth; rubbed & soiled, shelf numbers on spines, 1 spine torn. Library markings. bba Feb 5 (349) £100 [Rainer]

Freud, Sigmund, 1856-1939
— Drei Abhandlung zur Sexualtheorie. Leipzig & Vienna, 1905. 8vo, orig wraps; backstrip worn. sg Dec 4 (74) $1,200
— Gesammelte Schriften. Vienna, 1925-34. Vols I-XI (of 12). 8vo, orig cloth; some covers dampstained. bba Oct 30 (384) £85 [Nosbuesch]
— Die infantile Cerebrallaehmung. Vienna, 1897. 8vo, half mor. Vol IX of Specielle Pathologie und Therapie. S May 28 (667) £160

Freville, Anne Francois Joachim de
— Histoire des nouvelles decouvertes faites dans la Mer du Sud.... Paris, 1774. 2 vols. 8vo, old calf gilt; spines rubbed. pnNY Sept 13 (219) $140

Frexneda, Bernardo de
— Estatutos de la Sancta Yglesia Cathedral de Cordova. Antequera: por Andres Lobato, 1577. Folio, contemp calf gilt with ecclesiastical arms in gilt with a vellum onlay; rubbed & wormed. Some worming affecting a small amount of ptd surface of several leaves; ff. 60-61 with a slit up the inner margin; margins of final leaf trimmed; some dampstains. S June 25 (22) £850

Freycinet, Louis Claude Desaulses de, 1799-1842
— Voyage de decouvertes aux Terres Australes.... Paris, 1811. Part 2 of Atlas vol only. Folio, orig bds; badly worn & shaken. With 2 folding maps & 12 single maps. Folding maps with separations at several fold-lines & foxed; 1st folding map waterstained. sg Nov 20 (188) $1,400

Frezier, Amedee Francois, 1682-1773
— Relation du voyage de la Mer du Sud.... Amst., 1717. 2 vols in 1. 12mo, old vellum bds; soiled. Marginal dampstaining. S July 14 (802) £220
— Traite des feux d'artifice. The Hague: Jean Neaulme, 1741. 12mo, contemp calf. With frontis & 8 folding plates. sg Jan 15 (346) $250

Anr Ed. Paris, 1747. 8vo, contemp sheep. With 13 folding plates. sg Jan 15 (347) $225

Anr copy. Contemp sheep; rebacked. sg Jan 15 (348) $200
— A Voyage to the South Sea.... L, 1717. 4to, contemp calf. With 37 maps, plans & views. Tp repaired touching letters; some marginal worming. S Nov 10 (1008) £400 [Cavendish]

Anr copy. 2 vols. 12mo, contemp calf; spine ends worn. With 37 plates & maps. Upper margin of 1 plate extended. S Apr 24 (301) £750 [Maggs]

Anr copy. Contemp calf; rebacked & repaired. Minor dampstaining to lower portion of outer margin. sg Mar 12 (119) $475

Frick, Childs
— Long Point Glimpses, Oh Don't Forget Your Gear and Old Fowler. By a Long Pointer. Long Island: Pvtly ptd, 1942. Inscr. sg Oct 23 (280) $80

Frick, Christoph —& Schewitzer, Christoph
— A Relation of Two Several Voyages Made into the East-Indies. L, 1700. 1st Ed in English. 8vo, modern half mor. Annotations in an 18th-cent hand. S Apr 24 (341) £400 [Schwager]

Fricx, Eugene Henri
— Atlas des Pays Bas. [Amst.: J. Coverns & C. Mortier, 1745?]. Folio, contemp calf; worn. With 23 maps mtd as 8 long strips. Lacking title sheet. S Nov 17 (853) £320 [Arjomanc]
— Cartes de Pays-Bas et des frontieres de France. [Brussels, 1712]. Folio, orig lea. With 25 double-page maps & 48 battle plans. Dampstained throughout. pn May 21 (183b) £500 [Greenwood]
— Table des cartes des Pay Bas et des frontieres de France.... [Brussels, 1712 or later]. Folio, contemp calf; worn. With 37 double-page or folding maps only. Lacking tp & 20 of the 24-sheet map of the Southern Netherlands, but including 2 states of the plan of Bethune. S Nov 27 (162) £160 [Marshall]

Friederichs, Hulda
— In the Evening of his Days.... L, 1896. 8vo, cloth; backstrip faded. sg Oct 30 (78) $175

Friedlaender, Max J., 1852-1934
— Die altniederlandische Malerei. Berlin & Leiden, 1924-37. 14 vols. 4to, orig half cloth; soiled. S May 6 (378) £220 [Zwemmer]

Friedlaender, Max J., 1852-1934 —& Rosenberg, Jakob
— Die Gemaelde von Lucas Cranach. Berlin, 1932. 4to, orig cloth; worn. O Jan 6 (75) $80

Friend, A. See: Mangin, Edward

Friendly...
— A Friendly Letter to Little Children, by a Lover of Children. L: for Richard Hett, 1741. 12mo, contemp wraps. C Dec 12 (329) £220 [Quaritch]

Fries, Elias Magnus, 1794-1878
— Icones selectae hymenomycetum nondun delineatorum.... Uppsala, 1867-84. 2 vols, 10 fasicules. 4to, sewn but stitching broken. With port & 200 colored plates. C Oct 15 (229) £1,800 [Wheldon & Wesley]

Frink, Margaret A.
— Journal of the Adventures of a Party of California Gold-Seekers.... [Oakland, 1897]. 12mo, orig cloth; front hinge split. sg Sept 18 (99) $800

Frith, Francis
— Egypt and Palestine Photographed and Described.... L: Virtue, 1857. 2 vols. Folio, contemp half mor; broken, spine of Vol II lacking. With 76 mtd albumen prints. Foxed throughout, affecting text leaves & plate margins. Library markings. sg May 7 (39) $1,500

FRITH

— The Gossiping Photographer on the Rhine. Reigate: Frith, [1864]. 4to, orig cloth; broken. With orig mtd photo on title, orig mtd photograph of Tombleson's map of the Rhine & 14 views. S Oct 23 (250) £400 [Quaritch]

— Lower Egypt, Thebes, and the Pyramids. L, [c.1862]. Folio, orig cloth; rebacked, rubbed. With 111 mtd photographs. bba May 28 (287) £950 [Dawson]

Frith, John, 1503-33

— A Boke Made by John Frith Prisoner in the Tower of London.... L: Anthony Scoloker & William Seres, 1548. 4th Ed. 8vo, old calf; rebacked. Dampstained; apparently lacking 1st 4 leaves, next few leaves chipped along fore-edge; last 2 leaves repaired in lower margin. sg Mar 26 (122) $175

— Vox Piscis: or, the Book-Fish Containing three Treatises.... L, 1627 [1626]. 1st Ed. 4 parts in 1 vol. 12mo, contemp vellum; slightly discolored. A few small holes (1 in 3E4 slightly affecting text) or marginal tears repaired; portion of 2E11 torn away, not affecting text. S July 24 (389) £320 [Drury]

Frith, John Henry

— Repository Exercise. Compiled for the Use of the Madras Artillery.... Madras, 1850. Folio, later cloth. Lithographed throughout including 45 explanatory plates. Some blindstamps. Inscr. S Apr 23 (342) £550 [Quaritch]

Frith, William Powell, 1819-1909

— John Leech: his Life and Work. L, 1891. 2d Ed. 2 vols. 8vo, mor gilt. Extra-illus. S July 14 (500) £200

Anr copy. Unbound gatherings & plates loose in 2 cloth folders as issued. sg Sept 11 (119) $130

Fritsch, Gustav, 1838-1927

— Drei Jahre in Suedafrika. Breslau, 1868. 8vo, orig cloth. With folding map & 7 colored lithos. SSA Oct 28 (582) R620

Fritsch, K. E. O.

— Denkmaeler Deutscher Renaissance. Berlin, 1882-91. 3 vols (lacking text vol). Folio, contemp half mor gilt. With 300 plates. C July 22 (77) £460

Frizzi, Benedetto

— Difesa contro gli attachi fatti alla nazione ebrea nel libro intitolato: Della influenza del ghetto nello stato. Paris, 1784. 8vo, vellum bds; small wormhole on upper cover. Tp & a few other leaves foxed. S Nov 27 (164) £480 [Cats]

Froelich, Erasmus

— Notitia elementaris, numismatum antiquorum illorum. Vienna & Prague, 1758. 1st Ed. 4to, contemp calf gilt; front joint cracked, corners worn. With 22 folding plates; upper margin of opening leaves dampstained. sg Oct 9 (282) $50

Frohawk, Frederick William

— Natural History of British Butterflies. L, [1914]. 2 vols. Folio, orig cloth; paint spots on spine. pn July 23 (21) £110 [Old Hall]

Anr Ed. L, [1926]. 2 vols. Folio, orig cloth; rubbed & stained. S Feb 24 (567) £115 [Ruckstrudhl]

Froissart, Jean, 1333?-1400?

— Chronicles. L: Wm. Middleton, 1548 & Richarde Pynson, 1525. ("The Cronycles of Englande....") 2d Ed in English of Vol I; 1st Ed in English of Vol II. 2 vols. Folio, 18th-cent calf gilt; rubbed. Title & A2 of Vol I supplied in facsimile as is final leaf of Vol II; minor marginal defs or soiling. T Mar 19 (381) £300

Anr Ed. L, 1803-5. 4 vols. 4to, contemp calf gilt; broken. S Mar 9 (745) £160 [Morgan]

Anr Ed. L, 1852. 2 vols. 4to, mor gilt by J. Wright; scuffed. pn Oct 23 (322) £140 [Coup]

Anr Ed. L, 1868. Trans by Thomas Johnes. 2 vols. 8vo, contemp half mor; extremities rubbed. Ck May 29 (45) £120

Anr Ed. Stratford: Shakespeare Head Press, 1927-28. ("Froissarts Cronycles....") One of 350. 8 vols. 4to, half cloth; spines darkened & bumped at ends. cb Sept 11 (217) $600

Anr copy. Mor gilt by Stikeman. sg Dec 4 (178) $550

— Chroniques. Paris: Anthoine Verard, [c.1503]. Vols I-II only (of 4) in 1 vol. Folio, 17th-cent vellum. Vol I title & a few head-margins stained; small wormhole in 1st 15 leaves; 2 blank corners torn away; Vol II with short tear at foot of K5; some margins at end with minor stains; lacking blank leaves at end of each vol. C Dec 12 (292) £400 [Claridge]

Fromentin, Eugene, 1820-76

— Dominique. Paris, 1863. 1st Issue with misprint on p 177, line 10. 12mo, mor gilt, orig wraps bound in. Port inserted. S June 25 (23) £200 [Greenwood]

Fronsperger, Leonhard

— Von Kayserl. Kriegsrechten Malefitz und Schuldhaendlen.... Frankfurt: S. Feyerabend & S. Hueter, 1596. Folio, contemp blindstamped pigskin. With 20 (of 22) double-page plates. Some worming.

FD Dec 2 (66) DM9,000

Frossard, Benoit Daniel Emilien —& Jourdan, J.
— Vues prises dans les Pyrenees Francaises.... Paris, 1829. Folio, orig wraps. With hand-colored chart & 18 plates only. Some spotting. Sold w.a.f. bba Dec 4 (305) £80 [Goodey]

Frost, Arthur Burdett, 1851-1928
— A Book of Drawings. NY, [1904]. Intro by Joel Chandler Harris; verse by Wallace Irwin. Folio, bds; worn. With 29 plates. Foxed. wd June 19 (125) $50

Frost, Robert, 1874-1963
— A Boy's Will. NY, 1915. 1st American Ed, 1st Ptg. Inscr. O Mar 24 (74) $170
— Collected Poems. NY, 1930. 1st Ed, one of 1,000, sgd. Sgd. kh Mar 16 (203) A$200
— The Cow's in the Corn: A One Act Irish Play in Rhyme. Gaylordsville, Conn.: The Slide Mountain Press, 1929. 1st Separate Ed, one of 91, sgd. Erratum slip not mentioned. O Mar 24 (75) $125
— A Masque of Mercy. NY, [1947]. 1st Ed, one of 751, sgd. Half cloth, in d/j. sg Dec 11 (36) $140
— North of Boston. NY, 1932. In torn d/j. Sgd. sg Mar 5 (80) $120

Fruchtbringenden. See: Ludwig

Frutaz, Amato Pietro
— Le Piante di Roma. Rome, 1962. 3 vols, including 2 Atlases. Folio, cloth. With 684 facsimile illusts. sg Apr 2 (82) $425

Fry, Christopher
— Root and Sky: Poetry from the Plays.... Cambr., 1975. One of 220. Illus by Charles Wadsworth. 4to, half cloth. sg June 11 (199) $150

Fry, Edmund & Co.
— A Specimen of Printing Types by Edmund Fry and Co. L, 1788. 8vo, contemp calf gilt. C Dec 12 (88) £1,100 [Marlborough]
— A Specimen of Printing Types by Fry and Steele.... L, 1794. Bound with: Specimen of Metal Cast Ornaments.... L, 1794. 8vo, contemp half calf. C Dec 12 (87) £1,900 [Marlborough]

Fry, Frederick
— Fry's Traveller's Guide and Descriptive Journal of the Great North-Western Territories.... Cincinnati, 1865. 1st Ed. 12mo, orig cloth; chipped. Dampstain to lower corners. Inscr. cb Apr 2 (102) $325
Anr copy. Orig cloth; back repaired. sg Mar 12 (121) $325

Fry, Joseph & Sons
— A Specimen of Printing Types.... L, 1785. Single sheet. Marginal tear. bba Oct 16 (484) £70 [Forster]

Fry, Joseph Storrs, d.1835
— An Essay on the Construction of Wheel-Carriages. L, 1820. 1st Ed. 8vo, contemp calf gilt; rebacked in mor. S May 28 (944) £110

Fry, Roger Eliot, 1866-1934
— Henri Matisse. L & Paris, [1935]. One of 150. 4to, wraps. Text in English. sg Feb 5 (215) $175
Out-of-series copy. Wraps. Text in English. sg Feb 5 (216) $90
Anr Ed. NY & Paris, [1935]. One of 650. 4to, wraps, in d/j. O Jan 6 (76) $100
— Twelve Original Woodcuts. Richmond: Hogarth Press, 1921. 1st Ed. Orig wraps; rubbed. Ck Dec 10 (271) £190; S Dec 18 (134) £420 [Somner]
2d impression, without titles. Orig wraps; soiled. S Dec 18 (135) £300 [Maggs]

Fryer, John, d.1733
— A New Account of East-India and Persia.... L, 1698. Folio, contemp calf; joints split, head of spine worn. With port, 3 maps & 5 plates, 3 double-page. Minor worming to a few inner blank margins; small tear to 2 table leaves at end. C Apr 8 (89) £650 [Brooke-Hitching]

Fryer, John, 1752-1817. See: Golden Cockerel Press

Fuchs, Eduard
— Illustrierte Sittengeschichte. Munich, [1909-12]. Vols I-III, each with Supplement (Ergaenzungsband). Together, 6 vols. 4to, orig cloth. bba Mar 12 (418) £170 [Franks]
Anr copy. Orig cloth; shaken. sg Feb 12 (86) $90
— Die Juden in der Karikatur. Munich, [1921]. 4to, cloth. With 31 plates. sg Apr 30 (172) $110

Fuchs, Eduard —& Kind, Alfred
— Die Weiberherrschaft in der Geschichte der Menschheit. Munich, [1913-14]. 2 vols, plus "Ergaenzungsband." Together, 3 vols. bba Mar 12 (419) £130 [Franks]

Fuchs, Leonhard, 1501-66
— De curandi ratione libri octo. Lyons: G. Rovillius, 1554. 16mo, contemp lea; worn. FD Dec 2 (542) DM2,200
— De historia stirpium. Basel: Isingrin, 1542. 1st Ed. Folio, 18th-cent half calf gilt. With port of Fuchs on verso of title, 3 ports of

artists on recto of penultimate leaf & 512 full-page woodcuts of plants in the text. Some leaves dampstained at head or foot; 1 leaf stained; tp soiled & with a few tiny holes touching letters. S Oct 23 (685) £6,500 [Fletcher]

Anr Ed. Basel: J. Bebel, 1545. ("Primi de stirpium historia....") 8vo, old calf; rebacked. Tp guarded; marginal stains; Ms German index bound in at end. Crahan copy. P Nov 25 (207) $1,500

Anr Ed. Basel, 1549. ("Primi de stirpium historia commentariorum tomi vivae imagines....") 8vo, vellum. Dampstains on tp & 1st few leaves. pnE Jan 28 (303) £330 [Gladstone]

Anr Ed. Lyons: B. Arnollet, 1551. 8vo, 17th-cent calf; worn. Some stains; lower margin of title cut away & renewed; some marginal annotations & scoring through of text. S Oct 23 (687) £500 [Junk]

— Neu Kreuterbuch. Basel, 1543. Folio, later half calf; joints split, worn. Tp torn & reinforced in margins; tears repaired in z3 & BB7; other marginal tears; a few small holes in text; some dampstains. S Apr 23 (36) £5,000 [Koch]

Fuchs, Leonhard, 1506-66

— Laebliche Abbildung und Contrafaytung aller Kreueter. Basel: Michel Isingrin, 1545. 8vo, half vellum. With 517 woodcuts, some hand-colored. Some staining & soiling; repair to lower margin of a2; piece torn from top of y3 affecting page numeral; tear repaired in hh8; wormhole in lower margins at beginning. S Apr 23 (38) £850 [Koch]

Fueloep-Miller, Rene, 1891-1963 —& Gregor, Joseph

— The Russian Theatre. L, 1930. 4to, orig cloth; rubbed. bba Jan 15 (295) £120

Fuentes, Alonso de

— Summa de Philosophia Natural.... Seville, 1547. 4to, 19th-cent half lea. Some worming, affecting text; stains in lower margins towards end; tp cropped at fore-edge. sg Oct 9 (50) $275

Fuerst-Adliche...

— Fuerst-Adliche neu-ersonnene Jagd-Lust, bestehend in zweiyen Haupt-Theiler.... Frankfurt: J. L. Buggel, 1711. 3 parts in 1 vol. 8vo, contemp vellum. Some rubbing. Jeanson copy. SM Mar 1 (246) FF10,800

Fuerstenberg, Hans

— Das Franzoesische Buch im achtzehnten Jahrhundert und in der Empirezeit. Weimar, 1929. 4to, wraps; spine ends frayed, loose. sg Oct 2 (146) $60

Fuessli, Johann Casper, 1743-86

— Archiv der Insectengeschichte.... Zurich & Winterthur, 1781-86. 2 vols. 4to, contemp half sheep; rebacked & rubbed. With 52 plates (1 duplicated), 47 hand-colored. Text vol incomplete. Sold w.a.f. bba Sept 25 (213) £320 [Mandl]

Fulke, William, 1538-89

— Meteors: or, a Plain Description....... L, 1655. 2 parts in 1 vol. 8vo, old sheep; rebacked, covers worn. Blank margin of title with loss. Ck Apr 24 (195) £80

Fuller, Francis, 1670-1706

— Medicina Gymnastica: or a Treatise Concerning the Power of Exercise.... L, 1705. 2d Ed. 8vo, contemp calf. S May 28 (669) £110

Fuller, Thomas, 1608-61

— The History of the Worthies of England. L, 1662. Folio, calf; corner of lower cover worn. pnE Jan 28 (93) £300 [Steedman]

Anr copy. Contemp calf; joints split, rubbed. Some rust-holes just affecting text. S Mar 10 (1068) £130 [Scott]

— The Holy State. Cambr., 1648. 2d Ed. 2 parts in 1 vol. Folio, contemp calf gilt with arms & repeated monogram of John Evelyn; spine def. Inner margin of engraved title split. John Evelyn's copy, bound for him. S Apr 24 (260) £1,400 [Thomas]

— A Pisgah-Sight of Palestine. L, 1650. 1st Ed. Folio, later calf; joints repaired, rubbed. With engraved title, frontis & 28 folding maps & plates; title trimmed & inlaid. P Dec 15 (195) $750

Anr copy. Contemp calf; rubbed, spine damaged at head & foot. With engraved title, frontis & 28 maps & plans. Portion of corner of R2 restored; 3 maps torn at fold; a few tears or holes, sometimes affecting letters. S Dec 18 (274) £350 [Hofmann]

Anr Ed. L, 1662. Folio, modern half mor. Lacking 6 maps; lower left corner of tp & 1 plate torn & crudely repaired with loss of text; sections of fore-edges gouged; plates occasionally worn, soiled or torn; Ccc2 & 3 lacking. sg Sept 25 (92) $300

Fulton, Robert, of Brockley

— The Illustrated Book of Pigeons. L, etc., [c.1886]. 4to, contemp half mor; worn. With 50 color plates. Ck June 5 (200) £80

Anr copy. Half calf. pn Oct 23 (211) £110 [Traxel]

Anr copy. Orig cloth; worn & recased. 1 plate torn; some leaves at beginning & end from anr copy; marginal staining. S Nov 10 (490) £150 [Traxel]

Anr copy. Later half cloth; worn & soiled. wa Sept 25 (114) $140

Fulton, Robert, 1765-1815
— Torpedo War, and Submarine Explosions. NY, 1810. Oblong 4to, modern calf gilt, orig wraps bound in. C May 13 (201) £2,200 [Bjorck & Borjesson]

Anr copy. 19th-cent half mor; worn, front joint starting, spine ends chipped. With 5 plates. sg Apr 2 (83) $1,500

— A Treatise on the Improvement of Canal Navigation. L, 1796. 1st Ed. 4to, 19th-cent calf by Carss of Glasgow; rubbed. With 17 plates. Name stamp on title; plates dampstained at outer edge. S May 29 (945) £260

Anr copy. Half mor; needs rebdg. Tp loose, each plate with inked library stamp, primarily in margins, but slightly affecting image. sg Mar 12 (122) $175

Fulvio, Andrea
— Antiquitates urbis. [Rome: Marcellus Silber, 1527]. Folio, modern mor. Washed; residual dampstains at end; possibly lacking final blank. sg Dec 4 (75) $450

Fumagalli, Giuseppe
— L'Arte della legatura alla corte degli estensi.... Florence, 1913. 1st Ed. 4to, half cloth. sg May 14 (105) $225

Funnell, William
— A Voyage Round the World.... L, 1707. 8vo, contemp calf; broken. With 15 maps. Some stains; 1 plate torn. Ck Feb 27 (29) £350

Anr copy. Contemp calf; worn. 2 plates & 1 map torn; some plates shaved; spotted. Ck May 15 (20) £110

Anr copy. Contemp calf; rebacked, extremities worn. With 15 maps & plates; 1 with minor repairs. sg Apr 2 (84) $700

Furst, Herbert Ernest Augustus
— The Decorative Art of Frank Brangwyn. L & NY, 1924. 4to, cloth. With 33 color plates. sg Feb 5 (48) $80

Anr copy. Cloth; partly loose in bdg. sg June 4 (49) $50

Anr copy. Orig cloth, in d/j. T Oct 15 (90) £42

One of 120. Cloth. With 33 color plates. cb Dec 4 (85) $180

Furtenbach, Joseph, 1591-1667
— Architectura navalis, das ist von dem Schiff-Gebau.... Ulm, 1629. Bound with: Architectura martialis. Ulm, 1630. And: Das Giornal [1630] & Schuld Buch [1630] & Buchsenmeisteren-Schul. Augsburg, 1643. 1st Ed. Folio, vellum bds; dampstained, spine defective. With 20 double-page plates in 1st work, 12 in 2d & 43 in last. S Nov 27 (166) £1,700

Fusillot. See: Reveilhac, Paul

Futagawa Yukio
— The Roots of Japanese Architecture: A Photographic Quest. Tokyo: Bijutsu Shuppan-Sha, [1963]. Commentaries by Teiji Itoh; foreword by Isamu Noguchi. Folio, linen, in d/j. cb Mar 5 (235) $90

Fyfe, Andrew, 1754-1824
— A System of the Anatomy of the Human Body. Edin., 1814. 3d Ed. 3 vols. 4to, contemp half calf; worn. Sold w.a.f. S Feb 24 (568) £230 [Bickersteth]

C

Gadbury, John, 1627-1704
— Natura Prodigiorum: or, Discourse Touching the Nature of Prodigies. L, 1660. 8vo, old calf; worn. Margins trimmed close; some headlines shaved; lacking 1st leaf. sg Mar 26 (123) $250

Gaffar...
— Gaffar Guess-at-em's First Volume of Puzzles. L: E. Wallis, [watermarked 1818]. 8vo, orig wraps. Engraved throughout & colored by hand. S Dec 5 (281) £120 [Wakefield]

Gaffarel, Jacques, 1601-81
— Curiositez Inouyes, sur la Sculpture Talismanique des Persans.... [Paris?], 1650. 8vo, old vellum. Some dampstaining at corners; some tears. sg Oct 9 (213) $250

— Curiositez inouyes, hoc est; Curiositates inauditae de figuris Persarum Talismanicis.... Hamburg, 1678. 8vo, contemp half vellum. With folding frontis & 14 folding woodcut plates. A few short tears at edges & on folds; possibly lacking 1 prelim leaf. S Sept 23 (338) £140 [Thotias]

— Unheard-of Curiosities: concerning the Talismanical Sculpture of the Persians.... L, 1650. 8vo, 19th-cent lea. With 1 folding plate, backed. sg Oct 9 (214) $275

Gage, John
— Remarks on the Louterell Psalter.... L: Society of Antiquaries, 1839. Folio, contemp half mor. With 6 plates in plain & hand-colored states. Extract from Vol VI of Vetusta Monumenta, but evidently only 3 copies with colored plates were produced. Author's own copy with bookplate. Crahan copy. P Nov 25 (396) $2,500

Gage, Thomas, d.1656
— Nieuwe ende seer Naeuwkeurige Reyse door de Spaensche West-Indien. Utrecht, 1682. 1st Ed in Dutch. 4to, contemp vellum. With engraved title & 11 plates & maps. B Feb 25 (786) HF800

GAGNON

Gagnon, Phileas
— Essai de bibliographie canadienne.... Quebec, 1895 & Montreal, 1913. 8vo, cloth. sg Oct 2 (82) $50

Gaignat de l'Aulnais, C. F.
— Promenade de Seaux-Penthievre, de ses depandances et de ses environs.... Amst.: P. Fr. Gueffier, 1778. 12mo, contemp mor gilt. Jeanson copy. SM Mar 1 (250) FF1,7000

Gailhabaud, Jules, 1810-88
— L'Architecture du Vme au XVIIme Siecle.... Paris, 1858. 4 vols. 4to, contemp half mor; rubbed. Ck Sept 5 (21) £100

Gaine, Hugh, 1726-87
— Journals. NY, 1902. One of 350. Ed by Paul Leicester Ford. 2 vols. O Mar 24 (78) $70

Anr copy. Victor Paltsits's copy. With related material tipped in. sg Oct 2 (147) $110

Gainsborough, Thomas
— A Collection of Prints, Illustrative of English Scenery. L, [1819]. Folio, mor gilt; scuffed. With 60 plates, some with hand-colored wash. pn Jan 22 (196) £360 [Marlborough]

Galbally, Ann
— Arthur Streeton. Melbourne, 1969. 4to, cloth, in torn d/j. CA Oct 7 (71) A$130
One of 250. Bds, in d/j. CA Apr 12 (103) A$190

Galenus, Claudius
— De sanitate tuenda.... Lyons: G. Rovillius, 1548. 32mo, contemp vellum; worn. Some soiling & Ms annotations. S July 14 (396) £100

Galerie...
— Galerie de Florence. Tableaux, Statues, Bas-Reliefs et Camees. Paris, 1819. 4 vols. Folio, mor gilt; rubbed. Marginal tear to 1 title; some soiling & staining. S Nov 10 (86) £320 [Barker]
— Galerie theatrale, ou collection des portraits en pied des principaux acteurs des trois premiers theatres de la capitale. Paris: chez Bance aine, [1812-33]. 36 orig parts. Folio, orig wraps; some wraps missing or torn. With 139 (of 144) hand-finished color plates. sg Feb 26 (137) $3,000

Galezowski, Xavier
— Traite des maladies des yeux. Paris, 1872. 8vo, half mor. S Nov 10 (421) £280 [Bickersteth]
— Traite iconographique d'ophthalmoscopie, comprenant la description des differents ophthalmoscopes.... Paris, 1886. 2d Ed.

AMERICAN BOOK PRICES CURRENT

8vo, orig cloth; upper hinge cracked. With 28 color plates. S Nov 10 (422) £350 [Klein]

Galgemair, Georg
— Kurtzer Underricht Zubereitung und Gebrauch der...Instrumenten Proportional Schregmaess und Circkels.... Ulm, 1615. 4to, modern mor. Lacking 1 plate; outer margins dampstained at beginning; folding diagram repaired. S June 25 (109) £200 [Archinard]

Galiano, Dionisio Alcala
— Relacion del viage hecho por las goletas sutil y mexicana...para reconocer el Estrecho de Fuca. Madrid, 1802. 2 vols. 4to & folio, calf. With 9 maps (1 with neatline cropped) & 6 (of 8) plates. Lacking the 2 folding views of Nootka. S Oct 23 (518) £580 [Browning]

Galilei, Galileo, 1564-1642
— Dialogo di Galileo Galilei Linceo matematico...sopra i due massimi sistemi del mondo Tolemaico e Copernico. Florence, 1632. 1st Ed. 4to, old blindstamped calf. Lacking last blank, Bb misbound, frontis guarded at inner edge. S Nov 27 (260) £2,500 [Philipp]

— Discorso al Serenissimo Don Cosimo II. Florence: C. Giunta, 1612. 4to, modern bds. S June 25 (110) £700 [Quaritch]

— Discorso delle Comete di Mario Guiducci. Florence: Pietro Cecconcelli, 1619. Thick paper issue. 4to, modern mor. Minor soiling; c.5 leaves with marginal repairs affecting but not obscuring some words on B4 only; some leaves reinforced at blank inner margin. Riccardi copy. P Sept 24 (163) $1,700

— Istoria e dimonstrazioni intorno alle macchie solari e loro accidenti. Rome, 1613. 1st Ed, 2d Issue with letters from Christoph Scheiner to Welser. 2 parts in 1 vol. 4to, contemp vellum gilt. With port, 38 plates of sunspots, 5 plates of the Jovian satellites & 2 other plates, 1 double-page. Slight stain to corner of port & a few leaves. C Dec 12 (281) £2,700 [Phelps]

— Le Operazioni del compasso geometrico, et militare. Padua, 1640. 4to, contemp vellum. S June 25 (111) £450 [Schwing]

— Opere. Padua, 1744. 4 vols. 4to, contemp sheep; worn, spines defective. sg Jan 15 (314) $275

Anr Ed. Florence, 1842-56. 16 vols in 17. 8vo, contemp half lea; worn & soiled. Franklin Institute copy. wa Nov 6 (177) $160

Galilei, Vincentio

— Dialogo...della musica antica, et della moderna. Florence: G. Marescotti, 1581. Folio, old vellum bds; worn, upper cover detached & bowed. Title & last leaf soiled & spotted; small punctures in tp & following lea; some dampstains & foxing, heavy in last 40 pp; corners of B5 & last leaf torn away. CNY May 11 (45) £1,800

Gall, Franz Joseph, 1758-1828 —& Spurzheim, Johann Gaspar, 1776-1832

— Anatomie et physiologie du system nerveux. Paris, 1810-19. Atlas vol only. Contemp half calf; rebacked & recornered in mor, rubbed. With 20 plates. Some plates torn & frayed at edges; 2 loose & badly torn; 1 repaired; library markings. bba May 14 (282) £65 [Hildebrandt]

Anr copy. Atlas vol only. Folio, bdg not indicated. Library markings. Sold w.a.f, Franklin Institute copy. F Sept 12 (156) $110

Gallaeus, Philippus

— Semideorum marinorum amnicorumque sigillariae imagines perelegantes.... Antwerp, 1586. 8vo, later bds; worn. With engraved title (laid down) & 17 plates. Some soiling. S May 21 (39) £400 [Sourget]

Gallagher, Frank

— Days of Fear. L, 1928. Inscr by Lady Gregory to Augustus John. sg Dec 11 (39) $225

Gallatin, Albert Eugene, 1881-1952

— Aubrey Beardsley's Drawings; a Catalogue.... NY, 1903. One of 30 interleaves & specially bound. Folio, orig vellum gilt; soiled. Inscr to Frederick H. Evans. Extra-illus with 18 platinotype facsimiles by F. H. Evans of Beardsley drawings, various proof & unpbd drawings, a clipped signature & the orig Beardsley drawings for the full-page border of p 879 of Le Morte Darthur inset with a platinum print of Evans's port of Beardsley, sgd by Evans on mount. P June 18 (13) $17,000

Galle, Theodor

— Illustrium imagines ex antiquis marmoribus.... Antwerp: Plantin, 1598. 4to, old vellum gilt, armorial bdg; early 18th-cent mor gilt. With title & 151 plates. sg Oct 9 (215) $300

Anr Ed. Antwerp: Plantin, 1606. 4to, early vellum. sg Mar 26 (124) $275

Gallery...

— Gallery of Landscape Painters.... NY, 1872. Folio, orig mor gilt; worn & scuffed. With 24 plates. sg Dec 18 (176) $450

Gallesio, Giorgio, 1772-1839

— Pomona Italiana. Pisa, 1817-39. 2 vols. Folio, contemp half calf; worn. With 2 ptd tables, 2 engraved tables & 157 (of 160) colored plates. Some spotting. de Belder copy. S Apr 27 (126) £16,000 [Arader]

Gallo, Agostino, of Brescia

— Secrets de la vraye agriculture.... Paris: Nicolas chesneau, 1571. 4to, contemp vellum. SM Mar 1 (251) FF9,500

— Le Vinti Giornate della agricoltura.... Venice: Domenico Imberti, 1610. 4to, 19th-cent half mor; rubbed. Dampstains to some lower outer edges at front of book; lacking last leaf, some shaving at bottom, affecting signatures & border of 2 woodcuts. Hunt copy. CNY Nov 21 (128) $240

Gallotti, Jean

— Moorish Houses and Gardens of Morocco. NY, [1926?]. 2 vols. 4to, half cloth; worn, partly soiled & stained. With 136 plates. wa Feb 19 (388) $120

Galsworthy, John, 1867-1933

— A Bit O' Love. L, 1915. Inscr to Madge McIntosh & with ALs to her laid in. sg Dec 11 (41) $200

— Caravan. L, 1923. In d/j. Inscr. sg Dec 11 (42) $50

— Five Tales. NY, 1918. 1st American Ed. Inscr to W. H. Hudson. sg Dec 11 (43) $400

— The Forsyte Saga. L, 1922. 1st Ed. In d/j. sg Dec 11 (44) $90

Ltd Issue, sgd. Calf. pnE June 17 (147) £60

— From the Four Winds. 1897. 1st Ed. 12mo, orig cloth; rubbed, stamp on front free endpaper. bba July 2 (193) £110 [Sumner]

— Jocelyn. L, 1898. 1st Ed. 8vo, orig cloth; rubbed. bba July 2 (194) £90 [Sumner]

— A Modern Comedy. L, 1929. One of 1,030. Orig vellum. Inscr.. sg Dec 11 (45) $80

— The Silver Spoon. L, [1926]. 1st Ed. In d/j. Inscr. sg Dec 11 (46) $60

— Two Essays on Conrad. Freelands OH: Pvtly ptd, 1930. One of 25. Inscr & with related material laid in. sg Dec 11 (49) $550

— The White Monkey. L, 1924. Inscr. sg Dec 11 (50) $50

— Works. NY, 1922-36. Manaton Ed, one of 750. Vols 1-29 (of 30). Half mor. ha May 22 (58) $950

Anr copy. Vols I-XXV (of 30). Mor. O May 12 (77) $450

Anr Ed. L, 1923-36. one of 530. 30 vols. Half vellum. bba July 2 (198) £550 [Fitzcarrald]

Anr copy. Mor gilt. sg Dec 4 (76) $1,900

Devon Ed. NY, 1926-29. 22 vols. O Mar

24 (79) $80

Galton, Sir Francis, 1822-1911
— Finger Prints. L, 1892. 1st Ed. 8vo, cloth; moderate wear. O Sept 23 (68) $220
— Hereditary Genius.... L, 1869. 1st Ed. 8vo, orig cloth; head of spine worn. With 2 folding plates. pnE Dec 17 (176) £95 [Phillips]

Gamba, Francesco
— 125 Ex-Libris. Bologna: Cesare Ratta, [c.1925]. One of 175. Pictorial wraps; spine repaired, stamp on front free endpaper. sg Jan 22 (51) $110

Gamba, Pietro, Count, 1801-26
— A Narrative of Lord Byron's Last Journey to Greece. L, 1825. 1st Ed. 8vo, half calf; worn, joints weak. bba Jan 15 (83) £65 [Frew Mackenzie]

Gambara, Lorenzo, 1506-96
— Theron. Rome: Valerium e Loisius fratres Doricos, Jan 1552. 4to, mor, armorial bdg of a cardinal. Jeanson copy. SM Mar 1 (252) FF12,000

Gamble, John
— An Essay on the Different Modes of Communication by Signals. L, 1797. 4to, contemp calf-back bds. Half-title inscr "From the author". C Dec 12 (91) £950 [Quaritch]

Gambrill, R. V. N. See: Derrydale Press

Gambrill, Richard V. N. See: Derrydale Press

Gamucci, Bernardo, 1522-92
— Le Antichita della citta di Roma. Venice, 1569. 8vo, contemp vellum; worn. Old marginal waterstains. T Oct 16 (607) £220
— Libri quattro dell'antichita della citta di Roma. Venice, 1565. 4to, half vellum; worn. Lacking last leaf; repair to blank portion of title removing name; tp discolored; name erased; tear in upper margin of E2; Sig. S1-4 browned; lacking last blank. S Sept 23 (339) £170 [Brenan]

Gandy, John Peter. See: Gell & Gandy

Gandy, Joseph
— Designs for Cottages, Cottage Farms and other Rural Buildings. L, 1805. 4to, orig bds; worn & def. Some staining. bba Sept 25 (274) £380 [Weinreb]

Ganilh, Charles
— Essai Politique sur le Revenu Publique. Paris, 1806. 8vo, contemp calf with stamp of the Signet Library; rubbed, 1 joint darkened. Small hole along inner margin of tp; some spotting & staining. P Sept 24 (290) $150
— An Inquiry into the Various Systems of

Political Economy. L, 1812. 8vo, 19th-cent half calf; rubbed, spine chipped at head. Marginal tear in K5. P Sept 24 (291) $225
— La Theorie de l'Economie Politique. Paris, 1815. 2 vols. 8vo, contemp calf with stamp of the Signet Library; spines worn, joints cracking. Some spotting or staining, mainly of endpapers. P Sept 24 (292) $225

Ganymed...
— Ganymed: Blaetter der Marees-Gesellschaft. Munich, 1919-25. Vols I-V. Bds. HN Nov 26 (1805) DM3,200

Garcia, Gregorio, d.1627
— Origen de los Indios de el nuevo mundo.... Madrid, 1729. 2d Ed. Folio, contemp vellum; soiled. Inner portion of tp damp-stained. With related material. sg Sept 18 (100) $325

Garcia y Garcia, Jose Antonio
— Relaciones de los Vireyes del Nuevo Reino de Granada.... NY, 1869. 8vo, orig cloth; hinges cracking, soiled. Tp with owner's rubberstamp at bottom. sg Sept 18 (110) $60

Garcilaso de la Vega. See: Lasso de la Vega, Garcia

Garden Companion. See: Henfrey & Others

Gardeners'...
— The Gardeners' Magazine of Botany. L, Jan 1850-Dec 1851. Ed by Thomas Moore & W. P. Ayres. 3 vols. 4to, half mor gilt; rubbed. pn Sept 18 (102) £680 [Map House]

Gardens...
— Gardens Old and New: The Country House & its Garden Environment. L: Country Life Library, [1900]. Vols I-III. Folio, orig cloth; rubbed, Vol II not uniform. Ck May 29 (22) £220

Gardiner, Allen Francis, 1794-1851
— Narrative of a Journey to the Zoolu Country in South Africa.... L, 1836. 8vo, old calf; worn. O May 12 (78) $200

Gardiner, John Smallman
— The Art and the Pleasures of Hare-Hunting. L: for R. Griffiths, 1750. 8vo, 19th-cent calf gilt. Schwerdt-Jeanson copy. SM Mar 1 (254) FF8,800

Gardiner, Samuel Rawson, 1829-1902
— Oliver Cromwell. L, 1899. Ltd Ed on japan vellum, but without duplicate set of plates. 4to, lev gilt. S July 13 (196) £150

Gardner, Alexander, 1821-82

— Gardner's Photographic Sketch Book of the War. Wash., 1866. 2 vols. Oblong folio, orig mor gilt; worn & rubbed. With 100 albumen photographs on their orig ptd mounts; all prints crisp & clean. Minor stains to text. wa June 25 (162) $12,500

Gardner, Erle Stanley, 1889-1970

— The Case of the Curious Bride. NY, 1934. In d/j. cb Nov 20 (202) $80

Gardner, Herbert

— Come Duck Shooting with Me. NY, 1917. Inscr. sg Oct 23 (282) $70

Gardner, Thomas, 1690?-1769

— A Pocket Guide to the English Traveller. L, 1719. 1st Ed. 2 vols in 1. 4to, old calf; rebacked & recornered. With 100 double-page maps. Several margins cut close; lacking title to Part 2; 1 map mtd. Ck Nov 21 (343) £700

Anr copy. Contemp calf; rebacked. pn May 21 (363) £1,150 [Burgess Browning]

Gardnor, John

— Views Taken On and Near the River Rhine.... L, 1791. 4to, 19th-cent half lea; worn. With engraved title & 32 colored plates. HN Nov 26 (459) DM3,600

Garidel, Pierre Joseph, 1658-1737

— Histoire des plantes qui naissent aux environs d'Aix.... Aix, 1715. Folio, contemp calf; rubbed. With frontis & 99 (of 100) plates. Tp soiled & with a small tear; some stains; some marginal annotations. S Oct 23 (696) £620 [McCarthy]

Anr copy. 19th-cent calf; upper joint split. With frontis & 100 plates, all but 1 hand-colored. Plesch—de Belder copy. S Apr 27 (127) £2,800 [Hamlyn]

Anr Ed. Paris, 1719. ("Histoire des plantes qui naissent en Provence et principalement aux environs d'Aix....") Folio, contemp calf; worn. With frontis & 105 plates. Horticultural Society of New York—de Belder copy. S Apr 27 (128) £2,200 [Shapero]

Garner, Thomas, d.1906 —& Stratton, Arthur

— The Domestic Architecture of England during the Tudor Period. L, 1908-11. 2 vols. Folio, cloth; worn & soiled. sg June 4 (142) $175

2d Ed. L, 1929. 2 vols. Folio, cloth, in d/js; 1 rear cover dampstained. sg June 4 (143) $50

Garnet, Henry, 1555-1606

[-] A True and Perfect Relation of the Whole Proceedings against...Garnet a Jesuite.... L, 1606. STC 11619a.5. 4to, contemp half vellum; worn. Lacking tp (supplied in later Ms); lacking Fff1 & Fff4; some leaves marginally torn or def; 1 leaf with small hole affecting text. bba Mar 26 (154) £40 [News Today]

Garnett, Porter

— The Fine Book: A Symposium.... Pittsburgh: Laboratory Press, 1934. One of 225. Mor by Grabau. cb Feb 5 (96) $85

— The Grove Plays of the Bohemian Club. San Francisco: Bohemian Club, 1918. One of 31. 3 vols. Mor; 1st 2 vols dampstained. cb Jan 8 (14) $80

Garnett, Richard, 1835-1906 —& Gosse, Sir Edmund W., 1849-1928

— English Literature: an Illustrated Record.... NY, 1905. 4 vols. Half lev; rubbed, 1 cover nearly detached. O Sept 23 (69) $50

Garnier, Edouard

— The Soft Porcelain of Sevres. L, 1892. Folio, orig mor gilt; rubbed. With 50 plates. pnNY Sept 13 (232) $330

Anr copy. Orig half cloth; spine torn. Some handling marks. pnNY Oct 11 (23) $550

Garnier, Pierre, b.1811

— Chasse du lievre en France. Paris: Auguste Aubry, 1879. 8vo, contemp half calf. Schwerdt-Jeanson copy. SM Mar 1 (255) FF4,400

— Traite complet de la chasse des alouettes au miroir avec le fusil. Paris: Auguste Aubry, 1866. Unique copy on vellum. 8vo, mor janseniste by Chambolle-Duru. SM Mar 1 (256) FF16,000

Garran, Andrew

— Picturesque Atlas of Australasia. Sydney, 1886. 3 vols. Folio, mor; Vol II cracked. CA Apr 12 (104) A$300

Anr copy. Half mor gilt; stained & rubbed. Lacking titles; some foxing. CA Apr 12 (105) A$420

Anr copy. Vols I-II only. Folio, orig mor; worn, 1 cover detached. Ck Nov 21 (93) £85

Anr copy. 3 vols. Folio, mor gilt; Vols II & III worn, Vol II lower cover detached. Minor marginal stains to 6 plates; early leaves of Vol II & final leaves of Vols II & III with marginal waterstain; final 4 leaves of Vol II detached. L Dec 11 (204) £70

Anr copy. Contemp half mor; rubbed. SSA Feb 11 (516) R320

Garrick, David, 1717-79
— The Private Correspondence of.... L, 1831. 2 vols. 4to, cloth; worn. Frontis & tp foxed. sg Feb 26 (153) $60

Garrison, Everett —& Carmichael, Hoagy B.
— A Master's Guide to Building a Bamboo Fly Rod. Katonah NY: Martha's Glen Publishing Co., [1977]. One of 128. 4to, lea gilt. With lea pouch containing a bamboo specimen. Inscr by Carmichael to Charles Wood. sg Oct 23 (284) $325

Garstin, Sir William Edmund
— Report upon the Basin of the Upper Nile.... Cairo, 1904. Folio, cloth, orig front wrap pasted onto upper cover. Ink & perforated library stamps on titles & plates. bba Dec 18 (152) £50 [Hay]

Garzoni, Thomas
— La Piazza universale di tutte le professioni del mondo.... Venice: Vincenzo Somasco, 1595. 4to, vellum; loose. Waterstained throughout. S Nov 10 (423) £150 [Patilucci]

Gascoyne, Caroline L.
— Belgravia. A Poem. L, 1851. 2d Ed. 8vo, contemp mor; rubbed. T Sept 18 (537) £44

Gascoyne, David
— The Sun at Midnight. L: Enitharmon Press, 1970. One of 75. Half mor. Inscr. sg Dec 11 (294) $140
— Three Poems. Pvtly ptd, 1976. One of 26. 4to, half cloth. sg Dec 11 (295) $200

Gaskell, Elizabeth Cleghorn, 1810-65
— The Life of Charlotte Bronte. L, 1857. 1st Ed. 2 vols. 12mo, modern half calf. Lacking ad leaves at end of Vol II. bba Mar 12 (164) £190 [Jarndyce]

Anr copy. Later half mor; worn & broken. T Jan 22 (358) £50

Gaskell, Philip
— John Baskerville: A Bibliography. Chicheley, 1973. 4to, orig cloth, in d/j. bba Oct 16 (377) £50 [Frew Mackenzie]

Gaspari, Gaetano
— Catalogo della Biblioteca Musicale G. B. Martini. Bologna, 1961. 4 vols. 4to, cloth. sg Oct 2 (229) $100

Gaspey, William
— Tallis's Illustrated London. L, [1851-52]. 2 vols. 12mo, half mor; lacking 1 cover, spines def. pn Dec 11 (36) £120 [Nicholson]

Anr copy. Half calf; rubbed. pn June 18 (58) pS120 [Tilleke]

Anr copy. Half calf gilt. pn July 23 (156)

£160 [Myers]

Gass, Patrick, 1771-1870
— A Journal of the Voyages and Travels.... Pittsburgh, 1807. 1st Ed. 12mo, old half calf; rubbed. Sold w.a.f. O June 9 (67) $90

Anr copy. Half lea. Lacking 2 leaves; some foxing; marginal notations. sg Mar 12 (125) $275

Gassendi, Pierre, 1592-1655
— The Mirrour of True Nobility & Gentility.... L, 1657. 8vo, early 19th-cent calf gilt; rubbed, rebacked, orig spine preserved. Port & a few headlines shaved; lacking ad leaf & 1 blank. S July 14 (315) £120

Gastineau, Henry, 1791-1876
— Wales Illustrated.... L, 1830. 2 parts in 1 vol. 4to, contemp calf; broken. With 176 views on 88 plates only. Some plates & some text leaves torn; 1 plate stained. bba Apr 9 (371) £85 [Palace]

Anr copy. Contemp carved wooden bds; spine worn. Sold w.a.f. Ck Sept 26 (318) £90

Anr copy. Contemp half calf; rubbed. With 212 views on 106 plates only. Ck June 5 (58) £220

Anr copy. Half mor gilt. With engraved titles & 224 views on 112 plates. Final plate in Vol I slightly spotted. L Dec 11 (112) £160

Anr copy. 4to, contemp half calf; spine torn. With 84 views on 42 sheets. pn Jan 22 (95) £50 [Bookroom]

Anr copy. Part 1 only. 4to, contemp half calf; corners rubbed. With engraved title & 88 views on 44 plates only. Corner of some leaves stained. S Nov 17 (787) £80 [Palace]

Anr copy. 2 parts in 1 vol. 4to, 19th-cent half calf; def. With 114 plates, including 2 additional titles. S Feb 24 (382) £120 [Palace]

Anr copy. Contemp half mor; worn. With 1 engraved title (of 2) & 216 views on 108 plates only (of 112). Some imprints cropped. S May 28 (869) £200

Anr copy. Mor; rubbed. With 176 views on 88 leaves only. T Nov 20 (48) £230

Gaston III Phoebus, Comte de Foix, 1331-91
— Phebus des deduiz de la chasse des bestes sauvaigeset des oyseaux de proy.... Paris: pour Anthoine Verard, [c.1507]. Folio, mor janseniste by Chambolle-Duru. Jeanson copy. SM Mar 1 (465) FF1,200,000

Anr Ed. Paris: Jehan Trepperel, [c.1508]. Folio, mor janseniste by Chambolle-Duru. Jeanson copy. SM Mar 1 (466) FF360,000

Gates, Eleanor
— Good-Night (Buenas Noches). NY, 1907. Illus by Arthur Rackham. Half cloth; rubbed, bumped. With 5 color plates. sg Oct 30 (79) $475

Gatford, Lionel
— Publick Good without Private Interest.... L: Henry Marsh, 1657. 4to, half calf. Some shaving; 1st 2 leaves with 2 tears repaired. S June 25 (423) £4,000

Gatti, Alessandro
— La Caccia.... L: J. Bill, 1619. 8vo, 17th-cent mor gilt. Jeanson copy. SM Mar 1 (257) FF14,000

Gatty, Mrs Alfred. See: Gatty, Margaret

Gatty, Margaret, 1809-73
— British Sea-Weeds. L, 1872. 2 vols in 1. 4to, contemp half calf gilt; rubbed. T Feb 19 (356) £56

Gauchet, Claude
— Le Plaisir des champs.... Paris: Abel l'Angelier, 1604. 4to, mor gilt. Jeanson copy. SM Mar 1 (258) FF16,000
Anr Ed. Paris, 1879. 2 parts in 1 vol. 4to, mor gilt by Chambolle-Duru. Jeanson copy. SM Mar 1 (259) FF2,600

Gauden, John, 1605-62
— A Discourse of Artificial Beauty.... L, 1662. 8vo, contemp calf; rebacked. T Sept 18 (368) £115

Gaudier-Brzeska, Henri, 1891-1915
— Henri Gaudier-Brzeska 1891-1915. L: Ovid Press, [1919]. One of 250. Folio, unbound as issued in orig portfolio; lacking ribbon ties. With 20 facsimile drawings on 19 plates. sg Dec 11 (296) $275

Gauguin, Paul, 1848-1903
— Avant et Apres. Paris, 1923. Orig bds; backstrip def. S June 17 (25) £250 [Grob]
— Noa Noa. [Munich, 1926]. One of 320. 4to, orig raffia over bds, in torn d/j, spine darkened & brittle. Facsimile of the Ms. sg Dec 4 (77) $1,100

Gaunt, William
— The Etchings of Frank Brangwyn. A Catalogue Raisonne. L, 1926. One of 125. 4to, vellum gilt; worn & chipped. sg Feb 5 (49) $475

Gauss, Karl Friedrich, 1777-1855
— Recherches arithmetiques. Paris, 1807. 4to, later cloth. Library stamp on tp & last leaf. bba May 14 (301) £160 [Gurney]

Gauthier, ——
— Nouvelle Chimie du gout et de l'odorat.... Paris, 1819. 1st Ed. 2 vols. 8vo, contemp calf gilt. With frontis & 9 plates. Crahan copy. P Nov 25 (211) $300

Gauthier, J. B.
— La Plomberie au XIXe Siecle. Paris, 1885. Folio, cloth; worn. With 64 plates, including 3 depicting the Statue of Liberty. Piece torn from half-title. O Oct 21 (68) $240

Gautier d'Agoty, Jacques, 1717-85
— Collection des plantes usuelles, curieuses et etrangeres.... Paris, 1767. Folio, recent half mor over older bds. With 26 (of 40) hand-finished color plates. Tp laid down. Sold w.a.f. Hunt copy 1. CNY Nov 21 (130) $2,000

Gautier, Theophile, 1811-72
See also: Golden Cockerel Press

— Le Capitaine Fracasse. Paris, 1863. 1st Ed. 2 vols. 12mo, mor gilt by Yseux Sr. de Thierry-Simier, orig wraps bound in. Some spotting & soiling. S Sept 23 (563) £130 [Tristan]
— La Morte amoureuse. Paris, 1904. One of 90 with 2 additional sets of plates, 1 colored, the other plain. Illus by A. P. Laurens. Mor with inlaid flowers by Affolter, orig wraps bound in. With ALs & bill from the binder loosely inserted. S Oct 6 (663) £140 [Sayhof]
— Works. NY: George D. Sproul, 1900-3. One of 300. 24 vols. Mor gilt extra by Blackwell's. With some plates in 2 states. P Dec 15 (196) $1,500

Gavarni
— Le Diable a Paris: Paris et les Parisiens. Paris, 1845-46. 2 vols in 1. 8vo, contemp half mor; spine scuffed, edges & joints rubbed. Some foxing & soiling; marginal tear to frontis. cb Feb 19 (109) $130
— Gavarni in London, Sketches of Life and Character. L, 1849. Ed by Albert Smith. 8vo, half calf; rubbed, head & foot of spine worn. With extra title in gold & 23 plates. Perforated stamp on title. bba Feb 5 (298) £55 [Woodruff]
— Oeuvres choisies. Paris, 1846-48. 4 vols. 8vo, bds, orig wraps bound in. With frontis & 240 plates. S Oct 6 (641) £130 [Rebocchi]

Gavin, Charles Murray
— Royal Yachts. L, 1932. 4to, cloth; rebacked preserving most of orig spine. O Nov 18 (71) $70

GAWSWORTH

Gawsworth, John, Pseud.

— Above the River. L, 1931. Out-of-series copy. Pbd bds; soiled. Gawsworth's own copy, with holograph corrections. sg Mar 5 (83) $100

Gay, Jean

— Bibliographie des ouvrages relatifs a l'Afrique et a l'Arabie. San Remo & Paris, 1875. One of 500. 8vo, half lea; joints rubbed, orig wraps bound in. sg Oct 2 (148) $70

Gay, John, 1685-1732

— Achilles, an Opera. L, 1733. 1st Ed. 8vo, mor gilt by Riviere. sg June 11 (201) $250

— The Beggar's Opera. L, 1921. One of 430. Illus by Claude Lovat Fraser. 4to, recent half mor. With 8 colored plates. cb Sept 11 (252) $60

— The Distress'd Wife. L, 1743. 8vo, mor gilt by Riviere. sg June 11 (202) $300

— Fables. L, 1727-38. 1st Ed. 2 vols in 1. 4to, mor gilt by Zaehnsdorf. With 51 head-pieces in Vol I & frontis & 16 plates in Vol II. Small tear at D1 & O2 affecting head-piece on verso; small repair to M3 just shaving 2 letters. C Dec 3 (121) £750 [Beres]
Anr copy. 2 vols. 4to, modern half mor & contemp calf. O May 12 (79) $190
Anr copy. Contemp calf gilt; extremities worn, several hinges starting. With 67 plates. sg June 11 (203) $800
Anr Ed. L, 1793. 2 vols. 8vo, contemp calf gilt; Vol I rebacked preserving spine, Vol II upper cover detached. Flourishes shaved on calligraphic titles. bba Apr 23 (195) £60 [Martin]
Anr copy. Contemp calf; rebacked, extremities worn. With engraved titles & 68 plates, 12 after Wm. Blake. sg Mar 26 (125) $250

— Poems on Several Occasions. L, 1720. 1st Collected Ed. 2 vols in 1. 4to, contemp half calf; worn. Forbes copy. bba Oct 30 (78) £190 [Bickersteth]
Anr copy. Contemp calf; joints split. Ck Jan 30 (13) £90

— Trivia. L, [1716]. 1st Ed. 8vo, calf gilt; rebacked retaining orig backstrip. L.p. copy. sg Apr 2 (85) $175

— The What D'Ye Call It. L, [1715]. 8vo, mor gilt by Riviere. sg June 11 (204) $325

— The Wife of Bath. L, 1713. 1st Ed, Issue with woodcut figure on half-title. 4to, mor by Riviere. sg June 11 (205) $350

AMERICAN BOOK PRICES CURRENT

Gay, John, 1685-1732 —& Others

— Three Hours after Marriage. L, 1717. 8vo, mor gilt. sg June 11 (206) $475

Gay, Jules, b.1807

— Bibliographie des ouvrages relatifs a l'amour.... Turin & L, 1871-73. 6 vols. 8vo, half mor; rubbed. bba Mar 12 (338) £160 [A. Stewart]
4th Ed. Paris & Lille, 1894-1900. 4 vols. 8vo, orig half mor; rubbed. bba Oct 16 (378) £310 [Hesketh & Ward]

Gay, Sydney H., 1814-88. See: Bryant & Gay

Gay, Theresa

— James W. Marshall: the Discoverer of California Gold. Georgetown, Calif., 1967. One of 250. Half mor. Sgd.. cb Oct 9 (79) $50

Gay, Theressa

— James W. Marshall: The Discoverer of California Gold. Georgetown CA: Talisman Press, 1967. One of 250. cb Oct 9 (79) $50

Gayton, Edmund, 1608-66

— Pleasant Notes upon Don Quixot. L, 1654. Folio, old sheep; joints starting. Marginal repairs in first few leaves. sg Oct 9 (43) $175

Gazette...

— Gazette des Chasseurs. Chasse a courre et a tir.... Paris: Veuve Pairault et fils, 1883. In 2 vols. 4to, contemp half mor, not uniform. With autograph material & c.450 artists' proofs inserted. Jeanson copy. SM Mar 1 (260) FF20,000

— Gazette du Bon Ton. Art, modes & frivolites. Paris, 1912-15 & 1920-25. No 1, 1912 to No 9, 1924/5 (lacking only Jan-May 1923), a run of 70 in 69 Nos. 4to, orig wraps, in contemp half calf; rubbed, lacking some wraps. bba Jan 15 (214) £13,000 [Sims]

Gazius, Antonius

— Corona florida medicinae sive de conservatione sanitatis. Venice: Joannes & Gregorius de Gregoriis, de Forlivio, 20 June 1491. Folio, mor gilt extra by Amand. Dampstained, small marginal smudges, occasional browning. 124 (of 126) leaves lacking errata leaf & final blank. Goff G-111. P Dec 15 (159) $1,500

Gebhart, Emile, 1839-1908

— La Derniere nuit de Judas. Paris, 1909. One of 350. 8vo, calf extra. Tp foxed. cb Feb 19 (110) $100

Gedde, John
— The English Apiary; or, the Compleat Bee-Master. L, 1722. 2 parts in 1 vol. 12mo, contemp calf; rebacked, endpapers removed. Fore-edge cropped. sg Jan 15 (149) $425

Gedenkboek...
— Gedenkboek uitgegeven ter gelegenheid der opening van den Delagoabaai-spoorweg.... Amst., 1895. 4to, cloth. B Oct 7 (19) HF180

Gee, Ernest Richard
See also: Derrydale Press
— Gee's Hunting Diary, to Record the Sport of the Season. Pvtly ptd at the Derrydale Press, [1937]. Half cloth. sg Oct 23 (52) $250
— The Sportsman's Library: Being a Descriptive List.... NY, 1940. One of 600. With 8 plates. sg Oct 23 (285) $60

Geel, Pierre Corneille van
— Sertum Botanicum. Collection des plants remarquables.... Brussels, 1828-32. 1st Issue. 4 vols in 8. Folio, contemp half calf; rubbed. With 600 hand-colored plates. Some spotting. de Belder copy. S Apr 27 (129) £7,000 [Israel]

Geel, Pierre Corneille von —& Others
— Encyclographie du regne vegetal. Brussels, 1827-32. 4 vols. 4to, contemp half mor gilt; upper joint of Vol I broken, other inner joints cracked, Vol IV bdg & contents damaged by damp. With 1 plain & 600 handcolored plates. Hunt copy. CNY Nov 21 (254) $16,000

Geel, Pierre Corneille van —& Others
— Encyclographie du regne vegetal. I. Sertum Botanicum.... Brussels, [1827]-28-32. 4 vols in 6. Folio, contemp half mor; rubbed. With 1 plain & 599 hand-colored plates. Some marginal stains & foxing; 2 orig part wraps bound as titles in Vols V & VI. S Oct 23 (702) £6,000 [Burden]

Geffroy, Gustave, 1855-1926
— L'Apprentie. Paris, 1924. One of 40 on japon with 2 suites of plates & with 2 sgd ink drawings. Illus by Auguste Brouet. 4to, mor extra by Semet & Plumelle, orig wraps bound in. S June 17 (5) £320 [Stermer]

Gehyn, Jacob de, 1565-1615
— Wapenhandelinghe van Roers Musquetten ende Spiessen. Amst., 1608. 3 parts in 1 vol. Folio, contemp vellum; soiled & loose. With engraved title & 105 (of 116) plates. Some marginal fraying & waterstaining. Library release stamp on verso of tp. Sold w.a.f. S Oct 23 (189) £1,900 [King]

Geiler von Kaisersberg, Johann, 1445-1510
— Navicula sive speculum fatuorum prestantissimi sacrarum literarum.... Strassburg: [J. Preuss], 1511. 4to, contemp half pigskin. With woodcut on title & 112 woodcuts in text. P Nov 25 (212) $3,000

Geisel, Theodore. See: Seuss, Dr.

Gelabert, Jose Antonio
— Glorias del Tablero Capablanca. Havana, [1923]. Inscr by Koltanowsky. pn Mar 26 (221) £90 [Rodriguez]

Geldner, Ferdinand
— Bucheinbaende aus elf Jahrhunderten. Munich, 1958. Folio, cloth, in frayed d/j. With 100 plates. O June 16 (87) $70

Gell, Sir William, 1777-1836
— Pompeiana: the Topography, Edifices, and Ornaments of Pompeii. L, 1837. 2 vols. 4to, later half mor gilt; rubbed. cb Feb 19 (111) $75
— The Topography of Troy and its Vicinity. L, 1804. 1st Ed. Folio, half calf. With 2 hand-colored maps & 28 hand-colored plates. S Apr 24 (220) £750 [Traylen]

Gell, Sir William, 1777-1836 —& Gandy, John Peter
— Pompeiana. L, 1817-19. 1st Ed. 8vo, contemp mor; joints worn. sg Apr 23 (59) $100
— Pompeiana. The Topography, Edifices, and Ornaments of Pompeii. L, 1852. 8vo, half mor; rubbed, worn. cb Nov 6 (139) $65

Gellert, Hugo
— Comrade Gulliver; an Illustrated Account of Travel into.... NY, [1935]. 1st Ed. sg Jan 8 (80) $60

Gellius, Aulus
— Noctes Atticae. Venice: Aldus, 1515. ("Noctium Atticarum libri undeviginti.") 1st 1515 Aldine Ed, with "duerniorem" on final leaf. 8vo, old half calf; worn. Tp soiled, with scored inscr. sg Mar 26 (127) $130
Anr Ed. Basel: Henricum Petri, [1565]. 12mo, goatskin; worn. Lacking any front & rear blanks. ha Dec 19 (294) $65
Anr Ed. Paris, 1681. 4to, contemp red mor gilt with arms of Louis XIV. Rosebery copy. C May 13 (144) £600 [Lyon]

Gemeenschap...
— De Gemeenschap. Nijmegen, 1925-41. Vols I-XVII, No 9; lacking year 3. Bound in 17 vols. All wraps preserved. B Oct 7 (165) HF900

Gemma, Cornelius, 1535-79
— De naturae divinis characterismus. Antwerp: Plantin, 1575. 8vo, 19th-cent half calf; spine rubbed, some leaves misbound. Some dampstains; 1 woodcut shaved. S June 25 (113) £250 [Lyon]

Gemma, Reinerus, Frisius, 1508-55
— De Astrolabo catholico liber. Antwerp, 1556. 8vo, old vellum; worn. Some marginalia cut close. S Apr 23 (186) £950 [Quaritch]

Gemmarum...
— Gemmarum antiquarum delectus ex praestantioribus desumptus quae in dactyliothecis Ducis Marlburiensis conservantur. L, 1845. 2 vols. Folio, cloth. With 102 plates, including frontises. pn Jan 22 (8) £130 [Marlborough]

Gems...
— Gems of American Scenery, Consisting of Stereoscopic Views among the White Mountains. NY: Harroun & Bierstadt, [1878]. 8vo, orig cloth; viewer hinged to verso of front cover; rubbed. With 24 stereographs & map. sg May 7 (6) $225

General Officer. See: Lambart, Richard

Genet, Edmond Charles, 1763-1834
— Memorial on the Upward Forces of Fluids. Albany, 1825. 1st Ed. 8vo, orig bds; worn. O May 12 (80) $900

Geneva. See: Patten, William

Genevoix, Maurice
— La Boite a peche. Paris: Editions Vialetay, 1957. One of 20 on Rives with a suite of the illusts in color on Rives, an uncolored suite with remarques on japon mince, a suite with remarques in bistre on Rives, a suite of the wood-engravings & a watercolor. Illus by Gaston Barret. 4to, unsewn in orig wraps. S June 17 (71) £350 [Schoeni]

Genga, Bernardino, 1655-1734
— Anatomy Improv'd and Illustrated. L: J. Senex, [1723]. Folio, half lea; worn. Some soiling; 1st & last leaves frayed. bba Jan 15 (391) £300 [Phelps]

Genius...
— Genius: Zeitschrift fuer werdende und alte Kunst. Munich, 1919-20-21. Vols I-III (all pbd). 3 vols. 4to, orig bdgs. HK Nov 4 (2959a) DM1,300

Anr copy. Vols II-III in 2 vols only. 4to, orig cloth; worn. HN May 20 (2442) DM950

Genlis, Stephanie Felicite de, 1746-1830
— Theatre a l'usage des jeunes personnes. Paris, 1779-80. 4 vols. 12mo, contemp calf gilt. Lacking half-title in Vol I. S June 25 (24) £260 [Schiller]

Gent, Thomas, 1693-1778
— Annales Regioduni Hullini: or, the History of...Kingston-upon-Hull. York, 1735. 8vo, later calf by Tout. Ck Sept 26 (306) £85

Genthe, Arnold
— As I Remember. NY, [1936]. 1st Ed. 4to, cloth. Sgd. sg Nov 13 (54) $50

Anr copy. Cloth. Inscr. sg Feb 26 (154) $90

— The Book of the Dance. NY, 1916. 1st Ed, One of 100 on japan vellum, with photographic print, sgd, laid in. 4to, bds; worn. Program for an Isadora Duncan Dress Rehearsal laid in. sg Feb 26 (155) $425

— Highlights and Shadows. NY, [1937]. 4to, spiral bd wraps. cb June 18 (99) $60

— Impressions of Old New Orleans. NY, [1926]. 1st Ed, 2d ptg. 4to, half cloth, in d/j. With 102 plates. sg Nov 13 (55) $90

— Isadora Duncan. NY, 1929. 4to, cloth; worn. O Oct 21 (71) $70; sg Feb 26 (156) $110

— Pictures of Old Chinatown. NY, 1913. ("Old Chinatown.") Text by Will Irwin. cb Jan 8 (64) $80

Gentle...
— The Gentle Cynic: Being a Translation of the Book of Koheleth Known as Ecclesiastes.... [San Francisco: Book Club of Calif., 1927]. One of 250. 8vo, vellum; warped & discolored. sg Jan 8 (110) $80

Gentleman...
— The Gentleman Angler: Containing Short, Plain and Easy Instructions.... L, 1736. 2d Ed. 12mo, mor gilt by Zaehnsdorf; spine chipped at head. With 3 page numerals just shaved. S July 23 (281) £250 [Figgis]

Gentleman of the Province, A. See: Peters, Samuel A.

Gentleman's...
— The Gentleman's Magazine, or Trader's Monthly Intelligencer [continued as the Historical Chronicle, etc.]. L, 1731-1868. 222 vols plus 6 vols of index. 8vo, contemp calf. bba May 14 (59) £5,400 [Quaritch]

Gentry, Thomas George, 1843-1905
— Nests and Eggs of Birds of the United States. Phila., 1882. 25 orig parts. 4to, wraps; worn, some chipped or loose. With color title & 54 colored plates. Lacking port. sg Jan 15 (213) $80

Anr copy. 4to, needs rebdg. With port,

color title & 54 colored plates.. sg Jan 15 (214) $80

Anr copy. Disbound. Lacking 1 plate. wa Mar 5 (255) $190

Geoffroy Saint-Hilaire, Etienne, 1772-1844 —& Cuvier, Frederic Georges, 1773-1838

— Histoire naturelle des mammiferes. Paris, [1819]-24-42. 7 vols in 5. Folio, contemp half mor; 1 hinge weak. With 431 hand-colored plates. One plate in Vol I & 2 plates in Vol IV mtd to size & possibly from a smaller copy; titles in Vols I-III & V only; half-titles in Vols I-IV. S Apr 23 (29) £6,500 [Robinson]

George, Prince of Wales. See: Albert Victor & George

George III of England's copy

— Rider's British Merlin for 1761. L, 1761. 12mo, contemp mor gilt with rose, thistle & crown & with the crowned monogram in center, 4 silver bosses with the King's monogram. With George's autograph notes in the calendar & on blanks. S Dec 18 (216) £1,500 [Quaritch]

Gerard, John, 1545-1612

— The Herball.... L, 1597. Bound with: Catalogus arborum fruticum ac plantarum.... L, 1599. 1st Ed. Folio, contemp calf gilt. Engraved title repaired; lacking 2 index leaves; some index leaves with margins repaired; 1 index leaf with small hole. C Oct 15 (192) £2,000 [Maggs]

Anr copy. Old half calf. Lacking 3 leaves of prelims & 2D2; tp def & mtd; a few other leaves def. Sold w.a.f. S July 28 (1076) £380

Anr copy. 19th-cent calf; spine worn at head. Last few leaves frayed. T Dec 18 (282) £340

Anr copy. Early hand-coloring; frayed at end; lacking tp. T Feb 19 (488) £360

2d Ed. L, 1633. Folio, contemp calf; worn, joints & head & foot of spine repaired. Lacking 1st & last blanks & 7A2-5 of tables at end; tp with small piece torn from lower inner corner & a single round wormhole affecting engraved surface; a few marginal wormholes through much of the volume; corners torn from 3M6 & 4A6; piece torn from top of 6Z5; a few small holes & marginal tears touching text; occasional stains. S Oct 23 (697) £350 [Sotheran]

Anr copy. Calf; worn & loose. Lacking engraved title & with Ms title inserted; lacking 1st & last blanks; some dampstaining & worming; a few leaves trimmed; dedication leaf def at outer margin; some leaves repaired at beginning & end. Sold w.a.f. S Nov 10 (492) £350 [Broseghini]

3d Ed. L, 1636. Folio, contemp calf; rebacked. Tp slightly trimmed; minor browning. pnE Dec 17 (247) £620 [Thin]

Anr Ed. L, 1927. 4to, cloth. Frank Brangwyn's copy, sgd by him. O Feb 24 (85) $50

One of 150. Vellum. pnE Dec 17 (248) £65 [Traylen]

Gerard, Louis

— Flora Gallo-Provincialis. Paris, 1761. 8vo, contemp half calf; lower cover detached. pn Jan 22 (229) £85 [Maggs]

Gerard, Marc. See: Saint-Amant, Marc Antoine gerard

Gerard, Max

— Dali. NY, [1968]. One of 1,500. 4to, cloth. In folding box with extra suite of color plates rolled up in a tube & a mtd bronze medallion. wa Mar 5 (112) $225

Gerbier, Sir Balthazar, 1592-1667

— A Sommary Description, Manifesting that Greater Profits are to bee done in the hott then in the could parts.... Rotterdam, 1660. 2 vworks in 1 vol. 4to, half calf. S June 25 (434) £1,500

Germ...

— The Germ: Thoughts towards Nature in Poetry, Literature, and Art. L, Jan-Apr 1850. Nos 1-4 (all pbd). 8vo, orig wraps, in cloth box. S Sept 22 (172) £520 [Swaltes]

Germain, Pierre

— Elements d'orfevrie. Paris, 1748. 4to, contemp calf; spine & extremities rubbed. With 100 plates plus 5 additional plates. Ck May 29 (126) £650

German...

— German Romance: Specimens of its Chief Authors.... Edin & L, 1827. Ed by Thomas Carlyle. 4 vols. 8vo, half cloth; scuffed. Some foxing; Pp 315-17 of Vol II inserted at end of Vol I & p 337 of Vol I inserted at end of Vol II. sg Sept 11 (55) $120

Gerning, Johann Isaac von, 1767-1837

— A Picturesque Tour along the Rhine.... L, 1820. 4to, mor gilt. With double-page map & 24 hand-colored plates. FD June 11 (821) DM11,000

Anr copy. Modern half mor gilt. With 24 hand-colored plates & colored folding map. Library stamp on dedication leaf. Extra-illus with 16 plates on india paper. S Apr 23 (164) £1,800 [Dussel]

Anr copy. Mor gilt. With folding map & 24 hand-colored plates, all before numbers. S June 25 (306) £1,400 [Marshall]

Gernsheim, Helmut
— Lewis Carroll, Photographer. NY, 1949. 1st Ed. In d/j. With 64 plates. wa June 25 (84) $65

Gernsheim, Helmut & Alison
— The History of Photography from the Camera Obscura.... NY, [1969]. 2 leaves of index detached. sg Nov 13 (57) $275; sg May 7 (42) $325

Gersaint, Edme Francoise, d.1750
— A Catalogue and description of the Etchings of Rembrandt Van-Rhyn.... L, 1752. 12mo, contemp calf; rubbed & rebacked. S Nov 10 (89) £65 [Sims]

Gerstenberg, Walter
— Composers' Autographs. L, 1968. 2 vols. 4to, cloth, in d/js. bba Dec 18 (22) £42 [Talbot]

Gesamtkatalog...
— Gesamtkatalog der Wiegendrucke. Leipzig, 1925-40. Vols I-VII. Cloth. Library markings. bba June 18 (4) £400 [Maggs]
Anr copy. Vols 1-7 plus Vol 8/1 of 1972. Cloth, 8/1 in wraps. sg May 14 (443) $550
Anr copy. Vols I-VII. Cloth. sg May 14 (444) $500

Geschichte...
— Geschichte und bildliche Vorstellung der Regimenter des Erzhauses Oesterreich [der Koenighlich Preussischen Regimenter]. Vienna, 1796. 2 vols. 8vo, modern mor. With 109 hand-colored plates only. Tp in facsimile; lacking sectional titles & index; all plates tipped onto a leaf tissue except for 1 which is loosely inserted; some plates with short tears or holes not affecting engraved surface; 1 plate torn across & laid down; some soiling or staining. S June 25 (204) £900 [Schmidt]

Gesner, Conrad, 1516-65
— Chirurgia: de chirurgia scriptores optimi quique veteres et recentiores.... Zurich: A. & J. Gessner, 1555. Folio, modern vellum bds. Lacking last blank, lower margin of title cut away & repaired. S Nov 27 (261) $1,100 [Koch]
— De remediis secretis. Liber physicus, medicus & partim etiam chymicus.... Venice, 1556. 12mo, mor extra by Bueno. Marginalia. sg June 11 (208) $425
— Historia plantarum. Faksimileausgabe...Aquarelle aus dem botanischen Nachlass...in der Universitatsbibliothek Erlangen. Zurich, 1927-78. One of 590. 5 vols. Folio, orig half vellum, in d/js. Crahan copy. P Nov 25 (216) $800
— Historiae animalium liber III qui est de Avium natura. Zurich: Christopher Froshover, 1555. Folio, modern mor gilt by A. Vatant. FD Dec 2 (746) DM5,800
Anr copy. Contemp pigskin; soiled. One leaf torn without loss; the first 39 leaves missing bits of 1 or 2 letters per page. P Dec 15 (197) $1,700
— The Newe Iewell of Health.... L: H. Denham, 1576. 4to, old calf; rebacked. Library stamps. Crahan copy. P Nov 25 (217) $1,500
— Opera botanica. Nuremberg, 1751-59. 3 parts in 1 vol. Folio, contemp calf; spine & joints damaged. With 15 hand-colored engraved plates, 20 engraved plates & 22 woodcut plates. Horticultural Society of New York—de Belder copy. S Apr 27 (130) £3,000 [Law]
Anr Ed. Nuremberg, 1751-71. 2d Issue, with the 2d Issue, dated 1770 of Schmiedel's 1st fasciculus, & the 1st Ed, dated 1771 of the 2d fasiculus, thus completing the work. 2 vols. Folio, contemp half calf gilt. With 32 hand-colored plates, 20 engraved plates & 22 woodcut plates. de Belder copy. S Apr 27 (131) £4,000 [Asher]
— Thierbuch. Zurich: Froschauer, 1583. Folio, vellum. Some stains & repairs. HK Nov 4 (638) DM4,000
— Vogelbuch. Zurich: C. Froschauer, 1557. 1st Ed in German. Folio, contemp blind-stamped pigskin over wooden bds. HK Nov 26 (637) DM9,000

Gessner, Salomon, 1730-88
— La Mort d'Abel. Paris, 1793. 4to, contemp calf gilt. With engraved port & 5 plates. FD Dec (3738) DM1,650
— New Idylles. L, 1776. Trans by W. Hooper. 4to, disbound. With 9 plates. Some waterstains. bba Jan 15 (57) £45 [Archdale]

Getlein, Frank
— Jack Levine. NY, [1966]. Oblong 4to, cloth, orig plastic wrap. With frontis & 169 plates, many tipped in. sg Jan 8 (153) $50

Gheyn, Jacob de, 1565-1615
— Waffenhandlung von der Roeren, Musquetten, und Spiessen. The Hague, 1608. Folio, 19th-cent half vellum. With engraved title & 102 (of 117) plates. Title corrected in ink from 1607 to 1608. Sold w.a.f. sg Nov 20 (114A) $1,700

Ghirshman, Roman
— Fouilles de Sialk. Paris, 1938-39. 2 vols. Folio, modern half cloth. bba Aug 28 (47) £100 [Graves Johnston]

Ghisi, Andrea
— Laberinto dato novamente in luce.... Venice: Evangelista Deuchino, 1616. Folio, modern calf. With 1,260 small woodcuts ptd in red on 22 leaves. Small hole in 4 leaves just touching borders of a woodcut; upper margin of f.3 repaired; some soiling. S May 21 (107) £3,200 [Sourget]

Giacometti, Francesco
— Nuova Giuoco di Scacchi Ossia il Giuoco della Guerra. Genova, 1801. Half calf. Small wormhole in lower margin of 1st few leaves. pn Mar 26 (400) £45 [Former]

Giafferri, Paul Louis de
— L'Histoire du costume feminin.... Paris, [1922-23]. Orig 10 parts. Folio, unbound as issued in orig wraps. Ck June 19 (175) £140
— The History of French Masculine Costume. NY: Foreign Publications, [1927]. Folio, cloth. With 100 colored plates. Library markings. sg June 4 (97) $175

Gianutio, Orazio
— Libro nel quale si tratta della maniera di giuocara scacchi. Turin: Antonio de Bianchi, 1597. Modern vellum. Inner lower margins repaired with occasional loss of part of woodcut border on 9 last leaves. pn Mar 26 (401) £2,000 [De Lucia]

Gibbings, Robert
— Twelve Wood Engravings. [L], 1921. One of 125. 4to, orig half cloth. With 12 plates. bba Aug 20 (174) £280 [Henderson]
— The Wood Engravings.... L, 1959. 4to, cloth. bba Oct 16 (417) £50 [Bookroom]; bba Dec 4 (211) £50 [Bowers]

Anr copy. Orig cloth, in d/j. Ck Oct 17 (180) £45

Gibbon, Edward, 1737-94
— The History of the Decline and Fall of the Roman Empire. L, 1776-88. 2d Ed of Vol I; 1st Eds of Vols II-VI. 6 vols. 4to, contemp calf; rubbed. Ck Feb 13 (143) £450

3d Ed of Vol I, 1st Ed of Vols II-VI. L, 1777-88. 6 vols. 4to, contemp calf; rubbed, 2 covers broken. With engraved frontis & 3 folding maps. Ck Nov 7 (244) £220

Anr Ed. L, 1791. 12 vols. 8vo, calf. pnE Nov 12 (268) £38

Anr Ed. L, 1797. 12 vols. 8vo, contemp calf gilt; rubbed. Last 2 leaves of Vol VI torn at corner with loss of page numbers. S Jan 13 (643) £110 [Maggs]

Anr Ed. L, 1815. 12 vols. 8vo, contemp calf gilt; scuffed. Some foxing. rubberstamp reading "Printed in Great Britain" on versos of titles. cb Feb 19 (112) $110

Anr Ed. L, 1882. Vols I-III only. Contemp half mor. bba Ma 29 (184) £100
— Miscellaneous Works. L, 1796-1815. 1st Ed. 3 vols. 4to, half calf; rubbed, inner hinges crudely repaired. bba Jan 15 (67) £85 [Frew Mackenzie]

Anr copy. 3 vols. Contemp half calf; joints weak. Ck Feb 13 (144) £75

Anr copy. 3 vols. 4to, calf; worn, broken. Corner of 1 leaf soiled; some foxing. K Mar 22 (120) $120; pnE Jan 28 (98) £220 [Thin]

Anr copy. Contemp calf gilt; rubbed, rebacked with mor. S Mar 9 (746) £85 [Hannas]
— Works. NY, [1906-7]. 15 vols. ha May 22 (59) $75

Gibbon, Lardner. See: Herndon & Gibbon

Gibbons, Alfred St. Hill, 1858-1916
— Exploration and Hunting in Central Africa 1895-96. L, 1898. 8vo, cloth; extremities rubbed. With frontis, map, 8 plates & 25 photos. Lacking front free endpaper. cb Nov 6 (141) $95

Gibbs, George
— The Gibbs Family of Rhode Island.... Pvtly ptd at the Derrydale Press, 1933. One of 150. Ns laid in. sg Oct 23 (53) $350

Gibbs, James, 1682-1754
— A Book of Architecture. L, 1728. 1st Ed. Folio, contemp half calf; rubbed, head of spine frayed. With 149 (of 150) plates. Plate 98 torn; Plate 54 inverted; waterstain to a few plates at end. C May 13 (109) £800 [Ramsay]

Anr copy. Bdg not indicated. Library markings. Sold w.a.f. Franklin Institute copy. F Sept 12 (17) $1,100

Anr copy. Contemp half calf gilt; worn, rebacked. With 149 (of 150) plates. HN May 20 (161) DM1,800

2d Ed. L, 1739. Folio, modern half calf preserving old bds; hinges strengthened with tape. bba Sept 25 (275) £520 [Dennistoun]

Gibson, James, fl.1873
— The Bibliography of Robert Burns. Kilmarnock, 1881. One of 600. 8vo, orig half cloth; rubbed. O June 16 (24) $50

Gibson, John, Merchant of Glasgow
— The History of Glasgow, from the Earliest Accounts.... Glasgow, 1777. 8vo, orig bds; broken, spine chipped. O Feb 24 (86) $70

Gibson, John Michael. See: Green & Gibson

GIBSON

Gibson, Reginald Walter
— Francis Bacon: a Bibliography.... Oxford, 1950. 4to, half cloth. Lacking Supplement. bba Dec 4 (234) £50 [Weiner]
Anr copy. Cloth. sg May 14 (595) $90

Gibson, Strickland
— Early Oxford Bindings. L, 1903. 4to, mor, orig wraps bound as endpapers. S May 6 (379) £110 [Foster]

Gibson, William Hamilton, 1850-96
— Our Edible Toadstools and Mushrooms and How to Distinguish Them. NY, 1895. 4to, orig cloth. With 30 color plates. sg Jan 15 (215) £110

Gilbert, Josiah —& Churchill, G.C.
— The Dolomite Mountains. L, 1864. 8vo, orig cloth; rubbed, lower hinge cracked. With 2 folding maps & 6 colored plates. Ck Sept 26 (137) £120

Gilbert, Thomas
— Voyage from New South Wales to Canton.... L, 1789. 4to, contemp calf; hinges cracked. With 4 folding plates. Some spotting & staining; plates stained. Manchester copy. S June 25 (493) £1,700 [Maggs]

Gilchrist, Alexander, 1828-61
— Life of William Blake. L, 1863. 2 vols. 8vo, cloth; frontis of Vol I detached. Some foxing. sg Feb 5 (40) $150

Gildas, 516?-70?
— The Epistle of Gildas, the Most Ancient British Author.... L, 1638. 12mo, modern half calf. Last leaf repaired. bba Nov 13 (186) £50 [Bennett & Ken]

Giles, Ernest, 1847-97
— Geographic Travels in Central Australia.... Melbourne, 1875. 8vo, orig cloth. Inscr to the Governor General of Victoria. Ck Sept 26 (215) £750

Gilio, Giovanni Andrea
— Due Dialogi.... Camerino, 1564. 4to, vellum. Some dampstaining; tp rehinged; outer margin restored. sg Mar 26 (128) $900

Gill, Brendan
— Wooings. Verona: Plain Wrapper Press, [1980]. One of 155. Illus by Fulvio Testa. Bds. cb Sept 11 (208) $60

Gill, Emlyn Metcalf
— Practical Dry-Fly Fishing. NY, 1912. Inscr. sg Oct 23 (288) $70

Gill, Eric, 1882-1940
See also: Golden Cockerel Press
— 25 Nudes. L, 1938. In repaired d/j. With 26 plates. bba Apr 23 (286) £80 [Dawson]
Anr copy. In d/j. With 26 plates. Sold with 5 prospectuses. Ck Jan 30 (162) £65
— Sculpture, with a Preface about God. Ditchling: St. Dominic's Press, [1923]. 2d Ed. 16mo, orig cloth; discolored. sg June 4 (145) $80

Gill, Samuel Thomas, d.1890
— The Diggers and Diggings of Victoria as they are in 1855. Melbourne, 1855. Oblong 8vo, orig wraps. With 18 plates. Foxed. CA Apr 12 (105A) A$1,200
— Paintings of S. T. Gill. Adelaide, 1962. 4to, cloth, in d/j. kh Mar 16 (211) A$80
— Victoria Illustrated. Melbourne, etc., 1857. Oblong 4to, contemp mor. With engraved title & 45 plates. kh Mar 16 (449) A$2,000
Anr copy. Mor gilt; soiled. Some waterstains; all plates loose. S July 14 (853) £600

Gille, Philippe
— Versailles et les deux Trianons. Tours, 1899-1900. One of 150. Illus by M. Lambert. 2 vols. Folio, mor; worn. S Nov 10 (91) £80 [Duffy]

Gillen, Francis J. See: Spencer & Gillen

Gillespie, Maj. Alexander
— Gleanings and Remarks.... Leeds, 1818. 1st Ed. 8vo, orig bds; rubbed, back endpaper torn & def. With 2 folding maps. Lacking index leaf. bba Aug 28 (297) £50 [Pordes]
Anr copy. Later half mor; spine worn. With 1 double-page map. Ck May 15 (121A) £120
Anr copy. Orig bds; rubbed. With 2 folding maps. pn Mar 5 (24) £150 [Maggs]

Gillingwater, Edmund
— An Historical Account of...Lowestoft.... L, [1790]. 1st Ed. 4to, calf; rubbed. Lacking half title; with 9 plates from other works. S Feb 23 (16) £180 [Gouldby]

Gilliss, James Melville, 1811-65
— The U. S. Naval Astronomical Expedition to the Southern Hemisphere. Wash., 1855. Vol I only. Contemp mor gilt. With hand-colored panorama, 9 maps & plans & 41 plates, many hand-colored or ptd in color. Some stains. bba June 18 (126) £180 [Arader]
Anr copy. 2 vols. Orig cloth; broken. With 6 maps, 3 plans & 42 plates. cb Apr 2 (115) $120

Gillmore, Parker
— Prairie Farms and Prairie Folk. L, 1872 [1871]. 2 vols. 8vo, modern half calf. Some spotting. C Oct 15 (37) £100 [Bickersteth]

Gillray, James, 1757-1815
— The Caricatures of Gillray. L, [1818]. Parts 1-9 in 1 vol. Oblong 4to, contemp half calf, orig wraps bound in; loose. With 63 hand-colored plates. S June 17 (239) £1,300 [Renard]
— Works. L: Bohn, [c.1849]. Folio, contemp half mor; worn. With port & 587 caricatures on 152 leaves. Port & last leaf detached & frayed. C Oct 15 (38) £700 [Evans]

Anr copy. Modern half mor. With 576 plates on 147 leaves only. Dampstained; some plates worn or repaired. Sold w.a,f. S Nov 10 (214) £210 [Russell]

Cilpin, Laura
— The Enduring Navaho. Austin, 1968. 4to, cloth, in chipped d/j; shelf numbers on spine. Inscr. sg Nov 13 (58) $800

Gilpin, Richard
— Demonologia Sacra: or, a Treatise of Satan's Temptations. Edin., 1735. 8vo, calf; worn. bba Mar 12 (390) £50 [Camberwell]

Gilpin, William, 1724-1804
— Observations Relative Chiefly to Picturesque Beauty...Mountains and Lakes of Cumberland and Westmorland. L, 1788. 2d Ed. 2 vols. 8vo, later mor gilt. With 31 plates. Lacking half-titles. cb June 4 (82) $250
— Observations, Relative Chiefly to Picturesque Beauty Made in 1776... the High-Lands of Scotland. L, 1789. 1st Ed. 2 vols. 8vo, contemp calf; needs rebdg. sg June 11 (209) $100
— Observations on the River Wye.... L, 1792. 3d Ed. 8vo, contemp half calf; rubbed. With 17 plates, some loose. Some spotting or soiling. S Nov 10 (788) £50 [Evans]
— Observations on the Western Parts of England, Relative Chiefly to Picturesque Beauty. L, 1798. 8vo, later mor gilt. With 18 plates. Lacking half-title. cb June 4 (85) $65
— Remarks on Forest Scenery.... L, 1818. 8vo, contemp calf gilt; joints split, rubbed. With hand-colored folding map & 31 plates. bba Sept 25 (276) £100 [Rainer]

Gilpin, William, 1822-94
— The Central Gold Region. Phila., 1860. 1st Ed. 8vo, disbound. With 6 folding maps, mostly hand-colored, 1 with 4-inch tear. wa Sept 25 (445) $80

Gilpin, William Sawrey, 1762-1843
— Practical Hints upon Landscape Gardening. L, 1835. 8vo, orig cloth. bba Sept 25 (277) £130 [Weinreb]

Gimson, Ernest
— Ernest Gimson: his Life and Work. Stratford: Shakespeare Head Press, 1924. One of 550. 4to, orig half cloth. S Nov 10 (92) £420 [Haynes]

Giorgi, Federigo
— Libro Giorgi del modo di conoscere i buoni falconi.... Venice: Gabriel Giolito, 1567. 8vo, 19th cent shagreen. Schwerdt Jeanson copy. SM Mar 1 (263) FF3,200

Giorgio, Marco Antonio
— Ex divi Joannis apostoli et evangelistae.... Rome: heirs of Antonio Blado, 1570. 4to, contemp vellum; worn & loose. Wormhole through 1st few leaves. Phillipps copy. sg Mar 26 (129) $140

Giovanni, Tito
— I quattro libri della caccia.... Venice, 1556. 2 parts in 1 vol. 4to, modern mor gilt. With 13 woodcuts, including a world map. Short wormhole in some inner margins; 2 small holes in the fore-margins of the first 3 pp. S May 21 (40) £400 [Hesketh & Ward]

Anr copy. Contemp vellum; spine def. S June 25 (25) £500 [Koch]

Giovio, Paolo. See: Jovius, Paulus

Giraldus Cambrensis, 1146?-1220?
— Itinerarium Cambriae seu laboriose Balduin Cantuariensis Archiepiscopi per Walliam Legationis. L, 1804. 4to, contemp calf; rebacked. With folding map & 4 plates. S Nov 10 (789) £55 [Jones]

Girard, Guillaume, d.1663
— The History of the Life of the Duke of Espernon. L, 1670. 1st Ed in English. Folio, contemp calf; worn. With 2 ports. T Sept 18 (348) £46

Girard, Pierre Jacques Francois
— Traite des armes.... Paris, 1737. 2d Ed. Oblong 4to, later half mor. With engraved title, frontis & 98 plates only. Some plates torn & repaired, 1 detached. Sold w.a.f. Ck Jan 16 (112) £380

Giraudier, Baltasar
— Expedicion a Jolo, 1876. [Madrid: J. M. Mateu, 1877]. Oblong folio, half calf. With litho title & 38 plates. S Oct 23 (484) £950 [Remmington]

GIRAUDOUX

Giraudoux, Jean, 1882-1944
— Judith, Tragodie in drei Acten. Stuttgart: Manus Presse, 1972. One of 500. Illus by Max Ernst & Dorothea Tanning. Folio, unsewn in orig wraps. S June 29 (92) £500 [Bolligar]
— Suzanne et le Pacifique. Paris, 1928. Illus by Daragnes. 4to, mor by Paul Bonet with mor onlays. Lacking the plates & proofs. SM Oct 20 (631) FF105,000

Giraudoux, Jean, 1882-1944 —& Others
— Les Sept Peches capitaux. Paris: Kra, 1926. One of 300. Illus by Marc Chagall. 4to, orig wraps. With 15 etchings. JG Oct 2 (1890) DM12,000

Girava, Hieronymus, d.1556
— Dos Libros de cosmographia. Milan: G. A. Castiglione & C. Caron, 1556. 1st Ed. 4to, 17th-cent calf gilt; rubbed. Waterstaining to upper third of text; inner marginal worming to Y2-Ee2 not affecting text; map with short marginal tear & some neat reinforcement on verso. S Apr 23 (185) £5,600 [Israel]

Gironi, Robustiano, 1769-1838
— Le Danze dei Greci. Milan, 1820. One of 80. 4to, contemp lea; rebacked preserving orig spine. With frontis & 5 plates, all hand-colored. S Oct 23 (336) £1,200 [Raban]

Girtanner, Christoph, 1760-1800
— Abhandlung ueber die Krankheiten der Kinder.... Berlin, 1794. 8vo, contemp bds. HK Nov 4 (993) DM560

Girtin, Thomas, 1775-1802
See also: Turner & Girtin
— A Selection of Twenty of the Most Picturesque Views in Paris and its Environs. L, 1803. Folio, contemp half mor; worn. With engraved title & 20 plates. First plate faintly creased. S May 29 (1047) £1,500

Gissing, George, 1857-1903
— Born in Exile. L, 1892. 3 vols. 8vo, later cloth. Library markings. T Feb 18 (96) £38
— New Grub Street. L, 1891. 1st Ed, 2d Issue. 3 vols. 8vo, orig cloth, variant bdg. S May 6 (433) £260 [Thorn]

2d Ed. 8vo, orig cloth; blistered, front hinge split in Vol I & starting in Vol II. With 2 A Ls s. T. J. Wise's copy. sg Apr 2 (87) $600
— Workers in the Dawn. L, 1880. 1st Ed. 3 vols. 12mo, orig cloth; worn & spotted. sg Apr 2 (88) $1,750

AMERICAN BOOK PRICES CURRENT

Glaisher, James, 1809-1903 —& Others
— Voyages aeriens.... Paris, 1870. 8vo, contemp half mor; worn & rubbed. With 6 plates & 15 maps and diagrams. wa Nov 6 (6) $180

Glanvil, Barthelemy de
— Bestiaire. Paris, 1955. One of 100. Illus by Abraham Krol. Folio, unbound as issued in orig wraps. With 15 plates. Ck Nov 28 (335) £80

Glanvill, Joseph, 1636-80
— Lux Orientalis, or an Enquiry. L, 1662. 8vo, modern calf. Several leaves repaired; some leaves cropped close, just affecting headline; some dampstaining. bba Nov 13 (193) £170 [Quaritch]
— Saducismus triumphatus: or Full and Plain Evidence Concerning Witches and Apparitions. L, 1681-82. 8vo, contemp calf; broken, worn. Marginal soiling; frontis to Part 2 only. bba July 16 (231) £85 [Keyes]

Anr copy. Contemp calf; worn & soiled. wa Dec 11 (703) $160

Anr Ed. L, 1682-81. 8vo, old calf; rebacked, broken. Several minor marginal tears. sg Oct 9 (216) $250

Glas, George
— The History of the Discovery and Conquest of the Canary Islands. L, 1764. 2 parts in 1 vol. 4to, cloth. With 3 maps. bba Dec 18 (153) £55 [Bailey]

Glaspell, Susan, 1882-1948
— A Jury of her Peers. L, 1927. One of 250. Wraps. cb Nov 20 (211) $95

Glasse, Hannah, fl.1747
— The Art of Cookery, Made Plain and Easy.... L, 1747. 1st Ed, 1st Issue, with 16 pp of prelims, "6d" entered by hand on title; without notice of the second place of sale & without O2. Folio, later 19th-cent mor gilt; rubbed. Interleaved throughout; with 5 pp of Ms notes; some leaves strengthened or with tears repaired, scarcely affecting text; some dampstains in lower margin. S Dec 18 (337) £2,100 [Joseph & Sawyer]

4th Ed. L, 1751. 8vo, contemp calf; rebacked. First leaf of Chapter I torn & repaired. pn Nov 20 (175) £55 [Coop]

5th Ed. L, 1755. 8vo, contemp calf; rebacked, endpapers renewed. sg Jan 15 (25) $150

8th Ed. L, 1763. 8vo, calf; worn. Some staining. pn Sept 18 (121) £70 [Culpin]

Anr Ed. Edin., 1774. 12mo, lea; rubbed & scuffed, joints cracked. Prelims foxed; stain at beginning. cb July 30 (264) $150

Anr Ed. L, 1778. 8vo, contemp calf;

rubbed, upper cover detached. Some stains; short tear in folding plate. bba May 28 (46) £90 [Elkin Mathews]

Anr Ed. L, 1788. 8vo, old calf; rebacked, new endleaves, corners worn. Tp, folding plate, F8 & G1 all with clean tears repaired. Hunt copy. CNY Nov 21 (70) $170

Glasspoole, Richard, 1788-1846. See: Golden Cockerel Press

Glauber, Johann Rudolf, 1604-62
— Works. L, 1689. 3 parts in 1 vol. Folio, old calf; broken. Library markings. Sold w.a.f. Franklin Institute copy. F Sept 12 (77) $500

Gleason's...
— Gleason's Pictorial Drawing-Room Companion. Bost., 1853. Vol V. 26 issues (July-Dec) in 1 vol. Folio, half lea; worn & soiled. wa Nov 6 (430) $70

Gleichen, Wilhelm Friedrich von
— Auserlesene mikroskopische Entdeckungen bey den Pflanzen, Blumen und Bluethen, Insekten.... Nuremberg, 1777-[81]. 4to, contemp vellum bds. With port & 83 hand-colored plates. de Belder copy. S Apr 27 (134) £3,000 [Jan Loock]

— Dissertation sur la generation, les animalcules spermatiques.... Paris, 1799. 1st Ed in French. 4to, recent half lea. With 32 plates & tables. Tp browned; 2 plates with minor defs. HN May 22 (1065) DM650

— Das Neueste aus dem Reiche der Pflanzen.... Nuremberg, 1764-[66]. Folio, later half vellum bds. With 51 hand-colored plates. Honeyman—de Belder copy. S Apr 27 (132) £950 [Lan]

— Les plus nouvelles decouvertes dans le regne vegetal.... Nuremberg, 1763-70. Folio, contemp calf. With 51 hand-colored plates & with 2 titles, 1 dated 1763, the other, 1770. Vilmorin—de Belder copy. S Apr 27 (133) £1,400 [Junk]

Glorieux, Genevieve. See: Cockx-Indestege & Glorieux

Glover, Dorothy —&
Greene, Graham
— Victorian Detective Fiction. L, 1966. One of 500, sgd by John Carter, Glover & Greene. In d/j. cb Nov 20 (316) $190

Glover, Richard, 1712-85
— Leonidas, a Poem. L, 1737. 1st Ed. 4to, contemp calf; rubbed, rebacked. First few leaves spotted. bba Jan 15 (39) £35 [Smallwood]

Gobler, Justin
— Spiegel der Rechten.... Frankfurt: Egenolff, 1573. Bound with: Seyler, Raphael. Der Roemischen Kaiserlichen Mayestat und gemeiner des heyligen Reichs. Folio, contemp blind-stamped pigskin; clasps lacking. Some browning & soiling. O Sept 23 (72) $850

Goddard, John —&
Clarke, Brian
— The Trout and the Fly; a New Aoproach. L, [1980]. One of 25. 4to, mor gilt. With 7 hand-tied flies by Stewart Canham in an oval sunken mount. sg Oct 23 (289) $500

Goddard, Josiah
— A Chinese and English Vocabulary.... Bangkok, 1847. 8vo, orig cloth. S Apr 23 (343) £750 [Ad Orientum]

Goddard, Paul B.
— The Anatomy, Physiology, and Pathology of the Human Teeth.... Phila., 1844. 8vo, orig cloth; lacking backstrip. With 30 plates. Tp soiled. sg Jan 15 (84) $350

Goddard, Robert H., 1882-1945
— The Papers of Robert H. Goddard, 1898-1945. NY: McGraw-Hill, [1970]. Ed by Esther C. Goddard & G. Edward Pendray. 3 vols. 8vo, orig cloth. wa Nov 6 (47) $80

Godde, Charles
— Piqu'avant Conflans.... A la Chandeau [Paris: Bonaventure et Ducessois], 1863. One of 2. 12mo, contemp mor gilt with arms of Charles de Mandre. Dedication copy. Jeanson copy. SM Mar 1 (265) FF2,200

Godersky, steven Owen. See: Levack & Godersky

Godinho, Consuelo
— Alphabeto Aboim Composto Desenhado e Gravado pela Calligrapha. [Portugal, c.1860]. Oblong 4to, cloth; worn, spine torn, loose. With Tp in red & gold surrounding mtd photographic port medallion & with 26 alphabet plates within borders ptd in gold & colors. O Sept 23 (73) $160

Godman, Eva M. See: Archer & Godman

Godman, John Davidson, 1794-1830
— American Natural History. Phila., 1826-28. Part I: Mastology [all pbd]. 3 vols. 4to, modern half cloth; worn. Some foxing. O June 9 (70) $60

Godolphin, John, 1617-78
— The Orphan's Legacy. L, 1701. 4th Ed. 4to, contemp calf; joints cracked, rubbed. bba Oct 30 (83) £95 [Reese]

GODWIN

Godwin, George, 1815-88
— The Churches of London.... L, 1838-39. 2 vols. 8vo, contemp calf gilt; some wear. With 59 plates. S May 28 (870) £150

Godwin, William, 1756-1836
— The Enquirer. Reflections on Education, Manners and Literature. L, 1797. 1st Ed. 8vo, contemp half mor gilt; rubbed, tears in marbled paper, corners knocked. Lacking errata leaf; some stains, mostly marginal. P Sept 24 (294) $425

— An Enquiry Concerning Political Justice. L, 1793. 1st Ed. 2 vols. 4to, modern half calf. Lacking errata leaf; some waterstaining & soiling; hole in blank margin of 2y3; hole in 3X1 affecting 2 letters. P Sept 24 (295) $1,600

2 vols. L, 1796. 8vo, contemp calf; rubbed. With signatures on half-titles. cb Oct 23 (92) $65

— Lives of the Necromancers. L, 1834. 1st Ed. 8vo, 19th-cent half calf; rebacked with cloth, orig backstrip laid down. sg Feb 12 (162) $90

— Mandeville. Edin., 1817. 1st Ed. 3 vols. 12mo, contemp half calf; rubbed. Some spots & dampstains. S Jan 13 (496) £210 [Joseph]

— Memoirs of the Author of A Vindication of the Rights of Woman. L, 1798. 1st Ed. 8vo, orig bds; rubbed, spine torn & def; port stained. bba Apr 23 (197) £160 [Finch]

— Of Population. An Enquiry concerning the Power of Increase...an Answer to Mr. Malthus. L, 1820. 8vo, modern half mor gilt. P Sept 24 (295A) $650

1st Ed. 8vo, orig bds; broken. sg Apr 2 (89) $900

— Recherches sur la population.... Paris, 1821. 2 vols. 8vo, half calf with gilt initials LLL at bottom of spine; joint wormed, rubbed. Tear repaired in upper margin of 1 leaf affecting a running head. P Sept 24 (296) $300

Goebelius, Joannes
— Hydriatria Wisensis: das ist, beschreibung des Weisen- oder S. Jobs-Bades.... St. Annaberg, 1675. 12mo, old bds; worn. Browned; 1st few leaves of each gathering wormed. sg Jan 15 (64) $90

Goedaerdt, Joannes, 1620-68
— Metamorphosis naturalis ofte historische Beschrijvinghe.... Middelburg, [1667]. Vol II (of 3) only. 8vo, needs rebdg. With additional title & 42 plates. sg Jan 15 (216) $50

AMERICAN BOOK PRICES CURRENT

Goedeke, Karl, 1814-87
— Grundriss zur Geschichte der deutschen Dichtung.... Dresden, 1884-1938. Mixed Ed. Vols 1-12 (of 15) in 17. Various bdgs; some worn, 1 backstrip partly detached. sg Oct 2 (151) $500

Goeldi, Emil August, 1859-1917
— Album de aves amazonica. Rio de Janeiro, 1900-6. 4to, orig wraps. With 48 color plates. Haverschmidt copy. B Feb 25 (292) HF550

Goerling, Adolph, 1821-77
— Stahlstich-Sammlung nach den vorzueglichsten Gemaelden der Dresdener Galerie. Leipzig & Dresden: A. H. Payne, [c.1850]. 2 vols. 4to, contemp half lea. With engraved title & 124 plates only. JG Oct 2 (551) DM500

Goetghebuer, P. J.
— Choix des monuments, edifices et maisons les plus remarquables du royaume des Pays Bas. Ghent, 1827. Folio, contemp half calf; worn, spine def. With 118 plates. HN Nov 26 (399) DM2,800

Goethe, Johann Wolfgang von, 1749-1832
See also: Doves Press
— De Leiden des jungen Werthers.... Leipzig, 1774. 1st Ed, issue with woodcut vignette at end. 2 parts in 1 vol. 16mo, contemp bds. Waterstains, browning & spotting. FD June 11 (3995) DM16,000

Anr copy. Modern calf gilt. HN May 20 (1803) DM16,000

— Faust. Berlin, 1924. One of 1,000. 4to, vellum; soiled. S Oct 6 (646) £50 [Nosbuesch]

Anr Ed. L, [1925]. Illus by Harry Clarke; trans by John Anster. 4to, orig half vellum; soiled. With 21 plates, 7 colored. sg Jan 8 (47) $225

— Die Feier. [1825]. Single leaf. 8vo. Sgd. S May 21 (148) £480 [Symonds]

— Rameau's Neffe. Leipzig, 1805. 8vo, contemp half calf. HK Nov 4 (2511) DM1,100

— Reineke Fuchs. Berlin, 1921. One of 200. Illus by Lovis Corinth. Folio, orig portfolio. JG Oct 2 (1893a) DM3,400

— Werke. Stuttgart & Tuebingen: Cotta, 1815-19. 20 vols. 8vo, contemp half calf gilt; worn & def. HK Nov 4 (2489) DM1,800

Anr Ed. Stuttgart & Tuebingen, 1827-34. 55 vols. 12mo, contemp bds. HK Nov 4 (2490) DKM1,350

Anr copy. Contemp half lea; worn. Some spotting & browning; some leaves loose. HN May 20 (1797) DM2,100

Anr Ed. Stuttgart & Tuebingen, 1828-35.

57 vols, including contents vol & supplement. Later cloth, supplement not uniform. S Mar 10 (942) £300 [Kiefer]

Anr Ed. Stuttgart, 1866-68. 36 vols in 18. 8vo, contemp half mor; rubbed. O Nov 18 (73) $50

— West-oestlicher Divan. Stuttgart, 1819. 1st Ed. 8vo, contemp half calf. HK Nov 4 (2504) DM1,400

Anr copy. Vellum. HN Nov 26 (1212) DM1,000

Anr copy. Contemp bds. HN May 20 (1807) DM2,000

— Works. Bost.: Francis A. Niccolls, [1902]. Edition de Grand Luxe, One of 250. 14 vols. 8vo, half mor gilt. cb Dec 4 (109) $120

Goetz, Hermann. See: Kuehnel & Goetz

Goff, Frederick R.
— Incunabula in American Libraries: A Third Census. NY, 1964. bba Oct 16 (379) £75 [Poel]; sg May 14 (445) $225; sg June 11 (212) $110

Gogarty, Oliver St. John, 1878-1957. See: Cuala Press

Gogol, Nicolai Vasil'evich, 1809-52
— The Over-Coat. Verona: Officina Bodoni, 1975. One of 160. Illus by Pietro Annigoni. 4to, orig half vellum. With 6 plates. S June 18 (334) £380 [Hocarti]

Goguet, Antoine Yves, 1716-58
— De l'Origine des loix, des arts, et des sciences.... Paris, 1758. 1st Ed. 3 vols. 4to, half calf. B Feb 25 (1003) HF300

Anr Ed. Paris, 1759. 6 vols. 4to, contemp calf gilt; rubbed. O Sept 23 (74) $180

Golden...
— The Golden Hind, a Quarterly Magazine of Art and Literature. L, 1923-24. Vol II, Nos 5-8 only. Ed by Clifford Bax & Austin Spare. Half cloth, orig wraps bound in; worn. Inscr by Spare on front endleaf with details of his contributions to these issues. S Oct 6 (864) £80 [Camberwell]

Golden Cockerel Press—Waltham Saint Lawrence, Berkshire
— The Book of Jonah. 1926. One of 175. S Dec 4 (104) £700 [Buzell-Ross]

Anr copy. Sgd by David Jones. With 7 proofs for the wood engravings (sgd & dated) loosely inserted. S Dec 4 (105) £1,100 [Maggs]; S June 18 (322) £350 [Pappermain]

— Chanticleer, a Bibliography of the Golden Cockerel Press. 1936. One of 300. bba Aug 20 (216) £160 [Bowers]

Anr copy. Inscr by Christopher Sandford to Frank Lewis. pn Apr 30 (297) £150 [Croslano]

— The Chester Play of the Deluge. 1927. One of 275. cb June 18 (104) $325

Anr copy. Worn. S Dec 4 (108) £300 [Sykes]

— Ecclesiastes, or the Preacher. 1934. One of 247. S Dec 4 (116) £260 [Sykes]

— The Golden Cockerel Greek Anthology. 1937. One of 200. bba Apr 23 (278) £85 [Crosland]

— Homeric Hymn to Aphrodite. 1948. One of 650. sg Sept 11 (193) $130

— Kalidasa. A Circle of the Seasons. 1929. One of 500. sg Jan 8 (89) $50

— Mabinoglon. 1948. One of 75 specially bound. Trans by Gwyn Jones & Thomas Jones. sg Sept 11 (194) $900

— Pervigilium Veneris, the Vigil of Venus. 1939. Out-of-series copy. Unbound. T June 18 (176) £100

— The Psalter, or Psalms of David. 1927. One of 500. Ck Nov 21 (113) £45

— Roses of Sharon... 1937. One of 10 specially bound. Ed by O.E. Oesterley. S June 18 (324) £350 [Marks]

— Samson and Delilah. 1925. One of 325. Sgd by Robert Gibbings on tp. bba Aug 20 (195) £220 [Arnold]; S Oct 6 (721) £100 [Bookroom]

— The Song of Songs... 1925. One of 720. Some leaves roughly opened. cb Sept 11 (102) $250; S Dec 4 (102) £520 [Blackwells]

Anr copy. Illus by Eric Gill. bba Oct 16 (202) £160 [Quaritch]

Anr Ed. 1936. One of 140. bba Apr 23 (277) £110 [Orssich]

One of 64 with 6 extra plates specially bound. pnNY Sept 13 (233) $325

Aesop. - The Fables. 1926. One of 350. sg Jan 8 (84) $110

— Barclay, John. - Euphormio's Satyricon. 1954. One of 260. cb Dec 4 (110) $70

— Bell, Gertrude. - The Arab War. 1940. One of 30 specially bound in mor. Streeter copy. C May 13 (173) £600 [Loman]

One of 30 specially bound with 6 pp collotype supplement of an essay by Bell. With a set of corrected galley proofs & page proofs in half mor box by Sangorski & Sutcliffe. S Dec 4 (128) £900 [Loman]

— Bligh, William. - The Log of the Bounty. 1937. One of 300. 2 vols. S Dec 4 (122) £460 [Hayes]

— Bligh, William. - Voyage in the Resource. 1937. One of 350. S Dec 4 (123) £280 [Old Hall]

— Bligh, William & Fryer, John. - The Voyage of the Bounty's Launch. 1934. One of 300. Sgd by Robert Gibbings on tp. bba Aug 20 (210) £260 [Thorp]; S Dec 4 (115) £240 [Blackwells]

GOLDEN COCKEREL PRESS

- BRANTOME, PIERRE DE BOURDEILLE. - The Lives of Gallant Ladies. 1924. One of 18 with an extra set of the illusts, but this copy without the set of illusts. 2 vols. bba Aug 20 (191) £200 [National Library of Ireland] One of 625. O Mar 24 (83) $70
- CAREY, HENRY. - Songs & Poems. 1924. One of 30, sgd by Robert Gibbings. Vellum. bba Aug 20 (192) £130 [Dawson] One of 350. Sgd by Gibbings on the title. bba Aug 20 (193) £70 [Dawson]
- CHASE, OWEN & OTHERS. - Narratives of the Wreck of the Whale-Ship Essex. 1935. One of 275. bba Aug 20 (213) £300 [Thorp]; S Dec 4 (119) £280 [Traylen]
- CHAUCER, GEOFFREY. - The Canterbury Tales. 1929-31. One of 485. 4 vols. pnNY Mar 12 (83) $2,300
- CIBBER, COLLEY. - An Apology for the Life of.... 1925. One of 450. 2 vols. Unopened. sg Jan 8 (88) $60
- CLAY, ENID. - The Constant Mistress. 1934. One of 300. S May 6 (47) £100 [Cox]
- CLAY, ENID. - Sonnets and Verses. 1925. One of 450. Inscr to Mme Cyan from Moira & Robert Gibbings. Ck Dec 10 (332A) £120
- COPPARD, ALFRED EDGAR. - The Hundredth Story. 1931. One of 1,000. ha May 22 (161) $60
- DE CHAIR, SOMERSET. - The First Crusade. 1945. One of 500. pnNY Sept 13 (235) $180
- FLAUBERT, GUSTAVE. - Salambo. 1931. One of 500. Sgd by Robert Gibbings on frontis. bba Aug 20 (204) £90 [Deighton Bell]
- FLINDERS, MATTHEW. - Narrative of his Voyage in the Schooner "Francis." 1946. One of 750. bba Oct 30 (250) £90 [Smallwood]
- FLINT, SIR WILLIAM RUSSELL. - Minxes Admonished, or Beauty Reproved. 1955. One of 150 specially bound. C May 13 (189) £200 [Sims]
- GAUTIER, THEOPHILE. - Mademoiselle de Maupin. 1938. One of 450. bba Aug 28 (261) £190 [Kin Bkunya] One of 50 specially bound, with 4 extra plates. S Dec 4 (126) £480 [Green]
- GILL, ERIC. - Clothing Without Cloth.... 1931. One of 500. S Oct 6 (719) £90 [Contemporary]
- GLASSPOOLE, RICHARD. - Mr. Glasspoole and the Chinese Pirates. 1935. One of 315. Sgd by Robert Gibbings on tp. bba Aug 20 (214) £90 [Thorp]
- GRIMM BROTHERS. - Grimms' Other Tales: A New Selection. 1956. One of 75 specially bound in mor. sg Sept 11 (197) $200
- HARTNOLL, PHYLLIS. - The Grecian Enchanted. 1952. One of 60, with a duplicate set of plates & specially bound. cb Sept 11 (101) $550

AMERICAN BOOK PRICES CURRENT

- HUGHES, RICHARD. - Gipsy-Night and Other Poems. 1922. One of 63 with proof of the Bianco litho. O Nov 18 (94) $80
- KEATS, JOHN. - Endymion. 1947. One of 100 specially bound. S May 6 (58) £340 [Henderson]; S June 18 (326) £520 [Barlow]
- KEATS, JOHN. - Lamia, Isabella, the Eve of Saint Agnes and Other Poems. 1928. One of 485. cb June 18 (106) $180; pn Dec 11 (284) £55 [Chelsea]; S Oct 6 (722) £160 [Thorp]; S May 6 (59) £210 [Chandor]
- LACOMBE, JEAN DE. - A Compendium of the East. 1937. One of 10 specially bound. S June 18 (323) £380 [Chandler]
- LASCARIS, EVADNE. - The Golden Bed of Kydno. 1935. One of 200. bba Feb 5 (283) £60 [Oram]
- LAWRENCE, T. E. - Crusader Castles. 1936. One of 1,000. 2 vols. bba May 14 (132) £420 [Bologna]; C May 13 (174) £450 [Stern]

Anr copy. Vol I recently rebacked by Sangorski & Sutcliffe. Ck Dec 10 (334) £250; pnNY Mar 12 (84) $425
- LAWRENCE, T. E. - Men in Print. 1940. One of 30 specially bound & with extra facsimiles. S Dec 4 (129) £200 [Buzer-Ross]; S June 18 (325) £450 [Maggs] One of 500. C May 13 (176) £250 [Stern]
- LAWRENCE, T. E. - Secret Despatches from Arabia. 1939. One of 30 specially bound. Orig white pigskin by Sangorski. C May 13 (179) £700 [Traylen] One of 970. pn Nov 20 (77) £200 [Maggs]; S Oct 6 (726) £130 [Maggs]; S Oct 6 (726) £140 [Wendler]; S May 6 (62) £180 [Hannas] One of 1,000. sg Jan 8 (91) $250
- LAWRENCE, T. E. - Shaw-Ede...Letters to H. S. Ede. 1942. One of 30 specially bound. S Oct 6 (725) £220 [Maggs] One of 470. C May 13 (182) £160 [Stern]
- LUCAS, FRANK LAURENCE. - Gilgamesh, King of Erech. 1948. One of 60 specially bound. With corrected proofs, paste-up sheets & other related material. S May 6 (69) £180 [Marks]
- LUCIAN OF SAMOSATA. - The True Historie.... 1927. One of 275. Sgd by Robert Gibbings on tp. bba Aug 20 (198) £190 [Cox]
- MILTON, JOHN. - Paradise Lost. 1937. One of 200. pn Apr 30 (158) £200 [Wayley]
- MONCRIF, FRANCOIS AUGUSTIN PARADIS DE. - Moncrif's Cats. 1961. One of 100 specially bound. sg Jan 8 (93) $200
- MORE, SIR THOMAS. - Utopia. 1929. One of 500. sg Jan 8 (93) $200
- MORRISON, JAMES. - The Journal of Boatswain's Mate of the Bounty. 1935. One of 325. S Dec 4 (118) £280 [Blackwell]
- MUSAEUS. - Hero and Leander. 1949. One

of 100 specially bound & with extra plate. S Dec 4 (136) £480 [Greer]
— NAPOLEON I. - Memoirs. 1945. One of 450. 2 vols. Worn & stained. pn Jan 22 (94) £55 [Joseph]
One of 500. pnNY Sept 13 (234) $180
— NELSON, HORATIO NELSON. - Letters from the Leeward Islands. 1953. One of 60 specially bound. S Dec 4 (138) £360 [Thorp]
— OMAR KHAYYAM. - The Golden Cockerel Rubaiyat. 1938. One of 270. S Oct 6 (737) £240 [Words]; sg Sept 11 (242) $225; SSA Feb 11 (617) R400
— OVID (PUBLIUS OVIDIUS NASO). - The Amores. 1932. One of 350. S Oct 6 (739) £100 [Cox]; sg Sept 11 (243) $150
— PHILBY, HARRY ST. JOHN BRIDGES. - A Pilgrim in Arabia. 1943. One of 350. Ck May 21 (336) £150; pn Nov 20 (79) £130 [Brook]
— PLATO. - The Phaedo. 1930. One of 500. sg Jan 8 (95) $50
— POWYS, LLEWELYN. Glory of Life. 1934. One of 275. Sgd by Robert Gibbings on tp. bba Aug 20 (211) £260 [Blackwell]
— POWYS, THEODORE FRANCIS. - Goat Green. 1937. One of 150. bba Apr 23 (279) £40 [Booklore]
— QUENNELL, NANCY. - The Epicure's Anthology. 1936. One of 150. sg Jan 15 (43) $60
— QUENNELL, PETER. - Masques and Poems. 1922. One of 375. Unopened copy. bba Oct 16 (195) £50 [Hay Cinema]
— RUTTER, OWEN. - The First Fleet. 1937. One of 370. CA Apr 12 (214) A$700; S Dec 4 (125) £220 [Blackwell]; S May 6 (74) £300 [Dawes]
— SHAKESPEARE, WILLIAM. - The Poems & Sonnets. 1960. One of 470. sg Jan 8 (96) $80
— STERNE, LAURENCE. - The Life and Opinions of Tristram Shandy. 1929-30. One of 500. 3 vols. Rubbed. cb Feb 5 (192) $100; sg Jan 8 (98) $90
— STERNE, LAURENCE. - A Sentimental Journey. 1928. One of 500. sg Jan 8 (98) $90
— SUCKLING, SIR JOHN. - A Ballad Upon a Wedding. 1927. One of 375. sg Jan 8 (99) $60
— SWIFT, JONATHAN. - Directions to Servants. 1925. One of 30. S Oct 6 (747) £120 [Bookroom]
— SWIFT, JONATHAN. - Gulliver's Travels. 1925. One of 450. 2 vols. sg Jan 8 (100) $250
— SWINBURNE, ALGERNON CHARLES. - Hymn to Proserpine. 1944. One of 350. Ck Sept 5 (22) £40
— SWINBURNE, ALGERNON CHARLES. - Laus Veneris. 1948. One of 100 specially bound, with an extra illus. S Dec 4 (133) £260 [Traylen]
— SWINBURNE, ALGERNON CHARLES. - Pasiphae. 1950. One of 100 specially bound, with an extra illus. S Dec 4 (137) £250 [Thorp]
— SWIRE, HERBERT. - The Voyage of the "Challenger". 1938. One of 300. 2 vols. pn July 23 (69) £380 [Dawson]; S Dec 4 (127) £300 [Thorp]
— TELLIER, JULES. - Abd-er-Rhaman in Paradise. 1928. One of 400. sg Jan 8 (101) $60
— THOREAU, HENRY DAVID. - Where I Lived and What I Lived For. 1924. One of 350. Inscr by Robert Gibbings. bba Aug 20 (194) £75 [Deighton Bell]
— TOUSSAINT, FRANZ. - The Garden of Caresses. 1934. One of 275, this 1 of an unspecified number specially bound with 6 additional engravings, sgd. S Dec 4 (117) £280 [Sadwell]
— WALPOLE, HUGH. - The Apple Trees. 1932. One of 500. sg Sept 11 (281) $90
— WELLS, H. G. - The Country of the Blind. 1939. Out-of-series copy. bba May 14 (133) £140 [Whiteson]

Golden Gate Bridge. See: Strauss, Joseph B.

Goldicutt, John
— Antiquities of Sicily. L. John Murray, 1819. Folio, contemp half calf gilt; rubbed. With pictorial title & 41 plates. Some discoloration. S Apr 23 (95) £950 [Goldschmidt]

Golding, Louis —& Others
— An Xmas Miscellany. L: Corvinus Press, 1936. One of 40. Orig cloth-backed German Christmas wrapping paper-covered bds. Inscr to Doublas Garrett. C May 13 (159) £150 [Maggs]

Golding, William
— The Inheritors. L, 1955. In d/j. T Oct 15 (175) £55
— Lord of the Flies. L, 1954. 1st Ed. In torn d/j. S Mar 9 (642) £260 [Sanders]
— Poems. L, 1934. 8vo, orig wraps. P Dec 15 (198) $1,200

Goldman Collection, Henry
— VALENTINER, WILHELM REINHOLD. - The Henry Goldman Collection. NY: Pvtly ptd, 1922. One of 200. Folio, half mor; rubbed. O Jan 6 (191) $70

Goldoni, Carlo, 1707-93
— The Good-Humoured Ladies.... L, 1922. Out-of-series copy. 8vo, half vellum; worn. sg Dec 11 (165) $225

Goldschmidt, Ernst Philip
— Gothic & Renaissance Bookbindings.... L, 1928. 2 vols. 4to, orig cloth; rubbed. Library stamps on some pages. bba Feb 5 (86) £90 [Fogg]

GOLDSCHMIDT

Anr copy. Cloth. sg May 14 (107) $225
One of 50 with 50 additional photographs. Orig cloth; Vol II partly loose in bdg, spine damaged. sg May 14 (106) $550
— The Printed Book of the Renaissance. Cambr., 1950. One of 750. 4to, orig cloth, in d/j. sg May 14 (446) $150

Goldschmidt, Lucien. See: Grolier Club

Goldsmid, Edmund Marsden
See also: Collectanea...
— A Complete Catalogue of all the Publications of the Elzevir Presses. Edin., 1885-88. One of 275. 3 vols in 4. 8vo, orig wraps; chipped. sg June 11 (183) $140

Goldsmid, Sir Frederic John, 1818-1908
— Eastern Persia: an Account of...the Persian Boundary Commission. L, 1876. 2 vols. 8vo, cloth; worn, shaken. sg Dec 18 (194) $400

Goldsmith, Oliver, 1728-74
— The Deserted Village. L, 1770. 1st Ed. 4to, lev gilt by Riviere; washed. sg Apr 2 (91) $550

Anr copy. Mor gilt by Riviere. sg June 11 (214) $375

Anr Ed. Venice: Ptd in the Armenian Monastery of S. Lazarus, 1871. 8vo, ptd wraps; soiled. In English & Armenian. sg Sept 11 (195) $60

— Edwin and Angelina. A Ballad.... L, [1764?]. Bound with: Churchill, Charles. Apology. L, 1763. And: Churchill. Night. L, 1763. And: Morgan, T. Poetry. Wakefield, 1797. And: Cave, Jane. Poems on Various Subjects. L, 1795. 8vo, 19th-cent half calf; joints weak at head of spine. S Dec 18 (22) £12,000 [Quaritch]

— An History of England, in a Series of Letters.... L, 1825. 6 vols. 8vo, contemp half calf; rubbed. SSA Feb 11 (519) R240

— A History of the Earth and Animated Nature.... L, 1870. 2 vols. 8vo, contemp half calf; spines worn. T Mar 19 (112) £52

— The Life of Richard Nash of Bath. L, 1762. 8vo, modern calf. Tp slightly soiled. bba Jan 15 (49) £75 [Clark]

Anr copy. Mor gilt by Lloyd. sg June 11 (213) $175

— She Stoops to Conquer. L, 1773. 1st Ed, early state. 8vo, mor gilt. pnE Jan 28 (101) £450 [Quaritch]

Anr Ed. L, [1912]. One of 350. Illus by Hugh Thomson. 4to, vellum gilt. pnNY Sept 22 (236) $190

— The Traveller, or a Prospect of Society. L, 1765. 1st Pbd Ed. 4to, calf gilt. Final leaf from anr copy & soiled, with short tear in gutter. sg Apr 2 (90) $225

AMERICAN BOOK PRICES CURRENT

— The Vicar of Wakefield. Salisbury, 1766. 1st Ed. 2 vols in 1. 12mo, contemp calf; rebacked. pnE Jan 28 (102) £1,400

Anr Ed. L, 1817. Illus by Thomas Rowlandson. 8vo, lev gilt by Riviere; front joint starting. With 24 hand-colored plates. sg Feb 12 (266) $325

Anr Ed. L: Ackermann, 1817. 8vo, modern calf by Worsfold. With 24 hand-colored plates. sg June 11 (352) $550

Anr Ed. L, 1843. Illus by William Mulready. 8vo, contemp mor gilt. bba Feb 5 (299) £60 [Whitman]

Anr Ed. L, 1890. Illus by Hugh Thomson. 8vo, mor gilt by Henderson & Bisset. pnE Nov 12 (72) £60

Anr copy. Half mor gilt by Hatchard; spine faded to brown from green. wa Dec 11 (363) $130

Anr Ed. L, 1929. Illus by Arthur Rackham. 4to, cloth. pn Sept 18 (327) £50 [Thorp]; pn May 21 (278) £190 [Joseph]

Anr copy. Cloth, in d/j. torn & chipped. sg Oct 30 (81) $80; wa June 25 (517) $100

One of 775. Orig vellum gilt. pn Mar 5 (328) £200 [Sotheran]

1st Ed Deluxe. 4to, orig vellum gilt; rubbed. sg Oct 30 (80) $175

— Works. L, 1854. 4 vols. 4to, calf; worn. wa Feb 19 (82) $95

Turk's Head Ed, one of—1000. NY, [1908]. 10 vols in 20. Mor gilt extra. pnNY Sept 13 (200) $1,200

Goldsmith, Oliver, 1728-74 —& Parnell, Thomas, 1679-1718
— Poems. L, 1804. Illus by Thomas & John Bewick. 8vo, contemp calf; joints starting. sg June 11 (215) $50

Goldston, Will
— Further Exclusive Magical Secrets. L, [1927]. Ltd Ed. 4to, orig mor with locking clasp. S Nov 10 (323) £130 [Price]
— More Exclusive Magical Secrets. L, [1920?]. Ltd Ed. 4to, orig cloth. S Nov 10 (325) £80 [Palace]

Goldwater, Barry
— The Face of Arizona. [N.p.]: Republican State Committee of Arizona, [1964]. One of 1,000. Folio, cloth. Inscr. sg Mar 12 (128) $120

Golfer, A. See: Robb, George

Goll, Claire
— Diary of a Horse. Brooklyn, [1946]. Copy marked "Printer's copy". Illus by Marc Chagall. sg June 11 (97) $60

Golovnin, Vasily Mikhailavich, 1776-1831
— Narrative of my Captivity in Japan. L, 1818. 2 vols. 8vo, contemp half russia. S June 25 (466) £380 [Fletcher]

Goltzius, Hubert, 1526-83
— Caesar Augustus, sive historiae Imperatorum Romanorum.... Bruges, 1574. Folio, contemp vellum; upper cover stained. With engraved title & 83 plates of coins on 42 leaves. Lower margins dampstained. Ck Sept 5 (212) £280
— Fastos magistratum et triumphorum Romanorum...restitutos. Bruges, 1566. Folio, later wraps; rubbed. ha Sept 19 (275) $225

Gomez Pedraza, Manuel, 1789-1851
— Al Publico El Ejercito Libertador qui Sostiene la Causa de los Pueblos.... [San Luis Potosi: Imprenta del Estado, 1832]. 4to, modern wraps. sg Sept 18 (105) $150

Gommer, Pierre de, Seigneur de Lusancy
— L'Autourserie. Chalons-sur-Marne: Claude Guyot, 1594. 8vo, mor janseniste by Trautz-Bauzonnet. Jeanson copy. SM Mar 1 (266) FF220,000

Anr Ed. Paris. Jean Houze, 1605. 8vo, mor janseniste by Huser. Jeanson copy. SM Mar 1 (267) FF34,000

Anr Ed. Paris: Jean Houze, 1608. 8vo, mor janseniste by Trautz-Bauzonnet. Jeanson copy. SM Mar 1 (268) FF30,000

Gongora y Argote, Luis de, 1561-1627
— Vingt Poemes. [Paris, 1948]. One of 235. Illus by Picasso. 4to, mor extra by Therese Moncey. With 41 etchings. FD Dec 2 (4614) DM44,000

Gonsalvius Montanus, Reginaldus
— A Discovery and Playne Declaration of Sundry Subtill Practises of the Holy Inquisition of Spayne. L: J. Day, 1568. 4to, 19th-cent sheep; rebacked. Title soiled; washed & restored. sg Oct 9 (53) $350

Gonse, Louis
— L'Art japonaise. Paris, 1883. Ltd Ed. 2 vols. 4to, mor; corners rubbed. S May 6 (381) £420 [Han Shan Tang]

Gonzales de Barcia, Andres
— Ensayo cronologica, para la historia general de la Florida.... Madrid, 1723. 1st Ed. Folio, old vellum. Folding table torn without loss. S Apr 24 (262) £600 [Quaritch]

Anr copy. Modern vellum. Lacking folding table. sg Sept 18 (106) $200

Anr copy. Contemp vellum; covers spotted. sg Sept 18 (107) $400

Good. See: R., R.

Good, Edward
— The Book of Affinity. L, 1933. One of 525. Illus by Jacob Epstein. 4to, orig cloth. Tp soiled. bba Jan 15 (216) £40 [Keegan]

Anr copy. Cloth. Inscr. S Oct 6 (800) £50 [Hetherington]

Good, John M. See: Polehampton & Good

Good, Peter Peyto, 1789-1875
— The Family Flora and Materia Medica Botanica. Cambr., Mass., & Elizabethtown, NJ, [1854-45]. 2 vols. 8vo, orig cloth; spine ends chipped. With 98 color plates. sg Jan 15 (217) $150

Goodall, T. F. See: Emerson & Goodall

Goodland, Roger
— A Bibliography of Sex Rites and Customs. L, 1931. 4to, cloth, in d/j. bba Mar 12 (339) £80 [Diba]

Anr copy. Cloth. sg Jan 15 (96) $50

Goodrich, Frank B., 1826-94
— The Court of Napoleon: or Society under the First Empire. NY, 1857. Illus by Jules Champagne. 4to, lea. sg Dec 18 (180) $50

Goodrich, Lloyd
— Edward Hopper. NY: Abrams, [1978]. Oblong folio, cloth, in d/j. wa Nov 6 (439) $80
— Reginald Marsh. NY: Abrams, [1972]. Oblong folio, cloth, in soiled & worn d/j. wa Nov 6 (456) $70

Goodrich, Samuel Griswold, 1793-1860
— The Manners, Customs, and Antiquities of the Indians of North and South America. Bost, 1844. 8vo, half mor, orig wraps bound in; rubbed, front flyleaf loose. sg Sept 18 (11) $80

Goodridge, Charles Medyett
— Narrative of a Voyage to the South Seas.... Exeter, 1843. 5th Ed. 8vo, orig cloth; rubbed. With frontis & 2 plates. T Feb 19 (242) £75

Goodspeed, Charles Eliot
— Angling in America: its Early History and Literature. Bost., 1939. 1st Ed, one of 795. Inscr. O Sept 23 (75) $160

Goodwin, Francis, 1784-1835
— Domestic Architecture Being a Series of Designs. L, 1833-34. Series 1 & 2. 2 vols. 4to, orig cloth; splits in upper joints. With 83 plates. One text leaf in Vol I torn without loss. S June 25 (216) £550 [Schuster]
— Rural Architecture. L, 1835. 2d Ed. 4 vols in 1. 4to, contemp half calf; rubbed. With

GOODWIN

99 plates & plans. With 1 leaf damaged affecting a few words. S Feb 28 (348) £380 [Pigeonhole]

Goodwin, Philip Lippincott —& Milliken, Henry Oothovt
— French Provincial Architecture. NY, 1924. Folio, half cloth; worn & stained. sg Feb 5 (151) $120

Gookin, Vincent
— The Great Case of Transplantation in Ireland Discussed. L, 1655. 4to, modern half mor. Tp laid down; lacking final blank. bba Apr 9 (302) £240 [Drury]

Goor, Thomas Ernst van
— Beschryving der stadt en lande van Breda. The Hague, 1744. Folio, recent half calf. With 4 folding plans & map, 15 views & other plates (11 folding); 3 plates damaged & repaired. B Feb 25 (652) HF1,200

Goos, Pieter
— De Zee-Atlas, ofte Water-Wereld.... Amst., 1669. Folio, bds; rebacked with sailcloth. With engraved title & 40 double-page or folding charts & maps, all colored by a contemp hand & heightened with gold, on thick paper. Small wormhole affecting 1st few charts; occasional splits neatly repaired without loss. S Apr 24 (206) £19,000 [Arader]

Gordon...
— The Gordon Garland: A Round of Devotions by his Followers. NY, 1965. One of 1,500. Ed by Arnold Gingrich. 8vo, half lea. sg Oct 23 (292) $70

Gordon, Adam Lindsay. See: Fore-Edge Paintings

Gordon, James, Parson of Rothiemay
— History of Scots Affairs from MDCXXXVII to MDCXLI. Aberdeen, 1841. 3 vols. 4to, modern half mor. O Feb 24 (91) $130

Gordon, Patrick, fl.1700
— Geography Anatomized: or, the Geographical Grammar. L, 1693. 1st Ed. 12mo, contemp calf; hinges cracked. With 16 folding maps. Marginal defs. T June 18 (28) £100

Gordon, Sir Robert, 1580-1656
— Genealogical History of the Earldom of Sutherland. Edin., 1813. Folio, half mor; worn. O Feb 24 (92) $95

Gordon, Theodore, 1854-1915
— The Complete Fly Fisherman: The Notes and Letters.... NY, 1970. One of 50. 4to, calf gilt. sg Oct 23 (291) $700

AMERICAN BOOK PRICES CURRENT

Gordon, Thomas F., 1787-1860
— Gazetteer of the State of New York.... Phila., 1836. 8vo, disbound. With hand-colored map; torn in folds at margin & detached from book. wa Sept 25 (501) $60

Gorer, Edgar —& Blacker, J. F.
— Chinese Porcelains and Hard Stones. L, 1911. One of 1,000. 2 vols. 4to, orig cloth; soiled & worn. Marginal annotations. cb Feb 19 (117) $375
— Chinese Porcelain and Hard Stones. L, 1911. One of 1,000. 2 vols. 4to, cloth. With 254 colored plates. S May 6 (382) £200 [Hannas]

Gori, Antonio Francisco, 1691-1757
— Monumentum sive columbarium libertorum et servorum Liviae Augustae et Caesarum Romae.... Florence, 1727. Folio, contemp calf; extremities worn, front joint cracked. Tp stamped. sg Oct 9 (217) $50

Gorlaeus, Abraham, 1549-1609
— Dactyliotheca seu annulorum sigillarium quorum apud priscos tam Graecos quam Romanos usus.... Leiden, 1601. 4to, later sheep. Engraved title cropped at outer edge; small wormholes, afffecting tp; lacking port & 3 plates. bba Dec 4 (4) £35 [Clark]

Gorringe, Henry H., 1841-85
— Egyptian Obelisks. NY, [1882]. 4to, cloth. Last 2 leaves with lower corners repaired. cb Nov 6 (112) $90

Gorris, Guillaume
— Scotus pauperum. Toulouse: Henricus Mayer, 1486. 4to, modern half mor. Repairs to margins of a few leaves; upper half of D4 recto strengthened; some dampstains at beginning & end; inkstain in margin of a3. 252 (of 256) leaves; lacking a1-2 & H7-8. Goff G-323. S Sept 23 (454) £280 [Thomas]

Gosden, Thomas, 1780-1840
— Impressions of a Series of Animals.... L, 1821. One of 6 on yellow paper. 8vo, contemp calf gilt. Jeanson copy. SM Mar 1 (270) FF16,000

Gosnell, Harpur A. See: Derrydale Press

Gosse, Sir Edmund W., 1849-1928. See: Garnett & Gosse

Gossellin, Pascal Francois Joseph
— Geographie des grecs analysee.... Paris, 1790. 4to, contemp half lea; worn, spine chipped at top. wa Sept 25 (491) $270

Gothein, Marie Luise
— A History of Garden Art. L & Toronto, 1928. 2 vols. 4to, orig cloth. cb June 4 (89) $110

Anr copy. Orig cloth; front free endapers stamped. sg June 4 (151) $225

Anr copy. Orig cloth, in chipped & torn d/js. wa Sept 25 (125) $160

Gottfried, Johann Ludwig. See: Abelin, Johann Philipp

Gottschalk, Paul
— The Earliest Diplomatic Documents on America.... Berlin, 1929. One of 172 on van Gelder. Folio, cloth. Some soiling & wear; minor foxing at fore-edges. sg Sept 18 (109) $300

Gottschall, Hermann von, 1862-1933
— Adolf Anderssen der Altmeister deutscher Schachspielkunst sein Leben und Schaffen. Leipzig, 1912. Modern half calf gilt. pn Mar 26 (209) £70 [De Lucia]

Goudeau, Emile
— Paris qui consomme. Paris, 1893. One of 138. Illus by Pierre Vidal. 4to, mor gilt. With 50 color illusts. Crahan copy. P Nov 25 (220) $250

Goudot, Pierre Thomas
— Le Prix de la beaute ou les couronnes.... Paris, 1760. 4to, contemp calf gilt; rebacked retaining orig spine. S Sept 23 (566) £150 [Thomas]

Gouffe, Jules, b.1807
— Le Livre de cuisine. Paris, 1873. 2 vols. 8vo, contemp half calf; worn & loose. HK Nov 4 (1796) DM800

— Le Livre de patisserie. Paris, 1873. 8vo, orig half mor; rubbed. Some leaves loose. S Mar 9 (732) £150 [Weiss]

Gouger, Robert, 1802-46
— South Australia in 1837; in a Series of Letters.... L, 1838. 1st Ed. 8vo, orig cloth; broken, stained. CA Apr 12 (110) A$120

Gough Library, John Bartholomew
— The Works of George Cruikshank...Collected by John B. Gough. Bost.: Club of Odd Volumes, 1890. One of 125. 4to, bds. O Mar 24 (49) $60

Gough, Richard, 1735-1809
— British Topography. L, 1780. 2 vols. 4to, contemp calf; worn. With 9 folding maps. Some holing affecting text. hba Apr 9 (373) £110 [Blake]

— Sepulchral Monuments in Great Britain.... L, 1786-96. 2 vols in 5. Folio, contemp russia; 2 covers detached. Sold w.a.f. Ck Nov 21 (447) £600

Goulburn, Edward Meyrick
— The Ancient Sculptures in the Roof of Norwich Cathedral.... L, 1876. Folio, contemp half mor; rubbed. Ck Nov 28 (177) £50

Gould, John, 1804-81
— The Birds of Asia. L, 1850-83. 7 vols. Folio, contemp mor gilt by Sotheran. With 530 hand-colored plates. 2 plates just shaved. Earl Fitzwilliam subscriber's copy. C Oct 15 (205) £44,000 [Mitchell]

Anr copy. Parts 1-30 bound in 6 vols & Parts 31-35 in 5 orig parts. Folio, contemp half mor gilt & orig half cloth. John Gould's copy. S Apr 23 (201) £35,000 [Schuster]

— The Birds of Australia. L, [1840]-69. 8 vols. Folio, contemp mor gilt, Supplement with slightly varying gilt tooling; 1 cover detached, short split to 2 joints. With 681 hand-colored plates. A few plates slightly trimmed by binder. C Oct 15 (203) £115,000 [Mitchell]

Anr Ed. L, [1840]-1848-69. 41 parts plus Supplement in 8 vols. Folio, contemp mor gilt by Clyde. With 681 hand-colored plates. Some repairs. John Gould's copy. S Apr 23 (20g) £110,000 [Ebes]

Facsimile Ed. Melbourne, 1972-75. 8 vols. Folio & 8vo, syn. CA Apr 12 (112) A$1,800

— The Birds of Europe. L, [1832]-37. 5 vols. Folio, contemp half mor gilt; joints & corners rubbed with some abrasions. With 448 hand-colored plates. Lady Harriet Clive's copy. C Oct 15 (193) £38,000 [Mitchell]

Anr copy. Contemp mor gilt by Clyde. John Gould's copy. S Apr 23 (20b) £32,000 [Zanzotto]

— The Birds of Great Britain. L, [1862]-73. 5 vols. Folio, contemp half mor gilt; spines rubbed. With 367 hand-colored plates. A few plates offset onto facing text; minor spotting to a few leaves & plates; short to blank margin of 1 leaf of text. Mark Grigg's subscriber's copy. C Oct 15 (231) £24,000 [Le Flanchec]

Anr copy. Contemp half mor gilt; rubbed. One leaf with small stain in blank margin; Vol IV list of plates creased. C Apr 8 (147) £26,000 [Burgess Browning]

Anr copy. Contemp mor gilt; 2 upper covers detached. C Apr 8 (179) £30,000 [Weinreb]

Anr copy. Mor extra; extremities rubbed. P June 18 (74) $45,000

Anr copy. 5 vols in orig 25 parts. Folio, orig half cloth; soiled, spines worn. John Gould's copy. S Apr 23 (20m) £32,000 [Helianthus]

Anr copy. 5 vols. Folio, contemp mor gilt. Markree Castle copy. S Apr 23 (37) £32,000 [Torre]

— The Birds of New Guinea and the Adjacent Papuan Islands.... L, 1875-88. 5 vols. Folio, contemp mor gilt. With 320 hand-colored plates. C Oct 15 (206) £26,000 [Wheldon & Wesley]

Anr copy. Parts 1-10 bound in 2 vols & Parts 11-25 in 15 orig parts. Folio, contemp half mor gilt or orig half cloth. John Gould's copy. S Apr 23 (20n) £30,000 [Ebes]

— A Century of Birds from the Himalaya Mountains. L, [1831]-32. 1st Issue, with backgrounds uncolored. Folio, 19th-cent mor. With 76 hand-colored plates (of 80); lacking plates 30, 47, 54 & 75. Also lacking list of subscribers & 2 leaves of text. C Oct 15 (186) £5,500 [Mitchell]

Anr copy. Half mor gilt by Clyde; joints rubbed. With 80 hand-colored plates. John Gould's copy. S Apr 23 (20a) £3,500 [Russell]

— Handbook to the Birds of Australia. L, 1865. 2 vols. 8vo, orig cloth. pn Oct 23 (213) £180 [Maggs]

— Humming-Birds. L, [1849]-61. ("A Monograph of the Trochilidae or Family of Humming-Birds.") 2 parts only. Folio, orig bds; broken. With 24 hand-colored plates, most with metallic highlighting. Sold w.a.f. C Oct 15 (230) £2,000 [Ollson]

Anr copy. With 23 hand-colored plates.. C Oct 15 (230B) £2,000 [Ollson]

Anr copy. With 24 hand-colored plates.. C Oct 15 (230A) £2,200 [Ollson]

Anr copy. 5 vols plus 1887 Supplement in orig 5 parts. Folio, contemp mor by Clyde. With 418 hand-colored plates. John Gould's copy. S Apr 23 (20k) £45,000 [Helianthus]

Anr copy. Sharpe's 1887 Supplement only. Folio, mor gilt by Morrell, orig wraps bound at end. With 58 plates with later hand-coloring. S June 25 (158) £4,500 [Arader]

— Macropodidae. 1841-42. ("A Monograph of the Macropodidae or Family of Kangaroos.") 2 parts in 1 vol. Folio, contemp half mor gilt by Clyde, orig part wraps bound as titles. With 30 hand-colored plates. John Gould's copy. S Apr 23 (20h) £5,500 [Ebes]

— The Mammals of Australia. L, [1845]-63. 3 vols. Folio, contemp mor gilt by H. Stamper; rubbed, 1 joint split. With 182 hand-colored plates. C Apr 15 (204) £48,000 [Mitchell]

Anr copy. Contemp mor gilt; rebacked preserving orig spines. John Gould's copy. S Apr 23 (20j) £35,000 [Ebes]

Anr copy. Contemp mor gilt; joints rubbed. Minor restoration. S Apr 23 (30) £38,000 [Sims]

— A Monograph of the Odontophorinae, or Partridges of America. L, [1844]-50. Folio, mor gilt; new endpapers. With 32 hand-colored plates. Marginal repairs to 2 plates. S Feb 24 (569) £5,000 [Wheldon]

Anr copy. Contemp mor gilt by Clyde. John Gould's copy. S Apr 23 (20i) £6,000 [Helianthus]

Anr copy. Orig 3 parts. Folio, orig bds; worn. Marginal tear in 1st plate in Part 2. S Apr 23 (39) £6,200 [Mitchell]

— Pittidae. L, 1880-81. ("Monograph of the Pittidae.") Part I (all pbd). Folio, orig half cloth. With 10 hand-colored plates. John Gould's copy. S Apr 23 (20p) £1,800 [Sotheran]

— Toucans. L, [1833]-34-35. ("A Monograph of the Ramphastidae, or Family of Toucans.") Folio, mor gilt by Clyde. With 1 plain & 33 colored plates. John Gould's copy. S Apr 23 (20c) £6,000 [Robinson]

2d Ed. L, 1852-54. Folio, contemp mor gilt by Clyde. With 1 plain & 51 hand-colored plates. John Gould's copy. S Apr 23 (20d) £8,000 [Marshall]

Anr copy. Mor gilt by Morrell. With 1 plain & 51 plates with later hand-coloring. S June 25 (157) £5,000 [Grosvenor]

— Trogons. L, [1836]-38. ("A Monograph of the Trogonidae, or Family of Trogons.") Folio, contemp mor gilt by Clyde. With 36 hand-colored plates. John Gould's copy. S Apr 23 (20c) £5,200 [Lambourne]

Anr Ed. L, [1858]-75. Folio, contemp mor gilt by Clyde. With 47 hand-colored plates. John Gould's copy. S Apr 23 (20f) £6,000 [Noble]

Gould, Robert Freke, 1836-1915

— The History of Freemasonry.... L, 1886-87. 3 vols. 4to, contemp half mor gilt. bba Oct 30 (74) £100 [Subunso]

Anr copy. Orig cloth; rubbed. T Oct 16 (677) £40

Gourmont, Remy de, 1858-1915

— Litanies de la rose. Paris: Kieffer, 1919. One of 500. Illus by Andre Domin. Orig wraps. With 59 hand-colored illusts. S Dec 4 (6) £250 [Mark Brutta]

One of 500 on papier velin. Orig vellum. sg June 4 (152) $400

Goury de Champgrand, Charles Jean
— Almanach du chasseur. Paris: Pissot, 1773. 12mo, contemp red mor gilt with mosaic arms of Louis-Philippe I, duc d'Orleans. Jeanson copy. SM Mar 1 (271) FF22,000

Goury, Jules. See: Jones & Goury

Gouste, Claude
— Traicte de la puissance et authorite des rois.... Paris 1561. 8vo, modern mor. Small tear in G6 neatly repaired. C Dec 12 (293) £180 [Israel]

Gowans, William, 1803-70
— A Catalogue of Books on Freemasonry and Kindred Subjects. N Y, 1858. 4th Ed. 12mo, cloth; spine chipped at head. sg Oct 2 (144) $100

Gower, Richard Hall, 1767-1833
— A Treatise on the Theory and Practice of Seamanship. L, 1796. 2d Ed. 8vo, contemp calf; worn. With 3 folding plates, 1 partially hand-colored. With engraved moveable plate of a ship attached by lea strip to inside upper cover. Tp stamped; 1 plate torn. S Nov 18 (950) £160 [Libris Antill]

Gower, Ronald, Lord, 1845-1916
— Sir Thomas Lawrence. L, 1900. One of 200. 2 vols. 4to, contemp mor gilt. bba Mar 26 (46) £80 [Check]

Goya y Lucientes, Francisco, 1746-1828
— Los Desastros de la guerra. Madrid, 1903. 3d Ed. 4to, half cloth. With 80 plates. sg June 18 (204) $3,000
— Los Proverbios. Madrid: Real Academia, 1923. 4to, disbound & stapled at left edge. With 18 plates. Stained in top margin not affecting images. sg June 18 (205) $1,100

Graba, Johann Andreas, d.1669
— Elaphographia sive cervi descriptio physico-medico-chymica.... Jena, 1668. 8vo, contemp vellum. Schwerdt-Jeanson copy. SM Mar 1 (273) FF14,000

Grabhorn, Edwin. See: Grabhorn Printing

Grabhorn, Edwin & Marjorie. See: Grabhorn Printing

Grabhorn, Jane B. See: Grabhorn Printing

Grabhorn Printing—San Francisco, etc.
— The Book of Job. 1926. One of 210. cb Dec 4 (134) $150; cb Dec 4 (1134) $150
— The Book of Ruth. 1927. One of 250. cb Dec 4 (135) $225

Anr copy. Sgd by Angelo under the frontis & by the Grabhorns on front free endpaper, May 1927. cb Dec 4 (136) $250; cb Dec 4 (137) $190

One of a few with variant colophon stating the limitation to be 300 & bound in white vellum. cb Dec 4 (135) $225
— A California Gold Rush Miscellany... 1934. One of 550. Rubbed, cover nicked. cb Oct 9 (88) $65
— The Crusader. 1928. One of 300. Bates School yearbook. cb Dec 4 (142) $75
— The History of Susanna. 1948. One of 400. cb June 18 (122) $50
— Hymns to Aphrodite. 1927. One of 200. cb Dec 4 (151) $60
— Joan the Maid of Orleans... 1938. One of 525. cb June 18 (123) $70
— Joaquin Murieta: the Brigand Chief of California. 1932. One of 500. cb Sept 11 (133) $60; cb Dec 4 (153) $65
— A Leaf from the 1611 King James Bible with "The Noblest Monument of English Prose" by J. L. Lowes & "The Printing of the King James Bible" by L. I. Newman. 1937. One of 300. cb Sept 11 (52) $95; cb Sept 11 (139) $350

Anr copy. Rubbed, 2 corners chipped. cb Feb 5 (197) $160; sg Apr 2 (94) $500

Anr copy. Book Club of California No 51. sg June 11 (218) $175
— A Lytell Geste of Robyn Hode and his Meiny.... 1932. One of 25 made for H. L. Rothschild. cb Dec 4 (158) $700

One of 255. cb Dec 4 (159) $140
— An Original Issue of "The Spectator," together with the Story of the Famous English Periodical.... 1939. One of 455. 4to, half cloth. With orig issue of The Spectator tipped in. cb Sept 11 (154) $95
— An Original Leaf from the Bible of the Revolution and an Essay concerning it... 1930. One of 515. Inscr to Arthur Swann by John Howell & with Ls of Howell. sg June 11 (217) $110
— An Original Leaf from the Polycronicon printed by William Caxton... 1938. One of 297. cb Sept 11 (129) $100

Anr copy. Book Club of California No 54. cb Sept 11 (136) $550; sg Apr 2 (95) $550
— Reglamento para el gobierno de la Provincia de Californias...[Regulations for Governing the Province of the Californias...]. 1929. One of 300. 2 vols. cb Dec 4 (165) $85; cb Dec 4 (166) $85
— The Spanish Occupation of California. 1934. One of 550. cb Sept 11 (174) $50
— What Europe Knew of China Three Hundred Years Ago. [1936]. One of 100. Orig wraps. cb Dec 4 (174) $100
— The XXIII Psalm of David. 1931. One of 100. Single sheet. cb Dec 4 (180) $80
— Aesop. - The Subtyl Historyes and Fables. 1930. One of 200. cb Sept 11 (105) $425

Anr copy. Bound in mor tooled in black &

aluminum by D. K. Stevens. cb Dec 4 (130) $1,800

Anr copy. Inscr by E. Grabhorn to David Magee. cb Dec 4 (131) $425; cb Dec 4 (132) $300

— BAIRD, JOSEPH ARMSTRONG. - California's Pictorial Letter Sheets 1849-1869. 1967. One of 475. In d/j. cb Oct 9 (100) $130; cb Apr 2 (15) $85

Anr copy. Folio, half mor. sg Jan 22 (26) $150; sg Mar 12 (23) $80

— BECKER, ROBERT H. - Designs on the Land, Disenos of California Ranchos and Their Makers. 1969. One of 500. cb Sept 11 (19) $225; cb Oct 9 (101) $225

Anr copy. Back cover dampstained. cb Apr 2 (23) $160

— BECKER, ROBERT H. - Disenos of California Ranchos... 1964. One of 400. cb June 18 (110) $225; sg Jan 8 (105) $425

— BEECHEY, FREDERICK WILLIAM. - An Account of a Visit to California... 1941. One of 350. cb June 18 (108) $95

— BOSQUI, EDWARD. - Memoirs. 1952. One of 350. cb Oct 9 (87) $60

— COIT, DANIEL WADSWORTH. - An Artist in El Dorado... 1937. One of 325. cb Sept 11 (111) $80; cb Oct 9 (47) $90

Anr copy. In tattered d/j. With 2 A Ls s of Edith Coulter inserted. O Sept 23 (76) $80

— CORONADO, FRANCISCO VASQUEZ DE. - The Journey of... 1933. One of 550. cb Jan 8 (30) $100

— CRANE, STEPHEN. - The Red Badge of Courage. 1931. One of 980. cb Sept 11 (112) $95; cb Dec 4 (140) $70

Anr copy. Review copy. sg Jan 8 (107) $60

— DE SOTO, HERNANDO. - The Discovery of Florida. 1946. One of 280. cb Sept 11 (120) $65

— DE VINNE, THEODORE LOW. - The Plantin-Moretus Museum. 1929. One of 425. cb Dec 4 (146) $50; cb Dec 4 (146) $50

— DEARDEN, ROBERT R. & WATSON, DOUGLAS S. - An Original Leaf from the Bible of the Revolution and an Essay Concerning It. 1930. One of 515. cb Sept 11 (115) $70

Out-of-series copy with orig leaf. cb Dec 4 (144) $80

— DERBY, GEORGE H. - Phoenixiana: a Collection of the Burlesques...of John Phoenix. 1937. One of 550. cb Oct 9 (89) $55

— ELKUS, RICHARD J. - Alamos: A Philosophy in Living. 1965. One of 487. With 24 plates, tipped in. sg Jan 8 (108) $80

— FAHEY, HERBERT. - Early Printing in California... 1956. One of 400. cb Sept 11 (121) $170

— FOGAZZARO, ANTONIO. - Eden Anto. 1930. One of 250. cb Sept 11 (124) $75

— GRABHORN, EDWIN. - Figure Prints of Old Japan... 1959. One of 400. cb Sept 11 (123) $375; cb June 18 (116) $325; sg Apr 2 (93) $475

— GRABHORN, EDWIN. - Landscape Prints of Old Japan. 1960. One of 450. cb Sept 11 (137) $400; cb July 30 (79) $275

— GRABHORN, EDWIN & MARJORIE. - Ukiyo-e, "The Floating World." 1960. One of 300. cb Sept 11 (170) $350

Anr Ed. 1962. One of 400. cb June 18 (119) $275; sg Jan 8 (120) $250

— GRABHORN, JANE B. - The Compleat Jane Grabhorn... 1968. One of 400. cb June 18 (107) $75

— GRABHORN, ROBERT. - Short Account of the Life and Work of Wynkyn de Worde with a Leaf from the Golden Legend... 1949. One of 375. cb Sept 11 (126) $190

Anr copy. Tipped-in orig leaf, damp-stained & chipped at lower corner. cb Feb 5 (196) $100

— HARLOW, NEAL. - The Maps of San Francisco Bay from the Discovery...to the American Occupation. 1950. One of 375. cb Sept 11 (128) $650

— HARTE, BRET. - San Francisco in 1866. San Francisco: Book Club of California, 1951. One of 400. cb Sept 11 (130) $70

Anr copy. Soiled, corners jammed. cb Oct 9 (90) $50

— HAWTHORNE, NATHANIEL. - The Golden Touch. 1927. One of 240. cb Dec 4 (148) $110

— HAWTHORNE, NATHANIEL. - The Scarlet Letter. 1928. One of 980. cb Sept 11 (131) $70

— HELLER, ELINOR R. & MAGEE, DAVID. - Bibliography of the Grabhorn Press, 1915-1940. 1940. One of 210. Eleanora Bosworth Black's annotated copy. cb Sept 11 (132) $350

— HITTELL, THEODORE H. - El Triunfo de la Cruz: A Description of the Building...of the First Ship Made in California. 1930. One of 50. cb Dec 4 (150) $110

— HOLMES BOOK CO. - A Descriptive & Priced Catalogue of Books...on California and the Far West.... 1948. One of 500. Folio, half cloth. Inscr by Harold C. Holmes. cb Sept 11 (119) $100

— HUTTON, WILLIAM RICH. - California 1847-1852. 1942. One of 700. cb Jan 8 (77) $55

— JASTRO, MORRIS. - The Gentle Cynic. Being a Translation of the Book of Keheleth known as Ecclesiastes.... 1927. One of 250. cb Dec 4 (147) $190

— KAISER, HENRY J. - Twenty-Six Addresses Delivered during the War Years. 1945. One of 30. cb Sept 11 (134) $400

— KITAGAWA, UTAMARO. - Twelve Woodblock Prints of Kitagawa Utamaro Illustrating the Process of Silk Culture. 1965. One of

450. Intro by Jack Hillier. cb Feb 5 (201) $110; sg Jan 8 (119) $150
— LAWRENCE, D. H. - Fire and Other Poems. 1940. One of 300. cb Dec 4 (154) $200
— LEWIS, OSCAR. - The Origin of the Celebrated Jumping Frog of Calaveras County. 1931. One of 250. Book Club of California, No 39. cb Dec 4 (156) $100
— LEWIS, OSCAR. - The Wonderful City of Carrie Van Wie... 1963. One of 525. cb Oct 9 (91) $95
— LITTLEJOHN, DAVID. - Dr. Johnson and Noah Webster. 1971. One of 500. With orig leaves from the J section of Johnson's 1755 & Webster's 1828 dictionaries. cb Sept 11 (175) $120; cb June 18 (34) $85
— LYMAN, GEORGE D. - The Book and the Doctor. 1933. One of 50. Inscr. cb Feb 4 (157) $60
— MAGEE, DAVID. - The Hundredth Book: a Bibliography of the Publications of the Book Club of California... 1958. One of 400. cb Sept 11 (144) $140; sg Jan 8 (113) $110
— MAGEE, DOROTHY & DAVID. - Bibliography of the Grabhorn Press, 1940-56. 1957. One of 225. Eleanora Bosworth Black's annotated copy. cb Sept 11 (143) $325
— MANDEVILLE, SIR JOHN. - The Voiage and Travaile. NY: Random House, 1928. One of 150. cb Sept 11 (146) $1,500; cb Dec 4 (160) $1,200
— MELVILLE, HERMAN. - The Encantadas, or, Enchanted Isles. 1940. One of 550. cb Sept 11 (147) $150; cb June 18 (129) $80
— MEYERS, WILLIAM H. - Journal of a Cruise to California and the Sandwich Islands... 1955. One of 400. cb Sept 11 (149) $190; cb June 18 (131) $200; sg Jan 8 (115) $110
— MEYERS, WILLIAM H. - Naval Sketches of the War in California. NY, 1939. One of 1,000. Half mor. cb Oct 9 (92) $75; cb Dec 18 (120) $200
— MEYERS, WILLIAM H. - Sketches of California and Hawaii... 1970. One of 450. cb Sept 11 (177) $80
— MILLER, HENRY. - Account of a Tour of the California Missions... 1952. One of 375. cb Sept 11 (150) $70; sg Jan 8 (104) $80
— M'ILVAINE, WILLIAM, JR. - Sketches of Scenery and Notes of Personal Adventure in California & Mexico. 1951. One of 400. cb June 18 (128) $55; sg Jan 8 (114) $100
— MINASIAN, KHATCHIK. - The Simple Songs.... 1950. One of 300. cb Dec 4 (161) $55
— NIESENWURZEL, PAUL ARTHUR AMADEUS. - Doomsday Books. 1928. One of 150. cb Sept 11 (152) $80
— NORRIS, FRANK. - The Letters... 1956. One of 350. cb Sept 11 (153) $80
— NUNEZ CABECA DE VACA, ALVAR. - Relation...of What Befel the Armament in the Indias... 1929. One of 300. cb Dec 4 (162) $250
— OLDFIELD, OTIS. - A Pictorial Journal of a Voyage.... 1969. One of 400. cb Dec 4 (182) $95
— PARSONS, GEORGE F. - The Life and Adventures of James W. Marshall. 1935. cb July 16 (209) $110
— PATTISON, MARK. - The Estiennes: A Biographical Essay... 1949. One of 390. cba Feb 5 (199) $120
— PHILLIPS, CATHERINE COFFIN. - Coulterville Chronicle.... 1942. One of 500. Corners & spine ends bumped. cb Oct 9 (93) $65; cb June 18 (133) $80
— POWELL, H. M. T. - The Santa Fe Trail to California. [1931]. One of 300. Lacking limitation leaf. sg Jan 8 (116) $550; sg Apr 2 (96) $1,100
— ROBERTSON, JOHN WOOSTER. - Francis Drake and Other Early Explorers Along the Pacific Coast. 1927. One of 1,000. Inscr by Robertson. cb Dec 4 (167) $160
— ROBERTSON, JOHN WOOSTER. - The Harbor of St. Francis.... 1926. One of 100. cb Dec 4 (168) $85
— ROTHCHILD, HERBERT L. - A Survey of Modern Bookmaking. 1931. One of 70. cb Dec 4 (1702) $85
— SAWYER, EUGENE T. - The Life and Career of Tiburcio Vasquez... 1944. One of 500. cb June 18 (135) $60
— SCHULZ, H. C. - A Monograph on the Italian Choir Book. 1941. One of 75. cb Dec 4 (169) $375
Anr copy. With portion of a 16th-cent choir-book leaf bearing a large illuminated initial. sg Apr 2 (97) $550
— SCHULZ, H.C. - French Illuminated Manuscripts. 1958. One of 200 with an orig leaf from a 15th cent illuminated Book of Hours. sg June 11 (219) $350
— SHAKESPEARE, WILLIAM. - The Taming of the Shrew. 1967. One of 375. cb Dec 4 (184) $85
— STEVENSON, ROBERT LOUIS. - Diogenes at the Savile Club. 1921. One of 150. cb Sept 11 (158) $75
— STEVENSON, ROBERT LOUIS. - Robert Louis Stevenson to his Good Friend M. Donat. 1925. One of 50. sg Jan 8 (118) $90
— STEVENSON, ROBERT LOUIS. - Silverado Journal. 1954. One of 400. cb Sept 11 (160) $90
— SUTTER, JOHN A. - New Helvetia Diary... 1939. One of 950. cb Sept 11 (165) $55; cb Oct 9 (95) $80; cb June 18 (138) $65
— SWINBURNE, ALGERNON C. - Two Unpublished Manuscripts. 1927. cb Dec 4 (151) $200
— TENNYSON, ALFRED. - To Virgil. 1930. One of 100. Single sheet, mtd cb Dec 4 (172) $110

GRABHORN PRINTING

— Toke, Monroe Tsa. - The Peyote Ritual....
1957. One of 325. cb June 18 (139) $190
— Utamaro, Kitagawa. - Twelve Wood-Block Prints... 1965. One of 450. cb June 18 (142) $150; cb June 18 (143) $140
— Vespucci, Amerigo. - Letter...describing his Four Voyages to the New World... 1926. One of 250. cb Dec 4 (173) $250
— Waseurtz, G.M. - A Sojourn in California by the King's Orphan... 1945. One of 300. cb Sept 11 (173) $75; cb Oct 9 (96) $65
— Wheat, Carl I. - Books of the California Gold Rush.... 1949. One of 500. cb Oct 9 (97) $140; sg Oct 2 (309) $200; sg Jan 22 (314) $200
— Wheat, Carl I. - Mapping the Transmississippi West. 1957-63. One of 1,000. 5 vols in 6. Inscr. cb July 16 (306) $1,500; sg Apr 2 (216) $1,100
— Wheat, Carl I. - The Maps of the California Gold Region. 1942. One of 300. sg Dec 4 (202) $1,400; sg Apr 2 (217) $1,600
— Whitman, Walt. - Leaves of Grass. NY, 1930. One of 400. cb Dec 4 (176) $1,400; cb Feb 19 (118) $1,100
— Wierzbicki, Felix Paul. - California as it is... 1933. One of 500. Sgd by the Grabhorns, Valenti Angelo & George D. Lyman. cb Dec 4 (177) $375
— Wiltsee, Ernest A. - Gold Rush Steamers of the Pacific. 1938. One of 500. cb Oct 9 (98) $80

Anr copy. Inscr. cb July 16 (291) $140
— Windsor, Edward. - Farewell Speech of King Edward the Eighth. 1938. One of 200. Half mor. cb Sept 11 (122) $110
— Wood, Ellen L. - George Yount, the Kindly Host of Caymus Rancho. 1941. One of 200. cb Oct 9 (247) $130

Grabhorn, Robert. See: Grabhorn Printing

Grace, Sheffield
— Memoirs of the Family of Grace. L, 1823. 8vo, contemp half mor; rubbed. Inscr. T Apr 16 (124) £62

Grace, William Gilbert, 1848-1915
— Cricket. Bristol & L, 1891. One of 662. 4to, orig half mor gilt; upper joint split, rubbed. bba Aug 20 (449) £160 [Valentine]

Anr copy. Orig half mor; worn. S Feb 24 (632) £150 [Coupe]

Graesse, Johann Georg Theodor, 1814-85
— Tresor de livres rares et precieux.... Berlin, 1922. 8 vols, including Supplement. 4to, half vellum; shaken. sg May 14 (300) $600

Anr Ed. Milan, 1950. 8 vols, including Supplement. 4to, orig cloth. FD June 11 (289) DM1,100; sg Jan 22 (169) $550

AMERICAN BOOK PRICES CURRENT

Grafton, Richard, d.c.1572
— A Chronicle at Large and Meere History of the Affayres of Englande.... L: Denham for R. Tottle & H. Toye, 1569. 2d Ed. 2 vols in 1. Folio, 19th-cent half calf; broken. Lacking title & all before D.iv; marginal defs. Sold w.a.f. T Mar 19 (388) £80

Graham, Elizabeth S.
— A Poetical Chronology of English History from the Conquest for the Use of Children. L: John Marshall, [1800]. 24mo, orig bds. With 32 ports. With holograph revisions on 9 pp. S Dec 5 (282) £320 [Quaritch]

Graham, Maria
— Journal of a Residence in India. Edin., 1812. 4to, contemp half calf; upper cover worn, spine chipped. With colored frontis & 15 plates. C Apr 8 (90) £400 [Guller]

Anr copy. Contemp half russia; rubbed, corners worn. Faint waterstain to corner of a few plates. C Apr 8 (91) £180 [Lennox Money]

— Journal of a Residence in Chile.... L, 1824. 4to, half mor; broken. With 14 plates. Ck May 15 (58) £120

Anr copy. 19th-cent half mor; rubbed & discolored. Library stamp & release stamp. S Jan 12 (280) £380 [Bomberg]

— Memoirs of the Life of Nicholas Poussin. L, 1820. 8vo, contemp calf gilt. bba Sept 25 (310) £50 [Frew Mackenzie]

Graham, Thomas John, 1795?-1876
— Sure Methods of Improving Health.... L, 1827. 12mo, mor gilt; extremities worn. 2 pp stained. sg Jan 15 (28) $90

Graham, Tom. See: Lewis, Sinclair

Grahame, Kenneth, 1859-1932
See also: Limited Editions Club
— Dream Days. L, 1930. One of 275. Illus by E. H. Shepard. Orig half vellum. L.p. copy. pnNY Sept 13 (237) $110
— The Golden Age. L, 1928. One of 275, sgd by author & artist. Illus by E. H. Shepard. Orig half vellum. pnNY Sept 13 (237) $110
— The Wind in the Willows. L, 1908. 1st Ed. Orig cloth. S June 18 (457) £620 [Joseph]

Anr copy. Tp stamped "presentation copy". S June 18 (458) £450 [Joseph]

Anr Ed. L, 1931. Illus by E. H. Shepard. bba Sept 25 (124) £75 [Maggs]

One of 200, sgd by author & artist. Orig half cloth, in d/j, unopened. sg Mar 5 (85) $950

Anr Ed. NY, 1940. Illus by Arthur Rackham. S Oct 7 (923) £260 [Vischer]

Anr Ed. L, 1951. One of 500. 4to, orig calf; spine spotted. With 12 color plates. S Dec 4 (215) £300 [Gorlin]

Deluxe Ed. 4to, calf; soiled & scuffed, spine ends worn. With 12 color plates. sg Oct 30 (84) $375

Graham's...
— Graham's Lady's and Gentleman's Magazine. Phila., 1843-48. Vols 22 & 32 in 7 vols. 8vo, contemp half mor or contemp mor gilt; worn. cb Feb 19 (120) $250

**Grammaire... —&
Grammaire francoise. Avec quelques remarques sur cette langue. Lyon, Michel Duhan, 1657.** 8vo, mor gilt by Chambolle-Duru. Pichon-Schwerdt-Jeanson copy. SM Mar 1 (274) FF17,000

Grammaire francoise. Avec quelques remarques sur cette langue. See: Grammaire... & Grammaire francoise. Avec quelques remarques sur cette langue....
— Lyon: Michel Duhan, 1657

Gran...
— Il Gran Teatro di Venezia, ovvero raccolta delle principali vedute e pitture.... [Venice: Domenico Louisa, c.1720]. Vol I only. 18th-cent calf, with binder Andrew Fountaine's invoice on front flyleaf; worn. With 65 plates. Thick paper copy. S June 25 (225) £4,200 [Fenice]

Grand...
— Grand Prix des Meilleurs Romans Etrangers. Paris: Andre Sauret, 1955-57. One of 300. 18 vols. 4to, orig wraps, unopened. S June 17 (138) £260 [Gardiner]

Grand Cuisinier...
— Le Grand Cuisinier tres-utile & profitable. Paris: Nicolas Bonfons, 1576. 12mo, vellum wraps from an old French Ms; worn. Quires E8 & S8 lacking A-F8 loose; tp detached & dust-soiled; some corners turned or frayed without loss. Hume-Kodgkin-Vehling copy. P Nov 25 (221A) $1,600

Grand, Gordon
See also: Derrydale Press
— The Banshee Shadow Flies. [N.p., 1st half of 20th cent]. Ptd wraps; soiled. sg Oct 23 (293) $100

Grand-Carteret, John, 1850-1927
— Les Almanachs francais: bibliographie, iconographie des almanachs.... Paris, 1896. 4to, later half cloth, orig wraps preserved; rubbed. bba Oct 16 (381) £110 [Hay Cinema]
Anr copy. Half sheep; worn & shaken. sg May 14 (231) $150

Grandmont, Francois Fortin de. See: Fortin, Francois

Grandpre, L de
— A Voyage in the Indian Ocean and to Bengal. L, 1803. 2 vols. 8vo, later half mor. Some tears or holes, just affecting text; some stains & soiling. S July 14 (864) £320

Grandville
— Album de 120 sujets tires des fables de La Fontaine. Paris: Garnier, [c.1859]. 8vo, orig cloth blocked in gilt over onlays of blue, green, red, yellow & pink papers. S Nov 27 (72) £130 [Henderson]

Grandville, 1803-47
— Un Autre monde: Transformations, Visions, Incarnations. Paris, 1844. Text by Taxile Delord. 4to, 19th-cent mor gilt. With frontis & 36 hand-colored plates. S Nov 27 (73) £600 [Marlborough]
— Scenes de la vie privee et publique des animaux. Paris, 1842. Part II only. 4to, recent half calf. Engraved title misbound. ha Dec 19 (196) $220
1st Ed in Book form. 2 vols. 8vo, orig half mor; rubbed. bba Aug 20 (261) £200 [Deighton Bell]

Grannis, Ruth S. See: Grolier Club

Grant, Frederick Dent. See: Forsyth & Grant

Grant, George F.
— Montana Trout Flies. Portland OR: Champoeg Press, [1981]. One of 1,950. 4to, cloth. With 7 plates in color of flies in sleeve affixed to rear pastedown. sg Oct 23 (295) $80

Grant, George Monro, 1835-1902
— Picturesque Canada: The Country as it Was and Is. Toronto, [1882]. 2 vols in orig 6 parts. 4to, orig cloth. bba Mar 12 (15) £55 [Schutze]

Grant, James, 1771-1833
— The Narrative of a Voyage of Discovery Performed in his Majesty's Vessel the Lady Nelson.... L, 1803. 1st Ed. 4to, later mor. Lacking folding plate of keels & colored bird plate. Inscr. CA Apr 12 (115) A$1,600
Anr copy. Contemp half calf; rubbed. With folding frontis, chart & 6 plates (Cockatoo colored). Manchester copy. S June 25 (494) £1,800 [Quaritch]
Facsimile Ed. Adelaide, 1973. 4to, cloth. kh Mar 16 (225) A$90

Grant, James, 1822-87
— The Tartans of the Clans of Scotland. Edin., 1886. Folio, orig cloth; worn, loose. sg June 4 (153) $200

GRANT

Grant, John. See: Seton & Grant

Grant, Maurice Harold
— A Chronological History of the Old English Landscape Painters. L, [1926]-47. Vols I-II only. Mor gilt by Worrall. S Nov 10 (94) £160 [Sims]

Grant, Ulysses S., 1822-85
— Personal Memoirs. NY, 1885-86. 2 vols. 8vo, orig sheep. cb Dec 18 (70) $65

Granville, Augustus Bozzi, 1783-1872
— St. Petersburgh. A Journal of Travels.... L, 1828. 2 vols. 8vo, contemp calf; rubbed, splits in joints. Titles soiled. bba Mar 26 (360) £90 [Cavendish]

1st Ed. 2 vols. 8vo, contemp half calf; rubbed. Some browning. bba Oct 30 (311) £90 [Beyer]

Grapaldi, Francesco Mario. See: Grapaldus, Franciscus Marius

Grapaldus, Franciscus Marius, 1465?-1515
— De partibus aedium.... [Parma]: F. Ugoleto, 10 May 1506. 4to, half vellum; soiled. Some foxing; tp soiled; some singeing of lower margins. Crahan copy. P Nov 25 (223) $350

Anr Ed. Venice: A. de Bindonis, 31 Jan 1517. 4to, old vellum bds; wormed at joints & front hinge cracked; corner of b5 torn away with loss of part of a shoulder note; u1 & u2 torn affecting several lines of text; single tiny wormhole to last 3 leaves. Hunt copy. CNY Nov 21 (131) $160

Grapheus, Cornille
— La Tresadmirable, tresmagnificque & triumphante entree du treshault...Prince Philipes.... Antwerp: Gillis van Diest, 1550. Folio, contemp vellum. Lacking final blank; small hole affecting 1 or 2 letters of text of the final 2 leaves. S May 21 (41) £1,400 [Sourget]

Graphic...
— The Graphic Arts and Crafts Year Book, 1908. Hamilton: Republican Publishing, [1908]. 4to, later cloth; worn. ha Dec 19 (170) $75

— Graphic Illustrations of Warwickshire. Birm., 1829. Folio, half mor; hinges cracked. With frontis & 31 plates. pn Jan 22 (150) £95 [Tilleke]

Graslin, Jean Joseph Louis
— Essai analytique sur la richesse et sur l'impot.... L, 1767. 8vo, half mor; rubbed. A8 & b1 reversed; wormed throughout; leaves backed or repaired; holes affecting letters. P Sept 24 (298) $650

AMERICAN BOOK PRICES CURRENT

Grasset de Saint-Sauveur, Jacques
— Les Fastes du people francais.... [Paris, c.1801]. Supplement only. 4to, mor gilt by Riviere. With frontis & 15 hand-colored plates. Lacking title, Plate 16 & 7 leaves of text; 1 leaf repaired. C Dec 3 (122) £800 [Beres]

Grasset, Eugene
— Histoire des Quatre Fils Aymon. Paris: H. Launette, 1883. One of 100 on japon. 4to, half mor gilt. B Oct 7 (313) HF950

Gratius, Nemesianus & Ovid
— Poetae tres egregii nunc primum in lucem editi. Venice: Aldus, 1534. 8vo, calf gilt by Vogel; worn. Jeanson 1013. SM Mar 1 (275) FF2,200

Anr copy. Recent bds. Tp soiled. T July 16 (412) £100

Graux, Lucien
— Le Tapis de Prieres. Paris: Pour les amis du Docteur Lucien-Graux, 1938. One of 125. Illus by F. L. Schmied. 4to, loose as issued in ptd wrap. cb Dec 4 (346) $500

Graves, Algernon — & Cronin, William Vine
— A History of the Works of Sir Joshua Reynolds. L, 1899-1901. One of 125. 4 vols. Folio, contemp half mor. S Nov 10 (95) £360 [Sims]

Graves, George, fl.1777-1834
— Hortus Medicus: or, Figures and Descriptions of the more Important Plants.... Edin., 1834. 4to, contemp calf; head & foot of spine worn, hinges strengthened. With 44 hand-colored plates on 38 leaves. A few margins just shaved. C Oct 15 (232) £420 [Greyfriars]

Anr copy. Orig half cloth; worn. Some stains & tears. Sold w.a.f. S Nov 10 (494) £220 [Wheldon]

Graves, Richard, 1715-1804
— Columella; or, the Distressed Anchoret. L, 1779. 2 vols. 12mo, contemp calf; rubbed. S Jan 13 (498) £225 [Burmester]

Graves, Robert
— The Feather Bed. L: Hogarth Press, 1923. 1st Ed, one of 250. Orig bds; rubbed. bba Oct 16 (171) £110 [Henderson]

— Good-bye to All That. L, 1929. 1st Ed. In d/j. sg Dec 11 (57) $175

2d Issue. In d/j. S Sept 22 (88) £110 [Maggs]

— The Marmosite's Miscellany. L: Hogarth Press, 1925. 1st Ed. Sgd on front free endpaper. bba Oct 16 (174) £160 [Rota]

— Mock Beggar Hall. L: Hogarth Press, 1924. 1st Ed. Orig bds; rubbed. bba Oct 16

(173) £95 [Edrich]
- On English Poetry. L, 1922. Orig bds, variant bdg, in d/j. kh Mar 16 (228) A$110 Anr copy. Orig bds; worn. kh Mar 16 (229) A$60
- Ten Poems More. Paris: Hours Press, 1930. One of 200. T May 20 (19) £110

  1st Ed. Orig half mor by Len Lye. bba Oct 16 (177) £100 [Bell, Book]
- Welchman's Hose. L: The Fleuron, 1925. 1st Ed, one of 525. 4to, orig bds. bba Oct 16 (175) £85 [Palladour]
- Whipperginny. L, 1923. 1st Ed. In repaired d/j. bba Oct 16 (172) £45 [Bell, Book]

Gray, Asa, 1810-88

- Elements of Botany. NY, 1836. 8vo, modern calf. S Feb 24 (570) £130 [19th-cent]
- Plates Prepared between the Years 1849 and 1850 to Accompany a Report on the Forest Trees of North America. Wash., 1891. Folio, orig wraps. With 23 hand-colored plates. Marginal dampstaining affecting upper cover, prelim leaf & the 1st 4 plates. de Belder copy. S Apr 27 (136) £2,400 [De Pater]

Gray, Basil

- Iran, Persian Miniatures—Imperial Library. NY, [1956]. Folio, orig half cloth, in torn d/j. With 34 colored plates. Unesco World Art Series. C Nov 21 (31) £38

Gray, David. See: Derrydale Press

Gray, George John

- A Bibliography of the Works of Sir Isaac Newton. Cambr., 1907. 2d Ed. Half cloth. sg Oct 2 (238) $80

Gray, George Robert, 1808-72

- The Genera of Birds.... L, [1837]-44-49. 3 vols. Folio, orig cloth; soiled. With 150 plain & 185 hand-colored plates. All plates stamped, perforated stamps affecting titles & some text leaves. bba Aug 28 (147) £850 [Rainer]

  Anr copy. Contemp half calf. With 185 hand-colored plates & 150 uncolored plates. Strickland copy, annotated by Hugh Edwin Strickland. C Oct 15 (233) £7,000 [Mitchell]

  Anr copy. Contemp half russia gilt; rubbed. With 185 hand-colored plates & 150 uncolored plates of detail. Some foxing of uncolored plates & text; a few plates just shaved; half-title in Vol I only. S Oct 23 (703) £6,000 [Wesley]

Gray, John, 1866-1934

- Silverpoints. L, 1893. 1st Ed, one of 250. 12mo, orig cloth; edges worn. ha Sept 19 (215) $150

Gray, John Edward, 1800-75

- Illustrations of Indian Zoology.... L, 1830-34 [35]. 2 vols in 1. Folio, unbound with several orig ptd part wraps. With 2 titles & 202 hand-colored plates. Some fraying. S Oct 23 (52) £3,800 [Shapero]

Gray, Prentiss N. See: Derrydale Press

Gray, Thomas, 1716-71

- Designs by Mr. R. Bentley for Six Poems. L, 1753. 1st Ed, 1st Ptg. Folio, contemp calf; rubbed, joints split. bba Nov 13 (220) £120 [Axe]

  Anr Ed. L, 1766. Folio, contemp half calf; worn, spine broken. With note on endleaf stating ownership by the Ladies of Llangollen. S Nov 17 (655) £120 [Simon]
- An Elegy Wrote in a Country Church Yard. L, 1846. ("Gray's Elegy.") Illus by Owen Jones. 8vo, papier mache bds. pnE June 17 (164) £60

  Anr Ed. L: Raven Press, 1938. ("Elegy Written in a Country Churchyard.") Illus by Agnes Miller Parker. cb June 18 (264) $70

  One of 1,500. bba July 16 (361) £150 [Clark]
- Ode Performed in the Senate-House at Cambridge, July 1, 1769.... L, 1769. 4to, mor gilt by Riviere. Kern copy. sg June 11 (221) $1,000
- Odes. Strawberry-Hill, 1757. 1st Ed. 4to, mor gilt by Morrell; joints starting. Half-title repaired & more than half of tp replaced. wa Mar 5 (263) $210
- Works. Glasgow: Foulis, 1768. ("Poems.") 4to, contemp calf gilt. pnE Jan 28 (100) £150 [Maggs]

  Anr Ed. L, 1874. ("Poems and Letters.") 4to, contemp calf gilt. With 4 mtd photos. Eton presentation copy. cb July 30 (81) $130

  Anr Ed. L, 1879. 4to, calf gilt; scuffed. Minor foxing. sg Sept 11 (196) $130

Gray, Thomas, 1787-1848

- Observations on a General Iron Rail-Way.... L, 1823. 4th Ed. 8vo, orig bds. With 5 plates. bba June 18 (98) £100

Grazzini, Antonio Francesco, 1503-85

- The Story of Doctor Manente.... Florence: Orioli, [1929]. 1st Ed, one of 200. Trans by D. H. Lawrence. Bdg soiled. S Jan 13 (580) £100 [Gekowski]

Great...

— Great Drawings of all Time. NY, [1962]. Ed by Ira Moskowitz. 4 vols. 4to, cloth. sg Feb 5 (153) $150

— Great Exhibition, 1851. L, 1852. ("Exhibition of the Works of Industry of all Nations. Reports by the Juries on the Subjects in the Thirty Classes into which the Exhibition was Divided.") 4to, half lea, armorial bdg; worn. sg Jan 15 (315) $200
Anr Ed. L, [1854]. ("Dickinsons' Recollections of the Great Exhibition 1851.") Folio, orig half mor; worn. With 55 hand-colored proof plates. S Feb 23 (674) £3,600 [Cons]

Grece, Charles Frederick

— Essays on Practical Husbandry.... Montreal, 1817. 8vo, contemp half calf, orig wraps bound in; warped & worn. bba Sept 25 (228) £200 [Morrell]

Greco, Gioachino

— Chess Made Easy, or the Games of.... L, 1750. 12mo, contemp calf; rubbed, hinges split. With frontis & folding plate (torn & repaired). pn Mar 26 (405) £160 [De Lucia]

— Le Jeu des eschets. Paris, 1714. Contemp calf; hinges cracked. pn Mar 26 (404) £70 [Caisso]

— The Royall Game of Chesse-Play. L, 1656. 8vo, half mor gilt. Bulstrode Whitelocke's copy. pn Mar 26 (403) £400 [De Lucia]

Greek Anthology

— Anthologia epigrammatura graecorum libri VII... Venice: Aldus, Nov 1503. ("Florilegium diversorum epigrammatum in septem libros.") 8vo, 19th-cent mor gilt; both covers detached, spine def. S Mar 10 (1062) £600 [Maggs]

Greeley, Horace, 1811-72

— An Overland Journey, from New York to San Francisco.... NY, 1860. 1st Ed. 12mo, orig cloth; worn, backstrip faded. ha Dec 19 (120) $55

Greely, Adolphus Washington, 1844-1935

— Report on the Proceedings of the United States Expedition to Lady Franklin Bay, Grinnell Land. Wash., 1888. 2 vols. 4to, orig cloth. cb June 4 (91) $150

— Three Years of Arctic Service. An Account of the Lady Franklin Bay Expedition.... NY, 1886. 1st Ed. 2 vols. 8vo, orig cloth. Ck May 15 (72) £100
Anr copy. Half calf gilt by Mudie. pn July 23 (248) £140 [Thorp]

Green...

— The Green Sheaf. L, 1903-4. Ed by Pamela Coleman Smith. Nos 1-8 only. Orig wraps; worn. bba May 28 (94) £180 [Marks]

Green, Charles R. See: Clymer & Green

Green, Henry, 1801-73

— Shakespeare and the Emblem Writers.... L, 1870. 8vo, calf gilt; rubbed, hinges cracked. cb Feb 19 (121) $55

Green, J. F.

— Ocean Birds. L, 1887. Folio, cloth; scuffed. With 6 colored plates. pn Dec 11 (180) £75 [Greyfriars]
Anr copy. With 6 colored plates, 4 loose. pn Mar 5 (191) £40 [Levine]

Green, Jacob, 1790-1841

— Astronomical Recreations; or Sketches.... Phila., 1824. 4to, contemp cloth; hinges repaired. With engraved title & 19 plates, most colored by hand. F Oct 30 (467) $100
Anr copy. Later half lea; worn & stained. sg Apr 23 (165) $100

Green, Julien

— Mont-Cinere. Paris: Editions Jeanne Walter, [1930]. One of 280. Illus by Maurice Vlaminck. 4to, wraps. FD June 11 (5288) DM1,500

Green, Richard Lancelyn —& Gibson, John Michael

— A Bibliography of A. Conan Doyle. Oxford, 1983. In d/j. Soho Bibliographies XXIII. Inscr. cb Apr 24 (1033) $55; cb Apr 24 (1034) $60; cb Apr 24 (1035) $50

— My Evening with Sherlock Holmes. L, 1981. Proof copy. Wraps. Ls of Green laid in. cb Apr 24 (1335) $80

Green, Thomas

— The Universal Herbal. L, [1824]. 2 vols. 4to, contemp half calf gilt; worn & foxed. With 1 hand-colored engraved title, 2 hand-colored frontises & 104 hand-colored plates. A few plates with some staining; 1 plate with minor marginal repair. Sold w.a.f. CNY May 11 (61) $650
Anr copy. 2 vols plus appendix. 4to, contemp calf & calf-backed stiff wraps; worn, covers detached, spine of appendix missing. With engraved title, frontises & 106 hand-colored plates. S May 28 (674) £700

Green, Thomas, Botanist

— The Universal Herbal, or Botanical, Medical and Agricultural Dictionary.... Liverpool, [1816-20]. 1st Ed. 2 vols. 4to, contemp calf; worn. Some browning & dampstaining; final index leaf of Vol II torn in half. Ck Apr 24 (178) £270

Anr copy. Half calf; rubbed. Some foxing. pn Sept 18 (299) £380 [Dennistoun]

Anr copy. Contemp calf; rebacked. pnE Dec 17 (250) £110 [Thin]

Green, Valentine, 1739-1813

— The History and Antiquities of the City and Suburbs of Worcester. L, 1796. 2 vols. 4to, contemp calf gilt; rubbed. With port, folding map & 23 plates. pn May 21 (247) £120 [Sanders]

Greenaway, Kate, 1846-1901

— A Apple Pie. L: Routledge, [1886]. Oblong 4to, orig half cloth; worn. With 20 colored plates. pn Oct 23 (390) £70 [Trocchi]

— Book of Games. L: Routledge, [1889]. 4to, orig half cloth; worn. L Dec 11 (66) £90

— Kate Greenaway Pictures from Originals Presented...to John Ruskin.... L, 1921. 4to, cloth; worn. With port & 20 mtd colored plates. O Apr 28 (81) $100

— Language of Flowers. L: Routledge, [1884]. 1st Ed. 12mo, bds. pn Jan 22 (318) £70 [Cavendish]

— Under the Window. L: Routledge, [1878]. 1st Ed, 1st Issue. 4to, orig half cloth. S Oct 7 (968) £55 [Peters]

Greene, Graham

See also: Glover & Greene

— Babbling April. Oxford, 1925. Orig ptd bds. bba Oct 30 (252) £580 [Maggs]

— The Great Jowett. L, [1981]. One of 525. T Oct 15 (215) £85

— The Man Within. L, 1929. 1st Ed. Hole in upper joint of bdg. bba Feb 5 (256) £50 [Brook]

Anr copy. Orig cloth; worn. A few leaves soiled. ANs laid in. cb May 7 (91) $150; cb May 15 (83) $80

Anr copy. In d/j. sg Mar 5 (87) $375

— May We Borrow Your Husband? L, 1967. Proof copy. Wraps. T Feb 18 (82) £65

— The Name of Action. L, 1930. 1st Ed. In d/j; slightly warped. First few leaves spotted. S Sept 22 (90) £85 [Heywood Hill]

Stamboul Train. L, 1932. 1st Ed. In d/j. cb May 7 (85) £425; T May 20 (11) £145

— The Third Man and the Fallen Idol. L, [1950]. In d/j. cb Nov 20 (220) $80

— A Visit to Morin. L, [1959]. One of 250. Inscr for the benefit of the Berkhamsted Town Hall. S Jan 13 (568) £300 [Lloyd] 1st Ed in English. In d/j. bba July 16 (331) £260 [Joseph]

— A Wedding among the Owls. L, 1977. 1st Ed, one of 250. Orig wraps. Inscr in the cause of the Berkhamsted Town Hall. S Jan 13 (569) £200 [Perrin]

Greene, Louisa Lilias

— The Grey House on the Hill. L, [1903]. Illus by Arthur Rackham. Backstrip faded & creased, 1 hinge starting. With 8 color plates. Stained throughout. sg Oct 30 (85) $60

Greene, Max

— The Kanzas Region: Forest, Prairie, Desert.... NY, 1856. 1st Ed. 12mo, cloth; rubbed. cb Jan 8 (81) $750

Greene, William Thomas

— Parrots in Captivity. L, 1884-87. 3 vols. 8vo, later cloth. With 81 colored plates; without the 9 supplementary plates. Library markings. cb June 4 (92) $250

Anr copy. Orig cloth; rubbed & soiled. Without the 9 supplementary plates. S Oct 23 (700) £800 [Thomson]

Anr copy. Later cloth; rubbed. With 80 (of 81) colored plates. Library markings. T Nov 20 (138) £620

— The Science of Gunnery. L, 1841. 1st Ed. 8vo, orig cloth; rubbed. With extra engraved title & 8 plates. Library copy. ha Sept 19 (263) $85

Greener, William

— The Gun: or, a Treatise on the Various Descriptions of Small Fire-Arms. L, 1835. 1st Ed. 8vo, orig half cloth. With 4 plates. pnE Nov 12 (193) £130

Greener, William Wellington

— The Gun and its Development.... L, [1881]. 8vo, cloth; rubbed, spine ends frayed. cb Oct 9 (102) $100

Greenewalt, Crawford H.

— Hummingbirds. Garden City, [1960]. 4to, cloth. Sgd. wa Feb 19 (264) $85

One of 500. Orig cloth. With 69 mtd color plates. Haverschmidt copy. B Feb 24 (170) HF475

Anr copy. Cloth, in d/j. With 69 mtd colored plates. sg Jan 15 (218) $100; SSA Feb 11 (525) R120

Anr copy. Cloth. wa Sept 25 (158) $80

Greenfield, John

— A Compleat Treatise of the Stone and Gravel.... L, 1710. 8vo, calf gilt. With 23 plates, 3 folding. pnE Dec 17 (97) £230 [Phillips]

Greenham, Richard

— Works. L: Felix Kingston for Robert Dexter, 1599. 4to, old sheep; worn. Minor marginal defs. T Sept 18 (497) £135

Greenway, James C. —& Ripley, A. Lassell
— The Laurel Brook Club, 1902-1957. [N.p., 1958]. One of 150. 4to, cloth. sg Oct 23 (386) $300

Greenwell, George C., 1821-1900
— A Practical Treatise on Mine Engineering. Newcastle, 1855. 4to, contemp half mor; soiled & rubbed. With litho frontis & 61 plates, wholly or partially colored by hand. Some cropping; lacking initial blank; some soiling. S Nov 18 (951) £160 [Traylen]

Greenwood, Charles & John
— Atlas of the Counties of England. L, 1834. Folio, wraps. With engraved title & 46 hand-colored maps. pn May 21 (365) £950 [Burgess]

Anr copy. Half russia; joints repaired. S June 25 (238) £1,500 [Warwick]

Anr copy. Contemp calf; worn. With engraved title & 45 double-page county maps, hand-colored & edge bound. S July 28 (974) £1,400

Gregg, Josiah, 1806-50?
— Commerce of the Prairies, or the Journal of.... NY, 1844. 1st Ed, 1st Issue. 2 vols. 12mo, orig cloth; Vol I spine chipped. With 2 maps & 6 plates. Some staining. J. W. Abert's copy. K Dec 13 (116) $900

Grego, Joseph, 1843-1908
— Rowlandson the Caricaturist. L, 1880. 2 vols. 4to, orig half mor; rubbed, soiled. Ck Oct 17 (160) £75

Anr copy. Orig half mor; worn. Some spotting; 2 leaves loose. S Nov 10 (96) £85 [Rebecchi]

Anr copy. Half lea; worn, hinges cracked. sg Feb 5 (70) $100

Anr copy. Half lea gilt. sg June 4 (290) $200

Gregor, Joseph. See: Fueloep-Miller & Gregor

Gregory, David, 1661-1708
— Astronomiae physicae & geometricae elementa. Oxford, 1702. Folio, contemp vellum. S July 28 (1078) £450

Gregory I, Saint, Pope, 540-604
— Dialogorum libri quattuor. [Strassburg: Heinrich Eggestein, c.1472-74]. Folio, modern half vellum. Some dampstaining to a few upper margins; stamps of Royal library at Monaco at foot of 1st leaf; some early Ms annotations discolored. 57 (of 58) leaves; lacking final blank. Goff G-399. S Nov 27 (171) £1,300 [Maggs]

Anr Ed. [Strassburg: Jacob Elber, not after 1481]. Folio, modern bds. First 2 leaves discolored & remargined; some early an-notations; some worming in lower margin at beginning & in text at end. 78 leaves. Goff G-403. S Nov 27 (170) £430 [Klein]
— Opera. Paris, 1705. 4 vols. Folio, contemp calf; worn. Some dampstaining & spotting. bba Oct 30 (193) £70 [Pembroke]

Gregory, Lady Isabella Augusta, 1859?-1932
— Kincora. NY, 1905. One of 50. Wraps. S Sept 22 (91) £80 [Sumner & Stillman]

Gregory IX, Pope, 1147?-1241
— Decretales. Venice: L. Giunta, 20 May 1514. 4to, 19th-cent half vellum gilt. Some dampstaining throughout; 2 small holes in title. T Mar 19 (383) £200

Anr copy. Marginal repairs to title & 1st leaves; some dampstains; lacking full-page wood engraving, ai & yyyi. T Mar 19 (384) £110

Gregory, John Walter, 1864-1932
— The Great Rift Valley. L, 1896. 1st Ed. 8vo, orig cloth; rubbed & bumped. With 2 folding maps. cb May 21 (119) $120

Gregory of Nanzianus, Saint, 329-389
— Orationes trigintaocto...tractatus, sermones & libri aliquot. Paris: Claude Chevallon, 1532. Folio, early 19th-cent half sheep. Lacking final blank. sg Oct 9 (218) $110

Gregson, Matthew, 1749-1824
— Portfolio of Fragments Relative to the History and Antiquities of the...Duchy of Lancaster. Liverpool, 1817. Folio, later half calf; rubbed, joints split. bba Apr 9 (385) £40 [Sanders]

Gregynog Press—Newtown, Wales
— ABERCROMBIE, LASCELLES. - Lyrics and Unfinished Poems. 1940. One of 175. S Jan 8 (123) $120
— AESOP. - Fables. 1931. One of 250. S June 18 (337) £1,180 [Contemporary]
— BLUNT, LADY ANNE & BLUNT, WILFRID SCAWEN. - The Celebrated Romance of the Stealing of the Mare. 1930. One of 275. S Dec 4 (139) £270 [Blythman]; sg Dec 4 (81) $400
— BRIDGES, ROBERT. - Eros and Psyche. 1935. One of 300. sg June 11 (224) $375
— BUTLER, SAMUEL. - Erewhon. 1932. One of 300. bba Mar 26 (259) £110 [Clark]
— JOINVILLE, JEAN. - The History of Saint Louis. 1937. One of 200. S Dec 4 (141) £800 [Owen]
— MILTON, JOHN. - Comus.... 1934. One of 250. sg Jan 8 (124) $200
— SAMPSON, JOHN. - XXI Welsh Gypsy Folk-Tales. 1933. One of 250. S Dec 4 (140) £280 [Samrim]
— SHAW, GEORGE BERNARD. - Shaw Gives Himself Away. 1939. One of 275. S Dec 4 (142) £400 [Thorp]

— Vansittart, Robert. - The Singing Caravan. 1932. One of 250. T Oct 15 (29) £95
— Xenophon. - Cyropaedia. 1936. One of 150. S June 18 (339) £640 [Blackwell]

Greig, John. See: Storer & Greig

Grenier, Francis
— Douze sujets de chasse au tir dessines sur pierre.... Paris, 1829. Folio, modern half mor. Jeanson copy. SM Mar 1 (276) FF5,500

Grenier, Jacques Remond
— Memoirs de sa campagne et de ses decouvertes dans les Mers des Indes. Brest. 1770. 4to, half calf. With folding map. S Apr 24 (344) £460 [Perrin]

Gresset, Jean Baptiste Louis, 1709-77
— Ver-Vert, Poeme en Quatre Chants.... Paris, 1832. Illus by C. Monnet. 8vo, morbacked vellum by Mercier Sr. de Cuzin, orig wraps bound in. With engraved title & 5 plates. Extra-illus with a duplicate set of the plates before letters & 3 orig sepia drawings (loosely inserted). C Dec 3 (125) £400 [Bibermuhle]

Greville, Charles C. F., 1794-1865
— Greville Memoirs. L, 1874-87. Ed by Henry Reeve. 8 vols. 8vo, half calf gilt. pnE Jan 28 (99) £70 [Hay]
Anr Ed. L, 1938. Ltd Ed. 8 vols, including Index vol. pn Oct 23 (338) £500 [Lyon]

Greville, Fulke, Baron Brooke, 1554-1628
— The Life of the Renowned Sir Philip Sidney. L: Caradoc Press, 1906. One of 11 on vellum. Vellum. C Dec 12 (367) £500 [Weil]

Greville, Robert Kaye, 1794-1866
— Scottish Cryptogamic Flora. Edin., [1822]-23-28. 6 vols. 8vo, lea gilt. With 3 half-titles & 360 hand-colored plates. C Apr 8 (180) £500 [Quaritch]

Grew, Nehemiah, 1641-1712
— The Anatomy of Plants. [L], 1682. 1st Ed. Folio, contemp calf; rebacked, spine preserved. With 81(of 83) plates; last 5 plates laid down, 2 others torn. Sold w.a.f. pn Jan 22 (97) £75 [Gladstone]
Anr copy. Contemp calf; rubbed, rebacked, preserving old spine. With 83 plates. Some spots & stains. Horticultural Society of New York—de Belder copy. S Apr 27 (137) £900 [Knohl]
— Musaeum Regalis Societatis, or a Catalogue.... L, 1681. 1st Ed. 2 parts in 1 vol. Folio, contemp calf; worn. With port & 26 (of 31) plates. S Feb 24 (571) £90 [Bloom]
Anr copy. Contemp calf; worn, broken.
With port & 31 plates. sg Jan 15 (219) $375
Anr Ed. L, 1694. Folio, contemp calf; rebacked. With 31 plates, 1 torn & repaired. pn Jan 22 (98) £140 [Frew]
— New Experiments and Useful Observations concerning Sea-Water made Fresh.... L, 1684. 4to, disbound. Tp soiled & with minor repair. C May 13 (124) £1,100 [Laget]

Grey, Edward, Viscount Grey of Fallodon, 1862-1933
— Fly Fishing. L, 1899. 8vo, cloth. With 7 plates. With an ALs mtd to recto of front free endpaper. sg Oct 30 (86) $50
One of 150. Vellum. With 9 plates including a duplicate frontis loosely inserted. Ck May 29 (148) $80
Anr Ed. L & Toronto, 1930. One of 150, sgd & with an extra wood-engraving sgd by the artist. Illus by Eric Daglish. 4to, orig vellum bds; rear cover torn. sg Oct 23 (296) $225

Grey, Sir George, 1812-98
— Journals of Two Expeditions of Discovery in North-West and Western Australia.... L, 1841. 2 vols. 8vo, modern half mor. Some stamps (partly erased from titles); some plates cleaned; bound without ads. kh Mar 16 (235) A$950

Grey Library, Sir George
— The Library...Philology. L & Leipzig, 1858-59. Vols I-II (of 4) bound in 1 vol. 8vo, contemp half lea; rubbed. Inscr. sg Jan 22 (172) $250

Grey, James T., Jr.
— Handbook for the Magaree. Yardley PA: Pvtly ptd, 1976. One of 25. Half lea. With ANs from Grey laid in. sg Oct 23 (297) $130

Grey, Zane, 1875-1939
— An American Angler in Australia. NY, 1937. wa Dec 11 (173) $120
— Tales of the Angler's Eldorado, New Zealand. NY & L, 1926. 4to, cloth, in chipped d/j. sg May 21 (111) $130

Gribble, Ernest. See: Cescinsky & Gribble

Gribble, Francis
— Madame de Stael and her Lovers. L, 1907. Mor extra by Bayntun with oval miniature port of Mme. de Stael framed in a broad gilt border of onlaid mor leaves & flowers. Sold w.a.f. Extra-illus with 5 plain & 5 color plates. CNY Dec 19 (7) $500

Grierson, J.
— Twelve Select Views of the Seat of War including Views taken in Rangoon, Cachar and Andaman Islands. [Calcutta, 1825]. Oblong folio, contemp bds; spine def. With 12 lithos. Prelims dampstained in lower margin. sg Apr 2 (99) $3,200

Grieshaber, HAP
— Totentanz von Basel. Dresden, 1966. Folio, orig cloth. FD June 11 (4956) DM1,500; JG Oct 2 (1985) DM2,000

Grieve, Maud
— A Modern Herbal. L, 1931. 2 vols. T Apr 16 (162) £50

Griffin, Appleton P. C. See: Boston Athenaeum

Griffin, Gregory, Pseud. See: Microcosm...

Griffin, Richard, Baron Braybrooke
— The History of Audley End.... L, 1836. Folio, contemp calf; rebacked. Ck Nov 7 (140) £550

Griffith, George
— Valdar the Oft-Born: A Saga of Seven Ages. L, 1895. Cloth, Currey's A bdg; rear cover rubbed, front hinge starting. cb Sept 28 (567) £60

Griffith, Samuel Young
— New Historical Description of Cheltenham and its Vicinity. L, 1826. 4to, half mor gilt. Extra-illus with plates. S May 28 (871) £180

Anr copy. Recent mor gilt. Lacking view of Monpellier Baths. T July 16 (26) £160

Griffiths, Arthur George Frederick, 1838-1908
— Mysteries of Police and Crime. L 1912. Illus by Arthur Rackham. 3 vols. 8vo, cloth; hinges starting, 1 free endpaper torn. sg Oct 30 (87) $175

Griffiths, John Willis, 1809?-82
— Treatise on Marine and Naval Architecture.... NY, 1853. 4to, modern calf gilt. With 1 litho & 45 engravings. Tp stamped; some foxing. pnNY Sept 13 (240) $180

Grijalva, Juan de
— The Discovery of New Spain in 1518.... Berkeley: Cortes Society, 1942. One of 200. Ed by Henry Raup Wagner. sg Oct 2 (302) $150

Grillet, Laurent, 1851-1901
— Les Ancetres du violon et du violoncelle.... Paris, 1901. 2 vols. Contemp half mor. Some marginalia. bba Feb 5 (140) £90 [Teoh]

Grilli, Elise
— The Art of the Japanese Screen. NY & Tokyo, [1971]. 2d ptg. Folio, silk. wa Nov 6 (452) $70

Grimble, Augustus
— Deer-Stalking and the Deer Forests of Scotland. L, 1888. 2d Ed, One of 250. 4to, orig bds. A few plates loose. pn Jan 22 (172) £55 [Furness]

Anr copy. Orig bds; worn. pnE Oct 15 (1) £95

— The Salmon and Sea Trout Waters of England and Wales. L, 1904. One of 350. 2 vols. 4to, half vellum. pn June 18 (14) £140 [Howell Williams]

Anr copy. Orig half vellum. Tear in each of the folding maps. S July 28 (1019) £100

— The Salmon Rivers of Scotland. L, 1899-1900. Ltd Ed. 4 vols. 4to, orig half vellum; rubbed & soiled. S July 28 (1021) £240

— The Salmon Rivers of Ireland. L, 1903. One of 250. 2 vols. 4to, orig half vellum; corners rubbed, soiled. S July 28 (1020) £100

— The Salmon Rivers of England and Wales [Ireland; Scotland]. L, 1913. 3 vols. pnE Dec 17 (291) £65 [Cadzow]

Grimm Brothers
See also: Golden Cockerel Press; Limited Editions Club
— Fairy Tales. L, 1909. Illus by Arthur Rackham. 4to, orig cloth. bba June 18 (250) £150 [Joseph]

Anr copy. Orig cloth; backstrip faded. With 40 mtd color plates. Inscr by Rackham & with orig pen sketch on half-title. sg Oct 30 (89) $1,100

One of 750. Vellum; rubbed. bba Apr 23 (288) £380 [Burton Garbett]

Anr copy. Vellum gilt. pnE Nov 17 (238) £190

Deluxe Ed. 4to, vellum; spotted, lacking ties. sg Oct 30 (88) $950

— German Popular Stories. L, 1825-26. Illus by George Cruikshank. 2 vols. 8vo, orig half cloth; rubbed. With 22 plates, including titles; soiled & stained. S Dec 5 (284) £400 [Hirsch]

Anr copy. Contemp calf; cracked on hinges. Some browning. T Mar 19 (280) £42

— Hansel and Gretel and Other Tales. L, 1920. Illus by Arthur Rackham. 4to, orig cloth; backstrip faded & worn. With 20 mtd color plates. sg Oct 30 (93) $80

— Hansel and Gretel. L, [1925]. One of 600. Illus by Kay Nielsen. cb June 18 (289) $425

— Koenig Drosselbart. Berlin, 1922. One of 95. Illus by Max Slevogt. Folio, orig portfolio. HN Nov 26 (2108) DM620
— Little Brother and Little Sister. L, [1917]. One of 525. Illus by Arthur Rackham. 4to, orig cloth. With 13 color plates. S Dec 4 (213) £200 [Stremson]

One of 525, sgd by Rackham. Cloth; soiled, minor stains. With 13 mtd color plates & with additional mtd impression of one plate, sgd, in envelope. sg Oct 30 (91) $700

— Die zwei Brueder. Berlin, [1924]. One of 100. Illus by Max Slevogt. Folio, orig portfolio. HN Nov 26 (2103) DM900

Grimod de la Reyniere, Alexandre, 1758-1838
— Manuel des Amphitryons.... Paris, 1808. 8vo, contemp half calf; rubbed. With 17 plates. Captions of most plates shaved; 1 fish plate & portion of the other with later coloring; some foxing & staining. P Nov 25 (103) $700

Anr copy. Half vellum. Crahan copy. P Nov 25 (224) $750

Grimwade, Russell
— An Anthology of the Eucalypts. Sydney, 1920. 4to, half cloth. With 79 plates. Some soiling. kh Mar 16 (237) A$90

Grindel, Eugene. See: Eluard, Paul

Grindlay, Robert Melville
— Scenery, Costumes and Architecture, Chiefly on the Western Side of India. L, 1826-30. Part 4 only. contemp cloth; spine torn. With Abbey's Plates 21-26 only. C Oct 15 (39) £200 [Shapero]

Anr copy. 6 parts in 1 vol. 4to, half mor. With engraved title & 36 hand-colored plates. Lacking the litho title to Vol II. With titles to Parts 2-6 & ad leaves in Parts 2, 4 & 6. S June 25 (465) £2,000 [Mansoor]

Anr Ed. L, 1830. Folio, 19th-cent half mor gilt; rubbed. With engraved title & 36 hand-colored plates. A few plate margins slightly dust soiled. S June 25 (217) £3,200 [Traylen]

Anr Ed. L, 1892. Folio, bdg not described. All plates with perforated library stamps. bba Mar 12 (8) £220 [Vandeleur Books]

Grinnell, George Bird, 1849-1938
See also: Derrydale Press; Roosevelt & Grinnell
— American Big Game in its Haunts. NY, 1904. Ed by Grinnell. cb Nov 6 (141) $95

American Duck Shooting. NY, [1901]. sg Oct 23 (298) $50

One of 600. cb May 21 (122) $95

— American Game-Bird Shooting. NY, [1910]. 1st Ed. Worn & foxed, front hinge cracked. With 50 plain & 2 colored plates. Creases to c.75 pp. cb May 21 (121) $55

— The Cheyenne Indians: Their History and Ways of Life. New Haven, 1923. 2 vols. Cloth; worn & soiled. wa June 25 (243) $105

— Hunting at High Altitudes. NY & L, 1913. cb May 21 (123) $55

— Two Great Scouts and Their Pawnee Battalion.... Cleveland, 1928. cb Oct 9 (103) $65

Grinnell, Joseph, 1877-1939 —& Others
— The Game Birds of California. Berkeley, 1918. cb May 21 (126) $55

Anr copy. With 16 color plates by Louis Agassiz Fuertes & Allan Brooks. cb June 4 (93) $95; pn Oct 23 (216) £50 [Maggs]

Grinnell, Joseph, 1877-1939 —& Storer, Tracy
— Animal Life in the Yosemite. Berkeley, 1924. Extra copy of Plate 62 laid in loose. Inscr. cb Apr 2 (122) $130; cb May 2 (123) $95

Griswold, Frank Gray, 1854-1937
— After Thoughts. [NY: Plimpton Press], 1936. One of 150. Inscr. sg Oct 23 (299) $60

— The Cascapedia Club. [N.p.: Pvtly ptd], 1920. Inscr. sg Oct 23 (300) $90

— Salmo Salar. [Norwood, Mass.], 1929. Mor gilt; worn. Inscr. sg Oct 23 (301) $70

— A Salmon River. NY, 1928. One of 250. sg Oct 23 (302) $80

— Salmon Score of F. Gray Griswold for Ten Seasons 1920-1930. Grand Cascapedia River, 1930. Inscr. sg Oct 23 (303) $70

Groenveldt, Joannes. See: Greenfield, John

Grohmann, Adolf. See: Arnold & Grohmann

Grohmann, Will
— Paul Klee. NY, [1929]. 4to, cloth, in d/j. sg June 4 (190) $250

Grolier Club—New York
— Catalogue of Books...with Arms or Devices Upon the Bindings... 1895. One of 350. sg May 14 (108) $130

— A Catalogue of Books Illustrated by Thomas Rowlandson. 1916. One of 200. sg June 4 (288) $150

— A Description of the Early Printed Books owned by the Grolier Club... 1895. One of 400. O May 12 (82) $100

— Facsimile of the Laws and Acts of the General Assembly...of New-York... 1894. One of 312. Ed by Robert Ludlow Fowler. sg Jan 22 (174) $130

— Fifty-Five Books Printed Before 1525...Paul Mellon. 1968. One of 1,650. sg Jan 22

GROLIER CLUB

(176) $50
— One Hundred Influential American Books Printed Before 1900. 1947. One of 600. cba Feb 5 (102) $65; sg May 14 (301) $225
— A Selection of American Press Books, 1968-1978. Printer's Choice.... 1983. One of 325. Intro by Ruth Fine & William Matheson; bibliographical descriptions & notes by W. Thomas Taylor. sg Jan 22 (178) $250
— BRESLAUER, BERNARD & FOLTER, ROLAND. - Bibliography: its History and Development. 1984. One of 600. sg Jan 22 (173) $100
— DE VINNE, THEODORE LOW. - Notable Printers of Italy.... 1910. One of 400. Half cloth. Holograph compliment slip from De Vinne tipped in. sg May 14 (430) $130
— FAY, BERNARD. - Notes on the American Press at the End of the Eighteenth Century... 1927. One of 325. sg Jan 22 (175) $60
— GOLDSCHMIDT, LUCIEN & NAEF, WESTON. - The Truthful Lens: A Survey of the Photographically Illustrated Book, 1844-1914. 1980. One of 1,000. sg Nov 13 (59) $175; sg Jan 22 (168) $120; sg May 7 (44) $225; wa June 25 (37) $210
— GRANNIS, RUTH S. - A Descriptive Catalogue of the First Editions in Book Form of Percy Bysshe Shelley. 1923. One of 350. sg Oct 2 (273) $80
— HALSEY, RICHARD T.H. - The Boston Port Bill as Pictured by a Contemporary London Cartoonist. 1904. One of 325. Several leaves with minor staining to outer edge. sg Mar 12 (132) $60
— HART, CHARLES HENRY. - Catalogue of the Engraved Portraits of George Washington. 1904. One of 425. 4to, half vellum bds. With 20 plates. sg Jan 22 (177) $225
— HENDERSON, ROBERT W. - Early American Sport: a Chronological Check-list... 1937. One of 400. cba Feb 5 (101) $50; sg Oct 23 (304) $110
— HOE, ROBERT. - A Lecture on Bookbinding as a Fine Art... 1886. One of 200. Tp stamped. O May 12 (83) $225
Anr copy. Small gouge mark in margins of c.12 plates. O June 15 (88) $80
— HORBLIT, HARRISON D. - One Hundred Books Famous in Science. 1964. One of 1,000. HN May 20 (8a) DM650; pnE Jan 28 (196) £280 [McKenzie]
— KENT, HENRY W. - Bibliographical Notes on One Hundred Books Famous in English Literature. 1903. One of 305. O June 16 (89) $90
— KENT, HENRY W. - Bibliographical Notes on One Hundred Books Famous in English Literature. 1903. One of 305. O June 16 (89) $90
— KEYNES, SIR GEOFFREY. - A Bibliography of

AMERICAN BOOK PRICES CURRENT

William Blake. 1921. One of 250. sg Oct 2 (62) $450
— KOEHLER, SYLVESTER ROSA. - A Chronological Catalogue of the Engravings, Dry-Points and Etchings of Albert Duerer. 1897. One of 400. sg June 11 (225) $150
— LE ROUX DE LINCY, ADRIEN JEAN VICTOR. - Researches Concerning Jean Grolier... 1907. One of 300. sg Apr 2 (100) $300
— MAGEE, DAVID. - Fine Printing and Bookbinding from San Francisco and its Environs. San Francisco: Grabhorn Press, 1961. One of 200. sg Jan 8 (112) $70
— MORISON, STANLEY. - Fra Luca de Pacioli of Borgo S. Sepolcro. 1933. One of 390. cb Dec 4 (287) $600
— OMAR KHAYYAM. - Rubaiyat. 1885. One of 150. A. E. Newton copy. sg June 11 (226) $425
— TORY, GEOFROY. - Champ Fleury. 1927. One of 390. S Mar 9 (718) £110 [Forster]; sg June 11 (227) $175
— WARREN, ARTHUR. - The Charles Whittinghams Printers. 1896. One of 385. O June 16 (91) $100
— WROTH, LAWRENCE C. - The Colonial Printer. 1931. One of 300. bba Oct 16 (453) £40 [Mills]

Grolier de Serviere, Nicolas, 1479-1565

— Recueil d'ouvrages curieux de mathematique et de mecanique.... Lyons, 1719. 1st Ed. 4to, contemp calf; worn & wormed. With 85 plates. Some worming. HK Nov 4 (995) DM1,500

Grooscup, Ben S. See: Ziegler & Grooscup

Groote...

— Het Groote Tafereel der Dwaasheid, vertoonende de Opkomst.... [Amst.], 1720. Folio, contemp half lea. With 73 (of 74) plates & with Cole's additional plate 1 & duplicate of 11. B Oct 7 (1157) HF3,100
Anr copy. Contemp calf gilt; joints splitting. With 72 (of 74) plates & 4 extra plates. 4 plates torn at folds; others repaired. B Feb 25 (550) HF3,000

Gropius, Walter

— Bauhausbauten Dessau. Munich, 1930. 4to, orig bdg. B Oct 7 (915) HF650

Gros de Boze, Claude

— Medailles sur les principaux evenements du regne entier de Louis le Grand.... Paris. 1723. Folio, mor gilt, armorial bdg; worn, rubbed & scratched. Lower edges of a few leaves dampstained. cb Oct 23 (33) $325

Grose, Francis, 1731?-91

— The Antiquarian Repertory: A Miscellaneous Assemblage of Topography.... L, 1780-84. ("The Antiquarian Repertory: A Miscellany intended to Preserve and Illustrate Several Valuable Remains of Old Times.") 2d Ed of Vol I, 1st Ed of other vols. 4 vols. 4to, contemp sheep; covers starting. sg Mar 26 (132) $150

Anr Ed. L, 1807-9. 4 vols. 4to, calf gilt; hinges cracked. pn May 21 (85) £160 [Shapiro]

Anr copy. Calf gilt; 3 covers detached. pn June 18 (178) £190 [Grosvenor]

The Antiquities of England and Wales. L, 1781-97. 8 vols. 4to, contemp bds; rebacked in lea. Lacking map of Hereford & 5 plates. T Oct 16 (362) £400

Anr Ed. L, [1783]-97. 8 vols, including Supplement. 8vo, bdg not indicated. Library markings. Sold w.a.f. F Sept 12 (132) $275

Anr copy. Contemp calf gilt; upper cover of Vol I detached, upper cover of Vol V stained, inner joint repaired & some wear to spine. L Dec 11 (115) £340

Anr copy. Calf; rebacked. Some stains. pn Apr 30 (189) £340 [Saville]

Anr copy. Calf; rubbed, 1 cover detached. 1st few leaves of Vol I repaired at inner margin. S Nov 17 (790) £380 [Nicholson]

— The Antiquities of Scotland. L, 1789-91. 1st Ed. 2 vols. Folio, contemp calf gilt. With engraved titles & 190 plates. pnE May 20 (23) £170

— The Antiquities of Ireland. L, 1791-95. 2 vols. 4to, contemp calf; worn. With engraved title, frontises & 267 plates & plans. Some stains. pn Apr 30 (187) £280 [Smith]

Anr copy. Calf gilt; soiled, 1 cover detached. With 2 engraved titles, 2 frontises & 258 plates & plans. Plates bound out of sequence. sg Dec 18 (182) $425

— The Antiquities of Scotland. L, 1797. 2 vols. 4to, contemp calf gilt; rubbed, joints split. bba Apr 9 (395) £35 [Elliott]

Anr copy. Contemp calf; rebacked with modern calf, worn. cb Dec 18 (73) $200

Anr copy. Half calf; spines rubbed. pn Oct 23 (130) £55 [Robertshaw]

— A Classical Dictionary of the Vulgar Tongue. L, 1785. 8vo, contemp calf gilt. Lacking half-title. pnE Jan 28 (155) £110 [McKenzie]

Anr Ed. L, 1823. 8vo, later half mor. sg Sept 11 (198) $225

— Military Antiquities Respecting a History of the English Army. L, 1786-88. 2 vols. 4to, calf gilt. pn Apr 30 (45) £190 [Freeman]

Anr Ed. L, 1801. 2 vols. 4to, contemp calf gilt; rubbed. S Feb 23 (17) £140 [Renard]

— A Treatise on Ancient Armour and Weapons. L, 1786. 4to, calf gilt. pn Apr 30 (46) £130 [Freeman]

Gross, Henning

— Magica de spectris et apparitionibus spiritum. Leiden, 1656. 12mo, contemp calf; rubbed. Outer margins dampstained. bba Mar 12 (440) £75 [Hay Cinema]

Grossmith, George & Weedon

— The Diary of a Nobody. Bristol, [1892]. 1st Ed. 8vo, orig cloth. pn Sept 18 (188) £70 [Finch]

Grosz, Georg, 1893-1959

— Ecce Homo. Berlin, [1923]. 1st Ed, Ausgabe C. Folio, orig bdg. With 84 plain & 14 colored plates. Some foxing. HN Nov 26 (1831) DM1,400

— Interregnum. NY: Black Sun Press, 1936. Out-of-series copy, sgd on tp. Folio, half cloth. sg Apr 2 (101) $2,000

— A Little Yes and a Big No. NY, 1946. sg Jan 8 (125) $80

Grote, George, 1794-1871

— A History of Greece. L, 1854-56. 12 vols. 8vo, contemp calf; rubbed. Ck Nov 7 (229) £70

Anr Ed. L, 1883. 12 vols. 8vo, calf; worn, spines faded. Presentation copy from President & Fellows of Christ Church, Oxford. wa Sept 25 (16) $100

Grote-Hasenbalg, Werner

— Der Orientteppich, seine Geschichte und seine Kultur. Berlin, 1922. 3 vols. 4to, orig cloth. HN Nov 26 (201) DM800

Anr copy. Cloth. JG Mar 20 (1583) DM1,500

Anr copy. Orig cloth. Inscr. S Nov 10 (97) £140 [Hasbach]

Grotius, Hugo, 1583-1645

— Annales et historiae de rebus Belgicis. Amst., 1658. 8vo, vellum. Lacking 7 prelim leaves. B Feb 25 (552) HF140

— De imperio summarum potestatum circa sacra. Paris, 1647. 8vo, vellum. D Feb 25 (557) HF450

— Le Droit de la guerre, et de la paix. Amst., 1724. 2 vols in 1. 4to, contemp calf. FD June 11 (2239) DM1,400

Grouse, G., Pseud. See: Cross, Gorham Lamont

Grout, Lewis
— The Isizulu. A Grammar of the Zulu Language. Natal, 1859. 4to, cloth; stained & loose. SSA Feb 11 (529) R260

Grove, Sir George, 1820-1900
— Dictionary of Music and Musicians. L, 1954. 9 vols. Orig cloth, in d/js. bba Sept 25 (30) £120 [Bookroom]
Anr Ed. L, 1954-61. 10 vols, including Supplement. Orig cloth with Supplement in mor; soiled. bba Dec 18 (27) £150 [Muns]
Anr Ed. L, 1954. 10 vols, including Supplement. Orig cloth. Library copy. Ck Dec 18 (79) £150 [Cox]

Grove, William Robert
— On the Correlation of Physical Forces.... L, 1846. Bound with: Grove. A Lecture on the Progress of Physical Science.... L, 1842. 8vo, new cloth. Library stamp on tp. S May 28 (677) £360

Gruau, Louys
— Nouvelle invention de chasse pour prendre et oster les loups de la France. Paris: Laurent Sonnius, 1613. 8vo, mor gilt by Chambolle-Duru. Pichon-Hoe-Jeanson copy. SM Mar 1 (277) FF90,000

Gruber, Jacques
— Le Vitrail. A L'Exposition Internationale des Arts Decoratifs. Paris: Moreau, [1926]. Folio, loose as issued in half cloth. wa Sept 25 (178) $240

Gruel, Leon, 1841-1923
— Manuel historique et bibliographique de l'amateur de reliures. Paris, 1887-1905. 2 vols. 4to, contemp lea. sg May 14 (109) $750

Gruenbeck, Joseph
— Practica de gegenwertigen grossen Truebsaln.... Strassburg: Jacob Cammer Lander, [1520?]. 4to, disbound & laid in old lea cover. Soiled throughout, mainly in margins. CNY Dec 19 (93) $200

Gruetzner, Eduard von, 1846-1925
— Charakterkoepfe. Munich: Ackermann, 1890. Folio, cloth; worn & soiled. With 12 ports. Waterstained, affecting images. wa Sept 25 (234) $50

Gruner, Lewis, 1801-82
— Specimens of Ornamental Art. L, 1850. 2 vols. Folio, half mor. With 80 plates. C July 22 (83) £1,000

Gruner, Ludwig, 1801-82
— Art Treasures Preserved in the Green Vaults at Dresden. Dresden, 1862. 4to, cloth; soiled. With 28 litho plates, some colored & 1 photographic plate mtd at end. S Nov 10 (98) £100 [Marks]

— The Green Vaults, Dresden. L, 1876. Folio, orig cloth; rebacked preserving orig spine, rubbed, front endpaper torn & repaired. bba Aug 28 (77) £50 [Blake]

Grynaeus, Simon, 1493-1541
— Novus orbis regionum ac insularum veteribus incognitarum. Basel, 1532. 1st Ed. Folio, old half lea. Lacking map & 7 prelims; old library stamps; marginal inkings on tp verso; some soiling. K June 7 (152) $425
Anr Ed. Basel: Joannes Hervagius, 1537. Folio, contemp calf over pastebd. Old stamp on title; dampstained at end; lacking map. sg Mar 26 (133) $550

Gsell-Fels, Theodor, 1818-98
— Switzerland: its Scenery and People. L, 1881. 4to, orig cloth; worn. With 63 plates. pn Apr 30 (108) £280 [Weber]

Guadet, Julien
— Elements et Theorie de l'Architecture. Paris, [1902]. 4 vols. 4to, later cloth, orig wraps bound in. sg Feb 5 (155) $225

Gualtieri, Niccolo, 1688-1747
— Index testarum conchyliorum.... Florence, 1742. Folio, half mor; joints starting, surface of rear cover def. With frontis & 110 plates. sg Apr 2 (102) $3,600

Guarini, Giovanni Battista, 1538-1612
— Il Pastor fido. Venice, 1602-3. 2 parts in 1 vol. 4to, contemp mor gilt; spine repaired at top. With port & 5 plates. Fletcher of Saltoun copy. S July 14 (398) £200
Anr Ed. venice, 1621. 4to, vellum. S Sept 23 (345) £110 [Zayas]

Guatemala
— Brief Statement, Supported by Original Documents, of the Important Grants Conceded to the Eastern Coast of Central America Commercial and Agricultural Company, by the State of Guatemala. L, 1839. 8vo, orig cloth. With folding map of San Tomas, hand-colored in outline. Lacking map of Vera Paz. sg Sept 18 (114) $90

Guazzo, Francesco Maria
— Compendium maleficarum. Milan, 1608. 8vo, later vellum. Some dampstains; possibly lacking final blank. sg Dec 4 (144) $400

Guazzo, Stefano, 1530-93
— La Civil Conversazione.... Venice: Gratioso Percacino, 1581. 8vo, 17th-cent mor gilt with arms of the Fugger family surmtd by the initials HE on both covers. Lower corner of Gg7 repaired affecting a few letters. S June 25 (28) £1,000

— The Civile Converstaion. L: Thomas East, 1586. 4to, 17th-cent calf; spine def, upper cover detached. Some dampstaining; short tear in R5; some dampstaining; lacking 1st leaf. S Mar 10 (1076) £240 [Robertshaw]

Guenee, Antoine, 1717-1808
— Lettres de quelques Juifs, Portugais et Allemands a M. de Voltaire. Paris, 1772. 8vo, contemp half vellum. Some dampstaining. bba Nov 13 (27) £60 [Hoffman]

Guenther, Albert Carl Ludwig Gotthilf
— The Reptiles of British India. L: Ray Society, 1864. 4to, orig half cloth; broken. With 26 plates. S Nov 17 (657) £130 [Negro]

Guenther, Johannes, of Andernach
— Institutionum anatomicarum secundum Galeni sententia ad candidatos medicine.... Venice: M. Sessa, 1538. 12mo, recent calf gilt. Lower outer section of F8 def with some words in pen facsimile. S May 21 (199) £1,100 [Quaritch]

Guer, Jean Antoine, 1713-64
— Histoire critique des ames des betes. Amst., 1749. 2 vols. 4to, contemp mor gilt, armorial bdg. Title of Vol I stained. S Nov 27 (77) £900 [Chaponniere]

Guericke, Otto von, 1602-86
— Experimenta nova (ut vocantur) Magdeburgica de vacuo spatio. Amst., 1672. Bound with: Archimedes. Kunst-Buecher oder Heutiges Tags befindliche Schrifften.... Nuremberg, 1670. Folio, contemp blindstamped pigskin over wooden bds, armorial bdg. HK Nov 4 (996) DM5,000
1st Ed. Folio, contemp vellum. Dampstain in inner margin & lower inner corner throughout. sg Apr 2 (103) $3,400

Guerin, Victor
La Terre Sainte. Paris, 1882-84. 2d Ed. 2 vols. Folio, orig half mor gilt; rubbed, 1 hinge split. With 2 engraved titles, 3 maps & 43 plates. pnNY Sept 13 (241) $400

Gueroult, Guillaume, d.c.1570
— La Description, forme et nature des bestes.... Rouen: Robert Masselin for Robert & Jean du Gort, 1554. Bound with: Le Blason et description des Oyseaux. Rouen, 1554. 16mo, mor gilt by Trautz-Bauzonnet. Jeanson copy. SM Mar 1 (279) FF110,000

Guerra, Francisco
— American Medical Bibliography. NY, 1962. cb July 30 (84) $70; sg Oct 2 (201) $80

Gueulette, Thomas Simon, 1683-1766
— Memoires de Mademoiselle Bontemps.... Amst., 1738. 12mo, contemp half sheep; joints splitting, rubbed. Lacking last leaf. bba Nov 13 (22) £60 [Hannas]

Guevara, Antonio de, 1480?-1545
— Epistres dorees moralles et familieres. Lyons: Mace Bonhomme, 1558-60. Bound with: Traite des travaux et privileges des galeres.... Lyons: Mace Bonhomme, 1560. 4to, 18th-cent calf; scuffed, new endpapers. Tp frayed. S May 21 (42) £500 [Israel]
— Vita, gesti, costumi discorsi, et lettere di Marco Aurelio. Venice: appresso Gabriel Gioliti de Ferrari e fratelli, 1553. 2 vols in 1. 8vo, half lea; worn. Margins trimmed close; some stains; tp rehinged; lacking last leaf. sg Mar 26 (134) $60

Guggenheim, Peggy
— Art of this Century. NY, 1942. 4to, orig cloth. S June 29 (48) £320 [Bolligar]

Guibert, Jacques Antoine Hippolyte de
— A General Essay on Tactics.... L, 1781. 2 vols. 8vo, modern cloth. With 27 folding plates. sg Nov 20 (115) $80

Guibours, Pierre de. See: Anselme de Sainte-Marie & Du Fourney

Guicciardini, Francesco
— La Historia d'Italia.... Venice, 1574. 2 parts in 1 vol. 8vo, orig vellum; spine rebacked with old vellum. Some browning & foxing; early ink annotations on tp. pnNY Mar 12 (86) $110

Guicciardini, Ludovico, 1521-89
— Description de touts les Pais-Bas.... Amst., 1609. Folio, contemp calf gilt; rebacked, joints cracking rubbed. With engraved title, half-title with engraved arms on verso & 92 maps, plans & plates. Lacking 4 plates & including 1 not called for by the list of plates. Sold w.a.f. C Apr 8 (129) £1,400 [Faupel]
— Descrittione...di tutti i Paesi Bassi. Antwerp: Plantin, 1581. Folio, modern vellum bds. With port & 48 double-page maps, including the plans of Tournai & Cambrai not listed by Voet but mentioned by him as having been prepared after the work went to press. Some worming affecting letters & surfaces in some instances; some small repairs. S June 25 (265) £1,000 [Forum]
Anr Ed. Antwerp, 1588. Folio, contemp vellum; soiled. With frontis (torn without loss) & 77 mostly double-page maps, plans & views (of 78).d A few centerfolds split without loss. Mailhos copy. S Oct 23 (252) £1,000 [Hooff]

GUICHARD

Guichard, Kenneth M.
— British Etchers 1850-1940. L, 1977. Illus by Robin Tanner. 4to, orig half mor gilt. T Feb 19 (506) £70

Guide...
— Guide to the Megantic, Spider and Upper Dead River Regions of Quebec and Maine. Bost., 1888. 2d Ed. Oblong 8vo, cloth. With 2 folding maps. Library bookplate on contents page. sg Oct 23 (437) $110

Guide-Book....
— Guide-Book of the Central Railroad of New Jersey, and its Connections through the Coal-Fields of Pennsylvania. NY, 1864. 12mo, orig cloth; worn. Some terminal leaves waterstained at top inner edge; contents clean & unworn. wa Nov 6 (70) $65

Guiffrey, Jules Marie Joseph, 1840-1918
— Comptes des batiments du Roi.... Paris, 1881-1901. 5 vols. 4to, orig bds. HN May 20 (185) DM520

Guigard, Joannis, 1825-92
— Nouvel Armorial du bibliophile. Paris, 1890. 2 vols in 1. 8vo, half lea. sg May 14 (110) $175

Anr copy. Half lea; extremities worn. sg May 14 (111) $225

Guignes, Louis de, 1759-1845
— Dictionnaire chinois, francais et latin. Paris, 1813. Folio, contemp half mor; def. S Oct 23 (485) £650 [Marlborough]

Guillain, Charles
— Documents sur l'histoire, la geographie et le commerce de l'Afrique orientale. Paris, [1857]. Atlas vol only; lacking 3 vols of text. Folio, contemp half mor gilt; spine def. With 10 maps & plans & 45 tinted lithos. Sold w.a.f. S Apr 24 (322) £600 [Shapero]

Guillemet, E.
— En Chasse. Notes et croquis. Pontpoint, 1887. One of 150 on japon imperial. 4to, mor gilt by Chambolle-Duru. Jeanson copy. SM Mar 1 (280) FF8,500

Guillemin, Amedee, 1826-93
— The World of Comets. L, 1877. 8vo, orig cloth; worn. wa Nov 6 (125) $75

Guillim, John, 1565-1621
— A Display of Heraldrie. L, 1660. 4th Ed. Folio, half calf; rubbed. pn Jan 22 (47) £75 [Barker]

AMERICAN BOOK PRICES CURRENT

Guillot, Ernest
— L'Ornementation des Manuscrits au Moyen-Age. XII-XVI Siecle. Paris: Laurens, [c.1920?]. 4 vols. 8vo, pictorial wraps; worn. O Nov 18 (78) $60

Guilmard, Desire, b.1810
— Les Maitres ornemanistes.... Paris, 1880-81. 2 vols, including vol of plates. 4to, half mor by Riviere, orig wraps bound in. C Dec 3 (25) £280 [Sourget]

Guirlande...
— La Guirlande: Album mensuel d'art et de litterature. Paris, 1920. One of 800. Fascicule 4 only. Loose as issued in wraps. ha May 22 (164) $190

Guise, Louis Marguerite de Lorraine, Princesse de Conty
— Les Amours du grand Alcandre.... Paris: Didot l'aine, 1786. 2 vols. 12mo, contemp mor gilt. S Nov 27 (78) £200 [Booth]

Guitry, Sacha
— Des Gouts et des couleurs. Paris: Galerie Charpentier, [1943]. One of 23 on velin d'arches with an ink drawing. Illus by Dignimont. Folio, loose as issued in wraps. Lacking at least 2 leaves. Sold w.a.f. sg Jan 8 (127) $60

Guizot, Francois Pierre Guillaume
— A Popular History of France. Bost., [1880?]. 6 vols. 8vo, half mor; worn. ha Mar 13 (275) $50

Guizot, Francois Pierre Guillaume, 1787-1874
— Collection des memoires relatifs a l'histoire de France.... Paris, 1823-35. 31 vols, including Index vol. 8vo, half calf; worn. bba Dec 4 (23) £100 [Archdale]

Gulden...
— Het gulden Boek voor de tuberculeuse kinderen. Rotterdam, 1908. 4to, vellum gilt. B Oct 7 (67) HF340

Gulielmus Hentisberus. See: Heytesbury, William

Gully, John
— New Zealand Scenery. L, 1877. Folio, orig cloth; worn & stained. With 15 colored plates, each trimmed to image & mtd with gilt borders as issued. Letterpress taped to versos of plates. Some spotting. bba Oct 16 (245) £200 [Shapero]

Gumuchian & Cie., Kirkor
— Catalogue de reliures du XVe au XIXe siecle.... Paris, [1930]. 4to, orig ptd wraps; stained & rubbed. bba Sept 25 (374) £70 [Forster]

Anr copy. Cloth. Tp stamped. bba Feb 5 (87) £75 [Kuyper]

Anr copy. Orig wraps; worn. HN May 20 (71) DM620

Anr copy. Cloth; worn. O June 16 (92) $160

Anr copy. Cloth, orig wraps bound in. sg May 14 (112) $90

Anr copy. Cloth. sg May 14 (113) $90

— Les Livres de l'enfance du XVe au XIXe siecle. Paris, [1930]. One of 900. 2 vols. 4to, orig wraps; broken. sg Jan 22 (183) $250

Anr Ed. L, 1979. One of 75 with hand-colored title. 2 vols. 4to, orig cloth, in d/js. wa June 25 (7) $100

One of 600. Orig cloth, in d/js. O Apr 28 (83) $90

Anr Ed. L, 1985. One of 900. 2 vols. 4to, orig wraps; shaken, 1 cover detached & spine partially worn away. Facsimile. O June 16 (94) $50

Gun

— The Gun at Home and Abroad. L, 1912-15. One of 500. 4 vols. 4to, orig mor; some covers soiled. S Nov 10 (596) £260 [Way]

Gunn, Hugh. See: Ross & Gunn

Gunn, Thom

— Mandrakes. L: Rainbow Press, 1973. One of 150. Illus by Leonard Baskin. 4to, orig half vellum. S Sept 22 (92) £90 [Libris Arti]; sg Mar 5 (89) $150

Gunner, Johan Ernst, 1718-73

— Flora Norvegica. Trondhjem & Copenhagen, 1766-72. 2 parts in 1 vol. Folio, unbound. With 12 plates. The last section of the index at end (24 leaves including errata) is in photographic facsimile. S May 28 (679) £100

Gunsaulus, Helen Cowen

— Japanese Textiles. NY, 1941. One of 1,000. Folio, half cloth. With 8 plain & 8 colored plates. sg Feb 6 (181) $70

Gunther, Robert William Theodore

— Rolfe Family Records. L & Aylesbury, 1914. One of 112. Vol II (all pbd). Syn. sg Dec 11 (401) $805

Guptill, Arthur Leighton

— Norman Rockwell, Illustrator. NY, 1946. Folio, cloth, in def d/j. Inscr by Rockwell on a card pasted to front free endpaper. sg Jan 8 (249) $70

Guthe, Hermann. See: Ebers & Guthe

Guthrie, James Joshua, 1859-1930

— The Elf: a Magazine of Drawings and Writings.... Ingrave, 1899-1900. Nos 1-4. 4to, mor gilt, orig wraps preserved. Plates hand-colored. With 4 ALs s from James Guthrie laid in. S Dec 4 (90) £800 [Mitchell]

— The Elf, a Sequence of the Seasons. L, 1902. One of 250. 4 vols (complete set). Orig half cloth. S May 6 (127) £95 [Cox]

Guthrie, William, 1708-70

— A New Geographical, Historical, and Commercial Grammar.... L, 1788. 11th Ed. 8vo, old calf; broken. With 20 folding maps. Some dampstains. O Mar 24 (88) $60

— A New System of Modern Geography. L, 1780. 4to, contemp calf; worn. With 17 folding maps only (of 21). Some maps torn & repaired. Sold w.a.f. bba July 16 (96) £140 [Faupel]

1st American Ed. Phila., 1794-95. 4to, contemp calf. Franklin Institute copy. F Sept 12 (129) $110

Guthry, Henry

— Memoirs...in Scotland. L, 1702. 8vo, old half calf; rubbed. Some pencilled marginalia. O Feb 24 (96) $50

Gutierrez Davila, Julian

— Memorias historicas de la congregacion de el oratorio de la ciudad de Mexico. Mexico, 1736. 3 vols in 1. Folio, later vellum; head of spine torn, free endpaper frayed at outer third. Some worming, mostly marginal, affecting a few words of text of final 60 pp of Part 1 & 6 prelims; paper repair in top inner margin of tp & following leaf. sg Sept 18 (117) $425

Gutierrez de la Vega, Jose, 1824-99

— Bibliografia venatoria espanola. Madrid: M. Tello, 1877. One of 25. 8vo, contemp cloth; worn. Jeanson copy. SM Mar 1 (587) FF5,500

Guttmann, Heinrich. See: Bossert & Guttmann

Guyot, Charles

— Le Printemps sur la neige.... Paris, [1922]. One of 1,300. Illus by Arthur Rackham. 4to, wraps. With 16 mtd color plates. sg Oct 30 (94) $425

— La Toison d'or. Paris, 1921. One of 1,300. Illus by Edmund Dulac. 4to, contemp half mor, orig wraps bound in. Ck Dec 10 (272) £70

Guyton de Morveau, Louis Bernard, Baron —& Lavoisier, Antoine Laurent, 1743-94

— Methode de Nomenclature Chimique.... Paris, 1787. 8vo, modern half calf. Some foxing & dampstaining. sg Jan 15 (325) $350

Gwynn, Stephen
— River to River. A Fisherman's Pilgrimage. L, 1937. One of 250. 4to, cloth, in worn d/j. sg Oct 23 (306) $80

H

H., H. See: Jackson, Helen Hunt

Haarlem...
— Haarlem in Hout. Eenentwintig houtgravures van Haarlem en omgeving omstreeks het jaar 1909. Haarlem, 1971. One of 60. Orig wraps. B Oct 7 (443) HF340

Haberly, Loyd
— Mediaeval English Pavingtiles. Oxford: Shakespeare Head Press, 1937. One of 425. 4to, half mor. bba July 2 (219) £130 [Morter]; pn June 18 (77) £150 [Dawson]

Habert, Pierre, Sieur d'Orgemont
— La Chasse du lievre acecques les levriers. [Paris: Jannet, 1849]. Unique copy on vellum made for Baron Pichon. 4to, mor gilt by Trautz-Bauzonnet. Jeanson copy. SM Mar 1 (281) FF36,000
— La Chasse du loup.... Paris: Veuve Bouchard-Huzard, 1866. One of 2 on peau de vélin for Baron Pichon. 4to, half mor. Jeanson copy. SM Mar 1 (282) FF4,600

Habington, William, 1605-54
— The Historie of Edward the Fourth, King of England. L, 1640. 1st Ed. Folio, contemp calf; rebacked & rubbed, old spine preserved. bba Apr 9 (11) £80 [Maggs]

Hachette, Jean Nicolas Pierre, 1769-1834
— Traite elementaire des machines. Paris, [1811]. 4to, contemp calf. With 28 folding plates. Tear in p 231. C Dec 12 (103) £380 [Pickering & Chatto]

Hachisuka, Masauji
— The Dodo and Kindred Birds. L, 1953. One of 485. 4to, cloth. pn Oct 23 (218) £240 [Bles]

Hacke, William
— A Collection of Original Voyages. L, 1699. 1st Ed. 3 parts in 1 vol. 8vo, later half calf. With 6 maps & plates. pn Nov 20 (194) £850 [Bonham]

Hackenbroch, Yvonne. See: Untermyer Collection, Irwin

Hackett, James
— Narrative of the Expedition which sailed from England in 1817.... L, 1818. 1st Ed. 8vo, orig bds; rubbed, spine def, upper inscr Duke of Baccleuch. bba Apr 9 (422) £240 [Maggs]

Hackney, Louise Wallace —& Yau, Chang-foo
— A Study of Chinese Paintings in the Collection of Ada Small Moore. L, 1940. Folio, orig cloth. bba Sept 25 (321) £80 [Han Shan Tang]
   Anr copy. Cloth; spine chipped. With supplement laid in. sg Feb 5 (90) $90

Hadley, George
— A New and Complete History of...Kingston-upon-Hull. Kingston-upon-Hull, 1788. 4to, contemp half calf gilt; rubbed. With 15 (of 17) plates. T Oct 16 (349) £52

Haebler, Konrad
— Bibliografia Iberica del siglo XV. Leipzig & The Hague, 1903-17. 2 vols. 8vo, cloth, orig wraps preserved. sg May 14 (451) $700
— Die deutschen Buchdrucker des XV. Jahrhunderts im Auslande. Munich, 1924. Folio, half cloth. sg May 14 (453) $100; sg May 14 (454) $120
— Typenrepertorium der Wiegendrucke. Halle & Leipzig, 1905-24. 5 parts in 4 vols. Half cloth. sg May 14 (452) $200

Haeften, Benedictus van, 1588-1648
— Regia via crucis. Antwerp: Plantin, 1635. 8vo, modern mor by Petibled. Lacking D7; 1st leaf soiled & frayed. cb July 30 (85) $75

Haer, Floris van der, 1547-1634
— Les Chastelains de Lille.... Lille, 1611. 4to, later half calf; joints cracked. 2M4 incorrectly folded. sg Mar 26 (135) $175

Haestens, H. de
— La Nouvelle Troye, ou Memorable Histoire du Siege d'Ostende.... Leiden: Elzevier, 1615. 4to, contemp vellum with yapp edges; soiled & rubbed. With coat-of-arms, plate of Mauritius de Nassau & 11 (of 14) double-page plans. Lacking all text after Oo3; wormed at top. T Sept 18 (499) £64

Hafen, Leroy R.
— The Overland Mail.... Cleveland, 1926. Cloth; worn. With folding map. O Oct 21 (76) $110

Haggard, Andrew Charles Parker
— Sporting Yarns Spun Off the Reel. L, 1903. Cloth; upper spine end torn. sg Oct 23 (307) $50

Haggard, Sir Henry Rider, 1856-1925
— King Solomon's Mines. L, 1885. 8vo, orig cloth; soiled. Frontis torn & spotted. bba Mar 26 (223) £50 [Stilwell]
— Queen Sheba's Ring. L; Eveleigh Nash, 1910. 8vo, bdg not described but leaning. cb Sept 28 (572) $60
— She: a History of Adventure. L, 1887. 1st

Ed. 8vo, orig cloth; top of spine nicked. With 2 colored frontises. bba Mar 26 (225) £50 [Sanders]

Hagger, Conrad

— Neues Saltzburgisches Koch-Buch. Augsburg, 1719. 2d Ed. 4 parts in 1 vol. 4to, contemp pigskin. Engraved title trimmed & mtd; tp repaired; losses to a few plates repaired; some repairs. Crahan copy. P Nov 25 (225) $550; P Nov 25 (228) $3,250

Haghe, Louis, 1806-85

— Sketches in Belgium and Germany. First Series. L, 1840. Folio, contemp half mor; rubbed. bba Jan 15 (468) £50 [Rainer]

— Sketches in Belgium and Germany. Third Series. L, 1850. Folio, half lea; disbound, worn. With litho title & 26 colored plates, all loose. ha Sept 19 (16) $120

Hahnemann, Samuel Christian Friedrich, 1755-1843

— Organon der rationellen Heilkunde. Dresden, 1810. 8vo, contemp bds. Spotted at beginning. FD Dec 2 (554) DM5,000

Haig-Brown, Roderick L.

See also: Derrydale Press

— Bright Waters, Bright Fish. Vancouver, [1980]. One of 1,100. 4to, half lea gilt. sg Oct 23 (308) $80

— Return to the River; a Story of the Chinook Run. NY, 1941. One of 520. Illus by Charles DeFeo. Half mor. sg Oct 23 (309) $175

— The Salmon. Ottowa, 1974. Includes text vol & 4 folders, loose as issued, of plates. sg Oct 23 (464) $800

Hain, Ludwig, 1781-1836

— Repertorium bibliographicum in quo libri omnes ab arte typographica inventa usque ad annum MD. L, 1895-1902 & Munich, 1905-14. 2 vols in 4 plus supplement by Copinger in 3 vols, ptr's index by Burger & appendixes by Reichling in 4 vols. Together 12 vols. sg May 14 (455) $1,000

Anr Ed. Berlin, 1925. 4 vols in 2. Half lea; worn. HN Nov 26 (15) DM560

Anr Ed. Milan, [1948]. 4 vols. O June 16 (95) $210

Anr copy. 4 vols in 2. Half calf; worn. sg May 14 (456) $130

Haines, Richard, 1633-85

— The Prevention of Poverty.... L, 1674. 4to, wraps. S July 23 (440) £380 [Riley-Smith]

Hake, Henry M. See: British Museum

Hakewill, George

— An Apologie or Declaration of the Power and Providence of God. Oxford, 1635. 3d Ed. Folio, modern calf. With engraved title. Heavily annotated & underlined. cb Oct 23 (99) $75

Hakewill, James, 1778-1843

— The History of Windsor and its Neighbourhood. L, 1813. 4to, later half mor. With frontis & 20 plans & plates. Some spotting. Ck Feb 27 (170) £90

— A Picturesque Tour of Italy.... L, 1820. Folio, cloth. With 3 plans & 60 plates. L..n. copy. C July 22 (88) £180

Anr copy. Contemp calf gilt; joints split. S Feb 23 (18) £210 [Erlini]

Hakluyt, Richard, 1552?-1616

— The Principall Navigations.... L, 1598-99-1600. 2d Ed, 1st Issue. 3 vols in 2. Folio, old calf gilt. Vol III with title trimmed & inlaid; 2G5-6 repaired in upper inner corner; lacking the map. sg Apr 2 (104) $4,200

Anr Ed. L, 1599-1600. 2d Issue of Vol I. Vols I & II in 1. later calf; rubbed, upper hinge breaking. Some stains; marginal wormhole towards end of Vol II. bba June 18 (303) £260 [Smith]

Anr copy. 3 vols in 2. Folio, old calf gilt; rubbed, corners knocked, joints cracking. Vol I with waterstain to Uu2-4 & tp repaired along inner margin; Vol I with some soiling; Vol III with L1 torn affecting text; 3G4 torn in margin; marginal holes in 3M5-6, 3N1, 3S1-3; 4A gathering torn at top of inner margin affecting text; Ms marginalia cropped; 4B5-6 & 4C gathering on stubs; 4C5-6 def; lacking map. Crahan copy. P Nov 25 (229) $1,300

Anr Ed. L, 1809-12. ("Collection of the Early Voyages, Travels and Discoveries of the English Nation.") 5 vols. 4to, contemp calf; rebacked. Ck Sept 26 (58) £160

One of 250 on royal paper. Contemp calf; rebacked, old spines laid down, 2 covers detached. Ck May 15 (67) £95

Anr Ed. Glasgow, 1903-5. 12 vols. S Feb 23 (19) £150 [Smiley]

Anr Ed. L, etc., 1927-28. 10 vols. sg Apr 23 (61) $175

Halberstadt, P. See: Duchamp & Halberstadt

Haldeman, Joe

— The Forever War. NY, [1974]. 1st Ed, with sewn signatures. In d/j. Inscr. cb Sept 28 (578) $95

Hale, Edward Everett, 1822-1909
— The Man Without a Country. Bost., 1865. 1st Ed. 12mo, orig wraps; minor wear. ALs to his son inserted. K Mar 22 (128) $400

Hale, John Peter, 1824-1902
— Trans-Allegheny Pioneers: Historical Sketches of the First White Settlements West of the Alleghenies.... Cincinnati, 1886. 1st Ed. 8vo, orig cloth; spine soiled. sg Mar 12 (130) $130

Hale, Lucretia Peabody, 1820-1900
— The Peterkin Papers. Bost., 1880. 1st Ed. 8vo, cloth; worn & shaken. With 8 plates. O Sept 23 (77) $50

Hale, Sir Matthew, 1609-76
— The Primitive Origination of Mankind. L, 1677. 1st Ed. 4to, contemp calf; rebacked & recornered. cb Oct 23 (101) $110
— Works. L, 1805. 2 vols. 8vo, contemp calf. cb Oct 23 (102) $60

Hale, Thomas, Writer on Husbandry
— A Compleat Body of Husbandry.... L, 1756. 1st Ed. Folio, contemp calf; upper joint worn. With frontis & 12 plates; gathering 7H browned. Crahan copy. P Nov 25 (230) $500
— Eden: or, a Compleat Body of Gardening.... L, 1757. Folio, contemp calf gilt with Signet crest; joints cracked. With frontis & 60 plates. Tp spotted & browned. Crahan copy. P Nov 25 (231) $350

Halen, Juan van, Count de Perecamps, 1788-1864
— Memoirs.... L, 1830. 2 vols. 8vo, orig cloth; worn & leaning a bit. cb Dec 18 (176) $60

Hales, John Groves
— Survey of Boston and its Vicinity. Bost., 1821. 12mo, modern cloth. Perforated library stamp on frontis; folding map torn. sg Mar 12 (131) $50

Hales, Stephen, 1677-1761
— Statical Essays: containing Vegetable Staticks. L, 1738-40. 3d Ed of Vol I; 2d Ed of Vol II. 8vo, contemp calf. pnE Dec 17 (99) £480 [Phelps]
— Vegetable Staticks; or, an Account of some Statical Experiments on the Sap in Vegetables. L, 1727. 8vo, contemp calf; joints split. With 19 plates. S Nov 27 (263) £400 [Quaritch]

Halevy, Ludovic, 1834-1908. See: Meilhac & Halevy

Haley, William
— The Loves of Hally and Sophy. L: A. C. de Poggi, 1796. Illus by Charlotte Milnes. Oblong 8vo, contemp mor gilt. With 4 colored plates. C Dec 12 (331) £1,100 [Quaritch]

Halford, Frederic M., 1844-1914
— Dry Fly Entomology: a Brief Description.... L, 1897. One of 100. 2 vols. 4to, mor; rubbed. With 18 plain & 10 hand-colored plates & with 100 flies in 12 sunken mounts. sg Oct 23 (310) $1,400
— Dry-Fly Fishing in Theory and Practice. L, 1889. 8vo, half mor; scuffed. With 26 mtd plates. Library copy. sg Oct 23 (313) $50
  One of 100. Lev; faded. With 26 mtd plates. sg Oct 23 (312) $200
  Revised Ed. L, 1899. 8vo, cloth; worn. With 14 plain & 4 hand-colored plates. sg Oct 23 (314) $110
— The Dry-Fly Man's Handbook. L, 1913. One of 100. Calf gilt. pnE Dec 17 (342) £200 [Head]
  Out-of-series copy. 4to, half mor. With 43 plates in mtd India-proof state. Inscr & with ALs from Halford to Emlyn Gill laid in. sg Oct 23 (315) $650
— Floating Flies and How to Dress Them. L, 1886. One of 150 L.p. copies. 8vo, half mor. With 9 hand-colored plates. sg Oct 23 (316) $275
  Anr Ed. NY, 1886. 8vo, half lea. With 10 colored plates. Library copy. sg Oct 23 (317) $110
— Making a Fishery. L, 1895. One of 150 L.p. copies. 4to, lea; worn. With port & 4 plates. sg Oct 23 (318) $275
— Modern Development of the Dry Fly. L, 1910. De Luxe Ed, One of 50. 2 vols. 8vo, half calf gilt. With port, 43 plates & 33 flies in 9 sunken mounts. With 6 flies in an envelope laid in. sg Oct 23 (319) $2,600

Halfpenny, John
— The Gentleman's Jockey and Approved Farrier. L, 1679. 8vo, modern sheep; rubbed. Marginal worming; 2 leaves repaired in margin; most leaves spotted or soiled. bba Nov 13 (198) £110 [Edmondson]

Halfpenny, Joseph, 1748-1811
— Fragmenta Vetusta; or the Remains of Ancient Buildings in York. York, 1807. 4to, contemp mor gilt; rubbed. With engraved title & 34 plates. S Feb 24 (384) £80 [Marsden]
— Gothic Ornaments in the Cathedral Church of York. [York] 1795-[1800]. 4to, mor gilt by Carpenter & Co, with ticket, armorial bdg. With engraved title & 105 plates. S Oct 23 (4) £280 [Spelmans]

Halfpenny, William

— Practical Architecture, or a Sure Guide.... L, 1736. 4th Ed. 8vo, contemp calf; worn, front cover detached. Some staining & foxing. wa Mar 5 (233) $300

Halfpenny, William & John

— Chinese and Gothic Architecture Properly Ornamented. L, 1752. 4to, contemp calf; worn & rebacked. With engraved title & 59 plates, 11 folding. Some stains. bba Sept 25 (278) £700 [Reed]

— Gothic Architecture. L, 1752. ("Rural Architecture in the Gothick Taste.") 8vo, half calf; joints rubbed. With engraved title & 59 plates, 11 folding. C Oct 15 (40) £800 [Ewart]

Hali

Hali: The International Journal of Oriental Carpets and Textiles. L, 1978. Vol I, No 1 only. Folio, orig wraps; upper corner with small tear. Ck Oct 17 (75) £75

Anr copy. Vol I, Nos 1-4 only. Folio, Ck Oct 17 (201) £160

Halkett, Samuel, 1814-71 — & Laing, John, 1809-80

— Dictionary of Anonymous and Pseudonymous English Literature. Edin., 1926-34. 7 vols. 4to, cloth. sg Oct 2 (29) $375

Anr Ed. L, 1926-62. Vols I-VII & IX. 4to, cloth; worn. sg Jan 22 (185) $375

Anr Ed. NY, 1971. 7 vols. Orig syn. bba Sept 25 (365) £400 [Jarndyce]; S July 13 (61) £300

Anr copy. 7 vols. Orig syn. T Feb 19 (552) £240

Hall, Anna Maria

— The Book of Royalty.... L, 1839. Folio, contemp mor gilt; spine rubbed. With pictorial title & 12 hand-colored lithos. Some margins spotted or dust-soiled. S Nov 10 (380) £250 [Ferguson]

Anr Ed. L: Ackermann, 1839. Folio, cloth; rebacked. With frontis & 12 colored plates. ha May 22 (165) $150

Anr copy. Mor gilt; rubbed. pn Dec 11 (215) £85 [Rostron]

Anr copy. Contemp mor gilt; upper hinge weak. With engraved title & 12 litho plates, colored by hand. S July 14 (508) £130

Anr copy. Mor gilt with onlay. With frontis & 12 colored plates. S July 14 (571) £120

Hall, B. Fairfax. See: Le Bas Collection, Edward

Hall, Basil

— The Great Polyglot Bibles: Including a Leaf from the Complutensian of Acala, 1914-17. San Francisco: Book Club of Calif., 1966. One of 400. Folio, loose as issued in ptd wraps. cb Sept 11 (2) $300

Hall, Basil, 1788-1844

— Forty Etchings from Sketches Made with the Camera Lucida, in North America. Edin., 1829. 4to, orig bds; rubbed & soiled. With folding map (torn) colored by hand & with 40 plates on 20 sheets. S Nov 18 (1105) £160 [Burden]

— Travels in North America in the Years 1827 and 1828. Edin., 1829. 1st Ed. 3 vols. 12mo, contemp half mor gilt. With colored folding map & folding table. Tear in map. S July 14 (778) £110

Ed not specified. 3 vols. 12mo, half lea; spine ends crudely repaired. Map torn & split at fold-line; some dampstains in Vol II. sg Apr 23 (62) $100

Hall, Carroll Douglas

— Donner Miscellany.... San Francisco, 1947. One of 350. Half cloth, in chipped d/j. cb Sept 11 (3) $160

Anr copy. Cloth. cb Mar 19 (11) $110

— Heraldry of New Helvetia.... San Francisco, 1945. One of 250. Half calf. sg Jan 8 (3) $150

Hall, George Eli, 1863-1911

— A Balloon Ascension at Midnight. San Francisco, 1902. One of 15 on vellum. Inscr. ha May 22 (166) $450

Hall, James, 1793-1868

See also: McKenney & Hall

— The Wilderness and the War-Path. NY, 1846. 1st Ed. 12mo, orig cloth; rebacked, orig backstrip laid down, endpapers renewed. sg Sept 18 (118) $100

Hall, Joseph, 1574-1656

— Mundus alter et idem.... Frankfurt: haeredes Ascanii di Rinialme [but some quires ptd in L by H. Lownes, c.1607]. STC 12685.3. 8vo, contemp blindstamped armorial vellum. Engraved title colored & laid down; minor tear in 1 map & tear in 1 plate, both without loss. C May 13 (126) £2,200 [Bjorck & Borjesson]

— Mundus alter et idem sive terra australis.... Hanau [but L], 1607. 8vo, contemp vellum, armorial bdg. With engraved title (colored & laid down), 7 folding maps & 1 plate. Minor tear in 1 map; tear in plate, both without loss of text. C May 13 (126) £2,200 [Bjorck & Borjesson]

Anr copy. Contemp vellum; def. With engraved title & 5 folding maps. FD June 11 (4010) DM8,000

Hall, Manly P.
— An Encyclopedic Outline of Masonic, Hermetic, Qabbalistic and Rosicrucian Symbolical Philosophy. San Francisco, 1928. One of 800. Folio, half vellum; extremities worn. Library markings. sg Apr 2 (105) $225

Hall, Peter, 1803-49
— Picturesque Memorials of Salisbury.... Salisbury, 1834. 4to, orig cloth; rubbed, lacking front free endpaper. bba Apr 9 (375) £130 [Blake]

Hall, Samuel Carter, 1800-89
— The Baronial Halls and Picturesque Edifices of England. L, 1848. 2 vols. Folio, half mor; both vols loose. With 72 plates. sg Dec 18 (185) $110
— The Baronial Halls and Ancient Picturesque Edifices of England. L, 1858. 2 vols. Folio, contemp mor gilt; rubbed. Lacking 1 plate. S Jan 12 (80) £180 [Edwards]
Anr Ed. L, 1881. 2 vols. Folio, half mor gilt; rubbed. pn Apr 30 (47) £160
— Selected Pictures from the Galleries and Private Collections of Great Britain. L, [1862-68]. 4 vols. Folio, contemp half lea; rubbed, Vol IV lacking free endpapers. sg Feb 5 (156) $425
— The Vernon Gallery of British Art. L, 1840-54. 4 vols. 8vo, orig cloth; worn & affected by damp. Outer margins of 1st 2 leaves of Vol IV torn & repaired. S Mar 9 (676) £240 [Erlini]

Hall, Samuel Carter & Anna Maria
— Ireland, its Scenery, Character.... L, 1841-43. 3 vols. 8vo, orig cloth; rubbed. bba Aug 28 (315) £95 [Clark]
Anr copy. Contemp calf; rebacked, orig spine preserved, worn. cb Feb 19 (122) $225
Anr copy. Orig cloth; spines rubbed. With engraved titles & 18 hand-colored maps. Some stains. Ck Feb 27 (47) £200
Anr copy. Vols I-II (of 3) only. Orig cloth; worn. sg Apr 23 (63) $90
Anr Ed. L, [c.1850]. 3 vols. 8vo, contemp calf gilt. With 3 engraved titles, 18 hand-colored maps & 100 views. pn Jan 22 (143) £110 [Tillence]

Hall, Sidney
— A New British Atlas. L, 1834. 4to, contemp half mor; rubbed. With 54 maps on 51 sheets. pn May 21 (366) £190 [Burden]
Anr copy. Half mor; shaken. With 47 colored maps. Folding map mtd on linen. pn May 21 (418) £100 [Postaprint]
Anr copy. Orig half mor; worn. With hand-colored map of England & 45 county maps. Lacking 4 inland navigation plates. T June 18 (30) £135

Halle, Johann Samuel, 1727-1810
— Magie; oder, Die Zauberkraefte der Natur. Vienna, 1785-87. 4 vols. 8vo, contemp cloth; spotted. Some foxing. HK Nov 4 (998) DM3,400

Hallenbeck, Cleve —& Williams, Juanita H.
— Legends of the Spanish Southwest. Glendale, 1938. With 8 plates & folding map. cb Oct 9 (106) $55

Haller, Albrecht, 1708-77
— Usong. An Oriental History. L, 1773. 12mo, contemp calf; joints starting. sg Oct 9 (218) $110

Haller, Albrecht von, 1708-77
— Icones plantarum Helvetiae.... Berne, 1813. Folio, contemp half calf. With 52 (on 46) hand-colored plates. Plates 28 & 38 a little discolored in upper margins. S Oct 23 (701) £1,500 [Laube]

Halley, Edmund. See: Cutler & Halley

Hallock, Charles, 1834-1917
— The Salmon Fisher. NY, 1890. 16mo, cloth. sg Oct 23 (322) $60

Halma, Frans
— Tooneel der Vereenigde Nederlanden. Leeuwarden, 1725. 2 vols. 4to, vellum; spine def. With engraved title, port of Halma, 26 double-page maps, 36 ports & 1 other plate. B June 2 (386) HF750

Halsey, Richard T. H.
— Pictures of Early New York on Dark Blue Staffordshire Pottery.... NY, 1899. One of 268. 8vo, cloth. sg June 4 (62) $175
See also: Grolier Club

Hamconius, Martinus, c.1550-1620
— Frisiae seu de viris rebusque Frisiae illustribus. Westph.: L. Rasfeldii, 1609. 4to, vellum. With 13 coats-of-arms. Prelims misbound; margins of 2 leaves repaired. B Feb 25 (654) HF350

Hambourg, Maria Morris. See: Szarkowski & Hambourg

Hamelmann, Hermann
— Oldenburgisch Chronicon.... Oldenburg: Warner Berendts Erben, 1599. 1st Ed. Folio, half lea. With engraved title, port, double-page plate of Oldenburg, & 3 double-page family trees. Some worming text & surfaces. JG Oct 2 (1090) DM3,700

Hamerton, Philip Gilbert, 1834-94
— Etching and Etchers. L, 1868. 8vo, orig half lea; rubbed, inner joint broken. C July 22 (89) £550

Anr copy. Contemp calf gilt by Tout, orig cloth bound in. Ck Dec 10 (284) £520

Anr Ed. L, 1876. 8vo, cloth; worn, hinges cracked. sg Feb 5 (157) $110

3d Ed. L, 1880. 4to, half mor gilt. With 44 plates, including orig etching. pn Dec 11 (277) £320 [Henderson]

— The Graphic Arts. L, 1882. 4to, orig bds; hinges cracked. sg June 11 (229) $100

Anr Ed. NY, 1882. 4to, orig vellum gilt; soiled. sg Feb 5 (158) $90

— Landscape. L, 1885. One of 525. Folio, orig bds; marked. pnNY Oct 11 (24) $130

Hamilton, Alexander, 1755-1804
— Observations on Certain Documents Contained in..."The History of the United States for the Year 1796".... Phila, 1797. 1st Ed. 8vo, later calf extra; front cover detached. sg Mar 12 (133) $120

— The Papers.... NY, 1961-79. Ed by Harold C. Syrett. Vols 1-21 only. K Mar 22 (129) $130

Hamilton, Anthony, 1646?-1720
— Memoirs du Comte de Grammont.... L, [1793]. 4to, early 19th-cent lea gilt extra; extremities rubbed. With 79 ports. sg Oct 9 (220) $110

Hamilton, Mrs. Cospatrick Baille
— A Series of Twelve Views in the Mediterranean.... L, 1857. Folio, loose in ptd wraps. With litho title & 11 hand-colored views. S Oct 23 (340) £2,300 [Martinos]

Hamilton, Edmond
— The Horror on the Asteroid. L, 1936. In chipped d/j. cb Sept 28 (586) $150

Hamilton, Edward
The Flora Homeopathica.... L, 1852-53. 2 vols. 8vo, half calf; worn. With 66 hand-colored plates. pn Apr 30 (179) £420 [Maggs]

Hamilton, Frederic
— La Botanique de la Bible.... Nice: Eugene Fleurdelys, 1871. 8vo, cloth; worn, joints torn. With 25 albumen photos. sg Nov 13 (60) $325

Hamilton, John Potter, 1777-1873
— Travels through the Interior Provinces of Colombia. L, 1827. 2 vols. 8vo, orig half cloth; rebacked. With folding map & 7 plates. bba Sept 25 (415) £190 [Burton Garbett]

Hamilton, Myra
— Kingdoms Curious. L, 1905. Illus by Arthur Rackham & others. 8vo, orig cloth; spine darkened, corner dampstained. sg Oct 30 (95) $120

Hamilton, Peter J.
— Colonial Mobile.... Bost., 1897. 8vo, orig cloth. Library markings. sg Sept 18 (119) $60

Hamilton, Sinclair
— Early American Book Illustrators and Wood Engravers.... Princeton, 1958-68. 2 vols, including Supplement. 4to, cloth. Inscr. cba Feb 5 (105) $200

— Early American Book Illustrators and Wood Engravers, 1670-1870. Princeton, 1958, 1968. 2 vols, including Supplement. 4to, cloth. sg Jan 22 (186) $250

Hamilton, Vereker M. —& Fasson, Stewart M.
— Scenes in Ceylon. L, [1881]. Oblong folio, orig half lea with large colored pastedown on upper cover; spine & corners worn. With 20 plates. Marginal tears to 2 plates; tp soiled. L Dec 11 (67) £100

Hamilton, William, d.1856
— Prodromus plantarum Indiae occidentalis.... L, 1825. 8vo, contemp half mor; rubbed. With folding hand-colored litho frontis. bba Nov 13 (57) £75 [Maggs]

Hamilton, Sir William, 1730-1803
— Campi Phlegraei. Naples, 1776-79. 2 vols. Folio, contemp mor gilt. With double-page map & 59 hand-colored plates, all hand-colored.. S Oct 23 (257) £12,000 [King]

Anr copy. 2 vols & Supplement in 1 vol. Folio, modern half mor with gilt shelf-mark on spine. Tp torn & mtd with rubberstamp on verso. S Feb 24 (505) £10,000 [Bifolco]

— Collection of Etruscan, Greek and Roman Antiquities. Naples 1766-67. Vol II only (of 4). Folio, contemp calf gilt; covers detached, worn. Lacking 1 plate; 1 plate with small marginal tear. bba Aug 20 (41) £2,000 [Henderson]

Collection of Engravings from Ancient Vases.... Naples, 1791-95. Vols I-III (of 4). Folio, modern half mor. With engraved titles & 191 plates only. Ck June 19 (96) £400

Anr copy. Bdg not indicated. Library markings. Sold w.a.f. Franklin Institute copy. F Sept 12 (120) $400

— Memorandum on the Subject of the Earl of Elgin's Pursuits in Greece. L, 1811. 8vo, orig bds; worn. pn Apr 30 (154) £180 [Maggs]

— Observations on Mount Vesuvius...and Other Volcanos. L, 1772. 1st Ed. 8vo,

HAMILTON

contemp calf; rubbed. With 2 plates & folding map. Ck Sept 26 (244) £75

Hamilton Collection, Sir William
— Outlines from the Figures and Compositions upon the Greek, Roman and Etruscan Vases. L, 1804. 4to, contemp calf gilt; joints worn. With 62 plates in 2 states. S Nov 10 (100) £280 [Tucker]
— HANCARVILLE, PIERRE FRANCOIS HUGUES D'. - Antiquites etrusques, grecques et romaines.... Naples, 1766-67. Vols I-II only, bound in 4 vols. Half calf; broken. Minor tears & soiling. C July 22 (92) £600 Anr copy. Vols I-II only. Contemp calf; def. With 4 colored titles, engraved dedications & 90 hand-colored plates. Sold w.a.f. S Oct 23 (199) £7,200 [Schuster]

Hamma, Fridolin
— Meisterwerke Italienischer Geigenbaukunst. Stuttgart, [n.d.]. One of 1,200. 4to, orig half vellum. sg Feb 26 (231) $550

Hammen y Leon, Lorenzo van der
— Don Juan de Austria. Historia. Madrid: Luis Sanchez, 1627. 4to, contemp vellum bds with gilt-tooled ornament. Some lower margins wormed, occasionally touching text. Sir William Stirling-Maxwell's copy. S June 25 (29) £350

Hammer, Victor
— Engravings and Woodcuts. Lexington KY, 1979. One of 50. In d/j. With 36 mtd plates. sg Jan 8 (129) $130

Hammett, Dashiell, 1894-1961
— The Dain Curse. NY, 1929. Bdg soiled, rubberstamp on front pastedown. cb May 7 (275) $90
— The Maltese Falcon. San Francisco: Arion Press, 1983. One of 400. Half mor with "black bird" mor onlay. sg Jan 8 (8) $200
— Red Harvest. NY, 1929. bba Aug 20 (160) £45 [C. Smith]; cb May 7 (278) $160

Hamnett, Nina
— Is She a Lady? A Problem in Autobiography. L, 1955. In chipped d/j. Inscr & annotated by Hamnett & with a sgd drawing laid in. sg Dec 11 (300) $100
— Laughing Torso. L, 1932. One of 92 L.p. copies, with pencil-drawing bound in. 4to, cloth. sg Dec 11 (299) $375

Hampden, John
— The Tryal of John Hampden, Esq.... L, 1719. Issue with Hampden's name spelt correctly. Folio, contemp calf; formerly a chained bdg (duplicate of Magdalen College Oxford, which chained books until 1799). cb Oct 23 (103) $80

AMERICAN BOOK PRICES CURRENT

Hampton, J. Fitzgerald
— Modern Angling Bibliography. L, 1947. In d/j. sg Oct 23 (324) $90

Hanbury, David
— Sport and Travel in the Northland of Canada. NY, 1904. Cloth; rubbed. cb Nov 6 (143) $85

Hanbury, William, 1725-78
— A Complete Body of Planting and Gardening. L, 1770-71. 2 vols. Folio, early 19th-cent russia; joints split, rubbed. With 2 hand-colored frontises & 20 hand-colored plates. de Belder copy. S Apr 27 (138) £2,500 [Hill]

Hancarville, Pierre Francois Hugues d'
See also: Hamilton Collection, Sir William
— Monumens de la vie privee des douze Cesars.... Capri: Sabellius, 1782. 8vo, contemp calf gilt; worn, spine ends chipped. With engraved title & 50 plates. sg Apr 2 (106) $550
— Monumens du culte secret des dames romaines.... Capree: Sabellus [but Nancy: Leclerc], 1784. 4to, 19th-cent mor gilt. With engraved title & 50 plates. S Nov 27 (173) £420 [Olschki]

Hanfstaengl, Francois
— Die Vorzueglichsten Gemaelde des Koeniglichen Galerie in Dresden. Dresden, 1836-41. Vol I only. Contemp half calf. FD Dec 2 (799) DM2,700

Hanger, George, Baron Coleraine
— The Life, Adventures and Opinions.... L, 1801. 2 vols. 8vo, contemp bds; rebacked in mor with orig calf backstrips laid down, spines & edges worn. sg Sept 18 (120) $325

Hanley, James
— The German Prisoner. L: Pvtly ptd, [1935?]. One of 500. bba Oct 16 (197) £50 [Palladour]
— The Last Voyage. L, 1931. One of 550, sgd. Orig cloth. sg Mar 5 (90) $50

Hanley, Sylvanus, 1819-99. See: Forbes & Hanley

Hannaford, Samuel
— The Wild Flowers of Tasmania.... Melbourne, 1866. 8vo, orig cloth. kh Mar 16 (243) A$170

Hansard, George Agar
— The Book of Archery, being the Complete History.... L, 1840. 8vo, contemp calf gilt; rubbed. Some plates stained, mainly in margins. bba Nov 13 (253) £55 [Trocchi]

Hanway, Jonas, 1712-86
— An Historical Account of the British Trade over the Caspian Sea.... L, 1753. 4 vols. 4to, contemp calf; rubbed, head & foot of spines worn. With half-titles in Vols III & IV & 28 plates & maps. C Apr 8 (92) £320 [Morrell]
— Letters on the Importance of the Rising Generation.... L, 1767. 1st Ed. 2 vols. 8vo, contemp calf; rubbed, rebacked. S July 14 (320) £350
— Proposal for County Naval Free-Schools.... [L], 1783. 1st Ed. 3 parts in 1 vol. Folio, contemp half calf; worn. With 2 engraved titles, 8 plates & plans & 48 pages of engraved music. C Dec 12 (107) £850 [Cavendish]

Hanzelet
— Recueil de plusieurs machines militaires et feux artificiels pour la guerre, & recreation. See: Appier & Thybourel

Happel, Eberhard Werner, 1647-90
— Groeste Denkwuerdigkeiten der Welt.... Hamburg, 1685-89. 5 vols. 4to, contemp vellum; worn & soiled. HN May 20 (1822) DM3,000
— Thesaurus exoticorum.... Hamburg, 1688. Folio, contemp calf gilt; rubbed. With engraved title, 14 plates of ports, 17 plates of maps, plans & views & 3 double-page or folding woodcuts. Some tears without loss. S Oct 23 (116) £1,000 [Crete]

Harangues...
— Harangues facetieuses, remplies de doctrines et sentence, sur la mort de divers animaux.... Lyon: Pierre Roussin, 1618. 12mo, 18th-cent mor gilt. SM Mar 1 (283) FF11,000

Haraszthy, Agostin, 1812-69
— Grape Culture, Wines, and Wine-Making. NY, 1862. 8vo, orig cloth; rubbed. Marginal pencil notations. cb July 30 (220) $750
Anr copy. Orig cloth; rebacked, orig spine laid down. Crahan copy. P Nov 25 (233) $1,200
Anr copy. Orig cloth; worn. Library copy. sg Jan 15 (30) $550

Harbour, Henry
— Where Flies the Flag. L, [1904]. Illus by Arthur Rackham. With 6 color plates. sg Oct 30 (96) $150

Harcourt, Raoul d' & Robert d'
— La Musique des Incas et ses survivances. Paris, 1925. 2 vols. 4to, cloth & half cloth. sg Feb 26 (163) $130

Harcourt-Smith, Simon
— The Last of Uptake. L, 1942. One of 100. Illus by Rex Whistler. 4to, orig half mor. bba Oct 30 (255) £90 [Henderson]

Harcus, William, d.1885
— South Australia, its History, Resources and Productions. Adelaide, 1876. 8vo, cloth; soiled & worn. With 67 plates & 2 folding maps. wa Nov 6 (132) $60

Hardie, Martin
— English Coloured Books. L & NY, [1906]. 4to orig cloth. Affected by damp. Ck Oct 17 (61) £35
— Water-Colour Painting in Britain. L, 1966-68. 3 vols. In d/js. S Mar 9 (677) £120 [Birgo]
Anr Ed. L, [1967-68]. 3 vols. 4to, orig cloth, in d/js. pn July 23 (95) £100 [Gorlin]

Hardie, Martin —& Sabin, Arthur K.
— War Posters Issued by Belligerent and Neutral Nations 1914-19. L, 1920. 1st Ed. 4to, cloth; rubbed & worn. With 80 plates. cb Dec 18 (79) $70
Anr copy. Cloth; soiled. sg Feb 5 (278) $100

Harding, James Duffield, 1798-1863
— Elementary Art; or, the Use of the Lead Pencil.... L, 1834. Folio, orig cloth; worn, lacking backstrip. With litho frontis & 27 plates.. With photo loosely inserted. bba Dec 4 (191) £60 [Rainer]
— The Principles and Practice of Art. L, 1845. Folio, orig cloth; rubbed. Lacking 1 plate. bba Apr 9 (470) £45 [Rainer]
— Sketches in North Wales. L, 1810. 4to, orig wraps. With 6 hand-colored plates. C Apr 8 (24) £1,000 [Howell Williams]

Hardouin, Seigneur de Fontaines-Guerin
— Tresor de venerie compose l'an M.CCC.LXXX.IV.... Metz: Rousseau-Pallez, 1856. One of 200. 8vo, later mor with arms of the comte de Beaufort. Jeanson copy. SM Mar 1 (230) FF3,000

Hardy, Thomas, 1840-1928
— A Changed Man.... L, 1913. 1st Ed in Book form. Orig cloth in frayed d/j. Embossed presentation stamp on tp. bba Jan 15 (118) £80 [Maggs]
Proof copy. Wraps; soiled. T Feb 18 (39) £50
— The Dynasts. L, 1927. One of 525. 3 vols. 4to, orig half vellum, unopened; warped.

wd June 19 (128) $150
— The Dynasts: a Drama of the Napoleonic War. L, 1927. One of 525. 3 vols. 4to, orig half vellum. sg Feb 12 (165) $250
— Tess of the D'Urbervilles.... [L, 1891]. 1st Ed in Book form. 3 vols. 8vo, orig cloth; rubbed & discolored. bba Jan 15 (117) £130 [Sotheran]
Anr copy. Orig cloth; soiled, some corners bumped. pnNY Sept 13 (242) $525
— The Trumpet-Major. L, 1880. 1st Ed. 3 vols. 8vo, orig cloth; soiled. pn Mar 5 (306) £420
— Wessex Tales. L, 1888. 1st Ed in Book form. 2 vols. 8vo, orig cloth; rubbed. Ck June 5 (116) £120
— Works. L, 1919-20. Mellstock Ed, one of 500. 37 vols. Orig cloth. ha May 22 (60) $1,700
Anr copy. Mor by Whitman Bennett. O May 12 (85) $3,600; P June 18 (80) $2,900

Hardy, Sir Thomas Duffus, 1804-78. See: Carlyle's copy, Thomas

Hare, James H.
— A Photographic Record of the Russo-Japanese War. NY, 1905. Oblong 4to, orig bds, rebacked with cloth; rubbed & worn. Some ink underlining. cb Dec 18 (157) $60

Hare, William Loftus
— The Court of the Printer's Guild. NY: Valenti Angelo, 1949. One of 200. Mor gilt. Inscr. cb Dec 4 (313) $300
Anr copy. Vellum. cb Dec 4 (314) $100
Anr copy. Wraps over bds. Inscr in colophon. cb Dec 4 (316) $55
Anr Ed. San Francisco: Valenti Angelo, 1975. One of 65. Bds. cb Dec 4 (315) $55

Hargrave, Catherine Perry
— A History of Playing Cards and a Bibliography.... Bost & NY, [1930]. 1st Ed. 4to orig cloth. cb Feb 19 (128) $150

Hargraves, Edward Hammond, 1816-91
— Australia and its Gold Fields.... L, 1855. 8vo, cloth. With port & folding map. kh Mar 16 (245) A$350

Hargreaves, Mary. See: MacDonald & Hargreaves

Harleian...
— Harleian Miscellany: A Collection of Scarce, Curious, and Entertaining Pamphlets and Tracts. L, 1744-46. 1st Ed. 8 vols. 4to, contemp half calf; rubbed. Ck Feb 13 (188) £130
Vol I, 2d Ed; Vols II-VIII, 1st Ed. 8 vols. 4to, contemp calf; rubbed. cb Oct 23 (104) $150

Anr Ed. L, 1808-13. 10 vols. 4to, contemp half calf; rubbed, joints split. Each title with top half-inch trimmed off. cb Feb 19 (129) $130
Anr copy. Modern cloth. sg Oct 9 (221) $150

Harlow, Neal. See: Grabhorn Printing

Harmont, Pierre
— Le Miroir de fauconnerie.... Paris: Claude Percheron, 1620. 8vo, 19th-cent shagreen. Jeanson copy. SM Mar 1 (284) FF45,000
Anr Ed. Paris: Cardin Besongne, 1635. 8vo, mor janseniste by Duru, sgd 3 Mar 1844. Jeanson copy. SM Mar 1 (285) FF19,000

Harmsworth Trust Library
— [Sale Catalogue] Catalogue of the Highly Important Collection of Americana. L, 1948-53. Sections 1-18 in 1 vol. Orig ptd wraps bound in red cloth. cb Feb 5 (106) $60

Harper, Malcolm McLachlan.
— Rambles in Galloway. Dalbeattie, 1896. One of 250 L.p. copies. 4to, cloth; soiled. bba Nov 13 (142) £35 [Clark]

Harper's...
— Harper's Pictorial History of the Great Rebellion. Chicago, [1866-68]. Ed by Alfred H. Guernsey & Henry M. Alden. 2 vols. Folio, later cloth; soiled. Some leaves torn or frayed; some soiling & foxing. sg June 18 (183) $80
— Harper's Weekly: A Journal of Civilization. NY, 1857. Vol I, Nos 27-52. Old half sheep. ha May 22 (289) $150
Vol IV, Nos 158-209. NY, 1860. Old half calf; cover panels detached, worn. ha May 22 (290) $225
Vol XVI, Nos 784-835. NY, 1872. Old half sheep; worn & loose. ha May 22 (292) $200
Anr Ed. NY, 1873. Issues for 4 Jan 1873 through 27 Dec 1873 bound in 1 vol. Folio, half lea; worn. Includes 10 single & double-page wood engravings after Winslow Homer Some soiling & damp-staining. Sold w.a.f. sg June 18 (208) $1,400
Vol XVIII only. NY, 1874. Folio, orig cloth; broken, worn, lacking spine. With some tearing & chipping. wa Sept 25 (564) $310
Vol XXII, Nos 1097-1148. NY, 1878. Recent cloth. ha May 22 (293) $200
Vol XXVII, Nos 1359-1410. NY, 1883. Recent cloth. ha May 22 (294) $175
Vol XXVII, Nos 1364-1410. Recent cloth. ha May 22 (295) $160

Harral, Thomas, d.1853
See also: Fearnside & Harral
— Picturesque Views of the Severn.... L, 1824. 2 vols. 4to, orig cloth; worn, spine frayed. With 52 plates. C Dec 12 (237) £100 [Maggs]

Anr copy. 2 vols in 1. 4to, contemp half calf gilt. With litho frontises & 50 plates. S May 28 (873) £130

Anr copy. 2 vols. 4to, recent bds. T Mar 19 (60) £150

Harriman...
— Harriman Alaska Expedition. NY, 1901. Vols I & II (of 14). 4to, cloth, in d/js. sg Nov 13 (39) $90

Harrington, James, 1611-77
— The Common-Wealth of Oceana. L, 1656. Folio, contemp calf; rubbed, joints cracking, spine chipped. Lacking the Epistle to the Reader & the errata leaf but with the corrections made in ink in the margins of the text; some stains; tear into text on Y2; marginal worming. P Sept 24 (299) $320

Anr Ed. L, 1700. Folio, modern cloth; worn. Some foxing; frontis loose & chipped. sg Mar 26 (137) $70

Harriot, Thomas, 1560-1621
— A Briefe and True Report of the New Found Land of Virginia.... Manchester: for the Holbein Society, 1888. Folio, orig cloth; spine ends frayed. Library markings. sg Sept 18 (296) $80

Harris, Frank, 1854-1931
— Oscar Wilde: his Life and Confessions. NY, 1916. 2 vols. Orig half mor; spines worn. Inscr to Tiny Schuster. bba Apr 9 (235) £85 [Maguire]

Anr Ed. NY, 1918. 2 vols. Inscr. cb May 7 (89) $100

Harris, James, 1709-80
— Philological Inquiries in Three Parts. L, 1781. 3 parts in 1 vol. 8vo contemp calf; rubbed. T Jan 22 (364) £64

Harris, Joel Chandler, 1848-1908
— Uncle Remus: his Songs and his Sayings. NY, 1881. 1st Ed, 1st Issue. 8vo, orig cloth; shaken, front hinge partly frayed. sg Sept 11 (199) $120; sg Feb 12 (166) $200

Anr Ed. NY, 1920. Illus by A. B. Frost & E. W. Kemble. Inscr by the author's son. cb Dec 4 (189) $60

Harris, John, 1667?-1719
— Gardens of Delight: The Rococo English Landscape of Thomas Robins the Elder. L: Basilisk Press, 1978. One of 515. 2 vols. Oblong folio, orig cloth. S Mar 9 (643) £160 [Henderson]

— The History of Kent. L, 1719. 1st Ed. Vol I (all pbd). Folio old calf with arms of 2d Duke of Buccleuch. Lacking 4 plates & maps. Sold w.a.f. C Apr 8 (130) £900 [Toscani]

Anr copy. Old calf; rubbed, rebacked. With port, folding map & 42 plates & plans. Some margins shaved; some worming affecting early margins. Ck Nov 21 (254) £1,300 [Toscani]

Anr copy. Contemp calf; rebacked. Ck Nov 21 (361) £1,200

— Lexicon Technicum: or an Universal English Dictionary.... L, 1708-10. 2d Ed of Vol I; 1st Ed of Vol II. 2 vols. Folio, contemp calf; rubbed, spines frayed. Sold w.a.f. C Dec 12 (108) £380 [Bookpress]

— Navigantium atque Itinerantium Bibliotheca; or, a Compleat Collection of Voyages and Travels.... L, 1705. 1st Ed. Vol I only. Folio, old calf; rubbed. With frontis, 5 folding maps & 8 plates only. Sold w.a.f. bba July 16 (105) £310 [Orssich]

2d Ed. L, 1744-48. 2 vols. Folio, later half calf; worn. Last leaves of Vol I torn & repaired; 2 maps torn without loss; some text leaves torn; some stains & browning; number stamps on titles. bba Jan 15 (438) £1,150 [Shapero]

Anr copy. 2 vols in 4. Folio, contemp calf; broken. With 22 maps (1 torn, 12 with perforated library stamps) & 39 plates (1 torn, 21 with ink library stamps). Some text leaves torn. bba Feb 5 (341) £550 [Noble]

Anr copy. 2 vols. Folio, contemp calf; worn, hinges split. With 61 plates. Some spotting; 1 folding map & plate closely trimmed slightly affecting text. With port of Capt Cook mtd on flyleaf above an Ms inscr "Presented by Captn James Cook...to Captn. Furneaux of H.M.S. Adventure on the 10th day of January 1779". C Apr 8 (25) £1,700 [Ebes]

Anr copy. Contemp calf; rubbed. With port & 58 plates & maps only. Ck May 15 (61) £1,700

Anr copy. Old calf gilt; rubbed, hinges & spine worn. With 38 plates & 21 (of 22) maps. pnNY Sept 13 (243) $750

Anr Ed. L, 1764. Vol I only. Contemp calf; rubbed & worn. With 27 plates & maps. Wormed in margin towards end; minor flaw in 9F. S Jan 12 (181) £550 [Faupel]

Harris, John Benyon. See: Wyndham, John

HARRIS

Harris, Moses, 1731?-85?

— The Aurelian. A Natural History of English Insects.... L, [plates watermarked 1794]. Folio, contemp mor gilt; corners bruised, edges scuffed. With title within hand-colored engraved wreath, uncolored engraved key-plate with facing single leaf, Table of the Terms & 44 hand-colored plates. CNY Nov 21 (132) $8,000

Anr Ed. L, 1794. Folio, contemp mor gilt; rebacked with orig backstrip laid down, corners & edges repaired. With French title within handcolored wreath, hand-colored key plate with facing page Table of Terms & 44 hand-colored plates without engraved dedications & all ptd in reverse. Some stains throughout. Hunt copy. CNY Nov 21 (133) $4,500

Anr Ed. L, 1840. 4to, modern half mor. With engraved title & frontis & 44 hand-colored plates. Plate 17 bound upside down. bba Dec 4 (259) £1,400 [Shapero]

Anr copy. Contemp mor gilt; extremities rubbed. With additional title, key plate & 44 plates, all hand-colored. Both titles & c.3 plates torn in margin. P Dec 15 (200) $3,250

— An Exposition of English Insects. L, 1776. 1st Ed. 4to, contemp calf gilt; joints cracked. With 1 plain & 51 hand-colored plates. S Jan 13 (382) £400 [Daley]

Anr Ed. L, 1782. 4to, contemp calf; rebacked. With engraved title, hand-colored frontis, key plate & 50 hand-colored plates. S May 28 (583) £260

Harris, Stanley

— Old Coaching Days.... L, 1882. 8vo, orig cloth; soiled, extremities rubbed. Ck May 15 (214) £45

Harris, Thaddeus Mason, 1768-1842

— The Journal of a Tour into the Territory Northwest of the Alleghany Mountains.... Bost., 1805. 8vo, modern cloth; inexpertly cased, affecting inner margins of several maps. With plan, view & 3 maps. Each plate with perforated library stamp; plates heavily foxed. sg Mar 12 (134) $130

Anr copy. Half cloth. Lacking the map of Marietta; library markings. sg Mar 12 (135) $80

Harris, Thomas Lake, 1823-1906

— God's Breath in Man and in Humane Society. Santa Rosa, 1891. cb Jan 8 (84) $55

Harris, Tomas

— Goya: Engravings and Lithographs. Oxford, [1964]. 1st Ed. 2 vols. Folio, orig cloth, in d/js. sg Feb 5 (159) $800

Harris, W. A.

— Record of Fort Sumter.... Columbia, 1863. 8vo, modern half mor, orig front wrap bound in. Extra-illus with mtd ephemera (all stamped by Brooklyn Public Library). sg Mar 12 (85A) $650

Harris, Sir William Cornwallis, 1807-48

— The Highlands of Aethiopia. L, 1844. 4th Ed. 3 vols. 8vo, orig cloth; spine worn & frayed. Tp torn affecting print. SSA Feb 11 (535) R400

— Portraits of the Game and Wild Animals of Southern Africa. L, 1840. Folio, contemp half mor gilt. With litho title having hand-colored vignette & with 30 colored plates. Some spotting. C Oct 15 (123) £4,500 [Holland & Holland]

Anr copy. Half calf; 1 joint splitting. With engraved title & 30 hand-colored plates. Lacking 1 leaf of text for hippopotamus; some dampstaining at beginning & end; minor spotting. C Apr 8 (211) £2,500 [Shuster]

Anr Ed. Mazoe, 1976. Ltd Ed. Folio, half calf. SSA Feb 11 (534) R1,000

— The Wild Sports of Southern Africa. L, 1844. 8vo, orig cloth; tears at head & tail of spine. With frontis, folding map & 24 colored plates. Some spotting. pn Apr 30 (48) £240 [Way]

5th Ed. L, 1852. 8vo, contemp half mor. With engraved title, map & 25 colored plates. S Oct 23 (459) £420 [Holland]

Harrison, David L.

— Mammals of Arabia. L, 1964-72. 3 vols. 4to, orig cloth, in d/js. S Oct 23 (305) £170 [Weldon & Wesley]

Harrison, Godfrey

— J. Whatman. Romford, 1931. Bds. Ptd in red & black on specimens of various Whatman papers. Ck Apr 24 (51) £110

Harrison, Harry

— The Ethical Engineer. L, 1964. In soiled d/j. cb Sept 28 (595) $100

— Make Room! Make Room! Garden City, 1966. In d/j. cb Sept 28 (597) $130

Harrison, J. C. —& Evans, David

— The Birds of Prey of the British Islands. L, 1980. One of 275. Folio, orig half mor. With 20 colored plates. Ck Oct 31 (188) £170; pn Oct 23 (201) £100

Harrison, Jane Ellen —& MacColl, Donald Sutherland
— Greek Vase Paintings. L, 1894. Folio, orig cloth; rubbed. pn Mar 5 (309) £60 [Elliott]

Harrison, John, 1693-1776
— The Principles of Mr. Harrison's Time-Keeper. L, 1767. Leroy, Pierre. A Succinct Account of the Attempts of Mess. Harrison and Le Roy for Finding the Longitude at Sea. 4to, contemp half calf. C Dec 12 (109) £4,500 [Brooke-Hitching]

Harrison, Joseph
— The Floricultural Cabinet, and Florist's Magazine. L, 1833-59. Vols I-XIII, XVI & XVII. Together, 15 vols. Half calf gilt. With 199 hand-colored plates. pn Jan 22 (202) £800 [Bayer]

Mixed Ed of Vols 1-27. 8vo, contemp half calf gilt; 1 spine chipped, some rubbing. With 14 engraved titles & 350 hand-colored plates. A few plates slightly cropped. Blunt—de Belder copy. S Apr 27 (139) £3,000 [Richards]

Vols 1-13. L, 1833-46. Orig cloth. With 173 hand-colored plates. pn Sept 18 (156) £820 [Richards]

Vols 1-5. L, 1833-37. Cloth; rubbed. One text leaf torn; 3 engraved titles only; some dampstains. Sold w.a.f. bba Jan 15 (408) £160 [Dennistoun]

Vols I-VI only. L, 1833-38. Contemp cloth. Sold w.a.f. C Apr 8 (177) £350 [Greyfriars]

Harrisse, Henry, 1830-1910
— Bibliotheca Americana Vetustissima: A Description of Works relating to America.... NY, 1866 & Paris, 1872. One of 99 ptd in 4to. 2 vols. Half sheep. sg May 14 (11) $200

Anr copy. Half mor. sg May 14 (12) $375

— Decouverte et evolution cartographique de Terre-Neuve.... L & Paris, 1900. One of 40 on Van Gelder. 4to, bds; unopened; rear joint cracked. sg Oct 2 (158) $325

One of 380. Cloth. sg May 14 (190) $275

— The Discovery of North America, a Critical, Documentary and Historic Investigation. Paris & L, 1892. One of 380. 4to, half lea; orig front wrap bound in, extremities worn. sg Oct 2 (157) $200

— Jean et Sebastien Cabot, leur origine et leurs voyages.... Paris, 1882. 8vo, half mor; worn, orig wraps bound in. L.p. copy. sg Oct 2 (156) $225

— Notes on Columbus. NY, 1866. One of 90. Folio, mor; rubbed. Some library markings. O Oct 21 (132) $70

— Notes pour servir a l'histoire, a la bibliographie et a la cartographie de la Nouvelle-France et des pays adjacents,

1545-1700.... Paris, 1872. 8vo, cloth, orig wraps bound in. sg Oct 2 (155) $200; sg May 14 (13) $175

Anr copy. Orig wraps; soiled & chipped. sg May 14 (14) $140

Hart, Charles Henry. See: Grolier Club

Hart, James David
— My First Publication: Eleven California Authors Describe their Earliest Appearances in Print. San Francisco: Book Club of Calif., 1961. One of 475. cb Sept 11 (43) $95; sg Jan 8 (32) $60

Hart, Joseph C.
— A Modern Atlas, of Fourteen Maps. NY, 1830. 7th Ed. Folio, old bds; worn. Some stains & browning. O Nov 18 (80) $80

Hart, William Surrey
— My Life East and West. Bost. & NY, 1929. 1st Ed. In soiled d/j. Inscr. sg Feb 26 (160) $30

Harte, Bret, 1836-1902
See also: Clemens & Harte; Grabhorn Printing

— The Lost Galleon and Other Tales. San Francisco, 1867. 1st Ed. 12mo, cloth; 2 small stains on rear. cb Jan 22 (20) $50

— The Luck of Roaring Camp.... Bost., 1870. 1st Ed, 1st Issue. 12mo orig cloth. sg Feb 12 (167) $80

Harte, Walter, 1709-74
— The History of Gustavus Adolphus.... L, 1807. 2 vols. 8vo, mor with arms of william Stirling Maxwell; rubbed. O Feb 24 (98) $110

Hartenfels, Georg Christoph Petri von, 1633-1718. See: Petri von Hartenfels, Georg Christoph

Hartert, Ernst Johann Otto
— Die Voegel der palaarktischen Fauna. Berlin, 1903-38. 3 vols & Ergaenzungsband. B Feb 24 (72) HF400

Harting, James Edmund, 1841-1928
— Bibliotheca Accipitraria: a Catalogue of Books...Relating to Falconry.... L, 1891. 8vo cloth. SM Mar 1 (588) FF4,200

Hartinger, Anton
— Endlicher's paradisus Vindobonensis, Abbildungen seltener und schoenbluehender Pflanzen der Wiener.... Vienna, 1844-60. Folio, contemp half mor; rubbed. With litho title & 80 color plates on 78 leaves, many hand-finished. S Apr 27 (140) £15,000 [Jagger]

Hartinger, Anton —& Dalla Torre, Karl Wilhelm von
— Atlas der Alpenflora. Graz, 1897. 5 vols. 8vo, loose as issued in orig cloth. With 500 colored plates. JG Mar 20 (548) DM650

Anr copy. Orig cloth. sg Jan 15 (131) $200

Hartley, David, 1732-1813
— The Budget. Inscribed to the Man who thinks himself Minister [George Grenville]. L: for J. Almon, 1764. 4to, 19th-cent half calf. Private owner's library card pocket on front pastedown. sg Oct 9 (222) $60

Hartlib, Samuel, d.1662
— His Legacie.... L, 1655. 3d Ed. 4to, contemp sheep; recased with spine & corners repaired, joints worn. Tp soiled & with upper right corners frayed. CNY Nov 21 (134) $350

Anr copy. 17th-cent calf gilt; rubbed, joints broken. Stained. S May 29 (1201) £160
— The Reformed Common-Wealth of Bees.... L, 1655. 2 parts in 1 vol. 4to, 19th-cent sheep gilt; broken. First 4 leaves remargined. Johannson copy. sg Jan 15 (150) $1,200

Hartnoll, Phyllis. See: Golden Cockerel Press

Hartshorne, Albert
— Old English Glasses. L & NY, 1897. 4to orig cloth. Ck Sept 5 (219) £75

Anr copy. Orig half vellum; marked. S Nov 17 (658) £130 [Ash]

Anr copy. Orig half vellum; orig backstrip relaid. T Feb 19 (516) £80

Harvard Law School. See: Harvard University

Harvard University
— The Houghton Library, 1942-1967. Cambr., Mass., 1967. Folio, cloth. ha Dec 19 (43) $70
— HARVARD LAW SCHOOL. - Catalogue of the Library.... Cambr MA, 1909. 2 vols. 4to, cloth; shaken. Both vols sgd by J. H. Beale. sg Jan 22 (190) $175

Harvey, James, fl.1700
— Praesagium Medicum: or, the Prognostick Signs of Acute Diseases. L, 1706. 1st Ed. 8vo, contemp calf; worn. S Nov 10 (496) £50 [Phelps]

Harvey, John D. M. See: Ramsey & Harvey

Harvey, William, 1578-1657
See also: Nonesuch Press
— Exercitationes de generatione animalium.... Amst: Elzevir, 1651. 12mo, contemp vellum; repaired. FD Dec 2 (560) DM9,000

Anr copy. Contemp calf; rubbed. Lacking 2 leaves of preface; inking flaw affecting text on p 337. S Nov 10 (497) £60 [Phelps]

Anr copy. Contemp calf; rubbed, covers loose. S May 28 (683) £200

Anr copy. Contemp calf; worn, front cover starting. Browned, dampstained. sg Jan 15 (316) $80

Harvey, William Henry, 1811-66
— Nereis Boreali-Americana. Wash., 1851-58. 3 parts in 1 vol. 4to, cloth; soiled & chipped, backstrips partly lacking. With 50 colored plates. Inscr. sg Jan 15 (222) $325
— Phycologia Britannica: or, a History of British Sea-Weeds. L, 1846-51. 4 vols. 8vo, half calf; rubbed. Library stamps on titles. pn Oct 23 (8) £240 [Junk]

Anr copy. Orig calf; defective. pn Jan 22 (230) £50 [Maggs]

Hasen...
— Hasen Jagt: auff welcher mancherley Hasen gefangen werden.... Gedruckt zu Hasleben, 1629. 4to, mor janseniste by Riviere. Schwerdt-Jeanson copy. SM Mar 1 (287) FF24,000

Haskell, Daniel Carl
See also: Stokes & Haskell
— The United States Exploring Expedition, 1838-42, and its Publications. NY, 1942. sg Sept 18 (124) $60

Haskell, Grace C. See: Latimore & Haskell

Haslam, John, 1764-1844
— Sound Mind or Contributions to the Natural History and Physiology of the Human Intellect. L, 1819. 8vo, half calf; worn, upper cover loose. Library stamp on tp & at end; lacking ad leaves. S May 28 (684) £130

Hassall, William Owen
— The Holkham Bible Picture Book. L, 1954. Folio, orig half mor. sg Jan 22 (188) $100

One of 100. Mor gilt. pn June 18 (214) £100 [Dawson]

Hassam, Childe
— Catalogue of the Etchings and Dry-Points.... NY, 1925. One of 375. 4to, half cloth. With orig etching. sg Apr 2 (107) $1,100

Hassell, John
— The Camera or Art of Drawing in Water Colours. L, 1823. 8vo, contemp half calf; rubbed. With 1 folding plate in 3 states. S Nov 10 (101) £220 [Weinreb]
— Tour of the Grand Junction. L, 1819. 8vo, calf gilt. With 24 hand-colored plates. Some foxing. pn Dec 11 (73) £240 [Morris]
— Tour of the Isle of Wight. L, 1790. 2 vols. 8vo, calf. With 2 engraved titles & 31 plates. pn Jan 22 (276) £40

Anr copy. Recent half calf. With engraved titles & 30 plates. Vol II washed & trimmed so that the text appears off-center. T Mar 19 (62) £54

Hassenfratz, Jean Henri
— La Siderotechnie.... Paris, 1812. 4 vols. 4to, bdg not described. Franklin Institute copy. F Sept 12 (369) $550

Hasted, Edward, 1732-1812
— The History and Topographical Survey of the County of Kent. Canterbury, 1778-99. 1st Ed. 4 vols. Folio, contemp calf gilt; rehinged. With 35 maps, 128 (of 129) plates & 13 additional plates. pn Mar 5 (114) £900 [Swift]

Anr Ed. Canterbury, 1778-79. 4 vols. Folio, contemp calf gilt; worn. With 35 maps, 129 plates & 3 additional plates. pn Mar 5 (115) £850 [McKenzie]

Anr Ed. Canterbury, 1778-99. Vols I-II only. Contemp calf; worn & scuffed, upper joint of Vol I weak. pnE Dec 17 (40) £410 [Marshall]

Hastie, Peter —& Tracy, Edward H.
— [Sale Catalogue] Catalogue of a Library constituting the Collections.... NY. Leavitt, 1877. 4to, modern cloth, orig wraps bound in. Priced in ink; 1 leaf remargined. sg Jan 22 (189) $60

Hasting, Thomas, fl.1813-31
— Etchings from the Works of Ric. Wilson.... L, 1825. 4to, contemp half mor; rubbed. With engraved title & 40 mtd plates. Ck June 19 (14) £120

Hastings, Warren, 1732-1818
— Minutes of the Evidence taken at the Trial of Warren Hastings.... L, 1788. Folio, orig wraps; spine worn. bba Oct 30 (89) £40 [Scott]

Hatch, Alden. See: Derrydale Press

Hatch, Benton L.
— A Check List of the Publications of Thomas Bird Mosher 1891-1923. Northampton, Mass.: Gehenna Press, 1966. 4to, half cloth. With port & 21 mtd plates. sg Jan 22 (191) $150

Hatton, Edward, b.1664?
— A Mathematical Manual: Or, Delightful Associate.... L, 1728. 8vo, contemp calf; spine restored. T Sept 18 (362) £105
— A New View of London. L, 1708. 2 vols. 8vo, contemp calf; joints weak, rubbed. With 2 armorial plates, 2 folding maps & 1 table. Ck Sept 26 (35) £140

Hau...
— Hau Kiou Choaan or the Pleasing History. L, 1761. 4 vols. 8vo, contemp calf; rubbed. One frontis torn. C Dec 12 (110) £170 [Quaritch]

Haudicquer de Blancourt, Francois
— De l'art de la verrerie.... Paris, 1697. 1st Ed. 12mo, contemp calf; joints cracked, spine worn at ends. Crahan copy. P Nov 25 (238) $350

Anr Ed. Paris, 1718. ("L'Art de la verrerie ou l'on apprend a faire le verre....") 2 vols. 12mo, calf; worn. With 8 plates. pn Oct 23 (324) £65 [Greenwood]

Hauy, Rene Just, 1743-1822
— Essai d'une theorie sur la structure des crystaux.... Paris, 1784. 8vo, contemp bds. With 8 folding plates. S Nov 27 (264) £1,200 [Claureuil]

Havard, Henry, 1838-1921
— Dictionnaire de l'ameublement et de la decoration.... Paris: Maison Quantin, [1887-90]. 4 vols. 4to, half mor; rubbed. S Mar 9 (679) £190 [Laget]
— La France artistique et monumentale. Paris, [1890s]. 6 vols. 4to, contemp half mor by Petit-Simier, orig wraps bound in. Ck Sept 5 (42) £110
— Histoire de l'orfevrerie francaise. Paris, 1896. 4to half mor gilt; rubbed. Ck Jan 16 (113) £65

Havell, Daniel. See: Brayley & Havell

Havell, Robert
— The Tour, or Select Views on the Southern Coast. L, 1827. Oblong 4to, orig half lea; stitching def, worn. With 25 hand-colored plates, 1 folding. Folds strengthened & 1 plate slightly torn. C Apr 8 (26) £320 [Old Hall]

Havell, William
— A Series of Picturesque Views of the Thames. L, 1818. 2d Ed. Oblong folio, half mor. With aquatint title & 12 colored plates, each within buff wash-borders & laid on card. S Oct 23 (175) £5,000 [Traylen]

Hawker, Peter, 1786-1853
— The Diary, 1802-1853. L, 1893. 1st Ed. 2 vols. 8vo orig cloth. pnE Dec 17 (352A) £120 [Steedman]
— Instructions to Young Sportsmen.... L, 1814. 1st Ed. 8vo orig bds; dampstained, broken. sg Oct 23 (326) $750

3d Ed. L, 1824. 8vo modern calf. With 10 plates. L.p. copy. pnE Dec 17 (366) £240 [Steedman]

Anr copy. Half calf gilt, backstrip partly detached. With 10 plates, 4 hand-colored.

sg May 21 (118) $120

Anr copy. Shagreen. Jeanson 1888. SM Mar 1 (288) FF3,000

5th Ed. L, 1826. 8vo, bdg not described but bumped. cb May 21 (147) $55

Anr copy. Recent half mor. Plates foxed. cb May 21 (148) $130

1st American Ed. Phila., 1846. 8vo cloth; worn. sg Oct 23 (327) $80

Hawker, Robert Stephen, 1803-75
— Reeds Shaken with the Wind. L, 1843. 12mo, orig cloth. C Dec 12 (332) £280 [Burmester]

Hawkesworth, John, 1715?-73. See: Cook, Capt. James

Hawkins, Sir Anthony Hope, 1863-1933
— The Dolly Dialogues. L, 1894. Illus by Arthur Rackham. 8vo, contemp half calf. Inscr. cb Feb 19 (224) $55

Anr copy. Wraps; backstrip lacking at spine end. With 4 plates. sg Oct 30 (102) $375

Hawkins, F. Bisset
— Elements of Medical Statistics. L, 1829. 8vo, orig bds; rebacked. Inscr cut from title. S May 28 (685) £220

Hawkins, Sir Richard, 1562?-1622
— The Observations of Sir Richard Hawkins. L: Argonaut Press, 1933. One of 475. 4to, half vellum gilt; spine creased. cb Nov 6 (144) $90

Hawley Collection, Royal de Forest
— The Hawley Collection of Violins. Chicago, 1904. Out-of-series copy. 4to, half cloth. With port & 36 plates. sg Feb 26 (232) $225

Hawley, Walter A.
— Oriental Rugs. NY, 1937. cb July 30 (88) $80

Anr copy. In d/j. sg Feb 5 (244) $100

Hawthorne, Nathaniel, 1804-64
See also: Grabhorn Printing; Limited Editions Club
— Life of Franklin Pierce. Bost., 1852. 1st Ed. 12mo, orig cloth; worn. O Jan 6 (82) $60
— The Marble Faun. Bost., 1860. 1st American Ed. 2 vols. 12mo, orig cloth; blistered, spine ends chipped. With ads dated Mar 1860. Vol I dampstained in upper inner corner throughout. sg Feb 12 (168) $60
— Our Old Home: a Series of English Sketches. Bost., 1863. 1st Ed. 12mo, orig cloth. Inscr to Franklin Pierce, to whom it was dedicated. sg Feb 12 (169) $3,000
— The Scarlet Letter.... Bost., 1850. 1st Ed, 1st Issue. 8vo, orig cloth; lacking front free endpaper. sg June 11 (232) $650

— Tanglewood Tales.... L, [1918]. Illus by Edmund Dulac. 4to, orig vellum. With 14 color plates. S Dec 4 (189) £400 [Hirsch]
— A Wonder-Book for Girls and Boys. Bost., 1852. 1st Ed. 8vo, orig cloth; rebacked, preserving orig spine, worn. O Jan 6 (83) $100

Anr Ed. L, 1922. Illus by Arthur Rackham. With 24 color plates (16 mtd). sg Oct 30 (98) $110

One of 600, sgd by Rackham. 4to, orig cloth; rear cover torn & crudely repaired. With 24 color plates (16 mtd). sg Oct 30 (97) $600

— Works. Bost., [1882-84]. Standard Library Ed. 15 vols. 8vo, half mor; worn & soiled. Some dampstains. wa Feb 19 (97) $55

Anr Ed. Bost., [1900]. 22 vols. 12mo, half mor gilt. sg Feb 12 (170) $550

Hay, Robert, 1799-1863
— Illustrations of Cairo. L, 1840. Folio, contemp half mor; spine def. With frontis, dedication & 30 views on 29 plates. Lacking tp; 1 plate torn. S Jan 12 (238) £880 [Shapero]

Haycraft, Howard —& Queen, Ellery, Pseud.
— The Haycraft-Queen Definitive Library of Detective-Crime-Mystery Fiction. NY: Pvtly ptd, 1951. One of 500. Wraps. cb Nov 20 (229) $90

Hayden, Arthur
— Spode and his Successors. L, 1925. cb July 30 (89) $90

Anr copy. In torn d/j. sg June 4 (63) $80

Hayden, Ferdinand V., 1829-87
— Preliminary Report of the United States Geological Survey of Wyoming and Portions of Contiguous Territories. Wash., 1872-78. 6 vols. 8vo, orig cloth; worn. Library stamps. pn Nov 20 (235) £60 [Waterloo]
— Twelfth Annual Report of the United States Geological Survey.... Wash., 1883. 2 vols. 8vo, cloth; worn, front hinge broken. With 18 maps & 250 plates. Some plates loose, maps with splits & tears. wa Sept 25 (480) $150

Haydon, Arthur Lincoln
— Stories of King Arthur. L, 1910. Illus by Arthur Rackham. With 4 color plates. sg Oct 30 (99) $80

Haydon, George Henry
— Five Years' Experience in Australia Felix. L, 1846. 8vo later mor. With 6 tinted lithos. CA Apr 12 (129) A$300

Hayes, Isaac Israel, 1832-81
— An Arctic Boat Journey in the Autumn of 1854. Bost. & NY, 1860. 8vo, cloth; rubbed. With 2 folding maps, one torn. ha Dec 19 (95) $60

Hayes, William, fl.1794
— A Natural History of British Birds. L, [1771]-75. Folio, disbound & unstitched. With 40 hand-colored plates. Lacking dedication & anr prelim leaf; some plates captioned in ink; a few labels shaved. C Apr 8 (181) £3,000 [Quaritch]

Hayley, William, 1745-1820
— The Life, and Posthumous Writings, of William Cowper. Chichester, 1803-3-4. 3 vols. 4to, recent bds. With 3 ports & 2 plates, all etched or engraved by William Blake. Some internal spotting. T Sept 18 (344) £88

— A Philosophical, Historical and Moral Essay on Old Maids. L, 1786. 2d Ed. 3 vols. 8vo, contemp sheep; rubbed, some joints splitting. Some foxing. bba Oct 16 (94) £65 [Duncan]

— The Triumphs of Temper. Chichester, 1803. 12th Ed. Illus by William Blake after Maria Flaxman. 8vo, mor. With 6 plates. S Dec 4 (168) £180 [Thomas]

Hayn, Hugo, 1843-1923
— Bibliotheca erotica et curiosa Monacensis.... Berlin, 1889. 16mo, old half cloth; worn. sg Jan 22 (193) $140

Hayne, Friedrich Gottlob
— Getreue Darstellung und Beschreibung der in der Arzneykunde gebraeuchlichen Gewaechse. Berlin, 1805-37-[46]. Fine-paper Issue. 14 vols. 4to, contemp half sheep, orig upper wraps bound in. With 648 hand-colored plates. Marginal stain to Plate 2 of Vol I; outer margin of Plate 29 in Vol IX soiled in the press; dedication-leaf & 2 subscribers' lists in Vol I bound out of place. P Sept 24 (166) $8,250

Anr Ed. Berlin, 1817. Vol V only. 4to contemp half lea; worn, joints starting. With 48 hand-colored plates, most lightly foxed. sg Dec 18 (186) $350

— Termini Botanici iconibus illustrati oder Botanische Kunstsprache.... Berlin, 1799-1807-[1812]. 2 vols in 14 parts. 4to, orig wraps; soiled, a few worn at spines. With 2 hand-colored titles & 69 hand-colored plates. Some spotting. de Belder copy. S Apr 27 (141) £2,600 [Israel]

Haywood, Eliza, 1693?-1756
— The Fortunate Foundlings; being, the Genuine History of Colonel M---rs.... L, 1744. 12mo, contemp calf; front joint cracked, spine chipped at head, lacking front free endpaper. sg Oct 9 (223) $80

Hazelton, William C.
— Ducking Days. Narratives of Duck Hunting. Chicago, 1919. sg Oct 23 (251) $50

Hazelwood, D.
— A Compendious Grammar of the Feejeean Language.... Vewa [Fiji], 1850. 8vo, modern bds. S June 25 (499) £400

Hazlitt, William, 1778-1830
— The Plain Speaker: Opinions on Books.... L, 1826. 1st Ed. 2 vols. 8vo, later half calf; rubbed. Lacking half-titles. cb Oct 23 (108) $55

Anr copy. Later half calf; bottom portion of covers dampstained, affecting text in Vol I. Lacking half-titles. sg Sept 11 (201) $100

— A Reply to the Essay on Population, by the Rev. T. R. Malthus. L, 1807. 8vo, modern calf. Without pp 40-41, as usual; blank marginal portion of tp repaired; small portion of ptr's imprint on verso of tp repaired; tp possibly supplied; browned throughout; library blindstamp on p 37; hole on pp 137 & 174 affecting letters; marginal tear in L1 & Z4. P Sept 24 (301) $500

Head, Sir Francis Bond, 1793-1875. See: Fore-Edge Paintings

Head, Henry
Studies in Neurology. L, 1920. 2 vols. 4to, orig cloth. S May 28 (686) £130

Head, Richard, 1637?-86?
— Proteus Redivivus: or the Art of Wheedling, or Insinuation. L, 1675. 1st Ed. 8vo, modern half lea. Title repaired, 1 leaf badly torn. bba Nov 13 (196) £75 [Clark]

Heads
— Heads of the People: An Illustrated Journal of Literature, Whims and Oddities. Sydney, 1847-48. 2 vols. 4to, contemp half calf; 1 cover detached, worn. bba Oct 30 (98) £45 [Beyer]

Heal, Sir Ambrose
— London Tradesmen's Cards of the XVIII Century. L, 1925. 4to, half cloth; worn. O Nov 18 (83) $80

— The Signboards of Old London Shops. L, 1947. One of 250 L.p. copies. Half mor; scuffed. sg Feb 5 (161) $110

Heaney, Seamus
— Bog Poems. L: Rainbow Press, 1975. One of 150. Illus by Barrie Cooke. 4to, orig half mor. S Sept 22 (94) £180 [Gamble]

Heap, Gwinn Harris, 1817-87
— Central Route to the Pacific... Phila., 1854. 8vo, orig cloth; recased, with new pastedowns although orig ptd pastedowns & free endpapers have been retained as flyleaves. With folding map & 13 plates. Map detached but unchipped. cb Apr 2 (132) $550

Hearn, Lafcadio, 1850-1904
— La Cuisine Creole. A Collection of Culinary Recipes.... NY, [1885]. 1st Ed, 1st State. 8vo, orig cloth; rubbed. Crahan copy. P Nov 25 (242) $750
— Some Chinese Ghosts. Bost., 1887. 1st Ed. 12mo, orig cloth; recased, joints splitting. cb May 7 (94) $75
— Two Years in the French West Indies. NY, 1890. 1st Ed. 12mo, orig cloth. sg Feb 12 (171) $50
— Works. Bost. & NY, 1922. One of 750. 16 vols. half mor. ha May 22 (62) $1,000
   Anr copy. Half clothilt. wa Mar 5 (78) $800

Hearne, Samuel, 1745-92
— A Journey from Prince of Wales's Fort in Hudson's Bay to the Northern Ocean.... L, 1795. 1st Ed. 4to, modern half mor gilt. With folding frontis (partially hand-colored & mtd on linen) & 8 plates & maps, all but 1 folding. Some browning to frontis. bba Oct 16 (235) £1,200 [Way]
   Anr copy. Contemp calf. With 9 folding plates & maps. S Oct 23 (418) £2,000 [Steedman]
   Anr copy. Half calf. With folding map & 8 plans & views, some folding. S May 29 (1086) £1,400
   2d Ed. Dublin, 1796. 8vo, orig bds; spine broken. With 5 folding maps & plans & 4 plates. Perforated & inked library stamps. sg Mar 12 (137) $110

Hearne, Thomas, 1744-1817
— Antiquities of Great-Britain, Illustrated in Views of Monasteries, Castles, and Churches. L, 1786-1807. 2 vols in 1. Oblong 4to, calf; rebacked, rubbed. With engraved title & 83 plates. pn Nov 20 (196) £350 [Mizon]
   Anr copy. Vol I only, in 2 vols. 19th-cent mor gilt, armorial bdg. With 83 plates. S Oct 23 (6) £350 [Walford]

Heath, Charles, 1785-1848. See: Pugin & Heath

Heath, James, 1629-64
— Flagellum, or the Life and Death...of Oliver Cromwell.... L, 1665. 3d Ed. 8vo, modern half mor. Trimmed close, affecting some page numerals. O Feb 24 (99) $700

Heath, Robert, d.1779
— A Natural and Historical Account of the Islands of Scilly. L, 1750. 1st Ed. 8vo, modern calf. L Dec 11 (116) £240

Heath, William, 1737-1814
— Oddities of London Life. By Paul Pry. L, 1838. 2 vols. 8vo, calf gilt by Riviere, orig cloth bound in; Vol I front cover loose. sg Feb 12 (172) $110

Heath, William, 1795-1840
— Fashion and Folly. L, [c.1822]. 4to, contemp mor gilt by Morrell. With 23 (on 12) plates. One plate repaired. T Jan 22 (346) £380

Hebard, Grace R.
— Washakie: An Account of Indian Resistance of the Covered Wagon.... Cleveland, 1930. cb Oct 9 (113) $100

Heber, Reginald, 1783-1826
— Narrative of a Journey through the Upper Provinces of India. L, 1828. 1st Ed. 2 vols. 4to, contemp calf; joints worn. With frontis, folding map & 10 plates. sg Nov 20 (79) $250

Hebrew Books
— The Book of Daily Prayers...According to the Custom of the German and Polish Jews. Phila., 1848. 8vo, contemp calf; scuffed. Minor stains. sg Apr 30 (42) $300
— Buonaventura Mazal Tov Moden. L'Augusto Anniversario dell Nascita di S. M. Napoleone il Grande. Paris, 1806. 8vo, modern lea. bba Feb 19 (158) £420 [Valmadonna]
— Chibur Hamaasiyoth Vehamidrashoth Vehahagadoth. Venice: Giovanni di Gara, 1605. 16mo, modern lea. Tp remargined; some worming. sg Apr 30 (149) $1,600
— L'Elohei Me'ozim Ranei Todot. [N.p.], 1789. 4to, modern cloth. Text in Hebrew & Italian. bba Feb 19 (22) £350 [Valmadonna]
— The Form of Daily Prayers, According to the Custom of the Spanish and Portuguese Jews.... NY, [1826]. 8vo, orig cloth; def, upper cover detached. English tp detached. "The first Hebrew-English prayerbook published in America.". bba Feb 19 (88) £40 [Valmadonna]
— Haggadah. Venice: Bragadini-Calleoni, 1641. 4to, half calf; rubbed. Lacking last 4 leaves; stains; library stamp on title. Yaari 44. bba Feb 19 (96) £260 [Loewy]

Anr Ed. Venice: Bragadin, 1695. Folio, bds; worn. Tp repaired affecting engraving; f.2b repaired affecting border; some inner margins crudely repaired with loss; some shaving & fraying. Yaari 61. S Feb 17 (48) £650 [Valmadonna]

Anr Ed. Franeker: Jacob Horreus, 1698. 8vo, contemp sheep; worn, back cover detached. In Hebrew & Latin. Bound with 3 other works by the translator, Johann Stephen Rittangelius. Yaari 66. sg Sept 25 (96) $7,000

Anr Ed. Berlin: Moshe Yehudah Leib Henau, 1701. 4to, old bds; partly misbound. Trimmed close; some remargining affects text; some worming. Yaari 67. sg Sept 25 (97) $110

Anr Ed. Frankfurt, 1710. Commentary of Aaron Teumim. Folio, modern half vellum. Several leaves remargined; worming to f45 repaired. St. 2710. CAM Dec 3 (64) HF1,300

Anr copy. Modern half mor. Outer margins repaired; some stains & browning. Yaari 71. S Feb 17 (49) £800 [Heiberg]

Anr Ed. Venice, 1716. Folio, modern mor. Some leaves shaved at foot with slight loss; a few margins repaired. Yaari 81. bba Feb 18 (97) £1,700 [Durchlag]

Anr copy. Bds; def. 2 leaves repaired; a few small holes with loss; wine-stained. Yaari 82. S Feb 17 (50) £550 [Rosenfeld]

Anr Ed. Venice, 1740. Folio, half mor. Margin of tp & a few other leaves repaired with some loss. Yaari 116. bba Feb 19 (98) £1,500 [Durchlag]

Anr Ed. Amst., 1764. Commentary of Mordecai ben Yose Yusfa. Folio, old half cloth. 12 rehinged; "heavy victual stains". Yaari 151. sg Sept 25 (98) $110

Anr Ed. Metz, 1767. 4to, old cloth; shaken, some leaves resewn. On O2 title of each of the Ten Plagues written in contemp ink; Ee1 with small tear in outer margin of plate; some stains. sg Sept 25 (101) $125

Anr Ed. Amst.. Gerhard Johann Janson, 1776. 8vo, contemp half vellum; worn. Lacking at least 1 leaf after title; dampwrinkled; stained. Yaari 180. sg Sept 25 (100) $150

Anr Ed. Amst., 1781. 4to, contemp calf; worn. Lacking map of Palestine; stained. bba Feb 19 (101) £180 [Hirschler]

Anr copy. Modern mor. Map mtd; wine stains. Yaari 199. S Feb 17 (52) £800 [Yudkin]

Anr copy. Contemp lea gilt; rebacked, scuffed. Large portion of folding map missing. sg Sept 25 (102) $225

Anr copy. Disbound. Lacking the map; some soiling & staining. Yaari 199. sg Sept 25 (103) $150

Anr Ed. Amst., 1783. 4to, contemp lea; worn & chipped. Some stains & soiling. Yaari 204. sg Sept 25 (104) $200

Anr Ed. Offenbach: Tsvi Hirsch Segal Spitz, [1795?]. 8vo, bds; upper cover detached. Some browning & staining; lower margins of several leaves wormed. Yaari 262. CAM Dec 3 (66) HF600

Anr Ed. L: A. Alexander, 1806. 4to, contemp lea with red mor inlaid label "Samuel Jacobs"; edges worn, rebacked, 1 metal clasp def. With frontis, 7 plates & 4 fold-out maps. Sinai plate with pencil markings; wine stains. Yaari 345. sg Sept 25 (109) $1,500

Anr Ed. L, 1813. 4to, contemp calf; rebacked, chipped, new endpapers. With 2 (of 7) plates; lacking the 3 maps. Plates browned & rebacked with marginal loss. Yaari 381. sg Sept 25 (111) $475

Anr Ed. Amst., 1815-16. 8vo, orig bds on vellum. Some stains. Yaari 399. S Feb 17 (54) £440 [Quaritch]

Anr Ed. Vienna, 1823. 4to, contemp half lea; worn. Some stains & soiling; wormholes at extremities; some taped repairs, affecting text on C2 & N3-4. Yaari 453. sg Sept 25 (112) $150

Anr Ed. Sulzbach: Zekel Orenstein, 1829. 16mo, old cloth; scuffed. Some staining. Yaari 498. sg Sept 25 (114) $250

Anr Ed. L, 1831. 4to, contemp cloth. 1st title & plate loose. Yaari 516. sg Sept 25 (115) $550

Anr Ed. L: Hyam Barnett, 1837. 4to, old cloth; rubbed. With frontis & 6 plates. Trimmed; clean tear at outer corner of final plate not affecting image; some wine stains. sg Sept 25 (117) $750

Anr Ed. Livorno: Ottolenghi, 1838. 4to, contemp half lea; worn. Hole in C2; nicks on outer corner affecting some letters; a few wine stains. Yaari 575. sg Sept 25 (118) $110

Anr Ed. L: J. Wertheimer, 1842. 8vo, contemp cloth; scuffed. Yaari 619. sg Sept 25 (121) $650

Anr Ed. Livorno, 1864. 4to, contemp half mor; shaken. Some tears repaired with tape without loss. sg Sept 25 (123) $325

Anr Ed. Poona, 1874. 8vo, orig cloth; worn. Some browning. In Hebrew & Marathi. Yaari 1077. CAM Dec 3 (68) HF4,500

Anr Ed. Cluj, 1938. Illus by Solomon Yedidiah Seelenfreund. 8vo, half cloth; backstrip frayed, shaken, worn. Some stains. Yaari 2264. sg Sept 25 (121) $650

Anr Ed. L: Beaconsfield Press, [1939]. One of 125, ptd on vellum. Illuminated by Arthur Szyk; ed by Cecil Roth. 4to, orig mor gilt extra by Sangorski & Sutcliffe. S Feb 17 (55) £3,200 [Romain]

Anr Ed. Jerusalem, 1956. Ed by Cecil Roth; illus by Arthur Szyk. 4to, orig velvet gilt. wa Dec 11 (590) $100

Anr Ed. L: Trianon Press, [1966]. One of 228, sgd by artist & with an orig sgd litho. Illus by Ben Shahn. Folio, loose as issued in wraps. sg Sept 25 (129) $1,300

— Kol Bo. Rimini: Gerson Soncino, [1526]. 3d Ed. Folio, half lea. Inner margins of tp & a few leaves strengthened; tp soiled & frayed. St. 3591. CAM Dec 3 (17) HF9,500

— Machsor Lipsiae. [Leipzig, 1964.] Ed by Elias Katz. 2 vols. Folio, mor. With 68 colored facsimile plates. sg Apr 30 (312) $1,400

— Machzor. Vaduz & Jerusalem, 1985. One of 330. Folio, orig bdg. With the introductory volume & the portfolio. sg Apr 30 (316) $1,500

— Machzor Ashkenaz Sha'ar Bat Rabbim. Venice, 1711-15. 2 vols. Folio, half lea. With 2 engraved titles. Cancelled stamps of Hebrew University; some worming with loss of single letters; some stains. St. 2529, cols 386-87. S Feb 17 (76) £850 [Pseisser]

— Machzor shel Kol ha-Shana. Venice: Stamperia Bragadina, 1772. 2 parts in 2 vols. 8vo, later velvet with silver corner mounts, clasps & hinges. sg Apr 30 (137) $600

— Midrash Ha'Mechilta. Venice: Bomberg, 1545. Folio, modern mor. Lacking tp (supplied in facsimile); inner margin of last leaf repaired; some worming at end. bba Feb 19 (142) £300 [Sol]

— Midrash Rabbah. L: Soncino Press, 1939. One of 50. Trans & Ed by H. Freedman & Maurice Simon. 10 vols. Contemp calf gilt. Ck Oct 17 (115) £130

— Midrash Tanchuma. Verona: Messer Francesco de le Donne, 1595. Folio, modern half vellum. Some leaves repaired; some staining & worming. sg Apr 30 (359) $475

— Mishnayot. Amst.: Menasseh ben Israel, 1646. 2 parts in 1 vol. 8vo, old calf; worn. Inner margin of title strengthened; some holes in last leaf. CAM Dec 3 (140) HF1,900

— Pirkei Rabbi Elieser. Venice: Giovanni Zanetti, 1608. 4to, modern half mor. Some stains. St. 4012, col 634. bba Feb 19 (25) £260 [Rosenfeld]

— Ruach Chen. Cremona: Vincenzo Cont, 1566. 4to, modern lea. First 5 leaves frayed, repaired, with some loss; small area of architectural detail on tp added by hand. sg Apr 30 (244) $350

— Seder Hatefilot Mikol Hashana Keminhag Ashkenaz.... Amst., 1804. 8vo, calf; scuffed. sg Apr 30 (306) $425

— Seder Ma'amadot Ve'tuikun Chatzot. Venice: Vendramin, 1687. 12mo, syn. Outer margins of 1st 10 leaves repaired; minor dampstains. Lacking frontis. sg Apr 30 (302) $425

— Seder Olam Zutah. Paris: Martin Juvenis, 1572. 8vo, half vellum. Some stains & spotting. bba Feb 19 (27) £220 [Rosenfeld]

— Sepher Atereth Hachaim. Salonika: Saadia Halevi Ashkenazi, 1841. 8vo, modern bds. Ben Yaakov Ayin 680. sg Sept 25 (81) $175

— Siddur Me'Ha'Ari Zal. Kol Yaakov. Slavita, 1804. 4to, orig lea; repaired. Some worming; tp rehinged & with repairs & stamp. sg Apr 30 (307) $950

— Sidur Mi'bracha Minhag Italiani. Ferrara, 1693. 12mo, modern mor gilt. Some cropping; small rusthole in 1 leaf; some stains & foxing. bba Feb 19 (193) £250 [Quaritch]

— Talmud Yerushalmi. Venice: Bomberg, 1523-24. 4 parts in 1 vol. Folio, modern calf. Washed; several leaves remargined or mtd; some stains; tp soiled, damaged & mtd; worming defs restored. St. 2039. CAM Dec 3 (166) HF16,000

Anr Ed. Krotoschin: Dov Ber Monasch, 1866. Folio, modern lea; front hinge starting. Foxed; tp stamped. sg Sept 25 (291) $250

— Tana De'Vei Eliyahu Rabba Ve'zuta. Venice: D. Zanetti, 1598. 4to, modern calf. Some stains. bba Feb 19 (30) £380 [Schreiber]

— Tefilot Mikol Ha'shanah. Amst.: Joseph & Jacob Proops, 1769. 12mo, orig mor gilt. Foxed. S Feb 17 (114) £350 [Pseisser]

Anr Ed. Amst.: Joseph & Jacob Proops, 1773. 12mo, made-up silver bdg. Sold w.a.f. bba Feb 19 (198) £750 [Schwartz]

— Tephilloth Yisroel/ Gebethe der Israeliten. Vienna: Anton von Schmid, 1835. 8vo, red velour & double metal hem enclosing a glass-fronted embroidery on silk; spine repaired, glass on reverse cracked, new endpapers. Sold as a bdg. sg Sept 25 (51) $1,300

— AARON BEN SAMUEL. - Sepher Beith Aharon. Frankfurt am Oder, 1690. Folio, modern half mor. Tp torn & repaired affecting 1st 5 lines. sg Sept 25 (1) $130

— ABOAB, SHMUEL. - Dvar Shmuel. Venice, 1702. Folio, modern cloth. Repaired worming; some dampstains & soiling;

cropped with occasional loss to headnotes; last leaf repaired on verso; tp stamped; made-up copy. St. 2401/2402. sg Sept 25 (3) $250
— ABRAHAM BEN MEIR ABEN EZRA. - Sepher Klei Nechosheth. Koenigsberg, 1845. 8vo, old half cloth, orig wraps bound in. Owner's stamp on tp. Zedner 21. sg Sept 25 (9) $175
— ABRAHAM BEN MORDECHAI. - Sepher Yair Nethiv. Constantinople, 1718. 4to, modern half calf. Tear at top of leaf 19 affecting a few letters; blank portion of final leaf cleanly torn. Yaari 293. sg Sept 25 (10) $110
— ABRAHAM ZACUTO. - Yuchasin. Cracow, 1581. 4to, modern mor. Outer margin of tp strengthened without loss; some browning & stains. St. 4303.3, col 707. bba Feb 19 (228) £500 [Rosenfeld]
— ABRAMOWITSCH, SHALOM JACOB. - Sepher Toldoth Hateva. Leipzig, 1862; Zhitomir, 1866 & Vilna, 1872. Folio, orig bds; broken. Some stains; scattered owner's stamps. Cowley 427. sg Sept 25 (239) $130
— ABRAVANEL, ISAK. - Ateret Zekeinim. Sabbioneta: Tuvia Foa, 1557. 4to, modern mor gilt. Some stains; stamp on title, uncensored but sgd by censor in 1607. bba Feb 19 (1) £500 [Field]
— ABRAVANEL, ISAK. - Mashmia Yeshua. Amst., 1644. 4to, old vellum; worn. Tp soiled; some stains & browning. St. 5302.36 & 6288.2. CAM Dec 3 (3) HF300
— ABRAVANEL, ISAK. - Peirush al Neviim Rishonim. Hamburg: Thomas Rose, 1686. Folio, contemp calf; rubbed. Library stamps; some stains & browning. St. 5302.6. CAM Dec 3 (4) HF650
Anr Ed. Leipzig & Frankfurt: Franciscus Varrentrapp, [1686-1736]. Folio, later half sheep. First 14 signatures with taped wormholes; tp remargined, with owner's stamp; lacking Latin preface & indexes. sg Apr 30 (3) $140
— ABRAVANEL, ISAK. - Peirush Ha'Torah. Venice: Juan Bragadin & Asher Frenzoni, 1579. Folio, lea. Inner margins repaired; owner's stamp on tp; some worming at end. St. 5301.1, col 1077. S Feb 17 (1) £550 [Heiner]
Anr Ed. Hanau, 1710. Folio, modern half lea. Stained & browned; lacking final leaf; small loss to 1st title; partially misbound. sg Sept 25 (5) $120
— ABRAVANEL, ISAK. - Pirush al Nevi'im Rishonim. Hamburg: Thomas Rose, 1687. Folio, modern lea. 1st 2 leaves with minor tears repaired. Cowley 255. sg Sept 25 (4) $150
— ABRAVANEL, ISAK. - Zevach Pessach. Venice: Marco Antonio Giustiniani, 1545. 4to,

modern mor. Trimmed; stained; upper margins repaired not affecting text. Yaari 10, p 2. S Feb 17 (2) £1,000 [Yudkin]
— ALBO, JOSEPH. - Ikkarim. Venice: P. & L. Bragadin, 1618. Folio, contemp calf over wooden bds; rubbed. St. 5882.7. CAM Dec 3 (9) HF850
— ALMOSNINO, MOSHE. - Ma'amatz Koach. Venice: Juan di Gara, 1588. 1st Ed. 4to, modern mor gilt. Tp mtd & repaired; some stains. St. 340c., col 57. S Feb 17 (6) £200 [Schreiber]
— ALSHEICH, MOSHE. - Chavatzelet Ha'Sharon. Venice: Giovanni di Gara, 1591. 4to, modern calf. Library stamp on tp. bba Feb 19 (13) £330 [Ben Schmuel]
— ALSHEICH, MOSHE. - Chelkat Mechokek...Job. Venice, 1603. 4to, old bds. Some shaving. sg Apr 30 (13) $250
— ALSHEICH, MOSHE. - Einei Moshe. Venice: Giovanni di Gara, 1601. 4to, modern vellum; dampstained. First 7 leaves apparently from anr copy. St. 340c, col 57. sg Apr 30 (12) $375
— ALSHEICH, MOSHE. - Rav Paninim. Venice: Giovanni di Gara, 1601. 4to, half lea; worn. Some stains. St. 346, col 58. S Feb 17 (8) £400 [Pseisser]
— ALSHEICH, MOSHE. - Shoshanat Ha'Amakim. Venice: Giovanni di Gara, 1591. 4to, modern mor. Contemp marginal notes; some stains. St. 296, col 51. bba Feb 19 (17) £240 [Sol]
— ARCHEVOLTI, SCHMUEL. - Arugat Ha'Bosem. Venice: Giovanni di Gara, 1602. 4to, modern calf. With 2 leaves wormed & repaired with slight loss; signature erased from title. St. 7004.3. bba Feb 19 (35) £260 [Schreiber]
— ARIPOL, SHMUEL. - Mizmor Letodah. Prague, 1610. 4to, modern mor. Tp soiled, damaged & inlaid; stamps on title; several leaves remargined or inlaid. St. 390. CAM Dec 3 (22) HF800
— ARIPOL, SHMUEL. - Sepher Mizmor Lethodah. Venice: Juan di Gara, 1576. 4to, needs rebdg. Wormed, affecting text; some stains. Cowley 606. sg Sept 25 (27) $250
— ARON BEREC HIA BEN MOSHE OF MODENA. - Maavar Yabek. Mantua: Yehuda Shmuel of Perugia, 1626. 4to, cloth. Some stains & worming; outer margin of 3 leaves torn with loss. St. 4348.1, col 718. bba Feb 19 (36) £190 [Schreiber]
— ARON SHIMON VEN YAKOV ABRAHAM. - Or Ha'yashar. Amst.: Janson & Mondavi, 1769. 8vo, contemp sheep; scuffed. Tear in margin of 1 leaf, affecting a few letters. sg Apr 30 (2) $200
— ASHER BEN YECHIEL, ROSH. - She'eilot U'Teshuvot. Venice, 1552. Folio, calf. St. 4455.28, col 751. bba Feb 19 (39) £700

HEBREW BOOKS

[Rosenfeld]
— ASHKENAZI, JUDAH SAMUEL. - Sepher Geza Yishai, Sepher Rishon. Livorno, 1842. Folio, orig half lea; worn. Some worming, affecting a few letters. Zedner 58. sg Sept 25 (30) $150
— ASHKENAZI, JUDAH SAMUEL. - Sepher Yisa Berachah. Livorno: Yaakov Tuviana, 1822. Folio, contemp half lea; worn. Some worming, affecting letters. Zedner 322. sg Sept 25 (31) $300
— ASHKENAZI, SAMUEL YAPHO. - Sepher Yephei Anaph. Frankfurt am Oder: Michel Gottschalk, 1696. Folio, contemp vellum. Zedner 541. sg Sept 25 (32) $200
— ASHKENAZI, TZVI. - Chacham Tzvi. Fuerth, 1767. Folio, modern bds. Gutter reinforced; dampstained; marginal punctures. Zedner 763. sg Sept 25 (33) $100
— AVERROES IBN RUSHD. - Kol Mlechet Higayon. Riva di Trento: Yakov Mercaria, 1559. 8vo, modern half vellum. First leaf repaired with loss of a few letters; 2 outer margins shaved; some small wormholes repaired; some waterstains. St. 4485.16. bba Feb 19 (45) £400 [Freedman]
— AZULAI, CHAIM JOSEPH DAVID. - Sepher Machzik Berachah. Livorno, 1785. Folio, syn. Dampstained; 1st few leaves rehinged. Roest 122; Zedner 68. sg Sept 25 (34) $150
— BARUCH BEN ISAAC IBN YAISH. - Sepher Mekor Baruch. Constantinople: Eliezer ben Yitzchak Aschkenazi, 1576. Folio, modern lea. Some worming & fraying; each leaf silked. sg Apr 30 (225) $4,800
— BARUCH IBN YA'ISH. - Mekor Baruch. Constantinople: Eliezer Ashkenzai, 1576. Folio, modern cloth. Some stains & soiling. sg Apr 30 (173) $350
— BARUCH, JACOB BEN MOSES CHAYIM. - Shivchei Yerushalayim. Livorno, 1785. 8vo, modern bds. Cowley 290. sg Sept 25 (35) $200
— BASS, SABTAI. - Siftei Yesheinim. Amst., 1680. 1st Ed. 4to, early calf; worn. Tp soiled & stamped; some stains. St. 6862.4. CAM Dec 3 (24) A$700

Anr copy. Modern cloth. Cellotape repairs to 2 pp; some notes. sg Apr 30 (113) $475
— BENJAMIN BEN JONA OF TUDELA. - Masa'ot Shel Rabi Benjamin.... Leiden: Elzevier, 1633. 12mo, old vellum. St. 4570.4. CAM Dec 3 (25) HF900
— BENJAMIN BEN JONAH OF TUDELA. - Masaoth shel Rabbi Binyamin. Leiden: Elzevir, 1633. 12mo, contemp vellum; headband starting. Contemp marginalia & annotations. sg Sept 25 (36) $350
— BENJAMIN OF ZALOSHITZ. - Amtachat Benjamin. Minkowitz, 1796. 4to, half cloth; worn. Some stains; inner margin of 1st 2 & lower margin of last leaf torn, slightly affecting text. bba Feb 19 (52) £130

AMERICAN BOOK PRICES CURRENT

[Landau]
— BENJAMIN OF ZOLOZITZ. - Torei Zahav. Mohilev, 1816. 4to, modern lea. Some worming; last few leaves heavily stained. bba Feb 19 (53) £180 [Schwartz]
— BEZALEL BEN SOLOMON DARSHAN. - Sepher Korban Shabbath. Dyhernfurth, 1691. 4to, modern half calf. Some leaves trimmed or wormed slightly, affecting text; tp stamped; final blank silked. sg Sept 25 (38) $175
— BRACHA, ISAK. - Beirach Yitzhak. Venice, 1763. Folio, modern cloth. Some margins frayed; some stains, particularly at beginning & end; lower margin torn without affecting border. St. 5321, col 1096. bba Feb 19 (224) £130 [Sol]
— BRODA, ABRAHAM BEN SAUL. - Eshel Avraham. Frankfurt, 1747. Folio, old bds; scuffed. Some worming & staining. sg Sept 25 (52) $100
— CANPANTON, ISAK. - Darchei Ha'Gemara. Mantua: Tomaso Rufinelli, 1593. 4to, modern lea. Some stains. St. 5326.3. bba Feb 19 (225) £180 [Schreiber]
— CASTRO, JACOB. - Sepher Mohrika'sh Hanikra Oruch Lechem. Constantinople, 1718. 4to, old half lea gilt; worn. Wormed; remargined, occasionally affecting a few letters. Yaari 294. sg Sept 25 (55) $250
— CHAGIZ, MOSES BEN JACOB. - Sefat Emet. Amst.: Shlomo Proops, 1707. 8vo, contemp vellum; warped & worn. Tiny wormhole in f28; short copy. St. 6447.17. CAM Dec 3 (52) HF400
— CHAIM VITAL. - Sepher Hagilgulim. Frankfurt, 1684. 4to, modern half calf. Browned; light dampstains. sg Sept 25 (333) $200
— CHAYUTH, EPHRAIM BEN ABRAHAM. - Sepher Eshel Avraham. Livorno, 1819. Folio, modern cloth. Some leaves rehinged or remargined; foxed. sg Sept 25 (66) $150
— COHEN, ABRAHAM. - Kehunat Abraham. Venice, 1719. 4to, recent calf. St. 4302.1, col 706. bba Feb 19 (76) £450 [Gans]

Anr copy. Old calf. With port & plate of the heavenly bodies. Some stains & worming, affecting single letters. St. 4302.1, col 706. CAM Dec 3 (6) HF800
— COHEN, ISAAC BEN MEIR. - Zivchei Cohen. Livorno, 1832. 4to, contemp half vellum. With 7 fold-out woodcuts, 1 sewed at opening. sg Sept 25 (67) $325
— DAVID BEN SOLOMON GANS. - Tzemah. Frankfurt, 1692. 2 parts in 1 vol. 4to, half lea. Tp stamped. St. 4805.4. sg Sept 25 (93) $130
— DROHOBICZER, ISRAEL NACHMAN. - Kuntres Pekudath Hamelech. Livorno, 1804. 2 vols in 1. 4to, Modern bds. Some worming. sg Sept 25 (79) $110

— ELIESER BEN ELIJAH ASHKENAZI. - Peirush Megillat Esther. Cremona: Cristofero Draconi, 1576. 4to, modern calf. Light stains; title border repaired with slight loss at foot. St. 4980.1, col 354. bba Feb 19 (41) £420 [Rosenfeld]
— ELIJAH BEN JOSEPH SHAMMA. - Kuntres Machshirei Milah. Livorno, 1793. 8vo, modern half calf. Zedner 695. sg Sept 25 (278) $110
— ELIJAH BEN KALONYMUS. - Sepher Adereth Eliyahu. Frankfurt am Oder, 1694. 4to, modern cloth. Some browning. Zedner 229. sg Sept 25 (83) $140
— ELIJAH GAON. - Peirush Al Jonah. Wilno: Wichnusnega Kanonika, 1000. 4to, modern half cloth. A few words def at beginning of last page; lower margin repaired without loss; some stains. bba Feb 19 2l82 £55 [Kahn]
— ELIJAH LEVITA. - Masoret Ha'masoret. Venice: D. Bomberg, 1538. 4to, old half lea; worn. Some stains. St. 4960.20. CAM Dec 3 (101) HF800
— ELIJAH LEVITA. - Pirkei Elijah. Basel: Froben, 1527. 8vo, modern half vellum. Tp extended & stained; several other leaves extended; some notes. St. 4960.37. CAM Dec 3 (102) HF1,300

Anr copy. Early vellum; worn & wormed. Some dampstaining. S Nov 27 (159) £550 [Valmadonna]

— ERGAS, JOSEPH. - Divrei Joseph. Livorno, 1742. Folio, contemp vellum; repaired & stained. Small piece from tp excised; puncture in last leaf. St. 1457. sg Sept 25 (87) $120
— ERGAS, JOSEPH. - Shomer Emunim; Mavo Petachim. Amst., 1736. 4to, contemp calf. Some worming in lower margin. St. 5915.2-3. CAM Dec 3 (58) HF600
— EYBESCHUETZ, JONATHAN BEN NATHAN NATA. - Sefer Kreiti u-Pleiti. Altona, 1763. Folio, contemp calf; broken & scuffed. Tp stamped. St. 5867.6, Col 1432. sg Sept 25 (88) $200
— EYBESCHUETZ, JONATHAN BEN NATHAN. - Sepher Ahavath Yohathan. Hamburg, 1765-66. 4to, contemp lea; worn. Lacking final blank, some browning. Cowley 324. sg Sept 25 (89) $250
— FRIEDLANDER, SOLOMON JUDAH. - Seder Kodshim; Chelek Rishon.... Szinervaralja: Jacob Vider, 1907-9. 2 vols. Folio, needs rebdg. First 4 pp heavily creased & shaved with occasional loss of text; at least 1 prelim leaf lacking; some prelim leaves may be from anr copy; sporadic fraying; 2 leaves misbound. Literary forgery. sg Sept 25 (292) $175
— GERSHOM BEN SHLOMO OF CATALONIA. - Sepher Shar Hashamayim. Zolkiew: Gershon Leteris, 1805. 8vo, contemp half lea; worn & scuffed. Censor's stamp on tp verso; clean tear in lower part of N1 not affecting text. Friedberg Shin 2042. sg Sept 25 (94) $150
— GERSHOM BEN SHLOMO OF CATALONIA. - Sha'ar Ha'Shamaim. Venice: Meir ben Yakov Parenzo, 1547. 4to, half lea. Lacking index; marginal repairs on last 2 leaves not affecting text; some stains. St. 5139.1, cols 1014-16. S Feb 17 (46) £300 [Wyler]
— HAI GAON. - Mekach Ve'hamemkar. Venice: G. Di Gara, 1602. 4to, old half lea. Tp soiled & inner margin strengthened; some stains & browning; inner margin of f.97 torn. St. 3183.1, Col 1027-28. CAM Dec 3 (72) HF900
— HEILPERN, YAKOV. - Nachlat Yakov. Padua, 1623. 4to, modern cloth. Stained. St. 5538.2, col 1214. bba Feb 19 (106) £260 [Rosenfeld]
— HOROWITZ, ISAIAH. - Shnei Luchot Ha'brit [Shelah]. Amst., 1698. Folio, modern half calf. Tp repaired without loss; some stains & browning; library stamps. St. 5808.6, col 1387-88. bba Feb 19 (107) £420 [Jungreis]

Anr copy. Contemp blind-stamped lea over wooden bds; worn, backstrip & clasps missing. Marginal worming; some stains; signature & library stamp on tp. bba Feb 19 (108) £700 [Sol]

Anr copy. Contemp calf gilt over wooden bds; worn, clasps missing. Marginal worming in 1st leaves. St. 5808.10, col 1388. CAM Dec 3 (77) HF2,200

Anr copy. Contemp blind-tooled calf over wooden bds; scuffed. Some staining. St. 5808.10, col 1388. CAM Dec 3 (78) HF2,400

— ISAAC ALFASI. - Sepher Shailoth Uteshuvoth. Livorno, 1781. 4to, modern bds. Stained & wormed, not affecting text. Cowley 260. sg Sept 25 (14) $100
— ISAAC BEN ABRAHAM AKRISH. - Kovetz Vikuchim. Breslau, 1844. 16mo, modern half calf. Pencil markings on 2d title; some stains. Roest 463; Zedner 362. sg Sept 25 (11) $110
— ISAAC BEN MOSES ARAMAH. Akedat Yitzhak. Venice: Bomberg, 1547. Folio, half calf. Marginal worming, uncensored but sgd by censor in 1685. St. 5312.5. bba Feb 19 (32) £1,000 [Field]
— ISAAC BEN MOSES ARAMAH. - Akedat Yizhak. Venice: Juan di Gara, 1573. Folio, modern calf. Outer margin of tp repaired affecting border; upper margin of 6 leaves repaired with loss of text; outer margins of index repaired without loss; some stains. St. 5312.7. bba Feb 19 (34) £400 [Kahn]
— ISAAC BEN MOSES. - Sepher Hachizayon.

HEBREW BOOKS

Berlin, 1775?. 8vo, half cloth. With 2 fold-out plates with 4 shaped poems. Tp stamped. Roest 478. sg Sept 25 (273) $130
— Isaac ibn Sahula. - Sepher Moshal Hakadmoni. Frankfurt: Professor Elsner, 1800. 8vo, needs rebdg. Lacking 1st table; some tears or marks occasionally affecting text. Friedberg Mem 3893. sg Sept 25 (161) $275
— Isachar Baer of Austerlitz. - Zeida La'Derech. Prague: Bnei Yakov Bak, 1621. Folio, modern half mor. Outer margin of last 4 leaves repaired; other margins cut close with occasional loss; some worming at beginning; tp stained yellow. St. 5279, 4 col 1061. bba Feb 19 (111) £300 [HIrschler]
— Israel ben Azriel of Shklov. - Pe'at Ha'shulchan. Safed, 1836. Folio, recent cloth. First 5 leaves from a shorter copy. St. 5449.1, col 1163. bba Feb 19 (112) £120 [Annenberg]
— Jacob ben Ascher. - Arba'a Turim. Soncino: Schlomo ben Moshe Soncino, [1490]. Parts 3 & 4 in 1 vol. Folio, half calf. Some worming, annotations & other defs. 112 leaves only. Goff Heb-48. FD Dec 2 (76) DM4,500
— Jacob ben Ascher. - Tur Choshen Mishpat. Sabbioneta: Tuvia Foa, 1559. Folio, modern cloth. Repairs to tp & 1st 4 leaves with loss; margins of last 2 leaves repaired with loss; some worming & other repairs with loss. St. 5500.41. S Feb 17 (119) £500 [Pseisser]
— Jacob ben Asher. - Tur Yore De'ah. Venice, 1574. Folio, bds; worn. Tp & anr leaf detached; headlines cropped at beginning. bba Feb 19 (211) £420 [Schreiber]

Anr copy. Cloth. Tp partly mutilated & repaired affecting engraving; 1 index leaf torn not affecting text; some worming. St. 5500.34, col 1189. S Feb 17 (125) £260 [Hoffman]
— Jeshua ben Joseph Halevi. - Halichoth Olam. Venice; Juani di Fari, 1544. 4to, modern calf. Some margins reinforced; wormed affecting text; owner's stamps on tp & E3. Cowley 319. sg Sept 25 (166) $225
— Jose ben Chalfta. - Seder Olam Rabba Ve'Seder Olam Zuta-Megillat Ta'anit. Mantua: [Samuel ibn Latig], 1513. 4to, modern calf. Some stains. bba Feb 19 (26) £950 [Heitner]
— Joseph ben Moshe. - Beur al Sefer Mitzvot Gadol. Venice, 1605. 4to, modern vellum. Margins of 1st 2 leaves & tp badly frayed; 1st 2 leaves detached; some stains. St. 5945.1, col 1501. bba Feb 19 (114) £140 [Schreiber]
— Joseph ibn Gikatilia. - Sha'arei Orah. Riva di Trento, [Yakov Mercaria, 1561].

AMERICAN BOOK PRICES CURRENT

4to, modern mor. Some worming & stains. St. 5923.10, cols 1465-66. bba Feb 19 (95) £380 [Schwarzschild]
— Judah ben Chanin. - Sepher Eitz Hachaim. Livorno, 1783. Folio, contemp half lea; spine ends torn. Some foxing. Friedberg Ayin 1024. sg Sept 25 (170) $120
— Kalonymos ben Kalonymos. - Even Bohan. Venice: Cornelio Adelkind, 1546. 4to, half lea. Marginal notes; ff. 57-88 only. St. 6068.2, col 1579. bba Feb 19 (118) £30 [Annenberg]
— Karo, Joseph. - Bedek Ha'Bayit. Venice: Zanetti, 1606. 4to, modern half mor. Lacking the 2 unnumbered leaves; some headlines shaved. St. 5940.105, col 1495. bba Feb 19 (120) £300 [Schreiber]
— Karo, Joseph. - Shulchan Aruch - Bet Joseph. Cracow: Yitzhak Prostitz, 1583-91. 4 parts in 1 vol. Folio, half lea. Some stains; margins of last 2 leaves repaired with loss. St. 5940.8 & 10, col 1482. S Feb 17 (68) £350 [Heitner]
— Karo, Joseph. - Shulchan Aruch. Mantua, 1722-23. Commentaries of Moshe Isserles & Gur Arye Ha'Levi. 4 vols. 4to, cloth. Some worming & staining. bba Feb 19 (121) £480 [Schreiber]
— Katzenellenbogen, Samuel Judah. - Shneim Asar Drashot. Venice: Giovanni di Gara, 1594. 4to, bds; rubbed. Some stains. St. 7047.1, col 2432-3. bba Feb 19 (124) £320 [Rosenfeld]
— Kimchi, David ben Joseph. - Sefer Michlol. Venice, 1545. 8vo, contemp vellum. Tp partly detached. St. 4821.41. CAM Dec 3 (92) HF1,900
— Kimchi, David ben Joseph. - Sefer Miklol: Helek ha-Dikduk. Constantinople: Soncino, 1532-34. 4to, lea; scuffed. Some stamps; tp margins damaged & mtd; browning & staining. St. 4821.37. CAM Dec 3 (91) HF6,000
— Landau, Jacob Baruch ben Judah. - Sefer Agur. [Rimini: Gershom ben Moses Soncino], 1526. 4to, syn. Several inner margins strengthened; tp border wormed, affecting words on verso; other worming affecting single letters on ff. 101 & 102; some stains. St. 5564.2. CAM Dec 3 (96) HF13,000
— Levi ben Gershon. - Milchamot Hashem. Riva di Trento, 1560. Folio, modern mor. Margins of tp & some other leaves repaired; some worming & stains; library stamp on tp. St. 6138.2. bba Feb 19 (131) £550 [Freedman]

Anr copy. Modern lea. Some stains & browning. St. 6138.8. CAM Dec 3 (100) HF700
— Levi ben Gershon. - Toaliyot Ha'ralbag. Riva di Trento: Joseph Ottolenghi, 1560. 1st Ed. 4to, modern half lea. Lacking last

blank; piece cut from blank margin of tp. St. 6138.3, col 1611. bba Feb 19 (130) £200 [Schreiber]
— LEVI IBN CHABIB. - She'eilot U'teshuvot. Venice: Juan di Gara, 1565. 1st Ed. Folio, modern mor. Lower margin wormed & repaired not affecting title; some worming, affecting a few letters. St. 6136.2. S Feb 17 (34) £400 [Stern]
— LIWA YEHUDA BEN BEZALEL. - Drush Na'e. Prague: Mordecai Kohen, 1589. 4to, later half cloth. Shaved. bba Feb 19 (217) £800 [Schwartz]
— LIWA YEHUDA BEN BEZALEL. - Gvurot Ha'Shem. Cracow: Isaac ben Aaron, 1581-82. Folio, modern half mor. Lacking the Kuntras Yayin Nesech; tp repaired, affecting border; last leaf repaired, affecting a few words; some blank corners torn or frayed; light stains. St. 6153.3, col 1620. bba Feb 19 (218) £1,100 [Landau]
— LIWA YEHUDA BEN BEZALEL. - Tiferet Israel. Venice: Daniel Zanetti, 1599. 1st Ed. Folio, half lea. Inner margin of tp repaired affecting engraving; outer margins of some leaves repaired; some worming with occasional loss of single letters. St. 6153.14, col 1622. S Feb 17 (127) £380 [Sol]
— LUZZATO, EPHRAIM. - Eile bne Ha'neurim. L, 1766. One of 100. 4to, bds; rubbed. Library stamps. CAM Dec 3 (121) HF2,800
— LUZZATTO, MOSES CHAYIM. - Leshon Limudim. Mantua: Raphael d'Italia, 1727. 8vo, old calf; rebacked. Minor worming in lower margin of some leaves; tp soiled. CAM Dec 3 (123) HF700
— LUZZATTO, MOSES CHAYIM. - Mesilat Yesharim. Mantua, 1781. 8vo, mor gilt. Some browning. St. 6511.6. CAM Dec 3 (124) HF1,000
— MARGALIOTH, EPHRAIM SOLOMON. - Sepher Shaarei Ephraim—Pithchei Shearim. Dubno, 1820. 4to, modern cloth. First few pages stained & soiled. sg Sept 25 (233) $110
— MEIR ARAMA. - Urim Ve'tumim. Venice, 1603. 4to, old calf over wooden bds. Some browning & discoloration. ST. 6291.1. CAM Dec 3 (21) HF800
— MEIR BEN BARUCH OF ROTHENBURG. - Sheilot U'Teshuvot. Prague: Mordecai & Moshe ben Joseph Bezalel Katz, 1608. Folio, modern half mor. Slight worming. St. 6323.3, col 1714. bba Feb 19 (138) £400 [Rosenfeld]
— MEIR BEN GEDALIAH OF LUBLIN. - Sheilot Uteshuvot. Venice, 1618. Folio, modern cloth. Minor staining; inner margin of tp repaired. St. 6314.5, col 1706. bba Feb 19 (139) £600 [Quaritch]
— MEIR BEN ZE'EV. - Kuntress Kiriath Sepher. Ostrog, 1860. 8vo, modern bds. Foxed.

Roest 780. sg Sept 25 (236) $150
— MEIR IBN ISAK ALDABI. - Shvilei Emunah. Amst.: Daniel de Fonseca, 1627. 4to, half vellum; rubbed. Library stamps; tp soiled; some worming. St. 6288.2, col 1691. CAM Dec 3 (10) HF2,200
— MENACHEM AZARIA DI FANO. - Teshuvot. Venice: Daniele Zanetti, [c.1600]. 4to, modern lea. Some worming affecting text; a few stains. St. 6342.30. bba Feb 19 (141) £160 [Hirschler]
— MENACHEM MANN BEN PHOEBUS. - Sepher Tzentzeneth Hamon. Offenbach, 1723. Folio, modern cloth. Some browning & dampstaining. Cowley 427. sg Sept 25 (238) $130
— MENASSEH BEN ISRAEL. - Nishmat Chaim. Amst., 1651. 4to, old vellum. Library stamp on both titles; some browning. St. 6205.1, cols 1645-46. CAM Dec 3 (138) HF2,400

Anr Ed. Amst., 1652. 4to, old lea. Lower margins cropped; lacking Latin title & 4 Latin pp. S Feb 17 (79) £600 [Mandanes]
— MORTERA, SAUL. - Givat Shaul. Amst., 1645. 4to, contemp lea; worn. Upper margin of title damaged; library stamps; some stains. St. 7100.1. CAM Dec 3 (143) HF650
— MOSHE. - Sefer Mitzvot Gadol-Semag. Venice: Daniel Bomberg, 1522. Folio, half lea; worn. Tp & first 8 leaves repaired; some fraying & staining. Steinschneider 6453.3, col 1797. S Feb 17 (86) £1,100 [Heitner]
— MOSHE BEN JACOB OF COUCY. - Sefer Mitsvot Gadol. Soncino: Gershom Soncino, 19 Dec 1488. Folio, modern half calf. Partly misbound; 1 leaf repaired with tape; some corners restored; last 13 leaves worn at top affecting a few words; some worming; some stamps. 237 (of 279) leaves. Goff Heb-85. sg Apr 30 (279) $6,750
— MOSHE BEN JOSEPH OF TRANI. - Bet Elohim. Venice: Juan di Gara, 1576. 1st Ed. Folio, modern lea. Tp remargined & with owner's signatures & stamp; final leaf mtd; stained & dampwrinkled. St. 2007.6577.2. sg Apr 30 (280) $325
— MOSHE RUMI. - Sha'arei Gan Eden. Venice: Giovanni di Gara, 1589. Part 1 only. 4to, modern half lea. Some worming with loss. S Feb 17 (89) £600 [Sol]
— MUSSAPHIA, BENJAMIN BEN IMMANUEL. - Zecher Rav / Memoria Multa. Hamburg, 1638. 4to, modern half mor. Cowley 66. sg Sept 25 (248) $325
— NAGARA, ISRAEL. - Zemirot Israel. Venice: Giovanni di Gara, 1599-1605. 4 parts in 1 vol. 4to, 19th-cent mor gilt. Lacking last leaf; library stamps on 1st title. St. 5475.2. bba Feb 19 (156) £1,000 [Heitner]
— NATHAN BEN JECHIEL. - He'aruch. Venice:

Aloys & Pietro Bragadin, 1553. Folio, half lea. 1 leaf in Ms; inner margin of 1 leaf repaired with loss; other repairs; some worming. St. 6632.4, col 2041-42. S Feb 17 (92) £260 [Schreiber]
— NATHAN BEN JEHIEL OF ROME. - Sefer ha-Arukh. Basel: Conrad Waldkirch, 1599. Folio, half lea; rubbed. Wormed throughout, affecting single letters; some stains. St. 6632.5. CAM Dec 3 (146) HF650

Anr copy. Orig vellum; rebacked. Inner margin repaired not affecting title; some worming with loss of single letters. St. 6632.5, col 2042. S Feb 17 (93) £200 [Pseisser]
— NIETO, DAVID BEN PHINEHAS. - Mateh Dan-Kuzari Sheini. L: Thomas Iliffe, 1714. 4to, early vellum; stained. Some foxing; wormed in inner margins of last few leaves. St. 4834.5. CAM Dec 3 (147) HF2,400
— NINO, JACOB SHEALTIEL. - Sepher Emeth Leya'akov. Livorno, 1843. Folio, modern bds. Inscr. sg Sept 25 (250) $140
— NISSIM GERONDI. - Shneim Asar Drashot. Venice: Juan di Gara & Juan Bragadin, 1596. 2d Ed. 4to, contemp blind-stamped calf over wooden bds. Some headlines or catchwords just shaved; light waterstains. bba Feb 19 (161) £350 [Rosenfeld]
— PARDO, DAVID BEN JACOB. - Sepher Michtam Ledavid. Salonika, 1772. Folio, half lea. Lower outer corners frayed; wormed with loss. sg Sept 25 (253) $150
— RECANATI, MENAHEM. - Piskei Halachot. Bologna, 1538. Folio, 4to, modern mor. Upper corner of tp & upper margin of last leaf restored without loss; some stains. St. 6363.3, col 1737. bba Feb 19 (168) £600 [Rosenfeld]
— REUVEN BEN HOESCHKE. - Yalkut Reuveni. Prague, 1655. 4to, contemp calf; rubbed, lacking clasps. Some worming; 4 leaves detached; inscr & library stamp on tp. bba Feb 19 (169) £280 [Leowy]
— RICCHI, RAPHAEL IMMANUEL CHAI. - Zeh Sepher Adereth Eliyahu. Livorno, 1742. 2 vols in 1. 4to, modern half calf. Small oval area of tp erased & restored with minor loss of border. sg Sept 25 (269) $110
— ROTHENBURG, MORDECAI ZISKIND. - Shailoth Teshuvoth Chelek Rishon. Hamburg: Johann Rose, 1716. 4to, modern half calf. Dampwrinkled; minor staining; 2 minimal tears not affecting text. Roest 974. sg Sept 25 (271) $130
— SAADIAH GAON. - Sefer Hatchia Ve'sefer Ha'pedut. Mantua: Venturi Rufinelli, 1556. 12mo, modern calf. Inner margins strengthened; last leaf in facsimile. St. 6855.8, col 2179-80. S Feb 17 (100) £650 [Sol]
— SAMIGA, JOSEPH. - Mikraei Kodesh. Venice, 1586. 4to, modern half mor. Dust-stained

& with short tear in margin. St. 5990.2, col 1523. bba Feb 19 (176) £320 [Hirschler] Anr copy. Modern mor. Some stains. S Feb 17 (101) £300 [Kimche]
— SASPORTAS, YAKOV. - Sepher Ohel Yaakov. Amst., 1737. Folio, modern lea. Owner's stamp & small area excised on tp not affecting letters; lacking, as usual the Kitzur Tzitzath Novel Tzvi. sg Sept 25 (272) $225
— SCHIFF, MEIR BEN JACOB. - Sepher Chidushei Halachoth. Homburg, 1737. Folio, modern lea. Tp creased; corners dog-eared; some stains. sg Sept 25 (276) $120
— SCHLOMO IBN ADRET. - Torat Ha'Bayit. Cremona: Vincenzo Conti, 1565. 4to, modern half mor. Last 3 leaves repaired with loss; trimmed, occasionally affecting headnotes; stained; some worming. sg Apr 30 (348) $475
— SHIMSHON MORPURGO. - Shemesh Zedakah. Venice, 1743. Folio, contemp vellum. Some staining & marginal worming; library stamp on 2d title. St. 7239.2, col 2638. bba Feb 19 (148) £160 [Rosenfeld]
— SHLOMO ALMOLI. - Pitron Halomot. Amst.: Manasseh ben Israel, 1637. 8vo, library bdg. Some stains; library stamps; 3 leaves mutilated. St. 6896.6. CAM Dec 3 (12) HF2,400
— SHMUEL YAFO ASHKENAZI. - Yefe Mar'eh. Venice: Giovanni di Gara - Asher Parenz, 1590. Folio, modern mor gilt. Tp laid down without loss; some stains; index lacking. St. 7037.1. bba Feb 19 (42) £400 [Ben Schmuel]
— SHMUEL YAFO ASHKENAZI. - Yefe To'Ar. Constantinople: Shlomo & Abraham Franko, 1648. Folio, modern mor. Margins of 1st & last leaves repaired, just affecting text; 2 headlines shaved; tp laid down & stained; library stamps on title. St. 3779, col 495. bba Feb 19 (43) £300 [Sol]
— SIMNER, ZECHARIAH BEN JACOB. - Sepher Zechirah. Wilhermsdorf, 1729. 8vo, modern cloth. Some remarking with text added in Ms where necessary; wormed at end. sg Sept 25 (279) $100
— SOLOMON BEN ISAAC YITZCHAKI, RASHI. - Sefer Ha'Pardes. Constantinople, 1802. Folio, half lea. Some stains. St. 6972.74, cols 2354-55. S Feb 17 (108) £150 [Annenberg]
— SOLOMON BEN ABRAHAM ALGAZI. - Sepher Ahavath Olam. Constantinople, 1642. Folio, old half lea; worn & chipped. Wormed & stained; some clean tears & crude repairs, occasionally affecting text. Yaari 243. sg Sept 25 (13) $200
— SOMMERHAUSEN, HIRSCH. - Haggadah Leleil Shikurim. Hamburg, 1844. 8vo, modern

half mor. Minor paper repair to tp. sg Sept 25 (265) $110
— TOBIA KOHEN. - Maase Tuvia. Venice: Bragadin, 1708. 3 parts in 1 vol. 4to, new calf. Small hole in 1st few pages mended; some stains & thumbmarks. St.7305.1, col 2676. S Nov 27 (255) £1,400 [Quaritch]
— WEIL, YAKOV. - She'eilot U'Teshuvot. Venice, 1549. 4to, modern cloth. Tp washed & silked; some annotations; stained. sg Sept 25 (337) $275
— YAKOV BEN ASHER. - Tur Even Ha'ezer. Venice: Juan di Gara, 1565. Folio, modern cloth. Last leaf repaired with loss; some worming at beginning & end; some stains; margin of tp repaired, affecting a few words. St. 5500.39, col 1190. bba Feb 19 (208) £550 [Freedman]
Anr copy. Modern mor. Marginal worming towards end not affecting text. St. 5500.38, col 1190. S Feb 17 (123) £600 [Schwarz]
— YECHIEL ASHKENAZI OF JERUSALEM. - Heichal Ha'Shem. Venice: Daniele Zanetti, 1596-1606. 4to, modern half mor. Slight worming in some inner margins; lacking 1 blank; some stains. St. 5654, col 1273-74. bba Feb 19 (213) £300 [Rosenfeld]
— YEHUDA HA LEVI. - Kuzari. Venice: Meir ben Jacob Parenzo, 1547. 2d Ed. 4to, modern half calf. A few lines censored, but legible. St. 5738.2, col 1340. bba Feb 19 (215) £500 [Field]
Anr copy. Half cloth; scuffed. Tp stamped; stained; lower outer corners of ff.38-44 damaged without affecting text. St. 5738.2, col 1340. CAM Dec 3 (89) HF1,200
— YERUCHAM BEN MESHULAM OF PROVENCE. - Toldot Adam Ve'Chava. Venice: Aloys Bragadin, 1553. Folio, modern half mor. With 2 small wormholes in last few leaves; some stains; a few short passages censored. St. 5801.2, col 1384. bba Feb 19 (222) £800 [Quaritch]
— YITZHAK BECHOR DAVID. - Divrei emet. Constantinople: Reuven & Nissim Ashkenazi, 1760. Folio, contemp lea; worn & wormed. Final leaf with loss at top outer corner affecting a few letters; sporadic worming sometimes affecting text. Yaari 441. sg Sept 25 (159) $120
— YITZHAK BEN ABBA MARI. - Hai'tur. Venice: Juan di Gara, 1608. 1st Ed. Folio, bds. Some stains on last few leaves. St. 5291.1. CAM Dec 3 (81) HF1,100
— ZACHARIA OF PLUNGIAN. - Sefer Zechirah Ve'inyenei Segulot [Galicia, c 1840] 12mo, bds. S Feb 17 (128) £35 [Schreiber]
— ZERACHIAH HA'LEVI HA'YEVANI. - Sefer Ha'Yashar. Cracow: Yitzhak Prostitz, 1586. 3d Ed. 4to, contemp calf; rubbed, rebacked. Small piece torn from lower margin of tp without affecting text; a few headlines shaved; some stains. St. 7180, col 2588. bba Feb 19 (230) £350 [Sol]

Heckewelder, John, 1743-1823
— A Narrative of the Mission of the United Brethren among the Delaware and Mohegan Indians.... Phila., 1820. 1st Ed. 8vo, contemp calf; worn, spine soiled, front joint split. wa June 25 (238) $115

Heddon, Jack
— Scotcher Notes. Bibliographical, Biographical and Historical Notes to George Scotcher's Fly Fisher's Legacy.... L, 1975. One of 150, sgd by Heddon & John Simpson, the artist. Half mor. With 6 hand-colored plates & a hand-tied artifical black gnat by Jack Heddon countersunk as frontis. sg Oct 23 (329) $150

Hedgeland, J. P.
A Description, Accompanied by Sixteen Coloured Plates, of the Splendid Decorations...Church of St. Neot.... L, 1830. 4to, contemp half calf; rubbed. bba Oct 30 (470) £45 [Fogg]

Hedin, Sven, 1865-1952
— Overland to India. L, 1910. 2 vols. cb Nov 6 (151) $140
— Through Asia. NY, 1899. 2 vols. 8vo, cloth. cb Nov 6 (152) $130
— Trans-Himalaya: Discoveries and Adventures in Tibet. L, 1909-13. 3 vols. Ck May 15 (73) £140
Vol I, 2d ptg; others, 1st Eds. 3 vols. cb Nov 6 (154) $110

Hedlinger, Johann Carl
— Collection complete de toutes les medailles du Chevallier Jean Charles Hedlinguer.... Augsburg, 1782. Folio, contemp half calf. With frontis, port & 79 plates. With 293 wax impressions (of 296, with 6 broken) of the medals described, on 15 trays in 3 boxes. C Dec 12 (111) £1,800 [Bookpress]

Hedwig, Johann, 1730-99
— Descriptio et adumbratio microscopico-analytica muscorum frondosorum. Leipzig, [1783]-87-97. 4 vols. Folio, contemp half calf; worn. With 160 hand-colored plates. Some spotting & browning. S Apr 27 (143) £1,900 [Stalder]
— Species muscorum frondoscorum. Leipzig, 1801-16. Vol I & 4 supplementary vols in 11 parts. Together, 12 vols. 4to, later bds; rubbed & stained. With 403 hand-colored plates; a few with slight discoloration. Horticultural Society of New York—de Belder copy. S Apr 24 (142) £1,200 [Asher]
— Theoria generationis et fructificationis plantarum cryptogamicarum.... St. Petersburg, 1784. 4to, contemp half calf; some

HEDWIG

wear. With 37 hand-colored plates. de Belder copy. S Apr 27 (144) £700 [Asher]

Heeringen, Gustav von
— Wanderungen durch Franken. Leipzig, [c.1840]. 4to, half cloth. With 30 plates. FD Dec 2 (836) DM1,600

Heiblocq, Jacob
— Farrago Latino-Belgica.... Amst., 1662. 8vo, contemp vellum gilt. sg Oct 9 (224) $90

Heiden, Jan van der, the Elder & the Younger
— Beschryving der Nieuwlyks uitgevonden en geoctrojeerde Slang-Brand-Spuiten.... Amst., 1690. Folio, new bds with vellum spine. With 21 plates (7 folding). Title dust-soiled, some plates dampstained. S Nov 27 (174) £1,350 [Marshall]

Heilner, Van Campen
— A Book on Duck Shooting. Phila., [1939]. Inscr. sg Oct 23 (330) $80
— Our American Game Birds. Garden City, 1941. Folio, orig cloth, in chipped d/j. cb Nov 6 (155) $65

Heine, Heinrich, 1797-1856
— Buch der Lieder. Hamburg, 1827. 1st Ed. 12mo, mor gilt, orig wraps bound in. FD Dec 2 (3520) DM3,800
— Der Rabbi von Bacherach. Berlin, 1923. One of 100 with a sgd suite on japan. Illus by Max Liebermann. Folio, orig mor gilt. HN Nov 26 (1941) DM6,200
— Spanische Romanzen. Berlin, 1921. One of 15 on japan with the etchings sgd. Illus by Hugo Steiner-Prag. 4to, orig mor gilt; extremities rubbed. Ck Dec 10 (326) £320
— Works. NY: Groscup & Sterling, [190?]. Ed de Luxe, one of 1,000. 20 vols. Half mor. cb Dec 4 (192) $120
Anr Ed. NY: Groscup & Sterling, [c.1900]. 20 vols. Half lea; some spine tips chipped. O Mar 24 (89) $140

Heinecken, Karl Heinrich von, 1706-91
— Idee generale d'une collection complette d'estampes. Leipzig & Vienna, 1771. 8vo, half mor; worn. With 32 plates. O May 12 (87) $275

Heinlein, Robert A.
— Citizen of the Galaxy. NY: Scribner's, [1957]. In repaired d/j. cb Sept 28 (610) $225
— The Door into Summer. Garden City, 1957. In rubbed & repaired d/j. cb Sept 28 (611) $200
— Double Star. Garden City, 1956. In rubbed d/j; spine ends bumped. cb Sept 28 (612) $600
— Farmer in the Sky. NY, 1950. In rubbed, stained & creased d/j. cb Sept 28 (613) $80

AMERICAN BOOK PRICES CURRENT

— Farnham's Freehold. NY: Putnam, [1964]. In d/j. Some rubbing from erasure at top of tp. cb Sept 28 (614) $275
— Friday. NY: Holt, Rinehart & Winston, [1982]. One of 500. cb Sept 28 (616) $100
— Glory Road. NY: Putnam, [1963]. In frayed & rubbed d/j. wa Mar 5 (79) $250
— The Green Hills of Earth. Chicago: Shasta, [1951]. In rubbed d/j; bdg with upper corners bumped. cb Sept 28 (618) $80
Anr copy. Lacking d/j. Sgd. wa June 25 (358) $105
— I Will Fear No Evil. NY: Putnam, [1970]. In d/j. cb Sept 28 (619) $50
— The Man Who Sold the Moon. Chicago: Shasta, [1950]. One of 200 pre-publication copies, sgd. In chipped d/j. cb Sept 28 (620) $200
One of 200 pre-publication copies. wa June 25 (360) $170
— Methuselah's Children. Hicksville: Gnome, [1958]. In 1st issue d/j. cb Sept 28 (622) $150
— The Moon is a Harsh Mistress. NY: Putnam, [1966]. In d/j. wa Mar 5 (80) $550
— Orphans of the Sky. L, 1963. In d/j, with wrap-around band reading "Gollancz SF Gollancz/ Choice for March". cb Sept 28 (626) $600
— The Puppet Masters. Garden City, 1951. In d/j with small tear & crease at spine foot. cb Sept 28 (628) $140
— Red Planet. NY, 1949. In chipped d/j. cb Sept 28 (629) $130
— Rocket Ship Galileo. NY: Scribner's, [1947]. 1st Ed. In rubbed d/j. wa Sept 25 (670) $190
— Sixth Column. NY: Gnome, [1949]. In d/j. cb Sept 28 (630) $160
— The Star Beast. NY: Scribner's, [1954]. In soiled & stained d/j; rear cover of bdg stained. wa June 25 (361) $75
— Stranger in a Strange Land. NY: Putnam, [1961]. In worn d/j. Lurton Blassingame's copy. cb Sept 28 (632) $275
— Time Enough for Love. NY: Putnam, [1973]. In d/j; stamp of Heinlein's agent on front endpaper. cb Sept 28 (633) $50
— Time for the Stars. NY: Scribner's, [1956]. 1st Ed, with code A-8.56(v) on copyright page. In creased d/j; spine head bumped. cb Sept 28 (635) $275
— Tunnel in the Sky. NY, 1955. In d/j. cb Sept 28 (636) $275
— The Unpleasant Profession of Jonathan Hoag. Hicksville: Gnome Press, [1959]. In d/j. Marginal darkening. cb Sept 28 (638) $70
— Waldo and Magic, Inc. Garden City, 1950. In d/j which has been damaged by earlier

jacket protector. cb Sept 28 (639) $120

Heinroth, Oskar August & Magdalena
— Die Voegel Mitteleuropas. Berlin: Bermuehler, [1926-33]. Vols I-III (of 4). Half mor gilt. pn Oct 23 (224) £55 [Weldon & Wesley]

Heins, Henry Hardy
— A Golden Anniversary Bibliography of Edgar Rice Burroughs. West Kingston, Rhode Island: Grant, 1964. In d/j. wa June 25 (304) $190

Heister, Laurentius, 1683-1758
— Beschreibung eines neuen Geschlechts von einer...Afrikanischen Pflanze.... Brunswick, 1755. Folio, orig bds; rubbed. With 3 hand-colored plates. Horticultural Society of New York—de Belder copy. S Apr 27 (146) £1,900 [Joseph & Sawyer]
— Compendium anatomicum. Altdorf & Nuremberg, 1719. 8vo, contemp vellum, armorial bdg; worn & soiled. Library markings. wa Mar 5 (294) $300
— Descriptio novi generis plantae rarissimae et speciosissimae Africanae ex bulbosarum classe. Brunswick, 1753. Folio, modern bds. With 3 hand-colored plates. S Apr 27 (145) £1,900 [Macdougall]
— A General System of Surgery.... L, 1768. 8th Ed. 4to, contemp calf. With 40 plates. pnE Dec 17 (52) £550 [Phillips]

Heller, Edmund, 1875-1939. See: Roosevelt & Heller

Heller, Elinor R. See: Grabhorn Printing

Hellinga, Wytze & Lotte
— The Fifteenth-Century Printing Types of the Low Countries. Amst., 1966. 2 vols. Folio, orig half mor. bba Oct 16 (487) £140 [Maggs]
Anr copy. Cloth. sg May 14 (466) $900

Hellinga, Wytze Gerbens
— Kopij en Druk in de Nederlanden. Amst., 1962. Folio, orig cloth. bba Oct 16 (486) £50 [Forster]

Hellman, Lillian
— Watch on the Rhine. NY, 1942. One of 50 specially bound in lea; this copy unnumbered. 4to, lea; spine ends rubbed, joints cracking. cb Dec 4 (229) $250

Hellwig, Christoph von
— Nosce te ipsum vel anatomicum vivum.... Frankfurt: H. P. Ritschel, [1720]. Bound with: Cesio, Carlo. Eine herrliche Anweisung und wolgegruendete Fuerstellung von der Anatomie dess gantzen Menschlichen Coerpers.... Augsburg, 1708. And: Vesalius, Andreas. Zergleiderung dess menschlichen Coerpers.... Augsburg: A.

Maschenbauer, 1723. Folio, 18th-cent half calf; worn. With 4 plates with many moveable parts superimposed in 1st work, 16 plates in 2d work & 10 full-page woodcuts in 3d work. Plates 3 & 4 in 1st work trimmed at outer edge & outer & lower margins extended throughout to make size uniform with the other works; 3d work with numeral on Plate 4 just shaved, no numeral on Plate 6 & top of male & female figures at end just shaved. S Nov 27 (267) £3,600 [Phelps]

Helman, Isidore Stanislas Henri
— Les Conquetes de l'Empereur de la Chine. Paris, [1788]. Bound with: Abrege historique des principaux traits de la vie de Confucius. Paris, 1788. Oblong folio, contemp calf; worn. With 24 plates in each work. 2d work with sheets edge-bound. A few marginal stains. S Oct 23 (55) £1,700 [Tang]

Helmholtz, Hermann L. F. von, 1821-94
— Die Lehre von den Tonempfindungen.... Braunschweig, 1863. 1st Ed. 8vo, half calf; upper hinge weak. S May 21 (201) £650 [Pickering]

Helper, Hinton Rowan, 1829-1909
— The Land of Gold: Reality Versus Fiction. Balt., 1855. 1st Ed. 8vo, orig cloth. Foxed. sg Mar 12 (138) $120

Helps, Sir Arthur, 1813-75
— The Spanish Conquest in America and its Relation to the History of Slavery and the Government of Colonies. L, 1855-61. 1st Ed. 4 vols. 8vo, contemp calf gilt. F Oct 30 (460) $95

Helvetius, Claude Adrien, 1715-71
— De l'Esprit. Paris: Durand, 1758. 8vo, contemp calf gilt. Soiled. sg Oct 9 (225) $450
Anr Ed. L, 1759. 4to, modern mor gilt. Some spotting & soiling, mostly marginal. P Sept 24 (303) $450

Helwig, Hellmuth
— Handbuch der Einbandkunde. Hamburg, 1953-54. 2 vols. 4to, orig cloth. HN Nov 26 (43) DM1,100
Anr Ed. Hamburg, 1953-55. 3 vols. 4to, orig cloth; worn & cracked. sg May 14 (115) $450

Helyot, Pierre, 1660-1716 —& Bullot, Maximilien, d.1748
— Histoire des ordres monastiques, religieux et militaires. Paris, 1714-19. 1st Ed. 8 vols. 4to, half mor; rubbed. Sold w.a.f. bba Apr 23 (114) £140 [Armstrong]

HEMINGWAY

Hemingway, Ernest, 1899-1961

— Across the River and into the Trees. L, 1950. 1st Ed. Cloth, in d/j. sg Mar 5 (92) $120

— Death in the Afternoon. L, 1932. 1st English Ed. Orig cloth, in d/j. cb May 7 (96) $250

1st Ed. NY, 1932. Inscr. sg Dec 11 (62) $200

— A Farewell to Arms. NY, 1929. 1st Ed, 1st Issue, without the legal disclaimer. In chipped d/j. cb May 7 (97) $375

Anr copy. In d/j; 1 corner bumped. sg Dec 11 (63) $150

One of 510, sgd. Orig bds with vellum backstrip; slip-case missing. S Dec 18 (127) £360 [Reuter]

Anr copy. Half vellum. L. p. copy. sg Mar 5 (93) $1,900

— For Whom the Bell Tolls. NY, 1940. 1st Ed. In 1st state d/j, rubbed. cb May 7 (98) $140

Anr copy. In d/j. sg Dec 11 (64) $150

Anr copy. Soiled; spine rubbed. Inscr and sgd as "Pappy" to Archibald MacLeish & with MacLeish's autograph notes. sg Mar 5 (94) $9,500

Anr copy. Calf. Sl scuffed, sl trimmed. wa Sept 25 (20) $160

— Green Hills of Africa. NY, 1935. 1st Ed. In soiled d/j. cb May 7 (99) $140

Anr copy. In d/j; faded & spotted. Inscr. wd Nov 12 (122) $325

— The Old Man and the Sea. NY, 1952. In d/j. sg Mar 5 (97) $375

— Three Stories & Ten Poems [Paris: Contact Publishing Co., 1923]. 1st Ed, one of 300. Orig wraps; stained. Inscr. sg Mar 5 (96) $8,000

— Winner Take Nothing. NY, 1922. 1st Ed. In d/j. sg Dec 11 (65) $225

Anr Ed. NY, 1933. sg Mar 5 (98) $100

Hemingway, Joseph

— The Northern Campaigns, and History of the War.... Manchester, [c.1820]. 2 vols. 8vo, modern mor gilt with Napoleonic monogram, bee & eagle. Extra-illus with 82 contemp ports of European notables. sg Sept 11 (121) $325

Hemsterhuis, Franciscus, 1721-90

— Oeuvres philosophiques. Paris, 1792. 2 vols. 8vo, contemp calf; rubbed. B Oct 7 (1216) HF550

AMERICAN BOOK PRICES CURRENT

Hemsterhuis, Siboldus

— Messis aurea triennalis exhibens anatomica novissima et utilissima experimenta. Leiden: Adrian Wyngaerden, 1654. 12mo, contemp vellum. Library stamp on tp. S May 21 (202) £580 [Phillips]

Henault, Charles Jean Francois, 1685-1770

— Nouvel Abrege chronologique de l'histoire de France.... Paris, 1768. 4to, mor gilt by Hardy. Extra-illus with a port, a proof of the head-piece before the port of Marie Leczinska, proof before letters of the title-vignette & 18 proofs before letters of some of the plates. C Dec 3 (126) £850 [Sourget]

Henderson, Ebenezer, 1784-1858

— The Annals of Dunfermline and vicinity.... Glasgow, 1879. 8vo, half calf. O Feb 24 (100) $50

— Iceland.... Edin., 1818. 1st Ed. 2 vols. 8vo, contemp mor gilt. With folding map & 16 plates. A few ink smudges in margins. S Oct 23 (253) £300 [Hosbach]

Henderson, Edward George & Andrew

— The Illustrated Bouquet, Consisting of Figures with Description of New Flowers.... L, 1857-79. 3 vols. 4to, Vols I-II in orig mor gilt (rebacked) & Vol III in orig cloth (loose). With 85 hand-colored plates. de Belder copy. S Apr 27 (147) £6,000 [Schuster]

Henderson, George —& Hume, Allan Octavian

— Lahore to Yarkand. L, 1873. 8vo, orig cloth. With 4 maps & geological profiles, 16 heliotype plates, 32 hand-colored ornithological plates & 6 hand-colored botanical plates. Tp with perforated stamp. S Apr 24 (345) £600 [Bonham]

Henderson, Harold Gould —& Ledoux, Louis Vernon

— The Surviving Works of Sharaku. NY, 1939. 4to, cloth, in soiled & chipped d/j. Foxed. sg Feb 5 (182) $80

Henderson, Robert W. See: Grolier Club

Henderson, Thomas, 1789-1854

— Hints on the Medical Examination of Recruits for the Army.... Phila.: Lippincott, 1856. 8vo, cloth; spine ends chipped with tears at upper joint. ha Sept 19 (153) $65

Henderson, William

— My Life as an Angler. L, 1879. L.p. copy. 4to, half mor; worn. sg Oct 23 (331) $60

Henderson, William Augustus
— The Housekeeper's Instructor.... L, [c.1790]. 5th Ed. 8vo, modern half calf. With 12 plates. sg Jan 15 (31) $150

— The Housekeeper's Instructor; or Universal Family Cook. L: W. & J. Stratford, [c. 1790-91]. 8vo, contemp sheep; rebacked. With frontis & 11 plates, 2 folding. Crahan copy. P Nov 25 (246) $350

Henderson, Zenna
— The People: No Different Flesh. L, 1966. Review copy. In rubbed d/j. cb Sept 28 (641) $160

— Pilgrimage: The Book of the People. Garden City, 1961. In d/j. cb Sept 28 (642) $100

Henfrey, Arthur —& Others
The Garden Companion and Florist's Guide. L, 1852. 4to, half calf gilt; rubbed. With 20 colored plates. pn June 18 (230) £120 [Orde]

Henkel, Arthur —& Schoene, Albrecht
— Emblemata: Handbuch der Sinnbildkunst des XVI und XVII Jahrhunderts. Stuttgart, [1967]. Folio, half mor, in d/j. sg Jan 22 (147) $200

Henkel, Max D.
— Le Dessin hollandais des origines au XVII siecle. Paris, 1931. Folio, loose as issued in orig portfolio. SSA Feb 11 (543) R140

Henley, William Ernest, 1849-1903
See also: Stevenson & Henley

— A London Garland. L, 1895. Ed by Henley. 4to, vellum; front joint starting. sg Oct 30 (137) $425

Anr copy. Vellum; front joint repaired with cellotape. Some wear. sg Oct 30 (138) $130

Hennepin, Louis, 1640-1705?
— Aenmerckelycke historische reys-beschryvinge door verscheyde Landen.... Utrecht, 1698. Bound with : Dampier, William. Nieuwe reystogt rondom de werreld.... The Hague, 1698. Sold with the 2d part of Dampier, Utrecht, 1700. 4to, vellum. With frontis, folding map & 4 plates in the Hennepin. B Feb 25 (787) HF2,500

Henrey, Blanche
— British Botanical and Horticultural Literature before 1800.... L, 1975. 3 vols. 4to, cloth. pnE Jan 28 (197) $85 [Smith]

Henrich, Manuel
— Iconografia de las Ediciones del Quijote.... Barcelona, 1905. 3 vols. 4to, half vellum; shaken, 1 spine damaged at foot. sg Jan 22 (109) $275

Henry, Augustine. See: Elwes & Henry

Henry, George Morrison Reid
— Coloured Plates of the Birds of Ceylon. L, 1927-35. Parts 1-4 in 1 vol. 4to, cloth. With 64 colored plates. pn Oct 23 (225) £160 [Graham]

Henry, Samuel
— A New and Complete American Medical Family Herbal.... NY, 1814. 1st Ed. 8vo, later cloth; rear cover stained. Lacking title & appendix. wa Sept 25 (128) $120

Henry, Samuel J. See: Derrydale Press

Henry, William Seaton, 1816-51
— Campaign Sketches of the War with Mexico. NY, 1847. 8vo, orig cloth; soiled, adhesion damage, rear joint tearing. Some foxing; a few signatures starting. cb Dec 18 (80) $95

Henshall, John
— A Practical Treatise on the Cultivation of Orchidaceous Plants. L, 1845. 8vo, orig cloth. S Nov 10 (499) £80 [Wayaritch]

Henslow, John Stevens, 1796-1861
— Le Bouquet des souvenirs. L, 1840. 8vo, mor gilt. With 25 hand-colored plates. pn Apr 30 (18) £130

Henty, George Alfred, 1832-1902 —& Others
— Brains and Bravery. L, 1903. Illus by Arthur Rackham. Several owners' signatures clumsily removed. sg Oct 30 (100) $175

Hepplewhite, Alice
— The Cabinet-Maker and Upholsterer's Guide.... L, 1789. 2d Ed. Folio, calf; joints weak. With 126 plates. Ad leaf waterstained; several plates at end soiled. S Apr 23 (96) £1,250 [Ramsay]

Hepworth, George Hughes
— Starboard and Port; The "Nettie" Along Shore. NY, 1876. 8vo, cloth; 19th-cent library label affixed to front cover, bookplate on front pastedown. sg Oct 23 (332) $60

Heraldry...
— The Heraldry of Nature. L, 1785. 8vo, late 19th-cent mor with gilt initials W. H. W. on upper cover; extremities scuffed. Some leaves spotted. Ck Oct 17 (194) £110

HERBAL

Herbal
— Herbarius Patavie. Passau: Johann Petri, 1485. 4to, blindstamped lea over wooden bds; repaired & renewed. Tp in old facsimile; some worming & other defs; old marginalia. VH Sept 12 (838) DM27,000

Herbelot, Barthelemy d', 1625-95
— Bibliotheque orientale, ou dictionnaire universel. Paris, 1697. 1st Ed. Folio, contemp vellum. C Apr 8 (94) £350 [Marlborough]

Herbert, Frank
— Children of Dune. NY, 1976. In d/j. Sgd. cb Sept 28 (643) $90
— The Dosadi Experiment. NY, 1977. In d/j with wrap-around band. Sgd on tp. cb Sept 28 (645) $70
  Uncorrected Proof. Wraps. Sgd on tp. cb Sept 28 (644) $50
— Dune. NY: Chilton, [1965]. 1st Ed. Cloth, in rubbed d/j. Sgd. cb Sept 28 (646) $600
  Anr copy. In rubbed d/j. cb May 7 (378) $375
— Dune Messiah. NY, [1969]. In d/j. Sgd on tp. cb Sept 28 (647) $190
— The Great Dune Trilogy. L, 1979. In d/j. Sgd on tp. cb Sept 28 (651) $50
— Heretics of Dune. NY, 1984. One of 1,500. Sgd on tp. cb Sept 28 (653) $50
— Whipping Star. NY, 1970. Ltd Ed. In d/j. cb Sept 28 (655) $110

Herbert, George, 1593-1633
— Herbert's Remains. Or, Sundry Pieces.... L, 1652. 1st Ed. 12mo, contemp calf; foot of spine restored. C Dec 12 (333) £400 [Maggs]
— The Temple. Cambr., 1641. 6th Ed. Bound with: Harvey, Christopher. The Synagogue, or, the Shadow of the Temple. L, 1647. 2d Ed. 12mo, contemp london bdg of calf gilt; broken. Inscr by Maurice Baring to Lady Diana Cooper, 1929. S Mar 9 (783) £420 [Kunkler]

Herbert, Henry William, 1807-58
— Field Sports in the United States. NY, 1849. ("Frank Forester's Field Sports of the United States.") 2 vols. 12mo, orig cloth; worn. Marginal dampstains. O Oct 21 (82) $50; sg May 21 (121) $100
— Frank Forester's Horse and Horsemanship of the United States.... NY, 1857. 2 vols. 4to, lea; worn, Vol I lacking backstrip. Owner's rubberstamp in both vols. sg May 21 (122) $100
— Hints to Horse-Keepers.... NY, 1859. 1st Ed. 12mo, later half mor; rubbed. O Feb 24 (101) $80
— My Shooting Box. Phila., 1846. 1st Ed. 8vo, half mor; light dampstaining. sg Oct 23

AMERICAN BOOK PRICES CURRENT

(336) $300

Herbert of Cherbury, Edward, Lord, 1583-1648
— A Dialogue Between a Tutor and his Pupil. L, 1768. 1st Ed. 4to, 19th-cent mor gilt; spine faded. sg Oct 9 (227) $175
— The Life of Edward Lord Herbert of Cherbury, Written by himself. Strawberry Hill, 1764. 4to, contemp calf gilt; rubbed. Lacking genealogical table. S Jan 13 (650) £120 [Maggs]

Herbert, Sir Thomas, 1606-82
— Memoirs of the Two Last Years of the Reign of...King Charles I.... L, 1702. 8vo, early 20th-cent mor gilt with earlier endpapers. Inscr by William Godwin to Archibald Constable. S Jan 13 (497) £120 [Bauman]

Herbert, William, 1718-95. See: Ames & Herbert

Herbert, William, 1778-1847
— Amaryllidaceae. L, 1837. 4to, half calf; rubbed. With 5 plain & 43 hand-colored plates. S Oct 23 (705) £500 [Schire]

Herckmans, Elias
— Der Zee-vaert lof, handelende vande gedenckwaerdighste Zee-vaerden.... Amst., 1634. Folio, contemp vellum. With engraved title & 17 etchings. Some staining & repairs. B Feb 25 (722) HF1,100

Herculanensium...
— Herculanensium voluminum quae supersunt. Naples, 1793-1827. 3 vols. Folio, contemp mor gilt extra. With 119 papyrological plates. With bookplate of Maria Christina of Spain. P Dec 15 (202) $500

Herculaneum
— Le Antichita di Ercolano esposte. Naples, 1757-92. Vol I only. Folio, contemp lea; worn. Some foxing & soiling. sg June 18 (176) $500
  Anr Ed. Naples, 1757. Vol I only. Folio, contemp calf; worn. With title, port, map & 50 plates. wd Nov 12 (86) $500

Herdman, William Gawin, 1805-82
— Pictorial Relics of Ancient Liverpool. Liverpool, 1878. 2 vols. Folio, contemp mor gilt; rubbed. Ck Feb 27 (123) £90
  Anr copy. Orig mor gilt. With 72 plates. L Dec 11 (117) £80
— Picturesque Views in Liverpool. Liverpool, 1864. 4to, orig half lea; spine & corners rubbed. With 36 colored lithos on 28 sheets. 2 plates waterstained; 4 plates spotted. C Oct 15 (43) £230 [Fletcher]
— Views of Fleetwood on Wyre.... [Manchester: T. Physick, c.1850]. Oblong folio,

mor extra by J. Law of Liverpool. With 8 hand-colored views heightened with gum arabic. S Oct 23 (180) £3,000 [Quaritch]

Here, Emmanuel

— Plans et elevations de la place royale de Nancy.... Paris, 1753. Folio, modern half mor. With frontis & 13 folding plates. On guards throughout; 1 plate with minor repairs; without the final leaf of Reflection. C Oct 15 (44) £1,200 [Weinreb]

Heredia Library, Ricardo

— [Sale Catalogue] Catalogue de la Bibliotheque. Paris, 1891-1913. 4 vols, without Index. 4to, cloth, orig wraps bound in. sg May 14 (63) $120

Heresbach, Conrad, 1496-1576

— Foure Bookes of Husbandry. L: For John Wight, 1578. 8vo, old calf; rebacked, some wear. Tp rehinged & with tears repaired, with slight loss; some other minor tears, slightly affecting text. O Oct 21 (84) $400

Anr Ed. L: John Wight, 1578. Trans by Barnaby Googe. 4to, contemp vellum; worn & lacking ties. Inkstain to extreme top of 1st 4 leaves; minor soiling; several leaves in quire C misbound. Hunt copy. CNY Nov 21 (142) $950

Anr Ed. L: Iohn Wight, 1586. Trans by Barnabe Googe. 4to, early 20th-cent mor by Riviere. Some small repairs to very small wormholes. pn June 18 (173) £680 [Comber]

5th Ed in English. L, 1601. 4to, contemp vellum; loose in bdg, front endpaper removed. Tp & last leaf soiled; some worming affecting text. Hunt copy. CNY Nov 21 (143) $180

Hering, George Edwards, 1805-79

— The Mountains and Lakes of Switzerland, the Tyrol and Italy. L, 1847. Folio, half mor gilt. With hand-colored litho title, dedication & 18 views. pn May 21 (37) £600 [Marinoni]

Anr copy. Contemp mor gilt; rubbed. With litho title, engraved dedication & 18 handcolored plates. S Oct 23 (254) £800 [Hasbach]

Heriot, George, 1766-1844

— Travels through the Canadas. L, 1807. 4to, cloth. With hand-colored folding map & 27 plates. Lacking ad leaves. S Apr 24 (264) £1,000 [Traylen]

Hermannidus, Rutgerus, d.1680

— Britannia magna. Amst., 1661. 12mo, contemp vellum. With folding general map & 31 folding miniature town plans. Lacking engraved title. S Jan 12 (65) £440 [George]

Hermes Trismegistus

— The Divine Pymander. L, 1650. 1st English Ed. 8vo, contemp sheep. Lower margin of I4 torn, F8 stained. S Nov 27 (265) £1,050 [Khozal]

— Poemander. Paris: Turnebum, 1554. Contemp vellum; soiled. bba May 28 (4) £320 [Maggs]

Anr copy. Contemp calf; rebacked. Lacking final blank. S May 6 (568) £320 [Parikian]

Hermite, Jacques l'

— Journael van de Nassausche Vloot ofte Beschrijvingh van Voyagie om den gantschen Aert-Kloot, Gedaen met elf Schepen.... Amst., 1648. 4to, modern half vellum. With double-page plate. Tp mtd on guard. C Dec 12 (240) £250 [Van Noord]

Hernandez, Francisco

— Nova plantarum, animalium et mineralium Mexicanorum historia. Rome, 1651. Folio, 19th-cent half calf gilt; joints rubbed, inner hinge cracked. Engraved tp torn; some foxing & browning; library stamp on tp & at end. Crahan copy. P Nov 25 (250) $3,500

Anr copy. Contemp mor gilt by Samuel Mearne with the crowned cipher of Charles II within palm leaves at corners of central panel & in 6 compartments of spine, foot of spine lettered J. M. (John Morris, c.1580-1658). A few minor flaws & wormholes; a few leaves just trimmed. de Belder copy. S Apr 27 (148) £13,500 [Israel]

Herndon, Sarah Raymond

— Days on the Road; Crossing the Plains in 1865. NY, 1902. 1st Ed. cb Jan 8 (87) $70

Herndon, William Lewis, 1813-57 —& Gibbon, Lardner

— Exploration of the Valley of the Amazon. Wash., 1853-54. 2 vols. 8vo, orig cloth. With 1 of the 2 folders of large maps. 32d Congress, 2d Session, Senate Exec. Doc. 36. cb June 4 (101) $140

Anr copy. Orig cloth. Lacking the 2 folders of large maps. 32d Congress, 2d Session, House Exec. Doc. 53. cb June 4 (102) $90

Hero of Alexandria

— De gli automati, overeo machine se moventi. Venice, 1589. 1st Ed. 2 parts in 1 vol. 4to, modern mor. Engraved title with hole at upper blank margin. S Mar 10 (1078) £380 [Hesketh]

HERODIAN

Herodian
— The History.... L: William Copeland, [c.1556]. 8vo, 18th-cent half calf; some wear. Small marginal tears in 1st 3 leaves & in f.11; some leaves soiled. C Dec 12 (334) £1,200 [Poole]

Herodotus
— Historiarum libri IX. Paris: Jodocus Badius & Jean Petit, 1528. ("Historiarum musae...") Folio, contemp mor over pastebd with Herodotus lettered in gilt on front cover. Marginal dampstains. sg Mar 26 (138) $500

Anr Ed. Amst., 1763. ("Historiae....") Folio, contemp vellum gilt; rubbed. bba Oct 30 (197) £70 [Frew Mackenzie]

Anr copy. Contemp vellum gilt with arms of Amsterdam on covers; rubbed & soiled. S Mar 10 (1079) £95 [Hasbach]

Heroine...
— L'Heroine du Texas, ou voyage de Madame /21/21/21 aux Etats-Unis et au Mexique. Paris, 1819. 8vo, orig wraps. Library stamp at foot of title. S Apr 23 (275) £2,200 [Arader]

Heron, Robert, 1764-1807
— Observations made in a Journey through the Western Counties of Scotland.... Perth, 1793. 1st Ed. 2 vols. 8vo, modern half mor. bba Aug 20 (514) £100 [Scott]

Heron-Allen, Edward
— De fidiculis bibliographia: being, an Attempt towards a Bibliography of the Violin.... L, 1890-94. One of 60. 2 vols. 4to, bds; worn. sg Oct 2 (230) $175

Herrera, Antonio de, 1559-1625
— Eerste Scheeps-Togt ter verder Ontdekking van de West-Indien.... Leiden: Pieter van der Aa, 1706. Folio, modern bds. Some spotting. sg Sept 18 (127) $60

— The General History of the Vast Continent and Islands of America. L, 1725-26. 1st Ed in English. 6 vols. 8vo, later half mor; 1 cover detached. With 3 folding maps & 15 plates. S Oct 23 (444) £1,300 [Frers]

— Histoire generale des voyages et conquestes...des Indes occidentales.... Paris, 1671. Vol III (of 3) only. 4to, contemp calf with arms of the Comtesse de Verrue [Olivier, fer 799]. Some browning & waterstaining. S June 25 (437) £550 [Perceval]

— Historia general de las Indias occidentales. Antwerp, 1728. 4 vols. Folio, old lea with arms of Carlos VI on 1 cover; spines worn. With folding color map & 43 plates. Lacking tp; various defs. Sold w.a.f. K June 7 (156) $140

— Nieuwe Werelt, Anders ghenaempt West-Indien. Amst., 1622. 3 parts in 1 vol.

AMERICAN BOOK PRICES CURRENT

Folio, vellum; soiled. With the engraved title incorporatiing a map of the Americas & 14 double-page maps in Part 1. Part e with small world map on title & port on verso, 3 maps (1 folding) & 5 illusts in the text. Some small tears touching letters repaired. S Oct 23 (322) £1,100 [Arader]

— Verscheide Zee en Land-Togten gedaan in de West-Indien.... Leiden, 1706. Folio, modern bds. sg Sept 18 (91) $150

— Vervolg de Roemwaardinge Zee en Land Reysen des dapperen Ferdinand Cortes.... Leiden, [1729]. Folio, modern bds. With 4 folding maps & 13 plates in text. pnNY Oct 11 (3) $350

— Vyf Verscheide Voyagen der Kastiliaanen en Portuguezen ter Ontdekking gedaan naar de West-Indien in Jahren 1500.... Leiden: Pieter van der Aa, 1706. Folio, modern bds. sg Sept 18 (128) $60

Herrera, Gabriel Alonso de
— Agricultura general. Madrid, 1620. Folio, later half calf; rubbed, joints split. Small portion removed from upper blank margin towards end. S May 29 (1202) £240

— El Libro de Agricultura. Medina del Campo, 1584. Folio, early 19th-cent sheep. Some browning & dampstaining. sg Oct 9 (51) $475

— Obra de agricultura copilada de.... Medina del Campo: Juan Boyer, 1584. ("Libro de agricultura....") Folio, mor gilt bound for Jacques Auguste de Thou with his arms as a bachelor in center & spine with monogram of de Thou & his 1st wife; later endpapers, joints cracked & repaired. Hunt copy. CNY Nov 21 (144) $1,900

Herrick, Robert, 1591-1674. See: Cresset Press; Kelmscott Press

Herschel, Sir John Frederick William, 1792-1821
— A Collection of Examples of the Application of the Calculus. Cambr., 1820. 2 parts in 1 vol. 8vo, modern cloth. Some foxing at beginning. bba Aug 28 (127) £100 [Hippo Books]

— Essays from the Edinburgh and Quarterly Reviews.... L 1857. 8vo, orig cloth; rubbed. ALs tipped in. bba Nov 13 (41) £50 [Axe]

Hertz, Emanuel, 1870-1940. See: Roosevelt's copy, Franklin D.

Hertzog, Bernhart
— Chronicon Alsatiae. Edelsasser Chronik und aussfuerliche Beschreibung des unteren Elsasses am Rheinstrom.... Strassburg: Bernhart Jobin, 1592. Folio, contemp vellum; worn. Some browning & spotting;

1st half wormed. FD June 11 (84) DM1,200

Hervey, John
— Messenger, the Great Progenitor. NY: Derrydale Press, 1935. One of 500. Unopened. sg Oct 23 (74) $100
Anr copy. Unopened. sg May 21 (70) $90

Hervey, John, 1870-1947
See also: Derrydale Press
— Racing in America, 1665-1865. NY: Pvtly ptd for the Jockey Club, [1944]. One of 800. 2 vols. 4to, half cloth; corners showing. cb May 21 (151) $150

Hervey, Lord John, 1696-1743
— Memoirs of the Reign of George the Second to the Death of Queen Caroline. L, 1884. 3 vols. 8vo, calf by Zaehnsdorf; rubbed. wa Dec 11 (230) $120
— Some Materials toward Memoirs of the Reign of King George II. L, 1931. One of 900. 3 vols. Worn. O Feb 24 (102) $60

Hervieu, Louise
— L'Ame du Cirque. Paris, 1924. One of 403. Folio, mor gilt, orig wraps bound in; rebacked. Inscr to Henri-Jean Laroche & with the Ms of a story, Le Tireur a la bougie, which was turned down for inclusion in this vol. S June 17 (107) £420 [Ash]

Hervieux de Chanteloup, J. C., 1683-1747
— Traite curieux des serins de Canarie.... Amst.: Hendrik Schelte, 1712. 8vo, mor mosaic bdg by Chatelin. SM Mar 1 (289) FF4,800

Herz, Henri
— Mes Voyages en Amerique. Paris, 1866. Orig wraps. sg Sept 18 (129) $90

Hesiod
— Works. L, 1728. 2 vols in 1. 4to, contemp calf gilt; rubbed, joints starting, front endpapers & rear leaves foxed. cb Oct 23 (110) $50

Hess, P. von
— The Album of Greek Heroism, or the Deliverance of Greece. [Munich: H. Kohler, c.1835]. Folio, loose in portfolio with ptd wrap in English on upper cover. With 38 (of 40) tinted plates. Lacking the dedication. S Oct 23 (338) £5,000 [Economides]
Anr Ed. Braila: Pericles Pestemalgiogla, 1895. Folio, 19th-cent half mor gilt; rubbed. With 40 plates. Lacking port; a few outer marginal corners damaged without loss of image. S Apr 24 (221) £1,800 [Tsigaras]

Hessel, Peter
— Hertzfliessende Betrachtungen von dem Elbe-strom. Hamburg: Victor de Leeu, 1675. Part 1 (all pbd). 4to, contemp calf; worn. With frontis, port & 25 plates, some folding. One double-page plate shaved to neat-lines; minor wormholes touching text & plates. S Oct 23 (110) £500 [Israel]

Hessus, Helius Eobanus
— De tuenda bona valetudine.... Frankfurt: C. Egenolph, 1556. 8vo, mor by Aussourd. SM Oct 20 (516) FF6,000

Hetherington, Arthur Londsdale
— The Early Ceramic Wares of China. L, 1922. One of 50, sgd. 4to, orig pigskin; rubbed. bba Dec 4 (221) £60 [Short]

Hetley, G. B.
— The Native Flowers of New Zealand. L, 1888. 3 orig parts. Folio, orig bds; gutta-percha perished. With 3 uncolored plates of dissections & 36 color plates. C Apr 8 (131) £320 [Graham]

Heuglin, Martin Theodor von, 1824-76
— Ornithologie Nordost-Afrika's der Nilquellen- und Kuesten-Gebiete des Rothen Meeres.... Cassel, 1869-73-[75]. 1st Ed in Book form. 5 parts in 2 vols. 8vo, cloth. With folding map & 51 plates. Haverschmidt copy. B Feb 24 (2465) HF850
Anr copy. 4 parts in 2 vols. 8vo, With hand-colored folding map (torn & repaired), 1 plain & 50 hand-colored plates. Some stain on last few plates. pn Oct 23 (226) £370 [Buteo]

Heussen, Hugo F. van, 1654-1719 —& Rijn, H. van
— Oudheden en gestichten van Zeeland. Leiden, 1721. 2 vols. 8vo, vellum. With 2 folding ports & 7 folding views. Library stamps on title. B Feb 25 (656) HF325

Hevelius, Joannes, 1611-87
— Cometographia, totam naturam cometarum.... Danzig: S. Reiniger, 1668. Folio, contemp vellum; soiled. With frontis & 38 plates. Neat restoration to lower fore-edge corners of half-title & frontis with a portion of 1 letter & a bit of ornamental border supplied in ink on the latter; rust hole to Hh4; hole costing several letters on Fff4; Plate M loose; Plate F with small repair; other defs. P June 18 (83) $2,600
Anr copy. Contemp calf; spine def at foot. Upper blank margin & lower blank corner of frontis repaired; tears in title mended with a few letters strengthened in ink; marginal repair to errata leaf. S May 21 (200) £3,000 [Quaritch]

Hewitson, William Chapman, 1806-78

— Coloured Illustrations of the Eggs of British Birds.... L, 1846. 2 vols. 4to, contemp half calf; rubbed. With 139 colored plates. L Dec 11 (284) £60

Anr Ed. L, 1856. 2 vols. 8vo, contemp half mor. A few leaves spotted; 1 leaf loose in Vol I. bba Oct 30 (390) £60 [Barker]

Anr copy. Half mor gilt. With 145 hand-colored plates. pn Oct 23 (227) £80 [McCourt]

— Illustrations of New Species of Exotic Butterflies. L, [1856]-76. Vols I-IV (of 5). Contemp half mor; rubbed. S Apr 23 (10) £1,050

Hewitt, Edward R.

— Secrets of the Salmon. NY, 1922. 1st Ed, one of 750. 8vo, half cloth. sg Oct 23 (340) $80

Hewitt, Graily

— The Pen and Type Design. L, 1928. One of 250. Folio, orig mor gilt. sg June 11 (235) $60

Hewlett, Maurice, 1861-1923

— Quattrocentisteria: How Sandro Botticelli Saw Simonetta in the Spring. NY: Golden Cross Press, 1937. One of 175. Illus by Valenti Angelo. cb Dec 4 (121) $170

Hewson, William

— Experimental Inquiries: Part the First [Part the Second]. L, 1772-74. 2d Ed of Part 1; 1st Ed of Part 2. 2 vols. 12mo, contemp calf; rubbed, joints cracked. With 6 folding plates. Part 1 affected by damp. Ck Nov 21 (13) £240 [Camberwell]

Heylyn, Peter, 1600-62

— Cosmographie. L, 1652. 1st Ed. Folio, later calf; broken. With engraved title & 4 folding maps. Some shaving; small tear to lower margin of dedication-leaf; 1 corner stained. S Nov 10 (382) £280 [Burden]

Anr copy. Contemp calf; broken. With engraved title & 4 folding maps, all hand-colored. Engraved title trimmed & mtd to contemp leaf; some dampstains; maps trimmed, occasionally within image. sg Apr 23 (66) $275

3d Ed. L, 1666. Folio, contemp calf; worn, hinges cracked. Ms marginalia; last index leaf trimmed & mtd to larger sheet; first 15 leaves dampstained; lacking frontis; Europe torn at center & rejointed with loss of image. sg Apr 23 (67) $150

Anr Ed. L, 1674. Folio, contemp calf; rebacked, joints cracked. With engraved title & 4 folding maps. Small corner tear to 3 maps; a few rust-holes affecting letters; 13 corner torn with loss. C Dec 12 (238) £300 [Burgess & Browning]

— A Help to English History.... L, 1671. 8vo, contemp calf; spine chipped & cracked, small blindstamp on front free endpaper. cb Oct 23 (111) $80

— The Historie of that most Famous Saint...St. George of Cappadocia.... L, 1631. 1st Ed. 4to, modern calf. Title chipped. cb Dec 18 (82) $160

Heym, G.

— Umbra vitae. Munich, 1924. One of 100. Illus by E. L. Kirchner. Orig cloth. FD Dec 2 (4458) DM68,000

Anr copy. Orig bdg. FD June 11 (5048) DM64,000

Heytesbury, William, fl.1340

— De sensu composito et diviso. Venice: Jacobus Pentius de Leucho, 17 July 1501. 4to, lev by Sangorski & Sutcliffe. bba Aug 20 (337) £130 [Clark]

Heywood, Daniel E.

— Diary of...a Parmachenee Guide.... Bristol NH: Ptd for R. W. Musgrove, 1891. Ptd wraps; lacking rear cover. sg Oct 23 (341) $200

Heywood, Gerald G. P.

— Charles Cotton and his River. Manchester, 1928. 4to, cloth. sg Oct 23 (75) $425

Heywood, Thomas, 1574?-1641

— The Hierarchie of the Blessed Angells. L, 1635. 1st Ed. Folio, old calf; rebacked. With engraved title & 9 plates. Lacking final blank. O May 12 (89) $300

— The Life of Merlin, sirnamed Ambrosius. L, 1641. 4to, old calf; worn. Some stains. wa Dec 11 (690) $160

Hibberd, Shirley, 1825-90

— Familiar Garden Flowers. L: Cassel, [1895-96]. Illus by F. Edward Hulme. Series 1-5 in 5 vols. 8vo, orig cloth; rubbed. bba Jan 15 (409) £55 [Keegan]

Hickman, William

— Sketches on the Nipisaguit.... Halifax & L, 1860. Folio, orig cloth; broken, spine lacking. With 8 colored litho plates. Perforated library stamps on tp & last leaf of text; ink stamps on tp, plates & other leaves. bba Dec 18 (157) £1,900 [Burgess Browning]

Hierakosophion....

— Hierakosophion. Rei accipitrariae scriptores nunc primum editi.... Paris: S. Cramoisy, 1612. Ed by Nicolas Rigault. 4to, contemp vellum. Jeanson copy. SM Mar 1 (494) FF5,500

Hietling, Conrad
— Peregrinus affectuose per Terram Sanctam et Jerusalem.... Graetz, 1713. 2 vols in 1. Folio, contemp pigskin over wooden bds; rebacked in mor. With frontis, folding map & 6 (of 7) plates & plans. bba May 28 (291) £120 [Trotter]

Higden, Ranulph, c.1299-c.1363
— Polycronicon. [Westminster]: William Caxton, [after 2 July 1482]. 1st Ed. Single leaf, the beginning of Liber quintus. Capitulum septimum. O Oct 21 (85) $190

Higgins, F. R. See: Cuala Press

Higgins, William Mullingar
— The House Painter or Decorator's Companion.... L, 1841. 4to, contemp half calf; rubbed & chipped at base of spine. With 30 full-page colored specimens, some slightly damaged. T Nov 20 (361) £570

Hightower, John
— Pheasant Hunting. NY, 1946. One of 350 L.p. copies, sgd by Hightower & with an extra color plate. Illus by Lynn Bogue Hunt. cb Nov 6 (156) $85; sg Oct 23 (342) $120

Hilder, Jesse Jewhurst
— The Art of J. J. Hilder. Sydney, 1918. Ed by Sydney Ure Smith & Bertram Stevens. 4to, half cloth; worn, cracked. Tp & some leaves offset. CA Apr 12 (133) A$85

Anr copy. Half cloth; bds stained. CA Apr 12 (134) A$100

Hildreth, Richard, 1807-65
— Despotism in America; or an Inquiry into the...Slave-Holding System.... Bost.: Mass. Anti-Slavery Society, 1840. 12mo, orig cloth. cb Oct 9 (273) $55

Hiler, Hilaire & Meyer
— Bibliography of Costume; a Dictionary Catalogue.... NY, 1939. 4to, cloth. sg Jan 22 (195) $250

Hill, George Birkbeck
— Footsteps of Dr. Johnson, Scotland.... L, 1890. 4to, half mor; moderately worn. wa Sept 25 (574) $100

Hill, Ira
— Antiquities of America Explained. Hagerstown, 1831. 1st Ed. 16mo, modern half cloth. Some foxing; introductory leaves misbound. sg Sept 25 (19) $175

Hill, Sir John, 1716?-75
— The British Herbal. L, 1756. Folio, contemp calf; repaired but joints broken, inner hinges strengthened with tape. With frontis & 75 plates. Hunt copy 2. CNY Nov 21 (145) $260

Anr copy. Contemp half calf; broken. Frontis, tp & Plate 24 loose; Plate 36 foxed; marginal worming but affecting 5P-6C; some foxing & soiling. Crahan copy. P Nov 25 (251) $300

Anr copy. Later half mor. With frontis & 75 plates, hand-colored throughout. Tp with owner's stamp; slight repair to frontis & title; minor foxing. pnE Dec 17 (252) £800 [Marshall]

Anr copy. Contemp calf; rubbed, rebacked. With hand-colored frontis & 75 hand-colored plates. Minor spotting. Lakin—de Belder copy. S Apr 27 (149) £4,000 [White]

Anr copy. New half calf. With frontis & 75 plates, 45 fully colored, the remainder partly colored. Lacking 3 leaves of index at end (replaced in Ms); frontis backed; tp backed with outer blank margin def; following leaf tissued; lower corners of pp 3-6 repaired; last plate mtd with slight defs to margins & corners. S May 28 (687) £320

— The Conduct of a Married Life. L, 1754. 2d Ed. 12mo, contemp calf. With 8 plates. pnE Dec 17 (253) £70 [Traylen]

— Decade di alberi curiosi ed eleganti piante.... Rome, 1786. 4to, contemp calf gilt; worn. Title & Plate 1 stained; all plates with inner margins strengthened or mended; some Ms notes on blank leaves at end. S Sept 23 (567) £100 [Quaritch]

— A Decade of Curious and Elegant Trees and Plants. L, 1773. Folio, later half calf. With 10 hand-colored plates. sg Apr 2 (109) $2,600

— Eden, or a Compleat Body of Gardening.... L, 1757. Folio, contemp half calf; spine repaired. With frontis & 60 plates. pnE Dec 17 (203) £880 [Traylen]

— The Family Herbal. Bungay, [c.1808]. 8vo, contemp calf; broken. Ck Apr 24 (157) £105

Anr copy. Later half cloth; worn, spine shabby. With 54 colored plates. wa Mar 5 (295) $140

— A General Natural History. L, 1748-52. 3 vols. Folio, contemp calf gilt; hinges cracked. Lacking a gathering in Fossil section. pn Apr 30 (311) £380 [Elliott]

— A Review of the Works of the Royal Society of London. L, 1751. 4to, contemp calf. pnE Jan 28 (290) £270 [Traylen]

— The Useful Family Herbal. Bungay: Brightly & Kinnersley, [c.1810]. ("The Family Herbal....") 8vo, old calf; rebacked. With 54 handcolored plates. Ff4 torn & repaired. Hunt copy. CNY Nov 21 (146) $220

— The Vegetable System. L, [1759]-75 & 1786. 1st Ed, except Vol 23. 26 vols in 24. Folio, 21 vols in contemp calf with gilt stamp

Lowther within an oak wreath surmounted by a coronet on sides, Vols 21-26 in recent calf gilt by Sangorski & Sutcliffe. With 361 plain & 1,222 hand-colored plates plus 1 plain plate which may be from anr set. Plesch—de Belder copy. S Apr 27 (150) £50,000 [Israel]

Hill, Jonathan A.

— The Hill Collection of Pacific Voyages. San Diego, Calif., 1974. One of 1,000. Ed by De Braganza & Oakes; annotated by Hill. Vol I (of 3) sg Jan 22 (196) $175

Hill, Lewis Webb. See: Phillips & Hill

Hill, Thomas, fl.1590

— The Profitable Arte of Gardening. L: Thos. Marshe, 1568. 2 parts in 1 vol. 8vo, 18th-cent calf; rubbed. Tp torn & repaired on verso; border of tp & a few headlines shaved; burnhole in dd2 costing several letters; some worming with loss. P Nov 25 (253) $450

Anr Ed. L, 1586-1608. 2 parts in 1 vol. 4to, sheep; cover detached. Some headlines shaved; 1st 4 leaves remargined. Part 2 is from the 1608 Ed & lacks the last 3 leaves, which have been replaced in Ms. sg Jan 15 (151) $300

Anr Ed. L: Robert Waldegraved, 1586. 2 parts in 1 vol. 4to, modern calf. Some leaves trimmed; some soiling; some old writing in margins. S June 25 (161) £380 [Lawes]

Anr Ed. L, 1608. ("The Arte of Gardening.") Bound with: Reid, John. The Scots Gardener. Edin., 1683. Calf with 16th-cent calf panel mtd on upper cover. Contemp Ms notes bound into both works. William Johnston's copy. Tp of Hill has autograph of Thomas Urquhart, Burges of Forres. pnE May 20 (72) £230

Hill, William Henry, of Shettleston

— History of the Hospital and School in Glasgow founded by George and Thomas Hutcheson.... Glasgow, 1881. One of 100. 4to, cloth; worn. O Feb 24 (103) $70

Hill, William Henry, Violin Maker —& Others

— Antonio Stradivari, his Life and Work, 1644-1737. L, 1902. 1st Ed. 4to, calf. About half of text leaves stained in lower right corner, not affecting text. sg Feb 26 (234) $175

— The Violin-Makers of the Guarneri Family.... L, 1931. 4to, orig half vellum. sg Feb 26 (233) $400

Hillary, William, d.1763

— Observations on the Changes of the Air.... L, 1766. 8vo, contemp calf gilt. S May 28 (688) £280

Hiller, Lejaren Arthur

— Surgery Through the Ages: A Pictorial Chronicle. NY, [1944]. 4to, cloth. sg Nov 13 (62) $90

Hills, John Waller, 1867-1938

— A Summer on the Test. L, [1924]. One of 300. Illus by Norman Wilkinson. 4to, half mor. With 12 plates. pnE Dec 17 (344) £200 [Traylen]

Anr copy. Orig cloth. S July 28 (1039) £70

Hills, Robert

— Sketches in Flanders and Holland. L, 1816. 4to, cloth; rubbed. Lacking some plates; others poorly colored. bba July 16 (135) £40 [Shankland]

Anr copy. Orig bds; rebacked. With 36 plates, 5 hand-colored. pn Apr 30 (49) £250

Hiltebrand, Andreas

— Genealogia serenissimorum, potentissimorumque regum Sueciae.... Stettin, 1631. 4to, calf gilt by Sangorski & Sutcliffe. Folding genealogical table cropped with some text gone. sg Mar 26 (139) $50

Hilton, Harold H. —& Smith, Garden G.

— The Royal and Ancient Game of Golf. L, 1912. One of 900. pnC Jan 23 (103) £820; pnC July 16 (65) £1,000

Anr copy. Orig mor gilt. S Nov 10 (598) £450 [Light]

Hind, Arthur Mayger

— The Etchings of D. Y. Cameron. L, 1924. Cloth. sg Feb 10 (65) $110

— Giovanni Battista Piranesi, a Critical Study. NY, 1922. Half cloth. sg Feb 5 (275) $150

— A History of Engraving & Etching. L, 1923. 4to, cloth. sg Feb 5 (162) $90

— An Introduction to a History of Woodcut.... Bost., 1935. 2 vols. 4to, cloth. pn Nov 20 (152) $75 [Brayley]

Anr copy. Later cloth. sg Feb 5 (163) $90

Anr copy. Cloth. sg May 14 (45) $110

Anr copy. Half calf. Some foxing. sg June 4 (162) $70

Anr copy. Cloth. sg June 11 (236) $60

— Wenceslaus Hollar and his Views of London.... L, 1922. 4to, orig cloth. pn Dec 11 (142) £50 [Burgess & Browning]

Hindley, Charles
— Miscellanea Antiqua Anglica. The Old Book Collector's Miscellany.... L, 1871-73. 3 vols. 8vo, half calf gilt by Sangorski & Sutcliffe. sg Jan 22 (197) $175

Hinton, John Howard, 1791-1873
— The History and Topography of the United States.... L, 1830-32. 2 vols. 4to, contemp half mor; rubbed. With engraved titles, port, 17 maps & 79 plates. Some browning & spotting. S July 14 (779) £380
Anr Ed. L: J. & F. Tallis, [c.1850]. ("History of the United States of America.") 2 vols, 4to, mor; rubbed, worn. Lacking 3 plates, 1 plate partially torn away. Sold w.a.f. O Feb 24 (104) $100
Anr Ed. Bost., 1854-56. 2 vols. 8vo, half mor; rubbed. O Oct 21 (86) $250

Hipkins, Alfred James, 1826-1903
— Musical Instruments.... L, 1945. 4to, orig cloth. Ck Sept 5 (107) £35

Hipkiss, Edwin James
— Eighteenth-Century American Arts: the M. and M. Karolik Collection. Bost., 1941. 4to, cloth; rubbed. cb July 30 (94) $130

Hippisley, Gustavus
— Songs in the Opera of Flora with the Humorous Scenes of Hob.... L: J. Cooper & G. Bickham, 1737. 8vo, half mor. With engraved title, dedication & 24 (of 26) plates. C Dec 12 (335) £170 [Quaritch]

Hippocrates, 460?-377? B.C.
— Opera. Venice: Hieronymus Scoto, 1546. Folio, later half lea; worn. With some deletions & blotches in brown ink; some dampstaining & worming; lacking the first 11 pp, including tp. wa Mar 5 (297) $100
Anr Ed. Venice, 1588. Folio, vellum bds; spine def. Some discoloration. S Sept 23 (349) £130 [Pampolini]

Hippolytus...
— Hippolytus Redivivus; id est, Remedium contemnendi sexum muliebrum. Autore S.I.E.D.U.M.W.A.S. [N.p., 1644]. 24mo, later calf; joints weak. sg Oct 9 (228) $80

Hirsch, August, 1817-94
— Biographisches Lexikon der hervorragenden Aerzte aller Zeiten und Voelker. Vienna, 1884-88. 1st Ed. 6 vols. 8vo, half lea; worn, Vol I crudely rebacked, other covers detached or starting. sg Oct 2 (203) $250

Hirsch Library, Paul
— Katalog der Musikbibliothek. Berlin, 1928-30, Frankfurt, 1936, Cambr., 1947. 4 vols. 4to, half vellum. sg May 14 (547) $400

Hirschfeld, Christian Cayus Lorenz
— Theorie de l'art des jardins. Leipzig, 1779-89. 5 vols. 4to, contemp calf gilt; worn. With 5 engraved titles & 7 plates. JG Oct 2 (1368) DM2,800
Anr Ed. Leipzig, 1779-85. 5 vols. 4to, contemp half calf; def. pn Jan 22 (261) £880

Hislop, Herbert Robert, 1853-1934
— An Englishman's Arizona: The Ranching Letters of.... Tucson: Overland Press, 1965. One of 510. Cloth. cb Jan 8 (90) $50

Histoire...
See also: Prevost d'Exiles, Antoine Francois
— Histoire d'Aboulhassan Ali ebn Becar et de Schemselnihar. Harlem, 1929. Unique copy with 159 orig watercolors. Illus by M. A. J. Bauer. Contemp mor extra. FD Dec 2 (4213) DM25,000
— Histoire du livre et de l'imprimerie en Belgique.... Brussels, 1923-34. 6 vols plus Index vol. Folio, wraps. sg May 14 (334) $110

Historical...
— Historical and Scientific Sketches of Michigan.... Detroit, 1834. 1st Ed. 12mo, orig cloth; worn, soiled & faded. wa Sept 25 (365) $80
— The Historical Record. A Monthly Periodical. Salt Lake City, 1886-90. Vols 5-9. Bound in 1 vol. 8vo, orig cloth. All pbd under this title as Vols 1-4 were in Danish as Morgenstjernen. sg Mar 12 (185) $90

Historie. See: Bible in Dutch

History...
— History of Del Norte County, California.... [N.p.: Elliott, 1882]. Folio, orig half calf; worn. Lacking tp; map of California torn. cb Oct 9 (56) $225
— History of Goody Two Shoes, otherwise Called Mrs. Margery Two Shoes.... L: H. Abel, [watermarked 1794]. 16mo, orig Dutch floral bds. S June 17 (465) £600 [Randolph]
— History of Napa and Lake Counties, California. San Francisco, 1881. Orig calf; rubbed, front joint started, spine lifting, broken. cb Oct 9 (114) $85
— The History of the Works of the Learned.... L, 1699-1701. Vols I-III in 36 Nos, bound in 3 vols. Contemp calf; rubbed. cb Oct 23 (26) $100
— The History of the Human Heart: or, the Adventures of a Young Gentleman. L, 1749. 8vo, later half calf; joints weak. Opening leaves stained in lower corners; marginal tear in C8. sg Oct 9 (229) $1,100
— The History of the British Dominions in

North America. L, 1773. 2 vols in 1. 4to, contemp calf; joints cracked. With folding map hand-colored in outline. S June 25 (390) £420 [Voorhees]
— History of the Connecticut Valley in Massachusetts.... Phila., 1879. 2 vols. Folio, orig half mor; worn, 1 bdg broken, 1 frontis loose & frayed. Sold w.a.f. O Oct 21 (88) $50

Hitchcock, Henry Russell
— In the Nature of Materials: The Buildings of Frank Lloyd Wright. NY, 1942. 4to, cloth; worn & soiled. Inscr. wa Mar 5 (443) $200

Hitchcock, James Ripley Wellman, 1857-1918
— Etching in America. NY, 1886. 12mo, cloth. wa Sept 25 (237) $80

Hitchcock, Ripley, 1857-1918
— Notable Etchings by American Artists. NY, 1886. Ltd Ed. Folio, orig cloth. cb Mar 5 (88) $85

Hitler, Adolf, 1889-1945
— Bilder aus dem Leben des Fuehrers. Hamburg, 1936. 4to, orig half cloth. Frontis torn in corner. bba Oct 30 (199) £50 [Fisher]

Hittell, John Shertzer
— Hittell on Gold Mines and Mining. Quebec, 1864. 8vo, modern half mor. sg Dec 4 (29) $300

Hittell, John Shertzer, 1825-1901
— A History of the City of San Francisco and Incidentally of the State of California. San Francisco, 1878. 1st Ed. 8vo, orig cloth; recased, rubbed, tape-repairs. Tp torn & tape-repaired & followed by an inserted facsimile of the tp. cb July 16 (127) $110

Hittell, Theodore H. See: Grabhorn Printing

Hittell, Theodore Henry, 1830-1917
— History of California. San Francisco, 1885-98. Vols I & II, 1st Ed; Vols III & IV, 2d Ed. 4 vols. 8vo, calf; rubbed, front joint of Vol I starting. cb Oct 9 (115) $250

Hoare, Sir Richard Colt, 1758-1838
— A Classical Tour through Italy and Sicily. L, 1819. 2 vols. 4to, half calf; scuffed. pnE Dec 17 (42) £50 [Tosi]
— A Collection of Forty-Eight Views. L: Boydell, [c.1800]. Oblong 4to, contemp mor gilt; worn. With 48 plates. wa Mar 5 (151) $225
— Journal of a Tour in Ireland.... L, 1807. 8vo, later half calf; rubbed. Lacking half-title. bba Apr 9 (351) £55 [Dawson]

Hoare, Sir Richard Colt, 1758-1838 —& Others
— The History of Modern Wiltshire. L, 1822-43. With: The History of Ancient Wiltshire. L, 1845. 14 vols. Folio, half lea on orig bds; scuffed. Inscr. pn Oct 23 (326) £720 [Old Hall]

Hobart, Noah, 1706-73
— An Attempt to Illustrate and Confirm the Ecclesiastical Constitution of the Consociated Churches, in...Connecticut.... New Haven, 1765. 8vo, sewn through orig stab-holes; in mor box. Title remargined, other leaves repaired. Nathan Hale's copy. P Dec 15 (199) $4,500

Hobbes, Thomas, 1588-1679
— Behemoth; or an Epitome of the Civil Wars of England.... L, 1679. ("The History of the Civil Wars of England.") 12mo, old half calf; disbound. Some browning & soiling. O Feb 24 (106) $60
— De mirabilibus pecci. L, 1678. 8vo, disbound. Port cut down & mtd; cropped at fore-edge; 1st few leaves stained at lower margin; corner of tp repaired; lacking last leaf. S Nov 10 (383) £100 [Scott]
— Decameron Physiologicum: or, Ten Dialogues of Natural Philosophy. L, 1678. 1st Ed. 8vo, contemp calf; rebacked. Some leaves browned; upper margin trimmed just touching some pagination. C May 13 (127) £550 [Malcolm]
— Elementa philosophica de cive. Amst.: Elzevir, 1647. 3d version of Elzevir Ed. 12mo, 19th-cent mor; spine chipped & rubbed. cb Oct 23 (66) $55

Anr copy. Contemp vellum. sg Mar 26 (142) $120
— Leviathan. L: Andrew Ckooke, 1651 [but Amst., c.1651]. 2d Ed, with "bear" ornament on t.p. 4to, contemp calf; worn, upper cover detached. Engraved title with a couple of short tears; 2E1 frayed. S July 23 (414) £350 [Lake]

3d Ed with "type" ornament on t.p. L: Andrew Crooke, 1651 [but Amst., c.1680]. Folio, modern calf. Engraved title cut down & mtd; tp & some leaves repaired. S Nov 10 (384) £250 [Seibu]
— Opera philosophica quae latine scripsit omnia. Amst., 1668. 8 parts in 1 vol. 4to, later mor; loose. Tp margin restored; port in facsimile; browned & brittle. Sold w.a.f. T Dec 18 (244) £100
— Philosophical Rudiments Concerning Government and Society. L, 1651. 1st Ed in English. 12mo, 18th-cent calf; spine split, worn. With engraved title & 3 plates. Lacking initial & final blanks; holes affecting text in G3 & Q12; short tear in A12. S July 23 (415) £300 [Quaritch]

Hobhouse, John Cam, 1st Baron Broughton
— A Journey through Albania.... L, 1813. 1st Ed. 4to, contemp calf; rebacked. With frontis, plan, 2 folding maps & 17 colored plates heightened with gold. S Oct 23 (341) £650 [Davies]

Anr copy. 2 vols. 4to, half calf. With 2 frontises, 2 folding maps, plan, 2 facsimiles, 2 leaves of Greek music & 16 hand-colored plates, the costume plates with added gold. S Nov 17 (908) £550 [Cumming]

Anr Ed. L, 1858. ("Travels in Albania and other Provinces of Turkey.") 2 vols. 8vo, orig cloth. S Feb 23 (87) £180 [Adamopoulos]

Hobson, Geoffrey D.
— English Binding before 1500. Cambr., 1929. Folio, orig cloth; worn. Inscr. sg May 14 (118) $350
— English Binding Before 1500: Sandars Lectures. Cambr., 1929. One of 500. Folio, cloth; worn. O May 12 (91) $180
— English Bindings 1490-1940 in the Library of J. R. Abbey. L, 1940. One of 180. Folio, half mor gilt by Sangorski & Sutcliffe. Lacking pp 107-8 but with pp 105-6 in duplicate. S Mar 9 (715) £350 [Forster]
— Maioli, Canevari and Others. Bost., 1926. 4to, orig cloth, in tattered d/j. With 64 plates. O June 16 (98) $100

Anr Ed. L, 1926. 4to, orig cloth. Perforated stamps on title. bba Feb 5 (89) £50 [Zeitlin]

Anr copy. Orig cloth. With 64 plates. Inscr. sg May 14 (117) $200
— Les Reliures a la fanfare. L, 1935. One of 215. 4to, orig cloth; rubbed. O May 12 (92) $220; sg May 14 (119) $400

Hobson, Robert Lockhart
See also: Eumorfopoulos Collection, George
— A Catalogue of Chinese Pottery and Porcelain in the Collection of Sir Percival David. L, 1934. One of 650. Folio, silk by Sangorski & Sutcliffe. S Nov 10 (104) £650 [Heneage]
— Chinese Art. L, 1927. 4to, orig cloth. With 100 colored plates. sg Feb 5 (91) $140
— Worcester Porcelain. L, 1910. 4to, cloth; spine ends worn. With mtd frontis & 109 plates. Library stamp on verso of all plates. sg June 4 (64) $250

Hobson, Robert Lockhart — & Morse, Edward S., 1838-1925
— Chinese, Corean and Japanese Potteries.... NY, 1914. One of 1,500. 4to, half cloth. O June 16 (99) $50

Hochstetter, Christian Ferdinand, 1787-1860
— Naturgeschichte des Pflanzenreichs. Esslingen: J. F. Schreiber, 1874. 4to, orig half cloth; corners chipped. With 53 double-page hand-colored plates. sg Jan 15 (224) $100

Hodder, Edwin
— The History of South Australia.... L, 1893. 2 vols. 8vo, cloth. Map torn & loose in Vol I; map with small tear in Vol II. CA Apr 12 (137) A$110

Hodge, Frederick Webb, 1864-1956
Handbook of American Indians North of Mexico. Wash., 1907-10. 2 vols. Orig cloth. Bureau of American Ethnology Bulletin 30. bba Mar 12 (306) £65 [Walton]

Hodge, Hugh Lenox, 1796-1873
— The Principles and Practice of Obstetrics. Phila., 1864. 4to, orig cloth. With 32 plates. Small dampstains in extreme upper corners of plates. S May 28 (690) £200

Hodges, James
— Considerations and Proposals for Supplying the Present Scarcity of Money.... Edin., 1705. 4to, wraps. S July 24 (443) £650 [Perceval]

Hodges, Nathaniel, 1629-88
— Loimologia, or an Historical Account of the Plague of London.... L, 1720. 8vo, disbound. Lacking initial blank. pn Mar 5 (26) £80 [Finch]

Anr copy. Contemp calf; back relaid. pnE Dec 17 (104) £150 [Traylen]

Hodges, William, 1744-97
— Select Views in India [Choix de vues de l'Inde]. L, 1785-88. 2 vols. Folio, contemp half calf; joints cracked, worn. With 48 plates. Waterstain to blank corners of some plates. C Apr 8 (96) £2,100 [Lennox Money]
— Travels in India.... L, 1793. 1st Ed. 4to, mor by H. Walther; rubbed. With folding map & 14 plates. L.p. copy. O May 12 (93) $260

Hodgkin, John Eliot
— Rariora. L, [1900]-2. 3 vols. 4to, orig cloth; rubbed & soiled. bba Oct 16 (425) £110 [Hay Cinema]

Anr copy. Cloth; soiled. sg May 14 (305) $70

Anr copy. Cloth; worn & soiled. Wtih 65 plates. wa Nov 6 (535) $65

Hodgskin, Thomas
— Travels in the North of Germany...Particularly in the Kingdom of Hanover. Edin., 1820. 2 vols. 8vo, modern cloth. Pencil call numbers erased from titles. P Sept 24 (304) $875

Hodgson, Christopher Pemberton
— A Residence at Nagasaki and Hakodate in 1859-1860. L, 1861. 8vo, half calf; def. pn Jan 22 (187) £85 [Denniston]

Hodgson, John Edmund
— The History of Aeronautics in Great Britain. L, 1924. One of 1,000. 4to, orig cloth. sg Jan 15 (272) $350; sg May 14 (561) $175

Hodgson, William Hope, 1875-1918
— The Ghost Pirates. L, 1909. Cloth; worn & stained, adhesion damage to front endpaper. Some soiling; tp foxed. cb Sept 28 (661) $110
— The House on the Borderland. Sauk City, 1946. In d/j. cb Sept 28 (662) $225
 Anr copy. In chipped d/j. wa June 25 (362) $120
— Poems of the Sea. L: Ferret, [1977]. One of 50 L.p. copies. In d/j. cb Sept 28 (664) $850

Hodson, Sir Arnold Wienholt, 1881-1944
— Trekking, the Great Thirst. L, 1912. cb May 21 (152) $55

Hodson, William Stephen Raikes
— Twelve Years of a Soldier's Life in India.... L, 1859. 8vo, orig cloth; rubbed & soiled. Some staining. cb Dec 18 (83) $75

Hoe, Robert, 1839-1909. See: Grolier Club
Hoe Library, Robert
— [Sale Catalogue] Catalogue of the Library.... NY, 1911-12. 8 parts in 4 vols. Half mor gilt; corners & edges rubbed. sg Jan 22 (198) $75
 Anr copy. 8 parts bound in 7 vols. Needs rebdg. sg May 14 (64) $130

Hoelderlin, Friedrich
— Saemtliche Werke und Briefe. Leipzig: Insel-Verlag, 1914-26. 5 vols. 4to, orig half lea. HK Nov 4 (2552) DM1,100

Hoffmann, Professor. See: Lewis, Angelo John

Hoffmann, Carl, 1802-83
— Das Buch der Welt. Stuttgart: Hoffmann, 1848. Folio, contemp half sheep; lacking backstrip, worn. With litho title & 47 (of 48) plates, most hand-colored. cb Oct 23 (113) $90
 Anr Ed. Stuttgart, 1851-54. 4 vols in 2. 4to, half lea; worn. With engraved titles & 162 plates only, many hand-colored. Sold w.a.f.

S Feb 23 (573) £700 [Trocchi]

Hoffmann, E. T. A. See: Hoffmann, Ernst Theodor Wilhelm

Hoffmann, Ernst Theodor Wilhelm, 1776-1822
— Contes fantastiques. Paris, 1861. Illus by Gavarni. 8vo, contemp half lea; extremities rubbed. sg Feb 12 (161) $175
— The Devil's Elixir. Edin., 1824. 2 vols. 12mo, contemp calf; scuffed. sg Sept 11 (203) $130
— Gesammelte Schriften. Berlin, 1844-45. 12 vols. 8vo, contemp cloth; worn. HN May 20 (1841) DM2,000
— Klein Zaches genannt Zinnober. Berlin, 1819. 8vo, contemp bds; worn. HK Nov 4 (2556) DM500
— Meister Floh. Ein Maehrchen in sieben Abentheurn.... Frankfurt, 1822. 8vo, orig bdg; worn. FD June 11 (4026) DM2,750; HK Nov 4 (2557) DM850
— Prinzessin Brambilla. Breslau, 1821. 8vo, late 19th-cent half lea. With 8 plates by Jacques Callot. HK Nov 4 (2558) DM1,100
— Die Serapions-Brueder. Gesammelte Erzaehlungen und Maehrchen. Berlin, 1819-21. 4 vols. 8vo, contemp half calf; 1 bdg def. HK Nov 4 (2559) DM2,100
— Weird Tales. L: Nimmo, 1885 [1884]. One of 50. 2 vols. 8vo, mor gilt by Sangorski & Sutcliffe. Some foxing. cb Sept 11 (255) $425

Hoffmann, Georg Franz, 1761-1826
— Descriptio et adumbratio plantarum.... Leipzig, 1790-1801. 3 vols in 5. Folio, orig bds; some spines worn. With 3 dedication leaves, 3 engraved vignettes on titles, 1 plain & 72 hand-colored plates. de Belder copy. S Apr 27 (151) £1,600 [Asher]

Hoffmann, Heinrich, 1809-94
See also: Limited Editions Club
— Een Nieuw Aardig Prentenboek als Vervolg op het Beroemde Hoogduitsche Kinderwerk "Der Struwwelpeter".... Schiedam: H. A. M. Roelants, [1849]. 4to, orig ptd bds; rubbed, soiled. P June 18 (84) $1,200

Hoffmann, J.
— La Becasse. Paris, 1877. 8vo, contemp half cloth; worn. Jeanson copy. SM Mar 1 (290) FF5,500

Hoffmann, Peter
— [In Russian: A Collection Worthy of Curiosity from the Realm of Plants....] Moscow, 1797-1803. 7 parts in 1 vol. Folio, contemp half calf; worn. With engraved title & 60 hand-colored plates plus 3 identical plates from anr work. de Belder copy. S Apr 27 (153) £4,000 [Israel]
 1st Ed. Moscow, 1797. 4 parts in 1 vol.

Folio, contemp half calf; worn. With engraved title, 2 engraved dedication leaves & 20 hand-colored plates. Tp inlaid; portion of engraved divisional title to Part 2 mtd; may be lacking engraved divisional titles to Parts 3 & 4; some soiling; some dampstaining in margins; some holing. de Belder copy. S Apr 27 (154) £2,200 [Paalsell]

Hoffmannsegg, Johann Centurius von —& Link, Heinrich Frederick
— Flore Portugaise, ou description de toutes les plantes...en Portugal.... Berlin, 1809-20-[40]. 22 parts in 2 vols. Folio, unsewn & uncut as issued in 2 canvas boxes. With 111 plates, ptd in colors & finished by hand, & 3 plain plates. Text spotted; some marginal dampstaining towards end of Vol. II. Horticultural Society of New York—de Belder copy. S Apr 27 (155) £20,000 [Israel]

Hofmann, Ernst, 1837-92
— Die Schmetterlinge Europas. Stuttgart, [1901]-1910. 3d Ed. 4 vols in 3. 4to, contemp half mor; spines rubbed. Leaf of description to Plate 17 in Vol III def. S Apr 23 (11) £380 [Marks]

Hofmann, Friedrich Hermann
— Frankenthaler Porzellan. Munich, 1911. One of 400. 2 vols. Folio, orig half vellum. FD June 11 (2217) DM2,800; HK Nov 4 (3198) DM3,900

Hofmannsthal, Hugo von, 1874-1929
— Der weisse Faecher. Leipzig: Insel Verlag, 1907. One of 50. 4to, orig vellum. FD June 11 (4866) DM1,250
One of 800. Orig half vellum, in d/j. sg Feb 26 (93) $350

Hofstatter, Hans H.
— Gustav Klimt: Erotic Drawings. NY: Abrams, [1980]. Folio, cloth. cb Mar 5 (106) $160

Hogarth, William, 1697-1764
— The Analysis of Beauty. L, 1753. 4to, contemp calf gilt; rubbed, joints cracking. A1 torn without loss; spotted & soiled. Warren Hastings' copy. S Jan 13 (386) £240 [Bickersteth]
— Works. L, [1790]. Folio, contemp half calf; worn. Lacking 1 plate; some spotting & chipping. FD June 11 (4291) DM12,000
Anr Ed. L, 1801. ("Hogarth Restored.") Folio, half calf. One sheet with marginal tear. pn Apr 30 (25) £440 [Walford]
Anr copy. Modern cloth; soiled. With port & 94 plates only. Some plates cut down; extensive repairs & tears; soiled & stained. Sold w.a.f. S Nov 10 (216) £320 [Erlini]

Anr Ed. L, 1802. Folio, half calf; broken. With 111 plates on 86 sheets, including 2 suppressed plates. Some plates laid down. pn Apr 30 (127) £480 [Valcke]
Anr Ed. L, 1806. Folio, half calf; broken. With port & 72 engravings on 55 sheets. pn June 18 (108) £220 [Forster]
Anr copy. With port frontis & 94 plates. pnE Dec 17 (10A) £1,050 [L'Acquaforte]
Anr Ed. L, 1822. Ed by John Nichols. Folio, contemp half mor; upper joint cracking. C Apr 8 (27) £1,200 [Gollmann]
Anr copy. Half mor. With port & 156 plates on 115 sheets. pn Apr 30 (124) £600 [Collmann]
Anr copy. Contemp mor gilt. pnE Nov 12 (186) £480
Anr copy. Contemp half mor; worn. With 2 suppressed plates in pouch inside the lower cover. Tp soiled; a few leaves of intro creased. S June 17 (248) £550 [McKenzie]
Anr Ed. L, 1824. 2 vols. 4to, contemp mor gilt; rubbed. With 158 plates. Marginal dampstaining at beginning of Vol II. S July 13 (199) £100
Anr Ed. L, 1827. Ed by John Trusler. 2 vols. 4to, mor gilt. With 158 plates. sg Dec 18 (190) $80
Anr Ed. L: Baldwin, Cradock & Joy, [c.1830]. 2 vols. Folio, half mor; 1 bdg broken. C July 22 (98) £650
Anr Ed. L, 1833. 2 vols. 4to, contemp calf; rebacked, corners rubbed. Ck Oct 17 (69) £45
Anr Ed. L: Baldwin & Craddock, [1835-37]. Folio, contemp half mor; worn & stained, front hinge cracked, flyleaf & frontis detached. With 116 plates. Prelims dampstained & some plates with light dampstain. cb Oct 23 (114) $550
Anr Ed. L: Baldwin & Cradock, [1835-37]. Folio, half mor gilt; rubbed, call number on spine. With frontis & 115 plates. Without the 3 suppressed plates; frontis extended; tp soiled & torn & repaired; preface leaves creased; some plates with marginal tears; 2 plates short & possibly supplied; library markings. P June 18 (85) $900
Anr copy. Contemp half russia; spine lacking, upper cover loose. With frontis & 114 plates. Tp & 4 plates torn. S Oct 6 (817) £300 [Hepner]
Anr copy. Modern cloth; soiled. With frontis & 118 plates, including the 3 suppressed plates. Minor tears; 1 plate severely torn. S Nov 10 (217) £240 [Darker]
Anr copy. Half mor; worn & broken. Lacking 1 plate; foxed throughout, occa-

HOGARTH

sionally affecting images. sg Dec 18 (189) $600

Anr Ed. L, [c.1850]. Ed by Trusler & E. F. Roberts. 2 vols in 1. Folio, contemp mor gilt by Budden; some wear, broken. T Feb 19 (515) £48

Anr Ed. L. [c.1860]. Intro by James Hannay. 4to, mor gilt; worn & soiled. wa Feb 19 (82) $95

Hogg, Robert, 1818-97 —& Bull, Henry Graves

— The Herefordshire Pomona. Hereford, 1876-85. 2 vols. 4to, half mor gilt; upper joint torn. With 77 colored plates. L July 2 (163) £2,200

Anr copy. Contemp mor gilt; rubbed. With 77 colored plates & 4 woodcut plates. Humfrys-de Belder copy. S Apr 27 (49) £6,500 [Devonshire]

Hogg, Robert, 1818-97 —& Johnson, George William

— The Wild Flowers of Great Britain. L, 1863-80. Vols I-V only. Orig cloth; rubbed & soiled. Ck May 29 (222) £250

Holbach, Paul Henri Thiry, Baron d', 1723-89

— Systeme de la nature.... L [Amst.], 1770. 2 vols in 1. 8vo, contemp calf gilt; worn. FD Dec 2 (2516) DM6,000

Anr copy. 2 vols. 8vo, contemp calf; worn. HN Nov 26 (1235) DM700

Holbein, Hans, 1497-1543

— The Dance of Death. L, 1803. 4to, contemp half calf; rubbed, rubberstamp to front free endpaper. With engraved prelims & 46 plates. cb Feb 19 (130) £70

Anr Ed. L, 1811. 8vo, orig bds; broken. Marginal foxing. sg Mar 26 (91) $120

Anr Ed. L, 1816. Engraved by Wenceslas Hollar. 8vo, contemp mor gilt; worn. With 33 hand-colored plates. Marginal tear to 1 leaf. S Mar 9 (748) £170 [Walford]

Anr copy. Contemp half calf; spine ends chipped, joints cracked. With 2 ports & 31 hand-colored plates. sg Mar 26 (92) $100

— Facsimiles of Original Drawings in the Collection of his Majesty, for the Portraits of Illustrious Persons of the Court of Henry VIII. L, 1884. Folio, contemp half mor gilt; worn. S July 14 (461) £100

— Imitations of Original Drawings for the Portraits...of the Court of Henry VIII. L, 1792-[1800]. Bound in 1 vol. Folio, 19th-cent half mor. Lacking 1 plate; most plates mtd. C Oct 15 (47) £1,700 [Marks]

Anr copy. Folio, early 19th-cent mor gilt; slightly worn & soiled. With 84 hand-colored ports. A few ports foxed or spotted in margins. S Dec 18 (232) £2,650 [Pollard]

AMERICAN BOOK PRICES CURRENT

Anr Ed. L, 1828. ("Portraits of Illustrious Personages of the Court of Henry VIII.") 4to, contemp half mor gilt; rubbed. S July 13 (29) £190

Anr Ed. L, 1884. ("Facsimiles of Original Drawings....") Folio, later half cloth; rubbed. 1 corner torn not affecting text. S Nov 10 (108) £70 [Levy]

Holbrook, Theodore S. See: Otto & Holbrook

Hole, Samuel Reynolds, 1819-1904

— Our Gardens. L, 1899. One of 150 on handmade paper. 8vo, vellum. Sgd & with additional plate laid in. sg Oct 30 (101) $300

Holinshed, Raphael, d.1580?

— The Firste [-Laste] Volume of the Chronicles.... L: [H. Bynneman] for J. Harrison, 1577. 1st Ed, STC 13568.5. 4 parts in 2 vols. Folio, 17th-cent blind-tooled panelled calf; rebacked. Additional leaf (pilcrow 2) inserted after pilcrow 6. Lacking 1 errata leaf, general title, map of Edinburgh & leaves t5-v1, v7-x2 & 3H3.6 in Part 4; t3-t5 mtd on guards; some dampstains; a few other leaves torn or def; some cropping; a few holes or short tears slightly affecting text. S July 23 (6) £1,050 [Leinweber]

Holland, Sir Henry, 1788-1873

— Travels in the Ionian Isles.... L, 1815. 4to, contemp calf; rebacked, old spine relaid. With map & 12 plates. Foxed. pnE Jan 28 (68) £140 [McKenzie]

Anr copy. Contemp russia; rubbed. Map repaired in margin with loss. S July 13 (240) £160

Holland, P——

— Select Views of the Lakes in Cumberland, Westmorland & Lancashire. Liverpool, 1792. Oblong 4to, later calf. With 21 hand-colored plates. Engraved title soiled & with repair to margin. S Oct 23 (168) £450 [Mason]

Holland, Ray P.

— Seven Grand Gun Dogs. NY, [1961]. One of 250. 4to, cloth. sg Oct 23 (344) $60

— Shotgunning in the Uplands. NY, [1944]. 1st Trade Ed. cb Nov 6 (161) $70

Anr Ed. West Hartford, VT[1944]. One of 250. sg Oct 23 (346) $175

— Shotgunning in the Lowlands. NY, [1945]. 1st Trade Ed, One of 3,500. cb Nov 6 (160) $65

Anr Ed. West Hartford, VT[1945]. One of 350. s Oct 23 (345) $110

Holland, Romain
— Liluli. Geneva, 1919. One of 30 on papier verge Ingres d'Arches. Illus by Frans Masereel. Inscr by Masereel. B Oct 7 (186) HF275

Hollar, Wenceslaus, 1607-77
— The Kingdome of England & Principality of Wales, Exactly Described. L, 1644. 8vo, early calf gilt; hinges cracked. With engraved title & 6 folding maps, hand-colored in outline. All maps trimmed to plate mark & laid down. pn May 21 (367) £880 [Traylen]

— Ornatus Muliebris Anglicanus, or the Severall Habits of English Women. L, 1640 [but L: R. Sayer, 1755]. Bound with: Hollar. Theatru mulierum sive varietas atq. differentia habituum foeminei sexus.... Folio, modern mor by Riviere; marked. With engraved titles & 74 plates. S Nov 18 (931) £400 [Marlborough]

Holloway, William. See: Fore-Edge Paintings

Holman, Louis, 1866-1939
— The Graphic Processes: Intaglio, Relief, Planographic. Bost., 1929. Folio, loose as issued, in cloth folder. This copy with 24 mtd specimens. sg June 4 (154) $425

Holme, Charles, 1848-1923
— The Art of the Book. L: The Studio, 1914. 4to, later cloth. Spotting. bba Dec 4 (235) £40 [Brailey]

— The "Old" Water-Colour Society, 1804-1904. L: The Studio, 1905. 4to, wraps & portfolio of 40 color plates. cb Mar 5 (92) $110

— The "Old" Water-Color Society, 1804-1904. L: The Studio, 1905. 4to, cloth. Minor soiling. sg Oct 30 (209) $90

— The Royal Institute of Painters in Water Colours. L: The Studio, 1906. 4to, wraps & portfolio of 40 color plates. cb Mar 5 (93) $85

Holme, Randle
— The Academy of Armory. L, 1701. Folio, contemp calf; rebacked. Engraved title in facsimile & torn; some tears & repairs. S Sept 22 (246) £220 [Quaritch]

Holmes, Abiel, 1763-1837
— American Annals. Cambr., Mass., 1829. ("The Annals of America.") 2d Ed. 8vo, 19th-cent half sheep; worn, joints weak. sg Oct 2 (165) $80

Holmes Book Co. See: Grabhorn Printing

Holmes, Sir Charles John, 1868-1936
— Constable and his Influence on Landscape Painting. L, 1902. Folio, cloth. Some foxing, marginally affecting a few plates. sg Feb 5 (100) $120

Holmes, Oliver Wendell, 1809-94
— The Autocrat of the Breakfast Table. Bost., 1858. 1st Ed, 1st Issue. 12mo, orig cloth, Blanck's A bdg. With engraved title & 8 plates. Signature erased on p [v]. sg Sept 11 (204) $130

— Works. Cambr. MA, 1891-92. One of 275 L.p. copies. 16 vols. 8vo, orig half cloth; worn. ALs inserted. O Sept 23 (82) $170

Anr Ed. Cambr., Mass., 1891-92. 16 vols. 8vo, calf gilt; some covers scuffed. sg Dec 4 (84) $650

Holstein, H. L. V. Ducoudray
— Memoirs of Simon Bolivar and of his Principal Generals.... L, 1830. 12mo, orig cloth; rubbed. With port & folding map (repaired). bba Sept 25 (417) £75 [Waggett]

Holub, Emil, 1847-1902
— Sieben Jahre in Sud-Afrika. Vienna, 1881. 2 vols. 8vo, orig cloth. SSA Oct 28 (636) R400

— Von der Capstadt ins Land der Maschukulumbe. Vienna, 1890. 2 vols. 8vo, contemp half calf. SSA Oct 28 (637) R500

Holub, Emil, 1847-1902 —& Pelzeln, August von, 1825-91
— Beitraege zur Ornithologie Suedafrikas. Vienna, 1882. 8vo, cloth. Haverschmidt copy. B Feb 24 (254) HF360

Homann, Johann Baptist, 1663-1724
— Atlas Novus. Nuremberg, [c.1740]. Tabularum Homanniarum etc. Contemp calf. With 36 double-page maps & tables, all colored in a contemp hand. Marginal waterstains. S Oct 23 (228) £2,300 [Fletcher]

— Kleiner Atlas scholasticus von Achtzehen Charten. Nuremberg, [1732 or later]. Folio, lea; worn. With engraved title & 12 (of 18) double-page maps. HN May 20 (1073) DM1,200

— Neuer Atlas bestehend in auserlesenen und allerneusten Land-Charten ueber die gantze Welt. Nuremberg, [1712-30 & later]. Folio, contemp half lea; def. With 77 mapsheets only. Many maps excised; tp & some maps with losses & patched with or partly laid down upon old paper. Sold w.a.f. CNY Dec 19 (94) $2,800

Home, Francis, 1719-1813
— Medical Facts and Experiments. L, 1759. 8vo, calf; spine worn. pnE Dec 17 (106) £60 [Aberdeen]

Home, Henry, Lord Kames, 1696-1782
— Sketches of the History of Man. Edin., 1774. 1st Ed. 2 vols. 4to, contemp calf, armorial bdg; rubbed, rebacked & repaired. P Sept 24 (305) $600

Home, Robert, 1750?-1836?
— Select Views in Mysore.... L, 1794. 1st Ed. 4to, contemp russia; rubbed. With double-page map, 3 folding plans & 29 plates. Plans creased, 2 with tear. C Apr 8 (98) £190 [Shapero]

Anr copy. Contemp half sheep. With 3 maps & 28 plates. With Ms plate list inserted at end. sg Nov 20 (80) $200

Homer
See also: Bremer Press; Fore-Edge Paintings

Iliad & Odyssey in English
— 1715-16. - L. Trans by Alexander Pope. 11 vols in 6. 4to, old calf; rebacked. Some foxing & browning; lacking plate of Achilles' shield & the 6 plates on 2 leaves in the Iliad & lacking frontis to the Odyssey. Sold w.a.f. O Nov 18 (148) $160
— 1763. - L. Trans by Alexander Pope. 7 vols. 12mo, contemp calf; spine ends chipped, hinges cracked. wa Sept 25 (40) $65

Iliad in English
— [c.1612]. - L: Nathaniel Butter Trans by George Chapman. Folio, 20th-cent calf. Engraved title in early facsimile. Lacking 2 leaves of unsgd sonnets at rear. ha May 22 (171) $250
— 1660. - Iliads Translated.... L. Trans by John Ogilby. Folio, contemp calf gilt; spine worn, upper joint broken. Port, frontis & 1 other plate shaved; small piece missing from frontis; marginal def to Ff4. L Dec 11 (409) £120
— 1715-20. - The Iliad. L. Trans by Alexander Pope. 6 vols. Folio, contemp calf; rubbed, rebacked. With port & map. Some browning & offsetting. bba Sept 25 (18) £170 [Mandl]

Anr copy. 6 vols in 3. Folio, contemp calf; broken. With 3 plates. pn Jan 22 (13) £55 [Wheldon & Wesley]

Odyssey in English
— 1932. - L. One of 530. Trans by T. E. Lawrence. 4to, lev. pnNY June 11 (126) $120

Anr copy. Orig mor. S Sept 22 (112) £300

Anr copy. Orig mor gilt; marked. S July 23 (157) £500 [Joseph]

Anr copy. Orig mor by W. H. Smith; scuffed. sg Sept 11 (205) $450

Anr copy. Mor by W. H. Smith. sg Dec 4 (85) $750

Odyssey in French
— 1930. - L'Odyssee. Paris One of 140. Trans by Victor Berard; illus by Theo Schmied. 4 vols. 4to, loose as issued. SM Oct 20 (666) FF22,000
— 1930. - Paris: Ambroise Vollard Illus by Emile Bernard. 2 vols. Folio, loose as issued. F Oct 30 (565) $425

Works in English
— [1616]. - The Whole Works of Homer.... L: Nathaniell Butter Trans by George Chapman. 2 parts in 1 vol. Folio, mor gilt by Riviere. Tp & dedication leaf a little discolored & restored, with repair touching engraving on title; divisional title a little cropped at fore-margin; 3 small rust-holes & a few short tears repaired, scarcely affecting text; some waterstains. S July 23 (10) £2,600 [Book Block]
— 1930-31. - Oxford: Shakespeare Head Press One of 450. Trans by George Chapman. 5 vols. Folio, orig half calf. bba Dec 4 (165) £140 [Wall]

Anr copy. Orig half mor, unopened. sg Jan 8 (272) $275

Works in Greek
— 1800. - Oxford One of 25 L.p. copies. 4 vols. 4to, contemp mor gilt by Staggemeier and Welcher with arms of Sir Mark Masterman Sykes. With 3 plates. S Nov 27 (177) £1,900

Homes...
— Homes of American Statesmen.... NY, 1854. 8vo, lea; worn. Lacking Whipple blind stamp below orig sun photo of Hancock House. wa Nov 6 (316) $110

Homespun, Priscilla, Pseud.
— The Universal Receipt Book: Being a Compendious Repository.... Phila.: Isaac Riley, 1818. 12mo, recent syn. Minor stains. ha Dec 19 (291) $95

Hommaire de Hell, Xavier
— Voyage en Turquie et en Perse.... [Paris: P. Bertrand, c.1860]. Folio, half mor. With 32 plates (of 119). S Oct 23 (344) £1,050 [Martinos]

Hondius, Henrik, the Younger
— Grondige onderrichtinge in de optica ofte perspective konste. Amst: de Weduwe Josua Ottens, [1640]. Folio, vellum bds. With engraved title & 36 plates. S May 21 (109) £280 [Goldschmidt]

Hondius, Jodocus, 1563-1611. See: Mercator & Hondius

Hondt, Pierre de
— Figures de la Bible. Amst., 1728. Folio, 18th-cent mor; rebacked. With 2 engraved titles & 211 plates. Minor repairs. S May 21 (300) £300 [Hoffman]

Honeyman Collection, Robert
— [Sale catalogue] The Honeyman Collection of Scientific Books and Manuscripts. L, 1978-81. 7 vols. 4to, wraps; worn. bba Oct 16 (456) £50 [Maggs]

Anr copy. With estimate lists for all parts & price lists for Parts 1, 2 & 4. sg Jan 15 (317) $250

Honorius Augustodunensis
— De imagine mundi. [Nuremberg: Anton Koberger, 1472?]. 1st Ed. Folio, mor gilt by Riviere; worn. With 2 initials decorated in colors & gold. 46 (ot 48) leaves; lacking 2 final blanks. Goff H-323. FD Dec 2 (72) DM26,000

Honterus, Joannes, 1498-1549
— Rudimentorum cosmographicorum. Zurich, 1549. 8vo, contemp vellum. With 3 woodcut diagrams & 13 woodcut maps. Small wormhole in title & 1st 2 leaves, not affecting text. C Oct 15 (49) £850 [Quaritch]

Honzu Zufu
— Honzu Zufu. Tokyo, [1921]. Kinjunbu only. 6 vols. 247mm by 175mm, wraps. Crahan copy. P Nov 25 (255) $800

Hood, Thomas, 1799-1845 — & Reynolds, John Hamilton
— Odes and Addresses to Great People. L, 1825. 1st Ed. 8vo, orig bds; rubbed. bba Dec 4 (96) £100 [Jarndyce]

Hooft, Pieter Cornelizoon, 1581-1647
— Neederlandsche Histoorien. Amst.: Elzevir, 1642 & Amst.: J. v. Someren, 1677. 2 vols. Folio, vellum; not uniform; Vol I damaged, Vol II loose. B Feb 25 (617) HF300

Hooge, Romein de, d.1708. See: Neptune...

Hoogstraeten, Frans van
— Het Voorhof der Ziele.... Rotterdam, 1668. Illus by Romeyn de Hooghe. 4to, modern mor; worn. With frontis & 60 plates. S May 21 (110) £500 [Bouvier]

Hoogstraten, Jan van
— Staat en zedekundige zinneprenten of leerzame fabelen.... Rotterdam, 1731. 4to, bds; lower margin of first & last leaf cut off; stained. With engraved title & 100 emblems. B Feb 25 (542) HF260

Hooke, Nathaniel, d.1763
— The Roman History, from the Building of Rome to the Ruin of the Commonwealth. L, 1738-71. 4 vols. 4to, contemp calf; rubbed. bba Jan 15 (40) £45 [Grants]

Anr copy. Contemp calf; rebacked. A few leaves in Vol I misbound. bba July 16 (250) £50 [Fisher]

Hooke, Robert, 1635-1702
— Micrographia, or Some Physiological Descriptions of Minute Bodies Made by Magnifying Glasses. L, 1665. 1st Ed. Folio, 19th-cent half calf; rubbed. Light soiling to tp; minor marginal stains to text & 1 plate, c.7 folding plates & the imprimatur leaf with small marginal tears at join; margins trimmed, affecting a few plate numerals & the extreme lower edge of several plates. cb Feb 19 (191) $3,250

Abridged Ed. L, 1780. ("Microscopic Observations....") Folio, contemp half calf. With 33 plates. pnE Dec 17 (358) £550 [Dickerstaff]

— Philosophical Experiments and Observations. L, 1726. 1st Ed. 8vo, modern half calf. With 4 plates, 2 folding. Some discoloration; 1 plate torn; short tear in 2A7-8. S May 28 (691) £260

Anr copy. Contemp calf gilt. S May 28 (693) £350

— The Posthumous Works.... L, 1705. Folio, later half mor; spine worn. With 16 plates. Library markings; 1 leaf holed because of natural paper fault; marginal dampstains at end. T Mar 19 (319) £135

Hooker, Sir Joseph Dalton, 1817-1911
— The Botany of the Antarctic Voyage of H.M. Discovery Ships.... L, [1844]-47. Part 3: Flora Tasmaniae. 2 vols. 4to, modern half mor. With 200 hand-colored plates. Lacking 1st leaf in each vol. de Belder copy. S Apr 27 (158) £4,000 [Weldon & Wesley]

Anr Ed. L, [1852]-1853-55. Part 2: Flora Novae-Zelandiae. 2 parts in 4 vols. 4to, contemp half mor; soiled. With 130 hand-colored plates on 127 leaves. Rule—de Belder copy. S Apr 27 (157) £5,000 [Brooke-Hitching]

— Himalayan Journals. L, 1854. 2 vols. 8vo, orig cloth; rebacked, orig spine relaid. With 2 folding maps & 12 colored plates. pnE Jan 28 (17) £360 [Hosains]

— Illustrations of Himalayan Plants. L, 1855. Folio, later half lev by Riviere; slightly marked. With colored title & 24 hand colored plates. Canning—de Belder copy. S Apr 27 (159) £5,000 [MacDougall]

— The Rhododendrons of Sikkim-Himalaya. L, 1849-[51]. Folio, half mor; spine worn.

HOOKER

With 30 hand-colored plates. Marginal tears repaired in last leaf of text. S June 25 (162) £3,600 [Schuster]
2d Ed of Part 1; 1st Ed of Parts 2 & 3. Folio, later half mor. With 30 hand-colored plates. de Belder copy. S Apr 27 (156) £5,000 [Sourget]

Hooker, Richard, 1554?-1600
— Of the Lawes of Ecclesiastical Politie. L, 1632-31. 6th Ed. Folio, contemp calf gilt; spine rubbed, repair to upper cover. Ck Jan 30 (19) £95
— Works. L, 1682. Folio, contemp calf; rebacked, worn. With engraved title & port; dampstained in lower margins. sg Oct 9 (230) $140

Hooker, Sir William Jackson, 1785-1865
— Exotic Flora. Edin., 1823-27. 3 vols. 8vo, modern cloth. With 233 hand-colored plates. Library markings. de Belder copy. S Apr 27 (160) £2,200 [Berg]

Hooker, Sir William Jackson, 1785-1865 —& Greville, Robert Kaye
— Icones Filicum: Ad eas Potissimum Species Illustrandas. Figures and Descriptions of Ferns.... L, [1827]-31. 2 vols. Folio, contemp calf; rebacked preserving orig spines. With 240 hand-colored plates. Stamp partly removed from each title without loss of text; marginal dust-soiling. de Belder copy. S Apr 27 (161) £1,400 [Woodburn]

Hoola van Nooten, Bertha
— Fleurs, fruits et feuillages choisies de...l'Ile de Java.... Brussels: Lib. C. Muquardt, [1885]. 3d Ed. Folio, later cloth. With 40 colored plates. Some spotting & marginal browning. de Belder copy. S Apr 27 (162) £2,500 [Schuster]

Hooper, William, M. D.
— Rational Recreations. L, 1783-82. 4 vols. 8vo, new cloth. Lacking half-title; port inserted. S May 28 (694) £450

Hooper, William Eden
— The Motor Car in the First Decade of the Twentieth Century. L & NY, 1908. One of 650. 4to, orig mor gilt; rubbed. S Nov 18 (952) £180 [Cumming]

Hoover, Herbert Clark, 1874-1964
— A Remedy for Disappearing Game Fishes. NY, 1930. One of 990. Half cloth. Sgd on front free endpaper. sg May 21 (127) $150
Anr copy. Half cloth, unopened. sg June 11 (240) $110

Hope, Anthony. See: Hawkins, Sir Anthony Hope

Hope, James, 1801-41
— Principles and Illustrations of Morbid Anatomy.... L, 1834. 1st Ed. 8vo, contemp half calf; worn, rebacked. With 48 colored plates. S May 28 (695) £340
— A Treatise on the Diseases of the Heart and Great Vessels.... L, 1832. 1st Ed. 8vo, new cloth. With 48 plates. S May 28 (695) £340

Hope, Thomas, 1770?-1831
— Costume of the Ancients. L, 1812. 2 vols. 4to, contemp mor gilt, armorial bdg. With 300 plates. S Oct 23 (8) £320 [Spelmans]
— Household Furniture and Interior Decoration. L, 1807. Folio, contemp mor gilt; rubbed. With engraved title & 60 plates. S Mar 9 (682) £580 [Maggs]

Hope, Sir William
— A New, Short and Easy Method of Fencing. Edin., 1707. 4to, calf; rubbed. Some browning; folding scheme of laws repaired. pn Oct 23 (368a) £300 [Walford]

Hopkins, Sarah Winnemucca, 1844-91
— Life Among the Piutes.... Bost., 1883. Orig cloth; extremities rubbed. cb Oct 9 (116) $150

Horace, 65-8 B.C.
— A Medicinable Morall, that is, the Two Bookes of Horace his Satyres.... L: Thomas Marshe, 1566. 8vo, later calf; rebacked & restored. Dampstained throughout; margins shaved, touching the occasional headline & letter in sidenotes; soiled. C Dec 12 (336) £1,300 [Poole]
— The Odes and Epodes. Bost., 1901-4. One of 467 on handmade paper. Ed by Clement L. Smith. 7 vols in 10. 4to, orig bds, in torn d/js. pnNY Oct 11 (4) $90
— Opera. Strassburg: Johann Grueninger, 12 Mar 1498. Folio, bds; upper cover detached. Several leaves at the beginning with portions of their margins cut away; some soiling. 218 (of 220) leaves; lacking K2 & 5 (supplied in Ms facsimile). Goff H-461. S Sept 23 (351) £800 [Fletcher]
Anr Ed. Venice: heirs of Marchio Sessa, 1587. 4to, later calf; broken. Latin text with Italian commentary. sg Mar 26 (143) $110
Anr Ed. Leiden: Elzevir, 1629. 2 vols in one, 8vo later mor. With 1 leaf holed, affecting text. bba Nov 13 (5) £88 [Stewart]
Anr Ed. L, 1733-37. 2d Issue. 2 vols. 8vo, mor gilt; worn, joints cracked. F Jan 15 (346) $200
Pine's 2d issue with "potest" on p. 108. Later mor; rubbed. O Sept 23 (83) £210
Anr copy. Contemp mor gilt; joints split, spines chipped at head & foot. S Sept 22

(247) £120 [Stewart]
Anr Ed. L, 1749. 2 vols. 8vo, contemp mor gilt. Some spotting. C May 13 (128) £1,300 [Lardonchet]
Anr copy. Contemp calf gilt, with lea armorial label mtd to head of spine of both vols. sg June 11 (241) $50
Anr Ed. Parma, 1793. 8vo, contemp calf gilt. FD Dec 2 (3450) DM2,700
Anr Ed. L: Riccardi Press, 1910. One of 1,000. Mor gilt by Bumpus. cb Sept 11 (214) $800
— Works. L: E. Cotes for H. Brome, 1666. ("The Poems.") 8vo, 19th-cent half calf. Some headlines & frontis shaved. C Dec 12 (337) £320 [Hannas]

Horae B. M. V.

— 1490, 20 Aug. - Horae Beate Marie Virginis Secundum Usum Romane curie. Paris: Anthoine Verard. 4to, contemp lea gilt. With 13 large & 36 small miniatures. 98 (of 106) leaves; lacking Sig. a. FD Dec 2 (73) DM13,000

— 1498, 16 Sept. - Heures a l'usaige de Rome. Paris: Philippe Pigouchet for Simon Vostre. 4to, 18th-cent mor gilt; rubbed, 3 wormholes to spine. Ptd on vellum. 72 leaves. Goff H-395. P Sept 24 (167) $3,500

— 1506, 23 Dec. - Use of Rome Paris: Thielman Kerver. 8vo, 18th-cent mor gilt. Ptd on vellum. Each page within full woodcut border; rubricated in terracotta & blue & highlighted in gold throughout 1 small wormhole at top of spine. S Nov 27 (79) £5,000 [Bourget]

— [almanach dated 1513-30]. - Paris: G. & G. Hardouin. 8vo, modern velvet. Ptd on vellum. With 16 full-page & 37 smaller miniatures illuminated in gold & colors. One leaf possibly restored, anr split & mended, 8 ink-stained at fore-edges. P Dec 15 (203) $3,750

— c.1520. - Paris: Germain Hardouyn. 4to, mor by McLeish With 6 full-page & 14 half-page woodcuts & 12 woodcut miniatures, all illuminated in gold & colors. Ptd on vellum. S Nov 27 (178) £3,000 [Pirages]

— [c.1521-33]. - Heures a lusaige de Besenson tout au long sans rerequerir. Paris: Guillaume Godard. 4to, contemp calf gilt over pastebd; joints starting, endpapers renewed. Some marginal stains or soiling; lacking B3 & N3.4. sg Dec 4 (86) $1,800

— 1923. - Ditchling: St. Dominic's Press One of 220. Illus by Eric Gill. 4to, cloth. sg Jan 8 (81) $225

— [1971]. - The Grandes Heures of Jean, Duke of Berry. NY Intro by Marcel Thomas. Folio, cloth. B Feb 25 (966) HF280

Horam, the Son of Asmar

— The Tales of the Genii. L, 1805. 2 vols. 8vo, contemp mor gilt; spine ends & joints rubbed. Ptd on blue paper. Bound without ptd titles or prelims. sg Feb 12 (255) $250

Horan, James D.

— The Life and Art of Charles Schreyvogel. NY, [1969]. One of 249, sgd by Horan & Schreyvogel's daughter. Folio, half lea, in d/j. sg Sept 18 (268) $250

Horblit, Harrison D. See: Grolier Club

Horgan, Paul

— Great River. The Rio Grande in American History. NY, 1954. One of 1,000. 2 vols. 8vo, cloth. Sgd. cb July 16 (132) $100

Horizon

— Horizon: A Review of Literature and Art. L, 1940-50. Ed by Cyril Connolly. Nos 1-121 in 119 vols plus index vol for Nos 1-108. Orig wraps. bba Oct 16 (180) £120 [Bologna]

Horn, Georg, 1620-70

— De originibus Americanis, libri quatuor. The Hague, 1652. 1st Ed. 8vo, modern lea; endpapers renewed. sg Mar 12 (140) $90

Horn, Hosea B.

— Horn's Overland Guide, from the U. S. Indian Sub-Agency...to...Sacramento. NY, 1852. 1st Ed, 2d Issue. 16mo, orig cloth. With folding map with routes hand-colored in red. sg Dec 4 (87) $325

Horn, Johannes von, 1621-70

— Versuch einer Darstellung der Verbrennung und Pluenderung Moskwas durch die Franzosen, im September 1812. St. Petersburg, 1813. 8vo, contemp lea gilt; loose, spine def. With hand-colored map with outer margin extended to size & with 2 plates. Tp stamped. sg Nov 20 (73) $110

Horne, Bernard S.

— The Complete Angler 1653-1967 A New Bibliography. Pittsburgh, 1970. One of 500. In d/j. sg May 21 (296) $225; sg May 21 (297) $175

Out-of-series copy. In d/j. sg Oct 23 (548) $150

Horne, Henry

— Essays concerning Iron and Steel.... L, 1773. 12mo, later calf. C Dec 12 (113) £480 [Quaritch]

Horne, Thomas Hartwell, 1780-1862. See: Finden & Horne

Horneman, Frederich Konrad, 1772-1800
— The Journal of F. Horneman's Travels from Cairo to Mourzouk.... L, 1802. 4to, contemp half calf. With 2 folding maps & 1 plate. Ck May 8 (338) £140

Horner, John
— Buildings in the Town and Parish of Halifax.... Halifax, 1835. Oblong folio, modern half calf. With litho title & 19 views. Title & a few plates spotted. Inscr to Alfred Howarth. C Oct 15 (50) £200 [Weinreb]

Hornius, Georgius
— Accuratissima Orbis antiqui delineatio sive geographis vetus. Amst.: Jansson, 1654. Folio, lea; worn. With 53 double-page maps. FD Dec 2 (780) DM11,000

Hornot, Antoine
— Traite raisonne de la distillation.... Paris, 1753. 12mo, contemp calf; knocked, spine wormed. Crahan copy. P Nov 25 (147) $300

Hornstein, Bernhard, Freiherr von
— Algoica rupicaprarum venatio. Augsbourg: M. S. Pinziger, 1749. 4to, calf gilt by Riviere. Schwerdt-Jeanson copy. SM Mar 1 (291) FF7,000

Hornung, Clarence P. See: Monaghan & Hornung

Horr, Norton Townshend
— A Bibliography of Card-Games and of the History of Playing-Cards. Cleveland, 1892. One of 250. 8vo, cloth. sg Oct 2 (252) $225

Horsburgh, James, 1762-1836
— Directions for Sailing to and from the East Indies, China, New Holland.... L, 1809-11. 2 parts in 1 vol. 4to, modern half calf. Some staining. S Feb 24 (420) £200 [Maggs]

Horsfield, Thomas, 1773-1859
— Plantae javanicae rariores descriptae iconibusque illustratae.... L, 1838-[52]. 4to, contemp half calf; joints rubbed. With folding map & 50 hand-colored plates. Tp stamped. Leipzig University Library—de Belder copy. S Apr 27 (163) £2,000 [Chong]

Horsfield, Thomas Walker, d.1837
— The History, Antiquities, and Topography of the County of Sussex. Lewes, 1835. 2 vols. 4to, contemp half lea. Some dampstains. pn Apr 30 (50) £120

Anr copy. Contemp half mor; 2 covers detached. Lacking frontis to Vol I; prelims of Vol II detached & frayed. T Apr 16 (86) £90

Horsley, John, d.1731
— Britannia Romana: or the Roman Antiquities of Britain. L, 1732. 1st Ed. Folio, modern half mor. With 105 plates & maps. Half-title repaired; marginal tear to title; some holes in blank margins; some stains. S May 29 (1001) £110

Horsmanden, Daniel, 1691-1778
— The New-York Conspiracy, or a History of the Negro Plot. NY, 1810. 8vo, contemp calf; worn, spine corroded. Some foxing & browning. O Oct 21 (89) $120

Horticultural Society of London
— Transactions. L, 1812-30. Vols I-VII. 4to, 19th-cent cloth. With 115 (of 128) plates, including 57 colored plates. Some cropping, foxing & offsetting; Vols III & V-VII imperf. Sold w.a.f. S June 25 (163) £1,600 [Schuster]

First Series Vols I-VII & Second Series Vol I. L, 1812-35. 4to, contemp half mor gilt. With uncolored plates & 81 colored plates, some finished by hand. Sold w.a.f. C Oct 15 (234) £3,400 [Adams]

3d Ed of Vols I-II, 2d Ed of Vol III. L, 1820-30. First Series, 7 vols. 4to, contemp half russia gilt; rubbed, 1 spine chipped at head. With 133 plates, 69 colored & finished by hand. Some shaving & foxing. Sold w.a.f. S Oct 23 (695) £3,800 [Thorp]

Horticulturist...
— The Horticulturist and Journal of Rural Art and Rural Taste.... Albany 1846-52. Vols 1-7. Contemp half mor; rubbed. bba Sept 25 (269) £420 [Weinreb]

Hortulus...
— Hortulus animae. Frankfurt, 1907-11. One of 75 & 125. 2 vols, including Plate vol. 8vo & folio, calf gilt in medieval style; worn, joints broken. O Nov 18 (92) $110

Hortus...
— Hortus sanitatis. De herbis et plantis.... [Strassburg: Johann Pruess, c.1497]. Folio, 19th-cent vellum bds. Sold with a 1954 facsimile of an English version of the Hortus Sanitatis, c.1521. E5, G3-4 & the last leaf of De Lapidibus def with loss of large portions of text; tear repaired in o6; some marginal stains. 358 (of 360) leaves; lacking A7 & the 6th leaf of the quire preceding De Urinis. Goff H-488. S June 25 (164) £3,200 [Schmidt]

— Hortus Sanitatis. Paris: pour Anthoine Verard, [c.1500]. ("Ortus Sanitatis translate de latin en francois.") 2 vols. Folio, mor janseniste by Chambolle-Duru. Last 14 leaves of Vol II from another copy; some repairs. 444 (of 446) leaves; lacking 2 blanks. Goff H-490. SM Mar 1 (292)

FF280,000

Hosack, David, 1769-1835
— An Inaugural Discourse, Delivered at the Opening of Rutgers Medical College. NY, 1826. 8vo, orig bds; spine frayed. Inscr. O Sept 23 (84) $180

Hoskins, George Alexander
— Travels in Ethiopia. L, 1835. 4to, orig cloth; soiled, bumped. CK May 8 (340) £320
— A Visit to the Great Oasis of the Libyan Desert. L, 1837. 8vo, orig cloth; spines rubbed. With folding map & 20 plates. cb Feb 19 (137) $120

Hossack, Buckham Hugh
— Kirkwall in the Orkneys. Kirkwall, 1900. 4to, orig half calf gilt; rubbed. T Sept 18 (76) £75

Host, Nicolaus Thomas, 1761-1834
— Icones et descriptiones graminum austriacorum. Vienna, 1801-9. 4 vols. Folio, contemp sheep; rubbed, Vol IV not uniform. With 400 hand-colored plates. Some holing. Plesch—de Belder copy. S Apr 27 (164) £8,000 [Tan]

Host, Nikolaus Thomas
— Salix. Vienna, 1828. Folio, contemp mor gilt; rubbed. With 105 hand-colored plates. Derby—de Belder copy. S Apr 27 (165) £14,000 [Israel]

Hottinger, Johann Heinrich, 1620-67
— Bibliothecarius quadripartitus. Zurich, 1664. 4to, contemp vellum. Last few leaves wormed in gutters. sg Mar 26 (145) $475

Houdetot, Cesar Francois Adolphe, comte d', 1799-1869
— Chasses exceptionelles. Paris: Au Depot de Librairie [A Lebrument], 1850. 8vo, later half shagreen. Jeanson copy. SM Mar 1 (293) FF1,200

Houdini, Harry, 1874-1926
— Handcuff Secrets. L & NY, 1910. 12mo, orig bds; rebacked. Inscr to Sydney R. Axford. S Nov 10 (334) £90 [Reuter]
— The Unmasking of Robert-Houdin. NY, 1908. Sgd. pn July 23 (217) £95 [Field]

Hough, Romeyn Beck, 1857-1924
— The American Woods. Lowville, NY, 1894-1910. 4 parts. 8vo, cloth & specimen box. With 312 specimens of wood. sg Jan 15 (225) $500

Houghton, William, 1829?-97
— British Fresh-Water Fishes. L, [1879]. 2 vols. Folio, contemp half lea; spine rubbed. With 41 colored plates. C Apr 8 (182) £420 [Geneva Archibald]
Anr copy. Orig cloth; rubbed. C Apr 8 (183) £420 [Old Hall]
Anr copy. Vol I only. contemp half mor; rubbed. Ck Jan 16 (223) £150
Anr copy. 2 vols. Folio, orig cloth. With 41 colored plates. Ck Jan 30 (118) £350
Anr copy. Orig cloth; extremities rubbed. Frontis & title to Vol I soiled. Ck Apr 24 (50) £350
Anr copy. Orig cloth; worn, 1 leaf loose. FD Dec 2 (752) DM1,500; pn Oct 23 (157) £320 [Tooley]; pn Nov 20 (211) £320 [Walford]; pn July 23 (60) £340 [Walford]; pn July 23 (196) £340 [Walford]
Anr copy. Half calf; worn. pnE Nov 12 (76) £340
Anr copy. Buckram-backed bds. pnE Dec 17 (347) £320 [Cadzow]
Anr copy. Vol I only. Orig cloth; worn. With 20 colored plates. Some soiling. S Nov 10 (500) £150 [Negro]
Anr copy. 2 vols. Folio, half mor gilt; old spine laid down. With 41 colored plates. S June 25 (165) £300 [Walford]
Anr copy. Orig cloth; rubbed. Some plates loose; 1 plate with fore-margin frayed. S July 28 (1084) £300; S July 28 (1085) £340
Anr copy. Contemp half mor; worn, broken on spine. T Sept 18 (113) £320
Anr copy. Contemp half mor; spine worn. With 40 plates. Waterstained, affecting some plates. T Oct 16 (416) £300

House, Homer Doliver, 1878-1949
— Wild Flowers of New York. Albany, 1918. 2 vols. 4to, cloth; worn. O Nov 18 (93) $70

Household Words
— Household Words: A Weekly Journal. L, 1850-59. Ed by Charles Dickens. 19 vols (complete run). 8vo, orig cloth; rubbed. bba July 16 (287) £300 [Thorp]

Housekeeper's...
— The Housekeeper's Assistant; and Necessary Companion.... L: for R. Snagg, 1775. 12mo, contemp marbled papers; rubbed & frayed. Some pencilled scrawls; light browning or spotting. P Nov 25 (257) $550

Housman, Alfred Edward, 1859-1936
— A Shropshire Lad. L, 1896. 1st Ed, one of 500. 8vo, orig bds; faded, edges worn. CNY Dec 19 (95) $750
Anr Ed. L: Riccardi Press, 1914. One of 12 on vellum. 4to, orig vellum. C Dec 12

HOUTMAN

(372) £700 [Weil]

Houtman, Cornelis
— Diarium nauticum itineris Batavorum in Indiam Orientalem. Middelburg: Barent Langenes for Adrianus Perier in Paris, 1598. 2 parts in 1 vol. Oblong 4to, 19th-cent half or gilt. With 13 plates & illusts & with map & woodcut coastal profiles in appendix. Tp repaired touching surface. Phillipps copy. S June 25 (469) £450 [Sweet]

Houttuyn, Martin, b.1720
— Houtkunde behelzende de afbeldingen van meest alle bekende, in- en uitlandische houten.... Amst., 1791-95. 4to, contemp calf. With hand-colored frontis & 106 hand-colored plates depicting c.650 cross-sections of woods. Van Havre—de Belder copy. S Apr 27 (166) £6,200 [Weiner]

Houville, Gerard d', Pseud.
— Le Diademe de Flore. Paris, 1928. One of 25 on hollande with 40 color woodcuts on japon imperial before text & a suite of proofs for the frontis on japon blanc. Lev janseniste by Georges Levitsky, orig wraps preserved. CNY Dec 19 (116) $1,400

Houzeau, Jean Charles —& Lancaster, Albert
— Bibliographie generale de l'astronomie. L, 1964. 2 vols in 3. 4to, orig cloth, in d/js. sg Oct 2 (39) $200

Howard, Brian
— God Save the King. Paris: Hours Press, [1931]. One of 150, sgd. 4to, orig half lea; worn. sg Dec 11 (304) $80

Howard, George W., 1814-88
— The Monumental City: its Past History and Present Resources. Balt., 1873 [1880]. 2d Ed. 8vo, cloth; hinges cracked, stamp on endpaper, frayed. ha Mar 13 (196) $75

Howard, Henry, Earl of Northampton. See: Northampton, Henry Howard

Howard, Henry, Earl of Surrey, 1517?-47
— Songes and Sonettes. L: John Windet, 1585. ("Songes and Sonnets.") 9th Ed. 8vo, mor gilt by Riviere. Washed. Marginal restoration of title & last 2 leaves, some corners restored, light marginal waterstains. P Dec 15 (204) $5,000

Howard, Henry Eliot
— The British Warblers. L, 1907-14. Parts 1-9 in 2 vols. 4to, half cloth. With 63 plain & 35 colored plates. Haverschmidt copy. B Feb 24 (400) HF850

Anr copy. Half mor gilt. pn Oct 23 (229) £460 [Graham]

Anr copy. In 9/10 parts. 4to, orig bds.

AMERICAN BOOK PRICES CURRENT

With 35 hand-colored plates & 51 plain plates & 12 maps. pnE Dec 17 (268) £280 [Hunt]

Anr copy. 2 vols. 4to, half mor gilt. With 51 plain & 35 color plates & 12 maps. Marginal spotting. S Apr 23 (41) £400 [Pandya]

Howard, John, 1726?-90
— An Account of the Principal Lazarettos in Europe.... With Appendix. Warrington, 1789-91. 2 vols. 4to, contemp calf & contemp half calf; Vol I rebakced. With 22 plates & plans, mostly double-page or folding. sg Jan 15 (100) $250
— The State of the Prisons in England and Wales.... Warrington, 1777-84. 1st Ed. 2 vols, including Appendix, in 1. 4to, contemp half calf; worn, marbled paper removed. S May 28 (697) £220

3d Ed. Warrington, 1784. 2 vols, with Appendix. 4to, modern cloth; Appendix, contemp bds. Library copy. sg Oct 9 (232) $100

Howard, Oliver O.
— Famous Indian Chiefs I Have Known. NY, 1908. 12mo, orig cloth. Partially erased rubberstamps on tp & front pastedown; ink name to half-title; some hinges tender. cb Jan 8 (266) $50
— My Life and Experiences among our Hostile Indians. Hartford, [1907]. Rear cover & spine dampstained & rubbed. cb Jan 8 (267) $50

Howard, Robert E.
— The Dark Man and Others. Sauk City: Arkham House, 1963. In d/j. cb Sept 28 (673) $75
— Echoes from an Iron Harp. West Kingston RI: Donald M. Grant, [1972]. In d/j. cb Sept 28 (675) $110
— Etchings in Ivory. Pasadena, Texas: Glenn Lord, 1968. One of 250. Inscr by Lord. cb Sept 28 (676) $100
— The Pride of Bear Creek. West Kingston RI: Donald M. Grant, 1966. In soiled d/j. cb Sept 28 (681) $70
— Red Shadows. West Kingston RI: Donald M. Grant, 1968. In d/j. cb Sept 28 (682) $80
— Skull-Face and Others. Sauk City, Wisconsin, 1946. 1st Ed. In chipped d/j. cb Sept 28 (688) $100

Howard, W. See: Lowe & Howard

Howe, Ellic
— A List of London Bookbinders, 1648-1815. L, 1950. 4to, half cloth; Soiled & worn. Howard Nixon's copy, annotated by him in ink & pencil. cba Feb 5 (107) $180

Howe, Henry, 1816-93. See: Barber & Howe

Howe, Maurice L. See: Kelly & Howe

Howe, Sir William, 1729-1814
— The Narrative of Lieut. Gen. Sir William Howe. Relative to his Conduct during his late Command of the King's Troops in North America. L, 1780. 1st Ed. 4to, later bds. Half-title & tp with tear at inner edge repaired on verso. sg Sept 18 (132) $150

Howell, James, c.1594-1666
— Instructions for Forreine Travell. L, 1642. 1st Ed. 12mo, old sheep. Inkstained on tp & last page; port with border shaved. C Dec 12 (338) £280 [Pressler]

Anr copy. Modern calf gilt. pn Dec 11 (265) £240 [Shapiro]

Anr copy. Calf gilt by Riviere, with cypher of William Henry Miller on spine & Miller arms on both covers; upper joint splitting. Some staining. Britwell Court copy. S Dec 18 (275) £250 [Knohl]

— Londinopolis; an Historicall Discourse.... L, 1657. Folio, contemp calf. A few tears at inner margins without loss; numerous pagination errors. S Nov 17 (792) £180 [Ash]

— Proedria-Basilike: A Discourse Concerning the Precendency of Kings.... L, 1664. 1st Ed. Folio, calf; upper cove missing. Lacking the 4 ports. bba Mar 26 (162) £50 [Parsons]

Howell, John
— The Life and Adventures of Alexander Selkirk.... Edin., 1829. 12mo, contemp calf gilt; joints splitting, rubbed. bba Sept 25 (64) £65 [Lovett & Lovett]

Howells, John Mead, 1868-1959
— The Architectural Heritage of the Merrimack. NY: Architectural Book Publishing Co, [1941]. One of 1,000. 4to, cloth, in chipped & soiled d/j; worn & soiled. wa Sept 25 (169) $55

Howells, William Dean, 1837-1920
— The Rise of Silas Lapham. Bost., 1885. 1st Ed, 1st Issue. 8vo, orig cloth. sg Feb 12 (178) $60

Howes, Wright
— U.S.-iana (1650-1950); a Selective Bibliography.... NY, 1962. sg Jan 22 (200) $70; sg Mar 12 (141) $110; sg May 14 (17) $100; sg June 11 (243) $100

— U.S.-iana (1700-1950); a Descriptive Checklist.... NY, 1954. 1st Ed. Cloth. cb July 16 (134) $55

Anr copy. Interleaved. cba Feb 5 (108) $80

Anr copy. Cloth; worn. Library markings. O June 16 (104) $60; sg June 11 (242) $100

Reprint of 2d Ed. NY: Bowker [1978]. cba Feb % (109) $50

Howitt, Mary
— Biographical Sketches of the Queens of Great Britain. L, 1862. 4to, half mor gilt; worn. sg Sept 11 (206) $80

Howitt, Richard, 1799-1869
— Impressions of Australia Felix During Four Years Residence.... L, 1845. 8vo, cloth; both free front endpapers removed; some defs. kh Mar 16 (260) A$200

Howitt, Samuel, 1763?-1822
See also: Williamson & Howitt

— The British Sportsman. L, 1812. 4to, half mor. With 71 plates. pn Mar 5 (27) £750 [Postaprint]

Anr copy. Orig cloth; worn. With frontis & 71 plates, all hand-colored. S May 29 (1206) £800

Anr copy. Contemp half shagreen; rubbed. Jeanson 1618. SM Mar 1 (294) Ff9,500

— A New Work of Animals. L, 1811. Ed with 56 plates. 4to, orig bds; rebacked with cloth tape. Frontis & tp remtd. sg June 11 (241) $130

Howitt, William, 1792-1879
— Land, Labour, and Gold; or, Two Years in Victoria.... Bost., 1855. 2 vols. 8vo, cloth with insignia of the European & Australian Royal Mail Company on covers & blind-stamped on title. Some foxing. CA Apr 12 (139) A$220

Anr copy. Cloth; def. kh Mar 16 (260) A$200

Howitt, William & Mary
— Ruined Abbeys and Castles of Great Britain. L, 1862-64. 1st & 2d Series. 2 vols. 4to, contemp mor gilt. Ck Nov 21 (246) £60

Howlett, Robert
— The Angler's Sure Guide.... L, 1706. 8vo, calf; rebacked. pnE Dec 17 (320) £85 [Colcby]

Anr copy. Calf; worn. One plate detached & reinserted. sg Oct 23 (350) $175

Howley, James Patrick
— The Beothucks or Red Indians. Cambr, 1915. 4to, orig cloth. AVP Nov 20 (148) C$200 [Lentz]

Hoyem, Andrew
— Shaped Poetry. San Francisco: Arion Press, 1981. One of 300. Folio, loose as issued in wrap & with plexiglass frame for display. With 30 prints. sg Jan 8 (10) $225

HOYLE

Hoyle, Edmond, 1672-69
— The Accurate Gamester's Companion. L: T. Osborne, 1748. Half calf. pn Mar 26 (417) £50 [Schmidt]
— Epitome of Hoyle with Beaufort.... L: C. Etherington, [1800?]. 12mo, contemp calf; rebacked. pn Mar 26 (421) £140 [Quaritch]

Hoyle, Edmond, 1672-1769
— A Short Treatise on the Game of Whist. L, 1748. 8th Ed. 8vo, contemp mor gilt; spine worn. Sgd on verso of title. bba Sept 25 (31) £100 [Cox]

Hoyt Collection, Charles B.
— TSENG HIEN-CH'I & DART, ROBERT PAUL. - The Charles B. Hoyt Collection in the Museum of Fine Arts: Boston. Bost., 1964. Vol I only: Chinese Art. Cloth. cb Mar 5 (244) $60

Hoytema, Theo van, 1863-1917
— Hoe de Vogels aan een Koning Kwamen. The Hague, 1892. Oblong 8vo, litho bds. B Oct 7 (7) HF440
— Kalenders. 1902-17. 204 leaves (17 years). Complete set. B Oct 7 (11) HF3,000
— Uilen-Geluk. Amst., 1895. Orig half cloth. B Oct 7 (8) HF460

Hozier, Henry Montague
— The Franco-Prussian War.... L, [1870-72]. 2 vols. 4to, calf gilt. pn Mar 5 (220) £190
   Anr copy. Half calf gilt. pn June 18 (202) £150 [Broseghini]

Hrabanus Magnentius, 784-856
— De laudibus sancte crucis opus. Profzheim: T. Anselm, Mar 1503. Folio, contemp pigskin over wooden bds; rubbed. Wormholed repaired. FD June 11 (134) DM2,800

Hroswitha
— Opera. Nuremberg: Printer for the Sodalitas Celtica, 1501. Issue with colophon corrected. Folio, modern bdg of bds covered with 2 15th-cent vellum leaves. With 8 full-page woodcuts (one a repeat), including 2 by Duerer. First 2 leaves, a4 & last leaf from anr copy; some worming affecting text; tear in penultimate leaf. S May 21 (18) £1,900 [Maggs]

Hsiang Yuan-pien
— Noted Porcelains of Successive Dynasties. Peking, 1931. Folio, silk wraps. sg June 11 (430) $375

Huarte, Juan
— Examen de ingenios. The Examination of Mens Wits. L: Adam Islip for Thomas Man, 1594. 4to, old calf; broken. sg Mar 26 (150) $1,100

AMERICAN BOOK PRICES CURRENT

Hubback, Theodore R.
— To Far Western Alaska for Big Game. L, 1929. In soiled & frayed d/j. wa Sept 25 (133) $120

Hubbard, Alice, 1861-1915
— Life Lessons: Truths Concerning People Who Have Lived. East Aurora, [1909]. Designed by Dard Hunter. 4to, half lea, unopened. sg Jan 8 (261) $80

Hubbard, Elbert, 1856-1915
— Little Journeys to the Homes of English Authors. East Aurora, 1900. One of 925, 940 or 947 copies. 12 vols plus New Series, Vols I-II. Lea & half lea. sg Jan 8 (257) $140
— Little Journeys to the Homes of Great Musicians. East Aurora, 1901. One of 940. 12 vols plus New Series, 2 vols. Lea & half lea. sg Jan 8 (256) $140
— Little Journeys to the Homes of Eminent Artists. East Aurora, 1902. One of 940. 12 vols plus New Series Vols I-II. Lea & half lea. sg Jan 8 (258) $140
— The Man of Sorrows. East Aurora, 1905. One of 100. Illuminated by Dard Hunter. Half mor gilt. sg Jan 8 (259) $130
— This, then, is the William Morris Book.... East Aurora: The Roycrofters, 1907. One of 203. Half mor gilt; worn. sg Feb 12 (179) $175
— Works. East Aurora, N.Y., [c.1908-15]. One of 1,000. 20 vols. 4to, mor gilt. With additional ownership leaf of Dr. A. R. Miller & with 2 tipped-in leaves of typescript with holograph corrections apparently in Hubbard's hand. Inscr to Miller by Elbert Hubbard II. wa June 25 (67) $750

Hubbard, L. Ron
— Two Novels.... NY: Gnome Press, [1951]. In d/j. cb Sept 28 (702) $70

Hubbard, Lucius Lee, 1849-1933
— Hubbard's Guide to Moosehead Lake and Northern Maine. Bost., 1882. 12mo, cloth; worn. With 3 folding maps, 2 in rear pocket & 1 attached to front free endpaper. sg Oct 23 (351) $60

Hubbard, William, 1621?-1704
— A Narrative of the Indian Wars in New-England.... Worcester, 1801. 12mo, contemp calf; front cover loose. Some foxing. sg Mar 12 (142) $60
— A Narrative of the Indian Wars in New England, 1607-1677. Roxbury, Mass., 1865. ("The History of the Indian Wars in New England....") One of 350. 2 vols. 8vo, cloth; worn & shaken. Marginal ink stains in Vol I. O Oct 21 (91) $50

Huber, Francois, 1750-1831
— Nouvelles Observations sur les abeilles.... Geneva, 1792. 8vo, orig wraps, unopened; spine ends worn. sg Jan 15 (153) $225

Anr Ed. Paris, 1814. 2 vols. 8vo, contemp half sheep; spines rubbed. sg Jan 15 (154) $250

Hubert, Saint, Order of
— Calendarium inclyti ordinis equestris D. Hubberto sacri.... [Augsburg, 1761]. 2 parts in 1 vol. 8vo, contemp mor gilt. With 2 engraved titles & 80 plates. Jeanson copy. SM Mar 1 (497) FF4,000

Anr Ed. [Augsburg, 1786]. 8vo, mor gilt. Jeanson copy. SM Mar 1 (499) FF9,000

Huberty
— Recueil, pour le cors de chasse, contenant cent fanfares en duo avec la game. Paris: Chez l'Editeur, [c.1750]. 2 vols. 12mo, contemp calf; worn. Schwerdt-Jeanson copy. SM Mar 1 (296) FF7,000

Hubrecht, Alphonse
— Grandeur et suprematie de Peking. Peking, 1928. One of 1,000. 4to, orig ptd wraps. sg Apr 23 (70) $110

Huc, Evariste Regis, 1813-60
— The Chinese Empire. NY, 1855. 2 vols. 8vo, orig cloth. With folding colored map. cb Nov 6 (168) $60
— Travels in Tartary, Thibet, and China during the Years 1844-5-6. L, [1852]. 1st Ed in English. Trans by William Hazlitt. 2 vols. 8vo, orig cloth. Signature in Vol I becoming detached. cb Nov 6 (169) $130

Anr copy. Orig cloth; hinges cracked, worn & soiled. Minor foxing. sg Apr 23 (71) $90

Hudson, Derek
— Arthur Rackham: his Life and Work. L, 1960. 4to, orig bdg, in d/j. With 40 mtd plates. sg Oct 30 (105) $100

Anr copy. Cloth, in d/j. With 41 mtd plates. sg Jan 8 (243) $100

Anr copy. Cloth. wd June 19 (172) $75

Anr Ed. NY, [1960]. 4to, cloth, in d/j. With 40 mtd plates. sg Oct 30 (106) $70; sg Oct 30 (107) $110

Hudson, William Henry, 1841-1922
See also: Sclater & Hudson
— The Birds of La Plata. L, 1895. 8vo, orig cloth; extremities rubbed. With 8 plain & 8 color plates. sg Jan 15 (226) $50

Anr Ed. L, 1920. 2 vols. 4to, orig cloth. bba Oct 30 (392) £100 [Wagner]
— British Birds. L, 1895. 8vo, orig cloth; extremities rubbed. With 8 plain & 8 color plates. sg Jan 15 (226) $500
— Idle Days in Patagonia. L, 1893. 1st Ed,

one of 1,750. 8vo, orig cloth; rubbed & stained. John Galsworthy's copy. T Feb 18 (40) £40
— The Purple Land. L, 1929. Purple calf. cb Feb 19 (138) $65
— Works. L, 1922-23. One of 750. 24 vols. All but 2 vols with d/js. S July 13 (182) £550

Hueffer, Ford Madox. See: Ford, Ford Madox

Huegell, Carl Alexander Anselm von, Baron
— Travels in Kashmir and the Punjab.... L, 1845. 4to, cloth. With 5 plates & with folding map in rear sleeve. Some foxing, errata slip mtd on front free endpaper. sg Nov 20 (81) $175

Hueso Rolland, Francisco
— Exposicion de Encuadernaciones Espanolas. Siglos XII al XIX. Madrid, 1934. Folio, cloth; worn. With 61 plates, some colored. O Jan 6 (172) $170
— Exposicion de encuadernaciones espanolas, siglos XII al XIX: Catalogo general. Madrid, 1934 [1935]. One of 100. Folio, orig cloth. sg May 14 (120) $200

Hufeland, Christoph Wilhelm von
— Die Kunst das menschliche Leben zu verlaengern. Jena, 1797. 2d Ed. 8vo, 19th-cent half calf. HK Nov 4 (1022) DM700

Anr copy. Contemp half calf; rubbed, 1st gathering misbound. Crahan copy. P Nov 25 (258) $350

Anr Ed. Prague: Haas, 1797. 2 parts in 1 vol. 8vo, contemp calf gilt; worn. HK Nov 4 (1023) DM650

Hughes, Griffith
— The Natural History of Barbados. L, 1750. Folio, contemp calf; worn. With hand-colored double-page map & 30 hand-colored plates. With 2 leaves of addenda at end. L.p. copy. de Belder copy. S Apr 27 (168) £1,700 [Bourget]

Hughes, John T., 1817-62
— Doniphan's Expedition, Containing an Account of the Conquest of New Mexico. Cincinnati, 1848. 2d Ed. 12mo, later half mor. With folding map & 2 ports. cb Mar 19 (131) $120

Hughes, Richard
See also: Golden Cockerel Press
— A High Wind in Jamaica. L, 1929. One of 150. Unopened. O Jan 6 (89) $90

633

HUGHES

Hughes, Sukey
— Washi; the World of Japanese Paper. Tokyo, [1978]. One of 1,000. 25 orig parts. 4to, orig wraps, in orig portfolio. bba Mar 26 (44) £60 [Marco]
Anr copy. 4to, half cloth. sg Jan 22 (247) $275

Hughes, Ted
— Crow, from the Life and Songs of the Crow. L, 1973. One of 400. Illus by Leonard Baskin. Folio, orig cloth. kh Mar 16 (262) A$90; S Sept 22 (96) £40 [Desmond]
— The Hawk in the Rain. L, [1957]. 1st Ed. In d/j. sg Dec 11 (305) $50
— Moortown Elegies. L: Rampant Lions Press for the Rainbow Press, 1978. One of 143. Illus by Leonard Baskin. 4to, vellum. sg Mar 5 (101) $140
— Orts. L: Rainbow Press, 1978. One of 200. Frontis by Leonard Baskin. 4to, lea by Zaehnsdorf. sg Mar 5 (102) $100
— Remains of Elmet. L: Rainbow Press, 1979. With photos by Fay Godwin. 4to, half cloth. sg Mar 5 (104) $120
One of 70, sgd by author & photographer. Calf. sg Mar 5 (103) $225

Hughes, Thomas Smart, 1786-1847
— Travels in Sicily, Greece and Albania. L, 1820. 2 vols. 4to, modern cloth. Library stamps. bba Feb 5 (362) £70 [Broseghini]
Anr copy. Contemp half calf; rubbed. bba Apr 9 (414) £180 [Brailey]
Anr copy. Contemp half calf; worn. With 14 maps & plates. S Jan 13 (390) £300 [Mansbach]
Anr copy. Orig bds; spines worn, 2 covers detached. With 12 plates & 3 maps & plans. S May 29 (1049) £280
2d Ed. L, 1830. 2 vols. 8vo, orig cloth; worn, hinges starting. Marginal stain on 1 plate. sg Nov 20 (75) $100

Hughes, W. E.
— Chronicle of Black Heath Golfers. L, 1897. pnC July 16 (67) £1,250

Hughes, William, fl.1665-83
— The Flower Garden and Compleat Vineyard. L, 1683. 3d Ed. 2 parts in 1 vol. 12mo, contemp calf; rubbed. Folding plate torn & crudely repaired. S May 28 (298) £180

Hughson, David, Pseud. of David Pugh
— London: Being a Description of the British Metropolis. L, 1805-9. 6 vols. 8vo, half calf; spines damaged. pn Sept 18 (267) £85 [Argyle]
Anr copy. Half mor; rubbed & soiled. Some tears. Sold w.a.f. S Nov 17 (793) £160 [Burden]

AMERICAN BOOK PRICES CURRENT

— Walks through London. L, 1817. 2 vols. 8vo, contemp mor gilt; rubbed. bba Feb 5 (382) £60 [Taylor]

Hugnet, Georges
— Onan. Paris, 1934. One of 7 on papier pontval a la cuve, with the etching. Illus by Salvador Dali. 4to, orig wraps; soiled. S June 17 (98) £650 [Dennistoun]

Hugo, Hermannus, 1588-1629
— Pia desideria emblematis elegiis.... Antwerp, 1628. 16mo, contemp calf; rubbed; rebacked & corners reinforced. Waterstained. bba Nov 13 (4) £80 [Robert Shaw]
Anr copy. Modern bds; soiled. bba Aug 20 (354) £60 [Elliott]
— Pia desideria.... Antwerp: Henricus Aertssens, 1629. 8vo, 17th-cent vellum. Margins trimmed; some sidenotes shaved. sg Mar 26 (151) $225
— Pia Desideria: or, Divine Addresses. L, 1686. 8vo, modern sheep. With 46 engraved plates. Some spotting, staining, holes & tears. S Nov 13 (200) £35 [Trocchi]

Hugo, Thomas, 1820-76
— The Bewick Collector: a Descriptive Catalogue.... L, 1866-68. 2 vols, including Supplement. 8vo, cloth; worn, joints cracked. sg Jan 22 (201) $110

Hugo, Victor, 1802-85
See also: Limited Editions Club
— L'Annee terrible. Paris: Michel Levy, 1872. 8vo, half mor, orig wraps bound in. Inscr to Theophile Gautier. S May 21 (151) £500 [Lyon]
— Les Miserables. Paris: J. Hetzel & A. Lacroix, 1866. Illus by Gustave Brion. 4to, contemp half lea; corners scuffed. sg Sept 11 (207) $80
— Les Orientales. Paris, 1829. 1st Ed. 8vo, mor gilt by Champs. C May 13 (57) £400 [Pilg]

Hugues, P. See: Jacob & Hugues

Huish, Marcus Bourne
— Happy England, as Painted by Helen Allingham. L, 1903. One of 750 sgd by the artist. Illus by Helen Allingham. 4to, orig cloth; soiled & worn. S May 6 (80) £110 [Beetles]
— The Seine and the Loire. L, 1895. Illus by J. M. W. Turner. 8vo, half mor over decorated cloth; worn, broken. With 61 plates. bba Dec 18 (258) £50 [Rainer]

Huizinga, J.
— Werken. Haarlem, 1948-53. ("Verzamelde werken.") 9 vols, including Index. B Feb 25 (968) HF350

Hulot, ——, Pere
— L'Art du tourneur mecanicien. Paris, 1775. Part 1. Folio, modern cloth. Franklin Institute copy. F Sept 12 (340) $600

Hulsen, Esias von
— Aigentliche Wahrhaffte Delineatio unnd Abbildung aller fuerstlichen Auffzueg und Ruetterspilen...in Stuetgartt.... Stuttgart: Esias von Hulsen, [1618]. Weckherlin, Georg Rodolf. Kurze Beschreibung dess zu Stuttgarten bey den Fuerstlichen Kindtauf und Hochzeit...Frewden-Fests.... Tuebingen: Dieterich Werlin, 1618 Oblong folio, contemp blind-stamped vellum; upper cover stained. S May 21 (111) £4,000 [Quaritch]

Hulton, Paul Hope —& Quinn, David Beers
— The American Drawings of John White. L, 1964. 2 vols. Folio, orig cloth; 1 bdg wrinkled. sg June 4 (349) $275

Humbert, Aime, 1819-1900
— Japan and the Japanese Illustrated. L, 1874. 4to, orig cloth. bba Feb 5 (351) £110 [Elliott]; bba Feb 5 (352) £110 [Check]
— Le Japon illustre. Paris, 1870. 2 vols. Folio, half mor; soiled & worn. Some foxing; 3-inch tear in folding map of Yedo. wa Nov 6 (451) $170

Humboldt, Alexander von, 1769-1859
— Cosmos: a Sketch of a Physical Description of the Universe. L, 1849-52. Vols I-IV (of 5). 12mo, contemp half calf. wa Sept 25 (567) $85
— Essai politique sur l'ile de Cuba. Paris, 1826. 2 vols. 8vo, later cloth. With folding map;. wa Sept 25 (446) $180

Humboldt, Alexander von, 1769-1859 —& Bonpland, Aime J. A., 1773-1858
— Essai politique sur le Royaume de la Nouvelle-Espagne. Paris, 1811. 3 vols, including Atlas vol. 4to, text in half cloth, unopened & Atlas in half calf. With 21 plates on 19 sheets; lacking Plate 11 but duplicate Plate 10 supplied. C Apr 8 (29) £800 [Brockhaus]
— Voyage aux regions equinoctiales du nouveau continent.... Paris, 1808-34. Vol III of the 3d section of Botanique only. Folio, contemp bds. With 108 hand-colored plates numbered 193-300. Sold w.a.f. C Oct 15 (236) £2,300 [Scott Sandilands]
Anr copy. Vol VI of the 3d section of Botanique only. Folio, With 93 hand-colored plates numbered 513-600.. C Oct 15 (237) £2,400 [Scott Sandilands]
Anr copy. Section 3, Vols 2 of C. S. Kunth's Nova Genera et Species Plantarum. Folio, contemp bds; joint worn, inside hinges broken. With 96 hand-colored plates. A few leters of text affected due to adhesion. C Apr 8 (184) £4,200 [Brockhaus]
Anr copy. Section 3, Vol 7 (of 7): C. S. Kunth's Nova Genera et Species Plantarum. Folio, contemp bds; rubbed, inside hinge broken. With 105 hand-colored plates. Some index leaves holed in margin. Sold w.a.f. C Apr 8 (185) £4,800 [Brockhaus]
Anr copy. 15 vols; lacking the 4 vols of Synopsis. Folio, Viennese neo-classical bdg in calf gilt; worn, 1 vol in half calf. With 896 ptd in colors & finished by hand, 220 hand-colored plates & 145 plain plates. A few leaves spotted. Plesch—de Belder copy. S Apr 27 (167) £85,000 [Israel]
— Vues des cordilleres et monumens des peuples indigenes de l'Amerique. Paris, 1810-[13]. 1st Ed. 2 vols. Folio, 19th-cent half mor gilt; extremities worn, inner joints cracked. With 69 (on 68) plates, 24 plates colored. Minor dampstains to upper & lower blank margins. Hunt copy. CNY Nov 21 (149) $7,500
Anr copy. 2 vols in 1. Folio, cloth. With 69 (on 68) plates, including 25 colored plates. This copy contains the supplementary notes on 9 leaves & index & errata on 14 leaves at end Some spotting of text. S Oct 23 (445) £5,000 [Klee]
Anr Ed. Paris, 1816. 2 vols. 8vo, contemp calf; spines rubbed. With 13 plain & 6 hand-colored plates. Stamps on half-titles & last leaves; some foxing or staining. P Oct 29 (9) $1,000

Hume, Allan Octavian. See: Henderson & Hume

Hume, Allan Octavian —& Marshall, C. H. T.
— The Game Birds of India, Burmah, and Ceylon. Calcutta, [1878]-81. 3 vols. 8vo, orig cloth; worn. With 144 (of 145) colored plates. S Feb 24 (575) £360 [Dowling]

Hume, David, 1711-76
— Dialogues concerning Natural Religion. L, 1779. 1st Ed. 8vo, contemp calf; rubbed. Lacking half-title. S July 23 (417) £1,400 [Riley-Smith]
— An Enquiry concerning the Principles of Morals.... L, 1751. 1st Ed, 1st Issue. 12mo, old calf; rebacked, scuffed. Browned. P Sept 24 (306) $1,000
— Four Dissertations. L, 1757. 1st Ed. 12mo, contemp calf; rebacked. pn Sept 18 (142) £270 [Finch]
— The History of England.... L, 1770. 8 vols. 4to, contemp calf; worn & soiled, some

joints started. wa Nov 6 (541) $750

Anr Ed. L, [c.1850]. 8 vols. 8vo, orig cloth; worn. Some maps stained. Sold w.a.f. Ck June 5 (173) £160

— A Treatise of Human Nature. L, 1739-40. 1st Ed. 3 vols. 8vo, later calf; spines of 2 vols very worn. Dampstained throughout; lacking ad leaves in Vol II. C Dec 12 (114) £4,200 [Riley-Smith]

Anr copy. Contemp calf; joints split at head in 2 vols. Small rusthole affecting ad leaf in Vol I; faint marginal stains in Vols II & III. F6 & P6 in Vol III uncancelled. S June 25 (70) £5,500 [Quaritch]

Humourist. See: Cruikshank, George

Humphrey, Maud

— Maud Humphrey's Book of Fairy Tales. NY: Stokes, 1892. 4to, half cloth; worn & soiled. wa Nov 6 (525) $150

Humphreys, Andrew A. —& Abbot, Henry L.

— Report upon the Physics and Hydraulics of the Mississippi River. Phila., 1861. 4to, contemp bds; poorly rebacked. With 20 folding plates. wa Nov 6 (586) $85

Humphreys, Arthur Lee

— A Handbook to County Bibliography. L, 1917. Half cloth; worn. bba Mar 12 (344) £70 [Sanders]
— Old Decorative Maps and Charts. L & NY, 1926. One of 1,500. 4to, orig cloth; rubbed. Perforated stamp on title. bba Mar 12 (271) £90 [Hashimoto]

Humphreys, David, 1689-1740

— An Historical Account of the Incorporated Society for the Propagation of the Gospel in Foreign Parts. L, 1730. 1st Ed. 8vo, contemp calf; rebacked. With 2 folding maps. S June 25 (392) £300 [Reese]

Humphreys, Henry Noel

— The Art of Illumination and Missal Painting. L, 1849. 8vo, pictorial bds with later mor back; corners bumped. O Sept 23 (85) $100
— A History of the Art of Printing.... L, 1868. 2d Issue. Folio, half lea; rubbed. Marginal dampstains. O June 16 (105) $75
— The Illuminated Books of the Middle Ages. L, 1849. Folio, contemp half mor. With color title, 10 color plates & 1 litho plate with 100 illusts. C July 22 (101) £700
— Illuminated Illustrations of Froissart.... L, 1844-45. 2 vols in 1. 4to, contemp sheep; scuffed. sg Feb 5 (99) $150
— The Miracles of Our Lord. L, 1848. 8vo, carved bdg of black papier mache, with 6 medallions on each cover. sg Sept 11 (11) $150

— The Origin and Progress of the Art of Writing. L, 1853. 4to, orig bds; corners worn, cracked, rebacked. With 28 plates. T Feb 19 (5530) £52

Anr copy. Orig papier mache; rehinged, 2 corners chipped. wa Mar 5 (21) $130

— A Record of the Black Prince. L, 1849. 8vo, orig armorial papier mache covers; broken. Ck Apr 24 (214) £65
— Sentiments and Similes of William Shakespeare.... L, 1851. 4to, orig mor-backed papier mache with central oval earthenware medallions; spine rubbed, lacking front free endpaper. Ck Sept 26 (72) £160

Anr copy. Orig papier-mache; worn, recased preserving most of orig spine. O May 12 (96) $300

Humphreys, Henry Noel —& Cooke, William B.

— Rome, and its Surrounding Scenery. L, 1845. 8vo, contemp half mor; rubbed. With double-page view of Rome & 29 plates. T Apr 16 (6) £70

Humphreys, Henry Noel —& Westwood, John Obadiah, 1805-93

— British Butterflies and their Transformations. L, 1841. 4to, contemp half cloth. With hand-colored litho title & 42 plates. Ck Sept 5 (54) £240

Anr copy. Modern half mor gilt. pn Oct 23 (119) £260 [Marasse]; pn June 18 (243) £450 [Dixon]

— British Moths and their Transformations. L, 1843-45. 2 vols. 4to, contemp half calf; rubbed. With 124 hand-colored plates. Some sections of Vol II detached. Ck Sept 5 (53) £200

Anr copy. Orig cloth; stained. Ck Oct 31 (123) £190

Hungerford, Edward

— The Story of the Baltimore & Ohio Railroad. NY, 1928. 2 vols. wa Nov 6 (229) $55

Hunneman, W.

— Chess, a Selection of Fifty Games from those Played by the Automaton Chess-Player.... L, 1820. Orig bds. pn Mar 26 (245) £70 [Walford]

Hunt, John, Engraver

— British Ornithology. Norwich, 1815-22. Vols I-II only (with some plates from Vol III bound in). Later cloth. With 142 hand-colored & 4 uncolored anatomical plates. Vol II lacking all text after p 359. Sold w.a.f. Ck May 29 (29) £250

Hunt, Leigh, 1784-1859

— The Autobiography. L, 1850. 1st Ed. 3 vols. 8vo, orig cloth; soiled, spines chipped. wa Sept 25 (673) $70

— Foliage; or Poems Original and Translated. L, 1818. 1st Ed. 8vo, modern half calf. sg Feb 12 (180) $70

— The Story of Rimini, a Poem. L, 1816. 1st Ed. 12mo, orig bds; corners frayed. S Jan 13 (502) £80 [Finch]

Hunt, Lynn Bogue. See: Derrydale Press

Hunt, R. C.

— Salmon in Low Water. NY; Anglers' Club, 1950. One of 500. With 2 hand-colored plates of flies. sg Oct 23 (353) $150

Hunt, Thomas, 1627?-88

— Mr. Emmertons Marriage with Mrs. Bridget Hyde Considered. L, 1682. 4to, modern half mor. sg Mar 26 (152) $120

Hunt, Thomas Frederick

— Designs for Parsonage Houses, Alms Houses.... L, 1827. 4to, bds; def. Spotted. pn Sept 18 (132) £60 [Bookroom]

Hunt, William Holman, 1827-1910

— Oxford Union Society: The Story of the Painting.... L, 1906. One of 378. Folio, orig cloth; lower cover dampstained. bba Jan 15 (280) £40 [Zwemmer]

Anr copy. Some stains. bba Mar 26 (48) £45 [Dawson]

Hunter, Alexander, 1729-1809

— Culina Famulatrix Medicinae: or, Receipts in Modern Cookery. York, 1806. 12mo, cloth. Lacking R6; some stains. S July 14 (512) £100

Hunter, Alexander, b.1843

— Johnny Reb and Billy Yank. NY & Wash., 1905. Paint streaks on spine, hinges cracked. wa Feb 19 (52) $200

Hunter, Anole. See: Derrydale Press

Hunter, Dard

— Before Life Began, 1883-1923. Cleveland: Rowfant Club, 1941. One of 219, designed & sgd by Bruce Rogers. Half vellum; spine ends bumped. sg Apr 2 (114) $400

— Papermaking by Hand in India. NY, 1939. One of 375. 4to, orig half lea. sg Apr 2 (115) $800

— Papermaking through Eighteen Centuries. NY, 1930. Unopened, in d/j. sg June 11 (246) $130

— Papermaking: the History and Technique of an Ancient Craft. NY, 1943. 1st Ed. cba Feb 5 (110) $70

Hunter, George Lelan, 1867-1927

— Decorative Furniture. Phila., L & Grand Rapids, 1923. Folio, cloth. With 29 color plates. cba Mar 5 (97) $80

Hunter, James

— Picturesque Scenery in the Kingdom of Mysore. L, 1805. 10 orig parts. Oblong folio, orig wraps with hexagonal engraved labels on upper covers. With port & 40 plates, all hand-colored; interleaved with tissue throughout. With ptd title, dedication & index leaves in Part 10. S June 25 (467) £8,000 [Traylen]

Hunter, John, 1728-93

— The Natural History of the Human Teeth. Phila., 1839. ("Treatise on the Natural History and Diseases of the Human Teeth.") Bound with: Horner, G.R.B.- Medical and Topographical Observations upon the Mediterranean.... Phila., 1839. And: Megendie, Francois. - Lectures on the Blood. Phila., 1839. 8vo, contemp half calf. With 9 plates. sg Jan 15 (85) $200

— Observations on Certain Parts of the Animal Oeconomy. L, 1792. 2d Ed. 4to, later half calf; joints cracked. With 19 plates. bba Sept 25 (217) £360 [Gurney]

— A Treatise on the Venereal Disease. L, 1786. 1st Ed. 4to, contemp calf. With 7 plates.. pnE Dec 17 (109) £1,500 [Phillips]

— A Treatise on the Blood, Inflammation, and Gun-Shot Wounds. Phila., 1796. 8vo, contemp sheep; worn & rubbed. Corner torn from Contents leaf. cb Oct 23 (120) $180

— A Treatise on the Venereal Disease. L, 1810. 3d Ed. 4to, old half cloth. With a port & 7 plates. S May 28 (699) £90

— Works. L, 1835-37. 5 vols, including plate vol. 8vo & 4to, modern half calf. Library markings; stamp on tp. pnE Dec 17 (108) £1,400 [Traylen]

Hunter, John, d.1809

— Observations on the Diseases of the Army in Jamaica.... L, 1796. 2d Ed. 8vo, contemp calf; joints cracked. Institutional rubberstamp on title. og Jan 15 (101) $225

Hunter, Capt. John, 1738-1821

— An Historical Journal of the Transactions at Port Jackson and Norfolk Island.... L, 1793. 4to, contemp half calf; rebacked. Tp stamped; fore-margin of title shaved with loss of date & a few letters; corner of map torn; plate creased with blank corner torn away. C Apr 8 (99) £120 [Colleary]

Anr copy. Cloth; spine torn. Tp trimmed & foxed; port foxed; tear in 1st map. CA Apr 12 (140) A$2,800

Anr copy. Half mor; stained. Tp shaved,

HUNTER

with loss of publication date. CA Apr 12 (141) A$1,400

Anr copy. 19th-cent calf gilt, armorial bdg; rebacked. With engraved title, port, 10 plates & 5 maps. Short fold break in 1 folding map; X4 with closed tear into text; last leaf with 2 closed tears; date of tp imprint just shaved. P Sept 24 (168) $1,200

Anr copy. Calf gilt. With engraved title (date in imprint shaved), port & 15 plates & maps. Neatline of 1 map shaved. S Oct 23 (520) £1,400 [Bonham]

Anr copy. Contemp half calf; def. With engraved title, port, 13 plates & 2 maps. Tp soiled & with library stamp; some spotting & soiling. S Nov 18 (1241) £440 [Maggs]

Hunter, Joseph, 1783-1861

— Hallamshire. The History and Topography of...Sheffield. L, 1819. Folio, contemp half calf; rubbed. With 9 plates. Ck Sept 26 (309) £65

Hunter, William, 1718-83

— Anatomia uteri humani gravidi.... Birm: Baskerville, 1774. 1st Ed, Issue not stated. Folio, modern half mor. With 34 plates. Some dampstaining & soiling, 1 plate repaired, 3 text leaves repaired. S Nov 27 (266) £2,300 [Scheon]

— Medical Commentaries. L, 1762. 1st Ed. 4to, old half mor. With 4 plates. Port inserted. University College, London, duplicate. S May 28 (700) £280

— Two Introductory Lectures Delivered by W. H. to his last Course of Anatomical Lectures.... L, 1784. 4to, new cloth. Lacking the ad leaf for the Gravid Uterus. S May 28 (701) £180

Huntington, Dwight W.

— In Brush, Sedge and Stubble. Cincinnati, 1898. Folio, cloth. sg Oct 23 (354) $175

Huquier, Gabriel

— Recueil contenant...Frises d'ornements, arabesques a divers usages. Paris, [c.1740]. 2 parts in 1 vol. Folio, contemp half lea gilt. With 24 plates. Sold w.a.f. Extra-illus with 109 French 18th-cent architectural plates. C Dec 12 (116) £1,000 [Weinreb]

Hurd, D. Hamilton

— History of Otsego County, New York. Phila., 1878. 4to, half lea; detached at front hinge. Scattered foxing. sg Mar 12 (195) $60

Hurley, Capt. Frank

— Argonauts of the South. NY & L, 1925. kh Mar 16 (266) A$180

AMERICAN BOOK PRICES CURRENT

Hussey, Christopher

— English Country Houses. L, 1955-58. 3 vols. In d/js. kh Mar 16 (268) A$400

Hussey, Elisha Charles

— Hussey's National Cottage Architecture.... NY, 1874. 4to, orig bds; rebacked with tape, worn & tape torn. Extra title nearly detached; some smudging; a few edge tears; library markings. ha Sept 19 (120) $100

Husson, Jules Francois Felix. See: Champfleury

Husson, Pieter

— Variae Tabulae geographicae in quibus loca in orbe bello flagrantio conspiciuntur.... The Hague, [1709?]. Folio, modern half calf. With 50 double-page or folding maps & tables, colored in a contemp hand. With Ms index; some discoloration; some repairs causing loss of engraved surface; tp repaired & mtd. S June 25 (308) £1,400 [Schmidt]

— Variae Tabulae geographicae in quibus loca in orbe bello flagranta conspiciuntur.... The Hague, [c.1709]. Folio, modern half calf. With 50 double-page or folding maps colored in a contemp hand. With Ms index in a contemp hand. Some repairs & browning, the repairs occasionally affecting surface; tp repaired & mtd. S June 25 (308) £1,400

Husung, Max Joseph

— Bucheinbande aus der Preussischen Staatsbibliothek zu Berlin. Leipzig, 1925. Folio, orig half cloth; inner hinges strengthened, rubbed. Some staining & soiling. P Sept 24 (120) $450

Hutcheson, Francis, 1694-1746

— A System of Moral Philosophy. Glasgow: Foulis, 1755. 1st Ed. 2 vols. 4to, contemp calf; rubbed. S June 25 (68) £680 [McCrow]

Hutchings, James Mason, 1820-1902

— Scenes of Wonder and Curiosity in California. NY & San Francisco, [1860]. 1st Ed. 8vo, orig cloth; worn & faded; joints wormed. cb Jan 8 (95) $50

Anr Ed. NY, 1872. Orig cloth; spine ends & corners worn. Some soiling. cb Feb 19 (139) $55

Hutchins, Henry C.

— Robinson Crusoe and its Printing. NY, 1925. One of 350. 4to, cloth. sg Oct 2 (116) $50

Hutchins, John, 1698-1773

— The History and Antiquities of the County of Dorset. L, 1774. 1st Ed. 2 vols. Folio, contemp calf; rubbed, rebacked. With folding map (loose) & 53 plates, some double-page. bba Aug 28 (317) £260 [British Arch'l Library]

Anr copy. Contemp half calf; rubbed, joints cracked. With folding map & 53 plates only. Ck Nov 21 (252) £170

Anr copy. Half calf. With folding map & 25 plates only. Several plates with marginal tears repaired; corners of 2 text leaves damaged; minor marginal staining to final leaves in Vol I. Sold w,a,f, L July 2 (89) £150

3d Ed. L, 1861-70. 4 vols. Folio, orig cloth, in d/js. L Dec 11 (119) £300

Anr copy. Half mor; rubbed. Some dust-soiling; 3 plates in Vol IV with marginal stain; 1 plate repaired in margin; final leaf of Vol IV torn & repaired; Vol II lacking pp 482-84. Sold w.a.f. L July 2 (90) £420

Anr copy. Contemp half mor. pn Sept 18 (114) £300 [Old Hall]

Hutchinson, Francis, 1660-1739

— An Historical Essay Concerning Witchcraft. L, 1718. 8vo, old calf; rebacked. O May 12 (98) $225

Anr copy. Contemp calf; rubbed, rebacked, new endpapers. Some dampstains. S July 14 (324) £130

Hutchinson, Horace

— British Golf Links. L, 1897. pnC Jan 23 (113) £380; pnC Jan 23 (114) £360; pnC July 16 (70) £240

— The Golfing Pilgrim on Many Links. NY, 1898. 8vo, orig bdg. pnC Jan 23 (111) £160

Hutchinson, John, b.1884

— A Botanist in Southern Africa. L, 1946. 1st Ed. Orig cloth. SSA Feb 11 (547) R100

Hutchinson, John Hely

— The Commercial Restraints of Ireland. Dublin, 1779. 8vo, later half calf; rubbed, upper joint cracked. With 3 folding tables. Marginal soiling. bba Apr 9 (323) £140 [Drury]

Hutchinson, Thomas, 1711-80

— The History of the Colony of Massachusetts-Bay. L, 1760 [but 1765]-68-1828. 3 vols. With: Hutchinson. A Collection of Original Papers relative to the History of...Massachusetts-Bay. Bost., 1769 Together, 4 vols. 8vo, later half mor. Title of Vol I def & repaired. sg Sept 18 (172) $500

— The Speeches of his Excellency Governor Hutchinson, to the General Assembly of the Massachusetts-Bay. Bost., 1773. 4to, orig wraps; rubbed. Tp with signature torn from top edge & with fore-edge soiled. sg Sept 18 (133) $120

Hutchinson, William, 1732-1814

— The History and Antiquities of the County Palatine of Durham. Newcastle & Carlisle, 1785-94. 3 vols. 4to, later mor; rubbed. bba Apr 9 (377) £75 [Smith]

Huth, Alfred Henry

— Catalogue of the fifty Manuscripts & Printed Books bequeathed to the British Museum. L, 1912. Preface by F G Kenyon; introduction by A. W. Pollard. Folio, orig cloth; spine head & 2 upper corners jammed, lower 2 bumped. With 18 plates. Some dampstaining to fore-edges not affecting text. cb Sept 11 (229) $65

Huth, Frederick

— Works on Horses and Equitation. L, 1887. 4to, half vellum. sg Oct 2 (133) $375

Huth Library, Henry

— A Catalogue of the Printed Books, Manuscripts.... L, 1880. One of 130. 5 vols. 4to, half lea; joints & spine ends rubbed. Vol I frontis loose. sg Oct 2 (167) $700

— Catalogue of the Woodcuts and Engravings in the Huth Library. L: Chiswick Press, 1910. Ltd Ed. 8vo, orig half lea. bba Jan 15 (281) £45 [Dawson]

Huth Library, Henry & Alfred H.

— [Sale Catalogue] Catalogue of the Famous Library of Printed Books, Illuminated Manuscripts.... L, 1911-20. Parts 1-9 (of 11). Wraps. bba Apr 23 (23) £350 [Joseph]

Anr copy. Parts 1-9 (of 11) bound in 4 vols. Half mor by John D. Gray; rubbed. A few clippings removed with loss on c.5 leaves in 2d part. O May 12 (99) $200

Anr Ed. L, 1911-22. 12 parts in 3 vols. Sold w.a.f. pn Oct 23 (93) £190 [Browning]

Hutten, Ulrich von, 1488-1523

— De unitate ecclesiae conservanda, et schismate.... [Mainz: Johann Schoeffer, Mar 1520]. 4to, modern vellum. Light marginal dampstaining; some early marginalia & underscoring; lacking final leaf. sg Apr 2 (116) $750

Hutton, Charles, 1737-1823

— A Mathematical and Philosophical Dictionary. L, 1796. 2 vols. 4to, contemp calf; rubbed, rebacked. With 37 plates. bba Jan 15 (377) £150 [Frew Mackenzie]

Hutton, Edward
— The Children's Christmas Treasury of Things New and Old. L, [1905]. 4to, cloth; worn & soiled. sg Oct 30 (108) $50

Hutton, William Rich
See also: Grabhorn Printing
— The Washington Bridge over the Harlem River, at 181st Street, New York City. NY: Leo von Rosenberg, [1889]. 4to, orig cloth; worn & soiled, front hinge repaired. Some short tears. wa Nov 6 (220) $140

Huxley, Aldous, 1894-1963
— After Many a Summer.... L, 1933. Advance Proof copy. Wraps; worn, spine creased. Clipped signature laid on front free endpaper. cb Sept 28 (706) $100
— Brave New World. L, 1932. 1st Ed. In d/j. Dusty. cb May 7 (109) $225; S Jan 13 (572) £280 [Cain]
One of 324 L.p. copies, sgd. sg Dec 11 (306) $500
— The Burning Wheel. Oxford, 1916. 1st Ed. Wraps; rubbed. bba Apr 9 (203) £130 [Lobb]
— Leda. Garden City, 1929. One of 361. Illus by Eric Gill. cb May 7 (110) $55
— Point Counter Point. L, 1928. 1st Ed. In frayed d/j. ALs loosely inserted. bba Oct 30 (257) £40 [Oram]

Huxley, Thomas Henry, 1825-95
— Evidence as to Man's Place in Nature. L, 1863. 1st Ed. 8vo, orig cloth; lower cover affected by damp. S Feb 24 (576) £180 [Trocchi]
Later Issue. Orig cloth; tears on spine. pnE Dec 17 (376) £50 [Bickerstaff]

Huygens, Christian, 1629-95
— The Celestial Worlds Discover'd.... L: Timothy Childe, 1698. Ed collating A3, B-L8. 8vo, modern half calf. With 4 (of 5) folding plates. bba Oct 16 (302) £80 [Maggs]
— Kosmotheoros, sive de terris coelestibus.... The Hague, 1699. 2d Ed. 4to, old half sheep; spine & corners worn. With 5 folding plates. sg Jan 15 (320) $375

Huygens, Constantyn, 1596-1687
— Koren-bloemen, Nederlandsche gedichten. The Hague, 1658. 1st Ed. 4to, contemp vellum. With frontis, port & folding plate. Some dampstains. S Mar 10 (947) £120 [Poel]
Anr Ed. Amst., 1672. 2 vols. 4to, blind-tooled vellum; 1 joint cracking. With port, engraved title & 2 folding plates. Some stains & foxing. L.p. copy. B Feb 25 (725) HF475

Hyatt, T. Hart
— Hyatt's Hand-Book of Grape Culture.... San Francisco, 1867. 8vo, orig cloth. Tp stamped. cb Apr 2 (143) $190

Hyde, Thomas, 1636-1703
— Mandragorias sue Historia Shahiludii. Oxford, 1694. 4 parts in 1 vol. 8vo, contemp vellum. Partly misbound. pn Mar 26 (424) £920 [Kaminsky]

**Hyett, Francis Adams —&
Austin, Roland**
— Supplement to the Bibliographer's Manual of Gloucestershire Literature. Gloucester, 1915-16. 4to, orig cloth; soiled. T Apr 16 (59) £80

Hymns...
— Hymns to Aphrodite. NY: Press of Valenti Angelo, [1949]. One of 150. cb Dec 4 (317) $85

I

I Fioretti. See: Ashendene Press

Iamblichus
— De mysteriis Aegyptiorum, Chaldaeorum, Assyriorum.... Rome: A. Bladus, 1556. 4to, old vellum. sg June 11 (249) $200

Ibbetson, Julius
— A Picturesque Guide to Bath, Bristol.... L, 1793. 4to, orig cloth; rubbed. With 16 hand-colored plates. T Mar 19 (59) £310

Ibis...
— The Ibis: A Magazine of General Ornithology. L, 1861-1918. Series 1-10 in 59 vols, including the 2 Jubilee Supplements 1909 & 1915, 2 vols; Index of Genera & Species for Series 4-6 & General Subject Index series 1-6. Orig cloth, mostly unopened, some orig wraps bound in. Lacking Vols I-II, V & VI of 1st Series. Sold w.a.f. C Apr 8 (148) £1,800 [Wheldon & Wesley]

Ibn Butlan. See: Elimithar, Elluchasem

Ibn Khaldun, 1332-1406
— The Muquaddimah: An Introduction to History. NY: Pantheon, [1958]. 3 vols. In d/js. Bollingen Series 43. cb Nov 6 (178) $50

Ibsen, Henrik, 1828-1906
— Peer Gynt. L, 1936. Illus by Arthur Rackham. 4to, orig cloth, in d/j. With 12 color plates. sg Oct 30 (110) $150; sg Oct 30 (111) $60
One of 460. Vellum gilt. With 12 color plates. pnNY Sept 13 (276) $475
One of 460, sgd by Rackham. Vellum gilt.

With 12 mtd color plates. sg Oct 30 (109) $700
— Works. NY, 1914-16. 13 vols. 12mo, half mor gilt; some spine ends worn, some joints rubbed. sg Sept 11 (208) $150

Icelandic. See: Edda

Icones. See: Zorn, Johannes

Ide, Simeon
— A Biographical Sketch of the Life of William B. Ide.... [Claremont, N.H.]; pbd by the Subscribers, [1880]. 16mo, orig half mor. sg Mar 12 (24) $700

Idler...
— The Idler. L, 1892-96. Vols 1-8. Orig cloth. cb Apr 24 (355) $200; cb Apr 24 (356) $600

Ignatius, Saint, of Loyola
— Exercitia spiritualia. Coimbra: Ioannem Barrerium, 1553. 16mo, 16th-cent calf; worn & shaken, backstrip detached but present. Minor marginal soiling & a few stains. James P. R. Lyell's copy. CNY Dec 19 (125) $17,000

Iliazd
— L'Art de voir de Guillaume Tempel. Paris: Au Point Cardinal, 1964. One of 70. Illus by Max ernst. Orig wraps. S June 29 (76) £600 [Naggar]

Illustrated...
See also: Martin, Robert Montgomery
— An Illustrated History of Sacramento County, California. Chicago, 1890. 8vo, mor gilt extra; extremities scuffed. cb Oct 9 (171) $65

Image...
— L'Image: Revue litteraire et artistique. Paris, 1896-97. Nos 1-12 (all pbd). 4to, orig wraps. B Oct 7 (327) HF400

Imago...
— Imago Mundi: A Review of Early Cartography. Berlin & Amst., 1935-68. Vols 1-22. 4to, ptd wraps. sg May 14 (192) $425
Vols 1-25. Berlin & Amst., 1935-71. 4to, wraps; worn. sg May 14 (191) $600

Imbert, Barthelemi, 1747-90
— Les Bienfaits du Sommeil ou les quatre reves accomplis.... Paris. Desnos, 1776. Bound with: Le Secretaire des dames et des messieurs. 18mo, contemp red mor gilt with arms of Christian VII, King of Denmark & Norway, with 3 pencil loops held by metal pin. Carnarvon copy. C Dec 3 (72) £1,900 [Quaritch]

Imitatione Christi. See: Thomas a Kempis

Imlay, Gilbert
— A Topographical Description of the Western Territory of North America. L, 1792. 1st Ed. 8vo, modern cloth. sg Mar 12 (143) $175
2d Ed. L, 1793. 8vo, modern cloth. With 3 folding maps & 1 table. Ck Nov 21 (220) £250
Anr copy. Contemp bds; rebacked with paper, rubbed. With 3 folding maps. Dampstained; frontis repaired at edges of 1 fold; tp reset on stub. sg Sept 18 (134) $300
1st American Ed. NY, 1793. Vol I (of 2). 12mo, contemp calf, worn & soiled. With 2 maps. Spotted. wa Sept 25 (447) $60
3d Ed. L, 1797. 8vo, modern half calf; worn. With 4 maps. First map with perforated library stamps; several maps with minor tears along hinge. sg Mar 12 (144) $700

Imperato, Ferrante
— Historia naturale. Venice, 1672. Folio, contemp vellum; soiled. With folding plate of the interior of the museum & 126 woodcuts in text. Small hole in outer blank margin; occasional spotting. Horticultural Society of New York—de Belder copy. S Apr 27 (169) £1,100 [Bishop]

Imperial...
— The Imperial Gazetteer: A General Dictionary of Geography.... Glasgow, 1855. 28 parts in 11 vols. 4to, contemp cloth; worn. Some foxing. sg Nov 20 (24) $100
Anr Ed. L, 1874. 4to, contemp sheep; scuffed. sg Dec 18 (192) $130

Indians, North American
— Cherokee Hymn Book. Phila., 1866. 16mo, cloth. sg Mar 12 (53) $100
Anr copy. Orig half lea; worn. sg Mar 12 (54) $100
— General Rules of the United Societies of the Methodist Episcopal Church. Park Hill: Mission Press, 1841. 24mo, wraps. sg Mar 12 (76) $150
— Speeches on the Passage of the Bill for the Removal of the Indians, Delivered in the Congress of the United States. Bost., 1830. 8vo, contemp half cloth. Minor dampstains. sg Mar 12 (71) $120
— CHEROKEES, - Constitution and Laws of the Cherokee Nation. St. Louis, 1875. 8vo, contemp calf; worn, hinges taped. Inscr by Principal Chief Will P. Ross. sg Mar 12 (60) $375
Anr Ed. Parsons KS, 1893. 8vo, contemp half calf; hinges broken, lacking front free endpaper. Pencil scrawl on front pastedown & tp. sg Mar 12 (61) $90

INDIANS

— CHEROKEES. - Letters and Conversations on the Cherokee Mission. Bost., 1830. Vol I. 12mo, contemp half calf. Foxed throughout; ink library stamp on tp. sg Mar 12 (68) $60
— MUSKOGEE INDIANS. - Constitution and Laws of the Muskogee Nations. Muskogee: F. C. Hubbard, 1893. 8vo, contemp half calf; front joint broken, extremities worn, 1st gathering loose. sg Mar 12 (188) $70

Indo-Chinese Gleaner...
— The Indo-Chinese Gleaner, containing Miscellaneous Communications on the Literature, History, Philosophy, Mythology, &c., of the Indo-Chinese Nations.... Malacca, 1818-22. Vols I-III, Nos 1-20 (all pbd). 8vo, cloth. Nos 1 & 7 in facsimile. Sold w.a.f. S Oct 23 (486) £1,900 [Maggs]

Infeld, Leopold. See: Einstein & Infeld

Ingalls, Fay
— About Dogs—and Me. Hot Springs VA, 1939. Bds. Inscr. sg Oct 23 (355) $110

Ingelow, Jean, 1820-97
— Poems. L, 1867. 4to, orig cloth elaborately blocked in gold & black with quadrilobe white paper onlay mtd in sunken center panel on covers (see McLean, plate 108). sg Sept 11 (12) $150

Ingen-Housz, Jan, 1730-99
— Experiments upon Vegetables. L, 1779. 8vo, contemp calf; spine rubbed. S May 28 (705) £260

Ingersoll-Smouse, Florence
— Joseph Vernet. Peintre de Marine.... Paris, 1926. 2 vols. 4to, orig wraps. HN May 20 (640) DM880

Inglis, Henry David, 1795-1835
— Rambles in the Footsteps of Don Quixote. L, 1837. 1st Ed. Illus by George Cruikshank. 12mo, orig cloth. With engraved title & 6 plates. sg June 11 (145) $90

Ingoldsby, Thomas. See: Barham, Richard Harris

Ingraham, Henry Andrews
— American Trout Streams.... NY, 1926. One of 350. 8vo, half cloth, unopened. With 5 plates. sg Oct 23 (79) $225

Ingram, James, 1774-1850
— Memorials of Oxford. Oxford, 1837. 3 vols. 4to, contemp half mor gilt; rubbed. S May 28 (877) £340

Anr copy. Cloth; worn. With 99 plates. sg Dec 18 (192A) $130

AMERICAN BOOK PRICES CURRENT

Ingres, Jean August Dominique
— Oeuvres. Paris, 1851. Ed by M. A. Magimel. 4to, contemp cloth; worn. Inscr. S Nov 10 (244) £110 [Marlborough]

Ingresso
— Ingresso del procurator di San Marco Antonio Cappello: Della guerre de'Veneziani nell' Asia. Venice, 1796. 4to, orig wraps. Some dampstains. S Feb 23 (76) £580 [Chrisdoulou]

Inman, Henry, 1837-99
— The Old Santa Fe Trail: The Story of a Great Highway. NY, 1898. Illus by Frederic Remington. 8vo, cloth; worn & soiled. With port, folding map & 8 plates. cb Jan 8 (275) $50

Inman, Henry, 1837-99 —& Cody, William F., 1846-97
— The Great Salt Lake Trail. NY, 1898. 1st Ed. 8vo, orig cloth; rubbed & waterspotted. AVP Nov 20 (150) C$75 [Ewens]

Insel...
— Die Insel. Monatsschrift mit Buchschmuck und Illustrationen. Berlin, 1899-1902. 36 issued in 34 vols. 4to, orig wraps. HN Nov 26 (1870) DM3,900

Anr copy. Vols I-III, 34 parts in 12 vols. Bds, orig wraps bound in. HN May 20 (2560) DM3,000

Institoris, Henricus, d.c.1500 —& Sprenger, Jacobus
— Malleus maleficarum. Nuremberg: Anton Koberger, 17 Jan 1496. 6th Ed. 4to, early sheep over wooden bds; worn, lacking clasp. Dampstained, occasional worming. 159 (of 160) leaves; lacking final blank. Goff I-168. P Dec 15 (160) $2,200

Anr Ed. Frankfurt: Nicolaus Bassaeus, 1580. 8vo, contemp calf with gilt arabesque plaque on covers incorporating initials IB; rebacked. Tp soiled & possibly from anr copy. sg Dec 4 (145) $225

Instructions...
— Instructions for the Guidance of the Captains and Commanding Officers of Her Majesty's Ships of War Employed in the Suppression of the Slave Trade. L, 1892. 2 vols. 4to, half calf gilt; rubbed. Some foxing; paper mark on title of Vol II. pnNY Sept 13 (287) $225

Instructive. See: Yonge, Charlotte Mary

International...
— International Exhibition at Philadelphia.... Phila., 1876. Oblong folio, half mor gilt, orig front wrap bound in; rubbed. With 10 litho plates. 2 slight tears on lower margin. pnNY Oct 11 (28) $800

— The International Post, No 1. L, 1939. Ed by Christopher Robinson & Tristram Pownall. Orig card wraps. Only issue produced; contributors included Lawrence Durrell, Swane Fox, Cyril Beaumont, John Gawsworth, Eric Halpenny & Geoffrey Mordaunt. S Dec 18 (120) £420 [Blackwell]

— International Auction Records. Paris, 1974-79. Ed by E. Mayer. Vols 8-13. Some hinges cracked, a few joints splitting. ha Dec 19 (71) $160

— International Chess Magazine. Zurich: Edition Olms, 1985. Vols 1-7 in 3 vols. Reprint. pn Mar 26 (183) £110 [British Chess Magazine]

International Boundary Commission

— Boundary between the United States and Mexico.... [Wash., 1899]. Folio, disbound. With 26 double-page maps & profiles. 55th Congress, 2d Session, Senate Doc. 247. wa Mar 5 (322) $220

International Ornithological Congress

— Proceedings of the [3d-16th] Congress. 1900-74. 14 vols in 16. B Feb 24 (26) HF600

International Shooting & Field Sports Exhibition

— Die erste internationale Jagd-Austellung, Wien, 1910. Vienna: Wilhelm Frick, 1912. 4to, modern half shagreen. Jeanson copy. SM Mar 1 (215) FF3,2000

— Exposition internationale de la chasse, Berlin, 1937. [Paris, 1937]. 4to, half shagreen. Jeanson copy. SM Mar 1 (216) FF1,600

Introduction...

— Introduction a la revolution des Pays-Bas et a l'histoire des Provinces-Unies. [N.p.], 1754. 3 vols in 1. 12mo, contemp mor gilt with arms of the States of the Netherlands. S June 25 (32) £280

Invalid, An. See: Winter...

Irby, Leonard Howard Lloyd

— The Ornithology of the Straits of Gibraltar. L, 1895. 4to, orig cloth. With 14 colored plates. pn Oct 23 (230) £320 [Greyfriars]

Iredale, Tom

— Birds of New Guinea. Melbourne, 1956. 2 vols. kh Mar 16 (273) A$160

Anr copy. Half mor gilt, in d/js. pn Oct 23 (231) £200 [Weldon & Wesley]

Anr copy. Half mor gilt. pn Dec 11 (235) £220 [Wheldon & Wesley]

— Birds of Paradise and Bower Birds. Melbourne, 1950. 4to, half lea. kh Mar 16 (274) A$120

One of 100. Orig mor, in d/j. Ck Jan 16 (69) £140

Anr copy. Mor. kh Mar 16 (275) A$200

Ireland, John, d.1808

— Hogarth Illustrated. L, 1812. 3 vols. 8vo, contemp calf gilt; hinges cracked. T Oct 16 (580) £70

Ireland, LeRoy

— The Works of George Innes. An Illustrated Catalogue Raisonne. Austin: Univ. of Texas Press, [1965]. Preface by Donald B. Goodall; Foreword by Robert G. McIntyre. 4to, cloth. pnNY June 11 (151A) $375

Ireland, Samuel, d.1800

See also: Fore Edge Paintings

— Graphic Illustrations of Hogarth. L, 1794-99. 2 vols. 4to, mor gilt. With 102 plates. S Nov 10 (106) £280 [Way]

— A Picturesque Tour through Holland, Brabant and part of France. L, 1790. 1st Ed. 2 vols. 4to, contemp half calf, rubbed. bba Oct 30 (322) £85 [Elliott]

Anr copy. Half calf gilt. With 45 plates in 2 states. Last leaf of table repaired; dampstains in Vol II. pn Nov 20 (34) £90 [Smith]

— Picturesque Views on the River Thames. L, 1792. 2 vols. 4to contemp mor gilt; joints & corners rubbed. With 2 hand-colored titles, 2 maps & 52 plates. C Apr 8 (30) £380 [Weinreb]

Anr copy. Contemp calf; worn. With 43 plates only. Lacking engraved titles. Ck Nov 21 (327) £300

— Picturesque Views on the River Medway. L, 1793. 4to calf; hinges def. With aquatint title, map & 27 plates. pn Sept 18 (74) £100 [Woodruff]

Anr copy. Later mor. With hand-colored frontis, map & 28 hand-colored plates. L.p. copy. S Oct 23 (177) £350 [Gibbs]

— Picturesque Views on the Upper, or Warwickshire Avon. L, 1795. 1st Ed. 8vo, later mor gilt by Root. With map, hand-colored engraved title & 30 plates. Ck Nov 21 (358) £250

Anr copy. Later mor. With frontis, map, 2 ports & 28 hand-colored plates. Lacking half-title. L.p. copy. S Oct 23 (178) £320 [Henderson]

— Picturesque Views on the River Wye. L, 1797. 4to, contemp half mor; joints cracked. With map, port & 30 plates. sg Apr 30 (74) £90

— Picturesque Views, with an Historical Account of the Inns of Court.... L, 1800. 4to, modern half mor. With 21 hand-colored plates. Small stain to blank margin of a few plates; marginal repair to 1 leaf; spotting in margins of last plate. C Apr 8 (31) £380

IRELAND

[Woodruff]
Anr copy. Mor gilt; lower cover detached. pn Mar 5 (81F) £420 [Howell]

Anr copy. Later mor. Lacking half-title. L.p. copy. S Oct 23 (176) £440 [Thorp]

Anr copy. Half mor; scuffed. sg Feb 12 (182) $100

— Picturesque Views on the River Thames. L, 1801-2. 2 vols. 8vo, contemp calf; re-backed. Lacking 1 title. Ck Sept 26 (81) £180

Anr copy. Contemp bds; worn. Sold w.a.f. Ck Sept 26 (152) £160

Anr copy. Bdg not described. With hand-colored frontis, 2 maps & 53 hand-colored plates, including the New Staines Bridge not listed by Abbey; several plate imprints dated 1799. Lacking half-titles. L.p. copy. S Oct 23 (179) £520 [Dennistoun]

Ireland, William Henry, 1777-1835

— England's Topographer: A New and Complete History of the County of Kent. L, 1828-30. 4 vols. 8vo, calf; def. With engraved title, folding county map & 123 plates. pn Mar 5 (118) £160 [McKenzie]

Anr copy. Calf; worn. Engraved title soiled. pn Mar 5 (119) £160 [McKenzie]

Anr copy. Orig cloth. pn May 21 (236) £140 [Croft]

— The Life of Napoleon Bonaparte. L, 1823-28. 1st Ed in orig 64/53 parts. Illus by George Cruikshank. Loose in 4 vols. 8vo, lev slipcases by Riviere. With 24 folding plates, 3 uncolored plates & 4 engraved titles. C June 18 (224) £450

Anr Ed. L, 1828. 4 vols. 8vo, modern half calf. Some soiling & fold wear; lacking titles. S May 6 (511) £320 [Camberwell]

— Miscellaneous Papers and Legal Instruments under the Hand and Seal of William Shakespeare...from the Original Manuscripts. L, 1796. 1st Ed. Folio, old bds; rebacked in lea, worn at tips & edges. Some foxing. O Oct 21 (93) $50

Iriarte, Juan de

— Obras sueltas. Madrid: Francisco Manuel de Mena, 1774. 2 vols. 4to, half calf. S Sept 23 (458) £110 [Baldwin]

Irish...

— The Irish Chess Chronicle. [N.p] 1887. Nos 1-7 & New Series Nos 1-16 (all pbd) in orig parts. pn Mar 26 (184) £140 [Schmidt]

Irving, Washington, 1783-1859

See also: Manuscript...

— The Angler. [N.p.]: Harbor Press, 1933. One of 180. Half cloth, unopened. sg Oct 23 (356) $60

— Astoria, or Anecdotes of an Enterprise beyond the Rocky Mountains. Phila., 1836. 1st Ed, 1st State. 2 vols. 8vo, contemp half mor; extremities worn. Lacking ads. F Jan 15 (329) $130

— Bracebridge Hall: or, the Humourists, by Geoffrey Crayon. L, 1822. 1st English Ed. 2 vols. 8vo, contemp calf; worn. F Jan 15 (326) $150

Anr Ed. L, 1877 [1876]. Illus by Randolph Caldecott. 8vo, mor gilt by Chivers. ha May 22 (143) $200

Anr Ed. L, 1896. 2 vols. 8vo, cloth. sg Oct 30 (113) $80

Anr Ed. NY, 1896. 2 vols. 8vo, cloth; hinges starting. sg Oct 30 (112) $50

— Bracebridge Hall. NY, 1896. Illus by Arthur Rackham. 2 vols. cb Feb 19 (141) $130

— A Chronicle of the Conquest of Granada. Paris: Galignani, 1829. 1st French Ed in English. 2 vols. 8vo, contemp half mor; worn & soiled. sg Sept 18 (136) $60

1st Ed. Phila., 1829. 2 vols. 8vo, orig half cloth; lacking rear flyleaf in Vol I. Some foxing & staining.. With Gouverneur Morris bookplate & Washington Irving First Day Issue cover. F Jan 15 (332) $120

— The Crayon Miscellany. L, 1835-36. Vols I-III. 8vo, contemp calf gilt; rubbed. F Jan 15 (330) $170

— Histoire de la vie et des voyages de Christophe Colomb. Paris, 1828. 4 vols. 8vo, orig bds; Vol I front hinge starting. With 2 colored folding maps. sg Mar 12 (149) $100

— A History of New York.... NY, 1809. 1st Ed. 2 vols. 12mo, orig sheep; rebacked, 1 cover detached. Folding view rebacked with linen. F Jan 15 (334) $230

— A History of New York. By Diedrich Knickerbocker. L, 1820. 8vo, calf gilt; worn. Extra-illus with 22 watercolors. sg Dec 4 (89) $500

— A History of the Life and Voyages of Christopher Columbus. L, 1828. 4 vols. 8vo, orig bds; 1 corner damaged. bba Feb 5 (177) £65 [Kamiliya]

Anr copy. Rebound in modern half cloth. With folding map. Lacking half-titles. pnE Dec 17 (34) £85 [Maggs]

Anr copy. Half lea; worn, some covers detached. With 2 folding maps. sg Sept 18 (137) $60

Anr Ed. NY, 1828. 3 vols. 8vo, contemp calf gilt. F Jan 15 (327) $200

— The Legend of Sleepy Hollow. L, [1928]. Illus by Arthur Rackham. 4to, cloth, in d/j. With 8 color plates. sg Oct 30 (115) $250

Copy marked "Special copy". Orig cloth.

S June 17 (275) £280 [Marzamo]
One of 250, sgd by Rackham. Orig vellum gilt. With 8 mtd color plates. sg Oct 30 (114) $1,000

— Life of George Washington. NY, 1855-59. 1st Ed. 5 vols. 8vo, later half mor; worn, hinges starting; some tears. Extra-illus with c.350 engravings. wa Feb 19 (85) $150

Anr copy. Half mor with name stamped on spine; rubbed, hinges weak. Extra-illus with ports & views & with extra pen title in Vol I. wd Nov 12 (126) $100

Anr Ed. NY, 1857-63. 5 vols. 4to, half mor gilt. sg Feb 12 (104) $120

Anr Ed. NY, 1866. 5 vols. 8vo, contemp half mor; worn. wa Feb 19 (86) $70

— Rip Van Winkle.... L, 1893. One of 250. Illus by George Boughton. 8vo, half mor gilt by Bayntun. pnE June 17 (4) £50

Anr Ed. L, 1905. Illus by Arthur Rackham. 4to, orig half vellum; worn, crudely repaired with tape. bba Mar 26 (268) £500 [Joseph]

One of 250, sgd by Rackham. Orig vellum gilt. With 51 mtd color plates. sg Oct 30 (116) $2,000

Anr Ed. L & NY, 1905. 4to, orig cloth; worn at extremities, front hinge cracked. With 52 colored plates. cb June 18 (307) $60

— Salmagundi; or the Whim-Whams and Opinions of Launcelot Langstaff.... NY, 1808. 20 parts in 2 vols. Contemp sheep. F Jan 15 (335) $200

— The Sketch Book of Geoffrey Crayon. NY, 1819-20. 1st Ed. 7 parts in 1 vol. 8vo, contemp half lea; worn. Minor marginal worming in opening leaves of 1st part. sg Feb 12 (183) $375

Westminster Ed. NY, 1895. Out-of-series copy. Illus by Arthur Rackham. 2 vols. 4to, mor gilt. sg Oct 30 (118) $80

— Tales of a Traveller. L, 1824. 2 vols. Later half lea; rubbed. Some stains & foxing. O Nov 18 (96) $70

Anr Ed. NY, 1895. Illus by Arthur Rackham. 2 vols. Later half lev gilt. Some foxing. cb Feb 19 (142) $160

— A Tour on the Prairies. L, 1835. 1st Ed. 8vo, orig bds; rebacked, with orig spine & endpapers retained. K Oct 4 (224) $120

— Works. L, 1854-59. 14 vols. 8vo, 19th-cent half mor gilt. sg Feb 12 (185) $700

Author's Autograph Ed. NY, 1895-97. One of 500. 40 vols. 8vo, half mor. With Ms leaf. wa Mar 5 (81) $190

Joseph Jefferson Ed. NY & L, [1901]. one of 250 with fragment of Ms. 40 vols. 8vo, mor, elaborately gilt. Sold w.a.f. Garbisch copy. CNY Dec 19 (98) $1,000

One of 250. 40 vols. Half vellum. pnNY Sept 13 (249) $275

Irwin, Eyles, 1751?-1817

— A Series of Adventures in the Course of a Voyage up the Red Sea.... L, 1780. 4to, contemp calf; rubbed, upper joint cracked. With folding map & 5 plates. Lacking half-title; marginal repair to 1 leaf. C Dec 12 (239) £220 [Shapero]

Anr copy. Contemp calf; worn, spine crudely repaired. With 4 folding maps & 4 plates, all trimmed & mtd. Sold w.a.f. Extra-illus with an Ink & wash sketch. Ck May 15 (36) £110

Irwin, Frederick Chidley

— The State and Position of Western Australia.... L, 1835. 8vo, orig cloth; rubbed. bba June 18 (315) £320 [Maggs]

Anr copy. Orig cloth; rebacked. C Oct 15 (156) £400 [Maggs]

Irwin, Will. See: Genthe, Arnold

Isenring, Johann Baptist

— Sammlung malerischer Ansichten der merkwuerdigsten Staedte und Flecken der Schweiz. [St. Gallen: Isenring, c.1831]. Oblong folio, contemp mor gilt with red & citron onlays on upper cover. With 19 views, all but that of St. Gallen finely hand-colored, each heightened with gum arabic & laid onto colored paper. Bound with a pair of views showing the suspension bridge at Fribourg, 2 views in Zurich, a general view of Zurich, a colored aquatint of the rescue of Tell, an aquatint of Schaffhausen surrounded by cantonal costume vignettes & 2 further engraved Swiss views. S Oct 23 (255) £38,000 [Laube]

Isherwood, Christopher

— The Memorial; Portrait of a Family. L: Hogarth Press, 1932. 1st Ed. In d/j. S Mar 9 (846) £160 [Libris]

Anr copy. Cloth, variant bdg, in soiled d/j. S Mar 9 (847) £110 [Whiteson]

— Mr. Norris Changes Trains. L: Hogarth Press, 1935. 1st Ed. In d/j. Some wear to half-title. S Dec 18 (136) £320 [Maggs]

Ishizawa Takeo. See: Kobayashi Keisuke & Ishizawa Takeo

Isocrates, 436-338 B.C.

— Opera. Basel, 1582. 8vo, contemp blind-stamped pigskin over wooden bds; rubbed. Wormhole in prelims not affecting text; some soiling. bba Sept 25 (240) £95 [Poel]

ITALIAN...

Italian...
— Italian Tales. Tales of Humour, Gallantry, and Romance. L, 1824. 1st Issue, with "creditor," on p 32, line 10 & with the Dead Rider plate. Illus by George Cruikshank. 8vo, calf gilt. With 16 plates. Spotting affecting a few plates. sg Feb 12 (65) $250

Italy
— Regolamento del Regio Arcispedale di Santa Maria Nuova.... Florence: G. Cambiagi, 1783. 4to, contemp vellum bds; wormed. With frontis, 5 folding plates & 22 ptd tables. Minor worming. S Nov 10 (435) £420 [Marlborough]

Ivchenko, Valerian
— Anna Pavlova. Paris, 1922. One of 325. Trans by W. Petroff. 4to, orig wraps; spine soiled, frayed & wormed. With 23 plates. Sgd by Pavlova on half-title. cb June 18 (319) $475
— Thamar Karsavina. L, 1922. Ltd Ed. Trans by H. de Vere Beauclerk & Nadia Errenor; Ed by Cyril W. Beaumont; illus by Claud Lovat Fraser. 4to, orig half cloth. With 31 plates. wd June 19 (179) $400

Ives, Edward, d.1786
— A Voyage from England to India.... L, 1773. 1st Ed. 4to, contemp calf; rebacked. With 2 folding maps (1 hand-colored) & 15 plates. Maps slightly creased at margins, 1 detached & tipped-in with corner tear & spotting; other minor stains & spotting. C Apr 8 (101) £240 [Joseph]

Ives, Joseph C.
— Report upon the Colorado River.... Wash., 1861. 4to, orig cloth; spine ends frayed. Library markings; each folding map with a tear. cb Mar 19 (141) $375

Anr copy. Cloth; extremities worn, lacking spine ends. 1 map torn; several fold-out plates with small tears at folds. sg Mar 12 (150) $130

J

Jackson, Abraham Valentine Williams, 1862-1937
— History of India. L, [1906-7]. One of 200. 9 vols. Half mor gilt. O May 12 (102) $300

One of 1,000. Half mor gilt. pn Oct 23 (5) £120 [Hosain]

Anr Ed. L: Grolier Society, [1906-7]. One of 200. 9 vols. Half mor gilt; rubbed. K Oct 4 (220) $375; wa Dec 11 (333) $140

AMERICAN BOOK PRICES CURRENT

Jackson, Lady Catherine Charlotte
— Works. L: Grolier Society, [c.1895-1900]. L.p. Ed, one of 1,000. 14 vols. 8vo, half mor by Blackwell. ha May 22 (63) $325

Jackson, Sir Charles James
— English Goldsmiths and their Marks. L, 1921. 4to, orig cloth; rubbed. cb July 30 (102) $85
— An Illustrated History of English Plate. L, 1911. 2 vols. 4to, orig half mor. S Nov 17 (659) £55 [Ash]

Jackson, Emily Nevill
— The History of Silhouettes. L, 1911. 4to, half mor; worn. With 7 leaves with mtd silhouettes. wa Nov 6 (489) $75

Jackson, Sir Frederick John, 1860-1929
— The Birds of Kenya Colony and the Uganda Protectorate. L, 1938. 3 vols. 4to, cloth. pn Oct 23 (232) £260 [Graham]

Jackson, Helen Hunt, 1830-85
— Ah-Wah-Ne Days.... San Francisco, 1971. One of 450. cb June 18 (27) $85

Jackson, Herbert J.
— European Hand Firearms of the Sixteenth, Seventeenth, & Eighteenth Centuries.... L, 1923. One of 350. 4to, orig half cloth, in d/j with minor tears. O May 12 (103) $125

Jackson, Sir Keith Alexander
— Views in Affghaunistaun Port. L, [1841]. Folio, orig half calf; rubbed. With litho title, colored port, map & 23 plates (of 25). C Dec 12 (119) £150 [Scott]

Anr copy. Half mor gilt; loose. With hand-colored frontis, litho title, map (trimmed at bottom) & 23 plates. pn May 21 (44) £280 [Shapero]

Jackson, Maria Elizabeth
— Botanical Dialogues, between Hortensia and her four Children. L, 1797. 8vo, calf; worn. pn Jan 22 (231) £55 [Gladstone]

Jackson, Shirley
— The Road Through the Wall. NY, 1948. In d/j. sg Mar 5 (106) $200

Jackson, William Alexander
— An Annotated List of the Publications of...the Reverend Thomas Frognall Dibdin. Cambr., Mass., 1965. One of 500. Folio, orig cloth. bba June 18 (6) £95 [Frew MacKenzie]; O June 16 (112) $60; sg May 14 (220) $80

Jackson, William H., 1983-84
— The Canyons of Colorado. Denver: Frank S. Thayer, [c.1900]. 8vo, orig cloth; rubbed. 16 photographs on 9 folding leaves. Title soiled. cb Oct 9 (314) $75

Jacob, Giles, 1686-1744
— A New Law-Dictionary.... L, 1744. Folio, contemp calf; worn. Final leaf creased. Ck Jan 30 (121) £100

Jacob, Nicholas Henri —& Hugues, P.
— Storia naturale delle scimie e dei maki. Milan, 1812. Folio, contemp half cloth; rebacked, new endpapers. With 73 plates. 1st & last few leaves creased. cb June 4 (113) $650

Jacob, William, 1762-1851
— Tracts relating to the Corn Trade.... L, 1828. 8vo, modern bds. Discard stamps on tp; numbers on a2. P Sept 24 (307) $150

Jacobsen, Jens Peter
— Die Pest in Bergamo. Vienna & Leipzig, 1922. One of 150 with plates sgd by engraver. Illus by Alois Kolb. 4to, calf; marked. S Oct 6 (652) £70 [Frankle]

Jacobsz, Theunis
— Le Grand & Nouveau Mirroir, ou Flambeau de la Mer. Amst., 1688. 5 parts in 1 vol, including Supplement. Folio, contemp vellum; soiled. With 36 double-page charts. Small library stamp on tp. S June 25 (292) £4,200

Jacobus de Guitroede
— Lavacrum conscientiae. Cologne: Heinrich Quentell, 28 June 1499. 4to, disbound. With 2 small holes in upper margin of tp. 60 leaves. Goff L-104. S Feb 23 (1085) £420 [Maggs]

Jacobus de Voragine. See: Voragine, Jacobus de

Jacobus Philippus de Bergamo
— Novissime hystoriarum omnium repercussiones. Venice: Albertino de Lessona, 1503. Folio, modern vellum gilt. FD Dec 2 (64) DM6,800

Jacquemont, Victor
— Voyage dans l'Inde.... Paris, 1835-41-44. 6 vols. 4to, contemp half cloth; marked. With 4 folding maps & 290 plates, 27 hand-colored. Text with some discoloration & a little marginal dampstaining, the plates & maps with some spotting. de Belder copy. S Apr 27 (170) £3,000 [Asher]

Jacques, D.
— A Visit to Goodwood.... Chichester, 1822. 8vo, later half cloth; rubbed. With 3 plates. Tp & several leaves stained. Inscr. Ck Sept 5 (242) £50

Jacquin, Joseph Franz von, 1766-1839
— Eclogae plantarum rariorum. Vienna, 1811-44. 2 vols. With: Jacquin. Eclogae graminum. Vienna, 1813-44. Folio, contemp half russia gilt. Together, 3 vols in 2. Folio. Contemp half russia gilt. With 167 hand-colored plates in 1st work & 40 hand-colored plates in the 2d work. Plesch —de Belder copy. S Apr 27 (171) £17,000 [Israel]

Jacquin, Nicolaus Joseph von, 1727-1817
— Collectanea ad botanicam, chemiam et historiam.... Vienna, 1786-96. 5 vols. 4to, contemp calf. With 8 plain & 98 hand-colored plates. Some spotting in the text of Vol I. S Apr 27 (176) £4,000 [Israel]
— Florae Austriacae. Vienna, 1773-78. 5 vols. Folio, early 19th-cent half calf; rubbed. With colored engraved view on each tp, 500 hand-colored plates & 1 uncolored plate. A few marginal annotations. Rudge—de Belder copy. S Apr 27 (177) £26,000 [Junk]
— Fragmenta botanica. Vienna, 1809. Folio, contemp russia; rebacked. With 2 plain & 136 hand-colored plates. de Belder copy. S Apr 27 (180) £15,000 [Israel]
— Icones plantarum rariorum. L, 1781-93-[95]. 3 vols. Folio, contemp half calf; rubbed. With 649 hand-colored plates, many folding. de Belder copy. S Apr 27 (181) £32,000 [Israel]
— Miscellanea Austriaca ad botanicam, chamiam, et historiam naturalem spectantia. Vienna, 1778-81. 2 vols in 1. 4to, contemp calf gilt, armorial bdg. With 44 hand-colored plates. pnE Dec 17 (207) £1,100 [Maggs]

Anr copy. 2 vols. 4to, contemp half calf. de Belder copy. S Apr 27 (174) £700 [Israel]
— Observationum botanicarum. Vienna, 1764-71. 4 parts in 1 vol. Folio, contemp half calf; worn. With engraved title-vignettes & 100 plates. Some spotting & browning; 1 plate torn at outer blank corner. Horticultural Society of New York—de Belder copy. S Apr 27 (173) £800 [Ramer]
— Oxalis. Vienna, 1794. 4to, contemp half calf. With folding table, 6 plain & 75 hand-colored plates. Palmer—de Belder copy. S Apr 27 (178) £5,000 [Minton]
— Plantarum rariorum horti caesarei Schoenbrunnensis descriptiones et icones. Vienna, 1797-1804. 4 vols. Folio, contemp calf gilt; rubbed. With 500 hand-colored plates. Copy 68. de Belder copy. S Apr 27 (182) £80,000 [Israel]
— Selectarum stirpium Americanarum historia.... Vienna, 1763. Folio, contemp

calf; repaired at head of spine, slightly torn & rubbed. With engraved frontis & 184 plates. de Belder copy. S Apr 27 (172) £1,900 [Gall]

Anr Ed. Vienna, 1780-81. One of c.12 to 18 copies with sgd watercolor & gouache title by Franz Bauer & 264 watercolor plates. Folio, contemp calf gilt, with arms of the Russian Imperial family; rubbed, foot of spine repaired. Inscr to Maria Feodorovna, Tsarina of Paul I. de Belder copy. S Apr 27 (179) £52,000 [Israel]

Jacquin, Nicolaus Joseph von, 1766-1839
— Hortus botanicus vindobonensis. Vienna, 1770-76. One of 162. 3 vols in 4. Folio, contemp half calf; rubbed. With colored plan & 300 hand-colored plates. Blank lower outer corner of 1st title torn; 1 folding plate torn & repaired; a few plates slightly soiled. Horticultural Society of New York—de Belder copy. S Apr 27 (175) £20,000 [Israel]

Jadin, Emmanuel & Godefroy
— La Venerie, 1852-79. Paris, 1905. One of 10 on japon. Folio, loose as issued in mor album. Jeanson copy. SM Mar 1 (297) FF36,000

Jaenisch, Charles Frederick de, 1813-72
— Traite des applications de l'analyse mathematique au jeu des echecs. St. Petersburg, 1862-63. 3 vols in 1. Half calf. pn Mar 26 (425) £180 [Steighter]

Jagd...
— Die par force Jagd der Haasen.... Coulmback, 1751. 8vo, mor gilt by Gruel. Jeanson copy. SM Feb 28 (178) FF32,000

Jahrbuch...
— Jahrbuch der Jungen Kunst. Leipzig, 1921. 4to, orig bdg. B Oct 7 (966) HF500

— Jahrbuch der Auktionspreise fuer Buecher und Autographen. Hamburg, 1950-82. Vols 1-32 plus Index vols for 1950-59, 1960-69 & 1970-79. 31 vols. FD June 11 (214) DM3,200

Vols 24-35. Hamburg, 1973-85. Ck Nov 7 (6) £400

Jaillot, Charles Hubert Alexis
— Atlas Nouveau, contenant toutes les parties du monde. Paris, 1728. Folio, contemp vellum; worn & soiled. With engraved title & 52 double-page mapsheets, several hand-colored in outline. 6 maps inlaid to size; minor repairs; some stains. S Oct 23 (59) £2,100 [Potter]

Jaillot, Charles Hubert Alexis —& Sanson d'Abbeville, Nicolas
— Atlas Nouveau. Contenant toutes les parties du Monde.... L, 1696. 2 vols. Folio, contemp half vellum; worn. With 101 engraved mapsheets, most double-page or folding, all hand-colored in outline. Some soiling; a few leaves detached. Manchester copy. S June 25 (293) £7,000 [Schmidt]

Jalovec, Karel
— Italian Violin Makers. NY, [1964]. 4to, orig cloth, in d/j. bba Feb 5 (142) £65 [Check]

James, Edward
— Phrase and Periphrasis or the Bones of My Hand. [N.p., n.d.]. Frontis by Paul Tchelitcheff. Inscr to Magritte with a drawing in Magritte's style. S July 2 (1025) £700 [Armbruster]

James, Edwin. See: Tanner, John

James, Edwin, 1797-1861
— Account of an Expedition from Pittsburgh to the Rocky Mountains. Phila., 1822. 3 vols. 8vo & 4to, lev gilt. One-inch tear in 1st map repaired; all but 1 of the plates have been trimmed & inlaid into 4to sheets. sg Mar 12 (152) $2,400

— A Narrative of the Captivity and Adventures of John Tanner.... NY, 1830. 1st Ed. 8vo, contemp calf; worn, front detached. Top margins dampstained. Library copy. cb Jan 8 (100) $325

Anr copy. Orig bds; front cover becoming detached. Some soiling, mostly to prelims. cb Apr 2 (153) $375

James, George Payne Rainsford, 1799-1860
— Works. L, 1844-49. 21 vols. Half calf gilt; spines & corners rubbed. pnNY Sept 13 (198) $375

James, Grace
— Green Willow and other Japanese Fairy Tales. L, 1910. One of 500. Illus by Warwick Goble. 4to, orig vellum; soiled & shaken. S May 6 (125) £100 [Fraser]

James, Henry, 1843-1916
— The Ambassadors. NY & L, 1903. 1st Pbd Ed. Orig bds, in worn d/j. wa Sept 25 (674) $60

— English Hours. Cambr., Mass., 1905. L.p. Ed, one of 421. Designed by Bruce Rogers; illus by Joseph Pennell. Half cloth; rubbed. sg Feb 5 (259) $50

— Italian Hours. Bost., 1909. 1st American Ed. Illus by Joseph Pennell. With 32 colored plates. sg Feb 5 (260) $60

— Notes of a Son and Brother. NY, 1914. 1st Ed. Unopened, in d/j. wa Dec 11 (265) $230; wa Feb 19 (348) $55

— The Portrait of a Lady. L, 1883. 8vo, later cloth. T Sept 18 (376) £110

— Works. NY, 1907-17. ("The Novels and Tales.") New York Ed. Vols 1-24 (of 26). orig "unlacquered smooth silky plum cloth"; some covers rubbed. ha May 22 (64) $1,200

Anr Ed. NY, 1907-09. 24 vols. Half mor; rebacked with new spines. wd Nov 12 (128) $950

Anr Ed. NY, 1907-17. One of 156 on Ruisdael paper. 26 vols. Orig half cloth; some covers soiled. With 26 frontises. Library markings. bba Feb 5 (209) £400 [Kunkle]

Anr Ed. L, 1921-23. 35 vols. pnNY June 11 (123) $275

Anr Ed. NY, 1922. Most frontises by A. L. Coburn. 26 vols. sg Sept 11 (214) $375; wa Dec 11 (264) $700

James I, King of England

— Opera. L, 1619. Folio, contemp calf; lacking backstrip, covers almost detached. Prelims torn & frayed; all leaves severely stained. bba Mar 26 (152) £35 [Clark]

James, John Angell, 1785-1859. See: Poe's copy, Edgar Allan

James, John T., 1786-1828

— Views in Russia, Sweden, Poland, and Germany. L, 1826-27. Folio, modern half mor gilt. With 20 hand-colored mtd litho views. S May 29 (1050) £450

James, Montague Rhodes, 1862-1936

— Ghost-Stories of an Antiquary. L, 1904. 1st Ed. 8vo, orig cloth; split on rear hinge. T Oct 15 (214) £75

James, P. D.

— The Skull Beneath the Skin. L, 1982. In d/j. Sgd. sg Mar 5 (107) $60

James, Robert, 1705-76

— A Dissertation on Fevers, and Inflammatory Distempers. L, 1778. 8th Ed. 8vo, calf. pnE Dec 17 (110) £340 [Quaritch]

James, William, d.1827

— A Full Account of the Chief Naval Occurences of the late War between Great Britain and the United States.... L, 1817. 8vo, contemp half calf; corners worn. T Feb 19 (282) £82

— The Naval History of Great Britain. L, 1837. 6 vols. 8vo, half mor; rubbed, rear cover of Vol I detached. T Sept 18 (40) £405

Jameson, Robert

— A System of Mineralogy. Edin., 1804-8. 3 vols. 8vo, contemp calf gilt; 1 joint cracked. With 16 folding plates & 2 folding tables. C Dec 12 (120) £550 [Birmingham Assay Office]

Jamieson, Alexander

— A Celestial Atlas, comprising a Systematic Display of the Heavens.... L, 1822. Oblong 4to, disbound. With engraved title, dedication & 30 maps. 1 plate stained. pn Dec 11 (408) £320 [Nicholson]

Jamieson, John, 1759-1838

— Select Views of the Royal Palaces of Scotland. Edin., 1830. 4to, mor gilt by Carss of Glasgow; rubbed. With 24 plates mtd on india paper. O Feb 24 (112) £90

Jamot, Paul, 1863-1939 —& Wildenstein, Georges

— Manet. Paris, 1932. 2 vols. 4to, half mor, orig wraps bound in. Inscr by Georges Wildenstein. S June 17 (36) £360 [Grob]

Jane's...

— Jane's All the World's Fighting Ships. L, 1898. S May 6 (512) £40 [Vorlich]

Jane's All the World's Fighting Ships. L, 1898-1984. Vols for 1898-1985 in 84 vols, including Supplement 1915, but lacking 1945/46, 1958/49 & 1978/79. 4to, orig cloth, some vols in d/js. Small blindstamp at head of titles. Sold w.a.f. C Apr 8 (32) £3,200 [Green]

Janis, Harriet & Sidney

— Picasso: The Recent Years, 1939-1946. NY, 1947. One of 350, sgd by Picasso. 4to, half cloth. With 135 plates. cb May 7 (129) $300

Janner, Ferdinand

— Das heilige Land und die heiligen Staetten. Regensburg, NY & Cincinnati, [1869]. 4to, orig cloth. With engraved title with gold & 25 hand-finished color plates. S Oct 23 (378) £450 [Fletcher]

Janson, Charles William

— The Stranger in America: containing Observations Made During a Long Residence.... L, 1807. 4to, contemp half calf; rubbed, joints cracked. Ck Nov 21 (200) £280

Janssonius, Joannes

— Atlas contractus, sive Atlantis Majoris compendium. Amst.: Heirs of Johannes Jansson, 1666. 2 vols. Folio, contemp calf gilt; rubbed. With engraved titles (heightened with gold) & 170 doublepage mapsheets colored in a contemp hand. Lacking Mechelen & Flanders in Vol I; titles repaired at lower outer corners; slight

JANSSONIUS

damage to 1 or 2 maps of France in Vol II; some short splits elsewhere without loss; some marginal stains. S Oct 23 (40) £12,000 [Nieuw]

— Novus Atlas. Amst., 1653. ("[Spanish version] Nuevo Atlas, o Teatro de todo el Mundo.") Vol III only [France, Switzerland & the Low Countries]. Folio, contemp vellum; stained. With 66 double-page maps mtd on guards. Some spotting & discoloration. C Oct 15 (52) £1,200 [Loose]

Janvier, Thomas A., 1849-1913

— The Aztec Treasure-House. NY, 1890. Illus by Frederic Remington. 8vo, cloth. cb Jan 8 (277) $90

Jaquet, Eugene. See: Chapuis & Jaquet

Jardine, Sir William, 1800-74

— British Salmonidae. L, 1976. One of 500. 2 parts in 1 vol. Folio, half cloth. With 12 hand-colored plates. Facsimile. pnE Dec 17 (350) £40 [Neil]

— The Natural History of Humming Birds. Edin., 1833-34. 2 vols. 8vo, half calf. With 65 hand-colored plates. Library stamps. pn Nov 20 (22) £60
Anr copy. Contemp half sheep; scuffed. Vol II with additional title & port bound after page 104. sg Jan 15 (228) $300

— The Naturalist's Library. Edin., 1833-43. 40 vols. 8vo, contemp half calf; rubbed. Ck Nov 21 (194) £1,200
Anr copy. 19th-cent half mor gilt; minor wear. Light foxing; lacking 1 plate. ha Mar 13 (278) $2,000
40 vols. Orig cloth; rubbed, some backstrips missing or def. bba Aug 20 (439) £1,300 [Walford]
Anr Ed. Edin., 1843. 40 vols. 8vo, half calf by Brentano; minor rubbing, 1 bdg water-damaged. With frontis ports, engraved titles & 1,469 plates, 1,269 of them hand-colored. Vols 32, 33, 36, 37 & 40 with each plate in 2 forms, colored & uncolored. CNY May 11 (64) $2,000
Anr Ed. Edin., [1852-64]. 42 vols. 8vo, orig cloth; rubbed. With engraved titles, ports & 1,286 plates, all but a few hand-colored. Some leaves of text torn, affecting text. bba June 18 (154) £1,200 [Elliott]

Jarrin, G. A.

— The Italian Confectioner, or Complete Economy of Desserts. L, 1823. 8vo, half cloth; worn & shaken. With port & 2 folding plates. Some soiling & foxing. O Nov 18 (101) £60

AMERICAN BOOK PRICES CURRENT

Jars, Gabriel, 1732-69

— Voyages metallurgiques, ou recherches et observations sur les mines & forges de fer.... Lyon & Paris, 1774-81. 4to, contemp half calf. With 52 plates, many folding. C Dec 12 (121) £1,250 [Israel]

Jasper, Theodore

— The Birds of North America * Ornithology. Columbus, Ohio, [1874]-78. Together, 2 vols. 4to, orig half lea. Extremities rubbed. sg Jan 15 (229) $400

Jastro, Morris. See: Grabhorn Printing

Jaubert, Jean Baptiste —& Barthelemy-Lapommeraye, Christophe Jerome

— Richesses ornithologiques du midi de la France.... Marseilles, 1859-[62]. 4to, contemp half mor; rubbed. With 21 hand-colored lithos. S July 28 (1087) £280

Jaume Saint-Hilaire, Jean Henri

— Plantes de la France. Paris, [1805]-9. Issue on laid paper. 4 vols. 4to, contemp half mor. With 400 colored plates. Kerchove de Denterghem—de Belder copy. S Apr 27 (185) £2,600 [Hayward Hill]
Anr Ed. Paris, [1805]-1808-22-[24]. One of a few L.p. copies. 10 vols. 4to, contemp half mor gilt with gilt crown & initials on the spine of Marie Louise, Empress of France. With 10 ports & 1,000 color plates. Some plates with slight discoloration. de Belder copy. S Apr 27 (184) £19,000 [Sourget]

— Traite des arbrisseaux et de arbustes.... Paris, 1825. 2 vols. 4to, half mor gilt. With 176 hand-finished colored plates. Slight marginal waterstaining scarcely affecting plates. L.p. copy. de Belder copy. S Apr 27 (183) £3,200 [Macdougall]

Jefferies, Richard, 1848-87

— Hodge and his Masters. L, 1880. 2 vols. 8vo, orig cloth; rubbed. bba Jan 15 (110) £90 [Waggett]; pn Dec 11 (325) £120 [Shepheard]

— A Memoir of the Goddards of North Wilts. Swindon, [1873]. 4to, orig cloth; soiled. pn Dec 11 (329) £120 [Jarndyce]

— Wood Magic.... L, 1881. 1st Ed. 2 vols. 8vo, cloth. pn Dec 11 (331) £80 [Burwood]

Jeffers, Robinson, 1887-1962

— Cawdor. [Covelo, CA], 1983. One of 240. Illus by Mark Livingston. Folio, half mor. sg Jan 8 (295) $200

— Give Your Heart to the Hawks.... NY, 1933. 1st Ed, One of 200. Half calf. sg June 11 (253) $150

— Granite & Cypress. Santa Cruz: Lime Kiln Press, 1975. One of 100. 4to, cloth. sg Apr 2 (120) $2,400

— Medea. NY, [1946]. 1st Ed. Orig half cloth, in d/j. Inscr to Andrea Cowdin. wd June 19 (135) $125

— Poems. San Francisco, 1928. One of 310. Frontis by Ansel Adams. Sgd by Adams on port. cb Dec 4 (152) $650

— The Selected Poetry of.... NY, 1937 [1938]. In soiled d/j. cb Jan 22 (26) $55

— Such Counsels You Gave to Me.... NY, [1937]. One of 300. Half mor. sg Dec 11 (69) $130

— Tamar, and Other Poems. NY, [1924]. 1st Ed, One of 500. Inscr. sg Mar 5 (109) $250

— Themes in my Poems. San Francisco: Book Club of Calif., 1956. One of 350. In wrap which is clipped to show spine label. cb Sept 11 (45) $225; cb Jan 22 (28) $110

Jefferson, Thomas, 1743-1826

— A Manual of Parliamentary Practice. Wash., 1801. 12mo, half cloth. sg Mar 12 (154) $700

— Memoirs, Correspondence, and Private Papers. L, 1829. 8vo, half mor; worn & soiled. Some dampstains at lower edge. wa Dec 11 (306) $110

— Notes on the State of Virginia. L, 1787. 8vo, contemp calf; upper joint worn. With folding map hand-colored in outline (short tear in fold). S June 25 (424) £2,500 [Voorhees]

Anr Ed. Balt., 1800. 8vo, old calf; worn, stained. With folding table. Some stains in text. Laid into half lea box. ha Dec 19 (125) $180

— Observations sur la Virginie.... Paris. Barrois, 1786. 1st Ed in French. 8vo, contemp bds; rebacked. Lacking map. Ck Feb 27 (130) £280

Anr copy. Early 19th-cent half calf; lacking backstrip, damaged along top of bds. With map & table. Badly dampstained along upper margins, affecting 1 fold of map & some text. sg Mar 12 (153) $1,500

— The Papers.... Princeton, 1950-65. Ed by J.P. Boyd. Vols 1-19 plus 3 Index vols. K Mar 22 (150) $250

Jefferson's copy, Thomas

— DIONYSIUS HALICARNASSUS. - Les Antiquites Romaines. Chaumont, 1799-1800. 6 vols. 8vo, calf gilt by Mayo of Richmond. Some leaves dampstained; several perforated library stamps in each vol. Each volume with Jefferson's characteristic library marks. Brief holograph directions to the binder tipped in. sg Apr 2 (121) $5,600

Jefferys, Thomas, d. 1771

See also: Kitchin & Jefferys

— The American Atlas. L, 1776. Folio, contemp half calf; worn. With 13 mapsheets only. Some creases. S July 14 (746) £1,400

— A Description of the Spanish Islands and Settlements on the Coast of the West Indies. L, 1762. 4to, contemp half calf. With 32 folding maps & plans. C Apr 8 (132) £1,100 [Maggs]

— The Natural and Civil History of the French Dominions in North and South America.... L, 1760. 2 parts in 1 vol. Folio, contemp calf; needs rebacking. With 18 folding maps & plans. Tear in 1 map. sg Mar 12 (155) $2,200

— The West-India Atlas.... L, 1775. Folio, contemp half calf; worn, backstrip missing. With double-page engraved title & 39 mostly double-page charts. Some charts frayed. S June 25 (427) £3,000 [Fisher]

Jeffreys, John Gwyn, 1809-85

— British Conchology.... L, 1862-63-65. 3 vols. 12mo, orig cloth; rubbed. With 24 plates. Library stamps. bba Mar 26 (297) £140 [Smith]

Anr Ed. L, 1862-69. 5 vols. 12mo, orig cloth; spine ends bumped. With 24 plates. Many plates with pencil notes. cb June 4 (117) $170

Jekyll, Gertrude, 1843-1932

— Garden Ornament. L, 1918. 1st Ed. Folio, orig cloth; worn. S Nov 10 (109) £50 [Chesborough]

2d Ed. L, 1927. Folio orig cloth. Ck Feb 19 (160) £80; Ck Apr 24 (204) £90

Jenkins, James. See: Martial...

Jenkins, John, d.1823

— The Art of Writing.... Cambr., Mass., [1813]. Book I (all pbd). 8vo, contemp half calf; worn. With frontis, engraved title, port & 10 plates. Frontis & title both heavily dampstained. sg Jan 22 (321) $60

Jenkins, Rhys. See: Dickinson & Jenkins

Jenner, G. C. See: England

Jennings, Oscar

— Early Woodcut Initials. L, 1908. 4to, orig cloth. bba Oct 16 (428) £65 [Mills]

Jennings, Otto Emery

— Wild Flowers of Western Pennsylvania.... Pittsburgh, 1953. 2 vols. Folio, cloth. With 200 color plates. wa Nov 6 (267) $160

Anr copy. Cloth, in torn d/js; worn. wa Dec 11 (553) $200

JENNINGS

Jennings, Preston J. See: Derrydale Press

Jennings, Samuel
— Orchids: and How to Grow Them in India.... L, 1875. 4to, cloth. With 48 hand-colored plates, all with perforated library stamps. bba Dec 18 (161) £300 [Cassidy]

Jerdon, Thomas C., 1811-72
— Illustrations of Indian Ornithology. Madras, 1847. 4to, contemp half mor; worn, lacking front free endpaper & initial blank. Some leaves def from damp or torn & repaired. S Feb 24 (579) £600 [Wheldon]

Jerrard, Paul
— Flower Painting in Twelve Progressive Lessons. L, [1852]. 8vo, disbound. With hand-colored litho title & 12 plates. Ck Jan 30 (200) £260
— Gatherings from the Orchard. [L, c.1850]. Unbound as issued in orig folder; worn, spine lacking. With 12 hand-colored plates. Ck Jan 30 (199) £950

Jerrold, Douglas, 1803-57
— A Man Made of Money. L, 1849. 1st Ed, in 6 monthly parts. Illus by John Leech. Together in 1 vol. 8vo, modern mor gilt, orig wraps & ads bound in. sg June 11 (271) $225

Jerrold, William Blanchard, 1826-84
See also: Dore & Jerrold
— The Life of George Cruikshank in Two Epochs. L, 1882. 1st Ed. 2 vols. 8vo, mor gilt by Morrell. Extra-illus with c.90 ports. sg Apr 2 (66) $400
— London, a Pilgrimage. L, 1872. Illus by Gustave Dore. Folio, mor gilt. pn Dec 11 (30) £160 [Jarndyce]

Jesse, George Richard
— Researches into the History of the British Dog. L, 1866. 2 vols. 8vo, modern half calf gilt. With 20 plates Some dampstains at bottom corners of 1 vol. sg Feb 12 (29) $175

Jessen, Peter, 1858-1926
— Der Ornamentstich. Geschichte der Vorlagen der Kunsthandwerks seit dem Mittelalter. Berlin, 1920. Half cloth. sg May 14 (46) $120

Jesty, Simon
— River Niger, a Novel.... L, 1935. 1st Ed, One of 25. S Sept 22 (103) £220 [Maggs]

Jesuit Relations
— Relation des Jesuites, contenant ce qui s'est passe de plus remarquable dans les Missions.... Quebec City, 1858. 3 vols. 8vo, half mor, unopened. Inscr in Vol I by Attorney General Cartier. sg Oct 2 (83)

AMERICAN BOOK PRICES CURRENT

$350

Jesuits
— Imago primi saeculi Societatis Iesu a Provincia Flandro Belgica. Antwerp: Plantin, 1640. Folio, lea gilt. Arenberg copy. FD Dec 2 (56) DM2,700
— The Travels of Several Learned Missioners of the Society of Jesus, into Divers Parts of the Archipelago, India, China, and America. L, 1714. 8vo, calf; rebacked, soiled. With 2 folding plates, the first with portion torn off. sg Apr 23 (146) $250

Jeunesse...
— La Jeunesse inalterable et la vie eternelle. Conte populaire.... Amst., 1897. One of 250. Illus by Marius Bauer & G. W. Dijsselhof. 4to, vellum. B Oct 7 (27) HF825

Jevons, William Stanley, 1835-82
— The Theory of Political Economy. L & NY, 1871. 8vo, orig cloth; joints torn at top, some fraying. Some spotting & marginal browning. P Sept 24 (309) $400
Anr Ed. L, 1879. 8vo, orig cloth; soiled & shaken. Marginal browning at beginning. P Sept 24 (310) $150

Jewell, J. Grey
— Among Our Sailors. NY, 1874. 8vo, orig cloth. FDR sgd copy. pnNY Sept 13 (282) $240

Jewish...
— Jewish Encyclopedia.... NY, 1901-6. 12 vols. 4to, orig half mor; extremities rubbed. Ck Feb 27 (220) £140

Jewish Historical Society of England
— Anglo-Jewish Notabilities. Their Arms and Testamentary Dispositions. L: University College, 1949. Orig wraps, unopened. sg Sept 25 (168) $100

Jimenez Pantoja, Tomas
— Por Adrian Sen, de nacion Olandes.... [Madrid, 1665]. Folio, modern half mor. S June 25 (326) £420

Joachim, Abbot of Fiore, 1132-1202
— Vaticinia, sive prophetiae. Venice: Hieronymum Porrum, 1589. 4to, mor gilt by Bedford; worn. With engraved title & 34 plates. Some spotting & fingermarking. HN May 20 (1646) DM2,200

Jobert de Lamballe, Antoine Joseph, 1799-1867
— Plaies d'armes a feu memoire sur la cauterisation.... Paris: Bechet, 1833. 8vo, half calf, orig wraps bound in. Inscr but with name of recipient cut away. S Nov 10 (503) £100 [Phillips]

Jode, Gerard de
— Thesaurus Novi Testamenti. Antwerp: G. de Jode, 1572. Oblong folio, half calf by Bourlon-Cluytmans. With engraved title & 106 plates, all hand-colored. Many leaves laid down or with repairs to margins; Plates 20, 77 & 101 with small portions missing which have been supplied by hand. S May 21 (43) £1,700 [Sourget]

Jodelle, Etienne
— Les Oeuvres et meslanges poetiques.... Paris: N. Chesneau & M. Pattison, 1574. Vol I (all pbd). 4to, mor gilt by Hardy. Jeanson copy. SM Mar 1 (299) FF44,000

Anr Ed. Paris, 1583. Vol I (all pbd). 12mo, old vellum. Lacking last blank; tp repaired. Jeanson 1051. SM Mar 1 (300) FF5,000

Joesting, Edward. See: Adams & Joesting

Johannes Chrysostomus, Saint, 345?-407
— Homiliae super Johannem. Rome: George Lauer, 29 Oct 1470. Folio, early 19th-cent sheep; spine wormed. With q2.9 in duplicate; lacking a10, b1-5, b7 & u4-7. 260 (of 280) leaves. Goff J-286. sg Oct 9 (335) $1,200

Johannsen, Albert, Bibliographer
— The House of Beadle and Adams and its Dime and Nickel Novels. Norman, Okla., [1950]. 2 vols. 4to, cloth. cba Feb 5 (113) $65

Anr Ed. Norman, OK, 1950-62. 3 vols. 4to, cloth, Vol III in d/j. sg Jan 22 (208) $60

Johlson, Joseph
— Instruction in the Mosaic Religion. Phila., [1830]. Trans by Isaac Leeser. 8vo, orig cloth; backstrip worn away. sg Apr 30 (39) $700

John, Augustus, 1878-1961
— Fifty-Two Drawings. L, 1957. Folio, cloth, in d/j. With ANs laid in. sg Dec 11 (309) $225

John of the Cross, Saint
— The Song of the Soul. Abergavenny: Francis Walterson, 1927. One of 150. Illus by Eric Gill. 4to, orig half cloth. sg Jan 8 (82) $275

John, William David
— Nantgarw Porcelain. Newport, 1948. 4to, lea; upper joint cracking. cba Mar 5 (102) $80
— Pontypool and Usk Japanned Wares. Newport, 1953. 4to, cloth; worn. O Nov 18 (102) £140
— Swansea Porcelain. Newport, 1958. 4to, orig cloth; minor wear. S Mar 9 (685) £70 [Trocchi]

John, William David —& Baker, Warren
— Old English Lustre Pottery. Newport, 1951. Folio, orig cloth gilt; soiled. S Mar 9 (683) £100 [Manheim]

Johns, Alas —& Butler, Francis
— Confracti Mundi Rudera; An Atlas of:for the Imagination. Berkeley: Poltroon Press, 1975. One of 60. Folio, cloth silkscreened by Goodstuffs Handprinted Fabrics. sg Jan 8 (214) $70

Johnson, Alexander Keith, 1804-71
— The Royal Atlas of Modern Geography.... Edin., 1863. Folio, modern half mor. With 48 double-page colored mapsheets; Africa with overslip showing the discoveries of Speke & Grant in the upper Nile region in 1863. S Nov 10 (979) £180 [Minsheu]

Johnson, Alfred Edwin
— The Russian Ballet. Bost. & NY, 1913. 4to, cloth; soiled. sg Feb 26 (200) $150

Johnson, Alfred Forbes
See also: Cresset Press
— One Hundred Title-Pages, 1500-1800. L, 1928. 4to, orig half cloth, in worn d/j. bba Oct 16 (429) £50 [Check Books]
— Selected Essays on Books and Printing. Amst., 1970. Ed by Percy H. Muir. In soiled d/j. bba Mar 26 (24) £60 [Hashimoto]

Anr copy. In chipped d/j. O June 16 (113) $50

Anr copy. In d/j. sg Jan 22 (209) $50

Johnson, C. Pierpoint, d.1893 —& Sowerby, John E., 1825-70
— British Wild Flowers.... L, 1876. 8vo, orig cloth; rebacked preserving orig spine, rubbed. With 2 plain & 90 hand-colored plates, including frontis. Some soiling. bba Oct 16 (318) £40 [Baldwin]

Johnson, Capt. Charles, Pseud.
A General History of the Robberies and Murders of the Most Notorious Pyrates. L, 1724. 1st Ed, 8vo, contemp calf; corners & spine reinforced. With 3 engraved plates. bba Nov 13 (206) £320 [Hannas]
— A General History of the Lives and Adventures of the Most Famous Highwaymen.... L, 1734. Folio, later mor gilt; joints rubbed. With frontis & 23 (of 25) plates only. A few plates cut close; outer blank corner of last 2 leaves torn. S Mar 9 (752) £130 [Finch]
— A General History of the Lives and Adventures of Highwaymen.... L, 1736. Folio, contemp calf; rubbed, stab holes in lower cover, rebacked retaining orig spine gilt.

With 26 plates. Repaired tears to 9 plates, that opposite p 92 with loss; last leaf repaired at foot. Sold w.a.f. S May 29 (1210) £200

Johnson, Edward, 1599-1672
— A History of New-England.... L, 1654. 1st Ed. 4to, 19th-cent half lea gilt. Browned, with scattered minor stains; tp mtd. sg Apr 2 (122) $2,400

Johnson, Edwin F., 1803-72
— Northern Pacific Railway Company. Report to the Board of Directors. Hartford, 1867. 8vo, modern cloth. Some foxing. wa Mar 5 (403) $150

Johnson, Frank M.
— Forest, Lake and River: the Fishes of New-England and Eastern Canada. Bost., 1902. One of 350. 2 vols. 4to, calf; worn, silk doublures loose in 1 vol. Foxed. With presentation ACs in both vols. sg Sept 18 (140) $110

Johnson, George William. See: Hogg & Johnson; Wingfield & Johnson

Johnson, John, 1777-1848
— Typographia, or the Printers' Instructor. L, 1824. 2 vols. 12mo, contemp cloth; rubbed, 1 cover & spine loose. bba Jan 15 (266) £40 [Grant's]

Anr copy. Modern half calf. bba June 18 (19) £50 [Clark]

Johnson, Lieut. Col. John
— A Journey from India to England. L, 1818. 4to, half mor; worn, broken. With engraved plan, 13 plain & 5 hand-colored plates & 1 extra plate. Some spotting. bba Dec 18 (162) £80 [Anderson]

Anr copy. Contemp calf; crudely rebacked. With 13 plates. Ck Nov 21 (214) £80

Johnson, Kenneth M.
— The Sting of the Wasp: Political & Satirical Cartoons.... San Francisco: Book Club of California, 1967. One of 450. Folio, cloth; With 20 colored plates. cb Sept 11 (67) $75

Johnson, Lionel
— Poems. L: Chiswick Press, 1895. 1st Ed, one of 750. 8vo, orig bds; lacking portion of backstrip, chipped, soiled. Johnson's copy, inscr, and with his autograph errata list. sg Dec 11 (310) $1,600

Johnson, Merle
— American First Editions: Bibliographic Check Lists.... NY, 1929. One of 1,000. Inscr. sg June 11 (254) $80
— High Spots of American Literature. NY, 1929. One of 500. Half mor. Ls from David Randall to Philip Duschnes inserted.

O June 16 (114) $50

Johnson, Robert Underwood, 1853-1937 —& Buel, Clarence Clough
— Battles and Leaders of the Civil War. NY, [1887-89]. 4 vols. 4to, cloth; worn & shaken, a few inner joints broken. O Nov 18 (103) $80

Anr copy. Half lea; rubbed. O Mar 24 (95) $70

Anr copy. Contemp sheep; worn, 1 joint split. wa Nov 6 (557) $50

Anr copy. Half lea; worn. With clipped ports of Washington & Lincoln on endpapers of Vol II, and with long Ms poem in hand of soldier in the Army of the Potomac. wa Nov 6 (558) $110

Anr copy. Orig cloth; worn, some hinges poorly repaired. wa Feb 19 (54) $60

Johnson, Samuel, 1709-84
— An Account of the Life of Mr. Richard Savage. L, 1744. 1st Ed, last page in state without erratum. 8vo, 19th-cent half mor. sg Oct 9 (236) $400
— A Diary of a Journey into North Wales. L, 1774. Bound with: Adolphus's "Letters to Richard Heber" 1st Ed. 8vo, half calf. With 2 plates. Lacking half title. S Sept 22 (32) £70 [Pearl]
— A Dictionary of the English Language.... L, 1755. 1st Ed. 2 vols. Folio, contemp calf; worn, some tears in lea. Vol II title & a few corners creased. C Dec 12 (340) £2,200 [Traylen]

Anr copy. Modern calf. 2 leaves of Vol I supplied from anr copy; occasional soiling & dampstaining. Ck Nov 7 (73) £1,100

Anr copy. Vol II only. Folio, contemp calf; worn, joints cracked, front endpaper detached. Sold w.a.f. Ck Feb 13 (187) £240

Anr copy. 2 vols. Folio, calf; broken. Tp & preface leaf of Vol I detached; marginal tear in Preface leaf; 1 leaf lacking lower blank corner; tp of Vol II attached along inner margin to 14A1, which is separated from 15A2; tear in margins of 21X1. P Sept 24 (171) $1,200

Anr copy. Modern half calf; rubbed. Title of Vol II & following leaf supplied, with some repair; marginal tears or repairs. P Dec 15 (205) $2,700

Anr copy. Contemp calf gilt. Some tears; hole in 7X1 of Vol I. S Dec 18 (23) £2,100 [Maggs]

Anr copy. Modern half calf; Vol II covers detached. Some foxing; marginal tears in 3 leaves mended; 3 leaves possibly supplied from anr copy. sg Apr 2 (124) $2,800

Anr copy. Old calf; rebacked. Marginal repair to B in Vol I; spine label detached but present; final leaf remargined. wd June 19 (136) $2,600

2d Ed. 2 vols. Folio, later half mor by Baker & Son, Clifton; rubbed. Library markings; prelims of each vol frayed from damp. T Dec 18 (268) £320

1st Abridged (8vo) Ed. L, 1756. 2 vols. Contemp calf; joints cracked. Ck May 29 (197) £170

Anr copy. Contemp calf gilt; spines worn. T Nov 20 (458) £150

3d Ed. L, 1765. 2 vols. Folio, contemp calf; worn. Some dampstains. S May 6 (437) £500 [Maggs]

Anr copy. Contemp calf; rebacked. Marginal dampstaining throughout; traces of mold in Vol I. sg Oct 9 (176) $450

4th Abridged (8vo) Ed. L, 1770. Contemp calf. SSA Oct 28 (603) R400

Anr Ed. Dublin, 1775. 2 vols. 4to, contemp calf; hinges split, 1 cover detached. pn July 23 (235) £120 [Axe]

5th Ed. L, 1784. 2 vols. Folio, worn & scraped, 1 joint splitting. wa Sept 25 (572) $270

Anr Ed. L, 1785. 2 vols. 4to, contemp calf; rubbed, joints split. bba Mar 26 (186) £180 [Jarndyce]

Anr copy. Modern half calf gilt. Some stains in margins. pn June 18 (179) £220 [King]

Anr copy. Contemp russia gilt. pnE Jan 28 (115A) £200 [Frost]

Anr copy. Modern half calf gilt, old bds preserved; rubbed. With engraved port & title strengthened. pnNY Sept 13 (250) $400

Harrison's Ed. L, 1786. Folio, contemp calf; upper cover detached, worn. Port stained; marginal tear to 4A2; final leaf creased. L Mar 11 (412) £180

Anr Ed. L, 1799. 2 vols. 8vo, contemp calf; needs rebdg. sg June 11 (255) $110

Anr Ed. L, 1810. 2 vols. 4to, calf; broken. With port. pn Jan 22 (30) £85 [Frew]

— Irene. L, 1749. 1st Ed. 8vo, modern cloth. sg Oct 9 (237) $200

— A Journey to the Western Islands of Scotland. L, 1775. 1st Ed, with 12-line errata. 8vo, old calf; rebacked preserving orig spine, rubbed. O Mar 24 (96) $160

Anr copy. Contemp half calf; rebacked, corners worn, head of spine chipped. pnE Jan 28 (69) £170 [Thin]

Anr copy. Contemp calf; rebacked retaining remnants of orig backstrip, joints starting. Some stains & foxing. sg Mar 26 (155) $150

1st Ed, with the 12-line errata. 8vo, contemp calf; needs rebdg. sg June 11 (256) $700

— The Lives of the Most Eminent English Poets. L, 1779-78. ("Prefaces, Biographical and Critical, to the Works of the English Poets.") 10 vols. 8vo, contemp calf gilt. C Dec 12 (341) £1,300 [Quaritch]

1st Separate London Ed. L, 1781. 4 vols. 8vo, contemp calf; few joints weak. sg Oct 9 (239) $110

Anr copy. Contemp calf; rebacked, extremities worn. Some foxing; Vol IV without inserted final ad leaf. sg Mar 26 (156) $150

Marmor Norfolciense. L, 1739. 1st Ed. 8vo, half calf. pnE Jan 28 (109) £900 [Mackenzie]

— The Plan of a Dictionary of the English Language.... L, 1747. 1st Ed, 2d Issue, without Chesterfield's name on A1 recto. 4to, 19th-cent half lea. sg Apr 2 (123) $2,600

— Political Tracts. L, 1776. 1st Collected Ed. 8vo, orig wraps; spine chipped. sg Oct 9 (238) $700

— Prayers and Meditations. L, 1785. 1st Ed. 8vo, mor gilt. sg Oct 9 (240) $275

— Rasselas. L, 1759. ("The Prince of Abissinia.") 1st Ed. 2 vols. 8vo, contemp calf; lacking all free endpapers but 1. sg Apr 2 (125) $850

3d Ed. L, 1760. 2 vols. 8vo, contemp calf; spine ends chipped, joints tender. cb Oct 23 (122) $70

— Works. L, 1792. 12 vols. 8vo, contemp russia gilt; spines rubbed. S Jan 13 (394) £75 [Meikle]

Anr Ed. L, 1810-11. 14 vols. 8vo, contemp calf; rubbed. S May 6 (438) £150 [Camberwell]

Anr Ed. L, 1820. 12 vols. 8vo, half mor gilt. sg Feb 12 (189) $450

Anr Ed. Oxford, 1825. 9 vols. 8vo, calf. S Sept 22 (33) £260 [Jarndyce]

Anr Ed. Troy. [1903]. Out-of-series copy. 16 vols. 8vo, cloth. pnE Oct 15 (214) £170

Johnston, Alexander Keith, 1804-71

— The National Atlas of Historical, Commercial, and Political Geography. Edin., [1844]. Folio, orig half mor gilt; worn. With engraved title & 46 double-page maps, hand-colored in outline, the final map partly hand-colored. Tp browned. L Dec 11 (226) £70

Anr Ed. Edin, 1846. Folio, half mor gilt. With 46 maps, hand-colored in outline. pn Mar 5 (366) £220 [Waterloo]

— The Royal Atlas of Modern Geography.... Edin. & L, 1861. Folio, orig half mor gilt. With 48 double-page maps, hand-colored in outline. Marginal soiling, sometimes affecting maps. bba Oct 16 (227) £90 [Beyer]; L Dec 11 (226) £70

Johnston, Sir Harry Hamilton, 1858-1927
— The River Congo. L, 1884. 1st Ed. 8vo, recent half calf. With 3 plates & 2 folding maps. T.p. stained. O June 16 (8) $100
Anr copy. Orig cloth; recased. Some spotting. T Mar 19 (7) £55

Johnston, Isabel McElheny
— The Jeweled Toad. Indianapolis, [1907]. Pictorial bds; lightly rubbed & bumped. A few leaves soiled in margins. cb Dec 4 (102) $70

Johnston, John, 1570?-1611
— Inscriptiones historicae regum Scotorum. Edin.: A. Hart [Amst. ptd], 1602. 1st Ed. 4to, 19th-cent mor gilt; hinges rubbed. With 10 ports & plate of royal coat of arms. Some repairs. T Feb 19 (573) £220

Johnston, Joseph E., 1807-91
— Reports of the Secretary of War, with Reconnaissances of Routes from San Antonio to El Paso.... Wash., 1850. 1st Ed. 8vo, modern half calf. With 2 folding maps & 73 plates, including a duplicate No 40. 31st Congress, 1st Session, Sen. Exec. Doc. 64. cb Mar 19 (150) $400
Anr copy. Later half mor. With 72 plates; lacking maps. 31st Congress, 1st Session, Sen. Exec. Doc. 64. wa Sept 25 (451) $170

Johnston, Robert, A.M.
— Travels through Part of the Russian Empire.... L, 1815. 1st Ed. 4to, half mor; rubbed. With hand-colored frontis, 2 maps & 17 (of 19) hand-colored plates & 1 plain plate. Lacking plate list; some stains. pn Mar 5 (81G) £85 [Bowdage]

Johnston, Robert, 1567?-1639
— Historia rerum Britannicarum. Amst., 1655. Folio, contemp calf; worn, joints split. Library copy with Ms note on front free endpaper & top of tp. bba Oct 30 (101) £45 [Clark]

Johnston, William G., b.1828
— Experiences of a Forty-Niner. Pittsburgh, 1892. 8vo, orig cloth; front hinge cracked, spine ends frayed. With port & folding blueprint map issued after publication & 13 plates. sg Sept 18 (142) $325
Anr copy. Orig cloth; spine ends worn, front hinge split. With 14 plates & photostat of blueprint map. sg Mar 12 (156) $225

Johnstone, James, Chevalier de, 1719-1800?
— Memoirs of the Rebellion in 1745 and 1746. L, 1820. 4to, contemp half calf; rebacked & rubbed, hinges cracking. Frontis creased. cb Dec 18 (92) $750

Johnstone, William Grosart —& Croall, Alexander
— The Nature-Printed British Sea-Weeds. L, 1859-60. 4 vols. 4to, orig cloth. pn Apr 30 (314) £130 [Maggs]

Johonnot, James, 1823-88
— School-Houses. NY: Schermerhorn, 1871. 8vo, orig cloth; worn & soiled, lacking endpaper. wa Nov 6 (374) $70

Johson, Samuel, 1709-84 —& Dodd, William, 1729-77
— The Convict's Address to his Unhappy Brethren. L, 1777. 8vo, modern calf. S Sept 22 (34) £550 [Maggs]

Joinville, Jean, Sieur de, 1224?-1317
See also: Gregynog Press
— Histoire de Saint Louis.... Paris, 1761. Folio, contemp calf; joints split, worn. bba Mar 12 (81) £80 [Greenwood]

Jollandia...
— Hollandia Regenerata. L, [1794]. 4to, modenr half mor. With title & 19 plates ptd in bistre. C Apr 8 (28) £280 [Shapero]

Jomini, Antoine Henri de, Baron
— Life of Napoleon. NY, 1864. 5 vols, including Atlas. Contemp half mor; extremities rubbed. With 60 hand-tinted litho maps. cb Dec 18 (91) $550

Jones & Co.
See also: National...
— Views of the Seats, Mansions, Castles.... L, 1829-31. Bound in 4 vols. Near-contemp half mor gilt. Lacking engraved titles & 4th ptd title & possibly lacking other plates & a few text leaves. cb Feb 19 (145) $750

Jones, A. M.
— Illustrations of Rare Varieties of British Ferns. [N.p.], 1888. Folio, contemp half mor; upper hinge broken. With Ms title & 296 nature-ptd plates. de Belder copy. S Apr 27 (186) £2,200 [Tan]

Jones, David
— The Chester Play of the Deluge. L, 1977. One of 80 on handmade paper, with a set of the wood-engravings on japon. 4to, orig half mor. With 10 illusts. S Oct 6 (826) £190 [Marks]
— An Introduction to the Rime of the Ancient Mariner. L, 1972. One of 115 sgd & dated by author. 4to, orig half vellum. S May 6 (57) £100 [Cox]
— The Sleeping Lord. L, [1974]. One of 150.

4to, cloth. sg Dec 11 (311) $100

Jones, David, fl.1676-1720
— The Secret History of White-Hall.... L, 1697. 8vo, old calf; later spine. O Feb 24 (115) $55

Jones, David Michael
— In Parenthesis. L, 1961. One of 70. Intro by T. S. Eliot. S July 23 (151) £750 [Blackwell]

Jones, Edward Alfred
— A Catalogue of the Objects in Gold and Silver...in the Collection of the Baroness James de Rothschild. L, 1912. One of 175. Folio, orig half cloth; soiled. Ck Nov 28 (160) £400
— The Old Silver of American Churches. Letchworth, 1913. One of 500. Folio, orig cloth. pnNY Oct 11 (29) $475

Jones, Harry Longueville, 1806-70. See: Wright & Jones

Jones, Inigo, 1573-1652
— Designs of Inigo Jones and others published by I. Ware. [L, 1757?]. 4to, contemp calf; rubbed, head of spine weak. With engraved title & 48 plates, including 6 double page, numbered 1-53. C July 22 (104) £520
Anr copy. Contemp calf; broken. S Nov 10 (110) £200 [Finch]
— The Designs of Inigo Jones consisting of Plans and Elevations for...Buildings. L, 1727. 1st Ed. 2 vols in 1. Folio, bdg not described. Lacking description of last 43 plates in Vol II. F Sept 12 (18) $850
2d Ed. L, 1770. 2 vols in 1. Folio, contemp half calf; rubbed, joints broken. With frontis & 99 plates & 2 large plates of the Palace of Whitehall loosely inserted (1 torn at fold). C July 22 (105) £1,900
— The Most Notable Antiquity of Great Britain, Vulgarly Called Stone-Heng.... L, 1655. Folio, old calf; hinges split. pn May 21 (87) £380 [Hagen]

Jones, John Beauchamp
— Elementary Arithmetic, in Cherokee and English.... Tehlequah. Cherokee National Press, 1870. 12mo, contemp half cloth; rear hinge starting. sg Mar 12 (65) $175
Anr copy. Orig bds; rebacked. sg Mar 12 (66) $175

Jones, Owen, 1809-74
— Examples of Chinese Ornament.... L, 1867. Folio, orig cloth; soiled. With color title & 99 plates, some loose & soiled in margins. Some marginal tears & spotting. S Nov 10 (111) £700 [Henderson]
— Examples of Chinese Ornament...in the South Kensington Museum. L, 1867.
Folio, half mor. sg Feb 5 (198) $1,000
— The Grammar of Ornament. L, 1856. Folio, contemp half mor. With 100 colored plates. C July 22 (106) £2,000
Anr copy. Half mor gilt; rubbed, spine torn. With color title & 100 color plates. Some tears on tp; handling marks. pnNY Oct 11 (30) $1,200
Anr Ed. L, [1865]. Folio, orig cloth; rubbed. Some foxing. T Feb 19 (536) £95
Anr copy. Modern half calf. With litho title & 112 plates. Marginal dampstaining. T June 18 (372) £90
Anr Ed. L, 1868. Folio, later cloth; portion of orig front cover laid down, library lettering on spine. With illuminated title & 112 plates. cb June 18 (165) $250
Anr copy. Old calf; worn. With illuminated title & 109 plates. S Sept 18 (469) £72
Anr copy. Half mor; worn. With illuminated title & 112 plates. Library markings; rubberstamp in margins of each plate. sg June 4 (185) $250
Anr copy. Orig cloth; rubbed & repaired. With litho title & 111 plates. T Feb 19 (537) £200
Anr copy. Orig cloth; rubbed. With illuminated title & 112 plates. T June 18 (373) £100
Anr Ed. L, 1910. Folio, orig cloth; shaken, with some plates loose. With 112 colored plates. Ck Jan 30 (210) £100; pn Apr 30 (139) £130 [Hetherington]
— One Thousand and One Initial Letters. L, 1864. Folio, modern cloth; worn. With engraved title & 27 plates in colors & gold. Ms library marking on tp & 2 small repaired tears on margin. pnNY Oct 11 (31) $600

Jones, Owen, 1809-74 —& Goury, Jules
— Plans, Elevations, Sections, and Details of the Alhambra.... L, 1842-45. 2 vols. Folio, contemp half mor; rubbed. With color titles & 102 plates, including 2 hand-colored plans. C July 22 (107) £3,600

Jones, Paul. See: Blunt & Jones

Jones, Raymond F.
— This Island Earth. Chicago: Shasta, [1952]. In d/j. Inscr. cb Sept 28 (716) $110

Jones, Richard, 1790-1855
— An Essay on the Distribution of Wealth.... L, 1831. 8vo, later cloth. Tear in lower margin of b2 & b7. P Sept 24 (312) $450

Jones, Sir William, 1746-94
— Dissertations...relating to the History and Antiquities...of Asia. Dublin, 1793. 8vo, contemp sheep; worn. bba Nov 13 (237) £120 [Quaritch]
— Works. L, 1807. 13 vols. 8vo, contemp calf gilt; worn. S Jan 13 (394) £75 [Meikle]

Jonson, Ben, 1573?-1637
See also: Dickens Association copy, Charles
— The Masque of Queenes. L: King's Printers, 1930. One of 350. Folio, vellum gilt. cb Feb 5 (207) $80
— The Staple of Newes. L, 1631. Folio, old sheep; broken, backstrip def. sg Mar 26 (157) $110
— Volpone. Berlin, 1910. One of 650. 4to, cloth. S May 6 (85) £100 [Henderson]
— Works. L, [1616]. Vol I (of 2) only. Folio, contemp calf; broken. Lacking 1 leaf; a few leaves torn or repaired, sometimes affecting text; last leaf trimmed & laid down; 3Y & 3Y6 duplicated. Sold w.a.f. STC 14751. bba Feb 5 (160) £320 [Maggs] Anr Ed. L, 1716. 6 vols. 8vo, contemp calf gilt; joints weak or starting. With port & 11 plates, 1 loose. sg Oct 9 (242) $60
— ATHANAEUS. - Deipnosophistarum.... Lyons: A. de Harsy, 1612. Bound with: Casaubon, Isaac. Animadversionum in Athen. Dipnosophistas. Lyons, 1621. Folio, disbound. Sgd by Jonson on each title & with his holograph notes in Greek & Latin. P Sept 24 (172) $1,600

Jonston, John, 1570?-1611. See: Johnston, John

Jonston, John, 1603-75
— Historiae naturalis de quadrupetibus. Amst., 1657. 6 parts in 1 vol. Folio, calf; broken. With 4 engraved titles & 243 (of 250) plates. Wormed at head with some loss of text. S Feb 24 (581) £420 [Bolognese]
— Naturgeschichte aus den besten Schriftstellern mit Merianischen und neuen Kupfern.... Heilbronn (Wuertemberg): Ekebrechtischen Buchhandlung, 1783. Folio, old bds. With 19 plates. Plate 1 torn. Sold w.a.f. Hunt copy. CNY Nov 21 (156) $220

Jordan, Alexis —& Fourreau, Jules
— Icones ad floram Europae novo fundamento instaurandam spectantes. Paris, 1866-1903. 3 vols in 5. Folio, contemp half mor, not uniform. With 501 plates, 208 of them hand-colored. Some spotting of text. Horticultural Society of New York—de Belder copy. S Apr 27 (187) £4,000 [McCarthy]

Jordan, David Starr, 1851-1931
— The Fur Seals and Fur-Seal Islands of the North Pacific Ocean. Wash., 1898. 4 parts in 2 vols. 4to, orig cloth; hinge cracked. Titles stamped. cb Apr 2 (159) $160

Jordanes, Bishop of Ravenna
— De rebus gothorum. Augsburg: Johannes Miller, 21 Mar 1515. Folio, half vellum. Some early notes & underlining. S Nov 27 (18) £950

Jorgensen, Poul
— Salmon Flies; Their Character, Style, and Dressing. Harrisburg: Stackpole Books, [1978]. One of 250. 4to, cowhide, in d/j. With a salmon fly mtd to limitation page. sg Oct 23 (359) $275
 Anr copy. Lea. sg May 21 (135) $200

Joseph, Michael
— A Book of Cats. NY, 1930. One of 500. Illus by Foujita. 4to, orig cloth; soiled & rubbed. With 20 plates; lacking the extra suite of illusts. sg Jan 8 (76) $300

Josephus, Flavius, 37-100?
— De antiquitate Judaica.... [Augsburg]: Johann Schuessler, 1470. 1st Ed. 2 parts in 1 vol. Folio, contemp calf over wooden bds righly tooled in blind, the 2 covers different, with 2 brass clasps & catches. With [a2] recto having an illuminated initial & part border with flowers & a coat-of-arms supported by a man; 23 other illuminated initials heightened with gold or silver with elaborate borders. With 7 leaves (ff. 39, 85, 93, 132, 194, 203 & 272) inserted from a shorter copy with colored initials without gold or silver heightening. With 233 (of 288) leaves; lacking initial blank but with a blank inserted between ff. 202 & 203. Goff J-481. S May 21 (5) £30,000 [Kraus]
— Della Guerra de' Giudei.... Venice: Giolito, 1581. 4to, contemp vellum gilt; rubbed, small holes in covers from ties, library label on base of spine, lacking front free endpaper. Stained; some marginal worming. bba Sept 25 (237) £170 [Coxs]
— Histoire de la bataille des juifs. Paris: Pierre Leber, 4 Oct 1530. Folio, 18th-cent calf gilt; joints repaired. Repairs to margins of A1, M6 & DD1; 1 small wormhole in text running through book; slight worming to lower margins at beginning & end; some stains. S Nov 27 (16) £1,800 [New York Public Library]
— Histoire des juifs.... Brussels, 1701-3. Trans by Arnauld d'Andilly. 5 vols. 8vo, contemp calf; joints worn. Vol V dampstained. S Sept 23 (568) £200 [Bucherstube]
— Historien und Buecher: von alten juedischen Geschichten. Frankfurt, 1569.

Folio, contemp blind-stamped pigskin over wooden bds; soiled, lacking 2 clasps. Some marginal tears & spotting; slight damage to the text on N2 verso & T6 recto; a few short marginal tears. S May 21 (44) £400 [Goldberg]

— Werken. Amst., 1722. Illus by J. Luyken. 2 parts in 1 vol. Folio, 19th-cent half lea; rubbed. With engraved title, frontis, 4 folding maps & plans, 8 double-page plates & 208 engravings. Tp frayed; 2 leaves damaged; some stains. B Oct 7 (1166) HF500

— Works. L, 1602. Trans by Thomas Lodge. Folio, later half mor; rubbed. First & last leaves frayed; tp laid down, stained & soiled. bba Jan 15 (7) £100 [Maggs]

Anr Ed. L, 1693. Folio, old calf with brass corner-pieces, upper cover with decorative brass panel; rebacked, worn. Ck June 5 (167) £50

Anr Ed. L, 1732. Folio, contemp calf; rebacked, endpapers renewed. Half-title repaired & remtd at gutter; some dampstains. sg June 11 (261) $350

Anr Ed. L: C. Cooke, c.1785. ("The Whole Genuine and Complete Works.") Trans by George Henry Maynard. Folio, contemp calf; broken, worn. With 60 plates. Some marginal tears & defs. bba Mar 12 (145) £35 [Fisher]

Anr Ed. NY: William Durell, 1792-[94]. Folio, contemp calf; worn. With 60 plates. Sold w.a.f. O Mar 24 (98) $400

Anr copy. Contemp calf; worn & stained, joints splitting. wa Sept 25 (576) $65

Anr Ed. Bost.: S. Walker, 1825. 2 vols in 1. 4to, contemp calf; worn, rebacked. sg Apr 30 (36) $200

Anr Ed. L, 1825. 6 vols. 12mo, half calf; spine extremities worn. sg Sept 25 (169) $100

Anr Ed. NY, 1825. 6 vols. 12mo, old calf; rebacked in mor gilt. wd June 19 (137) $200

Josselyn, John

New-Englands Rarities Discovered.... L, 1672. 1st Ed. 16mo, contemp sheep; rear cover restored. Final 3 leaves of text, ad leaf & leaf with printer's woodcut device all in facsimile; running wormhole or nick affecting upper margin of tp & 1st 20 leaves, with loss of few letters from running titles; some marginal soiling. T July 16 (76) £1,000

Jostes, Barbara Donohoe

— John Parrott, Consul, 1881-1884. San Francisco, 1972. 4to, cloth. cb Jan 8 (102) $55

Joubert, Francois Etienne

— Manuel de l'amateur d'estampes. Paris, 1821. 1st Ed. 3 vols. 8vo, contemp calf; rubbed. Each vol sgd. Ck Nov 7 (32A) £85

Jouffroy, Alain

— Aube a l'Antipode. Paris, 1966. One of 15 hors commerce & 1 of 77 in a specially designed case. Illus by Rene Magritte. Wraps, unopened. S July 2 (1027) £600 [Rothberg]

Anr copy. Without the 7 postcards reproducing the illusts. S July 2 (1028) £450 [McCinsky]

Jouhandeau, Marcel

— Descente aux enfers. Paris, 1961. One of 30 reserved for the artist & author. Illus by Georges Braque. 4to, loose as issued. Lacking the supplementary suite of lithos. Sgd by Braque & Jouhandeau. P Dec 15 (181) $1,000

— Endymion. Paris, 1953. One of 50 on Auvergne. Illus by P. Y. Trémois. Folio, unsewn in orig wraps. SM Oct 20 (669) FF3,200

Jourdan, J. See: Frossard & Jourdan

Journal...

— Journal fuer Ornithologie. Kassel, 1909-86. Vols 57-127. 70 (of 71) vols; lacking Vol 64. B Feb 24 (27) HF1,400

Jousse, Mathurin, b.1607

— Nouveau Commentaire sur L'Ordonnance criminelle du mois d'Aout 1670. Paris, 1763. 12mo, contemp calf; rubbed, spine head chipped. cb Oct 23 (123) $60

Joutel, Henri, 1640?-1735

Journal historique du dernier voyage que feu M. de la Sale.... Paris, 1713. 12mo, contemp calf; joints starting. With folding map, which has been rehinged & repaired on verso. sg Dec 4 (92) $2,200

Jovius, Paulus, 1483-1552

— Elogia virorum bellica virtute illustrium. Basel, 1575. Bound with: Jovius. Elogia virorum literis illustrium. Basel, 1577. Folio, contemp calf gilt, dated 1579; rebacked & with small repairs. One small wormhole in fore-margin of tp of 1st work. S May 21 (45) £500 [Marlborough]

— Elogia virorum literis illustrium. Basel: Petrus Perna, 1577. Folio, 19th-cent half vellum. sg Dec 4 (78) $500

Joy, Norman Humbert
— A Practical Handbook of British Beetles....
L, 1932. 2 vols. S Feb 24 (582) £70
[Huggel]

Joyant, Maurice
— Henri de Toulouse-Lautrec. Paris, 1926-27.
2 vols. 4to, later cloth. sg Feb 5 (317) $400
Anr Ed. Paris, 1927. 2 vols. 4to, orig
wraps. S June 17 (55) £500 [Marks]

Joyce, James, 1882-1941
See also: Limited Editions Club
— Anna Livia Plurabelle. NY, 1928. One of
800, sgd. bba May 28 (103) £500 [Hosains]
One of 800. cb May 7 (113) $550; Ck Dec
10 (347) £300
One of 800, sgd. In d/j. F Jan 15 (115)
$500; sg Mar 5 (110) $600
— Chamber Music. L, 1907. 1st Ed, 2d bdg
variant. one of 509. Inscr to Cyril
Corrigan. bba May 28 (97) £3,200
Anr copy. With a note in the hand of Elkin
Mathews about W. B. Yeats' reaction. Ck
Dec 10 (348) £1,500
Anr Ed. NY, 1918. Bds; worn. O Jan 6
(98) $70
— Collected Poems. NY: The Black Sun
Press, 1936. 1st Ed, one of 50. Orig bds. O
May 12 (105) $2,600
— Dubliners. L, [1914]. 1st Ed. Ck Dec 10
(349) £140; kh Mar 16 (278A) A$380
Anr copy. Library markings. O Mar 24
(100) $340
— Exiles. L, 1918. 1st English Ed. Orig half
cloth. bba May 28 (99) £120 [Hildebrandt]
Anr copy. Orig half cloth; rubbed. Inscr to
Ezra Pound. Ck June 5 (117) £12,000
Anr Ed. NY, 1918. Half cloth. O May 12
(106) $160
1st Ed in German. Zurich, 1919.
("Verbannte.") Orig wraps; spine faded.
Inscr to Scofield Thayer. P June 18 (93)
$1,800
— Finnegans Wake. NY: Donald Friede,
1927. ("Work in Progress. Volume I.") One
of 15 or 20 copies. Folio, orig cloth;
rubbed. P June 18 (94) $8,000
Anr Ed. [NY, 1928]. ("Work in Progress.
Part 13.") One of 5 to secure American
copyright. Orig wraps; soiled & chipped,
with small loss to rear wrap & final blank.
P June 18 (95) $20,000
Anr Ed. [NY, 1929]. ("Work in Progress.
Part 15.") Orig wraps; soiled & chipped. P
June 18 (96) $24,000
Anr Ed. L, 1939. One of 425. S July 23
(154) £2,100 [Rocklin]
1st Ed. In torn d/j. Last leaf browned.
bba Apr 9 (205) £120 [Spencer]; S Sept 22

(104) £150 [Leimweber]
Anr copy. In frayed d/j. Sold with Skeleton Key.... wa Dec 11 (190) $325
One of 425. bba May 28 (106) £950
[Catnach]; pn Mar 5 (96) £620
Anr Ed. L & NY, 1939. One of 425, sgd.
Cover stained. sg Dec 11 (70) $1,000
1st American Ed. NY, 1939. In d/j. sg
Dec 11 (312) $50
Anr Ed. L, 1946. In torn d/j. Graham
Greene's copy, sgd by him. S July 13 (156)
£110
— Haveth Childers Everywhere. Paris, 1930.
1st Ed, one of 100 on japan. Folio, orig
wraps. O May 12 (108) $1,450
One of 500. Orig wraps. B Oct 7 (304)
HF340
Anr copy. Orig wraps; soiled. pn Sept 18
(288) £80 [Hildebrandt]
Anr copy. Orig wraps; spine torn. sg Dec
11 (71) $110
— Ibsen's New Drama. L: Ulysses Bookshop,
[1930]. 1st Ed, one of 40. 16mo, orig half
cloth. Inscr to H.H. Richardson by Jacob
Schwartz. bba May 28 (105) £1,300
[Gekoski]
— The Mime of Mick, Nick and the Maggies.
The Hague: Servire Press, 1934. 1st Ed,
one of 1,000. Orig wraps, unopened. O Jan
6 (102) $170
Out-of-series copy. Orig wraps; broken. T
July 16 (140) £180
[-] Our Exagmination round his Factification
for Incamination of Work in Progress.
Paris, 1929. 1st Ed. Orig wraps. bba May
28 (85) £220 [Clark]; O Jan 6 (103) $200
— Pomes Penyeach. Paris: Shakespeare &
Co., 1927. 1st Ed. Orig bds. With the
errata slip. bba May 28 (102) £70
[Holstrup]
Anr copy. Orig bds; hinge split. cb May 7
(114) $65
Anr copy. Orig bds; scuffed, spine frayed.
O Jan 6 (104) $60
Anr copy. Orig bds; spine def. With the
errata slip. S Jan 13 (576) £35 [Catnach]
— A Portrait of the Artist as a Young Man.
NY, 1916. 1st Ed. Orig cloth. O May 12
(109) $425
— Storiella As She Is Syung. [L: Corvinus
Press], Oct 1937. 1st Ed, one of 150. 4to,
orig vellum. O May 12 (110) $1,000
— Tales Told of Shem and Shaun. Paris:
Black Sun Press, 1929. 1st Ed, one of 400.
Orig wraps, in glassine d/j. Crosby Gaige's
copy. O May 12 (111) $400
One of 500. Orig wraps. bba May 28 (104)
£220 [D & G]
— Two Essays: A Forgotten Aspect...and "The

Day of the Rabblement...." Dublin, [1901]. 1st Ed. Orig wraps; some wear. O May 12 (112) $3,000

Anr copy. Orig wraps; lower cover discolored. S July 23 (153) £3,200 [Deeny]

— Ulysses. Paris, 1922. 1st Ed, One of 100 on Van Gelder Zonen, sgd. 4to, orig wraps; worn & broken. Some spots & tears. S Dec 18 (156) £5,900 [de Frietas]

One of 150 on verge d'Arches. Orig wraps; joints worn. bba May 28 (100) £3,500 [Catnach]

One of 750 on handmade paper. Later half mor gilt; spine rubbed. cb May 7 (115) $800

Anr copy. Recent mor. O May 12 (113) $1,000

Anr copy. Orig wraps; minor discoloration, repair to joints & spine extremities. P June 18 (92) $4,250

Anr copy. Lea, orig wraps bound in; rear cover detached. sg Dec 11 (72) $1,700

Anr copy. Orig wraps; rebacked in paper; with orig endpapers detached & laid in. Inscr. sg Dec 11 (73) $1,300

Anr copy. Later half mor, orig wraps bound in at end. T Feb 18 (109) £420

2d Ptg (1st English Ed). Paris: Pbd for the Egoist Press, L, by John Rodker, 1922. 4to, orig wraps, unopened. Lacking errata leaves. bba May 28 (101) £700 [Joseph]

Anr copy. Ptd wraps; defective, backstrip worn. Lacking initial blanks & errata leaves; final blank torn. S Sept 22 (105) £120 [Libris Antik]

8th Ptg. Paris, 1926. 4to, contemp cloth. Inscr to Harvey Rogers. bba Apr 23 (260) £650 [Manal]

Anr copy. Later cloth, orig wraps bound in. F Oct 30 (214) $90

Anr Ed. Hamburg: Odyssey Press, [1932]. 2 vols. orig wraps; edges slightly marked. S Jan 13 (577) £60 [Catnach]

1st Ptg in England. L, 1936. one of 100 on mould-made paper, specially bound & sgd. Orig vellum gilt, unopened. C May 13 (162) £1,800 [Joseph]

One of 900. Orig cloth; spine buckled. sg Dec 11 (75) $60

Juan de la Cruz, San

— Obras espirituales que encamian a una alma a la perfecta union con Dios.... Alcala: la vivda de Andres Sanches Ezpeleta, 1618. 4to, modern mor gilt by Brugalla. Engraved title remargined; plate foxed; some dampstains; 2 wormholes in tp; 1st few leaves repaired; small hole in A1 repaired. S Nov 27 (19) £1,000 [Quaritch]

Juan de los Angeles, Fray

— Dialogos de la conquista del espiritual y secreto Reyno de Dios.... Madrid: viuda de Madrigal, 1595. 4to, modern vellum. Worming in tp repaired; library stamp on tp. S Nov 27 (17) £750 [Baldur]

Juan y Santacilla, Jorge, 1712-73. See: Ulloa & Juan y Santacilla

Juanes Collection, Juan de

— Drawings and Lithographs of Joan Miro in the Collection.... Greenwich, CT: New York Graphic Society, [1960]. One of 700. 4to, pictorial wraps. sg Feb 5 (226) $350

Jukes, Joseph Beete, 1811-69

— Narrative of the Surveying Voyage of H. M. S. Fly.... L, 1847. 1st Ed. 2 vols. 8vo, orig cloth; rubbed, Vol I rebacked. Ck May 15 (50) £520

Julia de Fontenelle, Jean Sebastien Eugene

— Nouveau Manuel complet des sorciers, ou la Magie Blanche. Paris, 1841. 12mo, contemp half sheep by Carss of Glasgow; joints weak. With 3 folding plates. sg Feb 26 (175) $150

Julianus, Emperor, 331-63

— Opera. Paris: D. Duval, 1583. 1st Collected Ed. 4 parts in 1 vol. 8vo, contemp vellum. Evelyn copy. C Dec 12 (296) £280 [Dobbs]

Julien, Henri

— Album. Montreal, 1916. Folio, orig cloth. AVP Nov 20 (160) C$240 [Woolmer]

Jullien, Adolphe, 1845-1932

— Hector Berlioz, sa vie et ses oeuvres. Paris, 1888. Illus by Fantin-Latour. 4to, contemp half mor; rubbed. Perforated library stamp on title. bba Feb 5 (296) £260 [Smith]

Julliot, C. F. See: Remy & Julliot

Juncker, Christian

— Das Guldene und silberne Ehren-Bedaechtniss.... Frankfurt, 1706. 8vo, contemp vellum. sg Oct 9 (283) $110

Jung, Carl Gustav, 1875-1961

[Collection of 27 multigraphed reports of his seminars in 50 vols, 1925-42, sold at S on 27 Nov 1986.] S Nov 27 (268) £3,200 [Quaritch]

Junius, Pseud.

— Stat nominus umbra. L, 1797-99. 2 vols. 8vo, contemp calf; rebacked, worn. wa Sept 25 (346) $55

JUNIUS

Junius, Franciscus, 1589-1677
— De pictura veterum.... Rotterdam, 1694. 2 vols in 1. Folio, old half lea; rubbed. With engraved title & port. S Sept 23 (354) £90 [Robertshaw]

Junius, Hadrianus, 1511-75
— Emblemata.... Antwerp: Plantin, 1565. 8vo, 19th-cent mor by A. Grieve; slight wear to hinges. pn Mar 5 (28) £650 [Thomson]
— Emblemata ad D. Arnoldum Cobellium. Antwerp: Plantin, 1566. 8vo, later calf gilt. Tp soiled & chipped, upper margin cropped. sg June 11 (262) $100

Just. See: Kipling, Rudyard

Justin Martyr, Saint
— Opera. Paris, 1636. Folio, contemp mor gilt, with arms of Francois de Rignac. sg Oct 9 (244) $150
Anr Ed. Cologne, 1686. Folio, contemp blind-stamped vellum; rubbed. Marginal worming, browning & spotting. bba Oct 30 (202) £50 [Frew Mackenzie]

Justinianus I, Emperor, 483-565
— Novellae constitutiones. Paris: Andre Boucard for Jean Petit, 15 Apr 1527. 4to, old vellum; rebacked with vellum, spine wormed, endpapers renewed. Marginal stains & soiling; some headlines shaved. sg Oct 9 (245) $150

Justinus, Marcus Junianus
— Epitome in Trogi Pompeii historias. Venice: Aldus, Jan 1522. ("Trogi Pompei externae historiae in compendium ab Justino redactae.") 8vo, mor gilt; joints worn. Margins of several leaves covered with scribblings. S Sept 23 (461) £160 [Tolomei]
— Justino vulgarizato.... [Venice: Johannes de Colonia & Johannes Manthen, (not before 12) Sept] 1477. Folio, modern half sheep. One leaf torn & mended without loss. 123 (of 124) leaves; lacking 1st blank. Goff J-625. P Dec 15 (155) $1,600

Justus. See: Campbell, Ambrose George

Juta, Betsy
— Jonge Ranken. Sonnetten en verzen. Leiden, 1896. Orig cloth. B Oct 7 (24) HF180

Juvenalis, Decimus Junius, 60-140 A.D. —& Persius Flaccus, Aulus, 34-62 A.D.
— Satires. L, 1647. ("Juvenal's Sixteen Satyrs, or, a Survey of the Manners and Actions of Mankind....") Ed by Sir Robert Stapylton. 8vo, mor gilt by Riviere. Kern copy. wa Dec 11 (701) $260
Anr Ed. L, 1660. ("Mores Hominum, the Manners of Men.") 8vo, contemp calf; broken. Most leaves marginally damp-stained; some leaves with other small defs. bba Mar 26 (161) £75 [Booklore]
Trans by John Dryden. L, 1693. Folio, calf; hinges strengthened, spine worn. S Sept 23 (357) £70 [Pearl]
Anr copy. Contemp calf; rebacked retaining part of orig spine. Stained at head of pages towards end; inner margin wormed at end not affecting text; some tears. S Mar 10 (1056) £100 [Finch]
Anr copy. Contemp calf; minor restoration to joints. Last 10 prelims from anr copy; minor wormholes discreetly repaired. sg Mar 26 (158) $175
— Satyrae. Venice: Aldus, 1501 [c.1517]. 8vo, vellum bds. Some repairs to title; some lower corners def. S Sept 23 (463) £220 [Pampolini]
Anr Ed. Birm.: Baskerville, 1761. 4to, old mor gilt. Staining at end. sg Oct 9 (96) $225
Anr Ed. Cambr., 1763. 8vo, contemp mor gilt. With 15 plates. Browned. sg Mar 26 (158A) $70
Anr Ed. L, 1845. 4to, contemp calf gilt; rubbed. bba Feb 5 (186) £50 [Wise]

K

Kaal Kadosh Mickve Israel
— Charter and By-Laws of the Kaal Kadosh Mickve Israel, of the City of Philadelphia. Phila., 1824. 8vo, contemp wraps. sg Apr 30 (47) $1,500

Kaden, Woldemar
— Das Schweizerland.... Stuttgart: J. Engelhorn, [c.1880]. Folio, orig cloth; rubbed. FD June 11 (860) DM1,200

Kadlubko, Vincent, Saint, Bishop of Cracow
— Scriptores historiae Polonae vetustissimi.... Gdansk, 1749. Folio, later half vellum. Lacking final blank. Phillipps copy. sg Mar 26 (159) $450

Kaempfer, Engelbert
— Geschichte und Beschreibung von Japan. Lemgo, 1777. 2 vols in 1. 4to, half calf. With 45 folding plates & maps. S Oct 23 (487) £1,300 [Tang]
— Histoire naturelle, civile et ecclesiastique de l'empire du Japon.... The Hague, 1729. 1st Ed in French. 2 vols. Folio, contemp calf. With engraved title & 45 maps & plates. Some browning or spotting. S June 25 (470) £1,500 [Shoten]
— The History of Japan. L, 1727-28. 2 vols. Folio, contemp calf; upper joints cracked. With engraved title & 45 plates & maps. C Dec 12 (241) £1,000 [Stadt Museum Mun-

ster]
Anr copy. Contemp calf; worn. With engraved title & 43 plates & maps. Lacking Plates 35 & 36 but with large folding map of Japan; hole in 1 plate without significant loss; some fraying; titles soiled. S June 25 (471) £1,800 [Fletcher]

Kafka, Franz, 1883-1924
— Un Divertissement. Paris: Guy Levis Mano, 1938. One of 455. Illus by Max Ernst. S June 29 (44) £750 [Rota]
— In der Strafkolonie. Leipzig, 1919. 1st Ed. Orig wraps. HN Nov 26 (1894) DM1,100
— Ein Landarzt. Munich & Leipzig: Kurt Wolf, [1919]. Orig half cloth. S Sept 23 (569) £160 [Quaritch]

Kagan, Bernhard
— III. Internationales Schachmeisterturnier zu Ostende vom 16. Mai bis 25. Juni 1907. Berlin, 1923. Orig wraps. pn Mar 26 (64) £150 [Furstenburg]

Kahn, Anton Friedrich
— Anfangsgrunde der Fechtkunst.... Helmstadt, 1761. 4to, later half mor; rubbed. With port (holed) & 24 (of 25) folding plates. Library stamp on tp; 1 plate def. bba Sept 25 (253) £90 [Nosbuesch]

Kahnweiler, Daniel Henry
— Juan Gris: his Life and Work. NY, 1947. Trans by Douglas Cooper. 4to, cloth, in d/j; worn. With 2 mtd color plates. O Jan 6 (105) $70
— Les Sculptures de Picasso. Paris, 1948 [1949]. 4to, half cloth. O Mar 24 (31) $60

Kain, Saul. See: Sassoon, Siegfried

Kaiser, Henry J. See: Grabhorn Printing

Kalidasa, fl. 5th century A.D.
— Sakoontala, or the Lost Ring, an Indian Drama. Hertford: Stephen Austin, 1855. One of 110 on japan. Trans by Monier Monier-Williams. 4to, cloth, orig wraps bound in. sg Sept 11 (211) $50

Kallir, Otto
— Grandma Moses: American Primitive. Garden City, 1947. 4to, cloth, in d/j. Inscr by Grandma Moses. wa Nov 6 (432) $110

Kalm, Peter, 1716-79
— Travels into North America. L, 1772. 2 vols. 8vo, modern cloth. With folding map & 6 plates. Map with perforated library stamp. sg Mar 12 (158) $300

Kampen, Nicolaas Godfried van, 1776-1839
— The History and Topography of Holland and Belgium. L, [1837]. Illus by W. H. Bartlett. 8vo, orig cloth; joints cracked. With engraved title & 58 plates only. Ck May 15 (26) £80

Kandinsky, Wassily, 1866-1944 —& Marc, Franz, 1880-1916
— Der Blaue Reiter. Munich: R. Piper, 1912. 1st Ed, one of 1,200. 4to, mor, orig wraps bound in. O May 12 (115) $1,850

Kane, Elisha Kent, 1820-57
— Arctic Explorations. NY, 1854. ("The U. S. Grinnell Expedition in Search of Sir John Franklin....") 8vo, orig cloth. pn Apr 30 (232) £140
   Anr Ed. Phila., 1856. 2 vols. 8vo, orig cloth; spine ends chipped, corners & edges rubbed. cb June 4 (119) $65
   Anr Ed. Phila., 1857. 2 vols. 8vo, orig cloth; worn. With 2 folding maps & 12 plates. wa Nov 6 (119) $80

Kane, Richard, 1666-1736?
— Campaigns of King William and Queen Anne.... L, 1745. 1st Ed. 8vo, contemp calf; rebacked. With folding colored map & 17 colored plates. pn Dec 11 (304) £75 [Trocchi]

Kant, Immanuel, 1724-1804
— Critik der reinen Vernunft. Riga, 1781. 1st Ed. 8vo, contemp calf. S Nov 27 (20) £2,300 [Quaritch]
— Zum ewigen Frieden. Koenigsberg, 1795. 8vo, contemp bds; spine worn. HN Nov 26 (1250) DM600

Karaka, Dosabhai Franji
— History of the Parsis.... L, 1884. 2 vols. 8vo, cloth. Minor worming in margins. sg Nov 20 (84) $100

Karolik Collection, M. & M.
— American Paintings 1815 to 1865. Bost., 1949 [but 1951]. 4to, cloth; worn. O Sept 23 (88) $210

Karpinski, Louis Charles. See: Spaulding & Karpinski

Karsten, Karl Heinrich Gustav Hermann
— Florae Columbiae terrarumque adiacentium specimina selecta. Berlin, 1858-69. 2 vols. Folio, orig wraps; spines def & a few covers torn. With 200 hand-colored plates. Blindstamp at foot of plates; many plates stained in Parts 2-5 of Vol I & Part 4 of Vol II. S June 25 (166) £3,600 [Rainer]

Kasparian, Genrikh Maiseevich
— 2,500 Finales. Buenos Aires, 1963. 2 vols. Orig wraps. pn Mar 26 (296) £90 [Chen]

Kauffer, E. McKnight
— The Art of the Poster. L, 1924. 4to, orig half cloth; worn. Inscr, with comments about the book. S Jan 13 (654) £130 [Jolliffe]

Kaukol, Maria Joseph Clement
— Christlicher Seelen-Schatz auserlesener Gebetter. [Bonn, 1729]. 4to, contemp mor gilt. HK Nov 4 (1674) DM1,000

Anr copy. Contemp mor gilt; worn. Some fingersoiling. HK Nov 4 (1675) DM850

Anr copy. Contemp sheep gilt; rubbed, spine chipped at head, spine def at bottom. Engraved throughout. sg Dec 4 (93) $375

Kautsky, Vaclav, d.1924
— Partie Mezinarodnich Turnaju Sachovych v Praze 1908. Prague, 1909. Half cloth. pn Mar 26 (66) £130 [De Lucia]

Kay, John, 1742-1826
— A Series of Original Portraits and Caricature Etchings. Edin., 1837-38. 2 vols. 4to, calf. pnE Oct 15 (213) £300

Anr copy. Later calf by Grieve. pnE June 17 (84) £190

Anr copy. Calf; marked. With 230 plates. L.p. plates. S July 13 (201) £300

Anr Ed. Edin., 1877. 2 vols. 4to, orig half mor. With 361 plates. pnE May 20 (11) £170

Anr copy. Orig half mor; rubbed. S Jan 13 (655) £85 [McKenzie]

Kayll, Robert
— The Trades Increase. L, 1615. 4to, half calf. Last leaf soiled; tear in B3; blank corners torn from prelims. S July 23 (445) £3,200 [Drury]

Keale, Robert. See: Kayll, Robert

Keate, George, 1729-97
— An Account of the Pelew Islands. Dublin, 1788. 1st Irish Ed. 8vo, cloth; broken & rubbed. With port, folding map & 16 plates, some folding. bba Dec 18 (164) £40 [Elliott]

3d Ed. L, 1789. 4to, contemp calf; upper joint cracked. With port, 15 plates & folding chart. Tp soiled. Ck May 15 (55) £80

Keating Collection, George T.
— A Conrad Memorial Library.... Garden City, 1929. One of 501. 4to, cloth; worn. Tipped in is a 1940 letter of Bertram Rota, attesting that this copy is from the library of Rudyard Kipling. O June 16 (116) $150

Keats, John, 1795-1821
See also: Eragny Press; Golden Cockerel Press

— Endymion. New Rochelle: Elston Press, 1902. One of 160. Orig cloth; rubbed. Lower edge of tp stained. cb Sept 11 (89) $65

— Isabella or the Pot of Basil. L, 1898. 4to, orig cloth. B Oct 7 (280) HF325

— Lamia, Isabella, The Eve of St. Agnes, and Other Poems. L, 1820. 1st Ed. 12mo, contemp half calf; joints weak. sg Apr 2 (127) $1,200

— Life, Letters, and Literary Remains. L, 1848. Ed by Richard Moncton Milnes. 2 vols. 8vo, contemp half calf; rubbed. Inscr "Matilda Tennyson from her affectionate brother Alfred". S Jan 13 (526) £260 [McKenzie]

— Poems. L: Vale Press, 1898. One of 210. Ed by Charles Holmes; illus by Charles Ricketts. 2 vols. 8vo,; mor gilt by Bayntun. FD June 11 (5040) DM3,000

Anr copy. 8vo,; mor gilt by Zaehnsdorf. pnE Oct 15 (141) £160

— Poetical Works. Oxford, 1925. Mor gilt by Riviere. sg Sept 11 (216) $130

Anr Ed. NY, 1938-39. One of 1,050. Intro by John Masefield. 8 vols. Half lev gilt. Sgd by Masefield. sg Feb 12 (190) $700

Keen Hand. See: Farnie, Henry Brougham

Keene, Foxhall. See: Derrydale Press

Keene, J. Harrington
— Fly-Fishing and Fly-making for Trout.... NY, 1887. 8vo, cloth; worn. sg Oct 23 (360) $100

Anr Ed. NY, 1891. 8vo, cloth. With 11-pp Forest & Stream Catalog. wa Sept 25 (88) $180

Anr Ed. NY, 1898. 8vo, cloth. With 2 plates of mtd fly-tying materials. sg Oct 23 (361) $60

Keere, Pieter van den
— Germania inferior. Amst., 1622. Folio, old calf; rebacked. With hand-colored engraved title & 25 double-page maps, all but 3 colored by hand with yellow wash borders. Leo Belgicus with 2 small tears at fold. C Oct 15 (54) £5,500 [Tooley Adams]

Kegel, Philip
— Tolf aandelige Betaenckninger...paa Danske udsat af N. M. Aalb. Copenhagen: Daniel Pauli, 1674. 12mo, contemp velvet with large raised floral cornerpieces & centerpiece elaborately worked in silverwire over silk thread & padding. C Dec 12 (312) £900 [Quaritch]

Kehimkar, Haeem Samuel
— The History of the Bene Israel of India. Tel Aviv, 1937. Orig wraps. sg Apr 30 (248) $350

Keill, James, 1671-1721
— The Anatomy of the Humane Body Abridged. L, 1698. 12mo, new half calf. Worming in some lower margins. S May 28 (709) £100

Keith, Alexander, 1791-1880
— The Land of Israel. According to The Covenant with Abraham.... NY, 1844. 12mo, orig cloth, Initial blank torn; minor scattered foxing. sg Sept 25 (21) $100

Keith, E. C.
— A Countryman's Creed. L, 1938. One of 250. Illus by Archibald Thorburn. sg Oct 23 (362) $60

Keith, Sir George Mouat
— A Voyage to South America and the Cape of Good Hope.... L, 1819. 4to, half calf. S Oct 23 (461) £350 [Bonham]

Kelland, Clarence Buddington
— Not Their Breed & The Forgotten Man. Pvtly ptd at the Derrydale Press, [1938]. Wraps. sg Oct 23 (81) $70

Keller, Ferdinand
— The Lake Dwellings of Switzerland.... L, 1878. 2d ed. 2 vols. 8vo, orig cloth; spine worn. With 206 plates. bba Oct 30 (324) £75 [Brailey]

Keller, Gottfried
— Der Schmied seines Glueckes. Leipzig. Insel-Verlag, 1921. One of 120. Calf gilt; worn. HN Nov 26 (1475) DM520

Keller, Helen
— Midstream. My Later Life. Garden City, 1929. Sgd. K June 7 (185) $75

Kellet, Susanna, Elizabeth & Mary
— A Complete Collection of Cookery Receipts. Newcastle, 1780. 1st Ed. 4to, modern bds; upper joint cracked at top. Some waterstains to last few gatherings. Crahan copy. P Nov 25 (267) $650

Kelley, J. D. Jerrold, 1847-1922
See also: Cozzens & Kelley; Wagner & Kelley
— Our Navy, its Growth and Achievements. Hartford: American Pbg, [1897]. Oblong 4to, cloth; soiled. With 24 colored plates. wa Nov 6 (404) $325

Kelley, James Douglas Jerrold, 1847-1922
— American Yachts, Their Clubs and Races. NY: Scribner's, 1884. 8vo, contemp half mor; worn & soiled. wa Nov 6 (29) $70

Kells, Book of. See: Codex...

Kelly, Charles —&
Howe, Maurice L.
— Miles Goodyear, First Citizen of Utah. Salt Lake City, 1937. One of 350. In d/j. cb Oct 9 (126) $80
Anr copy. In d/j partly slit along fore-edge. sg Mar 12 (254) $80

Kelly, Christopher
— A New and Complete System of Universal Geography. L, 1814-17. 2 vols. 4to, calf; def. With frontis, 2 engraved titles, 33 maps & 47 plates. pn June 18 (12) £120 [Sweet]

Kelly, Fred Charters, 1882-1959. See: Wright presentation copy, Orville

Kelly, Howard Atwood, 1858-1943
— Some American Medical Botanists.... Troy, 1914. K June 7 (220) $60

Kelly, Patrick, 1756-1842
A Practical Introduction to Spherics and Nautical Astronomy.... L, 1822. 5th Ed. Orig bds; spine worn. With 2 tables & 18 folding plates. sg Jan 15 (322) $100

Kelly, William
— An Excursion to California over the Prairie.... L, 1851. 1st Ed. 2 vols. 8vo, orig cloth, unopened; rear hinge starting. Lacking ads. sg Mar 12 (159) $400
— Life in Victoria, or Victoria in 1853-1858. L, 1859. 2 vols. 8vo, early half mor; rubbed. Map backed & tipped to lower endpaper. kh Mar 16 (280) A$300
— A Stroll through the Diggings of California. L, 1852. 8vo, bds; rubbed. Bookcase Library, Vol IV. sg Mar 12 (160) $110

Kelmscott Press—London
— The Floure and the Leafe.... 1896. One of 300. S Dec 4 (74) £200 [Bruce Marmall]
— The History of Godefrey of Boloyne.... 1893. One of 300. S Dec 4 (47) £420 [Perceval]; S June 18 (300) £300 [Cox]
— Laudes Beatae Mariae Virginis. 1896. One of 250. S Dec 4 (73) £280 [Fletcher]; T June 18 (178) £155
— Of the Friendship of Amis and Amile. 1894. One of 500. S Dec 4 (55) £200 [Old Hall Bks]
The Order of Chivalry. 1893. One of 225. cb Feb 5 (206) £300
— Psalmi Penitentiales. 1894. One of 300. cb June 18 (167) $190
— Sire Degrevaunt. 1896 [1897]. One of 350.

KELMSCOTT PRESS

    cb Sept 11 (185) $250; S Dec 4 (77) £340 [Hirsch]
— Some German Woodcuts of the Fifteenth Century. 1897 [pbd 1898]. One of 225. ALs of William Morris laid in along with a proof. wd June 19 (140) $425
— Syr Perecyvelle of Gales. 1895. One of 350. Unopened. S Dec 4 (65) £250 [Fletcher]; S Dec 4 (88) £340 [Hirsch]
— Syr Ysambrace. 1897. One of 350. S Dec 4 (78) £280 [Fletcher]
    Anr copy. F. S. Ellis's copy. S Dec 4 (89) £220 [Fletcher]
— The Tale of Beowulf. 1895. One of 300. S Dec 4 (64) £700 [McMubis]; S June 18 (310) £500 [Ash]
— The Tale of King Florus and the Fair Jehane. 1893. One of 350. S Dec 4 (53) £200 [Fletcher]
— The Tale of the Emperor Coustans and of Over Sea. 1894. One of 525. Contemp lea by Frank Murray with embossed design of a galleon in full sail. T Feb 19 (590) £95
— BLUNT, WILFRID SCAWEN. - The Love-Lyrics and Songs of Proteus.... 1892. One of 300. bba Apr 9 (240) £220 [Swales]; cb Sept 11 (182) $475; S Dec 4 (40) £350 [Monk Bretton]
— CAVENDISH, GEORGE. - The Life of Thomas Wolsey. 1893. One of 250. sg Jan 8 (140) $350
— CAXTON, WILLIAM. - The History of Reynard the Foxe. 1892. One of 300. Unopened. S Dec 4 (46) £400 [Perceval]
— CHAUCER, GEOFFREY. - Works. 1896. One of 425. P June 18 (98) $12,500; S Dec 4 (71) £6,200; sg Apr 2 (47) $14,000
— COLERIDGE, SAMUEL TAYLOR. - Poems Chosen out of the Works of Samuel Taylor Coleridge. 1896. One of 300. S Dec 4 (69) £350 [Thorp]
— HERRICK, ROBERT. - Poems. 1895. One of 250. S Dec 4 (68) £400 [Old Hall Bks]
— LE FEVRE, RAOUL. - The Recuyell of the Historyes of Troye. 1892. One of 300. 3 vols in 2. S June 18 (299) £400 [Ash]; sg Apr 2 (128) $650
— MACKAIL, JOHN WILLIAM. - Biblia Innocentium: Being the Story of God's Chosen People.... 1892. One of 200. S Dec 4 (45) £280 [Old Hall Bks]
— MEINHOLD, WILLIAM. - Sidonia the Sorceress. 1893. One of 300. S Dec 4 (51) £380 [Percival]
    Anr copy. 2 ties missing, 2 repaired. S Dec 4 (86) £200 [Fletcher]; wd June 19 (139) $225
— MORE, SIR THOMAS. - Utopia. 1893. One of 300. S Dec 4 (48) £420 [Percival]
— MORRIS, WILLIAM. - Child Christopher and Goldilind the Fair. 1895. One of 600. 2 vols. Bdg worn. Inscr by Sydney Cockerell. S June 18 (309) £250 [Cox]; sg Sept 11 (217) $425
— MORRIS, WILLIAM. - The Defence of Guenevere.... 1892. One of 300. Unopened. S Dec 4 (42) £400 [Thomas]
— MORRIS, WILLIAM. - A Dream of John Ball and a King's Lesson. 1892. One of 300. S Dec 4 (43) £400 [Thomas]
— MORRIS, WILLIAM. - The Earthly Paradise. 1896-97. One of 225. 8 vols. Buxton Forman—Kalbfleisch copy. CNY May 11 (65) $2,800; FD June 11 (5046) DM3,200; S Dec 4 (72) £480 [Percevial]
— MORRIS, WILLIAM. - Gothic Architecture.... 1893. One of 1,500. In contemp loose cover of Morris fabric. Inscr to John and Margaret Mackail from the Kelmscott Fellowship. S Dec 4 (85) £360 [Maggs]
— MORRIS, WILLIAM. - The Life and Death of Jason.... 1895. One of 200. A few prelims spotted. S Dec 4 (66) £500 [Trinity Fine Art]
— MORRIS, WILLIAM. - Love is Enough, or the Freeing of Pharamond: A Morality. 1897. One of 300. S Dec 4 (81) £400 [Perceval]
— MORRIS, WILLIAM. - News from Nowhere: or, an Epoch of Rest.... 1893. One of 300. S Oct 6 (733) £220 [Swales]
— MORRIS, WILLIAM. - A Note on his Aims in Founding the Kelmscott Press. 1898. One of 525. S Dec 4 (82) £380 [Thomas]; S June 18 (312) £400 [Mr. K]
— MORRIS, WILLIAM. - Poems by the Way. 1891. pn June 18 (172) £240 [Dawson]
— MORRIS, WILLIAM. - The Story of Sigurd the Volsung. 1898. One of 160. S Dec 4 (79) £380 [Perceval]; S June 18 (311) £820 [Maggs]
— MORRIS, WILLIAM. - The Story of the Glittering Plain. 1891. One of 200. S Dec 4 (39) £420 [Perceval]
    Anr Ed. 1894. One of 250. Vellum; dampstained & wrinkled. O June 9 (89) $225; S Dec 4 (54) £740 [Dover Publications]; S June 18 (305) £520 [Lechti]
— MORRIS, WILLIAM. - The Sundering Flood. 1897. One of 300. S Dec 4 (80) £880 [Fletcher]
    Anr copy. In mor gilt by the Doves Bindery, 1899. sg June 11 (264) $2,800
— MORRIS, WILLIAM. - The Water of the Wondrous Isles. 1897. One of 250. S Dec 4 (76) £380 [Sims Reed]
— MORRIS, WILLIAM. - The Well at the World's End. 1896. One of 350. S Dec 4 (70) £520 [Thorp]
— MORRIS, WILLIAM. - The Wood beyond the World. 1894. One of 350. S Dec 4 (59) £420 [Thorp]
— ORBELIANI, SULKHAN SABA. - The Book of Wisdom and Lies. 1894. One of 250. Inscr by H. L. Corbett to C. E. S. Wood. cb Sept 11 (183) $225; S June 18 (307) £220

[Joseph]
— ROSSETTI, DANTE GABRIEL. - Ballads and Narrative Poems. 1893. One of 310. S Dec 4 (52) £380 [Fletcher]
— ROSSETTI, DANTE GABRIEL. - Sonnets and Lyrical Poems. 1894. One of 310. S Dec 4 (57) £300 [Fletcher]
— RUSKIN, JOHN. - The Nature of Gothic. 1892. One of 500. S Dec 4 (41) £300 [Thatcher]; sg Jan 8 (141) $250
— SAVONAROLA, GIROLAMO. - Epistola de contemptu mundi. 1894. One of 150. S Dec 4 (63) £300 [Saibu]
— SHAKESPEARE, WILLIAM. - The Poems of William Shakespeare. 1893. One of 500. Inscr by the Ed, F. S. Ellis. S June 18 (303) £400 [Joseph]
— SHELLEY, PERCY BYSSHE. - The Poetical Works. [1894]-95. One of 250. 3 vols. FD June 11 (6047) DM4,000
Anr copy. Unopened. S Dec 4 (61) £480; S June 18 (308) £550 [Joseph]
— SPENSER, EDMUND - The Shepheards Calendar. 1896. One of 225. S Dec 4 (75) £500 [Srurrim]
— SWINBURNE, ALGERNON CHARLES. - Atalanta in Calydon. 1894. One of 250. S Dec 4 (58) £350 [Fletcher]; S Dec 4 (87) £300 [Fletcher]
— TENNYSON, ALFRED. - Maud, a Monodrama. 1893. One of 500. S Dec 4 (49) £300 [Thomas]; S Dec 4 (83) £280 [Old Hall]; S June 18 (301) £300 [Maggs]
Anr copy. Inscr by William Morris with initials, 6 Oct 1893. sg Dec 4 (95) $750
— VORAGINE, JACOBUS DE. - The Golden Legend. 1892. One of 500. 3 vols. S Dec 4 (44) £800 [Thomas]; sg Dec 4 (94) $850

Kelson, George M.
— The Salmon Fly. L, 1895. 4to, half mor gilt. With port & 8 colored plates. Some soiling; minor marginal tears. pn Sept 18 (17) £160 [Furniss]
Anr copy. Orig cloth. pnE Dec 17 (349) £200 [Codzow]
Anr copy. Half mor. sg Oct 23 (363) $250
Anr copy. Cloth. wa Feb 19 (5) $140
— Tips, by the Author of The Salmon Fly. L, 1901. wa Feb 19 (6) $140

Keltie, Sir John Scott, 1840-1927
— A History of the Scottish Highlands, Clans and Regiments. Edin. & L, 1875. 2 vols. 8vo, half mor; extremities rubbed. sg Dec 18 (193) $80

Kemble, Frances Anne, 1809-93
— Journal of a Residence on a Georgian Plantation in 1838-1839. NY, 1863. 12mo, orig cloth; spine ends frayed, front joint starting. sg Mar 12 (126) $60

Kendall, George Wilkins, 1809-67
— Narrative of the Texan Santa Fe Expedition.... NY, 1844. 1st Ed. 2 vols. 12mo, orig cloth. With folding map & 5 plates; with 2-inch tear to map. cb Jan 8 (104) $300
Anr copy. Orig cloth; worn & soiled. With folding map & 4 plates. wa Sept 25 (397) $110

Kendall, Paul Green. See: Derrydale Press

Kendall, William Converse
— The Fishes of New England. Bost., 1935. Vol II only. 4to, cloth. sg Oct 23 (364) $90

Kendrick, Albert Frank —& Tattersall, Creassey Edward Cecil
— Fine Carpets in the Victoria and Albert Museum. L, 1924. One of 450. Folio, cloth. With 20 colored plates. sg Feb 5 (246) $225
— Hand-Woven Carpets, Oriental & European. NY, 1922. One of 1,000. 2 vols. 4to, orig cloth; soiled. S Nov 10 (114) £140 [Quaritch]

Kennedy, Edward Shirley
— Peaks, Passes and Glaciers. Second Series. L, 1862. 2 vols. 8vo, half calf gilt; rubbed. pn Apr 30 (340) £100 [Smith]

Kennedy, R. A.
— The Triuneverse: A Scientific Romance. L: Charles Knight, 1962 [1912]. Inscr. cb Sept 28 (725) $95

Kennett, White, 1660-1728
— Parochial Antiquities Attempted in the History of Ambrosden, Burcester.... Oxford, 1695. 1st Ed. 4to, contemp calf; spine & extremities worn. With 9 plates. Some spotting; 2 plates torn. Ck May 15 (134) £80

Kent, Henry W. See: Grolier Club

Kent, Rockwell
— After Long Years... Ausable Forks: Asgaard Press, 1968. One of 250. Half cloth. Inscr. cb Dec 4 (214) $75
— Alaska Drawings. NY, 1919. One of 1,500. Wraps; toxed & creased. cb Dec 4 (217) $110
Anr copy. Pictorial wraps; some soiling. cb June 18 (173) $140
— A Birthday Book. [NY], 1931. One of 1,850 sgd. cb Dec 4 (220) $65
One of 1,850. sg Jan 8 (142) $90
One of 1,850 sgd. sg June 11 (265) $50
— The Bookplates & Marks of Rockwell Kent. NY, 1929. One of 1,250. Cloth, in d/j. Inscr. cb Dec 4 (222) $140; cb June 18 (175) $160
— Greenland Journal. NY, [1962]. One of

KENT

1,000. With a suite of 6 lithos, 1 sgd. cb June 18 (177) $65
— Later Bookplates & Marks. NY, 1937. One of 1,250. In d/j. cb Dec 4 (231) $160
Anr copy. Unopened. sg Jan 8 (143) $130
— N by E. NY, 1930. One of 900, sgd. 4to, cloth. cb Dec 4 (233) $130; cb Feb 19 (150) $170; cb June 18 (184) $180; cb July 30 (108) $90
— Of Men and Mountains. NY, 1959. One of 250. Half cloth. Inscr. cb Dec 4 (234) $120
— Rockwell Kent's Greenland Journal. NY, [1962]. One of 1,000. With extra suite of 6 litho plates. cb Dec 4 (239) $65
— Salamina. NY, 1935. 1st Ed. Sgd. sg Mar 5 (112) $80
— This Is my Own. NY, [1940]. 1st Ed. In d/j. cb June 18 (192) $55
— Voyaging Southward from the Strait of Magellan. NY, 1924. 1st Ed, One of 100. 4to, half vellum. Inscr to his wife, Christmas 1924. cb Dec 4 (251) $400
— Wilderness; a Journal of Quiet Adventure in Alaska. NY, 1920. 1st Ed. 4to, cloth, 1st Issue bdg. cb Dec 4 (253) $75

Kent's copy, Rockwell

— Litho Media: A Demonstration of the Selling Power of Lithography. NY, 1939. Folio, cloth, in chipped d/j. O June 16 (125) $100

Kent, William Saville, d.1908

— The Naturalist in Australia. L, 1897. 4to, orig cloth; inner hinge cracked. Ck Sept 24 (211) £130

Kenyon, C. R.

— The Argonauts of the Amazon. L, 1901. Illus by Arthur Rackham. sg Oct 30 (121) $130

Kepler, Johannes, 1571-1630

— De cometis libelli tres. Augsburg, 1619-[20]. 4to, 18th-cent bds. P Sept 24 (183) $4,500
— Phaenomenon signulare seu Mercurius in sole. Leipzig, 1609. 4to, modern bds. S June 25 (115) £700
— Strena seu de nive sexangula. Frankfurt: G. Tampach, 1611. 4to, modern half vellum. S June 25 (116) £1,300 [Lan]

Keppel, George Thomas, Earl of Albemarle, 1799-1891

— Personal Narrative of a Journey from India to England. L, 1827. 1st Ed. 4to, contemp calf; rebacked. With folding map & 3 colored plates. sg Apr 23 (79) $150

AMERICAN BOOK PRICES CURRENT

Keppel, Sir Henry, 1809-1904

— A Visit to the Indian Archipelago.... L, 1853. 2 vols. 8vo, orig cloth; soiled, rebacked preserving orig spines. With folding chart & 8 litho plates. C Apr 8 (102) £220 [Gaston]

Ker, Charles Henry Bellenden

— Icones plantarum sponte China nascentium.... L, 1821. Folio, modern half mor. With 28 (of 30) hand-colored plates. Lacking tp, preface & Plates 22 & 28 (these present in photographic facsimile). Sheets irregularly trimmed with some cropping. Sold w.a.f. Hunt copy. CNY Nov 21 (158) $600

Anr copy. Modern half mor by Sangorski & Sutcliffe. With 30 hand-colored plates. Slight browning & spotting. Plesch—de Belder copy. S Apr 27 (188) £3,000 [Minton]

Kerdyk, Rene

— Les femmes de ce temps. Paris, 1920. One of 500. Illus by Guy Arnoux. 4to, bds; slightly stained. With 10 plates. cb Dec 4 (31) $80

Kerguelen-Tremarec, Yves Joseph de, 1734?-97

— Relation de deux voyages dans les mers Australes & des Indes.... Paris, 1782. 8vo, half calf; rubbed. With folding chart. S Oct 23 (503) £2,700 [Perrin]

Kern, Huldrich

— Eyn new kunstlichs wolgegruends Visierbuech.... Strassburg: Peter Schaeffer bei Hansen Schwyntzern, 1531. Folio, 19th-cent bds; spine def. Lacking final blank; a few leaves trimmed; some stains & discoloration. S June 25 (117) £1,800

Kerner, Johann Simon

— Abbildung aller oekonomischen Pflanzen. Stuttgart, 1786-96. ("Figures des plantes economiques.") 8 vols. 4to, contemp calf; rubbed. With hand-colored engraved vignettes on titles & 800 folding hand-colored plates. Some plates creased at fore-edge. S June 25 (167) £14,000 [Burgess]

— Hortus sempervirens. Stuttgart, 1795-1830. Parts 52-55 only (of 71). 4to, old half cloth; worn & loose. With 38 orig watercolor plates. Lacking tp & contents leaves, the 1st 6 plates & text leaves of Part 52; Plates 638, 648 & 650/51 & the text-leaf for Plate 629 restored without loss; 3 plates stained; Plate 630 scarred & 649 detached. P June 18 (100) $11,000

Kerners, J. S.
— Beschreibung und Ubbildung der Baeume und Gestrauche. Stuttgart, 1783-92. 9 parts in 1 vol. 4to, contemp bds; rubbed. With 71 hand-colored plates. Minor dampstaining at head of 1st few leaves & to the upper margin of a few plates at end; repairs to title & following leaf. de Belder copy. S Apr 27 (189) £2,500 [Harley]

Kerouac, Jack
— Doctor Sax. NY, [1959]. One of 26. Half cloth. sg Mar 5 (114) $1,200

Kerr, John, 1852-1920
— The Golf-Book of East Lothian. Edin., 1896. One of 250 L.p. copies. 4to. half lea. Inscr. pnC July 16 (80) £750; pnC July 16 (81) £900; pnC July 16 (82) £950

One of 500. Orig cloth. pnC Jan 23 (125) £680; pnC Jan 23 (126) £660

— The History of Curling. Edin., 1890. 8vo, orig half lea gilt. S Nov 10 (599) £85 [McCarthy]

Anr copy. Orig half lea gilt; worn & broken on hinges. T Oct 16 (660) £46

Kerr, Robert, 1755-1813
— History of Scotland during the Reign of Robert I.... Edin., 1811. 2 vols. 8vo, contemp calf; scuffed & worn. cb Dec 18 (93) $130

Kerridge, Philip Markham
— An Address on Angling Literature. Fullerton, [1970]. One of 350. Half lea with fly in sunken mount set in front cover. sg Oct 23 (366) $90

Kersey, John, 1616-90?
— The Elements of that Mathematical Art Commonly Called Algebra. L, 1673-74. 1st Ed. 2 vols in 1. Folio, contemp calf; spine rubbed. Marginal worming not affecting text; some leaves soiled or stained. S Nov 10 (504) £320 [Phillips]

Kertesz, Andre
— Day of Paris. NY, [1945]. sg Nov 13 (70) $90

Kester, Jesse Y.
— The American Shooter's Manual. Phila., 1827. 1st Ed. 8vo, calf; worn. With 3 plates. sg Oct 23 (367) $325

Ketchum, Arthur
— Roads & Harbours; Pieces in Cadence and Rhyme. NY: ptd at the Derrydale press for Harry Roberts, Jr., 1927. One of 150. Bds; minor wear. sg Oct 23 (83) $350

Kettell, Russell Hawes
— The Pine Furniture of Early New England. Garden City, 1929. One of 999. 4to, orig cloth. sg June 4 (188) $50

Kettilby, Mary
— A Collection of Above Three Hundred Receipts in Cookery, Physick.... L, 1714. 1st Ed. 8vo, modern half mor; endpapers renewed. sg Jan 15 (32) $275

4th Ed. L, 1728. 8vo, modern half calf. Several leaves spotted. Ck Sept 5 (217) £120

Keulemans, John Gerrard, 1842-1912
— Onze Vogels in huis en tuin. Leiden, 1869-76. 3 vols. 4to, cloth; def, worn. With 200 color lithos, some browning & foxing. Haverschmidt copy. B Feb 24 (350) HF4,600

Keynes, Sir Geoffrey
See also: Nonesuch Press

— The Complete Portraiture of William and Catherine Blake. L, 1977. One of 500. 4to, half mor. O May 12 (116) $125

— Engravings by William Blake. The Separate Plates. Dublin, 1956. One of 500. 4to, cloth. bba July 2 (258) £100 [Dawson]; S Oct 6 (771) £800 [Kerr]

— A Study of the Illuminated Books of William Blake. L, 1964. 4to, cloth. With 32 color plates. cba Mar 5 (24) $50

One of 525. Half mor. O May 12 (117) $100

Anr Ed. NY, [1964]. 4to, half mor. O Mar 24 (101) $90

— William Blake's Laocoon, a Last Testament. Paris: Trianon Press, 1976. One of 438. 4to, half mor. O May 12 (118) $90

Keynes, John Maynard, 1883-1946
— The General Theory of Employment, Interest and Money. L, 1936. Lacking front endpaper. bba Oct 30 (395) £70 [Woollam]

Anr copy. In chipped d/j. P Sept 24 (314) $375; sg Sept 11 (218) $225

— Indian Currency and Finance. L, 1913. 1st Ed. 8vo, orig cloth; rubbed. Some stains & spotting. P Sept 24 (315) $900

— A Revision of the Treaty. L, 1922. Bdg rubbed & buckled. bba Apr 23 (261) £60 [Birgo]

Keys, John
— The Antient Bee-Master's Farewell.... L, 1796. 8vo, modern calf by Crahan. Crahan copy. P Nov 25 (269) $250

KEYSLER

Keysler, Johann Georg, 1693-1743
— Travels through Germany, Bohemia, Hungary, Switzerland.... L, 1760. 4 vols. 8vo, contemp calf; rubbed, joints split. bba Oct 30 (327) £85 [Shapero]

Khlebnikov, Velemir
See also: Kruchenykh & Khlebnikov
— Izbornik Stikhov 1907-1914. St. Petersburg, 1915. One of 1,000. Orig wraps. S June 17 (181) £500 [Rabinovich]

Kidd, Capt. William, 1645?-1701
[-] The Arraignment, Tryal, and Condemnation of Captain William Kidd, for Murther and Piracy. L, 1701. Folio, half calf. First 3 leaves with minor marginal repair; closely trimmed at head, not affecting text. wd Nov 12 (130) $350

Kidder, Daniel Parish, 1815-91
— Sketches of Residence and Travels in Brazil. Phila., 1845. 2 vols. 12mo, cloth. With 10 plates. wa Nov 6 (139) $70

Kidder, Edward
— Receipts of Pastry and Cookery.... L, [c.1740]. 8vo, contemp sheep; rebacked, new endpapers, surface worming. With port. Crahan copy. P Nov 25 (270) $750

Anr copy. Contemp calf gilt; rubbed, waterstained at fore-edge corners. Some shaving, affecting signature marks & 2 final lines of text; 1 plate laid down with minor loss; 2 other plates with minor repairs. P Nov 25 (271) $600

Kidder, Jonathan Edward
— Japanese Temples: Sculpture, Paintings, Gardens, and Architecture. Tokyo, [1964]. 4to, cloth; worn. O Jan 6 (107) $60

Kieseritzky, Lionel Adalbert Bagration Felix, 1805-53
— Cinquante Parties, jouees au Cercle des Echecs et au Cafe de la Regence. Paris, 1846. Half calf; rebacked. pn Mar 26 (432) £50 [Moran]

Kikuchi Sadao
— A Treasury of Japanese Wood Block Prints.... NY: Crown, [1969]. In frayed d/j. cb Mar 5 (254) $50

Kilby, Thomas, 1794-1868
— Scenery in the Vicinity of Wakefield. Wakefield, 1843. Folio, orig cloth; rubbed & rebacked. With pictorial title & 15 plates. Some spotting & staining, mostly marginal. bba June 18 (392) £130 [Shapero]

Killian, James R. See: Edgerton & Killian

AMERICAN BOOK PRICES CURRENT

Kilmer, Joyce, 1886-1918
— Summer of Love. NY, 1911. 1st Issue. sg Mar 5 (115) $140

Kilner, Dorothy, d.1836
— The Histories of More Children than One.... L: John Marshall, [c.1785]. 24mo, orig bds; rebacked, backstrip defective. S Dec 5 (283) £260 [Hirsch]
— The Holiday Present, Containing Anecdotes of Mr. and Mrs. Jennet.... L: John Marshall, [c.1788]. 3d Ed. 12mo, orig half sheep. S June 18 (411) £1,000 [Randolph]
— Jingles, or Original Rhymes for Children. L, 1806. 16mo, orig wraps. S June 17 (415) £300 [Moon]
— Little Stories for Little Folks.... L: John Marshall, [c.1790]. 24mo, contemp calf gilt. S June 18 (412) £600 [Quaritch]
— The Village School, or a Collection of Entertaining Histories.... L: John Marshall, [1785?]. 2 vols. 12mo, contemp calf gilt. 2 ad leaves removed at end of Vol I. S June 17 (413) £580 [Vincent]

Kimball, Charles P.
— The San Francisco City Directory...1850. San Francisco, [1890]. 24mo, cloth; spine faded. Reprint of 1850 Ed. cb Oct 9 (127) $70

Kind, Alfred. See: Fuchs & Kind

King, Charles, 1844-1933
— A Daughter of the Sioux. NY, 1903. Illus by Frederic Remington & E. W. Deming. 12mo, calf; rubbed, spines corroded. O Oct 21 (100) $75

King, Edward, 1735?-1807. See: Fore-Edge Paintings

King, James, 1750-84. See: Cook, Capt. James

King, Jessie M.
— How Cinderella was able to go to the Ball. L, [1924?]. Orig bds; soiled. With 17 plates. bba Oct 16 (206) £60 [Korn]

King, John Glen, 1732-87
— The Rites and Ceremonies of the Greek Church in Russia. L, 1772. L.p. copy. 4to, contemp half mor; spine worn, rubbed. With double-page frontis & 12 plates. bba Nov 13 (228) £65 [P & P]

King, Phillip Parker, 1793-1856
— Narrative of a Survey of the Intertropical and Western Coasts of Australia.... L, 1826. 1st Ed, 1st Issue. 2 vols. 8vo, contemp calf gilt by Henington. With 2 charts, 4 plates & 10 views on 9 leaves. Some spotting. C Oct 15 (157) £2,600 [Quaritch]
— Narrative of Survey of the Intertropical and Western Coasts of Australia.... L, 1827. 2

vols. 8vo, half calf gilt; modern cloth. With 2 charts & 13 plates. Some margins cut close. bba Dec 18 (165) £250 [Smith]
Anr copy. Contemp half calf gilt; rubbed. With 2 folding charts & 12 (of 13) plates. One chart detached & torn with loss at lower right margin. Ck May 15 (54) £650

King, Stephen
See also: McCauley, Kirby
— Black Magic & Music. Bangor ME: Bangor Historical Society, 1983. Wraps. Without the ads. sg Sept 28 (729) $110
— Carrie. Garden City, 1974. In d/j. Sgd, 1979. cb Sept 28 (730) $275
Advance copy in ptd wraps. wa June 25 (366) $400
Advance proof copy. Orig wraps. O May 12 (119) $375
— Christine. West Kingston RI: Donald M. Grant, [1983]. One of 1,000. In d/j. cb Sept 28 (731) $170
— Cujo. NY: Mysterious Press, [1981]. One of 750. cb Sept 28 (733) $160; cb May 7 (186) $180
Anr Ed. NY: Viking, [1981]. In d/j. Inscr. cb May 7 (387) $70
— Danse Macabre. NY: Everest House, [1981]. One of 250. cb Sept 28 (735) $475
— The Dark Tower: The Gunslinger. West Kingston, Rhode Island: Grant, [1982]. In d/j. Inscr. cb May 7 (389) $180
— The Eyes of the Dragon. Bangor ME: Philtrum Press, 1984. One of 1,000. Illus by Kenneth R. Linkhauser. Half cloth. cb May 7 (390) $375
— Firestarter. Huntington Woods, Michigan: Phantasia Press, 1980. One of 26. Aluminum-coated asbestos. cb Sept 28 (739) $2,250
One of 725. In d/j. This copy sgd on 5 July. cb Sept 28 (740) $325
— The Plant.... Bangor: Philtrum Press, 1982. Out-of-series copy. Wraps. cb Sept 28 (741) $400
— The Plant...Part Two. Bangor ME: Philtrum Press, 1983. Out-of-series designer copy. Ptd wraps. cb Sept 28 (742) $500
— Salem's Lot. Garden City, 1975. In creased d/j; bdg bumped. Minor soiling to top & bottom page edges. cb Sept 28 (743) $375
Anr copy. In chipped & frayed 1st Issue d/j. A few words crossed out with blank marker on endpaper. wa June 25 (368) $140
— The Shining. Garden City, 1977. In d/j. cb Sept 28 (744) $190; cb May 7 (391) $90
— The Stand. Garden City, 1978. In chipped d/j. cb May 7 (394) $55
— Thinner. NY: New American Library,

[1984]. Special ABA Ed of uncorrected advance proofs. Wraps. cb Sept 28 (728) $100
[-] Whispers. Binghamton: David Schiff, [1983]. One of 350. Vol V, Nos 1-2. Cloth, orig wraps bound in. Special King issue, sgd by pbr & King. cb Sept 28 (749) $160

King, Stephen —& Straub, Peter
— The Talisman. NY, 1984. In d/j for Christine. Inscr by King, who thought he was signing Christine. wa May 30 (177) $60
Anr Ed. West Kingston: Donald M. Grant, 1984. T Feb 19 (73) £120

King, Thomas Butler —& Browne, J. Vincent
— Correspondence on the Subject of Appraisements.... Wash., 1852. Half mor, orig wraps bound in. cb Jan 8 (105) $50

King, William, 1650-1729
— State of the Protestants of Ireland. L, 1692. 4th Ed. 8vo, contemp calf; rebacked. Marginal worming. bba Apr 9 (311) £50 [Catnach]

King, William Ross
— Campaigning in Kaffirland, or Scenes and Adventures.... L, 1853. 8vo, modern half mor. SSA Oct 28 (668) R370
— The Sportsman and Naturalist in Canada. L, 1866. 8vo, orig cloth; rubbed, hinges starting. With 6 plates. AVP Nov 20 (162) C$150 [Wright]
Anr copy. Modern half mor. sg Oct 23 (368) $70

Kinglake, Alexander William, 1809-91
— Eothen, or Traces of Travel brought Home from the East. L, 1844. 1st Ed. 8vo, half calf. With 2 colored lithos, 1 folding. Lacking half-title; some foxing. bba Jan 15 (459) £45 [Hunt]
Anr Ed. L, 1913. One of 100. Illus by Frank Brangwyn. 4to, half vellum; soiled. cb Dec 4 (86) $200
— The Invasion of the Crimea. L, 1863-87. 8 vols. 8vo, half mor; corners bumped. cb Dec 18 (95) $180
Anr Ed. Edin., 1888-89. 9 vols. 8vo, contemp half calf; scuffed, corners worn. cb Feb 19 (151) $130

Kingsborough, Edward, Viscount
— Antiquities of Mexico: Comprising Facsimiles of Ancient Mexican Paintings and Hieroglyphics.... L, 1830-38. Illus by Augustine Aglio. 9 vols. Folio, contemp half mor. With 742 plates, including 547 hand-colored lithos, the uncolored lithos on india paper. With the 60-page section for

the intended Vol X bound in at end of Vol IX. With 2 litho tables. Some discoloration & foxing. Stoke Rochford copy. S Apr 24 (303) £35,000 [Israel]

Kingsley, Charles, 1819-75
See also: Limited Editions Club
— The Water-Babies. L & Cambr., 1863. 1st Ed. 8vo, mor gilt by Bayntun; soiled & frayed. Lacking prelim blank, L'Envoi leaf & final ad leaf. S May 6 (208) £150 [Peters] 1st Issue. Orig cloth. S Jan 13 (507) £140 [Daley]

Anr Ed. L, 1909. One of 250. Illus by Warwick Goble. 4to, orig vellum gilt. With 42 colored plates. pn Mar 5 (334) £120 [Frazer]

Anr copy. Orig vellum gilt; soiled. S Nov 17 (654) £80 [Marks]

Anr Ed. NY, [1916]. Illus by Jessie Willcox Smith. O Oct 21 (165) $130

— Works. L, 1901-3. One of 525 L.p. sets. 19 vols. 8vo, calf gilt. pnE Oct 15 (212) £380

Kingsley, Henry
— The Recollections of Geoffry Hamlyn. Cambr., 1859. 3 vols. 8vo, orig cloth; ends rubbed. sg Feb 12 (191) $90

Kininger, Vincenz George —& Mansfeld, Jos. Georg
— Abbildung der neuen Adjustirung der K.K. Armee. Vienna: Tranquillo Mollo, [1796-98]. Folio, contemp half russia gilt. With colored title, port & 46 hand-colored plates. S Oct 23 (190) £5,000 [Marks]

Kinloch, Alexander Angus Airlie
— Large Game Shooting in Thibet.... L, 1869. Vol I (of 2). 4to, orig cloth; worn, corners showing, joints frayed. With map, folding plate & 12 photos; front free endpaper detached. cb Nov 6 (187) £120

Anr Ed. Calcutta & L, 1885. 4to, orig cloth; worn, rear cover stained, hinges cracked. A few plates & page edges chipped. cb Nov 6 (188) £90

Kinsey, William Morgan
— Portugal Illustrated in a Series of Letters. L, 1829. 2d Ed. 8vo, mor gilt; With engraved title, 9 hand-colored & 23 plain plates & 10 leaves of music. pn June 18 (40) £150 [Shapero]

Kip, Joannes
— Britannia Illustrata or Views of Several of the Queens Palaces.... L: David Mortier, 1707. Folio, modern mor. With 79 double-page or folding views. Tp & index leaf repaired without loss. S June 25 (218) £3,600

Anr Ed. L, 1709. Folio, contemp calf; upper cover detached. With engraved title & 80 double-page views, 2 also folding. Minor repairs; a few plates browned. C Apr 8 (140) £3,500 [Mediolanum]

— Nouveau Theatre de la Grande Bretagne. L, 1724-15. Vol III only. Disbound. With 35 (of 49) plates mtd on guards. Some foxing; minor staining to edges. Sold w.a.f. C Oct 15 (57) £1,500 [Gilbert]

Anr copy. Vol IV only. With 1 map & 45 plates only (of 73). Mtd on guards; lacking title & text; some shaving & repairs. Sold w.a.f. C Oct 15 (58) £1,800 [Stafford]

Kipling, Rudyard, 1865-1936
— An Almanac of Twelve Sports.... L, 1898. Illus by William Nicholson. 4to, orig half cloth; rubbed. bba May 14 (159) £120 [Oram]; HN Nov 26 (2019) DM600

Anr copy. Orig half cloth; rubbed. pn Sept 18 (233) £140 [Ayres]; pnC Jan 23 (149) £90

Anr copy. Orig bds; worn. S Oct 6 (839) £80 [Elliott]

Anr copy. Orig half cloth; loose, spine def. S Mar 9 (759) £130 [Arjomane]

Anr copy. Pictorial bds; rubbed, front free endpaper lacking. sg June 4 (230) $175

Anr copy. Ptd bds; extremities worn & bumped, front free endpaper torn out & laid in. Lacking plate for March. sg June 18 (214) $130

One of 150. Orig half cloth; spine worn. Ck Apr 24 (39) £140

— American Notes. NY, [1891]. 1st Ed, 1st Issue. 8vo, half mor, orig wraps bound in. Half title chipped & detached; 1st page chipped. sg Sept 11 (219) $80

— "Captains Courageous." L, 1897. 1st English Pbd Ed. 8vo, orig cloth. sg Feb 12 (193) $150

— Departmental Ditties and Other Verses. Calcutta, 1888. 8vo, gray cloth variant bdg; rubbed. sg June 11 (267) $150

— The Five Nations. L, 1903. 1st Ed, one of 200. Half vellum; soiled. sg Sept 11 (220) $70

— The Jungle Book. With: The Second Jungle Book. L, 1894-95. 2 vols. 8vo, orig cloth; extremities worn, spines leaning, some hinges cracking. cb Sept 28 (752) $200

Anr copy. Orig cloth; rubbed. S Oct 7 (972) £100 [Bentley]

Anr copy. Mor gilt by Riviere with "Irene Xmas 1922" stamped in gilt in the center of the upper covers. S July 23 (84) £320 [Traylen]

Anr copy. Orig cloth; 1 cover blistered. sg Feb 12 (192) $225

— Just So Stories.... L, 1902. 1st Ed. Ck Oct 31 (174) £50

Anr copy. In d/j. S Dec 5 (319) £2,600 [de

Zayas]; wd June 19 (141) $250
— Kim. Paris, 1936. One of 15 on japon with illusts in color & in sepia & each vol with an orig watercolor bound in. Illus by Auguste Leroux. 2 vols. 4to, mor gilt by Fernarnd Gampert front covers gilt with head of Buddha & red mor onlay butterfly, orig wraps bound in; extremities rubbed, lower front joint of Vol II abraded. P Dec 15 (178) $600
— Poems, 1886-1929. L, 1929. One of 525, sgd. 3 vols. 4to, mor, in d/js. Etched port by Francis Dodd. pn Sept 28 (307) £280 [Maggs]

Anr copy. Mor gilt. Etched port by Francis Dodd, sgd in pencil. pnNY Sept 13 (251) $575

Anr copy. Mor; scuffed. Etched port by Francis Dodd. sg Dec 4 (99) $225

1st American Ed. Garden City, 1930. 3 vols. 4to, bds; soiled. sg June 11 (268) $130

— Puck of Pook's Hill. NY, 1906. Illus by Arthur Rackham. With 4 colored plates. sg Feb 12 (194) $80

— Sea and Sussex. L, 1926. One of 500. Illus by Donald Maxwell. 4to, half vellum, in d/j. bba Oct 30 (103) £120 [Edwards]

Anr copy. Half vellum. pnE Nov 12 (40) £55

— The Sin of Witchcraft. From The Times, March 15, 1900. L: The Times Office, 1901. 1st Separate Ed. 8 pp, 8vo, orig wraps; soiled & with ink marks on lower wrap. S July 23 (154) £250 [Maggs]

— A Song of the English. L, [1909]. One of 50. Illus by W. Heath Robinson. 4to, orig mor gilt. pnE Nov 12 (41) £280

One of 500. Vellum gilt. pnE Nov 17 (240) £85

— Songs of the Sea. L, 1927. One of 500, sgd. Illus by Donald Maxwell. 4to, half vellum. bba Oct 30 (102) £110 [Edwards]; pnE Nov 12 (39) £65

— Twenty Poems from Rudyard Kipling. L, 1918. 12mo, calf gilt by Sangorski & Sutcliffe; rubbed. cb Dec 4 (258) $60

— Works. L, 1913-38. Bombay Ed. 31 vols. Orig bdgs & d/js. Vol I sgd. pnE Oct 15 (215) £900

Anr Ed. L, 1913-20. One of 1,050; Vols 27-31 are 1 of 500. 31 vols. Mor gilt by Bayntun. sg Dec 4 (100) $3,800

Seven Seas Ed. Garden City, 1914-26. one of 1,050. 27 vols. cb Dec 4 (257) $170

Anr copy. Vols 1-26 (of 27). O May 12 (120) $300

Sussex Ed. L, 1937-39. one of 525. Orig mor by James Burn. pn Nov 20 (87) £3,800 [Sotheran]

Kippis, Andrew, 1725-95
— The Life of Captain James Cook. L, 1788. 4to, contemp calf; upper joint cracked. kh Mar 16 (283) A$480

Kirby, Frederick Vaughan
— In Haunts of Wild Game.... Edin. & L, 1896. 8vo, half lev gilt; spine faded. With frontis, folding colored map & 15 plates. cb Nov 6 (189) $95
— Sport in East Central Africa.... L: Rowland Ward, 1899. 8vo, orig cloth; stained, frayed, bookplate removed from front pastedown with stain & adhesion damage. cb Nov 6 (190) $350

Kirby, John Joshua, 1716-74
— Dr. Brook Taylor's Method of Perspective Made Easy.... Ipswich, 1755. 2d Ed. 2 parts in 1 vol. 4to, later half calf. With frontis & 50 folding plates. Ck May 29 (238) £150

Anr copy. Contemp half calf; rubbed. With frontis & 51 folding plates. T Feb 19 (533) £220

Kirby, William, 1759-1850
— On the Power, Wisdom, and Goodness of God.... L, 1835. 2 vols. 8vo, contemp calf; rubbed. With 19 plates. Bridgewater Treatise VII, Vols 10 & 11. O Oct 21 (97) £70

Kirby, William, 1759-1850 — & Spence, William
— An Introduction to Entomology.... L, 1826. 4 vols. 8vo, contemp half calf; scuffed. With 32 plates, some hand-colored. Some plates foxed. cb Oct 23 (124) $70

Kirby, William F., 1844-1912
— European Butterflies and Moths. L, [c.1880]. In orig 61 parts. 4to, orig wraps; some torn. pn Sept 18 (290) £150 [Pardny]

Anr Ed. L, 1882. 4to, cloth. With 1 plain & 61 hand-colored plates. A few leaves loose. bba Dec 18 (166) £55 [Grenville]

Anr copy. Half mor. Some spotting & soiling. S May 28 (588) £170

Anr Ed. L, 1889. 4to, orig cloth; rubbed. With 61 colored plates. pnE June 17 (105) £130

Anr copy. Orig cloth; rubbed, frayed & partially split on hinges. Library markings. T Mar 19 (118) £100

Anr Ed. L, 1903. ("The Butterflies and Moths of Europe.") 4to, half calf gilt. With 55 color plates. pn Jan 22 (115) £40 [Trottor]

Anr copy. Cloth. pn Jan 22 (272) £40 [Elliott]
— The Hero of Esthonia.... L, 1895. 2 vols. 8vo, calf gilt by Zaehnsdorf; rubbed. With folding map. O Oct 21 (96) $60

KIRCHER

Kircher, Athanasius, 1601-80

— Arca Noe. Amst., 1675. Folio, new half calf. With 9 plates only. Also lacking frontis, port & several leaves of text; some rough repairs in some lower margins; small hole in 13 affecting text. Sold w.a.f. S May 28 (711) £140

— Ars magna lucis et umbrae.... Rome, 1646. 1st Ed. Folio, contemp blindstamped pigskin; rebacked. Some spotting. FD Dec 2 (418) DM2,800

Anr copy. Contemp calf; rebacked, corners renewed. With engraved title, 34 plates & 2 leaves of tables. Lacking f.4; tear in inner blank margin of N1. Sold w.a.f. S May 21 (203) £450 [Hildebrandt]

— Ars magna sciendi, in XII libros digesta. Amst., 1669. 2 vols in 1. Folio, modern bds; new endpapers, bds tape-repaired. With engraved titles, port, plate of the Arbor Philosophica, plate with movable parts to be cut out, 1 volvelle & 5 large folding tables. Tp & port frayed, soiled & thumbed. cb June 4 (125) $200

— D'onder-aardse wereld. Amst., 1682. 2 vols. Folio, vellum. With engraved title & 13 (of 15) plates or maps. B Feb 25 (993) HF2,200

Anr copy. 2 vols in 1. Folio, vellum; back damaged. With engraved title & 15 plates or maps. B June 2 (1084) HF1,600

— Historia Eustachio-Mariana. Rome, 1665. 4to, contemp vellum; rebacked. With frontis & 6 plates, 5 folding & with 2 folding tables. Schwerdt-Jeanson copy. SM Mar 1 (302) FF3,800

— Magnes, sive de arte magnetica.... Rome, 1654. 3d Ed. Folio, contemp vellum with arms of Maximilian, Abbot of Lambach. Lacking 2 leaves of text. S May 28 (712) £300

— Mundus subterraneus.... Amst., 1665. 2 vols in 1. Folio, 18th-cent calf; restored & rebacked. With 2 engraved title, 2 ports & 21 plates & maps, 12 folding, all with contemp hand-coloring. Some leaves browned; a few marginal tears. C Dec 12 (242) £3,000 [Quaritch]

— Obeliscus Pamphilius. Rome, 1650. 1st Ed. Folio, contemp vellum; soiled, 1 corner worn. Tear to corner of engraved title, causing slight loss; paper flaw in title with slight loss. S May 6 (569) £1,000 [Pagan]

— Scrutinium physico-medicum contagiosae luis quae dicitur pestis. Leipzig, 1659. 4to, contemp calf. HK Nov 4 (1036) DM650

AMERICAN BOOK PRICES CURRENT

Kirchweger, Anton Joseph

— Miscroscopium Basilii Valentini sive commentariolum et cribrellum.... Berlin, 1790. 8vo, orig half cloth. FD Dec 2 (482) DM1,200

Kirk, Thomas, 1828-98

— The Forest Flora of New Zealand. Wellington, 1889. Folio, orig cloth; rubbed. pn Oct 23 (29) £90 [Browning]

Kirmse, Marguerite. See: Derrydale Press

Kitagawa, Utamaro, 1753?-1806. See: Grabhorn Printing

Kitaibel, Paul. See: Waldstein & Kitaibel

Kitchin, Thomas, d.1784

See also: Bowen & Kitchin

— Geographia Scotiae. L, 1749. 8vo, modern half mor. With 28 (of 33) hand-colored maps. Lacking tp & prelims. pn May 21 (368) £260 [Franks]

Anr Ed. L, 1756. 8vo, contemp calf; rubbed. With 33 double-page maps. Small wormholes touching neatlines. S Nov 17 (752) £250 [Nicholson]

— Pocket Atlas of the Counties of South Britain. L, 1769. Oblong 8vo, modern half mor gilt. With 51 maps on 45 sheets (10 laid down) plus 6 facsimile maps. pn May 21 (369) £320 [Green]

— Post-Chaise Companion through England and Wales.... L, 1767. Oblong 4to, half mor gilt; rubbed. With 104 maps on 52 plates. Tp & first few leaves of text browned with upper margin trimmed. pn May 21 (370) £160 [Postaprint]

Anr copy. Disbound. With 103 leaves of maps. Tp repaired. S July 28 (973) £260

Kitchin, Thomas, d.1784 —& Others

— A New Universal Atlas.... L: Laurie & Whittle, 1796. Folio, contemp calf; def. With 66 maps, several folding, hand-colored in outline. Some margins frayed & 1 or 2 def. S Oct 23 (229) £1,300 [Postaprint]

Kitchin, Thomas, d.1784 —& Jefferys, Thomas, d.1771

— Small English Atlas. L: R. Sayer, [1785]. 4to, modern half mor gilt. With engraved title & 50 maps. pn May 21 (372) £750 [Intercol]

Kitchiner, William, 1775?-1827

— The Cook's Oracle.... L, 1817. ("Apicius Redivivus; or, the Cook's Oracle....") 1st Ed. 12mo, contemp half lea; worn, spine ends damaged. sg Jan 15 (33) $175

Anr Ed. NY, 1825. 12mo, calf; rebound.

sg Jan 15 (34) $70

Kitto, John
— Palestine: the Bible History of he Holy Land. L. 1841. 3 vols. Contemp calf; rubbed. bba May 28 (293) £80 [Steinberg]

Klauber, Joseph & Johann
— Historiae Biblicae Veteris et Novi Testamenti...Biblische Geschichten, des Alten und Neuen Testaments.... Augsburg, [c.1750]. Oblong folio, later vellum. With 100 plates, a few loose; dampstained toward end. sg Oct 9 (118) $350

Klauber, Laurence Monroe
— Rattlesnakes: Their Habits, Life Histories, and Influence on Mankind. Berkeley, 1956. 2 vols. 4to, cloth, in frayed d/js. Sgd. sg Jan 15 (231) $100

Klebs, Arnold Carl
— Incunabula scientifica et medica. Bruges, 1938. Issued as Vol IV, Part 1, of Sarton's Osiris. sg May 14 (598) $80

Klein, William
— Moscow. NY, [1964]. Folio, cloth, in worn d/j; soiled. sg Nov 13 (72) $140; sg May 7 (51) $175
— New York. Geneva, 1956. 4to, cloth, in torn & repaired d/j. sg Nov 13 (73) $250
— Rome: The City and its People. NY, [1959]. 4to, cloth, in chipped d/j. sg Nov 13 (74) $175

Kleiner, Salomon, 1703-59
— Francofurtum ad Moenum floridum.... Augsburg: Johann Andreas Pfeffel, 1738. Oblong folio, 18th- or 19th-cent bds, rubbed. With engraved title, dedication & 8 plates. The views formerly matted & showing some discoloration in the margins beyond the plate marks; 4 plates trimmed narrower than the rest; folding plate chipped & browned at 1 corner beyond the plate-mark; nick in Plate 2. P Sept 24 (184) $4,750
— Representation exacte du chateau de chasse de...l'Eveque de Bamberg, nome Marquardsbourg ou Seehof.... Augsburg, 1731. Oblong folio, modern bds. With engraved title & 6 plates. Marginal repairs. Jeanson 1656. SM Mar 1 (303) FF38,000

Kleines...
— Kleines Bilder-Cabinet, zu Erhöung der Vier Spruchen. Augsburg: Johann Andreas Pfeffel, 1735. 8vo, half calf. Engraved throughout. Lacking pp 3 & 92. S June 17 (466) £400 [Buchholz]

Kleist, Heinrich von
— 54 Steindrucke zu kleinen Schriften von Heinrich von Kleist. Berlin: Bruno Cassirer, [1917]. One of 270, sgd by artist. Illus by Max Liebermann. 4to, orig vellum. With frontis & 54 illusts. HN Nov 26 (1942) DM1,600

Kleist, Heinrich von, 1777-1811
— Hinterlassene Schriften. Berlin, 1821. 8vo, unbound in modern half lea portfolio. FD June 11 (4048) DM2,800

Anr copy. Half calf. JG Oct 2 (1630) DM850
— Penthesilea, ein Trauerspiel. Stuttgart & Tuebingen: Cotta, [1808]. 8vo, contemp wraps; worn. FD Dec 2 (3538) DM5,000

Anr copy. Bds. Some browning & spotting; last leaves with some waterstaining. FD June 11 (4045) DM5,800

Klimt, Gustav, 1862-1918
— Fuenfundzwanzig Handzeichnungen. Vienna: Gilhoffer & Ranschburg, [1919]. One of 500. Folio, unbound as issued in bd folder. HN May 20 (2615) DM1,700

Kling, Joseph, 1811-76
— The Chess Euclid. L, 1849. Orig cloth; rebacked. pn Mar 26 (298) £45 [DeLucia]

Kmoch, Hans
— Rubinstein Gewinnt. Vienna, 1933. Orig cloth. Sgd by Rubinstein. pn Mar 26 (253) £160 [Kalinsky]

Knecht, Edmund
— A Manual of Dyeing for the Use of Practical Dyers.... L, 1893. 3 vols. 8vo, orig cloth; rubbed. bba Dec 4 (275) £70 [Maggs]

Kneeland, Samuel
— The Wonders of the Yosemite Valley.... Bost., 1871. ("The Wonders of Yosemite Valley and California.") 1st Ed. Illus by John Soule. 8vo, orig cloth; frayed. With 10 albumen prints. Prelims foxed. Inscr by Pbr. cb May 2 (165) $475

Knickerbocker, Diedrich. See: Irving, Washington

Knigge, Adolph Franz Friedrick, Baron von
— Ueber den Umgang mit Menschen.... Leipzig, 1789. 4to, contemp half calf gilt; worn. HK Nov 4 (2593) DM650

Knight, Charles, 1791-1873
— Old England: A Pictorial Museum of Regal, Ecclesiastical, Baronial, Municipal, and Popular Antiquities. L, 1845-[46]. 2 vols. Folio, contemp half lea. Some plates spotted; lacking 2 plates. sg Apr 23 (102) $150
— The Popular History of England. L, 1856-

62. 8 vols. 8vo, half calf. With 68 plates. Library copy, edges worn. wa Sept 25 (9) $85

Knight, Charles Raleigh

— Scenery on the Rhine. L: Dickinson & Son, [c.1850]. One of 130. Folio, contemp calf gilt; broken. With litho title & 17 plates. One plate imprint shaved; anr cropped. C Oct 15 (59) £1,800 [Chaponniere]

Anr copy. Oblong folio, contemp half lea; worn & broken. With litho title & 16 plates. Some spotting; a few blanks & text leaves have vertical folds; marginal repair on bottom edge of plate list leaf. K June 7 (188) $2,650

Knight, Cornelia, 1757-1837

— A Description of Latium, or La Campagna di Roma. L, 1805. 4to, contemp half calf; worn. With map & 20 tinted plates. S Jan 13 (397) £140 [Tosi]

Knight, Henry Gally

— The Ecclesiastical Architecture of Italy. L: Henry Bohn, 1842-44. 2 vols. Folio, half mor gilt; rubbed. With 2 chromolitho titles & 81 plates. S Apr 23 (92) £750 [Rainer]

Knight, John Alden

— Ruffed Grouse. NY, 1947. One of 210. 4to, half mor. Extra color plate laid in. sg Oct 23 (370) $325

— Woodcock. NY, 1944. One of 275. sg Oct 23 (371) $200

Knight, Richard Payne, 1750-1824

— An Account of the Remains of the Worship of Priapus...in the Kingdom of Naples. L, 1786. 4to, modern mor gilt. With port, 12 plates & 6 text illusts. sg Dec 4 (101) $325

Anr copy. Orig bds; backstrip deficient. With 18 plates. With 2 extra plates loosely inserted. T Sept 18 (521) £330

— An Inquiry into the Symbolical Language of Ancient Art and Mythology. Pvtly ptd, 1818. 8vo, contemp half calf; upper joint split, rubbed. bba Oct 16 (112) £140 [Mills]

— The Landscape, a Didactic Poem. L, 1794. 4to, orig wraps; worn & broken. With 3 plates, 2 folding. Plates & some other leaves dampstained. L.p. copy. bba Sept 25 (44) £150 [Bickersteth]

Knight, Thomas, 1759-1838

— Pomona Herefordiensis.... L, 1811. 4to, orig bds; worn. With 30 hand-colored plates. Some leaves spotted. Horticultural Society of New York—de Belder copy. S Apr 27 (190) £2,000 [Taylor]

Knip, Antoinette Pauline Jacqueline —& Temminck, Coenraad Jacob

— Les Pigeons. Paris, [1809]-11-[1835-43]. 2 vols. Folio, 19th-cent half mor gilt, not quite uniform. With 147 hand-finished color plates, nearly half of those in Vol II supplied from proof impressions. Some plates in Vol II stained or spotted & 2 are of smaller format. Godman-Dearden copy. S Apr 23 (42) £11,000 [Israel]

Kniphof, Johann Hieronymus

— Botanica in originali seu herbarium vivum. Erfurt: Johann Michael Funcke, 1747. Bound in 1 vol. Folio, contemp vellum gilt with arms of the Deutsche Akademie der Naturforscher on front cover. With 686 uncolored nature-ptd plates numbered 501-1186 & with 44-page Ms index. sg Dec 4 (102) $5,500

Anr Ed. Halle, 1757-64. 8 (of 12) parts in 4 vols. Folio, old sheep gilt; worn. With 5 letterpress titles within color-ptd nature-ptd floral & lepidopterous borders & 800 color-ptd nature-ptd plates, finished in colors by hand. One title torn without loss. Osberghaus-Arzt copy. P June 18 (102) $6,000

Anr copy. 12 vols in 4. Folio, contemp calf gilt; rebacked preserving orig spines. With 1,200 colored nature-ptd plates; index leaf to Vols III & IV & Plate 656 mtd before bdg. Massachusetts Horticultural Society —de Belder copy. S Apr 27 (193) £18,000 [Israel]

Knoch, August Wilhelm, 1742-1818

— Beitraege zur Insektengeschichte. Leipzig, 1718-83. 3 vols in 1. 8vo, 19th-cent half mor; worn. With 19 hand-colored plates. O Sept 23 (91) $290

Knoop, Johann Hermann

— Fructologie, ou description des arbres fruitiers. Amst., 1771. Bound with: Knoop. Pomologie. Amst., 1771. Folio, contemp calf; rebacked, orig spine preserved. With 39 folding handcolored plates. Some browning. Crahan copy. P Nov 25 (275) $500

— Fructologie, ou description des arbres frutieres. Amst., 1771. Bound with: Knoop. Pomologie. Amst., 1771. Folio, contemp half calf; rubbed. With 39 folding handcolored plates. Horticultural Society of New York—de Belder copy. S Apr 27 (192) £800 [Arader]

— Pomologia. Fructologia. Dendrologia. Leeuwarden, [1758-63]. Folio, contemp half calf; repaired & rebacked preserving old spine. With 39 hand-colored plates. Marginal stain to Plate 19 of Fructologia. Horticultural Society of New York—de

Belder copy. S Apr 27 (191) £2,200 [Arader]

Knorr, Christian, Baron von Rosenroth
— Kabbalah Denudata. Sulzbach: Abraham Lichtenthaler, 1677 & Frankfurt: Joannes David Zunner, 1684. 4 parts in 2 vols. 4to, calf; worn. Lacking 1 plate & 1 blank; some stains. S Feb 17 (71) £2,300 [Khazal]

Knorr, Georg Wolfgang, 1705-61
— Thesaurus rei herbariae hortensisque universalis.... Nuremberg, 1750-52. 2 vols in 3 parts. Folio, contemp calf; worn. With 301 hand-colored plates on 300 leaves. Slight surface wear to engraved title. Plesch—de Belder copy. S Apr 27 (194) £43,000 [Israel]

Knox, John, d.1778
— An Historical Journal of the Campaigns in North-America. L, 1769. 1st Ed. 2 vols. 4to, half mor. With folding map & frontis ports. S Oct 23 (419) £700 [Lake]

Anr copy. Contemp calf; joints cracked. With folding map. S June 25 (395) £750 [Voorhees]

Knox, John, d.1790
— A New Collection of Voyages, Discoveries and Travels.... L, 1767. 7 vols. 8vo, contemp sheep; worn. With 49 maps & plates. sg Dec 4 (103) $400

Knox, Robert, 1640?-1720
— An Historical Relation of the Island Ceylon.... L, 1681. 1st Ed. Folio, modern calf. With folding map & 15 plates. Lacking port; tears in outer blank margin but occasionally affecting text or touching platemark. S May 29 (1129) £220

Knox, Ronald Arbuthnott, 1888-1957
— Essays in Satire. L, [1928]. One of 250. Spine soiled. cb Apr 24 (1418) $50

— A Selection from the Occasional Sermons. L: Dropmore Press, 1949. One of 50. 4to, orig mor gilt, in d/j. S Oct 6 (724) £320 [Wendler]

Knuttel, Willem Pieter Cornelis
— Catalogus van de Pamfletten-Verzameling berustende in de Koninklijke Bibliotheek. The Hague, 1889-1920. 9 vols bound in 11. 4to, bds; several vols broken. sg Oct 2 (177) $300

Kobayashi Keisuke —& Ishizawa Takeo
— The Eggs of Japanese Birds. Kobe, 1932-40. One of 300. 2 vols in 15 parts. 4to, cloth. pn Oct 23 (235) £300 [Junk]

Kobbe, Theodor von —& Cornelius, Wilhelm
— Wanderungen an der Nord- und Ostsee. Leipzig: Wigand, [c.1840]. 2 vols in 1. 8vo, contemp cloth. With 28 (of 30) plates. Vol X of "Malerisches und romantisches Deutschland". JG Oct 2 (1088) DM1,000

Anr copy. Contemp half lea. With 29 (of 30) plates. Vol X of "Malerisches und romantisches Deutschland". JG Mar 20 (448) DM1,050

Kobell, Ferdinand
— Radierungen.... Nuremberg: Carl Mayer's Kunstanstalt, [1841]. 1st Ed, Issue not stated. Folio, cloth. With 178 plates on 79 leaves. A few pages chipped. bba Dec 18 (167) £220 [Erlini]

Kober, George M.
— Reminiscences of.... Wash., 1930. Vol I (all pbd). cb Jan 8 (280) $60

Koch, Rudolf
— The Book of Signs.... L, 1930. One of 500. Worn. O Jan 6 (108) $70

Koch, Rudolf —& Kredel, Fritz
— Das Blumenbuch. [Darmstadt], 1929-30. One of 1,000. 3 vols. 4to, orig bdgs. With 250 colored plates. JG Oct 2 (2095) DM1,900

Anr Ed. Mainz: Ptd by the Mainzer Presse for Insel-Verlag, 1929-30. 3 vols. 4to, orig bds. With 250 hand-colored plates. FD June 11 (5055) DM2,350

Kochno, Boris
— Le Ballet. [Paris, 1954]. 4to, orig cloth. With frontis by Picasso. B June 2 (987) HF500

Anr copy. Library markings. sg Feb 26 (125) $110; sg Feb 26 (170) $200

Kock, Charles Paul de, 1794-1850
— Madame Pantalon. Bost.; Frederick J. Quinby, [1904]. One of 100. Vol II only. Mor extra by the Harcourt Bindery. With 2 sgd etchings & 2 ink drawings by John Sloan. sg Apr 2 (129) $3,000

— Works. NY: Quinby, [1902-4]. One of 1,000. 25 vols only. Half mor gilt. sg Feb 12 (195) $700

Koehler, Sylvester Rosa. See: Grolier Club

Koeman, Cornelis
— Atlantes Neerlandici: Bibliography of Terrestrial, Maritime and Celestial Atlases and Pilot Books.... Amst., 1967-71. 5 vols. Folio, orig cloth. pn Dec 11 (6) £220 [Berryman]

Koenig, Alexander Ferdinand
— Katalog der nodo-oologischen Sammlung im Museum Alexander Koenig in Bonn. Bonn, 1931-32. 4 vols. 4to, orig wraps. B Feb 24 (223) HF260
— Die Voegel am Nil.... Bonn, 1937. Vol II: Raubvoegel, only. 4to, orig wraps. B Feb 24 (236) HF500

Koenig, Frans Niklaus
— Collection de costumes suisses tires du cabinet de M. Meyer d'Aarau. [Unterseen, 1804?]. 4to, contemp bds; spine def. With 24 hand-colored plates. HN May 20 (1432) DM5,300

Anr copy. Contemp bds; chipped at head & tail of spine. S Oct 23 (259) £3,500 [Chaponniere]

Koenig, Frans Nikolaus
— Neue Sammlung von Schweizertrachten. Zurich: Orell fussli, 1811. 4to, half mor preserving orig wraps. With 50 hand-colored plates. S Apr 23 (72) £1,200 [Maliye]

Koenig, Georg Matthias
— Bibliotheca vetus et nova...scriptorum, theologorum.... Altdorf, 1678. Folio, old bds. Tp mtd; lacking initial blank; profusely annotated. sg Mar 26 (160) $600

Koester, August
— Ship Models of the Seventeenth to the Nineteenth Centuries. NY, 1926. 4to, cloth; worn. With 124 plates. O Sept 23 (92) $100

Kohl, Johann Georg, 1808-78
— Die Donau von ihrem Ursprunge bis Pesth. Trieste, 1854. 4to, contemp half calf; worn. With engraved title, map & 27 plates. Tp frayed & with perforated stamp. bba Dec 18 (168) £160 [Elliott]

Kohn, Pinchas Jacob
— Osar Ha-Beurim We-ha-Perushim. Thesaurus of Hebrew Halachic Literature. L, 1952. 4to, cloth, in d/j. sg Sept 25 (46) $150

Kokoschka, Oskar
— Der gefesselte Columbus. [Berlin, 1921]. One of 70 on laid paper. 4to, orig bds. S Oct 6 (658) £70 [Zwemmer]
— Hiob, ein Drama. Berlin, 1917. Folio, orig half vellum; rubbed. S June 17 (121) £880 [Mytze]
— Die Traeumenden Knaben. Vienna, 1908. 4to, orig cloth. With 2 plain & 8 colored lithos. C Dec 12 (378) £4,200 [Joseph]; FD June 11 (5057) DM15,000

Anr copy. Orig cloth; soiled. With 11 lithos. S Dec 9 (11) £5,000 [Remingmore]

Anr Ed. Leipzig, 1917. One of 275. 4to, orig cloth. With 11 lithos. Reissue of 1908 Ed. S Dec 4 (12) £5,000 [Hrubich]

Kolben, Peter
— Caput Bonae Spei hodiernum; das ist: vollstaendige Beschreibung des Africanischen Vorguebuerges der Guten Hofnung. Nuremberg, 1719. 1st Ed. Folio, contemp vellum. SSA Oct 28 (674) R4,000
— Description du Cap de Bonne-Esperance.... Amst., 1741. 3 vols. 12mo, contemp calf. With 22 plates & 4 folding maps. SSA Oct 28 (672) R550
— Naaukeurige en uitvoerige Beschryving van de Kaap de Goede Hoop.... Amst., 1727. 1st Ed. 2 vols. Folio, contemp half calf; spine worn & splitting on Part I. With port & 44 plates & 5 folding maps. SSA Oct 28 (673) R3,200
— The Present State of the Cape of Good Hope.... L, 1731. Vol I only. contemp calf; spine rubbed. With frontis & 17 plates. C Oct 15 (48) £1,800 [Scott]

Koldewey, Karl, 1837-1908
— The German Arctic Expedition of 1869-70 and Narrative of the Wreck of the "Hansa" in the Ice. L, 1874. 1st Ed in English. 8vo, half calf gilt. pn Apr 30 (233) £260

Kondakov, Nikodim Pavlovich
— The Russian Icon. Prague: Seminarium Kondakovianum, 1928-33. Vol I only. Folio, loose in cloth portfolio as issued. With 65 mtd color plates. O Jan 6 (109) $130

Koop, Albert J.
— Early Chinese Bronzes. NY, 1924. 4to, cloth. With 110 plates. Tp stamped. cb July 30 (115) $150

Koops, Matthias
— Historical Account of the Substances which have been used to Describe Events.... L, 1801. 2d Ed. 8vo, half lea; front joint starting. Library markings, with perforated stamps on plate & title. sg Mar 26 (161) $550

Kops, Jan, 1765-1849
— Flora Batava. Amst., 1800-46. Vols I-IX (of 28). 4to, unbound sheets in 6 portfolios. With engraved titles to Vols I-VII & c.670 hand-colored plates. Sold w.a.f. S Apr 23 (40) £2,400 [Walford]

Koran
— The Koran. Hamburg, 1694. ("Al-Coranus s. Lex Islamitica Muhammedis.") 4to, contemp vellum bds; spine head damaged. S Nov 20 (414) £1,400

Anr Ed. L, 1734. Trans by George Sale. 4to, contemp calf; rebacked. With a folding map & 4 plates (3 folding). sg Dec 4 (104) $375

Anr copy. Modern lea. sg Mar 26 (162) $200

Kornbluth, C. M. See: Pohl & Kornbluth

Koster, Henry
— Travels in Brazil. L, 1816. 1st Ed. 4to, orig bds; rubbed & soiled. With 2 engraved maps & 8 hand-colored aquatint plates. T Feb 19 (222) £210

Kotschy, Karl & Georg Theodor
Plantae sive descriptio plantarum in expeditoine Tinneanae ad flumen Bahl-el-Ghasal.... Vienna, 1867. Folio, orig half cloth; rubbed & soiled, spine a little torn. With litho frontis, port, 3 tinted engraved illusts & 27 lithos, 26 wholly or partly hand-colored. Half-title spotted. de Belder copy. S Apr 27 (195) £1,400 [Solomon]

Kotschy, Theodor, c.1813-66
— Die Eichen Europas und des Orients. Vienna & Olmuetz, 1862. Folio, contemp cloth, armorial bdg. With 40 color plates. Library stamp at foot of each plate. S Oct 23 (710) £1,150 [Heues]

Kottenkamp, Franz
— History of Chivalry and Ancient Armour. L, 1857. Oblong 8vo, orig cloth; worn. With 62 hand-colored plates. 2 plates with marginal tears. S Sept 22 (250) £220 [Randall]

Kotzebue, Otto von, 1787-1846
— Neue Reise um die Welt.... Weimar & St. Petersburg, 1830. 2 vols in 1. 8vo, calf. With 2 frontises, 2 folding maps & 1 folding chart. FD June 11 (908) DM1,900

Anr copy. Contemp vellum over bds; endpapers renewed. sg Dec 4 (105) $550

— A New Voyage round the World. L, 1830. 2 vols. 12mo, contemp cloth; worn. With frontis & 3 folding maps. HN Nov 26 (340) DM1,600

Anr copy. Half mor gilt. With 2 plates & 3 maps. Some soiling. S Apr 24 (378) £350 [Maggs]

Kouchakji, Fahim. See: Eisen & Kouchakji

Krafft, Michael
— The American Distiller.... Phila., 1804. 1st Ed. 8vo, contemp sheep; rebacked, later endpapers. With 2 folding plates; 1 torn along margin; some tears & spotting. Crahan copy. P Nov 25 (276) $400

Kramer, Hilton
— Richard Lindner. Bost.: NY Graphic Society, [1975]. In d/j. With errata slip laid in. cb Mar 5 (117) $95

Krascheninnikoff, Stephan Petrovich
— The History of Kamtschatka and the Kurilski Islands. L & Gloucester, 1764. 1st Ed in English. 4to, contemp calf gilt; rebacked. With 2 maps & 5 plates. Some spotting. S June 25 (501) £600 [Sellers]

Krause, Georg A. J., 1858-1901
— Oologia universalis Palearctica. Stuttgart, 1906-13. 78 parts in 3 vols. 4to, orig wraps. pn Oct 23 (237) £360 [Quaritch]

Krauss, Friedrich Salomon
— Das Geschlechtleben in Glauben, Sitte und Brauch der Japaner. Leipzig, 1907. sg Feb 12 (92) $110

Krauss, Johann Ulrich
— Historischer Bilder Bibel. Augsburg, 1705. 5 parts in 1 vol. Folio, 18th-cent half calf gilt. With frontis & 126 (of 136) plates. FD June 11 (60) DM700

Anr copy. Contemp calf gilt. With 5 engraved titles, 5 frontises & 136 plates. HK Nov 4 (1710) DM1,900

Krazeisen, Carl
— Bildnisse augezeichneter Greichen und Philhellenen.... Munich, 1828-31. Folio, contemp bds. With 28 plates. Ptd title cut from one of the orig wraps & pasted on upper cover; litho map of Athens from the lower wrap of the last part loosely inserted. S Oct 23 (343) £7,000 [Tzarina]

Kredel, Fritz. See: Koch & Kredel

Kreider, Claude M.
— The Bamboo Rod and How to Build It. NY, 1951. In tape-repaired d/j. sg Oct 23 (373) $60

Kren, Thomas
— Renaissance Painting in Manuscripts: Treasures from the British Library. NY, [1983]. 4to, cloth. sg Jan 22 (202) $70

Kress...
— Kress Library of Business and Economics: Catalogue.... Bost., [1940]-64. Vol I only. 4to, cloth; worn. sg May 14 (324) $200

Krestinin, Vasili Vasilevich, 1729-95
— Kratkaya Istoriya o Gorode Arkhangelskom. St. Petersburg, 1792. 8vo, contemp mor gilt; scraped. With library blindstamp. S Apr 23 (168) £1,000

Kretschmer, Albert
— Deutsche Volkstrachten. Leipzig, [1887-90]. 4to, half lea gilt. With 90 plates. JG Oct 2 (656) DM2,000

Anr copy. Half calf gilt; worn. JG Mar 2 (659) DM2,000

Anr copy. Orig cloth; worn, spine def. JG Mar 20 (489) DM2,000

Kroniek...
— De Kroniek. Een Algemeen Weekblad. Amst., 1895-98. Vols I-IV (Nos 1-209) in 4 vols. 4to, orig cloth. With 157 (of 162) plates. One leaf torn. B Oct 7 (20) HF1,500

Kropotkin, Peter Alexeivich, Prince
— L'Anarchie, sa philosophie, son ideal. Paris, 1896. 8vo, orig wraps, unopened; torn. S Sept 23 (573) £120 [Libris]

Kruchenykh, A. —& Khlebnikov, Velemir
— Igra v adu. Svet [St. Petersburg], 1915. Orig wraps; backstrip repaired. S June 17 (184) £700 [Ex Libris]

Anr copy. Orig wraps; repaired. S June 17 (185) £420 [Gilbert]

— Mirskontsa. Moscow, [1912]. 4to, orig wraps; litho title & collaged design replaced. "An excellent copy, with the collage cut from embossed silver paper". S June 17 (186) £1,000 [Gilbert]

Krul, Jan Hermansz, 1602-46
— Pampiere Wereld, ofte Wereldsche Oeffeninge.... Amst., 1681. Folio, contemp calf; worn. Some browning; minimal worming. HK Nov 4 (1759) DM600

Kubin, Alfred
— Rauhnacht. Berlin, 1925. Folio, orig cloth folder. HK Nov 4 (3012) DM500

Anr copy. Loose as issued in orig folder. Text leaves minimally frayed. Sgd. sg Feb 5 (200) $175

— Von verschiedenen Ebenen. Berlin, 1922. One of 400. 4to, orig half cloth. HK Nov 4 (3012a) DM1,900

Kuehnel, Ernst —& Goetz, Hermann
— Indian Book Painting. L, 1926. Folio, cloth, in d/j. sg June 11 (269) $150

Kuhlemann, Johannes Th.
— Consolamini: Dichtungen. Cologne: Kairos Verlag, 1919. Illus by Max Ernst. Orig wraps. Inscr by Kuhlemann. S June 29 (3) £1,900 [Trinity Fine Arts]

Kume Yasuo
— Fine Handmade Papers of Japan. Tokyo, 1980. One of 200. 3 vols. Orig wraps. bba Oct 16 (431A) £320 [Mackay]

Kunz, George Frederick, 1856-1932
— The Curious Lore of Precious Stones. Phila., 1913. 1st Ed. Hinges cracking. cba Mar 5 (108) $55

— The Magic of Jewels and Charms. Phila. & L, 1915. 1st Ed. Inscr to Louis C. Tiffany. sg June 4 (193) $275

— Rings for the Finger.... Phila. & L, 1917. O Oct 21 (98) $90

Kurz, Martin
— Handbuch der Iberichen Bilddruke des XV. Jahrhunderts. Leipzig, 1931. 4to, wraps; torn. S Nov 10 (14) £60 [Maggs]

Kuttner, Henry. See: Padgett, Lewis

Kyriss, Ernst
— Verzierte gotische Einbaende im alten deutschen Sprachgebiet. Stuttgart, 1951-58. 4 vols. Wraps; worn. With 364 plates. sg May 14 (121) $400

Kyster, Anker. See: Larsen & Kyster

L

L. D. H. See: Mirabeau, Honore Gabriel Riquetti

La Bedoyere, Henri de
— Journal d'un voyage en Savoie.... Paris, 1849. 8vo, contemp half mor gilt. With frontis by Devilliers after Moreau le jeune in 3 states. L.p. copy. C Oct 15 (60) £140 [Cavendish]

La Blanchere, Henri de, 1821-80
— Les Oiseaux gibier. Paris: J. Rothschild, 1876. 4to, contemp half mor. Jeanson copy. SM Mar 1 (304) FF11,000

La Branche, George M. L.
— The Dry Fly and Fast Water. NY, 1914. sg Oct 23 (374) $70

Anr copy. Soiled & worn. wa Nov 6 (106) $55; wa Nov 6 (106) $55

— The Salmon and the Dry Fly. Bost., 1924. One of 775. Half lea. Inscr. sg Oct 23 (375) $90

La Caille, Nicholas Louis de, 1713-62
— Journal historique du voyage fait au Cap de Bonne-Esperance.... Paris, 1763. 16mo, contemp calf. With 2 folding maps. SSA Oct 28 (509) R720

La Calprenede, Gaultier de Cortes, Seigneur de

— Cassandra: the Fam'd Romance.... L, 1652. Folio, contemp calf gilt; spine ends restored. sg Apr 2 (130) $550

La Chambre, Marin Cureau de

— L'Art de connoitre les hommes. Amst., 1660. 12mo, vellum. B Feb 25 (912) HF220

— Traite de la connoissance des animaux.... Paris; Pierre Rocolet, 1647. 4to, contemp Parisian bdg of red mor decorated to a center & corner pattern with massed volutes & fleurons inside roll-tooled borders. S May 21 (103) £850 [Kraus]

Anr Ed. Paris: Pierre Rocolet, 1647 [colophon 1648]. 4to, contemp mor gilt. Jeanson copy. SM Mar 1 (306) FF18,000

La Chapelle, Vincent

— The Modern Cook. L, 1736. 3 vols. 8vo, contemp calf; rubbed. With folding frontises & 8 folding plates accompanied by 7 folding tables. Some plates frayed or separated at folds; O2 in Vol I with paper flaw affecting 1 letter. P Nov 25 (277) $1,000

La Condamine, Charles Marie de, 1701-74

— Journal du voyage fait par ordre du Roi a l'equateur. Paris, 1751-52. 3 parts in 1 vol. 4to, contemp calf; rebacked. With 3 folding maps & plans, 2 folding views, 1 full-page plate & 1 folding table. S Apr 24 (306) £250 [Crabtree]

Anr copy. Bound with: Supplement au Journal hHistorique du Voyage a l'Equateur. Paris, 1754. 4to, contemp calf; joints cracked, clumsy glue-repairs to joints & spine. With 7 maps & plates, 6 folding. Library copy. sg Nov 20 (90) $300

— Relation abregee d'un voyage fait dans l'interieur de l'Amerique meridionale. Maestricht, 1778. 8vo, contemp calf; rebacked, with orig backstrip laid down. With folding frontis & map. sg Nov 20 (92) $150

La Conterie, Jean Baptiste Jacques Le Verrier de. See: Le Verrier de la Conterie, Jean Baptiste Jacques

La Curne de Siant-Palaye, Jean Baptiste de

— Memoires sur l'ancienne chevalerie.... Paris, 1753. 4to, contemp mor gilt with arms of the Marquise de Pompadour [Olivier 2399, fer 1]. Jeanson copy. SM Mar 1 (310) FF28,000

Anr Ed. Paris: N. B. Duchesne, 1759-81. 3 vols. 12mo, contemp mor gilt. Jeanson 1520. SM Mar 1 (311) FF8,500

La Devansaye, A. de

— Les Chasses de l'Anjou. Paris: Delarue, [n.d.]. Folio, contemp silk with arms of Henri V. With 6 colored plates. Dedication copy. Jeanson copy. SM Mar 1 (312) FF28,000

La Faille, Clement

— Essai sur l'histoire naturelle de la taupe.... La Rochelle: Jerome Legier, 1769. 8vo, contemp mor gilt. Jeanson copy. SM Mar 1 (313) FF9,500

La Feuille, Daniel de

— Devises et emblemes anciennes & modernes.... Amst., 1691. 4to, later mor. With engraved title & 50 plates. 1 leaf repaired at inner margin; several leaves with tears along plate mark; some tears; tp holed with loss of signature. bba Nov 13 (16) £120 [P & P Books]

La Fontaine, Jean de, 1621-95

— 1685. - Contes et nouvelles en vers. Amst 2 vols in 1. 12mo, later mor. C Dec 3 (129) £420 [Vancook]

Anr copy. 2 vols. 12mo, modern mor gilt; upper cover of Vol I detached. pn Jan 22 (145) £180 [Tracchi]

Anr copy. 2 vols in 1. 12mo, mor gilt by Harvey. S May 21 (113) £420 [Bouvier]

— 1688-87. - Fables choisies mises en vers. Antwerp 4 parts in 1 vol. 8vo, 18th-cent calf; joints worn. S July 14 (407) £200

— 1699. - Contes et nouvelles en vers. Amst.: P. Brunel. 2 vols in 1. 12mo, 18th-cent calf; rebacked. Tear in lower margin of G7 just touching text; anr tear in fore-margin of B4 in Vol II; engraving on P4 recto in Vol II pasted down. S July 14 (406) £180

— 1718. - Amst. Illus by Romeyn de Hooghe. 2 vols in 1. 8vo, contemp vellum. sg Mar 26 (165) $100

— 1721. - Amst.: N. Etienne Lucas Illus by Romain de Hooge. 2 vols in 1. 8vo, contemp calf gilt. S July 28 (1202) £240

— 1755-59. - Fables choisies mises en vers. Paris 4 vols. Folio, mor by Raparlier. With frontis & 275 plates, that of Le Singe et le Leopard in Vol II in 1st state. Some plates reinserted; that of Fable 165 torn & expertly repaired. Port of Oudry by Tardieu after de l'Argilliere loosely inserted. C Dec 3 (135) £1,700 [Beres]

Anr copy. Contemp calf gilt; some joints repaired, scuffed, spines chipped. With frontis & 276 plates ("Le singe et le leopard" plate in 2 states). Some browning; front endpaper of Vol I waterstained. P Sept 24 (185) $2,100

Anr copy. Contemp calf gilt; artlessly restored, extremities rubbed. With frontis

LA FONTAINE

& 267 (of 275) plates. Some tears, chiefly marginal. P June 4 (103) $2,000

Anr copy. Contemp calf gilt; worn. With 273 (of 275) plates; Fore-edge of Plate 20 lightly shaved. sg Dec 18 (194) $400

Anr copy. Illus by Jean Baptiste Oudry. Late 19th-cent half mor gilt; worn. With frontis, port & 275 plates Some staining throughout. Sold w.a.f. CNY Dec 19 (112) $1,000

— 1762. - Contes et nouvelles en vers. Amst. [i.e., Paris] Trial issue for the Fermiers Generaux Ed. 2 vols. 8vo, contemp mor gilt. With 2 ports & 80 plates, 4 in 2 states & 12 other engravings inserted. C Dec 3 (130) £1,200 [Beres]

Fermiers-Generaux Ed. 2 vols. 8vo, contemp mor gilt. With 2 ports & 80 plates before letters. Inserted are 19 plates before letters. C Dec 3 (178) £2,600 [Chaponniere]

Anr copy. Contemp mor gilt; bds just showing through at several corners. With 2 ports & 80 plates. Frontis port in Vol I a bit shorter than the rest of the leaves. cb Feb 19 (153) $2,500

— 1764. - Amst. 2 vols. 8vo, contemp mor gilt; rubbed. With port & 80 plates, all before letters. C Dec 3 (132) £1,000 [Beres]

Anr copy. With 80 plates, all before letters. C Dec 3 (132) £1,000 [Beres]

Anr copy. Lacking 1 plate; tear in H6 in Vol II repaired. C May 13 (129) £200 [Greenwood]

Anr copy. 19th-cent calf; rubbed, joints split. With 80 plates. Lacking port. S Jan 13 (398) £170 [Archdale]

— 1777. - Paris 2 vols. 8vo, contemp calf gilt. With 2 engraved titles, port & 80 plates. C May 13 (24) £160 [O'Keefe]

— 1786. - Fabelen. Amst. 5 vols. 8vo, contemp half calf; rubbed. With engraved frontis, titles, port & 275 plates. bba Oct 16 (36) £250 [Archdale]

— 1786. - Fables choisies, mises en vers. Leiden 6 vols. Contemp half calf. With frontis & 271 (on 275) plates. B Oct 7 (874) HF800

— 1795. - Contes et nouvelles en vers. Paris 2 vols. 4to, mor gilt by Zaehnsdorf. L.p. copy on papier velin, extra-illus with 98 plates, all proofs before letters. C Dec 3 (134) £1,000 [Beres]

— 1814. - Oeuvres. Paris: imprimerie de Crapelet. 6 vols. 8vo, half mor gilt. With port & 25 plates. S Nov 27 (81) £150 [Olschki]

— 1838. - Fables. Paris: H. Fournier aine Illus by J. J. Grandville. 2 vols. 8vo, contemp half lea; rubbed. Some foxing; damp-wrinkled; marginal dampstains in 1st volume. O Oct 21 (99) $90

— 1839. - Paris Illus by Grandville. 2 vols. 8vo, contemp half sheep; worn. sg Dec 18 (181) $90

— 1842. - Paris: Daguin Freres. 2 vols. 8vo, contemp half lea. With 13 half-titles & 120 plates. B Feb 25 (937) HF260

— 1842. - Paris: H. Fournier Aine. 2 vols. 8vo, contemp calf. sg Feb 12 (164) $110

— 1929. - Tales and Novels of.... Nijmegen Holland: Pvtly ptd at G. J. Thieme One of 100. 2 vols. With 12 hand-colored etchings. cb Sept 11 (321) $700

— 1931. - The Fables. L. One of 525. Illus by Stephen Gooden. 2 vols. Vellum. Ck Dec 10 (275) £75

Anr copy. Vellum; soiled. pnNY Sept 13 (253) $350

— 1940-41. - Contes et Nouvelles en vers. Paris Ltd Ed. Illus by Brunelleschi. 5 vols in 2. 4to, orig wraps, unopened. pnNY Sept 13 (252) $200

— Les Amours de Psyche et de Cupidon. Paris: Didot le jeune, [1795]. Folio, contemp mor gilt extra; worn. With 8 plates. L.p. copy. S Nov 27 (82) £500 [Teuscher]

— Oeuvres. Paris, 1822-23. 6 vols. 8vo, contemp half lea gilt. Marginal dampstaining at end of Vol VI. sg Feb 12 (197) $150

La Fuye, Maurice de
— La Chasse des becassines. Blois: R. Duguet, 1922. One of 150. 8vo, half mor by Saulnier. Jeanson copy. SM Mar 1 (314) FF8,500

La Gueriniere, Francois Robichon de
— Ecole de cavalerie.... Paris, 1733. Folio, contemp calf; loose, spine def. Lacking 1 plate. JG Mar 20 (691) DM1,400

Anr Ed. Paris, 1751. Folio, 19th-cent cloth; worn & damaged. With engraved title & 24 plates. HN Nov 26 (267) DM1,800

Anr copy. Contemp calf; worn. With engraved title, frontis & 23/24 plates. A few plates with tears; some stains. S Apr 23 (67) £700 [Roncalli]

Anr Ed. Paris, 1769. 2 vols. 8vo, contemp calf gilt. HK Nov 4 (2047) DM750

La Harpe, Jean Francois de
— Abrege de l'histoire generale des voyages. Paris, 1820. 24 vols, (lacking Atlas). 8vo, contemp half sheep; worn, spines partly discolored. sg Nov 20 (93) $50

La Lande, Joseph Jerome le Francais de
— The Art of Papermaking. 1761. Mountcashel Castle: Ashling Press, 1976. One of 405, sgd by ptr. Trans by R. MacI. Atkinson. Folio, half calf. sg Jan 22 (212) $110
— Astronomie. Paris, 1771-81. 2d Ed. 4 vols. 4to, modern half calf. With 43 folding plates some stained. Ck Nov 7 (103) £250
— Des canaux de navigation et specialement du Canal de Languedoc. Paris, 1778. Folio, bdg not described. F Sept 12 (329) $200

La Live d'Epinay, Louise Florence Petronille de. See: D'Epinay, Louise Florence Petronille

La Marche, F. D.
— Dess musicalischen Jegerhorns Text oder Vers. Ohne die Musik. Neuberg an der Thonau: Johann Strasser, 1656. 4to, modern vellum. 1p repaired. Jeanson copy. SM Mar 1 (318) FF10,000

La Marre, L. H. de. See: Duhamel du Monceau & La Marre

La Mesangere, Pierre de
— Voyages en France. Paris: Chaigneau aine [1796-98]. 4 vols. 12mo, mor by Zaehnsdorf. Ptd on papier velin. With 8 ports, frontis & 23 plates, all proofs before letters. Extra-illus with 21 eau-forte proof plates. C May 13 (26) £220 [Greenwood]

La Mettrie, Julien Jean Offray de
— L'Homme machine. Leiden, 1748. Bound with: Luzac, Elie. L'homme plus que machine. 1748. 12mo, contemp calf; rubbed. S Mar 10 (956) £950 [Quaritch]

La Mothe le Vayer, Francois de, 1588-1672
— Hexameron rustique. Amst., 1698. 12mo, contemp calf gilt, with arms of Madame de Pompadour. C Dec 3 (178A) £150 [Beres]

La Motraye, Aubrey de
— Voyages en Anglois et en Francois.... L, 1732. Folio, contemp calf gilt, worn, joints split. With frontis & 9 plates & maps. Some dampwrinkling; library markings. sg Apr 23 (81) $175

La Motte-Fouque, Friedrich H. C. de, 1777-1843
— Undine. L, 1909. Illus by Arthur Rackham. 4to, orig cloth. B Oct 7 (284) HF250

Anr copy. Orig cloth. Inscr by Rackham to his sister in law, with an ink drawing. B June 17 (268) £580 [Gandolf]

One of 1,000. Vellum gilt; soiled. Outer edges of text leaves slightly dustsoiled. L Dec 11 (91) $200; pn Mar 5 (329) £180

[Sotheran]; pn May 21 (290) £120 [Joseph]; S May 6 (145) £200 [Hannas]

One of 1,000, sgd by Rackham. Orig vellum; rubbed & excessively spotted. With 15 mtd color plates. sg Oct 30 (129) $425

La Neuville, Adolphe, vicomte de
— La Chasse au chien d'arret. Blois: Typographie Giraud, 1860. 12mo, contemp shagreen with arms of Henri V. Inscr. Jeanson copy. SM Mar 1 (319) FF9,000

La Neziere, Joseph de
— Les Monuments Mauresques du Maroc. Paris: Albert Levy, [c.1922]. Folio, loose in bd portfolio, as issued. O Jan 6 (140) $100

La Noue, Francois de, 1531-91
— The Politicke and Militarie Discourses. L: T. Orwin, 1587. 4to, mor; wormed. With title & last leaf soiled & silked; A2 supplied in photocopy. sg Nov 20 (117) $250

La Perouse, Jean Francois Galaup de, 1741-88
— Voyage de La Perouse autour du monde.... Paris, 1797. 5 vols, including Atlas. 4to & folio, orig bds; covers of Atlas detached, worn, edges uncut. With port, engraved title & 69 charts & plates, many doublepage or folding. Marginal waterstains. S Oct 23 (64) £4,200 [Postaprint]

Anr copy. Atlas vol only. Folio, orig bds; scuffed. Some imprints shaved. S Jan 12 (328) £600 [Shapero]

Anr Ed. Nice: Editions les Chants des Spheres, 1971-72. ("Le Voyage extraordinaire.") Unique copy with pbr's certificate, suite of the illusts, suite of the illusts in bistre outline, watercolor drawings for 3 of the full-page illusts, 3 other large watercolors & 3 large ink drawings. Illus by H. Da Ros. 3 vols. 4to, mor gilt. With watercolor drawing for the double-page illust, sgd & framed. S June 17 (95) £1,300 [Schoeni]

— A Voyage Round the World in the Years 1785.... L, 1798. ("The Voyage of M. de la Perouse round the World....") 2 vols. 8vo, contemp half russia gilt, upper joints splitting, head of 1 spine worn. With 51 plates & maps. 1 plate imprint shaved. C Oct 15 (159) £340 [Heynes]

Anr copy. Atlas only. Orig bds; spine def. With engraved title & 68 charts & plates. Sold w.a.f. pn Apr 30 (100) £680 [Maggs]

Anr copy. 2 vols. 8vo, contemp calf; broken. With 48 (of 51) plates & maps. sg Nov 20 (95) $800

Anr copy. Contemp calf gilt; spines partly cracked. With 44 plates & 7 folding maps. Foxed. sg Apr 23 (82) $475

La Peyrere, Isaac de, 1594-1676
— Praeadamitae sive exercitatio super versibus.... [Amst.: Elzivir], 1655. 4to, contemp vellum; soiled. cb Oct 23 (131) $200

La Pilorgerie, Jules de. See: De La Pilorgerie, Jules

La Quintinye, Jean de
— The Compleat Gard'ner. L, 1693. 2 vols. Folio, contemp calf; worn & soiled. Lacking port. wa Sept 25 (124) $250
Anr copy. Trans by John Evelyn. Folio, contemp calf; rebacked, repaired & rubbed. With port & 11 plates, 2 double-page. H4 carefully attached along inner margin of H3; some browning & staining to margins. Crahan copy. P Nov 25 (281) $450
Anr copy. Calf. With port & 11 plates. pnE Dec 17 (213) £500 [Head]
— Instruction pour les jardins fruitiers et potagers.... Paris, 1690. 1st Ed. 2 vols. 4to, contemp calf; repaired, a few small holes in gilt spines. Some repairs & marginal worming. S Feb 24 (527) £320 [Wesley]
Anr Ed. Amst., 1697. Bound with: L'Art ou la Maniere Particuliere & seure de Tailler les Arbres Frutiers. Amst., 1699. 2 vols. 4to, contemp calf gilt with Garter crest of the 3d Duke of Buccleuch. C Apr 8 (133) £260 [Perrin Thomas]
Anr copy. 2 vols in 1. 4to, contemp calf; scuffed, ink notes on front endpages. With frontis & 13 plates, 2 folding. Small puncture to frontis; dampstains to c.20 pp at end. Hunt copy. CNY Nov 21 (164) $700
Anr Ed. Paris, 1715. 2 vols. 4to, contemp calf gilt; worn. With 13 plates. JG Mar 20 (673) DM1,300
Anr Ed. Paris, 1746. 2 vols. 4to, contemp calf; top of spines & corners worn or chipped. With 13 plates, 2 folding (1 folding plate torn). Hunt copy. CNY Nov 21 (166) $220
Anr Ed. Paris, 1839. 2 vols. 4to, old calf; rebacked & with bd edges renewed, new pastedowns. With 12 plates. Hunt copy. CNY Nov 21 (165) $220

La Rocque, Andre Jean
— Sommaire de considerations sur les possessions de l'Espagne dans le grand Archipel de l'Amerique.... Phila.: Jean Oswald, [1794]. Bound with: Examen sommaire de questions relatives a l'influence de la decouverte du nouveau monde.... Phila.: Jean Oswald, [1794]. And: Memoire sur cenne Question: La Louisiane peut-celle etre peuplee, par les moyens que l'Angleterre a employes pour etablis la partie de l'Amerique Septentrionale....

Phila.: Jean Oswald, [1794]. Modern vellum bds. S Apr 23 (267) £4,300 [Perrin]

La Roque Jean de
— Voyage fait par ordre du Roy Louis XIV dans la Palestine.... Paris, 1717. 12mo, contemp calf; worn. With 4 plates; 1 repaired on verso. sg Mar 26 (168) $175

La Rouliere, Louis de
— Traite de la chasse du lievre a courre en Poitou. Paris, 1888. One of 336. 4to, modern half shagreen. Jeanson copy. SM Mar 1 (322) FF1,900

La Serre, Jean Puget de. See: Puget de la Serre, Jean

La Taysonniere, Guillaume de, Seigneur de Chancin
— Sourdine royale, sonnant le boutesselle.... Paris: Frederic Morel, 1569. 8vo, mor gilt by Trautz-Bauzonnet. Jeanson copy. SM Mar 1 (327) FF14,000

La Touche, J. D. D.
— Handbook of the Birds of Eastern China. L, 1925-34. 2 vols. 8vo, half cloth. pn Oct 23 (239) £190 [Weldon & Wesley]

La Vallee, Joseph, 1801-78
— Technologie cynegetique. Origine et signification des termes.... Paris: Balitout, Questroy et Cie, [1863]. 8vo, half shagreen. Jeanson copy. SM Mar 1 (332) FF4,000

La Valliere, L. C. de la Baume-le-Blanc, Duc de. See: De Bure, Guillaume Francois

La Vardin, Jacques de
— The Historie of George Castriot, surnamed Scanderbeg, King of Albanie. L: William Ponsonby, 1596. 1st Ed in English. Folio, 18th-cent half calf; broken. Stained. STC 15318. sg Oct 9 (249) $325

La Varenne, Francois Pierre
— Le Cuisinier francois.... Lyon, 1663. 12mo, contemp vellum; soiled. Marginal tears. Crahan copy. P Nov 25 (282) $800

Labat, Jean Baptiste, 1663-1738
— Nouveau voyage aux Isles de l'Amerique. The Hague, 1724. 6 vols. 12mo, contemp half mor. With 62 (of 68) engraved maps & plates. Lacking table & 4 leaves at end and with a few marginal tears. bba Dec 171 £110 [Elliott]

Labaume, Eugene, 1783-1849
— A Circumstantial Narrative of the Campaign in Russia.... L, 1815. 8vo, later half vellum; worn, hinges cracking. cb Dec 18 (97) $65

Labillardiere, Jacques Julien Houton de, 1755-1834

— An Account of a Voyage in Search of La Perouse.... L, 1800. 2 vols. 8vo, modern half calf. Vol II lacking first blank, some staining. bba Nov 13 (95) £220 [Robertshaw]

Anr copy. Later mor. CA Apr 12 (154) A$600

— Novae Hollandiae plantarum specimen. Paris, 1804-6. Vol I only. contemp half mor; rubbed. With 142 plates. Some worming; some dampstains in lower margins; half-title foxed. S Oct 23 (711) £1,050 [Drowning]

— Relation du voyage a la recherche de La Perouse.... Paris, An VIII [1800]. 3 vols, including Atlas. 4to & folio, text in orig wraps, rebacked with cloth & Atlas in contemp half calf. With engraved title, folding maps & 43 plates. S Oct 23 (60) £900 [Perrin]

Atlas vol only. Paris, 1817. Folio, half calf; joints worn. With engraved title, double-page chart & 43 plates. Lower margin of title abraded. S Oct 23 (61) £800 [Browning]

Laborde, Alexandre L., Comte de, 1774-1842

— Descripcion de un Pavimento en Mosayco. Madrid, 1806. Folio, bdg not described but worn & def. With engraved title, 4 plain & 17 hand-colored plates. Affected by damp; 1st 20 pp with small hole. Sold w.a.f. S Nov 10 (115) £450 [Tucherson]

Laborde, Jean Benjamin de

— Choix de Chansons, mises en musique. Rouen: L. Lemonnyer, 1881. 4 vols. 8vo, modern mor gilt, orig wraps bound in. Facsimile of the 1773 Ed. cb Feb 19 (154) $375

Laborde, Leon de, 1807-69

— Journey through Arabia Petraea to Mount Sinai..., L, 1836. 8vo, orig cloth. With folding map & 24 plates. bba May 28 (294) £95 [Check]

Anr copy. Half calf gilt. bba May 28 (295) £70 [Shankland]

Anr copy. Contemp calf gilt; worn. With folding map & 26 plates. T Oct 16 (271) £50

Anr Ed. L, 1838. 8vo, orig cloth; slight wear, 1 signature starting. cb Feb 19 (155) $80

— Voyage de l'Arabie Petree. Paris, 1830. Folio, contemp half mor; spine worn. With 69 plates & maps, 2 hand-colored. Minor stains; 1 map detached. Ck Feb 27 (92) £1,250

Labruyerre, L., b.1723

— Les Ruses du braconage, mises a decouvert.... Paris: Lottin l'aine, 1771. 8vo, contemp red mor gilt with arms of Louis-Charles de Bourbon, comte d'Eu [Olivier 2606, fer 9]. Jeanson copy. SM Mar 1 (305) FF52,000

Lacepede, Bernard de la Ville, Comte de, 1756-1825

— Oeuvres. Paris: F. D. Pillot, 1832-31-32-33. 13 vols in 12. 8vo, contemp half calf; 3 backstrips def; some rubbing. Some discoloration throughout affecting most plates; 1 leaf with inkblot. CNY Nov 21 (160) $750

Lacepede, Bernard de La Ville sur Illon, Comte de, 1756-1825 —& Cuvier, Georges L. C., Baron, 1769-1832

— La Menagerie du Museum National d'Histoire Naturelle. Paris, 1801 [An X]. Folio, half mor. With 39 plates in colored & plain states. Some foxing of plates; text browned in places; 1 plate ink-stained in upper margin; some marginal repairs. S Oct 23 (712) £4,400 [Robinson]

Lacerda e Almeida, Francisco Jose Maria de

— The Lands of Cazembe. L, 1873. Ed by Sir Richard F. Burton. 8vo, orig cloth; lower edges of covers dampstained. With 2 marginal tears to map. cb June 8 (127) $55

Lacets...

— Les Lacets de Venus. Paris: Bailly, [c.1787]. 24mo, contemp calf with maroon onlays gilt over tinsel, with hand-painted miniatures on tinsel of 2 boys playing with boats & with ships & a house in the background on upper cover. Pichon copy. With related material. C Dec 3 (73) £2,000 [Sourget]

Laclos, Pierre A. F. Choderlos de, 1741-1803

Les Liaisons dangereuses. Paris, 1908. One of 40 on Japon with 3 suites of plates. 8vo, mor gilt, orig wraps bound in. S Oct 6 (615) £210 [Thorp]

Anr Ed. Paris: Black Sun Press, 1929. One of 1,000. Illus by Alastair. 2 vols. 4to, orig wraps. With 14 color plates. S Dec 4 (2) £400 [Maggs]

Anr copy. Wraps, unopened; Vol II in d/j. With 14 colored plates. sg Jan 8 (27) $70

Lacollombe, —— de

— Nouveaux Desseins d'arqueburesies. Pairs: Chez de Marteau, 1730. 4to, 19th-cent half shagreen. With 12 plates. SM Mar 1 (308) FF21,000

LACOMBE

Lacombe, Jacques, 1724-1811
— Dictionnaire de toutes les especes de chasses. Paris: H. Agasse, 1795-1811. 2 vols. 4to, text in half mor & Atlas in mor by Stroobants. Jeanson copy. SM Mar 1 (309) FF4,600

Lacombe, Jean de, Sieur de Quercy. See: Golden Cockerel Press

Lacombe, Paul, 1834-1919
— Livres d'heures imprimes au XVe et au XVIe siecle. Paris, 1907. 8vo, half mor, orig wraps bound in. sg May 14 (486) $140

Lacroix, Eugene
— Bibliographie des Ingenieurs, des Architectes.... Paris, 1863-67. Series I-III in 3 vols. 4to, bdg not described. Franklin Institute copy. F Sept 12 (60) $325

Lacroix, Paul, 1806-84
— Les Arts au moyen age et a l'epoque de la Renaissance. Paris, 1869-91. 9 vols. 8vo, half mor gilt. With 144 plates. B Oct 7 (1164) HF700
— Directoire, Consulat et Empire, moeurs et usages.... Paris, 1884. 8vo, half mor gilt; spine ends worn. sg Dec 18 (175) $50
— The Eighteenth Century: its Institutions, Customs, and Costumes. France, 1700-1789. NY, 1876. 8vo, recent half mor. With 21 color lithos & 351 wood-engravings. Tp foxed. cb Oct 23 (128) $75
— Moeurs, usages et costumes au moyen age et a l'epoque de la renaissance. Paris, 1871. 1st Ed. 4to, cloth; spine rubbed, front hinge cracking. With 15 plates. Lower margin dampstained, not affecting text. cb Oct 23 (127) $140

Anr copy. Mor extra; spine rubbed. With 15 color plates. cb Dec 4 (259) $80

4th Ed. Paris, 1874. 4to, cloth; rebacked. With 19 color plates. S Nov 10 (116) £130 [Hetherington]
— XVIIeme Siecle, Institutions, Usages et Costumes. Paris, 1880. 4to, cloth. With 16 color plates. sg Feb 5 (203) $110
— XVIIIme siecle: institutions, usages, et costumes.... Paris, 1875. 8vo, contemp half mor, orig wraps preserved. bba Oct 16 (386) £90 [Maggs]

Lada-Mocarski, Valerian
— Bibliography of Books on Alaska Published before 1868. New Haven, 1968. 4to, orig cloth, in d/j. cba Feb 5 (4) $130; O Sept 23 (93) $110; sg Oct 2 (3) $325; sg Jan 22 (211) $225; sg May 14 (18) $375

Ladd, William. See: Coleman, William

AMERICAN BOOK PRICES CURRENT

Ladies...
— The Ladies Cabinet Enlarged and Opened: Containing, Many Rare Secrets, and Rich Ornaments.... L: for G. Bedel & T. Collins, 1658. 12mo, contemp calf, armorial bdg; rebacked, free endpapers loose. Tp soiled. sg Dec 4 (106) $850

Laehr, Heinrich
— Die Literatur der Psychiatrie.... Berlin, 1900. 3 vols in 4. 8vo, half lea; spines scuffed; opening leaves of Vol I wrinkled. sg Oct 2 (204) $250

Lafitau, Joseph Francois, 1670-1740
— De Zeden der Wilden van Amerika. The Hague, 1731. 2 vols in 1. Folio, half lea; rubbed. With map & 42 plates. Some marginal dampstaining. L.p. copy. B Feb 25 (788) HF900
— Histoire des decouvertes et conquestes des Portugais dans le nouveau monde. Paris, 1733. 1st Ed. 2 vols. 4to, contemp calf; spines rubbed. With frontis, folding map & 14 plates, 1 folding. C Dec 12 (244) £450 [Israel]

Lafuente Ferrari, Enrique
— Goya: His Complete Etchings, Aquatints and Lithographs. NY: Abrams, [c.1962]. Folio, cloth, in d/j. Marginal streaks on Plate 1. cb Mar 5 (79) $60

Lahontan, Louis Armand, Baron de, 1666-1715
— New Voyages to North America. L, 1735. 2 vols. 8vo, contemp calf; worn. With 4 maps & 16 plates. ha Sept 19 (163) $650
— Nouveaux voyages de Mr. le Baron de Lahontan dans l'Amerique septentrionale.... The Hague, 1703. 2 vols in 1. 12mo, contemp sheep; spine def, rubbed. Lacking 2 plates; some tears. S Jan 12 (263) £240 [Ruddell]

Laigue, Estienne de
— Encomium brassicarum sive caulium.... Paris: Christian Wechel, 1531. 8vo, mor by Cape. Hunt copy. CNY Nov 21 (161) $2,200

Laing, David, Architect
— Plans, Elevations and Sections of Buildings Public and Private.... L, 1818. Folio, bdg not indicated. Library markings. Sold w.a.f. Franklin Institute copy. F Sept 12 (9) $300

Anr copy. Bds; worn. With 46 plates, some double-page. Slightly affected by damp. S May 29 (950) £230

Laing, John, 1809-80. See: Halkett & Laing

Laking, Sir Guy Francis
— A Record of European Armour and Arms through Seven Centuries. L, 1920-22. 5 vols. 4to, orig cloth; soiled. pnE June 17 (154) £280

Lally Tollendal, Thomas Arthur de, Count
— Memoirs of Count Lally.... L, 1766. 8vo, contemp calf; rubbed. bba Apr 9 (70) £85 [Hannas]

L'Alouete, Francois de
— Traite des nobles et des vertus dont ils sont formes.... Paris: Robert le Manier, 1577. 4to, contemp vellum with colored flowers. Jeanson copy. SM Mar 1 (316) FF19,000

Lamartine de Prat, Marie Louis Alphonse de, 1790-1869
— Cours familier de litterature. Paris, 1856-65. 20 vols. Contemp half mor; some spines chipped. Ck Sept 5 (191) £700

Lamb, Charles, 1775-1834
See also: Falstaff, Sir John; Fore-Edge Paintings
— Essays of Elia. Edin., 1885. 8vo, half mor by Bayntun. sg Sept 11 (221) $60
— Satan in Search of a Wife.... L, 1831. 12mo, mor gilt by Riviere. S Jan 13 (508) £120 [Bickersteth]
— Works. L, 1903. One of 300. Ed by William Macdonald. 12 vols. Half mor gilt. L.p. copy. wd Nov 12 (95) $325

Lamb, Charles & Mary
— Tales from Shakespeare. L, 1899. Illus by Arthur Rackham. 12mo, calf. With frontis & 11 plates. sg Oct 30 (125) $80

Anr Ed. L, 1909. One of 750. 4to, cloth. pnNY Sept 13 (277) $450

Anr copy. Orig cloth; soiled. With 12 colored plates. S Oct 6 (850) £300 [Storey]

One of 750, sgd by Rackham. Cloth. With 12 color plates. With the additional color plate. sg Oct 30 (126) $450

Lamb, Patrick
— Royal Cookery; or, the Complete Court-Cook.... L, 1710. 8vo, contemp sheep; loose, joints & front hinge crudely tape-reinforced. With 35 plates. sg Jan 15 (35) $400

Lambard, William, 1536-1601
— A Perambulation of Kent.... L, 1596. 2d Ed. 4to, modern mor. With 2 maps. Final leaf repaired. Ck Nov 21 (408) £350 [Tooley]

Anr copy. Vellum. Lacking map. pn May 21 (262) £100

Anr Ed. L, 1656. 8vo, old calf; worn. With 2 title pages, 1 lacking upper margin with no loss of text; 1st 12 leaves with worm to outer lower margin not affecting text. pn Mar 5 (120) £80 [Clarke]

Lambart, Richard, 6th Earl of Cavan
— A New System of Military Discipline....By a General Officer. Phila.: R. Aitken, 1776. 8vo, modern cloth. Foxed & dampstained; upper portion of tp & lower portion of last leaf torn away. sg Mar 12 (162) $400

Lambert, Canon of St. Omer
— Liber Floridus. Codex Autographus Bibliothecae Universitatis Gandavensis.... Ghent: Story-Scientia, 1968. One of 75 for the University Council. Ed by Alberto Derolez. Hunt copy. CNY Nov 21 (162) $200

Lambert, Aylmer Bouke
— A Description of the Genus Cinchona.... L, 1797. 4to, orig bds. With 13 folding plates. Library stamp on half-title. pnE Dec 17 (211) £280 [Traylen]
— A Description of the Genus Pinus. L, 1803-7. One of 25 colored copies. Folio, contemp russia gilt by Staggemeier with his ticket; slightly rubbed. With 47 plates, all but 3 colored by hand; some browning. Horticultural Society of New York—de Belder copy. S Apr 28 (199) £17,000 [Israel]

Anr Ed. L, 1828-37. 3 vols. 8vo, mor gilt by Bedford. With port & 100 plates, all but 2 hand-colored & heightened with varnish. C Oct 15 (238) £6,500 [Traylen]

Anr copy. 3 vols. Folio, contemp half mor; head of 1 spine missing. With port & 100 engraved & watercolor plates, all but 2 of the engraved plates colored by hand. Port & 1st title spotted & browned. Derby—de Belder copy. S Apr 28 (201) £8,000 [Israel]

Anr Ed. L, 1832. 2 vols. 8vo, contemp half mor; worn, head of 1 spine def. With port & 75 hand-colored plates. A few captions slightly cropped; 1 plate cut close; some discoloration at folds; some spotting. de Belder copy. S Apr 28 (200) £1,700 [Henly]

Anr copy. 19th-cent half calf. With port & 73 plates, 71 colored by hand. A few plates shaved. de Belder copy. S Apr 28 (202) £1,600 [Maiers]

Anr copy. Contemp half mor; minor wear. With port & 75 plates, 73 colored by hand. de Belder copy. S Apr 28 (203) £3,200 [Wilson]

Lambert, Edward
— The Art of Confectionary. Shewing the Various Methods.... L: T. Payne, 1761. 12mo, later mor; joints rubbed. Tp browned. Hunt copy. CNY Nov 21 (73) $550

Lambert, George Washington
— The Art of George W. Lambert. Sydney, 1924. One of 750. 4to, half cloth; spine poorly reinforced. Some leaves foxed at beginning. CA Oct 7 (100) A$260

Lambert, John
— Travels through Lower Canada and the United States of North America in the Years 1806, 1807, and 1808.... L, 1816. 3d Ed. 2 vols. 8vo, contemp mor gilt; spines rubbed. With 2 hand-colored maps & 16 plates, 6 colored by hand. S Feb 23 (26) £250 [McCall]

Lambert, Samuel W.
— The Oquossoc Angling Association, 1870-1970. Pvtly Ptd, 1970. One of 150. Half cloth. With TLs from Lambert laid in. sg Oct 23 (380) $250

Lampman, Ben Hur, 1886-1954
— A Leaf from French Eddy. Portland OR: Touchstone Press, 1965. One of 950. Syn, in d/j. sg Oct 23 (382) $70

Lancaster, Albert. See: Houzeau & Lancaster

Lanckoronska, Anna M. I. —& Oehler, Richard
— Die Buchillustration des XVIII Jahrhunderts in Deutschland, Oesterreich und der Schweiz. Leipzig, 1932-34. 3 vols. Folio, bds; Vols I and II, backstrip detached. sg Oct 2 (179) $400

Lande Collection, Lawrence M.
— The Lawrence Lande Collection of Canadiana in the Redpath Library of McGill University. Montreal, 1965. Folio, orig half lea. AVP Nov 20 (183) C$200 [Falconi]
Anr Ed. Montreal, 1965-71. One of 950 & 500. 2 vols, including Supplement. Half pigskin; foot of spine stained. O June 9 (94) $120

Lander, Richard & John
— Journal of an Expedition to Explore the Course and Termination of the Niger. L, 1832. 12mo, half lea; worn. With 2 maps & 6 plates, affected by foxing. sg Nov 20 (94) $120

Landi, Ortensio
— Commentario dele piu notabili & mostruose cose d'Italia...inventori de le cose, che si mangiano. Venice: 'al segno del pozzo,' 1550. 8vo, modern half vellum. Lacking final blank; E4.5 transposed; tp may be supplied from anr copy; A2 damaged in gutters & mended costing bits of a few letters; some leaves guarded with tissue occasionally touching text; some dampstains. P Nov 25 (278) $250

Landon, Charles Paul, 1760-1826
— Annales du Musee et de l'Ecole Moderne des Beaux-Arts. Paris, 1902-8. Vols 1-35 (of 42). 8vo, orig cloth; soiled. Ck Nov 7 (196) £130

Landor, A. Henry Savage
— Across Widest Africa. L, 1907. 2 vols. orig cloth; rubbed, spines torn; Vol II hinges cracked. cb Nov 6 (191) $95
— In the Forbidden Land: An Account of a Journey into Tibet.... NY, 1899. 2 vols. 8vo, orig cloth. sg Apr 23 (86) $110

Landor, Walter Savage, 1775-1864
See also: Limited Editions Club
— Imaginary Conversations of Literary Men and Statesmen. L, 1824-29. Series 1 & 2 in 5 vols. 8vo, orig bds; 2d Series bdgs fragile. Hogan copy. sg Apr 2 (131) $325
— Poemata et inscriptiones. L, 1847. 12mo, contemp calf gilt; rubbed. Inscr. bba Aug 28 (220) £50 [Quaritch]

Landscape...
See also: Finden, William
— The Landscape Annual. L, 1830-39. 10 vols (all pbd). 8vo, mor; joints rubbed, library numbers pasted onto base of spines. Library markings, including perforated stamps. bba Jan 15 (242) £500 [Ashcroft]

Landseer, Thomas, 1795-1880. See: Lowry & Landseer

Lane, William Coolidge —& Browne, Nina E.
— A.L.A. Portrait Index. Wash., 1906. Orig cloth; rubbed. bba Nov 13 (67) £40 [Watkins]

Lanery d'Arc, Pierre
— Le Livre d'Or de Jeanne d'Arc.... Paris, 1894. One of 330. 8vo, contemp half calf, orig wraps bound in; broken. With 18-page pamphlet bound in at end. sg Jan 22 (207) $90

Lanfrancus, Mediolanensis
— La Cirugia de Maestre Lanfranco Mediolanense. Seville: tres alemanes companeros, 15 May 1495. Folio, 19th-cent calf with ptr's mark reproduced in blind on sides; spine def. Last 2 leaves lightly stained at head. Unpressed copy. 132 leaves. Goff L-52. S June 25 (119) £17,000 [Quaritch]

Lang, Andrew, 1844-1912
— The Princess Nobody. A Tale of Fairyland. L: Longmans Green & Co., [1884]. Illus by Richard Doyle. 4to, orig half cloth. 2 leaves torn & repaired. L July 2 (62) £70

Lang, Carl
— Sammlung mahlerisch gezeichneter und nach der Natur ausgemahlter Blumen, bluethen und fruechte. Heilbronn am Nekar, 1796. 4to, disbound, orig wraps trimmed & mtd to front & rear endpapers. With 12 hand-colored plates & 12 uncolored duplicates. sg Dec 18 (173) $700

Lang, Henry Charles
— Rhopalocera Europae. L, 1884. 2 vols. 4to, contemp half mor. With 82 colored plates. S May 28 (590) £170
Anr copy. Cloth. xxx

Lang, John Dunmore
— An Historical and Statistical Account of New South Wales. L, 1834. 1st Ed. 2 vols. 8vo, orig cloth. With folding map colored in outline. CA Apr 12 (156) A$350

Langbaine, Gerard, 1656-92
An Account of the English Dramatick Poets. Oxford, 1691. 1st Ed. 8vo, modern half calf. A few leaves torn, not affecting text; wormed, mostly marginal, but affecting text near end. S Sept 22 (36) £55 [Vine]
Anr copy. Mor gilt; broken. sg Mar 26 (167) $60

Lange, Ludwig
— Der Rhein und der Rheinlande. Darmstadt, 1855-[59]. 3 vols. 8vo, modern half calf gilt; worn. With 3 engraved titles & 439 plates. VH Sept 12 (125) DM14,000

Langford, Thomas
— Plain and Full Instructions to Raise all sorts of Fruit-Trees. L, 1681. 1st Ed. 8vo, modern calf. With 2 plates. pn Mar 5 (29) £100 [Traylen]

Langland, William, 1332?-1400?
See also: Fore-Edge Paintings
— The Vision of Pierce Plowman. [New Rochelle: Elston Press, 1901]. ("The Vision of William concerning Piers the Plowman.") One of 210. Folio, half cloth; soiled & stained. sg June 11 (181) $50

Langley, Batty, 1696-1751
— New Principles of Gardening. L, 1728. 1st Ed. 4to, contemp calf; rebacked in mor, with new endpapers. With 28 folding plates. Several plates with clean tears at fold; Plate X with repaired tear to image; several plates cropped to within platemark on 1 edge, affecting engraver's name in 1 case. Hunt copy. CNY Nov 21 (163) $850
Anr copy. Contemp calf; scuffed; lower cover wormed. Lacking Plate 22; some tears to folds of plates; marginal stain to a few leaves. Crahan copy. P Nov 25 (279) $500

Anr copy. Contemp calf; broken. With frontis & 25 plates only. Some tears & repairs. S Feb 24 (585) £220 [Hunnersdorf]
— Pomona: or the Fruit-Garden Illustrated.... L, 1729. Folio, cloth. With 68 plates, some double-page. A few plates torn & repaired, some marginally defective or shaved. bba Dec 18 (172) £650 [Grenville]
Anr copy. Calf; rubbed. With 68 plates numbered as 79; 1 torn in fold. Crahan copy. P Nov 25 (280) $1,200
— A Sure Method of Improving Estates. L, 1728. 8vo, contemp calf. Ck Jan 16 (55) £160

Langley, Batty & Thomas
— Ancient Architecture, Restored and Improved.... [L, 1742]. 4to, contemp half calf; rubbed. With engraved title & 64 plates. S May 29 (1214) £900
— Gothic Architecture.... L, 1747. 4to, contemp half calf; joints split, rubbed. With 32 plates. bba Sept 25 (280) £440 [Weinreb]

Langley, Henry G.
— Langley's San Francisco Directory for the Year 1882. San Francisco, 1882. Orig bds; rubbed, spine worn & chipped. Lacking the map. cb Oct 9 (198) $110
— Langley's San Francisco Directory for the Year 1883. San Francisco, 1883. Orig bds, rebacked with modern cloth; rubbed. Lacking the map. b Oct 9 (199) $110
— The Pacific Coast Business Directory for 1867.... San Francisco, 1867. Orig bds with lea spine; hinge cracking, spine chipped, rubbed. cb Oct 9 (66) $200
— The San Francisco Directory for the Year 1858 San Francisco, 1858. Modern half mor. Top margins dampstained throughout. cb Oct 9 (177) $160
— The San Francisco Directory for the Year 1859. San Francisco, 1859. Orig bds, crudely rebacked; rubbed, worn. cb Oct 9 (178) $170
— The San Francisco Directory for the Year 1860. San Francisco, 1860. Modern cloth. cb Oct 9 (179) $120
— The San Francisco Directory for the Year 1864. San Francisco, 1864. Orig bds rebacked with modern cloth; rubbed & soiled. Pp 129-30 supplied in facsimile. cb Oct 9 (182) $55
— The San Francisco Directory for the Year 1865 San Francisco, 1865. Modern cloth. Map torn in several places. cb Oct 9 (183) $55
— The San Francisco Directory for the Year 1867 San Francisco, 1867. Rebound in modern cloth, orig bd covering laid on. Lacking the map. cb Oct 9 (184) $140

LANGLEY

— The San Francisco Directory for the Year 1868. San Francisco, 1868. Orig bds; rubbed & worn. cb Oct 9 (185) $100
— The San Francisco Directory for the Year 1869 San Francisco, 1869. Orig bds. cb Oct 9 (186) $160

Anr copy. Contemp bds, rebacked with modern cloth. Lacking the map. cb Oct 9 (187) $100

— The San Francisco Directory for the Year 1871. San Francisco, 1871. Orig bds. "In exceptionally good condition". Inscr. cb Oct 9 (188) $400
— The San Francisco Directory for the Year 1874. San Francisco, 1874. Orig bds, rebacked with cloth; rubbed, worn, several hinges cracked. Lacking the mpa. cb Oct 9 (191) $60
— The San Francisco Directory for the Year 1876. San Francisco, 1876. Orig bds. Lacking the map. cb Oct 9 (192) $65

Langley, Samuel Pierpont, 1834-1906
— Experiments in Aerodynamics.... Wash., 1891. 4to, orig cloth; spine chipped. Inscr. sg Jan 15 (274) $225
— Langley Memoir on Mechanical Flight. Wash., 1911. Cloth; worn, inner joint broken. Smithsonian Contributions to Knowledge, Vol 27, No 3. O Sept 23 (94) $80

Anr copy. 2 parts in one. Wraps; chipped & soiled. wa Nov 6 (8) $70

Langlois, Jean Julien
— Dictionnaire des chasses, contenant l'explication des termes.... Paris: Prault, 1739. 12mo, contemp mor with arms of Louis XV. Jeanson copy. SM Mar 1 (321) FF12,000

Langsdorff, Georg Heinrich von
— Voyages and Travels in Various Parts of the World.... L, 1813-14. 2 vols. 4to, half calf. With port & 14 plates only. pn Apr 30 (272) £260

Anr copy. Vol I only. 4to, contemp calf; rebacked. sg Apr 23 (87) $100

Langstroth, Lorenzo Lorraine, 1810-95
— Langstroth on the Hive and the Honey-Bee.... Northampton MA, 1853. 8vo, modern cloth. Library markings on tp. sg Jan 15 (157) $200

Languet, Hubert, 1518-81
— Vindiciae contra tyrannos. Edin. [but Basel?], 1579. 8vo, 18th-cent calf; rebacked. Lacking final blank. S Nov 27 (185) £750 [Abrams]

Anr Ed. Hanau: Guiliemus Antonius, 1595. 8vo, modern half vellum. sg Oct 9 (247) $110

AMERICAN BOOK PRICES CURRENT

Lanier, Henry W.
See also: Derrydale Press
— Greenwich Village, Today & Yesterday. NY, [1949]. 1st Ed. Illus by Berenice Abbott. In d/j. wa Nov 6 (274) $65

Lanman, Charles, 1819-95
— Adventures of an Angler in Canada.... L, 1848. 8vo, cloth; worn. With title & margin of frontis dampstained. sg Oct 23 (383) $150

Lansing, Abraham
— Recollections. [NY]: Pvtly ptd, 1909. Ltd Ed. Ed by Charles E. Fitch. sg Oct 23 (384) $130

Lapauze, Henry, 1867-1925
— Ingres. Sa Vie et son oeuvre. Paris, 1911. 4to, half lea, orig wraps bound in; rubbed. O Jan 6 (110) $80

Laplace, Cyrille Pierre Theodore
— Voyage autour du monde, par les mers de l'Inde et de Chine.... Paris, 1833-35. Atlas only. Half calf; broken. With engraved title & 11 charts. S Jan 12 (330) £400 [Maggs]

Lark...
— The Lark. San Francisco, 1895-97. Nos 1-24 plus Epilark in 2 vols. Orig cloth; some chipping. Sold w.a.f. O Mar 24 (102) $70

Larkin, Philip
— The Less Deceived. Hessle: Marvell Press, 1955. In d/j. Ck Dec 10 (356) £100

Anr copy. In d/j. Inscr. Ck Jan 30 (155A) £180; T Feb 18 (118) £85

Larrey, Isaac de
— Geschiedenis van Engelandt, Schotlandt en Ierlandt. Amst., 1728-41. 4 vols. Folio, contemp vellum; soiled, minor defs. With 2 frontises, 4 vignette titles, 4 large folding plates, 67 ports & 4 folding maps. wa Sept 25 (539) $220

Larsen, Sofus Christian —& Kyster, Anker
— Danish Eighteenth Century Bindings. Copenhagen & L, 1930. 4to, half cloth; worn. With 102 plates. O June 16 (120) $130

Lartigue, J. H.
— Boyhood Photos of J. H. Lartigue: The Family Album of a Gilded Age. [Lausanne]: Ami Guichard, [1966]. Oblong 4to, cloth; rubbed. O Sept 23 (95) $130; sg May 7 (52) $150

Anr copy. Cloth; upper cover stained. wa June 25 (98) $100; wa NOv 6 (322) $120

Las Casas, Bartolome de. See: Casas, Bartolome de las

690

Lascaris, Evadne. See: Golden Cockerel Press

Lasker, Emanuel, 1868-1944
— Common Sense in Chess. L, 1896. 1st Ed. Half calf gilt. Inscr. pn Mar 26 (434) £95 [De Lucia]
— Der Internationale Schachkongress zu St. Petersburg, 1909. Berlin, 1909. Orig cloth. pn Mar 26 (67) £80 [Finestein]

Lassaigne, Jacques
— The Ceiling of the Paris Opera. NY, [1966]. Illus by Marc Chagall. 4to, cloth, in d/j. Folding study of the ceiling laid in. sg Sept 25 (58) $60
— Chagall. [Paris]: Maeght, [1957]. 4to, wraps. With 15 lithographs by Chagall. FD June 11 (4855) DM1,700; HN Nov 26 (1760) DM1,100

Anr copy. Orig bds; spine ends worn. Inscr, 1965. pn Mar 5 (146) £800 [Marks]
— Marc Chagall: dessins et aquarelles pour le ballet. Paris, [1969]. 4to, cloth, in d/j. With orig colored lithograph. JG Oct 2 (1887) DM900

Lassels, Richard, 1603?-68
— The Voyage of Italy.... Paris & L, 1670. 2 parts in 1 vol. 12mo, contemp calf; rubbed, rebacked. Some browning & pencillings. S July 14 (329) £220

Lasso de la Vega, Garcia, 1539?-1616
— La Florida del Inca.... Madrid, 1723. Folio, old vellum. S Apr 24 (261) £700 [Perrin]

Anr copy. Part 1 only. Contemp vellum; hinges split. Tp rebacked with paper; most of text dampstained at outer margins; library bookplate. sg Sept 18 (101) $90; sg Mar 12 (123) $150
— Histoire de la conquete de la Floride. Leiden, 1731. 2 vols. 8vo, contemp calf; spine ends worn. With 9 folding plates & folding map with 2 minor tears. Vol I lacking last leaves; Vol II with final index leaves wormed & lacking front free endpaper. sg Sept 18 (102) $425
— Historia general del Peru.... Cordova, 1617. 1st Ed, 2d Issue. Folio, old vellum; worn. Tp stained & torn at inner margin; K8 torn at margin & small hole in O7 with slight loss; minor marginal tears at beginning; some stains to margins. S Apr 24 (305) £1,700 [Fleming]

2d Ed. Madrid, 1722. Folio, vellum; tear at fore-edge of front cover & at spine ends. Small wormhole in bottom corner from Bbb1-Hhh1. sg Sept 18 (103) $175
— Primera parte de los commentarios reales....

Madrid, 1723. Folio, contemp vellum. Tp creased without tears; Index with light dampstains in outer edges. sg Sept 18 (104) $225
— The Royal Commentaries of Peru. L: Miles Flesher for Christopher Wilkinson, 1688. Folio, contemp calf; rebacked, corners worn. With frontis & 9 (of 10) plates & an extraneous plate laid in. sg Sept 18 (104A) $225

Last...
— The Last Newes from Ireland.... L, 1641. 4to, modern half mor. Library label pasted to title ft with stamp on verso. bba Apr 9 (298) £120 [Lawson]

Latham, Charles
— In English Homes. L, 1907-9. 2d Ed. 3 vols. Folio, orig cloth; rubbed. Some soiling to Vol III. S Nov 10 (118) £90 [Woodroffe]; S May 6 (387) £75 [Stodard]

Latham, John, 1740-1837
— A General Synopsis of Birds. L, 1781-85. 3 vols in 6. Together with: Supplement to the General Synopsis.... L, 1787. And: Supplement II.... L, 1801. And: Index ornithologicus.... L, 1790. 2 vols. Together, 10 vols. 4to. Cloth. Plates all perforated or library-stamped on engraved surface. bba Jan 15 (411) £200 [Barker]

Anr copy. 5 (of 6) parts in 3 vols; lacking Vol II, Part 2. Modern cloth. Library markings. bba Feb 5 (313A) £130 [Rainer]

Anr copy. 3 vols in 6. Together with: Supplement to the General Synopsis.... L, 1787. 7 vols. Later half mor; worn. With 119 hand-colored plates & 7 hand-colored titles. cb Feb 19 (157) $900

Anr copy. 3 vols in 6. Together with: Supplement to the General Synopsis.... L, 1787. And: Supplement II.... L, 1801. And: Index ornithologicus.... L, 1790. 2 vols. Together, 10 vols. 4to. Contemp half calf; worn, some joints split, 1 cover detached. With 142 hand-colored plates. Some foxing; 4 leaves with holes. S Jan 13 (399) £1,200 [Vitale]

Latham, Simon
— Falconry. L, 1633. 2 parts in 1 vol. 4to, 18th-cent calf; rubbed. Jeanson 1695. SM Mar 1 (328) FF4,000

Anr Ed. L: R. Hodgkinsonne for Thomas Rooks, 1658. ("Lathams faulconry, or the faulcons lure and cure.") 8vo, 19th-cent shagreen. Jeanson copy. SM Mar 1 (329) FF6,500

Latham's. See: Latham, Simon

Lathy, Thomas Pike
— The Angler; A Poem in Ten Cantos.... L, 1820. 8vo, lea gilt; front free endpaper detached. Frontis & tp foxed. sg Oct 23 (385) $140

Latimer, Hugh
— 27 Sermons Preached by the Ryght Reverende.... L: J. Day, 1562. Part 1 only: The Seven Sermons.... 4to in 8's, later sheep; broken. Lacking final leaf; browned throughout. T Sept 18 (498) £72

Latimore, Sarah B. —& Haskell, Grace C.
— Arthur Rackham: a Bibliography. Los Angeles, 1936. One of 550. Bds. sg Oct 30 (133) $325
Anr copy. Half cloth. sg Jan 22 (214) $250

Latini, Brunetto
— Il Tesoro.... Venice: Marchio Sessa, 1533. 8vo, 17th-cent vellum bds. Some dampstaining; 2 holes in text of P1. S Sept 23 (465) £260 [De Zayas]

Latini, Brunetto, 1220-95
— Li Livres Dou Tresor...publie pour la premiere fois.... Paris, 1863. 4to, orig bds; worn. Jeanson copy. SM Mar 1 (330) FF500

Latomus, Sigismund
— Schon newes Modelbuch von 600 ausserwehlten kunstlichen so wol Italianischen, Franzosischen, Nederlandischen, Engellandischen als Teutschen Modeln. Frankfurt, 1606. Oblong folio, sewn. With 33 woodcut plates & hand-colored woodcut title (holed with slight loss). Ck Oct 31 (66) £4,000

Latrobe, Christian Ignatius, 1758-1836
— Journal of a Visit to South Africa.... L, 1818. 4to, contemp half mor gilt; backstrip inserted, worn. With folding map & 16 plates, 12 hand-colored. Library stamps on all plates, tp & other leaves. Sold w.a.f. bba Aug 28 (302) £160 [Grosvenor]
Anr copy. Contemp half calf. Library markings; plates stamped. Ck May 8 (293) £180
Anr copy. Contemp half calf; broken on front hinge. With folding map & 16 plates, 12 hand-colored. O Oct 16 (268) £55
Anr copy. Half mor. S Nov 18 (1190) £300 [Negro]
Anr copy. Orig bds; worn & broken. S May 29 (1116) £340

Laud, William, 1573-1645
— The History of the Troubles and Tryal.... L, 1695. 1st Ed. Folio, contemp calf; spine defective. sg Oct 9 (248) $140
— A Relation of the Conference betweene William Lawd...and Mr. Fisher the Jesuite. L, 1639. 1st Ed. Folio, contemp calf; upper joint cracked. Some annotations. Ck Feb 13 (140) £95

Lauder, Sir John, of Fountainhall
— The Decisions of the Lords of Council and Session, from June 6th, 1678, to July 30th, 1712. Edin., 1759-61. 2 vols. Folio, half calf. pnE Nov 12 (143) £65

Lauder, William, d.1771
— An Essay on Milton's Use and Imitation of the Moderns in his Paradise Lost. L, 1750. 1st Issue. 8vo, contemp calf; rebacked, portion of old spine preserved. S Jan 13 (506) £320 [Murray]

Lauderdale, James Maitland, 8th Earl of. See: Maitland, James

Laughlin, Ledlie Irwin
— Pewter in America.... Bost., 1940. 2 vols. Folio, cloth. sg June 4 (251) $70

Laughton, L. G. Carr
— Old Ship Figure-Heads & Sterns. L & NY, 1925. One of 1,500. 4to, cloth; rear cover detached. sg Nov 20 (96) $60

Laumer, Keith
— Galactic Diplomat. Garden City, 1965. Increased d/j. cb Sept 28 (780) $65
— Reteif and the Warlords. Garden City, 1968. In d/j. cb Sept 28 (782) $60
— Reteif's War. Garden City, [1965]. Increased d/j. Some staining to fore-edges. cb Sept 28 (785) $70

Laumer, Keith —& Brown, Rosel George
— Earthblood. Garden City, 1966. In rubbed d/j. cb Sept 28 (779) $85

Launhardt, Wilhelm, 1832-1918
— Mathematische Begruendung der Volkswirthschaftslehre. Leipzig, 1885. 8vo, half cloth; rubbed. Library markings; some soiling. P Sept 24 (320) $1,600

Lauremberg, Peter, 1585-1639
— Apparatus plantarius primus, tributus in duos libros.... Frankfurt, [1632]. Bound with: Horticultura, libris II. Frankfurt: Merian, [1631]. 4to, contemp vellum bds. With 29 plates. de Belder copy. S Apr 28 (204) £1,000 [Robinson]

Laurence, Edward, d.1740?
— The Duty of a Steward to his Lord. L, 1727. 4to, contemp calf; joints cracked. With folding frontis & plate. Interleaved; K2 cleanly torn. Ck Nov 21 (205) £100

Laurent, Henri, 1779-1844
— Le Musee Napoleon. Paris, 1816-18. 2 vols. 4to, contemp half mor; 1 cover detached. S Nov 10 (221) £900 [Palgrave]

Lauri, Jacobus
— Antiquae urbis splendor.... Rome, 1612-[41]. 4 parts in 1 vol. Oblong 4to, contemp vellum; worn. With engraved title & 172 plates, including table at end. Main title dust-soiled; marginal tears or slight creases elsewhere. S Oct 23 (200) £400 [Barker]

Laurie, Robert —& Whittle, James
— A New and Elegant Imperial Sheet Atlas. L, 1798. Folio, disbound. With 51 hand-colored maps. A few splits or frayed margins without loss. S Oct 23 (231) £1,300 [King]
— New and Elegant General Atlas. L, 1804. 4to, old calf; worn. wd June 19 (58) $275

Lautensack, H.
— es Cirkels uund Richtscheyts, auch der Perspectiva.... Frankfurt: Georg Raben, 1564. Folio, vellum wraps from a Ms with musical notation. Some dampstaining. S May 21 (47) £1,800 [Rota]

Laval, Antoine Jean de
— Voyage de la Louisiane.... Paris, 1728. 4to, contemp calf gilt; chipped. With 15 maps (4 folding), 4 engraved folding tables & diagrams & 11 ptd folding tables. Some browning. S Oct 23 (142) £900 [Cavendish]

Lavalee, Joseph, 1747-1816 —& Filhol, Antoine Michel
— Galerie du Musee Napoleon. Paris, 1804-28. 11 vols. 8vo, contemp half mor; some joints cracked & backstrips torn. Some foxing. sg Dec 18 (171) $700

Lavater, Johann Caspar, 1741-1801
— Essays on Physiognomy. L, 1792. 3 vols in 5. 4to, contemp calf gilt; some covers detached. bba Aug 28 (130) £110 [Shapero]

Anr Ed. L, 1797. 4 vols. 8vo, later half calf. pnE Nov 12 (37) £75

Anr Ed. L, 1804. 3 vols in 4. 4to, contemp calf; rebacked & rubbed. Lacking 3 plates. Sold w.a.f. bba Oct 16 (303) £40 [Rainer]

Anr Ed. L, 1810. 3 vols in 5. 4to, contemp calf gilt; rubbed, spines chipped. Ck Feb 13 (203) £130

Anr copy. Contemp russia gilt; rebacked

with mor gilt. sg Feb 12 (200) $375

Laverack, Edward
— The Setter. L, 1872. 8vo, half mor. With 2 color plates. sg Oct 23 (387) $200

Lavoisier, Antoine Laurent, 1743-94
See also: Guyton de Morveau & Lavoisier
— Resultats extraits d'un ouvrage intitule: De la richesse territoriale du Royaume de France. Paris, 1791. 8vo, modern bds. Library stamp on tp & last page. S Nov 27 (271) £450 [Perriana]

Lavoisne, C. V.
— A Complete Genealogical, Historical, Chronological, & Geographical Atlas. Phila, 1820. 2d American Ed. Folio, disbound. With 68 maps & charts, all hand-colored. Some stains; 4 maps & charts damaged or torn & creased. sg Apr 23 (177) $350
— Complete Genealogical, Historical, Chronological and Geographical Atlas. 1840. 4th Ed. Folio, contemp half lea; worn. With 69 hand-colored maps & tables, 1 plain double-page historical map & 3 double-page plain appendices. S Jan 12 (92) £230 [George]

Lawlor, C. F.
— The Mixicologist; or, How to Mix All Kinds of Fancy Drinks. Cincinnati & Cleveland, [1899] 12mo, orig wraps; chipped, spine repaired. sg Jan 15 (36) $60

Lawrance, Mary
— A Collection of Roses from Nature. L, 1799 [1796-1810]. Folio, contemp half mor; rubbed & soiled. With engraved title & dedication, hand-colored frontis & 90 colored plates. Engraved title creased; some spotting. de Belder copy. S Apr 28 (205) £32,000 [Hill]
— A Collection of Passion Flowers. L, [1799]-1802. Folio, 19th-cent half cloth. With 18 hand-colored plates. Issued without text. Plesch—de Belder copy. S Apr 28 (206) £13,000 [Earhart]

Lawrence, D. H., 1885-1930
See also: Cresset Press; Grabhorn Printing
— The Escaped Cock. L, 1931. ("The Man Who Died.") Half cloth. pn Dec 11 (20) £40

One of 1,000, sgd. Cloth, unopened. sg Mar 5 (118) $100
— Lady Chatterley's Lover. Florence, 1928. One of 1,000, sgd. Orig bds; spine & hinges worn. Title & a few leaves stained. pnNY Sept 13 (254) $500

Anr copy. Orig bds, unopened; foot of spine & 2 corners chipped. S Dec 18 (158) £480 [Walker]

LAWRENCE

1st Ed. Orig bds; rubbed & soiled, spine def. bba Sept 25 (127) £200 [Heritage]; sg Mar 5 (117) $600
— The Paintings.... L: Mandrake Press, [1929]. 1st Ed, One of 510. Folio, orig half mor gilt; worn. bba Aug 28 (20) £350 [Subunso]
Anr copy. Orig half mor; rubbed & stained, front endpapers dampstained. S Nov 10 (247) £60 [Sims]
Anr copy. Half mor; worn. sg Mar 5 (119) $375
— Pansies. L, 1929. 1st Ed, one of 250. In d/j. kh Mar 16 (292) A$400; pn Mar 5 (156) £160 [Henderson]
Anr copy. In d/j. S Jan 13 (579) £120 [McDonald]
Anr copy. Wraps. sg Mar 5 (120) $140
— The Prussian Officer and Other Stories. L, 1914. 1st Ed, 1st Issue. Orig cloth; worn. bba July 2 (263) £110 [Forster]
— Tortoises. Williamsburg MA: Cheloniidae Press, 1983. One of 200. Illus by Alan James Robinson. 4to, half vellum. sg Jan 8 (44) $90
— The Virgin and the Gipsy. Florence, 1930. One of 810 on handmade paper. pnNY Sept 13 (255) $140
— The Widowing of Mrs. Holroyd. NY, 1914. ha May 22 (179) $70

Lawrence, Frieda von Richthofen
— "Not I, But the Wind...." Santa Fe, [1934]. 1st Ed, one of 1,000, sgd. Half cloth, unopened. sg Mar 5 (121) $50

Lawrence, H. W. —&
Dighton, Basil L.
— French Line Engravings of the late XVIII Century. L, 1910. One of 1,050. 4to, orig cloth. pn Mar 5 (81H) £40 [Elliott]
One of 1,050, but this copy lacks extra suite of plates. Orig cloth. wa June 25 (452) $130

Lawrence, John, 1753-1839
— British Field Sports. L, 1818. 8vo, contemp calf; broken. bba oct 30 (329) £120 [Sanders]
Anr copy. Later half calf; worn. With 34 plates (including 1 extra). Shaved. Ck Sept 5 (6) £60
Anr copy. Mor gilt. With engraved title & 34 plates. pnE Dec 17 (353) £380 [McEwan]
Anr copy. Contemp calf; rebacked preserving old spine. Some soiling; 1 caption cropped. S Nov 10 (610) £130 [Nagel]
— The History and Delineation of the Horse. L, 1809. 4to, modern cloth. Sold w.a.f. Extra-illus with plates. Ck June 5 (22) £140

— The Sportsman's Repository. L, 1820. 4to, contemp half mor; rubbed. With engraved title & 37 plates. Stained, affecting some plates. bba Oct 30 (398) £280 [Sanders]

Lawrence, Richard, Veterinary Surgeon
— The Complete Farrier, and British Sportsman. L, [1816]. 4to, contemp calf gilt; worn. With frontis & 12 plates. JG Oct 2 (1406) DM900
— An Inquiry into the Structure and Animal Economy of the Horse. Birm., 1801. 4to, contemp half russia gilt. With 18 plates. C Dec 12 (126) £180 [Old Hall]

Lawrence, Richard Hoe
— History of the Society of Iconophiles of the City of New York. NY, 1930. One of 186. 4to, half lea; soiled, endpapers stained. O June 9 (95) $50

Lawrence, T. E., 1888-1935
See also: Golden Cockerel Press; Woolley & Lawrence
— The Diary of T. E. Lawrence 1911. L: Corvinus Press, 1937. 1st Ed, one of 100 on parchment substitute paper. 4to, orig half mor. C May 13 (175) £850 [Loman]
— An Essay on Flecker. NY, 1937. 1st American Ed. Orig wraps; loose. Helle Flecker's copy, with letters of A. W. Lawrence to herabout the work. S Dec 18 (161) £600 [Rota]
— A Letter from T. E. Lawrence to his Mother. Pvtly ptd by the Corvinus Press for Mrs. Lawrence, Aug 1936. One of 23 on Barcham Green Medway paper. 4to, orig half cloth. S Dec 18 (162) £900 [Rota]
— Letters. L, 1938. Ed by David Garnett. In soiled & chipped d/j. cb May 7 (117) $55
— The Mint. L, [1955]. 1st Ed, one of 2,000. Orig half mor. bba Dec 4 (143) £50 [Laffont]; S Sept 22 (110) £35 [Thomas]
Anr copy. Half mor. sg Dec 11 (322) $120
— Prospectus for Seven Pillars of Wisdom. [L, 1925]. 4to, wraps. With a colored frontis & 40 pp of text & with a ptd sheet explaining delay in publication. C May 13 (181) £500 [Dailey]
Anr copy. Mor gilt by Riviere. With color plate. pnNY Mar 12 (96) $350
— Revolt in the Desert. L, 1927. 1st Ed, One of 315 L.p. copies. Orig half cloth. C May 13 (178) £320 [Maggs]
One of 315. Orig half mor, in soiled d/j. cb May 7 (119) $300
Out-of-series copy. Orig half pigskin; spine worn. S Sept 22 (107) £130 [Sotheran]
— Seven Pillars of Wisdom. L, 1926. 1st Ed, one of 170 complete copies, so inscr. 4to, orig mor by Sangorski. C May 13 (180) £15,000 [Maggs]

Anr copy. Lea gilt by Sangorski & Sutcliffe. With the 2 leaves, "Some Notes..." but without the 2 line drawings on pp 92 & 208 & without the Ms correction in the list of illusts as it is correctly ptd in this copy. P Sept 24 (186) $16,000

1st Trade Ed. L, 1935. 4to, half mor gilt. pnNY Mar 12 (99) $90

Anr copy. Orig half pigskin; upper cover stained. S Sept 22 (108) £220 [Maggs]

One of 750. Half pigskin, in d/j. C May 13 (185) £220 [Burton]

— To his Biographer Robert Graves. With: To his Biographer Liddell Hart. L, 1938. Out-of-series copies, sgd by Graves & Hart. 2 vols. S Sept 22 (111) £85 [Irwin]

Lawson, Thomas W. See: Thompson & Lawson

Lawson, William, fl.1618. See: Cresset Press

Layard, Sir Austen Henry, 1817-94
— The Monuments of Nineveh. Series I & II. L, 1849-53. 6th Thousand. 2 vols. Folio & oblong folio, half calf; not uniform. With 171 plates & 2 plans, some plates colored. A few marginal tears; some stains & soiling. S Nov 18 (1070) £380 [Maggs]
— Nineveh and Its Remains. L, 1849. 2 vols. 8vo, contemp half calf; rubbed. Map torn without loss. T Oct 16 (279) £42

Anr Ed. NY, 1849. 2 vols. 8vo, modern half mor. sg Nov 20 (97) $50

Layard, George Somes, 1857-1925. See: Spielmann & Layard

Laye, Elizabeth P. Ramsay
— Social Life and Manners in Australia...by a Resident. L, 1861. 8vo, half mor. CA Apr 12 (165) A$170

Le Bas Collection, Edward
— Paintings and Drawings by Harold Gilman and Charles Ginner in the Collection.... L: Pvtly ptd, 1965. One of 105. Text by B. Fairfax Hall. 4to & folio, text in half mor, plates loose in half mor box. S Dec 4 (153) £200 [Sims Reed]

Le Bey de Batilly, Denis
— Emblemata. Frankfurt, 1596. Engravings by Theodore de Bry after Jean Boissard. 4to, later bds; broken. With engraved title, port & 63 plates. S Nov 27 (187) £1,250 [Lib. Valette]

Le Blanc, Charles, 1817-65
— Manuel de l'amateur d'estampes. Paris, 1854-89. 4 vols. 8vo, half mor. C Dec 3 (27) £350 [Stogdon]

Anr Ed. Paris, 1854-88. 4 vols. 8vo, contemp half mor. C May 13 (105) £240 [Maggs]

Le Blanc, Guillaume. See: Blancus, Guilielmus

Le Blond, Jean, Sieur de Branville, 1502-53
— Le Printemps de l'humble esperant.... Paris, 1536. 8vo, mor gilt by Chambolle-Duru. Repair to 1 leaf; stamp on tp. Jeanson copy. SM Mar 1 (334) FF28,000

Le Brun, Charles, 1619-90
— Le Grand Escalier du Chateau de Versailles des Ambassadeurs. Paris, [1725]. Folio, contemp calf; rubbed, short splits to joints. With 24 plates. Engraved throughout. C May 13 (110) £850 [Weinreb]
— Receuil de divers desseins de fontaines. Paris, [c.1660]. Folio, half lea, rubbed. With engraved title & 27 plates. S Oct 23 (208) £1,600 [Fletcher]

Le Brun, Cornelius
— Reizen over Moskovie, door Persie en Indie. Amst., 1714. Folio, modern half mor. With frontis, port, 2 folding maps & 260 plates on 108 sheets. Lacking engraved title C Apr 8 (103) £650 [Mackenzie]

Anr copy. Contemp calf; spine chipped at head & repaired at foot, hinges reinforced with cloth tape. Lacking Plate 74; some edge tears or chips. cb Nov 6 (40) $550
— Travels into Muscovy, Persia.... L, 1737. 2 vols. Folio, contemp half mor; worn. With 1 frontis (of 2), port, 3 folding maps & 112 (of 114) plates. Sold w.a.f. bba Dec 18 (174) £150 [Elliott]

Anr copy. Contemp calf; joints split, head & foot of spine worn. With frontis, port, 3 maps & 123 plates. Minor repair in margin of final leaf; Vol II with short tear in O2 affecting 1 illust. C Dec 12 (245) £950 [Von Hunersdorff]

Anr copy. 19th-cent calf gilt; worn. Minor repairs without loss. S Jan 12 (313) £580 [George]

Anr copy. Vol I only. Contemp calf; joints split, worn. Some worming & browning. S May 29 (1059) £160
— Voyage au Levant. Delft, 1700. Folio, modern calf. With engraved title, port, folding map & 97 plates. Stamp at foot of tp. Sold w.a.f. C Oct 15 (63) £1,500 [Remington]

Anr copy. Contemp calf gilt; rubbed. With engraved title, port, folding general map, allegorical plate & 210 plates. Some browning. S Oct 23 (119) £1,500 [Perrin]

Anr copy. 19th-cent calf gilt. With port, folding map & 97 plates. S Apr 24 (232) £1,300 [Tooley]
— Voyages de Corneille Le Brun par la Moscovie, en Perse, et aux Indes orientales. Amst., 1718. 2 vols. Folio, contemp calf gilt; rubbed. With frontis, port, 3 double-

page maps & 114 plates. S Oct 21 (145) £1,300 [Marshall]

Le Bruyn, Cornelius. See: Le Brun, Cornelius

Le Camus de Mezieres, Nicolas
— Le Guide de ceux qui veulent batir. Yverdon, 1782-81. 2 parts in 1 vol. 8vo, old half vellum. Library markings, including perforated stamps. sg Mar 26 (169) $150

Le Carre, John, Pseud.
— The Spy Who Came In From the Cold. L, 1963. In d/j with small tear. pn Nov 20 (239) £75 [Conway]
Anr copy. In d/j. pn June 18 (145) £75 [Berryman]; pnE June 17 (85) £95; T May 20 (6) £170

Le Clerc, Chrestien, 1641-99?
— Nouvelle Relation de la Gaspesie.... Paris, 1691. 12mo, contemp calf. SM Oct 20 (471) FF21,000

Le Clerc, Jean, 1657-1736
— Atlas de la Geographie ancienne, sacree, ecclesiastique et profane. Amst.: J. Covens & C. Mortier, [1705]. Folio, contemp half calf; def. With engraved title & 94 maps, all hand-colored in outline. Some creasing; Ms index. S Nov 10 (967) £1,100 [Burden]
— Histoire des Province-Unies des Pays Bas. Amst., 1723-28. 4 vols in 2. Folio, calf; joints cracked. With frontis & 103 plates. B Feb 5 (625) HF300
— Theatre geographique du Royaume de France.... Paris, 1631. Folio, contemp vellum; soiled & worn. With 52 maps on 50 double-page mapsheets. Lacking engraved title, 2 ports & all text leaves following maps; some worming affecting lower centerfolds of maps 3, 4 & 9 occasioning some loss. S Oct 23 (288) £1,700 [Schmidt]

Le Clerc, Nicolas Gabriel
— Atlas du commerce. Paris, 1786. 4to, contemp half vellum; soiled. With 11 folding charts, some hand-colored in outline. S june 25 (303) £500 [Martinos]
— Histoire de la Russie ancienne et moderne. Paris, 1783-94. 3 vols. 4to, 19th-cent half sheep, rebacked with syn. With 47 engraved plates, most folding; not collated. sg Dec 18 (196) $225

Le Clerc, Sebastien, 1637-1714
— Traite de geometrie. Paris: J. Jombert, 1690. 8vo, contemp calf; rubbed, joints split. bba Aug 20 (414) £70 [Weiner]
— A Treatise of Architecture.... L, 1732. 2 vols. 8vo, contemp calf; rebacked. Some browning. T June 18 (358) £140

Le Clert, Louis
— Le Papier: Recherches et notes.... Paris, 1926. One of 675. 2 vols. Folio, cloth, orig wraps bound in. bba Dec 18 (176) £220 [Erlini]
Anr copy. Orig wraps. Hunt copy. CNY Nov 21 (209) $350

Le Comte, Pierre
— Afbeeldingen van Schepen en Vaartuigen in Verschillende Bewegingen. Amst., 1831. Oblong 4to, loose in orig wraps. With 50 plates. Minor marginal stains. Sgd. C Dec 12 (246) £1,200 [Warnecke]

Le Corbusier, 1887-1965
— La Ville radieuse. Boulogne, 1933. Folio, orig bdg. B Oct 7 (918) HF900

Le Couteulx de Canteleu, John Baptiste Emmanuel Hector, comte de, b.1827
— La Chasse du loup. Paris: Veuve Bouchard-Huzard, 1861. One of 50 on vellum. 4to mor gilt by Chambolle-Duru. Jeanson copy. SM Mar 1 (335) FF11,000
— La Venerie francaise. Paris: Veuve Bouchard-Huzard, 1858. 4to, mor gilt by Gruel. Jeanson copy. SM Mar 1 (336) FF7,000

Le Fanu, Joseph Sheridan, 1814-73
— Green Tea and other Ghost Stories. Sauk City: Arkham House, 1945. In rubbed d/j. cb Sept 28 (788) $75

Le Fevre, Raoul. See: Kelmscott Press

Le Francq van Berkhey, Joannes
— Natuurlyke historie van Holland. Amst., 1769-1806. Vol I through Vol IV, Part 1 & Vol V, Part 2, in 12 vols. 8vo, bds. B Feb 25 (627) HF1,200

Le Gallienne, Richard, 1866-1947
— The Romance of Perfume. NY & Paris, 1928. Illus by Georges Barbier. 4to, bds; soiled. cb Sept 11 (261) $50; ha Dec 19 (206) $90
Anr copy. Bds; stained. wa Mar 5 (103) $55

Le Gentil de la Galaisiere, Guillaume Joseph
— Voyage dans les mers de l'Inde.... Paris, 1779-81. 2 vols. 4to, contemp calf; 1 cover stained. With 27 folding plates. Some spotting; 1 plate with marginal tear. S Apr 24 (348) £700 [Perrin]

Le Gouz de la Boullaye, Francois
— Les Voyages et observations ou sone decrits...Italie, Greece.... Paris, 1653. 4to, contemp calf; spine rubbed. S Oct 23 (320) £700 [Rota]
— Les Voyages et observations ou sont decrits...Italie, Grece.... Troyes & Paris, 1657. 4to, 19th-cent calf; rebacked with

orig spine. Some tears affecting text. C Dec 12 (247) £400 [Smitskamp]

Le Grand d'Aussy, Pierre Jean Baptiste
— Fabliaux or Tales, Abridged from French Manuscripts. L, 1815. 3 vols. 8vo, mor by David. O May 12 (69) $200

Le Guin, Ursula K.
— City of Illusions. L, 1971. In d/j. cb Sept 28 (789) $65
— The Dispossessed: An Ambiguous Utopia. NY: Harper, [1974]. In mildly creased d/j. Inscr. sg Sept 28 (791) $130
— Gwilaln's Harp. Northridge: Lord John Press, 1981. One of 50. Half mor. cb Sept 28 (796) $90

Le Hay, ——
— Recueil de cent estampes representant differentes nations du Levant. Paris, 1714. Folio, contemp mor extra with arms of Pavee de Vandeuve. With engraved title, preface, 7 leaves of text, leaf of music & 102 plates, hand-colored, heightened with gold & with mica chips added to simulate jewels in buckles. S Oct 23 (337) £11,500 [Traylen]

Anr copy. Bound with: Le Hay. Explication des cent estampes. Paris, 1715. calf; rubbed & def. Lacking 1 plate; slight damage by adhesion to inner margin of title. S Jan 12 (218) £1,600 [Pantazelos]

Le Keux, John
— Memorials of Cambridge. L, 1841-42. 2 vols. 8vo, contemp half mor. With engraved titles, double-page map & 74 plates. C July 22 (113) £200

Anr copy. Contemp mor gilt. With engraved titles, map (frayed) & 73 plates on india paper mtd. S May 28 (933) £280

Le Long, Isaac
— Boek-Zaal der Nederduytsche Bybels. Amst., 1732. 4to, later half calf; rubbed. bba Oct 16 (419) £90 [Maggs]

Le Long, Jacques, 1665-1721
— Bibliotheque historique de la France. Paris, 1719. Folio, contemp calf; worn. bba Mar 12 (345) £90 [Hashimoto]

Le Masson, Edmond
— Nouvelle Venerie normande, ou essai sur la chasse du lievre.... Avranches: E. Tostain, 1847. 8vo, contemp bds. Jeanson copy. SM Mar 1 (340) FF1,500

Le Mercier de La Riviere, Pierre Paul, 1720-93
— L'Ordre naturel et essentiel des societes politiques. L & Paris, 1767. 2 vols. 4to, contemp calf; rubbed & scuffed, Vol number labels lacking. Margin tear in N4 of Vol I. P Sept 24 (347) $400

Le Muet, Pierre, 1591-1669
— Maniere de bastir pour touttes sortes de personne. Paris, 1623. 1st Ed. Folio, contemp calf gilt; worn & waterdamaged. With engraved title & 53 plates. Last leaves with worming; tp stamped. HN May 20 (189) DM800

Le Normand, Marie Anne Adelaide
— The Historical and Secret Memoirs of the Empress Josephine. L, 1895. One of 500. 2 vols in 4. 8vo, mor. Stamp on each front free endpaper. Extra-illus with engravings. sg Sept 11 (18) $250

Le Normant, Jean, Sieur de Chiremont
— Histoire veritable et memorable de ce qui s'est passe sous l'exorcisme de trois filles possedees es pais de Flandre.... Paris: Nicolas Buon, 1623. 2 vols in 1. 8vo, contemp vellum. Some worming & browning. bba Mar 12 (443) £140 [Korn]

Le Pautre, Antoine, 1621-91
— Les Oeuvres d'architecture. Paris, [1652]. 2 parts in 1 vol. Folio, contemp half calf; worn. With 62 plates. S May 6 (388) £480 [Margi]

Le Petit, Jean Francois
— La Grande Chronique ancienne et moderne.... Dordrecht, 1601. Illus by Christoffel van Sichem. 2 vols. Folio, disbound. Some browning. sg Mar 26 (173) $100

Le Pois, Antoine
— Discours sur les medalles et graveures antiques.... Paris: Mamert Patisson, 1579. 4to, contemp calf; rubbed. With 20 plates. Plate of Priapus unmutilated. bba Dec 4 (3) £90 [Drury]

Le Prestre de Vauban, Sebastien
— De l'attaque et de la defense des places. The Hague, 1737-42. 2 parts in 1 vol. 4to, contemp calf. Some spotting & browning. FD June 11 (2667) DM2,000

Anr Ed. The Hague, 1737. 2 parts in 1 vol. 4to, later half calf; warped. Some stains & soiling. S Nov 18 (943) £100 [Dennistoun]

Anr copy. Vol I (of 2) only. 4to, contemp calf; worn. With 36 folding maps. sg Nov 20 (118) $90

Anr copy. 2 vols in 1. 4to, early 19th-cent half lea; worn. First title stained, with old signature & stamp; worming in lower inner corner through 1st quarter of volume, affecting text & plates. sg Mar 26 (174) $150

— Projet d'une dixme royale. Paris, 1707. 12mo, contemp calf gilt; worn & repaired. With 4 folding tables. Minor soiling & foxing; tables browned; 1 table with 2 short

LE PRESTRE DE VAUBAN

fold separations; anr with caption just shaved. P Sept 24 (416) $650

Le Prevost, Hubert

— La Vie de Monseigneur Sainct Hubert Dardeine.... Paris: Chez les de Marnef, [c.1520]. 8vo, mor janseniste by Koehler. Jeanson copy. SM Mar 1 (342) FF65,000

Le Rouge, George Louis

— Atlas nouveau portatif.... Paris, [1748]. 8vo, lea; worn & dried. With engraved title & 91 maps & plates, hand-colored in outline. One corner torn, not affecting image. sg Apr 23 (178) $600

Le Roux de Lincy, Adrien Jean Victor. See: Grolier Club

Le Roy, Jacques, 1633-1719

— Notitia marchionatus Sacri Romani Imperii.... Amst., 1678. Folio. contemp calf; rubbed. Lacking some leaves. HN Nov 26 (380) DM2,200

Le Sage, Alain Rene, 1668-1747
See also: Fore-Edge Paintings; Washington's copy, George

— The Adventures of Gil Blas of Santillane. L, 1819. Trans by Tobias Smollett. 3 vols. 8vo, half calf. Lacking half-titles. bba Dec 4 (92) £55 [Guenter]
Anr copy. Calf gilt by Zaehnsdorf. sg Feb 12 (202) $140
Anr copy. Contemp half calf gilt; hinges cracked. T Oct 16 (491) £55
Anr Ed. L: Nimmo & Bain, 1881. One of 100. 8vo, recent half lev gilt. cb Feb 19 (159) $65
Anr copy. Mor gilt by Bayntun with multi-colored mor inlays of text characters in various costumes. Extra-illus with 134 hand-colored plates. sg Sept 11 (118) $400

— Histoire de Gil Blas de Santillane. Paris: Didot le jeune, [1795]. 4 vols. 8vo, mor gilt by Riviere. With 100 plates, all proofs before letters. L.p. copy. C May 13 (28) £350 [Lardanchet]
Anr Ed. Paris: Chaigneau Aine, [1801]. 4 vols. 8vo, mor gilt by Cuzin. With port & 28 plates, all in 2 states, proofs before letters & eaux-fortes. Date of An IV in Vol I only. L.p. copy. C May 13 (29) £400 [Landarchet]

— Oeuvres. Paris, 1818-21. 16 vols. 12mo, contemp calf gilt. With 40 plates. Some foxing. S Nov 27 (84) £140 [Booth]
See also: Limited Editions Club

AMERICAN BOOK PRICES CURRENT

Le Trosne, Guillaume Francois

— De l'ordre social, ouvrage suive d'un traite elementaire sur la valeur.... Paris, 1777. 8vo, contemp calf; rubbed & wormed, some stitching loose. Wormholes along inner margin; paper flaw affecting corners of V1 & Hh4; light soiling in a few places. P Sept 24 (321) $1,200

Le Verrier de la Conterie, Jean Baptiste Jacques

— L'Ecole de la chasse aux chiens courans.... Rouen: Nicolas & Richard Lallemant, 1763. 2 vols. 8vo, contemp calf. Jeanson copy. SM Mar 1 (344) FF18,000

— Venerie normande, ou l'ecole de la chasse aux chiens courants. Rouen, 1778. 8vo, contemp calf gilt. With 19 wood-engravings, most folding. Jeanson 1285. SM Mar 1 (345) FF9,500

Lea, Isaac, 1792-1886

— Contributions to Geology. Phila., 1833. 1st Ed. 4to, orig bds; worn, covers nearly detached. With 6 plates. sg Jan 15 (326) $70

Lea, Matthew Carey

— A Manual of Photography Intended as a Text Book.... Phila., 1871. 2d Ed. 8vo, cloth; worn, spine frayed, hinges cracked. ha Nov 7 (174) $90

Lea, Tom

— The King Ranch. Bost., [1957]. 1st Trade Ed. 2 vols. cb Jan 8 (110) $75
Anr Ed. Kingsville, TX, 1957. Ltd Ed. 2 vols. cb Jan 8 (109) $800

— Peleliu Landing. El Paso, 1945. One of 500. 4to, cloth. With 10 plates. cb Sept 11 (187) $500

Leadbetter, Charles

— Mechanick Dialling, or, the New Art of Shadows. L, 1737. 8vo, contemp calf; broken. With 12 (of 13) folding plates. Some wormholes in margins. S Nov 10 (199) £60 [Sperman]

Leake, Stephen Martin, 1702-73

— Nummi Britannici Historia: or an Account of English Money. L, 1626 [but 1726]. 8vo, contemp calf; rubbed. With 8 plates. Dampstained; a few plates stained. bba Aug 28 (192) £44 [Titles]

Leake, William Martin, 1777-1860

— The Topography of Athens. L, 1821. 8vo, orig half cloth. bba Oct 30 (330) £230 [Frew Mackenzie]

698

Leakey, Louis Seymour Bazett
— The Stone Age Cultures of Kenya Colony. Cambr., 1931. 4to, orig cloth. SSA Oct 28 (689) R130

Leales...
— Leales Demostraciones, Amantes Finezas, y Festivas Aclamaciones...Luis Fernando Joseph. Manila: en la Compania de Jesus por D. Gaspar Aquino de Belen, 1709. 4to, modern vellum gilt. Ptd on rice paper. Some tears & repairs caused by brittleness. sg Dec 4 (120) $6,200

Lear, Edward, 1812-88
— A Book of Nonsense. L, 1855. 2d Ed. Oblong 8vo, old half calf; upper cover detached. With litho title & 72 plates. Some cropping & brown spotting. Cranmore Hall copy. L July 2 (63) £950
— Journal of a Landscape Painter in Corsica.... L, 1870. 1st Ed. 8vo, orig cloth; rubbed, loose. bba Jan 15 (471) £60 [Dawson]

Anr copy. Contemp vellum gilt, upper cover with owner's name encircled by paper onlay in the form of a belt & with borders of red mor inlay. S Nov 17 (660) £120 [Thorp]
— Journals of a Landscape Painter in Albania. L, 1851. 1st Ed. 8vo, orig cloth; head & tail of spine slightly torn, soiled. With map & 20 plates, all stained. pn July 23 (177) £210 [Noakes]

Anr copy. Orig cloth; worn. With map & 20 plates. S Mar 9 (754) £320 [Brinded]
— Journals of a Landscape Painter in Southern Calabria.... L, 1852. 1st Ed. 8vo, half calf; rubbed. pn May 21 (227) £170 [Callea]
— Views in Rome and its Environs. L, 1841. Folio, contemp half mor. With engraved title & 25 tinted plates. bba Apr 23 (354) £750 [Swales]

Anr copy. Orig cloth; rebacked with mor. Tp detached; occasional spotting. C Oct 15 (62) £1,150 [d'Arcy]

Leared, Arthur
— Marocco and the Moors.... L, 1891. Ed by Sir Richard F. Burton. 8vo, orig cloth; spine ends worn, hinges cracked. sg Nov 20 (39) $80

Learned...
— A Learned and Necessary Argument to prove that each Subject hath a Propriety in his Goods.... L: John Burroughes, 1641. 4to, wraps. S July 24 (467) £580 [Quaritch]

Lebas, J.
— Festin Joyeux ou, la cuisine en musique, en vers libres. Paris: Chez Lesclapart Pere, 1738. 2 parts in 1 vol. 12mo, contemp calf; spine repaired. Deuzel-Lambert-Crahan copy. P Nov 25 (286) $350

Lebrun, Frederico
— Drawings for Dante's Inferno.... [N.p]: Kanthos Press, 1963. Folio, cloth. sg Jan 8 (139) $130

Leckey, Edward
— Fictions Connected with the Indian Outbreak of 1857. Bombay, 1859. 8vo, orig cloth; rubbed, hinges cracked. cb Dec 18 (100) $80

Leclerc, Nicolas Gabriel
— Histoire physique, morale, civile et politique de la Russie moderne. Paris, 1783-[94]. 6 vols. 4to, cloth; soiled. With 4 engraved maps & 74 plates. Some spotting. bba Dec 18 (175) £500 [Anderson]

LeClerc, Sebastien. See: Le Clerc, Sebastien

Leclerq, Lena
— La Rose est nu. [Paris], 1961. One of 90 with the etchings. Illus by Max Ernst. Folio, unsewn in wraps. With 6 plates. VH Sept 12 (2357) DM5,000

Lecluse, Charles de, 1526-1609
— Exoticorum libri decem.... [Leiden], 1605. Folio, vellum; spine worn, rubbed. Tp mtd & repaired; tear to p 109 & top corner of p 119; some foxing. Crahan copy. P Nov 25 (114) $550
— Rariorum aliquot stirpium, per Hispanias observatarum historia. Antwerp, 1576. 1st Ed. 8vo, modern calf. 1st 24 leaves wormed in lower outer corner, affecting catchwords; perforated library stamp on tp. sg Dec 4 (108) $1,400

Lecomte, Hippolyte
— Costumes francais, de 1200 a 1715. L: C. Hullmandel, [c.1830]. 8vo, contemp half vellum. With 100 hand-colored plates, including title. pn Mar 5 (594) £50 [Walford]

Anr copy. Mor gilt. sg Sept 11 (68) $350

Lecuyer, Raymond
— Histoire de la photographie. Paris, 1945. 1st Ed. 4to, later cloth; rubbed. With 3-dimensional glasses in endpocket. sg May 7 (53) $550

Ledebour, Karl Friedrich von, 1785-1851
— Icones plantarum novarum vel imperfecte cognitarum floram Rossicam.... Riga, 1829-34. 5 vols. Folio, contemp half russia; spines def. With 500 hand-colored plates. Massachusetts Horticultural Society—de Belder copy. S Apr 28 (208) £19,000 [Israel]

LEDERMUELLER

Ledermueller, Martin Frobenius, 1719-69
— Versuch bey angehender Fruehlings Zeit.... Nuremberg, 1764. Folio, contemp half calf; rubbed, spine torn. With hand-colored engraved title & 12 hand-colored plates. Plesch—de Belder copy. S Apr 28 (207) £850 [Arader]

Ledoux, Louis Vernon. See: Henderson & Ledoux

Ledyard, John, 1751-89. See: Cook, Capt. James

Lee, Amy Freeman. See: Derrydale Press

Lee, Gypsy Rose
— The G-String Murders. NY, 1941. In d/j. Inscr. sg Mar 5 (122) $140

Lee, Henry, 1756-1818
— Memoirs of the War in the Southern Department of the United States.... NY, 1869. Ed by Robert E. Lee. 8vo, orig cloth, unopened; front hinge split, spine ends frayed, backstrip soiled. Some dampstaining. Sgd on half-title verso by R. E. Lee. sg Sept 18 (148) $750

Lee, John Doyle, 1812-1877
— Journals of...1846-47 & 1859. Salt Lake City, 1938. One of 250. Ed by Charles Kelly. 4to, in d/j. cb Oct 9 (129) $110

Lee, Nathaniel, 1653?-92
— The Tragedy of Nero, Emperour of Rome. L, 1675. 1st Ed. 4to, disbound. bba Mar 12 (452) £55 [Hannas]
— Works. L, 1694. 4to, contemp calf; rebacked, rubbed. Lacking final play. T Sept 18 (354) £39

Lee, Ronald Alfred
— The Knibb Family Clockmakers. L, 1964. 4to, orig cloth, in torn d/j. Ck June 5 (41) £250

Lee, William, Health Official
— Daniel Defoe; his Life, and Recently Discovered Writings.... L, 1869. 3 vols. 8vo, contemp half mor; rubbed. bba Apr 23 (32) £80 [Clark]

Leech, John, 1817-64
— Pictures of Life and Character...from the Collection of Mr. Punch. L, [1854-63]. 1st Eds. Series 1-5 in 2 vols. Oblong folio, half mor; spotted. wd June 19 (144) $225

Leech, John, 1817-64 —& Smith, Albert Richard, 1816-60
— The Month. L, 1851. Nos 1-6 [all pbd]. 16mo, orig wraps; 2 spines restored. Without Advertiser in No 2. sg Sept 11 (222) $200

AMERICAN BOOK PRICES CURRENT

Leech, John Henry, 1862-1900
— Butterflies from China, Japan and Corea. L, 1892-94. 3 vols. 4to, half mor gilt. With 43 colored plates, 5 litho views & a colored folding map. S Apr 23 (13) £1,100 [Ackroyd]

Leeper, David R., 1832-1900
— The Argonauts of 'Forty-Nine.... South Bend, 1894. 1st Ed. 8vo, orig cloth; front hinge cracking. cb Jan 8 (111) $60

Leeser, Isaac
— The Claims of the Jews to an Equality of Rights.... Phila., [1841]. 8vo, modern cloth. Some pencil underlining; 1 word crossed out in ink on p 72. sg Sept 25 (24) $450
— Discourses Argumentative and Devotional on the Subject of the Jewish Religion.... Phila., [1836-41]. 2d Series only. 8vo, contemp lea; worn & broken. Minor stains. sg Apr 30 (41) $110
— Instruction in the Mosaic Religion. Phila., 1830. 8vo, orig cloth; spine worn. Some browning. sg Sept 25 (22) $425
— The Jews and the Mosaic Law.... Phila., [1833]. 8vo, contemp cloth; hinges reinforced. Some foxing. sg Sept 25 (23) $300

Leeuwen, Simon van
— Batavia illustrata, ofte verhandelinge vanden oorspronk...van oud Batavien. The Hague, 1685. Folio, calf. Waterstained. B Feb 25 (626) HF360

Leeuwenhoek, Anthony van, 1632-1723
— Arcana naturae. Delft, 1695. 4to, contemp calf. With engraved title & 27 plates; lacking port, light dampstaining at beginning & end. sg Jan 15 (329) $140
— The Select Works of.... L, 1800. 2 vols. 8vo, later half calf; rubbed, 1 spine chipped. Marginal dampstains; margins trimmed. cb Feb 19 (192) $170
— Send-Brieven zoo aan de...Koninklyke Societeit te Londen.... Delft, 1718. 1st Ed. 4to, contemp calf. With 31 plates; 2d leaf loose, lacking frontis & title. sg Jan 15 (329) $140

Lefebure-Durufle, N. J.
— Voyage pittoresque dans les ports sur les cotes de France. [Paris, c.1823]. Folio, half russia; rebacked. With 45 colored plates. S Oct 23 (256) £10,000 [Arader]

Leffel, James & Co.
— The Construction of Mill Dams. Springfield, Ohio, 1874. 8vo, cloth. wa Nov 6 (28) $85

Leffingwell, William Bruce
— Shooting on Upland, Marsh, and Stream. Chicago, 1890. 8vo, cloth; rubbed, small stain on front cover. cb May 21 (175) $65

Legallois, Julien Jean Cesar, 1770-1814
— Experiments on the Principle of Life.... Phila., 1813. 8vo, contemp sheep. Browned; marginal dampstaining. sg Jan 15 (103) $90

LeGear, Clara E. See: Phillips & LeGear

Leger, Fernand, 1881-1955
— Mes Voyages.... Paris, 1960. One of 281. Folio, loose in orig wraps. With 18 plain & 10 color lithos. S Dec 4 (19) £300 [Perceval]

Legh, Gerard, d.1563
— The Accedens of Armory. L: Richard Tottill, 1562. 1st Ed. 8vo, contemp calf; rebacked. Title cropped; small tear repaired with slight loss; folding woodcut plate shaved; 1 leaf laid down; final leaf supplied from anr Ed; several headlines shaved. Sold w.a.f. S Sept 23 (359) £85 [Elliott]

Anr Ed. L: Henry Ballard, 1597. 4to, contemp calf; rebacked, corners reinforced, rubbed. Top outer corner of tp def, just affecting woodcut; G3 & G4 marginally def, affecting 1 illust; marginal dampstaining to some leaves. bba Aug 28 (165) £85 [Robertshaw]

Legman, Gershon
— The Limerick: 1700 Examples, with Notes.... Paris: Les Hautes Etudes, 1953. 8vo, orig wraps. sg Feb 12 (94) $90
— Oragenitalism. [N.p.], 1940. Part 1 only. sg Feb 12 (93) $375

Legrand, Augustin
— Album de la Jeunesse, Melange d'Histoire Naturelle, Mineraux, Plantes, Animaux. Paris: Gide fils, [c.1830]. Oblong 4to, contemp half lea; rubbed. With 60 plates. Lacking tp; text spotted; 1 plate lacking volvelles. S Oct 7 (975) £70 [Hildebrandt]

Legrand, Edy
— Macau & cosmage. Paris, [1919]. 4to, bds; worn & rubbed. cb Dec 4 (261) $110

Legrand, Francin
— La Chasse au gabion ou a la hutte. Caen. E. Adeline, 1906. 8vo, half shagreen. Jeanson copy. SM Mar 1 (338) FF2,200

Legrand, Gerard. See: Breton & Legrand

Legros, Alphonse
— Histoire du bonhomme misere. L, 1877. One of 60, sgd. Folio, orig vellum. With 6 plates. S Nov 10 (391) £100 [Fogg]

Lehmann, Friedrich Ernst
— Tractatus juridicus theoretico-practicus de variis ludendi generibus.... Bautzen, 1680. 4to, disbound. Blank corner of 1 leaf torn & repaired. sg Mar 26 (170) $100

Lehmann-Haupt, Hellmut —& Others
— Bookbinding in America: Three Essays. Portland, Maine, 1941. 1st Ed. sg June 11 (273) $80

Lehner, Hermann
— Der Erste Wiener Internationale Schachcongress in Jahre 1873. Leipzig, 1874. 8vo, cloth. pn Mar 26 (39) £50 [Farmer]

Lehrs, Max
— Geschichte und kritischer Katalog des deutschen, niederlaendischen und franzoesischen Kupferstichs im XV Jahrhundert. NY, [n.d]. 10 vols. Folio & 8vo, cloth. Facsimile reprint. S Nov 10 (112) £65 [Mas]

Leiber, Fritz
— The Swords of Lankhmar. L, 1969. In d/j. cb Sept 28 (812) $55
— The Wanderer. L: Dennis Dobson, [1967]. In d/j which is soiled at back. cb Sept 28 (813) $50
[-] Whispers. Browns Mills NJ: Stuart David Schiff, Oct 1979. Special Fritz Leiber Issue. Vol IV, No 1-2 cb Sept 28 (814) $50

Leibnitz, Gottfried Wilhelm von, 1646-1716 —& Bernoulli, Jean, 1667-1748
— Commercium philosophicum et mathematicum ab anno 1694 ad annum 1716. Lausanne & Geneva, 1745. 2 vols. 4to, contemp vellum. With 23 folding plates; lacking port; 1 plate & Aa2 in Vol I cleanly torn. Ck Feb 13 (186) £180

Leibnitz, Gottfried Wilhelm von, 1646-1716 —& Clarke, Samuel, 1675-1729
[ ] A Collection of Papers, which Passed between the Late Learned Mr. Leibnitz and Dr. Clarke in the Years 1715 and 1716.... L, 1717. 1st Ed. 2 parts in 1 vol. 8vo, modern cloth; stained. All but 1 ad leaves lacking; wormed, slightly affecting some text. bba Sept 25 (17) £210 [Bickersteth]

Leichardt, Ludwig, 1813-48
— Journal of an Overland Expedition in Australia.... L, 1847. 8vo, orig cloth; marked. One folding plates repaired & reinserted. Without the accompanying set of 3 maps. kh Mar 16 (297) A$600

Leigh, Charles, 1662-1701?

— The Natural History of Lancashire, Chesire and the Peak in Derbyshire. Oxford, 1700. 1st Ed. 3 parts in 1 vol. Folio, contemp calf; broken. Index leaf torn without loss; library markings. T Mar 19 (328) £165

Anr copy. Contemp calf; rebacked, upper cover detached. T June 18 (36) £110

Leigh, Edward, 1602-71

— A Systeme or Body and Divinity.... L: A. M. for William Lee, 1662. Folio, old calf; rubbed. bba Nov 13 (194) £60 [Lachman]

Leigh, Richard. See: Cecil, William

Leigh, W. H.

— Reconnoitering Voyages and Travels, with Adventures in...South Australia. L, 1839. 8vo, contemp half calf; rubbed. With litho title & 7 plates. Lacking half-title; 1 caption cropped. C Oct 15 (160) £120 [Green]

Anr copy. Later half calf. Some stains & soiling. kh Mar 16 (298) A$100

Leighton, Clare

— Growing New Roots: An Essay with Fourteen Wood Engravings. San Francisco: Book Club of Calif., 1976. One of 50 sgd, numbered & ptd by Leighton. sg Jan 8 (33) $80

Leighton, J. M. See: Swan & Leighton

Leinster, Murray

— Operation Outer Space. Reading: Fantasy Press, [1954]. One of 300. In d/j. Sgd on inserted nebula leaf. cb Sept 28 (818) $50

Leiris, Michel. See: Miro, Joan

Leisenring, James E.

— The Leisenring Color & Materials Book for Fly Tying.... [N.p.], 1966. One of 8. 12mo, ostrich. With specimens mtd & with title & all captions hand-lettered. sg Oct 23 (389) $1,000

Leith, Sir George

— A Short Account of the Settlement, Produce, and Commerce, of Prince of Wales Island, in the Straits of Malacca. L, 1805. Lacking last blank. Bound with: Stanley, John Thomas. An Account of the Hot Springs in Iceland. [Edin.? 1791]. And: Black, Joseph. An Analysis of the Waters of some Hot Springs in Iceland. [N.p., c.1791]. 8vo, contemp calf, armorial bdg; worn. Stuart de Rothesay copy. S Oct 23 (488) £1,200 [Hannas]

Leland, John, 1506?-52

— The Itinerary... Oxford, 1744-45. One of 350. 9 vols. 8vo, half calf. sg Oct 9 (253) $150

2d Ed. Oxford, 1745-44. 9 vols. 8vo, calf in the style of Edwards of Halifax. S Jan 16 (400) £360 [Daley]

Leland, Thomas, 1722-85

— The History of Ireland. L, 1773. 1st Ed. 3 vols. 4to, contemp calf; rubbed. Slight marginal worming. bba Apr 9 (320) £50 [Catnach]

Leloir, Maurice

— Une Femme de Qualite du Siecle Passe. Paris, 1899. One of 200. 4to, mor extra with gilt foliate rococo decoration, by Zaehnsdorf. Illusts hand-colored. S Dec 4 (17) £1,200 [Mitchell]

Lemaire, Charles, 1801-71

— L'Horticulteur universel; Journal general des jardiniers.... Paris, 1839-45. 8 vols. 8vo, half calf. With 260 (of 264) color plates. SM Oct 20 (473) FF5,000

— Iconographie descriptive des cactees.... Paris, 1841-47. Parts 1-7 (of 8). Folio, loose in 12 orig ptd wraps only. With 14 (of 16) hand-finished color plates. Paper fragile; some plates with marginal tears not affecting image. de Belder copy. S Apr 28 (209) £4,800 [Elliott]

Lemaire, Charles, 1801-71 —& Others

— Flore des serres et des jardins de l'Europe. Ghent, 1845-88. Vols VII-X (of 10) & Second Series Vols I-IV (of 5) only. 8vo, contemp calf. Sold w.a.f. C Oct 15 (228) £2,600 [Walford]

Anr copy. 23 vols (all pbd). 8vo, contemp half mor; spines rubbed or faded. de Belder copy. S Apr 28 (210) £17,000 [Antipodean Books]

— L'Illustration horticole, journal special des serres et des jardins. Ghent, 1854-86. Vols 1-33 (of 43). 8vo, contemp half mor; rubbed. de Belder copy. S Apr 28 (211) £7,500 [Berg]

Lemberger, Ernst

— Die Bildnis Miniatur in Deutschland von 1550-1850. Munich: F. Bruckmann, [1909]. One of 400. 2 vols. Folio, cloth; soiled. With 65 plates. bba Dec 18 (178) £100 [Crisford]

Lemery, Louis, 1677-1743

— A Treatise of Foods in General. L, 1704. 1st Ed in English. 8vo, contemp calf; front cover detached. Some stains & soiling; tear to A1. cb July 30 (271) $275

Lemery, Nicholas, 1645-1715
— A Course of Chymistry.... L, 1698. 8vo, contemp calf; repaired, rebacked. With 7 full-page woodcuts. Small piece torn from 1 margin; neat tear in 1 leaf. bba May 14 (302) £180 [P & P Books]

Lemnius, Levinus, 1505-68
— Occulta naturae miracula. Antwerp, 1564. 8vo, contemp blindstamped calf over wooden bds. Some browning & other defs. HK Nov 4 (659) DM800
— Similitudinum ac parabolarum quae in Bibliis ex herbis atque arboribus desumuntur.... Frankfurt, 1596. 16mo, old vellum. Margins trimmed; some browning; paper flaw in B1 affecting 2 words. sg Jan 15 (232) $110

Lemoisne, Paul Andre
— Gavarni, peintre et lithographe. Paris, 1924. 4to, contemp half mor. cba Mar 5 (75) $110

Lemonnier, Camille, 1844-1913
— Felicien Rops: l'homme et l'artiste. Paris, 1908. 1st Ed. 4to, contemp half mor, orig wraps bound in; worn. bba Sept 25 (312) £80 [Oram]

Lempe, Johann Friedrich
— Magazin der Bergbaukunde. Dresden, 1785-90. Vols I-VII. 8vo, contemp half calf. C Dec 12 (128) £260 [Quaritch]

Lenin, Vladimir Il'ich, 1870-1924
— Doklad ob obedinitel'nom sezde Rossiiskoi sotsialdemocraticheskoi rabochei partii. Moscow, 1906. 8vo, loose as issued in orig wraps; marginal fraying & chipping. P Sept 24 (322) $150
— Works. Moscow, 1960-70. 45 vols. bba Oct 30 (206) £75 [Smith]

Lenroot, Clara C.
— Will You Walk Into My Garden? NY: Derrydale Press, 1936. One of 200. Inscr. sg Oct 23 (88) $275

Lenygon, Francis
— Furniture in England from 1660 to 1760. L, [1914]. Folio, cloth; worn & shaken. O Feb 24 (122) $80

Leo I, Pope, 390?-461
— Sermones. Rome: Conrad Sweynheym & Arnold Pannartz, after 30 Aug 1470. Folio, wooden bds with blind-tooled lea spine, 2 clasps & catches; new endpapers. With a three-quarter border by a contemp Roman hand on f.5 recto of white vinework infilled with blue, green, yellow & red, framed in gold & incorporating large initial L. Foot of decoration slightly shaved by the binder; repaired tear with no loss in ff. 3 & 4; minor repairs in last leaf; occasional spotting mainly in margins. 133 (of 134) leaves; lacking initial blank. Goff L-129. S May 21 (8) £8,500 [Fletcher]

Leo, Johannes
— A Geographical Historie of Africa. L, 1600. 1st Ed in English. Folio, contemp calf; repaired but broken. Some dampstaining; minor worming. S June 25 (485) £1,250 [Maggs]

Leon & Brother
— Catalogue of First Editions of American Authors.... NY, 1885. 8vo, def wraps. sg Oct 2 (5) $70

Leon, Luis de, d.1591
— De los nombres de Cristo en dos libros.... Salamanca: Juan Fernandez, 1583. 4to, modern vellum bds. S May 21 (48) £1,400 [Quaritch]
— La Perfecta Casada.... Salamanca: Juan fernandez, 1583. 4to, modern vellum bds. S May 21 (49) £1,400 [Quaritch]

Leon, Nicolas, 1859-1929
— Bibliografia Mexicana del Siglo XVIII. Mexico City, 1902-8. 5 vols in 6, without indexes. 4to, cloth; soiled. sg Sept 18 (27) $200
Anr Ed. Mexico City, 1902-46. 5 parts in 10 vols. With vol containing 3 index pamphlets by Robert Valles. Lea gilt, orig wraps bound in. sg Oct 2 (216) $375

Leonard, Zenas
— Leonard's Narrative, Adventures of Zenas Leonard, Fur Trader and Trapper.... Cleveland, 1904. One of 520. 8vo, orig cloth; rubbed. cb Mar 19 (168) $150

Leonardo da Vinci, 1452-1519
— Quaderni d'anatomia, I-V: della Royal Library di Windsor. Christiania, 1911-16. Ltd Ed. 6 vols. Folio, bds; worn. sg Jan 15 (104) $700
— Traite de la peinture. Paris, 1651. Folio, half lea. Dampstained. SM Oct 20 (571) FF4,000
A Treatise of Painting. L, 1721. 1st Ed in English. 8vo, contemp calf; rebacked. Some plates dampstained. sg Mar 26 (172) $250

Leonhardi, Friedrich Gottlieb, d.1814
— Forst und Jagd Taschenbuch fuer das Jahr 1794 [-1803]. Leipzig, 1794-1803. 10 vols. 16mo, orig bdg. Jeanson copy. SM Mar 1 (341) FF40,000

Leopold, Jan Hendrik
— Verzen. Brugge: E. Verbeke, 1912. One of 80. Orig wraps. B Oct 7 (659) HF1,250

Lepere, Auguste, 1849-1918
— Nantes en dix-neuf cent. Nantes: Emile Grimaud & fils, [1900]. One of 20. 4to, mosaic bdg in mor by Levitsky. FD Dec 2 (4524) DM4,600

Lermontov, Mikhail Yurievitch, 1814-41
— A Song about Tsar Ivan Vasilyevitch. L: Aquila Press, 1929. One of 750. Illus by Paul Nash. Mor with mor onlays. cb Dec 4 (29) $75

Leroux, Gaston, 1868-1927
— The Phantom of the Opera. NY: Bobbs Merrill, [1911]. Cloth. cb Sept 28 (826) $65

Lery, Jean de, 1534-1611
— Historia navigationis in Brasiliam.... [Geneva]: Eustathius Vignon, 1586. 8vo, contemp vellum from an Ms leaf; rubbed. FD Dec 2 (1085) DM2,900

Leslie, Charles, of Jamaica
— A New History of Jamaica. L, 1740. 8vo, later calf. With 2 folding maps. Small ptd area of title adhering to the facing map. C Dec 12 (248) £380 [Von Hunersdorf]

Anr copy. Contemp calf gilt; worn. With 2 maps. Small piece cut from upper blank margin of preface leaf. pn Mar 5 (30) £250 [Maggs]

Leslie, Eliza, 1787-1858
— Seventy-five Receipts for Pastry, Cakes and Sweetmeats. Bost., 1828. Lowenstein's 1st Ed. 12mo, orig cloth; worn & soiled. Crahan copy. P Nov 25 (292) $300

Leslie, John, 1527-96
— De origine, moribus & rebus gestis Scotorum, libri decem. Rome, 1578. 4to, old lea; rebacked, joints cracked. Lacking the map. sg Oct 9 (255) $130

Lessing, Gotthold Ephraim, 1729-81
— Saemmtliche Schriften. Berlin, 1784-94. 30 vols. 8vo, calf gilt; 2 vols broken. HN Nov 26 (1265) DM2,600

Lessing, Julius
— Alt Orientalisch Teppichmuster. Berlin, 1877. Folio, cloth, in chipped d/j. With 30 colored plates. sg Feb 5 (241) $400

Lesson, Rene Primevere, 1794-1849
— Histoire naturelle des colobris.... Paris, [1830-32]. 8vo, later half sheep; joints & extremities rubbed. With 66 hand-colored plates. sg Jan 15 (233) $950
— Histoire naturelle des oiseaux de paradis et des epimaques. Paris, [1834-35]. 8vo, 19th-cent half calf; joints starting. With 43 hand-colored plates, a few spotted. sg Jan 15 (234) $850
— Les Trochilidees ou les colibris et les oiseaux-mouches. Paris, [1832-33]. 8vo, half mor gilt; rubbed. With 66 hand-colored plates. pn Dec 11 (210) £400 [Burgess & Browning]

Letarouilly, Paul, 1795-1855
— Edifices de Rome moderne. Paris, 1860-50-57. 4 vols. Folio & 4to, contemp half mor. With 354 plates. C July 22 (115) £500
— Le Vatican et la Basilique de Saint-Pierre de Rome. Paris, 1882. 2 vols. Folio, contemp half mor. With 264 plates. C July 22 (116) £750

Leth, Andries de
— De zegepraalende Vecht, vertoonende verscheidene Gesichten van Lustplaatsen.... Amst., 1719. 1st Ed. Folio, contemp vellum. With engraved title, map & 98 views on 49 leaves. S Oct 23 (115) £1,500 [Goldschmidt]

Leth, Hendrik de
— Nieuwe geographische en historische Atlas van de Zeven Vereenigde Nederlandsche Provintien. Amst., [1740]. Oblong 8vo, half calf. With engraved title, 35 maps, colored in outline, 13 plans, 2 tables & a plate, all folding; lacking plan of Arnhem. B Oct 7 (1362) HF2,400

Lettere...
— Lettere di principi. Venice: Ziletti, 1564-81. 3 vols. 4to, bdg not described. Some dampstaining; hole in 2Q4 of Vol II with loss & in margin of 3N1 with slight loss of text. S Jan 16 (401) £50 [Zayas]

Lettre...
— Lettre a un ami, sur l'utilite des globes volans, de M. de Montgolfier & sur la possibilite de la Prise de Gibraltar. Amst.: Gueffier, 1783. 8vo, wraps; spine crudely reinforced with tape. Tp soiled. sg Mar 26 (209) $250

Lettres...
— Lettres edifiantes et curieuses, ecrites des missions etrangeres. Paris, 1780-83. 26 vols. 12mo, contemp calf. With 56 ports, plates & maps. S June 25 (327) £850 [Remington]

Lettsom, John Coakley
— History of the Origin of Medicine.... L, 1778. 4to, half calf. With 2 plate in colored & uncolored states. S May 28 (718) £220

Letty, Cynthia
— Wild Flowers of the Transvaal. Johannesburg, 1962. Ltd Ed. 4to, cloth, in d/j. SSA Feb 11 (560) R220

Leupold, Jacob
— Theatrum machinarum generale, Schau-Platz des Grundes mechanischer Wissenschafften. Leipzig, 1724-35. Parts 1-8 (of 12) in 4 vols. Folio, contemp calf; rubbed, head of 1 spine torn. With 447 plates, 1 with detached volvelle. C Dec 12 (129) £3,800 [Quaritch]

Anr copy. Part 1 only. calf. With 51 plates. HK Nov 4 (1049) DM1,400

— Theatrum Pontificiale, oder Schau-Platz der Bruecken und Bruechen-Baues.... Leipzig, 1726. 1st Ed. Folio, contemp half calf gilt. With 60 folding plates. FD June 11 (3437) DM1,500

Levack, Daniel J. H. —& Godersky, steven Owen
— PDK: A Philip K. Dick Bibliography. San Francisco, 1981. One of 200. As new in orig shrink wrap. cb Sept 28 (441) $75

Levaillant, Francois, 1753-1824
— Oiseaux d'Afrique. Paris, [1796]-99-1808-[12]. ("Histoire naturelle des oiseaux d'Afrique.") Vols I-III only (Vol III incomplete). Old half calf; rebacked. With 144 color plates. Sold w.a.f. C Oct 15 (240) £1,900 [Davies]

Anr Ed. Paris, [1796]-1799-1808-[12]. 6 vols. 4to, half mor gilt. With 300 hand-colored plates Some repairs. pn Jan 22 (201) £2,700 [Pitt]

— Oiseaux de paradis. Paris, [1801]-06. ("Histoire naturelle des oiseaux de paradis et des rolliers....") 2 vols. Folio, contemp mor gilt. With 103 plates only. Marginal foxing. P Sept 24 (191) $10,500

Anr copy. Sold with: Levaillant. Histoire naturelle des promerops et des guepiers. Paris, 1807-[18]. 3 vols. Folio, 19th-cent mor gilt; rubbed. With 197 hand-finished color plates. P June 18 (109) $21,000

Anr copy. 2 vols. Folio, contemp mor gilt; rubbed, joints split. With 114 colored plates. Some foxing & offsetting affecting a few plates; a few plates just trimmed; small repair to Plate 3 of Vol II. S Oct 23 (713) £6,000 [Grahame]

— Traveller in South Africa. Cape Town, 1973. Ltd Ed. 2 vols. 4to, calf. SSA Feb 11 (561) R440

— Voyage dans l'interieur de l'Afrique.... Paris, 1790. 1st Ed. 2 vols. 8vo, contemp calf. With frontis & 10 hand-colored plates. SSA Oct 28 (697) R560

Levanto, Francesco Maria
— Prima Parte dello specchio del mare.... Venice, 1698. Revised by Vincenzo Maria Coronelli. Folio, contemp calf; worn. With 25 charts (all but 1 double-page), 3 argonauti plates, double-page allegorical plate (wormed at fold), 3 double-page naval plates, port of Coronelli & with 10 naval plates & diagrams including some from the Dudley dell'Arcano del Mare. A few leaves & plates slightly waterstained; minor repairs without loss. S Apr 24 (205) £5,000 [Martinos]

Levanto, Leonardo
— Cathecismo de la Doctrina Christiana, en lengua Zaapoteca. Puebla, 1776. 4to, contemp limp vellum; front cover spotted. Text in Spanish & Zapotecan. sg Sept 18 (151) $325

Levayer de Boutigny, Roland
— Tarsis et Zelie. The Hague, 1720. 6 parts in 3 vols. 8vo, contemp calf, armorial bdg. A few borders shaved. S Mar 10 (957) £50 [Robertshaw]

L'Eveque, Henry
— Campaigns of the British Army in Portugal.... L, 1812. Folio, half calf. With port & 17 plates. Marginal waterstain at end. S Oct 23 (193) £1,100 [Marshall]

Lever, Charles James, 1806-72
— Works. L, [1897-99]. One of 1,000. 37 vols. 8vo, orig cloth; worn. pn June 18 (193) £140 [Shapero]

Levett, John
— The Ordering of Bees.... L, 1634. 4to, 19th-cent half lea; rebacked. Johannson copy. sg Jan 15 (159) $800

Levi, Eliphas
— Dogme et Rituel de la Haute Magie. Paris, 1861. 2 vols in 1. 8vo, contemp half mor. Some spotting. Ck Jan 30 (160) £45

Levinsohn, Isaac Baer
— Efes Dammim: A Series of Conversations at Jerusalem.... L, 1841. 8vo, orig cloth, unopened; hinge split. Some stains. sg Sept 25 (181) $140

Levinson, Andre, 1887-1933
— Bakst: The Story of the Artist's Life. L, 1923. One of 315. Folio, orig vellum; soiled. pn July 23 (164) £280

Anr copy. Orig vellum; worn & soiled. With 67 plates, 51 in color. S June 17 (72) £420 [Lewinson]

Anr copy. Orig vellum; slightly discolored. With 68 colored plates. sg Feb 26 (123) $700

— The Designs of Leon Bakst for The Sleeping Princess. L, 1923. One of 1,000. Folio, half vellum; spotted & rubbed. With port by Picasso & 54 colored plates by Bakst. wd June 19 (63) $650

— Histoire de Leon Bakst. Paris, [1924]. One

of 160. 4to, mor by Elias. With 68 plates. FD June 11'(4794) DM2,500

Levis, Howard C.
— A Descriptive Bibliography of the most Important Books in the English Language Relating to...Engraving. L, 1912-13. 1st Ed, one of 350. 2 vols, including Supplement, in 1. 4to, half cloth; shaken. Inscr. sg May 14 (48) $325

Levy, Julien
— Surrealism. NY: Black Sun Press, 1936. Bds. Inscr to Rene Magritte. S July 2 (1031) £400 [Takahata]

Lewenklau, Hans
— Neuwe Chronica Tuerckischer Nation.... Frankfurt, 1595. Bound with: Neuwer Musulmanischer Histori, Tuerckischer Nation.... Frankfurt, 1595. Folio, vellum bds. Some worming & stains; tp stamped. S Oct 23 (348) £1,400 [Wood]

Lewin, John William
— A Natural History of the Birds of New South Wales. L, 1822. 4to, contemp half lea; worn. With 26 hand-colored plates. Marginal tear in last plate. S Oct 23 (716) £3,200 [Quaritch]
Anr Ed. Melbourne, 1978. One of 500. Folio, mor. pn Oct 23 (240) £65 [Bles]

Lewin, William
— The Birds of Great Britain. L, 1789-94. 7 vols. 4to, contemp mor gilt with arms of the 3d Duke of Roxburghe. With 324 orig watercolor drawings. C Oct 15 (241) £25,000 [Sims]
Anr Ed. L, 1795-1801. 8 vols. 4to, half calf; rubbed. With 336 hand-colored plates, including 58 plates of eggs. All plates linen-backed & E. Williams Library written in ink across each. pn Mar 5 (31) £680 [Johnson]
— The Insects of Great Britain. L, 1795. 1st Ed. Vol I (all pbd). 4to, contemp half calf gilt; joints split. With 46 hand-colored plates. S Apr 23 (14) £850 [Dunbar]

Lewine, J.
— Bibliography of Eighteenth Century Art and Illustrated Books. L, 1898. Ltd Ed. 8vo, cloth. sg May 14 (49) $150

Lewis, Angelo John, 1839-1919
— Modern Magic, a Practical Treatise on the Art of Conjuring. L, [1876]. 8vo, orig cloth; worn, front endpapers removed. Half-title & 1 leaf of contents loose. S Nov 10 (330) £60 [Walker]

Lewis, Cecil Day
— Collected Poems. L, 1954. Proof copy. Ptd wraps. Numerous corrections in several hands. sg Dec 11 (18) $120

Lewis, Charles Thomas Courtney
— George Baxter, Colour Printer, his Life and Work. L, 1908. Orig cloth; rubbed. O June 16 (121) $50
— The Story Book of Picture Printing in England during the Nineteenth Century. L, 1928. 4to, orig cloth; shaken. O June 16 (122) $70

Lewis, Elisha Jarrett, 1820-77
— The American Sportsman: Containing Hints to Sportsmen.... Phila., 1855. 8vo, orig cloth; worn. Prelims foxed. cb Nov 6 (194) $80

Lewis, Frederick Christian
— Scenery of the River Exe. L, 1827. Folio, later half calf; rebacked preserving old spine. With engraved title & 29 views on 27 plates, all on india paper. S May 29 (1004) £130

Lewis, Henry
— Das Illustrirte Mississippithal.... Dusseldorf, [1854-58]. 4to, modern half mor; old spine laid down. With litho pictorial half-title & 76 hand-finished color plates. Lacking 2 plates, including the double-page view of New Orleans; 2 other plates trimmed to image & mtd; half-title, tp, last few leaves & a few plates extended; some foxing. P Oct 29 (12) $9,000

Lewis, James O., 1799-1858
— The Aboriginal Port-folio. Phila., 1835-36. Folio, orig half calf. With 60 plates only. Lacking tp; some chips & marginal tears; stamp on 1 of the 3 Advertisement leaves present. ha May 22 (298) $4,100

Lewis, John, 1675-1747
— The History and Antiquities, Ecclesiastical and Civil, of the Isle of Tenet, in Kent. L, 1723. 1st Ed. 2 parts in 1 vol. 4to, calf; rebacked. With 25 plates. pn Mar 5 (122) £100 [Camberley]

Lewis, John Frederick, 1860-1932
— Sketches and Drawings of the Alhambra.... L, [1835]. Folio, contemp half mor; rubbed & loose. With engraved title, dedication, frontis & 23 (of 24) plates. bba May 14 (415) £380 [Kamiliya]
— Sketches of Spain and Spanish Character. L, [1836]. 1st Ed. Folio, half mor gilt. With 20 (of 25) plates, 3 hand-colored. pn Jan 22 (208) £280 [Orssich]

Lewis, Matthew Gregory, 1775-1818
— Tales of Terror. L, 1801. 19th-cent half calf worn; With engraved title & 3 colored folding plates.. Some foxing & minor stains.. Sokmetimes attributed to Lewis. sg Feb 12 (301) $150

Lewis, Meriwether, 1774-1809. See: Limited Editions Club

Lewis, Meriwether, 1774-1809 —& Clark, William, 1770-1838
— History of the Expedition.... L, 1814. ("Travels to the Source of the Missouri River and across the American Continent to the Pacific Ocean,,,,") 1st English Ed, 4to, old calf; worn & spotted. With folding map & 5 maps on 3 plates. Folding map torn & detached; text browned. wd June 19 (146) $3,000

Anr Ed. Phila., 1814. 2 vols. 8vo, later mor gilt; several covers loose. With folding map & 5 plates. Map backed with paper; 1 small tear along fold & anr near hinge; perforated library stamp on tp of Vol I. sg Mar 12 (165) $4,500

— Message from the President of the United States, Communicating Discoveries Made in Exploring the Missouri, Red River, and Washita.... L, 1807. ("Travels in the Interior Parts of America....") 8vo, half mor; joints worn, rear cover stained. With folding table. Ink library acquisition number on A2. sg Mar 12 (164) $275

Anr Ed. Dayton, Ohio, 1840. ("The Journal of Lewis and Clarke....") 12mo, contemp calf; front cover detached. sg Mar 12 (166) $150

Lewis, Oscar. See: Grabhorn Printing

Lewis, Samuel, d.1862
— An Atlas, Comprising Maps of the Several Counties.... L, 1842. 4to, contemp half calf; worn, head of spine partially missing. With 56 maps, hand-colored in outline, & 1 plan. 2 maps repaired. S May 29 (975) £260

— Atlas to the Topographical Dictionary of England and Wales. L, 1844. 4to, cloth; torn. With 42 maps only. pn May 21 (377) £90 [Eisler]

— Atlas to the Topographical Dictionary of England & Wales. L, 1845. 4to, cloth. With 55 maps, colored in outline. pn Jan 22 (349) £140 [Franks]

— A Topographical Dictionary of England. L, 1835. 5 vols, including Atlas vol. 4to, orig cloth. With 110 maps, colored in outline. pn May 21 (376) £100 [Bowdage]

Anr Ed. L, 1849-48. 5 vols, including plate vol. 4to, orig cloth; spines repaired at head & base, joints split. With 57 maps, all but 1 hand-colored in outline. Some maps torn along folds. bba Mar 26 (366) £80 [Franks]

Anr copy. Atlas vol only. 4to, With folding plan of London & 55 county maps, colored in outline. pn Jan 22 (344) £120 [Kentich]

Anr copy. Plate vol only. 4to, With folding general map & 32 county maps colored in outline. pn Mar 5 (367) £85

— A Topographical Dictionary of Scotland. L, 1846. 3 vols, including Atlas. 4to, orig cloth. bba Apr 9 (356) £120 [Catnach]

Lewis, Sinclair, 1885-1951
See also: Limited Editions Club

— Arrowsmith. NY, [1925]. 1st Ed, one of 500 L.p. copies, sgd. sg Mar 5 (126) $275

— Babbitt. NY, [1922]. 1st Ed, 1st State. Bdg worn. Inscr. O June 9 (101) $90

Anr copy. In d/j. sg Mar 5 (130) $300

— Dodsworth. NY. Harcourt, Brace, [1929]. Advance copy. sg Mar 5 (127) $150

— Elmer Gantry. NY, [1927]. 1st Ed, 1st Bdg. In chipped d/j. sg Mar 5 (131) $100

— Free Air. NY, 1919. Worn. sg Mar 5 (128) $50

— Hike and the Aeroplane. By Tom Graham. NY, [1912]. 1st Ed. Orig cloth; soiled, hinges repaired. wa June 25 (374) $330

— John Dos Passos' Manhattan Transfer. NY, 1926. One of 975. Unopened copy. sg Mar 5 (129) $100

— Our Mr. Wrenn. NY, 1914. 1st Ed. wa June 25 (373) $110

Lewis, William, 1714-81
— An Experimental History of the Materia Medica.... L, 1791. 4th Ed. 2 vols. 8vo, bds. pnE Dec 17 (119) £55 [Steedman]

Lewis, William, 1787-1870
— Chess Problems. L, 1827. 1st Issue (without solutions). Cloth. pn Mar 26 (303) £130 [De Lucia]

Fifty Games at Chess. L, 1832. Orig bds; rebacked. Upper margin of tp torn & repaired. pn Mar 26 (235) £35 [British Chess Magazine]

— Oriental Chess or Specimens of Hindoostanee Excellence in that Celebrated Game. L, 1817. 2 vols. Contemp calf; rebacked. pn Mar 26 (305) £75 [Hoffman]

— A Selection of Games at Chess...L. C. de la Bourdonnais and an English Amateur [Alexander McDonnell]. L, 1835. Orig wraps; spine repaired. pn Mar 26 (113) £55 [Furstenberg]

Lewis, William S. —& Phillips, Paul C.
— The Journal of John Work. Cleveland, 1923. cb Oct 9 (130) $60

Lewis, Wyndham, 1884-1957
— The Apes of God. L, 1902. 1st Ed, One of 750, sgd. 4to, cloth, in d/j. sg Dec 11 (327) $140

Anr Ed. L, 1930. One of 750. 4to, cloth. T Feb 18 (71) £42

— Thirty Personalities and a Self-Portrait. L, 1932. One of 200. Folio, unbound as issued. S June 17 (252) £280 [Sims]

Ley, Willy
— Die Moeglichkeit der Weltraumfahrt: Allgemeinverstaendliche Beitraege zum Raumschiffahrtsproblem. Leipzig, 1928. Later cloth, orig wraps bound in. sg Jan 15 (357) $250

Leybourn, William, 1626-1700?
— Arithmetical Recreations: or, Enchiridion of Arithmetical Questions.... L: J. C. for Hen. Brome & Sam. Speed, 1667. 12mo, contemp half vellum; short split to head of upper joint. Small piece torn from corner of G5 & 6, affecting page numeral; a few small stains on A7v & A8r. C May 13 (164) £850 [Goldschmidt]

— Dialling: Plain, Concave, Convex... L, 1700. Folio, contemp calf; rebacked, worn. With 30 plates only. Some soiling. Sold w.a.f. Ck Jan 30 (43) £70

Leyes...
— Las Leyes de Toro Glosadas. Burgos, 1527. Folio, later vellum. Dampstaining in lower margins throughout; slight worming in gutters not affecting legibility; scattered early marginalia & underscoring; tp frayed; portion of lower margin excised from last leaf. sg Mar 26 (175) $350

Leymarie, Jean
— The Jerusalem Windows. NY, [1962]. 4to, cloth, in d/j. sg Jan 8 (43) $300

— Picasso, the Artist of the Century. NY, 1972. 4to, cloth, in d/j; worn. O Jan 6 (112) $50

L'Heritier de Brutelle, Charles Louis
— Cornus. Specimen botanicum sistens descriptiones.... Paris, 1788-[89]. Bound with: Sertum Anglicum, seu plantae rariores quas in hortis juxta Londinum.... Paris, 1788-[92]. Folio, contemp calf gilt; rubbed. With 35 plates. Simpson—de Belder copy. S Apr 28 (214) £7,000 [Israel]

— Geraniologia, seu Erodii, Pelargonii, Geranii, Monsoniae et Grieli historia. Paris, 1787-88. Folio, orig bds, uncut. With 44 plates. Some spotting. de Belder copy. S Apr 28 (213) £2,200 [Krohn]

— Stirpes novae aut minus cognitae. Paris, 1784-[91]. Folio, early 19th-cent half calf; rubbed, spine repaired. With 91 plates. Horticultural Society of New York—de Belder copy. S Apr 28 (216) £3,000 [Berg] Anr copy. 2 vols. Folio, contemp russia gilt extra, armorial bdg, bound for George Spencer, 5th Duke of Marlborough with his arms as Marquis of Blandford on sides, in glazed mahogany case. With 91 plates, 1 plain, the others hand-colored, 4 of which are orig watercolors; Plate 30 bis is in uncolored state only. Some spotting. Linnean Society—de Belder copy. S Apr 28 (218) £98,000 [Israel]

L'Hospital, Guillaume Francois Antoine, Marquis de, 1661-1704. See: Washington's copy, George

Liber...
— Liber Scriptorum. The First Book of the Author's Club. NY, 1893. One of 251. 4to, syn; front hinge cracked, spine partly perished. With 109 contributions, each sgd by its author. wd June 19 (98) $650

— Liber Scriptorum: The Second Book of the Author's Club. NY, 1921. One of 251. Folio, orig lea gilt. With each article sgd by the contributor. O May 12 (123) $300

Liboschitz, Joseph —& Trinius, Charles
— Flore des environs de St. Petersbourg et de Moscou. St. Petersburg, 1811. Vol I (all pbd). 4to, calf, orig wraps bound in. With 40 hand-colored plates. de Belder copy. S Apr 28 (212) £3,500 [Mcdougall]

Library of Congress—Washington, D.C.
— Children's Books in the Rare Book Division of the Library.... Totowa, N.J., 1975. 2 vols. 4to, orig cloth. O Apr 28 (42) $50

Libri, Guillaume, 1803-69
— Histoire des sciences mathematiques en Italie depuis la renaissance des lettres jusqu'a la fin du dix-septieme siecle. Paris, 1838-41. 1st Ed. 4 vols. 8vo, wraps; worn. sg May 14 (600) $200

— Monuments inedits ou peu connus.... L, 1862-64. 2 vols (including Supplement) in 1. Folio, half cloth; worn. With 65 plates in gold or silver & color. HK Nov 4 (3155) DM700

Libro...
— Libro de la natura di cavalli: & el modo di relevarli: medicarli: & domarli.... Venice: G. B. Sessa, 29 Jan 1502. 4to, mor janseniste by Chambolle-Duru. Jeanson copy. SM Mar 1 (346) FF42,000

— Libro de la natura di cavalli.... Venice:

Melchoir Sessa, 4 Mar 1517. 4to, mor gilt by Chambolle-Duru. Jeanson copy. SM Mar 1 (347) FF11,500

Licetus, Fortunius, 1577-1657
— De spontaneo viventium ortu.... Vicenza: D. Amadei, 1617. Folio, modern half vellum. Hole in tp affecting 1 letter; lacking final leaf. Hunt copy. CNY Nov 21 (170) $240

Lichtenberger, Johannes
— Prognosticatio in Latino. [Cologne:] Peter Quentel, May 1526. 4to, vellum. Some finger-soiling & worming. FD June 11 (110) DM4,500

Liddell, Donald Macy
— Chessmen. NY, 1937. 4to, cloth, in d/j. pn Mar 26 (447) £110 [Furstenberg]

Liebault, Jean, d.1596. See: Estienne & Liebault

Liebault, Jean, d.1796. See: Estienne & Liebault

Liebig, Justus von, 1803-73 —& Others
— Handwoerterbuch der reinen und angewandten Chemie. Braunschweig, 1842-50. 10 vols, including Supplement. 8vo, disbound. HK Nov 4 (1055) DM1,200

Liebmann, Louis —& Wahl, Gustave
— Katalog der Historischen Abteilung der Ersten Internationalen Luftschiffahrts-Ausstellung.... Frankfurt, 1912. sg May 14 (562) $200

Liebreich, Richard
— Atlas der Ophtalmoscopie. Berlin, 1863. 1st Ed. Folio, orig bds; sides soiled. With 12 colored plates. S Nov 10 (424) £900 [Pickering]

Anr copy. Orig bds; worn & soiled, lower cover wormed. With 12 plates. Some margins discolored or stained. S Nov 27 (272) £950 [Phillips]

Lietze, Ernst
— Modern Heliographic Processes. NY, 1888. One of 1,000 with 10 specimen heliograms mtd on 5 leaves. 8vo, cloth; new endpapers. pnE June 25 (40) $110

Lieure, Jules
— Jacques Callot. NY, 1969. 8 vols. 4to, orig cloth. sg Oct 2 (79) $90

Lieutaud, Joseph, 1703-80
— Essais anatomiques, contenant l'histoire exacte de toutes les parties qui composent le corps de l'homme.... Paris, 1766. 8vo, contemp calf; rubbed, spine chipped. With 6 folding plates. Some plates soiled. Ck Jan 30 (181) £90

Lifar, Serge
— Pensees sur la danse. [Paris, 1946]. One of 450 on velin de rives. Illus by Aristide Maillol. 4to, orig ptd wraps. With 7 plates. S May 6 (21) £80 [Sutherland]

Life...
— The Life and Death of Miss Deborah Diddle of Daisy Mead Green and Sir Gilbert Go-Softly of Gooseberry Hall. L: R. Macdonald, [c.1820]. 8vo, mor gilt, orig wraps bound in. With frontis, pictorial title & 11 pp each with illust & accompanying verses; engraved throughout & colored by hand. S Dec 5 (322) £200 [Stone]

Liger, Louis, 1658-1717
— Le Jardinier fleuriste et historiographe, ou la culture universelle des fleurs, arbres.... Amst., 1748. 2 vols. 8vo, contemp calf; rubbed, joints cracked. With 20 folding plates. bba Apr 9 (444) £150 [Greenwood]

— Le Nouveau Theatre d'agriculture menage des champs. Paris, 1723. 4to, contemp calf gilt with crest of Duke of Buccleuch. With 29 plates. Minor discoloration. C Apr 8 (134) £260 [Weinreb]

La Nouvelle Maison rustique. Paris, 1768. 9th Ed. 2 vols. 4to, contemp calf gilt; joints cracked, corners bumped & rubbed. With frontis & 35 plates. Small rip in margin of tp; 1 plate with clean tear, 2 plates in Vol II loose. Hunt copy. CNY Nov 21 (171) $350

Anr Ed. Paris, 1790. 2 vols. 4to, calf; worn. Minor dampstaining to 1 vol, occasionally affecting text & images. sg Feb 5 (210) $80

Light, Sir Henry, 1783-1870
— Travels in Egypt, Nubia, the Holy Land.... L, 1818. 4to, later half cloth. Stained. bba May 28 (298) £140 [Heater]

Anr copy. Contemp half calf; rubbed, spine worn. Ck May 15 (16) £320

Light, William, 1785?-1839 —& De Wint, Peter, 1784-1849
— Sicilian Scenery. L, 1823. 4to, cloth. With engraved title & 61 plates. bba Dec 18 (181) £60 [Elliott]

Lightfoot, John, 1735-88
— Flora Scotica. L, 1777. ("Flora Scotica: or, a Systematic Arrangement...of the Native Plants of Scotland and the Hebrides.") 1st Ed. 2 vols. 8vo, contemp calf. With engraved title & 42 plates, including 7 inserted from anr work. Short tear in 1 leaf; 1 leaf torn in fold. bba May 14 (308) £100 [Greyfriars]

LIGNIVILLE

Ligniville, Jean de, comte de Bey, d. c.1645
— La Meutte et venerie pour le chevreuil. Nancy: Anthoine Charlot, 1655. 4to, mor gilt by Trautz-Bauzonnet. Jeanson copy. SM Mar 1 (352) FF200,000

Anr Ed. Paris, 1844. ("Les Meuttes et veneries.") 8vo, contemp calf with arms of the Comte de Beaufort. Jeanson copy. SM Mar 1 (353) FF2,100

Anr Ed. Nancy: Aubry et Veuve Bouchard-Huzard, 1861. One of 111. 4to, contemp shagreen. Jeanson copy. SM Mar 1 (354) FF2,800

Anr Ed. Paris: Damascene Morgand, 1892. 2 vols. 4to, half mor by Saulnier. Jeanson copy. SM Mar 1 (356) FF4,000

Anr copy. Half mor by Champs. Jeanson copy. SM Mar 1 (357) FF4,500

Unique copy on japon for henri Gallice. 4to, mor janseniste by Chambolle-Duru. Jeanson copy. SM Mar 1 (355) FF45,000

Anr Ed. Paris: Plume et Presse, 1947-48. One of 300. 4to, half mor. Jeanson copy. SM Mar 1 (358) FF3,400

Ligon, Richard
— A True & Exact History of the Island of Barbados.... L, 1657. 1st Ed. Folio, old calf; rebacked. With folding map, 6 engraved plates & 3 folding plans, 1 torn & repaired. Title & A1 repaired along margin, C2 with small hole. pnNY Sept 13 (256) $550

Lilford, Thomas L. Powys, 4th Baron
— Coloured Figures of the Birds of the British Islands. L, 1885-97. 7 vols. 8vo, later half mor, orig wraps bound in. With port & 421 plates. bba Oct 30 (399) £850 [Greyfriars]

Anr copy. 7 vols in 8. 8vo, contemp mor gilt. Vol VIII contains the index & all the wraps to the 36 orig parts & the list of subscribers. Lacking the extra plate of the Turtle Dove, but with 8 other duplicates. bba Apr 23 (149) £1,300 [Greyfriars]

Anr copy. 7 vols. 8vo, contemp half mor, orig wraps bound in. With port & 421 colored plates on linen guards throughout. Vol III, p 4 with loss of text due to adhesion. C Apr 8 (149) £2,200 [Gaston]

Anr copy. Half mor gilt; spines rubbed. With port & 421 colored plates. S Oct 23 (719) £1,600 [Wesley]

Anr copy. 7 vols plus Index, which is bound separately with the wraps to the orig 36 parts & lists of subscribers. 8vo, half mor gilt; rubbed. S Apr 23 (43) £1,450 [Grahame]

Anr Ed. L, 1891-97. 7 vols. 4to, half mor, orig wraps bound in. With frontis & 421 colored plates. pnE Dec 17 (272) £1,400

AMERICAN BOOK PRICES CURRENT

[Quaritch]
— Lord Lilford on Birds. L, 1903. T Oct 16 (383) £65
— Notes on the Birds of Northamptonshire.... L, 1895. 2 vols. 8vo, orig cloth. With folding map & 17 plates. pn Oct 23 (241) £90 [Bewder]

Anr copy. Half mor. pn Dec 11 (237) £85 [Old Hall]

One of 100 L.p. copies. Contemp half mor gilt; rubbed. S May 28 (720) £120

Lilienthal, Otto, 1848-96
— Birdflight as the Basis of Aviation. L, 1911. Orig cloth; soiled & worn. With 8 folding plates (browned at edges). wa Nov 6 (9) $90

Lilius, Zacharias
— De gloria et gaudiis beatorum Venice: Simon Bevilaqua, 24 Sept 1501. 1st Ed. 4to, vellum gilt. Text inlaid on tp; some foxing & worming; margin note shaved on 42 verso; 2 leaves from a shorter copy. S Mar 10 (1091) £160 [Scarre]

— Orbis breviarium. Florence: Antonio di Bartolommeo Miscomini, 5 June 1493. 1st Ed. 4to, contemp blind-stamped calf over wooden bds; repaired, bds a little wormed. First 4 leaves repaired without loss; marginal repairs elsewhere; marginal annotations in ink in a contemp hand. 130 leaves. Goff L-218. S Apr 24 (187) £5,000 [Thomas]

Lillingston, Luke, 1653-1713
— Reflections on Mr. Burchet's Memoirs.... L, 1704. 8vo, old calf; rebacked. Some stains, tears & soiling. O May 12 (124) $300

Lilliputian...
— The Lilliputian Conjuror, or an Account of the Signs and Planets.... L: H. Roberts, 1777. 16mo, contemp limp cloth; spine def. Lacking frontis, B8, C1-2 & C5-8. S Oct 7 (976) £70 [Quaritch]

Lilly, Eli
— Prehistoric Antiquities of Indiana.... Indianapolis, 1937. 4to, cloth. sg Sept 18 (152) $150

Lilly, William, 1602-81
— Mr. William Lilly's History of his Life and Times.... L, 1715. 12mo, disbound. Some fraying. T Sept 18 (514) £50

Lima
— Concilium Limensi. Celebratum anno. 1583. Madrid: P. Madrigal, 1591. 4to, later calf; spine & edges rubbed. Some dampstains; minor wormholing with paper repairs on final 15 leaves; blank corner of title replaced. sg Sept 18 (63) $50

Lima, Eladio de Cruz. See: Cruz Lima, Eladio de

Limborch, Philippus van, 1633-1712
— Historia inquisitionis; cui subjungitur.... Amst., 1692. 2 parts in 1 vol. Folio, contemp calf. Minor worming to lower outer corner of 1st several leaves. sg Oct 9 (54) $130

Limited Editions Club—New York
See also: Dolphin...
— The Arabian Nights. 1934. Burton's trans. 6 vols. cb Dec 421267 $110; O Sept 23 (100) $70; S Oct 7 (903) £40 [Bell]
— Bhagavad Gita, the Song Celestial. 1964. cb Sept 11 (266) $30
— Bible (King James Version). 1935-36. O Sept 23 (116) $80
— Book of Job. 1946. One of 1,950. sg Sept 25 (288) $225; sg Apr 30 (357) $200
— The Book of Ruth. 1947. One of 1,950. sg Apr 30 (358) $175
— The Koran; Selected Sutras. 1958. cb Dec 4 (275) $70
— Quarto-Millenary: the First 250 Publications.... 1959. O Nov 18 (113) $160; wa Mar 5 (55) $190
— The Song of Roland. 1938. O Sept 23 (132) $60
— ANDERSEN, HANS CHRISTIAN. - The Complete Andersen.... 1949. 6 vols. S Oct 7 (937) £160 [Libris]
— ANDERSEN, HANS CHRISTIAN. - Fairy Tales. 1942. 2 vols. S Oct 7 (927) £120 [Adams]
— ARISTOPHANES. - Lysistrata. 1934. Illus by Picasso. O Sept 23 (99) $725; P June 18 (151) $1,300; sg Dec 4 (156) $1,200 Anr copy. With 6 etchings. sg Jan 8 (204) $1,200
One of 1,500, sgd by Picasso. P Dec 15 (213) $1,000
— ARISTOTLE. - Politics & Poetics. 1964. O Nov 18 (110) $50
— BACON, SIR FRANCIS. - The Essays or Counsels.... 1944. cb June 18 (252) $55
— BIERCE, AMBROSE. - The Devil's Dictionary. 1972. cb Sept 11 (267) $80
— BIERCE, AMBROSE. - Tales of Soldiers and Civilians. 1943. cb June 18 (254) $50; O Nov 18 (111) $60
— BOCCACCIO, GIOVANNI. - Decameron. 1930. 2 vols. cba Feb 5 (208) $110
— BORROW, GEORGE HENRY. - Lavengro. 1936. 2 vols. O Sept 23 (101) $50; S Oct 7 (914) £55 [Bell]
— BOSWELL, JAMES. - The Life of Samuel Johnson. 1938. 3 vols. O Sept 23 (102) $60
— BRADBURY, RAY. - The Martian Chronicles. 1974. In d/j. cb May 7 (318) $140
— BRILLAT-SAVARIN, JEAN ANTHELME. - The Physiology of Taste. 1949. cb Sept 11 (268) $100

— BROWNING, ELIZABETH BARRETT. - Sonnets from the Portuguese. 1948. K Dec 13 (147) $110
— BROWNING, ROBERT. - The Ring and the Book. 1949. 2 vols. S Oct 7 (936) £40 [Bell]
— BURNS, ROBERT. - Poems. 1965. cb Sept 11 (269) $50
— BUTLER, SAMUEL. - Erewhon. 1934. O Sept 23 (103) $60
— BUTLER, SAMUEL. - The Way of All Flesh. 1936. 2 vols. cb June 18 (257) $55; O Sept 23 (104) $50
— CAESAR, CAIUS JULIUS. - The Gallic Wars. 1954. cb Feb 19 (46) $75
— CASANOVA DE SEINGALT, GIACOMO GIROLAMO. Memoirs. 1940. 8 vols. O Jan 6 (113) $80; S Oct 7 (922) £40 [Bell]
— CELLINI, BENVENUTO. - The Life of Benvenuto Cellini Written by Himself. 1937. O Sept 23 (119) $70
— CHAUCER, GEOFFREY. - The Canterbury Tales. 1934. 2 vols. O Sept 23 (107) $70
— CONFUCIUS. - The Analects. 1970. cb Sept 11 (272) $85
— DANA, RICHARD HENRY, JR. - Two Years Before the Mast. 1947. With ALs from Dana to H. Bokum, 1840, laid in. sg Jan 8 (59) $120
— DANTE ALIGHIERI. - The Divine Comedy 1932. S Oct 7 (895) £100 [Thorp]
— DEFOE, DANIEL. - Robinson Crusoe. 1930. cb June 18 (114) $80
— DIAZ DEL CASTILLO, BERNAL. - The Discovery and Conquest of Mexico. 1942. cb June 4 (48) $90; cb June 18 (258) $80
— DICKENS, CHARLES. - The Chimes. 1931. bba June 18 (272) £300 [Oram]; cb June 18 (259) $190
Anr copy. With "The Ideal Book" by Francis P. Dill & Porter Garnet laid into slipcase. ha Dec 19 (212) $265; S Oct 7 (889) £110 [Thorp]; sg Oct 30 (62) $130; sg Jan 8 (228) $225
— DICKENS, CHARLES. - A Christmas Carol. 1934. O Sept 23 (109) $70
— DICKENS, CHARLES. - The Cricket on the Hearth. 1933. S Oct 7 (899) £40 [Dickens]
— DODGSON, CHARLES LUTWIDGE. - Alice's Adventures in Wonderland. 1932. One of 500 sgd by Alice Hargreaves. wd June 19 (148) $400
— DODGSON, CHARLES LUTWIDGE. - Through the Looking Glass. 1935. One of 1,150 sgd by Alice Hargreaves. sg June 11 (92) $375
— DUMAS, ALEXANDRE. - Camille. 1937. S Oct 7 (916) £80 [Bell]
— EPICURUS. - [Works]. 1947. cb Dec 4 (271) $80; S Oct 7 (934) £50 [Bell]
— FRANCE, ANATOLE. - The Crime of Sylvestre Bonnard. 1937. O Sept 23 (111) $50
— FRANCIS OF ASSISI. - The Little Flowers. 1930. cba Feb 5 (210) $90
— FRANKLIN, BENJAMIN. - Poor Richard's

LIMITED EDITIONS CLUB

Almanacs.... 1964. sg June 4 (281) $140
— GRAHAME, KENNETH. - The Wind in the Willows. 1940. One of 2,020. sg Oct 30 (83) $450
— GRIMM BROTHERS. - Fairy Tales. 1931. ha Dec 10 (218) $70
— HAWTHORNE, NATHANIEL. - The House of the Seven Gables. 1935. O Sept 23 (113) $50
— HOFFMANN, HEINRICH. - Slovenly Peter. 1935. cb Dec 4 (273) $55
— HUGO, VICTOR. - Notre-Dame de Paris. 1930. 2 vols. Untrimmed. ha Dec 19 (221) $70
— JOYCE, JAMES. - Ulysses. 1935. O Sept 23 (115) $900

Anr copy. This copy sgd by both Matisse & Joyce. sg Apr 2 (126) $3,200
— KINGSLEY, CHARLES. - Westward Ho! 1947. 2 vols. S Oct 7 (933) £40 [Bell]
— LANDOR, WALTER SAVAGE. - Imaginary Conversations. 1936. cb Sept 11 (280) $110; cb June 18 (266) $75; O Sept 23 (117) $70; S Oct 7 (912) £70 [Liechti]
— LE SAGE, ALAIN-RENE. - The Adventures of Gil Blas of Santillane. 1937. 2 vols. cb Sept 11 (281) $200; O Sept 23 (118) $60
— LEWIS, MERIWETHER & CLARK, WILLIAM. - The Journals of the Expedition. 1962. 2 vols. wa May 5 (49) $160
— LEWIS, SINCLAIR. - Main Street. 1937. sg June 4 (350) $380
— MANZONI, ALESSANDRO. - I Promessi Sposi [The Betrothed]. 1951. cb June 18 (268) $70
— MARAN, RENE. - Batouala. 1932. Rubbed. ha Dec 19 (223) $75
— MAUGHAM, W. SOMERSET. - Of Human Bondage. 1938. 2 vols. Inscr by John Sloan to Thomas Harvey & with all the etchings sgd in pencil by Sloan. F Jan 15 (279) $1,700; O Sept 23 (122) $200; S Oct 7 (918) £100 [Marks]; wa Mar 5 (51) $260; wd Nov 12 (163) $100
— MELVILLE, HERMAN. - Typee. 1935. cb June 18 (269) $55; O Sept 23 (123) $70
— MERIMEE, PROSPER. - Carmen. 1941. cb June 18 (270) $95
— MILTON, JOHN. - Paradise Lost and Paradise Regain'd. 1936. O Sept 23 (124) $60
— MOLIERE, JEAN BAPTISTE POQUELIN DE. - Tartuffe, or The Hypocrite. 1930. B Oct 7 (386) HF220; ha Dec 19 (224) $85
— MORE, SIR THOMAS. - Utopia. 1934. O Sept 23 (125) $70
— OMAR KHAYYAM. - The Rubaiyat. 1935. cb Dec 4 (278) $95
— PAINE, THOMAS. - Rights of Man. 1961. cb Sept 11 (284) $140
— PLATO. - The Republic. 1944. 2 vols. cb Sept 11 (286) $70; S Oct 7 (930) £45 [Liechtl]

One of 15 presentation copies. sg June 11

AMERICAN BOOK PRICES CURRENT

(320) $90
— PORTER, WILLIAM SYDNEY. - The Voice of the City and Other Stories. 1935. cb June 18 (265) $140; O Sept 23 (136) $110; S Oct 7 (909) £100 [Zindenberg]
— RABELAIS, FRANCOIS. - Gargantua and Pantagruel. 1936. 5 vols. O Sept 23 (127) $60
— SHAKESPEARE, WILLIAM. - Hamlet. 1933. S Oct 7 (896) £120 [Branners]
— SHAKESPEARE, WILLIAM. - The Poems and Sonnets. 1941. 2 vols. cb Feb 19 (245) $170
— SHAKESPEARE, WILLIAM. - Works. 1939-41. 39 vols. plus the Review & Preview sg Oct 30 (193) $650
— SHELLEY, MARY WOLLSTONECRAFT. - Frankenstein, or the Modern Prometheus. 1934. O Sept 23 (129) $60
— SHERIDAN, RICHARD BRINSLEY. - The School for Scandal. 1934. O Sept 23 (130) $50
— SIENKIEWICZ, HENRYK. - Quo Vadis? 1959. cb Sept 111 (290) $70
— SMOLLETT, TOBIAS. - The Adventures of Peregrine Pickle. 1936. 2 vols. cb Sept 11 (291) $275; O Sept 23 (131) $60
— STERNE, LAURENCE. - A Sentimental Journey.... 1936. O Sept 23 (134) $80; S Oct 7 (915) £110 [Libris]
— STEVENSON, ROBERT LOUIS. - Strange Case of Dr. Jekyll and Mr. Hyde. 1952. cb Nov 20 (301) $70
— SUETONIUS TRANQUILLUS, CAIUS. - The Lives of the Twelve Caesars. 1963. cb Feb 19 (255) $110
— SWIFT, JONATHAN. - Gulliver's Travels. 1929. S Oct 7 (871) £45 [Liechti]
— THACKERAY, WILLIAM MAKEPEACE. - Vanity Fair. 1931. 2 vols. S Oct 7 (886) £40 [Allen]
— TOLSTOY, LEO. - Anna Karenina. 1951. Dummy copy with proofs of lithos & textual vignettes. 2 vols. Presentation copy, sgd by Barnett Freedman, the illustrator. bba Nov 13 (317) £130 [Marks]
— TOLSTOY, LEO. - War and Peace. 1938. 6 vols. S Oct 7 (920) £130 [Contemporary]
— WHITMAN, WALT. - Leaves of Grass. 1929. S Oct 7 (872) £40 [Bell]

Anr Ed. 1942. 2 vols. sg May 7 (83) $650
— WILDE, OSCAR. - The Ballad of Reading Gaol. 1937. O Sept 23 (137) $60
— WILDE, OSCAR. - Salome: A Tragedy in One Act. 1938. One of 1,500 sgd by the artist. bba Nov 13 (319) £80 [Stransky]
— WILDE, OSCAR. - Salome: Drame en un acte. *Salome: A Tragedy. 1938. Trans by Lord Alfred Douglas. 2 vols. O Sept 23 (128) $110
— WROTH, LAWRENCE C. - A History of the Printed Book. 1938. sg Jan 22 (321) $80

Lincoln, Abraham, 1809-65
— Emancipation Proclamation. [Bost., Dec 1862]. ("The Proclamation of Emancipation, by the President of the United States....") 74mm by 51mm, orig ptd wraps. Lower fore-corner of text stained. CNY May 11 (101) $1,600

Anr Ed. Wash., 2 Jan 1863. ("General Orders No. 1, War Department, Adjutant General's Office...A Proclamation....") 12mo, disbound but sewn with c.200 other General Orders from the War Department. 2 spindle holes at inner margin of both leaves. sg Sept 18 (154) $225

— Political Debates between Hon. Abraham Lincoln and Hon. Stephen A. Douglas.... Columbus, 1860. 1st Ed, Issue not indicated. 8vo, orig cloth; rubbed. S Sept 22 (253) £100 [Martin]

Lind, James
An Answer to the Declaration of the American Congress. Dublin: P. Highly, 1777. Bound with: Pownall, Thomas. Report from the Committee Appointed to Consider of the Methods Practiced in making Flour from Wheat. Dublin: George Faulkner, 1774. 8vo, contemp bds; broken. og Sept 18 (159) $150

Lind, John
— Defence of Lord Pigot. L, 1777. 4to, contemp calf gilt; rubbed. T Sept 18 (44) £145

Anr copy. Contemp half calf; hinges cracked. T Sept 18 (45) £95

Lindberg, Pehr
— Architectura mechanica of moole-boek. Amst., 1727. Folio, contemp calf; rebacked. With 32 plates. S Apr 23 (93) £1,000

Lindbergh, Charles A.
— The Spirit of St. Louis. NY, 1953. In d/j. Inscr. wd Nov 12 (135) $250

Linde, Antonius van der, 1833-97
— Bibliotheca van der Linde-Niemeijeriana; a Catalogue of the Chess Collection in the Royal Library, The Hague. The Hague, 1955. pn Mar 26 (448) £50 [Kitz]

— Geschichte und Litteratur des Schachspiels. Berlin, 1874. 2 vols. Half calf; scuffed. pn Mar 26 (449) £120 [Furstenberg]

Linden, Jean Jules, 1817-98
— Lindenia: Iconographie des Orchidees. Ghent, 1885-98. 20 vols in 14. Folio, later cloth; rubbed. With 024 color plates. bba Mar 12 (43) £3,800 [Elliott]

Anr Ed. Ghent, 1885-96. Vol VIII only. Folio, contemp half mor by H. Wood; scuffed at top & bottom of spines. T Nov 20 (133) £380

Lindenbrog, Friedrich
— Codex legum antiquarum.... Frankfurt, 1613. One vol in 2. Folio, later 17th-cent calf, armorial bdg; front joints cracked. sg Oct 9 (159) $250

Lindley, John, 1799-1865
See also: Bauer, Franz Andreas; Edwards, Sydenham Teak

— Collectanea Botanica; or, Figures and Botanical Illustrations of Rare and Curious Exotic Plants.... L, 1821-[26]. Folio, half mor gilt; rubbed. With 41 plates, all but 1 hand-colored, several double-page. Bound at end is a fragment of Blume's Florae Javae, with plates 1-6. de Belder copy. S Apr 28 (217) £6,000 [Junk]

— Digitalium monographia; sistens historiam botanicum generis.... L, 1821. Folio, half mor; joints & corners rubbed. With 28 hand-colored plates, several with ptd slips correcting the captions. Horticultural Society of New York—de Belder copy. S Apr 28 (218) £5,500 [Phelps]

— Pomologia Britannica; or Figures and Descriptions...of Fruit.... L, 1841. 3 vols. 8vo, half mor. With 152 colored plates. Fairfax Rhodes Library—de Belder copy. S Apr 28 (219) £3,800 [Sourget]

— The Pomological Magazine. L, 1828-30. Vols I-III (all pbd). 8vo, contemp half calf gilt; repaired. With 152 hand-colored plates. HK Nov 12 (1093) DM 11,000

Anr copy. Half mor; rubbed. Crahan copy. P Nov 25 (296) $3,500

— Sertum Orchidaceum: a Wreath of the Most Beautiful Orchidaceous Flowers. L, 1838. Folio, modern half mor gilt. With colored litho half-title & 49 hand-colored plates. C Apr 8 (186) £5,000 [Earhart]

Lindley, John, 1799-1865 —& Paxton, Sir Joseph, 1801-65
— Paxton's Flower Garden. L, 1850-53. Vol I only. Contemp half mor; rubbed. With 25 hand-colored plates only. Library stamps on plates. bba Aug 20 (442) £130 [York]

Anr copy. 3 vols in 1. 4to, contemp half calf; worn, joints partially broken. With 46 hand-colored plates only & tp in Vol II only. Vol I lacking all before Y1 except 1 leaf preface; Vol III lacking all before B1 & after E3; a few plates cut close. S Nov 10 (544) £320 [McCarthy]

Lindsay, Colin, Earl of Balcarras
— An Account of the Affairs of Scotland.... L, 1714. 1st Ed. 8vo, modern calf. O Feb 24 (12) $60

Lindsay, Sir Lionel Arthur
— Conrad Martens, the Man and his Art. Sydney, 1920. Bdg with spine torn & covers stained. CA Apr 12 (170) A$100

Lindsay, Norman, 1879-1969
— The Magic Pudding. Sydney, 1918. 4to, half cloth; soiled. CA Oct 7 (105) A$450
— Micomicana. Melbourne, 1979. One of 527. Folio, lea. kh Mar 16 (304) A$420

Line, Les. See: Amuchastegui, Axel

Ling, Nicholas
— Politeuphuia, Wits Common-Wealth. L: M. Flesher, to be sold by George Badger, 1647. 12mo, later calf; broken, rubbed. O Feb 24 (123) $70

Anr Ed. L, 1650. 12mo, recent calf. Tp soiled & repaired; soiled. T Mar 19 (398) £38

Lingenfelter, Richard E.
— Presses of the Pacific Islands, 1817-1867. Los Angeles, 1967. Ltd Ed. sg Jan 8 (156) $100

Link, Heinrich Frederick. See: Hoffmannsegg & Link

Linnaeus, Carolus, 1707-78
— Ad Memoriam...Caroli Linnaei...Systema Naturae per tria regna dispositae explicavit Regia Academia Scientiarum Svecica biseculari natali auctoris denuo editit. Stockholm, 1907. Folio, half lea. With port, tp, preface leaf, 8 leaves of full-size facsimile of 1st Ed & 1 stub of 24 facsimile engravings. Hunt copy. CNY Nov 21 (172) $400
— Amoenitates academicae, seu dissertationes variae.... Leiden or Amst., 1749-60. Vol I, 2d Ed; Vols II-VII, 1st Ed. 7 vols. 8vo, contemp calf; worn. With 43 folding plates, 2 trimmed or torn, 2 leaves in Vol V misbound. S Nov 27 (273) £350 [Israel]
— A Genuine and Universal System of Natural History.... L, [1802-6?]. 7 vols. 8vo, half calf gilt; upper inner joint of Vol I broken & crudely repaired, corners rubbed. One leaf torn & anr repaired in Vol I. L Dec 11 (295) £240
— Hortus Cliffortianus. Amst., 1737. Folio, contemp calf; joints renewed, extremities worn. With frontis & 36 plates. Hunt copy. CNY Nov 21 (173) $4,800
— Lachesis Lapponica, or a Tour in Lapland.... L, 1811. 1st Ed in English. 2 vols. 8vo, cloth. bba Dec 18 (182) £80 [Hannas]
— Species plantarum exhibentes plantas rite cognitas...secumdum systema sexuale digestas.... Stockholm, 1753. 1st Ed. 2 vols in 1. 8vo, contemp calf; joints wormed, front free endpaper removed. Last 4 leaves with wormhole at extreme inner upper corners. Hunt copy. CNY Nov 21 (174) $3,400

Linschoten, Jan Huygen van, 1563-1611
— His Discours of Voyages unto ye Easte & West Indies.... L: John Wolfe, [1598]. 1st Ed in English. Folio, 19th-cent mor gilt. With 3 divisional titles & 12 folding maps. FD Dec 2 (916A) DM32,000

Anr copy. Old calf; shellacked & needs rebdg. Lacking maps & plates, 2F6 & 2Q8. Sold w.a.f. sg Sept 18 (160) $450

Anr copy. 19th-cent russia gilt by J. Brooks; front cover detached. With 12 folding maps & plates. Maps & plates washed. sg Apr 2 (134) $12,000
— Itinerarium. Ofte Schip-Vaert naer Oost ofte Portugael's Indien. Amst.: Cloppenburch, 1644. 3 parts in 1 vol, plus the 1924 Voyasie, Ofte Schip-Vaert...van by Noorden om langes Noorwegen de Noordt-Caep.... Together, 4 parts in 1 vol. Folio, contemp vellum; head of backstrip torn. Dampstained throughout; some maps torn & backed. Sold w.a.f. CNY Dec 19 (122) $5,500

Linton, William James, 1812-97
— The Masters of Wood-Engraving. L, 1889. One of 600. 4to, half mor, orig cloth bound in. C Dec 12 (371) £180 [Maggs]

Lipchitz, Jacques
— The Drawings. NY: Curt Valentin, 1944. One of 765. Folio, unbound as issued. S Oct 6 (669) £60 [Wendler]

Lipperheide Library, Franz Joseph von
— Katalog der Freiherrlich von Lipperheide'schen Kostuembibliothek. NY, 1963. ("Katalog der Kostuembibliothek.") 2 vols. 4to, cloth. S Feb 24 (338) £280 [Diba]

Lippmann, Friedrich, 1838-1903
— Kupferistiche und Holzschnitte alter Meister in Nachbildungen. Berlin, 1889-99. 10 vols. Folio, unbound as issued in orig half-cloth portfolios. Ck Jan 30 (220) £900
— Zeichnungen von Albrecht duerer in Nachbildungen. Berlin: Grotesche, 1883-1904. One of 300. Parts 1-49 only in 5 vols. Folio, orig cloth. Ck Jan 30 (219) £1,100

Lippold, Georg
— Gemmen und Kameen des Altertums und der Neuzeit. Stuttgart: Hoffman, [c.1925]. 4to, half cloth; worn. O Jan 6 (117) $90

Lipsius, Justus, 1547-1606
— De cruce.... Antwerp: Plantin, 1594. 4to, contemp calf with flowers & leaves & with animals being hunted along the border, the center panel bearing the words in gilt "Jacobus Guerrier, Bello sed Palladis Armis"; worn. Jeanson 1528. SM Mar 1 (359) FF220,000

— Saturnalium sermonum libri duo.... Antwerp: Christopher Plantin, 1582. 4to, contemp vellum. Some foxing. sg Mar 26 (176) $120

Liron d'Airoles, Jules de
— Album de la civeliere. Brussels, 1855. Vol I (of 2) only. 4to, later half cloth. With frontis (bound after copy) & 26 colored plates. 1 plate mtd. C Oct 15 (242) £1,400 [Adams]

Lisbon
— Colleçao de algumas ruinas de Lisboa causadas pelo terremoto e pelo fogo do primeiro de novembro do anno 1755. Paris, 1757. Folio, sewn. With engraved title & 6 plates. S Oct 23 (258) £700 [Goldschmidt]

Lisle de Moncel, —— de. See: Delisle de Moncel

Lisle, Edward, 1666?-1722
— Observations on Husbandry. L, 1757. 2d Ed. 2 vols. 8vo, contemp calf; rebacked, corners renewed, rubbed. Heertje copy. P Nov 25 (297) $150

List, Freidrich, 1789-1846
— Das Nationale System der Politischen Oekonomie.... Stuttgart & Tuebingen, 1841. 8vo, half lea. Some browning. P Sept 24 (323) $1,400

Lister, Joseph Lister, 1st Baron, 1827-1912
— The Collected Papers. Oxford, 1909. 1st Ed. 2 vols. 4to, orig cloth; rubbed & soiled. bba May 14 (400) £190 [Old South]

Lister, Martin, 1638?-1712
— De fontibus medicatis Angliae.... L, 1684. 2 parts in 1 vol. 8vo, contemp calf, upper joint repaired. Lacking blank before plate; 1st title with piece cut from outer margin & repaired; some dampstains. S Nov 10 (510) £100 [Phelps]

— A Journey to Paris in the Year 1698. L, 1699. 1st Ed. 8vo, contemp calf. With 6 plates. pnE June 17 (146) £85

Littauer, Vladimir S. See: Derrydale Press

Little, Thomas. See: Fore-Edge Paintings

Littlejohn, David. See: Grabhorn Printing

Littleton, Sir Thomas
— Les Tenures. L, 1612. 8vo, modern lea. Some shaving or cropping. STC 15756. bba Jan 15 (8) £90 [Baumann]

Littmann, Enno
— Vom morgenlaendischen Floh. Dichtung und Wahrheit.... Leipzig: Insel-Verlag, 1925. One of 300. Illus by M. Behmer. Orig half vellum. HN Nov26 (1732) DM1,000

Littret, Claude Antoine de
— Uniformes militaires ou se trouvent graves en taille-douce les uniformes de la Maison du Roy.... Paris: chez Chereau, 1772 [1773?]. 12mo, contemp calf gilt; spine chipped at head. With engraved title having hand-colored border & 175 hand-colored plates. S June 25 (207) £2,000

Livermore, George, 1809-65
— An Historical Research Respecting the Opinions of the Founders of the Republic on Negroes as Slaves, as Citizens, and as Soldiers. Bost., 1862. One of 50 L.p. copies. 4to, cloth. Inscr. cb Oct 9 (280) $65

Lives...
— Lives of Distinguished Shoemakers. Portland: Davis & Southland, 1849. 12mo, orig cloth; worn, spine head chipped. O Jan 6 (118) $60

Living...
— Living English Poets. L, 1883. 8vo, orig syn. Tipped in are cut signatures of the 31 contributors. sg Dec 4 (111) $225

Livingston, Luther Samuel, 1864-1914
— Auction Prices of Books: a Representative Record. 1886-1904. NY, 1905. One of 750. 4 vols. 4to, cloth; worn, hinges cracked; Vol III loose. sg Oct 2 (184) $40

Livingston, P.
— Other Side of the Question: or, A Defence of the Liberties of North-America. NY, 1774. 8vo, modern half calf. Lacking ad leaf; library markings. sg Mar 12 (169) $120

Livingstone, David, 1813-73
— Missionary Travels and Researches in South Africa. L, 1857. 1st Ed, 1st Issue. 8vo, cloth; hinges repaired. With port & 2 folding maps. sg Apr 23 (91) $250

2d Issue. Orig cloth; broken. With folding map in pocket. bba Dec 4 (290) £60 [Cavendish]

Issue not given. Later half lea. With folding frontis, port, & 24 plates. B Feb 25 (782) HF475

Anr Ed. NY, 1858. 8vo, cloth. Library

LIVINGSTONE

markings. SSA Feb 11 (564) R100

Livius, Titus, 59 B.C.-17 A.D.

Decades

— 1511, 16 Apr. - Deche vulgare hystoriate. Venice: Bartholomeo de Zanni de Portesio. Folio, modern half mor over wooden bds; lacking 2 clasps & catches, new endpapers. Fore-margin of title repaired with some text of the contents on the verso supplied in Ms; lacking final blank; border & woodcut on B1 recto soiled & with short tear at bottom; a few letters in the text of m3 damaged; some dampstains. S May 21 (50) £480 [Lojewski]

— 1527. - Historiae romanae decades. Paris: Bernard Aubri. ("Gestarum populi Romani....") Folio, old calf; worn, endpapers renewed. Marginal dampstaining; wormed at beginning & end. sg Mar 26 (177) $150

— 1554. - Basel: apud Episcopium iuniorem. 8vo, contemp blind-stamped pigskin over wooden bds; 2 clasps & catches. S Nov 27 (85) £150 [Poel]

— 1600. - The Romane Historie. L: Adam Islip. 1st Ed in English. Trans by Philemon Holland. Folio, contemp calf; spine ends chipped. Scattered marginal stains; lacking initial blank. sg mar 26 (178) $225

— 1646. - Romainsche Historien. Amst. 2 parts in 1 vol. Folio, contemp blind-stamped vellum. B Oct 7 (1341) HF600

— 1665-64. - Historiae romanae decades. Amst.: Elzevir. ("Historiarum quod extat.") 3 vols. 8vo, contemp vellum. With engraved title. B Feb 25 (849) HF200

— 1678-79. - Historiarum libri quod extat. Amst.: Elzevir. 3 vols. 8vo, later calf; rebacked, orig spines laid down, joints & extremities rubbed. cb Oct 23 (67) $110

Livre...

— Le Livre des Rois. Lausanne, 1930. One of 195. Illus by F. L. Schmied. 4to, unsewn in orig wraps. S Dec 4 (32) £3,000 [Maggs]

— Le Livre du faulcon des dames. [Paris: Alain Lotrian, c.1530]. 8vo, mor gilt by Bauzonnet-Trautz. Jeanson copy. SM Mar 1 (363) FF55,000

— Livre pour un Petit Garcon Bien Sage. Paris, 1817. 16mo, half lea. With 14 hand-colored plates. Some plates discolored. S Dec 5 (323) £480 [Huber]

Livret...

— Livret des chasses du Roi. [Paris, 1816-28]. 13 vols. 4to, 7 vols in red mor gilt with royal arms, 1 vol in 1829 & other vols in contemp bds. Jeanson copy. SM Mar 1 (367) FF160,000

AMERICAN BOOK PRICES CURRENT

Lizars, Daniel

— The Edinburgh Geographical and Historical Atlas. Edin.: John Hamilton, successor to Daniel Lizars, [c.1830]. Folio, contemp half calf; rubbed. With double-page tabular view of the principal mountain chains & 68 hand-colored maps with colored wash borders, some joined forming large folding maps. Mtd on guards. C Oct 15 (64) £260 [Potter]

Lizars, John

— A System of Anatomical Plates of the Human Body. Edin.: W.H. Lizars, [c.1840?]. 2 vols. Folio, contemp half mor; worn, 1 spine torn. With engraved title & 103 plates, most hand-colored, a few with annotations. bba May 14 (284) £350 [Hildebrandt]

Anr copy. Folio, half calf; upper joint cracked. With engraved title & 103 colored plates. pn Oct 23 (375) £580 [McCarthy]

Lizars, William Home, 1788-1859 —& Brown, James

— Views of Edinburgh. L, 1825. 4to, half mor gilt. pnE Nov 12 (259) £140

Llewellyn, Martin

— Men-Miracles, with Other Poems. [Oxford: Henry Hall], 1646. 8vo, modern sheep. Washed, margins trimmed close; lacking initial blank. sg Oct 9 (259) $325

Lloyd, Edward, Publisher

— Natural History. L, 1896-97. 16 vols. 8vo, orig half lea; rubbed, 1 spine def. S Feb 24 (587) £130 [Bifalco]

Anr copy. Various bdgs. S Feb 24 (588) £130 [Bifolco]

Lloyd, Llewellyn, 1792-1876

— Field Sports of the North of Europe. L, 1831. 2 vols. 8vo, contemp half calf; rubbed. bba Oct 30 (334) £45 [Smith]

Lloyd, Nathaniel, 1867-1933

— A History of English Brickwork. L, 1925. 4to, orig cloth; broken on front hinge. T oct 16 (587) £74

Lloyd, Robert, 1733-64

— The Poetical Works. L, 1774. 2 vols. 8vo, contemp calf; rubbed, 1 cover detached. Some stains. bba Apr 9 (72) £55 [Axe]

L'Obel, Matthias, 1533-1616 —& Pena, Petrus

— Plantarum, seu stirpium historia. Antwerp: Plantin, 1576. 2 parts in 1 vol. Folio, contemp calf. NSTC 19595.3. Candolle-plesch copy. FD Dec 2 (362) DM6,000

Anr copy. 4to, vellum. Lacking the Nova Stirpium adversari & Formulae aliquot. HK Nov 4 (1057) DM2400

Anr copy. 2 parts in 1 vol. Folio, later vellum. Page 17 of Part 1 soiled; some dampstains to lower margins of Part 2. sg Dec 4 (112) $1,300

Lobera de Avila, Luis
— Ein nutzlich Regiment der Gesundtheyt, genant das Vanquete, oder Gastmal der edlen Diener von der Complexion, Eigenschefft, Schad, und Nutz allerley Speys.... Augsburg: Heinrich Steyner, 1531. 4to, modern bds. Lacking leaf A4 with port; tp cropped at fore-edge; some stains; early annotations. Crahan copy. P Nov 25 (298) $950

Lobo, Jerome, 1593-1678
— Voyage historique d'Abissinie. Paris, 1728. 4to, contemp calf gilt; rubbed. One map torn without loss. S Feb 23 (221) £220 [Brill]
— A Voyage to Abyssinia. L, 1735. 1st Ed. Trans by Samuel Johnson. 8vo, contemp calf; upper joint tender, lower cover loose. Some foxing. pnE Jan 28 (70) £250 [Maggs]

Anr copy. Contemp calf; rebacked, front cover loose. sg June 11 (259) $225

Loccenius, Johannis
— Rerum Suecicarum historia.... Stockholm, 1654. 2 parts in 1 vol. 8vo, old vellum. Light dampstaining. sg Oct 9 (326) $50

Lochmaier, Michael
— Sermones de sanctis cum vigintitribus Pauli Wann sermonibus. [Passau: Johann Petri, 1490-91]. Folio, contemp pigskin over wooden bds; worn & wormed. Wormed, slightly affecting text; corner of last 2 leaves def. Sold w.a.f. 400 (of 402) leaves; lacking rrrl & last blank. Goff L-170. bba Sept 25 (233) £400 [Mandl]

Locke, Harold
— A Bibliographical Catalogue of the Writings of Sir Arthur Conan Doyle. Tunbridge Wells, 1928. Half cloth. Harold Mortlake's annotated working copy. cb Apr 24 (1002) $50

Locke, John, 1632-1704
See also: Roxburghe Club
— An Essay concerning Humane Understanding. L, 1690. 1st Ed, 1st Issue. Folio, modern calf. Some browning & spotting. P Dec 15 (208) $2,000
2d Ed. L, 1694. Folio, contemp calf; rubbed & repaired, recased. With port (frayed & repaired). Fore-edge margin of tp repaired, last 9 leaves repaired with loss to index; waterstained. S Mar 10 (1092) £160 [Scott]
3d Ed. L, 1695. Folio, contemp calf; worn. Tp torn with partial loss of border; with 14 pp Ms additional text; some tears. S May 6 (515) £150 [Hassbach]
4th Ed. L, 1700. Folio, orig calf. pnE Jan 28 (120) £400 [Thin]
Anr Ed. L, 1706. Folio, orig calf; worn & broken. 2 Ms leaves tipped in before title. pnNY Oct 11 (7) $160
— A Letter to the Right Reverend Edward Ld. Bishop of Worcester.... L, 1697. 1st Ed. 8vo, contemp calf. pnE Jan 28 (123) £280 [Maggs]

Anr copy. Modern lea; scuffed. Half-title soiled. sg Oct 9 (260) $175
— A New Method of Making Common Place-Books.... L, 1706. 1st Ed. 8vo, contemp sheep; spine worn. Ck Jan 30 (123) £300
— Observations upon the Growth and Culture of Vines and Olives.... L, 1766. 8vo, old calf; joints rubbed. Lacking front blank; tp soiled. Hunt copy. CNY Nov 21 (176) $480
— Posthumous Works. L, 1706. 1st Ed. 8vo, contemp calf gilt, with shield of the Bibliotheque Bignon; rebacked, old spine preserved, lacking front pastedown. Graham Pollard's copy. S Jan 13 (510) £190 [Meikle]
— Some Familiar Letters between Mr. Locke, and Several of his Friends. L, 1708. 8vo, contemp calf. pnE Jan 28 (122) £260 [Steedman]
— Some Thoughts concerning Education. L, 1693. 1st Ed. 8vo, contemp calf gilt. pnE Jan 28 (121) £880 [Maggs]
— Two Treatises of Government. L, 1690. 1st Ed. 8vo, contemp calf; joints rubbed. Some browning; errata scored through. C Dec 12 (344) £600 [Pickering & Chatto]
— Works. L, 1751. 5th Ed. 3 vols. Folio, contemp calf; hinges split. Some spotting. C Dec 12 (131) £300 [Pressler]

Locker-Lampson, Frederick, 1821-95
— Poems. L, 1868. One of 100. 8vo, mor. With frontis by George Cruikshank. C Dec 12 (345) £80 [Spelman]

Lockhart, John Gibson, 1794-1854
— Ancient Spanish Ballads. L, 1842. Illus by Owen Jones. 4to, mor gilt; worn & soiled. wa Sept 25 (24) $55

Lockhart, Sir Robert Hamilton Bruce, 1887-1970
— The Marines Were There: The Story of the Royal Marines.... L, [1950]. Mor gilt by Zaehnsdorf. Inscr. cb Dec 18 (103) $75

Lockman, John
— Travels of the Jesuits. L, 1762. 2 vols. 8vo, contemp calf. With 6 folding maps & plates. sg Mar 12 (170) $275

Lockwood, Francis Cummins, 1864-1948
— Pioneer Days in Arizona.... NY, 1932. ALs tipped to front pastedown. O June 9 (103) $70

Loddiges, Conrad & Sons
— The Botanical Cabinet. L, [1817]-24. Vols I-IX. 9 vols. 4to, contemp half calf gilt. With engraved titles & 900 hand-colored plates. A few plates shaved. C Oct 15 (194) £2,300 [Scott Sandilands]
Vols I-V. L, [1817]-20. 5 vols. 8vo, contemp half calf; rubbed. With 469 (of 500) partly hand-colored plates. Vols III & V lacking the 2-leaf index (supplied in Ms in Vol III). S Nov 10 (663) £460 [Dorger]
Vols I-XIII. L, [1817]-33. 4to, contemp calf; some covers detached. With 1,301 plates, all but 1 hand-colored. de Belder copy. S Apr 28 (220) £4,500 [McCarthy]
Vols I-XVI. L, [1817]-29. 16 vols. 4to, contemp half calf; rebacked. With 1 uncolored & 1,600 hand-colored plates; ad for Hothouses with 2 engraved plates at end of Vol III. Titles spotted; 1 text leaf with a few letters defaced. C Oct 15 (243) £3,600 [Walford]

Loddington, William
— Plantation Work the Work of this Generation.... L, 1682. 4to, half calf. S June 25 (396) £1,700

Lodewyk, Van Velthem
— Spiegel historiaal, of rympspiegel.... Amst., 1727. Folio, vellum. B Feb 25 (628A) HF450

Lodge, Edmund, 1756-1839
— Portraits of Illustrious Personages of Great Britain. L, 1823-34. 12 vols. 4to, contemp half mor; rubbed. Some staining. bba Jan 15 (243) £40 [Elliott]
Anr copy. Contemp mor gilt by Clark. Plates on india paper, mtd. Vol XII affected by damp. Ck June 19 (1) £110
Anr copy. Old half calf gilt; rubbed, some spines torn. pnNY Oct 11 (7A) $225
Anr copy. 12 vols in six. 4to, contemp half lea; soiled & worn. With 240 ports. wa Nov 6 (455) $130
Anr Ed. L, 1835. 12 vols. 8vo, orig mor gilt. bba Aug 28 (280) £140 [Shapero]
Anr copy. Later half mor; rubbed, joints worn. O Feb 24 (124) $60
Anr Ed. L, 1840. 10 vols. 8vo, half mor; rubbed. Some dampstaining. S Nov 10 (393) £65 [Russell]

Lodge, George E. See: Bannerman & Lodge

Lodge, John, d.1774
— The Peerage of Ireland.... Dublin, 1789. 7 vols. 8vo, contemp calf; rubbed. With 86 plates; some with platemarks cropped. Some browning & stains. S Nov 10 (394) £120 [Heraldry]

Lodge, Thomas, 1558?-1625
— Rosalynde, or Euphues Golden Legacie, 1592. New Rochelle [NY]: Elston Press, 1902. One of 160. sg Jan 8 (68) $60

Lodi
— Ordines novi civitatis Laudae super victualiis et damnis agrorum. Milan, 1562. Folio, 19th-cent mor; spine def. Inscr on tp deleted; lower margin of title strengthened & with an early inscr; lower margin of 1st 4 leaves wormed; wormhole in the inner margin of title just touching border; extra leaf added at end in a contemp hand. S May 21 (51) £380 [Parikian]

Lofft, Capel
— Laura: or an Anthology of Sonnets.... L, 1813-14. 5 vols. 12mo, orig bds; soiled, backstrips chipped. Some soiling. Ck Jan 30 (1) £220

Loftie, William John
— Windsor, a Description... L, 1886. One of 100 with proof plates. Folio, orig half mor; spine worn. bba Apr 23 (360) £55 [Wise]

Loftus, Edward
— Joyfull Newes from Ireland.... L, 1642. 4to, modern half mor gilt. Library markings. bba Apr 9 (299) £120 [Emerald Isle]

Logan, James, 1674-1751
— The Scottish Gael: or, Celtic Manners.... L, 1831. 2 vols. 8vo, cloth; worn. O May 12 (125) $160
Anr copy. Contemp half calf; scuffed. With 8 plates, 7 colored. T Feb 19 (296) £50

Logan, James, 1794?-1872 —& McIan, Robert Ronald, d.1856
— The Clans of the Scottish Highlands. L, 1845-47. 2 vols. Folio, old half mor & modern cloth; def. With 2 colored armorial frontises & 72 plates. 1 title torn & detached, the other repaired; many plates torn along edges & creased. Sold w.a.f. pnNY Oct 11 (33) $300
Anr copy. Mor gilt, armorial design. S Apr 23 (70) £2,300 [McEwan]
Anr Ed. L: Ackermann, 1857. 2 vols. Folio, half mor gilt with Scottish arms; upper cover of Vol I slightly dampstained. With 2 frontises & 72 colored plates. Some spotting; 2 plates supplied from a smaller

copy. S May 28 (884) £1,200

Loggan, David, 1635-1700?
— Cantabrigia illustrata. Cambr., [1688]. 1st Ed. Folio, old calf; worn & broken. Library markings. Sold w.a.f. Franklin Institute copy. F Sept 12 (10) $650

Anr copy. Contemp calf; rubbed. With engraved title & 30 plates. pn Jan 22 (185) £1,700 [Hadland]

— Oxonia illustrata. Oxford, 1675. Folio, contemp mor gilt; rubbed, minor loss to spine. With engraved title, 39 double-page & 1 folding engravings. Tp trimmed & laid down; some soiling, staining & browning; a few tears & repairs. P June 18 (112) $1,300

Lohde, Ludwig
— Schinkel's...Mobel Entwurfe. Berlin, 1835. Folio, bdg not described. Some dampstains. Franklin Institute copy. F Sept 12 (111) $4,000

Lohmeier, Phillipp, d.1680
— Exercitatio physica de artificio navigandi per aerem.... Rinteln, [1676]. 4to, old wraps. sg Mar 26 (179) $250

Loiseleur-Deslongchamps, Jean Louis Auguste. See: Mordaunt de Launay & Loiseleur-Deslongchamps

Lolli, Giovanni Battista
— Osservazioni teorico-pratiche sopra il giuoco degli scacchi.... Bologna, 1763. Folio, half mor. pn Mar 26 (451) £300 [Furstenberg]

Lom d'Arce, Louis Armand. See: Lahontan, Louis Armand

Lomax, Virginia, b.1831
— The Old Capitol and its Inmates. NY, 1867. 12mo, orig cloth; shaken. sg Sept 18 (60) $700

Lomenie de Brienne, Louis Henri de, Count
— Itinerarium.... Paris, 1662. 8vo, 18th-cent mor gilt. With engraved title, port, plate & folding map (torn). S Nov 27 (86) £240 [Hannas]

Lonchamp, Frederic Charles
— Manuel du bibliophile francais (1470-1920). Paris & Lausanne, 1927. 8vo, orig wraps; shaken. sg May 14 (236) $110

London...
— The London and Country Brewer.... L, 1737. 5th Ed. 8vo, contemp calf; rebacked. bba July 16 (71) £70 [Port]

4th Ed. L, 1742. 8vo, contemp calf; front cover detached, rear cover split. sg Jan 15 (37) $90

London and its Environs Described. L, 1761. 6 vols. 8vo, contemp calf. With 4 half-titles & 79 (of 80) maps & plates, 1 hand-colored in outline, & folding plan of Windsor. Sold w.a.f. C Dec 12 (132) £240 [Scott]

— The London Aphrodite. L: Fanfrolico Press, 1928-29. Nos 1-6 in orig parts. pn Mar 5 (321) £50 [Burwood]

— The London Chair-Makers' and Carvers' Book of Prices.... L, 1802-8. 3 parts in 1 vol, including 1811 Supplement. 4to, later half calf. With 29 plates. bba May 14 (242) £520 [Axe]

— The London Encyclopaedia. L, 1829. 22 vols. 8vo, contemp half calf gilt; rubbed. Sold w,a,f. pn Jan 22 (163) £90 [Wadel]

— London Interiors: A Grand National Exhibition. L, [1841]. 2 vols in one. 4to, old half lea; worn. With extra engraved title & 75 plates. ha Dec 19 (228) $90

— The Several Plans and Drawings referred to in the Third Report from the Select Committee upon the Improvement of the Port of London. L, 1800. Folio, orig wraps. With 21 plates, some colored in wash & outline. Ck Jan 16 (94) £1,000

London, Charmian
— The Book of Jack London. NY, 1921. 1st Ed. 2 vols. Cloth; extremities worn. cb Jan 22 (32) $130

Anr copy. Vol I (of 2) only. Cloth, in tape-repaired d/j. Inscr. cb Jan 22 (33) $65

— The Log of the Snark. NY, 1925. 3d ptg. In d/j. Inscr "From the 'Mate' of the Beloved Skipper....". cb Jan 22 (34) $70

— Our Hawaii. NY, 1917. 1st Ed, Review copy, so stamped on tp. cb Jan 22 (35) $60

London, Jack, 1876-1916
— The Acorn-Planter: A California Forest Play.... NY, 1916. Orig cloth; rubbed. cb Jan 22 (40) $1,000

— Adventure. NY, 1911. cb Jan 22 (42) $225

— Before Adam. NY, 1907. 1st Trade Ed. cb Jan 22 (48) $80

— Burning Daylight. NY, 1910. 3d Issue. cb Jan 22 (50) $200; cb Jan 22 (51) $70

4th Issue. cb Jan 22 (52) $80

— The Call of the Wild. NY, 1903. 1st Ed. Cloth; spine worn. sg Mar 5 (133) $175

Anr Ed. L, 1908. Later Issue. cb Jan 22 (54) $55

— Children of the Frost. NY, 1902. 1st Ed. Front cover dampstained. cb Jan 22 (55) $275

— The Cruise of the Dazzler. NY, 1902. 1st Ed. Rubbed & soiled; spine worn & fraying; a few joints loose. cb Jan 22 (56) $600

Anr copy. Rubbed & soiled; front & rear

hinges loose, front endpaper chipped through to bds. cb Jan 22 (57) $350
— The Cruise of the Snark. NY, 1911. Rear hinge cracked & repaired. cb Jan 22 (58) $400
— A Daughter of the Snows. Phila., 1902. 8vo, cloth; worn. Check, sgd by London, tipped to front endpaper. O Oct 21 (104) $275

1st Ed. Illus by Frederick C. Yohn. With lettering missing from spine. With frontis & 3 colored plates. cb Jan 22 (59) $200
— Dutch Courage and Other Stories. NY, 1922. Front hinge cracked, missing flyleaf. cb Jan 22 (60) $190

Anr copy. Cloth; minor dampstain to lower right corner of front cover. cb May 7 (122) $225
— The Faith of Men. NY, 1904. 1st Ed. Cloth; rubbed & soiled, front hinge starting. cb Jan 22 (61) $130
— The Game. NY, 1905. 1st Ed. With 1/16 inch rubberstamp. cb Jan 22 (63) $75; sg Dec 11 (78) $50
— The God of his Fathers. NY, 1901. 1st Ed. Cloth; rubbed, leaning. cb Jan 22 (65) $225
— The House of Pride. NY, 1912. 1st Ed. In d/j. cb Jan 22 (68) $1,500
— The Human Drift. NY, 1917. cb Jan 22 (69) $400
— The Iron Heel. NY, 1908. cb Jan 22 (71) $180

Anr copy. Rubbed, 2 hinges starting. cb Jan 22 (72) $120
— Jack London Reports: War Correspondence.... Garden City, 1970. In repaired d/j. cb Jan 22 (73) $60
— Jerry of the Islands. NY, 1917. 1st Ed. Cloth, in d/j; rubbed. cb Jan 22 (75) $1,100

Anr copy. Cloth. Tp foxed. sg Feb 12 (209) $90
— John Barleycorn. NY, 1913. 1st Ed. Cloth, in d/j (chipped). cb Jan 22 (76) $500
— The Kempton-Wace Letters. NY, 1903. 1st Ed. Cloth; rubbed, rear cover soiled. cb Jan 22 (79) $250
— A Klondike Trilogy: Three Uncollected Stories. Santa Barbara, 1983. One of 300. cb Jan 22 (82) $55
— The Little Lady of the Big House. NY, 1916. In d/j. cb Jan 22 (84) $1,000
— London's Essays of Revolt. NY, 1926. In d/j. cb Jan 22 (85) $140
— Love of Life. NY, 1907. 1st Ed. cb Jan 22 (87) 60
— Martin Eden. NY, 1909. 1st Pbd Ed. cb Jan 22 (88) $190

Anr copy. Corners worn. cb Jan 22 (89) $170
— Michael, Brother of Jerry. NY, 1917. Extremities rubbed. cb Jan 22 (92) $110
— The Night-Born. NY, 1913. 1st Ed, 1st Issue. Cloth, in d/j. cb Jan 22 (95) $1,000
— An Old Lie Finally Nailed. [Minneapolis, 1916]. Wraps; soiled & with chip. cb Jan 22 (155) $140
— On the Makaloa Mat. NY, 1919. 1st Ed. Cloth, in d/j. cb Jan 22 (96) $1,000
— The People of the Abyss. NY, 1903. 1st Ed. Rear cover dampstained. cb Jan 22 (97) $225
— Revolution. NY, 1910. 1st Ed. Cloth; worn. cb Jan 22 (99) $250
— The Road. NY, 1907. 3d Issue. Covers soiled. cb Jan 22 (202) $100
— The Scarlet Plague. NY, 1915. 1st Ed. In d/j. cb Jan 22 (102) $800
— Scorn of Women. NY, 1906. Chip missing from the J of Jack London on front cover, corners slightly worn, rubberstamp on front flyleaf. cb Jan 22 (103) $1,100
— The Sea Wolf. NY, 1904. 1st Ed, 2d Issue. Illus by W. J. Aylward. Cloth; rubbed, soiled, front hinge starting, 2 pp tape-repaired. cb Jan 22 (105) $50
— Smoke Bellew. NY, 1912. 1st Ed. Cloth; worn. With frontis & 7 plates. cb Jan 22 (106) $120
— A Son of the Sun. Garden City, 1912. 1st Ed. Cloth; corners worn. With frontis & 3 plates. cb Jan 22 (108) $180
— The Son of the Wolf. Tales of the Far North. Bost. & NY, 1900. 1st Ed. 8vo, cloth. wa Dec 11 (194) $160

1st Issue. Cloth; corners rubbed. cb Jan 22 (109) $425

3d Issue. Cloth; front hinge repaired, covers & spine rubbed. cb Jan 22 (111) $140
— South Sea Tales. NY, 1911. 1st Ed. Cloth; corners worn. cb Jan 22 (112) $120
— The Star Rover. L, 1915. ("The Jacket.") 1st Ed. Cloth; some wear to front cover. Prelims darkened at lower margin. cb Jan 22 (74) $150

Anr Ed. NY, 1915. Rubbed. cb Jan 22 (113) $130

1st American Ed. Orig cloth; spine stained. cb Sept 28 (836) $140
— The Strength of the Strong. NY, 1914. 1st Ed. Wraps. cb Jan 22 (114) $60
— Theft. NY, 1910. 1st Ed. Cloth; front hinge cracked. ha May 22 (186) $130

1st Issue. Cloth. Inscr to Ferrari. cb Jan 22 (118) $2,000
— The Tramp. Chicago: Charles H. Kerr, [n.d.]. Ptd wraps. Dampstain to upper corner throughout. cb Jan 22 (119) $130

— The Valley of the Moon. NY, 1913. 1st Ed. Cloth; rear hinge poorly repaired. cb Jan 22 (121) $130

Anr Ed. Santa Barbara, 1975. In d/j. cb Jan 22 (122) $50

— War of the Classes. NY, 1905. 1st Ed. Bdg rubbed. Inscr. S Jan 13 (586) £520 [Bauman]

1st Issue. cb Jan 22 (123) $400

— What Life Means to Me. San Francisco, 1916. Wraps. With George Sterling's Tribute to Jack London as Intro. cb Jan 22 (126) $150

Anr Ed. Chicago: Charles H. Kerr [n.d.]. Wraps. cb Jan 22 (125) $130

— When God Laughs. NY, 1911. 1st Ed. With frontis & 5 plates. b Jan 22 (127) $375

— White Fang. NY, 1906. 1st Pbd Ed. Cloth; some wear. Tp is an integral part of gathering. O Oct 21 (105) $50

1st Issue. Title not tipped in. cb Jan 22 (129) $80

Long, Frank Belknap

— The Hounds of Tindalos. Sauk City: Arkham House, 1946. 1st Ed. In d/j. cb Sept 28 (838) $55

Long, G.

— Voyages and Travels of an Indian Interpreter and Trader.... L, 1791. 4to, contemp calf. With folding map. Short tear in S4. S June 25 (397) £500 [Sellers]

Long, John, Indian Trader

— Voyages and Travels of an Indian Interpreter and Trader.... L, 1791. 1st Ed. 4to, contemp calf; rebacked. Fitzwilliam copy. S Ot 23 (420) £900 [Sadlon]

Long Pointer. See: Frick, Childs

Longfellow, Henry Wadsworth, 1807-82
See also: Fore-Edge Paintings

The Courtship of Miles Standish and Other Poems. Bost., 1858. 1st American Ed, 1st Issue. 12mo, orig cloth; rubbed. bba Oct 16 (131) £60 [Mandl]

Anr copy. Cloth. cb Oct 23 (138) $55

Anr copy. Cloth, pbr's "Gilt Extra" bdg; spine-tips frayed. O Oct 21 (108) $90

2d Issue. Cloth. Jerome Kern—Barton Currie copy. O May 12 (127) $600

— Poems of Places. Bost., 1877. 2 vols. 12mo, orig cloth, spine ends frayed. Inscr. sg June 11 (278) $225

— Works. Bost., [1904]. One of 750. 11 vols. 8vo, half mor gilt. sg Sept 11 (230) $500; sg Sept 11 (231) $225

Longpre, Alexandre de, 1795-1856

— Une Saint-Hubert, comedie en un acte.... Paris: Barba 1838. 8vo, mor gilt. Jeanson copy. SM Mar 1 (368) FF1,600

Longstreet, James, 1821-1904

— From Manassas to Appomattox.... Phila., 1896. 1st Ed. 8vo, orig cloth; worn & soiled, shaken. wa Feb 19 (56) $130

Longus

— Daphnis and Chloe. L, 1925. Illus by John Austen. 4to, cloth. With 12 mtd color plates. sg Jan 8 (13) $50

— Daphnis et Chloe. [Paris] 1718. 8vo, lev extra with color-ptd gilt endpapers lettered in relief J. K. F. R. H. M. Fyrth & Johan. Kochel. With engraved title, 15 single- & 13 ddouble-page plates. 1 leaf foxed. Leopold, Duke of Albany's copy. P June 18 (114) $1,000

Anr Ed. L, 1779. ("Les Amours pastorales de Daphnis et Chloe.") 4to, half calf. With engraved title & 29 plates. S July 28 (1209) £250

Anr Ed. Paris, 1937. One of 250. Illus by Aristide Maillol. Orig vellum; soiled. With a suite of 53 woodcuts in half-vellum folder. P Sept 24 (195) $1,500

— Pastoralium de Daphnide et Chloe. Paris [but Amst.], 1754. 4to, contemp mor gilt. Lacking 1 plate. S July 28 (1140) £200

Lonicer, Adam, 1528-86

— Kreuterbuch.... Frankfurt: Egenolf, 1577. Folio, disbound. Plates "artlessly" hand-colored. Imperfect copy with scattered miscellaneous defects. Lacking c.50 pp at beginning. Sold w.a.f. sg Jan 15 (235) $350

Anr Ed. Augsburg, 1783. ("Kraeuter-Buch, oder Das Buch ueber alle Drey Reiche der Natur.") Folio, 19th-cent half vellum. Lacking 2 leaves; some spotting. HK Nov 4 (1059) DM1,100

Lonicerus, Philippus

— Chronicorum turcicorum. Frankfurt, 1578. 3 vols in 1. Folio, contemp vellum bds; soiled. Lacking 2 leaves in Vol I; Index to Vol I bound at end of Vol III; some repairs & holes; slight worming to margins towards the end of Vol III. S May 21 (52) £300 [Burgess Browning]

— Icones Livianae: Praecipuas romanorum historias magno artificio ad vivum.... Frankfurt, 1572-73. Illus by Jost Amman. 8vo, modern bds. With 98 (of 103) full-page woodcuts. sg June 11 (14) $300

Lonnberg, Einar. See: Wright, Magnus· fWilhelm·f& Ferdinand von

Loomis, Alfred F. See: Derrydale Press

Lopez de Altuna, Pedro
— Primera Parte de la Coronica General de la Orden de la Santissima Trinidad. Segovia, 1637. Folio, old vellum; loose. Browned & dampstained; some worming in lower inner corners affecting text. sg Mar 26 (181) $175

Lopez de Gomara, Francisco, 1510-60?
— Historia dell Illustriss. et Valorosiss. Capitano Don Ferdinando Cortes.... Rome: Valerio & Luigi Dorici, 1556. 4to, vellum. Small hole in C2 & tear in YY1 with loss of text; tear in tp repaired; adhesion affecting a few letters of KK3. S Nov 18 (1165) £180 [Philadelphia]
— The Pleasant Historie of the Conquest of the Weast India.... L: Henry Bynneman, 1578. 8vo, contemp vellum; worn. Lacking 3F4; 2 leaves torn; tp & several other leaves at beginning & end marginally def, affecting text in places; several other leaves at beginning & end marginally def, affecting text in plates; headline of last few leaves def; ink annotations on title & marginalia to most leaves; some dampstains. bba Oct 16 (230) £550 [Maggs]

Lopez de Sigura, Ruy
— Il Giuoco de gli scacchi. Venice, 1584. 4to, contemp vellum. C Dec 12 (297) £550 [Lanfranchi]
— Il Giuoco de gli scaachi.... Venice: Presso C. Arrivabene, 1584. 4to, modern vellum. Some staining. pn Mar 26 (452) £700 [Furstenberg]

Lorenzana, Francesco Antonio, 1722-1804
— Concilios provinciales primero, y segundo, celebrados en...Mexico.... Mexico, 1769. Folio, early 20th-cent half vellum bds; rubbed & dust-soiled. S Nov 10 (1166) £280 [Quaritch]

Loring, Rosamond Bowditch
— Decorated Book Papers.... Cambr., Mass., 1942. One of 250. Half cloth. With 25 mtd specimens of papers. sg May 14 (123) $400

L'Orme, Philibert de
— Le Premier Tome de l'architecture [all pbd]. Paris: Federic Morel, 1567. 1st Ed, 1st Issue. Folio, old calf; rebacked, joints cracked. Lacking 11 text leaves & 1 blank. Sold w.a.f. C Apr 8 (121) £200 [Weinreb]

Lorrain, Pierre le
— La Physique occulte, ou traide de la baguette divinatoire. The Hague, 1762. 2 vols. 12mo, contemp calf; rubbed. O Nov 18 (116) $300

Lorris, Guillaume de —& Meung, Jean de
— Le Romant de la rose. Paris: [Antoine Verard, c.1511]. 4to, 18th-cent calf gilt, armorial bdg. Some wear; lacking last leaf. FD June 11 (137) DM24,500

Lory, Gabriel, The Younger
— Voyage pittoresque de l'Oberland.... Paris & Strasbourg, 1812. 1st Ed. Folio, 19th-cent bds; extremities rubbed, spine def. With colored frontis & 14 colored plates. Lacking map. P Sept 24 (193) $16,000
Anr copy. Later calf. With map, colored frontis & 14 colored plates. Marginal tears repaired. S Oct 23 (260) £4,500 [Burkhard]

Los Angeles
— Los Angeles Cookery. The Ladies' Aid Society of the Fort Street M. E. Church.... Los Angeles, 1881. 8vo, orig cloth; upper joint cracked. Crahan copy. P Nov 25 (300) $1,500

Lossing, Benson John, 1813-91
— The History of American Industries and Arts. Phila.: Porter & Coates, [1878]. 4to, orig cloth; hinge repaired. With 58 plates. wa Nov 6 (196) $110
— Pictorial Field Book of the Revolution. NY, 1851-52. 1st Ed. 2 vols. 8vo, old half calf; rubbed & worn. cb Dec 18 (104) $60

Lothian, Philip Henry Kerr, 11th Marquis of
— Illuminated Manuscripts, Incunabula and Americana; from the Famous Libraries of.... NY: American Art Association, 1932. 4to, modern cloth. ALs & other material tipped in. pn Oct 23 (96) £50 [Fogg]

Loti, Pierre, 1850-1923
— Un Pelerin d'Angkor. Paris, 1930. One of 25. Illus by Paul Jouve. 4to, mor gilt extra by Max Fonseque with onlaid design of elephant's head, orig wraps preserved. With 2 extra suits of all the illusts. CNY Dec 19 (86) $3,200

Lottery...
— The Lottery; A Comedy. L, 1728. 8vo, modern lea. Lower outer corner of last 2 leaves torn & repaired. sg Mar 26 (182) $250

Lotz, Arthur
— Bibliographie der Modelbuecher. Leipzig, 1933. sg May 14 (330) $80

Loubat, Joseph Florimond de
— The Medallic History of the United States.... NY, 1878. Illus by Jules Jacquemart. 2 vols. 4to, cloth; minor wear. Library markings. Inscr. O Sept 23 (140) $150

Loudon, Jane Webb

[A set of Annuals, Bulbous Plants, Greenhouse Plants & Perennials, sold in the de Belder sale at S on 28 Apr 1987] S Apr 28 (221) £8,000 [Newmann]

— Annuals. L, 1840. ("The Ladies' Flower-Garden of Ornamental Annuals.") 1st Ed. 4to, orig cloth; rebacked, old backstrip laid down. With 48 hand-colored plates. S Oct 23 (726) £1,300 [Adams]

Anr copy. Modern half calf. Some cropping to plate imprints or numerals. S Apr 23 (47) £1,200 [McCarthy]

"2d Ed". L, [1849]. 4to, orig cloth; worn & stained, upper half of spine missing. With 50 colored plates. Plates 1, 16, 25, 38, & 42 detached & torn in margins, as is 1 leaf of text. S Nov 10 (511) £900 [McCarthy]

— British Wild Flowers. L, [1849]. 2d Ed. 4to, disbound. Lacking 1 plate. Ck Apr 24 (70) £280

Anr copy. Orig cloth; rubbed. Lacking 2 plates; Plates 11 & 32 detached & frayed. T Mar 19 (110) £400

3d Ed. L, 1859. 4to, orig cloth; broken. pn Mar 5 (225) £680 [Adams]

Anr copy. Half mor gilt. pn June 18 (130) £500 [Adams]

— Ladies' Magazine of Gardening. L, 1842. Vol I, Nos 1-12 (all pbd). 8vo, contemp half calf. With 13 colored plates. pnE June 17 (143) £160

Loudon, John Claudius, 1783-1843

— An Encyclopaedia of Cottage, Farm, and Villa Architecture... L, 1833. 1st Ed. 8vo, contemp half mor; rubbed. bba Sept 25 (282) £220 [Weinreb]

Anr Ed. L, 1835. 8vo, half sheep; scuffed. ha Sept 29 (124) $80

— The Suburban Gardener, and Villa Companion.... L, 1838. 8vo, orig cloth; recased & rubbed. Tears in tp repaired. bba Sept 25 (281) £180 [Carter]

— A Treatise on Forming, Improving, and Managing Country Residences.... L, 1806. 2 vols. 4to, contemp half calf; joints split. With 32 plates, 1 double-page rubbed. bba Sept 25 (280) £440 [Weinreb]

Anr copy. 2 vols in 1. 4to, early 20th-cent half mor. With 32 plates, 1 with overlay. T May 21 (294) £360

Louis XIV, King of France

[-] L'Entree triomphante de leurs maiestez Louis XIV...et Marie Therese d'Autriche... dans la ville de Paris. Paris, 1662. Folio, 19th-cent half vellum; spine torn. With frontis, dedication & 21 plates. Lacking port; some leaves soiled; 3 leaves torn & repaired. C May 13 (75) £400 [Traylen]

[-] Medailles sur les principaux evenements du regne de Louis le Grand. Paris, 1702. Folio, contemp mor gilt with arms of Louis XIV; spine wormed & repaired at head & foot. With port of Louis XIV inserted. C May 13 (35) £1,300 [Quaritch]

Anr copy. Contemp calf, armorial bdg; corners repaired with lea. With 285 plates. cb Dec 18 (105) $275

Anr Ed. Paris, 1723. folio, contemp mor gilt, with French royal arms on covers; extremities worn, rear joint starting. Perforated stamp in margin of tp & a few other leaves. sg Mar 26 (183) $450

Louis XV, King of France

[-] Relation de l'arrivee du Roi au Havre-de-Grace, le 19. Septembre 1749. Paris, 1753. Folio, contemp mor gilt, with arms of Louis XV; rubbed. With 6 double-page plates. SM Oct 20 (550) FF9,000

[-] Le Sacre de Louis XV...dans l'Eglise de Reims.... [Paris], 1723. Folio, contemp calf; worn. With 9 double-page plates & 30 costume plates. Library stamp on engraved title. Engraved throughout. S Oct 23 (62) £600 [Gilbert]

Louisiana

— Code Civil de L'Etat de la Louisiane. [N.p: L'Imprimerie de E. Duverger, 1825]. 8vo, contemp calf; rebacked. Bottom forecorner of leaves dampstained. sg Mar 12 (172) $120

Lousbergh, F. J. H.

— Verzen en fragmenten. Maastricht, 1920. One of 40, this copy for Alex Stols, Jr. 4to, wraps. B Oct 7 (108) HF300

Loutherbourg, Philippe Jacques de, 1740-1812

— The Romantic and Picturesque Scenery of England and Wales. L, 1805. Folio, contemp half mor; rubbed. With hand-colored frontis & 18 plates. T Feb 19 (328) £560

Louys, Pierre, 1870-1925

— Aphrodite. Paris, 1896. 8vo, contemp mor gilt, orig wraps bound in. bba Dec 4 (184) £80 [Joseph]

— Collected Tales. Chicago: Argus, 1930. Illus by John Austen. 4to, cloth, in d/j. cb Dec 4 (36) $55

— Le Crepescule des nymphes. Paris, 1926. One of 10 on Whatman with an orig sketch. Illus by Bosshard. 4to, mor by Schroeder with mor onlays. With 10 lithos. SM Oct 20 (645) FF8,000

— La Femme et le pantin. Paris, 1903. One of 260. Mor extra by Noulhac, orig wraps bound in. S May 6 (25) £240 [Hannas]

— Leda: In Praise of the Blessings of Dark-

LOUYS

ness. Easthampton MA: Cheloniidae Press, 1985. One of 60 but with the extra suite of sgd prints usually accompanying the 15-copy issue. Illus by Alan James Robinson. 4to, bds. sg Dec 4 (37) $375
— Les Poesies de Meleagre. [Paris, 1926]. One of 135. Illus by Edouard Chimot. 4to, mor gilt extra by Pierre Legrain, orig wraps bound in. With 15 etchings in 2 states & extra-illus with 10 orig pencil and watercolor drawings by Pierre Mercelly. P Dec 15 (179) $5,750
— The Songs of Bilitis. NY, [1926]. One of 2,000, sgd by the artist. Illus by Willy Pogany. Cloth. cb Feb 19 (215) $70; sg Jan 8 (211) $130
— The Twilight of the Nymphs. N.p.: pvtly ptd, 1927. One of 1,250. Illus by Clara Tice. 4to, half cloth. CA Oct 7 (108) A$100
Anr copy. Mor with multi-colored onlay of a cavorting nymph, by Sangorski & Sutcliffe. cb Sept 11 (322) $375

Love...
— Love Ballads of the XVIth Century. East Aurora, 1897. Half cloth. With watercolor on title page. sg Jan 8 (263) $225

Lovecraft, Howard Phillips
— At the Mountains of Madness.... Sauk City: Arkham House, 1964. 1st Issue. In d/j. cb Sept 28 (844) $65
— Beyond the Wall of Sleep. Sauk City: Arkham House, 1943. 1st Ed. In chipped & repaired d/j. cb Sept 28 (845) $250
— The Outsider and Others. Sauk City: Arkham House, 1939. 1st Ed. Worn, Shaken, spine rubbed. sg Mar 5 (134) $250
— The Shunned House. Athol, Mass.: Pbd by W. Paul Cook/The Recluse Press, 1928. 1st Ed, Arkham House Remainder Issue. Cloth, bound in 1961. cb Sept 28 (854) $1,100
[-] The Vagrant: The Sixth Number. Athol MA: [W. Paul Cook, Nov 1917]. Wraps; rubbed. Contains Lovecraft's poem To Greece. cb Sept 28 (859) $55
— DAVIS, SONIA H. - Howard Phillips Lovecraft as his Wife Remembers Him. Providence: Friends of the Library of Brown Univ, 1949. Wraps. In: Books at Brown, Vol XI, Nos 1-. Inscr to Mr & Mrs Eddy by Davis. cb Sept 28 (862) $170

Lovecraft, Howard Phillips —& Derleth, August
— The Lurker at the Threshold. Sauk City: Arkham House, 1945. In repaired d/j. cb Sept 28 (852) $55

AMERICAN BOOK PRICES CURRENT

Lover of Children. See: Friendly...

Lover of his Country's Peace. See: Mystery...

Lover of his Country. See: Prat, Samuel

Lover, Samuel, 1797-1868
— Works. Bost., 1901-2. Treasure Trove Ed, one of 900. 10 vols. Half mor. cb Dec 4 (284) $75

Lovett, Richard, Lay Clerk of Worcester Cathedral
— The Electrical Philosopher. Containing a New System of Physics.... Worcester, 1774. 8vo, modern cloth. Marginal tears; library markings, including perforated stamp on tp & 1 plate. sg Mar 26 (184) $130

Low, Charles Rathbone, 1837-1918
— Her Majesty's Navy. L, 1890-93. 3 vols. 4to, orig cloth; rubbed. Ck Nov 21 (354) £220
Anr copy. 22 orig parts. 4to, orig wraps; spotted. Ck May 15 (193) £170
Anr copy. In 22 orig parts. 4to, orig wraps; worn. Ck June 5 (11) £170
Anr copy. 3 vols in 6. 4to, orig cloth; worn. With 3 ports, 3 titles & 39 colored plates. pn Dec 11 (279) £240 [Walford]
Anr copy. 3 vols in 6. 4to, half mor. pn July 23 (63) £220 [Walford]
Anr copy. 3 vols in 6. 4to, orig cloth; soiled, 2 vols marked by damp at 1 corner. S July 14 (581) £260

Low, David, 1786-1859
— The Breeds of the Domestic Animals of the British Islands. L, 1842. Illus by W. Nicholson. 2 vols. Folio, old half mor gilt; 1 spine def, scuffed. With 56 hand-finished colored plates. pnNY June 11 (128) $5,000

Low, Capt. James, d.1852
— A Dissertation on the Soil and Agriculture of the British Settlement of Penang.... Singapore, 1836. 8vo, cloth. With folding table & hand-colored folding plate. Some tears; interleaved throughout; marginal & other notes in a contemp hand; some light stains. S Oct 23 (489) £1,300 [Randall]

Lowe, Edward Joseph, 1825-1900
— Ferns: British and Exotic. L, 1867-68. 8 vols. 8vo, orig cloth; spines faded. Ck Oct 31 (94) £45
Anr Ed. L, 1872. 8 vols. 8vo, contemp half mor. With 479 plates. S May 28 (591) £220

Lowe, Edward Joseph, 1825-1900 —& Howard, W.
— Beautiful Leaved Plants. L, 1872. 8vo, orig cloth; spine ends frayed. With 60 colored plates. sg June 11 (279) $100

Lowe, Peter
— A Discourse of the Whole Art of Chyrurgerie.... L: T. Purfoot, 1634. 3d Ed. 4to, 19th-cent half calf; worn. Ck Oct 31 (179) £350

Lowell, James Russell, 1819-91
— Conversations on Some of the Old Poets. Cambr., Mass., 1845. 1st Ed. 12mo, wraps; soiled, spine reinforced with glue, lacking lower portion of spine. cb Oct 23 (141) $55
— Works. Bost., 1899-1901. 13 vols. 12mo, half mor. cb Oct 23 (142) $55
Elmwood Ed. Bost, 1904. 16 vols. Cloth. ha May 22 (65) $75
Edition de Luxe. Cambr., 1904. One of 1,000. 16 vols. mor gilt. With ADs & Ls tipped in. O May 12 (128) $650

Lowenfels, Walter
— Apollinaire, an Elegy. Paris: Hours Press, 1930. One of 150. 4to, bds; soiled & rubbed. sg Dec 11 (329) $110
Anr copy. Half lea. T May 20 (18) £110

Lower, Mark Antony, 1813-76
— A Compendious History of Sussex. Lewes, 1870. 2 vols. 8vo, half mor; rubbed. pn June 18 (134) £140 [Campbell]

Lowery, F. W.
— History of a Fishing Trip. [N.p., 1933]. One of 100. Bds. Bottom margin of some pp dampstained. sg Oct 23 (169) $110

Lowery, Woodbury. See: Phillips, Philip Lee

Lowndes, John
— The Coffee-Planter; or an Essay on the Cultivation and Manufacturing of that Article.... L, 1807. 8vo, modern vellum. With 6 folding plates (misbound). S June 25 (432) £550 [Maggs]

Lowndes, William, 1652-1724
— A Report containing an Essay for the Amendment of the Silver Coins. L, 1695. 1st Ed. 8vo, contemp calf gilt; joints cracking, spine & corners chipped. B1 a cancel & with small burn mark at back; G5r with inked underlinings; lower endpaper removed; stamp on front free endpaper; marginal tear on B2; K6 wrinkled. P Sept 24 (324) $300

Lowndes, William Thomas, d.1843
— The Bibliographer's Manual of English Literature. L, 1857-64. 11 parts. 8vo, orig cloth; rubbed & stained. bba Sept 25 (367) £95 [Hay Cinema]
Anr copy. 11 vols. 8vo, orig cloth; spines stained. Ck Nov 7 (12) £50
Anr copy. 11 parts in 4 vols. 8vo, new cloth. sg Oct 2 (185) $60
Anr copy. 11 vols. 8vo, cloth; worn. sg May 14 (221) $140
Anr Ed. L, 1862-64. 7 vols, including appendix. 8vo, half mor, appendix in orig cloth; worn. bba Mar 12 (347) £50 [English]
Anr Ed. L, 1864. Ed by Henry G. Bohn. 4 vols. 8vo, half mor; rubbed. cb Sept 11 (231) $120
Anr copy. 6 vols. 8vo, contemp half sheep; worn. sg Jan 22 (220) $200

Lowry, Joseph Wilson —& Landseer, Thomas, 1795-1880
— Illustrations of Zoology. L & Glasgow, 1851. Folio, orig cloth; worn. bba Dec 4 (262) £35 [Rainer]

Lowry, Malcolm
— Ultramarine: a Novel. L, [1933]. 1st Ed. S Jan 13 (588) £50 [Leinweber]

Lowth, Robert, 1710-87
— De sacra Poesi Hebraeorum. Oxford, 1753. 1st Ed. 4to, contemp calf; broken. bba Jan 15 (43) £45 [Teoh]

Lowther, Barbara J.
— A Bibliography of British Columbia. [Victoria, B.C., 1968-75]. 2 vols. 4to, cloth. O Sept 23 (141) $90

Loyd, Samuel, 1841-1911
— Chess Strategy. Elizabeth NJ, 1878. Orig cloth. pn Mar 26 (306) £200 [De Lucia]

Lozano, Pedro, 1697-1759
— A True and Particular Relation of the Dreadful Earthquake...at Lima. L, 1748. 8vo, contemp calf; worn, spine ends chipped, joints cracked. With 8 folding maps & plates, some with later hand-coloring. cb Feb 19 (165) $65
Anr copy. Modern calf. With 9 folding maps & plates. Some fraying. O May 12 (129) $275

Luard, Lowes Dalbiac
See also: Derrydale Press
— The Anatomy and Action of the Horse. Woodstock VT: Countryman Press, [1950s]. 4to, cloth, in torn d/j. sg Oct 23 (391) $50

Lubin, Augustin, 1624-96
— Orbis augustinianus sive conventuum ordinis eremitarum Sancti Augustini chorographica et topographica descriptio. Paris: Pierre Baudouin, 1659. Oblong 4to, later bds. With engraved title, table & 59 full-pge maps. S Oct 23 (220) £1,500 [Martayan]

Luc, Jean Andre de, 1727-1817
— Idees sur la meteorologie. Londres, 1786-87. 2 vols. 8vo, contemp calf; spine of Vol I scuffed. With 2 folding plates. C Dec 12 (133) £240 [Quaritch]

Lucanus, Marcus Annaeus, 39-65 A.D.
— Pharsalia. Venice: Guerinus, 14 May 1477. Folio, vellum bds; broken. Some worming. 116 (of 120) leaves. Goff L-296. S Sept 23 (361) £360 [Barber]

Anr Ed. Venice: Aldus, Apr 1502. ("Civilis belli.") 8vo, orig calf over wooden bds; front joint starting, spine ends chipped; lacking clasps. Stained. sg Oct 9 (82) $375

Anr copy. Modern vellum. Minor stains. sg Mar 26 (185) $275

Anr Ed. Burgos: Phelippe de Punta, 1588. ("Lucano traduzido de verso Latino en prosa Castellana....") Folio, old vellum; loose in bdg. Some foxing & soiling; early marginalia. sg Mar 26 (186) $425

Lucas, Fielding, 1781-1854
— A General Atlas.... Balt, [1823]. Folio, contemp mor; torn, broken, lacking spine. With engraved title, frontis & 97 (of 98) hand-colored maps. Sold w.a.f. P Dec 15 (174) $1,000

Lucas, Frank Laurence, 1894-1967. See: Golden Cockerel Press

Lucas, Paul, 1664-1737
— Voyage fait en 1714 par ordre du roi dans la Turquie.... Amst., 1720. 2 vols. 12mo, contemp calf; rubbed. bba Nov 13 (120) £130 [Frew Mackenzie]

Lucas, Theophilus
— Memoirs of the Lives, Intrigues and Comical Adventures of the most Famous Gamesters.... L, 1714. 12mo, contemp calf; rubbed. Corner of tp torn away with loss. T Sept 18 (369) £75

Lucas, Thomas J.
— Camp Life and Sport in South Africa. L, 1878. 8vo, orig cloth. With frontis & 3 plates. SSA Oct 28 (710) R460

Lucatt, Edward
— Rovings in the Pacific from 1837 to 1849.... L, 1851. 2 vols. 8vo, half calf gilt. With 4 colored plates. pn Dec 11 (266) £180 [Phillips]

Lucian of Samosata
— I dilettevoli dialogi: le vere narrationi: le facete epistole. Venice: Zoppino, 1525. 8vo, 19th-cent mor gilt; upper joint def. S Sept 23 (466) £160 [Pampolini]

— Oeuvres. Amst.: Wetstein, 1712. 2 vols. 8vo, mor by Derome le jeune with his ticket in Vol II. With 2 frontises, port & 12 folding plates. C May 13 (30) £500 [O'Keefe]

Lucien-Graux, ——, Docteur
— Le Tapis de Prieres. [N.p.], 1938. One of 125. Illus by F. L. Schmied. 4to, unsewn in orig wraps. S June 17 (50) £600 [Dailey]

Luckombe, Philip
— A Concise History of...Printing. L, 1770. 1st Ed. 8vo, disbound. Tp stamped. sg Mar 26 (187) $150

Lucretius Carus, Titus, 96?-55 B.C.
— De rerum natura. L, 1712. 4to, modern cloth. Some browning. sg Mar 26 (188) $80

Anr Ed. Birm: Baskerville, 1772. 4to, contemp mor gilt; worn. Hole at inner margin of tp; 1st 2 leaves stained in margins; some leaves spotted. S Nov 10 (395) £70 [Vine]

Anr copy. Contemp mor gilt; joints rubbed. S Jan 13 (624) £110 [McKenzie]

Ludlam, William
— Astronomical Observations Made in St. John's College, Cambridge.... Cambr., 1769. 4to, contemp calf. With 8 folding plates. 1 plate spotted. C Dec 12 (135) £320 [Quaritch]

Anr copy. Contemp bds; rubbed. With 7 folding plates. Ownership stamp on tp. S Feb 24 (592) £160 [Penny]

Ludlow, Edmund, 1617?-92
— Memoirs. Vevay, 1698-99. 3 vols. 8vo, 19th-cent mor; rubbed. O Feb 24 (126) $210

Anr copy. Contemp calf; rubbed. O Feb 24 (127) $90

Anr copy. Contemp calf; spines worn. Vol I tp frayed. T Apr 16 (115) £80

Anr Ed. Vevey, 1698. 2 vols. 8vo, old calf; worn, broken. sg Oct 9 (261) $80

Ludlow, William
— Report of a Reconnaissance from Carroll, Montana.... Wash., 1876. 4to, orig cloth; worn & soiled. Library markings. wa Sept 25 (479) $75

Ludolf, Hiob, 1624-1704
— Historia Aethiopica. Frankfurt, 1681. Folio, contemp calf gilt; joints weak. With folding table & 8 folding plates & 2 double-page ptd genealogies. Some shaving & browning. S June 25 (486) £550 [Kahn]

— Lexicon Aethiopico-Latinum. L: Thomas Roycroft, 1661. Bound with: Grammatica Aethiopica. And: Confessio fidei Claudii regis Aethiopicae. 4to, modern cloth by Maltby. S May 21 (114) £280 [Thomas]

Ludolphus de Saxonia

— Vita Christi. Cologne:[Ludwig von Renschen], 1487. ("Meditationes vite Jhesu Christi.") Folio, contemp blindstamped calf over woden bds; rebacked, wormed, upper cover repaired. One leaf holed, anr stained. 348 (of 352) leaves; lacking title, C4-5, and final blank. Goff L-344. S Nov 27 (190) £1,000 [Mauss]

Anr Ed. Zwolle: Pieter van Os, 20 Nov [1495]. ("Dat Boeck vanden leven ons Heren Jhesu Cristi anderwerven gheprint.") Folio, contemp blind-tooled calf over oak bds with later clasps; rebacked. 355 (of 356) leaves; lacking last blank. Goff L-356. pn Oct 23 (37) £12,500 [N. Israel]

Anr Ed. Seville: Juan Cromberger, 1537-44. Vol II only. Folio, 17th-cent calf; uppermost compartment of spine off. Some worming in gutters; short tear through center of tp affecting vignette of the Virgin. sg Mar 26 (189) $90

Anr Ed. Venice: nella stamperia della luna, 1576. ("Vita di Giesu Christo nostro redentore.") Folio, later half lea. Tp strengthened on verso; final leaf repaired in margins; some stains & soiling. O Nov 18 (105) $140

Ludwig, Prince of Anhalt

— Der fruchtbringenden Gesellschaft nahmen, vorhaben Gemaehlde und Woerter. Frankfurt, 1646. 4 parts in 1 vol. 4to, contemp vellum bds; soiled. With 4 engraved titles & 400 plates. Library stamp on 1st title; 1st few leaves dampstained. de Belder copy. S Apr 28 (222) £10,500 [Israel]

Ludwig, Christian Gottlieb

— Ectypa vegetabilium, usibus medicis praecipue.... Halle & Leipzig, 1769-[64]. Folio, contemp calf gilt; repaired at head & foot, rubbed & holed. With 200 colored nature-ptd plates. Portion torn from tp with loss of 2 letters. Horticultural Society of New York—de Belder copy. S Apr 28 (223) £11,000 [Maggs]

Lugar, Robert

— The Country Gentleman's Architect. L, 1807. ("The Country Gentleman's Architect; Containing a Variety of Designs for Farm Houses and Farm Yards.") 4to, old bds; worn. With 22 plates. Tp soiled; marginal worming. S Feb 23 (349) £220 - [Shapero]

Lugt, Frits

— Les Marques de collections de dessins & d'estampes. Amst., 1921. Half mor gilt. C Dec 3 (28) £100 [Tulkens]

Anr copy. 2 vols including Supplement, 1956. Orig cloth; blistered. sg May 14 (50) $175

— Les Marques de Collections de Dessins et d'Estampes. The Hague, 1956 & San Francisco, 1975. 2 vols, including Supplement. 4to, orig cloth. S Nov 10 (124) £230 [Zwemmer]

Luis de Granada, 1504-88

— Rosario della...Vergine Maria.... Rome, 1573. 4to, contemp mor gilt, bound for the Carafa family; spine repaired, new endleaves. Furstenberg copy. S June 25 (26) £1,300 [Hannas]

Lull, Ramon, 1235-1315

— De Secretis naturae sive guinta essentia libri duo. Venice: Peter Schoeffer, 1542. 8vo, 18th-cent vellum. Lacking colophon leaf; signature scored at foot of title. C Dec 12 (282) £300 [Quaritch]

Lumholtz, Carl, 1851-1922

— Among Cannibals: An Account of Four Years' Travels in Australia.... NY, 1889. 8vo, orig cloth; worn. pn Dec 11 (267) £80 [Trocchi]

— Through Central Borneo: Two Years' Travel in the Land of the Head Hunters. L & NY, 1920. 2 vols. cb June 4 (137) $110

Lumisden, Andrew, 1720-1801

— Remarks on the Antiquities of Rome.... L, 1797. 1st Ed. 4to, modern half calf gilt; corners bent. sg Apr 2 (135) $475

Lumpkin, Wilson

— The Removal of the Cherokee Indians from Georgia. Wormsloe GA, 1907. One of 500. 2 vols in 1. 8vo, modern cloth. Half-title of 2d part repaired. sg Mar 12 (70) $70

Luna, Alvaro de

[-] CHACON, GONZALO. - La Coronica de Don Alvaro de Luna.... Milan: Juan Antonio de Castellono, 23 Oct 1546. Folio, vellum. S Nov 27 (10) £10,500 [Quaritch]

Lunardi, Vincent, 1759-1806

— An Account of the First Aerial Voyage in England. L, 1784. 8vo, orig wraps. Lacking port. bba Jan 15 (381) £160 [Phelps]

Lupton, Thomas

— A Thousand Notable Things of Sundry Sorts, Enlarged. L, 1675. 4th Ed. 8vo, modern blind-stamped calf. Some headlines shaved; wormed; waterstained. bba Jan 15 (392) £150 [Phelps]

Lupus, Johannes
— Quaestiones super confoederationes. Siena: Henricus de Haarlem, [c.1492]. 4to, modern bds. Minor worming in some lower margins repaired, occasionally touching text; inner margin of 1st leaf strengthened; library stamps. 32 leaves. Goff L-401. S Nov 27 (191) £1,800 [De Zayas]

Lustiger Spruch...
— Ein Lustiger von der Buelschafft, inn Jagens weiss gestellet.... [Nuremberg, c.1530]. 4to, modern vellum. With 5 woodcuts, that on the title is repeated on B1v. Huth-Jeanson copy. SM Mar 1 (382) FF82,000

Luther, Martin, 1483-1546
— Colloquia Mensalia: or, Dr. Martin Luther's Divine Discourses. L, 1652. 1st Ed in English. Folio, modern cloth. Lacking last leaf. bba Aug 28 (174) £50 [Munday]

Anr copy. Later calf; rubbed. Title relaid; last few leaves stained. T Sept 18 (300) £50

— A Commentarie upon the Epistle of S Paule to the Galathians. L, 1580. 4to, contemp calf; rebacked. Dampstaining in upper portion of 1st half of vol. sg Oct 9 (262) $325

— Contra Henricum Regem Angliae. Wittenberg: Johann Rhau-Gruenberg, 1522. 4to, wraps. Dampstain to lower margin of last leaf. sg June 11 (280) $1,000

— Disputatio domini Johannis Eccii et Pa. Martini Luther in studio Lipsensi futura. [Leipzig: Martin Landsberg, 1519]. 4to, 20th-cent mor gilt; lacking spine. Library stamp of Heidelberg University on tp verso; 1 wormhole in text. H. W. Poor copy. S June 25 (31) £450

— Opera. Jena: Christian Rhoidius, 1570. ("Tomus quartus et idem ultimus omnium operum....") Contemp pigskin over bds with inset medallion port of Luther; worn. Browned. cb Oct 23 (143) $250

— Operationes in duas psalmorum decades. Basel: Adam Petri, 1521. Folio, blindstamped contemp pigskin with metal fittings. Benzing 518. FD Dec 2 (80) DM13,000

— Resolution Lutheriana super propositione decia tertia: de potestate pape. [Leipzig: Valentin Schumann, 1520]. 4to, half vellum. Tear in tp. sg June 11 (281) $650

— Das windliecht Gottes. Heerenveen, 1942. One of 100. Orig wraps. B Oct 7 (238) HF1,200

Luyken, Jan
— Afbeeldingen der Merkwaardigste Geschiedenissen van het Oude en Nieuwe Testament.... Amst., 1729. 2 parts in 1 vol. Folio, 19th-cent half mor; loose. With engraved title & 66 double-page plates including a World map. S Jan 12 (239) £440 [Dennistoun]

— Beschouwing der Wereld, bestaande in hondert konstige Figuuren.... Amst., 1708. 12mo, vellum. With engraved title & 100 plates. B Feb 25 (543) HF440

— Die bykorf des Gemoeds.... Amst., 1711. 8vo, vellum. With engraved title & 101 plates. B Feb 25 (544) HF460

— De onwaardige wereld. Amst., 1710. 8vo, vellum; damaged. With engraved title & 60 plates. Some stains. B Feb 25 (545) HF225

Luyts, Joannes
— Introductio ad geographiam. Utrecht, 1692. 4to, contemp calf; spine & extremities worn & repaired. With engraved title & 66 double-page maps hand-colored in outline. Some dampstaining to upper margins; some soiling; about half of the maps loose. P June 18 (116) $2,200

Anr copy. Contemp vellum. With frontis & 2 folding plates. With 2 stamps on title. S July 28 (1091) £360

Luzzatto, Aldo — & Otto-Lenghi, Luisa Mortar
— Hebraica Ambrosiana. Catalogue of Undescribed Hebrew Manuscripts in the Ambrosiana Library. [Milan], 1972. Ltd Ed. 4to, cloth, in d/j. With 12 colored plates. sg Sept 25 (44) $150

Lyall, Robert, d.1831
— The Character of the Russians, and a Detailed History of Moscow. L, 1823. 4to, half calf; broken, lacking backstrip. With folding plan (torn at fold) & 23 plates, some colored. Title & plates stamped. bba Mar 12 (30) £40 [Hetherington]

Anr copy. Calf; rebacked. With folding plan & 23 plates, 13 hand-colored. Tear to plan; a few plate imprints shaved. S Oct 23 (262) £320 [Walford]

Lycett, Joseph
— Views in Australia, or New South Wales.... L, 1824. Oblong 4to, half lea; spine def. With litho title & 48 hand-colored plates. Lacking maps & 2 prelims; 2 text leaves def; paint scribblings on 2 plates; 3 other plates with very small crayon marks; Plate 48 crumpled & corner def; tp stained. bba Apr 23 (332) £7,500 [Jones]

Anr copy. Modern mor gilt. With pictorial title & 24 hand-colored plates & 2 maps. Tears in 1 folding map repaired; same map slightly def in lower right-hand corner. C Oct 15 (184) £22,000 [Hewlett Gallery]

Lydekker, Richard, 1849-1915
— Animal Portraiture. L, [1912]. 1st Ed. Folio, loose in orig folder. pn Apr 30 (51) £130 [Greyfriars]

Anr copy. Orig cloth. With 50 colored plates. S Oct 23 21306 £120 [Holland & Holland]

— The Deer of all Lands: a History of the Family Cervidae, Living and Extinct. L, 1898. 1st Ed, One of 500. Illus by J. Smit. 4to, orig cloth. With 24 colored plates. L July 2 (166) £900; sg Dec 4 (116) $1,400

— The Game Animals of Africa. L, 1908. 4to, orig cloth. T May 21 (235) £115

Anr Ed. L, 1926. 33A Feb 11 (303) R320

— The Royal Natural History. L, 1893-96. 6 vols. 8vo, half mor. Some foxing. O June 9 (104) $130

— Wild Oxen, Sheep & Goats of all Lands. L, 1898. 1st Ed, One of 500. Illus by J. Smit. 4to, orig cloth. sg Dec 4 (117) $1,300

Lye, Edward, 1694-1767
— Dictionarium Saxonico et Gothico-Latinum.... L, 1772. 1st Ed. 2 vols. Folio, contemp calf; rebacked, 1 cover detached. sg Oct 9 (177) $120

Lyell, Sir Charles, 1797-1875
— The Geological Evidences of the Antiquity of Man. L, 1863. 1st Ed. 8vo, orig cloth; spine partly restored, but joints cracked. With 2 plates. sg Jan 15 (330) $90

— Principles of Geology. L, 1835. 4 vols. 8vo, orig bds. S July 28 (1092) £190

Lyell, Denis D.
— The Hunting & Spoor of Central African Game. L, 1929. Index leaves lacking or torn away. ch May 21 (181) $85

Lyell, James P. R.
— Early Book Illustration in Spain. L, 1926. One of 500. 4to, orig cloth. bba Feb 5 (55) £120 [Check Books]

Anr copy. Orig cloth; spine damaged. Perforated stamp on title. bba Feb 5 (56) £60 [Hodgson]

Anr copy. Orig cloth; rubbed & soiled. Inscr & with Ls pasted to front free endpaper. bba Apr 9 (458) £100 [Brook]; sg May 14 (645) $250

Anr copy. Orig cloth; backstrip darkened. sg May 14 (646) $200

Lyman, George D. See: Grabhorn Printing

Lyman, Phineas
— General Orders [at Ft. Edward in 1757]. NY, 1899. One of 250. 12mo, half cloth. Some leaves roughly opened. Webb Series, Vol I. ha Dec 19 (127) $60

Lymington, Gerard Vernon Wallop, Viscount
— Git le Coeur. Paris: Editions Narcisse, 1928. One of 200. 4to, ptd wraps; spine cracked. sg Dec 11 (8) $70

Lynch, Bohun
— The Prize Ring. L, 1925. One of 1,000. 4to, orig half vellum; rubbed. S Nov 10 (600) £120 [Townsend]

Anr copy. Half lea; joints & spine ends worn. sg May 21 (29) $100

Lynch, John Roy, 1847-1939
— The Facts of Reconstruction. NY, 1913. Inscr. cb Oct 9 (281) $75

Lynch, William F., 1801-65
— Official Report of the United States' Expedition to Explore the Dead Sea and the River Jordan. Balt.: John Murphy, 1852. 4to, contemp half lea; worn & soiled. With 16 plates, 1 diagram & 1 large folding map. Library markings. wa Sept 25 (585) $80

Lynd, John. See: Lind, John

Lyon, Charles Jobson
— History of St. Andrews.... Edin., 1843. 2 vols. 8vo, calf. O Feb 24 (128) $100

Lyon, George Francis, 1795-1832
— Journal of a Residence and Tour in...Mexico. L, 1828. 2 vols in 1. 8vo, modern half cloth; worn. O Oct 21 (108) $90

— A Narrative of Travels in Northern Africa. L, 1821. 4to, modern half calf. With folding map & 17 colored plates. One plate shaved. C Apr 8 (37) £320 [Brockhaus]

Anr copy. Half calf. Fold tear in map. S Oct 23 (463) £440 [McKenzie]

Lyons, Jacques J. —& De Sola, Abraham
— A Jewish Calendar for Fifty Years. Montreal, 1854. 12mo, orig cloth; frayed, hinge starting. Stained; soiled; pencil marginalia. sg Sept 25 (54) $550

Lysons, Daniel, 1762-1834
— The Environs of London. L, 1792-1811. 5 vols, including the Account of Middlesex. 4to, contemp calf; joints rubbed. Ck Feb 27 (51) £90

Anr Ed. L, 1792-1800. 5 vols. 4to, contemp lea; lacking one cover. Extra-illustrated. Sold w.a.f. pn Jan 22 (164) £160 [Talbot]

Lysons, Daniel & Samuel
— Magna Britannia, being a Concise Topographical Account.... L, 1814. Vol III: Cornwall. 4to, contemp half mor; rubbed, partially split on hinges. Lacking half-title. T Mar 19 (65) £70

Anr Ed. L, 1817. Vol V: Derbyshire. 4to,

LYSONS

early 20th-cent mor gilt by Riviere; discolored. S Jan 12 (83) £60 [Marsden]

Lysons, Samuel, 1763-1879
— A Collection of Gloucestershire Antiquities. L, 1804. Folio, recent half calf gilt. With 110 plates. T Jan 22 (46) £70

Lyttelton, George Lyttelton, 1st Baron
— Dialogues of the Dead. L, 1760. 1st Ed. 8vo, contemp calf. Corner off C4. sg Mar 26 (190) $70

Lyttelton, Robert Henry
— Out-Door Games: Cricket & Golf. L, 1901. One of 150 on handmade paper. Vellum. With 9 color plates. sg Oct 30 (139) $275

Lyttleton, Thomas, 2d Baron, 1744-79
— Poems by a Young Nobleman of Distinguished Abilities.... L: G. Kearsley, 1780. Folio, later half mor; rubbed, spine ends chipped, joints cracking. Some foxing. cb Feb 19 (167) $80

Lytton, Edward George Earle Bulwer, 1st Baron Lytton, 1803-73
See also: Fore-Edge Paintings
— St. Stephen's. A Poem. L, 1860. 8vo, orig cloth; rubbed. bba Dec 4 (105) £60 [Hannas]

M

M., G. See: Markham, Gervase

M., W.
— The Queens Closet Opened. L: Nathaniel Brooks, 1658. Bound with: The Compleat Cook, Expertly Prescribing.... L: E. B. For Nathaniel Brooks, 1658. 12mo, modern calf by M. Ziegler. Hunt copy. CNY Nov 21 (74) $950

Anr Ed. L: J. G. for Nath. Brook, 1663. Bound with: The Compleat Cook, Expertly Prescribing.... L, 1663. 12mo, contemp calf; rebacked, later endpapers. Tear in lower margin of E5 not affecting text; tear in D10 of 1st work causing some loss; some stains & soiling. Crahan copy. P Nov 25 (304) $1,200

Maaskamp, Evert
— Afbeeldingen van de kleeding.... Amst., [1823]. 4to, modern mor gilt. With handcolored allegorical frontis & 24 handcolored plates. Frontis possibly from anr copy. S June 25 (193) £500 [Jonge]

Maberly, Joseph
— The Print Collector. NY, 1880. 4to, orig cloth. With 8 plates. wa Sept 25 (269) $110

Anr copy. Cloth; worn. O Feb 24 (129) $60

Mabille, Pierre
— Le Miroir des Merveilleux. Paris, 1962. One of 118. Orig wraps, unopened. S June 29 (73) £1,800 [Rota]

Mabillon, Jean, 1632-1707
— De re diplomatica libri VI.... Paris, 1709-4. 2 parts in 1 vol, including Supplement. Folio, later 18th-cent russia gilt, armorial bdg; joints starting. With title & 69 plates. sg Oct 9 (263) $450
— Praefationes in acta sanctorum ordinis Sancti Benedicti conjunctim editae. Venice, 1740. Folio, contemp vellum. Damp-wrinkled. sg Oct 9 (264) $90

Mac Orlan, Pierre, 1882-1970
— Paris. Paris: Plon, [1934]. Illus by Andre Kertesz. 4to, pictorial wraps; worn, spine & hinges repaired with cellotape. sg Nov 13 (71) $100
— Vlaminck. Monte Carlo & NY, 1958. Trans by J. B. Sidgwick. Folio, wraps. With 5 orig lithos. cba Mar 5 (200) $80

McAdam, John Loudon, 1756-1836
— Remarks on the Present System of Road Making. L, 1820. 8vo, orig bds; marked & rubbed. bba Oct 30 (402) £50 [Axe]

Macaulay, Thomas Babington, 1st Baron Macaulay, 1800-59
— The History of England. L, 1913-15. 6 vols. cloth, in d/j. pnE Jan 28 (147) £50 [McKenzie]

McBey, James. See: Salaman, Malcolm Charles

Macbride, David, 1726-78
— A Methodical Introduction to the Theory and Practice of Physic. L, 1772. 4to, contemp calf; rebacked. bba May 14 (401) £90 [National Library of Ireland]

Anr copy. Calf; rebacked. pnE Dec 17 (127) £180 [Thin]

McCaffrey, Anne
— The Coelura. Columbia PA: Underwood-Miller, 1983. One of 7 bound galleys. Wraps. With presentation letter from pbr, Tim Underwood, sgd as Yoganathan. cb Sept 28 (873) $180
— Dragonflight. NY: Walker, [1968]. In d/j. Sgd on tp. cb Sept 28 (879) $150
— The Smallest Dragonboy. Kilquade: Drogonhold Ltd, [1976]. One of 200. Wraps. cb Sept 28 (888) $65
— A Time When. Cambr. MA: Nefsa Press, 1975. One of 20 bound in half mor by Harcourt Bindery. In d/j with slight soil. cb Sept 28 (889) $325

One of 800. In d/j. cb Sept 28 (890) $65
— To Ride Pegasus. L: Dent, [1974]. In d/j.

Sgd on tp. cb Sept 28 (891) $65
— The White Dragon. NY: Ballantine, 1978. In d/j. Sgd on tp. cb Sept 28 (893) $50

McCall, Ansel J.
— Pick and Pan. Trip to the Digging's in 1849.... Bath NY, 1883. 8vo, ptd wraps; rear wrap lacking, front backed with tissue. sg Dec 4 (128) $325

McCauley, Kirby
— Dark Forces: New Stories of Suspense and Supernatural Horror. NY: Viking, [1980]. In d/j. Contains Stephen King's The Mist. cb Sept 28 (747) $55

McCauley, Lois B.
— Maryland Historical Prints, 1752-1889. Balt.: Maryland Historical Society, [1975]. 4to, cloth, in rubbed d/j with price torn off. ha Sept 19 (167) $100

McCausland, Elizabeth. See: Abbott & McCausland

Macchiavelli, Niccolo. See: Machiavelli, Niccolo

McChyne, Robert Murray, 1813-43. See: Bonar & McChyne

McClellan, George Brinton, 1865-1940
— Report on the Organization and Campaigns of the Army of the Potomac.... NY, 1864. 8vo, orig cloth; rubbed. sg Sept 18 (163) $50

McClellan, Henry Brainerd
— The Life and Campaigns of Major-General J. E. B. Stuart. Bost., 1885. 8vo, later cloth. With port & 7 folding maps. wa Feb 19 (57) $140

MacClure, Sir Robert John LeMesurier, 1807-73
— The North-West Passage. Capt. M'Clure's Despatches.... L, 1853. 8vo, disbound. With folding map. Marginal dampstaining to tp & 1st few leaves. bba Sept 25 (422) £110 [Gilbert]

MacColl, Donald Sutherland. See: Harrison & MacColl

McCoy, James Comly, 1862-1934
— Jesuit Relations of Canada, 1632-1673, a Bibliography.... Paris, 1937. One of 325. sg May 14 (19) $90

McCracken, Harold
— The American Cowboy. NY, 1973. One of 300. 4to, lea. Sgd. cb Jan 8 (284) $85
— The Charles M. Russell Book. Garden City, 1957. One of 250, sgd. Folio, mor with lea cattle skull inlay. sg Feb 5 (219) $250
   Anr copy. Mor with lea cattle skull inlay on front cover. sg June 4 (293) $275

— Frederic Remington's Own West. NY, 1960. One of 167. 4to, lea. With 2 colored plates Pp 143-44 with large marginal chip. Sgd. cb Jan 8 (289) $150
— The Frederic Remington Book. Garden City, 1966. 1st Ed, One of 500. Folio, calf. With 33 colored plates, 1 tipped in. Sgd. cb Jan 8 (286) $150
   One of 1,000. Calf. Sgd. cb Jan 8 (287) $120

McCrae, Thomas. See: Osler & McCrae

McCrary, George Washington, 1835-90
— El Paso Troubles in Texas. Letter from the Secretary of War.... Wash., 1878. 8vo, disbound. Short tears at lower edge. 5th Congress, 2d Session, H of R Exec Doc 93. wa Sept 25 (475) $130

McCullers, Carson
— The Heart is a Lonely Hunter. Bost., 1940. 1st Ed. In frayed d/j. wa Dec 11 (76) $160

Macculloch, John, 1773-1835
— The Highlands and Western Isles of Scotland. L, 1824. 4 vols. 8vo, calf gilt. pnE Jan 28 (148) £180 [Thin]

McCulloch, John Ramsey, 1789-1864
— A Dictionary...of Commerce and Commercial Navigation.... L, 1854. 8vo, orig cloth; soiled. T Sept 18 (355) £80
— The Principles of Political Economy. Edin., 1825. 1st Ed. 8vo, later half mor; inner hinges strengthened. Some staining & spotting. P Sept 24 (327) $500
   2d Ed. L, 1830. 8vo, 19th-cent half calf; spine chipped at head. P Sept 24 (328) $300

MacDiarmid, Hugh
— Direadh I, II and III. Frenich: Kulgin Duval & Colin H. Hamilton, 1974. One of 200. 4to, half lea gilt. sg Mar 5 (141) $110

MacDonald, George, 1824-1905
— At the Back of the North Wind. NY, 1871. 1st Ed, 1st Issue. 8vo, half mor, covers & spine of orig cloth bdg bound in. With author's signature loosely inserted. S Dec 5 (331) £600 [J. Schiller]
   2d Issue. Orig cloth; rebacked, orig spine preserved. S Dec 5 (330) £350 [Subun-So]

MacDonald, Hugh, Bibliographer —& Hargreaves, Mary
— Thomas Hobbes: a Bibliography. L, 1952. 4to, half cloth. sg May 14 (222) $50

MacDonald, Ross, Pseud.
— The Drowning Pool. NY, 1950. In rubbed d/j. cb Nov 20 (243) $225
— The Moving Target. NY, 1949. In chipped & repaired d/j. cb May 7 (286) $65

MACDONALD

— The Way Some People Die. NY, 1951. In d/j. cb Nov 20 (250) $110

M'Dougall, Capt George Frederick

— The Eventful Voyage of H. M. Discovery Ship "Resolute".... L, 1857. 8vo, half calf; broken. With 8 colored plates & folding map. wd Nov 12 (137) $50

Macfall, Haldane, 1860-1928

— The Book of Lovat Claud Fraser. L, 1922. "Apparently comprising a publisher's mock-up in preparation for the first editon of 1923". 4to, bds, in d/j. O Mar 24 (111) $110

Anr Ed. L, 1923. One of 150. 4to, bds, in d/j (piece clupped from d/j spine). With 23 mtd plates. O Mar 24 (110) $90

— A History of Painting. Bost., [1916?]. One of 124. 8 vols. half mor; spines faded, corners & edges rubbed. With 200 tipped-in color plates. cb Oct 23 (146) $170

— The Splendid Wayfaring. L, 1913. 4to, orig cloth. ALs inserted. S Oct 6 (831) £50 [Thorp]

MacFarlane, Charles, 1799-1858

— Constantinople in 1828. L, 1829. 1st Ed. 4to, modern half mor. With 4 plates; frontis & title margins trimmed & laid down. pn Jan 22 (91) £50 [Harrison]

McGarrahan, William

— Proceedings of the Committee on Public Lands.... Wash., 1878. Half lea. 45th Congress, 2d Session, Sen. Misc. Doc. 85. cb Jan 8 (113) $110

MacGibbon, David —& Ross, Thomas

— The Castellated and Domestic Architecture of Scotland. Edin., 1887-92. 5 vols. 8vo, cloth. pnE May 20 (13) £250

— The Ecclesiastical Architecture of Scotland. L, 1896-97. 3 vols. 8vo, cloth; worn. O Feb 24 (130) $120

Anr copy. Orig cloth. S Nov 17 (801) £75 [Scott]

Macgillivray, William, 1796-1852

— A History of British Birds Indigenous and Migratory. L, 1837-52. 5 vols. 8vo, half mor; joints & corners rubbed. With 29 plates. Haverschmidt copy. B Feb 24 (401) HF420

— The Natural History of Dee Side and Braemar. L, 1855. 8vo, half mor gilt. With folding frontis map. pnE Nov 12 (191) £90

McGrath, Daniel F.

— Bookman's Price Index. Detroit, [1964-73]. Vols I-VIII. Orig cloth; worn. O June 16 (126) $110

McGraw, Eloise Jarvis —& Wagner, Lauren McGraw

— Merry Go Round in Oz. Chicago: Reilly & Lee, [1963]. 1st Ed. Illus by Dick Martin. In lst bdg, in d/j. cb Sept 28 (111) $180

M'Gregor, John, 1796-1857

— Commercial Statistics.... L, 1844-48. 4 vols. 8vo, orig cloth; rebacked, orig spines laid down, Vol III loose in bdg. Library stamps; bottom edges dust-soiled. P Sept 24 (329) $200

M'Gregor, John, 1797-1857

— British America. L, 1833. 2d Ed. 2 vols. 8vo, half calf gilt; rubbed. With 13 maps & 2 folding plans. 1 map repaired, anr with small tear. pn July 23 (23) £110 [Faupel]

McGuire, J. A.

— In the Alaska-Yukon Gamelands. Cincinnati: Kidd, [1921]. Inscr. wa Sept 25 (134) $50

Machen, Arthur Llewelyn Jones, 1863-1947

— The Anatomy of Tobacco, or Smoking Methodised.... [L], 1884. 1st Ed. 8vo, orig vellum. sg Mar 5 (145) $80

— Works. L, 1923. One of 1,000. 9 vols. In d/js. sg Feb 12 (214) $120

Machiavelli, Niccolo, 1469-1527

— L'Asino d'oro con alcuni altri capitoli & novelle del medesimo. Florence: Bernardo Giunta, 24 Nov 1549. 8vo, 19th-cent mor gilt with crowned D at head of spine. Lacking final leaf; top of tp repaired; some dampstains in upper portion of 1st few leaves. S Nov 27 (194) £700 [Ghengi]

— Discourses, upon the First Decade of T. Livius. L, 1636. 1st Ed in English. 12mo, old vellum. B1 cancelled & not replaced. S July 14 (332) £260

— The Florentine Historie. L, 1595. 1st Ed in English. Folio, early vellum bds. Lacking V4; some soiling; dampstained towards end. S May 29 (1218) £310

Anr copy. Trans by Thomas Bedingfeld. Contemp calf; spine ends chipped, covers detached. Tp supplied from anr copy; lacking last leaf. sg Mar 26 (191) $300

— Opere. [Geneva], 1550 [but 1609-19]. 1st "Testina" Ed. 5 parts in 1 vol. 4to, old vellum. With Ms genealogical table tipped in. sg Oct 9 (265) $175

— Il Principe. Venice: Aldus, 1540. 8vo, later calf; joints reinforced, spine ends chipped. sg Oct 9 (83) $375

— Il Principe [& other works]. Florence: B.

Giunta, 8 May 1532. 4to, modern vellum.
A few leaves stained. S Nov 27 (193)
£3,600 [Pickering & Chatto]

— Works. L, 1695. Folio, contemp calf;
worn, joints split. Some waterstaining.
bba Oct 30 (209) £35 [Clark]

McIan, Robert Ronald, d.1856. See: Logan &
McIan

McIlvaine, Charles

— Toadstools, Mushrooms, Fungi, Edible and
Poisonous.... Indianapolis, [1900]. Author's Ed, One of 750. 4to, cloth; worn,
inner joints repaired. O Mar 24 (112) $80

M'Ilvaine, William, Jr. See: Grabhorn Printing

McIntosh, Charles, 1794-1864

— The Greenhouse. L, 1838. 8vo, orig cloth.
With 17 hand-colored plates. pnE Dec 17
(220) £95 [Graham]

— The Orchard: Including the Management
of...Fruit Trees.... L, 1839. 8vo, half calf;
worn. With colored title & 17 hand-colored
plates. S May 28 (731) £100

— The Practical Gardener, and Modern Horticulturist.... L, 1828-29. 2 vols. 8vo,
contemp mor gilt; rubbed, hinges cracked,
top of spine of Vol I chipped. With frontis,
16 hand-colored plates & 15 uncolored
plans. Some spotting; several of the
uncolored plates with captions shaved.
Hunt copy. CNY Nov 21 (187) $200

Anr copy. Contemp calf. With 15 handcolored plates. pnE Dec 17 (221) £120
[Thin]

Anr Ed. L, 1832. 2 vols. 8vo, contemp half
calf; rebacked in calf. With engraved title,
frontis, 15 plain & 16 handcolored plates.
Some spotting & browning at ends. Hunt
copy. CNY Nov 21 (188) $170

Anr Ed. L, 1849. 2 vols. 8vo, contemp half
calf gilt; rubbed. With frontis & 31
uncolored plates. Frontis & engraved title
with dampstain; plates spotted; some plates
with captions shaved. Hunt copy. CNY
Nov 21 (189) $50

Macintyre, Donald, 1831-1903

— Hindu-Koh; Wanderings and Wild Sport on
and beyond the Himalayas. Edin. & L,
1889. 8vo, cloth; recased, with new
endpaeprs & flyleaves. Tp stamped on
verso. cb May 21 (103) $110

McIntyre, Vonda N.

— Dreamsnake. Bost., 1978. Uncorrected
proof. Wraps. cb Sept 28 (903) $90

Mackail, John William, 1859-1945
See also: Doves Press; Kelmscott Press
— The Life of William Morris. L, 1899. 2
vols. 8vo, orig cloth. bba Feb 5 (200) £60
[Burmester]

Mackay, Alexander, 1849-90
— The Western World.... L, 1849. 2d Ed. 3
vols. 12mo, orig cloth. With 2 folding
maps. cb Mar 19 (183) $140

Mackay, George Henry
— Shooting Journal. Cambr.: Pvtly ptd, 1929.
One of 300. Cloth; unopened. Inscr. sg
Oct 23 (393) $110

McKay, George Leslie
— A Stevenson Library. Catalogue of a Collection...Formed by Edwin J. Beinecke.
New Haven, 1951-64. One of 500. 6 vols.
sg Jan 22 (288) $275

McKelvey, Susan Delano
— The Lilac. NY, 1928. 1st Ed. 4to, cloth;
worn. O Oct 21 (110) $130

Anr copy. With 4 color charts inside rear
cover pocket. O Jan 6 (120) $90; O Mar 24
(113) $90

**McKenney, Thomas L., 1785-1859 —&
Hall, James, 1793-1868**
— History of the Indian Tribes of North
America. Phila: F. W. Greenough [Vol I] &
D. Rice & J. G. Clark, 1838-44. State not
given. 3 vols. Folio, contemp half mor gilt;
worn. With map & 120 hand-finished
plates; text foxed. CNY Dec 19 (128)
$17,000

1st 8vo Ed. Phila., 1848-49-50. 3 vols. 8vo,
contemp half mor; rubbed. With colored
litho dedication & 120 colored plates. S
Oct 23 (423) £2,000 [Phelps]

Anr copy. Mor gilt; extremities worn, 1
cover loose. Some foxing. sg Apr 2 (136)
$2,800

Anr Ed. Phila., 1855. 3 vols. 8vo, contemp
mor. With 121 hand-colored plates. Plate
of Caatousee loose with tear & chip in
blank margin; Ongpatunga & Waatopenot
with short tears in blank margins. P May
13 (15) $2,900

Anr Ed. Phila.: D. Rice, [c.1870]. 3 vols.
8vo & folio, contemp half russia gilt;
rubbed, upper cover of Vol I of text
detached. With 121 hand-finished colored
plates, including a 4to version of the Billy
Bowlegs port serving as a frontis to Vol II
of text. Without the litho map, table & pp
of facsimile signatures of subscribers; Red
Jacket with small dampstain in extreme
lower margin; Opothle Yoholo with pale
dampstaining in lower right corner; 16
other plates with minor spotting or foxing,
mostly to blank margins; titles of text vols

with library stamps. CNY Nov 21 (192) $18,000

Anr Ed. Edin., 1933-34. ("The Indian Tribes of North America.") 3 vols. 4to, orig cloth. Ck Nov 21 (206) £160

Anr copy. Cloth. sg Mar 12 (173) $250

MacKenzie, Sir Alexander, 1764-1820

— Voyages from Montreal on the River St. Laurence.... L, 1801. 1st Ed. 4to, contemp half calf; joints splitting, head of spine worn. With port & 3 folding maps with 1 colored route. Spotting to tp, dedication leaf & port margins; lacking half-title; 1 map with tear repaired at margin. C Oct 15 (66) £900 [Thorp]

Anr copy. Contemp half calf; spine worn. With port & 3 folding maps (1 colored in outline but with tear). S Oct 23 (421) £800 [Traylen]

Anr copy. Modern half mor; worn. With port & 3 folding maps. Each map with inked & perforated library stamps; 1 map entirely torn along fold but complete. sg Mar 12 (174) $375

Anr copy. Contemp half calf; head of spine chipped. sg Apr 2 (137) $1,100

Mackenzie, Alfred Robert Davidson

— Mutiny Memoirs: Being Personal Reminiscences of the Great Sepoy Revolt of 1857. Allahabad, 1891. Contemp half mor; scuffed. Rubberstamp at top of title. Sgd. cb Dec 18 (107) $55

Mackenzie, Arthur Ford, 1861-1905

— Chess: Its Poetry and Its Prose. Kingston, Jamaica, 1887. Orig cloth; new endpapers. pn Mar 26 (308) £110 [De Lucia]

Mackenzie, Compton. See: Mackenzie, Sir Edward Montague Compton

Mackenzie, Sir Edward Montague Compton

— Poems. Oxford, 1907. Wraps; chipped. Inscr. wa Sept 25 (680) $500

Mackenzie, Eneas, 1778-1832

— An...View of the County fo Northumberland. Newcastle, 1825. 2d Ed. 3 vols. 4to, contemp half calf; rubbed. T Oct 16 (347) £56

Mackenzie, Eneas, 1778-1832 —& Ross, M.

— An Historical, Topographical, and Descriptive View of the County of Durham. Newcastle, 1834. 2 vols. 4to, mor gilt. L.P. copy. Extra-illus copy. pnE Jan 28 (245) £340 [Steedman]

Mackenzie, Sir George, 1636-91

— Memoirs of the Affairs of Scotland from the Restoration of King Charles II. Edin., 1821. 4to, contemp half mor; rubbed. O Feb 24 (131) $50

Mackenzie, Sir George Steuart, 1780-1848

— Travels in the Islands of Iceland. Edin, 1811. 4to, contemp calf gilt; rebacked, orig spine laid down. With 2 maps, 4 folding tables & 14 plates. Lacking map of the South West Coast of Iceland; half-title & tp stained; other minor staining; 1st leaf of index re-margined. C Oct 15 (67) £120 [Heynes]

Anr copy. 19th-cent half calf; rubbed, joints worn. With 2 maps, 4 folding tables & 15 plates. O May 12 (130) £350

Anr copy. Contemp half calf; spine rubbed. With 3 maps & 13 plates, 8 being mtd hand-colored plates. S Nov 17 (913) £200 [Porter]

2d Ed. Edin., 1812. 4to, new cloth. With 16 plates & maps. bba Dec 18 (186) £90 [Gustaisson]

Anr copy. Calf gilt; rebacked. Library markings. T Mar 19 (2) £180

Mackenzie, James C. See: Derrydale Press

MacKenzie, John, 1835-99

— Austral Africa, Losing It or Ruling It. L, 1887. 2 vols. 8vo, orig cloth. SSA Oct 28 (715) R240

Mackenzie, Keith Stewart

— Narrative of the Second Campaign in China. L, 1842. 12mo, 19th-cent half mor. With folding map (partially hand-tinted). cb Dec 18 (108) $50

McKillip, Patricia A.

— Heir of Sea & Fire. NY, 1977. In d/j. cb Sept 28 (910) $55

McKim, Mead & White

— A Monograph of the Work of.... NY, [1915-18]. 4 vols. Folio, loose in half cloth folder; badly worn. sg June 4 (206) $50

McKinlay, John, 1819-72

— Journal of Exploration in the Interior of Australia. (Burke Relief Expedition). Melbourne, [c.1862]. 8vo, modern half calf. kh Mar 16 (322) A$700

McKinley, William, 1843-1901

— Speeches and Addresses from March 1, 1897, to May 30, 1900. NY, 1900. 8vo, half mor; worn. Inscr. A. Edward Newton's copy. O June 9 (113) $160

Mackinnon, Daniel, Colonel
— Origin and Services of the Coldstream Guards. L, 1833. 2 vols. 8vo, contemp calf gilt. bba Oct 30 (112) £70 [Hayneer]

Mackintosh, James, 1765-1832
— Vindiciae Gallicae: Defence of the French Revolution. Phila., 1792. Bound with: The French Constitution. Phila., 1791. 8vo, orig bds; loose. Foxed. sg Oct 9 (212) $140

Mackworth, Sir Humphrey, 1657-1727
— Sir H. Mackworth's Proposal in Miniature.... L, 1720. 8vo, wraps. Some cropping. S June 25 (398) £350

Macky, John, d.1726
— Memoirs of the Secret Services of.... L, 1733. 1st Ed. 8vo, modern wraps. Lacking final blank. bba Mar 26 (60) £80 [Stewart]

MacLaurin, Colin, 1698-1746
— An Account of Sir Isaac Newton's Philosophical Discoveries. L, 1748. 1st Ed. 4to, contemp calf; worn, joints weak. With 6 plates. Some browning. bba Jan 15 (382) £120 [Frew Mackenzie]

Anr copy. Half calf. With 6 folding plates. Title & all leaves strengthened on outer margins. pn Jan 22 (216) £55 [Gladstone]

Anr copy. Contemp calf; worn. With 6 plates. pn Mar 5 (32) £140 [Demetzy]

Anr copy. Contemp sheep; worn, covers detached, opening leaves loose. sg Mar 26 (192) $100

Maclehose, James
— The Picture of Sydney.... Sydney, [1839]. ("Maclehose's Picture of Sydney; and Stranger's Guide in New South Wales, for 1839.") 8vo, orig cloth. With folding map & 42 plates. Map creased at fold & slightly frayed at head margin. C Oct 15 (161) £1,150 [Maggs]

MacLeod, Donald
— Memoirs of the Life and Gallant Exploits of.... L, 1791. 8vo, later half mor. Minor soiling on half-title & last leaf. AVP Nov 20 (401) £260 [Mappin]

M'Leod, John, 1777?-1820
— Voyage of his Majesty's Ship Alceste.... L, 1817. ("Narrative of a Voyage in His Majesty's late ship Alceste to the Yellow Sea.") 1st Ed. 8vo, contemp sheep; rebacked, worn, rear cover detached. With port & 4 colored plates. sg Nov 20 (129) $70

2d Ed. L, 1818. 8vo, modern bds; worn. Some stains; frontis chipped in gutter margin. O Oct 21 (111) $60

Anr copy. Disbound. With port & 5 hand-colored plates. sg Apr 23 (92) $130

Anr Ed. L, 1820. 8vo, disbound. With frontis, 5 hand-colored aquatint plates, 4 folding litho plates, 1 folding litho map & 1 folding engraved map. sg Apr 23 (93) $275

MacLeod, Norman, 1812-72
— In Memoriam...Darmstadt, December 14, 1864. L: Bradbury & Evans, [1864]. 4to, orig wraps; soiled. Memorial sermon dated on the 3d anniversary of the death of Prince Albert. Inscr to Charles Kingsley by Queen Victoria, 1865. CNY Dec 19 (129) $200

Maclise, Joseph
— Surgical Anatomy. L, 1851. 1st Ed. Folio, contemp calf; rubbed. S Nov 27 (270) £450 [Phelps]

MacMahon, Charles Laure, Marquis de
— La Saint-Hubert, ou quinze jours d'automne dans un vieux chateau de Bourgogne. Paris, 1827. 18mo, contemp mor gilt. Jeanson copy. SM Mar 1 (383) FF6,000

Anr Ed. Paris, 1842. Bound with: Lancosme-Breves, Comte Savary de. La Verite a cheval. Paris 1843. 8vo, contemp half shagreen. Jeanson copy. SM Mar 1 (384) FF2,800

McMullan, Joseph V.
— Islamic Carpets. NY, 1965. 4to, orig cloth, in chipped d/j. sg Feb 5 (242) $275

McMurtrie, Douglas Crawford
— Early Printing in Wisconsin.... Seattle, 1931. One of 300. Folio, orig cloth. bba Oct 16 (433) £45 [Mills]

Anr copy. Cloth. sg Mar 12 (175) $90

— The First Printers of Chicago.... Chicago, 1927. One of 650. Cloth-backed bds. O June 16 (127) $60

— The Golden Book. Chicago, 1927. One of 220, sgd. 4to, orig cloth. bba Oct 16 (432) £50 [Hay Cinema]

A History of Printing in the United States. NY, 1936. Vol II (all pbd). bba Oct 16 (491) £55 [Mills]

Anr copy. Corners bumped. cba Feb 5 (120) $75

McNabb, Vincent Joseph
— Geoffrey Chaucer: A Study in Genius & Ethics. Ditchling: Pepler & Sewell, 1934. One of 300. Half cloth. cb Sept 11 (98) $65

McNail, Stanley
— Something breathing. Sauk City: Arkham House, 1965. (Ptd & pbd in England by Villiers Corp. for Arkham House). cb Sept 28 (912) $60

Macomb, John N.
— Report of the Exploring Expedition from Santa Fe.... Wash., 1876. 4to, orig half sheep; hinges cracked. With 11 plain & 11 colored plates & folding map; map torn twice & with brief separation at fold. ha Sept 19 (164) $375

MacPherson, H. A.
— A History of Fowling. Edin., 1897. 4to, orig cloth; stained. Haverschmidt copy. B Feb 24 (230) HF260

Macpherson, James, 1736-96
See also: Fore-Edge Paintings
— The Poems of Ossian. L, 1807. 3 vols. 4to, contemp calf; rubbed. sg Feb 12 (215) $140

Macquoid, Percy
— A History of English Furniture. L, 1904-8. 4 vols. Folio, cloth; worn. pn Oct 23 (330) £130 [Elliott]
Anr copy. Cloth; worn & soiled, 1 spine broken. pn Jan 22 (140) £110 [Bailey]
Anr copy. Cloth; worn. S May 6 (390) £140 [Stodart]
Anr copy. Orig cloth. Tears & repairs. Sold w.a.f. S May 6 (391) £100 [Smith]
Anr Ed. L, 1938. 4 vols. Folio, orig cloth. Ck Oct 31 (24) £140

Macquoid, Percy —& Edwards, Ralph
— The Dictionary of English Furniture. L, 1924-27. 3 vols. Folio, orig cloth. cb July 30 (129) $375
Anr copy. Modern cloth. Some crudely-repaired tears. Sold w.a.f. Ck Oct 17 (45) £100
Anr copy. Orig cloth. Occasional spotting. Ck Oct 31 (23) £260; pn Jan 22 (68) £190 [Tracchi]
Anr copy. Disbound. pn May 21 (213) £70 [Clarke]
Anr copy. Orig cloth; soiled. S Nov 10 (126) £100 [Russell]; S May 6 (392) £200 [Goldstein]
Anr copy. Orig cloth; scuffed. S May 28 (886) £160
2d Ed. L, 1954. 3 vols. Folio, orig cloth. Ck Jan 30 (95) £350
Anr copy. Cloth, in worn d/js. kh Mar 16 (333) A$1,700
Anr copy. Cloth, in d/js. pn Apr 30 (356) £300
Anr copy. Orig cloth, in d/j. pn July 23 (94) £400 [Phillips]
Anr copy. Orig cloth, torn d/js. pnE Jan 28 (304) £350 [McKenzie]

Macrobius, Ambrosius Theodosius
— In Somnium Scipionis.... Venice: Joannes Tacuinus de Tridino, 18 July 1521. ("Interpretatio in somnium Scipionis....") Folio, bds; rebacked & worn. Some stains. S Feb 23 (1097) £380 [King]

McWilliam, Robert
— An Essay on...Dry Rot. L, 1818. 4to, calf gilt. pnE Jan 28 (162) £150 [Bradley]

Macy, Obed. See: Melville's copy, Herman

Madden, Sir Frederic, 1801-73
— Illuminated Ornaments Selected from Manuscripts and Early Printed Books.... L: Pickering, 1833. 4to, contemp half mor; worn, loose. With engraved title & 59 plates, hand-finished & illuminated in gold & colors, by Henry Shaw. Foxed. cba Mar 5 (120) $225
Anr copy. Cloth. Library stamps on titles & on plate versos. sg Feb 5 (166) $200

Maddock, James
— The Florist's Directory; or a Treatise on the Culture of Flowers. L, 1792. 8vo, calf gilt; recased preserving orig spine. With 6 plates. T Feb 19 (442) £50

Maddow, Ben
— Faces. A Narrative History of the Portrait in Photography. Bost., [1977]. 4to, cloth, in d/j. O Oct 21 (112) $60

Madeira, Percy
— Hunting in British East Africa. Phila. & L, 1909. Hinges cracked at endpapers, map pocket torn. cb Nov 6 (197) $95
Anr copy. Orig cloth. cb May 21 (184) $200

Madol, Roger. See: Sitwell & Madol

Madou, Jean Baptiste
— Vie de Napoleon, redigee pare une societe de gens de lettres.... Brussels, 1827. 2 vols. Oblong folio, contemp half calf; worn. With 2 ports (1 partly detached) & 142 plates. S June 25 (33) £350

Madox, Thomas, 1666-1727
— Formulare Anglicanum, or, a Collection of Ancient Charters. L, 1702. 1st Ed. Folio, contemp calf; rebacked, covers & title crudely rehinged. sg Oct 9 (266) $80
— The History and Antiquities of the Exchequer. L, 1711. Folio, contemp calf; joints splitting, rubbed. bba Aug 28 (188) £140 [Titles]

Madrigal, Alonso de, Bishop of Avila
— Tratado al conde don Alvaro de Stuniga sobre la forma qui avie de tener en el oyr de la missa. Alcala de Henares: Arnao Guillem de Brocar, 26 Feb 1511. 4to, modern blind-stamped mor. S May 21 (53) £2,600 [Quaritch]

Maeterlinck, Maurice, 1862-1949
— Hours of Gladness. L & NY, 1912. Illus by E. J. Detmold. 4to, orig cloth; soiled. With 20 colored plates. Ck Jan 30 (195) £65

Anr copy. Orig cloth; spine soiled, corners bumped. Ck Apr 24 (54) £55; pn Sept 18 (328) £65 [Maggs]

— The Life of the Bee. L, 1911. Trans by Alfred Sutro; illus by Edward J. Detmold. 4to, orig bds; rubbed. bba Apr 9 (250) £65 [Spencer]

— The Swarm. From the Life of the Bee.... NY, 1906. Mor gilt by Macdonald. Frontis recto bears a full-page autograph excerpt from an essay, Les Parfums, dated 10 Dec 1906 & sgd by Maeterlinck. sg Feb 12 (216) $175

— Le Tresor des humbles. Paris, 1896. One of 29. 12mo, mor by Noulhac, 1912, orig wraps bound in. S Sept 23 (583) £120 [Warrack & Perkins]

Maffei, Giovanni Pietro, 1533-1603
— Le Istorie delle Indie Orientali.... Florence: Giunta, 1589. 4to, 17th-cent mor gilt. S Apr 24 (349) £650 [Borjesson]

Anr copy. Later half vellum. Occasional worming. sg Nov 20 (100) $50

Maffei, Raffaello, 1451-1522
— Commentariorum urbanorum.... Basel: Froben, 1530. Folio, half lea; worn. Tp & colophon defaced; some browning & staining. bba Mar 12 (58) £75 [Robertshaw]

Magdeburg, C. van
— Wonderen der Natury, of een beschryvingh van...des Hemelsche firmaments.... The Hague, 1694. 4to, contemp vellum. With engraved title & 23 (of 30) plates. Haverschmidt copy. B Feb 24 (464) HF260

Magee, David
See also: Grabhorn Printing; Grolier Club
— Victoria R. I.: A Collection.... San Francisco, [1969-70]. One of 625. 3 vols. Half cloth. Vol I inscr. cba Feb 5 (204) £65

Anr copy. Wraps, Vol III in half cloth. O June 16 (128) $60

Anr copy. Bds. sg Jan 22 (223) $80

Magee, David & Dorothy
— The Ballad of the Hollow Leg. San Francisco: Lewis & Dorothy Allen, 1955. Single sheet ptg, 20 by 15 inches. Framed. cb Sept 11 (5) $160

Magee, Dorothy & David. See: Grabhorn Printing

Maggi, Giovanni
— Nuova Raccolta di fontane...di Roma, Tivoli e Frascati. Rome: Giovanni Iacomo Rossi, [c.1645]. Bound with: Sadeler, Marco. Vestigi delle antichita di Roma.... Rome: Rossi, [1660] Oblong folio, contemp calf; tear across cover. Some spotting; wormed in fore-margin at beginning. S Apr 23 (165) £1,300 [Zanzotto]

Maggi, Girolamo, d.1572
— De tintinnabulis liber posthumus. Asmt., 1689. 12mo, 18th-cent vellum; spine worn. With extra title & 7 plates. With 1 leaf remargined. bba Dec 4 (11) £110 [Poole]

Maggi, Girolamo, d.1572 —& Others
— Della fortificatione delle citta.... Venice: Rutilio Borgominiero, 1564. Folio, new bds; a few small inkstains on upper cover, loose. Some leaves discolored or browned. S Sept 23 (364) £420 [Breman]

Maggio, Bartolomeo
— Trattato delle ferite delli arcobugi et artigliarie.... Bologna: Jacobus Montius, 1666. 4to, calf gilt. S May 21 (205) £2,500 [Pickering & Chatto]

Maggs Brothers
— Bibliotheca Americana et Philippina. L, 1922-28. ("Bibliotheca Americana.") Parts 1-7 in 6 vols. 4to, new cloth, orig wraps bound in. sg Oct 2 (185) $60

Anr copy. Half cloth, orig wraps bound in. sg May 14 (20) $175

Magic...
— Magic. The Magician's Monthly Magazine. L, 1900-20. Vol I, No 1-Vol XV, No 9. Contemp cloth. Some leaves spotted or soiled. s Nov 10 (354) £90 [Tarakan]

Magician's...
— The Magician's Own Book, or the Whole Art of Conjuring.... NY, [1857]. 12mo, orig cloth. sg Feb 26 (178) $60

Magius, Hieronymous. See: Maggi, Girolamo

Magna Carta
See also: Young, Noel Denholm
— Magna Carta. L: T. Berthelet, 1531-32. 8vo, later calf; rubbed, covers detached. Lacking title to 1st part & last leaf; some spots & stains; early marginalia. bba Jan 15 (1) £140 [Rix]

MAGNAN

Magnan, P.
— Elegantiores statuae antiquae in variis Romanorum palatiis asservatae. Rome: Barbiellini, 1776. 4to, old calf. With engraved title & 42 plates. Some plates foxed in margins. S Nov 27 (188) £150 [Olschki]

Magne de Marolles, G. F.
— La Chasse au fusil. Paris, 1788. 8vo, contemp pigskin gilt. Jeanson copy. SM Mar 1 (385) FF15,000

Anr Ed. Paris, 1836. 8vo, contemp half calf; worn. Jeanson copy. SM Mar 1 (387) FF2,400

— Supplement au traite de la chasse au fusil. Paris, 1791. 8vo, contemp pigskin gilt. Jeanson copy. SM Mar 1 (388) FF2,600

Magninus, Mediolanensis
— Regimen sanitatis. [Lyon: Francois Fradin, c.1505]. 4to, contemp sheep; worn. Last few leaves frayed & dampstained. bba Aug 20 (415) £600 [Phelps]

Magnus, Olaus, 1490-1558
— A Compendious History of the Goths, Swedes & Vandals. L, 1658. Folio, modern half mor gilt. Tp strengthened; 3 prelims misbound; some discoloration; 2 holes not affecting text. S July 14 (415) £300

— Historia de gentibus septentrionalibus. Rome, 1555. 1st Ed. Folio, 18th-cent calf; worn. Some corners repaired. Jeanson 1080. SM Mar 1 (389) FF34,000

Anr Ed. Antwerp: Christopher Plantin, 1558. 8vo, old calf; rebacked, lacking front endpaper. 2 small holes in last leaf. sg Mar 26 (194) $300

Anr Ed. Antwerp: apud Ioannem Bellerum, 1562. 8vo, half vellum; soiled & worn. FD June 11 (1014) DM1,800

Anr copy. Later vellum; soiled, front free endpaper stamped. Some browning & foxing; single wormhole from T1-Aa8. P Nov 25 (309) $400

Magritte, Rene
— La Fidelite des Images. Brussels: Lebeer Hossmann, 1976. One of 10 hors commerce. Folio, orig fitted case. S July 2 (1036) £420 [Den Tind]; S July 2 (1037) £450 [Somenflod]

Mahony, Bertha Everett —& Others
— Illustrators of Children's Books, 1744-1945 Bost.: The Horn Book, 1947. 1st Ed. 4to, half cloth. cba Feb 5 (122) $60

AMERICAN BOOK PRICES CURRENT

Mahony, Francis Sylvester, 1804-66
— The Reliques of Father Prout.... L, 1836. Ed by Oliver Yorke; illus by Alfred Croquis. 2 vols. 8vo, contemp half mor by Potter & Sons. T Feb 19 (457) £44

Mailer, Norman
— The Faith of Graffiti. NY, 1974. One of 350. 4to, syn. sg Mar 5 (146) $80

— Marilyn. NY, 1973. Ltd Ed, sgd. In d/j. sg June 11 (284) $70

Maillard, Leon
— Les Menus et programmes illustres. Paris, 1898. One of 25. 4to, half mor by Riviere. C Dec 3 (29) £500 [Sims]

Mailly, ——, Chevalier de, d. c1724
— L'Eloge de la chasse.... Paris, 1723. 12mo, mor gilt by Tripon. Jeanson copy. SM Mar 1 (390) FF3,800

Mailly, Jean de
— Les Illustres Fees. Amst.: Michel Charles Le Cene, 1727. 12mo, wraps; stitching def. With frontis & 11 illusts. S Dec 5 (324) £200 [Hirsch]

Maimbourg, Louis, 1620?-86
— The History of the Crusade.... L, 1685-84. Trans by John Nalson. 2 vols. Folio, contemp calf; worn. bba Apr 23 (108) £50 [Thomson]

Maimonides, Moses, 1135-1204
— De sacrificiis liber.... L, 1683. 4to, vellum. Some stains & foxing. St. 6513.52, col 1878. S Feb 17 (88) £240 [Shane]

Anr copy. Old calf; rebacked. Lacking prelim leaf A2. S Mar 10 (1099) £100 [Nosbusch]

— More Nebuchim. Sabbioneta: Cornelio Adelkind & Tobia Foa, 1553. 3d Ed. Folio, calf gilt. Wormed with loss of single letters; last 5 leaves trimmed with loss of single letters. St. 6513.102, col 1895-96. S Feb 17 (87) £600 [Wyler]

— Yad Ha'chazaka-Mishneh Torah. Venice: Alviso Bragadin & Meir Frenzoni, 1574-76. 4 vols. Folio, 18th-cent half vellum; worn & wormed at edges. Some leaves from anr copy; some stains, worming & repairs. sg Apr 30 (281) $130

Maindardi, Arlotto
— Facetie, fabule, motti.... Venice: Bernardino di Bondoni, 1538. 8vo, 18th-cent mor gilt. Minor wormholes in margin of a few leaves. C Dec 12 (298) £360 [Lanfranchi]

Maindron, Ernest, 1838-1908
— Les Affiches illustrees. Paris, 1886. One of 525. 4to, modern cloth, orig wraps bound in. sg Dec 4 (119) $375
— Les Affiches illustrees 1886-1895. Paris, 1896. 4to, half mor gilt; worn, spine torn. With 72 color plates. pnNY Sept 13 (257) $400

One of 1,000. Modern cloth, orig wraps bound in; soiled. sg Dec 4 (118) $850

Mainfray, Pierre, c.1580-1630
— La Chasse royalle comedie.... Troyes: Nicolas Oudot, 1625. 8vo, calf. Lacking the last leaf. Jeanson copy. SM Mar 1 (391) FF3,800

Mainwaring, Sir Thomas
— The Legitimacy of Amicia.... L, 1679. 8vo, contemp calf; spine & corners damaged, rubbed. G7 torn; final leaf stuck to lower cover; lacking front free endpaper. bba Apr 9 (34) £40 [Clark]

Mairobert, Pidansat de
— L'Espion anglois, ou correspondance secrete entre Mylord All-Eye et Mylord All-Ear. L: John Adamson, 1784-86. 10 vols. 8vo, contemp calf gilt. S May 21 (155) £200 [Greenwood]

Maison, Karl Eric
— Honore Daumier: Catalogue Raisonne of the Paintings, Watercolours, and Drawings. L, 1968. One of 1,500. 4to, orig cloth. S July 13 (36) $300

Maitland, James, 8th Earl of Lauderdale, 1759-1839
See also: Canard, Nicolas Francois
— An Inquiry into the Nature and Origin of Public Wealth.... Edin., 1804. 1st Ed. 8vo, contemp half mor gilt; rubbed, frayed along top. Table browned & frayed along outer edge; some creasing in C gathering. P Sept 24 (318) $450

Anr copy. Contemp calf; rubbed. S May 29 (1222) £380
— An Inquiry into the Practical Merits of the System for the Government of India. Edin., 1809. 8vo, later half calf; rubbed. Lacking A1. P Sept 24 (319) $150

Maitland, William, 1693?-1757
— The History of Edinburgh. Edin., 1753. 1st Ed. Folio, calf gilt; badly worn. pnE Nov 12 (255) £110

Anr copy. Contemp calf; rebacked. With folding map (rebacked) & 20 plates. pnE May 20 (22) £200

Anr copy. Later calf gilt; rubbed. With folding map & 20 plates. 6 extra plates inserted; folding map mtd on linen; with the suppressed passages at p 123 & 175 & an extra leaf inserted at each with the later, altered text; marginal tears. S Nov 17 (804) £260 [Peterson]
— The History of London. L, 1756. ("The History and Survey of London.") 2 vols. Folio, contemp calf; spines worn. Sold w.a.f. CK May 15 (135) £380

Maitres...
— Maitres de la venerie. Paris: Emile Nourry, 1928-34. One of 50 on vellum Annam. 10 vols in 11. 8vo, half shagreen. Inscr to Marcel Jeanson. SM Mar 1 (392) FF17,000

Major, Thomas
— The Ruins of Paestum, otherwise Posidonia.... L, 1768. Folio, contemp mor gilt; rubbed. With 25 plates (1 repeated). S Oct 23 (207) £1,200 [Weinreb]

Makryjannis, K. D. —& Zographos, D.
— Histoire picturale de la guerre de l'independance hellenique. Geneva & Paris, [1926]. One of 140. Folio, text in wrap plus plates, together within orig portfolio. With 24 colored plates, 2 extra proofs for Plate 2 & 3 photogravure plates in the text vol. S Apr 23 (224) £3,000 [Pervannas]

Malcolm, Sir John, 1769-1833
— The History of Persia. L, 1815. 2 vols. 4to, half calf; rubbed. pn Dec 11 (144) £210 [Holmes]

Anr copy. Calf; rebacked, rehinged, worn. With folding map, torn. Title loose. sg Nov 20 (101) $425

Malegue, Hippolyte
— Album photographique d'Archeologie Religieuse. Puy & Paris, 1857. Folio, later mor gilt, with all leaves rehinged with linen. With 32 mtd salt prints. Some foxing; 1 plate margin repaired on verso. Inscr. sg May 7 (54) $3,750

Malgaigne, Joseph Francois, 1806-65
— Traite des fractures et des luxations. Paris, 1847-55. 2 vols, including Atlas vol. 8vo & folio, text, half lea; atlas, half calf; both vols rubbed. With 30 plates.. S Nov 27 (274) £350 [Lange & Springer]

Malherbe, Francois de
— Poesies. Paris, 1776. 8vo, contemp silk embroidered with a hand holding a spray of flowers, the hand rising from a cloud over a metal pedestal, surrounded by flowers & a scroll & motto & border of metallic thread & colored sequins on upper cover, the lower cover stitched in metallic thread & sequins of sprays & flourishes & the initials CL, the spine dated Anno 1789 in metallic thread &

sequins. C Dec 3 (74) £3,600 [Sourget]

Malinowski, Bronislaw
— The Sexual Life of Savages in North-Western Melanesia.... NY, 1929. 2 vols. In d/js. cb Nov 6 (198) $50

Malleson, George Bruce, 1825-98
— The Indian Mutiny of 1857. L, 1891. One of 250. 4to, half mor. With 7 plates. sg Nov 20 (84) $100
— The Mutiny of the Bengal Army.... L, 1857-58. 2 parts in 1 vol. 8vo, modern cloth. Tp soiled. cb Dec 18 (109) $90

Mallet, Allain Menesson
— Description de l'univers. Paris, 1683. 5 vols. 8vo, contemp calf gilt. With engraved titles, 2 ports & 677 maps & plates. N2 in Vol II torn & repaired; a few other marginal tears; some leaves soiled. C Dec 12 (249) £2,400 [Franks]
Anr Ed. Frankfurt: J. D. Zunner, 1685-86. 5 vols. 8vo, contemp calf; rubbed. With engraved titles, 2 ports & 595 maps & plates. Occasional small wormholes touching text; 1 plate in last vol laid down; some discoloration. S Apr 23 (137) £2,600 [Map]

Mallet Dupan, Jacques Francois
— The History of the Destruction of the Helvetic Union and Liberty. Bost.: Manning & Loring for J. Nancrede, Aug 1799. 12mo, contemp pigskin; loose, spine cracked, frontis & tp detached. sg Sept 18 (33) $80

Malleville, Claudius
— In regias aquarum et silvarum constitutiones.... Paris: Vincent Sertenas, 1561. 8vo, contemp vellum. Jeanson copy. SM Mar 1 (393) FF2,900

Mallory, Wheeler & Co.
— Door Locks, Knobs, Padlocks.... New Haven, 1871. Folio, bdg not described. Franklin Institute copy. F Sept 12 (376) $2,500

Malo, Charles, 1790-1871
— Histoire des tulipes. Paris: Janet, [1821]. 12mo, half vellum; worn. O May 12 (131) $225
Anr copy. 19th-cent calf; joints split, rubbed. With 12 hand-finished colored plates. Inscr to Juliet Duff by Lady Diana Cooper. S Mar 9 (786) £130 [Sabben]

Malo de Luque, E. See: Raynal, Guillaume Thomas Francois

Malory, Sir Thomas, fl.1470
Le Morte Darthur
— 1889-91. - L.Ed by H. Oskar Sommer. 3 vols. 8vo, contemp mor gilt by Zaehnsdorf; scuffed. Ck May 29 (242) £280
— 1910-11. - L: Riccardi Press One of 12 ptd on vellum. Illus by W. Russell Flint. 4 vols. 4to, orig vellum gilt. FD Dec 2 (4544) DM2,800
One of 500. 2 vols. 4to, orig half cloth. pn Mar 5 (272) £160 [Walford]
Anr copy. Orig vellum gilt; soiled. S June 17 (235) £380 [Joseph]
— 1917. - L. One of 500. Abridged by A. W. Pollard; illus by Arthur Rackham. 4to, orig vellum; worn. pnNY Sept 13 (272) $450
Anr copy. With 16 mtd color plates. sg Oct 30 (142) $700
— 1917. - The Romance of King Arthur. L. Illus by Arthur Rackham. 4to, orig cloth; foot of spine rebacked. With 16 color plates. sg Oct 30 (143) $110
— 1972. - L. Illus by Aubrey Beardsley. 4to, cloth, in d/j. sg Jan 8 (159) $50

Malpighi, Marcello, 1628-94
— Dissertatio epistolica de formatione pulli in ovo. L, 1673. 4to, new half calf. With 4 folding plates. S May 28 (728) £1,100
— Opera posthuma.... Amst., 1698. 4to, old vellum. With 19 folding plates & a duplicate of Plate 14; lacking frontis. sg Jan 15 (105) $350

Malraux, Andre
— Psychologie de l'art. [Geneva] 1947-48-[50]. 3 vols. 4to, wraps. S Nov 10 (127) £50 [Eumopoulos]
— Saturne; essai sur Goya. Paris, 1950. 4to, ptd wraps; spine ends with tears. sg Feb 5 (152) $50

Malte-Brun, Conrad, 1775-1826
— A New General Atlas.... Phila., 1828. 4to, orig half mor; rubbed & worn. With 40 hand-colored maps, 2 with marginal tears & chipping. cb Nov 6 (199) $190
— Precis de la geographie universelle.... Paris, 1831-37. Atlas vol only. Folio, contemp half calf; upper joint split. With colored geological chart & 70 maps, all but 1 hand-colored, mostly in outline. Lackng map of ancient Spain. C Oct 15 (68) £270 [Van Noord]
— Universal Geography.... Bost., 1834. ("A System of Universal Geography: or, a Description of all the Parts of the World....") Vols I & II (of 3). 4to, contemp calf; scuffed & worn. Prelims of Vol I dampstained. cb Nov 6 (200) $120

Malthus, Thomas Robert, 1766-1834
— Definitions in Political Economy.... L, 1827. 8vo, half calf; rubbed, label lacking, spine chipped at head. Some smearing on pp 124-25; spotted at front & back. P Sept 24 (331) $600

Anr copy. Half calf; worn. pnE Oct 15 (183) £480

— An Essay on the Principle of Population.... L, 1803. 4to, contemp calf gilt; rebacked. pnE Jan 28 (126) £980 [Thin]

Anr copy. Contemp half calf; rubbed. Some tears & holes. S July 23 (446) £1,300 [Gless]

3d Ed. L, 1806. 2 vols. 8vo, modern cloth, rubbed & soiled. Half-titles hinged along inner margins; B2 in Vol I torn into text; marginal tear in I3 of Vol I & Mm8 of Vol II. P Sept 24 (333) $200

Anr copy. Contemp calf. Some leaves spotted. S May 29 (1220) £230

4th Ed. L, 1807. 2 vols. 8vo, calf; rubbed & scuffed, tear in lea along lower joint of Vol II. P Sept 24 (334) $175

5th Ed. L, 1817. 3 vols. 8vo, contemp half calf; rubbed. S Jan 16 (406) £350 [Cavendish]

— The Grounds of an Opinion on the Policy of Restricting the Importation of Foreign Corn.... L, 1815. 4to, modern half cloth. P Sept 24 (335) $600

Anr copy. Disbound. Some browning. P Sept 24 (336) $500

— The Measure of Value Stated and Illustrated. L, 1823. Bound with: Definitions in Political Economy. L, 1827. 8vo, contemp half russia; split in upper hinge. C Dec 12 (140) £550 [Pressler]

— Principes d'economie politique.... Paris, 1820. 1st Ed in French. 2 vols. 8vo, contemp sheep; rubbed. Marginal tear on 21-6. P Sept 24 (337) $300

— Principles of Political Economy.... L, 1820. 1st Ed. 8vo, contemp half russia; upper hinge split, rubbed. C Dec 12 (140) £550 [Pressler]

Anr copy. Modern half calf gilt. Library stamp & signature on tp. P Sept 24 (338) $800

Anr copy. Calf. pnE Jan 28 (125) £520 [Steedman]

Malton, James, d. 1803
— An Essay on British Cottage Architecture. L, 1798. 4to, contemp half calf; rebacked & cornered. With 21 plates. Some spotting. bba Apr 23 (56) £600 [Jones]

— The Young Painter's Maulstick.... L, 1800. 4to, contemp half lea; rubbed. With 23 plates. AVP Nov 20 (239) C$150 [Art 45]

Malton, Thomas, 1748-1804
— A Picturesque Tour through the Cities of London and Westminster. L, 1792-[1801]. 2 vols in 1. Folio, contemp mor gilt by Riley, with his ticket. With 100 hand-finished color plates. C Oct 15 (69) £16,000 [Maggs]

Anr copy. Contemp russia, armorial bdg; small piece missing from head of spine. With plates in uncolored state. S Oct 23 (10) £7,000 [Robinson]

Malvezzi, Virgilio, 1599-1654
— Discourses upon Cornelius Tacitus. L, 1642. 1st Ed in English. Folio, contemp sheep; rebacked, rubbed. bba July 16 (220) £40 [Hirsh]

Anr copy. Contemp calf; foot of spine restored. Opening leaves dampstained in lower inner corner. sg Mar 26 (195) $175

Man, Felix H. See: Bauman, Hans F. S.

Manchester, Herbert. See: Derrydale Press

Mandelslo, Johann Albrecht von
— Voyages celebres et remarquables, faits de Perse aux Indes Orientales.... Amst., 1727. 2 vols. Folio, contemp calf, rubbed, joints split. With 19 maps & 27 plates. FD June 11 (1188) DM1,800

Mander, Carel van
— Het schilder Boeck.... Amst., 1618. 4to, vellum. B Feb 25 (539) HF2,200

Anr Ed. Haarlem, 1604. 4 parts in 1 vol. 4to, contemp vellum; upper hinge broken, spine torn. With port & 2 engraved titles. S Mar 10 (1100) £550 [Juiper]

Mandeville, Bernard de, 1670?-1733
— The Fable of the Bees. L, 1724. 8vo, early 19th-cent half calf; rubbed. 1 leaf torn without loss. bba Sept 25 (20) £130 [Quaritch]

Mandeville, Sir John, d.1372
See also: Grabhorn Printing

— Itinerarius. [Cologne: Cornelis de Zierikzee, c.1495]. 4to, modern calf. Small stain to a few blank corners at end. 48 leaves. Goff M-162. C Dec 12 (299) £6,500 [Quaritch]

Manec, Pierre Joseph, 1799-1884
— A Theoretical and Practical Treatise upon the Ligature of Arteries. Halifax, 1838. 4to, half calf; worn. With 14 hand-colored plates. Library stamp on tp. S Nov 10 (516) £350 [Phillips]

Manet, Edouard, 1823-83
— Letters with Aquarelles. NY: Pantheon, [n.d.]. One of 345. sg Feb 5 (213) $130

Manetti, Xaverio —& Others
— Ornithologia methodice digesta atque iconibus aeneis ad vivum illuminatis ornata. Florence: Stamperia Mouckiana, 1767-76. Folio, contemp half calf; rubbed & slightly wormed. With 5 frontises, port & 600 hand-colored plates. Marginal tear in Plate 208 of Vol II; small holes repaired in plates 129 & 135 of Vol II. S Oct 23 (708) £38,000 [Quaritch]

Mangin, Edward
— Piozziana; or, Recollections of the later Mrs. Piozzi....By a Friend. L, 1833. 12mo, contemp calf; broken, rebacked. With ALs of Piozzi tipped in. sg Feb 12 (249) $150

Manifiesto...
— Manifiesto historico de los procedimientos del tribunal del santo Oficio, de la Inquisicion de Cartagena de las Indias en los Sucessos de los Anos de 1681...1687. Cadiz, 1688. Folio, later vellum; front cover warped. Wormholed, affecting some text. sg Sept 18 (135) $90

Manilius, Marcus
— Astronomicon. Paris, 1679. ("Astronomicon libri quinque.") 4to, later vellum over bds; rebacked, orig spine laid down. cb Feb 19 (172) $130

Manley, Mary de la Riviere, 1663?-1724
— Secret Memoirs and Manners...from the New Atalantis. L, 1709. 1st Ed. 8vo, contemp calf; rubbed, joints cracked. With Ms key to the characters at end. Ck Nov 21 (23) £100

Manly, William Lewis
— Death Valley in '49: Important Chapter of California Pioneer History. San Jose, 1894. 1st Ed. 8vo, cloth; rubbed & soiled. With port & 3 plates. cb Oct 9 (135) $65; cb Jan 8 (114) $110

Mann, Daniel Dickenson
— The Present Picture of New South Wales.... L, 1811. 4to, contemp calf; rebacked. With folding hand-colored plan. Lacking 4 plates; map offset onto title. C Oct 15 (162) £290 [Maggs]

Mann, James, 1759-1832
— Medical Sketches of the Campaigns of 1812, 13, 14.... Dedham, Mass., 1816. 1st Ed. 8vo, modern bds. Foxed throughout, dampstained at end. sg Jan 15 (106) $275

Mann, Johann Gottlieb
— Die auslaendischen Arzney-Pflanzen. Stuttgart, 1830-[33?]. Orig 22 parts in 13. Folio, orig wraps. With 130 (of 132) hand-colored plates. Some dampstaining. de Belder copy. S Apr 28 (224) £2,200 [Maggs]

— Deutschlands wildwachsende Arzney-Pflanzen. Stuttgart, [1823]-28. Folio, contemp half vellum; worn. With port & 186 hand-colored plates Some spotting & soiling; Plate 11 shaved at head; blank corner torn from Plate 22; Plate 147 stained; contents leaf torn in inner margin. S Oct 23 (729) £2,500 [Walford]

Anr copy. Contemp half calf; rubbed. Some staining, mostly marginal but affecting some plates, particularly 49-69. de Belder copy. S Apr 28 (225) £3,000 [Arader]

Mann, Thomas, 1875-1955
— The Beloved Returns. NY, 1940. 1st American Ed, one of 395. Trans by H. T. Lowe-Porter. 4to, half cloth. pnNY Mar 12 (100) $80

Anr copy. Bds. Sgd. wd Nov 12 (138) $75

— Death in Venice. Balt. & NY: Aquarius Press, 1971. One of 25. Illus by Warrington Colescott. Folio, portfolio with copy of the 1965 Knopf Ed inlaid. With a suite of the "Principal Edition". sg Dec 4 (121) $500

— Der junge Joseph. Berlin, 1934. Inscr. O Mar 24 (116) $100

Manners, John Henry, 5th Duke of Rutland
— A Tour through Part of Belgium and the Rhenish Provinces. L, 1822. Illus by Elizabeth, Duchess of Rutland. 4to, disbound. With 13 plates. wa Sept 25 (629) $270

Manners, Lady Victoria —& Williamson, George Charles
— Angelica Kauffmann, R. A., her Life and her Works. L, 1924. One of 75, with 3 extra plates. 4to, half cloth. cb Feb 19 (173) $225

Manning, Anne. See: Fore-Edge Paintings

Manning, Frederic
— The Middle Parts of Fortune. L, 1929. One of 500. 2 vols. S Jan 13 (589) £100 [Gekoski]

Manning, Samuel
— American Pictures Drawn with Pen and Pencil. L: Religious Tract Society, [1876]. 8vo, orig cloth; spine ends chipped. Sgd, July 1886. cb Jan 22 (26) $75

Mansfeld, Jos. Georg. See: Kininger & Mansfeld

Mansfield, Charles Blachford
— Aerial Navigation. L, 1877. 8vo, orig cloth, unopened. Ck Jan 30 (194) £65

Anr copy. Orig cloth. sg Jan 15 (275) $110

Mansfield, Katherine, 1888-1923
— The Garden Party and Other Stories. L: Verona Press, 1939 [1947]. One of 1,200. Illus by Marie Laurencin. 4to, bds, in d/j. With 16 colored plates. kh Mar 16 (336) A$350; S June 18 (332) £900 [Sayle]; sg Jan 8 (151) $500
— Prelude. Richmond: Hogarth Press, [1918]. 1st Ed. Orig wraps; upper cover torn with loss. T Oct 15 (74) £195
Later issue without the Fergusson line block on the wraps. Orig wraps; short tears at edges, 1 joint torn. Some spotting at beginning & endd. S Dec 18 (137) £800 [Maggs]

Manstein, Christoph Hermann von
— Memoirs of Russia.... L, 1783. 2d Ed. 4to, contemp half sheep; joints split. With 10 folding maps. One text leaf torn & repaired; some maps torn & repaired, most with small tears at folds. bba Mar 26 (184) £80 [Bickersteth]

Mantle, Robert Burns
— The Best Plays of.... NY, [1940s-1960s]. For the years 1894 to 1963. Bound in 47 vols. With the Index for 1899-1950. O Feb 24 (133) $110

Mantuano, Pedro
— Advertencias a la historia del Padre Ivan de Mariana.... Madrid: Imprenta Real, [1613]. 4to, contemp vellum; loose. Some leaves dog-eared at beginning & end; wormholes at top of inner margin. sg Sept 18 (166) $70

Manuel II, King of Portugal
— Livros Antigos Portuguezes 1489-1600. L: Maggs, 1929-35. One of 650. 3 vols. 4to, orig cloth, in d/js; minor wear. O May 12 (132) $800

Manuscript...
— The Manuscript of Diedrich Knickerbocker, Jun. NY, 1824. 8vo, half mor. Tp & errata leaf soiled; last leaf torn & repaired without loss. Sometimes attributed to Washington Irving. sg Sept 11 (213) $80

Manzini, Cesare
— Instruction pour elever, nourrir, dresser...toutes sortes de petits oyseaux de voliere.... Paris: Charles de Sercy, [1665]. 12mo, 19th-cent bdg. Tp restored at bottom with the 2 last lines in facsimile. Jeanson copy. SM Mar 1 (395) FF3,400

Manzoni, Alessandro, 1785-1873
See also: Limited Editions Club
— Adelchi. Milan, 1822. 8vo, contemp wraps; spine def. S Sept 23 (585) £160 [King]

Map...
— Map Collectors' Circle. L, 1963-75. Ed by R. V. Tooley. Parts 1-110 in 11 vols [all pbd]. Cloth. S May 29 (979) £360

Mapei, Camillo
— Italy: Classical, Historical and Picturesque. Glasgow, 1856. 4to, old calf. With 60 plates. One plate defaced. ha Dec 19 (232) $225

Maps & Charts

Africa
— BERTIUS, P. - Carte de l'Afrique. [Paris, 1639 or later]. 380mm by 495mm, hand-colored in outline. Ck May 8 (5) £300
— BLAEU, JAN. - Aethiopia inferior vel exterior. [Amst., 1635, or later]. 380mm by 500mm, in card mount. Hand-colored in outline. Ck May 8 (221) £320
Anr copy. Hand-colored. Short split without loss. S Jan 12 (293) £120 [Taback]
— BLAEU, WILLEM & JAN. - Africae nova descriptio. [Amst., c.1640]. 410mm by 550mm, hand-colored. Some discoloration. S July 14 (8117) £350
Anr Ed. [Amst., c.1650]. 410mm by 540mm. Stained, clean tear to fold. Ck May 8 (9) £320
Anr Ed. [Amst., c.1662]. 410mm by 555mm, colored in a contemp hand, framed. S Nov 10 (1171) £520 [Pantuzelous]
Anr Ed. [Amst., c.1663]. 560mm by 415mm, hand-colored. pn Apr 30 (544) £500 [Maliye]
— BLAEU, WILLEM. - Guinea. [Amst., after 1640]. 387mm by 530mm, hand-colored in outline, with fully colored title & cartouches. Paper tape on recto; some browning. sg Apr 23 (259) $100
— BRAUN, GEORG & HOGENBERG, FRANZ. - Hierosolyma urbs sancta.... [Cologne, 1575]. 324mm by 412mm, colored in a contemp hand. S Jan 12 (224) £350 [Patterson]
— CORONELLI, VINCENZO MARIA. - L'Africa divisa nelle sue Parti.... [1691]. 2 sheets, totalling 610mm by 900mm, hand-colored, framed. Ck May 8 (21) £500
— CORONELLI, VINCENZO MARIA. - Route Maritime de Brest a Siam.... Paris: J. B. Nolin, 1687 [or later]. 450mm by 730mm. Right margin cut away & repaired. Ck May 8 (22) £260
— DE JODE, GERARD. - Africae vera formis, et situs. Antwerp, 1593. 325mm by 440mm. S Apr 23 (319) £900 [George]
— DE WIT, FREDERICK. - Nova Africa Descriptio. Amst., 1660. 35cm by 55.6cm, early hand-coloring. pnNY Sept 13 (355A) $550

MAPS & CHARTS

— DE WIT, FREDERICK. - Nova et Accurata totius Africae tabula.... Amst., [c.1660]. 19.25 by 23.75 inches Early hand-coloring. Strengthened on back, slight loss of image along center-fold. pnNY Sept 13 (357) $600

— DE WIT, FREDERICK. - Totius Africae Accuratissima Tabula. Amst., [17th cent]. 489mm by 580mm, hand-colored in outline with fully colored cartouche. Abrasions with minor loss of image at center fold-line; some paper repairs on verso. sg Nov 20 (272) $150

Anr copy. 487mm by 575mm, hand-colored in outline, uncolored cartouche. Minor marginal tears. sg Nov 20 (273) $130

— DELISLE, GUILLAUME. - Africa accurate in imperia. Amst., [c.1730]. 49.5cm by 57.8cm, hand-colored. Tp strengthened on surface. pnNY Sept 13 (345) $200

— FER, NICHOLAS DE. - L'Afrique.... [1786]. 4 sheets mtd as 1 on linen, 1,000mm by 1,180mm, repaired, framed & glazed. Ck May 8 (33) £1,600

— HOMANN, JOHANN BAPTIST. - Totius Africae Nova Repraesentatio.... Nuremberg, [1707 or later]. 485mm by 560mm, early hand-coloring. pnNY Sept 13 (369) $175

Anr Ed. Nuremberg, [1715]. 485mm by 565mm, hand-colored. Crease at fold. S July 14 (742) pS160

— HONDIUS, JODOCUS. - Africa nova tabula. [Amst., 1632]. 400mm by 550mm. S July 14 (811) £380

— JANSSONIUS, JOANNES. - Aethiopia inferior, vel exterior. [Amst., c.1650]. 383mm by 505mm. Small marginal stain. S Jan 12 (294) £110 [Taback]

Anr copy. 15 by 20 inches, hand-colored in outline. T Jan 22 (132) £100

— LINSCHOTEN, JAN HUYGEN VAN. - Typus orarum maritimarum Guineae et Angola. [L, 1598]. 390mm by 525mm. Faint traces of wear at fold without apparent loss; shaved to plate-mark in places. S Oct 23 (457) £350 [Putnam]

— MERCATOR, GERARD. - Abissinio Rumsive. Amst., [c.1600]. 34.3cm by 48.9cm, early hand-coloring. pnNY Sept 13 (404) $190

— MERCATOR, GERARD. - Africa. [Duisberg, c.1600]. 38cm by 47cm, hand-colored. Some browning. pnNY Sept 13 (403) $450

Anr Ed. Amst., [c.1623]. 380mm by 470mm, colored in a contemp hand, framed. S Nov 10 (1174) £340 [Goldbaum]

— MERCATOR, GERARD. - Africa, ex magna orbis terre descriptione.... [Amst, c.1609]. 387mm by 475mm, old hand-coloring. Some wear down centerfold; tear with loss at lower corner; foxed. pnNY Dec 10 (222) $275

AMERICAN BOOK PRICES CURRENT

Anr Ed. [Amst, 1613?]. 380mm by 475mm. Small section of lower margin excised. Ck May 8 (53) £180

— MERCATOR, GERARD. - Guineae nova descriptio.... Amst., 1636. 350mm by 500mm, hand-colored. Framed. Ck May 8 (130) £160

— MERCATOR, GERARD & HONDIUS JODOCUS. - Nova Africae tabula. Amst., [1630, or later]. 380mm by 500mm. French text on verso. Lower fold repaired. Ck May 8 (39) £180

— ORTELIUS, ABRAHAM. - Aegyptus antiqua. [Antwerp], [1590]. 2 sheets joined, 895mm by 482mm, fully hand-colored. S July 14 (725) £120

— ORTELIUS, ABRAHAM. - Africae tabula nova.... Antwerp, 1570. 370mm by 500mm, hand-colored. Margins stained. Ck May 8 (58) £280

Anr copy. 50cm by 37cm, early hand-coloring. Latin text on verso. Browned. pnNY Sept 13 (435) $300

Anr copy. Center-fold worn, thin lower margins. pnNY Sept 13 (436) $300; pnNY Sept 13 (437) $425

Anr copy. Overall browning, trimmed with loss of image on lower edge. pnNY Sept 13 (438) $250

Anr copy. 372mm by 500mm, colored in a contemp hand. S July 14 (l817) £350

Anr copy. 14.5 by 20 inches, hand-colored, framed. T Mar 19 (173) £240

— ORTELIUS, ABRAHAM. - Presbiteri Johannis, sive Abissinorum imperii descriptio. Antwerp, [1572 or later]. 371mm by 440mm, uncolored. Small split at center fold-line; partly paper-reinforced on verso; paper tape on verso of margin edges. sg Nov 20 (270) $150

— ORTELIUS, ABRAHAM. - Terra Sancta. [Amst., c.1570]. 367mm by 503mm. French text on verso. Margins foxed. pnNY Sept 13 (451) $350

Anr Ed. [Antwerp, c.1590]. 370mm by 510mm. pn June 18 (376) £200 [Faupel]

— PTOLEMAEUS, CLAUDIUS. - Affrice tabule quatuor. Ulm: Leonardus Hol, 1482. 354mm by 476mm, colored in a contemp hand, framed. S Apr 23 (321) £650 [Grand Rue]

— PTOLEMAEUS, CLAUDIUS. - Africae-Pars. Basel, [c.1542]. 40cm by 48.4cm, early hand-coloring. Trimmed to edge of image. pnNY Sept 13 (458) $200

— PTOLEMAEUS, CLAUDIUS. - Sexta Asie tabula [Arabian Peninsula]. Ulm: L. Hol, 1482. 286mm by 497mm, fully colored by a contemp hand. Framed. Very small water-stain touching upper border. S Apr 24 (225) £2,800 [Arader]

— PTOLEMAEUS, CLAUDIUS. - Tabula nova

1986 - 1987 · BOOKS

partis Africae. Basel, [c.1542]. 30.5cm by 42.5cm, early hand-coloring. Strengthened on verso; centerfold browned. pnNY Sept 13 (457) $225
— RENNELL, JAMES. - A Chart of the Bank of Lagullus; and Southern Coast of Africa. L, 1778-97. 330mm by 630mm, with ptd 8-page pilot attached. Inscr to Henry Dundas. S Nov 10 (1178) £240 [Potter]
— SCHENK, PETER. - Nieuwe Naauwkeurige Land- en Zee-kaart van het Voornaamste Gedeelte der Kaffersche Kust.... [Amst., c.1700]. 575mm by 488mm, colored in a contemp hand. S Nov 10 (1180) £880 [Porter]
— SENEX, JOHN - A New Map of Africa from the Latest Observations. [L, 1721]. 500mm by 575mm, colored in outline. Light stain down centerfold. Ck May 8 (71) £170

Anr copy. 500mm by 580mm. Colored in outline, framed. SSA Feb 11 (627) R480
— TEIXEIRA, LUIS - Effigies ampli Regni auriferi Guineae in Africa siti. Amst.: Carel Allard, [c.1690]. 46100 by 600mm, colored in a contemp hand & with marginal annotations in a contemp hand. Some restoration. S June 25 (482) £1,900
— VISSCHER, NICOLAS. - Africae Accurata Tabula. [Amst., 1690 or later]. 438mm by 552mm, early hand-coloring. pnNY Sept 13 (491) $200
— VISSCHER, NICOLAS. - Carte de l'Afrique meridionale.... [Amst., 1710]. 510mm by 580mm, hand-colored. Ck May 8 (254) £190

Americas

— Amerique. Paris: Crepy, 1735. 52.1cm by 66cm, early hand-coloring. Frayed & repaired along lower border & lower portion of centerfold. pnNY Sept 13 (334) $350
— Chart of the Atlantic Ocean, with the British, French & Spanish Settlements in North America.... L: Thomas Jefferys, [1762]. 2d Issue. 470mm by 610mm, hand-colored in wash & outline. With 2 overlays. S Oct 23 (132) £700 [Martayan]
— Nova Totius Americae Descriptio. Amst., 1660 [or later]. 43.8cm by 55.9cm, hand-colored. Repaired along lower part of centerfold. pnNY Sept 13 (356) $850
— ANVILLE, JEAN BAPTISTE BOURGUIGNON D'. - L'Amerique septentrionale. Paris, 1746. 4 sheets joined as 2, each 450mm by 870mm, hand-colored in outline. Lower right corner below cartouche torn, creased & repaired on verso. sg Apr 23 (191) $120
— ANVILLE, JEAN BAPTISTE BOURGUIGNON D'. - Canada, Louisiane et terres angloises. Paris, 1755. 4 sheets, totalling 940mm by 1,100mm. S July 14 (267) £220
— ANVILLE, JEAN BAPTISTE BOURGUIGNON D'. - Carte du Mexique et de la Nouvelle

MAPS & CHARTS

Espagne.... Venice, 1779. 448mm by 580mm, partly hand-colored in outline. sg Apr 23 (192) $110
— ANVILLE, JEAN BAPTISTE BOURGUIGNON D'. - Carte generale du Canada, de la Floride, de la Caroline.... Venice: Santini, 1775. 47.5cm by 65cm, hand-colored in outline with inset map in corner. Trimmed & frayed at lower edge. pnNY Sept 13 (337) $375
— ANVILLE, JEAN BAPTISTE BOURGUIGNON D'. - Partie meridionale de la Louisiane avec la Floride.... Venice: P. Santini, 1776. 482mm by 575mm, hand-colored in outline. One small hole. pnNY Sept 13 (336) $225

Anr Ed. Venice: G. Remondini, [1784 or later]. 482mm by 575mm, early hand-coloring. Lower part of center-fold torn. pnNY Sept 13 (335) $225

Anr copy. 489mm by 575mm. pnNY Sept 13 (338) $325
— ARROWSMITH, AARON. - Chart of the West Indies and Spanish Dominions in North America. L, 1803. 1,210mm by 1,420mm, folding to 4to, contemp mor gilt with ticket of Picquet of Paris. S June 25 (426) £1,000
— BECK, J. M. - Tilforladelig Kort over Eylandet St. Croix udi America.... Copenhagen, 1754. 472mm by 734mm, hand-colored by quarters & plantations. With Ms annotations showing individual proprietors & the locations of windmills, in a contemp hand. S Oct 23 (112) £2,200 [R.O.H.R.]

Anr copy. Hand-colored in outline. S Feb 23 (302) £1,100 [Potter]
— BELLIN, J. N. - Carte reduite des Costes Orientales de l'Amerique Septentrionale. [Paris] 1778. 609mm by 115mm, hand-coloring Torn & repaired along margins & partly into plate. pnNY Sepp 13 (500) $475
— BLAEU, WILLEM & JAN. - Americae nova tabula. [Amst., 1631, or later]. 410mm by 550mm. Dutch text on verso.. S July 14 (740) £750

Anr Ed. [Amst., 1630 but c.1650]. 42cm by 56cm, old hand-coloring. Foxed. pnNY Dec 10 (201) $750
— BLAEU, WILLEM & JAN. - Brasilia. [Amst., 1642, or later]. 380mm by 490mm, hand-colored in outline. Adhesion flaw at fold; some discoloration. S Jan 12 (267) £150 [Map]
— BLAEU, WILLEM & JAN. - Mappa aestivarum insularum, alias Barmudas.... Amst., [c.1640 or later]. 400mm by 510mm, hand-colored. German text on verso. Stained; 1 clean tear. CK May 15 (259) £130

Anr copy. 400mm by 530mm. S Jan 12 (247) £340 [George]

MAPS & CHARTS

Anr copy. 16 by 21 inches, hand-colored in outline, with cartouches, etc, fully colored. German text on verso. Some repairsl tears. T Jan 22 (113) £200

— BLAEU, WILLEM. - Nova Hispania et Nova Gallica. [c.1660]. Double-page folio. Early hand-coloring. Dutch text on verso. pnNY Sept 13 (310) $250

Anr copy. Early hand-coloring. Center-fold repaired. pnNY Sept 13 (311) $275

Anr copy. Early hand-coloring. Latin text on verso. pnNY Sept 13 (312) $250

— BLAEU, WILLEM & JAN. - Paraguay o Prov. de Rio de la Plata. Amst., [c.1650]. 36.8cm by 48.3cm, early hand-coloring. Slight crease along centerfold. pnNY Sept 13 (313) $250

— BLAEU, WILLEM & JAN. - Venezuela, cum parte australi Novae Andalusia. Amst., [1630, but 1642 or later]. 378mm by 486mm, hand-colored pnNY Sept 13 (314) $300

— BOEHMIUS, A. G. - Americae mappa generalis. [Nuremberg: Homann's heirs, 1746. 525mm by 465mm, hand-colored in outline pn Sept 18 (387) £150 [Richards]

— BONTEIN, ARCHIBALD. - A Map of the Island of Jamaica. L, Mar 1 1753. 485mm by 735mm, hand-colored in full. Short tears repaired. S Nov 10 (1149) £160 [Burgess]

— BOWLES, CARINGTON. - America. L, [1790]. 100.4cm by 120cm, 4 sheets laid down on canvas, hand-colored. Some creasing & browning. pnNY Sept 13 (323) $750

Anr Ed. L, [c.1800]. 57.2cm by 56.5cm, partly hand-colored. Some foxing; trimmed to edge of platemarks. pnNY Sept 13 (324) $140

— BUACHE, PHILIPPE. - Carte d'une partie de l'Amerique pour la navigation des Isles et du Golfe du Mexique.... Paris, [1740]. 490mm by 920mm, colored in outline. S Feb 23 (329) £200 [Marsden]

— CHATELAIN, HENRI ABRAHAM. - Carte tres curieuse de la Mer du Sud. [Amst., c.1719]. 780mm by 1,400mm, in 4 sheets joined as 2. S Oct 23 (387) £3,800 [Radin]

— CORONELLI, VINCENZO MARIA. - America Meridionale. Venice, [c.1696]. 2 sheets, total 606mm by 900mm. S Nov 10 (1125) £200 [Goldbaum]

— CORONELLI, VINCENZO MARIA. - Archipelague du Mexique, ou sont les Isles de cuba.... Paris, 1742. 45.1cm by 59.7cm, hand-colored in outline. pnNY Sept 13 (331) $550

— COSTANSO, MIGUEL. - Chart of California by Miguel Costanso 1770. L: Alexander Dalrymple, 21 June 1790. 625mm by 480mm. S June 25 (362) £2,200

— CRUZ CANO Y HOLMEDILLA, JUAN DE LA. - Mapa geographico de America meridional.

AMERICAN BOOK PRICES CURRENT

L: Wm. Faden, 1 Jan 1799. 8 sheets, hand-colored, mtd on linen & dissected in 120 sections, total dimensions being 2,460mm by 3,120mm, folding into contemp mor gilt slipcase with ticket of Picquet of Paris S June 25 (425) £720 [Houle]

— DE BRY, THEODOR. - Neuwe landtaffel...das gewaltige und Goldtreiche Kunigreich Guiana. [Frankfurt, 1599]. Proof state. 335mm by 450mm. S Oct 23 (431) £850 [Israel]

— DE JODE, GERARD. - Brasilia et Peruvia. [Antwerp, 1593]. 357mm by 425mm. Fold repaired. S Oct 23 (430) £750 [Franks]

— DE LA TOUR, B. - Amerique Septentrionale. Paris, 1779. 52.1cm by 75cm, hand-colored in outline. Trimmed to within plate along lower margin. pnNY Sept 13 (341) $250

— DE LETH, HENDRICK. - La Nouvelle Grande Carte des Indes Orientales. Amst.: Ottens, [c.1735]. 4 uncut sheets, 1,000 by 1,200mm, colored in a contemp hand S Oct 23 (147) £900 [Browning]

— DE WIT, FREDERICK. - Nova totius Americae descriptio. [Amst., c.1670]. State 2. 440mm by 555mm. S Oct 23 (383) £850 [Burden]

— DE WIT, FREDERICK. - Novissima et accuratissima septentrionalis ac meridionalis Americae Descriptio. Amst., [c.1680]. 490mm by 585mm, colored in a contemp hand. S Apr 24 (248) £650 [Arader]

— DELISLE, GUILLAUME. - L'Amerique septentrionale. Paris, 1700 [1708]. 455mm by 605mm. Remargined. S Feb 24 (449) £150 [Franks]

— DELISLE, GUILLAUME. - Carte d'Amerique. Paris: Dezanche, 1790. 48.9cm by 60.9cm, hand-colored. Some creasing in centerfold. pnNY Sept 13 (342) $400

— DELISLE, J. N. - Nouvelle Carte des decouvertes faites par les vaisseaux Russiens.... St. Petersburg, 1758. 455mm by 630mm, colored in outline. S Feb 23 (264) £520 [Smiley]

— EVANS, LEWIS. - A General Map of the Middle British Colonies in America.... L, 1758. 485mm by 660mm, unfolded, hand-colored in outline. Short tear in lower margin without loss. S Feb 23 (259) £600 [Smiley]

— FORLANI, PEOLO. - La Descrittione di tutto il Peru. [Venice, c.1566?]. 508mm by 370mm. With 1 small wormhole in sea area. S Oct 23 (427) £5,000 [Map]

— GREEN, JOHN. - A Chart of North and South America. L: Robert Sayer & Thomas Jefferys, [1768?]. 6 sheets with totally uncut margins, total dimensions if joined, 1,140mm by 1,115mm. Small stain touching plate mark. S Oct 23 (124) £1,400 [Berryman]

Anr Ed. L: Sayer & Bennett, 10 June 1775. 6 sheets joined 2 to a frame, in 3 frames measuring 16.75, 17.75 & 17.25 inches all by 44 inches wide. AVP Nov 20 (248) C$1,075 [Sloan]

— HOBBS, J. S. - The Island of Trinidad. L, 1881. 635mm by 780mm, canvas-backed. S Nov 10 (1135) £120 [Quaritch]

— HOBBS, J. S. - Porto Rico and Virgin Islands. L, 1880-[81]. 640mm by 940mm, canvas-backed. S Nov 10 (1124) £120 [Quaritch]

— HOMANN HEIRS. - De Gros-Britannische Colonie-Lander in Nord America. [Nuremberg, c.1760]. 50.8cm by 55.9cm, hand-colored. Torn & repaired along left margin. pnNY Sept 13 (373) $170

— HOMANN HEIRS. - Dominia Anglorum Die/ Gros Britannische Colonie-Lander in Nord America. [Nuremberg, c.1760]. 51.4cm by 56.5cm, hand-colored. Some stains in margin. pnNY Sept 13 (374) $170

— HOMANN, JOHANN BAPTIST. - Regni Mexicani seu Novae Hispaniae, Floridae, Novae Angliae.... Nuremberg, [1714]. 480mm by 575mm, principal areas fully hand-colored, with uncolored engraved title cartouche. sg Nov 20 (209) $350

Anr Ed. Nuremberg, [c.1725]. 47.5cm by 57.4cm, early hand-coloring. pnNY Sept 13 (370) $550

Anr copy. 480mm by 575mm, hand-colored. S Jan 12 (255) £200 [George]

— HOMANN, JOHANN BAPTIST. - Totius Americae Septentrionalis et Meridionalis. Nuremberg, [c.1700]. 490mm by 570mm, hand-colored, split at fold without loss. S Jan 12 (243) £200 [George]

Anr copy. 484mm by 565mm, hand-colored, with uncolored engraved title & cartouches. sg Nov 20 (211) $300

Anr copy. 20 by 23 inches, framed. wd June 19 (153) $150

Anr Ed. Nuremberg, [c.1714]. 490mm by 570mm, hand-colored in outline. sg Nov 20 (211) $300

— HONDIUS, JODOCUS. - America Meridionalis. [Amst., c.1623]. 355mm by 490mm, colored in a contemp hand, framed. S Nov 10 (1128) £450 [Goldbaum]

— HONDIUS, JODOCUS. - America noviter delineata.... Amst., Jansson, [1630]. Early issue with the broken upper right-hand corner. 470mm by 565mm, colored in a contemp hand, framed. S Nov 10 (1082) £1,600 [Map House]

Anr Ed. Amst., 1631. 19½ by 23½ inches, early hand-coloring. With 2 small inset maps of the polar regions. Creased down center-fold. pnNY Sept 13 (378) $1,000

Anr copy. 380mm by 500mm, hand-colored. Some browning. S Oct 23 (384) £450 [Arader]

Anr copy. 375mm by 495mm. S Jan 12 (244) £260 [George]

Issue with the broken upper right-hand corner. 470mm by 565mm, hand-colored. Short split at lower fold without loss; marginal browning. S Oct 23 (385) £1,450 [Burden]

Anr Ed. Amst., [c.1633]. 470mm by 565mm, colored in a contemp hand. German text on verso. Short split at lower fold without loss. S Apr 24 (249) £1,050 [Burgess]

Anr Ed. Amst.: Jansson, [c.1658]. 380mm by 500mm, hand-colored. Some discoloration. S Nov 10 (1081) £500 [Ash]

— HONDIUS, JODOCUS. - America septentrionalis. Amst., [c.1628]. 375mm by 500mm, colored in a contemp hand. S July 14 (749) £700

— JANSSONIUS, JOANNES. - America noviter delineata. Amst., [c.1650]. 37.5cm by 49.5cm, hand-colored & heightened with gilt. Strengthening to 2 areas. pnNY Sept 13 (384) $650

— JANSSONIUS, JOANNES. - America Septentrionalis. [Amst., 1636]. 465mm by 550mm. Hand-colored. Latin text on verso.. S Oct 23 (407) £500 [Smiley]

Anr Ed. L, [c.1650]. 465mm by 550mm, hand-colored. Lower margin restored. S July 14 (756) £460

Anr Ed. Amst., [c.1660]. 465mm by 550mm, hand-colored. Tissued. S Nov 18 (1089) £500 [Minishul]

— JANSSONIUS, JOANNES. - Indiae Orientalis Nova Descriptio. Amst., [c.1650]. 14½ by 19 inches, early hand-coloring. French text on verso. Lower margin torn. pnNY Sept 13 (390) $200

— JANSSONIUS, JOANNES. - Insulae Americanae in oceano septentrionali, cum terris adjacentibus. Amst., [c.1640, or later]. 377mm by 518mm, early hand-coloring. Latin text on verso. Strengthened on verso, foxed. pnNY Sept 13 (385) $300

— JANSSONIUS, JOANNES. - Magellanica qua Tierrae del Fuego. [Amst., c.1670]. 405mm by 520mm, colored in a contemp hand. S Nov 10 (1134) £150 [Map House]

— JANSSONIUS, JOANNES. - Mappa Aestivarum insularum, alias Barmudas. Amst., [c.1658]. 390mm by 510mm, hand-colored. Tissued. S Nov 10 (1113) £200 [Druett]

— JANSSONIUS, JOANNES. - Nova Anglia Novum Belgium et Virginia. Amst., [c.1636]. 385mm by 500mm, colored in a contemp hand. S Apr 24 (255) £500

MAPS & CHARTS

[George] Anr Ed. Amst., [c.1650]. 390mm by 505mm, hand-colored in outline. S May 29 (1080) £400

— Janssonius, Joannes. - Venezuela com parte Australi Novae Andalusiae. Amst., [c.1650]. 37.5cm by 48.9cm, early hand-coloring. pnNY Sept 13 (386) $300

— Janvier, Antide. - L'Amerique divisee en ses principaux etats. Venice: F. Santini, [c.1780]. 48.3cm by 66.7cm, hand-colored in outline. A few slight surface marks. pnNY Sept 13 (398) $325

— Jefferys, Thomas. - Plan de l'Isle de la Grenade.... L: T. Jefferys, 1763. 485mm by 625mm, hand-colored in outline. With the ptd Explication in French & English. S Oct 23 (140) £600 [Clavreuil]

— Keulen, Gerard van. - Carte Nouvelle contenant la partie d'Amerique le plus septentrionale. Amst., [c.1710]. 52.1cm by 59.7cm, early hand-coloring. Trimmed along upper margin. pnNY Sept 13 (489) $350

— Keulen, Gerard van. - Pas-Kaart van de Grande Banq by terra Neuff. Amst., [c.1680]. 71.8cm by 59.1cm. pnNY Sept 13 (487) $275

— Keulen, Gerard van. - Pas-Kaart van de Zee Kusten in de Boght van Nieuw-Engeland. Amst., [c.1680]. 71.8cm by 59.1cm, early outline hand-coloring. Trimmed within plate along upper edge. pnNY Sept 13 (488) $800

— Laurie, Robert & Whittle, James. - A New Map of the Whole Continent of America.... L, 1794. 4 sheets joined, 1,035mm by 1,180mm, boundaries colored by hand, cartouche uncolored. Lower left corner dampstained affecting inset; 2 tears at right affecting 40mm of image; some cellotape repairs on verso. sg Apr 23 (193) $175

— Le Moyne de Morgues, Jacques. - Chorographia nobilis & opulentae Peruanae Provinciae, atque Brasiliae, quas a decimo ad quintum & quinquagesimum ferre gradum ultra aequatorem in longitudinem patere.... Frankfurt, 1592. 365mm by 444mm, completely uncolored. Map taped to overmap with tape; stains from previous cellotape at margin dges; a few clean tears in margins; 1 small hole with small loss of text on scale cartouche. sg Nov 20 (214) $1,300

— Le Moyne de Morgues, Jacques. - Florida Americae Provinciae Recens.... Frankfurt, c.1591. 370mm by 454mm. Tissue repairs without loss. S June 25 (391) £1,800

— Le Rouge, Georges Louis. - Canada et Louisiane. Paris, 1755. 24 by 20 inches, hand-coloring. Upper corner repaired. Trimmed inside plate mark. pnNY Sept 13

AMERICAN BOOK PRICES CURRENT

(399) $325

Anr copy. Strengthened on back & around margins. Trimmed to edge of map. pnNY Sept 13 (400) $225

— Lea, Philip. - A New Mapp of the Island of Jamaica. L: George Willdey, [c.1710]. 480mm by 550mm. Small hole at additional fold without loss. S Nov 10 (1144) £240 [Potter]

— Lotter, Conrad. - Carte nouvelle de l'Amerique Angloise.... Augsburg, [c.1780]. 492mm by 602mm, hand-colored in outline. pnNY Sept 13 (401) $325

Anr copy. Margins creased. pnNY Sept 13 (402) $400

— Marggraff, Georg. - Brasilia qua parte paret Belgis. Amst., 1659. 9 sheets joined as 3, trimmed to plate marks & laid on large paper as folding sections, 1,170mm by 1,560mm. S Oct 23 (141) £7,000 [Israel]

— Mercator, Gerard. - America Meridionalis. [Amst., c.1610, or later]. 362mm by 500mm, old hand-coloring. French text on verso Some worming around edges. pnNY Dec 10 (224) $275

— Mercator, Gerard. - America sive India Nova. [Duisberg, 1595, or later]. 365mm by 456mm. Hand-colored Centerfold repaired. pnNY Sept 13 (405) $1,900

Anr Ed. [Amst., c.1628]. 375mm by 470mm, old hand-coloring. Some browning & staining, mainly in margins; torn with loss in upper cover. French text on verso. pnNY Dec 10 (223) $1,000

Anr copy. 368mm by 462mm, colored. Some discoloration. French text on verso. S Oct 23 (386) £850 [Burden]

— Mercator, Gerard. - Mappa aestivarum insularum, alias Bermudas.... Amst., [c.1633, or later]. 390mm by 520mm, hand-colored, split at fold. S May 29 (1078) £170

— Mitchell, John. - A Map of the British and French Dominions in North America. L, 1755. 8 sheets mtd & dissected in 2 parts each of 36 sections, totalling 1,350mm by 1,980mm, folding into 4t0 paper-covered slipcase. Hand-colored in outline. Small tear in western part at a sectional joint without apparent loss. S June 25 (369) £11,000 [Voorhees]

Anr Ed. [L], 13 Feb 1755. 8 sheets totalling 1,320mm by 1,940mm. Traces of outline color, mtd on linen, framed. Some surface abrasions, tears & closed tears & stains; some defs affecting image. Sold w.a.f. P May 13 (13) $8,000

— Moll, Hermann. - Map of South America. L, [c.1720]. 580mm by 960mm, hand-colored in outline, hand-colored title cartouche. Few tears in margins, affecting image. sg Nov 20 (219) $275

1986 - 1987 · BOOKS

— MOLL, HERMANN. - A New and Exact Map of the Dominions of the King of Great Britain on ye Continent of North America. [L, c.1755]. 1,015 mm by 610mm, colored in outline. Def at 1 margin affecting neatline. S Oct 23 (405) £1,400 [Map]
— MORTIER, PIERRE. - Cartier nouvelle de l'Amerique angloise. Amst., [c.1700]. 585mm by 905mm, hand-colored in outline. Marginal repairs without loss of surface. S June 25 (370) £1,000 [Voorhees]
— MORTIER, PIERRE. - Le Golfe de Mexique et les Isles Voisine. Amst., [1700 or later]. 600mm by 850mm, colored in wash & outline in a contemp hand. S Oct 23 (429) £500 [Berryman]
— MUENSTER, SEBASTIAN. - Tabola dell'Isole nuove.... Bascl: H. Petri, [1571]. 254mm by 336mm. Browned & creased at centerfold. S Jan 12 (246) £750 [George]
— MUENSTER, SEBASTIAN. - Tabula novarum insularum - Die Nieuw Welt [Basel, c.1550]. 26cm by 34.25cm. 4 worm holes in image; marginal foxing; taped to mat. pnNY Dec 10 (234) $600
— NOLIN, JEAN BAPTISTE THE YOUNGER. - L'Amerique dressee sur les relations les plus recentes. Paris, 1775. 4 sheets joined in 1, with attached border, 1,225mm by 1,425mm, hand-colored by a contemp hand. Some strengthening & restoration at folds. S Oct 23 (391) £2,400 [Potter]
— OGILBY, JOHN. - Portus Acapulco. L, [c.1670]. 29.1cm by 35.6cm, early hand-coloring. Some foxing. pnNY Sept 13 (433) $170
— ORTELIUS, ABRAHAM. - Americae sive novi orbis, nova descriptio. [Antwerp, c.1579]. 370mm by 505mm, hand-colored. Faint marginal browning. S Oct 23 (392) £950 [Ross]
Anr Ed. [Antwerp, 1579-84]. 350mm by 480mm, hand-colored. Hole & stain in margin. sg Apr 23 (226) $1,200
Anr Ed. [Antwerp, 1603]. 352mm by 457mm. Center-fold browned, lower part torn at fold. pnNY Sept 13 (439) $2,000
Anr copy. 370mm by 505mm. Latin text on verso. S Jan 12 (245) £900 [Pantezelos]
Anr copy. 368mm by 500mm. Repaired at fold without loss. S July 14 (745) £550
Anr Ed. [Antwerp, c.1612]. 368mm by 500mm, colored in a contemp hand. Latin text on verso. S Apr 24 (250) £850 [George]
— ORTELIUS, ABRAHAM. - La Florida, Guastecan, Peruviae, Auriferae Regionis typus. [Antwerp, c.1570]. 33cm by 45.7cm. pnNY Sept 13 (440) $300
Anr copy. Early hand-coloring. pnNY Sept 13 (441) $650
— ORTELIUS, ABRAHAM. - La Florida; Guastecan Reg.; Peruviae auriferae regionis. [Antwerp, c.1595]. 341mm by 462mm, colored in a contemp hand. S July 14 (761) £320
— ORTELIUS, ABRAHAM. - Hispaniae Novae.... [Antwerp, c.1580]. 340mm by 500mm, hand-colored. S Nov 10 (1123) £240 [McCann]
— PALAIRET, JEAN. - Carte des possessions angloises.... Amst., 1755. 410mm by 565mm, hand-colored in outline with several areas fully hand-colored. sg Apr 23 (227) $225
Anr Ed. [N.p., 1775]. 417mm by 575mm, hand-colored. S May 29 (1082) £300
— PTOLEMAEUS, CLAUDIUS. - Novae Insulae XVII Nova Tabula. Basel, [c.1542]. 25.4cm by 34.3cm, early hand-coloring. Repaired. pnNY Sept 13 (459) $1,500
— PTOLEMAEUS, CLAUDIUS. - Tabula Terre Nova. Basel, [c.1542]. 28.5cm by 41.9cm, early hand-coloring. Centerfold repaired at upper margin; 2 wormholes along lower margin. pnNY Sept 13 (460) $1,600
— SANSON D'ABBEVILLE, NICOLAS. - Amerique septentrionale.... [Paris,] 1674. 470mm by 590mm, hand-colored. Backed with tissue. S Feb 24 (450) £380 [Smiley]
Anr Ed. Paris, 1685. 543mm by 872mm, hand-colored in outline. S Oct 23 (406) £480 [Potter]
Anr Ed. [Paris,] 1691. 584mm by 887mm, early hand-coloring. Center-fold strengthened. Trimmed to within plate along lower margin. pnNY Sept 13 (464) $700
Anr Ed. Paris: H. Jaillot, 1696. 557mm by 865mm, early hand-coloring Foxed. pnNY Sept 13 (465) $375
Anr Ed. Amst.: P. Portier, [c.1710]. 445mm by 585mm, hand-colored in wash & outline; framed. Split at fold without loss. S July 14 (768) £160
— SANSON, N. - Le Nouveau Mexique, et la Floride.... Paris, 1656. 310mm by 545mm, hand-colored in outline. S Oct 23 (395) £1,050 [Burden]
— SCHENK, PETER & VALK, GERARD. - America Septentrionalis. Amst, [early 18th cent]. 49cm by 57cm, partly hand-colored. Strengthened, slight foxing. pnNY Sept 13 (470) $650
Anr Ed. Amst., [c.1730]. 45.7cm by 54.6cm, partly hand-colored. Torn & repaired on lower part of centerfold. pnNY Sept 13 (471) $750
— SELLER, JOHN. - Novissima et Accuratissima Insulae Jamaicae descriptio. L, [1670-71]. Proof copy before coats-of-arms, rhumb lines, Septentrio in upper margin & the banner lettered Insulae Insignia. 425mm by 540mm, hand-colored in outline with embellishments fully colored. Lower blank

MAPS & CHARTS

margin a little frayed. S Nov 10 (11141) £2,200 [Quaritch]
— SENEX, JOHN. - A New Map of America. L, [1721 or later]. 476mm by 579mm, early hand-coloring. Slight wormholes in lower corner. pnNY Sept 13 (472) $500
— SEUTTER, MATTHAEUS. - Novus Orbis sive America meridionalis et septentrionalis. Augsburg, [c.1720, or later]. 495mm by 570mm, hand-colored; cartouches may be later hand-coloring. With 2 small wormholes in image. sg Apr 23 (233) $600
Anr Ed. Augsburg, [c.1745]. 495mm by 570mm, partially hand-colored. Discoloration & short tear at fold without loss. S July 14 (743) £280
— SLANEY, EDWARD. - Tabula Iamaicae Insulae.... L, 1678. 1st State. 442mm by 621mm, partly colored, laid on thick paper. S Nov 10 (1118) £360 [Burgess]
— SPEED, JOHN. - America.... L, [1676]. 410mm by 515mm, hand-colored in outline, framed. Soiled at lower fold. Ck May 15 (242) £600
— SPEED, JOHN. - A Map of Jamaica & Barbados. L: Basset & Chiswell, [1676]. 395mm by 410mm. Some discoloration. S Oct 23 (389) £900 [Marsden]
— VAN LANGEREN, A. - Delineatio omnium orarum totius australis partis Americae. [Amst., 1596 or later]. 386mm by 545mm. Fold wear. S Oct 23 (433) £400 [Franks]
— VISSCHER, CARL JANSZ. - Verovering vande Silver-Vloot inde Bay Matanca. Amst., 1628. 365mm by 400mm. Marginal tear. S Nov 10 (1159) £180 [Potter]
— VISSCHER, NIKOLAUS JANSSON. - Insulae Americanae in Oceano Septentrionali.... [Amst., c.1670]. 47.6cm by 57.2cm, early hand-coloring. Sheet strengthened. pnNY Sept 13 (492) $425
— VISSCHER, NIKOLAUS JANSSON. - Jamaica, Americae Septentrionalis ampla insula. Amst., [1680?]. 1st State. 510mm by 590mm, hand-colored. Added upper margin. S Nov 10 (1119) £220 [Map House]
— VISSCHER, NIKOLAUS JANSSON. - Nova Tabula Geographica complectens Boreraliorem AMericae partem.... [Amst., c.1692]. 595mm by 900mm, hand-colored. S Oct 23 (402) £850 [Potter]
— WALDSEEMUELLER, MARTIN. - Tabula terre nova. Strassburg, [c.1520]. 370mm by 445mm, Hand-colored. With small neatly infilled wormhole at fold. S Oct 23 (390) £3,400 [Map]
— WILSON, C. - Barbadoes. L, 1881. 645mm by 455mm, canvas-backed. S Nov 10 (1112) £240 [Quaritch]
— WYLD, JAMES. - Map of North America.... L, 1824-25. 2d Ed. 585mm by 535mm, hand-colored in outline. pn Mar 5 (411) £110 [Whiteson]

AMERICAN BOOK PRICES CURRENT

— ZATTA, ANTONIO. - Il Canada, le colonie inglesi con La Luiglana e Floridu. Venice, 1778. 12 by 16 inches, hand-colored in outline. T Jan 22 (143) £100
— ZATTA, ANTONIO. - Messico ovvero Nuova Spagna. Venice, 1785. 12 by 16 inches, hand-colored in outline. T Mar 19 (203) £130

Asia

— Asia, partium orbis maxima. Antwerp: Heirs of Gerard de Jode, 1593. 370mm by 450mm. S Apr 23 (324) £1,200 [Potter]
— AA, PIETER VAN DER. - L'Asie selon les nouvelles observations. Leiden, [c.1720]. 49.5cm by 66cm, early hand-coloring. Trimmed into plate along upper margin; centerfold repaired. pnNY Sept 13 (486) $275
— ADRICHOM, CHRISTIANUS. - Palestine sive Terrae Sanctae. Paris, 1646. 40cm by 54.6cm, early hand-coloring. Trimmed along horizontal margins; repaired along other margins. pnNY Sept 13 (304) $120
— ANVILLE, JEAN BAPTISTE BOURGUIGON D'. - La Palestine, les tribus, et Jerusalem. Venice, 1783. 45.1cm by 55.2cm, hand-colored. pnNY Sept 13 (339) $275
— BLAEU, WILLEM & JAN. - Asia noviter delineata. [Amst., c.1640, or later]. 408mm by 550mm. French text on verso. Hand-colored. Repaired along lower margin. pnNY Sept 13 (319A) $700; pnNY Sept 13 (319) $700
Anr copy. 410mm by 558mm, hand-colroed in outline, borders fully-hand-colored. Margins trimmed. sg Apr 23 (255) $650
Anr Ed. [Amst., c.1662]. 410mm by 550mm. Framed. S Nov 18 (1195) £400 [Hendrick]
— BLAEU, WILLEM & JAN. - Cyprus insula. [Amst., c.1650]. 380mm by 500mm, hand-colored in outline. Marginal stains. S Feb 23 (115) £180 [Hadji]
— BLAEU, WILLEM & JAN. - Moluccae insulae celeberrimae. Amst., [1635 or later]. 373mm by 488mm, principal areas fully hand-colored, as are title & scale cartouches & decorative inset of Bachian Island. sg Nov 20 (260) $175
— BLAEU, WILLEM & JAN. - Terra Sancta quae in Sacris Terra promissionis olim Palestina. Amst., 1629. 379mm by 495mm, hand-colored. Center creased; tear in lower part. pnNY Sept 13 (320) $300
Anr Ed. Amst., [1663]. 384mm by 487mm, hand-colored in outline, framed. Minor discoloration. S Feb 24 (432) £160 [Swaen]
— BOWLES, CARINGTON. - New and Accurate Map of Asia. L, [1789]. 101.6cm by 120.7cm, hand-colored, 4 sheets laid down

on canvas. One tear reparied. pnNY Sept 13 (325) $300
— BRAUN, GEORG & HOGENBERG, FRANZ. - Aden; Mombaza; Quiloa; Cefala. Amst., 1575. 340mm by 470mm, Ck May 8 (203) £180
— BRAUN, GEORG & HOGENBERG, FRANZ. - Byzantium, nunc Constantinopolis. [Cologne, c.1590]. 325mm by 475mm, hand-colored. S Nov 10 (1024) £240 [Shalabi]
— BRAUN, GEORG & HOGENBERG, FRANZ. - Hierosolyma. [Cologne, c.1590]. 342mm by 490mm, framed. Some creases. S July 14 (726) £120
— BRIET, PHILIPPE. - Palestinae delineatio ad geographiae canones revocata. Paris: P Mariette, [c.1641]. 395mm by 548mm, colored in outline. S Nov 10 (1034) £140 [Kurymann]
— BRIET, PHILIPPE. - Royaume du Japon. Paris, [c.1660]. 37.5cm by 52.7cm, hand-colored in outline. pnNY Sept 13 (326) $400
— BUENTING, HEINRICH. - Reisen der Kinder von Israel aus Egypten. [Helmstadt: Jacob Lucius, c.1582]. 263mm by 394mm, hand-colored in outline with seas fully colored. Margins trimmed; corners rounded; fold breaks; silked; some rubbing; coloring probably later. sg Sept 25 (199) $450
— CORONELLI, V. M. - Isola del Giapone e Penisola di Corea. Venice, [c.1696]. 455mm by 610mm. S Oct 23 (469) £620 [Map]
— CORONELLI, V. M. - Royaume de Siam.... Paris, 1742. 610mm by 450mm. S Feb 23 (295) £400 [Potter]
— DE JODE, CORNELIS. - China. Antwerp, [1593]. 360mm by 440mm, hand-colored. S Apr 23 (326) £1,300 [Potter]
— DE WIT, FREDERICK. - Aegypti recentior descriptio. [Amst., c.1670]. 40.6cm by 50.8cm, early hand-coloring. Slight tear at centerfold along lower margin. pnNY Sept 13 (358) $190
— DE WIT, FREDERICK. - Nova Orbia Tabula. [Amst., c.1680]. 463mm by 563mm, early hand-coloring. Strengthened on back; center-fp;d × ptjer s[pts stremgtjemed pm sirface. pnNY Sept 13 (366) $1,200
— DE WIT, FREDERICK. - Tabula Indiae Orientalis. [Amst., 1662, but 1680 or later]. 18 by 22 inches, hand-colored in wash & outline. Some browning. T Mar 19 (152) £180
— DE WIT, FREDERICK. - Tabula Tartariae et majoris partis Regni Chinae. Amst., [c.1680]. 43.8cm by 52.7cm, hand-colored. pnNY Sept 13 (362) $200
— DE WIT, FREDERICK. - Terra Sancta. [Amst.], 1670. 18 by 22 inches. Slight wear to lower fold. Ck Feb 27 (143) £100
Anr copy. 463mm by 563mm, early hand-coloring. Sheet strengthened, a few holes & thin tears. pnNY Sept 13 (359) $425
Anr copy. Creased along center-fold, repaired at lower corner, strengthened, some spotting. pnNY Sept 13 (360) $200
— DE WIT, FREDERICK. - Terra Sancta Promissionis olim Palestina. Paris, 1664. 40cm by 52.1cm, early hand-coloring. pnNY Sept 13 (361) $225
— DUDLEY, SIR ROBERT. - Carta particolare della Grande Isola del'Giapone e di Iezo.... [Florence, c.1647]. 485mm by 755mm S June 25 (452) £1,700
— FER, NICOLAS DE. - Descriptio acurata Terrae Promissae.... Paris, 1720. 45.7cm by 72.4cm, early hand-coloring. pnNY Sept 13 (340) $375
— FORLANI, PAOLO. - La Nuova et esatta desrittione del la Soria.... Venice, 1566. 263mm by 342mm. Trimmed to platemark; broad margins added. S Oct 23 (358) £1,000 [Arader]
— GASTALDI, GIACOMO. - Il Disegno della primm parte del Asia.... Venice. Fabio Licinus, 1559. 2 sheets joined, c.435mm by 735mm. S Oct 23 (366) £1,700 [Arader]
— GASTALDI, GIACOMO. - Il Disegno della seconda parte dell'Asia.... Venice, 1561. 470mm by 745mm, 2 sheets joined. S Oct 23 (361) £2,200 [Map]
— GASTALDI, GIACOMO. - Il Disegno della terza parte dell'Asia. Venice, [1561]. 629mm by 732mm, in 2 sheets joined Some waterstain to margins. S Oct 23 (467) £2,500 [Map]
— GERMANUS, NICOLAUS. - Tabula Moderna Terre Sancte. Ulm: Leonardus Hol, 1482. 248mm by 527mm, in contemp color, with the seas & lakes painted a dark blue, tribal boundaries in red & mountain ranges emphasized in sepia. Repair & browning at fold. S Apr 23 (226) £4,500 [Lewin]
— HARENBERG, I. C. - Palaestina seu Terra olim Sancta.... Nuremberg: Heredes Homaniani, 1744. 463mm by 545mm, hand-colored in outline, cartouches fully colored. Margins browned & stained. sg Sept 25 (206) $100
— HARENBURG, J. C. - Palestina. Nuremberg, 1750. 49.5cm by 57.2cm, partly hand-colored. Some foxing. pnNY Sept 13 (367) $140
— HASIUS, JOHANN MATTHIAS. - Asia. Nuremberg, 1744. 50.8cm by 58.4cm, early hand-coloring. Marginal foxing. pnNY Sept 13 (368) $150
— HOMANN, JOHANN BAPTIST. - Judaea seu Palaestina.... Nuremberg, [c.1720]. 490mm by 570mm, hand-colored, with uncolored title cartouche. A few wormholes in border repaired. sg Nov 20 (331) $100
Anr copy. 483mm by 492mm, hand-col-

ored in outline, with fully hand-colored title, scale & informational cartouches. Paper tape on margin edges; a few scuffed areas. sg Nov 20 (332) $130
— HONDIUS, HENRICUS & JANSSON, J. - Asia, recens summa cura delineata. Amst., [1633]. 375mm by 500mm, early hand-coloring; strengthened, some browning. Latin text on verso. pnNY Sept 13 (381) $300
— HONDIUS, JODOCUS. - Situs terrae promissionis.... [Amst., c.1630]. 14½ by 19½ inches, Early hand-coloring. French text on verso. pnNY Sept 13 (376) $425
Anr copy. Early hand-coloring. Repaired along upper part. Latin text on verso. pnNY Sept 13 (377) $300
Anr copy. Early hand-coloring. Lower margin holed. Dutch text on verso. pnNY Sept 13 (383) $275
— HONDIUS, JODOCUS. - Tartaria. [Amst., c.1613]. 367mm by 493mm, uncolored. Tear in lower margin not affecting imae; cellotape-repaired on verso. sg Nov 20 (333) $110
— JANSSON, JAN. - Indiae orientalis nova descriptio. Amst., [1630, but 1638 or later]. 390mm by 510mm. German text on verso. S Oct 23 (508) £350 [Snow]
— JANSSONIUS, JOANNES. - China. [Amst., c.1642]. 405mm by 494mm, colored in an early hand. S Jan 12 (306) £240 [George]
Anr Ed. Amst., [c.1650]. 40.6cm by 50.2cm, early hand-coloring. Some staining; centerfold browned & backed. pnNY Sept 13 (387) $225
Anr copy. 41.3cm by 50.2cm, Some worming. pnNY Sept 13 (388) $375
— JANSSONIUS, JOANNES. - Japoniae. Amst., [c.1650]. 33.7cm by 44.5cm, early hand-coloring. Some browning down centerfold; slight stains to lower margin; wormhole in upper margin. pnNY Sept 13 (391) $350
— JANSSONIUS, JOANNES. - Japoniae Nova Descriptio. Amst., [c.1650]. 34.3cm by 45.1cm, early hand-coloring. Many repairs to surface. pnNY Sept 13 (392) $170
— JANSSONIUS, JOANNES. - Japoniae Terrae Esonis. Amst., [c.1650]. 45.7cm by 55.9cm, early hand-coloring. Lower portion of centerfold slightly torn & repaired. pnNY Sept 13 (393) $375
— JANSSONIUS, JOHANNES. - Nova et accurata Iaponiae, terrae Esonis...descriptio. [Amst., 1659 or later]. 455mm by 555mm, hand-colored in outline Minor flaws repaired. French text. S Nov 18 (1205) £180 [Hendrick]
— JANSSONIUS, JOANNES. - Situs Terrae Promissionis. Amst., [c.1650]. 37.5cm by 49.5cm, early hand-coloring. Centerfold worn & creased in lower margin. pnNY Sept 13 (394) $250
Anr Ed. Amst., [1658 or later]. 368mm by 488mm, hand-colored in outline. Margins trimmed; some browning at centerfold line. sg Sept 25 (207) $375
— JANSSONIUS, JOANNES. - Tribus Juda. Amst., [c.1650]. 8 sheets joined, 85.1cm by 176.5cm, early hand-coloring & gold leaf. Tear on 1st sheet at lower left margin. pnNY Sept 13 (395) $1,700
— KAEMPFER, ENGELBERT. - Regni Japoniae. Augsburg: Seutter, [c.1745]. 480mm by 560mm, hand-colored. Split at fold without loss. S Jan 12 (308) £320 [Potter]
— MERCATOR, GERARD. - Asia. Amst., [c.1609]. 38cm by 47.5cm, old hand-coloring. pnNY Dec 10 (227) $200
Anr Ed. Amst., [c.1610]. 38.1cm by 47cm, early hand-coloring. Marginal soiling. pnNY Sept 13 (406) $275; pnNY Sept 13 (407) $300
— MERCATOR, GERARD. - Japonia. [Amst., 1606, or later]. 340mm by 442mm. hand-colored. Torn & repaired, strenthened along back of center-fold. French text on verso. pnNY Sept 13 (408) $500
— MERCATOR, GERARD. - Tataria. Amst., [c.1610]. 34.3cm by 49.5cm, early hand-coloring. Marginal tears. pnNY Sept 13 (409) $375
— MERCATOR, GERARD. - Terra Sancta quae in Sacris Terra promissionis olim Palestina. [Amst.: Hondius, 1606]. 355mm by 500mm, old hand-coloring. Some wear down centerfold. pnNY Dec 10 (230) $475
— MOLL, HERMANN. - Asia. L: Bowles & Overton, [c.1725]. 580mm by 950mm, hand-colored in outline. Additional folds strengthened. S Nov 10 (1198) £200 [Castle]
— MOXON, JOSEPH. - Canaan or the Land of Promise. L, [c.1680]. 31.7cm by 435.1cm, early hand-coloring. Some foxing. pnNY Sept 13 (422) $250
— MOXON, JOSEPH. - Israel's Peregrination. L, [c.1680]. 32.4cm by 47cm, early hand-coloring. Slight tears on margins; sheet strengthened. pnNY Sept 13 (423) $160
— MOXON, JOSEPH. - Paradise or the Garden of Eden. L, [c.1680]. 29.1cm by 47cm, hand-colored. pnNY Sept 13 (424) $130
— MUENSTER, SEBASTIAN. - Destruccio Jherosolime. [N.p., c.1560]. 44.5cm by 62.23cm, early hand-coloring. Wear along centerfold; some marginal soiling. pnNY Sept 13 (428) $350
Anr copy. 44.5cm by 62.2cm, Centerfold worn & repaired. pnNY Sept 13 (429) $275
— MUENSTER, SEBASTIAN. - Das heylig juedisch Land.... [N.p., c.1560]. 25.4cm by 34.3cm, early hand-coloring. Fold breaks. pnNY Sept 13 (425) $200

1986 - 1987 · BOOKS

— MUENSTER, SEBASTIAN. - India Extrema. [Basel, after 1531]. 11 by 13 inches, hand-colored, framed. cb Nov 6 (14) $750

— ORTELIUS, ABRAHAM. - Abrahami Patriarchae Peregrinatio et Vita. Antwerp, [c.1590]. 356mm by 465mm, colored. S Nov 10 (1041) £460 [Van de Broodicol]

Anr Ed. Antwerp, [1624]. 350mm by 455mm, completely uncolored. sg Nov 20 (335) $300

— ORTELIUS, ABRAHAM. - Asia nova descriptio. [Antwerp, c.1584]. 370mm by 486mm. Marginal stains. S Jan 12 (303) £190 [Perini]

— ORTELIUS, ABRAHAM. - Asiae nova descriptio. [Antwerp, c.1570]. 368mm by 502mm, early hand-coloring Small burn hole; overall browning. Latin text on verso.. pnNY Sept 13 (443) $300; pnNY Sept 13 (444) $400

Anr copy. 368mm by 495mm, early hand-coloring pnNY Sept 13 (445) $350

Anr Ed. [Antwerp, 1574]. 375mm by 485mm, hand-colored. Some surface dirt. S Feb 24 (476) £140 [Orient]

Anr Ed. [Antwerp, 1595]. 370mm by 485mm, hand-colored Latin text on verso. S Nov 18 (1200) £280 [McCann]

Anr copy. 370mm by 485mm, colored in a contemp hand. Latin text on verso. S July 14 (827) £300

Anr copy. 14.5 by 19.5 inches, hand-colored T Mar 19 (176) £180

— ORTELIUS, ABRAHAM. - Chinae, olim Sinarum regionis, nova descriptio. Antwerp, 1584. 365mm by 470mm. Small stains; light browning. S Nov 18 (1202) £240 [Burgess]

— ORTELIUS, ABRAHAM. - Iaponiae insulae descriptio.... L: for Norton & Bill, [1606]. 355mm by 485mm. With English text. S Nov 10 (1206) £420 [Potter]

— ORTELIUS, ABRAHAM. - Indiae orientalis insularumque adiacentium typus. [Antwerp, 1570, or later]. 350mm by 495mm, hand-colored in outline with fully colored cartouche. Small hole in image at fold line; lower portion of fold line paper-reinforced on verso. sg Apr 23 (267) $300

Anr Ed. [Antwerp, 1603]. 345mm by 495mm. S Feb 24 (483) £380 [Orient]

— ORTELIUS, ABRAHAM. - Palestinae sive totius terrae promissionis. [Antwerp, 1570 or later]. 350mm by 460mm. pn June 18 (375) £220 [Goodall]

Anr copy. 13.5 by 18 inches, hand-colored. Strengthened along centerfold. Latin text on verso. T Mar 19 (181) £110

— ORTELIUS, ABRAHAM. - Peregrinationis Divi Pauli Typus Corographicus. [Antwerp, 1579]. 35cm by 50cm, early hand-coloring

MAPS & CHARTS

Latin text on verso. pnNY Sept 13 (446) $350

— ORTELIUS, ABRAHAM. - Tartary. [Antwerp, 1579]. 470mm by 350mm. Discolored along center fold. pn Nov 20 (348) £200 [Barbican]

Anr copy. 35cm by 47cm, early hand-coloring. Spanish text on verso. Torn in lower part of center-fold. pnNY Sept 13 (448) $385

Anr Ed. [Antwerp,c.1590]. 347mm by 470mm. S Feb 24 (482) £260 [Subunso]

Anr Ed. [Antwerp, c.1595]. 347mm by 470mm, hand-colored. S Feb 24 (442) £140 [Arens]

Anr Ed. [L: Norton & Bill, 1606]. 347mm by 470mm. S Feb 24 (441) £200 [Potter]

— ORTELIUS, ABRAHAM. - Terra Sancta.... [Amst., c.1572 or later]. 14 by 20 inches, early hand coloring. Latin text on verso. Slight hole at center-fold. pnNY Sept 13 (449) $500

Anr copy. Center-fold holed & browned. pnNY Sept 13 (450) $300

Anr Ed. [Antwerp, 1584]. 367mm by 505mm. Framed Marginal worming. S Jan 12 (230) £180 [Potter]

— ORTELIUS, ABRAHAM. - Typus Chorographicus, celebrium locorum in regno Iudae et Israhel. [Antwerp, 1586, or later]. 356mm by 463mm, early hand-coloring. pnNY Sept 13 (453) $350

— PRICE, CHARLES. - Asia. L, 1714 [but 1715]. 625mm by 970mm, hand-colored in outline. S Oct 23 (466) £350 [Duchauffour]

— PTOLEMAEUS, CLAUDIUS. - Geographica: quarta Asie tabula [Iraq, Syria, Lebanon & Northern Arabia]. [Ulm, 1482]. 286mm by 497mm, in contemp color, framed. Waterstain touching upper border. S Apr 24 (225) £2,800 [Arader]

— PTOLEMAEUS, CLAUDIUS. - Quarta Asiae Tabula. [Venice: J. Pentius de Leucho, 1511]. 2 leaves, 398mm by 523mm. Marginal waterstain. S Apr 24 (227) £900 [Leach]

— PTOLEMAEUS, CLAUDIUS. - Sexta Asie tabula. [Venice: J. Pentius de Leucho, 1511]. 332mm by 490mm. S Oct 23 (363) £900 [Map]

— ROBERT DE VAUGONDY, GILLES. - Carte de la terre des Hebreux ou Israelites.... Paris: Delamarche, [c.1750]. 490mm by 673mm, hand-colored in outline, cartouche uncolored. sg Sept 25 (224) $225

— ROBERT DE VAUGONDY, G. & D. - L'Empire du Japon. Venice, 1750. 48.3cm by 55.9cm Hand-coloring. pnNY Sept 13 (350) $200

Anr Ed. Venice, 1778. 18.25 by 21 inches Early hand-coloring. pnNY Sept 13 (351)

MAPS & CHARTS

$250
— ROBERT DE VAUGONDY. - La Judee ou Terre Sainte. Venice, 1779. 48.3cm by 60.9cm, hand-colored. pnNY Sept 13 (352) $225
Anr copy. 59cm by 61.6cm, early hand-coloring. pnNY Sept 13 (353) $200
— ROBERT DE VAUGONDY, GILLES & DIDIER. - Terre de chanaan ou Terre Promise a Abraham.... Paris, c.1750. 425mm by 560mm, hand-colored in outline. Small portions of verso mended or tape-reinforced; mat burn outside platemark. sg Apr 23 (269) $100
— SANSON D'ABBEVILLE, NICOLAS. - L'Asia. Rome: G. G. Rossi, [c.1687 or later]. 406mm by 559mm, early hand-coloring. Repaired & touched up on upper centerfold. Minor worming. pnNY Sept 13 (466) $350
— SANSON D'ABBEVILLE, NICOLAS. - L'Asie. [Paris, c.1690]. 572mm by 876mm, early hand-coloring Text along upper edge of map; slight spotting. pnNY Sept 13 (467) $300
— SANSON D'ABBEVILLE, NICOLAS EDME. - Judea seu Terra Sancta.... Paris: H. Jaillot, 1691. 572mm by 835mm, hand-colored. Small tear in lower centerfold line, affecting image. sg Sept 25 (228) $400
— SANSON D'ABBEVILLE, GUILLAUME. - Judea seu terra Sancta quae hebraeorum.... Amst: P. Schenk, [c.1705]. 49cm by 58.5cm, early hand-coloring. Slight surface wear, centerfold strengthened. pnNY Sept 13 (468) $325
— SCHEDEL, HARTMANN. - Destruccio Iherosolime. [Nuremberg: A. Koberger, 1493]. 255mm by 530mm. S Nov 10 (1030) £300 [Potter]
— SENEX, JOHN. - A New Map of Asia. [L, c.1720]. 559mm by 483mm. hand-colored. pnNY Sept 13 (473) $300
Anr copy. 572mm by 483mm. Partly hand-colored Torn & repaired at bottom of center-fold; frayed along bottom margin. pnNY Sept 13 (474) $225
— SEUTTER, MATTHAEUS. - Regio Canaan seu Terra Promissionis.... [Augsberg, c.1730]. 50.2cm by 58.4cm, early hand-coloring. Centerfold repaired at lower edge; library stamp on left edge. pnNY Sept 13 (475) $325
— SPEED, JOHN. - Asia.... L: T. Bassett & R. Chiswell, 1626 [but 1676, or later]. 520mm by 400mm. pn Oct 23 (427) £170 [Antiques]
Anr copy. 515mm by 400mm. pn Oct 23 (440) £260 [Antiques]
— SPEED, JOHN. - Canaan. L: T. Bassett & R. Chiswell, [1676]. 387mm by 520mm, hand-colored in outline, framed. Minor discoloration. S Feb 23 (434) £240 [Halpenn]

AMERICAN BOOK PRICES CURRENT

— SPEED, JOHN. - The Kingdom of Persia.... L: Bassett & Chiswell, [1676]. 15.5 by 20.5 inches Ck Feb 27 (13) £150
Anr copy. 15.5 by 20.5 inches, early hand-coloring pnNY Sept 13 (479) $475
— SPEED, JOHN. - Oxfordshire.... L: J. Sudbury & G. Humble, [1614]. 380mm by 520mm, partly colored, framed. Minor repair at fold without loss. S Nov 17 (736) £280 [Swift]
— STOLZ, TILEMANN. - Typus Chorographicus, celebrium locorum in Regno Iudae et Israhel. [Antwerp, c.1595]. 350mm by 460mm, hand-colored. S Nov 10 (1047) £260 [Halperin]
— VALCK, GERALD. - L'Asie. Amst., c[c.1720 or later]. 49.5cm by 59.7cm, early hand-coloring. Centerfold strengthened. pnNY Sept 13 (485) $275
— VAN ADRICHOM, C. - Ierusalem, et suburbia eius. Cologne, 1584 [or later]. 727mm by 477mm, hand-colored. S Oct 23 (365) £620 [Tooley]
Anr Ed. [Cologne, c.1588]. 727mm by 477mm, framed. S Nov 10 (1026) £260 [Halperin]
— VAN ADRICHOM, C. - Pianta della Regia Citta di Gerusalemme. [Verona, 1620?]. 275mm by 470mm. Imprint a little weak. S Nov 10 (1028) £450 [Naytalin]
— VAN DEN KEERE, PIETER. - Asiae nova descriptio. Amst., [1614]. 435mm by 560mm, colored in a contemp hand. Laid down & shaved at neatlines. S Jan 12 (302) £360 [Israel]
— VAN KEULEN, JOHANNES. - Pas-Kaart van het in-en opkomen van de Rivier van Quantong.... Amst., [c.1730]. 500mm by 570mm, colored in a contemp hand. S June 25 (155) £1,050
— VAN LANGREN, A. F. - Exacta & accurata delineatio cum orarum maritimorum tum etiam locorum terrestrium...China, Cauchinchina.... [Amst., 1595 or later]. 385mm by 525mm. Some fold wear; shaved to plate-mark in places. S Oct 23 (468) £900 [Potter]
— VAN LINSCHOTEN, J. H. - Deliniantur in hac tabula.... [Amst.: C. Claesz, 1595 or later]. 390mm by 540mm. Some wear at folds without apparent loss. S Oct 23 (362) £550 [Map]
— VAN MEURS, JACOB. - Pars Maxima Tribus Juda versa Orientem. [c.1670]. 58.5cm by 120.7cm, early hand-coloring. Some waterstaining; trimmed to plate mark. pnNY Sept 13 (490) $900
— VISSCHER, NICOLAUS. - Asiae in Tabula Geographica Delineatio. Amst.: Peter Schenk, [c.1740]. 488mm by 580mm, hand-colored, with uncolored cartouche. Small area of verso paper-reinforced. sg Nov 20 (339) $130

- VISSCHER, NICOLAUS. - Asiae Nova Delineatio. Amst., [late 17th cent]. 44cm by 55cm, early hand-coloringline. pnNY Sept 13 (493) $190

  Anr copy. 550mm by 445mm, early hand-coloring. Lower part of center-fold repaired. pnNY Sept 13 (494) $140

  Anr copy. 44cm by 55cm, Rowned. pnNY Sept 13 (495) $250
- VISSCHER, NICOLAUS. - Indiae orientalis, nec non insularum adiacentium. Amst., [c.1678]. 460mm by 560mm, hand-colored. Tissued. S Nov 18 (1202) £240 [Burgess]
- VISSCHER, NICOLAUS. - Indiae Orientalis. [Amst., c.1680]. 460mm by 560mm, hand-colored in full. Tissued. S Nov 10 (1203) £280 [Deloit]
- VISSCHER, NICOLAUS. - Terra Sancta.... [Amst.], 1659. 462mm by 552mm, hand-colored. Short split at lower fold. S Nov 10 (1051) £100 [Lervin]
- VISSCHER, NIKOLAUS JANSSON. - Hierusalem. [Amst., c.1680]. 29.9cm by 38.7cm, hand-colored. Centerfold repaired & strengthened; some browning. pnNY Sept 13 (498) $500
- WALDSEEMUELLER, MARTIN. - India Orientalis. [Lyons, 1535]. 310mm by 423mm, hand-colored. S Nov 10 (1204) £300 [Map House]
- WALDSEEMUELLER, MARTIN. - Tabula Terre Sanctae. [Lyons, 1535]. 280mm by 415mm, hand-colored. S Nov 18 (1058) £400 [Lenin]

Atlantic Ocean

- BLAEU, WILLEM. - West Indische Paskaert.... Amst.: Jacobus Robyn, [c.1695?]. 790mm by 970mm, 4 sheets joined, colored in a contemp hand & heightened with gold. Folds repaired; margins repaired & strengthened; minor stains. S Apr 23 (246) £7,000 [Burgess]
- CORONELLI, VINCENZO MARIA. - Mare del Nord. Venice, [c.1690]. 450mm by 600mm. Lower corners repaired; center-fold torn & repaired. Imprint loss supplied by hand. pnNY Sept 13 (332) $400

  Anr copy. 448mm by 600mm. S Nov 18 (1092) £200 [Feldbaum]
- HONDIUS, JODOCUS. - Mappa Aestivarum Insularum, alias Barmudas. Amst., [1633 or later]. 390mm by 520mm, early hand-coloringline. Latin text on verso. pnNY Sept 13 (379) $750

  Anr copy. 390mm by 520mm, early hand-coloring Strengthened down center-fold & anr part. pnNY Sept 13 (380) $550

  Anr copy. 390mm by 520mm, hand-colored in outline. Dutch text on verso. S Jan 12 (248) £280 [George]
- SELLER, JOHN. - A General Chart of the West India's. L, [c.1675]. 428mm by 535mm, hand-colored. Margins frayed without loss. S Apr 23 (247) £600 [Hagstrom]
- VAN KEULEN, GERARD. - Nieuwe en aldereeste Afteekening.... Amst., [c.1719]. 590mm by 100mm, hand-colored. S June 25 (450) £1,600
- VAN KEULEN, JOHANNES. - Pascaerte vande Caribes. Amst., [c.1690]. 515mm by 590mm, colored in a contemp hand. S Apr 23 (284) £600 [Pulido]

Australasia

- Carte tres curieuse de la Mer du Sud contenant des remarques nouvelles...sur les ports et iles de cette mer. [Amst.: L'Honore & Chatelain, 1719 or later]. 410mm by 1,405mm, uncolored. Some stains; a few areas rubbed & very thin, 3 small areas paper-reinforced on verso. sg Nov 20 (205) $1,800
- Map of Victoria Constructed & Engraved at the Surveyor General's Office, Melbourne....bc joints breaking, corners scuffed. 72.5 by 78.5 inches, in 16 sections folded & backed orig half mor with upper cover lettered in gilt with royal arms. C Oct 15 (180) £550 [Mitchell]
- BRUE, ADRIEN HUBERT. - Oceanie ou cinquieme partie du monde.... Paris, [1817]. 980mm by 1,480mm, 4 sheets, colored in outline. S Oct 23 (507) £500 [Quaritch]
- DE WIT, FREDERICK. - Terra Australis Incognita. Amst., 1644. 43.2cm by 50.2cm, early hand-coloring. Torn down lower part of centerfold; 1 other slight tear. pnNY Sept 13 (363) $250
- DONCKER, HENDRICK. - Pascaerte van Oost Indien.... AMst., [c.1664]. 710mm by 905mm, 4 sheets joined, colored in a contemp hand & heightened with gold, richly embellished with numerous vignettes by J. Leupenius.. Some fold repairs with occasional very slight loss mostly confined to sea areas; some stains elsewhere. S Apr 23 (368) £12,500 [Arader]
- GOOS, PIETER. - Oost Indien. Wassendegraade Paskaart.... Amst., [c.1680]. 605mm by 880mm. S June 25 (489) £1,400
- SELLER, JOHN. - A Chart of the Eastermost Part of the East Indies. Wapping, [c.1676]. 445mm by 500mm, hand-colored in outline. Upper neatline shaved touching border. S June 25 (490) £900
- VAN KEULEN, JOHANNES. - Nieuwe Pascaert van Oost Indien. Amst., 1689. 500mm by 580mm, colored in a contemp hand. S July 28 (957) £380
- VISSCHER, NICOLAUS. - Indiae orientalis. Amst., [c.1682]. 18.5 inches by 22 inches, hand colored in outline. Ck Feb 27 (137) £260

MAPS & CHARTS

Canada

— BELLIN, JACQUES NICOLAS. - Partie occidentale de la Nouvelle France ou du Canada.... [Nuremberg], 1755. 44.5cm by 57.2cm, hand-colored in outline. pnNY Sept 13 (305) $400

Anr copy. 425mm by 535mm, hand-colored in outline, with uncolored cartouche. sg Nov 20 (199) $300

— BOUCHETTE, JOSEPH. - Map of the Provinces of Lower and Upper Canada.... L, 1831. 48 by 30 inches, mtd on linen & folded into bd slipcase. AVP Nov 20 (27) C$1,200 [Bib. Nat. Quebec]

— CARVER, JONATHAN. - A New Map of the Province of Quebec.... L: Sayer & Bennett, 16 Feb 1776. 490mm by 670mm, uncut & unfolded, colored in a contemp hand. S Oct 23 (136) £600 [Crete]

— CORONELLI, MARCO VINCENZO. - Canada orientale nell' America settentrionale.... [Venice, 1695]. 610mm by 465mm, hand-colored. pn Apr 30 (617) £180 [Ruddell]

— DES BARRES, J. F. W. - Annapolis Royal - St. Mary's Bay. L, 1 Jan 1781. 71.75cm by 103cm, 2 sheets joined. pnNY Dec 10 (213) $450

— DU VAL, PIERRE. - Le Canada faict par le Sieur de Champlain. Paris, 1664. 360mm by 540mm, hand-colored in outline. S Oct 23 (396) £1,800 [Martayan]

— JAILLOT, HUBERT. - Le Canada ou Partie de la Nouvelle France. Paris, 1696 [but Amst., 1700 or later]. 460mm by 605mm, hand-colored in outline. Some dampstain. S Feb 23 (154) £190 [Potter]

— JEFFERYS, THOMAS. - An Exact Chart of the River St. Laurence.... L, 1775. 945mm by 600mm, colored in outline. Small tear in center. pn Nov 20 (347) £110 [Faupel]

Celestial

— HOMANN, JOHANN BAPTIST. - Tabula Selenographica. Nuremberg, [c.1730]. 49.5cm by 58.4cm, early hand-coloring. pnNY Sept 13 (372) $325

— SEUTTER, MATTHAEUS. - Planisphaerium Coeleste. [Augsberg, c.1735]. 48.9cm by 55.9cm, early hand-coloring. pnNY Sept 13 (477) $325

Europe

— BACLER D'ALBE, LOUIS ALBERT GUILLAIN. - Carte generale du theatre de la guerre en Italie.... Paris, 1798 [An VI]. On 30 folding sheets & Carte Generale on separate folding sheet, all linen backed, in 2 contemp calf boxes. C Dec 12 (9) £240 [Israel]

— BARENTSZOON, WILLEM. - Hydrographica descriptio maris Mediterranei.... Amst., [c.1600]. 370mm by 520mm. Fold repairs. S Oct 23 (283) £500 [Orssich]

— BLAEU, WILLEM & JAN. - Europa recens descripta. [Amst., c.1662]. 410mm by 550mm, colored in a contemp hand, framed. S Nov 10 (848) £480 [Potter]

— BLAEU, WILLEM & JAN. - Pascaarte van alle de Zee-custen van Europa. Amst., 1677. 2 sheets joined, 690mm by 870mm, colored in a contemp hand & heightened with gold, embellished with imperial & royal arms in mainland areas. S Apr 23 (146) £4,900 [Arader]

— BRAUN, GEORG & HOGENBERG, FRANZ. - Moscovia. [Cologne, c.1575]. 350mm by 490mm, colored in a contemp hand. Margins faintly browned. S Nov 10 (874) £120 [Rabinovitch]

— BRUCKNER, DANIEL. - Canton Basel. Basel, 1766. 425mm by 515mm, hand-colored in wash & outline. S Oct 23 (95) £400 [Crete]

— BRUNET, R. - Carte de France levee par ordre du Roy. Paris, 1756-67. 182 sheets (some joined, each about 600mm by 930mm, all linen-backed & folding. In 13 contemp half russia wooden boxes. With carte trigonometrique & hand-colored key map in 4 sections. C Dec 12 (39) £2,000 [Israel]

— CHAFRION, JOSE. - Carta de la Rivera de Genova.... Milan, 1685. 12 sheets joined as 4 sections, 865mm by 1,900mm. S Oct 23 (89) £1,500 [Israel]

— CORONELLI, V. - Isola Regno di Candia. Venice, [c.1696]. 615mm by 460mm, uncolored. pn Apr 30 (577) £180 [Potter]

— COUTANS, GUILLAUME. - Reduction du tableau topographique de la Forest de Senart.... [N.p., c.1780]. 341mm by 445mm, folded into 8vo, hand-colored, in mor case with arms of Louis XVIII as Comte de Provence. Jeanson copy. SM Feb 28 (146) FF62,000

— DANCKERTS, JUSTUS. - Europa. AMst., [c.1670]. 4 sheets joined & laid on canvas, 880mm by 1,060mm, colored in full & heightened with gold in a contemp hand.. Slight fraying of outer blank margins; slight abrasion at junction of folds without apparent loss. S Oct 23 (100) £2,600 [Israel]

— DE FER, NICOLAS. - Principaute de Piemont Seigneurie de Verceil Duche.... Paris, 1743. 1,040mm by 390mm, in 4 uncut & unfolded sheets S Feb 23 (256) £480 [Nino]

— DE JODE, CORNELIS. - Valesiae provinciae montanae.... [Antwerp, 1593]. 385mm by 480mm. S Oct 23 (275) £250 [Mohler]

— DE JODE, GERARD. - Septentrionalium regionum Svetiae Gothiae Norvegiae Daniae.... [Antwerp, 1593]. 470mm by 495mm. Small adhesion mark at lower neatline. S Oct 23 (282) £1,700 [Map]

— DE JODE, GERARD. - Septentrionalium regionum Svetiae Gothiae Norvegiae.... Antwerp, 1593. 370mm by 495mm, colored in a contemp hand. S June 25 (261)

1986 - 1987 · BOOKS

£2,400
— DE PALMEUS, A. F. G. - Carte generale de la principaute souveraine des Isles de Malte.... Paris, [1752]. 580mm by 1,330mm, 2 sheets joined. Minor waterstain. S Jan 12 (138) £460 [Mason]
— DE RAM, JOHANNES. - Belgium Foederatum emendate auctum te novissime editum. Amst., [1689?]. 6 uncut sheets, 1,060mm by 1,260mm, hand-colored in outline. S Oct 23 (97) £850 [Cremers]
— DE WIT, FREDERICK. - Tabula Portugalliae et Algarbia. Amst., [c.1680]. 47cm by 55.9cm, contemp hand-coloring. Some repairs. pnNY Sept 13 (364) $190
— DESNOS, LOUIS CHARLES. - L'Europe, divisee selon l'etendue de ses principales parties. Paris, 1786. 930mm by 1,050mm, 4 sheets joined, partly colored, mtd on linen between wooden rollers. S Oct 23 (278) £750 [Israel]
DEUTSCH, HANS RUDOLF MANUEL. Berna Helvetiae... [Basel, 1549?]. Image size 210mm by 300mm. S Oct 23 (276) £400 [Burkhard]
— DIETZ, C. W. - Carte over den Kongel: Residencz-Stad Kioebenhavn.... Copenhagen, 1769. 450mm by 645mm, hand-colored & heightened in gold & silver in a contemp hand. S Oct 23 (94) £950 [R.O.H.R.]
— DUCHETTI, CLAUDIO. - Rhodi. Venice, 1570. 263mm by 176mm. Trimmed to neatlines but with broad added margins. S Oct 23 (326) £280 [Finopoulos]
— FERRARIS, JOSEPH JEAN. - Cart chorographique des Pays-Bas Autrichiens.... Brussels, 1777. 24 mapsheets (lacking index sheet), 650mm by 520mm, contemp half calf; worn. S Apr 23 (144) £1,050 [Braun]
— FERRARIS JOSEPH JEAN. - Carte chorographique des Pays-Bas Autrichiennes. Brussels, 1777. 24 (of 25) mapsheets (lacking the dedication sheet), 620mm by 520mm. A few repairs & creases. S Oct 23 (18) £800 [Nieuw]
— FERRARIS, JOSEPH JEAN. - Carte chorographique des Pays-Bas Autrichiens.... [N.p.], 1777. On 25 sheets, large folio, contemp half russia; spine chipped, corners rubbed. C Dec 12 (78) £800 [Hildebrandt]
Anr Ed. [Paris, 1777]. In 25 parts. Mtd & dissected, hand-colored within the area of Belgium except for the plan of Brussels, the index map & dedication sheet, & folded into 2 4to slipcases. S July 14 (606) £600
— GEIGER, JOHANN CONRAD & MEYER, JOHANNES. - Nova Descriptionis Tigurina. Zug, 1685. 6 sheets joined, 915mm by 970mm, boundary & costume vignettes colored in a contemp hand. S Oct 23 (109) £4,600 [Niew]

MAPS & CHARTS

— HOMANN, JOHANN BAPTIST. - Accurater Grundriss und Prospect...Stockholm. Nuremberg, [c.1720]. 487mm by 583mm, hand-colored. Small split at lower fold without loss; some surface dirt. S Nov 10 (885) £150 [Damms]
— HOMANN, JOHANN BAPTIST. - Geographische Vorstellung der jaemerlichen Wasser-Flutt in Nieder-Teutschland.... Nuremberg, [c.1720]. 470mm by 575mm, hand-colored. S Jan 12 (145) £250 [Ochs]
— HOMANN, JOHANN BAPTIST. - Hiberniae Regnum tam im praecipuas Ultoniae, Connaciae, Laceniae et Momoniae. Nuremberg, [1714]. 573mm by 480mm, hand-colored, with uncolored cartouches. sg Nov 20 (306) $120
— HOMANN, JOHANN BAPTIST. - Insularum Maltae et Gozae. Nuremberg, [c.1760, or later]. 480mm by 580mm, uncut & unfolded, hand-colored. Marginal waterstain. S Feb 23 (237) £180 [Ash]
— HOMANN, JOHANN BAPTIST. - Prospect und Grund-riss der Kayserl. Residenz-Stadt Wien. Nuremberg, [1712-30]. 490mm by 570mm, principal areas fully-hand-colored, with uncolored panoramicview of the city. sg Nov 20 (302) $150
Anr Ed. Nuremberg, [c.1720]. 490mm by 570mm, hand-colored. Split at fold without loss. S Nov 10 (889) £170 [Maliye]
— HOMANN, JOHANN BAPTIST. - Regni Norvegiae. Nuremberg, [c.1720]. 580mm by 495mm, hand-colored. S Jan 12 (147) £260 [Noble]
— HOMANN, JOHANN BAPTIST. - Status Reipublicae Genuensis. Nuremberg, [c.1725, or later]. 485mm by 561mm, hand-colored in outline, principal area fully colored. S Jan 12 (120) £200 [Perini]
— HONDIUS, HENRICUS. - Europa exactissime descripta. Amst.: Jansson, [c.1660]. Size not given but double-page S Feb 23 (175) £130 [Franks]
— HONDIUS, HENRICUS. - Galliae. Amst., 1631. 36.8cm by 49.5cm, early handcoloring. pnNY Sept 13 (382) $250
— JAILLOT, B. A. - Carte particuliere des Isles de Malte du Goze et du Cuming. Paris, 1734. 435mm by 730mm, uncut 7 unfolded. S Feb 23 (238) £150 [Marsden]
— JAILLOT, HUBERT. - La Suisse. [Amst.: P. Mortier, c.1700]. 475mm by 612mm, hand-colored in full & heightened with gold. Fold repair. S Oct 23 (284) £780 [Maliye]
— JANSSONIUS, JOANNES. - Portugallia et Algarbia quae olim Lusitania. Amst., [c.1650]. 33.6cm by 49.5cm, early handcoloring. Centerfold repaired. pnNY Sept 13 (396) $140
— JODE, GERARD DE. - Nova Totius Europae Tabula. Antwerp, 1593. 33cm by 43.8cm.

MAPS & CHARTS

early hand-coloring. Slight tear on centerfold in upper margin. pnNY Sept 13 (346) $1,600

Anr Ed. Antwerp, 1613. 33cm by43.8cm, early hand-coloring. Some tears along margins & into plate. pnNY Sept 13 (347) $750

— MERCATOR, GERARD. - Belgii. Amst., [c.1610]. 35.6cm by 45.7cm, early hand-coloring. Slight wear on centerfold. pnNY Sept 13 (411) $250

— MERCATOR, GERARD. - Daniae Regnum. Amst.:[c.1610]. 375mm by 445mm, hand-colored French text on verso. pnNY Sept 13 (412) $375

— MERCATOR, GERARD. - Europa. Duisberg, [c.1600]. 38.1cm by 46.4cm, early hand-coloring. pnNY Sept 13 (413) $300

Anr copy. 38.7cm by 47cm, Crease by centerfold; some fraying. pnNY Sept 13 (414) $225

— MERCATOR, GERARD. - Islandia. [Amst., 1633, or later]. 381mm by 492mm, hand-colored. Slight overall browning. pnNY Sept 13 (416) $250

— MERCATOR, GERARD. - Turcici imperii imago. [Amst., 1613, or later]. 360mm by 485mm, early hand-coloring. French text on verso.. pnNY Sept 13 (410) $400

Anr copy. 370mm by 495mm, old hand-coloring. Slight loss of image; slight wear on centerfold. pnNY Dec 10 (231) $250

— ORTELIUS, ABRAHAM. - Lutzenburgensis Ducatus.... [Antwerp, c.1590]. 370mm by 495mm, hand-colored. Stain & tear at lower left without loss; framed. S May 29 (1028) £130

Anr Ed. [Antwerp, 1603]. 362mm by 490mm. Browned. S Jan 12 (136) £170 [Ganesha]

— ORTELIUS, ABRAHAM. - Oost ende West Vrieslandt beschryvinghe...1568. [Antwerp, c.1580]. 340mm by 510mm, hand-colored. S Nov 10 (854) £130 [Faupel]

— ORTELIUS, ABRAHAM. - Transilvania. [Antwerp, c.1570]. 33cm by 45cm, early hand-coloring. pnNY Sept 13 (454) $160

— PETRINI, PAOLO. - Pianta ed Alzata della Citta di Napoli.... Naples, 1718. 3 sheets joined, 500mm by 1,030mm. S Oct 23 (92) £1,400 [King]

— PEYER, HEINRICH. - Schaffhauser Gebiet samt den Grentzen und umbligenden Orten...1685. Schaffhausen, 1685. 520mm by 720mm, 4 sheets joined, boundary hand-colored. Faint waterstains; slight marginal fraying. S Oct 23 (104) £1,700 [Payer]

— PTOLEMAEUS, CLAUDIUS. - Decima Europa tabula. Ulm: Johannes Reger, 1586. 370mm by 445mm, colored in a contemp hand. Headline shaved with partial loss of

AMERICAN BOOK PRICES CURRENT

running title; centerfold strengthened. S Oct 23 (325) £300 [Martoyan]

— PTOLEMAEUS, CLAUDIUS. - Quarta Europae tabula. [Strassburg: Leonardus Hol, 1482]. 374mm by 403mm, colored in a contemp hand, the sea in an ochre tint, framed Centerfold strengthened without loss. S Apr 23 (18) £1,000 [Niewodniczanski]

Anr Ed. [Strassburg: Johannes Schott, 1513 or 1520]. 370mm by 400mm, colored in a contemp hand, framed. S Apr 23 (145) £1,200 [Fogg]

— PTOLEMAEUS, CLAUDIUS. - Septima Europe Tabula. Strassburg, [1513 or 1520]. 320mm by 540mm. S Nov 10 (884) £120 [Lassalle]

— PTOLEMAEUS, CLAUDIUS. - Tabula Neoterica Crete sive Candie insule. Strassburg: Jacob Eszler & Georgius Ubelin, 1513. 370mm by 530mm, uncolored. Some soiling in margins. sg Nov 20 (313) $250

— SALAMANCA, ANTONIO. - Tabula Moderna Poloniae Ungariae Boemiae Germaniae.... [Rome, c.1572]. 383mm by 513mm. Some discoloration at fold. S Jan 12 (115) £1,400 [Israel]

— SALAMANCA, FRANCESCO. - Graeciae chorographia. [Rome, c.1560?]. 2 sheets joined, 408mm by 617mm. Small flaw at bottom center repaired without loss. S Apr 23 (219) £1,500 [Arader]

— SCHEDA JOSEF. - General-Karte des Oesterreichischen Kaiserstaates mit einem grossen Theile der Angrenzenden Laender. [N.p., 1856 or later]. 20 parts, each 500mm by 560mm, hand-colored in outline. With key, scales & tables, text leaf & 2 sheets showing map when all 20 parts are assembled. sg Nov 20 (317) $400

— SCHEUCHZER, J. J. - Nouvelle carte de la Suisse divisees en ses treize cantons.... Amst.: J. Covens & C. Mortier, [c.1740]. 4 sheets, total dimensions 900mm by 1,020mm, with boundaries colored in outline. S Oct 23 (106) £2,100 [Lehmann]

— SCHOENEMANN, FRIEDRICH. - Lissabon. Hamburg, 1756. 2 sheets joined, 405mm by 1,160mm. S Oct 23 (90) £1,600 [Arader]

— SELLER, JOHN. - A Chart of the North Sea. L, [c.1675]. 428mm by 535mm, hand-colored. Thick-paper copy. S June 25 (360) £900 [Tooley]

— SPEED, JOHN. - The Map of Hungary. L, 1676. 520mm by 395mm, hand-colored. pn Mar 5 (388) £120 [Burgess Browning]

— STRAHLENBERG, PHILIPP JOHANN VON. - Nova Descriptio Geographia Tattariae Magnae.... [Stockholm, 1730]. 650mm by 1,000mm, in 2 sheets joined. Marginal waterstains. S Oct 23 (281) £850 [Heckrotte]

— UGHI, LODOVICO. - Iconografica rappresentatione della Citta di Venezia. Venice,

[c.1790]. 1,320mm by 1,760mm, 8 sheets joined. Small tears at additional folds. S Jan 12 (154) £1,600 [Casali]
— VALENTYN, FRANCOIS. - Kaart der Reyse van Abel Tasman volgens syn eygen opstel. Amst.: J. van Braam & G. onder de Linden, [1726]. 305mm by 465mm, uncolored. sg Nov 20 (324) $850
— VAN KEULEN, JOANNES. - Paskaarte van de Zuyder Zee met alle des Zelfs inkomende. AMst., [c.1590]. 510mm by 600mm, colored in a contemp hand. Light crease & minor strengthening without loss. S Apr 24 (252) £950 [Arader]
— VASI, GIUSEPPE. - Prospetto d'Alma Citta di Roma visto dal Monte Gianicolo. Roma, 1765. 6 sheets mtd & dissected on linen in 24 sections, total 1,015mm by 2,260mm. S Jan 12 (154) £1,600 [Casali]
— VERBIEST, PETER. - Antverpia, constructionis eius primordia et incrementa. Antwerp, [1648?]. 2 sheets joined & laid on linen, 480mm by 665mm. A few small repairs wihtout loss; hsaved to plate mark; some discoloration. S Oct 23 (91) £600 [Cremers]
— VISSCHER, NICOLAUS. - Palatinatus Rheni nova, et accurata descriptio.... Amst., 1652. 440mm by 550mm. S Jan 12 (152) £550 [Nagel]
— VISSCHER, NIKOLAUS JANSSON. - Europa. [Amst., c.1680]. 43.8cm by 54.6cm, early hand-coloring. pnNY Sept 13 (496) $250
— VISSCHER, NIKOLAUS JANSSON. - Portugalliae et Algarbiae Regna. [Amst., c.1680]. 47.6cm by 57.2cm, early hand-coloring. Slight centra crease. pnNY Sept 13 (497) $225
— WALDSEEMUELLER, MARTIN. - Ducatus Lotharingie. [Strassburg: Johannes Schott, 1513 or 1520]. 360mm by 260mm, pted in 3 colors. S Apr 23 (150) £550 [Israel]
— WALDSEEMUELLER, MARTIN. - Norbegia et Gottia. [Lyons, 1535]. 340mm by 450mm, hand-colored. Small repair at lower blank margin without loss. S Nov 10 (883) £550 [Damms]
— WALDSEEMUELLER, MARTIN. - Tabula Moderna Bossine Servie Gretiae et Sclavonie. [Strassburg: J. Schott, 1513 or 1520]. 418mm by 550mm. S Nov 10 (863) £350 [Pantazelous]
— WALSER, G. - Canton Lucern. Nuremberg: Homann's Heirs, 1763. 470mm by 560mm, hand-colored.. Some surface dirt. S Nov 10 (870) £210 [H. Cristopher]

Great Britain

— A Balloon View of London as seen from Hampstead. L, 1851. 72cm by 107cm. Orig case. Some stains along folds. pn Jan 22 (354) £170 [J. Woods]
— ADAMS JOHN. - The Design of this map is to Given and Account Roads & of Distances without Scale or Compass. L, 1688. 2d state. 2 sheets joined, 610mm by 860mm hand-colored in outline, framed. Upper margin just shaved. S Nov 10 (711) £320 [Quaritch]
— AGAS, RALPH. - Civitas Londinium Anno Domini circiter MDLX. L: Society of Antiquaries, 1737. 690mm by 1,880mm, in 8 sheets joined & mtd on linen, colored. S Nov 10 (731) £380 [Goulden]
— AINSLIE, JOHN. - Map of the County of Forfar or Shire of Angus. Edin., 1794. 545mm by 350mm, 4 sheets, hand-colored in outline. S Nov 10 (692) £190 [Cambridge University Library]
— ARMSTRONG & SON. - A New Map of Ayr Shire.... L, Jan 10 1775. 550mm by 335mm, 6 sheets. Hand-colored in outline, in contemp bds. S Nov 10 (693) £150 [Marshall]
— ARROWSMITH, AARON. - Map of England and Wales. L, 1815. Folio, contemp half russia; broken. With outline hand-coloring on 18 double-page sheets, including title. Hand-colored key map pasted on flyleaf. C Oct 15 (1) £150 [Shapero]
— BAUGH, ROBERT. - Shropshire. Llanymynech, 1 Aug 1808. 1,370mm by 1,410mm, in 9 sheets joined & mtd on linen. S Nov 10 (744) £120 [Burgess]
— BLAEU, WILLEM & JAN. - Britannia prout divisa fuit temporibus Anglo-Saxonum. Amst., [1645 or later]. 410mm by 520mm, hand-colored, framed. S July 28 (904) £150; S July 28 (969) £320
— BLAEU, WILLEM & JAN. - Cornubia, sive Cornwallia. [Amst., c.1645]. 505mm by 390mm, hand-colored in outline, decorations fully colored. pn May 21 (533) £150 [Goodall]

Anr Ed. [Amst., 1663]. 19.75 by 23.75 inches, hand-colored in outline, decorations fully colored. Small tears at margins; minor spotting. L Dec 11 (192) £120

Anr Ed. [Amst., c.1700]. 390mm by 510mm, hand-colored. Ck May 15 (247) £110
— BLAEU, WILLEM & JAN. - Cornwallia. [Amst., c.1645]. 390mm by 495mm, hand colored. Slight adhesion damage at fold without loss. French text. S Nov 10 (702) £110 [Price]
— BLAEU, WILLEM & JAN. - Ducatus Eboracensis, anglice York Shire. [Amst., 1648]. 15 by 20 inches. Laid down on card. T Mar 19 (162) £100
— BLAEU, WILLEM & JAN. - Glocestershire & Monmouthshire. Amst., [c.1660]. 38.3/cm by 51.4cm, early hand-coloring. Repaired along lower part of centerfold. pnNY Sept 13 (321) $120
— BLAEU, WILLEM & JAN. - Gloucestria

MAPS & CHARTS

Ducatus, vulgo Glocester Shire. [Amst., 1663]. 500mm by 410mm, hand-colored in outline, decorations fully colored. pn Dec 11 (480) £120 [Baker]
— BLAEU, WILLEM. - Hantonia, sive Southantonensis comitatus, vulgo Hantshire. [Amst., 1648]. 16 by 19.5 inches, hand-colored in outline, with decorations fully colored. Latin text on verso. T Jan 22 (120) £120
— BLAEU, WILLEM & JAN. - Magnae Britanniae et Hiberniae tabula. Amst., [1631, or later]. 385mm by 490mm, hand-colored in outline. S Nov 17 (695) £120 [Whittaker]
 Anr Ed. Amst., [c.1650]. 505mm by 395mm, hand-colored in outline, with decorations fully colored. pn May 21 (535) £130
— BLAEU, WILLEM & JAN. - Monumenthensis comitatus. [Amst., 1645]. 380mm by 495mm, hand-colored, framed. S Nov 10 (732) £100 [Howell-Morton]
— BLAEU, WILLEM & JAN. - Oxonium comitatus. [Amst., c.1650]. 500mm by 380mm. pn Oct 23 (453) £120 [Goodall]
— BLAEU, WILLEM & JAN. - Somersettensis Comitatus. SomersetShire. [1648]. 15 by 20 inches. T Jan 22 (118) £105
— BOAZIO, BAPTISTA. - Irlandiae accurata descriptio. Antwerp: J. B. Vrints, [1606, or later]. 439mm by 572mm, S Apr 23 (115) £1,200 [Hughes]
— BOWEN, EMANUEL. - An Accurate Map of the County of Surrey. L, [c.1760]. 520mm by 700mm, hand-colored in outline, framed. CK May 15 (234) £180
— BRAUN, GEORG & HOGENBERG, FRANZ. - Cantebrigia.... [Cologne, c.1590]. 325mm by 440mm. Sold w.a.f. S July 28 (907) pS150
— BRAUN, GEORG & HOGENBERG, FRANZ. - Edenburg. [Cologne, 1581, or later]. 340mm by 450mm. Some worming. S Jan 12 (31) £180 [Nelson]
— BRAUN, GEORG & HOGENBERG, FRANZ. - Londinum feracissimi Angliae regni metropolis. Cologne, [c.1590]. 328mm by 435mm, colored in a contemp hand. S July 28 (942) £500
— BRAUN, GEORG & HOGENBERG, FRANZ. - Nordovicum Angliae civitas. [Cologne, c.1580]. 420mm by 295mm, hand-colored. Slight wear to centerfold. pn Oct 23 (445) £100 [Goodall]
— BRYANT, A. - Map of the County of Surrey... L, 1823. Size not given, hand-colored. On linen, folded into calf box. pn May 21 (432) £220 [Traylen]
— BRYANT, A. - A Map of the County of Northampton. L, 1827. 6 sheets mtd, totalling 1,800mm by 1,990mm, dissected in 96 sections & folding into 4to size contemp calf case. Rubbed. S Jan 12 (49) £140

AMERICAN BOOK PRICES CURRENT

[Hall]
— DANCKERTS, JUSTUS. - Nova totius Angliae, Scotiae et Hiberniae tabula. Amst., [c.1685]. 4 sheets joined, 870mm by 1,040mm, hand-colored in outline. S Oct 23 (88) £2,600 [Israel]
— DE WIT, FREDERICK. - Nova Totius Angliae Scotiae et Hiberniae. Amst., [c.1680]. 48.3cm by 55.9cm, hand-colored. Some repairs & tears; 1 ink mark; some foxing. pnNY Sept 13 (365) $200
— DIGHTON, R. - Geography Bewitched! or, droll Caricature Map of Ireland. [c.1800]. Map in the form of a seated female figure, brightly colored, cut round & mtd on a folio leaf with Ms notes, total dimensions 365mm by 265mm, framed. S Nov 10 (722) £110 [Lassille]
— DONCKER, H. - Pas-Caart van 't Canaal vertoonende in 't Geheel Engelandt.... Amst., [c.1665]. 440mm by 535mm, hand colored. Margins cut close. S Nov 10 (696) £170 [Ash]
— DORRET, JAMES. - A General Map of Scotland.... [N.p.], 1750. 1,803mm by 1,346mm, in 5 entirely uncut sheets S Feb 23 (289) £400 [Quaritch]
— GREENWOOD, C. & J. - Map of the County of Surrey. L, 1823. 1,230mm by 1,020mm, hand-colored, on linen. pn May 21 (435) £150 [Traylen]
— GREENWOOD, CHRISTOPHER & JOHN. - Map of London. L, 1827. 6 sheets mtd & dissected in 60 sections, 1,235mm by 1,850mm, hand-colored. S Nov 17 (728) £340 [Lipton]
— GREENWOOD, CHARLES. - Map of the County of Yorkshire. L, 1817. Map in 9 sheets bound in 2 parts, total dimensions if joined 2,400mm by 1,420mm, in wraps. S Nov 17 (747) £200 [Old Hall]
— GREENWOOD, CHARLES & JOHN. - Map of the County of Kent. L, 1821. 1,755mm by 1,150mm, hand-colored, folding into contemp calf box. bba Nov 13 (90) £240 [Check]
— HOMANN, JOHANN BAPTIST. - Hiberniae Regnum.... Nuremberg, [c.1730]. 565mm by 470mm, hand-colored. Slight cockling at fold. S Nov 17 (719) £160 [Burden]
— HONDIUS, JODOCUS. - Magnae Britanniae et Hiberniae tabula. Amst., 1631 [but c.1633]. 380mm by 510mm, hand-colored in outline, framed. Split at fold without loss. S Nov 10 (697) £280 [Brure-Lyster]
— JANSSONIUS, JOANNES. - Comitatis Cantabrigiensis.... Amst., [c.1650]. 525mm by 425mm. Sold w.a.f. pn July 23 (338) £120 [Wayman]
— JANSSONIUS, JOANNES. - Comitatus Dorcestria, vulgo anglice Dorsetshire. Amst, [c.1700, or later]. 15 by 19 inches, hand-colored in outline. T Jan 22 (162)

£110
- JANSSONIUS, JOANNES. - Scotia Regnum. Amst., [c.1650]. 38.7cm by 50.8cm, hand-colored. pnNY Sept 13 (397) $140
- JANSSONIUS, JOANNES. - Suthsexia vernacule Sussex. AMst., [c.1650]. 525mm by 390mm. pn July 23 (339) £150 [Faupel]
- LHUYD, HUMPHREY. - Angliae Regni Florentissimi Nova descriptio. [Antwerp, c.1590]. 370mm by 460mm, colored in a contemp hand, framed. S July 28 (964) £220
- MERCATOR, GERARD. - Irlandiae Regnum. [Amst.: Hondius, 1609]. double sheet. 62.9cm by 47cm, early hand-coloring French text on verso. Center-folds repaired & joined; lower margin torn. pnNY Sept 13 (415) $225
- MERCATOR, GERARD. - Scotiae Tabula. [Amst., c.1610]. 14 by 18.75 inches, early hand-coloring. Crease along upper corner; waterstains along lower margin. pnNY Sept 13 (420) $200
- ORTELIUS, ABRAHAM. - Angliae, Scotiae, et Hiberniae.... [Antwerp, 1573, or later]. 13.5 by 19.5 inches, hand-colored. Stained at base of centerfold; some repairs to verso. T Jan 22 (126) £270
- ORTELIUS, ABRAHAM. - Britannicarum Insularm Typus. [Antwerp] 1595. 370mm by 510mm, early hand-coloring. Latin text on verso. Center-fold wormed. Browned. pnNY Sept 13 (456) $300
- ORTELIUS, ABRAHAM. - Britannicarum Insularum Typus. [Antwerp?], 1595. 510mm by 370mm, uncolored. pn Apr 30 (614) £160 [Griffiths]
- ORTELIUS, ABRAHAM. - Hiberniae Britanicae Insulae nova descriptio. [Antwerp, 1592 or later]. 355mm by 480mm. S July 28 (935) £160
- ORTELIUS, ABRAHAM. - Insularum Britannicarum acurata delineatio.... Amst., [c.1658]. 390mm by 500mm, hand-colored, framed. Trimmed to plate-mark & laid down. S July 28 (903) £100
- ORTELIUS, ABRAHAM. - Scotiae tabula. [Antwerp, 1573, or later]. 355mm by 475m. S Jan 12 (55) £110 [Marsden]
- ORTELIUS, ABRAHAM & SAXTON, CHRISTOPHER. - Anglia regnum.... [Antwerp, 1603]. 375mm by 465mm, colored. S July 28 (917) £130
- PACKE, CHRISTOPHER. - A New Philosophico-Chorographical Chart of East-Kent. L, 1743. 4 sheets, totalling 1,202mm by 1,304mm, joined & laid on linen between rollers (lower roller lacking). S June 25 (236) £2,500 [Maggs]
- PARSONS, SAMUEL. - A New Map of Staffordshire.... Newcastle, 1747. 1,015mm by 708mm, 4 sheets joined, outer edges uncut. S Feb 23 (305) £440 [Sabin]

- PTOLEMAEUS, CLAUDIUS. - Tabula I Europae. [Lyons, 1535]. 298mm by 410mm, hand-colored. S Nov 10 (701) £160 [Bruce-Lystan]
- ROCQUE, JOHN. - A Topographical Map of the County of Middlesex. L, 1754. 4 sheets totalling 1,400mm by 1,000mm. pn Nov 20 (362) £280 [Goodall]
- ROCQUE, JOHN. - A Topographical Map of the County of Surrey. L, [c.1760]. Size not given, but large hand-colored map on linen. pn May 21 (443) £220 [Traylen]
- ROWE, ROBERT. - A New Map of Yorkshire. L, 4 June 1810. 410mm by 520mm, in 4 sheets, hand-colored & bound in half mor with an index & gazetteer. S Nov 10 (748) £220 [Quaritch]
- SAXTON, CHRISTOPHER. - Dunelmensis Episcopatus.... L, [1576]. 373mm by 480mm, hand-colored in outline. Minor def at fold without significant loss. S Nov 10 (709) £300 [Burgess]
- SAXTON, CHRISTOPHER. - Glamorgan comitatus.... L, 1579. 330mm by 480mm, colored in an early hand. Some restoration affecting green-painted area. S Jan 12 (36) £400 [Kentish]

  Anr Ed. L, [c.1690]. 13 by 19 inches, hand-colored in outline. T Jan 22 (167) £210
- SAXTON, CHRISTOPHER. - Glamorgan Shire Described.... L, [1690]. 13 by 19 inches, framed. Repair to top left corner. T Sept 18 (104) £110
- SAXTON, CHRISTOPHER. - Hartfordiae comitatus.... L, 1577 [but 1579]. 395mm by 490mm, hand-colored in outline, laid on paper backing. S Feb 24 (364) £280 [Burgess]
- SAXTON, CHRISTOPHER. - Monumethensis Comitatus.... L, [1579]. 390mm by 484mm, colored in a contemp hand. S Nov 10 (733) £850 [Michael]
- SAXTON, CHRISTOPHER & LEA, PHILIP. - Sommersetshire. L, 1575. 15.5 by 18.5 inches, hand-colored. Slight damage to lower fold. Ck Feb 27 (24A) £650
- SAXTON, CHRISTOPHER. - Wigorniensis Comitatus.... L, [1579]. 368mm by 483mm, colored in a contemp hand. Faint discoloration. S Nov 17 (746) £700 [Merry]
- SEUTTER, MATTHAEUS. - Londinum celeberrima Metropolis. Augsburg, [c.1740]. 500mm by 576mm, uncut & unfolded & finly colored in a contemp hand. S Feb 23 (225) £520 [Ash]
- SEUTTER, MATTHAEUS. - Regnum Hiberniae. Augsburg, [c.1745]. 578mm by 495mm, hand-colored in wash & outline. Margins faintly discolored. S Nov 10 (721) £130 [Bruce-Lysten]
- SPEED, JOHN. - Caernarvon both Shyre and Shire-towne.... L, 1676. 15 by 20 inches. T

MAPS & CHARTS

Jan 22 (111) £110

— SPEED, JOHN. - Cardigan Shyre.... L: J. Sudbury & G. Humble, 1610 [1646]. 380mm by 498mm, hand-colored in outline, with cartouches, etc, fully hand-colored. Backed with contemp laid paper. sg Apr 23 (252) $200

— SPEED, JOHN. - The Countie of Leinster. L; Sudbury & Humble, [1616]. 385mm by 515mm, colored in a contemp hand. S Feb 24 (368) £210 [Ash]

— SPEED, JOHN. - The County Palatine of Chester.... L: J. Sudbury & G. Humbell, [1611]. 16½ by 21 inches, framed & double glazed. pn Jan 22 (376) £200 [Goodall]

— SPEED, JOHN. - The County Pallatine of Lancaster Described. L: T. Bassett & R. Chiswell, [1676, or later]. Size not given, hand-colored. pn July 23 (352) £160 [Burgess Browning]

Anr Ed. L: G. Humble, [1611]. 380mm by 520mm, framed. Several small holes along fold. Ck May 15 (223) £260

Anr Ed. L: G. Humbell [1627]. 390mm by 515mm, hand-colored. Framed and double glazed. pn Jan 22 (377) £280 [Goodall]

Anr Ed. L: Roger Rea, 1662. Size not given, hand-colored, framed. pn Mar 5 (439) £280 [Kidd]

— SPEED, JOHN. - Devonshire. L: Sudbury & Humble, [1611]. Size not given. Hand-colored & framed. pn Mar 5 (438) £180 [Kidd]

— SPEED, JOHN. - Dorsetshyre.... L: Sudbury & Humble, 1610 [1611-12]. 380mm by 510mm, framed. Ck May 15 (227) £120

— SPEED, JOHN. - Glamorganshire. L: Sudbury & Humble, [1627]. 15 by 20 inches, hand-colored, framed. Ck Feb 27 (3) £110

— SPEED, JOHN. - Hartfordshire. L: Sudbury & Humble, 1611. 395mm by 520mm, hand-colored in outline. Repaired at top & bottom of centerfold; stains in lower margin. pn July 23 (350) £140 [Goodall]

— SPEED, JOHN. - Hereford-shire Described. L: Humble, 1627. 15 by 20 inches, hand-colored in outline, framed. Wear at lower fold. Ck Feb 27 (2) £120

— SPEED, JOHN. - Holy Iland; Farne Iland; Garnsay; Jarsey. L: J. Sudbury & G. Humbell, 1610 [but 1614, or later]. 510mm by 390mm. pn oct 23 (424) £110 [Whitford]

— SPEED, JOHN. - The Invasions of England and Ireland...since the Conquest. L: Bassett & Chiswell, [1676]. 375mm by 515mm, framed. Faint waterstain. S July 28 (972) £240

— SPEED, JOHN. - The Isle of Man. L: Bassett & Chiswell, [1676]. 510mm by 390mm. Framed. pn Mar 5 (378) £210 [Burgess Browning]

— SPEED, JOHN. - Kent.... L: G. Humble, [1611, but 1627 or later]. 380mm by 510mm, framed. Ck May 15 (224) £220

— SPEED, JOHN. - The Kingdome of England. L: T. Bassett & R. Chiswell, 1646 [but 1676, or later]. 385mm by 515mm, hand-colored in outline. Framed. English text on verso. S july 28 (915) £240

— SPEED, JOHN. - The Kingdome of Great Britanie and Ireland. L, 1610 [but 1614, or later]. 380mm by 510mm, hand-colored, framed. English text on verso. S July 28 (968) £450

— SPEED, JOHN. - The Kingdome of Irland.... L: William Humble, 1651. 15.25 inches by 19.75 inches, framed. Small repaired area in sea off northeast coast. L Dec 11 (220) £120

— SPEED, JOHN. - Midle-sex Described.... L: G. Humble, [1611]. Size not given, hand-colored, framed. Some weat to centerfold; dampstains; 1 small hole. pn July 23 (382) £160 [Goodall]

— SPEED, JOHN. - Northumberland L: T. Bassett & R. Chiswell, [1676, or later]. Size not given, but colored & framed. pn Mar 5 (437) £110 [Wayman]

— SPEED, JOHN. - Nottingham. L: Sudbury & Humble, [c.1610]. 510mm by 380mm. pn Oct 23 (425) £100 [Saville]

— SPEED, JOHN. - The Province of Connaugh, with the Citie of Galwaye. L: Sudbury & Humble, [1616]. 385mm by 515mm, colored in a contemp hand. S Feb 24 (369) £160 [Ash]

— SPEED, JOHN. - Suffolk. L: G. Humble, [1611]. Size not given, hand-colored.. pn Jan 22 (380) £170 [Goodall]

— SPEED, JOHN. - Sussex. L: F. & G. [1627]. 515mm by 390mm, hand-colored Laid down on card. pn Jan 22 (378) £190 [Goodard]

Anr Ed. L: Bassett & Chiswell, [1676]. Size not given, hand-colored,. framed. pn May 21 (524) £220 [Goodall]

— SPEED, JOHN. - Wales. L: R. Chiswell & T. Bassett, [1676, or later]. 380mm by 510mm, hand-colored, framed. S July 28 (961) £280

— SPEED, JOHN. - Wilshire. L: Sudbury & Humble, [1611 or later]. Size not given. Hand-colored. pn Mar 5 (380) £180 [Sands]

Anr Ed. L: Humble, [c.1627]. 15 by 20 inches, Hand-colored, framed. Ck Feb 27 (5) £120

— SPEED, JOHN. - Wiltshire. L, [1611]. 380mm by 510mm, framed. Ck May 15 (228) £130

— STANFORD, EDWARD. - Stanford's Large Railway Map of England and Wales. L, 1867. 4 parts mtd on linen & folded in sections to 4to, hand-colored, in orig mor

slipcase; worn. bba Sept 25 (381) £65 [Brayley]
— STOCKDALE, JOHN. - A New Plan of London.... L, 1797 [but c.1809]. 1,010mm by 1,380mm, in 4 sheets joined. Marginal tears touching engraved surface. S Nov 10 (730) £150 [Lipton]
— WAGHENAER, LUCAS JANSZ. - Zee Caerte van Engelants Eijndt.... [Leiden], 158[6]. 342mm by 532mm, uncolored. Centerfold strengthened on verso. pnNY Dec 10 (238) $300

Pacific Ocean

— GOOS, PIETER. - Pascaerte vande Zuyd-Zee tussche California, en Ilhas de Ladrones. Amst., 1666. 510mm by 600mm, hand-colored in outline. Upper margin shaved just touching outer neatline. S June 25 (368) £4,500 [Arader]
— MORTIER, PIETER. - Mer du Sud, ou pacifique.... Amst., [c.1700]. 595mm by 740mm, hand-colored in wash & outline in a contemp hand. S June 25 (491) £680
— ORTELIUS, ABRAHAM. - Maris Pacifici.... [Antwerp], 1589 [but 1603]. 13 by 16 inches, Latin text on verso. pnNY Sept 13 (442) $1,500

Anr Ed. [Antwerp, c.1612] 344mm by 497mm, colored in a contemp hand. S Apr 23 (366) £700 [George]
— TATTON, GABRIEL. - Maris Pacifici quod vulgo Mar del Zur.... L, 1600. State 1. 405mm by 523mm, untrimmed. Engraved by Benjamin Wright. S Oct 23 (149) £18,000 [Arader]
— VAN KEULEN, GERARD. - Mer du Sud of De Zuyd Zee. Amst., [c.1720]. 505mm by 600mm. S June 25 (492) £900

Polar Regions

— AA, PIETER VAN DER. - Planisphere terrestre. [c.1713]. 665mm by 545mm, uncolored. pn Jan 22 (362) £650 [Tooley]
— BARENTS, WILLEM. - Delineatio cartae trium navigantium per Batavos.... [Frankfurt, 1601]. 275mm by 350mm. S Apr 24 (361) £500 [Fisher]
— BELLIN, JACQUES NICOLAS. - Carte reduite des Mers du Nord. [Genoa: Y. Gravier, 1780 or later]. 560mm by 860mm. Faint discoloration. s Feb 24 (497) £240 [Orsssich]
— BLAEU, WILLEM & JAN. - Regiones sub polo arctico. [Amst., 1640]. 410mm by 530mm, hand-colored. French text on verso.. pnNY Sept 13 (322) $300

Anr copy. 413mm by 535mm, hand-colored in outline, with cartouches, etc., fully colored. Mtd to heavy bd; foxed & browned. sg Apr 23 (254) $225
— BRY, THEODOR DE. - Delineatio cartae trium navigationum per Batavos ad Septentrionalem plagem.... Frankfurt, 1601. 275mm by 350mm. Narrow margins. S Apr 23 (361) £500 [Fisher]
— CORONELLI, VINCENZO MARIA. - Terre artiche. Venice, [c.1696]. 448mm by 600mm. S Nov 10 (1218) £240 [Goldbaum]
— DELISLE, GUILLAUME. - Hemisphere meridional pour voir plus distinctement les Terres Australes. Amst.: Ottens, [c.1745]. 460mm by 605mm, hand-colored. Some surface dirt. S Nov 10 (1217) £200 [Orsich]
— MERCATOR, GERARD. - Septentrionalium terrarum descriptio. [Amst.: H. Hondius, 1619, or later]. 366mm by 394mm, early hand-coloring. pnNY Sept 13 (418) $800

Anr copy. French text on verso. pnNY Sept 13 (419) $750
— VAN KEULEN, JOANNES. - Nieuwe Paskaart inhoudende 't Noorder deel van Europa sijnde seer Dienstigh voorde Groenlandse en Moskovise Scheepvaart.... Amst., 1701. 2 sheets joined & backed with blue paper, 590mm by 990mm. Small portion torn from upper margin to just within neatline; small stamp. S Nov 10 (1222) £220 [Tooley]

United States

— Colton's New Sectional Map of Nebraska and Part of Dakota. NY, 1870. 710mm by 940mm, hand-colored, folded into 8vo cloth covers, which are broken. Some foldbreaks. sg Nov 20 (249) $175
— Map of the States of California and Nevada. San Francisco: Warren Holt, 1869. 1,440mm by 1,190mm, in 4 sheets joined as 2, folded to 8v. In cloth covers; worn. Fully hand-colored. Some dampstaining; large separations at several horizontal fold-lines; some small tears. sg Nov 20 (204) $750
— ANVILLE, JEAN BAPTISTE BOURGUIGNON D'. - Carte de la Louisiane. Paris, 1752. 515mm by 915mm. Small tear without loss. S Nov 18 (1085) £280 [Map House]
— BELLIN, J. N. - Carte reduite des costes de la Louisiane et de la Floride.... [Paris], 1764. 540mm by 870mm. Minor stains. S Feb 24 (443) £170 [Smilers]
— BLAEU, WILLEM & JAN. - Americae nova tabula. Amst., [1663]. 412mm by 560mm, colored in a contemp hand. S Jan 12 (242) £1,300 [Pantazelos]
— BLAEU, WILLEM & JAN. - Nova Belgica et Anglia nova. [Amst., 1663]. 385mm by 493mm, early hand-cp,promg. Dutch text on verso. Lower portion of center-fold repaired. pnNY Sept 13 (308) $950

Anr copy. Early hand-coloring. French text on verso. Lower margin torn at centerfold. pnNY Sept 13 (309) $750

Anr copy. 390mm by 500mm, hand-colored. Latin text on vers. S Jan 12 (250)

MAPS & CHARTS

£550 [Pantazelos]
— BLAEU, WILLEM & JAN. - Nova Virginiae tabula. [Amst., 1663]. 370mm by 475mm, colored in a contemp hand. Latin text on verso. S Nov 18 (1100) £300 [Potter]
Anr copy. Hand-colored. Latin text on vers. S Jan 12 (259) £420 [George]
— BLAEU, WILLEM & JAN. - Virginiae partis australis, et Floridae, partis orientalis.... [Amst., 1640]. 19½ by 23 inches, hand-colored. Latin text on verso. English royal coat-of-arms. pnNY Sept 13 (317) $400; pnNY Sept 13 (318) $400
Anr copy. French text on verso.. pnNY Sept 13 (3125) $550
Anr copy. 388mm by 506mm, Latin text on vers. S Jan 12 (257) £260 [George]
— BLANCHARD, JOSEPH & LANGDON, SAMUEL. - An Accurate Map of His Majesty's Province of New Hampshire.... L: Thomas Jefferys, [1761]. 2 sheets, 680mm by 730mm, hand-colored, entirely uncut & unfolded as issued. S Oct 23 (129) £2,400 [Arader]
— BOHN, CASIMIR. - Map of the City of Washington in the District of Columbia. Wash.: C. Bohn, 1854. 295mm by 400mm, uncolored, folded within 18mo cloth covers. Fold breaks. sg Nov 20 (254) $140
— BONNE, RIGOBERT. - Carte des Isles Sandwich. [Geneva, 1781]. 9.25 by 13.33 inches, hand-colored. cb Feb 19 (177) $180
— BRASSIER, WILLIAM. - A Survey of Lake Champlain including Lake George, Crown Point.... L, 5 Aug 1776. 656mm by 475mm, hand-colored in outline. About 10 brown spots; tear at top right not affecting surface; mtd on linen. sg Apr 23 (195) $750
— COLTON, J. H. - Map of the Country Thirty Three Miles Around the City of New York. NY, 1858. 625mm by 580mm, hand-colored, folded into 8vo cloth covers, front cover detached. sg Nov 20 (252) $275
— CORONELLI, VINCENZO MARIA. - America Settentrionale colle Nuove Scoperte.... [Venice, 1691-95]. 2 sheets joined, 610mm by 900mm. Faint discoloration caused by guard adhesive at folds. S Oct 23 (404) £1,900 [Map]
— DE BRAHM, WILLIAM GERARD. - A Map of South Carolina and a Part of Georgia. L: Thomas Jefferys, 20 Oct 1757. 1st Issue. 6 entirely uncut sheets, 1,340mm by 1,220mm. S Oct 233 (125) £5,000 [Browning]
— DE L'ISLE, GUILLAUME. - L'Amerique septentrionale. Amst., [c.1708]. 485mm by 570mm, early hand-coloring. Some foxing & creasing. pnNY Sept 13 (343) $750
— DE WIT, FREDERICK. - Novissima et accuratissima totius americae descriptio. Amst., [c.1680]. 492mm by 580mm. Margins trimmed close; rubbed, with loss of surface in Canada; fold break. sg Nov 20 (246) $225
— DES BARRES, J. F. W. - A Chart of Delawar Bay.... L, 1 June 1779. 78cm by 56.5cm. pnNY Dec 10 (210) $2,300
— DES BARRES, J. F. W. - The Coast Rivers and Inlets of the Province of Georgia. L, 1 Feb 1780. 60.25cm by 76cm, partly hand-colored. pnNY Dec 10 (215) $2,900
— DES BARRES, J. F. W. - Falmouth. L, 1 Jan 1781. 75cm by 54cm. Partly hand-colored. Margin torn & repaired. pnNY Dec 10 (214) $700
— DES BARRES, J. F. W. - A Plan of Fort Montgomery and Fort Clinton.... L, 1 Jan 1779. 54.5cm by 78.75cm, partly hand-colored & with wash. Faint central crease. pnNY Dec 10 (211) $2,000
— DES BARRES, J. F. W. - A View of the East End of the Isle Sable.... L, 1 June 1779. 50.25cm by 72.5cm. Some browning. pnNY Dec 10 (212) $400
— DES BARRES, J. F. W. - Vineyard Sound and Buzzard's Bay. L, 1 Nov 1781. 105.5cm by 75cm, 2 sheets jointed. Some browning. pnNY Dec 10 (217) $1,000
— EVANS, LEWIS. - Carte generale des etats de Virginie, Maryland, Delaware.... Paris, [late 18th or early 19th cent]. 485mm by 565mm, hand-colored. Tears at top & right entering engraved border; reinforced with paper on verso. sg Nov 20 (207) $650
— FILSON, JOHN. - Carte de Kentucke. Paris, 1785. 14 by 13 inches plus margins. Minor defs. wa Sept 25 (498) $210
— FRY, JOSHUA & JEFFERSON, PETER. - A Map of the Most Inhabited Part of Virginia.... L, [1755]. 4 sheets joined as 2, 780mm by 1,220mm, colored in outline. Some discoloration. S Oct 23 (410) £2,000 [Vorles]
— GOOS, PIETER. - Paskaerte van Nova Granada en t'Eylandt California. Amst.: P. Goos, 1666. 440mm by 545mm, colored & heightened with gold in a contemp hand. Upper margin extended; small blemish at upper fold. S June 25 (363) £2,000 [Arader]
— HOLMES, J. B. - Map of Property in Harlem.... NY, 1885. 880mm by 1,000mm, hand-colored, linen-backed. Creased with some tears. sg Nov 20 (225) $100
— HOLMES, J. B. - Map of the Louvre Farm.... NY, 1868. 815mm by 1,050mm, linen-backed. Some creases & dust-soiling. sg Nov 20 (222) $110
— HOLMES, J. B. - Map of the Murray Hill Farm, Ogden Place Farm.... NY, 1867. 690mm by 640mm, hand-colored, linen-backed. Some creases & dust-soiling. sg Nov 20 (223) $225
— HOLMES, J. B. - Map of the Rutger's Farm....

NY, 1874. 540mm by 1,000mm, hand-colored, linen-backed. Puncture at outer edge. sg Nov 20 (228) $100
— HOLMES, J. B. - A Map Showing all the Farm and Boundary Lines of the Estates as they Existed when in Possession of the Apthorpe's, Vanderheuvel's, Somerindike's.... NY, [c.1870]. 700mm by 900mm, hand-colored, linen-backed. Some creasing; puncture at outer edge. sg Nov 20 (228) $100
— HOLMES, J. B. - Map Showing the Perimeters of Farms in Bloomingdale. NY, 1880. 740mm by 1,150mm, hand-colored, linen-backed. sg Nov 20 (231) $275
— HOLMES, J. B. - Maps of the James W. Beekman, Catherine Livingston, Breevoort and Odell Estates. NY, 1880. 780mm by 620mm, hand-colored, linen-backed. sg Nov 20 (236) $275
— HOLMES, J. B. - Maps Showing the Original Boundaries of the Varian, Horn, and Samler Estates. NY, 1884. 790mm by 870mm, hand-colored, linen-backed. sg Nov 20 (230) $120
— HOLMES, JOHN BUTE. - Map of the Turtle Bay Farm.... NY, 1867. 600mm by 770mm, principal areas fully hand-colored. Linen-backed; a few creases & tears. sg Nov 20 (233) $100
— HOMANN, JOHANN BAPTIST. - Nova Anglia. Nuremberg, [c.1720]. ("Nova Anglia septentrionali Americae implantata Anglorumque Coloniis Florentissima.") 484mm by 570mm, hand-colored. S May 29 (1079) £300
— HOMANN, JOHANN BAPTIST. - Virginia, Marylandia et Carolina. Nuremberg, [c.1720]. 480mm by 575mm, hand-colored in wash & outline. S May 29 (1077) £180
— HONDIUS, JODOCUS. - Nova Virginiae tabula. Amst., [1639]. 38.5cm by 49.5cm. Early hand-coloring. Latin text on verso. With English royal coat-of-arms. pnNY Sept 13 (375) $500
— JANSSONIUS, JOANNES. - Nova Belgica et Anglia Nova. Amst., [c.1636]. 385mm by 500mm, hand-colored. S Oct 23 (398) £480 [Arader]
— JEFFERYS, THOMAS. - A Map of the most Inhabited Part of New England. L, 29 Nov 1774. 1,040mm by 975mm, 4 sheets joined as 2 hand-colored in outline. S Oct 23 (399) £700 [Arader]
— MATHER, W W. - Geological Map of Long & Staten Islands with the Environs of New York.... NY, 1842. 22.5 by 50.7 inches, partly hand-colored. Minor stains. wa Sept 25 (515) $160
— MERCATOR, GERARD. - Virginiae item et Floridae Americae provinciarum.... [Amst.: J. Hondius, c.1609]. 340mm by 495mm, old hand-coloring. Some marginal worming & staining. pnNY Dec 10 (226) $375

Anr Ed. [Amst.: J. Hondius, c.1610]. 340mm by 481mm. French text on verso. Early hand-coloring Center-fold torn & repaired, slight loss of image along upper part of fold. Wide margins. pnNY Sept 13 (405A) $800

Anr copy. 340mm by 490mm. Hand-colored in outline, framed. Some worming in sea area. S Oct 23 (409) £320 [Strausburgh]

Anr copy. Colored in a contemp hand, framed. Latin text on verso. S Nov 18 (1098) £250 [Potter]

— MITCHELL, JOHN. - Amerique septentrionale. Paris, 1777. 8 map sheets jointed in 4 each 1,400mm by 525mm, partially hand-colored in outline. P May 13 (14) $1,600
— OGILBY, JOHN. - Arx Carolina. L, [c.1670]. 27.9cm by 34.3cm, hand-colored. pnNY Sept 13 (432) $275
— ROBERT DE VAUGONDY. - Partie de l'Amerique septentrionale.... [Paris, c.1758]. 19 by 24.5 inches, hand-colored in outline. T Jan 22 (149) £140
— SANSON D'ABBEVILLE, NICHOLAS. - Amerique septentrionale. Paris, 1650. 386mm by 550mm, hand-colored in outline. Some browning. sg Nov 20 (240) $800
— SAUTHIER, CLAUDE JOSEPH. - A Map of the Provinces of New-York.... Augsburg, 1777. 730mm by 560mm, 2 sheets joined, hand-colored. S Oct 23 (401) £400 [Keating]
— SCULL, NICHOLAS. - Map of the Improved Part of the Province of Pennsylvania. Phila., 1759. In 6 sheets, total if joined being 760mm by 1,500mm S Oct 23 (139) £4,400 [Arader]
— SCULL, NICHOLAS & HEAP, GEORGE. - A Plan of the City and Environs of Philadelphia.... L: Faden, 12 Mar 1777. 1st Issue with unnamed island between Hog & Mug Islands & no soundings in the River. 625mm by 460mm, Elevation of the Statehouse uncolored but with Delaware & Schuylkill Rivers hand colored as well as buildings in eastern portion of the city & a few outlying areas. sg Nov 20 (241) $1,900
— SCULL, WILLIAM. - A Map of Pennsylvania exhibiting not only the Improved Parts of that Province.... L: Sayer & Bennett, June 10 1775. 3 sheets joined, 675mm by 1,330mm, colored in outline S Nov 10 (1093) £500 [Faupel]
— SMITH, CAPT. JOHN. - New England.... [Frankfurt, 1617 or later]. 300mm by 348mm, uncolored. Tear at leaf affecting 25mm of engraved text; trimmed close, affecting border. sg Nov 20 (242) $6,000
— SOTZMANN, DANIEL FRIEDRICH. - Connecticut.... Hamburg: Carl Ernst Bohn, 1796.

MAPS & CHARTS

358mm by 440mm, hand-colored, entirely uncut & unfolded as issued. S Oct 23 (126) £750 [Elliott]
— SOTZMANN, DANIEL FRIEDRICH. - Maine.... Hamburg: Carl Ernst Bohn, 1798. 638mm by 438mm, hand-colored, entirely uncut & unfolded as issued. S Oct 23 (127) £720 [Potter]
— SOTZMANN, DANIEL FRIEDRICH. - Maryland and Delaware.... Hamburg: Carl Ernst Bohn, 1797. 446mm by 656mm, hand-colored, entirely uncut & unfolded as issued. S Oct 23 (128) £1,500 [Smiley]
— SOTZMANN, DANIEL FRIEDRICH. - New Hampshire.... Hamburg: Carl Ernst Bohn, 1796. 673mm by 450mm, hand-colored, entirely uncut & unfolded as issued. S Oct 23 (130) £600 [Schuster]
— SOTZMANN, DANIEL FRIEDRICH. - New Jersey.... Hamburg: Carl Ernst Bohn, 1797. 654mm by 471mm, hand-colored, entirely uncut & unfolded as issued. S Oct 23 (131) £950 [Schuster]
— SOTZMANN, DANIEL FRIEDRICH. - New York.... Hamburg: Carl Ernst Bohn, 1799. 486mm by 637mm, hand-colored, entirely uncut & unfolded as issued. S Oct 23 (133) £1,200 [Hubbard]
— SOTZMANN, DANIEL FRIEDRICH. - Pennsylvania.... Hamburg: Carl Ernst Bohn, 1797. 408mm by 695mm, hand-colored, entirely uncut & unfolded as issued. S Oct 23 (134) £950 [Patterson]
— SOTZMANN, DANIEL FRIEDRICH. - Rhode Island.... Hamburg: Carl Ernst Bohn, 1797. 484mm by 358mm, hand-colored, entirely uncut & unfolded as issued. S Oct 23 (137) £400 [Arader]
— SOTZMANN, DANIEL FRIEDRICH. - Vermont.... Hamburg: Carl Ernst Bohn, 1796. 685mm by 462mm, hand-colored, entirely uncut & unfolded as issued. S Oct 23 (138) £700 [Elliott]
— SPEED, JOHN. - A Map of Virginia and Maryland. L: Bassett & Chiswell, [1676]. 38.7cm by 50.2cm, early hand-coloring. pnNY Sept 13 (478) $850
— TANNER, HENRY S. - Map of the United States of America. [Phila., 1832]. 1,165mm by 1,540mm,, colored in outline, folded to fit 8vo bd case. Mtd on linen; minor worming in northern Arkansas. sg Nov 20 (243) $1,100

Anr Ed. [Phila., 1834]. 1,190mm by 1,540mm, colored in outline, folded to fit 8vo lea case. Minor offsetting; 1 brown spot in Virginia mountains. sg Nov 20 (244) $1,200
— TIDDEMAN, M. - A Draught of Virginia from the Capes to York.... Dublin: George Grierson, [c.1740]. 47cm by 59.7cm, hand-colored. Strengthened along margins; trimmed along lower margin. pnNY

AMERICAN BOOK PRICES CURRENT

Sept 13 (482) $900
— TIRION, ISAAK. - Kaart van het Nieuw Mexico en van California. Amst., 1765. 33cm by 35.6cm, hand-colored. pnNY Sept 13 (483) $300
— VISSCHER, C. J. - Novi Belgii Novaeque Angliae nec non partis Virginiae tabula.... [Amst., c.1650 or later]. 465mm by 555mm, hand-colored in outline, with view fully colored & heightened with gold. Short split without loss. S Oct 23 (400) £1,600 [Potter]
— WALKER, JOHN & ALEXANDER. - Map of the United States.... L, 1827. 4 sheets mtd & dissected on linen in 64 sections, 1,040mm by 1,920mm folding to 8vo, hand-colored. "Fine copy". S Nov 10 (1094) £360 [Tooley]
— WYLD, JAMES. - Wyld's Military Map of the United States.... L, 1861. 35 by 24 inches, colored in outline, linen-backed. wa Sept 25 (494) $180

World

— Orbis terrarum tabula recens emendata. [Amst., c.1729]. 14 by 18 inches, matted, framed. cb June 4 (37) $225
— AA, PIETER VAN DER. - Nova Orbis terraquei tabula accuratissime delineata. Leiden, [1713 or later]. 505mm by 665mm, pn Jan 22 (760) £760 [Map House]
— ALLARD, CAROLUS. - Novissima totius orbis tabula. Amst., [c.1690]. 490mm by 585mm, with ptd gazetteer leaf attached. S Oct 23 (303) £1,000 [Arader]
— BELLIN, JACQUES NICOLAS. - Carte des variations de la Boussole et des vents generaux.... Paris: Depot de la Marine, 1765 [but c.1790]. 552mm by 884mm. S Nov 10 (1018) £210 [Fisher]
— BELLIN, JACQUES NICOLAS. - Carte reduite des parties connues du Globe Terrestre.... Paris: Depot de la Marine, 1784 [but c.1790]. 540mm by 820mm, creased at centerfold. S Nov 10 (1020) £220 [Shapero]
— BELLIN, JACQUES NICOLAS. - Essay d'une carte reduite contenant les parties connues du globe terrestre. Paris, 1748. 48.9cm by 65.4cm, early hand-coloring. 4 sheets overlaid, but corner of 1 slightly detached; some creasing in upper corner. pnNY Sept 13 (306) $200

Anr copy. 52.1cm by 71.1cm, 4 sheets overlaid. With 2 tears on left edge with other tears along edge repaired. pnNY Sept 13 (307) $235
— BLAEU, JAN. - Novus Planiglobii Terrestris per utrumque polum conspectus. Amst., [c.1695]. 400mm by 535mm, colored in a contemp hand. With Valck imprint imposed over that of Blaeu. Unfolded copy. S Oct 23 (301) £2,000 [Map]
— BLAEU, WILLEM & JAN. - Nova et

accuratissima totius terrarum orbis tabula. [Amst., 1662]. 400mm by 540mm, finely colored in a contemp han; framed. S Oct 23 (299) £2,400 [Map]
— BLAEU, WILLEM. - Nova totius terrarum orbis.... [Amst., 1630, or later]. 417mm by 540mm. Minor discoloration. S Oct 23 (298) £1,300 [Sneyd]
— BLAEU, WILLEM & JAN. - Nova Totius Terrarum Orbis Georgaphica Ac Hydrographia Tabula. [Amst., c.1630-55]. 50cm by 60.5cm, hand-colored. HN Nov 26 (475) DM1,500

Anr copy. 412mm by 545mm, colored in a contemp hand. Some wear & a few slight holes down centerfold; browned; laid down. pnNY Dec 10 (206) $750

Anr copy. 417mm by 540mm, Backed with tissue repairing split at fold. S June 25 (336) £900 [Arader]
— BRUE, ADRIEN HUBERT. - Mappe-Monde sur la projection de Mercator.... Paris, 1816. 1,110mm by 1,550mm, in 4 sheets, colored in outline. S Oct 23 (312) £500 [Monckton]
— CHATELAIN, HENRI. - Mappe-Monde. Paris, [c.1760]. 13 by 18 inches, early hand-coloring. pnNY Sept 13 (329) $225
— CHATELAIN, HENRI. - Nouveau Mappe monde. Paris, [c.1760]. 47.6cm by 67.3cm, early hand-coloring. Tear along fold. pnNY Sept 13 (330) $275
— COVENS, JOHANNES & MORTIER, C. - Carte Generale de toutes les costes du monde et les pays nouvellement decouvert. Amst., [c.1715]. 585mm by 895mm, colored in wash & outline in a contemp hand. S Oct 23 (305) £850 [Arader]

Anr copy. Hand-colored in outline. Faint crease at fold. S June 25 (337) £700 [Hagstrom]
— DANCKERTS, J. - Nova Totius Terrarum orbis tabula. [Amst., 1680 or later]. 475mm by 550mm, hand-colored. Some discoloration & minor repairs. S July 14 (702) £800
— FRISIUS, LAURENT. - Orbis typus universalis iuxta hydrographorum.... [Lyons, 1535]]. 315mm by 480mm. Some restoration affecting ptd surface. From Ptolemy's Geographia. S Oct 23 (293) £400 [Damms]
— GRYNAEUS, SIMON. - Typus cosmographicus universalis. [Basel, 1532 or later]. Harrisse's B state. 360mm by 556mm, 2 sheets joined S Oct 23 (294) £1,800 [Monckton]
— JAILLOT, H. - Mappe-Monde geo-hydrographique. Paris, 1696. 540mm by 900mm, hand-colored in outline.. Repaired at outer margin & centerfold without apparent loss. S Oct 23 (304) £420 [Potter]
— JAUGEON, N. & PARIS, 1688. - Sciences du jeu du monde ou la carte generale contenante les mondes coeleste terrestre et civile.... State 1. 1,230mm by 920mm, in 6 sheets joined. Repaired at junction of folds; some repairs. S Oct 23 (300) £2,500 [Browning]
— MERULA, PAULUS. - Totius Orbis cogniti universalis descriptio. [Leiden, 1605]. 295mm by 495mm. Traces of folds skilfully strengthened; 1 margin a little close as usual. S Apr 23 (210) £1,300 [Burgess]
— MOLL, HERMANN. - A New and Corrected Map of the Whole World. L, [1730]. 565mm by 970mm, hand-colored in outline. Minor marginal repairs without loss. S May 29 (1067) £350
— MORTIER, PIETER. - Carte generale du Monde.... Amst., [c.1700]. 395mm by 470mm, hand-colored. S Nov 10 (1015) £360 [Shapero]
— MOXON, JOSEPH. - A Map of all the Earth and how after the Flood it was Divided among the Sons of Noah. [Amst., c.1680?]. 31.7cm by 45.1cm, early hand-coloring. Creased & soiled, thin upper margin. pnNY Sept 13 (421) $300
— MOXON, JOSEPH. - A Mapp of all the Earth.... L, [1671?]. 315mm by 460mm, hand-colored in outline, on thick paper. S Nov 10 (1014) £260 [Shapero]
— MUENSTER, SEBASTIAN. - Typus Orbis universalis. [N.p., c.1560]. 26cm by 37.5cm, early hand-coloring. Tear along lower margin repaired. pnNY Sept 13 (430) $500

Anr copy. 31cm by 40cm, hand-colored. Tear in upper margin; 2 wormholes. pnNY Sept 13 (431) $550
— ORTELIUS, ABRAHAM. - Typus orbis terrarum. [Antwerp, 1571 or later]. 342mm by 502mm, old hand-coloring. Tear in lower corner repaired; small tear on margin. pnNY Dec 10 (237) $750

Anr Ed. [Antwerp, 1574]. 330mm by 485mm, colored in a contemp hand. Light creasing at lower fold. S Oct 23 (295) £1,100 [Arader]

Anr Ed. [Antwerp, 1579]. 333mm by 495mm, fully colored in a contemp hand. Short split at lower fold without apparent loss. S June 25 (335) £1,300 [Moore]

Anr Ed. [Antwerp, 1588 or later]. 355mm by 485mm, hand-colored, framed. Small split at centerfold. S Oct 23 (297) £980 [Wittaker]

Anr copy. 14 by 19.5 inches. T Mar 19 (138) £600

Anr Ed. [Antwerp, c.1590]. 355mm by 485mm, hand-colored, framed. Small repair at fold. S Jan 12 (195) £1,300 [Pantazelos]

Anr Ed. [Antwerp, c.1612]. 355mm by

MAPS & CHARTS

485mm, colored in a contemp hand. Marginal browning. S Apr 24 (209) £900 [George]
— PLANCIUS, P. - Orbis Terrarum typus de integro multis in locis emendatus...1594. [Amst., c.1599]. 404mm by 576mm, hand-colored. Trimmed to platemark & with added blank margins, framed. S Oct 23 (296) £2,800 [Map]
— PRICE, CHARLES. - A New and Correct Map of the World.... L: George Willdey, [c.1715?]. State 2. 635mm by 965mm, 2 sheets joined, colored in outline. Additional folds reinforced. S Oct 23 (310) £1,700 [Smiley]
— PTOLEMAEUS, CLAUDIUS. - Tabula nova totius orbis. Basel, [c.1542]. 28.5cm by 34.29cm, early hand-coloring. Centerfold strengthened. pnNY Sept 13 (462) $700
— PTOLEMAEUS, CLAUDIUS. - Typus orbis descriptione.... [c.1550]. 30.5cm by 45.7cm,, early hand-coloring. Centerfold strengthened; surface repaired. pnNY Sept 13 (463) $800
— ROBERT DE VAUGONDY. - Mappe-Monde. Paris, [c.1780]. 48.3cm by 74cm, hand-colored. pnNY Sept 13 (354) $250
— ROBERT DE VAUGONDY, GILLES & DIDIER. - Orbis vetus. Venice, 1752. 477mm by 710mm, early hand-coloring. Creased, trimmed to within plate. pnNY Sept 13 (355) $250
— SANSON D'ABBEVILLE, NICOLAS. - Mappamondo.. Rome: Caleographia Camerale [c.1690]. 375mm by 508mm, contemp hand-coloring. Thin margins. pnNY Sept 13 (469) $375
— SANTINI, FRANCOIS. - Nouvelle mappe monde. Venice, [c.1777]. 20 by 25½ inches, early hand-coloring pnNY Sept 13 (469A) $400
— SEUTTER, MATTHEW. - Diversi globe terraquei.... Augsburg, [c.1735]. 492mm by 575mm, colored in wash & outline in a contemp hand. S Oct 23 (308) £480 [Hendry]
— SEUTTER, MATTHAEUS. - Diversi Globi Terr-Aquei.... [Augsberg, c.1735]. 50.2cm by 57.8cm, hand-colored. Centerfold worn. pnNY Sept 13 (476) $750
— THOMPSON, GEORGE. - A New Map of the World, with all the New Discoveries.... L, 1 Jan 1798. 630mm by 940mm, 2 sheets joined, hand-colored in outline. Small hole at lower right touching engraved surface. S Apr 23 (211) £1,600 [Quaritch]
— VALCK, GERARD. - Orbis Terrarum Nova et Accurata Tabula. Amst., [c.1700]. 483mm by 572mm, early hand-coloring. Strengthened down center-fold. pnNY Sept 13 (484) $1,200
— VEZOU, LOUIS CLAUDE DE. - Mappe-monde Geo-spherique ou Nouvelle Carte.... Paris,

AMERICAN BOOK PRICES CURRENT

1754. 604mm by 910mm, coloed in a contemp hand. Small marginal waterstain not affecting colors; short split without loss. S Oct 23 (118) £600 [Monckton]
— VISSCHER, NIKOLAUS. - Orbis terrarum nova et accuratissima tabula. [Amst., c.1660]. 470mm by 560mm, hand-colored in outline. Faint creases & small repair at fold. S Jan 12 (198) pS1,100 [Pantazelos]
— WELLS, EDWARD. - A New Map of the Terraqueous Globe. Oxford, [c.1700]. 37.5cm by 51.4cm, crude early hand-coloring. Creased along central fold. pnNY Sept 13 (499) $425
— ZUERNER, ADAM FRIEDRICH. - Planisphaerium Terrestre cum utroque Coelesti Hemisphaerio.... Amst.: Pieter Schenk, [c.1700]. 576mm by 504mm, hand-colored. Short split without loss. S Oct 23 (302) £550 [Arader]

Maps & Charts, Europe
— DUDLEY, SIR ROBERT. - Carta particolare dell'Isole di Islandia.... [Florence, c.1661]. 475mm by 755mm. S June 25 (251) £700

Marais, Paul —&
Dufresne de Saint-Leon, A.
— Catalogue des Incunables de la Bibliotheque Mazarine. Paris, 1893. 8vo, half cloth; worn. sg May 14 (492) $150

Maran, Rene, 1887-1960. See: Limited Editions Club

Marbault,—
— Essai sur le commerce de Russie.... Amst., 1777. 8vo, contemp calf; rubbed, bowed. With folding map. O May 12 (135) $450

Marbecke, John
— A Concordance.... [L]: Richard Grafton, July 1550. 1st Ed. Folio, modern calf. 3 leaves short; 5 leaves remargined; tp discolored & with 2 small holes in border; 2 small rust-holes in margins of H4 & 3P1; some tears, those in 2P6 & 3B4 affecting text; some marginal dampstains. S Dec 18 (320) £350 [Knohl]

Marbot, Alfred de
— Costumes militaires francais, depuis l'organisation des premieres troupes regulieres.... Paris, [1830-60]. 3 vols. Folio, loose in 23 folders in 3 portfolios within 3 slipcases; worn & broken. With 450 plates. Lacking text. Sold with a copy of Marbot's Tableaux synoptiques, 1826. S June 25 (208) £3,200

Marbury, Mary Orvis
— Favorite Flies and their Histories. Bost., 1892. 4to, orig cloth. Library copy. sg Oct 23 (394) $150

Anr copy. Orig cloth; soiled & worn. With

32 color plates. wa Sept 25 (89) $160

Marc, Franz, 1880-1916. See: Kandinsky & Marc

Marcelli, Francesco Antonio
— Regole della scherma insegnate da Lelio e Titta Marcelli. Rome: D. A. Ercole, 1686. 4to, modern half vellum. With frontis & 34 half-page engravings. A few blank margins strengthened slightly affecting a few letters on a3v; minor spotting to 3 leaves; small tear in f2 & n4. C Dec 12 (300) £400 [Lanfranchi]

Marcellinus, Ammianus
— Rerum gestarum.... Leiden, 1693. Folio, blind-stamped vellum. With engraved title & 15 plates. Some stains. pn Sept 18 (217) £65 [Poel]

Anr copy. Contemp vellum; soiled. Lacking tp; folding plates with short tears. S Mar 10 (1101) £100 [Hasbach]

Anr copy. Contemp calf; rubbed, joints worn. Library stamp on tp verso; some dampstaining in upper margins. S July 14 (416) £100

Marcgravius, Georglus. See: Piso & Marcgravius

Marchand, Jean Henri, d. c.1785
— Calendrier ou essai historique et legal sur la chasse.... Paris: Le Jay, 1770. 12mo, mor gilt by Petit. Jeanson copy. SM Mar 1 (396) FF1,700

Marchand, Prosper, d.1756
— Histoire de l'origine et des premiers progres de l'imprimerie. The Hague, 1740. 2 parts in 1 vol. 4to, contemp calf gilt. C Dec 12 (283) £200 [Greenwood]

Anr Ed. The Hague, 1742. 2 parts in 1 vol. 4to, contemp calf; worn. Lacking half-title or initial blank; perforated stamp on tp & other leaves. sg Mar 26 (197) $120

Marchesinus, Joannes
— Mammotrectus super Bibliam. Venice: Franciscus Renner de Heilbronn & Nicolaus de Frankfordia, 1476. 4to, contemp vellum; worn. 225 (of 228) leaves. Goff M-236. HN May 20 (1657) DM1,500

Marchetti, Alessandro, 1632-1714
— De resistentia solidorum. Florence: V. Vangelisti & P. Matini, 1669. 4to, contemp vellum. Some browning; tear in foremargin of D4 touching a few letters. Inscr to Count Giulio Cesare Gonzaga on tp. S June 25 (120) £550 [Kraus]

Marco, Georg —& Schlechter, C.
— Das Internationale Schachmeisterturnier in Karlsbad 1907. Vienna: Verlag der Wiener Schachzeitung, [1907]. Cloth, orig upper wrap bound in. pn Mar 26 (62) £100 [DeLucia]

Marcus Aurelius Antoninus, 121-180
— The Thoughts. L: Medici Society, 1912. Illus by W. Russell Flint. Mor by Sangorski & Sutcliffe. sg Feb 12 (217) $200
— Wisdom of the Emperor Marcus Aurelius. Bost.: Pvtly ptd by Nathan Haskell Dole, [1903]. One of 100. Mor gilt. cb Sept 11 (304) $130

Marcy, Randolph Barnes, 1812-87
— Exploration of the Red River of Louisiana.... Wash., 1854. House Issue. 8vo, orig cloth; worn. With 65 plates, some torn. wa Sept 25 (456) $80
— The Prairie Traveller: a Hand-Book for Overland Expeditions. NY, 1859. 1st Ed. 8vo, orig cloth; rubbed. cb Jan 8 (117) $190

Mardersteig, Giovanni
— The Officina Bodoni. Verona, 1980. One of 125. 4to, orig half mor gilt. With separate vol of orig leaves from book of the press. bba Oct 16 (492) £420 [Georges]

One of 1,500. Orig cloth; worn. O June 16 (129) $50

One of 99 with 10 orig leaves. Orig half mor. S Nov 10 (17) £320 [Forster]

Mardrus, Joseph Charles Victor
— Histoire charmante de l'adolescente sucre d'amour. Paris, 1927. 1st Ed, One of 170 on velin d'Arches. Illus by Schmied. 4to, unsewn in orig wraps. Sgd by Schmied. S Dec 4 (30) £1,080 [Marks]
— Le Livre de la verite de parole. Paris, 1929. One of 150. Illus by F. L. Schmied. 4to, unsewn in orig wraps. S Dec 4 (31) £1,000 [Joseph & Sawyer]

Marez, Hendrik de
— Mijn herte weet. Antwerp, 1898. Ltd Ed. Designed by K. Doudelet. Orig wraps; rebacked. B Oct 7 (41a) HF850

Marguerite d'Angouleme, 1492-1549
— L'Heptameron. Berne, 1780-81. ("Les Nouvelles....") 3 vols. 8vo, contemp mor gilt. Some foxing. Wilmerding copy. sg Apr 2 (138) $850

Mariana, Juan de, 1536-1623?
— The General History of Spain. L, 1699. Folio. old calf. Contents bound out of order, heavily foxed. sg Nov 20 (106) $80

MARIANO

Mariano, Vincent C.
— In the Ring of the Rise. NY, [1976]. One of 175. 4to, syn. sg Oct 23 (395) $90

Mariette, Jean
— L'Architecture francaise. Paris & Brussels, 1927-29. Ed by Louis Hautecoeur. 3 vols. Folio, modern half vellum; soiled. With 166 plates. HN May 20 (194) DM2,600
Anr copy. Loose as issued in orig wraps. HN May 20 (195) DM1,300

Mariette Library, Pierre Jean
— Catalogue raisonne des differens objets de curiosites dans les sciences et arts.... Paris, 1775. Compiled by Francois Basan. 8vo, half calf; worn. Priced in ink throughout. S NOv 27 (91) £250 [Quaritch]

Marinaro, Vincent
— A Modern Dry-Fly Code. NY: Crown, [1970]. One of 350. In d/j. sg Oct 23 (397) $175
Anr copy. Lea. sg Oct 23 (397) $175

Mariner's...
— The Mariner's Chronicle: Containing Narratives of the Most Remarkable Disasters at Sea.... New Haven, 1834. Contemp sheep; worn. Foxed. cb Nov 6 (201) $70
— The Mariner's Library or Voyager's Companion. Bost., 1834. Later calf. Several engravings colored by a former owner; lacking 1 prelim leaf & final leaves. cb Nov 6 (203) $55

Marinis, Tammaro de
— Catalogue d'un collection anciens livres a figures italiens. Milan: Ulrich Hoepli, [1925]. One of 440. Folio, cloth. sg May 14 (493) $325
— Die Italienischen Renaissance—Einbande der Bibliothek Furstenberg.... Hamburg, [1966]. Folio, orig cloth. With 79 plates. bba Oct 16 (471) £55 [Forsterough]

Marinoni, Giovanni Jacopo de
— De astronomia specula domestica et organico apparatus astronomico.... Vienna, 1745. Folio, contemp calf. Some worming. HK Nov 4 (1061) DM4,600

Marionette...
— The Marionette. Florence, 1918-19. Ed by Edward Gordon Craig. Vol I, Nos. 1-12 & Special Issue, "The Three Men of Gotham" (complete set). Half vellum. sg Feb 26 (103) $1,200

Mariotte, Edme, 1620-85
— Oeuvres. Leiden, 1717. 2 parts in 1 vol. 4to, contemp vellum. With 26 folding plates. pn June 18 (197) £260 [Campbell]
— Recueil de plusieurs traitez de mathematique de l'Academie Royal des Sciences.

AMERICAN BOOK PRICES CURRENT

Paris, 1676-77. 4 parts (of 6) in 1 vol. Folio, bds; broken. L.p. copy. bba Oct 16 (306) £160 [Pickering & Chatto]

Mariz Carneiro, Antonio de
— Roteiro da India Oriental. Lisbon: Domingos Carneyro, 1666. 4to, modern mor gilt. C Apr 8 (38) £1,200 [Ramer]

Markham, Edwin, 1852-1940
[-] A Wreath for Edwin Markham; Tributes from the Poets of America on his Seventieth Birthday, April 23, 1922. Chicago: The Bookfellows, 1922. One of 300. Half cloth. Inscr by Markham, 1923. sg Dec 11 (81) $80

Markham, Francis, 1565-1627
— Five Decades of Epistles of Warre. L, 1622. 1st Ed. Folio, contemp calf; rubbed, rebacked, old spine preserved. Lacking 1st & last blanks. S July 14 (333) £230

Markham, Col. Frederick
— Shooting in the Himalayas: a Journal of Sporting Adventures and Travel. L, 1854. 8vo, contemp half calf; rubbed. With map & 8 plates. bba May 14 (103) £120 [Check]

Markham, Gervase, 1568?-1637
— Cheape and Good Husbandry for the Well-Ordering of all Beasts.... L: T.S., 1623. 3d Ed. 4to, modern calf. 3 leaves with tear in upper margin; some stains & soiling. S Nov 10 (522) £50 [Vine]
6th Ed. L: Anne Griffin for John Harrison, 1631. 4to, modern half calf. Fore-margins of O3 & O4 frayed; lacking prelim blank A1 & final blank O6. Hunt copy. CNY Nov 21 (193) $220
Anr Ed. L, 1653. 4to, calf; worn & rebacked. Lacking initial blank; 1 corner stained throughout. S Nov 10 (524) £50 [Randall]
— Country Contentments.... L: I. B. for R. Jackson, 1623. 4to, modern half mor; worn at extremities. Lacking last leaf. Hunt copy. CNY Nov 21 (75) $130
Anr Ed. L, 1654. 4to, calf. Lacking last 2 blanks. S Nov 10 (519) £50 [Bookroom]
10th Ed. L, 1669. 4to, recent half calf. T Oct 16 (386) £140
— The English Hous-Wife.... L, 1653. "5th" Ed. 4to, contemp calf; worn & rebacked. Lacking pp 139-50; margins frayed; stained. S Nov 10 (521) £60 [Bine]
— The Inrichment of the Weald of Kent. L: Anne Griffin for John Harrison, 1636. Bound with: Markhams Farewell to Husbandry.... L: Edward Griffin for John Harrison, 1638. 4to, contemp calf; rebacked, corners repaired. Hunt copy. CNY Nov 21 (194) $350
— Markham's Farewell to Husbandry. L,

1653. 4to, calf. Marginal staining. S Nov 10 (520) £50 [Bookroom]
— A Way to Get Wealth.... L: Nicholas Okes for John Harison, 1631. 8vo, contemp calf; worn. Lacking general title, C6 & G5. S Mar 10 (1103) £190 [Wise]

13th Ed. L: E. H., 1676. 4to, contemp calf. General title torn. P Nov 25 (310) $450

Markland, George
See also: Derrydale Press
— Pteryplegia; or the Art of Shooting-Flying.... L, 1727. 8vo, disbound. Tp foxed. sg Oct 23 (398) $150

Marklove, H.
— Views of Berkeley Castle. L, 1840. Folio, half mor gilt; rubbed. With double-page frontis & 12 plates. Some plates spotted. L July 2 (93) £320

Marloth, Rudolf
— The Flora of South Africa.... Cape Town, 1913-32. 4 vols in 6. 4to, cloth; marked. Vol IV lacking fig 59 as usual. SSA Feb 11 (566) R1,500

Marlowe, Christopher, 1564-93
— The Famous Tragedy of the Rich Jew of Malta. L, 1933. One of the copies taken over by Hollis & Carter & numbered with a number plus an (a). Illus by Eric Ravilious. 4to, orig cloth. cb Dec 4 (129) $95
— The Tragicall History of Doctor Faustus. L: Golden Hours Press, 1932. One of 250. Illus by Blair Hughes-Stanton. 4to, half mor; spine rubbed at foot. cb Sept 11 (103) $80

Marlowe, Christopher, 1564-93 —& Chapman, George, 1559?-1634
— Hero and Leander. L: Golden Hours Press, 1933. One of 206. Illus by Lettice Sandford. 4to, orig half mor. cb Sept 11 (104) $110

Marmaduke...
— Marmaduke Multiply's Merry Method of Making Minor Mathematicians. L: J. Harris, [imprints dated 1816-17]. Issue not specified. 16mo, mor gilt with the name Sarah Napier to each cover; rubbed & gnawed. T July 16 (432) £150

Marmol Carvajal, Luis del
— L'Afrique de Marmol.... Paris, 1667. 3 vols. 4to, contemp & modern calf; rebacked. Lacking tp to Vol III & half-title to Vol I; first few leaves of Vol III affected by worming. Sold w.a.f. Ck May 8 (361) £280

Marmont du Hautchamp, Barthelemy
— Histoire du systeme des finances, sous la minorite de Louis XV. The Hague, 1739. 6 vols in 3. 12mo, contemp half calf; corners knocked. Lacking 3 blanks; half-title in Vol I only; some minor stains & foxing. P Sept 24 (339) $2,400

Marmontel, Jean Francois, 1723-99
— Les Contes moraux. Paris, 1765. 1st Issue, with errata at foot of contents leaves. 3 vols. 12mo, mor gilt by Zaehnsdorf. With port (with reversed proof loosely inserted) engraved titles (with 2 eaux-fortes, 1 reversed) & 23 plates (12 proofs before letters, 1 in 2 states & 8 eaux-fortes in different states bound in). L.p. copy on papier velin. C May 13 (34) £800 [Joseph]

Marnette, ——
— The Perfect Cook, being the Most Exact Directions for the making all Kinds of Pastes.... L: for Nath. Brooks, 1656. 12mo, modern calf. With frontis; with blank O12 & longitudinal half-title on A12. Marginal tears & fraying at beginning; L5 with page numeral punched through; some headlines shaved; some soiling; some dampstaining to lower margins. P Nov 25 (311) $900

Marolles, gaston de
— Langage et termes de venerie. Paris, 1906. 4to, half cloth. Jeanson copy. SM Mar 1 (398) FF4,000

Marolois, Samuel
— Artis Muniendi, sive fortificationis.... Amst.: Jansson, 1633. 2 parts in 1 vol. Folio, contemp vellum; soiled. With 42 double-page plates & 1 double-page table. Wormhole affecting 1st few leaves (touching letters). S Nov 10 (945) £170 [Dennistoun]

Marra, John
— Journal of the Resolution's Voyage.... L: for F. Newbery, 1775. 8vo, contemp calf; rebacked. With folding chart & 5 plates. D2 a cancel, chart shaved at neatline & laid on tissue. S Apr 24 (376) £800 [Quaritch]

Marraccio, Hippolyto
— De Diva Virgine, Copacavana, in Pervano Novi Mundi Regno Celeberrima. Liber Unus. Rome: H. Colini, 1656. 8vo, later vellum. Some dampstains, mostly marginal. sg Sept 18 (168) $60

Marroni, Salvatore
— Raccolta dei principali costumi religiosi e militari della Corte Pontificia. Rome, [c.1845]. Bound with: Nuova Raccolta principali Costumi di Roma. Rome [n.d.] Folio, cloth; stained, soiled. 1st work with title & 18 plates; 2d work with title & 43

MARRONI

plates -- all in both works hand-colored. bba Dec 18 (190) £600 [Rostron]

Marryat, Francis S., 1826-55
— Borneo and the Indian Archipelago.... L, 1848. 1st Ed. 8vo, orig cloth; joints cracked. With engraved title, colored frontis & 20 plates. Phillipps copy. S Feb 24 (492) £260 [McKenzie]

Marryat, Capt. Frederick, 1792-1848
See also: Moore & Marryat
— Works. L, [c.1900]. Ltd Ed. 24 vols. Lev gilt. sg Feb 12 (218) $275

Marschall von Bieberstein, Friedrich August
— Centuria plantarum rariorum Rossiae meridionalis. Charkov, 1810. One of 70. Part I (of 2). Folio, contemp half mor; rubbed. With 50 colored plates. Ouseley —de Belder copy. S Apr 28 (226) £6,000 [Asher]

Marseillais. See: Blanc, Mathieu

Marshall, C. H. T. See: Hume & Marshall

Marshall, Frances & Hugh
— Old English Embroidery: Its Technique and Symbolism. L, 1894. 4to, cloth; worn. O Nov 18 (118) $80

Marshall, Henry Rissik
— Coloured Worcester Porcelain of the First Period.... Newport, 1954. One of 1,200. 4to, orig cloth. S Mar 9 (690) £65 [Stodart]

Marshall, John, 1755-1835
— The Life of George Washington. L, 1804-7. 6 vols, including Atlas. 8vo & 4to, contemp half lea; rubbed, a few joints broken. With port & 14 plates & maps. O Nov 18 (119) $230

Anr copy. Atlas only. Orig bds; rebacked with modern cloth. With 10 maps. Minor snag at top edge of 5 maps & 3 text leaves; dampstain on top inner edge of tp. sg Sept 18 (169) $275

Marshall, William, 1745-1818
— A Review of the Landscape.... L, 1795. 8vo, old calf; rebacked. Lacking half-title or initial blank. sg Mar 26 (198) $130
— The Rural Economy of Norfolk.... L, 1787. 1st Ed. 2 vols. 8vo, contemp calf; rubbed, joints split. T Sept 18 (126) £95
— The Rural Economy of Glocestershire.... Gloucester, 1789. 1st Ed. 2 vols. 8vo, contemp half mor; rubbed. Sept 18 (125) £180
— Rural Economy.... L, 1795-99. 6 works in 12 vols. 8vo, contemp half calf. C Dec 12 (145) £900 [McCrow]

AMERICAN BOOK PRICES CURRENT

Marsigli, Luigi Ferdinando, Count, 1658-1730
— Description du Danube, depuis la montagne de Kalenberg.... The Hague, 1744. Vol V only. Folio, contemp calf; worn & def. With frontis & 73 (of 74) color plates. FD June 11 (721) DM6,600
— Histoire physique de la mer. Amst., 1725. 8vo, contemp vellum. With frontis, 12 maps & 40 plates. Frontis def. FD June 11 (722) DM3,100

Marston, Anne Lee
— Records of a California Family: Journals and Letters of Lewis C. Gunn and Elizabeth Le Breton Gunn. San Diego, 1928. One of 300. Half cloth; spine ends rubbed & creased. With map & 15 plates. Inscr. cb Mar 19 (187) $110

Anr copy. Half cloth. Inscr by the Gunns' daughter. cb Ja 8 (118) $110

Marston, George. See: Murray & Marston

Marsyas
— Eine Zweimonatsschrift. Berlin, 1917-19. One of 235. Vol I, Nos 1-6 (all pbd). Folio, orig wraps. With 86 lithos (21 sgd by the artists). S Dec 4 (20) £1,300 [Gardiner]

Marta, Luigi
— Costumi della Festa data da S. Maesta' il di 20 Feb 1854. Paris: Bertauts, 1854. Oblong folio, half mor. With litho title & 31 hand-colored plates. Dedication & text leaf stained. S Oct 23 (153) £1,200 [Lyon]

Martens, Robert W. See: Sisson & Martens

Martial...
— The Martial Achievements of Great Britain. L: James Jenkins, [1815]. 4to, half mor gilt; spine def. With 54 hand-colored plates, including titles & dedication. Frontis & tp soiled; lacking list of subscribers; some margins frayed. pn May 21 (226) £420 [Shapiro]

Anr copy. Moden half calf gilt. With engraved title, colored dedication leaf & 52 hand-colored plates. Lacking port & subscribers list. pn June 28 (72) £480 [Campbell]

Anr copy. Contemp half mor; rubbed. With uncolored engraved title, colored dedication with arms, frontis & 51 hand-colored plates. Margins of 2 plates repaired; some browning throughout, upper hinge cracked. S Apr 23 (80) £780

Anr Ed. L: James Jenkins, [plates watermarked 1830-31]. 4to, contemp half mor; joints & corners rubbed. With engraved title haing colored vignette, engraved dedication having hand-colored coat-of-arms & with 52 colored plates. C Dec 12 (33) £1,000 [Armero]

MARTIN

Martial de Paris, dit d'Auvergne
— Droictz nouveaux publiez de par messieurs les Senateurs du temple de Cupido.... [N.p., 1540]. 8vo, 19th-cent mor gilt. First few leaves very lightly discolored. S Nov 27 (192) £900 [Sarti]

Martialis, Marcus Valerius
— Opera. Amst.: Joannes Jansson, 1628. ("M. Val. Martialis. ex Museo Petri Scriverii.") 16mo, later mor. Tp dusty. cb Oct 23 (148) $80

Martin, Alexandre
— Manuel de l'amateur de truffes.... Paris, 1829. 2d Ed. 8vo, mor by Crahan, orig wraps bound in. With folding colored frontis by Henry Monnier. Crahan copy. P Nov 25 (453) $350

Martin, Charles & Leopold
— The Civil Costume of England from the Conquest to the Present Period. L, 1842. 4to, cloth. With engraved title & 60 hand-colored plates. bba Dec 18 (191) £55 [Smith]

Martin, David, 1639-1721
— Historie de ouden en nieuwen Testamenten. Amst., 1700. 2 vols in 3. Folio, half calf; def. With 2 engraved titles, 5 double-page maps & 214 plates. B Feb 25 (744) HF1,600

Martin de Argenta, Vincente
— Album de la flora medico-farmaceutica.... Madrid, 1862-64. 3 vols. Folio, contemp calf; rubbed. With 3 litho titles, 3 litho ports & 300 hand-colored litho plates. de Belder copy. S Apr 28 (227) £2,200 [Preciadas]

Martin, Fred
— A Travel Book. San Francisco: Arion Press, 1976. One of 200. Folio, cloth in Lucite slipcase. sg Jan 8 (9) $130

Martin, Fredrik Robert
— A History of Oriental Carpets before 1800. Vienna, 1908. One of 300. 3 vols. Folio, orig half cloth; stained, spine worn. With 33 plates, many colored & mtd. All leaves loose, dampstains in inner margin of many leaves. bba Oct 16 (250) £2,000 [Abingdon]

Martin, Gregory, d.1582
— A Discoverie of the Manifold Corruptions of the Holy Scriptures.... Rheims: John Fogny, 1582. 8vo, contemp vellum. Some dampstains; outer corners of prelim & final leaves creased & torn. Ck Apr 24 (24) £160

Anr copy. 19th-cent sheep; front hinge cracked, crudely reinforced. Soiled & dampstained; first 7 leaves possibly from anr copy. sg Oct 9 (268) $175

Martin, Henry, 1852-1927 —& Others
— Le Livre francais, des origines a la fin du Second Empire. Paris, 1924. 4to, half mor; joints & corners rubbed. cba Feb 5 (124) $160

Anr copy. Cloth. sg May 14 (238) $100

Martin, John, 1789-1869
— An Account of the Natives of the Tonga Islands. L, 1817. 1st Ed. 2 vols. 8vo, contemp calf; joints cracked. With frontis. S July 14 (851) £220

Martin, John, 1789?-1854
— Illustrations of the Bible. L, 1838. Folio, orig cloth; faded & rubed. With 20 plates; plates & leaves loose. S Dec 4 (201) £700 [Joseph & Sawyer]

Martin, John, 1791-1855
— A Bibliographical Catalogue of Books Privately Printed. L, 1834. 8vo, contemp half mor; rubbed. bba Feb 5 (17) £240 [Henderson]

2d Ed. L, 1854. 8vo, contemp mor gilt; rubbed. A few leaves spotted. bba Feb 5 (18) £130 [Dawson]

Martin, Martin, d.1719
— A Description of the Western Islands of Scotland. L, 1703. 8vo, calf gilt. With folding map & plate Folding map & outer margins of last leaf repaired; plate margin cropped without loss. pnE Jan 28 (72) £190 [Frost]

Anr copy. Contemp calf; upper hinge broken, crudely repaired with tape at top & bottom of spine. Lacking map & folding plate. T Feb 19 (341) £35

2d Ed. L, 1716. 8vo, contemp calf; rebacked. With folding map & 1 plate. Folding map with slight tear. S Nov 17 (805) £110 [Russell]

Martin, Richard
A Seach Delivered to the Kings...Majestie.... L: for T. Thorppe, 1603. Mor gilt by Bedford with Britwell arms. Lacking A1. S Sept 23 (366) £360 [Quaritch]

Martin, Robert Montgomery, 1803?-68
— The British Colonies, their History, Extent.... L, [1855]. 12 orig parts. 4to, orig cloth; spines chipped. With 40 double-page maps colored in outline. pn Mar 5 (33) £750 [Leadley]
— History of the British Colonies. L, 1834-35. 5 vols in 6. 8vo, contemp calf gilt. With folding chart & 26 maps, some hand-colored in outline, some folding. Lacking half-titles; maps backed with linen. C Oct

MARTIN

15 (70) £450 [Cavendish]
Anr copy. 5 vols. 8vo, orig cloth. With 26 maps, colored in outline. Some tears without loss. S Feb 24 (421) £360 [Orient]
— The Indian Empire; History, Topography, Geology. L, [1858-61]. 3 vols in 2. 4to, contemp half calf; worn, 1 spine crudely repaired. Some plates soiled in margin. bba Aug 20 (478) £130 [Henderson]
— Tallis's Illustrated Atlas. L, 1851. Folio, contemp half calf; rubbed. With engraved title & 81 hand-colored maps & 2 plates. Ck Nov 21 (400) £1,400

Anr copy. Orig half lea; def. With frontis, 81 colored maps & 2 plain plates. SMall tears to 2 maps. pn Dec 11 (405) £1,300 [Sweet]

Anr copy. Modern half mor gilt. With engraved title, frontis & 81 maps, hand-colored in outline, & 2 plates. One or 2 plates marked faintly. S Oct 23 (236) £1,500 [Marsden]

Anr copy. Contemp half mor; worn. With engraved title & 110 maps & plans, most hand-colored in outline. Some plates loose & torn with loss. Sold w.a.f. S Nov 18 (977) £1,200 [Whiteson]

Anr copy. Orig half mor gilt; rubbed, inner hinge broken. With 80 hand-colored maps & double-page uncolored town plan of Liverpool. T May 21 (262) £1,400

Martin, Thomas Commerford, 1856-1924 —& Wetzler, Joseph
— The Electric Motor and its Applications. NY: Johnston, 1888. 2d Ed. 4to, orig cloth; worn & soiled, front hinge cracked. wa Nov 6 (54) $50

Martin, Violet. See: Derrydale Press

Martinelli, Domenico
— Horologi elementari divisi in quattro-parti. Venice, 1669. 1st Ed. 4to, early 19th-cent wraps. With 16 plates. Imprint at foot of tp & heading of final leaf affected by small wormholes. S May 19 (118) £900 [King]

Martinez de Espinar, Alonso
— Arte de ballesteria, y monteria.... Madrid, 1644. 4to, mor gilt by Duru. Jeanson copy. SM Mar 1 (399) FF190,000

Anr Ed. Madrid: Antonio Marin, 1761. 4to, contemp vellum. With 5 plates plus a duplicate of Plate 1 at the end. Jeanson 1482. SM Mar 1 (400) FF24,000

Martinez de la Puente, Jose
— Compendio de las historias de los descubrimentos, conquistas, y guerras de la India Oriental.... Madrid: Widow of Joseph Fernandez de Buendia, 1681. 4to, 19th-cent half sheep. Marginal worming &

AMERICAN BOOK PRICES CURRENT

scattered paper flaws, occasionally affecting sidenotes; marginal dampstaining at beginning & end; lacking half-title, pp 279-82 & penultimate index leaf (text for these supplied in Ms). sg Sept 18 (170) $225

Martingale, Pseud.
— Sporting Scenes and Country Characters.... L, 1840. 8vo, later half mor. cb May 21 (187) $55

Martini, Martinus, 1614-61
— Sinicae historiae. Munich, 1658. 4to, contemp calf gilt; worn. S Oct 23 (63) £300 [Bernard]

Martinoff, Andre Evthimievich
— Voyage pittoresque de Moscou aux frontieres de la Chine. St. Petersburg, 1819. Oblong 4to, contemp calf; rebacked & repaired. With 25 (of 30) hand-colored plates. Small damage in upper margins of 7 leaves. S Feb 24 (493) £700 [Anderson]

Martinus, Joannes, of Paris
— Praelectiones in librum Hippocratis...de morbis internis. Paris: Joannes Libert, 1637. 4to, contemp vellum; soiled. With bookplate of Constant Dumeril. cb Oct 23 (112) $225

Martius, Carl Friedrich Philipp von
See also: Spix & Martius
— Flora brasiliensis. Leipzig, 1840-1906. 15 vols in 56. Folio, 49 vols in near contemp pigskin, the remaining 7 in a similar-looking half cloth. With 2 maps & 3,805 plates. Horticultural Society of New York —de Belder copy. S Apr 28 (228) £20,000 [Elliott]
— Historia naturalis palmarum. Leipzig, 1823-53. 3 vols. Folio, contemp half russia; worn. With port, 25 plain & 220 hand-colored lithos. Horticultural Society of New York—de Belder copy. S Apr 28 (229) £23,000 [Israel]
— Nova Genera et species plantarum.... Munich, 1823. Folio, contemp half calf; worn. With 300 plates, all but 9 hand-colored. Plate 39 duplicated in Vol I. General title inserted, short in upper margin & apparently from anr copy; 2 small wormholes in inner margin of text to Vol III. S Oct 23 (709) £10,000 [Marshall]

Martuinov, Andrei Eythimievich. See: Martinoff, Andre Evthimievich

Martyn, John, 1699-1768
— Historia plantarum rariorum. L, 1728-[37]. Folio, contemp calf; rebacked. With 50 hand-finished color plates plus an orig watercolor drawing inserted before title. Slight abrasion on surface of 1 plate.

Derby—de Belder copy. S Apr 28 (231) £12,500 [Israel]

Anr Ed. Nuremberg, 1752. Folio, bds; rebacked with cloth spine & corners. With 50 hand-finished color plates. A few marginal spots & stains. Horticultural Society of New York—de Belder copy. S Apr 28 (232) £6,000 [Burgess Browning]

Martyn, Thomas, 1735-1825

— Thirty-Eight Plates with Explanations: Intended to Illustrate Linnaeus's System of Vegetables. L, 1794. 8vo, calf; rebacked. With 38 hand-colored plates. pnE Dec 17 (215) £110 [Traylen]

Martyn, Thomas, fl.1760-1816

— The English Entomologist, Exhibiting all the Coleopterous Insects.... L, 1792. 4to, later half mor gilt. With engraved title & 2 uncolored plates of medals & 42 hand-colored plates heightened with varnish. C Oct 15 (244) £500 [Greyfriars]

Anr copy. Contemp half vellum bds; worn. With engraved titles, 2 plates of medals & 42 hand-colored plates. Some soiling. S Oct 23 (730) £350 [Marshall]

— Entomologist Anglois ouvrage ou l'on a rassemble tous les Insectes Colcopteres.... L, 1792. 4to, contemp mor; rubbed & broken. With 2 plain & 42 hand-colored plates. S Nov 17 (666) £280 [Negro]

Martyn, William Frederick

— The Geographical Magazine. L, 1782-83. 2 vols. 4to, contemp half calf; rubbed. Frontises repaired; titles shaved. Ck May 15 (70) £130

Martyr, Peter. See: Vermigli, Pietro Martire

Martyr, Peter, d.1525

— De rebus oceanicis & orbe novo decades tres.... Basel: J. Bebel, 1533. Folio, modern half vellum. Bottom margin replaced & a few small wormholes repaired in final leaf; outer margins spotted or foxed; marginal ink notes & underlinings. sg Sept 18 (171) $900

— The Decades of the Newe Worlde or West India.... L, 1555. 1st Ed, 1st Issue. Trans by Rycharde Eden. 4to, later calf gilt; rebacked, rubbed. Lacking 5A3-5; 3R1 torn & repaired; 4S1 repaired; many leaves shaved at outer margin, affecting sidenotes; some dampstaining & soiling throughout. bba Oct 16 (229) £850 [Maggs]

— The History of Travayle in the West and East Indies.... L: Richard Jugge, 1577. 4to, 18th-cent blind-stamped calf; repaired & rabacked. First 5 leaves slightly soiled; ink stain on 2S1 & 2T2-3; some other soiling; outer margin of F5-6 & O7 cropped touching 7 letters of ptd marginalia. C Dec 12 (250) £4,200 [Quaritch]

Marvell, Andrew, 1621-78

— Works. L, 1776. 3 vols. 4to, contemp calf gilt; joints cracked. sg Oct 9 (269) $130

Marx, Karl, 1818-83

— Le Capital. Paris: Maurice Lachatre, [1872-75]. In Book form. 4to, 19th-cent half mor; rubbed. Marginal tear to facsimile. P Sept 24 (343) $1,000

Orig parts bound in 1 vol. 4to, contemp cloth. P Sept 24 (342) $2,600

— Capital. NY: Humboldt Publishing Co., [1886]. 8vo, half lea; extremities rubbed. Tp soiled & frayed at upper outer corner; some spotting in upper margin. S Nov 10 (396) £350 [Drury]

Anr Ed. L, 1887. 8vo, orig cloth; worn, spine-tips chipped, rear cover of Vol I cracked. Library markings. O May 12 (137) $325

— Das Kapital. Hamburg, 1867-94. 1st Ed. 3 vols in 4. 8vo, modern half calf & half mor; rubbed. Vol I lacking gathering 5 & with a duplicate of gathering 26 bound in its stead; some waterstains at end. P Sept 24 (340) $9,250

2d Ed of Book I, 1st Ed of Books II & III. Hamburg, 1872-94. 3 books in 5 vols. 8vo, 19th-cent half calf by the London socialist Cooperative Society Bindery; index to Book I misbound. S June 25 (72) £2,100 [Neidhardt]

— Kapital. Kritika Poleticeskoj Ekonomii. St. Petersburg: N. P. Poliakov, 1872. 8vo, half lea; rubbed. FD June 11 (2697) DM42,000

Mary, Princess of Liechtenstein

— Holland House. L, 1874. 2 vols. 4to, contemp mor; rubbed. Extra-illus with ports, plates & autographs, mtd. bba Dec 18 (189) £130 [Grosvenor]

Anr copy. Contemp mor; worn, 1 cover detached. Library markings. Sold w.a.f. Extra-illus with ports & plates. Ck June 5 (36) £40

Maryland

— The City Hall, Baltimore; History of Construction and Dedication. Balt., 1877. 4to, mor gilt extra; scuffed. ha Sept 19 (143) $85

Mas, Simon Alphonse

— Le Verger, ou histoire, culture et description...des varietes de fruits.... Paris, [1873]. 8 vols. 8vo, contemp half mor; rubbed. With 384 color plates. Neame—de Belder copy. S Apr 28 (233) £3,800 [Junk]

Mas, Simon Alphonse —& Pulliat, M.
— Le Vignoble ou histoire, culture...des vignes.... Paris, 1874-79. 3 vols. 8vo, half mor; inner hinges cracked. With 288 colored plates. 1 plate damaged by adhesion. Crahan copy. P Nov 25 (312) $1,300

Mascagni, Paolo, 1752-1815
— Vasorum lymphaticorum corporis humani historia et ichnographia. Siena, 1787. 1st Ed. Folio, contemp calf; spine & corners badly worn, joints cracked. Dampstaining in lower inner corners throughout. sg Apr 22|141 $1,300

Masefield, John, 1878-1967
— Right Royal. L, 1922. Ltd Ed. Illus by Cecil Aldin. Orig half vellum. pn Mar 5 (200) £50 [Donovan]
— Salt-Water Ballads. L, 1902. 1st Ed, 1st Issue. O Sept 23 (142) $230
— The Wanderer of Liverpool. L, 1930. 4to, orig calf gilt by Wood. With orig ink drawings & verse inscr by Masefield. S July 23 (161) £400 [Libris]

Masereel, Frans
— La Ville. Paris, 1928. One of 630. 4to, ptd wraps; soiled & broken. wa June 25 (512) $130

Maseres, Francis, 1731-1824
— Select Tracts relating to the Civil Wars in England. L, 1815. 2 vols. 8vo, contemp calf gilt; worn. bba Nov 13 (243) £60 [Hay]

Mask...
— The Mask: A Monthly Journal of the Art of the Theatre. L, 1908-29. Vols 1-15 (complete) plus vol containing wraps, ads & insertions for Vols 4-7. Together 16 vols. 4to & 8vo, orig half vellum. sg Feb 26 (99) $3,400

Anr copy. Vols 1-15 plus vol containing wraps, ads & insertions for Vols 4-7. Together, 16 vols. 4to & 8vo, half vellum, cloth, or orig wraps. sg Feb 26 (100) $2,000

Maskell, Alfred
— Wood Sculpture. L, 1911. 8vo, mor gilt. With frontis & 59 plates. pn Jan 22 (36) £45 [Bookroom]

Mason, George Henry
— The Costume of China. L, 1804 [plates watermarked 1818-20]. Folio, contemp mor gilt; rubbed. With 60 colored plates. C Apr 8 (158) £550 [Gaston]
— The Punishments of China. L, 1801. Folio, contemp mor gilt; joints rubbed, spine ends chipped. Some foxing & browning; Plate 19 torn & reinforced on verso. sg June 18 (219) $150

Anr Ed. L, 1804. Folio, mor gilt; spine rubbed. With 22 colored plates. pn Sept 18 (301) £120 [Waxman]

Anr Ed. L, 1808. Folio, contemp mor gilt. With 22 hand-colored plates. C Oct 15 (71) £150 [Van Noord]

Anr copy. Old mor; worn & def. S Jan 12 (314) £110 [Grants]

Anr Ed. L, 1801 [plates watermarked 1819]. Folio, contemp mor gilt. With 22 colored plates. C Apr 4 (158) £550 [Gaston]

Mason, I. J. See: Schodde & Mason

Mason, John, of Leicester
— Paper Making as an Artistic Craft. Leicester: Twelve by Eight Press, 1963. 2d Ed. Illus by Rigby Graham. 4to, orig wraps. With 8 specimens of handmade paper. bba Sept 25 (376) £35 [Brayley]
— The Twelve by Eight Papers. L: Maggs, 1959. Ltd Ed. 4to, half vellum. With 35 leaves ptd in various colors. sg Jan 8 (160) $130

Mason, Richard
— The Gentleman's New Pocket Farrier.... Richmond, 1828. 12mo, contemp calf; spine ends worn. With frontis & 4 plates. Heavily foxed. sg Dec 4 (123) $1,900

Mason, Stuart. See: Millard, Christopher Sclater

Maspero, Gaston
— History of Egypt, Chaldea, Syria Babylonia, and Assyria. L, [1903-6]. One of 200. 13 vols. 4to, half mor gilt; worn. wa Dec 11 (318) $230

One of 1,000. Orig half mor. ha May 22 (67) $450

Anr copy. 4to, cloth; worn & soiled. wa Sept 25 (31) $110

Masque...
— A Masque of Poets. Bost., 1878. 8vo, orig cloth; rebacked, orig backstrip laid down. Contains Emily Dickinson's 1st appearance in print & only work pbd during her lifetime. F Oct 30 (195) $100

Massachusetts
— A Collection of the Proceedings of the Great and General Court or Assembly.... Bost.: T. Fleet, 1729. 4to, wraps. 1st & last leaves soiled. S June 25 (411) £800
— The Perpetual Laws of the Commonwealth of Massachusetts. [Bost.: Adams & Nourse, 1789]. Folio, contemp calf; rubbed. Minor stains & foxing. O June 9 (109) $160
— Private and Special Statutes of the Commonwealth of Massachusetts, from the Year 1780 to...1805. Bost.: Manning &

Loring, 1805. 3 vols. 8vo, contemp lea; rubbed. O Nov 18 (120) $60
— Rules and Regulations for the Massachusetts Army. Watertown, 1775. 8vo, sewn. Small tear on 1 leaf not affecting text. pnNY June 11 (133) $325

Massary, Isabel. See: Laye, Elizabeth P. Ramsay

Massialot, Francois
— Le Cuisinier royal et bourgeois. Paris: Charles de Sercy, 1693. 2d Ed. 12mo, contemp calf; upper joint cracked. Corner of T2 torn away with loss; library stamp on tp; some browning. Crahan copy. P Nov 23 (314) $300

Massinger, Philip, 1583-1640
— The Unnaturall Combat. L, 1639. 1st Ed. 4to, mor by Riviere. C Dec 12 (347) £260 [Hannas]

Mast, D. Heymansz
— Practique des notarischaps, seer nut, profijtelijck ende noodigh alle jonckheyt.... Rotterdam, 1642. 8vo, vellum; soiled. B Feb 25 (705) HF1,500

Masterman, Walter S.
— The Flying Beast. NY: Dutton, [1932]. In soiled & chipped d/j. Marginal tear to pp 285-86. cb Sept 28 (923) $50

Masterpieces...
— The Masterpieces of the Centennial International Exhibition Illustrated.... Phila., [1876-78]. 3 vols. Folio, half mor; worn, scuffed. Some margins dampstained in Vols I & III. ha Sept 19 (112) $65

Masters, Edgar Lee, 1869-1950
— Mitch Miller. NY, 1920. 1st Ed, 1st State. Illus by John Sloan. Inscr by Masters & Sloan. F Jan 15 (260) $150
— Spoon River Anthology. NY, 1925. In chipped d/j. Sgd. sg Dec 11 (82) $80

Mateos, Juan
— Origen y dignidada de la caca. Madrid, 1634. 4to, mor gilt with arms of Baron Pichon, by Duru, 1843. With frontis, port & 6 plates, all double-page. Jeanson 1457. SM Mar 1 (401) FF100,000

Mather, Cotton, 1663-1728
— Boanerges. A Short Essay to Preserve and Strengthen the Good Impressions Produced by Earthquakes. Bost., 1727. 8vo, modern half mor. Library markings; well-thumbed copy. sg Mar 12 (177) $800
— Magnalia Christi Americana; or, the Ecclesiastical History of New England.... L, 1702. Folio, modern calf; worn. Some stains toward the end; 1 leaf torn without loss; map in modern color facsimile. O May 12 (138) $975
Anr copy. 19th-cent calf; joint rubbed. Map soiled & backed with linen & with a few minor repairs; a few leaves with rust holes or small losses to blank margins; occasional minor soiling or browning; lacking blank 6M2; lacking errata leaves. P Oct 29 (14) $1,600
— The Triumphs of the Reformed Religion, in America. Bost.: Benjamin Harris & John Allen for Joseph Brunning, 1691. 1st Ed. 8vo, mor gilt by Francis Bedford; joints repaired. D2 torn & repaired; 2 headlines & 1 catchword cropped; a few minor restorations. With port of Mather & facsimile signature laid down on recto & verso of 1st flyleaf and with facsimile of note sgd by Eliot bound in at front. CNY Dec 19 (81) $4,000

Mather, Increase, 1639-1723
— A Brief Relation of the State of New England.... L, 1689. 4to, half calf. Some catchwords shaved; some soiling. S June 25 (406) £1,500
— A Discourse Proving that the Christian Religion is the Only True Religion.... Bost., 1702. 12mo, contemp calf; worn with loss to head & foot of spine. Stained & browned; C4 & D12 with short marginal tears into 1 letter. P Oct 29 (16) $4,000

Mather, Samuel, 1706-85
— The Life of the Very Reverend and Learned Cotton Mather. Bost., 1729. 8vo, 18th-cent calf; rebacked with mor, outer corners nicked. Rust hole in tp not affecting type. Isaac Watts's annotated copy. sg Dec 4 (124) $1,500
— Life of...Dr. Cotton Mather. L, 1744. 12mo, mor gilt. Library markings. sg Mar 12 (178) $150

Mathes, W. Michael
— Spanish Approaches to the Island of California, 1628-1632. San Francisco: Book Club of Calif., 1975. One of 400. cb Sept 11 (66) $75

Matheson, Ewing
— Works in Iron. Bridge and Roof Structures. L, 1877. 8vo, cloth; shaken. O Jan 6 (121) $50

Mathews, Alfred E.
— Pencil Sketches of Montana. NY, 1868. 1st Ed. 8vo, orig cloth; spine discolored, a few stains on front cover. With 31 plates, 4 folding. sg Apr 2 (142) $3,800

Mathews, Anne
— Memoirs of Charles Mathews, Comedian. L, 1838-39. 4 vols. 8vo, contemp calf; rubbed, joints cracked. With 17 plates. bba Jan 15 (90) £100 [Bookroom]

Mathison, Gilbert Farquhar
— Narrative of a Visit To Brazil, Chile, Peru, and the Sandwich Islands. L, 1825. 8vo, orig bds. With folding map, 1 plain & 3 colored plates. Lacking dedication leaf. S Jan 12 (282) £440 [Brooke]

Mathison, Thomas
— The Goff. An Heroi-Comical Poem. Edin., 1793. 3d Ed. pnC Jan 23 (146) £9,600

Matisse, Henri, 1869-1954
— Jazz. NY: Braziller, [1983]. Folio, cloth, in d/j. wa Nov 6 (457) $55
— The Last Works of.... NY, [1958]. Folio, bds; rubbed. Verve No 35/36. bba Oct 16 (330) £90 [Coultas]
 Anr copy. Bds, in d/j. Verve No 35/36. O Mar 24 (118) $160

Matsell, George Washington
— Vocabulum; or, the Rogue's Lexicon. NY, 1857. 12mo, orig cloth. Blank upper margin excised from title. sg Feb 12 (220) $225

Matthew, Sir Tobie
— The Flaming Hart, or the Life of...S. Teresa. Antwerp, 1642. 8vo, contemp calf gilt; rubbed. Some headlines shaved; slight worming, not affecting text. S July 14 (348) £120

Mattioli, Pietro Andrea, 1500-77
— I Discorsi...nelli sei libri di Pedacio Dioscoride Anazarbeo della materia medicinale. Venice: Valgrisi, 1673. Bound in 2 vols. Folio, 19th-cent half calf; rubbed. Tp browned & brittle with some losses; browned; foxed & stained throughout; some tears & repairs. P Nov 25 (319) $350
— New Kreuterbuch...durch Georgium Handsch...verdeutscht. Prague: Georg Malantrich of Absenberg for himself & Vincenzo Valgrisi of Venice, 1563. Folio, contemp blindstamped vellum over wooden bds with front cover stamped kreuterbuch & 1659 & with gilt heraldic stamp of the Deutsche Akademie der Naturforscher added in the 18th cent, 5 (of 8) brass cornerpieces; spine ends worn, rear cover rubbed. Marginal imperfections; C1 loose; stains in gutter of title & several other leaves, possibly caused by bleach. sg Dec 4 (125) $2,400
— Opera. Frankfurt: Nicolaus Bassaeus, 1598. Folio, contemp vellum over wooden bds with stamp of the deutsche Akademie der Naturforscher added in 18th cent, with 5 (of 8) brass cornerpieces; spine ends worn, rear cover rubbed; lacking clasps & catches.. Marginal imperfections; C1 loose; bleach stains in gutter of tp & several other leaves. sg Dec 4 (125) $2,400
 Anr copy. Contemp blindstamped calf over wooden bds; backstrip def, lacking 1 clasp. Some browning, scattered early underscoring & marginalia; bleach stains on tp & 2 other leaves. sg Dec 4 (126) $900

Maugham, W. Somerset, 1874-1965
See also: Limited Editions Club
— Ah King. L, 1933. One of 175, sgd. Spine faded & soiled. L.p. copy. Inscr. wd Nov 12 (144) $400
— Ashenden, or the British Agent. L, 1928. In d/j with some wear & 2 small tears. cb Nov 20 (257) $375
 Anr copy. In repaired d/j. cb May 7 (287) $200
 Anr copy. In d/j; spine worn. sg Mar 5 (157) $325
 Anr copy. In d/j. Inscr. wd Nov 12 (145) $1,300
— Cakes and Ale.... L, 1930. 1st Ed. In d/j. Inscr & with a small correction on p. 47 initialed by Maugham. wd Nov 12 (147) $250
 Anr copy. In d/j. Inscr. wd Nov 12 (148) $100
 Anr Ed. L, [1954]. One of 1,000, sgd by author & artist. Illus by Graham Sutherland. Lea; spine rubbed & soiled. sg Dec 11 (83) $275
— The Casuarina Tree. L, 1926. In half mor slipcase. Inscr. wd Nov 12 (149) $125
— Don Fernando. L, 1935. 1st Ed, One of 175, sgd. sg Mar 5 (152) $200
— The Explorer. L, 1908. In half mor slipcase. Inscr. wd Nov 12 (150) $150
— First Person Singular. L, [1931]. In d/j. In half mor slipcase. Inscr. wd Nov 12 (151) $175
— The Gentleman in the Parlour. L, [1930]. In d/j. In half mor slipcase. Inscr. wd Nov 12 (152) $325
— The Hero. L, 1901. In half mor slipcase. Inscr. wd Nov 12 (153) $500
— The Letter: a Play in Three Acts. L, [1927]. Inscr. sg Mar 5 (153) $175
— Liza of Lambeth. L, 1897. 1st Ed, 1st Issue. 8vo, orig cloth. In half mor slipcase. Inscr. wd Nov 12 (154) $850
 Jublilee Ed. L, 1947. One of 1,000, sgd. Half vellum, in d/j. sg Dec 11 (84) $60
— The Making of a Saint. L, 1898. 8vo, orig cloth. Inscr. wd Nov 12 (157) $350
— A Man of Honour. A Play in Four Acts. L, 1903. Orig wraps. In half mor slipcase.

Inscr. wd Nov 12 (158) $1,200
Anr copy. Orig wraps. In half mor slipcase. Sgd. wd Nov 12 (159) $650
— The Moon and Sixpence. L, [1919]. 1st Ed, 1st Issue. Orig cloth. In half mor slipcase. Inscr. wd Nov 12 (160) $175
— The Narrow Corner. L, 1932. 1st Ed. In d/j. In half mor slipcase. Inscr. wd Nov 12 (161) $250
— Of Human Bondage. L, [1915]. 1st English Ed. Orig cloth. In half mor slipcase. Inscr. Library stamp on half title. wd Nov 12 (154) $175

1st American Ed. NY, [1915]. Orig cloth; spine worn. pnNY Sept 13 (258) $110

Anr Ed. Garden City, 1936. One of 751. wd Nov 12 (162) $150
— The Painted Veil. L, 1925. 1st English Ed, 1st Issue, 2d State. In soiled d/j. Sgd. One of a few with text in unaltered state. S July 23 (163) £1,100 [Manyon]

1st Issue, 3d State. In d/j. In half mor slipcase. Inscr. wd Nov 12 (165) $850

Issue not indicated. In chipped d/j. sg Mar 5 (160) $70
— Strictly Personal. Garden City, 1941. 1st Ed, One of 515. sg Mar 5 (155) $175
— The Summing Up. L, [1938]. In d/j. In half mor slipcase. Inscr. wd Nov 12 (166) $325

Anr Ed. Garden City, 1954. One of 391. In d/j. sg Mar 5 (155) $175
— Theatre. L & Toronto, 1937. In half mor slipcase. Inscr. wd Nov 12 (167) $300
— The Trembling of a Leaf. L, 1921. In worn d/j. sg Mar 5 (161) $80
— The Vagrant Mood. L, 1952. One of 500. Orig calf; warped. ha May 22 (192) $110

Anr copy. Lea. sg Mar 5 (156) $80

Maund, Benjamin, 1790-1863. See: Botanic...; Botanist...

Maundrell, Henry
— A Journey from Aleppo to Jerusalem.... Oxford, 1703. 1st Ed. 8vo, contemp calf; rubbed. With 9 plates. bba May 28 (303) £110 [Dawes]

4th Ed. Oxford, 1721. 8vo, contemp calf; rubbed. bba Oct 30 (338) £75 [Wagner]

Maupassant, Guy de, 1850-93
— Contes de la becasse. Paris, 1883. 1st Ed. 12mo, mor gilt janseniste by Chambolle-Duru. Unique copy with the 34 orig aquarelles of Pierre Vidal. Jeanson 1917. SM Mar 1 (102) FF90,000
— Oeuvres. Paris, 1908-10. 29 vols. Contemp half mor by Canape, orig wraps bound in; rubbed. Ck Sept 5 (189) £380

Anr Ed. Paris, 1934-38. 15 vols. 4to, half mor, orig wraps bound in. SM Oct 20 (654) FF5,000
— Sur l'eau. Paris, [1888]. 1st Ed, one of 50 on japon. 12mo, bdg not described. S May 21 (158) £200 [Maggs]
— Works. L & NY, [1903]. One of 50 with plates in 2 states. 17 vols. Mor extra by MacDonald. O May 12 (140) $1,100

Anr copy. Mor extra. wd Nov 12 (96) $500

Cambridge Ed. L & NY: M. W. Dunne, 1903. 17 vols. Contemp half mor; rubbed. bba Mar 12 (129) £110 [Burton Garbett]

Anr copy. Cloth. ha May 22 (68) $75

Maupertius, Pierre Louis Moreau de, 1698-1759
— The Figure of the Earth.... L, 1738. 8vo, old calf; rebacked. With folding map & 9 folding plates, torn & browned at fold lines. sg Nov 20 (107) $200

Maurice, Sir John Frederick
— History of the War in South Africa.... L, 1906-10. 4 vols in 8 (including 4 of folding maps). 8vo, orig cloth; 1 upper cover rubbed. S Nov 10 (946) £270 [Maggs]

Maurois, Andre, 1885-1967
— Climats. Paris, 1929. One of 30 on japon, with an extra suite of plates. Illus by Jean Hugo. 4to, orig wraps. With 24 colored gouaches. sg Jan 8 (161) $325
— Les Erophages. Paris, 1960. One of 104 on vellum. Illus by Andre Masson. Folio, unsewn as issued in orig wraps. With 16 plates & 2 etched cover designs. SM Oct 20 (651) FF7,000

Maury, Matthew Fountaine, 1806-73
— The Physical Geography of the Sea. NY, 1855. 8vo, orig cloth; marked. With 8 folding plates. S Nov 10 (526) £180 [Wheldon]

Maverick Augustus. See: Briggs & Maverick Augustus

Maw, George, 1832-1912
— A Monograph of the Genus Crocus.... L, 1886. 4to, orig cloth; rubbed & soiled. With 81 hand-colored pltes, 1 colored double page map & 2 double page ptd tables. de Belder copy. S Apr 28 (230) £2,500 [Woodburn]

Mawe, John, 1764-1829
— Travels in the Interior of Brazil. L, 1812. 4to, cloth; soiled. With map & 8 plates, 1 hand-colored. bba Dec 18 (192) £100 [Crisford]
— A Treatise on Diamonds and Precious Stones.... L, 1813. 1st Ed. 8vo, contemp mor gilt; soiled. With 3 hand-colored plates. Lacking final leaf. bba Aug 28 (130) £110 [Shapero]

Mawson, Sir Douglas, 1882-1958
— The Home of the Blizzard. L, [1915]. 2 vols. kh Mar 16 (344) A$520; sg Apr 23 (96) $150

Maxim, Sir Hiram Steven
— Artificial and Natural Flight. L & NY, 1908. 1st Ed. wa Nov 6 (12) $50

Maximilian zu Wied-Neuwied, Prince
— Reise nach Brasilien in den Jahren 1815 bis 1817. Frankfurt, 1820-21. 3 vols, including Atlas vol. 4to & folio, contemp half lea; spines def, Atlas contents loose. With 3 maps & 22 plates, including 2 maps with outline color & several colored plates. Text vols discolored; 2 plates with tears repaired; tears affecting pp 251-54 in Vol II; waterstain affecting Vol I. S Oct 23 (446) £2,000 [Levy]
— Verzeichniss der Reptilien.... Dresden, 1865. 4to, modern half lea; new endpapers. With 7 hand-colored plates by E. Lange after Carl Bodmer; some plates foxed or spotted. sg Jan 15 (237) $750
— Voyage au Bresil.... Paris, 1822. Atlas only. Half mor. With 22 plates, 3 maps & 19 engraved vignettes (1 torn & repaired). S Apr 23 (308) £1,200 [Fleming]

Maxwell, Sir Herbert Eustace
— Fishing at Home and Abroad. L, 1913. One of 750. Mor. pnE Dec 17 (346) £80 [Cadzow]
— The Story of the Tweed. L, 1905. One of 375. Folio, orig cloth gilt. pnE June 17 (127) £55

Maxwell, James Clerk, 1831-79
— On the Theory of Three Primary Colours. L, [1861]. 8vo, disbound. Extracted from the Proceedings of the Royal Institution, Vol II, pp 370-74. S May 21 (206) £400 [Ganz]

Maxwell, William Hamilton, 1792-1850
— Wild Sports of the West. L, 1832. 1st Ed. 2 vols. 8vo, orig bds; joints cracked, backstrip chipped. With 5 plates. sg June 11 (291) $70

May, Julian
— The Nonborn King. Bost., 1983. Uncorrected proof. Wraps. Inscr. cb Sept 28 (931) $65

May, Robert, b.1588
— The Accomplisht Cook, or the Art and Mystery of Cookery.... L, 1665. 2d Ed. 8vo, old calf; rebacked, corners renewed. Frontis in facsimile; tears to O1 & T4; portion of T3 torn away affecting 8 lines of text; some browning. Crahan copy. P Nov 25 (321) $350

Anr copy. Contemp calf; rubbed. Minor worming in a few blank margins; some fraying; corner torn from Cc6 costing c.20 letters; plates soiled, torn & separated at centerfolds. Vehling copy. P Nov 25 (322) $700

May, Thomas
— The Old Couple. L, 1658. 4to, old half sheep; broken. Chew-Clawson-van Dyke copy. sg Dec 4 (127) $300

May, Thomas, 1595-1650
— Arbitrary Government Display'd to the Life.... L, 1683. 2d Ed. 12mo, contemp calf; rebacked, rubbed. Frontis stained in margin & repaired; F2 torn; some cropping, just affecting text. bba Nov 13 (199) £65 [Quaritch]

Maydman, Henry
— Naval Speculations, and Maritime Politicks.... L, 1691. 1st Ed. 8vo, contemp calf; rubbed. C Dec 12 (348) £700 [Warnecke]

Mayer, Alfred Marshall, 1836-97
— Sport with Gun and Rod...in American Woods and Waters. NY, [1883]. 1st Ed. 4to, cloth; worn. sg Oct 23 (399) $80

Mayer, Anton
— Wiens Buchdrucker-Geschichte, 1482-1882. Vienna, 1883-87. 2 vols. 4to, cloth; shaken. Owner's stamp on titles. sg Oct 2 (200) $60

Anr copy. Half vellum; worn. sg May 14 (389) $175

Mayer, August Liebmann
— Dominico Theotocopuli El Greco. Munich: Hanfstaengl, 1926. Folio, half lea; rubbed. O Jan 6 (122) $50

Mayer, Brantz
— Baltimore Past and Present. Balt., 1871. 8vo, mor. With 62 photos. ha Nov 7 (139) $70

Mayer, Johann of Wurzburg, 1804
— Pomona Franconica. Description des arbres fruitiers.... Nuremberg, 1776-79. Vols I & II (of 3). 4to, contemp calf; some scratches, joints weak. With frontis, folding map, 11 plain & 101 hand-colored plates. Derby —de Belder copy. S Apr 28 (235) £8,500 [Israel]

Mayer, Luigi
— A Selection of...Sir Robert Ainslie's...Collection of Views in Turkey in Europe, and in Asia.... L, 1811. Folio, later half calf. With 24 hand-colored plates, including a folding view of Constantinople. Folding view with tear. C Oct 15 (72) £460 [Schrire]
— Views in Egypt, Palestine, and Other Parts of the Ottoman Empire. L, 1801-3. 3 vols in 2. Folio, contemp half mor; rubbed. With 96 hand-colored plates. Without

general title & port; French title with tear in blank margin. C Apr 8 (150) £3,000 [Chalabi]
Anr Ed. L, 1804. Folio, later bds. With 48 hand-colored plates. S Oct 23 (379) £1,000 [Quaritch]

Mayhew, Augustus & Henry

— The Good Genius that turned Everything into Gold.... L, 1847. 1st Ed. Illus by George Cruikshank. 16mo, modern mor gilt, orig cloth bound in. With 4 etchings & 4 glyphographs. sg June 11 (146) $110

— The Greatest Plague of life, or the Adventures of a Lady in Search of a Good Servant. L, [1847]. Illus by George Cruikshank. 8vo, mor by Bedford, orig wraps bound in at end. O June 9 (112) $100

Mayhew, Henry, 1812-87

— 1851: or the Adventures of Mr. and Mrs. Sandboys.... L, [1851]. Illus by George Cruikshank. 8 orig parts. 8vo, orig wraps; some spine ends chipped. With engraved title & 10 plates. One plate loose; anr partly separated at fold. sg Sept 11 (77) $175
Anr copy. 8vo, lev. With 10 plates, 8 folding; dampstaining affecting plates. sg Dec 18 (161) $90
Anr copy. Half mor gilt by Whitman Bennett. sg Feb 12 (61) $130
Anr copy. Calf gilt, orig covers bound in. sg June 18 (148) $300

— The Upper Rhine. L, 1860. 8vo, orig cloth; soiled & worn. With 22 plates. wa Nov 6 (425) $190

Mayhew, Horace

— The Tooth-Ache. L, [1849]. Illus by George Cruikshank. 12mo, orig bds; back cover loose, backstrip def. With 43 plates. Without ads on pastedowns. H. W. Bruton copy. sg June 11 (147) $375

Mayhew, Thomas. See: Eliot & Mayhew

Maynard, Charles Johnson, 1845-1929

— The Birds of Eastern North America. West Newton, Mass., 1906-[10]. ("An Atlas of Plates for the Directory to the Birds of Eastern North America.") 10 parts in 1 vol. Folio, cloth, orig wraps bound in. With 51 hand-colored plates. 2 wraps sgd. sg Sept 18 (173) $500

— The Butterflies of New England. Bost., 1886. Folio, cloth; worn & soiled. With 8 hand-colored plates. Minor pencilling in text. wa Sept 25 (112) $95

Mayne, Richard Charles, 1835-92

— Four Years in British Columbia...and Vancouver Island. L, 1862. 8vo, orig cloth. With folding map. pn Mar 5 (34) £180 [Maggs]

Mayo, Charles Herbert

— Bibliotheca Dorsetiensis. L: Chiswick Press, 1885. 4to, orig cloth. L Dec 11 (28) £60

Mayo, John Horsley

— Medals and Decorations of the British Army and Navy. Westminster, 1897. 1st Ed. 2 vols. 8vo, cloth; soiled, hinges weak. With 55 colored plates. cb Dec 18 (113) $55

Mayow, John, 1643-79

— Tractatus duo quorum prior agit de respiratione.... Leiden: F. López de Haro & C. Driehuysen, 1671. 8vo, modern half calf. Piece torn from outer margin of A6. S Nov 27 (296) £480 [Phelpse]

Mayr, H. von

— Malerische ansichten aus dem Orient, gesammelt auf der Reise...Herzogs Maximilian in Bayern im jahre MDCCCXXXVIII. Munich, [1839-40]. Folio, loose in orig pictorial wraps with frame borders hand-colored. With hand-colored litho title & 60 hand-colored views. Clean tear in 1 margin. S June 25 (353) £3,000 [David]

Mazois, Francois —& Others

— Les Ruines de Pompei. Paris, 1812. Part 1 only. Modern cloth. With engraved title 2 plans & 37 plates. Some spotting & waterstains. FD June 11 (848) DM600

Mazuchelli, Nina Elizabeth

— The Indian Alps and How We Crossed Them. L, 1876. 4to, gilt-pictorial cloth. Ck Feb 27 (37) £130

Mazzinelli, Alessandro

— Uffizio della settimana santa. Rome, 1758. 8vo, mor gilt. With 14 plates. S June 25 (36) £500

Mazzocchius, Jacobus

— Epigrammata antiquae urbis. Rome: Jacobus Mazochius, 1521. Folio, contemp blindstamped calf. Du Chôul copy. FD Dec 2 (85) DM6,100
Anr copy. 15th-cent vellum; worn & repaired. Some worming & browning. HK Nov 4 (679) DM1,100

Mead, Richard, 1673-1754
— De imperio solis ac lunae in corpora humana.... L, 1746. 2d Ed. 8vo, contemp calf; rubbed, rebacked. K2 & 3 torn, affecting text; duplicate perfect leaves bound in at end. bba Jan 15 (393) £100 [Maggs]
— A Mechanical Account of Poisons. L, 1702. 1st Ed. 8vo, contemp calf gilt. S May 28 (732) £120
   Anr copy. Orig calf; soiled & worn. wa Nov 6 (203) $120
— The Medical Works. Edin., 1763. 3 vols. 8vo, contemp calf gilt. With 5 folding plates. pnE Dec 17 (123) £380 [Traylen]
   Anr Ed. Edin., 1765. 3 vols. 12mo, contemp calf; worn. With 5 folding plates. Port lacking. Ck Apr 24 (74) £95

Meadows, Sir Philip
— Observations Concerning the Dominion and Sovereignty of the Seas. L, 1689. 1st Ed. 4to, wraps. Light stains affecting tp & prelims. S July 23 (341) £220 [Wood]

Meager, Leonard
— The English Gardener.... L, 1670. 1st Ed. 4to, contemp calf; free endpapers removed. With 24 plates. Dedication leaf trimmed at outer margin; some waterstain, mostly marginal; minor marginal tears. Crahan copy. P Nov 25 (325) $550

Meares, John, 1756?-1809
— Voyages Made in the Years 1788 and 1789.... L, 1790. 4to, cloth. With port, 10 maps & 16 plates. bba Dec 18 (194) £500 [Barnett]
   Anr copy. Half mor, with Wharncliffe arms. With port, 10 maps & 17 (of 18) plates. Lacking a folding view of the Philippines. S Oct 23 (522) £600 [Perrin]

Mechnikov, Il'ia Il'ich, 1845-1916
— Lecons sur la pathologie comparee de l'inflammation faites a l'Institut Pasteur. Paris, 1892. 8vo, half cloth; 1 gathering loose, half-title starting. With 3 colored plates. sg Jan 15 (108) $100

Medailles. See: Louis XIV

Meder, Joseph
— Duerer-Katalog. Vienna, 1932. 4to, half mor gilt. sg May 14 (51) $300

Medhurst, Walter Henry
— General Description of Shanghae and its Environs.... Shanghai: Mission Press, 1850. 8vo, later wraps. With 6 folding maps in Chinese style (1 loose with tear & slight loss at folds). S Apr 23 (350) £1,800 [Fletcher]

Medical...
— Medical Observations and Inquiries, by a Society of Physicians in London. L, L, 1757-84. Mixed Ed. 6 vols. 8vo, contemp calf. With 29 plates. Part of outer margin of D2 torn away. pnE Dec 17 (50) £320 [Phillips]
— Medical Transactions, Published by the College of Physicians in London. L, 1768-1820. 6 vols. 8vo, modern half calf. Some leaves stamped. pnE Dec 17 (153) £280 [Phillips]
   Mixed Ed. L, 1785-72-85. 3 vols. 8vo, contemp calf. With 2 folding plates in Vol III. pnE Dec 17 (43) £500 [Phillips]

Medina, Balthasar de
— Vida, martyrio, y beatificacion del invicto proto-martyr de el Japan San Felipe de Jesus, Patron de Mexico.... Madrid, 1751. 4to, vellum. S Apr 24 (351) £800 [Saweres]

Medina, Jose Toribio, 1852-1930
— Los Aborigenes de Chile. Santiago, 1882. 4to, contemp half mor; front joint with tear at top & small wormholes at bottom. With 40 plates. Library markings erased. sg Sept 18 (56) $90
— Bibliografia Numismatica Colonial Hispano-Americana. Santiago, 1912. One of 120. 4to, cloth, orig front wrap bound in. sg Oct 2 (210) $200
— Biblioteca Hispan-Chilena, 1523-1817. Santiago de Chile, 1897-99. 3 vols. 4to, wraps; unopened; worn. sg Oct 2 (209) $225
— Biblioteca Hispanoamericana, 1493-1810. Santiago de Chile, 1958-62. One of 250. 7 vols. 8vo, cloth. sg Jan 22 (230) $275
— Ensayo acerca de una Mapoteca Chilena. Santiago, 1889. 8vo, half lea; extremities worn. sg Oct 2 (91) $200
— Historia del Tribunal del Santo Oficio de la Inquisicion de Lima.... Santiago, 1887. 2 vols. 4to, wraps, unopened; fragile. sg Oct 2 (208) $150
— La Imprenta en Manila desde sus origenes hasta 1810. Santiago de Chile, 1896. One of 300. 8vo, half lea; worn, spine taped. Some margins chipped. sg May 14 (672) $200
— La Imprenta en Mexico, 1539-1821. Santiago de Chile, 1908-12. One of 250. 8 vols. 4to, cloth; Vols II & VI loose; others partly loose. sg Oct 2 (217) $475

Medley, Julius George, 1829-84
— A Year's Campaigning in India.... L, 1858. 8vo, orig cloth; spine rubbed, some hinges cracking. With color frontis & 4 folding maps & plans. Some soiling; 1 map with repair on verso; rubberstamps to front endpapers. cb Dec 18 (119) $110

Mee, Margaret
— Flowers of the Brazilian Forest.... L, [1968]. One of 100 with orig hand-colored drawing tipped in. Folio, vellum gilt. pn Oct 23 (362) £380 [Guest]

Out-of-series copy. Orig cloth. Ck June 19 (174) £110

Meehan, Thomas, 1826-1901
— The Native Flowers and Ferns of the United States.... Bost., 1878-[80]. First Series in orig 24 parts. Wraps; worn. With 96 color plates. O May 12 (141) $300

Anr copy. Series I-II. 24 parts in 4 vols. 4to, orig cloth; worn. With 192 color plates. S May 28 (736) £340

Anr copy. Vol I & Series II, Vol II. 4to, orig cloth; worn, backstrips torn, Vol II partly disbound. With 96 plates. sg Dec 18 (197) $140

Anr copy. Series I-II. 4 vols. 4to, orig half lea; scuffed. With 192 color plates. sg Jan 15 (238) $325

Meeker, Nathan Cook, 1814-79
— First Annual Report of the Union Colony of Colorado.... NY, 1871. Modern half mor, orig wraps bound in. cb Jan 8 (119) $85

Meerburgh, Nicolaas
— Afbeeldingen van zeldzaame Gewassen. Leiden, 1775. Folio, contemp half calf. With 55 hand-colored plates. Plesch—de Belder copy. S Apr 28 (236) £5,000 [Schoern]

Meerman, Gerard, 1722-71
— Origines typographicae. The Hague, Paris & L, 1765. 1st Ed. 2 vols. 4to, vellum bds; torn & soiled. With 10 plates but without the 2 ports. S Nov 10 (21) £65 [Maggs]

Mehegan, Guillaume Alexandre de
— Considerations sur les revolutions des arts. Paris, 1755. 8vo, contemp calf; extremities worn. sg Mar 26 (200) $175

Meheut, Mathurin
— Etude de la Foret. Paris: Albert Levy, [early 20th-cent]. With Texts by Julien Noel Costantin & L, Plantefol. 2 vols. Folio, loose as issued in pictorial bd folders. sg Dec 18 (198) $150

Meibom, Marcus, d.1711
— Antiquae musicae.... Amst., 1652. 1st Ed. 2 vols in one. 4to, contemp Dutch vellum bds with arms of city of Amsterdam; lacking ties. With 5 folding tables. S Nov 27 (98) £600 [Cristad]

Meier-Graefe, Julius, 1867-1935
— Modern Art being a Contribution to a New System of Aesthetics. L, 1908. 2 vols. 4to, cloth; worn. sg Feb 5 (220) $140
— Vincent Van Gogh. A Biographical Study. L: Medici Society, 1922. One of 200. 2 vols. 4to, cloth; worn. O Jan 6 (124) $100

Meikle, Desmond
— Wild Flowers of Cyprus. L, 1973. One of 200. Folio, orig half mor. With 40 colored plates. S Nov 10 (527) £200 [Meikle]

Meilhac, Henri —& Halevy, Ludovic, 1834-1908
— La Mi-Careme. Paris, 1874. Illus by Henriot. 12mo, mor by Carayon, orig wraps bound in. With all the marginal illusts hand-colored. Sgd dedication by Meilhac on front wrap; sgd dedication by Henriot on half-title; ALs of Henriot bound in at end. S Nov 27 (99) £200 [Henderson]

Meinertzhagen, Richard
See also: Nicoll & Meinertzhagen
— Birds of Arabia. L, 1954. 4to, cloth. With 19 color plates. Haverschmidt copy. B Feb 24 (446) HF600

Anr copy. Orig cloth, in d/j. pn Oct 23 (245) £270 [Bles]
— Nicoll's Birds of Egypt. L, 1930. 2 vols. 4to, cloth. With 7 plain & 30 color plates. Haverschmidt copy. B Feb 24 (244) HF750

Anr copy. Half mor gilt. pn Oct 23 (246) £220 [Holmes]

Anr copy. Orig cloth. S Feb 24 (595) £190 [Bookroom]

Meinhold, William
See also: Kelmscott Press
— Sidonia the Sorceress. L, 1849. 2 vols in 1. 12mo, contemp half calf; spine brittle. sg Feb 12 (221) $100

Meisel, Max
— A Bibliography of American Natural History, 1769-1865. Brooklyn, 1924-29. 3 vols. sg Oct 2 (211) $325

Meisl, Willy —& Others
— Die Olympischen Spiele in Los Angeles 1932. Altona-Bahrenfeld, 1932. 4to, orig cloth, in worn d/j; bdg broken. bba Oct 30 (214) £55 [Goldman]

Mejer, Johannes. See: Danckwerth & Mejer

Mejer, Wolfgang
— Bibliographie der Buchbinderei-Literatur. Leipzig, 1925. Vol I. Unopened. O Nov 18 (122) $70

Bibliographie der Buchbinderei Literatur 1924-1932. Leipzig, 1925-33. Vol I only.

sg May 14 (126) $100

Mela, Pomponius
— Cosmographia. Venice: Bernhard Malor & others, 1478. ("Cosmographi de situ orbis.") 4to, vellum bds. A few leaves repaired. 48 leaves.. S Nov 27 (196) £950 [Olschki]

Anr Ed. Basel: Andreas Cratander, 1522. ("De orbis situ libri tres.") Folio, contemp blind-stamped pigskin; soiled & rubbed, foot of spine repaired. With double-page woodcut cordiform world map (restored at outer margins & backed with tissue). Last few leaves dampstained at foot. S Apr 24 (208) £2,000 [Tooley]

— De situ orbis libri tres. Paris: Jacob Kerver, 1557. 4to, modern calf. Lower outer corner of several leaves gnawed. sg Mar 26 (201) $175

Melancthon, Philipp, 1497-1560
— Corpus doctrinae Christianae. Frankfurt: Martin Lechler for Hieronymus Feyerabend, 1569. Bound with: Sarcerius, Wilhelm. Pastorale, oder Hirtenbuch. Frankfurt, 1566. Folio, contemp blind-tooled pigskin over wooden bds, brass studs & clasps. Marginal tears & repairs with occasional text loss; minor stains. sg Oct 9 (270) $475

Meldrum, Max
— The Science of Appearances as Formulated and Taught by Max Meldrum. Sydney, 1950. Ed by Russell R. Foreman. Cloth, in d/. CA Apr 12 (181) A$800

Melish, John, 1771-1822
— Travels in the United States of America.... Phila., 1812. 1st Ed. 2 vols. 8vo, modern cloth. With 8 maps & plans. Several maps with perforated library stamps; several with small tears along folds. sg Mar 12 (179) $90

Mellerio, Andre
— La Lithographie Originale en Couleurs. Paris, 1898. One of 1,000. 4to, half cloth, orig wraps preserved. With litho frontis on chine & cover in color by Pierre Bonnard. S Dec 4 (3) £1,050 [Sims & Reed]

— Odilon Redon. Paris, 1913. One of 550. 4to, cloth. S Dec 4 (28) £300 [SimsReed]

— Odilon Redon, peintre, dessinateur et graveur. Paris, 1923. 4to, pictorial wraps. sg June 4 (269) $300

Melling, Antoine Ignace
— Voyage pittoresque de Constantinople et des rives du Bosphore.... Paris, 1809-19. 2 vols. Folio, contemp half lea; rubbed. With engraved title, port & 48 double-page views & 3 double-page maps at end. Library stamp on titles & pastedowns; text vol

spotted & stained at outer margin. S Apr 24 (235) £4,500 [Hantzis]

Melon, Jean Francois
— Essai politique sur le commerce. Amst.: Chez Francois Chanquion, 1735. 8vo, calf; rebacked with mor with orig spine laid down. Lacking half-title; marginal tear in Q5. P Sept 24 (345) $200

Melville, Herman, 1819-91
See also: Grabhorn Printing; Limited Editions Club; Nonesuch Press

— Israel Potter: His Fifty Years of Exile. NY, 1855. 1st Ed, 1st Ptg. 12mo, orig cloth. A few leaves stained at end. sg Feb 12 (223) $150

— Mardi: and a Voyage Thither. NY, 1849. 1st American Ed. 2 vols. 12mo, orig cloth. Some foxing. sg Apr 2 (145) $600

— Moby Dick. NY, 1851. ("Moby Dick; or, the Whale.") 1st American Ed. 12mo, orig gray-green cloth with orange endpapers; front joint broken, corners rubbed, spine dull & frayed. CNY Dec 19 (132) $1,400

Anr copy. Recent syn. Old marginal dampstains, half-title tape-repaired. ha Dec 19 (234) $1,000

Anr Ed. L, 1853. ("The Whale.") 3 vols. 8vo, contemp calf; rubbed. Lacking half-title in Vol I. G. L. Clarke copy. sg Dec 4 (129) $2,200

Anr Ed. Chicago, 1930. One of 1,000. Illus by Rockwell Kent. 3 vols. 4to, cloth, unopened, in aluminum slipcase. cb Dec 4 (232) $900

Anr copy. Cloth, without aluminum slipcase; spine ends rubbed. cb June 18 (214) $900

Anr copy. Cloth, in aluminum slipcase. sg Dec 4 (96) $900

Anr Ed. NY, 1930. Rubbed. sg Jan 8 (147) $60

Anr Ed. Mt. Vernon, 1975. One of 1,500. Preface by Jacques Cousteau; illus by LeRoy Neiman. Folio, mor by George Wieck. O Nov 18 (123) $275

Anr copy. Mor. With 12 double-page plates. sg Jan 8 (163) $550

Anr Ed. San Francisco: Arion Press, 1979. ("Moby-Dick, or the Whale.") One of 265. Illus by Barry Moser. Folio, orig mor. sg Apr 2 (143) $2,600

California Deluxe Ed. Berkeley, [1981]. One of 750. cb Feb 5 (213) $100

Anr copy. Folio, cloth. sg Jan 8 (164) $90

— Omoo: A Narrative of Adventures in the South Seas. L, 1847. 1st Ed. 12mo, cloth; extremities worn. sg Apr 2 (144) $200

Anr copy. Orig cloth; spine chipped. wa June 25 (384) $325

— White-Jacket; or the World in a Man-of-War. NY, 1850. 1st American Ed. 2 vols. 12mo, orig cloth; spine nicked at head. Some foxing & dampstaining. sg Feb 12 (222) $250

— Works. L, 1922-24. Standard Ed, one of 750. 16 vols. bba Nov 13 (282) £280 [Joseph]; O May 12 (142) $1,800
Anr copy. Half mor gilt. sg Dec 4 (130) $2,200

Melville's copy, Herman
— MACY, OBED. - The History of Nantucket.... Bost., 1835. 1st Ed. 8vo, orig cloth; broken, backstrip loose. With map & plate Title & frontis detached. Herman Melville's copy, inscr to him, and with his markings. CNY Dec 19 (133) $9,500

Melzo, Lodovico
— Regole militari sopra il governo a servitio.... Antwerp: Gioachino Trognaesio, 1611. 1st Ed. Folio, contemp vellum; some worming at hinges. With engraved title & 16 (on 15) double-page folding plates. Date erased at foot of engraved title & inserted in ink; piece cut from blank margin at foot of engraved title; minor worming at foremargin of 11 leaves, affecting a few letters; inor fold tears to a few plates. C Dec 12 (301) £380 [Griffiths]
Anr copy. Old calf; rubbed. Lacking Plates 2 & 3; most plates cropped; a few tears & repairs. S Sept 23 (868) £230 [McNaul]

Memoir. See: Raffles, Lady Sophia

Men...
— Men and Women of the Day: A Picture Gallery of Contemporary Portraiture. L, 1888-92. 8 vols. Folio, half mor; not uniform. With 190 Woodburytypes, each mtd. ha Nov 7 (208) $225

Mena, Juan de
— Copilacion de Todas las Obras.... Seville: Juan Varela, 1534. 2 parts in 1 vol. Folio, 19th-cent sheep; worn. General title & last leaf remargined. sg Oct 9 (60) $450

Menagier ...
— Le Menagier de Paris, traite de morale et d'economie domestique compose vers 1393,.... Paris: Crapelet, 1846. 8vo, lev gilt by Closs with the Imperial Eagle. Napoleon III's copy. Jeanson 1741. SM Mar 1 (405) FF28,000

Menander
— Ex veterem comicorum fabulis.... Paris: G. Morel, 1553-[54]. 8vo, 19th-cent vellum. C Dec 12 (301A) £300 [Maggs]

Menasseh ben Israel
— De Resurrectione Mortuorum Libri III. Amst., 1636. 8vo, bds; rubbed. Some stains. CAM Dec 3 (137) HF1,300
— The Hope of Israel.... L, 1652. 2d Ed. 4to, disbound. S Feb 17 (78) £2,100 [Shane]
— Humas o Cinco Libros de la Ley Divina. Amst.: Menasseh ben Israel, 1654-55. 8vo, orig lea mtd on wood; worn, spine cracked. S Feb 17 (21) £1,600 [Mandanes]

Mencken, Henry Louis, 1880-1956
— Damn! A Book of Calumny. NY: Philip Goodman, 1918. 12mo, cloth; rubbed. ha Dec 19 (235) $55
— A Monograph of the New Baltimore Court House. [Balt.: Frank D. Thomas, 1899]. Oblong folio, orig cloth (presentation bdg?), with orig front wrap bound in; minor edge wear. ha Mar 13 (202) $1,200

Mendelsohn, Erich
— Russland, Europa, Amerika. Ein Architektonischer Querschnitt. Berlin, 1929. 4to, half cloth; rubbed. bba Dec 4 (215) £85 [Henderson]

Mendelssohn, Sidney
— South African Bibliography. L, 1910. One of 450. 2 vols. 4to, orig cloth; worn. sg Oct 2 (212) $110; SSA Oct 28 (727) R700

Mendelssohn-Bartholdy's copy, Felix
— WILSON, THOMAS. - A Descriptive Catalogue of the Prints of Rembrandt. By an Amateur L, 1836. 8vo, contemp half calf; rubbed, interleaved throughout. Annotated in pencil. Ck June 19 (13) £75

Mendes da Costa, Emanuel. See: Costa, Emanuel Mendes da

Mendieta, Geronimo de
— Historia Eclesiastica Indiana. Mexico City: Antigua Libreria, 1870. One of-420. 4to, contemp half mor, orig wraps bound in; joints & hinges starting. Crudely opened. sg Sept 18 (174) $275

Mendoza, Diego Hurtado de
— Leben des Lazarillo von Tormes. Berlin: Propylaen, [1924]. One of 125. Illus by H. Meid. 4to, orig half lea. With 28 plates. S Oct 6 (679) £130 [Zwemmer]

Menefee, C. A.
— Historical and Descriptive Sketch Book of Napa, Sonoma.... Napa City, 1873. 8vo, orig cloth; loose. cb Jan 8 (120) $55

Menestrier, Claude Francois
— La Nouvelle Methode raisonnee du Blason.... Lyon: Thomas Amaulry, 1696. 12mo, contemp calf; worn, upper joint cracking. Lacking front blank; upper corners of final 36 leaves dampstained. cb

MENESTRIER

Oct 23 (149) $65

Menger, Carl
— Untersuchungen ueber die methode der Socialwissenschaften.... Leipzig, 1883. 8vo, modern half mor. Lacking half-title; ownership stamp on tp; last leaf browned. P Sept 24 (346) $650

Mennessier de la Lance, Gabriel Rene
— Essai de bibliographie hippique. Paris, 1915-21. 2 vols & Supplement. Cloth; shaken. sg May 14 (358) $110
Anr copy. Cloth, Supplement in wraps. sg May 14 (359) $275

Mennie, Donald
— The Grandeur of the Gorges. Shanghai, 1926. One of 1,000. 4to, orig silk; rubbed & soiled. bba Apr 9 (424) £60 [Elliott]
Anr copy. Orig silk; rubbed. Ck Sept 26 (66) £110

Menon, ——
— La Cuisiniere bourgeoise.... Paris: Guillyn, 1750. 3d Ed. 12mo, contemp calf; worn. S Nov 27 (100) £160 [Booth]
— La Nouvelle Cuisine avec de nouveaux menus pour chaque saison.... Paris: Joseph Saugrain, 1742. 12mo, contemp sheep, spine chipped & with wormhole. With 4 folding plates. Some soiling. Crahan copy. P Nov 25 (327) $350
— Les Soupers de la coeur.... Paris, 1755. 4 vols. 12mo, contemp sheep gilt extra. A few leaves stained; lower forecorners of some others dampstained. P Nov 25 (328) $1,400

Menpes, Mortimer, 1859-1938
— Whistler as I Knew Him. L, 1904. One of 500, sgd. 4to, orig cloth. With 125 plates. With an orig etching. B Oct 7 (979) HF550

Men's...
— Men's Wear. Chicago, 1929-30. Vols 67-69 in 5 vols. 4to, cloth. bba Dec 18 (102) £140 [Ives]

Mentet de Salmonet, Robert
— Histoire des Troubles de la Grand' Bretagne. Paris, 1661. Bound with: Riordan de Muscry, D. Relation des veritables causes...qui ont contribue au restablissement du Roy de la Bretagne. Paris, 1661. Folio, 17th-cent calf gilt. S Sept 23 (369) £100 [Veyemans]

Menzies Library, William
— Catalogue of Books, Manuscripts, and Engravings. NY, 1875. Compiled by Joseph Sabin. 4to, cloth; worn. sg May 14 (22) $150

Mercator, Gerard, 1512-94 —& Hondius, Jodocus, 1563-1611
— Atlas Minor. Amst. [1610?]. Oblong 8vo, contemp vellum; worn. With 70 engraved hand-colored maps; with foxing, creasing & some tears in margin. Lacking port. pnNY Sept 13 (508) $275
— Atlas ofte afbeeldinge vande gantsche Weereld.... Amst.: Janson & Hondius, 1634. Folio, vellum; rebacked. With engraved title, double-page port & 177 (of 182) doublepage maps. Repaired; some spotting & foxing. VH Sept 12 (10) DM18,100
— Atlas sive cosmographicae meditationes.... Amst.: Hondius, 1613. 5 parts in 1 vol. 4to, contemp calf; worn. With engraved title, 4 engraved section titles, double-page port & 150 double-page maps with contemp hand-coloring. Occasional damage by adhesion; some splits without loss; browned. S Oct 23 (222) £11,000 [Tooley]
Anr Ed. Amst., 1619. 5 parts in 1 vol. Folio, 19th-cent half calf. With engraved general title & 164 maps on 156 plates. Lacking the port & the divisional titles; some leaves repaired at margins; browned throughout; some stains. French text. S Oct 23 (65) £7,000 [Lemuers]
Anr Ed. Amst., 1623. Folio, contemp calf. With engraved title, 4 engraved sub-titles, double-page port, 1 full-page & 155 double-page maps. Some worming & other minor defs. Text in Latin. FD Dec 2 (783) DM22,000
— Historia mundi: or Mercator's Atlas.... L, 1635. 1st English Ed, 1st Issue. Folio, modern half calf; def. With 181 maps, some colored. Lacking engraved title; New Spain repeated at Hhhh4; lacking engraved tile; some maps shaved at neatlines; last leaf def; minor marginal repairs. S Oct 23 (221) £1,700 [Postaprint]
2d Issue [frontis dated 1637]. Disbound. With frontis & 176 (of 183) full-page maps. Lacking frontis, tp, A2 & other leaves; some waterstains. Sold w.a.f. bba Aug 20 (455) £1,900 [Fisher]

Mercer, Asa Shinn
— The Banditti of the Plains.... [Cheyenne, Wyoming], 1894. 8vo, later cloth; hinges broken; small nail hole through outer margin of 16 leaves. sg Mar 12 (180) $1,200

Mercier, A.
— [Sale Catalogue] Catalogue de livres sur la chasse provenant de la bibliotheque de M. A. Mercier. Paris: Labitte, 1889. 8vo, half cloth. With the prices written in by hand. Jeanson copy. SM Mar 1 (589) FF2,000

Mercier de la Riviere, Paul Pierre. See: Le Mercier de La Riviere, Pierre Paul

Mercurialis, Hieronymus, 1530-1606
— De arte gymnastica, libri sex. Venice: Juntas, 1573. 2d Ed. 4to, modern vellum bds. Marginal dampstaining with occasional traces of mold; minor worming not affecting text; corner of 1st 2 leaves restored; last few leaves gnawed. sg Jan 15 (107) $60

Anr Ed. Paris: Jacques du Puys, 1577. 4to, 18th-cent calf. Margins dampstained. S June 25 (37) £480 [King]

Anr Ed. Venice: Giunta, 1601. Bound with: De decoratione liber. Venice, 1601. 4to, contemp vellum; worn & repaired. Stained. bba Aug 28 (92) £140 [P & P Books]

Anr Ed. Amst., 1672. 4to, vellum bds. With 6 folding plates & 21 full-page woodcuts. Lacking Y1 & Cc4. S Sept 23 (370) £160 [Pampolini]

Anr copy. Modern calf. With engraved title & 6 double-page or folding plates. Some worming, slightly affecting text & plates. S Mar 10 (1109) £220 [Poole]
— Praelectiones Pisanae.... Venice: Giunta, 1597. Folio, contemp vellum. Prince of Liechtenstein copy. Crahan copy. P Nov 25 (329) $450

Meredith, George, 1828-1909
— Works. L, 1896-98. Ltd Ed. 32 vols. 8vo, orig mor gilt extra. pnNY Sept 13 (197) $800

Anr copy. Half mor gilt. sg Sept 11 (233) $475

Memorial Ed. L, 1909-11. 27 vols. pnE Nov 12 (175) £75

Meredith, Louisa Anne Twamley
— The Romance of Nature. L, 1839. 3d Ed. 8vo, orig mor gilt; rubbed. With 26 hand-colored plates. T Apr 16 (158) £110

Meredith, Owen. See: Fore-Edge Paintings

Meredith, William
— Love Letter from an Impossible Land. New Haven, 1944. In d/j. sg Mar 5 (165) $60

Merian, Maria Sibylla, 1647-1717
— De Europische Insecten. Amst., 1730. Folio, half lea; worn, joints cracked. With 184 plates on 47 leaves. HN May 20 (990) DM19,000
— Dissertatio de generatione et metamorphosibus insectorum Surinamensium. Amst., 1719. ("De generatione et metamorphosibus insectorum Surinamensium.") Bound with: De Europische Insecten. Amst., 1730. Folio, contemp vellum bds; soiled & stained. 1st work with hand-colored frontis, colored vignette on title & coat-of-arms at head of dedication & 72 hand-colored plates; short marginal tear repaired in frontis & small piece torn from lower margin of Plate 61. 2d work with 184 hand-colored plates on 47 leaves. de Belder copy. S Apr 28 (238) £110,000 [Arader]
— Schmetterlinge, Kaefer und andere Insekten.... Leipzig, 1976. 2 vols. 4to, half lea. B Feb 24 (481) HF700

Merian, Matthaeus, 1593-1650
See also: Abelin & Others

— La Danse des Morts.... Basel: Johann Rudolph Imhof, 1756. 4to, mor by Nicolini with gilt arms of the Marquis de Villeneuve; extremities worn. sg Mar 26 (93) $375
— Todten-Tanz. Basel, 1744. 4to, half mor. S May 6 (517) £220 [Hill]
— Topographia Germaniae inferioris.... Frankfurt, [1659]. Text by Martin Zeiler; engravings by Merian. Folio, contemp mor gilt. With engraved title, 12 double-page maps & 108 plates. Ludwig XIV's copy. FD Dec 2 (816) DM10,000

Anr Ed. Frankfurt: Merian, [c.1660]. Folio, later half vellum; worn & soiled. With engraved title, 12 double-page maps & 107 plates containing 158 plans & views. Lacking 1 plate. HN Nov 26 (322) DM3,000

— Topographia Saxoniae Inferioris, das ist Beschreibung der vornehmsten Staette unnd Plaetz.... Frankfurt, 1653. Bound with: Topographia Electorat. Brandenburgici. et Ducatus Pomeraniae. Frankfurt, 1652. Folio, old half vellum; rubbed. FD Dec 2 (845) DM22,000

Anr copy. Text by Martin Zeiler; plates by Merian. 19th-cent half lea. With engraved title, 3 double-page maps, 1 folding map & 36 plates & plans. JG May 20 (458) DM7,000

Anr Ed. Frankfurt, [c.1700]. Folio, modern bds. With engraved title & 42 double-page or folding plates; 1 map & the views of Hildesheim & Rostock each on 2 plates bound separately. S Oct 23 (274) £1,500 [Schmidt]

— Topographia Westphaliae. Das ist Beschreibung der vornembsten und bekantisten Staette un Plaetz.... [Frankfurt, 1648]. Folio, 18th-cent half calf; extremities worn, joints cracked. With engraved title, double-page map & 50 plates; lacking ptd title; all plates on guards, minor dampstaining & spotting. Sold w.a.f. CNY Dec 19 (124) $6,000

MERIDA

Merida, Carlos
— Mexican Costume. [Chicago, 1941]. One of 1,000. Folio, loose as issued in bds. With 25 plates. sg Sept 18 (176) $700

Merigot, James
— A Select Collection of Views and Ruins in Rome.... L, 1797-99. 2 parts in 1 vol. Folio, disbound. With 61 plates. pn Dec 11 (42) £130 [Walford]

Merimee, Prosper, 1803-70
See also: Limited Editions Club
— Carmen. Paris, 1846. 1st Ed in Book form. 8vo, orig wraps. FD Dec 2 (3560) DM5,000
Anr Ed. Winchester, Mass., 1896. One of 50 on japan. Illus by E. H. Garrett. 8vo, mor gilt by Blackwell. Inscr to Paul Lemperly by Garrett with orig sketch. cb Sept 11 (87) $170

Merino de Jesu-Christo, Andres
— Escuela Paleographica o de leer letras cursivas antiguas y modernas. Madrid, 1780. 1st Ed. Folio, contemp calf. With engraved title & 58 plates. S Sept 23 (469) £240 [Palido]

Merken, Johann
— Liber artificiosus alphabeti maioris. Muelheim am Rhein, 1782-85. 2 vols. Oblong folio, contemp half calf; upper cover of Vol I damaged. With 56 plates. S May 21 (159) £1,000 [Marlborough]
Anr Ed. Mulheim, 1782-85. 2 parts in 1 vol. Oblong folio, contemp half lea. With 56 plates. FD June 11 (455) DM2,700
Anr Ed. Mulheim, 1782. 2 parts in one. Oblong folio, half calf; rebacked, lower cover repaired. With 56 plates, including title; some plates soiled. S Nov 27 (200) £1,000 [Bourget]

Merle d'Aubigne, Jean Henri. See: Fore-Edge Paintings

Merrill, Eliphalet & Phinehas
— A Gazetteer of the State of New Hampshire. Exeter, N.H., 1817. 1st Ed. 8vo, cloth. Some browning throughout. sg Mar 12 (192) $50

Merrill, James
— The Black Swan and Other Poems. Athens, 1946. One of 100. 4to, orig wraps; small chip at top of spine. Inscr to Kenneth Heuer. CNY May 11 (73) $2,400

Merriman, Henry Seton —& Tallentyre, Stephen G.
— The Money-Spinner, and Other Character Notes. L, 1896. Illus by Arthur Rackham. 8vo, orig cloth; front cover spotted. With 12 plates. sg Oct 30 (145) $90

AMERICAN BOOK PRICES CURRENT

Merriman, Henry Seton, 1862-1903
— The Grey Lady. L, 1897. Illus by Arthur Rackham. 8vo, cloth; rear hinge cracked. sg Oct 30 (146) $100

Merritt, Abraham, 1884-1943
— Dwellers in the Mirage. NY: Liveright, [1932]. Covers rubbed & stained, lower corners bumped. With Ls. cb Sept 28 (938) $225

Mershon, William Butts
— The Passenger Pigeon. NY, 1907. Minor dampstains. Inscr by the author's son. cb Nov 6 (207) $70
Anr copy. 4to, cloth, unopened. Inscr. sg Oct 23 (401) $80

Meryman, Richard
— Andrew Wyeth. Bost., 1968. Oblong 4to, orig cloth, in pictorial d/j. With 121 plates. K Dec 13 (173) $160
Anr copy. Orig cloth, in d/j. O June 9 (115) $90
Anr copy. With 165 color reproductions. wa Nov 6 (459) $110; wa Nov 6 (513) $95

Mesens, E. L. T.
— Poemes, 1923-1958. Paris: Le Terrain Vague, 1959. One of 1,100. Illus by Rene Magritte. Inscr to Georgette & Rene Magritte. S July 2 (1047) £420 [McCinsky]

Mesens, Edouard L. T.
— Troisieme Front.... L: Gallery Editions, 1944. One of 500. In ptd wraps & d/j. Inscr to Pablo Picasso. sg Mar 5 (166) $400

Meserve, Frederick Hill
— The Photographs of Abraham Lincoln. NY: Pvtly ptd, 1911. With the 1917 & 1938 Supplement. One of 102. 4to, later cloth. Library markings but no stamps on mtd numbered ports. sg May 7 (56) $475

Mesmer, Friedrich Anton, 1734-1815
— Memoire sur la decouverte du magnetisme animal. Geneva & Paris, 1779. 1st Ed. 8vo, half calf. FD June 11 (635) DM4,500

Messel, Oliver
— Stage Designs and Costumes. L, 1933. Ltd Ed. 4to, bds; spine worn & frayed. wd June 19 (157) $100

Messi Sbugo, Christoforo di
— Banchetti compositioni di vivande.... Ferrara: G. de Buglhat & A. Hucher, 1549. 4to, 19th-cent half vellum. With woodcut port & 2 large woodcuts. Tp loosening at lower gutter; minor stains & fingersoiling; last 3 leaves of index with thin strip at top edge renewed; lacking last blank; border of 1 large woodcut shaved by binder. Hunt copy. CNY Nov 21 (76) $5,000

Messi Sbugo, Cristoforo di
— Banchetti compositione di vivande.... Ferrara: G. de Bulghat & A. Hucher, 1549. 4to, later vellum. Lacking final blank; inner & upper margin of tp renewed affecting ornaments. Vehling-Crahan copy. P Nov 25 (331) $7,000

Messingham, Thomas
— Florilegium insulae sanctorum seu vitae et acta sanctorum Hiberniae. Paris, 1624. Folio, 19th-cent mor; rubbed. Minor wormed to corners of last few leaves. Huth Library copy. cb Oct 23 (150) $400

Mestrovic, Ivan
— Mestrovic. Zagreb, 1935. 4to, orig cloth. Sgd on frontis. bba Aug 28 (263) £55 [C. G. Agents]

Mesue, Joannes. See: Elimithar, Elluchasem

Metastasio, Pietro, 1698-1782
— Opere. Paris: Vedova Herissant, 1780-82. 12 vols, 8vo, contemp mor gilt; worn. With port & 37 plates. L.p. copy. HK Nov 4 (2855) DM900

Metchnikoff, Elie. See: Mechnikov, Il'ia Il'ich

Meteren, Emkmanuel van, 1535-1612
— Commentarien ofte memorien van den Nederlandtschen staet/handel/oorloggen ende gheschiedenissen van onsen tyden.... L, 1610. Folio, calf gilt; damaged. Lacking map; some stains & browning; 2 holes in 1 leaf. B Oct 7 (1351) HF750

Meung, Jean de. See: Lorris & Meung

Meurer, Noe
— Jag und Forstrecht, das ist Undericht.... Frankfurt: Peter Schmid for Sigmund Feyerabend, 1581. Folio, contemp vellum. Jeanson copy. SM Mar 1 (406) FF20,000

Meursius, Joannes, 1579-1639
— Athenae Batavae. Leiden, 1625. 1st Ed. 4to, half calf. With engraved title & 9 plates & plans. Hole in tp affecting 3 letters; plate on p. 170 shaved at top & bottom; some folding plates shaved by binder. S May 28 (738) £200
— Graecia ludibunda; sive, de ludis graecorum liber.... Leiden: Elzevir, 1625. 2 parts in 1 vol. 8vo, contemp vellum. sg Mar 26 (202) $150

Mexico
— Bases organicas de la republica Mexicana.... Mexico, 1843. 12mo, orig wraps; extremities chipped. Foxed. sg Sept 10 (66) $175
— Manifesto del Congreso General en el Presente Ano. Mexico City, 1836. 8vo, orig wraps. sg Sept 18 (279) $275
— Mexico y sus aldrededores, colleccion de monumentos, trajes y paisajes.... Mexico, 1855-56. Folio, half cloth; rubbed. With double-page plan loosely inserted, partially hand-colored & with litho title & 25 plates. S Apr 24 (296) £1,800 [Arader]
2d Ed. Mexico, 1864. Folio, modern cloth. With color litho title & 45 litho plates & with folding map hand-colored in outline. bba Dec 18 (137) £500 [Bailey]
Anr Ed. Mexico: Decaen, 1864. Folio, contemp cloth; worn. With folding plan, tinted litho title & 38 plates. Last few plates with tears at lower blank margin; last plate detached; half-title with small hole affecting text; some stains. S Apr 24 (297) £2,800 [Arader]

Meyer, Adolf Bernhard
— Unser Auer- Rackel- und Birkwild und seine Abarten. Vienna, 1887. Atlas vol only. Folio, modern cloth. With 17 hand-colored plates. Tp spotted; edges of margins spotted; 2 blank corners def. C Oct 15 (246) £1,200 [Marshall]

Meyer, Conrad Ferdinand
— Die Richterin. Hellerau & Vienna, 1923. One of 50 with an orig sgd etching. Illus by A. Kolb. 4to, orig vellum by Enders of Leipzig. HN Nov 26 (1488) DM580

Meyer, Franz
— Marc Chagall: Life and Works. [Paris]: Flammarion [1964]. 4to, cloth, in d/j. sg Jan 8 (42) $250

Meyer, Henry Leonard
— Illustrations of British Birds. L, [1837-44]. 4 vols. Folio, later half mor gilt; Vol II with small split at foot of upper joint, other vols rebacked preserving orig spines. With litho titles & 313 hand-colored lithos. Very small hole in 1 plate. C Oct 15 (247) £3,800 [Quaritch]
Anr Ed. L, 1842-50. ("Coloured Illustrations of British Birds.") Vols I-II only. Contemp mor gilt; rubbed. bba Jan 15 (415) £120 [Barker]
Anr Ed. L, 1853-57. 7 vols. 8vo, contemp half lea; worn. Some staining. S Feb 24 (596) £440 [Osborne]
Anr Ed. L, 1857. ("Colored Illustrations of British Birds and their Eggs.") 7 vols. 8vo, contemp half calf; spines rubbed. With 433 plates, most hand-colored. Some spotting; 1 plate & 2 leaves torn. bba Oct 30 (406) £550 [Greyfriars]

Meyer, Johann Daniel, b.1713
— Angenehmer und nuetzlicher Zeit-vertreib mit Betrachtung curioser vorstellungen allerhand...Thiere. Nuremberg, 1748-56. 3 vols in 2. Folio, contemp calf gilt, with arms of the Stahl family of Prussia; rubbed, 1

spine chipped, anr spine repaired. With port, 3 engraved titles & 240 plates, all hand-colored. S Oct 23 (735) £2,700 [Marlborough]

Anr copy. 3 vols in 1. Folio, 19th-cent half mor; rubbed & repaired. Repair to inner margin of last leaf just touching text; a little discolored by damp at beginning. S Apr 23 (44) £4,200 [Antik]

Meyer, Johann Jacob. See: Ebel & Meyer

Meyer, Rudolf & Conrad
— Die menschliche Sterblichkeit unter dem Titel Todten-Tanz, in LXI Original-Kupfern.... Hamburg, 1759. 4to, contemp lea. With frontis & 61 plates. JG Oct 2 (743) DM2,400

Meyers, William H. See: Grabhorn Printing

Meyrick, Sir Samuel Rush. See: Shaw & Meyrick

Micalori, Giacomo
— Della sfera mondiale. Urbino, 1626. 8vo, vellum. Outer margin of title shaved with loss; some wormholes in inner upper margins; a few wormholes elsewhere affecting letters. S Sept 23 (371) £120 [Robertshaw]

Michaelis, J. D.
— Recueil de questions, proposees a une societe de savants.... Amst., 1774. 4to, contemp calf; edges & joints rubbed. cb Feb 19 (207) $85

Michaud, Joseph Francois, 1767-1839
— History of the Crusades. Phila., [c.1880]. Illus by Gustave Dore. 2 vols. Folio, orig half lea gilt. sg Sept 11 (105) $120

Michaux, Andre, 1746-1802
— Geschichte der amerikanischen Eichen.... Stuttgart, 1802-4. 2 parts in 1 vol. Folio, modern half calf. With 14 plates, all but 3 hand-colored. de Belder copy. S Apr 28 (240) £1,600 [Maggs]

— Histoire des chenes de l'Amerique. Paris, An IX [1801]. Folio, later 19th-cent half cloth; rubbed. With 36 plates. Minor creasing. Jussieu—de Belder copy. S Apr 28 (239) £2,800 [Henderson]

Michaux, Francois Andre, 1770-1855
— Histoire des arbres forestiers de l'Amerique septentrionale.... Paris, 1810-13. 4 parts in 3 vols. 8vo, modern half calf. With 138 hand-finished color plates. Horticultural Society of New York—de Belder copy. S Apr 28 (241) £2,200 [Swann]

Anr copy. Contemp half mor; rubbed. S June 25 (169) £2,700 [Israel]

— The North American Sylva.... Paris, 1819-18-19. Part 3 only: A Treatise on the Resinous Trees of North America. modern cloth. With 23 colored plates, numbered 134-156. Library markings. O Nov 18 (125) $180

Anr Ed. Paris, 1819. 3 vols. 8vo, contemp calf gilt. With 156 hand-finished color plates. This copy an intermediate between Macphail's 17a & 17b, having titles as 17b but text as 17a. Vilmorin—de Belder copy. S Apr 28 (242) £6,000 [Brittain]

— Voyage a l'ouest des monts alleghanys.... Paris, An XII [1804]. 1st Ed. 8vo, later half calf. With a folding map, lacking 1 small corner. cb Nov 6 (209) $70

Michaux, Francois Andre, 1770-1855 —& Nuttall, Thomas, 1786-1859
— The North American Sylva.... Phila.: Robert P. Smith, 1852. 6 vols, including Nuttall's Supplement. 8vo, contemp mor gilt; rubbed. CNY Nov 21 (198) $2,200

Anr Ed. Phila., 1865. 3 vols. 8vo, modern half mor. With 156 hand-colored plates. Library copy. sg Jan 15 (239) $150

Anr Ed. Phila., 1871. 5 vols, including Nuttall's Supplement. 8vo, orig mor; rubbed. With port & 276 hand-colored plates. S Oct 23 (736) £1,200 [Mr. Henly]

Anr copy. Orig mor; rubbed, spines blackened. With port & 277 hand-colored plates. Some foxing of text & plates; 1 plate detached in Vol III. S Oct 23 (737) £750 [Vorles]

Michel, Adolphe
— L'Ancienne Auvergne et le Velay.... Moulins, 1843-47. 4 vols. Folio, half cloth. With 138 plates. SM Oct 20 (483) FF8,000

Michel, Guillaume
— La Forest de conscience.... Paris: Michel Le Noir, 30 Sept 1516. 8vo, mor gilt by Raparlier. Jeanson copy. SM Mar 1 (407) FF75,000

Michel, Marius
— La Reliure francaise. Paris, 1880. 1st Ed. 4to, contemp mor extra with inlay designs of a shield & of a fleur-de-lis; extremities worn. sg Dec 4 (132) $325

Anr Ed. Paris, 1881. 4to, contemp lea extra with inlaid center panels of mor blind-tooled to a weave pattern on front cover & vellum painted with red & green arabesque interlaces in a center-and-corner design on rear. sg Dec 4 (131) $275

Micheli, Pier Antonio
— Catalogus plantarum horti Caesarei Florentini. Florence, 1748. 4to, new half mor gilt. With folding frontis & 7 plates. Crahan copy. P Nov 25 (332) $950

— Nova Plantarum genera juxta Tournefortii methodum disposita.... Florence, 1729.

Folio, contemp bds; rubbed. With 108 plates. Tp browned; tp & some other leaves guarded, occasionally causing stains along inner margins. Crahan copy. P Nov 25 (333) $700

Michener, James A.
— Facing East. NY, 1970. Illus by Jack Levine. 2 parts in 1 vol. Folio, loose in silk folding-case. With 54 plates. sg Jan 8 (154) $250

Anr copy. Loose in satin folding-case. With 4 orig colored lithos. sg June 4 (199) $225

— Japanese Prints from the Early Masters to the Modern. Tokyo & Rutland, [1959]. 4to, cloth, in d/j; rubbed, spine creased. cba Mar 5 (256) $60

— The Modern Japanese Print. Rutland, [1962]. One of 510, sgd. Folio, orig cloth. With 10 plates, each sgd by artist. sg Feb 5 (184) $900; sg Apr 2 (146) $850

Anr copy. Cloth. sg June 4 (211) $750

Michetschlager, Heinrich F.
— das Ordenbuch des gewesenen Oester-reichischungarischen Monarchie.... Vienna, 1918-19. Folio, loose as issued in folding mor portfolio. Lacking pp 1-2 of text. cb Dec 18 (121) $110

Microcosm...
— The Microcosm. A Periodical Work, by Gregory Griffin. Windsor, 1787. Nos 1-40 in 1 vol. 8vo, modern half calf. bba Apr 9 (77) £85 [Clark]

Micyllus, Jacobus
— Elegia de duobus falconibus. Wittemberg, 1539. 8vo, mor janseniste by Chambolle-Duru. Jeanson copy. SM Mar 1 (408) FF40,000

Middleton, Charles Theodore
— A New and Complete System of Geography. L, [1777-78]. 2 vols. Folio, contemp calf; rubbed. With frontis, 98 plates & 20 maps. Ck Feb 27 (158) £460

Anr Ed I, 1778-79. Vol II only. Contemp calf; rubbed & worn, joints repaired. Portion of tp torn away. Sold w.a.f. O Oct 21 (116) $310

Middleton, Conyers, 1683-1750
— The History of the Life of Marcus Tullius Cicero. L, 1741. 1st Ed. 2 vols. 4to, contemp calf; worn & rubbed, joints repaired. O Oct 21 (117) $50

— The Origin of Printing, in Two Essays. L, 1776-81. 8vo, 19th-cent half lea; worn. Accession stamp on tp verso, visible on recto. sg Mar 26 (46) $150

Middleton, Erasmus, 1739-1805
— The New Complete Dictionary of Arts and Sciences. L, 1778. 2 vols in 1. Folio, contemp calf; upper joint worn. Tp torn & def at 1 corner; 4 plates def, anr with a small hole. Sold w.a.f. L July 2 (23) £60

Anr copy. Modern calf. With frontis & 80 plates. Lacking Aa1-2; 4a bound in its place; some marginal tears; 1 plate with 2 small holes. S Nov 10 (398) £105 [Negro]

Middleton, J. J.
— Grecian Remains in Italy. L, 1812. Folio, contemp half calf; broken. With 2 plain & 23 colored plates. bba Feb 5 (302) £650 [Rainer]

Anr copy. Half lea; def & loose. S Apr 23 (98) £800 [Shapero]

Middleton, John
— Five Hundred New Receipts.... L: Thomas Astley, 1734. Ed by Henry Howard. 8vo, 19th-cent half calf; rubbed, front joint starting. Some soiling & staining, occasionally heavy at lower margin. P Nov 25 (334) $500

— For the Good of the Publick.... Edin. [1700?]. 4to, wraps. S July 24 (447) £900 [Institute of Actuaries]

Middleton, Thomas, 1570?-1627
— Works. L, 1885-86. 8 vols. 8vo, half mor gilt. sg Feb 12 (224) $250

Midgely, Alfred
— The Queensland Illustrated Guide.... Brisbane, 1888. 8vo, orig cloth; rubbed. With 9 mtd photographs & folding map in pocket at end. bba Oct 16 (247) £170 [Bonham]

Midolle, Jean
— Galerie. Compositions avec ecritures anciennes et modernes.... Strasbourg, [1834-35]. Oblong folio, unbound as issued in orig wraps. With 36 plates only. Lithographed throughout. Sold w.a.f. Ck Sept 5 (4) £500

Migeon, Gaston, 1861-1930
— Manuel d'Art Musulman: Arts Plastiques et Industriels. Paris, 1927. 2d Ed. 2 vols. New cloth, orig wraps bound in; worn. O Jan 6 (126) $75

Mikan, Johann Christoph
— Delectus Florae et Faunae Brasiliensis. Vienna: A. Strauss, 1820-23. Parts 1-3 (of 4). Folio, unbound as issued in ptd bd portfolios. With 18 hand-colored plates. Four plates stained in outer margins; 2 with marginal tears. S Oct 23 (738) £850 [Marks]

Milanuzzi, Carlo
— Celeste Origine e miracolose grazie del pane benedetto del glorioso Padre S. Nicola da Tolentino. Venice: G. A. Giuliani, 1632. 8vo, later 17th-cent mor with arms of Mary of Modena; small puncture in head of spine. cb Oct 23 (151) $95

Milbert, Jacques Gerard
— Itineraire pittoresque du Fleuve Hudson.... Paris, 1828-29. 2 vols in 1 of text & Atlas vol. 4to & folio, half mor. WIth hand-colored double-page map & 43 plates. Atlas with blindstamp at foot of litho title. S Oct 23 (422) £6,600 [Smith]
— Voyage pittoresque a l'Ile-de France, au cap de Bonne-Esperance, et a l'ile de Teneriffe. Paris, 1812. Atlas only. Oblong folio, contemp bds; spine def. With 45 plates & maps. S Apr 23 (188) £1,050 [Joseph]

Miles, Henry Downes, 1806-89
— British Field Sports. L: Wm. Mackenzie, [n.d.].. 4to, later half mor incorporating orig bds. Ck Oct 31 (188) £170

Miles, Nelson Appleton
— Personal Recollections and Observations...Civil War.... Chicago, 1896. 1st Ed, 1st Issue, with "General" at frontis port. Illus by Frederic Remington. 4to, cloth; rubbed. cb Jan 8 (293) $100
 2d Ed. Chicago, 1897. 4to, cloth; worn, rear cover slightly stained. cb Jan 8 (294) $60

Miles, William J.
— Modern Practical Farriery.... L, [1873-74]. 4to, half calf. pnE nov 12 (79) £42

Military...
— The Military Costume of Europe. L: T. Goddard & J. Booth, 1812. 1st Ed. 4to, half calf. With 97 hand-colored plates. Lacking title & contents leaf to Vol II; some margins soiled. S Apr 23 (75) £650 [Thorp]
 Anr Ed. L, 1822. 2 vols. Folio, half mor gilt; rubbed. With 96 hand-colored plates, some heightened with gum arabic. Some spotting affecting margins. S June 25 (199) £1,200 [Neidhardt]
— The Military Costume of Turkey. L, 1818. Folio, contemp mor gilt; rubbed. With engraved title & 30 colored plates. C Apr 8 (160) £500 [Rome]
 Anr copy. Mor. pn Apr 30 (56) £290 [Ariel]
 Anr copy. Orig bds; rebacked & recornered with pigskin. S Feb 24 (339) £260 [Metaxes]
 Anr copy. Contemp calf gilt; rubbed, broken. With engraved title, frontis & 29 (of 30) plates, hand-colored. S July 14 (575) £520

Military Order of Christ
— Diffinicoens, & Estatutos dos Cavalleyros, e Freyres da Orden de Nosso Senhor Jesu Christo.... Lisbon: Pascoal da Sylvani, 1717. Folio, contemp vellum; upper cover split cleanly across center. Phillipps copy. sg Mar 26 (204) $325

Mill, James, 1773-1836
— Analysis of the Phenomena of the Human Mind. L, 1829. 2 vols in 1. 8vo, contemp calf; rebacked with orig spine laid down, part of 1 raised band lacking. P Sept 24 (348) $450
— Elemens d'economie politique.... Paris, 1823. 8vo, calf; scuffed, rubbed, head of spine pulled, surface worming. Minor soiling & spotting; final leaf sliced out with free endpaper. P Sept 24 (349) $175
— Elements of Political Economy. L, 1824. 2d Ed. 8vo, bds; rubbed, affecting imprint, rebacked, worn. Repair along inner margin; soiled at front & back; stamp on tp & endpapers; Some Ms corrections. P Sept 24 (350) $325

Mill, John Stuart, 1806-73
— Autobiography. L, 1873. 1st Ed, 1st Issue. 8vo, orig cloth; splits in hinges, tear at foot of joint. Inscr by Florence Nightingale. S Jan 13 (513) £150 [Bauman]
— Essays on Some Unsettled Questions of Political Economy. L, 1844. 1st Ed. 8vo, contemmp calf; rubbed, joints worn. O Nov 18 (127) $140
 Anr copy. Orig bds; spine damaged. A few fore-margins soiled. S June 25 (73) £300 [Quaritch]
— On Liberty. L, 1859. 1st Ed. 8vo, orig cloth; rubbed, torn along lower joint. P Sept 24 (352) $600
— Principles of Political Economy. L, 1848. 1st Ed. 2 vols. 8vo, orig cloth. C Dec 12 (152) £1,500 [Martin]
 Anr copy. Orig cloth; worn, later labels. Pencilled notes on endpapers of Vol I; some underscoring in text. P Sept 24 (353) $1,100
— The Subjection of Women. L, 1869. 1st Ed. 8vo, orig cloth; rear hinge cracked. sg Feb 12 (225) $225
— Three Essays on Religion. L, 1874. 1st Ed. 8vo, orig cloth. T Oct 16 (478) £46

Millais, John Everett, 1829-96
— Millais's Illustrations. A Collection of Drawings on Wood. L & NY, 1866. 4to, half mor. With frontis & 80 wood-engravings. Tp & contents leaf repaired with loss; other marginal repairs. bba Aug 20 (266) £40 [Rainer]

Millais, John Guille, 1865-1931
— A Breath from the Veldt. L, 1895. 4to, orig cloth; soiled, extremities worn, contents coming loose because of poor glue. cb Nov 6 (212) $350

— British Deer and their Horns. L, 1897. Folio, cloth; rubbed, front joint starting. cb Nov 6 (213) $110

Anr copy. Orig cloth; soiled. pn Sept 18 (24) £130 [McEwan]

Anr copy. Orig cloth; repaired. pn Oct 23 (159) £120 [Holland & Holland]

— Game Birds and Shooting-Sketches. L, 1892. Folio, orig half calf. With port, 18 plain & 16 colored plates. Jeanson 1623. SM Mar 1 (410) FF4,200

— The Mammals of Great Britain and Ireland. L, 1904-6. One of 1,025. 3 vols. 4to, buckram-backed cloth; spine extremities rubbed. With 62 colored plates. Vol I with faint waterstain to a few margins. C Oct 15 (248) £150 [Shapero]

Anr copy. Cloth; rubbed, corners bumped. cb Nov 6 (214) $350

Anr copy. With 52 color plates. cb June 4 (155) $350

Anr copy. Half mor gilt. Marginal spotting in Vol I; frontis & 2 plates in Vol II have small inkstain in margin; in Vol III 1 uncolored plate cut round, torn & repaired & a few leaves & plates have marginal tear. L July 2 (169) £200

— The Natural History of the British Surface-Feeding Ducks. L, 1902. One of 600 L.p. copies. 4to, orig cloth; def. With 41 color plates. Haverschmidt copy. B Feb 24 (402) HF900

Anr copy. Orig cloth; rubbed. With 41 color & 6 plain plates. bba Oct 30 (409) £260 [Greyfriars]

— The Natural History of British Game Birds. L, 1909. One of 550. Folio, orig cloth. With 17 plain & 18 color plates. bba Oct 30 (408) £200 [Rainer]; S Nov 10 (528) £320 [Tryan]

Millar, George Henry
— The New and Universal System of Geography. L, 1783. Folio, old calf; rebacked with more recent half calf, scuffed. Some stains; a few tears. cb Feb 19 (196) $550

Millar, John, 1733-1805
— Observations on the Asthma and on the Hooping Cough. L, 1769. 8vo, later half sheep; worn. Some soiling. bba Sept 25 (190) £230 [Phillips]

— Observations Concerning the Distinction of Ranks in Society. L, 1771. 4to, half calf; worn, upper cover broken. Contents page misbound, considerably foxed & with ink smears. cb Oct 23 (153) $65

Anr copy. Calf; spine worn, joints worn. Some spotting. P Sept 24 (355) $950

Millar, Kenneth
See also: MacDonald, Ross

— The Dark Tunnel. NY, 1944. cb Nov 20 (258) $250

— The Three Roads. NY, 1948. In soiled & frayed d/j. cb Nov 20 (259) $110

Millar, Margaret
— The Weak-Eyed Bat. Garden City, 1942. In chipped d/j. cb May 7 (289) $80

Millard, Christopher Sclater
— Bibliography of Oscar Wilde. L, [1914]. One of 100, sgd "Mason". 2 vols. sg Jan 22 (316) $175

Millay, Edna St. Vincent, 1892-1950
[-] A Book of Vassar Verse. Poughkeepsie, 1916. In torn d/j. Contains Millay's "Interim," "Why Did I Ever Come to This Place," & "The Suicide". sg Dec 11 (86) $70

— Renascence and Other Poems. NY, 1917. 1st Ed, 1st Issue. In d/j. sg Mar 5 (167) $175

Miller, Alfred W.
— Fishless Days, by Sparse Grey Hackle. NY, 1954. One of 591. sg Oct 23 (403) $100

Miller, Arthur
— After the Fall. NY, 1964. One of 999, sgd. sg Mar 5 (168) $90

Miller, C. William
— Franklin's Philadelphia Printing, 1728-1766: a Descriptive Bibliography. Phila., 1974. 4to, cloth, in d/j. wa June 25 (21) $95

Miller, Chuck. See: Underwood & Miller

Miller, Francis Trevelyan
See also: Photographic...

— The World in the Air,... NY, 1930. 2 vols. 4to, cloth. wa Sept 25 (98) $210

Miller, Henry
— Black Spring. Paris: Obelisk Press, [1936]. 1st Ed. Orig wraps. sg Mar 5 (173) $80

— Max and the White Phagocytes. Paris, [1938]. 1st Ed. Orig wraps; spne worn. T Feb 18 (111) £35

— Tropic of Capricorn. Paris: Obelisk Press, [1939]. 1st Ed. Orig wraps; frayed. T Oct 15 (83) £70

Miller, Henry, fl. 1856. See: Grabhorn Printing

MILLER

Miller, John, 1715?-90?
— Illustratio systematis sexualis Linnaei. An Illustration of the Sexual System of the genera plantarum of Linnaeus. L, [1770]-77. Folio, contemp russia gilt; upper cover detached, lower cover worn & with joint broken. With frontis, 4 handcolored plates of leaves & 104 plates of plants in 2 states, uncolored & ptd in black & handcolored. Frontis detached & with extreme blank margin chipped; colored plate 72 with ptr's crease. Hunt copy. CNY Nov 21 (199) $11,000

Anr copy. 1 vol in 2. Folio, old half calf gilt; rubbed & loose. With 4 hand-colored plates of leaves, 104 hand-colored plates & 104 duplicate uncolored plates. A few marks. pnNY Oct 11 (34) $8,500

Anr copy. 2 vols. Folio, contemp half russia. With frontis, 4 hand-colored plates of botanical detail & 104 plates, each in 2 states, 1 hand-colored before letters. Northwick—de Belder copy. S Apr 28 (245) £11,000 [V. F. White]

Miller, John Frederick. See: Shaw & Miller

Miller, John Samuel
— A Natural History of the Crinoidea, or Lily-Shaped Animals. Bristol, 1821. 4to, calf; rebacked, corners repaired. With 50 colored plates. Inscr to Sir Humphry Davy. S Nov 10 (529) £220 [Wheldon]

Miller, Joseph, fl.1722-48
— Botanicum Officinale, or a Compendious Herbal.... L, 1722. 8vo, contemp calf gilt; worn. pnE Dec 17 (254) £140 [Maggs]

Miller, P. Schuyler. See: De Camp & Miller

Miller, Philip, 1691-1771
— Catalogus plantarum tum exoticarum tum domesticarum...a Catalogue of Trees.... L, 1730. Folio, old calf; rubbed. With 14 hand-colored & 7 colored plates. Some foxing. pn May 21 (201) £280 [Maggs]

Anr copy. Contemp calf; chipped. With engraved frontis & 21 plates, of which 7 are hand-finished color mezzotints & 14 are hand-colored engravings. Horticultural Society of New York—de Belder copy. S Apr 28 (339) £5,000 [Hill]

— Dictionnaire des jardiniers. Paris, 1785-90. 8th Ed. 8 (of 10) vols. 4to, bdg not described. Franklin Institute copy. F Sept 12 (265) $175

— Figures of Plants.... L, 1771. ("Figures of the Most Beautiful, Useful...Plants Described in the Gardeners Dictionary.") 1st Ed, 2d Issue. 2 vols. Folio, contemp russia gilt. With 300 hand-colored plates. Cuthbert—de Belder copy. S Apr 28 (243) £6,500 [Pavlov]

2d Ed. Vol I (of 2). Half cloth; worn. Some discoloration; Plates 2 & 3 creased. Sold w.a.f. S June 25 (170) £1,950 [Bifolco]

— The Gardener's Dictionary.... L, 1731. Folio, contemp calf; rubbed, rebacked & repaired. Marginally waterstained. bba June 18 (159) £110 [Clark]

Anr copy. Modern cloth. With frontis & 4 plates. S Feb 24 (530) £110 [Wesley]

2d Ed. L, 1733. Folio, contemp calf; rubbed. Text & plates loose. pn Jan 22 (235) £135 [Frew]

8th Ed. L, 1768. 2 vols. Folio, contemp calf; joints split & crudely repaired with tape. Frontis torn & repaired; library markings. bba Feb 5 (316) £90 [Lloyds of Kew]

Anr Ed. L, 1807. ("The Gardener's and Botanist's Dictionary.") 2 vols in 4. Folio, contemp calf; worn, 2 covers detached. With 17 plates. Some marginal repairs to margins. S Nov 10 (530) £50 [Greyfriars]

Anr copy. Contemp half calf; worn. With 20 plates. S Feb 24 (529) £60 [Wesley]

Anr copy. Contemp calf; rubbed. With frontis & 15 plates. Marginal worming. S Feb 24 (597) £120 [HIll]

Miller, Thomas, 1807-74
— The Poetical Language of Flowers. L, 1855. 8vo, mor gilt; rubbed. With 11 hand-colored plates. Lacking upper blank. pn Dec 11 (339) £160

Miller, Walter M.
— A Canticle for Liebowitz. Phila., 1960. 1st Ed. In 1st jacket. cb Sept 28 (946) $750

Milliken, Henry Oothovt. See: Goodwin & Milliken

Millin de Grandmaison, Aubin Louis
— Antiquites nationales, ou recueil de monumens pour servir a l'histoire de l'Empire Francais. Paris, 1790-99 [An VII]. 5 vols. Folio, contemp half sheep; worn. Lacking 4 plates but with 7 additional plates. L.p. copy. bba Aug 20 (310) £160 [Blake]

Mills, John, d.1784
— D'Horsay; or, the Follies of the Day. L, 1844. 8vo, mor gilt by Riviere. With engraved title & 10 plates. Extra-illus with 2 ports of the Count d'Orsay & related material. sg Feb 12 (126) $175

— An Essay on the Management of Bees. L, 1766. 8vo, contemp half sheep; extremities rubbed, front free endpaper loose. sg Jan 15 (161) $200

Mills, John, d. c.1885
— D'Horsay; or, the Follies of the Day. L, 1844. 8vo, calf gilt by Murrell; orig cloth bound in. sg Sept 11 (234) $80
— The Sportsman's Library. Edin., 1845. 1st Ed. 5 parts in 1 vol. 8vo, mor gilt. Lacking half-title. pnE Dec 17 (354) £70 [Traylen]

Mills, Robert, 1781-1855
— Statistics of South Carolina.... Charleston, 1826. 8vo, modern cloth. Lacking 1 map. sg Mar 12 (237) $60

Millspaugh, Charles Frederick
— Medicinal Plants..... NY & Phila.: Boericke & Tafel, [1882-87]. ("American Medicinal Plants.") 6 vols. 4to, orig half cloth. S Feb 24 (531) £260 [Wesley]

Milman, Helen Rose Anne
— In the Garden of Peace. L, 1896. 8vo, contemp embroidered bdg of white satin with front cover worked to an all-over floral design in colors. bba Sept 25 (88) £50 [Wren]

Milne, Alan Alexander, 1882-1956
— A Gallery of Children. L, [1925]. One of 500. Illus by H. W. Le Mair. 4to, cloth; soiled. S Oct 7 (978) £200 [Thorp]
Anr copy. With 12 color plates. S Dec 5 (328) £480 [P. Cope]
— The House at Pooh Corner. L, 1928. 1st Ed. Illus by E. H. Shepard. In chipped & soiled d/j. bba Jan 15 (187) £75 [Damms]
Anr copy. Calf gilt. pn Dec 11 (348) £75 [Henderson]
Anr copy. Lea gilt, prize label inserted inside upper cover. S Oct 7 (979) £120 [Vischer]
One of 350. In d/j. With orig ink drawing of Christopher Robin & Eeyore by E. H. Shepard pasted to front free endpaper. P June 18 (126) $6,000
Anr copy. 4to, half cloth. pn May 21 (279) £420 [Burton Garbett]
Anr copy. Orig half cloth, in d/j; soiled. pnNY Sept 13 (260) $275
Anr copy. Orig half cloth, unopened, in d/j. S June 18 (469) £330 [Sotheran]
— Michael and Mary. L, 1930. 1st Ed, One of 260. sg Mar 5 (177) $100
— Now We Are Six. L, 1927. one of 200. Illus by E. H. Shepard. Orig half cloth, in d/j, unopened. pnNY Sept 13 (261) $325
1st Ed. In chipped d/j. bba Sept 25 (130) £65 [Lovett & Lovett]
Anr copy. Orig lea. pn Sept 18 (312) £60 [Walford]
— Those were the Days. L, 1929. 1st Ed, One of 250. In d/j. wa Nov 6 (526) $90
— When We Were Very Young. L, 1924. 1st Ed. Illus by E. H. Shepard. Orig cloth, in soiled & repaired d/j. Sgd by Milne & Shepard on tp & with ALs from Milne to Mrs Steel, 1 Sept 1918, laid in. P Sept 24 (196) $900
— Winnie-the-Pooh. L, 1926. 1st Ed. Illus by E. H. Shepard. In chipped & soiled d/j. bba Jan 15 (186) £95 [Lovett & Lovett]
Anr copy. In d/j from a later Ed with portion torn from lower cover. S Jan 13 (662) £70 [Subin]
Anr copy. Inscr. S May 6 (215) £360 [Brandreth]; SSA Feb 11 (567) R140
Anr copy. In frayed d/j. T Oct 15 (223) £120; T July 16 (452) £140
One of 350, sgd by author & artist. 4to, orig half cloth, in d/j, unopened. S Dec 5 (329) £500 [S. Randall]
Anr copy. Orig half cloth, unopened, in d/j. S June 18 (472) £600 [Nagami]

Milnor, William, Jr., 1769-1848
— An Authentic Historical Memoir of the Schuylkill Fishing Company.... Phila., 1830. 2 parts in 1 vol. 8vo, half lea; joint worn. s Oct 478 $500
— Memoirs of the Gloucester Fox Hunting Club.... NY: Derrydale Press, 1927. One of 375. With 2 mtd plates. sg May 21 (75) $70

Milton, John, 1608-74
See also: Cresset Press; Fore-Edge Paintings; Golden Cockerel Press; Gregynog Press; Limited Editions Club; Nonesuch Press
— Areopagitica. L: Rampant Lions Press, [1973]. One of 100 specially bound. Folio, orig mor. S Oct 6 (730) £40 [Thorp]
— Comus. L & NY, [1921]. Illus by Arthur Rackham. 4to, orig cloth. With 24 mtd color plates. sg Oct 30 (149) $90
Anr copy. Cloth; backstrip faded. sg Oct 30 (150) $90
One of 550, sgd by Rackham. Vellum; discolored & spotted. With 24 mtd color plates. sg Oct 30 (148) $500
— Of Prelatical Episcopacy... L, 1641. 1st Ed. 4to, mor by Riviere. C Dec 12 (350) £380 [Maggs]
— Of Reformation Touching Church-Discipline in England.... L: For Thomas Underhill, 1641. 4to, modern bds. Small hole in I4, not affecting text. S July 23 (12) £650 [Finch]
— Paradise Lost. L, 1688. 4th Ed. Folio, contemp calf gilt, worn. With port & 12 plates. Marginal dampstains; some fraying. S Mar 10 (1112) £500 [Kohler]
Anr Ed. L, 1794. 4to, contemp mor gilt. With port, dedication & 13 (of 12 - 1 in

MILTON

duplicate) plates. One text leaf torn & repaired. sg Apr 2 (149) $375

Anr Ed. L, 1827. Illus by John Martin. 2 vols. Folio, contemp lev gilt by Charles Murton. L.p. copy. C May 13 (131) £950 [Sims]

Anr copy. Contemp mor gilt; rubbed. Some spotting, browning & repairs. HK Nov 4 (2857) DM2,800

Anr copy. Contemp lea gilt; worn. S June 17 (254) £600 [Campbell]

Anr copy. Contemp calf; worn & broken. Lacking 1 plate; browned. T Apr 16 (282) £100

Anr Ed. L, 1849. Illus by John Margin. 4to, later calf. Frontis waterstained. bba Aug 28 (282) £150 [Rainer]

Anr Ed. Liverpool, 1906. Illus by William Blake. 4to, mor with raised colored bands by Marianne Ishibashi. With 12 plates. Some leaves repaired. S Oct 6 (773) £60 [Bookroom]

— Paradise Regain'd L, 1680. 2d Ed. 8vo, old calf; rebacked & recornered. Some browning of margins. Ck Nov 21 (39) £95

— Poetical Works. L, 1794-97. 3 vols. Folio, lev extra by Tout; Vol I loose in bdg, Vol III joints cracked. Some foxing; 1 text leaf torn; accession number stamped on titles. Extra-illus with c.212 plates. sg Dec 4 (133) $475

Anr Ed. Phila., 1895. One of 60. 2 vols in 4. 4to, padded lea extra. With 50 plates in mtd india-proof state. sg Feb 12 (228) $350

— Pro populo Anglicano defensio contra Claudii Anonymi, alias Salmasii, defensionem regiam. L, [i.e., Utrecht], 1652. 12mo, old calf; worn, broken. bba Nov 13 (190) £35 [Cameron]

— Samson Agonistes. Harrow Weald: Raven Press, 1931. One of 275. Illus by R. A. Maynard. 4to, orig half vellum; soiled. bba Oct 30 (119) £65 [Marks]

— The Shorter Poems. L, 1889. One of 135. Illus by Samuel Palmer. Folio, cloth. With 12 plates. sg Feb 5 (248) $100

— Works. L, 1851. 8 vols. 8vo, contemp mor gilt gift bdg; some corners worn, extremities rubbed. sg Sept 11 (235) $200

Paradise Lost bound with or accompanied by Paradise Regain'd

— 1758. - Birm.: Baskerville. 2 vols. 4to, old calf gilt. pnNY June 11 (133A) uS250

Anr copy. Contemp calf gilt; rubbed, hinges tender. T Feb 19 (450) £110

— 1759. - Birm.: Baskerville. 2 vols. 4to, 19th-cent calf gilt; rebacked. sg Feb 12 (227) $250

— 1760. - Birm.: Baskerville. 2 vols. 8vo,

AMERICAN BOOK PRICES CURRENT

contemp calf; rebacked, spine ends chipped, joints starting. Marginal dampstaining. sg Oct 9 (271) $175

Minasian, Khatchik. See: Grabhorn Printing

Minchin, James Innes, 1825-1903
— Games Played in the London International Chess Tournament, 1883. L, 1885. 2d Ed. 8vo, cloth. pn Mar 26 (46) £55 [De Lucia]

Miner, Charles
— History of Wyoming.... Phila., 1845. 8vo, orig cloth; joints cracked, spine ends chipped. With 2 folding maps & 2 plates. One map separated at fold. sg Mar 12 (213) $50

Miniature Books
— Abrege de l'histoire des Provinces Unies. Amst.: T. Crajenschot, 1756. 2 parts in 1 vol. 24mm by 25mm, contemp calf gilt. With engraved title & 36 plates. S Dec 5 (367) £1,600 [J. Schiller]

— The Aeolian Harp, or Songster's Cabinet. NY, 1820. 2 vols in 1. 68mm by 50mm, orig bds; spotted. Houghton copy. CNY May 11 (74) $700

— The Bible in Miniature. L, 1778. 45mm by 27mm, orig mor gilt; wormhole in spine, upper cover loose. S May 6 (239) £130 [Fletcher]

Anr Ed. L, 1780. 40mm by 30mm, orig mor gilt with central onlay, lower cover lacking onlay. Engraved title with word Miniature reworked. Ck Apr 24 (125) £70

Anr copy. 41mm by 29mm, contemp mor gilt. CNY May 11 (77) $300

Anr copy. 45mm by 31mm, orig mor gilt. With 2 engraved titles & 14 plates. S Oct 7 (1006) £220 [Seibu]

— [Bible] La Sainte Bible, mise en vers par J. P. J. Du Bois. The Hague: P. Servas, 1752. 52mm by 32mm, contemp calf gilt; rubbed & broken. CNY May 11 (75) $380

— The Child's Book Case. L, 1840. 3 vols only. 135mm by 101mm, orig half mor in orig mor box. CNY May 11 (83) $380

— English Bijou Almanac for 1841. L: A. Schloss, [1840]. 20mm by 12mm, orig bdg. Ck Apr 24 (123) £70

— The Form and Order of the Service...to be Observed in the Coronation of Her Majesty Queen Elizabeth II. Worcester: Achille J. St. Onge, 1953. 2.75 by 1.8 inches, mor by Sangorski & Sutcliffe. O Jan 6 (128) $125

— The Golden Alphabet; or Parents' Guide an dChild's instructor. L: Robert Taylor, 1846. 22mm by 20mm, orig wraps; worn. A few leaves cropped. CNY May 11 (88) $380

— Horae dicendae singulis diebus hebdomadae. Paris: Thomas Hardouyn [almanac dated 1544-52]. 55mm by 40mm, modern mor. Ptd on vellum. Lacking F3 & K1; minor stains. CNY May 11 (93) $6,500

— Journee du Chretien. Rouen: Besongue, [c.1784]. 37mm by 23mm, contemp mor gilt. CNY May 11 (97) $850

— Kern der kerkelyke Historie. AMst.: T. Crajenschot, 1753. 2 vols. 45mm by 26mm & 44mm by 29mm, contemp calf gilt, not uniform. With 36 plates. Some plates cropped at fore-edge; folding plates creased. CNY May 11 (99) $300

Anr Ed. Dordrecht: A. Blusse, 1755. 2 vols. 41mm by 30mm, contemp calf gilt. With 36 plates. Folding plate creased. CNY May 11 (98) $450

— Koh Tebarku Bnei Israel. Livorno: Jedidiah ben Isaac Gabbai, 1671. 50mm by 35mm, modern mor gilt. CNY May 11 (100) $2,500

— Lobster's Voyage to the Brazils. L, 1808. 1st Ed. 4¾ by 4 inches. Sewn. With 8 plates. FD Dec 2 (3356) DM1,200

— London Almanack for the Year 1851. L, [1850]. 2.25 by 1.25 inches. Contemp mor gilt; rubbed. Ck Jan 16 (49) £95

— [New Testament in Greek]. Sedan: J. Jannon, 1628. 72mm by 52mm, 18th-cent mor gilt; corners worn. Tp def; NN5 & NN6 torn with slight loss. CNY May 11 (78) $180

— [New Testament in Shorthand] L: Wm. Marshall & Jno. Marshall, [1700?]. 68mm by 40mm, mor gilt. S June 18 (545) £350 [Bondy]

— Il Piccolo parochiano dell' infanzia. Milan, 1837. 27mm by 22mm, contemp mor gilt; rubbed. CNY May 11 (94) $480

— Powesci Moralne. Warsaw: Nakladem N. Gluecksberga, 1824. 75mm by 52mm, orig ptd wraps; soiled, ink stain to lower spine. CNY May 11 (111) $150

— The Psalms of David in Metre.... Edin., 1779. 72mm by 42mm, contemp mor gilt. Houghton-Marcus copy. CNY May 11 (112) $100

— Les Pseaumes de David. Sedan: Pierre Jannon, 1644. 60mm by 38mm, contemp mor with silver clasp monogrammed I.F.. S June 18 (544) £850 [Fletcher]

— Seder Tephiloth. Amst.: Naphtali Herz Levi, 1739. 55mm by 35mm, contemp blind-tooled vellum. CNY May 11 (114) $2,600

— Septem Psalmi Poenitentiales. Rome, 1592. 33mm by 25mm, 19th-cent mor gilt enclosing the letters L & M on the 2 covers. CNY May 11 (113) $2,500

— Tehillim. Tel Aviv, [c.1947]. Illus by Solomon Cohen. 62mm by 40mm,

Bezalel-style bdg of cloth-back olivewood bds. sg Sept 25 (242) $275

— Tom Thumb's Play-Book to Teach Children their Letters.... Birmingham: T. Warren, 1755. 71mm by 46mm orig wraps; worn, restitched. 2 corners torn away, not affecting ptd surface. S Dec 5 (383) £8,000 [J. Schiller]

Anr Ed. Birmingham: H. Butler [not after 1758]. 78mm by 51mm orig Dutch wraps; worn. S Dec 5 (384) £4,200 [Birmingham Lib.]

— A Travelling Library of Classics. Amst., 1627-37. 14 vols, some 104mm by 51mm & others 86mm by 46mm, contemp mor gilt. Engraved titles in 12 vols. CNY May 11 (96) $1,600

— Walsprack och Werser. Stockholm, 1790. 46mm by 77mm, contemp bds. Tp detached. CNY May 11 (117) $130

— Who's Who 1922. L: A. & C. Black, [1923?]. 65mm by 42mm, orig cloth, in repaired d/j. CNY May 11 (120) $420

— BENOIT, P. A. - Meurs. Ales, [1960]. One of 40, sgd by author & artist. Illus by Picasso. 31mm by 42mm, sewn in orig wraps, in d/j. With engraved frontis by Picasso. CNY May 11 (109) $1,800

— BOREMAN, THOMAS. - Curiosities in the Tower of London. L, 1741. 2d Ed. 2 vols. 57mm by 46mm, orig Dutch bds. S Dec 5 (372) £1,300 [J. Schiller]

— BOYE, FRIDERICH. - Nogle faae udvalgte og med Blod Gesprengte Blomster.... Copenhagen, 1759. 53mm by 94mm, contemp sharkskin gilt. CNY May 11 (80) $150

— BUFFON, GEORGES LOUIS MARIE LECLERC. - Buffon in Miniatuur, of Natuurlijke Historie voor de Jeugd. Amst.: M. Westerman, [c.1830]. 5 vols. 100mm by 63mm, orig bds, in box with inset glass. CNY May 11 (82) $200

— CICERO, MARCUS TULLIUS. - De Officiis. Paris, 1773. 87mm by 53mm, contemp mor gilt with arms of Lord Stuart de Rothesay. L.p. copy. CNY May 11 (85) $420

— DANTE ALIGHIERI. - Galleria Dantesca Microscopica. Milan: Ulrico Hoepli, 1880. 51mm by 39mm, contemp mor gilt. With 30 photographic plates. CNY May 11 (86) $380

— EISENHOWER, DWIGHT DAVID. - The Inaugural Address of.... Worcester: Achille J. St. Onge, 1954. One of 100. 2.75 by 1.8 inches, mor by Sangorski & Sutcliffe. O Jan 6 (127) $70

— GALILEI, G. - Galileo a Madama Cristina di Lorena. Padua: Salmin, 1896 [1897]. 16mm by 11mm, orig mor gilt. C Dec 3 (94) £4,000 [Tulkens]

— GRESSET, JEAN BAPTISTE LOUIS. - Ver-Vert

797

MINIATURE BOOKS

suivi de La Chartreuse.... Paris, 1855. Size not specified, mor gilt by David. CNY May 11 (89) $380
— HARROP, RENE POUL JORGENSON & OTHERS. - A Book of Small Flies. Arlington VT: Isaac Oelgart, 1983. One of 60. 2 vols. including folding box containing 8 miniature flies on mounts. 73mm by 55mm, orig mor gilt. With advance order acknowledgment in wraps, inscr by Oelgart, 2 hand-colored etchings by Al Barker. CNY May 11 (90) $1,200
— HOMER. - Ilias. Odysseia. L, 1831. 2 vols. 87mm by 48mm, mor janseniste by Hardy. cNY May 11 (92) $280
— LINCOLN, ABRAHAM. - Addresses. Kingsport, Tenn., 1929. One of 150 copies set, ptd & bound by students in training at the Kingsport Press. $7/8$ by $5/8$ inches sg Feb 12 (232) $70
— MAY, JULIAN. - Brede's Tale. Mercer Island: Starmont House, [1982]. One of 100. Illus by Fabian. 2.75 by 2 inches, lea with gilded silver casting of torc emblem attached to front cover. cb Sept 28 (926) $75
— OMAR KHAYYAM. - The Rose Garden. Worcester, Mass., 1932. 4mm by 6mm, mor. In orig box with magnifying glass, 2 other copies in larger format & the 8vo A Thimbleful of Books. sg Dec 4 (134) $550
— PETRARCA, FRANCESCO. - Le Rime. Venice: Ferd. Ongania, 1879. One of 1,000. 2 vols. 54mm by 34mm, contemp vellum gilt with inlaid panel. Houghton copy. S June 1821536 £300 [Bandy]
— PINDAR. - [Odes in Greek]. Glasgow: Foulis, 1754-58. 4 vols in 3, 73mm by 46mm, contemp mor gilt. Houghton copy. CNY May 11 (110) $450
— SHAKESPEARE, WILLIAM. - Works. L: Allied Newspapers, [n.d.]. 40 vols. 2 by $1\frac{1}{2}$ inches orig mor, in wooden bookcase. Ck Jan 30 (89) £60
— WESLEY, JOHN. - Hymns for the Use of the People Called Methodists. L: T. Blanshard, [c.1820]. 62mm by 40mm, contemp mor gilt with silver lock. With engraved title & port. Houghton copy. CNY May 11 (119) $1,400

Minkowski, Hermann, 1864-1909
— Raum und Zeit. Leipzig & Berlin, 1909. 1st Ed. Orig wraps; soiled. Some foxing. S June 25 (121) £400 [Seibu]

Minnigerode, Meade
— Some Personal Letters of Herman Melville and a Bibliography. NY, 1922. One of 1,500. Half cloth, in d/j; worn & soiled. O Jan 6 (132) $70

Minorsky, V. See: Beatty Library, Sir A. Chester

Minotaure...
— Minotaure: Revue artistique et litteraire. Paris, 1933-39. Nos 1-13 (complete set) in 11 issues. 4to, orig wraps. S June 29 (30) £1,900 [Seibu]

Mins, Peter
— A Narrative of the Naval Part of the Expedition to Portugal.... L, 1833. 8vo, later half cloth, amateurishly rebound. Foxed at beginnning. cb Dec 18 (126) $85

Minsheu, John, fl.1617
— Hegemon eis tas glossus; id est, ductor in linguas, the Guide into Tongues. L, 1617. 1st Ed. 2 parts in 1 vol. Folio, contemp calf; rebacked, lacking free endpapers, hinges reinforced. Some dampstaining; outer margin of general title reinforced on verso; short tear in G5 of 2d part, causing loss. sg Mar 26 (205) $175

Minucius Felix, Marcus
— Octavius et Caecilli Cypriani De Vanitate Idolorum.... Halle: Zeitler & Mussel, 1699. 8vo, contemp vellum; soiled & yawning with 3 corners bumped, front hinge just starting. Text soiled with minor dampstain at lower margins. cb Oct 23 (156) $50

Miquel, Frederik Anton Willem
— De Noord-Nederlandsche vergiftige gewassen. Amst., 1836. 8vo, orig bds. With 28 (of 30) hand-colored plates. Haverschmidt copy. B Feb 24 (520) HF200

Mirabeau, Honore Gabriel Riquetti, Comte de, 1749-91
— Des lettres de cachet et des prisons d'etat. Hamburg, 1782. 8vo, early wraps; spine chipped at foot. Dampstaining in upper outer corner throughout. sg Oct 9 (273) $140
— Les Economiques. Par L. D. H. [i.e., L'Ami des Hommes]. Amst., 1769. 4to, contemp half calf. Light waterstain affecting a few leaves. S June 25 (74) £650

Mirabeau Library, Honore Gabriel Riquetti, Comte de
— [Sale catalogue] Catalogue...de la bibliotheque de...Mirabeau.... Paris, 1791. 8vo, 19th-cent half lea. Priced in ink throughout in a contemp hand. sg May 14 (67) $450

Miranda, Francisco
— Catecismo breve en lengua Otomi.... Mexico, 1759. 12mo, later half calf. Stain on top edge of tp & following 2 pages. sg Sept 18 (184) $350

Mirbeau, Octave, 1850-1917
— Dingo. Paris: Ambroise Vollard, 1924. One of 20 hors commerce on Arches. Illus by Pierre Bonnard. 4to, mor extra by Henningsen. With 14 full-page illusts. With sketches & drawings related to the bdg. FD Dec 2 (4240) DM10,000

Miro, Joan
See also: Juanes Collection, Juan de
— Lithographs. NY: Tudor Publishing, [1972]. Ed by Michel Leiris & Fernand Mourlot. Vols I-III. Folio, orig cloth; in d/j. Dec 4 (22) £280 [Sayle]

Anr Ed. Paris [1977]. Vol III only. Folio, in d/j. cba Mar 5 (129) $150

Mirrlees, Hope
— Paris. A Poem. Richmond: Hogarth Press, 1919 [1920]. One of 175. 4to, orig wraps; spine worn. S Dec 18 (138) £250 [Gekoskill]

Mirtil
— Les Amours de Mirtil. Constantinople [Paris?], 1761. 18mo, contemp calf gilt; rubbed, joints split. With engraved title & 6 plates. S Mar 9 (894) £80 [Luia]

Miscellanea...
— Miscellanea Curiosa. Containing a Collection of some of the Principal Phaenomena in Nature.... L, 1726-27. 3 vols. 8vo, contemp calf; rubbed, 1 cover detached. O Sept 23 (146) $100

Missal
— 1549. - Missale Romanum.... Venice; Johannes Gryphius 8vo, contemp mor over bds with remnants of clasps; scuffed & wormed. Contents soiled with some staining & scorch marks; final blanks lacking. cb Oct 23 (157) $550
— 1555. - Missale ad usum insignis ecclesie Sarisburiensis. Paris: Guillaume Merlin. Folio, 19th-cent russia gilt. With 2 prelims laid down; some repairs & worming; lacking 6 leaves. Ptd on vellum. S Feb 23 (1113) £1,300 [Noble]
— 1555. - Missale ad usum insignis ecclesiae sarisburiensis. Paris. Guillaume Merlin. Folio, 19th-cent russia gilt. Some worming at beginning & end; 2 prelim leaves laid down; repairs to a few margins; worming at the beginning & end. S Sept 23 (470) £700 [Rix]
— 1571. - Missale Romanum ex decreto sacrosancti Concilii Tridentini restitutum. Venice Folio, contemp mor of South German origin; rubbed. Sold w.a.f. S Nov 10 (402) £100 [Tucker]
— 1722. - Canon missale ad usum episcoporum, ac prelatorum...sub auspiciis Innocentii XIII. Rome Folio, contemp mor gilt; rebacked, edges with brass reinforcements, worn. Ink annotations; small tears & soiling to margins; some leaves slightly stained; later extra leaf in red & blank Ms at end. bba Mar 26 (118) £120 [Callea]

Misselden, Edward
— The Circle of Commerce. Or the Ballance of Trade.... L: John Dawson, 1623. 4to, half calf. Some cropping. S July 24 (448) £5,100 [Riley Smith]

Missionary...
— A Missionary Voyage to the Southern Pacific Ocean...in the Ship Duff. L, 1799. 4to, modern calf. Paper discolored. kh Mar 16 (536B) A$320

Mitchell, Margaret, 1900-49
— Gone with the Wind. NY, 1936. 1st Ed, 1st Issue, with May 1936 date. In d/j. sg Mar 5 (178) $1,800

Mitchell, Samuel Augustus, 1792-1868
— Mitchell's Traveller's Guide Through the United States. Phila., 1836. 12mo, orig lea wallet-style bdg. Map hand-colored. O Oct 21 (118) $180

Mitchell, Silas Weir, 1829-1914
— Gunshot Wounds and other Injuries of Nerves. Phila., 1864. 1st Ed. 12mo, new cloth. S May 28 (740) £340
— Injuries of Nerves and their Consequences. Phila., 1872. 8vo, orig cloth. S May 28 (739) £240

Mitchell, Sir Thomas Livingstone, 1792-1855
— Journal of an Expedition into the Interior of Tropical Australia. L, 1848. 8vo, modern half mor. Maps set down on linen & 1 repaired. kh Mar 16 (360) A$900
— Three Expeditions into the Interior of Eastern Australia. L, 1839. 2d Ed. 2 vols. 8vo, old half mor. Some repairs to folding map; some foxing. kh Mar 16 (361B) A$1,050

Anr copy. Early half calf; rubbed. Titles stamped; folding map set down on linen; lacking ads. kh Mar 16 (361) A$1,150

Mitelli, Giuseppe Maria, 1634-1718
— Caccia giocosa, invenzioni.... Bologna: Lelio dalla Volpe, 1745. 4to, modern half vellum. Jeanson copy. SM Mar 1 (409) FF23,000

Mitford, John, 1781-1859
— The Adventures of Johnny Newcome in the Navy. L, 1818. 1st Ed. Illus by Thomas Rowlandson. 8vo, lev gilt by Riviere, broken. With 16 colored plates. sg Feb 12 (262) $200

Anr Ed. L, 1819. 8vo, mor gilt by Stern & Dess. With 20 hand-colored plates. O May

12 (143) $300
  Anr Ed. L, 1823. Illus by Thomas Rowlandson. 8vo, calf gilt by Worsfold; recased. With 20 hand-finished color plates. wa Mar 5 (108) $100

Mitford, Mary Russell, 1787-1855
— Our Village. L, 1904. Illus by C. E. Brock. Contemp vellum with painted & gilt view of a village, by Chivers of Bath. S Dec 4 (222) £500 [Greer]
— Recollections of a Literary Life. L, 1852. 1st Ed. 3 vols. 12mo, orig cloth; broken. bba Oct 30 (120) £40 [Wise]

Moat, Louis Shepheard
— Frank Leslie's Illustrated Famous Leaders and Battle Scenes of the Civil War. NY, [1896]. Folio, cloth; worn, some cover stains, endpapers affected by adhesion. O Oct 21 (119) $50

Mocatta Library, Frederic David
— Catalogue of the Printed Books and Manuscripts.... L, 1904. Compiled by Reginald Arthur Rye. 4to, orig half cloth. Library markings. bba Apr 23 (34) £50 [Rosenthal]

Mode...
— La Mode Illustree. Paris, 1875-1093. Vols 16-44, lacking Vol 37. 11 vols. Folio, contemp half calf or library buckram; rubbed or worn. With c.1,400 colored plates. Sold w.a.f. bba Jan 15 (246) £5,200 [Walford]

Modern. See: Shepherd, Thomas Hosmer

Modest...
— A Modest Enquiry into the Grounds and Occasions of a late Pamphlet intitled, a Memorial of the Present Deplorable State of New England. L, 1707. 4to, wraps. Some cropping. S June 25 (409) £1,150

Moe, Jorgen I, 1813-82. See: Asbjornsen & Moe

Moellhausen, Balduin, 1825-1905
— Resor i Norra Amerikas Klippberg til Ny—Mexikos Hogslatt. Stockholm, 1867. 2 vols in 1. 8vo, later half cloth; spine rubbed. With folding map & 6 colored plates. cb Jan 8 (125) $170

Moerus...
— Les Moeurs des premiers ages ou l'ecole de l'antiquite. Paris: Janet, [n.d.]. 32mo, contemp mor gilt with 2 hand-painted miniatures on ivory inset; mirror inside upper cover with glass broken. With engraved title & 12 plates, all hand-colored. C Dec 3 (76) £800 [Sourget]

Moeurs...
— Moeurs et coutumes des peuples. Paris: Hocquart, [1811-14]. 2 vols. 4to, contemp half calf; worn. With 142 (of 144) hand-colored plates.. wa June 25 (491) $800

Moffat, Robert, 1795-1883
— Missionary Labours and Scenes in Southern Africa. L, 1842. 8vo, orig cloth. SSA Feb 11 (569) R230

Moffett, Thomas, 1553-1604
— Healths Improvement.... L, 1655. 4to, orig half calf. pnE Jan 28 (300) £560 [Grant]
  Anr copy. New cloth. Some stains. S May 28 (747) £220
— Healths Imrpovement.... L, 1655. 4to, contemp calf; rebacked. Waterstain in margins of title & 3 leaves at the front; short tear to T4; a few catchwords cropped. C May 13 (165) £650 [Thomas]

Moholy-Nagy, Laszlo
— Vision in Motion. Chicago, 1947. 4to, cloth; some wear. O Oct 21 (123) $70

Moir, David Macbeth. See: Fore-Edge Paintings

Molesworth, Robert, Viscount, 1656-1725
— An Account of Denmark.... L, 1694. 1st Ed. 8vo, contemp calf gilt; rubbed. Marginal worming to last few leaves. bba Aug 28 (183) £80 [Northcote]

Moleville, Antoine Francois Bertrand de
— The Costume of the Hereditary States of the House of Austria.... L, 1804. 4to, contemp mor; corner torn. With 50 hand-colored plates. 1 plate detached. C Oct 15 (75) £260 [Marshall]
  Anr copy. Calf gilt; scuffed. pn Dec 11 (44) £300 [Walford]
  Anr copy. Modern half mor gilt. 1 torn. In English & French. pnNY Sept 13 (220) $475
  Anr Ed. L, 1804 [but plates watermarked 1815-19]. 4to, contemp mor gilt. With 50 hand-colored plates. C Apr 8 (161) £320 [Gaston]
  Anr Ed. L, 1804 [plates watermarked 1817]. 4to, contemp mor gilt. With 50 hand-colored plates. C Oct 15 (74) £320 [Traylen]

Moliere, Jean Baptiste Poquelin de, 1622-73
See also: Cabinet...; Limited Editions Club
— Les Essais. Paris, 1872-1900. 5 vols. 8vo, contemp half mor by Ruzicka, Balto; worn. cb Oct 23 (159) $80
— Les Femmes scavantes. Paris, 1673. 1st Ed. 12mo, 19th-cent mor. Short tears in tp repaired; margins cropped, affecting a few letters & page numerals. bba Sept 25 (248)

£50 [Quaritch]
— Les Oeuvres. Paris, 1734. 6 vols. 4to, contemp calf gilt; rubbed. With 33 plates & 198 vignettes & culs-de-lamp. Lacking port. C May 13 (58) £450 [Hasback]

Anr copy. Contemp calf; rubbed. With engraved frontis & 32 plates after Boucher. Occasional dampstaining. Ck Oct 31 (69) £280

Anr copy. Contemp mor gilt. Some worming at beginning & end of each vol. S Mar 10 (970) £220 [Maggs]

Anr Ed. Paris, 1773. 6 vols. 8vo, contemp calf gilt; joints rubbed or cracked, Vol V worn. S May 29 (1227) £320

— Oeuvres. Paris, 1819-25. 9 vols. 8vo, contemp half mor; rubbed. Lacking frontis to Vol VIII. cb Oct 23 (158) $65

Anr Ed. Paris, 1863-64. 7 vols. 8vo, half mor gilt. sg Feb 12 (238) $100

— Le Sicilien, ou l'amour peintre. Paris, 1668. 1st Ed. 12mo, mor by Aussourd. SM Oct 20 (485) FF14,000

— Theatre complet. Paris, 1876-83. One of 100 on papier verge with plates in 2 states, before & after letters. Illus by Louis Leloir after Leopole Flameng. 8 vols. 8vo, mor extra by Magnin. Extra-illus with c.400 plates from earlier Eds & 3 orig ink drawings by Choquet. C Dec 3 (145) £3,400 [Tenschert]

— [Works] The Dramatic Works. Edin, 1875-76. 6 vols. 8vo, mor gilt by Andrew Grieve. S July 13 (202) £170

Molina, Alonso de, d.1535
— Vocabulario en lengua castellana y mexicana.... Mexico: Antonio de Spinoza, 1571. 2d Ed. 2 parts in 1 vol. Folio, vellum; soiled. Tp & the last leaf of Part 2 in facsimile; minor tears repaired without loss. S Oct 23 (448) £5,200 [Quaritch]

Moll, Herman, d.1732
— Atlas Minor: or a New and Curious Set of Sixty-Two Maps. L, [1732?]. Oblong folio, contemp half lea. With 62 maps, colored in outline; a few torn. bba Dec 195 £750 [Kentish]

— A Set of Fifty New and Correct Maps of England and Wales.... L, 1724. Oblong folio, contemp calf; worn. With 2 colored folding maps & 48 double-page county maps. pn May 21 (380) £1,230 [Intercol]

— A System of Geography. L, 1701. 1st Ed. 2 parts in 1 vol. Folio, old calf; worn. With engraved title & 41 maps. sg Dec 4 (135) $2,200

Mollard, John
— The Art of Cookery Made Easy and Refined.... L, 1801. 8vo, modern half calf. Minor spotting & soiling. Hunt copy. CNY Nov 21 (77) $200

Mollet, Claude
— Theatre des Jardinages. Paris: Charles de Sercy, 1663. 4to, contemp vellum. Tp & 2 following leaves with 2 minute wormholes. Hunt copy. CNY Nov 21 (200) $600

Mollhausen, Balduin
— Tagebuch einer Reise vom Mississippi nach den Kuesten der Suedsee.... Leipzig, 1858. 4to, contemp half mor gilt. With 13 plates & folding map. With 6 plates cut round & mtd. CNY May 11 (124) $1,400

Moltoni, Edgardo —& Ruscone, G. G.
— Gli Uccelli dell'Africa orientale italiana. Milan, 1940-44. 4 vols. Bdgs dampstained. With 152 color plates. B Feb 24 (240) HF220

Momaday, N. Scott
— Before an Old Painting of the Crucifixion. San Francisco. Valenti Angelo, 1975. One of 100. Bds. cb Dec 4 (322) $55

Monaghan, James —& Hornung, Clarence P.
— The Book of the American West. NY, [1963]. 4to, lea; spine rubbed & fading. cb Jan 8 (297) $110

Monaghan, Jay
— Lincoln Bibliography, 1839-1939. Springfield, Ill., 1943-45. 2 vols. sg Jan 22 (231) $100

Monardes, Nicholas, 1498-1588
— Joyful Newes Out of the New-Found Worlde.... L: assign of Bonham Norton, 1596. 3d Ed in English. Trans by John Frampton. 4to, contemp calf; front joint inexpertly repaired, corners bumped. Lacking last 16 leaves. sg June 11 (294) $225

Monceau, Henri Louis Duhamel du. See: Duhamel du Monceau, Henri Louis

Moncel, Delisle de. See: Delisle de Moncel

Moncrif, Francois Augustin Paradis de. See: Golden Cockerel Press

Mongez, Antoine, 1747-1835
— Tableaux, Statues, Bas-Reliefs et Camees, de la Galerie de Florence et du Palais Pitti. Paris, 1819. 4 vols. Folio, contemp mor gilt; rubbed. S Nov 10 (132) £360 [Tucker]

Monier, Pierre, 1641-1703
— The History of Painting, Sculpture, Architecture, Graving.... L, 1699. 8vo, contemp calf; joints split, rubbed. Small portion torn from blank margin of frontis. S Mar 10 (1114) £140 [Sims]

Monier-Williams, Monier. See: Kalidasa

Monigilia, Giovanni Andrea
— Descrizione della presa d'Argo e degli amori di Linceo con Hipermestra.... [Florence, 1658]. Folio, later half calf. With 13 double-page plates (most repaired along fold). S Nov 27 (198) £2,400

Monipennie, John
— The Abridgement or Summarie of the Scots Chronicles.... Edin.: J. W[reittoun] for J. Wood, 1633. 2 parts in 1 vol. 4to, 19th-cent half calf. Some shaving & browning. S July 14 (335) £320

Moniteur...
— Le Moniteur des Architectes: Revue mensuelle de l'art architectural et moderne. Nouvelle Serie.... Paris, 1866-89. Vols I-XXII, lacking Vol XXII. 23 vols, including the 2 parts of Vol IV. 4to, half mor or orig ptd bds. C July 22 (128) £1,600

Monkhouse, William Cosmo, 1840-1901
— The Turner Gallery.... L, [1878]. 3 vols. Folio, contemp half mor; rubbed. bba Nov 13 (70) £320 [B. Bailey]

Anr copy. 3 vols in 6. Folio, orig cloth; spines bumped. With engraved title. Some light spotting.. Ck Nov 28 (89) £280

Anr copy. 6 orig parts. Folio, pn Mar 5 (138) £400 [Walford]

Anr copy. 3 vols in 1. Folio, mor gilt with initials R.J.S. on upper cover. With engraved title, port & 119 plates. S Nov 10 (177) £300 [Bailey]

Monro, Alexander, 1733-1817
— Works. Edin, 1781. 1st Ed. 4to, contemp half lea gilt with cipher of Duncan on spine; rubbed. With port & 7 plates. Lacking half-title. Inscr by the Ed, the younger Alexander Monro. S May 28 (743) £440

Monroe, Harriet, 1860-1936
— Valeria and Other Poems. Chicago, 1891. Half vellum. sg Mar 5 (179) $80

Mont, Karel Maria Polydoor de, 1857-1937
— Van Jezus. Antwerp, 1897. One of 270. Oblong 8vo, bds. B Oct 7 (16) HF160

Mont, Pol de. See: Mont, Karel Maria Polydoor de

Montagne, Prosper
— Larousse gastronomique.... Paris, [1938]. 4to, vellum; worn. cb July 30 (276) $95

Montagu, Lady Mary Wortley, 1689-1762
— Letters.... L, 1763. 1st Ed. Vols I-III (of 4) in 1 vol. 8vo, contemp calf; worn & broken. Some staining. bba Oct 16 (78) £45 [Hay Cinema]
— Select Passages from...Letters.... L, 1892. 8vo, mor gilt by the Guild of Women Binders; front joint cracked. Extra-illus with 86 plates, inscr by Lord Belham & ANs of Lord Brougham. sg Sept 11 (120) $130

Montaigne, Michel Eyquem de, 1533-92
See also: Nonesuch Press
— Discorsi morali, politici et militari. Ferrara: Benedetto Mamarello, 1590. 8vo, modern calf; new endpapers. S May 21 (56) £650 [Quaritch]
— Les Essais. Paris, 1635. Folio, 17th-cent calf; rebacked retaining orig backstrip, corners restored. Marginal staining. sg Mar 26 (207) $175

Anr Ed. Nice: Editions d'Art Sefer, 1973-74. Unique copy with suite of the plates ptd in blue outline, decomposition of 1 colored plate, 4 watercolor drawings for full-page plates, 4 watercolor drawings not used in the book & 4 ink drawings not used in the book, all the drawings sgd & bound at end of each vol. Illus by H. Da Ros. 4 vols. 4to, mor gilt with gilt metal centerpiece on each upper cover. With the watercolor draawing for the double-page plate, framed & inscr. S June 17 (96) £1,500 [Schoeni]
— The Essayes.... L, 1603. 1st Ed in English. Trans by John Florio. 3 parts in 1 vol. Folio, contemp calf with gilt badge of Tudor rose; inner hinges strengthened, rubbed, scraped; spine & covers restored. Several leaves repaired along inner margins, a few burnholes & a little worming. Some waterstaining. P Dec 15 (211) $1,900

2d Ed of Florio's trans. L, 1613. 8vo, contemp calf gilt; rubbed, joints split. Some dampstains & soiling; a few tears. S Mar 10 (1115) £260 [Claridge]

Anr copy. Contemp vellum; soiled. Logan Pearsall Smith's copy with his notes & underscoring throughout. T Sept 18 (352) £58

Anr Ed. L, 1700. ("Essays....") Trans by Charles Cotton. 8vo, old calf; worn. Minor stains; some foxing & soiling. O Nov 18 (132) $50

Anr Ed. L, 1743. Trans by Cotton. 3 vols. 8vo, 19th-cent half calf. sg Oct 9 (274) $80

Anr Ed. Bost., 1904. ("Essays of Michael, Lord of Montaigne.") One of 265. 3 vols.

In d/js. cb Feb 19 (197) $800
Anr Ed. Garden City, 1947. One of 1,0000. Illus by Salvador Dali. wa Mar 5 (113) $100

— Journal du voyage...en Italie.... Rome, 1774. 2 vols. 4to, contemp calf gilt; rubbed. Outer margins cut close. bba Dec 4 (19) £110 [Cavendish]

Montanus, Arnoldus, 1625?-83
— Atlas Chinensis.... L, 1671. 1st Ed in English. Folio, calf; worn. Lower inner corner of first 188 pp burnt away, affecting text on many pages. Sold w.a.f. S Nov 17 (667) £320 [Remmington]
— Atlas Japannensis.... L, 1670. 1st Ed in English. Trans by John Ogilby. Folio, contemp calf; worn. With engraved title, folding map (with small tears) & 24 double-page plates. Some dampstaining & occasional small tears. C Dec 12 (251) £400 [Israel]

Anr copy. Contemp calf gilt. With engraved title, folding map & 24 (of 25) views & plans. Aa4 torn across text without loss; 1 plate with scrape at centerfold; 1 plate repaired on verso; some foxing. CNY May 11 (125) $2,100

— Gedenkwaerdige Gesantschappen der Oost-Indische Maetschappy in't Vereenigde Nederland.... Amst., 1669. Folio, later calf gilt. With engraved title, folding map & 25 plates. Map mtd on linen & def in folds; lacking A3; Sig. Hh misbound; a few leaves crudely repaired with loss; some headlines shaved; some worming. bba Oct 16 (15) £500 [Isseiao]

Montanus, Pieter. See: Van den Keere & Montanus

Monte Simoncelli, Baldovino di
— Il Simoncello, o vero della caccia. Florence: Zanobi Pignoni, 1616. 4to, contemp vellum. Some dampstains. Jeanson copy. SM Mar 1 (414) FF2,400

Montecalerio, Joannis a
— Chorographica descriptio provinciarum, et conventuum...S. Francisci Capucinorum. Milan: J. P. Malatesta, 1712. Oblong folio, contemp vellum; def. With engraved title & 63 maps, including folding general map (detached). Some soiling. S Oct 23 (287) £1,300 [Israel]

Monteiro Baena, Antonio Ladislau
— Compendio das Eras da Provincia do Para.... Para: Typographia de Santos, 1838. 4to, orig wraps; front wrap detached, shaken. Library markings. sg Sept 18 (38) $130

Monteith, Robert, fl.1660-1713
— An Theater of Mortality: or a Further Collection of Funeral-Inscriptions over Scotland.... Edin., 1713. 8vo, contemmp calf; rubbed. O Feb 24 (140) $50

Montemayor [y Cordoba] de Cuenca, Juan Francisco
— Summaria Investigacion del origen, y privilegios, de los Ricos Hombres.... [Mexico, 1664]. 2 parts in 1 vol. 4to, contemp calf by Marcos Antonio Varangot of Pamplona. sg Sept 18 (185) $400

Montes de Oca, Rafael
— Hummingbirds and Orchids of Mexico. Mexico, [1963]. One of 1,500. Folio, cloth. sg Sept 18 (74) $100

Montesquieu, Charles de Secondat, Baron de, 1689-1755
— De l'esprit de loix. Geneva: Barillot, [but Paris: Prault, c.1748]. 2 vols 4to, contemp calf. B Feb 25 (1007) HF1,300

Anr copy. Contemp calf gilt, worn & repaired. FD June 11 (4102) DM17,200

Anr copy. 18th-cent calf; joints worn. Lower margins in Vol II stained. S Nov 27 (201) £700 [Rota]

— Miscellaneous pieces.... L, 1759. 8vo, contemp calf; rubbed, spine worn at head. S Nov 10 (403) £150 [Quaritch]

— Oeuvres. L, 1767. 3 vols. 4to, contemp calf. With engraved title & port & 2 folding engraved maps. Occasional spotting. bba Dec 4 (17) £110 [Greenwood]

Anr copy. Contemp calf; worn & loose. Some worming, occasionally affecting text. S Jan 16 (411) £150 [Cavendish]

— The Spirit of Laws. L, 1750. 2 vols. 8vo, contemp calf; rebacked, worn, covers brittle. sg Apr 2 (150) $600

— Le Temple de Gnide. Paris, 1772. 8vo, contemp mor gilt. With engraved title & 10 plates. C Dec 3 (179) £1,400 [Stern]

Anr Ed. Paris, [1795]. One of 100 L.p. copies on papier velin. 12mo, mor gilt by Joly. With 12 plates in 2 states, proofs before letters & eaux-fortes & with additional plate by de Launay after Marillier bound in. C May 13 (36) £280 [Greenwood]

Anr Ed. Paris, 1796. 4to, half mor gilt. With 7 hand-finished color plates. Some foxing. sg Mar 26 (208) $325

Montfaucon, Bernard de, 1665-1741
— L'Antiquite expliquee et representee en figures. Paris, 1722-57. 5 vols in 10. Folio, contemp calf gilt; worn & repaired. Lacking 1 plate. HK Nov 4 (1653) DM1,400

2d Ed. Paris, 1722. 5 vols in 10 plus 1757

MONTFAUCON

Supplement in 5 vols. Folio, contemp vellum. Sold w.a.f. With bookplate of Consul Smith. C July 22 (129) £1,300
— The Antiquities of Italy.... L, 1725. 2d Ed. Folio, contemp calf; rebacked. T Nov 20 (300) £135
— A Collection of Regal and Ecclesiastical Antiquities of France. L, 1750. 2 vols in 1. Folio, contemp calf; worn & broken. T July 16 (2) £160

Montgomery, Sir Archibald
— The Story of the Fourth Army in the Battles of the Hundred Days.... L, [1920]. 4to, calf gilt. With 24 folding maps & plates. sg Feb 12 (239) $80

Montgomery, Bernard Law, 1st Viscount Montgomery of Alamein
— El Alamein to the River Sangro.... L, 1971. One of 265, sgd & specially bound. Mor by Zaehnsdorf. pn July 23 (213) £110 [Connor]

Montgomery, Rutherford G. See: Derrydale Press

Month. See: Leech & Smith

Monthly...
— The Monthly Microscopical Journal. Transactions of the Royal Microscopical Society. L, 1869-77. Vols 1-18. 8vo, orig cloth; soiled. Ck Nov 7 (132) £300

Monthois, Robert
— La Noble et furieuse chasse du loup.... Ath: Jean Maes, 1642. 4to, mor janseniste by Chambolle-Duru. Jeanson copy. SM Mar 1 (411) FF110,000

Anr Ed. Paris: Veuve Bouchard-Huzard, 1863. One of 10 on vellum. 4to, mor gilt by Chambolle-Duru. Jeanson copy. SM Mar 1 (412) FF14,000

Anr Ed. [Paris: L. Techener, 1865]. Copy on vellum. 8vo, mor gilt by Chambolle-Duru, 1869. Jeanson copy. SM Mar 1 (413) FF2,800

Montigny, Sieur de. See: Littret, Claude Antoine de

Montigny, Writer on Chess
— Les Stratagemes des Echecs. Paris: A. Koenig, [1801-2]. 2 parts in 1 vol. 16mo, half mor. pn Mar 26 (317) £75 [Caissa]

Montmort, Pierre Remond de
— Essai d'analyse sur les jeux de hazards. Paris, 1714. 2d Ed. 4to, contemp mor; upper cover dented. With 5 folding plates. Some worming & dampstaining. S Nov 27 (102) £650 [Sanieri]

Montorgueil, Georges
— Louis XI. Paris, 1905. Illus by Job. 4to, orig cloth; worn. O Apr 28 (143) $160
— La Vie des boulevards Madeleine-Bastille. Paris, 1896. Illus by Pierre Vidal. 8vo, half mor gilt; worn. HN May 20 (2014) DM1,200

Montpetit, Andre Napoleon
— Les Poissons d'eau douce du Canada. Montreal, 1897. 8vo, half lea; worn, spine torn, inner joints broken. Library markings; plates stamped on versos. Sold w.a.f. O Nov 18 (133) $50

Montucla, Jean Etienne, 1725-99
— Histoire des mathematiques. Paris, 1758. 2 vols. 4to, contemp calf; spine ends worn. With 15 folding plates. sg May 14 (601) $250

Anr Ed. Paris, 1799-1802. 4 vols. 4to, modern half calf. With 2 ports & 44 (of 45) folding plates. Some staining. bba Mar 26 (322) £130 [Check]

Montule, Edouard de
— A Voyage to North America and the West Indies.... L, 1821. 8vo, old bds. With 6 plates. Library markings. O June 9 (117) $80

Monumens. See: Hancarville, Pierre Francois Hugues d'

Monumenta...
— Monumenta Palaeographica Vindobonensia: Denkmaeler der Schreibkunst aus der Handschriftensammlung des Habsburg-Lothringischen Erzhauses. Leipzig: Karl W. Hiersemann, 1910-13. Fascicles 1-2 [all pbd]. 2 vols. Folio, loose in half cloth portfolios as issued. sg Oct 2 (190) $275

Moodie, Duncan Campbell Francis
— The History of the Battles and Adventures of the British, the Boers, and the Zulus. Cape Town, 1888. 2 vols. 8vo, mor. With frontis, 5 plates & folding map. SSA Oct 28 (729) R250

Anr copy. Cloth. SSA Oct 28 (744) R310

Moodie, John Wedderburn Dunbar
— Ten Years in South Africa. L, 1835. 1st Ed. 2 vols. 8vo, contemp half calf; rubbed. Lacking ads. Ck May 8 (313) £140

Moor, Edward, 1771-1848
— Bealings Bells. An Account of the Mysterious Ringing.... Woodbridge, 1841. 12mo, orig cloth; worn. bba Mar 12 (466) £60 [Iredell]

Moorcock, Michael
— The Stealer of Souls and Other Stories. L, 1963. In d/j & in Currey's A bdg. cb Sept 28 (954) $50
— Stormbringer. L, 1965. In d/j. cb Sept 28 (955) $55

Moorcroft, W. —& Trebeck, George
— Travels in the Himalayan Provinces of Hindustan and the Panjab. L, 1841. 2 vols. 8vo, orig cloth; 1 joint repaired. With frontises & folding map. S Apr 24 (352) £1,150 [Quaritch]

Moore, Ada Small. See: Hackney & Yau

Moore, Andrew
— A Compendious History of the Turks. L, 1660. 8vo, contemp calf; spine ends damaged. Minor worming in lower outer corners towards end. sg Nov 20 (130) $350

Moore, Catherine
See also: Padgett, Lewis
— Doomsday Morning. Garden City, 1957. Review copy. In rubbed d/j. Sgd on tp. cb Sept 28 (957) $75
— Jirel of Joiry. West Kingston, Rhode Island: Donald M. Grant, 1977. ("Black God's Shadow.") One of 150. In d/j. cb Sept 28 (956) $85
— Judgment Night. NY: Gnome Press, [1952]. In rubbed & reinforced d/j. Sgd on tp. cb Sept 28 (958) $75
— Northwest of Earth. NY: Gnome Press, [1954]. In chipped d/j. cb May 7 (400) $65
— Shambleau and Others. NY: Gnome Press, [1953]. In d/j. With 2 Ls s laid in. cb Sept 28 (959) $140

Moore, Charles, Rector of Custon
— A Full Inquiry in to the Subject of Suicide. L, 1790. 2 vols. 8vo, modern half mor gilt. sg Jan 15 (123) $300

Moore, Clement Clarke, 1779-1863
— Night Before Christmas L, 1931. Illus by Arthur Rackham. Wraps, in d/j. With 4 color plates. sg Oct 30 (153) $140

One of 275, sgd by Rackham. Vellum gilt. With an orig watercolor by Rackham. sg Oct 30 (152) $5,500

One of 550, sgd by artist. Orig vellum. With 4 colored plates. sg June 11 (327) $650

Anr Ed. Phila., [1931]. Cloth; soiled. With 4 color plates. sg Oct 30 (154) $130

Moore, Edward. See: Muir, Edwin

Moore, Edward Alexander
— The Story of a Cannoneer under Stonewall Jackson.... NY, 1907. ha Nov 7 (29) $75

Moore, Frederic, 1830-1907
— The Leipdoptera of Ceylon. L, 1880-87. 3 vols in 4. 4to, half mor. With 215 colored plates. Some spotting of 1st few pages of Vol I & II but plates mostly unaffected; Plate 85 in Vol II a little soiled. S Apr 23 (15) £1,900 [Schneider]

Moore, George, 1852-1933
— Works. NY, 1922-24. Carra Ed, One of 1,000. 21 vols. ha May 22 (70) $130

Moore, Henry Spencer
— Heads, Figures, and Ideas. L & Greenwich, Conn., 1958. Folio, orig half cloth, in frayed d/j. S Oct 6 (836) £130 [Gardiner]
Anr copy. Half cloth, in d/j. S Jan 13 (666) £140 [Fogg]; T May 20 (86) £105
— Shelter Sketch Book. [L, 1940?]. Oblong 8vo, cloth; shaken. Sgd & dated Oct 1940. sg Jan 8 (166) $90

Moore, James Carrick, 1763-1834
— A Narrative of the Campaign of the British Army in Spain. L, 1809. 4to, later half mor; rubbed. With port, plate & 2 folding maps, partially hand-colored. Lacking half-title. bba Apr 9 (95) £50 [Turner]

Moore, John C. See: Sheringham & Moore

Moore, John Hamilton
— A New and Complete Collection of Voyages and Travels. L, 1778-[80]. 2 vols. Folio, contemp half mor; worn. With 2 frontises, 20 maps & 78 plates; 1 plate cropped & mtd, both titles defective. bba Dec 18 (196) £200 [Graton & Graton]
Anr copy. Half calf, 1 bdg def. With 98 (of 100) plates. Sold w.a.f. S Jan 12 (187) £260 [Noble]

Moore, Lieut. Joseph —& Marryat, Capt. Frederick, 1792-1848
— Rangoon Views, and Combined Operations in the Birman Empire. L: T. Clay, [1825-26]. Folio, modern lev gilt portfolio, 2 text vols in orig wraps. With folding map & 24 hand-colored plates. Plate 19 with tear repaired; tp, dedication, list of subscribers & all prelims to 1st series are lacking. Sold w.a.f. C Oct 15 (125) £3,200 [Chang]

Moore, Marianne
— Poems. L: Egoist Press, 1921. 1st Ed. Orig wraps. Inscr to Scofield Thayer & with holograph revisions. P June 18 (133) $1,400
— Tell Me, Tell Me. NY, [1966]. 1st Ed. Half cloth, in d/j; worn. Inscr to Frances Steloff. sg Dec 11 (88) $250

Anr copy. Half cloth, in d/j. Inscr to Miriam Benkovitz. sg Dec 11 (337) $60

Moore, Merrill
— Illegitimate Sonnets. NY, [1950]. Illus by Edward Gorey. Sgd by Moore. sg Dec 11 (90) $150

Moore, Thomas, 1779-1852
— Memoirs of the Life of the Right Hon. R. B. Sheridan. L, 1825. 1st Ed. 8vo, half mor gilt; rubbed. Extra-illus with c.50 ports. S July 13 (111) £80
— Paradise and the Peri. L, [1860]. 4to, orig cloth; worn. Foxed throughout. O May 12 (146) $50
— A Selection of Irish Melodies.... L, [c.1834]. 5 parts in 2 vols. Folio, modern half mor. pnNY Sept 13 (264) $225

Moore, Thomas, 1821-87
See also: Floral...
— The Ferns of Great Britain and Ireland. L, 1855. Folio, contemp half mor; upper hinge broken, rubbed. With 51 color nature-ptd plates. bba Nov 13 (59) £550 [Maggs]
Anr copy. Contemp half mor gilt; scuffed, corners bruised. With 48 (of 51) nature-ptd plates. ALso lacking text to Plates 49-51. Sold w.a.f. Hunt copy. CNY Nov 21 (201) $750
Anr copy. Old half mor gilt; rubbed. With 51 colored nature-ptd plates. Library stamps on tp & on 1 other page. pnNY Oct 11 (35) $1,200
Anr copy. Contemp half mor; corners rubbed. de Belder copy. S Apr 28 (237) £1,800 [Arader]
Anr copy. Half mor; joints weak. SM Oct 20 (487) FF5,000
Anr copy. Bound in is the 1856 Supplement, The Fern Allies. Folio, contemp half mor gilt; rubbed & partially split at head of rear hinge. T Mar 19 (116) £52

Moore, Ward, 1903-78
— Bring the Jubilee. NY, [1953]. In d/j. cb Sept 28 (961) $50

Morais, C. de
— Le Veritable fauconnier. Paris, 1683. 12mo, contemp mor gilt. Jeanson 1118. SM Mar 1 (415) FF24,000

Moralite...
— Moralite des blasphemateurs de Dieu. Paris: Silvestre, 1831. One of 90. Folio, contemp lea; rubbed, endpaper torn. O June 16 (133) $90

Morand, S.
— Memoir on Acupuncturation, Embracing a Series of Cases.... Phila., 1825. 12mo, contemp sheep; broken. sg Jan 15 (61) $225

Morant, Philip, 1700-70
— The History and Antiquities of the Most Ancient Town and Borough of Colchester.... L, 1748. 1st Ed. Folio, later half mor with initials J.T.S. onlaid in mor to center of upper cover; rubbed. T Feb 19 (331) £60
— The History and Antiquities of the County of Essex. L, 1768. 1st Ed. 2 vols. Folio, contemp calf; rubbed. With 33 plates & maps. CK Nov 21 (253) £300

Mordaunt de Launay, Jean Claude Michel —& Loiseleur-Deslongchamps, Jean Louis Auguste
— Herbier general de l'amateur. Paris, [1810]-16-27. 8 vols. 8vo, 19th-cent half mor gilt. With 573 (of 575) handcolored plates. Ink stain to margin of 2 plates in Vol I; some foxing; smudge to corner of Plate 423 in Vol VI. Hunt copy. CNY Nov 21 (202) $9,500
Anr copy. Contemp bds; rubbed, heads of some spines chipped. With 575 handcolored plates. Titles stamped by Philippe de Vilmorin. Vilmorin—de Belder copy. S Apr 28 (246) £5,500 [Burden]
Anr Ed. Brussels, 1828-35. ("Herbier de l'amateur de fleurs.") 8 vols. 4to, contemp half calf. With 600 hand-colored plates. Some spotting; Dampstain in margins at beginning of Vol III & the text at end of Vol VIII. S Apr 27 (108) £5,500 [Pavlov]

Morden, Robert
— Magna Britannica et Hibernia.... L, 1738. 6 vols. 4to, calf gilt; worn. With engraved title & 47 maps, 1 folding plate & 36 full-page tables of road distances. Maps in Vol I with worn margins. pn May 21 (381) £680 [Traylen]
— The New Description and State of England... L, 1701. 1st Ed. 8vo, contemp calf; upper cover detached. With general map & 53 folding county maps. Tp loose; stain on 1st few leaves; wormhole through 1st 23 leaves. pn May 21 (420) £700 [Burgess Browning]

Morden, William James
— Across Asia's Snows and Deserts. NY, 1927. wa June 25 (112) $90

More, Hannah, 1745-1833
— Strictures on the Modern System of Female Education.... L, 1799. 2 vols. 8vo, contemp calf; rubbed. bba May 14 (191) £120 [Bickersteth]
Anr Ed. NY, 1813. 2 vols in 1. 12mo,

contemp calf. Some foxing. sg Sept 18 (187) $100

More, Henry, 1614-87
— An Antidote against Atheism.... L, 1655. Bound with: Conjectura Cabbalistica; or, a Conjectural Essay....L, 1653. 8vo, modern half lea; joints rubbed & weak. Opening leaves of 1st work wormed in lower inner corner, not affecting legibility. Library stamp on tp. sg Mar 26 (210) $340
— The Immortality of the Soul.... L, 1659. 8vo, contemp calf. sg Oct 9 (275) $300

More, Sir Thomas, 1478-1535
See also: Golden Cockerel Press; Kelmscott Press; Limited Editions Club
— De optimo reip. statu deque nova insula utopia libellus vere aureus.... Basel: Johann Froben, Nov-Dec 1518. 3 parts in 1 vol. 4to, mor gilt by J. Faulkner. Tp remargined with small portion of woodcut border rule supplied in facsimile; wormholes or filled wormholes in blank margins of a2-b1 & U4-U6; rust hole affecting 2 letters on l2; marginal discoloration to final gathering; Harvard release stamps; washed; some underscoring. P Sept 24 (356) $2,600
  La Description de l'Isle d'Utopie. Paris: Charles l'Angelier, 1550. 8vo, mor gilt by Masson-de Ronnelle; spine head & corners with wear. Tp & 2 other leaves in 1st gathering short; some lower outer margins at front with repairs. CNY Dec 19 (136) $3,500
— The Historie of the Pitifull Life and Unfortunate Death of Edward the Fifth.... L, 1641. 12mo, 19th-cent mor; rubbed. Some shaving; lacking the 2 leaves of publisher's preface; some stains. S Mar 10 (1116) £160 [Helm]
— Lucubrationes. Basel, 1563. 8vo, later 19th-cent mor. Library stamp. sg Oct 9 (276) $1,100
— Utopia. L, 1685. 8vo, calf; upper cover loose. Small piece torn from top margin of tp. pnE Jan 28 (181) £440 [Galbraith]
  Anr Ed. L, 1808. ("A Most Pleasant, Fruitful, and Witty Work....") One of 250 L.p. copies with an extra plate of More's family. 2 vols. 8vo, calf gilt; worn. sg Sept 11 (236) $200
— Works. Louvain, 1566. ("Omnia opera Latina.") Folio, modern calf blind-stamped in the old style; spine rubbed. Some margins dampstained; tp & final leaf soiled & covered with early inscrs; portions of blank margins of 1st & final leaves torn away. S May 21 (57) £750 [Pickering]
— The XII Propertees or Condicyons of a Lover. Ditchling: St. Dominic's Press, 1928. One of 250. Half mor; bds rubbed. cb Sept 11 (97) $50

Anr copy. Orig cloth. sg Jan 8 (268) $100

Moreau, Hegesippe
— Le Mossotis: Petits Contes et petits vers. Paris, 1893. One of 150 with plates in 2 states. 8vo, mor extra by the Club Bindery, 1898. cb Feb 19 (199) $250

Moreau-Nelaton, Etienne
— Jongkind raconte par lui-meme. Paris, 1918. One of 600. 4to, orig wraps, unopened. S Nov 10 (253) £150 [Sims]
— Millet raconte par lui-meme. Paris, 1921. One of 600. 3 vols. 4to, orig wraps. Inscr. S July 14 (534) £160

Morecamp, Arthur, Pseud.
— Live Boys; or Charley and Nasho in Texas. Bost., [1878]. 8vo, orig cloth; worn. O May 12 (157) $140

Morellet, Andre, 1727-1819
— Theorie du Paradoxe. Amst. [but Paris], 1775. 12mo, modern mor; scuffed. Some browning. P Sept 24 (357) $150

Moreri, Louis, 1643-80
— The Great Historical, Geographical and Poetical Dictionary. L, 1694. Folio, contemp calf; rebacked. T Sept 18 (338) £120

Morgagni, Giovanni Battista, 1682-1771
— Adversaria anatomica omnia. Padua, 1717-19. 6 vols in 2. 4to, contemp vellum; worn. With frontis & 11 plates. sg Jan 15 (111) $325
  1st Ed of Parts 2-6; later Ed of Part 1. Padua, 1719-17. 6 parts in 1 vol. 4to, vellum; soiled, 1 corner 7 top of 1 spine damaged. With frontis & 11 plates. S May 28 (745) £180
— The Seats and Causes of Diseases.... L, 1769. 1st Ed in English. 3 vols. 4to, modern half mor. Marginal dampstaining throughout; 1st & last leaves of each vol remargined. sg Jan 15 (112) $600

Morgan, Dale Lowell —& Wheat, Carl I.
— Jedediah Smith and His Maps of the American West. San Francisco, 1954. One of 530. Faded. With 7 folding maps, 3 in pocket. cb Jan 8 (128) $300; cb July 16 (183) $425
  Anr copy. Faded. sg Jan 22 (92) $275; sg Jan 22 (93) $250

Morgan, John Hill —& Fielding, Mantle
— The Life Portraits of Washington and their Replicas. Phila., [1931]. One of 1,000. 4to, cloth. sg June 11 (421) $70

MORGAN COLLECTION

Morgan Collection, John Pierpont
— Chinese Porcelains. NY, 1904-11. 2 vols. Contemp mor. Rubberstamps of G. de Batz & his inked comments in margins of intro to Vol I. cb Feb 19 (201) $400
— Porcelaines francaises. Paris, 1910. One of 150. Ed by the Comte X. de Chavagnac. Folio, mor extra by Pagnant; extremities rubbed. Christmas card from Morgan tipped to front endpaper. cb Feb 19 (200) $550
— PORADA, EDITH. - Corpus of Ancient Near Eastern Seals in North American Collections: The Collection of the Pierpont Morgan Library. [NY, 1948]. 2 vols. 4to, cloth. O Mar 24 (125) $100

Morgan, Joseph, Miscellaneous Writer
— Phoenix Britannicus: A Miscellaneous Collection of Scarce and Curious Tracts.... L, 1732. Sq 4to, contemp calf; rubbed & rebacked. bba Sept 25 (23) £45 [Vine]

Morgan, Sylvanus, 1620-93
— Armilogia sive Ars Chromocritica, the Language of Arms.... L, 1666. 1st Ed. 4to, contemp calf; worn. Some browning & soiling. S July 14 (336) £130

Morgan, T., of Wakefield. See: Goldsmith, Oliver

Morgan, Thomas, d.1743
— Philosophical Principles of Medicine. L, 1725. 8vo, contemp calf; rubbed. Top of A2 cut away, affecting headline; marginal annotations. bba Mar 12 (55) £110 [Korn]

Morghen, Raffaelo. See: Volpato & Morghen

Morier, Sir James Justinian, 1780?-1849
— The Adventures of Hajji Baba, of Ispahan, in England. L, 1828. 1st Ed. 2 vols. 8vo, orig bds. sg Feb 12 (241) $120
— A Journey through Persia, Armenia, and Asia Minor.... L, 1812. With: Morier. A Second Journey.... L, 1818. Together, 2 vols. Both works, 4to, modern half calf. sg Nov 20 (32) $425

Anr copy. Lacking half-title. With: Morier. A Second Journey.... L, 1818. Together, 2 vols. 4to, 19th-cent half sheep; broken. sg Dec 4 (136) $600
— A Second Journey through Persia, Armenia, and Asia Minor.... L, 1818. 4to, contemp calf gilt; rebacked, corners rubbed. With 2 maps & 17 plates, including 4-hand-colored Frontis offset onto title; 1 plate repaired at foot of fold; minor waterstians to maps & blank margins of uncolored plates. C May 8 (106) £380 [Lennox Money]
— Second Voyage en Perse.... Paris, 1818. 2 vols. 8vo, half lea; library stamps on front free endpapers. sg Nov 20 (131) $140

AMERICAN BOOK PRICES CURRENT

Morin, Louis
— Les Cousettes: Physiologie des couturieres de Paris. Paris, 1895. One of 100 on japon, this being the pbr's own copy. Illus by Henry Somm. 8vo, orig wraps. Accompanied by a vol containing 97 proof impressions in several states & 89 preparatory drawings. S June 17 (151) £420 [Edbe]

Morin, Pierre, Horticulturist
— Nouveau Traite des orangers et citronniers. Paris: Charles de Sercy, 1692. 12mo, contemp calf; rebacked, corners renewed. Hunt copy. CNY Nov 21 (203) $350

Morison, Douglas, 1814-47
— Views of Haddon Hall. L, 1842. Folio, loose in orig half mor gilt; gutta-percha perished. Some spotting. T Sept 18 (71) £70

Morison, Robert, 1620-83
— Hortus regius Blesensis.... L, 1669. 2 parts in 1 vol. 8vo, vellum. Dedication bound at front; tp browned with small paper loss at corner. Crahan copy. P Nov 25 (337) $450
— Plantarum historiae universalis Oxoniensis. Oxford, 1680-99. Vols II & III (all pbd) bound in 3 vols. Folio, contemp calf gilt; rubbed, 1 vol with joints split at foot. With port & 292 plates. Some browning. Plesch —de Belder copy. S Apr 28 (248) £11,000 [Schuster]

Morison, Stanley
See also: Grolier Club
— The Art of the Printer. L, 1925. 4to, orig cloth, in worn d/j. bba Oct 16 (495) £40 [Hay Cinema]

Anr copy. Cloth; worn. O June 16 (134) $70
— The English Newspaper. Cambr., 1932. 1st Ed. Folio, orig cloth; worn. Perforated stamps. bba Feb 5 (57) £65 [Diba]

Anr copy. Orig cloth, in d/j; rubbed & frayed. bba Mar 12 (27) £120 [Check]
— Modern Fine Printing. L, 1925. One of 650 with English text. Folio, orig cloth, in worn d/j. bba Oct 16 (496) £120 [Forster]

Anr copy. Cloth; rubbed. sg June 11 (295) $100
— On Type Faces. L, 1923. One of 750. Folio, half cloth, in worn d/j. bba Oct 16 (494) £35 [Hay Cinema]

Anr copy. Orig half cloth; rubbed. bba Feb 5 (20) £40 [Kuyper]
— The Typographic Book, 1450-1935. L, 1963. 4to, orig cloth, in d/j. sg May 14 (333) $150

Anr copy. Orig cloth. wa June 25 (42) $90
— Typographic Design in Relation to Photographic Composition. San Francisco:

Book Club of California, 1959. 1st Ed, One of 400. Bds, in d/j. cb Sept 11 (55) $65
Anr copy. Orig half vellum. cba Feb 5 (184) $65

Morison, Stanley —& Carter, Harry
— John Fell.... Oxford, 1967. One of 1,000. Folio, cloth, in soiled d/j. bba Oct 16 (499) £95 [Brill]
Anr copy. Orig cloth, in d/j. bba Feb 5 (108) £110 [Questor]

Morisot, Claude Barthelemy
— Orbis maritimi sive rerum in mari et littoribus gestarum generalis historia. Dijon, 1643. Folio, half vellum. Inner margin of A2 & last leaf of index torn; some waterstains. S Feb 24 (342) £260 [Brooklyn]

Morley, Christopher
— Where the Blue Begins. L & NY, [1925]. Illus by Arthur Rackham. Cloth. With 4 colored plates. B Oct 7 (288) HF230
Anr copy. Cloth; soiled. With 4 color plates. sg Oct 30 (156) $50
One of 100, sgd by author & artist. Half cloth; worn. sg Oct 30 (155) $800
One of 175, sgd by the artist. Half cloth, in d/j; spotted. S Dec 4 (214) £450 [Rosenblatt]

Mornay, ——
— Une Annee de Saint-Petersbourg ou douze vues pittoresques.... [Paris, 1812]. Folio, contemp half cloth; rebacked & recornered with mor. With uncolored map & 12 hand-colored plates. Marginal tears repaired. C Apr 8 (39) £20,000 [Smith]
— A Picture of St. Petersburgh, represented in a Collection of Twenty Interesting Views of the City.... L, [c.1834]. Folio, contemp half lea; rubbed, hinges def. With engraved title & 17 (of 20) hand-colored plates; lacking uncolored frontis & Abbey's plates 5, 11 & 14. One plate spotted in blank margin; anr with short tear entering blank plate frame. C Oct 15 (76) £800 [Shapero]

Mornay, Philippe de, 1549-1623
— A Woorke concerning the Trewnesse of the Christian Religion.... L: George Robinson for Thomas Cadman, 1587. 4to, modern cloth. With engraved title having port of Robert Dudley affixed to verso. Corners or margins of 4 leaves strengthened or restored; portion of A8 detaced in ink; some tears; 1 rusthole in margin of 2O4 just touching 2 letters of a sidenote; some dampstaining. S Dec 18 (321) £230 [Quaritch]

Morphy, Paul Charles, 1837-84
— Izbrannyya shakmatnyya partii. St. Petersburg, 1884. Modern cloth. pn Mar 26 (241) £40 [Hoffman]

Morris, Beverley Robinson
— British Game Birds and Wildfowl. L, 1855. 4to, contemp half mor. With 60 hand-colored plates. C Oct 15 (249) £1,300 [Thompson]
Anr copy. Contemp calf gilt. pnE Dec 17 (276) £1,100 [L'Aquaforte]
Anr copy. Contemp half mor; rubbed & soiled. S Oct 23 (739) £900 [Schire]
Anr copy. Contemp half mor; rubbed. Tp & contents leaf detached; frayed. S Oct 23 (740) £1,150 [Map]
Anr copy. Contemp mor gilt. Some soiling & discoloration; 1 leaf of text torn. S June 25 (171) £850 [Houle]
Anr Ed. L, [c,1860]. 4to, 19th-cent lea. With 20 colored plates only. Sold w.a.f. bba Dec 4 (266) £200 [Erlini]
Anr Ed. L, [1889]. 4to, orig cloth; worn. With 57 (of 60) hand-colored plates. Marginal soiling. S Apr 23 (49) £850 [Premier]
Anr copy. With 56 (of 60) hand-colored plates. S Apr 23 (50) £850 [Premier]

Morris, Earl Halstead —& Others
— The Temple of the Warriors at Chichenitza, Yucatan. Wash., 1931. Vol I (of 2). 4to, cloth. Library markings; dampstained on lower edge throughout; tp clipped. wa Sept 25 (362) $60

Morris, Edmund, 1804-74
— Derrick and Drill.... NY, 1865. 12mo, orig cloth; worn, edges of covers stained. With folding map ptd in blue. wa Nov 6 (61) $55

Morris, Edward Ellis. See: Cassell's...

Morris, Francis Orpen, 1810-93
— A History of British Birds. L, 1851-57. 1st Ed. 6 vols. 8vo, contemp half calf gilt; ribbed. With 3 engraved titles & 8 folding plates, all hand-colored. Plates soiled along folds; Vol I lacking front free endpaper. bba Oct 16 (322) £80 [Hannas]
Anr copy. Contemp half calf; rubbed. With hand-colored plates. Ck Sept 5 (58) £300
Anr copy. Contemp half mor gilt; worn. With 358 colored plates. L July 2 (170) £180
Anr copy. Half calf gilt; rubbed. pn Sept 18 (71) £300 [Smith]
Anr copy. Half calf. pn Sept 18 (177) £400 [Thorp]
Anr copy. Contemp lea gilt; rubbed. S Feb 24 (598) £320 [Tievision]

Anr copy. Contemp half lea; extremities rubbed. sg Dec 4 (137) $450

Anr Ed. L, 1863-64. 6 vols. 8vo, orig cloth. S Nov 17 (668) £340 [Boyd]

Anr Ed. L, 1865. 6 vols. 8vo, cloth; soiled. With 356 (of 358) colored paltes. Library markings; ink stamps on plates; pages brittle; some leaves frayed or torn. bba Jan 15 (420) £100 [Smith]

Anr Ed. L, 1868. 6 vols. 8vo, orig cloth; def, worn. With 358 hand-colored plates. Haverschmidt copy. B Feb 24 (404) HF2,000

"2d" Ed. L, 1870. 6 vols. Cloth; worn. bba Apr 9 (448) £320 [Vitale]

Anr copy. 6 vols. 8vo, orig cloth. bba May 14 (309) £340 [Beyer]; pn Oct 23 (250) £300 [Paul]

Anr copy. 6 vols. Orig cloth; spines worn. T Feb 19 (353) £280

— A History of British Butterflies. L, 1876. 4to, orig cloth; rubbed. pn Sept 18 (251) £80 [Piel]

— A History of British Birds. L, 1880. 8 vols. 8vo, orig cloth; loose. With 358 hand-colored plates. pn Mar 5 (235) £250 [Loose]

Anr Ed. L, [1888]. 8 vols. 8vo, orig cloth; tear in 1 spine. With 358 hand-colored plates. L July 2 (172) £220

Anr copy. Cloth; soiled. A few marginal tears. S Nov 10 (533) £380 [Campbell]

"3d" Ed. L, 1891. 6 vols. 8vo, orig cloth; front endpapers trimmed. With 394 hand-colored plates. Ck Jan 16 (209) £310; pnE Dec 17 (275) £300 [Coss]

"4th" Ed. L, 1895-97. 6 vols. 8vo, orig cloth. With 394 hand-colored plates. pn Oct 23 (251) £280 [Walford]

"5th" Ed. L, 1903. 6 vols. With 400 hand-colored plates. L July 2 (173) £300

Anr copy. Half calf; rubbed. With 396 hand-colored plates. Titles & endpapers stamped. pn Oct 23 (12) £820 [Egee]

— A History of British Butterflies. L, 1857. 8vo, half calf gilt. With 71 hand-colored plates. Tp stamped. pn Oct 23 (11) £65 [Lamb]

Anr Ed. L, 1870. 8vo, orig cloth. With 72 colored plates. pn Dec 11 (293) £80 [Book]

Anr Ed. L, 1876. 4to, orig cloth; rebacked, orig backstrip laid down. With 72 color plates & 2 plain plates. L Dec 11 (299) £50

— A Natural History of British Moths. L, 1871. 4 vols. 8vo, half mor gilt. With 132 colored plates. Stamps on titles & endpapers. pn Oct 23 (10) £80 [Bookroom]

3d Ed. L, 1891. 4 vols. 8vo, half mor gilt. With 132 hand-colored plates. A few plates soiled. S May 28 (593) £120

— A Natural History of the Nests and Eggs of British Birds. L, 1853-56. 1st Ed. 3 vols. 8vo, half mor gilt. With 223 colored plates. pn Oct 23 (252) £60 [Riff]

Anr Ed. L, 1870. 3 vols. 8vo, cloth. Library stamps on titles; pages brittle. bba Jan 15 (422) £40 [Barker]

"2d" Ed. L, 1875. 3 vols. 8vo, orig cloth; rubbed & soiled. bba Sept 25 (218) £40 [Greyfriars]

— A Series of Picturesque Views of Seats of the Noblemen and Gentlemen of Great Britain and Ireland. L, [c.1880]. 7 vols. 4to, orig cloth; rubbed. With 240 colored plates. bba Mar 26 (280) £120 [Marco]

Anr copy. Some marginal staining; a few leaves browned. bba Apr 9 (392) £85 [Elliott]

Anr copy. 6 vols. 4to, contemp mor gilt; inner hinges strengthened. C Oct 15 (77) £200 [Sifton Pread]

Anr copy. Orig cloth. Ck May 15 (177) £70

Anr copy. 7 vols, including facsimile of Autographs. Mor gilt; scuffed. pn Mar 5 (139) £120 [Walford]

Anr copy. 6 vols. 4to, orig cloth; most hinges broken or reinforced. S Nov 17 (806) £70 [Marinoni]

Anr copy. 7 vols, including vol of facsimile autographs. 4to, orig cloth; scuffed. T Mar 19 (52) £95

Morris, Frank T.

— Birds of the Australian Swamps. Vol I. Grebes-Cormorants. Melbourne, 1978. Ltd Ed. Folio, orig half lea. With 10 colored plates. kh Mar 16 (365) A$120

— Robins and Wrens of Australia: a Selection. Melbourne, [1979]. One of 500, sgd. Folio, orig bdg. pn Dec 11 (240) £55 [Gowland]

Morris, Henry

See also: Taylor & Morris

— Bird & Bull Pepper Pot.... [North Hills, Pa.]: Bird & Bull Press, 1977. Half lev; rubbed at edges & margins of front cover. cb Sept 11 (10) $95

Anr copy. Half cloth. sg Jan 8 (21) $120

— Omnibus: Instructions for Amateur Papermakers. [North Hills, Penna.], 1967. One of 500. Orig half mor by Sangorski & Sutcliffe. Hunt copy. CNY Nov 21 (212) $100

— A Visit to Hayle Mill.... North Hills PA, 1970. One of 210. Orig half lea. Hunt copy. CNY Nov 21 (213) $100

Morris, May
— William Morris, Artist, Writer, Socialist. Oxford, 1936. One of 750. 2 vols. 8vo, orig half cloth. With 2 A Ls s loosely inserted. S Nov 10 (23) $210 [Spelman]

Morris, Robert, Surveyor
— Select Architecture.... L, 1755. 4to, contemp calf; rebacked. With engraved title & 50 plates. Marginal worming repaired. John Betjeman's copy. bba Apr 23 (58) £650 [Henderson]

Morris, William, 1834-96
See also: Kelmscott Press

— An Address Delivered by William Morris at the Distribution of Prizes to Students of the Birmingham Municipal School of Art on Feb. 21. 1894. L, 1898. 8vo, ptd bds; bookplate removed from front pastedown. sg Sept 11 (237) $90

— A Book of Verse. L: Scolar Press, 1980. 4to, mor, inlaid with floral design. Facsimile of 1870 Ms. T Sept 18 (528) £85

— The Defence of Guenevere.... L, 1904. Illus by Jessie M. King. sg Jan 8 (150) $150

— Love is Enough. L, 1873 [1872]. 8vo, orig cloth; rubbed & soiled. bba Feb 5 (192) £50 [Bermester]

— Some Hints on Pattern Designing. L: Chiswick Press, 1899. 8vo, orig half cloth. pn mar 5 (36) £70 [Withercombe]

— The Two Sides of the River.... L, 1876. 8vo, orig wraps in contemp mor case. T. J. Wise forgery. Todd 184f. With 11 Ms lines of Hapless Love in Morris's hand tipped onto verso of upper cover.. Ck Oct 17 (111) £350

— Works. L: Chiswick Press, 1901-2. One of 315. 8 vols. S Oct 6 (734) £120 [Hetherington]

Anr Ed. L, 1910-15. 23 vols; lacking Vol I. Orig half cloth. bba Feb 5 (195) £300 [Subunso]

Anr copy. 23 vols; lacking Vol 24. Later lea or orig half cloth; some spines soiled. bba Feb 5 (196) £180 [Upper Street]

Morrison Collection, Alfred
— Catalogue of the Collection of Autograph Letters and Historical Documents.... Pvtly ptd, 1883-92. One of 200. Compiled by A. W. Thibaudeau. 6 vols. Folio, orig half cloth; soiled. S Nov 10 (669) £440 [Burgess]

Morrison, James, 1763-1807. See: Golden Cockerel Press

Morrison, Robert
— A Grammar of the Chinese Language. Serampore, 1815. 4to, contemp cloth. S Apr 23 (353) £650 [Elte]

Morrison, William
— The Dictionary of Decisions of the Court of Session. Edin. 1811. 21 vols. 4to, contemp calf; worn. pnE Nov 12 (128) £45

Morse, Edward S., 1838-1925. See: Hobson & Morse

Morse, Jedidiah, 1761-1826
— The American Gazetteer.... Bost., 1797. 1st Ed. 8vo, contemp calf; loose. With 7 maps. Separation in fold of 1 map. AVP Nov 20 (284) C$175 [Woolmer]

— The American Geography. Elizabethtown, N.J., 1789. 1st Ed. 8vo, old calf. With 2 folding maps. With related material. K Dec 13 (190) $250

Morse, Peter
— John Sloan's Prints: a Catalogue Raisonne.... New Haven, 1969. Folio, cloth, in d/j. sg June 4 (220) $100; sg June 4 (313) $100

Mortensen, William
— Monsters and Madonnas: A Book of Methods. San Francisco, 1936. 4to, spiral-bound wraps. sg Nov 13 (80) $70

Mortier, Cornelis. See: Covens & Mortier

Mortier, Pieter
See also: Neptune...

— Atlas Nouveau des cartes geographiques choisies ou le grand theatre de la guerre. Amst., 1703. Folio, contemp half vellum. With hand-colored allegorical title by Romein de Hooghe & 64 double-page maps, most with contemp outline hand-coloring. Tears in 2d ptd title, map of Europe & a few margins, all repaired. C Apr 8 (40) £3,200 [Postaprint]

— Atlas Royal a l'usage de Monseigneur le Duc de Bourgogne. Paris: N. de Fer, 1695 [but Amst., 1695?]. Folio, calf; def. With engraved allegorical title & 33 double-page maps only, most hand colored in outline. Stained; some defs affecting engraved surface. S Nov 10 (873) £200 [Arjomane]

Mortimer, Ruth
— French 16th Century Books. Cambr., Mass., 1964. 2 vols. 4to, cloth. bba Oct 16 (389) £95 [Georges]

Anr copy. Cloth; worn. sg Jan 22 (234) $130; sg May 14 (498) $175; sg May 14 (499) $175

— Italian 16th Century Books. Cambr., 1974. 2 vols. 4to, cloth; worn. O June 16 (134) $70; sg May 14 (500) $175

Morton, Henry —& Others
— Report of the Committee [of the Philomathean Society of the University of Pennsylvania] Appointed...to Translate the Inscription on the Rosetta Stone. [Phila., 1859]. 2d Ed. 4to, orig cloth. Lithographed throughout in black & colors. sg Sept 18 (259) $275

Morton, Nathaniel, 1613-85
— New-Englands Memoriall. Bost.: Nicholas Boone, 1721. ("New-England's Memorial....") 2d Ed. 12mo, contemp calf. Some soiling & foxing; several leaves with small portions missing, affecting some text. sg Mar 12 (186) $600

Morton, Richard, 1637-99
— Phthisiologia or, a Treatise of Consumptions. L, 1694. 8vo, half mor. Port cut round & mtd. S May 28 (746) £180

Morton, Samuel George, 1799-1851
— Crania americana. Phila., 1839. Folio, contemp half mor; backstrip detached. Tipped in are 2 ink drawings by J. Collins of George Morton & John Collins. F Oct 30 (547) $400
Anr copy. Cloth; worn. wd June 19 (158) $250

Morton, Thomas, 1564-1659
— The Grand Imposture of the (now) Church of Rome. L: G. Miller for Robert Mylbourne, [1626?]. 4to, contemp vellum gilt. Ck Sept 5 (207) £180

Morton, William James, 1845-1920
— The X Ray or Photography of the Invisible. NY, 1896. 8vo, orig cloth; stained, worn. wa Nov 6 (62) $130

Moschetti, Alessandro
— Raccolta delle principali vedute di Roma. Rome: F. Ducro, [1848]. Oblong folio, half calf. With pictorial engraved title (repeated), plan of Rome & 33 plates. Some spotting. S Nov 10 (914) £125 [Erlini]

Moser, Barry
— Fifty Wood Engravings. Northampton MA: Pennyroyal Press, 1978. One of 100. Folio, loose as issued in folder. Inscr. sg Jan 8 (168) $550

Moser, Friedrich Carl von, Baron
— Der Herr und der Diener geschildert mit patriotischer Freiheit. Frankfurt, 1759. 8vo, contemp sheep. sg Oct 9 (277) $140

Moses, Henry. See: Englefield Collection, Sir Henry Charles

Moses, Henry, 1782?-1870
— A Collection of Antique Vases, Altars, Paterae, Tripods.... L: Bohn, [c.1814]. 4to, contemp cloth; rubbed. With engraved title & 151 plates, 8 colored. wa Feb 19 (399) $130

Moskowitz, Ira
— Great Drawings of All Time. NY, 1962. 4 vols. 4to, cloth. sg June 4 (155) $80; sg June 11 (297) $110; wa Dec 11 (547) $110

Mossman, Samuel
— Narrative of the Shipwreck of the "Admella" Inter-Colonial Steamer.... Melbourne, 1859. 1st Ed. 8vo, wraps; worn & broken. With frontis & folding map. Sgd by Edw. Henty. kh Mar 16 (369) A$200

Mothe le Vayer, Francois de la. See: La Mothe le Vayer, Francois de

Mother...
— Morther Chipton. L: Wm. Tringham, 1771. 8vo, orig wrap. On folded sheet in 4 shections each with 2 flaps to alter the illust & continue the story, colored by hand. S Dec 5 (398) £1,000 [Hirsch]

Mott, J. L.
— J. L. Mott Iron Works. Illustrated Catalogue of Statuary.... NY, 1875. Folio, bdg not described. Franklin Institute copy. F Sept 12 (31) $1,800
— J. L. Mott Iron Works. Illustrated Catalogue of Wrought & Cast Iron Railing. NY, 1883. Folio, orig wraps; worn. Franklin Institute copy. F Sept 12 (30) $400

Mottelay, Paul Fleury
— Bibliographical History of Electricity & Magnetism. L, 1922. sg Oct 2 (227) $120
— The Soldier in Our Civil War.... NY, 1884-85. 2 vols. Folio, cloth; worn, backstrips torn. sg Dec 18 (153) $120

Mottin de la Balme
— Essais sur l'equitation, ou principes raisonnes sur l'art de monter et de dresser les chevaux. Amst.: Jombert & Ruault, 1773. 12mo, contemp mor gilt with arms of Marie-Louise de Rohan-Soubise, comtesse de Lorraine-Marsan (Olivier 55, fer 1). S Nov 27 (101) £900 [Chaponniere]

Mouchon, Pierre
— La Chasse des oiseaux d'eau en France. Paris, 1931. One of 15 on japan imperial. 4to, half mor gilt by Saulnier. Sold with a folio volume containing orig drawings by Leliepvr & bound similarly by Saulnier. Jeanson 1599 & 1915. S Mar 1 (418) FF50,000

Moufet, Thomas
— Healths Improvement.... See: Moffett, Thomas

Moule, Horace Frederick. See: Darlow & Moule

Moule, Thomas
— Bibliotheca heraldica Magnae Britanniae. L, 1822. 4to, contemp bds; rebacked. Ck Jan 30 (106) £48

Anr copy. Half lea; rear joint cracked, crudely rehinged. sg Jan 22 (235) $90

— The English Counties Delineated.... L, 1837. 2 vols. 4to, contemp half mor; worn & broken. With 2 engraved titles & 59 plates & maps. Sold w.a.f. Ck Nov 21 (350) £550

Anr Ed. L, 1838. 2 vols. 4to, contemp calf; worn. With 2 engraved titles & 60 plates & maps. Some shaving; folding plates def. S Nov 17 (761) £550 [Boyd]

— Great Britain Illustrated. L, 1830. Illus by William Westall. 4to, contemp half mor; rubbed. With engraved title & 118 (on 59) plates. bba Sept 25 (451) £140 [Mandl]

Anr copy. Contemp half calf; rubbed, upper cover detached. Ck Nov 21 (455) £120

Anr copy. Cloth. With 89 views only. pn Dec 11 (76) £75 [Fines]

Anr copy. Calf gilt; rebacked. With engraved title & 118 (on 59) plates. pn Mar 5 (221) £180 [Map House]

— Winkles's Architectural and Picturesque Illustrations of the Cathedral Churches of England and Wales. L, 1836-42. 3 vols. 8vo, orig cloth; def. With engraved titles & 169 plates. pn Dec 11 (77) £90 [Fines]

Anr copy. Contemp calf gilt; worn. T Apr 16 (73) £80

Mountbatten, Louis, Earl Mountbatten of Burma
— Speeches. [New Delhi, 1949]. Contemp mor; soiled, inner hinges reinforced. Inscr to his private secretary Ian Scott. bba Oct 16 (156) £50 [Douglas]

Mountgomery, Sir Robert
— A Discourse concerning the Design'd Establishment of a New Colony to the South of Carolina.... L, 1717. 8vo, wraps. Tp soiled. S June 25 (393) £3,800

Mourelle, Francisco Antonio
— Voyage of the Sonora in the Second Bucareli Expedition.... San Francisco, 1920. One of 230. 4to, half cloth. With port & 2 maps. cb Oct 9 (147) $190

Anr copy. Half cloth, in d/j. Frontis & smaller map detached but present. cb July 16 (187) $225

Mouret, Simon Francois
— Chasses du Roy, et la quantite des lieues que le Roy a fait tant a cheval qu'en carosse. Pendant l'annee 1725. Paris: Collombat, [1726]. 8vo, mor janseniste by Trautz-Bauzonnet. Jeanson copy. SM Mar 1 (419) FF13,000

Mourlot, Fernand. See: Buffet, Bernard; Miro, Joan

Mourt, George
— A Relation or Journall of the beginning and proceedings of the English Plantation setled at Plimoth in New England.... L: for John Bellamie, 1622. 4to, modern mor; spine repaired. First 6 leaves in facsimile; some annotations in ink. Penrose copy. S Apr 23 (270) £2,300 [Maggs]

Moxon, Elizabeth
— English Housewifery. Exemplified in about Four Hundred and Fifty Receipts.... Leeds, 1749. 12mo, contemp sheep; rebacked with calf, new endpapers. With 2 folding woodcut plates; 1 torn along fold. Marginal inkstain; some browning. Crahan copy. P Nov 25 (339) $600

Anr Ed. Leeds, 1790. 2 parts in 1 vol, including Supplement. 12mo, contemp sheep; rebacked. With folding table (backed) & with 2 folding plates in Supplement, 1 with fold tear. Crahan copy. P Nov 25 (339) $600

Moxon, Joseph, 1627-1700
— Mechanick Exercises, or the Doctrine of Handy-Works, applied to the Art of Printing. NY, 1896. One of 450. 2 vols. 8vo, orig half lea. Type-facsimile of 1683 Ed. bba Apr 9 (459) £50 [Moreton]

Mr. See: Hunt, Thomas

Mucha, Alphonse, 1860-1939
— Le Pater. Paris: H. Piazza, [1899]. One of 510. 4to, wraps; chipped, spine tape-repaired. With 23 illusts. sg Dec 18 (202) $1,200

Mudford, William, 1782-1848
— An Historical Account of the Campaign in the Netherlands.... L, 1817. 4to, half mor gilt. With hand-colored frontis & title, 2 folding plans & 26 hand-colored plates. Some repairs with linen; slight spotting. pn Apr 30 (57) £400 [Shapero]

Mudie, Robert, 1777-1842
— The Feathered Tribes of the British Islands. L, 1834. 1st Ed. 2 vols. 8vo, cloth; worn. With 18 hand-colored plates. bba July 16 (82) £45 [Shapero]

Anr copy. Orig cloth; worn, joints splitting. cb Nov 6 (216) $75

Anr copy. Orig cloth; tears in spine of Vol I with loss. T Feb 19 (368) £40

Mueller, Ferdinand J. H. von, Baron
— Eucalyptographia.; A Descriptive Atlas of the Eucalypts of Australia.... Melbourne & L, 1879-84. Parts 1-9 (of 10). 4to, orig wraps. Some dampstains. Ck Sept 26 (213) £180

Mueller, Gerhard Friedrich
— Voyages from Asia to America for Completing the Discoveries of the North West Coast of America.... L, 1761. 1st Ed in English. 4to, contemp calf; rebacked. With 2 folding maps hand-colored in outline & 2 other maps. Tears repaired in folding maps; soiled & stained at beginning & end; lacking G1. S June 25 (328) £700 [Anderson]

Mueller, Hans Alexander
— Woodcuts and Wood Engravings: How I Make Them. NY, 1939. one of 250. Folio, loose as issued, in cloth box. O Mar 24 (127) $95

Muenchener...
— Muenchener Bilderbogen. Munich, [1900?]. Vols I-V. Folio. B Feb 25 (906) HF700

Muenster, Sebastian, 1489-1552
— Cosmographia. Basel: H. Petri, 1552. ("Cosmographiae universalis libri VI.") Folio, contemp blindstamped pigskin over wooden bds, with 2 clasp & catches. With 14 double-page maps & port & 39 double-page illusts. HK Nov 4 (687) DM16,500

1st Ed in Italian. Basel: Henrigo Pietro, 1558. ("Sei Libri della cosmografia universale.") Folio, contemp vellum; soiled. Lacking a few plates & leaves. Sold w.a.f. C Apr 8 (107) £2,200 [Rossley]

Anr Ed. Basel: S. Henricpetri, 1574. ("Cosmographia, das ist: Beschreibung der gantzen Welt.") Folio, contemp blindstamped vellum over wooden bds; worn & soiled, lacking 1 clasp. With 26 double-page woodcut maps with ptd titles within elaborate borders on versos, 53 other double-page maps, plans & views & c.825 woodcuts in the text. Lacking tp; browned & stained throughout; the 3 folding views very def or missing; some repairs. Sold w.a.f. S June 25 (274) £1,700 [Schmidt]

Anr Ed. Basel: Officina Henricpetrina, 1578. ("Cosmography oder Beschreibung aller Laender, Herrschafften....") Folio, contemp vellum; repaired. Tp laid down; 2 panoramas torn & repaired; 1 view torn lacking small portion; many small tears; some underlinings in text. pn Apr 30 (326) £2,500 [Weston]

Anr Ed. Basel: Sebastian Henricpetri, 1592.

("Cosmographia, das ist: Beschreibung der gantzen Welt.") Folio, half calf; worn. With 26 double-page woodcut maps with ptd & woodcut headpiece on verso of each, 65 other double-page maps, plans & views (2 folding, damaged) & c.1,280 woodcuts in the text. Lacking the title with port on verso & the last leaf; browned throughout; marginal repairs. Sold w.a.f. S June 25 (276) £2,200 [Schmidt]

— Organum Uranicum.... Basel: H. Petrus, 1536. Folio, half vellum. With large woodcut on tp, woodcut of author on f4 verso & 34 woodcuts in the text of which 14 (should be 15) have volvelles & threads attached. Colophon leaf repaired at outer blank corners; minor marginal repairs; some small stains. S Nov 27 (277) £1,200 [Kraus]

Muenz, Ludwig
— Rembrandt's Etchings. L, 1952. 2 vols. Folio, orig cloth; upper joints split, inner hinges split. Titles affected by damp; frontis to Vol I lacking small blank section; frontis to Vol II detached but tipped in. Ck Jan 30 (135) £45

Anr copy. Orig cloth, in d/js. S July 13 (41) £170

Muffett, Thomas. See: Moffett, Thomas

Muhammad, of Baghdad
— De superficierum divisionibus liber.... Pesaro: G. Concordia, 1570. 4to, contemp vellum. Some stains & spotting. HK Nov 4 (689) DM900

Muhlenberg, Henry
— Descriptio uberior graminum et plantarum calamariarum America Septentrionalis indigenarum et circurum. Phila., 1817. 8vo, contemp calf; worn, joints starting. sg Jan 15 (241) $70

Muir, Edwin, 1887-1959
— We Moderns: Enigmas and Guesses, by Edward Moore L, [1918]. 1st Ed. pn Nov 20 (96) £55 [Henderson]

Muir, John, 1838-1914
— Arctic Cruise of the Revenue Steamer Corwin in Alaska.... Wash., 1883. 4to, orig cloth; worn. With 12 plates, some colored. S Nov 10 (1229) £220 [Negro]
— The Mountains of California. NY, 1894. 1st Ed. 8vo, orig cloth. cb Mar 19 (201) $180

Anr copy. Cloth. With 51 plates & 2 maps. cb July 16 (189) $180

Anr copy. Cloth; worn. O June 9 (121) $120

— Travels in Alaska. Bost. & NY, 1915. One of 450. Cloth; lacking free endpaper. sg

Sept 18 (190) $50

Muir, Percy H.
See also: Carter & Muir
— Points. [First Series]: 1874-1930. Second Series: 1866-1934. L, 1931-34. 1st Eds, One of 500 & 750. Orig half vellum. bba July 2 (45) £150 [Updyke]

Muirhead, James Patrick
— The Origin and Progress of the Mechanical Inventions of James Watt.... L, 1854. 3 vols. 4to, orig cloth; Vol I with tear at head of spine & rear cover warped. With 34 plates. sg Jan 15 (379) $175

Mullan, Capt. John, 1830-1909
— Letter from the Secretary of War Transmitting the Report of Lt. Mullan in Charge of the Construction of a Military Road from Fort Benton to Fort Walla-Walla.... Wash., 1861. 8vo, later calf. With folding map. 36th Congress, 2d Session, II of R Exec. Doc. 44. cb Jan 8 (130) $200

Mullen, Allan
— An Anatomical Account of the Elephant Accidentally Burnt in Dublin.... L: Sam. Smith, 1682. 4to, wraps; stained. With 2 folding plates. Tp & several leaves cropped affecting sidenotes or text; tp soiled & stained; marginal worming at end. S Nov 10 (539) £240 [Phelps]

Mullens, William H. —& Swann, H. Kirke
— A Bibliography of British Ornithology.... L, 1917-23. 2 parts in 1 vol. pnE Jan 28 (318) £100 [Greyfriars]

Muller, Andreas. See: Valckenier & Muller

Multatuli, Pseud.
— Max Havelaar, of de koffij-veilingen der Nederlandsche Handel-Maatschappij. Amst., 1860. 2 vols. Orig bds; 1 bdg broken, the other with damaged back. B Oct 7 (562) HF1,000

Mumey, Nolie
— A Study of Rare Books.... Denver, 1930. One of 1,000, sgd. 4to, half cloth. Library markings. bba Feb 5 (59) £60 [Hashimoto]; sg Jan 22 (236) $110

Mummery, Alfred F.
— My Climbs in the Alps and Caucasus. L, 1895. 8vo, cloth; soiled. pn Mar 5 (249A) £50 [Taylor]

Mun, A. de
— Histoire de la grande et de la petite chasse.... Brussels: J. Geruzet, [c.1850]. 4to, 19th-cent half shagreen. Jeanson copy. SM Mar 1 (420) FF7,000

Mun, Thomas, 1571-1641
— England's Treasure by Forraign Trade.... L, 1669. 2d Ed. 8vo, old sheep; restored, new endpapers. Marginal browning & staining; tissue repairs in blank areas at end & in inner margins; tight inner margins not affecting legibility; blank at end with contemp notations. P Sept 24 (359) $1,000

Munby, Alan Noel Latimer
— Sale Catalogues of Libraries of Eminent Persons. L, 1972-75. 12 vols. 4to, cloth, 2 vols in d/js. bba Oct 16 (392) £80 [Baldwin]

Munchausen, Baron. See: Raspe, Rudolph Erich

Muncq, Alexander de, 1655-1719
— Ecclesiastes ofte Prediker. In Duytse vaarzen overgesett. Rotterdam, 1708. Bound with: Muncq. Eenzaame bezigheden. Amst., 1711. And: Wintervrugt gesasschen op het hov Niet altyd Zomer. Middelburg, 1712. And: 4-page poetical pamphlet on Simon Simonsen, who had tried to murder Muncq & committed suicide in prison. 4to, contemp mor over wooden bds gilt. B Feb 25 (727a) HF6,500

Mundy, Godfrey Charles
— Our Antipodes: or, Residence and Rambles in the Australian Colonies. L, 1852. 2d Ed. 3 vols. 8vo, contemp half calf gilt. With 15 plates. Small repair to 1 plate; a few leaves spotted at end of Vol III. C Oct 15 (165) £190 [Thorp]

Munnings, Sir Alfred James, 1878-1959
— Pictures of Horses and English Life. L, 1927. One of 250. 4to, orig vellum gilt. S May 6 (395) £450 [Sims]
Anr Ed. L, 1939. 4to, orig cloth, in soiled & torn d/j. S Nov 10 (603) £90 [Ilcad]

Munoz, Filadelfo
— I Raguagli Historici del Vespro Siciliano.... Palermo, 1669. 4to, old vellum. With 2 small portions of title excised & restored. sg Mar 26 (211) $140

Munting, Abraham, 1626-83
— Naauwkeurige beschryving der aardgewassen. Leiden & Utrecht, 1696. 3 parts in 1 vol. Folio, contemp blind-stamped vellum; soiled, 1 corner slightly damaged. With engraved title, vignette on ptd title & 243 plates. de Belder copy. S Apr 28 (252) £6,500 [Burgess Browning]
— Phytographia curiosa. Leiden & Amst., 1702. Folio, contemp calf; rubbed. With frontis, engraved dedication & 245 plates. Minor spotting & soiling. Vilmorin—de Belder copy. S Apr 28 (253) £5,800 [Burgess Browning]
Anr Ed. Amst., 1713. Folio, later calf.

With engraved frontis & dedication & 245 plates. Repair to tear in lower margin of 1 leaf. Horticultural Society of New York —de Belder copy. S Apr 28 (254) £6,200 [Burgess Browning]
— Waare Oeffening der Planten.... Amst.: Jan Rieuwertsz, 1672. 4to, calf; new endpapers. With engraved title & 40 hand-colored plates. Some stains; half-title & tp repaired. B Feb 24 (516) HF2,600
Anr.copy. Modern calf. With frontis & 40 plates. de Belder copy. S Apr 28 (251) £1,400 [E. McDougall]

Murasaki, Lady
— The Tale of Genji Scroll. [Tokyo, 1971]. One of 1,500. Ed by Ivan Morris. Oblong folio, padded cloth, tie, box. With 63 colored plates. A facsimile Ed. sg June 4 (222) $275

Muratori, Ludovico Antonio, 1672-1750
— Antiquitates Italiciae medii aevi L, 1738-42. 6 vols. Folio, half calf; rubbed. B Oct 7 (1068) HF600
— Della Publica Felicita, Oggetto di Buoni Principi. Lucca, 1749. 4to, contemp vellum. Foxed; some leaves wormed with loss. sg Mar 26 (212) $500
— A Relation of the Missions of Paraguay. L, 1759. 8vo, contemp calf; rebacked. With folding map (loose). sg Mar 12 (204) $110

Murchison, Sir Roderick Impey, 1792-1871
— The Silurian System. L, 1839. 1st Ed. 2 vols. 4to, mor gilt; rubbed, 1 joint split. With 45 plates & 12 maps. S Nov 27 (278) £650 [Maggs]

Murchison, Sir Roderick Impey, 1792-1871 —& Others
— The Geology of Russia in Europe and the Ural Mountains. L & Paris, 1845. 2 vols. 4to, orig cloth; worn, joints & hinges splitting. With 2 folding color maps, 12 views & 68 plates. Some pp loose. Library copy. wa Nov 6 (245) $300

Mure, William, 1799-1860
— Journal of a Tour in Greece and the Ionian Islands.... Edin. & L, 1842. 2 vols. 8vo, orig cloth. With 15 plates and maps. Vol II with short tear in 1 plate & small portion torn from front free endpaper. S Jan 12 (172) £80 [pantazelos]

Murphy, James Cavanagh. See: Sousa Coutinho, Manuel de

Murphy, Robert Cushman
— Oceanic Birds of South America. NY, 1936. 2 vols. 4to, cloth. With 72 plain & 16 colored plates. Inscr. cb June 4 (158) $160
Anr copy. Cloth; worn. O Mar 24 (128) $95

Anr copy. With 72 plain & 16 colored plates. pn Oct 23 (255) £130 [Greyfriars]; pn Dec 11 (241) £95 [Graham]

Murphy, Stanley
— Martha's Vineyard Decoys. Bost., [1978]. Oblong 4to, cloth, in d/j. sg Oct 23 (245) $120
One of 55. Half calf. sg Oct 23 (405) $150

Murray, Alexander Sutherland
— Twelve Hundred Miles on the River Murray. L, 1898. Oblong 4to, orig cloth; loose. With 15 colored plates. Lacking 2 plates. CA Apr 12 (190) A$110

Murray, Andrew & Robert
— The Theory and Practice of Ship-Building.... Edin., 1861. 4to, orig cloth; worn at top & bottom of spine. T Mar 19 (36) £48

Murray, Archibald K.
— History of the Scottish Regiments. Glasgow, 1862. 2 vols. 4to, contemp mor; rubbed. T July 16 (63) £180

Murray, Sir Charles Augustus
— Travels in North America. L, 1839. 1st Ed. 2 vols. 8vo, orig cloth; rebacked & bumped. O Oct 21 (125) $175

Murray, Harold James Ruthven
— A History of Board-Games other than Chess. Oxford, 1952. pn Mar 26 (460) £65 [Kitz]
— A History of Chess. Oxford, 1913. Bdg repaired. pn Mar 26 (459) £110

Murray, Hugh, 1779-1846
— Historical Account of Discoveries and Travels in North America. L, 1829. 1st Ed. 2 vols. 8vo, disbound. Library markings. wa Sept 25 (458) $90

Murray, James —& Marston, George
— Antarctic Days. L, 1913. One of 280. Intro by Sir Ernest Shackleton. One plate guard torn & marked. S Nov 18 (1227) £420 [Simper]

Murray, James, 1721-94
— Impartial History of the Present War in America. Newcastle, 1779-84?. 2 vols. 8vo, modern cloth. With fold-out map & 23 ports. Library markings on each plate, affecting image; map with additional perforated stamp. sg Mar 12 (187) $200

Murray, Sir John, 1841-1914 —& Pullar, Laurence
— Bathymetrical Survey of the Scottish Fresh-Water Lochs. Edin., 1910. 6 vols. 8vo, half pigskin; worn. pn July 23 (98) £130 [Elliott]

Murray, T. L.
— An Atlas of the English Counties. L, 1830. Folio, orig half lea; worn. With engraved title & 43 (of 44) maps. pn Sept 18 (348) £420 [Taylor]

Murray, Sir Thomas
— The Laws and Acts of Parliament...of Scotland. Edin., 1681. Folio, old bds; broken. With engraved title, coat-of-arms & 8 ports.. O Feb 24 (117) $80

Murray-Oliver, Anthony
— Captain Cook's Artists in the Pacific.... Christchurch, 1969. One of 2,000. Oblong folio, half syn. sg Apr 23 (100) $225

Murrell, John
— Murrels Two Bookes of Cookerie and Carving. L, 1641. 8vo, contemp calf; rubbed, rebacked. Rust hole to general title touching 1 letter; final leaf extended; lacking last blank; some waterstaining to lower fore-edge corners; some browning. P Nov 25 (342) $750

Musaeus. See: Golden Cockerel Press

Musee...
— Musee Francais. Recueil des plus beaux tableaux, statues, et bas-reliefs qui existaient au Louvre.... Paris: Galignani, [1829-30]. 3 (of 4) vols. Folio, half mor gilt; worn. Sold w.a.f. S Mar 9 (693) £1,200 [Barker]

Anr copy. 4 vols. Folio, contemp half mor gilt; worn. Some foxing. sg Feb 5 (231) $2,200

Musee du Louvre
— Les Tapisseries des chasses de Maximilien.... Paris, 1920. Folio, half shagreen. Jeanson copy. SM Mar 1 (421) FF1,800

Muselli, Vincent
— Les Travaux et les jeux. Paris, 1929. One of 11 hors commerce. Illus by Andre Derain. 4to, orig wraps. S May 6 (4) £260 [Gabus]

Musil, Robert
— Der Mann ohne Eigenschaften. Berlin & Lausanne, 1930-33-43. 3 vols. Orig bdg. HN May 20 (2738) DM1,000

Muskogee Indians. See: Indians, North American

Muspratt, James Sheridan
Chemistry, Theoretical, Practical and Analytical.... Glasgow, etc., [1853-61]. 1st Ed. 2 vols. 4to, half calf; worn & stained, broken. With 2 engraved titles & 31 ports, many waterstained. wa Nov 6 (27) $55

Musschenbroek, Peter van, 1692-1761
— Essai de physique.... Leiden, 1739. 1st Ed. 2 vols. 4to, contemp calf. With port & 33 folding plates. Paper browned & discolored in places. S May 28 (748) £190

Musset, Alfred de, 1810-57
— La Nuit venetienne. Paris, [1913]. One of 500 on japon. Illus by U. Brunelleschi. 4to, contemp half mor, orig wraps bound in. bba Dec 4 (170) £70 [Check]
— On ne Badine pas avec l'amour. Paris, 1904. Illus by Louis Morin. Mor gilt. S May 6 (30) £120 [Hannas]

Mussolini, Benito, 1883-1945
— NIETZSCHE, FRIEDRICH WILHELM. - Cosi parlo Zarathustra. Rome, 1910. Cloth; worn. Sgd by Mussolini on verso of half-title, 1917. P Sept 24 (197) $1,600

Muthesius, Hermann
— Das englische Haus. Berlin, 1908-11. 3 vols. Folio, orig bdg. B Oct 7 (921) HF500

Muybridge, Eadweard, 1830-1904
— Animal Locomotion. An Electro-Photographic Investigation of Consecutive Phases of Animal Movements. L, 1899. ("Animals in Motion.") Oblong 4to, orig cloth; rubbed. Some soiling. pn Dec 11 (198) £60 [Elliott]

Anr Ed. L, 1902. Oblong 4to, orig cloth; stained. S July 28 (1099) £110

Myers, Francis
— The Coastal Scenery, Harbours, Mountains, and Rivers, of New South Wales. Sydney, 1886. 4to, contemp mor gilt. Ck Sept 26 (222) £110

Mylius, Christian Friedrich
— Malerische Fussreise durch das Suedliche Frankreich.... Carlsruhe, 1818-19. 8 parts in 4 vols. 8vo & oblong folio, contemp half calf. With 8 litho titles, 4 frontises & 84 plates only. FD Dec 2 (821) DM1,500

Mynsicht, Adrian von, 1603-38
— Thesaurus et armamentarium medico chymicum.... Luebeck, 1662. 4to, contemp vellum bds; rubbed. Many leaves spotted & browned. bba Nov 13 (46) £60 [P & P Books]

Mystery...
— The Mystery of Ambras Merlins, Standard-bearer Wolf, and Last Boar of Cornwal With sundry Other Misterious Prophecys...on the Signification...of that Prodigious Comet, seen by Most of the World Anno 1680, with the Blazing Star Anno 1682...written by a Lover of his Country's Peace.... L: for Benjamin Billingsley, 1683. Folio, modern wraps. Upper margins unevenly trimmed. sg Mar 26 (136) $175

N

N., M. See: Anatomy...

N., N.
— Che la Platina Americana era un Metallo Conosciuto dagli Antichi, Dissertazione.... Bassano, 1790. 8vo, modern half vellum. Erasures on tp. sg Sept 18 (183) $50
— A Short Account of the Present State of New-England. [L, 1690]. 4to, wraps. Discolored throughout; some cropping. S June 25 (408) £1,400

Nabokov, Vladimir
— Lolita. Paris, 1955. 1st Ed. 2 vols. Wraps. sg Mar 5 (186) $425; sg Mar 5 (187) $425

Nadel, Arno
— Das Jahr des Juden. Berlin, 1920. 4to, ptd wraps. Some foxing. sg Apr 30 (140) $120

Naef, Weston. See: Grolier Club

Nagayev, Aleksey Ivanovich
— Atlas vsego Baltiyskago morya s'Finskim i Botnicheskim zalivami, s' Shkager Rakom, kategatom, Zundom, i Beltami. St. Petersburg: Admiralsheiskoi Kollegii, 1757. Folio, contemp calf gilt; worn. With 29 sea charts, 24 double-page, 2 folding & 3 full-page. S Oct 23 (117) £4,500 [Germudson]

Nagler, Georg Kaspar, 1801-66
— Die Monogrammisten und diejenigen bekannten und unbekannten Kuenstler aller Schulen. Munich, 1858-79. 5 vols. 8vo, half calf; rebacked. sg Feb 5 (232) $175

Nairn, Thomas
— A Letter from South Carolina.... L, 1718. 8vo, wraps. S June 25 (379) £900

Najera, Antonio de
— Navegacion especulativa, y Practica.... Lisbon: for Pedro Crasebeeck, 1628. 4to, modern calf gilt. Some waterstains & browning. S Apr 23 (192) £2,500 [Quaritch]

Nalson, John, 1638?-86
— An Impartial Collection of the Great Affairs of State...to the Murther of King Charles I. L, 1682-83. 2 vols. Folio, contemp calf; rubbed, 2 covers detached. O Feb 24 (144) $90

Nance, Ernest Morton
— The Pottery and Porcelain of Swansea and Nantgarw. L, 1942. 4to, mor; lower hinge broken, rubbed. Some stains in lower margins. S Nov 10 (136) £60 [Pariser]

AMERICAN BOOK PRICES CURRENT

Nancy...
— Nancy Cock's Song Book, being a Collection of Old Songs with which most Young Wits have been Delighted, to which is added the Death and Burial of Cock Robin. L, 1795. 32mo, orig Dutch floral wraps; resewn. Lacking A9; 2 other leaves loose. S Sept 23 (981) £1,600 [Moon]

Nansen, Fridtjof, 1861-1930
— Farthest North. L, 1898. 2 vols. 8vo, orig cloth. bba Dec 4 (281) £40 [Bruton]
— Fram over polhavet den norske polarfaerd.... Oslo, 1897. 1st Ed. 2 vols. 8vo, orig cloth. S Nov 18 (1230) £100 [Sim]
— In Northern Mists. L, 1911. 2 vols. 4to, orig cloth. Inscr. S Oct 23 (506) £300 [Thorp]

Napier, Archibald, 1st Lord Napier
— Memoirs.... Edin., 1793. 4to, orig bds; spine chipped. O Feb 24 (145) $75

Napier, Charles James
— Memoir on the Roads of Cefalonia. L, 1825. 8vo, orig bds; upper cover detached. With folding frontis & 4 plates & charts, 3 hand-colored. Ck Nov 21 (211) £160

Napier, Mark
— Memorials and Letters Illustrative of the Life and Times of John Graham of Claverhouse.... Edin., 1859-62. 3 vols. 8vo, orig cloth. O Feb 24 (146) $70

Napoleon...
— Napoleon in the Other World; a Narrative Written by Himself and Found near his Tomb in the Island of St. Helena, by Xongo-Tee-Foh-Tchi, Mandarin of the Third Class. L, 1827. 8vo, orig half cloth; broken, backstrip worn away & shaken. Frontis soiled & detached; signature clipped from blank top edge of title. sg Sept 11 (238) $60

Napoleon I, 1769-1821. See: Golden Cockerel Press

Narazaki Muneshige
— The Japanese Print: Its Evolution and Essence. Tokyo & Palo Alto, 1966. Folio, cloth, in d/j. With 107 color plates. cba Mar 5 (260) $60

Narbrough, Sir John, 1640-88 —& Others
— An Account of Several Late Voyages & Discoveries.... L, 1711. 8vo, contemp calf; rebacked. With 3 folding maps & 19 plates. C Oct 15 (166) £500 [McCormick]
  Anr copy. Later half mor. kh Mar 16 (377) A$750

Nardini, Famiano
— Roma antica. Rome, 1666. 1st Ed. 2 parts in 1 vol. 4to, contemp vellum; soiled. T Oct 16 (523) £85

Nares, Robert
— Elements of Orthoepy.... L, 1784. 8vo, contemp sheep gilt; worn. sg Oct 9 (193) $120

Narrenspiegel
— Wol-Geschliffener Narren-Spiegel, worinnen hundert und vierzehn Arten allerley Narren ihr Eben-Bild.... Freystadt, gedruckt in diesem Jahr [Nuremberg?, c.1730?]. Folio, modern half mor. With 115 illusts after Matthaeus Merian. C Dec 12 (302) £1,300 [Pressler]

Nash, Frederick
— A Series of Views Interior and Exterior of the Collegiate Chapel of St. George at Windsor. L, 1805. Folio, wraps; hinges worn. With vignette title & 9 aquatints. pn Dec 11 (197) £300 [Orssich]

Nash, Frederick —& Others
— Picturesque Views of the City of Paris and its Environs. L, 1820-23. 2 vols in one. Folio, contemp half mor; worn. With the 7 supplementary plates. Vol II lacking title. bba Dec 18 (200) £100 [Rainer]

Nash, Joseph, 1809-78
— The Mansions of England in the Olden Time. L, 1839-49. Series 1-3. Folio, disbound. With 3 litho titles, dedications & 75 plates. Sold w.a.f. Ck nov 21 (359) £320

Anr copy. Series 1-4 in 4 vols. Folio, contemp cloth; worn. With 100 plates. Some fraying & marginal spotting. Ck Feb 27 (164) £280

Anr copy. Series 1 & 2. 2 vols. Folio, disbound. With tinted litho title & 50 plates. Sold w.a.f. Ck Feb 27 (198) £130

Anr Ed. L, 1869-72. 4 vols. Folio, orig cloth; broken. With 104 plates. Litho titles in Vols I & IV torn & frayed; 5 other plates soiled & frayed in margins. L July 2 (96) £110

Anr copy. 4 vols in 2. Folio, mor gilt by Sotheran. With 104 colored plates. L July 2 (97) £600

Anr copy. In 4 vols. Folio, orig cloth. pn Apr 30 (58) £130 [Shapero]

— Views of the Interior and Exterior of Windsor Castle. L, 1848. Folio, modern half calf. With colored title & 25 colored plates. Tp cropped at head & with small stain at margin; plates mtd on card with Ms captions in margins & guarded throughout; last plate torn at foot & slightly def at corner. C Oct 15 (78) £400 [Brewin]

Nash, Paul, 1889-1946. See: Postan, Alexander

Nash, Thomas, 1588-1648
— Quaternio, or a Fourefold Way to a Happie Life. L, 1633. 1st Ed, 1st Issue. 4to, contemp calf; covers stained, spine def. Some dampstaining; a little worming in 2 corners, affecting 3 letters of text. S July 23 (14) £360 [Lawson]

Nast, Thomas
— Christmas Drawings for the Human Race. NY, 1890 [1889]. 1st Ed. 4to, cloth; soiled, foot of spine torn. With 60 plates. sg June 4 (224) $175

Natalis, Hieronymus
— Evangelicae historiae imagines. Antwerp, 1593. Bound with Adnotationes et meditationes.... Antwerp, 1595. Folio, 18th-cent mor extra. Some plates in 1st work thumbed, 1 rehinged, 3 trimmed & mtd, 1 prelim leaf possibly lacking; last leaf of 2d work rehinged & remargined. sg Oct 9 (279) $400

Anr Ed. Antwerp: [Martinus Nutius?], 1593. Folio, 17th-cent mor gilt, armorial bdg. With 152 (of 155) plates. HK Nov 4 (692) DM1,750

National...
— National Antarctic Expedition, 1901-1904: Natural History. L, 1907-10. One of 25 on special paper. Vol II (of 6) only. 4to, cloth; dampstained. With 35 plates. Haverschmidt copy. B Feb 24 (319) HF420

— The National Gallery of Pictures of the Great Masters. L: Jones & Co., [c.1840]. 2 vols. 4to, mor gilt by Chambolle-Duru. With 2 engraved titles, frontis & 114 plates. Lacking ptd title. sg Feb 12 (242) $350

— National Geographic Magazine. Wash., 1940-54. Vols 77-106. 30 vols plus Indexes for 1899-1963 & 4 files with maps. B June 2 (1129) HF850

National Library of Medicine. See: Durling, Richard J.

Natrus, Leendert van —& Others
— Groot volkomen moolenboek; of naauwkeurig Ontwerp, van allerhande tot nog toe bekende soorten van moolens. Amst., 1734-36. Folio, bdg not indicated. Library markings. Sold w.a.f. Franklin Institute copy. F Sept 12 (343) $1,100

Natura...
— Natura Brevium.... L: Richard Tottel, 1580. ("La Vieux Natura brevium, dernierment corrigee....") 8vo, contemp blind-stamped calf; worn, backstrip def. STC 18401. bba Sept 25 (2) £140 [Meyer Boswell]

Natural...

— The Natural History of Birds, from the Works of the Best Authors.... Bungay, 1815. Vol II only. Later half lea; worn. Sold w.a.f. O Mar 24 (131) $240

Naude, Gabriel, 1600-53
— Instructions Concerning Erecting of a Library.... L, 1661. Trans by John Evelyn. 8vo, old calf; rebacked, corner off front free endpaper. sg Mar 26 (213) $1,600

Naumann, Johann Andreas, 1747-1826
— Naturgeschichte der Voegel Deutschlands. Leipzig, 1822-60. 13 vols. Contemp half lea. B Feb 24 (378) HF700
— Naturgeschichte der Voegel Mitteleuropas. Gera-Untermhaus: Koehler, [1895]-97-1905. 12 vols. Folio, orig bdg. With 10 plain & 439 colored lithos. B Feb 24 (421) HF3,100

Anr copy. 12 vols text & 3 portfolios of plates. Folio, contemp half cloth; 1 spine chipped at head; short splits in portfolios. With 10 plain & 429 color plates. A few text leaves creased & with small marginal tears in Vol IX. S Oct 23 (741) £2,000 [Dorge]

Naunton, Sir Robert, 1563-1635
— Fragmenta regalia. [L], 1641. 4to, 19th-cent calf. Each leaf inlaid to folio & bound with port of Queen Elizabeth I & 22 ports of her statesmen & courtiers & with an AD of Prime Minister Burleigh. F Jan 15 (345) $230

Naval...
— The Naval Achievements of Great Britain.... L: James Jenkins, 1817 [plates watermarked 1812-17]. 4to, mor gilt; rebacked. With engraved title, 2 hand-colored ports, uncolored plan (detached) & 55 hand-colored plates. C Oct 15 (53) £3,800 [Sifton Pread]

Anr Ed. L: James Jenkins, 1817 [plates watermarked 1812-16]. 4to, disbound; worn. With engraved title & 55 hand-colored plates. Lacking list of subscribers & 2 ports. pn Apr 30 (123A) £3,600 [Burgess]

Anr Ed. L: J. Jenkins, [watermarked 1835]. 4to, contemp half mor; sides rubbed. With engraved title & 55 hand-colored plates. Lacking list of subscribers & uncolored plan. C Oct 15 (124) £3,400 [Scott Sandilands]

— Naval Anecdotes: Illustrating the Character of British Seamen.... L, 1806. 8vo, later half calf; worn. O June 9 (122) $50

— Naval Documents related to the Quasi-War between the United States and France.... Wash., 1935-38. 7 vols. cb Dec 18 (138) $160

AMERICAN BOOK PRICES CURRENT

Naville, Henri Edouard
— The Temple of Deir el Bahara. L, [1895]-1908. Text, plus 3 vols of plates; together, 4 vols. Folio, half cloth. cb Nov 6 (118) $200

Nayler, Sir George
— The Coronation of His Most Sacred Majesty King George the Fourth.... L, 1839. Folio, mor gilt by J. Wright. With 40 hand-colored plates heightened with gold, 3 uncolored plans, engraved title with hand-colored vignette & colored explanatory key plate. C Apr 8 (41) £2,800 [Woodruff]

Neale, Adam, d.1832
— Travels through some Parts of Germany, Poland, Moldavia, and Turkey. L, 1818. 4to, contemp calf gilt; rebacked in calf, corners worn. Some foxing. pnE Jan 28 (75) £240 [McNaughton]

Neale, John Preston
— Views of the Seats of Noblemen and Gentlemen.... L, 1818-23. 1st Series only. 6 vols. 4to, contemp russia gilt; spines def, some cover detached. S Nov 10 (807) £360 [Boyd]

Anr Ed. L, 1822-29. First Series only. 6 vols. 8vo, contemp half lea; worn, spines def. L.p. copy. S Nov 17 (671) £320 [Roberts]

Neamet Ullah. See: Ni'mat Allah

Nebrija, Antonio de, 1444-1532
— Ex grammatico rhetoris...atque Historici Regii Apologia. Granada: Nebrija, 1535. Bound with: Melendez de Valdes, Franciscus. Exhortatio. [Granada?] 1544. 4to, half cloth S Nov 27 (202) £2,200 [De Zayas].
— Opuscula quae in hoc volumine continentus sunt haec: Passio domini hexametris versibus composita.... Logrono: Miguel Eguia, 13 Aug 1528. 8vo, old vellum. Some stains & browning. sg Oct 9 (63) $450
— Rerum a Fernando & Elisabe Hispaniarum.... Granada, 1550. 8vo, 19th-cent half lea. sg Oct 9 (62) $225

Necker, Jacques, 1732-1804
— Comte rendu au roi.... Paris, 1781. 4to, contemp half calf. With 1 folding table & 1 hand-colored folding map. S Nov 27 (205) £200 [Dreesman]

Nederlandsche...
— Nederlandsche Bloemwerk, door een Gezelschap geleerden. Amst., 1794. 4to, orig bds; spine worn. With engraved title & 53 hand-colored plates. S Apr 23 (45) £4,200 [Israel]

Needham, Paul
— Twelve Centuries of Bookbindings 400-1600. NY, [1979]. 4to, cloth, in d/j. O June 9 (123) $90

Nees von Esenbeck, Theodor Friedrich Ludwig —& Others
— Plantae officinales oder Sammlung officineller Pflanzen. Duesseldorf, [1821]-28. 3 vols plus Supplement in 2 vols. Folio, half calf & half cloth bdgs. With 545 (of 552) colored plates. HK Nov 4 (1077) DM9,000

Anr copy. 3 vols. Folio, half calf; worn. With engraved title, 5 plain & 387 colored plates only. Some soiling & foxing; a few leaves loose. JG Mai 20 (552) DM4,000

Anr copy. 6 vols, including 1833 Supplement. Folio, contemp half calf; rubbed, text in half cloth. With 552 plates, most hand-colored. A few plates with tears, mostly marginal; occasional dampstaining. S Apr 23 (51) £5,200 [Walford]

Anr copy. 4 vols, including 1833 Supplement. Folio, contemp half mor; rubbed. With 552 hand-colored & 6 plain plates & with 3 litho titles (1 mtd & all with rubber stamps). Numerous marginal tears & repairs, affecting figure on 1 plate. Horticultural Society of New York—de Belder copy. S Apr 28 (256) £3,200 [Rainer]

Nees von Esenbeck, Theodor Friedrich Ludwig —& Sinning, Wilhelm
— Sammlund schoenbluehender gewaechse fuer Blumen- und Gartenfreunde nach lebenden Examplaren des K. Botanischengartens zu Bonn gezeichnet.... Duesseldorf, [1823]-31. 10 parts in 2 vols. Folio, contemp half calf; rubbed, orig wraps to Parts 1-4 bound in. With 100 hand-colored plates. One plate torn at outer margin; a number with outer margins strengthened or repaired. de Belder copy. S Apr 28 (255) £13,000 [Israel]

Neill, John R.
— Lucky Bucky in Oz. Chicago: Reilly & Lee, [1942]. cb Dec 4 (43) $80

The Scalawagons of Oz. Chicago: Reilly & Lee, [1941]. cb Dec 4 (44) $110

— The Wonder City of Oz. Chicago: Reilly & Lee, [1940]. In chipped d/j. cb Dec 4 (45) $110

Nelson, Edward William, 1855-1934
— Report upon Natural History Collections made in Alaska.... Wash., 1887. 4to, orig cloth; chipped. With 9 plain & 12 colored plates. wa Sept 25 (295) $75

Nelson, Horatio Nelson, Viscount, 1758-1805.
See: Golden Cockerel Press

Nelson, James
— An Essay on the Government of Children. L, 1753. 8vo, contemp calf gilt; hinges cracked. T Oct 16 (494) £220

Nelson, John, of Islington
— The History and Antiquities of the Parish of Islington.... L, 1829. 3d Ed. 8vo, modern half sheep; rubbed. Extra-illus with plates & Ms notes. bba May 14 (419) £120 [Dyson]

Neptune...
— Le Neptune francois, ou atlas marine nouveau. Amst., 1693-94. ("De Fransche Naptunus.") 2 parts in 1 vol (Part 2 being Romein de Hooge's Zee Atlas). Folio, contemp calf gilt with onlaid panel with Atlas device centerpiece. With engraved title, table of comparative nautical scales, 3 shipping plates, 29 double-page charts & 9 charts by de Hooge, all hand-colored & with heighteneing in gold. Faint stain on Mediterranean chart; 1 shipping plate damaged by adhesion. S June 25 (291) £15,000 [Martinos]

Neralco, Pastore Arcade, Pseud.
— I Tre Ordini d'Architettura dorico, ionico e corintio.... Rome, 1744. Folio, contemp half calf; spine wormed. sg apr 2 (78) $1,600

Neri, Antonio
— Art de la verrerie. Paris, 1752. 4to, contemp calf; spine worn & def. With 16 plates. bba July 16 (156) £220 [Thorp]

Nericault-Destouches, Philippe, 1680-1754
— Oeuvres. Amst. & Leipzig, 1755-59. 5 vols. 12mo, mor gilt by Zaehnsdorf. With port, frontis & 23 plates. C May 13 (38) £200 [Head]

— Oeuvres dramatiques. Paris, 1822. One of 80 on grand raisin velin. 6 vols. 8vo, half mor. Extra-illus with 30 orig drawings by Baudet-Bauderval, a port & 9 plates, eaux-forte, by Fragonard fils & 76 other ports & plates. C Dec 3 (150) £400 [Tenschert]

Nescio, Pseud.
— Dichtertje, De uitvreter, Titaantjes. Haarlem: J. H. de Bois, [1918]. Orig half cloth; inner joint cracking. B Oct 7 (673) HF550

Nettle, Richard
— The Salmon Fisheries of the St. Lawrence and its Tributaries. Montreal, 1857. 8vo, orig cloth. Lacking front endpaper. sg Oct 23 (407) $50

Neue...

— Neue Berliner Schachzeitung. Berlin, 1864-71. Vols 1-8 (all pbd). pn Mar 26 (189) £440 [Adams]

Neu-entsprungene...

— Neu-entsprungene Wasser-Quelle vor Gottes ergebene und geistlich-durstige Seelen. Goettingen: J. H. Schmiedt, 1676. 12mo, 18th-cent silver over shagreen. bba Sept 25 (249) £320 [Maggs]

Neugebauer, Salomon

— Historia rerum polonicarum. Hannover, 1618. 4to, contemp vellum bds. Stamp of Prince Czartoryski on tp verso. S June 25 (45) £300

— Selectorum symbolorum heroicorum centuria. Frankfurt, 1619. 8vo, later half vellum; rubbed. Engraved title cropped. bba Oct 16 (14) £130 [Robertshaw]

Neumann, Caspar, 1683-1737

— The Chemical Works.... L, 1759. 4to, contemp calf; rubbed, spine worn at extremities. Sgd by Matthew Boulton. C Dec 12 (156) £450 [Mackenzie]

Neumann, Gustav Richard, 1838-81 —& Arnous de Riviere, J.

— Le Jeu des echecs. Paris: Delarue, 1868. Cloth. pn Mar 26 (461) £35 [Hoffman]

Neustadt, Egon

— The Lamps of Tiffany. NY: Fairfield Press, [1970]. Ltd Ed. Folio, cloth, in chipped d/j. wa Sept 25 (282) $170

Anr copy. With extra suite of 16 color plates. wa Nov 6 (496) $180

Neve, Richard

— The City and Country Purchaser's and Builder's Dictionary. L, 1736. 3d Ed. 8vo, contemp calf; rebacked. bba Mar 26 (59) £120 [RIBA]

Neves, Diocleciano Fernandes das

— A Hunting Expedition to the Transvaal. L, 1879. 8vo, cloth; worn. Library markings; worm-holed with 1 hole affecting 1st 8 pages. SSA Oct 28 (505) R360

Nevill, Ralph

— British Military Prints. L, 1909. 4to, cloth; faded, worn & soiled. wa Nov 6 (461) $80

— Old English Sporting Books. L, 1924. One of 1,500. 4to, orig cloth. pnE Jan 28 (285) £80 [McEwan]

Neville, Alexander White

— The Red River Valley; Then and Now. Paris TX: Hertzog, 1948. Illus by Jose Cisneros. In d/j. Inscr by Neville, also sgd by Cisneros. sg Sept 18 (194) $100

New...

See also: Dickson, R. W.; Latham, Simon

— A New and Accurate Account of the Provinces of South-Carolina and Georgia. L, 1732. 8vo, wraps. Some headlines shaved. S June 25 (399) £1,600

— A New Book of Instruments. L: for William Jacobs & T. Dring, 1680. 2 parts in 1 vol. Contemp calf; rubbed. Tp soiled. Ck Sept 5 (196) £400

— New Discoveries Concerning the World and its Inhabitants.... L, 1778. 1st Ed. 2 parts in 1 vol. 8vo, modern half calf. kh Mar 16 (9B) A$380

— A New Riddle Book for Good Boys and Girls. Gainsborough, 1802. 32mo, orig bds; lacking backstrip. S Dec 5 (286) £180

— The New Royal Primer, or an Easy and Pleasant Guide to the ARt of Reading. L: J. Fuller, [c.1765]. 24mo, orig bds; loose, lacking lower cover. Some shaving at outer mragin of 2 leaves. S June 17 (476) £1,500 [Randolph]

New Charge...

— A New Charge given by the Queenes Commandement, to all Justices of Peace...for Execution of Sundry Orderes Published Last Yeere for the Staie of dearth of Graine.... L: Deputies of Christopher Barker, 1595. 4to, wraps. Black letter. Side-notes shaved. S July 24 (439) £420 [Lawson]

New England Primer

— 1776. - New-England Primer Improved.... Paisley: A. Weir. 16mo, wraps; worn, restitched. Stained. S Dec 5 (332) £1,500 [Quaritch]

New Hampshire

— The Act of Incorporation, Constitution, and By-Laws, of the New-Hampshire Historical Society.... Concord, 1823. 8vo, lea; backstrip chipped & scuffed. ha Sept 19 (177) $80

New Jersey

— Acts of the Council and General Assembly. Trenton: Isaac Collins, 1784. Folio, contemp half calf; worn. Ccc1 & Ccc2 replaced with contemp blank leaves; A1-K1 dampstained; brittle at fore-edges, with small wormholes; stains on some other leaves. sg Sept 18 (197) $120

— Acts of the General Assembly of the Province of New Jersey, 17 April 1702 to 14 January 1776. Burlington, 1776. Compiled by Samuel Allinson. Folio, contemp calf; worn, front cover detached. Ms annotations in margins; some foxing. sg Sept 18 (196) $120

— Atlas of Monmouth County. NY: Beers, Comstock & Cline, 1873. Folio, contemp

bds; rebacked. With hand-colored maps of New Jersey, Monmouth County & 65 maps of townships, towns & villages. 3 maps repaired; some tears. wa Nov 6 (626) $260
— Atlas of the City of Plainfield, Union County, and Borough of North Plainfield, Somerset County, New Jersey. Plainfield: Dunham, 1894. Folio, orig half lea; worn, spine lacking. With 12 double-page colored maps & index map. With 2 zone maps of Plainfield, 1921 & c.1945, laid in. Maps backed. wa Nov 6 (621) $65
— Combination Atlas Map of Middlesex County New Jersey. Phila., 1876. Folio, orig half lea; worn, lacking spine. With hand-colored Railroad map & 36 other maps. Some edges soiled & worn. wa Nov 6 (630) $200
— County Atlas of Warren.... NY: Beers, 174. Folio, orig half lea; worn, hinges cracked. With 60 maps, 3 double-page, all hand-colored. wa Nov 6 (627) $160

Anr copy. Orig half lea; front cover nearly detached. wa Nov 6 (628) $200

— Historical and Biographical Atlas of the New Jersey Coast. Phila.: Woolman & Rose, 1878. Folio, orig half lea; worn & stained. With 44 maps & 76 views. wa Nov 6 (631) $400

Anr copy. Orig half lea; worn, broken, with all pp loose. With 43 (of 44) maps & 75 (of 76) views. wa Nov 6 (632) $130

New York (City)
— Atlas of New York and Vicinity.... NY, 1867. Folio, orig half lea; worn & soiled. With 50 color maps. Endpaper, title, contents leaf & State map wrinkled & torn. wa Mar 5 (320) $170

Anr copy. Orig half lea; worn & stained, joints cracked. With 62 hand-colored maps. Some tape-repairs; several maps stained. wa Mar 5 (321) $260

Anr Ed. NY, 1873. Folio, half lea. With 52 single-page maps, 35 double-page maps & 10 folding maps, principal areas fully hand-colored. Apparently lacking pp 84-85; some tears in margins. sg Apr 23 (159) $300

— An Index to the Illustrations in the Manuals of the Corporation of the City of New York 1841-1870. NY: Society of Iconophiles, 1906. One of 250. 8vo, orig cloth. sg Sept 18 (209) $50
— New York Illustrated. NY, 1881. 8vo, contemp half mor gilt; rubbed & soiled. bba Oct 16 (239) £40 [Cape]
— Robinson's Atlas of the City of New York. NY, 1885. Folio, orig half lea; worn & soiled, spine shabby. With 42 double-page, hand-colored maps. wa Nov 6 (637) $90

New York (Colony & State)
— Atlas of Nassau County, Long Island, N.Y. Brooklyn, 1914. Folio, half lea; bdcoming disbound. With 120 maps, hand-colored in outline. Pencil notes & soiling to 10 maps; 1 map detached at centerfold line. sg Apr 23 (183) $140
— Atlas of Niagara and Orleans Counties.... Phila.: Beers et al, 1875. Folio, cloth; broken & worn. Some soiling. O Sept 23 (10) $70
— Atlas of the Hudson River Valley.... NY, 1891. Folio, orig half lea; worn, joints splitting. With Index map & 35 double-page colored maps, all hand-colored. wa Nov 624 $160
— First Annual Report of the Commissioners of Fisheries, Game and Forests.... Albany, 1896. 4to, cloth. With 13 color plates. sg Oct 23 (408) $150
— Journal of the Votes and Proceedings of the General Assembly of the Colony of New York NY, 1764-66. 2 vols. Folio, modern half calf gilt. pnNY Sept 13 (265) $275
— Laws of New-York, from the Year 1691, to 1751.... NY, 1752. Folio, modern half mor. Lacks leaf following title & 8 Ordinance pp. With errata leaf. sg Mar 12 (196) $350

Newberry, Arthur St. John
— A Fisherman's Paradise. Cleveland: Pvtly Ptd, [1914]. One of 150. Worn. sg Oct 23 (411) $80

Newbolt, Sir Henry John, 1862-1938
— Drake's Drum, and other Songs of the Sea. [L, 1914]. One of 250 L.p. copies, sgd by the artist. Illus by A. D. McCormick. 4to, orig vellum gilt; soiled. With 12 color plates. S Oct 6 (830) £60 [Cavendish]

Newcastle, William Cavendish, Duke of
— A General System of Horsemanship. L, 1743. 2 vols. Folio, contemp calf gilt; rubbed, joints cracked. With 62 plates. A few plates with short splits at foot of centerfold; 1 plate torn. C Apr 8 (141) £2,600 [Traylen]

Anr copy. Contemp calf; worn. With double-page engraved title & 62 plates, 44 double-page. Guarded throughout; Vol I with tear repaired in Plate 36 & a few plates wormed at end; marginal worming & dampstaining in Vol II; last leaf creased. S Apr 23 (69) £2,700 [Traylen]

Newhouse, C. B.
— The Roadster's Album. L, 1845. Folio, half mor; soiled. With hand-colored title & 16 hand-colored views, each heightened with gum arabic. Tp & final plate slightly spotted. S Oct 23 (184) £3,200 [Ross]

Newman, Frederick
— The Curiosities and Beauties of England Displayed. L: Alex. Hogg, [c.1790]. Folio, old sheep; spine def. With frontis & 280 views on 106 sheets. pn July 23 (180) £170 [Howell-Williams]

Anr copy. Contemp calf; broken. With frontis & 102 plates. tp creased & torn; frontis detached & frayed; marginal dampstains. Sold w.a.f. T Oct 16 (323) £95

Newman, John Henry, Cardinal, 1801-90
— The Dream of Gerontius. L, 1866. 16mo, orig blind-panelled brown cloth, variant bdg (see John Carter in The Book Collector, Summer, 1956). C Dec 12 (351) £700 [Burmester]

Newman, Neil. See: Derrydale Press

Newton, Alfred Edward, 1863-1940
— Derby Day and Other Adventures. Bost., 1934. 1st Ed. O June 9 (124) $60
— End Papers. Bost., 1933. One of 1,351 L.p. copies. Inscr. O June 9 (125) $60
— Mr. Strahan's Dinner Party. San Francisco: Book Club of California, 1930. One of 350. Half cloth. cb Sept 11 (58) $65
— This Book-Collecting Game. Bost., 1928. One of 990, sgd. Half cloth; worn. O June 9 (126) $60; sg June 11 (300) $80

Newton, Sir Charles Thomas, 1816-94
— Travels and Discoveries in the Levant. L, 1865. 2 vols. 8vo, orig cloth; rubbed, 1 joint torn. With 44 plates & maps. S Feb 23 (99) £100 [Ash]

Anr copy. Orig cloth; rubbed, hinges cracked. sg Nov 13 (13) $60

Anr copy. Orig cloth; hinges cracked. With 9 maps & plans & 32 plates. sg Nov 20 (134) $50

Newton, Sir Isaac, 1642-1727
— The Chronology of Ancient Kingdoms Amended.... L, 1728. 1st Ed. 4to, later half calf. Hole affecting inner margins of early leaves. Ck Feb 13 (80) £80

Anr copy. Contemp bds; rebacked, worn. With 3 folding plates; title dusted & with some ink splotches. Henry Thomas Buckle's copy. ha Dec 19 (97) $325
— The Mathematical Principles of Natural Philosophy. L, 1729. 1st Ed in English. Trans by Andrew Motte. 2 vols. 8vo, contemp calf; hinges cracked. With 47 folding plates. Lacking the 2 frontises. S May 29 (1230) £200

Anr Ed. L, 1803. Trans by Motte. 3 vols. 8vo, calf; rebacked. Vol II with brown stain on blank margin. bba Apr 9 (433) £35 [Elliott]
— Observations upon the Prophecies of Dan-

iel.... L, 1733. 1st Ed. 2 parts in 1 vol. 4to, contemp calf; worn, repaired & rebacked. S May 28 (751) £60
— Opticks.... L, 1718. 2d Ed, 2d Issue. 8vo, contemp calf; rebacked. Lacking 3 prelim leaves. C May 13 (203) £160 [Tovey]

4th Ed. L, 1730. 8vo, old calf; worn. With 12 folding plates. Title repaired with adhesive tape at inner margin; browned. Ck Apr 24 (129) £110
— Philosophiae naturalis principia mathematica. Cambr., 1713. 2d Ed. 4to, blind-stamped calf; worn. Some marginal notes, mostly in pencil. C. V. L. Charlier's copy with holograph notes inserted. pn Dec 11 (347) £1,650 [Rota]

Anr Ed. Geneva, 1760. 3 vols. 4to, contemp calf; rubbed. A few leaves discolored. S Nov 27 (106) £320 [Quaritch]
[-] TELESCOPE, TOM. - The Newtonian System of Philosophy. L, 1798. 12mo, orig bds; broken & worn. With 5 plates. O Apr 28 (147) $50

Newton, John, 1622-78
— Cosmographia, or a View of the Terrestrial and Coelestial Globes.... L, 1679. 8vo, contemp calf; rebacked. Some cropping at fore-edge, affecting 2 plates. T Sept 18 (361) £90

Nichol, John
— Byron. L, 1880. 8vo, mor gilt extra by Riviere with inlaid miniature port. Extra-illus with 26 additional plates. Sold w.a.f. CNY Dec 19 (217) $850

Nicholles, John
— The Teeth in Relation to Beauty, Voice and Health. L, 1833. 8vo, orig cloth; broken. Old stamp on tp. sg Jan 15 (86) $100

Nicholls, William Henry
— Orchids of Australia.... Melbourne, 1951. 4to, half mor bdg from Parts 1-3 of the orig Ed. kh Mar 16 (380) A$170

Nichols, John, 1745-1826
— Biographical and Literary Anecdotes of William Bowyer.... L, 1782. 1st Ed. 4to, contemp calf; rubbed, joints split. bba Apr 9 (460) £120 [Frew Mackenzie]
— The Progresses, and Public Processions of Queen Elizabeth. L, 1788-1805. 1st Ed. 3 vols. 4to, contemp calf; rebacked. Library markings. T Mar 19 (317) £210

Nicholson, William, 1753-1815
— The British Encyclopaedia or Dictionary of Arts and Sciences. L, 1807-9. 7 vols. 8vo, contemp calf; rubbed. Ck June 5 (60) £200
— An Introduction to Natural Philosophy. L, 1787. 2 vols. 8vo, contemp calf. With 25 folding plates. S May 28 (752) £160

Nicholson, William, 1872-1949
— An Alphabet. L, 1898. 4to, orig half cloth; worn, lacking front free endpaper. Ck Dec 10 (280A) £120; pn May 21 (209) £160 [Leadley]

Anr copy. Orig half cloth; worn, backstrip damaged. sg June 4 (229) $175

Deluxe issue, with each leaf inserted between brown art paper. Orig cloth; spine def, upper cover slightly stained. bba May 14 (158) £240 [Subunso]

— The Book of Blokes. L, [1929]. Orig bds; soiled. wa Dec 11 (636) $110
— London Types, Quatorzains by W. E. Henley. L, 1898. 4to, orig half cloth; worn. With 12 colored plates. HN Nov 26 (2020) DM750; pn Sept 18 (234) £140, [West]

Anr copy. Later cloth with orig pictorial upper cover pasted on. S Oct 6 (838) £85 [Manheim]

Anr Ed. NY, 1898. 4to, orig half cloth. With 12 colored plates. B Oct 7 (281) HF550; sg Jan 8 (173) $80

Nickson, Geoffrey
— A Portrait of Salmon Fishing. Rugby: Anthony Atha, [1976]. One of 200. Oblong 4to, mor gilt. With 37 color plates. sg Oct 23 (412) $600

Nicolas, Sir Nicholas Harris
— History of the Orders of Knighthood of the British Empire. L, 1842. 4 vols. 4to, contemp calf; rubbed. With engraved title, 4 ports & 21 plates, colored by hand & heightened with gold. S July 14 (540) £280

Nicolaus de Lyra, 1270?-1340?
— Postilla super totam Bibliam. Rome: C. Sweynheym & A. Pannartz, 1471-72. Vols I only (of 5). Folio, modern half vellum. Large capitals in blue with penwork decoration in red, other capitals in red or blue. Sold w.a.f. 331 (of 452) leaves only. Goff N-131. bba Oct 30 (218) £560 [Smallwood]

Anr Ed. Venice: [B. Locatellus] for O. Scotus, 9 Aug 1488. Vol III only. Folio, modern half sheep. Some marginal staining throughout; lacking initial & final blanks. 326 (of 328) leaves; lacking initial & final blanks. Goff N-132. sg Mar 26 (214A) $550

— Postilla super epistolas et evangelia quadragesimalia.... Ferrara: Laurentius de Rubeis de Valentia, 10 Mar 1490. 4to, modern half calf. Minor worming to 1st few leaves; small repair to fore-margin of m3; waterstain to a few margins at the end. 180 leaves. Goff N-117. C Dec 12 (303) £650 [Rivara]

Nicolay, Nicolas de, 1517-83
— Les Navigations, peregrinations, et voyages, faicts en la Turquie. Antwerp, 1576. 4to, later half calf; rubbed. With 47 (of 60) plates. Tp & first & last few leaves wormed; marginal dampstains. Sold w.a.f. bba Aug 20 (486) £140 [Walford]

Anr copy. Later calf; repaired. With 60 plates. Wormhole in lower blank margin throughout; some leaves stained. S Apr 23 (172) £900 [Wood]

Nicoll, Michael J. —& Meinertzhagen, Richard
— Birds of Egypt. L, 1930. 2 vols. 4to, orig cloth; inner hinge weak. Ck Oct 31 (159) £200

Anr copy. Orig cloth; soiled. With 37 plates, 31 colored & with 3 colored folding maps. S Nov 10 (542) £170 [Palace]

Nicolson, Harold
— Some People. L, 1927. In d/j. sg Dec 11 (345) $60

Nicolson, Joseph —& Burn, Richard
— The History and Antiquities of the Counties of Westmorland and Cumberland. L, 1777. 2 vols. 4to, contemp half calf; worn, rebacked. With 2 folding maps. bba Dec 4 (344) £60 [Smith]

Niebuhr, Barthold Georg
— The Greek Heroes. L, 1910. Illus by Arthur Rackham. With 4 color plates. Interior spotted & soiled; several pp loose. sg Oct 30 (163) $110

Niebuhr, Carsten, 1733-1815
— Beschreibung von Arabien aus eigenen Beobachtungen. Copenhagen, 1772. 1st Ed. 4to, contemp calf gilt; rubbed. With folding map hand-colored in outline, & 24 plates & maps, 2 colored. S Oct 23 (120) £600 [Koch]
— Description de l'Arabie. Amst. & Utrecht, 1774. 4to, contemp calf gilt; rubbed, corners showing. With 25 plates & maps. cb Feb 19 (205) $225
— Reisebeschreibung nach Arabien und andern umliegenden Landern. Copenhagen, 1774-78. 4to, contemp calf gilt; rubbed. With folding map (hand-colored in outline) & 124 plates & maps. S Oct 23 (121) £650 [Koch]
— Reize naar Arabie en andere omliggende landen. Amst. & Utrecht, 1776-80. 2 vols. 4to, contemp half calf; worn. With engraved titles, folding map of Yemen & 124 maps & plates, many folding. One plate repaired at inner margin; anr plate browned; hole in Dd4 of Vol I with loss. S Apr 24 (233) £700 [Hagstrom]

NIEBUHR

— Travels through Arabia, and other Countries in the East.... Edin., 1792. 1st Ed in English. 2 vols. 8vo, contemp cal; joints weak. With 3 folding maps & 10 plates. bba May 28 (260) £190 [Wagner]

Anr copy. Contemp cal; rubbed, rebacked. With 3 folding maps & 9 plates. Maps cropped & torn; 1 plate torn at upper blank margin; A4 in Vol I repaired at inner margin. S July 14 (873) £190

— Voyage en Arabie et en d'autres pays de l'orient. Amst: J. S. Baalde, 1780. 2 vols. 8vo, contemp calf gilt; rubbed. With 135 plates & maps. cb Feb 19 (206) $375

Niedeck, Paul
— Kreuzfahrten im Beringmeer. Berlin, 1907. sg Nov 20 (139) $50

Nielsen, Lauritz Martin
— Dansk typografisk atlas, 1482-1600. Copenhagen, 1934. Folio, orig half vellum bds. sg May 14 (507) $110

Nieremberg, Joannes Eusebius, 1595?-1658
— Historia naturae maxime peregrinae libris XVI distincta.... Antwerp: Plantin, 1635. Folio, contemp blind-stamped pigskin over wooden bds with 2 clasps. Horticultural Society of New York—de Belder copy. S Apr 28 (257) £2,000 [Bjork]

Niesenwurzel, Paul Arthur Amadeus. See: Grabhorn Printing

Nietzsche, Friedrich Wilhelm, 1844-1900
See also: Mussolini, Benito
— Goetzen-Daemmerung oder wie man mit dem Hammer philosophirt. Leipzig, 1889. 8vo, cloth; rubbed & stained. Repair along inner margin of title; marginal browning; stitching loose following title & p 142. P Sept 24 (198) $175

Nieuhoff, Jan
— An Embassy from the East-India Company of the United Provinces, to the Grand Tartar Cham, Emperor of China.... L, 1669. 1st Ed in English. Folio, contemp calf; worn, joints cracked. With engraved title & 18 plates. Lacking port, map & 1 plate; occasional small tears. Sold w.a.f. C Dec 12 (252) £350 [Sweet]

Anr copy. Contemp calf gilt with Evelyn arms. With port, engraved title, double-page map & 19 plates. Lower marginal tears at Cc1-2 touching letters; inner marginal waterstain towards end. S Oct 23 (491) £1,700 [Duchauffor]

— Die Gesantschaft der Ost-Indischen Geselschaft in den Vereinigten Niederlaendern, an den Tartarischen Cham.... Amst., 1669. Folio, contemp vellum; soiled. With engraved title, port, folding map of China & 34 double-page plates.

Some tears & stains. S Feb 23 (258) £500 [Quaritch]

— Het gezantschap der Neerlandtsche Oost-Indische Compagnie.... Amst., 1665. Folio, contemp calf; upper joints cracked, extremities worn. With 2 engraved plates of coats-of-arms, engraved port & 33 (of 35) engraved double-page plates. Sold w.a.f. CNY Dec 19 (211) $550

Nieuwe...
See also: Leth, Hendrik de
— De Nieuwe Gemeenschap. Hilversum, 1934-36. Years I-III in orig parts; lacking Part 8/9 of Vol III. 4to, orig wraps. B Oct 7 (176) HF220

Nieuwenkamp, Wijnand Otto Jan, 1874-1950
— Oude Hollandsche steden aan de Zuiderzee. Haarlem, 1897. 4to, orig wraps. B Oct 7 (29) HF400

Nieuwentijdt, Bernard
— L'Existence de Dieu demontree par les mervilles de la nature.... Paris, 1725. 4to, half sheep gilt. With 28 (of 29) folding plates. Owner's stamp on tp. sg Jan 15 (334) $100

Nifo, Agostino
— Philosophorum hac nostra tempestate Monarche Augustini.... Venice: heirs of Octavianus Scotus, 12 Feb 1518. Folio, early vellum Ms wraps; repaired, new endpapers. S May 21 (60) £250 [Quaritch]

Nightingale, Florence, 1820-1910
— Notes on Nursing.... NY, 1860. 1st American Ed. 12mo, cloth. sg Jan 15 (115) $70

Nightingale, Joseph
— English Topography. L, 1816. Folio, half mor; rubbed. With 58 maps. bba Dec 4 (348) £120 [Smith]

Anr copy. Half calf; def. With 58 hand-colored maps. Middlesex from anr atlas. pn May 21 (382) £340 [Postaprint]

Nijhoff, Martinus, 1894-1953
— Het jaar 1572. Heerenveen: De Blauwe Schuit, 1941. One of 100. Folio, orig bdg; back stained. B Oct 7 (236) HF340

— Holland [en In plaats van foto...]. Heerenveen, 1942. One of 120. 4to, wraps. B Oct 7 (235) HF1,250

Nijhoff, Wouter
— L'Art typographique dans les Pays-Bas. The Hague, 1926-35. Vols I & II. Folio, loose in half cloth portfolio. Sold w.a.f. sg May 14 (508) $100

— Nederlandsche Bibliographie van 1500 tot 1540. The Hague, 1923-40. 3 vols in 7. Contemp half mor. bba Oct 16 (393) £160 [Maggs]

Ni'mat Allah
— History of the Afghans, translated from the Persian of Neamet Ullah by Bernhard Dorn. L, 1829-36. 2 vols. 4to, wraps & cloth. pn Dec 11 (113) £170 [Hosain]

Nimmo, Joseph, Jr., 1837-1909
— Report on the Internal Commerce of the United States.... Wash., 1885. 8vo, recent half lea. With 5 folding maps. Bound with anr work, identified as H. R. Ex. Doc 7, Pt 2, which has 2 folding maps. cb Mar 19 (206) $1,300

Nimrod. See: Apperley, Charles J.

Nin, Anais
— Cities of the Interior. Denver: Alan Swallow, [1959]. Cloth by Ian Hugo. Inscr. sg Mar 5 (193) $70
— D. H. Lawrence: an Unprofessional Study. Paris: Black Manikin Press, 1932. 1st Ed, one of 500. In d/j, unopened. S July 13 (162) £50
— The Four-Chambered Heart. nY, [1950]. In chipped d/j. Inscr. sg Mar 5 (194) $100
— House of Incest. NY: Gemor Press, 1947. Inscr. sg Mar 5 (195) $225
— Nuances. [Cambr., Mass.]: San Souci Press, [1970]. 1st Ed, one of 99, sgd. 4to, raw silk by William Ferguson. Inscr. sg Mar 5 (197) $130

Nisbet, Alexander, 1657-1725
— A System of Heraldry.... Edin., 1804. 2d Ed. 2 vols. Folio, later half mor; rubbed. Title of Vol II relaid & prelims repaired with archival tape; internal dampstains. T Feb 19 (541) £60

Nisbet, John
— Our Forests and Woodlands. L, 1900. One of 150. 8vo, cloth. With 12 plates. sg Oct 30 (164) $70

Nissen, Claus
— Die botanische Buchillustration.... Stuttgart, 1951. 2 vols in 1. Folio, cloth. sg May 14 (613) $425
— Die illustrierten Vogelbuecher. Stuttgart, 1953. 4to, orig cloth; rubbed. bba Oct 16 (394) £60 [Hay Cinema]
Anr copy. Orig cloth, in d/j. cba Feb 5 (134) $120

Nivelon, F,
— The Rudiments of Genteel Behavior. [L], 1737. 4to, contemp calf; broken, worn. Lacking engraved title & text. bba July 16 (396) £190 [Crisp]

Niven, Larry
— The Flight of the Horse. NY, 1973. Uncorrected galley proof. Wraps. Sgd. cb Sept 28 (975) $65
— Neutron Star. L: Macdonald, [1969]. In slightly rubbed d/j. cb Sept 28 (982) $100
— Protector. Tisbury: Compton Russell, [1976]. In d/j. cb Sept 28 (987) $110
— The Ringworld Engineers. Huntington Woods, Michigan: Phantasia Press, 1979. One of 500. In d/j. cb Sept 28 (991) $90
Anr Ed. Huntington Woods: Phantasia, 1979. cb Sept 28 (991) $90

Niven, Larry —& Barnes, Steven
— Dream Park. Huntington Woods MI: Phantasia, 1981. One of 600. In d/j. cb Sept 28 (974) $55

Niven, Larry —& Pournelle, Jerry
— Inferno. L, 1977. In d/j. Sgd by both on tp. cb Sept 28 (977) $65
— The Mote in God's Eye. NY, 1974. In d/j with a few short tears. Inscr by Niven & sgd by both. cb Sept 28 (981) $120
— Oath of Fealty. Huntington Woods MI: Phantasia, 1981. One of 750. In d/j. cb Sept 28 (984) $55

Nixon, Howard M.
— Broxbourne Library: Styles and Designs of Bookbindings from the Twelfth to the Twentieth Century. L, 1956. One of 300. 4to, orig half vellum. sg May 14 (128) $900
— Sixteenth-Century Gold-Tooled Bookbindings in the Pierpont Morgan Library. NY, 1971. 4to, cloth; worn. O June 16 (138) $100

Noah, Mordecai M.
— Travels in England, France, Spain, and the Barbary States.... NY & L, 1819. 8vo, orig bds; rebacked. Some stains; small tear at upper edge of tp. sg Apr 30 (52) $275

Noailles, Anna Elisabeth, Comtesse de
— Les Climats. Paris, 1924. One of 125. Illus by F. L. Schmied. 4to, mor extra mosaic bdg by Levitzky. SM Oct 20 (656) FF130,000

Nobbes, Robert
— The Compleat Troller.... L, 1682 [but c.1814]. 8vo, half calf. Library stamps. pnE Dec 17 (310) £110 [Coleby]

Noble, Thomas —& Rose, Thomas
— The Counties of Chester, Derby, Leicester, Lincoln, and Rutland. L, 1836-[37]. 4to, half calf gilt; rubbed. With engraved title & 72 (on 36) plates. L Dec 11 (125) £120

Noble, W. B.
— A Guide to the Watering Places on the Coast between the Exe and the Dart. Teignmouth, 1817. 4 parts in 1 vol. 8vo, contemp half calf; rubbed, rebacked retaining spine. With map (tear repaired) & 15 (of 16) hand-colored plates. Sold w.a.f. S Nov 17 (808) £140 [Vine]

Anr copy. Contemp calf gilt; rubbed. With engraved title & 76 views on 36 plates. S May 28 (887) £180

Noco, Henry —& Others
— Orfeverie civile francaise du XVIe au debut du XIXe siecle. Paris, [c.1927]. 2 vols. Folio, loose as issued in orig cloth. S Nov 10 (138) £100 [Robertshaw]

Nodder, Frederick P. See: Shaw & Nodder

Nodier, Charles, 1780-1844
— Journal de l'expedition des Portes de Fer. Paris, 1844. 8vo, contemp bds; worn. With folding map & 40 plates in india-proof state. sg Apr 23 (3) £150

Noe, Louis Panteleon Jules Amedee, Comte de
— Memoires relatifs a l'expedition anglaise partie du Bengale en 1800.... Paris, 1826. 8vo, modern half mor. With 2 colored fold-out maps & 19 colored plates. sg June 11 (303) $150

Noel, E. B. —& Clark, J. O. M.
— A History of Tennis. Oxford, 1924. 2 vols. 4to, orig cloth. bba Oct 30 (123) £400 [Lumley]

Noel, Theophilus, b.1804
— Autobiography and Reminiscences.... Chicago, 1904. Orig cloth; extremities rubbed. cb Dec 18 (140) $80

Nogaret, Francois Felix
— L'Aristenete francais. Paris, 1897. One of 150. 2 vols. 16mo, mor extra by Chambolle-Duru. Extra-illus with a set of the illusts in eau-forte state & further 2 sets of the illusts in 2 proof states before text. Inserted are 49 orig drawings by Durand. M. L. Claude Lafontaine's copy. C Dec 3 (151) £4,200 [Tenschert]

Noguchi Yone, 1875-1947
— Hiroshige. NY, 1921. One of 750. String-bound wraps. With color frontis & 19 colotype plates. cb Mar 5 (261) $85

Noisette, Louis Claude
— Le Jardin fruitier, histoire et culture des arbres fruitiers.... Paris, 1839. 2d Ed. 2 vols. 8vo, mor gilt by H. Duhayon. With 152 hand-finished color plates. S Apr 28 (258) £5,500 [Luby]

Nolan, Edward Henry
— The Illustrated History of the British Empire in India and the East. L, [1855-57]. Orig 40 parts. 4to, pictorial wraps; worn, frayed, or soiled, a few loose. wa Mar 5 (196) $210
— The Illustrated History of the War Against Russia. L: Virtue, [c.1857]. 2 vols. 8vo, half calf. pnE Nov 12 (261) £40

Nonesuch Press—London
— Bible, The Holy. 1963. 3 vols. pn Mar 5 (176) £75 [Gorlin]
— The Nonesuch Century. 1936. One of 750. pnE Jan 28 (172) £250 [Updike]; S Nov 10 (25) £140 [Cox]; sg Jan 8 (189) $175
— ANACREON. - Poems. 1923. One of 725. Rubbed. cb June 18 (290) $65; sg Jan 8 (177) $60
— BECKFORD, WILLIAM THOMAS. - Vathek. 1929. One of 1,050. cba Feb 5 (218) $55
— BLAKE, WILLIAM. - The Notebook...called the Rossetti Manuscript. 1935. One of 650. cba Feb 5 (219) $60
— BLAKE, WILLIAM. - Pencil Drawings. 1927. One of 1,550. sg Jan 8 (178) $200
— BLAKE, WILLIAM. - Pencil Drawings. 2d Series. 1956. One of 1,440. K June 7 (58) $85; T Oct 15 (89) £48
— BLAKE, WILLIAM. - The Writings. 1925. One of 1,500. 3 vols. B Oct 7 (302) HF320; sg Feb 5 (39) £140
— BURTON, ROBERT. - The Anatomy of Melancholy. 1925. One of 750. pnE Jan 28 (173) £140 [Smith]
— COLERIDGE, SAMUEL TAYLOR. - Selected Poems. 1935. One of 500. Bound in orange vellum gilt by Ernest Ingham at the Fanfare Press. cb Sept 11 (199) $225
— COLLIER, JOHN. - The Devil and All. 1934. One of 1,000. cb Sept 28 (340) $75
— CONGREVE, WILLIAM. - The Complete Works. 1923. One of 75 on handmade paper. 4 vols. sg Jan 8 (180) $150
— DANTE ALIGHIERI. - La Divina Commedia. 1928. One of 1,475. bba Apr 23 (276) £180 [Whetman]; pn Mar 5 (99) £70 [Sotheran]; S May 6 (48) £90 [Thorp]; S July 14 (491) £140; sg Jan 8 (181) $140
— DICKENS, CHARLES. - Works. 1937-38. One of 877. 25 vols including Dickensiana & steel plate pn May 21110 £2,400

Anr copy. 25 vols. S Dec 4 (144) £2,600 [Ross]

Anr copy. With related ephemera. S Dec 4 (145) £2,400 [Maggs]

Anr copy. 25 vols, including prospectus & steel plate S June 18 (348) £2,400 [Old Hall]

Anr copy. 24 vols, including steel plate S June 18 (349) £2,600 [Blackwell]
— DONNE, JOHN. - Complete Poetry and

Selected Prose. 1929. One of 675. cba Feb 5 (222) $50
— DREYFUS, JOHN. - A History of the Nonesuch Press. 1981. One of 950. bba Feb 5 (49) £110 [Whatman]; bba Feb 5 (50) £110 [Forster]

Anr copy. Sgd. cb Feb 5 (136) $150; cb June 18 (292) $110; S Nov 10 (9) £110 [Cox]

Anr copy. In d/j. sg Jan 22 (142) $130

— EVELYN, JOHN. - Directions for the Gardiner at Says-Court. 1932. One of 800. In d/j. sg Jan 8 (182) $100
— FONTENELLE, BERNARD LE BOVIER DE. - A Plurality of Worlds. 1929. One of 1,200. cb Feb 5 (224) $55

Anr copy. Worn. sg Jan 8 (183) $100
— HARVEY, WILLIAM. - The Anatomical Exercises.... 1928. One of 1,450. sg Sept 11 (200) $140; sg Jan 8 (184) $130
— KEYNES, SIR GEOFFREY. - Jane Austen: A Bibliography. 1929. One of 875. bba Apr 23 (28) £65 [Wise]; O Jan 6 (106) $160
— KEYNES, SIR GEOFFREY. - William Hazlitt: A Bibliography. 1931. One of 750. bba Apr 23 (29) £45 [Collinge]
— MELVILLE, HERMAN. - Benito Cereno. 1926. One of 1,650. bba Nov 13 (311) £35 [Henderson]
— MILTON, JOHN. - Poems in English. 1926. One of 1,450. 2 vols. Unopened. pnNY Sept 13 (267) $160; sg Jan 8 (188) $150
— MONTAIGNE, MICHEL EYQUEM DE. - Essays. 1931. One of 1,375. cb Sept 11 (202) $70; wa Dec 11 (337) $130
— PLUTARCH. - The Lives of the Noble Grecians and Romans. 1929-30. One of 1,550. 5 vols. pn Sept 18 (152) £95 [Meynell]; sg Jan 8 (190) $70
— RICKETTS, CHARLES DE SOUSY. - Some Recollections of Oscar Wilde. 1932. One of 800. bba Feb 5 (286) £60 [Clark]; S May 6 (73) £120 [Henderson]
— ROCHESTER, JOHN WILMOT. - Works. 1926. One of 975. pn Sept 18 (151) £55 [Meynell]; pn Nov 20 (104) £80 [Temperley]

Out-of-series copy. cba Feb 5 (228) $100
— SHAKESPEARE, WILLIAM. - The Sonnets. [1928]. Out-of-series copy. With an ALs from Francis Meynell to T.A. Jackson inserted. S Dec 4 (143) £420 [Subun-So]
— SHAKESPEARE, WILLIAM. - Works. 1929-33. One of 1,600. 7 vols. bba Jan 15 (204) £420 [Subunso]; sg Dec 4 (138) $425; wd June 19 (161) $550

Coronation Ed. 1953. 4 vols. bba Dec 4 (160) £85 [West]; S May 6 (75) £65 [Joseph]
— VANBRUGH, SIR JOHN. - Collected Works. 1927. One of 110 on hand-made paper. 4 vols. bba July 16 (364) £140 [Dawson] One of 1,300. HN May 20 (168) DM950
— WALTON, IZAAK. - Works. 1929. One of 1,600. cba Feb 5 (227) $65; sg May 21

(278) $60; wa Sept 25 (92) $95
— WHITE, GILBERT. - The Writings. 1938. One of 850. 2 vols. pnE Jan 28 (175) £320 [Smith]; S July 28 (1131) £380

Nonnius, Ludovicus
— Diatecticon, sive de re cibaria, libri IV. Antwerp, 1645. 2d Ed. 4to, 17th-cent vellum gilt; spine soiled & wormed. Some marginal worming affecting text. S Mar 10 (973) £160 [Phelps]

Norden, Friderik Ludwig
— Travels in Egypt and Nubia.... L, 1757. 1st Ed in English. 2 vols. Folio, cloth; soiled. With port & 162 plates & maps Pages brittle. bba Dec 18 (202) £320 [Rainer]

Anr copy. Contemp calf; joints cracking, corners rubbed. With port, frontis & 162 plates. C Oct 15 (132) £500 [Marshall]

— Voyage d'Egypte et de Nubie. Copenhagen, 1755. 3 vols in 2. Folio, orig half calf; worn. With port, frontis & 162 plates & maps. Minor browning. S Apr 24 (234) £1,500 [Rosenkilde]

Norden, John, 1548-1625?
— Speculum Britaniae: An Historical and Chorographical Description of Middlesex and Hartfordshire. L, 1723. 3d Ed. 4to, half mor gilt; rubbed. With 3 engraved titles, 1 plate of arms, 2 town plans & 2 maps. pn Oct 23 (120) £190 [Sawyer]

Anr copy. 2 parts in 1 vol. 4to, With 3 engraved titles & 4 folding maps. pn Jan 22 (118) £210

Anr copy. 4to, contemp calf; rubbed. With 2 engraved titles & 4 folding maps. S Jan 12 (47) £220 [Shapero]

Nordhoff, Charles, 1830-1901
— California: for Health, Pleasure, and Residence.... NY, 1873. 1st Ed. 4to, orig cloth; blistered, spine ends chipped, front free endpaper pasted down; lacking rear free endpaper. Marginal soiling. sg Mar 12 (28) $90
— The Communistic Societies of the United States. NY, 1875. 8vo, cloth. sg Oct 2 (239) $70

Norris, Frank, 1870-1902
See also: Grabhorn Printing

McTeague: a Story of San Francisco. San Francisco: Colt Press, 1941. Half cloth. sg Jan 8 (195) $50

Norris, Thaddeus
— The American Angler's Book.... Phila., 1865. New Ed, with a Supplement. 8vo, cloth; spine ends frayed. sg May 21 (157) $110

North American...

North American...
- North American Big Game. Official Measurement Records Compiled...for the Boone and Crockett Club.... Bridgeport CT: Remington Arms Co, 1934. Pictorial wraps. sg May 21 (65) $1,500
- North American Big Game. A Book of the Boone and Crockett Club.... NY & L, 1939. In d/j. cb Nov 6 (31) $300
  Anr copy. In d/j. Related material inserted. sg May 21 (158) $120

North, Andrew, Pseud. See: Norton, Alice Mary

North, Sir Dudley, 1641-91
- Discourses upon Trade.... L: Thomas Basset, 1691. 4to, wraps. Some headlines shaved. S July 24 (449) £3,000 [Riley Smith]

North, Joseph
- Men in the Ranks. [NY, 1939]. Foreword by Hemingway. Orig wraps. sg Dec 11 (66) $100

North, Roger, 1653-1743
- The Life of...Francis North, Baron of Guildford.... L, 1742. 4to, contemp calf; joints split, spine chipped. Ck Jan 30 (18) £40

North, William, 1824-54
- The Slaves of the Lamp. Phila., [1877]. ("The Man of the World.") 12mo, orig cloth; spine ends worn. With related material. sg Feb 12 (246) $60

Northampton, Henry Howard, Earl of, 1540-1614
- A Defensative Against the Poyson of Supposed Prophecies.... L, 1620. Folio, 19th-cent half mor; rubbed. One corner of title frayed, shaving border; marginal worming; lacking A1. O May 12 (95) $325

Northcote, James, 1746-1831
- One Hundred Fables, Original and Selected.... L, 1828. 8vo, contemp half calf; rubbed. bba Nov 13 (330) £55 [Trocchi]
  2d Ed. L, 1829. 8vo, mor gilt. ha Dec 19 (243) $55

Northern...
- Northern Lights. [N.p.]: Palaemon Press, 1983. One of 75. Folio, in half cloth portfolio. Set of 15 broadside poems, each sgd. sg Mar 5 (211) $400

Norton, Mrs., Pseud.
- Mrs. Norton's Story Book.... L: John Marshall, [c.1790]. 12mo, orig bds; backstrip worn. S June 18 (473) $260 [Mugee]

Norton, Mrs ——. See: Fore-Edge Paintings

Norton, Alice Mary
- At Swords' Point. NY: Harcourt, [1954]. In d/j. cb Sept 28 (996) $85
- The Beast Master. NY: Harcourt, [1959]. In d/j. cb Sept 28 (997) $50
- Catseye. NY: Harcourt, [1961]. In soiled d/j. cb Sept 28 (998) $75
- The Crystal Gryphon. NY, 1972. In d/j. cb Sept 28 (999) $55
- Galactic Derelict. Cleveland: World, [1959]. In d/j. cb Sept 28 (1003) $65
- Judgment on Janus. NY: Harcourt, [1963]. In d/j. ANs tipped to front endpaper. cb Sept 28 (1005) $80
- Night of Masks. NY: Harcourt, 1964. In rubbed d/j. ANs affixed to front endpaper. cb Sept 28 (1009) $50
- Quest Crosstime. NY: Viking, [1965]. Currey's A bdg in d/j with 1 small tear. cb Sept 28 (1013) $65
- Sargasso of Space. NY: Gnome Press, [1955]. In d/j. cb Sept 28 (1014) $80
- Space Police. Cleveland: World, 1956. Ed by Norton. In d/j. cb Sept 28 (1022) $80
- Storm over Warlock. Cleveland: World, [1960]. In d/j. cb Sept 28 (1017) $85
- The Time Traders. Cleveland: World, [1958]. In d/j. cb Sept 28 (1018) $80
- Victory on Janus. NY: Harcourt, [1966]. In d/j. cb Sept 28 (1019) $80

Norton, Andre, Pseud. See: Norton, Alice Mary

Norton, Charles Benjamin, 1825-91
- Treasures of Art, Industry, and Manufacture represented in the American Centennial Exhibition.... Phila., 1877-78. Folio, half mor; worn. With engraved title & 50 plates. wa Nov 6 (401) $200

Nostredame, Cesar de
- L'Histoire et chronique de Provence.... Lyon, 1614. Folio, contemp calf; rebacked & rubbed. Some leaves at beginning & end stained at inner margin; some marginal worming. S Nov 10 (672) £170 [Seibu]

Nostredame, Jean de
- Les Vies des plus celebres et anciens poetes provensaux.... Lyons: [Basile Bouquet] for Alexandre Marsilii, 1575. 1st Ed. 8vo, calf; worn. First 2 pages disbound. SM Oct 20 (548) FF3,500

Notitia...
- Notitia utraque cum orientis tum occidentis ultra Arcadii Honoriique Caesarum tempora.... Basel: Froben, 1552. Bound with: Panvinius, Onuphrius.- Fasti et triumpho Rom. a Romulo rege.... Venice, 1557. Folio, 18th-cent calf. S Nov 27 (21) £1,150 [Thomas]

Notizia...
— Notizia e maniera per la gran caccia de'cignali.... Naples: Gennaro e Muzio, 1739. 4to, contemp vellum; worn. Sometimes attributed to Giuseppe Carafa. Jeanson copy. SM Feb 28 (105) FF3,200

Nott, Stanley Charles
— A Catalogue of Rare Chinese Jade Carvings. St. Augustine, 1940. 4to, cloth; rubbed. sg Feb 5 (176) $90
— Chinese Jade Throughout the Ages. L, 1936. 4to, orig cloth. cba Mar 5 (262) $75

Nouhuys, Willem Gerard van, 1854-1914
— Egidius en de vreemdelling. Haarlem, 1899. Illus by J. Th. Toorop. 4to, wraps. B Oct 7 (45) HF250

Nourse, Joseph Everett, 1819-89
— American Explorations in the Ice Zones. Bost.: D. Lothrop, [1884]. 3d Ed. cb Nov 6 (218) $65

Nouvelle...
— La Nouvelle Omphale, comedie representee par les comediens italiens ordinaires du Roi, devand leur Majestes le 22 November 1782.... [Paris: Valleyre, 1785]. 12mo, mor gilt by Riviere, orig wraps bound in. With engraved hand-colored title & 4 folding plates, each in the nature of an overslip disclosing anr scene below on unfolding. C Dec 3 (81) £1,300 [Boaretto]

Novena...
— Novena al Sacratisimo Corazon de Jesus. Buenos Aires: Ninos Espositos, 1785. 16mo, modern vellum. Extreme corners of final 4 leaves dog-eared. sg Sept 18 (18) $130
— Novena del Santo de los Santos Nuestro Senor Jesu-Christo Sacramentado. Buenos Aires: Ninos Espositos, 1784. 16mo, modern vellum, contemp wraps bound in. With 2 wormholes in tp & following 2 leaves affecting a few words; 2 small rubberstamps. sg Sept 18 (17) $150

Novisimo...
— Novisimo Arte de cocina, o escelente coleccion de las mejores recetas, para que al menor costo posible.... Mexico, 1831. 12mo, recent calf. Some stains. crahan copy. P Nov 25 (350) $500

N.,T. See: Social...

Nuevo...
— Nuevo Cocinero Mejicana en forma de diccionario. Paris & Mexico, 1858. Folio, contemp calf; upper joint repaired & cracking. With colored frontis & 2 plates. Crahan copy. P Nov 25 (351) $450

Nuix, Giovanni
— Reflexiones imparciales sobre la humanidad de los Espanoles en las Indias.... Madrid, 1782. 4to, contemp calf; corners & spine ends frayed. sg Sept 18 (211) $100

Nummi. See: Leake, Stephen Martin

Nunez Cabeca de Vaca, Alvar, 1490?-1557?. See: Grabhorn Printing

Nunez de Avendano, Pedro
— Aviso de cacadores y de caca. Alcala de Henares: Joan de Brocar, 18 Dec 1543. 4to, mor extra by Marius Michel. Jeanson copy. SM Mar 1 (422) FF85,000
   Anr Ed. Madrid: Pedro Madrigal, 1593. Folio, 19th-cent vellum. Jeanson copy. SM Mar 1 (423) FF38,000

Nuremberg Chronicle
— SCHEDEL, HARTMANN. - Liber Chronicarum.... Nuremberg: Anton Koberger, 12 July 1493. Folio, 16th-cent blind-stamped calf over wooden bds, with remnants of 3 brass cornerpieces & hasps; worn, spine detached. Map def; several leaves torn affecting text; other leaves repaired; map & some leaves detached; some waterstaining. Sold w.a.f. 326 leaves. Goff S-307. C Dec 12 (307) £7,000 [Marshall]
   Anr copy. Modern mor gilt in the style of the 18th cent. 325 (of 326) leaves; lacking final blank. FD Dec 2 (96) DM66,000
   Anr copy. Old mor; rebacked with orig spine laid down. First few leaves washed; ff. 57 & 58 short at fore-edges; marginal repair to f.72 just affecting border of a woodcut & to f.186 not affecting ptd area; map of Europe also repaired. 325 (of 326) leaves; lacking final blank. Goff S-307. P Sept 24 (212) $15,000
   Anr copy. World map only. 360mm by 510mm. S Oct 23 (291) £2,400 [Map]
   Anr copy. Folio, 18th-cent calf gilt. Tp backed; lower & foremargins of 1 leav repaired, 2 leaves with paper pasted over early inscrs on verso; some dampstains & annotations. 326 leaves (5 unnumbered leaves "De Sarmacia" inserted at end). Goff S-307. S May 21 (14) £8,800 [Burgess Browning]
   Anr copy. 18th-cent calf gilt. Several leaves supplied from anr copy; long knife slit through 1 leaf; 1 leaf torn; modern blanks inserted after 2 leaves; many margins repaired, occasionally affecting edge of text; some headlines shaved; some soiling. 321 (of 326) leaves; lacking leaves 259-261, 264 & final blank. Goff S-307. S June 25 (53) £6,000 [King]
   Anr copy. 1 leaf only. World map. S June

25 (334) £2,000 [Pantazelo]
Anr copy. Folio, old vellum; worn, loose in bdg. Lacking title, blank leaf following and ff 6, 7 & 30. Marginal dampstaining & soiling, scattered tears & repairs, minor worming. 326 leaves. Goff S-307. sg Dec 18 (217) $7,750
Anr Ed. Augsburg: Johann Schoensperger, 1 Feb 1497. Folio, old calf; rubbed, rebacked. Double-page map cropped; small holes in E2 & GG4; part of tp torn away from a5 with loss; some leaves repaired in margins; light waterstaining in lower margins. 366 leaves; lacking b1 & b4. Goff S-308 Goff S-308. bba Sept 25 (234) £2,600 [Mandl]

Nutt, Frederick
— The Complete Confectioner. L, 1809. 6th Ed. 8vo, rebound in modern cloth. With frontis & 10 plates, 3 folding. Ink mark to tp; some soiling. cb July 30 (277) £110
— The Imperial and Royal Cook. L, 1819. 2d Ed. 8vo, orig bds; rebacked. Occasional ink stains. pn Nov 20 (180) £160 [Clark]

Nuttall, Thomas, 1786-1859
See also: Michaux & Nuttall
— Manual of Ornithology of the United States and Canada. The Land Birds. Cambr., 1832. With: Nuttall. The Water Birds. Bost., 1834. 12mo, modern half mor. Some stains. sg Sept 18 (212) $350

Nutter, M. E.
— Carlisle in the Olden Time. Carlisle, 1835. Folio, orig half mor. With litho title & 17 litho plates on india paper. pn June 18 (131) £120 [Mizon]

Nutting, Wallace, 1861-1941
— Furniture Treasury. Framingham, [1928-33]. Vols I-II. Cloth. cba Mar 5 (140) $80
Anr copy. Cloth; worn. Sgd. wa June 25 (457) $160

Nuyens, A.
— De Vogelwereld. Groningen, 1886. 2 vols in 1. Folio, orig cloth. Lacking 1 plate; several plates repaired. Ck Jan 16 (208) £220

Nye, Russell Scudder
— Scientific Duck Shooting in Eastern Waters. Falmouth, 1895. sg Oct 23 (416) $150

O

Oakes, Alma
— The National Costumes of Holland. L, 1932. One of 525. Illus by Gratiane de Gardilanne & Elizabeth Whitney Moffat. Folio, half mor. With 50 colored plates. sg Dec 18 (158) $175

Oakley, Edward
— The Magazine of Architecture, Perspective, & Sculpture. L, 1730. Folio, contemp calf; worn. With engraved title, frontis & 95 plates. Corner torn from 1 plate, anr with tear along platemark; a few leaves of text with perforated library stamps. bba Feb 5 (128) £350 [Beyer]
Anr copy. Contemp calf; rebacked & repaired, rubbed. With engraved title, frontis, 1st p of dedication & 95 plates (Plate 57 in duplicate; Plate 59 missing). S Nov 10 (139) £380 [Tucker]

Oakley, Violet
— Samuel F. B. Morse. Phila.: Cogslea Studio Publications, [1939]. One of 500. wa Sept 25 (255) $50

Oates, Frank
— Matabele Land and the Victoria Falls.... L, 1889. 2d Ed. 8vo, orig cloth gilt. Inscr by Robert Washington Oates. S Apr 24 (323) £360 [Mitchell]

Oates, John Claud Trewinard
— A Catalogue of the Fifteenth-Century Printed Books in the University Library, Cambridge. Cambr., 1954. 4to, orig cloth, in d/j; marked. sg Jan 22 (242) $175
Anr copy. Orig cloth. sg Jan 22 (243) $150

Oates, Joyce Carol
— By the North Gate. NY, [1963]. In d/j. cb May 7 (127) $60

Obsequiale...
— Obsequiale, simul ac Benedictionale, juxta ritum...Constantiensis. Ingolstadt: Alexander & Samuel Weissenhorn, 1560. 4to, later 18th-cent vellum, with arms of Pope Pius VI. sg Oct 9 (284) $450

O'Callaghan, Edmund Bailey, 1797-1880
— The Documentary History of the State of New York. Albany, 1849-51. 4 vols. 8vo, cloth. Some foxing throughout. wd June 19 (162) $150

Ocampo, Victoria
— 338171 T.E. Buenos Aires, 1942. Ptd wraps; soiled. sg Dec 11 (325) $250

Ochsenbrunner, Thomas
— Memorabilia gesta virorum illustrium arboris Capitoline. Paris: Jean de Gourmont, [c.1512]. 4to, half vellum. With large woodcut of the Capitoline oak & 74 woodcut vignettes in the text. S June 25 (39) £1,000

Ockham, William of
— Tractatus de sacramento altaris. Strassburg: Ptr of the 1483 Jordanus de Quedlinburg, after 6 Jan 1491. Bound with: Quodlibeta septem (Polain B 2903). Folio, unbound. 36 leaves. Goff O-18. S Nov 27 (203) £300 [Dinter]

O'Clery, Michael, 1575-1643 —& Others
— Annals of the Kingdom of Ireland. Dublin, 1856. 2d Ed. 7 vols, including Index. 4to, contemp half mor. Text in Gaelic with English trans on facing page. sg Nov 20 (6) $110

O'Connell, James
— A Residence of Eleven Years in New Holland and the Caroline Islands. Bost., 1836. 8vo, cloth; spine chipped. S June 25 (502) £750

O'Connell, Mary Anne
— The Last Colonel of the Irish Brigade. L, 1892. 2 vols. 8vo, contemp half calf; rubbed. bba Apr 9 (343) £50 [Hay Cinema]

O'Connell, Mrs Morgan John. See: O'Connell, Mary Anne

O'Connor, Frank. See: Cuala Press

O'Connor, Jack. See: Derrydale Press

O'Connor, Vincent Clarence Scott
— The Silken East. L, 1904. 2 vols. Front hinge cracked on both vols. sg Nov 20 (37) $100

O'Connor, William Douglas, 1832-89
— The Good Gray Poet: A Vindication. NY, 1866. 8vo, orig wraps; soiled, split at front joint. P Dec 15 (123) $650
— [Newspaper review of the 4th Ed of Leaves of Grass] NY, 2 Dec 1866. ("Walt Whitman.") 8 pp, folio. Unopened. In: The New-York Times, Vol XVI, No 4738. Annotated by Whitman in blue pencil. P Dec 15 (124) $600

Oddi, Muzio
— Degli horologi solari. Venice, 1638. 4to, modern wraps; worn. Blank margins of 1st 3 & last 2 leaves holed & repaired. Ck Jan 30 (36) £260

Odieuvre, L.
— Receuil d'oiseux, insects et animaux.... Paris [n.d.] & 1742. 2 parts in 1 vol. Folio, modern calf. Jeanson copy. SM Mar 1 (424) FF26,000

O'Donoghue, Freeman. See: British Museum

O'Donovan, Edmond
— The Merv Oasis. L, 1882. 2 vols. 8vo, contemp half calf; 1 vol broken, worn. bba Nov 13 (97) £140 [Hosains]

O'Donovan, John, 1809-61. See: O'Clery & Others

Oeconomy...
— The Oeconomy of Human Life. L, 1751. 1st Ed. 8vo, contemp calf; spine ends chipped, front cover loose. sg Mar 26 (101) $90

Oeder, Georg Christian von
— Flora Danica. Copenhagen, 1761-1883. ("Icones plantarum sponte nascentium in regnis daniae et norvegiae....") 54 fasicules bound in 18 vols, including Supplement (1-51; 1-3). Complete set. Folio, contemp & near-contemp half calf; a few vols rebacked preserving old spines. With 3,240 hand-colored plates. Minor spotting & discoloration. Horticultural Society of New York—de Belder copy. S Apr 28 (259) £60,000 [White]

Fascicles 1-2, in 1 vol. Folio, contemp calf gilt; worn. With 120 colored plates. Some spotting & worming. HN May 20 (1040) DM1,500

Oehler, Andrew
— The Life, Adventures, and Unparalleled Sufferings of.... Trenton, 1811. 1st Ed. 12mo, contemp calf; rubbed. Some browning, soiling & staining; piece torn from blank margin of title. O Nov 18 (137) $125

Oehler, Richard. See: Lanckoronska & Oehler

Oertli, Ad
— Le Decorateur moderne. Lausanne: Ches l'Autheur, [1915]. Oblong 4to, cloth; shaken. O Nov 18 (138) $200

Oertli, Adolf
— Neue Tortenverzierungen im modernen Stile. [Lausanne, 1915]. Oblong 4to, cloth; shaken. Tp soiled, upper corner excised. sg Jan 15 (40) $110

Oettinger, Eduard Maria
— Moniteur des dates, contenant un million de reseignements biographiques.... Dresden, 1866-82. 6 vols in 2 plus 3 supplements in 1 vol. Together, 3 vols. 4to, half lea; worn, 1st vol partly loose in bdg. 2 leaves supplied in photostat facsimile; some stains. sg Oct 2 (241) $110

Officer, An. See: Roberts, Col. David

Officium

— 1623. - Officium Beatae ariae Virginis. Paris: Sebastien Hure. 12mo, in mor bdg inlaid with semi-precious stones. SM Oct 20 (531) FF120,000

— 1646. - L'Office de la Semaine Saincte.... Paris 8vo, 17th-cent French calf elaborately gilt; lacking clasps. sg June 11 (60) $250

— 1707. - Office de l'eglise, en latin & en francois. Paris: Pierre le Petit. 8vo, contemp mor gilt by either Luc-Antonie Boyet or Louis-Joseph Dubois, border inlaid with olive mor & tooled with a continuous fillet forming a complex pattern of triangular, small circular & shaped compartments, all filled with pointille tooling. S Nov 27 (111) £1,200 [Torre]

— 1728. - L'Office de la semaine sainte.... Paris 8vo, lea gilt bound for Marie Leczinska, Queen of Louis XV, with her arms; spine repaired. Some dampstaining. S Nov 27 (107) £340 [Greenwood]

— 1732. - Office de la Semaine Sainte. Paris: Jacques Colombat. 8vo, contemp mor gilt with arms of Louis XV, bound for presentation by the King to the members of the court at Easter. S Nov 27 (109) £300 [Tenschert]

— 1776. - L'Office de l'eglise a l'usage de Rome. Paris 12mo, contemp mor gilt. sg June 11 (59) $250

O'Flaherty, Liam

— The Assassin. L, 1928. One of 150. bba May 28 (110) £40 [Catnach]

Anr copy. In frayed & stained d/j. O Oct 21 (134) $70

— Red Barbara and Other Stories. NY & L, 1928. One of 600, sgd. O Oct 21 (135) $50

— The Tent. L, [1926]. 1st Ed. In torn & stained d/j. Inscr. O Oct 21 (136) $60

— Thy Neighbour's Wife. L, [1923]. 1st Ed. In chipped d/j. O Oct 21 (137) $80

Ogawa Kazumasa

— Chrysanthemums of Japan. Tokyo, [1900?]. Folio, pictorial wraps; soiled, corners chipped. With 1 color & 13 plain collotype plates. sg Nov 13 (84) $60

Ogden, Henry Alexander, 1856-1936

— Uniform of the Army of the United States, from 1774 to 1889. [NY]: Quartermaster General, [1890]. Folio, contemp mor; broken, worn, lacking backstrip. With 44 colored plates; with additional 3 plates pbd in 1901. wa Sept 25 (207) $450

Ogden, James, Angler

— Ogden on Fly Tying, etc. Cheltenham, 1879. 1st Ed. 8vo, orig cloth; worn, lacking endpapers. Frontis & title loose. T Oct 16 (411) £80

Ogilby, John, 1600-76

— Africa, being an Accurate Description.... L, 1670. Folio, contemp calf; rebacked, very worn. Lacking 3 maps: Balzom, the Fight & Tripoli; some browning. L.p. copy. C Dec 12 (253) £260 [Shapero]

— Asia, the First Part.... L, 1673. 1st Ed. Vol I (all pbd). Folio, contemp calf gilt; joints cracked, rubbed. With 33 plates. C Dec 12 (254) £780 [Israel]

— Britannia.... L, 1675. 1st Ed. Vol I (all pbd). Folio, recent vellum gilt. With frontis, general map & 100 double-page road maps, mtd on guards. Map 45 with small strip missing at fold; Map 58 inserted from a smaller copy with vertical creases; some staining & discoloration in margins. C Oct 15 (138) £3,500 [Nicholson]

Anr copy. Old calf; joints cracking head & foot of spine & corners scuffed. With frontis, general map & 100 road maps, all mtd on guards. One plate with small hole; a few vertical creases. C Apr 8 (69) £3,800 [Traylen]

— Itinerarium Angliae, or, a Book of Roads.... L, 1675. Folio, old calf; worn. With 100 double-page strip maps. Crease to 1 map; a few later margins lightly wormed. Ck Nov 21 (360) £3,000

Ogilby, John, 1600-76 —& Senex, John, d.1740

— An Actual Survey of All the Principal Roads of England and Wales. L, 1719. 2 vols in 1. 8vo, modern half mor gilt; corners rubbed. With 2 titles, engraved dedication & 99 engraved maps (plus 1 in facsimile), all partly hand-colored. Inscr by Denis Wheatley. pnNY Sept 13 (511) $800

Ogilvie, John, 1797-1867

— The Imperial Gazetteer. Glasgow, [c.1855]. 11 vols. 4to, orig cloth. Library markings. wa Sept 25 (502) $60

Ogilvie, Katharine Nairn —& Ogilvie, Patrick

[-] The Trial of Katharine Narin and Patrick Ogilvie for the Crimes of Incest and Murder. Edin., 1765. 8vo, rebound in modern cloth. pnE Nov 12 (171) £50

Ogilvie, Patrick. See: Ogilvie & Ogilvie

Ogle, George, 1704-46
— Antiquities Explained. Being a Collection of Figured Gems. L, 1737. Vol I (all pbd). 4to, contemp calf; worn, covers detached. Extra-illus with engravings. bba Aug 20 (32) £140 [Pagan]

O'Hara, Frank
— In Memory of my Feelings: a Selection of Poems. NY, [1967]. Folio, loose in covers. O Nov 18 (139) $70

Ohm, Georg Simon, 1787-1854
— Die galvanische Kette, mathematisch Bearbeitet. Berlin, 1827. 1st Ed. 8vo, modern half calf. bba May 14 (303) £1,600 [Rootenberg]

Oijen, A. A. V. van
— Stam- en Wapenboek van aanzienlijke Nederlandsche Familien.... Groningen, 1885-90. 3 vols. Folio, half mor; defective. With 104 plates. B Oct 7 (1349) HF1,100

Oinophilus, Boniface. See: Sallengre, Albert Henri de

O'Keeffe, Georgia
— Georgia O'Keeffe. NY, 1976. One of 175. Folio, cloth. With 108 color plates. wa Nov 6 (471) $120

Old...
— The Old Country: A Book of Love & Praise of England. L, [1929]. Ed by Ernest Rhys. Lev gilt by Sangorski & Sutcliffe. sg Feb 12 (247) $120
— Old Daddy Gander's Fairy Tales. L: S. Fisher, [1804]. 8vo, modern half calf. S Dec 5 (334) $200 [Hirsch]
— The Old Man Young Again.... Paris, 1898. One of 500 on papier de Chine. 8vo, half lea gilt; rubbed. sg Feb 12 (99) $70
— Old Master Drawings: A Quarterly Magazine for Students and Collectors. NY, 1970. 14 vols. 4to, orig cloth. sg June 11 (305) $130
— Old Miscellany Days: A Selection of Stories from Bentley's Miscellany. L, 1885. 8vo, half lev by Bayntun. With 33 hand-colored plates. sg Feb 12 (62) $110

Old Sailor. See: Barker, Matthew Henry

Oldfield, Otis. See: Grabhorn Printing

Oldfield, Thomas Hinton Burley
— An Entire and Complete History, Political and Personal, of the Boroughs of Great Britain.... L, 1792. 3 vols. 8vo, contemp calf gilt; rubbed, library stamps on back pastedown. bba Oct 16 (95) £80 [Hay]
  Anr copy. Contemp calf gilt; rubbed, 1 cover detached. S Jan 16 (417) £120 [Arnold]

Oldham, James Basil
— Blind Panels of English Binders. Cambr., 1958. 1st Ed. Folio, orig cloth, in torn d/j. O June 16 (138) $100
— English Blind-Stamped Bindings. Cambr., 1952. 1st Ed, one of 750. Folio, orig cloth, in torn d/j. Some pencilled marginalia. O June 16 (140) $130
  Anr copy. Orig cloth, in d/j. sg Jan 22 (44) $100
— Shrewsbury School Library Bindings. Catalogue Raisonne. Oxford, 1943. 1st Ed, one of 200. 4to, orig cloth; soiled & frayed at top of spine. T Oct 16 (556) £260

Oldmixon, John, 1673-1742
— Memoirs of North-Britain.... L, 1715. 8vo, contemp calf; rubbed. O Feb 24 (159) $100

Oldys, William, 1696-1761
— The British Librarian. L, 1738. Nos I-VI (all pbd) in 1 vol. 8vo, contemp calf. bba Mar 12 (352) £80 [Fogg]
  Anr copy. Contemp half calf. Contents leaves misbound. bba Apr 23 (38) £60 [Frost]

Olearius, Adam
— Offt begehrte Beschreibung der Newen Orientalischen Reisen. Schleswig: Jacob zur Glocken, 1647. Folio, contemp vellum; soiled. With engraved title, 11 ports, folding map & 10 double-page plates. Minor tears without loss; folding map torn at folds without loss; wormhole affecting lower blank margin of a few leaves. Inscr to Claus von Qualen, Landrat of Schleswig-Holstein. S Oct 23 (492) £2,200 [Tang]
— The Voyages and Travels of the Ambassadors Sent by Frederick Duke of Holstein to the Great Duke of Muscovy.... L, 1662. 1st Ed in English. 2 vols in 1. Folio, contemp calf; rebacked & repaired. With 3 ports & 8 folding or double-page maps. C Dec 12 (255) £500 [Von Hunersdorff]
  Anr copy. Contemp calf; rubbed, joints worn. Some plates & maps shaved & torn at fold; frontis & final leaf backed; Vol I title with small hole in blank area. C Apr 8 (108) £400 [Joseph]
  Anr copy. Contemp calf; rubbed, joints split. Minor tears; soiled; stained in margin towards end. S May 29 (1233) £480
  2d Ed in English. L, 1669. 2 parts in 1 vol. Folio, half mor gilt. pn Mar 5 (262) £450

Olina, Giovanni Pietro
— Uccelliera overo discorso della natura.... Rome, 1622. Bound with: Cavalerio, Giovanni Battista. Aves Aeneis typis incisas. 4to, 17th-cent mor with initials HD. Jeanson copy. SM Mar 1 (425) FF44,000

OLINA

Anr Ed. Rome, 1684. 4to, calf with arms of Jerome Bignon. Jeanson copy. SM Mar 1 (426) FF30,000

Oliphant, Laurence, 1829-88
— Narrative of the Earl of Elgin's Mission to China and Japan.... L, 1859. 1st Ed. 2 vols. 8vo, bdg not described; but worn. Inscr "From the Author". S Nov 18 (1214) £300 [Cavendish]

2d Ed. L, 1860. 2 vols. 8vo, half mor gilt. pn Oct 23 (38) £160 [Maggs]

Oliver, Daniel, 1830-1916
— Botany of the Speke and Grant Expedition. L, 1872. Issue with colored plates. 4to, contemp mor gilt; slightly rubbed. With 136 plates, partly colored by hand. Grant —de Belder copy. S Apr 27 (135) £2,800 [Pernanas]

Oliver, Peter
— A New Chronicle of the Compleat Angler. NY, 1936. O June 16 (141) $50

Oliver, Richard Aldworth
— A Series of Lithographic Drawings from Sketches in New Zealand.... L: Dickinson Bros., [1852]. Folio, orig wraps. With 8 hand-finished colored plates. S Jan 12 (331) £240 [Doaks]

Olivier, Eugene —& Others
— Manuel de l'amateur de reliures armoriees francaises. Paris, 1924-38. One of 1,000 on velin. 30 vols, including Index. 4to, loose in orig wraps; Index vol rebound in cloth. sg Oct 2 (66) $650

Olivier, Guillaume Antoine
— Entomologie, ou histoire naturelle des insectes. Paris, 1789-1808. 6 vols. 4to, 19th-cent half mor. With colored frontis & 362 hand-colored plates. Marginal stains in Vol IV; 1 text leaf repaired. S Oct 23 (742) £3,200 [Smith]

Olivier, J., Fencing Master
— Fencing Familiarized.... L & York, 1771. 1st Ed. 8vo, contemp half calf; worn. With folding frontis & 8 plates. S Nov 10 (605) £90 [Head]

Olschki, Leo Samuel
— Choix de livres anciens rares et curieux.... Florence, 1907-34. 10 vols. bba Oct 16 (437) £450 [Parikian]
— Le Livre en Italie a travers les siecles. Florence, 1914. Mor. bba Sept 25 (369) £100 [Alice]

Anr copy. 4to, half lea, orig wraps bound in. sg May 14 (313) $150
— Le Livre illustre au XVe siecle. Florence, 1926. Half lea, orig wrap bound in. With 220 plates. sg May 14 (510) $70

AMERICAN BOOK PRICES CURRENT

Olson, Anton
— J. H. Zukertort...201 Partier. Stockholm, 1912. pn Mar 26 (269) £35 [Adams]

Olson, Toby
— Maps; Poems. Mt. Horeb WI: Perishable Press, [1970]. One of 132. Half mor. sg Jan 8 (200) $80

Omar Khayyam, d. c.1123
See also: Golden Cockerel Press; Grolier Club; Limited Editions Club

The Rubaiyat
— 1859. - The Rubaiyat. L: Bernard Quaritch. 4to, modern vellum gilt. With London Library blindstamp on tp. S July 23 (91) £1,750 [Marshall]
— 1897. - Springfield One of 1,250. Trans by Fitzgerald; illus by Will Bradley. Bds; worn. O Jan 6 (30) $70
— 1898. - L: Macmillan. 8vo, lev extra by J. H. Collins. pn July 23 (107) £320
— L: Hodder & Stoughton [1909]. - Illus by Edmund Dulac. 4to, orig cloth. WIth 20 tipped-in color plates. cb June 18 (86) $50

Anr copy. Half mor; rubbed. O Apr 28 (60) $90

Anr copy. Orig cloth; soiled, spine frayed. With 20 colored plates. T Jan 22 (259) £50

Anr copy. Orig cloth; spine worn. T Feb 18 (173) £60

Anr copy. Orig cloth; soiled & rubbed, spine brayed. T Mar 19 (433) £48

One of 200. Vellum gilt; worn. O Apr 28 (173) $180
— [1909]. - L. One of 750. Illus by Edmund Dulac. 4to, orig vellum gilt; soiled. T Dec 18 (135) £190

Anr copy. Illus by Gilbert James. Cloth. With 16 colored plates. bba Oct 16 (207) £40 [Nutter]

One of 750. Illus by Willy Pogany. Folio, orig mor gilt. L July 2 (65) £140
— [1909]. - L: Hodder & Stoughton One of 750. Illus by Edmund Dulac. 4to, orig vellum gilt; top portion of upper cover soiled. With 20 colored plates. pn Dec 11 (354) £160 [McKenzie]
— [1910]. - L. Illus by Rene Bull. 4to, orig cloth; worn. bba Mar 26 (267) £85 [Peters]

Anr copy. Orig vellum bds gilt; soiled. With 29 colored plates. S Oct 6 (775) £150 [Marks]
— [1911]. - L. Reproduced from a calligraphic Ms written & illuminated by Sangorski & Sutcliffe. 4to, lev extra with colored mor inlays gilt, the upper cover with a peacock jewelled with 31 turquoises, set in a recessed cartouche a la turque centered in a ground of dense floral sprays of colored

836

morocco inlays elaborately gilt, all within a fancy panel border of gilt fillets & dotted rules with green mor corner ornaments inlaid & gilt; upper joint split, hinge tender, gilt extra doublures mildewed, extremities rubbed. Sold as a bdg. P Sept 24 (113) $1,500

Anr copy. Orig vellum gilt. S Nov 10 (405) £130 [Head]

One of 550. Vellum gilt; loose in bdg. sg Sept 11 (241) $175

— 1930. - L. One of 750. Illus by Willy Pogany. 4to, mor extra with oval panel containing Eve in the Garden of Eden, by Riviere. pn Nov 20 (81) £700 [Maggs]

One of 1,250. Orig mor gilt. With 12 color plates. S Dec 4 (209) £300 [Peters]

Omar Khayyam Club
— The Book of the Omar Khayyam Club 1892-1910. L, 1910. Ltd Ed. 4to, orig half cloth; soiled. bba Aug 28 (239) £80 [London Library]

On Human Rights
— On Human Rights. Bronxville: Valenti Angelo, 1963. One of 50. Wraps. cb Dec 4 (324) $70

On the Ambitious Projects...
— On the Ambitious Projects in Regard to North West America...by an Englishman. San Francisco: Book Club of Calif., 1955. One of 400. cb Sept 11 (6) $90

Onassis, Jacqueline Bouvier Kennedy —& Radziwill, Lee Bouvier
— One Special Summer. NY, 1974. One of 500. wa May 30 (175) $130

Onderdonk, Henry, Jr., 1804-86
— Revolutionary Incidents of Suffolk and Kings Counties.... NY, 1849. 1st Ed. 12mo, orig cloth; worn, spine-tips frayed. Inscr. O Oct 21 (138) $110

O'Neill, Eugene, 1888-1953
The Hairy Ape. NY, 1929. One of 775 L.p. copies, sgd. Illus by Alexander King. 4to, half cloth, in d/j, unopened. With 9 colored plates. sg Mar 5 (206) $175

— Plays. NY, 1934-35. Wilderness Ed, One of 770. 12 vols. sg Mar 5 (207) $500

— Strange Interlude. NY, 1928. One of 775, sgd. Orig vellum over bds. sg Mar 5 (208) $150

Anr copy. Orig vellum over bds, with orig plain wrap. wd June 19 (164) $175

— Thirst. Bost., [1914]. 1st Ed. Orig bds, in d/j. wd June 19 (165) $350

Ongania, Ferdinando, 1842-1911
— L'Arte della Stampa nel Rinascimento Italiano Venezia. Venice, 1894. 2 vols in 1. 4to, modern cloth. Library markings. bba Feb 5 (60) £90 [Acquaforte]

Anr copy. Wraps; worn. sg May 14 (511) $150

— Streets and Canals in Venice. Venice, 1893. Text by Pompeo Molmenti. Folio, orig half lea. With litho title & 100 photographic plates. C July 22 (140) £300

Anr copy. Orig half lea; broken & shabby. With 100 plates. sg May 7 (60) $300

Oort, Edward Daniel van
— Ornithologia Neerlandica. De vogels van Nederland. The Hague, 1922-35. 5 vols. Folio, cloth. pn Oct 23 (260) £620 [Dennistoun]

Oppe, Adolf Paul
Thomas Rowlandson: His Drawings and Water-Colours. L: The Studio, 1923. Folio, half vellum; worn. With 96 plates. O June 16 (142) $90

Oppianus
See also: Arrianus & Oppianus
— La Chasse, Poem d'Oppien.... Strasbourg: A La librairie academique, 1787. 8vo, calf gilt by Meslant. Jeanson copy. SM Mar 1 (431) FF1,100

— De piscibus libri V. Eiusdem de venatione libri IIII. Venice: Aldus, 1517. 8vo, 18th-cent calf gilt with unidentified arms. Jeanson 1392. SM Mar 1 (427) FF15,000

Anr Ed. Paris, 1555. ("De piscatu libri V. De venatione.") 2 parts in 1 vol. 4to, 18th-cent calf; rubbed. S May 21 (63) £250 [Poole]

— De venatione libri IIII. Leiden: Plantin, 1597. 8vo, vellum gilt. Jeanson copy. SM Mar 1 (428) FF4,200

— Les Quatre Livres de la venerie.... Paris: R. Estienne, 1575. 4to, calf gilt by Niedree. Jeanson copy. SM Mar 1 (430) FF8,500

Opsopoeus, Johannes, 1556-96
— Sybyllina oracula. Paris, 1607. 3 parts in 1 vol. 8vo, later half calf. Title to Vol I frayed; some upper margins cut close. S Sept 23 (397) £75; S Mar 10 (1151) £60 [Maggs]

Orange, James. See: Chater Collection, Sir Catchick P.

Oratio...
— Oratio Dominica in CLV linguas versa et exoticis characteribus plerumque expressa. Parma: Bodoni, 1806. Folio, old half calf; worn, loose, lacking backstrip. Perforated & ink stamps on titles. Prelims & dedication in Latin, Italian & French; the

ORATIO...

Lord's Prayer in 150 languages, presented in 97 exotic alphabets, all designed by Bodoni. bba Jan 15 (364) £60 [Robertshaw]

Orbeliani, Sulkhan Saba. See: Kelmscott Press

Orbigny, Charles Dessalines d'
— Dictionnaire universel d'histoire naturelle.... Paris, [1839]-49. 16 vols, including 3 vols of plates. 8vo, later half mor; rubbed. With 287 plates, all but a few hand-colored. Ink & perforated library stamps on titles; ink stamps on plates; hinges of plate vol broken. bba Jan 15 (405) £150

Orchardist's...
— The Orchardist's Companion. Phila., 1841. Ed by Alfred Hoffy. 4to, modern half mor by Crahan. With 48 color plates. Plate 41 stained from pressed flower. Sold w.a.f as a periodical, this apparently being the 4 nos of the 1st year's publication. Crahan copy. P Nov 25 (354) $1,100

Orcutt, William Dana
— The Book in Italy during the Fifteenth and Sixteenth Centuries. L, [1928]. One of 750. 4to, orig half vellum; rubbed. sg May 14 (512) $150
— The Magic of the Book. Bost., 1930. One of 25 hors commerce with 6 extra plates. cb Sept 11 (232) $65
One of 375. 8vo, half vellum gilt. pnNY Mar 12 (106) $80

Ord, Harry St. George
— Account of a Visit to the King of Siam.... Singapore, 1868. 8vo, orig wraps; def. With 15 orig photographs mtd in at end. S Oct 23 (493) £950 [Randall]

O'Reilly, Bernard, Arctic Explorer
— Greenland, the Adjacent Seas, and the Northwest Passage.... L, 1818. 4to, modern half calf. With 3 charts and 18 plates. Some browning & staining; 1 folding chart repaired. bba Oct 30 (345) £110 [Elliott]
Anr copy. Contemp calf; worn. With 3 maps & 18 plates. bba Dec 18 (204) £70 [Hannas]
Anr copy. Contemp half mor; worn, broken. bba Dec 18 (205) £55 [Smith]
Anr copy. Modern mor; rubbed. With 3 folding maps. O Nov 18 (140) $150
Anr copy. Contemp half calf; rubbed, joints worn. With 3 charts and 18 plates. Fold breaks. O Nov 18 (141) $110
Anr copy. Bound with: Barrington, Daines. The Possibility of Approaching the North Pole Asserted. NY, 1818. 8vo, contemp half calf; rubbed. sg Sept 18 (214) $250
Anr copy. 4to, contemp half sheep; extremities worn, endpapers renewed. With 3 charts and 18 plates. sg Apr 23 (103) $350

O'Reilly, John
— The Placenta, the Organic Nervous System, the Blood.... NY, 1861. 8vo, orig cloth; spine chipped at head. Stamp on tp. Inscr. sg Jan 15 (117) $140

Oribasius Sardianus
— Collectorum medicinalium libri xvii.... Venice: Aldus, [c.1554]. 8vo, 19th-cent half calf; rubbed. S Nov 27 (279) £300 [Quaritch]

Original...
See also: Ege, Otto F.
— Original Etchings by American Artists. NY: Cassell, [1883]. Folio, cloth. With 20 plates. Dampstained throughout. O Mar 24 (133) $250

Orioli, Giuseppe
— Adventures of a Bookseller. L, 1938. With 7pp of holograph reminiscences which could not be pbd. sg Dec 11 (347) $1,000
— Moving Along, Just a Diary. L, 1934. In d/j. sg Dec 11 (348) $70
— Some Letters...to Mrs. Gordon Crotch. Edin.: Tragara Press, 1974. One of 120. 4to, half cloth. sg Dec 11 (349) $90

Orlandi, Pellegrino Antonio
— Abecedario Pittorico.... Venice, 1753. 4to, contemp vellum. Institutional stamps on rear blank & top & bottom edges. sg Mar 26 (217) $150

Orleans, Henri d', Duc d'Aumale. See: Aumale, Henri Eugene Philippe Louis d'Orleans

Orleans Collection, Louis Philip Joseph, Duc d'
— Description des principales pierres gravees du cabinet de.... Paris, 1780-84. 2 vols. Folio, contemp calf gilt; joints cracked. With frontis & 179 plates. A few leaves with tiny holes; some soiling & spotting. S Nov 10 (143) £180 [Russell]
Anr copy. Modern half mor. Titles stamped. S July 13 (44) £190

Orlers, Jan
— Beschrijvinge der Stad Leyden. Leiden, 1614. 4to, later half mor; rubbed, lacking upper endleaf. With 3 plans (2 folding & repaired) & 6 double-page plates. S Nov 10 (916) £130 [F. Loose]

Orlowski, G.
— Russian Cries, in Correct Portraiture; from Drawings Done on the Spot.... L: Edward Orme, 1809 [watermarked 1815]. Folio, orig bds; rebacked in mor. With engraved title & 8 hand-colored plates. P June 18 (146) $1,000

Orme, Edward
— An Essay on Transparent Prints, and on Transparencies in General. L, 1807. 1st Ed. 4to, contemp half mor; rubbed. Some browning. S Nov 10 (144) £200 [Spelman]
— Graphic History of the Life, Exploits and Death of Horatio Nelson.... L, [1806]. Folio, contemp half mor; broken. Lacking final 3 key plates. Sold w.a.f. Ck Nov 21 (217) £260
— Historic, Military, and Naval Anecdotes.... L, [1819]. 4to, half mor gilt. With 40 hand-colored plates. Some spotting; 1 leaf of text torn & repaired. pn Apr 30 (59) £980

Anr copy. Half mor by Riviere. sg Apr 23 (106) $600
— A Picture of St. Petersburgh. L, [c.1834]. Folio, contemp half lea; rubbed, hinges def. With engraved title & 17 (of 20) colored plates, lacking uncolored frontis & Abbey's plates 5, 11 & 14. One plate spotted in blank margin, anr with short tear entering blank plate frame. C Oct 15 (76) £800 [Shapero]

Orme, Robert, 1728-1801
Historical Fragments of the Mogul Empire.... L, 1805. 4to, contemp calf with arms of East India College; rubbed, rebacked. With port & 3 maps. bba July 16 (127) £80 [Thorp]

Ormerod, George, 1785-1873
— The History of the County Palatine and City of Chester. L, 1819. 3 vols. Folio, contemp russia gilt; joints rubbed. A few plates colored by hand. S Nov 17 (809) £200 [Nicholson]

2d Ed. L, 1882. 3 vols. Folio, contemp half cloth; rubbed. Ck Nov 21 (250) £130

Anr copy. Orig half cloth; shaken. F Oct 30 (544) $275

Anr copy. Contemp half mor; worn. A few plates colored by hand. S Nov 17 (810) £220 [Huntley]

Anr copy. Marginal tears; some leaves loose. Sold w.a.f. S Nov 17 (811) £180 [Nicholson]

Anr copy. Some tears; some leaves lacking; a few leaves loose & torn. Sold w.a.f. S Nov 17 (812) £80 [Nicholson]

Anr copy. Orig bds; worn. L.p. copy. T Jan 22 (36) £195

Ornamental...
— The Ornamental Flower Garden and Shrubbery.... L, 1852-54. 4 vols. 4to, cloth; not uniform. With 288 hand-colored plates. Some browning. de Belder copy. S Apr 28 (352) £3,200 [McDougall]

Orosius, Paulus
— Historiae adversus paganos. Venice: Octavianus Scotu, 30 July 1483. Folio, later half mor. Scattered worming to text & margins; dampstaining in lower margin of many leaves; several leaves with marginal repairs. 78 leaves. Goff O-98. sg June 11 (309) $650

Orpen, Francis H. S. See: Arnot & Orpen

Orpen, Sir William
— Stories of Old Ireland & Myself. L, 1924. 4to, cloth; worn. Some stains. With ink & wash drawing, inscr by Orpen, on the front free endpaper. sg Dec 11 (352) $130

Orpheus, Junior. See: Vaughan, William

Orta, Garcia da —& Acosta, Cristoval de, 1597-1676?
— Tractado de las drogas y medicinas de las Indias orientales. Burgos, 1578. 1st Ed. 4to, vellum in the style of the epoch. Waterstained at beginning. FD Dec 2 (445) DM6,000

Ortelius, Abraham, 1527-98
— Abrege du Theatre.... Antwerp: B. Vrients, 1602. Oblong 32mo, contemp vellum gilt; soiled. With engraved arms, 2 plates of globes, view & 125 maps. S Oct 23 (218) £1,200 [Franks]
— Epitome du Theatre du Monde. Antwerp: Plantin, 1590. 8vo, contemp lea; chipped & wormed, front cover detached, backstrip lacking. Lacking 1 map; dampstained throughout. Houdini's sgd copy. sg Nov 20 (193) $900

Anr copy. Old pigskin; rubbed. With 93 (of 94) plates by Phillip Galle in the test; lacking map of England & Wales. T Sept 18 (41) £820
— An Epitome of Ortelius, his Theatre of the World.... L, 1603. Oblong 8vo, contemp vellum; def. With 119 (of 123) maps. Partially misbound; some shaving; numerous annotations throughout the text; some stains. S June 25 (280) £800 [Hildenbrandt]

Epitome theatri Orteliani..... Antwerp: C. Plantin, 1589. Oblong 16mo, vellum; soiled. With plate & 94 maps, hand-colored throughout & many maps heightened with gold. S Oct 23 (217) £1,350 [Burden]
— Theatro de la Tierra universal. Antwerp: Plantin, 1588. Folio, later vellum gilt. With engraved title, port & 100 double-page maps, colored throughout in a contemp hand. Somewhat faded & discolored throughout; a few maps brittle & tornl; port & a few maps def; many marginal repairs; a few maps shaved. C

ORTELIUS

Apr 8 (43) £7,000 [Giuller Frers]
— Theatrum oder Schawplatz des Erdtbodems. Antwerp: Gilles van Diest, 1572-[73]. Folio, 18th-cent bdg; worn. With 69 double-page mapsheets, including 16 from the Additamentum, colored throughout in a contemp hand. On facing pages is a complete holograph English trans of the German text by William Smith (1550?-1618). S Oct 23 (216) £6,800 [Israel]
Anr copy. Modern vellum gilt. With 53 double-page mapsheets colored in full in an early hand. Maps 39-53 dampstained with occasional adhesion damage; lacking colophon leaf; tp stamped. S Nov 10 (963) £5,500 [Feldbaum]
— Theatrum orbis terrarum. Antwerp, 1573. Folio, modern vellum. With engraved hand-colored title & 70 double-page maps all with full early hand-coloring. 8 maps def & neatly repaired; a few other tears repaired; tp & maps expertly restored & resized; mtd on guards throughout. C Apr 8 (42) £5,800 [Lemmers]
Anr copy. Calf; worn. With frontis & 70 maps, hand-colored. With 1 extra map by Ortelius & 4 inserted maps by de Jode & an Ms map of Artois. 10 maps damaged with portions cut away. Koeman III, Ort 12, pp 41-43. S Apr 23 (133) £3,750 [Broecke]
Anr Ed. Antwerp: C. Plantin, 1579. Bound with: Ortelius. Nomenclator Ptolemaicus. Antwerp, 1579 Folio, contemp vellum; worn. With engraved title & 62 (of 93) maps. Lacking port; some browning & minor defs. HN May 22 (1076) DM18,000
Anr Ed. Antwerp: Plantin, 1591 [colophon reads 1592]. 3 parts in 3 vols. Folio, 19th-cent calf. With 2 engraved titles, port & 134 double-page maps. Vols II & III heavily dampstained; a few maps def. S Oct 23 (67) £5,500 [Sagen]
Anr Ed. Antwerp: Plantin, 1595. With engraved title, port & 115 maps. Bound with: Ortelius. Parergon.... Antwerp: Plantin, 1595. 2 parts. With 32 mapsheets. And: Nomenclator ptolemaicus. Antwerp: Plantin, 1595. Folio, contemp calf gilt; rebacked preserving orig spine. Hand-colored in full throughout with titles & port heightened with gold. Mtd on guards. C Oct 15 (80) £25,000 [Dreesman]
Anr copy. With engraved title, port & 115 maps. Bound with: Ortelius. Parergon.... Antwerp: Plantin, 1595. 2 parts. With 31 (of 32) mapsheets. And: Nomenclator ptolemaicus. Antwerp: Plantin, 1595. modern vellum. Hand-colored in full throughout in a contemp hand. Some browning & fingersoiling. VH Sept 12 (a8) DM43,000
Anr Ed. Antwerp, 1598. ("Theatrum orbis terrarum, dit tonneel des aert-bodems.") Folio, contemp vellum; worn & soiled. Lacking tp & an unknown number of leaves at end including colophon; Map 35 lacking & replaced with a folding map by M. Lotter; some dampstains & discolorations to margins, heavy at end causing some damage to paper; last 42 maps with tissue reinforcements to fore-margins, the final 7 maps with paper loss at edges; other defs. Sold w.a.f. CNY May 11 (126) $9,000
Anr Ed. Antwerp, 1610. Folio, disbound. With engraved title, port & 124 maps on 121 double-page plates. Some dampstains. pn Apr 30 (479) £8,200 [Weston]
Anr copy. With engraved title, port & 121 (of 128) sheets of maps.. pn June 18 (352A) £8,200 [Burgess]
Anr Ed. Antwerp, 1612. ("Theatro d'el orbe de la tierra.") Bound with: Ortelius. Parergon.... And: Ortelius. Nomenclator Ptolemaicus. Both: Antwerp, 1609. Folio, old sheep; rubbed & worn. With hand-colored title with hand-colored arms on verso (torn & def), port of Ortelius & 6 small maps in text all colored by a contemp hand & 127 (of 128, lacking Portugal) maps. Lacking 2 maps in Parergon. At least 34 maps torn or def or both; a further 8 with splits at centerfold. C Apr 8 (45) £6,500 [Redelmeier]
Anr Ed. Antwerp: Plantin, 1624. ("Theatri orbis terrarum parergon....") Folio, modern bds. With engraved title & 44 double-page maps & plates. A few text headlines shaved. S Oct 23 (66) £1,700 [Sagen]
Anr Ed. [Cleveland, 1964]. Folio, half mor. Facsimile of the Antwerp, 1570, Ed. sg Apr 23 (184) $225

Ortiz, Lorenzo
— Origen y Instituto de la Compania de Jesus en la Vida de San Ignacio de Loyola. Seville, 1679. Folio, later half mor. sg Sept 18 (215) $200

Orvis, Charles F. —& Cheney, A. Nelson
— Fishing with the Fly.... Manchester, Vt., 1883. 1st Ed. 8vo, cloth. With 15 color plates. Sl worn. wa Sept 25 (90) $105

Orwell, George
— Animal Farm. L, 1945. 1st Ed. In d/j. S July 13 (164) £240
— Down and Out in Paris and London. L, 1933. Uncorrected proof copy. Orig wraps; soiled. Pencil sketch of Orwell pasted onto verso of title. bba Jan 15 (190) £750 [Gekoski]
— Nineteen Eighty Four. L, 1949. 1st Ed. Orig cloth, in red d/j. kh Mar 16 (393B) A$220

Anr copy. Orig cloth, in d/j; spine ends & corners chipped. sg Dec 11 (92) $250

Proof copy, with the name of the work expressed numerically. Orig wraps. S Dec 18 (171) £1,600 [Beres]

Osbaldiston, William Augustus

— The British Sportsman. L, [1792]. 4to, contemp calf gilt. With 42 plates. Minor defs. HK Nov 4 (1898) DM1,000

Anr copy. Contemp calf; spine worn at head & foot. With 42 plates in contemp color. Some plates trimmed within platemark at outer edge; a few plates slightly oxidised; a few spots on pp 322-23 obscuring letters of text. S Oct 23 (767) £1,250 [Armouries]

Osbeck, Pehr

— A Voyage to China and the East Indies. L, 1771. Trans by John Reinhold Forster. 2 vols. 8vo, contemp calf; joints weak; Vol I spine cracked. With 13 plates. sg Nov 20 (140) $500

Osborn, Sherard, 1822-75

— Stray Leaves from an Arctic Journal. L, 1852. 8vo, orig cloth. sg Apr 23 (107) $100

Osborne Collection, Edgar

— The Osborne Collection of Early Children's Books. Toronto, 1958-75. Compiled by Judith St. John. 2 vols. 4to, orig cloth. O Mar 24 (135) $140

Osborne, Edward, Pseud. See: Fore-Edge Paintings

Osborne, Sidney Godolphin, 1808-89

— Scutari and its Hospitals. L, 1855. 4to, later half mor. With 5 colored plates. pnE Jan 28 (311) £210 [Traylen]

Anr copy. Orig cloth; loose in bdg. sg Apr 23 (108) $400

Osborne, Thomas, d.1767

— A Collection of Voyages and Travels.... L, 1745. 2 vols. Folio, modern cloth. Library stamps on plates & maps. bba Feb 5 (342) £120 [Whiteson]

— Geographia Magane Britanniae. or, Correct Maps of...England, Scotland and Wales. L, 1748. Oblong 4to, modern half calf gilt. With engraved title, folding map & 60 double-page maps. General map lacking lower portion; Kent with tears; some stains. pn May 21 (383) £380 [Burden]

Anr copy. Contemp half calf. With engraved title, folding map & 60 double-page map. Lacking general view of the roads. pn May 21 (384) £500 [Nicholson]

Osbourne, Katharine Durham

— Robert Louis Stevenson in California. Chicago, 1911. Bds; soiled. ALs of Stevenson, sgd with initials, laid in. wa Dec 11 (112) $300

Osgood, Frances Sargent

— The Floral Offering: a Token of Friendship. Phila., 1847. 4to, cloth; loose, spine damaged. With 10 hand-colored plates. sg Dec 18 (204) $325

Osler, Sir William, 1849-1919

— Bibliotheca Osleriana: a Catalogue of Books.... Oxford, 1929. 4to, orig cloth. S May 28 (821) £240

Anr copy. Cloth. sg May 14 (614) $325

— Incunabula Medica: a Study of the Earliest Printed Medical Books, 1467-1480. Oxford, 1923. 4to, orig bdg. pnE Dec 17 (129) £70 [Weiner]

— The Principles and Practice of Medicine. NY, 1892. 1st Ed. 8vo, orig sheep; rubbed, joints cracked. F Oct 30 (147) $75

Osler, Sir William, 1849-1919 —& McCrae, Thomas

— Modern Medicine: its Theory and Practice. Phila., 1907-10. 7 vols. Orig sheep; soiled. wa Mar 5 (305) $190

Osmond, Ranulph Marie Eustache, Marquis deti Les Hommes des bois. —&
Paris, 1892 8o, half mor gilt by Saulnier. Jeanson copy. SM Mar 1 (441) FF2,800

Osorio da Fonseca, Jeronimo, 1506-80

— De rebus Emmanuelis regis Lusitaniae.... Lisbon, 1571. 1st Ed. Folio, contemp calf; rebacked retaining orig cpint with gilt-crowned Ns. Some worming & tears repaired; hole in text of K6 repaired obscuring 1 or 2 letters; wormhole in foremargin towards the end repaired; some underlining & early marginal annotations. S May 21 (64) £400 [Baldwin]

Ossian. See: Macpherson, James

Ostayen, Paul van, 1896-1928

— Bezette stad. ANtwerp: Het Sienjaal, 1921. One of 540. 4to, wraps. B Oct 7 (211) HF1,700

Others. See: Dement'ev & Others

Otis, Fessenden Nott, 1825-1900

— Illustrated History of the Panama Railroad. NY, 1861. 12mo, orig cloth; loose, some spine wear. Some marginalia. sg Sept 18 (216) $60

Ottley, William Young, 1771-1836

— A Collection of 129 Fac-Similes.... L, 1828. L.p. Issue. Folio, contemp half vellum; worn. Some mounts foxed or dampstained. sg June 4 (235) $350

— An Inquiry into the Origin and Early History of Engraving upon Copper and in Wood. L, 1816. 2 vols. 4to, half cloth; rubbed; joints split. bba Oct 30 (485) £120 [Erlini]

— The Italian School of Design. L, 1823. Folio, cloth. Perforated library stamp on tp. bba Feb 5 (115) £260 [Acquaforte]

Ottley, William Young, 1771-1836 —& Tomkins, Peltro William

— Engravings of the most Noble Marquis of Stafford's Collection of Pictures. L, 1818. 4 vols in 2. Folio, cloth. bba Dec 18 (207) £150 [Elliott]

Otto, Alexander F. —& Holbrook, Theodore S.

— Mythological Japan. Phila., 1902. One of 950. 4to, Japanese-style bdg in padded raw silk. wa Mar 5 (197) $110

Otto-Lenghi, Luisa Mortar. See: Luzzatto & Otto-Lenghi

Oudegherst, Pierre d', 1540-92

— Les Chroniques et annales de Flandres.... Antwerp: C. Plantin, 1571. 4to, old vellum; worn. S Sept 23 (373) £160 [Delvoe]

Oudry, Jean Baptiste, 1686-1755

— Chasse par J-B. Oudry a Mr. le Chevalier de Breteuil. [N.p., c.1760]. 4to, half pigskin by Stroobants. With 17 plates. Jeanson copy. SM Mar 1 (442) FF29,000

— Recueil de divers animaux de chasse tire du cabinet de Monsieur le Comte de Tessin. Paris: J. P. Le Bas, [c.1760]. Oblong folio, modern half vellum. With 12 plates. Jeanson copy. SM Mar 1 (443) FF17,500

Oughtred, William, 1575-1660

— The Circles of Proportion and the Horizontall Instrument.... Oxford, 1660. 8vo, contemp calf; rebacked with orig backstrip retained. With 8 folding plates; margins trimmed, some soiling, 1 corner torn (with loss of text). sg Jan 15 (335) $425

Ovalle, Alonso de, 1601-51

— Historica relacion del Reyno di Chile.... Rome, 1646. 4to, contemp vellum; loose. With folding map & 14 plates.. FD Dec 2 (1087) DM2,200

Overbeke, Bonaventura ab

— Reliquiae antiquae urbis Romae.... Amst., 1708. In 1 vol. Folio, contemp russia gilt; upper cover worn, spine rubbed. With frontis, dedication plate with port of Queen Anne, port of Overbeke & 147 plates, including 2 double-page. C Apr 8 (46) £1,200 [Weinreb]

— Les Restes de L'ancienne Rome. Amst., 1709. Ed by Michael ab Overbeke. 3 vols. Folio, bdg not indicated. Library markings. Sold w.a.f. Franklin Institute copy. F Sept 12 (20) $900

Overbury, Thomas, d.1684

— A True and Perfect Account of the Examination, Confession, Tryal...of Joan Perry...for the supposed Murder of William Harrison.... L, 1676. 4to, modern calf; worn. Lacking prelim leaf; last few page numbers cropped. S May 6 (526) £100 [Quaritch]

Overfield, T. Donald. See: Skues & Overfield

Overloop, Eugene van

— Dentelles anciennes des Musees Royaux des Arts Decoratifs et Industriels a Bruxelles. Brussels & Paris, 1912. 4to, half mor gilt by Zaehnsdorf, orig wraps to Fasicules I-V bound in at end. With 100 plates on linen-hinged guards. C Dec 3 (31) £400 [Marks]

Ovid (Publius Ovidius Naso), 43B.C.-17?A.D. See also: Golden Cockerel Press

— De Remedio Amoris. Rouen: Martin Morin, [c.1497]. 4to, disbound. In gothic letter (types: 73G, leaded: 120G); large ptr's device (Davies 161) at end. Wormhole in fnial leaf just touching 1 or 2 letters; some lower margins lightly dampstained. 20 leaves. Apparently unrecorded. S May 21 (10) £1,250 [Bibliogheque de Caron]

— Heroides. Paris, 1938. One of 100. Illus by Andre Derain. 4to, mor extra by Therese Moncey. With 15 plates. SM Oct 20 (657) FF55,000

— Lehrbuch der Liebe. Berlin, 1921. One of 100 with an extra suite of sgd lithos on japan. Illus by Max Slevogt. 4to, orig pigskin gilt. HN Nov 26 (2123) DM1,300

English Versions of Metamorphoses

— Metamorphoses. L, 1717. Folio, later russia; rebacked. Some browning. sg Mar 26 (219) $150

— Ovid's Metamorphosis Englished.... Oxford, 1632. Trans by George Sandys. Folio, late 19th-cent half calf. Lacking tp & final 2 leaves of text; ingraved title inlaid & several corners renewed. Sold w.a.f. cb July 30 (141) $110

Anr copy. Calf; rebacked, corners repaired.

With title from 1626 Ed and engraved frontis & 14 (of 15) plates. Title mtd. With 1970 reprint. sg Dec 18 (205) $200

French Versions of Metamorphoses

— Les Metamorphoses. Amst., 1702. Folio, contemp calf; rebacked, endpapers renewed. Some browning. sg Mar 26 (218) $275

Anr Ed. Amst., 1732. 2 parts in 1 vol. Folio, contemp calf gilt. Some fingersoiling. HK Nov 4 (2860) DM2,700

Anr Ed. Paris, 1738. 2 vols. 4to, 18th-cent calf gilt; worn. 2 leaves torn without loss; small hole in 1 plate in Vol I; lacking Ss1 in Vol II. S July 28 (1224) £80

Anr Ed. Lausanne, 1931. One of 95. Illus by Pablo Picasso. 4to, unsewn in orig wraps. HK Nov 4 (3057) DM28,000

Italian Versions of Metamorphoses

— La Vita et metamorfoseo.... Lyons: G. de Tournes, 1559. 8vo, 18th-cent calf. Some stains & browning; some marginalia shaved. S Mar 10 (1120) £340 [Maggs]

Anr copy. Modern calf. Final 8 leaves in facsimile; many leaves dampstained & soiled. sg May 21 (311) $80

Latin & French Versions

— Les Metamorphoses. Paris, 1767-71. 4 vols. 4to, contemp half calf. With 139 plates. Last vol lacks tp. O May 12 (150) $325

Anr copy. Contemp calf gilt; rubbed, joints split. With engraved title, dedication & 140 plates. Some spotting & discoloration. S May 29 (1234) £420

Latin & Greek Versions

Paris: for Nicolas Elio Lemaire, 1822. One of 2 ptd on vellum throughout. 1 vol bound in 2. 8vo, 19th-cent bds gilt extra. P Dec 15 (234) $1,700

Latin Versions of Metamorphoses

— Metamorphoses. Toscolano: A. Paganini, 1526. 4to, modern bds. A few leaves lacking or misbound; some worming, affecting text. Sold w.a.f. bba Oct 16 (4) £75 [Rix]

Anr Ed. Frankfurt: S. Feyerabend & W. Gall, 1563. 8vo, contemp blindstamped pigskin dated 1566 & with letters IHLM on upper cover. Some marginal numbering & underlining. S Sept 23 (475) £190 [Smallwood]

Oviedo, Juan Antonio de

See also: Florencia & Oviedo

— Vida admirable, apostolicos ministeros.... Mexico, 1752. contemp vellum S June 25 (446) £550

Owen, Charles, d.1746

— An Essay towards a Natural History of Serpents. L, 1742. 4to, contemp bds; rebacked. With 7 plates. Some corners stained. S May 28 (755) £220

Owen, David Dale

— Report of a Geological Exploration of Part of Iowa, Wisconsin, and Illinois. Phila., 1852. 4to, orig cloth; worn. O June 9 (133) $160

Owen, John, of the Middle Temple —& Bowen, Emanuel, d.1767

— Britannia Depicta or Ogilby Improv'd. L, 1720. 4to, modern calf. With engraved title, 2 leaves of "Table" & 273 road maps, hand-colored throughout. C Apr 8 (70) £700 [Faupel]

Anr copy. Calf; rebacked. With engraved title, 2 leaves of "Table" & 273 road maps. pn May 21 (328) £450 [Way]

Anr Ed. L, 1731. 4to, contemp calf; worn. With 273 road map. Engraved throughout. One foremargin shaved. C Apr 8 (47) £400 [Ingol]

Anr Ed. L, 1736. 4to, later calf. With engraved title, 4 tables & 273 road maps. Ink stamp to verso of title & outer margins of 2 leaves; single wormhole affecting top margins; some waterstains; last leaf frayed. T Mar 19 (55) £460

Anr Ed. L, 1753. 4to, contemp calf; joints repaired. With engraved title, 2 leaves of "Table" & 273 road maps. Pp 23/24 with small tear & marginal def; 1 leaf of tables with short tear & shaved affecting a few numerals. L July 2 (145) £380

Anr copy. Old calf; worn. pn May 21 (329) £380 [Saville]

Anr Ed. L, 1764. 8vo, modern half calf. With ptd title, 12 pages of tables & 273 pages, including 54 maps. pn May 21 (330) £120 [Map House]

Anr copy. Modern calf. With ptd title, 5 leaves of tables & 273 pages, including 54 maps. S June 25 (234) £450 [Hagstrom]

Owen, John, 1616-83

— The Doctrine of the Saint's Perseverance.... Oxford, 1654. Folio, contemp calf; lacking rear endpapers. Partial dampstaining throughout. sg Mar 26 (220) $130

Owen, Major John, 1818-89

— The Journals and Letters of.... NY, 1927. One of 550. 2 vols. With 2 folding maps & 30 plates. cb Jan 8 (152) $75

Owen, Robert, 1771-1858
— Report to the County of Lanark, of a Plan for Relieving Public Distress. Glasgow, 1821. 4to, contemp half calf. With a leaf of Autograph Ms. JG Mar 20 (146) DM7,800

Owen, Samuel. See: Cooke & Owen

Owen, Wilfred, 1893-1918
— Poems. L, 1920. 1st Ed. Worn. sg Dec 11 (355) $120

Anr Ed. L, 1931. One of 160 L.p. copies, sgd by Blunden. With essay by Edmund Blunden. Discolored. sg Dec 11 (356) $90

— Thirteen Poems, with Drawings by Ben Shahn. Northampton, Mass: Gehenna Press, 1956. One of 400, sgd by Leonard Baskin. Folio, half lea. O Sept 23 (70) $120

Owens, Harry J. See: Caxton Club

Owings, Mark
— The Necronomicon: A Study. Balt.: Mirage, 1967. One of 600. Wraps; soiled. cb Sept 28 (866) $15

Owl...
— The Owl: A Miscellany L, 1919. One of 24 sgd by the contributors. Ed by Robert Graves. No 1 only. Wraps. S Dec 18 (172) £650 [Maggs]

Oxenham, John. See: Dunkerley, William Arthur

Oxford English Dictionary
— A New English Dictionary on Historical Principles. Oxford, 1888-1933. 10 vols in 1. Without Supplement. Folio, orig half mor gilt; some vols worn. bba Aug 28 (230) £150 [Subunso]

Anr copy. Bound in 32 vols. 4to, half mor gilt; worn. P June 18 (148) $2,600

Anr copy. 11 vols in 13, including Supplement. Folio, half mor; some spines damaged. pn Sept 18 (277) £70 [Weiner]

Anr copy. 12 vols, including Supplement. Folio, vellum; 2 hinges cracked. pn Jan 22 (184) £190 [Wade]

Anr copy. 10 vols in 15. Folio, half mor gilt. pn Apr 30 (319) £160

Anr copy. 10 vols in 20. Folio, orig half lea; shaken. sg Jan 22 (244) $500

Anr Ed. Oxford, 1961. 13 vols, including Supplement. 4to, cloth; spines faded, a few corners dampstained. bba Dec 18 (43) £200 [Skoob]

Oxford University Press
[A collection of 158 issues of the Oxford Almanack, the annual broadsheets issued by the Press between 1674 & 1850, with an additional 13 sheets of annual issued published in 2 states sold at C on 15 Oct 1986 to Goldschmidt] C Oct 15 (81) £750 [Goldschmidt]

Oxley, John, 1781-1828
— Journals of Two Expeditions into the Interior of New South Wales.... L, 1820. 4to, later half mor. Some foxing; folding maps & plate strengthened on verso. kh Mar 16 (396) A$3,000

Oyved, Moysheh. See: Good, Edward

P

P., D.
— The Rise and Progress of Australia, Tasmania, and New Zealand.... See: Puseley, Daniel

P., M.
— A Character of Coffee and Coffee-Houses. L: for John Starkey, 1661. 4to, new calf. Cropped affecting pagination & a few ptd marginalia. Crahan copy. P Nov 25 (118) $1,600

Pacific...
— Pacific Coast Annual Mining Review.... San Francisco, 1878. 8vo, orig wraps; worn, soiled, chipped; lacking bottom inch of front. cb Oct 9 (153) $80

Pack, Reynell
— Sebastopol Trenches and Five Months in Them. L, 1878. Orig cloth. With 2 folding panoramas & double-page color frontis of decorations. cb Dec 18 (142) $65

Packe, Christopher
— Medela chymica; or, an Account of the Vertues and Uses of a Select Number of Chymical Medicines.... L, 1708. 8vo, new cloth. Upper outer corner of tp mended with loss of letter A & affecting lineborders; worming in lower corner of tp; some page-numerals shaved. S Nov 10 (543) £50 [Elliott]

Packman, Ana Begue
— Early California Hospitality.... Glendale, 1938. 1st Ed. sg Jan 15 (41) $100

Pacot, Jean
— Figures de la Passion de Notre Seigneur Jesus-Christ.... Paris: Chereau, [1743]. 8vo, contemp calf gilt; brittle, joints cracked. Some worming, occasionally affecting text. sg Mar 26 (221) $100

Padgett, Lewis, Pseud.
— A Gnome There Was. NY, 1950. In d/j. cb Sept 28 (1029) $85
— Robots Have No Tails. NY: Gnome Press, [1952]. In d/j. Sgd by Catherine Moore on tp. cb Sept 28 (1031) $65

Padmore, George. See: Cunard & Padmore

Padovani, Fabrizio
— Tractatus duo, alter de Ventis, alter perbrevis de terrae motu. Bologna, 1601. 4to, contemp vellum bds; spine worn. Some browning. S May 21 (119) £1,600 [Goldschmidt]

Padovani, Giovanni
— De compositione et usu multiformium horologiorum.... Venice, 1582. 4to, old vellum; soiled. Final leaf with hole to blank margin; lacking 2 leaves of errata at end. Ck Jan 30 (30) £220

Paduanius, Fabricius. See: Padovani, Fabrizio

Paff, Adam E. M. See: Benson, Frank Weston

Page, John Lloyd Warden
— The Church Towers of Somerset. Bristol, [c.1900]. One of 175. 4to, orig wraps; soiled & frayed. With 51 plates. T Oct 16 (324) £125

Pages...
— Pages from the Past: A Collection of Original Leaves from Rare Books and Manuscripts. NY: Foliophiles, [c.1920]. Folio, loose in 2 boxes. With 35 leaves. sg Jan 22 (157) $450

Pages, Pierre Marie Francois, Vicomte de
— Voyages autour du monde.... Paris, 1782. 1st Ed. 2 vols. 8vo, contemp calf gilt; rubbed. With 10 folding plates & charts. FD June 11 (1107) DM1,300

Paget, J. Otho
— Hunting. L, 1900. One of 150 on handmade paper. Vellum. With 12 plates. sg Oct 30 (165) $275

Pain, William, 1730?-90?
— The Practical Builder. L, 1778. 4to, modern lea. With 83 plates. S Nov 10 (145) £55 [Archdale]

Paine, Albert Bigelow, 1861-1937
See also: Clemens's copy, Samuel Langhorne
— Thomas Nast: his Period and his Pictures. NY, 1904. 8vo, orig cloth. O Nov 18 (142) $50

Paine, Thomas, 1737-1809
See also: Limited Editions Club
— Lettre adressee a l'abbe Raynal.... [N.p.], 1783. 8vo, calf. Corners of 2 final leaves repaired; library stamp. S Sept 23 (521) £170 [Booth]
— The Political and Miscellaneous Works. L, 1819. 2 vols. 8vo, half mor; rubbed. sg Sept 18 (218) $90
— Rights of Man. L: J. S. Jordan, 1791. 1st Jordan Ed, 2d Issue. Bound with: Part the Second, 1792. 8vo, bds; rebacked with stained vellum, rubbed & scuffed. Tp of 1st work cut round & laid down; marginal tear in G4 affecting letters; only 3 leaves in last gathering of 1st work; lacking half-title to 2d work & probably N2. P Sept 24 (199A) $250
— Works. NY, [1908]. One of 500. Ed by D. E. Wheeler. 10 vols. ha May 22 (72) $55; sg Sept 18 (217) $400

Painter, William, 1540?-94. See: Cresset Press

Palatino, Giovanni Battista
— Compendio del gran volume dell'arte del bene & leggiadramente scrivere.... Venice: heirs of Marchio Sessa, 1578. 4to, modern half mor. S May 21 (68) £520 [Lanfranchi]

Palau y Dulcet, Antonio
— Manual del librero hispano-americano. Barcelona, 1948-85. 28 vols, with Index Vols 1-5. 4to, half cloth & wraps. sg May 14 (648) $2,200

Anr copy. 28 vols. Cloth. sg May 24 (647) $1,900

Palgrave, Olive H. C.
— Trees of Central Africa. L, 1956. 4to, cloth. SSA Feb 11 (583) R100

Palisot de Beauvois, Ambroise Marie Francois Joseph, 1752-1820
— Flore d'Oware et de Benin.... Paris, 1804-7 [An XII]. 2 vols. Folio, contemp half calf; rubbed, hinges repaired, upper covers detached, rebacked, 1 spine def. With 120 hand-finished colored plates. de Belder copy. S Apr 28 (260) £5,000 [Brittain]

Palladio, Andrea, 1518-80
— The Architecture. L, 1735. 4 parts in 1 vol. Folio, calf; def. With engraved title & 208 (of 209) plates. Lacking Plate 45 of 2d Book; some soiling; marginal tears. pn Jan 22 (199) £480 [Pitt]

Anr Ed. L, 1738. ("The Four Books of....") 4 parts in 1 vol. Folio, contemp calf; rubbed. With 4 engraved titles & 205 plates. Some leaves dust-soiled. S Nov 10 (148) £500 [Finch]

Anr copy. In 2 vols. Folio, contemp half calf; broken. With engraved title (torn

PALLADIO

without loss) & 215 plates.. T Sept 18 (482) £255
— L'Architettura. Venice, 1642. Folio, contemp calf; worn, upper cover detached. bba Jan 15 (346) £370 [Axe]
Anr Ed. Venice, 1711. Folio, modern cloth. First & last few leaves repaired with loss. Sold w.a.f. Ck Feb 13 (137) £70
— The First Book of Architecture.... L, 1728. 4to, modern mor; rubbed. With engraved title & 31 plates. Lacking final blank; some soiling. S Mar 9 (647) £280 [Walford]

Palladius, Rutilius Taurus Aemilianus
— Della agricultura.... Venice: Bernardino de Viano de Lexona Vercellese, 1538. Bound with: Venuti, Antonio. De agricultura opusculum. Venice: Marchio Sessa, 1541. 8vo, 18th-cent vellum. Minor marginal dampstains. Hunt copy. CNY Nov 21 (208) $550

Pallas, Peter Simon, 1741-1811
— Bemerkungen auf einer Reise in die Suedlichen Statthalterschaften des Russischen Reichs in den Jahren 1793 und 1794. Leipzig, 1799-1801. 2 vols plus Atlas. 4to & oblong folio, contemp lea gilt; worn. With 3 maps & 52 plates, 43 colored. FD Dec 2 (981) DM7,500
— Flora Rossica.... St. Petersburg, 1784-88. Vol I, parts 1 & 2. Folio, half calf gilt. With hand-colored engraved dedication & 101 hand-colored plates. Library stamp & cancellation stamp on tp. Horticultural Society of New York—de Belder copy. S Apr 28 (261) £3,200 [Goldschmidt]
— Illustrationes plantarum imperfecte vel nondum cognitarum cum centuria iconum. Leipzig, 1803-[6]. Folio, loose in contemp half lea; rubbed. With 59 hand-colored plates. Horticultural Society of New York —de Belder copy. S Apr 28 (263) £3,000 [Minton]
— Species Astragalorum descriptae et iconibus coloratis illustratae.... Leipzig, 1800. Folio, contemp half calf; recornered, worn. With 99 hand-colored plates.. Plesch—de Belder copy. S Apr 28 (262) £3,000 [Van Loock]
— Travels through the Southern Provinces of the Russian Empire.... L, 1802-3. 2 vols. 4to, contemp half lea; worn, hinges repaired. With 4 folding maps & 51 plates. bba Dec 18 (207) £150 [Elliott]
Anr copy. Contemp half calf gilt; broken. With 52 plates, most hand-colored, & 3 maps. Old stamp on some text leaves. sg Dec 4 (149) $325
— Voyages dans les gouvernemens meridionaux de l'Empire de Russie. Paris, 1805. Atlas only. Contemp half calf; rubbed.

AMERICAN BOOK PRICES CURRENT

With 55 plates & maps. sg Apr 23 (109) $225
— Voyages...dans plusiers provences de l'Empire de Russie.... Paris, 1788-93. 6 vols, including Atlas. 4to & folio, contemp lea gilt. With folding map & 107 plates. FD Dec 2 (982) DM2,000
Anr copy. 5 (of 6) vols;lacking Atlas. 4to, modern half calf. S Jan 12 (174) £70 [Shapero]

Pallavicino, Ferrante, 1615-44
— Il Divortio celeste.... Villafranca [Geneva?] 1643. 12mo, early calf-backed vellum. sg June 11 (337) $60

Palliere, Leon
— Album Palliere Escenas Americanas. Buenos Aires: Fusoni Hermanos, [c.1860]. Folio, contemp mor gilt, orig wraps preserved. With 52 tinted plates. S Oct 23 (450) £8,000 [Quaritch]
Anr copy. Orig cloth; rebacked. With 52 hand-colored plates. 1 plate repaired at outer margin. S Apr 23 (309) £10,000 [Guller]

Palmedo, Roland. See: Derrydale Press

Palmer, E. —& Pitman, N.
— Trees of Southern Africa. Cape Town, 1972. 3 vols. 4to, cloth. SSA Feb 11 (583) R100

Palmer, Joel
— Journal of Travels over the Rocky Mountains, to the Mouth of the Columbia River.... Cincinnati, 1847. 12mo, orig wraps; front wrap chipped, rear wrap & spine eroded. Some leaves dampstained & with mildew traces; a few tiny holes in last leaf. K June 7 (256) $2,500

Palmerin of England
— The First Part, Shewing the Mirrour of Nobilitie.... L, 1639. 2 parts in 1 vol. 4to, later calf gilt; lacking backstrip. Lacking final blank to Part 2; several leaves torn & repaired affecting text with slight loss on several leaves; 1 leaf badly torn with substantial loss of text; wormed towards end. S Sept 23 (375) £120 [Rix]

Palmireno, Lorenzo
— El Estudioso Cortesano. Acala, 1587. 8vo, old vellum; worn. Some stains & soiling; outer portion of last leaf torn & restored with text supplied in Ms. sg Oct 9 (64) $225

846

Palmstruch, Johann Wilhelm
— Svensk Botanik. Stockholm, 1802-43. 11 vols. 8vo, contemp & later half calf. With 774 hand-colored plates. This copy includes the Register. de Belder copy. S Apr 28 (264) £4,200 [Douglas]

Palou, Francisco, 1722?-89?
— Relacion historica de la vida y apostolicas tareas del venerable Padre Fray Junipero Serra.... Mexico, 1787. 4to, contemp vellum. With full-page port & folding map; map soiled & wormed along top margin. Presented by John Carter Brown to John Bartlett. cb Jan 8 (157) $1,900

Paltock, Robert, 1697-1767
— The Life and Adventures of Peter Wilkins.... L, 1751. 1st Ed. 2 vols. 12mo, contemp calf; rebacked using old spine. With 2 frontises & 4 plates. cb Sept 28 (1032) $450

Panckow, Thomas. See: Pancovius, Thomas

Pancovius, Thomas
— Herbarium oder Kraeuter- und Gewaechs-Buch. Coeln an der Spree, 1673. 4to, contemp vellum. HK Nov 4 (1085) DM4,500

Pantzer, Katharine F. See: Short-Title Catalogue

Panvinio, Onofrio, 1529-68
— Fasti et triumphi...a Romulo...ad Carolum V. Venice, 1557. Folio, half lea; orn & broken. Tp & first few leaves detached; lacking final blank; some waterstains. bba May 28 (7) £60 [Tosi]

Panvinius, Onuphrius. See: Notitia...

Panzer, Georg Wolfgang
Aelteste Buchdruckergeschichte Nuernbergs oder Verzeichnis aller...bis 1500 in Nuernberg.... Nuremberg, 1789. 4to, old bds; spine worn. sg May 14 (513) $275

Papin, Denys, 1647-1712?
— A New Digester...for Softning Bones.... L, 1681. 4to, modern half calf over bds. Piece torn from margin of tp. Andrade-Crahan copy. P Nov 25 (357) $1,400

Papworth, John Buonarotti
— Hints on Ornamental Gardening. L: Ackermann, 1823. 8vo, half calf gilt. With 27 hand-colored plates, 1 with overlay. Lacking half-title as usual; some foxing. pn Sept 18 (103) £340 [Thorp]
— Rural Residences... L: Ackermann, 1818. 1st Ed. 8vo, orig bds; rubbed, rebacked. With 27 hand-colored plates. bba Sept 25 (283) £740 [Reed]
2d Ed. L, 1832. 8vo, orig cloth. With 27 colored plates. S Nov 10 (149) £420

[Henderson]
— Select Views of London. L: Ackerman, 1816. 1st Ed in Book form. 8vo, contemp calf; rebacked. With 76 hand-colored plates, 5 folding. Plate 25 remargined. S Apr 23 (127) £2,000 [Sims]

Papworth, John Buonarotti —& Others
— Poetical Sketches of Scarborough. L, 1813. Illus by Thomas Rowlandson. 8vo, lev gilt by Riviere. With 21 hand-colored plates. sg Feb 12 (267) $275

Paquet, Marcel
La Philosophie et la peinture de Rene Magritte. Paris, 1980. One of 200. Folio, text & plates in separate transparent envelopes bound in mor-backed cloth folder. S July 2 (1055) £900 [Smaver]

Parabosco, Girolamo
— L'Oracolo. Venice: Griffio, 1551. 4to, wraps; spine split. S Sept 23 (476) £240 [Parikian]

Paracelsus, 1493?-1541
— The Hermetic and Alchemical Writings.... L, 1894. 2 vols. 4to, orig cloth, scuffed. S July 28 (1102) £80

Paradin, Claude
— The Heroicall Devises.... L: William Kearney, 1591. 16mo, contemp calf; rebacked & relined. Tp laid down & part of its outer margin clipped away; next leaf torn; last leaf frayed & mended; headlines of L4,5 & a few sidenotes shaved; corner off X7 costing the page-numerals. P Sept 24 (200) $1,200

Paradin, Claude —& Others
— Princelijcke devijsen. Leiden, 1615. 12mo, vellum. B Feb 25 (546) HF1,300

Paramo, Ludovicus a
— Responsum...pro defensione iurisdictionis sancti Offici.... Madrid: Ludovicus Sanchez, 1594. 4to, contemp vellum. sg Oct 9 (55) $200

Paramore, Edward E., Jr.
— The Ballad of Yukon Jake. NY, 1928. Inscr. cb June 18 (216) $85

Parboni, Achille
— Nuova raccolta delle principali vedute antiche, e moderne dell'alma citta di Roma e sue vicinanze. Rome, [plates dated 1824-29]. Oblong 8vo, modern half cloth. With 100 plates. Engraved title stained. Ck Feb 27 (72) £130

PARDOE

Pardoe, Julia, 1806-62

— The Beauties of the Bosphorus. L, 1838. Illus by W. H. Bartlett. 4to, contemp half mor gilt. With engraved title frontis, map & 85 plates. bba June 18 (335) £120 [Nicholas]

Anr copy. Contemp mor gilt. With port, map, engraved title & 78 plates. Ck Nov 21 (453) £170

Anr copy. Contemp mor; rubbed. With frontis (detached & cut down), map & 78 plates. Plates soiled. Sold w.a.f. Ck Feb 27 (152) £110

Anr copy. Old half calf; worn & broken. Some foxing & minor stains. O Nov 18 (143) $120

Anr copy. Disbound. pn Mar 5 (55) £80 [Waterloo]

Anr copy. Mor gilt. pn June 18 (61) £140 [Holmes]

Anr copy. Contemp half calf; hinges cracked. Lacking 2 plates. T Oct 16 (261) £95

Anr Ed. L, 1839. 4to, disbound. With engraved title, map & 73 plates only. pn Dec 11 (46) £80 [Taylor]

Anr Ed. L, [c.1840]. 4to, contemp half mor. bba Sept 25 (405) £100 [Bailey]

Anr copy. Mor gilt; rubbed. With port, engraved title, map & 85 plates. pn Mar 5 (260) £110

Anr copy. Contemp half mor gilt; rubbed. With engraved title, map & 86 plates. S May 28 (889) £95

Anr copy. Contemp calf; rubbed. With port, 3 maps & 165 plates. T Dec 18 (1) £220

Pare, Ambroise, 1510?-90

— Works. L, 1634. 1st Ed in English. Folio, contemp calf; rebacked. Lower blank corner of title torn away; small tear in upper outer corner of H2 affecting ptd line only; small tear in lower margin of M2 just affecting a few letters; small tear in lower margin of Z3 mended; tear in outer margin of 3E6; lower margins from ff. 88 to 916 wormed affecting occasional letters; stains on 5A3-4. S May 21 (208) £2,400 [Quaritch]

Anr Ed. L, 1678. Folio, contemp calf; rebacked. Paper flaws in 3 leaves. S May 28 (756) £800

Paredes, Ignacio de

— Promptuario manual mexicano.... Mexico, 1759. 4to, later half calf. sg Sept 18 (220) $325

AMERICAN BOOK PRICES CURRENT

Parent, Louis

— Le Tableau des merveilles de l'univers. Franequer: Jean Wellens, 1661. 4to, mor janseniste by Duru & Chambolle, 1862. Jeanson copy. SM Mar 1 (448) FF3,400

Paris...

— Paris et ses environs.... Paris, [1855]. Oblong folio, orig cloth; worn. With litho title & 20 colored plates. Some foxing & soiling. O May 12 (53) $250

— Paris et ses environs, 1859.... Paris, [1859]. Oblong folio, orig cloth; broken. With 61 plates, all with library stamps. bba Feb 5 (356) £280 [Rainer]

— EXPOSITION INTERNATIONALE DES ARTS DECORATIFS ET INDUSTRIELS MODERNES. - L'Art Hollandais a l'Exposition.... Paris & Haarlem, 1925. 4to, cloth. First use of Van Krimpen's Lutetia. B Oct 7 (83) HF250

Paris, 1892. See: Osmond & Paris

Paris Comique...

— Paris comique: Revue amusante. Paris, [1844]. 4to, half cloth. With 20 hand-colored lithos. JG Oct 2 (1559) DM580

Park, John James

— The Topography and Natural History of Hampstead. L, 1818. 8vo, contemp half calf; joints split, worn. Some spotting & offsetting. Extra-illus with plates. bba Aug 28 (320) £110 [British Arch'l Library]

Park, Mungo, 1771-1806

— The Journal of a Mission to the Interior of Africa.... L, 1815. 1st Ed. 4to, contemp half calf; spine rubbed & worn. With folding map. One leaf torn & repaired. T Feb19 (224) £60

— Travels in the Interior Districts of Africa. L, 1799. 1st Ed. 4to, contemp calf; rebacked & corners repaired. With port, 3 folding maps (1 hand-colored in outline & laid down, anr torn), 5 plates & 2 leaves of music. 2 leaves laid down; some stains. bba Mar 26 (353) £75 [Fisher]

Park, Thomas

— The British Poets.... L, 1810-24. In 100 vols. 12mo, mor gilt; rubbed. sg Sept 11 (38) $550

— Cupid Turned Volunteer. L, 1804. 4to, contemp half calf; rebacked, corners restored, hinges strengthened. With 12 hand-colored plates, including frontis. C Dec 12 (368) £150 [Henderson]

Parker, Charles, 1800-81

— Villa Rustica. L, 1848. 4to, later half calf. With 72 plans & plates Tp browned. bba Sept 25 (284) £130 [Demetzy]

Parker, Henry, 1604-52?

— The Generall Junto; or, the Councell of Union.... L, 1642. Folio, contemp presentation bdg of citron lev extra lettered for the 3d Earl of Lothian. P June 18 (149) $1,800

— The Generall Junto, or the Councell of Union. L, 1642. Folio, contemp mor gilt with central oval bearing a presentation inscr to Edward, Lord Herbert of Cherbury. Manchester copy. S July 24 (261) £800 [Maggs]

— Of a Free Trade. L: Fr. Neile for Robert Bostock, 1648. 4to, wraps. Head of rule-border on title & a few headlines shaved. S July 24 (451) £2,200 [Drury]

Parker, John Henry

— A Glossary of Terms Used in Grecian, Roman, Italian and Gothic Architecture. Oxford, 1850. 3 vols. 8vo, mor gilt extra; rubbed & worn. cb Oct 23 (169) $60

Parker, Samuel, 1779-1866

— Journal of an Exploring Tour Beyond the Rocky Mountains. Ithaca, NY, 1842. 12mo, orig cloth. Folding map with 3-inch tear repaired when map was linen-backed. sg Mar 12 (205) $130

Parker, Theodore, 1810-60

— The Trial of Theodore Parker for the "Misdemeanor" of a Speech in Faneuil Hall against Kidnapping.... Bost., 1855. 8vo, orig cloth. bba Nov 13 (110) £40 [Goldman]; cb Oct 9 (286) $85

Parker, Thomas Lister

— Description of Browsholme Hall in the West Riding of the County of York.... L, 1815. 4to, old bds; rubbed, upper joint broken. With 20 plates. O Feb 24 (63) $60

Parker, Thomas N.

— Leaves out of the Book of a Country Gentleman. Oswestry, 1847. Ltd Ed. Folio, half lea; def. With 22 plates on 18 sheets. Minor dampstains. S Mar 9 (762) £250 [Sims]

Parkinson, James, d.1824

— Organic Remains of a Former World.... L, 1820-11. 3 vols. 4to, modern cloth. Some plates in Vol III a little stained; text leaves of Vols II & III with occasional staining. L Dec 11 (302) £260

Parkinson, John, 1567-1650

— Paradisi in sole paradisus terrestris.... L, 1629. 1st Ed. Folio, contemp calf, armorial bdg; rebacked, rubbed. Marginal repairs to 4 leaves; stain in O4; library stamps on tp & several other leaves. Crahan copy. P Nov 25 (358) $1,500

Anr copy. Contemp calf. With port & 110 full-page woodcuts. "Fine copy". pnE Dec 17 (222) £1,500 [Steedman]

Anr copy. Contemp calf; worn, rebacked & recornered. With allegorical title (with small tear), woodcut port & 3 small & 110 full page woodcuts. Small stain to lower blank margin of final leaves Ggg1-2. Luttrell—Lambert—Jussieu—de Belder copy. S Apr 28 (266) £2,600 [Wilson]

Anr Ed. L, 1656. Folio, old calf by Birdshall; lower cover detached. Small repair to woodcut title; final leaf strengthened at gutter; many leaves browned; some old ink annotations cropped; small holes in S4 & Mm1; some blank foremargins dampstained. Hunt copy. CNY Nov 21 (216) $850

— Theatrum botanicum.... L, 1640. Folio, 19th-cent calf; rubbed, joints cracked, head & foot of spine worn. Lacking intial blank; errata leaf backed; short tear in 4Y3; minor worming in a few inner blank margins; faint waterstain in a few upper corners. C Apr 8 (151) £800 [Wheldon & Wesley]

Anr copy. Calf; rebacked with mor, rubbed, scuffed. Waterstaining; tear on 4G6 into text; marginal tears & soiling. Crahan copy. P Nov 25 (359) $950

Anr copy. Modern half mor gilt. Browned; tp & 1st 5 leaves repaired; lacking 2L1-2L6, 2A1, 4V6 & 5Z3; last leaves of index repaired with loss; lacking last leaf of index. Sold w.a.f. pn Sept 18 (257) £260 [Edmunds]

Anr copy. Modern half calf gilt. Engraved title trimmed & laid down; some stains in margins & occasional small tears; index stained & repaired. pn June 18 (117) £380 [Dunsheath]

Anr copy. Bound in 2 vols. Folio, 18th-cent calf with arms of Duke of Newcastle; spines & joints worn. Vol II wormed at beginning; errata leaf torn & backed; holes in 4K6 & 6K4 affecting text; piece torn from outer margin of 4V6. Clumber Library copy. S Oct 23 (743) £800 [Bur-

den]
  Anr copy. Folio, contemp calf; rebacked & worn. Engraved title & final errata leaf partly backed; last 2 gatherings frayed & trimmed in outer margins; piece torn from 7I4 affecting text. S Oct 23 (744) £250 [Walford]
  Anr copy. Contemp calf bound for John Evelyn with his gilt arms on sides; spine def at foot, repaired. Some rust-stains. John Evelyn's annotated copy. de Belder copy. S Apr 28 (267) £6,800 [Israel]

Parkinson, Richard
— A Tour in America, in 1798, 1799, and 1800.... L, 1805. 2 vols. 8vo, orig half calf; worn, minor worming to inside of 1 rear cover. Library markings. ha May 22 (313) $250

Parkinson, Sydney. See: Cook, Capt. James

Parkinson, Thomas, Artist
— Flower Painting Made Easy. L: Robt. Sayer, [1766?]. 4to, contemp half calf; worn, upper cover recornered. With 70 (of 72) hand-colored plates. Plesch—de Belder copy. S Apr 28 (265) £4,200 [Krohn]

Parkman, Francis, 1823-93
— The California and Oregon Trail. Bost., 1925. ("The Oregon Trail.") One of 975. Illus by Frederic Remington & N. C. Wyeth. Half cloth. With 5 plain & 5 color plates, all tipped-in. cb Jan 8 (301) $170
— Works. Bost., 1897-98. Champlain Ed. 20 vols. 8vo, half mor gilt; joints rubbed. With plates in mtd India-proof state. sg Sept 11 (244) $275
  Anr Ed. Bost., 1902. 17 vols, including Life by C. H. Farnham. 8vo, cloth, in d/js. sg Sept 11 (245) $175

Parkyns, George Isham
— Monastic and Baronial Remains. L, 1816. 2 vols. 8vo, orig bds; worn, 1 spine partially def. With 100 plates. The first few plates in Vol II stained in margin. S Nov 17 (813) £55 [Rankin]

Parmentier, Antoine Augustin, 1737-1813
— Examen chymique des pommes de terre. Paris, 1773. 12mo, modern bds. Some soiling. Crahan copy. P Nov 25 (361) $500
— Memoire sur les avantages que la province de Languedoc peut retirer de ses grains.... Paris, 1786. 4to, contemp half calf; spine worn at head & foot. C Dec 12 (159) £320 [Spelman]

Parnell, Thomas, 1679-1718. See: Goldsmith & Parnell

Paroles...
— Paroles peintes V. Paris,1 1975. One of 50 on Arches, with each engraving sgd. Folio, unbound as issued in ptd wraps. With 9 color engravings. sg Apr 2 (152) $3,000

Parry, Sir Edward Abbott. See: Cervantes Saavedra, Miguel de

Parry, Sir William Edward, 1790-1855
— Journal of a Voyage for the Discovery of a North-West Passage.... L, 1821. 1st Ed. 4to, contemp half calf gilt; rubbed. Tp & prelims dampstained. pn Apr 30 (235) £140 [Ruddell]
  Anr copy. Modern cloth. Some perforated library stamps; 1 map crudely repaired. sg Mar 12 (206) $250
— Journal of a Second Voyage for the Discovery of a North-West Passage.... L, 1824-25. Lacking Appendix. 4to, cloth. With 39 maps & charts. bba Dec 18 (209) £70 [Elliott]
  Anr copy. 2 vols, including Appendix. 4to, orig half cloth; worn. With 41 plates & charts. Vol I upper cover & tp detached. S July 14 (846) £320

Parsifal. See: Wagner, Richard

Parsons, George F. See: Grabhorn Printing

Parsons, Robert, 1546-1610
— Elizabethae reginae Angliae edictum promulgatum Londini 29 Novemb. anni M.D.XCI. [N.p., 1573]. 8vo, old vellum; front hinge cracked & repaired. Some browning. sg Oct 9 (286) $150

Particularitez...
— Les Particularitez de la chasse royale faite par Sa Majeste le jour de St Hubert.... Paris: Alexandre Lesselin, 1649. 4to, modern half calf. Jeanson copy. SM Mar 1 (449) FF2,800

Pascal, Blaise, 1623-62
— Monsieur Pascall's Thoughts.... L: Jacob Tonson, 1688. 8o, modern half calf; new endpapers. Repair to the lower margin of T4 just affecting text. S July 23 (15) £500 [Quaritch]
— Oeuvres. The Hague [Paris], 1779. 5 vols. 8vo, contemp calf gilt; worn & rebacked. HN Nov 26 (264) DM520
— Pensees sur la religion et sur quelques autres sujets. Paris, 1670. 1st Ed, Issue not stated. 12mo, contemp calf; rebacked. F2 supplied in photocopy; small hole in text of G4; tear at top of O11 just affecting 2 lines of text; small hole in headline of P7; some stains. S Mar 10 (1121) £130 [Burden]

Pasquier, Etienne, 1529-1615
— Les Lettres. Paris: Abel l'Angelier, 1586. 4to, old calf; rebacked, orig spine laid down, front cover detached. sg Oct 9 (288) $300

Pasquin, Peter. See: Pyne, William Henry

Pass, Crispin van de
— Hortus floridus. Utrecht & Arnheim, 1614-[16]. Dutch text issue. 4 parts in 1 vol (lacking "Altera pars"). Oblong folio, modern vellum bds; discolored. With engraved title 2 garden views, 1 allegorical plate & 112 plates. Small hole in border of Latin title; some dampstains; occasional ink sketches on versos of plates; portion of lower border of 1 plate torn away. de Belder copy. S Apr 28 (270) £5,000 [Schuster]

English text issue. 5 parts in 1 vol. Oblong folio, contemp vellum; worn. With 2 engraved title, 2 garden views, 1 allegorical plates & 163 plates. Some soiling & marginal scribbles; 2 plates inlaid; 1 inner margin strengthened; a number of tears repaired but occasionally affecting text or plates; 1 wormhole running through lower margin. de Belder copy. S Apr 28 (271) £7,500 [Israel]

Latin text issue. Oblong folio, contemp calf; joints rubbed. With engraved title, 4 engraved garden views, 1 allegorical plate & 154 plates. Some dampstain in outer margins; small stain in Plate 9 affecting ruled border only; 1 plate in Alter pars with hole not affecting engraving & anr plate inlaid. Linnean Society—de Belder copy. S Apr 28 (272) £8,500 [Forum]

Savage's State 1c. 4 parts in 1 vol (lacking "Altera pars"). Oblong folio, early vellum; stained. With 61 complete plates only; lacking some & others deformed. pnE Oct 15 (81) £520

Passages...
— Passages from Modern English Poets, illustrated by the Junior Etching Club. L: W. Tegg, [1862]. 4to, early half mor; scuffed, joints tender. With 38 (of 45) plates. ha Sept 19 (220) $300

Passavant, Johann David
— Le Peintre-graveur. Leipzig, 1860-64. 6 vols in 3. 8vo, cloth; hinges split. sg May 14 (52) $90

Passerat, Jean, 1534-1602
— Le Premier Livre des poemes. Paris: Veuve Mamert Patisson, 1602. Bound with: Bertaut, J. Recueile quelques vers amoureux. Paris, 1602. 8vo, mor gilt with arms of de Thou & of his first wife, Marie de Barbancon. Jeanson copy. SM Mar 1 (450) FF24,000

— Recueil des oeuvres poetiques.... Paris: Abel L'Angelier, 1606. 2 parts in 1 vol. 8vo, contemp vellum. Without the port on the verso of the 8th leaf of the 2d part. Jeanson copy. SM Mar 1 (451) FF6,500

Pasteur, Louis, 1822-95
— Etudes sur la biere.... Paris, 1876. 1st Ed. 8vo, contemp half mor; cover detached but present & lacking top 2 inches. With 12 plates. cb July 30 (227) $160

Anr Ed. Paris, 1920. 8vo, wraps. With 12 plates. Facsimile of 1876 Ed. sg Jan 15 (337) $50

— Etudes sur le vin.... Paris, 1866. 1st Ed. 8vo, modern cloth; dampstained. With 32 colored plates, slightly foxed. sg Jan 15 (336) $200

2d Ed. Paris, 1873. 8vo, orig half cloth; rubbed. Some foxing, mostly marginal. cb July 30 (228) $300

— Memoire sur la fermentation appelee lactique. Paris, 1858. 8vo, orig ptd wraps, unopened. Offprint from: Annales de dhimie et de physique, 3e serie, LII, [1858]. S Nov 27 (282) £1,700 [Freidman]

Pastissier...
— Le Pastissier Francois. Ou est enseigne la maniere de faire toute sorte de Pastisserie.... Amst.: Elzevier, 1655. 12mo, mor gilt by Trautz-Bauzonnet; joints rubbed, 1 cracking. Silver-Crahan copy. P Nov 25 (365A) $10,000

Paston, George. See: Symonds, Emily Morse

Pastrana, Francisco
— Catecismo de Geografia de la Isla de Puerto-Rico. Puerto-Rico: Marquez, 1852. 8vo, orig wraps; spine chipped. With folding map. sg Sept 18 (241) $70

Pater, Walter, 1839-94
— Sebastian Van Storck. Vienna: Avalun, 1924. One of 480. Illus by Alastair. 4to, orig bds; soiled. With 8 colored illusts. HN Nov 26 (1661) DM500

Anr Ed. L & NY, 1927. One of 1,050, with 1 plate sgd. 4to, orig cloth; soiled. With 8 colored illusts. S Oct 6 (753) £100 [Fantasy]

Paterson, Daniel, 1739-1825
— British Itinerary, being a New and Accurate Delineation.... L, 1785. 2 vols. 8vo, modern mor gilt. pn Nov 20 (270) £110

Anr copy. Calf; rubbed. pn Mar 5 (369) £180 [Saville]

Anr copy. Calf; loose. pn May 21 (385) £90 [Saville]

Paton, Hugh
— Etching, Drypoint, Mezzotint. The Whole Art of the Painter-Etcher. L, 1909. 2d Ed. ha Dec 19 (74) $70

Patri, Giacomo
— White Collar: Novel in Linocuts. [N.p., c.1940]. 2d Ed. Spiral-bound wraps. Inscr. cb Dec 4 (295) $65

Anr copy. Intro by Rockwell Kent. Wraps. Small tear to fore-edge of intro leaf. cb Dec 4 (294) $75

Patricius Piccolomineus, Augustinus
— Rituum ecclesiasticorum sive sacrarum cerimoniarum S. S. Romanae ecclesiae.... Venice: Gregorii de Gregoriis, 21 Nov 1516. ("Sacrum cerimoniarum Romanae ecclesiae libri tres.") Folio, bds; hinges def. Some worming & dampstaining; tp discolored & detached. S Sept 23 (478) £340 [Thomas]

Patte, Pierre, 1723-1814
— Monumens eriges en France a la gloire de Louis XV. Paris, 1767. Folio, contemp calf; rubbed. With 57 plates. With 1 small wormhole. HN May 20 (199) DM1,000

Patten, William, Londoner
— The Expedicion into Scotlande of Edward, Duke of Soomerset. L, 30 June 1548. Blank margin of t.p. holed. New STC 19476.5. Bound with: Proctor, John. The Hstorie [sic] of Wyates Rebellion. L, 10 Jan 1555, Wormed, affecting woodcut border & sidenotes. STC 20408. And: The Lawes and Statutes of Geneva.... L, 16 Apr 1562. STC 11725. 8vo, late 18th-cent calf gilt; rubbed. C Dec 12 (352) £1,300 [Maggs]

Pattison, Emilia Francis Strong. See: Dilke, Emilia Francis Strong Pattison

Pattison, Mark, 1813-84. See: Grabhorn Printing

Paul, Elliot. See: Quintanilla, Luis

Paul, Herbert, 1853-1935
— Queen Anne. L, 1906. One of 200 with plates in duplicate. 4to, mor gilt with royal arms. S July 13 (203) £160

Paul, Sir James Balfour
— The Scots Peerage. Edin., 1904-14. 9 vols, including Index. Orig cloth. Ck Nov 21 (271) £260

Paul Pry, Pseud. See: Heath, William

Paul the Servite. See: Sarpi, Paolo

Paul, William, 1822-1905
— The Rose Garden. L, 1848. 1st Ed. 8vo, orig cloth; bumped & frayed, hinges & lower joint repaired. With 15 hand-colored plates. cb Feb 19 (210) $325

Anr copy. Contemp mor gilt. pn Dec 11 (306) £280 [Greyfriars]

Anr copy. Half mor by Sangorski & Sutcliffe. pnE Dec 17 (223) £500 [Steedman]

Paulhan, Jean
— De mauvais sujets. [Paris], 1958. One of 112. Illus by Marc Chagall. Folio, unsewn in orig wraps. With 10 colored plates. SM Oct 20 (600) FF65,000

— Les Hain-Teny. [Paris, 1956]. One of 116 on Auvergne. Illus by Andre Masson. Folio, unsewn in orig wraps. With 9 orig watercolors by Masson. SM Oct 20 (652) FF8,050

— Les Paroles transparentes. Paris: Bibliophiles de l'Union Francaise, 1955. One of 132, sgd by author & artist. Illus by Georges Braque. Folio, unsewn in orig wraps. With 4 lithos. SM Oct 20 (594) FF8,000

Paulinus a Sancto Bartholomaeo, 1748-1806
— Mumiographia Musei Obiciniani. Pavia: Typographia Seminarii, 1799. 4to, 19th-cent mor, blindstamped arms on covers; worn. Marginal dampstaining; some mildew at end. sg Jan 15 (113) $175

Paulison, C. M. K.
— Arizona; the Wonderful Country.... Tucson, 1881. 8vo, orig wraps; rebacked with gray paper, brittle. Small chip at title fore-edge. sg Sept 18 (19) $1,500

Paulli, Simon, 1603-80
— A Treatise on Tobacco, Tea, Coffee, and Chocolate.... L, 1746. 8vo, half mor. With 2 folding plates (mtd). S May 28 (757) £320

Pausanias
— Opera. Venice: Aldus, July 1516. Folio, mor gilt by Bedford; joints rubbed. Tiny puncture to blank margin of i5. Hoe copy. CNY May 11 (1) $1,500

Paxton, Sir Joseph, 1801-65
See also: Lindley & Paxton
— The Magazine of Botany, and Register of Flowering Plants. L, 1834-37. Vols I-III only. 3 vols. 8vo, contemp half mor; rubbed, spine of Vol I chipped. Ck Oct 31 (120) £650

Vols I-IV only. L, 1834-49. Half mor; worn. pnE June 17 (142) £820

Vols I-VIII only. L, 1834-43. Modern half mor. Some plates torn, def or cropped. Sold w.a.f. S Oct 23 (745) £1,600 [Sablon]

Anr Ed. L, 1841-49. 16 vols. 8vo, contemp half mor; soiled. With 717 hand-finished colored plates. Sold w.a.f. de Belder copy. S Apr 28 (274) £6,000 [Krohn]

Payer, Julius von
— New Lands within the Arctic Circle. L, 1876. 2 vols. 8vo, orig cloth; spine ends frayed. Frontis detached. cb June 4 (166) $110

Payne, Albert Henry
— The Royal Dresden Gallery. Dresden, [1845?-50]. 2 vols. 4to, half mor. bba Apr 23 (64) £130 [Frew Mackenzie]

Anr copy. Orig calf gilt. Some foxing & browning to text; a few plates slightly cropped. ha Mar 13 (140) $300

Anr copy. Half calf gilt. pn May 21 (100) £110 [Grimstad]

Payne, William
— Picturesque Views in Devonshire, Cornwall &c. L, 1826. Oblong 4to, orig half mor; soiled, corners & spine worn. With 16 colored plates. Plate 1 with brown spotting in blank margin; tp, list of plates & descriptions of Plates 1 & 16 stained. L July 2 (98) £700

Anr copy. Contemp half lea; extremities worn, rear joint starting. sg Apr 2 (154) $850

Payne-Gallwey, Sir Ralph
— The Book of Duck Decoys. L, 1886. 4to, orig cloth. S Nov 17 (673) £220 [Tzarina]

Anr copy. Half mor. sg Oct 23 (246) $100

Peacham, Henry, 1576?-1643?
— The Valley of Varietie: or, Discourse Fitting for the Times. L: M. Parsons for James Becket, 1638. 12mo, 19th-cent mor gilt; rubbed. Upper margin shaved affecting border of headline on some leaves. C Dec 12 (353) £480 [Lawson]

Peacock, Thomas Love, 1785-1866
— Sir Hornbook; or, Childe Launcelot's Expedition.... L, 1815. 2d Ed. 16mo, orig wraps. With 7 hand-colored plates. S Dec 5 (287) £400 [Maggs]

Peake, Mervyn
— A Reverie of Bone. L, 1967. Ltd Ed. In d/j. T Oct 15 (18) £40

— Shapes & Sounds. L, [1941]. Orig half cloth, in torn d/j. Inscr to Ruthven Todd & with orig pencil & wash drawing on front endpaper of a semi-nude female dancer. T Oct 15 (9) £500

Peake, Richard Brinsley
— The Characteristic Costume of France. L, 1819. 4to, contemp half calf; worn & broken. With 19 hand-colored plates. Ck Sept 26 (175) £160

— Memoirs of the Colman Family.... L, 1841. 2 vols extended to 4. 8vo, mor gilt by Riviere. Extra-illus with 170 ports & with plates. ha May 22 (73) $350

— Snobson's Seasons.... L: M. A. Nattali, [c.1838]. Illus by R. Seymour. 8vo, calf gilt. With 92 plates. Some plates repaired on verso. sg June 11 (314) $275

Pearse, Geoffrey Eastcott
— Eighteenth Century Furniture in South Africa. Pretoria, 1960. 4to, cloth, in d/j. cba Mar 5 (142) $65; SSA Oct 28 (799) R260

Pearson, Henry J.
— Beyond Petsora Eastward. Two Summer Voyages.... L, 1899. 4to, orig cloth. pn Oct 23 (261) £60 [Bewder]

Pearson, Karl, 1857-1936
— The Life, Letters and Labours of Francis Galton. Cambr., 1914-30. 3 vols in 4. 4to, orig cloth. Ck Nov 7 (98) £300

Pearson's...
— Pearson's Magazine. L, 1896-1901. Vols 1-12. 12 vols. Orig cloth. Contains a number of Arthur Conan Doyle stories & H. G. Wells' War of the Worlds. cb Apr 24 (424) $450

Peary, Robert Edwin, 1856-1920
— The North Pole. L, 1910. One of 500. 4to, orig cloth. S Oct 23 (318) £220 [Thomson]

Pechstein, Max, 1881-1955
— Reisebilder: Italien-Suedsee. Berlin, 1919. One of 800. Oblong 4to, orig cloth. HN Nov 26 (2032) DM1,000

Peck, Charles Horton, 1833-1917
— Annual Report of the State Botanist of the State of New York. Albany, 1897. 4to, orig cloth. With 43 color plates. sg Dec 18 (203) $60

Pecquet, Antoine, 1704-62
— Loix forestieres de France.... Paris: Prault, 1753. 2 vols. 4to, contemp mor gilt. Jeanson copy. SM Mar 1 (452) FF5,500

Pedrusi, Paolo
— I Cesari in oro.... Parma: Stamperia di S.A.S., 1694-1727. 10 vols. Folio, contemp bdg; a few spines wormed. With 10 frontises & 263 folding numismatic plates. Tear in lower portion of title to Vol X repaired; corner of 1 leaf in Vol VIII torn away; occasional light marginal worming; some short tears in margins. S Nov 27

(208) £1,200 [Goldschmidt]

Peel, Charles Victor Alexander
— Somaliland: Being an Account of Two Expeditions.... L, 1900. 8vo, orig cloth; bumped, hinge cracked. Library markings. cb Nov 6 (225) $50

Peep...
— A Peep at the Esquimaux. L, 1825. 2d Ed. 8vo, orig half lea; spine repaired. With 40 hand-colored woodcuts. Stained, 1 leaf misbound. S Dec 5 (356) $200 [J. Peters]

Peguy, Charles Pierre, 1873-1914
— Presentation de la Beauce a Nostre-Dame de Chartres. Paris, 1964. One of 100 on vellum. Illus by Alfred Manessier. Oblong folio, unsewn in orig wraps. SM Oct 20 (649) FF3,000
— La Tapisserie de Notre Dame 1912. The Hague, 1929. One of 105. 4to, orig vellum. B Oct 7 (123) HF850
— La Tapisserie de Notre Dame. The Hague, 1929. One of 105. 4to, vellum. B Oct 7 (123) HF850

Peignot, Gabriel, 1767-1849
— Dictionnaire critique, litteraire et bibliographique des principaux livres condamnes au feu, suprimes ou censures. Paris, 1806. 1st Ed. 2 vols in 1. 8vo, contemp mor; rebacked, extremities worn. sg May 14 (345) $500

Pelham, M. See: Kilner, Dorothy

Pelican, Mr. See: Pellisson-Fontanier, Paul

Pell, Daniel
— Nec inter vivos, nec inter mortuos...Improvement of the Sea. L, 1659. 8vo, disbound. Lacking initial blank; worming at beginning affecting some text; running heads of last few leaves shaved; scribbling on tp. S Nov 10 (406) £55 [Burmester]

Pellechet, Marie
— Catalogue general des incunables des bibliotheques publiques de France. Paris, 1897-1909. Vols I-III (all pbd) in 1 vol. 8vo, cloth, orig wraps bound in. sg May 14 (515) $350

Pellenc, Cesar
— Les Plaisirs de la vie. Aix: Jean Roize, 1654. 8vo, mor gilt by Duru & Chambolle, 1862. Jeanson copy. SM Mar 1 (454) FF100,000

Pellisson-Fontanier, Paul, 1624-93
— La Feste d'Erbaud. Du 8 Oct 1668, descrite par Mr. Pelicon. [N.p., n.d.]. 12mo, mor janseniste by Cape. Jeanson copy. SM Mar 1 (473) FF7,000

Pelzeln, August von, 1825-91. See: Holub & Pelzeln

Pemberton, Henry, 1694-1771
— A View of Sir Isaac Newton's Philosophy. L, 1728. 4to, contemp calf; joints & edges taped. With 12 folding plates. sg Jan 15 (333) $150

Anr copy. Contemp calf; hinges cracked. T Nov 20 (439) £100

Pena, Petrus. See: L'Obel & Pena

Penafiel, Antonio
— Nombres Geograficos de Mexico: Catalogo alfabetico.... Mexico, 1885. 2 vols. Folio, orig wraps, plates unbound in wraps. With 39 color plates. sg Sept·18 (223) $350

Pendleton, Nathaniel Greene
— Military Posts - Council Bluffs to the Pacific Ocean. Wash., 1843. 8vo, recent half mor. With folding map. 27th Congress. 3d Session, House Doc 31. cb Jan 8 (158) $70

Penfield, Edward
— Holland Sketches. NY, 1907. 1st Ed. Bds; soiled. With 30 mtd color plates. O Oct 21 (140) $60

Anr copy. Bds; light wear. O Apr 28 (154) $150

Penn, Irving
— Moments Preserved. L, 1960. 1st English Ed. 4to, cloth, in d/j. sg Nov 13 (86) $175

Anr Ed. NY, 1960. 4to, cloth, in d/j. ha Nov 7 (185) $120

Anr copy. Cloth, in d/j. Inscr. sg May 7 (61) $375; wa Nov 6 (333) $150

Penn, William, 1644-1718
— A Further Account of the Province of Pennsylvania.... [L, 1685]. 4to, wraps. S June 25 (415) £1,100
— A Letter from William Penn...to the Committee of the Free Society of Traders.... L, 1683. 3d Ed. Folio, disbound. With folding map. Last leaf loose & torn with loss of c.150 words of text; map soiled with some marginal fraying & loss. P Oct 29 (6) $18,500
— Quakerism a New Nick-Name for Old Christianity. [L], 1672. 8vo, contemp calf; worn. Contents dampstained; marginal worming. T Apr 16 (372) £52

Pennant, Thomas, 1726-99
— British Zoology. L: J. & J. March, [1761]-66. Folio, contemp calf gilt; spine repaired at head & foot. With 133 hand-colored plates. Tear in N1. S Apr 23 (53) £9,000 [Schuster]

Pennant, Thomas, 1726-98
— British Zoology. L, 1766. Folio, contemp calf gilt. With 132 hand-colored plates, including those in the Supplement & with 1 small engraving. 1 plate with tear, not affecting ptd area; a few marginal tears. C Oct 15 (195) £9,000 [Maggs]
 Anr Ed. L, 1812. 4 vols. 8vo, contemp half calf; rubbed. With 4 engraved titles & 297 plates. pn July 23 (239) £110 [Smith]
— History of London, Westminster, and Southwark. L, 1814. 2 vols. 4to, disbound. Sold w.a.f. Extra-illus with views & ports. S July 28 (1000) £160
— History of Quadrupeds. L, 1793. 3d Ed. 2 vols. 4to, contemp calf; worn, rebacked, 1 cover loose. Lacking frontises. bba Apr 23 (152) £80 [Rainer]
 Anr copy. Contemp russia gilt; rubbed, upper cover detached. With engraved titles & 111 plates. 1 marginal tear. S Nov 10 (545) £95 [Wheldon]
 The History of the Parishes of Whiteford and Holywell. L, 1796. 4to, 19th-cent russia gilt; spine chipped. L.p. copy. Author's copy, extra-illus with watercolors, engravings, sketches & related Ms material. S Dec 18 (268) £2,000 [Quaritch]
— A Journey from London to the Isle of Wight. L, 1801. 2 vols. 4to, half mor gilt by Bayntun. With 2 folding maps, colored in outline, & 47 plates. pn Mar 5 (140) £160 [Camberley]
— Of London. L, 1790. 1st Ed. Extended to 6 vols. 4to, 19th-cent half mor; worn. All leaves mtd. Sold w.a.f. bba Oct 16 (263) £480 [Jeffery]
— A Tour in Scotland. Chester, 1774. 2d Ed. 4to, calf gilt. With engraved titles & 129 plates & maps. S Feb 23 (392) £200 [Beasley]
 4th Ed. L, 1776. 4to, contemp russia; rubbed, 1 cover detached. bba Oct 30 (346) £75 [Smith]
— A Tour in Wales. L, 1778. 1st Ed. 4to, contemp calf; rebacked & recornered in 19th-cent mor. With frontis & 26 plates. cb July 30 (144) £95
 Anr Ed. L, 1784. 2 vols. 4to, contemp calf gilt; spines worn, upper cover of Vol I detached. T Apr 16 (81) £80
— A View of Hindoostan. L, 1798-1800. Vol II only. Orig bds; worn & soiled. bba July 16 (128) £85 [Tritton]
 Anr Ed. L, 1798. 2 vols in 1. 4to, contemp half mor; rubbed. With folding map & 20 plates. Map with small corner tear; Vol II lacking Plate 8. C Apr 8 (109) £200 [Joseph]
 Anr copy. 2 vols. 4to, contemp calf gilt. With folding map & 21 plates. Lacking half-titles & final blank in Vol I; small tear in 2 leaves. C Apr 8 (110) £280 [Lennox Money]

Pennell, Elizabeth Robins & Joseph
— The Glory of New York. NY, 1926. One of 355. Folio, cloth. With 24 colored plates. Sgd by Elizabeth Pennell. sg Sept 18 (203) $100
— The Life of James McNeill Whistler. L: Heinemann, 1908. 2 vols. 4to, orig half cloth; worn. cb Feb 19 (277) $65
 One of 150. Half mor gilt; extremities worn, endpapers soiled. sg Feb 5 (255) $150
 Anr Ed. Phila., 1909. 2 vols. 4to, half cloth. sg Feb 5 (326) $50
— Lithography and Lithographers: Some Chapters in the History of the Art. L, 1898. Folio, orig bds; rubbed & soiled. With 7 orig lithos. cb July 30 (145) $250
 Anr Ed. NY, 1898. Folio, orig cloth; joints split, hinges repaired. Library stamps on title, plates & some leaves of text. bba Dec 18 (210) £60 [King]
— Our Philadelphia. Phila. & L, 1914. One of 289, sgd by both Pennells & with 10 extra drawings. sg Sept 18 (224) $130

Pennell, Elizabeth Robins, 1855-1936
— The Delights of Delicate Eating. NY, 1901. sg Jan 15 (42) $80
— My Cookery Books. Bost. & NY, 1903. One of 330. sg Jan 15 (42A) $175; sg Feb 5 (250) $300

Pennell, Joseph, 1857-1926
— The Adventures of an Illustrator.... Bost., 1925. 4to, half sheep, in torn d/j. sg Feb 5 (251) $100
— Pen Drawing and Pen Draughtsmen. NY & L, [1920]. One of 250. 4to, half mor gilt. With orig ink drawing mtd to sheet. sg Feb 5 (254) $150

Pennsylvania
— FREE SOCIETY OF TRADERS IN PENNSYLVANIA. - The Articles, Settlement and Offices of the Free Society of Traders in Pennsylvania.... L, 1682. Folio, disbound. Stained & soiled; C2 torn affecting letters; some other leaves torn in blank inner margin. P Oct 29 (5) $1,200

Pennsylvania Packet, and Daily Advertiser. See: Constitution of the United States

Penrose, Francis Cranmer, 1817-1903
— An Investigation of the Principles of Athenian Architecture. L, 1851. Folio, orig half mor; rubbed. With 49 plates & plans, some colored. S Feb 23 (100) £160 [Martinos]

Pepler, Hilary Douglas Clerk

— In Petra, Being a Sequel to Nisi Dominus. Ditchling: St. Dominic's Press, 1923. Half mor. cb Sept 11 (93) $90

— Libellus lapidum. L: St. Dominic's Press, 1924. Illus by David Jones. Orig wraps; worn. With 17 wood-engravings, including upper cover. Dampstain at lower corner of some leaves. cb Sept 11 (94) $55

Pepler, Hilary Douglas Clerk —& Others

— Pertinent and Impertinent, an Assortment of Verse. Ditchling: St. Dominic's Press, 1926. One of 200. Half cloth; rubbed. cb Sept 11 (95) $75

Pepys, Samuel, 1633-1703

— Memoires relating to the State of the Royal Navy of England.... [L], 1690. 1st Ed. 8vo, late calf. pnE Jan 28 (145) £850 [McDowell]

Anr copy. Contemp blind-panelled calf; rubbed, joints weak. Manchester copy. S July 23 (345) £1,600 [Woolfe]

Anr copy. Old calf; rebacked. wd June 19 (166) $100

— Memoirs. L, 1893-99. ("Diary....") Ed by Henry B. Wheatley. 10 vols, including Index & Pepysiana. 8vo, half vellum gilt. pn May 21 (89) £95 [Traylen]

Anr Ed. L, 1899-1900. ("The Diary.") 10 vols. 8vo, half mor gilt. pnNY Sept 13 (268) $325

Anr Ed. L, 1926. ("Everybody's Pepys, the Diary....") One of 350. Illus by E. H. Shepard. pn Jan 22 (190) £30 [Mackenzie]

Peralta Barnuevo Rocha y Benavides, Pedro de

— Lima Triumphante, glorias de la America.... Lima: Joseph de Conteras y Alvarado, 1708. 4to, contemp vellum; loose. Dampstaining in top outer corner of a number of leaves. sg Sept 18 (227) $175

Perceau, Louis

— Bibliographie du roman erotique au XIXe siecle. Paris, 1930. 2 vols. Bdg not described, but orig wraps bound in. bba Mar 12 (353) £95 [George's]

Percier, Charles, 1764-1838 —& Fontaine, Pierre Francois Leonard, 1762-1853

— Recueil de decorations interieures.... Paris, 1812. 1st Ed. Folio, half lea; worn. With 72 plates. SM Oct 20 (538) FF3,400

Anr Ed. Paris, 1827. Folio, modern cloth; rubbed & soiled. bba Sept 25 (285) £210 [Weinreb]

Percival, Robert, 1765-1826

— An Account of the Island of Ceylon. L, 1803. 4to, contemp half russia. With 4 folding maps & charts. C Dec 12 (162) £300 [Old Hall]

— Account of the Cape of Good Hope. L, 1804. 4to, contemp calf. SSA Oct 28 (803) R600

— An Account of the Island of Ceylon. L, 1805. 2d Ed. 4to, contemp calf; worn, broken. bba Dec 18 (211) £80 [Hay]

Percival, Thomas, 1740-1804

— Medical Ethics; or a Code of Institutes.... Manchester, 1803. 8vo, contemp half calf; extremities rubbed. Half-title & title browned. Ck Nov 21 (4) £240

Percy, Henry Algernon, 5th Earl of Northumberland

— The Regulations and Establishment of the Household of Henry Algernon Percy.... L: [Pvtly ptd], 1770. 8vo, calf; spine chipped. Clanbrassill-Crahan copy. P Nov 25 (367) $250

Percy, Sholto & Reuben

— The Percy Anecdotes. L, 1826. 40 vols in 20. 16mo, contemp half mor; rubbed. cb July 30 (33) $95

Percy, Thomas, 1729-1811

— Reliques of Ancient English Poetry. L, 1765. 1st Ed. 3 vols. 8vo, contemp calf gilt; joints cracking. Vol II wormed & 1 leaf stained; marginal stain to a few leaves in Vol I. L Dec 11 (424) £70

Percyvall, Richard

— A Dictionarie in Spanish and English. L: Edm. Bollifant, 1599. Bound with: Percyvall. A Spanish Grammar. L: Edm. Bollifant, 1599. 1st Eds. Folio, contemp calf; worn. Some dampstaining. S May 29 (1244) £260

Perefixe, Hardouin de Beaumont de

— The Life of Henry the Fourth of France.... Paris: Didot l'aine, 1785. 8vo, calf. bba Dec 4 (22) £50 [Laffont]

Pereira, Jonathan, 1804-53

— A Treatise on Food and Diet.... L, 1843. 8vo, orig cloth; broken. S Nov 10 (546) £95 [Wheldon]

Perelle, Gabriel

— Vues des belles maisons de France.... Paris, [c.1700]. Oblong folio, modern mor gilt. With 328 views (including 7 titles) on 289 plates, 1 folding. A few repaired tears; last leaf creased. Sold w.a.f. C May 13 (81) £2,800 [Traylen]

Perelle, Nicolas
— Le Premier [Second; Troisieme] Livre de Lecons donnees a SAS Monseigneur le Duc de Bourbon pour apprendre a dessiner.... Paris: I. Mariette, [c.1675]. 3 vols in 1. Oblong folio, contemp calf gilt; restored. With 60 plates. C May 13 (80) £1,300 [Beres]

Peret, Benjamin
— Au 125 du Boulevard Saint-Germain. Paris, 1923. Out-of-series presentation copy. Frontis by Max Ernst. Orig wraps. Inscr to P. Andre May. S June 29 (15) £1,800 [Sims]
— Mourir de ne pas mourir. Paris, 1924. One of 545. Illus by Max Ernst. Orig wraps, unopened. S June 29 (16) £350 [Retuke]

Perez Calama, Jose
— Politica Christiana para toda Clase de Personas.... Nueva Cuidad de la Asuncion de Guatemala, 1782. 4to, contemp vellum; loose in bdg, spine chewed at foot, portion of fore-edges chewed. Some worming in inner margin. sg Sept 18 (225) $70

Perez, Francisco, Mexican Priest
— Catecismo de la doctrina Cristiana en lengua otomi.... Mexico, 1834. 4to, later vellum bds; dust-soiled. S May 29 (1109) £170

Perez, Luis
— Del can, y del cavallo, y de sus calidades.... Valladolid: Adrian Ghemart, 1568. 8vo, 19th-cent calf with arms of Salva. Jeanson copy. SM Mar 1 (455) FF11,000

Perez Rosales, Vicente, 1807-86
— California Adventure. San Francisco: Book Club of California, 1947. One of 250. Trans by E. S. Morby & Arturo Torres-Rioseco. In d/j clipped to show spine title. cb Sept 11 (63) $70

Pergolesi, Michele Angelo
— Designs for Various Ornaments. L., 1777-85. Folio, contemp half russia; def. With Proposals for Publishing sheet mtd in place of title (torn & repaired affecting text), engraved dedication & 66 plates, including the dedication to the Duchess of Buccleuch, some ptd in sepia. Some imprint dates altered in Ms; Plate 43 torn & repaired; lacking tp & text. C July 22 (142) £1,300

Periander, Aegidius, Pseud.
— Noctuae Speculum, omnes res memorabiles.... Frankfurt: G. Rab for S. Feyrabendt & S. Hutter, 1567. 8vo, 17th-cent vellum. Last leaf stained & blank outer corner repaired. C Dec 12 (304) £750 [Schwing]

Perk, Jacques Fabrice Herman, 1859-81
— Gedichten. Amst., 1897. 2d Ed. Orig cloth. B Oct 7 (32) HF550

Perkins, James H.
— Annals of the West. Cincinnati, 1847. 8vo, contemp sheep; broken. Some foxing. sg Sept 18 (226) $50

Perkins, William, 1558-1602
— How to Live and That Well. L: John Legatt, 1621. Bound with: Two Treatises. And: A Direction for the Government of the Tongue.... And: A Graine of Musterdseede.... And: A Declaration of the True Manner of Knowing Christ Crucified And A Salve for a Sicke Man. All: L, 162. 12mo, contemp vellum gilt; inner hinges broken; some sidenotes cropped; small rust-hole in H1 of last work, touching 2 letters of text. STC 19687.5, 19693, 19726.5, 19730.3, 19746.3 & 19761.9. S Dec 18 (322) £450 [Knohl]

Perley, Moses Henry, 1804-62
— Reports on the Sea and River Fisheries of New Brunswick. Fredericton, 1852. 2d Ed. 8vo, disbound. Tp torn, stained & with pencil notations. sg Oct 23 (420) $50

Pernau, F. A.
— Gruendliche Anweisung alle Arten voegel zu fangen. Nuremberg, 1754. 8vo, 19th-cent half vellum. Jeanson 1411. SM Mar 1 (278) FF5500

Peron, Francois —& Others
[A set of the Voyage de Decouvertes aux Terres Australes, with Atlas plus Freycinet's Voyage, with Atlas sold at S on 25 June 1987] S June 25 (500) £14,000 [Borges]

Perpetuum...
— Perpetuum Calendarium. [Augsburg?, early 18th cent]. 6 ivory sheets, 45mm by 84mm, in silver bdg with a revolving rondelle giving the days & date on upper cover, & the feast-days & other dates on the lower cover, held with a silver pivot. C Dec 3 (82) £3,000 [Quaritch]

Perrault, Charles, 1628-1703
See also: Eragny Press
— La Chasse.... Paris: Veuve J. B. Coignard et J. B. Coignard fils, 1692. 12mo, mor gilt by Huser. Jeanson copy. SM Mar 1 (456) FF32,000
Anr Ed. Paris: Auguste Aubry, 1862. 8vo, mor gilt by Smeers. This copy on peau de velin. Jeanson copy. SM Mar 1 (457) FF11,000
— Courses de testes et de bague faites par le roy.... Paris, 1670. Folio, 18th-cent mor gilt with arms of Louis XIV; worn. With

PERRAULT

engraved title & 95 plates. S Nov 27 (210) £5,800 [Marlborough]
— Histoires ou contes du temps passe. The Hague [Paris], 1742. 12mo, mor gilt by Cape. With frontis & 8 headpieces by Fokke after de Seve. C Dec 3 (155) £3,200 [Schiller]
— Histories, or Tales of Passed Times.... L; R. Montague & J. Pote, 1741. 12mo, contemp sheep; joints split. S June 17 (478) £3,800 [Randolph]

Anr Ed. L: Fortune Press, [c.1925]. Trans by G. M. Gent. 12mo, mor. sg Jan 8 (74) $50
— Les Hommes illustres qui ont paru en France pendant ce siecle.... Paris, 1696-1700. 2 vols. Folio, contemp calf gilt; rubbed. With 103 ports (ports of Thomassin & Du Cagne instead of suppressed ports of Arnauld & Pascal). Short tear in head margin of 2d plate of Vol I; a few leaves discolored. S Sept 23 (522) £260 [Maggs]

Anr copy. 19th-cent mor gilt. With port & 102 plates, including the 2 suppressed ports of Pascal & Arnauld bound in at end. S May 21 (121pPS450) [Maggs]
— Labyrinte de Versailles. Paris, 1679. 8vo, mor gilt. With plan & 40 plates. C Dec 3 (156) £1,400 [Schiller]

Anr Ed. Paris, 1693. Oblong 4to, contemp half calf; worn. With plan & 40 plates. pn Apr 30 (246) £460 [Marlborough]
— Le Petit Chaperon Rouge. [N.p.]: Cyril Beaumont sur la Press de l'Imagier, 1918. One of 50. Illus by Edgard Tijtgat. 4to, orig bds. With 16 illusts in outline with a suite ptd in color bound in. S Dec 4 (35) £800 [Perceval]

Perrault, Claude, 1613-88
— Memoires pour servir a l'histoire naturelle des animaux. Paris, 1671-76. Vol II only. Folio, contemp calf; rebacked & recorndered. Marginal stains throughout; tp soiled & holed; British Museum duplicate. bba May 14 (287) £550 [Pickering]

Perret, P. See: Eyries & Perret

Perrier, Francois, 1590-1656
— Icones nobilium signorum et statuarum. [Rome], 1638. Folio, 19th-cent half calf; rubbed. With engraved title & 100 plates. Engraved title torn & mtd; hole in Plate 20; Plate 100 torn & repaired; last leaf restored. S July 22 (144) £220

Anr copy. 18th-cent calf gilt; joints worn. sg June 18 (231) $375

Perrin, Ida Southwell. See: Boulger & Perrin

Perrin, Jean
— Nouvelles proprietes des rayons cathodiques. Paris, 1895. In: Comptes rendus mensuels de travaux chimiques, 121, pp 1130-39. wa Nov 6 (1158) $55

Perrin, Jean Paul
— Luther's Fore-Runners; or, a Cloud of Witnesses.... L: for Nathanael Newbery, 1624. 4 parts in 1 vol. 4to, contemp vellum. Library markings. Ck Sept 5 (206) £160

Perrin, William, d.1892?
— History of Summit County.... Chicago: Baskin & Battey, 1881. 4to, orig half mor; worn, spine partly torn. wa Sept 25 (459) $50

Perrinet D'Orval, Jean Charles
— Essay sur les feux d'artifice pour le spectacle et pour la guerre. Paris, 1745. 1st Ed. 8vo, early 19th-cent half sheep. With 13 folding plates. Title soiled. sg Jan 15 (350) $225

Anr copy. Contemp sheep gilt; spine ends worn. sg Jan 15 (351) $200

Perrins Library, C. W. Dyson
— POLLARD, ALFRED WILLIAM. - Italian Book-Illustrations and Early Printing. A Catalogue.... L, 1914. One of 125. 4to, orig cloth. sg May 14 (516) $400

Perry, Charles, 1698-1780
— A View of the Levant: Particularly of Constantinople.... L, 1743. 1st Ed. Folio, contemp calf; rubbed, joints breaking. With map & 19 plates. S May 29 (1074) £190

Anr copy. Calf; needs rebdg. With 19 plates. sg Nov 20 (142) $200

Perry, George, Conchologist
— Conchology, or the Natural History of Shells. L, 1811. Folio, modern half calf gilt. With 61 hand-colored plates. A few foremargins thumbed with minor tears; a few plate numerals altered in pencil. C Apr 8 (188) £1,300 [Geneva Archibald]

Perry, John, 1670-1732
— The State of Russia under the present Czar. L, 1716. 1st Ed. 8vo, contemp calf; rubbed. With folding map. O May 12 (155) $200

Anr copy. Contemp calf; rebacked. With folding map with tear Some dampstains. S May 6 (557) £110 [Sanderson]

Perry, Matthew Calbraith, 1794-1858
— Narrative of the Expedition of an American Squadron to the China Seas and Japan.... Wash., 1856. 1st Ed. 3 vols. 4to, contemp half mor, Vol II in orig cloth; all rebacked & rubbed. Bathing plate not mentioned. bba Apr 9 (427) £190 [Elliott]

Anr copy. Orig cloth; Vol II rebacked with mor. Includes the nude bathing plate. Some stains. cb June 4 (169) $700

Anr copy. Vol II only. Orig cloth; worn, shaken. Sold w.a.f. O June 9 (134) $140

Anr copy. 3 vols. 4to, modern cloth. With the bathing plate & with the view of the photographer at work. Stamp, call number & notatations on titles; folding plates reinforced with cellotape on verso. sg Dec 4 (153) $1,000

Anr copy. Vol I only. Modern library cloth. Library stamp on tp. sg Apr 23 (113) $350

Anr copy. 3 vols. 4to, Vol I disbound, Vol II broken, Vol III lacking of spine. With 116 plates & 13 (of 15) charts. With large map (wrinkled, worn) bound into Vol I. wa Sept 25 (607) $100

Anr copy. Orig cloth; worn. With 6 maps & 90 plates (including the bathing plate). wa Nov 6 (225) $140

Anr copy. With the bathing plate but lacking Yedo Bay & the folding color plate. wa Dec 11 (692) $260

Persius Flaccus, Aulus, 34-62 A.D.
See also: Juvenalis & Persius Flaccus

— Persio tradotto in verso.... Rome, 1630. Trans by F. Stelluti. 4to, 17th-cent calf. Lacking final blank. Johannson copy. sg Jan 15 (162) $1,100

Person, David

— Varieties, or a Surveigh of Rare and Excellent Matters.... L, 1635. 5 parts in 1 vol. 4to, 19th-cent half vellum. Old inscriptions on title; last leaf mtd. sg Jan 15 (338) $250

Perthshire...

— Perthshire Illustrated. L, 1843. 4to, contemp half mor. With engraved title & 63 plates on india paper, mtd. A few marginal tears. S May 28 (874) £140

Peterdi, Gabor

— Black Bull. Paris, 1939. One of 57. Oblong folio, unbound as issued. S June 17 (141) £380 [Griffiths]

Peters, DeWitt Clinton

— The Life and Adventures of Kit Carson. NY, 1858. 1st Ed. 8vo, contemp half calf; worn & soiled. With 10 plates. wa Nov 6 (548) $80

Peters, Fred J.

— Railroad, Indian and Pioneer Prints by N. Currier and Currier & Ives. NY, 1930. One of 750. Cloth. With prospectus laid in. sg Oct 23 (231) $100

Peters, Harry Twyford

— America on Stone.... Garden City, 1931. One of 751. 4to, cloth; covers foxed. First signature detached. ha Mar 13 (240) $200

Anr copy. Cloth, in d/j. sg Feb 5 (268) $400

Anr copy. Orig cloth; front hinge cracked. sg June 4 (248) $250

— California on Stone. Garden City, 1935. One of 501. 4to, orig cloth, in d/j. sg Feb 5 (269) $275

Anr copy. Cloth. sg June 4 (249) $200

— Currier & Ives.... Garden City, 1929-31. One of 501. 2 vols. 4to, orig cloth. sg Apr 2 (156) $650

Anr copy. Cloth. wd Nov 12 (181) $75

Peters, Samuel A.

— A General History of Connecticut. L, 1781. 8vo, contemp calf; loose. Foxed; penciled biography of the author on front endpapers. sg Mar 12 (214) $375

Petit...

— Petit Courrier des dames.... Paris, 1858. Vol 72. Half mor; scuffed. Sold w.a.f. pn July 23 (113) £210 [Lewis]

Petit, John Louis

— Remarks on Church Architecture. L, 1841. 2 vols. 8vo, later mor gilt by Hayday; spine ends rubbed, front cover of Vol II scratched. Most plates foxed. cb Oct 23 (171) $70

Petit, Paul

— Anciens souvenirs de venerie. Evreux: Herissey 1914. One of 100. 8vo, half shagreen. Jeanson copy. SM Mar 1 (458) FF1,600

— Quelques additions a la bibliographie generale des ouvrages sur la chasse.... Louviers: E. Izambert, 1888. 8vo, bds. Jeanson copy. SM Mar 1 (590) FF1,800

Petit, Victor

— Chateaux de la vallee de la Loire des XVe, XVIe et XVIIe siecles. Paris, 1861. 2 vols in 1. Folio, contemp half mor. With 100 tinted plates. Tp foxed; some foxing to plates. C July 22 (145) £520

Petite...

— Petite Galerie Dramatique, ou recueil de differents costumes d'acteurs des theatres de la capitale.... Paris, 1796. 4 vols. 8vo, mor gilt by Zaehnsdorf. With engraved titles & 426 hand-colored plates on 419 leaves only. C Oct 15 (84) £3,800 [Chaponniere]

Petitot, Ennemond Alexandre. See: Bossi, Benigno

Petiver, James
— Opera, historiam naturalem spectantia, or Gazophylacium.... L, 1764. 2 vols. Folio, contemp calf gilt; rubbed. With 292 plates. Some text browned & spotted. de Belder copy. S Apr 28 (275) £2,800 [Junk]

Petrakis, Harry Mark
— Chapter Seven from the Hour of the Bell.... Mt. Horeb WI: Perishable Press, [1976]. One of 150. Half mor. cb Sept 11 (205) $65

Petrarca, Francesco, 1304-74
— De remediis fortunae. Cremona: Bernardinus de Misintis & Caesar Parmensis, 17 Nov 1492. Folio, 17th-cent vellum; both covers damaged. Some marginalia; 5 lines scored out on n1 verso; short tear in n2 just touching catchword. 164 (of 166) leaves; lacking initial & final blanks. Goff P-409. S May 21 (11) £1,000 [Bossi]
— Opera. Venice: per Simon Papiensem dictum Bivilaquam, 1503. Folio, old vellum. Corner off title; old inscriptions scored; dampstains at end; 1 leaf misbound. sg Mar 26 (226) $250
— The Triumphs. Bost., [1906]. One of 100. Folio, mor, unopened. sg Sept 11 (248) $200
— Trotspiegel in Glueck und Unglueck. Frankfurt, 1604. Illus by Hans Weiditz. Folio, contemp vellum. HK Nov 4 (701) DM4,600

Canzonieri
— 1528, Feb. - Il Petrarcha.... Venice: Bernardino di Vidali. 2 parts in 1 vol. 4to, old vellum. Map partly separated at fold; marginal dampstaining; lacking final blank & rear free endpaper. sg Mar 26 (227) $200
— 1533. - Il Petrarca. Venice: heirs of Aldus Manutius & Andreas Torresanus. 8vo, mor gilt by J. Wright. Marginal stains; tiny marginal wormholes restored. sg Mar 26 (228) $300
— 1756. - Le Rime. Venice 2 vols. 4to, later calf gilt; spines wormed, ends badly chipped. cb Feb 19 (211) $85

Petri von Hartenfels, Georg Christoph, 1633-1718
— Elephantographia curiosa, seu elephanti descriptio. Erford, 1715. 4to, old calf; repaired. Library stamp on tp. Jeanson copy. SM Mar 1 (286) FF20,000

Petrides, Paul
— L'Oeuvre complet de Maurice Utrillo. Paris, 1959-74. One of 1,000. 5 vols, including supplement. 4to, orig wraps or bds, unopened. S Nov 10 (266) £580 [Joseph]

Petrie, Sir William Matthew Flinders
— Abydos.... L, 1902-3. Parts 1 & 2 (of 3) in 2 vols. Orig half cloth. 22d & 24th Memoirs of the Egypt Exploration Fund. cb Nov 6 (121) $85
— The Royal Tombs of the First Dynasty. L, 1900-1. Parts 1 & 2 in 2 vols. Half cloth. 18th & 21st Memoirs of the Egypt Exploration Fund. cb Nov 6 (124) $70

Petrizky, Anatol
— Theater-Trachten. Staatsverlag der Ukraine, 1929. Text by B. Chmury. 4to, orig wraps, in torn d/j; spine ends chipped. sg Feb 26 (195) $400

Petronius, Alexander Trajanus
— De victu romanorum et de sanitate tuenda.... Rome, 1581-82. 2 parts in 1 vol. Folio, 18th-cent vellum gilt. Library stamps on tp; stained. Crahan copy. P Nov 25 (369) $650

Petronius Arbiter
— Satyricon. L, 1694. ("The Satyr....") 1st Ed of Burnaby's trans. 8vo; contemp calf; worn. sg Oct 9 (289) $80

Anr Ed. Amst., 1743. 2 vols. 4to, later 19th-cent mor gilt. sg Oct 9 (290) $200
— Works. L: Fanfrolico Press, [1927]. One of 650. Trans by Jack Lindsay; illus by Norman Lindsay. Folio, half vellum. bba Sept 25 (160) £110

Anr copy. Half vellum; spine rubbed. S Oct 6 (829) £80 [Nosbuesch]

Anr copy. Half vellum; worn. sg Jan 8 (202) $120

Petrus Comestor. See: Rolewinck, Werner

Pettigrew, Thomas Joseph
— A History of Egyptian Mummies. L, 1834. 4to, contemp half mor; rubbed. Ck Feb 13 (1) £200

Anr copy. Orig half cloth; worn. S Mar 9 (696) £120 [Walford]
— Medical Portrait Gallery. L, [1838-40]. 4 vols. 4to, half calf. pnE Dec 17 (174) £150 [Maggs]

Pettingill, Olin Sewall, Jr.
— The American Woodcock. Bost., 1926. 4to, cloth; spine & extremities faded. Memoirs of the Boston Society of Natural History, Vol IX, No 2. sg Oct 23 (421) $70

Pettus, Sir John, 1613-90
— Fleta Minor. The Laws of Art and Nature, in...Metals. L, 1683. 1st Ed. Folio, contemp calf; rubbed, short split to head of upper joint. C May 13 (112) £1,700 [Goldschmidt]

Anr copy. Contemp calf; worn. Lacking port; Rrr2 verso worn; some soiling. S

Nov 10 (547) £200 [Wheldon]

Petty, Sir William, 1623-87
— The Political Anatomy of Ireland.... L, 1719. ("Political Survey of Ireland....") 2d Ed. 8vo, contemp calf; rebacked. bba Apr 9 (313) £200 [Drury]
— Political Arithmetick, or a Discourse Concerning the Extent and Value of Lands, People.... L, 1691. 8vo, sheep; worn, joints cracked, endpapers removed. Upper blank portion of tp cut away affecting rule; tear in margin of E4 from paper flaw; marginal browning. P Sept 24 (369) $1,000

Petzholdt, Julius
— Bibliotheca Bibliographica. Leipzig, 1866. 8vo, contemp half mor; rubbed. bba Mar 12 (354) £55 [Questor]

Peurbach, Georg
— Tabulae eclypsium.... Vienna: J. Winterburger for L. & L. Alantsee, 1514. Folio, modern vellum bds. Repair to outer blank margin; some stains. S June 25 (126) £1,650
— Theoricae novae planetarum.... Paris: Carolus Perier, 1557. 8vo, old vellum; soiled, inner hinges broken. Some damp stains; wormed in lower margins through most of the book, hardly affecting text. S July 28 (1104) £280

Pevsner, Nikolaus
— The Buildings of England. L: Penguin Books, 1951-74. 44 vols. bba Feb 5 (129) £300 [Axe]

Peyre, Joseph
— Sang et lumieres. Paris: Pierre de Tartas, 1962. One of 4 on japon nacre with a suite of the 1st 5 lithos on velin de Rives, a suite of the 6 double-page illusts on japon imperial, a decomposition of 1 of the lithos, 4 planches refusees & the gouache drawing for 1 of the lithos, sgd. Illus by Hans Erni. Unsewn in orig wraps. S June 17 (110) £1,000 [Fenteman]

Peyritch, Johann
— Aroideae Maximilianae. Vienna, 1879. Folio, orig bds; rebacked & soiled. With 43 color plates. Marginal tear to Plate 37. S Apr 23 (54) £950 [Walford]
— Aroidaeae Maximilanae. Die auf der Reise Sr. Majestaet des Kaisers maximilian I.... Vienna, 1879. Folio, contemp half mor; corners rubbed. With color frontis & 42 plates. Horticultural Society of New York —de Belder copy. S Apr 28 (276) £4,200 [Ross]
— Aroideae Maximilianae. Die auf der Reise Majestaet des Kaisers Maximilian I....

Vienna, 1879. Folio, orig mor gilt. With 43 color plates. Marginal tear in Plate 38. S Oct 23 (746) £1,100 [Arader]

Pezuela, Jacobo de la, 1811-82
— Diccionario geografico, estadistico, historico de la isla de Cuba. Madrid, 1863-66. 4 vols. 4to, contemp sheep; rubbed. bba Dec 18 (212) £120 [von Hunersdorf]

Pezzi, Lorenzo
— La Vigna del Signore. Venice, 1599. 4to, 18th-cent calf; joints repaired. With engraved title, port, folding plate & 16 engravings Lacking L1. S June 25 (40) £250 [Weiss]

Pfannstiel, Arthur
— Modigliani. Paris, [1929]. 4to, orig wraps; worn. With 6 color plates. O June 9 (135) $50

Pfeiffer, Ludwig G. C.
— Abbildung und Beschreibung bluehender Cacteen.... Cassel, [1838]-43-50. 2 vols in 1. 4to, contemp half lea; rubbed, joints split. With 60 hand-colored plates. Lacking text leaf for Cereus coccineus, supplied in photo-facsimile; some discoloration. Wawrinsky—de Belder copy. S Apr 28 (278) £2,500 [Asher]

Pfister, Kurt
— Deutsche Graphiker der Gegenwart. Leipzig, 1920. 4to, orig bds; worn. With 23 orig graphics & 9 plates. HK Nov 4 (3056a) DM3,800

Anr copy. Orig half cloth; worn. HN Nov 26 (2035) DM4,200

Anr copy. Orig bds; worn. HN Nov 26 (2036) DM5,200

Pforzheimer Library, Carl Howard
— The Carl H. Pforzheimer Library: English Literature, 1475-1700. NY, 1940. 1st Ed, one of 150. 3 vols. Folio, orig cloth; slightly soiled. sg Dec 4 (155) $4,800

Phair, Charles. See: Derrydale Press

Phebus, Gaston, Comte de Foix. See: Gaston III Phoebus

Phelps'...
— Phelps' Traveller's Guide Through the United States.... NY, 1849. 16mo, lea gilt; broken. With folding colored map (split at folds; some tape repairs on verso). O Oct 21 (141) $50

Phenix. See: Dunton, John

PHILADELPHIA...

Philadelphia...
— The Ordinances of the City of Philadelphia.... Phila.: Zacariah Poulson, 1798. 8vo, orig wraps; worn & chipped, spine paper worn off. Some chipping & foxing. ha Sept 19 (182) $70
— CONGREGATION KAAL KADOSH MICKVE ISRAEL. - Charter and By-Laws.... Phila.: Barrington & Haswell, 1841. 8vo, contemp wraps. Minor foxing. Rosenbach 481. sg Sept 25 (18) $250

Philalethes. See: Fellowes, Robert

Philalethes, Eugenius. See: Vaughan, Thomas

Philby, Harry St. John Bridges, 1885-1960. See: Golden Cockerel Press

Philiater, Euonymus. See: Gesner, Conrad

Philibert, J. C.
— Introduction a l'etude de la botanique. Paris, 1799 [An VII]. 3 vols. 8vo, contemp calf gilt; rubbed. With 10 hand-colored plates. S Feb 24 (534) £150 [Hunnersdorf]

Philidor, Francois Andre Danican, 1726-95
— Analysis of the Game of Chess. L, 1790. 2 vols in 1. Contemp calf gilt. pn Mar 26 (471) £65 [Hoffman]
— L'Analyze des echecs. L, 1749. 1st Ed, 1st Issue. Contemp calf gilt; rebacked. Subscriber's copy with Earl of Sandwich's bookplate. pn Mar 26 (465) £980 [De Lucia]

Anr Ed. L, 1777. ("Analyse du Jeu des Eches.") Contemp calf; rebacked, orig spine preserved. pn Mar 26 (468) £130 [Furstenberg]

— Chess Analysed. L, 1762. Bound with: Lambe, Robert. The History of Chess. L, 1764. Calf; hinges cracked. pn Mar 26 (467) £110 [Williams]

Philidorian...
— The Philidorian. A Magazine of Chess..... L, [1837]-38. 6 nos in 1 vol. Modern bds. pn Mar 26 (191) £75 [De Lucia]

Anr copy. Half mor; worn. pn Mar 26 (192) £55 [Farmer]

Philipot, Thomas, d.1682
— Villare Cantianum, or Kent Surveyed.... L, 1776. Folio, modern cloth. With 2 plates. Lacking map; 1 plate laid down on free endpaper. Extra-illus with 1 watercolor drawing & 41 views of Kent. L Dec 11 (127) £150

Philippart, John
— The Royal Military Calendar.... L, [1815]. 3 vols. 8vo, contemp bds; rebacked in calf, corners worn. cb Dec 18 (145) $120

AMERICAN BOOK PRICES CURRENT

Philippi, Rudolfo Armando
— Reise durch die Wueste Atacama.... Halle, 1860. 4to, orig bds; rubbed. With folding map, 10 tinted views (2 folding) & 15 natural history plates (7 hand-colored). Some foxing. S June 25 (444) £350 [Becker]

Philippovich von Philippsberg, Eugen, 1858-1917
— Die Entwicklung der wirtschaftspolitischen Ideen im 19 Jahrhundert...Sechs Vortrage..... Tuebingen: J. C. B. Mohr, 1910. Orig wraps; rubbed. P Sept 24 (370) $200

Philips, John, 1631-1709
— Cyder, a Poem. L, 1708. 1st Ed. 8vo, contemp calf; upper joint split. bba Aug 28 (187) £60 [Francis]

Anr copy. Contemp calf; upper cover detached. T Sept 18 (510) £34

Phillip, Arthur, 1738-1814
— The Voyage of Governor Phillip to Botany Bay. L, 1789. 1st Ed. 4to, calf. Lacking 4 plates; tp & frontis foxed. CA Apr 12 (195) A$1,700

Anr copy. Later half calf gilt. With port, engraved title, 6 maps & 47 plates. Some tears in margins repaired; frontis laid down. CA Apr 12 (196) A$2,500

Anr copy. Old calf; rubbed & rehinged. Frontis & tp foxed. kh Mar 16 (416) A$2,300

Anr Ed. Dublin, 1790. 8vo, contemp calf; rehinged. kh Mar 16 (417) A$600

Anr copy. Contemp calf; rubbed, joint split. Lacking plan of Port Jackson & 1 plate but with 2 others not called for; some soiling. S July 14 (852) £140

2d Ed. L, 1790. 8vo, calf; rebacked, corners worn. With engraved title, port & 55 plates, maps & charts. Frontis & title creased & foxed. CA Apr 12 (198) A$3,000

Anr Ed. Melbourne, 1950. One of 1,000. 4to, mor. Australiana Facsimiles, Vol I. A facsimile reprint of the 1789 Ed. CA Oct 7 (136) A$140

Anr copy. Bds, in d/j. Australiana Facsimiles, Vol I. A facsimile reprint of the 1789 Ed. CA Apr 12 (199) A$95

Phillipps-Wolley, Sir Clive, 1854-1918
— Big Game Shooting. L, 1894. One of 250 L.p. copies. 2 vols. 4to, half lea; spines & corners faded. cb Nov 6 (229) $110
— Sport in the Crimea and Caucasus. L, 1881. 8vo, orig cloth; extremities worn, spine leaning. Last leaf of text & ad leaves detached. cb Nov 6 (230) $50

Phillips, Catherine Coffin. See: Grabhorn Printing

Phillips, John Charles
— A Bibliography of American Sporting Books. Bost., [1930]. O Nov 18 (145) $120
— John Rowe, an Eighteenth Century Boston Angler. Cambr., Mass., 1929. One of 150. Half cloth, in d/j. sg Oct 23 (422) $100
— A Natural History of the Ducks. Cambr., Mass., 1922-26. 4 vols. 4to, half cloth; rubbed, corners worn. With 220 maps & plates. bba Dec 18 (213) £420 [Greyfriars]
Anr copy. Half cloth. Library copy. sg Oct 23 (423) $650
— The Sands of Muskeget; A Christmas Holiday. Cambr. MA, 1931. One of 250. Bds; spine chipped, extremities worn. sg Oct 23 (427) $80
— Shooting-Stands of Eastern Massachusetts. Cambr., Mass., 1929. Unopened. sg Oct 23 (424) $130

Phillips, John Charles —& Hill, Lewis Webb
— Classics of the American Shooting Field. Bost. & NY, 1930. One of 150. cb May 21 (206) $85

Phillips, Paul C. See: Lewis & Phillips

Phillips, Philip A. S.
— John Obrisset: Huguenot, Carver, Medallist.... L, 1931. One of 250. 4to, cloth. cba Mar 5 (143) $120
— Paul de Lamerie, Citizen and Goldsmith of London. L, 1935. One of 250. Folio, orig cloth. sg June 4 (311) $425

Phillips, Philip Lee
— A List of Geographical Atlases in the Library of Congress.... Wash., 1909-20. 4 vols. 4to, orig cloth. sg May 14 (194) $300
Anr copy. Vols I-III (of 5). 4to, cloth; worn & soiled. wa Sept 25 (488) $120
A List of the Maps of America in the Library of Congress. Wash., 1901. 4to, cloth; orig backstrip laid down. sg Oct 2 (92) $120
— Lowery Collection: a Descriptive List.... Wash., 1912. sg Oct 2 (90) $250

Phillips, Philip Lee —& LeGear, Clara E.
— A List of Geographical Atlases in the Library of Congress.... Wash., 1909-58. 5 vols. 4to, cloth; Vols I-IV loose. sg Oct 2 (93) $125
Anr Ed. Wash., 1971-74. 8 vols in 6. Cloth; 2 bdgs lack back. pn Dec 11 (5) £85 [Maggs]

Phillips, Sir Richard, 1767-1840
— Modern London: Being the History and the Present State of the British Metropolis. L, 1804. 4to, calf gilt; rebacked. With 54 plates 7 maps. Frontis & map torn in folds. S May 29 (1015) £500
Anr Ed. L, 1805. 4to, half calf gilt. Browned. pn Sept 18 (167) £240 [Map House]
— New Voyages and Travels.... L, [1819-23]. 9 vols. 8vo, orig half mor gilt; rubbed. With 215 plates & maps, 4 hand-colored. Some soiling. S Apr 24 (193) £900 [Traylen]

Phillips, Thomas, d.1815
— The History and Antiquities of Shrewsbury. Shrewsbury, 1779. 1st Ed. 4to, contemp half calf; rubbed. With 15 plates. Ck Nov 21 (296) £100

Phillips, Walter J.
— The Techniques of the Color Wood-Cut. [NY, 1926]. In d/j. O Sept 23 (159) $190; O June 9 (136) $160

Phillpott, Nicholas
— Reasons & Proposals for a Registry or Remembrancer of all Deeds and Incumbrances of Real Estates.... Oxford: W. Hall, 1671. 4to, wraps. S July 24 (450) £400 [Quaritch]

Phillpotts, Eden, 1862-1960
— The Dartmoor Novels. L, 1927-28. One of 1,500, sgd. 20 vols. Cloth. Sgd. pn June 18 (194) £130 [Traylen]
— A Dish of Apples. L & NY, [1921]. Illus by Arthur Rackham. 4to, orig cloth, in soiled d/j. With 3 colored plates. cb July 30 (157) $300
Anr copy. Orig cloth. With 3 color plates. With sgd dedication & pen and ink sketch on half title. pnNY Sept 13 (280) $600
Anr copy. Orig cloth; shaken. sg Oct 30 (167) $40
One of 500. Orig cloth. With 3 colored plates. bba Apr 23 (289) £70 [Smith]
Anr copy. With 3 color plates. pnNY Sept 13 (272) $450; sg Oct 30 (166) $450

Philobiblon...
— Philobiblon: Eine Vierteljahrschrift fuer Buch- und Graphiksammler Hamburg, 1957-83. Vols 1-27; lacking 2 nos. Wraps. sg Oct 2 (250) $80

Philomathean Society. See: Morton & Others

Philopatri, Andreae. See: Parsons, Robert

Philopolites. See: Nash, Thomas

Philosophical...
— The Philosophical Dictionary: or, the Opinions of Modern Philosophers on Metaphysical, Moral, and Political Subjects. L, 1786. 4 vols. 12mo, contemp half calf; worn. cb Oct 23 (173) $80

Philostratus, Flavius
— Les Images ou tableaux de platte peinture des deux Philostrates.... Paris, 1629. Folio, contemp lea; worn, joints cracked. With 68 plates. Some waterstains & spotting. FD Dec 2 (59) DM1,600

Phipps, Constantine John, Baron Mulgrave, 1744-92
— A Voyage towards the North Pole. L, 1774. 1st Ed. 4to, cloth; stained. With 3 folding charts, 12 plates & 11 folding tables. bba Dec 18 (199) £200 [Elliott]

Anr copy. Half calf; rubbed, rebound. Lacking half-title. bba Dec 18 (215) £45 [Elliott]

Anr copy. Half lea; worn, lower cover detached. With 15 plates & charts, all but 1 folding & 1ith 10 folding tables. Lacking half-title; perforated library stamp on tp & plates. bba Mar 26 (340) £110 [Rainer]

Anr copy. Orig calf; needs rebdg. With 3 folding charts, 12 plates & 11 folding tables. Some dampstaining & chips in margins of several plates. sg Nov 20 (144) $400

Photographic...
— The Photographic History of the Civil War. NY, 1911-12. Ed by Francis Trevelyan Miller. 10 vols. 4to, cloth; soiled & shaken, some hinges cracked. sg Nov 13 (77) $350

Anr copy. Cloth; soiled & shaken, some leaves detached. sg May 7 (58) $300

Anr copy. Half mor gilt; worn & soiled, some spine ends chipped. wa June 25 (181) $170

Physiologus...
— Physiologus: The Very Ancient Book of Beasts.... San Francisco: Book Club of Calif., 1953. One of 325. sg June 11 (65) $175

Anr copy. In d/j which is worn & clipped to expose spine title. cb Sept 11 (28) $150

Piazza, Girolamo Bartolomeo
— A Short and True Account of the Inquisition.... L, 1722. 4to, old half sheep; spine chipped at head. Lower corner of 2 leaves torn & restored. sg Oct 9 (56) $225

Pibrac, Guy de Faur, Seigneur de, 1529-84
— Les Plaisirs de la vie rustique. [Paris, 1573]. 4to, mor janseniste by Trautz-Bauzonnet. Jeanson copy. SM Mar 1 (467) FF16,500

Picard, Etienne
— La venerie et la fauconnerie des ducs de Bourgogne d'apres des documents inedits. Paris: Honore Champion, 1881. One of 100. 8vo, half shagreen. Jeanson copy. SM Mar 1 (468) FF1,200

Picart, Bernard
— Ceremonies et coutumes religieuses de tous les peuples du monde. Amst., 1723-43. Vols I-VII only. Folio, cloth. With 199 plates (in 2 vols only). With 1 plate & 1 text leaf torn. Dampstained. bba Dec 18 (217) £320 [Hirschler]

Anr copy. 4 (of 9) vols plus 1 (of 2) supplements. Folio, contemp blindstamped vellum. FD Dec 2 (822) DM3,300

Anr copy. Vols I-III only. Contemp calf; Vol III not uniform. Lacking half-title of Vol I & Ss2 of Vol III; some marginal tears. S May 21 (161) £380 [Cohen]

— Naaukeruige Beschryving der uitwendige Godtsdeinst-Plichten.... The Hague, 1727-38. 6 vols. Folio, vellum; a few joints def, 3 vols staned. With frontis & 225 plates. B Feb 25 (1150) HF1,200

— The Religious Ceremonies and Customs of the...World. L, 1733-39. ("The Ceremonies and Religious Customs of the...World....") 7 vols in 6. Folio, old calf gilt; rubbed, hinges & some corners & edges worn. With 205 plates only. Library stamp on titles & on a few other leaves. pnNY Oct 11 (38) $600

— Le Temple des muses. Amst., 1749. Folio, contemp calf gilt; wormed. With 60 plates, titles in French, English, German & Dutch. Some text leaves stained, wormed or browned. Extra-illus with 11 contemp plates. sg Mar 26 (164) $275

— The Temple of the Muses. Amst., 1742. Folio, contemp calf gilt; worn. pnNY June 11 (140) $250

Picasso, Pablo
— Couleur de Picasso. Paris, [1948]. Folio, bds; shaken. O Mar 24 (139) $60

— Picasso 347. NY, [1947]. 2 vols. Oblong 4to, cloth; rubbed. cba Mar 5 (149) $75

Anr Ed. NY, [1970]. 2 vols. Oblong 4to, orig half cloth. sg Jan 8 (203) $130; sg Feb 5 (271) $80; sg June 4 (254) $140; wa Nov 6 (474) $120

— Picasso lithographe. Monte Carlo, 1949-50-56-64. Text by Fernand Mourlot. 4 vols. Folio, orig wraps. HN Nov 26 (2042) DM3,000

Vol I only. Orig wraps. FD Dec 2 (4619) DM1,200

— A Suite of 180 Drawings, 1953-54. NY, [1954]. Folio, orig bds; shaken. Some penned marginalia. Verve Nos 29/30. O Mar 24 (138) $110

- ZERVOS, CHRISTIAN. - Picasso: Oeuvres de 1895-1972. Paris, 1942-78. Parts 1-28 in 29 vols. 4to, orig wraps; some chipped. With 185 plates. S June 17 (140) £12,000 [Uppstrom]

Picatoste y Rodriguez, Felipe
- Apuntes para una biblioteca cientifica espanola del siglo XVI. Madrid, 1891. 8vo, cloth; backstrip partly loose. sg May 14 (615) $200

Piccolomini, Alessandro, 1508-78
- De la sfera del mondo.... Venice, 1540. 1st Ed. 2 parts in 1 vol. 4to, old bds. Partly misbound; some stains. S July 28 (1106) £600

Anr Ed. Venice, 1595. 2 parts in 1 vol. 4to, contemp vellum; warped. S July 28 (1107) £130

Pickering, Harold G. See: Derrydale Press

Pickersgill, Richard
- A Concise Account of Voyages for the Discovery of a North-West Passage.... L, 1782. 12mo, calf. sg Apr 2 (157) $2,400

Pico de la Mirandola, Giovanni Francesco, 1469?-1533
- Dialogo intitolato la Strega.... Pescia: Lorenzo Torrentino, 1555. 4to, modern blind-stamped mor. Lacking A6; some spotting & annotations. S May 21 (69) £340 [Jung]

Pico della Mirandola, Giovanni, 1463-94
- Opera. Reggio: Ludovicus de Mazalis, 15 Nov 1506. Folio, contemp calf gilt; heavily restored. Minor worming to a few blank margins. C May 13 (145) £950 [Maggs]

Picotrial...
- Pictorial Photography in America. NY, 1929. Vol 5 of 2d Ed, one of 1,500. Folio, half cloth. cb July 30 (149) $75

Pictorial...
- Pictorial Photography in America. NY, 1926. Vol 4 of 2d Ed, one of 1,500. Folio, half cloth; rubbed. cb July 30 (148) $80

Picture See: Prim, Peter

Picturesque...
See also: Grant, George Monro
- Picturesque America.... NY, [1872-74]. Ed by William Cullen Bryant. Orig 48 parts. Wraps; soiled & chipped. O Oct 21 (144) $180

Anr copy. 2 vols. 4to, mor & half mor; rubbed. O June 9 (139) $170

Anr copy. Disbound. pn Dec 11 (26) £80 [Taylor]

Anr copy. Mor, orig covers retained; rubbed. pnNY Mar 12 (107) $200

Anr copy. Orig mor gilt; rubbed. With engraved titles & 47 plates. S May 29 (1087) £170

Anr copy. 48 parts. Folio, orig wraps; several loose. sg Dec 18 (210) $225

Anr copy. 2 vols. 4to, lea gilt. With engraved titles & 47 plates. sg June 18 (232) $250

Anr copy. Half lea; worn, hinges cracked. With 49 engraved titles & plates. With 9 loose issues in wraps. wa Sept 25 (286) $170

Anr copy. Contemp half mor; worn. With 2 engraved titles & 47 plates. wa Nov 6 (503) $160

Anr copy. Half mor; worn. wa Nov 6 (503) $190

Anr copy. Contemp mor gilt; rubbed. wa Dec 11 (597) $180

- Picturesque Europe: A Delineation by Pen and Pencil.... NY, [1875-79]. Ed by Bayard Taylor. Vols I-II. Half lea. O June 9 (140) $100

Anr copy. 3 vols. Folio, half mor; rubbed, several hinges starting. sg Nov 20 (146) £120

Anr copy. Orig mor gilt, front cover of Vol I stained. With engraved titles & 60 plates. sg June 18 (233) $225

Anr Ed. L, [1876-79]. 10 vols. 4to, orig cloth or wraps; rubbed. bba Jan 15 (472) £120 [Beyer]

Anr copy. 5 vols. 4to, contemp half mor gilt; rubbed. bba Mar 26 (281) £150 [Backus]

Anr copy. 5 vols in 10. 4to, mor gilt; rubbed. S Jan 12 (175) £125 [Hill]

- Picturesque Europe. With Illustrations on Steel and Wood. L: Cassell, [1876-79]. 5 vols. 4to, half calf gilt; rubbed. Lacking tp & list of plates in 1 vol of the British Isles. L Dec 11 (179) £75

Anr copy. 3 vols. 4to, orig cloth; worn. pn Jan 22 (76) £100 [Bailey]

- Picturesque Representations of the Dress and Manners of the English. L, 1814. 8vo, half lea; rubbed. With 50 colored plates. pn Mar 5 (38) £260

- Picturesque Views of the Principal Seats of the Nobility and Gentry in England and Wales. L: Harrison & Co., [c.1788]. Oblong 4to, contemp half mor. With engraved title & 100 plates. Ck Sept 26 (315) £370

Picus de Mirandula, Johannes, 1463-94
- Opera. Strassburg: J. Prus, 1504. Folio, old vellum. Marginal dampstains throughout; hole in tp affecting several words. sg Mar 26 (229) $275

PIEROTTI

Pierotti, Ermete
— Jerusalem Explored. L, 1864. 2 vols. Folio, half calf. With folding panorama of Jerusalem & 63 plates & plans. pn Mar 5 (39) £340 [Trotter]
    Anr copy. Orig half mor; rubbed. With 63 plates; many becoming detached from bdg. S Nov 18 (1071) £320 [Khalib]

Pierre de Ste. Marie Magdeleine
— Traitte d'Horlogiographie, contentant plusieurs manieres de construire sur toutes surfaces.... Paris, 1663. 8vo, old vellum. With engraved title & 72 plates & tables, 2 folding. Some tears with loss. Ck Jan 30 (38) £140

Piesse, George William Septimus, 1820-82
— The Art of Perfumery and the Methods of Obtaining Odours of Plants.... L, 1879. 8vo, cloth; worn. Pbr's embossed stamp on tp. sg Jan 15 (245) $50

Pigafetta, Antonio, 1491-1534?
— Primo viaggio intorno al globo terracqueo.... Milan, 1800. Trans by Carlo Amoretti. 4to, contemp wraps. With 2 folding charts & 4 hand-colored woodcut maps. FD June 25 (329) £600 [Quaritch]

Pigal, Edme Jean
— Collection de costumes des diverses provinces de l'Espagne. Paris: Langlume for Clement Freres, [c.1825]. 4to, half mor; def. With litho title (cut round & mtd) & 96 hand-colored plates of 100; lacking Nos 97-100). S June 25 (194) £1,150

Pigandet, Paul Ambroise, 1813-94
— The Life, or Legend of Gaudama.... Rangoon, 1866. 8vo, contemp half mor. Inscr to the King of Siam. S Apr 23 (333) £1,250 [Ad Orientum]

Piggot, Charles
— A Political Dictionary.... L, 1795. 18mo, later half lea; worn & broken. Library markings; last leaf trimmed 7 mtd; possibly lacking half-title or initial blank. sg Mar 26 (231) $60

Pigna, Giovanni Battista
— Historia de Principi di Este. Ferrara: F. Rossi, 1570. Folio, old calf gilt; worn. Stains in upper margin of opening leaves. sg Mar 26 (229) $275

Pigot & Co., James
— British Atlas of the Counties of England... L, [c.1834]. Folio, orig half cloth. With 39 hand-colored maps only. Ck Nov 21 (368) £400

Pigot, George, Baron Pigot. See: Lind, John

AMERICAN BOOK PRICES CURRENT

Pike, Douglas
— Australian Dictionary of Biography. Melbourne, 1966-77. 7 vols. Cloth, in d/js. kh Mar 16 (423) A$150

Pike, Nicolas
— A New and Complete System of Arithmetic.... Newburyport, 1788. 8vo, contemp calf; worn, a few signatures sprung. O Nov 18 (146) $130

Pike, Samuel, 1717?-73
— A Compendious Hebrew Lexicon. Adapted to the English Language.... Cambr. MA, 1802. 8vo, orig calf. sg Apr 30 (55) $650
    Anr Ed. Cambr. MA, 1811. 8vo, old calf; worn at edges. Some foxing & browning. ha Sept 19 (272) $50

Pilgrim, Thomas, d.1882. See: Morecamp, Arthur

Pilkington, Matthew
— Poems on Several Occasions. L, 1731. 8vo, contemp calf; rubbed. With S3-4 cancelled & not replaced. Some stains at beginning & end. S Jan 13 (515) £180 [Hannas]

Pillet, Roger
— Les Oraisons amoureuses de Jeanne-Aurelie Grivolin Lyonnaise. Paris, 1926. Out-of-series copy on japon. Illus by Yan B. Dyl. Mor gilt extra by Creuzevault. With 2 drawings by Dyl. CNY Dec 19 (53) $400

Pilote...
— Le Pilote de l'Isle de Saint-Domingue et des debouqements de cette isle. Paris, 1787. Folio, disbound. With 2 double-page charts & 4 plates Some worming & soiling. S July 14 (789) £240

Pinder, Ulrich
— Speculum passionis domini nostri Jesu Christi. Nuremberg: Ptr for the Sodalitas Celtica, 30 Aug 1507. Illus by Hans Schaeufelein & Hans Baldung Grien. Folio, contemp calf; rebacked, repaired, lacking 2 clasps. With 37 woodcuts by Schaeufelein & 3 large cuts by Grien. Some underlining & a few early notes in the margins in brown ink; O1 & 6 discolored. S Nov 27 (213) £7,500 [Lardanchet]

Pinedo, Encarnacion
— El Cocinero espanol, obra que contiene mil recetas.... San Francisco, 1898. 8vo, orig cloth; rubbed. Crahan copy. P Nov 25 (373) $400

Pinel, Philippe, 1745-1826
— Traite medico-philosophique sur l'alienation mentale.... Paris, An IX [1801]. 8vo, contemp calf gilt; worn. HN May 20 (1023) DM1,600

Pinelli, Bartolomeo
— Nuova Raccolta di cinquanta motivi pittoreschi e costumi di Roma. Rome, 1810. 4to, half lea. With engraved title & 49 plates. FD June 11 (850) DM1,300
— Nuova Raccolta di cinquanta costumi pittoreschi. Rome, 1817. Oblong 8vo, 19th-cent cloth gilt. With engraved title & 50 hand-colored plates. HK Nov 4 (1940) DM680

Anr copy. Contemp bds; rubbed. With engraved title & 50 plates. Dampstain affecting title & 1st 7 plates. sg June 18 (234) $450

Raccolta di cinquanta costumi pittoreschi. Rome, 1809. 1st Ed. Oblong 4to, 19th-cent half lea; joints worn. With etched title & 50 plates, which are numbered. Some damp-staining & marginal foxing throughout. sg Nov 20 (147) $300

Raccolta di quindici costumi li piu interessanti...Suizzera. Rome: L. Fabri, 1813. 8vo, wraps. With engraved title & 15 plates. Some foxing. B Feb 25 (830) HF7250

— Raccolta di soggetti li piu rimarchevoli dell' istoria greca. Rome, 1821. Oblong folio, orig wraps. With 100 plates. B Feb 25 (883) HF350
— Tasso figurato. Rome, 1826-27. Oblong folio, contemp half calf. With frontis & 72 plates. Some plates stained in margins; lacking tp. bba May 28 (29) £360 [Mugnaini]

Pinelli Library, Maffei
— [Sale Catalogue] Bibliotheca Pinelliana. A Catalogue of.... [L, 1789]. 8vo, orig bds. sg Dec 4 (158) $250

Pingre, Alexandre Guy
— Cometographie ou traite historique et theorique des cometes. Paris, 1783-84. 2 vols. 4to, contemp calf; split in joints of Vol I. Vol II lacking final leaf. C Dec 12 (165) £1,000 [Zeitlin]

Pinkerton, John, 1758-1826
— A General Collection of the Best and Most Interesting Voyages.... L, 1808-14. 17 vols. 4to, contemp half calf; spines worn, broken. Sold w.a.f. C Apr 8 (48A) £500 [Maggs]

Anr copy. Contemp calf; rubbed. dWith 195 plates, including frontises. S Oct 23 (321) £1,400 [Cavendish]

— A Modern Atlas. L, 1815. Folio, contemp half russia; rebacked in calf. With 61 hand-colored maps. Small wormholes in 2 maps of Latin America without significant loss. S June 25 (299) £1,300 [Burgess]

Pinkerton, Robert
— Russia: or, Miscellaneous Observations on the Past.... L, 1833. 8vo, orig half cloth; rubbed, joints split. bba Oct 30 (347) £80 [Check]

Anr copy. Orig half cloth; spine worn, soiled. With 8 hand-colored plates. sg Nov 20 (154) $90

Anr copy. Half cloth; front joint split, rear joint crudely repaired. sg Nov 20 (155) $80

Anr copy. Later calf; rebacked with cloth retaining orig chipped backstrip. One plate dampstained. sg Apr 23 (116) $50

Pinter, Harold
— Monologue. L: Covent Garden Press, 1973. One of 100. Calf. sg Mar 5 (213) $140
— Poems. L: Enitharmon Press, 1968. One of 200. Half mor. sg Dec 11 (359) $80

Anr Ed. L: Enitharmon Press, 1971. One of 100. Half mor. Inscr. sg Dec 11 (360) $80

Pinto, Isaac de, 1715-87
— Traite de la circulation.... Amst., 1771. 8vo, contemp bds; chipped. Marginal staining in the M gathering; marginal soiling at front & back; some discoloration. P Sept 24 (373) $2,800

Piozzi, Hester Lynch Thrale, 1741-1821
— Anecdotes of the late Samuel Johnson. L, 1786. 1st Ed. 8vo, contemp sheep; joints split, spine chipped. Ck Nov 21 (193) £60

Anr copy. Contemp half calf; rubbed, upper cover detached. 2 leaves flawed with loss of a few letters. S Nov 10 (407) £60 [Burmester]

— Autobiography, Letters, and Literary Remains.... L, 1861. 2d Ed. 2 vols. 8vo, calf gilt. sg Feb 12 (248) $175
— Letters to and from the late Samuel Johnson. L, 1788. 1st Ed. 2 vols. 8vo, contemp half calf. pnE Jan 28 (115) £400 [Aberdeen]

Anr copy. Contemp calf gilt; rubbed, joints cracked. S Jan 16 (420) £80 [Scott]

Anr copy. Orig bds; rebacked with contemp green paper tape, 1 cover loose, 1st 5 gatherings of Vol I loose. sg June 11 (257) $425

— Observations and Reflections made in the Course of a Journey through France.... L, 1789. 1st Ed. 2 vols. 8vo, contemp sheep gilt; Vol I broken. sg Oct 9 (291) $110

Anr copy. Contemp half calf; rubbed. 1 Feb 19 (238) £125

— Retrospection.... L, 1801. 2 vols. 4to, contemp calf; rebacked. T June 18 (420) £105

Piper, Henry Beam, 1904-64
— Four-Day Planet. NY: Putnam, [1961]. In rubbed d/j. cb Sept 28 (1043) $650

Piper, John
— Brighton Aquatints. L, 1939. One of 55 with the plates sgd & hand-colored by the artist. Oblong folio, orig half cloth. With 12 plates; 3 plates & 2 leaves of text loose. S Dec 4 (210) £950 [Marks]

Anr copy. Intro by Lord Alfred Douglas. Half cloth; scuffed. pn July 23 (149) £330 [Henderson]

Piranesi, Francesco, 1748-1810
See also: Piranesi & Piranesi
— Raccolta de' Tempi Antichi. Prima Parte.... Rome, [c.1780]. Folio, 19th-cent half russia; broken, spine lacking. With 20 (of 21) plates. C July 22 (147) £950

Piranesi, Giovanni Battista, 1720-78
— Antichita d'Albano e di Castel Gandolfo. Paris, [1764]. Bound with Piranesi. Descrizione e disegno dell'Emissario del Lago Albano. Rome, [1762]. And: Piranesi. Di due Spelonche ornate. Rome, [1762-64]. Folio, contemp calf; rubbed. S Apr 23 (97) £3,200 [Marcus]
— Le Antichita Romane. Rome, 1756. 4 vols. Folio, contemp calf gilt; rubbed, a few strips torn from covers. With port & 212 plates only. Vol I frontis contains the dedication to Lord Charlemont found in early copies. Marginal spotting. Sold w.a.f. C July 22 (153) £7,000

Anr copy. Vols II-IV. Contemp half calf; rubbed. With 160 plates, including engraved titles & 2 contents leaves. Sold w.a.f. S Apr 23 (99) £5,000
— Il Campo marzio dell'antica Roma. Rome, 1762. 1st Ed. Folio, contemp half lea; worn, covers detached. With 2 engraved titles & 48 plates (4 folding, including 1 which comprises Plates 5-10). Folding plan of Rome torn; some soiling & marginal dampstains. C July 22 (148) £3,400
— Della magnificenza e d'architettura de Romani. Rome, 1761-65. 2 parts in 1 vol. Folio, contemp half russia; worn, spine & joints split. With 2 engraved titles, port & 38 plates in Part 1; 9 plates in Osservazione. Port & Latin title of 1st part bound before Osservazione; engraved title of 2d part bound before its plates; 1 plate with tear repaired; a few plates def at fold; some marginal repairs. C July 22 (149) £1,900

Anr copy. Part 1 only. Old russia; rubbed & worn, broken. With 2 engraved titles, port & 38 plates. C July 22 (150) £1,600

Anr copy. Bound with Osservazione.... Rome, 1765. With engraved title & 9 plates, without text. Folio, contemp half mor with blindstamp on upper cover & small gilt stamp on spine; worn. Italian title with stamp on verso; blindstamps on plates. S Feb 24 (506) £1,900 [Pigeonhole]
— Raccolte di varie vedute di Roma.... Rome, 1752. Folio, contemp vellum bds. With 92 views on 46 leaves (some soiled). C July 22 (157) £1,600
— Le Rovine dell' Castello dell'Acqua Giulia.... Rome, [after 1761]. Folio, contemp half calf; worn & broken. With engraved title & 19 plates on 18 leaves. C July 22 (154) £1,300
— Vasi, candelabri, cippi... [Rome], 1778. 2 vols. Folio, contemp half russia; worn. With title engraved on 2 double-page sheets, double-page dedication as title to Vol II & 94 plates only. Some waterstain to a few plates; a few creases; stain to Plate 62. C July 22 (155) £4,600

Anr Ed. [Paris, c.1836]. 3 vols. Folio, half vellum. With engraved title & 111 plates. S Oct 23 (210) £4,000 [Raban]

Piranesi, Giovanni Battista, 1720-78
Piranesi, Francesco, 1748-1810
— Differentes Vues de quelques restes de trois grands edifices qui subistent encore dans le milieu...de Pesto autrement Posidonia.... [Rome, 1778]. Folio, 19th-cent half mor. With frontis & 20 plates. Small hole in bottom left corner of last plate repaired with slight loss of surface. C July 22 (156) £9,000

Pirie-Gordon, Harry
See also: Rolfe & Pirie-Gordon
— Innocent the Great; An Essay on his Life and Times. L 1907. 8vo, cloth; worn, inner hinge cracked. Inscr to Cecil Woolf & with ALs to Sir Harry Luke laid in. sg Mar 5 (226) $250

Pisanus Fraxi. See: Ashbee, Henry Spencer

Piso, Gulielmus
— De Indiae utriusque re naturali et medica.... Amst.: Elzevir, 1658. Folio, recent calf gilt. Dampstained at head; a few small holes in text. S Apr 23 (55) £900 [Ramer]

Anr copy. Later half vellum; soiled. Tear at inner blank margin at beginning; some staining at beginning & some spotting. Horticultural Society of New York—de Belder copy. S Apr 28 (280) £1,000 [Preciados]

Piso, Gulielmus —&
Marcgravius, Georgius
— Historia naturalis Brasiliae. Leiden & Amst., 1648. 1st Ed. 2 parts in 1 vol. Folio, contemp calf; rebacked. L.p. copy. Horticultural Society of New York—de Belder

copy. S Apr 28 (279) £1,800 [Preciado]

Pissaro, Lucovic-Rodo —& Venturi, Lionello
— Camille Pissaro. Paris, 1939. Ltd Ed. 2 vols. 4to, cloth, orig upper covers bound in. S June 17 (134) £2,200 [Uppstrom]

Pistolesi, Erasmo
— Il Vaticano descritto ed illustrato.... Rome, 1829-38. 8 vols. Folio, bdg not indicated. Library markings. Sold w.a.f. F Sept 12 (118) $110

Pitati, Pietro
— Almanach novum ad annos quinque supra ultimas hactenus in luce.... Tuebingen: Ulricum Morhardum, 1552. 4to, early limp vellum. Small wormhole in foremargin of 1st 2 leaves. S May 21 (211) £350 [Quaritch]

Pitman, Charles Robert Senhouse
— A Guide to the Snakes of Uganda. Kampala, 1938. 4to, orig cloth, in d/j. SSA Feb 11 (584) R460

Pitman, N See: Palmer & Pitman

Pitou, Louis Ange
— Voyage a Cayenne, dans les deux Ameriques.... Paris, [1805]. 2 vols. 8vo, contemp half calf; rubbed, lower cover of Vol I severely rubbed. S Feb 24 (464) £140 [Greenwood]

Pitt, William, 1749-1823
— General View of the Agriculture of the County of Stafford. L, 1796. 8vo, orig bds; spine worn, stained, new endpapers. With folding hand-colored map & 14 plates. bba Sept 25 (110) £55 [Chesters]

Pitt-Rivers, Augustus Henry Lane Fox, 1827-1900
— Antique Works of Art from Benin. L, 1900. 4to, orig cloth; rubbed. Library stamp on tp & margins of each plate. S Nov 10 (151) £65 [Negro]
— Excavations in Cranborne Chase near Rushmore. L, 1887-97. Vols I-III. 4to, orig cloth. With 3 linen-backed folding maps & 232 fulther maps, plates & plans, many double-page or folding. Tp of Vol I stained. L Dec 11 (128) £100
Anr Ed. L, 1887-1905. 5 vols. 4to, orig cloth; worn. T June 18 (58) £280

Pius II, Pope. See: Aeneas Sylvius

Pius II, Pope, 1405-64. See: Aeneas Sylvius

Planiscig, Leo
— Andrea Riccio. Vienna, 1927. 4to, orig half cloth. HN May 20 (591) DM1,300
— Die Bronzeplastiken Statuetten, Reliefs, Geraete und Plaketten. Vienna, 1924. 4to, orig cloth. HN May 20 (714) DM1,000
— Piccoli bronzi italiani de rinascimento. Milan, 1930. 4to, orig cloth, in d/j; rubbed. HN May 20 (716) DM560
— Venezianische Bildhauer der Renaissance. Vienna, 1921. Folio, orig cloth; rubbed. HN May 20 (717) DM1,150

Plans...
— Plans. Revue mensuelle. Paris, 1931-32. Nos 1-13 (complete set). Orig wraps. S June 29 (28) £2,800 [Arginthan]

Plantarum...
— Plantarum indigenarum et exoticarum icones...Sammlung...inn- und auslaendischer Pflanzzen.... Vienna, 1789-90. Parts 3 & 4 (of 8). 8vo, contemp half lea. With 2 color title vignettes & 120 colred plates. FD June 11 (560) DM2,100

Plath, Sylvia
— The Colossus. L, 1960. 1st Ed. Orig bds, in soiled d/j with Ms notes on front & rear flaps. T May 20 (96) £110
— Dialogue over a Ouija Board. Cambr.: Rampant Lions Press for Rainbow Press, 1981. One of 100. Orig vellum. Frontis by Leonard Baskin. S Sept 22 (130) £70 [Maggs]
— Lyonesse: Poems. L: Rainbow Press, 1971. One of 400. Folio, orig half calf. S Sept 22 (132) £100 [Leimweber]

Platina, Bartholomaeus Sacchi de, 1421-81
— De honesta voluptate et valetudine. Venice: Laurentius de Aquila & Sibylinus Umber, 13 June 1475. Folio, modern vellum. Some capitals supplied in ink. Inner margins of leaves 5, 15 & 32 repaired; inkstain to f.42; minor worming & staining at margins. 93 (of 94) leaves; lacking last blank. Goff P 762. Crahan copy. P Nov 25 (377) $20,000
Anr Ed. Bologna: Ioannes Antonius de Benedictis, 11 May 1499. 2d Issue. 4to, half mor; wormed. About 10 leaves partly stained; some marginal worming; tp dust-soiled. 96 leaves. Goff P-766. Crahan copy. P Nov 25 (380) $2,100
— Le Livre de honeste volupte et sante. Paris: Michel le Noir, 18 Sept 1509. 4to, vellum; spine def at foot. Some inner margins repaired; lacking 4 prelims, G1 & final leaf; a1 repaired; some worming; a title & table of contents supplied in Ms. S Sept 23 (378) £280 [Weiss]
— Vitae pontificum. Venice: Johannes de

PLATINA

Colonia & Johannes Manthen, 11 June 1479. Folio, later vellum. Light marginal stains or soiling; last leaf torn & mtd; d4.5 supplied from anr copy. 238 (of 240) leaves. Goff P-768. Heber copy. sg Dec 4 (159) $1,100

Plato, 427?-347 B.C.

See also: Golden Cockerel Press; Limited Editions Club

— Opera. Basel, 1534. Folio, early vellum bds; soiled. Final leaf of Vol II partly detached. S May 21 (70) £550 [Sokol Books]

Anr copy. 17th-cent vellum; spine defective, front cover loose. Scattered marginalia & marginal dampstains. sg Oct 9 (292) $425

Anr copy. In 2 vols. Folio, old calf; recased. Some marginal repairs & soiling. T Sept 18 (339) £150

Anr Ed. Lyon: Franciscus le Preux, 1590. Folio, contemp calf; worn, spine lacking. Tp detached; some leaves frayed. Sold w.a.f. bba Mar 12 (61) £50 [Poole]

Platt, Charles Adams

[-] Monograph of the Work of Charles A. Platt. NY, 1913. Folio, orig cloth; hinge cracking. cb July 30 (150) $130

Platt, Sir Hugh

— Delights for Ladies to Adorne their Persons, Tables.... L, 1628. 4to, old calf; rebacked. Tp restored; lacking final leaf; 1st leaves soiled. Hunt copy. CNY Nov 21 (219) $500

— The Jewel House of Art and Nature.... L, 1594. 1st Ed. 4to, old calf; worn, spine & corners repaired. With the woodcut arms of the Earl of Essex on verso of tp. Folding plate repaired & guarded; some stains & soiling; some fraying; marginalia. Crahan copy. P Nov 25 (376) $1,000

Anr Ed. L, 1653. 4to, old half calf; rebacked, new endleaves. Extreme margins of tp restored; small patch to bottom corner of last leaf; tp & following leaf with small rust-hole; ink stamp of Royal Society on tp. Hunt copy. CNY Nov 21 (220) $380

Anr copy. New half mor. Some worming in inner lower blank margins; rusthole in upper margin of I1. S May 28 (763) £260

Plaut, James Sachs

— Oskar Kokoschka. Bost. & L, [1948]. With 2 lithos, 8 colored & 48 plain plates. S May 6 (16) £110

Plautus, Titus Maccius, 254?-184 B.C.

— Comoediae. Strasbourg: W. Meissner pour Z. Schurer, 1605. 4to, contemp calf gilt; extremities rubbed, spine chipped at head. sg Mar 26 (232) $60

Plaw, John

— Ferme Ornee; or Rural Improvements. L, 1795. 4to, orig bds; lacking backstrip. With 38 plates. Some soiling. S Feb 24 (350) £440 [Hunnersdorf]

2d Ed. L, 1800. 4to, half cloth; rubbed & soiled. With 38 plates. bba Sept 25 (286) £130 [Weinreb]

Playfair, William

— British Family Antiquity. L, 1809-11. 9 vols. 8vo, contemp bds; rebacked, rubbed. Ck Jan 30 (186) £220

— An Inquiry into the Permanent Causes of the Decline and Fall of Powerful and Wealthy Nations. L, 1805. 4to, contemp calf; upper cover detached. T Oct 16 (500) £400

— The Statistical Breviary; shewing on a Principle entirely New.... L, 1801. 8vo, orig bds; spine def. With 5 folding colored plates. S June 25 (74) £650

Pleasonton, Augustus James, 1808-94

— The Influence of the Blue Ray of the Sunlight.... Phila., 1877. 8vo, orig cloth; worn. sg Jan 15 (119) $150

Plenck, Joseph Jakob von

— Icones plantarum medicinalium. Vienna, 1788-1803. Vols I-VII. Folio, contemp calf; repaired, worn. With 700 hand-colored plates. A few plates browned in Vol VII; 1 or 2 plates slightly cropped, 1 plate with slight marginal repair. Plesch—de Belder copy. S Apr 28 (281) £19,000 [Junk]

Plesch Library, Arpad

— Mille et un Livres botaniques.... Brussels, 1973. 3 parts in 1 vol. 4to, cloth, in d/j. sg Jan 15 (246) $250

— [Sale Catalogue] The Magnificent Botanical Library.... L, 1975-76. Parts 1-3 (complete set) in 3 vols. 4to, bds. With price lists. With scholarly annotations. O June 9 (142) $80

Pleske, Theodor D.

— Birds of the Eurasian Tundra. Bost., 1928. Contemp cloth. Memoirs of the Boston Society of Natural History, Vol VI, No 3. Sgd. pn Oct 23 (263) £90 [Bewder]

Anr copy. Orig cloth. pn Dec 11 (243) £95 [Gowland]

Pleske, Theodor D. —& Others
— Birds of the Eurasian Tundra. Bost., 1928. Wraps. Haverschmidt copy. B Feb 24 (323) HF375

Plimsoll, Samuel
— Our Seamen, an Appeal. L, 1873. 4to, recent cloth. T Oct 16 (668) £64

Plinius Secundus, Gaius, 23-79
— Historia naturalis. Frankfurt: for Johann Feyerabendt, 1599. ("Historiae mundi libri XXXVII.") Folio, contemp blind-tooled pigskin over wooden bds with center panel-stamp of Melanchthon ove date 1617 on front cover & arms of the city of Goerlitz on rear cover. sg Mar 26 (233) $325

Plinius Secundus, Gaius, 23-79
— Historia naturalis. Basel: Froben, 1525. ("Historia mundi.") Folio, contemp calf over wooden bds; worn. Some fingersoiling & waterstains. JG Mar 20 (265) DM850

Anr Ed. Basel: Froben, 1549. ("Historia mundi, libri XXXVII....") Folio, later calf; worn. Leaves dampstained, more severely at end. bba Mar 26 (96) £80 [Poole]

Anr Ed. Venice: Aldus, 1559 [1558]. ("Naturalis historiae.....") Folio, later vellum. With 2 leaves of the Index repeated. S Sept 23 (379) £150 [Thomas]

Anr Ed. Venice: Aldus, 1559-58. Folio, 18th-cent vellum. Wormed at beginning. HK Nov 4 (704) DM650

Anr Ed. Paris, 1723. 3 vols. Folio, contemp calf; worn. Some leaves in Vol II with marginal worming. S May 6 (529) £160 [Shapero]

— The Historie of the World.... L: Adam Islip, 1601. 1st Ed in English. Trans by Philemon Holland. 2 vols in 1. Folio, contemp calf; rebacked, new endpapers. Marginal dampstaining at beginning & end; tp creased; lacking 1st & final leaves, 1 leaf supplied in duplicate. sg Apr 2 (158) $650

— Sommaire des singularitez de Pline. Paris: Richard Breton, 1559. Ed by Pierre de Changy. 8vo, mor gilt by Lortic. Jeanson copy. SM Feb 28 (118) FF17,000

Plomer, William
— At Home. L, 1958. In d/j. Inscr & with ALs laid in. sg Dec 11 (361) $80
— Double Lives. L, 1943. ALs laid in. sg Dec 11 (362) $80

Plomley, Norman James Brian. See: Robinson, George Augustus

Ploss, Hermann Heinrich —& Bartels, Max & Paul
— Woman. L, 1935. 3 vols. bba Mar 12 (474) £70 [Nosbuesch]

Plot, Robert
— The Natural History of Oxfordshire. Oxford, [1676]. Folio, 19th-cent half calf; rubbed. With folding map (repaired without loss) & 16 plates. Occasional stains; tp shaved & laid down. S Nov 17 (815) £240 [Young]

Anr Ed. Oxford, 1677. Folio, calf; rebacked. With folding map (strengthened at fold) & 16 plates. Some browning through out; last few leaves wormed at fore-margin. S Jan 12 (51) £240 [Shapero]

— The Natural History of Staffordshire. Oxford, 1686. Folio, contemp calf; hinges cracked, rubbed. With double-page map, plate of arms & 37 plates, many double-page. Some plates with minor tears & stained in margins. pn Nov 20 (21) £460 [Weston]

Anr copy. Contemp calf; rebacked & rubbed. Lacking leaf "Armes omitted"; some leaves & plates cropped & torn. T July 16 (23) £380

Plumier, Charles, 1645-1704
— L'Art de tourner ou de fair en perfection toutes sourtes d'ouvrages au tour. Lyons, 1701. Folio, contemp vellum. Franklin Institute copy. F Sept 12 (317) $1,000

Anr Ed. Lyons, 1706. Folio, contemp calf; spine ends chipped, joints cracked. With engraved title & 72 plates. sg June 4 (259) $600

Anr Ed. Paris, 1749. Folio, contemp calf; worn. With engraved title & 80 plates. S June 25 (127) £380 [Phelps]

— Description des plantes de l'Amerique. Paris, 1693. Folio, later russia; rubbed. With 108 plates. Occasional slight marginal spotting. Broussonet—de Belder copy. S Apr 28 (282) £1,500 [Preciados]

— Plantarum Americanarum. Amst., 1755-[60]. 10 parts in 1 vol. Folio, contemp half calf; worn. With 263 plates. Text at beginning somewhat browned. Horticultural Society of New York—de Belder copy. S Apr 28 (283) £3,000 [Preciados]

Anr Ed. Amst. & Leiden, 1755-60. 10 parts in 1 vol. Folio, contemp calf; upper cover wormed. With port & 263 plates. C Oct 15 (196) £1,400 [Lalce]

— Traite des fougeres de l'Amerique. Paris, 1705. Folio, contemp calf; spine chipped at head & foot. With 172 plates. de Belder copy. S Apr 28 (284) £2,600 [McDougall]

Plumley, Ladd
— With the Trout Fly. NY, 1929. In d/j. sg Oct 23 (430) $50

Plumptre, Anne
— Narrative of a Residence in Ireland.... L, 1817. 4to, orig bds; worn. With port (loose) & 11 plates. S Nov 10 (816) £130 [Henderson]

Plutarch, 46?-120?
See also: Fore-Edge Paintings; Nonesuch Press
— Lives. L, 1657. ("The Lives of the Noble Grecians and Romains....") Folio, old calf; worn & marked. bba Oct 30 (131) £40 [Axe]

Anr Ed. Cambr., 1676. ("The Lives of the Noble Grecians and Romans.") Trans by Thomas North. Folio, contemp calf; joints split, rubbed. Lacking last leaf; a few small holes. S Mar 10 (1124) £170 [Scott]

Anr Ed. L, 1819. 6 vols. 8vo, modern calf gilt by Bayntun of Bath. Extra-illus with 77 plates. pn Apr 30 (130) £320

— Opera. [Geneva]: H. Estienne, 1572. 13 vols, including Appendix. 8vo, 18th-cent mor. Some foxing & discoloration. S Sept 23 (482) £1,100 [Maggs]

Anr Ed. Paris, 1624. 2 vols. Folio, contemp sheep; worn. Marginal repairs. bba Mar 26 (109) £40 [Stewart]

— Les Vies des hommes illustres grecs et romains.... Geneva: pour les Heritiers d'Eustache Vignon, 1594. Folio, later sheep; joints splitting. Inner margin of tp repaired; some dampstaining & spotting. bba Dec 4 (6) £110 [Robertshaw]

— Vitae parallelae. Basel: Bebel, 1533. ("Parallela.") 3d Ed in Greek. Folio, contemp pigskin over wooden bds with 2 clasps & catches. Small tear in fore-margin of O5 not affecting text; 2 wormholes in fore-margins of final leaves; early marginal notes & underlining. S Nov 27 (112) £620 [Maggs]

Anr Ed. Basel: Froben, 1533. Folio, old calf; worn. ha Dec 19 (306) $300

Pocock, Isaac, 1782-1835
— The Miller and his Men. L, 1820. 8vo, mor gilt by royal coat-of-arms, by George Mullen of Dublin. Georgiana Paget's copy. S Sept 22 (205) £220 [Lyon]

Pocock, William Fuller
— Architectural Designs for Rustic Cottages, Picturesque Dwellings, Villas.... L, 1807. 1st Ed. 4to, orig bds; rubbed. S Feb 24 (351) £460 [Pigeonhole]

— Modern Finishings for Rooms: A Series of Designs.... L, 1823. 4to, contemp calf gilt; rubbed. With 86 plates, a few with pen-cilled annotations. bba Sept 25 (287) £460 [Demetzy]

Pococke, Richard, 1704-65
— A Description of the East. L, 1743-45. Vol I only. Contemp calf; broken. Inner margins of opening leaves dampstained; 3 plates torn & some plates foxed. sg Nov 20 (148) $250

Poe, Edgar Allan, 1809-49
See also: American...; Baltimore; Graham's...
— The Bells, and other Poems. L, [1912]. Illus by Edmund Dulac. 4to, orig cloth; foot of spine with 1 small crease. cb Sept 11 (242) $130

Anr copy. Orig cloth; rubbed, some hinges cracked. With 28 colored plates Marginal pencil notes. cb Feb 19 (90) $65; pn Oct 23 (383) £100 [McKazie]

Anr copy. Orig vellum gilt; soiled. S Oct 6 (790) £200 [MPL]

Anr copy. Orig cloth; soiled. S Oct 6 (795) £120 [Sanzin]

One of 1,000. Orig vellum gilt. S June 17 (227) £420 [Immas]

— The Black Cat. [N.p.]: Cheloniidae Press, 1984. One of 60 in quarter lea with drypoint & extra suite of the wood engravings. Illus by Alan James Robinson. sg Jan 8 (46) $250

— The Fall of the House of Usher. Paris, 1928. One of 300. Illus by Alastair. 4to, orig wraps. With 5 plates, mtd on silver paper. HN Nov 26 (1663) DM800

— The Masque of the Red Death. Phila., 1841-42. 8vo contemp half mor; rubbed, corners showing, spine end gouged. In: Graham's Lady's and Gentleman's Magazine, Vols XIX & XX. cb Oct 23 (180) $110

Anr Ed. Balt.: Aquarius Press, 1969. ("The Mask of the Red Death.") One of 500. Illus by Federico Castellon. Folio, cloth. With 16 lithos. s Jan 8 (210) $200

— Mesmerism, "In Articulo Mortis...." L, 1846. 8vo, self-cover; 2 hinges starting. cb Sept 28 (1046) $400

— The Narrative of Arthur Gordon Pym. Bost.: David Godine, [1973]. One of 150. Illus by Gerry Hoover. Half mor by Arno Werner. cb Sept 11 (308) $100

— The Pit and the Pendulum. Phila.: Carey & Hart, [1842]. 8vo, calf; rubbed. With extra title & 8 plates. In: The Gift: A Christmas and New Year's Present, for 1843.. ha Sept 19 (229) $75

— The Purloined Letter. Phila., 1845. Contemp calf; rubbed. In: The Gift: A Christmas, New Year, and Birthday Present With 6 (of 8) plates. cb Oct 23 (182) $100

1986 - 1987 · BOOKS

— The Raven. Easthampton MA: Cheloniidae Press, 1985. One of 50 in mor with an extra suite of prints, working proofs of the wood engravings, state proofs of the etching & a drawing, all sgd. Illus by Alan James Robinson. sg Dec 4 (38) $375

— Tales of Mystery and Imagination. L, 1919. Illus by Harry Clarke. 4to, cloth; soiled. Inscr by Clarke. Ck Feb 13 (110) £120

Anr Ed. NY, 1933. 4to, orig cloth, in worn d/j. sg Jan 8 (48) $50

Anr Ed. L, 1935. Illus by Arthur Rackham. 4to, orig cloth, in d/j. bba June 18 (275) £110 [Lydian]

Anr copy. Orig mor gilt, rubbed. Ck Sept 5 (38) £75

Anr copy. Mor. With 12 color plates. sg Oct 30 (169) $275

Anr copy. Cloth. Endpaper spotted. sg Oct 30 (170) $60

One of 460. Orig vellum gilt; bowed & soiled. S June 17 (276) £480 [Immer]

Anr copy. Orig vellum gilt; spine head rubbed & repaired. With 12 mtd color plates. sg Oct 30 (168) $800

— Works. Chicago, 1894-95. 10 vols. 8vo, half calf gilt; spine ends worn. sg Sept 11 (249) $500

Anr copy. Orig cloth; worn. wa Mar 5 (85) $140

Virginia Ed. NY, [1902]. Ed by James A. Harrison. 17 vols. ha May 22 (74) $450

Manuscript Ed. NY & Pittsburgh, 1903. One of 30 on handmade japan vellum. 10 vols. mor gilt extra. With autograph Ms fragment of Poe's Marginalia bound in Vol I. CNY Dec 19 (215) $8,000

Anr Ed. NY, 1914. Ltd Ed. 10 vols. Half cloth; rubbed. cb Sept 11 (309) $225

Poe's copy, Edgar Allan

— JAMES, JOHN ANGELL. - The Marriage Ring: or How to Make a Home Happy. Bost., [1842]. 12mo, orig cloth; rubbed & soiled, front free endpaper lacking. Inscr to Poe by Nathaniel Parker Willis, 25 Dec 1846. P Dec 15 (214) $600

Poems...

— Poems from Italy Verses written by Members of the Eighth Army.... L, 1945. One of 110, sgd by Siegfried Sassoon. Intro by Siegfried Sassoon. Mor. sg Dec 11 (429) $175

— Poems on Affairs of State. [L], 1697. 1st Ed. 8vo, recent mor gilt by Waters. T Oct 16 (473) £120

POIRET

Poetae...

See also: Gratius, Nemesianus & Ovid

— Poetae Graeci veteres carminis heroici scriptores.... Geneva: Pierre de la Roviere, 1606. 2 parts in 1 vol. Folio, 17th-cent vellum with brass cornerpieces, fore-edges restored. Tp soiled. sg Oct 9 (198) $100

— Poetae Latini rei venaticae scriptores et bucolici antiqui.... Leiden: J. A. Langerak, 1728. 4to, contemp vellum. Jeanson copy. SM Mar 1 (470) FF1,400

Poetical...

— A Poetical Description of Beasts, with Moral Reflections for the Amusement of Children. L, 1777. 2d Ed. 12mo, orig pictorial bds; backstrip def. With port & 32 woodcut illusts. Roscoe J298 (2). S June 17 (421) £3,000 [Randolph]

— The Poetical Magazine. L: R. Ackermann, 1809-11. Vols I-IV. 8vo, lev gilt by Morrell. With engraved titles, 2 plain & 50 colored plates. sg Apr 2 (159) $750

Poets...

— The Poets of Great Britain. Edin., 1777-92. Ed by John Bell. 107 vols only. 18mo, contemp calf gilt; 1 spine damaged. Sold w.a.f. Ck Feb 13 (61) £850

Poggius Florentinus, d.1459. See: Bruni, Leonardo·fAretinus

Pohl, Frederik

— Gateway. NY, 1977. In d/j. cb Sept 28 (1051) $130

— Star Short Novels. NY: Ballantine, [1954]. Hardcover Issue. Ed by Pohl. In soiled d/j. cb Sept 28 (1062) $65

Pohl, Frederik — & Kornbluth, C. M.

— Gladiator-at-Law. NY: Ballantine, [1955]. In d/j. cb Sept 28 (1053) $200

Pohl, Johann Baptist Emanuel

— Plantarum Brasiliae icones et descriptiones.... Vienna, 1827-31. Folio, later 19th-cent half mor. With 200 hand-colored plates. Plate margins stamped. L.p. copy. Massachusetts Horticultural Society—de Belder copy. S Apr 28 (285) £10,000 [Brittain]

Poiret, Jean Louis Marie

— Lecons de flore. Paris, 1819-20. 4to Ed. 3 vols in 2. Contemp half calf gilt; rubbed. With 64 hand-colored plates & 3 folding plates (1 torn & cropped). S Feb 24 (535) £220 [Wesley]

Anr copy. Contemp half calf. With 64 hand-finished color plates, 1 folding hand-finished color chart & 1 table. Aiguet—de Belder copy. S Apr 28 (286) £1,500 [Hill]

Poiteau, Pierre Antoine, 1766-1854
See also: Risso & Poiteau
— Flora parisiensis.... Paris, [1808-13]. Folio, modern half calf gilt by Sangorski & Sutcliffe. With 101 plates, 11 hand-colored. Lacking tp; some dampstains. pn Apr 30 (120F) £400 [Burgess]

Polain, Marie-Louis
— Catalogue des livres imprimes au quinzieme siecle des Bibliotheques Belgique. Brussels, 1932. 4 vols in 2. Folio, contemp half mor; torn. bba Oct 16 (395) £170 [Georges]
Anr Ed. Brussels, 1932-78. 5 vols. Folio, cloth. sg May 14 (519) $450

Pole, Reginald, Cardinal, 1500-58
— De concilio liber. Rome: Aldus, 1562. 4to, 19th-cent mor; worn. Lacking 2 blanks at end. sg Mar 26 (234) $110
— De summo pontifice Christi in terris vicario.... Louvain: Joannes Fouler, Anglus, 1569. 8vo, calf; upper hinge split. Some leaves soiled. C Dec 12 (305) £280 [Maggs]

Polehampton, Edward —&
Good, John M.
— The Gallery of Nature and Art.... L, 1821. 2 vols. 8vo, modern cloth. bba Dec 18 (218) £45 [Kaplan]

Polite...
— The Polite Academy, or Complete Instructions for a Genteel Behaviour.... L & Salisbury, [c.1790]. ("The Polite Academy, or School of Behaviour....") 10th Ed. 12mo, contemp Dutch floral bds; spine worn. Closely shaved on lower margins with loss of description; frontis & final leaf of text pasted to bds. T Feb 19 (585) £120

Pollard, Alfred Frederick
— Henry VIII. L, 1902. One of 250 on japon with plates in 2 states, the port-frontis in 1 state in colors. 4to, mor gilt with royal arms. S July 13 (204) £160

Pollard, Alfred William
See also: Caxton Club; Perrins Library, C. W. Dyson
— Cobden-Sanderson and the Doves Press. San Francisco: John Henry Nash, 1929. One of 339. Folio, vellum gilt. cb Sept 11 (197) $160

Pollard, Graham. See: Carter & Pollard

Pollard, Hugh Bertie Campbell
See also: Derrydale Press
— Game Birds. L, 1929. One of 99. 4to, cloth; worn & soiled. sg Oct 23 (431) $100
— The Gun Room Guide. Bost. & NY, 1930. One of 225. 4to, orig half vellum. sg Oct 23 (432) $80
Anr Ed. L, 1930. 4to, orig half vellum; stain on front cover. Some staining to extreme top margins of several leaves. cb May 21 (211) $160
— Wildfowl & Waders; Nature & Sport in the Coastlands. L, 1928. One of 950. Illus by Frank Southgate. 4to, orig cloth. With 16 mtd colored plates & 48 plain plates. pn Mar 5 (308) £75 [Furness]
Anr copy. Half vellum; worn. With 16 color plates. sg Oct 23 (433) $60

Pollen, Maria Margaret
— Seven Centuries of Lace. L & NY, 1908. 4to, cloth; worn. With 120 plates. Inscr. sg Feb 5 (201) $130

Polo, Marco, 1254?-1324?
— The Travels.... L, 1929. ("The Book of Ser Marco Polo, the Venetian, concerning the Kingdoms and Marvels of the East.") 2 vols. pnE Jan 28 (79) £90 [Prof. Bruck]
Anr Ed. L: Argonaut Press, 1929. ("The Most Noble and Famous Travels....") One of 1,050. Trans by John Frampton. 4to, half vellum; soiled. pn Mar 5 (100) £35 [Bookroom]

Polonsky, Vyacheslav
— Russky revolyutsionny plakat. Moskow, 1925. Folio, orig bds; worn & def. VH Sept 12 (2509) DM8,000

Polybius, 205?-125? B.C.
— De legationibus.... Antwerp: Plantin, 1582. 4to, mor gilt by Charles lewis. Tear in D1 repaired; repair in lower margin of m2; some stains. S May 21 (72) £750 [Thomas]

Pomet, Pierre
— A Compleat History of Druggs.... L, 1712. 2 vols in 1. 4to, modern calf. 2 leaves of dedication to Vol I & tp to Vol II def with loss of lower sections (the latter supplied in facsimile); R4 & S1-2 torn & repaired & last leaf remargined in Vol II. Sold w.a.f. S Nov 10 (549) £90 [Hindmarch]
Anr Ed. L, 1737. 4to, contemp calf gilt; corners worn. pnE Dec 17 (255) £380 [Traylen]
— Histoire generale des drogues.... Paris, 1694. 1st Ed. 4 parts in 1 vol. Folio, contemp calf; rebacked, covers laid down. Outer margin of port shaved; some stains; lacking 1 plate, 8 prelims & last leaf. Ck Jan 30 (179) £110
Anr Ed. Paris, 1735. 2 vols. 4to, contemp calf; rubbed. With 91 plates. Some plates cropped; occasional stains. S Nov 10 (550) £250 [Gillard]

Pomi, David de
— Tsemakh David. Venice: Juan di Gara, 1589. Folio, old vellum; stained. Tp soiled & damaged, affecting 2 words; some stains & browning; marginal worming, affecting single letters. St. 4841.1. CAM Dec 3 (151) HF2,200

Pompadour Library, Marquise de
— [Sale Catalogue] Catalogue des livres de la bibliotheque de...la Marquise de Pompadour. Paris, 1765. 8vo, contemp calf; worn. Priced throughout in contemp hand. S Nov 10 (259) £420 [Dawson]

Anr copy. Half calf. Priced throughout in ink. S Nov 27 (113) £420 [Quaritch]

Anr copy. Priced throughout in ink; 3C2 supplied in Ms. S July 28 (1228) £200

Ponce de Leon, Eduardo. See: Zamora & Ponce de Leon

Poncelet, Polycarpe
— Chimie du gout et de l'odorat. Paris, 1755. 1st Ed. 8vo, calf; rubbed. With frontis & 6 plates;. SM Oct 20 (518) FF2,000

Poncetton, Francois. See: Portier & Poncetton

Pond, James I.
— History of Life-Saving Appliances and Military and Naval Constructions... NY, 1885. 8vo, cloth; worn, spine-tips frayed. O Oct 21 (146) $110

Pontanus, Johannes Isaac, 1571-1640
— Rerum et urbis Amstelodamensium historia.... Amst., 1611. Folio, vellum. A few small wormholes touching text & plates. S Oct 23 (323) £1,300 [Browning]

Pontifical
— Pontificale Romanum ad omnes ceremonias...accomodatum. Venice: Giunta, 1561. Folio, later calf; worn. Some leaves stained & repaired in lower right corner. wa Dec 11 (698) $240
— Pontificales Romanum Clementis VIII primum. Rome, 1645. Folio, 17th-cent mor; extremities worn. sg Oct 9 (295) $110

Pontoppidan, Erik, 1698-1764
— The Natural History of Norway. L, 1755. Folio, contemp calf; joints cracked. With folding map hand-colored in outline & 28 plates. sg Apr 2 (160) $450

Ponziani, Domenico Lorenzo, 1719-96
— Il Giuoco incomparabile degli scacchi. Modena, 1782. 2d Ed. Half calf; scuffed. pn Mar 26 (481) £110 [Furstenberg]
— The Incomparable Game of Chess. L, 1820. Half calf; scuffed. pn Mar 26 (483) £35 [Drury]

Pool, Robert
— Views of the Most Remarkable Public Buildings...in the City of Dublin.... Dublin, 1780. 8vo, contemp calf; worn. With engraved title, 2 folding plans (slightly torn) & 29 plates. S Nov 17 (817) £320 [Neptune]

Poor, Charles Lane. See: Derrydale Press

Poore, Benjamin Perley, 1820-87
— A Descriptive Catalogue of the Government Publications of the United States.... Wash., 1885. 4to, modern half cloth; worn. O June 9 (144) $60

Poortenaar, Jan
— The Art of the Book and its Illustration. L, [1935]. 4to, cloth. bba Dec 4 (240) £95 [Brailey]

Anr copy. Cloth, in d/j. cba Feb 5 (141) $90

Pope, Alexander, 1688-1744
See also: Fore-Edge Paintings
— The Dunciad. L, 1729. ("The Dunciad Variorum. With the Prolegomena of Scriblerus.") 1st Complete Ed of 1st 3 books. 4to, contemp calf; joints split, rubbed. Inscr "C F 1729 given me by Mr. Pope" & with Charles Ford's bookplate opposite. S Nov 17 (675) £160 [Quaritch]
— An Essay on Man. L, 1819. Folio, contemp mor gilt. With port & 4 plates, all mtd india-proofs. sg Feb 12 (250) $150
— Der Lockenraub. Leipzig: Insel-Verlag, 1908. One of 100. Illus by Aubrey Beardsley. 4to, orig calf gilt. FD June 11 (4810) DM1,800
— [Of False Taste]. An Epistle to the...Earl of Burlington. L, 1731. 1st Ed, 1st Issue. Folio, orig wraps; frayed. Tp repaired; waterstained throughout. bba May 28 (39) £60 [Wood]
— Of the Characters of Women.... L, 1735. 1st Ed. Folio, later bds; spine worn, rubbed. Lacking half-title & final ad & with title in 2d state. bba Nov 13 (216) £50 [Hannas]
— The Rape of the Lock. L, 1714. 1st Separate Ed. 8vo, modern half mor. With frontis & 5 plates. Portion cut from title (repaired). bba Sept 25 (15) £180 [Martin]

Anr copy. Contemp wraps; worn. With 4 (of 5) engraved plates. bba Nov 13 (209) £40 [Axe]

Anr Ed. L, 1896. Illus by Aubrey Beardsley. 4to, orig cloth. B Oct 7 (273) HF525

Anr copy. Orig cloth; rubbed. bba Nov 13 (313) £70 [Sherman]; S Jan 16 (433) £220 [Sartin]
— Works. L, 1717-35. 2 vols. Folio, contemp calf; 1 cover loose. pnE Jan 28 (130) £190 [Traylen]

POPE

Anr Ed. L, 1797. 9 vols. 8vo, contemp calf gilt; joints cracking, rubbed. S July 13 (113) £80

Anr Ed. L, 1847. 8 vols. 8vo, contemp calf. S May 28 (892) £130

Pope, Alexander, Jr., 1849-1924
— Celebrated Dogs of America, Imported and Native. Bost., [1879]. Oblong folio, covers detached, orig pictorial wraps bound in. With 20 mtd colored plates. sg May 21 (168) $1,700

Pope, Arthur Upham —& Ackerman, Phyllis
— A Survey of Persian Art. L & NY, 1938-39. 6 vols plus 1958 vol. Folio, cloth. SSA Feb 11 (596) R3,800

Pope-Hennessy, Una, 1876-1949
— Early Chinese Jades. L, 1923. 4to, orig cloth; soiled. Library markings. sg Feb 6 (177) $200

Popham, Arthur Ewart. See: British Museum

Popish Plot
[A collection comprising more than 1,400 broadsides & pamphlets relating to the Popish Plot, indexed in 13 vols & annotated throughout in the same hand that produced the contemp index, sold at S on 24 July 1987] S July 24 (262) £100,000 [Quaritch]

Porada, Edith. See: Morgan Collection, John Pierpont

Porphyrius, Publius Optatianus
— Panegyricus dictus Constantino Augusto..... Augsburg, 1595. Folio, half mor; front cover cracked. An early owner has traced the solution in red ink on 18 (of 25) of the text pages. sg Oct 9 (297) $275

Porta, Giovanni Battista della, 1538-1615
— Della fisionomia dell'huomo. Padua, 1613. 4to, contemp vellum. Tear in 1 leaf. bba Aug 20 (353) £300 [Henderson]

— La Fisonomia dell' huomo.... Venice, 1652. 8vo, contemp half vellum; peeling. sg Jan 15 (341) $225

— Magiae naturalis, sive de miraculis rerum naturalium libri IIII. Naples: H. Salviani, 1589. ("Magiae naturalis libri XX.") Folio, old vellum. sg Jan 15 (339) $650

Anr Ed. Leiden: Hieronymus de Vogel, 1644. 12mo, contemp calf gilt; rebacked. With additional title. sg Jan 15 (340) $200

Anr Ed. Rouen, 1650. ("Magiae naturalis libri viginti.") 8vo, old calf gilt; joints cracked. sg Mar 26 (238) $120

Portalis, Roger
— Les Dessinateurs d'illustrations au dix-huitieme siecle. Paris, 1877. 2 vols extended to 4. 8vo, contemp half mor. Extra-illus with c.280 plates & drawings. C Dec 3 (32) £1,700 [St. Morritz]

Portalis, Roger —& Beraldi, Henri
— Les Graveurs du dixhuitieme siecle. Paris, 1880-82. 3 vols extended to 11. 8vo, contemp half mor. Extra-illus with c.705 plates. C Dec 3 (33) £2,100 [Tenschere]

Porter, Eugene
— San Erizario: A History. Austin, 1973. One of 50. Illus by Jose Cisneros. 4to, half lea. With pen drawing on limitation page showing the Comandante del Presidio. sg Sept 18 (236) $100

Porter, Sir James, 1710-86
— Observations on the Religion, Law, Government and Manners, of the Turks. L, 1771. 8vo, contemp sheep; joints & spine broken. S4-8 wrinkled & soiled. sg Nov 20 (149) $60

Porter, Jane, 1776-1850
— The Scottish Chiefs, a Romance. L, 1810. 1st Ed. 5 vols. 12mo, later half mor; rubbed. Minor paper flaws; lacking half-titles. O Oct 21 (148) $60

Porter, Katherine Anne
See also: F., M. T.
— Hacienda. [NY]: Harrison of Paris, [1934]. One of 895. S Sept 22 (133) £60 [Salima]

Porter, Sir Robert Ker, 1777-1842
— Travelling Sketches in Russia and Sweden.... L, 1809. 2 vols in 1. 4to, contemp calf gilt; worn. With 41 plates, many hand-colored. bba Dec 18 (219) £60 [Elliott]

Anr copy. 2 vols in one. 4to, bba Dec 18 (219) £60 [Elliott]

Anr Ed. L, 1813. 2 vols in 1. 4to, half calf; def. With 41 plates, 28 hand-colored. pn July 23 (66) £180 [Plinke]

— Travels in Georgia, Persia, Armenia, Ancient Babylonia. L, 1821-22. 2 vols. 4to, half calf; rebacked. With frontises, 2 folding maps (repaired) & 87 plates, 5 hand-colored Lacking half-titles, map & list of plates. Sold w.a.f. pn Dec 11 (145) £200 [Haye]

Porter, William Sydney, 1862-1910
See also: Limited Editions Club
— Works. NY, 1912. One of 125. 12 vols. Mor gilt. O May 12 (158) $1,400

Anr Ed. Garden City, 1917. One of 1,075. Illus by Gordon Grant. 14 vols. Half vellum. S July 23 (170) £720 [Joseph]

Portier, Andre —& Poncetton, Francois
— Les Arts Sauvages. Paris, [1930]. Oceanie only. Folio, cloth. With 50 plates, 5 colored. Library stamps. bba Mar 12 (298) £45 [C. G. Agents]

Portius, Simon, 1496-1554
— De rerum naturalium principiis, libri duo. Naples, 1561. 4to, vellum. S Sept 23 (380) £230 [King]

Portlock, Nathaniel
— A Voyage Round the World. L, 1789. 1st Ed. 4to, calf gilt; rebacked. With port & 19 charts & plates, 5 colored. Tp & most plates foxed. CA Apr 12 (203) A$1,100

Anr copy. Contemp calf; rebacked, front cover detached. With port & 19 charts & plates. Tears in 5 maps mended on verso. sg Apr 23 (119) $800

Portlock, William Henry
— A New Complete and Universal Collection of...Voyages and Travels.... L, [1794]. Folio, contemp calf; upper cover detached. with frontis (worn) & 97 (of 90) plates, maps & charts. Some cropping; tears in pp 659-62 with loss. Sold w.a.f. S Jan 12 (188) £220 [Shapero]

Anr copy. Needs rebdg. Frontis damaged; folding map creased & reinforced. Sold w.a.f. sg Nov 20 (150) $350

Portraits...
— Portraits des grands hommes, femmes illustres.... Paris, 1786-91. 4to, mor gilt by Riviere. With engraved title & 192 color plates.. Extra-illus with 35 ports & plates, most laid down. C May 13 (52) £2,200 [Beres]

Post...
— The Post Chaise Companion: or, Travellers Directory through Ireland.... Dublin, 1803. 3d Ed. 8vo, contemp half calf; rebacked, new endpapers. Inner margins cut close; some waterstains; map torn along folds. bba Apr 9 (358) £80 [Mullott]

Post Boy
— The Post Boy [continued as The Daily Post Boy]. L, 1706-35. Nos 1780-8004, in 10 vols. Folio, contemp half calf; worn. Lacking Nos 2167, 2635, 2664, 2684, 2871, 5442, 6885-90 & 7691; some defs. Sold w.a.f. S July 24 (270) £17,500 [Burgess Browning]

Postan, Alexander
— The Complete Graphic Work of Paul Nash. L, 1973. One of 43. Half mor. With 4 unpbd woodcuts. S Dec 4 (203) £180 [Sherlock]

Poster...
— The Poster: An Illustrated Monthly Chronicle. L, 1898-1901. Vols I-III only. cloth, orig wraps bound in; soiled & rubbed. S Oct 6 (842) £160 [Stone]

Posthius, Joannes
— Tetrasticha in Ovidii metamor. lib XV. Frankfurt: G. Corvinum, 1563. 8vo, contemp calf gilt; rebacked. Lacking 2 leaves; some wear. HK Nov 4 (720) DM1,500

Postlethwayt, Malachy
See also: Savary des Bruslons, Jacques
— Great-Britain's True System. L, 1757. 8vo, contemp calf; worn. S May 29 (1248) £280
— The Universal Dictionary of Trade and Commerce.... L, 1766. 2 vols. Folio, modern mor. First few leaves of Vol I stained at upper margin & with slight worming in lower margin. S Feb 24 (422) £700 [Traylen]

Pote, Joseph, 1703?-87
— The History and Antiquities of Windsor Castle.... L, 1749. 4to, contemp calf; rubbed, joints cracked. With 12 plates. cb Dec 18 (149) $65

Pott, Percival, 1714-88
— The Chirurgical Works. L, 1779. 3 vols. 8vo, contemp calf. pnE Dec 17 (51) £220 [Phelps]

Potter, Beatrix
— Appley Dapply's Nursery Rhymes. L, 1917. 16mo, orig bds. pn Jan 22 (294) £100 [Peterss]
— Cecily Parsley's Nursery Rhymers. L, [1922]. 16mo, orig bds. Inscr. S Dec 5 (348) £700 [Joseph & Sawyer]
— Changing Pictures, a Book of Transformation PIctures. L: Nister, [c.1894]. 4to, orig half cloth. S June 17 (479) £300 [Yablon]
— The Fairy Caravan. L, 1929. One of 100 with the 1st 9 leaves ptd in Ambleside. 4to, orig half cloth. Small tear in 1 leaf. With prelim leaves for the American Ed in a separate folder. S June 17 (488) £1,100 [Hough]
— Ginger and Pickles. L, [1909]. 1st Ed. 4to, orig bds. pn Sept 18 (320) £60 [Thorp]
— The Roly-Poly Pudding. L, 1908. 1st Ed. 4to, orig cloth; upper portion faded. pn Jan 22 (295) £95 [Cavendish]; pnE Oct 15 (140) £110
— The Story of Miss Moppet. L, 1906. 1st Ed. 16mo, orig cloth wallet-type bdg. Minor creasing. S Oct 7 (986) £60 [Bale]
— The Tailor of Gloucester. L, 1902. 1st Ed. One of 500. 16mo, orig bds; faintly

POTTER

spotted. S June 18 (482) £1,150 [Peters]

1st Pbd Ed. L & NY, 1903. 16mo, orig cloth. S Oct 7 (990) £240 [Quaritch] One of a few specially bound. Flower-patterned cambric from the Potter family textile mill. C May 13 (166) £320 [Sumner & Stillman]

— The Tale of Benjamin Bunny. L, 1904. 1st Ed. 16mo, orig bds; soiled. pn Jan 22 (298) £50 [Day]

— The Tale of Johnny Town-Mouse. L & NY, [1918]. 1st Ed. 4to, orig bds; faded. pn Jan 22 (300) £50 [Peters]

— The Tale of Little Pig Robinson. L & NY, [1930]. 1st Ed. With 6 color plates. pn Jan 22 (301) £55 [Joseph]

— The Tale of Mr. Jeremy Fisher. L, 1906. 1st Ed. 16mo, orig bds. pn Jan 22 (302) £100 [Roberts]

— The Tale of Mr. Tod. L & NY, 1912. 1st Ed. 16mo, orig bds. pn Jan 22 (303) £80 [Joseph]

— The Tale of Mrs. Tiggy-Winkle. L, 1905. 1st Ed. 16mo, orig bds. pn Sept 18 (322) £65 [Demetzy]

— The Tale of Mrs. Tittlemouse. L & NY, 1910. 1st Ed. 16mo, orig bds. pn Sept 18 (323) £60 [Peters]

Anr copy. Orig bds; faded. pn Jan 22 (304) £35 [Peters]

— The Tale of Peter Rabbit. [L], Feb 1902. 1st Pbd Ed, 2d copyright Ed. 16mo, orig bds. Frontis loose; tear affecting 1 plate & leaf of text. S Oct 7 (992) £65 [Lovett]

Anr copy. Orig bds; soiled & worn. Inscr. S June 18 (480) £1,400 [Joseph]

— The Tale of Pigling Bland. L, [1913]. 1st Ed. 16mo, orig bds; faded. pn Jan 22 (305) £70 [Joseph]

— The Tale of Squirrel Nutkin. L, 1903. 1st Ed. 16mo, orig bds. pn Jan 22 Day (307) £100

— The Tale of the Flopsy Bunnies. L, 1909. 1st Ed. 16mo, orig bds. pn Jan 22 (299) £100 [Peters]

— The Tale of Timmy Tiptoes. L, 1911. 1st Ed. 16mo, orig bds. pn Jan 22 (306) £65 [Stone]

Pottier, Andre Ariodant

— Monuments francais inedits pour servir a l'histoire des arts depuis le VIe siecle.... Paris, 1839. Illus by Nicolas Xavier Willemin. 2 vols. Folio, 19th-cent half lea; joints & spine ends worn. With 2 hand-colored engraved titles & 300 plates, 179 hand-colored. sg Apr 2 (161) $1,700

AMERICAN BOOK PRICES CURRENT

Pottier, Eugene, 1816-87

— L'Internationale. Belves: Pierre Vorms, 1970. One of 160. Illus by Frans Masereel. B Oct 7 (197) HF220

Pottinger, Sir Henry, 1789-1856

— Travels in Beloochistan and Sinde. L, 1816. 1st Ed. 4to, modern half calf. With hand-colored frontis & folding map (fold slightly torn & reinforced). bba Oct 30 (350) £300 [Hosains]

Potts, Thomas, 1778-1842

— The British Farmer's Cyclopaedia. L, 1807. 4to, contemp calf; upper cover detached, lower joint split. With engraved title & 42 plates, 24 hand-colored. Ck Jan 16 (17) £160

Poulson, George, 1783-1858

— Beverlac; or, the Antiquities and History of the Town of Beverley.... Beverley, 1829. 2 vols. 8vo, contemp half calf; hinges cracked, spines torn. T Oct 16 (343) £40

Pouncey, Philip. See: British Museum

Pouncy, John

— Dorsetshire Photographically Illustrated.... L & Dorchester, [1857]. 4 vols in 2. Oblong folio, orig cloth; worn. With litho title & 76 tinted photolitho plates only. Leaf of intro in Vol I detached & frayed. L July 2 (101) £180

Pound, Ezra

— A Draft of the Cantos 17-27. L: John Rodker, 1928. 1st Ed, one of 70 on Roma. Folio, half mor. P June 18 (162) $1,100

— A Draft of XVI Cantos. Paris: Three Mountains Press, 1925. One of 70. Folio, half mor. P June 18 (161) $1,000

— A Draft of XXX Cantos. Paris: Hours Press, 1930. 1st Ed, One of 200. Orig cloth; soiled. T Oct 15 (70) £420

— Drafts & Fragments of Cantos CX-CXVII. NY: New Directions, [1968]. 1st Ed, one of 310. Folio, orig cloth. pnNY Sept 13 (269) $225

— Gaudier-Brzeska, a Memoir. L, 1916. 1st Ed. wa Dec 11 (89) $130

— Hugh Selwyn Mauberley. L, 1920. 1st Ed, One of 165. Orig unbound sheets; soiled. Inscr to Scofield Thayer. P June 18 (163) $2,500

— Indiscretions. Paris: Three Mountains Press, 1923. One of 300. 4 bi-folio ptd sheets unfolded & unbound sg Mar 5 (220) $425

— Lustra. NY, 1917. Bds, in chipped d/j. wa Dec 11 (91) $140

— Quia pauper amavi. L: The Egoist, [1919]. 1st Ed, one of 100. Orig half cloth. ALs inserted. O May 12 (159) $1,000

Anr copy. Orig half cloth. With holograph correction. pnNY June 11 (142) $300

One of 100, sgd. Orig half cloth. wa Sept 25 (686) $450

One of 500. Half mor gilt. pnNY Sept 13 (270) $130

Pournelle, Jerry. See: Niven & Pournelle

Povey, Charles
— A Discovery of Indirect Practices in the Coal-Trade.... L: H. Hills, 1700. 4to, wraps. Tp soiled. S July 24 (458) £500 [Lawson]

Powell, Anthony
— A Dance to the Music of Time. L, 1951-75. 12 vols. In d/js. bba July 2 (416) £520 [Fitzcaraldo]

Powell, H. M. T. See: Grabhorn Printing

Powell, John Wesley
— Exploration of the Colorado River of the West and its Tributaries.... Wash., 1875. 1st Ed. 8vo, orig cloth; spine ends & corners worn. With 72 plates & 2 folding charts. Library markings. cb Mar 19 (219) $150

Anr copy. Orig cloth; worn. wa Mar 5 (401) $120

Powell, Lawrence Clark
— Robinson Jeffers: the Man & His Work. Los Angeles, 1934. Ltd Ed. Cloth, in d/j. cb June 18 (217) $75

Power, Henry
— Experimental Philosophy, in Three Books. L, 1664. 1st Ed. 4to, 19th-cent half calf; rubbed & worn. Some soiling to tp & preceding leaf; folding plate with tear repaired. cb Feb 19 (194) $750

Power, Sir William James Tyrone
— Sketches in New Zealand. L, 1849. 8vo, half mor. With frontis (foxed) & 7 plates. pn Dec 11 (268) £65 [Scott]

Pownall, Thomas, 1722-1805
— A Topographical Description of Such Parts of North America as are Contained in the (Annexed) Map of the Middle British Colonies, &c in North America. L, 1776. Folio, sewn in wraps; frayed & broken. With the Lewis Evans map, hyaving a few outlines added in colored wash. L.p. copy. CNY May 11 (128) $7,000

Anr copy. Modern bds. With the Evans map (with 1 small hole & a few very small worm holes). Sold with a modern Ed. sg June 11 (323) $3,800

Powys, Llewelyn, 1884-1939. See: Golden Cockerel Press

Powys, Theodore Francis, 1875-1953. See: Golden Cockerel Press

Poynting, Frank
— Eggs of British Birds with an Account of their Breeding-Habits, Limicolae. L, 1895-96. 4to, half mor. With 54 colored plates. pn Oct 23 (264) £190 [Bles]

Anr copy. Half mor gilt, orig wraps bound in. pnE Dec 17 (278) £180 [Egglishaw]

Poyntz, John
— The Present Prospect of the Famous and Fertile Island of Tobago. L, 1695. 2d Ed. 4to, wraps. First & last leaves soiled. S June 23 (449) £500 [Maggs]

Pozzo, Andrea, 1642-1709
— Perspectiva pictorum et architectorum. Rome, 1693-1700. 1st Ed. 2 parts in 2 vols. Folio, contemp calf. With 3 engraved titles & 222 plates. Opening leaves of Vol II minimally dampstained in corners. sg Apr 2 (162) $5,000

— Rules and Examples of Perspective Proper for Painters and Architects. L, 1707. Folio, vellum gilt; spine torn at top & bottom. With 2 engraved titles, dedication, frontis & 101 plates. S May 6 (530) £95 [Barker]

Pradt, Dominique Dufour de, 1759-1837
— Des Colonies, et de la Revolution actuelle de l'Amerique. Paris, 1817. 2 vols in 1. 8vo, contemp half·sheep; rubbed. P Sept 24 (374) $175

Prarond, Ernest, 1821-1909
— Les Chasses de la Somme. Paris, 1858. One of 300. 8vo, half mor gilt by Magnier. Jeanson copy. SM Mar 1 (472) FF2,200

Prat, Samuel, 1659-1723
— The Regulating Silver Coin, Made Practicable and Easie. L: Henry Bonwick, 1696. 8vo, contemp calf; joints splitting, spine damaged. Some dampstains. bba Aug 28 (185) £65 [Bickersteth]

Pratt, Anne, 1806-93
— The Flowering Plants, Grasses, Sedges, and Ferns of Great Britain. L, [c.1873]. 7 vols in 4. 8vo, mor gilt. pn July 23 (76) £170 [Lewis]

Anr copy. 6 vols. 8vo, orig cloth. S Nov 17 (676) £160 [Broseghini]

Anr copy. Half mor; spines darkened. "Not collated but likely complete". sg Jan 15 (247) $300

Anr Ed. L, 1899-1900. 4 vols. 8vo, half mor gilt; worn. sg June 18 (235) $350

Pratt, Fletcher. See: De Camp & Pratt

Pratt, Peter, fl.1810
— The Theory of Chess. L, 1799. Half calf. pn Mar 26 (485) £55 [Caissa]

Preece, Louisa. See: Symonds & Preece

Prendergast, Maurice, 1859-1924
— Water-color Sketchbook 1899. Bost., 1960. Text in wraps, sketchbook in cloth. wa Sept 25 (268) $55

Prenner, Anton Joseph von. See: Stampart & Prenner

Prescott, George Bartlett
— The Speaking Telephone, Talking Phonograph and other Novelties. NY, 1878. 8vo, cloth; worn. wa Nov 6 (93) $110

Prescott, William Hickling, 1796-1859
— History of the Conquest of Mexico. L, 1843. 3 vols. 8vo, orig cloth; recased. With 2 folding maps & plate of Cortes' signature. cb June 4 (172) $110

Anr copy. Orig cloth; soiled & worn. With 2 folding maps. wa Nov 6 (227) $200

Present...
— The Present State of Ireland.... L, 1673. 8vo, later calf over bds; scuffed. With folding map. Trimmed with occasional loss of a few letters at fore-edge; later front & rear blanks. ha May 22 (346) $650

— The Present State of New-England.... L, 1675. 1st Issue. Folio, modern mor gilt. 2 leaves transposed. sg Dec 4 (164) $3,000

Preti, Jean, 1798-1881
— Traite complet, theorique et pratique sur les fins de parties jeu des echecs. Paris, 1858. Half calf gilt. pn Mar 26 (321) £35 [Courtney]

Pretty, Edward
— A Practical Essay on Flower Painting in Water Colours. L: D. N. Shury for S & J. Fuller, 1812. 4to, contemp half lea; worn. With 10 plain & 14 hand-colored plates. Some staining & soiling. S Apr 23 (56) £450 [Sims]

Preussische...
— Preussische Armee-Uniformen unter der Regierung Friedrich Wilhelm II.... Potsdam, 1796. 8vo, old bds; worn & loose. With 154 hand-colored plates. HN May 20 (1615) DM12,000

Prevert, Jacques
— Les Chiens on soif. Paris, 1964. One of 250. Illus by Max Ernst. Folio, loose in orig wraps. With 26 colored lithos & 2 orig colored etchings. sg Dec 4 (67) $200

Anr copy. Unbound as issued in pictorial wraps. sg Apr 2 (79) $1,100

Prevost d'Exiles, Antoine Francois, 1697-1763
— Histoire generale des voyages.... Paris & Amst., 1746-70. Vols 1-19 (of 20). 4to, contemp calf gilt; rubbed. C Dec 12 (256) £2,200 [Strasser]

— Manon Lescaut. Paris: Didot l'aine, 1797. ("Histoire du chevalier Des Grieux, et de Manon Lescaut.") One of 100 L.p. copies on grand papier velin, with the plates in 4 states. 2 vols. 8vo, mor extra by Lortic with his ticket. With 8 plates. C Dec 3 (157) £3,200 [Camille]

Anr Ed. L, 1841. Illus by Tony Johannot. 8vo, mor gilt; minor wear at joints. sg Sept 11 (215) $70

Prevost, Jean Louis
— Collection des fleurs et des fruits. Paris, 1805. Folio, contemp half mor gilt; worn. With 48 plates, ptd in colors & finished by hand. Linnean Society—de Belder copy. S Apr 28 (287) £140,000 [Ursus]

Priapeia...
— Priapeia, sive diversorum poetarum in Priapum lusus. Padua: Gerhardum Nicholaum V, 1664. 8vo, 19th-cent half mor; rubbed. Dampstained. cb Oct 23 (184) $55

Price, Charles Matlack
— Posters: a Critical Study of the Development of Poster Design.... NY, 1913. One of 250. 4to, orig cloth; rubbed. S Oct 6 (843) £110 [Marks]

Price, Elizabeth
— The New Book of Cookery.... L: Alex. Hogg, [c.1780]. 12mo, 19th-cent half mor. Frontis torn & frayed at inner margin; some browning. Crahan copy. P Nov 25 (384) $400

Price, Francis, d.1753
— The British Carpenter: or, A Treatise on Carpentry.... L, 1735. 2 parts, including Supplement, in 1 vol. 4to, contemp calf; worn. Foxed & heavily dampstained. sg June 4 (264) $375

Price, Capt. George F.
— Across the Continent with the Fifth Cavalry. NY, 1883. 8vo, orig cloth; stained, endpaper torn. With 4 ports. wa Feb 19 (58) $70

Price, John Edward
— A Descriptive Account of the Guildhall of the City of London. L, 1886. Folio, modern cloth preserving orig upper cover & spine. With 4 colored maps, double-page genealogy & 43 plates. bba Apr 9 (389) £60 [Rainer]

Price, Lake
— Interiors and Exteriors in Venice. L, 1843. Folio, modern cloth. With engraved title & 25 hand-colored plates. Plates mtd on card & with Ms captions; guarded throughout. Lacking tp & dedication leaf. C Oct 15 (88) £800 [Sims]

Anr copy. Unbound as issued in orig cloth portfolio. With hand-colored title & 23 plates only, all mtd on card with titles in Ms. Lower margin soiled throughout; lacking dedication, text & 2 plates. Ck Nov 21 (249A) £350 [Toscani]

Anr copy. Orig half mor; rubbed. With litho title, dedication & 25 views. S Nov 17 (917) £300 [Marshall]
— Tauromachia, or the Bull-Fights of Spain.... L, 1852. Folio, half mor preserving orig cloth sides. With engraved title & 25 plates. Short tear repaired; some foxing; some margins frayed with a few small stains & 1 short tear repaired. S Oct 23 (269) £1,200 [Level]

Price, Owen. See: Russell & Price

Price, Richard, 1723-91
— Additional Observations on the Nature and Value of Civil Liberty,.... L, 1777. 3d Ed. 8vo, later half mor; corners worn. Tp soiled; tear at blank right edge. sg Sept 18 (239) $100

Price, Sarah
— Illustrations of the Fungi of Our Fields and Woods. L, 1864-65. Series I & II in 1 vol. 4to, orig cloth. With 20 hand-colored plates. C Oct 15 (197) £460 [Sotheran]

Anr copy. 2 vols in 1. 4to, mor; worn, lower joint splitting. With 20 colored plates. Lacking some text. S Nov 17 (677) £260 [Greyfriars]

Anr copy. 2 vols. 4to, orig cloth. T Nov 20 (125) £360

Price, Sir Uvedale
— A Letter to H. Repton, Esq., on the Application of the Practice as well as the Principles of Landscape-Painting.... L, 1795. 1st Ed. 8vo, contemp calf; rubbed. bba Sept 25 (288) £280 [Shapero]

Prichard, Hesketh Vernon
— Through Trackless Labrador. L, 1911. 4to, modern cloth. sg Sept 18 (146) $80

Prichard, James Cowles, 1786-1848
— Histoire naturelle de l'homme. Paris, 1843. 2 vols. 8vo, contemp half lea gilt. With 39 (of 40) plates, most hand-colored. Marginal dampstains. sg Jan 15 (342) $150
— The Natural History of Man. L, 1845. 2d Ed. 8vo, orig cloth; rubbed. Some spotting & staining. bba Oct 30 (415) £75 [Sanders]

Prideaux, Mathias
— An easy and Compendious Introduction for Reading.... Oxford, 1664. 4th Ed. 4to, contemp calf; rebacked. B4 of Synopsis incorrectly folded. sg Mar 26 (239) $130

Prideaux, Sara T.
— Aquatint Engraving. L, 1909. 1st Ed. sg Feb 5 (280) $150

Prideaux, William Francis
— A Bibliography of the Works of Robert Louis Stevenson. L, 1917. sg May 14 (224) $50

Anr copy. Ed by Flora V. Livingston. sg Oct 2 (285) $100

Priest, Cecil Damer
— The Birds of Southern Rhodesia. L, 1933-36. 4 vols. 4to, orig cloth; rubbed. With folding map & 10 colored plates. pn Oct 23 (265) £180 [Graham]

Anr copy. With folding map & 40 colored plates. pn Dec 11 (244) £170 [Wakeley]

Priestley, Joseph, 1733-1804
— Discourses relating to the Evidences of Revealed Religion. Phila., 1796. 8vo, old calf; rubbed. Some foxing; minor stains & soiling. O Oct 21 (150) $60
— Histoire de l'electricite. Paris, 1771. 3 vols. 12mo, contemp calf. With 9 folding plates. Minor worming. FD June 11 (688) DM850
— The History and Present State of Electricity.... L, 1767. 1st Ed. 4to, 19th-cent calf; wormholes at foot of joints, 1 corner rubbed. With 8 plates. Tear repaired at blank margin of title; some spotting; a few plates with soft crease; offest from bookmark on 2 leaves. C Dec 12 (168) £1,300 [Keating]

2d Ed. L, 1769. 4to, contemp calf gilt. With 8 plates. HK Nov 4 (972) DM1,350

Anr copy. Contemp calf; spine ends chipped, joints cracked. With 8 plates & 2 tables. sg Jan 15 (343) $250
— The History and Present State of Discoveries Relating to Vision, Light and Colours. L, 1772. 1st Ed. 2 vols. 4to, contemp calf; worn, 1 cover detached. With folding chart & 24 folding plates. Vol I lacking S1; library stamp of Trinity College, Dublin. Sold w.a.f. bba Aug 28 (134) £120 [Rainer]
— Lectures on History, and General Policy. Birm., 1788. 1st Ed. 4to, contemp calf; broken. Minor dampstains to inner margins of 1st few leaves. T Nov 20 (438) £120

Prieur, Claude
— Dialogue de la lycanthropie.... Louvain: J. Maes & P. Zangre, 1596. 8vo, late 19th- or early 20th-cent mor gilt. Jeanson 1117. SM Mar 1 (473) FF19,000

Priezac, Salomon de, Sieur de Sauges
— L'Histoire des elephants. Paris: Charles Sercy, 1650. 12mo, 17th-cent mor gilt. Jeanson copy. SM Mar 1 (474) FF15,000

Prim, Peter, Pseud.
— The Picture Gallery, or Peter Prim's Portraits of Good and Bad Girls and Boys. L, 1814. 1st Ed. 16mo, modern calf gilt, orig wraps bound in. Engraved & hand-colored throughout. S Dec 5 (339) £320 [Mrs. Moon]

Prince, Thomas, 1687-1758
— A Chronological History of New-England in the Form of Annals. Bost.: Kneeland & Green for Gerrish, 1736. 1st Ed. Vol I only. 8vo, contemp calf gilt; rubbed. Some browning; front flyleaf damaged. S Apr 24 (272) £250 [Steinbock]

Prince, William Robert, 1795-1869
— A Treatise on the Vine.... NY, 1830. 1st Ed. 8vo, half mor gilt. Library stamp on tp; foxed throughout. Hunt copy. CNY Nov 21 (230) $380

Anr copy. Orig bds; rubbed, rebacked. Inscr. P Nov 25 (48) $600

Anr copy. New calf. Library stamp on tp. Crahan copy. P Nov 25 (385) $350

Principall. See: Hakluyt, Richard

Pringle, Sir John, 1707-82
— A Discourse upon some Late Improvements...for...Preserving the Health of Mariners.... L, 1776. 4to, calf; rebacked. pnE Dec 17 (135) £1,500 [Quaritch]
— Observations on the Diseases of the Army.... L, 1753. 2d Ed. 8vo, contemp calf; rebacked, orig spine relaid. pnE Dec 17 (171) £340 [McCormack]

3d Ed. L, 1761. 8vo, contemp calf gilt; joints cracked. Marginal dampstaining. sg Jan 15 (120) $100

Prinsep, Henry Thoby, the Elder
— A Narrative of the Political and Military Transactions of British India.... L, 1820. 4to, modern cloth; soiled. Half-title repaired; 1 page clipped along lower margin. wa Sept 25 (139) $80

Print...
— Print: A Quarterly Journal of the Graphic Arts. New Haven, 1940-46. Vols I-V. 4to, wraps; worn. With 5 miscellaneous duplicates. O Jan 6 (150) $60

Priscianus, fl.500 A.D.
— Libri de nummis, ponderibus, mensuris.... Paris: Rouille, 1565. 8vo, bds. 1 leaf soiled. sg Jan 15 (380) $80
— Octavii Horatiani rerum medicarum lib. quatuor.... Strassburg: Joannes Schott, 1532. Folio, recent mor. Piece torn from lower margin of u l. S May 21 (214) £2,400 [Thomas]
— Opera. Venice: Philippus Pincius, 20 June 1492. Folio, contemp Cambridge bdg by W. G. of blind-tooled calf over wooden bds. With illuminated ecclesiastical arms at foot of a2 recto, being those of Potier de la Morandiere, Seigneur de Novion et de Montauglan. Slight worming to upper outer corner of final 3 leaves; minor marginal dampstaining. 308 leaves. Goff P-969. S Nov 27 (22) £2,800 [Kraus]

Prisse d'Avennes, Achille Constant T. Emile
— L'Art Arabe, d'apres les monuments du Kaire.... Paris, 1877. 3 plate vols, folio & text vol, 4to, contemp half mor. With 234 plates. C July 22 (163) £5,800

Pritt, Thomas Evan
— The Book of the Grayling. Leeds, 1888. 4to, orig cloth. With 3 colored plates. pn Dec 11 (256) £60 [Peltz]

Pritts, Joseph
— Mirror of Olden Time Border Life. Abingdon VA, 1849. 8vo, orig cloth; rebacked with backstrip laid down, worn. ha Mar 13 (165) $90

Pritzel, Georg August
— Thesaurus literaturae botanicae, omnium gentium. Milan, [1950]. 4to, cloth; front cover warped. Facsimile of the 1871 Ed. sg May 14 (617) $155

Probus Britannicus. See: Johnson, Samuel

Probus, Marcus Valerius
— De notis Roma.... Venice: Joannes Tacuinus, Feb 1525. 4to, wraps. FD June 11 (129) DM1,350

Processo...
— Processo formado de Order del Rey N. Senor por la Junta de Generales...sobre la conducta, que tuvieron en la Defensa...de la Habana.... Madrid, 1763-64. 2 vols. Folio, calf. S Oct 23 (447) £4,800 [Hodgson]

Proclamation...
— A Proclamation for the Observation of Certayne Statutes, with a Fourme howe the same shalbe Executed. L: [R. Jugge, 1567?]. 4to, wraps. Black letter. Head of title & a few headlines cut close. S July 24 (444) £750 [Lesker]

Procopius, of Caesarea

— Historiarum Procopii libri VIII. Augsburg, 1607. Folio, vellum bds. Soiling. S Sept 23 (483) £100 [Maggs]
— The History of the Warres of the Emperour Justinian.... L, 1653. Folio, contemp calf; rebacked. sg Mar 26 (240) $225

Proctor, John. See: Patten, William

Proctor, Robert George Collier, 1868-1903

— An Index to the Early Printed Books in the British Museum, from the Invention of Printing to 1500. L, 1898-1938. 2 vols plus 5 supplements in 1 vol. 8vo, cloth. sg May 14 (413) $350
— The Printing of Greek in the Fifteenth Century. Oxford, 1900. 4to, cloth, orig wraps bound in. sg May 14 (521) $150

Proedria-Basilike. See: Howell, James

Proehl, Carl William

— The Fourth Marine Division in World War II. Wash.: Infantry Journal Press, [1946]. 1st Ed. Bdg worn. wa Sept 25 (401) $60

Pronti, Domenico

Nuova Raccolta di 100 vedutine antiche [moderne] della citta di Roma... Rome [1795]. 2 vols in 1. 4to, half calf; rubbed. With 2 engraved titles, port & 170 views on 85 plates. Lacking port. S Jan 16 (423) £110 [Casali]
— Nuova Raccolta rappresentante i costumi religiosi, civili e militari degli antichi Egiziani, Etruschi.... Rome, [c.1800]. 4to, contemp mor gilt; drubbed. With engraved title, plan & 48 plates. Some staining. bba Sept 25 (175A) £50 [Magnaini]

Prony, Gaspard Clair Francois Marie Riche, Baron de

— Nouvelle architecture hydraulique.... Paris, 1790-96. 2 vols. 4to, contemp half calf. With half-title in Vol I & 55 folding plates. Lacking Plate 46 but 48 supplied in duplicate; 1 plate headline shaved. Tp inscr by Mathew Boulton. C Dec 12 (170) £450 [Keating]

Propert, John Lumsden

— A History of Miniature Art. L, 1887. 4to, orig cloth; loose. sg Feb 5 (225) $150

Propert, Walter Archibald

— The Russian Ballet in Western Europe, 1909-1920.... L, 1921. 1st Ed, One of 500. 4to, orig half cloth; rubbed. Ck Sept 26 (82) £100; Ck Jan 16 (240) £150

Propertius, Sextus

— Opera. See: Catullus, Tibullus & Propertius

Propriete...

— De la Propriete en nature d'aucuns oiseaux. Paris: Nicolas Bonfons, 1584. 16mo, mor gilt by Cape. Jeanson copy. SM Mar 1 (476) FF38,000

Prospect. See: Speed, John

Prosper

— De vita contemplativa. Speier: Peter Drach, 1486. 4to, modern bds. 50 leaves. Goff P-1022. sg Dec 4 (165) $800

Proust, Marcel

See also: Atget, Eugene

— 47 lettres inedites a Walter Berry. Paris: Black Sun Press, 1930. One of 50 on japon. 4to, wraps. sg Jan 8 (28) $250
One of 200. Half lea; rubbed. O Mar 24 (141) $120
— Un Amour de Swann. Paris, [1930]. One of 15 on Whatman, with 2 suites of the plates; in black & in sanguine. Illus by Pierre Laprade. Orig wraps. With orig watercolor by Laprade laid in. FD Dec 2 (4516) DM2,100
— A la recherche du temps perdu. Paris: Bernard Grasset & Editions de la Nouvelle Revue Francaise, [1913]-27. 1st Ed. Vols IV & V only. Half leaps. Inscr to Alec W. Randal. HN May 20 (2773) DM2,000

Prout, Samuel, 1783-1852

— Facsimiles of Sketches made in Flanders and Germany. L, [1833?]. Folio, orig half mor. With litho title, dedication & 50 plates. Title & dedication spotted. C July 22 (164) £2,200
— Rudiments of Landscape. L: Ackermann, 1813. Oblong 4to, later mor gilt. With 64 plates, 16 hand-colored. Some dampstains. Possibly a made-up copy. bba July 16 (397) £300 [Thorp]
— Sketches at Home and Abroad. L, 1844. Folio, half mor gilt; worn. With 48 plates. pn May 21 (56) £130
— Sketches in France, Switzerland and Italy. L, [1839]. Folio, orig half mor. With litho title & 25 plates. C July 22 (167) £700

Provis, John

— Tables of the Most Useful Kind to Facilitate Business...Copper Trade. Truro, 1801. 4to, contemp half lea; spine worn at extremities, joints cracked. C Dec 12 (171) £300 [Birmingham Assay Office]

Pry, Paul. See: Heath, William

Pryce, William

— Mineralogia Cornubiensis, a Treatise on Mining.... L, 1788. Folio, contemp calf; head of spine worn, slight worming to upper joint. With port, 7 plates & 2 folding tables. Plate IV with slightly flawed impression. C Dec 12 (172) £850 [Quaritch]

Prynne, William, 1600-69
— A Declaration and Protestation against the...New Tax and Extortion of Excise in General.... L, 1654. 4to, wraps. S July 24 (454) £260 [Quaritch]
— Histrio-mastix. L, 1633. 1st Ed, 2d State, with list of "Errataes". 2 parts in 1 vol. 4to, contemp calf; rebacked & bumped. Lacking initial blank; tp guarded; some browning & rustmarks; marginal tears & holes affecting text on 5 leaves; inner margin of final leaf restored. Halliwell-Phillipps copy. S Dec 18 (10) £700 [Quaritch]
— An Humble Remonstrance to His Majesty against the Tax of Ship-money.... L, 1641. 4to, wraps. S July 24 (455) £250 [Pickering]

Psalms & Psalters

Dutch Versions
— 1928. - Het Boeck der Psalmen. Haarlem One of 150. Half vellum. B Oct 7 (86) HF850

English Versions
— 1632. - The Psalmes of David, translated into Lyrick-Verse...by George Wither. "In the Neatherlands": Cornelis gerrits van Breughel. 16mo, sheep gilt; broken. Margins trimmed close; tp & Q6 restored with loss; small piece of title outer margin loose. Sophisticated copy. sg Oct 9 (103) $130
— 1861. - The Psalms of David, Illuminated. L. Illus by Owen Jones. Folio, orig calf; broken. Some spotting. bba Sept 25 (176) £150 [Demetzy]

German & Hebrew Versions
— 1804-5. - Sepher Zemiroth Yisroel—Sepher Tehillim. Offenbach 5 parts in 2 vols. 8vo, contemp calf; worn & scuffed. sg Sept 25 (41) $140

Latin Versions
— c.1485. - Wurezburg: George Reyser. Folio, contemp pigskin over wooden bds. 278 (of 280) leaves; 1 leaf on photocopy. Goff P-1046. HK Nov 4 (613) DM4,000

Polyglot Versions
— 1516. - Genoa: Petrus Paulus Porrus. Folio, 19th-cent half calf; broken. Library markings; tp soiled & with minor marginal repair; single wormhole in blank margins of 1st 14 leaves; hole to inner margins of Q1-2 & V1-3 touching a few characters. P Sept 24 (203) $3,000

Anr copy. 17th-cent vellum bds. Early bibliographical notes on front fly-leaf. S Nov 27 (26) £8,400 [Kraus]

Psnnsylvania Journal
— Postscript to the Pennsylvania Journal, March 22. No 1424 [Middle-colony Report on the Boston Massacre]. Phila.: William & Thomas Bradford, 22 mar 1775. Single leaf ptd on both sides, 16 by 10 inches. P May 13 (21) $2,000

Ptolemaeus, Claudius
— Almagestum.... Venice: Petrus Liechtenstein, 10 Jan 1515. Folio, 17th-cent calf; rebacked, joints cracked. Marginal worming, occasionally affecting a few letters. C May 13 (147) £1,500 [Quaritch]

Anr copy. Contemp blindstamped calf; rebacked & repaired. Minor worming. FD June 11 (528) DM12,500

Anr Ed. Venice: L. A. Giunta, 1528. Folio, contemp vellum bds; worn & stained. Some staining to lower margins; tp a little discolored. S June 25 (128) £1,050 [Kraus]
— Mathematicae constructionis liber primus. Wittenberg: J. Lufft, 1549. 8vo, vellum. Lacking a folding table; lower outer blank corner of title repaired; some staining. S july 28 (1109) £150

Geographia
— 1525. - Geographicae enarrationis libri octo.... Strasbourg: Johannes Grueninger for J. Koberger. Folio, vellum; soiled. With 27 double-page maps of the ancient world, 22 double-page maps of the modern world & 1 full-page map of Lotharingia on verso of Map 46, all woodcut. On vellum guards cut from a contemp Ms; marginal repairs. s Oct 23 (215) £6,200 [Nieuw]

Anr copy. Mor. On new guards throughout. "A fine copy". S June 25 (271) £8,000 [Tooley]
— 1541. - Vienna: Gaspar Trechsel. Folio, 19th-cent half calf. With 27 double-page maps of the ancient world, 22 double-page maps of the modern world & 1 full-page map of Lotharingia on verso of Map 46. A few marginal wormholes. Annotated by Abraham Ortelius, with his autograph ownership inscr at foot of title. Kloss copy. S Apr 23 (131) £28,000 [Niewodnik]
— 1545. - Geographia universalis. Basel: H. Petrum. Folio, modern lea. With 54 double-page maps. JG Mar 20 (267) DM8,500

Anr copy. Half lea. Lacking tp. FDR copy, inscr by him in 1905 "A remarkably fine copy of this rare Ptolemy". pn Dec 11 (47) £210 [Mackenzie]

Anr copy. 17th-cent calf; def. With 53 (of 54) double-page maps; without the American maps. Some leaves repaired or slightly marked; some side-notes shaved. S June 25 (273) £2,000 [Shoten]
— 1578. - Geographia Cologne Koeman's

Issue without ptd privilegio dated Brussels 3 Feb 1578 pasted on verso of title. Folio, contemp calf gilt, armorial bdg. With hand-colored engraved title & 28 maps colored in a contemp hand. Without Privilegio; tp & blank following torn affecting lower portion of engraved surface; some maps transposed. S Feb 24 (402) £2,700 [Shapero]

— 1584. - Geographiae libri octo.... Cologne: G. von Kempen. Folio, modern half mor. Lacking Iberia; some marginal wormholes; occasional creases. S June 25 (275) £900 [Hagstrom]

— 1597. - Geographiae universiae. Cologne: Petrus Keschedt. 2 parts in 1 vol. 4to, contemp calf gilt; rebacked. With titles within engraved borders & 64 maps. Marginal wormholes; some browning. S June 25 (277) £750

— 1598-97. - Venice: G. B. & G. Galignani. 2 parts in 1 vol. 4to, old vellum bds. With 2 titles & 47 half-page maps only; two leaves loose, 1 torn with loss of text. Foxing & staining. pnNY Sept 13 (509) $750

— 1704. - Tabulae geographicae Orbis Terrarum veteribus cogniti. Amst. & Utrecht Folio, half sheep; worn. With engraved title & 28 double-page maps. Some spotting & creasing. S Nov 10 (966) £500 [Tooleybaum]

— 1730. - Orbis antiqui tabulae geographicae secundum. Amst. Folio, contemp calf; rubbed. With frontis & 28 double-page maps. S June 25 (286) £800 [Martinos]

— 1932. - Geography.... NY One of 250. Trans by Edward Luther Stevenson. Folio, half lea. sg Oct 2 (94) $275

Publicius, Jacobus

— Artes orandi, epistolandi, memorandi. Venice: Erhard Ratdolt, 31 Jan 1485. ("Oratoriae artis epitoma.") 4to, 19th-cent half calf. First leaf silked with some loss of text; 8 leaves at beginning extended; some dampstains; last few leaves just separating at foot of gutter. 65 (of 66) leaves; lacking initial blank & 1 volvelle. Goff P-1097. cb Feb 19 (221) $300

Puebla de Los Angeles

— ACADEMIA MEDICO-QUIRURGICA. - Ensayo para la materia medica Mexicana.... Puebla: oficina del hospital de S. Pedro, 1832. 4to, contemp mor gilt. Library markings. sg Sept 18 (87) $700

Pufendorf, Samuel, Baron von, 1632-94

— Of the Law of Nature and Nations. Oxford, 1717. 3d Ed in English. Folio, contemp calf; upper cover def & loose. 1 leaf soiled in upper margin. bba Sept 25 (113) £85 [Quaritch]

Anr copy. Contemp calf; later rebacking & endpapers, worn. Tp soiled; some foxing & marginal worming. cb Feb 19 (222) $55

4th Ed in English. L, 1729. Folio, contemp calf; joints split, rubbed. bba Aug 28 (193) £110 [Titles]

Puget de la Serre, Jean

— Histoire de l'entree de la Reyne Mere du Roy Tres-Chrestien, dans la Grande-Bretaigne. L, 1639. Bound with: Histoire de l'entree de la Reyne Mere du Roy Tres-Chrestien dans la Grande-Bretaigne. Londres, 1639. And: Barleus, gaspar. Marie de Medicis, engrant dans Amsterdam,.... Amst., 1638. Folio, 19th-cent mor gilt. C May 13 (132) £4,200 [Zola]

Pugh, Edward, d.1813

— Cambria Depicta: a Tour through North Wales. L, 1816. 4to, calf gilt; upper joint split. With /1 hand-colored plates. Marginal tears to text. S July 28 (1003) £350

Pugin, Augustus Charles, 1762-1832

— Gothic Furniture. L, [c.1828]. 4to, orig bds; spine broken. With 27 colored engravings & 27 hand-colored plates. Last plates & a few leaves of text soiled. pn Dec 11 (185) £350 [Fogg]

— Gothic Ornaments.... L, 1854. 4to, contemp half mor; rubbed. bba Sept 25 (290) £80 [Dover]

Pugin, Augustus Charles, 1762-1832 —& Heath, Charles, 1785-1848

— Paris and its Environs. L, 1829-31. 2 vols. 4to, cloth. With 2 additional titles & 202 views on 101 plates. bba Dec 18 (221) £60 [Rainer]

Anr copy. With 2 additional titles & 202 views on 101 engraved plates. bba Dec 18 (221) £60 [Rainer]

Anr Ed. L, 1831. 2 vols. 4to, mor; rubbed, extremities chipped. With title & first 2 pp of text detached, but present. cb Oct 23 (168) $85

Anr copy. 2 vols in 1. 4to, orig mor gilt; spines broken. With 202 views on 101 plates.. pnNY Sept 13 (271) $250

Anr copy. Contemp half calf; rubbed. T Oct 16 (263) £100

Anr copy. Contemp mor gilt; rubbed. With 2 engraved titles & 200 views on 100 plates. T Apr 16 (5) £70

Pugin, Augustus Welby, 1812-52

— Glossary of Ecclesiastical Ornament and Costume.... L, 1856. 4to, contemp mor; rubbed. With 70 color plates. Ck Jan 16 (83) £130

PULLAR

Pullar, Laurence. See: Murray & Pullar

Pulliat, M. See: Mas & Pulliat

Pulman, George Philip Rigney
— The Book of the Axe. L, 1875. 4th Ed. 8vo, orig cloth; rubbed. Dampstained, not affecting contents. Inscr. T Apr 16 (57) £52

Pulteney, Richard, 1730-1801
— A General View of the Writings of Linnaeus. L, 1781. 8vo, contemp calf gilt. pn Jan 22 (237) £85 [Burns]
— Revue generale des ecrits de Linne.... Londres, 1789. 2 vols. Lea; corners rubbed. B Feb 24 (463) HF2200

Pumpelly, Raphael, 1837-1923
— Explorations in Turkestan, Expedition of 1904.... Wash., 1908. 2 vols. Folio, half mor; scuffed, minor stains to fore-edges of Vol II. cb Nov 6 (234) $225
Anr copy. 2 vols. 4to, ptd wraps; worn & broken. Library markings. wa Sept 25 (622) $100

Punch...
— Punch: Or the London Charivari. L, 1841-1933. Vols 1-185 plus Spielmann's History of Punch in 70 vols. 4to, mor gilt; some covers detached. S Sept 22 (265) £260 [Leinweber]
Anr Ed. L, 1841-1971. Vols 1-261 plus duplicates of Vols 15 & 32, bound in 251. various bdgs. Sold w.a.f. S Sept 22 (266) £450 [Punchy Publications]
Anr Ed. L, 1841-1932. 108 vols. 4to, mor gilt. T Feb 19 (385) £480
Vols 1-41. L, 1841-81. Half mor gilt. pn Dec 11 (170) £300 [Map House]

Punt, Jan
— Lyk-staetsie van zyne doorluchtigste hoogheid den heere Willem Carel Hendrik Friso, Prince van Orange en Nassau. The Hague, 1755. Bound with: Afbeelding van de Zaal en't Praalbed waar op het lyk van zyne doorluchtige Hoogheid den Heere Willem Karel Hendrik Friso Prince van Orange en Nassau. Amst., 1752. Folio, contemp bds; rubbed & stained. With 41 double-page plates in 1st work & 4 double-page plates in 2d work. C Apr 8 (49) £260 [Pagan]

Purcell, John, 1674?-1730
— A Treatise of the Cholick.... L, 1715. 2d Ed. 8vo, contemp calf; rebacked. wa Mar 5 (309) $135

AMERICAN BOOK PRICES CURRENT

Purchas, Samuel, 1575?-1626
— Purchas his Pilgrimage.... L, 1617. 3d Ed. Folio, 19th-cent calf gilt; rebacked with earlier gilt backstrip laid down. ha May 22 (315) $1,500
Anr copy. Old calf; rebacked, retaining orig backstrip. Last leaf soiled & stained, with reinforcement in lower margin on verso. Quiller-Couch copy. sg Apr 2 (163) $550
— Purchas his Pilgrimes. Glasgow, 1905-7. ("Hakluytus Posthumus or Purchas His Pilgrimes.") One of 100. 20 vols. Orig cloth; rubbed. bba Oct 16 (151) £130 [Hashimoto]
— A Theatre of Political Flying-Insects. L: R. I. for Thomas Parkhurst, 1657. 4to, 19th-cent lea; broken. Johannson copy. sg Jan 15 (163) $275

Purey-Cust, Arthur Percival
— The Heraldry of York Minster. Leeds, 1896. One of 300. 4to, cloth; rubbed. pn Jan 22 (215) £35 [Mackenzie]

Purmann, Matthaeus Gottfried
— Chirurgia Curiosa.... L, 1706. Folio, contemp calf; worn, rebacked & repaired. With 5 folding plates. Paper flaw in Tt1; 2 plates shaved at top. S May 28 (767) £600

Pusch, C. G.
— Geognostyscher Atlas von Polen. Stuttgart, 1836-37. Folio, loose as issued in portfolio. With 7 folding hand-colored maps & charts in 10 sheets, all laid on linen. S June 25 (260) £800

Puseley, Daniel
— The Rise and Progress of Australia, Tasmania, and New Zealand.... L, 1857. 1st Ed. 8vo, orig cloth; chipped at head of spine & cracked on rear hinge. T Apr 16 (21) £45

Puteo, Paris de
— Duello: libro de re: imperatori, principi.... Venice: Marchio Sessa & Piero della Serena, 10 Mar 1525. 8vo, later vellum over bds; new endpapers, rubbed. Tp rubbed & smudged. ha Mar 13 (262) $390

Putnam, Samuel
— The World of Jean de Bosschere. L: Fortune Press, [1932]. One of 900 but with the orig std etching supposedly reserved for the issue of 100. In d/j. O Mar 24 (142) $100

Puydt, Paul Emile de
— Les Orchidees. Paris, 1880. 8vo, half cloth. With 50 hand-finished color plates. Some spotting, leaves brittle. bba Dec 18 (222) £150 [Rainer]
Anr copy. Orig half mor. xxx

Pyle, Howard, 1853-1911

— Otto of the Silver Hand. NY, 1888. 1st Ed. 8vo, half lea; rubbed. sg Sept 11 (251) $110

— Yankee Doodle. An Old Friend in a New Dress. NY, 1881. 1st Ed. 4to, orig bds; lacking backstrip, worn & soiled. wa Nov 6 (528) $55

Pyne, James Baker

— The English Lake District. Manchester, 1853. Folio, disbound. With tinted litho title (torn affecting plate area) & 23 plates only. Some margins torn, spotted & soiled. Ck May 15 (127) £520

— Windsor, with its Surrounding Scenery.... L, [c.1839]. Folio, contemp half mor; stained. With colored litho title & 12 plates. Ck Nov 21 (401) £480

Pyne, William Henry

— The Costume of Great Britain. L, 1808 [some plates watermarked 1819]. Folio, contemp mor gilt; rubbed. With 60 hand-colored plates. Lacking tp. Sold w.a.f. C Apr 8 (162) £520 [Gaston]

Anr copy. Contemp mor gilt, armorial bdg. With 100 hand-colored plates. S Oct 23 (9) £3,500 [Raban]

Anr Ed. L, 1804 [plates watermarked 1823]. Folio, contemp mor gilt; rubbed. With hand-colored vignette on title & 59 hand-colored plates (of 60); lacking Plate 42. S Nov 18 (933) £340 [Nicolson]

— Etchings of Rustic Figures.... L, 1815. 4to, orig cloth; spine chipped. With 59 (of 60) plates, a few detached. Ck Nov 21 (183) £55

— The History of the Royal Residences.... L, 1819. 3 vols. 4to, contemp mor gilt; joints repaired, Vol II rebacked preserving orig backstrip. With 100 hand-colored plates. Lacking sub-titles & list of plates. C Oct 15 (90) £3,200 [Traylen]

Anr copy. Contemp mor gilt; head & foot of spines rubbed. C Oct 15 (91) £2,800 [Weinreb]

Anr copy. Half calf gilt; rubbed. Tear to 1 plate repaired. ph Apr 30 (254) £3,000 [Dennistoun]

Anr copy. Modern half mor gilt. With 67 (of 100) hand-colored plates only. Plates stamped; Vol I lacking 2d fly-title & final blank; Vol III lacking final blank & slip; dampstain in Vol III. S Feb 24 (507) £950 [Barker]

Anr copy. Contemp mor gilt; rubbed. With 100 hand-colored plates. S Apr 23 (128) £3,800 [Map]

Anr copy. Modern half mor. S June 25 (243) £3,400 [Joseph]

Anr Ed. L, 1819 [1 plate watermarked 1835]. Plate vol only. contemp mor gilt; rebacked. With 100 hand-colored plates plus a later litho title reading Pyne's One Hundred Views of Royal Residences in England. Ck Feb 27 (131) £1,400

Pyne, William Henry —& Others

— Picturesque Groups for the Embellishment of Landscape. L, 1845. 2 vols in 1. 4to, contemp half lea. With frontis & 160 plates. C Oct 15 (139) £400 [Temperly]

Q

Quackenbos, John D.

— Geological Ancestors of the Brook Trout.... NY, 1916. One of 300. Lea; worn. sg Oct 23 (436) $225

Quain, Richard

— The Anatomy of the Arteries of the Human Body. L, 1844. Plate vol only. Folio, loose in contemp half mor portfolio. With 87 plates on india paper, some outline-colored in red or blue. Tp & prelims soiled & badly frayed. Sold w.a.f. T Jan 22 (274) £70

Quaritch, Bernard, 1819-89

— A Catalogue of English and Foreign Bookbindings. L, 1921. 4to, orig bds; worn. O June 16 (54) $50

— Contributions Towards a Dictionary of English Book-Collectors.... NY: Burt Franklin, [1968]. Reprint. cb Feb 5 (150) $50

Quayle, Eric

— The Collector's Book of Detective Fiction. [L, 1972]. Folio, cloth, in d/j. With Ls laid in. cb Nov 20 (271) $85

Anr copy. Cloth, in d/j. With ALs, Ls & related material laid in. cb Apr 24 (1012) $55, cb Apr 24 (1013) $55

Quebec...

— The Quebec Gazette. Quebec: Brown & Gilmore, 1764-72. Nos 1-417 plus 73 supplements & other inserted items, including broadside prospectus, bound in 4 vols. Folio, contemp half calf 6worn, 2 spines def. Dark stain to lower corners of Nos 414-17; portions clipped from 1 column in Nos 15, 61, 94, 118 & 156; lower edges of both leaves of No 300 torn away; many issues neatly holed in center; a few headlines or lower edges cropped; lacking Nos 30, 63, 67, 68, 166, 253, 288, 289, 298 & 362. CNY May 11 (129) $28,000

Queen...
— Queen Mab, or Fairy Adventures, being a Series of Incidents Wonderful and Surprizing.... L: W. Lane, [c.1780]. 12mo, orig sheep. Some leaves stained. S Dec 5 (352) £500 [Quaritch]
— Queen Mab's Fairy Realm. L, 1901. Orig cloth; front hinge cracked, front endpapers scuffed. sg Oct 30 (173) $80

Queen, Ellery, Pseud.
See also: Haycraft & Queen
— The Chinese Orange Mystery. NY, 1934. In chipped & soiled d/j. cb Nov 20 (272) $85
— The Detective Short Story: A Bibliography. Bost., 1942. One of 1,060. cb Nov 20 (273) $65
— The French Powder Mystery. NY, 1930. Bdg rubbed & soiled. cb Nov 20 (276) $100
— The Misadventures of Sherlock Holmes. Bost., 1944. Jay Finlay Christ's copy. cb Apr 24 (1178) $255
— Queen's Awards. L, 1949-53. Vols 2-6. In d/js. Each vol sgd "Barnaby Ross Ellery Queen". sg Dec 11 (104) $60

Queeny, Edgar M.
— Prairie Wings: Pen and Camera Flight Studies. NY, 1946. 1st Ed. Illus by Richard E. Bishop. 4to, cloth, in d/j; worn. sg Oct 23 (438) $100
Anr copy. Cloth. sg May 21 (172) $120
One of 225. Pigskin gilt. With the etching "They're off!" bound in. sg May 21 (171) $800
Anr Ed. NY, 1947. 4to, cloth. cb Nov 6 (236) $65

Quennell, Nancy. See: Golden Cockerel Press

Quennell, Peter. See: Golden Cockerel Press

Querard, Joseph Marie, 1797-1865
— Les Supercheries litteraires devoilees. Paris, 1869-70. 6 vols. 8vo, half mor; extremities worn. sg May 14 (239) $100

Quiller-Couch, Sir Arthur, 1863-1944
— In Powder and Crinoline: Old Fairy Tales.... L, [1913]. Illus by Kay Nielsen. 4to, orig half cloth; soiled & shaken. With 24 colored plates. cb Sept 11 (307) $75
Anr copy. Orig half cloth; worn. S Oct 6 (840) £170 [Trocchi]
One of 500. Orig half cloth; soiled & marked. With 24 color plates. S Dec 4 (206) £650 [Hirsch]
Anr copy. Orig vellum gilt; bowed & marked. With 24 colored plates. S June 17 (258) £550 [Marzamo]
— The Sleeping Beauty and Other Fairy Tales.... L, [1910]. One of 100. Illus by Edmund Dulac. 4to, mor; spine def. S May 6B (107) £150 [Marks]
One of 1,000. Orig mor gilt; rubbed. S Jan 13 (367) £110 [Thornton]
Anr copy. Cloth. sg Jan 8 (65) $80
— The Twelve Dancing Princesses, and other Tales. Garden City, 1930. Illus by Kay Nielsen. In frayed & repaired d/j. O Apr 28 (163) $90

Quimby, M.
— Mysteries of Bee-Keeping Explained. NY, 1853. 12mo, orig cloth; ends worn, lacking front free endpaper. Marginal dampstaining. sg Jan 15 (165) $275

Quinn, David Beers. See: Hulton & Quinn

Quinn, Seabury
— Roads. Sauk City: Arkham House, 1948. Illus by Virgil Finlay. In d/j. Inscr. cb Sept 28 (1075) $80; cb Sept 28 (1076) $55

Quintanilla, Luis
— All the Brave. NY, [1939]. One of 440. Text by Elliot Paul & Jay Allen; preface by Ernest Hemingway. 4to, pictorial wraps; worn, small tear in front cover. sg June 4 (317) $250

Quintilianus, Marcus Fabius
— Declamationes. Parma: Angelus Ugoletus, 3 July 1493. 4to, 18th-cent vellum; minor worming to front cover, pastedown & free endpaper. Some marginal dampstains; final 6 leaves damaged with loss. 96 leaves. HC13659. cb Oct 23 (185) $190
— The Declamations. L, 1686. 8vo, contemp calf; broken. sg Mar 26 (241) $700
— Institutiones oratoriae. Paris: J. Badius & J. Petit, 1516. ("Oratoriarum institutionum.") Folio, later russia gilt; rubbed, rebacked. Lacking D3 & D6. bba Aug 20 (340) £130 [Rix]
Anr Ed. Paris, 1538. ("Institutionum oratoriarum libri xii....") Folio, old calf; worn. Some marginal tears; tp soiled; 1 leaf torn; anr leaf with corner torn & repaired; lacking all after z10 (that is, without the additional text by Mosellani & Camerarii). S Mar 10 (1131) £40 [Minsky]
Anr Ed. Paris: Audoenus Parvus, 1549. ("De institutione oratoria libri XII.") Folio, 16th-cent calf gilt to an all-over fanfare design, with center cartouche containing the (obliterated) name of the orig owner. C May 13 (133) £1,600 [Zola]
Anr Ed. Oxford: Henry Cruttenden, 1693. ("De institutione oratoria libri duodecim.") 4to, contemp calf; upper joint cracking. Some foxing. cb Oct 23 (186) $50

Quirini, Angelo Maria, Bishop of Brescia
— Primordia Corcyrae post editionem lyciensem.... Brescia, 1738. 2 parts in 1 vol. 4to, contemp vellum; cracked. S Oct 23 (346) £600 [Johns]

Quiz, Peter. See: Egerton, Daniel Thomas

Quizem, Caleb, Pseud.
— Annals of Sporting. L, 1809. 8vo, mor gilt by Root; front joint & head of spine rubbed. Frontis backed with linen; outer margin of tp torn away & restored. sg Feb 12 (268) $175

R

R., L. S.
— L'Art de bien traiter.... Paris: for Jean du Puis, 1674. 12mo, old vellum; upper hinge weak & free endpaper lost. Paper faults in margins of I2 & L5 without loss; tear at fore-edge of S3 affecting a few letters mended without loss. P Nov 25 (392) $1,000

R., R.
— The Good Boy's Soliloquy, Containing his Parent's Instructions.... L, 1811. 1st Ed. 16mo, wraps. With 16 plates; soiled. S Dec 5 (353) £280 [Dipple]

Rabel, Daniel
— Theatrum florae.... Paris: N. de Mathoniere, 1622. 4to, later mor gilt; joints split, worn. With engraved title, frontis & 60 plates, all with contemp hand-coloring by William Theodore. Plus 5 contemp watercolors in similar style inserted at end. A few marginal stains. de Belder copy. S Apr 28 (289) £170,000 [Hill]

Rabelais, Francois, 1494?-1553
See also: Limited Editions Club
— Les Horribles et espovantables faictz et prouesses du tres renomme Pantagruel. Paris, [1943]. One of 50 sgd & numbered on velin d'Arches with separate folder of 128 figures & ornaments on Madagaskar. Illus by Andre Derain. 4to, unsewn in orig wraps. FD June 11 (4874) DM46,000
Anr Ed. Paris: Skira, 1943. One of 275, sgd by artist. 4to, Orig wraps. With 180 colored woodcuts, including 39 large illusts. S June 17 (105) £5,800 [Sims]
— Oeuvres. Amst., 1741. Ed by Le Duchat. 3 vols. 4to, mor gilt by Trautz Bauzonnet. With 2 engraved titles, 2 ports, folding map & 16 plates. L.p. copy. C May 13 (45) £1,700 [Lardanchet]
Anr copy. Contemp mor gilt. With port, 3 frontises, folding map, 3 folding plates & 13 plates. C May 13 (134) £1,700 [Lardanchet]

Anr copy. Contemp calf gilt. With 2 engraved titles, 1 folding map & 13 plates. S Nov 27 (115) £420 [Valette]
Anr Ed. Geneva, 1782. 4 vols. 12mo, contemp calf gilt. S Nov 27 (114) £180 [Greenwood]
Anr Ed. Paris, 1798 [An VI]. 3 vols. 4to, contemp mor gilt. With port & 75 plates, proofs before letters. L.p. copy. C Dec 3 (158) £600 [Sourgetrt]
— Works. L: for Richard Baldwin, 1694. 2 parts in 1 vol. 12mo, contemp calf; spine ends chipped, rear cover loose. Marginal repairs; old scrawls on front endpapers & frontis. sg Mar 26 (242) $150
Anr Ed. L, 1904. Illus by W. Heath Robinson. 2 vols. 4to, orig cloth; soiled. pn Sept 18 (187) £55 [Stevenson]; sg Jan 8 (247) $120
Anr Ed. NY, 1929. One of 200. Illus by Alexander King. 3 vols. 4to, half cloth, joints worn. sg June 11 (326) $225

Racine, Jean, 1639-99
— Oeuvres. Paris, 1760. 3 vols. 4to, contemp calf gilt; rebacked, corners reinforced, rubbed. With port & 12 plates. H2 in Vol II def in margin; some foxing. Strachey Senhouse copy. bba Oct 16 (27) £500 [Quevedo]
Anr copy. Later mor gilt. Port margins repaired. S Nov 27 (214) £3,000 [Bonna]
Anr Ed. Paris, 1768. 7 vols. 8vo, contemp calf gilt; repaired. With port & 12 plates, proofs before letters. C May 13 (47) £180 [Beres]
Anr Ed. Paris: Didot l'Aine, 1783. 3 vols. 4to, contemp mor gilt; joints cracked. Lacking B1 in Vol I. Sold w.a.f. bba Sept 25 (260) £95 [Way]
Anr Ed. Paris: Didot L'Aine, 1801-5. One of 200. 3 vols. Folio, contemp half mor; rubbed. bba Oct 30 (223) £440 [Maggs]
— Phedre & Hippolyte. Paris: Jean Ribou, 1677. 12mo, 19th-cent mor; joints weak. sg Oct 9 (299) $700

Racinet, Auguste
— Le Costume historique. Paris, [1876-88]. 2 vols. Folio, loose in folders. With 200 plates "en camaieu" & 300 in colors, gold & silver plus some duplicate plates. Plate list lacking. Sold w.a.f. ha May 22 (207) $475
Anr Ed. Paris, 1888. 6 vols. 4to, contemp half mor; worn. With 200 plates "en camaieu" & 300 in colors, gold & silver. S Feb 24 (340) £780 [Dennistoun]
Anr copy. Contemp half lea; extremities worn. With 200 plates "en camaieu" & 300 in colors, gold & silver, on 453 leaves. Wharncliffe copy. sg Dec 4 (166) $1,000

Anr copy. Half mor. With 200 plates "en camaieu" & 300 in colorrs, gold & silver. sg Feb 5 (284) $500

— L'Ornement polychrome. Paris, [1869-87]. Series 1 & 2 in 2 vols. Folio, later cloth; worn. With 220 color plates; a few plates with minor stains or tears repaired. Sold w.a.f. O May 12 (160) $650

Anr copy. Later cloth; soiled. With 219 (of 220) plates. wa Mar 5 (140) $550

Anr Ed. Paris, [c.1870]. Folio, cloth; rebacked, repaired, orig spine laid down & ocvers preserved. With 100 plates. cb Oct 23 (188) $160

Rackham, Arthur, 1867-1939

— Arthur Rackham's Book of Pictures. L, 1913. 4to, orig cloth. With 44 color plates. sg Oct 30 (13) $100

Anr copy. Orig cloth. With 3 additional black & white Rackham plates mtd in book by owner. sg Oct 30 (14) $90

— The Arthur Rackham Fairy Book. L, 1933. 4to, cloth; soiled. With 8 color plates. sg Oct 30 (10) $100

One of 460, sgd by Rackham. Orig vellum gilt, unopened. With 8 color plates. With the orig ribbon bookmark. sg Oct 30 (9) $900

— Britsche Balladen. Amst., [1920]. One of 550. 4to, mor gilt; stained. B Oct 7 (289) HF220

— Mother Goose: The Old Nursery Rhymes. L, [1913]. One of 1,130. 4to, cloth. S May 6 (148) £170 [Hannas]

One of 1,130, sgd. Cloth; soiled. With 13 mtd color plates. With announcement of a Rackham exhibition of Mother Goose watercolors laid in. sg Oct 30 (159) $1,100

Anr Ed. NY, 1913. 4to, cloth. With frontis & 13 color plates. sg Oct 30 (162) $200

— The Peter Pan Portfolio. L, [1912]. One of 100 with each mount sgd by the artist. 4to, orig vellum; soiled. With 12 colored plates. S June 17 (267) £6,200 [Joseph & Sawyer]

One of 500. Orig half vellum; worn & crudely repaired with tape. With 12 mtd colored plates. bba Mar 26 (269) £420 [Henderson]

— Some British Ballads. L, [1919]. One of 575, sgd. 4to, orig half vellum gilt. With 16 colored plates. L July 2 (67) £140

One of 575. Orig half vellum; soiled. pnNY Sept 13 (278) $425

Anr copy. Illus by ArthurRackham. Orig cloth. sg Oct 30 (200) $80

One of 575. Orig half vellum; rubbed, backstrip discolored. sg Oct 30 (199) $325

Rackham, Bernard

— Catalogue of the Glaisher Collection of Pottery and Porcelain. Cambr., 1935. 2 vols. 4to, orig cloth, in d/js. T Apr 16 (311) £340

Radcliffe, Ann, 1764-1823

— The Italian, or the Confessional of the Black Penitents. L, 1797. 1st Ed. 3 vols. 12mo, contemp half sheep; spine worn, a few covers partly detached. sg Oct 9 (300) $100

— The Mysteries of Udolpho. L, 1794. 1st Ed. 4 vols. 12mo, contemp half calf; rubbed. Corners torn from E2, Q1 & Q7 without loss. S Jan 13 (516) £230 [Hannas]

Radcliffe, Frederick Peter Delme

— The Noble Science: A Few General Ideas on Fox-Hunting. L, 1893 [1892]. 8vo, orig cloth; rubbed. With 10 hand-colored plates. bba Oct 30 (416) £40 [Greyfriars]

Radclyffe, Charles Robert Eustace

— Big Game Shooting in Alaska. L, 1904. Rubbed & soiled, front hinge weakening. cb Nov 6 (237) $170

Radclyffe, Charles W.

— Memorials of Rugby. Rugby, 1843. Folio, contemp half mor; corners rubbed. With 28 views on 24 plates. S May 28 (897) £340

— Memorials of Shrewsbury School, with Views.... Shrewsbury, 1843. Folio, later cloth. Some spoting & staining. S May 28 (898) £80

Rademaker, Abraham

— Versameling van hondert vijftig nederlantse outheeden en Gesigten. L, [1770]. 2 vols in 1. Oblong folio, contemp vellum; soiled. With 2 engraved titles (both cut down & mtd) & 300 views on 75 leaves. A few wormholes in inner margin. Paul Sandby's copy. O'Byrne copy. C July 22 (174) £850

Rademaker, Abraham —& Others

— Hollandsche Arkadia, in Zeshonderd en meer Afbeeldingen van Land- en Watergezichten.... Amst., 1807. 12 orig parts. Folio, contemp half calf, orig wraps bound in. With 2 engraved titles & 608 views on 311 plates. Title with 2 small erased patches & with outer margin frayed. bba Dec 18 (224) £2,600 [Israel]

Raden, Woldemar

— Switzerland. L, 1878. 4to, orig cloth; worn & shaken, endpapers stained. O Nov 18 (152) $300

Anr copy. Orig cloth; rubbed. With 90 plates. pn Jan 22 (252) £220 [Grayling]

Anr copy. Orig cloth; worn & soiled. S May 29 (1053) £220

Radford, George
— Rambles by Yorkshire Rivers. Leeds, [1880]. Ltd Ed. 8vo, pictorial cloth; rubbed. sg May 21 (174) $100

Radiguet, Raymond, 1903-23
— Le Bal du Comte d'Orgel. Monaco, [1953]. One of 250. Illus by Jean Cocteau. Loose as issued in wraps. With 33 etchings. FD Dec 2 (4295) DM1,900

Radziwill, Lee Bouvier. See: Onassis & Radziwill

Rae, John
— New Adventures of "Alice." Chicago: P. F. Volland, [1917]. Half cloth, extremities rubbed. cb Sept 28 (289) $65

Rae, John, 1796-1872
— Statement of some New Principles on the Subject of Political Economy.... Bost., 1834. 8vo, cloth; joints repaired; some discoloration. Marginal browning. P Sept 24 (376) $900

Rae, John, 1813-93
— Narrative of an Expedition to the Shores of the Arctic Sea in 1846 and 1847.... L, 1850. 8vo, orig cloth; lower joint splitting. With 2 folding maps hand-colored in outline. 1st 3 leaves & large map spotted. C Apr 8 (50) £650 [Gilbert]

Raff, Georg Christian, 1748-88
— Natuurlyke Historie voor Kinderen. Leiden, 1781. 3 vols. 8vo, contemp half calf gilt; rubbed. With 3 engraved titles & 8 folding plates, all hand-colored.. bba Oct 16 (322) £80 [Hannas]

Raffles, Lady Sophia
— Memoir of the Life and Public Services of Sir T. S. Raffles.... L, 1830. 1st Ed. 2 parts in 1 vol. 4to, orig cloth; rubbed & soiled. With 4 maps, 5 plates & folding panorama of Singapore. bba May 14 (6) £300 [Grosvenor]

Raffles, Sir Thomas Stamford, 1781-1826
— Description geographique, historique et commerciale de Java,.... Brussels, 1824-25. 4to, contemp half calf. With 2 folding hand-colored maps & 46 plates, including 10 hand-colored costume plates (2 plates are ptd recto & verso). Occasional spotting. S June 25 (474) £280 [Griffiths]

— The History of Java. L, 1817. 1st Ed. 2 vols. 4to, contemp calf; rebacked. with folding hand-colored map, 10 hand-colored costume plates & 56 plates including 2 pages of engraved music, 9 illusts in text & 2 folding tables. Lacking half-titles. Brodie of Brodie copy. S Oct 23 (497) £1,250 [Chang]

Ragged, Hyder, Pseud.
— King Solomon's Wives; or, the Phantom Mines. L, 1887. Cloth, orig wraps bound in. cb Sept 28 (575) $80

Rahir, Edouard
— La Collection Dutuit. Paris, 1899. One of 350. Folio, half mor gilt, orig wraps bound in. C Dec 3 (36) £600 [Beres]

Rahir Collection, Edouard
— [Sale Catalogue]. La Bibliotheque de feu Edouard Rahir.... Paris, 1930-31. 2 vols. 4to, half mor, wraps preserved. bba Sept 25 (370) £220 [Maggs]

Anr copy. Cloth. sg May 14 (72) $250; sg May 14 (73) $300

Raikes, Thomas, 1777-1848
— A Portion of the Journal Kept by.... L, 1858. 2 vols. 8vo, orig cloth; some wear. Library markings. With 2 ink port sketches by Alfred Guillaume Gabriel, Comte d'Orsay, tipped in. ha Dec 19 (248) $50

Raimondi, Eugenio
— Le Caccie fiere armate e disarmate. Naples: Lazaro Scoriggio, 1626. ("Delle Caccie....") 4to, 17th-cent calf; worn & repaired. With engraved title & 21 plates. H2 repaired. Jeanson 1448. SM Mar 1 (479) FF13,000
— Delle caccie.... Venice: G. B. Catani, 1675. 4to, 18th-cent bds. With 12 plates. Jeanson copy. SM Mar 1 (480) FF4,000

Raine, Herbert
— Old Montreal. Montreal, 1921. One of 500. Folio, orig bds; stained. AVP Nov 20 (320) C$100 [Wolfe]

Raine, James
— The History and Antiquities of North-Durham. L, 1852. Folio, later cloth; rebacked, worn. bba Sept 25 (447) £40 [Old Hall]

Anr copy. Mor gilt by Hammond. Frontis foxed. T Feb 19 (329) £70

Raines, Caldwell Walton
— A Bibliography of Texas. Austin, 1896. One of 500. 4to, later cloth, orig wraps bound in. Some annotations. sg Oct 2 (288) $120

Raleigh, Sir Walter, 1552?-1618
— The History of the World. L, 1614. Folio, old calf; needs rebdg. With engraved title & 7 (of 8) double-page maps. Initial leaf & title mtd; lacking last 4 leaves. sg Nov 20 (151) $140

Anr copy. Contemp calf, armorial bdg; rebacked. Initial leaf repaired along gutter. sg June 11 (329) $1,500

Anr Ed. L, 1621. Folio, old calf; rebacked,

RALEIGH

rubbed. Engraved title trimmed & mtd; some dampstains. O May 12 (161) $350

Anr Ed. L, 1666. Folio, contemp calf; broken. With hand-colored frontis (loose), port & 8 hand-colored maps & plates. pn Sept 18 (303) £90 [Culpin]

Anr Ed. L, 1736. 2 vols. Folio, contemp calf; joints split, worn. bba Dec 4 (63) £70 [F. Mackenzie]

— Judicious and Select Essayes and Observations upon the First Invention of Shipping.... L, 1650. 8vo, modern calf. Title of Part 3 & 2 other leaves in same part frayed. L July 2 (240) £120

— Works. L: R. Dodsley, 1751. 2 vols. 8vo, contemp calf; spines rubbed, joints repaired. cb Oct 23 (189) $75

Ralfe, James

— The Naval Chronology of Great Britain. L, 1820. 3 vols. 8vo, contemp half cloth. With colored port, 2 sepia frontises & 57 colored plates; inscrs above some plates ptd in blue. C Oct 15 (126) £2,000 [Traylen]

Ralph, James. See: Sidney & Ralph

Ramiro, Erastene, Pseud.

— Catalogue descriptif et analytique de l'oeuvre gravé de Felicien Rops. With: Supplement. Paris, 1887 & 1895. One of 40 on Hollande; Supplement one of 50 on Hollande. 2 vols. 4to, mor gilt extra; doublures ptd with Rops illust in black. Orig wraps presrved. Extra-illust with over 70 inserted etchings & other illusts by Rops. Hoe copies. Sold as a bdg. Sold w.a.f. CNY Dec 19 (221) $1,500

— Felicien Rops. Paris, 1905. One of 125 with plates in 2 states. Contemp half mor, orig wraps bound in. Ck Dec 10 (325) £160

Ramsay, David, 1749-1815

— The History of South Carolina.... Charleston, 1809. 2 vols. 8vo, lea; needs rebdg. With 2 folding maps, with ink & perforated library stamps. sg Mar 12 (238) $225

Ramsden, Charles

— French Bookbinders 1789-1848. L, 1950. 4to, orig cloth; worn. sg May 14 (131) $140

Ramsey, Stanley Churchill —& Harvey, John D. M.

— Small Houses of the Late Georgian Period. L, 1924. 2 vols. 4to, orig cloth; worn. S Mar 9 (698) £65 [Camden]

Ramuz, Charles Ferdinand, 1878-1947. See: Stravinsky, Igor

Rand, Ayn

— Atlas Shrugged. NY: Random House, [1957]. In d/j with 2-inch tear. cb May 7 (423) $50

Randall, David A. See: Van Winkle & Randall

Randall, Joseph

— A Course of Lectures in the Most Easy, Useful and Entertaining Parts of Geography...Academy at Heath.... L, 1750. 8vo, old calf; rubbed, worn at joints. O Mar 24 (144) $75

Randolph, Georgiana Ann, 1908-57. See: Rice, Craig

Randolph, Thomas, 1605-35

— Poems, with the Muses Looking-Glasse: and Amyntas. Oxford, 1638. 1st Ed. 4to, contemp calf; rubbed. Some soiling. S Mar 10 (1132) £170 [Martin]

2d Ed. Oxford, 1640. 8vo, later half calf; worn. Ck Jan 16 (252) £75

Rankine, William John Macquorn, 1820-72

— Shipbuilding, Theoretical and Practical. L, 1866. Folio, bdg not indicated. Library markings. Sold w.a.f. Franklin Institute copy. F Sept 12 (352) $175

Ransome, John Crowe

— Grace after Meat. L: Hogarth Press, 1924. One of 400. Intro by Robert Graves. Orig bds. S Dec 18 (143) £250 [Blackwell]

Anr copy. Orig bds; rear cover stained. T Feb 18 (116) £60

Ransonnet-Villez, Eugene de, Baron

— Reise von Kairo nach Tor zu dem Korallenbanken des Rothen Meeres. Vienna, 1863. 4to, half lea. With 5 colored or tinted plates. bba Oct 16 (286) £110 [Mytze]

— Sketches of the Inhabitants, Animal Life and Vegetation in...Ceylon. Vienna, 1867. Folio, orig cloth; loose. With 26 plates. Some dampstains. pn May 21 (57) £300 [Shapiro]

Raphael Sanzio d'Urbino, 1483-1520

— Imagines Veteris ac Novi Testamenti.... Rome, 1674. Oblong 4to, early 19th-cent half lea. With 2 engraved titles, & 51 plates only.. sg Feb 5 (285) $375

— Les Loges de Raphael... [Rome, 1772-77?]. Folio, old bds. With 43 plates. Sold w.a.f. C July 22 (175) £4,600

— Loggie de Rafaele nel Vaticano, Parts 1 and 2 [of 3]. Rome, 1772-[76]. Part 1 only. Oblong folio, contemp calf, with arms of King Gustav III of Sweden; rubbed. With frontis, port, folding plan, 14 arabesques plates, each of 2 sheets joined, 2 plates of doorways, each of 2 sheets joined. Copy with plates hand-colored. S Oct 23 (201) £9,000 [Cain]

Anr copy. 2 parts in 1 vol. Mor; spine rubbed. With frontis, folding plan, 2 plates or doorways, each of 2 sheets; 14 plates of arabesques, each of 2 sheets, 13 plates of small arches, each of 2 sheets. Lacking title to Part 2. S Oct 23 (202) £3,000 [Schuster]

Anr copy. Part 1 only. half lea. With frontis, 2 plates of doorways, each of 2 sheets; 14 plates of arabesques, each of 2 sheets but wanting the upper sheet of No 3; & large folding plan of the gallery (dustsoiled & with creases). S Oct 23 (203) £1,200 [Schuster]

— Psyches amoris nuptiae ac fabula.... Rome: Domenico de Rossi, 1693. Bound with: Berretini, Pietro. Barberinae aulae fornix Romae. Rome: de Rossi, [1691?]. And: Heroicae Vitutis imagines. Rome, [1691?]. Folio, contemp calf; worn. 1st work with double-page engraved title & 10 (of 11) plates; 2d work with double-page engraved title & 19 plates; 3d work with 16 (of 17) plates. Some waterstain affecting lower margins. S Oct 23 (85) £1,600 [Giunta]

Raphall, Morris Jacob, 1798-1868

— Bible View of Slavery. NY, 1861. 8vo, orig wraps sewn into modern protective paper cover. Some stains & spotting, not affecting text. sg Sept 25 (25) $550

Rapin de Thoyras, Paul, 1661-1725

— Histoire d'Angleterre. The Hague, 1724-27. 10 vols. 4to, contemp calf; rubbed. bba July 16 (26) £80 [Wade]

— The History of England. L, 1723-51. Tindal's continuation only. 2 vols in 1. Folio, half calf; worn. pn Jan 22 (289) £270 [Burgess]

"2d" Ed. L, 1732-47. 4 vols in 5. Folio, calf gilt; hinges cracked, not uniform. With frontis, ports, plates of medals & 73 folding maps, plans & views. pn Mar 5 (56) £800 [Burgess]

3d Ed. L, 1743-47. 5 vols, including Tindal's continuation. Folio, contemp calf; broken. S Sept 22 (267) £500 [Framed]

Rappard-Boon, Charlotte van. See: Rijksmuseum, Amsterdam

Rasmussen, Louis J.

— San Francisco Ship Passenger Lists. Colma: San Francisco Historic Records, 1965-70. Vols I-IV (Vol II is a 2d ptg). In d/js. cb Oct 9 (160) $55

Raspe, Rudolf Erich, 1737-94

— Gulliver Revived; Containing Singular Travels...by Baron Munchausen. L, 1827. ("The Surprising Adventures...of the Renowned Baron Munchausen.") 12mo, half mor; extremities worn. sg Feb 12 (63) $80

— Aventures du Baron de Munchhausen. Paris: Furne, Jouvet, [1862]. Trans by Theophile Gautier fils; illus by Gustave Dore. 4to, orig lea gilt; corners scuffed. Some foxing at extremities. sg Sept 11 (106) $200

— Gulliver Revived; Containing Singular Travels...by Baron Munchausen. L, 1809. ("The Travels and Surprising Adventures of the Renowned Baron Munchausen....") Illus by Thomas Rowlandson. 12mo, mor gilt by Riviere. With 90 hand-colored plates. Tp & half-title washed. sg Feb 12 (269) $300

Anr Ed. L, 1811. ("The Surprising Adventures of the Renowned Baron Munchausen....") 12mo, 19th-cent half mor. With folding frontis & 8 hand-colored plates. S Dec 5 (354) £280 [Kendle]

Anr copy. Calf gilt; joints starting. Lacking half-title. sg June 11 (353) $150

Anr Ed. L, 1868. ("The Travels and Surprising Adventures of Baron Munchausen.") 8vo, mor bdg with port of Munchhausen by Bayntun-Riviere, orig wraps bound in. With 22 hand-colored plates; some double-page. FD Dec 2 (3705) DM2,100

Rastell, John, d.1536

— The Pastime of People, or, the Chronicles of Divers Realms.... L, 1811. 4to, contemp half lea; corners worn. Thick paper copy. O May 12 (162) $125

Rathbone, Hannah Mary Reynolds

— The Poetry of Birds Selected from Various Authors.... Liverpool & L, 1833. One of c.25. 4to, contemp mor gilt. With 21 hand-colored plates. C Oct 15 (252) £600 [Thorp]

Anr copy. Half mor by Sangorski & Sutcliffe, orig wraps bound in at end with inscr to Lady Jardine from W.K.. S Apr 23 (64) £950 [Greyfriars]

Anr copy. Contemp calf gilt, orig wraps bound in; rubbed, joints repaired. Inscr to Lady Cornwallis by Princess Augusta, 1834. S June 25 (174) £500 [Greyfriars]

Ratta, Cesare
— L'Arte de libro e della rivista nei paesi d'Europa e d'America. Bologna, 1927. Ltd Ed. 2 vols. Folio, orig bds; worn, 1 spine def. Some leaves stamped. bba Feb 5 (67) £80 [Acquaforte]

Ratzeburg, J. T. C. See: Brandt & Ratzeburg

Rauch, J.
— Vidiy Mel'nitsiy podmoscovnoi prinadlyeashchei knyazyu Sergiyu Mikhailovichu Golitsinu v' & verstakh' ot' Moskviy. [Moscow, c.1820]. Oblong folio, disbound with orig ptd upper wrap. With 17 hand-colored views. Some short tears repaired. S June 25 (316) £1,200 [Galitzine]

Rauwolf, Leonhard
— Aigentliche beschreibung der Raiss.... Laugingen: L. Reinmichel, 1582-83. 4 parts in 1 vol. 4to, contemp pigskin over wooden bds with monogram H.W. (for Hans Waiblinger, Augsburg). HK Nov 4 (707) DM3,000

Raven, Henry Cushier, 1889-1944
— The Anatomy of the Gorilla.... NY, 1950. cb Nov 6 (240) $55

Raveneau de Lussan, ——, Sieur de
— Journal du voyage fait a la Mer de Sud. Paris, 1690. 12mo, early bds. sg Sept 18 (244) $200

Ravenscroft, Edward James
— The Pinetum Britannicum. L, [1863]-84. 3 vols. Folio, contemp half calf gilt. With 48 colored lithos & 5 photos. Some spotting, mainly affecting margins of text. C Oct 15 (253) £1,800 [Walford]

Anr copy. Contemp half mor; rubbed. With 48 hand-colored plates, 4 mtd albumen prints & 1 engraved plate of maps. Some spotting. de Belder copy. S Apr 28 (288) £3,000 [Woodburn]

Anr copy. Half mor; worn. With 54 plates, 4 hand-colored & with 4 mtd albumen prints. S June 25 (175) £450 [Shapero]

Ravilious, Eric William, 1903-42
— The Wood Engravings. L: Lion & Unicorn Press, 1972. One of 13. Folio, orig cloth. S Oct 6 (741) £170 [Elliott]

Rawlings, Marjorie Kinnan
— The Yearling. NY, 1939. One of 770 L.p. copies. Illus by N. C. Wyeth. sg Mar 5 (223) $325

Rawstorne, Lawrence
— Gamonia: or, the Art of Preserving Game. L: Ackermann, 1837. 8vo, orig mor gilt. With 15 hand-colored plates. Some foxing; several imprints concealing in binding; imprint shaved on plate at p 184; lacking half-title. Schwerdt copy. S Oct 23 (768) £850 [Sotheran]

Anr copy. Orig mor gilt; spine torn & lacking base. Some imprints cropped; some leaves spotted or offset. S Nov 10 (608) £380 [Blest]

Anr copy. Half mor. sg Apr 2 (164) $750

Ray, Gordon N.
— The Art of the French Illustrated Book.... NY, 1982. 2 vols. 4to, cloth, in d/j. O Mar 24 (145) $110

Anr copy. Cloth, in d/js. sg Jan 22 (258) $140

— The Illustrator and the Book in England from 1790 to 1914. NY, 1976. 4to, cloth. sg Jan 22 (257) $130

Ray, John, 1628-1705
— Catalogus plantarum circa Cantabrigiam nascentium.... L, 1660. 1st Ed, 1st Issue. 2 parts in 1 vol. 8vo, contemp calf; rebacked, old spine laid down. Ck Oct 31 (206) £700

— A Collection of English Proverbs.... Cambr., 1678. 2d Ed. 8vo, 19th-cent calf; rubbed. cb Oct 23 (190) $95

— Historia plantarum species hactenus editas.... L, 1686-1704. 1st Ed, 1st State of Vol I. Vols I-II (of 3). Folio, contemp calf; worn. S Feb 24 (536) £140 [Balduin]

— Observations Topographical, Moral & Physiological, Made in a Journey through Part of the Low-Countries, Germany, Italy and France.... L, 1673. 1st Ed. 2 parts in 1 vol. 8vo, modern half mor. With 4 plates, 2 folding. Tp stamped on verso. S Feb 24 (537) £360 [Bald]

— Select Remains.... L, 1760. 8vo, contemp calf. pnE Jan 28 (157) £120 [McKenzie]

— The Wisdom of God Manifested.... L, 1743. 8vo, contemp calf; worn. bba Oct 30 (417) £40 [Bickersteth]

Ray, Man
— Mr. and Mrs. Woodman. The Netherlands: Unida Editions, 1970. One of 65. 4to, orig mor. With 1 engraving & 27 silver prints. S June 17 (142) £1,500 [Perass]

— Photographs by Man Ray, Paris 1920-1934. Hartford, [1934]. 4to, spiral bound; spiral cracked, lacking bottom ring. cb May 7 (133) $400

Ray, Patrick Henry
— Report of the International Polar Expedition to Point Barrow, Alaska. Wash., 1885. 4to, contemp half mor; worn. 48th Congress 2d Session, House Ex Doc No 44. wa Sept 25 (529) $90

Raymond, Alex
— Flash Gordon in the Caverns of Mongo. NY: Grosset & Dunlap, [1937]. In chipped d/j. cb Sept 28 (1084) $55

Raymond, George B.
— Catalogue of Books on Angling, Shooting, Field Sports.... NY, 1904. One of 150. Interleaved with blank paper. sg Oct 23 (439) $150

Raymundus de Penaforte
— Summula. Strassburg: Johann Knobloch, 3 July 1504. 4to, modern vellum. Some stains & marginalia; lacking final blank. sg Oct 9 (65) $225

Raymundus de Sabunde
— Theologia naturalis sive liber creaturarum. Strassburg: Martin Flach, 21 Jan 1496. Folio, vellum. Some spotting & waterstaining. 162 leaves. Goff R-33. JG Mar 20 (238) DM2,500

Raynal, Guillaume Thomas Francois, 1713-96
— Histoire philosophique et politique des etablissemens et du commerce des Europeens dans les deux Indes. Geneva, 1781. 10 vols (lacking Atlas). 8vo, contemp calf; rubbed. O Nov 18 (152) $300
— Historica politica de los establecimientos ultramarinos de las naciones Europeas. Madrid, 1784-90. 5 vols. 8vo, contemp calf. With 7 folding tables & 13 folding maps; some maps torn. FD June 11 (911) DM710

Anr copy. Old calf; worn. kh Mar 16 (313) A$120
— The Revolution of America. L, 1781. 12mo, contemp calf; broken. O Mar 24 (146) $80

Rea, John, d.1681
— Flora: seu De Florum Cultura.... L, 1665. 1st Ed. Folio, later half calf. With engraved title & 8 plates. With The Mind of the Front leaf. Loosely inserted is an additional dedication leaf from possibly a later Ed. pnE Dec 17 (225) £320 [Marshall]

Read, Herbert, 1893-1968
— English Stained Glass. L & NY, [1926]. 4to, cloth; worn. sg June 4 (268) $140
— Mutations of the Phoenix. Richmond, 1923. 4to, orig half cloth; corners rubbed. Inscr to A. W. G. Randall. S Mar 9 (862) £90 [Sumner]

Reage, Pauline
— Histoire d'O. Paris: Au Cercle du Livre Precieux, 1962. One of 314. Illus by Leonor Fini. 4to, unsewn in orig wraps. S June 17 (24) £320 [Peeper]

Real...
— Real ordenanza para el establecimiento...de intendentes de exercito y provincia en...Nueva-Espana. Madrid, 1786. 4to, contemp calf; worn. Marginal staining; some worming affecting letters. sg Sept 18 (272) $225

Reamy, Tom
— San Diego Lightfoot Sue. Kansas City: Earthlight Publishers, [1979]. One of 100. In d/j. Sgd by the artists & by Harlan Ellison & Howard Waldrop. cb Sept 28 (1087) $140

Reasons
— Reasons for a Limited Exportation of Wooll. Oxford, 1677. 4to, wraps. S July 24 (470) £800 [Riley-Smith]
— Reasons for Continuing the Duty of Eight Pence upon each One-hundred and twenty Pounds weight of Rock Salt.... L, 1697. 4to, wraps. Minor staining. S July 24 (457) £600 [Quaritch]
— Reasons humbly Offered to the Consideration of Parliament, for the suppressing such of the Stage-Coaches and Caravans now travelling upon the Roads of England.... L, [c.1670]. 4to, modern half mor. Evelyn Library copy. S Dec 18 (243) £400 [Horseman's]

Reau, Louis
— Etienne-Maurice Falconet. Paris, 1922. One of 500. 2 vols. Folio, orig wraps. HN May 20 (450) DM620

Reaumur, Rene Antoine Ferchault, 1683-1757
— L'Art de convertir le fer forge en acier.... Paris, 1722. 4to, contemp calf; head of spine chipped. With 17 folding plates. C Dec 12 (174) £750 [Bookpress]
— The Natural History of Bees. L, 1744. 8vo, contemp calf; rebacked. With 12 folding plates, a few brownspotted. Johannson copy. sg Jan 15 (166) $175

Rechberg, Charles de —& Depping, George Bernhard
— Les Peuples de la Russie.... Paris, 1812-13. 2 vols. Folio, contemp half mor; upper cover of Vol I damaged. With 88 handcolored plates & 18 orig watercolors in place of 18 others. L.p. copy. S Apr 23 (174) £6,000 [Traylen]

Rechten...
— Rechten ende costumen van Antwerpen.... Antwerp: Plantin, 1582. One of 400. 2 parts (including Supplement) in 1 vol. Folio, later half lea. Lacking map; waterstain in lower margin. B Feb 25 (676) HF1,600

RECIT...

Recit...
— Recit veritable de la venue d'une canne sauvage depuis longtemps en la Ville de Montfort.... Rennes: Michel Hellot, 1652. 8vo, 19th-cent russia gilt. Beckford-Rahir-Jeanson copy. SM Mar 1 (481) FF3,000

Recollections. See: Beckford, William Thomas

Recueil...
— Recueil des tiltres du baillage et capitainerie des chasses de la Varenne et chasteau du Louvre.... Paris, 1676. 4to, contemp mor gilt. Jeanson copy. SM Mar 1 (483) FF17,000
— Recueil d'estampes representant les differents evenemens de la guerre qui a procure l'independance aux Etats de l'Amerique. Paris, [1784?]. 4to, contemp bds. With engraved title, 2 maps & 13 plates. FD June 11 (1110) DM1,200
Anr copy. Later half lea; scuffed. Several plates foxed or dampstained, generally not affecting image; Plate 12 torn with small loss of engraved text; Plate 1 torn not affecting text & with corner supplied in paper facsimile; margins soiled; child's scribbling on verso of last plate & rear endpaper. sg Dec 4 (162) $325

Redding, Cyrus
— A History and Description of Modern Wines. L, 1836. 2d Ed. 8vo, orig cloth; front joint partly torn. sg Jan 15 (45) $100

Redoute, Pierre Joseph, 1759-1840
— Le Bouquet royal. Paris, 1844. Folio, orig wraps. With port & 4 hand-colored plates. de Belder copy. S Apr 28 (293) £3,800 [Moorthamers]
— Choix des plus belles fleurs. Paris, 1827-[33]. Folio, contemp half mor; edges & corners worn, inner hinges strengthened with tape. With 144 hand-finished colored plates. Plate 127 torn across & repaired; Plate 22 cracked along left edge of plate mark; some soiling; possibly lacking a half-title & ad leaf. Hunt copy. CNY Nov 21 (240) $32,000
Anr copy. Contemp calf gilt; rubbed. Some plates spotted or discolored; flaw in margin of plate of Gnapalium csimium. S Oct 23 (714) £50,000 [Arader]
Anr copy. 19th-cent half mor; rubbed. With 80 (of 144) hand-finished colored plates. On guards throughout. S Apr 23 (52) £15,000 [Ackermann]
Anr copy. Bound in 2 vols. Folio, contemp half calf; joints worn. With 144 hand-finished colored plates. The paper of a few plates discolored or with faint spotting. L.p. copy. Vilmorin—de Belder copy. S Apr 28 (294) £45,000 [Beres]

Anr Ed. Paris, 1939. Folio, loose in bd portfolio as issued. With 12 color plates. O Jan 6 (153) $50
— Les Liliacees. Paris, 1802-[16]. 8 vols. Folio, contemp half mor gilt. With port & 487 hand-finished color plates & uncolored plate of Amaryllis bulb. Some foxing; port spotted; some plate numerals trimmed. This copy contains 2 extra plates, being other versions of Plate 427, Narcissus intermedius & 428, Narcissus laetus. de Belder copy. S Apr 28 (292) £140,000 [Brittain]

Redoute, Pierre Joseph, 1759-1840 —& Thory, Claude Antoine
— Les Roses. Paris: Didot, 1817-21-24. 1st Ed. Folio, contemp half mor; upper hinge of 1st vol split, several joints rubbed or with short splits. With port, engraved wreath & 169 hand-finished color plates.. Inscr "Cette exemplaire est un des premier tirage et des plus beaux." This is the copy from which the de Schutter facsimile was prepaired. de Belder copy. S Apr 28 (290) £130,000 [Ursus]
1st 8vo Ed. Paris, 1824-26. 3 vols in 2. Contemp half calf; worn. With 159 (of 160) hand-finished color plates & with prospectus bound after the title. S Apr 23 (57) £6,000 [Schuster]
2d 8vo Ed. Paris, 1828-29. Contemp half calf; rubbed. With 2 ports, hand-finished floral wreath & 182 hand-finished color plates. Slight spotting. Copy from which the De Schutter facsimile reproduced the octavo plates. de Belder copy. S Apr 28 (291) £10,000 [Laby]
3d 8vo Ed. Paris & St. Petersburg, 1835. 2d Issue. 3 vols. Half mor gilt; broken or loose. With 2 ports & 178 hand-finished color plate only. Minor background soiling. sg Apr 2 (165) $11,000
Anr Ed. Antwerp, 1974-78. One of 510. 4 vols. Orig half mor. Facsimile of 1st Ed. S Oct 23 (750) £1,150 [Wesley]

Reed, Henry M.
— The A. B. Frost Book. Rutland VT, [1967]. 4to, cloth, in d/j. Sgd by Reed. sg Oct 23 (281) $110

Reed, John, 1887-1920
— Ten Days that Shook the World. NY, 1919. 1st Ed. O June 9 (148) $70

Rees, Abraham
— The Cyclopaedia.... L, 1819-20. 45 vols. 4to, contemp half calf; joints rubbed. bba Apr 9 (114) £320 [Fisher]
Anr copy. Contemp calf; 1 cover detached. S Feb 23 (34) £820 [Grant]

Reese, Albert Moore
— The Alligator and its Allies. NY, 1915. cb Nov 6 (241) $50

Reese, Charles Lee. See: Bissell & Reese

Reeve, J. Stanley. See: Derrydale Press

Reeve, Lovell Augustus
— Conchologia Systematica, or Complete System of Conchology. L, 1841-42. 1st Ed. 2 vols. 4to, orig cloth; gutta-percha perished. With folding table & 301 hand-colored plates. C Dec 12 (177) £2,800 [Marshall]

Reflections...
— Reflections on Courtship and Marriage: In Two Letters to a Friend.... L: J. James 1759. 12mo, recent half calf gilt. With port of Jonathan Swift. Some old dampstains & marginal soiling. T Sept 18 (512) £100

Reginaldetus, Petrus
— Speculum finalis retributionis. [N.p., 10 Apr 1498]. 8vo, contemp blindstamped calf over wooden bds; lea very worn. 124 leaves. Goff R-89. C May 13 (148) £950 [Rivara]

Regiomontanus, Johannes, 1436-76
— Ephemerides sive almanach perpetuum. Venice: Petrus Liechtenstein for Johannes Lucilius Santritter, 15 Oct 1498. 4to, vellum. Tp soiled; upper margin of following leaf restored. 122 leaves. Goff R-110. sg Apr 2 (166) $1,600

Registre...
— Le Registre des ans passez depuis la creation du monde.... Paris: Anthoine Couteau for Galliot du Pre, 1532. 2 parts in 1 vol. 4to, 17th-cent calf. Some browning & waterstaining; minor defs. Lacking 34 leaves. FD June 11 (75) DM3,200

Reglement...
— Reglement de la confrerie de l'adoration perpetuelle du S. Sacrement, et de la bonne mort. Montreal: F. Mesplet & C. Berger, 1776. 16mo, orig bds in damask wallpaper. AVP Nov 20 (263) C$550 [Pope]

Regnard, Jean Francois, 1655-1709
— Oeuvres. Paris, 1810. 6 vols. 8vo, contemp calf gilt. With port & 11 plates. Some foxing. S Nov 27 (118) £100 [Booth]

Regnault, Nicolas Francois
— La Botanique mise a la portee de tout le monde.... Paris, [1770]-74-[80]. 3 vols. Folio, contemp calf; rubbed. WIth engraved titles surrounded by a hand-colored floral wreath, engraved Introduction leaf & 472 hand-colored plates. Tp to Vol II & a few leaves creased; minor dampstaining at end of Vol III; Ms Table generale des trois volumes at end of Vol III; lacking the ptd Table des noms. S Apr 23 (58) £7,500 [Antik]

Anr copy. Contemp calf; rubbed. With 3 engraved titles & 472 plates, all hand-colored. Minor spotting. Plesch—de Belder copy. S Apr 28 (295) £11,000 [Israel]

Anr Ed. Paris, 1774. One vol only (of 3). Folio, contemp calf. With engraved colored title & 138 colored plates. Sold w.a.f. C Oct 15 (254) £2,000 [Shapero]

Anr copy. One vol only. Folio, contemp half calf. With 80 hand-colored plates. Lacking title. Sold w.a.f. C Oct 15 (255) £1,800 [Scott Sandilands]

Regnier, Marie Louise Antoinette de Heredia de. See: Houville, Gerard d'

Regulations...
— Regulations for the Field Exercise, Manoeuvres, and Conduct of the Infantry of the United States. Phila., 1812. 8vo, contemp calf; worn. With 34 folding plates. wa Nov 6 (585) $75

Reibisch, Friedrich
— Der Rittersaal. Stuttgart, 1842. Oblong 4to, contemp cloth; worn, rebacked preserving old spine. With 62 hand-colored plates. Some soiling. S July 14 (582) £300

Reichenbach, Anton Benedikt
— Bildergallerie der Thierwelt oder Abbildungen des...Thierreichs. Leipzig, 1835. 4to, bds; worn & repaired. B Feb 24 (490) HF650

Reichenbach, Heinrich Gottlieb Ludwig, 1793-1879
— Flora Exotica. Die Prachtpflanzen des Auslandes in naturgetreuen Abbildungen herausgegeben von einer Gesellschaft von Gartenfreuden in Brussel. Leipzig: Hofmeister, 1834-36. 5 vols. Folio, contemp half mor. With 359 (of 360) hand-colored plates. Lacking Plate 171; Plate 145 torn; some spotting. C Oct 15 (256) £5,000 [Geibdon & Wesley]

— Iconographia botanica.... Leipzig, 1822-32. 3 vols. 4to, contemp bds; worn & loose. With 250 hand-colored plates. Some discoloration. Horticultural Society of New York—de Belder copy. S Apr 28 (298) £5,200 [Macdougall]

Anr Ed. Leipzig, 1823-34. 11 vols. 4to, contemp calf; joints rubbed, a few split. With 1,110 hand-colored plates. The 11th vol is devoted to grasses & cyperoids & contains 110 plates. Horticultural Society of New York—de Belder copy. S Apr 28 (297) £5,200 [Leinweber]

— Illustratio specierum Aconiti generis. Leipzig, 1823-27. Folio, later 19th-cent bds. With 1 plain & 71 hand-colored plates. Some leaves slightly discolored or spotted. de Belder copy. S Apr 28 (299) £2,200 [Krohn]

Reichenbach, Heinrich Gottlieb Ludwig, 1793-1879 —&
Reichenbach, Heinrich Gustav, 1824-89
— Icones florae Germanicae et Helveticae.... Leipzig 1837-1912. 2d Ed [1850] of Vol I, 1st Ed of Vols 2-25. 25 vols. 4to, contemp half mor; rubbed, a few vols with foot of spine chipped. L.p. copy with text in Latin & fully colored plates. Horticultural Society of New York—de Belder copy. S Apr 28 (296) £11,000 [Israel]

Reichenbach, Heinrich Gustav, 1824-89. See: Reichenbach & Reichenbach

Reichenow, Anton, 1847-1941
— Vogelbilder aus fernen zonen.... Cassel, 1878-83. 4to, cloth. With 33 color plates. Haverschmidt copy. B Feb 24 (175) HF1,700

Reichhelm, Gustavus Charles
— Chess in Philadelphia. Phila., 1898. Half mor; repaired. pn Mar 26 (488A) £40 [Wildey]

Reid, John
— The Scots Gard'ner. Edin.: David Lindsay & his Partners, 1683. 4to, contemp blind-stamped sheep; broken. Wormhole in lower margin of B1-D3; tear with loss to F1 not affecting text; some dampstains. Hunt copy. CNY Nov 21 (245) $1,200

Reid, John, Bookseller
— The American Atlas. NY: John Reid, 1796. Folio, contemp bds; worn with some loss. With 20 maps, all but 3 folding & with the unlisted double-page plan of Washington. Maine with marginal loss affecting image; soiled & stained; some tears, chips & holes. Sold w.a.f. P May 13 (17) $1,500

Reid, Thomas, Clockmaker
— Treatise on Clock and Watch Making. L, 1852. 5th Ed. 8vo, later cloth. With engraved title & 20 plates. Ck Sept 5 (171) £40

Reid, Thomas, 1791-1825
— Two Voyages to New South Wales and Van Diemen's Land.... L, 1822. 8vo, orig bds; spine torn. CA Apr 12 (209) A$500

Reigart, J. Franklin
— The Life of Robert Fulton. Phila., 1856. 8vo, orig cloth; spine chipped. With 27 plates.. wa Nov 6 (46) $90

Reinagle, George Philip
— Illustrations of the Battle of Navarin. L, 1828. Folio, half mor, orig wrap bound in. With plan & 12 plates on india paper. Slight abrasion affecting caption to the final plate; 1 mount torn & repaired; battle plan soiled & with some loss affecting neatline only. S Oct 23 (347) £3,500 [Martinos]

Reinhardt, Johann Christian
— A Collection of Swiss Costumes. L, 1822. 4to, half mor; spine rubbed. With 30 colored plaes. T May 21 (227) £2,200
Anr Ed. L, [watermarked 1825]. 4to, half mor; rubbed. With 30 colored plates. pn Nov 20 (32) £1,700 [Traylen]

Reisch, Gregorius, d.1525
— Margarita Filosofica.... Venice: Jacomo Antonio Somascho, 1599. 4to, old vellum. sg Mar 26 (244) $300
— Margarita philosophica. [Freiburg im Breisgau: Johann Schott, 16 Mar 1504]. ("Aepitoma omnis phylosophiae. alias Margarita phylosophica tractans....") 4to, old vellum; worn. With 2 folding plates; map supplied in facsimile. sg Jan 15 (353) $800
Anr Ed. Basel: H. Petrus, 1535. 4to, contemp pigskin over wooden bds; rubbed. FD June 11 (133) DM16,500

Reiser, Othmar
— Materialien zu einer Ornis balcanica. Vienna, 1894-1939. 4 vols. Folio, orig bdg; worn. B Feb 24 (365) HF375

Reiset, Marie Antoin de, Vicomte
— Marie-Caroline, Duchesse de Berry, 1816-1830. Paris, 1906. One of 80 with plates in 2 states. 4to, mor extra by Survand, orig wraps bound in; rubbed. wa Feb 19 (772pUS95)

Reiss, Johann Wilhelm —&
Stuebel, Alphonse
— The Necropolis of Ancon in Peru. Berlin, 1880-87. 3 vols. Folio, loose. With 10 plain & 132 color plates. Library stamps throughout. S Oct 23 (451) £1,500 [Israel]

Reitter, Edmund
— Fauna Germanica. Die Kaefer des Deutschen Reiches. Stuttgart, 1908-16. 1st Ed. 5 vols. Orig cloth. With 166 (of 168) plates on 83 leaves only. S Feb 24 (608) £140 [Berdcaunt]

Relacion...
— Relacion cierta y verdadera de la feliz Vitoria sucessos que en la India Oriental han consequido los Portugueses.... Madrid, 1625. Folio, modern bds. Dust-soiling on final page. sg Sept 18 (44) $375

Reland, Adrian
— Palaestina ex monumentis veteribus illustrata. Utrecht, 1714. 2 vols. 4to, contemp blind-stamped vellum. Library stamps on titles; 2 maps torn. bba May 28 (316) £220 [Ungar]

Anr copy. Disbound. Some browning; tears in folding plates. CAM Dec 3 (156) HF950

Anr copy. Orig vellum; soiled. WIth 12 maps & plates. Def in 1 map. Sold w.a.f. pn June 18 (56) £150 [Campbell]

Anr copy. 2 vols in 1. 4to, contemp calf; scuffed, rebacked, new endpapers. sg Apr 30 (326) $600

Relhan, Richard
— Flora cantabrigiensis. Cambr., 1785. Half calf gilt; rubbed. With 7 plates. pn Jan 22 (238) £85 [Maggs]

Reliques See: Mahony, Francis Sylvester

Remarks...
— Remarks on the Comparative Merits of Cast Metal and Malleable Iron Railways. Newcastle, 1827. Half cloth. With 1 folding litho view & 2 litho plates. bba June 18 (99) £340 [Elton]

Anr copy. Orig half cloth. With 3 folding plates. Tear in 1 plate; a few leaves coming loose or torn in inner margin. S May 28 (954) £280

Remington, Frederic, 1861-1909
— A Bunch of Buckskins. NY, 1901. Intro by Owen Wister. Folio, orig half cloth portfolio. With 6 (of 8) color lithos. All plates restored & backed with archival paper, 4 taped on versos to mats; several were previously torn & with paper loss around edges. cb Jan 8 (310) $2,000

— Crooked Trails. NY, 1898. 1st Ed. 8vo, orig cloth; soiled, corners rubbed. cb Jan 8 (311) $130

— Drawings. NY, 1897. Oblong folio, half cloth; waterstains on front cover, spine ends frayed. sg June 4 (271) $375

One of 250. Suede. Fore-edges of latter leaves dampstained. Sgd. cb Jan 8 (313) $1,600

— Frontier Sketches. Chicago, [1898]. Oblong 4to, orig bds; soiled. With pictorial title & 15 plates. bba Apr 9 (417) £65 [Brailey]

Anr copy. Pictorial cloth; soiled. sg Mar 12 (216) $120

— Pony Tracks. NY, 1895. 1st Ed. 8vo, cloth; soiled & rubbed. cb Jan 8 (319) $110

— A Rogers Ranger in the French and Indian War.... [NY: Harper, 1897]. 12 pp. Orig wraps. cb Jan 8 (322) $130

Remmelin, Johann —& Spaher, Michael, of Tyrol
— A Survey of the Microcosme.... L: James Moxon, 1675. folio, contemp half calf; broken. With 4 plates, 3 with hinged flaps. All plates with some tears; margins frayed & soiled; text leaves also torn. Sold w.a.f. bba Sept 25 (195) £1,400 [Phelps]

Anr Ed. L, 1702. Folio, contemp bds; worn. With 4 plates, 3 with moveable parts. HK Nov 4 (1103) DM3,600

Remond de Montmort, Pierre. See: Montmort, Pierre Remond de

Remond des Cours, Nicolas
— The True Conduct of Persons of Quality. L, 1694. 8vo, contemp mor gilt. Browned. sg Mar 26 (245) $150

Rems, Jack. See: Frane & Rems

Remy, Jules
— Champignons et truffes. Paris, 1861. 12mo, contemp half lea; worn. With 12 color lithos. Old dampstain throughout. Sold w.a.f. wa Nov 6 (63) $65

Remy, Jules —& Brenchley, Julius L., 1816-73
— A Journey to Great-Salt-Lake City. L, 1861. 2 vols. 8vo, modern half calf. Inscr. cb Oct 9 (163) $300

Anr copy. Cloth; stained. O May 12 (164) $400

Anr copy. Orig cloth; 1 spine torn at head. With frontises, folding map & 8 plates. S May 29 (1088) £130

Remy, Pierre
— [Sale Catalogue] Catalogue de tableaux precieux; miniatures & gouaches...le cabinet de feu M. Blondel de Gagny.... Paris, 1776. Contemp calf. Interleaved. cb Feb 19 (7) $200

[Sale Catalogue] Catalogue d'une riche collection de tableaux...le cabinet de feu son Altesse serenissime Monseigneur le Prince de Conti.... Paris, 1777. Later calf. Priced throughout in a contemp hand. cb Feb 19 (8) $225

Remy, Pierre —& Julliot, C. F.
— [Sale Catalogue] Catalogue des tableaux & desseins precieux des maitres celebres...cabinet de feu M. Randon de Boisset.... Paris, 1777. Contemp half calf; upper joint cracking. Priced in a contemp hand. Includes the supplement & errata. cb Feb 19 (9) $170

Renard, Louis
— Atlas de la navigation et du commerce.... Amst., 1715. Folio, contemp vellum gilt; dust-soiled. With frontis, port & 30 sea-charts, hand-colored in wash & outline except for the plates at end. Chart of Europe torn & repaired at folds without loss; some splits repaired elsewhere. S Oct 23 (240) £6,600 [Browning]

Renaudot, Esuebius, the Elder
— A General Collection of Discourses of the Virtuosi of France. L, 1664-65. 2 parts in 1 vol. Folio, old calf; spine ends chipped, front cover partly detached. sg Mar 26 (246) $120

Rendella, Prospero
— Tractatus de vinea, vindemia, et vino. Venice: Giunta, 1629. Folio, contemp vellum; spine worn. SM Oct 20 (520) FF3,000
Anr Ed. Naples: Stephanus Abbate, 1739. Folio, contemp vellum; stained. Browned. S Nov 27 (283) £380 [Olschki]

Rene d'Anjou
— Livre du cuer d'amours espris. Vienna, 1926. 2 vols, plus portfolio of plates. Together, 3 vols. Folio, bds; plates loose as issued, in box. FD Dec 2 (388) DM1,500

Reneaulme, Paul
— Specimen historiae plantarum. Paris, 1611. 2 parts in 1 vol. 4to, early half vellum; lower cover split, upper cover splitting. With 25 etched illusts. Some browning. Horticultural Society of New York—de Belder copy. S Apr 28 (300) £1,200 [Segal]

Renger-Patzsch, Albert
— Die Halligen. Berlin: Alertus, [1927]. 4to, pictorial wraps over wraps; worn. With 144 plates. sg Nov 13 (92) $110
— Hamburg: Photographische Augnahmen. Hamburg, [1930]. 4to, cloth over flexible bds; rubbed. With 80 plates. sg May 7 (67) $120

Rennell, James, 1742-1830
— A Bengal Atlas. L, 1781. Folio, modern cloth. With 23 maps & plates on 20 sheets, some hand-colored. Some soiling. S Oct 23 (470) £200 [Marshall]
Anr copy. Contemp half calf; rubbed. WIth 22 maps & plates, some hand-colored in outline. S Apr 24 (329) £400 [Maggs]
— Memoir of a Map of Hindoostan.... L, 1788. 4to, contemp calf; worn. With 2 folding maps. bba Oct 30 (351) £65 [Shapero]

Renneville, Rene Augustin Constantin de. See: East India Company, Dutch

Rennie, George, 1791-1866. See: Cooke & Rennie

Renny, Robert
— A History of Jamaica. L: J. Cawthorn, 1807. 4to, modern mor gilt. With folding map. Some browning. Hunt copy. CNY Nov 21 (248) $160

Renoir, Auguste, 1841-1919
— L'Atelier de Renoir. Paris, [1931]. One of 500. 2 vols. Folio, orig wraps; backstrips def. S June 17 (45) £2,600

Renouard, Antoine Augustin
— Annales de l'Imprimerie des Alde.... Paris, 1803-12. 1st Ed. 3 vols. 8vo, contemp half calf; rubbed, spines worn. With 2 engraved ports. Ck Oct 31 (175) £110
2d Ed. Paris, 1825. 3 vols. 8vo, half mor; joints weak. sg May 14 (523) $500
— Catalogue de la bibliotheque d'un amateur. Paris, 1819. 1st Ed. 4 vols. 8vo, half calf; 2 spines damaged at head. Cancelled stamp on titles. sg May 14 (74) $325

Renouard de Bussierre, M. T.
— Lettres sur l'Orient, ecrites pendant les annees 1827 et 1828. [N.p.], 1829. 2 vols plus Atlas. 8vo & folio, text in contemp half mor, Atlas in contemp half calf. S Oct 23 (350) £1,000 [Wood]

Renouard, Philippe
— Bibliographie des editions de Simon de Colines, 1520-1546. Paris, 1894. 8vo, cloth, orig wraps preserved. sg May 14 (525) $250

Repertoire...
— Repertoire du theatre francois.... Paris, 1803-5. 23 vols. 8vo, contemp calf. bba Sept 25 (261) £120 [Greenwaldt]

Repertory...
— The Repertory of Arts and Manufactures. L, 1794-1800. 12 vols in 6. 8vo, contemp calf. Sold w.a.f. S June 25 (129) £450 [Traylen]

Reports...
— Reports of Explorations and Surveys...for a Railroad from the Mississippi River to the Pacific Ocean.... Wash., 1855-61. 12 vols in 13. 4to, contemp calf or sheep; various defs. Some foxing & stains; tears in maps. wa Mar 5 (405) $2,200
Mixed Issue. Vol II (of 13) only. Orig cloth; worn, joint repaired. With 38 plates. wa Nov 6 (605) $65
Vol II. Wash., 1855. Half lea; worn. Some stains. O June 9 (149) $70
Vol III. Wash., 1856. Half calf. 1 plate loose & browned. Sold w.a.f. O June 9 (151) $130

Vol V. Contemp half calf; worn. Some dampstaining, affecting some uncolored natural history plates. Sold w.a.f. House Exec. Doc. 91, 33d Congress, 2d Session. O June 9 (152) $190

Vol X. Wash, 1859. 8vo, cloth; worn. Some dampstaining. Sold w.a.f. O June 9 (153) $150

Anr copy. Cloth; broken, spotted & worn. With 122 color plates.. wa Nov 6 (606) $80

Vol XII, Books 1 & 2. Wash, 1860. 2 vols. Half lea; worn. Some foxing. O June 9 (154) $90

Vol XII, Book 1 only. 4to, half lea; joints cracked, spine chipped. With 2 folding maps & 70 color lithos & 1 folding chart. sg Sept 18 (308) $200

Vol XI. Wash, 1861. Orig cloth; worn. Some foxing & spotting with some tears & fold breaks. wa June 25 (251) $280

Representations...
— Representations of the Embossed Chased & Engraved Subjects....which Decorate the Tobacco Box and Cases, Belonging to the Past Overseers Society.... L, 1824. Folio, orig half cloth; worn. bba May 14 (263) £110 [Bowers]

Reps, John W.
— Views and Viewmakers of Urban America. Columbia: U. of Missouri Press, 1984. In d/j. wa Nov 6 (501) $65

Repton, Humphry
— Designs for the Pavillon at Brighton. L, 1808. Folio, contemp half cloth; rebacked & recornered preserving orig backstrip & corners. With 20 plates, 7 with hinged overslips (hinges reinforced), some hand-colored. bba Sept 25 (292) £3,000 [Reed]

Anr copy. Orig bds; spine def. With 20 plates. pn Apr 30 (62) £2,500 [Henderson]

Anr Ed. L, [c.1822]. Folio, half mor; rubbed. Minor repairs; some faint soiling. S Apr 23 (100) £1,500 [Pagan]

— Observations on the Theory and Practice of Landscape Gardening. L, 1803. 4to, contemp calf; rebacked, old spine preserved, corners repaired. With port & 25 plates, 10 hand-colored & 11 with overslips; 2 maps, 1 hand-colored; other illusts, 1 hand-colored, 2 with overslips. Tear in 1 folding plate repaired. bba Sept 25 (291) £2,200 [Reed]

2d Ed. L, 1805. 4to, contemp half calf gilt. With frontis & 27 plates, some colored, some with overslips. S Apr 23 (129) £2,300 [Traylen]

— Sketches and Hints on Landscape Gardening. L, [1794]. Oblong folio, disbound; restored. With 16 plates, 10 hand-colored. Lacking half-title; some stains & soiling;

some larger plates refolded. Sold w.a.f. P June 18 (168) $1,800

Repton, Humphry & John Adey
— Fragments on the Theory and Practice of Landscape Gardening.... L, 1816. 4to, contemp half calf; rubbed, rebacked, inner hinges repaired. With 42 plates, 21 hand-colored, 13 with hinged overslips; 9 text illusts, 2 with overslips. 1 plate becoming loose; some stains. bba Sept 25 (293) £2,400 [Reed]

Reresby, Sir John
— The Travels and Memoirs of.... L, 1813. 8vo, modern calf. With 40 ports & views, some hand-colored. O Nov 18 (133) $130

Anr copy. Contemp calf gilt. With 40 plates & ports, 12 colored. S Nov 17 (919) £70 [Mackenzie]

Reresby, Tamworth
A Miscellany of Ingenious Thoughts and Reflections.... L, 1721. 4to, contemp calf gilt; broken. bba Nov 13 (213) £48 [Drury]

Resident, A. See: Alexander, Sir James Edward

Restif de la Bretonne, Nicolas-Edme, 1734-1806
— Le Quadragenaire, ou l'age de renoncer aux passions. Geneva [Paris], 1777. 2 vols. 12mo, calf. Hole in T1-4 of Vol I with loss of text; small cut in margin of final leaves of Vol I. S Mar 9 (788) pS260 [Dailey]

Restle, Marcell
— Byzantine Wall Painting in Asia Minor. Shannon, 1969. 3 vols. 4to, orig cloth, in d/js. bba Oct 30 (490) £85 [Check]

Retana y Gamboa, Wenceslao Emilio, 1862-1924
— Aparato Bibliografico de la Historia general de Filipinas.... Madrid, 1964. 3 vols. 4to, syn. Reprint of 1906 Ed. sg Oct 2 (247) $50

Reuilly, Jean de, Baron
— Voyage en Crimee et sur les bords de la Mer Noire, pendant l'annee 1803.... Paris, 1806. 8vo, contemp calf; backstrip nearly detached. With 2 folding maps, 3 folding plates & 3 folding tables. Stamp on front blank. sg Apr 23 (40) $50

Reveilhac, Paul
— Un Debut au marais, par Fusillot. Paris: A. Ferroud, 1892. One of 50 on chine. 8vo, half vellum. Jeanson copy. SM Mar 1 (484) FF3,000

Revere, Joseph Warren
— Keel and Saddle. Bost., 1872. 8vo, orig cloth. Some foxing. Ls from T. W. Streeter mtd to front pastedown. sg Mar 12 (219) $300

REVERE

— A Tour of Duty in California.... NY, 1849. 1st Ed. 12mo, orig cloth. With folding map & 6 plates. With 1-inch tear in front flyleaf & frontis. sg Mar 12 (218) $250

Revett, Nicholas, 1720-1804. See: Stuart & Revett

Revoil, Benedict Henry

— Chasses dans l'Amerique du Nord. Tours: A. Mame, 1869. 8vo, contemp shagreen; worn. Jeanson copy. SM Mar 1 (484) FF3,000

— Le Reve du chasseur. Paris, 1873. One of 100. Folio, contemp half shagreen. Jeanson copy. SM Mar 1 (486) FF4,500

Revolution...

— The Revolution. NY, 1868-69. Ed by Elizabeth Cady Stanton & Parker Pillsbury. Susan B. Anthony, Proprietor. Vol I, no 24 to Vol IV, No 2 bound in 1 vol. 4to, cloth; broken, spine taped. O Sept 23 (169) $250

Revue...

— Revue generale de l'architecture et des travaux publics.... Paris, 1865-72. 6 vols. Folio, half modern cloth; worn. Library markings. O Feb 24 (158) $160

Reynard the Fox

— Reinaert de Vos. Amst.: L. J. Veen, 1911. Version by S. Streuvels (pseud. of Frank Lateur); illus by G. van de Woestijne. 4to, orig cloth. B Oct 7 (70) HF250

— Reynaert den Vos ofte het oordeel der dieren.... Antwerp: J. H. Heyliger, [1670?]. 4to, modern bds. With partly-colored woodcut on title. Some discoloration. S Nov 27 (215) £250 [Forum]

Reynardson, Charles Thomas Samuel Birch

— "Down the Road." Or Reminiscences of a Gentleman Coachman. L, 1875. 2d Ed. 8vo, orig cloth. pn Mar 5 (65) £65 [Druett]

Reynaud, Leonce

— Memoire sur l'eclairage et le balisage des cotes de France. Paris, 1864. 2 vols. 4to, cloth. bba Oct 16 (287) £400 [Elton Engineering Books]

Reynell, Carew, 1636-90

— The True English Interest: or an Account of the Chief National Improvements.... L: Giles Widdowes, 1674. 1st Ed. 8vo, later half calf. Lower blank corner of tp restored; slightly dust-stained. bba Jan 15 (22) £360 [Quaritch]

Anr copy. Sheep; rubbed. G1 burn hole affecting parts of 3 words. P Sept 24 (377) $950

AMERICAN BOOK PRICES CURRENT

Reynier, Jean Louis Ebenezer

— Campaign between the French Army of the East.... L, 1802. 8vo, contemp calf; rebacked. cb Nov 6 (242) $250

Reynolds, Bruce

— A Cocktail Continentale. Concocted in 24 Countries.... NY, [1926]. Half mor gilt. sg Jan 15 (46) $100

Reynolds, Helen Wilkinson

— Dutch Houses in the Hudson Valley before 1776. NY, 1929. 1st Ed, One of 250. Intro by Franklin D. Roosevelt. 4to, cloth. With 151 plates. Foxed. sg June 4 (276) $110

Reynolds, John Hamilton. See: Hood & Reynolds

Reynolds, Sir Joshua, 1723-92

— Engravings from the Works. L, [1833-39]. 3 vols. Folio, 19th-cent lea gilt; worn. Lacking 1 plate in Vol I. sg Feb 5 (286) $400

— Seven Discourses Delivered in the Royal Academy. L, 1842. ("The Discourses....") 4to, old mor gilt; rubbed. With vignette title & 11 plates. Tp stamped. pnNY Oct 11 (40) $90

Reynolds, Osborne, 1842-1912

— Papers on Mechanical and Physical Subjects. Cambr., 1900-1-3. 3 vols. Folio, orig cloth; worn, soiled. Library copy. wa Nov 6 (79) $150

Reyrac, Francois Philippe de Laurens de

— Poesies tirees des Saintes Ecritures.... Paris, 1770. 8vo, contemp red mor with arms of Mercy-Argenteau. C Dec 3 (160) £300 [Chaponniere]

Rezanov, Nikolai Petrovich

— Rezanov Reconnoiters California, 1806.... San Francisco: Book Club of Calif., 1972. One of 450. cb Sept 11 (60) $65

— The Rezanov Voyage to Nueva California.... San Francisco, 1926. One of 260. Half cloth. cb Oct 9 (164) $160

Rhabanus Maurus. See: Hrabanus Magnentius

Rhead, George Woolliscroft

— History of the Fan. Phila., 1910. One of 180. Folio, orig cloth; shaken. O Jan 6 (155) $210

Rhead, Louis John

— American Trout-Stream Insects: a Guide.... NY, [1916]. sg Oct 23 (441) $80

— The Speckled Brook Trout. NY, [1902]. Half lea; worn. sg Oct 23 (442) $90

Rheede tot Draakestein, Henrik Adrian van

— Hortus indicus malabaricus, continens regni malabarici apud Indos celeberrimi omnis generis.... Amst., 1678-1703. Vol X only (of 12): De Herbis et diversis illarum specibus. Folio, contemp blind-stamped vellum; soiled. With 94 plates. Tp stamped on verso. C Apr 8 (189) £1,100 [Renard]

— Hortus Indicus Malabaricus, continens regni malabarici apud Indos celeberrimi omnis generis plantas rariores.... Amst., 1678-1703. 12 vols. Folio, contemp vellum. With 795 double-page plates, stamped in margins. Massachusetts Horticultural Society—de Belder copy.. S Apr 28 (301) £10,500 [Asher]

— Malabaarse Kruidhof, vervattende het raarste Slag van allerlei Zoort van Planten.... Amst., 1689. Folio, contemp half calf; rubbed. With frontis & 113 double-page plates. S Apr 28 (302) £2,500 [Macdougall]

Rhodes, Ebenezer

— Peak Scenery.... L, 1818-23. 4 parts in 2 vols. Folio, orig bds; rubbed & soiled. bba Sept 25 (448) £100 [Cox]

Rhodius, Ambrosius

— Optica, cui additus est tractatus de crepusculis. Wittenberg: Laurentius Seuberlich for Samuel Seelfisch, 1611. 2 parts in 1 vol. 8vo, recent bds; paper on spine partly torn. Some leaves in Sig. P misbound. S Nov 10 (426) £580 [Quaritch]

Riat, Georges

— Gustave Courbet, peintre. Paris, 1906. 4to, cloth, orig wraps bound in; worn. O Jan 6 (156) $50

Ribadeneyra y Barrientos, Antonio Joaquin de

— Manual compendio de el Regio Patronato Indiano.... Madrid, 1755. 1st Ed. 4to, contemp vellum; hinges weak, spine torn. Minor worming in top outer corner of first 150 pp & in bottom margin of Lll3-Vvv2, affecting a few words from Mmm to end. sg Set 18 (247) $150

Ricard, Samuel

— Traite general du commerce. Amst., 1781. 4to, contemp half calf. Some dampstains; lacking half-title in Vol I. S June 25 (79) £350

Ricardo, David, 1772-1823

— On the Principles of Political Economy and Taxation. L, 1817. 8vo, 19th-cent half mor; rubbed. G8 torn without loss. P Sept 24 (230) $4,000

Anr copy. Calf gilt, with gilt Signet stamp; rebacked, new endpapers. Pencilled notations in margins; marginal stain in F & G gatherings. P Sept 24 (378) $4,000

2d Ed. L, 1819. 8vo, disbound. Dampstaining to 1st few leaves; some foxing. bba Sept 25 (114) £580 [Stern]

Anr copy. Modern cloth. A2 & 3 reversed; marginal tear on L4 affecting 2 letters. P Feb 24 (379) $750

3d Ed. L, 1821. 8vo, contemp calf gilt; rubbed, joints cracked. Some pencilled notes. P Sept 24 (380) $800

— Proposals for an Economical and Secure Economy.... L, 1816. 2d Ed. 8vo, modern half calf. H1 with tear along blank inner margin; strengthening added between half-title & tp. P Sept 24 (381) $550

— Reply to Mr. Bosanquet's Practical Observations of the Report of the Bullion Committee. L, 1811. 8vo, modern cloth. Pencilled underlinings. P Sept 24 (382) $1,300

Riccardi, Pietro

— Biblioteca matematica Italiana.... Modena, 1870-93. One of 250. 4 vols. 4to, half lea; worn, Vol I lacking backstrip. sg May 14 (602) $250

Anr Ed. Milan, 1952. 2 vols. S Sept 23 (595) £110 [Farfouille]; S Nov 10 (26) £140 [Quaritch]

Rice, Craig, Pseud.

— 8 Faces at 3. NY, 1939. In d/j. cb Nov 20 (281) $65

Rice, David Talbot. See: Byron & Rice

Rice, Maj. Gen. William

— "Indian Game" (from Quail to Tiger). L, 1884. 8vo, cloth. Library markings. cb Nov 6 (243) $80

Rich, Claudius James

— Narrative of a Journey to the Site of Babylon.... L, 1839. 1st Ed. 8vo, modern cloth. Old stamp on title. sg Apr 23 (122) $110

Rich, Obadiah

— Bibliotheca Americana Nova; or, A Catalogue of Books...relating to America. L, 1832. 8vo, orig cloth; covers loose, backstrip defective. Inscr to the Hakluyt Society. sg Oct 2 (262) $110

Richard, Jules, 1825-99. See: Detaille & Richard

Richards, Anna Matlock

— A New Alice in the Old Wonderland. Phila., 1895. cb Sept 28 (290) $55

Richards, Walter
— Her Majesty's Army.... L, [1888-91]. In 6 vols. Orig cloth; rubbed. With 3 colored titles & 44 plates. Ck Nov 21 (355) £170

Anr copy. 3 vols. 4to, cloth; worn. With 31 color plates. O Nov 18 (156) $160

Anr copy. Cloth; worn & broken, spines gone. Library markings. Sold w.a.f. O Nov 18 (157) $160

Anr copy. Half mor gilt. With 3 color titles & 43 color plates. pn Sept 18 (176) £100 [Sanders]

Anr copy. Orig cloth. With 3 color titles & 44 colored plates. pn July 23 (120) £160 [Walford]

— His Majesty's Territorial Army: a Descriptive Account.... L: Virtue & Co., [c.1910]. Illus by R. Caton Woodville. 4 vols. 4to, pictorial cloth. L Dec 11 (351) £55

Richardson, Albert Deane
— Beyond the Mississippi.... Hartford, 1867. 1st Ed. Cloth; rubbed, front hinge starting. cb Oct 9 (165) $75

Richardson, Charles James, 1806-71
— Studies from Old English Mansions.... L, 1841-48. Series 1-4. 4 vols. Folio, orig half mor gilt. With litho titles & 133 plates, some tinted, a few hand-finished. C July 22 (178) £160

— Studies in Ornamental Design. L, 1851. 2 parts in 1 vol. Folio, contemp half lea; worn & loose. With 16 lithos, some in color. cb Feb 19 (231) $190

Richardson, George, 1736?-1817?
— A Book of Ceilings Composed in the Style of the Antique Grotesque. L, 1776. Folio, modern half calf. With 48 hand-colored plates. C Apr 8 (51) £2,100 [Weinreb]

Richardson, James
— Travels in the Great Desert of Sahara. L, 1848. 2 vols. 8vo, orig cloth; bumped, spine ends chipped & frayed. With folding map & 2 plates. cb Feb 19 (232) $75

Richardson, Sir John, 1787-1865
— Fauna Boreali-Americana; or the Zoology of the Northern Parts of British America. L, 1829-37. Vols I & III only (Quadrupeds & Birds). Contemp calf; rubbed, spines lacking. Ck May 29 (223) £700

— The Museum of Natural History. Glasgow, [1859-62]. 2 vols. 4to, contemp half calf; rubbed. Some plates loose. bba Dec 4 (269) £50 [Barley]

Anr Ed. L, [1859-62?]. 3 vols. 8vo, half calf gilt; rubbed. pn Jan 22 (269) £50 [Bowdage]

Anr Ed. Glasgow [c.1870]. 2 vols. 8vo, contemp calf; rubbed, 1 cover weakening.

With 136 plates, many hand-colored. cb Nov 6 (244) $120

Richardson, R. H. —& Others
— Chesapeake Bay Decoys; The Men Who Made and Used Them. Cambridge MD: Tidewater Publishers, 1973. One of 100. 4to, lea gilt. sg Oct 23 (444) $175

Richardson, R. J. See: Extraordinary...

Richardson, Rupert Norval
— The Comanche Barrier to South Plains Settlement. Glendale, 1933. cb Oct 9 (166) $160

Richardson, Samuel, 1689-1761
— Clarissa, or the History of a Young Lady. L, 1748. 1st Ed. 7 vols. 12mo, contemp calf with Leveson Gower crest on spines; upper cover of Vol II detached. Titles of Vols III & IV transposed; hole in C1 of Vol VI with loss of text. S Jan 13 (517) £50 [Freeman]

Anr copy. Contemp calf; worn, spine ends chipped. Lady Dorothy Bradshaigh's set, annotated by her & by Richardson. sg Apr 2 (167) $38,000

2d Ed of Vol I; 1st Ed of Vols II-VII. L, 1749-48. 7 vols. 12mo, contemp calf; worn. Last 2 gatherings loose in Vol III. sg Feb 12 (254) $130

— The History of Sir Charles Grandison. L, 1754. 1st Ed. 7 vols. 8vo, contemp calf; rubbed. Some soiling. S Jan 13 (518) £100 [McKenzie]

— Works. NY, [1901-2]. ("The Novels.") Ed de Luxe. 19 vols. Half mor gilt. cb Dec 4 (338) $160

Richardson, William, Architect —& Churton, Edward, 1800-74
— The Monastic Ruins of Yorkshire. L, 1834. 2 vols. Folio, half mor; worn & rubbed, Vol I bdg broken. With map & 55 plates only. K June 7 (319) $120

Richardson, William H., of Boston
— The Boot and Shoe Manufacturers' Assistant and Guide. Bost.: Higgins, Bradley & Dayton, 1858. 8vo, orig cloth; spine ends frayed. O Jan 6 (29) $135

Richter, Gisela Marie Augusta
— Red-Figured Athenian Vases in the Metropolitan Museum of Art. New Haven, 1936. One of 500. 2 vols. Folio, cloth; worn. O Jan 6 (157) $250

— The Sculpture and Sculptors of the Greeks. New Haven, 1929. 4to, cloth; worn. Some pencilled marginalia & underscoring. O Jan 6 (158) $60

Richter, Jean Paul
— Saemmtliche Werke. Berlin, 1826-28. 65 vols in 20. 8vo, half calf gilt. FD Dec 2 (3412) DM4,000

Anr copy. 60 vols in 30. 8vo, half cloth. Some spotting. HK Nov 4 (2568) DM800

Richter, Kurt
— Schach-Olympia Muenchen 1936. Berlin, 1936-37. 2 vols. Vol VI of Buecherei des Gross deutschen Schachbundes. pn Mar 26 (93) £80 [MacDonald Ross]

Rickett, Harold William
— Wild Flowers of the United States. NY, 1966-73. Vols I-VI in 14 vols. sg Sept 18 (248) $500

Ricketts, Charles de Sousy
See also: Nonesuch Press
— A Catalogue of Mr. Shannon's Lithographs. L: Vale Press, [1902]. One of 200. 8vo, orig bds; worn & soiled. O Nov 18 (158) $70

Ricketts, Edward F. See: Steinbeck & Ricketts

Rickman, John. See: Cook, Capt. James

Rickman, Philip
A Bird Painter's Sketch Book. L & NY, 1931. One of 125. 4to, half vellum. Pencil sketch of woodcock loosely inserted. pn Oct 23 (269) £230 [Graham]
— A Selection of Bird Paintings and Sketches.... L, 1979. One of 500. Folio, orig half mor gilt. Ck Oct 31 (187) £250; Ck May 29 (113) £320; pnNY Sept 13 (281) $300

Rider, Cardanus. See: Almanacs

Riding, Laura
— Four Unposted Letters to Catherine. Paris: Hours Press, [1930]. One of 200, sgd. 4to, half lea; spine worn. sg Dec 11 (372) $150
— Twenty Poems Less. Paris: Hours Press, 1930. One of 200, sgd. Half lea; extremities worn. sg Dec 11 (372) $150
— Voltaire: a Biographical Phantasy. L: Hogarth Press, 1927. 1st Ed. Orig wraps; spine torn. S Mar 9 (865) £90 [Whiteson]

Ridinger, Johann Elias, 1698-1767
— Abbildung der Jagtbaren Thiere mit derselben angefugten Faehrten und Spuhren. Augsbourg: Ridinger, 1740. Folio, old vellum. Jeanson copy. SM Mar 1 (487) FF22,000

Anr copy. Modern half shagreen. Jeanson copy. SM Mar 1 (488) FF19,000
— Chasseurs et Fauconniers. [Augsburg, c.1764]. Folio, half mor by Saulnier. With 25 plates. Jeanson copy. SM Mar 1 (489) FF35,000

— Estampes cynegetiques. [Augsburg, c.1745]. Folio, old bds. Jeanson copy. SM Mar 1 (492) FF9,000
— Der Par Force Jagt. [Augsburg, 1756]. Folio, modern half shagreen. With 16 plates. Jeanson copy. SM Mar 1 (490) FF38,000
— Vollkommene und gruendliche Vorstellungen der vortreflichen Fuersten-Lust oder der Edlen Jagdbarkwit.... Augsburg: J. E. Ridinger, 1729. Folio, half mor. With 35 plates. Jeanson copy. SM Mar 1 (493) FF60,000

Ridings, Sam P.
The Chisholm Trail: a History.... Guthrie, Okla., [1936]. In d/j. Inscr. O Oct 21 (154) $220

Riefstahl, Rudolf Meyer
— The Parish-Watson Collection of Mohammadan Potteries. NY, 1922. cb July 30 (164) $250

One of 500. O Jan 6 (159) $180

Out-of-series copy. sg June 11 (332) $150

Rienits, Rex & Thea
— Early Artists of Australia. Sydney, 1963. In d/j. kh Mar 16 (434) A$120

Riesenthal, J. A. Oskar von
— Die Raubvoegel Deutschlands und des angrenzenden Mittel-Europas. Cassel, 1876-[78]. With 60 color plates. B Feb 24 (373) HF1,100

Rietsch, F. G.
— Abbildungen der wichtigsten deutschen Holzpflanzen.... Prague, [1825]-26. The 16 issues together with German & Czech titles & 2 leaves of dedication that make up Vol I plus 3 other parts, all bound in 1 vol. With 38 (of at least 48) hand-colored plates. Some fore-margins toward end dampstained. de Belder copy. S Apr 28 (303) £1,600 [Elliott]

Rieu, Charles
— Catalogue of the Persian Manuscripts. L, 1879-95. 4 vols, including Supplement. 4to, orig cloth, unopened; rubbed. Spotted; library markings. bba Apr 23 (7) £160 [Check]

Rifaud, J. J.
— Voyage en Egypte, en Nubie.... Paris, [1830]. Folio, bds; spine reinforced with later crude cloth. With litho title, dedication & 211 plates only, including 62 partly or fully hand-colored. Dampstaining in lower right corner & fore-edges; foxed & browned throughout; tp & 7 plates torn affecting image. sg Apr 2 (169) $5,000

Rigeneratione...
— La Rigeneratione dell' olanda, specchio a tutti popli rigenerati. Venice, 1799. Folio, recent half lea. With engraved title & 19 plates, ptd in red. B Feb 25 (909) HF1,000

Riis, Jacob August
— How the Other Half Lives.... NY, 1890. 8vo, cloth; soiled. wa Nov 6 (340) $50

Rijksmuseum, Amsterdam
— RAPPARD-BOON, CHARLOTTE VAN. - Catalogue of the Collection of Japanese Prints.... Amst., 1977-84. 3 parts in 4 vols. Pictorial wraps. cb Mar 5 (251) $60

Rijn, H. van. See: Heussen & Rijn

Riley, Frank. See: Clifton & Riley

Riley, James Whitcomb, 1849-1916
— All the Year Round. Indianapolis: Bobbs Merrill, [1916]. 4to, half cloth. With 12 full-page color woodblock prints. wa Sept 25 (184) $240

Riling, Ray
— Guns and Shooting: a Selected Chronological Bibliography. NY, [1951]. One of 1,500. In chipped d/j. cb May 21 (214) $110

Anr copy. In d/j. sg Oct 23 (445) $70

Rilke, Rainer Maria, 1875-1926
See also: Cranach Press
— Gesammelte Gedichte. Leipzig, 1930-34. One of 200. Vol I only. Orig half vellum. HN May 20 (2157) DM950
— Primal Sound & Other Prose Pieces. [Cummington, Mass., 1943]. One of 175. sg Jan 8 (54) $350

Rimbaud, Arthur, 1854-91
— Une Saison en Enfer. The Hague, 1949. One of 150. Illus by Louis Favre. 4to, unsewn as issued in orig wraps. B Oct 7 (131) HF1,100

Rimmel, Eugene
— The Book of Perfumes. L, 1865. 4to, orig cloth; corners worn. pnE Jan 28 (154) £120 [Gladstone]
— Le Livre des parfums. Paris, [1870]. 8vo, orig cloth; rubbed, hinge weak. Engraved title spotted. bba Aug 28 (117) £50 [Greenwood]

Rinder, Frank
— D. Y. Cameron: An Illustrated Catalogue.... Glasgow, 1912. One of 200 on handmade paper, with plates on Japan vellum & with a sgd etching by Cameron. 4to, half vellum; soiled. pn Jan 22 (188) £40 [Trocchi]

Anr Ed. Glasgow, 1932. One of 600. 4to, orig cloth, in d/j. pn Oct 23 (72) £70 [Whitford]

Rinehart, Frank
— Rinehart's Indians. Omaha, 1899. 8vo, wraps. sg Nov 13 (93) $250

Ringhieri, Innocentio
— Cento giuochi liberali, et d'ingegno. Venice: G. M. Bonelli, 1553. 4to, needs rebdg. Dampwrinkled; lacking final blank. sg Mar 26 (247) $200

Ringwalt, John Luther
— American Encyclopaedia of Printing. Phila., 1871. 4to, cloth. Library markings. K Oct 4 (387) $110

Rintoul, Leonora Jeffrey. See: Baxter & Rintoul

Rio, Antonio del
— Description of the Ruins of an Ancient City.... L: Henry Berthoud, 1822. 4to, orig bds; worn. With 17 litho plates. S Apr 23 (311) £600 [Gott]

Ripalda, Geronimo de
— Catecismo mexicano.... Mexico, 1758. 4to, vellum. A few leaves soiled; some lower margins shaved affecting borders of titles & catchwords. S Apr 23 (312) £350 [Israel]

Anr copy. 8vo, contemp vellum. Lacking frontis; inserted final leaf possibly from anr copy; Y1 with bottom outer corner portion restored with plain paper, affecting text. sg Sept 18 (55) $325

Ripley, A. Lasseli
— Sporting Etchings. Barre MA, 1970. One of 500. Commentary by Dana S. Lamb; intro by Guido Perera. Oblong 4to, half cloth. cb May 21 (215) $80

Ripley, A. Lassell. See: Greenway & Ripley

Ripley, S. Dillon
— Rails of the World. Toronto, 1977. One of 400. Folio, orig cloth, in d/j. pn Oct 23 (270) £55 [Tryon]

Ripley, Sidney Dillon —& Scribner, Lynette L.
— Ornithological Books in the Yale University Library.... New Haven, 1961. In d/j; worn. sg Jan 15 (250) $175

Anr copy. Cloth, in d/j. sg Jan 22 (260) $150

Risso, J. Antoine —& Poiteau, Pierre Antoine, 1766-1854
— Histoire naturelle des orangers. Paris, 1818-[20]. Folio, contemp half calf; worn. With 109 hand-colored plates. Plate 12 with small marginal tear repaired & stained; a few plates slightly discolored. C Apr 8 (190) £2,800 [Marks]

Risso, J. Antoine —& Poiteau, Pierre Antoine
— Histoire naturelle des orangers. Paris, 1818-[20]. Folio, contemp half mor by Du Castin; rubbed. With 109 hand-finished color plates. Some spotting & browning. de Belder copy. S Apr 28 (304) £4,900 [Sourget]

Rister, Carl Coke
— The Southwestern Frontier - 1865-1881. Cleveland, 1928. cb Oct 9 (167) $60

Ritchie, Leitch, 1800-65
— Ireland Picturesque and Romantic. L, 1837-38, 2 vols, 8vo, contemp velvet. With 2 engraved titles & 36 plates only. Ck May 15 (168) £50
— Wanderings by the Loire. L, 1833. Illus by J. M. W. Turner. 8vo, mor gilt; worn, hinges cracked. With engraved title & 20 plates. sg Dec 18 (227) $90
— Wanderings by the Seine.... L, 1835. Illus by J. M. W. Turner. 8vo, recent half mor & contemp mor gilt. T Feb 19 (230) £48

Ritson, Joseph, 1752-1803
— The Letters.... L, 1833. 2 vols. 8vo, later calf; rubbed at extremities. cb Oct 23 (194) $85

Rittenhouse, David
— Memoirs. Phila., 1813. 8vo, modern cloth. Library markings. ADs of David Rittenhouse laid in. sg June 11 (333) $200

Ritz, Charles
— A Fly Fisher's Life. NY, [1960]. One of 250. Soiled & worn. sg Oct 23 (449) $50

Rives, Reginald W. See: Derrydale Press

Rivinus, August Quirinus, 1652-1723
— Introductio generalis in rem herbariam. Leipzig, 1690. Vols I-III (of 6)in 1 vol. Folio, contemp vellum; soiled. With 244 plates. Browned & spotted. Horticultural Society of New York—de Belder copy. S Apr 28 (305) £1,600 [Rainer]

Rizzi-Zannoni, Giovanni Antonio
— Atlas geographique contenant la mappemonde et les quatre parties avec les differents etats d'Europe. Paris, 1762. 24mo, contemp calf gilt; joints split, rubbed. With engraved title, double-page frontis & 29 double-page maps, hand-colored in outline. bba Mar 26 (326) £70 [David]

Roback, Charles W.
— The Mysteries of Astrology and the Wonders of Magic.... Bost., 1854. 8vo, cloth; spine ends frayed. ha Dec 19 (304) $55

Robb, George
— Historical Gossip about Gold and Golfers. By a Golfer. Edin.: Ptd by John Hughes, 1863. Card cover. pnC Jan 23 (167) £11,200

Robberds, J. W. See: Stark & Robberds

Robert de Vaugondy, Gilles & Didier
— Atlas portatif, universal et militaire. Paris, 1748. 2 vols, including Supplement. 4to, early calf gilt; rubbed, slight tears on 1 spine. With 2 hand-colored engraved titles & 208 (of 210) hand colored double page maps; 1 map loose & a few torn at central folds, some worn. pnNY Sept 13 (510) $650

Anr copy. 4to, contemp calf; worn & crudely repaired. With engraved title & 209 maps, all but title & 1st map hand-colored in outline. Some wormholes towards end; some soiling, a few tears in lower margins at end affecting 1 map; 1 map cropped. S Feb 24 (403) £1,000 [Postaprint]

Anr copy. One vol in 3. 4to, contemp mor gilt; joints weak. With double-page engraved title & 109 double-page maps & plans. Some waterstains & foxing. S Apr 23 (140) £1,300 [Franks]

— Atlas universel. Paris, 1757-[58]. Folio, contemp calf; broken. With engraved title & 108 double-page maps colored in outline. Centerfold tears to 8 maps. pn Mar 5 (371) £1,700 [Coss]

Anr copy. Contemp calf gilt; worn. With engraved title & 108 maps, hand-colored in outline. A few faint marks or short splits without loss. S Oct 23 (72) £2,800 [Perrin]

Anr copy. 18th-cent russia gilt; broken. With engraved title & 107 (of 108) maps, hand-colored in outline. S June 25 (295) £1,900 [Voorhees]

Anr Ed. Paris, 1757 [but 1783 or later]. Folio, half vellum; def. With 90 double page maps only, hand-colored in outline. Some fold breaks & waterstains. S July 14 (594) £1,000

Anr Ed. Paris: Delamarche, [1793?]. Folio, contemp half calf; def. With engraved title, 4 tables & 111 double-page maps, hand-colored in outline. Most dates erased; marginal fraying or creasing. S Oct 23 (71) £1,600 [Frann]

— Nouvel Atlas portatif. Paris, 1762. 4to, contemp calf gilt; worn. Engraved throughout. With 53 double-page maps, hand-colored in outline, principal areas fully colored. pn Sept 18 (349) £420 [Isler]

ROBERT

Robert, Francois
— Methode pour laver et fondre avec economie les mines de fer. Paris, 1757. 12mo, contemp sheep; worn. With 4 folding plates. C Dec 12 (178) £240 [Quaritch]

Robert, Hubert
— Le Soirees de Rome.... Paris: Basan Freres, [c.1765]. 8vo, half mor by Zaehnsdorf. With engraved title & 9 plates, hinged into album. C Dec 3 (161) £3,800 [Tunick]

Robert, Nicolas
— Estampes pour servir a l'histoire des plantes. [Paris, c.1685]. Folio, later vellum over orig bds. With 271 plates, 1 pen-and-wash drawing bound in. de Belder copy. S Apr 28 (307) £24,000 [Israel]

Anr copy. 3 vols. Folio, contemp red mor gilt, stamped in gilt on upper cover Donne par le Roi a M. le Comte de Bily, with the arms of Louis XVI below. With 319 plates. Some spotting & a few plates lightly discolored. de Belder copy. S Apr 28 (308) £46,000 [Israel]

— Variae ac multiformes florum species.... Rome, 1665. Folio, contemp calf gilt; rebacked preserving old spine. With engraved title & 29 plates, 2 partly hand-colored. Some discoloration or foxing. Horticultural Society of New York—de Belder copy. S Apr 28 (306) £4,500 [Paulsell]

Roberts, Austin
— The Mammals of South Africa. Johannesburg, 1951. Ltd Ed. 4to, cloth, in d/j. SSA Feb 11 (613) R190

One of 500. Half calf, in torn & repaired d/j. cb July 30 (165) $75

Roberts, David, 1796-1864

Egypt and Nubia

— Egypt and Nubia, from Drawings made on the Spot.... L, 1846-49-49. 3 vols. Folio, orig half mor gilt; rubbed, 1 hinge detached. With map & with 3 titles & 121 plates finely colored by hand & mtd as originals on card. On linen guards throughout; Vol I tp spotted at margin; a few plates slightly cockled; 2 plates with minor repairs; 3 plates with small stain. Subscriber's colored copy. C Oct 15 (94) £28,000 [Weinreb]

Anr copy. Bdgs not described but broken & lacking backstrips. With 3 litho titles, map & 108 (of 121) plates. Some plates mtd; 1 plate with tear repaired. Sold w.a.f. C Oct 15 (95) £3,600 [Scott Sandilands]

Anr copy. Contemp half mor gilt; spine head restored, 2 joints cracked. With 3 litho titles with hand-colored vignettes, map & 121 hand-colored plates mtd on card & guarded throughout. A few plates cockled; 2 plates spotted; a few plates & leaves detached; 1 tinted plate from anr issue finished by hand. Colored copy. C Apr 8 (53) £27,000 [Weinreb]

Anr copy. 3 vols in 2. Folio, 19th-cent half mor. With 3 titles, map & 121 tinted views. Some marginal dampstaining; c.5 views with marginal chips not affecting images. P June 18 (170) $6,500

Anr copy. 3 vols. Folio, contemp half mor gilt. With 3 litho titles, map & 121 plates. pn Apr 30 (121) £5,000 [Walford]

Sets of Both Works

— The Holy Land, Syria, Idumea, Arabia, Egypt and Nubia. With: Egypt and Nubia. L, 1842-49. 6 vols. Folio, contemp half mor; rubbed. Some vols affected by damp. Inscr by the pbr. bba Sept 25 (407) £8,900 [Burgess Browning]

Anr copy. 6 vols in 4. Folio, mor gilt by Ramage; rubbed, 1 inner hinge broken. With 6 litho titles with hand-colored vignettes, 2 maps & 241 tinted litho plates, all hand-colored. The 121 full-page plates cut round & mtd on thick card, the 120 half-page plates with text ptd beneath as issued. Lacking the port & list of subscribers; some spotting throughout. Colored copy. C Apr 8 (52) £18,000 [Perrin Thomas]

Anr copy. 6 vols in 2. Folio, modern half cloth; scuffed. With 6 tinted titles, port, 2 maps & 241 tinted plates. Lacking list of subscribers; 1 plate with tear repaired; anr plate with small marginal tear; dampstaining affecting some text & c.17 plates. Sold w.a.f. C Apr 8 (54) £7,500 [Burgess Browning]

Anr copy. 6 vols. Folio, 19th-cent half mor; worn, some joints cracked, some spines missing; 2 vols loose. With 247 plates, including titles, 2 maps & port. P Dec 15 (220) $10,500

Anr copy. Contemp half mor gilt. With 247 plates, including titles, 2 maps & port, colored by hand. Some spotting, chiefly in margins. S Nov 18 (1072) £15,500 [Burgess]

Anr copy. 6 vols in 4. Folio, contemp half mor gilt; spotted & with some wear. Stain throughout at outer margin & with some leaves loose. S Jan 12 (232) £1,000 [Burgess]

Anr copy. 6 vols. Folio, contemp mor gilt. With 6 litho titles, 2 maps & 241 plates (121 full-page). S Apr 23 (238) £9,500 [Slade]

Anr copy. Contemp half mor gilt, with arms of the Duke of Northumberland. With 6 litho titles, 241 tinted plates, uncolored port

& 2 maps. Guarded throughout; some spotting. S June 25 (356) £12,500 [Shirvany]

Anr Ed. L, 1855-56. 6 vols. 4to, half mor; rubbed. With port, 6 litho titles, 2 maps & 241 plates. Some spotting & staining. bba May 28 (319) £900 [Ungar]

Anr copy. 6 vols in 3. 4to, contemp half mor; worn. Most plates with library stamps; port def. bba Aug 20 (488) £150 [Trotter]

Anr copy. Contemp mor gilt. With 2 maps, port, 6 titles & 241 plates. C Apr 8 (55) £1,700 [Joseph]

Anr copy. Half mor; rubbed. With 6 litho titles & 242 plates only. Sold w.a.f. pn Nov 20 (190) £720 [Wood]

Anr copy. Old half calf gilt; rubbed, 2 covers detached. With 250 plates, including titles & maps. pnNY Oct 11 (41) $1,300

Anr copy. Contemp half mor gilt; rubbed. With 250 plates. S Oct 23 (357) £1,200 [Hasbach]

Anr copy. Half mor gilt; 1 vol rejointed. With 6 litho titles, port, 2 maps & 241 plates. S Apr 24 (239) £1,800 [Sims]

Anr copy. Loose in orig cloth; joints rubbed, 1 torn. With port, 2 pictorial titles, 2 maps & 241 views. Plate 130 torn across. S May 29 (275) £1,200

The Holy Land

— The Holy Land, Syria, Idumea, Arabia, Egypt and Nubia. L, 1842-43-[45]. 20 orig parts in 18. Folio, loose in pbr's cloth covers; lea spines. With port, 2 litho titles, 60 full-page & 60 smaller litho plates, all on india paper, hand-colored & mtd on card. Without Vol III title, map & leaf of description of Vol II & III title-vignettes. Colored copy. C Oct 15 (93) £19,000 [Sims]

Anr copy. Orig 20 parts in 18. Folio, orig mor-backed cloth portfolios gilt; gutta-percha perished. With uncolored port, 2 colored litho titles & 120 hand-colored plates mtd on card. Lacking leaves of subscribers & description of title-pages; c.15 plates spotted or foxed; c.4 plates with minor cockling; without map as issued. Colored copy. P Sept 24 (209) $46,000

Roberts, Col. David, 1757-1819

The Military Adventures of Johnny Newcombe. L, 1816. 2d Ed. Illus by Thomas Rowlandson. 8vo, lev gilt by Riviere. With 15 colored plates. Marginal soiling of text leaves. sg Feb 12 (270) $275

Roberts, Emma

— Views in India, China, and on the Shores of the Red Sea. L, 1835. 2 vols in 1. 4to, contemp mor gilt. With colored frontis, engraved titles & 61 plates. Ck May 15 (75) £90

Anr copy. Contemp half calf; rubbed. With engraved titles, colored frontis & 61 plates. T Feb 19 (226) £100

Roberts, Frederick Sleigh, 1832-1914

— Forty-One Years in India.... L, 1897. 1st Ed. 2 vols. 8vo, orig cloth; inner hinges repaired at endpapers, extremities rubbed & worn. cb Dec 18 (152) $55

Roberts, John S.

— The Life and Explorations of David Livingstone, LL.D. L, [1875?]. 8vo, orig mor gilt; rubbed. Some spotting. bba Dec 4 (289) £80 [Trophy]

Roberts, Kenneth, 1885-1957

— Oliver Wiswell. NY, 1940. One of 1,050. 2 vols. O Sept 23 (171) $60

— Trending Into Maine. Bost., 1938. One of 1,075. Illus by N. C. Wyeth. With an extra suite of the 14 Wyeth plates in an envelope. wd June 19 (198) $275

Roberts, Lewes, 1596-1640

— The Merchants Mappe of Commerce.... L: for R. Mabb, 1638. ("The Marchants Mapp of Commerce.") 1st Ed. Folio, modern half calf. Lacking title; lacking all before a3 & several leaves at end; some worming or damage affecting ptd surfaces. S Jan 12 (192) £240 [Schmidt]

Anr copy. Contemp calf; rubbed & broken. With additional title & 5 maps on versos of divisional titles. Lacking port; wormed in lower margins at end. S June 25 (80) £1,550 [McCrow]

— The Treasure of Traffike, or a Discourse of Forraigne Trade. L, 1641. 4to, wraps. S July 23 (456) £3,800 [Riley-Smith]

Roberts, S. C.

— Holmes & Watson: A Miscellany. L, 1953. In d/j. Roberts' own copy with 3 pp of his notes loosely inserted. cb Apr 24 (1505) $80

— A Note on the Watson Problem. Cambr., 1929. One of 100. Orig wraps. cb Apr 24 (1421) $180

Roberts, William. See: Ward & Roberts

Robertson, Edward Graeme

— Early Buildings of Southern Tasmania. Melbourne, 1970. 2 vols. 4to, wraps. kh Mar 16 (131) A$160

— Sydney Lace. Ornamental Cast Iron in Architecture.... Melbourne, 1962. 4to, syn, in d/j. kh Mar 16 (437) A$150

Robertson, Edward Graeme —& **Craig, Edith N.**
— Early Houses of Northern Tasmania.... Melbourne, 1964. One of 1,000. 2 vols. 4to, cloth, in d/js. kh Mar 16 (437) A$150

Robertson, John Wooster. See: Grabhorn Printing

Robertson, William, Architect
— Collection de differentes especes de serres chaudes, pour forcer des ananas.... L: Ackermann, 1798. Oblong 4to, contemp half sheep. With 24 hand-colored plates. bba Sept 25 (294) £800 [Reed]

Anr copy. Contemp wraps. Some browning. S Nov 18 (956) £440 [Marlborough]

Robertson, William, 1721-93
— The History of America. Dublin, 1777. 2 vols. 8vo, contemp calf; joints cracked. sg Sept 18 (251) $200

2d Ed. L, 1778. 2 vols. 4to, calf; broken, edges worn. With 2 maps. wa Sept 25 (385) $80

11th Ed. L, 1808. 4 vols. 8vo, old calf; worn, some panels detached. ha Mar 13 (168) $90

— Works. Oxford, 1825. 8 vols. 19th-cent half mor gilt. sg Feb 12 (256) $90

Robin, Claude C., b.1750
— Nouveau Voyage dans l'Amerique septentrionale, en l'annee 1781.... Phila. & Paris, 1782. 8vo, contemp calf; rubbed, hinges cracked. T Sept 18 (46) £65

Robins, Benjamin, 1707-51
— Mathematical Tracts.... L, 1761. 2 vols. 8vo, modern half calf. Some foxing; dampstains in Vol I. O Oct 21 (156) $70

Robins, William Palmer
— Etching Craft. L, 1922. Inscr. T Feb 19 (58) £50

Robinson, Alfred, 1806-95
— Life in California before the Conquest. San Francisco, 1925. One of 250. Half cloth. With 7 colored plates. cb Oct 9 (168) $120

Robinson, Charles N.
— Old Naval Prints, their Artists and Engravers. L: The Studio, 1924. One of 1,500. 4to, orig cloth. sg June 4 (280) $100

Robinson, Conway, 1805-94
— An Account of Discoveries in the West until 1519. Richmond, 1848. 1st Ed. 8vo, modern half sheep. sg Mar 12 (220) $130

Robinson, Fayette
— California and its Gold Regions. NY, 1849. 8vo, old half lea. sg Dec 4 (168) $600

2d Issue, with Appendix added. Modern half calf. Some foxing. sg Mar 12 (221) $400

Robinson, George Augustus
— Friendly Mission: The Tasmanian Journals and Papers.... [Hobart], Tasmania, 1966. Ed by Norman J. B. Plomley. Cloth. CA Oct 7 (138) A$150

Robinson, Mary, 1758-1800
— Memoirs of the late Mrs. Robinson.... L, 1801. 4 vols. 12mo, contemp calf; rebacked, rubbed. bba Jan 15 (71) £90 [Sutherland]

Robinson, Paul. See: Robinson, Spider

Robinson, Peter Frederick
— Village Architecture.... L, 1837. 4th Ed. 4to, contemp half mor; rubbed. With 41 plates. T Mar 19 (363) £64

Robinson, Selma
— City Child: Poems. NY: The Colophon, 1931. One of 300. Illus by Rockwell Kent. In d/j. cb June 18 (219) $90

Robinson, Spider
— Callahan's Crosstime Saloon. Short Hills NJ: Ridley Enslow, [1978]. Sgd on tp. cb Sept 28 (1101) $65

Robinson, William
— An Attempt to Elucidate the Principles of Malay Orthography. Fort marlborough: Mission Press, 1823. 8vo, half mor. S Oct 23 (496) £3,400 [Orientum]

Robinson, William, Barrister
— The History and Antiquities of Enfield. L, 1823. 2 vols. 8vo, contemp half calf; worn. With port, hand-colored folding map (torn at folds) & 15 plates & plans (1 handcolored in outline). S Nov 17 (820) £80 [Young]

Robinson, William, 1838-1935
— Flora and Sylva. L, 1903-5. 3 vols. 4to, cloth. S Feb 24 (539) £120 [Brosi]

Anr copy. Vol I (of 3). 4to, half cloth; worn, soiled. wa Nov 6 (44) $100

Robinson, William Heath, 1872-1944
— Bill the Minder. L, 1912. 4to, orig vellum; soiled, lacking ties. With 16 color plates. pnNY Mar 12 (108) $275

— Railway Ribaldry. L, 1935. 4to, orig wraps. S Oct 6 (861) £40 [Thorp]

Anr copy. Orig wraps; worn. Sgd on endleaf with a small ink drawing of a bird & egg. S Oct 6 (862) £50 [Thorp]

Robison, John
— Proofs of a Conspiracy Against All the Religions and Governments of Europe, carried on in the Secret Meetings of Free Masons.... L, 1797. 2d Ed. 8vo, orig bds; broken. sg Oct 9 (303) $50
4th Ed. L, 1798. 8vo, contemp calf. pnE Jan 28 (27) £70 [McCormack]

Robson, George Fennell
— Scenery of the Grampian Mountains. L, 1814. 1st Ed. Oblong folio, recent calf; rubbed. With map & 41 hand-colored plates. T Oct 16 (321) £500

Roccha, Angelo, Bishop of Tagasti
— De campanils commentarius. Rome: Facciottus, 1612. 4to, modern calf. With 4 plates. Woodcut border to title repaired at outer margin & with rubber-stamp; of the 4 plates, 1 is repaired & the others are cropped or cut very close; lacking final blank; some stains. S Sept 23 (384) £190 [Robertshaw]
Anr copy. Calf by Evans & Short. Some leaves spotted. S Nov 27 (216) £350 [Quaritch]

Rochefort, Charles de, b.1605
— The History of the Carriby Islands, viz., Barbados, St. Christophers.... L, 1666. 1st Ed in English. Folio, contemp calf; re-backed. With 9 plates. Tp cut round & mtd; a few short tears without loss; some browning. S Apr 24 (313) £600 [Perrin]

Rochester, John Wilmot, Earl of, 1647-80
See also: Nonesuch Press
— Poetical Works. [Halifax]: Haworth Press, 1933. One of 50 on handmade paper & specially bound. Ed by Quilter Johns. 4to, mor by Sangorski & Sutcliffe. S Sept 22 (42) £70 [Taylor]

Rochowanski, Leopold Wolfgang
— Wiener Keramik. Leipzig & Vienna, 1923. One of 150 with watercolor drawing by Egon Schiele. 8vo, orig vellum. S Nov 10 (158) £210 [Frankel]

Rocque, John
— A Plan of the Cities of London and Westminister.... L, 1746. 1st Ed. Folio, contemp half calf; worn. With 24 double-page sheets & key-map, mtd on guards. One sheet cleanly torn down fold. With an alphabetical index, 1755. Engraved throughout. Ck May 15 (218) £2,600
— The Small British Atlas. L, 1753. 4to, half calf. With 2 engraved titles, 2 general maps & 52 double-page maps. pn May 21 (389) £650 [Burgess Browning]
Anr copy. Half calf gilt. With engraved title, 2 general maps & 52 county maps.

Extra-illus with 19 maps from Jefferies, 3 plates from Seale's Globes & other maps. pn May 21 (390) £620 [Burgess Browning]
— A Topographical Survey of the County of Berks. L, 1761. Folio, bdg not described. With title & 12 sheets of text & 18 sectional maps, 3 with tears. pn Dec 11 (414) £220 [Magna]

Rodenberg, Julius. See: Simon & Rodenberg

Rodker, John
— Collected Poems, 1912-1925. Paris: Hours Press, 1930. One of 200. Half lea. sg Dec 11 (373) $150

Rodrigues, Eugene. See: Ramiro, Erastene

Rodriguez de Castro, Joseph
— Biblioteca espanola. Madrid, 1781-86. 2 vols. Folio, contemp wraps; spines worn, Vol I rear wrap loose. sg Mar 26 (249) $475

Rodriguez, Manuel
— El Maranon, y Amazonas. Historia de los descubrimientos.... Madrid, 1684. Folio, contemp vellum. A few perforations in the upper blank margin of tp & final leaf; some browning & foxing. S Apr 24 (316) £2,500 [Israel]

Rodriguez, Mathias
— Explicacion de las Sesenta y Cinco Proposiciones Prohibidas por la Santidad de N.M.S.P. Innocencio XI. Puebla: Diego Fernandez de Leon, 1684. 4to, old vellum; loose & stained. Tp stained; 1st 35 leaves chewed at bottom corners not affecting text. sg Sept 18 (252) $200

Roe, Fred
— Ancient Coffers and Cupboards: their History and Description.... L, 1902. 4to, cloth; rubbed. O Oct 21 (157) $90

Roeding, Johann Hinrich
— Allgemeines Woerterbuch der Marine. Hamburg, etc., [1794-98]. 4 vols. 4to, contemp half russia; foot of 1 spine chipped. With engraved title & 115 plates. Some plate numerals cropped. C Dec 12 (179) £2,300 [Warneke]

Roentgen, Wilhelm Conrad, 1845-1923
— Eine neue Art von Strahlen. Wuerzburg, 1895-96. Part 1 only. Orig wraps. Offprint from the Sitzungberichte der Physik.-Med. Gesellschaft zu Wuerzburg. S May 21 (213) £1,200 [Prevanas]

Roesel von Rosenhof, August Johann
— De natuurlyke historie der insecten. Haarlem & Amst., [1764-68]. 9 parts in 5 vols bound in 8, plus Kleeman's 1770 continuation. 4to, old half russia gilt; rubbed. With 3 hand-colored frontises & 288 hand-

colored plates plus 26 hand-colored plates in Kleeman. Some fore-edges stained or frayed. P June 18 (172) $3,750

Anr Ed. Haarlem & Amst., [1765-88]. 5 parts in 9 vols, including Kleemann's continuation. 4to, contemp calf, Supplement in half calf. With hand-colored frontises in Vols I-III, uncolored port in Vol I & 384 subjects on 314 hand-colored plates. Vol V in Landwehr's 3d state without tp & with the text breaking off abruptly on p 192. S June 25 (177) £3,600 [Marshall]

— Historia naturalis ranarum nostratium. Nuremberg, [1753]-58. Folio, bdg not described. With 19 (of 24) colored & 20 (of 24) plain plates. HK Nov 4 (1104) DM1,500

— Der monatlich-herausgegebenen Insecten-Belustigung. Nuremberg, [1740]-61. Vols 1-4 in 3 only. Contemp mor,l armorial bdg. With 3 frontises & 316 color plates on 247 leaves. FD June 11 (726) DM19,000

Anr Ed. Nuremberg, 1746-[59]. Vol I only. Contemp calf gilt. HK Nov 4 (977) DM1,800

Anr copy. 4 vols. 4to, contemp calf; worn. With hand-colored frontises in Vols I-III, uncolored port in Vol IV & 357 subjects on 286 hand-colored plates. A few plates browned, mainly in Vol IV; Vol II with tp cut close at outer edge & a little worming at beginning. S Oct 23 (751) £2,500 [Fletcher]

Roger, Abraham
— Le Theatre de l'idolatrie, ou la porte ouverte. Amst., 1670. 4to, contemp half calf; spine worn & defective, rubbed. With additional engraved title & folding plate. bba Nov 13 (8) £50 [Bennett & Kerr]

Roger-Marx, Claude
— Bonnard: Lithographe. Monte Carlo, 1952. 4to, orig wraps. O May 12 (167) $275
— French Original Engravings from Manet to the Present Time. L & NY, 1939. 4to, cloth, in d/j. O Mar 24 (151) $60

Rogers, Bruce, 1870-1957
— Four Unpublished Letters to S. H. de Roos. Haarlem: Tuinwijkpers, 1975. One of 20. With calligraphed initial by S. L. Hartz. Orig wraps. B Oct 7 (44) HF260
— Report on the Typography of the Cambridge University Press.... Cambr., 1950. One of 500. Folio, orig half cloth. Inscr. sg Jan 22 (262) $80
— The Work of Bruce Rogers: Catalogue of an Exhibition Arranged by the A.I.G.A. NY, 1939. In repaired d/j. cb June 18 (309) $70; O Nov 18 (163) $70

Anr copy. In d/j. Sgd by Rogers. sg Jan 22 (261) $50

Rogers, Charles, 1711-84
— A Collection of Prints in Imitation of Drawings.... L, 1778. 2 vols. Folio, 19th-cent mor; rubbed. With engraved titles, port, dedication & 114 plates on 105 leaves. C July 22 (180) £3,200

Rogers, Meyric Reynold
— Carl Milles: An Interpretation of his Work. New Haven, 1940. Folio, cloth; worn. With 163 plates. Corner clipped from first few leaves. O Jan 6 (163) $50

Rogers, Nehemiah
— The True Convert; or, an Exposition upon the XV Chapter of St. Luke's Gospell.... L, 1632. 3 parts in 1 vol, here bound in reverse order. 4to, 19th-cent sheep; joints cracked. Part 1 lacking prelims. sg Oct 9 (305) $90

Rogers, Robert, 1731-95
— Journals of Major Robert Rogers.... L, 1765. 1st Ed. 8vo, modern half mor gilt. sg Mar 12 (222) $600

Anr Ed. Concord, N.H., 1831. ("Reminiscences of the French War....") 12mo, half cloth; worn. O Mar 24 (152) $70

Rogers, Samuel, 1763-1855
See also: Fore-Edge Paintings
— Italy, a Poem. L, 1830. 8vo, contemp mor by C. Smith; rubbed; some foxing. O Oct 21 (158) $50
— The Pleasures of Memory. L, 1810. 8vo, contemp mor gilt; spine rubbed. Unique copy ptd on india paper. sg Feb 12 (259) $325

Rogers, Capt. Woodes, d.1732
— A Cruising Voyage Round the World.... L, 1712. 1st Ed. 2 parts in 1 vol. 8vo, contemp calf; upper cover detached. With 5 folding maps. Some margins soiled; 1 map torn with loss; 2 maps cleanly torn; tp soiled & frayed. Ck Feb 27 (155) £160

Anr copy. Calf gilt by Zaehnsdorf. With 5 folding maps, linen-backed. sg Apr 23 (125) $950

Rohmer, Sax, Pseud.
— The Island of Fu Manchu. L, 1941. In d/j which is rubbed at extremities. cb Nov 20 (283) $150

Rokewode, John Gage. See: Gage, John

Roland Holst, Adrianus
— De Vagebond. Rotterdam, 1930. One of 100. Orig wraps. B Oct 7 (119) HF300

Roland Holst, Henriette van der Schalk. See: Schalk, Henriette van der

Rolando, Guzman
— A Treatise on the Theory and Practice of the Art of Fencing. Edin., 1823. 1st Ed. 8vo, orig bds; rebacked. With 12 plates. sg June 11 (336) $50

Rolewinck, Werner, 1425-1502
— Fasciculus temporum. Louvain: Johann Veldener, 29 Dec 1476. Folio, later half calf; spine worn. 70 (of 72) leaves. Goff R-256. T Nov 20 (504) £280
Anr Ed. [Strassburg: Johann Pruess, not before 1490]. Contemp blindstamped lea over wooden bds. 96 leaves. Goff R-275. FD Dec 2 (93) DM7,000

Rolfe, Frederick William
See also: Thomas, Owen
— Amico di Sandro. A Fragment of a Novel. Harrow: Pvtly ptd, 1951. One of 150. sg Dec 11 (376) $275
— Ballade of Boys Bathing. L., 1972. One of 200. Wraps. sg Dec 11 (377) $140
— The Bull Against the Enemy of the Anglican Race. L: Pvtly ptd, 1929. One of 50. Wraps. "A superb copy". sg Dec 11 (379) $500
— The Cardinal Prefect of Propaganda.... L, 1957. 1st Ed, Out of series copy. sg Dec 11 (380) $80
— Collected Poems. L, 1974. One of 200. sg Dec 11 (382) $100
— Don Renato, an Ideal Content. L, 1963. 1st Ed, One of 200 with frontis of Corvo's working notes. Orig cloth. Lacking title & half-title. sg Dec 11 (383) $120
— In His Own Image. L, 1901. sg Mar 5 (225) $600
— A Letter to a Small Nephew Named Claud. Iowa City: Typographic Laboratory of the U of Iowa School of Journalism, 1964. One of 134. 4to, wraps. sg Dec 11 (385) $350
— A Letter to Father Beauclerk. Edin.: Tragara Press, 1960. One of 20 or less. Wraps, in d/j. sg Dec 11 (384) $900
Letters. L: Nicholas Vane, [1959-62]. 3 vols. Vol I is 1 of 30; Vol II is 1 of 260; Vol III is 1 of 30. sg Dec 11 (381) $325
— Letters of Baron Corvo to Kenneth Grahame. Hurst: Peacocks Press, 1962. One of 40. 4to, ptd wraps. sg Dec 11 (386) $400
— Three Tales of Venice. L, [1950]. 1st Ed, one of 140. Half cloth; spine worn. sg Dec 11 (392) $200
— The Venice Letters. L, 1974. One of 200. sg Dec 11 (393) $70
— Without Prejudice: One Hundred Letters from Frederick William Rolfe...to John Lane. L, 1963. 1st Ed, One of 600 on handmade paper. Bds. sg Dec 11 (394) $80

Rolfe, Frederick William —&
Pirie-Gordon, Harry
— The Weird of the Wanderer.... L, 1912. In d/j. sg Dec 11 (399) $400

Rolland, Romain
See also: Fore-Edge Paintings
— Jean-Christophe. Paris: Albin Michel, [1925-27]. One of 100 on Van Gelder. Illus by Frans Masereel. 5 vols. 4to, wraps. bba Aug 28 (267) £40 [Leichti]

Rollin, Charles
— The Ancient History of the Egyptians, Carthaginians, Assyrians...., Bost,, 1823, 2 vols. 4to, lea; rubbed, stained. O Jan 6 (4) $170
— Philosophy for Children, Extracted from the universally admired Belles Lettres.... L: W. Lane, [c.1780]. 32mo, orig Dutch floral bds; rebacked. Sydney Roscoe's copy. S Dec 5 (356) £1,500 [Schiller]

Romance...
See also: Malory, Sir Thomas
— The Romance of Violette. Toronto, [20th cent]. 12mo, syn. With 4 mtd photos. sg Feb 12 (100) $110

Romanus, Adrianus
— Parvum theatrum urbium sive urbium praecipuarum totius orbis...descriptio. Frankfurt: Nicolaus Bassaeus, 1595. 4to, contemp pigskin over wooden bds stamped ICLBAP 1596. Library stamp on tp. S Apr 23 (134) £2,000 [Tieger]

Rombauer, Irma S.
— The Joy of Cooking.... [St. Louis, 1931]. 1st Ed. Cloth; hinges cracked, shaken. P Nov 25 (397) $550

Romero, Jose Guadalupe
— Noticias para formar la historia y la estadistica del Obispado de Michocan. Mexico City: Vicente Garcia Torres, 1682. 4to, contemp calf gilt. With 3 folding maps, 2 partly hand-colored. Browned. sg Sept 18 (255) $50

Romney Collection, George
— [Sale Catalogue] A Catalogue of the Select and Reserved Collection of Paintings.... L: Christie's, 1807. 4to, unbound in orig wraps. John Romney's copy. CNY Dec 19 (219) $750

Romoli, Domenico
— La Singolare Dotrina...dell'Ufficio dello Scalco.... Venice: D. Farri, 1587. 8vo, contemp vellum. Some stains; last few leaves with marginal repairs. Crahan copy. P Nov 25 (398) $1,100

Ronalds, Alfred

— The Fly-Fisher's Entomology. L, 1836. 1st Ed. 8vo, half lea; worn. With 19 hand-colored plates. sg Oct 23 (452) $80

5th Ed. L, 1856. 8vo, cloth; worn. With 20 hand-colored plates. sg Oct 23 (453) $90

8th Ed. L, 1877. 8vo, orig cloth; rubbed. With 20 hand-colored plates. T oct 16 (407) £75

Anr Ed. L, 1901. With 20 hand-colored plates. pn Dec 11 (272) £60 [Chelsea Rare Books]

Anr Ed. Liverpool, 1913. One of 250. 2 vols. 4to, orig half mor. With 7 plates of rivers & 13 hand-colored plates; 48 flies on 9 leaves of sunken mounts. pn Sept 18 (20) £440

11th Ed. 4to, cloth. With hand-colored plates & with 48 flies in sunken mounts. sg Oct 23 (454) $1,700

Ronalds, Hugh, 1759-1833

— Pyrus Malus Brentfordiensis: or, a Concise Description of Selected Apples. L, 1831. Folio, later mor gilt. With 42 hand-colored plates. Plesch—de Belder copy. S Apr 28 (309) £3,000 [Keser]

Ronsard, Pierre de, 1524-85

— Les quartre premiers livres des Odes...Ensemble son Bocage. Paris: Cavellat, 1550. Bound with: L'Hymne de France. Paris, 1549. And: Ode de la Paix. Paris, 1550. 1st Ed of all 3 works. 8vo, orig calf with blind-stamped panels; repaired, joints defective, some scuffing. With the 2 errata leaves. The Eugene Piot-Herpin-Robert Hoe-W.A. White copy. S Nov 27 (218) £6,000 [Kraus]

Roo, Gerard von

— Annales rerum belli domique ab Austriacis Habspurgicae gentis principibus a Rudolpho primo, usque ad Carolum V. Gestarum.... Innsbruck: Joannes Agricola, 1592. 1st Ed. Folio, old vellum bds. 2 small holes in margin of title; lacking final blank. S Sept 23 (385) £200

Anr copy. With 2 small holes in margin of title; lacking final blank. S Mar 10 (1133) £100 [Pavlov]

Roosch, Kurt

— Sprig and Turfy. Mount Vernon: Golden Eagle Press, [1938]. One of 108. 4to, cloth; worn. With 15 plates, all but the last colored in water color over a key plate in black. O Jan 6 (164) $160

Rooses, Max, 1839-1914

— Le Musee Plantin Moretus. Antwerp, 1913-14. One of 60 with a duplicate suite of the plates engraved on copper. 26 parts in 7 orig fasicules. 4to, loose as issued in wraps; 1 spine frayed. Some plates hand-colored. C Dec 3 (38) £550 [Hildebrandt]

Roosevelt Franklin D., 1882-1945

— Addresses...from July 19, 1940 to January 20, 1941. Wash: The White House, Christmas 1941. One of 75. 4to, half vellum. Inscr to Archibald MacLeish. sg Apr 2 (170) $2,400

Roosevelt's copy, Franklin D.

— BRANT, IRVING. - James Madison. Indianapolis, [1941]. Inscr to Roosevelt by Brant, sgd by Roosevelt, 1941 & with ANs of Robert Hopkins stating that Roosevelt gave the book to his father, Harry Hopkins. P Oct 29 (18) $1,400

— HERTZ, EMANUEL. - Lincoln Talks: A Biography in Anecdote. NY, 1939. Sgd by Roosevelt, 1939 & inscr by him to Harry Hopkins, 1942. P Oct 29 (19) $3,000

Roosevelt, Theodore, 1858-1919

— African Game Trails. L, 1910. Orig cloth; rubbed. cb May 21 (218) $55

One of 500. Half lea; worn & soiled. wa Mar 5 (277) $500

Anr Ed. NY, 1910. 2 vols. 8vo, modern half mor gilt. pnNY Sept 13 (285) $475

— Big Game Hunting in the Rockies and on the Great Plains. NY & L, 1899. One of 1,000 L.p. copies, sgd. Contemp mor; recased, with portions of spine laid down. wa Nov 6 (191) $280

— Hunting Trips of a Ranchman. NY, 1885. Medora Ed, one of 500. 4to, orig cloth; worn, corners showing. Annotated by an owner. cb May 21 (220) $80

— Ranch Life and the Hunting-Trail. NY, [1888]. Illus by Frederick Remington. Folio, cloth; worn, shaken. One signature loosening; those pp creased & browned. cb Jan 8 (328) $130

— The Wilderness Hunter: An Account of the Big Game of the United States.... NY, [1893]. 8vo, orig cloth; worn. O June 9 (157) $80

— Works. NY, 1923-26. Memorial Ed, one of 1,050. 24 vols. Orig cloth. Sgd by Edith Kermit Roosevelt. K June 7 (319) $120

Roosevelt, Theodore, 1858-1919 —& Grinnell, George Bird, 1849-1938

— Hunting in Many Lands. NY, 1895. Hinges cracking. cb Nov 6 (248) $95

— Trail and Camp Fire. NY, 1897. cb May 21 (124) $55

Roosevelt, Theodore, 1858-1919 —& **Heller, Edmund, 1875-1939**
— Life Histories of African Game Animals. NY, 1914. 2 vols. 8vo, orig cloth. cb Nov 6 (249) $150

Roper, J. See: Cole & Roper

Roques, Joseph
— Plantes usuelles, indigenes et exotiques. Paris, 1809. 2d Ed. 2 vols. 4to, later bds; worn. With colored engraved title & 132 colored plates. C Apr 8 (191) £1,000 [Walford]

Roquet, Antoine Ernest. See: Thoinan, Ernest

Rosaccio, Giuseppe
— Viaggio da Venetia, a Constantinopoli per Mare, e per Terra.... Venice: Giacomo Franco, 1617. Oblong 4to, vellum bds; soiled. With 2 (of 3?) leaves of text & 72 full-page plates. Head of title cropped; several leaves wormed at inner margin touching surface. S Apr 23 (203) £1,300 [Franks]

Rosales, Vicente Perez. See: Perez Rosales, Vicente

Rosborough, F. H. ("Polly")
— Tying and Fishing the Fuzzy Nymphs. Harrisburg: Stackpole, [1978]. One of 300, with artificial fly in sunken mount on front cover. Lea gilt. sg Oct 23 (457) $140

Roscius, Julius Hortinus
— Icones operum misericordiae cum J. Roscii Hortini, sententiis et explicationibus. Rome: B. Grassi, 1586. 2 parts in 1 vol. Folio, old vellum. With 2 engraved titles, frontis & 14 plates. Some marginal stains; 2 blank corners torn. S Mar 10 (1134) £130 [Noble]

Anr copy. 17th-cent calf; worn. Marginal soiling & stains; 1st title with old signatures & tiny hole; lacking final blank. sg Mar 26 (251) $275

Roscoe, Sydney
— John Newbery and his Successors, 1780-1814. [Wormley, Herts.]: Five Owls Press [1973]. bba Oct 16 (397) £40 [Francis]

Roscoe, Thomas, 1791-1871
— The Tourist in Italy. L, 1831-33. Vol I only. Contemp mor. L.p. copy. bba Oct 16 (222) £70 [Scott]
— Views of Cities and Scenery in Italy, France and Switzerland. L, 1836-38. 3 vols in 2. 4to, contemp half mor. S May 28 (902) £220
— Wanderings and Excursions in South Wales. L, [1837]. 8vo, orig mor gilt; worn. O June 9 (158) $80

Roscoe, William, 1753-1831
— Monandrian Plants of the Order Scitamineae.... Liverpool, [1824]-28. One of 150. Folio, contemp half mor. With 112 hand-colored plates. Some spotting. de Belder copy. S Apr 28 (311) £5,000 [Brittain]

Roscommon, Wentworth Dillon, Earl of, 1633?-85
— Poems.... L, 1717. 8vo, contemp calf; rubbed. Tp frayed; a few leaves loose. bba Mar 26 (53) £80 [Hannas]

Rose, Thomas. See: Noble & Rose

Rose, Thomas, Topographer
— Picturesque Rambles in Westmorland, Cumberland, Durham and Northumberland. L, 1847 [49]. Illus by Thomas Allom. 3 parts in 2 vols. 4to, half mor. With engraved title & 215 plates. bba Dec 4 (347) £80 [Elliott]
— Westmoreland, Cumberland, Durham and Northumberland. L, 1832-[35]. Vol I only. 4to, contemp half calf; rubbed. bba Dec 4 (347) £80 [Elliott]

Anr copy. 3 vols. 4to, half mor; rubbed. With engraved title & 108 plates only. bba May 14 (50) £150 [Bookroom]

Anr copy. Half mor gilt; rubbed. With engraved title & 215 views on 110 plates. Some spotting to 14 plates; many plates with lower edge of margin waterstained. L Dec 11 (131) £100

Anr copy. 2 vols. 4to, contemp half calf; rubbed. With engraved title & 212 views on 107 plates. With 2 views stained in 1 corner. L July 2 (103) £100

Anr copy. 3 vols in 2. 4to, bdgs not described but def. With engraved title & 109 plates (of 110). pn Dec 11 (50) £180 [Nicholson]

Anr copy. 2 vols. 4to, contemp half mor gilt, many of the part wraps & ads bound in. With engraved title & 215 views on 110 plates, with 1 map. S May 28 (903) £170

Anr copy. 3 vols. 4to, contemp half calf gilt. With engraved title & 215 views on 110 plates. S July 28 (1004) £190

Anr copy. Contemp half mor. T Nov 20 (46) £210

Rosello, Lucio Paolo
— Il Ritratto del Vero Governo del Prencipe dal l'Essempio Vivo del Gran Cosimo de' Medici. Vinegia: Bonelli, 1552. 8vo, old bds; worn. O Nov 18 (164) $80

ROSENBACH

Rosenbach, A. S. W., 1876-1952
See also: Widener Library, Harry Elkins
— The All-Embracing Doctor Franklin. Phila., 1932. Out-of-series copy. Half mor. sg Jan 22 (265) $200
— Books and Bidders: the Adventures of a Bibliophile. Bost., 1927. Half cloth. Lower margins of prelims slightly rippled. cb Sept 11 (233) $80
Anr copy. Cloth, in d/j. cb June 18 (310) $95
One of 760. sg Jan 22 (264) $150
One of 785. Half cloth. cb Feb 19 (236) $50
— The Collected Catalogues.... NY, [1967]. 10 vols. sg Jan 22 (266) $75; sg Jan 22 (267) $75
— Early American Children's Books. Portland, 1933. One of 88 on Zerkall Halle. 4to, half cloth. HN May 20 (87) DM860
One of 585. Half lea; worn, joints broken. O Apr 28 (171) $110
Anr copy. Half mor. O May 12 (168) $200
Anr Ed. NY, 1966. In d/j; worn. O Jan 6 (165) $50
— An Introduction to Herman Melville's Moby-Dick. NY, 1924. One of 250. Bds. sg Oct 2 (265) $60

Rosenberg, Isaac
— Moses, a Play. Stepney Green: Paragon Printing Works, 1916. 4to, orig wraps. With corrections in unidentified hand. sg Dec 11 (404) $650
— Poems.... L, 1922. 1st Ed. In d/j. sg Dec 11 (405) $120
— Youth. L, 1915. 1st Ed. Orig wraps. sg Dec 11 (406) $425; T Feb 18 (113) £380

Rosenberg, Jakob. See: Friedlaender & Rosenberg

Rosene, Walter
— The Bobwhite Quail; Its Life and Management. New Brunswick NJ, [1969]. One of 250. Illus by Richard A. Parks. 4to, syn. sg Oct 23 (458) $175

Rosenthal, Leonard
— Au Jardin des Gemmes. Paris, [1924]. Illus by Leon Carre. 4to, vellum, with orig wraps bound in. SM Oct 20 (597) FF700
— The Kingdom of the Pearl. L, [1920]. Special copy No 3 without text & with presentation inscr by Dulac. Illus by Edmund Dulac. Orig half vellum gilt. With 10 colored plates. pn Nov 20 (255) £300 [Joseph]

Rose's...
— The Rose's Breakfast. L, 1808. 1st Ed. 16mo, orig wraps; loose. With frontis & 7 plates. ha May 22 (176) $65

Rosey, Gui
— Les Moyens d'Existence. Paris, 1969. One of 25 hors commerce with etchings in 2 states. Illus by Rene Magritte. Orig wraps. S July 2 (1062) £620 [Gordon]
— Signe de Survie au Temps d'Amour. Paris, 1968. One of 25 hors commerce with etchings in 2 states. Illus by Rene Magritte. Orig wraps. Inscr to Georgette Magritte. S July 2 (1061) £1,900 [Gordon]

Rosoi, Barnabe Farmain de. See: Farmain de Rosoi, Barnabe

Ross, Alexander, 1591-1654
— Pansebeia: or a View of all Religions.... L: John Williams, 1683. 8vo, contemp calf; joints repaired with glue, rehinged. cb Oct 23 (196) $50

Ross, Sir James Clark, 1800-62
— A Voyage of Discovery and Research in the Southern and Antarctic Regions... L, 1847. 1st Ed. 2 vols. 8vo, bdg not described. Repair to 1 folding plate. kh Mar 16 (441) A$1,150

Ross, John —& Gunn, Hugh
— The Book of the Red Deer and Empire Big Game. L, 1925. One of 500. 4to, orig cloth; soiled, spine ends & corners bumped. cb Nov 6 (254) $80

Ross, Sir John, 1777-1856
— Narrative of a Second Voyage in Search of a North-West Passage.... L, 1835. 8vo, later half calf. With 31 maps & plates. Folding map with several tears repaired. cb June 4 (177) $700
Anr copy. Vol I only. Contemp half mor; worn. Frontis & tp wormed; some spotting. S Nov 18 (1231) £130 [Negro]
Anr copy. With frontis & 28 plates & charts, some colored by hand. S May 29 (1064) £180
Anr copy. 2 vols (including Appendix). 8vo, modern cloth. With folding map & 50 plates & maps. Library stamps on titles & plates. sg June 11 (338) $90

Ross, M. See: Mackenzie & Ross

Ross, Thomas. See: MacGibbon & Ross

Rossetti, Christina Georgina, 1830-94

— Goblin Market.... Phila. [1933]. Illus by Arthur Rackham. 8vo, cloth, in d/j. sg Oct 30 (182) $130

Anr Ed. L, 1933. 8vo, wraps, in d/j. sr Oct 30 (181) $175

One of 410, sgd by Rackham. Orig vellum. With 4 color plates. sg Oct 30 (180) $350

Rossetti, Dante Gabriel, 1828-82
See also: Kelmscott Press

— Poems. L, 1870. 8vo, lev extra in exhibition bdg by Zaehnsdorf. With ALs to William Allingham laid in. sg Dec 4 (169) $750

Rossetti, Giovanni Battista

— Dello scalco. Ferrara: Domenico Mammarello, 1584. 4to, old vellum; relined, spine mended, stained. Marginal worming; inkstain on 2E2r affecting c.20 letters; a few other stains & early Ms notes. P Nov 25 (399) $1,900

Rossi, Domenico

— Studio d'architettura civile sopra gli ornamenti di porte e finestre tratti da alcune fabbriche insigni de Roma. Rome, 1702-[21]. 3 vols. Folio, orig bds; worn, spine torn & def. With 3 engraved titles, engraved dedication & 282 plates. Some worming of inner margin of Vols I & III affecting engraved area of a few plates; hole in Plate 60 of Vol II. C Oct 15 (96) £2,400 [Weinreb]

Anr copy. 3 vols in 2. Folio, 19th-cent calf; rebacked, joints broken. C July 22 (184) £3,000

Anr copy. Part 1 only. Folio, contemp calf over wooden bds; def. With engraved title, dedication & 140 plates. Marginal waterstains; some worming. S Oct 23 (86) £620 [Dennistoun]

Rossi, Giovanni Bernardo de

— De Hebraicae typographiae origine ac primitiis... Parma, 1776. 1st Ed. 4to, modern half mor; scuffed. sg Sept 25 (270) $130

— De typographia Hebraeo-Ferrariensi.... Parma: Bodoni, 1780. 8vo, orig half vellum. First few leaves lightly dampstained. S Nov 10 (2) £180 [Kota]

— Dizionario storico degli autori ebrei.... Parma: Bodoni, 1802. 2 vols in 1. 8vo, cloth. sg May 14 (319) $350

Rossi, Giovanni Gherardo de

— Scherzi poetici e pittorici. Parma: Bodoni, 1795. 4to, contemp mor gilt. With engraved title & 40 plates. Some worming. S Jan 16 (426) £300 [Erlini]

Rossi, Giovanni Giacomo de

— Insignium Romae templorum prospectus.... Rome, 1648. Bound with: Disegni vari altari e capelle nelle chiese di Roma.... Rome, [n.d.]. Folio, later calf; rebacked & restored. With engraved frontis & 70 plates in 1st work & engraved 49 plates in 2d work. C May 13 (86) £550 [Thomas]

Anr Ed. Rome, [1684]. Folio, disbound. With engraved title & 54 (of 72) plates only. Some worming in margins; engraved title soiled. Sold w.a.f. C Oct 15 (97) £600 [Weinreb]

Anr copy. Wraps; spine def. With 72 plates including title. Some waterstains. S Oct 23 (73) £700 [Vaes]

Rossi, Giovanni Giacomo de —& Falda, Giovanni Battista

— Le Fontane di Roma nelle piazze.... Rome, [1675]. Bound with: Le Fontane delle Ville di Frascati.... Rome, [c.1687]. And: Le Fontane ne'palazzi e ne'giardini di Roma.... [Rome, c.1689]. 3 works in 1 vol. Oblong folio, later calf, with arms of Sir Hugh Wyndham; restored & rebacked. Plates unnumbered. With engraved title dedication & 31 plates in 1st work; engraved title, dedication & 16 plates only in 2d work; engraved title, dedication & 25 plates in 3d work. C May 13 (87) £1,800 [Walford]

— Il Nuovo Teatro delle fabriche et edificii, in prospettiva di Roma moderna. Rome, 1665. Parts 1-3 (of 4) in 1 vol. Oblong folio, later calf, with arms of Sir Hugh Wyndham; rebacked with mor. With 82 plates before numbers only. C May 13 (88) £1,200 [Galen]

Anr Ed. Rome, 1665-99. Parts 1-4 in 1 vol. 4to, contemp calf; worn. With 142 plates. S Apr 23 (94) £1,700 [Shapero]

Rossini, Giovanni Pietro, the Elder

— Il Mercurio Errante delle Grandezze di Roma.... Rome, 1732. 12mo, 19th-cent vellum. With engraved title & 70 plates, some folding, the rest trimmed & inlaid to size. sg Dec 18 (213) $60

Rostand, Edmond, 1868-1918

— Cyrano de Bergerac. Paris, 1898. 8vo, mor gilt by Rene Kieffer, orig wraps bound in. Cornelia Otis Skinner's copy, with watercolor illusts throughout by Eugene Grivaz. sg Feb 26 (199) $800

Anr Ed. Paris: Magnier, 1899. 4to, mor extra by Affolter, orig wraps bound in.

ROSTAND

With wrapper vignette & port in 4 states, dedication & 6 titles in 3 states, 5 plates in 4 states & 41 illusts in 3 states. With 3 A Ls s from the binder laid in. S Oct 6 (703) £85 [Thorp]

One of 400 with plates in 2 states. Half mor gilt by Carayon, orig wraps preserved. With an extra suite of the cover & the illusts. B Oct 7 (331) HF420

Rostovtzeff, Mikhail Ivanovich

— The Social and Economic History of the Hellenistic World. Oxford, 1959-64. 3 vols. O Sept 23 (172) $170

Rosvita. See: Hroswitha

Roth, Henry Ling

— The Discovery and Settlement of Port Mackay, Queensland. Halifax, 1908. One of 250. 4to, orig cloth; spine head frayed. C Oct 15 (169) £170 [Maggs]

Rothchild, Herbert L. See: Grabhorn Printing

Rothschild Library, Nathan James Edouard

— Catalogue des livres composant la bibliotheque.... Paris, 1884-1920. Ed by Emile Picot. 5 vols. Vols I-IV in half mor by Riviere, Vol V in wraps, unopened. C Dec 3 (39) £700 [Maggs]

Anr Ed. Paris, 1884-1912. 5 vols. Cloth. sg May 14 (240) $375

Anr Ed. NY: Burt Franklin, [1965]. 5 vols. Reprint of the 1884-1920 Ed. O June 16 (147) $70

Rothschild Library, Victor Nathan Meyer

— Rothschild Library: a Catalogue of the Eighteenth-Century Printed Books and Manuscripts. Cambr.: Pvtly ptd, 1954. 1st Ed. 2 vols. 4to, orig half cloth. pnE Jan 28 (316) £280 [Smith]

Rottiers, Bernard Eugene Antoine

— Description des monumens de Rhodes. Brussels, 1830-28. 2 vols. 4to & folio, contemp half mor. Atlas with engraved title & 75 plates, several colored. S Oct 23 (351) £800 [Fletcher]

Rouault, Georges, 1871-1958

— Souvenirs intimes. Paris, 1927. One of 350. Ed by A. Suares. Folio, broche; broken. SM Oct 20 (664) FF6,000

Roubo, Andre Jacob

— L'Art du Menuisier. Paris, 1769-75. 4 parts in 2 vols. Folio, modern calf. With 383 plates. C Apr 8 (57) £1,800 [Schuster]

AMERICAN BOOK PRICES CURRENT

Rouille, Guillaume

— Promptuarii Iconum insigniorum a seculo hominum.... Lyons, 1553. 1st Ed. 2 parts in 1 vol. 4to, old calf; worn. Some dampstaining. Ck Oct 17 (145) £85

Rouse, Henry Clark, 1853-1906

— Traveling Around the World with General Nelson A. Miles. NY, 1904. 4to, cloth; spine ends frayed. With c.175 mtd gelatin photos & 2 maps. sg Nov 13 (94) $200

Rousseau, Jean Jacques, 1712-78

— La Botanique. Paris, 1805. Illus by P. J. Redoute. Folio, early 19th-cent calf gilt; rubbed, rebacked, old spine preserved. With 64 (of 65) hand-finished colored plates. Lacking Plate 38 & half-title; some spotting, mainly marginal. Ponsonby—de Belder copy. S Apr 28 (310) £6,000 [Van Loock]

— Les Confessions.... Geneva, 1782. 1st Ed. 2 vols. 8vo, wraps. S July 28 (1141) £100

— The Confessions.... Phila.: Gebbie, 1902. Astral Ed, One of 56. 12 vols in 6. Mor extra with inlays. cb Feb 19 (237) $750

Anr copy. Mor extra with onlays; 1 vol broken, corners worn, 2 joints starting. wa Sept 25 (43) $160

— Le Devin du Village. Paris, [1753]. Folio, mor gilt. Unique copy inscr to Denis Diderot, who gave the book to Sophie Vollond (inscr below that of Rousseau). SM Oct 20 (551) FF200,000

— Emile, ou de l'education. "A La Haye: Chez Jean Neaulme," 1762. 4 vols. 8vo, contemp calf. bba May 14 (200) £580 [Rota]

Anr Ed. [Paris], 1762. 4 vols. 8vo, contemp calf; broken. Vol III waterstained. bba Sept 25 (115) £75 [Merrion Book Co.]

— Oeuvres. Londres [but Brussels], 1774-83. 12 vols. 4to, contemp calf. With port & 37 plates by Moreau le Jeune & Le Barbier.. SM Oct 20 (552) FF8,000

Anr Ed. Geneva, 1782. Vols I-XII, lacking 3-vol Supplement. 4to, orig wraps; rubbed. bba Mar 12 (86) £110 [Clark]

Anr Ed. Paris, 1825-24-25. 27 vols. 8vo, half calf. pnE Oct 15 (20) £260

Anr copy. Contemp half calf; rubbed. Some leaves loose. S July 28 (1233) £150

Rousselet, Louis

— India and its Native Princes.... L, 1876 [1875]. 4to, orig mor gilt; soiled & worn. With 6 maps & 317 plates. wa Nov 6 (444) $110

Anr Ed. NY, 1876. 4to, cloth; spine spotted. sg Nov 20 (88) $80

Anr copy. With 6 maps & 317 plates. sg Nov 20 (88) $80

Rousset de Missy, Jean. See: Dumont & Rousset de Missy

Rousset, Francois. See: Dodoens, Rembert

Rousset, Leonce
— Les Grands Chefs de l'Armee Francaise. Paris: J. Tallandier, [1923]. 4to, ptd wraps. With 70 tipped-in ports. ha Nov 7 (209) $65

Rouveyre, Edouard
— Connaissances necessaires a un bibliophile. Paris, 1899. 5th Ed. 10 vols. 8vo, modern cloth, orig wraps bound in. O June 16 (167) $70

Roux, Augustin, 1726-76 —& Others
— Dictionnaire domestique portatif, contenant toutes les connoissances relative a l'oeconomie domestique et rurale.... Paris: Lottin le jeune, 1769. 8vo, contemp mor gilt with arms of the comtesse de Provence [Olivier 2549]. Jeanson copy. SM Mar 1 (307) FF24,000

Roux, Joseph
— Recueil des principaux plans des ports et rades de la Mer Mediterranee. Genoa, 1779. Oblong 8vo, contemp calf; repaired & rubbed. With engraved title & 120 charts (of 121) plus a duplicate of Plate 114. Engraved title soiled. S Feb 23 (103) £400 [Broseghini]

Rovelli, Filippo
— Emo. Canti due. Venice: A. Zatta, 1787. 8vo, contemp mor gilt, armorial bdg. S Nov 27 (217) £120 [Olschi]

Rovinsky, Dmitri Alexandrovich
— Dostovernye portrety Moskoviskikh gosudarei. St. Petersburg, 1882. Folio, contemp half mor. With 44 (of 45) ports & views mtd on card. S Nov 17 (921) £190 [Lewinson]

Rowe, George
— Forty-Eight Views of Cottages and Scenery at Sidmouth, Devon. Sidmouth: John Wallis [1826]. Oblong 4to, orig half mor gilt. L July 2 (105) £380

Rowlands, Richard
— A Restitution of Decayed Intelligence. L, 1628. 4to, later mor gilt; rubbed. Lacking final leaf; slightly dampstained at end. S Sept 23 (388) £60 [Rix]
— A Restitution of Decayed Intelligence. L, 1628. 4to, mor gilt by James Toovey; rubbed. Lower corner of final leaf restored. T Mar 19 (400) £100

Rowlandson, Thomas, 1756-1827
— Hungarian and Highland Broad Sword. L, 1799. Oblong folio, half lea. With 24 colored plates. Marginal repair to 1 plate. sg June 11 (339) $3,000
— Medical Caricatures.... NY: Editions Medicina Rara, [1971]. Foreword by Morris H. Saffron. Folio, loose in folding case as issued. With 12 color plates, mtd. sg Jan 15 (121) $500
— Miseries of Human Life. L: Ackermann, 1808 [watermarked 1823]. Oblong 4to, contemp half lea; extremities worn. With 50 hand-colored plates, including title. sg Apr 2 (171) $800
— Rowlandson's World in Miniature. L, 1816. 8 parts in 1 vol. 4to, lev by Riviere, with mor inlay of 2 women on front cover. sg Apr 2 (172) $4,000

Roxburghe...
— The Roxburghe Ballads. L, 1873-74. Ed by Charles Hindley. 2 vols. 4to, orig half mor; joints worn, front joint broken. Mark Twain set, so stated by A. B. Paine. sg Sept 11 (256) $60

Roxburghe Club—London
— Architectural Drawings in the Library of Elton Hall. 1964. C Dec 12 (373) £450 [Weinreb]
— Titus & Vespasian, or the Destruction of Jerusalem.... 1905. cb July 30 (170) $130
— LOCKE, JOHN. - Directions Concerning Education. Being the First Draft of his Thoughts.... 1933. Sydney Cockerell's copy, sgd by him. Ck Sept 5 (18) £100
— SKELTON, RALEIGH ASHLIN & SUMMERSON, JOHN. - A Description of Maps and Architectural Drawings.... 1971. Folio, orig half mor. T Jan 22 (297) £110

Roxburghe Library, John Ker, Duke of
— [Sale Catalogue] A Catalogue of the Library.... L, 1812. Bound with: A Supplement to the Catalogue of the Library. L, 1812. Contemp calf. Priced, with buyers' names in Ms. C Dec 12 (181) £380 [Rota]

Roxburghe, William
— Plants of the Coast of Coromandel.... L, 1795-1819. Vol III only. Contemp half calf gilt; corners rubbed, joints cracking. With 50 hand-colored plates. Sold w.a.f. C Oct 15 (198) £2,300 [Gilbert's]
Anr copy. 3 vols. Folio, contemp russia gilt; broken. With 300 hand-colored plates. Derby—de Belder copy. S Apr 28 (312) £14,000 [Junk]

Roy, Claude
— La France de profil. Lausanne, [1952]. Ltd Ed. 4to, wraps over bds; chipped, spine damaged, 1 fold-out leaf detached. sg Nov 13 (103) $175

Roy, William
— Rede me and be not wrothe, for I saye no thynge but trothe.... Chiswick: Reprinted by Charles Whittingham, 1845. 8vo, orig cloth; spine chipped. Some soiling. Ck Oct 17 (166) £40

Roy, William, 1726-90
— The Military Antiquities of the Romans in Britain. L, 1793. 1st Ed. Folio, modern half mor. With 51 plates, some with marginal dampstaining. cb Dec 18 (154) $325

Anr copy. Contemp half calf; spine rubbed, lower cover detached. With 50 plates. S Jan 16 (427) £55 [Arnold]

Anr copy. Half mor; soiled. With 51 plates. S May 6 (400) £100 [Camberwell]

Royal...
— The Royal Charter of Confirmation granted to the City of London. L: for Samuel Lee & Benjamin Alsop, [1680]. 8vo, later calf; rear cover def. Browned; some marginal repairs. T Mar 19 (271) £42

Royal Horticultural Society. See: Horticultural Society of London

Royal Institute of British Architects
— Catalogue of the Library. L, 1937-38. 2 vols. 4to, orig cloth; rubbed. T July 16 (382) £125

Royal Society of Edinburgh
— Transactions.... Edin., 1788-98. Vols I-IV. 4to, contemp calf. With 48 plates. Includes James Hutton's Theory of the Earth. C Dec 12 (207) £900 [Wheldon & Wesley]

Royaumont, Sieur de. See: Fontaine, Nicolas

Royle, John Forbes
— Illustrations of the Botany and...Natural History of the Himalayan Mountains.... L, 1839. 2 vols. 4to, contemp half mor gilt. With frontis, colored plan, 3 plain & 97 colored plates. One plate cropped with loss of plate numeral. C Oct 15 (199) £2,700 [Joseph]

Anr copy. Contemp half mor. Barclay—de Belder copy. S Apr 28 (314) £4,800 [Burton—Garbett]

Rubens, Peter Paul, 1577-1640
— La Gallerie du Palais de Luxembourg. Paris, 1710. Folio, calf; worn, edges frayed, spine def. With engraved title, 2 ports & 23 plates. Most leaves soiled. S Mar 10 (985) £650 [Clark]

Anr copy. Later half calf; upper cover detached. Marginal repair just touching 1 plate. S May 6 (402) £520 [Margi]

Ruchat, Abraham —& Others
— Etat et delices de la Suisse. Berne, 1776. 4 vols. 12mo, contemp calf; joints worn. With folding map & 34 plates. S Oct 23 (248) £2,800 [Mohler]

Rudbeck, Johannes Reinhold Gustaf
— Svenska Bokband. Stockholm, 1912 [1913]-13-14. Ltd Ed. 3 vols. Folio, contemp half mor. bba June 18 (16) £220 [Quaritch]

Rudder, Samuel, d.1801
— A New History of Gloucestershire. Cirencester, 1779. Folio, later half mor; spine worn. T Dec 18 (32) £140

Anr copy. Contemp half calf; rubbed. With folding map & 17 folding plates. Folding map torn & frayed along fold. T June 18 (55) £350

Rudge, Thomas, 1754-1825
— The History of the County of Gloucester. Gloucester, 1803. 2 vols. 8vo, contemp mor gilt; Vol I recased & inner hinges strengthened. With folding map & 2 plates. T Apr 16 (91) £62

Rudimentum...
— Rudimentum Novitiorum. Luebeck: Lucas Brandis de Schass, 5 Aug 1475. Folio, 19th-cent half mor; lower hinge def. With 2 double-page woodcut maps fully colored in a contemp hand; several initial letters illuminated. Both maps slightly shaved at upper & lower margins; marginalia; repair to penultimate leaf affecting letters of last word. S June 25 (272) £50,000

Ruding, Rogers
— Annals of the Coinage of Britain and its Dependencies.... L, 1819. 6 vols including 1 vol of plates, 8vo & 4to, contemp half mor; joints worn; plate vol broken. With map, plan & 118 plates. bba Oct 30 (492) £55 [Shapero]

Ruemann, Arthur
— Das illustrierte Buch des XIX Jahrhunderts in England, Frankreich und Deutschland, 1790-1860 Leipzig, 1930. sg May 14 (353) $90

Rueppell, Eduard, 1794-1884
— Atlas zu der Reise in nordlichen Afrika...Zoologie [all pbd]. Frankfurt, 1826. 5 parts in 1 vol. Folio, contemp bds; broken, lower cover & backstrip detached. With 6 plain & 113 hand-colored plates. Some plate numerals just shaved. C Apr 8 (193) £1,050 [Quaritch]
— Systematische Uebersicht der Voegel Nord-Ost Afrika's. Frankfurt, 1845. Illus by

Joseph Wolf. 8vo, orig bds. With 50 hand-colored litho plates. Haverschmidt copy. B Feb 24 (252) HF1,600

Ruffhead, Owen
— The Statutes at Large from Magna Charta to 1761. L, 1763. 8 vols. Folio, contemp calf; worn. pnE Nov 12 (139) £50

Ruffi, Antoine de
— Histoire de la ville de Marseille. Marseilles: Henri Martel, 1696. 2 vols. Folio, contemp mor gilt with arms of Marseilles. S Nov 27 (96) £400 [Greenwood]

Ruggle, George, 1575-1622
— Ignoramus.... L, 1630. 1st Ed. 12mo, old vellum; some wear. T Mar 19 (395) £40

Ruiz de Montoya, Antonio
— Conquista espiritual hecha por los religiosos de la Compania de Jesus.... Madrid, 1639. 4to, contemp calf; lacking front free endpaper. Minor dampstains at bottom of inner portion of 1st 25 & few final leaves. sg Sept 18 (260) $275

Rules...
— Rules and Regulations for the Sword Exercise of the Cavalry.... L, 1796. 8vo, contemp half vellum; spine lacking. With 29 folding plates. Prelims spotted. Ck Jan 30 (124) £100

Rummonds, Richard Gabriel. See: Fletcher, Cora C.

Rumpf, Georg Eberhard
— Herbarium Amboinense plurimas conplectens arbores frutices,.,., Amst.: M. Uytwerf, [1741]-50-55. 7 vols, including Auctuarium. Folio, contemp calf with arms of the Earl of Bute. With frontis, ports of Rumpf & Burmann & 700 plates. 2 plates coming loose, some discolored. Derby—de Belder copy. S Apr 28 (315) £7,000 [Chong]

Rumpolt, Marx
— Ein new Kochbuch, das ist ein gruendtliche Beschreibung.... Frankfurt: J. Feyerabend, 1587. 2 parts in 1 vol. Folio, old half calf; rubbed. Wormed at blank inner upper margin; lacking blank leaf following p 41. Westbury-Crahan copy. P Nov 25 (402) $4,500

Runge, Heinrich, 1817-86
— Die Schweiz in Original-Ansichten.... Darmstadt, 1866-70. Vols I & III (of 3). Orig cloth; worn. HN Nov 26 (409) DM3,800

Rusca, Louis
— Recueil des dessins de differens batimans construits a Saint-Petersbourg. St. Petersburg, 1810. 2 parts in 1 vol. Folio, contemp half mor; worn. Tear to some inner blank margins; last few plates slightly wormed; some stains & soiling. S Feb 24 (408) £1,700 [Weinreb]

Ruscelli, Girolamo
— Prima [seconda, terza] Parte de Secreti.... Venice: G. Bariletto, 1575. 8vo, contemp vellum. Tp stained & with owner's stamp. S Nov 10 (433) £210 [Phelps]

Ruscone, G. G. See: Moltoni & Ruscone

Rusconi, Giovanni Antonio
— Della architettura. Venice: Gioliti, 1590. 1st Ed, Issue not indicated. Folio, modern bds. Tp & dedication in facsimile. FD June 11 (2114) DM1,800

Rusden, George William
— History of Australia. Melbourne & L, 1897. 2d Ed. 3 vols. 8vo, cloth. Minor defs. kh Mar 16 (444B) A$150

Rusden, Moses
— A Further Discovery of Bees. L, 1679. 8vo, early 19th-cent mor; rebacked. With frontis & 3 folding plates. Some worming in upper inner corners. Johannson copy. sg Jan 15 (168) $350

Rush, Benjamin, 1745-1813
— An Account of the Bilious Remitting Yellow Fever.... Phila., 1794. 1st Ed. 8vo, new cloth. S May 28 (773) £180
— An Eulogium, Intended to Perpetuate the Memory of David Rittenhouse.... Phila., [1796]. 1st Ed. 8vo, orig wraps; lacking rear wrap. wa Sept 23 (387) $100

Rushworth, John, 1612?-90
— Historical Collections. L, 1659-80-92-1722-21-1680. Mixed Ed. 8 vols. Folio, old calf; rebacked. With 2 double-page plates & 8 ports. O May 12 (169) $400
Anr Ed. L, 1721. 8 vols. 8vo, contemp calf; hinges cracked, not uniform. pn Mar 5 (57) £70 [Camberley]
— The Tryal of Thomas, Earl of Strafford.... L, 1680. Folio, contemp calf; rubbed, joints worn. O Feb 24 (163) £110

Ruskin, John, 1819-1900
See also: Doves Press; Fore-Edge Paintings; Kelmscott Press
— Catalogue of the Sketches and Drawings by J. M. W. Turner...in Marlborough House.... L, 1857. 8vo, mor by the Doves Bindery, dated 1910. sg Apr 2 (173) $500
— Circular Respecting Memorial Studies of St. Mark's, Venice. L, [n.d.]. 8vo, mor gilt by

the Doves Bindery, 1911. sg June 11 (166) $325
— Fors Clavigera. Letters to the Workmen and Labourers of Great Britain. Keston & Orpington, 1871-87. 1st Ed. 9 vols (including Index). 8vo, calf; spines rubbed at extremities, some corners bumped. cb Sept 11 (311) $130
— General Statement Explaining the Nature and Purposes of St. George's Guild.... Orpington, 1882. 8vo, mor gilt with flourishes. sg Apr 2 (175) $425
— The King of the Golden River. L, 1851. 1st Ed. Illus by Richard Doyle. 4to, orig bds; worn, rebacked. S Oct 6 (789) £115 [Quaritch]
Anr Ed. L, 1932. Illus by Arthur Rackham. Wraps, in d/j. With 4 color plates. sg Oct 30 (184) $130
One of 570. Orig vellum. With 4 color plates. With an orig pen & wash sketch. sg Oct 30 (183) $3,400
Anr copy. Vellum gilt. With 4 colored plates. sg June 11 (328) $225
— Modern Painters. Orpington, 1888. 6 vols, including Index. 8vo, orig cloth; slightly rubbed & stained. Some spotting. bba Apr 23 (65) £35 [Axe]
— The Queen's Gardens: a Lecture.... Manchester, 1864. 8vo, lev gilt by Doves Bindery dated 1911. sg Apr 2 (174) $650
— The Seven Lamps of Architecture. L, 1849. 1st Ed. 8vo, contemp cloth; worn. With 14 plates. HN Nov 26 (109) DM660
— The Storm Cloud of the Nineteenth Century. Orpington, 1884. 4to, mor gilt by the Doves Binder, 1909. sg Apr 2 (176) $850
— Works. L, 1903-12. Library Ed. 39 vols. Orig cloth; soiled, 1 spine torn & repaired. Ck Nov 7 (34) £600; S Feb 23 (40) £750 [McKenzie]
Anr copy. Half mor. sg Dec 4 (170) $1,800

Russell, Alexander, 1715?-68
— The Natural History of Aleppo.... L, 1794. 2d Ed. 2 vols. 4to, contemp half lea; worn. bba Dec 18 (228) £75 [Greyfriars]

Russell, Bertrand, 1872-1970
— A Critical Exposition of the Philosophy of Leibnitz. Cambr., 1900. 1st Ed. 8vo, orig cloth; extremities rubbed. Some spotting of margins. Ck Nov 21 (60) £150

Russell, Charles Marion
— More Rawhides. Great Falls, 1925. 1st Ed. 4to, orig wraps; chipped. wa Mar 5 (407) $140
— Pen and Ink Drawings.... Pasadena: Trail's End Publishing, [1946]. Nos 1 & 2. 2 vols. cb Jan 8 (166) $200
— Rawhide Rawlins Rides Again.... Pasadena: Trail's End, [1948]. One of 300. Calf. wa June 25 (270) $130

Russell, Eric Frank
— Sinister Barrier. Reading: Fantasy Press, 1948. One of 500. Currey's A State bdg, in d/j. cb Sept 28 (1108) $50

Russell, John Scott, 1808-82
— The Modern System of Naval Architecture. L, 1865. 3 vols. Folio, bdg not indicated. Library markings. Sold w.a.f. Franklin Institute copy. F Sept 12 (353) $1,500

Russell, Kenneth Fitzpatrick
— British Anatomy, 1525-1800. Melbourne, [1963]. One of 750, sgd. bba June 18 (9) £70 [Goldman]; CA Apr 12 (213) A$75

Russell, P. —& Price, Owen
— England Displayed. L, 1769. 2 vols. Folio, contemp calf; rubbed. pn May 21 (392) £580 [Nicholson]
Anr copy. 2 vols in 1. Folio, contemp calf; hinges split. With frontis, 54 county maps & 83 plates. pn May 21 (423) £650 [Nicholson]

Russell, Richard, d.1771
— Dissertation on the Use of Sea-Water.... L, 1752. 12mo, contemp calf. pnE Dec 17 (172) £110 [Quaritch]
— A Dissertation on the Use of Sea Water.... L, 1769. 8vo, contemp sheep; joints cracked, spine ends restored. Marginal foxing. sg Jan 15 (122) $100

Russell, Samuel
— History and Notes Relating to the Currituck Shooting Club. [N.p.]: Pelton & King, 1925. sg Oct 23 (232) $300

Russell, Sir William Howard
— The Atlantic Telegraph. L: Day & Son, [1865]. 4to, cloth. With 25 plates & 1 chart. pn Dec 11 (181) £200 [Nicholson]
Anr copy. Orig cloth; worn. With litho title & 24 tinted plates & 1 plain plate. Clean tear to 1 plate. pn Apr 30 (345) £100 [Bookroom]
— The British Expedition to the Crimea. L, 1858. 8vo, later half mor; bumped & rubbed. Some tears & creases to maps; some repairs. cb Dec 18 (155) $95
— A Diary in the East during the Tour of the Prince and Princess of Wales. L, 1869. 8vo, half calf; rubbed. With 6 colored plates. O Sept 23 (173) $50

Russell, Sir William Howard —& Dudley, Robert

— A Memorial of the Marriage of Albert Edward, Prince of Wales, and...Alexandra, Princess of Denmark.... L: Day & Son, [1864]. 2 vols. Folio, contemp cloth; spine defective. With 2 ports & 41 plates; text & plates loose. pn Jan 22 (109) £90 [Russell]

Russians...

— The Russians in California. San Francisco: California Historical Society, 1933. cb Oct 9 (170) $70

Rutherford, Samuel

— The Due Right of Presbyteries. L, 1644. 4to, old half calf, new endpapers. Some leaves repaired in blank gutters; marginal repairs. O May 12 (170) $210

Ruthven, Patrick, Lord. See: Ladies

Rutland, John Henry Manners, 5th Duke of. See: Manners, John Henry

Rutledge, Archibald Hamilton

— Hunter's Choice. West Hartford, Vermont, 1946. One of 475. Illus by Paul Bransom. 4to, cloth. sg Oct 23 (460) $60

Rutter, John

— Delineations of Fonthill and its Abbey. L, 1823. 4to, bdg not described. With hand-colored engraved title, folding map & 14 plates, a few hand-colored. bba Apr 9 (265) £160 [Dawson]

Anr copy. Contemp half mor; rubbed, lacking head of spine. With engraved title, 15 plates & folding map; title & 2 plates hand-colored. L.p. copy. S Nov 17 (678) £240 [Clegg]

Anr copy. Contemp half sheep; spine badly rubbed. With additional title & 13 plates, all mtd India-proofs. L.p. copy. sg Dec 18 (215) $150

Rutter, Owen, 1889-1944. See: Golden Cockerel Press

Ruxton, George Frederick

— Life in the Far West. Edin., 1849. 1st Ed. 8vo, orig cloth; rubbed. bba Nov 13 (113) £55 [Axe]

Ruytinck, Symeon

— Gulden Legende vande Roomsche Kercke.... L, 1612. 2 parts in 1 vol. 4to, contemp vellum bds; rubbed & soiled. Small burn hole in R4 affecting a few letters. bba Oct 16 (54) £420 [Sokol]

Ryan, William Redmond

— Personal Adventures in Upper and Lower California in 1848-9.... L, 1850. 1st Ed. 2 vols. 12mo, mor gilt. With 23 plates. sg Dec 4 (171) $325

Rycke, Josse de, 1587-1627

— De Capitolio Romano Commentarius. Ghent: C. Marius, 1617. Folio, 18th-cent calf gilt. S July 14 (428) £100

Anr Ed. Leiden, 1669. 12mo, contemp vellum. With engraved title & 16 plates. sg Mar 26 (253) $50

Ryff, Walther Hermann

— Confect Buechlin, und Hauss Apoteck.... Frankfurt: C. Egenolph, 1544. 8vo, new vellum. Tp & next 17 leaves crudely repaired at upper margin affecting text; a1 short at fore-edge & possibly from anr copy; browned; last few leaves damp-damaged at upper margins. Crahan copy. P Nov 25 (405) $1,600

— Des aller furtreflichsten hochsten unnd adelichsten gscoepffs aller Creaturen.... Strassburg: Balthassar Beck, 1541. Folio, old vellum. With 25 full-page woodcuts. Lacking last blank (replaced with anr leaf of old blank paper); repair to outer margin of B5 just affecting a few letters; short tear in G6 mended without loss; some thumbmarks & stains. S Nov 27 (284) £8,500 [Quaritch]

— Der furnembsten, notwendigsten, der gantzen Architectur. Nuremberg: G. Heyn, 1558. ("Der Architectur furnembsten, notwendigsten....") Folio, contemp blind-stamped pigskin. Some browning. HK Nov 4 (710) DM5,200

— Das new grosse distillier Buch. Frankfurt: Christian Egenolff, 1545. 4to, contemp blindstamped pigskin over wooden bds; worn. Lacking 2 unnumbered leaves & 21 numbered leaves. HK Nov 4 (1106) DM1,300

— New Kochbuech fuer die Krancken. Frankfurt: Christian Egenolff, 1545. 4to, contemp blindstamped calf; restored. Some browning. Crahan copy. P Nov 25 (406) $4,500

— Von Richtem Verstandt, Wag und Gewicht.... N.p., [1540]. Folio, later bds. Franklin Institute copy. F Sept 12 (245) $3,250

Ryley, Arthur Beresford

— Old Paste. L, 1913. 4to, cloth. bba Aug 28 (61) £85 [Graves Johnston]

RYORI...

Ryori...
— Ryori Monogatori. [N.p.], 1643. 270mm by 170mm, wraps. Worm trails repaired. Crahan copy. P Nov 25 (407) $5,750

Anr Ed. [N.p.], 1664. 192mm by 136mm, wraps. Crahan copy. P Nov 25 (408) $8,750

Ryoyi...
— Ryoyi Taizen. Tokyo, 1714. 250mm by 185mm, wraps Some worming & waterstains. Crahan copy. P Nov 25 (409) $1,500

Ryusui Katsuma
— Umi No Sachi. [N.p., 1762]. 2 vols in 1. 286mm by 203mm, wraps. With 72 color illusts. Repaired. This copy with 111 pp. Crahan copy. P Nov 25 (410) $2,000

Ryves, Bruno
— Angliae Ruina: or, Englands Ruine. [L], 1647. 3 parts in 1 vol. 8vo, 19th-cent calf; spine soiled. A8 & 1st 2 leaves torn & repaired. Ck Oct 17 (162) £50

S

S., I. F.
— Algemeine Geschichte der Laender und Voelker von America. Halle, 1752-53. In 2 vols. 4to, contemp vellum; worn. With 66 maps & plates. sg Dec 18 (218) $225

S., N. See: Present...

S., S.
— Representations of the Embossed Chased & Engraved Subjects...which Decorate the Tobacco Box and Cases, Belonging to the Past Overseers Society.... See: Representations...

Saalmuller, Max
— Lepidopteren von Madagascar. Frankfurt, 1884-91. 4to, contemp half mor. With port & 14 colored plates. S May 28 (597) £400

Saavedra Fajarda, Diego de, 1584-1648
— Idea principis christiano-politici.... Pest: J. G. Mauss, 1748. Folio, contemp mor gilt. Beckford copy. S May 21 (165) £1,200 [Goldschmidt]

Sabartes, Jaime
— Picasso: Toreros. L & Monte Carlo, 1961. Oblong 4to, orig cloth. S Oct 6 (688) £160 [Eliopoulos]

Anr copy. With 4 lithos, 1 colored. sg Feb 5 (274) $150

Anr copy. Orig cloth, in d/j. sg June 11 (318) $175

— A los Toros mit Picasso. Monte Carlo, 1961. 4to, orig cloth. S Sept 23 (689) £120 [Eliopoulos]

Sabatini, Rafael, 1875-1950
— Works. Bost., 1924-37. Definitive Ed. 34 vols. 8vo, half calf. ha May 22 (77) $375

Sabellicus, Marcus Antonius Coccius
— De Venetis magistratibus. Venice: Antonius de Strata de Cremona, 19 Jan 1488/89. 4to, 19th-cent mor gilt; rubbed. Two wormholes restored, 1 leaf misprinted, obscuring c.20 letters, anr forecorner restored without loss. 26 leaves. Goff S-9. P Dec 15 (157) $1,200

Sabin, Arthur K. See: Hardie & Sabin

Sabin, Joseph, 1821-81
— A Dictionary of Books Relating to America. Amst., 1961-62. ("Bibliotheca Americana: A Dictionary of Books....") 29 vols in 15 Worn. sg Jan 22 (271) $650

Mini-Print Ed. NY, [1967]. 29 vols in 2. Oblong 4to, orig cloth; soiled. Library markings. O June 16 (169) $310; S July 13 (70) £350

Readex Microprint Ed. NY, [c.1967]. 29 vols in 1. 8vo, cards loose in cloth solander case; rubbed. sg May 14 (24) $110

Sacheverell, Henry
[-] The Tryal of Dr. Henry Sacheverell.... L, 1710. Folio, contemp calf; spine chipped. With 4 speeches on the Sacheverell affair, 1710. sg Oct 9 (307) $70

Sackville-West, Victoria, 1892-1962
— Collected Poems. L: Hogarth Press, 1933. One of 150. Vol I only. Half vellum, in def d/j. S Mar 9 (868) £160 [Whiteson]

— The Heir. L, [1922]. 1st Ed, One of 50. Orig half cloth; soiled. Ck Apr 24 (184) £160

— Sissinghurst. L: Hogarth Press, 1931. 1st Ed, Out-of-series copy. Orig bds. S Mar 9 (370) £170 [Whiteson]

Sacrobosco, Johannes
— La Sfera. Florence: Giunti, 1571. 4to, contemp vellum; soiled. Small hole at top of title; tear in fore-margin of F3; some marginal stains. S June 25 (130) £330

— Sphaera mundi. Venice, 1508. ("Textus Sphaerae....") Bound with: Julius Firmicus Maternus. De nativitatibus. Venice, 1490. 124 (of 126) leaves. Goff F-190. Folio, old calf; joints starting, dampstained. Title holed, affecting text; last leaf lacking. sg Jan 15 (362) $450

Sade, Donatien Alphonse Francois, Marquis de, 1740-1814

— Eugenie de Franval. Paris: Georges Artigues, 1948. One of 50. Illus by Valentine Hugo. 8vo, loose as issued in wraps. With 9 drypoints. sg Feb 12 (103) $350

— Opus Sadicum: A Philosophical Romance. Paris, 1889. One of 250. 8vo, syn. Reprint of the Holland, 1791 Ed of Justine. sg Feb 12 (101) $60; sg Feb 12 (102) $50

Sadeler, Marco

— Vestigi delle antichita di Roma.... Prague, 1606. Oblong folio, 19th-cent vellum bds, with arms of William Stirling Maxwell. With engraved title & 50 plates. Some outer margins repaired. C May 13 (90) £600 [Thomas]

Sadleir, Michael, 1888-1957

— XIX Century Fiction. A Bibliographical Record. L, 1951. One of 1,025. 2 vols. 4to, cloth; covers dampstained. bba Aug 20 (289) £160 [Hashimoto]

Anr copy. Cloth, in d/js. cba Feb 5 (153) $350; pnE Jan 28 (320) £240 [Smith]; sg Jan 22 (272) $275

Saenger, Eugen

— Raketen-Flugtechnik. Berlin & Munich, 1933. 8vo, cloth, orig front wrap laid in. Inscr. sg Jan 15 (358) $100

Sagard-Theodat, Gabriel

— Le Grand Voyage du pays des Hurons. Paris, 1632. 2 parts in 1 vol. 8vo, modern vellum. Ptd & engraved titles & 3 other leaves in facsimile. Signature N inserted from another copy. Sold w.a.f. CNY Dec 19 (225) $700

Sage, Dean

— The Ristigouche and its Salmon Fishing.... Edin., 1888. One of 105. Folio, cloth; worn. With 20 etchings. Inscr to Mr. and Mrs. Lansing & with an ALs to Mr. Lansing laid in. sg Oct 23 (461) $8,000

One of 250 with 2 sgd color plates. Lea gilt. Cornelius Ryan's copy. sg May 21 (180) $425

Anr Ed. Goshen, CT, 1973. One of 205. 4to, mor; worn. With 2 color plates sgd by the artists. sg Oct 23 (462) $475

Sage, Dean —& Others

— Salmon and Trout. NY, 1902. One of 100. Illus by A. B. Frost. Half mor. sg Oct 23 (466) $100

Sailland, Maurice Edmond. See: Curnonsky, M. Ed.

Sainctyon, Louis de

— Les Edicts et orgonnances des roys.... Paris: Veuve Abel Langelier, 1610. Folio, contemp mor gilt with arms of Henri IV [Olivier, 2492, fers 7, 9 & 10]. Dedication copy. Jeanson copy. SM Mar 1 (495) FF80,000

St. Clair, Philip R.

— Frederic Remington: The American West. Kent, 1978. Oblong 4to, cloth; soiled. Sgd. cb Jan 8 (331) $55

Saint German, Christopher

— The Dialogue in English.... L, 1623. 8vo, contemp sheep, broken, no endpapers. Marginalia. bba Mar 26 (155) £35 [Fletcher]

St. John, J. Hector. See: Crevecoeur, Michel Guillaume St. Jean de

Saint-Amant, Marc Antoine gerard, Sieur de, 1594-1661?

— Animalium quadrupedum omnis generis verae et artificiosissimae delineationes. Anvers: Everard Hoeswinckel, 1583. 8vo, contemp vellum; worn. With frontis & 20 plates. Jeanson copy. SM Mar 1 (261) FF17,000

Saint-Andre, Francois de

— Reflexions nouvelles sur les causes des maladies et de leurs symptomes. Paris, 1687. 12mo, contemp calf; rubbed. bba Nov 13 (48) £55 [P & P Books]

Saint-Chamans, August de, Vicomte

— Du systeme d'impot fonde sur les principes de l'economie politique. Paris, 1820. 8vo, calf gilt, with Signet arms; spine chipped, rubbed. Inscribed leaf 4I partially stuck to previous page along inner margin; spotted. P Sept 24 (384) $175

Saint-Gelais, Octovien de, 1468-1502

— Sensuyt la chasse & le dapart damours.... Paris: Veuve Jehan Trepperel, [c.1515]. 2 parts in 1 vol. 4to, mor gilt by Joly. Jeanson copy. SM Mar 1 (496) FF170,000

Saint-Lambert, Jean Francois de

— Les Saisons. Amst., 1769. 8vo, modern calf gilt by A. Winstanley. With 5 plates. S Sept 23 (596) £35 [Archdale]

7th Ed. Amst. [Paris?], 1775. 8vo, With 7 plates. C May 13 (50) £150 [Greenwood]

Anr copy. Mor gilt by Bayntun. S July 28 (1142) £150

Anr Ed. Paris, 1823. 3 vols. 8vo, mor gilt by Masson-Debonnelle. L.p. copy on papier velin, extra-illus with 100 plates. C Dec 3 (163) £750 [Braunschweig]

Saint-Marc, Camille de. See: Sourbets & Saint-Marc

Saint-Non, Jean Claude Richard de
— Voyage pittoresque ou description des royaumes de Naples et de Sicile. Paris, 1781-86. 4 vols in 5. Folio, half calf; rebacked. With 285 plates & maps only. Small stamps on half-titles. S Oct 23 (264) £2,400 [Marinoni]

Saint-Pierre, Bernardin de, 1713-1814
— Paul and Virginia, an Indian Story. L, 1839. ("Paul and Virginia.") 8vo, mor gilt by Zaehnsdorf; extremities worn. With port & 28 plates in india-proof state. Extra-illus with 8 plates after Albert Lalauze, each in 2 states. sg Feb 12 (273) $100
— Paul et Virginie. Paris, 1789. Copy on papier velin d'essone with 4 proof plates before letters & a suite eau-forte. 18mo, mor extra by Mercier Sr. de Cuzin. C Dec 3 (164) £2,600 [Lardenchet]

Anr Ed. Paris, 1838. 8vo, 19th-cent calf gilt; joints rubbed. With 34 plates. S Nov 27 (121) £110 [Tensehart]
— Voyage a l'isle de France, a l'isle de Bourbon.... Amst. & Paris, 1773. 1st Ed. 2 vols in 1. 8vo, mor extra by Mercier. Sold as a bdg. FD June 11 (1056) DM22,000

Saint-Victor, Jacques M. B. Bins de
— Tableau historique et pittoresque de Paris. Paris, 1809. 3 vols. 4to, contemp half mor; top of 1 spine damaged. Titles stamped; some leaves loose; some stains. bba Feb 5 (357) £350 [Shapero]

Salaman, Malcolm Charles
— British Book Illustration Yesterday and To-Day. L: The Studio, 1923. Folio, cloth. With c.100 plates. sg Oct 30 (186) $300
— The Etchings of James McBey. L, 1929. sg Feb 5 (219) $100; sg June 4 (203) $225
— Masters of Modern Etching: Frank W. Benson. L, 1925. Oblong 4to, bds. Tp & half-title foxed. sg Oct 23 (183) $120
— Modern Book Illustrators and their Work. L, 1914. 4to, modern half mor. Pen notations on contents page. sg Oct 30 (185) $130

Salel, Hugues, 1504-53
— Les Oeuvres. Paris: Pour Etienne Roffet, [1540]. 8vo, mor gilt by Bauzonnet. Jeanson copy. SM Mar 1 (500) FF37,000

Saliceto, Guilielmus de
— De salute corporis. Leipzig: Wolfgang Stoeckel, 1495. 2 parts in 1 vol. 4to, later half calf; rubbed. Bound with anr work. Some worming throughout, affecting c.12 letters per page; tp sprung. 9 (of 10) leaves; lacking final blank. HC 14153. P Sept 24 (208) $1,400

Salinas, Miguel
— Rhetorica en lengua castellana. Alcala de Henares: Juan de Brocar, 8 Feb 1541. 4to, 19th-cent calf gilt, armorial bdg; worn. FD June 11 (136) DM10,000

Salinger, J. D.
— The Catcher in the Rye. Bost., 1951. 1st Ed. In chipped d/j. cb May 7 (135) $475

Salisbury, Richard Anthony
— The Paradisus Londinensis Containing Plants Cultivated in the Vicinity of the Metropolis. L, 1806-[9]. Vol I, Parts 1 & 2 bound in 2 vols. Half calf; rubbed. With 119 hand-colored plates. pn Apr 30 (120) £2,000 [Weldon & Wesley]

Anr copy. 3 parts in 1 vol. 4to, half calf; partially preserving old spine, vellum corners. Lacking the text to the unpbd plates 118-122. With Ms index added at end. Plesch—de Belder copy. S Apr 28 (316) £2,800 [Hill]

Salisbury, William
— The Botanist's Companion. L, 1816. 2 vols. 8vo, orig bds; marked & rubbed. With folding frontis. bba Sept 25 (219) £95 [Maggs]

Sallander, Hans
— Bibliotheca Walleriana.... Stockholm, 1955. 2 vols. bba Oct 16 (398) £160 [Dawson]

Sallengre, Albert Henri de
— Ebrietatis Encomium, or the Praise of Drunkenness. L: E. Curll, 1723. 12mo, contemp calf; worn & broken. cb Feb 19 (208) $110
— Novus Thesaurus Antiquitatum Romanarum. The Hague, 1716-19. 3 vols. Folio, contemp calf; broken. sg Oct 9 (308) $50

Sallustius Crispus, Caius, 86-34 B.C.
— The Famous Cronicle of Warre.... L, 1557. 4to, 19th-cent mor; broken. Minor marginal repairs to tp; small worming repair to head margin of a2 just touching 1 letter. Part of STC 10752. C Dec 12 (356) £380 [Finch]
— Liber de bello Iugurtino. Liber de coniuratione. Leipzig: Martinus Herbipolensis, 1510. Folio, later wraps. Wormhole in fore-margin throughout most of the book just touching some text; a few small wormholes at end; copious interlinear & arginal notes in a contemp hand throughout; some dampstains at end. S May 21 (74) £300 [Quaritch]
— Opera. Venice: Aldus, 1509. 8vo, 19th-cent half mor; front joint weak. Marginal

dampstaining & minor worming at beginning & end; 1st few leaves remargined. sg Oct 9 (84) $225
— Works. Dublin, 1744. 2 parts in 1 vol. 4to, contemp calf. pnE Dec 17 (12) £70 [McCormack]

Sallwigt, Gregorius Anglus. See: Welling, Georg von

Salmon...
— Salmon Fishing on the Great Wacheeshoo. [Montreal, n.d.]. 12 pp. 8vo, ptd wraps; broken. Map torn in several places; some cellotape repairs. sg Oct 23 (465) $500

Salmon, Andre
— Le Manuscrit trouve dans un chapeau. Paris, 1919. One of 750 but this copy with a suite of the plates on velin bleu. Illus by Pablo Picasso. 4to, half mor, orig wraps bound in. S Oct 6 (690) £60 [Luia]
— Modigliani, sa vie et son oeuvre. Paris, 1926. 4to, orig wraps; worn. With 50 plates. U Jan 6 (166) $80
— Rive Gauche: Quartier Latin, Plaisance Montparnasse.... Paris, 1951. One of 30 on japon imperial with the self-port sgd, with an orig sgd etching & an extra suite of the illusts on arches. Illus by Maurice de Vlaminck. 4to, vellum, orig wraps bound in. With 15 plates, including cover, & 2 facsimiles of drawings. This copy with anr uncolored suite on chine & anr state of the port on vellum mtd on upper cover. S June 17 (60) £1,500 [Marks]
One of 10 on japon nacre with the etched self-port sgd, 2 suites of the port & illusts on arches (in color) & on chine, a cancelled copper plate & a sgd etching. Orig wraps, unsewn. With 15 plates, including cover, & 2 facsimiles of drawings. S June 17 (59) £2,100 [Dennistoun]

Salmon, Richard
— Trout Flies. NY, 1975. One of 560. 4to, lea. With mtd samples of fly-tying materials. sg Oct 23 (468) $225

Salmon, Thomas, 1679-1767
Modern History. L, 1725-39. Vols I-VI only. Contemp calf; rubbed. Ck Nov 21 (362) £170
Anr Ed. L, 1739. Vols I-II only (of 3). 4to, modern cloth. Library stamps, some perforated; tears in a few leaves. bba Feb 5 (336) £200 [Whiteson]

Salmon, William, 1644-1713
— Ars Anatomica, or the Anatomy of Humane Bodies.... L, 1714. 8vo, contemp calf; worn. With port & 29 plates. Tp inserted, possibly from anr copy; last leaf loose. S May 28 (774) £140

— Ars Chirurgica: a Compendium.... L, 1698. 8vo, later half mor. Library markings. Sold w.a.f. Franklin Institute copy. F Sept 12 (154) $350
— Botanologia. The English Herbal. L, 1710-11. 2 vols. Folio, orig calf; rebacked. pnE Dec 17 (257) £520 [Traylen]
Anr copy. Half mor; rubbed. Lacking index at end; 2H1 def; some other leaves frayed & repaired; some browning & soiling; tp dust-soiled; some worming affecting text. Sold w.a.f. S Nov 10 (552) £220 [Russell]
— Doron Medicum: or, a Supplement to the New London Dispensatory. L, 1690. 8vo, calf; hinges weak. Lacking 1st leaf; port loosely inserted; worming in some inner margins in 2 sections of the book; some lines in upper margins shaved; lower outer corners of 3 leaves def; small tear in Uu4. S May 28 (776) £120
— Medicina Practica: or, Practical Physick.... L, 1692. 8vo, half calf gilt. With 8 plates of alchemy; port inserted (mtd). Tp mtd; upper outer corner of H3 torn; rust-hole in Tt6; closely cut affecting some headlines. S May 28 (775) £140

Salm-Reifferscheidt-Dick, Joseph von
— Monographia generum aloes et mesmebryanthemi. Duesseldorf & Bonn, 1836-63. 1st Ed. 7 parts in 2 vols. 4to, contemp half calf. With 352 hand-colored plates. Some captions cropped. Horticultural Society of New York—de Belder copy. S Apr 28 (317) £5,500 [Joseph & Sawyer]

Salnove, Robert de, d. c.1690
— La Venerie royale.... Paris: Antoine de Sommaville, 1665. 4to, mor gilt by Marius Michel. Jeanson copy. SM Mar 1 (502) FF7,000
Anr Ed. Paris: Mille de Beaujeu, 1672. 2 vols. 12mo, 18th-cent mor gilt. Jeanson copy. SM Mar 1 (503) FF4,500

Salomon, Bishop
— Glossae ex illustrissimis collectae auctoribus. [Augsburg: Monastery of SS. Ulrich & Afra, c.1474]. Folio, contemp blind-stamped pigskin over wooden bds; spine damaged, 1 clasp def. Arms of the Planta family emblazoned in lower margin of 1st text leaf. ff. 145-50 & 263-70 supplied from a shorter copy. 288 leaves. Goff S-21. S June 25 (52) £5,600

Salomons, Sir David Lionel
— Breguet (1747-1823). L, 1921. One of 1,000. 2 vols, with Supplement but lacking Addenda. Orig wraps; rubbed. bba Dec 4 (226) £40 [Hay]

Salomonsen, Finn
— Gronlands fugle. The Birds of Greenland. Copenhagen, 1949-51. 3 vols. 4to. With 52 color plates. Serious insect damage to 10 leaves. B Feb 24 (326) HF260

Salt, Sir Henry
— A Voyage to Abyssinia. L, 1814. 4to, contemp half calf. With 7 maps & 27 plates, 1 map hand-colored. Ck May 8 (299) £250

Anr copy. Contemp calf; bumped, rebacked. With 7 maps & charts & 27 plates. Some stains; lacking half-title. Ck May 8 (362) £170

Anr copy. Contemp calf; rubbed, broken. With 34 plates & maps. Some stains. Ck May 15 (74) £170

Anr copy. Contemp calf; rebacked. With 7 maps & 27 plates. FD Dec 2 (1045) DM2,000

Anr copy. Contemp bds; rubbed, edges worn. With 7 maps & charts & 27 plates. Several signatures dampstained, affecting text & plates in margins. ha Sept 19 (276) $50

Anr copy. Half calf. With 7 maps (1 hand-colored) & 27 plates. Lacking half-title; last leaf repaired. S Oct 23 (464) £250 [Vecseri]

Salt Lake City
— The Salt Lake City Directory and Business Guide, for 1869. Salt Lake City, 1869. Compiled by Edward L. Sloan. 8vo, half cloth; rubbed, joint cracked. Some soiling & staining to corners. cb Mar 19 (240) $600

Salva Y Mallen, Pedro
— Catalogo de la Biblioteca de Salva. Valencia, 1872. 2 vols. 8vo, cloth. sg May 14 (650) $275

Anr Ed. Barcelona, 1963 & Madrid, 1968. 2 vols plus separately issued Index. 4to, half mor. Facsimile of the 1872 Ed. sg Sept 18 (262) $70

Salvado, Rudesindo, Bishop
— Memorie storiche dell' Australia.... Rome, 1851. 8vo, contemp mor gilt. With folding map. C Oct 15 (170) £150 [McCormick]

Salviani, Ippolito
— Aquatilium animalium historiae.... Rome, 1554 [colophon dated Jan 1558]. Folio, late 17th-cent calf gilt; restored. With engraved title & 98 engravings on 81 plates. Some foxing; tp grazed & with small piece cut from lower blank corner; marginal tear in Q3; small tear in CC3. S Oct 23 (748) £1,600 [Bishop]

Salvin, Francis Henry —& Brodrick, William
— Falconry in the British Isles. L, 1873. 8vo, cloth. With 28 colored plates. sg May 21 (103) $900

Salvin, Osbert. See: Sclater & Salvin

Salvio, Alessandro
— Il Giuoco degli scacchi. Naples, 1723. Half calf. Browned & spotted throughout. pn Mar 26 (491) £160 [Furstenberg]

Samain, Albert Victor, 1858-1900
— Contes. Paris, 1926. One of 25 with 2 suites of proofs in sanguine & in colors & with the suppressed plate. 4to, text in mor extra, extra plates loose in folding case & slipcase. sg Jan 8 (271) $900

Sampson, John. See: Gregynog Press

San Francisco
See also: Colville, Samuel
— The Bay of San Francisco.... Chicago, 1892. 2 vols. 4to, orig mor; scuffed. cb Oct 9 (172) $60

— Business Directory of San Francisco and Principal Towns of California and Nevada, 1877. San Francisco: L. M. McKenney, 1877. Orig bds; worn & stained, spine ends chipped. Minor tearing to tp along gutter edge. cb Oct 9 (211) $65

— Handy Block Book of San Francisco.... San Francisco, 1894. 8vo, orig cloth; hinge cracking at front endpapers. With occasional pencil notes & a few laid-on newspaper clippings. cb Oct 9 (174) $100

— Lecount & Strong's San Francisco City Directory for the Year 1854.... San Francisco, 1854. Modern half mor. Lacking lower 3d of tp; with entire title reproduced in facsimile; also in facsimile are pp 17-18 & ad pp iii-x; some running heads cropped. cb Oct 9 (175) $150

— Relief Business Directory, May 1906. Giving Names, Business and Address of San Francisco Firms and Business Men who were Compelled to Change their Location by the Disaster.... Berkeley, 1906. Cloth, orig ptd wraps bound in. Somewhat brittle. cb Oct 9 (213) $110

San Miguel, Fray Isidro de. See: Serra's copy, Fray Junipero

Sanchez, Juan Manuel
— Bibliografia Aragonese del siglo XVI. Madrid, 1913-14. 2 vols. Folio, orig wraps; soiled. bba Feb 5 (75) £130 [Dawson]

Sancroft, William, 1617-93 —& Others
[-] The Proceedings and Tryal in the Case of...William, Lord Archbishop of Canterbury.... L, 1689. Folio, old half sheep; rebacked, joints cracked. sg Oct 9 (309) $110

Sand, Maurice, Pseud., 1823-89
— The History of the Harlequinade. L, 1915. 2 vols. 8vo, orig cloth; soiled & worn, head of spine torn. With 16 color plates. wa Nov 6 (495) $60

Sandburg, Carl, 1878-1967
— Steichen the Photographer. NY, [1929]. One of 925. 4to, orig cloth. bba Apr 23 (290) £150 [Jones]

Anr copy. Cloth; worn. sg Nov 13 (99) $375

Sandby, Paul, 1725-1809
— A Collection of One Hundred and Fifty Select Views in England, Wales, Scotland and Ireland. L, 1783-82. 2 vols in 1. Folio, later half mor; worn. bba Apr 23 (230) £160 [Erlini]

Sandeman, Fraser
— Angling Travels in Norway. L, 1895. 4to, orig half vellum; soiled. L.p. copy. sg Oct 23 (469) $100

— By Hook and by Crook. L, 1892. Out-of-series copy. 8vo, mor. sg Oct 23 (470) $60

Sander, Henry Frederick Conrad
— Reichenbachia. Orchids Illustrated and Described. L & St. Albans, [1886-95]. 1st & 2d Series. 4 vols. Folio, half mor; rubbed, foot of 1 spine missing. With 192 colored plates, some finished by hand. Marginal browning. Candolle—Horticultural Society of New York—de Belder copy. S Apr 28 (318) £5,200 [Brittain]

Anr copy. Second Series only. 2 vols. Folio, contemp half mor; rubbed. With 95 (of 96) color plates. S June 25 (176) £1,900 [McCarthy]

Anr Ed. L & St. Albans, 1888-94. 1st & 2d Series in 4 vols. Folio, unbound in 6 cloth portfolios. With 192 color plates. Some plates adhering to tissues. S Oct 23 (753) £5,000 [Shapero]

Anr copy. Contemp half mor gilt; rubbed. A few plates adhering to tissues. S Apr 23 (59) £3,800 [Antik]

Sanders, Nicholas
— Les Trois Livres.... [N.p.], 1587. 8vo, old vellum; front pastedown imperf. sg Oct 9 (310) $70

Sanders, Prince
— A Memoir Presented to the American Convention for Promoting the Abolition of Slavery.... Phila.: Dennis Heartt, 1818. 8vo, disobund. Foxed; some stains. cb Oct 9 (301) $275

Sanders, Robert, 1727-83
— The Complete English Traveller. L, 1773. Folio, contemp calf; spine & joints worn. With frontis (frayed & loosening), single-page map by T. Bowen, 2 folding maps (1 torn) & 56 plates. Final index leaf torn & creased. L Dec 11 (137) $200

Sanderson, J,
— An Ocean Cruise and Deep Water Regatta of the Pacific Yacht Club, July, 1884. San Francisco, 1884. 4to, orig cloth; rubbed & soiled, rear dampstained. With 8 color plates. Lacking leaf before title, occasional marginal dampstains, affecting a few plates. cb Oct 9 (215) $325

Sanderson, Sir William, 1586-1676
— A Compleat History of the Life and Raigne of King Charles from his Cradle to his Grave. L, 1658. 1st Ed. Folio, contemp calf gilt with arms of Charles II; rebacked with mor. F Jan 15 (354) $600

Anr copy. Contemp calf; rubbed. Lacking the port of Charles. O Feb 24 (163) £110

Sandford, Francis, 1630-94
— A Genealogical History of the Kings and Queens of England.... L, 1677. ("A Genealogical History of the Kings of England.") Folio, modern half calf. Blank corner torn from 2C2; some tears & holes, just affecting text & 1 plate. S July 14 (344) £100

Anr copy. Contemp calf; worn, rebacked. Annotated by John Longes. sg Dec 4 (173) $350

Anr Ed. L, 1707. Folio, contemp calf; worn. pnE Dec 17 (30) £115 [McKenzie]

— The History of the Coronation of James II and Queen Mary. L, 1687. Folio, contemp calf gilt; worn, later endpapers. Lacking the 20th processional plate & the fireworks plate; last leaf mtd. S Sept 23 (394) £230

Sandrart, Joachim von, 1606-88
— L'Academia Todesca della architectura, scultura & pittura: oder Deutsche Academie. Nuremberg, 1675-79. 6 parts in 1 vol. Folio, modern lea; rubbed. With 5 (of 6) engraved titles, frontis, 2 ports & 237 (of 264) plates. HN Nov 26 (1331) DM1,800

Anr copy. 6 parts in 2 vols. Folio, half calf; worn & def. With 2 frontises, 2 ports & 268 double page plates & plans. VII Sept 12 (893) DM5,400

SANDS

Sands, Benjamin
— Metamorphosis; or a Transformation of Pictures.... Phila., 1847. 12mo, orig wraps. S Dec 5 (401) £200 [J. Schiller]

Sands, Kenny & Co. See: Australia

Sands, Ledyard
— The Bird, the Gun and the Dog. NY, 1939. Illus by Courtenay Brandreth. 4to, cloth, in d/j. sg Oct 23 (471) $50

Sandwich, John Montagu, 4th Earl of
— A Voyage Round the Mediterranean in 1738 and 1739. L, 1799. 4to, contemp calf; rubbed, upper cover detached. With port & 25 plates & 1 hand-colored map. Some cropping. S Jan 16 (429) £190 [Martinos]

Sandys, Sir Edwin, 1516?-88
— Europae Speculum; or, a View or Survey of the State of Religion.... L, 1632. 4to, 19th-cent half sheep; joints racked. Minor stains. sg Oct 9 (311) $70

Sandys, George, 1578-1644
— A Paraphrase upon the Psalmes of David.... L, 1638. ("A Paraphrase upon the Divine Poems.") Folio, old calf; rebacked. S Sept 22 (45) £70 [Knohl]
— A Relation of a Journey.... L, 1615. ("A Relation of a Journey begun An. Dom 1610...Description of the Turkish Empire.") 1st Ed. Folio, contemp calf gilt; spine worn. With double-page map (repaired & mtd), folding plate of the Seraglio at Constantinople mtd on D4v & 47 illusts in text. Some waterstains. S Oct 23 (381) £420 [Maggs]
Anr copy. Contemp calf; rebacked. 2d leaf rehinged & remargined; lacking last leaf; engraved title trimmed & mtd. sg Sept 25 (296) $425
3d Ed. L, 1627. Folio, contemp vellum; soiled. Library markings; 1 leaf with small burn hole. bba May 28 (322) £110 [Bologna]
7th Ed. L, 1673. ("Travels....") Folio, contemp calf; rubbed, spine chipped. With engraved title from 6th Ed, folding map & plate. Some dampstaining; rust-holes with minimal loss. S Nov 10 (1073) £150 [Nesro]
Anr copy. Contemp calf; worn. Folding map detached & torn; hole in E3; rusthole in margin of G1; X3 & X4 transposed; lacking last blank. S Nov 18 (1074) £180 [A Zegian]
Anr copy. Contemp calf; broken. Map torn without loss. T Jan 22 (1) £95

Sansom, Joseph
— Travels in Lower Canada. L, 1820. 8vo, wraps. sg Mar 12 (41) $70

Sanson d'Abbeville, Nicolas
See also: Jaillot & Sanson d'Abbeville
— L'Asie en plusieurs cartes. Paris, 1658. 2d Ed. 4to, contemp vellum. With 17 double-page maps, colored in outline. Marginal waterstains. S Oct 23 (75) £450 [Duchautfour]
— Atlas Nouveau. Paris, 1692-93. ("Nouvelle Introduction a la geographie pour l'usage de Monseigneur le Dauphin.") Folio, old half calf; worn & broken. With 80 hand-colored maps & 8 additional later maps. Tp & table of maps laid down & slightly def. C Apr 8 (136) £4,000 [Colleary]
— L'Europe [l'Asie, l'Afrique, et l'Amerique] en plusieurs cartes.... Paris, 1683. 4 parts in 1 vol. 4to, modern calf. With folding engraved title, 10 double-page & 52 folding maps. Browned; small repair to tp; small library stamp on verso of tp & at end. S June 25 (283) £1,600 [Orssich]

Sansovino, Francesco
— Venetia citta novilissima et singolare. Venice, 1581. 4to, contemp vellum. Some dampstaining of margins. This copy includes an additional part headed Cronico Pareticolare della cose fatte da i Veneti dal Principio della citta fino all'anno 1581. Ck Jan 16 (151) £180

Santa Teresa, Giovanni Giuseppe di
— Istoria delle guerre del regno del Brasile.... Rome, 1698. 1st Ed. 2 parts in 2 vols. Folio, vellum bds. With frontis, 2 ports & 23 folding maps, plans & views, hand-colored throughout. Aa4 in part 1 repaired; facsimile Ms title to Part 2; 1st tp stamped. S Apr 24 (314) £2,500 [George]

Santander, Carlos Antonio de la Serna. See: Serna Santander, Carlos Antonio de la

Santini, Piero. See: Derrydale Press

Santos, Joao dos
— Ethiopia Oriental, e varia historia de cousas, notaveis do Oriente. Convento de S. Domingos de Evora, 1609. 2 parts in 1 vol. folio, contemp calf with Signet arms; upper cover detached. Lacking 3 prelim leaves; small areas of engraved title expertly restored. C Apr 8 (59) £520 [Maggs]

Santucci, Luigi
— La Donna con la bocca aperta.... [Verona, 1980]. One of 110. Illus by Emilio Tadini. 4to, vellum. sg Jan 8 (207) $130

Sappho
— Fragments. Paris, 1933. One of 40 on japon. Illus by Mariette Lydis. 4to, unsewn in orig wraps. With 15 etched plates, each sgd in pencil. Inscr by the artist. CNY Dec 19 (126) $1,200

Sarayna, Torellus
— Dell'Origine et Ampiezza della Citta di Verona. Verona: Francesco de Rossi, 1649. 4to, orig bds; worn. Inner margins of tp & 1st few leaves repaired; some waterstains. bba Sept 25 (246) £120 [Shapero]

Sardou, Victorien
— Costumes of the Time of the French Revolution.... NY, 1889. Folio, orig cloth. With 65 hand-colored plates. Tp stamped. S Jan 12 (4) £220 [Daley]

Sargent, Charles Sprague, 1841-1927
— Forest Flora of Japan. Bost., 1894. Folio, orig bds; worn. Library copy. sg Jan 15 (253) $225

Sarkowski, Heinz
— Der Insel-Verlag: Eine Bibliographie, 1899-1969. Frankfurt, 1970. sg Jan 22 (273) $70

Saroyan, William
— The Fiscal Hoboes. NY: Press of Valenti Angelo, 1949. One of 250. Bds, 1st bdg. cb Dec 4 (325) $140

Anr copy. Wraps. cb Dec 4 (326) $65

— Three Times Three. Los Angeles: Conference Press, 1936. Inscr. sg Mar 5 (229) $60

Sarpi, Paolo, 1552-1623
— Historia del Concilio Tridentino. L, 1619. Folio, later bds; worn. S Nov 27 (221) £650

— The History of the Quarrels of Pope Paul V. with the State of Venice. L, 1626. 1st Ed in English. 4to, contemp vellum, with arms of Sir Robert Naunton; rubbed. Ck Jan 16 (148) £200

— The Maxims of the Government of Venice in an Advice to the Republick.... L, 1707. 8vo, contemp calf; rubbed & wormed. Tp shorter at fore-edge. P Sept 24 (385) $175

Sarratt, J. H.
— A Treatise on the Game of Chess. L, 1808. 2 vols. Half calf gilt. pn Mar 26 (493) £50 [Mittelbach]

— The Works of Damiano, Ruy-Lopez & Salvio. L, 1813. Half calf gilt. pn Mar 26 (494) £75 [Chen]

— The Works of Gianutio and Gustavus Selenus.... L, 18117. 2 vols. Modern half calf. pn Mar 26 (495) £60 [Hoffman]

Sarre, Friedrich, 1865-1945
— Islamic Bookbindings. Berlin, [1923]. Trans by F. D. O'Byrne. Folio, orig cloth. C May 13 (206) £250 [Beres]

Sarre, Friedrich, 1865-1945 —& Trenkwald, Hermann
— Alt-Orientalische Teppiche. Vienna & Leipzig, 1926-28. 2 vols. Folio, orig half calf. With 120 plates. FD Dec 2 (2130) DM4,000

Anr copy. Orig cloth. JG Mar 20 (1564) DM4,000

Sarton, May
— Encounter in April. Bost., 1937. In re paired d/j. Inscr & with inscr poem & 4-page typescript of poems, initialled, inserted. O Sept 23 (174) $230

Sartorius, Carl Christian Wilhelm, 1796-1872
— Mexico. Landscapes and Popular Sketches. NY, [c. 1859]. 4to, cloth; worn & chipped. With 18 plates. Library markings. Sold w.a.f. O Nov 18 (165) $110

Sartre, Jean Paul
— La Nausee. Paris: Gallimard, [1938]. 1st Ed, One of 15. Lea avantgarde bdg by J. de Gonet. Inscr to M. Ripault. FD June 11 (4700) DM4,000

— Oeuvre Romanesque. Paris, [1964-65]. One of 12 on japon nacre with a suite of the lithos on velin d'arches & watercolor drawings for 5 of the full-page lithos, each titled & sgd. Illus by Walter Spitzer. 5 vols. 4to, unsewn in orig wraps. S June 17 (153) £500 [Peeper]

Sassoon Collection, Sir Ellice V.
— The Catalogue of Sassoon Chinese Ivories. L, 1950. One of 250. Compiled by S. E. Lucas. 3 vols. Folio, half vellum. S July 13 (49) £350

Sassoon, Siegfried, 1886-1967
— An Adjustment. Royston: Golden Head Press, 1955. One of 150, initialled by Sassoon. Orig wraps. With 5 poems by Sassoon, each ptd on a single sheet by Stanbrook Abbey Press. sg Dec 11 (417) $140

— Common Chords. Stanford Dingley: Mill House Press, 1950. One of 7 ptd on parchment. sg Dec 11 (418) $1,100

— Counter-Attack and Other Poems. L, 1918. Orig wraps. Inscr & with 7 autograph corrections of the text. sg Dec 11 (419) $325

— The Daffodil Murderer. L, 1913. Wraps. spine chipped, dust-soiled. Inscr to Roderick Meiklejohn. S Dec 18 (176) £300 [Bell, Book]

— Emblems of Experience. Cambr.: The

SASSOON

Rampant Lions Press, 1951. One of 75, sgd. sg Dec 11 (420) $250

— Four Poems. Cambr., 1918. Wraps. No 7 in the Reprints from the Cambridge Magazine Series. sg Dec 11 (421) $110

— In Sicily. L, 1930. 1st Ed, One of 400. sg Dec 11 (422) $50

— Memoirs of an Infantry Officer. L, 1930. 1st Ed, One of 750, sgd. bba Feb 5 (269) £100 [Mandler]; sg Mar 5 (230) $200

— Rhymed Ruminations. L, 1939. 1st Ed, One of 75. Inscr. sg Dec 11 (424) $350

— To My Mother. L, [1928]. One of 500 L.p. copies, sgd. Illus by Stephen Tennant. Bds. sg Dec 11 (425) $50

— To the Red Rose. L, 1931. One of 400. Bds. sg Dec 11 (426) $50

— Vigils. [Bristol] 1934. One of 8 on vellum. Illus by Stephen Gooden. Orig mor gilt. Engraved throughout. S July 23 (177) £600 [Maggs]

Satan. See: Lamb, Charles

Satchell, Thomas. See: Westwood & Satchell

Satchwell, Richard

— Scripture Costume Exhibited in a Series of Engravings. L, 1819. 4to, contemp half mor; worn. With 20 hand-colored plates. Some spotting. kh Mar 16 (450) A$520

Sato Shozo

— The Art of Arranging Flowers. NY: Abrams, [1966]. cb Mar 5 (265) $40

Satyre...

— Satyre menippee, de la vertue du Catholicon d'Espagne.... Ratisbon: heirs of Matthias Kerner, 1752. 3 vols. 8vo, contemp calf gilt. With 9 plates only. sg Mar 26 (254) $120

Sauer, Martin

— An Account of a Geographical and Astronomical Expedition to the Northern Parts of Russia.... L, 1802. 1st Ed. 2 parts in 1 vol. 4to, old bds. Some foxing & wear. O May 12 (171) $450

Anr copy. Contemp half russia; joints cracked, head of spine def. With folding map & 14 plates. Minor worming at end. S Oct 23 (524) £280 [Steldart]

Saugrain, Claude Marin

— Code des chasses, ou nouveau traite du droit des chasses.... Paris: Prault, 1753. 2 vols. 12mo, contemp mor gilt with arms of Louis-Philippe I, Duc d'Orleans. Jeanson copy. SM Mar 1 (504) FF17,000

Saul, Arthur

— The Famous Game of Chesse-Play.... L: B. Alsop for Roger Jackson, [1618]. 12mo, contemp vellum; hinges detached. With woodcut diagram on F6 & folding table. Tp slightly stained & def; imprint date cropped; folding table pasted to endpaper & with short tears at folds; last 2 leaves with headline shaved; lacking A1 & G4. C May 13 (167) £850 [Lawson]

Saulat des Marez, Jacob

— Mutus liber, in quo tamen tota philosophia hermetica.... La Rochelle, 1677. 1st Ed. Folio, old wraps; corners creased. With 15 plates. "Au lecteur" leaf lacking; tears in tp & 3 other plates repaired roughly at an early date; Plate 14 torn in half; Plate 15 & privilege leaf def at lower outer corner with loss of small portion of engraving & a few letters. Honeyman copy. S May 21 (215) £2,800 [Bouvier]

Saunders, Daniel

— Journal of the Travels and Sufferings of.... Salem, 1794. 12mo, contemp calf. Library markings. sg Mar 12 (226) $60

Saunders, George

— A Treatise on Theatres. L, 1790. 1st Ed. 4to, contemp half calf. With 13 plates, 4 folding. One plate trimmed just affecting image. C Dec 12 (185) £2,100 [Quaritch]

Saunders, James, of Newton Awbery

— The Compleat Fisherman. L, 1724. 12mo, mor gilt by Zaehnsdorf. With folding plate. S July 24 (280) £270 [Figgis]

Saunders, Louise

— The Knave of Hearts. NY, 1925. Illus by Maxfield Parrish. Folio, spiral-bound wraps; bookplates removed from endpapers, spine ends chipped. cb Dec 4 (293) $325

Anr copy. Cloth. sg Sept 11 (246) $375; sg Dec 4 (151) $375

Saunders, Richard

— Physiognomie, and Chiromancie, Metoposcopie. L, 1653. Folio, contemp calf; joints cracked, rubbed. Short tear without loss; lacking Gg4; a few leaves repaired at margin mostly not affecting text; some lower margins cropped affecting catchwords & occasionally a few words of text; a few small rust-holes & tears; a few leaves dampstained or soiled. S Sept 23 (396) £220 [McNaul]

Saunier, Claudius
— Treatise on Modern Horology.... L, [1878-81]. 8vo, orig half mor; joint splitting, rubbed. With 21 folding plates, partly colored. S Nov 10 (200) £65 [Traylen]
Anr copy. Recent cloth; worn. Foxed. T Oct 16 (565) £56

Saur, Abraham
— Fasciculus de Poenis, vulgo Straffbuch. Frankfurt, [1590]. Bound with: Peinlich Halsgericht des Allerdurchleuchtigsten... Keyser Carols des Fuenfften...auff den Reichstaegen zu Augspurg und Regenspurg. Frankfurt, 1587. Folio, old calf; worn. Tp detached & frayed with some loss to imprint; 1st few leaves with stains, tears & fraying. Sold w.a.f. O Sept 23 (175) $500

Saussure, Horace Benedicte de, 1740-99
— Voyages dans les Alpes, precede d'un essai sur histoire naturelle des environs de Geneve. Neuchatel, 1779-96. 4 vols. 4to, contemp half calf gilt; worn. With engraved title vignettes, 1 map & 23 plates, most folding; Vol I with frontis ink drawing of de Saussure seated on a rock. Plates 6 & 7 with small holes along central margin; T2 in Vol II with small loss from marginal paper def; MM4 with marginal repair; Vol IV has leaf XX3 with 6-inch repaired tear. CNY May 11 (130) $2,200
Anr Ed. Geneva, 1786 & Neuchatel 1796. 8 vols. 8vo, contemp calf. With 22 maps & plates on 21 sheets. C Dec 12 (186) £1,600 [Cavendish]

Sauvan, Jean Baptiste Balthazar
— Picturesque Tour of the Seine.... L: Ackermann, 1821. 4to, half calf gilt. With hand-colored vignette title, 24 plates & 1 map. pn Apr 30 (64) £1,200 [Shapero]
Anr copy. With map & 24 hand-colored plates. Tp & 1st plate loose. S Oct 23 (265) £1,300 [Marshall]

Savage, John, Surgeon
— Some Account of New Zealand. L, 1807. 8vo, calf by Sangorski. With frontis & 2 plates, 1 colored. C Dec 12 (258) £200 [Cavendish]

Savary des Bruslons, Jacques
— The Universal Dictionary of Trade and Commerce. L, 1751-55. 1st Ed in English. 2 vols. Folio, contemp calf. With frontis, 23 (of 24) folding maps & 25 folding tables. Sold w.a.f. C Dec 12 (187) £900 [McCrow]
Anr copy. Contemp calf; worn, joints split. With frontis, 24 folding maps & 25 folding tables. With 1 fold severed. C May 13 (113) £650 [Traylen]
Anr copy. 2 vols in 4. Folio, contemp half calf. With frontis & 24 folding maps. 2d title torn. Ck Nov 7 (95) £550
Anr copy. 2 vols. Folio, contemp calf; worn, broken. With frontis, 24 folding maps & 25 folding tables. Some tears to maps. wa Mar 5 (358) $160
4th Ed in English. L, 1774. Trans by Malachy Postlethwayt. 2 vols. Folio, contemp calf; worn. With frontis & 7 maps on 24 double-page mapsheets. S June 24 (330) £600 [Lake]

Savary, Jacques Timent
— Venationis cervinae, capreolinae, aprugnae et lupinae leges. Caen: Jean Cavelier, 1659. 4to, contemp calf gilt with arms of Pierre-Danuel Huet, bishop of Avranches [Olivier 1684, fer 2]. Jeanson copy. SM Mar 1 (505) FF6,500

Saven, W. Henry
— The Grand International Centennial Chess Congress, Held in Philadelphia in August, 1876. Phila., 1876. 8vo, cloth. pn Mar 26 (40) £75 [Hoffman]

Savi, Gaetano
— Flora italiana, ossia raccolta delle piante piu belle.... Pisa, 1818-24. 3 vols. Folio, contemp half calf. With 120 hand-finished color plates. Some spotting. S Apr 28 (320) £18,000 [McDougall]
— Materia medica vegetabile della Toscana. Florence, 1805. Folio, later bds. With 60 hand-colored plates. Tp soiled & mtd, with loss of text; dedication leaf repaired. Plesch—de Belder copy. S Apr 28 (319) £1,700 [Tulkins]

Savonarola, Girolamo, 1452-98
See also: Kelmscott Press
— Confessionale pro instructione confessorum. Venice: F. Bindani, 21 Apr 1524. Bound with: Corradonus, Matthaeus. Speculum confessorum & lumen conscientiae. Venice, 1535. 8vo, contemp vellum; spine worn. Some marginalia. bba Aug 28 (86) £280 [Sokol]
— De simplicitate vita Christiane. Acala, 1529. 8vo, old vellum; pastedowns lifted. sg Oct 9 (67) $300
— Triumphis crucis. [Florence: Bartolommeo di Libri, 1497?]. Folio, calf. Short tear to 1 leaf of table; some headlines & initial flourishes shaved; waterstain in lower margins; wormholes repaired in last 2 leaves with loss of a few letters. 98 leaves. Goff S-274. C Dec 12 (306) £480 [Pressler]

Savoy...
— The Savoy: an Illustrated Quarterly. L, 1896. Ed by Arthur Symons; illus by Aubrey Beardsley. Nos 1-8 (complete set). Orig bds & orig wraps. bba Sept 24 (133) £200 [Warreck & Perkins]

Anr copy. Nos 1-8 (complete set). 8vo, orig bds & orig wwraps; worn & frayed. pn Sept 18 (123) £170 [Walford]

Anr copy. Nos 1-8 (all pbd) in 1 vol. 4to, half calf, orig wraps bound in, Christmas card tipped in. S Oct 6 (760) £220 [Wendler]

Anr copy. Nos 1-8 (all pbd) Orig cloth; rubbed, 1 upper joint torn. S Jan 16 (452) £300 [Walford]

Sawyer, Charles J. —& Darton, F. J. Harvey

— English Books, 1475-1900. L, 1927. 2 vols. O June 16 (82) $50; sg Jan 22 (274) $100; sg Jan 22 (275) $50; sg June 11 (356) $70

Sawyer, Eugene T. See: Grabhorn Printing

Saxby, Henry L.

— The Birds of Shetland.... Edin., 1874. 1st Ed. 8vo, orig cloth; rubbed. With 8 plates. pn Oct 23 (272) £95 [Bewder]

Saxby, Jessie M. E.

— Joseph Bell...An Appreciation by an Old Friend. Edin., 1913. cb Apr 24 (1998) $100

Saxe, Maurice, Comte de, 1696-1750

— Mes Reveries, ouvrage postume. Amst. & Leipzig, 1757. Vol I only. Calf; worn. S Jan 12 (8) £75 [Shapero]

— Reveries, or Memoires upon the Art of War. L, 1757. 4to, later half calf; rubbed. Lacking 1 plate. bba Apr 9 (66) £65 [Turner]

Anr copy. Contemp calf; rubbed. With 40 (on 34) folding plates. S Nov 18 (949) £110 [Filbert]

Saxton, Christopher

— An Atlas of England and Wales. L, [1579]. Folio, contemp calf gilt; rebacked. With 34 double-page or folding maps (of 35 - lacking the general map of England & Wales) fully colored in a contemp hand. Lacking the doublepage coats-of-arms & gazetteer plate & ptd index leaf but with Ms index & 10 leaves of Ms tables; folding map torn without much loss; a few splits elsewhere; some discoloration; 1 or 2 neatlines just shaved. S Apr 23 (104) £32,000 [Knohl]

Anr Ed. L, 1936. Folio, half mor gilt. Facsimile of 1574-79 Ed. pn May 21 (393) £150 [Map House]

Say, Jean Baptiste, 1767-1832

— Lettres a M. Malthus, sur differens sujets d'economie politique.... Paris, 1820. 1st Ed. 8vo, modern calf. Loss in upper margin of half-title. P Sept 24 (389) $400

— Traite d'economie politique.... Paris, 1803. 2 vols. 8vo, contemp calf gilt; rubbed & chipped. Minor foxing & soiling. P Sept 24 (390) $2,100

Say, Thomas, 1787-1834

— American Entomology. Phila., 1824-28. Vols I-II (of 3). Orig bds; worn, spines def, 2 covers detached. With engraved title & 36 hand-colored plates. Sold w.a.f. C Apr 8 (195) £400 [Maggs]

Anr copy. 3 vols. 8vo, orig bds; front covers & backstrips detached. With 54 hand-colored plates. Top of 1 leaf torn in Vol III. sg Apr 2 (177) $1,300

Saybrook Platform

— A Confession of Faith Owned and Consented to by the Elders and Messengers of the Churches in the Colony of Connecticut. New London: Timothy Green, 1760. 8vo, old calf; worn. Some stains & soiling. O Feb 24 (164) $80

Sayers, Dorothy Leigh

— The Devil to Pay. L, 1939. Inscr. cb Nov 20 (285) $225

— Op. 1. Oxford: Blackwell, 1916. 1st Ed. Orig wraps; broken. S Sept 22 (138) £100 [Libris Antik]

Sayers, Dorothy Leigh —& Byrne, Muriel Saint Clare

— Busman's Honeymoon. L, 1937. In repaired d/j. cb Nov 20 (284) $400

Scaccia, Sigismund

— Tractatus de Commerciis et Cambio. Venice, 1669. Folio, contemp red mor gilt with arms of Jean-Baptiste Colbert on sides & his crowned cypher gilt in compartments of spine. C Dec 3 (180) £1,600 [Quaritch]

Scale, Bernard

— An Hibernian Atlas, or General Description of the Kingdom of Ireland. L, 1776. 4to, contemp calf; rebacked. With engraved title, dedication & 37 hand-colored maps. S Jan 12 (69) £420 [Map]

Anr Ed. L, 1798. 4to, later half calf. With engraved title, dedication & 37 hand-colored maps. 1 map foxed. bba Apr 9 (359) £440 [Monckton]

Scalichius, Paulus

— Encyclopaediae, seu orbis disciplinarum. Basel: Oporinus, Feb 1559. 4to, later calf, with Signet arms; worn, joints cracked. With 1 woodcut diagram only, cleanly torn along fold. Ck Jan 30 (183) £80

Scammon, Charles M.

— The Marine Mammals of the North-Western Coast of North America.... San Francisco & NY, 1874. 4to, orig cloth. S May 29 (1252) £500

Scamozzi, Ottavio Bertotti

— Il Forestiere istruito delle cose piu rare di archittetura...della citta di Vicenza.... Vicenza, 1761. 4to, modern calf. With port & 36 plates. One plate torn & repaired; anr soiled on back of fold. Ck June 5 (75) £350

Scamozzi, Vincenzo, 1552-1616

— Les Cinq Ordres d'architecture. Paris, 1685. Folio, contemp calf; rubbed. With 38 plates. C July 22 (189) £300

— Discorsi sopra l'antichita di Roma.... Venice: Francesco Ziletti, 1583. Folio, 19th-cent half vellum. With engraved title (mtd on guard) & 40 double page plates. Plate 13 torn & neatly repaired; some stains. C July 22 (190) £900

Scandianese, Tito Giovanni. See: Giovanni, Tito

Scappi, Bartolommeo

— Dell'Arte del cucinare con il mastro di casa e trinciante. Venice, 1643. 4to, contemp vellum. With engraved title & 27 plates. Some waterstains at end affecting plates. P Nov 25 (418) $1,500

— Opera. Venice: Alessandro Vecchi, 1596. 2d Issue. 4to, calf gilt by Y. Laengner of Milan; upper joints cracked. Some restoration to blank corners; hole in 2T2 mended costing a few letters. Vehling copy. P Nov 25 (417) $2,100

Scapula, Johann

— Lexicon Graeco-Latinum.... Amst & Leiden [ptd]: J. Blaeu & L. Elzevir, 1652. 2 parts in 1 vol. Folio, contemp calf gilt; rebacked, corners repaired, joints split. bba Mar 26 (112) £70 [Subunso]

Scarlett, Peter Campbell

— South America and the Pacific.... L, 1838. 2 vols. 12mo, orig cloth; rubbed, spines frayed. With 4 folding maps & 5 plates Contents leaf in Vol II torn without loss. T Oct 16 (287) £50

Scarpa, Antonio, 1747-1832

— Tabulae neurologicae.... Ticini, 1794. Folio, orig bds; rebacked & recornered in calf. With 7 plates, each with accompanying outline plate. Tp badly spotted; library markings. bba May 14 (290) £1,000 [Phelps]

Scarron, Paul, 1610-60

— Oeuvres. Amst., 1752. 7 vols. 12mo, mor gilt by Bozerian jeune. Half-titles in Vols I & III. C Dec 3 (165) £1,200 [Maggs]

Scaruffi, Gasparo

— L'Alitinonfo di M. Gasparo Scaruffiper fare ragione, et concordanza d'oro et d'argento.... Reggio: H. Bartoli, 1582. 2 parts in 1 vol. Folio, modern blind-stamped calf. S May 21 (76) £2,200 [King]

Schaeffer, Jacob Christian

— Fungorum, qui in Bavaria et Palatinatu circa Ratisbonam nascuntur icones nativis coloribus expressae. Erlangen, 1800. 5 vols in 3. 4to, later half calf; rubbed. With 2 frontises & 330 hand-colored plates. Minor spotting. Joubert—de Belder copy. S Apr 28 (322) £3,500 [Marshall]

Schaldach, William J.

— Carl Rungius, Big Game Painter. West Hartford, Vt., [1945]. One of 160. 4to, cloth. sg May 21 (179) $3,200

Out-of-series copy. Cloth; spine rubbed. With frontis etching sgd. sg Oct 23 (159) $1,700

— Currents & Eddies. Chips from the Log of an Artist-Angler. West Hartford, Vermont, 1944. One of 250. 4to, cloth, in d/j. sg Oct 23 (472) $50

— Fish by Schaldach. Phila., 1937. One of 157. Folio, vellum. With frontis etching, sgd. sg Oct 23 (473) $300

One of 1,500. Cloth; soiled. cb Nov 6 (256) $80; sg Oct 23 (474) $140

— Upland Gunning. West Hartford, VT[1946]. One of 160. 4to, cloth. With 8 colored & 48 plain plates. With frontis etching, sgd. sg Oct 23 (475) $325

Schalk, Henriette van der, 1869-1952

— Sonnetten en verzen in terzinen geschreven. Amst., 1895. 4to, orig half cloth. B Oct 7 (21) HF320

Schallopp, Emil, 1843-1919

[-] Emil Schallopp ein Gedenkblatt zum 70 Geburtstage. Potsdam, 1913. Ed by M. Lewitt. Half mor gilt, orig upper wrap bound in. pn Mar 26 (254) £35 [Caissa]

Schammade...

— Die Schammade. Cologne: Schloemilch Verlag, 1920. Ed by Max Ernst & J. T. Baargeld (Alfred Gruenewald). 4to, loose in orig wraps. S June 29 (6) £3,800 [Bolliger]

Schatzbehalter...

— Schatzbehalter oder Schrein der wahren Reichtuemer des Heils und ewiger Seligkeit. Nuremberg: Anton Koberger, 8 Nov 1491. Folio, contemp blindstamped pigskin over wooden bds. Minor defs; paper fault in the margin of B1. 352 (of 354) leaves; lacking 1st & final blanks. Goff S-306. Jeanson D5. SM Mar 1 (245) FF220,000

Schauer, Georg Kurt

— Deutsche Buchkunst 1890-1960. Hamburg, 1963. 4to, orig cloth. bba Oct 16 (441) £160 [Check Books]

Schauplatz....

— Schauplatz des Gegenwaertigen Kriegs. Nuremberg: Raspe, [1756-62]. 10 parts in 1 vol. Oblong folio, disbound. With 10 engraved titles (some hand-colored), 1 table & 157 partly hand-colored plates & maps (of 159, lacking Plates 12 & 16). Library markings; tp to part 1 soiled & with ink & perforated library stamps; some stains. bba Dec 18 (233) £380 [Maggs]

Schedel, Hartmann. See: Nuremberg Chronicle

Scheele, Carl Wilhelm, 1742-86

— Traite chimique de l'air et du feu.... Paris, 1781-85. 2 vols with Supplement. 12mo, contemp calf gilt. With folding plate. C Dec 12 (188) £480 [Quaritch]

Scheible, Johann

— Das Kloster. Weltlich und geistlich. Stuttgart, 1845-49. 12 vols in 24. 8vo, half cloth. With 8 ports, 3 plates of facsimiles, 2 folding plates & 341 plates. S May 21 (167) £400 [Quaritch]

Schellhammer, Maria Sophia

— Die wol unterwiesene Koechinn. Braunschweig: Caspar Gruber, 1697. Bound with: Der wohl-unterwiesenen Koechinn zufaelliger Confect-Tisch.... Braunschweig: Caspar Gruber, 1699. 1st Eds. 4to, old half calf with new lea spine labels. With frontis in each work & with 9 plates in 2d work. Sold w.a.f due to inability to verify proper plate count. Crahan copy. P Nov 25 (419) $2,100

Schelling, Pieter van der

— Histori van het notarisschap.... Rotterdam, 1745. 8vo, vellum. With folding plate. B Feb 25 (706) HF700

Schelstrate, Emanuel A.

— Sacrum Antiochenum Concilium. Antwerp: J. B. Verdussen, 1681. 4to, contemp mor gilt with arms of Pope Innocent XI surmounted by the triple tiara & crosskeys in the center inside a complex frame. S Nov 27 (123) £1,800 [Torre]

Schema...

— Schema aller Uniform der Kaiserl. Koenigl. Kriegsvoelkern. Vienna, 1793. 8vo, contemp bds; rubbed. With engraved title & 131 (of 132) hand-colored plates. HK Nov 4 (1982) DM2,000

Schenk, Peter

See also: Valck & Schenk

— Afbeeldinge der voornaamste gebouwen van Amsterdam. Amst., [c.1700]. Oblong 4to, modern mor gilt. With 100 plates. Single wormhole through 1st few leaves, not affecting text; without title. C Dec 12 (269) £480 [Kornfeld]

Anr copy. Bds; broken. With 97 (of 100) plates. HN Nov 26 (398) DM1,100

Scherschevsky, Alexander Boris

— Die Rakete fuer Fahrt und Flug.... Berlin, 1929. Wraps; spine ends chipped. sg Jan 15 (359) $100

Scheuchzer, Johann Jacob, 1672-1733

— Helveticus.... Leiden, 1723. 4 vols in 1. 4to, contemp calf; rubbed. With port & 132 plates. Shuckburgh—Horticultural Society of New York—de Belder copy. S Apr 28 (323) £7,200 [Bourlot]

— Herbarium diluvianum. Leiden, 1723. Folio, contemp half calf; rubbed. With engraved title, port & 14 plates. pn Jan 22 (239) £230 [Maggs]

— Kupfer-Bibel. Augsberg & Ulm, 1731-35. 1st Ed. Text, 2 vols; plates, 2 vols. Together, 4 vols. Folio, contemp panelled calf. With frontis, 2 ports & 760 plates. Horticultural Society of New York—de Belder copy. S Apr 28 (324) £6,000 [Minton]

— Ouresiphoites Helveticus, sive itinera Alpina tria.... Leiden, 1723. ("Ouresiphoites Helveticus, sive itinera per Helvetiae alpinas regiones facta.") Vols I & II, 2d Ed; Vols III & IV, 1st Ed. Together, 4 vols in 1. 4to, contemp vellum. With port, engraved title & 131 plates, 2 with overslips. Minor tears. S June 25 (314) £6,800 [Maliye]

Schewitzer, Christoph. See: Frick & Schewitzer

Scheyb, Franz Christoph von

— Peuteringeriana Tabula Itineraria.... Vienna, 1753. Folio, contemp half calf; spine damaged & glue-mended. With 12 double-page maps. sg Nov 20 (196) $300

Schiefler, Gustav

— Das graphische Werk von Max Liebermann. Berlin, 1907. One of 100. Orig bdg. HN Nov 26 (1951) DM1,400

One of 300. Orig bdg. HN Nov 26 (1949) DM750

Schiele, Egon

— Das Egon Schiele Buch. Vienna & Leipzig, 1921. One of 1,000. 8vo, orig mor; rubbed. C May 13 (195) £260 [Dreesman] Anr copy. Orig wraps. S May 6 (33) £60 [Bobok]

— Zeichnungen. Vienna, 1917. One of 400, sgd. Folio, Loose as issued; worn. With 12 plates. HN May 20 (2802) DM2,500

Schiff Collection, Mortimer L.

— [Sale Catalogue] Catalogue of a Selected Portion of the Famous Library.... L, 1938. 3 vols. 4to, wraps; worn. Priced in pencil throughout. sg May 14 (132) $140

Schiller, Friedrich von, 1759-1805

— Don Karlos. Leipzig, 1787. 8vo, contemp bds; rubbed, joints split. Tear in tp; Vol II tp shaved at foot; small hole at head of U7 just affecting text. S July 28 (1235) £100

— Geschichte des dreyssigjaehrigen Krieges.... Leipzig, 1793. 3 vols. 16mo, contemp calf; 1st bdg abraded. With 49 plates & ports. Engraved title Historischer Calender fuer Damen fuer 1792 bound into Vol III. C Dec 12 (189) £300 [Hannas]

— Die Horen, eine Monatsschrift. Tuebingen, 1795. Ed by Schiller. Vol I, Nos 1-12 in 2 vols. 8vo, half mor; worn. ha Sept 19 (235) $325

— Die Raeuber. Hellerau, 1923. One of 150 with a sgd litho. Illus by Lovis Corinth. 4to, half vellum. HN Nov 26 (1767) DM2,200

— Wallenstein. Tuebingen, 1800. 2 vols. 8vo, half calf gilt. HK Nov 4 (2698) DM550

— Wallensteins Lager. Berlin, 1922. One of 300, with last plate sgd by artist. Illus by Lovis Corinth. 4to, orig half calf. With 6 plates. HN May 20 (2393) DM1,000

Werke. Stuttgart & Tuebingen, 1812-15. 12 vols. 8vo, contemp half calf. B Oct 7 (861) HF1,150

Anr copy. Early 20th-cent half calf gilt. HK Nov 4 (2691) DM1,500

Anr Ed. Stuttgart & Tuebingen, 1835-36. 12 vols. 8vo, contemp half calf gilt; worn. HN May 20 (1957) DM2,000

— Wilhelm Tell: Schauspiel.... Tuebingen, 1804. 1st Ed. 12mo, contemp bd; backstrip imperf. Some foxing; corner off title. sg Apr 2 (178) $700

— Works. Bost.: Francis A. Niccolls, [1902]. Ed de Grand Luxe, One of 250. 10 vols. Half mor. cb Dec 4 (345) $140

Schinz, Salomon

— Anleitung zu der Pflanzenkenntnis und derselben nuetzlichsten Anwendung. Zurich, 1774. Folio, contemp vellum bds. With 2 hand-colored plates of floral detail & 101 hand-colored woodcut plates. Vilmorin—de Belder copy. S Apr 28 (325) £4,000 [Bucher-Kabinet]

Schioler, Lehn, 1874-1929

— Danmarks Fugle.... Copenhagen, 1925-31. 3 vols. 4to, orig half vellum; new endpapers. B Feb 24 (426) HF700

Anr copy. 3 vols. Folio, half vellum. With 276 plates, some colored. pn Oct 23 (273) £400 [Junk]

Schlangintweit, Emil

— Buddhism in Tibet. Leipzig, 1863. Atlas only. Folio, orig cloth-backed portfolio; worn. With 20 plates. C Dec 12 (270) £1,100 [Knuttel]

Schlechtendal, Diedrich Franz Leonhard von —& Others

— Flora von Deutschland.... Gera, 1880-88. 31 vols. 8vo, orig half mor; rubbed. Minor defs. FD June 11 (563) DM3,100

Schlechter, C. See: Marco & Schlechter

Schlegel, Frederick

— Saemmtliche Werke. Vienna, 1822-25. 10 vols. 8vo, contemp half calf gilt; worn. HK Nov 4 (2705) DM800

Schlegel, Hermann, 1804-84 —& Verster de Wulverhorst, A. H.

— Traite de fauconnerie. Leiden & Dusseldorf, 1844-53. Folio, contemp mor gilt; minor defs. With litho title, 2 tinted views & 14 colored plates. Jeanson 1692. SM Mar 1 (506) FF110,000

Schlegel, Hermann, 1804-84 —& Westerman, Gerardus Friedrich

— De Toerako's afgebeeld en beschreven. Amst., 1860. Folio. With 13 text leaves & 2 sets of plates, 1 plain, 1 hand-colored; colored set lacking 1 plate. Haverschmidt copy. B Feb 25 (187) HF3,400

Anr copy. Contemp cloth; spine def at head & foot. With 17 hand-colored plates. Small tears in margins of title & text; some spotting. Bookplate of Prince Roland Bonaparte. S Apr 23 (60) £4,500 [St. James]

Schley, Winfield Scott, 1839-1911

— Report of...Greely Relief Expedition of 1884. Wash., 1887. 4to, cloth; soiled & worn. With port & 3 maps. Some pp waterstained. wa Nov 6 (123) $55

Schloss, Albert. See: Miniature Books

Schlueter, Christoph Andreas
— De la fonte, des mines, des fonderies.... Paris, 1764-53. 2d Ed of Vol I, 1st Ed of Vol II. 2 vols. 4to, contemp calf; worn. With frontis & 58 folding plates. O May 12 (172) $225

Schmalen, Johann Christoph Hermann von
— Accurate Vorstellung der saemtlichen Koeniglich Preussischen armee. Nuremberg, 1759. 8vo, modern calf; scratches. With hand-colored frontis, engraved title, 2 dedication leaves & 117 hand-colored plates heightened with gold & silver. S June 25 (210) £1,500

Schmidel, Casimir Christoph
— Icones plantarum et analyses partium.... Nuremburg, 1793-96. Folio, modern half calf. With 75 hand-colored plates. Marginal dampstaining, affecting a few leaves of text & 1 or 2 plates. S Apr 28 (326) £1,800 [Volbracht]

Schmidt, Adolf, of Darmstadt
— Bucheinbaende aus dem XIV-XIX Jahrhundert in der Landesbibliothek zu Darmstadt. Leipzig, 1921. Folio, orig cloth; worn & shaken. sg May 14 (133) $375

Schmidtmeyer, Peter
— Travels into Chile. L, 1824. 4to, cloth. With 10 hand-colored & 18 plain plates. bba Dec 18 (234) £100 [Remington]

Schmit, Robert
— Eugene Boudin, 1824-1898. Paris, 1973. One of 1,200. 3 vols. 4to, orig cloth. S Nov 10 (262) £450 [Heneage]

Schmitt, Annegrit. See: Degenhart & Schmitt

Schmitz, James H.
— A Nice Day for Screaming.... Phila.: Chilton, [1965]. In d/j. cb Sept 28 (1119) $200

Schmoller, Hans
— Mr. Gladstone's Washi: A Survey of Reports.... Newton PA, 1984. One of 500. 4to, half mor. With extra set of prints in portfolio. sg Jan 8 (22) $140

Schnackenberg, Walthur —& Bie, Oskar
— Kostueme, Plakate und Dekorationen.... Munich, 1920. 4to, orig bds; spine torn. pn Jan 22 (209) £210 [Orssich]

Schneevoogt, G. Voorhelm
— Icones plantarum rariorum. Haarlem: C. Plaat, 1792-93-[95].. 16 parts. Folio, unbound in orig sheets, orig wraps to Part 11 & upper wrap to Part 2 included. With 48 hand-colored plates. Occasional spotting or soiling; a few marginal repairs. de Belder copy. S Apr 28 (321) £6,000 [Arader]

Schnitzler, Arthur, 1862-1931
— Die Hirtenfloete. Vienna, 1912. One of 400. Orig mor gilt. JG Oct 2 (2343) DM950

Schoberl, Frederick
— Picturesque Tour from Geneva to Milan.... L: Ackermann, 1820. 8vo, later calf. With map & 36 hand-colored plates. Some margins soiled; short tears in fore-margins of K1 reinforced. S Oct 23 (267) £1,250 [Browning]
  Anr copy. Half lea. With plan & 36 colored plates. S Nov 17 (922) £1,100 [Healford]
— Voyage pittoresque de Geneve a Milan par le Simplon. Basel, 1819. 2d Ed. Folio, later half mor gilt; extremities rubbed. With 35 hand-colored plates. Plate 31 short; background of Plate 33 soiled. P Sept 24 (194) $9,500
— The World in Miniature: The Asiatic Islands and New Holland. L: Ackermann [plates dated 1824]. 2 vols. 12mo, calf; worn. With 26 hand-colored plates. sg Apr 23 (134) $225
— The World in Miniature: Austria. L: Ackermann, [1823]. Ed by Schoberl. 2 vols in one. 12mo, calf; spine damaged. With 32 hand-colored plates. Lacking ads. pn Jan 22 (110) £70 [Neale]
— The World in Miniature: Hindoostan. L: Ackermann [imprints dated 1822]. Ed by Schoberl. 6 vols. 12mo, contemp calf; worn, 1 spine lacking. With 100 (of 103) colored plates. Stained; 2 plates def. bba Jan 15 (458) £75 [Cumming]
— The World in Miniature: Japan. L: Ackermann, [1823]. Ed by Schoberl. 12mo, orig cloth. With 20 hand-colored plates. Tp spotted with small tear & loosening; Z3 & 4 detached. L Dec 11 (184) £120
— The World in Miniature: Persia. L: Ackermann, [1822]. 3 vols. 12mo, orig bds; rubbed. With 30 colored plates. O May 12 (177) $190
— The World in Miniature: Switzerland. L: Ackermann, [1824]. 12mo, orig cloth. Lacking 1 plate & 1 leaf of text; 1 leaf torn. L Dec 11 (185) £220

Schodde, Richard —& Mason, I. J.
— Nocturnal Birds of Australia.... Melbourne, 1980. One of 750. Folio, orig lea. kh Mar 16 (454) A$120
  Anr copy. Mor gilt. pn Oct 23 (274) £50 [Grant]

Schoene, Albrecht. See: Henkel & Schoene

Schoener, Johann
— Opusculum astrologicum.... Nuremberg, 1539. 4to, modern vellum. S July 28 (114) £320

Schoettgen, Christian, 1687-1751
— Historie derer Dressdnischen Buchdrucker. Dresden: F. Hekels, [1740]. Bound in the middle of: Schoettgen. Der loeblichen Buchdrucket-Gesellschafft zu Dressden Jubel-Geschichte. 1740. And: Historische beschreibung des Dressdnischen Buch-drucker-Jubilaei....Dresden, 1740. 4to, later half mor; edges worn. Browned; publication information cut from title with blank restoration to entire title. Hoe-Columbia copy. ha Sept 19 (74) $800

Schomburgk, Sir Robert Hermann
— A Description of British Guiana. L., 1840. 8vo, orig bds; def. With colored litho title (loose & soiled), map & 12 hand-colored plates. Small portion of 1 text leaf lacking. pn June 18 (166) £600 [Faupel]
— The History of Barbados. L, 1848. 3 parts in 1 vol. 8vo, contemp half mor gilt; rubbed. With litho title, frontis & 7 plates, 1 partially hand-colored. bba Oct 16 (231) £200 [Burton Garbett]

Anr copy. Orig cloth; rubbed. With tinted litho title & 6 plates only. Ck Feb 27 (210) £300

Anr copy. Orig cloth; worn, spine def. With litho additional title, frontis, 6 plates, folding table & hand-colored map. Frontis & litho title stained. S Nov 18 (1169) £200

Schookius, Martin
— Tractatus de turffis ceu cespitibus bituminosis. Groningen, 1658. 12mo, old calf; worn. Cropped with occasional loss; wormed with some loss; G5 torn with loss of a few words; bound with 2 unidentified works. S Nov 10 (554) £80 [Rota]

Schoolcraft, Henry Rowe, 1793-1864
See also: Allen & Schoolcraft
— Archives of Aboriginal Knowledge.... Phila., 1860. 6 vols. 8vo, modern cloth. With engraved titles, port & 362 plates, some partly hand-colored. pnNY Oct 11 (42) $900
— Historical and Statistical Information Respecting...the Indian Tribes of the United States. Phila., 1853-56. ("Information Respecting the History...of the Indian Tribes of the United States....") Part 1 only. 4to, orig cloth; worn & soiled. Some foxing & stains. Laid in are 18 plates ptd in brown ink, from anr Ed. sg Mar 12 (227) $130

Schoonhovius, Florentius
— Emblemata. Leiden: Elzevir, 1626. 2d Ed. 4to, old vellum. S Nov 17 (679) £170 [Vine]

Schopper, Hartmann
— Panoplia omnium illiberalium mechanicarum.... Frankfurt: Georgius Corvinus for Sigismund Feyerabend, 1568. 8vo, contemp vellum. I4-L8 wormed at top of inner margin, in some cases just touching the border of the woodcut; S1-4 torn & damaged by a large hole in the text. S June 25 (54) £3,800 [Sourget]
— Speculum vitae aulicae. De admirabili fallacia et astutia vulpeculae Reinikes. Frankfurt, 1584. 12mo, vellum. FD June 11 (141) DM980

Schorr, J.
— Schachkongress Teplitz-Schoenau im Oktober 1922. Teplitz-Schoenau-Turn, 1923. Orig cloth. pn Mar 26 (73) £50 [Hoffman]

Schott, Gaspar
— Joco-seriorum naturae et artis.... [Wuerzburg, 1666?]. 4to, contemp calf; joints cracked. With engraved title & 22 plates. Ck June 19 (169) £126
— Schola Steganographica. Nuremberg, 1665. 4to, modern half pigskin; spine ends chipped, covers detached. Some dampstaining & browning; marginal repairs to 1st 3 leaves. sg Mar 26 (255) $325

Schottenloher, Karl
— Bibliographie zur deutschen Geschichte im Zeitalter der Glaubensspaltung, 1517-1585. Stuttgart, 1956-66. 7 vols. 4to, half lea; 2 vols with worn joints. sg Oct 2 (259) $500

Schottus, Franciscus
— Itinerario overo nuova descrittione de viaggi principali d'Italia. Rome: Filippo de' Rossi, 1650. 8vo, old vellum; worn. With 20 folding maps; 1 repaired. Most leaves browned; some spotting or soiling; cut in outer margin from Z1 to end, touching text after Hh2. S Nov 10 (924) £260 [Faupel]

Schouten, Wouter
— Ost-Indische Reyse: worin erzehlt wird viel gedenckwuerdiges und ungemeine seltsame Sachen.... Amst., 1676. 2 parts in 1 vol. Folio, contemp vellum; soiled. With engraved title, port & 27 plates. Some discoloration. S Oct 23 (148) £1,050 [Fletcher]

Schrader, Heinrich Adolph —& Wendland, Johann Christoph
— Sertum Hannoveranum, seu plantae rariores.... Goettingen/Hanover, 1795-1800. Bound with: Wendland, J. C. Hortus Herrenhusanus.... Parts 1-3 (of 4).

SCHRADER

Together 7 parts in 1 vol. Folio, 19th-cent half calf, orig fasicule wraps preserved. With 1 hand-colored garden plan & 42 hand-colored plates. de Belder copy. S Apr 28 (327) £6,000 [Macdougall]

Schrank, Franz von Paula von
— Plantae rariores horti academici Monacensis.... Munich, [1817]-19-[22]. 2 vols in 10 parts. Folio, orig wraps; worn. With 100 hand-colored plates. Titles to Parts 5 & 6 only. de Belder copy. S Apr 28 (328) £12,500 [Israel]

Schreiber, Wilhelm Ludwig
— Handbuch der Holz- und Metallschnitte des XV. Jahrhunderts. Leipzig, 1926-30. 8 vols. 4to, cloth. sg May 14 (54) $700

Schreiner, William H.
— Schreiner's Sporting Manual: a Complete Treatise.... Phila., 1841. 12mo, cloth; worn. "Unusally crisp, clean copy". sg Oct 23 (477) $1,600

Schrevelius, Theodorus
— Harlemias of Eerste Stichting der Stad Haarlem. Haarlem, 1754. 2d Ed. 2 parts in 1 vol. 4to, half calf. With engraved title, plan & 47 folding plates. Lacking ptd titles, 5 leaves of text & 7 prelim leaves; loose, stained. B Oct 7 (1373) HF1,050

Schreyvogel, Charles
— My Bunkie and Others. NY, 1909. Oblong folio, pictorial bds; back cover water-stained. With 36 plates. sg Sept 18 (267) $300

Schroeder, Johann
— The Compleat Chymical Dispensatory. L, 1669. 1st Ed in English. Folio, loose in contemp calf; worn. Several leaves torn in outer blank margin; some stains. S Nov 10 (555) £130 [Phelps]

Anr copy. Contemp calf; rebacked, new endpapers. Lacking 1st & last blanks; some worming in upper margins from p 263 to end affecting text on several pages. S May 28 (777) £110

— Vollstaendige und Nutzreiche Apotheke.... Frankfurt & Leipzig, 1718. 3d Ed. Folio, contemp pigskin over wooden bds; worn. HK Nov 4 (848) DM2,200

Schubert, Gotthilf Heinrich von
— Naturgeschichte des Pflanzenreichs. Stuttgart, [n.d.]. Folio, orig cloth with pasted down colored illust on upper cover; slightly soiled. With 54 double-page colored plates. Plate 6 damaged in margins. L Dec 11 (308) £50

Schuecking, Christoph Bernhard Levin. See: Freiligrath & Schuecking

AMERICAN BOOK PRICES CURRENT

Schultens, Henricus Albertus
— Meidanii Proverbiorum Arabicorum.... L, 1795. 4to, contemp calf; broken. pn Jan 22 (63) £140 [Pooleom]

Schulte-Strathaus, E. See: Bremer Press

Schultz, Franz Johann
— Abbildung der in- und auslaendischen Baeume, Stauden und Strauche.... Vienna, 1792-1804. 3 vols. Folio, contemp half cloth; rubbed, some joints partly split. With 390 (of 400) hand-colored engraved & watercolor plates. Some spotting, almost entirely to text; a few leaves browned. Liechtenstein—de Belder copy. S Apr 28 (329) £6,200 [Junk]

Schultze, Walter. See: Schouten, Wouter

Schulz, H. C. See: Grabhorn Printing

Schumpeter, Joseph Alois
— Das Wesen und der Haupinhalt der theoretischen National-okonomie. Leipzig, 1908. Half cloth; rubbed, joints wormed, spine chipped. Marginal browning. P Sept 24 (395) $900

Schurig, Martin
— Gynaecologia historico-medica.... Dresden & Leipzig, 1730. 4to, later half vellum. Small hole in 1 leaf. bba Mar 12 (461) £90 [Nosbuesch]
— Spermatologia historico-medica. Frankfurt, 1720. 1st Ed. 4to, contemp vellum; rubbed. Some browning. bba Mar 12 (458) £220 [Whiteson]

Schuyler, Eugene
— Turkistan. NY, 1877. 2 vols. Orig cloth; spine ends bumped or frayed. Foxing & soiling; maps with tears. cb Nov 6 (259) $55

Schweiger-Lerchenfeld, Amand von
— Aus dem Sueden. Vienna, [1880]. Illus by Ludwig Hans Fischer. Oblong folio, orig cloth. With engraved title & 20 plates. S Oct 23 (352) £150 [Nicolas]

Schweinfurth, Georg, 1836-1925
— The Heart of Africa. NY, 1874. 2 vols. 8vo, orig cloth. Frontis & upper blank loose. pn Oct 23 (17) £120 [Stewart]

Schwerdt, C. F. G. R.
— Hunting, Hawking, Shooting.... L, 1928-37. One of 300. 4 vols. 4to, orig half mor gilt; joints rubbed. sg June 11 (357) $1,300

Anr copy. Orig bdg. Jeanson copy. SM Mar 1 (592) FF30,000

Schwerdt Library, C.F.G.R.
— [Sale Catalogue] The Schwerdt Collection...relating to Hunting, Hawking & Shooting. L, 1939-46. Issue without

plates. 6 parts. 4to, orig wraps; worn. sg May 14 (351) $150

Schwerin, Ellwood William

— Salmonitis. A Treatise on its Symptomology.... [N.p.], 1927. 4to, half cloth; minor wear. sg Oct 23 (480) $200

Schwiebert, Ernest George

— Matching the Hatch. NY, 1955. Proof copy. Folio, loose as issued. sg Oct 23 (481) $100

— Salmon of the World. NY: Winchester Press, [1970]. One of 750. Folio, half cloth. With 30 color plates loose in port folio. sg Oct 482 $175

— Trout. NY, [1978]. One of 750, with an artificial fly in sunken mount. 2 vols. 4to, cloth. sg Oct 23 (483) $150

Schwitters, Kurt

— Anna Blume. Dichtungen. Hannover, 1919. 8vo, orig bds. JG Mar 20 (1297) DM1,300
Anr copy. Bds. Sgd inside upper cover & with related material. S May 6 (35) £140 [Gabus]

Scicluna, Sir Hannibal Publius

— The Church of St. John in Valletta. Rome: Pvtly ptd, 1955. Folio, orig cloth, in d/j. Ck Sept 5 (20) £35

Scidmore, Eliza Ruhamah, 1856-1928

— Alaska: Its Southern Coast and the Sitkan Archipelago. Bost.: D. Lothrop, [1885]. Orig cloth; rubbed. cb Jan 8 (4) $55

Scilla, Agostino

— De corporibus marinis lapidescentibus.... [N.p.]: Venantius Monaldinus, 1759. 4to, contemp calf; spine wormed. With frontis & 31 plates. Some dampstaining to lower portion of text throughout. S June 25 (55) £350

Scilly

— A Petition from the Island of Silley, 1, 12 Aug 1642. 4to, disbound. Some worming in inner margin; frayed; 1 leaf torn, affecting page numeral. S July 24 (264) £320 [Maggs]

Sclater, Philip Lutley
See also: Wolf, Joseph

— A Monograph of the Jacamars and Puff-Birds. L, [1079-82]. 4to, contemp half mor gilt, orig wraps to the 7 parts bound in; spine def at top. With 55 hand-colored plates. Some foxing of text; tp creased. S Oct 23 (755) £1,500 [Mitchell]

Sclater, Philip Lutley —& Hudson, William Henry, 1841-1922

— Argentine Ornithology. L, 1888-89. 2 vols. 8vo, orig bds; spines lacking. With 20 hand-colored plates. Titles stamped. pn Oct 23 (15) £520 [Thorp]
One of 200. Orig bds; rubbed & soiled, spines repaired. With 20 hand-colored plates. Cancelled library stamps on titles; a few leaves brittle at edges. S Oct 23 (756) £1,100 [Frers]

Sclater, Philip Lutley —& Salvin, Osbert

— Exotic Ornithology...New or Rare Species of American Birds. L, [1866]-69. Folio, contemp half mor gilt; upper joint broken. With 100 hand-colored plates. C Apr 8 (196) £2,800 [Phelps]

Sclater, Philip Lutley —& Thomas, Michael R. Oldfield

— The Book of Antelopes. L, 1894-1900. 4 vols. 4to, cloth; worn, 1st leaves of Vol I detached. With 100 colored plates. Titles stamped; ink stamps on plates. bba Jan 15 (424) £750 [Maggs]
Anr copy. Half calf. C Oct 15 (257) £5,000 [Foxworth]
Anr copy. Cloth. sg Dec 4 (174) $5,500

Sclater, William Lutley
See also: Shelley & Sclater

— System avium Aethiopicarum. A Systematic List.... L, [1924]-30. B Feb 24 (241) HF400

Scoffern, John

— Chemistry No Mystery: or a Lecturer's Bequest.... L, 1839. 8vo, half mor gilt. sg Sept 11 (79) $90

Scopoli, Johann Anton, 1723-88

— Deliciae Florae et faunae insubricae.... Ticini [Pavia], 1786-88. 3 parts in 3 vols. Folio, contemp calf, with Hapsburg royal arms; 2d vol not quite uniform, a few scrapes. With 4 frontises (1 in 2 states) & 74 (of 75) plates, all but 1 in 2 states, 1 plain & the other ptd in colors & finished by hand. This copy has pp 103-14 in Vol II which are usually absent. de Belder copy. S Apr 28 (331) £3,200 [Marks]

Scoresby, William, 1789-1857

— Journal of a Voyage to Australia and Round the World.... L, 1859. 8vo, half calf; worn. Frontis foxed. CA Apr 12 (218) A$80

Scot, Reginald, 1538-99

— The Discoverie of Witchcraft. L, 1651. ("The Discovery of Witchcraft.") 2d Ed. 4to, old bds; worn. Tear in a1 mended; some shaving. S May 6 (572) £300 [Jung]
Reprint of 1584 Ed. [L]: John Rodker,

SCOT

1930. One of 1,275. Folio, orig cloth; soiled. bba Mar 26 (262) £35 [Cox]

Scotcher, George
— The Fly Fisher's Legacy. L: Honey Dun Press, 1974. One of 380. Half mor. sg Oct 23 (485) $90

L.p. DeLuxe Ed, One of 55. Mor. With 30 hand-tied trout flies in sunken compartments. sg Oct 23 (484) $650

Scotland
— Acts and Proceedings of the General Assemblies of the Kirk of Scotland.... Edin.: Bannatyne Club, 1839-45. One of 100 on special club paper. 4 vols. 4to, half mor; rubbed. O Feb 24 (1) £60
— Cases Decided in the Court of Session.... Edin., 1821-1981. 158 vols; lacking that for 1973. 4to, half calf; some bdgs slightly worn. pnE Nov 12 (146) £2,400

Church of Scotland
— A True Copy of the Whole Printed Acts of the Generall Assemblies of the Church of Scotland. [Edin.?], 1682. 8vo, old calf; rubbed. O Feb 24 (46) £70

Scots...
— Scots Law Times. Edin., 1893-1985. No of vols not stated but complete for this period. Orig cloth, Vols I-X in contemp half calf. pnE Nov 12 (145) £1,200

Anr Ed. Edin., 1925-75. 75 vols. 4to, half calf. pnE Nov 12 (119) £300

76 vols. Edin., 1925-82. 4to, orig cloth. pnE Nov 12 (120) £540

Scott, Hew
— Fasti ecclesiae scoticanae. Edin., 1866-71. 6 parts in 3 vols. 4to, half mor gilt by Grieve. pnE Oct 15 (175) £180

Scott, Hugh S. See: Merriman & Tallentyre

Scott, James Edward
— A Bibliography of the Works of Sir Henry Rider Haggard. Takeley, 1947. One of 500. T Oct 15 (98) £40; T Oct 15 (99) £40

Scott, John
— British Field Sports. See: Lawrence, John

Scott, Peter
— Wild Chorus. L, 1938. One of 1,250, sgd. 4to, orig cloth; soiled. S Nov 17 (680) £90 [Tryon]

Scott, Capt. Robert Falcon
— Scott's Last Expedition. L, 1913. 2 vols. Orig cloth; rubbed. Some foxing. CA Apr 12 (219) A$100; kh Mar 16 (460) A$220
— The Voyage of the "Discovery." L, 1905. 2 vols. Orig cloth. kh Mar 16 (459) A$180

AMERICAN BOOK PRICES CURRENT

Scott, Sir Walter, 1771-1832
See also: Fore-Edge Paintings
— The Border Antiquities.... L, 1814-17. 2 vols. 4to, contemp mor gilt; rubbed. Ck Sept 26 (296) £65

Anr copy. Orig half mor. L.p. copy. pnE Jan 28 (262) £120 [Thin]

Anr copy. Contemp mor gilt, armorial bdg. With plates on india paper. L.p. copy. S Oct 23 (11) £360 [Spelmans]

Anr copy. Contemp half lea gilt. With engraved titles & 92 plates, all mtd india-proofs. L.p. copy. sg Feb 12 (279) $70

Anr copy. Contemp mor gilt; rebacked with orig backstrips preserved. T Oct 16 (351) £105
— The Lady of the Lake. L, 1810. 1st Ed. 4to, mor gilt by Fazakerley of Liverpool. Extra-illus with plates from the 1811 Westall Ed; with fore-edge painting of Loch Katrine; with ALs, 18 Aug 1806, to Mrs. George Ellis. P Sept 24 (213) $1,000

Anr Ed. Edin., 1834. 12mo, half mor with small view of Scott Monument painted on front cover. sg Feb 12 (281) $175
— Letters on Demonology and Witchcraft.... L, 1830. 1st Ed. 12mo, recent calf gilt; joints rubbed. cb Feb 19 (241) $130

Anr copy. Calf gilt. Frontis loose. sg Feb 12 (66) $175

Anr copy. Mor gilt. With frontis & 12 plates in 3 states. sg June 11 (149) $450
— The Life of Napoleon.... Edin., 1827. 9 vols. 8vo, orig cloth; 1 cover gouged. cb Dec 18 (160) $110

2d Ed. 9 vols. 8vo, orig bds; spines worn, inner hinge of Vol I broken. ALs to James Ballantyne tipped in, referring to the publication of this work. C June 18 (228) £450
— Marmion: A Tale of Flodden Field. Edin., 1866. 4to, orig mor gilt; rubbed. With 15 mtd photos by Thomas Annan. bba Oct 16 (134) £40 [Quaritch]
— Tales of the Crusaders. Edin., 1825. 1st Ed. 4 vols. 8vo, orig bds. pnE Jan 28 (140) £220 [Johnston]
— Waverley.... Edin., 1814. 1st Ed, 1st Issue. 3 vols. 12mo, half mor. pnE Jan 28 (136) £900 [Johnston]
— Works. Edin., 1829-33. ("Waverley Novels.") 48 vols. 12mo, contemp half mor gilt; rubbed. bba Feb 5 (180) £380 [Fletcher]

Anr copy. Contemp mor gilt. pn May 21 (99) £160 [Bailey]

Abbotsford Ed. Edin. & L, 1842-47. 12 vols. 8vo, contemp half calf; 1 spine damaged, several others soiled. Ck Jan 30 (101) £150

Anr copy. Half mor gilt. pnE Oct 15 (83)

£100
Anr copy. Half mor. With ALs to "James" pasted into Vol I. S Sept 22 (46) £190 [Thorp]

Anr Ed. Edin, 1853-52. 48 vols. 8vo, contemp half calf. T Oct 16 (642) £300

Library Ed. Edin., 1857. 25 vols. 8vo, half mor gilt. pnE Oct 15 (71) £340

Centenary Ed. L, 1871. 25 vols. 8vo, contemp half mor. S May 28 (908) £180

Anr Ed. Edin., 1877-79. 48 vols. 8vo, contemp half calf. pnE May 20 (77) £270

Ed de Grand Luxe. Phila., 1893-94. 8vo, mor gilt; rubbed. O May 12 (173) $800

Edinburgh Ed. Edin., 1901-3. One of 1,040. 48 vols. Orig cloth. pnE Oct 15 (205) £140

Scott, William Henry. See: Lawrence, John

Scotti, Francesco. See: Schottus, Franciscus

Scottish...
— Scottish Current Law Statutes.... Edin., 1949-82. 41 vols. 4to, cloth. pnE Nov 12 (121) £140

Anr Ed. Edin., 1949-85. 48 vols. 4to, orig cloth. With service file. pnE Nov 12 (148) £250

Scribner, Lynette L. See: Ripley & Scribner

Scrope, Frederic B.
— Scrope; or, the Lost Library. Bost., 1874. 8vo, orig cloth; spine ends chipped, hinges cracked. sg Jan 22 (276) $60

Scrope, William
— The Art of Deer Stalking. L, 1838. 1st Ed. 8vo, contemp calf gilt; small stain on upper cover. With engraved title, frontis & 10 tinted plates. Most plates stained. bba Mar 26 (209) £110 [Check]

Anr Ed. L, 1839. 8vo, cloth; small tear at head of spine. With 13 plates. Fresh copy. O Nov 18 (167) $110

Anr copy. Contemp half calf. Some foxing. pnE Oct 15 (2) £110

Anr copy. Mor gilt. With engraved title & 11 plates. sg May 21 (189) $200

— Days and Nights of Salmon Fishing in the Tweed. L, 1843. 1st Ed. 8vo, cloth; rubbed. With frontis & 11 plates. pn Mar 5 (40) £140 [Furness]

Anr copy. Mor gilt; scuffed. pnE Dec 17 (368) £260 [Steedman]

Anr copy. Orig cloth; worn. With additional title & 12 plates, 3 hand-colored. S Nov 17 (681) £100 [Negro]

Anr copy. Cloth; spine faded & worn. sg Oct 23 (486) $225

Scudery, Madeleine de, 1697-1701
— Almahide; or, the Captive Queen. L, 1677. Trans by J. Phillips. Folio, contemp calf; rebacked, inner hinges repaired. Short tear in 2d B2. S July 14 (345) £110

Scutenaire, Louis
— Les Enfants Trouves. Paris, 1968. Out-of-series copy for Georgette Magritte. Illus by Rene Magritte. Folio, unsewn in orig wraps. S July 2 (1065) £1,500 [Concept Art]

— Le Lien de Paille. Paris, 1969. One of 25 with etchings in 2 states. Illus by Rene Magritte. 4to, unsewn in orig wraps. Lacking 2 plates. Inscr to Georgette Magritte. S July 2 (1063) £1,400 [Gordon]

Anr copy. Lacking 3 plates. S July 2 (1064) £1,000 [Seibu]

Searle, Ronald
— Ronald Searle in Perspective. L, 1984. One of 250. 4to, orig mor. With sgd color litho loosely inserted. T Sept 18 (435) £55

Seasonable...
— Seasonable Remarks on the Act lately pass'd in Favour of the Jews.... L, 1753. 8vo, disbound. S Feb 17 (64) £200 [Shane]

Seaver, James E.
— A Narrative of the Life of Mrs. Mary Jemison.... Howden, 1826. 1st English Ed. 16mo, orig bds; backstrip torn. Ck Nov 21 (178) £140

Seba, Albert, 1665-1736
— Locupletissimi rerum naturalium thesauri. Amst., 1734-65. 4 vols. Folio, contemp half calf over bds; worn. With 449 plates. Some spotting. Horticultural Society of New York—de Belder copy. S Apr 28 (330) £8,500 [Schuster]

Seccombe, Joseph, 1706-60
Business and Diversion inoffensive to God.... Bost.: for S. Kneeland & T. Green, 1743. Bound with: Robbins, Chandler. A Reply to Some Essays lately Published by Joseph Cotton, Esq. 1773. And: Seccombe, Joseph. Reflections on Hypocrisy. 1741. And: Bellamy, Joseph. The Half-way Covenant. 1749. 8vo, half calf. Tp soiled. sg Oct 23 (487) $14,000

Second...
— A Second Collection of the Newest and most Ingenious Poems...Against Popery and Tyranny.... L, 1689. 4to, modern calf. Some paper-flaws & marginal corrosion. O Feb 24 (169) $70

Secousse, Denis Francois
— [Sale Catalogue] Catalogue des livres de la bibliotheque.... Paris: Barrois, 1755. Contemp half vellum; rubbed. Priced throughout in a contemp hand. Some marginal dampstains. cb Feb 5 (156) $110

See, Robert Rene Meyer
— English Pastels 1750-1830. L, 1911. Ltd Ed. 4to, vellum gilt; soiled. O Nov 18 (168) $50

Seebohm, Henry, 1832-95
— The Birds of Siberia.... L, 1901. 8vo, orig cloth. pn Oct 23 (275) £60 [Bewder]
— The Geographical Distribution of the Family Charadriidae, or the Plovers, Sandpipers.... L, [1887-88]. 4to, orig cloth; stained. With 21 plates. B Feb 24 (155) HF1,100

Anr copy. Contemp mor gilt. With 21 color plates. C Apr 8 (152) £500 [Traylen]
— A History of British Birds. L, 1883-85. 1st Ed. 4 vols. 8vo, contemp half mor; faded & rubbed. With 68 color plates. bba Oct 30 (421) £60 [Rainer]

Anr copy. Contemp half calf; rubbed. Ck Jan 16 (93) £50

Anr copy. Bdg not described. With 68 colored plates. pnE Dec 17 (279) £75 [Polwarth]

Anr Ed. L, 1896. 4 vols extended to 7. 8vo, half mor gilt. With 68 colored plates. Sold w.a.f. Extra-illus with 356 hand-colored plates extracted from Morris's History of British Birds. S May 28 (598) £380

Seguier, Jean Francois
— Bibliotheca botanica. The Hague, 1740. 4to, contemp calf; rehinged. pn Jan 22 (240) £280 [Maggs]

Segur, Sophie, Comtesse de, 1799-1874
— Old French Fairy Tales. Phila.: Penn Publishing Co., [1920]. Illus by Virginia Frances Sterrett. Cloth; rubbed, soiled & shaken. cb Sept 11 (314) $60

Seguy, E. A.
— Papillons. Paris, [1925]. Folio, cloth. With 20 colored plates. Bound with a Paint and Color Book of Butterflies; library markings. sg June 4 (304) $1,100
— Prismes. Paris: Moreau, [c.1930]. 4to, loose as issued in orig portfolio. Lacking 4 plates. sg Feb 5 (118) $350

Seitz, Adalbert
— The Macrolepidoptera of the World. I. Division Palaearctic Fauna. Stuttgart, 1906-32. Vol I only: The Palaearctic Butterflies. With Supplement. 2 vols. 4to, cloth; 1 spine damaged. S May 29 (1255) £160

— The Macrolepidoptera of the World. Stuttgart, 1909-38. Vols I-XVI in 27, including Supplements to Vols I-IV. 4to, orig half lea gilt. A few plates adhering to each other; Vol IV lacking 3 plates; Vol VI lacking 4 plates; Vol VII lacking 9 plates; Vol VIII lacking 3 plates; Vol XI lacking 2 plates; Vol XII lacking 1 plate; Vol XV lacking Plate 20; Vol XVI lacking 4 plates. Sold w.a.f. S Apr 23 (16) £5,200 [Rigout]

Selby, Prideaux John
— Illustrations of British Ornithology. Edin., [1819]-34. 4 vols. 8vo & folio, contemp half russia; lacking backstrips, broken. With engraved titles, 4 plates of detail & 218 uncolored plates. 1 plate just shaved; 5 plates with stains; small portion at foot of folding plates removed to facilitate fold. C Oct 15 (187) £5,800 [Heald]

Anr copy. Contemp russia gilt (broken); text in contemp half calf gilt. With engraved titles & 223 plates with early watermarks. Some tears; last plate of both plate vol mtd; tp to 1st plate vol creased. C Oct 15 (188) £25,000 [Mitchell]

Anr copy. Vol I only in 7 orig parts. Orig bds. With engraved title & 88 plates. 2 plates in Part 3 with small marginal tears. Sold w.a.f. C Oct 15 (200) £3,200 [Heald]

Anr copy. 4 vols. 8vo & folio, contemp bds, text in contemp half mor; bds rebacked & recornered with green calf. With 2 engraved titles, 4 uncolored plates of detail & 218 hand-colored plates. C Apr 8 (197) £14,000 [Coode-Adams]

Selden, John, 1584-1654
— De anno civili & calendario veteris ecclesiae seu republicae Judaicae, dissertatio.... L, 1644. 4to, modern lea. Marginal notes; light waterstains. bba Feb 19 (181) £350 [Valmadonna]
— De jure naturali & gentium. L, 1640. 1st Ed. Folio, vellum. B Feb 25 (1012) HF850
— De successionibus ad leges ebraeorum in bona defunctorum liber singularis.... Leiden: Elzevir, 1638. 12mo, contemp vellum; soiled. cb Oct 23 (69) $75
— The Historie of Tithes. L, 1618. 4to, contemp calf; rebacked. Light dampstaining in outer corners. sg Oct 9 (314) $150
— Of the Dominion, or, Ownership of the Sea. L, 1652. 1st Ed in English. 2 parts in 1 vol. Folio, sheep; def. pn June 18 (32) £240 [Traylen]
— Opera. L, 1726. 3 vols in 6. Folio, contemp calf gilt. sg Oct 9 (313) $400
— Titles of Honor. L, 1631. 2d Ed. 4to, contemp calf; hinges cracked. Title soiled. T Sept 18 (328) £64
— Titles of Honour. L, 1632. Folio, contemp

calf gilt; upper joint split, extremities bumped, head of spine chipped. Ck Jan 30 (16) £260
— Uxor Ebraica, seu de nuptiis & divortiis ex jure civili.... Frankfurt on Oder, 1673. 2 vols in 1. 4to, contemp calf; broken, worn. bba Nov 13 (10) £55 [Rees]

Select...
— Select Views of London and its Environs. L, 1804-5. 2 vols in 1. 4to, later half mor gilt. L.p. copy. bba Aug 20 (510) £120 [Axe]

Selection. See: Mayer, Luigi

Selfridge, Thomas Oliver, d.1818
— Report of Explorations and Surveys to Ascertain the Practicability of a Ship-Canal...by the Way of the Isthmus of Darien. Wash., 1874. 4to, modern half mor. With 14 plates & 17 folding maps & plans, some with crease tears. cb Jan 8 (178) $95

Anr copy. Orig cloth; bumped. With 14 plates & 17 maps. Minor foxing. cb Apr 2 (229) $160

Seligmann, Johann Michael. See: Edwards, George

Selincourt, Jean de Sacquespée, Vicomte de, c.1695
— Le Parfait Chasseur, pour l'instruction des personnes de qualite.... Paris: Gabriel Quinet, 1683. 12mo, contemp mor gilt; worn. Jeanson copy. SM Mar 1 (507) FF13,000

Selkirk, Thomas Douglas, 5th Earl of
— Observations on the Present State of the Highlands of Scotland.... L, 1805. 1st Ed. 8vo, old half calf, joints broken. O Mar 24 (156) $120

Anr copy. Modern calf gilt. pn Mar 5 (41) £90 [Walford]

Sella, Antonio
— Calligrafia di Antonio Sella.... Rome, 1840. Oblong folio, contemp half sheep; worn. With 52 plates. Engraved throughout. Two plates with purple ink stains. Sold w.a.f. Ck Sept 5 (2) £120

Seller, John, Hydrographer
— Atlas Caelestis.... L, [1680]. 12mo, contemp calf; worn. With allegorical title & 59 mostly double-page plates. Lacking frontis & South Polar chart; 1 plate torn without loss; some waterstains. S Oct 23 (224) £550 [Smiley]
— Atlas Maritimus, or the Sea-Atlas.... L, 1675. Folio, 19th-cent half calf gilt; rubbed. With engraved title & 28 double-page maps, colored in a contemp hand.

Minor damage & repairs; 1 or 2 maps just shaved within plate marks; minor worming affecting engraved surface. S Oct 23 (239) £28,000 [Arader]
— A Book of the Principal Cityes, Townes, and Bridges, in Hungary. L, [c.1686]. 8vo, wraps. With engraved title & 39 plans on 24 full-page or folding plates. S June 25 (315) £900
— Practical Navigation. L, 1702. 4to, old calf; worn, rebacked. With engraved title & 8 folding plates. bba Jan 15 (384) £85 [Phillips]

Selous, Edmund
— Bird Watching. L, 1901. One of 150 on handmade paper. Vellum. With additional color copy of the frontis laid-in. sg Oct 30 (187) $350

Selous, Frederick Courteney, 1851-1917
— Recent Hunting Trips in British North America. L, 1907. With 65 plates. cb Nov 6 (261) $110

Popular Ed. L, 1909. Contemp half mor. cb May 21 (228) $80
— Sunshine and Storm in Rhodesia. L, 1896. 2d Ed. 8vo, cloth; soiled. cb Nov 6 (262) $65
— Travel and Adventure in South-East Africa. L, 1893. 8vo, orig cloth; soiled, a few hinges cracking. cb May 21 (230) $140; pn Sept 18 (125) £75 [Trophy Room]

Semper, Gottfried
— Der Stil in den technischen und tektonischen Kuensten oder praktische Aesthetik. Munich, 1878-79. 2 vols. 8vo, half lea. B Oct 7 (925) HF600

Seneca, Lucius Annaeus, 54? B.C.-39 A.D.
See also: Shelley's copy, Percy Bysshe
— De Benifizii. Florence: Lorenzo Torrentino, 1554. 1st Ed in Italian. Trans by Benedetto Varchi. 4to, modern bds. Some browning. S Sept 23 (490) £180 [Zayas]
— Opera. Paris: for Antoine Verard, [not before 1500]. Folio, modern vellum by L. Pouillet for G. Duval. With large woodcut on a2r of a sainted author delivering his book to several persons; text initials touched with yellow; ruled in red throughout; in batarde types with French text 40 lines flanked by the Latin text 50 lines. 120 leaves. Goff S-373. P Dec 15 (163) $1,400
— Opera philosophicae. Basel: Froben, 1529. Folio, blind-stamped calf; regilded. Some dampstains; some leaves loose; writing on tp affecting text; pp 457-66 mis-numbered. pn Sept 18 (218) £50 [Tosi]

Anr Ed. Antwerp: Plantin, 1652. Folio, vellum; soiled, def. With engraved title, port & 2 plates. B Feb 25 (859) HF350

SENECA

— Works. L, 1614. 1st Complete Ed in English. Folio, needs rebdg. Index leaves wrinkled; lacking errata/colophon leaf & initial & final blanks; b1-3 & b6 not present. sg Mar 26 (257) $140

Senex, John, d.1740
See also: Ogilby & Senex

— Jeffery's Itinerary; or Travellers Companion through England, Wales and Part of Scotland.... L, 1775. Oblong 8vo,, disbound. With general map & 104 strip maps. pn May 21 (397) £300 [Postaprint]

— Modern Geography: or all the Known Countries of the World. L, [1708-25]. Folio, contemp russia; broken. With plate & 33 maps & additional map of the Netherlands, hand-colored in outline. Most maps detached; 3 maps dust-soiled with marginal tears; 4 maps with splits at fold. C Oct 15 (133) £1,000 [Burgess]

Anr copy. Contemp bds; worn. With 29 (of 34) maps, most hand-colored. Most maps damaged with some loss of surface. S July 14 (593) £700

Senior, Nassau William, 1790-1864

— Three Lectures on the Transmission of the Precious Metals from Country to Country and the Mercantile Theory of Wealth. L, 1828. 8vo, disbound. Inscr on tp. bba Sept 25 (116) £160 [Quaritch]

— Three Lectures on the Cost of Obtaining Money.... L, 1830. 8vo, modern half mor. Some stains. P Sept 24 (396) $300

Sententiae...

— Sententiae singulis versibus contentae...ex diversis poetis. Paris: R. Estienne, 1566. Bound with: Loysel, Christophorus. Etopaedia, sive morum institutio. Paris, 1580. And: Dicta septem sapientum & eorum qui cum iis numerantur. Paris: Etienne Prevosteau, [n.d.]. 8vo, 19th-cent mor. S May 21 (77) £500 [Kraus]

Sepp, Christiaan

— Beschouwing der Wonderen Gods, in de minstgeachte Schepzelen.... Amst., [1762-95] & The Hague, 1928. Series I-III in 12 vols plus 5 parts. 4to, contemp half calf; some spines & joints worn, 1 cover detached. With hand-colored engraved titles in First Series & 610 colored plates. Vol IV of First Series apparently lacking 12 pp at end; Third Series lacking tp. S June 25 (178) £4,600 [Israel]

Sept. See: Giraudoux & Others

AMERICAN BOOK PRICES CURRENT

Sepulveda, Juan Gines de

— Opera. Madrid, 1780. 4 vols. 4to, contemp calf; rubbed, 1 joint broken. O May 12 (174) $150

Seriman, Zaccaria

— Viaggi di Enrico Wanton.... Berne, 1764. 4 vols. 8vo, contemp vellum; rubbed. With folding map & 31 plates. Some worming; 1 gathering loose in Vol I. bba Oct 30 (228) £110 [Korn]

Serlio, Sebastiano, 1475-1554

— De Architectura libri quinque. Venice: Francesco de' Franceschi & Giovanni Chriegher, 1568-69. 2d Issue. Folio, 18th-cent vellum. S Apr 23 (101) £1,000 [Sims]

— Extraordinario Libro di architettura.... Venice: G.B. & M. Sessa, 1557. Folio, old bds; worn. With 50 plates. Lower blank corner of text & 17 plates restored; small stamp on tp. pn Apr 30 (333) £440 [Walford]

— Il Primo [-secundo] Libro d'Architettura....Le Premier [-second] livre d'architecture. Paris: J. Barbe, 22 Aug 1545. French trans by Jehan Martin. Folio, 18th-cent calf gilt; rebacked, corners restored. Lacking blank leaf c8; f2 with dampstain; some browning; fore-edge of diagrams on d3, g4 & h1 cropped. CNY Dec 19 (226) $2,800

— Regole generali di architettura. Venice, 1544. Folio, vellum bds; spine damaged. Tp discolored & repaired; lacking B1 & T4; several margins repaired; long tear in P3 repaired; T1 loose; some worming & soiling. S Sept 23 (523) £220 [Pesaro]

— Tutte l'opere d'architettura.... Venice, 1584. 4to, old vellum. Some browning; Index waterstained. FD June 11 (142) DM5,400

Anr Ed. Venice, 1619. 7 parts in 1 vol. 4to, contemp vellum. sg Apr 2 (179) $1,600

Sermonete, Alexander. See: Heytesbury, William

Serna Santander, Carlos Antonio de la

— Dictionnaire bibliographique choisi du quinzieme siecle. Brussels, 1805-7. 3 vols. 8vo, contemp half lea; rebacked, old backstrips laid down. sg May 14 (487) $275

Seroux D'Agincourt, Jean Baptiste L. G.

— Histoire de l'art par les monumens. Paris, 1823. 6 vols. Folio, later half cloth; rubbed. Ck June 19 (142) £260

Anr copy. Half mor gilt; rubbed. pn Apr 30 (303) £160 [Walford]

Serra's copy, Fray Junipero

— SAN MIGUEL, FRAY ISIDRO DE. - Parayso cultivado de la mas senzilla prudencia Virtudes practicadas en la Inocentissima Vida del V. Siervo de Dios.... Naples: Juan de Vernuccio & Nicolas Layno, 1695. 8vo, vellum; rebacked in calf. Port torn & repaired at margins; text browned throughout; some leaves cut close touching sidenotes. With 2-line ownership inscr by Serra at foot of title. S Apr 23 (273) £4,000 [Joseph]

Serre de Rieux, Jean de

— Les Dons des enfans de latone.... Paris, 1734. 8vo, contemp mor gilt with arms of Louis XV. Dedication copy. Hoe-Bishop-Jeanson copy. SM Mar 1 (508) FF65,000

Serres, Dominick & John Thomas

— Liber Nauticum, and Instructor in the Art of Marine Drawing. L, 1805-6. 1st Ed. 2 parts in 1. Folio, contemp half calf; blindstamp on lower cover. With 41 plates, 1 colored by hand. Lacking list of plates at end; tp mtd on linen & stamped on verso; plates stamped. S Feb 24 (510) £3,800 [Pigeonhole]

Serres, Olivier de, Seigneur du Pradel, 1539-1619

— Le Theatre d'agriculture et mesnage des champs. Paris: Jamet Metayer, 1600. Folio, contemp vellum with crowned H at corners & the arms of Henri IV at the center of the upper cover [Olivier 2492, fers 6, 10, 11 & 13]. Dedication copy. Jeanson copy. SM Mar 1 (509) FF950,000

Serrurier, J. F.

— Fruitkundig Woordenboek.... Amst.: J. Allart, 1805-6. 2 vols. 8vo, orig wraps, unopened; spines & joints worn. With 18 folding plates. Rectangular piece cut away from a prelim leaf in Vol I bearing a ptd spine label. Hunt copy. CNY Nov 21 (253) $90

Sertum...

— Sertum Botanicum. Collection choisie de plantes les plus remarquables par leur elegance, leur eclat ou leur utilite. Brussels, 1828-30. Ed by P. C. van Geel. Livraisons 1-42 (of 100). Folio, loose as issued. With 252 hand-colored plates. Text in French & Dutch. Lacking 3 text leaves. B Feb 24 (529) HF4,600

Set...

— A Set of Cuts for Children. L: [John Marshall, c.1797]. 8vo, orig bds; backstrip split. Engraved throughout. S June 17 (422) £1,050 [Randolph]

Seth-Smith, David

— Parrakeets, a Handbook to the Imported Species. L, 1926. Cloth. pn Oct 23 (276) £280 [Walford]

Seton, Sir Bruce Gordon, b.1868 —& Grant, John

— The Pipes of War: A Record of the Achievements of Pipers.... Glasgow, 1920. One of 200. Half vellum; soiled, ends creased. Lacking the separate portfolio of Pipe Tunes. cb Dec 18 (163) $65

Seton, Ernest Thompson, 1860-1946

— Life-Histories of Northern Animals. NY, 1909. 2 vols. 4to, cloth; soiled. Inscr. O Mar 24 (158) $225

Anr Ed. L, 1910. 2 vols. 4to, orig cloth; rubbed. Christmas card, sgd, loosely inserted. T Apr 16 (152) £100

— Lives of Game Animals. Bost., 1953. 4 vols in 8. cb Nov 6 (263) $225

Settle, Elkanah, 1648-1724

— Carmen irenicum. The Union of the Imperial Crowns of Great Britain. L, 1707. 1st Ed. Folio, contemp mor gilt, with the arms of the Sheffield family, bound for the author; short split at head of joints. C Dec 12 (358) £350 [Hannas]

Seuss, Dr.

— Horton Hears a Who! NY: Random House, [1954]. 4to, pictorial bds; worn. Inscr. wa Sept 25 (196) $60

Seutter, Matthaeus

— Atlas minor.... Augsburg, [1744?]. Oblong 8vo, modern half calf. With double-page hand-colored title & 63 double-page hand-colored maps. Lacking Europe & Alsace but including a map of Genoa not called for; some waterstaining throughout; top edges browned by fire just affecting ptd border of a few maps; title & world maps with tears repaired; world map def; France laid down; some splits at folds; 1 map torn. C Oct 15 (99) £800 [Faupel]

— Atlas novus indicibus instructus oder neur mit Wort-Registern versehener Atlas. Augsburg, [1740?]. Folio, lea. With 62 hand-colored maps. Some margins trimmed; some maps repaired. S Oct 23 (413) £1,600 [Hildebrand]

Severino, Marco Aurelio

— Zootomia democritaea: Id est, anatome generalis totius animantium opificii. Nuremberg: Endterianis, 1645. 4to, vellum bds. Browned throughout. S Nov 27 (286) £320 [Israel]

Severn Wildfowl Trust
— Annual Report. Slimbridge, 1948-84. Nos 1-35. 35 vols. B Feb 24 (44) HF200

Sevigne, Marie de Rabutin-Chantal, Marquise de, 1626-96
— Letters. Phila., 1927. Intro by A. E. Newton. 7 vols. Mor gilt; joints & corners worn. wa Sept 25 (44) $50
— Lettres.... Paris, 1818. ("Lettres de Madame de Sevigne de sa famille et de ses amis.") 11 vols including the Collection de Vingt Portraits du Siecle de Louis XIV. Contemp half mor gilt; rubbed. bba Oct 30 (229) £100 [Maggs]

Sewall, Stephen
— An Hebrew Grammar Collected.... Bost.: R. & S. Draper, 1763. 8vo, contemp half lea; worn. Annotations & defacement to a few words. sg Apr 30 (58) $800

Seward, Anna, 1742-1809
— Llangollen Vale. L, 1796. 4to, orig wraps; soiled. bba Oct 16 (99) £80 [Mills]

Seward, William Wenman
— Topographia Hibernica; or the Topography of Ireland. L, 1795. 4to, contemp half calf; worn, spine def. Some leaves torn in margins; 1 leaf torn across, affecting text; small hole in title. bba Apr 9 (360) £40 [Maguire]

Sewell, Brocard. See: Woolf & Sewell

Sexton, J. J. O'Brien. See: Binyon & Sexton

Seyer, Samuel
— Memoirs Historical and Topographical of Bristol.... Bristol, 1821-23. 2 vols in 1. 4to, later half mor gilt; rubbed. T Jan 22 (55) £48

Anr copy. 2 vols. 4to, modern half mor, retaining orig bds. Lacking 3 plates. T Feb 19 (298) £46

Seymour, Richard
— The Court Gamester, or, Full and Easy Instructions.... L, 1722. 3d Ed. 8vo, early 19th-cent half mor; worn, white ink call numbers on spine. Tp soiled & mtd & supplied from anr copy. sg Mar 26 (258) $100

Seymour, Robert
— Sketches. L, [c.1840]. 2 vols in 1. 8vo, contemp half mor; scuffed & worn. ha Sept 19 (236) $140

Sfortunati, Giovanni
— Novo Lume, libro di arithmetica. Venice: [Francesco del Leno], 1561. 4to, modern calf. Minor worming to title & 2 leaves, slightly affecting a few letters; 2 leaves with waterstain. C Dec 12 (284) £130 [Martin]

Shackleton, Sir Ernest Henry, 1874-1922
— The Heart of the Antarctic. L, 1909. 2 vols. 4to, cloth; worn, 1 joint split. kh Mar 16 (462) A$150

Anr copy. Cloth; worn. Inscr to J. P. Stewart & with photo of Shackleton & Stewart on board ship. pn May 21 (239) £180 [Sotheran]

— South.... NY, 1920. cb Nov 6 (265) $80

Anr copy. Lacking 1 plate; tp & prelims wormed. Inscr. Ck Nov 21 (73) £80

Shadbolt, Sydney Henry
— The Afghan Campaigns. L, 1882. 2 vols. 4to, half calf; rubbed. pn July 23 (282) £95 [Maggs]

Shadwell, Thomas, 1642?-92
— Works. L: Fortune Press, 1927. 5 vols. 4to, half mor; spines stained. CA Oct 7 (157) A$240

Shaffer, Ellen Kate
— The Garden of Health. An Account of Two Herbals. [San Francisco]: Ptd for the Book Club of California, 1957. Folio, orig bds. With an orig leaf from the 1499 Hortus Sanitatis bound in. cb Sept 11 (65) $150

Anr copy. Half cloth. With an orig leaf from the 1499 Hortus Sanitatis bound in. cb Oct 23 (206) $120

Shaftesbury, Anthony Ashley Cooper, 3d Earl of, 1671-1713
— Characteristicks of Men, Manners, Opinions, Times. [L], 1723. 3d Ed. 3 vols. 8vo, contemp calf. pnE Jan 28 (131) £160 [Thin]

4th Ed. L, 1727. 3 vols. 8vo, early 19th-cent mor gilt; joints & spine ends rubbed. sg Mar 26 (259) $80

6th Ed. L, 1737-38-37. 3 vols. 8vo, contemp calf gilt; worn, joints cracked. Some dampstains. cb Feb 19 (244) $130

Shahn, Ben
— An Alphabet of Creation.... NY, [1954]. One of 50, with a sgd ink drawing. 4to, cloth. sg Apr 2 (180) $900

SHAKESPEARE

Shakespeare, William, 1564-1616
See also: Cranach Press; Golden Cockerel Press; Grabhorn Printing; Kelmscott Press; Limited Editions Club; Nonesuch Press

— Antony and Cleopatra. Guildford: Circle Press, 1979. One of 300. Illus by Ronald King. Folio, unsewn as issued. sg June 11 (106) $110

— The Chronicle History of Henry the Fift.... L: William Jaggard for Thomas Pavier, 1608 [1619]. 4to, mor gilt by Riviere. A1.4 slightly discolored; tp neatly guarded at inner edge but with a short split along the guard. Wallace-Terry copy. S July 23 (18) £30,000 [Pickering]

Hamlet. L. Selwyn & Blount, [1922]. ("Hamlet, Prince of Denmark.") One of 60, sgd by the artist. Illus by John Austen. 4to, half vellum gilt. With extra title. S Dec 4 (160) £520 [Mitchell]

One of 60. Orig half cloth, in repaired d/j. S June 17 (204) £1,100 [Mesti]

— Julius Caesar. L, 1684. 4to, early wraps. Small blank corner piece torn from tp. C May 13 (169) £2,400 [Joseph]

— King Lear. San Francisco, [1930]. One of 200. cb Sept 11 (324) $85

— A Midsummer-Night's Dream. L, 1908. Illus by Arthur Rackham. 4to, cloth. Some foxing at beginning & end. bba June 18 (249) £100 [Oram]

Anr copy. Contemp vellum; soiled. pn Jan 22 (314) £110 [Mackenzie]

Anr copy. Orig cloth. pn Mar 5 (337) £120 [Henderson]

Anr copy. Cloth. With 40 mtd color plates. sg Oct 30 (189) $120

Anr copy. Half cloth; worn & soiled. sg Jan 8 (233) $50

One of 1,000, sgd by Rackham. Orig vellum gilt; rubbed. With 40 mtd color plates. sg Oct 30 (188) $850

One of 1,000. Orig vellum gilt; soiled. With 40 colored plates. sg Jan 8 (232) $450

— Othello. L, 1695. 4to, disbound. Tears to prelims & several gatherings. sg June 11 (359) $130

— Romeo and Juliet. L & NY, [1912]. One of 250, sgd by artist. Illus by W. Hatherell. 4to, orig vellum gilt. With 22 colored plates. S Oct 6 (815) £70 [Marks]

— Sentiments and Similes.... L, 1857. Decorated by Henry Noel Humphreys. 4to, orig half lea on papier mache bds; rebacked retaining part of orig spine. S Nov 10 (385) £65 [Barker]

— Le Songe d'une nuite d'ete. Paris, 1909. One of 30 on japan vellum. Illus by Arthur Rackham. 4to, pictorial vellum gilt. With 40 mtd color plates. sg Oct 30 (190) $700

— The Tempest. L, [1908]. One of 500. Illus by Edmund Dulac. 4to, orig vellum gilt; soiled. With 40 colored plates. S May 6 (109) £100 [Dawes]

Anr Ed. L, [1926]. Illus by Arthur Rackham. With 20 mtd color plates. sg Oct 30 (192) $225

One of 520. 4to, vellum gilt; worn & stained. K Oct 4 (377) $200

Anr copy. Orig half vellum. With the additional color plate. sg Oct 30 (191) $750

— The Whole Contention betweene the Two Famous Houses, Lancaster and Yorke.... [Henry VI. Parts 2 & 3]. L: William Jaggard for Thomas Pavier, [1619]. 4to, 19th-cent mor gilt; joints repaired. A few headlines just shaved; without Pericles. Clawson-Hogan copy. S July 23 (19) £30,000 [Quaritch]

1st Folio

Comedies, Histories, & Tragedies. L, 1623. Cloth by Zaehnsdorf. Fragment of 26 leaves comprising 2 discontinuous leaves of As You Like It and the complete text of The Taming of the Shrew and All's Well That Ends Well. sg Apr 2 (181) $3,000

2d Folio

1st Issue, 1st state of imprint; 2d variant of Effigies leaf. Modern half calf. Lacking tp, 1 other prelim & all after 3A6; severely damaged by damp in inner margin, affecting text; some tears & holes. Sold w.a.f. S Dec 18 (13) £1,500 [Sotheran]

3d Folio

— Comedies, Histories & Tragedies. L, [1663]-64. 2d Issue. 19th-cent mor; rebacked, old backstrip laid down. Scattered stains; minor marginal repairs; tp soiled; 5 leaves supplied from anr copy; leaf A1 from 1st or 2d Folio inserted after A4. Wing S2914. sg Apr 2 (182) $42,000

2d Issue. L, 1664. Mor by Zaehnsdorf, 1905. Frontis, title, A3-4, b4, A1, R2 & Z6 in facsimile; K1-2 with minor adhesion flaws & a few words in ink facsimile; margins of 2 leaves repaired with a few lines supplied in ink facsimile; margins of b6 & 3M5 cropped affecting a few letters; b1 head-margin restored shaving 1 initial. C May 13 (168) £2,400 [Joseph]

4th Folio

— Comedies, Histories, and Tragedies. L, 1685. Contemp calf gilt; worn. Short tears in a few leaves occasionally extending into text; corner torn from Hh4 & small holes in

SHAKESPEARE

Bbb3 & Ppp6 affecting a few letters; small wormholes in lower margin of a few leaves towards end; stains in some inner margins; some signatures in second section corrected in ink. bba June 18 (176) £15,000 [Quaritch]

Collected Works

— 1765. - L. 8 vols. 8vo, contemp calf; joints cracked. T Nov 21 (52) £170
— 1768. - The Plays. L. Ed by Samuel Johnson. 8 vols. 8vo, contemp calf gilt; worn, 1 cover loose. Some worming. S Jan 16 (433) £120 [Maggs]
— 1788. - L. 20 vols. 12mo, contemp calf; worn. Ck Feb 13 (60) £320
— 1791. - The Dramatic Works. L. Ed by George Steevens. 9 vols. Folio, contemp calf; rubbed. Ck Nov 7 (41) £260
— 1793. - L. Notes by Samuel Johnson & George Steevens. 16 vols. 8vo, early 19th-cent russia gilt. sg Feb 12 (284) $500
— 1802. - The Dramatic Works.... L.Boydell Ed. Ed by George Steevens. 9 vols. Folio, mor gilt. Browned. L Dec 11 (430) £320
— 1832-34. - L: A. J. Valpy. 15 vols. 12mo, half lea by Root; broken. O Mar 24 (160) $70

Anr copy. Half mor; rubbed. Minor stains. O June 9 (164) $80
— 1880-81. - Works. L. Ed by Alexander Dyce. 10 vols. 8vo, half mor; rubbed. cb July 30 (172) $150
— 1900-03. - L: Vale Press One of 310. 39 vols. Orig cloth. sg June 11 (417) $325
— 1901-4. - L. One of 1,000. Ed by W. E. Henley. 10 vols in 5. Folio, half mor gilt. pnNY Mar 12 (109) $250
— 1904-7. - Stratford: Shakespeare Head Press One of 1,000. 10 vols. 4to, half mor gilt; rubbed. O May 12 (176) $400
— 1909. - NY One of 1,000. 10 vols. Half mor; extremities worn. cb Oct 23 (208) $65
— 1936. - Garden City One of 750. Ed by W. A. Wright; illus by Rockwell Kent. 2 vols. 4to, cloth. Inscr by Christopher Morley. cb June 18 (211) $475

Anr copy. Illus by Rockwell Kent. Cloth; rubbed & bumped. cb Dec 4 (243) $150; cb Feb 19 (149) $150; sg Dec 4 (97) $300; sg Jan 8 (148) $450

Facsimile Editions

— The National Shakespeare. L: W. Mackenzie, [n.d.]. Illus by J. Noel Paton. 3 vols. Folio, orig mor gilt. Facsimile of 1st Folio. Ck Apr 24 (215) £95
— 1864. - L. Folio, half mor; rubbed, joints starting. Ellen Terry's copy, with the bookplate designed for her by Edward Gordon Craig. sg Feb 26 (203) $350
— 1902. - L. One of 1,000, sgd by Sir Sidney Lee. Folio, orig half lea. K June 7 (341) $160
— 1968. - NY Folio, orig half mor. The Norton Facsimile. O Nov 18 (169) $80

Poems, Sonnets, etc.

— Of Imagination All Compact. Four Sonnets.... San Francisco, 1971. One of 35. 4 leaves, 11 by 18 inches, loose as issued in portfolio. sg Jan 8 (117) $200
— The Poems. L: Essex House, 1899. One of 450. 8vo, orig vellum. sg June 11 (189) $200
— Songs and Sonnets. Harrow Weald: Raven Press, 1931. ("Venus and Adonis.") One of 295. cb June 18 (223) $160
— The Sonnets. Birm.: Birmingham Guild of Handicraft, 1895. 4to, mor gilt. S Sept 22 (186) £85 [Sotheran]
— The Sonnets of Shakespeare. East Aurora, 1899. One of 980. 8vo, half lea; worn. With hand-colored woodcut initials. sg Jan 8 (264) $60
— Venus and Adonis. Rochester, 1931. One of 1,175, sgd by the artist. Illus by Rockwell Kent. 4to, half calf. cb Dec 4 (244) $110

Shand, A. I.
— Shooting. L, 1902. One of 150 on handmade paper. Vellum. With a copy of the frontis laid in. sg Oct 30 (194) $325

Shapiro, Elliott. See: Dichter & Shapiro

Shapiro, Karl
— Poems. Balt.: Waverly Press, 1935. Out-of-series copy. With Poem Jazz Hit annotated in Shapiro's hand. sg Mar 5 (232) $400

Sharp, Samuel, 1700?-78
— A Critical Enquiry into the Present State of Surgery. L, 1750. 8vo, contemp calf. pnE Dec 17 (49) £65 [Maggs]
— A Treatise on the Operations of Surgery. L, 1739. 1st Ed. 8vo, contemp calf. pnE Dec 17 (48) £200 [Hunt]

Sharpe, Richard Bowdler, 1847-1909
— An Analytical Index to the Works of the Late John Gould. L, 1893. 4to, orig cloth; worn. S Apr 23 (20q) £350 [Smit]

One of 100 L.p. copies. Orig half mor; rubbed. C Oct 15 (207) £1,500 [Mitchell]
— A Monograph of the Alcedinidae: or, Family of Kingfishers. L, 1868-71. 4to, modern mor gilt. With folding map & 120 hand-colored plates. pn Apr 30 (225) £3,000 [Phelps]

Anr copy. Contemp half mor gilt; rubbed. With hand-colored map & 121 plates, all but 1 hand-colored. S Oct 23 (757) £2,800 [Wesley]

Anr copy. Contemp mor gilt; worn & stained. Several plates foxed or slightly stained in extreme lower margins; stain on Plate 89; plates numbered in upper corner in pencil or pen. S Oct 23 (758) £2,700 [Zanzotte]
— A Monograph of the Paradiseidae, or Birds of Paradise. L, 1891-98. 2 vols. Folio, mor gilt by Morrell, orig wraps bound in. With 79 hand-finished colored plates (coloring may be later). S June 25 (179) £7,500 [Klein]

Sharpe, Richard Bowdler, 1847-1909 —& Wyatt, Claude Wilmott
— A Monograph of the Hirundinidae or Family of Swallows. L, 1885-94. 2 vols. 4to, contemp half mor gilt; rubbed, 2 joints split. With 103 hand-colored plates. S Oct 23 (760) £3,500 [Vischer]

Shaul, H. Edwin
— The Golden Retriever. Bost.: Indian Springs Press, 1954. Ltd Ed. Lea, in torn d/j. sg Oct 23 (491) $90

Shaw, George, 1751-1813 —& Miller, John Frederick
— Cimelia Physica. Figures of Rare and Curious Quadrupeds, Birds.... L, 1796. 1st Ed. Folio, contemp half mor; rubbed. With 60 hand-colored plates. Grote—Brooke —de Belder copy. S Apr 28 (244) £8,500 [Elliott]

Shaw, George, 1751-1813 —& Nodder, Frederick P.
— The Naturalist's Miscellany. L, [1789]-1790-[99]. Vols I-V (of 24). 8vo, contemp calf; broken. Plates & text generally rather grubby & soiled; Plate 23 def; 2 folding plates repaired; some plates out of sequence. L Dec 11 (307) £380

Anr copy. Vols I-VI (of 24). 8vo, calf; worn. Sold w.a.f. S Feb 23 (42) £850 [Edge]

Shaw, George Bernard, 1856-1950
See also: Gregynog Press
— The Apple Cart. L, 1930. 1st Ed. In d/j; upper hinge broken, cover wormed. Inscr. S Sept 22 (40) £180 [Libris Antik]
— Augustus Does his Bit; an Unofficial Dramatic Tract on War Saving.... [L, 1916]. Wraps; worn, front cover tape-repaired. Proof copy. sg Dec 11 (111) $175
— Buoyant Billions. [L], [1949]. 1st Ed, one of 1,000. Cloth. sg Mar 5 (233) $50
— Great Catherine: a Thumbnail Sketch of Court Life in St. Petersburg.... L, 1914. 1st Ed. "Rough proof - unpublished.". sg Dec 11 (108) $250
— O'Flaherty V. C. An Interlude in the Great War of 1914. [N.p., 1915]. "Rough Proof Unpublished". Ptd wraps. sg Dec 11 (109) $300
— Plays: Pleasant and Unpleasant. L, 1901. 2 vols. Each vol inscr to Sir Sydney Cockerell. Vol I with autograph postcard & Vol II with ALs, both from Shaw to Cockerell. S Sept 22 (141) £440 [Joseph]
— Saint Joan. L, 1924. One of 750. Folio, bds; extremities worn. With 16 tipped-in color plates. sg Jan 8 (246) $70

Anr copy. Illus by Charles Ricketts. Orig half mor by Zaehnsdorf. With 4 plain & 12 color plates. S Dec 4 (218) £220 [Thorp]
— War Issues for Irishmen.... Dublin, 1918. Suppressed 1st Ed. Wraps; spine & edges worn. sg Dec 11 (110) $800
— Works. NY, 1930-32. Ayot St. Lawrence Ed, one of 1,790. Half cloth. pn Nov 20 (89) £180 [Shaw]

One of—1,790. Half cloth; spines soiled, some stained. wa Sept 25 (45) $80

Shaw, Henry, 1800-73
— Dresses and Decorations of the Middle Ages. L, 1843. 2 vols. 4to, half mor gilt by Bickers. pn Mar 5 (296) £110 [Elliott]

Anr copy. Mor gilt. Hand-colored copy. S Nov 18 (934) £250 [Sims]

Anr copy. Mor; worn, cracked, loose in bdg. sg Dec 18 (219) $110

Anr copy. Mor; needs rebdg. sg Feb 5 (297) $400

Anr Ed. L, 1858. 2 vols. 4to, 19th-cent half lea. With 94 color plates. Stain in corner of Vol II opening leaves. sg June 4 (309) $225

Shaw, Henry, 1800-73 —& Meyrick, Sir Samuel Rush
— Specimens of Ancient Furniture.... L, 1866. 4to, modern half lea; worn. Minor dampstains. O Nov 18 (170) $60

Shaw, John Mackay
— Childhood in Poetry: A Catalogue.... Detroit, 1967. 5 vols. 4to, cloth. sg Jan 22 (277) $60

Shaw, Peter
— The Dispensatory of the Royal College of Physicians in Edinburgh. L, 1727. 8vo, contemp calf; joints cracked, rubbed. bba Oct 30 (423) £120 [Cavendish]
— An Enquiry into the Contents, Virtues, and Uses, of the Scarborough Spaw-Waters.... L, 1734. 4to, contemp half lea; hinges cracked. T Sept 18 (363) £425

Shaw, Ralph R. —& Shoemaker, Richard H.
— American Bibliography; a Preliminary Checklist for 1801-1819.... [Methuen, N.J.], 1958-66. 22 vols. O June 16 (172) $300

Anr Ed. [Methuen, N.J.], 1958-75. 36 vols,

SHAW

including Indexes & Addenda. sg Jan 22 (278) $475

Shaw, Simeon
— History of the Staffordshire Potteries. Hanley, 1829. 1st Ed. 8vo, calf gilt. P Nov 25 (421) $350

Shaw, Thomas, 1694-1757
— Reizen en aanmerkingen door en over Barbaryen en het Oosten. Amst., 1780. 2 parts in 1 vol. 4to, contemp half calf. With engraved titles & 40 maps & plates. bba Mar 26 (354) £160 [Poel]
— Travels or Observations relating to Several Parts of Barbary and the Levant. Oxford, 1738-46. Without Supplement. Folio, bds preserving contemp calf spine, unpressed copy. With 12 maps & plans & 21 plates. S Nov 18 (1075) £260 [Mackenzie]
  Anr copy. 2 vols, including Supplement, in 1. Folio, contemp calf gilt; joints broken. A few leaves torn; some tears. S Jan 12 (241) £200 [Demetzy]
  Anr Ed. L, 1757. 4to, contemp calf; rebacked. With 36 maps & plates. Ck Sept 26 (80) £160

Shaw, Vero Kemball
— The Illustrated Book of the Dog. L, [1881]. 4to, orig cloth; rubbed & soiled, lacking endpapers. bba Mar 26 (302) £250 [Shapero]
  Anr copy. Half mor; rubbed. Lacking 2 plates; some plates loose; 1 leaf torn at inner margin. S Feb 24 (611) £320 [Dowling]

Sheets, Millard
[-] Millard Sheets. Articles by Arthur Millier, Dr. Hartley Burr Alexander and Merle Armitage. Los Angeles, 1935. One of 1,000. Mor gilt by Hazel Dreis. With port by Edward Weston, orig sgd litho by Sheets & 28 plates. cb Dec 4 (347) $180

Sheldon, Harold P.
  See also: Derrydale Press
— A Private Affair. Pvtly ptd by the Derrydale Press for Col. Woods King, [1941]. Bds. sg Oct 23 (117) $550

Sheldrake, Timothy
— Botanicum Medicinale: an Herbal of Medicinal Plants. L, 1759. Folio, contemp half sheep; worn & rubbed. With 111 (of 118) leaves, each with hand-colored figure of a plant surrounded by engraved text. Sold w.a.f. C Apr 8 (142) £3,800 [Shapero]
  Anr copy. Modern half mor gilt. With 104 (of 118) leaves, each with hand-colored figure of a plant surrounded by engraved text. L.p. copy. Harewood—de Belder copy. S Apr 28 (333) £4,500 [Shapiro]

AMERICAN BOOK PRICES CURRENT

Shelley, George Ernest
— A Monograph of the Nectariniidae, or Family of Sun-Birds. L, 1876-80. 4to, contemp half mor gilt. With 121 hand-colored plates. Tp & some leaves spotted. C Apr 8 (153) £3,500 [Wheldon & Wesley]

Shelley, George Ernest —& Sclater, William Lutley
— The Birds of Africa, Comprising all the Species...in the Ethiopian Region. L, 1896-1912. Vols I-IV (of 5) bound in 5 vols. 4to, contemp cloth. With 42 hand-colored plates. Sold w.a.f. C Oct 15 (258) £600 [Barrell]

Shelley, Henry C.
— The Homes and Haunts of Thomas Carlyle. L, 1895. 8vo, cloth; spine faded. sg Oct 30 (195) $60

Shelley, Mary Wollstonecraft
  See also: Limited Editions Club
— Frankenstein; or, the Modern Prometheus. L, 1831. 8vo, late 19th-cent calf by Mansell; slightly rubbed. Minor spotting. S Dec 18 (89) £300 [Joseph & Sawyer]
  Anr Ed. West Hatfield MA: Pennyroyal Press, 1983. One of 5 specially bound by Daniel Kelm in mor with front cover panel of spray-cast fiber with goatskin onlay of the monster's hand, after an orig wax sculpture by Moser. Illus by Barry Moser. sg Dec 4 (152) $3,400
— Mounseer Nontongpaw: a New Version. L: The Juvenile Library, 1808. Illus by William Mulready. 16mo, orig ptd wraps. With frontis & 11 plates, 2 colored by a former owner. Some stains. S Dec 5 (290) £1,600 [Quaritch]
  4th Ed. L: M. J. Godwin & Co at The Juvenile Library, 1816. 16mo, orig ptd wraps. With 12 colored plates. S Dec 5 (291) £250 [Schiller]
— Mountseer Nontongpaw: a New Version. L, 1808. Illus by William Mulready. 16mo, contemp half lea; rubbed. With frontis & 11 plates, 4 partly colored by a former owner. Some waterstains; a few margins strengthened or restored; several leaves short; 1 line of verse cropped on pp 5 & 6. S Dec 18 (90) £700 [Quaritch]
— Valperga: or, the Life...of Castruccio, Prince of Lucca. L, 1823. 1st Ed. 3 vols. 12mo, contemp calf; needs rebdg. sg Sept 11 (260) $250

Shelley, Percy Bysshe, 1792-1822
  See also: Fore-Edge Paintings; Kelmscott Press
— The Cenci. Italy [Leghorn]: Ptd for C. & J. Ollier of London, 1819. 1st Ed. 8vo, mor gilt by Zaehnsdorf. Lacking initial blank; a few spots or marks. Esher copy. S Dec 18

(84) £1,050 [Quaritch]
— Hellas, a Lyrical Drama. L, 1822. 1st Ed. 8vo, lev gilt by Riviere. S July 23 (96) £450 [Maggs]
— Letters to J. H. Leigh Hunt. L, 1894. 1st Ed, one of 6 on vellum. Ed by T. J. Wise. 2 vols. 8vo, modern mor by Ramage; rubbed. S Dec 18 (86) £700 [Blackwell]
— Note Books.... St. Louis, 1911. One of 250. 3 vols. 4to, half vellum, unopened. Inscr by William Bixby. sg June 11 (360) $100
— Posthumous Poems. L, [1824]. 8vo, orig bds; spine worn. Lacking errata leaf. S Dec 18 (85) £500 [Blackwell]

Anr copy. 19th-cent calf; rubbed, spine def. Inscr to Duff Cooper by Venetia & Edwin Montagu. S Mar 9 (791) £220 [Quaritch]

— Prometheus Unbound. L, 1820. 1st Ed, 2d Issue. 8vo, modern half mor. Lacking half-title & ad leaf. S Jan 13 (521) £80 [Bauman]

Anr Ed. L: Essex House Press, 1904. One of 200. S Oct 6 (743) £130 [Thorp]

— Queen Mab. L, 1813. 1st Ed. 8vo, mor gilt by Pratt; broken. Unmutilated copy with dedication and imprints on title and verso of last leaf. Tp repaired. S Dec 1 (81) £1,200

1st Pbd Ed. L, 1821. Later calf; rubbed. Prelims browned. Ck Jan 16 (140) £70

Unauthorized Benbow Ed with the false imprint. NY, 1821. Later mor gilt. Terry copy. sg June 11 (361) $100

— Rosalind and Helen. L, 1819. 1st Ed. 8vo, mor by Sangorski. C May 13 (170) £380 [Blackwell]

Anr copy. Calf gilt by Bedford. First few leaves spotted. Hibbert-Esher copy. S Dec 18 (83) £420 [Blackwell]

— The Sensitive Plant. L, 1911. 4to, vellum; rubbed. cb Feb 19 (246) $150
— Works. L, 1927. Ed by Roger Ingpen & Walter E. Peck. 10 vols. 8vo, half vellum. wa Dec 11 (214) $220
— Zastrozzi, a Romance. L, 1810. 12mo, mor gilt by Douglas Cockerell with his monogram. Tinker copy. sg Apr 2 (183) $7,000

Shelley's copy, Percy Bysshe
— SENECA, LUCIUS ANNAEUS. - Opera philosophicae. Antwerp: Plantin, 1615. Folio, early 19th-cent calf; rebacked. Extensively annotated by Shelley, who received the book from Clare Clairmont. S Dec 18 (87) £9,500 [Quaritch]

Shelvocke, Capt. George
— A Voyage Round the World.... L, 1726. 8vo, contemp calf. With folding map & 4 plates. Map & 1 plate torn with loss. Sold w.a.f. Ck May 21 (56) £85

2d Ed. L, 1757. 8vo, contemp calf; worn.

With frontis map on 2 leaves, title vignette & 4 plates. Map torn at fold; some leaves soiled. S June 25 (415) £400 [Griffiths]

Anr copy. Contemp calf; rebacked. sg Dec 4 (179) $425

Shepard, E. Clarence. See: Fore-Edge Paintings

Shepard, Thomas, 1605-49
— The Clear Sun-shine of the Gospel. L, 1648. 4to, mor gilt; joints & corners rubbed. Upper margin of title patched with slight loss; A3 and a1 torn & repaired; lacking 1st blank. CNY Dec 19 (73) $2,000

Shephard, Charles
— An Historical Account of the Island of Saint Vincent. L, 1831. 1st Ed. 2 parts in 1 vol. 8vo, orig cloth; extremities frayed in a few places. With 2 plates. sg Apr 23 (132) $175

Shepherd, Thomas Hosmer
— Bath and Bristol, with the Counties of Somerset and Gloucester.... L, 1829. 4to, modern cloth. With 2 engraved titles & 82 views on 41 sheets. T Nov 20 (57) £200

Anr copy. Contemp cloth; spine worn. With 40 (of 48) views on 20 leaves. T Dec 18 (36) £230

Modern Athens. Displayed.... L, 1829. 4to, modern calf gilt. Frontis with some adhesion damaged. O June 9 (165) $70

Anr copy. Half calf. With 100 views on 48 sheets. Engraved title stained. pn Dec 11 (80) £80 [Nicholson]

Shepherd, Thomas Hosmer — & Elmes, James, 1782-1862
— London and its Environs in the Nineteenth Century. L, 1829. 4to, contemp mor gilt; hinges worn. With engraved title & 195 views on 81 leaves. T May 21 (292) £140
— Metropolitan Improvements; or London in the Nineteenth Century. L, 1827. 4to, half mor; rubbed, broken. With 158 views on 79 plates. With perforated stamp on 2 pp. bba Dec 4 (351) £140 [Barker]

Anr copy. Half calf gilt. pn Sept 18 (166) £180 [Nicholson]

Anr copy. Half lea gilt. With engraved title, plan & 158 views on 79 sheets. pn Apr 18 (104) £190 [Gill]

Anr copy. Contemp half calf; rubbed. Lacking 1 plate. S Nov 17 (825) £200 [Boyd]

Anr Ed. L, 1828. 4to, modern cloth. Engraved title misbound & repaired in margin. bba Dec 352 £50 [Elliott]

Anr copy. With engraved title, plan & 162 views on 81 plates. Perforated stamps on title & plates. bba Feb 5 (385) £50 [Rainer]

Anr copy. Contemp half mor; front joint

Shepherd

starting. With engraved title, folding plan & 62 mtd india-proof plates. L.p. copy. sg Nov 20 (158) $250

Shepperd, Tad. See: Derrydale Press

Sherer, John
— The Classic Lands of Europe. L, [1879-81]. 2 vols. 4to, half lea; worn. Sold as collection of plates. Sold w.a.f. sg Dec 18 (219) $110
— Europe Illustrated: its Picturesque Scenes and Places of Note. 1st Series. L & NY, [1876-79]. 2 vols. Folio, half lea gilt. sg Apr 23 (133) $250
— The Gold-Finder of Australia. L, [1853]. 8vo, orig cloth. With vignette title & 47 plates. Contents leaves spotted. C Oct 15 (172) £280 [Mall Gallery]

Anr copy. Half calf; worn. Some stains. pn Mar 5 (317) £110 [Knowles]

Sheridan, Richard Brinsley, 1751-1816
See also: Limited Editions Club
— The Critic.... L, 1781. Bound with: Pizarro; a Tragedy. L, 1799. 11th Ed. 8vo, later half calf. bba Jan 15 (61) £45 [Cathach]
— Dramatic Works. NY, 1883. One of 348. 3 vols. 8vo, calf gilt. sg Feb 12 (287) $110

Anr copy. Calf gilt; 1 cover faded. sg Feb 12 (287) $110
— Pizarro. L, 1799. 1st Ed. 8vo, calf gilt; front joint cracked. sg Sept 11 (261) $100

Anr copy. Modern calf gilt by Wood. sg June 11 (362) $80
— The School for Scandal. L, [1911]. Illus by Hugh Thomson. 4to, orig cloth. pn Jan 22 (322) £130 [Joseph]

Sheridan, Thomas, 1719-88
— British Education: or, the Source of the Disorders of Great Britain. L, 1756. 1st Ed. 8vo, contemp calf. bba May 14 (202) £180 [Drury]

Sheringham, Hugh Tempest
— Trout Fishing. Memories and Morals. L, [1920]. Calf by Sangorski & Sutcliffe. ANs from the pbr tipped in. sg Oct 23 (497) $175

Sheringham, Hugh Tempest —& Moore, John C.
— The Book of the Fly-Rod. Bost. & NY, 1931. One of 195. Orig half vellum. Library stamp. sg Oct 23 (494) $100

Sherlock, H. H.
— The Practical Christian or the Devout Penitent. Oxford, 1846. 2 vols in 1. 8vo, later mor gilt. pnE Nov 12 (90) £45

Sherman, William Tecumseh, 1820-91
— Supplemental Report of the Joint Committee on the Conduct of the War. Wash., 1866. 2 vols. 8vo, orig cloth; rubbed. With 13 folding maps & plans. Some foxing & offsetting; some plates soiled. sg Sept 18 (269) $50

Shields, George Oliver
— Cruisings in the Cascades. Chicago & NY, 1889. 8vo, orig cloth; scuffed. pn Oct 23 (323) £50

Anr copy. Orig cloth; worn. wa Sept 25 (148) $50

Shillibeer, Lieut. John
— A Narrative of the Briton's Voyage to Pitcairn's Island.... L, 1817. 2d Ed. 8vo, contemp bds; rebacked with cloth. With frontis & 11 plates. With bookseller's catalogue description mtd to tp. sg June 11 (298) $80

Shipley, Conway
— Sketches in the Pacific: The South Sea Islands. L, 1851. Folio, orig cloth; spine lacking, loose. With litho title & 25 plates. Marginal waterstain affecting 1st plate. S Apr 24 (380) £2,400 [Hitching]

Shipley, M. A.
— Artificial Flies and How to Make Them. Phila., 1888. 12mo, cloth; worn. sg Oct 23 (496) $150

Shipp, Lieut. John
— Memoirs of the Extraordinary Military Career of.... L, 1829. 3 vols. 12mo, contemp half mor; rubbed. bba Aug 28 (217) £70 [Geng]

Shirakawa, Yoshikazu
— Himalayas. NY, [1971]. Folio, cloth, in d/j. With 248 color plates, 6 folding plates & 6 maps. wa Nov 6 (341) $160

Shirley, James, 1596-1666
— The Constant Maid. A Comedy. L, 1640. 4to, lev gilt by the French Bindery; front joint weak. Margins trimmed close; lacking final blank. J. P. Kemble's copy. sg Mar 26 (260) $450
— The Court Secret. L, 1653. 8vo, later half mor; rubbed. Most leaves soiled or spotted. bba Sept 25 (6) £50 [Martin]
— The Grateful Servant. L, [c.1660]. 3d Ed. 4to, sewn. Tp soiled & frayed; some dampstaining of lower margins. Ck Jan 30 (128) £70

Shirley, Thomas, Angler
— The Angler's Museum.... L, 1784. 12mo, calf. pnE Dec 17 (311) £85 [Graham]
— The Angler's Museum. Or, the Whole Art of Float and Fly Fishing. L, [c.1790]. 12mo,

recent half calf. Port in facsimile. T Oct 16 (412) £90

Shoberl, Frederick. See: Schoberl, Frederick

Shoemaker, Richard H. See: Shaw & Shoemaker

Shop...
— Shop Signs of Peking. Peking: Chinese Painting Association, [1931]. One of 100. Preface by H. J. Fung. Oblong folio, cloth. sg Nov 20 (50) $200

Shortridge, Guy Chester
— The Mammals of South West Africa. L, 1934. 2 vols. 4to, cloth. SSA Oct 28 (844) R230

Shortt, Angela
— The Hunting If. NY: Derrydale Press, 1932. One of 100. 16mo, orig lea. Inscr. sg Oct 23 (121) $400

Short-Title Catalogue
— A Short-Title Catalogue of Books Printed in England, Scotland & Ireland...1475-1640. L, 1976-86. 2d Ed. Ed by W. A. Jackson, F. S. Ferguson & Katharine F. Pantzer. 4to, cloth, in d/js. bba Oct 16 (399) £180 [Shapero]

Anr copy. 2 vols. 4to, orig cloth, in d/js. bba Apr 9 (466) £150 [Poole]

Anr copy. Vol II. 4to, cloth, in d/j. sg May 14 (223) $80

Shunami, Shlomo
— Bibliography of Jewish Bibliographies. Jerusalem, 1969. 4to, cloth, in frayed d/j. Reprint of 1965 Ed. sg Sept 25 (47) $600

Siant-Exupery, Antoine de
— Vol de Nuit. Paris, 1931. One of 100 on papier verge lafuma. 4to, orig wraps. C May 13 (59) £350 [Beres]

Sibley, John Langdon, 1804-85 —& Others
— Biographical Sketches of Graduates of Harvard University.... Cambr. & Bost., 1873-1972. 16 vols. All but 4 in d/js; 1st 3 vols worn. sg Oct 2 (160) $300

Sibly, Ebenezer
A New and Complete Illustration of the Occult Sciences. L, [c.1795]. 2 vols. 4to, contemp half calf; broken, worn. With engraved frontis, 26 engraved plates & 2 full-page woodcuts. Ink annotations & underlining. bba Nov 13 (272) £60 [Cameron]

Anr copy. Modern cloth. First 11 leaves laid down & washed, with some loss of text & affecting frontis & title; some other leaves with marginal defs. bba Mar 26 (189) £45 [Goulden]

Anr copy. New cloth. With frontis & 28 (of 29) plates. Lacking last 2 leaves; final catchword obscured; tp dust-soiled. S Nov 10 (556) £60

Sibthorp, John —& Smith, Sir James Edward
— Flora Graeca; sive Plantarum rariorum historia.... L, 1806-40 [some plates watermarked 1847]. 2d Issue. 10 vols. Folio, contemp half mor by J. Wright. With 10 engraved titles & 966 plates, all handcolored. Plesch—de Belder copy. S Apr 28 (332) £105,000 [Israel]

Siddons, Henry
— Practical Illustrations of Rhetorical Gesture and Action.... L, 1822. 8vo, contemp half calf. With 66 plates. Ck Nov 21 (185) £65

Siddons, Sarah
— The Story of our First Parents. L, 1822. 8vo, mor gilt; rubbed, upper cover detached. pn Jan 22 (22) £55 [Talbot]

Sidney, Algernon, 1622-83
— Discourses Concerning Government.... L, 1763. 4to, contemp calf; joints cracked. Some staining. bba Oct 30 (159) £70 [Cavendish]

Sidney, Algernon, 1622-83 & Ralph, James
— Of the Use and Abuse of Parliament.... L, 1744. 2 vols. 8vo, contemp sheep; worn. sg Oct 9 (317) $150

Sidney, Sir Philip, 1554-86
— Certain Sonets. Bost. & NY, 1904. One of 430. Designed by Bruce Rogers. Half vellum. O Nov 18 (162) $50

— The Countesse of Pembrokes Arcadia. L, 1613. "4th" Ed. Folio, old calf gilt; some wear. With ornamental title for the 1605 Ed in place of the 1613 title. O Nov 18 (172) $180

Anr Ed. Dublin, 1621. Folio, old calf; worn, joints split. Tp cropped & laid down; 3B6 torn & repaired, slightly affecting text; some stains. bba Oct 16 (56) £80 [Mellor & Baxter]

"9th" Ed. L, 1638. Folio, contemp calf gilt; rubbed. D3-E4 ruststained at inner margin; D4-E2 holes at inner margin; 5 leaves cleanly torn; some browning. Ck Jan 30 (15) £180

Sidney, Samuel
— The Book of the Horse. L, [1884-86]. 3d Ed. 4to, contemp half mor; worn, rebacked, old spine preserved. bba June 18 (150) £100 [Shapero]

Anr copy. Half calf; def. pn Nov 20 (217) £90 [Nicholson]

Anr copy. Half mor gilt. With 28 plates.

pn June 18 (132) £170 [Walford]

Siebeck, Rudolph
— The Elements of the Art of Landscape-Gardening. L, 1862. 2 vols. Oblong folio & 12mo, bdg not described. Franklin Institute copy. F Sept 12 (32) $300

Siegel, Henry A. —& Others
— The Derrydale Press: A Bibliography. Goshen, Conn.: The Angler's & Shooter's Press, 1981. One of 1,250. cb May 21 (85) $110

Sienkiewicz, Henryk, 1846-1916. See: Limited Editions Club

Siestrunck, R. —& Fabri, Jean
— Recherches historiques sur l'origine des Sarmates.... St. Petersburg, 1812-13. 4 vols in 2. 8vo, contemp lea gilt; backstrips def. Titles stamped. sg Nov 20 (161) $120

Sieveking, Lancelot de Giberne
— Beyond This Point. L: Duckworth [1929]. Illus by Francis Bruguiere. 4to, cloth; soiled. Inscr. cb June 18 (315) $110

Signature...
— Signature: A Quadrimestrial of Typography and Graphic Arts. L, 1935-40. Nos 1-15, lacking 1 issue. Orig wraps; spine ends frayed. sg June 11 (366) $200

Sigonius, Carolus
— Emendationum libri duo.... Venice: Aldus, 1557. 4to, old vellum; spine wormed. sg Oct 9 (85) $60

Siguenza y Gongora, Carlos de, 1645-1700
— The Mercurio Volante of Don Carlos de Siguenze y Gongora.... Los Angeles: Quivira Society, 1932. One of 665. Bds; spine ribbed. With 12 plates. cb Jan 8 (180) $50

Silence, Samuel, Pseud.
— The Foundling Hospital for Wit. L, 1743-64. Mixed Ed. 6 parts in 1 vol. 8vo, contemp calf; rebacked & repaired. Contemp annotations. S Sept 22 (27) £120 [Vine]

Silesio, Mariano
— The Arcadian Princesse.... L, 1635. 1st Ed of Richard Brathwaite's trans. 8vo, mor gilt by F. Bedford. C Dec 12 (359) £350 [Hannas]

Silliman, Benjamin, 1816-85 —& Others
— The World of Science, Art and Industry, illustrated from Examples in the New-York Exhibition, 1853-54. NY, 1854. 2 parts in 1 vol. Folio, orig cloth; needs rebdg, 1st few leaves detached. Library markings. sg Mar 12 (230) $325

Silliphant, Sterling. See: Chandler & Silliphant

Sillitoe, Alan —& Fainlight, Ruth
— Poems. L: Rainbow Press, 1971. One of 300. Lea gilt with hand-painted Japanese endpapers. sg Mar 5 (105) $120

Siltzer, Frank
— The Story of British Sporting Prints. L, 1929. 4to, cloth; worn, backstrip gouged. With 8 color plates tipped in. ha Dec 19 (256) $55

Anr copy. Orig cloth. T Jan 22 (281) £48

Silva. See: Evelyn, John

Silver, Jacob Mortimer Wier
— Sketches of Japanese Manners and Customs. L, 1867. 4to, cloth; soiled. With additional title & with 27 plates. bba Dec 18 (235) £160 [Marks]

Silverberg, Robert
— Lord Valentine's Castle. NY: Harper & Row, [1980]. One of 250. cb Sept 28 (1143) $50; cb Sept 28 (1144) $50

Simak, Clifford D.
— City. NY: Gnome Press, [1952]. In d/j lightly soiled at back. Sgd. cb Sept 28 (1161) $225
— The Werewolf Principle. NY: Putnam, [1967]. In d/j. cb Sept 28 (1169) $75

Simenon, Georges
— Maigret. Paris: Artheme Fayard, [1934]. One of 50. Wraps. cb Nov 20 (288) $65
— The Patience of Maigret. NY: Harcourt, Brace, [1940]. 1st American Ed. Trans by Geoffrey Sainsbury. In d/j. cb Nov 20 (291) $95

Simeoni, Gabriele
— Dialogo pio et speculativo. Lyons, 1560. 4to, contemp vellum. Very small wormhole affecting the final leaves; some leaves discolored. The map of the Auvergne belonging to Description de la Limagne d'Auvergne inserted. S Sept 23 (492) £180 [Farbouille]

Simes, Thomas
— The Military Guide for Young Officers. Phila.: Humphreys, Bell & Aitken, 1776. ("A New Military, Historical and Explanatory Dictionary....") Vol II (of 2) only. 8vo, old calf; worn, joints broken. Some worming; browned. O Mar 24 (163) $110

Simmons, Albert Dixon. See: Derrydale Press

Simmons, Amelia
— American Cookery, or the Art of Dressing Viands.... Hartford, 1798. 3d Ed. 8vo, later bds, old wraps bound in. Some light dampstain throughout; perforation stamp in title. O May 12 (178) $3,700

Anr copy. Sewn in contemp wraps. Waterstain to upper inner margin of 1st few leaves; some foxing; margin of E4 holed. Crahan copy. P Nov 25 (423) $6,000

Simon, Andre Louis
— Bibliotheca Bacchica. L, 1927-32. One of 250 & 275. Vol II only. Half cloth, in d/j. Inscr. cb July 30 (233) $150

Anr copy. 2 vols. 4to, half cloth, in rubbed d/js. Inscr to Phil Townsend Hanna. Crahan copy. P Nov 25 (424) $400

Anr Ed. L: Holland Press, [1972]. 2 vols in 1. Facsimile of 1927 Ed. cba Feb 5 (158) $55

— Bibliotheca Gastronomica. L, 1953. 4to, cloth. SM Oct 20 (525) FF1,100

One of 750. Cloth, in d/j. cb July 30 (282) $100

Anr copy. Cloth. sg Jan 15 (50) $90

Anr copy. Cloth, in d/j. Inscr. sg Jan 22 (279) $120

Simon, Howard
— 500 Years of Art in Illustration: From Albrecht Durer to Rockwell Kent. Garden City, [1949]. 2d Ed. 4to, cloth. sg Oct 30 (197) $120

Simon, Oliver —& Rodenberg, Julius
— Printing of To-day.... L, 1928. 4to, orig half cloth, in worn d/j. Material from private presses tipped in to various pages or loosely inserted; 1 leaf torn at inner margin. bba Jan 15 (32) £140 [Smallwood & Randall]

Simons, Mathew
— A Direction for the English Traviller. L, 1643. 8vo, contemp calf; rebacked, old spine laid down. With engraved title & 38 county maps only. Lacking map of England & table of roads; 1 map detached; anr cleanly torn. Ck Nov 21 (409) £750

Anr copy. Contemp calf; worn. With engraved title & 39 maps, 2 folding. pn May 21 (398) £620 [Burgess]

Anr copy. Old calf; worn. With 37 maps & folding map of England. pn May 21 (399) £600 [Way]

Anr Ed. L: Thomas Jenner, 1657 [engraved title dated 1643]. ("A Book of the Names of All Parishes, Market Towns....") 8vo, modern half calf. Lacking tp & map of England. pn May 21 (400) £400 [Burgess]

Anr copy. Modern half calf gilt. With engraved title & 37 maps only. Lacking table of roads & maps of England, Wales & Yorkshire. pn May 21 (401) £480 [Burgess]

Anr Ed. L, 1668. 4to, contemp calf; rebacked. Yorkshire & Wales with margins trimmed. pn May 21 (402) £400 [Burgess]

Anr Ed. L: J. Garret, 1677. 4to, modern half calf gilt. With 39 partly colored maps. Tables trimmed; 1 table laid down. pn May 21 (403) £420 [Burgess]

Simons, Menno
— Opera. Amst., 1681. Folio, contemp calf over wooden bds; back def. B Feb 25 (774) HF850

Simpson, Christopher
— A Compendium of Practical Musick. L, 1678. 3d Ed. 8vo, contemp calf; worn. Lacking port. Ck Dec 18 (51) £100 [Ransom]

Simpson, G.
— The Anatomy of the Bones and Muscles, Exhibiting the Parts as they Appear on Dissection.... L, 1825. 4to, half calf; spine corroded & partially rebacked. With 30 mtd plates on india paper. A few plates with marginal repairs. Inscr. O Oct 21 (163) $60

Simpson, Sir George, 1792-1860
— Narrative of a Journey Round the World. L, 1847. 1st Ed. 2 vols. 8vo, orig cloth. With port & folding map. S Apr 24 (381) £500 [Quaritch]

Anr Ed. San Francisco, 1930. ("Narrative of a Voyage to California Ports.") One of 250. 4to, half cloth. Sgd. cb Oct 9 (221) $150

Simpson, James, 1813-83
— Report and Map of the Route from Fort Smith, Arkansas, to Santa Fe, New Mexico. Wash., 1850. 1st Ed. 8vo, disbound. With 4 folding maps. wa Sept 25 (391) $100

— Report of Explorations Across the Great Basin of the Territory of Utah.... Wash., 1876. 4to, orig cloth; spine bumped. cb Apr 2 (235) $225

Anr copy. Orig cloth; worn, soiled, hinges cracked. With folding map & 24 plates. wa Sept 25 (468) $85

Simpson, T. See: Wethered & Simpson

Simpson, Sir Walter Grindlay
— The Art of Golf. Edin., 1887. 1st Ed. 8vo, half mor. pnC Jan 23 (170) £260

Anr copy. Calf. pnC Jan 23 (172) £250

Anr copy. Orig half mor. pnE Oct 15 (204) £360

SIMPSON

Simpson, William, 1823-99
— The Seat of the War in the East. First and Second Series. L, 1855-56. Series 1 & 2 bound together. Folio, later half mor gilt with orig cloth sides. With 2 litho titles & 79 plates. Title of 1st Series soiled & torn with 1 corner def; Plate 22 detached; Plate 35 torn affecting illust; 5 other plates with marginal tears; Plates 36-39 with stain in margin; title of 2d series torn in margin & 2 others with small marginal tears; Plate 9 frayed; many plates lacking their tissue guards with ptd key; a few plates cropped. L Dec 11 (353) £180

Anr copy. 1st Series only. Folio, orig half cloth portfolio; worn. With colored litho title & 40 plates. pn Apr 30 (129) £180 [Greenaway]

Anr copy. Half mor gilt. With colored litho title & 39 plates. pn July 23 (283) £80 [Connor]

Anr copy. First and Second Series. Folio, orig half cloth portfolio; worn. WIth 70 plates only. Dampstains & foxing. Sold w.a.f. T Apr 16 (25) £190

Anr Ed. L, 1856. Bound in 1 vol. Folio, half calf; def. With 2 litho titles & 70 (of 79) plates. Some margins frayed. pn June 18 (190) £240 [Tilleke]

Sincerus, J.
— Itinerarium Galliae. Amst., 1649. 12mo, vellum. With 22 folding views. B Oct 7 (1336) HF500

Sinclair, Catherine
— Holiday House. Edin., 1839. 8vo, contemp calf gilt; rebacked. Inscr to her sister & with a series of 31 watercolor drawings made by her to accompany the work. S Dec 5 (359) £3,600 [Schiller]

Sinclair, Hugh
— The Whole Process of Marbling Paper.... L, 1820. 12mo, contemp half lea; rubbed. bba Sept 25 (377) £1,600 [Dennistoun]

Sinclair, Isabella
— Indigenous Flowers of the Hawaiian Islands. L, 1885. Folio, later cloth; worn. With 44 color plates. pnNY Oct 11 (43) $850

Sinclair, Sir John, 1754-1835
— The Statistical Account of Scotland. Edin., 1791-99. 1st Ed. 21 vols. 8vo, contemp half calf. With 18 plates & maps, some folding. Short fold tear in 1 plate. C Dec 12 (191) £950 [Quaritch]

Anr copy. Contemp calf; worn. pnE Nov 12 (266) £300

AMERICAN BOOK PRICES CURRENT

Sinclair, Jr., Mrs. Francis. See: Sinclair, Isabella

Sinclair, Upton, 1878-1968
— The Jungle. NY, 1906. 1st Ed, 1st Issue. Orig cloth; hinges cracked. wa Dec 11 (291) $130

Sinel, Joseph
— A Book of American Trade-Marks and Devices. NY, 1924. 4to, half cloth; worn. O Mar 24 (164) $50

Singer, Charles Joseph
[-] Science, Medicine, and History: Essays on the Evolution of Scientific Thought and Medical Practice in Honour of.... Oxford, 1953. 2 vols. In d/js, torn & tape-repaired. sg Oct 2 (275) $80

Anr copy. George Sarton's set, with note in his hand. sg Jan 15 (369) $275

— Studies in the History and Method of Science. Oxford, 1917-21. 2 vols. 8vo, cloth; rubbed. sg May 14 (627) $140

Singer, Charles Joseph —& Others
— A History of Technology. Oxford, 1954-58. 5 vols. 4to, cloth; stamps on pastedowns. cb June 4 (187) $100

Anr copy. Cloth, in d/js. With colored frontises & 204 plates. sg Jan 22 (280) $175

Anr copy. Cloth, in d/js; 1 d/j torn & repaired. sg May 14 (628) $350

Anr Ed. NY, 1957-59. 5 vols. 4to. sg Jan 15 (368) $150

Anr Ed. Oxford, 1957-58. 5 vols. 4to, cloth, in d/js. sg Oct 2 (273) $80

Singer, Isaac Bashevis
— Satan in Goray. NY, [1981]. One of 50 bound in mor with additional suite of etchings & ink frontis. This out-of-series & marked "Publisher's copy". Illus by Ira Moskowitz. 4to, mor gilt with extra suite in cloth folding case. sg June 11 (367) $500

Sinning, Wilhelm. See: Nees von Esenbeck & Sinning

Siodmak, Curt
— Donovan's Brain. NY, 1943. In repaired d/j; spine ends bumped, leaning a bit. cb Sept 28 (1170) $55

Sipes, William B.
— Pennsylvania Railroad; its Origin, Construction.... Phila., 1875. 1st Ed. 8vo, orig cloth; worn. wa Nov 6 (233) $65

Siquerios, David Alfaro
— Mural del Hospital de la Raza. [Mexico City: Imprenta Nueva Mundo, 1954]. One of 200. Folio, loose in portfolio. With 5 plain & 3 color plates. cb Mar 5 (183) $75

Siren, Osvald, 1879-1966
— Early Chinese Painting from the A. W. Bahr Collection. L, 1938. One of 750. bba Sept 25 (327) £80 [Alice]

Anr copy. Rubbed. bba Dec 18 (236) £60 [Hay]

Anr copy. Inscr. Ck 80 £120; sg June 4 (312) $150

— A History of Early Chinese Art. L, 1929-30. 4 vols. Folio, orig cloth, in d/js. cb July 30 (173) $1,100; sg Feb 5 (94) $375

— The Imperial Palaces of Peking. Paris & Brussels, 1926. 3 vols. Folio, modern half lea. cb July 30 (174) $80

— La Sculpture Chinoise du Ve au XIVe siecle Paris & Brussels, 1925-26. 5 vols. 4to, orig wraps; backstrips worn. HN May 20 (249) DM620

— The Walls and Gates of Peking. L, 1924. One of 800. 4to, orig half cloth. bba Sept 25 (326) £260 [Weinreb]

Siringo, Charles A., 1855-1928
— Riata and Spurs: The Story of a Lifetime Spent in the Saddle.... Bost., 1927. Cloth, in chipped d/j. cb Mar 19 (239) $225

Siskind, Aaron
— Photographs. NY, 1959. Intro by Harold Rosenberg. Folio, cloth; rubbed. Sgd by Siskind on front free endpaper. sg Nov 13 (95) $80

Sismondi, Jean Charles Leonard Simonde de, 1773-1842
— De la richesse commerciale.... Geneva, 1803 [An X]. 2 vols in 1. 8vo, old calf; rebacked. Hole in blank portion of margin of P1 in Vol II. P Sept 24 (397) $400

— Etudes sur l'economie politique. Brussels, 1837-38. 2 vols. 8vo, contemp half vellum; rubbed. bba Dec 4 (33) £40 [Drury]

Sisson, James E., III. See: Walker & Sisson

Sisson, James E., III —& Martens, Robert W.
— Jack London First Editions. Oakland: Star Rover House, 1979. One of 1,000. cb Jan 22 (180) $50

Sitgreaves, Lorenzo
— Report of an Expedition Down the Zuni and Colorado Rivers. Wash., 1853. 1st Ed, 1st Issue. 8vo, orig sheep. With 76 (of 78) plates. wa Sept 25 (470) $90

Anr copy. Modern cloth. With folding map & 78 plates. Some tears. wa Mar 5 (408) $190

Anr Ed. Wash., 1854. 2d Issue. 8vo, orig cloth; worn. With folding map & 77 (of 78) plates. Some foxing. wa Sept 25 (470) $90

Sitwell, Dame Edith
— Facade. L, [1922]. Unrecorded Ed. Pinkish-gray wraps. 9 single leaves typed on the recto only. With 7 fewer poems than Fifoot EA6a & numbered differently. S July 23 (184) £1,000 [Currie]

— Five Poems. L, 1928. 1st Ed, One of 275. Worn. Inscr. sg Dec 11 (431) $110

— Five Variations on a Theme. L, 1933. One of 100. In d/j. Inscr. sg Dec 11 (432) $100

— Poem for a Christmas Card. L: Fleuron, [c.1925]. Illus by Albert Rutherston. 4to, Christmas card with self-wraps. Fifoot EA14b. sg Dec 11 (433) $150

— The Sleeping Beauty. L, 1924. In d/j. Inscr by Siegfried Sassoon. sg Dec 11 (435) $250

Sitwell, Dame Edith —& Walton, Sir William
— Facade. L, 1922. One of 150, sgd by Sitwell. Bds. sg Dec 11 (430) $200

Anr Ed. L, 1972. One of 1,000. Orig half mor, with 45 rpm record in pocket. S Sept 22 (142) £110 [Emery]

Sitwell, Edith, Osbert & Sacheverell
— Poor Young People. L, 1925. 1st Ed, one of 375. 4to, orig cloth, in d/j. sg Dec 11 (439) $150

Sitwell, Sacheverell. See: Beaumont & Sitwell

Sitwell, Sacheverell —& Others
— Fine Bird Books. L, 1953. Folio, orig half cloth. L Dec 11 (42) £250

Anr copy. Orig half cloth, in d/j. pnE Dec 17 (282) £300 [Polwarth]; S Nov 10 (557) £300 [Lan]

Anr copy. Half cloth; worn. sg Jan 15 (254) $375

— Old Garden Roses. L, 1955-57. 2 vols. Folio, orig cloth in d/j. pnE Dec 17 (228) £35 [Maggs]

Sitwell, Sacheverell —& Blunt, Wilfrid Jasper Walter
— Great Flower Books.... L, 1956. Folio, half cloth in d/j. pnE Dec 17 (230) £260 [Greyfriars]

Anr copy. Orig half cloth, in torn d/j. S Nov 10 (559) £320 [Traylen]

Anr copy. Orig half cloth. S July 13 (73) £310

Anr copy. Half cloth. sg Oct 2 (276) $450

Anr copy. Half cloth; worn. sg Jan 15

SITWELL

(255) $450

**Sitwell, Sacheverell —&
Madol, Roger**
— Album de Redoute. L, 1954. One of 250. Folio, half mor by Mansell. With 25 colored plates. sg June 18 (237) $650

Six...
— Six Sketches in Lithography, representing the Common Actions of the Horse. L: Day & Hague, [c.1842]. Folio, orig wraps; rebacked. With litho title & 6 hand-colored plates. Marginal dampstains. S Oct 23 (770) £800 [Rostron]

Skelton, Sir John, 1831-97
— Charles I. L, 1898. 4to, mor gilt, armorial bdg; worn, edges scuffed. ha Dec 19 (257) $110

One of 500. Folio, orig wraps & extra portfolio of 23 prints in orig ptd box. K June 7 (345) $100

Skelton, Joseph
— Engraved Illustrations of the Principal Antiquities of Oxfordshire.... Oxford, 1823. 4to, half calf; broken. With frontis & 50 plates & maps. pn June 18 (11) £140 [Croft]

Anr copy. Contemp half mor gilt; rubbed, inner front hinge broken. Minor marginal dampstains, mainly to prelims. T Oct 16 (365) £140

— Oxonia antiqua restaurata. Oxford, 1823. 2 vols. 4to, contemp half mor gilt. With 132 plates & plans. Some dampstains. S Nov 17 (826) £850 [Boyd]

— Skelton's Etchings of the Antiquities of Bristol.... [Oxford?, 1825]. 4to, contemp calf; stained, spine chipped. With engraved title & 31 plates only. Sold w.a.f. Ck Nov 21 (420) £60

Skelton, Raleigh Ashlin
See also: Roxburghe Club
— Decorative Printed Maps of the 15th to 18th Centuries. L & NY, [1952]. 4to, cloth; worn. With 84 plates. sg Jan 22 (95) $100

Sketches...
See also: Home, Henry
— Sketches in New Brunswick.... L: Ackermann, 1 Mar 1836. Folio, half mor, orig wrap bound in. With 12 hand-colored plates, several heightened with varnish. S Apr 24 (274) £3,000 [Lake]

Sketchley, Rose E. D.
— English Book-Illustration of To-Day. L, 1903. One of 50 on japan. Vellum gilt; warped & stained. sg Oct 30 (198) $350

Skinner, Andrew. See: Taylor & Skinner

AMERICAN BOOK PRICES CURRENT

Skinner, John
— The Present State of Peru.... L, 1805. 1st Ed. 4to, contemp calf; rebacked. With 20 hand-colored plates. Some foxing & soiling. O May 12 (179) $475

Skinner, Stephen, 1623-67
— Etymologicon linguae Anglicanae.... L, 1671. 1st Ed. 2 parts in 1 vol. Folio, contemp calf; broken. Marginal staining & worming. bba July 16 (227) £90 [Thomson]

Skogman, Carl Johan Alfred
— Fregatten Eugenies Resa Omkring Jorden aren 1851-1853.... Stockholm: Adolf Bonnier, [1854-55]. 1st Ed. 2 vols. 8vo, modern half lea. With 23 colored plates & 3 folding maps. kh Mar 16 (470B) A$200

Anr copy. Contemp half calf. With 3 folding maps & 24 plates. Marginal stains affecting a few leaves at end of Vol I. S Jan 12 (333) £530 [Hagstrom]

Skues, G. E. M.
— Nymph Fishing for Chalk Stream Trout. L, 1939. In d/j. sg Oct 23 (496) $150

**Skues, G. E. M. —&
Overfield, T. Donald**
— The Way of a Man with a Trout. L, [1977]. One of 150. 2 vols. Vol I, mor; Vol II, half mor. With 20 nymphs on 4 sunken mounts. sg Oct 23 (501) $600

Slater, John
— Prospectus for his Patent Steam Kitchen. Birm., c.1810. Oblong folio, orig leabacked wraps. With frontis & 11 plates (Plates 6-11 with engraved table of dimensions). Mtd on versos of plates are text of patent, leaf of directions, 3 slips of explanation & price lists with prices in Ms. Variant of leaf of directions loosely inserted. C Dec 12 (192) £1,200 [Weinreb]

Slauerhoff, Jan Jacob
— Arhipel. Chaumont-Gistoux, 1929. One of 60. B Oct 7 (697) HF800
— Fleurs de marecage. Poemes. Brussels, 1929. One of 75 hors commerce. B Oct 7 (132) HF340

Sleidanus, Johannes, 1506?-56
— De statu religionis et reipublicae.... [Strassburg: Josias Rihel], 1561. 8vo, later vellum; Occasional early underscoring & annotations. sg Oct 9 (318) $90

Sloan, Edward L. See: Salt Lake City

Sloan, Samuel, 1817-1907
— The Model Architect: a Series of Original Designs for Cottages, Villas, Suburban Residences.... Phila., [1852]. 1st Ed. 2 vols. Folio, contemp half calf; rubbed, joints split. bba Sept 25 (295) £360 [Weinreb]; bba Sept 25 (295) £360 [Weinreb]

Sloane, Sir Hans, 1660-1753
— A Voyage to the Islands Madera, Barbados, Nieves, S. Christophers and Jamaica.... L, 1707-25. 1st Ed. 2 vols. Folio, contemp calf; rebacked & repaired. With 284 double-page or folding plates & folding map; mtd on guards as usual throughout. Corner of Plate 134 in Vol I torn away with loss of just the top of a few letters. C Dec 12 (259) £3,200 [Maggs]

Anr copy. Contemp calf gilt; joints renewed, 1 joint beginning to split. With 284 folding or double page plates & folding map, mtd on guards. Some plates trimmed; a few with short tears, 1 leaf of introduction misbound in Vol II; small hole in 1 leaf & short tear repaired in errata leaf in Vol I; 6C2v soiled & piece torn from margin of 6D2 in Vol II; titles a little soiled & spotted. S Oct 23 (452) £2,000 [Marshall]

Anr copy. Contemp mor gilt; not uniform. With 240 plates; some shaved. Plesch—de Belder copy. S Apr 28 (334) £6,000 [Israel]

Slothrop, William
— On Preterition. L: James Moxon, 1650. 8vo, orig pigskin; rebacked in syn gilt. S June 25 (39) £1,100

Slush, Barnaby, Pseud.
— Navy Royal: or a Sea-Cook turned Projector.... L, 1709. 12mo, modern calf. Tp remargined affecting a few letters; last leaf backed almost obscuring the 7 lines of text; some marginal tears; browned throughout. C Dec 12 (360) £400 [Warnecke]

Small, James
— A Treatise on Ploughs and Wheel Carriages. Edin., 1784. 8vo, orig bds; worn. Ck Jan 16 (15) £220

Small, John, M.A.
— The Castles and Mansions of the Lothians. Edin., 1883. 2 vols. Folio, orig cloth. With 103 photographic plates. pnE May 20 (29) £135

Small, John William
— Scottish Market Crosses. Stirling: Eneas Mackay, 1900. One of 500. Folio, cloth; spine-tips frayed. With 118 plates. O Feb 24 (175) $70
— Scottish Woodwork of the Sixteenth and Seventeenth Centuries. Stirling & L: Mackay & Quaritch, [1878]. One of 500. Folio, cloth; worn. O Feb 24 (176) $60

Smalley, Eugene Virgil, 1841-99
— History of the Northern Pacific Railroad. NY, 1883. Contemp half mor; rubbed at joints & extremities. cb Oct 9 (222) $75

Smart, Christopher, 1722-71
— Poems on Several Occasions. L, 1752. 4to, contemp half calf; worn. Tp & last leaf soiled; 1 plate only. Ck Feb 13 (141A) £45

Smeaton, John, 1724-92
— Reports of the late John Smeaton on various occasions in the Course of his Employment as a Civil Engineer. L, 1812. 3 vols. 4to, contemp calf gilt; joints rubbed. With port & 72 plates. C Dec 12 (193) £750 [Phillips]

Smedley, Robert C.
— History of the Underground Railroad in Chester and the Neighboring Counties of Pennsylvania. Lancaster, 1883. Orig cloth; spine ends frayed. cb Oct 9 (299) $50

Smellie, William, 1697-1763
— Anatomical Tables with Explanations.... Edin., 1787. Folio, new half calf. With 40 plates; title & 1st 2 pp of text in photocopy, tears repaired in preface & 2 plates. S Nov 27 (287) £320 [Phelps]
— A Sett of Anatomical Tables.... Worcester, Mass.: Isaiah Thomas, 1793. ("A Set of Anatomical Tables....") 8vo, contemp calf; worn, joint splitting, lacking free endpaper. With 40 plates, but with Plate 19 duplicated & Plate 28 lacking. wa Mar 5 (311) $210
— A Treatise on the Theory and Practice of Midwifery. L, 1752. 2d Ed. 8vo, contemp calf; worn, joints split. Tp soiled; browned. bba Jan 15 (398) £300 [Phillips]

Anr copy. Contemp calf; worn. Some leaves soiled. S Feb 24 (613) £320 [Phillips]

Smibert, Thomas
— The Clans of the Highlands of Scotland. Edin., 1850. 8vo, mor gilt. pnE June 17 (157) £80

Smids, Ludolph
— Schatkamer der Nederlandsse oudheden.... Amst., 1711. 8vo, wraps. With engraved title & 60 folding plates. Light waterstains, mainly in margins. B Feb 25 (658) HF450

Smiles, Samuel, 1812-1904. See: Fore-Edge Paintings

Smith, Adam, 1723-90
[-] A Catalogue of the Library of Adam Smith. L, 1894. Ed by James Bonar. 8vo, contemp cloth; rubbed. T Sept 18 (447) £180
— Essays on Philosophical Subjects. L, 1795. 8vo, modern half calf, earlier label laid

down. P Sept 24 (398) $1,000

1st Ed. 4to, contemp half calf; scuffed. Signature of Matthew Boulton on title cropped. C Dec 12 (194) £1,900 [Pickering & Chatto]

Anr Ed. Dublin, 1795. 8vo, contemp half calf. "A fine copy". S June 25 (78) £1,850 [Traylen]

— An Inquiry into the Nature and Causes of the Wealth of Nations. L, 1776. 1st Ed. 2 vols. 4to, old calf; rebacked. Lacking final blank in Vol I; corners off Vol I leaves P4 & 3T3 without loss; paper fault in U3 of Vol I costing most of the page-numbers; paper fault in M1 of Vol II affecting a few letters. Sutherland copy. P Sept 24 (231) $11,000

Anr copy. Contemp calf; spines repaired, joints cracked. With 6 leaves on stubs; half-title & tp of Vol I with marginal staining. P Sept 24 (399) $11,000

Anr copy. Contemp calf; rebacked preserving orig spine, joints rubbed. 4 leaves on stubs; 3 leaves with marginal tears or losses; hole in 2H4 costing a few words. P June 18 (180) $8,500

Anr copy. Contemp calf; spine ends worn, Vol II joints starting. Minor worming in opening leaves of both vols; Vol II with lower outer corners of Q4 & H4 torn & repaired; 2C2.3 bound after 4B1; lacking half-title. sg Dec 4 (181) $4,000

Anr Ed. L, 1784. 3 vols. 8vo, contemp calf; worn, upper joint of Vol I crudely repaired with adhesive tape. Some staining. S Jan 13 (679) £380 [Boyle]

1st American Ed. Phila., 1789. 3 vols. 8vo, contemp sheep; joints cracked, heads & tails chipped, lower cover of Vol I detached. P Dec 15 (228) $2,600

Anr Ed. L, 1791. 3 vols. 8vo, contemp calf; spines rubbed, broken. S Mar 9 (765) £110 [Demetzy]

Anr copy. Modern cloth. wa Nov 6 (540) $65

Anr Ed. Edin., 1806. 3 vols. 8vo, contemp calf; rubbed. S Sept 22 (273) £40 [Garrett]

— The Theory of Moral Sentiments. L, 1759. 1st Ed. 8vo, contemp calf gilt; rubbed, spine chipped. P Sept 24 (402) $3,750

Anr Ed. L, 1804. 2 vols. 8vo, contemp calf; spines & corners rubbed. Some foxing. cb Oct 23 (210) $70

Smith, Albert Richard, 1816-60. See: Leech & Smith

Smith, Sir Andrew, 1797-1872
— Illustrations of the Zoology of South Africa. Johannesburg, 1977. Facsimile Ed, one of 350. 3 vols. 4to, orig syn. bba Dec 4 (271) £200 [Ritchie]

Smith, Bernard William
— European Vision and the South Pacific 1768-1850. Oxford, 1960. In d/j. CA Apr 12 (221) A$110

Smith, Charles, Bookseller
— New English Atlas being a Complete Set of County Maps. L, 1804. Folio, contemp half mor; rubbed. With engraved title (slightly waterstained) & 43 maps on 47 sheets, all hand-colored with colored wash borders & mtd on guards. C Oct 15 (100) £550 [Leadley]

Anr copy. Contemp calf; worn. With engraved title, general map & 45 double-page hand-colored county maps. Some discoloration. Ck Sept 26 (122) £420

Anr copy. Contemp russia gilt; hinges cracked. With 3 hand-colored folding maps of England, Scotland & Ireland & 46 hand-colored county maps. Some foxing. pn May 21 (404) £550 [Goodall]

Anr copy. Orig half calf gilt. With hand-colored general map & 42 hand-colored maps. pn May 21 (405) £550 [Burden]

4th Ed. L, 1821. Folio, modern half calf. With engraved title & 43 hand-colored double-page maps on 47 sheets. S Jan 12 (70) £550 [Wells]

Smith, Charles, Topographer
— The Ancient and Present State of the County of Kerry. Dublin, 1774. 8vo, contemp calf; rubbed. With port & 14 plates & maps, some folding. Marginal worming; a few plates torn or loose. bba Apr 9 (361) £110 [Catnach]

— The Antient and Present State of...Waterford. Dublin, 1746. 8vo, half calf. pnE Dec 17 (32) £75 [Traylen]

Smith, Charles, 1713-77
— Three Tracts of the Corn-Trade and Corn-Laws.... L, 1766. 8vo, contemp calf; rubbed & soiled "from dressing buildup," with top of spine repaired. Library & discard stamps on endpaper. P Sept 24 (403) $175

Anr copy. Old calf; rebacked & repaired, rubbed. Some browning, staining & offsetting. P Sept 24 (404) $175

Smith, Charles Hamilton
— Selections of the Ancient Costume of Great Britain and Ireland.... L, 1814. Folio, modern half mor. With 61 colored plates, including frontis. Lacking dedication; some soiling. Sold w.a.f. bba Aug 28 (288) £240

[Ege]
Anr copy. Later half lea; rubbed. Some foxing & browning. O May 12 (180) $350

Smith, Charles John
— Historical and Literary Curiosities.... L, 1840. 4to, contemp half mor; rubbed. S Sept 22 (274) £35 [Cox]

Smith, Clark Ashton, 1893-1961
— The Dark Chateau and Other Poems. Sauk City: Arkham House, 1951. In d/j. cb Sept 28 (1172) $200

Smith, David Seth. See: Seth-Smith, David

Smith, Edgar W.
— Introducing Mr. Sherlock Holmes. Morristown NJ: Baker Street Irregulars, 1959. One of 350. cb Apr 24 (1527) $85
— Profile by Gaslight: An Irregular Reader about the Private Life of Sherlock Holmes. NY, 1944. In d/j. cb Apr 24 (1519) $130

Smith, Edmund Ware. See: Derrydale Press

Smith, Edward E., 1890-1965
— The Skylark of Space. Providence: Buffalo Book Co, 1946. In d/j. cb Sept 28 (1180) $150

Smith, Edwin, The Edwin Smith Surgical Papyrus, Published in Facsimile.... 1930
— The Edwin Smith Surgical Papyrus.... See: Breasted, James Henry

Smith, Elizabeth, of Burnhall. See: Fore-Edge Paintings

Smith, Ernest Bramah, 1868-1942. See: Bramah, Ernest

Smith, Frederick William
— The Florist's Magazine.... L, 1836. 2 parts in 1 vol. 4to, disbound. With 59 hand-colored plates only. pn May 21 (65) £240 [Elliott]

Smith, Garden G. See: Hilton & Smith

Smith, George, of Kendal
— A Compleat Body of Distilling. L, 1731. 2d Ed. 8vo, modern half calf; rubbed. Marginal worming; soiled; lacking initial leaf. S Nov 10 (561) £70 [Bookman]

Smith, George, Upholsterer
— Cabinet-Maker and Upholsterer's Guide. L, 1826. 4to, contemp half calf; rubbed, rebacked, old spine preserved. bba Sept 25 (297) £560 [Weinreb]
— A Collection of Designs for Household Furniture and Interior Decoration. L, 1808. 1st Ed. 4to, orig bds; rebacked, rubbed. With 158 hand-colored plates. 1 plate soiled; anr with outer margin repaired; frontis & text spotted; some stains.

bba Sept 25 (296) £2,000 [Weinreb]

Smith, George Oliver
— Venus Equilateral. Phila.: Prime Press, 1947. Illus by Sol Levin. In chipped d/j. Inscr to the pbr by the author & sgd by the artist on title; sgd again by both on front endpaper. cb Sept 28 (1187) $80

Smith, Gerard C.
— All at Sea. NY: Pvtly ptd, 1939. One of 200. 4to, half mor gilt; extremities rubbed. sg Oct 23 (504) $60

Smith, Harold Clifford
— Buckingham Palace. L, 1931. Folio, orig cloth, in soiled d/j. bba July 16 (131) £45 [Allan]
Anr copy. Orig cloth. Inscr by King George VI and Queen Mary. Ck Sept 5 (29) £90
— Jewellery. L, [1908]. Later cloth. With 54 plates. Library markings. sg Feb 5 (190) $70

Smith, Harry Worcester
See also: Derrydale Press
— A Sporting Family of the Old South. Albany: J. B. Lyon, 1936. 4to, cloth, in torn d/j. sg Oct 23 (505) $50

Smith, Miss J.
— Studies of Flowers from Nature. Adwick Hall, near Doncaster, 1818. Folio, half calf; rubbed. With hand-colored title & 19 (of 20) color plates. pn Jan 22 (165) £250 [Thorp]
Anr copy. Half calf. With hand-colored title & 20 plates in 2 states, colored & plain. de Belder copy. S Apr 28 (338) £8,000 [Burgess Browning]

Smith, Sir James Edward. See: Sibthorp & Smith

Smith, Sir James Edward, 1759-1828
See also: Sowerby & Smith
— Exotic Botany.... L, 1804-5-[8]. 2 vols. 4to, contemp half calf gilt; rubbed. With 120 hand-colored plates. Tp & last leaf of text spotted. L.p. copy. de Belder copy. S Apr 28 (336) £4,500 [Burton Garbett]
— Icones pictae plantarum rariorum. L, 1790-[93]. 3 parts. Folio, uncut & unsewn in orig wraps; lacking the 3 lower covers. With 18 hand-colored plates. Lacking the English preface leaf & 14 leaves of descriptions of plates; 1 plate mtd; the 2 dedication leaves repaired in corner; small wormhole in a few leaves with loss of text; some dampstaining throughout. L.p. copy. de Belder copy. S Apr 28 (337) £4,500 [Burgess Browning]
— A Specimen of the Botany of New Holland. L, 1793-[95]. Vol I (all pbd). 4to, modern half mor, orig wraps to Part 1 & front wrap

to Part 4 bound in. L.p. copy. Plesch—de Belder copy. S Apr 28 (335) £5,600 [Ross]

Smith, Jerome V.C. See: Derrydale Press

Smith, John, LL.B.
— Chronicon Rusticum-Commerciale; or, Memoirs of Wool.... L, 1747. 2 vols. 8vo, contemp calf; rebacked, restored. P Sept 24 (405) $325

Smith, John, M.D., Inoculator of Small Pox
— Choir Gaur; The Grand Orrery of the Ancient Druids.... Salisbury, 1771. 4to, orig wraps; soiled & worn. With 3 plates. T Feb 19 (324) £105

Anr copy. Orig wraps; worn & soiled. T June 18 (65) £120

Smith, John, Picture Dealer
— A Catalogue Raisonne of the Works of the Most Eminent Dutch, Flemish and French Painters. L, 1908. One of 1,250. 9 vols, including Supplement. Facsimile reprint of the 1829-42 Ed. S Nov 10 (165) £100 [Schmidt]

Smith, John, fl.1633-70
— England's Improvement Reviv'd. L, 1673. 8vo, mor by MacDonald; joints rubbed. To the Reader leaf & tp backed; tp partially washed; lacking 1st & final blanks; some running heads closely cropped. Hunt copy. CNY Nov 21 (257) $190

Smith, Capt. John, 1580-1631
— The Generall Historie of Virginia, New-England, and the Summer Isles.... L, 1624. 1st Ed. Folio, 19th-cent calf; rubbed, rebacked. Engraved title in Sabin's 1st state, with Prince Charles uncrowned; folding map of Virginia in Sabin's 10th state; folding map of New England in 4th state; double-page plate with map of Ould Virginia in 3d state; double-page plate with map of the Summer Isles in 1st state; errata slip pasted to foot of final page. Ports of the Duchess of Richmond & Pocahontas in facsimile; tp shaved at fore-edge; maps with slight defs & repairs & 2 with rust holes costing 3 letters; E4-F2 with repaired wormhole in inner blank margin; T1, Y1 & Y2 with paper flaws affecting several letters; Y4 with closed marginal tear into text & internal tear in text; some soiling & staining. Stanley-Wilbraham-Crane-Vail-de Coppett copy. P Oct 29 (20) $17,000

Anr copy. Modern half mor. With the 4 maps in facsimile, mtd; a few leaves repaired or holed. Final leaf restored with some loss. P Dec 15 (229) $1,400

Anr Ed. Glasgow, 1907. One of 100 on handmade paper. 2 vols. Orig half vellum gilt; spines soiled. wa Dec 11 (674) £130

— The True Travels, Adventures and Observations.... Richmond, 1819. 2 vols. 8vo, old calf; rubbed, rebacked. With port, coat-of-arms, 1 folding map & 2 folding plates. Some foxing & browning. pnNY Sept 13 (288) $275

Smith, John Chaloner
— British Mezzotinto Portraits. L, 1884. 4 vols. 8vo, cloth; shaken, spine ends chipped. sg Feb 5 (300) $400

Smith, John Thomas, 1766-1833
— Antiquities of London and its Environs. L, 1791-[1800]. 4to, modern half mor. Some dampstaining & marginal tears. bba Aug 28 (320) £85 [Egee]

Anr copy. Contemp mor gilt. Some spotting. sg June 4 (314) $350

— Antiquities of Westminster. L, 1807-9. 2 vols in 1. 4to, mor gilt by Zaehnsdorf. With 102 plates, some colored. pn May 21 (66) £420 [Frost]

Anr copy. Contemp russia; hinges rubbed. With engraved title to Vol II & 100 plates. pn July 23 (67) £360 [Henderson]

— The Cries of London. L, 1839. 4to, cloth; rebacked. With port & 30 plates. pn Jan 22 (141) £65 [Shapero]

— Etchings of Remarkable Beggars.... L, 1815. 4to, orig cloth; spine repaired. With pictorial title & 23 plates. Tp foxed. sg June 28 (242) $600

Smith, Joseph, 1805-44
— The Book of Mormon. Palmyra, NY, 1830. 1st Ed. 8vo, contemp calf; worn, lacking rear free endpaper. Some wear to page corners; 1 leaf with piece lacking from margin, affecting text. cb Apr 2 (240) $3,800

Anr copy. Contemp calf; spine ends nicked. Some foxing. sg Apr 2 (184) $3,800

— Document Showing the Testimony given Before the Judge of the Fifth Judicial Circuit.... Wash., 1841. Disbound. Some foxing. 26th Congress, 2d Session, Senate Doc 189. cb Jan 8 (182) $55

— The Pearl of Great Price. Salt Lake City, 1878. 8vo, orig wraps; soiled, some wear & marginal loss & with stamp of a Salt Lake City bookseller. Some corners worn or soiled. P Oct 29 (21) $450

Smith, Meredith, J.
— Marsupials of Australia. Melbourne, 1980. One of 1,000. Illus by Rosemary Woodford Ganf. Vol I. Folio, orig bdg. kh Mar 16 (474) A$150

Smith, Nathan Ryno, 1797-1877
— Treatment of Fractures of the Lower Extremity by the Use of the Anterior Suspensory Apparatus. Balt., 1867. 8vo, orig cloth; worn. wa Mar 5 (312) $130

Smith, Robert, 1689-1768
— A Compleat System of Opticks. Cambr., 1738. 2 vols. 4to, contemp calf; upper joints split. With 83 folding plates. C Dec 12 (196) £700 [Phelps]

Smith, Samuel, 1720-76
— The History of the Colony of Nova-Caesaria, or New-Jersey... Burlington, 1765. 1st Ed, 1st Issue. 8vo, calf; stained. With 2 small holes in tp restored. se Apr ? (185) $475

Smith, Thomas, Accountant, of London
— An Essay on the Theory of Money and Exchange. L, 1811. 2d Ed. 8vo, calf gilt; hinges rubbed. pn Jan 22 (147) £160

Smith, Walter E.
— Charles Dickens in the Original Cloth.... Los Angeles, 1982-83. 2 vols. 4to, cloth, in d/js. sg June 11 (163) $110

Smith, William, 1550?-1618. See: Ortelius, Abraham

Smith, William, 1727-1803, Provost
— Eulogium on Benjamin Franklin L.L.D., President of the American Philosophical Society...delivered March 1, 1791.... Phila.: Benjamin Franklin Bache, 1792. 8vo, modern wraps. Tiny closed marginal tear to tp; blank corner of final leaf loose. P May 13 (22) $250
— An Historical Account of the Expedition against the Ohio Indians.... L, 1766. 4to, modern calf. With folding map, 2 full-page maps & plans & 2 full-page plates. Folding map shaved & repaired at fold; C-C2 repaired touching headline; hole at G affecting page number; H2v shaved at margin affecting ptd diagram; last leaf repaired affecting letters. S June 25 (414) £1,300 [Lake]
— Oration in Memory of General Montgomery. Phila: John Dunlap, 1776. 8vo, modern half mor gilt. sg Mar 12 (231) $200

Smith, William, 1728-93
— The History of the Province of New-York.... L, 1776. 8vo, contemp calf; rubbed. S Oct 23 (426) £450 [Maggs]

Smith, William, 1769-1839
— Observations on the Utility, Form and Management of Water Meadows, and the Draining and Irrigating of Peat Bogs. Norwich, 1806. 8vo, contemp sheep; rebacked & worn. With 2 folding plates, 1 with slight tear. bba Sept 25 (232) £75

[Maggs]
— Observations on...Water Meadows and...Peat Bogs. Norwich, 1806. 8vo, orig bds; worn. S Nov 10 (563) £120 [Maggs]

Smithers, Leonard. See: Burton & Smithers

Smollett, Tobias, 1721-71
See also: Limited Editions Club
— The Adventures of Roderick Random. L, 1748. 1st Ed. 2 vols. 12mo, later calf; rebacked. sg June 11 (370) $200
— The Adventures of Peregrine Pickle. L, 1751. 1st Ed. 4 vols. 12mo, contemp calf; worn, joints split, Vol III broken. Some stains. bba Aug 28 (198) £140 [Bickersteth]
— The Adventures of Ferdinand Count Fathom. L, 1753. 1st Ed. 2 vols. 12mo, contemp calf; 1 cover detached. bba Jan 15 (44) £160 [Scott]
— Travels through France and Italy. L, 1766. 1st Ed. 2 vols. 8vo, contemp calf; spine worn, joints cracking. P Sept 24 (406) $275
Anr copy. Contemp calf; Vol I joints weak. sg Oct 9 (319) $200
Anr copy. Later mor gilt, contemp calf bound in. With extraneous engraved port of author bound in. sg June 11 (371) $200
— Works. L, 1899-1901. 12 vols. 8vo, half mor. pnE Jan 28 (132) £300 [Hay]
Anr Ed. NY: George D. Sproul, 1902. One of 150. 12 vols. 8vo, mor extra. F Jan 15 (4) $550
Anr Ed. Bost., 1926. One of 500. 11 vols. Orig half cloth. bba Dec 4 (162) £240 [Dr. Pyke]

Smyth, Henry De Wolf
— Atomic Energy for Military Purposes. Princeton: Princeton University Press, 1945. cb Dec 18 (164) $225
— A General Account of the Development of Methods of Using Atomic Energy for Military Purposes.... Princeton, 1945. In chipped & torn d/j. sg Jan 15 (369) $275

Smyth, Robert Brough
— The Gold Fields and Mineral Districts of Victoria.... Melbourne & L, 1869. 4to, orig cloth. Library stamp. bba Oct 16 (288) £100 [Check Books]; kh Mar 16 (478) A$320

Smythies, Bertram Evelyn
— The Birds of Borneo. Edin. & L, 1960. In d/j. pn Oct 23 (279) £55 [Graham]
— the Birds of Burma. Rangoon, 1940. 1st Ed. Orig cloth, in repaired d/j. With 50 colored plates. pn Oct 23 (279) £55 [Graham]
Anr copy. Orig cloth; worn. With map & 30 colored plates. pn July 23 (33) £160 [Graham]

SMYTHIES

Anr Ed. Edin., 1953. pn Dec 11 (247) £65 [Gowland]

Snelling, William Joseph, 1804-48

— Brief and Impartial History of the Life and Actions of Andrew Jackson. Bost., 1831. 12mo inlaid onto 4to sheets, mor; joints starting. Library markings. Extra-illus with 5 color prints from an early 8vo Ed of the McKenney & Hall History of the Indian Tribes of North America. sg Mar 12 (232) $425

Snellius, Willebrord, 1591-1626

— Descriptio cometae qui anno 1618 mense Novembro primum effulsit.... Leiden: Elzevir, 1619. 1st Ed. 4to, modern half vellum. Inscr. S July 28 (1118) £1,800

Snow, Jack

— The Magical Mimics in Oz. Chicago: Reilly & Lee, [1946]. Cloth, in d/j. sg Dec 4 (53) $110

— The Shaggy Man of Oz. Chicago: Reilly & Lee, [1949]. Cloth, in d/j. cb Dec 4 (54) $65

Snow, William Parker

— Voyage of the Prince Albert in Search of Sir John Franklin. L, 1851. 8vo, orig cloth; spine worn. With folding map bound in. T Sept 18 (58) £90

Snowman, Abraham Kenneth

— Eighteenth Century Gold Boxes of Europe. Bost., 1966. In d/j. bba Jan 15 (312) £80 [Wartski]

Soane, Sir John, 1753-1837

— Description of the House and Museum on the North Side of Lincoln's Inn Fields. L, [1835]. One of 150. 4to, orig half lea by J. Smith; rubbed. Inscr. S July 13 (50) £1,900

— Plans, Elevations and Sections of Buildings Executed in...Norfolk, Suffolk.... L, 1788. Folio, disbound. Tp loose & soiled; marginal wormholes. bba Mar 26 (61) £750 [Henderson]

Anr copy. Contemp bds; rebacked & worn. Some soiling; most plates stained. bba Aug 28 (37) £650 [Weinreb]

Anr copy. Bdg not indicated. Library markings. Franklin Institute copy. F Sept 11 (22) $1,400

— Sketches in Architecture. L, 1798. 2d Ed. 2 parts in 1 vol. Folio, contemp half calf; rubbed, rebacked. With 54 plates. bba Sept 25 (298) £700 [Weinreb]

AMERICAN BOOK PRICES CURRENT

Soby, James Thrall

— Ben Shahn: his Graphic Art. NY, 1957. One of 250. 4to, half cloth. With orig mtd litho frontis by Shahn, sgd. sg June 4 (306) $3,000

Social...

— The Social Pipe; or, Gentleman's Recreation. L, 1826. 12mo, later half mor. Minor foxing. sg Oct 23 (269) $110

Society...

— Society, Instituted at London, for the Encouragement of Arts, Manufactures, and Commerce: Transactions. L, 1789-99. 17 vols in 9. 8vo, contemp half calf. Sold w.a.f. S June 25 (132) £1,000

— Society of Dilettanti: The Unedited Antiquities of Attica. L, 1817. Folio, half mor; rubbed. With 78 plates & plans. S Mar 9 (704) £550 [Sims]

Anr copy. Mor gilt. Some spotting. S Mar 9 (705) £500 [Sims]

Anr Ed. L, 1833. Folio, contemp half calf; spine worn, upper joint weak. With 78 maps & plates. C July 22 (198) £240

— SOCIETY OF DILETTANTI. - Ionian Antiquities. L, 1821-1797-1840-1881-1915. ("Antiquities of Ionia.") Vols I-II only. Folio, mor gilt; rubbed. With 105 plates & plans. Bedford copy. S Mar 9 (702) £550 [Sims]

Society for the Diffusion of Useful Knowledge

— The Complete Atlas of Modern Classical and Celestial Maps.... L, 1860. 2 vols. 4to, contemp half calf; worn. With 167 maps (6 double-page), 51 town plans (1 double-page & several on 2 sheets) & 6 star maps, all hand-colored in outline. Ck May 15 (320) £800

— Complete Atlas of Modern Classical and Celestial Maps. L: Edward Stanford, 1874. Folio, contemp half mor; rubbed. With 224 maps, hand-colored. S Nov 10 (980) £550 [Jago]

— The Gallery of Portraits: with Memoirs. L, 1833-37. 7 vols. 4to, half lea; rubbed, spines starting. With 168 ports. sg Dec 18 (177) $60

— Maps. L, 1844. 2 vols. 4to, contemp half mor; gutta-percha perishing. With 118 maps, hand-colored in outline. C Dec 12 (199) £950 [Franks]

Anr copy. Contemp half mor; broken, worn. Ck Sept 26 (229) £340

Anr copy. Half calf; broken. With 161 partly colored maps, 48 town plans & 6 celestial maps. pn Oct 23 (414) £480 [Waterloo]

Anr copy. With 161 maps colored in outline, 50 town plans, 6 celestial maps. pn May 21 (395) £520 [Sweet]

Anr copy. Half calf; worn. With 151 maps colored in outline, 48 town plans, 6 celestial maps. pn May 21 (424) £500 [Way]

Anr copy. Old half calf; rubbed, rebacked. With 121 engraved maps, hand-colored in outline; some browning, some frayed along edges, loose. pnNY Sept 13 (512) $150

Anr copy. Modern half mor. With 219 mapsheets, mostly hand-colored in outline. S Oct 23 (234) £600 [Ash]

Anr copy. 2 vols in 1. Folio, contemp half mor; def. With 174 mapsheets only, hand-colored. S Nov 28 (976) £300 [Nicholson]

Anr copy. 2 vols in 1. 4to, half calf; def. With 212 mostly full-page mapsheets only, neatly hand-colored, many detached. S June 25 (300) £480 [Santa]

Society of Dilettanti. See: Society...

Society of Foliophiles
— Specimens of Oriental Manuscripts and Printing. NY, [1928]. One of 220. Compiled by G. M. L. Brown. 15 parts. Folio, loose as issued in folders. Some worming to some specimens. S Sept 23 (493) £180 [Sahth]

Socinus, Faustus, 1539-1604
— Epistolae. Racov: Sebastian Sternach, 1618. 8vo, old calf; 2 holes in upper cover, both joints very weak. A few margins with small portions torn away or torn along the edge of the text but without affecting text; a few small holes at the top of the text of A5a; tear in A7 going into the text. S May 21 (126) £200 [Kraus]

Sole, William
— Menthae Britannicae: being a new Botanical Arrangement of...British Mints. Bath, 1798. Folio, orig bds; spine def, 2 corners worn. With 24 plates. Two plates wormed in inner blank margins. L July 2 (177) £440

Anr copy. Contemp half calf; upper cover detached. With the 26 orig watercolors for the plates bound in place of the plates. Sole—Lingwood—de Belder copy. S Apr 28 (340) £4,800 [Arader]

Soliday, George W. See: Decker, Peter

Solinus, Caius Julius
— Polyhistor. Venice: [Joannes Rubeus Vercellensis], 10 Mar 1498. ("De mirabilibus mundi.") 4to, modern blind-stamped mor. Margin of final & penultimate leaves repaired, affecting 1 or 2 letters of the text of the final leaf, some discoloration; early Ms marginal notes; some fore-margins just shaved. 46 leaves. Goff S-622. S Apr 24 (198) £900 [Thomas]
— Polyhistor...huic...Pomponii Melae de situ orbis...adiunximus. Basel: M. Isingrinius & H. Petrus, 1538. Folio, vellum bds; head of spine def. Some waterstaining. S Nov 18 (962) £550 [Farley]

Solis y Ribadaneyra, Antonio de, 1610-86
— Histoire de la conquete du Mexique.... Paris, 1691. 4to, contemp calf; lacking portion of backstrip. Marginal dampstaining to a few leaves; lacking 5 plates. sg Mar 12 (234) $100
— Historia de la conquista de Mexico.... Madrid: Blas Roman, 1776. 4to, contemp calf. Soiling on bottom corner tip of tp & following few leaves. sg Sept 18 (271) $60
— The History of the Conquest of Mexico.... L, 1724. 1st Ed in English. Folio, contemp calf. Some fraying. O May 12 (181) $375

Anr copy. Contemp calf; rebacked. Tp soiled; minor tears repaired on verso; marginal dampstaining, occasionally affecting text & plates. sg Mar 12 (235) $325

Anr Ed. L, 1738. 2 vols. 8vo, contemp calf gilt; rubbed. With 9 plates & maps. pn Sept 18 (108) £100 [Culpin]

Solleysell, Jacques, Sieur de
— The Compleat Horseman.... L, 1717. Folio, contemp calf; rubbed, rebacked. With frontis & 6 folding plates. Some holes from rust & paper-flaws. S Nov 10 (564) £150 [Head]

Solly, Nathanael Neal
— Memoir of the Life of David Cox. L, 1875. 8vo, orig cloth; hinges broken. With mtd photos. T Sept 18 (467) £66

Solon, Louis Marie Emmanuel
— The Art of the Old English Potter. Derby, 1885. 2d Ed, One of 250 L.p. copies. 4to, orig half mor gilt. T July 16 (363) £60
— Ceramic Literature: An Analytic Index to the Works Published in all Languages.... L, 1910. 4to, half pigskin; broken, worn. sg Oct 2 (101) $70

Solvyns, Frans Baltasar
— The Costume of Hindostan. L, [text watermarked 1823, plates watermarked 1832]. Folio, contemp mor gilt; rubbed. With 60 hand-colored plates. C Apr 8 (114) £700 [Roome]
— Les Hindous. Paris, 1808-12. 4 vols. Folio, contemp half mor. With 288 hand colored plates. Some spotting. S June 25 (195) £4,000 [Lennox]

Somaveda
— Katha Sarit Sagara...The Ocean of Story. L, 1924-28. One of 1,500. Trans by C. H. Tawney; Ed by N. M. Penzer. 10 vols. Newer buckram. O Oct 21 (133) $50

Some...

— Some Account of the Conduct of the Religious Society of Friends towards the Indian Tribes.... L, 1844. 8vo, modern half mor; rubbed. With 2 colored maps. O Oct 21 (11) $130

— Some British Ballads. NY, [1919]. Illus by Arthur Rackham. O Sept 23 (167) $90

— Some Observations on the Assiento Trade. L, 1728. 8vo, modern half mor. Library markings. sg Mar 12 (151) $200

— Some Southwestern Trails. El Paso, 1948. Illus by Harold Bugbee. 4to, cloth; rubbed, loose. cb Apr 2 (246) $110

Somers, John, Baron Somers, 1651-1716

— A Collection of Scarce and Valuable Tracts. L, 1809-15. 13 vols. 4to, contemp calf gilt; hinges cracked, rubbed, a few covers loose. bba July 16 (273) £460 [Subunso]

Anr copy. Contemp calf gilt; rubbed, joints of last vol split. bba Aug 20 (52) £500 [Jarndyce]

Somerset, Edward, Marquis of Worcester. See: Worcester, Edward Somerset

Somervile, William, 1675-1742

See also: Fore-Edge Paintings

— The Chase. L, 1735. 1st Ed. 4to, contemp calf; rubbed. S Jan 13 (522) £80 [Tarakan]

Anr copy. Contemp calf; rubbed. Jeanson 1516. SM Mar 1 (510) FF4,000

Anr Ed. L, 1796. Illus by Thomas Bewick. 8vo, contemp calf Etruscan bdg. L.p. copy. Jeanson 1258. SM Mar 1 (511) FF17,000

Somerville, Edith. See: Derrydale Press

Sommer, Johann Gottfried, d.1848

— Taschenbuch zur Verbreitung Geographischer Kenntnisse. Prague, 1823-45. Nos 1-24 (of 25). 12mo, contemp half calf; marked. With 146 maps & plates. Some captions cropped; a few leaves in Vol 18 loose; some dampstains in a few vols. S Nov 10 (1012) £320 [Noshiub]

Sonn, Albert H.

— Early American Wrought Iron. NY, 1928. 3 vols. 4to, cloth; worn, Vol III joints strengthened. O June 9 (172) $250

Anr copy. Cloth; soiled & worn, hinges tender. wa Nov 6 (450) $140

Sonnerat, Pierre

— Voyage aux Indes Orientales et a la Chine.... Paris, 1782. 1st Ed. 2 vols. 4to, contemp calf gilt; rubbed. With folding map, hand-colored in outline (repaired) & 140 plates. Vol I lacking final blank & with some light staining; 1 plate torn at outer margin. S Apr 24 (355) £650 [Orient]

Sonnini, Charles Nicolas

— Travels in Upper and Lower Egypt. L, 1807. 3 vols. 8vo, modern half lea. With 40 plates. Some foxing & browning. sg Apr 23 (138) $175

Sophocles, 496?-406 B.C.

— King Oedipus. NY, [1968]. One of 105, sgd by artist. Illus by Giacomo Manzu. 4to, loose in wraps as issued. With 7 etchings. wd Nov 12 (98) $800

— Koning Oidipoes. Haarlem, 1929. One of 150. B Oct 7 (91) HF320

— Scholia. Rome: Angelus Collotius, 1518. ("Commentarii in septem tragedias Sophoclis.") 4to, half calf. A few leaves repaired or spotted. In Greek. S Nov 27 (228) £700 [Schal]

— Tragoediae septem. Florence, 1522. 4to, contemp vellum; soiled, lacking ties, spine damaged. A few leaves dampstained in lower portion. In Greek. S Nov 27 (229) £900 [Maggs]

Anr Ed. [Geneva]: Paulus Stephanus, 1603. 4to, contemp vellum; waterstained. B Feb 25 (860) HF380

Sorlier, Charles

— The Ceramics and Sculptures of Chagall. Monaco, 1972. 4to, orig cloth, in d/j. S Nov 10 (62) £55 [Fitton]

Sotheby, Samuel Leigh, 1805-61

— Principia Typographia.... L, 1858. 3 vols. Folio. contemp half lea; needs rebdg. sg Jan 22 (281) $225

Sotheby, William, 1757-1838

— A Tour through Parts of Wales.... L, 1794. 4to, orig bds; broken, lacking backstrip. With 13 plates, some washed with color. bba Oct 16 (265) £60 [Hetherington]

Anr copy. With 13 plates. O May 12 (182) $175

Anr copy. Contemp lea; rebacked, worn. With 11 aquatints tinted with watercolor wash. sg Nov 20 (163) $60

Sotheran, Henry

— Bibliotheca Chemico-Mathematica.... L, 1921-52. 6 vols, including 4 Supplement vols. Ck Nov 7 (20) £350

Anr copy. 5 vols, including 1st & 2d Supplements. sg May 14 (629) $325; sg May 14 (630) $350

Anr copy. Vols I-II. Library markings. wa Mar 5 (11) $110

Souhart, Roger Francois

— Bibliographie general des ouvrages sur la chasse, la venerie et la fauconnerie. Paris, 1886. 8vo, half mor by Saulnier. Jeanson 1348. SM Mar 1 (593) FF3,800

One of 550. Sheep; rear cover chafed. sg Oct 2 (166) $225

Soule, Frank —& Others
— The Annals of San Francisco NY, 1855. 1st Ed. 8vo, later half mor; front hinge cracking. With 2 maps. Folding map torn. cb Oct 9 (224) $150

Anr copy. Orig mor presentation bdg; rebacked in cloth with gilt spine lettering laid down, new endpapers. With 2 views, 4 ports & 2 maps. Folded map with a few tears; plates with mild foxing. ha May 22 (319) $100

Anr copy. Lea. With 6 plates & 2 maps, 1 with short tear. sg Mar 12 (30) $175

Sourbets, G. —& Saint-Marc, Camille de
— Precis de fauconnerie.... Niort: L. Clouzot, 1887. One of 150. 8vo, contemp half cloth. Jeanson copy. SM Mar 1 (512) FF4,50000

Sousa, Antonio de
— Aphorismi inquisitorum.... Tournon, 1633. 8vo, contemp vellum. Some foxing. sg Oct 9 (57) $50

Sousa Coutinho, Manuel de, 1555-1632
— Plans, Elevations, Sections and Views of the Church of Batalha.... L, 1795. Folio, contemp half calf; rubbed, joints cracking. With engraved title & 25 plates. S Jan 16 (435) £100 [Weinreb]

Anr Ed. L, 1836. Folio, bdg not indicated. Lacking tp. Sold w.a.f. Franklin Institute copy. F Sept 12 (19) $50

South...
— The South Vindicated from the Treason and Fanaticism of the Northern Abolitionists. Bost., 1836. Orig cloth; worn. Foxed. cb Oct 9 (300) $60

Southall, John
— A Treatise of Buggs: Shewing When and How they were first brought into England.... L: J. Roberts, 1730. 4to, modern half vellum. Hunt copy. CNY Nov 21 (259) $420

Southard, Charles Z.
— Trout Fly-Fishing in America. NY, 1914. 4to, cloth; worn, discolored. With 20 color plates. Inscr. wa Nov 6 (110) $120

One of 100. Cloth; worn, discolored. With 20 color plates. wa Nov 6 (110) $120

Southesk, James Carnegie, 9th Earl of
— Saskatchewan and the Rocky Mountains.... Edin., 1875. 8vo, orig cloth. cb July 16 (242) $110

Southey, Robert, 1774-1843
See also: Annual...

— The Curse of Kehama. L, 1810. 1st Ed, L.p. copy. 4to, contemp half calf; needs rebdg. Endpapers spotted. bba Nov 13 (241) £65 [Bindman]

— Letters from England. L, 1807. 3 vols. 12mo, russia; backstrips def. Southey's own interleaved & annotated copy. S July 23 (99) £3,200 [Quaritch]

— Poetical Works. L 1812-15. 13 vols. 12mo, contemp calf gilt; joints & spine ends worn. sg Feb 12 (290) $150

Souvenir...
— Souvenir des dames. [N.p., c.1830]. 97mm by 72mm, sides of mother-of-pearl with engraved border of flourishes & the word souvenir on upper cover, with pink silk doublures & liners & gilt wire holders with pencil, the calendar for 1826 loose in a gilt metal frame. C Dec 3 (88) £800 [Tenschert]

Sowerby, James, 1757-1822
— The British Miscellany: or Colored Figures of New, Rare, or Little Known Animal Subjects. L, 1804-6. 12 parts in 1 vol. 8vo, half lea, orig wraps bound in. With 76 hand-colored plates. pn July 23 (181) £360 [Maggs]

— Coloured Figures of English Fungi. L, [1795]-1797-1803. 3 vols & Supplement, bound in 2 vols. Folio, contemp calf; rebacked, corners & hinges worn. With 440 hand-colored plates on 436 leaves, including 4 plates with double numeration. Vol II title & a few leaves spotted. C Oct 15 (259) £2,200 [Walford]

Anr copy. 3 vols plus 1815 Supplement in 2 vols. Folio, later half mor. With 440 on 436 handcolored plates, some from anr copy. Some foxing or spotting at beginning of Vol II. Crahan copy. P Nov 25 (431) $2,700

Anr copy. 3 vols. Folio, contemp half calf; rebacked. With 440 hand-colored or color-ptd plates on 436 leaves. Some spotting; a few with browning. de Belder copy S Apr 28 (342) £3,200 [Phelps]

— Flora Luxurians or the Florist's Delight. L, 1789. Parts 1 & 2 (of 3) only. Folio, orig wraps; worn, 1 torn. With 12 hand-colored plates. de Belder copy. S Apr 28 (341) £8,000 [Arader]

— The Genera of Recent and Fossil Shells. L, [1820-34]. 42 parts bound in 3 vols. Contemp cloth; worn, joints cracked, 3 covers detached. With 1 plain & 256 hand-colored plates only. cb June 4 (192) $650

SOWERBY

Sowerby, James, 1757-1822 —& Smith, Sir James Edward, 1759-1828

— English Botany. L, 1790-1814. 36 vols, including Index but without Supplement vols. 8vo, contemp half mor; rubbed, 2 covers detached. With 2,592 hand-colored plates. Tear to Plates 324 & 325. Sold w.a.f. C Apr 8 (154) £2,600 [Gaston]
Anr copy. Vols 1-8 only. Half calf; hinges cracked. pn Oct 23 (379) £520 [Plinke]
Anr copy. 36 vols. 8vo, contemp calf; 1 spine chipped at head, joints of last vol repaired. A few plates stained in Vol I; some foxing & offsetting; a few plates trimmed. Sold w.a.f. S Oct 23 (761) £2,200 [Wesley]
Anr copy. 41 vols in 23, including 5-vol supplement to 1866. 8vo, contemp half calf, calf & orig wraps; rubbed, some covers detached. With 3,018 hand-colored plates. Vol V of the supplement is made up, in part, with some of the orig fascicles & is partially duplicated in the same manner. Bagge—Lawrence—de Belder set. S Apr 28 (343) £4,500 [Berg]
Anr Ed. L, [1832]-46. 13 vols, including Supplementary vol of plates. 8vo, contemp half calf. C Apr 8 (209) £680 [Russell]
Anr copy. 12 vols. 8vo, contemp cloth; spines worn. Sold w.a.f. S Feb 24 (615) £700 [Kidd]

Vols I-VI only. L, 1835-39. Contemp half cloth; worn. Sold w.a.f. Ck May 29 (152) £240
Anr Ed. L, 1863-1902. 11 vols. 8vo, orig cloth. With 1,824 color plates. pn Jan 22 (11) £460 [Ramsey]
Anr copy. Vols I-XI. 8vo, contemp half calf; defective. With 1,838 hand-colored plates. pn Jan 22 (29) £380 [Garrard]
Anr copy. 12 vols, without Supplement. Half mor; library numbers on spines. With 1,939 hand-colored plates, including 17 bis plates. Marginal tear in Plate 1906. S June 25 (180) £650 [Ferrini]
Anr Ed. L, 1899. 13 vols, including Supplement. 8vo, mor gilt. With 1,922 hand-colored plates with 31 additional plates. Contents loose in some vols. pnE Dec 17 (231) £780 [Traylen]
Anr Ed. L, 1913. 13 vols. Sold w.a.f. S Feb 24 (614) £360 [Russel]

Sowerby, John E., 1825-70. See: Johnson & Sowerby

AMERICAN BOOK PRICES CURRENT

Soyer, Alexis, 1809-58

— The Gastronomic Regenerator. L, 1846. 8vo, orig cloth. Some stains. pn Nov 20 (183) £55 [Clark]
— Soyer's Culinary Campaign.... L, 1857. 1st Ed. 8vo, cloth; rebacked with orig spine laid on, new endpapers. Foxed. cb July 30 (284) $75

Soyer, Raphael

[-] Raphael Soyer; Fifty Years of Printmaking.... NY, 1967. One of 100, with a numbered, sgd etching bound in. By Sylvan Cole, Jr. 4to, cloth, in d/j. sg June 4 (315) $175

Spaendonck, Gernit van

— Fleurs dessinees d'apres nature.... Paris, [c.1800]. Folio, orig bds; worn. With 21 (of 24) plates. Upper blank margins strengthened or repaired; some soiling & occasional marginal staining. de Belder copy. S Apr 28 (344) £14,000 [Strauss]

Spaher, Michael, of Tyrol. See: Remmelin & Spaher

Spain

— Recopilacion de las leyes destos Reynos, hecha por mandado de la Magestad Catolica del Rey Don Felipe Segundo. Madrid, 1640. 3 vols. Folio, contemp vellum. sg Mar 26 (262) $425

Spalding, Albert Goodwill, 1850-1915

— America's National Game; Historic Facts Concerning...Baseball. NY, 1911. Lower corner dampstained throughout. wa Sept 25 (157) $50

Spalding, John, of Aberdeen

— The History of the Troubles and Memorable Transactions in Scotland and England.... Edin.: Bannatyne Club, 1828-29. One of 100. 2 vols. 4to, half mor; rubbed. O Feb 24 (180) $50

Spallanzani, Lazzaro

— De' fenomeni della circolazione.... Modena, 1773. 1st Ed. 8vo, contemp bds; lower cover wormed. A few leaves wormed, affecting text. S Nov 27 (287) £320 [Phelps]
— Dissertations Relative to the Natural History of Animals and Vegetables. L, 1789. 2 vols. 8vo, recent half calf. Some stains, mainly at beginning & end of Vol I. S July 28 (1119) £120
— Voyages dans les deux Siciles.... Paris, 1800, [An VIII]. 6 vols in 3. 8vo, later half calf; rubbed. Library markings. cb June 4 (193) $225

Spangenberg, Cyriacus, 1528-1604
— Bestendiger und wolgegruendter Bericht, wie ferrn die Jagten rechtmessig und zuebelassen.... Frankfurt, 1561. Folio, modern half calf. Lower margin of the 2d leaf repaired. Jeanson copy. SM Mar 1 (513) FF10,0000

Sparks, Jared, 1789-1866
— Diplomatic Correspondence of the American Revolution. See: Diplomatic...

Sparling, Henry Halliday
— The Kelmscott Press and William Morris.... L, 1924. bba Feb 5 (203) £100 [Burmester]; S Nov 10 (29) £90 [Traylen]

Sparrman, Anders
— Voyage au Cap de Bonne-Esperance, autour du monde avec le Capitaine Cook. Paris, 1787. 1st Ed in French. 3 vols. 8vo, contemp calf. With folding map & 15 plates. SM Oct 20 (559) FF2,500
— A Voyage to the Cape of Good Hope.... Dublin, 1785. 2 vols. 4to, contemp calf. With frontis, folding map & 9 plates. S Oct 23 (465) £700 [Bonham]
2d Ed. L, 1786. 2 vols. 4to, contemp calf, stained, rebacked. With frontis, folding map & 9 plates. Some soiling. Ck Sept 26 (79) £160

Sparrow, Walter Shaw
— Advertising and British Art.... L, [1924]. 4to, half cloth. sg Feb 5 (2) $110
— Angling in British Art. L, 1923. 4to, orig cloth. pnE Dec 17 (293) £42 [Head]
Anr copy. Orig cloth, in d/j; worn. sg Oct 23 (508) $80
— Ben Alken. L & NY, 1927. 4to, cloth, in def d/j. cb May 21 (244) $60
— A Book of British Etching. L, 1926. 4to, cloth. sg Feb 5 (303) $60
— A Book of Sporting Painters. L, 1931. 4to, cloth, in d/j. pn Jan 22 (100) £40 [Pearson]
— Frank Brangwyn and His Work. Bost., 1911. Folio, cloth, rubbed, top spine end torn. sg Feb 5 (50) $140
— John Lavery and his Work. L, [1911]. Ltd Ed. Folio, orig half vellum bds; soiled. With an unbound set of duplicate plates in orig portfolio. Ck Nov 25 (90) £80

Spaulding, Thomas Marshall —& Karpinski, Louis Charles
— Early Military Books in the University of Michigan Libraries. Ann Arbor, 1941. 4to, cloth. With frontis & 37 plates. sg Oct 2 (223) $175; sg May 14 (356) $300

Speaking...
— The Speaking Picture Book. NY [Ptd in Germany, c.1890]. 4to, orig pictorial bds; repaired. With 8 colored plates & 9 string-pull tabs. Some repairs; 1 pull-tab detached but present. O Apr 28 (181) $190

Spears, John R., 1850-1936
— Illustrated Sketches of Death Valley.... Chicago, 1892. 12mo, pictorial wraps; spine worn, shaken. sg Sept 18 (273) $120

Spectator...
— The Spectator [By Addison, Steele & others]. Dublin, 1753. 8 vols. 16mo, contemp calf; rubbed. Ck Sept 5 (106) £60
Anr Ed. L, 1819. Nos 1-635 in 8 vols. 8vo, calf gilt. S Jan 16 (436) £70 [Cavendish]

Speculum...
— Speculum Humanae Salvationis. Kritische Ausgabe. Leipzig: Karl W. Hiersemann, 1907. 2 vols. Folio, cloth, plates loose in cloth portfolio as issued. sg Oct 2 (191) $275

Speechly, William
— A Treatise on the Culture of the Pine Apple.... York, 1779. 8vo, contemp half calf, with Signet seal on covers; rubbed, upper joint cracking. Worming to upper margin of folding plate; marginal worming affecting final few leaves & folding plan; some browning. Crahan copy. P Nov 25 (434) $350

Speed, John, 1552-1629

Abridgement of Theatre
— England, Wales, Scotland and Ireland Described. L, [1627, or later]. 2 parts in 1 vol, including "A Prospect of the World." Oblong 8vo, old calf; worn. With 83 maps. Tears to 2 folding maps with a little loss; some soiling; some margins tattered. Ck May 15 (308) £950

Anr copy. Part 1 (of 2) only; lacking "A Prospect of the World". Oblong 8vo, 17th-cent mor gilt; rebacked. With 1 plate & 63 maps. Anr copy of engraved title cut round & mtd on front flyleaf; final text leaves cropped. S Jan 12 (64) £680 [Franks]

Anr Ed. L, 1627. 2 parts in 1 vol. Oblong 8vo, contemp calf; rebacked. With engraved title (holed) & 62 (of 63) maps. Middlesex with small hole; 4 maps with dampstains; last 3 leaves of text torn with loss. pn Sept 18 (350) £800 [Saville]

Anr copy. Disbound. With engraved title & 37 maps only. pn Apr 30 (482) £300 [Burgess]

Anr copy. Oblong 8vo, contemp vellum. With engraved title (lower margin trimmed) & 63 maps. pn May 21 (430) £780 [Traylen]

SPEED

Anr copy. 2 parts in 1 vol. Oblong 8vo, contemp vellum; soiled. With engraved title & 63 maps. Corners of 1st few leaves dog-eared; final leaf frayed with slight loss of table. S Oct 23 (161) £750 [Postaprint]

Continuation of Theatre

— The Historie of Great Britaine under the Conquests.... L, 1627. "2d" Ed. Folio, contemp calf gilt; rehinged. pn May 21 (190) £110 [Speed]

3d Ed. L, 1632. Folio, crude modern cloth. Lacking 1st leaf; small hole in tp with slight loss. Sold w.a.f. O Nov 18 (178) $100

— The History of Great Britaine.... L, 1650. "3d" Ed. Folio, contemp calf; rebacked, orig spine preserved. Light stain in outer margin. pn May 21 (193) £110 [Speed]

Theatre

— The Theatre of the Empire of Great Britaine. L, 1611-12. 1st Ed. 4 (of 5) parts in 1 vol; lacking the "Prospect." Folio, modern half calf over wooden bds. With 67 double-page maps. Some guards renewed; tp with short tear; plate of arms trimmed to frame & inset; dedication leaf def; Devonshire inverted; Connaught detached; a few folds def; some marginal tears & waterstains. C Oct 15 (102) £8,500 [Kentish]

Anr copy. Mor gilt by Riviere. With 67 double-page maps, all partly hand-colored. Wight Island with small central tear; 7 maps with foremargins just shaved. Sold w.a.f. Sold with The History of Great Britaine, 1611, in 2 vols, with title & text illusts hand-colored & heightened with gold. C Apr 8 (71) £10,000 [Ingol]

Anr copy. Early 19th-cent russia gilt; rebacked preserving spine. With engraved title & royal achievement & 67 double-page maps. A few maps damaged at centerfold with slight loss; tp mtd; a few marginal repairs. Henry Yates Thompson —Hopwell Hall copy. S Apr 23 (105) £14,000 [Arader]

2d Ed. L, 1614. 4 (of 5) parts in 1 vol; lacking the "Prospect." Folio, contemp calf gilt with Northampton crest; rebacked with orig spine preserved. With 67 double-page maps, engraved title, illus & woodcut coat-of-arms, all hand-colored. Minor repairs without loss. S Oct 23 (158) £14,000 [Kentish]

Anr Ed. L, 1616. ("Theatrum imperii magnae Britanniae....") 4 parts in 1 vol. Folio, contemp calf; upper joint broken. With 67 double-page maps, hand-colored in outline. Engraved title & achievement soiled & repaired at outer margins. S Oct 23 (159) £8,500 [Browning]

Anr Ed. L, 1627-[31]. 4 parts in 1 vol. With engraved title & 67 double-page maps. Bound with: Speed. A Prospect of the Most Famous Parts of the World. L, 1631. With port & 20 (of 21) double-page maps. Together, 87 maps. Folio, old calf; broken. Port & title to Prospect cut round & laid down; lacking map of America; some staining; a few maps with tears, some with slight loss; some maps split at fold; some creased. C Apr 8 (72) £9,500 [Burgess Browning]

Anr Ed. L, 1676. ("The Theatre of the Empire of Great Britain.") 2 parts in 1 vol. Folio, old calf; rebacked. With 94 (of 96) double-page maps & 5 double-page tables. Lacking engraved title, frontis, Italy & the Roman Empire; a few maps split at fold including world map; Greece laid down; minor marginal dampstaining; hole in France & Hertfordshire; Essex def, lacking left half. C Oct 15 (140) £17,000 [Sweet]

Speer, Joseph Smith
— The West-India Pilot. L, 1771. 2d Ed. Folio, contemp calf; portions of backstrip lacking, joints cracked. With 28 plates, including hand-colored double-page view. Some foxing, browning & dampstaining; tear at bottom of inner edge of F1; portion of margin edges of 2 leaves lacking; Ms corrections in a contemp hand throughout. sg Dec 4 (184) $2,400

Speke, John Hanning, 1827-64
— Journal of the Discovery of the Source of the Nile. Edin & L, 1863. 8vo, half calf gilt; rubbed. pn May 21 (105) £130 [Joseph]

Anr copy. Contemp calf. pnE June 17 (52) £90

Spelen...
— Spelen van Sinne, vol scoone moralisacien wtleggingen ende Bedienissen op all loeflijcke Consten. Antwerp: W. Silvius, 1562. Bound with: Spelen van Sinne waer inne Oirboirlijcke ende Eerlijcke Handwercken ghepresen ende verhaelt Worden. Antwerp: Silvius, 1562. 4to, vellum. With 32 (of 37) woodcuts. B Feb 25 (728) HF1,500

Spelman, Sir Henry, 1564-1641
— Archaeologus, in modum glosarii... L, 1687. ("Glossarium archaiologicum; continens Latino & Barbara...vocabula.") 3d Ed. Folio, contemp calf; rebacked, lower cover detached. bba Mar 26 (169) £60 [Roter-Kasten]

— Concilia, decreta, leges, constitutiones.... L, 1639-64. 2 vols. Folio, later calf; rebacked. sg Oct 9 (321) $175

— The English Works.... L, 1723. Folio, contemp calf; chafed, front cover detached. sg Oct 9 (322) $225

Spence, James Lewis Thomas Chalmers
— The Myths of the North American Indians.... L, 1914. With 32 color plates. cb Jan 8 (184) $50

Spence, William. See: Kirby & Spence

Spencer, Sir Baldwin
— Report on the Work of the Horn Scientific Expedition to Central Australia. L & Melbourne, Sept 1896. 4 vols. 8vo, cloth. Library markings. bba Feb 5 (312) £380 [Morrell]
— Wanderings in Wild Australia. L, 1928. 2 vols. pn Jan 22 (254) £110 [Fabian]

Spencer, Sir Baldwin —& Gillen, Francis J.
— Across Australia. L, 1912. 2 vols. pn Dec 11 (224) £65 [Bowen]
— The Northern Tribes of Central Australia L, 1904. 1st Ed. CA Oct 7 (150) A$300

Spencer, Nathaniel
See also: Sanders, Robert
— The Complete English Traveller. L, 1772. Folio, half calf; hinges split. pn July 23 (200) £240 [Walford]

Spenser, Edmund, 1552?-99
See also: Ashendene Press; Cresset Press; Kelmscott Press
— The Faerie Queene. L: William Ponsonby, 1590-96. 1st Ed, STC 23081, 23082. 2 vols. 4to, lev gilt by Riviere. First title rehinged; old signature washed out of 2d; Vol I lacks last 12 leaves. Terry copy. sg Apr 2 (186) $3,800
  2d Ed of Part 1; 1st Ed of Part 2. L: R. Field for William Ponsonbie, 1596. 2 vols in 1. 4to, contemp embroidered bdg of gilt & colored threads on purple velvet worked to a large floral design with initials E & T; worn & def. Part 1 lacking all before C3 & lacking H1 & Bb1; Part 2 lacking last 4 leaves. Large hole in C3 in Part 1; other minor defs. Sold w.a.f. bba Aug 28 (164) £200 [Nudelman]
— Works. L, 1611-12. ("The Faerie Queene: The Shepheards Calendar: Together with Other Works of England's Arch-Poet.") 1st Collected Ed, NSTC 23083.7. Folio, contemp calf gilt; rubbed. A few tears & rust-holes, scarcely affecting text. S Mar 10 (155) £700 [Henderson]
  Anr copy. Early 20th-cent lev gilt. General title possibly inserted from anr copy; some small holes. S July 14 (438) £380
  Anr Ed. L, 1679. Folio, contemp calf; rebacked, corners repaired. Some rust-marks or holes. This copy annotated by Matthew Prior & with his presentation inscr to Lord Harley. S July 23 (16) £2,400 [Quaritch]
  Anr copy. Old calf; rebacked. sg Oct 9 (323) $275
  Anr copy. Old calf; front cover detached. sg Mar 26 (263) $225
  Anr Ed. L, 1715. 6 vols. 8vo, contemp calf gilt; some joints split, rubbed. bba Oct 30 (149) £50 [Bailey]

Spiegel, Jacob
— Iuris civilis lexicon. Strassburg: Johann Schott, 1538. Bound with: Oldendorp, Johannes. Variarum lectionum libri ad iuris civilis interpretationem. Cologne: Joannes Gymnicus, 1540. Folio, contemp blind-tooled pigskin over wooden bds, brass catches & clasps. sg Oct 9 (251) $400

Spielmann, Mabel Henrietta
— The Rainbow Book: Tales of Fun & Fancy. L, 1909. sg Oct 30 (201) £110

Spielmann, Marion Harry —& Layard, George Somes, 1857-1925
— Kate Greenaway. NY & L, 1905. One of 500, sgd by John Greenaway & with pencil sketch by Kate laid in. Cloth; soiled. Ck Feb 13 (117) £400
  Anr copy. Half mor gilt; rubbed. pnNY Sept 13 (239) $500
  Anr copy. Cloth. S Dec 5 (314) £320 [Benemix]
  Anr copy. 4to, orig cloth. S May 6 (224) £100 [Hayes]
  Anr copy. Cloth. S June 18 (461) £400 [Peters]

Spies, Werner
— Max Ernst: Collagen. Cologne, 1974. Folio, orig cloth, in d/j. S June 29 (99) £340 [Henderson]
— Max Ernst Oeuvre-Katalog. Houston & Cologne, 1975-79. One of 1,500. 4 vols. Folio, orig half cloth, in d/js. S June 29 (100) £1,100 [Kede]

Spiller, Burton L. See: Derrydale Press

Spilsbury, Francis B.
— Picturesque Scenery in the Holy Land and Syria. L, 1803. 1st Ed. Folio, half cloth. With 19 hand-colored plates. Lacking port; library stamp at foot of title; 1 plate cropped. S Feb 24 (440) £640 [Khatib]
  Anr copy. Later half mor; broken. With port & 19 hand-colored plates. A few tears repaired; imprint on port cropped; 1 plate cropped to plate mark. S Apr 24 (244) £550 [Ungar]
  Anr Ed. L, 1823. 4to, modern half mor.

SPILSBURY

With 19 hand-colored plates. Ck Feb 27 (107) £280

Anr copy. Cloth; rebacked with tape, some leaves loosening. Minor faults to margins of plates. wa June 25 (523) $260

Spinoza, Baruch, 1632-77
— Opera posthuma. [Amst.?], 1677. 2 parts in 1 vol. 8vo, calf; worn, joints cracked. HN Nov 26 (1377) DM2,400

Anr copy. Contemp vellum; hole in spine. Tp stained & stamped. sg Dec 4 (185) $1,200

Anr copy. Contemp calf; rebacked. sg Apr 30 (352) $1,100

— Tractatus theologico-politicus.... Hamburg, 1670. Bound with: Spinoza. Opera Posthuma. [Amst., 1677] 4to, contemp calf; rubbed, upper back joint split. Tp of 1st work torn. CAM Dec 3 (164) HF9,000

— Traite des ceremonies superstitieuses des Juifs. Amst., 1678. 12mo, calf gilt. Some browning. CAM Dec 3 (165) HF2,800

— Traitte des ceremonies superstitieuses des Juifs. Amst., 1678. 12mo, orig lea. Worming at beginning & end; some stains; stamp of former owner on tp. S Feb 17 (112) £600 [Mandanes]

Spix, Johann Baptist von
— Caphalogenesis; sive, Capitis ossei structura.... Munich, 1815. Folio, disbound. With 18 litho plates. Tp margin dampstained. sg Jan 15 (257) $130

— Testacea Fluviatilia quae in ininere per Brasiliam.... Munich, 1827. 4to, contemp half russia; worn. With 29 colored plates. S Apr 23 (61) £850 [Antik]

Spix, Johann Baptist von —& Martius, Carl Friedrich Philipp von
— Reise in Brasilien auf Befehl Sr. Majestaete Maximilian Joseph I.... Munich, 1823-31. 3 vols text plus Atlas. 4to & oblong folio, text in recent mor, Atlas in orig wraps & orig bds. With frontis, 5 maps on 8 sheets & 41 plates, 3 colored. Lacking a folding map & 30 pp of music called for by Palau. S Oct 23 (454) £2,000 [Geyerhahn]

Text vols only. 3 vols. 4to, modern cloth. With large folding map at end of Vol III. S July 14 (807) £350

Spon, Jacob, 1647-85
— Histoire de Geneve. Geneva, 1730. 2 vols. 4to, contemp calf; worn. FD June 11 (985) DM1,500

Sporting...
— Sporting Magazine: Or, Monthly Calendar.... L, 1792-1892. 157 vols, including Index of Engravings. 8vo, half calf gilt; 14 covers detached, spine of index vol def.

AMERICAN BOOK PRICES CURRENT

Sold w.a.f. S Oct 23 (769) £4,800 [Armouries]

— The Sporting Repository, containing Horse-Racing, Hunting, Coursing, Shooting, Archery.... L, 1822. Vol I, Nos 1-6 (all pbd). 8vo, contemp half mor gilt; rubbed. With 19 hand-colored plates. C Apr 8 (202) £600 [Blest]

— The Sporting Repository. L, 1822. Vol I, Nos 1-6 (all pbd). 8vo, mor gilt by Bickers; joints renewed. With 19 hand-colored plates. Small holes in Y3 & 2E2; 2 plates with imprints cropped or obscured in bdg. S Apr 23 (68) £1,600 [Ackermann]

Anr copy. Lev gilt by Lloyd. sg Apr 2 (4) $1,100

Sportsman's...
— The Sportsman's Dictionary. L, 1735. 2 vols. 8vo, contemp calf. With 24 (of 25) plates. Vol I lacking 1st gathering, including title & frontis. cb Nov 6 (271) $170

3d Ed. L, 1785. ("The Sportsman's Dictionary, or the Gentleman's Companion for Town and Country....") 4to, contemp calf gilt. With frontis & 15 plates. pn Apr 30 (339) £110

Sprat, Thomas, 1635-1713
— The History of the Royal Society of London. L, 1667. 1st Ed. 4to, modern half calf. Licence leaf waterstained. bba Oct 30 (150) £140 [Shapero]

Anr copy. Contemp calf; hinges weak, spine tender. With frontis & 2 folding plates. pnE Jan 28 (307) £260 [Traylen]

3d Ed. L, 1722. 4to, contemp calf; rebacked. With frontis & 2 folding plates. pnE Jan 28 (308) £160 [Traylen]

— A True Account and Declaration of the Horrid Conspiracy against the late King.... L, 1685. Folio, contemp calf; rubbed, rebacked, joints split. Port inserted. bba Apr 9 (40) £40 [Frazer]

Anr copy. Bound with: Copies of the Informations and Original Papers relating to the Proof of the Horrid Conspiracy. L, 1685. Folio. Contemp calf; rubbed, foot of spine chipped. O Feb 24 (182) $70

Spratt, George
— Obstetric Tables.... L, 1835. 2d Ed. 2 vols. 4to, cloth; soiled. With 19 plates, 8 with movable slips. pnNY Sept 13 (290) $275

Sprengel, Christian Konrad
— Das entdeckte Geheimniss der Natur.... Berlin, 1793. 4to, contemp bds; worn. With engraved title & 25 plates. C Oct 15 (259A) £1,600 [Burden]

974

Sprengel, Kurt, 1766-1833
— An Introduction to the Study of Cryptogamous Plants. L, 1807. 8vo, orig bds. With 10 folding plates. pn Jan 22 (241) £35 [Maggs]

Sprenger, Jacobus. See: Institoris & Sprenger

Sprunt, Alexander
— Florida Bird Life. NY, [1954]. 4to, cloth; worn. O Mar 24 (166) $60

Spurzheim, Johann Gaspar, 1776-1832. See: Gall & Spurzheim

Squires, Frederick
— Architec-Tonics; The Tales of Tom Thumtack, Architect. NY, 1914. 1st Ed. Illus by Rockwell Kent. In d/j. cb Dec 4 (247) $170

Anr copy. In repaired d/j. cb June 18 (227) $190

Staats, Henry Philip
— African Journal, 1953-1954. New Haven: Pvtly ptd, 1954. sg Oct 23 (511) $70

Stackelberg, Otto Magnus von, 1787-1837
— Vestiture ed Usi de Popoli della moderna Grecia. Naples, 1827. Folio, mor, orig wrap bound in. With litho title & 40 hand-colored plates, each with pbr's blindstamp in lower margin. S Oct 23 (331) £3,500 [Martins]

Stackhouse, Thomas, 1677-1752
— A New History of the Holy Bible. L, 1752. 2 vols. Folio, bdg not given. Some dampstaining & tears. Sold w.a.f. pn Jan 22 (173) £60
— An Universal Atlas.... L, 1790. 4th Ed. Folio, cloth. With 39 hand-colored maps. Light stain in upper margin; lacking title. pn Jan 22 (340) £320 [Tooley]

Stael-Holstein, Anne Louise Germaine de
— Oeuvres. Paris, 1820-21. 17 vols. 8vo, contemp half sheep; some spines crudely repaired with tape, some joints split, rubbed. bba Mar 12 (105) £50 [Skoob]

Anr copy. Half calf gilt; worn. HN Nov 26 (1378) DM650

Stafford, Thomas, fl.1633
— Pacata Hibernia, Ireland Appeased and Reduced. L, 1633. Folio, later russia gilt; rubbed, joints worn. Lacking map of Munster. bba Apr 9 (296) £150 [Emerald Isle]

Anr copy. Old calf; rubbed, rebacked. With 18 maps & plans. Most plates torn or frayed; wormed in outer margin towards end. Sold w.a.f. S Feb 24 (397) £160 [Smith]

Stage...
— The Stage and its Stars. Phila., [c.1890]. Ed by H. P. & G. Gebbie. 2 vols. Folio, half mor; worn. sg Feb 26 (209) $225

Stainton, Henry Tibbats —& Others
— The Natural History of the Tineina. L, 1855-73. 8vo, modern half mor gilt. With 104 hand-colored plates. S Apr 23 (17) £440 [Rigout]

Stalin, Josef, 1879-1953
— Works. Moscow, 1952-55. 13 vols. bba Oct 30 (230) £40 [Cyclamen]

Stalkartt, Marmaduke
— Naval Architecture, or the Rudiments and Rules of Ship-Building.... L, 1781. Folio, bdg not described. With frontis. With portfolio of 14 plates. Franklin Institute copy. F Sept 12 (200) $400

Stamler, Johann
— Dyalogus de diversarum gentium sectis et mundi religionibus. Augsburg: Erhard Ogllin & Georg Nadler, 29 May 1508. Folio, 19th-calf; scuffed. Margins trimmed close, affecting top line of title & some sidenotes. sg Oct 9 (324) $500

Stamma, Philip, fl.1737
— Essai sur le jeu des echecs. The Hague, 1741. 12mo, modern calf. pn Mar 26 (499) £100 [Furstenberg]
— The Noble Game of Chess. L, 1745. 2 parts in 1 vol. Calf; hinges cracked. Sgd on p 115. pn Mar 26 (500) £300 [De Lucia]
— Stamma on the Game of Chess. L, 1819. Ed by W. Lewis. Half calf gilt. With diagrams ptd in 3 colors. pn Mar 26 (439) £40 [Walford]

Stampart, Frans van —& Prenner, Anton Joseph von
— Prodromus...seu praembulare lumen.... Vienna, 1735. Folio, contemp wraps. Some plates dampstained at margins; tp slightly soiled. Ck June 19 (109) £600

Stanard, Mary Newton
— Edgar Allan Poe Letters...in the Valentine Museum. Richmond VA, 1925. One of 1,500. 4to, half cloth. wa Nov 6 (657) $60

Stanfield, Clarkson, 1793-1867
— Sketches on the Moselle, the Rhine and the Meuse. L, 1838. Folio, orig half mor. With litho title, dedication & 29 hand-colored views on 25 sheets. S Oct 23 (272) £1,900 [Maliye]
— Stanfield's Coast Scenery: a Series of Views in the British Channel. L, 1836. 4to, orig cloth; rubbed. With frontis, engraved title & 38 plates. Some stains. bba Oct 30 (357) £40 [Shapero]

Anr copy. Mor gilt. pn Dec 11 (81) £80 [Nicholson]

Anr Ed. L, 1847. 8vo, cloth; def. pn Dec 11 (82) £80 [Nicholson]

Stanhope, Leicester Fitzgerald Charles, 5th Earl of Harrington

— Greece in 1823 and 1824.... L, 1824. 8vo, calf gilt; soiled. With hand-colored frontis & 6 facsimile letters. L July 2 (123) £100

Stanley, Sir Henry Morton, 1841-1904

— How I Found Livingstone. L, 1872. 1st Ed. 8vo, half calf gilt; rubbed, hinge split. pnE Oct 15 (75) £100

— In Darkest Africa. L, 1890. 1st Ed. 2 vols. 8vo, cloth; rubbed; front hinge of Vol I cracked, partially repaired. cb Nov 6 (272) $55

Anr copy. Half mor; worn. Some repaired tears to maps. cb Feb 19 (252) $130

Anr copy. Orig cloth; rubbed. One map torn without loss. T Jan 22 (7) £44

One of 250 L.p. copies. Orig half mor. bba Dec 18 (242) £130 [Hay]

Anr copy. 2 vols. 4to, orig half mor over vellum bds; rubbed & soiled. S Nov 18 (1192) £320 [Joseph]

1st American Ed. NY, 1890. One of 250. 4to, orig half mor; scuffed. sg Apr 23 (139) $550

Stanley, John Thomas, 1st Baron Stanley of Alderley. See: Leith, Sir George

Stansbury, Howard

— Exploration and Survey of the Valley of the Great Salt Lake.... Phila., 1852. 1st Ed. 8vo, orig cloth; worn. Lacking folder with 2 maps. O Oct 21 (168) $65

Anr copy. Contemp sheep; joints splitting. With 2 folding maps & 59 plates, With 5-inch tear in 1 plate. wa Sept 25 (472) $160

Anr Ed. Wash., 1853. 8vo, orig cloth; worn & faded. With 56 (of 59) plates. With separate folder containing 2 folding maps. wa Sept 25 (473) $75

House Issue. 2 vols. 8vo, orig cloth; worn & shaken. Foxed, variously affecting plates; With 2 large folding maps; 1 map loose with portion repaired on verso. sg Mar 12 (241) $150

Stanyan, Temple

— An Account of Switzerland.... L, 1714. 8vo, contemp calf gilt; broken. bba Sept 25 (434) £65 [Brayley]

Stapley, Mildred. See: Byrne & Stapley

Stark, James —& Robberds, J. W.

— Picturesque Views on and Near the Eastern Coast of England. L, 1834. 1st Ed. Folio, cloth; worn. Some foxing. O Oct 21 (169) $90

Anr copy. Contemp half mor; worn. With engraved title & 24 plates on india paper mtd. Some soiling & staining. L.p. copy. S May 28 (913) £200

Stark, Peter

— Tomorrow's Ghosts. Guildford: Circle Press, [c.1973]. One of 50. Illus by Arthur Boyd. Folio, unsewn in orig wraps. Inscr by Stark. S June 17 (214) £440 [Arnold]

Starkey, George, d.1666

— Die behaupt- und erlaeuterte Pyrotechnie.... Frankfurt, 1711. 8vo, contemp bds. Tp stamped; some wear. HK Nov 4 (877) DM1,600

Starr, Frederick, 1858-1933

— Indians of Southern Mexico.... Chicago, 1899. One of 60 on japan. Oblong 4to, cloth; rubbed. With 141 plates. Some plates imperfectly ptd. sg Nov 13 (97) $425

Starrett, Vincent

— Bookman's Holiday. NY, [1942]. In d/j. cb Apr 24 (1176) $50

— Buried Caesars: Essays in Literary Appreciation. Chicago, 1923. In d/j. cb Nov 20 (295) $50

— Midnight and Percy Jones. NY, [1936]. In rubbed & repaired d/j. Inscr. cb Nov 20 (298) $75

— Murder on "B" Deck. NY, 1929. In chipped d/j; endpapers soiled. Inscr. cb Nov 20 (299) $65

Statius, Publius Papinius, 45?-96? A.D.

— Opera. Leiden, 1671. ("Sylvarum; Thebaidos; Achilleidos.") 8vo, contemp vellum; soiled & discolored. Some stains in margin. cb Oct 23 (217) $100

Staton, Frances M. —& Tremaine, Marie

— A Bibliography of Canadiana. Toronto, 1934. Cloth; rubbed. ha Dec 19 (54) $90; sg Oct 2 (84) $200

Anr Ed. Toronto, 1934-59. 2 vols, with First Supplement. sg Jan 22 (284) $150

Anr Ed. Toronto, 1934. Cloth. sg May 14 (25) $140

Statten, Paul von

— Herren Paul von Stetten des Juengern Erlaeuterungen der in kupfer gestochenen Vorstellungen aus der Geschichte der Reichsstadt Augsburg. Augsburg: C. H. Stage, 1765-67. 4to, 18th-cent half calf;

worn. With engraved title & 18 plates showing 36 subjects. S Oct 23 (268) £380 [Clarke]

Staunton, George Leonard, 1737-1801

— An Authentic Account of an Embassy from the King of Great Britain to the Emperor of China. L, 1797 [plates dated 1796]. Atlas vol only. Folio, contemp half calf; worn, joints split. With 44 maps, charts & plates. S Jan 16 (430) £1,100 [Davies]

Anr Ed. L, 1797. Atlas vol only. Folio, modern half cloth. 1 map detached; several spotted; stain affecting lower margins. Sold w.a.f. Ck Nov 21 (238) £800 [Toscani]

Anr copy. 2 vols plus Atlas, 4to & folio, calf gilt rebacked, Atlas in orig bds uncut. S Oct 23 (498) £1,450 [Walford]

Anr copy. Half calf, Atlas in half russia; text vols rebacked. With 2 ports; Atlas with 44 charts, plans & views. Some spotting & staining. S June 25 (479) £1,650 [Gregory]

Anr copy. Atlas vol only. Disbound. With 41 (of 44) maps & views. sg Nov 20 (197) $900

Anr copy. 2 vols plus atlas, 4to & folio, half lea; worn, atlas bdg repaired. Titles stamped. sg Dec 4 (186) $1,600

Anr Ed. Dublin, 1798. 2 vols. 8vo, text in half calf, broken. Foxed. wd June 19 (178) $750

Anr Ed. Phila., 1799. 2 vols in 1. 8vo, contemp calf; worn. With folding table & 8 plates. Foxed; browned. sg Nov 20 (165) $60

Staunton, Sir George Thomas

— Ta-Tsing-Leu-Lee, ou les lois fondamentales du code penal de la Chine. Paris, 1812. 2 vols. 8vo, orig bds; rubbed. Some leaves with slight marginal worming; 1 gathering loose. S Apr 23 (356) £300 [Perrin]

Staunton, Howard, 1810-74

The Chess Tournament. L, 1852. Modern cloth. pn Mar 26 (28) £180 [Furstenberg]

Anr Ed. L, 1873. Orig cloth; soiled. pn Mar 26 (29) £35 [Blair]

— The Chess-Player's Handbook. L, 1847. 8vo, half mor with Signet arms. pn Mar 26 (502) £40 [Thompson]

Stearns, Edward Josiah, 1810-90

— Notes on Uncle Tom's Cabin.... Phila., 1853. 8vo, orig cloth; rubbed, spine chipped. ha Dec 19 (260) $55

Stebbing, Henry, 1799-1883

— The Christian in Palestine. L, [1847]. Illus by W. H. Bartlett. 4to, contemp half mor; worn. bba Sept 25 (409) £90 [Bailey]

Stedman, John Gabriel

— Narrative of a Five Years' Expedition against the Revolted Negroes of Surinam.... L, 1796. 2 vols. 4to, modern lea. Some waterstaining & browning. JG Mar 20 (307) DM2,600

Anr copy. Contemp calf gilt; rebacked, corners renewed. With engraved titles having hand-colored vignettes & 81 hand-colored plates & maps. Some soiling; a few plates & text leaves with marginal tears; G3 of Vol II torn into text. P Sept 24 (214) $1,600

Anr copy. Contemp sheep; rebacked, extremities worn, Vol II spine ends chipped. sg Dec 4 (187) $800

Anr Ed. L, 1813. 2 vols. 4to, contemp half calf; rebacked & restored preserving orig spine. With engraved titles, port & 80 plates & maps. C Dec 12 (260) £400 [Griffiths]

Steedman, Andrew

— Wanderings and Adventures in the Interior of Southern Africa. L, 1835. 2 vols. 8vo, half calf. With frontis, 9 (of 10) plates & folding map. Plates foxed. Inscr. SSA Oct 28 (869) R650

Steel, David

— The Elements and Practice of Naval Architecture. L, 1805. 4to, bdg not described. With portfolio of 38 plates. Franklin Institute copy. F Sept 12 (201) $1,200

Steel, Flora Annie, 1847-1929

— English Fairy Tales. L, 1918. One of 500, sgd by Rackham. Illus by Arthur Rackham. 4to, vellum; soiled & rubbed. With 16 color plates. sg Oct 30 (204) $750

Anr Ed. NY, 1918. 4to, cloth. sg Oct 30 (206) $80

One of 250. Calf; soiled, hinges cracked. sg Oct 30 (205) $450

Steele, H. Milford

— Sporting Incidents being a Collection of Sixteen Plates.... NY: Henry T. Thomas 1893-[94]. One of 1,000. Illus by W. S. Vanderbilt Allen. Folio, loose as issued in portfolio. Plates dampstained in corners; some text leaves chipped. Sold w.a.f. sg May 21 (4) $950

Steele, Richard, of York
— An Essay Upon Gardening, Containing a Catalogue of Exotic Plants.... York, 1793. 4to, contemp mor gilt with Signet arms; edges & spine ends rubbed. With 3 large folding plates, 1 with trifling tear. Hunt copy. CNY Nov 21 (263) $1,600

Steele, Sir Richard, 1672-1729. See: Spectator...

Steele, Thomas Sedgwick
— Canoe and Camera; A Two Hundred Mile Tour through the Maine Forests. NY, 1880. With 9 artificial flies mtd on front flyleaf. Some wear & dampstaining. Inscr. sg Oct 23 (513) $100

Steichen, Edward
— A Life in Photography. Garden City, 1963. 4to, cloth; scuffed. Inscr. sg Nov 13 (98) $60

Steiger, Ernst, 1832-1917
— The Periodical Literature of the United States of America. NY, 1873. 4to, orig cloth; spine ends frayed. Tp stamped. sg Jan 22 (285) $70

Stein, Elias, 1748-1812
— Nouvel Essai sur les jeu des echecs. The Hague, 1789. Half calf gilt. Tp browned. pn Mar 26 (505) $95 [Hoffman]

Stein, Friedrich
— Der Organismus der Infusionsthiere.... Leipzig, 1859-83. 3 vols. Folio, cloth. bba Oct 16 (289) £550 [Wheldon & Wesley]

Stein, Gertrude, 1874-1946
— The Autobiography of Alice B. Toklas. NY, [1933]. 1st Ed. Bdg soiled & stained. Inscr by Alice Toklas to John Malcolm Brinnen. cb May 7 (154) $95
— Four Saints in Three Acts. NY, 1934. 1st Ed. Sgd. O Mar 24 (167) $60
  Anr copy. Inscr to Mignon Eberhart. sg June 11 (374) $425
— The Making of Americans, being a History of a Family's Progress. Paris, [1925]. 1st Ed. Orig wraps, unopened. sg Mar 5 (238) $130
  Abridged Ed. NY, [1934]. ("The Making of Americans: the Hersland Family.") In chipped d/j. cb May 7 (143) $55
— Portrait of Mabel Dodge at the Villa Curonia. [Florence, 1912]. 1st Ed, one of 300. 4to, orig wraps. sg Mar 5 (239) $750
— A Primer for the Gradual Understanding of Gertrude Stein. Los Angeles, 1971. One of 60 with tipped-in signature. Half cloth. cb May 7 (145) $70
— The World is Round. NY, [1939]. 1st Ed. Illus by Clement Hurd. 4to, half cloth, in d/j. O Jan 6 (178) $60

One of 350. Half cloth, in d/j. sg Dec 11 (114) $80

Stein, Sir Marc Aurel, 1862-1943
— An Archaeological Tour in Upper Swat.... Calcutta, 1930. Folio, mor. Memoirs of the Archaeological Survey of India, No 42. sg Nov 20 (85) $225
— Memoirs of the Archaeological Survey of India. Calcutta, 1931. Ck Sept 26 (74) £90
— Old Routes of Western Iran. L, 1940. S Jan 12 (317) £220 [Randall]
— On Alexander's Track to the Indus. L, 1929. Worn, covers wormed. sg Nov 20 (86) $175
— On Ancient Central-Asian Tracks. L, 1933. sg Apr 23 (140) $175
— Ruins of Desert Cathay. L, 1912. Hinges weak or cracking. cb Nov 6 (273) $275
  Anr copy. 2 vols. Rubbed, extremities bumped & with hinges cracked in both vols. cb Nov 6 (274) $150
  Anr copy. Orig cloth; 1 hinge weak. S Nov 17 (682) £300 [Sawers]

Steinbeck, John, 1902-68
— Bombs Away: The Story of a Bomber Team. NY, 1942. Cloth, in worn d/j. cb Jan 22 (192) $85
— East of Eden. NY, 1952. 1st Ed. In chipped d/j. Sgd. sg Mar 5 (242) $175
  One of 1,500. bba Mar 12 (229) £220 [Burton Garbett]; sg Mar 5 (241) $400
— The First Watch. [Los Angeles: Ward Ritchie Press], 1947. 1st Ed, one of 60. 16mo, orig wraps, with a mailing envelope. sg Dec 11 (115) $1,100
— Flight. Covelo CA: Yolly Bolly Press, 1984. One of 260. 4to, cloth. sg Jan 8 (296) $150
— The Grapes of Wrath. NY, [1939]. 1st Ed. In d/j. bba Mar 12 (228) £140 [Whiteson]; ha Mar 13 (251) $85
— The Moon is Down. NY, 1942. 1st Ed. In d/j; worn. Inscr. pnNY Sept 13 (291) $350
— The Red Pony. NY, 1937. 1st Ed, one of 699. sg June 11 (376) $400
  Anr copy. Lower corners bumped, endpapers tapestained. wa Sept 25 (695) $240
— Saint Katy the Virgin. [NY: Covici-Friede, 1936]. 1st Ed, one of 199. Orig bds, in d/j; extremities rubbed. sg June 11 (375) $350
— Tortilla Flat. NY, [1935]. 1st Ed. Orig cloth; with jacket flaps tipped & laid on front pastedown. Inscr. cb Jan 22 (196) $425
— The Winter of our Discontent. NY, 1961. One of 500. In d/j. wa Sept 25 (696) $750

Steinbeck, John, 1902-68 —& Ricketts, Edward F.
— Sea of Cortez. NY, 1941. In chipped & creased d/j. cb May 7 (149) $150

Steindorff, Georg, 1861-1951
— Egypt. NY, [1943]. Illus by George Hoyningen-Huene. 4to, cloth, in d/j; front hinge cracked. Inscr by Hoyningen-Huene. sg Nov 13 (65) $110

Steinert, Otto
— Akt International. Munich: Bruder Auer, [1954]. 4to, cloth; scuffed. With 78 plates. sg Nov 13 (82) $110
— Subjektive Fotografie; Ein Bildband moderner europaeischer Fotografie. Bonn, [1952]. 4to, cloth; rubbed, front hinge cracked. With 111 plates. sg May 7 (69) $650
— Subjektive Fotografie 2; Ein Bildband moderner europaeischer Fotografie. Bonn, [1955]. 4to, cloth, in d/j. With 111 plates. sg Nov 13 (100) $150

Steinilber-Oberlin, Emile, b.1878
— Chansons de Geishas.... Paris, 1926. One of 87 on japan. Illus by Leonard Foujita. Mor, orig wraps bound in. With 14 ink drawings for the vignettes & the artist's ink and wash drawings (1 sgd) for 9 of the plates bound in; drawing for frontis removed. S Dec 4 (10) £3,500 [Garber]

Steinitz, William, 1836-1900
— The Book of the Sixth American Chess Congress. NY, 1891. One of 500. 8vo, orig cloth; hinges repaired. pn Mar 26 (50) £160 [Levine]

Steinlen, Theophile Alexandre, 1859-1923
— Des Chats: images sans paroles. Paris, [1898]. Folio, orig half cloth; worn. Ck Jan 16 (116) £85; S May 6 (179) £130 [Henderson]
  Anr copy. Marginal fraying; some soiling. S July 14 (559) £180
— Steinlen and his Art. Twenty-Four Cartoons. L, 1911. Folio, cloth; spine torn. With 24 plates. ha Mar 13 (146) $55

Steinlin, Theophile Alexandre, 1859-1923
— Dans la Vie: cent dessins en couleurs. Paris, 1901. 12mo, contemp half shagreen, orig wraps preserved. With 100 color plates. B Oct 7 (334) HF280

Steinmetz, Charles Proteus, 1865-1923
— Four Lectures on Relativity and Space. NY, 1923. With 6 stereoscopic views in rear pocket. wa Nov 6 (86) $65

Steinschneider, Moritz
— Hebraeische Ueberestzungen des Mittelalters. Berlin, 1893. Ltd Ed. 4to, half mor; tape-repaired, some leaves detached at beginning. sg Sept 25 (283) $130

Stella, Joannes
— Vita romanorum imperatorum. Venice: Bernardino de Vitali, 26 Nov 1503. 1st Ed. 4to, later wraps. Fore-margins stained & repaired, just touching tp woodcut & some ptd margin notes. S Mar 10 (1158) £100 [Hesketh]

Stelliola, Nicolo
— Il Telescopio over Ispecillo celeste. Naples, 1627. 4to, old bds. S July 28 (1121) £1,200

Stendhal. See: Beyle, Marie Henri ("Stendhal")

Stenger, Erich
— The History of Photography. Easton, Penna., 1939. Trans by Edward Epstean. 4to, cloth, in remnants of d/j. sg Nov 13 (101) $50

Stennett, Samuel. See: Fore-Edge Paintings

Step, Edward
— Favourite Flowers of Garden and Greenhouse. L, [1896-97], 4 vols, 8vo, half mor; extremities worn. sg Feb 5 (308) $475

Stephano Junio Bruto. See: Languet, Hubert

Stephanus Byzantius
— Peri Poleon. De Urbibus. Amst.: Jacob de Jonge, 1678. Folio, contemp vellum over bds, school prize bdg; soiled, joints splitting. Some dampstain to lower corners of several leaves. cb Oct 23 (218) $200

Stephen, Henry John, Serjeant-at-Law
— New Commentaries on the Laws of England.... L, 1880. 8th Ed. 4 vols. 8vo, half mor; worn & scraped. wa Sept 25 (580) $60

Stephens, Frederic George
— Flemish Relics. L, 1866. 8vo, orig mor by Suttaby; rubbed. With 15 mtd photos; 1 loose. O May 12 (170) $170

Stephens, George, 1813-95
— Handbook of the Old-Northern Runic Monuments.... L, 1884. Folio, half cloth, orig wraps bound in. cb July 30 (180) $55

Stephens, James, 1882-1950
— The Crock of Gold. L, 1926. One of 525. Illus by Thomas Mackenzie. 4to, orig half vellum; rubbed. ha May 22 (215) $120
  Irish Fairy Tales. L, 1920. Illus by Arthur Rackham. 4to, orig cloth. With 16 color plates. sg Oct 30 (208) $60
  One of 520, sgd by Rackham. Half vellum; corners bumped. Scattered foxing. sg Oct

30 (207) $375

Stephens, James Francis, 1792-1852
— Illustrations of British Entymology; or a Synopsis of Indigenous Insects... Mandibulata [Haustellata]. With: Supplement. L, 1827-46. Vols I-IV (of 7) of Mandibulata & all 4 vols of Haustellata. Together, 8 vols. 8vo, later cloth. With 64 (of 80) hand-colored plates. Ink stamps on titles. bba Jan 15 (425) £120 [Trotter]

Stephens, John Lloyd, 1805-52
— Yucatan. NY, 1843. ("Incidents of Travel in Yucatan.") 2 vols. 8vo, later mor. sg Dec 19 (99) $350

Anr copy. Illus by F. Catherwood. Orig cloth; joints cracked, spine of Vol II chipped. Sold w.a.f. Ck Feb 27 (244) £110

Stephenson, David
— Medicine Made to Agree with the Institutions of Nature... L, 1744. Folio, contemp calf; rebacked. With 3 folding plates. pnE Dec 17 (167) £240 [Phillips]

Stephenson, John, 1790-1864 —& Churchill, James Morss
— Medical Botany. L, [1828]-31. 4 vols. 8vo, calf; rebacked. With 185 colored plates. pnE Dec 17 (233) £880 [Egglishaw]

Anr Ed. L, 1834-36. 3 vols. 8vo, half calf; lacking spines. With 187 hand-colored plates. 1 plate loose & soiled. pn Dec 11 (205) £680 [Major Graham]

Anr copy. Half mor gilt. With 185 hand-colored plates plus 2 additional plates. pnE Dec 17 (234) £600 [Hughes]

Stephenson, Simon. See: Representations...

Sterbeeck, Francis van
— Theatrum fungorum, oft het tooneel der campernoelien. Antwerp, 1675. 4to, contemp vellum bds; soiled. With frontis, folding port & 36 plates. Minor spotting. Darbishire—de Belder copy. S Apr 28 (345) £3,000 [Ursus]

Sterling Library, Louis
— The Sterling Library. A Catalogue of the Printed Books and Literary Manuscripts.... L, 1954. 1st Ed, one of 500. bba Feb 5 (33) £65 [Barker]

Stern, Frederic Claude
— A Study of the Genus Paeonia. L, 1946. Folio, orig cloth. With 15 color plates. Ck Oct 31 (200) £100

Anr copy. WIth 15 colored plates. pnE Dec 17 (235) £85 [Greyfriars]

Sternberg, Kaspar M., Graf von
— Revisio saxifragum iconibus illustrata. Ratisbon, 1810. Bound with: Supplementum. Ratisbon, 1822. With 10 hand-colored plates. And: Supplementum secundum. Prague, 1831. With 6 plain & 10 hand-colored plates. Folio, contemp half russia; repaired. With 3 plain & 28 hand-colored plates in orig work. Plesch—de Belder copy. S Apr 28 (346) £3,200 [Kisther]

Sterne, Laurence, 1713-68
See also: Golden Cockerel Press; Limited Editions Club
— Letters...to his Most Intimate Friends. L, 1775. 1st Ed. 3 vols in 1. 8vo, half calf; scuffed. pnE Jan 28 (135) £150 [Traylen]
— The Life and Opinions of Tristram Shandy. L, 1775. 6 vols. 12mo, calf gilt. sg Feb 12 (292A) $275
— A Sentimental Journey.... L, 1768. 1st Ed. 2 vols. 12mo, contemp calf gilt; rebacked retaining orig backstrips. sg Apr 2 (187) $900

Anr Ed. L, 1809. 12mo, half calf gilt. With 2 hand-colored plates. sg Feb 12 (271) $100

Anr Ed. NY: J. W. Bouton, 1884. One of 100 with an orig watercolor drawing. Illus by Maurice Leloir. Contemp mor gilt. cb Sept 11 (318) $375

Anr Ed. L & NY, 1885. One of 550. Folio, mor gilt extra; worn & soiled. wa Sept 25 (47) $90

Sterry, Consider & John
— American Youth: being a New and Complete Course of Introductory Mathematics. Providence, 1790. Vol I (all pbd). 8vo, contemp calf; worn, small portions missing from front free endpaper & last leaf; library markings. sg Mar 12 (176) $60

Steuart, Sir Henry, 1759-1836
— The Planter's Guide; or a Practical Essay.... Edin., 1828. 8vo, contemp calf; rubbed. With 5 mtd plates, 1 double-page. Margins stained. bba Sept 25 (299) £65 [Hay Cinema]

Steuart, Sir James. See: Denham, Sir James Steuart

Steuben, Friedrich W. A., Baron von, 1730-94
— Regulations for the Order and Discipline of the Troops of the United States. Vermont: Anthony Haswell, 1794. 12mo, orig paper over wooden bds; worn, spine defective. With 8 folding plates; plates poorly folded. CNY Dec 19 (234) $50

Anr Ed. Bost., 1894. 8vo, contemp wooden bds covered with paper; worn, lacking much of the paper covering, broken. Lacking Plate 1 & all leaves before tp. cb Dec 18 (166) $60

Stevens, Charles W.
— Fly-Fishing in Maine Lakes.... Bost., 1881. 8vo, cloth; worn, spine-tips frayed, inner joint broken. O Oct 21 (172) $100

Stevens, Frank Everett, b. 1856
— The Black Hawk War. Chicago, 1903. Cloth; worn. Small library blindstamp on tp. Inscr. O Oct 21 (173) $150

Stevens, Henry, 1819-86
— Benjamin Franklin's LIfe and Writings.... L, 1881. 4to, orig cloth; spine ends worn. sg Jan 22 (287) $80

— Historical Nuggets: Bibliotheca Americana.... L, 1862. 2 vols. 16mo, orig cloth, several corners bumped, hinges starting. sg Mar 12 (242) $120

Stevens, Isaac Ingalls. See: Reports...

Stevens, Wallace
— Harmonium. NY, 1923. 1st bdg, in d/j. P June 18 (186) $1,500

Anr copy. In mended d/j. sg Mar 5 (245) $375

Anr copy. Half cloth, in chipped & def d/j. wa Dec 11 (108) $375

2d Issue. Sgd. sg Mar 5 (246) $200

Stevens, William Bacon
— A History of Georgia.... NY, 1847 & Phila, 1859. 2 vols. 8vo, modern half calf gilt. With 2 engraved ports, hand-colored engraved map & 3 engraved plates & plans; slight staining. pnNY Sept 13 (292) $190

Stevens-Nelson Paper Corp.
— Paper and Printing Specimens [of handmade and mouldmade paper]. [NY, c.1953]. 4to, orig half mor. cb June 19 (299) $130

Stevenson, Edward Luther, 1858-1944
Terrestrial and Celestial Globes: Their History and Construction.... New Haven, 1921. 2 vols. sg May 14 (196) $225

Stevenson, John Robert Horne
— Heraldry in Scotland. Glasgow, 1914. One of 210. 2 vols. 4to, orig half vellum, in torn d/js. S Mar 9 (768) £40 [Heraldry]

Stevenson, Matthew
— The Twelve Moneths or, a Pleasant and Profitable Discourse.... L, 1661. 4to, calf by Riviere. Final leaf in facsimile; some paper restoration to tp & ink strengthening to a few letters. Hunt copy. CNY Nov 21 (264) $1,800

Anr copy. 19th-cent half mor. Jeanson 1212. SM Mar 1 (514) FF35,000

Stevenson, Robert, 1772-1850
— An Account of the Bell Rock Light-House. Edin., 1824. 4to, contemp half mor. With frontis after Turner & additional engraved title on india paper mtd & 21 plates. Adhesion affecting a few words on pp 528-29. Inscr to Matthew Boulton. C Dec 12 (201) £1,200 [Elton]

Anr copy. Contemp half lea; rubbed. With frontis additional title (bound after H4) & 21 plates & maps. Plates spotted. S Nov 10 (958) £260 [Traylen]

Stevenson, Robert Louis. See: Grabhorn Printing

Stevenson, Robert Louis, 1830-94
See also: Limited Editions Club
— Across the Plains. L, 1892. One of 100 L.p. copies. 4to, half mor gilt. S Sept 22 (145) £80 [Glendall]

Anr Ed. Hillsborough: Allen, 1950. One of 200. Illus by Mallette Dean. cb Oct 9 (5) $95

— The Charity Bazaar: an Allegorical Dialogue. [Edin., 1868]. 4to, folded, laid into mor gilt covers. Sgd by Stevenson at the end. sg June 11 (379) $1,200

— Father Damien: An Open Letter to the Reverend Dr. Hyde of Honolulu.... Sydney: Pvtly ptd, 1890. 1st Ed. 8vo, selfwraps; small chip from corner of front wrap. Minor staining to recto of final leaf. sg June 11 (381) $475

1st Trade Ed. L, 1890. ("Father Damien: An Open Letter to the Reverend Doctor Hyde of Honolulu.") 8vo, wraps. Sgd on tp. Eugene Field's copy. sg June 11 (380) $1,000

— Island Nights' Entertainments. L, 1893. 8vo, orig cloth. Quinn copy. With signatures of Stevenson & Eugene Field on tp. sg Feb 12 (294) $275

— The Letters. L, 1911. In 2 vols. Contemp mor gilt; rubbed. bba Sept 25 (92) £360 [Joseph]

— The Pentland Rising. A Page of History. Edin., 1866. 8vo, orig wraps. sg June 11 (382) $1,600

— La Porte de maletroit. Cagnes-sur-Mer, 1952. One of 300. Wraps. sg Jan 8 (34) $550

— San Francisco: A Modern Cosmopolis. San Francisco: Book Club of California, 1963. One of 450. sg Jan 8 (35) $50

— The Strange Case of Dr. Jekyll and Mr. Hyde. L, 1886. 1st English Ed. 8vo, orig wraps, with date on front wrap changed in ink to 1886; rubbed & creased, spine worn & partially perished. cb Nov 20 (300) $475

Anr copy. Contemp half calf. Lacking half-title. kh Mar 16 (482B) A$100

STEVENSON

Anr Ed. NY: G. Munro, 1886. 8vo, orig ptd wraps; frayed & soiled. O Mar 24 (173) $350
— Ticonderoga. Edin., 1887. Wise—Buxton Forman Forgery. 4to, orig bds; rubbed. H. Buxton Forman's copy with an 11-line note in Forman's hand. sg June 11 (384) $750
— Travels with a Donkey in the Cevennes. L, 1879. 1st Ed. 8vo, orig cloth. pnNY Sept 13 (293) $100
— Treasure Island. L, 1883. 1st Ed. 8vo, orig cloth; spine repaired. S Dec 5 (360) £350 [Kendle]
— Works. Edin., 1895-1903. One of 1,035. 35 vols. 8vo, orig cloth; rubbed. bba Mar 12 (180) £60 [Burton Garbett]
Swanston Ed. L, 1911-12. 25 vols. Half mor gilt by Riviere. pn Mar 5 (1) £700 [Joseph]
Vailima Ed. L, 1922-23. One of 1,060. 26 vols. 21 vols in d/js. S Sept 22 (53) £220 [Joseph]
Skerryvore Ed. L, [1924-26]. 35 vols. Orig cloth. pnE June 17 (9) £55

Stevenson, Robert Louis, 1850-94 —& Henley, William Ernest, 1849-1903
— Deacon Brodie or the Double Life. Edin., 1888. 8vo, orig wraps; front joint starting. sg June 11 (386) £425

Stevenson, Robert Louis & Fanny
— More New Arabian Nights: The Dynamiter. L, 1885. 1st Ed. 8vo, orig cloth; rubbed & soiled. bba Jan 15 (113) £40 [Klute]

Stevenson-Hamilton, James, 1867-1957
— Animal Life in Africa. NY, 1912. 1st American Ed. Hinges cracked at endpapers. cb Nov 6 (276) $50

Steward, Julian H.
— Handbook of South American Indians. NY, 1963. Vols I-VI. Lacking pocket map in Vol VI. wa Sept 25 (328) $100

Stewart, Basil
— Japanese Colour-Prints. L, 1920. One of 125. Cloth. O Nov 18 (182) $70
— Subjects Portrayed in Japanese Colour-Prints. L, 1922. Folio, cloth; soiled. bba Dec 18 (244) £45 [Hay]
Anr copy. Orig bds; soiled & scuffed. T Jan 22 (287) £85

Stewart, Charles William, 3d Marquess of Londonderry
— Narrative of the Peninsular War.... L, 1828. 2d Ed. 4to, orig bds. With folding colored map & 6 plans. With 9 ports of officers in the campaign laid in loose. cb Dec 18 (168) $140

Stewart, Donald William
— Old and Rare Scottish Tartans. Edin., 1893. Ltd Ed on Whatman paper. 4to, orig cloth; rubbed. With 45 tartan specimens mtd. pn Dec 11 (136) £170 [McEwan]

Stewart, Dugald, 1753-1828
— Philosophical Essays. Edin., 1810. 1st Ed. 4to, calf; rebacked, some wear, new endpapers. Lacking half-title; repair along lower margin of tp; marginal tear in b2; 3X gathering & adjacent leaves spotted. P Sept 24 (408) $200

Stewart, George R.
— Earth Abides. NY: Random House, [1949]. In d/j; spine leaning, adhesion damage to pastedowns. cb Sept 28 (1206) $55

Stewart, J. Lindsay —& Brandis, D.
— The Forest Flora of North-West and Central India. L, 1874. 2 vols, including Atlas. 8vo & 4to, half lea; worn. With 70 plates. bba Oct 16 (290) £75 [Maggs]

Stewart, Sir James, Lord Advocate of Scotland
— The Index or Abridgement, of the Acts of Parliament, and Convention.... Edin., 1707. 12mo, contemp calf; worn. O Feb 24 (185) $100

Stewart, John, Millwright
— Plan and Description of Mr. John Stewart's Fire Engine Mill. L, [1766]. 8vo, contemp half sheep; hinges split. With 2 folding woodcut plates. Outer edge of tp cropped with loss of a few letters. C Dec 12 (202) £1,200 [Martin]

Stickley, Gustav
— Craftsman Homes. NY, [1909]. 4to, cloth; soiled. With 4 color plates. wa Nov 6 (493) $150
Anr copy. Pictorial bds; worn, spine frayed. Ownership stamps & bookplate. wa June 25 (431) $120

Stieglitz, Alfred
— Picturesque Bits of New York & Other Studies. NY, 1897. Folio, unbound as issued. With 12 photogravures. sg May 7 (70) $24,000

Stieler, Adolph, 1775-1836
— Hand Atlas ueber alle Theile der Erde.... Gotha: Perthes, [1879-82]. Folio, half lea. With 95 double-page maps & charts (including engraved title), colored in outline. wa Sept 25 (485) $115

Stieler, Karl
— Italy: from the Alps to Mount Etna. L, 1877 [1876]. Trans by Frances Eleanor Trollope. 4to, half mor; joints starting. sg Apr 23 (76) £100

Stillingfleet, Edward, 1635-99
— The Bishop of Worcester's Answer to Mr. Locke's Letter.... L, 1697. 1st Ed. 8vo, contemp sheep; rubbed, spine worn & chipped, joints cracking. Burnhole affecting a few letters on B4; marginal stain. P Sept 24 (409) $175

Stillman, Jacob D. B., 1819-88
— The Horse in Motion.... Bost., 1882. Illus by Eadweard Muybridge. 4to, orig cloth; rubbed. bba Mar 12 (47) £240 [Henderson]

Anr copy. Orig cloth; spine ends chipped. Elihu Thomson's copy. K Dec 13 (193) $275

Anr copy. Orig cloth; rubbed, front hinge cracked. Frontis detached. sg Nov 13 (81) $200

Stillman, William James
— Poetic Localities of Cambridge. Bost., 1876. 4to, orig cloth; becoming disbound. With 12 plates. sg Nov 13 (102) $175

Stillwell, Margaret Bingham
— Gutenberg and the Catholicon of 1460.... NY, 1936. Folio, calf gilt; rubbed, front joint starting. With 2 conjugate leaves from Johannes Balbus's encyclopedia (Mainz, 1460) laid in. P Dec 15 (154) $2,100

— Incunabula and Americana.... NY, 1931. In chipped d/j. sg Jan 22 (289) $110

Stirling, William, 1851-1932
— Some Apostles of Physiology.... L, 1902. Folio, cloth; corners bumped, back cover wrinkled. sg May 14 (631) $70

Stirrup, Thomas
— Horometria: or the Compleat Diallist. L, 1652. 1st Ed. 4to, modern calf. Frontis misbound; N3 & last 5 leaves holed or wormed with loss; last 5 leaves repaired. Sold w.a.f. Ck Jan 30 (37) £420

Stock...
— The Stock Exchange in Caricature: A Private Collection of Caricatures, Cartoons, and Character Sketches of Members of the New York Stock Exchange.... NY: Abram Stone, 1904. One of 177. 2 vols. Folio, cloth; backstrip of Part 1 torn & repaired. sg Mar 12 (243) $110

Stockdale, Frederick Wilton Litchfield
— Excursions in the County of Cornwall. L, 1824. 8vo, half lea; rebacked, spine flaked. With engraved title & 48 plates. C Dec 12 (262) £140 [Griffiths]

Stockdale, John. See: Cary & Stockdale

Stockdale, John Joseph
— The History of the Inquisitions.... L, 1810. 1st Ed. 4to, contemp half calf; broken. With 12 plates. Some foxing. sg Sept 11 (212) $150

Stockum, W. P. Van, the Younger
— La Librairie, l'imprimerie et la presse en Hollande à travers quatre siecles.... The Hague, 1910. 4to, lea; extremities worn, joints cracked. sg May 14 (367) $100

Stoddard, Herbert L.
— The Bobwhite Quail: its Habits, Preservation, and Increase. NY, 1931. DeLuxe Ed. One of 260. 4to, half vellum. With a sgd etching by Frank W. Benson. sg Oct 23 (514) $650

Stoeffler, Johann
— Calendarium Romanum magnum. Oppenheim: J. Koebel, 1518. Folio, early 19th-cent bds. Fragment, consisting of A1-E8 & last 18 unsigned leaves. sg Jan 15 (371) $500

Stoker, Bram, 1847-1912
— Dracula. L, 1897. 1st Ed. 8vo, orig cloth; soiled. Without ads. cb Sept 28 (1209) $1,400

Anr copy. Orig cloth; soiled & stained, spine split. Some leaves carelessly opened; portion torn from upper corner of C5. Inscr to George Alexander. S Dec 18 (91) £800 [Sothcran]

Anr copy. Orig cloth; soiled. S July 23 (116) £1,000 [Joseph]

Anr Ed. L, 1897 [1898]. later issue. 8vo, orig cloth; rubbed & bumped. S Dec 18 (92) £400 [Minerva]

— The Mystery of the Sea. L, 1902. Cloth; rubbed, inner hinges repaired by cracking. Tp, copyright page & half-title foxed. Inscr to Sir Walter Gilly. cb Sept 28 (1210) $500

— Personal Reminiscences of Henry Irving. L, 1906. 2 vols. 8vo, cloth; rubbed. Inscr. sg Feb 26 (164) $50

Stokes, Isaac Newton Phelps —& Haskell, Daniel Carl
— American Historical Prints.... NY, 1933. 4to, cloth. ha Mar 13 (172) $100

Anr copy. With 118 plates. sg Oct 2 (286) $175; sg Feb 5 (310) $225; wa Nov 6 (494) $110

Stokes, John Lort
— Discoveries in Australia. L, 1846. 2 vols. 8vo, orig cloth, variant bdg with kangaroo vignette at foot of Vol I; head of 1 spine frayed, foot of spines rubbed. With 8 folding maps & 26 plates. 6 maps loose. C Oct 15 (173) £1,700 [Lenon]

Stoll, Caspar, d.1795
— Natuurlyke en naar't leeven naaukeurig gekleurde Afbeeldingen...der Cicaden. Amst., [1780]-88. 2 vols. 4to, 19th-cent half calf. With 2 hand-colored titles & 70 hand-colored plates. FD June 11 (729) DM2,800

Stoltz, J. L.
— Amphelographie Rhenane ou description...cepages...dans la vallee du Rhin. Paris & Mulhouse, 1852. 4to, half mor gilt by Crahan, orig wraps restored & preserved. With 32 plates, most colored. Crahan copy. P Nov 25 (437) $750

Stone, Herbert L. See: Derrydale Press

Stone, William L.
— The Life and Times of Sa-go-ye-wat-ha, or Red Jacket.... Albany, N.Y., 1866. 2d Ed, One of 75 L.p. copies. 8vo, half mor. O Oct 21 (174) $270

Stonehill, Charles A. —& Others
— Anonyma and Pseudonyma. L, 1926-27. One of 325. 4 vols. cba Feb 5 (162) $55

Stoneman, Vernon C.
— John and Thomas Seymour: Cabinetmakers in Boston, 1794-1816. Bost., 1959. 2 vols, including 1965 Supplement. 4to, cloth; worn. O Mar 24 (178) $120; sg June 4 (7) $120

Stones, Margaret —& Curtis, Winifred
— The Endemic Flora of Tasmania. L, 1967-68. 6 vols. Folio, cloth, in d/js. kh Mar 16 (142) A$1,400

Anr Ed. L, 1967-75. Vols I-V (of 6). Folio, cloth, in d/js. sg Jan 15 (258) $400

Stoney, Henry Butler
— A Residence in Tasmania, with a Descriptive Tour.... L, 1856. 8vo, contemp calf gilt. With double-page map & 8 plates. Lacking pbr's catalogue at end. Ck Feb 27 (32) £160

Stonham, Charles
— The Birds of the British Islands. L, 1906-11. 5 vols. 4to, later half mor gilt. Some foxing. bba Apr 9 (449) £140 [Greyfriars]

Anr copy. 20 orig parts. 4to, orig wraps; some stained. pn Mar 5 (43) £240 [Erlini]

Anr copy. 5 vols. 4to, half mor gilt. pnE Dec 17 (280) £260 [Marshall]

Anr copy. Contemp cloth; rubbed. T Feb 19 (351) £1,150

Storer, James S.
— The Antiquarian Itinerary.... L, 1815-18. 7 vols. 8vo, orig bds; spines worn. bba Oct 30 (497) £60 [Fogg]

Storer, James S. —& Brewer, James Norris
— Delineations of Gloucestershire. L, 1824. 4to, contemp half mor; rubbed. With engraved title & 48 plates on india paper. S May 28 (845) £180

Storer, James S. —& Greig, John
— Antiquarian and Topical Cabinet. L, 1807-11. 10 vols. 8vo, contemp calf; rubbed. With engraved titles & 490 plates. Ck June 5 (69) £170

Anr copy. Calf gilt; scuffed, lower cover of Vol I detached, lacking 1 backstrip. Some stains, mostly minor & marginal. L Dec 11 (138) £90

Anr copy. Cloth. Most plates with marginal dampstains. pn Dec 11 (83) £80 [Crofts]

Anr Ed. L: J. Murray, etc., [1817]-19. 6 vols. 8vo, syn. Some foxing. sg Nov 20 (166) $60

Storer, Tracy. See: Grinnell & Storer

Storrow, Charles Storer, 1809-1904
— A Treatise on Water-Works for Conveying and Distributing Supplies of Water.... Bost.: Hilliard, Gray, 1835. 12mo, orig cloth; worn & soiled, repairs along joint. wa Nov 6 (256) $100

Stothard, Anna Eliza
— Letters Written during a Tour through Normandy, Brittany.... L, 1820. 4to, bdg not described. With folding map & 6 hand-colored plates & 17 views. C Dec 12 (261) £1,300 [Griffiths]

Stothard, Thomas
— Shakespeare's Seven Ages of Man...Illustrated. L, 1799. Folio, half calf; rubbed. With engraved title & 7 plates. bba Dec 4 (188) £40 [Barker]

Stott, Raymond Toole
— Circus and Allied Arts, a World Bibliography.... Derby, 1958-62. One of 1,200. 3 vols. 4to, cloth. Library copy. ha Sept 19 (75) $55

Anr Ed. Derby, 1958-71. 4 vols. 4to, orig cloth, 3 vols in d/js. T Apr 16 (333) £65

Stout, Rex, 1886-1975
— Fer-de-lance. NY, [1934]. Bdg worn. cb Nov 20 (302) $120
— Mountain Cat. NY: Farrar & Rinehart, [1939]. In chipped & tape-repaired d/j. cb Nov 20 (303) $70
— Too Many Cooks. NY, [1938]. In worn & chipped d/j. wa Dec 11 (220) $100

Stow, John, 1525?-1605
— The Annales. L: Ralfe Newbery, [1592]. ("The Annales of England....") 4to, later half calf; rubbed. Hhh8 torn & repaired with slight loss; lacking Qqqq5; hole in b3 & c3 affecting several words; slightly wormed at inner margin with some loss; cropped affecting mainly headlines but also some text; some dampstains. S Sept 23 (400) £700 [Knohl]
— A Survay of London. L, 1618. 4to, contemp calf; spine worn. T Sept 18 (81) £75

Anr Ed. L, 1633. ("The Survey of London.") Folio, calf; worn. pn Dec 11 (108) £140 [Cavendish]

Anr Ed. L, 1754-55. ("A Survey of the Cities of London and Westminster....") 2 vols. Folio, contemp calf; worn, rebacked. With 80 plates (35 folding) & 52 maps (37 folding). 1 map cut out & remounted, a few with margins cut close. bba Dec 18 (245) £950 [Burgess Browning]

Anr copy. 3 vols. Folio, contemp calf; rubbed. With 132 plates & plans. Ck May 15 (192) £2,000

Stowe, Harriet Beecher, 1811-96
— A Key to Uncle Tom's Cabin. Bost., 1853. 1st Ed. 8vo, orig cloth; spine chipped at head. sg Feb 12 (298) $130

Strabo, 63 B.C.-24 A.D.
— De situ orbis. Basel: Henricus Petri, 1549. Folio, old sheep; corners worn, backstrip def. sg Dec 4 (188) $275
— Geographia. Basel: Valentinus Curio, 1523. Folio, later half calf; def. 1st 4 leaves & last leaf repaired. B Feb 25 (861) IIΓ550

Anr Ed. Paris, 1620. ("Rerum geographicarum.") 2 parts in 1 vol. Folio, contemp mor gilt; spine chipped, tear along upper joint. Tp soiled; some rust-holes affecting text. Chatsworth copy. S Feb 23 (107) £300 [Burnet]

Strada, Famiano, 1572-1649
— De Bello Belgico. L, 1650. 1st Ed in English. Folio, contemp calf; broken. Frontis torn & repaired without loss. T Sept 18 (327) £50
— Prolusiones academicae... Lyons, 1617. 8vo, modern bds. Browned. sg Mar 26 (265) $50

Strada, Giovanni della. See: Straet, Jan van der

Strada, Jacobus de, d.1588
— Epitome thesauri antiquitatum; hoc est, Impp. Rom. orientalium et occidentalium iconum.... Zurich, 1557. 8vo, contemp vellum. sg Mar 26 (266) $120

Stradanus. See: Straet, Jan van der

Straet, Jan van der, 1536-1605
— Venationes ferarum, avium, piscium.... [Antwerp: P. Galle, 1578]. Part 1. Folio, 17th-cent bdg. With Plates 1-31. Lacking title-frontis. Jeanson copy. SM Mar 1 (540) FF26,000

Anr copy. Part 2. Folio, With 31 plates. SM Mar 1 (541) FF30,000

Anr Ed. [Antwerp: J. Galle, c.1585]. Bound with: Equile, seu speculum equorum....Antwerp, [c.1585] Folio, contemp vellum. With title-frontis & 104 plates in 1st work & 41 plates in 2d work. Jeanson copy. SM Mar 1 (542) FF110,000

Straker, David Augustus, d.1908
— A Trip to the Windward Islands.... Detroit: James H. Stone, [1896]. Cloth. cb Oct 9 (302) $50

Strand...
— Strand Magazine: An Illustrated Monthly. L, 1891-. Issue 1. Wraps. cb Apr 24 (137) $150

Issue 1. Orig wraps; soiled & chipped. cb Apr 24 (138) $55

Anr copy. Wraps; soiled, spine extremities def. cb Apr 24 (139) $50

Vols 1-50. L, 1891-1915. Orig cloth. cb Apr 24 (133) $1,200

Vols 1-6. L, 1891-93. Orig cloth. cb Apr 24 (134) $550

Anr copy. Orig cloth; some wear. cb Apr 24 (135) $350

Vols 1-88. L, 1891-1934. Orig cloth. cb Apr 24 (132) $5,500

Strand, Paul
— Paul Strand: A Retrospective Monograph.... Phila.: Phila. Museum of Art, [1971]. 2 vols in 1. 4to, pictorial cloth. sg May 7 (72) $130
— Tir a'Mhurain: Outer Hebrides. L, [1962]. 4to, cloth, in chipped d/j. sg May 7 (73) $140

Strang, William, 1859-1921
— The Earth Fiend A Ballad. L, 1892. Ltd Ed. 4to, cloth. With 11 plates. B Oct 7 (271) HF300

Strangford, Emily Anne, Viscountess. See: Beaufort, Emily Anne

Straparola, Giovanni Francesco, d.c.1557
— Le Piaceuoli Notti. San Luca: al segno del Diamante, 1551-54. 8vo, 18th-cent mor. Small repair to 1st title slightly affecting woodcut with small portion supplied in ink. C Dec 12 (308) £600 [Quaritch]

Stratton, Arthur. See: Garner & Stratton

Straub, Peter
See also: King & Straub
— Floating Dragon. San Francisco, 1982. One of 500. In d/j. cb Sept 28 (1213) $85

Straus, Ralph
— The Unspeakable Curll.... L, 1927. One of 535. O June 16 (176) $60

Strauss, Joseph B.
— Bridging "The Golden Gate." [N.p., c.1920s]. 16 pp, folio, orig wraps. With sketches & plans of the proposed bridge. cb Jan 8 (69) $120
— The Golden Gate Bridge: Report of the Chief Engineer.... [San Francisco: Golden Gate Bridge & Highway District], 1937. Folio, cloth, in d/j. Inscr by the general manager of the district. cb Jan 8 (71) $55

Stravinsky, Igor, 1882-1971
— De geschiedenis van den Soldaat. Maastricht, 1930. One of 251. Illus by E. Tijtgat. Bds. With 8 full-page illusts, all colored by hand. B Oct 7 (226) HF340
— Die Geschichte vom Soldaten. Zurich, 1951. Illus by Frans Masereel. With orig drawing & proof. B Oct 7 (193) HF1,200

Streeter, Burnett Hillman
— The Chained Library.... L, 1931. In d/j. cba Feb 5 (163) $70

Streeter, Floyd Benjamin
— Michigan Bibliography. Lansing, 1921. 2 vols. Worn. sg Oct 2 (219) $100

Streeter Library, Thomas Winthrop
— Bibliography of Texas. Cambr., Mass, 1955-60. 3 parts in 5 vols. 4 vols in d/js. sg Oct 2 (289) $700
    Anr copy. In d/js. sg Jan 22 (289) $110
— [Sale Catalogue] The Celebrated Collection of Americana. NY, 1966-70. 8 vols, including Index, bds. cb July 16 (252) $450; O May 12 (184) $350
    Anr copy. Bds; Vols II & VI worn at spine ends; others worn & soiled. Includes price lists for Vols II, IV, VI & VII. sg Nov 6 (536) $550; sg Dec 4 (189) $425
    Anr copy. Bds; Index, cloth. sg Jan 22 (291) $325
    Anr copy. Bds. sg Mar 12 (244) $450
    Anr copy. Vols I & III priced in ink. sg Apr 2 (189) $400; sg May 14 (28) $300

Streeton, Arthur
— The Art of Arthur Streeton. Sydney, 1919. 4to, half cloth. Special No of Art in Australia. kh Mar 16 (487) A$220; kh Mar 16 (487) A$220

Streeton, Sir Arthur, 1867-1943
— The Arthur Streeton Catalogue.... Melbourne, 1935. One of 500. 4to, later cloth retaining orig cloth covers; def. Lacking Illus 496; piece torn from Illus 786. CA Oct 7 (153) A$1,500
— Smike to Bulldog. Letters from Sir Arthur Streeton to Tom Roberts. Sydney, 1946. Library stamps on some leaves. CA Apr 12 (81) A$320

Streett, William B. See: Derrydale Press

Stresemann, Erwin
— Sauropsida: Aves. Berlin, 1927-34. 2 vols. 4to, orig bdg. B Feb 24 (66) HF380

Stretch, Richard H.
— Illustrations of the Zygaenidae & Bombycidae of North America.... [San Francisco, 1872-74]. Vol I, Parts 1-9. 8vo, later 19th-cent half lea. With 10 color plates. sg Jan 15 (259) $225

Strickland, Agnes, 1796-1874
— Lives of the Queens of England. L, 1841-48. 12 vols in six. 12mo, sheep; worn, extremities scraped. wa Sept 25 (10) $80

Strickland, Walter G.
— Dictionary of Irish Artists. Dublin & L, 1913. 2 vols. Cloth; Vol I front hinges cracked. sg Feb 5 (311) $150

Strickland, William —& Others
— Public Works of the United States. L, 1841. Parts 1 & 2. Folio, bdg not described. Franklin Institute copy. F Sept 12 (312) $850

Stridbeck, Johann
— Curioses Staats und Kriegs Theatrum Dermahliger Begebenheiten...in Niederland. Augsburg, [1710-30?]. Oblong folio, contemp bds; worn. With engraved title & 45 plates. One plate repaired without loss. S Sept 23 (597) £420 [Christoph]

Stringer, Arthur, Huntsman
— The Experienced Huntsman.... Belfast, 1714. 16mo, later calf gilt by Winckworth, armorial bdg; rubbed, upper hinge broken. S Nov 10 (616) £800 [Quaritch]

Strobl, Alice
— Gustav Klimt: 25 Zeichnungen. Graz, 1964. Folio, unsewn in orig folder. With 25 facsimile reproductions in separate mounts. S June 17 (30) £250 [Marks]

Strong, Asa B.
— The American Flora.... NY, 1848-50. Vols I-III., Half mor gilt. With 3 engraved titles & 145 hand-colored plates & 1 port. Some browning; 1 engraved title torn with loss; some cropping. CNY May 11 (132) $1,300
— Illustrated Natural History of the Three Kingdoms.... NY, 1853. Vol I - New Series. Orig mor gilt; spine disintegrated, worn. cb Nov 6 (278) $55

Strong, Leonard Alfred George, 1896-1958
— Two Stories. L, [1936]. One of 60. Half vellum gilt. pn Mar 5 (101) £40 [Quaritch]

Strong, Reuben Myron
— A Bibliography of Birds. Chicago, 1939-46. 3 vols. Zoological Series, Field Museum of Natural History, No 25. B Feb 24 (62) HF260

Strother, David H.
— Virginia Illustrated: Containing a Visit to the Virginia Canaan and the Adventures of Porte Crayon and his Cousins. NY, 1857. 8vo, contemp half calf; rubbed. O June 9 (178) $60

Strozzi, Ercole, 1471-1508
La Partie de chasse.... Paris: Leon Techener, 1876. 8vo, contemp vellum. This copy on vellum. Jeanson copy. SM Mar 1 (543) FF6,000

Strozzi, Filippo
— Le Discours du deduit de la chasse.... Paris, 1601. 8vo, mor janseniste by Chambolle-Duru. Jeanson copy. SM Mar 1 (544) FF18,000
— Le Guidon des capitaines utile et necessaire a toutes personnes.... Rouen: Claude le Villain, 1609. 3 parts in 1 vol. 12mo, mor janseniste by Duru. Jeanson copy. SM Mar 1 (545) FF7,500

Strozzi, Tito Vespasiano
— Strozzi poetae pater et filius. Venice: Aldus, 1513. 2 parts in 1 vol. 8vo, 18th-cent half calf. Some stains & soiling. S Sept 23 (401) £220 [Peel]
Anr copy. 8vo, contemp wooden bds recovered with lea stamped with the Aldine anchor. Some spotting & browning. Jeanson 1188. SM Mar 1 (546) FF15,000

Struck, Hermann
— Die Kunst des Radierens. Berlin, 1919. 4to, orig bds. With 5 plates. C May 13 (197) £200 [London]
Anr copy. Bds; backstrip frayed, hinge starting. sg Sept 25 (285) $175
Anr Ed. Berlin, [1920]. 4to, orig bds. S Oct 6 (701) £180 [Gowdine]

Strutt, Jacob George
— Sylva Britannica. L, 1822-26. Folio, contemp half mor; rubbed. With 50 mtd india-proofs. Ck Apr 24 (69) £450

Strutt, Joseph, 1749-1802
See also: Fore-Edge Paintings
— Biographical Dictionary...of all the Engravers.... L, 1785-86. 2 parts in 1 vol. 4to, modern half lea. Some slight spotting. bba Dec 4 (80) £75 [Goulden]
— A Complete View of the Dress and Habits of the People of England. L, 1796-99. 1st Ed. 2 vols, 4to, later half mor. With 152 colored plates. S Nov 18 (935) £130 [Dennistoun]
Anr Ed. L, 1842. 2 vols. 4to, half lea; worn, cover of Vol II detached. wa June 25 (492) $280
Glig Gamena Angel-Deod.... L, 1801. 1st Ed. 4to, mor gilt by Root. With 40 plates, 39 hand-colored. Some spotting. Jeanson 1508. SM Mar 1 (547) FF6,000
2d Ed. L, 1810. ("The Sports and Pastimes of the People of England.") 4to, 19th-cent half sheep; scuffed. With hand-colored frontis & 39 plates. sg May 21 (199) $130
Anr Ed. L, 1831. 8vo, calf. L.p. copy with the cuts colored. pnE Jan 28 (358) £200 [Bradley]
Anr Ed. L, 1845. 4to, cloth. sg May 21 (200) $120

Strzelecki, Sir Paul Edmund de
— Gold and Silver: a Supplement to Strzelecki's Physical Description of New South Wales and Van Diemen's Land. L, 1856. 8vo, orig cloth. L July 2 (124) £380
— Physical Description of New South Wales and Van Diemen's Land. L, 1845. Bdg not described. Some repairs; outer margin of folding map frayed; small stain at foot of tp. kh Mar 16 (489) A$300

Stuart, Lieut.-Col. Charles
— Journal of a Residence in Northern Persia. L, 1854. 1st Ed. 8vo, orig cloth; recased. bba May 28 (250) £160 [Ad Orientem]

Stuart, Charles Beebe
— Lives and Works of Civil and Military Engineers of America. NY, 1871. 8vo, contemp mor gilt; broken. With frontis & 9 ports. wa Nov 6 (87) $65

Stuart, Gilbert, 1742-86
— A View of Society in Europe. L, 1778. 4to, half calf. S June 25 (84) £450 [Traylen]

STUART

Stuart, Granville
— Forty Years on the Frontier.... Cleveland, 1925. 2 vols. Unopened. sg Mar 12 (245) $150

Stuart, James, 1713-88 —& Revett, Nicholas, 1720-1804
— Les Antiquites d'Athenes. L, 1762-1830. 4 vols. Folio, Orig bds. S Apr 23 (102) £900 [Handtiz]
— The Antiquities of Athens. L, 1762-1830. 4 vols plus Supplement. Folio, contemp half calf; spines worn & def, covers loose. Lacking 5 plates; some spotting. bba Apr 23 (356) £1,000 [Rainer]

Anr copy. 4 vols, without Supplement. Folio, later half calf. With double-page folding hand-colored map & 317 maps & plates. Lacking 1 plate; minor worming affecting corner of 1 plate; a few minor tears; lacking list of subscribers. C July 22 (204) £2,200

Anr copy. Mor; rubbed. With 2 ports, folding hand-colored map of Greece & 316 plates. S Apr 23 (103) £2,500 [Rainer]

Stuart, Martinus
— De Mensch, zoo als hij voorkomt op den bekenden Aardbol. Amst., 1802-7. Illus by Jacques Kuyper. 6 vols. 8vo, contemp half lea; worn. With hand-colored titles & frontis, 2 plain & 41 hand-colored plates. Some foxing. O May 12 (185) $425

Stubbe, Henry, 1632-76
— The Miraculous Conformist.... Oxford, 1666. 4to, disbound. Tp & last leaf soiled; upper corners torn from leaves to G4 affecting tp margin & page numbers. bba July 16 (226) £65 [Elliott]

Stubbs, Harry C. See: Clement, Hal

Stubbs, Harry Clement. See: Clement, Hal

Studer, Jacob Henry
— The Birds of North America. NY, 1897. 4to, orig half lea; joints weak. With port & 119 colored plates. K Oct 4 (58) $170

Anr copy. Disbound. sg Dec 18 (224) $150; sg June 18 (245) $325

Anr copy. Contemp half mor; worn, front joint broken. wa Dec 11 (544) $230

Anr Ed. NY, 1903. Folio, modern cloth. With 119 colored plates. Library stamp on tp. pnNY Oct 11 (45) $300

Anr copy. Half lea; joints & spine ends worn. With port & 119 colored plates. sg Sept 18 (276) $150

Anr copy. Cloth; worn & shaken. sg June 18 (244) $200

— Studer's Popular Ornithology: The Birds of North America. Columbus, Ohio, & NY,

1881. Folio, orig lea; worn, backstrip renewed, hinges reinforced. With litho title & 119 colored plates. sg Sept 18 (275) $1,300

Anr copy. Mor gilt; cover & backstrip detached. sg June 18 (212) $425

Studio...
— The Studio. L, 1898-1903. Vols 14-27. 4to, modern half cloth, orig wraps bound in. bba Sept 25 (317) £280 [Reed]
— The Studio: An Illustrated Magazine of Fine and Applied Art. L, 1893-1917. Vols 1-72 (No 297). 4to, orig cloth. FD June 11 (5262) DM6,000
— The Studio: An Illustrated Magazine of Finae and Applied Art. L, 1913-16. Vols 59-68. 10 vols. 4to, half mor gilt. pn Apr 30 (259) £160 [Henderson]

Stuebel, Alphonse. See: Reiss & Stuebel

Stukeley, William, 1687-1765
— Itinerarium curiosum. L, 1724-76. 2 vols. Folio, contemp calf gilt; rubbed. With 206 plates & maps. Some spotting; 1 map repaired at folds; a few cropped. S Jan 16 (437) £340 [Weinreb]

Anr Ed. L, 1724. Folio, contemp calf; rebacked but broken. With frontis & 100 plates. Library markings. T Mar 19 (327) £120

Sturgeon, Launcelot
— Essays, Moral, Philosophical, and Stomachical.... L, 1822. 8vo, later half calf. sg Jan 15 (51) $100

Sturgeon, Theodore
— Without Sorcery. Phila.: Prime Press, 1948. 1st Trade Ed. In rubbed d/j. cb Sept 28 (1221) $55

One of c.88 l.p. copies. Intro by Ray Bradbury; illus by L. Robert Tschirsky. Cloth. Without holograph limitation notice. Sgd by Sturgeon, Bradbury & Tchirsky. cb Sept 28 (1220) $600

Sturges, Lee
— Salmon Fishing on Cain River, New Brunswick. [Chicago]: Pvtly ptd, 1919. One of 50. Bds. With frontis etching sgd by Sturges. Inscr. sg Oct 23 (515) $2,000

Sturgis, William B. See: Derrydale Press

Sturt, Capt. Charles, 1795-1869
— Narrative of an Expedition into Central Australia. L, 1849. 1st Ed. 2 vols. 8vo, early half calf; rubbed. Lacking the separately-pbd map. Frontises foxed & 1 stained. kh Mar 16 (492) A$1,050
— Two Expeditions into the Interior of Southern Australia.... L, 1833. 1st Ed. 2 vols. 8vo, early half mor; rubbed. Titles

stamped, bound without ads. kh Mar 16 (493) A$1,000

2d Ed. L, 1834. 2 vols. 8vo, orig cloth; recased, rebacked preserving orig spines, new endpapers. With folding map in pocket, chart, 9 plates & 4 hand-colored plates of birds. Lacking ads at end of Vol I; map wormed & spotted; a few uncolored plates spotted mainly in margins; library stamp on titles. C Oct 15 (175) £320 [Bonham]

Stutfield, Hugh E.M. —& Collie, John Norman
— Climbs and Exploration in the Canadian Rockies. L, 1903. pp Nov 20 (202) £150 [Cavendish]

Stylianou, A. & J.
— The History of the Cartography of Cyprus. Nicosia, 1980. Folio, cloth, in d/j. S Nov 10 (997) £65 [Hicknet]

Styward, Thomas
— The Pathwaie to Martiall Discipline.... L, 1581. 4to, disbound. Lacking 2 folding woodcut plates; other plates torn; lacking Sig. I. Sold w.a.f. bba Nov 13 (183) £90 [Burgess Browning]

Suares, Joseph Marie
— Praenestes antiquae. Rome, 1655. 4to, contemp calf gilt; upper cover detached. With 8 plates, 5 folding. Some leaves spotted or dampstained; 1 leaf repaired in margin. bba Sept 25 (247) £110 [P & P Books]

Suarez, Pablo Antonio
— Por D. Francisco Justiniano Chavarri, Cavallero de la Orden de Santiago.... [Madrid, c.1650]. Folio, modern half vellum. S June 25 (332) £520

Suckling, Alfred
— The History and Antiquities of the County of Suffolk. L, 1846-48. 1st Ed. 2 vols. 4to, contemp half calf gilt; spine & corners rubbed. S Feb 23 (46) £220 [Beasley]

Anr copy. Later half calf; some orig wraps bound in. T Feb 19 (302) £155

Suckling, Sir John, 1609-42
See also: Golden Cockerel Press
— Works. L, 1646. ("Fragmenta Aurea. A Collection of all the Incomparable Peeces.") 1st Ed. 4 parts in 1 vol. 8vo, calf by Kalthoeber. C Dec 12 (361) £320 [Barden]

Sudek, Josef
— Janacek-Hukvaldy. Prague, 1971. 4to, cloth, in d/j. ha Nov 7 (190) $50
— Sudek. Czechoslovakia, 1964. 4to, cloth, in worn d/j. sg May 7 (75) $600

Sue, Eugene, 1804-57
— Le Juif errant. Paris: Paulin, 1845. 4 vols. 8vo, half mor gilt. With 84 plates. Foxed. sg Sept 11 (266) $120
— The Mysteries of Paris. L, 1845-46. 3 vols. 8vo, half mor gilt by Root; 1 joint starting. With engraved title & 20 plates, trimmed & inlaid to size. sg Sept 11 (267) $120

Suetonius Tranquillus, Caius
See also: Limited Editions Club
— De vitae XII Caesarum. Bologna: Benedictus Hectoris, 5 Apr 1493. ("Vitae Caesarum.") Folio, modern calf preserving fragments of 18th-cent calf covers. Roman type. Minor worming to a few leaves at front & at end. 333 (of 334) leaves; lacking final blank. Goff S-825. C May 13 (149) £1,000 [Fletcher]
— Opera. Leeuwarden, 1714-15. 2 vols. 4to, contemp vellum; 1 joint split, rubbed. Some marginal tears. bba Oct 30 (153) £95 [P & P Books]

Anr Ed. Amst., 1736. 2 vols. 4to, vellum; lacking ties. With engraved title. B Feb 25 (863) HF260

Anr copy. Contemp calf gilt; worn, joints cracked. cb Feb 19 (256) $70

Sugden, Alan Victor —& Edmondson, John Ludlam
— A History of English Wallpaper. L, [1925]. 4to, orig cloth. S Nov 10 (170) £200 [Woodruff]

Suhr, Christoph
— Der Ausruf in Hamburg.... Hamburg, 1808. 8vo, calf gilt; worn. With 120 hand-colored plates. HN Nov 26 (435) DM8,500

Anr copy. Contemp calf; def. With 118 (of 120) hand-colored plates. Lacking 4 pp of ptd index. S Apr 23 (73) £1,650 [Braun]
— Hamburgische Trachten Gezeichnet und Gestochen. [Hamburg?], 1815. Folio, modern mor gilt. With 36 hand-colored plates. FD Dec 2 (1310) DM12,000

Suidas
— Lexikon. Milan: Johannes Bissolus & Benedictus Mangius, 15 Nov 1499. Folio, 18th-cent calf gilt; rebacked & worn. Some staining & browning; wormed at end. In Greek. 515 leaves. Goff S-829. HN May 20 (1668) DM5,600

Suliman Ben Ibrahaim Baemer. See: Dinet & Suliman Ben Ibrahaim Baemer

Sullivan, Sir Edward Robert
— Rambles and Scrambles in North and South America. L, 1852. 1st Ed. 12mo, modern half cloth. Lacking errata slip. cb Jan 8 (189) $70

Sully, Maximilien de Bethune, Duc de
— Memoires des sages et royales oeconomies d'estat, domestiques, politiques...de Henry le Grand. Amst., 1638. 1st Ed. 2 vols in 1. Folio, contemp vellum; worn & soiled. HN Nov 26 (949) DM1,000

Anr copy. Contemp calf; rubbed, joints broken. Minor staining & soiling. O Feb 24 (187) $130

Anr Ed. Londres [Paris], 1745. 3 vols. 4to, contemp calf gilt; Vol II def. Some staining. bba July 16 (31) £50 [Shankland]

Sulzer, Johann Heinrich
— Die Kennzeichen der Insekten, nach Anleitung...Karl Linnaeus. Zurich, 1761. 4to, modern vellum. With frontis & 24 hand-colored plates. Small library stamp in tp margin. C Apr 8 (203) £520 [Quaritch]

Sumbel, Mary Leah Wells
— Memoirs of the Life of.... L, 1811. 1st Ed. 3 vols. 12mo, contemp half calf; rubbed, rebacked, new endpapers. Library stamps on titles. bba Jan 15 (75) £80 [Sutherland]

Summerhayes, Martha
— Vanished Arizona. Phila., 1908. Cloth. Sgd. cb Jan 8 (190) $80; cb Jan 8 (191) $90

Summers, Lewis Preston
— Annals of Southwest Virginia, 1769-1800. Abingdon, 1929. 8vo, cloth. With 3 folding maps. wa Nov 6 (617) $55

Summerson, John. See: Roxburghe Club

Sunset...
— Sunset City and Sunset Scenes. [San Francisco, c.1893]. Folio, orig cloth. cb Oct 9 (320) $160

Surirey de Saint Remy, Pierre
— Memoires d'artillerie. Paris, 1745. 3d Ed. 3 vols. 4to, bdg not indicated. Library markings. Sold w.a.f. Franklin Institute copy. F Sept 12 (347) $130

Surprises...
— Les Surprises, ou le bien et le mal. Paris: Guerin-Muller, [c.1880]. Folio, loose in orig half cloth. With 6 hand-colored illusts. HK Nov 4 (2820) DM520

Surtees, Robert Smith, 1803-64
— The Analysis of the Hunting Field. L: Ackermann, 1846. 1st Ed, 1st Issue. 8vo, orig cloth; spine relaid. With engraved title & 6 hand-finished color plates. pnE Jan 28 (266) £140 [Traylen]; pnE Jan 28 (267) £230 [Josephs]

Anr copy. Later russia; rebacked & recornered. S Feb 24 (63) £210 [Trocchi]

Anr copy. Orig cloth; worn. S July 28 (1043) £320

Anr copy. Orig cloth; spine ends & corners worn. sg Apr 2 (190) $300

— "Ask Mama...." L, 1857-58. 1st Ed, 1st Issue. Orig 13 parts. 8vo, orig wraps. With 13 hand-colored plates. pnE Jan 28 (273) £500 [Traylen]

1st Ed in Book form. L, 1858. Illus by John Leech. 8vo, orig cloth. pnE Jan 28 (274) £85 [Grant]

— Handley Cross, or the Spa Hunt. L, 1853-54. In 17 monthly parts. 8vo, orig wraps. pnE Jan 28 (271) £750 [Traylen]

Anr Ed. L, 1854. 2d Issue. 8vo, orig cloth. pnE Jan 28 (272) £80 [Maggs]

— Hillingdon Hall.... L, 1888. 8vo, orig cloth. With 12 hand-colored plates. pnE Jan 28 (279) £95 [Josephs]

— Jorrocks' Jaunts and Jollities. L: Ackermann, 1843. 2d Ed. Illus by Henry Alken. 8vo, orig cloth; spine relaid. pnE Jan 28 (265) £240 [Steedman]

Anr copy. Orig cloth; hinges broken. With 15 hand-colored plates. S Nov 17 (683) £150 [Boyd]

Anr copy. Calf gilt by Riviere, orig cloth bound in. With 12 plates. sg Feb 12 (299) $475

— Mr. Facey Romford's Hounds. L, 1864-65. 1st Ed, 1st Issue. In orig 12 parts. 8vo, orig wraps. With 24 hand-colored plates. pnE Jan 28 (277) £740 [Traylen]

1st Ed in Book form. L, 1865. 8vo, orig cloth. With 24 hand-colored plates. pnE Jan 28 (278) £50 [Polworth]

— Mr. Jorrocks' Lectors.... L, 1910. One of 350 sgd by artist. Illus by G. Denholm Armour. 4to, orig pigskin. Ck Dec 10 (262) £85

— Mr. Sponge's Sporting Tour. L, 1853. 1st Ed. In orig 13/12 parts. 8vo, orig wraps. pnE Jan 28 (269) £550 [Traylen]

Anr copy. Cloth. pnE Jan 28 (270) £200 [Steedman]

— "Plain or Ringlets?" L, 1860. 1st Ed in Book form. Illus by John Leech. 8vo, cloth. With 13 hand-colored plates. pnE Jan 28 (276) £75 [Steedman]

1st Ed, in orig 13/12 parts. 8vo, orig wraps. With 13 hand-colored plates. Inserted in Part 1 is a proof on white paper of the design for the wraps. pnE Jan 28 (275) £520 [Traylen]

— [Sporting Novels]. L, 1843-65. 6 vols. 8vo, mor gilt. Minor foxing; tp & next 2 leaves of Handley Cross supplied from anr copy. sg Apr 2 (191) $1,300

Anr Ed. L, 1854-69. 6 vols. 8vo, half mor gilt. S July 28 (1041) £320

M.F.H. Ed. L, 1899-1900. 11 vols. 8vo, contemp half mor gilt; rubbed. bba Oct 30

(155) £200 [Russell]

Anr Ed. [L: Ptd for subscribers, 1926]. 6 vols. 8vo, cloth. ha May 22 (79) $90

Anr copy. 6 vols. pnE Nov 12 (44) £65

Susemihl, Johann Conrad

— Teutsche Ornithologie oder Naturgeschichte aller Voegel Teutschlands.... Darmstadt, 1800-17. 2 vols. Folio, half calf with wraps bound in. With 125 (of 132) hand-colored plates. Some spotting & minor defs. HK Nov 4 (1157) DM 16,000

Sutcliffe, Matthew

— A Ful and Round Answer to N D alias Robert Parsons.... L, 1604. 4to, contemp vellum. sg Oct 9 (325) $150

Sutherland, A. R.

— The Knight Crusaders' Games. L, 1839. Cloth. With folding frontis & 2 plates. pn Mar 26 (332) £40 [Schmidt]

Sutherland, Alexander

— Victoria and its Metropolis, Past and Present.... Melbourne, 1888. 2 vols. 4to, old mor; restored. Stains to some leaves of Vol II. kh Mar 16 (494) A$190

Sutherland, Elizabeth, Duchess of

— Views on the Northern and Western Coasts of Sutherland. [Pvtly ptd, not before 1833]. Folio, half mor. With engraved contents leaf, engraved map (tears repaired) & 22 hand-colored plates mtd on card as issued. S Apr 23 (130) £1,050 [Tegner]

Sutherland, James, Hunter

— The Adventures of an Elephant Hunter. L, 1912. cb Nov 6 (279) $275; cb May 21 (250) $160

Sutro, Adolph Heinrich Joseph, 1830-98

— The Advantages and Necessity of a Deep Drain Tunnel, for the Great Comstock Ledge. San Francisco, Feb 1865. Orig wraps; lower wrap with corner chipped. Some discoloration to wraps & tp. cb Oct 9 (236) $100

Sutter, John A. See: Grabhorn Printing

Sutton, Thomas

— King James his Hospitall: Founded in the Charter-house.... L: for Thomas Thorpe, 1618. 4to, vellum by Riviere. Tp restored in outer & lower margins touching 1 letter & date; small rust hole in G2 slightly affecting text. Britwell Court copy. S Dec 18 (244) £550 [Knoll]

Sutton, Thomas, of Caius College, Cambridge

— A Dictionary of Photography.... L, 1858. 8vo, cloth; worn, spine chipped. ha Nov 7 (191) $150

Suyin, Han. See: Cartier-Bresson, Henri

Svenska Vetenskaps-Akademien

— Kongliga Svenska Fregatten Eugenies Resa Omkring Jorden under befal af C. A. Virgin. Aren 1851-1853.... Uppsala & Stockholm, 1847-1910. 3 vols in 5. 4to, orig wraps. With folding map & 54 plates. sg Jan 15 (373) $275

Svenskt...

— Svenskt Silversmide, 1520-1850. Stockholm, [1941-45, 1963]. Vols I-III. Vellum. wa Mar 5 (143) $250

Svetlov, Valerian. See: Ivchenko, Valerian

Svin'in, Pavel Petrovich

— Sketches of Russia. L, 1831. 2d Ed. 8vo, contemp half cloth; worn, upper hinge weak. With 15 colored plates. bba Jan 15 (473) £90 [Dyson]

Swainson, William, 1789-1855

— Exotic Conchology. L, 1841. 4to, cloth; spine. With 48 hand-colored plates, a few soiled. bba Dec 18 (246) £260 [Burgess Browning]

Anr copy. Modern half mor; new endpapers. sg Apr 2 (192) $1,000

Swammerdam, Jan, 1637-80

— The Book of Nature; or, the History of Insects.... L, 1758. Folio, contemp calf; rubbed, joints breaking. With 53 plates. Small hole in 1 plate with slight loss; tp coming loose; some worming in margin. S July 28 (1122) £400

— Bybel der natuure, of historie der insecten.... Leiden, 1737-38. 2 vols. Folio, half calf; rubbed. With 53 plates. pn June 18 (218) £800 [Maggs]

Swan, Abraham

— The British Architect. Bost., 1794. Folio, bdg not described. Franklin Institute copy. F Sept 12 (11) $2,700

Swan, James

— The Northwest Coast; or, Three Years' Residence in Wahsington Territory. NY, 1857. 8vo, orig cloth; front hinge cracked. sg Mar 12 (246) $300

Swan, John

— Speculum Mundi or, a Glass Representing the Face of the World. Cambr., 1643 [1644]. 2d Ed. 4to, contemp calf; joints rubbed, corners repaired. CNY Nov 21 (266) $160

Swan, Joseph —& Leighton, J. M.
— Select Views on the River Clyde. Glasgow, 1830. 4to, contemp mor gilt; rubbed. With engraved title & 42 plates on india paper. Perforated library stamp & small tears in title. bba Dec 4 (353) £70 [West]

Swann, H. Kirke. See: Mullens & Swann

Swann, Harry Kirke
— A Monograph of the Birds of Prey. L, [1924-25]. 16 parts in 14 vols. Folio, orig wraps; some damaged. With 56 plates. Haverschmidt copy. B Feb 24 (142) HF700

Anr Ed. L, 1930-45 [1924-45]. 2 vols. Folio, modern half calf gilt. pn Oct 23 (285) £400 [Traylen]

Swarbreck, Samuel D.
— Sketches in Scotland. L, 1845. Folio, orig half mor. With 25 plates, including title. C July 22 (206) £550

Anr copy. Orig bds; loose. Lacking 1 plate. pnE Oct 15 (128) £440

Swarzenski, Georg
— Die illuminierten Handschriften und Einzelminiaturen des Mittelalters und der Renaissance in Frankfurter Besitz.... Frankfurt, 1929. Folio, wraps with plates loose in portfolio. sg Oct 2 (192) $250

Swayne, George
— Gramina pascua.... Bristol, 1790. Folio, orig bds; worn. With 6 plates containing actual specimens of dried grass. Ck Apr 24 (201) £320

Swayne, Harold George Carlos
— Seventeen Trips through Somaliland.... L, 1895. 8vo, orig cloth; rubbed, spine ends chipped, front joint started, contents shaken. cb Nov 6 (280) $85

Swebach, Edouard
— Desagremens de la chasse a courre. Brussels: De Wasne, [c.1840]. Folio, 6 modern bdg Jeanson copy. SM Mar 1 (548) FF19,000

Sweert, Emanuel
— Florilegium amplissimum et selectissimum. Amst. [1631?]. Folio, contemp calf; rebacked & repaired. With engraved title & 110 plates. Engraved title stained in margin. Horticultural Society of New York—de Belder copy. S Apr 28 (348) £3,800 [Handler]

— Florilegium, tractans de variis floribus.... Frankfurt, 1612. 2 parts in 1 vol. Folio, contemp vellum; stained, inner hinges broken. With engraved title & 110 plates, all in contemp hand-coloring, the title heightened with gold. Some browning & discoloration; lower corner of f.5 repaired touching catchword. Vilmorin—de Belder copy. S Apr 28 (347) £8,500 [Arader]

Anr copy. Old half calf gilt; inner hinges broken. With engraved title & 108 (of 110) plates, some apparently sgd by the colorist. Lacking Plates 10 & 15 of Part 1 & engraved titles & 2 prelims; some browning & discoloration; a few marginal tears & a few plates trimmed. S June 25 (181) £13,500 [Burgess]

Anr copy. Old vellum. With engraved title, port & 110 plates, many browned & foxed. sg Dec 4 (192) $3,800

Sweet, Robert, 1783-1835
See also: Ornamental...

— The British Flower Garden. L, 1823-38. Series I-II. 7 vols. 8vo, late 19th-cent half mor gilt; rubbed. With 712 hand-colored plates. Minor dampstaining affecting a few prelims in Vol II of 1st Series & a few leaves & plates in Vol II of 2d Series; head of some leaves & plates in Vols I & IV of 2d Series edged by binder. Colville—de Belder copy. S Apr 28 (353) £7,000 [Lan]

— Cistineae: The Natural Order of Cistus.... L, 1825-30. 8vo, library cloth. With 112 hand-colored plates. All plates stamped; other library markings. bba Feb 5 (321) £300 [Elliott]

Anr copy. Contemp mor gilt; spine rubbed. C Oct 15 (260) £1,400 [Davies]

Anr copy. Half mor gilt. pnE Dec 17 (236) £1,100 [Steedman]

Anr copy. Contemp mor; marked. de Belder copy. S Apr 28 (349) £1,950 [Krohn]

Anr copy. Later half mor. Upper blank corner of tp renewed; repair to l2. S June 25 (182) £1,100 [Heuer]

— Flora Australasica.... L, 1827-28. 8vo, contemp half mor; rubbed. With 56 hand-colored plates. Some spotting. Johnston—de Belder copy. S Apr 28 (350) £5,500 [Ross]

— The Florist's Guide, and Cultivator's Directory. L, 1827-32. 2 vols. 8vo, orig cloth; rubbed, rebacked, old spines preserved. With 200 hand-colored plates. A few plates with spotting, mostly marginal. Krelage—de Belder copy. S Apr 28 (354) £3,200 [Shapiro]

— Geraniaceae. L, 1820-30. 5 vols. 8vo, cloth. With 500 hand-colored plates, all with ink library stamps. Library markings. bba Feb 5 (320) £500 [Elliott]

Anr copy. Late 19th-cent half mor gilt; corners rubbed. de Belder copy. S Apr 28 (351) £4,200 [Krohn]

Swift, Jonathan, 1667-1745
See also: Cresset Press; Golden Cockerel Press; Limited Editions Club

— A Complete Collection of Genteel and Ingenious Conversation. L, 1738. 1st English Ed with Neptune ornament. 8vo, contemp half calf; spine worn at extremities. Uncut copy. Lacking ad leaf. C Dec 12 (362) £400 [Pirages]

— Gullivers Reise ins Land der Reisen. Berlin, 1922. One of 25. Illus by Lovis Corinth. With 25 sgd lithos & a sgd etching. HN Nov 26 (1768) DM2,600

One of 175. With 25 lithos & a sgd etching. FD Dec 2 (4301) DM11,000; FD June 11 (4864) DM1,650

— Gulliver's Travels. L, 1726. ("Travels into Several Remote Nations of the World.") Teerink's "A" Ed (1st 8vo Ed). 2 vols. Mor gilt by Leichton. With frontis & 6 maps & plans. Minor staining & discoloration. S July 23 (26) £3,800 [Bull]

Teerink's "AA" Ed (2d 8vo Ed). ("Travels into Several Remote Nations of the World...by Lemuel Gulliver.") 2 vols. Contemp calf; rubbed, rebacked. With port & 6 plates. Port in 2d state & with vertical chain lines. bba Mar 12 (140) £290 [Jarndyce]

Teerink's "B" Ed (3d 8vo Ed). ("Travels into Several Remote Nations of the World.") 2 vols. Modern calf. Titles torn & repaired at upper edge, affecting title-borders. bba Oct 16 (68) £150 [Carhoch]

Anr copy. Contemp calf; not uniform, rubbed, spines worn. With 7 engraved maps & plates. A few leaves loose. S Sept 22 (55) £100 [Sotheran]

Teerink's "B" Ed. 2 vols. contemp calf; rubbed. With port & 6 plates. Some browning. Duff Cooper's copy. S Mar 9 (792) £220 [Bennett]

Teerink's 2d (4th 8vo) Ed. L, 1727. 2 vols. Modern calf. 2 leaves repaired. bba Aug 20 (23) £160 [Murray Hill]

Anr copy. 3 vols (including the spurious 3d vol). Modern mor gilt. With port, 4 maps & 2 plans. S May 29 (1266) £260

Anr copy. 3 vols. Modern calf. Opening Ode in Vol I supplied from anr copy, with outer margins shaved, affecting text. sg June 11 (392) $400

Anr Ed. L & NY, 1909. Illus by Arthur Rackham. 4to, orig cloth. With 12 color plates. sg Oct 30 (213) $70

One of 750. Cloth; backstrip darkened. With 13 mtd color plates. sg Oct 30 (211) $550

Anr copy. Cloth; soiled. Foxed. sg Oct 30 (212) $150

Anr copy. Orig cloth; rubbed & soiled. With 13 colored plates. T Mar 19 (429) £230

— The History of the Four Last Years of the Queen. L, 1758. 1st Ed. 8vo, contemp calf; broken. sg June 11 (380) $70

— A Modest Proposal. Dublin, 1729. 1st Ed. 8vo, modern half vellum. Some discoloration; edges frayed; half-title torn. S July 23 (28) £1,650 [Quaritch]

— A Tale of a Tub. L, 1704. 8vo, contemp calf gilt; joints repaired. Some browning & spotting; last leaf repaired. FD Dec 2 (3635) DM3,000

Anr copy. Calf; broken. Lacking final blank. Bound with A Complete Key..., 1710. sg Apr 2 (193) $750

— Works. L, 1755-79. 14 vols. 4to, late 18th-cent calf gilt; worn, joints of Vol I split. Lacking the final blank in Vol I & II & the blank at the end of Part 1 of Vol VIII & IX; portions torn from margins of tp of Vol IV without affecting text; tp of Vol VI torn & repaired affecting 4 letters of the title; 1 leaf restored; a few leaves short, some holes. S May 6 (446) £300 [Shapero]

Anr Ed. L, 1765-79. 26 (of 27) vols; lacking Vol 27. Calf; worn. sg Sept 11 (269) $200

Anr Ed. L, 1801. 19 vols. 8vo, half calf gilt by Zaehnsdorf. sg Sept 11 (270) $850

Anr Ed. Edin., 1814. 19 vols. 8vo, 19th-cent half calf gilt; some joints weak. sg Dec 4 (194) $400

Anr Ed. Edin., 1824. Ed by Sir Walter Scott. 19 vols. 8vo, calf. Port spotted & offset. S Sept 22 (54) £440 [Thorp]

Anr copy. 18 vols; lacking Vol II. Contemp calf; scuffed. S Feb 23 (47) £120 [Dailey]

Swinburne, Algernon C. See: Grabhorn Printing

Swinburne, Algernon Charles, 1837-1909
See also: Golden Cockerel Press; Kelmscott Press

— Atalanta in Calydon. L, 1865. 1st Ed. 8vo, orig cloth. ALs tipped to front free endpaper. bba July 2 (368) £350 [Kent]

— Laus Veneris. Portland ME: Mosher, 1899. One of 25. Mor gilt by Toof; upper joint repaired. O Mar 24 (179) $140

— Notes on Poems and Reviews. L, 1866. 8vo, orig wraps; soiled. Waterstained. bba Mar 12 (166) £35 [Wise]

— Poems and Ballads. L: J.C. Hotten, 1866. 8vo, mor gilt exhibition bdg by Zaehnsdorf. sg Apr 2 (194) $700

— The Springtide of Life. L, 1918. Illus by Arthur Rackham. 4to, half vellum. With 9 colored plates. sg Jan 8 (236) $150

One of 765. Orig half vellum gilt. S Oct 6 (852) £180 [Storey]

Anr copy. Half vellum; spine rubbed. With 8 colored plates. sg Oct 30 (214) $175

— Works. L, 1925-27. Bonchurch Ed, One of 780. Ed by Sir Edmund Gosse & T. J. Wise. 20 vols. sg Sept 11 (271) $375

Swinburne, Henry, 1743-1803

— Picturesque Tour through Spain. L, 1810. Oblong folio, contemp half mor; broken, worn. With frontis, 20 plates & 1 map. bba Dec 18 (247) £130 [Clarke]

— Travels in the Two Sicilies. L, 1783-85. 1st Ed. 2 vols. 4to, contemp calf; worn, covers detached. With folding map & table & 21 (of 22) plates. Perforated stamp & ink number on titles; perforated stamp on map. bba Mar 12 (33) £110 [Callea]

— Travels through Spain. L, 1779. 4to, contemp calf; worn, broken. With 13 plates. pnE June 17 (123) £120

Anr Ed. L, 1787. 2 vols. 8vo, modern half calf. With port, 2 folding maps & 10 folding plates mtd on linen. A few plates cut close. Extra-illus with 2 pencil & brown wash drawings. S Nov 10 (925) £135 [Duran]

Anr copy. Modern half mor gilt. sg Mar 26 (268) $150

Swinden, Henry, 1716-72

— The History and Antiquities of the Ancient Burgh of Great Yarmouth. Norwich, 1772. 4to, calf gilt; worn. Folding map torn & mtd. S Feb 23 (48) £170 [Wells]

Swinney, Myles

— Specimen of Printing Types.... Birm.: Swinney & Collins, 1795. 4to, contemp half calf; spine head frayed, lower joint splitting. C Dec 12 (203) £1,300 [Marlborough]

Swire, Herbert, d. 1934. See: Golden Cockerel Press

Sydenham, Thomas, 1624-89

— The Entire Works. L, 1742. 8vo, calf gilt. pnE Dec 17 (142) £200 [Maggs]

— Opera. L, 1705. 3d Ed. 8vo, contemp calf; rebacked, rubbed. bba Mar 26 (315) £45 [Maggs]

Sylva. See: Evelyn, John

Syme, Patrick

— A Treatise on British Song-Birds. Edin., 1823. 8vo, modern half cloth. With 15 hand-colored plates. pn Oct 23 (286) £70 [Hay Cinema]

Anr copy. Orig half cloth. pnE May 20 (91) £210

Symes, Michael

— An Account of an Embassy to the Kingdom of Ava.... L, 1800. 4to, disbound. With 17 plates only. Dampstained. pn Dec 11 (52) £80 [Waterloo]

Symonds, Emily Morse

— Social Caricature in the Eighteenth Century. L, 1905. Folio, cloth; backstrip nearly detached, shaken. sg Feb 5 (72) $60

Anr copy. Cloth; worn. sg June 4 (237) $50

Symonds, John Addington, 1840-93

— The Escorial; A Prize Poem.... Oxford, 1860. 8vo, ptd wraps. sg Mar 5 (259) $80

— The Life of Michelangelo Buonarroti. L, 1893. 4to, half lea; spines dry & worn, joints starting. wa Feb 19 (396) $50

— Mediaeval Latin Students Songs. San Francisco: Windsor Press, 1928. One of 250. Ed by Symonds. Contemp vellum; soiled. With 2 hand-colored & hand-illuminated woodcuts & hand-painted initials by Howard Simon. cb Feb 19 (281) $55

Symonds, Mary —& Preece, Louisa

— Needlework through the Ages. L, 1928. 4to, orig half vellum. sg Apr 2 (195) $325

Symonds, Robert Wemyss

— English Furniture from Charles II to George II. L, 1929. One of 1,000. 4to, orig cloth; rubbed. bba July 16 (193) £100 [Hannan]

— Furniture Making in Seventeenth and Eighteenth Century England. L, 1955. Folio, orig cloth, in d/j. S July 13 (51) £200

— Masterpieces of English Furniture and Clocks. L, 1940. One of 750. 4to, orig cloth. pn Dec 11 (595) £50 [Phillips]

— Thomas Tompion. L, 1951. One of 350. 4to, orig half mor gilt. S Nov 10 (202) £100 [Traylen]

Symons, A. J. A.

— The Quest for Corvo. L, 1934. 1st Ed. In frayed d/j. Initialled on front endpaper. T Feb 18 (103) £70

Symons, Arthur, 1865-1945

— The Cafe Royal and Other Essays. L: Beaumont Press, 1923. One of 80. Bds. sg Dec 11 (445) $600

— Mes Souvenirs. Chapelle-Reanville: Hours Press, [1931]. Out of series copy for The New Statesman. Bds. sg Dec 11 (446) $140

Symons, George James

— The Eruption of Krakatoa and Subsequent Phenomena.... L, 1888. 4to, cloth; hinges weak. With double-page chromolitho frontis & 3 chromolitho plates, maps, plates & tables. Library stamps. bba Dec 18

(248) £55 [Randall]

Synge, John Millington, 1871-1909. See: Cuala Press

Synodo...
— Synodo diocesana que celebro...Manuel de Alday y Aspee, obispo de Santiago de Chile.... Lima, 1764. Folio, contemp vellum; loose in bdg, snag to top of front joint. Small blank piece torn from half-title; blank bottom corner of final 2 leaves chewed. Unrecorded variant with 2d part title in red, green & black within 3-color ornamental borders. sg Sept 18 (58) $325

System...
— A System of Anatomy and Physiology, from the Latest...Authors.... Edin., 1787. 2d Ed. 3 vols. 8vo, calf. With 16 plates. pnE Dec 17 (44) £320 [Phillips]

Szarkowski, John —&
Hambourg, Maria Morris
— The Work of Atget. NY: Museum of Modern Art, [1981-82]. Vols I-II (of 4). 4to,. cloth, in d/j. wa Nov 6 (285) $50

Szyk, Arthur
— Ink & Blood: a Book of Drawings. NY, 1946. One of 1,000, sgd. Folio, half mor; spine rubbed. With 7 mtd colored plates. sg Sept 25 (287) $400

T

T., R.
— Good Husbandry, or, the Improvement of Time.... L, 1675. 4to, wraps. Some margins shaved with slight loss. S July 24 (461) £1,050 [Hunersdorf]

Tabella...
— Tabella Cibaria. The Bill of Fare.... L, 1820. Trans by A. D. Macquin. 4to, old half lea. Opening leaves browned; final blank torn. sg Jan 15 (52) $70

Tabernaemontanus, Jacobus Theodorus
— Eicones plantarum. Frankfurt: N. Bassaeus, 1590. 4to, old calf; portions of lea renewed, part of spine lea torn away. Some worming to inner portions of 1st 18 leaves, 9 leaves at end & leaves 3G2 to 3I6, affecting a few letters in index; marginal dampstains; Dd3-4 with tears to lower margins; 3T7-8 stained; 3Z6 with clean tear affecting 1 woodcut; 3I2-4 with small wormtrail affecting headlines. Hunt copy. CNY Nov 21 (267) $1,500
— Neu vollkommentlich Krauter Buch. Frankfurt, 1613. Folio, old vellum; worn & def. VH Sept 12 (897) DM3,200
  Anr Ed. Frankfurt: P. Jacobi, 1625. 3 parts in 1 vol. Folio, contemp vellum; worn.

Some spotting & repairs. HK Nov 4 (1131) DM5,000
  Anr Ed. Basel, 1664. Folio, contemp pigskin with brass catches; lacking clasps, worn & torn at head of spine & corners. Wormhole affecting title & following 3 leaves; more severe worming to last leaves; some leaves loose; some browning & dampstains. Sold w.a.f. Hunt copy. CNY Nov 21 (268) $1,100

Table...
— The Table Fruits of India. Calcutta: Ballin & Co., 1842. Oblong folio, modern half mor, orig wraps bound in. With 16 hand-colored plates. de Belder copy. S Apr 27 (12) £1,200 [Ursus]

Tableaux...
— Tableaux historiques de la Revolution Francaise. Paris, 1817. 2 vols. Folio, contemp calf; rubbed. With 2 allegorical frontises, 61 ports & 154 views. One plate split at plate-mark. S May 6 (498) £380 [Shapero]

Tablettes...
— Les Tablettes guerrieres, ou Cartes choisies pour la commodite des officiers et des voyageurs, contenant toutes les cartes generales du monde.... Amst.: Paul de la Feuille, 1709. 8vo, half mor. With 31 double-page folding maps. Without maps of Denmark but with map of Scotland, not called for. pn Apr 30 (328) £470

Tacitus, Publius Cornelius
— The Annales...the Description of Germanie. L, 1598. Bound with: Tacitus. The Ende of Nero and Beginning of Galba.... L, 1598. 2d Ed. 1st Ed in English. Later half calf; hinges cracked. Some leaves trimmed, touching marginal notes, underscoring throughout. I Sept 18 (329) £78
— Oeuvres. Paris: la veuve Jean Camusat & Pierre le Petit, 1644. Folio, 17th-cent mor with arms of Louis XIV on both covers; some scratches. Short tear in tp & A4; occasional spotting; M4 & N4 misbound. S Nov 27 (231) £200 [Peck]
— Opera. Basel: J. Froben, 1533. ("Annalium.....") Folio, mor gilt, armorial bdg; rebacked, scratched. B Feb 25 (864) HF400
  Anr Ed. Leiden: Elzevir, 1634. 16mo, later mor gilt extra; rubbed. Willems 415. cb Oct 23 (71) $100

Taeubel, Christian Gottlob
— Allgemeines theoretisch-practisches Woerterbuch der Buchdruckerkunst und Schriftgiesserey. Vienna, 1805. 2 vols, including 1809 Supplement. 4to, old half cloth; not uniform. With 2 frontises, 10 plates & 27 folding tables. sg Apr 2 (196)

995

TAFT

$1,500

Taft, Jonathan, b.1820
— A Practical Treatise on Operative Dentistry. Phila., 1859. 1st Ed. 8vo, orig sheep; spine chipped & repaired. Light dampstaining at end. sg Jan 15 (87) $100

Tagore, Rabindranath, 1861-1941
— Nationalism. San Francisco: Book Club of California, 1917. One of 250. Mor gilt. cb Sept 11 (69) $85

Tahitian...
— Tahitian and English Dictionary with Introductory Remarks on the Polynesian Language.... [Papeete], Tahiti: London Missionary Society's Press, 1851. 8vo, modern half mor gilt. S Apr 24 (383) £300 [Marlborough]
  Anr copy. Contemp cloth, preserving orig wrap; soiled. S June 25 (504) £200 [Lawson]

Taisnier, Joannes, b.1509
— De Usu annuli sphaerici libri tres. Palermo, 1550. 4to, modern bds. Cl & 4 supplied in facsimile & crudely tipped in with adhesive tape; tp & last 2 leaves holed with loss; dampstained. Ck Jan 30 (28) £170
— Opus mathematicum.... Cologne: T. Baum, 1583. Folio, old bds. S July 28 (1125) £500

Tait, Arthur Fitzwilliam. See: Butterworth & Tait

Taiwan
— The Illustrated Catalogue of Sung Dynasty Porcelain in the National Palace Museum. Taipei, 1973-74. One of 300. 4 vols. Folio, bds. cba Mar 5 (269) $1,100

Takahashi Seiichiro
— The Japanese Wood-Block Prints Through Two Hundred and Fifty Years. Tokyo: Chuo-Koron Bijutsu Shuppan, [1965]. One of 1,000. In repaired d/j. Sgd on tp. cb Mar 5 (271) $85

Talbot, Edward Allen
— Five Years Residence in the Canadas. L, 1824. 2 vols. 8vo, orig bds; worn. pn Sept 18 (229) £170 [Thorp]

Tale. See: Murasaki, Lady

Tallentyre, Stephen G. See: Merriman & Tallentyre

Talleyrand-Perigord, Charles Maurice, Prince de, 1754-1838
— Memoirs.... L: Grolier Society, [c.1900]. Connoisseur Ed, one of 75. 5 vols. 8vo, half mor gilt. sg Sept 11 (272) $425

Talleyrand-Perigord Library, Charles Maurice, Prince de
— [Sale Catalogue] Bibliotheca Splendid-

AMERICAN BOOK PRICES CURRENT

issima. A Catalogue.... L, 1816. 8vo, half calf gilt. L Dec 11 (25) £180

Tallis, John & Co.
See also: Gaspey, William
— History and Description of the Crystal Palace. L, [1851]. 3 vols. 4to, old half mor. K June 7 (96) $100

Tally-Ho, Ben. See: Alken, Henry

Tancred, George
— Historical Record of Medals and Honorary Distinctions.... L, 1891. 4to, half calf gilt; rubbed. pn Apr 23 (288) £90 [Drury]

Tanner, Henry Schenck
— A Description of the Canals and Rail Roads of the United States. NY, 1840. 8vo, cloth; soiled, worn; head of spine chpped. With 2 tipped-in profiles & folding color map. wa Nov 6 (90) $160
— A New American Atlas.... Phila., 1823. 1st Ed. Folio, bdg not described but broken. With 18 (of 22) double-page colored maps. Prelims torn & partly lacking; heavily foxed & soiled. wd June 19 (181) $650

Tanner, John, 1780?-1847
— A Narrative of the Captivity and Adventures of John Tanner...during Thirty Years Residence among the Indians. NY, 1830. Ed by Edwin James. 8vo, contemp bds; rebacked in cloth. sg Sept 18 (278) $350

Tans'ur, William, 1699?-1783
— The American Harmony; or Royal Melody Complete. Newbury-Port, 1771. 6th Ed. 2 vols in 1. Oblong 16mo, contemp calf. Vol I lacking 1 leaf; Vol II lacking 3 leaves; some leaves stained at top edge. sg Sept 18 (7) $90

Tapia y Salcedo, Gregorio, d.1671
— Exercicios de la ginet. Madrid: Diego Diaz, 1643. 8vo, contemp vellum; worn. Jeanson copy. SM Mar 1 (549) FF100,000

Tapisseries...
— Tapisseries du Roy, ou sont representez les quatre elements et les quatre saisons. Paris, 1670. Folio, contemp calf gilt, with arms of Louis XIV; spine restored, worn. HN Nov 26 (1175) DM700
  Anr copy. Modern mor. Lower half dampstained & many lower margins reinforced. S Sept 23 (402) £160 [Hetherington]

Taplin, William
— The Sportsman's Cabinet.... L, 1803-4. 2 vols. 4to, calf; lower cover of Vol I almost detached, spines worn, corners rubbed. Some foxing & staining. Lacking to the binder leaf at end. L July 2 (179) £190

Taraval, Sigismundo, 1700-63
— The Indian Uprising in Lower California, 1734-1737. Los Angeles: Quivira Society, 1931. One of 665. cb Jan 8 (194) $65

Tardif, Guillaume, b. c.1400
— L'Art de faulconerie. Et des chiens de chasse. Paris: pour Anthoine Verard, 17 Jan 1506. Bound with: Lozenne, Marechal de. La Medecine des cheuaulx et des bestes cheualines. Paris: Jehan trepperel, [c.1506] 4to, 18th-cent calf. Schwerdt-Jeanson copy. SM Mar 1 (550) FF200,000

Tarkington, Booth, 1869-1946
— The Gentleman from Indiana. NY, 1899. 1st Ed, 1st State. 8vo, orig cloth with ear of corn pointing down. ANs inserted. K Oct 4 (420) $130
— Penrod. Garden City, 1914. 1st Ed, 1st State. sg Dec 11 (119) $100
— Penrod and Sam. Garden City, 1916. 1st State. sg Dec 11 (120) $90

Anr copy. Illus by Worth Brehm. sg Dec 11 (120) $90

— Works. NY, 1918-32. Autograph Ed, one of 565. 27 vols. Half cloth. ha May 22 (81) $200

Tarleton, Sir Banastre, 1754-1833
— A History of the Campaigns of 1780 and 1781 in the Southern Provinces of North America. L, 1787. 4to, modern calf gilt. With folding map & 4 folding plans. 2 plans laid down on canvas, 2 torn & repaired. pnNY Sept 13 (294) $650

Tarling, Alan
— Will Carter, Printer: An Illustrated Study. L: Galahad Press, [1968]. One of 100. 4to, cloth. sg Jan 22 (91) $70

Tarpon...
— The Tarpon. By C. A. D. [N.p., early 20th cent]. Oblong 12mo, ptd wraps; rubbed. sg Oct 23 (516) $300

Tarrasch, Siegbert, 1862-1934
— Das Champion-Turnier zu Ostende im Jahre 1907. Leipzig, 1907. Orig wraps. pn Mar 26 (63) £60 [Furstenburg]

Tassie, James, 1735-99
— A Descriptive Catalogue of a General Collection of Ancient and Modern Engraved Gems.... L, 1791. 2 vols. 4to, half calf; broken. pn Sept 18 (302) £260 [Baldwin]

Tassin, Nicolas
— Les Plans et profils de toutes les principales villes et lieux considerables de France. Paris, 1634. 2 vols. Oblong 4to, contemp mor gilt, later arms added. Minor foxing. sg Apr 2 (197) $3,400

Tasso, Torquato, 1544-95
See also: Fore-Edge Paintings
— La Gerusalemme liberata. Genoa, 1617. Folio, 17th-cent mor gilt. With engraved title, frontis & 20 plates. C Dec 12 (308A) £350 [Pilo]

Anr copy. Vellum gilt; soiled. With 2 engraved titles & 20 plates. Lacking 1 leaf; dampstaining in lower margin of some leaves. S Sept 23 (403) £120 [Vine]

Anr copy. Later vellum; endpapers renewed. Some worming in inner margins, occasionally affecting illusts & text; 1st engraved title remargined. sg Mar 26 (269) $90

Anr Ed. Venice: Albrizzi, 1745. Illus by G. B. Piazzetta. Folio, contemp sheep. With engraved title, frontis, port & 20 plates. P Dec 15 (231) $4,500

Anr Ed. Venice: A. Groppo, 1760-61. ("Il Goffredo....") 2 vols. 4to, half vellum; worn. pnE Jan 28 (16) £340 [McKenzie]

Anr Ed. Paris, 1771. ("La Gierusalemme liberata.") 2 vols. 8vo, mor gilt, relieure de present designed by Gravelot, probably bound by Derome le jeune. On papier de Hollande. C Dec 3 (181) £1,800 [Stern]

Anr Ed. Paris: Didot l'aîné, [1784]. 2 vols. 4to, later calf; rubbed. With 40 plates. Some marginal tears. S Mar 10 (991) £170 [Robertshaw]

Anr copy. Lacking 1 plate; some marginal tears. S July 28 (1240) £90

Anr Ed. Parma, 1807. 2 vols. 4to, vellum gilt; soiled. Date altered on Vol II to read 1794. S Sept 23 (536) £150 [Smallwood]

— Ierusalem Libertada. Madrid, 1587. 4to, contemp calf; rubbed, head of spine chipped. Title soiled. cb Oct 23 (222) $85

Tate, Allen
— Reason in Madness. NY, [1941]. Alfred Kazin's annotated copy. sg Dec 11 (122) $60
— Stonewall Jackson; The Good Soldier. NY, 1928. sg Mar 5 (260) $150

Tattersall, Creassey Edward Cecil. See:
Kendrick & Tattersall

Tattersall, George
— The Cracks of the Day, Edited by Wildrake. L, 1844. 8vo, contemp mor gilt; rear hinge split. T June 18 (78) £220
— The Pictorial Gallery of English Race Horses. L, 1850. 8vo, orig cloth; soiled & rebacked with old spine preserved, new endpapers. Some plates stained; 1 plate torn. bba Sept 25 (318) £230 [Shapero]

Anr copy. With 73 plates. FD Dec 2 (3018) DM1,400

TATTERSALL

Anr copy. Half mor. sg May 21 (201) $400

Taubert, Sigfred
— Bibliopola. Hamburg, L & NY, 1966. 2 vols. Folio, orig cloth. bba Oct 16 (444) £45 [Hay Cinema]
Anr copy. Cloth. bba Feb 5 (34) £85 [Kuyper]; bba Feb 5 (72) £60 [Dawson]
Anr copy. Cloth; moderate wear. O June 16 (182) $50

Tauler, Johann
— Sermonen und historia. Leipzig: Conrad Kachelofen, 17 Mar 1498. Contemp pigskin over wooden bds. Occasional underlining in text. 1 leaf repaired, a few wormed or soiled. 290 leaves. Goff T-48. S Nov 27 (27) £4,800 [Goldschmidt]

Taullard, Alfredo
— El Mueble Colonial Sudamericano. Buenos Aires, 1947. 4to, modern cloth. Ck Oct 31 (132) £85

Taunton, Thomas Henry
— Portraits of Celebrated Racehorses of the Past and Present.... L, 1887-88. 4 vols. 4to, orig half mor. A few leaves detached. Ck Sept 5 (70) £400
Anr copy. Cloth; worn & stained. pnE Jan 28 (42) £320 [McKenzie]

Tavares de Velles Guerreiro, Joao
— Jornada que o Senhor Antonio de Albuquerque Coelho Governador...de Macao na China. [Macao, 1718]. 1st Ed. 8vo, calf. Ptd xylographically on 1 side of leaf only. "A fine copy". S Oct 23 (499) £16,000 [Israel]

Taverner, Eric —& Others
— Salmon Fishing. L, 1931. One of 275. With 7 orig flies mtd at end. Ck June 5 (54) £280
Anr copy. Orig mor gilt. S Nov 10 (624) £300 [Head]; sg Oct 23 (517) $475
Anr copy. Syn; chipped, spine damaged. wd Nov 12 (192) $150
— Trout Fishing from all Angles. L, 1929. With 30 specimen flies, bound in cloth folder. "A modern FAKE -- these flies were tied at a later date". sg Oct 23 (519) $225
One of 375. Orig mor. With 30 specimen flies on sunken mounts. Ck June 5 (53) £180
Anr copy. Orig mor gilt. S Nov 10 (625) £300 [Traylen]; sg Oct 23 (518) $500
Anr copy. Orig mor gilt; rubbed. T Oct 16 (405) £210
Anr Ed. Phila., [1929]. sg May 21 (202) $200

AMERICAN BOOK PRICES CURRENT

Tavernier, Jean Baptiste, 1605-89
— A Collection of Several Relations & Treatises.... L, 1680. 1st Ed in English. 2 parts in 1 vol. Folio contemp calf; rebacked & repaired, head of spine worn. With folding map (torn) & 8 folding plates. Some leaves with small marginal wormholes. C Dec 12 (264) £380 [Maggs]
— The Six Voyages.... L, 1678. Folio, contemp calf; restored & rebacked. With 25 plates & maps. Stain on upper margin of some leaves at end. C Dec 12 (263) £700 [Shapero]

Taylor, Archer
— Book Catalogues: Their Varieties and Uses. Chicago: Newberry Library, 1957. In d/j with piece chipped from spine. O June 16 (183) $50

Taylor, Bayard, 1825-78
— Eldorado, or Adventures in the Path of Empire. NY, 1850. 1st Ed. 2 vols. 12mo, orig cloth. With 8 plates. cb Mar 19 (251) $160
2d Ed. 2 vols. 12mo, orig cloth; stained, worn. With 8 plates. Marginal soiling or staining. cb Jan 8 (195) $50
8th Ed. NY, 1856. 12mo, orig cloth; worn & soiled. Foxed. wa Sept 25 (302) $50

Taylor, Deems
— Fantasia. NY, 1940. 4to, cloth. cb May 7 (430) $50; sg June 4 (117) $50

Taylor, Edward Samuel
— The History of Playing Cards. L, 1865. 8vo, orig cloth; rubbed & worn, split along front joint. Houdini's copy. cb Oct 23 (177) $100

Taylor, Frederick Winslow
— The Principles of Scientific Management. NY & L, 1911. wa Nov 6 (90) $160
1st Issue. K Mar 22 (344) $700
Ltd 1st Ed with foreword & appendix. P Sept 24 (410) $1,400

Taylor, George —& Skinner, Andrew
— Maps of the Roads of Ireland. L, 1778. 8vo, contemp half calf; worn & loose, spine def. bba Apr 9 (362) £120 [Catnach]
Anr copy. Lacking folding map; some soiling. bba Apr 9 (363) £80 [Franks]
Anr copy. Half lea. With engraved title, dedication & 284 maps only. Engraved title repaired & margin cut at top; lacking 4 maps & general map. L Dec 11 (240) £60
Anr copy. Contemp calf; rebacked & recornered. With engraved title, dedication, folding map & key & 288 road maps on 144 leaves. S Nov 17 (754) £220 [Swift]

Anr copy. Contemp calf gilt. With engraved title, folding general map (torn without loss), dedication with key verso, 6 leaves of tables & 288 strip maps ptd recto & verso. S July 28 (955) £280

— Survey and Maps of the Roads of North Britain or Scotland. L, 1776. Oblong folio, contemp half calf; worn, hinge broken. 1 map torn; some worming; tp marked. bba July 16 (99) £110 [Shapero]

Anr copy. Contemp calf; upper cover stabbed through to title & 1st map. Some short tears without loss. S July 28 (956) £150

Taylor, Jeremy, 1613-67. See: Fore-Edge Paintings

Taylor, John, 1753-1824

— The Identity of Junius, with a Distinguished Living Character Established.... NY, 1818. 8vo, contemp half sheep; broken. Extensively annotated by a mid-19th cent owner. sg Oct 9 (243) $200

— An Inquiry into the Principles and Policy of the Government of the United States.... Fredericksburg, 1814. 8vo, contemp calf; rubbed. Some foxing. O Oct 21 (175) $140

Taylor, Joseph, c.1761-1844

— Apparitions; or, The Mystery of Ghosts. L, 1814. 1st Ed. 12mo, orig bds; spine def, rubbed. Some stains & browning. bba Jan 15 (77) £55 [Murray-Hill]

Taylor, Samuel, Angler

— Angler in all its Branches.... L, 1800. 1st Ed. 8vo, contemp calf. pnE Dec 17 (321) £40 [McCormack]

Taylor, Thomas, fl.1715

— England Exactly Described. L, [1715]. 8vo, disbound. With engraved title & 41 folding county maps. England, Essex & Lancashire with tears at folds; a few maps shaved. C Oct 15 (103) £520 [Mackenzie]

Anr copy. Contemp calf. pn May 21 (406) £850 [Burgess Browning]

Anr copy. Calf; rebacked. With engraved title & 51 double-page maps hand-colored in outline. Oxfordshire from anr Atlas & annotated; some spotting. pn May 21 (407) £580 [Traylen]

Anr copy. With engraved title, 4 folding tables & 42 folding maps. pn May 21 (408) £620 [Burgess Browning]

Anr Ed. L: Thomas Bakewell, [1735?]. 8vo, disbound. With 40 (of 42) double-page colored county maps; lacking England & Ireland. S Jan 12 (67) £680 [Map]

Taylor, Thomas, 1758-1835

— A Dissertation on the Eleusinian and Bacchic Mysteries. L, [1790]. 8vo, 19th-cent half sheep. sg Oct 9 (327) $150

Taylor, W. Thomas —& Morris, Henry

— Twenty-One Years of Bird & Bull. [North Hills, Pa.]: Bird & Bull Press, 1980. One of 350. Half mor. With cloth folder containing Bird & Bull specimens & ephemera. sg Jan 8 (23) $150; sg Jan 8 (24) $100

Taylor, Zachary, 1784-1850

— Message of the President...Transmitting the Correspondence with General Taylor since the Commencement of Hostilities with Mexico.... Wash., 1847. 8vo, modern half calf. 29th Congress, 2d session, House Exec. Doc 119. cb Jan 8 (197) $55

Tchemerzine, Stephane & Avenir

— Bibliographie d'editions originales et rares d'auteurs francais des XVe, XVIe, XVIIe et XVIIIe siecles. Paris, 1927-33. One of 800. 10 vols. 8vo, half mor. bba Sept 25 (371) £320 [Alice]

Anr copy. Half lea; worn, some joints starting. sg May 14 (242) $500

Anr Ed. Paris, [1936]. 10 vols. 8vo, half lea; worn, some spine ends chipped. sg May 14 (243) $300

Tchigorin, Mikhail I. See: Chigorin, Mikhail I.

Tebbel, John William

— A History of Book Publishing in the United States. NY, 1972-81. 4 vols. 4to, cloth. cba Feb 5 (166) $80

Teerink, Herman

— A Bibliography of the Writings of Jonathan Swift. Phila.,. [1963]. 2d Ed. S July 13 (76) £110

Anr copy. In d/j. sg Jan 22 (293) $150; sg Jan 22 (294) $80

Teesdale, Henry

— New British Atlas. L, 1829. 4to, half calf gilt. With engraved title, 3 general maps (linen-backed) & 45 hand-colored county maps. pn May 21 (409) £480 [Burgess Browning]

Teirlinck, Herman, 1879-1967

— Ave. Antwerp, 1938. One of 100 on handmade paper. Illus by Frans Masereel. B Oct 7 (192) HF240

Teixeira da Mota, Avellinus. See: Cortesao & Teixeira da Mota

Telescope, Tom. See: Newton, Sir Isaac

Telford, Thomas, 1757-1834
— Life of Thomas Telford Civil Engineer. L, 1838. Atlas vol only. Half calf; def. With double-page map & 82 plates. Some dampstains to outer fore-edge. pn May 21 (272) £300

Tellier, Jules. See: Golden Cockerel Press

Tellier, N.
— Manuel du veneur.... Paris: au Menestrel, Heugel & Cie, [n.d.]. ("Nouveau Manuel du veneur....") 8vo, modern half shagreen. Jeanson copy. SM Mar 1 (552) FF1,600

Temminck, Coenraad Jacob
See also: Knip & Temminck
— Nouveau Recueil de planches coloriees d'oiseaux. Paris: F. G. Levrault, [1820]-38-[39]. 5 vols. Folio, contemp half mor; rubbed. With 600 hand-colored plates, some heightened in gold. Stain on 2 plates. S Oct 23 (722) £12,500 [Marshall]
— Verhandelingen over de Natuurlijke Geschiedenis der Nederlandsche overseesche bezittingen.... Leiden, 1839-44. Botanical vol only: Korthals' Verhandelingen over de natuurlijke geschiedenis der Nederlandsche overzeesche bezittigen... botanie. Folio, contemp mor gilt. With 2 plain & 68 hand-colored plates. Spotted badly in text & much less so in plates. Derby—de Belder copy. S Apr 27 (197) £1,400 [Minton]

Tempesta, Antonio
— Nuova Raccolta de li animali piu curiosi del mondo.... Rome, [c.1650?]. Oblong folio, half vellum; worn. With 206 plates only. Tear repaired in Plate 84. S Oct 23 (759) £600 [Shapero]

Tempesta, Antonio, 1550-1630
— Icones venatum species varias representantes. Frankfurt: de Bry, 1598. Bound with: Icones venantum species varias representantes. Frankfurt, 1656. 8vo, 19th-cent vellum. Jeanson copy. SM Mar 1 (553) FF8,000
— Venationes ferarum, avium, piscium pugnae bestiariorum et mutuae bestiarum delineatae. Amst.: Justus danckerts, [c.1627]. 4to, 19th-cent vellum. Jeanson copy. SM Mar 1 (555) FF9,500

Anr Ed. Amst.: Pieter Goos, [c.1627]. 4to, 19th-cent half vellum. With 30 plates. Jeanson copy. SM Mar 1 (556) FF7,500

Temple, Sir John, 1600-77
— The Irish Rebellion or, an History.... L, 1646. 1st Ed. 4to, modern half calf. Title & last leaf repaired; some browning. bba Apr 9 (301) £85 [Catnach]

Temple, Sir Richard
— Palestine Illustrated. L, 1888. 8vo, orig cloth; worn, rebacked, preserving most of orig spine. With 32 color plates, a few with minor adhesion. Sold w.a.f. O Jan 6 (183) $70

Temple, Sir William, 1628-99
— An Essay upon Taxes. L, 1693. 4to, wraps. S July 23 (464) £550 [Riley-Smith]
— Works. L, 1720. 2 vols. Folio, calf; def. B Feb 25 (638) HF320

Anr Ed. L, 1740. 2 vols. Folio contemp calf; rubbed. Some marginal soiling; lower margins of final leaves of Vol II wormed. Ck Nov 7 (69) £80

Tempsky, G. F. von
— Mitla: A Narrative of Incidents on...a Journey in Mexico, Guatemala.... L, 1858. 8vo, contemp calf; rebacked. With folding map & 14 plates, 5 colored. pn Mar 5 (44) £170 [Maggs]

Tench, Capt. Watkin
— A Narrative of the Expedition to Botany Bay. Dublin, 1789. 1st Dublin Ed. 8vo, disbound. Lacking final text leaf; final blank repaired. sg June 11 (395) $600
1st Ed. L, 1789. 8vo, later calf. Lacking all before title; tp soiled; some waterstains. CA Apr 12 (231) A$1,700

Tengler, Ulrich
— Der neue Layenspiegel vo rechtmaessigen ordnungen in Burgerlichen.... Strassburg, 1518. Folio, half lea. FD Dec 2 (98) DM5,800

Teniers, David, 1610-92
— Schilder-Thooneel.... Brussels & Antwerp, 1660. Folio, 19th-cent mor; rubbed. With 225 plates. SM Oct 20 (564) FF15,000

Tennant, Edward
— The Royal Deccan Horse in the Great War. Aldershot: Gale & Polden, [1939]. Half mor. cb Dec 18 (172) $50

Tennyson, Alfred, Lord, 1809-92
See also: Doves Press; Fore-Edge Paintings; Grabhorn Printing; Kelmscott Press
— The Cup and the Falcon. L, 1884. 1st Ed. 8vo, orig cloth. Inscr to Laura Tennant & with holograph notation on p 80 to see 7 additional lines of text on blank p 86. sg June 11 (396) $850
— Enoch Arden. L, 1864. 1st Ed. 8vo, orig cloth; rear cover puckered, front hinge cracked. Inscr to Harriet Wright. sg June 11 (397) $1,000
— Idylls of the King. L, 1868. Illus by Gustave Dore. Folio, contemp calf gilt; rubbed, upper joint weak. S Oct 6 (787) £60 [Studd]

— Poems. L, 1889. One of 100. Illus by Edward Lear. 4to, orig half mor. S July 13 (277) £720

— Poems, 1842. L, 1842. 1st Ed. 2 vols. 8vo, contemp calf. bba Dec 4 (98) £170 [Hannas]

— The Promise of May. L, 1882. 8vo, orig wraps; spine torn. Some soiling. Wise-Forman forgery. S Sept 22 (62) £220 [Jarndyce]

— Queen Mary, a Drama. L, 1875. 1st Ed. 8vo, orig cloth. Inscr to his son Hallam. sg June 11 (400) $750

— Song of the Brook. Bronxville: Valenti Angelo, [1959]. One of 50. Wraps over flexible bds. cb Dec 4 (329) $50

— The Throstle. L, 1889. 4 pp, 8vo, mor by Riviere. Esher copy. S Dec 18 (100) £300 [Maggsch]

— [Timbuctoo] Prolusiones Academicae.... Cambr : John Smith, [1829]. 1st Ed. 8vo, mor gilt, armorial bdg. sg June 11 (401) $300

— Tiresias, and other Poems. L, 1885. 1st Ed, 2d Issue, with ptr's imprint at foot of p 204. 8vo, orig cloth; corners bumped. Inscr to Frederic & Jane Locker-Lampson. sg June 11 (402) $1,100

— Works. L, 1870. 10 vols. 8vo, contemp mor. Ck June 5 (66) £60

Anr Ed. L, 1884. 7 vols. 8vo, half mor gilt by Zaehnsdorf. sg Sept 11 (273) $150

Anr Ed. Bost.: Estes & Lauriat, 1895-98. One of 1,000. 12 vols. 8vo, half mor gilt; worn. wa Feb 19 (94) $160

Anr Ed. L, 1898-99. One of 1,050. 12 vols. 8vo, contemp vellum with painted decoration depicting Arthur & Guinevere kneeling, by Chivers of Bath. S June 17 (295) £440 [Hannas]

Anr Ed. Bost., 1929. One of 500. 7 vols. Half mor. sg Sept 11 (274) $50

Terentius Afer, Publius, 185-159 B.C.
See also: Fore-Edge Paintings

— Andria. Verona: Bodoni, 1971. One of 160. 4to, orig half vellum gilt. HN Nov 26 (1616) DM820; pnNY Mar 12 (104) $400

— Le Comedie...volgare. Venice: Aldus, 1546. 8vo, 18th-cent mor gilt; rubbed. S Jan 16 (441) £95 [Bouchard]

— Comoediae. Venice: Aldus, 1575. 3 parts in 1 vol. 8vo, half vellum. Final blank with short tear. S Sept 23 (496) £70 [Poel]

Anr Ed. Paris, 1753. 2 vols. 12mo, contemp mor gilt. With 6 plates. FD Dec 2 (3841) DM2,600

Anr Ed. Edin., 1758. 12mo, late 18th-cent mor gilt by Roger Payne. Payne-Hoe copy. CNY May 11 (127) $2,500

Anr Ed. Birm.: Baskerville, 1772. 4to, mor gilt; scuffed. pnE Dec 17 (14) £85 [Traylen]

— Comoediae sex. Leiden, 1635. 12mo, contemp mor gilt extra. With engraved title. Lacking 16 pages of prelims. B Feb 25 (866) HF200

— Opera. Lyons: P. Mareschal & B. Chaussard, 30 May 1513. 4to, 16th-cent mor gilt. S May 21 (19) £500 [Newbury Library]

— Terentius cum quinque commentis.... Venice: Lazarum de Soardis, 1511. 8vo, later blindstamped vellum. Some dampstains & thumbprints; 1st 6 leaves possibly from anr copy; tp with small hole & early signatures. sg Mar 26 (271) $500

Terrace, Claude, 1867-1923
— Petit Solfege illustre. Paris: Libraires reunis, [1893]. Illus by Pierre Bonnard. 4to, orig bds. With 30 lithos. Gould copy. S June 17 (73) £750 [Zoffany]

Terrasse, Charles
— Bonnard. Paris, 1927. One of 200. 4to, orig wraps. S June 17 (3) £290 [Sims]

Terry, Ellen, 1847-1928
The Story of My Life. L, 1908. Orig cloth; spotted. Cut signature mtd to front pastedown. sg Feb 27 (216) $50

Tertius, Franciscus
— Austriacae gentis imaginum pars prima.... Innsbruck, 1569-[73]. 5 parts in 1 vol. Folio, contemp calf; rubbed, spine def, 1 hinge broken. With 5 engraved titles & 52 plates. Some plates trimmed; wormed at beginning & end affecting plates; some dampstains. S May 21 (80) £750 [Lanfranchi]

Tertullianus, Quintus Septimus Florens, 160?-230?
— Opera. [Basel: J. Froben, 1521]. Folio, contemp vellum over wooden bds. Corner of upper margin repaired in 2 leaves. pn Jan 22 (103) £270 [King]

Tesauro, Emmanuele, Conte
— Il Cannocchiale Aristotelico o sia idea dell'arguta et ingeniosa elocutione.... Turin: Bartolomeo Zavatta, 1670. Folio, contemp calf; worn, hinges cracked. With frontis & port. S Nov 10 (428) £120 [Quaritch]

— Il Cannocchiale Aristotelico.... Venice, 1696. 4to, contemp vellum. Lacking final blank; opening leaves dampstained in margins. sg Mar 26 (272) $225

— De Regno d'Italia sotto i barbari epitome.... Venice, 1672. 12mo, vellum bds. With 3 folding maps & 63 plates. Worming in some lower margins occasionally touching the lower line of text; short tear just touching the top edge of the plate on P11. S Mar 10 (1162) £95 [McKenzie]

Texier, Charles Felix Marie
— Description de l'Asie Mineure faite par ordre du Gouvernement Francais de 1833 a 1837. Paris, 1839-49. 3 vols. Folio, half cloth; worn. With map in 2 double-page sheets & 251 plates, 6 in color. Some spotting. pn Apr 30 (123) £2,100 [Martinos]

Thacher, James, 1754-1844
— Observations on Hydrophobia.... Plymouth, Mass., 1812. 8vo, old sheep; worn & rubbed. Considerable browning & foxing with marginal dampstaining. cb Oct 23 (223) $110

Thacher, John Boyd, 1847-1909
— The Continent of America.... NY, 1896. One of 250. Folio, half imitation vellum. sg Oct 2 (290) $150

Thackeray, William Makepeace, 1811-63
See also: Limited Editions Club
— Doctor Birch and his Young Friends. L, 1849. 1st Ed. 8vo, contemp cloth. With 14 hand-colored plates. cb Oct 23 (224) $50
   Anr copy. Calf gilt by Cross. With 16 hand-colored plates. sg Feb 12 (307) $50
— The English Humourists of the Eighteenth Century. L, 1853. 1st Ed. 8vo, calf gilt; worn & faded. Extra-illus with 29 engravings. wa Sept 25 (48a) £110
— Etchings...while at Cambridge.... L, 1878. 8vo, orig bds; soiled & chipped at corners. With engraved titles & 8 hand-colored plates. Tp browned. S July 13 (120) £90
— The Four Georges.... L, 1861. 1st English Ed in Book form, 1st Issue. 8vo, lev by Riviere, orig covers bound in. Lacking ads. O Oct 21 (176) $50
   Anr Ed. L, 1866. 8vo, calf gilt; spine rubbed, front joint split. Lacking frontis. Extra-illus with c.140 ports & views. sg Feb 12 (309) $120
— The Loving Ballad of Lord Bateman. L, 1839. 1st Ed, 2d Issue. Preface & notes by Charles Dickens; illus by George Cruikshank. 16mo, mor gilt, orig wraps bound in; soiled. S Oct 6 (783) £50 [Valentine]
— Mrs. Perkins's Ball. [L, 1847]. 1st Ed. 4to, mor gilt by Riviere, orig wraps bound in. With 22 colored plates. sg June 11 (403) $60
— Notes of a Journey from Cornhill to Grand Cairo. L, 1846. 1st Ed. 12mo, calf gilt by Cross. sg Feb 12 (305) $50
— Rebecca and Rowena.... L, 1850. 1st Ed in Book form. Illus by Richard Doyle. 12mo, half mor gilt, wraps bound in. With 8 colored plates. pn Nov 20 (98) £140 [Jarndyce]
   Anr copy. Half calf. wd June 19 (182) $100
— The Second Funeral of Napoleon.... L, 1841. 1st Ed. 16mo, lev extra with Imperial coat-of-arms, by Zaehnsdorf, orig front wrap bound in. C June 18 (229) £170
— Vanity Fair. L, 1848. 1st Ed in Book form, 1st Issue. 8vo, modern mor gilt by Sangorski & Sutcliffe. Final leaf of text with marginal tear not affecting text. S May 6 (448) £240 [Shimougush-Shobo]
   Anr copy. Half sheep gilt; worn. Foxed. sg Sept 11 (275) $110
   Anr copy. Half mor gilt by Tout. wa Dec 11 (356) $200
   Anr copy. Mor gilt by Root; spine ends chipped. Theodore Roosevelt's copy. wa Dec 11 (361) $100
   Issue not specified. In 2 vols. 8vo, mor gilt by Root and Son. With 48 plates. Extra-illus with 12 orig drawings by Kyd (J. Clayton Clarke). B Oct 7 (897) HF1,250
— The Virginians. L, 1857-59. 1st Ed. Orig 24 parts. 8vo, orig wraps; Part 1 rebacked. Plates foxed. sg June 11 (405) $120
   1st Ed in Book form. L, 1858-59. 2 vols. 8vo, contemp half calf. Some foxing throughout. O Mar 24 (181) $60

Thackrah, Charles Turner
— The Effects of the Principal Arts, Trades and Professions...on Health and Longevity.... L, 1831. 8vo, disbound. S May 28 (791) £650

Tharaud, Jerome & Jean
— La Fete Arabe. Paris, 1926. One of 300. Illus by Andre Sureda. 4to, mor gilt by Rene Kieffer. With 22 colored woodcuts by Sureda, engraved by Aubert. FD June 11 (5270) DM1,900
— La Maitresse servante. Paris, 1924. One of 300. 4to, mor by Paul Bonet with cubist design of light brown, chocolate brown & black mor onlays heightened with blind line, hatching & silver decoration & irregularly set with 10 lines of large circular onlays of green mor (Bonet, Carnets 1924-1971, no 70). CNY Dec 19 (13) $2,600

Thatcher, Benjamin B.
— A Retrospect of the Boston Tea-Party.... NY, 1834. 12mo, contemp half cloth; worn & soiled. Some foxing. wa Sept 25 (382) $50

Thayer, Emma Homan
— Wild Flowers of Colorado × Wild Flowers of the Pacific Coast. NY, [1885] & 1887. Together, 2 vols. 4to, cloth; worn & soiled, Vol I def. With 48 plates. sg Dec 18 (225) $120

Thayer, Gerald Handerson
— Concealing-Coloration in the Animal Kingdom. NY, 1909. 4to, cloth; rubbed. With 16 colored & 139 plain plates. cb Dec 4 (245) $95; sg Jan 15 (260) $80

Theatre. See: Le Clerc, Jean

Thelwall, Algernon Sydney
— The Iniquities of the Opium Trade with China. L, 1839. 12mo, orig cloth; rubbed & soiled. T Sept 18 (357) £52

Theobaldus Episcopus
— Physiologus Theobaldi Episconi, Bloomington: Indiana University Press, [1964]. One of 325. Illus by Rudy Bozzatti. Folio, unbound as issued. sg Jan 8 (215) $120

Theocritus, Bion & Moschus
Idylls
— 1922. - The Idyls. L; Riccardi Press One of 500. Trans by Andrew Lang; illus by W. Russell Flint. 2 vols. 4to, orig half cloth. S May 6 (122) £80 [Santin]

Theodoretus, Bishop of Cyrus
— Dialogi tres contra quasdam Haereses. Rome: P. de Nicolini, 1547. 4to, modern calf. With 2 leaves misbound; loosely inserted are 2 Ms fragments apparently from the orig bdg. S July 14 (443) £160

Theodosius II, Emperor of the East
— Codicis Theodosianis libri XVI. Basel: Henricus Petrus, Mar 1528. Folio, contemp bdg by the KL-LK Bidder of blind-stamped calf over wooden bds Henry VIII's copy with press mark of Royal Library on tp. S June 25 (57) £2,600

Theophrastus, d.c.287 B.C.
— Characteres Ethici, sive descriptiones morum Graece. Lyons: Franciscum le Preux, 1592. 8vo, old vellum; soiled. Small tears to K6 & 7. Ck Jan 30 (2) £95

De historia plantarum.... [Lyons, c.1505]. 8vo, contemp mor over pastebd; worn, spine wormed, ends chipped, loose. sg Mar 26 (273) $500

Anr Ed. Amst., 1644. Folio, modern half calf. Engraved title soiled & laid down; some stains; 2 leaves misbound; some worming affecting index. Ck Apr 24 (168) £350

Anr copy. Contemp vellum bds; spine torn at head. Paper loss in Xx6 affecting letters; some soiling. Crahan copy. P Nov 25 (449) $900

Theophylactus
— Enarrationes in epistolas S. Pauli. Rome: Udalricus Gallus, 25 Jan 1477. Folio, modern mor. Marginal repairs at beginning & end; 1 inner margin strengthened; modern ink initials washed or masked. 278 leaves. Goff T-156. bba Apr 23 (91) £900 [Thomas]

Thevenot, Jean de
— Les Voyages.... Amst., 1727. 5 vols. 12mo, contemp calf; joints split, rubbed. S May 29 (1065) £150

Thevenot, Melchisedec
— Relations de divers voyages curieux.... Paris, 1696. 2 vols. Folio, contemp calf, rebacked. With 10 folding maps & 27 plates, many folding. Part 2 of Vol I lacking prelim leaf O3 & a map of Pegu & Japan; 1 plate with numeral cropped; 1 map with neat corner repair; lacking frontises & possibly ptd titles to 5 sections. Without Routier des Indes orientales (9 pp), privilege (2 pp), explication de la carte de Telmar & the 3 final fragments listed by Brunet. Sold w.a.f. C Dec 12 (265) £1,700 [Israel]

Thibault, Jacques Anatole. See: France, Anatole

Thiberge
— Fanfares et tons de chasse ou manuel abrege du chasseur.... Paris, 1848. 8vo, half shagreen. Jeanson copy. SM Mar 1 (558) FF2,600

Thickenesse, Philip
[-] Memoirs and Anecdotes of.... L, 1788. 2 vols. 8vo, contemp half sheep; worn. C Dec 12 (204) £260 [Hannas]

Thicknesse, Philip
— Year's Journey through the Pays Bas; or, Austrian Netherlands. L, 1786. 2d Ed. 8vo, contemp half calf; rubbed. bba Nov 13 (136) £90 [Hannas]

Thiebaud, J.
— Bibliographie des ouvrages francais sur la chasse. Paris, 1934. Half shagreen by Saulnier. Inscr by Thiebaud & by E. Nourry to Marcel Jeanson & with Jeanson's annotations. SM Mar 1 (594) FF4,000

Thiers, Jean Baptiste, 1636-1703
— Traite des jeux et des divertissements.... Paris, 1686. 12mo, contemp calf gilt; corners & spine reinforced. bba Nov 13 (14) £65 [Poole]

— Traite des superstitions selon l'ecriture Sainte.... Paris: Antoine Dezallier, 1679. 8vo, 18th-cent mor gilt, armorial bdg. Piece cut from lower blank margin of tp & from

THIERS

last text leaf, affecting letters. S May 6 (577) £280 [Hannas]

Thiers, Louis Adolphe, 1797-1877
— History of the Consulate and the Empire of France under Napoleon. L, 1845-62. 20 vols in 10. 8vo, calf gilt. pn Sept 18 (7) £190 [Rogers]

Thiery, Augustin
— Histoire de la conquete de l'Angleterre par les Normands.... Paris, 1843. 5 vols. 8vo & oblong 4to, contemp calf; rubbed. bba Dec 4 (35) £60 [Hashimoto]

Thimm, Carl Albert
— A Complete Bibliography of Fencing and Duelling. L, 1896. 8vo, cloth; spine worn. sg Oct 2 (136) $110

Anr copy. Half mor; front joint starting. sg May 14 (363) $175

Thiout, Antoine
— Traite de l'horlogerie, mechanique et pratique. Paris, 1741. 4to, contemp calf; rubbed. With 91 folding plates. 1st title with tear. S Nov 10 (203) £480 [Phillips]

Thoinan, Ernest, Pseud.
— Les Relieurs francais (1500-1800). Paris, 1893. One of 20 on japon. 4to, mor, orig wraps bound in. C Dec 3 (40) £420 [Tenschert]

One of 650. Half lea; worn & shaken. sg May 14 (136) $130

Thom, Adam
— The Claims to the Oregon Territory Considered. L 1844. 4to, sewn. Slight soiling to tp & last page. cb Jan 8 (201) $70

Thomas a Kempis, Saint, 1380-1471
See also: Fore-Edge Paintings
— Contemptus mundi, nuevamente romancado. Seville, 1542. 8vo, old vellum; loose. Some stains. sg Oct 9 (46) $225
— De imitatione Christi. [Paris: Philippe Pigouchet for E., J. & G de Marnef, c.1491]. ("Imitatio Christi.") 8vo, 19th-cent vellum with yapp edges. Some inner margins strengthened with tissue; some dampstains, chiefly marginal. 96 leaves. Apparently unrecorded. P Sept 24 (169) $800

Anr Ed. Paris: Philippe Pigouchet, 15 July 1492. 8vo, modern mor gilt. Margins trimmed; some headlines shaved; some stains; tp replaced by extraneous leaf with full-page de Marnef device. 95 (of 96) leaves. Goff I-25. sg Dec 4 (196) $375

Anr Ed. Florence: Philippo di Giunta & Agnolo Cartolaio, 23 Jan 1509. ("Della imitatione di Giesu Xpo....") 4to, old calf; worn. Lacking tp; some soiling. S Nov 27 (129) £280 [Quaritch]

AMERICAN BOOK PRICES CURRENT

Anr Ed. Rouen, 1656. ("L'Imitation de Jesus-Christ.") Trans & paraphrased in verse by Pierre Corneille; illus by Chauveau. 4to, contemp mor gilt; lacking endpapers. pn Nov 20 (117) £95 [Lyon]
— Opera. Nuremberg: Caspar Hochfeder, 29 Nov 1494. Folio, 19th-cent calf, armorial bdg; edges & joints worn. Corner of B1 torn away, some dampstaining at beginning and end. 184 leaves; Goff T-352. S Nov 27 (239) £650 [Stewart]

Thomas Aquinas, Saint, 1225?-74
— Commentaria in omnes epistolas Sancti Pauli. Basel: M. Furter for W. Lachner, 1495. Folio, in Italian Rennaissance mor relief bdg. Sold as a bdg. 291 leaves only. Goff T-234. FD June 11 (154) DM26,500
— Expositio (Postilla) in Job. [Esslingen]: Conrad Fyner, 1474. Folio, contemp blindstamped pigskin over wooden bds; soiled & rubbed, lacking clasp & catch. A few upper margins dampstained. 107 leaves. Goff T-236. S Nov 27 (25) £4,800 [Abrams]

Thomas, Daniel
— Sali Herman. Sydney, 1971. One of 50. 4to, cloth, in d/j. CA Apr 12 (233) A$55

Thomas, Dylan, 1914-53
— Eighteen Poems. L: Fortune Press, 1934. 1st Ed, Issue not indicated. Inscr. pn Dec 11 (308) £700 [Rota]
— Twenty-Six Poems. L [ptd Verona, 1949]. One of 140. Folio, half cloth. Stamped "File" on the half-title & front free endpaper. S July 23 (195) £800 [Dylan]
— Under Milk Wood. L, 1954. In d/j. S July 13 (173) £160

Thomas, Sir Henry
— Early Spanish Bookbindings.... L, 1939. 4to, orig half cloth; rubbed. With erased stamp on front free endpaper & upper cover. bba Oct 16 (473) £54 [Quaritch]; bba Dec 4 (242) £65 [Oresich]

Anr copy. Perforated stamp on 1 margin. bba Feb 5 (92) £60 [Kuyper]

Anr copy. Perforated stamp on tp & 2 text leaves. bba Feb 5 (95) £65 [Hetherington]

Thomas, Isaiah, 1750-1831
— A Grammar of the Greek Language.... Bost.: Thomas & Andrews, Apr 1800. 12mo, contemp calf; rebacked, corners restored. sg Sept 18 (283) $110
— The History of Printing in America.... Worcester, 1810. 1st Ed. 2 vols. 8vo, contemp lea; spine & edges worn. Some browning & soiling to 1 vol. sg Sept 18 (281) $200

Thomas, Joseph B. See: Derrydale Press

Thomas, Lowell
— The First World Flight. Bost., 1925. One of 575, sgd. Half vellum, unopened. pnNY Sept 13 (295) $190

Thomas, Michael R. Oldfield. See: Sclater & Thomas

Thomas, Owen
— Agricultural and Pastoral Prospects of South Africa. L, 1904. Folding map mtd on rear free endpaper. Ghost-written by Frederick William Rolfe. sg Dec 11 (398) $225

Thomas, Pascoe
— A True and Impartial Journal of a Voyage to the South-Seas.... L, 1745. 8vo, modern mor by Stern & Dess. Some browning & foxing; later port of Anson inserted. O May 12 (187) $450

Thomas, William, d.1554
— Principal Rules of the Italian Grammar.... L, 1550. 4to, 18th-cent calf gilt; joints weak. Tp spotted; blank corner torn from 2D3; 2L3 & 4 misbound before 2L1; small hole in 2M4 just touching text; slight worming in 2N3-2O2 affecting text. S July 23 (8) £1,100 [Pickering]

Thomason Collection, George
— Catalogue of the Pamphlets, Books, Newspapers....Relating to the Civil War.... L, 1908. 2 vols. Library markings. bba Apr 23 (44) £90 [Clark]

Anr copy. H. M. Nixon's signature on flyleaves. bba June 18 (11) £120 [Hannas]

Anr copy. Shaken, spine ends nicked. 1 leaf torn in Vol 1. sg Oct 2 (71) $250

Thomassin, Simon
— Recueil des figures, groupes, thermes, fontaines...de Versailles. Paris, 1694. 8vo, contemp calf; rebacked with modern calf. With engraved title, engraved allegorical title & 218 plates. Lacking a folding plan. C May 13 (97) £200 [Weinreb]

Thomas-Stanford, Charles
— Early Editions of Euclid's Elements. L, 1926. 4to, half cloth. sg May 14 (605) $80

Thome, Otto Wilhelm
— Flora von Deutschland, Oesterreich und der Schweiz. L, 1904. 2 vols. 8vo, half mor gilt. With 322 colored plates. pn Jan 22 (114) £120

Thompson, Edward G. See: Woodward & Thompson

Thompson, George, d.1893
— Travels and Adventures in Southern Africa. L, 1827. 2 vols. 8vo, contemp calf; spine rubbed. With folding frontis, 20 plates, 2 folding maps & folding plan. SSA Oct 28 (907) R520

Thompson, Robert, Horticulturist
— The Gardener's Assistant. Glasgow, [1859]. 8vo, contemp half calf; worn. With 12 hand-colored plates. pnE Dec 12 (238) £55 [Greyfriars]

Anr Ed. L, 1909. 6 vols. B Feb 24 (506) HF200

Thompson, Ruth Plumly
— The Enchanted Island of Oz. [Kinderhook, Ill.]: The International Wizard of Oz Club, [1976]. Illus by Dick Martin. 4to, wraps. cb Sept 28 (114) $85
— The Giant Horse of Oz. Chicago, [1928]. 1st Ed, 1st State. cb Dec 4 (59) $100
— The Gnome King of Oz. Chicago, [1927]. 1st Ed. Emerald green cloth; bumped. Rear pages with half-inch tear on lower edge near hinge. cb Dec 4 (60) $60
— Grampa in Oz. Chicago, [1924]. 1st Ed, early state. cb Dec 4 (61) $65
— Handy Mandy in Oz. Chicago: Reilly & Lee, [1937]. Illus by John R. Neill. In d/j (issued later). cb Sept 28 (115) $200
— The Hungry Tiger of Oz. Chicago, [1926]. 1st Ed, earliest state. Lacking 1 plate. cb Dec 4 (62) $55
— Jack Pumpkinhead of Oz. Chicago, [1929]. 1st Ed. Cloth; rubbed, rear cover rippling slightly. cb Dec 4 (63) $75
— The Lost King of Oz. Chicago, [1925]. 1st Ed, early state, plates coated only on the ptd side. Contents shaken. cb Dec 4 (64) $60
— Ojo in Oz. Chicago, [1933]. 1st Ed. cb Dec 4 (65) $90
— Ozoplaning with the Wizard of Oz. Chicago: Reilly & Lee, [1938]. 1st Ed. Illus by John R. Neill. In creased & chipped d/j. cb Dec 4 (66) $150
— Pirates in Oz. Chicago, [1931]. 1st Ed. A few leaves marginally soiled. cb Dec 4 (67) $90
— The Purple Prince of Oz. Chicago, [1932]. 1st Ed. Lacking plate opposite p 24. cb Dec 4 (68) $80
— The Silver Princess in Oz. Chicago: Reilly & Lee, [1938]. 1st Ed. Illus by John R. Neill. Bdg rubbed & soiled. cb Dec 4 (69) $120
— Speedy in Oz. Chicago, [1934]. 1st Ed. cb Dec 4 (70) $70
— The Wishing Horse of Oz. Chicago, [1935]. 1st Ed. 1 plate with marginal chipping & detached. cb Dec 4 (71) $100

THOMPSON

— The Yellow Knight of Oz. Chicago, [1930]. 1st Ed. cb Dec 4 (72) $120

Thompson, Theophilus A.
— Chess Problems. Dubuque IA, 1873. Orig wraps. pn Mar 26 (336) £40 [Levine]

Thompson, William, 1805-52
— The English Flower Garden. L, 1852-53. 2 vols. 4to, orig cloth; soiled. With 23 colored plates. S Feb 23 (51) £180 [Shapero]

Thompson, Winfield M. —& Lawson, Thomas W.
— The Lawson History of the America's Cup. Bost., 1902. 4to, cloth; soiled & shaken. A few leaves loose. pn Jan 22 (182) £480 [Cavendish]

Thompson, Zadock
— Gazetteer of the State of Vermont. Montpelier, 1824. 12mo, modern cloth. With fold-out map & 3 plates. Foxed throughout. sg Mar 12 (256) $50

Thomson, Arthur S.
— The Story of New Zealand. L, 1859. 2 vols. 8vo, half mor gilt. pnE Jan 28 (158) £150 [Cole]

Thomson, James, 1700-48
See also: Fore-Edge Paintings
— The Castle of Indolence: an Allegorical Poem. L, 1748. 4to, mor gilt extra by the Club Bindery; rubbed, hinge cracked. With the leaf of explanation at the end. cb Oct 23 (225) $225

Anr copy. Modern half sheep; joints weak. sg Oct 9 (330) $60

— The Poetical Works. Glasgow: Andrew Foulis, 1784. 2 vols. Folio, modern cloth. sg Oct 9 (329) $70

— The Seasons. L, 1730. 4to, calf gilt; rubbed. With engraved plates. bba Nov 13 (215) £110 [Murray-Hill]

Anr copy. Bound with: Britannia. A Poem. L, 1730. contemp calf gilt; rebacked, some wear. With 5 plates. Tp & 1 other leaf with neat repair to blank margins. L Dec 11 (441) £80

Anr copy. Vellum c.1800 in the style of Edwards of Halifax. sg Apr 2 (199) $600

Anr Ed. L, 1793. Ed by Percival Stockdale. 8vo, calf. pnE Feb 17 (165) £70

Anr copy. Contemp calf; rebacked. With engraved title & 5 hand-colored plates. Marginal foxing. sg Mar 26 (274) $70

Anr Ed. Perth, 1793. 8vo, modern mor gilt. With engraved title, port & 6 plates. Extra-illus with 60 thematically related plates, either inlaid to size or mtd. sg Sept 11 (122) $175

AMERICAN BOOK PRICES CURRENT

Thomson, James, 1800-83
— Retreats: a Series of Designs.... L, 1833. 4to, modern half mor. With 41 plans & plates. Some staining. bba Sept 25 (300) £460 [Weinreb]

Thomson, John, Cartographer
— A New General Atlas. [Edin., 1814]. Folio, contemp calf gilt; worn. With engraved table & 40 double-page maps (of 74; lacking the World maps & the European section), hand-colored. S Oct 23 2178 £750 [Moncaron]

Anr Ed. Edin., 1817. Folio, contemp half russia; worn, lower joint cracked. With 74 hand-colored maps on 88 double-page sheets & 2 double-page plates of mountains & rivers. Some fold tears & creases. C Oct 15 (106) £700 [Nicholson]

Anr Ed. Edin., 1821. Folio, half mor gilt. With 76 double-page hand-colored maps. Some browning; 1 map torn. pn Oct 23 (413a) £920 [Berg]

Anr copy. Modern half mor. With engraved dedication, 2 engraved tables & 75 double-page mapsheets, hand-colored in wash & outline. A few creases; occasional dust-soiling. S Oct 23 (233) £800 [Burden]

Anr copy. Contemp half russia gilt; repaired. With 75 double-page mapsheets. Occasional marginal stains. S Nov 18 (973) £850 [Hayelstaum]

Thomson, Sir Joseph John
— Conduction of Electricity through Gases. Cambr., 1903. Soiled & worn. wa Nov 6 (37) $100

Thomson, Peter Gibson
— A Bibliography of the State of Ohio. Cincinnati, 1880. 4to, cloth; rebacked, shaken, crudely rehinged. sg Oct 2 (242) $150

Thomson, S. Harrison
— Latin Bookhands of the Later Middle Ages. Cambr., 1969. Folio, cloth, in d/j. sg Jan 22 (297) $90

Thomson, William Rodger, 1832-67. See: Bowler, Thomas William

Thorburn, Archibald
— British Birds. L, 1915-16. 4 vols. 4to, orig cloth; faded & rubbed. With 80 color plates. bba Oct 30 (428) £200 [Greyfriars]

Anr copy. 4 vols plus 1918 Supplement. 4to, orig cloth, Supplement in wraps. With 80 colored plates. pn Oct 23 (290) £480

Anr copy. Orig cloth; worn. With 82 colored plates. pn July 23 (158) £400 [Graham]; pnE Dec 17 (283) £370 [Marshall]

Anr Ed. L, 1916. 4 vols plus Supplement, L, 1918. 4to, orig cloth. With 82 colored plates. pn Sept 18 (76) £260 [Way]

Anr copy. 4 vols (without Supplement). 4to, orig cloth; worn. With 80 colored plates. pn Mar 5 (228) £300 [Grahame]

One of 105 L.p. copies. 4 vols plus 1918 Supplement. 4to, orig cloth. pn Oct 23 (289) £1,250 [Old Hall]

3d Ed of Vols I & II; 2d Ed of Vols II & IV. L, 1917-18. 4 vols. 4to, half mor. C Oct 15 (261) £400 [Thorp]

Anr Ed. L, 1918. 4 vols. 4to, orig cloth; dampstained. With 192 color plates. Haverschmidt copy. B Feb 24 (411) HF650

Anr Ed. L, 1925-26. 4 vols. With 192 color plates. Haverschmidt copy. B Feb 24 (412) HF475

Anr copy. In frayed d/js. bba Sept 25 (223) £50 [Keegan]

Anr copy. Extremities soiled. Ck Oct 17 (20) £80; Ck Nov 21 (118) £80; pn Sept 18 (19) £60 [Smith]; pn Jan 22 (70) £50 [Mackenzie]; T Jan 22 (92) £50

Anr Ed. L, 1931. 4 vols. With 192 colored plates. L Dec 11 (313) £70

Mixed Ed. L, 1931-26. 4 vols. In torn d/js. S July 28 (1127) £120

— British Mammals. L, 1920-21. 2 vols. 4to, orig cloth; rubbed & stained, newspaper cutting taped to front free endpaper of Vol I. bba Sept 25 (222) £190 [Greyfriars]

Anr copy. Orig cloth; rubbed. With 50 colored plates. bba Jan 15 (427) £180 [Greyfriars]

Anr copy. Modern half mor. Ck Sept 5 (152) £300

Anr copy. Cloth, in d/j; faded. With 50 color plates. pn Jan 22 (69) £280 [Graham Galleries]

Anr copy. Orig cloth; worn. With 50 colored plates. pn July 23 (159) £300 [McEwan]

Anr copy. Cloth. pnE Dec 17 (285) £200 [Grahams]

— Game Birds and Wild-Fowl of Great Britain and Ireland. L, 1923. Folio, orig cloth; worn. With 30 colored plates. pn July 23 (160) £360 [Graham]; pnE Dec 17 (284) £340 [Greyfriars]

Anr copy. Half mor gilt; spine scuffed. S Feb 24 (618) £320 [Grahams]

One of 155. Orig cloth; spine rubbed & faded. With 30 colored plates. Ck Jan 16 (129) £160

— A Naturalist's Sketch Book. L, 1919. 4to, orig cloth; bumped. With 36 plain & 24 colored plates. Ck Oct 31 (191) £160; pn Mar 5 (307) £230 [Sotheran]; pnE Oct 15 (58) £150; pnE Dec 17 (286) £200 [Greyfriars]

Anr copy. Half mor; joints cracked. sg Jan 15 (261) $300

Thoreau, Henry David, 1817-62
See also: Golden Cockerel Press

— Essay on Friendship. East Aurora, NY, 1903. One of 50 on Japan vellum. Folio, mor extra. wa Mar 5 (27) $330

— In the Maine Woods. Bost., 1864. 8vo, half calf. Lacking ads. sg Oct 23 (520) $80

— Walden. Bost., 1854. 1st Ed. 8vo, orig cloth; faded & rubbed, corners bumped. Ads dated June 1854. cb Oct 23 (226) $800

Anr Ed. Chicago, 1930. One of 1,000. Illus by Rudolph Ruzicka. 8vo, bds, unopened. cb Dec 4 (340) $85

— A Week on the Concord and Merrimack Rivers. Bost. & Cambr., 1849. 1st Ed. 8vo, orig cloth. sg Apr 2 (200) $3,400

Thoresby, Ralph, 1658-1725

— Ducatus Leodiensis: or, The Topography of...Leedes. Leeds, 1816. 2d Ed. 2 vols. Folio, contemp half calf gilt; hinges splitting. T Feb 19 (330) £95

Thornbury, Walter —& Walford, Edward

— Old and New London. L, [c.1880]. 6 vols. 4to, contemp half calf; worn & rubbed, 1 cover nearly detached. cb Oct 23 (137) $95

Anr copy. Contemp half calf; scuffed. Ck Feb 27 (150) £95

Anr Ed. L, 1897-98. In 6 vols. With: Thornbury & Walford. Greater London. 2 vols. Together, 8 vols bound in 4. 4to, half calf, rubbed. pn Mar 5 (76) £90

Thorndike, Lynn, 1882-1965

— A History of Magic and Experimental Science. NY, 1934-58. 8 vols. sg Jan 15 (375) $150; sg May 14 (634) $225

Thornhill, Richard Badham

— The Shooting Directory. L, 1804. 1st Ed, 1st Issue. 4to, half mor. With 3 folding tables, 1 plain & 7 colored plates. sg Oct 23 (521) $350

Thornton, Alfred, fl.1820

— Don Juan. L, 1821-22. 1st Ed. 2 vols. 8vo, mor gilt by Tout; joints rubbed. With 31 colored plates. S Sept 22 (279) £100 [Cox]

Thornton, Henry, 1760-1815

— An Enquiry into the Nature and Effects of the Paper Credit of Great Britain. L, 1802. 8vo, calf gilt, with Signet stamp; worn & repaired. P Sept 24 (412) $700

Thornton, Robert John

— A New Family Herbal. L, 1810. 1st Ed. 8vo, half mor. pnE Dec 17 (378) £110 [McNaughton]

— New Illustration of the Sexual System of...Linnaeus. Comprehending...The Temple of Flora.... L, [1799]-1807-[10]. 4to, later half calf; rubbed. With port of Linnaeus in Lapland dress, 24 ports of botanists & 31 plates ptd in colors & finished by hand. Plates 9, 11, 12, 13 & 24 are Buchanan's A plates; Plate 21 is engraved by Earlom; most plates are in Buchanan's 2d or 3d state. Lacking the 1st leaf of the engraved title, 1 dedication leaf & the half-title Select Plants; several plates show signs of cracking along the plate line; 3 plates strengthened on verso where this has occurred; Plates 9A & 13 with small pieces torn from blank margins; Plate 16 with marginal tear repaired; some stains & soiling of prelims & ports; 1st 2 engraved leaves repaired. Sold w.a.f. S Oct 23 (733) £28,000 [Robinson]

Anr copy. 3 parts in 1 vol. Folio, contemp russia gilt; rebacked preserving orig spine. With 31 hand-finished color plates to the Temple of Flora, preceded by 6 ports, 11 engraved calligraphic titles & half-titles & 6 engraved plates & tables. Northampton —de Belder copy. S Apr 28 (355) £170,000 [Israel]

— New Illustration of the Sexual System of...Linnaeus. L, [1799]. Vol I, Part 2 only. Folio, contemp bds, crudely rebacked with cloth. With 97 plates. sg Dec 18 (226) $1,000

— The Temple of Flora, or Garden of the Botanist. L, 1812 [plates dated 1798-1812; watermarked 1810]. 4to, contemp mor gilt; rebacked & corners renewed, lower cover worn. With engraved contents leaf, engraved title on 2 sheets, engraved dedication on 2 sheets, leaf of Select Plants & 31 colored plates, mostly in Dunthorne & Buchanan's later states except for the 10 plates issued in 1 state only & including their plates 9a, 11a, 12a & 24a proving later issue, but Plate 13 in 1st state. Foremargin of Flora dispensing her Favours renewed over image; Plate 16 with the right edge of platemark cracked & the sheet backed at right & left margins; Plate 17 similarly backed at right & left margins; Plate 28 with small repair to lower blank margin on verso; minor soiling. Sold w.a.f. Hunt copy. CNY Nov 21 (269) $30,000

Anr Ed. L, 1799-[1812]. 4to, contemp mor gilt; rebacked. With engraved title with vignette on 2 leaves, engraved list of plates, colored port of Linnaeus in Lapland Dress, colored stipple or aquatint plates of Flora & Cupid (Flora inserted on guard) & 28 colored plates, finished by hand, of which c.20 are in 1st state. With contemp mor label inside front cover stating that the work was presented by Sir Patrick Inglis to his grandniece on 14 Dec 1808 Sold w.a.f. C Oct 15 (262) £48,000 [Sotheran]

Anr Ed. L, 1812. 4to, modern half mor gilt by Sangorski & Sutcliffe; 1 corner rubbed. With engraved title with vignette on 2 leaves, colored frontis, 2 plain & 28 hand-finished colored plates. Title & plain plates foxed; imprint cropped from frontis & the plate of the Indian Reed; lacking ptd title & engraved dedication. S Oct 23 (762) £2,300 [Arader]

Anr Ed. L, 1951. Ed by G. Grigson & H. Buchanan. Folio, half cloth; worn. O Mar 24 (185) $70

Anr copy. Orig half coth, in d/j. pnE Dec 17 (237) £60 [Hughes]

Anr copy. Orig half cloth, in torn d/j. S Nov 10 (568) £80 [Traylen]

Anr copy. Orig half cloth, in d/j. S Nov 10 (569) £90 [McCarthy]

Thornton, Col. Thomas, 1757-1823

— Sporting Tour through the Northern Parts of England.... L, 1804. 4to, later mor; new endpapers. With 16 plates. pnE Dec 17 (355) £120 [Thin]

Anr copy. Contemp half mor gilt. With 16 plates 2 states, before & after letters. William Beckford's annotated copy. Jeanson 1500. SM Mar 1 (559) FF4,800

Thornton, William, Topographer

— The New, Complete, and Universal History, Description, and Survey of...London and Westminster. L, [1784]. Folio, contemp calf; ubbed, joints split. With 1 of the plates torn & repaired. bba Apr 23 (364) £170 [Axe]

Thoroton, Robert, 1623-78

— The Antiquities of Nottinghamshire. L, 1677. 1st Ed. Folio, early 19th-cent russia gilt, armorial bdg; rubbed. With 25 plates, maps & plans, some misbound. S Oct 23 (14) £300 [BAL]

Anr copy. Contemp calf; rubbed, joints broken, endpapers detached. With double-page map, 16 plates & 8 plates of arms on 4 leaves & a slip bearing coats-of-arms. Upper margins of first few leaves frayed. S May 29 (1019) £240

— Thoroton's History of Nottinghamshire. L, 1797. 3 vols. 4to, early 19th-cent mor gilt by Kalthoeber with his ticket, armorial bdg. Some discoloration. S Oct 23 (15) £480 [Traylen]

Thorowgood, Thomas

— Jewes in America, or Probabilities that the Americans are of that Race. L, 1650. 1st Ed. 4to, 19th-cent calf gilt; edges rubbed. Some minor holes & cropping, prelims dampstained; ptd instruction to bdr lost in bdg. CNY Dec 19 (82) $4,500

— Jews in America, or Probabilities, that those Indians ar Judaical.... L: for Henry Brome, 1160. 4to, mor gilt by Riviere. Port of Charles II bound as frontis; trimmed close with many shoulder notes & some headlines, numerals & catchwords cropped; 2D2 with rust hole just touching 1 letter; gathering F heavily washed, with some repairs & wormholes & evidently supplied. P May 13 (23) $3,250

— Vindiciae Judaeorum, or, a True Account of the Jews. L: for Henry Brome, 1660. 4o, 19th-cent calf gilt by J. Mackenzie. Imprint on tp, several signatures & catchwords & a few ptd marginalia cropped with loss, last 2 & last 3 lines lost on B3 & final page respectively & supplied on stubs in pen & ink; C3 with paper thin & 2 tears not affecting legibility; some dampstaining affecting upper portions of some leaves & upper cover. "Apparently the only recorded copy with the Latin title." Murphy-Eliot copy. CNY Dec 19 (83) $2,200

Thory, Claude Antoine. See: Redoute & Thory

Thou, Jacques Auguste de, 1553-1617

— Il Falconiere.... Venice, 1735. 4to, contemp vellum. Jeanson 1531. SM Mar 1 (561) FF1,300

— Hieracosophioy, sive de re accipitraria libri tres. Paris: M. Patisson et R. Estienne, 1584. 4to, contemp vellum gilt with arms of de Thou as a bachelor [Olivier 216, fer 1]. Some dampstaining of lower margin. Jeanson copy. SM Mar 1 (560) FF22,000

Thou, Nicolas de, Bishop of Chartres

— Les Ceremonies observees au sacre et Coronement du...Henri IIII. Paris: Jamet Mettayer & Pierre L'Huillier, 1594. Bound with: Ronsard, Pierre. Les Destinees de la France And: Le Juste Banissement des Jesuites. Paris, 1594-95. 4to, old vellum; hinges cracked. sg Oct 9 (226) $750

Thoumas, Charles Antoine

— Les Anciennes Armees Françaises. Paris, 1890. 2 vols. 4to, contemp half mor, orig wraps bound in; spine ends worn. Some foxing. sg Nov 20 (123) $130

Thrale, Hester Lynch Salusbury

— Letters to and from the late Samuel Johnson. See: Piozzi, Hester Lynch Thrale

Three...

— Three Erfurt Tales, 1497-1498. North Hills PA: Bird & Bull Press, 1962. One of 310. sg May 14 (533) $300

Threlkeld, Lancelot Edward

— An Australian Language as Spoken by the Awabakal, the People of Awaba or Lake Macquarie. Sydney, 1892. 8vo, mor gilt. With folding map. kh Mar 16 (504B) A$100

Throsby, John

— Select Views in Leicestershire from Original Drawings. Leicester & L, 1789-90. 2 vols. including Supplementary Vol. 4to, contemp half calf; worn. With engraved title (holed at inner margin), 79 plates & 1 folding map. Ck May 15 (125) £110

Thucydides, 471?-400? B.C.

See also: Ashendene Press

— De bello Peloponnesiaco, libri octo. [Treviso: Johannes Rubeus Vercellensis, 1483?]. Folio, contemp half calf; rebacked but broken, clasps lost. First quire loose & fore-edge of a2 frayed without loss; small stains on b2v & b8r; other scattered light stains, chiefly marginal; marginal worming; early marginalia; early Ms corrections in text on l6. 135 (of 136) leaves; lacking final blank. Goff T-359. P Sept 24 (217) $3,100

Anr Ed. Venice: Aldus, May 1502. Folio, 19th-cent mor gilt extra; extremities rubbed. Washed. A few margins strengthened or dampstained. P Dec 15 (232) $3,250

Anr Ed. Amst., 1731. Folio, half lea; back damaged. With frontis & 2 double-page maps. B Feb 25 (868) HF400

Thudichum, John Louis William — & Dupre, August

— A Treatise on the Origin, Nature and Varieties of Wine. L, 1872 [1871]. 8vo, orig cloth, rubbed, spine ends chipped & frayed, front free endpaper detached & chipped but present. Some foxing. cb July 30 (241) $110

Thumtack, Tom. See: Squires, Frederick

Thunberg, Carl Peter, 1743-1828

— Voyages au Japon. Paris, An IV [1796]. 4 vols. 4to, contemp calf; rubbed. With port & 28 plates. C Dec 12 (266) £440 [Perrin-Thomas]

Thurber, James

— Men, Women and Dogs. NY, [1943]. Inscr twice. sg Dec 11 (124) $175

THUYS

Thuys, J.
— Ars notariatus, dat is: conste ende stijl van notarischap.... Antwerp, 1590. 8vo, vellum; dust-soiled. Some stains. B Feb 25 (707) HF2,200

Thybourel, Francois. See: Appier & Thybourel

Thyraeus, Petrus
— Daemoniaci. Cologne, 1598. 2 parts in 1 vol. 4to, 19th-cent calf; rubbed. Library markings; dampstains at end. S July 14 (444) £130

Tibullus, Albius, 54?-18 B.C.
— Elegies. Amst. & Paris, 1776. Bound with: Bernard, Pierre Joseph. L'Art d'aimer et poesies diverses. 8vo, contemp mor gilt by Derome le jeune, with his ticket. C Dec 3 (182) £650 [Maggs]

Tieck, Ludwig
— Minnelieder aus dem Schwaebischen Zeitalter. Berlin, 1803. 8vo, contemp half lea gilt; worn & def. With engraved title & 2 plates. HN May 20 (1996) DM3,900

Tiffany, John K., 1843-97
— The Philatelical Library. A Catalogue of Stamp Publications.... St. Louis: Pvtly ptd, 1874. One of 150. 4to, contemp half mor. bba Oct 30 (501) £55 [Axe]

Tiffany, Louis Comfort
[-] The Art Work of Louis Comfort Tiffany. Garden City, 1914. One of 492 on japon vellum. 4to, syn gilt. sg June 4 (326) $750

Tight...
— Tight Lines and a Happy Landing. Anticosti, 1937. One of 300. Half cloth; worn. sg Oct 23 (170) $110

Tilander, Gunnar
— Glanures lexicographiques. Lund: C. Gleerup, 1932. 8vo, half shagreen. Jeanson copy. SM Mar 1 (595) FF800

Tiliobroga. See: Lindenbrog, Friedrich

Tilke, Max
— Orientalische Kostueme.... Berlin, 1923. 4to, cloth; worn. With 128 colored plates. pn Dec 11 (132) £90 [Egee]

AMERICAN BOOK PRICES CURRENT

Tilley, Frank
— Teapots and Tea. Newport, England, 1957. One of 1,000. 4to, orig cloth. bba Oct 30 (362) £40 [Nosbuesch]

Tilloch, Alexander
— The Mechanic's Oracle and Artisan's Laboratory.... L, 1825. 4to, contemp half lea gilt; joints cracked. With 28 plates. Some foxing. sg Jan 15 (376) $70

Timbs, John
— A Picturesque Promenade round Dorking. L, 1823. Modern half calf. Interleaved throughout. Author's own copy, with annotations in text. bba Feb 5 (390) £55 [Jarndyce]

Timlin, William M.
— The Ship that Sailed to Mars. L, [1923]. 4to, half vellum; worn & soiled, adhesion remnants to front pastedown. With calligraphic text & 48 colored plates. cb Sept 28 (1237) $475

Anr copy. Orig half vellum, in torn d/j. S May 6 (161) £240 [Frazer]

Timperley, Charles H.
— A Dictionary of Printers and Printing.... L, 1839. 8vo, orig cloth; rebacked, orig backstrip laid down, endpapers renewed, 1st gathering loose. sg Jan 22 (299) $200

Tindal, Nicholas. See: Rapin de Thoyras, Paul

Tindal, William, 1756-1804
— The History and Antiquities of the Abbey and Borough of Evesham. Evesham, 1794. 4to, modern half calf. With 7 plates. bba Aug 20 (517) £120 [Hay Cinema]

Tindale, Thomas K. & Harriett R.
— The Handmade Papers of Japan. Rutland, Vt., 1952. Foreword by Dard Hunter. 4 vols. 4to, orig wraps. wd June 19 (184) $2,800

Ting, Wallasse
— One-Cent Life. Berne, 1964. Folio, unsewn in orig cloth folder. HK Nov 4 (3087) DM1,600

Anr copy. Unsewn in orig cloth folder & d/j. S June 17 (292) £480 [Joseph]

Tinker Library, Chauncery Brewster
— The Tinker Library; Bibliographical Catalogue. New Haven, [1959]. One of 500. Compiled by Robert Metzdorf. sg Oct 2 (292) $90

Tipping, Henry Avray
— English Homes. L, 1920-34. 9 vols. Folio, cloth. One vol with library markings. S Mar 9 (651) £750 [Harrington]

Anr Ed. L, 1921-37. 9 vols. Folio, orig cloth; soiled, 1 vol shaken. S May 28 (918)

£550
Anr Ed. L, 1922. Vol I (of 9) only. Folio, cloth; worn. O Feb 24 (190) $70
— English Homes. Period II. L, 1924. Vol I (of 9) only. Folio, cloth; worn. O Feb 24 (191) $70

Tir...
— Le Tir a l'arc. [Paris, 1960]. One of 20 with a signed & numbered separate folder of the graphics on japon nacre. Illus by Georges Braque. 4to, unsewn in wraps. FD June 11 (4830) DM22,500

Tirel, Guillaume, called Taillevent
Le Viandier de Guillaume Tirel dit Taillevent.... Paris, 1892. One of 50 on Hollande. Ed by Baron Jerome Pichon & Georges Vicaire. 2 vols, including Supplement. 8vo, half mor. Westbury-Crahan copy. P Nov 25 (371) $450

Tissot, James Joseph Jacques
— The Life of Our Saviour Jesus Christ. L & Paris, 1897-98. 2 vols. Folio, contemp vellucent bdg by Cedric Chivers. S Dec 4 (223) £1,200 [Maggs]

Titford, William Jowit
— Sketches towards a Hortus Botanicus Americanus. L, 1811-12. 4to, orig cloth; rubbed. With colored frontis & 17 hand-colored plates. Frontis & title coming loose; tp & last few leaves spotted. S Apr 28 (356) £800 [Maggs]

Titsingh, Isaac
— Illustrations of Japan. L, 1822. 4to, cloth; soiled. With frontis & 12 plates, 1 folding, all hand-colored. Library stamps on titles & plates, some perforated; folding plate soiled, torn & repaired. bba Dec 18 (252) £720 [Isseido]

Tjader, Richard, 1869-1916
— The Big Game of Africa. NY, 1910. cb May 21 (253) $55; O June 9 (182) $50

Tobin, Lady Catherine
— The Land of Inheritance, or Bible Scenes Revisited. L, 1863 [1862]. 8vo, orig cloth; worn. With frontis & 8 plates. S Nov 10 (1077) £160 [Wood]
— Shadows of the East. L, 1855. 8vo, orig cloth; worn, spine partially def. With 3 hand-colored double-page maps & 17 plates. One plate loose & frayed. S Nov 10 (1076) £300 [Wood]
Anr copy. Cloth; front joint torn. With 17 tinted plates, 1 loose & 3 double-page maps hand-colored in outline. sg Nov 20 (167) $350

Tod, W. M.
— Farming. L, 1903. One of 150 on handmade paper. Vellum. With 8 plates; 1 mtd color plate duplicating frontis. sg Oct 30 (217) $275

Todd, Frank Morton
— The Story of the Exposition. NY, 1921. 5 vols. 4to, cloth; worn, edges soiled. cb Oct 9 (155) $110

Todd, James Henthorn
— Descriptive Remarks in Illuminations in Certain Ancient Irish Manuscripts. L, 1869. Folio, orig wraps; backstrip split. Some browning. sg Jan 22 (203) $110

Tofino de San Miguel, Vicente
— Atlas maritimo de Espana. Madrid, 1789. Vol I (of 2) only. Folio, contemp calf gilt; rubbed. With 30 charts, 28 double-page. Lacking the plan of Cadiz but including a plate showing coastal profiles in north western Africa; minor waterstains. S Apr 24 (207) £800 [Armuro]

Toke, Monroe Tsa. See: Grabhorn Printing

Toland, John, 1670-1722
— A Critical History of the Celtic Religion and Learning.... L, [1740?]. 8vo, orig bds, rubbed. bba Nov 13 (273) £80 [Catbach]
— The Life of John Milton.... L, 1699. 1st Ed. 8vo, contemp calf; rebacked. sg Oct 9 (272) $100

Toledano, Miguel
— Minerva Sacra. Madrid: Juan de la Cuesta, 1616. 8vo, modern vellum. Dampstained at beginning. sg Oct 9 (44) $400

Toledo Osorio y Mendoza, Fadrique de
— Feliz. Vitoria que ha tenido Don Fadrique de Toledo, General de la Real Armada.... Seville: Francisco de Lira, 1630. Folio, modern half mor. Palau 333530. S June 25 (321) £380

Tolfrey, Frederic
— The Sportsman in Canada. L, 1845. 2 vols. 8vo, half calf; edges worn. sg Oct 23 (522) $275

Tolkien, John Ronald Reuel
— The Fellowship of the Ring. L, 1953. Advance proof copy. Folding map in earliest state. cb Sept 28 (1241) $4,250
— The Hobbit. L, 1937. 1st Ed. 1st Ed. d/j with the misprint Dodgeson & with pbr's handwritten correction on rear flap, d/j repaired. cb Sept 28 (1242) $2,000
Anr copy. In d/j. S June 18 (495) £2,800 [Randolph]
1st American Ed. Bost., 1938. O June 9 (183) $70
— The Lord of the Rings. L, 1954-55. 1st Ed.

3 vols. In d/js. bba Oct 30 (270) £1,200 [Bologna]
Anr copy. In d/js. With ALs laid in. cb Sept 28 (1244) $3,250
Anr copy. Orig cloth, in d/js. Ck Dec 10 (360) £1,400
Anr copy. In d/js; soiled, 1 spine repaired. pnNY Sept 13 (296) $600
Anr copy. In slightly soiled d/js with a few short tears. S Dec 18 (182) £1,100 [Beres]
Anr copy. In d/js. S July 23 (198) £750 [Wendler]
2d impression of Vol I. In d/js. bba Aug 20 (169) £250 [Burton Garbett]
— The Return of the King. L, 1955. In d/j. With folding map at end. S Sept 22 (147) £60 [Libris Antik]

Tollenare, L. F. de
— Essai sur les Entraves que le commerce eprouve en Europe. Paris, 1820. 8vo, contemp calf with Signet stamp; rebacked & rubbed. Ms correction on 1st line of p 481; 1st gathering heavily spotted. P Sept 24 (413) $150

Tolstoy, Leo, 1828-1910
— Works. NY, 1923. 24 vols. Half mor gilt. sg Dec 4 (197) $600

Tom...
— Tom Thumb's Folio for Little Giants, to which is Prefixed an Abstract of the Life of Mr. Thumb.... Bost: Sold at the Bible & Heart in Cornhill, [c.1780]. 16mo, orig lower wrap. S Dec 5 (364) £2,600 [Schiller]

Tombleson, William
— Eighty Picturesque Views on the Thames and Medway. L, [1834]. 4to, contemp mor gilt. With engraved title, 79 plates & folding panorama. Some staining. Ck Feb 27 (81) £340
Anr copy. Modern half calf. Folding map torn & repaired; lacking tp. Sold w.a.f. CK May 15 (198) £250
Anr copy. Orig cloth; worn. With engraved title, frontis (stained) & 78 plates. pn Oct 23 (42) £380 [Lewis]
Anr copy. Half mor gilt. pn Dec 11 (84) £480 [Goodall]
Anr copy. Orig cloth; worn. With engraved title & 79 plates; lacking dedication. Dampstained at 1 corner. S Nov 17 (829) £300 [Boyd]
Anr copy. Contemp mor gilt. With engraved title, dedication & 79 plates. Marginal repair to 1 plate. S May 28 (919) £420

Tombleson, William —& Fearnside, William Gray
— The Upper Rhine. L, [1834]. 8vo, orig cloth; worn & stained. WIth engraved title, folding map & 69 plates. Marginal dampstains. T May 21 (230) £310
— Views of the Rhine. L, [1830-34]. 8vo, orig cloth. With engraved title, folding panorama & 68 plates. pn Sept 18 (105) £210 [Ortman]
Anr Ed. L, 1832. 8vo, orig cloth. With engraved title, 68 plates & folding panorama. Lacking half-title. B Feb 25 (809) HF650
Anr Ed. L, 1832-[34]. 2 vols, including The Upper Rhine. 8vo, modern cloth. bba Sept 25 (436) £200 [Mandl]
Anr copy. 8vo, contemp calf; rubbed. With engraved title & folding map.. bba Nov 13 (124) £220 [Hoff]
Anr copy. 2 vols, including The Upper Rhine. 8vo, contemp mor gilt. With engraved titles, folding map of the Upper Rhine & 136 plates. 3 plates detached; most of Rhine panorama torn away; apparently lacking a view at p 173. C Oct 15 (107) £520 [Gorwood]
Anr copy. 8vo, bdg not described but def. With engraved title, panorama & 62 plates only. Panorama torn & loose. Sold w.a.f. pn Sept 18 (253) £150 [Smith]
Anr copy. Half lea; rubbed. With engraved title, 69 plates & folding panorama. Some foxing. pn June 18 (60) £180 [Plinke]
Anr Ed. L, [c.1840]. 2 vols, including The Upper Rhine. 8vo, contemp half lea gilt; worn. With 139 plates, including titles, & 2 maps. HN Nov 26 (464) DM1,600

Tomes, Robert
— Panama in 1855.... NY, 1855. 16mo, orig cloth; spine ends worn. wa Sept 25 (461) $55

Tomes, Robert, 1817-82
— Battles of America by Sea and Land.... NY, [1861]. Vols I-III (of 8). 4to, half mor; rubbed. Some foxing. O Oct 21 (179) $150
— The War with the South.... NY, [1862]. 4to, half mor; worn & soiled. With 66 (of 70) plates. wa Mar 5 (371) $160
Anr Ed. NY: Virtue & Yorston, [1882-67]. 4to, contemp half calf; worn & scuffed. ha Dec 19 (115) $70

Tomkins, Peltro William. See: Ottley & Tomkins

Tomkinson, Geoffrey Stewart
— A Select Bibliography of the Principal Modern Presses.... L, 1928. One of 1,000. 4to, orig half cloth; worn & soiled, spine ends frayed, front hinge cracking. cb Sept 11 (218) $55

Anr copy. Half cloth; rubbed. sg June 11 (409) $70

Tomlinson, Charles, 1808-97
— Cyclopaedia of Useful Arts.... L & NY, 1854. 2 vols. 8vo, orig cloth; rubbed, frayed at top & bottom of spines. With 40 plates. T Feb 19 (406) £64
— Illustrations of the Useful Arts. The Manufacture of a Needle. L, 1855. 12mo, cloth. With 10 mtd specimens of needle wire in various states. Library markings. sg Oct 23 (523) $600

Tomlinson, Henry Major, 1873-1958
— The Sea and the Jungle. NY, 1930. Calf extra by Riviere. cb Feb 19 (263) $95

Toms, William Henry. See: Badeslade & Toms

Tone, Theobald Wolfe
— Life of Theobald Wolfe Tone. Wash., 1826. Ed by his son, William Theobald Tone. 2 vols. 8vo, half mor gilt. Rosebery copy. pn Nov 20 (149) £220 [Black]

Anr copy. Contemp half calf gilt. pn Nov 20 (150) £85 [Traylen]

Tooke, William
— History of Russia from the Foundation.... L, 1800. 1st Ed. 2 vols. 8vo, contemp calf gilt; joints rubbed, new endpapers. Some staining. bba Jan 15 (474) £80 [Frew Mackenzie]

Tooley, Ronald Vere
— Some English Books with Coloured Plates. L, 1935. 1st Ed. 4to, orig cloth; worn. sg Jan 22 (300) $60

Anr copy. Orig cloth; shaken. sg June 11 (410) $100

Anr Ed. NY, 1973. ("English Books with Coloured Plates.") In d/j. O Nov 18 (186) $80; O June 9 (184) $120

Tootell, Hugh, Pseud.
— The Church History of England.... Brussels [but England], 1737. 8 parts in 3 vols. folio, sheep gilt by Riviere. sg Oct 9 (331) $80

Tornieri, Lorenzo
— La Caccia della lepre poemetto. Parma: Bodoni, 1802. 16mo, contemp half mor with crowned monogram of Princesse Augusta Amelie de Bavaria, wife of Prince Eugene-Napoleon. Jeanson copy. SM Mar 1 (562) FF2,800

Torquemada, Antonio de
— Hexameron ou six journees contenans plusiers doctes discours.... Lyon: Anthoine de Harsy, 1582. 8vo, 19th-cent calf gilt. Jeanson copy. SM Mar 1 (563) FF3,400

Torre, Carlos
— Development of Chess Ability. NY, 1926. Orig wraps. Inscr. pn Mar 26 (260) £50 [DeLucia]

Torreblanca Villapando, Francisco
— Epitomes delictorum in quibus aperta.... Seville, 1618. 3 parts in 1 vol. Folio, old vellum. Browned; some worming, affecting text. sg Oct 9 (71) $225

Torrecilla, Andrew Avelino Salabert y Arteaga, Marques de la
— Indice de bibliografia hipica espanola y portuguesa.... Madrid, 1916-21. Folio, half lea, orig wraps bound in; spine worn. sg Oct 2 (134) $300

Torrens, Robert
— Colonisation of South Australia. L, 1835. 8vo, orig bds. With folding map. pnE Oct 15 (196) £220

Torrens, Robert, 1780-1864
— Colonisation of South Australia. L, 1835. 8vo, orig bds; broken. With folding map. CA Apr 12 (235) A$380
— An Essay on the External Corn Trade. L, 1815. 8vo, half calf with Signet stamp; spine & joints worn. P Sept 24 (415) $800

Torrente, Mariano, 1792-1856
— Bosquejo Economico Politico de la Isla de Cuba.... Madrid, 1852 & Havana, 1853. 2 vols. 8vo, contemp half calf; worn. Wormhole at extreme inner margin throughout Vol I; minor dampstains to top corner of some final leaves of Vol II. sg Sept 18 (71) $130

Torres y Pena, Joseph Antonio de & Santiago de
— Oracion que en la Solemne Fiesta de Accion de Gracias a Dio...por la Senaladas Victorias.... Bogota, 1809. 4to, later sheep inlaid with mor gilt; lacking free endpapers. sg Sept 18 (286) $60

Torrington, Otto M.
— A Catalogue of the Etchings of Levon West. NY, 1930. One of 810. sg Feb 5 (322) $300

Tory, Geofroy, 1480?-1533?. See: Grolier Club

Tott, Francois, Baron de
— Memoires...sur les Turcs et les Tartares. Amst., 1785. 4 parts in 2 vols. 8vo, modern calf. With 16 plates, all but 1 double-page. S July 14 (721) £240

Toulet, Paul Jean, 1867-1920
— Les Contrerimes. Paris, 1930. One of 301. Illus by J. E. Laboureur. 4to, in box by Creuzevault. With double suite of plates. SM Oct 20 (668) FF20,000

Tourchet de Boismele, Jean Baptiste —& Others
— Histoire generale de la marine. Paris, 1744-58. 3 vols. 4to, contemp calf; rubbed. Ck Jan 16 (79) £110

Tournefort, Joseph Pitton de
— Relation d'une voyage du Levant.... Amst., 1718. 2 vols in 1. 4to, contemp calf; upper joint split. With 89 maps & plates. Stamp on verso of 1st title. S Feb 23 (110) £290 [McKenzie]; S June 25 (345) £480 [Houle]
Anr Ed. Lyons, 1727. 3 vols. 8vo, contemp calf; rubbed. With 150 plates & maps only, 6 supplied in watercolor facsimile. Some plates cropped; 1 plate with hole with loss; a few plates torn. S Feb 24 (541) £150 [Broseghini]
— A Voyage into the Levant. L, 1718. 2 vols. 4to, contemp calf gilt, armorial bdg; rubbed. With folding map & 150 (of 152) plates. bba May 28 (329) £300 [Ad Orientem]

Toussaint, Franz. See: Golden Cockerel Press

Townley, Edward
— A Practical Treatise on Humanity to Honey-Bees.... NY, 1843. 18mo, orig cloth. Johannson copy. sg Jan 15 (170) $150

Townsend, John Kirk, 1809-51
— Narrative of a Journey Across the Rocky Mountains to the Columbia River.... Phila., 1839. 1st Ed. 8vo, orig cloth; spine ends chipped, backstrip torn. ha Sept 19 (192) $210

Townsend, P. S.
— Memoir of the Topography, Weather, and Diseases of the Bahama Islands. NY, 1826. Cloth. Inscr to his brother. sg Mar 12 (6) $150

Townshend, John
— The Universal Cook, or Lady's Complete Assistant.... L, 1773. 1st Ed. 8vo, contemp sheep; rubbed, joints cracked. Crahan copy. P Nov 25 (452) $900

Townson, Robert
— Travels in Hungary.... L, 1797. 4to, half mor; rubbed. With folding chart, folding map, hand-colored in outline & 16 plates. Map torn in folds. bba Dec 18 (253) £90 [Rainer]

Tractatus...
— Tractatus de expositione misteriorum misse Christi passionem figurantium. Augsburg: Johannes Froschauer, 1501. 4to, modern vellum gilt. Some dampstaining in center margins. 24 leaves, 37 & 17 lines; gothic letter. S Sept 23 (404) £140 [McMaul]

Tracy, Edward H. See: Hastie & Tracy

Tradivaux, Rene. See: Boylesve, Rene

Tragical History. See: Affecting...

Traite...
See also: Frezier, Amedee Francois
— Traite theorique et pratique du jeu des echecs, par une Societe d'Amateurs. Paris, 1775. Contemp calf gilt. Wormholes throughout last 20 leaves. pn Mar 26 (371) £130 [Farmer]
2d Ed. Paris, 1786. Contemp calf gilt. pn Mar 26 (372) £75 [Hoffman]

Transition...
— Transition. Paris, 1927-30, 1948-50. Nos 1-20 & New Series, Nos 1-6. Orig wraps; spine worn. T Oct 15 (65) £270

Trattinnick, Leopold
— Archiv der Gewaechskunde. Vienna, 1812-14. 2 vols in 3. 4to, contemp calf. With 296 plates. de Belder copy. S Apr 28 (358) £3,500 [Macdougall]
— Ausgemalte Tafeln aus dem Archiv der Gewaechskunde. Vienna, 1812-14. 4 vols in orig 40 parts. 4to, orig wraps. With 4 ports, 1 plain & 480 hand-colored plates. Marginal spotting. S Apr 28 (357) £13,500 [Book Service]
— Flora des Oesterreichischen Kaiserthumes. Vienna, 1816-20. 4to, contemp half calf. With 2 ports & 219 hand-colored plates. Some foxing of text. Armorial stamp of the Tetschner Bibliothek on verso of titles. de Belder copy. S Apr 28 (358) £4,200 [Krohn]
— Neue Arten von Pelargonien deutschen Ursprunges.... Vienna, 1825-43. 6 vols in 2. 8vo, contemp calf. With 263 hand-colored plates on 202 leaves (plate 197 was not published). de Belder copy. S Apr 28 (361) £5,000 [Krohn]
— Thesaurus botanicus. Vienna, [1805]-19. Folio, 19th-cent cloth; rubbed, Ms index in red ink on back free endpaper. With 80 hand-colored plates. de Belder copy. S Apr 28 (360) £20,000 [Burgess Browning]

Travers, Benjamin, 1783-1858. See: Cooper & Travers

Travers, William T. L., 1819-1903. See: Barraud & Travers

Travies, Edouard
— Les Oiseaux les plus remarquables par leurs formes et leurs couleurs.... Paris & L, [c.1857]. Folio, half mor, orig upper wrap bound in. With 42 (of 79) hand-colored plates only. Some foxing or smudging; Plates 17 & 41 slightly mildewed. P June 18 (197) $12,000
— La Venerie* La Chasse. Paris: Ledot, [c.1850]. 2 parts in 1 vol. Folio, half shagreen. With 25 hand-colored lithos in Part 1 & 11 hand-colored lithos in Part 2. SM Mar 1 (566) FF260,000

Treatise. See: Colquhoun, Patrick; Hume, David

Trebeck, George. See: Moorcroft & Trebeck

Trechslin, Anne Marie —& Coggiatti, Stelvio
— Old Garden Roses. Berne: Editions Le Moulin, 1975. One of 250 hors commerce. Folio, orig wraps (plates mtd on same paper). Hunt copy. CNY Nov 21 (270) $450

Tredgold, Thomas
— The Steam Engine, comprising an Account of its Invention.... L, 1827. 4to, contemp calf. With 20 plates. Tp creased; 1 plate with small ink spot. C Dec 12 (208) £380 [Quaritch]

Anr copy. Orig bds; broken, soiled. wa Nov 6 (262) $170

Tremaine, Marie. See: Staton & Tremaine

Trembley, Abraham, 1700-84
— Memoires pour servir a l'histoire d'un genre de polypes d'eau douce.... Leiden, 1744. 2 vols. 8vo, half calf; hinges rubbed. With 13 folding plates. S May 28 (796) £160

Trench, Richard Chenevix. See: Fore-Edge Paintings

Trenkwald, Hermann. See: Sarre & Trenkwald

Tresham, Henry —& Others
— The British Gallery of Pictures.... L, 1818. Folio, contemp russia gilt; spine ends & corners worn. With 25 plates. Some foxing. sg June 18 (249) $225

Trew, Abdias. See: Velsch, Georg Hieronymus

Trew, Christoph Jakob
— Plantae rariores quas maximam partem ipse in horto domestico.... Nuremberg, 1763. Folio, 19th-cent mor gilt; rubbed, hinges reinforced. With 10 hand-colored plates. Some soiling. Vilmorin—de Belder copy. S Apr 28 (365) £3,000 [Israel]

Anr Ed. Nuremberg, 1763-79. 2 parts in 1 vol. Folio, contemp bds; backstrip def,

loose. With 1 double-page & 19 single-page plates in Part 1 & with 10 single-page plates in 2d part Extreme fore-edges of 1st 8 plates slightly browned & chipped. Without Decas III. sg Dec 4 (198) $3,600

— Plantae selectae. Augsburg, 1750-73. 3 vols in 1. Folio, contemp calf; rebacked, retaining orig spine. With 180 hand-colored plates. Short tear in lower margin of Plate 61/62; a few leaves of text lightly discolored. Horticultural Society of New York—de Belder copy. S Apr 28 (362) £280,000 [Brendz]

Anr Ed. Augsburg, 1750-92. 12 parts. Folio, unbound or in contemp bds. With 10 engraved titles (in red, black & gold) 4 ports & 120 hand-colored plates. de Belder copy. S Apr 28 (363) £90,000 [Israel]

— Uitgezochte Planten. Amst.: J. C. Sepp, [1769]-71-[74]. Folio, contemp calf gilt; repaired at head & foot. With 100 hand-colored plates with captions in gold. de Belder copy. S Apr 28 (364) £26,000 [Sourget]

Treyazychnaya...
— Treyazychnaya Kinga; Lesebuch in drei Sprachen; Le Livre en Trois Langues. Riga, 1786. 4to, contemp calf. Some discoloration. S Dec 5 (361) £380 [Glendale]

Triggs, Henry Inigo
— Formal Gardens in England and Scotland. L, 1902. 2 vols in one. Folio half mor; rubbed. O Feb 24 (193) $160

Trimen, Roland —& Bowker, J. H.
— South-African Butterflies. L, 1887-89. 3 vols. 8vo, half mor. Some spotting at beginning & end. Vols I & III inscr. S May 28 (602) £190

Trimmer, Sarah
— The Guardian of Education, a Periodical Work.... L, 1802-6. 5 vols 8vo, contemp calf; rubbed, 1 vol worn. bba Sept 25 (117) £600 [Quaritch]

Trinius, Charles. See: Liboschitz & Trinius

Trismosin, Salomon, Pseud.
— La Toyson d'or, ou la fleur des tresors.... Paris: Charles Sevestre, 1613. Bound with: Meung, Jean de. Le miroir d'alquimie. Paris: Charles Sevestre, 1612. 8vo, 18th-cent mor gilt. With 22 woodcuts in 1st work, all colored by a contemp hand. S Nov 27 (130) £1,450 [Biblioteca Hermetica]

TRISSINO

Trissino, Giovanni Giorgio, 1478-1550

— Dialogo del Trissino intitulato il Castellano.... [Vicenza: T. Janiculo da Bressa, 1529]. Folio, modern half mor. First & last leaf discolored. S May 21 (82) £600 [Maggs]

— La Poetica. Vicenza: Tolomeo Ianiculo, Apr 1529. Bound with: Dante Alighieri. - De la volgare eloquenzia. Vicenza, 1529. And: Trissino. - Dialogo initulato il Castellano.... 4to, 18th-cent calf gilt; edges worn. One leaf misbound, upper portion of text dampstained. S Nov 27 (236) £1,500 [DeZayas]

Anr copy. Folio, new vellum. S May 21 (83) £400 [Thomas]

Anr copy. Old vellum bds; new endpapers. S May 21 (84) £450 [Thomas]

— La Sophonisba. Vicenza: Tolomeo Ianiculo, 1529. 8vo, vellum. Some leaves soiled. S Sept 23 (498) £220 [Pampolay]

Tristram, W. Outram

— Coaching Days and Coaching Ways. L, 1888. Illus by Herbert Railton & Hugh Thomson. 4to, orig cloth; rubbed. bba Oct 16 (224) £60 [Brailey]

Anr copy. Cloth; worn. O Feb 24 (194) $60

Anr copy. Mor gilt. sg Feb 12 (311) $200

Tritheim, Johann. See: Trithemius, Joannes

Trithemius, Joannes, 1462-1516

— Polygraphiae libri sex. [Oppenheim: J. Koebel], 1518. 2 parts in 1 vol. Folio, 16th-cent half calf; rubbed. Some worming, slightly affecting text; lower outer corners stained, lower margin excised from B1, first a6 supplied from a shorter copy; lacking Part 1 title & blank r6. sg Jan 15 (377) $275

— Polygraphie et universelle escriture cabalistique.... Paris: Kerver, 1561. 1st Ed in French. 4to, calf gilt, with arms of the Gramont family added. With 13 woodcuts with movable parts. Strip on M5 recto is folded & this figure is slightly shaved at outer margin. S May 21 (81) £1,850 [Kraus]

— Steganographia: hoc est: ars per occultam scripturam animi voluntatem absentibus.... Darmstadt, 1621. 3 parts in 1 vol. 4to, later vellum. Last few leaves stained. S Mar 10 (1168) £420 [Hesketh]

Trittenheim, Johannes. See: Trithemius, Joannes

AMERICAN BOOK PRICES CURRENT

Troil, Uno von, 1746-1803

— Letters on Iceland. L, 1780. 8vo, contemp calf; worn, broken. Library markings. Sold w.a.f. sg Mar 26 (276) $50

Troili, Giulio

— Paradossi per pratticare la prospettiva senza saperla.... Bologna, 1683. 3 parts in 1 vol. Folio, lea. HK Nov 4 (2152) DM2,500

Trois...

— Les Trois Muses Reunies; recueil agreable de chansons anacreontiques, romances, ariettes, vaudevilles, et airs d'operas. Paris, [n.d.]. 12mo, French Revolutionary red mor bdg with liberty bonnet cornerpieces & the initials of Therovique de Mericourt on covers. C Dec 3 (89) £950 [Sourget]

Troisieme...

— Troisieme Tournoi international d'echecs. Moscow, 1936. Orig cloth. Text & added tp in Russian. pn Mar 26 (91) £75 [Brandreth]

Trollope, Anthony, 1815-82

— Barchester Novels. Stratford: Shakespeare Head Press, 1929. One of 525. Ed by Michael Sadleir. 14 vols. ha May 22 (84) $550

— Can You Forgive Her? L, 1864-65. 1st Ed in Book form. 2 vols. 8vo, modern half calf. Lacking half-titles. S May 6 (449) £60 [Hannas]

— An Editor's Tales. L, 1870. 1st Ed. 8vo, modern half mor gilt by Root. Lacking initial blank. S Jan 13 (529) £100 [McKenzie]

— Framley Parsonage. L, 1861. 1st Ed in Book form. 3 vols. 8vo, orig cloth; worn, library label on upper cover of Vol II, 1 hinge split. pn Sept 18 (124) £80 [Scott]

— He Knew He Was Right. L, 1869. 1st English Ed in Book form. 2 vols. 8vo, later half calf; 2 joints repaired. Spotted. bba Mar 12 (168) £40 [Scott]

— How the "Mastiffs" Went to Iceland. L, 1878. 1st Ed. 4to, orig cloth. pn Mar 5 (46) £230

— The Last Chronicle of Barset. L, 1867. 1st English Ed in Book form. 2 vols. 8vo, half calf by Hale of Berkeley Square. bba Mar 26 (219) £90 [Peters]

— Orley Farm. L, 1862. 1st Ed in Book form, 1st Issue. 2 vols. 8vo, later half mor; worn. With 40 plates by J. E. Millais. O Sept 23 (181) $60

— Phineas Finn. L, 1869. 1st English Ed in Book form. 2 vols. 8vo, orig cloth; rebacked perserving orig spines. bba Mar 12 (167) £80 [Marin]

— The Prime Minister. L, 1876. 1st English Ed in Book form. 4 vols in 2. 8vo, contemp

half calf; rubbed. cb Feb 19 (265) $55
— The Three Clerks. L, 1858. 3 vols. 8vo, contemp half lea; worn, Vol I joints cracked, spine chipped at foot. sg Feb 12 (312) $175
— The Way We Live Now. L, 1875 [1874-75]. 1st Ed in Book form. 2 vols. 8vo, orig cloth; soiled. Lacking half titles; 2 titles & 2 contents leaves from smaller copies. pn Jan 22 (157) £95 [Burmester]
— The West Indies and the Spanish Main. L, 1859. 1st Ed. 8vo, contemp calf. With hand-colored litho map. Ck Sept 26 (54) £130
— Works. Stratford: Shakespeare Head Press, 1929. ("Barchester Novels.") One of 525. Ed by Michael Sadleir. 14 vols. Orig cloth. S May 28 (920) £440
Anr Ed. L, 1948-54. 15 vols. In d/js. Ck June 19 (177) £280

Trollope, Frances, 1780-1863
— The Refugee in America. L, 1932. 3 vols. 12mo, orig bds; head of 1 spine chipped. O Nov 18 (187) $110

Trollope, Thomas Adolphus, 1774-1835
— A Summer in Britanny. L, 1840. 1st Ed. Ed by Frances Trollope. 8vo, recent half mor. T Apr 16 (12) £55

Trotter, William Edward
See also: Fearnside & Harral
— Select Illustrated Topography of Thirty Miles Round London. L, 1839. 8vo, orig cloth. With engraved title, map & 33 plates. pn Mar 5 (81L) £80 [Walford]

Troupes...
— Troupes Francaises (Premier Empire). Paris: Martinet, 1807-14. 2 vols. 8vo, contemp mor; worn. With 227 (of 296) hand-colored plates. Without title or text. S June 25 (209) £2,400

True...
— A True Relation of Divers Great Defeats Given Against the Rebells of Ireland.... L, 1642. 1st Ed. 4to, half mor. Folding map def & repaired; library markings. bba Apr 9 (300) £120 [Catnach]
— A True Transcript and Publication of His Majesties Letters Pattent. For an Office to be erected, and called the Publicke Register for generall Commerce. L: John Budge, 1611. 4to, half calf. S July 24 (463) £1,00 [Drury]
— The True Way of Preserving and Candying, and Making Several Sorts of Sweet-Meats.... L, 1695. 8vo, contemp sheep gilt; broken & worn. Minor foxing; G2-7 loose; thumbed. P Nov 25 (448) $550

True, Frederick W.
— The Whalebone Whales of the Western North Atlantic. Wash.: Smithsonian, 1904. 4to, cloth; worn & soiled. wa Nov 6 (265) $50

Truefit, Henry Paul
— New Views on Baldness. L, 1863. 12mo, orig cloth; rubbed. Some spotting; tp becoming loose. bba Aug 28 (137) £60 [Bickersteth]

Truesdell, Stephen Riggs
— The Rifle: Its development for Big Game Hunting. Harrisburg: Military Service Publishing Co, 1947. In chipped & soiled d/j. wa Nov 6 (183) $80

Truesdell, Winfred Porter
— Engraved and Lithographed Portraits of Abraham Lincoln. Champlain: Pvtly ptd at Troutsdale Press, 1933. One of 200 on "suede laid" paper. Vol II [all pbd]. 4to, bds. ha Nov 7 (24) $275

Trumbull, Henry, Jr.
— History of the Discovery of America.... Brooklyn, [1802]. 8vo, later half mor. With frontis & 17 plates & 2 added maps. Frontis repaired; browned & foxed. sg Sept 18 (287) $110

Trusler, John, 1735-1820
— Hogarth Moralised.... L, 1831. 8vo, recent half mor. Some foxing & dampstaining. cb Oct 23 (115) $65
— The Honours of the Table.... Bath, 1803. 3d Ed. 12mo, later half lea; worn. Some stains. bba Jan 15 (72) £95 [Korn]

Tryon, Thomas, 1634-1703
— The Way to Health.... L: Andrew Sowle, 1683. 8vo, old sheep; broken. Marginal worming at end; some browning. Crahan copy. P Nov 25 (454) $550
— The Way to Save Wealth.... L: G. Conyers, [c.1695]. 12mo, contemp half calf. Loss of text in E2 recto; some browning. Crahan copy. P Nov 25 (456) $350

Tseng Hien-ch'i. See: Hoyt Collection, Charles B.

Tucker, Ethelyn Maria. See: Arnold Arboretum

Tucker, Wilson
— The Long Loud Silence. NY: Rinehart, [1952]. In worn d/j with tear at bottom front. Inscr. cb Sept 28 (1252) $75

Tuckerman, Henry T., 1813-71
— The Character and Portraits of Washington. NY, 1859. Out-of-series copy. 4to, later half calf. Some foxing. wa Sept 25 (409) $160

Tuckey, James Kingston, 1776-1816
— An Account of a Voyage to Establish a Colony at Port Philip in Bass's Strait. L, 1805. 8vo, orig lea. kh Mar 16 (507B) A$3,300

Anr Ed. Melbourne, 1974. One of 500. Lea. kh Mar 16 (507) A$120

— Narrative of an Expedition to Explore the River Zaire. L, 1818. 1st Ed. 4to, contemp calf; rebacked. FD Dec 2 (1056) DM1,600

Tudal, Antoine
— Souspente. Paris, 1945. One of 125. 4to, orig wraps. With colored litho by Georges Braque. S June 17 (76) £440 [Dennistoun]

Tudor, Henry
— Narrative of a Tour in North America.... L, 1834. 2 vols. 12mo, orig cloth; stained or spotted. sg Mar 12 (251) $110

Tuer, Andrew White, 1838-1900
— The Follies and Fashions of our Grandfathers.... L, 1886-87. One of 250 L.p. copies. 8vo, contemp half mor; rubbed. cb Oct 23 (227) $190

— Forgotten Children's Books. L, 1898-99. 1st Ed, One of 112 L.p. copies. 8vo, cloth; broken. Inscr & with 2 A Ls s. O Apr 28 (193) $55

— History of the Horn-Book. L, 1896. 2 vols. 4to, orig vellum gilt. With 7 facsimile horn books & 1 actual horn book in end pocket. C July 22 (208) £320

Anr copy. Vellum gilt; soiled. With the complete set of 7 facsimile horn-books & battledores. S June 18 (497) £250 [Subunso]

Tull, Jethro, 1671-1741
— The New Horse-Houghing Husbandry.... Dublin: A. Rhames et al, 1733. ("The Horse-Hoing Husbandry....") 8vo, contemp calf; rebacked in mor, orig endleaves preserved. With 6 folding plates. Hunt copy. CNY Nov 21 (273) $340

Anr Ed. L, 1733. 2 parts in 1 vol, including 1740 Supplement. Folio, contemp calf; front endpaper detached, joints cracked. With 7 folding plates. Ck June 19 (190) £380

Anr copy. Folio, old calf; rebacked, orig spine laid down. With 6 folding plates. Fitzwilliam-Crahan copy. P Nov 25 (457) $250

Anr Ed. L, 1751. 8vo, contemp calf; rebacked, orig backstrip laid down on rear pastedown. With 7 folding plates. Library stamp on top fore-edge & margin of p iii; some dampstains. Hunt copy. CNY Nov 21 (274) $180

Anr Ed. L, 1822. 8vo, contemp half calf; rebacked. Hunt copy. CNY Nov 21 (275) $70

Tully, Richard
— Narrative of a Ten Years' Residence at Tripoli in Africa. L, 1816. 1st Ed. 4to, contemp half calf; worn, crudely backed, loose. With folding map & 4 hand-colored plates. bba Dec 18 (256) £42 [Smith]

2d Ed. L, 1817. 4to, modern cloth. With folding map & 7 colored plates. bba Dec 18 (256) £42 [Smith]

Tunnicliff, William
— A Topographical Survey of the Counties of Stafford, Chester and Lancaster.... Nantwich, 1787. Folio, orig bds; spine rubbed. With e folding maps. bba Apr 9 (401) £70 [Cox]

Turnbull, George
— A Treatise on Ancient Painting. L, 1740. 1st Ed. Folio, contemp half sheep; rubbed. With 54 plates. Tear to lower blank margin of 1 plate. S Nov 10 (176) £110 [Russell]

Turnbull, John, fl.1800-13
— A Voyage Round the World.... L, 1805. 1st Ed. 3 vols. 16mo, contemp half calf; worn. Some spotting & browning. bba Oct 30 (364) £80 [Bonham]

2d Ed. L, 1813. 4to, contemp mor gilt. S Oct 23 (529) £1,500 [Hitching]

Turner, A. A.
— Villas on the Hudson. NY, 1860. Oblong folio, modern cloth. bba Sept 25 (302) £740 [Weinreb]

Turner, Dawson
— Account of a Tour in Normandy. L, 1820. 2 vols. 8vo, cloth. With 50 plates. pn Dec 11 (85) £75 [Thorp]

Anr copy. Calf gilt; spines rubbed. T Feb 19 (231) £58

Turner, Elizabeth, 1775-1846
— The Daisy, or Cautionary Stories in Verse.... L, 1807. 1st Ed. Part 1 only. 12mo, orig wraps; worn. With 16 plates. Piece torn from blank margin of 1 leaf. O Apr 28 (38) $60

Turner, Sir James, 1615-86?
— Pallas Armata. Military Essayes.... L, 1683. Folio, contemp calf; spine & corners worn. Lacking frontis. Sold w.a.f. bba Mar 26 (168) £45 [Trottman]

Turner, Joseph M. W., 1775-1851
— An Antiquarian and Picturesque Tour round the Southern Coast of England. L, 1849. 4to, half mor; worn, covers loose, backstrip detached. Library markings; ink stamps on plates. bba Jan 15 (489) £80 [Baldwin]

Anr copy. Contemp half mor; worn, joints split. bba May 28 (218) £320 [Croft]

Anr copy. Orig cloth; upper cover detached. With 48 plates. Ck Sept 26 (85) £160

Anr copy. Contemp half mor gilt; rubbed. Lacking 1 plate; anr plate repaired with adhesive tape at inner margin. S May 28 (923) £250

— Liber Fluviorum, or River Scenery of France. L, 1853. 8vo, contemp half mor. 1 leaf of text torn; last few leaves loose. bba Apr 9 (267) £50 [Fisher]

Anr copy. Orig cloth. pn Dec 11 (86) £60 [Thorp]

Anr copy. 2 vols. 4to, contemp half mor; rubbed. With engraved title & 60 plates. S Nov 10 (926) £50 [Robertshaw]

Anr copy. 8vo, contemp mor gilt; worn. S May 28 (924) £60

Anr Ed. L, 1857. 8vo, orig cloth; rubbed, hinge starting. With title & 60 engraved plates. cb Oct 23 (228) $75

— Picturesque Views on the Southern Coast of England. L, 1826. 2 vols. 4to, mor gilt; worn, 1 vol broken. With 48 plates. Perforated stamp on titles & a few text leaves. bba Dec 4 (354) £85 [Rainer]

Anr copy. Old calf gilt; rebacked, rubbed. Library stamp on tp. pnNY Oct 11 (48) $275

Anr copy. 2 vols in 1. 4to, 19th-cent mor gilt; rubbed. With 48 plates. Lacking titles to the individual volumes. S Nov 17 (831) £500 [Thorp]

— Picturesque Views in England and Wales. L, 1838. 2 vols. 4to, contemp calf gilt; rebacked, rubbed, corners worn, 1 hinge cracked. With 96 plates. Faint spotting to a few plates; 1 plate with engraver's name erased. C Dec 12 (271) £700 [Yamanaka]

Anr copy. Old half mor gilt, orig front wraps bound in. Library stamp on title & wraps. pnNY Oct 11 (47) $425

Anr copy. Contemp half mor; worn. S Feb 23 (52) £700 [Cox]

— The Rivers of France. L, 1837. 4to, contemp calf; worn. With engraved title & 60 plates. Some foxing. O May 12 (188) $140

Anr copy. Contemp russia gilt. Tp & a few plates heavily foxed; marginal foxing of other plates. sg June 4 (331) $110

Anr copy. Later mor gilt by Potter. Some spotting. T Oct 16 (265) £70

— The Turner Gallery: a Series of Sixty Engravings.... L: J. S. Virtue, [c.1865]. Folio, contemp mor gilt; rubbed. With port & 60 plates. S Mar 9 (710) £190 [Erlini]

Anr Ed. L, 1875. Folio, orig mor gilt; edges rubbed. Library stamp on tp. pnNY Oct 11 (49) $180

Anr copy. Contemp lea gilt; worn. Some foxing. sg Feb 5 (318) $325

Turner, Joseph M. W., 1775-1851 — & Girtin, Thomas, 1775-1802

— River Scenery. L, [1823-30]. Folio, later half lev; worn. With 20 plates. C Oct 15 (108) £500 [Yamanaka]

Turner, Laurence Arthur

— Decorative Plasterwork in Great Britain. L, 1927. Folio, orig cloth. T Feb 19 (517) £60

Turnor, Christopher Hatton, 1840-1914

— Astra Castra. Experiments and Adventures in the Atmosphere. L, 1865. Folio, orig cloth; rubbed. C Dec 12 (209) £230 [Phelps]

Tuscarora...

— Tuscarora Club's Forty-Year History, 1901-41. [N.p.], 1941. One of 100. Club president Homer E. Fraser's copy. sg Oct 23 (527) $500

Tuson, Edward William

— Myology. L, 1828. 2d Ed. 2 vols, including Supplement, in 1. Folio, contemp half calf; worn & recovered. With 17 hand-colored plates with hinged overlays. Lacking tp; dedication very soiled & with small tear affecting text. bba Oct 16 (310) £480 [Phelps]

Tussac, F. Richard de

— Flore des Antilles, ou Histoire generale botanique.... Paris, 1808-27. 4 vols in 2. Folio, contemp bds; worn. With 137 (of 140) hand-finished colored plates. Foxed. L.p. copy. Plesch—de Belder copy. S Apr 28 (366) £20,000 [Arader]

Tusser, Thomas, 1524?-80

— Five Hundreth Pointes of good Husbandrie.... L: Henrie Denham, 1585. 4to, early calf; rubbed, corners & spine extremities repaired. Slight fingersoiling. Hunt copy. CNY Nov 21 (276) $1,100

Anr Ed. L, 1672. ("Five Hundred Points of Good Husbandry....") 4to, early 19th-cent half calf; broken. Britwell-Hunt copy. CNY Nov 21 (277) $110

— Tusser Redivivus: Being Part of Mr. Thomas Tusser's Five Hundred Pointes of Husbandry.... L: J. Morphew, 1710. 12 orig monthly parts in 11. 8vo, disbound. Hunt copy. CNY Nov 21 (278) $160

Twain, Mark. See: Clemens, Samuel Langhorne

Twice a Year...

— Twice a Year: A Book of Literature, the Arts & Civil Liberties. NY, 1947. ("Stieglitz Memorial Portfolio.") sg May 7 (71) $200

Twining, Elizabeth, 1805-89

— Illustrations of the Natural Order of Plants. L, 1849-55. 2 vols. Folio, contemp half mor gilt; soiled. With 160 hand-colored plates. de Belder copy. S Apr 28 (367) £16,000 [Rostron]

Twiss, Richard

— Chess. L, 1787. 2 vols in 1. 8vo, modern calf. pn Mar 26 (513) £130 [De Lucia]
— Miscellanies. L, 1805. 2 vols. Half calf gilt. pn Mar 26 (514) £190 [De Lucia]
— A Tour of Ireland in 1775. L, 1776. 8vo, contemp calf; rubbed. bba Mar 26 (373) £65 [Camberwell]
— Travels through Portugal and Spain. L, 1775. 4to, contemp calf; rubbed, joints weak. With folding map, engraved sheet of music & 6 plates. bba Dec 4 (299) £130 [Orssich]

Anr copy. Contemp russia gilt; rubbed, joints broken. With folding map & 6 plates. S Jan 16 (444) £190 [Orssich]

Twitchell, Ralph Emerson

— The Leading Facts of New Mexican History. Cedar Rapids, 1911-12. One of 1,500. 2 vols. Half mor. Vol II opening leaves dampstained. sg Oct 2 (234) $200

Tyler, John, 1790-1862

— Message from the President, Communicating...Information touching the Proceedings of the Convention of 11 April 1839, between the United States and the Mexican Republic. Wash., 1842. 8vo, modern half lea; spine torn at foot. 27th Congress, 2d Session, Senate Doc. 320. sg Sept 18 (289) $50

Tyler, Royall, Counsellor at Law

— The Algerine Captive.... Hartford, 1816. 2 vols in 1. 18mo, contemp calf; worn. sg Apr 23 (148) $200

Tymms, William Robert —& Wyatt, Sir Matthew Digby, 1820-77

— The Art of Illuminating as Practised in Europe.... L, [1859] 1860. Folio, orig cloth; soiled, inner joints broken. Minor foxing. O June 16 (187) $120

Anr copy. Orig cloth; worn, backstrip almost detached. Lacking 2 plates; Plate 64 torn with loss. T Feb 19 (535) £45

Anr copy. Orig cloth; recased in buckram. With litho title & 99 color plates. wa Mar 5 (124) $170

Anr Ed. L, [1866]. 8vo, orig cloth; worn & shaken. With colored title & 95 plates. O Sept 23 (183) $60

Tyndale, William, d.1536

— The Whole Workes of W. Tyndall, John Frith, and Doct. Barnes, Three Worthy Martyrs. L: John Daye, 1573-72. 1st Collected Ed. Folio, modern vellum bds; 1 clasp broken, part of old bdg preserved inside upper cover. First 7 leaves & last 4 leaves torn & repaired with some loss; last leaf def; small hole in QQ6g; a few leaves dampstained or soiled. Sold w.a.f. S Sept 23 (405) £280 [Sotheran]

Tyrell, Henry

— The History of the War with Russia.... L, [c.1856]. 3 vols in 6. 4to, cloth; worn, some hinges broken. Some foxing & other minor defs. Vols IV-VI of F. Williams's England's Battles by Sea and Land. sg Nov 20 (156) $200

Tyrrell, Sir James, 1642-1718

— Bibliotheca Politica. L, 1691-1702. 4to, contemp calf; rebacked, front cover detached. Some foxing; front blank imperf. sg Oct 9 (333) $90

Tyson, Henry

— The Plan for the Improvement of the Channel of Jones' Falls.... Balt., 1871. 4to, cloth; spine frayed, tears along upper joint. With 1 folding plan chipped & dusted, the other linen-backed. ha Dec 19 (109) $50

Tyson, Philip T.

— Report of the Secretary of War Communicating Information in Relation to the Geology and Topography of California. Wash., 1850. 2 parts in one. 8vo, modern half calf. With 13 folding maps. 31st Congress, 1st Session, Sen. Exec. Doc. 47. cb Jan 8 (204) $55

Tyszkiewicz, Eustachy

— Listy o Szweiji. Wilno, 1846-47. 2 vols. 8vo, cloth, orig wraps bound in; soiled. With 8 plates, 1 mtd. Some repairs. S Nov 10 (927) £70 [Meir]

Tytler, William

— An Historical and Critical Enquiry into the Evidence...against Mary Queen of Scots. Edin., 1760. 8vo, contemp calf; rubbed. bba Oct 16 (76) £65 [Scott]

Tzara, Tristan, 1896-1963

— L'Antitete. Paris, 1949. One of 200. 3 vols. 4to, orig vellum wraps. S June 29 (56) £5,500 [Ursus]
— L'Arbre des voyageurs. Paris, [1930]. One of 25 on Holland. Illus by Joan Miro. 4to, ptd wraps; spine ends worn. With 4 sgd plates. sg Apr 2 (202) $4,000
— Parler seul. Paris: Maeght, 1948-50. One

of 253. Illus by Joan Miro. Folio, mor gilt by J. F. Barbance, orig wraps bound in. FD Dec 2 (4587) DM26,500
— La Premiere aventure celest de Mr. Antipyrine. Zurich: J. Heuberger, 1916. Illus by Marcel Janco. Orig ptd wraps. With 6 colored illusts. C Dec 12 (379) £900 [Weinreb]

U

Ubaldini, Petruccio, 1524?-1600?
— Le Vite delle donne illustri del regno d'Inghilterra.... L: G. Wolf, 1591. 4to, later vellum; soiled. Tp soiled; marginal repairs to lower right corner of 1st few leaves with loss of ptd marginal note on A2. T Mar 19 (389) £65

Uchteritz, H. von
— Kurtze Reise Beschreibung.... Weissenfels: Johann Christian Wohlfarten, 1705. 4to, calf gilt by Pratt. With 3 margins neatly repaired; some discoloration. Huth copy. S Apr 24 (315) £300 [Fleming]

Udall, William
— The Historie of the Life and Death of Mary Stuart Queene of Scotland. L, 1636. 2d Ed. 8vo, contemp mor; worn. T Sept 18 (501) £70

Ulitius, Janus. See: Vliet, Jan van

Ulloa, Antonio de, 1716-95
— Noticias Americanas. Madrid, 1772. 4to, contemp vellum; spine rubbed at head. S May 29 (1111) £190
— A Voyage to South America.... L, 1807. 2 vols. 8vo, orig bds; rubbed. With folding map & 6 folding plates Title of Vol I torn & repaired; lacking last leaf of Vol II. bba Sept 25 (419) £70 [Burton Garbett]

Ulloa, Antonio de, 1716-95 —& Juan y Santacilla, Jorge, 1712-73
— Voyage historique de l'Amerique meridionale. Amst. & Leipzig, 1752. 2 vols 4to, cloth. With 2 frontises & 45 plates & maps. With 25 extra plates, many from a work on China. Some leaves soiled. bba Dec 18 (163) £280 [Rainer]
— A Voyage to South-America.... L, 1760. 2 vols. 8vo, contemp calf; spines scuffed. With 7 folding plates. C Dec 12 (210) £200 [Griffiths]

Underwood, L. M. See: Cook & Underwood

Underwood, Michael, 1736-1820
— Traite des maladies des enfans.... Paris, 1786. 8vo, contemp calf; rubbed. T Feb 19 (444) £46

Underwood, Tim —& Miller, Chuck
— Fear Itself: The Horror Fiction of Stephen King. San Francisco, Underwood Miller, 1982. One of 225. In d/j. Sgd on front flyleaf by 11 contributors. cb Sept 28 (748) $225

Unedited. See: Society...

Union...
— Union des sentences de philosophie. Paris: Guillaume le noir, 1570. 8vo, calf gilt by Gruel. S June 25 (58) £1,500

United Brethren
— Confessio fidei et religionis Christianae.... Wittenberg, 1573. 8vo, contemp blind-tooled pigskin over pastebd stamped 1573 on front cover; wormed. Contemp notes on endpapers by Hieronymus Zanchius. William Jackson booklabel. sg Mar 26 (44) $600

United States of America
— Acts Passed at the Second Congress...24 October, 1791. Phila.: Francis Childs & John Swaine, [1792]. Bound with: Acts Passed at the Second Session.... And: Acts Passed at the Third Session.... 8vo, modern cloth. Library markings. sg Mar 12 (87) $475
— Journals of Congress, Containing the Proceedings from Sept 5, 1774 to Jan 1, 1776 Phila.: R. Aitken, 1777. Vol I. 8vo, orig bds; lacking back, worn & soiled. wa Sept 25 (439) $200
— Plans of Public Buildings. Wash., 1855-56. Folio, bdg not described. Franklin Institute copy. F Sept 12 (25) $4,500
— Report of the Commissioner of Patents for 1849. Part I: Arts and Manufactures. Wash., 1850. 8vo, orig half lea; rubbed. With statement by Abraham Lincoln on p 262. sg Sept 18 (158) $50

Universal...
— An Universal History, from the Earliest Account of Time.... L: T. Osborne, 1747-54. 21 vols. 8vo, contemp calf; worn, some covers detached. Sold w.a.f. O June 9 (188) $180
— The Universal Jewish Encyclopedia. NY, 1939-44. One of 761. Ed by Isaac Landman. 11 vols, including Index. 4to, cloth. Minor dampwrinkling & slight adhesion in some blank margins. O June 16 (188) $140; sg Sept 25 (84) $100
— The Universal Songster: or, Museum of Mirth. L, 1828-29. 3 vols. 8vo, modern half mor gilt. sg Sept 11 (81) $100
  Anr Ed. L: George Routledge, [c.1850]. 3 vols. 8vo, later half mor gilt. sg Sept11 (82) $90

UNKNOWN

Unknown
— Unknown. [N.p., 1939-43]. Vols I-VII, complete run of 39 Issues, including name alterations to Unknown Fantasy Fiction & Unknown Worlds. 8vo & 4to, orig wraps; 1 front wrap lacking, 1 rear wrap detached. ha Mar 13 (45) $350

Unknown Fantasy Fiction. See: Unknown

Unknown Worlds. See: Unknown

Unlawfulness...
— The Unlawfulness of Polygamy Evinced; or, Observations Occasioned by the Erroneous Interpretations of the Passages of the New Testament.... L, 1780. 8vo, modern cloth. Lacking half-title or initial blank. sg Oct 9 (293) $50

Untermyer Collection, Irwin
— HACKENBROCH, YVONNE. - Chelsea and Other English Porcelain in the Irwin Untermyer Collection. Cambr., Mass., 1957. 4to, orig half cloth, in d/j. CA Apr 12 (123) A$95
— HACKENBROCH, YVONNE. - Meissen and other Continental Porcelain, Faience and Enamel.... L, 1956. 4to, orig half cloth, in torn d/j. O Mar 24 (191) $50

Upcott, William
— A Bibliographical Account of the Principal Works relating to English Topography. L, 1818. 3 vols. 8vo, contemp calf; worn & loose. bba Mar 12 (360) £50 [Bailey]
Anr Ed. NY, [1968]. 3 vols. 8vo, cloth. Ck Sept 26 (235) £55

Updike, Daniel Berkeley
— Printing Types. Cambr., Mass., 1922. 2 vols. In d/js. bba Feb 5 (35) £55 [Kuyper]
2d Ed. Cambr., Mass., 1937. In worn d/js. bba Oct 16 (506) £50 [Check Books]; bba Dec 4 (249) £40 [Goldman]; S Nov 10 (32) £42 [Forster]
Anr Ed. Cambr., Mass., 1966. 2 vols. In d/js. bba Oct 16 (507) £40 [Forster]

Updike, John
— The Coup. NY, 1978. One of 350. In d/j. wa Nov 6 (668) $55

Upham, Charles Wentworth
— Lectures on Witchcraft.... Bost., 1831. 1st Ed. 12mo, cloth. sg Sept 11 (287) $70

Upham, Edward, 1776-1834
— The History and Doctrine of Budhism. L: Ackermann, 1829. Folio, orig bds; upper cover almost detached. T Apr 16 (292) £95
Anr copy. Orig bds; hinges cracked, upper cover almost detached. T July 16 (320) £135

AMERICAN BOOK PRICES CURRENT

Upton, John
— Critical Observations on Shakespeare. L, 1746. 8vo, disbound. sg Mar 26 (277) $70

Ure, Andrew
— A Dictionary of Arts, Manufactures, and Mines. NY, 1858. 2 vols. 8vo, orig cloth; worn, faded & soiled. Endpapers & prelims waterstained. wa Nov 6 (33) $50

Urquhart, Beryl Leslie
— The Rhododendron. Sharpthorne, 1958-62. Illus by Carlos Riefel. 2 vols. Folio, half cloth, in d/js. With 36 colored plates. pnE Dec 17 (240) £70 [Maggs]

Usage...
— De l'usage du caphe, du the, et du chocolate. Lyons: J. Girin & B. Riviere, 1671. 12mo, contemp calf; spine repaired at foot. Sometimes attributed to Philippe Dufour or Jacob Spon. Westbury-Crahan copy. P Nov 25 (164) $450

Usher, James
— Gravissimae quaestionis, de Christianarum ecclesiarum.... L, 1613. 1st Ed. 4to, contemp vellum gilt with sunflower design; soiled. Final 2 leaves almost detached. Ck Sept 5 (208) £80

Usurie...
— Usurie arraigned and condemned. Or a Discoverie of the infinite Injuries this Kingdome endureth.... L: W. S. for John Smethwicke, 1625. 4to, half calf. S July 24 (465) £850 [Lawson]

Utamaro, Kitagawa, 1754?-1806. See: Grabhorn Printing

Utrillo, Maurice. See: Petrides, Paul

Uzanne, Octave, 1852-1931
See also: Caxton Club
— Fashion in Paris: the Various Phases of Feminine Taste. L, 1898. Illus by Francois Courboin. 8vo, orig cloth; upper cover soiled. With 100 hand-colored plates. Ck Jan 16 (110) £120
— La Femme a Paris: Nos contemporaines.... Paris, 1894. One of 110 on Japan vellum, with plates in 2 states, colored & plain. Illus by Pierre Vidal. 4to, calf gilt. With 20 plates. B Oct 7 (311) HF360
— The Frenchwoman of the Century. L, 1886. Ltd Ed. 4to, cloth; soiled, frontis loose. O Nov 18 (192) $80
Anr Ed. NY, 1887. 4to, mor. O June 16 (190) $70

V

Vaenius, Ernestus
— Tractatus physiologicus de pulchritudine.... Brussels, 1662. 8vo, 19th-cent mor gilt; rubbed, upper portion of flyleaf cut away. T June 18 (413) £180

Vaenius, Otto
— Batavorum cum Romanis bellum.... Antwerp: Philipp Lisaert, 1612. Oblong folio, early half vellum; bowed, partly loose in bdg. Tp soiled. sg Oct 9 (334) $350
— Vita D. Thomas Aquinatis. Antwerp, 1610. Folio, half calf; rubbed. S July 14 (445) £380

Vagrant. See: Lovecraft, Howard Phillips

Vahl, Martin
— Eclogae Americanae seu Descriptiones Plantarum...., Copenhagen, 1796-1807. 3 parts in 1 vol. Folio, half mor gilt; worn. sg Apr 2 (203) $850

Vail, Alfred
— Description of the American Electro-Magnetic Telegraph.... Phila., 1845. 1st Ed. 8vo, contemp half lea; worn, broken. Endpaper stained. wa Nov 6 (259) $110

Vaillant, Sebastien
— Botanicon parisiense. Leiden & Amst., 1727. Folio, contemp calf; rubbed. With port map & 33 plates. Short tear repaired in port. S Oct 23 (763) £300 [Volbracht]

Vaillat, Leandre
— L'Hotel-Dieu de Beaune. Paris, 1921. One of 25 on hollande. Illus by F. L. Schmied. Orig wraps. Inscr by Schmied to Charles Linguet. S Dec 4 (33) £580 [Monk Bretton]

Vaines, Francois Joseph de
— Dictionnaire raisonne de diplomatique. Paris, 1774. 2 vols. 8vo, contemp sheep gilt; extremities worn, joints cracked. With 49 plates. sg Oct 9 (335) $130

Valadon, Suzanne
— L'Oeuvre complet. Paris, 1971. Ltd Ed. Text by Paul Petrides. 4to, orig syn. S Nov 10 (260) £220 [Sims]

Valck, Gerard
— Nova totius geographica Telluris projectio. Amst., [c.1708]. Folio, contemp calf gilt. With engraved title & 107 double-page or folding maps colored in a contemp hand. Most maps accompanied by loosely inserted notes in a contemp hand; Ms indexes at end. S Apr 23 (141) £11,000 [George]

Valck, Gerard —&
Schenk, Peter
— Novissima...Regnorum Angliae, scotiae, Hiberniae tabula. Amst., [1706]. Folio, 19th-cent half calf; rubbed. With 60 hand-colored double-page maps within yellow wash frames, mtd on guards throughout. Lacking title & text; minor tears. With additional maps on smaller paper inserted. C Apr 8 (60) £5,000 [Burgess Browning]

Valckenier, Petrus —&
Muller, Andreas
— Das vervirrte Europa.... Amst.: Jacob von Meurs, 1677-80. 2 vols in 1 (of 3). Folio, contemp blind-stamped vellum; scuffed & stained. With frontis, 33 ports & 38 double-page plates. Fold tears to 2 plates. C Dec 12 (267) £320 [Stadt Museum Munster]

Valentia, George Annesley, Viscount. See: Annesley, George

Valentijn, Francois, 1656-1727
— Oud en Nieuw Oost-Indien.... Dordrecht, 1724-26. 5 vols. Folio, orig half vellum, uncut & unpressed. With frontis, engraved dedication, port, 60 maps & plans (44 folding) & 182 plates (51 folding), 21 ports & 9 ptd folding tables. Some plates loose or misbound; lacking general map in Vol I. s Oct 23 (146) £4,200 [Chong]

Valentiner, Wilhelm Reinhold. See: Goldman Collection, Henry

Valentini, Michael Bernard
— Museum museorum, oder Vollstaendige Schau-Buehne aller Materialien und Specereyen. Frankfurt, 1714. 2d Ed. 2 parts in 1 vol. Folio, contemp lea. FD Dec 2 (428) DM1,600

Anr copy. Contemp vellum. With 2 engraved titles, 297 engraved illusts & 97 engraved plates, many double-page. Vol II with some staining in upper margin & corner, affecting a few plates. Horticultural Society of New York—de Belder copy. S Apr 28 (369) £3,800 [Israel]

— Viridarium reformatum, seu regnum vegetabile.... Frankfurt, 1719. 2 parts in 1 vol. Folio, contemp calf with 19th-cent press-mark on fore-edge. With 223 emplem plates in text, 304 botanical plates & 10 "occult" plates to the 2d part. Lower margins dampstained. Horticultural Society of New York—de Belder copy. S Apr 28 (368) £6,000 [Schuster]

VALERA

Valera, Diego de
— La Chronica de Espana Abreviada. Seville: Sebastian Trugillo, 1562. Folio, later vellum. Margins trimmed; scattered minor stains; some worming in upper corners in 1st half of volume, occasionally affecting text. sg Oct 9 (72) $350

Valeriani, Domenico
— Atlante del basso ed alto egitto illustrato... sui disegni di Denon.... Florence, 1835-37. 3 vols. 8vo & Folio, contemp half calf & modern half mor. With 159 plates, many hand-colored. Ck May 8 (335) £1,000

Valeriano Bolzano, Giovanni Pietro
— Hieroglyphica, sive de sacris Aegyptiorum literis commentarii. Basel, 1556. Folio, contemp calf over wooden bds; worn, spine lacking. Tp & a few leaves waterstained; forecorners of title frayed affecting port border on verso; corner of C6 def with loss of text; some leaves loose; library stamp on tp. C May 13 (150) £220 [Bifolco]

Valerius Flaccus, Caius
— Argonautica. Venice: christophorus de Pensis de Mandello, 1501. 4to, old vellum. Marginal dampstaining; some worming. sg Mar 26 (278) $175
— Argonauticon, libri octo. Venice: Aldus, May 1523. ("Argonautica. Orphei Argonautica.") 8vo, mor gilt. pn Mar 5 (292) £260 [Hesketh & Ward]

Valerius Maximus, Gaius
— Opere. Venice: Albertino da Lissona, 6 Nov 1504. Folio, contemp Venetian bdg of blind-stamped or over wooden bds; rebacked, small repairs, 2 small wormholes in upper cover. Lower outer corner of a1 repaired; some marginal dampstains. S May 21 (86) £850 [Maggs]

Valery, Paul, 1871-1945
— Charmes ou poemes. Paris, 1922. 1st Ed, one of 27 on japon. 4to, in box by Martin, 1958. SM Oct 20 (671) FF11,000
— Le Cimetiere marin. L, 1946. ("Le Cimetiere marin. The Graveyard by the Sea.") One of 500. Trans by C. Day Lewis; ptd at the Officina Bodoni, Verona. bba July 16 (365) £140 [Helliman]
— Degas, danse, dessin. Paris, 1936. One of 305. 4to, unsewn in orig wraps. S June 17 (16) £480 [Marks]
— La Jeune Parque. Maestricht, 1926. One of 190. 4to, orig cloth. B Oct 7 (89) HF200

Valery, Paul, 1871-1945 —& Others
— Paul Bonet. Paris, 1945. One of 300. 4to, loose as issued in orig wraps. FD Dec 2 (321) DM1,300

AMERICAN BOOK PRICES CURRENT

Valicourt, Joseph de, Comte
— La Picardie et ses chasses. Paris: Nouvelles Editions de la Toison d'Or, [1947]. One of 36. 4to, bdg not described. Jeanson copy. SM Mar 1 (569) FF2,000

Valier, Max
— Vorstoss in den Weltenraum. Munich & Berlin, 1930. ("Raketenfahrt.") Later half lea. sg Jan 15 (360) $500

Valla, Georgius
— De corporis commodis et incommodis. Strassburg: Henricum Sybold, [1530?]. 8vo, newer limp vellum. Some stains & browning. O Sept 23 (184) $230

Valla, Laurentius, 1406-57
— Elegantiarum libri sex. Lyons: Joannes David, 2 Sept 1531. 4to, old lea over pastebd; worn. Marginal soiling & stains; some worming in inner margins, variously affecting text. sg Oct 9 (336) $90

Vallance, Aylmer
— The Art of William Morris. L, 1897. One of 220. Folio, orig half cloth. C July 22 (130) £1,000

Valle, Pietro della, 1586-1652
— Reise-Beschreibung...in Tuerckey, Etypten.... Geneva: Johann Herman Widerhold 1674. Folio, contemp vellum; worn & woiled. With engraved title, plate of Swiss cantonal arms, 2 ports, allegorical plate & 26 plates (all but 1 full-page). Occasional faint discoloration. S Oct 23 (122) £950 [Loman]

Valleriola, Franciscus
— Loci medicinae communes, tribus libris digesti. Lyons: S. Gryphii, 1562. Folio, mor gilt. Marginal repairs to last few leaves. S Nov 10 (571) £120 [Way]

Vallet, Pierre
— Le Jardin du roy tres chrestien Henry IV.... [Paris], 1608. Folio, modern vellum. With engraved title, 2 ports & 73 plates. Some marginal dampstaining & spotting to plates; tp trimmed at inner edge & guarded; library stamp in margin of 1 port; some wormholes & corners repaired at beginning. de Belder copy. S Apr 28 (370) £7,500 [Hill]

Valvasone, Erasmo di, 1523-93
— Della Caccia. Bergamo, 1591. 8vo, 18th-cent mor gilt in the syle of Padeloup. Jeanson 1132. SM Mar 1 (570) FF18,000

1024

Valverde de Hamusco, Juan
See also: Vesalius & Valverde de Hamusco
— Anatome corporis humano.... Venice: Giunta, 1607. Folio, contemp vellum; soiled, spine cracked. With engraved title, port & 46 full-page anatomical engravings. Title with tear repaired in lower outer margin; some dampstains; a little worming, mostly marginal. S June 25 (136) £650 [Phelps]
— De animi et corporis sanitate tuenda libellus. Paris: C. Estienne, 1552. 8vo, mor gilt by R. Melton, 1932. Library stamp & 2 ownership signatures on title; corner of 1 leaf repaired. Crahan copy. P Nov 25 (439) $650
— Historia de la composicion del cuerpo humano. Rome: Antonio Salamanca & Antonio Lafrerius, 1556. Folio, modern vellum. Lacking the errata leaf; some repairs; marginalia in an early hand FD June 11 (659) DM25,000

Vambery, Armin, 1832?-1913
— Travels in Central Asia. NY, 1865. Orig cloth; soiled, minor glue repairs. With 12 plates & with folding map loose in rear pocket. cb Nov 6 (283) $65

Van de Velde. C. W. M.
— Le Pays d'Israel. Paris, 1857-[59]. Folio, contemp half mor gilt by Elias P. V. Bommel; rubbed. With litho title, map & plan, plate of architectural detail & 98 tinted views, on linen guards throughout. C Apr 8 (63) £4,500 [Wood]

Van de Vennes, Adrian. See: Venne, Adriaen van de

Van den Keere, Pieter — & Montanus, Pieter
— Germania Inferior id est, XVII Provinciarum.... Amst., 1617. Folio, contemp half vellum. With engraved title & 24 (of 25) double-page mapsheets, all colored in a contemp hand & with gold heightening to the title. Lacking Typus Frisiae Orientalis; some creases or small fold tears. S June 25 (267) £12,000

Van den Velde, Jan
— Spieghel der Schrijfkonste, Inden welcken ghesien worden veelderhand gheschriften.... Amst., [after 1605]. Oblong folio, half mor; worn. With engraved title & 53 plates. Most leaves remargined, affecting plates in some cases; dampstained. S Sept 23 (406) £240 [Tristan]

Van der Straet, Jan. See: Straet, Jan van der

Van Duzer Library, Henry Sayre
— Thackeray Library: First Editions and First Publications. NY, 1919. One of 175. Compiled by Edward Turnbull. sg Oct 2 (291) $90

Van Gogh, Vincent, 1853-90
— The Complete Letters of.... Greenwich CT: New York Graphic Society, [c.1955]. 3 vols. cb Mar 5 (197) $130

2d Ed. Greenwich CT: New York Graphic Society, [1959]. cb Mar 5 (198) $80
— Correspondance complete. Paris, 1960. 3 vols. S Nov 10 (267) £100 [Finch]

Van Gulik, Robert, 1910-67
— The Chinese Bell Murders. L, [1958]. 1st Ed. In d/j; Spine rubbed. sg Dec 11 (59) $150
— The Chinese Lake Murders. L, [1960]. 1st Ed. In repaired d/j. cb Nov 20 (311) $95
— The Chinese Maze Murders. The Hague, 1956. 1st Ed. In chipped & stained d/j. cb May 7 (299) $140

Van Laar, G.
— Magazijn van tuin-sieraaden. Amst., 1802. 4to, modern half calf. With engraved title & 190 hand-colored plates. Library stamp on tp. S June 25 (224) £2,000 [Branners]

Van Loon, Gerard
— Aloude Hollandsche histori der keyzeren, koningen, hertogen en Graaven.... The Hague, 1734. 2 vols. Folio, contemp vellum bds; soiled. With frontis, engraved dedication, 13 double-page maps, 21 genealogical tables & 10 plates. Some browning & marginal waterstaining. C July 22 (212) £250

Van Nostrand, Jeanne
— The First Hundred Years of Painting in California.... San Francisco, 1980. In d/j. With 42 colored plates. cb Oct 9 (240) $60
— San Francisco, 1806-1906 in Contemporary Paintings, Drawings.... San Francisco: Book Club of California, 1975. One of 500. Book Club of California No 150. cb Sept 11 (72) $100

Van Nu...
— Van Nu en Straks. Brussels, 1893-95. First Series, Parts 1-10. Wraps. B Oct 7 (17) HF2,200

Van Rensselaer, May King, 1848-1925
— The Devil's Picture-Books: A History of Playing-Cards. NY, [1890]. 8vo, orig cloth; spine frayed. With 24 plates. wa Nov 6 (476) $70

Van Riebeck Society—Cape Town
— Publications. Cape Town, 1918-69. First Series, Nos 1-50 (complete set). SSA Oct 28 (925) R1,400; SSA Oct 28 (927) R1,300; SSA Feb 11 (654) R1,600

Van Urk, John Blan. See: Derrydale Press

Van Vogt, Alfred Elton
— Empire of the Atom. Chicago: Shasta, [1956]. In rubbed d/j. cb Sept 28 (1261) $65
— Slan. Sauk City, 1946. 1st Ed. In worn d/j. Inscr. cb Sept 28 (1268) $100; cb May 7 (432) $50
Anr copy. In worn d/j. cb May 7 (433) $70

Van Winkle, William Mitchell —& Randall, David A.
— Henry W. Herbert: a Bibliography.... Portland, Me., 1936. sg Oct 23 (339) $80

Van Zyl, Johannes
— Theatrum machinarum universale; of groot algemeemen Moolen-Bock. Amst., 1761. Folio, bdg not given. Franklin Institute copy. F Sept 12 (345) $1,300

Vanbrugh, Sir John, 1664-1726
See also: Nonesuch Press
— The Provok'd Wife. L, 1709. 8vo, mor gilt by Douglas Cockerell, 1903. Sold w.a.f. With related material laid in. CNY Dec 19 (51) $480

Vance, Jack
— The Languages of Pao. NY: Avalon, [1958]. In worn d/j. cb Sept 28 (1281) $50
— The Seventeen Virgins. The Bagful of Dreams. San Francisco: Underwood-Miller, 1979. One of 600. In d/j. Sgd on front flyleaf. cb Sept 28 (1288) $80
— To Live Forever. NY: Ballantine Books, 1956. In soiled d/j. cb Sept 28 (1290) $150
— The Tschai Series. San Francisco: Underwood-Miller, 1979-81. ("City of the Chasch * Servants of the Wahkh * The Dirdir * The Pnume.") One of 111. 4 vols. cb Sept 28 (1292) $130

Vancouver, George, 1757-98
— Voyage de decouvertes, a l'Ocean Pacifique du Nord, et autour du monde.... Paris, 1799-1800 [An VIII]. 4 vols. 8vo, orig bds. Text with engraved map & 17 views; Atlas with 10 double-page maps & 6 coastal profiles. Some spotting. S Oct 23 (528) £1,800 [Clavreuil]
Anr copy. 3 vols, lacking Atlas. 4to, orig wraps. S May 29 (1090) £180
Anr Ed. Paris, 1800-2 [An X]. 4 vols. 8vo, contemp bds, unopened, Atlas in orig bds. Text with engraved map & 17 views; Atlas with 10 double-page maps & 6 coastal profiles. Some foxing to plates in text vols. S Oct 23 (80) £2,000 [Perrin]
Anr copy. Atlas only. Half cloth; worn. With 10 double-page maps & 6 coastal profiles, some double-page. Margins stained at ends. S Oct 23 (81) £800 [Quaritch]
— A Voyage of Discovery to the North Pacific Ocean and Round the World. L, 1801. 6 vols. 8vo, later half mor. Some library stamps. kh Mar 16 (514B) A$600

Vanel, ——
— Histoire et description ancienne et moderne du Royaume de Hongrie.... Paris, 1688. 8vo, contemp calf gilt; rubbed. Engraved title frayed. bba Sept 25 (250) £70 [Morrell]

Vanity...
— Vanity Fair. L, 1907-8. Vols 39-40. 2 vols. Folio, orig cloth; dampstained. With 106 colored plates. Minor marginal staining. S Nov 10 (414) £680 [Blest]
— Vanity Fair: A Weekly Show of Political, Social & Literary Wares. L, 1869-96. Vols 1-55 & Index of ports. Together, 56 vols. Folio, orig cloth. Sold w.a.f. C July 22 (213) £7,000

Vansittart, Robert. See: Gregynog Press

Vargas, Ignacio
— Elogio Historico de Maria Santisima de Guadalupe de Mexico. Mexico City: Jauregui,1 798. 4to, modern calf. With the word "aprecio" corrected by a pasteover on p 10, line 6. Tp foxed. sg Sept 18 (290) $120

Varin, A. & E.
— L'Architecture pittoresque en Suisse. Paris, 1861. Folio, contemp half mor; rebacked with old spine preserved. With 48 plates. S May 29 (1055) £450

Varley, John
— The Persistence of Vision. NY: Dial Press, 1978. Review copy. In d/j. cb Sept 28 (1295) $60

Vasari, Giorgio, 1511-74
— Lives of the Most Eminent Painters, Sculptors, and Architects. L: Medici Society, 1912-15. 10 vols. 4to, orig cloth. bba Dec 4 (209) £100 [Hetherington]; S Feb 23 (54) £140 [McKenzie]; sg Feb 12 (323) $90
— Opere. Florence, 1822-23. 6 vols. 12mo, contemp half calf; rubbed. Some staining. bba Oct 30 (235) £80 [Frew Mackenzie]
— Le Vite de' piu eccellenti pittori, scultori, e architettori. Livorno & Florence, 1767-72. 7 vols. 8vo, old vellum bds; torn on spine. S Nov 10 (180) £150 [Barker]

Vasey, George, 1822-93

— Illustrations of North American Grasses. Wash., 1891-93. 2 vols in 1. 4to, contemp half lea; joints & corners worn. With 200 litho plates. Some text leaves & plate rectos stamped. sg Sept 18 (291) $140

Vasi, Giuseppe Agostino

— Delle magnificenze di Roma antica e moderna. Rome, 1747-61. 10 vols. Oblong 4to, contemp bds; extremities worn. With 10 title-vignettes & 216 plates; last leaf in Vol VII detached. P Dec 15 (233) $5,500

Anr Ed. Rome, 1786. ("Raccolta delle piu belle vedute antiche e moderne di Roma.") 2 vols. Oblong folio, contemp half calf. With engraved title vignettes & 202 plates. Plates & & 13 are abound at end of Vol I; Plate 105 is a duplicate of PLate 102 with numbering altered in ink; tp with 3 letters of pbr's address rubbed & re-supplied in ink. C Oct 15 (110) £3,200 [Zanzotto]

Vauban, Sebastien, Le Prestre de. See: Le Prestre de Vauban, Sebastien

Vaughan, J. D.

— The Manners and Customs of the Chinese of the Straits Settlements. Singapore, 1879. 8vo, mor gilt by Sangorski & Sutcliffe. A few small private library stamps. S Apr 23 (357) £800 [Orient]

Vaughan, Rice

— A Discourse of Coin and Coinage. L, 1675. 12mo, early 19th-cent calf. C Dec 12 (211) £500 [Martin]

Anr copy. Contemp calf; spine worn. C Dec 12 (285) £400 [Rota]

Vaughan, Thomas, 1622-66

— Anthroposophia Theomagica; or, a Discourse.... L, 1650. Bound with: Vaughan. Anima Magica Abscondita; or, a Discourse.... L, 1650. 8vo, 19th-cent mor gilt; joints & corners worn. Margins trimmed; 1st title mtd. sg Oct 9 (337) $350

— Long Livers, a Curious History...by Eugenius Philalethes. L, 1722. 8vo, contemp calf; rebacked, endpapers renewed. Lacking g4. sg Jan 15 (97) $175

— Magia Adamica: or the Antiquitie of Magic.... L, 1650. 8vo, modern calf. Tp & some other leaves slightly soiled; outer margin of L3 holed. Ck Jan 16 (123) £240

Vaughan, William, 1577-1641

— The Church Militant.... L, 1640. 8vo, old sheep; spine wormed. Portion torn from Y4 with slight loss of text; lacking 1st blank & final leaf. S July 14 (350) £100

Vaurie, Charles

— The Birds of the Palearctic Fauna. L, 1959-65. 2 vols. B Feb 24 (80) HF340

Vaux, Calvert, 1824-95

— Villas and Cottages. NY, 1857. 8vo, orig cloth; worn. O May 12 (192) $200

Anr Ed. NY, 1864. 8vo, orig cloth; spine faded. bba Sept 25 (301) £60 [Weinreb]; bba Sept 25 (301) £60 [Weinreb]

Anr copy. Orig cloth; worn. Some foxing. O Mar 24 (192) $50

Vaux, Charles Maurice, Baron de

— Les Grands Fusils de France. Paris, 1898. One of 50 on japon. 4to, half shagreen. With 50 hand-colored plates. Jeanson 1712. SM Mar 1 (571) FF12,000

— Les Grands Veneurs de France.... Paris, 1895. One of 500. Folio, half shagreen. With 20 color plates. Jeanson copy. SM Mar 1 (572) FF5,500

Vaz Coutinho, Goncalo

— Historia do successo que na Ilha de S. Miguel ovve com armada ingresa que sobre a ditta Ilha foy.... Lisbon: Pedro Crasebeeck, 1630. 8vo, 19th-cent mor gilt; spine damaged at foot. S Apr 23 (200) £400 [Ramer]

Vaz D'Almada, Francisco

— Tratado do successo que teve a nao S. Joam Baptista.... Lisbon, 1625. 4to, modern mor gilt; head of spine torn. Library stamp at foot of dedication; some underlining. C Apr 8 (64) £600 [May]

Vazquez, Andres Clemente, 1844-1901

— El Ajedrez en Cuba: J. H. Blackburne en la Habana. Habana, 1891. Orig wraps; repaired. pn Mar 26 (215) £40 [Winter]

Vecellio, Cesare, 1530-1600

— Corona delle nobili et virtuose donne.... Venice: Vecellio, 1600-1. Parts 1-4 (of 5) in 1 vol. 4to, mor gilt by Asper. FD June 11 (152) DM7,600

Veen, Jan van der

— Zinne-beelden, ofte adams appel...... Amst., 1745. 8vo, vellum. With 50 half-page plates. B Feb 25 (548) HF425

Veer, Gerrit de

— Warhafftige Relation. Der dreyen newen unerhorten seltzamen Schiffart.... Nuremberg, 1598. 4to, contemp vellum; soiled. Stained throughout; 1 plate with small tear & small repair; anr plate with larger repair. CNY Dec 19 (97) $3,200

Vega, Pedro de la

— La Rosa de Alexandria.... Mexico City: Francisco R. Lupercio, 1672. 4to, later vellum; stained in top corner of front cover. Marginal worming throughout, affecting some marginal notes; lacking port. sg Sept 18 (292) $80

Vegetius Renatus, Flavius

— De re militari, libri quatuor [& other works]. Paris: C. Wechel, 1535. Folio, contemp vellum; soiled. With 123 woodcut. FD Dec 2 (101) DM5,000

— Du Fait de guerre, et fleur de chevalerie.... Paris, 1536. 1st Ed of Nicole Volkyr de Serouville's trans. Folio, contemp vellum bds; lower inside hinge broken. With full-page woodcut of a lansquenet, cut of a military council before a tent (both of these repeated) & 119 full-page woodcuts. A few leaves marginally stained. S June 25 (138) £2,400 [Sourget]

Vehling, Joseph Dommers

— Apicius. Cooking and Dining in Imperial Rome. A Bibliography.... Chicago, 1936. One of 30 on handmade paper. Orig half cloth, in d/j. Crahan copy. P Nov 25 (26) $250

Veitch, James Herbert

— A Manual of Orchidaceous Plants Cultivated under Glass in Great Britain. L, 1887-94. L.p. Ed. 10 parts in 2 vols. 8vo, loose in orig wraps & cloth. T Oct 16 (395) £110

Veitia Linage, Jose

— Norte de la contratacion de las Indias Occidentales. Sevile, 1672. 2 parts in 1 vol. Folio, old sheep; worn, rebacked with vellum. Lacking frontis. sg Mar 12 (255) $80

Velsch, Georg Hieronymus

— Commentarius in Ruzname Naurus.... Augsburg, 1676. 4to, modern bds. With engraved frontis & 22 plates. bba Aug 20 (399) £280 [Maggs]

Venables, Robert, 1612-87

— The Experienc'd Angler.... L, 1668. 3d Ed. 8vo, contemp calf; worn, broken. A few pp stained. sg Oct 23 (530) $475

Venel, Jean Andre

— Essai sur la sante et sur l'education medicinale des filles destinees au mariage. Yverdon, 1776. 2 parts in 1 vol. 8vo, modern bds. bba Nov 13 (50) £50 [Laywood]

Veniard, John

— Fly-Dressing Materials. L, [1977]. One of 100. 4to, half lea. sg Oct 23 (531) $70

Venne, Adriaen van de

— Tafereel van de belacchende werelt en des self geluckige Eeuwe. The Hague, 1635. 4to, contemp calf. With engraved title & 12 plates. Ink stain at foot of inner margin throughout. With bookplate reading "Ex libris Vincent van Gogh". S May 21 (128) £400 [Wolf]

Anr copy. Later 127th-cent vellum. With 12 illusts, 3 mtd; inner margins wormed. sg Oct 9 (338) p$375

Venner, Tobias

— Via recta ad vitam longam: or, a plaine Philosophicall Demonstration.... L: Felix Kyngston for Richard Moore, 1628. 2 parts in 1 vol. 4to, contemp vellum; soiled. Section excised from 1st title with loss of date; 1st gathering almost detached; some staining or worming of margins. Ck Jan 30 (122) £130

Ventenat, Etienne Pierre

— Choix de plantes.... Paris, 1803-[8]. Folio, contemp half mor; rubbed. With 60 hand-finished colored plates. Half-title spotted. de Belder copy. S Apr 28 (372) £4,200 [Brittain]

— Description des plantes nouvelles et peu connues, cultivees dans le jardin de J. M. Cels. Paris, 1800. 4to, contemp calf gilt; rubbed, rebacked partially preserving old spine. With 100 plates. Some spotting. L.p. copy on papier velin. de Belder copy. S Apr 28 (373) £4,500 [Brittain]

— Jardin de la Malmaison. Paris, An XI [1803-5]. 2 vols. Folio, 19th-cent half mor gilt; spine ends & lower bd edges worn, upper joint of plate vol cracked. With 120 plates after P. J. Redoute, ptd in color & finished by hand & with uncolored dissections . Some foxing, mostly to 1st 19 & last 10 plates; most of the upper plate marks & the plate numerals & many outer plate marks cropped by the binder; PLates 53 & 61 with marginal stains; Plate 59 with small repaired tear to blank margin. Hunt copy. CNY Nov 21 (282) $18,000

Anr copy. 2 vols in 1. Folio, later mor gilt. Some spotting. de Belder copy. S Apr 28 (371) £32,000 [Brittain]

Venturi, Lionello
See also: Pissaro & Venturi

— Cezanne, son art, son oeuvre. Paris, 1936. One of 1,000. 2 vols. 4to, orig wraps; backstrips chipped. S June 17 (11) £3,400 [Uppstromm]
Anr copy. Cloth, orig upper covers loosely inserted, worn, spines def. A few leaves loose in Vol II. S June 17 (85) £1,900 [Sims]
Anr copy. Cloth. sg Dec 4 (33) $2,200

Venusti, Antonio Maria

— Compendio utilissimo di quelle cose.... Milan: Antonio degli Antonii, 1561. 8vo, vellum; spine wormed. Some marginal worming repaired. S Sept 23 (407) £330 [Tristram]

Venuti, Ridolfino

— Accurata e succincta descrizione topografica delle antichita di Roma. Rome, 1763. 2 parts in 1 vol. 4to, 19th-cent half mor; rubbed. With folding map & 96 plates. Ck Sept 26 (51) £350

Ver Sacrum...

— Ver Sacrum, Organ der Vereinigung bildender Kuenstler Oesterreichs. Vienna, 1898. Vol I, Parts 1-12. 4to, orig wraps; worn & def. JG Mar 20 (1182) DM1,700
Anr Ed. Vienna, 1898-99. Vol I only. orig cloth, orig wraps for the 12 issues bound in. S June 17 (120) £460 [Sims]

Vera y Figueroa, Juan Antonio de

— Resultas de la vida de Don Fernando Alvarez de Toledo, tercero Duque de Alba. Milan, 1643. 4to, contemp vellum. Wormhole in blank top outer corner of tp & following 3 leaves. sg Sept 18 (294) $50

Verdet, Andre

— Georges Braque le solitaire. Paris, [1959]. Ltd Ed. 4to, cloth. With 8 plates. sg June 11 (75) $50

Verdier, Antoine du. See: Du Verdier, Antoine

Verelst, Harry

— A View of the Rise, Progress, and Present State of the English Government in Bengal. L, 1772. 1st Ed. 4to, modern half calf. bba Nov 13 (106) £100 [Drury]

Vergil, Polydore, 1470?-1555

— Urbinatis Anglicae historiae libri vigintisex Basel: Michael Isingrinius, 1546. Folio, later calf with arms of Nicolas Chevalier; worn, joints starting. Last few leaves stained. sg Mar 27 (279) $200

Vergilius Maro, Publius, 70-19 B.C.

— Antiquissimi Virgiliani Codicis fragmenta et picturae ex Bibliotheca Vaticana. Rome, 1741. Folio, mor gilt, armorial bdg. S Oct 23 (16) £240 [Schuster]

— Opera. Strassburg: J. Gruninger, 25 Sept 1502. Folio, 17th-cent vellum gilt; worn. FD Dec 2 (102) DM13,000
Anr Ed. Lyons: Jacobo Sachon, 1517. 2 parts in 1 vol. Folio, later vellum bds; upper cover wormed. With 207 woodcuts, the 1st 18 colored "in an early hand." Margins of 1st title repaired, some leaves misbound or loose, some marginal dampstaining. S Nov 27 (238) £2,200 [Thomas]
Anr copy. Disbound. Sold for woodcuts only. Sold w.a.f. sg Dec 18 (229) $700
Anr Ed. Lyons, 1529. 2 parts in one. Folio, 18th-cent calf; worn & scraped. A few leaves slightly discolored. S Nov 27 (131) £2,000 [Abrams]
Anr Ed. Leiden: Elzevir, 1636. 12mo, contemp mor gilt with arms of Philip V. Schiff copy. S Mar 10 (994) £320 [Museon]
Anr Ed. Florence, 1741. ("Codex antiquissimus....") 4to, 19th-cent mor gilt. S Sept 23 (499) £170 [Laywood]
Anr Ed. Birm: Baskerville, 1757. ("Bucolica, Georgica, et Aeneis....") 1st Issue. 4to, contemp mor gilt. Some staining to margins. bba June 18 (181) £340 [Goldman]
Anr Ed. Rome, 1763-65. 3 vols. Folio, contemp half vellum; worn. L.p. copy. HK Nov 4 (2888) DM900
Anr Ed. Birm: Baskerville, 1766. 8vo, old mor gilt; rubbed. Hoe copy. S Nov 10 (415) £55 [Bookroom]
Anr Ed. Glasgow: Foulis, 1778. 2 vols in 1. Folio, later half calf; worn. Marginal staining. S Jan 13 (682) £60 [Thornton]
Anr Ed. Brussels: J. L. de Loubers, [c.1800]. 5 vols. 8vo, contemp calf; rebacked. Engraved throughout by Marcus Pitteri Vol I frontis mtd; Vol II top edges stained. sg Dec 18 (228) $110
Anr Ed. L, 1800. ("Bucolica, Georgica et Aeneis.") 2 vols. 8vo, contemp mor gilt; rebacked, preserving orig spines. C Dec 12 (310) £160 [Callea]
Anr copy. ("Bucolica, Georgica et Aenis.") Contemp mor; rubbed. Some foxing. O Nov 18 (194) $230
Anr copy. Mor; rubbed. W. H. Winship's copy. O June 9 (192) $190

— Works. L, 1698. "2d" Ed. Trans by John Dryden. Folio, contemp calf; joints splitting, rubbed. bba Oct 30 (161) £170 [Axe]

VERGILIUS MARO

Aeneid in French
— L'Eneide. Rome, 1819. 2 vols. Folio, half mor. With port & 50 plates. HK Nov 4 (2889) DM950

Bucolica in English
— The Pastorals. L, 1821. 2 vols. 8vo, half calf. With some plates by William Blake. acking frontis in Vol II; tear to K2 repaired with loss of 4 letters. Tipped in is ALs by R. J. Thornton (the editor) presenting the volume. pn Sept 18 (138) £1,900 [Lott & Gerrish]

Anr copy. Vol I only. 8vo, orig sheep. S Dec 4 (164) £2,200 [Swales]

Georgica in French
— Les Georgiques. Paris, 1937-43-[50]. One of 750. Illus by Aristide Maillol. 2 vols. 4to, loose as issued in orig wraps. HN Nov 26 (1955) DM1,900

Verity, Roger
— Le Farfalle diurne d'Italia. Florence, 1940-53. One of 1000 (Vols IV & V are 1 of 800). 5 vols in 4. 4to, half mor. With 27 plain & 74 colored plates. S Apr 23 (19) £1,150 [Antik]
— Rhopalocera palaerarctica. Iconographie et description des papilionidae et pieridae. Florence, 1905-11. 2 vols in 1. Folio, half mor gilt, orig wraps bound in. With 2 maps & 86 plates. S Apr 23 (18) £700 [Antik]

Verlaine, Paul, 1844-96
— Clair de lune. Florence: Henri Ariani, [1895]. 2 leaves. 12mo, mor gilt by Riviere. S May 21 (170) £300 [Maggs]
— Fetes galantes. Paris, 1928. Ltd Ed. 4to, half mor gilt. With 20 plates & with a 2d suite of plates. FD Dec 2 (4203) DM6,400

Anr copy. Wraps, lacking backstrip, shaken. With 20 (of 22) plates. sg Jan 8 (15) $375

Anr Ed. Paris, 1944. One of 5 on Portugese paper. Illus by Marie Laurencin. 4to, orig mor. S Mar 10 (995) £50 [McKenzie]
— Parallelement. Paris: Guillot, 1949. One of 70 with an extra suite of plates in black & 5 of the rejected plates in 2 forms: black & in color. 4to, unbound in orig wraps. CNY Dec 19 (127) $250
— Sagesse. Paris, 1911. One of 210 on Hollande. Illus by Maurice Denis. 4to, high-tech relief bdg by Jean de Gonet. FD Dec 2 (4317) DM5,200

AMERICAN BOOK PRICES CURRENT

Vermeylen, August
— Der Ewige Jude. Leipzig: Insel Verlag, 1921. Out-of-series copy. Illus by Frans Masereel. 4to, half cloth. ha Dec 19 (233) $75

Vermigli, Pietro Martire, 1500-62
— Loci Communes.... L: T. Vautrollerius, 1583. Folio, contemp calf over wooden bds; lacking clasps. Some worming, mostly to tp & 1st few leaves; stamps. T Sept 18 (299) £52

Vermont
— County Atlas of Washington Vermont. NY, 1873. Folio, cloth; spine backed with tape, loose in bdg. Plates brittle & with marginal tape-repairs. Sold w.a.f. O Sept 23 (17) $70

Vermorel, Victor. See: Viala & Vermorel

Verner, William Willoughby Cole
— Sketches in the Soudan. L, 1885. Oblong folio, orig bds. With engraved title, plan & 37 plates. pn Oct 15 (149) £170

Anr copy. Recent cloth. With litho titles, map & 37 plates. One plate torn without loss. T Oct 16 (299) £75

Vernet, Carle, 1758-1835
— Accidents de la chasse et des voitures. Paris: Delpech, [c.1825]. Folio, 19th-cent cloth. With 16 mtd hand-colored plates. Jeanson copy. SM Mar 1 (575) FF28,000
— Chasse au cerf. Paris: Depose a la Bibliotheque Imperiale, [c.1830]. Folio, modern cloth. Jeanson copy. SM Mar 1 (574) FF10,000
— La Chasse au renard.... Paris, [c.1820]. Folio, half shagreen. With 6 colored plates. Jeanson copy. SM Mar 1 (576) FF30,000
— Cris de Paris. Paris, [c.1820]. 2 vols in 1. Folio, contemp half mor; head of spine scuffed. With litho title & 100 hamd-colored plates. Tp spotted; Plate 21 torn across & repaired. C Oct 15 (141) £2,700 [Marlborough]
— Recueil de chevaux de tous genres.... Paris, [1794-1807]. Folio, contemp bds; worn. With engraved title & 52 plates, all hand-colored. Rosebery-Cockerell-Jeanson copy. SM Mar 1 (577) FF90,000

Verniere, Laure
— Geographie du regard. Verona: Plain Wrapper Press, [1976]. One of 71. Illus by Jacques Verniere. Half vellum. cb Sept 11 (210) $110

Verrill, A. Hyatt
— The Bridge of Light. Reading: Fantasy Press, 1950. One of 300. In worn d/j. Inscr. cb Sept 28 (1300) $50

Verschaffelt, Ambroise, 1825-86

— Nouvelle Iconographie des camellias. Ghent, 1848-58. Vols I-X (of 13). 4to, contemp half lea. A few plates trimmed affecting lithographer's name in Vol I; marginal stain on 2 plates in Vol III; 1 plate stained in Vol VI; some paper discoloration; a few plates creased in margins; no titles in Vols II & III. S Apr 23 (62) £6,500 [Burden]

Anr Ed. Ghent, 1848-60. 13 vols in 7. 8vo, contemp half calf; some bdgs rubbed, 1 vol with joints broken. With 624 hand-colored plates. Some spotting. de Belder copy. S Apr 28 (374) £10,500 [Duke of Devonshire]

Versor, Johannes

— Questiones...super metaphisicam Arestotelis cum textu eiusdem. [ologne: Heinrich Quentell, 1489-94, but before 28 Apr 1498]. Folio, contemp lea & wooden bds. Some soiling & waterstaining. 116 (of 118) leaves. Goff V-258. JG Mar 20 (232) DM1,100

Verster de Wulverhorst, A. H. See: Schlegel & Verster de Wulverhorst

Vertes, Marcel

— Nous les Abstraits. Paris, [1960]. One of 278. Loose in portfolio, as issued. With a pencil drawing of the painter slumped in front of his easel & sgd inscr on tp. sg June 4 (337) $225

— The Stronger Sex. NY, [1941]. Text by Janet Flanner. Folio, library cloth. Perforated library stamp on title. bba Feb 5 (294) £150 [Elliott]

Vertex, Jean

— Le Village inspire. Paris, 1950. One of 35 with the 12 views by Utrillo in color on velin d'Arches. Illus by Maurice Utrillo. 4to, unsewn in orig wraps. S June 17 (57) £2,600 [Marks]

Vertot, Rene Aubert de, 1655-1735

— The History of the Knights of Malta. L, 1728. 2 vols. Folio, contemp calf; worn. L.p. copy. pnE Jan 28 (55) £540 [McKenzie]

Anr copy. With 5 maps & plans & 71 ports. Marginal worming to prelims of both vols not affecting text. S Oct 23 (310) £300 [Dupont]

Anr copy. Contemp calf; broken. With 70 (of 71) ports & 5 maps & plans. sg Nov 20 (172) $325

Vertue, George, 1684-1756

— Medals, Coins, Great-Seals.... [L], 1753. 1st Ed. 4to, contemp half calf; worn. With 38 plates. S Nov 10 (183) £95 [Drury]

Verve...

[For Issues on individuals, See Bonnard, Braque, Chagall, etc.]

— Verve: Revue artistique et litteraire. Paris, 1937. No 1. 4to, orig wraps. cb June 18 (323) $90

Nos 1-5/6 in 5 vols. Wraps. HN Nov 26 (2165) DM1,800

No 3. Paris, 1938. 4to, orig bds. In English. JG Oct 2 (2317) DM600; JG Oct 2 (2318) DM500

Nos 2-4. Paris, 1938-39. 4to, orig cloth, with orig wraps. wa Sept 25 (285) $210

No 5/6. Paris, 1939. Wraps; worn, spine torn. O Jan 6 (193) $80

Nos 3, 4 & 5/6. Wraps; spines taped. Stamp & tape stains on titles. sg June 4 (339) $225

Nos 5-6. 4to, orig bdgs. JG Oct 2 (2321) DM500

Nos 5-8. Paris, 1939-40. 4to, orig wraps; worn. ha Sept 19 (139) $150

Nos 27/28. Paris, 1952. Bds. O Mar 24 (194) $390

Vervliet, Hendrik D. L.

— The Book through 5,000 Years. L & NY, [1972]. 4to, orig cloth, in d/j. bba Feb 5 (36) £110 [Dawson]

Verwey, Albert, 1865-1937

— Aarde. Amst., 1896. Orig cloth. B Oct 7 (25) HF120

Vesalius, Andreas, 1514-64

— De humani corporis fabrica.... Basel: Johannes Oporinus, June 1543. 1st Ed. Folio, modern vellum. Short tear repaired in 2 leaves; some marginal repairs & spotting; very small hole in 2 leaves; minor worming to inner blank margin of a few leaves slightly affecting a few letters of sidenotes. C Dec 12 (286) £16,000 [Schindler]

Anr copy. Vellum bds; lower cover repaired. Title rebacked, some margins repaired. S Nov 27 (291) £25,000 [Elte]

Anr copy. Recent calf gilt. Tp backed & with tiny wormhole at lower corner; 11 leaves in quires O-Q with margins repaired or strengthened; tear in k6 repaired; marginal tear in T6; other defs. S May 21 (218) £1,700 [Thomas]

Anr Ed. Venice: Franciscium & Criegher, 1568. Folio, contemp vellum; worn. Some staining & spotting. S June 25 (140) £3,200 [King]

VESALIUS

— Epistola rationem modumque propinandi radicis chymae decocti.... Basel, [Johannes Oporinus, 1546]. Bound with: Alexander of Tralles. - De singularum corporis partium. Basel,[1533] & Andrea Gallo. - Gascis de peste. Brescia, 1565. Folio contemp pigskin; clasps partly lost. With port of au from Fabrica woodblook & 4 capitals also from Fabrica blocks. P Dec 15 (235) $8,500

— Epitome anatomica.... Leiden, 1616. 4to, half syn. Title stamped. sg Jan 15 (125) $2,200

**Vesalius, Andreas, 1514-64 —&
Valverde de Hamusco, Juan**

— Anatomie ofte Af-beeldinghe van de deelen des menschelijken lichaems en derselver Verklaringhe.... Amst.: Cornelis dankertz, 1647. Bound with: Mauden, David van. Bedieninghe der Anatomien....Amst.: Cornelis Dankertz, 1646. Folio, vellum. Partial dampstaining of text throughout; title stamped. sg Jan 15 (126) $850

Vesling, Johann, 1598-1649

— Syntagma anatomicum. Padua, 1647. 2d Ed. 4to, contemp vellum; spine with tear. With engraved title & 24 plates. One plate with small hole; library stamp at foot of tp. C May 13 (205) £400 [Maggs]

Vespucci, Amerigo, 1454-1512
See also: Grabhorn Printing

— Mundus novus. [Rome: Eucharius Silber, 1504]. 4to, modern mor. 4 leaves, with 2 woodcut initials & 3 woodcut diagrams. S Apr 24 (318) £20,000 [Kraus]

Vetromile, Eugene, 1819-81

— Indian Good Book.... NY, 1857. 2d Ed. 12mo, orig lea. O Nov 18 (195) $150

Vezins, Elie de Levezou de, Comte

— Les Chiens courants francais pour la chasse du lievre.... Paris, 1890. One of 200. Illus by Ch. Boyer. 8vo, mor gilt by Chambolle-Duru. With 18 orig aquarelles. Jeanson copy. SM Mar 1 (573) FF11,000

**Viala, Pierre —&
Vermorel, Victor**

— Traite general de viticulture. Paris, 1901-10. 7 vols. Folio, orig bdg. With 70 plain & 500 colored plates. FD Dec 2 (472) DM3,800

Anr copy. Ptd wraps; some spines chipped. Surfaces of c.5 plates damaged; 2 plates adhered to preceding versos; 1 plate badly torn & mended; some marginal tears. Crahan copy. P Nov 25 (465) $2,400

AMERICAN BOOK PRICES CURRENT

Viardel, Cosme

— Observations sur la pratique des acouchemens.... Paris, 1674. 8vo, contemp vellum; worn. With folding port & 16 folding plates; stained & soiled. S Nov 27 (292) £380 [Gurney]

Vicaire, Georges

— Bibliographie gastronomique. L, 1954. cb July 30 (296) $75

Anr copy. In torn d/j. sg Jan 15 (54) $70

Anr copy. In d/j. sg Jan 22 (307) $70; SM Oct 20 (520) FF1,000

— Manuel de l'amateur de livres du XIXe Siecle.... Paris, 1894-1920. One of 1,000. 8 vols. 8vo, half vellum, orig wraps bound in; some covers warped. sg May 14 (244) $600

Victoria...

— Victoria Illustrated. Second Series. Melbourne & Sydney, 1862. Oblong 4to, orig cloth; rebacked, preserving orig spine. With engraved title & 43 plates, some detached. C Oct 15 (181) £1,100 [Mall Gallery]

Victoria, Queen of England

— Leaves from the Journal of Our Life in the Highlands. L, 1868. 1st Pbd Ed. Ed by Arthur Helps. 8vo, later mor gilt, orig bdg preserved; worn. With 2 plates. Inscr to Lady Belhaven. cb Dec 4 (333) $300

Anr copy. Mor gilt; rubbed. Inscr. S Jan 13 (683) £120 [Maggs]

— The Letters of Queen Victoria. L, 1907-32. 9 vols. orig cloth. sg Feb 12 (325) $250

Victoria History of the Counties of England

— Bedfordshire. L, 1904-14. 4 vols, including Index. Folio, orig cloth; hinges weak, rubbed. Titles stamped. bba Dec 4 (307) £85 [Quaritch]

— Berkshire. L, 1906-27. 5 vols, including Index. Folio, orig cloth; hinges weak, rubbed, 1 bdg broken. Titles stamped. bba Dec 4 (308) £90 [Quaritch]

— Buckinghamshire. L, 1905-28. 5 vols. 4to, orig cloth. bba Dec 4 (309) £130 [Quaritch]

— Cambridge and the Isle of Ely. L, 1938-59. Vols I-IV (of 6). Folio, orig cloth; hinges weak, rubbed. Titles stamped. bba Dec 4 (310) £110 [Quaritch]

— Hampshire and the Isle of Wight. L, 1900-14. 6 vols. Folio, cloth; some joints split, lacking 1 backstrip. bba Dec 4 (313) £150 [Quaritch]

— Hertfordshire. L, 1902-23. 5 vols, including Index. Folio, orig cloth; some vols broken, 1 lacking backstrip. bba Dec 4 (314) £75 [Quaritch]

— Kent. L, 1908-32. 3 vols. Folio, orig cloth; hinges weak, rubbed. Titles stamped. bba

Dec 4 (316) £190 [Quaritch]
- Lancashire. L, 1901-14. Vols I-VIII. Folio, orig cloth; some spines torn. Pages brittle with a few tears. bba Dec 4 (317) £250 [Quaritch]
- Leicestershire. L, 1907-64. 5 vols. Folio, orig cloth; hinges weak, rubbed. Titles stamped. bba Dec 4 (318) £110 [Quaritch]
- Northamptonshire. L, 1902-37. 4 vols. 4to, orig cloth; some joints split, lacking 1 backstrip. bba Dec 4 (321) £80 [Quaritch]
- Rutland. L, 1908-36. 3 vols, including Index. Folio, orig cloth; hinges weak, rubbed. Titles stamped. bba Dec 4 (324) £160 [Quaritch]
- Shropshire. L, 1908-68. 3 vols. Folio, orig cloth; hinges weak, rubbed. Titles stamped. bba Dec 4 (325) £150 [Quaritch]
- Staffordshire. L, 1908-63. 5 (of 6) vols; lacking Vol III. Folio, orig cloth; hinges weak, rubbed. Titles stamped. bba Dec 4 (327) £170 [Quaritch]
- Surrey. L, 1902-14. 5 vols, including Index. 4to, orig cloth; 2 vols lacking backstrip. bba Dec 4 (3238) £150 [Quaritch]

Vida, Marcus Hieronymus, 1480?-1566
- De arte poetica libri tres. Oxford, 1723. 3 parts in 1 vol. Contemp calf; rebacked. pn Mar 26 (518) £80 [Furstenberg]
- Poemata. L, 1732. 2 vols in 1. 12mo, contemp calf; rebacked. pn Mar 26 (519) £35 [Blain]

Vidal, Emeric Essex
- Picturesque Illustrations of Buenos Ayres and Monte Video.... L: Ackermann, 1820. 4to, mor gilt by Sangorski & Sutcliffe. With 24 plates, 4 double-page & colored. FD June 11 (1161) DM12,500

Vidmar, M.
- Pol Stoletja ob Sahovnici. Ljubljana, 1951. pn Mar 26 (266) £60 [Chen]

Vie...
- Vie de Guillaume de Gimaches... Paris: Prault, 1786. 4to, contemp calf; worn. L.p. copy. Jeanson copy. SM Mar 1 (578) FF2,800

Vieillot, Louis Jean Pierre. See. Audebert & Vieillot

Viel de Saint Maux, Charles Francois
- Projet d'un monument consacre a l'histoire naturelle. Paris, 1779. 4to, bdg not described but loose. Franklin Institute copy. F Sept 12 (24) $700

Vietz, Ferdinand Bernhard
- Icones plantarum medico-oeconomico-technologicarum.... Vienna, [1800-6]. 11 vols in 10, including 1822 Supplement. 4to, contemp half calf; rubbed. With 11 engraved titles with hand-colored borders & 1185 (of 1187?) hand-colored plates. Lacking Plate 21 in Vol I & Plate 73 in Supplement; some discoloration; some plates slightly trimmed; a few small holes. S Apr 23 (63) £4,200 [Antik]

Vigne, Godfrey Thomas
- Travels in Kashmir, Ladak, Iskardo.... L, 1842. 2 vols. 8vo, cloth; spines worn. With folding map in Vol I front cover pocket. Some foxing & soiling. sg Nov 20 (87) $350

Vigny, Alfred de, 1797-1863
- Les Destinees: Poemes philosophiques. Paris: Leon Pichon, 1930. One of 290 on papier d'Arches. Illus by Pedro Centeno Vallenilla. Folio, mor gilt extra by Marot-Rodde, orig wraps bound in. With 27 orig pencil drawings, sgd. Inscr by Vallenilla. P Dec 15 (180) $700

Vilaplana, Hermenegildo
- Vida portentosa del Americano septentrional apostol.... Madrid, 1775. 4to, vellum. Port & 1st 9 leaves of text inserted from a shorter copy. S Apr 24 (276) £950 [Arader]

Villers, Clemence de
- Dialogues sur la musique. Paris, 1774. 8vo, contemp wraps gilt with arms of Louise-Marie-Adelaide de Bourbon Pantievre, duchesse de Chartres. S June 25 (59) £480

Villette, Charles Michel de, Marquis
- Oeuvres. Londres [i.e. Paris], 1786. 12mo, contemp mor gilt; rubbed. Ptd on Ecorce de Tilluel paper. With 20 paper samples at end, some torn or def. bba Mar 26 (135) £800 [Questor]

Villon, Francois, b.1431
See also: Eragny Press
- Oeuvres. Paris, [1933]. 4to, mor, orig wraps bound in; joints starting. sg Jan 8 (288) $50
  Anr Ed. Paris, 1942. Mor by Courtney Sheehan. cb Sept 11 (315) $200
- Le Testament. Paris, 1930. Out-of-series copy, unsgd. Illus by Frans Masereel. 4to, orig folders. B Oct 7 (191) HF440

Vilmorin, Louise de
- L'Echo des Fantaisies. [N.p, n.d.]. Out-of-series copy marked "de Rene Magritte". 2 vols. Unbound as issued in orig cases. Inscr to Georgette & Rene Magritte. S July 2 (1076) £200 [Rota]
- Madame de.... Paris & Bievres: Gallimard

VILMORIN

& Pierre de Tartas, 1975. One of 185 on grand velin d'Arches with 2 sgd double-page plates. Illus by Pecnard. 4to, loose as issued in litho cover & plexiglass box. With 23 color lithos. sg Jan 8 (289) $175

Vilnay, Zev
— The Holy Land in Old Prints and Maps. Jerusalem, 1965. 4to, cloth, in worn d/j; front free endpaper removed. sg Apr 30 (364) $150

Vilvain, Robert
— Theoremata Theologica: Theological Treatises. L, 1654. Bound with: A Compend of Chronography. L, 1654. 4to, later calf; joints split. Ck Jan 30 (10) £65

Vince, Samuel
— A Treatise on Practical Astronomy. Cambridge, 1790. 4to, contemp calf; broken, spine defective. With 8 folding plates. sg Jan 15 (378) $200

Vincent, Henriette Antoinette
— Etudes de fleurs et de fruits.... [N.p., c.1810]. Folio, contemp half mor; rubbed. With 24 hand-finished color plates. Some spotting to Plate 1; tear in outer margin of Plate 23. de Belder copy. S Apr 28 (375) £3,200 [Arader]
— Studies of Fruits and Flowers, Painted from Nature. L: Ackermann, 1814. Folio, orig bds; rebacked in calf & recornered. With hand-colored frontis & 23 hand-finished color plates, each accompanied by an uncolored outline plate, 1 with a partly colored state. Also 1 plate of flower detail. Altogether, 48 plates. de Belder copy. S Apr 28 (376) £5,000 [Hill]

Vinciolo, Federico di
— Les Singuliers et nouveaux Pourtraicts.... Paris: Jean Le Clerc, 1599. Bound with: Vinciolo. Les Secondes oeuvres, et subtiles inventions de lingerie.... Paris: Jean Le Clerc, 1599 4to, mor gilt extra. One leaf shaved, with loss of signatures & bits of woodcuts. Skillful restorations in both works, affecting 2 or 3 woodcuts. Huth copy. P Dec 15 (236) $3,000

Vindel, Francisco
— Manual grafico-descriptivo del bibliofilo Hispano-Americano. Madrid, 1930-34. 11 (of 12) vols; lacking Vol XI. Folio, contemp calf, orig wraps bound in. Owner's stamp on verso of each title. sg Sept 18 (295) $500

Anr copy. 12 vols. Folio, lea gilt, orig wraps bound in; scuffed. sg Oct 2 (295) $750

— Mapas de America en los Libros Espanoles.... Madrid, 1959. One of 520. Vol II only. Folio, lea gilt, orig wraps bound in. sg Oct 2 (96) $60

Vindel, Pedro
— Bibliografia grafica. Madrid, 1910. 2 vols. Half sheep. sg May 14 (652) $475
— Biblioteca Oriental.... Madrid, 1911-12. 2 vols. 8vo, sheep, orig wraps bound in. sg Oct 2 (296) $70

Vingboons, Philip, 1608-88
— Gronden en afbeeldsels der voornaamste gebouwen.... Amst., 1680. Folio, old bds with lea back; worn. With 58 (of 62) plates; 1 plate torn; part of Plate 32 torn away. Sold w.a.f. O Sept 23 (185) $230

Vinge, Joan
— The Snow Queen. NY: Dial Press, 1980. Uncorrected proof used as review copy. Wraps. cb Sept 28 (1303) $150

Vingtieme Siecle
— XXe Siecle: Cahiers d'art. Paris, 1959-75. Nos 12-45. Wraps. JG Oct 2 (2323) DM3,600

Viollet-le-Duc, Eugene Emmanuel, 1814-79
— Dictionnaire raisonne de l'architecture francais du XIe au XVIe siecle. Paris, 1858-68. 10 vols. 8vo, contemp lea; worn. S Nov 17 (685) £180 [Diwan]
— Dictionnaire raisonne de l'architecture francaise du XIe au XVIe siecle. Paris, 1867-70. 10 vols. 8vo, half calf gilt. HN May 20 (800) DM680
— Dictionnaire raisonne de l'architecture francais du XIe au XVIe siecle. Paris, 1875. 10 vols. 8vo, contemp half lea; extremities worn, spine ends of 1st & last vols reinforced with tape. sg Feb 5 (320) $300
— Dictionnaire raisonne du mobilier francais.... Paris, 1863-75. 6 vols. 8vo, contemp mor; spines dry, Vol VI torn. C July 22 (219) £150

Anr Ed. Paris, 1872-75. 6 vols. 8vo, contemp half mor. S Nov 17 (686) £140 [Diwan]

— Habitations modernes. Paris, 1874-75. Orig 10 parts. Folio, loose as issued in orig ptd cloth folders & with 4 of the orig wraps. With 200 plates. C July 22 (221) £850

Viollis, Jean
— Bonne-Fille. Paris: Editions Mornay, 1926. One of 18 on japon with 2 large ink & watercolor drawings & 2 smaller designs, each sgd by the artist. 8vo, mor extra by Canape, orig wraps bound in. S June 17 (19) £360 [Stemer]

Virchow, Rudolf, 1821-1902
— Der Cellularpathologie.... Berlin, 1858. 1st Ed. 8vo, contemp bds; worn & broken. HN Nov 26 (259) DM2,000

Virginia
— A True and Sincere Declaration of the Purpose and Ends of the Plantation begun in Virginia. L: I. Stepneth, 1610. 2d Issue. 4to, mor. Some shaving. S June 25 (418) £13,500

Viribus...
— Viribus Unitis. Das Buch vom Kaiser. Budapest, etc. [c.1908]. Folio, orig mor gilt with gilt centerpiece with enamelling & stones. S May 6 (31) £100 [Hannas]

Virtue...
— Virtue in a Cottage, or a Mirror for Children in Humble Life. L: John Marshall, [c.1790]. 32mo, orig floral bds. With wood-engraved frontis & 14 illusts. S June 17 (419) £250 [Magee]

Vischer, Edwardoanne
— Drawings of the California Missions, 1861-1878. San Francisco: Book Club of California, 1982. One of 600. Oblong 4to, orig cloth. sg Mar 12 (25) $50

Vishniac, Roman
— Polish Jews: A Pictorial Record. NY, 1947. 4to, cloth. sg Sept 25 (332) $70

Vision...
— Vision, a Literary Quarterly. Sydney, 1923-24. Nos 1-4 in 4 vols. 4to, cloth, orig wraps retained. Some foxing. CA Apr 12 (146) A$130

Visit...
— A Visit to Texas; being the Journal of a Traveller.... NY: Goodrich & Wiley, 1834. 12mo, orig cloth; worn, lacking free endpapers. Foxed throughout; lacking folding color map. wa Sept 25 (396) $85

Visscher, Jan de
— Diversa Animalia. Berghem delineavit. Amst., [c.1670]. 8vo, old wraps. With pictorial title & 11 plates. Some crude hand-coloring; 7 plates with 1 small worm hole. sg Apr 2 (205) $500

Visscher, Nikolaus Jansson
— Atlas Mayor sive totius orbis terrarum contracta delineata. Amst., [c.1710]. Folio, contemp calf; rebacked. With engraved title & 143 double-page or folding maps & 1 loosely inserted Ms map, all colored in a contemp hand, the title heightened with gold. Minor discoloration & repairs. S Apr 23 (139) £22,000 [George]
— Atlas minor sive totius orbis terrarum contracta delineata. Amst., [1689 or later]. Folio, contemp vellum; soiled & scuffed. With engraved title & 172 double-page maps, all fully hand-colored by a contemp hand, title heightened with gold. Ms index at end; some mapsheets with appended folding gazetteer leaves; mtd on guards throughout; both titles torn, def & creased; c.13 maps with tears & defs; some thumbing. C Oct 15 (112) £12,500 [Tooley Adams]

Visscher, Roemer
— Zinne-Poppen. Alle verciert met Rijmen.... Amst., 1678. 12mo, contemp vellum. With engraved title & 193 emblematical plates. Waterstained, 1 leaf defective. B Oct 7 (1141) HF2,500

Vita. See: Guevara, Antonio de

Vitringa, Campegius
— De synagoga vetere libri tres. Franequer, 1696. 2 parts in 1 vol. 4to, contemp calf; backstrip lacking, worn. Marginal tears & holes not affecting text; library stamps, 1 plate cropped at upper margin. bba May 28 (371) £100 [Valmadonna]

Vitruvius Pollio, Marcus

In English
— The Architecture. L, 1791. 2 vols. Folio, contemp half calf; worn. With port & 46 plates. Dampstained. L.p. copy. Ck Nov 21 (36) £130

Anr copy. Bdg not indicated. Library markings. Sold w.a.f. Franklin Institute copy. F Sept 11 (27) $300

In French
— Les Dix Livres d'architecture. Paris, 1683. 1st Ed of Perrault's trans. Folio, contemp calf; spine worn & chipped. Some dampstain in margins at beginning. sg Apr 2 (206) $900

2d Ed of Perrault's trans. Paris, 1684. Folio, contemp calf gilt. With engraved title & 68 plates. Occasional minor discoloration. S Oct 23 (205) £520 [Quaritch]

Anr copy. Half calf gilt. With frontis & 68 plates. Small tears in 1 leaf repaired with paper tape; waterstain in lower outside corner throughout; outer corner of last 7 leaves repaired. sg Apr 2 (207) $900

In Italian
— De architectura.... Venice, 1535. ("Di architettura....") Folio, 18th-cent vellum over bds; soiled. Title with small tears & repairs, corners & gutters dampstained. cb Dec 18 (177) $500

Anr Ed. Perugia, 1536. ("Architettura.") Folio, vellum bds. Tp cropped; wormed at beginning; contemp marginal annotations

VITRUVIUS POLLIO

cropped; some headlines shaved; some dampstains. S Nov 10 (185) £330 [Tose]

Anr Ed. Venice: Francesco Marcolini, 1556. ("Il Dieci libri dell' architettura.") Folio, recent half sheep. With 8 double-page woodcuts, 6 pasted extensions, 1 volvelle & pointer on Q2. Nine leaves with severe marginal repairs; lacking volvelles at V2 & V3. CNY Dec 19 (245) $500

Anr Ed. Venice, 1567. ("I Dieci Libri del architettura.") 4to, new vellum; new endpapers. Lower outer corner of final leaf strengthened. S June 25 (223) £500 [Perceval]

Anr Ed. Naples, 1758. ("L'Architettura.") Folio, bdg not indicated. Library markings. Sold w.a.f. Franklin Institute copy. F Sept 12 (26) $220

In Latin

Anr Ed. Florence: Giunta, 1522. 8vo, contemp Italian calf; joints cracked, backstrip defective. Upper cover & 1st 75 leaves with extreme blank corers gnawed away; some upper margins stained. CNY Dec 19 (244) $350

Anr Ed. Strassburg: In Officina Knoblochiana per Georgium Machaeropioeum, 1543. ("De architectura, libri decem.") 3 parts in 1 vol. 4to, vellum gilt. Some dampstains. pn Apr 3021125 £420

Anr Ed. Lyons, 1586. 4to, later half mor; rubbed. Some running heads & page numerals cropped; ink annotations in margin at beginning; stained. S Nov 10 (186) £220 [Hasbach]

Anr Ed. Amst.: Elzevir, 1649. Folio, contemp vellum; worn. Large sections lacking; some stains; final leaf torn with loss. Sold w.a.f. Ck Jan 16 (10) £140

Anr copy. Contemp vellum; worn & wormed. Some worming. FD June 11 (2119) DM1,200

Vivaldus, Johannes Ludovicus

— Opus regale in quo continentur infrascripta opuscula. Lyons: Etienne Gueynard, 7 Aug 1512. 8vo, contemp blind-stamped pigskin; lacking clasps. Minor worming to bottom of inner margin towards beginning. S Nov 27 (28) £800 [Thomas]

Vives, Johannes Ludovicus, 1492-1540

— L'Institution de la Femme Chrestienne. Cologne: Petrus HOrst, 1579. 8vo, 19th-cent half vellum; worn. Sidenotes shaved. sg Mar 26 (280) $60

Vizetelly, Henry, 1820-94

— Four Months among the Gold Finders of Alta California.... L, 1849. 2d Ed. 8vo, orig cloth. With map. sg Mar 12 (259) $110

— A History of Champagne.... L, 1882. 4to, orig cloth; worn & soiled. Library markings. wa Mar 5 (229) $130

— Vier Monate under den Goldfindern in Obercalifornien. Hamburg, 1849. 12mo, unbound. cb Jan 8 (17) $50

Vlaminck, Maurice, 1876-1958

— En Noir et en couleur. Paris, [1962]. One of 40 on japon nacre with an extra suite of the illusts on Arches & a decomposition of 1 double-page illust on Rives. 4to, unsewn as issued in orig wraps. S June 17 (58) £420 [Marks]

Vliet, Jan van, 1620-66

— Venatio novantiqua. Leiden: Elxevir, 1645. 12mo, l8th-cent mor gilt. Jeanson copy. SM Mar 1 (567) FF1,800

Voellinger, Joseph

— Grossherzoglich Badisches Militar. Karlsruhe: J. Velten, 1824. Folio, modern half cloth. With 30 hand-colored plates. Tp & contents leaf trimmed; some foxing. S June 25 (211) £1,800

Vogt, Johann, 1695-1764

— Catalogus historico-criticus librorum rariorum. Hamburg, 1753. 8vo, modern half calf. Some spotting. pn Sept 18 (182) £60 [Forster]

Voice...

— The Voice of Jacob. L: B. Steill, 1843-44. Vol III. Folio, loose in contemp cloth. sg Apr 30 (80) $130

Voight, Hans Henning

— Fifty Drawings. NY, 1925. One of 1,025. 4to, half cloth. With 50 plates. Ck Dec 10 (250) £75

Voigtel, Nicolaus

— Vermehrte geometria subterranea, oder Marckscheide-Kunst. Eisleben, 1713. Folio, contemp calf; spine & corners worn. With 10 double-page plates. Marginal worming at beginning & end. S June 25 (141) £600

Voiture, Vincent de, 1597-1648

— Letters of Affaires Love and Courtship.... L, 1657. Trans by J. Davies. 8vo, early calf; worn. Frontis scratched; 2 small holes in frontis & 1st 4 leaves; rust-hole in D8; stain in outer margins. S Sept 23 (409) £110 [Bennett & Kerr]

Volkman, Daniel G.
— Fifty Years of the McCloud River Club. San Francisco: Pvtly ptd, 1951. One of 150. 4to, half cloth. sg Oct 23 (392) $225

Volkmann, Daniel G.
— Memories of a Fishing Journey to New Zealand Made in 1950 by Dean and Helen Witter.... San Francisco, 1950. One of 100. Bds. sg Oct 23 (410) $350

Vollard, Ambroise
— La Vie et l'oeuvre de Pierre-Auguste Renoir. Paris, 1919. One of 100 on japon imperial. Folio, mor gilt extra by Peuser. With 51 plates, each in 2 states. P Dec 15 (237) $1,900

One of 1,000. Half mor. S June 17 (46) £1,200 [Sayle]

Volney, Constantin Francois, Comte de
— Oeuvres. Paris, 1826. 8 vols. 8vo, contemp half mor gilt. sg Feb 12 (326) $90
— Tableau du climat et du sol des Etats-Unis d'Amerique. Paris, 1803 [An XII]. 1st Ed, Issue not indicated. 2 vols. 8vo, contemp calf, with gilt arms of Napoleon on sides. 1 torn. With Ms note indicating that this came from Napoleon's library. C June 18 (230) £1,000

Volpato, Giovanni —&
Morghen, Raffaelo
— Principes du dessein tires apres les antiques statues. Rome, 1786. Folio, new half lea. With 36 plates; lightly dampstained, affecting images. sg Dec 18 (230) $350

Voltaire, Francois Marie Arouet de
— Candide. NY, 1928. One of 95 hand-colored copies. Illus by Rockwell Kent. 4to, orig half mor. cb Dec 4 (249) $600

One of 1,470. Cloth. cb Dec 4 (250) $65; cb June 18 (229) $55

Anr Ed. NY: Pantheon, [1944]. One of 50 hand bound by Gerlach & with 2 extra suites of the illusts, on white & yellow paper. Illus by Paul Klee. 4to, half lev. 1 leaf affected by stain. cb Feb 19 (272) $250; cb June 18 (246) $225

— Candide, ou l'optimisme. [Amst.: Marc Michel Rey], 1759. ("Candide traduit de l'allemand. De Mr, le Docteur Ralph.") Wade's 1st Ed. 8vo, contemp calf; front cover detached. sg Oct 9 (340) $120

Anr Ed. Paris, 1932. One of 100. Illus by Gus Bofa. 4to, bdg not described. With 33 colored plates. B Oct 7 (357) HF350

— La Henriade. Kehl, 1789. 4to, mor extra by Zaehnsdorf. With 2 ports, 10 plates in 2 states, 5 eaux-fortes & 8 proofs. On papier velin. Extra-illus with 136 plates from other Eds. C Dec 3 (166) £1,600 [Tenschert]

— Histoire de Charles XII. Basel: C. Revis [L], 1731. 1st Ed. 2 vols in 1. 8vo, contemp calf gilt; rebacked. Lacking the 2 errata leaves. S Sept 23 (502) £170 [Libris]

— The History of the War of Seventeen Hundred and Forty One. L, 1756. Contemp calf; extremities worn, front joint cracked. cb Dec 18 (178) $65

— Letters Concerning the English Nation. L, 1733. 1st Ed. 8vo, calf; rebacked, rubbed, corners knocked. Marginal tears on G3 not affecting text. P Sept 24 (417) $325

— Memoires.... L, 1784. 8vo, orig bds. sg Mar 26 (281) $350

— Oeuvres. Geneva: 1756-63. 17 vols, plus 4 supplementary Vols. 8vo, contemp calf; rubbed. bba Oct 30 (239) £80 [Shapero]

Anr Ed. Geneva, 1768-77. 30 vols. 4to, half calf. B Oct 7 (883) HF1,900

Anr Ed. Kehl, 1785-89. 70 vols. 8vo, contemp calf gilt; rebacked & worn. No plates; browned & stained. bba Oct 16 (35) £280 [Meilor & Baxter]

Anr copy. Contemp calf gilt; some spine ends chipped. C Dec 3 (184) £1,500 [Heyward]

Anr copy. Contemp half russia gilt; rubbed. With port & 93 plates & 14 ports. C Dec 12 (212) £1,000 [McCrow]

Anr Ed. Kehl, 1785-89-1082. 72 vols, including 2 vols of Tables. 8vo, contemp calf by Delorme with his ticket; some repairs, last 4 vols not uniform. Sold w.a.f. C May 13 (60) £500 [Van Doorn]

Anr Ed. Kehl, 1785-89. 70 vols. 8vo, contemp calf. Small tear in tp of Vol XXX repaired. S May 21 (171) £2,000 [Lyon]

— La Pucelle d'Orleans. Londres [Paris], 1780. 2 vols. 4to, mor extra by Chambolle Duru. L.p. copy with plates in 2 states. C Dec 3 (167) £1,800 [Camille]

Anr copy. 12mo, mor gilt by David. Extra-illus with 70 plates. S Mar 10 (1000) [360] [Maggs]

Anr Ed. Londres [but Paris: Cazin], 1790. 12mo, contemp mor gilt. With 2 ports & 22 plates heightened with a wash & mtd "a la glomy" within blue & yellow wash borders. C Dec 3 (170) £3,000 [Beres]

Anr Ed. Paris: Didot Jeune, [1795]. 2 vols in 1. 4to, mor gilt by Zaehnsdorf. L.p. copy with plates in 2 states. C Dec 3 (168) £950 [Heyward]

— Works. L, 1762-73. 35 vols. 8vo, calf; worn. sg Sept 11 (279) $150

— Zadig, ou la destine. L: J. Brindley, 1749. 12mo, contemp calf; rubbed. Frontis torn at fold. S Nov 10 (417) £200 [Quaritch]

Vondel, Joost van den, 1587-1679
— Gysbregt van Aemstel. De ondergang van syn stad...Treurspel. Haarlem, 1893-[94-1901]. Vol I only. Folio, half lea. B Oct 7 (18) HF550

Vonnegut, Kurt, Jr.
— Slaughterhouse-Five or the Children's Crusade. NY, 1969. In d/j with date stamp at foot of rear flap. cb May 7 (159) $55

Voorn, Hendrick
— Old Ream Wrappers. [North Hills, Pa.]: Bird & Bull Press, 1969. One of 375. Half lea. sg Sept 11 (31) $175

Voorsnydinge...
— De Cierlijck Voorsnydinge aller Tafel-Gerechten. Amst.: Hieronymus Sweerts, [c.1664]. Oblong 8vo, wraps. Some waterstains; folding plate torn & repaired. Deuzel-Lambert-Crahan copy. P Nov 25 (146) $1,100

Voragine, Jacobus de, 1230?-98?
See also: Kelmscott Press
— Legenda aurea. Cologne: Ulrich Zel, 19 May 1482. Folio, contemp blind-tooled calf voer wooden bds. 280 leaves; lacking 1st blank. Goff J-102. sg Apr 12 (118) $1,600

Anr Ed. Cologne: [Ulrich Zel], 1483. Folio, 18th-cent mor gilt. Small hole in c4, S4 & X4 affecting a few letters; small wormhole in H8 & 11 affecting a few letters; color from a few initials transferred to facing page; hole in blank lower margin of B4; faint waterstain to portion of lower blank margins; final leaf backed. 462 leaves. Goff J-108. C Dec 12 (295) £2,400 [Schwing]

Anr Ed. Strassburg: Printer of the 1483 Jordanus de Quedlinburg, May 1496. ("Lombardica historia que a plerisque aurea legenda sanctorum appelatur.") Folio, contemp half vellum over wooden bds; with catch, lacking clasp, spine chipped at head. Marginal dampstains; contemp marginalia throughout; lacking D3-5. 261 (of 264) leaves; lacking D3-5. Goff J-133. sg Dec 4 (90) $550

— Legendario di sancti. Venice: N. & D. dal Jesu, 2 Aug 1518. Folio, 19th-cent calf; scraped & rubbed. Most borders shaved, 1 leaf torn, title repaired & stained. S Nov 27 (183) £600 [Marshall]

Vosburgh, W.S. See: Derrydale Press

Vosmeer, Michael
— Principes Hollandiae et Zelandiae.... Antwerp, 1578. Folio, 19th-cent half calf. With 36 ports. Interleaved copy of Gerrit Poelgheest. B Feb 25 (640) HF1,400

Vossius, Gerardus Joannes
— De quatuor artibus popularibus.... Amst.: J. Blaeu, 1650. 3 parts in 1 vol. 4to, calf; worn. pn Jan 22 (51) £85 [Poole]

Voyage...
— Voyage fair par ordre du Roi en 1771 et 1772.... Paris, 1778. 2 vols. 4to, 19th-cent half lea gilt. Some stains & foxing. sg Apr 2 (204) $700

— The Voyage of the Racoon: A "Secret" Journal of a Visit to Oregon, California & Hawaii, 1813-1814. San Francisco: Book Club of Calif., 1958. cb Sept 11 (74) $75

Voyages. See: Acuna, Christoval

Vredeman de Vries, Jan
— Perspective die Weitberuhmte Kunst. Amst., 1628. Bound with: Albrecht, Andreas. Zwey Bueche: Das erst von der...Perspectiva. Folio, 18th-cent vellum. First work with 74 double-page plates; 2d work with engraved titles & 14 plates. 2d work with 1 engraved title cropped & a small hole in the 2d affecting surface. S Oct 23 (213) £650 [Rota]

Vries, Hugo de. See: De Vries, Hugo

Vries, Jan Vredemann, b.1527
— Variae architecturae formae.... Antwerp: Theodorus Gallaeus, 1601. Oblong 4to, modern bds; spine loose. With engraved title & 48 plates. Margins of tp frayed; Plate 42 inserted from anr copy; marginal tears or repairs to c.10 plates; Plate 24 spotted; some finger-soiling. Hunt copy. CNY Nov 21 (283) $140

Vues...
— Vues des villes, edifices & autre choses remarquables de l'Ecosse & d'Irlande. Leiden: Pieter van der Aa, [c.1720]. 2 vols in 1. 8vo, later cloth. With 63 (of 64) plates Ms plate numbers added in lower margins, in some cases affecting image; a few margins dampstained. sg Nov 20 (1) $200

— Vues remarquables tirees des montagnes de la Suisse.... Berne, 1776 & Paris, [c.1780]. 2 parts in 1 vol. Folio, contemp calf; worn. WIth 8 (of 10) hand-colored plates in Part 1 & 7 color plates & 1 plain plate in Part 2. Premiere partie erased from 1st tp. Sold w.a.f. S Oct 23 (82) £4,200 [Mohler]

Vuillier, Gaston
— A History of Dancing. L, 1898. 4to, orig cloth; corners frayed, hinges reinforced. With 20 plates. Library markings. sg Feb 26 (239) $100

Anr copy. Orig cloth; rubbed & soiled. T Oct 16 (662) £48

VVV

— VVV. NY, 1942-44. Ed by David Hare. Nos 1-4 in 3. 4to, orig wraps. S June 29 (47) £620 [Ursus]

Vyse, Howard

— Operations carried on at the Pyramids of Gizeh in 1837. L, 1840-42. 3 vols, including Appendix. 8vo, half calf; worn & soiled, 1 spine torn. With 5 maps & 122 plates. wa Sept 25 (554) $310

Anr copy. 2 vols. 4to, orig cloth; tape repairs to head of spines. wa Mar 5 (183) $210

W

Waechter, Georg Philipp Ludwig Leonhard

— The Sorcerer: A Tale. L, 1795. contemp lea gilt extremities rubbed. sg Oct 9 (341) $150

Wafer, Lionel, 1660?-1705?

— A New Voyage and Description of the Isthmus of America.... L, 1704. 2d Ed. 8vo, old calf; rebacked. With folding map & 3 folding plates.. O May 12 (195) $325

Wagenaar, Jan

— Amsterdam, in zyne opkomst, aanwas, geschiedenissen.... Amst., 1760-94. 4 vols. Folio, half calf. With frontis & 94 ports, maps, plans & plates.. B Feb 25 (630) HF2,400

Anr Ed. Amst., 1760-88. Vols I-III. vellum; soiled, back of Vols I-II damaged. Lacking 1 plate. B june 2 (462) HF750

Anr copy. Vols I-III only. Contemp half calf. With 66 plates & maps only. Vol II with 1 plate torn, anr stained. Sold w.a.f. sg June 18 (250) $600

— Vaderlandsche Historie, vervattende de Geschiedenissen der Vereenigde Nederlanden.... Amst., 1749-59. 21 vols. 8vo, half calf. With frontis, 6 maps, 53 folding plates & 147 ports.. Extra-illus with 2 maps, 14 plates & 74 ports. B Feb 25 (641) HF1,200

Anr copy. 22 vols, including Index, bound in 21. Vol I, later Ed (1790). 8vo, half calf (Vol I, bds). With frontis, 6 folding maps, 40 folding plates & views & 93 ports. B Feb 25 (642) HF575

Anr Ed. Amst., 1782. 21 vols. 8vo, half calf; corners def. With frontis, 4 (of 6) maps, 40 folding plates & 106 ports. Some foxing; minor stians. B Oct 7 (1355) HF800

Wagenseil, Johann Christof

— Sota, hoc est liber mischnicus de uxore adulterii suspecta.... Altdorf, 1674. 4to, old vellum. Some worming, affecting single letters. St. 7356.1. CAM Dec 3 (170) HF600

Waghenaer, Lucas Janssen

— Speculum nauticum super navigatione maris occidentalis confectum.... Leidin, 1586. Folio, contemp vellum; rubbed. With 45 double-page maps, all but 1 in Koeman's b state. Some spotting & marginal dampstaining; some wormholes & repaired wormholes at beginning & end, affecting text or charts, marginal dampstains; 1st chart shaved at neatlines. S Apr 24 (202) £1,250 [Sourget]

— Spieghel der Zeevaerdt. Amst., 1964. Folio, half lea. Facsimile of the Utrecht copy. sg Apr 23 (189) $250

Wagner, Arthur L. —&
Kelley, J. D, Jerrold, 1847-1922

— The United States Army and Navy. Akron, 1899. Folio, orig cloth; dented. With 43 colored plates. sg Sept 18 (297) $400

Wagner, Daniel

— Pharmaceutisch-medicinische Botanik. Vienna, 1828-29. 2 vols. Folio, unsewn in orig wraps. With 249 hand-colored plates. Last plate with small marginal tear. C Oct 15 (263) £8,500 [d'Arcy]

Anr copy. Contemp half calf; rubbed, 1 joint split. Bibliotheca Albertina—de Belder copy. S Apr 28 (377) £2,800 [Israel]

Wagner, Henry Raup

— California Imprints, August 1846-June 1851. Berkeley, 1922. One of 25. 4to, bds. Facsimile plates tipped in. sg Oct 2 (299) $150

— The Cartography of the Northwest Coast of America to the Year 1800. Berkeley, 1937. 2 vols. 4to, cloth; cacked. sg Oct 2 (97) $425

— The Plains and the Rockies. San Francisco, 1920. One of 45 distributed of the suppressed issue of 300. Half cloth. cb Oct 9 (241) $325

Anr Ed. San Francisco: John Howell, 1920. Suppressed 1st Issue. Half cloth; hinges cracked. sg Oct 2 (297) $325

Anr Ed. San Francisco, 1921. One of 50 with the photstat plates. Half vellum; worn. With photostat facsimile of title of work not in this ed. Sgd. sg Oct 2 (298) $400

— The Plains and the Rockies, a Bibliography of Original Narratives of Travel and Adventures. Columbus, 1953. Revised by Charles L. Camp. O Sept 23 (187) $75; O

Oct 21 (187) $80

Anr copy. Half cloth; backstrip soiled. sg Mar 12 (260) $60

— The Plains and the Rockies.... San Francisco, 1982. 4th Ed. Revised by Charles L. Camp & then by Robert H. Becker. cb Oct 9 (242) $110; cba Feb 5 (172) $110; K Oct 4 (450) $100; K June 7 (53) $130; sg Jan 22 (309) $110

— The Spanish Southwest, 1542-1794. An Annotated Bibliography. Albuquerque: Quivera Society, 1937. One of 401. 2 vols. Folio, half cloth; worn, Vol I joints partly cracked. sg Oct 2 (301) $300

— Spanish Voyages to the Northwest Coast of America in the Sixteenth Century. San Francisco, 1929. With 15 plates. sg Oct 2 (300) $175

Wagner, Johann-Friedrich
— Ansichten Saemtlicher Burgen, Schloesser und Ruinen der Schweiz.... Berne, 1840. 2 vols. 8vo, contemp mor gilt. With 219 plates. Lacking tp. C Oct 15 (113) £5,800 [Schidlof]

Wagner, Lauren McGraw. See: McGraw & Wagner

Wagner, Ludwig
— Der Szeniker Ludwig Sievert. Berlin, 1926. 4to, orig bds; rubbed, rebacked. bba Jan 15 (297) £75 [Weinreb]

Wagner, Richard, 1813-83
— Parsifal. L, 1912. Illus by Willy Pogany. Folio, half mor. With 16 colored plates. sg Jan 8 (212) $150

Anr copy. Orig cloth; rubbed. sg June 4 (260) $130

— Das Rheingold und die Walkyre. Frankfurt, 1910. Illus by Arthur Rackham. 4to, orig half vellum; rubbed. One plate loose. ha Sept 19 (231) $55

Anr Ed. L, 1910. One of 1,150, sgd by Rackham. 4to, vellum. With 34 mtd color plates. sg Oct 30 (219) $325

— The Rhinegold & the Valkyrie. L, 1910. Illus by Arthur Rackham. 4to, orig cloth; front hinge cracked. With 34 mtd color plates. With 2 contemp Rackham ads laid in. sg Oct 30 (220) $175

One of 1,150. Vellum gilt. pnNY Sept 13 (274) $375

Anr copy. Half vellum. With 34 mtd color plates. sg Jan 8 (237) $70

Anr Ed. NY, 1910. 4to, vellum gilt; soiled. With 34 colored plates. cb Sept 11 (310) $200

Anr Ed. L, [1920]. T Feb 18 (175) £40

— The Ring of the Niblung. L, 1939. Illus by Arthur Rackham. 4to, cloth. With 48 color plates. sg Oct 30 (224) $50

Anr copy. Orig cloth, in repaired d/j. T Oct 15 (110) £42

— Siegfried & The Twilight of the Gods. L, 1911. Illus by Arthur Rackham. 4to, orig cloth. With 30 mtd color plates. sg Oct 30 (222) $200

Anr copy. Half mor gilt. sg Oct 30 (223) $130

Anr copy. Illus by Arthur Rackham. Orig cloth. cb Feb 19 (228) $85

Anr copy. Orig cloth; spine rubbed. T Feb 18 (174) £65

One of 1,150. Orig vellum; worn. K Oct 4 (378) $170

Anr copy. Half vellum. O Sept 23 (166) $310

Anr copy. Vellum gilt. pnNY Sept 13 (275) $375; S May 6 (151) £180 [Hannas]

One of 1,150, sgd by Rackham. Vellum; rubbed. With 30 mtd color plates. sg Oct 30 (221) $400

— Tannhauser. NY: Crowell [n.d.]. One of 525. Illus by Willy Pogany. Pictorial lea. sg Sept 11 (280) $450

Wahl, Gustave. See: Liebmann & Wahl

Wahl, Ralph
— Come Wade the River. Seattle: Salisbury Press, [1971]. One of 250. Folio, cloth. sg Oct 23 (533) $70

Wain, Louis
— Big Dogs, Little Dogs, Cats and Kittens. L: Tuck, [1902]. Folio, orig half cloth. pn Dec 11 (350) £130 [Henderson]

Wait, Frona Eunice. See: Colburn, Frona Eunice Wait

Wakefield, Edward Gibbon, 1796-1862
— The New British Province of South Australia. L, 1834. 12mo, orig cloth; rebacked. Tears in folding map; waterstains; lacking half-title. CA Apr 12 (244) A$100

Walch, Garnet
— Victoria in 1880. Melbourne, [1880]. 1st Ed. 4to, bdg not described. Tp detached & chipped on inner margin. kh Mar 16 (519C) A$380

Walch, Johannes
— Australien (Suedland), auch Polynesien oder Inselwelt.... Augsburg, 1802. 470mm by 590mm, hand-colored. Laid down. S Jan 12 (327) £130 [Potter]

Walcott, Mary Vaux, 1860-1940

— North American Wild Flowers. Wash., 1925-29. 5 vols. In portfolios. With 400 plates. sg Sept 18 (299) $250

Anr copy. Vols I, II & IV. Loose, as issued in cloth box. With 240 plates. wa Sept 25 (110) $80

Anr copy. 5 vols. In portfolios. With 393 colored plates. Lacking 7 plates in final volume. wa Dec 11 (555) $160

Waldberg, Patrick

— Aux Petits Agneaux. Paris: Galerie Lucie Weill, 1971. One of 174. Folio, unsewn in orig wraps. S June 29 (90) £4,500 [Naggar]

Max Ernst. Paris, 1958. Inscr to Rene Magritte by Waldberg & Ernst. S July 2 (1015) £320 [Ulrissen]

Walden, Howard T. See: Derrydale Press

Waldmann, Emil

— Edouard Manet. Berlin, 1923. 4to, half vellum, in tattered d/j. With 2 orig etchings by Manet. sg Feb 5 (214) $1,000

Waldrop, Keith

— Songs from the Decline of the West. Mount Horeb: Perishable Press, 1970. One of 120. Half mor. cb Sept 11 (206) $65

Waldseemueller, Martin

— Cosmographiae introductio: cum quibusdam geometriae.... Lyons: Jean de la Place, [1517-18?]. 4to, later vellum. Tp with 2 small wormholes not affecting text; double-page woodcut shaved at foot. S Apr 23 (201) £10,000 [Burgess]

Waldstein, Franz de Paula Adam, Graf von —& Kitaibel, Paul

— Descriptiones et icones plantarum rariorum Hungariae. Vienna, [1800]-2-12. 3 vols. Folio, contemp bds. With sepia aquatint view & 280 hand-colored plates, some folding. Horticultural Society of New York—de Belder copy. S Apr 28 (378) £15,000 [Kistner]

Waldung, Wolfgang

— Lagographia. Natura leporum. Amberg, 1619. 4to, half calf. Upper margin of tp & of A4 repaired not affecting text. Jeanson 1151. SM Mar 12 (579) FF5,500

Walford, Edward. See: Thornbury & Walford

Walker, Alexander

— Woman Physiologically Considered as to Mind, Morals, Marriage.... L, 1839. 12mo, contemp half mor gilt; rubbed. Some spotting. bba Oct 30 (430) £55 [Goldman]

Walker, Dale L. —& Sisson, James E., III

— The Fiction of Jack London: A Chronological Bibliography. El Paso, 1972. Sgd by Walker. cb Jan 22 (184) $50

Walker, Donald

— British Manly Exercises. Phila., [1837]. 8vo, orig cloth. With 50 hand-colored plates. Foxed throughout. sg Dec 18 (231) $100

Walker, Francis A., 1840-97

— Statistical Atlas of the United States.... Wash., 1874. Folio, half lea; front cover nearly detached. With 54 color maps, charts & tables. sg Nov 20 (198) $200

Walker, George, 1781-1856. See: Costume...

Walker, George, 1803-79

— Chess and Chess-Players. L, 1850. Modern cloth. pn Mar 26 (521a) £35 [Caissa]

— A Selection of Games at Chess actually played by Philidor. L, 1835. Orig cloth. pn Mar 26 (247A) £70 [DeLucia]

Walker, James, 1748-1808. See: Atkinson & Walker

Walker, John & Charles

— Hobson's Fox-Hunting Atlas. L, [c.1848]. Folio, half lea; rubbed. With 42 double-page colored maps. pn May 21 (431) £240 [Nicholson]

Walker, John Charles

— Hobson's Fox-Hunting Atlas. L, [c.1860]. Folio, half mor gilt. With 42 maps colored in outline. pn May 21 (426) £220 [Map House]

Anr copy. Half mor; rubbed. With 42 partly colored maps. pn May 21 (427) £210 [Nicholson]

Wall, Bernhardt

— Following General Sam Houston 1793-1863. Lime Rock CT: Bernhardt Wall, [1935] Texas Centennial Ed, One of 100. In d/j. Inscr, 1936 & with ALs stating that "This is the first copy in which I countersigned each and every plate....". cb Sept 11 (221) $1,200

Wallace, Alfred R.

— The Geographical Distribution of Animals.... L, 1876. 1st Ed. 2 vols. 8vo, orig cloth; joints & extremities rubbed. With 20 maps & plates. cb June 4 (202) $170

Wallace, Edgar, 1875-1932

— The Four Just Men. L, 1905. Orig cloth; rubbed & soiled. Dr. Crippen's copy. bba Mar 12 (230) £110 [Kendall]

Wallace, Philip B.
— Colonial Ironwork in Old Philadelphia. NY: Architectural Book Publishing Co., [1930]. 4to, cloth. wa Nov 6 (449) $50

Waller Collection, Francois Gerard. See: Dronckers, Emily

Waller, Edmund, 1606-87
— A Poem on St. James's Park.... L, 1661. Folio, lev gilt by Riviere. sg Apr 2 (209) $750
— The Second Part of Mr. Waller's Poems Containing his Alteration of the Maids Tragedy.... L, 1690. 8vo, mor gilt by Riviere. Lacking final blank. sg Mar 26 (282) $90

Waller, Erik, 1875-1955
— Bibliotheca Walleriana. Stockholm, 1955. Compiled by Hans Sallander. 2 vols. Cloth. sg May 14 (635) $400

Waller, Pickford
— Bookplates. L: Pear Tree Press, 1916. One of 30. 4to, orig half cloth. bba Aug 20 (292) £180 [Stone]

Wallhausen, Johann Jacobi von
— L'Art militaire pour l'infanterie. Oppenheim, 1615. Bound with: Furtenbach, Joseph. Architectura navalis. Ulm, 1629. Folio, 17th-cent vellum bds. First work with 35 plates (some repaired) & folding table. 2d work with 20 double-page plates (tear in Plate 7). Hole in text of P4 of 1st work & 1 leaf partly detached. S Nov 27 (243) £600 [Lib. Valette]

Anr Ed. Franeker, [1638]. Folio, later half calf; spine & corners rubbed. With 31 (of 33) plates. Some plate-marks cropped; a few plates shaved. S Sept 23 (412) £160 [McNaul]
— Romanische Kriegskunst.... Frankfurt: Paul Jacobi, 1616. 2 vols in 1. Folio, contemp vellum. With engraved title & 21 double-page plates. HK Nov 4 (1987) DM600

Wallich, Nathaniel
— Plantae Asiaticae Rariores; or, Descriptions and Figures of a Select Number of Unpublished East Indian Plants. L, 1829-31-[32]. 3 vols. Folio, contemp half mor gilt. With 295 hand-colored plates. Earl of Plymouth's subscriber's copy. C Oct 15 (201) £12,500 [Baskett & Day]

Anr copy. 3 vols in 12 parts. Folio, orig cloth-backed wraps; Part 1 lacking lower cover, rather soiled & torn. With 295 hand-colored litho plates & 1 folding map. Plates 23-25 loose & soiled & torn in margins. de Belder copy. S Apr 28 (380) £15,000 [Sourget]

Wallis, Henry, b.1830
— Persian Ceramic Art in the Collection of Mr. F. DuCane Godman: the Thirteenth Century Lustred Vases. L, 1891. Ltd Ed. 4to, half mor gilt. pn Apr 30 (126) £150 [Dennistoun]

Wallis, James
— An Historical Account of the Colony of New South Wales.... L: R. Ackermann, 1821. 1st Ed. Folio, half mor, uncut. With map & 12 plates. Marginal tears in map repaired; minor restoration to upper margin of title. S Oct 23 (527) £6,000 [N. Keating]

Wallis, James, Publisher
— Wallis's New Pocket Edition of the English Counties: or, Travellers Companion. L, [c.1810]. 12mo, half mor gilt. With engraved title & 44 hand-colored maps. pn May 21 (410) £180 [Map House]

Wallis, John, 1616-1703
— Grammatica linguae Anglicanae.... L, 1765. 4to, mor gilt with seated Britannia on upper cover; worn, hinges dry. Cortlandt Bishop copy. pn Nov 20 (74) £220 [Marlborough]

Wallner, Mary Cole
— Pydie's Poems. NY: Derrydale Press, 1928. One of 100. Half vellum, unopened. sg Oct 23 (147) $550

Wallop, Gerald Vernon, Earl of Portsmouth. See: Lymington, Gerard Vernon Wallop

Wallwork, James
— The Modern Angler; Comprising Angling in All Its Branches. Manchester, 1847. 8vo, modern cloth. Library markings. sg May 21 (209) $175

Walpole, Horace, 4th Earl of Orford
— Aedes Walpolianae: or, a Description of the Collection of Pictures at Houghton-Hall in Norfolk.... L, 1747. 1st Ed, 3d setting of Sig. G. 4to, modern mor. With 2 ports & 4 folding plates. S Nov 10 (190) £210 [Quaritch]

2d Ed. L, 1752. 4to, mor gilt; rubbed. With 2 ports & 4 folding plans. pn Mar 5 (240) £65 [Comberley]

Anr copy. Old bds rebacked in calf. T Jan 22 (294) £40
— Anecdotes of Painting in England. Strawberry Hill, 1762-71. 4 vols. Plus: A Catalogue of Engravers. Strawberry Hill, 1763. Together, 5 vols. 4to, contemp calf; rubbed & loose, 1 cover detached. bba Sept 25 (21) £50 [Hay]

Anr copy. Contemp calf; joints cracked, corners bumped. sg Apr 2 (210) $375

Anr Ed. L, 1828. 5 vols. 8vo, later half mor gilt extra; spine ends rubbed. cb Oct 23

(235) $150

Anr copy. Contemp half calf. S July 13 (54) £100

Anr copy. Contemp calf gilt. Foxed. sg Feb 12 (327) $200

— The Castle of Otranto. Parma: Bodoni for J. Edwards, 1791. One of 300. 8vo, contemp mor; extremities rubbed. With frontis in Hazen's A & B states. O Sept 23 (27) $250

6th Ed. Parma: Bodoni, 1791. 4to, modern half mor; rubbed. With frontis, port & 6 plates. Foxed. O Oct 21 (30) $90

Anr Ed. L, 1800. Illus by Mrs. Clarke. 8vo, orig bds; worn, broken. With 7 plates. T Sept 18 (522) £62

— A Description of the Villa of Mr. Horace Walpole...at Strawberry-Hill. Strawberry Hill, 1784. 4to, contemp calf gilt; joints rubbed. With frontis & 26 plates, 5 double-page. Marginal tear in K1 repaired. S Feb 24 (356) £1,000 [Glegg]

— Fugitive Pieces in Verse and Prose, Strawberry Hill, 1758. 1st Ed. 8vo, contemp calf. Lacking inserted "note" leaf; upper blank portion of tp cut away. S Jan 16 (446) £100 [Vine]

Anr copy. Modern cloth. Title chipped; outer margin browned. sg Mar 26 (283) $140

Anr copy. Contemp half mor; spne rubbed. Lacking inserted "note" leaf. T Jan 22 (224) £110

— Hieroglyphic Tales. L [ptd at Officina Bodoni, Montagnola], 1926. One of 250. Ck Jan 30 (110) £100

— Historic Doubts on the Life and Reign of King Richard the Third. L, 1768. 4to, contemp calf; rubbed, joints split. bba Apr 9 (71) £45 [Francis]

— Horace Walpole and his World. L, 1884. Ed by L. B. Seeley. 2 vols. 8vo, lev extra by Bradstreet. Extra-illus with c.200 ports & views, inlaid to size. sg Feb 12 (328) $275

— The Letters of Horace Walpole.... Oxford, 1903-18. Ed by Mrs. Paget Toynbee. 18 vols, including 2 Supplements cloth; worn. Frontises foxed. cb Oct 23 (236) $80

— Strawberry Hill Accounts: a Record of Expenditure.... Oxford, 1927. One of 500. 4to, half vellum, in d/js; browned & frayed. bba Dec 18 (260) £40 [Bookroom]

— Works. L, 1798. 5 vols. 4to, contemp half russia; scuffed. C Dec 12 (213) £200 [Arnon]

Anr copy. Early 19th-cent russia; joints cracked or starting. sg Oct 9 (343) $60

Walpole Library, Horace

— [Sale Catalogue] A Catalogue of the Classic Contents of Strawberry Hill. L, [1842]. 4to, orig wraps; stained. T Sept 18 (445) £52

Walpole, Hugh, 1884-1941. See: Golden Cockerel Press

Walpole-Bond, John

— A History of Sussex Birds. L, 1938. 3 vols. Contemp cloth. With 53 colored plates. Ck Jan 16 (243) £120

Anr copy. In d/js. Marginal annotations in ink. Inscr & with sgd photo inserted. pn Oct 23 (296) £130 [Old Hall]

Walpoole, George Augustus

— The New British Traveller. L,[1782]. Folio, contemp calf; worn. With frontis, maps on 23 leaves only & views on 85 leaves only. Shaving with loss to marginal decorations; last few leaves torn with loss. Sold w.a.f. Ck May 15 (143) £240

Anr copy. Modern half lea. Some soiling; some maps laid down. Sold w.a.f. Ck May 15 (138) £320

Anr Ed. L, [maps dated 1784]. Folio, old calf; worn & broken. Sold w.a.f. T May 21 (325) £430

Anr Ed. L, [c.1790]. Folio, calf gilt. With frontis & 130 maps & views on 69 plates. pn Oct 23 (374) £300 [Saville]

Walras, Antoine Auguste

— Theorie de la richesse sociale.... Paris, 1849. 12mo, orig wraps; spine chipped. Waterstained at beginning. P Sept 24 (422) $800

Walras, Leon

— Etudes d'economie politique appliquee.... Lausanne & Paris, 1898. 8vo, half mor; rubbed. With 6 tables on 4 folding sheets. Some browning. P Sept 24 (421) $1,000

Walser, Robert

— Fritz Kocher's Aufsaetze. Leipzig: Insel-Verlag, 1904. Orig calf. HN Nov 26 (2174) DM1,100

Walsh, Edward, 1756-1832

— A Narrative of the Expedition to Holland. L, 1800. 4to, contemp calf; rubbed. With double-page map & 7 plates. S May 29 (1274) £190

2d Ed. 4to, contemp calf; spine rubbed. With double-page plan & 7 plates. Some underscoring & marginal notes in ink. T Sept 18 (43) £70

Walsh, John Henry, 1810-88

— The Modern Sportsman's Gun and Rifle. L, 1882-84. 2 vols. 8vo, orig cloth; rubbed. Ck Oct 31 (126) £1400

WALSH

Walsh, Robert, 1772-1852
— Constantinople and the Scenery of the Seven Churches of Asia Minor. L, [c.1839]. 2 vols in 1. 4to, mor gilt; def. With 94 plates, 2 engraved titles & 2 maps. Vignette title stained. pn Nov 20 (216) £120 [Dupont]

Anr copy. 2 vols. 4to, mor gilt; rubbed. Some staining. pn Dec 11 (54) £300

Anr copy. Mor gilt; scuffed. Some spotting. pn May 21 (71) £220 [Chalabi]

Anr copy. Contemp mor gilt; rubbed. S Nov 18 (1078) £130 [Osbek]

Anr copy. Contemp calf gilt; rubbed. S May 28 (926) £170

Walsh, Capt. Thomas
— Journal of the Late Campaign in Egypt. L, 1803. 4to, contemp half cloth; worn. With 44 plates & plans including 2 not belonging to this work, some colored by hand. S Nov 18 (1193) £60 [Trotter]

Anr copy. Half calf; rubbed, rebacked. With 42 plates & maps, some hand-colored. Some cropping, tears 7 repairs. Extra-illus with 4 ink & watercolor drawings inserted. S July 14 (888) £150

Walsingham, Thomas, d.1422?. See: Asser, Joannes

Walter, of Henley. See: Donne, John

Walter, Johann Ernst Christian
— Flora eller colorerede Afbildninger af Pragt-Blomster. Copenhagen, 1835-47. 4to, later 19th-cent half calf, orig wraps bound in. With 306 hand-colored plates. Plates 290 & 292 in watercolor copy; lacking the leaf of text to Plates 289-94. de Belder copy. S Apr 28 (379) £15,000 [Douglas]

Walter, Richard. See: Anson, George

Walter, S. See: Bromley & Walter

Walters Art Gallery
— The History of Bookbinding, 525-1950 A.D.: An Exhibition. Balt., 1957. 4to, cloth; worn. O June 9 (193) £70

Walton, Izaak, 1593-1683
See also: Fore-Edge Paintings; Nonesuch Press
— The Life of Dr. Sanderson.... L, 1678. 2 parts in 1 vol. 8vo, modern calf by Sanford. O May 12 (196) $100

Anr copy. Contemp calf. Presentation copy. pnE Jan 28 (146) £580 [Traylen]
— The Lives of Doctor John Donne, Sir Henry Wotton.... NY: Brentano's, 1907. One of 210. Folio, half mor; corners dented. sg Sept 11 (282) $50

— The Lives of Dr. John Donne, Sir Henry Wotton.... York, 1796. 4to, calf gilt. sg May 21 (293) $80

Walton, Izaak, 1593-1683 —& Cotton, Charles, 1603-87
[A collection of the 1st 5 editions of the Compleat Angler, L, 1653-76, sold at sg on Apr 2, 1987, for $20,000] sg Apr 2 (211) $20.000

Compleat Angler

— 1655. - L.2d Ed. 12mo, mor gilt by Bedford. sg May 21 (215) $4,800
— 1661. - L.3d Ed. 8vo, mor gilt by Bedford. sg May 21 (216) $2,200
— 1668. - L.4th Ed. 8vo, mor by Riviere. sg Oct 23 (534) $1,500

Anr copy. Calf. sg May 21 (217) $175
— 1676. - L: Marriott & Brome. 8vo, modern calf. First 3 & last 5 leaves in facsimile as are license leaf before Part 2, engraved title to Part 3 & G1 in Part 3; lacking a blank leaf at end of Parts 1 & 3; tp to Part 2 repaited & mtd; corner torn from B1; repaire to E2 of Part 3; some leaves trimmed; some dampstains. Sold w.a.f. S Nov 10 (628) £70 [Head]

Anr copy. Calf gilt; front joint starting. Gosden copy. sg May 21 (218) $2,000
— 1676. - The Universal Angler. L: Marriott & Brome. 8vo, later mor; rubbed. Lacking last leaf; margins cropped, occasionally affecting text. bba Jan 15 (24) £360 [Head]
— 1750. - L.1st Moses Brown Ed. 16mo, calf; rebacked. sg May 21 (219) $175
— 1766. - L.2d Hawkins Ed. 8vo, calf; worn. sg May 21 (222) $130
— 1772. - L. 12mo, calf; rebacked. sg May 21 (223) $50
— 1775. - L.3d Hawkins Ed. 8vo, calf; worn. With frontis, port & 14 plates. sg May 21 (224) $130
— 1792. - L. 8vo, contemp calf; rebacked. sg May 21 (227) £70
— 1797. - L. 8vo, calf; rebacked. sg May 21 (228) $100
— 1808. - L. 8vo, contemp calf gilt; rubbed. With 2 ports & 15 plates; with contemp Ms notes on endpapers. bba Oct 30 (431) £70 [Cavendish]

Anr copy. Calf gilt; rebacked. Extra-illus with plates in color. sg May 21 (230) $150
4to Ed. Cloth; rebacked. sg May 21 (231) $175
— 1810. - L. 16mo, mor gilt. Hoe copy. sg May 21 (232) $150
— 1815. - L: Samuel Bagster. 2 parts in 1 vol.

8vo, modern half mor. sg May 21 (233) $70

Anr copy. Mor gilt. sg May 21 (234) $70

— 1822. - L. 8vo, mor gilt wiht fore-edge painting of 2 18th-cent gentlemen fishing. sg May 21 (235) $800

Anr copy. Bds; worn. Heavily annotated in a contemp hand. sg May 21 (236) $70

Anr copy. Mor gilt. sg May 21 (237) $70

— 1823. - L. Intro by John Major. 16mo, mor gilt. With extra plate, Mrs Walton's Tombstone, a proof, not called for. L Dec 11 (316) £60

Anr copy. Lea with piscatorial decorations. With frontis & 11 plates.. sg Oct 23 (536) $60

Anr copy. Mor gilt. Extra-illus wiht 35 plates. sg May 21 (239) $350

Anr copy. 8vo, mor gilt; worn. With 14 mtd india-proof plates. L.p. copy. sg May 21 (241) $200

— 1824. - L.2d Major Ed. 8vo, mor. L.p. copy. sg Oct 23 (537) $275

— 1825. - L. 8vo, mor gilt with fore-edge painting of Chatsworth & a fisherman. sg May 21 (244) $325

Anr copy. Cloth; front hinge cracked. sg May 21 (245) $70

1836. - L. Ed by Sir Harris Nicolas. 2 vols. 4to, mor gilt. S Nov 10 (627) £170 [Head]

Anr copy. Mor gilt; spines faded. With engraved titles & 13 plates. sg Oct 23 (538) $475

Anr copy. 2 vols extended to 6. 4to, mor gilt by Zaehnsdorf, 1903. Extra-illus with hundreds of plates. sg Apr 2 (212) $3,200

Anr copy. 2 vols. 4to, mor gilt. sg May 21 (249) $325

— 1844. - L. 16mo, cloth; worn. sg May 21 (251) $80

— 1847. - NY1st American Ed. 2 vols in 1. 12mo, half morth. Dampstained & foxed. sg Oct 23 (540) $110

Anr copy. 8vo, orig cloth; rebacked. sg May 21 (253) $70

One of 50 L.p copies. 2 vols in 1. 12mo, half mor. sg Oct 23 (539) $750

Anr copy. 4to, half mor gilt by Riviere. sg May 21 (252) $750

— 1866. - Bost.7th Major Ed. Bound in 3 vols. 4to, mor. Extra-illus with plates. sg Oct 23 (541) $350

— [1878]. - L: Frederick Warne & Co 1st Davies Ed. 12mo, cloth, unopened, with Chandos Library on front cover; edges worn. wa Sept 25 (91) $70

— [1880]. - L: Elliott Stock One of 6 on vellum. 8vo, mor gilt. sg May 21 (258) $1,500

— 1883. - L.12th Major Ed. 8vo, cloth with gilt vellum back. With 8 plates in 2 states & 74 text wood-illusts, each a mtd india proof. O Sept 23 (190) $70

— 1888. - L. One of 250 with all illusts in mtd india-proof state. 2 vols. 4to, mor gilt; extremities rubbed. With 54 mtd photogravures, 3 maps & c.100 woodcuts on india paper. sg Nov 13 (47) $1,100

One of 250. Half cloth; rubbed. sg May 21 (263) $650

One of 500. Orig mor gilt; rubbed. S May 28 (801) £360

Anr copy. Half cloth; rubbed. sg May 21 (264) $300

— 1893. - L.Tercentenary Ed, one of 350. 2 vols, 4to, half vellum, in d/j. pn Jan 22 (176) £100

Anr copy. Half vellum. S July 28 (1044) £220

— 1902. - L.Winchester Ed, one of 150, sgd by the artists William Strang & D. Y. Cameron, & with plates in 2 states. 2 vols. 4to, half mor. sg May 21 (270) $300

— [1903]. - L. Ed by Richard Le Gallienne; illus by Edmund H. New. Half mor. Extra-illus with plates. sg May 21 (271) $200

— 1905. - Chiswick: Caradoc Press One of 350. Mor gilt, unopened. sg May 21 (272) $110

— [1911]. - L. One of 250, sgd by the artist, James Thorpe. 4to, mor gilt with pictorial mor inlay of an angler. sg May 21 (274) $1,100

— [1927]. - L. One of 100 L.p. copies with an extra plate. Illus by E. Fitch Daglish. 4to, half vellum. sg May 21 (275) $140

Anr copy. Half vellum, unopened. sg May 21 (275) $140

— 1928. - Bost.: GoodspeedMor with piscatorial decorations. Inscr by Charles Goodspeed, Bliss Perry & D. B. Updike to Frank S. Hatch. Also sgd by A. de Sauty & 3 craftsmen from the bindery. Extra-illus with a sgd watercolor of a fish by Marion H. Hatch & a small ink sketch of a fish by W. A. Dwiggins. sg Oct 23 (545) $3,600

— 1931. - L. Illus by Arthur Rackham. 4to, cloth, in d/j. With 12 colored plates. cb May 21 (257) $65

Anr copy. Cloth. With 12 color plates. pn Jan 22 (320) £65 [Joseph]

Anr copy. Orig mor. With 12 colored plates. S Oct 6 (855) £60 [Massey]

Anr copy. Cloth, in tattered d/j. With 12 color plates. sg Oct 30 (227) $80

Anr copy. Cloth, in d/j. With 12 colored plates. sg May 21 (282) $80

One of 750. Mor gilt by Monastery Hill Bindery. With 12 colored plates. cb Dec 4 (337) $325

One of 775. Orig vellum gilt; soiled. pn

Sept 18 (316) £150 [Culpin]

Anr copy. With 12 colored plates. pn May 21 (296) £280

Anr copy. Vellum; soiled. Wtih 12 color plates. sg Oct 23 (546) $425

Anr copy. Orig vellum gilt; yellowed. With 12 color plates. sg Oct 30 (226) $750

Anr copy. Vellum, unopened. With 12 colored plates. sg Jan 8 (240) $600

Anr copy. Vellum gilt, unopened. sg May 21 (280) $475

— 1943. - Den Fuldkomne Fisker: The Compleat Angler [in Danish]. Copenhagen 1st Danish Ed, one of 1,000. Lea, orig wraps bound in. sg May 21 (283) $325

Walton, J. See: Fielding & Walton

Walton, William, 1843-1915

— World's Columbian Exposition...Official Illustrated Publication: Art and Architecture. Phila., [1893]. 2 vols. Folio, mor; rubbed. O Feb 24 (195) $60

Anr copy. Mor gilt; joints worn. With 130 plates. wa Nov 6 (402) $130

Walton, William, fl. 1890

— The Army and Navy of the United States, from the Period of the Revolution to the Present Day. Phila., [1889-95]. 12 parts in 2 vols. Folio, orig half mor gilt; rubbed & loose. With 44 hand-colored plates. pnNY Oct 11 (52) $275

— The Army and Navy of the United States, from the Peiord of the Revolution to the Present Day. Phila., [1889-95]. 12 parts in 11. Folio, loose as issued in cloth folders. With 44 colored india-proof mtd plates. wa Mar 5 (154) $450

Walton, Sir William. See: Sitwell & Walton

Wang Kai

— The Tao of Painting: A Study of the Ritual Disposition of Chinese Painting. NY: Pantheon, 1956. Trans by Mai-Mai Sze. 2 vols. In d/js. Bollingen Series No 49. cb Mar 5 (270) $55

Wann, Paulus

— Sermones de tempore. Passau: Johann Petri, 1491. Folio, contemp half pigskin over wooden bds; torn & wormed, spine def, lacking 2 clasps. Some worming & dampstains; tear in lower blank margin of 13 & L8; some inner margins repaired. 377 (of 430) leaves only. Goff W-5. S July 14 (449) £180

Wappenbuch

— Das erneuerte und vermehrte Teutsche Wappenbuch. Nuremberg, 1657-56-[67]. 5 vols in 3. Oblong 4to, contemp vellum; worn. With 1,147 plates. Vol I wormed. HN May 20 (1404) DM2,700

Warburg Institute

— Journal of the Warburg and Courtauld Institutes. L, 1937-85. Vols 1-43. 4to, orig wraps. B Oct 7 (1061) HF4,400

Warburton, John, of Dublin —& Others

— History of the City of Dublin. L, 1818. 2 vols. 4to, later half calf; worn. With 5 maps & plans, 21 plates & 2 facsimiles. S Nov 17 (832) £260 [Boyd]

Ward, Sir Adolphus William

— The Electress Sophia and the Hanoverian Succession. L, 1903. One of 250 on japon. 4to, mor gilt by Zaehnsdorf. CA Oct 7 (169) A$200

Ward, Henry George

— Mexico in 1827. L, 1828. 1st Ed. 2 vols. 8vo, orig bds; broken. With 13 plates (1 hand-colored) & 2 folding maps. S Nov 18 (1170) £300 [Maggs]

Anr copy. Half calf; rubbed. With folding frontises (1 almost detached), 2 folding maps & 11 plates, 1 colored. Some plates cut close; 1 plate stained. S Jan 16 (448) £190 [Caley]

Ward, Humphry —& Roberts, William

— Romney: a Biographical and Critical Essay. L, 1904. One of 350. 2 vols. 4to, half lea; spines worn. sg June 4 (283) $140

Ward, Maria

— The Complete Cook-maid, or Housewife's Assistant.... L, [c.1766]. 12mo, half sheep; worn & wormed. "Apparently the only recorded copy." Crahan copy. P Nov 25 (470) $2,500

Ward, Rowland

— The English Angler in Florida.... L, 1898. 8vo, cloth; hinges cracked, 1 signature starting. cb Nov 6 (287) $55

— Records of Big Game.... L, 1899. 3d Ed. 8vo, orig cloth; worn & soiled. cb May 21 (259) $180

4th Ed. L, 1903. cb Nov 6 (288) $160

— Rowland Ward's Records of Big Game. L, 1935. 10th Ed. Ed by G. Dollman & J. B. Burlace. 4to, orig cloth. cb NOv 6 (289) $375; SSA Feb 11 (615) R400

Warde, Frederic

— Printers Ornaments. L, 1928. 4to, orig cloth. bba Jan 15 (37) £50 [Forestow]

Warden, Davie Baillie, 1778-1845

— Description statistique, historique et politique des Etats-Unis de L'Amerique Septentrionale.... Paris: Rey et Gravier, 1820. 5 vols. 8vo, contemp half mor gilt; rubbed. With folding view, folding map, folding plan & 2 folding tables. Hunt copy. CNY Nov 21 (284) $140

Wardrop, James, 1782-1869

— On the Nature and Treatment of the Diseases of the Heart. L, 1851. 8vo, cloth. pnE Dec 17 (158) £240 [Phelps]

Ware, Isaac, d.1766

— A Complete Body of Architecture.... L, 1756. 1st Ed. Folio, contemp calf, worn, hinges cracked. With frontis & 114 plates in 1st state. C Dec 12 (214) £550 [Sillerman]

Anr copy. Contemp lea; rebacked. FD June 11 (2120) DM1,400

Anr copy. Old calf; worn & broken. Lacking 3 plates; 2 plates shaved; frontis, title & preface stained red; 1st leaf of preface & XI torn; lacking 1 index leaf. Sold w.a.f. L Dec 11 (47) £200

Anr copy. Old calf; repaired. With frontis & 114 plates. Outer margin of 1st 2 blanks & title strengthened; some browning. pn Sept 18 (157) £500 [Toscani]

Anr copy. Contemp calf; defective. With 114 plates, some folding; some margins of text stained, lacking last few leaves of index. Sold w.a.f. pn Jan 22 (200) £380 [Shapero]

Anr copy. Disbound. Some plates stained or with short tears. sg Feb 5 (321) $600

Anr copy. Contemp calf; worn & def T Nov 20 (315) £400

— The Plans, Elevations, and Sections, Chimney-Pieces, and Ceilings of Houghton in Norfolk.... [L], 1735. Folio, half russia; spine def. With engraved title & 28 plates. Discoloration affecting 1 or 2 plates. S Oct 23 (211) £320 [Raban]

Ware, James, Surgeon

— Chirurgical Observations relative to the Eye.... L, 1805-12. 2 vols. 8vo, orig bds; worn, spine of Vol I torn. Lacking Z1 in Vol I. Sold w.a.f. S Nov 10 (573) £80 [Phelps]

Ware, Sir James, 1594-1666

— The Antiquities and History of Ireland. Dublin, 1705. 8vo, contemp calf; rubbed. With frontis & 4 plates. Frontis cropped; some worming at inner & outer margins towards beginning. S Feb 24 (399) £140 [Ware]

— Works. Dublin, 1764. 3 vols in 2. Folio, contemp calf; joints split. bba Apr 9 (318) £180 [Webb-Ware]

Warhol, Andy

— The Philosophy of Andy Warhol (from A to B & Back Again). NY; Harcourt Brace Jovanovich, [1975]. 2d Ptg. Half cloth, in d/j. Inscr & with sketch of a soup can on half-title & anr on contents leaf. wa Sept 25 (288) $140

Waring, Edward Scott

— A Tour to Sheeraz by the Rout of Kazroon.... L, 1807. 4to, contemp calf; hinge cracked, rubbed. pn Dec 11 (102) £260 [Cavendish]

Waring, John Burnley

— Art Treasures of the United Kingdom. L, 1858. Folio, orig calf; rubbed. Many leaves detached, some margins tattered. Ck Oct 17 (86) £90

Anr copy. Orig calf gilt in walnut box. Presentation leaf bound in. Ck Dec 10 (372) £420

— Examples of Stained Glass, Fresco Ornament.... L, [c.1853]. Folio, modern cloth. Library markings; engraved title with corner repaired. bba Feb 5 (154) £170 [Marts]

— Masterpieces of Industrial Art and Sculpture.... L, 1863. 3 vols. Folio, orig mor gilt; worn. With 298 (of 301) plates, many dampstained or loose. Sold w.a.f. bba Oct 30 (505) £260 [Russell]

Anr copy. Early half mor; worn & water-damaged. Most plates with waterstaining to upper or lower blank margins, affecting a number of captions & a small minority of a the plates themselves. kh Mar 16 (525) A$250

Anr copy. Loose in orig mor gilt. With color titles & 298 (of 301) plates. A few plates with minor marginal tears; some plates stained. S Nov 10 (223) £290 [Gilbert]

Warne, Charles

— Ancient Dorset. The Celtic, Roman, Saxon and Danish Antiquities.... Bournemouth, 1872. Folio, half mor gilt. With 18 plates. L Dec 11 (145) $500

Warner, Charles Dudley
See also: Clemens & Warner
— Works. Hartford, 1904. One of 612. 15 vols. Orig cloth. Leaf of autograph Ms & ALs tipped in. sg Feb 12 (329) $225

Warner, Sir George Frederic. See: British Museum

Warner, Richard, 1713?-75
— The History of Bath [with Appendix]. L, 1801. 2 parts in 1 vol. 4to, contemp half calf; rubbed. Ck May 15 (197) £55

Anr copy. Contemp calf gilt. Library markings. Inscr by Anne Warner. T Mar 19 (56) £110

— An History of the Abbey of Glaston; and of...Glastonbury. Bath, 1826. 4to, orig bds; worn & split on upper hinge. With 20 plates. Some waterstaining at beginning. T Jan 22 (45) £54

Warner, Richard, 1763-1857
— Antiquitates Culinariae, or Curious Tracts Relating to the Culinary Affairs of the Old English. L, 1791. 1st Ed. 4to, half mor; spine rubbed. With hand-colored frontis & doublepage Peacock Feast plate. Marginal browning. Crahan copy. P Nov 25 (472) $350

Anr copy. Contemp half mor; rubbed, partially split at top of hinges. T Dec 18 (250) £180

Warner, Robert
— The Orchid Album. L, 1882. 11 vols. 4to, orig cloth; worn, 1 backstrip missing. With 528 colored plates Perforated stamps on plates. bba Jan 15 (429) £1,350 [Shapero]

Anr copy. Vols I & II only. 4to, orig cloth; spines split at head and foot. With 95 hand-finished color plates. Ck Oct 31 (93) £1,000

Anr copy. Vols I-V (of 11). 4to, orig cloth; stained, some covers detached or def. Sold w.a.f. S June 25 (184) £3,200 [Arader]

Anr Ed. L, 1882-97. 11 vols. 4to, half calf gilt; worn, joints cracked. With 528 colored plates, many partially hand-colored. Some foxing, mainly to text; a few plates creased; library blinkstamp on titles & on each plate, occasionally affecting image. CNY May 11 (135) $4,500

— Select Orchidaceous Plants. First series: Fort Caroline Orchids. Jacksonville, 1975. Folio, syn. With 40 color plates. Haverschmidt copy. B Feb 24 (524) HF180

Warren, Arthur. See: Grolier Club

Warren, Benjamin Harry
— Report on the Birds of Pennsylvania. Harrisburg, 1890. 2d Ed. 8vo, half mor; rubbed. With 100 colored plates. pn June 18 (199) £95 [Faupel]

Warren, John
— The Conchologist. Bost., 1834. 8vo, bds; worn, joints cracked. With frontis & 16 plates, most colored. sg Jan 15 (264) $110

Warrington, William, Glass Stainer
— The History of Stained Glass. L, 1848. Folio, old half mor gilt, part of earlier cloth covers stuck down on inside of upper & lower covers. With color title & 25 color plates. Some fraying; some tears with loss. pnNY Oct 11 (54) $350

Waseurtz, G.M. See: Grabhorn Printing

Washington, George, 1732-99
— A Message...to Congress: Relative to France and Great Britain, delivered December 5, 1793...[The Genet Affair]. Phila.: M. Carey, 4 Oct 1795. 8vo, cloth. sg Sept 18 (302) $70

Anr Ed. Phila., Oct 24 1795. 8vo, modern half cloth. Marginal tears repaired on 1st 10 leaves; paper brittle; some foxing. sg Sept 18 (175) $90

— Official Letters to the Honorable American Congress.... NY: Samuel Campbell, 1796. 2 vols in 1. 8vo, later calf; worn. Some browning. wd June 19 (188) $125

— The President's Address to the People of the United States, Announcing his Intention of Retiring from Public Life.... Phila.: D. Hogan S. Longcope & Co, 20 Sept 1796. Variant imprint of a very early publication. 8vo, stabbed as issued. Marginal fraying; a few pencilled notes & rules. P May 13 (24) $700

— Writings.... Wash., 1931-44. Ed by John C. Fitzpatrick. 39-vol, including 2-vol Index. O Sept 23 (191) $160; sg Sept 18 (303) $300

Washington's copy, George
— FREDERICK II. - Posthumous Works. L, 1789. Vol XII only. 8vo, contemp calf; rubbed. Sgd by Washington on tp. O May 12 (75) $3,100

— LE SAGE, ALAIN RENE. - The Adventures of Gil Blas of Santillane. L, 1785. Vol IV (of 4) only. Contemp sheep; rebacked with most of orig spine laid down, corners restored. Sgd on tp. P Oct 29 (22) $7,500

— L'HOSPITAL, GUILLAUME FRANCOIS ANTOINE. - An Analytick Treatise of Conick Sections.... L, 1723. 4to, old calf; rebacked. Sold w.a.f. Sgd by Washington on front blank & dated March 1750. K Oct 4 (453) $1,400

Wasserstrom, William
— The Time of the Dial. Syracuse, 1963. In d/j. Inscr by Marianne Moore below her photograph. sg Dec 11 (89) $50

Wasson, Robert Gordon
— The Hall Carbine Affair. An Essay in Historiography. Danbury, 1971. One of 250. 4to, half mor. cb Sept 11 (223) $75
— Soma: Divine Mushroom of Immortality. NY: Harcourt, Brace & World [ptd at Officina Bodoni, Verona], 1968. 3 parts in 1 vol. Orig half mor. With 11 plain & 13 mtd color plates. sg Jan 8 (291) $120
Anr copy. With 24 plates, including 13 mtd color plates. sg Jan 15 (266) $150
— The Wondrous Mushroom: Mycolatry in Mesoamerica. NY: McGraw-Hill, [1980]. One of 475. Half mor. cb Sept 11 (224) $150

Wasson, Robert Gordon —& Others
— Maria Sabina and her Mazatec Mushroom Velada. NY, [1974]. One of 50, this copy ptd for the Crahans. 4to, half mor. With separate box containing the 4 records & the musical score. P Nov 25 (475) $250

Wasson, Valentina P. & Robert G.
— Mushrooms, Russia and History. NY, 1957. One of 510. 2 vols. 4to, orig cloth. Inscr by R. G. Wasson to Marcus Crahan. P Nov 25 (476) $950

Waterhouse, Edward
— A Declaration of the State of the Colony and Affaires in Virginia. L, 1622. 4to, mor. With the folding broadside. S June 25 (421) £13,000

Waterman, Thomas Tileston —& Barrows, John A.
— Domestic Colonial Architecture of Tidewater Virginia. NY, 1932. Folio, cloth; rubbed. cba Mar 5 (203) $55

Wathen, James
— A Series of Views, Illustrative of the Island of St. Helena. L, 1821. 4to, contemp half calf; def. With port, engraved title & 7 (of 9) hand-colored plates. Port spotted. C July 22 (226) £240

Watin, Jean Felix
— L'Art du peintre, doreur, vernisseur.... Paris, 1773. 8vo, later bds. Half-title & Supplement present. A few stains. bba Oct 16 (31) £80 [Mills]

Watkins, John
— The Important Results of an Elaborate Investigation into the Mysterious Case of E. Fenning. L, 1815. vo, later cloth. pnE Nov 12 (22) £42

Watson, A. E. T. See: Beaufort & Watson

Watson, Alfred Edward Thomas
— King Edward VII, as a Sportsman. L, 1911. One of 250. Folio, orig vellum gilt; soiled. Ck Oct 17 (184) £65

Watson, Douglas S.
See also: Grabhorn Printing
— California in the Fifties. San Francisco, 1936. One of 50 on Alexandra japan. Oblong 4to, half mor; lacking accompanying portfolio. cb Oct 9 (35) $190
One of 850. Cloth; rubbed, unevenly faded. Several numerals on contents page ink-circled. cb Oct 9 (36) $120
Anr copy. Cloth, in d/j. cb July 16 (43) $110

Watson, Frederick, 1885-1935. See: Derrydale Press

Watson, John Forbes, 1827-92
— The Textile Manufactures and the Costumes of the People of India. L, 1866. Folio, cloth. With 3 plates & 9 photos. bba Dec 18 (262) £190 [Burgess Browning]

Watson, Peter William, 1761-1830
— Dendrologia Britannica.... L, 1825. 2 vol. 4to, mor. With 172 hand-colored plates. pn Sept 18 (119) £360 [Greyfriars]

Watson, William, F.A.S.
— An Historical Account of the Ancient Town...of Wisbech. Wisbech, 1827. 8vo, orig bds; worn. S July 28 (1009) £80

Watson, William, 1858-1925 —& Bean, W.
— Orchids; their Culture and Management. L, [1890]. 8vo, modern half mor. With 58 plates, 16 colored. CK Nov 21 (160) £70

Watt, Robert, 1774-1819
— Bibliotheca Britannica. Edin., 1824. 4 vols. 4to, half calf; rubbed, joint cracked. bba Mar 12 (362) £80 [Stewart]
Anr copy. Contemp half calf gilt; worn. T Nov 20 (384) £110

Watts, George
— A Sermon Preached before the Trustees for Establishing the Colony of Georgia.... L, 1736. 4to, 19th-cent half mor; rubbed. Tp soiled. P May 13 (25) $80

Watts, Isaac, 1674-1748
— Divine Songs Attempted in Easy Language for the Use of Children. L: H. Turpin, 1784. 32mo, orig dutch floral bds; backstrip def. With port & 12 plates. S June 17 (499) £650 [Moen]

Watts, William, 1752-1851
— The Seats of the Nobility and Gentry.... L, [1779-86]. Oblong 4to, disbound. With 83 (of 84) plates; lacking Plate 68. pn Dec 11 (55) £200 [Watson]

Watts, William Henry
— Chess Pie. L: British Chess Federation, 1922-36. Nos 1-3 (all pbd) in 2 vols. 4to,. cloth. rubbed pn Mar 26 (175A) £40 [Squires]

Waugh, Evelyn, 1903-66
— Basil Seal Rides Again. L, [1963]. 1st Ed, one of 750. bba July 2 (389) £110 [Fitzcarralde]
— Black Mischief. L, 1932. 1st Ed. In frayed d/j. T Feb 18 (101) £55
One of 250, sgd. Inscr to Lord David Cecil, 1 Oct 1932. S Sept 22 (195) £420 [Maggs]
— Brideshead Revisited. L, 1945. 1st Ed. In def d/j. Inscr. S May 6 (467) £260 [Henderson]
— Decline and Fall. L, 1928. 1st Ed. Orig cloth; spine rubbed, joints split. Library stamps. S Sept 22 (148) £30 [Deeny]
— A Handful of Dust. L, 1934. Inscr to Lord & Lady David Cecil. S Sept 22 (194) £160 [Studd]
— Helena. L, 1950. 1st Ed. Inscr to Lord & Lady David Cecil. S Sept 22 (196) £260 [Libris Antik]
— Love Among the Ruins. L, 1953. 1st Ed. In d/j. pn Nov 20 (90) £85 [Henderson]
One of 350. In severely torn d/j. S May 6 (468) £90 [O'Neill]; sg Dec 11 (453) $80
— The Loved One. L, [1948]. 1st Ed, one of 250. Illus by Stuart Boyle. Inscr to William Davis. S Mar 9 (828) £280 [Whiteson]
Anr copy. Orig cloth, corners bumped. T May 20 (94) £105
— Robbery under Law. L, 1939. 1st Ed. In torn d/j. Inscr. bba Sept 25 (138) £340 [Maggs]

Way, Thomas R.
— The Lithographs by Whistler. NY, 1914. One of 400. 4to, orig portfolio. wa June 25 (481) $280

Wayland, Virginia & Harold
— Of Carving, Cards & Cookery.... Arcadia CA: Raccoon Press, 1962. One of 275. Bds. sg Jan 15 (55) $70

Weaver, George Sumner, 1818-1908
— Lectures on Mental Science.... NY: Fowlers & Wells, 1852. 8vo, orig cloth. cb Oct 23 (175) $55

Weaver, Sir Lawrence
— Houses and Gardens by E. L. Lutyens. L, 1914. Folio, half cloth; worn & shaken. O Nov 18 (196) $130
Anr Ed. L, 1925. ("Houses & Gardens by Sir Edwin Lutyens....") Folio, cloth. sg Feb 5 (211) $150

Weaver, William D.
[-] Catalogue of the Wheeler Gift of Books, Pamphlets and Periodicals in the Library of the American Institute of Electrical Engineers. NY, 1909. 2 vols. cb June 4 (54) $110; sg May 14 (636) $150

Webb, Peter
— The Erotic Arts. L, 1975. Ltd Ed. With colored screenprint by Allen Jones & etching by David Hockney, each sgd & numbered. sg Feb 12 (87A) $1,000

Webber, Charles Wilkins
— The Gold Mines of the Gila. NY, 1849. 1st Ed. 2 vols. 12mo, half mor; rubbed, front joint cracked. cb Jan 8 (211) $200
— Wild Scenes and Song-Birds. NY & L, 1854 [1853]. 8vo, cloth; loose. With 20 colored plates. Some fraying. Sold w.a.f. O Sept 23 (193) $60

Weber, Carl Jefferson
— Fore-Edge Painting. Irvington, NY, 1966. Orig cloth, in d/j. O Sept 23 (194) $100; sg Jan 22 (310) $100
— A Thousand and One Fore-Edge Paintings. Waterville, Me., 1949. Orig cloth, in d/j. O Sept 23 (195) $130

Weber, Max, 1881-1961
— Primitives: Poems and Woodcuts. NY, 1926. One of 350. Intro by Benjamin de Casseres. Bds; worn, lacking backstrip. Inscr. sg Apr 2 (213) $600

Weber, Veit, Pseud. See: Waechter, Georg Philipp Ludwig Leonhard

Webster, Daniel, 1782-1852
— Mr Webster's Speech on the Greek Revolution. Washington, 1824. 8vo, disbound. S Feb 23 (113) pS160 [Alldoc]
— The Private Correspondence.... Bost., 1857. 2 vols. 8vo, cloth; worn, spines torn. Interleaved with news clippings, etc. Sold w.a.f. ALs to Attorney General Henry D. Gilpin tipped in. O Sept 23 (196) $650
— Works. Bost., [1903]. ("Writings and Speeches.") National Ed, Franklin Issue. One of 10. 18 vols. Mor gilt with library shelf numbers in gilt. With 2 A Ls s tipped in Vol I & a vol of 103 plates relating to Webster. sg Apr 2 (214) $1,000

Webster, Noah, 1758-1843

— An American Dictionary of the English Language. NY, 1828. 2 vols. 4to, calf; 1 bdg broken. Some stains & foxing. Benjamin Waterhouse's copy, with his clipped signature affixed to each front endpaper; also sgd by Waterhouse's grandson, J. F. W. Ware. O Sept 23 (197) $850

Anr copy. Calf; covers loosening, worn. Vol II dampstained. sg Sept 18 (307) $425

Anr copy. Orig half cloth; worn & soiled, Vol II frayed & torn. Port foxed. wa Mar 5 (413) $2,500

— A Compendious Dictionary of the English Language. Hartford & New Haven, 1806. 12mo, contemp calf. Some foxing & browning. wd June 19 (191) $750

Wedekind, Frank, 1864-1914

— Der Greise Freier. Berlin, [1924]. One of 200, sgd & each plate sgd by artist. Illus by Alfred Kubin. Orig half lea gilt. With 6 plates. HK Nov 4 (3018) DM2,200

Weegee

— Naked City. NY, [1945]. 1st Ed. Inscr. wa Nov 6 (357) $65

Weeks, Edward

— The Moisie Salmon Club. Barre, 1971. One of 1,500. 4to, cloth. sg Oct 23 (553) $50

Weeks, John Moseley, 1788-1838

— A Manual: or an Easy Method of Managing Bees. Middlebury VT: Knapp & Jewett, 1836. 24mo, contemp half lea; spine worn, front cover loose. Some dampstaining. sg Jan 15 (172) $130

Weibel, Adele Covlin

— Two Thousand Years of Textiles. NY, 1952. 4to, orig cloth; rear hinge broken. sg Feb 5 (313) $110

Weigel, Christoph, 1654-1725

Historiae celebriores Veteris [Novi] Testamenti.... Nuremberg, [1708]. 2 parts in 1 vol, Folio, contemp vellum gilt. With 2 engraved titles & 250 plates. HK Nov 4 (1711) DM2,000

Anr Ed. Nuremberg, [1712]. ("Historiae celebriores Veteris Testamenti iconibus repraesentatae.") 2 vols. Folio, contemp vellum; upper joint cracked. With 2 engraved titles & 251 plates.. Ck Sept 5 (93) £150

— La Passione del nostro signore Giesu Christo.... Augsburg, 1694. 8vo, mor; scuffed. With engraved title, frontis & 100 text illusts. sg Oct 9 (119) $100

Weigel, Johann Christoph

— Continuirter Atlas Portatilis germanicus.... Nuremberg: J. C. Weigel, 1733. 8vo, contemp calf gilt. With 36 maps & 1 distance table all colored in a contemp hand. S Apr 23 (173) £700 [Koch]

Weiler, Milton C.

— Classic Shorebird Decoys. NY, 1971. Ltd Ed, sgd. Half mor gilt. With 24 uncolored plates. Laid into front cover are 24 color plates. sg May 21 (210) $400

Weinbaum, Stanley Graumann, 1900-35

— Dawn of Flame and Other Stories. [Milwaukee: American Fiction Guild, 1936]. Syn; rubbed. With the Keating foreword. cb Sept 28 (1315) $400

Weinmann, Johann Wilhelm, d.1741

— Phytanthoza iconographia sive conspectus aliquot milium.... Regensburg, [1735]-37-45. 3 vols only. Contemp lea gilt. With frontis, 2 ports & 773 (of 775) plates. FD Dec 2 (471) DM53,000

Anr copy. 8 vols. Folio, contemp calf. With mezzotint frontis, 2 ports & 1,025 plates partly ptd in colors & finished by hand. Potocki—Vilmorin—de Belder copy. S Apr 28 (382) £35,000 [Israel]

— Thesaurus Rei Herbariae locupletissimus indice systematis et emendatus.... Augsburg: J. E. Haid, 1787. 8vo, contemp calf gilt; scored. Hunt copy. CNY Nov 21 (286) $80

Weinstein, S. O.

— Mezhdunarodnyy Shakhmatnyy turnir. Moscow, 1936. Orig cloth. pn Mar 26 (90) £160 [De Lucia]

Weirter, Louis

— The Story of Edinburgh Castle. Phila., [1913]. 4to, cloth; worn. With frontis & 24 mtd plates. O Feb 24 (197) $50

Weiss, Franz

— Die malerische und romantische Pfalz.... Neustadt, 1840. 8vo, contemp half cloth HN May 20 (1221) DM1,800

Weissenborn, Hellmuth

— Hellmuth Weissenborn: Painter and Graphic Artist. L: Bachman & Turner, [1976]. One of 200. T May 20 (72) £100

Welby, Adlard

— A Visit to North America and the English Settlements in Illinois.... L, 1821. 1st Ed. 8vo, modern half calf. With 14 hand-colored plates. Some dampstaining S July 14 (780) £300

Welch, d'Alte A.
— A Bibliography of American Children's Books Printed Prior to 1821. [Worcester, Mass.]: American Antiquarian Society, 1963-67. Orig 6 parts. Wraps. sg Jan 22 (311) $175

Weld, Isaac, 1774-1856
— Travels through the States of North America.... L, 1799. 1st Ed. 4to, modern half lea; rubbed. O May 12 (198) $600

Anr copy. Needs rebdg. With 16 fold-out maps & plates, each with perforated library stamp; 1 map repaired. Lacking ads. sg Mar 12 (264) $100

3d Ed. L, 1800. 2 vols. 8vo, half calf; rebacked. With 3 folding maps & 5 engraved plates. pnNY Sept 13 (298) $225

Well...
— Well Dressed Lines Stripped from the Reels of Five New Englanders. NY: Anglers' Club, 1962. One of 500. sg Oct 23 (166) $70

Wellcome Historical Medical Library
— Catalogue of Printed Books.... L, 1962-66. 3 vols. pnE Jan 28 (322) £160 [McKenzie]

Anr Ed. L, 1962-76. 3 vols. S July 13 (79) £340

Weller, Emil
— Die falschen un fingirten Druckorte.... Leipzig, 1864. 2 vols. 8vo, cloth. sg May 14 (376) $225

Weller, John B.
— First Annual Message of John B. Weller, Governor.... Sacramento, 1859. Recent half mor, orig front wrap bound in. Inscr. cb Jan 8 (213) $65

Welles, Gideon, 1802-78
— Diary of Gideon Welles. Bost., 1911. 3 vols. 8vo, cloth; worn. Some foxing. sg Mar 12 (265) $120

Welling, Georg von
— Opus mago-cabalisticum et theologicum.... Frankfurt, 1760. Folio, contemp half vellum; worn & soiled, lacking free endpapers. Some short closed tears. wa Mar 5 (160) $210

Wellington, Arthur Wellesley, 1st Duke of
— The Dispatches of Field Marshal the Duke of Wellington.... L, 1837-39. 13 vols. 8vo, orig half cloth; lower joint split, rubbed. bba Jan 15 (89) £120 [Trotman]

Wells, Edward, 1667-1727
— A New Sett of Maps both of Antient and Present Geography. L, 1714. Folio, old half calf. With 33 maps only. Dampstained; soiled; some maps torn with loss; title & contents leaves torn, the tp with loss. Ck May 15 (328) £320

Anr copy. Early half calf; def. With 24 (of 41) engraved hand-colored maps. A few maps detached. pnNY Sept 13 (513) $650

Wells, H. G., 1866-1946
See also: Golden Cockerel Press
— The Door in the Wall and Other Stories. NY & L, 1911. One of 600. Folio, half cloth; soiled & worn. With frontis & 9 plates after A. L. Coburn. wa Sept 25 (262) $1,150

— The Invisible Man: A Grotesque Romance. L, 1897. 1st Ed in Book form. 8vo, orig cloth; rubbed, hinge cracked. bba Dec 4 (146) £60 [Martin]

Anr copy. Orig cloth; rubbed. kh May 16 (527B) A$140

— The Island of Doctor Moreau. L, 1896. 1st Ed. 8vo, orig cloth; rubbed & soiled, hinges cracking. cb Sept 28 (1332) £110

Anr copy. Orig cloth, variant bdg. S Jan 13 (605) £160 [Perrin]

— The Sea Lady: A Tissue of Moonshine. L: Methuen, 1902. 2d State. 1st bdg. cb Sept 28 (1335) $60

— The Stolen Bacillus and Other Incidents. L, 1895. 1st Ed. 8vo, orig cloth; rubbed, spine darkened. cb Sept 28 (1336) $225

— The Time Machine. An Invention. L, 1895. 1st Ed, 1st Issue. Inscr to Cosmo Rowe & by Rowe to Neville Lynn. With ALs inserted & other related material. S July 23 (122) £1,500 [Quaritch]

1st American Ed. NY, 1895. 8vo, orig cloth, Currey's B State; soiled & rubbed, front hinge starting. Tp & prelims foxed. cb May 7 (437) $325

— Tono-Bungay. L, 1909. 1st Ed, 1st Issue. Inscr. S Sept 22 (150) £80 [Sotheran]

— The War of the Worlds. L, 1898. 1st Ed. 8vo, orig cloth; rubbed & soiled, 1 signature started. With pbr's catalogue dated Autumn MDCCXCVII inserted at rear. cb Sept 28 (1343) $350

1st Illustrated & 1st American Ed. NY, 1898. 8vo, orig cloth. cb Sept 28 (1344) $85

— Works. L, 1924-27. Atlantic Ed, One of 620. bba Oct 30 (163) £480 [Joseph]; cb Feb 19 (274) $250; pn Sept 18 (83) £420 [Thorp]

One of 1,050. 28 vols. Calf; scuffed. sg Feb 12 (330) $650

— The World of William Clissold. A Novel at a New Angle. L, 1926. 1st Ed, one of 198. 3 vols. half vellum. pnNY Sept 13 (299) $140

Wells, Henry P.
— Fly-Rods and Fly-Tackle: Suggestions as to their Manufacture.... NY, 1885. 8vo, cloth; worn. sg Oct 23 (554) $50

Wells, J. R.
— The Family Companion.... Bost., 1846. 12mo, ptd self-wraps; stained. Lower portion of tp torn away & ragged edges reinforced with cellotape. sg Jan 15 (56) $50

Wells, William Charles, 1757-1817
— Two Essays: One upon Single Vision with Two Eyes; the Other on Dew.... L, 1818. 8vo, orig bds; soiled, rebacked. S May 28 (804) £240

Welty, Eudora
— The Bride of the Innisfallen and other Stories. NY, [1955]. In d/j. Inscr. sg Mar 5 (270) $175
— A Curtain of Green. Garden City, [1943]. Inscr. O Jan 6 (195) $100
— The Optimist's Daughter. NY, [1972]. One of 300. sg Mar 5 (271) $150
— A Pageant of Birds. NY: Albondocani Press, 1974. One of 300. Wraps in d/j. sg Mar 5 (272) $60

Wendingen...
— Wendingen. An International Magazine of Arts. Amst., 1921. Frank Lloyd Wright Special No. 4to, orig wraps; soiled & chipped. Cover design by El Lissitsky. S May 6 (22) £180 [Julien]

Wendland, Johann Christoph. See: Schrader & Wendland

Wenlock, John
— To the Most Illustrious...Charles II...the Humble Declaration of John Wenlock.... L, 1662. 1st Ed. 4to, early 20th-cent mor by J. Mackenzie. Some shaving, browning & soiling. S July 14 (354) £110

Wentworth, Thomas, Earl of Strafford, 1672-1739
— Letters and Dispatches.... L, 1739. 2 vols. Folio, contemp calf; rubbed, joints broken, 1 signature bound upside down. O Feb 24 (186) $50

Wentworth, William Charles, 1793-1872
— New South Wales. L, 1819. ("A Statistical, Historical, and Political Description of the Colony of New South Wales....") 1st Ed. 8vo, contemp calf gilt; worn, joints cracked. Some foxing & soiling. cb June 4 (206) $160

Anr copy. Half calf; rubbed. Lacking appendix leaves. Sold w.a.f. pn June 18 (5) £100 [Arnold]

2d Ed. L, 1820. 8vo, modern half mor. With frontis & folding map. Plate & map waterstained; map fold backed. C Oct 15 (182) £120 [Hitchens]
— A Statistical Account of the British Settlements in Australasia.... L, 1824. 3d Ed. 2 vols. 8vo, early calf; rebacked. Folding map set down on linen. kh Mar 16 (528B) A$380

Wentz, Roby
— The Grabhorn Press: A Biography. San Francisco: Book Club of California, 1981. One of 750. Half cloth, in d/j; soiled. Book Club of California No 168. cb Sept 11 (75) $130; cb Feb 5 (186) $75

Wertheim, Maurice, 1886-1950
— Salmon on the Dry-Fly. NY, 1948. One of 500. Half cloth; worn. sg Oct 23 (555) $40

Wescott, Glenway
— The Babe's Bed. Paris, 1930. 1st Ed, one of 375. Worn. O Jan 6 (194) $80

Wesley, John, 1703-91
— The Doctrine of Original Sin.... Bristol, 1757. 8vo, modern half calf. Gg6 torn. bba Feb 5 (168) £90 [Parsons]

Anr copy. Contemp calf; spine & corners worn. Tear to Aa4. L July 2 (251) £60

West, John, 1778-1845
— The Substance of a Journal during a Residence at the Red River Colony.... Vancouver: Alcuin Society, 1967. One of 500. Half lea. cb Oct 9 (244) $70

West, John, 1809-73
— The History of Tasmania. Launceston, 1852. 2 vols. 8vo, orig cloth; hinges cracked, 1 spine torn, covers stained. CA Apr 12 (245) A$300

West, Michael Philip
— Claire de Lune and Other Troubadour Romances. [L. Harrap, 1913]. Illus by Evelyn Paul. 4to, cloth with mtd color plate by Evelyn Paul. sg Dec 18 (207) $90

West, Rebecca
— The Modern "Rake's Progress." L, 1934. One of 250. Illus by David Low. 4to, half cloth; worn. With 12 double-page plates. sg Jan 8 (157) $90

West, William, fl.1568-94
— The First Part of Simboleography [The Second Part....]. L, 1603-1. 2 vols in 1. 4to, old half calf; joints cracked. 1st title with minor tear at inner corner. sg Oct 9 (345) $200

West, William, 1770-1854
— Picturesque Views and Descriptions of Cities, Towns, Castles...in Staffordshire and Shropshire. Birm., 1830-31. 2 parts in 1 vol. 4to, contemp half mor; rubbed. With engraved titles & 69 (of 70) plates. Tear in 1 plate. S May 28 (927) £120

Westall, Richard
— Victories of the Duke of Wellington. L, 1819. Folio, modern cloth. Lacking 4 plates & prelims; text margins repaired. Sold w.a.f. bba Apr 23 (316) £70 [Oissich]

Anr copy. Later calf; rubbed. With 12 hand-colored plates. Some soiling; 1 plate repaired. S July 14 (583) £150

Anr copy. Contemp hlaf mor gilt. Somewhat affected by damp; 1 leaf of text torn & repaired. S July 14 (584) £250

Westall, William
— Drawings. L, 1962. Ed by T. M. Perry & D. H. Simpson. Folio, cloth. CA Apr 12 (246) A$160

— Thirty-five Views on the Thames, at Richmond, Eton, Windsor, and Oxford. L: Rodwell & Martin, 1824. 7 orig parts. Folio, orig wraps; worn. Most plates foxed. pn Sept 18 (297) £750 [Grosvenor]

Westall, William —& Others
— Views of Country Seats of the Royal Family, Nobility and Gentry of England. L: Ackermann, 1830. Vol I only., With folding hand-colored map. With 146 colored plates. O May 12 (198) £600

Westcott, Thompson, 1820-88
— Centennial Portfolio: A Souvenir of the International Exhibition at Philadelphia. Phila., 1876. Oblong folio, orig cloth; shaken. With 52 plates. sg Mar 12 (268) $110

Westerman, Gerardus Friedrich. See: Schlegel & Westerman

Westmacott, Charles Molloy
— The English Spy. L, 1825-26. 2 vols. 8vo, contemp mor gilt. With hand-colored frontis & 71 plates, 1 uncolored. Ck Sept 26 (174) £500

Anr copy. Mor gilt by Riviere; small stain on lower cover of Vol II. With 1 plain & 71 hand-colored plates. Some plates repaired or cut down & mtd. S Nov 10 (419) £350 [Seibu]

Anr copy. Late 19th-cent mor gilt by Riviere; stain on lower cover of Vol I. S July 23 (483) £500 [Ash]

Anr copy. Mor gilt by Riviere; joints & spine ends rubbed. sg Feb 12 (332) $550

Anr copy. Mor gilt by Root. Several plates spotted in margins. sg Apr 2 (215) $1,100

1st Issue. Contemp half mor gilt; upper cover of Vol I detached, rubbed. With 1 plain & 70 hand-colored plates. Marginal tears repaired; 1 leaf of text def. bba Aug 20 (274) £350 [Hay Cinema]

Anr copy. Illus by Cruikshank. Contemp half mor. With 69 hand-colored plates. cb Oct 23 (50) $180

— Points of Misery, or Fables for Mankind.... L, 1823. Illus by Robert Cruikshank. 8vo, modern half calf; new endpapers. Some soiling. bba Jan 15 (256) £35 [Heneage]

Anr copy. Half mor by Riviere; front joint weak. With frontis, 8 plates & 11 text illusts. Lacking half-title. sg Sept 11 (85) $60

Anr copy. Lev by Bayntun in imitation Doves style. Wilmerding copy. sg Feb 12 (331) $425

Anr copy. Half calf; worn. wa Sept 25 (213) $75

Weston, Edward
— The Daybooks of Edward Weston. Rochester, [1961-66]. Ed by Nancy Newhall. 2 vols. 4to, cloth, Vol II in rubbed d/j; rubbed. wa Nov 6 (363) $70

[-] Edward Weston. NY, 1932. One of 550, sgd by Weston. Folio, half cloth. With 40 plates. sg May 7 (80) $850

— My Camera on Point Lobos. Yosemite National Park & Bost., 1950. Folio, spiral bdg, in torn d/j. Inscr. cb Oct 9 (321) $300

Weston, Edward & Charis W.
— California and the West. NY, [1940]. 4to, cloth; stained & worn. cb Oct 9 (322) $75

Weston, Robert Harcourt
— Letters and Important Documents Relative to Eddystone Lighthouse.... L, 1811. 4to, half calf. With 2 plates. Caption of 1 plate cropped. S Nov 18 (959) £90 [Traylen]

Westrumb, Johann Friedrich
— Kleine Physikalisch-chemische Abhandlungen. Leipzig, 1786-95. 8 parts in 4 vols. 8vo, contemp half calf. C Dec 12 (217) £1,000 [Rota]

Westwood, John Obadiah, 1805-93
See also: Humphreys & Westwood
— Arcana Entomologica; or Illustrations of...Insects. L, [1841]-45. 2 vols. 8vo, orig cloth. With 96 hand-colored plates. pn Apr 30 (226) £460 [Wheldon]

— British Butterflies and their Transformations. L, 1848. 4to, orig cloth; rebacked, loose. With additional title & 42 colored plates. Ck Oct 31 (122) £190

— The Butterflies of Great Britain. L, 1855.

1st Ed. 8vo, mor gilt; hinges rubbed. With colored engraved title & 19 colored & 2 plain plates. pn Sept 18 (73) £110 [Culpin]
— Fac-Similes of the Miniatures and Ornaments of Anglo-Saxon and Irish Manuscripts. L, 1868. Folio, contemp half mor; rubbed. With 53 litho plates, most colored. Inscr to Alderman Sir Stuart Knill by "The Odd Volumes". S Nov 10 (33) £600 [Fogg]

Westwood, Thomas —& Satchell, Thomas
— Bibliotheca Piscatoria: a Catalogue of Books on Angling.... L, 1883. 8vo, cloth; spine ends chipped. 1 p copy. With interleaved copy of the 1901 supplement. sg Oct 2 (308) $300

Wethered, H. Newton —& Simpson, T.
— The Architectural Side of Golf. L, 1929. pnC July 16 (116) £420

Wetmore, Alphonso
— Gazetteer of the State of Missouri.... St. Louis, 1837. 1st Ed. 8vo, orig cloth. With plate & folding map. Ck May 15 (76) $95

Wetzel, Charles M.
— American Fishing Books: A Bibliography.... Newark, Del., 1950. One of 200. 4to, half calf. sg Oct 23 (556) $650

Wetzler, Joseph. See: Martin & Wetzler

Weyland, John, 1774-1854
— The Principles of Population and Production.... L, 1816. 8vo, bds; rebacked in mor endpapers replaced. Lacking half-title; stamp on free endpaper reading Greening Bequest. P Sept 24 (423) $500

Weyman, Stanley John, 1855-1928
— The Castle Inn. L, 1898. Frontis by Arthur Rackham. Some foxing. sg Oct 30 (229) $70

Wezel, Johann Karl, 1747-1834
— Belphegor, oder die wahrscheinlichste Geschichte unter der Sonne. Leipzig, 1776. 2 vols. 8vo, contemp wraps. HK Nov 4 (2763) DM4,600

Whalley, Peter. See: Bridges, John

Wharton, Edith, 1862-1937
— Italian Villas and their Gardens. NY, 1904. 1st Ed. Illus by Maxfield Parrish. 4to, orig cloth; edges worn. wa Sept 25 (259) $85
Anr Ed. NY, 1905. Worn. O Jan 6 (196) $90

Whately, Richard, 1787-1863
— Remarks on Transportation and on a Recent Defence of the System.... L, 1834. 8vo, later cloth. Contents leaf reinforced. CA Oct 7 (171) A$100

Whear, Diggory, 1573-1647
— The Method and Order of Reading both Civil and Ecclesiastical Histories.... L, 1685. 1st Ed in English. Trans by Edmund Bohun. 8vo, modern half calf. Opening leaves soiled; A7 punctured. sg Oct 9 (346) $80

Wheat, Carl I. See: Grabhorn Printing; Morgan & Wheat

Wheatley, Henry Benjamin, 1838-1917
— Remarkable Bindings in the British Museum. Paris & L, 1889. One of 150. 4to, cloth. With 62 plates. Perforated stamp & ink number of title. bba Feb 5 (93) £90 [Zeitlin]

Wheatley, Phillis, 1753?-84
— Poems on Various Subjects.... L, 1773. 8vo, contemp calf; spine & cover edges worn or rubbed. Marginal soiling on tp, following leaf & final 2 leaves; top corner of final leaf frayed; old owner's stamp in upper margin of frontis. sg Dec 4 (203) $1,200

Wheeler, Alfred
— Land Titles in San Francisco.... San Francisco, 1852. 8vo, orig bds; rebacked in calf. With folding map. sg Mar 12 (225) $800

Wheeler, George M.
— Preliminary Report Concerning Explorations...in Nevada and Arizona. Wash., 1872. 4to, orig cloth; worn, library markings. Tear in folding map. wa Sept 25 (412) $55

Wheeler, Gervase
— Homes for the People.... NY, 1855. 12mo, orig cloth; rubbed & soiled. Some browning. bba Sept 25 (303) £50 [Weinreb]

Wheeler, John, fl.1601-8
— A Treatise of Commerce, wherein are Shewed the Commodities.... L: Harison, 1601. 1st Ed. 4to, half calf. S July 23 (466) £6,100 [Riley-Smith]

Wheeler, Joseph Towne
— The Maryland Press, 1777-1790. Balt., 1938. 1st Ed. 4to, cloth. sg Oct 2 (194) $70

Wheels...
— Wheels: An Anthology of Verse [Wheels: a Second (-Sixth) Cycle]. Oxford, 1916-21. Ed by Edith Sitwell. Nos 1-6 (all pbd). sg Dec 11 (455) $275

Whipple, George
— George Eastman: A Picture Story of an Out-of-Doors Man.... [N.p., 1930s]. Oblong 4to, half cloth; soiled & scuffed. sg Oct 23 (252) $175

Whistler, James Abbott McNeill, 1834-1903
— Eden versus Whistler: The Baronet & the Butterfly. Paris, [1899]. 8vo, bds, unopened. sg Feb 12 (333) $60

Whistler, Rex, 1905-44
— The New Forget-Me-Not. L, 1929. Orig half cloth, in def d/j. With 4 colored plates. Inscr with a drawing to Ernest Armstrong. S June 17 (293) £900 [Edberg]

Whiston, William, 1667-1752
— Memoirs of the Life and Writings of.... L, 1753. 3 parts in 2 vols. 8vo, contemp calf; extremities rubbed, spines repaired. cb Oct 23 (238) $50

Whitaker, Joseph Isaac
— The Birds of Tunisia. L, 1905. One of 250. 2 vols. 8vo, cloth. With the 26-page Supplement, 1924. Haverschmidt copy. B Feb 24 (246) HF850

Whitaker, Joseph Vernon
— Art Treasures of England. Phila., 1875. 4to, contemp mor; rubbed. Ck Sept 5 (146) £55

Whitaker, Thomas Dunham
— The History and Antiquities of the Deanery of Craven. L, 1805. 4to, contemp half calf; rubbed, upper cover virtually detached, new endpapers. With 35 plates only, 2 colored by hand. Some tears. S Nov 17 (834) £50 [Neptune]
2d Ed. L, 1812. 4to, contemp mor gilt; rubbed. With engraved plates & folding charts. William Boyne copy with additional plates added by him. bba Nov 13 (139) £100 [Quaritch]
Anr copy. With hand-colored frontis, folding map, 69 plates (including 24 hand-colored) & 19 folding table. Some foxing affecting port. cb Feb 19 (278) $500
Anr copy. Contemp half russia gilt; worn, front cover detached. Some minor browning. L Dec 11 (147) £80
Anr copy. Contemp half mor gilt; worn. Tear along fold of folding map. T Feb 19 (301) £90
— An History of Richmondshire.... L, 1823. 2 vols. Folio, contemp russia; spines gilt. Some spotting. Ck Nov 21 (251) £160
Anr copy. Mor gilt; some scuffing. With 6 plates a little stained. L Dec 11 (149) £180
Anr copy. Contemp calf gilt; rubbed, Vol I hinges cracked. T June 18 (57) £170
— An History of the Original Parish of Whalley and Honor of Clitheroe. L, 1818. Folio, contemp calf; rear cover & last few leaves detached. Folding map torn without loss. T Feb 19 (300) £70

White, Alain Campbell
— Les Tours de force sur l'echiquier. Paris, 1906. Orig cloth. pn Mar 26 (339) £35 [Levine]

White, Alain Campbell —& Others
— The Stapelieae. Pasadena, 1937. 3 vols. 4to, cloth; rubbed. Marginal dampstaining & adhesion damage to Vols I & II. cb June 4 (208) $130; SSA Oct 28 (963) R420
— The Succulent Euphorbieae. Pasadena, 1941. 2 vols. 4to, cloth. SSA Oct 23 (962) R540

White, Charles. See: Martingale

White, Charles, 1728-1813
— A Treatise on the Management of Pregnant and Lying-In Women.... Worcester, Mass.: Isaiah Thomas, 1793. 8vo, contemp sheep; worn. With 2 plates, 1 loose. sg Jan 15 (127) $120

White, Elwyn Brooks
— Stuart Little. NY, 1945]. Illus by Garth Williams. In d/j. sg June 11 (424) $60

White, Frederick. See: Derrydale Press

White, George Francis
— Views in India, Chiefly among the Himalaya Mountains. L, 1838. 2 vols. Folio, orig half mor; small dampstain to 1 lower cover. With engraved dedication, engraved title & 29 proof plates on india paper. Engraved title & a few blank margins spotted; 1 plate frayed at margins. C Apr 8 (118) £350 [Bahra]
Anr copy. 4to, half calf; rubbed. pn Mar 5 (230) £75 [Traylen]
Anr copy. Contemp mor gilt; rubbed. With engraved title & 36 plates. S Feb 24 (494) £120 [Shankland]

White, Gilbert, 1720-93
See also: Nonesuch Press
— The Natural History and Antiquities of Selborne. L, 1789. 1st Ed. 4to, 19th-cent half calf; corners worn. With engraved title, folding frontis & 7 plates. pnE Dec 17 (359) £620 [Marshall]
Anr copy. Contemp calf; rebacked & rehinged. With folding frontis (repaired) & 6 plates. A few plates dampstained at corner. sg Dec 4 (204) $400
Anr Ed. L, [1837]. 8vo, lev gilt by Kelliegram. sg Dec 4 (205) $750
Anr Ed. L, 1876. 2 vols. 4to, orig half mor gilt; spine faded & rubbed. pnNY Sept 13 (300) $60

Anr Ed. L, 1900. 2 vols. 4to, mor by the Guild of Women-Binders, orig wraps bound in. bba July 2 (394) £140 [Dawson]
— A Naturalist's Calendar. L, 1795. 8vo, modern half calf. Margin of frontis cropped. bba Apr 9 (450) £50 [Whetman]
Anr copy. Modern calf gilt. pnE Dec 17 (371) £95 [Grant]
Anr copy. Later half calf; spine chipped. Title stained. sg Jan 15 (267) $50

White, James
— The Dream Millenium. L, 1974. In d/j. With ALs. cb Sept 28 (1347) $60

White, James, Newspaper Agent. See: Falstaff, Sir John

White, John, fl.1788-96
— Journal of a Voyage to New South Wales. L, 1790. 4to, calf; rebacked. With engraved title & 65 hand-colored plates. Some plates foxed. CA Apr 12 (252) A$2,200
Anr copy. Modern mor. kh Mar 16 (529C) A$3,500
Anr copy. Modern half mor gilt. With engraved title & 65 plate, the Pennantian Parrot plate colored. P Sept 24 (223) $1,400
Anr copy. Calf; worn. With engraved title & 65 hand-colored plates. pn Apr 30 (71) £1,250 [Maggs]
Anr copy. Half mor. S Oct 23 (530) £1,800 [Perrin]
— Voyage a la Nouvelles Galles du Sud, a Botany Bay.... Paris, 1798 [An VI]. 8vo, orig bdg. With 2 plates. FD June 11 (1201) DM2,500

White, Minor
— Mirrors, Messages, Manifestations. [NY, 1969]. 4to, cloth, in d/j. With pamphlet of commentary in back cover pocket. sg May 7 (84) $110

White, Samuel Alexander
— Into the Dead Heart: An Ornithological Trip.... Adelaide, 1914. Wraps. Corner cut from tp. kh Mar 16 (533) A$100

White, Terence Hanbury
— The Green Bay Tree; or, the Wicked Man Touches Wood. Cambr: Heffer, 1929. Pictorial wraps by Raymond McGrath; minor wear. sg Mar 5 (273) $130

White, William Anthony Parker, 1911-68. See: Boucher, Anthony

White, William Smith
— The Professional: Lyndon B. Johnson. Bost., 1964. In d/j. Inscr by Johnson. sg Sept 18 (141) $90

Whitefield, Henry
— The Light Appearing More and More towards the Perfect Day.... L: by T. R. & E.M. for John Bartlet, 1651. 4to, calf gilt by Bedford; joints cracked. Title with H. Whitfeld & the word church mis-spelled Chuch all on line 12 Catchword on A4 cropped; page numerals on B1, E2v, G2-3 caught by binder. Eliot's Indian Tract No 5. CNY Dec 19 (75) $1,500
— Strength out of Weaknesse.... L: M. Simmons for John Blague, 1652. 4to, calf gilt by Bedford; broken. With 15 pp of prelims & 40 numbered text pages; Sabin's variant a of the title with the spelling "Pulished" in line 15; variant a of the Epistle Dedicatory leaves sgd by John Owen & 11 others; variant a of 1st preface To the Reader leaves sgd by W. Gouge & 13 others; variant a of 2d preface To the Christian Reader with 3 pages; variant a of the last page of text with heading The Corporation to the reader; variant a of p 1 with headline type ornament; variant b of the text & ornamental initial settings on pp 6, 20, 27 & 33; variant b1 of p 36 with no floriated initial & line 17 beginning "word of English"; variant b2 of the last 2 leaves with signature mark G & heading The Corporation to the Reader on p 40. Signature 7 catchword on A2 & the word Finis on G2v cropped; tiny tear in tp repaired. Eliot's Indian Tract No 6. Brinley copy. CNY Dec 19 (76) $2,000

Whitehead, Charles Edward
— The Camp-Fires of the Everglades. Edin., 1891. 8vo, cloth; worn, endpapers damp-stained. O Oct 21 (196) $50

Whitehead, Henry S.
— Jumbee and Other Uncanny Tales. Sauk City, 1944. In d/j. cb Sept 28 (1349) $110

Whitehead, John, 1860-99
— Exploration of Mount Kina Balu. L, 1893. Folio, orig cloth; small tear to lower hinge of spine. With 11 colored & 21 plain plates. pn Oct 23 (18) £600 [Antiques]

Whitehouse, Francis Reginald Beaman
— Table Games of Georgian and Victorian Days. L, 1951. Orig cloth. O Apr 28 (200) $70

Whitehurst, John
— Works. L, 1792. 4to, contemp half sheep; corners reinforced, rubbed. With port & 9 plates. bba Aug 28 (138) £130 [P & P Books]

Whitelocke, Sir Bulstrode, 1605-75
— Memorials of the English Affairs.... L, 1709. Folio, contemp calf gilt, armorial bdg; rubbed. bba Oct 30 (165) £70 [Shapero]
Anr Ed. L: Tonson, 1732. Folio, contemp calf; broken. O Feb 24 (199) $50
— Monarchy Asserted.... L, 1660. 1st Ed. 8vo, early 19th-cent half lea; extremities worn. Lower margins wormed, corners dampstained. sg Oct 9 (169) $120

Whitgift, John, 1530?-1604
— An Answere to a Certen Libel Intituled, An Admonition to the Parliament. L: Henrie Bynneman for Humfrey Toy, 1572. 4to, 19th-cent mor gilt, armorial bdg. Old ink stain to title & small tear just affecting border; 2 other leaves with small marginal tears not affecting text; minute worming in lower margins. Sir Mark Masterman Sykes' copy. L Dec 11 (446) £260

Whiting, John
— A Catalogue of Friends' Books Written by Many...Quakers.... L, 1708. 1st Ed. 8vo, contemp calf; worn & broken. bba Mar 1221331 £200 [Murray Hill]

Whiting, Sydney
— Memoirs of a Stomach. L, [c.1856?]. 3d Ed. 8vo, orig cloth; spine worn. sg Jan 15 (57) $60

Whitman, Malcolm D. See: Derrydale Press

Whitman, Walt, 1819-92
See also: Grabhorn Printing; Limited Editions Club
— After All, Not to Create Only. Bost., 1871. 1st Pbd Ed. 8vo, orig cloth in half mor slipcase. With a set of uncorrected proofs of the poem in folio sheets, broadside form. P Dec 15 (111) $800
— As a Strong Bird on Pinyons Free. And Other Poems. Wash., 1872. 1st Ed. 8vo, cloth; head & foot of spine worn. With ptd preface from this Ed in duplicate loose leaves. P Dec 15 (113) $300
— Complete Poems and Prose...1855-1888. [Phila., 1888-89]. One of 600. 8vo, orig half cloth; upper hinge torn. With 2 ports, 1 spotted. pn Dec 11 (280) £130 [Sanders]
— Good-Bye My Fancy. Phila., 1891. 1st Ed. Title-page only. With emendations by Whitman, using this as proof for section-title of this work in the 1891-92 Ed of Leaves of Grass. Soiled, ragged margin. P Dec 15 (131) $250
L.p. copy. 8vo, cloth; rubbed. With fragment of Whitman Ms (6 words) tipped to front pastedown. With a proof of Gordon Craig's port of Whitman, stained. P Dec 15 (130) $300
— Leaves of Grass. Brooklyn, NY, 1856. 2d Ed. 12mo, orig cloth; corners bumped. Horace Traubel's copy, sgd & dated Oct 1897. P Dec 15 (132) $900
Anr copy. Contemp mor; rubbed. P Dec 15 (133) $350
3d Ed. Bost.: Thayer & Eldridge, 1860-61. 1st Issue. 8vo, orig cloth; worn & shaken, partly sprung. O Oct 21 (197) $110
6th Ed. Camden, N.J., 1876. 8vo, orig half calf; soiled, rubbed, front joint cracked. Sgd by Whitman on title. P Dec 15 (135) $600
Anr copy. Orig half calf gilt. Sgd by Whitman on title & with an orig undivided sheet of the "Intercalations". P Dec 15 (136) $1,100
Anr Ed. [Phila., 1889]. One of 300. 8vo, orig mor gilt; rubbed, extremities chipped. Sgd by Whitman on title. P Dec 15 (138) $700
— Notes and Fragments Left by.... London, Ontario: Pvtly ptd, 1899. One of 225. Ed by Dr. Richard Maurice Bucke. Folio, orig cloth; spine frayed, front hinge worn. Inscr by Bucke to Horace Traubel. P Dec 15 (143) $650
— November Boughs. Phila., 1888. 1st Ed. 8vo, cloth; front cover paint-spattered. sg Feb 12 (334) $60
[-] Poster designed by Walt Whitman, advertising his books. 630mm by 480mm,. ("Walt Whitman's Books/ Leaves of Grass...Democratic Vistas....") framed Print composed of 8 different type faces, headed by a simulated signature of Walt Whitman..... P Dec 15 (110A) $800
— Two Rivulets. Camden, 1876. 1st Ed. 8vo, orig half mor; hinges cracked. Frontis sgd. T Feb 18 (108) £70
— Works. [Phila., 1888-89]. ("Complete Poems & Prose, 1855-1888.") One 16 pp gathering only. Contains section-title to Leaves of Grass with Whitman's signature and limitation notice. 8vo. P Dec 15 (127) $300
One of 50, sgd, specially bound for presentation. Half calf gilt; spine faded. With 2 copies (one orig ptg, one revised) of R.M. Bucke's "Criticism" of the vol, 1888. P Dec 15 (126) $800
One of 600. Single gathering only, beginning with the section-title to Leaves of Grass. Sgd by Whitman with handwritten limitation noticed. P Dec 15 (127) $300
Author's Ms Ed. NY, [1902]. one of 10. 10 vols. Mor extra. Lacking the Whitman ALs with which the set was issued. P Dec 15 (128) $550
Camden Ed, One of 500. 10 vols. Half vellum. sg Feb 12 (335) $500
Whitman's copy, Walt

— ALGER, WILLIAM ROUNSEVILLE. - The Poetry of the East. Bost., 1856. 8vo, orig cloth; rebacked with portion of orig spine laid down. Tp detached & pinned to following leaf; some browning; stained at upper margins. With holograph notes, including that about the staining of the book through breaking a bottle of Virginia wine. P Dec 15 (112) $1,300

Whitney, Asa, 1797-1872
— Memorial of Asa Whitney, Praying a Grant of Public Land to Enable him to Construct a Railroad.... Wash., 1846. 8vo, disbound. With folding map. 29th Congress, 1st Session, Senate Doc. 161. wa Sept 25 (463) $50

Whitney, Casper —& Others
— Musk-Ox, Bison, Sheep and Goat. NY, 1904. Bdg bumped. cb Nov 6 (291) $65

Whitney, Charles Smith
— Bridges; A Study in their Art, Science and Evolution. NY: Rudge, 1929. One of 75. 4to, half lea; worn. O Sept 23 (198) $110

Whitney, Joel P.
— Silver Mining Regions of Colorado. NY, 1865. 16mo, ptd wraps. cb Jan 8 (217) $150

Whitney, Josiah D., 1819-96
— The Yosemite Guide-Book. NY, 1869. 8vo, orig cloth. With 2 maps. wa Mar 5 (415) $190

Whittier, John Greenleaf, 1807-92
— Works. Bost. & NY: Houghton, Mifflin, 1892-[94]. Artists' Ed. 9 vols. 8vo, half mor; spines rubbed. cb July 30 (195) $70

Whittle, James. See: Laurie & Whittle

Whittock, Nathaniel
— The Oxford Drawing Book. Oxford, [c.1825]. Oblong 4to, orig half mor; worn. With 107 plates. Some detached or cut-down, some soiling. Ck Oct 17 (144) £40

Whitworth, Charles Whitworth, Baron
— An Account of Russia.... Strawberry-Hill, 1758. 1st Ed. 8vo, calf, armorial bdg. pn Sept 18 (105) £210 [Ortman]

Whitworth, Geoffrey Arundell
— The Art of Nijinsky. L, 1913. Illus by Dorothy Mullock. Orig cloth. With 10 colored plates. Ck Apr 24 (132) £45

Whole...
— The Whole Art of Bookbinding. Oswestry, 1811. 1st Ed. 12mo, orig bds; worn, lacking upper free endleaf. Some pencil marks in margins; some soiling. S July 14 (453) £1,500

Why...
— Why Colored People in Philadelphia Are Excluded from the Street Cars. Phila., 1866. Orig wraps; soiled. 1 leaf stamped; the whole creased once vertically. cb Oct 9 (306) $50

Whymper, Edward, 1840-1911
— Scrambles Amongst the Alps in the years 1860-69. L, 1871. 1st Ed. 8vo, cloth; worn. S July 14 (680) £65
— Travels Amongst the Great Andes of the Equator. L, 1892-91. 2 vols, including Supplementary Appendix. 8vo, orig cloth; spines stained. Ck Sept 26 (130) £65

Whytt, Robert, 1714-66
— An Essay on the Vital and Other Involuntary Motions of Animals. Edin., 1751. 8vo, disbound. O Nov 18 (199) $100
— Works. Edin., 1768. 1st Collected Ed. 4to, later calf gilt. pnE Dec 17 (175) £730 [Harding-Brookes]
Anr copy. New cloth. S May 28 (806) £480

Wichmann, Hans & Siegfried
— Chess; the Story of Chesspieces from Antiquity to Modern Times. L, 1964. 4to, orig cloth, in d/j. pn Mar 26 (523) £90 [Furstenberg]

Wichmann, Siegfried
— Japonisme: The Japanese Influence on Western Art.... NY: Harmony Books, [1981]. In rubbed d/j; Cover chewed. cb Mar 5 (274) $55

Wickersham, James
— A Bibliography of Alaskan Literature. Cordova, 1927. Worn. sg Oct 2 (4) $175

Wickes, Charles
— Illustrations of the Spires and Towers of the Mediaeval Churches of England. L, 1853-59. 3 vols, including Supplement. Folio, orig half lea. C July 22 (229) £170

Wicquefort, Abraham van
— Advis fidelle aux veritables Hollandois.... The Hague: Steucker, 1673. Illus by Romeyn de Hooghe. 4to, 18th-cent calf gilt; scratched. With 8 double-page plates. Marginal repairs; inner margin of Cc1 repaired. S May 21 (129) £500 [Israel]

Widener Library, Harry Elkins
— A Catalogue of Some of the More Important Books.... Phila., 1910. One of 102. 4to, half mor; extremities scuffed, front joint weak. sg Oct 2 (310) $425
— A Catalogue of the Books and Manuscripts of Robert Louis Stevenson in the Library.... Phila.: Pvtly ptd, 1913. One of 150. With a Memoir by A. S. W. Rosenbach. 4to, half mor gilt. sg Oct 2 (311) $150

— A Catalogue of the Writings of Charles Dickens in the Library.... Phila: Pvtly ptd, 1918. Compiled by A. S. W. Rosenbach. 4to, cloth. sg Oct 2 (312) $130

Widman, Johann
— Regimen durch den Hochgelerten unnd uebertreffenlichen der artznei Doctor Johann Wydman.... Strassburg: Matthias Schuerer, 1511. 4to, cloth. Small reapir to inner margin of last leaf; marginal tear in title crudely repaired; stamp at end. S June 25 (137) £3,000

Widmanstadt, Johann Albrecht von
— Syriacae linguae prima elementa. Antwerp: Plantin, 1572. 4to, old half sheep; worn. 2 marginal tears repaired at end. sg Oct 9 (347) $325

Widmanstetter, Johann Albrecht. See: Widmanstadt, Johann Albrecht von

Wiener, Norbert
— Cybernetics, or Control and Communication in the Animal and the Machine. NY: John Wiley, [1948]. 8vo, orig cloth. Perforated library stamp on tp. S May 21 (219) £250 [Haas]

Wier, Johannes
— De praestigiis daemonum, et incantationibus ac ueneficiis. Basel: J. Oporinus, 1564. 2d Ed. 8vo, vellum; upper cover wormed. Upper corners of 1st few leaves damaged; small hole in text of tp & following 2 leaves & b8; foremargins of n7-8 damaged. S Nov 27 (242) £340 [Israel]
— De Praestigiis daemonum et incantationibus ac veneficii libri sex.... Basel: Oporinus, 1583. 4to, 18th-cent calf gilt; joints cracked at either end. Some browning & dampstaining; minor worming in outer margins; paper flaw in 2H1 causing loss. sg Oct 9 (348) $400

Wierzbicki, Felix Paul, 1815-60. See: Grabhorn Printing

Wight, John
— More Mornings at Bow Street. L, 1827. 8vo, mor gilt by Riviere; front cover loose. Lacking ads. sg June 11 (151) $200
— Mornings at Bow Street. L, 1824. 1st Ed, 1st Issue. Illus by George Cruikshank. 8vo, half calf gilt. sg June 11 (150) £110

Wight, Robert, 1796-1872
— Illustrations of Indian Botany Principally of the Southern Parts. Madras, [1838]-40-50. Vol I only. Contemp half mor gilt; rubbed. With 101 hand-colored plates. Tp creased; some discoloration of text. S Nov 10 (575) £240 [Walford]

Wigstead, Henry
— Remarks on a Tour to North and South Wales.... L, 1800. 1st Ed. 8vo, mor gilt; joints starting. With engraved title & 22 plates. Lacking tp. sg Feb 12 (336) $175

Wikgren, Allen P.
— The Coverdale Bible. San Francisco: Book Club of California, 1974. One of 425. With facsimile reproductions & an orig leaf. sg Jan 22 (315) $100

Wilberforce, William, 1759-1833
— A Letter on the Abolition of the Slave Trade. L, 1807. 1st Ed. 8vo, old calf; rebacked. Library markings; last 2 leaves wormed in margin. Inscr "From the Author" on half-title. L Dec 11 (447) £180
Anr copy. Contemp half calf; spine & joints worn, rubbed. Marginal tear in P8; lacking initial blank. P Sept 24 (424) $600

Wilbur, Richard
— A Bestiary. NY, [1955]. One of 750. Illus by Alexander Calder. Folio, cloth; spine rubbed. sg Jan 8 (39) $200

Wild, Frank
— Shackleton's Last Voyage. The Story of the Quest. L, 1923. 1st Ed. sg Nov 20 (8) $130

Wild, J. C.
— Panorama and Views of Philadelphia, and its Vicinity. Phila., 1838. 1st Ed. Folio, contemp cloth; broken. With 24 plates. Tp torn & lacking lower blank corner. wa Dec 11 (649) $1,200

Wild, John James
— At Anchor: a Narrative of Experiences Afloat and Ashore.... L, 1878. Folio, orig cloth; worn. With double-page map & 12 colored plates. S Jan 12 (334) £75 [Grant]

Wilde Oscar, 1854-1900
See also: Limited Editions Club
— L'Anniversaire de l'Infante. Paris: Black Sun Press, 1928. One of 110. Illus by Alastair. 4to, orig wraps. With 9 plates. S Dec 4 (1) £600 [Arwas]
— The Ballad of Reading Gaol. L, 1898. 1st Ed, one of 800. 8vo, cloth; soiled. bba Apr 9 (229) £180 [Stern]
Anr Ed. Munich, 1923. One of 250. Illus by Frans Masereel. 4to, half calf; rubbed. B Oct 7 (184) HF675
— De Profundis. L, [1905]. Cloth. pn Mar 5 (253) £75 [Whiteson]
One of 200. Orig cloth; slightly rubbed. Inscr to Tiny Schuster by Robert Ross. bba Apr 9 (232) £160 [Sumner & Stillman]
— The Happy Prince and Other Tales. L, 1888. 1st Ed. Illus by Walter Crane & Jacomb Hood. 4to, orig vellum. Inscr by Tiny Schuster. bba Apr 9 (225) £300

[Johns]
Anr Ed. L, 1913. One of 260. Illus by Charles Robinson. 4to, cloth; worn, small tear in edge of spine, library circulation pocket at end. O Apr 28 (201) $60

Anr copy. Vellum; extremities worn. sg Jan 8 (29) $200

— A House of Pomegranates. L, 1891. 1st Ed. Illus by Charles Ricketts. 4to, orig cloth; rear cover spotted, hinges cracked. With colored engraved title & 16 colored plates. sg Dec 11 (1132) $150

Anr Ed. L, 1915. Illus by Jessie M. King. 4to, orig cloth; worn. With colored engraved title & 16 colored plates. pn Oct 23 (330) £130 [Elliott]

— An Ideal Husband. L, 1899. 1st Ed, one of 1,000. 4to, orig cloth; spine soiled. bba Apr 9 (230) £60 [Ash]

Anr copy. Orig cloth; unopened. sg Dec 11 (133) $80

— The Importance of Being Earnest. L, 1899. 1st Ed, one of 1,000. 4to, orig cloth; rubbed. Sgd by Tiny Schuster. bba Apr 9 (231) £220 [Ash]

— Intentions. L, 1891. 1st Ed. 8vo, orig cloth; soiled. Inscr by Tiny Schuster. bba Apr 9 (228) £50 [Pagoda]

— Lady Windermere's Fan. L, 1893. 1st Ed. 4to, orig cloth; rubbed. bba Apr 9 (226) £100 [Stern]

— The Picture of Dorian Gray. L, [1891]. 1st Ed, Issue not given. 8vo, orig half vellum; rubbed & soiled, lower hinge broken. S Sept 22 (152) £40 [Leimweber]

1st Ed in Book form, One of 250 L.p. copies, sgd. 4to, orig half vellum bds; rubbed. bba July 2 (399) £700 [Hever]

Ed A. L, [1968]. but lacking the suite of 6 lithos sgd in separate folder & facsimile of typescript. Illus by Jim Dine. Folio, orig velvet. With 12 colored plates. wa Mar 5 (115) $80

Ed B, one of 225 with 4 sgd etchings in separate folder. Folio, velvet. With 12 color plates.. S Dec 4 (186) £700 [Finch]

— Poems. L, 1892. One of 220. 8vo, modern calf; new endpapers. S July 23 (126) £380 [Deeny]

— Prose Poems. Belfast: Crannog Press, 1973. One of 100. sg Mar 5 (275) $50

— Salome. A Tragedy in One Act. L & Bost., 1894. One of 500. Trans by Lord Alfred Douglas; illus by Aubrey Beardsley. 4to, orig cloth. S Jan 16 (457) £460 [Shobo]

— Salome, drame en un acte. Paris & L, 1893. 1st Ed, one of 600. orig wraps S Jan 16 (460) £500 [Shobo]

Pirated Ed. Paris, 1907. one of 400. Illus by Aubrey Beardsley. 4to, vellum & mor mosaic bdg by Charles Benoit, orig wraps bound in. FD Dec 2 (4221) DM1,800

Anr Ed. Paris, 1922. Illus by Alastair. With 9 plates. HN Nov 26 (1665) DM500

— The Sphinx. L, 1894. 1st Ed, one of 200. Illus by Charles Ricketts. 4to, orig vellum gilt; bowed & soiled. S June 17 (282) £900 [Joseph]

Anr Ed. L, 1920. One of 1,000. Illus by Alastair. 4to, orig cloth. S May 6 (79) £110 [Goldsmith]

— A Woman of No Importance. L, 1894. 1st Ed, One of 500. 4to, orig cloth; spine rubbed. bba Apr 9 (227) £220 [Ash]

— Works. L, 1908. One of 1,000. 14 vols. pn Jan 22 (142) £380 [Joseph]

Wildenstein, Georges
See also: Jamot & Wildenstein

— The Paintings of Fragonard. L, 1960. 4to, cloth. HN May 20 (454) DM520

Wilder, Thornton

— The Bridge of San Luis Rey. L, 1927. In d/j. sg Mar 5 (278) $90

Anr Ed. NY, 1929. One of 1,100. Illus by Rockwell Kent. 4to, cloth; spine ends def. cb June 18 (231) $80

Anr copy. With 16 mtd woodcuts. sg Jan 8 (149) $175

— Our Town. NY, [1938]. Inscr. sg Mar 5 (279) $550

Wildman, Thomas

— A Treatise on the Management of Bees. L, 1768. 1st Ed. 4to, contemp calf; spine ends chipped, joints cracked. With 3 folding plates. sg Jan 15 (174) $100

Wildrake

— The Cracks of the Day, Edited by Wildrake. See: Tattersall, George

Wilhelm, Gottlieb Tobias

— Unterhaltungen aus der Naturgeschichte. Insekten (Vols 6-8). Fische (Vols 9-10). Wuermer (Vols 11-12). Augsburg, 1796-1802. 1st Ed. 7 vols. 8vo, contemp half lea; worn & def. HK Nov 4 (1161) DM2,200

— Unterhaltungen aus der Naturgeschichte. Die Pflanzenreich. Augsburg, 1810-20. 10 vols. 8vo, contemp mor. With port, 10 engraved titles & 608 hand colored plates. Horticultural Society of New York—de Belder copy. P Apr 28 (381) £13,000 [Israel]

Anr Ed. Augsburg, 1821. Vol X (of 10) only. 8vo, contemp half calf; spine chipped & cracking. Lacking final leaf but with the Register. cb Oct 23 (239) $110

Wilkes, Benjamin
— The English Moths and Butterflies. L, 1773. ("One Hundred and Twenty Copper-Plates of English Moths and Butterflies.") 4to, contemp half russia; some wear. With 120 hand-colored plates. McLeod—de Belder copy. S Apr 28 (384) £5,000 [Arader]

Wilkes, Charles, 1798-1877
— Narrative of the United States Exploring Expedition, during the Years 1838-42.... Phila., 1845. 5 vols. 4to, orig cloth; spine ends chipped. With 8 (of 11) maps. sg Nov 20 (173) $175

Anr copy. 5 vols, plus Atlas. 4to, With 5 folding maps, 1 hand-colored, in Atlas; 9 mtd double-page maps in text vols. sg Dec 4 (207) $900

Anr copy. 2 vols only. 4to, wd June 19 (191) $750

— Narrative of the United States Exploring Expedition.... NY, 1851. 5 vols. 8vo, contemp half calf gilt; 1 cover detached, small tear to 1 spine. With 11 maps & 64 plates. C Oct 15 (114) £380 [Cavendish]

Wilkins, Ernest Hatch. See: Caxton Club

Wilkins, John, 1614-72
— An Essay towards a Real Character.... L, 1668. 1st Ed. Folio, modern half calf. Lacking 3 folding tables & final blank; some marginal annotations & staining; licence leaf frayed without loss. S July 28 (1132) £120

— Mathematicall Magick.... L, 1648. 8vo, calf. Lacking blank before title. pn Apr 30 (335) £240 [Demetzy]

Anr copy. Modern half mor. Upper margins trimmed close; lacking initial blank. sg Mar 26 (287) $200

Anr copy. Contemp calf; spine ends restored, varnished. sg Apr 2 (218) $375

4th Ed. L, 1691. 8vo, contemp calf; spine rubbed. S May 28 (807) £140

Wilkins, William, 1778-1839
— The Antiquities of Magna Graecia. Cambr., 1807. Folio, modern half mor. Wtih 73 plans & plates. Some spotting; waterstained towards end. S Oct 23 (354) £350 [Crete]

Wilkinson, Charles Henry
— Elements of Galvanism in Theory and Practice. L, 1804. 1st Ed. 2 vols. 8vo, contemp half russia. With frontis & 12 plates, 1 hand-colored. Some plate numerals cropped. C Dec 12 (220) £300 [Travis]

Wilkinson, Sir John Gardner, 1797-1875
— The Manners and Customs of the Ancient Egyptians. L, 1878. Ed by Samuel Birch. 3 vols. 8vo, half mor gilt. pn Oct 23 (26) £130 [Walford]

Wilkinson, Robert, Publisher
— A General Atlas. L, 1809. 4to, contemp half calf; worn. With engraved title, platelist & 48 colored maps. Ck Nov 21 (341) £150

— Londina Illustrata. L, 1819-25. 2 vols. Folio, half mor gilt. pn Apr 30 (260) £240 [Woodruff]

Willard, Samuel, 1640-1707
— A Compleat Body of Divinity.... Bost., 1726. Folio, contemp sheep; worn, joints starting. Lacking port. sg Sept 18 (309) $150

Willdenow, Karl Ludwig
— Hortus Berolinensis. Berlin, 1816. 2 vols in 1. Folio, contemp half calf; hinges cracking, 1 joints partly torn. With 2 colored plans & 108 hand-colored plates. Plesch—de Belder copy. S Apr 28 (383) £13,000 [Israel]

Willems, Alphonse
— Les Elzevier. Histoire et annales typographiques. Brussels, Paris & The Hague, 1880-97. 2 vols, including Supplement. 8vo, contemp half calf & orig wraps. Some stains. bba Oct 16 (402) £80 [Hay Cinema]

Willett Library, Ralph
— A Description of the Library at Merly in the County of Dorset. L, 1785. Folio, contemp half mor; worn. With 14 plates only. Sold w.a.f. Ck Jan 30 (85) £350

William, Elijah, d.1854. See: Bristol Chess Club

Williams, Ben Ames. See: Derrydale Press

Williams, Carl M.
— Silversmiths of New Jersey, 1700-1825.... Phila.: MacManus, 1949. 4to, cloth. wa Nov 6 (491) $90

Williams, Sir Charles Hanbury
— The New Foundling Hospital for Wit.... L, 1784. 6 vols. 12mo, contemp sheep; rubbed, joints weak, Vol I front cover detached. sg Oct 9 (349) $60

Williams, Edward
— Virginia's Discovery of Silk-Wormes.... L: T. H. for John Stephenson, 1650. 4to, 19th-cent mor gilt, armorial bdg. First 3 leaves may be from a shorter copy, with several letters of title shaved; some other shaving; lacking A1 blank & 2L2-4; L12 & 3 partially supplied in ink facsimile. Hunt copy. CNY Nov 21 (288) $750

— Virgo Triumphans: or, Virginia.... L: Thomas Harper for John Stephenson, 1650. 4to, half mor. Some cropping. S June 25 (422) £7,500

Williams, Elijah, d.1854
— Horae Divanianae. L, 1852. Orig cloth; worn. Library stamp on title. pn Mar 26 (525) £35 [Caissa]

Williams, Frederick Smeeton
— Our Iron Roads: Their History, Construction, and Social Influence. L, 1852. 8vo, orig cloth; worn, spine chipped, hinges cracked. wa Nov 6 (73) $55

Williams, Hugh W., 1773-1829
— Select Views in Greece. L, 1829. 2 vols in one. 4to, half mor gilt; worn, crudeley rebacked. With 64 plates. Title browned. bba Dec 18 (265) £150 [Cassidy]

Williams, James Leon
— The Home and Haunts of Shakespeare. NY, 1894. Stratford Ed. Folio, cloth; worn. O Oct 21 (198) $130

Williams, John, 1796-1839
— A Narrative of Missionary Enterprises in the South Sea Islands. L, 1840. 24th thousand. 8vo, contemp half calf; upper joint split, rubbed. With frontis & map. bba Oct 30 (366) £45 [Hashimoto]

Williams, Juanita H. See: Hallenbeck & Williams

Williams, Sidney Herbert
— Bibliography of the Writings of Lewis Carroll. L, 1924. One of 700. O Sept 23 (199) $70
— A Handbook of the Literature of the Rev. C. L. Dodgson. L, 1931. One of 750. In d/j. bba Apr 23 (47) £40 [Forster]

Williams, Tennessee
— Androgyne, Mon Amour. NY, 1977. One of 200. sg Mar 5 (280) $175
— Hard Candy. [NY]: New Directions, [1954]. Ltd Ed. Half cloth. Sgd. cb May 7 (162) $65
— It Happened the Day the Sun Rose. Los Angeles: Sylvester & Orphanos, 1981. One of 300. 4to, cloth. sg Mar 5 (281) $150
— Memoirs. NY, 1975. Ltd Ed, sgd. cb May 7 (163) $95; sg Mar 5 (282) $175
— Moise and the World of Reason. NY, [1975. One of 350. Syn. sg Mar 5 (283) $150
— One Arm, and Other Stories. [NY]: New Directions, [1954]. In d/j. Sgd. cb May 7 (164) $65
— Out Cry. NY, 1973. In d/j. Inscr. sg Mar 5 (284) $275
— The Rose Tattoo. [NY]: New Directions,

[1951]. In d/j. Sgd. cb May 7 (165) $60
— Shooting script "Revised Final White". [N.p.], 22 Oct 1954. In black cloth pressure-binder. Williams' own copy with a few pencil notes. Inscr to Gene Brooks. With related material. cb May 7 (166) $1,000
— Suddenly Last Summer. NY, 1958. In d/j. Inscr. sg Mar 5 (285) $425
— Summer and Smoke. NY, 1948. Inscr. sg Mar 5 (286) $325
— Sweet Bird of Youth. NY, 1969. One of 350. 4to, cloth. sg Mar 5 (288) $175
— The Two-Character Play. [NY, 1969]. One of 350. sg Dec 11 (141) $130

Williams, Thomas Lanier. See: Williams, Tennessee

Williams, William Carlos, 1883-1963
— The Great American Novel. Paris, 1923. 1st Ed, One of 300. Half cloth, soiled. T Feb 18 (166) £120
— White Mule. [Norfolk, Conn.]: New Directions, 1937. 1st Ed. 8vo, cloth, in frayed d/j. wa Dec 11 (125) $95

Williams, William Mattieu, 1820-92
— The Chemistry of Cookery. NY, 1885. 12mo, orig cloth. sg Jan 15 (58) $50

Williamson, George Charles. See: Manners & Williamson

Williamson, George Charles, 1858-1942
— The Book of the Famille Rose. Rutland VT: Charles E. Tuttle, [1970]. In d/j. cb Mar 5 (275) $90
— The History of Portrait Miniatures. L, 1904. One of 520. 2 vols. Folio, orig cloth, in d/js. pnE Jan 28 (218) £110 [Spearman]
— Life and Works of Ozias Humphry, R.A. L, 1918. One of 400. 4to, orig half vellum; rubbed. bba Feb 5 (117) £50 [Hay]

Williamson, Henry
— The Patriot's Progress.... L, 1930. 1st Ed, One of 350. Orig half vellum. S Jan 13 (614) £50 [Perrin]
— The Village Book. L, [1930]. 1st Ed, one of 504. T Oct 15 (39) £42

Williamson, Jack
— Darker Than You Think. Reading PA: Fantasy Press, 1948. One of 500. Illus by Edd Cartier. In d/j. Inscr to Alistair Cameron. cb Sept 28 (1354) $100

Williamson, James Alexander
— The Voyages of the Cabots.... L, 1929. One of 1,050 on Japanese vellum. 4to, cloth. sg Mar 12 (274) $60

Williamson, John, M.D.
— Medical and Miscellaneous Observations, Relative to the West India Islands. Edin., 1817. 1st Ed. 2 vols. 8vo, half calf; rubbed, joints split. S May 29 (1275) £190

Williamson, Joseph
— A Bibliography of the State of Maine.... Portland, 1896. 2 vols. 8vo, half lea; extremities chafed. sg Oct 2 (189) $130

Williamson, Robert Stockton
— Report of Explorations in California for Railroad Routes. Wash., 1856. Folio, later half calf; spine & extremities rubbed. With 22 plain & 19 color plates, 7 fold-out sectional drawings & 4 color maps, 1 folding. Foxing affecting some plates. b Jan 8 (220) $425

Williamson, Capt. Thomas
— The Complete Angler's Vade-Mecum.... L, 1808. 8vo, half mor gilt. With 10 plates. pnE Dec 17 (332) £110 [Head]

Williamson, Capt. Thomas —& Blagdon, Francis, William, 1778-1819
— The European in India. L, 1813. 4to, contemp mor gilt; rubbed. With 20 colored plates. Tp with minor stain & spotting; Plate I mtd on front pastedown; finger-soiling to some margins. C Apr 8 (84) £350 [Joseph]

Anr copy. Modern half mor. With 20 colored plates, all with perforated library stamps. Library markings. Sold w.a.f. Ck Feb 27 (122) £75

Anr copy. Half calf; rubbed. With 20 colored plates. Title & plates soiled. pn June 18 (240) £190 [Brown]

Williamson, Capt. Thomas —& Howitt, Samuel, 1765?-1822
— Oriental Field Sports. L, 1807. Oblong folio, contemp half mor. With colored engraved title & 40 colored plates. This copy with Plate 31 lettered Hunting Jackalls. C Oct 15 (127) £5,200 [Rostron]

Anr copy. Half mor; worn. With colored engraved title & 40 colored plates. Frontis creased; some soiling. S June 25 (475) £12,500 [Musso]

Anr copy. Contemp russia; worn. Jeanson 1567. SM Mar 1 (580) FF190,000

Anr Ed. L, 1808. 2 vols. 4to, contemp half calf; worn. With 2 engraved titles & 40 plates, all colored by hand. bba Dec 4 (189) £400 [Smith]

Anr copy. 2 vols in 1. 4to, contemp half calf; rubbed, hinges worn. With 2 engraved titles & 40 plates. Small waterstain to frontis; minor spotting to Vol I title. C Apr 8 (119) £350 [Christenson]

Anr Ed. L, 1819. In 2 vols. Oblong folio, contemp half Russia; 1 backstrip def. With 40 hand-colored plates. Jeanson 1617. SM Mar 1 (581) FF5,500

Willich, Anthony Florian Madinger
— Lectures on Diet and Regimen.... Bost., 1800. 2 vols. 12mo, contemp half calf; spine worn. Pencil marks in margins. S Nov 10 (420) £65 [Weiss]

Willis, Browne
— A Survey of the Cathedrals of York, Durham, Carlisle.... L, 1727-30. 2 vols. 4to, orig calf; upper covers detached. With 20 plates. pn Jan 22 (21) £40 [Clegg]

Willis, Henry
— Specimen of Printing Types from the New England Type Foundry. Bost., 1834. 4to, contemp half lea; worn. With 7 plates lacking considerable portions; some tears. wa Nov 6 (538) $350

Willis, Nathaniel Parker, 1806-67
— American Scenery. L, 1840. 2 vols. 4to, contemp half mor; rubbed. With 2 engraved titles, port, map & 117 plates. C Oct 15 (115) £290 [Walford]

Anr copy. Vol I only. Mor; spine torn, partly sprung. Foxed; minor stains. O Oct 21 (199) $160

Anr copy. 2 vols. 4to, orig wraps; def. Lacking 1 plate. Sold w.a.f. pn Nov 20 (227) £300 [Walford]

Anr copy. Bdgs not described but def. With 2 engraved titles, port, map & 117 plates. pn Dec 11 (56) £260 [Walford]

Anr copy. Half mor gilt; not uniform. pn Dec 11 (59) £220 [Walford]

Anr copy. Half calf gilt. S Oct 23 (317) £220 [Lewis]

Anr copy. Orig cloth. S May 28 (929) £320

Anr copy. Contemp mor gilt. With port, 2 engraved titles, map & 117 plates. Dampstained. S May 29 (1091) £260

Anr copy. Orig mor gilt; front cover of Vol I detached, spine defective. With 2 engraved titles, port, map & 117 plates. sg Dec 18 (144) $400

Anr copy. Contemp lea gilt. sg Mar 12 (276) $350

Anr copy. Half lea. With 2 engraved titles, port, map & 116 plates. sg Apr 23 (154) $500

Anr copy. Contemp half mor; 1 backstrip def. With 2 engraved titles, map & 117 plate. Lacking port. T Oct 16 (316) £220

Anr copy. Illus by W. H. Bartlett. Vol I (of 2) only. 4to, contemp mor gilt; rubbed. 1 plate torn. O Feb 24 (5) $210

Anr Ed. L, 1852. 2 vols. 4to, half mor; worn & chipped. wd June 19 (192) $300

— Canadian Scenery. L, 1842. Illus by W. H. Bartlett. 2 vols. 4to, contemp half calf; joints rubbed. With engraved titles, map & 117 plates. Lacking port. C Oct 15 (116) £450 [Green]

Anr copy. Contemp calf; worn, spines def, 1 cover detached. Lacking port; 1 plate loose & frayed. S Nov 18 (1110) £400 [Michelsen]

Anr copy. Orig cloth; worn & shaken. Most plates clean; institutional stamp on some versos. Sold w.a.f. sg Mar 12 (43) $225

Anr copy. 2 vols in 1. 4to, contemp half mor; worn, lacking most of spine. With engraved titles, port, map & 117 plates. 9 plates stained. wa Dec 11 (598) $400

— Pencillings by the Way. L, 1835. 3 vols. 12mo, orig half cloth; endpapers browned. sg Sept 11 (284) $70

Willis, Nathaniel Parker, 1806-67 —& Coyne, Joseph Stirling, 1803-68

— The Scenery and Antiquities of Ireland. L: Virtue, [1841]. 2 vols. 4to, modern cloth. With 118 plates by W. H. Bartlett. Map detached, ink stains on plates & titles. bba Dec 4 (355) £85 [Rainer]

Anr copy. 2 vols in one. 4to, contemp mor; worn. bba Dec 4 (356) £85 [Schuetze]

Anr copy. 2 vols. 4to, contemp half mor; soiled. With engraved titles, map & 116 plates. Lacking port. Ck Feb 27 (45) £90

Anr copy. 2 vols in 1. 4to, contemp half calf; worn. With engraved titles, map & 116 (of 118) plates.. S Nov 17 (836) £90 [Henderson]

Anr copy. Orig 6 parts. 4to, orig lea-backed bds; rubbed & soiled. With 2 engraved titles, port, map & 19 plates. S Nov 17 (837) £130 [Boyd]

Anr copy. 2 vols in 1. 4to, contemp half mor. With engraved titles, map & 118 plates. Lacking port. S Feb 23 (56) £90 [Smith]

Anr copy. 2 vols. 4to, mor; rubbed. S May 28 (930) £110

Anr copy. Contemp mor gilt; worn. With 120 (of 121) plates. sg Nov 20 (174) $200

Anr copy. Contemp calf; Vol I loose. SSA Feb 11 (448) R260

Anr Ed. L, [c.1845]. 2 vols. 4to, contemp half calf; rubbed. With 2 engraved titles, map & 118 plates. Minor dampstaining. T Apr 16 (111) £95

Willis, Thomas, 1621-75

— Cerebri anatome, cui accessit nervorum descriptio et usus. L, 1664. 8vo, contemp calf; rebacked. With 15 plates. A few marginal tears in some plates. Owner's name cut from upper margin of title. S Nov 27 (297) £2,400 [Canape]

Issue with the errata & an extra leaf of text (p. 56). Vellum bds. With 15 plates. Small burn hole in a3 affecting 1 letter; library stamp on tp erased; some spotting at beginning. S June 25 (139) £1,500 [Phelps]

— Dr. Willis's Practise of Physick. L, 1684. Folio, calf. With 40 plates. pnE Dec 17 (161) £1,400 [Phelps]

— The London Practice of Physick.... L: T. Basset & W. Crooke, 1685. 8vo, contemp calf; rebacked, corners worn. Extreme upper corner of title & few following leaves stained & slightly def; marginal tear in Y4 & Z2. S May 28 (809) £260

— Opera. Geneva, 1676. 2 vols. 4to, contemp calf; worn. With 40 plates. Lacking port. S Nov 27 (298) £260 [Lehman]

— The Remaining Medical Works.... L: T. Dring et al, 1681. Folio, half calf. With port (in facsimile) & 16 plates. Plate 8 in facsimile; plate at p 70 soiled; some tears in the 4 folding plates. S Nov 10 (577) pS460 [Ebers]

Willmott, Ellen Ann

— The Genus Rosa. L, 1910-14. 2 vols. Folio, contemp half lea, orig wraps bound in; worn, 1 spine imperf. Some browning & leaf def. HN Nov 26 (284) DM3,000

Anr Ed. L, 1914. 2 vols. Folio, half mor, orig wraps bound in. With 132 colored plates. A few plates adhering to tissue guards. S Oct 23 (764) £580 [Sablon]

Willsford, Thomas

— Natures Secrets, of the Admirable and Wonderfull History of the Generation of Meteors. L, 1658. 8vo, old calf; rubbed. Some worming to inner margin; repairable tear to p 96. pn Mar 5 (17) £85 [Camberley]

Willughby, Francis

— The Ornithology.... L, 1678. 1st Ed in English. 3 parts in 1 vol. Folio, contemp calf; worn, upper joint cracked. With 2 tables & 78 (of 80) plates. Lacking the 2 unnumbered plates; minor tear in 1st leaf of index; paper flaw in 3K2v affecting 2 words. C Dec 12 (287) £280 [Rix]

Anr copy. Calf gilt; upper bd split. pnE Dec 17 (288) £680 [Maggs]

Anr copy. New cloth. With 2 tables & 80 plates. Plates 60, 70 & 78 are in facsimile. Tiny wormhole throughouter blank margins in 1st section; some worming in inner margins of about half the plates affecting little engraved surface; rough repair in lower outer section of Plate 75; Plate 77 mtd. Sold w.a.f. S May 28 (810) £160

Wilmot, Alexander
— History of the Zulu War. L & Cape of Good Hope, 1880. 8vo, cloth. SSA Oct 28 (965) R210

Wilmott, Ellen Ann
— The Genus Rosa.... L: John Murray, 1914. Illus by Alfred Parsons. 2 vols. Folio, orig half mor with orig wraps preserved at end of each vol; bdgs broken. With 132 color plates. Some plates & text detached with edges frayed or chipped. Sold w.a.f. CNY Nov 21 (289) $1,500

Wilpert, Joseph
— I Sarcofagi Cristiani antichi. Rome, 1929-36. 5 vols. Folio, cloth. With 300 plates. sg Apr 2 (219) $800

Wilson, Adrian
— Printing for the Theater. San Francisco, 1957. One of 250. sg Dec 4 (208) $650
— The Work and Play.... Austin: W. Thomas Taylor, 1983. One of 325. Folio, half mor. sg Jan 22 (317) $300

Wilson, Alexander, 1766-1813 —& Bonaparte, Charles Lucien, 1803-57
— The American Ornithology. L, 1832. 3 vols. 8vo, later half mor gilt. With 97 hand-colored plates. sg June 11 (425) $1,200
 Anr Ed. L, 1876. 3 vols. 4to, orig cloth; rubbed, crudely rebacked. With port & 103 color plates. Library stamps. P Dec 15 (238) $200
 Anr copy. Half mor gilt; soiled. Some spotting. pn Oct 23 (321) £130 [Tooley]

Wilson, Arthur, 1595-1652
— The History of Great Britain, being the Life of King James the First. L, 1653. 1st Ed. Folio, old half lea; front cover detached. sg Mar 26 (289) $175

Wilson, Benjamin, 1721-88
— An Account of the Experiments Made at the Pantheon.... L, 1778. 4to, contemp half sheep. With frontis & 2 plates. C Dec 12 (222) £380 [Quaritch]

Wilson, Sir Charles William
— Picturesque Palestine. L, [1880-84]. 4 vols. 4to, orig cloth; worn. bba Oct 30 (367) £85 [Boyer]
 Anr copy. 5 vols, including Supplement. 4to, orig cloth; rubbed. bba Nov 13 (123) £90 [Goldman]
 Anr copy. 4 vols. 4to, Ck May 15 (95) £800
 Anr copy. 5 vols, including Supplement.

4to, cloth; worn. pn Dec 11 (163) £190 [F& S]
 Anr copy. 4 vols. 4to, half mor. pnE June 17 (169) £50
 Anr copy. Contemp half mor; worn. S Nov 18 (1079) £180 [Vecseri]
 Anr copy. Contemp mor gilt; worn. T Feb 19 (226) £100
 Anr Ed. NY, [1881]-84. 2 vols. Folio, half mor gilt. Titles with some foxing. sg Sept 25 (251) $300
 Anr copy. Orig lea; scuffed, Vol II front cover starting. sg Apr 30 (293) $250

Wilson, Colin
— The Mind Parasites. L, 1967. In d/j. Inscr. cb Sept 28 (1363) $70

Wilson, Edmund
— Note-Books of Night. San Francisco, 1942. 1st Ed. Cloth, in d/j. Weldon Kees's copy. sg Mar 5 (296) $140
— The Rats of Rutland Grange. NY: Gotham Book Mart, 1961. Illus by Edward Gorey. Sgd by Gorey. sg Mar 5 (297) $150
— To the Finland Station. NY, [1940]. 1st Ed. In d/j. cb May 7 (174) $225

Wilson, Edward
— The Book of.... NY, 1948. 4to, half cloth, in d/j. ha Dec 19 (285) $55

Wilson, Elijah Nicholas
— Among the Shoshones. Salt Lake City, [1910]. 1st Ed, 1st Issue. Orig cloth; worn, front free endpaper missing, marginal tear to flyleaf. With 8 plates Tears in 2 leaves, affecting text on 1. cb Mar 19 (280) $225

Wilson, Ernest Henry
— A Naturalist in Western China with Vasculum, Camera and Gun.... NY, 1913. 2 vols. Some soiling to Vol II prelims & tp. cb June 4 (209) $170

Wilson, Harriette
— Memoirs of Harriette Wilson, Written by Herself. L, 1825. 3 vols. 8vo, orig bds; worn, Vol I front cover detached. With engraved title in Vol I, port & 10 hand-colored plates. Lacking the folding plates. sg Sept 11 (285) $70

Wilson, Harry
— Fugitive Sketches in Rome, Venice.... L, 1838. Folio, orig half mor; broken & worn. With litho title & 12 plates, all but 1 stamped. bba Feb 5 (363) £110 [Elliott]

Wilson, Horace Hayman, 1786-1860. See: Moorcroft & Trebeck

Wilson, Capt James. See: Wilson, William

Wilson, James Grant, 1832-1914
— Bryant and his friends.... NY, 1886. 3 vols. 4to, contemp half mor by R. W. Smith. Extra-illus with A Ls s of Bryant & Wilson & with c.400 inlaid plates. sg Sept 18 (45) $300

Wilson, John Marius
— The Rural Cyclopedia. Edin., 1847-49. 4 vols. 8vo, contemp half calf; rubbed. Ck Sept 5 (197) £70

Wilson, Sir John Mitchell H.
— The Royal Philatelic Collection.... L, 1952. Ed by Clarence Winchester. Folio, orig mor. bba Nov 13 (78) £90 [Renard]; Ck Sept 5 (91) £160

Anr copy. Orig mor gilt. Ck Oct 31 (125) £70; pn July 23 (162) £110 [Joseph]

Wilson, Richard, 1714-82
— Studies and Designs...done at Rome in the Year 1752. Oxford, 1811. 4to, contemp half calf; worn, joints cracked. With title & 51 litho plates. C July 22 (232) £100

Wilson, Robert Forrest. See: Crowell & Wilson

Wilson, Sir Robert Thomas, 1777-1849
— Brief Remarks on the Character and Composition of the Russian Army.... L, 1810. 4to, half lea; worn, covers nearly detached. With folding & 7 folding plans, each with some hand-coloring. L.p. copy. sg NOv 20 (125) $60

— History of the British Expedition to Egypt. L, 1803. 2d Ed. 4to, contemp calf; worn, front joint splitting. With port, 3 folding maps & 2 folding tables. Lacking half-title. cb Nov 6 (294) $160

Wilson, Samuel
— An Account of the Province of Carolina in America. L: G. Larkin, 1682. 1st Issue. 4to, half mor. Some page numerals cut close; lacking map. S June 25 (381) £1,500

Wilson, Scott B. —& Evans, Arthur Humble
— Aves Hawaiienses: The Birds of the Sandwich Islands. L, 1890-99. In orig 8 parts. 4to, orig wraps; most spines frayed or split, blank portion of rear wrap of Part 2 lost. P Sept 24 (224) $3,200

Wilson, Thomas, Solicitor
See also: Mendelssohn-Barthodly's copy, Felix
— A Catalogue Raisonne of the Select Collection of Engravings of an Amateur. L: [Pvtly ptd], 1828. One of 100 L.p. copies. 4to, later 19th-cent mor gilt; rubbed. Extra-illus with engravings & etchings. P Feb 24 (225) $1,000

Wilson, Thomas Fourness
— The Defense of Lucknow: A Diary.... L, 1858. 16mo, later cloth. Frontis creased with 2 small pinholes. cb Dec 18 (181) $60

Wilson, W. J. See: De Ricci & Wilson

Wilson, William, Chief Mate of the Ship Duff
— A Missionary Voyage to the Southern Pacific Ocean. L, 1799. 1st Ed. 4to, later cloth; rubbed. With 6 plates & 7 folding maps. bba Oct 30 (368) £170 [Shapero]

Anr copy. Cloth; soiled. With 7 maps (5 folding) & 6 plates. Plates stamped & stained. bba Dec 18 (266) £100 [Elliott]

Anr copy. Calf; rebacked. With 7 folding maps or charts & 6 plates. Lacking all before title; tear in 1st map; some foxing. CA Apr 12 (254) A$380

Anr copy. Contemp half cloth; worn. With 2 folding maps & 11 other maps & views. Tp repaired. S Nov 18 (1243) £270 [Remington]

Anr copy. Contemp half calf; worn. With 7 maps & 6 plates. Most maps torn and/or repaired to some extent; 1 map shaved; some worming at beginning & end in margin. S Feb 24 (500) £160 [Cox]

Anr copy. Contemp calf; rubbed, hinges weak. With 7 folding maps & 6 plates. A few imprints cropped. S June 25 (505) £300 [Bonham]

Anr copy. Contemp half sheep; worn, covers detached. sg Apr 23 (155) $150

Wiltsee, Ernest A. See: Grabhorn Printing

Wimmer, G. A.
— Das pittoreske Oesterreich, oder Album der oesterreichischen Monarchie. Vienna, 1840-46. Vols I-III. Contemp half lea With 32 maps & 148 (of 155) colored plates. 3 maps loose & worn. FD Dec 2 (880) DM8,000

Winckelmann, Johann Joachim, 1717-68
— Histoire de l'art chez les anciens. Paris, [1794]-1803. 2 vols in 3. 4to, contemp half calf; rebacked, old spines laid down, covers of Vol I detached. With frontises (1 detached) & 65 plates. Ck Sept 5 (165) £50

— Monumenti antichi inediti. Rome, 1767. 2 vols plus Supplement of 1779. Folio, contemp calf. With 208 illusts on 105 plates plus 15 plates in the Albani Supplement. S Oct 23 (212) £300 [Raban]

Windsor...
— The Windsor Magazine. L, 1895. Vol II, No 12, Christmas No, Wraps ptd "Given away to each Purchaser: a Copy of Conan Doyle's Novel, A Study in Scarlet, the first book about Sherlock Holmes". cb Apr 24 (54) $355

WINDSOR

Windsor, Edward, Duke of
— A King's Story. L, 1951. 1st Ed, one of 250. 8vo, orig mor by Zaehnsdorf. With 22 plates. pn Nov 20 (83) £150 [Joseph]
Out-of-series copy. Mor with Butler arms, portion of cloth cover pasted onto inside lower cover. Inscr to R. A. Butler, July 1959. S Dec 18 (220) £650 [Woods]

Windus, John
— A Journey to Mequinez.... L, 1725. 8vo, modern half mor. With 6 folding plates. Tp defaced; lacking half-title & final blank. bba Feb 5 (344) £85 [Elliott]
Anr copy. Later sheep; front cover detached. 1 plate frayed; foxed. sg Nov 20 (175) $175

Wing, Donald
— Short-Title Catalogue of Books Printed in England...1641-1700. NY, 1945-51. 3 vols. 4to, orig cloth; rubbed. bba Aug 20 (295) £320 [Bookroom]; sg May 14 (225) $750

**Wingfield, William —&
Johnson, George William**
— The Poultry Book. L, 1853. 4to, contemp calf gilt. With colored title & 21 (of 22) colored plates. 1 plate with small tear. C Oct 15 (264) £170 [Thompson]

Winkler, Eduard
— Saemmtliche Giftgewaechse Deutschland, naturgetrue dargestellt und fasslich Beschrieben. Berlin, 1831. 8vo, contemp bds; worn, broken. With 96 hand-colored plates. HN May 20 (1045a) DM1,200

Winkler, Ernest W.
— Manuscript Letters and Documents of Early Texians 1821-1845. Austin, [1937]. 4to, cloth. sg Sept 18 (280) $150

Winkler, Friedrich
— Die Zeichnungen Albrecht Duerers. Berlin, 1936-39. 4 vols. 4to, orig cloth; rubbed. HN May 20 (444) DM600

Winsemius, Pierius
— Chronique ofte historische geschiedenisse van Vrieslant.... Frankfurt, 1622. Folio, calf; back & 2 corners damaged. With engraved title, armorial engraving, 3 folding plans & 58 engravings. Lacking map; some browning. B Oct 7 (1418a) HF1,000

Winship, George Parker
— Cabot Bibliography. L, 1900. 8vo, cloth. sg May 14 (29) $80

Winslow, Edward
— The Glorious Progress of the Gospel. L: for Hannah Allen 1649. 4to, mor gilt by W. Pratt for Henry Stevens, 1883. Headlines of A2, A3, B4v, C1v & E1 just cropped but legible; tiny hole to a2 not touching text;

AMERICAN BOOK PRICES CURRENT

some old creases to last 2 leaves & occasional soiling. Eliot's Indian Tract No 4. Hoe copy. CNY Dec 19 (63) $1,700

Winslow, Forbes Benignus
— The Anatomy of Suicide. L, 1840. 8vo, modern half cloth. sg Jan 15 (124) $150

Winslow, Jacques Benigne, 1669-1760
— Exposition anatomique de la structure du corps humain. Paris, 1732. 1st Ed. 4to, contemp sheep; worn; spine & gutters wormed with some text affected. With 4 folding plates; minor tears in plates. sg Jan 15 (128) $225

Winsor, Justin, 1831-97
— Narrative and Critical History of America. Bost., [1884-89]. 8 vols. 4to, cloth; some vols shaken. sg Oct 4 (316) $110
1st Ed. Bost., 1889. 8 vols. 4to, cloth; worn. O Nov 18 (200) $70
Anr copy. 8 vols in 16. 4to, half lea; extremities worn. sg Jan 22 (318) $110
Anr copy. 8 vols. 4to, sg May 14 (30) $60

Winter...
— A Winter in the West Indies and Florida.... By an Invalid. NY, 1839. 12mo, cloth; faded. Library markings. sg Sept 18 (92) $150

Winterbotham, William. See: Fore-Edge Paintings

Wirsung, Christoph. See: Wirtzung, Christoph

Wirt, Mrs. E. W.
— Flora's Dictionary. Balt: Fielding Lucas, [after 1837]. Folio, orig mor gilt; scuffed & worn, lacking front free endpaper. With 42 hand-colored plates only. Some plates torn or chipped. cb Feb 19 (281) $55

Wirt, William
— Opinion on the Right of the State of Georgia to Extend her Laws over the Cherokee Nation. New Echota GA: Cherokee Phoenix, 1830. 8vo, self-wraps; rear wrap loose. sg Mar 12 (72) $650

Wirtzung, Christoph
— Ein new Artzney Buch.... Neustadt: M. Harrnisch, 1582. Folio, contemp calf over wooden bds; worn & def. Minor defs. HK Nov 4 (1166) Dm3,600

Wise, Capt Hugh D.. See: Derrydale Press

Wise, John, 1808-79
— A System of Aeronautics, Comprehending its Earliest Investigations.... Phila., 1850. 1st Ed. 8vo, cloth; spine ends & corners chipped. With port & 12 plates. sg Jan 15 (277) $250

Wise, Thomas James, 1859-1937
— A Bibliography of the Writings in Prose and Verse of George Borrow. L: Privately ptd, 1914. One of 100. 4to, orig bds. bba Apr 23 (48) £75 [Clark]
— A Bibliography of the Writings in Prose and Verse of Algernon Charles Swinburne. L: Privately ptd, 1919-20. 1st Ed, one of 125. 2 vols. 8vo, orig bds. Inscr. bba Apr 23 (50) £130 [Forster]
— A Bibliography...Wordsworth. L, 1916. One of 100. bba Apr 23 (49) £55 [Wise]
— A Byron Library. L: Privately ptd, 1928. One of 200. 4to, cloth. cba Feb 5 (175) $80
— A Complete Bibliography of the Writings in Prose and Verse of John Ruskin. L, 1893. One of 250. 2 vols. 4to, contemp half calf; rubbed. S Nov 10 (27) £120 [Tarakan]
— A Conrad Library. L: Privately ptd, 1928. One of 25. 4to, cloth. bba Apr 23 (51) £150 [Henderson]
— A Pope Library. Edin., 1931. One of 160. 4to, orig cloth. bba Apr 23 (52) £50 [Forster]

Wislizenus, Frederick
— A Journey to the Rocky Mountains.... St. Louis, 1912. One of 500. Half cloth, unopened. sg Sept 18 (310) $100
— Memoir of a Tour to Northern Mexico...with Col. Doniphan's Expedition. Wash., 1848. 8vo, disbound. Minor worming, mostly at lower gutter edge. cb Jan 8 (221) $95

Wister, Owen, 1860-1938
— The Virginian. NY, 1902. 1st Ed, Sgd on half-title. Cloth. sg Apr 2 (220) $325

Wit, Frederick de
— Atlas. See: De Wit, Frederick

Withals, John, fl.1556
— A Dictionarie in English and Latine for Children.... L, 1602. 8vo, contemp calf; worn, backstrip def, loose. Minor marginal stains & soiling; last leaf pasted on inside rear cover. sg Mar 26 (290) $550

Witham, Henry Thomas Marc
— The Internal Structure of Fossil Vegetables. Edin., 1833. 4to, orig half lea; spine def. pn Jan 22 (243) £65 [Maggs]

Wither, George, 1588-1667
— A Collection of Emblemes, Ancient and Moderne. L, 1635-34. 1st Ed. 4 parts in 1 vol. Folio, modern mor gilt. Engraved title shaved; N1 & 2K2 with repair; last leaf supplied in pen facsimile, including movable parts. Sold w.a.f. C Dec 12 (363) £400 [Forum]
— Speculum Speculativum: or, A Considering-Glass. L, 1660. 8vo, 19th-cent half mor gilt; rubbed. With duplicates of the last 2 leaves which contain variations in the text. Last leaf repaired. T Mar 19 (407) £46

Witherby, H. F. —& Others
— The Handbook of British Birds. L, 1938-41. 5 vols. 4 vols in d/js. Ck Sept 5 (94) £65
Anr copy. In d/js. pn Oct 23 (299) £50 [Harrel]; pnE Dec 17 (287) £85 [Polwarth]

Withering, William, 1741-99
— An Account of the Foxglove and some of its Medical Uses.... Birm., 1785. 8vo, orig bds. With colored folding frontis in 1st state. pnE Dec 17 (243) £6,700 [Phelps]
— The Miscellaneous Tracts to which is Prefixed a Memoir of his Life. L, 1822. 2 vols. 8vo, new cloth. S May 28 (811) £240

Withers, Alexander S.
— Chronicles of Border Warfare, or a History.... Clarksburg, Va., 1831. 12mo, contemp sheep; worn. cb Mar 19 (281) $140
Anr copy. Contemp calf. Contents stained. wa Sept 25 (404) $65
Anr copy. Contemp sheep; worn, lacking front free endpaper. Some staining. wa June 25 (286) $190

Witt, C.
— Die tapferen Zehntausend. Berlin, 1921. One of 50 with a 2d suite of lithos on japan, sgd. Illus by Max Slevogt. 4to, orig vellum. With litho title & 32 illusts. HN Nov 26 (2132) DM1,400

Witt, Richard
— Arithmeticall Questions, touching the Buying or Exchange of Annuities.... L: H. L. for Richard Redmer, 1613. 4to, half calf. A few foremargins shaved. S July 24 (469) £950 [Lawson]

Wittman, William
— Travels in Turkey, Asia-Minor, Syria.... L, 1803. 1st Ed. 4to, mor-backed modern cloth. With folding frontis, 1 folding map & 20 plates. pnE Jan 28 (77) £260 [Thin]
Anr copy. Contemp calf; rubbed. With folding frontis, map & facsimile plate (all torn) & 20 plates, of which 16 are hand-colored. S Jan 16 (450) £340 [McKenzie]

Wodehouse, Pelham Grenville
— The Head of Kay's. L, 1905. 1st Ed. Orig cloth; rubbed. With 8 plates. Some spotting. T Feb 18 (54) £250
— My Man Jeeves. L, [1919]. 1st Ed. Orig cloth; rubbed & soiled, joints split. S Sept 22 (153) £60 [Sumner & Stillman]
— The Pothunters. L, 1902. Illus by R. Noel

WODEHOUSE

Pocock. Bdg soiled & shaken. S Mar 9 (820) £75 [Whiteson]
— Anr copy. Inscr. S May 6 (470) £250 [Sumner]
— Psmith, Journalist. L, 1915. Tp spotted. bba July 16 (349) £80 [Clute]
  Anr copy. Orig cloth; rubbed, recased, new endpapers. bba July 16 (350) £40 [Mullett]
— William Tell Told Again.... L, 1904. Ck Feb 13 (154) £65; T Oct 15 (43) £210

Wolf, Edwin, 2d —& Fleming, John F.
— Rosenbach: a Biography. Cleveland, [1960]. In d/j. sg Jan 22 (269) $80
  One of 250. Sgd by both authors. sg Jan 22 (268) $110

Wolf, Joseph
— Zoological Sketches by J. W. Made for the Zoological Society.... L, 1861-67. 2 vols. Folio, contemp mor gilt; joints of Vol I repaired, upper joint of Vol II breaking; hinges & corners worn. With 2 pictorial titles & 100 colored plates. All of the plates cut round & mtd (as issued) with captions in gold print on mounts; text leaves of 1st series cut round & mtd; text of 1st series revised. CNY June 11 (138) $8,000

Wolfe, Gene
— The Citadel of the Autarch. NY: Timescape Books, [1982]. Uncorrected proof. Wraps. cb Sept 28 (1369) $55
— The Shadow of the Torturer. NY: Simon & Schuster, [1980]. In d/j. cb Sept 28 (1372) $60
— The Sword of the Lictor. NY: Timescape Books, [1981]. In d/j. cb Sept 28 (1373) $55

Wolfe, James, 1727-59
— Instructions to Young Officers.... L, 1768. ("General Wolfe's Instructions to Young Officers....") 1st Ed. 12mo, contemp calf; rebacked. AVP Nov 20 (402) C$1,600 [Ewens]

Wolfe, Richard J.
— Jacob Bigelow's American Medical Botany..... [North Hills, Pa.]: Bird & Bull Press, 1979. Half mohand-. With 1 colored & 1 plain plate. wa Nov 6 (17) $230

Wollaston, Thomas Vernon, 1822-78
— Insecta Maderensia. L, 1854. 4to, cloth; worn. With 13 colored plates. bba Oct 16 (293) £120 [Wheldon & Wesley]

Wollaston, William
— The Religion of Nature Delineated. L, 1726. 4to, contemp calf; worn. Some leaves dampstained. S Sept 22 (285) £80 [Stewart]

AMERICAN BOOK PRICES CURRENT

Wolley, Sir Clive Phillipps, 1854-1918. See: Phillipps-Wolley, Sir Clive

Wolley, Hannah
— The Accomplish'd Ladies Delight in Preserving, Physick.... L: Benjamin Harris, 1684. 4th Ed. 12mo, contemp sheep; rubbed & repaired. Engraved title & E11 repaired in margins; some fraying. Crahan copy. P Nov 25 (493) $900
— New and Excellent Experiments and Secrets in the Art of Angling. L, 1685. 8vo, mor gilt. Each leaf mtd. sg May 21 (213) $800
— The Queen-Like Closet; or Rich Cabinet.... L, 1684. 5th Ed. 2 parts in 1 vol. 12mo, modern calf gilt by Bayntun; rubbed. Engraved title shaved along fore-margin. CNY Nov 21 (79) $950

Wolley, John
— Ootheca Wolleyana: an Illustrated Catalogue of the Collection of (Lapland) Birds' Eggs.... L, 1864-1907. 4 parts in 2 vols. 8vo, cloth; back damaged. B Feb 24 (226) HF1,000

Wollstonecraft, Mary, 1759-97
— Letters Written during a Short Residence in Sweden, Norway and Denmark. L, 1796. 1st Ed. 8vo, orig half vellum; worn, spine def. bba May 28 (50) £130 [Stern]
— Original Stories, from Real Life. L, 1788. 16mo, contemp calf; joints & spine partly cracked, ends chipped. Clean tear across C9. sg Mar 26 (291) $200
  Anr Ed. L, 1791. 12mo, contemp calf; rubbed, rebacked. Lacking the frontis & 5 plates. bba Jan 15 (63) £45 [Korn]
  Anr copy. Later mor gilt; rubbed. With 6 plates plus an additional set of plates bound facing, often showing a variant state. Port supplied from anr work. P Sept 24 (117) $1,300
— Thoughts on the Education of Daughters. L, 1787. 8vo, contemp calf gilt; rubbed, joints cracked. Manchester copy. S July 23 (32) $1,200 [Stern]

Wolters, Richard A.
— The Labrador Retriever; The History.... Los Angeles, [1981]. One of 300. 4to, lea. sg Oct 23 (562) $325

Wood, Anthony a, 1632-95
— Athenae Oxoniensis. L, 1813-20. 4 vols. 4to, contemp calf; spines rubbed & chipped. Ck Oct 31 (111) £150
— The History & Antiquities of the Colleges and Halls in the University of Oxford. Oxford, 1786. 4to, 19th-cent calf; spine & joints worn, front cover detached. sg Feb 5 (247) £70

Wood, Arnold
— A Bibliography of "The Complete Angler." NY, 1900. One of 120. 4to, half vellum; soiled. sg Oct 23 (550) $225

Wood, Casey Albert
— An Introduction to the Literature of Vertebrate Zoology. L, 1931. 4to, orig cloth. McGill University Publications. Series XI (Zoology). No 24. pn Oct 23 (301) £100 [Graham]; sg Oct 2 (317) $200

Wood, Ellen L. See: Grabhorn Printing

Wood, Harry B.
— Golfing Curios and the Like. L, 1910. pnC Jan 23 (197) £380; pnC Jan 23 (198) £400
Anr copy. L.p. copy. pnC Jan 23 (199) £1,250; pnC July 16 (120) £600

Wood, John
— [Town Atlas of Scotland.] Edin., 1818-27. Folio, contemp half calf; rubbed & worn, With 47 double-page plans on 48 leaves, the streets on most with pale yellow wash. Glasgow slightly creased at centerfold; 6 plans with margins slightly shaved; all maps mtd on guards. C Apr 8 (138) £5,200 [Quaritch]

Wood, John, 1705?-54
— The Origin of Building.... Bath, 1741. Folio, later half calf; rebacked & re?s. bba Apr 23 (59) £600 [Frew Mackenzie]
Anr copy. Bdg not indicated. Library markings. Sold w.a.f. Franklin Institute copy. F Sept 12 (12) $1,100

Wood, John George, 1827-89
— Animate Creation. NY, [1885]. Ed by Joseph B. Holder. 3 vols. Folio, contemp half lea; spines worn, joints starting. With 30 mtd color plates. sg June 18 (251) $90
— The Principal Rivers of Wales. L, 1813. 2 vols bound in 4 (of 5) parts; lacking the end of Vol I (Part 3). 4to, orig wraps; spotted. With 4 colored maps & 158 plates. S Nov 17 (687) £140 [Palace]
Views in Kent. L, 1800. Oblong folio, contemp half mor. With 36 hand-colored plates. C Oct 15 (128) £8,000 [Traylen]

Wood, Robert, 1717?-71
— The Ruins of Balbec. L, 1757. 1st Ed. Folio, contemp calf gilt; rebacked. With 46 plates. bba apr 23 (346) £550 [Rainer]
— Ruins of Palmyra, Otherwise Tedmor, in the Desert. L, 1753. 1st Ed. Folio, modern half mor. With 56 (of 57) plates on 58 sheets & 3 full-page tables. Marginal soiling. bba Oct 16 (256) £350 [Boston]
Anr copy. Contemp calf gilt; rebacked. With 57 plates, including 1 double-page panorama. bba Apr 23 (345) £550 [Rainer]

Woodbridge, William Channing, 1794-1845
— He Hoikehonua, he mea ia e hoakaka' i ke ano o ka honua nei. Oahu, 1845. 12mo, half cloth; worn. Minor stains & browning. O Sept 23 (79) $150

Woodforde, James
— Diary of a Country Parson. Cambr., 1926-31. 5 vols. pnE Jan 28 (179) £160 [Quaritch]

Woodville, William, 1752-1805
— Medical Botany. L, 1790-94. 4 vols. 4to, contemp half calf; broken. With 274 colored plates. Title of Vol III torn & loose. bba Jan 15 (431) £270 [Grants]
Anr copy. Vols I-III (of 4). Calf gilt; repaired. pn Sept 18 21|20 £750
Anr copy. 4 vols. 4to, contemp calf; broken, 1 cover lacking. With 274 colored plates. Some stains to text. pn Mar 5 (48) £980 [Boston]
Anr copy. Contemp calf; loose. With 210 colored plates. pn Apr 30 (221) £860 [Demetzy]
Anr copy. Vols I-III (of 4). Various bdgs; some broken. With 206 plates only, some colored. Lacking Plates 19,35, 59 & 102; Plates 172 & 185 duplicated. sg June 18 (852) $800
2d Ed. L, 1810. 4 vols. 4to, modern half mor gilt. With 275 hand-colored plates. pnE Dec 17 (244) £900 [Traylen]

Woodward, Bernard Bolingbroke
— The History of Wales. L, 1853. 8vo, orig cloth; rubbed. bba Nov 13 (146) £55 [Clark]

Woodward, Calvin Milton, 1837-1914
— A History of the Saint Louis Bridge. St. Louis, 1881. Folio, orig cloth. Franklin Institute copy. F Sept 12 (323) $550

Woodward, Charles L.
— [Sale Catalogue] Bibliothica Scallawagiana · Catalogue of a Matchless Collection of Books...Relating to Mormonism and the Mormons. [NY, 1880]. 8vo, rebound in half cloth, orig front wrap bound inhed. Priced throughout in pencil. sg Oct 2 (226) $150

Woodward, George Evertson —& Thompson, Edward G
— Woorward's National Architect; Containing 1000 Original Designs.... NY, [1869]. 4to, cloth; broken. Some dampstains, affecting c.10 plates. O Jan 6 (3) $100

Woodward, George Moutard
— Something Concerning Nobody. L, 1814. 8vo, later sheep. With 14 plates. With 1 plate shaved. bba Dec 4 (89) £40 [Wise]

Woolf, C. N. Sidney
— Poems. Richmond: Pvtly ptd at the Hogarth Press, [1918]. 4to, disbound, upper wrap preserved. Tp soiled with portions missing from inner corners, not affecting text. S Dec 18 (146) £2,800 [Brown]

Woolf, Cecil —& Sewell, Brocard
— Corvo, 1860-1960: A Collection of Essays.... Aylesford: Saint Albert's Press, 1961. One of 300. sg Dec 11 (403) $50

Woolf, Leonard, 1880-1969
— Stories of the East. Richmond: Hogarth Press, 1921. 8vo, orig wraps. Some spotting; small hole in final leaf. S Dec 18 (145) £250 [Somner]

Woolf, Virginia, 1882-1941
— Beau Brummell. NY, 1930. 1st Ed, one of 550. Folio, half cloth; soiled. cb June 18 (330) $130

Anr copy. Orig half cloth. pn Apr 30 (90) £130 [Pilcher]; pnNY Sept 13 (301) $350; S Sept 22 (154) £110 [Bell, Book & Radmell]

Anr copy. Orig half cloth; marked. S Mar 9 (881) £140 [Hill]

Anr copy. Orig half cloth; soiled. S May 6 (471) £110 [O'Neill]; sg Mar 5 (301) $175

— A Haunted House and Other Short Stories. L: Hogarth Press, 1943. In d/j by Vanessa Bell; spine ends chipped. sg Mar 5 (302) $50

— Jacob's Room. Richmond: Hogarth Press, 1922. 1st Ed, One of 40 with ptd slip sgd by author tipped in on front endpaper. H. G. Wells's subscriber copy. S Dec 18 (150) £1,200 [Blackwell]

— Kew Gardens. Richmond: Hogarth Press, 1919. 1st Ed, 2d State of woodcut. Cancel slip over imprint. With postcard from Virginia Woolf to Frank Harris loosely inserted. S Dec 18 (151) £1,300 [Brown]

Anr Ed. Richmond: Hogarth Press, 1927. One of 500. Illus by Vanessa Bell. 4to, orig bds; spine chipped at foot. S July 23 (204) £350 [Crozier]

— The Mark on the Wall. Richmond, Surrey: Hogarth Press, 1919. 2d (1st separate) Ed. Orig wraps; soiled. S Dec 18 (154) £400 [O'Neill]

— Monday or Tuesday. L, 1921. 1st Ed. Bdg rubbed & soiled. S Mar 9 (885) £240. [Libris]

— Mrs. Dalloway. L: Hogarth Press, 1925. 1st Ed. S Mar 9 (883) £100 [Schindler]

— On Being Ill. L: Hogarth Press, 1930. 1st Ed, one of 250. Orig half vellum, unopened, in d/j. S Dec 18 (147) £500 [Bell, Book]

Out-of-series copy with holograph correction by Leonard Woolf changing the limitation number. Orig half vellum. S Dec 18 (148) £540 [Doaks]

— Orlando. NY, 1928. ("Orlando, a Biography.") 1st Ed, One of 800. T Feb 18 (2) £180

1st American Ed. NY: Crosby Gaige, 1928. One of 861, sgd. In orig glassine d/j. Inscr. wa Sept 25 (711) $310

— Street Haunting. San Francisco, 1930. one of 500, sgd. Half mor; worn & soiled. Extra-illus with 4 mtd plates. sg Dec 11 (142) $130

Anr copy. Half lea, unopened. sg Mar 5 (303) $425

— To the Lighthouse. L: Hogarth Press, 1927. 1st Ed. In strengthened d/j with a few short tears. S Dec 18 (152) £400 [Gekoski]

— The Voyage Out. L, 1915. 1st Ed. S Mar 9 (886) £200 [Rota]

— Walter Sickert: a Conversation. L: Hogarth Press, 1934. Wraps. bba Oct 16 (192) £50 [Hessey]

— The Waves. L, 1931. 1st Ed. In chipped d/j. cb May 7 (176) $60

Anr copy. In d/j. F Oct 30 (399) $80

— The Years. L: Hogarth Press, 1937. 1st Ed. In d/j. F Jan 15 (398) $75; S Mar 9 (887) £95 [Clark]

Woollams, John. See: Collinwood & Woollams

Woolley, Sir Charles Leonard, 1880-1960
— Ur Excavations. NY, 1934. Vol II: The Royal Cemetery. 2 vols. Folio, orig half cloth; soiled. S Nov 18 (1080) £75 [Negro]

Woolley, Sir Charles Leonard, 1880-1960 —& Lawrence, T. E., 1888-1935
— The Wilderness of Zin. L, [1915]. 4to, orig half cloth; rubbed. bba May 28 (311) £80 [Hirschler]; C May 13 (183) £260 [Maggs]

Anr copy. Orig half cloth; soiled. pnNY Mar 12 (98) $275

Woolnough, C. W.
— The Whole Art of Marbling as Applied to Paper Book-Edges. L, 1881. 8vo, orig cloth; rubbed, hinges repaired. With 38 examples of marbled paper. bba Sept 25 (378) £540 [Maggs]

Anr copy. Loose in orig cloth; worn. With 39 examples of marbled paper. S Nov 10 (35) £290 [Sims]

Anr Ed. Oxford: Plough Press, 1985. Reprint of 1881 Ed. sg Jan 22 (319) $175

Woolrich, Cornell, 1903-68
— Rendezvous in Black. NY, [1948]. In d/j. cb Nov 20 (329) $110

Woolward, Florence H.
— The Genus Masdevallia. L, [1890]-96. One of 250. Folio, contemp half mor; broken, rubbed, portion of front endpaper torn away. With double-page colored map & 87 hand-colored plates. de Belder copy. S Apr 28 (385) £4,500 [Swann]

Wooster, David
— Alpine Plants. L, 1872. 1st & 2d Series. 2 vols. 8vo, orig cloth; scuffed. With 108 plates plates. C Apr 8 (205) £200 [Heuer]

Anr Ed. L, 1872-74. 8vo, orig cloth. With 108 color plates. Some spotting. S Feb 24 (621) £160 [Burgess]; S Feb 24 (622) £170 [Burgess]

1st Series. L, 1872. 8vo, orig cloth; spine darkened, ends chipped. With 54 colored plates. sg Jan 15 (268) $100

2d Ed of 1st Series, 1st Ed of 2d Series. L, 1874. 2 vols. 8vo, cloth; worn. With 108 colored plates. pn Oct 23 (368A) £130 [Walford]

Anr copy. Orig cloth; affected by damp, rubbed. S Nov 10 (580) £110 [Walford]

Anr copy. Orig cloth; marked. S Nov 17 (688) £140 [Negro]

Anr copy. Half mor gilt. S May 28 (605) £220

Anr copy. Orig cloth; rubbed. T Apr 16 (158) £110

Wooster, Nora
— Semi-Precious Stones. Harmondsworth: Penguin Books, 1952. Mor gilt by Peter Fahey. cb Sept 11 (249) $170

Worcester, Edward Somerset, Marquis of
— A Century of the Names and Scantlings of...Inventions. L, 1663. 12mo, 18th-cent calf. A few rule-borders shaved. C Dec 12 (223) £550 [Quaritch]

Worcester, Samuel, 1770-1821
— California. Outlines of an Address Before the Naumkeag Mutual Trading and Mining Company, at the Tabernacle Church in Salem, on Sabbath Evening, Jan 14, 1849. [N.p., 1849]. Orig wraps; upper wrap chipped. Some soil & dampstain. Streeter copy. cb Jan 8 (223) $110

Wordsworth, Christopher, 1807-85
— Greece. L, 1859. 8vo, vellum gilt. With 20 plates. pn Oct 23 (355) £70 [Walford]

Anr copy. Mor gilt. With engraved title & 20 maps & views. Marginal stains. pn Mar 5 (61) £75 [Waterloo]

Wordsworth, William, 1770-1850
See also: Fore-Edge Paintings
— The Excursion. L, 1814. 1st Ed. 4to, contemp half calf; rubbed. Lacking half-title. S Sept 22 (64) £60 [Kikko Bks]
— Our English Lakes, Mountains, and Waterfalls.... L, 1868. Illus by Thomas Ogle. 4to, orig cloth. O May 12 (202) $125
— The Prelude, or Growth of a Poet's Mind. L, 1850. 1st Ed. 8vo, orig cloth; faded, spine worn. pnNY Sept 13 (302) $120
— Works. Bost., 1910. One of 500 L.p. copies. 10 vols. Orig cloth, unopened. bba Aug 20 (227) £110 [Hay Cinema]

Wordsworth, William, 1770-1850 —& Coleridge, Samuel Taylor, 1772-1834
— Lyrical Ballads. L, 1798. 1st Ed, 2d Issue. 8vo, contemp calf gilt; joints split, rubbed. Lacking ad leaf at end; some soiling; 1 leaf marginally torn. bba Mar 12 (148) £350 [jarndyce]

Anr copy. Bds. Leaf containing pp 49/50 & leaves containing 77/80 lacking & supplied in type facsimile; lacking ad leaf. wd June 18 (197) $175

World...
— The World Displayed; or, a Curious Collection of Voyages and Travels... L, 1757-68. Intro by Samuel Johnson. 20 vols. 18mo, contemp calf; some joints & covers worn. sg Dec 4 (209) $375

6th Ed. Dublin, 1779. 20 vols. 18mo, contemp calf gilt; worn. Ink accession number on titles; some leaves loose. sg Dec 18 (234) $175

Anr Ed. L, 1788. 20 vols in 10. 8vo, old calf; rubbed. cb June 4 (212) $160

World War II
— International Military Tribunal. Trials of the Major Criminals.... Nuremberg & L, 1946-51. 23 parts. Wraps. SSA Feb 11 (550) R260

World's...
— The World's Worst Marbled Papers; being a Collection of Ten Contemporary San Serriffean Marbled Papers Showing the Lowest Level of Technique, the Worst Combination of Colors, the most Inferior Execution Known since the Dawn of the Art of Marbling. [N.p.]: San Serriffe Publishing Co [but ptd at the Bird & Bull Press], 1978. One of 400, all numbered 1. 4to, wraps. sg Jan 22 (226) $120

Worlidge, John
— Dictionarium Rusticum, Urbanicum & Botanicum: or a Dictionary of Husbandry.... L, 1717. 2d Ed. 2 vols. 8vo, contemp calf. With 2 plates, 1 torn. sg Jan 15 (269) $70

Worlidge, John, fl.1669-98

— Systema Agriculturae, the Mystery of Husbandry Discovered. L, 1669. 1st Ed. Folio, modern half cloth; soiled. Browned. Hunt copy. CNY Nov 21 (291) $120

3d Ed. L, 1681. 3 parts in 1 vol. Folio, contemp calf; joints rubbed, hinges split. Hunt copy. CNY Nov 21 (292) $180

4th Ed. L, 1687. 3 parts in 1 vol. Folio, contemp calf; rubbed. K2 with small rust hole costing 1 letter & affecting several others; S3 with paper flaw costing several letters; Nn1 with corner lost costing catchword & several letters of text & with marginal paper flaw affecting shoulder note; b2 with blank corner lost; some stains & foxing. P Nov 25 (494) $450

— Vinetum Britannicum, or a Treatise of Cider.... L: Thomas Dring, 1678. 8vo, old calf; rebacked, worn, new endpapers. Lacking 1 blank; some leaves repaired along inner margins; marginal tears not affecting text. Crahan copy. P Nov 25 (495) $500; P Nov 25 (495) $500

Anr copy. Contemp calf; rubbed. Minor soiling; some worming in lower blank margin. P Nov 25 (496) $750

3d Ed. L, 1691. 2 parts in 1 vol. 8vo, contemp sheep; broken. With 2 frontises, 1 just shaved at outer margin & with 3 illusts. Marginal worming; some leaves stained. bba Sept 25 (11) £250 [Phelps]

Anr copy. Contemp calf; worn. Some tears; frontis & general title repaired; some headlines shaved. S May 28 (813) £280

Worlidge, Thomas

— A Select Collection of Drawings from Curious Antique Gems.... L, 1768. 4to, contemp mor gilt; Vol II chipped at base of spine. Lacking port. T Feb 19 (575) £40

Worsley, Sir Richard

— The History of the Isle of Wight. L, 1781. 4to, contemp half calf; hinges broken. Folding colored map torn & partly repaired; partly interleaves; some ink marginalia to Appendix. T Oct 16 (326) £95

Wotton, Sir Henry, 1568-1699

— Reliquiae Wottonianae.... L, 1654. 12mo, later calf; spine worn. With 4 ports, all shaved with loss; O1 torn with loss of a few characters; tp shaved; some spotting. Ck Jan 30 (22) £50

Wotton, William, 1666-1727

— Reflections upon Ancient and Modern Learning. L, 1694. 1st Ed. 8vo, vellum. pnE Jan 28 (183) £130 [Traylen]

Wren, Christopher, 1675-1747

[-] Christopher Wren, 1632-1723. L, 1923. Folio, cloth. cba Mar 5 (209) $90

— Parentalia: or Memoirs of the Family of the Wrens.... L, 1750. 1st Ed. Folio, contemp calf; rubbed, rebacked. With port & 11 plates. Some spots & stains; 1 plate bound upside down, anr shaved at head & foot. S May 6 (411) £340 [Finch]

Wren Society

— The First [-Twentieth] Volume of the Wren Society. Oxford 1924-43. 20 vols. 4to, orig half cloth; dampstained at lower corners. S Mar 9 (712) £180 [Sims]

Wright, Albert Hazen

— Life-Histories of the Frogs of Okefinokee Swamp, Georgia. NY, 1931. wa Sept 25 (123) $50

Wright, Frank Lloyd, 1869-1959

— Ausgefuehrte Bauten un Entwuerfe.... Berlin, 1924. Folio, loose in orig folder with German text. With 100 plates. Re-issue of the 1910 Ed. S Dec 4 (36) £300 [Grypmen Gall]

— An Autobiography. L & NY, 1932. 1st Ed. 4to, cloth; spine head rubbed. cb July 30 (201) $100

— Drawings for a Living Architecture. NY, 1959. 1st Ed. In d/j, chipped. wa Mar 5 (439) $700

— Genius and the Mobocracy. NY, [1949]. 1st Ed. 4to, cloth, in wrinkled d/j. wa Mar 5 (440) $110

— The Japanese Print: An Interpretation. NY: Horizon Press, [1967]. Folio, cloth. cba Mar 5 (277) $130

[-] The Life-Work.... Santpoort (Holland), 1925-[26]. 1st Ed. 7 parts. 4t. B Oct 7 (243) HF1,500

— Modern Architecture. Princeton, 1931. Bds; soiled & worn. wa Nov 6 (379) $210

— The Natural House. NY: Horizon Press, 1954. In repaired d/j. Stamped. cb Mar 5 (213) $60

— Studies and Executed Buildings.... [Berlin, 1910]. 1st Ed. 2 vols. Oblong folio, ptd wraps; rear cover torn in half. With 71 plates, with tissue overlays; 1 tissue torn. wa Mar 5 (446) $260

Wright, George Newenham

— Belgium, The Rhine, Italy, Greece, and the Shores and Island of the Mediterranean. L, [c.1840]. Vol II only. 4to, cloth; worn. O Jan 6 (199) $90

Anr copy. Vol I & part of Vol II, in 1 vol. Contemp calf gilt; upper cover detached. With 79 plates. T Feb 19 (228) £110

— Belgium, The Rhine, Italy, Greece, and the Shores and Islands of the Mediterranean.

L, [1851]. 2 vols in 1. 4to, half calf; worn & loose. Library stamps, including perforated stamps on plates. bba Feb 5 (371) £140 [Kimakarakos]

— China in a Series of Views. L, [1843]. 4 vols in 2. 4to, contemp half mor; broken. Perforated stamps throughout. bba Mar 26 (330) £50 [Marco]

Anr copy. 4 vols. 4to, contemp half calf. With engraved titles & 124 plates. Engraved title to Vol I foxed. C July 22 (233) £280

Anr copy. 4 vols in 2. 4to, contemp half mor. With engraved titles & 123 (of 124) plates. Ck Nov 21 (215) £260

Anr copy. 4 vols. 4to, bdgs not described but def. Sold w.a.f. pn Nov 20 (229) £190 [Bayer]

Anr copy. 4 vols in 2. 4to, contemp half mor. With engraved titles & 124 plates. S May 28 (931) £300

Anr copy. Contemp lea gilt. With engraved titles & 123 (of 124) plates. Vokl II lacks pp 9-12 as well as 1 plate. sg Nov 20 (177) $275

Anr Ed. L: London Ptg & Pbg Co., [1858-59]. ("The Chinese Empire Illustrated: Being a Series of Views....") 2 vols. 4to, half lea; scuffed. With 151 engravings. sg Nov 20 (51) $275

— The Chinese Empire Illustrated. L, [c.1860]. 7 vols. 4to, orig cloth; soiled. With 4 engraved titles, 159 plates & 3 hand-colored folding maps. S Jan 12 (319) £320 [Demetzy]

Anr copy. 2 vols. 4to, later half mor gilt; broken. With 3 vignette titles, 3 double-page engraved maps (colored in outline), 12 uncolored costume plates & 146 views. T May 21 (222) £300

— France Illustrated. L., [1845-47]. 4 vols. 4to, contemp half calf. Ck Sept 26 (86) £130

Anr copy. 4 vols in 2. 4to, half calf; rubbed. With 4 vignette titles & 128 plates. Dampstained. pn June 18 (34) £100 [Watson]

— France Illustrated, Exhibiting Landscape Scenery.... L, [1845-47]. Illus by Thomas Allom. 4 vols in 2. 4to, contemp calf; worn, broken, lacking most of 1 spine. Plates with library stamps. bba Mar 12 (37) £50 [Jeffery]

— The Gallery of Engravings. L: Fisher, Son & Co., [1845-46]. 3 vols. 4to, mor gilt; scuffed, head of 1 spine torn. Some staining, mostly minor & marginal. L Dec 11 (90) £50

Anr copy. 3 vols in 2. 4to, half calf; spines rubbed. Internal spotting. T Sept 18 (448) £65

— Ireland Illustrated from Original Drawings.... L, 1831. 4to, mor gilt; rubbed. With engraved title (with marginal tear) & 80 views on 40 plates. S July 28 (1012) £80

Anr copy. Contemp half mor gilt; rubbed. Some spotting & marginal dampstains. T Jan 22 (51) £70

Anr Ed. L, 1832. 4to, contemp half lea. With engraved title & 78 views on 39 plates. Ck Nov 21 (92) £60

Anr copy. Contemp half lea; joints rubbed. With engraved title & 40 plates. S Nov 17 (838) £150 [Boyd]

Anr Ed. L, 1839. 4to, orig cloth; frayed. Some foxing & stains. T Jan 22 (52) £70

— A New and Comprehensive Gazetteer.... L, 1834-38. 5 vols, including Supplement vol but without Atlas. 8vo, contemp half calf; rubbed. bba June 18 (306) £240 [Garwood]

— The Rhine, Italy and Greece. L, [1841]. 2 vols, 4to, contemp mor gilt; rubbed. With engraved titles & 71 plates. Some staining. S Feb 24 (417) £190 [Walford]

— The Shores and Islands of the Mediterranean. L, [1840]. 4to, contemp half mor. With engraved title, folding map & 63 plates. Some spotting. Ck Nov 21 (452) £160

Anr copy. Contemp mor gilt; broken. A few plates stained. L Dec 11 (188) £120

Anr copy. Orig cloth; worn. Some soiling. S Nov 17 (929) £100 [Doran]

Anr copy. Contemp half calf. Some spotting. T Dec 18 (2) £105

Wright, Hendrick Bradley

— Historical Sketches of Plymouth, Luzerne Co, Penna. Phila., [1873]. 8vo, cloth. With 25 mtd photos. wa Nov 6 (364) $65

Anr copy. Orig cloth; worn & soiled. wa Mar 5 (400) $105

Wright, James, 1643-1713

— The History and Antiquities of the County of Rutland. L, 1684. Folio, modern half mor gilt. L Dec 11 (151) £120

Wright, John, Horticulturist

— The Fruit Growers' Guide. L: Virtue, [1891-94]. 3 vols in 6. 4to, orig cloth. With color titles & 42 (of 43) color plates. C Oct 15 (265) £350 [Cork Street]

Anr copy. Parts 1-4 only. 4to, orig cloth; rubbed. With 2 colored titles & 30 plates. Ck May 29 (221) £250

Anr copy. 3 vols. 4to, orig cloth; dampstained & warped. Some dampstaining affecting text at end of Vol I. L July 2 (184) £280

Anr copy. 6 orig parts. 4to, cloth; spines worn. T Jan 22 (82) £300

Anr copy. 3 vols. 4to, orig cloth; rubbed. T Mar 19 (111) £350

Wright, John Michael
— An Account of His Excellency Roger, Earl of Castlemaine's Embassy, from...James the IId.... L, 1688. Folio, later calf; rebacked & restored. With port, frontis & 15 plates. C May 13 (100) £500 [Lanfranchi]

Anr copy. Contemp calf; upper joint cracked. With port, frontis & 16 plates. Small hole in frontis. S June 25 (85) £420 [Traylen]

Wright, Lewis
— The Illustrated Book of Poultry. L, 1880. 4to, orig cloth; loose. With colored frontis (loose) & 49 colored plates. pn June 18 (62) £460 [Green]

Anr copy. Contemp half mor; worn. With 50 colored plates. 1 plate numeral cropped. S Nov 17 (689) £360 [Grahame]

Anr copy. Orig cloth; worn & affected by damp. With 41 (of 50) colored plates only. Lacking title & all before lists of illusts, which is torn. Sold w.a.f. S Feb 24 (623) £400 [Dowling]

Anr Ed. L, 1890. 4to, orig cloth; rubbed. bba June 18 (164) £480 [Shapero]

Wright, Magnus, Wilhelm & Ferdinand von
— Svenska faglar efter naturen och pa sten ritade. Stockholm, [1917]-29. 3 vols. 4to, half calf gilt; rubbed. With 364 color plates. B Feb 24 (434) HF2,200

Anr copy. Text by Einar Lonnberg. Old half cloth. With 342 (of 364) colored lithos. HK Nov 4 (1158) DMK1,700

Wright presentation copy, Orville
— KELLY, FRED CHARTERS. - The Wright Brothers: A Biography Authorized by Orville Wright. NY, [1943]. Inscr to Porter Adams. O Sept 23 (89) $185

Wright, Thomas, 1810-77
— England under the House of Hanover. L, [1868]. ("Caricature History of the Georges....") 8vo, contemp calf; rebacked, endpapers renewed. sg Sept 11 (288) $60

— The History and Topography of the County of Essex. L, [1831]-36. 2 vols. 4to, contemp half calf; rubbed. With 43 plates. Some foxing, soiling & discoloration to plates. cb Feb 19 (283) $65

Anr copy. Contemp calf; spines worn. With engraved titles, 1 folding map (torn) & 98 plates (2 torn). Dampstained. Ck May 15 (142) £280

Anr copy. Calf; def. pn Sept 18 (295) £240 [Roberts]

— Universal Pronouncing Dictionary.... L, [1852-56]. In 25 vols. 4to, orig cloth. pnE Nov 12 (55) £780

— The Works of James Gillray the Caricaturist. L, [1873]. 4to, cloth; inner hinges cracked. sg Feb 5 (73) $225

Wright, Thomas, 1810-77 —&
Jones, Harry Longueville, 1806-70
— Memorials of Cambridge. L, 1841-42. 2 vols. 4to, later half mor; bumped. With engraved titles, map & 73 plates; several stained. Ck Sept 26 (288) £220

Wroth, Lawrence C.
See also: Grolier Club; Limited Editions Club
— A History of Printing in Colonial Maryland.... Balt., 1922. One of 500. sg Oct 2 (195) $100

Wuerth, Louis A.
— Catalogue of the Etchings of Joseph Pennell. Bost., 1928. One of 465. Half sheep, in d/j. sg Feb 5 (262) $475

Anr copy. Cloth. With an orig etching by Pennell. wa Mar 5 (130) $370

Wulff, Lee
— The Atlantic Salmon. NY, 1958. One of 200. 4to, half mor. sg Oct 23 (565) $250
— Leaping Silver: Words and Pictures on the Atlantic Salmon. NY, [1940]. In d/j. sg Oct 23 (567) $70

Out-of-series copy. 4to, half mor. sg Oct 23 (566) $175

Wurzbach, Alfred Wolfgang von, 1846-1915
— Niederlaendisches Kuenstler-Lexicon. Vienna & Leipzig, 1906-11. 3 vols in 5. Contemp half mor. B Oct 7 (1130) HF680

Anr copy. 3 vols. Half mor; backstrips scuffed. sg May 14 (58) $200

Wyandanch Club
— Constitution and By-Laws, Officers and Members. Smithtown NY, 1918. sg Oct 23 (568) $250

Wyatt, Claude Wilmott
See also: Sharpe & Wyatt
— British Birds. L, 1894-99. 2 vols in 1. 4to, contemp half mor; rubbed. With 67 colored lithos. S Apr 23 (65) £1,000 [Marshall]

Wyatt, Sir Matthew Digby, 1820-77
See also: Tymms & Wyatt
— The Industrial Arts of the Nineteenth Century. L, 1851-53. 2 vols. Folio, half mor gilt; rubbed, spines torn. With 2 color titles & 158 plates. Library stamps. pnNY Oct 11 (57) $500

— Metal Work and its Artistic Design. L, 1852. Folio, orig half mor; wornen, spine def. With 50 colored plates. Library markings. Inscr. O May 2 (203) $275

Anr copy. Modern half mor. With colored

frontis & 50 colored plates. S Mar 9 (713) £110 [Sneyd]

— Specimens of Ornamental Art Workmanship.... L, 1853. Folio, cloth; misbound, partially bound upside down. Tp dampstained at lower margin; some foxing. cb Feb 19 (284) $120

Wycherley, William, 1640-1716

— Miscellany Poems. L, 1704. 1st Ed, 1st Issue. Folio, contemp calf; rebacked, corners rubbed. Port repaired; a few leaves soiled. S Sept 22 (65) £280 [Cox]

— Works. L, 1713. 8vo, contemp calf; joints starting. sg Oct 9 (351) $110

Wyeth, John Allan, 1845-1922

— With Sabre and Scalpel. NY, 1914. Inscr. cb Dec 18 (212) $75

Wyeth, Samuel Douglas

— The Rotunda and Dome of the U. S. Capitol.... Wash., [1869]. 8vo, cloth; worn, hinges cracked. Dampstained at beginning. sg Nov 13 (110) $175

Wyld, James, 1812-87

— A General Atlas. Edin., 1819. Folio, contemp half calf; worn, stitching broken. With engraved title, 2 charts & 41 colored maps. Some browning; 1 map detached with margins tattered. Ck May 15 (312) £190

Anr Ed. Edin.: J. Thomson & Co., [c.1820]. Folio, contemp half calf; worn, upper cover detached. With engraved title, frontis, table & 44 maps, hand-colored in outline. Ck Nov 21 (472) £170

Anr copy. Contemp half calf; worn. Marginal soiling. S Jan 12 (96) £500 [Goodall]

— A New General Atlas of Modern Geography. L, [1842]. Folio, half lea; def. With 68 partly-colored maps. pn Sept 18 (357) £820 [Burgess Browning]

— Notes on the Distribution of Gold Throughout the World... L, [1851]. 8vo, orig self-wraps; spine reinforced. With 4 folding maps. World map with gold regions hand-tinted. Minor tears. cb Jan 8 (225) $300

— A Popular Atlas of the World. L, 1849. Folio, contemp half calf; def. With 48 hand-colored mapsheets plus a may of Cyprus pasted in. All maps backed with linen. S Oct 23 (235) £450 [Tooley]

Wyman, Charles William Henry. See: Bigmore & Wyman

Wyndham, Guy Richard Charles

— A Book of Towers and Other Buildings of Southern Europe. L, 1928. One of 350. 4to, half vellum; soiled & worn. With 25 plates. sg Jan 8 (294) p$70

Wyndham, John, Pseud.

— The Day of the Triffids. Garden City, 1951. In d/j. cb Sept 28 (1380) $130

1st English Ed. L, [1951]. In d/j; soiled at rear. Sgd as Wyndham & as John Benyon Harris on front free endpaper. cb Sept 28 (1381) $170

— The Kraken Wakes. NY: Ballantine, [1953]. ("Out of the Deeps.") In d/j. cb Sept 28 (1384) $65

— Re-Birth. L, 1955. ("The Chrysalids.") In d/j. cb Sept 28 (1379) $50

Anr Ed. NY: Ballantine, [1955]. In d/j. cb Sept 28 (1386) $150

Wyse, Sir Thomas

— An Excursion in the Peloponnesus.... L, 1865. 2 vols. 8vo, orig cloth; worn. With 24 plates. wa Sept 25 (562) $65

Wyss, Johann David, 1743-1818

— Swiss Family Robinson. L, 1814-16. ("The Family Robinson Crusoe....") 2 vols. 12mo, contemp calf; lower cover of Vol I loose. Corners missing from 2 leaves & small tears in margins of 2 others; folding map repaired. S June 17 (501) £400 [Joseph]

Wytsman, Philogene Auguste Galilee

— Genera avium. Brussels, 1905-14. 26 parts (all pbd) in 2 vols. 4to, modern half calf, orig upper wraps bound in. With 43 color plates. Typed list of plates inserted at front of each vol; typed index inserted at end of text vol C Oct 15 (266) £280 [Greyfriars]

Anr copy. 26 parts (all pbd) in 1 vol. 4to, modern half mor, orig upper wraps bound in. n Oct 23 (302) £160 [Maggs]

X

Xenophon, c.430-c.355 B.C.

See also: Gregynog Press

— Opera minore. [Lyons, c.1511]. Counterfeit of an Aldine Ed. 8vo, later calf; worn, spine def. Some browning & staining. bba Apr 23 (92) £100 [Poole]

Xeres, Francisco de

— Libro primo de la conquista del Peru.... Venice: Stephano de Sabbio, 1535. 4to, mor gilt by Bayntun of Bath. Some marginalia. FD June 11 (1162) DM13,000

Xongo-Tee-Foh-Tchi, Mandarin of the Third Class. See: Napoleon...

XXe Siecle. See: Vingtieme Siecle

Y

Yaari, Abraham
— Bibliografya shel Haggadot Pesah. Jerusalem, 1960. Folio, cloth, in d/j. With 20 plates & with facsimile of 1st ptd Haggadah laid in. sg Apr 30 (123) $100
— Bibliography of the Passover Haggadah.... Jerusalem, 1960. Folio, cloth, in d/j. Facsimile of copy of the 1st ptd Haggadah laid into rear cover. bba Feb 19 (68) £100 [19th-Cent shop]; sg Sept 25 (48) $120

Yague de Salas, Juan
— Los Amantes de Tereul.... Valencia: por Pedro Patricio May, 1616. 8vo, contemp vellum. Some spotting. S May 21 (130) £4,000 [Quaritch]

Yarbro, Chelsea Quinn
— On Saint Hubert's Thing. New Castle VA: Cheap Street, [1982]. One of 60. Wraps in Barcham green outer wrap. With related material. cb Sept 28 (1389) $50

Yarranton, Andrew, 1616-84?
— England's Improvement by Sea and Land.... L, 1677.. 1st Ed. 4to, contemp half vellum. With 5 (of 8) folding plates. 1 plate very defective. Sold w.a.f. bba Nov 13 (197) £40 [Subunso]

Yarrell, William, 1784-1856
— A History of British Fishes. L, 1836. L.p. copy. 2 vols. 8vo, cloth; worn. With the 1839 Supplement bound in. sg Oct 23 (569) $150
— A History of British Birds. L, 1843. 3 vols. 8vo, later cloth. Haverschmidt copy. B Feb 24 (416) HF250

Anr Ed. L, 1871-85. 4 vols. 8vo, contemp calf gilt; spines faded. bba Oct 30 (435) £40 [Head]

Anr copy. Orig cloth; worn. T Apr 16 (143) £45
— On the Growth of the Salmon in Fresh Water. L, 1839. Oblong folio, orig wraps. With 3 colored plates. sg Oct 23 (570) $350

Yashiro, Yukio
— Sandro Botticelli. L: Medici Society, 1925. One of 630. 3 vols. Folio, orig cloth; worn. O Jan 6 (200) $110

Anr copy. Cloth; torn. pn Jan 22 (4) £55 [Thorp]

Anr copy. Cloth, in frayed d/js. sg Feb 5 (46) $200

Anr copy. Cloth, in chipped d/js. sg June 4 (47) $200

Yates, William, of Sidney Sussex College, Cambridge
— An Illustration of the Monastic History and Antiquities...of St. Edmund's Bury. L, 1805. 4to, russia gilt; joints rubbed. WIth 15 plates, 1 partly hand-colored. S Feb 23 (59) £90 [Rankin]

Yau, Chang-foo. See: Hackney & Yau

Yauville, ——— d'
— Traite de venerie. Paris: Imprimerie Royale, 1788. 4to, contemp red mor gilt with arms of Louis Joseph Xavier Francois, Dauphin [Olivier 2530 fer 1]. L.p. copy. Jeanson copy. SM Mar 1 (582) FF140,000

Anr copy. Calf gilt with arms of Napoleon I [Olivier 2652, fer 7]. Jeanson copy. SM Mar 1 (583) FF70,000

Year-Book...
— The Year-Book of Chess. L, 1907-18. Vols for 1907-16. 9 vols. Orig cloth; soiled. pn Mar 26 (202) £75

Yeats, Jack Butler, 1871-1957
— The Treasure of the Garden.... L, [1902]. 4to, orig wraps. With 7 hand-colored plates. bba May 28 (121) £75 [Gestetner]

Yeats, William Butler, 1865-1939
See also: Cuala Press
— Cathleen ni Hoolihan. L: Caradoc Press, 1902. Orig half pigskin; lower cover soiled. S Jan 13 (618) £75 [Daley]
— Eight Poems. L: Morland Press, 1916. Out-of-series copy on handmade paper. 4to, orig wraps. S May 6 (475) £90 [Whiteson]
— John Sherman and Dhoya. L, 1891. Vellum. bba May 28 (124) £280 [Maggs]
— The King's Threshold. NY, 1904. One of 100. Orig bds, in tissue d/j. bba July 2 (411) £280 [Updike]
— The Land of Heart's Desire. L, 1894. 4to, later mor. bba May 28 (125) £60 [Clark]
— The Poems of W. B. Yeats. L, 1949. One of 375. 2 vols. 4to, orig cloth. bba May 28 (153) £450 [Cathnach]

Anr copy. Orig cloth; soiled. pnNY Sept 13 (303) $225

Anr copy. Orig cloth, unopened. S Jan 13 (622) £280 [Maggs]
— Reveries over Childhood and Youth. L, 1916. Unopened. With colored frontis & 2 plates. bba May 28 (130) £45 [Clark]
— The Secret Rose. L, 1897. 8vo, orig cloth. bba May 28 (126) £110 [Sumner]
— The Shadowy Waters. L, 1900. 1st Ed. 4to, orig cloth. bba may 28 (127) £75 [Bologna]
— A Speech and Two Poems. Dublin, 1937. One of 70. Inscr by George Yeats, 1942. S Dec 18 (201) £400 [Bernard Stone]

— Three Things. L, 1929. 1st Ed. bba May 28 (145) £45 [Somebet]

One of 500 L.p. copies. Spine def. bba May 28 (144) £70 [Cathach]; sg June 11 (428) $300

— The Tower. L, 1928. 1st Ed. bba May 28 (142) £45 [Maggs]

— The Trembling of the Veil. L, 1922. 1st Ed, one of 1,000, sgd. bba may 28 (134) £140 [Goddard]

— A Vision. L, 1925. 1st Ed, One of 600, sgd. Orig bds, in soiled d/j. bba May 28 (137) £220 [Goddard]

— The Wanderings of Oisin and Other Poems. L, 1889. 1st Ed. 8vo, orig cloth variant bdg with no pbr's monogram on lower cover & Paul, Trench, Trubner & Co gilt-stamped at foot of spine; rubbed & stained, spine slightly def, 1 inner hinge split. Some pencil markings. S Dec 18 (190) £150 [Hughes]

Anr copy. Orig cloth with pbr's monogram blind-stamped on lower cover & Kegan Paul Trench & Co gilt-stamped at foot of spine. S Dec 18 (200) £300 [Somner]

— Wheels and Butterflies. L, 1934. 1st Ed, Proof copy. Wraps; spine worn. T Feb 18 (14) £60

— The Wild Swans at Coole. L, 1919. 1st Ed. Inscr to Frederic Prokosch. S Dec 18 (192) £250 [Quaritch]

— The Winding Stair and Other Poems. NY: Crosby Gaige, 1929. ("The Winding Stair.") Sgd by Yeats on half-title. S Sept 22 (158) £50 [Treadwell]

— Works. Stratford: Shakespeare Head Press, 1908. 8 vols. 8vo, orig half vellum; soiled. Ck Jan 30 (156) £150

Anr copy. Vol I (of 8) only. Orig half cloth; Ex-library copy, worn & soiled. Inscr by Yeats on front blank: "Only the wasteful virtues earn the sun". wa Sept 25 (713) $110

Ye'hia, Ezra & Aben

— Delices Royales ou Le Jeu des Echecs... Paris, 1864. Modern half cloth, orig wraps bound in. Some stains at beginning. sg Apr 30 (148) $150

Yellow...

— The Yellow Book: an Illustrated Quarterly. L, 1894-97. Vols 1-12 (of 13). 8vo, orig cloth. pn Jan 22 (77) £160 [Thorp]

Vols 1-13 (all pbd). 3d Ed of Vols 1-2, 1st Eds of other parts. 8vo, orig cloth; soiled. S Oct 23 (309) £90 [Walford]

Vols 1-13 (all pbd). 8vo, orig cloth; faded & worn. S Dec 4 (161) £200 [Thorp]

Anr copy. Orig cloth; soiled. S Jan 16 (453) £300 [Maggs]; T June 18 (159) £200

Yerkes Collection, Charles Tyson

— The Yerkes Collection of Oriental Carpets. [NY, 1910]. Folio, loose in half cloth portfolio; corners bumped. With 27 colored plates. sg June 4 (353) $225

Ymagier...

— L'Ymagier. Revue Trimestrielle. Paris, 1894-96. Nos I-VIII (all pbd). 4to, wraps. Lacking 3 plates. B Oct 7 (323) HF7,600

Yonge, Charlotte Mary, 1823-1901

— The Instructive Picture Book.... Edin., 1867. Folio, orig half cloth; broken. With 60 colored plates. pn May 21 (42) £95 [Barker]

York, Alvin Cullum, b.1887

— Sergeant York: His Own Life Story and War Diary. Garden City, 1928. In chipped d/j. Sgd. cb Dec 18 (213) $60

Yoshiwara...

— Yoshiwara: The Nightless City. Paris: Charles Carrington, 1907. One of 500. 8vo, bds bound in the Oriental manner. With 5 plates. sg Feb 12 (113) $140

Young, Arthur, 1741-1820

— Annals of Agriculture and other Useful Arts. Bury St. Edmunds, 1790-99. Vols 1-33 (of 46) in 17. 8vo, contemp calf. Sold w.a.f. S June 25 (86) £1,000

— The Example of France, a Warning to Britain. Dublin, 1793. 8vo, disbound. Tp spotted; some marginal staining. bba Sept 25 (43) £50 [Burmester]

— The Farmer's Tour through the East of England. L, 1771. 4 vols. 8vo, contemp calf; worn. wa Dec 11 (706) $240

— General View of the Agriculture of the County of Essex. L, 1807. 1st Ed. 2 vols. 8vo, later half mor; worn. With colored folding map & 58 plates (1 slightly torn). S Nov 17 (691) £140 [Vine]

— A Six Months Tour through the North of England. L, 1770. 1st Ed. 4 vols. 8vo, contemp calf. pnE Jan 28 (78) £220 [Thin]

— A Six Weeks Tour through the Southern Counties of England and Wales. L, 1768. 8vo, calf gilt. T Dec 18 (71) £100

— A Tour in Ireland. L, 1780. 4to, contemp calf; rubbed, hinges repaired. bba Apr 9 (365) £170 [Catnach]

Anr copy. Contemp calf; worn. wa Dec 11 (707) $170

— Travels during the Years 1787, 1788 and 1789 in the Kingdom of France. Bury St. Edmunds, 1792. 4to, later calf. With 3 folding maps, 1 hand-colored. Ms index of towns inserted; title creased. Sadleir copy. C Dec 12 (288) £220 [Martin]

Anr copy. Old calf; rebacked, ll rubbed. Minor with minor tears. O Mar 24 (198)

YOUNG

$130
2d Ed. Bury St. Edmunds, 1794. 2 vols. 4to, orig bds; broken. With 3 folding maps. Some foxing. O Oct 21 (200) $130

Young, Charles Frederick T.
— The Economy of Steam Power on Common Roads.... L: Atchley, [1861]. 8vo, orig cloth; worn, hinges strengthened. wa Nov 6 (97) $50

Young, Edward, 1683-1765
See also: Fore-Edge Paintings
— The Complaint, and the Consolation; or Night Thoughts. L, 1797. Illus by William Blake. Folio, contemp half calf; worn. Pencil note by former owner in lower margin of each engraving. S Dec 4 (166) £1,000 [Shopa]

Anr copy. Contemp half mor. Explanation leaf repaired; some soiling; 1st gathering misbound. S June 17 (208) £1,700 [Subunso]

Young, G. O.
— Alaskan Yukon Trophies Won and Lost. Huntington WV: Standard, 1947. 4to, cloth; worn, hinges starting. wa Sept 25 (86) $120

Young, George
— A Treatise on Opium.... L, 1753. 8vo, new half calf. S May 28 (814) £130

Young, John Philip
— San Francisco.... San Francisco & Chicago, [1912]. Ltd Ed, sgd. 2 vols. Folio, half mor; hinges reinforced. cb Jan 8 (228) $130

Young, Morris N.
— Bibliography of Memory. Phila., 1961. In d/j. sg Jan 22 (323) $110

Young, Noel Denholm
— Magna Carta and Other Charters of English Liberty. L: Guyon House Press, 1938. Folio, mor. Some soiling. sg Jan 8 (128) $70

Young, Thomas, 1773-1829
— A Course of Lectures on Natural Philosophy and the Mechanical Arts. L, 1807. 1st Ed. 2 vols. 4to, contemp half sheep. With 43 double-page plates, 2 colored. bba May 14 (305) £140 [Fenelon]

Young, Sir William, 1749-1815
— The West India Common Place Book.... L, 1807. 1st Ed. 4to, contemp half calf. With 2 folding maps & 2 folding tables. S June 25 (451) £380 [Quaritch]

AMERICAN BOOK PRICES CURRENT

Yourcenar, Marguerite
— The Alms of Alcippe. NY: Targ, 1982. One of 250. Half cloth. cb Feb 5 (241) $55

Ypres...
— The Ypres Times. L: Ypres League, 1921-39. Vol I, No 1 to Vol 9, No 3 (complete run) bound in 4 vols. Cloth or bds. cb Dec 18 (205) $110

Yriarte, Charles Emile, 1832-98
— Florence. Paris, 1881. Orig half mor; rubbed. Ck Oct 17 (186) £50

Y-Worth, William
— The Britannian Magazine: or, a New Art of Making...English Wines. L, [1700]. 3d Ed. 12mo, modern lea; endpapers renewed. sg Jan 15 (60) $150
— Cerevisiarii Comes; or the New and true Art of Brewing.... L: J. Taylor & S. Clement, 1692. 12mo, modern calf. Crahan copy. P Nov 25 (497) $350
— Introitus Apertus ad Artem Distillationis.... L: John Taylor, 1692. 1st Ed. 8vo, contemp sheep; worn & repaired. Marginal browning & chipping. Crahan copy. P Nov 25 (498) $450

Z

Z., K. Y. See: Almanacs

Zabaglia, Niccola
— Castelli, e ponti.... Rome, 1743. 1st Ed. Folio, contemp half calf; rubbed. With port & 54 plates. C July 22 (235) £1,200

Zach, ——, Baron de
— Correspondence astronomique, geographique, hydrographique et statistique. Geneva, 1818-26. 14 (of 15) vols. 8vo, half mor; rubbed. bba Oct 16 (294) £110 [Maggs]

Zahn, Wilhelm
— Die Schoensten Ornamente und merkwuerdigsten Gemaelde aus Pompeii, Herkulanum und Stabiae. Berlin, 1828-59. 2d Series, Parts 1-10 in 1 vol(of 3 series of 10 parts each). Folio, half calf. With 100 plates, some in color. Some plates affected by waterstaining & spotting. C Oct 15 (117) £1,200 [Sims]

Zamora, Lucas Florentine —& Ponce de Leon, Eduardo
— Bibliografia espanola de arquitectura (1526-1850). Madrid, 1947. One of 300. 4to, half lea, orig wraps bound in. sg Oct 2 (36) $120

Zamorano...
— The Zamorano 80: a Selection of Distinguished California Books... Los Angeles: Zamorano Club, 1945. One of 500. cb Mar 19 (286) $160; sg June 11 (84) $80

Zampetti, Pietro
— A Dictionary of Venetian Painters.... Leigh-on-Sea, 1969-79. 5 vols. 4to, cloth, in d/js. bba Feb 5 (118) £65 [hay]; Ck Oct 31 (48) £65

Zanchi, Girolamo, 1516-90
— Operum Theologicorum. [Heidelberg]: Stephanus Gamonetus, 1613. 4 parts in 1 vol. Folio, old vellum. Some soiling & shelf-wear. Sold w,a,f. O Mar 24 (199) $60

Zangwill, Israel, 1864-1926
— Works. L, 1925. One of 1,000. 14 vols. Contemp half mor. Ck Nov 7 (79) £110
Anr copy. Orig half calf. pn Apr 30 (149) £130 [Traylen]
Am copy. Orig half mor. S Sept 22 (159) £65 [Molan]

Zant, Johan Wilhelm van der. See: Cobra

Zappullo, Michele
— Sommario Istorico...oue con occasione de Celebrare i successi di quattro gran Citta.... Naples: Carlino & Vitale, 1609. 4to, 18th-cent vellum. Some foxing & dampstains. sg Sept 18 (313) $200

Zarate, Augustin de, b.1514
— Historia del descubrimiento y conquista del Peru. Seville: Alonso Escrivano, 1577. Folio, 17th-cent calf gilt; spine ends chipped, owner's library card pocket on front pastedown. Marginal worming; blank lower portion of last leaf torn away & restored. sg Dec 4 (210) $1,600

Zedner, Joseph
— Catalogue of Hebrew Printed Books in the British Museum. [L], 1867. Orig cloth; rubbed. bba Feb 19 (69) £100 [Sofer]

Zeiler, Martin, 1589-1661
— Itinerarium Italiae non-antiquae: oder, Raiss-Beschreibung durch Italien. Frankfurt: M. Merian, 1640. Folio, contemp vellum; worn. With 4 double-page maps & 38 double-page plates. FD June 11 (849) DM3,300
— Topographia Electoratus Brandenburgici et Ducatus Pomeraniae.... Frankfurt: Heirs of M. Merian, [1652]. 3 parts in 1 vol. Folio, modern blindstamped calf. With engraved title, 4 double-page maps & 100 views on 70 plates. FD June 11 (802) DM15,000
— Topographia Galliae. Frankfurt, 1655-61. Vol I only. Folio, vellum, armorial bdg. HN Nov 26 (319) DM2,000
Anr copy. Parts 3-13 in 2 vols. Folio, contemp calf gilt; spine repaired. Lacking 8 plates. HN Nov 26 (320) DM3,000

Zelazny, Roger
— Eye of Cat. San Francisco: Underwood-Miller, 1982. One of 20 rubberstamped Presentation Copy on limitation page. cb Sept 28 (1397) $60
— The Guns of Avalon. Garden City: Doubleday, 1972. 1st Ed. In d/j; spine ends rubbed. cb Sept 28 (1399) $450
— Jack of Shadows. NY: Walker, [1971]. In d/j. cb Sept 28 (1402) $70
— Lord of Light. Garden City, 1967. In d/j with tear & creases at bottom front. cb Sept 28 (1404) $600
— Nine Princes in Amber. Garden City, 1970. In d/j. Sgd on tp. cb Sept 28 (1407) $475

Zenger, John Peter, 1697-1746
[-] Remarks on the Trial of...Printer of the New-York Weekly Journal.... L: J. Roberts, 1738. With: The Tryal of John Peter Zenger, of New-York, Printer.... [L? 1738?] Title lacking. Both works disbound from anr vol. 4to. Sold w.a.f. CNY Dec 19 (257) $420

Zervos, Christian
See also: Picasso, Pablo
— Naissance de la civilisation en grece. Paris, 1962-63. 2 vols. Folio, orig cloth, in torn d/js. bba Oct 30 (240) £75 [Check]
— Pablo Picasso. Paris, 1957-49-78. Mixed Ed, Vol 1 is one of 50 hors commerce, Vol 2 is one of 400, the remainder are 1st Ed. Vols 1-33 in 34 vols. Orig wraps. C May 13 (194) f10,500 [Green]

Zettler, F. X. —& Others
— Ausgewahlte Kunstwerke aus dem Schatze der Reichen Capelle in der Koeniglichen Residenz zu Munchen. Munich, 1876. Folio, unbound as issued in orig cloth portfolio, with metal clasps & supports; rubbed. With 37 color plates. Some soiling. S Mar 9 (714) £240 [Marks]

Ziegler, Wilbur G. —& Grooscup, Ben S.
— The Heart of the Alleganies,... Raleigh: Alfred Williams, [1883]. 8vo, orig cloth; soiled. With folding map. O June 9 (200) $140

Zimmer, John Todd
— Catalogue of the Edward E. Ayer Ornithological Library. Chicago, 1926. 2 vols. pnE Jan 28 (186) £110 [Maggs]

ZIMMERMANN

Zimmermann, Johann Georg, 1728-95
— Ueber die Einsamkeit. Leipzig, 1784-85. 4 vols. 8vo, contemp calf gilt. HK Nov 4 (2769) DM1,150

Zinner, Ernst
— Geschichte und Bibliographie der astronomischen Literatur.... Leipzig, 1941. sg May 14 (639) $200
— Verzeichnis der astronomischen Handschriften des deutschen Kulturgebietes Munich, 1925. Half lea, orig wraps bound in. sg Oct 2 (40) $80

Zittel, Karl Alfred von
— Handbuch der Palaeontologie. Munich & Leipzig, 1876-93. 5 vols. 8vo, later half mor; joints & ends rubbed. cb June 4 (213) $65

Zoethoet, D. A.
— Amsterdams brandweer zooals zij is en zooals zij was. Amst., 1899. 4to, half mor gilt. B Oct 7 (46) HF220

Zographos, D. See: Makryjannis & Zographos

Zoist...
— Zoist: A Journal of Cerebral Physiology & Mesmerism. L, 1844-45. Vols 1-10 (of 13). 8vo, contemp half calf. Sold w.a.f. C Dec 12 (225) £1,100 [Phelps]

Zola, Emile, 1840-1902
— Oeuvres. Paris, 1907-24. 68 vols. Half lea. B Oct 7 (840) HF600

Zollikofer, Georgius Joachimus de. See: Fore-Edge Paintings

Zonca, Vittorio
— Nova teatro di machine et edificii. Padua, 1656. Folio, contemp vellum bds. With engraved title & 42 plates. Some staining & discoloration; last leaf with wormhole in upper margin catching headline. S June 25 (142) £1,600 [Fletcher]

Zoological Society of London
— Transactions. L, 1835-1910. Vols 1-19. 4to, contemp half mor gilt. With 1,243 plates, including 180 hand-colored plates. Sold w.a.f. C Apr 8 (155) £4,800 [May]

Zorn, Johannes
— Afbeeldingen der artseny-gewassen met derzelver nederduitsche en latynsche beschryvingen. Amst., 1796-1800. 6 vols. 8vo, contemp half lea; rubbed. With 600 hand-colored plates. Some spotting; title & half title of Vol III with slight dampstaining. Stamps on titles. de Belder copy. S Apr 28 (388) £4,000 [Krohn]
— Dreyhundert auserlesene amerikanische Gewaechse. Nuremberg, 1785-88. 6 parts in 2 vols. 8vo, contemp calf; rubbed,

AMERICAN BOOK PRICES CURRENT

rebacked, old spines preserved. With 300 hand-colored plates. Library stamp of the Societe d'Agriculture, Douai. de Belder copy. S Apr 28 (387) £4,200 [Krohn]
— Icones plantarum medicinalium; Abbildungen von Arzneygewaechsen. Nuremberg, 1779-84. Vols I-VI. 8vo, contemp calf; rubbed. With frontis & 600 hand-colored plates. Horticultural Society of New York—de Belder copy. S Apr 28 (386) £4,200 [Dick]

Zouch, Thomas, 1737-1815
— The Life of Isaac Walton; including Notices of his Contemporaries. L, 1823. 4to, mor extra by Bayntun; upper hinge weak. With frontis & 20 plates. pn Nov 20 (109) £85 [Peters]
Anr copy. Lea gilt by Gosden with blind-stamped ports of Walton & Cotton on covers; scuffed, worn. With 20 mtd India-proofs of plates. With an extra engraving mtd on flyleaf. sg Oct 23 (551) $1,300

Zschokke, Johann Heinrich Daniel
— Die klassischen Stellen der schweiz und deren Hauptorte in Originalansichten dargestellt.... Karlsruhe & Leipzig, 1836. 8vo, contemp cloth. With engraved title & 85 plates. S Oct 23 (273) £550 [Walford]
— Die Schweiz in ihren klassischen Stellen un Hauptorten. Stuttgart & St. Gallen, 1858. 4to, calf. With 72 plates. C Oct 15 (118) £520 [Maus]

Zuccolo, Gregoria
— I Discorsi.... Venice: Giovanni Bariletto, 1575. 8vo, old vellum; endpapers renewed; bottom edge shaved. sg Mar 26 (294) $130

Zuchetta, Giovanni Battista
— Prima parte della arimmetica. Brescia, 1600. Part I (all pbd). Folio, contemp vellum. Some waterstaining, stamps & worming. HK Nov 4 (1172) DM900

Zuckerkandl, Robert
— Zur Theorie des Preises.... Leipzig, 1889. 8vo, contemp half mor; rubbed. Tp & half-title with short tear in blank margin. P Sept 24 (425) $400

Zukertort, Johannes Hermann, 1842-88. See: Olson, Anton

Zuniga y Sotomayor, Fadrique de
— Libro de cetreria de caca de acor.... Salamanca: Juan de Canova, 1565. 4to, 19th-cent calf. Jeanson copy. SM Mar 1 (584) FF65,000

Zurla, Placido
— Il Mappamondo di Fra Mauro Camaldolese. Venice, 1806. Folio, contemp calf; worn. With plate & folding map. FD June 11 (892) DM1,200

Zwang, Gerard
— Le Sexe de la Femme. Paris, 1967. 4to, mor gilt. sg Feb 12 (114) $120; sg Feb 12 (338) $80

Zweig, Paul
— Images & Footsteps: A Poem. [Verona, 1970-71]. One of 200. Illus by Berta Moltke. Folio, half syn. sg Jan 8 (208) $175

Images & Footsteps. Verona: Plain Wrapper Press, [1971]. One of 200. Illus by Bertha Moltke. Half mor. cb Sept 11 (211) $120

Zwinger, Theodor
— Theatrum botanicum, das ist, neu vollkommenes Kraeuter-Buch. Basel: Bertsche, 1696. Folio, contemp calf; worn & def. Woodcuts with contemp coloring. HK Nov 4 (1132) DM7,200

Zyl, Jan van
— Theatrum machinarum universale, of groot algemeen moolenboek. Amst., [1734]. 2 parts in 1 vol. Folio, bdg not indicated. Library markings. Sold w.a.f. Franklin Institute copy. F Sept 12 (344) $1,100

A book sale at Sotheby's, circa 1800, by Thomas Rowlandson, collection Sotheby Parke Bernet & Co.